PUBLIC LIBRARY CORE COLLECTION:

NONFICTION

THIRTEENTH EDITION

CORE COLLECTION SERIES

Formerly
STANDARD CATALOG SERIES

JOHN GREENFIELDT, GENERAL EDITOR

CHILDREN'S CORE COLLECTION

MIDDLE & JUNIOR HIGH CORE COLLECTION

SENIOR HIGH CORE COLLECTION

PUBLIC LIBRARY CORE COLLECTION: NONFICTION

PUBLIC LIBRARY CORE COLLECTION: FICTION

PUBLIC LIBRARY CORE COLLECTION: NONFICTION

A Selection Guide to Reference Books
and
Adult Nonfiction

THIRTEENTH EDITION

Former title:

Public Library Catalog

EDITED BY

JOHN GREENFIELDT

AND

PATRICE BARTELL

THE H. W. WILSON COMPANY
NEW YORK AND DUBLIN
2008

Printed in the United States of America

ISBN 978-0-8242-1094-6

Library of Congress Cataloging-in-Publication Data

Public library core collection. Nonfiction : a selection guide to reference books and adult nonfiction. — 13th ed. / edited by John Greenfieldt and Patrice Bartell.
    p. cm. — (Core collection series)
 Updated ed. of: Public library catalog. 12th ed. 2004.
 Kept up to date between editions by annual supplements.
 Includes index.
 ISBN 978-0-8242-1094-6 (alk. paper)
 1. Public libraries—United States—Book lists. I. Greenfieldt, John. II. Bartell, Patrice. III. Public library catalog.
 Z1035.P934 2008
 025.2'187473—dc22   2008042489

Visit H.W. Wilson's Web site at: www.hwwilson.com

CONTENTS

CONTENTS

PREFACE

PUBLIC LIBRARY CORE COLLECTION, formerly entitled Public Library Catalog, is a list of recommended reference and nonfiction books for adults, in classified order. The Public Library Core Collection service consists of this basic volume and three annual supplements for the years 2009-2011. They will be distributed on publication to purchasers of the thirteenth edition without further charge. The Wilson Core Collections are also available in electronic format on the Web, updated daily.

What's new in this Edition?

Each new edition of PUBLIC LIBRARY CORE COLLECTION is a mixture of the old and the new. Older titles, some in updated versions, are included if they remain the best titles in their field. Newer titles reflect new topics of interest and new interpretations of traditional knowledge. This edition of the Core Collection features extensive revision in the areas of psychology and philosophy, religion, science, crafts and sports, cooking, and art. Biography, drama, poetry, and literary criticism have also received comprehensive revision and expansion. Reference materials in all subject fields have been updated.

History

The first of several installments of the "Standard Catalog" for the general library was published in 1918. It was called STANDARD CATALOG: SOCIOLOGY SECTION. Additional installments were issued over the next fourteen years, covering Biography; Fiction; Fine Arts; History and Travel; Science and Useful Arts; Literature and Philology; and Philosophy, Religion and General Works. Finally, a fully integrated first edition of the STANDARD CATALOG FOR PUBLIC LIBRARIES was assembled and published in 1934. The contents were displayed in classified order, according to the Dewey Decimal Classification. The name was changed to PUBLIC LIBRARY CATALOG with the publication of the fifth edition in 1969, and then to PUBLIC LIBRARY CORE COLLECTION: NONFICTION with this edition.

Although a Fiction Section was issued in 1923, followed by supplements in 1928 and 1931, fiction was omitted from the first edition of the complete Catalog in 1934. A new expanded edition of the Fiction Section was published as FICTION CATALOG in 1942. In its preface that Catalog was referred to as "a companion volume to the Standard Catalog for Public Libraries." This complementary relationship has continued to the present. PUBLIC LIBRARY CORE COLLECTION: NONFICTION has always listed works of literary criticism and literary history and books about literary technique.

Scope and Purpose

This volume lists nonfiction books published in the United States, or published in other countries and distributed in the United States. It excludes non-print materials; periodicals; non-English items (with the exception of dictionaries), aids to language learning, and similar materials; and works of an ephemeral nature. All books were in print at the time of listing. Original paperback editions are included. Entries for hardcover editions provide information about the availability of paperback reprints where possible. This volume comprises over 9,000 book titles with multiple subject access. The three annual supplements will expand the coverage by several thousand additional titles.

The Core Collection is intended to serve the needs of public and undergraduate libraries and stand as a basic or "opening day" collection. The newer titles help in identifying areas in a collection that can be updated or strengthened. Retention of useful material from the previous edition enables the librarian to make informed decisions about weeding a collection. With its classified arrangement, complete bibliographical data, and descriptive and critical annotations, the Core Collection provides useful information for the acquisitions librarian, the reference librarian, and the cataloger. Entries provide information about the availability of electronic versions of books listed.

Preparation

Books included in this edition were elected by experienced librarians representing public library systems across the United States, a committee of advisors on policy and trends and a roster of nominators who recommend titles in specialized areas. The names of participating librarians and their affiliations are listed in the Acknowledgments.

Organization

The Core Collection is organized into two parts: the Classified Collection; and an Author, Title, and Subject Index.

Part 1. Classified Collection. This is arranged according to the Dewey Decimal Classification. Within classes, arrangement is by main entry, with complete bibliographical and cataloging information given for each book. The classified arrangement, along with the descriptive and critical annotations, provides a useful guide to book selection. Entries include such information as price and ISBN to facilitate acquisitions.

Part 2. Author, Title, and Subject Index. This is a comprehensive key to the Classified List with entries for authors, titles, and subjects.

For further information consult the Directions for Use of the Core Collection.

ACKNOWLEDGMENTS

The H. W. Wilson Company expresses its special gratitude to the following librarians who both advised the company in matters of editorial and assisted in the selection of titles for this Core Collection:

Committee of Advisors

James E. Bobick
Author and Consultant
Pittsburgh, Pennsylvania

Pat Dempsey
Cuyahoga County Public Library
Parma, Ohio

Mary Griffin
Omaha Public Library
Omaha, Nebraska

Steven Jablonski
Skokie Public Library
Skokie, Illinois

Brett W. Lear
Jefferson Public Library
Jefferson, Colorado

Charlene Rue
Brooklyn Public Library
Brooklyn, New York

Gregg Sapp
Evergreen State College
Olympia, Washington

Nominators

James E. Bobick
Author and Consultant
Pittsburgh, Pennsylvania

Barbara Palmer Cassini
Formerly, Radnor Memorial Library
Radnor, Pennsylvania

Pat Dempsey
Cuyahoga County Public Library
Parma, Ohio

Mary Griffin
Omaha Public Library
Omaha, Nebraska

Steven Jablonski
Shokie Public Library
Skokie, Illinois

Katharine L. Kan
Reviewer and consultant
Panama City, Florida

Brett W. Lear
Lakewood Library Manager
Jefferson Public Library

Elizabeth Lowther
Formerly, Free Library of
    Philadelphia
Philadelphia, Pennsylvania

Charlene Rue
Brooklyn Public Library
Brooklyn, New York

Gregg Sapp
Evergreen State College
Olympia, Washington

Tim Siftar
Drexel University
Philadelphia, Pennsylvania

David Soltész
Cuyahoga County Public Library
Parma, Ohio

Doreen Velnich
Worcester Public Library
Worcester, Massachusetts

DIRECTIONS FOR USE OF THE CORE COLLECTION

Part 1. Classified Collection

The Classified Collection is arranged by the Dewey Decimal Classification in numerical order from 000 to 999. Individual biographies are classed at 92 and follow the 920s (collective biography). An Outline of Classification, which serves as a table of contents for the Classified Collection, is reproduced below. It should be noted that many topics can be classified in more than one discipline. If a particular title is not found where it might be expected, the Index should be consulted to determine if it is classified elsewhere.

Within classes, works are arranged alphabetically under main entry, usually the author. Works of individual biography are arranged alphabetically under the name of the person written about.

Each listing consists of a full bibliographical description. Prices, which are always subject to change, have been obtained from the publisher and are as current as possible. Entries include recommended subject headings derived from the *Sears List of Subject Headings*, a suggested classification number from the *Abridged Dewey Decimal Classification and Relative Index*, a brief description of the contents, and, whenever possible, an evaluation from a quoted source. The key to the abbreviations of the journal sources can be found on the Web at: www.corecollections.net. An asterisk (*) after the price indicates that a book is a "most highly recommended" title.

Part 2. Author, Title, and Subject Index

The Index is a single alphabetical list of all the books entered in the Core Collection. Each book is entered under author; title (if distinctive); and subject. The classification number, displayed in boldface type, is the key to the location of the main entry for the book in the Classified Collection.

Appropriate added entries are made for joint authors and editors. "See" references are made from forms of names or subjects that are not used as headings. "See also" references are made to related or more specific headings.

Outline of Classification

Reproduced below is the Second Summary of the Dewey Decimal Classification. * As Part 1 of this Core Collection is arranged according to this classification, the outline will serve as a table of contents for it. Please note, however, that the inclusion of this outline is not to be considered a substitute for consulting the Dewey Decimal Classification itself.

PUBLIC LIBRARY CORE COLLECTION: NONFICTION

THIRTEENTH EDITION

CLASSIFIED COLLECTION

000 COMPUTER SCIENCE, KNOWLEDGE & SYSTEMS

Levine, Lawrence W., 1933-2006
The opening of the American mind; canons, culture, and history. Beacon Press 1996 xxiv, 212p pa $18 hardcover o.p. **001.1**
1. Higher education 2. United States—Intellectual life
ISBN 0-8070-3119-4 (pa)   LC 96-33866
The author "examines the current critique of higher education, the major debates over the curriculum and the canon over two centuries, and changes in the perceptions of the national culture. . . . Levine insists that there is no stable canon of writers; that universities have always mirrored dominant cultural attitudes toward gender, race, and ethnicity; and that diversity, pluralism, and multiculturalism have been present throughout American history." Choice
"Levine's presentation is eloquent, eminently reasonable, and gratifyingly optimistic." Booklist
Includes bibliographical references

001.4 Research; statistical methods

Awards, honors, & prizes. 28th ed. Gale Res. 2v
v1 $385; v2 $420 *   **001.4**
1. Awards
ISSN 0196-6316
ISBN 978-1-414419-00-8 (v1); 1-414419-00-7 (v1); 978-1-414419-01-5 (v2); 1-414419-01-5 (v2)
First published 1969. Frequently revised
Contents: v1 United States and Canada; v2 International and foreign
Volume one is an alphabetical directory of organizations in the United States and Canada sponsoring awards, honors and prizes in a wide range of endeavors from academic awards to prizes in sports. Volume two provides coverage of awards originating in other countries

Feldman, Burton
The Nobel Prize; a history of genius, controversy, and prestige. Arcade Pub. 2000 489p il $29.95; pa $15.95   **001.4**
1. Nobel Prizes
ISBN 1-55970-537-X; 1-55970-592-2 (pa)
          LC 00-42002
The author provides a "history of the prizes awarded in the sciences, literature, social sciences, and humankind's . . . peace efforts. This is the first comprehensive critical history of the prizes to appear, and it's very good." Libr J
Includes bibliographical references

Tufte, Edward R., 1942-
The visual display of quantitative information. 2nd ed. Graphics Press 2001 197p il $40
          001.4
1. Statistics—Graphic methods
ISBN 0-9613921-4-2   LC 2001-271866
First published 1983
This book focuses "on statistical graphics, charts, tables. Theory and practice in the design of data graphics, 250 illustrations of the best (and a few of the worst) statistical graphics, with . . . analysis of how to display data for precise, effective, quick analysis." Publisher's note

001.9 Controversial knowledge

Clark, Jerome
Unnatural phenomena; a guide to the bizarre wonders of North America; illustrations by John Clark. ABC-CLIO 2005 xxxiv, 369p il $85
          001.9
1. Curiosities and wonders
ISBN 1-57607-430-7   LC 2005-11206
"Organized geographically, . . . [this book] explores the history of bizarre natural phenomena in virtually every U.S. state." Publisher's note
Includes bibliographical references

Ellis, Richard, 1938-
Imagining Atlantis. Knopf 1998 322p il maps pa $13 hardcover o.p. *   **001.9**
1. Atlantis
ISBN 0-375-70582-1 (pa)   LC 97-48432
"Chronicles the rarely examined history of the dream of Atlantis, a centuries-long quest for evidence of the existence of a lost continent that has involved philosophers, historians, scientists, and mystics." Booklist
"Engaging, lucid, and full of lore, Ellis's book makes a convincing case that Atlantis was merely a morality tale of Plato's, and along the way provides insight into our enduring preoccupation with things vanished and lost." New Yorker
Includes bibliographical references

Shermer, Michael
Why people believe weird things; pseudoscience, superstition, and other confusions of our time; foreword by Stephen Jay Gould. rev and expanded. Freeman, W.H. 2002 xxvi, 349p il pa $16   **001.9**
1. Science 2. Belief and doubt 3. Parapsychology
ISBN 0-8050-7089-3   LC 2002-68784

Shermer, Michael—*Continued*

"First Owl Books edition"

First published 1997

Contents: Science and skepticism; Pseudoscience and superstition; Evolution and creationism; History and pseudohistory; Hope springs eternal

The author "explores the very human reasons people find otherworldly phenomena, conspiracy theories, and cults so appealing. In . . . [the] chapter, 'Why Smart People Believe in Weird Things' he takes on science luminaries like physicist Frank Tippler and others, who hide their spiritual beliefs behind the trappings of science." Publisher's note

Includes bibliographical references

Wilson, Colin, 1931-

The Atlantis blueprint; unlocking the ancient mysteries of a long-lost civilization; [by] Colin Wilson and Rand Flem-Ath. Delacorte Press 2001 xxv, 415p il maps hardcover o.p. pa $16

001.9

1. Atlantis

ISBN 0-385-33479-6; 0-440-50898-3 (pa)

LC 00-47449

The authors "propose a single, geo-historical theory that links the Egyptian, Chinese and South American pyramids and other sacred sites. According to this argument, these civilizations received templates from Atlantis that contained crucial geodesic, geological and geometric information. Furthermore, Atlantean mariners, based in Antarctica, sailed the globe over 100,000 years ago and established more than 60 sacred sites around the world." Publ Wkly

002   The book

Basbanes, Nicholas A., 1943-

Patience & fortitude; a roving chronicle of book people, book places, and book culture. HarperCollins Pubs. 2001 636p il hardcover o.p. pa $19.95 *   **002**

1. Book collecting 2. Books and reading 3. Libraries

ISBN 0-06-019695-5; 0-06-051446-9 (pa)

LC 2001-16935

The author "traces the crucial role that book collectors, librarians and scholars have played in the 'transmission and preservation of knowledge,' starting with the vast ancient library at Alexandria, Egypt, and ending with our current, not always book-friendly, era of computer technology." N Y Times Book Rev

"Basbanes's fund of stories will delight readers who value books for more than just a good story, have a yen for second-hand books plucked from dusty shops or look to book catalogs for suspense and excitement." Publ Wkly

Includes bibliographical references

Buzbee, Lewis, 1957-

The yellow-lighted bookshop; a memoir, a history. Graywolf Press 2006 216p $17

002

1. Booksellers and bookselling

ISBN 1-55597-450-3   LC 2005-938151

The author "tells the story of his lifelong obsession [with books], from his elementary school Weekly Reader orders to his first jobs clerking in bookstores and his short career as a publisher's rep. Woven into these personal essays is a tangential discourse on the history of bookmaking and bookselling, from the ancient Romans and Chinese to the modern era." Publ Wkly

This "is a tribute to those who crave the cozy confines of a bookshop." Booklist

Kelly, Stuart

The book of lost books; an incomplete history of all the great books you will never read. Random House 2006 344p $24.95   **002**

1. Books and reading

ISBN 1-4000-6297-7   LC 2005-51653

The author "covers manuscripts of stories, poems, and plays that have been destroyed (e.g., Shakespeare's Cardenio), misplaced or stolen (e.g., Malcolm Lowry's Ultramarine), unfinished (e.g., Chaucer's The Canterbury Tales), and even one simply too illegible to read (for which we have Ezra Pound to thank). Also featured are notes by authors who intended to write stories they never began (e.g., Dylan Thomas and Adventures in the Skin Trade). The writers under discussion span 3000 years of literary history and include Homer, Franz Kafka, Sylvia Plath, Robert Louis Stevenson, Jane Austen, and William Burroughs." Libr J

"Prodigiously informative, if occasionally dense, 'The Book of Lost Books' is less a book one reads than a vade mecum one consults. But every page is a garden of delights." N Y Times Book Rev

002.075   Book collecting

Lansky, Aaron, 1955-

Outwitting history; the amazing adventures of a man who rescued a million Yiddish books. Algonquin Books of Chapel Hill 2004 316p

002.075

1. National Yiddish Book Center 2. Book collecting 3. Yiddish language

ISBN 1-56512-429-4   LC 2004-51587

"Part memoir and part history, this is the . . . tale of how Lansky retrieved thousands of books from dumpsters and abandoned buildings across America. He also rescued books from the aftermath of the 1994 terrorist bombing of the Jewish Community Center in Buenos Aires and went to Havana to save the few remaining Yiddish books of a vestigial Jewish community there." Libr J

"The book is a testimony to [Lansky's] love of Judaism and literature and his desire to make a difference in the world." Publ Wkly

Includes bibliographical references

004 Data processing. Computer science

Baig, Edward C.

Macs for dummies. 9th ed. Wiley 2006 386p il (--For dummies) pa $21.99 * **004**
1. Macintosh (Computer)
ISBN 0-470-04849-2; 978-0-470-04849-8
LC 2006-926376
First published 1992 by IDG Books. Frequently revised

In addition to assembly instructions and explanation of parts, this guide to Macintosh computers discusses customizing workspaces, Mac OS X, going online, iLife applications, e-mail, and security issues.

Computer sciences; Roger R. Flynn, editor in chief. Macmillan 2002 4v set $325 **004**
1. Computer science
ISBN 0-02-865566-4
LC 2002-754
Contents: v1 Foundations; v2 Software and hardware; v3 Social applications; v4 Electronic universe

This set "includes 286 signed entries written by more than 125 contributors. . . . Many articles are enhanced by sidebars, glossary definitions, black-and-white illustrations, cross-references, and bibliographic or Internet resources. Additional features include time lines, a glossary, and an index to the set. Intended for general readers and high school students, this encyclopedia will appeal to anyone curious about this complex field or its impact on today's world." Choice

Downing, Douglas

Dictionary of computer and Internet terms; [by] Douglas A. Downing, Michael A. Covington, Melody Mauldin Covington; with the assistance of Catherine Anne Covington. 9th ed. Barron's 2006 587p il (Barron's business guides) pa $12.99 *
004
1. Computers—Dictionaries 2. Internet—Dictionaries
ISBN 0-7641-3417-5
LC 2005-52175
First published 1986 with title: Dictionary of computer terms

This work defines approximately 2,500 computer terms. Topics explained "include finding information with search tools on the Web, creating a home page with HTML, communicating via e-mail, tuning in to multimedia applications, and the technical details involved in connecting a computer with a modem to other computers and the Internet." Publisher's note

The **Facts** on File dictionary of computer science; edited by John Daintith, Edmund Wright. Rev. ed. Facts on File 2006 273p il (Facts on File science library) $49.50 * **004**
1. Computer science—Dictionaries
ISBN 0-8160-5999-3; 978-0-8160-5999-7
LC 2006-42004
First published 2001; based on the Minidictionary of computing, published 1986 by Oxford University Press

This dictionary provides over 2400 "entries that explain such fundamental concepts as hardware, software,

and applications." Publisher's note

"The book will prove a handy reference for budding computer scientists." Voice Youth Advocates

Includes bibliographical references

Gookin, Dan

PCs for dummies. 11th ed. Wiley 2007 xx, 383p il (--For dummies) pa $21.99 * **004**
1. Microcomputers
ISBN 978-0-470-13728-4; 0-470-13728-2
First published 1992. Frequently revised. Publisher varies

Starting with the assembly and plug-in operation, the author goes on to outline how to use Windows. He explains concepts and procedures (virus protection, spam blocking and digital imaging as well as Internet use).

Hally, Mike

Electronic brains; stories from the dawn of the computer age. Joseph Henry 2005 xxiii, 275p $27.95 **004**
1. Computers—History
ISBN 0-309-09630-8
LC 2005-16583
"Inspired by a popular BBC radio series of the same name, this book details the postwar computer development boom, concentrating on the personalities instead of the technology. . . . Major historical events serve as the backdrop to Hally's history; The Manhattan Project's atomic researches, presidential elections, wars and revolutions all figure into the computer's development. The book has its techie moments, but this is an informative and entertaining read." Publ Wkly

High definition; an A to Z guide to personal technology. Houghton Mifflin 2006 361p il pa $14.95 * **004**
1. Electric household appliances—Dictionaries
ISBN 0-618-71489-8; 978-0-618-71489-6
LC 2006-19549
This dictionary "brings together more than 3000 terms used to describe the components, functions, and applications of devices found in today's homes and offices: cell phones, computers, MP3 players, gaming systems, CD and DVD players, and more. . . . This very affordable volume should be part of every reference collection, large and small." Libr J

Ifrah, Georges

The universal history of computing; from the abacus to the quantum computer; translated from the French, and with notes by E.F. Harding, assisted by Sophie Wood {et al.}. Wiley 2000 410p il hardcover o.p. pa $16.95 **004**
1. Computers—History 2. Data processing—History
ISBN 0-471-39671-0; 0-471-44147-3 (pa)
LC 00-47771
The author covers "the history of computing from its earliest time to today's supercomputers. After extensive coverage of numbers and the calculating techniques of early history, he discusses in great detail modern calculating machines. . . . Ifrah's erudite book adds new and interesting findings to the topic." Libr J

Includes bibliographical references

Johnson, George, 1952-
A shortcut through time; the path to a quantum
computer. Knopf 2003 204p il hardcover o.p. pa
$13   **004**
1. Quantum theory 2. Computers
ISBN 0-375-41193-3; 0-375-72618-7 (pa)
LC 2002-73013
The author "communicates some of the propositions
offered by theorists about the virtually unlimited computing power that may follow certain practical triumphs that
are not quite in sight." N Y Times Book Rev
"Johnson has presented the fascinating science of
quantum computing and its future development in a
down-to-earth style." Libr J
Includes bibliographical references

Levy, David N. L.
Love + sex with robots; the evolution of
human-robot relationships; [by] David Levy.
HarperCollins 2007 334p il $24.95   **004**
1. Computers and civilization 2. Robots
ISBN 978-0-06-135975-0; 0-06-135975-0
LC 2007-27508
The author "shows how automata have evolved from
the mechanical marvels of centuries past to the electronic
androids of the modern age, and how human interactions
with technology have changed over the years. Along the
way, Levy explores many aspects of human relationships—the reasons why we fall in love, why we form emotional attachments to animals and to virtual pets such as
the Tamagotchi, and why these same attachments could
extend to love for robots." Publisher's note
Includes bibliographical references

Markoff, John
What the dormouse said—; how the sixties
counterculture shaped the personal computer
industry. Viking Penguin 2005 xxiii, 310p il
$25.95; pa $16 *   **004**
1. Computers—History 2. Computers and civilization
3. Counter culture
ISBN 0-670-03382-0; 0-14-303676-9 (pa)
LC 2004-61181
"This is the story of the political, social, and cultural
forces in the 1960s and 1970s that ultimately shaped the
birth of the personal computer." Sci Books Films
"This book is a rare treat and a must-read for everyone who has had the pleasure of using the mysterious
friend called the PC." Choice
Includes bibliographical references

Miller, Michael, 1958-
Absolute beginner's guide to computer basics.
4th ed. Que 2007 430p il pa $21.99 *
004
1. Microcomputers
ISBN 0-7897-3673-X; 978-0-7897-3673-4
LC 2006-103336
Annual. First published 2003
This beginner's computer guidebook covers initial
computer set up, connecting to the Internet, altering digital photos, downloading music to an mp3 player, burning

CDs, watching DVDs on the computer, making presentations, and other information. Windows Vista and XP are
covered.

White, Ron, 1944-
How computers work; illustrated by Timothy
Edward Downs. 9th ed. Que Pub. 2007 452p il pa
$34.99 *   **004**
1. Microcomputers
ISBN 0-7897-3613-6; 978-0-7897-3613-0
LC 2007-46236
First published 1993 by Ziff-Davis Press. Frequently
revised
In addition to information about the different hardware
parts of the computer, this guide also features "explanations about home networking, the Internet, PC security,
and even how cell phone networks operate." Publisher's
note

004.6 Interfacing and communications

Handbook of computer networks; key concepts,
data transmission, and digital and optical
networks; edited by Hossein Bidgoli. John
Wiley & Sons, Inc. 2008 3v il set $900
004.6
1. Computer networks
ISBN 978-0-471-78461-6   LC 2007-12619
Volumes also available separately ea $270
"Each volume incorporates . . . core information and
networking topics, practical applications and coverage of
the emerging issues in the computer networking and data
communications fields." Publisher's note
Includes bibliographical references

The **Internet**; a historical encyclopedia; edited by
Hilary W. Poole. ABC-CLIO 2005 3v il set
$285   **004.6**
1. Internet 2. Telecommunication
ISBN 1-85109-659-0   LC 2005-22156
This set contains a volume of biographical profiles,
another with a chronology, and a third with discussions
of important issues surrounding the Internet. The chronology volume is the second edition of History of the
Internet: a chronology, 1843 to the present, published
1999 under the authorship of Christos J. P. Moschovitis
"This well-organized and clearly written work is an
excellent resource to begin research on the topic." SLJ
Includes bibliographical references

Levine, John R.
The Internet for dummies; [by] John Levine,
Margaret Levine Young, Carol Baroudi. 11th ed.
Wiley 2007 386p pa $21.99 *   **004.6**
1. Internet
ISBN 978-0-470-12174-0; 0-470-12174-2
First published 1993 by IDG Books. Frequently re-
vised
This guide to the Internet includes information on the
Web, Internet service providers, sending e-mail as well
as other benefits of electronic communication.

Lowe, Doug

Networking for dummies. 8th ed. Wiley 2007 412p il (--For dummies) pa $24.99 *

004.6

1. Computer networks

ISBN 978-0-470-05620-2; 0-470-05620-7

First published 1994 by IDG Books. Frequently revised

This describes how to set up local area networks (LANs) enabling workers to share files, internet access, printers and other peripherals. Discusses operating systems, network architectures, cabling systems, and security issues.

Magid, Lawrence J.

MySpace unraveled; a parent's guide to teen social networking from the directors of BlogSafety.com; [by] Larry Magid and Anne Collier. Peachpit Press 2007 184p il pa $14.99 *

004.6

1. MySpace (Web site) 2. Internet and teenagers 3. Parenting

ISBN 0-321-48018-X; 978-0-321-48018-7

LC 2006-298800

This is a "look at what MySpace is, why teens use it, and what parents should know to help guarantee that their teen is safe when using MySpace or other social networking sites. . . . The book is easy to read, filled with colorful screenshots, and sure to help parents understand what their role is in their teen's involvement in social networking." Voice Youth Advocates

005 Computer programming, programs, data

Wang, Wally

Beginning programming for dummies; [by] Wallace Wang. 4th ed. Wiley Pub., Inc 2007 384p il (--For dummies) pa $24.99 *

005

1. Computer programming

ISBN 978-0-470-08870-8; 0-470-08870-2

LC 2006-932692

First published 1999 by IDG Books Worldwide

Includes CD-ROM

This guide explains "how computer programming works. . . . It explores the common parts of every computer programming language and how to write for multiple platforms like Windows, Mac OS X, or Linux." Publisher's note

005.8 Data security

Jennings, Charles

The hundredth window; protecting your privacy and security in the age of the Internet; {by} Charles Jennings and Lori Fena; foreword by Esther Dyson. Free Press 2000 xxv, 278p hardcover o.p. pa $19.95

005.8

1. Computer security

ISBN 0-684-83944-X; 978-0-7432-5498-4 (pa); 0-7432-5498-8 (pa)

LC 00-22527

The authors "look at the typical day of a high-tech user, noting the myriad ways in which such an individual exposes information about personal income, health, buying preferences, and daily activities. They counsel online consumers on how to protect their privacy by encrypting e-mail, checking for security provisions on Web sites, and updating browsers." Booklist

006.3 Artificial intelligence

Kurzweil, Raymond, 1948-

The age of spiritual machines; when computers exceed human intelligence; [by] Ray Kurzweil. Viking 1999 388p pa $16 hardcover o.p.

006.3

1. Artificial intelligence 2. Computers

ISBN 0-14-028202-5 (pa)   LC 98-38804

"Kurzweil's contention is that artifical intelligence will surpass human intelligence by 2100, and this work outlines the incipient technical developments, such as quantum computing and nanobots (atom-sized robots), that will enable it." Booklist

"This superb work is a thoughtful melding of technology, philosophy, ethics, and humanism." Libr J

Includes bibliographical references

Seife, Charles

Decoding the universe; how the new science of information is explaining everything in the cosmos, from our brains to black holes. Viking 2006 296p il $24.95 *

006.3

1. Information theory

ISBN 0-670-03441-X   LC 2005-42093

The author "explains how the concepts of information theory have begun to unlock many of the mysteries of the universe, from quantum mechanics to black holes and the likely end of the universe." Publ Wkly

Seife "does a good job of explaining many difficult concepts in ways that should be quite understandable to an interested layperson." Sci Books Films

Includes bibliographical references

006.7 Multimedia systems

Coombs, Karen A.

Library blogging; [by] Karen A. Coombs and Jason Griffey. Linworth Pub. 2008 151p il pa $39.95 *

006.7

1. Librarians—Weblogs

ISBN 978-1-58683-331-2; 1-58683-331-6

"This book is an overview of the world of blogs in libraries, including both use and technological discussions. The authors bring you the 'whys' and 'how to' of using a blog in a library context, including the different options available for a library blog, the appropriateness of each option, and the possibilities of each program or service." Publisher's note

Stone, Biz

Who let the blogs out? a hyperconnected peek at the world of Weblogs; with a foreword by Wil Wheaton. St. Martin's Griffin 2004 244p pa $13.95 *   **006.7**

1. Weblogs

ISBN 0-312-33000-6   LC 2004-50860

The author "presents a brief history of blogging in addition to covering the growth of the 'participatory web,' blogging in businesses, political blogging, and the 'blogosphere.' But he is at his best when providing advice to veteran and aspiring bloggers about blogrolling, blog culture dos and don'ts, easy HTML editing, and adding subtle advertising to blogs to create revenue. Stone's enthusiasm for his subject is infectious, and anyone who has toyed with the idea of starting a blog will be inspired to begin." Libr J

Includes bibliographical references

011 Bibliographies

American reference books annual 2008 edition, volume 39; Shannon Graff Hysell, associate editor. Libraries Unlimited 2008 xxv, 697p $135 *   **011**

1. Reference books—Bibliography

ISSN 0065-9959

ISBN 978-1-59158-691-3; 1-59158-691-7

Cumulative indexes available 1990-1994; 2000-2004

Annual. First published 1970

Editor: 1970-2001 Bohdan S. Wynar

"Each issue covers the reference book output (including reprints) of the previous year (i.e., the 1970 volume covers 1969 publications). Offers descriptive and evaluative notes (many of them signed by contributors), with references to selected reviews. Limited to titles in English. Classed arrangement; author-subject-title index." Guide to Ref Books. 11th edition

Guide to reference books; edited by Robert Balay; associate editor, Vee Friesner Carrington; with special editorial assistance by Murray S. Martin. 11th ed. American Lib. Assn. 1996 xxvii, 2020p $275   **011**

1. Reference books—Bibliography

ISBN 0-8389-0669-9   LC 95-26322

First published 1902

Nearly 16,000 entries provide details on general reference works and on reference books in the humanities, social and behavioral sciences, history and area studies, and science, technology, and medicine. Electronic resources are included

Includes bibliographical references

Magazines for libraries; for the general reader and school, junior college, college, university and public libraries; reviewing the best publications for serials collections since 1969; edited by Cheryl LaGuardia; created by Bill Katz. 16th ed. Bowker 2007 lii, 1045p $305 *

011

1. Periodicals—Bibliography

ISSN 0000-0914

ISBN 1-60030-105-3; 978-1-60030-105-6

First published 1969. Frequently revised

First-tenth edition edited by Bill Katz

"Annotated classified guide to recommended periodicals for the general reader and school, college, and public libraries. Provides comparative evaluations and grade and age-level recommendations for all periodicals included." N Y Public Libr Book of How & Where to Look It Up

Recommended reference books for small and medium-sized libraries and media centers; Shannon Graff Hysell, associate editor. Volume 28, 2008 ed. Libraries Unlimited 2008 xxi, 343p $70 *   **011**

1. Reference books—Bibliography 2. Reference books—Reviews

ISSN 0277-5948

ISBN 978-1-59158-692-0; 1-59158-692-5

Annual. First published 1981

Each annual volume includes reviews of about 550 titles chosen by the editor as the most valuable reference titles published during the previous year.

"Where budget restrictions are a consideration, this is an invaluable asset; for small libraries, a superior selection/acquisitions tool. Highly recommended." Voice Youth Advocates

Reference sources for small and medium-sized libraries; Jack O'Gorman, editor. 7th ed. American Library Association 2008 329p pa $88

011

1. Reference books—Bibliography

ISBN 978-0-8389-0943-0; 0-8389-0943-4

LC 2007-40026

First published 1969 with title: Reference books for small and medium-sized libraries

"Intended as a guide for college and large secondary school libraries as well as for public libraries. Items are grouped in subject categories and further subdivided by type of reference source or other suitable subdivision. Sections were prepared by individual compilers or teams of compilers. Good annotations; coverage of various subject fields is unusually even for a work of this kind; index of names and titles." Guide to Ref Books. 11th edition

Includes bibliographical references

Rosow, La Vergne

Accessing the classics; great reads for adults, teens, and English language learners. Libraries Unlimited 2006 301p pa $40 *   **011**

1. Best books 2. Reading—Remedial teaching

ISBN 1-56308-891-6; 978-1-56308-891-9

LC 2005-30838

"This collection of annotated titles aims at providing resources for anyone who works with inexperienced or low-literacy teenagers or adults." Voice Youth Advocates

"The intended audience is wide-ranging and includes anyone who wishes to foster language and literacy skills. Essential reading." Booklist

Includes bibliographical references

The **Standard** periodical directory. 31st ed. Oxbridge Communications Inc; distributed by Gale Res. 2008 $1795 **011**
1. Periodicals—Bibliography 2. Periodicals—Directories
ISSN 0085-6630
ISBN 978-1-89178-340-1; 1-89178-340-8
Annual. First published 1964/1965
A guide to more than 75,000 publications published in the United States and Canada.
"Alphabetical subject arrangement with index of titles and subjects. Information given includes name and address of publisher, editorial content and scope, year founded, frequency, subscription rate, total circulation, advertising rate, etc." Guide to Ref Books. 11th edition

Ulrich's periodicals directory 2008. Bowker 2007 4v $920 * **011**
1. Periodicals—Bibliography 2. Periodicals—Directories
ISSN 0000-2100
ISBN 978-1-6003-0104-5
Also available CD-ROM version and online
Annual since 1980. First published 1932 with title: Periodicals directory. Variant title: Ulrich's international periodicals directory
"Arranged by subject classification, includes magazines, journals, newsletters, newspapers, annuals and irregular serials published worldwide. Separate indices list refereed serials, serials available on CD-ROM, CD-ROM producers, serials available online, online services, cessations, publications of international organizations, International Standard Serial Numbers, and titles. Entries include title, circulation, frequency, complete publisher address, telephone, fax, email and URL, description, subscription price, with subscription and distribution addresses, telephone and fax information. Also includes bibliographic classification . . . abstracting and indexing information, document type notations, document delivery service availability, advertising rates and contact name, among other data." Publisher's note

011.6 General bibliographies of works for specific kinds of users and libraries

Children's catalog. 19th ed.; edited by Anne Price. H. W. Wilson Co. 2006 1670p (Core collection series) $195 * **011.6**
1. Children's literature—Bibliography 2. Classified catalogs 3. School libraries—Catalogs
ISBN 0-8242-1073-5; 978-0-8242-1073-1
Also available online
First published 1909
Kept up to date by annual supplements included in the price of main volume
This collection of recommended materials includes approximately 9,000 entries of books for children from preschool to grade six including fiction and nonfiction works, story collections, picture books, and graphic novels. Entries contain full bibliographic information, Dewey Decimal Classification number, subject headings, reading level, descriptive, and when possible, critical annotations.

Also included are professional literature for the children's librarian, lists of recommended periodicals for children and for professionals, and of Web resources.
"This work as been a mainstay for almost 100 years . . . in supplying authoritative and dependable information on collection evaluation and development for children's libraries in elementary schools and public libraries. . . . An essential professional tool for all libraries serving children." Am Ref Book Annu, 2007

Senior high core collection; a selection guide; edited by Raymond W. Barber and Patrice Bartell. 17th ed. H.W. Wilson Co. 2007 1456p (Core Collections series) $245 * **011.6**
1. Classified catalogs 2. High school libraries—Catalogs 3. Young adult literature—Bibliography
ISBN 978-0-8242-1086-1   LC 2007-31812
Also available online
First published 1926-28 with title: Standard catalog for high school libraries; previous edition published 2002 with title: Senior high school library catalog
Kept up to date by annual supplements included in price of main volume
This collection of recommended materials includes more than 6,200 titles and over 4,500 analytical entries of books for grades nine through twelve. Entries contain full bibliographic information, Abridged Dewey Decimal Classification number, subject headings, rosettes for most highly recommended titles, descriptive, and when available, critical annotations. Includes lists of recommended periodicals and electronic resources.

Silvey, Anita
100 best books for children. Houghton Mifflin 2004 184p $20 **011.6**
1. Children's literature—Bibliography 2. Best books
ISBN 0-618-27889-3   LC 2003-56899
"A former editor and reviewer for The Horn Book Magazine recommends one hundred of the best books for children, including a variety of works to suit diverse interests, reading levels, and special needs." Publisher's note
The author's "long experience as a book reviewer and editor makes her list pretty much spot-on. . . . Each title gets a short essay that not only discusses the book and what it has meant to its audience but that also supplies wonderful behind-the-scenes information. . . . A helpful list, 'Beyond the 100 Best,' points parents in the right direction for more good reads." Booklist
Includes bibliographical references

015.73 Bibliographies and catalogs of works issued or printed in the United States

Books in print 2008-2009. Bowker 2008 7v set $980 **015.73**
1. Bibliography
ISSN 0068-0214
ISBN 978-0-8352-4922-5
Also available CD-ROM version and online
Annual. First published 1948

Books in print 2008-2009—*Continued*

Updated by Books in print Supplement (3v) published annually in Spring, available at $546 (ISBN 978-0-8352-4937-9)

Lists titles available during the current year from American publishers, supplying such information as authors, co-authors, title, price, publisher, year of publication, and International Standard Book Numbers of cooperating publishers

The **Complete** directory of large print books and serials 2008. Bowker 2008 $375   **015.73**
1. Large print books—Bibliography
ISSN 0000-1120
ISBN 978-0-8352-4941-6
Annual. First published 1970 with title: Large type books in print

This directory covers books, periodicals, and newspapers printed in 14 point type or larger. Books are indexed by subject, author and title, with complete bibliographic and ordering information

Forthcoming books. Bowker $299.95 per year
015.73
1. Bibliography
ISSN 0015-8119
Bimonthly. First published 1966

This supplement to Books in print, and Subject guide to Books in print, provides a cumulative author-title-subject index to books that are to appear in the next five-month period. Information includes price, publisher, ISBN and LC control numbers and expected publication date

016.327   Bibliographies of foreign relations

American foreign relations since 1600; a guide to the literature; Robert L. Beisner, editor. 2nd ed. ABC-CLIO 2003 2v set $255   **016.327**
1. United States—Foreign relations—Bibliography
ISBN 1-57607-080-8   LC 2003-8684
Also available online

First published 1983 under the editorship of Richard Dean Burns with title: Guide to American foreign relations since 1700

"The arrangement is essentially chronological, with the first of 32 chapters covering reference works and bibliographies and the second chapter, overviews and synthesis. Individual chapter editors . . . include journal articles, essays in collections, and dissertations. . . . Each chapter begins with a brief statement of the editor's selection criteria. Works in related specialties are listed for their influence on foreign relations, including Native American relations, gender and ethnic issues, and religious groups. . . . This is an excellent book; imaginative users will find ways to apply these listings to a wide variety of projects." Libr J

Includes bibliographical references

016.381   Bibliographies of internal commerce (Domestic trade)

The **directory** of mail order catalogs 2008; [editor: Richard Gottlieb] 22nd ed. Grey House Pub. 2007 1199p $250 *   **016.381**
1. Mail-order business
ISSN 0899-5710
ISBN 1-59237-202-3; 978-1-59237-202-7
Also available online
Annual. First published 1981. Editors vary. New edition in preparation
On cover: Includes separate section on business to business catalogs
"Lists companies by categories that sell directly to consumers; indexed by product and company name." Guide to Ref Books. 11th edition

016.39426   Bibliographies of holidays

World holiday, festival, and calendar books; edited by Tanya Gulevich. Omnigraphics 1998 477p $55   **016.39426**
1. Holidays—Bibliography
ISBN 0-7808-0073-7   LC 97-37784
Subtitle: An annotated bibliography of more than 1,000 books on contemporary and historic religious, folk, ethnic, and national holidays, festivals, celebrations, holy days, commemorations, seasonal celebrations, and calendar systems from around the world, arranged by topic, supplemented by descriptive lists of periodicals, associations, and web sites, and indexed by author, title, and subject

016.613   Bibliographies of general and personal hygiene

Consumer health information source book; edited by Alan M. Rees. 7th ed. Greenwood Press 2003 325p pa $65   **016.613**
1. Health—Information services 2. Medicine—Information services
ISBN 1-57356-509-1   LC 2003-40871
"An Oryx book"
First published 1981 by Bowker
"The book contains more than 2,000 descriptive evaluations of 385 books, 165 popular health magazines and newsletters, 1,500 English-language pamphlets, 850 Spanish-language pamphlets, 215 toll-free information hotlines, 325 health resource and referral organizations, 31 online and fax-based information services and CD-ROMs, and 40 medical textbooks, monographs, and journals. . . . The *Consumer Health Information Source Book* remains a key resource for all libraries that provide health information to the general public." Booklist

Includes bibliographical references

016.7 Bibliographies of the arts

Pawuk, Michael G.
Graphic novels; a genre guide to comic books, manga, and more; foreword by Brian K. Vaughn. Libraries Unlimited 2007 xxxv, 633p il (Genreflecting advisory series) $65 *

016.7

1. Graphic novels—Bibliography
ISBN 1-59158-132-X; 978-1-59158-132-1

LC 2006-34156

"This guide is intended to help you start, update, or maintain a graphic novel collection and advise readers about the genre. It covers more than 2,400 titles, including series titles, and organizes them according to genre, subgenre, and theme—from super-heroes and adventure to crime, humor, and nonfiction. Reading levels, awards/recognition, and core titles are identified; and tie-ins with gaming, film, anime, and television are noted." Publisher's note
Includes bibliographical references

016.79143 Bibliographies of motion pictures

Beck, Jerry
The animated movie guide; contributing writers, Martin Goodman . . . [et al.] Chicago Review Press 2005 xx, 348p il pa $26.95 *

016.79143

1. Animated films
ISBN 1-55652-591-5

LC 2005-8629

Also available online in an abbreviated version
"An A Cappella book"
"The book offers a chronological list of the included films, followed by an alphabetical list of entries for each. Each entry includes title and production credits, consumer tips, star and MPAA ratings, story synopses, film comments, and additional credits." Choice
"A good choice for collections of popular culture, film studies, and graphic arts, this will also be a popular title for fans of animated film and parents who want quality entertainment for the kids." Booklist

016.8 Bibliographies of literature

Anatomy of wonder; a critical guide to science fiction; [edited by] Neil Barron. 5th ed. Libraries Unlimited 2004 995p $80 *

016.8

1. Science fiction—Bibliography 2. Science fiction—History and criticism
ISBN 1-59158-171-0

First published 1976 by Bowker
"Critical discussions of more than 1,400 science fiction novels, story collections, and anthologies, along with a . . . survey of the 'secondary' literature, chapters on teaching science fiction, titles appropriate for—or appealing to—teens, a directory of libraries containing significant collections of science fiction, and award-winning titles and titles of literary merit. Author, title, and theme indexes [are provided]." Publisher's note

Bleiler, Richard
Reference and research guide to mystery and detective fiction; [by] Richard J. Bleiler. 2nd ed. Libraries Unlimited 2003 828p (Reference sources in the humanities series) $78 *

016.8

1. Mystery fiction—Bibliography
ISBN 1-56308-924-6

LC 2003-58905

First published 1999 with title: Reference guide to mystery and detective fiction
"Separate chapters cover sources as diverse as maps and atlases, writers' associations and awards, character indexes, calendars, and quotations in addition to guides, encyclopedias, and dictionaries." Choice
Includes bibliographical references

Bouricius, Ann
The romance readers' advisory; the librarian's guide to love in the stacks. American Lib. Assn. 2000 107p pa $56

016.8

1. Love stories—Bibliography 2. Love stories—History and criticism
ISBN 0-8389-0779-2

LC 99-57295

The author provides "information about the highly popular romance genre and its diverse subgenres; addresses key issues regarding the establishment of a romance collection; and, in a series of reading lists, recommends outstanding romances of all flavors for avid fans and new converts." Booklist

Burgess, Michael, 1948-
Reference guide to science fiction, fantasy, and horror; [by] Michael Burgess, Lisa R. Bartle. 2nd ed. Libraries Unlimited 2002 605p (Reference sources in the humanities series) $75

016.8

1. Science fiction—Bibliography
ISBN 1-56308-548-8

LC 2002-151707

First published 1992
A guide to "amateur and professional reference materials in the related fields of science fiction, fantasy, and horror. . . . The book is divided into 32 sections . . . including 'Encyclopedias and Dictionaries,' 'Magazine and Anthology Indexes,' 'Subject Bibliographies,' 'Character Dictionaries and Author Cyclopedias,' and 'Film and Television Catalogs.' . . . Complete bibliographic citations are followed by literature and readable annotations that vary from a brief note to three or four lengthy paragraphs. The annotations consist of description and succinct analysis of the strengths and weaknesses of each item. . . . 'Major On-Line Resources,' is a particularly valuable examination of 20 Web sites." Booklist
Includes bibliographical references

Fiction catalog; edited by John Greenfieldt. 15th ed. H. W. Wilson 2006 1317p $240 *

016.8

1. Fiction—Bibliography 2. Best books
ISBN 0-8242-1055-7; 978-0-8242-1055-7

LC 2006-549

Also available online
"Standard catalog series"
First published 1908
Kept up to date by annual supplements included in price of main catalog

Fiction catalog—*Continued*

This catalog "features classic and contemporary works of fiction recommended for a general adult audience, written in or translated into English. . . . Fiction Catalog provides entries for individual novels and analytic entries for novellas and novels contained in composite works. More than 8,000 titles are listed in the main hardcover volume, and more than 2,000 new titles are listed in three annual paperback supplements. Entries provide complete bibliographic data, price, descriptive annotations, and evaluative quotations from a review when available." Publisher's note

Fonseca, Anthony J.

Hooked on horror; a guide to reading interests in horror fiction. 2nd ed. Libraries Unlimited 2003 xxiii, 464p il $55   **016.8**

1. Horror films
ISBN 1-56308-904-1
First published 1999

"Although we . . . refer to this guide as a second edition . . . it is, for all practical purposes, volume 2 of Hooked on horror. This is because space constraints make it impossible for us to list most of the titles that are found in the first edition. Therefore, readers' advisors . . . who own the first edition are advised to use this guide as a supplement rather than as a stand-alone product." pxxii

"Focusing on titles published in the last decade and older classics that are currently in print or commonly available in libraries, the authors cover 13 popular subgenres of horror fiction, including vampires and werewolves, techno horror, ghosts and haunted houses, and small town horror. . . . Special features of this book . . . {include} the inclusion of graphic novels; indications of audio, e-book, and large print formats." Publisher's note

Frolund, Tina

Genrefied classics; a guide to reading interests in classical literature. Libraries Unlimited 2007 xxiv, 365p (Genreflecting advisory series) $45 *
     016.8

1. Fiction—Bibliography
ISBN 1-59158-172-9; 978-1-59158-172-7
     LC 2006-33740

"By identifying the genre characteristics of more than 400 classic fiction works, and organizing titles according to these features, this guide helps readers find the type of books they enjoy." Publisher's note
Includes bibliographical references

Herald, Diana Tixier

Fluent in fantasy; the next generation; [by] Diana Tixier Herald and Bonnie Kunzel. Libraries Unlimited 2008 312p (Genreflecting advisory series) $52   **016.8**

1. Fantasy fiction—Bibliography
ISBN 978-1-59158-198-7; 1-59158-198-2
     LC 2007-28840
First published 1999

"More than 2,000 titles are arranged by author in 14 thematic chapters, including 'Epic Fantasy,' 'Arthurian Legend,' and 'Time Travel Romance.' . . . An essential collection development and readers'-advisory tool." Booklist
Includes bibliographical references

Genreflecting; a guide to popular reading interests; edited by Wayne A. Wiegand. 6th ed. Libraries Unlimited 2006 562p (Genreflecting advisory series) $60; pa $45 *   **016.8**

1. Fiction—Bibliography 2. Fiction—History and criticism 3. Books and reading
ISBN 1-59158-224-5; 1-59158-286-5 (pa)
     LC 2005-30804

First published 1982 under the authorship of Betty Rosenberg

A listing of recommended titles in such genres as crime, adventure, romance, science fiction, Christian fiction, fantasy, horror, and their subgenres. Besides information on authors and titles, the volume provides information on anthologies, bibliographies, critical works, encyclopedias, organizations, and publishers.

Includes bibliographical references

Strictly science fiction; a guide to reading interests; [by] Diana Tixier Herald, Bonnie Kunzel. Libraries Unlimited 2002 xxii, 297p (Genreflecting advisory series) $55 *   **016.8**

1. Science fiction—Bibliography 2. Science fiction—History and criticism
ISBN 1-56308-893-2   LC 2002-3186

"The purpose of this volume is to serve as both a readers' advisory tool and as a guide for collection development. It lists approximately 900 mainly adult titles currently in print or likely to be found in library collections, and is organized by subgenres such as action/adventure, high tech, and short stories." SLJ

"Good indexing, by author, title, subject, and character name, along with chapters devoted to books written for children and young adults and genre-blended books (such as science fiction/ romance or science fiction/mystery), sets this reference apart." Libr J

Includes bibliographical references

Hollands, Neil

Read on . . . fantasy fiction; reading lists for every taste. Libraries Unlimited 2007 210p (Read on series) pa $30   **016.8**

1. Fantasy fiction—Bibliography
ISBN 978-1-59158-330-1; 1-59158-330-6
     LC 2007-7841

This book "organizes more than 800 titles into over 100 lists, in such categories as 'The Magic of Threes: Fantasy's Best Trilogies,' 'The Fellowship is the Thing: Companions on a Quest,' 'Fan-to-Sea-Nautical Fantasy,' and 'When Groan Men Scry: Puns as a Fantasy Tradition.'" Publisher's note

"Librarians who do readers advisory for teens or adults will wonder how they ever got along without this funny, opinionated, wide-angle guide." SLJ

Johnson, Sarah L., 1969-
Historical fiction; a guide to the genre. Libraries Unlimited 2005 xxi, 813p (Genreflecting advisory series) $75 *   **016.8**
1. Historical fiction—Bibliography
ISBN 1-59158-129-X   LC 2005-47483
"Each category, e.g., 'Traditional Historical Novels,' 'Historical Thrillers,' 'Time-Slip Novels,' is subdivided further by world region and historical era. . . . The annotations also indicate benchmarks of the genre, award winners, and titles recommended for young adults and reading groups. . . . This is an excellent resource." Choice
For a fuller review, see: Booklist, Sept. 15, 2005
Includes bibliographical references

Pearl, Nancy
Now read this II; a guide to mainstream fiction, 1990-2001. Libraries Unlimited 2002 300p il $55
016.8
1. Fiction—Bibliography 2. Best books
ISBN 1-56038-867-3   LC 2002-274079
Also available Now read this, published 1999 covering the years 1978-1998
This is an annotated list of 500 books categorized by setting, story, characterization, or language. "New features include a YA designation for selected titles, a section on fiction trends, and two appendixes, one on genre bridges (books that share elements with genre fiction) and one on book groups. Like others in the Genreflecting series, this work is a truly useful tool." Booklist

Ramsdell, Kristin, 1940-
Romance fiction; a guide to the genre. Libraries Unlimited 1999 435p (Genreflecting advisory series) $47.50   **016.8**
1. Love stories—Bibliography 2. Love stories—History and criticism
ISBN 1-56308-335-3   LC 99-10207
First published 1987 with title: Happily ever after: a guide to reading interests in romance fiction
"Part 1 has several chapters that discuss the definition and appeal of romance and contain general information about advising readers and building collections. Part 2, 'The Literature,' has chapters devoted to 13 specific subgenres of romance, from contemporary to ethnic/multicultural. . . . Part 3, 'Research Aids,' surveys the secondary literature (histories and critical guides, dissertations, biographical sources, etc.), periodicals, organizations, awards, publishers, and other resources. . . . Libraries will want to hold on to their copies of *Happily Ever After,* which this new edition builds upon rather than supersedes." Booklist

Trott, Barry
Read on . . . crime fiction; reading lists for every taste. Libraries Unlimited 2008 146p (Read on series) pa $30   **016.8**
1. Mystery fiction—Bibliography
ISBN 978-1-59158-373-8   LC 2007-33858
The author organizes recommended crime fiction titles by "five 'appeal characteristics' commonly employed by

RA professionals: story, character, setting, mood, and language. Under these broad categories, he offers an assortment of creatively titled reading lists ('Serf and Turf: Medieval Mysteries') that illustrate aspects of one of the appeal factors. Arrows designate one title per list selected as a good starting point for that category. . . . Both readers' advisors and crime-fiction fans will find all sorts of inventive ways to use this book, including, of course, compiling their own lists of titles or categories that should have been represented." Booklist

What do I read next? 2007; a reader's guide to current genre fiction, fantasy, western, romance, horror, mystery, science fiction; [by] Neil Barron [et al.] Gale Res. 2007 2v ea $185
016.8
1. Fiction—Bibliography
ISSN 1052-2212
ISBN 978-0-7876-9025-0 (v1); 0-7876-9025-2 (v1); 978-0-7876-9026-7 (v2); 0-7876-9026-0 (v2)
Also available online
Annual. First published 1991 for 1989-1990
A guide to locating new fiction titles in specific genres. Arranged by author within six genre sections, each entry provides publisher and publication date, series name, major characters, time period, geographic setting, review citations, and related books.

020.5 Library and information sciences—Serial publications

The **Bowker** annual library and book trade almanac 2008. 53rd ed. Information Today 2008 863p $199.95   **020.5**
1. Libraries 2. Book industry
ISSN 0068-0540
ISBN 978-1-57387-321-5; 1-57387-321-7
Annual. First published 1956 by Bowker. Title varies
"A compendium of statistical and directory information relating to most aspects of librarianship and the book trade. Professional reports from the field; international library news; library legislation; grants; survey articles of developments during the preceding year." Ref Sources for Small & Medium-sized Libr. 6th edition

021.7 Promotion of libraries, archives, information centers

Thenell, Jan
The library's crisis communications planner; a PR guide for handling every emergency. American Library Association 2004 77p il pa $25
021.7
1. Libraries—Public relations
ISBN 0-8389-0870-5   LC 2004-10891
Offering "advice, firsthand experience, scenarios, and guidelines for communicating effectively before, during, and after a crisis or crisis-producing events, ... [the author's] guide is a ready-made workshop on how to establish and maintain relationships with the media, including how to write a press release, how to keep all staff

Thenell, Jan—*Continued*
informed and aware of what to do when an emergency occurs, and how to make sure library board members and other community stakeholders are notified and/or involved. Whether or not you have a public relations office or officer, this slim volume is a must for your professional shelf." Libr J
Includes bibliographical references

Wolfe, Lisa Ann
Library public relations, promotions, and communications; a how-to-do-it manual. 2nd ed. Neal-Schuman Publishers 2005 230p (How-to-do-it manuals for librarians) pa $65 *   **021.7**
1. Libraries—Public relations
ISBN 1-55570-471-9   LC 2004-25944
First published 1997
"The book is divided into two parts—'Planning and Evaluation' and 'Strategies and Methodologies'—with many examples of successful communicating and the impact and changes brought by technology. Ideas on putting together a communications plan, creating clear signage and print products, effectively using a library's Web site, and communicating during a crisis will be helpful for all types of libraries and positions." Booklist
Includes bibliographical references

023 Personnel management (Human resource management)

Cohn, John M., 1943-
Staffing the modern library; a how-to-do-it manual; by John M. Cohn [and] Ann L. Kelsey. Neal-Schuman Publishers 2005 105p pa $75 *
                                          023
1. Librarians 2. Libraries—Automation
ISBN 1-55570-511-1   LC 2004-53174
"Comprised of 10 parts, the text discusses staffing as it relates to libraries as 'lean' organizations (ones that are flexible, adaptable, and resourceful), staff competencies, competency-based job descriptions, out and in sourcing, Web site development, digital resources, staffing options, and the expanding definition of the term staff. In addition to its well-organized design, clear content, and focused scope, the book provides practical, hands-on information in worksheets, tables, and planning tools." Booklist
Includes bibliographical references

Giesecke, Joan
Fundamentals of library supervision. American Library Association 2005 166p il (ALA fundamental series) pa $42 *   **023**
1. Libraries—Administration 2. Personnel management
ISBN 0-8389-0895-0   LC 2004-24654
This book teaches library "supervisors how to motivate staff, encourage a positive work ethic, and build teams. The advice on interviewing, hiring, training, and working with new employees is highly relevant. . . . New managers needing an outline of the fundamental principles of supervision as well as old hands who can

benefit from a refresher course will find all the practical advice they need to accomplish their jobs." Libr J
Includes bibliographical references

025 Operations of libraries, archives, information centers

Bolan, Kimberly
Technology made simple; an improvement guide for small and medium libraries; [by] Kimberly Bolan and Robert Cullin. American Library Association 2007 213p il $40   **025**
1. Libraries—Automation 2. Information technology
ISBN 0-8389-0920-5; 978-0-8389-0920-1
                                          LC 2006-13191
The authors present an "overview of basic public library technologies. . . . Using examples from a plethora of small- and medium-sized libraries to illustrate how such specific issues as self-check, hiring for attitude, tech policies, staff and public training, and formal planning can be approached as doable and nonthreatening to the non-specialist, this guide is an excellent demonstration of how order can make big issues approachable. . . . Libraries should purchase it for their staff collections but also make reading and implementing various suggestions part of their work plans." Voice Youth Advocates
Includes bibliographical references

Technology for the rest of us; a primer on computer technologies for the low-tech librarian; edited by Nancy Courtney. Libraries Unlimited 2005 184p pa $40   **025**
1. Library information networks 2. Libraries—Automation 3. Computers 4. Telecommunication
ISBN 1-59158-233-4   LC 2005-18009
"The essays here are not meant to make you an expert but to give you a basic introduction to some of the current technologies impacting libraries and their patrons, including computer networks, wireless networks, network security, OpenURL, RFID (radio frequency identification), blogs and RSS, XML, Open Archive Initiatives Protocol for Metadata Harvesting, local digital repositories, adaptive or assistive technology, and digital image management. . . . The articles are brief and clearly written, and computer jargon is defined and explained. Each chapter lists references for further information for both print and online resources, and there is a selected bibliography and glossary at the end of the book." Libr J

Ward, Diane, 1971-
The complete RFID handbook; a manual and DVD for assessing, implementing, and managing radio frequency identification technologies in libraries. Neal-Schuman Publishers 2007 261p il pa $75   **025**
1. Radio frequency identification systems
ISBN 978-1-55570-602-9; 1-55570-602-9
                                          LC 2007-7651
Includes DVD
"Containing 10 chapters, each with references, this guide is a very timely resource on . . . [radio frequency identification] technology, with much practical informa-

Ward, Diane, 1971-—*Continued*

tion, including real-life situations gathered from interviews. For libraries even remotely considering RFID, this is the book to have, since it incorporates everything from developing a plan for specific types of libraries to vendor selection, installation, and implementation." Booklist

Includes bibliographical references

025.04 Information storage and retrieval systems

Dornfest, Rael

Google hacks; [by] Rael Dornfest, Paul Bausch, and Tara Calishain. 3rd ed. O'Reilly 2006 xxxii, 510p il $24.99   **025.04**

1. Google (Web site) 2. Internet searching

ISBN 0-596-52706-3; 978-0-596-52706-8

LC 2006-285771

First published 2003 under the authorship of Tara Calishain and Rael Dornfest

This guide to the search engine Google gives instructions on how to use such tools as Google Earth, Google Maps, Google Blog Search, Video Search, and Music Search, as well as different ways of using Google products, such as using Google to keep track of new blog posts and building customized Google maps.

Includes bibliographical references

Gale directory of databases. Gale Res. 2008 2v in 4 parts set $585   **025.04**

1. Information systems—Directories

ISSN 1066-8934

ISBN 978-0-7876-9755-6; 0-7876-9755-9

Also available online as part of the Gale directory library

Annual. First published 1993. Formed by the merger of Directory of online databases, Directory of portable databases, and Computer-readable databases

Contents: v1 Online databases; v2 CD-ROM, diskette, magnetic tape, handheld, and batch access database products

"Descriptive entries include such details as producer name and contact information, summary of content, database language, geographic coverage, year first available, time span, updating, availability, rates, and more." Publisher's note

Hernon, Peter, 1944-

U.S. government on the Web; getting the information you need; [by] Peter Hernon, Robert E. Dugan, John A. Shuler. 3rd ed. Libraries Unlimited 2003 xxvi, 465p il pa $50

025.04

1. Government information—Directories 2. Internet 3. Web sites

ISBN 1-59158-086-2   LC 2003-51584

First published 1999

This guide to U.S. government information on the Web contains information from the current administration and includes material on the Patriot Act, the E-Government Act of 2002, and the Department of Homeland Security. The authors provide Web sites and suggest

strategies for effectively accessing and using government information online.

Includes bibliographical references

The **Medical** Library Association encyclopedic guide to searching and finding health information on the Web; edited by P.F. Anderson and Nancy J. Allee. Neal-Schuman Publishers 2004 3v pa set $395   **025.04**

1. Medicine—Internet resources 2. Health—Internet resources 3. Medical care—Internet resources

ISBN 1-55570-494-8   LC 2004-42862

Also available CD-ROM edition $395 (ISBN 1-55570-495-6) and print and CD-ROM edition $495 (ISBN 1-55570-496-4)

Contents: v1 Search strategies/quick reference guide; v2 Diseases and disorders/mental health and mental disorders; v3 Health and wellness/life stages and reproduction/cumulative index

"The three volumes cover search techniques as well as information about research on specific subject areas. . . . [This set] lives up to its title. Covering a wide range of health and medical topics, it will help both librarians and consumers search with confidence." Booklist

Includes bibliographical references

Norlin, Elaina

Usability testing for library websites; a hands-on guide; [by] Elaina Norlin, CM! Winters. American Lib. Assn. 2002 69p il pa $35   **025.04**

1. Web sites

ISBN 0-8389-3511-7   LC 2001-33817

"Four goals are explored in improving library sites: usefulness, effectiveness, learn-ability, and user satisfaction. . . . Steps for recruitment of a testing team, development of sample questions and tasks, and evaluation of results are included." SLJ

Includes bibliographical references

Smith, J. Douglas, 1965-

World War II on the Web; a guide to the very best sites; [by] J. Douglas Smith and Richard Jensen. Scholarly Resources 2003 207p $65; pa $23.95   **025.04**

1. World War, 1939-1945—Internet resources 2. Web sites

ISBN 0-8420-5020-5; 0-8420-5021-3 (pa)

LC 2002-29236

"Provides descriptions and ratings for 'the top 100+' sites, plus listings for an additional 140 'sites worth a visit.' Arrangement is topical, and separate ratings are given for content, aesthetics, and navigation. Each topical chapter includes a fairly extensive list of suggested readings, a nice addition that we don't often find in Web site guides. A CD-ROM, included with the guide, links to all the sites that are listed." Booklist

Includes bibliographical references

The **United** States government Internet manual 2007. Bernan 2007 pa $59 *   **025.04**

1. Government information—Directories 2. Internet 3. Web sites

ISSN 1547-2892

ISBN 1-59888-073-X; 978-1-59888-073-1

Annual. First published 2004

The United States government Internet manual 2007—*Continued*

Continues Government information on the Internet

This is a resource to "federal government data online, including laws, pamphlets, press releases, numerous statistics, grant and fellowship information, dictionaries, and much more. . . . This reference is suitable for libraries offering Internet access, but it will also prove valuable to teachers, students, and even children (included are government sites containing online educational games, quizzes, and resources)." Libr J

025.1　Administration

Block, Marylaine, 1943-

The thriving library; successful strategies for challenging times. Information Today 2007 xxi, 324p il pa $39.50　　　　　**025.1**

1. Public libraries 2. Libraries and community

ISBN 978-1-57387-277-5　　　　LC 2007-1170

Contents: Focusing on children and teens — The library as place — Partnerships — Marketing the library — Emphasizing the economic value of the library — Library 2.0 — Outreach to nontraditional users — Helping the community achieve its aspirations

To write this book, the author "identified over 100 thriving libraries. . . . She then designed a survey, asking directors of the selected libraries about their strategies for success. The libraries represent small towns, urban areas, modest and sizable budgets, and systems scattered over multiple towns. The result is an excellent volume of tried-and-true ideas for public libraries of all sizes seeking to garner community support and funding." Libr J

Includes bibliographical references

Casey, Michael E., 1967-

Library 2.0; a guide to participatory library service; [by] Michael E. Casey, Laura C. Savastinuk. Information Today, Inc. 2007 xxv, 172p il pa $29.50　　　　　**025.1**

1. Library services 2. Libraries—Public relations

ISBN 978-1-57387-297-3; 1-57387-297-0

LC 2007-5247

"The authors emphasize regular evaluation and retooling of existing services and provide a model for identifying and implementing new services with input from library users, nonusers, and all levels of staff. Topics covered include instituting and managing change, incorporating technology into the Library 2.0 model, and getting buy-in from administrators, staff, and users. The focus is on public libraries, but the concepts could be applied to any type of institution." Libr J

"This title should be required reading for professional library staffs struggling with change and organizational restructure." Libr Media Connect

Includes bibliographical references

Curzon, Susan Carol

Managing change; a how-to-do-it manual for librarians. rev. ed. Neal-Schuman Publishers 2005 129p (How-to-do-it manuals for librarians) pa $55　　　　　**025.1**

1. Libraries—Administration

ISBN 1-55570-553-7　　　　LC 2005-22846

First published 1989

The author "outlines the step-by-step processes and . . . instructions necessary for conceptualizing the issues; planning; preparing; decision-making; controlling resistance; and implementing changes. Practical guidance for dealing with technology's impact on libraries, applying the latest research in change management, and developing new strategies for coping with change are included." Publisher's note

"The real-world approach makes the book a valuable addition to the professional collection." Booklist

Includes bibliographical references

Gerding, Stephanie K.

Grants for libraries; a how-to-do-it manual. Neal-Schuman Publishers 2006 xxiii, 252p il (How-to-do-it manuals for librarians) $99.95　　　　　**025.1**

1. Grants-in-aid 2. Fund raising

ISBN 1-55570-535-9　　　　LC 2005-27980

Includes CD-ROM

"The authors of this book take the reader through every phase of the grant-writing cycle, offering details, examples, and relevant tools. Dividing the process into 10 steps, each covered in a separate chapter, the book offers practical advice and easy-to-follow suggestions appropriate for every type of library. . . . This book should be at the side of every grant-writing librarian." Booklist

Includes bibliographical references

Hallam, Arlita

Managing budgets and finances; a how-to-do-it manual for librarians and information professionals. Neal-Schuman Publishers 2005 233p il (How-to-do-it manuals for librarians) pa $65 *　　　　　**025.1**

1. Library finance

ISBN 1-55570-519-7

"This budgeting manual . . . offers the new or seasoned library administrators, board members, department heads, or finance professionals a way to budget carefully and clearly by offering a variety of strategies, definitions, and suggestions. The manual is divided into three parts: basics for librarians, special topics in financial management for libraries, and alternative library funding." Booklist

Includes bibliographical references

Matthews, Joseph R.

Strategic planning and management for library managers. Libraries Unlimited 2005 150p il pa $40　　　　　**025.1**

1. Libraries—Administration

ISBN 1-59158-231-8　　　　LC 2005-10099

Matthews, Joseph R.—*Continued*
"Part 1 defines a strategy, addresses the need for one, and presents 10 distinct schools of strategic thought. Part 2 differentiates between strategic planning and long-range planning, discusses the benefits of strategic planning, and identifies approaches to preparing and implementing such plans. Part 3 focuses on performance measures, ways to communicate the value of libraries to others, and the 'culture of assessment,' an environment where all library staff are routinely involved in the evaluation process. Information presented throughout the book is clear, practical, readily accessible, well documented, and amply supported by notes, tables, figures, diagrams, and quotes." Booklist

Our new public, a changing clientele; bewildering issues or new challenges for managing libraries? edited by James R. Kennedy, Lisa Vardaman, and Gerard B. McCabe. Libraries Unlimited 2008 305p (Libraries Unlimited library management collection) $45 **025.1**
1. Libraries—Administration 2. Libraries and students
ISBN 978-1-59158-407-0 LC 2007-35907
"Several chapters in this . . . title discuss the milennials—children of the baby boomers—and digital natives and how they have already had an impact on library service. . . . Each chapter offers practical advice based on experiences, and each includes a list of references. Library managers and those aspiring to be managers will find help in providing services for a younger demographic." Booklist
Includes bibliographical references

Stueart, Robert D.
Library and information center management. 7th ed. Libraries Unlimited 2007 xxviii, 492p (Library and information science text series) $70; pa $50 * **025.1**
1. Libraries—Administration
ISBN 978-1-59158-408-7; 978-1-59158-406-3 (pa) LC 2007-7922
This "covers all the essential functions involved in library management. New theories, concepts, and practices currently being developed and used are included. . . . Both novices and veteran managers will find this to be a valuable tool." Booklist
Includes bibliographical references

025.2 Acquisitions and collection development

Baker, Nicholson
Double fold; libraries and the assault on paper. Random House 2001 370p il pa $14 hardcover o.p. **025.2**
1. Libraries—Special collections 2. Paper 3. Library resources—Conservation and restoration
ISBN 0-375-72621-7 (pa) LC 00-59171
Baker criticizes libraries for discarding books, magazines and newspapers and disputes the arguments for doing so "that libraries are running out of space, and that

paper, because of its acid content, is rapidly turning to dust. . . . What the Library of Congress spends in a year on microfilming would, (according to Baker), buy a storage facility 'the size of a Home Depot, which would hold a century of newsprint.' . . . Librarians, he says, 'have lied to us shamelessly about the extent of paper's fragility, and they continue to lie about it.'" N Y Times Book Rev
Includes bibliographical references

Brenner, Robin E., 1977-
Understanding manga and anime. Libraries Unlimited 2007 335p il $40 * **025.2**
1. Manga 2. Anime 3. Libraries—Special collections—Graphic novels 4. Libraries—Collection development
ISBN 978-1-59158-332-5 LC 2007-9773
Contents: Short history of manga and anime — Manga and anime vocabulary — Culture clash: East meets West — Adventures with ninjas and schoolgirls: humor and realism — Samurai and shogun: action, war, and historical fiction — Giant robots and nature spirits: science fiction, fantasy, and legends — Understanding fans and fan culture — Draw in a crowd: promotion and programs — Collection development
The author "provides thorough explanations of manga and anime vocabulary, potential censorship issues because of cultural disparities, and typical Manga conventions. . . . No professional collection could possibly be complete without this all-inclusive and exceptional work." Voice Youth Advocates

Foerstel, Herbert N.
Banned in the U.S.A; a reference guide to book censorship in schools and public libraries. rev and expanded ed. Greenwood Press 2002 xxvii, 296p $54.95 * **025.2**
1. Books—Censorship 2. Libraries—Censorship
ISBN 0-313-31166-8 LC 2001-55620
First published 1994
This volume provides "a survey of major book-banning incidents in the United States, accessible background material on the legal history of book banning . . . interviews with banned writers, and a synopsis of the 50 most frequently challenged books from the period 1996-2000." Libr J
"Librarians and teachers need this book, but patrons who want to better understand the threats to their First Amendment rights should be led to it as well." SLJ
Includes bibliographical references

Greiner, Tony
Analyzing library collection use with Excel. American Library Association 2007 167p il pa $40 * **025.2**
1. Library circulation 2. Libraries—Collection development 3. Excel (Computer program)
ISBN 0-8389-0933-7 (pa); 978-0-8389-0933-1 LC 2006-101539
The authors "show how to use Excel® to translate circulation and collection data into meaningful reports for making collection management decisions." Publisher's note
Includes bibliographical references

Slote, Stanley J.

Weeding library collections; library weeding methods. 4th ed. Libraries Unlimited 1997 xxi, 240p il $69 *   **025.2**

1. Libraries—Collection development

ISBN 1-56308-511-9   LC 96-54865

First published 1975

"The author demonstrates how weeding strengthens a collection and increases circulation. . . . Four weeding methods are presented: the book card method, the spine-marking method, the historical reconstruction method, and the computer-assisted method. Slote gives precise instructions for each method, enhanced with illustrations." Book Rep

Includes bibliographical references

White, Andrew C., 1966-

E-metrics for library and information professionals; how to use data for managing and evaluating electronic resource collections. Neal-Schuman Publishers 2006 249p il pa $75 *   **025.2**

1. Digital libraries

ISBN 1-55570-514-6   LC 2004-54678

"Designed to introduce readers to e-metrics ('the measurements of the use and activity of networked information'), this book is made up of 10 chapters that are divided among three major sections. Part 1 supplies a definition of e-metrics, explores their use in libraries, and discusses vendor-supplied electronic data reports. Part 2 explains why libraries need e-metrics, focusing on how they can be used for public relations, collection management, and library administration. Part 3 offers ways that libraries can build local e-metrics. Chapters cover the capturing and processing of statistics, infrastructure and technical requirements, and staffing needs. With its coherent structure, well-articulated language, and illustrative material (tables, figures, and examples), this book has much to recommend it." Booklist

Includes bibliographical references

025.3 Bibliographic analysis and control

Gorman, Michael, 1941-

The concise AACR2; prepared by Michael Gorman. 4th ed. American Library Association 2004 179p pa $40 *   **025.3**

1. Anglo-American cataloguing rules 2. Cataloging

ISBN 0-8389-3548-6   LC 2004-16088

First published 1981

On cover: Fourth edition

"This practical guidebook . . . [is] in concordance with AACR2, 2002 Revision 2004 Update. Michael Gorman . . . explains the more generally applicable AACR2 rules for cataloging library materials in simplified terms that make the rules more accessible and practical for practitioners and students who are in less complex library and bibliographic environments." Publisher's note

Intner, Sheila S., 1935-

Standard cataloging for school and public libraries; [by] Sheila S. Intner and Jean Weihs. 4th ed. Libraries Unlimited 2007 286p il pa $50 *   **025.3**

1. Cataloging 2. Library classification

ISBN 978-1-59158-378-3; 1-59158-378-0   LC 2007-9009

First published 1990

This explains the Anglo-American Cataloging Rules (AACR2), Sears and Library of Congress subject headings, Dewey decimal and Library of Congress classification systems, MARC format, large computer networks, policy manuals, and how to manage a cataloging department.

Includes bibliographical references

Maxwell, Robert L., 1957-

FRBR; a guide for the perplexed. American Library Association 2008 151p il pa $50   **025.3**

1. FRBR (Conceptual model)

ISBN 978-0-8389-0950-8; 0-8389-0950-7   LC 2007-27845

This book explains "Functional Requirements for Bibliographic Records (FRBR), an evolving conceptual model developed to assist users in navigating library catalogs to find the information they want and need. Maxwell . . . explains and illustrates the FRBR model, details why the document and model are important for the future of information organization, and explains what a catalog based on FRBR principles might look like. He also briefly illustrates the use of Functional Requirements for Authority Data (FRAD)." Booklist

Includes bibliographic references

Mitchell, Anne M., 1972-

Cataloging and organizing digital resources; a how-to-do-it manual for librarians. Neal-Schuman Publishers 2005 219p il (How-to-do-it manuals for librarians) pa $75 *   **025.3**

1. Information systems 2. Cataloging 3. Digital libraries

ISBN 1-55570-521-9   LC 2005-903

This "volume addresses the ways a library can manage electronic collections. The goal is to provide an overview of management concerns and issues regarding bibliographic control in an online environment and to suggest tools that are available. The 10 chapters address such topics as development of digital libraries, organization of work flow, alternatives to cataloging, cataloging rules and records, online monographs and serials, integration of resources, and trends. Each chapter offers an introduction; guidelines, instructions, or strategies; and a summary and references. The writing is clear, with plentiful examples that include figures and titles." Booklist

Understanding FRBR; what it is and how it will affect our retrieval tools; edited by Arlene G. Taylor. Libraries Unlimited 2007 186p il pa $45   **025.3**

1. FRBR (Conceptual model)

ISBN 978-1-59158-509-1   LC 2007-13558

Understanding FRBR—*Continued*
This book "offers a basic introduction to FRBR, discussions about FRBR, FRAD (functional requirement for authority data), and RDA (resource description and access), and the issues involved in using FRBR in nontraditional library settings such as with cartographic materials and music." Libr J
Includes bibliographical references

025.4 Subject analysis and control

Dewey, Melvil, 1851-1931
Dewey decimal classification and relative index; devised by Melvil Dewey. ed 22, edited by Joan S. Mitchell, Julianne Beall, Giles Martin, Winton E. Matthews, Jr., Gregory R. New. OCLC 2003 4v set $375 * **025.4**
1. Dewey Decimal Classification
ISBN 0-910608-70-9   LC 2003-50872
Also available online
First published anonymously in 1876
Contents: v1 Manual, tables; v2 Schedules 000-599; v3 Schedules 600-999; v4 Relative index

Library of Congress. Cataloging Policy and Support Office
Library of Congress subject headings; prepared by the Cataloging Policy and Support Office, Library Services. 30th ed. Library of Congress 2007 5v set $295   **025.4**
1. Subject headings
Also available online
Annual. Variant title: Subject headings used in the dictionary catalogs of the Library of Congress. Issued previously by the Subject Cataloging Division and later by the Office for Subject Cataloging Policy
New edition in preparation
This work contains the headings and cross-references established and applied by the Library of Congress.

Sears list of subject headings; Joseph Miller, editor; Barbara A. Bristow, associate editor. 19th ed. Wilson, H. W. 2007 li, 823p $145 * **025.4**
1. Subject headings
ISBN 978-0-8242-1076-2
Also available Canadian companion. 6th edition published 2001
First published 1923 with title: List of subject headings for small libraries, by Minnie Earl Sears
This is "a standard authority list for subject cataloging in small and medium-sized libraries. It contains more than 8,000 established subject terms and . . . provisions for establishing further terms as needed. It also contains more than 500 authorized subdivisions with instructions in their application, scope notes, suggested cross-references, and suggestions for classification." Publisher's note

025.5 Services for users

Buker, Derek M.
The science-fiction and fantasy readers' advisory; the librarian's guide to cyborgs, aliens, and sorcerers. American Lib. Assn. 2002 230p (ALA readers' advisory series) pa $50   **025.5**
1. Science fiction—Bibliography 2. Fantasy fiction—Bibliography 3. Reference services (Libraries)
ISBN 0-8389-0831-4; 978-0-8389-0831-0
LC 2002-1494
A "well-organized, humorous guide to providing readers' advisory to customers wanting science fiction or fantasy recommendations. . . . The book is divided into two parts, one dealing with science fiction and one with fantasy, and further divides these genres into their many subgenres, providing short annotated lists of recommended titles as well as longer lists without annotations. . . . What this guide does best is demonstrate the wide scope of science fiction and fantasy literature; it gives many suggestions and recommendations across this broad range." SLJ
Includes bibliographical references

Charles, John A., 1962-
The mystery readers' advisory; the librarian's clues to murder and mayhem; [by] John Charles, Joanna Morrison, [and] Candace Clark. American Library Association 2002 227p (ALA readers' advisory series) pa $45   **025.5**
1. Mystery fiction—Bibliography 2. Reference services (Libraries)
ISBN 0-8389-0811-X; 978-0-8389-0811-2
LC 01-45083
"Covering everything a librarian would need to know to successfully build and promote a mystery collection, the authors include chapters on weeding and marketing the collection, with a great section on how to do a readers' advisory interview. . . . The text is peppered with authors and titles to know and plenty of plot teasers to fill your reading list. There are thorough discussions of the different subgenres, from police procedural to romantic suspense and other genre blends. . . . The lists of mystery periodicals, reference sources, and Web sites are well-rounded and up-to-date." Voice Youth Advocates
Includes bibliographical references

Cords, Sarah Statz, 1974-
The real story; a guide to nonfiction reading interests; edited by Robert Burgin. Libraries Unlimited 2006 xxxii, 460p (Genreflecting advisory series) $55 * **025.5**
1. Books and reading 2. Reference services (Libraries)
ISBN 1-59158-283-0   LC 2006-3712
The author "describes more than 555 popular nonfiction titles published over the last 15 years, along with classic titles such as Truman Capote's In Cold Blood. . . . Cords has identified 11 broad categories based on subjects, genres, and appeal factors. Among the categories are 'Biography,' 'Travel,' 'True Adventure,' and 'True Crime.' . . . A must-read for any librarian who

Cords, Sarah Statz, 1974-—*Continued*
recommends popular reading titles, it belongs at the reference and readers'-advisory desks of most libraries."
Booklist
Includes bibliographical references

Farkas, Meredith, 1977-
Social software in libraries; building collaboration, communication, and community online. Information Today, Inc. 2007 xxiv, 320p il pa $39.50 **025.5**
1. Libraries and community 2. Telecommunication 3. Information technology
ISBN 978-1-57387-275-1 LC 2007-4515
This "guide provides librarians with the information and skills necessary to implement the most popular and effective social software technologies: blogs, RSS, wikis, social networking software, screencasting, photo-sharing, podcasting, instant messaging, gaming, and more." Publisher's note
Includes bibliographical references

Ford, Charlotte
Crash course in reference. Libraries Unlimited 2008 143p il (Crash course) pa $30 **025.5**
1. Reference services (Libraries)
ISBN 978-1-59158-463-6 LC 2007-52948
"A basic explanation of reference services for those with little formal LIS training working in small rural libraries or others who have been working in other areas and wish to brush up on their skills, this author provides an introduction to reference services including search strategies." Publisher's note
Includes bibliographical references

Katz, William A., 1924-2004
Introduction to reference work. 8th ed. McGraw-Hill 2001 c2002 2v v1 $82.81; v2 $85 *
025.5
1. Reference services (Libraries) 2. Reference books—Bibliography
ISBN 978-0-07-244107-9 (v1); 0-07-244107-0 (v1); 978-0-07-244143-7 (v2); 0-07-244143-7 (v2)
First published 1969. Periodically revised
Contents: v1 Basic information services; v2 Reference services and reference processes
Volume one opens with a general introduction to the reference process and online reference services. Types of services include: bibliographies; indexing and abstracting services; encyclopedias; ready-reference; biographies; government documents. Volume two covers community reference services; interviewing; online searching; and library and bibliographic instruction, as well as evaluation of reference services

Moyer, Jessica E.
Research-based readers' advisory; with contributions by Amanda Blau . . . [et al.] American Library Association 2008 278p (ALA readers' advisory series) pa $50 **025.5**
1. Reference services (Libraries)
ISBN 978-0-8389-0959-1; 0-8389-0959-0
LC 2007-49421

"Following a survey of the current state of RA, 11 chapters cover topics such as 'Nonfiction Readers and Nonfiction Advisory,' 'Romance and Genre Readers,' and 'Tools for Readers' Advisory.' Each chapter begins with a 'Research View,' in which Moyer summarizes the latest literature. Following the 'Research View' is a 'Librarian's View,' in which an impressive array of contributors talk about practical applications." Booklist
Includes bibliographical references

Nonfiction readers' advisory; edited by Robert Burgin. Libraries Unlimited 2004 250p pa $39.95 **025.5**
1. Reference services (Libraries)
ISBN 1-591-58115-X LC 2004-48642
This is a "collection of essays on the challenges of readers' advisory librarians who strive to meet the nonfiction reading needs of patrons." Booklist
Includes bibliographical references

Saricks, Joyce G.
Readers' advisory service in the public library. 3rd ed. American Library Association 2005 211p il pa $38 **025.5**
1. Reference services (Libraries) 2. Public libraries
ISBN 0-8389-0897-7 LC 2004-29271
First published 1989
In this guide to readers' advisory, "online tools for identifying and evaluating titles to suggest to today's new adult leisure readers are described, in addition to . . . tried-and-true print sources. The value of personal reading suggestions from staff and patrons is addressed. Topics for discussion and techniques for marketing good reading material are offered. . . . A priority for all libraries involved in readers' advisory." Booklist
Includes bibliographical references

Spratford, Becky Siegel
The horror readers' advisory; the librarian's guide to vampires, killer tomatoes, and haunted houses; [by] Becky Siegel Spratford [and] Tammy Hennigh Clausen. American Library Association 2004 161p il (ALA readers' advisory series) pa $36 **025.5**
1. Horror fiction—History and criticism 2. Reference services (Libraries)
ISBN 0-8389-0871-3 LC 2003-25530
This is a "guide to horror fiction, explaining its appeal and advising on how librarians unfamiliar with the genre can broaden their own knowledge and build a viable collection. The text briefly outlines the characteristics of the main categories, or subgenres, including the usual monsters and occult creatures; extreme suspense of all types; hauntings and possession; and a section on classic works of horror, along with tips for interviewing readers of each subgenre. . . . [This] small, helpful book will be a boon to readers' advisors needing fresh meat for horror fans." Libr J
Includes bibliographical references

Virtual reference service; from competencies to assessment; edited by R. David Lankes . . . [et al.] Neal-Schuman Publishers 2008 206p il (Virtual reference desk series) $75

025.5

1. Reference services (Libraries)
ISBN 978-1-55570-528-2   LC 2007-24104

"Featuring essays from the 2005 7th Annual Virtual Reference Desk Conference, this book focuses on the evolving aspects of virtual reference theory, research, and practice. . . . The topics explored include the implementation and expansion of virtual reference programs, and the training and assessment that is necessary to ensure the success of these services. . . . This is a valuable resource for library practitioners involved with reference services." Am Ref Books Annu, 2008

Includes bibliographical references

Willis, Mark R.
Dealing with difficult people in the library. American Lib. Assn. 1999 195p pa $28 *

025.5

1. Public libraries
ISBN 0-8389-0760-1   LC 99-20426

"Besides the angry patron, [Willis] considers situations including suspected child abuse, censorship, problems with Internet users, homeless persons in the library, and parents who treat the library as a convenient, free baby-sitting service. In separate sections he focuses on communicating and preventing problems from occurring, and he includes sample policy statements." Booklist

Includes bibliographical references

Woodward, Jeannette A.
What every librarian should know about electronic privacy. Libraries Unlimited 2007 222p pa $40 *

025.5

1. Right of privacy 2. Computer security 3. Internet—Security measures 4. Libraries—Security measures
ISBN 978-1-59158-489-6; 1-59158-489-2

LC 2007-13566

Contents: Portrait of a library computer user — Protecting library users from identity theft — Privacy threats from the business world — Protecting children and teenagers — Government surveillance, data mining, and just plain carelessness — RFID systems in libraries — The challenge of library records: what to keep and how long to keep it — The Patriot Act quandary: obeying the law and protecting library users — Protecting electronic privacy: a step-by-step plan — Education and advocacy

"Beginning with a breakdown of the types of library clients and their often blasé attitude toward Internet privacy and security, author Jeannette Woodward then proceeds to use those client types as examples for real-world impact of how privacy could be an issue to librarians. . . . Well written and well researched, this book certainly lives up to its title." Libr Media Connect

Includes bibliographical references

Wyatt, Neal
The readers' advisory guide to nonfiction. American Library Association 2007 318p (ALA reader's advisory series) pa $48   **025.5**

1. Reference services (Libraries) 2. Public libraries
ISBN 978-0-8389-0936-2; 0-8389-0936-1 (pa)

LC 2006-102318

Wyatt "focuses on eight popular categories: history, true crime, true adventure, science, memoir, food/cooking, travel, and sports. Within each, she explains the scope, popularity, style, major authors and works, and the subject's position in readers' advisory interviews. Wyatt addresses who is reading nonfiction and why, while providing RAs with the tools and language to incorporate nonfiction into discussions that point readers to what to read next. . . . [This] guide includes nonfiction bibliography, key authors, benchmark books with annotations, and core collections." Publisher's note

Includes bibliographical references

025.7   Physical preparation for storage and use

Lavender, Kenneth
Book repair; a how-to-do-it manual. 2nd ed. Neal-Schuman 2001 xxiv, 269p il (How-to-do-it manuals for libraries) pa $55 *   **025.7**

1. Books—Conservation and restoration
ISBN 1-55570-408-5   LC 00-48206

First published 1992

"Covering both basic book repair techniques and . . . conservation practices, this . . . manual offers illustrated sections on cleaning, mending, hinge and spine repair, strengthening paperbacks, [etc.]. . . . Chapters cover: wet and water-damaged books; mold and mildew; repair of book linings and pamphlet bindings; using acid-free materials to repair damaged books; lining paper objects; affordable repair tools and supplies. . . . A full discussion of when and how to make repairs, and alternative conservation practices that enable each librarian to develop procedures appropriate to his or her library are also provided." Publisher's note

Includes bibliographical references

Schechter, Abraham A.
Basic book repair methods; illustrated by the author. Libraries Unlimited 1999 102p il pa $37

025.7

1. Books—Conservation and restoration
ISBN 1-56308-700-6   LC 98-50950

Photographs accompany step-by-step instructions for common preservation techniques, from the cleaning of pages and their readhesion, to case reattachment and rebacking.

Includes bibliographical references

025.8 Maintenance and preservation of collections

Halsted, Deborah D.
Disaster planning; a how-to-do-it manual for librarians with planning templates on CD-ROM. Neal-Schuman Publishers 2005 xx, 247p il (How-to-do-it manuals for librarians) pa $85 *
025.8
1. Disaster relief 2. Accidents—Prevention 3. Library resources—Conservation and restoration
ISBN 1-55570-486-7   LC 2003-65152
Includes CD-ROM
"Step-by-step instructions discuss creating a working disaster team, establishing a communications strategy, identifying relief and recovery agencies, developing response plans, and examining issues of cutting-edge library security. . . . This valuable resource is an important addition to most professional collections." Booklist
Includes bibliographical references

026 Libraries, archives, information centers devoted to specific subjects and disciplines

Directory of special libraries and information centers, [2008]; a guide to more than 35,000 special libraries, research libraries, information centers, archives, and data centers maintained by government agencies . . .; Matthew Miskelly, content project editor. 34th ed. Thompson/Gale 2008 3v set $1260 *   **026**
1. Special libraries—Directories
ISBN 978-0-7876-9679-5; 0-7876-9679-X
Annual. First published 1963. Volume one is kept up to date by mid-year supplementary volume (v3)
"Volume 1, in three parts, provides . . . contact and descriptive information on more than 35,800 subject-specific resource collections maintained by various government agencies, businesses, publishers, educational and nonprofit organizations, and associations around the world. . . . Volume 2, Geographic and Personnel Indexes, provides access to profiled libraries by geographic region, as well as by the professional staff that are cited in each listing." Publisher's note

027 General libraries, archives, information centers

American library directory 2008-2009. 61st ed. Information Today 2008 2v set $299.95 *
027
1. Libraries—Directories
ISSN 0065-910X
ISBN 978-1-57387-320-8; 1-57387-320-9
Also available online
Annual. First published 1923 by Bowker
"Includes U.S. and Canadian public, academic, and special libraries arranged by state or province, city, and

institution. Gives personnel and statistical data, subject interests, and special collections." Ref Sources for Small & Medium-sized Libr. 6th edition

The **whole** library handbook 4; current data, professional advice, and curiosa about libraries and library services; edited by George M. Eberhart. American Library Association 2006 585p il map pa $42   **027**
1. Library science 2. Libraries—United States 3. Library services
ISBN 0-8389-0915-9; 978-0-8389-0915-7
LC 2005-33619
First published 1991
This is an "encyclopedic collection of factual data covering all aspects of the library world, together with readable excerpts from recent books and articles on 'librariana.'" Choice
Includes bibliographical references

027.4 Public libraries

McCook, Kathleen de la Peña
Introduction to public librarianship. Neal-Schuman Publishers 2004 406p il pa $59.95 *   **027.4**
1. Public libraries
ISBN 1-55570-475-1   LC 2004-46012
"The first portion of the book reviews the literature on the history of public library development in the United States. Later chapters explore organizational structures, funding, laws and politics, architecture, administration and staffing, programs, and services. Throughout, McCook makes references to divisions and sections of the American Library Association and Public Library Association that are relevant to each topic." Ref & User Services Quarterly
"The book is a necessary addition to all professional collections, not to collect dust, but to become respectfully dog-eared and coffee-stained through repeated use." Florida Libraries
Includes bibliographical references

027.5 Government libraries

Conaway, James, 1941-
America's library; the story of the Library of Congress, 1800-2000; foreword by James Billington; introduction by Edmund Morris. Yale Univ. Press 2000 226p il $48   **027.5**
1. Library of Congress
ISBN 978-0-300-08308-8; 0-300-08308-4
LC 99-58751
Published "in association with the Library of Congress."
This history of the Library of Congress is organized "around that tiny, hardy band of men and women who have used both political acumen and intellectual vision to build the library's collections and establish those services that make the LC library to both Congress and nation. Richly supplemented with photographs, this history reaches out to touch all who love libraries." Booklist
Includes bibliographical references

027.6 Libraries for special groups and organizations

Alire, Camila
Serving Latino communities; a how-to-do-it manual for librarians. 2nd ed. Neal-Schuman Publishers 2007 229p bibl il (How-to-do-it manuals for libraries) pa $59.95 *   **027.6**
1. Libraries and Hispanic Americans
ISBN 978-1-55570-606-7 (pa); 1-55570-606-1
LC 2007-7783
First published 1998
"The information covered helps library staff understand the needs of their library's Latino community; develop successful programs and services; obtain funding for projects and programs; prepare staff to work more effectively with Latinos; establish partnerships with relevant external agencies and organizations; improve collection development; and perform effective outreach and public relations. . . . There are few resources widely available on this topic and none as complete." Libr Media Connect
Includes bibliographical references

Moller, Sharon Chickering
Library service to Spanish speaking patrons; a practical guide. Libraries Unlimited 2001 207p pa $30   **027.6**
1. Libraries and Hispanic Americans 2. Public libraries
ISBN 1-56308-719-7   LC 00-45090
Chapters "cover the history of Spanish speakers in the U.S., adult, children, and teen services; how to help access library resources; and helpful Internet sites. Some of the chapters include examples of what other library systems or librarians have done to try and meet the needs of Spanish-speaking patrons." SLJ
"Intended to stimulate discussion among library service planners and to offer counsel to service providers, this book should become required reading in any jurisdiction with an underserved Latino population." Voice Youth Advocates
Includes bibliographical references

027.62 Libraries for specific age groups

Cullum, Carolyn N.
The storytime sourcebook II; [a compendium of 3500+ new ideas and resources for storytellers] Neal-Schuman Publishers 2007 489p pa $75
027.62
1. Storytelling 2. Children's libraries
ISBN 1-55570-589-8; 978-1-55570-589-3
LC 2006-35096
First published 1990 with title: The storytime sourcebook
Subtitle from cover
"Each of the 146 themed programs, designed for children ages two to eight, appears on two facing pages that include appropriate calendar tie-ins, videos, books, music,

movements, crafts, activities, and songs. . . . [The author] presents clear and simple directions for crafts and activities, quick and uncomplicated for librarians to prepare, and easy for children to follow. . . . This sourcebook is an essential purchase for libraries serving this audience." SLJ
Includes bibliographical references

Fiore, Carole D.
Fiore's summer library reading program handbook. Neal-Schuman Publishers 2005 xxiii, 312p pa $65 *   **027.62**
1. Children's libraries 2. Books and reading
ISBN 1-55570-513-8   LC 2004-31104
"This research-laden handbook . . . serves as a 'comprehensive program-planning and implementation tool' for public libraries seeking to revamp, revise, or develop a summer library reading program. . . . This is an invaluable resource, both for its concrete guidance and its abstract exploration of the meaning of summer library programs." Bull Cent Child Books
Includes bibliographical references

Vaillancourt, Renée J.
Bare bones young adult services; tips for public library generalists. American Lib. Assn. 2000 142p il pa $33   **027.62**
1. Young adults' libraries 2. Libraries and students 3. Public libraries
ISBN 0-8389-3497-8   LC 99-35643
The author "provides guidelines for forming Teen Advisory Boards and focus groups, dealing with unruly adolescent patrons, providing homework support, as well as some basic programming ideas. She also discusses collection development and suggests resources that specialize in reviewing teen-level materials." SLJ
Includes bibliographical references

028 Reading and use of other information media

Basbanes, Nicholas A., 1943-
Every book its reader; the power of the printed word to stir the world. HarperCollins 2005 360p il $29.95; pa $15.95 *   **028**
1. Best books 2. Books and reading
ISBN   0-06-059323-7;   978-0-06-059323-0; 0-06-059324-5 (pa); 978-0-06-059324-7 (pa)
LC 2005-46164
The author "focuses on peoples' reading habits and on the books they have read, both obscure and renowned, as well as on the importance of particular books in specific contexts. Basbanes begins by interviewing some of the best-read people alive, among them David McCullough, Harold Bloom, Helen Vendler, and Elaine Pagels; he also mentions a wide variety of contemporary and historical personages. The loosely related stories are often inspirational, making this an engrossing read." Libr J
Includes bibliographical references

Dirda, Michael, 1948-
Book by book; notes on reading and life. Henry Holt 2006 c2005 170p $17　　**028**
1. Books and reading 2. Best books
ISBN 978-0-8050-7877-0; 0-8050-7877-0
LC 2005-55451
The author "writes a guide to reading and its life lessons ranging widely and pithily through the universal themes of learning, school, work, love, childhood and spiritual guidance. Dirda's message is simple: if reading is to be life enhancing, we need to focus our attention on books that are rewarding. . . . For those who enjoy books about reading, and for all those seeking to encourage others to read, Dirda's brief yet suggestive book will inspire." Publ Wkly

Edmundson, Mark, 1952-
Why read? Bloomsbury 2004 146p $21.95
　　028
1. Books and reading 2. Literature—Study and teaching 3. Higher education
ISBN 1-582-34425-6　　LC 2004-2401
The author "calls for a new humanist education that stresses the importance of literary reading and teaching in making a life and ethical decisions. . . . He discusses the interpretation of literature as a process of understanding, identification, impersonation, and spiritual truth, which leads to the reader's developing a final narrative or life vision. . . . Engaging and controversial, this book will lead to discussion and debate." Libr J

Ellington, Elisabeth
A year of reading; a month-by-month guide to classics and crowd-pleasers for you and your book group; by H. Elisabeth Ellington and Jane Freimiller. Sourcebooks 2002 314p pa $14.95
　　028
1. Best books 2. Books and reading
ISBN 1-57071-935-7　　LC 2002-6926
"Five titles designated as crowd pleasers, classics, challenges, memoirs, or potluck options are provided for each month. . . . There are brief descriptions of each book, thought-provoking discussion questions, information about the authors, video and Internet resources, and lists of related readings. Literary discussion groups will welcome this invaluable resource." Booklist

Major, David C., 1938-
100 one-night reads; a book lover's guide; [by] David C. Major and John S. Major. Ballantine Bks. 2001 312p pa $12.95　　**028**
1. Best books 2. Books and reading
ISBN 0-345-43994-5　　LC 2001-16135
The authors "offer recommendations in nonfiction, general fiction, fantasy, humor, mystery, history, public affairs, memoirs, science, and travel. Most are by English or U.S. authors and were published in the 20th century. Each three-page entry includes a description of the book, information about the author, and an evaluation of what makes the book distinctive. Suggestions for additional writings by the author are often included." Libr J
Includes bibliographical references

Pearl, Nancy
Book lust; recommended reading for every mood, moment, and reason. Sasquatch Books 2003 287p pa $16.95　　**028**
1. Books and reading 2. Best books
ISBN 1-57061-381-8　　LC 2003-45796
Pearl's "recommendations are arranged under an alphabetical, subjective, but certainly comprehensive system of categories, which range from 'Academic Mysteries' to 'World War II Nonfiction' and from 'First Novels' to 'Three-Hanky Readers.' Within each category, Pearl's commentaries are concise and sound. A book difficult to put down and easy to be guided by." Booklist

More book lust; recommended reading for every mood, moment, and reason. Sasquatch Books 2005 286p pa $16.95　　**028**
1. Books and reading 2. Best books
ISBN 1-57061-435-0　　LC 2004-66292
Sequel to: Book lust (2003)
The author presents a list of "books she or someone else really enjoyed reading, presented in more than 100 lists covering a delightful range of topics, from the biographical or geographical (Winston Churchill, Africa) to favorite writers categorized as 'too good to miss'. . . . If you're clueless about what to read next, you'll find something to pique your interest here." Publ Wkly
Includes bibliographical references

028.1　Reviews

Szymborska, Wisława, 1923-
Nonrequired reading; prose pieces; translated from the Polish by Clare Cavanagh. Harcourt 2002 233p $24　　**028.1**
1. Books and reading
ISBN 0-15-100660-1　　LC 2002-2440
The Nobel laureate's "essays are musings with unexpected twists on topics as diverse as Korean fairy tales, paleontology and the hygiene of the nobility." N Y Times Book Rev
"The skillful simplicity and lyric quality of these essays make them distinctive. With her poet's gift for compression, Szymborska captures large concepts and brilliantly reduces them to pithy, two-page essays." Libr J
Includes bibliographical references

028.5　Reading and use of other information media by young people

The **Cambridge** guide to children's books in English; [edited by] Victor Watson; advisory editors, Elizabeth L. Keyser, Juliet Partridge, Morag Styles. Cambridge Univ. Press 2001 814p il $75　　**028.5**
1. Children's literature—Encyclopedias
ISBN 0-521-55064-5　　LC 00-65163
This reference provides an "overview of historic and contemporary children's books published in English. The entries include authors, illustrators, and significant works primarily from Britain, the US, Canada, Australia, New

The Cambridge guide to children's books in English—*Continued*
Zealand, India, and Africa. . . . Major themes, such as fairy tales, fantasy, folktales, legends, mythology, and young adult fiction, are covered as well as less-expected entries on topics such as bias, the bush, disability, ecology, and nudity in children's books. Nonbook media are also covered by entries on animated cartoons, comics, superheroes, and television for children." Choice

Includes bibliographical references

Gillespie, John Thomas, 1928-
The Newbery/Printz companion; booktalk and related materials for award winners and honor books; [by] John T. Gillespie and Corinne J. Naden. 3rd ed. Libraries Unlimited 2006 503p $75
*   028.5
1. Newbery Medal 2. Michael L. Printz award 3. Children's literature—History and criticism 4. Authors
ISBN 1-59158-313-6   LC 2006-14955
First published 1996 with title: The Newbery companion

This guide to the "Newbery and Printz awards for children's and young adult literature provides information on each year's winners and honor books, as well as on the awards themselves and the librarians for whom they are named. For each award-winning book, there is a plot summary, list of characters and themes, background on the author, incidents for booktalking, related reads, and . . . ideas for introducing the book to young readers." Publisher's note

"This invaluable source should be in every school and public library." Booklist

Includes bibliographical references

Helbig, Alethea
Dictionary of American children's fiction, 1995-1999; books of recognized merit; [by] Alethea K. Helbig and Agnes Regan Perkins. Greenwood Press 2002 614p $115   028.5
1. Children's literature—Dictionaries 2. Best books
ISBN 0-313-30389-4   LC 2001-23871
Also available volumes in series covering the years 1859-1959, 1960-1984, 1985-1989 and 1990-1994

"This dictionary is arranged alphabetically by title entries, author entries, character entries, and miscellaneous entries. . . . Entries include award winning and notable books from 1995-1999, as well as a few from previous years. Descriptions of each book are concise and include an overview of the characters, plot, setting, and awards received." Book Rep

"The extensive, detailed index is an excellent resource for locating fiction about a wide range of specific topics, characters, authors, and genres." Booklist

Includes bibliographical references

Dictionary of American young adult fiction, 1997-2001; books of recognized merit; {by} Alethea K. Helbig and Agnes Regan Perkins. Greenwood Press 2004 xxii, 558p $75
                                                     028.5
1. Young adult literature—Dictionaries 2. Young adult literature—Bio-bibliography 3. Youth—Books and reading 4. Best books
ISBN 0-313-32430-1   LC 2003-56804

"The 290 books included {in this volume} have been recognized by one or more of the following: Alex Award, ALA Best Books for Young Adults, Booklist, NYPL, and the Michael L. Printz Award. Approximately 60 of the listed books are adult books considered appropriate for young adults by the award committees. The 741 entries, which include books, their authors, major characters, and settings, are listed alphabetically and range in length from a couple of paragraphs to a bit more than a page. Book entries describe plot, themes, and characters, as well as relevant literary awards, while author entries consist of a brief biography and bibliography. . . . {The information is collected} usefully for selectors of young adult fiction, reader's advisers, teachers, and libraries supporting young adult fiction teaching." Libr J

Includes bibliographical references

Trelease, Jim
The read-aloud handbook. 6th ed. Penguin Books 2006 xxvi, 340p il pa $15 *
                                                     028.5
1. Books and reading 2. Children's literature—Bibliography
ISBN 0-14-303739-0   LC 2006-41773
First published 1982

This handbook explains the importance of reading aloud to children, offers guidance on how to set up a read-aloud atmosphere in the home or classroom and suggests 1,500 titles for reading aloud.

Includes bibliographical references

031 General encyclopedic works in American English

The **Encyclopedia** Americana. Grolier 30v il maps set $349 *   031
1. Encyclopedias and dictionaries
ISBN 0-7172-0139-2
Also available online
First published 1829. Frequently revised

"An encyclopedia suitable for junior and senior high school students as well as adults and college-level students. Cross-references are plentiful throughout the 45,000 articles. The index is comprehensive and analytical. *Americana* contains an exceptionally large number of U.S. place-names and biographies. The sciences, mathematics, American history, and the social sciences are particularly well developed. There are bibliographies at the end of major articles, nearly 400 of which have been updated for this edition." Ref Sources for Small & Medium-sized Libr. 6th edition

Hirsch, E. D. (Eric Donald), 1928-
The new dictionary of cultural literacy; {by}
E.D. Hirsch, Joseph F. Kett, James Trefil.
Completely rev and updated, 3rd ed. Houghton
Mifflin 2002 647p il maps $29.95   **031**
1. English language—Dictionaries
ISBN 0-618-22647-8   LC 2002-27609
First published 1988 with title: The dictionary of cultural literacy
Includes index
"The text is divided into sections by subject—e.g.,
fine arts, world politics, life sciences—each with a brief
introduction; access is also aided by a thorough index.
The entries themselves are complete, concise, and clearly
written as well as extensively and effectively cross-
referenced." Libr J

Jacobs, A. J., 1968-
The know-it-all; one man's humble quest to
become the smartest person in the world. Simon &
Schuster 2004 386p $25   **031**
1. Encyclopaedia Britannica
ISBN 0-7432-5060-5   LC 2004-48233
This "book stems from the author's herculean effort to
read every volume of the majestic Encyclopaedia
Britannica. . . . Jacobs turns his quest for intellectual enlightenment into alphabetically ordered, humorous ruminations on all persons and events of his life. . . . Plenty
of good fun pours out of this prose." Booklist
Includes bibliographical references

The **New** Encyclopaedia Britannica. Encyclopaedia
Britannica 2007 32v il maps apply to publisher
for price *   **031**
1. Encyclopedias and dictionaries
ISBN 1-59339-292-3; 978-1-59339-292-5
Also available CD-ROM version and online
First published 1768 in England; in the United States
1902. Now published with the editorial advice of the
University of Chicago. First published with current title
with the fifteenth edition in 1974. Frequently revised
"In three sections: Propaedia, or outline of knowledge;
Macropaedia, with longer in-depth articles covering major topics; and Micropaedia, with shorter A-to-Z ready
reference entries. *Britannica's* reputation as the basic encyclopedia for all libraries and reference collections is
based on the writing and knowledge of thousands of expert contributors and consultants. Updated between major
editions by the Britannica *Book of the Year.*" NY Public
Libr Book of How & Where to Look It Up

Webster's new explorer desk encyclopedia.
Federal Street Press 2003 1349p il map $19.98
          031
1. Encyclopedias and dictionaries
ISBN 1-892859-43-2   LC 2002-115261
"With more than 17,500 entries, this useful work provides very basic information on a wide variety of topics,
from geography and biography to history, science, and
literature. Additional features include photographs, diagrams, and maps, all in black and white." SLJ

The **World** Book encyclopedia. World Book 2008
22v il map set $999 *   **031**
1. Encyclopedias and dictionaries
ISBN 978-0-7166-0108-1   LC 2007-22003
Also available CD-ROM version and online
First published 1917-1918 by Field Enterprises. Frequently revised
Supplemented by: World Book's year in review; another available annual supplement is World Book's science year in review
"Curriculum-oriented, this superior encyclopedia is
well-edited and produced to meet the reference and informational needs of students from grade four through high
school. Long standing tradition of excellence for readability, accuracy, authoritativeness, objectivity, judicious
and extensive use of outstanding graphics and timeli-
ness." N Y Public Libr. Ref Books for Child Collect
Includes bibliographical references

031.02 American books of miscellaneous facts

Brahms, William B.
Notable last facts; a compendium of endings,
conclusions, terminations and final events
throughout history; compiled by William B.
Brahms. Reference Desk Press 2005 834p $145 *
          031.02
1. Encyclopedias and dictionaries
ISBN 0-9765325-0-6   LC 2005-901194
"Notable last facts, as defined by the compiler, are
'any historically significant event, person, place or thing
that marks the end of its kind or its era.' These facts [in-
clude] the last self-service Horn & Hardart Automat in
Manhattan, the last theatrical performance of Sir John
Gielgud, the last year hurricanes had no name, the last
game played by Red Sox legend Ted Williams, and so
forth." Booklist
"This extensive compilation is a groundbreaking core
reference work for libraries of all kinds." Choice
Includes bibliographical references

Encyclopaedia Britannica almanac, 2006.
Encyclopaedia Britannica 2005 pa $11.95
          031.02
1. Almanacs 2. Statistics 3. United States—Statistics
ISSN 1540-8868
ISBN 1-4022-0604-6; 978-1-4022-0604-7
2008 edition available as an e-book
Annual. First published 2002
"Features include biographies of notable figures, from
the past as well as the present; a lookup of thousands of
facts covering various branches of knowledge (e.g., science, business, history, entertainment, sports, and the
arts). . . . There are also entries for countries and their
leaders, with maps, flags, and various statistics; for
awards and award winners; for sporting events; and
much more." Libr J

Famous first facts, international edition; a record of first happenings, discoveries, and inventions in world history; {edited by} Steven Anzovin & Janet Podell. Wilson, H.W. 2000 837p $140

031.02

1. Encyclopedias and dictionaries
ISBN 0-8242-0958-3   LC 99-86869

This work "contains more than 5000 firsts from hundreds of countries and ranging in time from 3.5 billion years ago (the age of the oldest continental land discovered) to 2001 (the scheduled date of completion of the first building over 1500 feet tall). . . . {It} groups related entries under broad subject categories (arranged alphabetically) and sub-categories. Within each category or sub-category, entries are arranged chronologically." Publisher's note

Feldman, David, 1950-
When do fish sleep? and other imponderables of everyday life; illustrated by Kassie Schwan. Harper & Row 1989 260p il hardcover o.p. pa $12.95   **031.02**

1. Questions and answers
ISBN 0-06-016161-2; 0-06-074093-0 (pa)
                                LC 89-45038

"Feldman offers answers to such 'imponderables' as Why are rented bowling shoes so ugly? and Why do doctors tap on our backs during physical exams? Delightful and informative browsing fare." Booklist

Why do clocks run clockwise? and other imponderables; mysteries of everyday life; explained by David Feldman; illustrated by Kas Schwan. Harper & Row 1987 251p il hardcover o.p. pa $12.95   **031.02**

1. Questions and answers
ISBN 0-06-015781-X; 0-06-074092-2 (pa)
                                LC 87-45045

The author "answers such recurring questions as 'What causes the ringing sound in your ears?' 'Why do nurses wear white?' and 'Why doesn't a "two-by-four" measure two inches by four inches?' Feldman answers them as authoritatively and truthfully as he can, relying on as trustworthy sources as he can find and sometimes, when the query submits to no single answer, fielding several different probable responses." Booklist

Kane, Joseph Nathan, 1899-2002
Famous first facts; a record of first happenings, discoveries, and inventions in American history; [by] Joseph Nathan Kane, Steven Anzovin, & Janet Podell. 6th ed. H.W. Wilson 2006 1307p il $185 *   **031.02**

1. Encyclopedias and dictionaries 2. United States—History—Dictionaries
ISBN 978-0-8242-1065-6; 0-8242-1065-4
                                LC 2006-3096

Also available CD-ROM version and online
First published 1933
Over 7500 entries cover first occurences in American history, organized into 16 chapters each divided into sections. Sections are alphabetically organized, and individual entries are organized chronologically within each section. Includes five indexes: subject index, index by years, index by days, index to personal names, and geographical index.

"Besides serving as an essential ready-reference source, the book is also fun to read out loud to colleagues—when was bubble gum first manufactured in the U.S.? When was the spray can introduced?" Booklist

The **New** York Public Library desk reference. 4th ed. Hyperion 2002 999p il maps $34.95 *
031.02

1. Encyclopedias and dictionaries
ISBN 0-7868-6846-5   LC 2002-27480
"A Stonesong Press book"
First published 1989 by Webster's New World
Divided into chapters, this reference features charts, tables, lists, and illustrations providing information in such categories as signs and symbols, mathematics and science basics, the arts, grammar and punctuation, etiquette, personal finance, first aid, and household tips.
Includes bibliographical references

The **New** York Times 2008 almanac; edited by John W. Wright with editors and reporters of the Times. Penguin Reference 2007 1004p il map pa $11.95   **031.02**
1. Almanacs 2. Statistics 3. United States—Statistics
ISSN 1523-7079
ISBN 978-0-14-311233-4; 0-14-311233-3
Annual. First published 1997
On cover: The almanac of record
This almanac contains a "chronology of the year; major news stories of the year; U.S. history; U.S. presidential biographies; world history; world geography; economic and climate data; major awards in the arts, sciences, and sports; and a wide variety of U.S. demographic information. . . . It is well organized, the table layout is easy to read, and the typeface does not invite eye strain." Am Ref Books Annu, 1998

The **New** York times guide to essential knowledge; a desk reference for the curious mind. Rev. and expanded 2nd ed. St. Martin's Press 2007 1320p il $35   **031.02**
1. Encyclopedias and dictionaries
ISBN 978-0-312-37659-8; 0-312-37659-6
                                LC 2007-38724
First published 2004
This book "defines nearly every facet of contemporary life—from arts, grammar, mythology, and culture to science, economics, and geopolitical issues. . . . An essential background reference for almost every subject." Libr J

Time almanac, 2008; powered by Encyclopedia Britannica. Time Home Entertainment 2008 992p il map hardcover o.p. pa $12.99
031.02
1. Almanacs 2. United States—Statistics
ISBN   978-1-93382-121-4;   1-93382-121-3;
978-1-60320-754-6 (pa); 1-60320-754-6 (pa)
Also available online
Annual. Time almanac began with 1998 edition; absorbed Information please in 1998

Time almanac, 2008—*Continued*

Also known as The Time almanac with Information please

Contains statistical and factual material with a general topical arrangement and subject index. Illustrated with news photos and maps.

The **world** almanac and book of facts, 2008; [editorial director, C. Alan Joyce; managing editor, Elizabeth J. Lazzara; editor, Sarah Janssen] 140th anniversary ed. World Almanac Books 2008 1008p il map $32.99; pa $12.99 *   **031.02**

1. Almanacs 2. Statistics 3. United States—Statistics
ISSN 0084-1382
ISBN 978-1-60057-073-5; 978-1-60057-072-8 (pa)

Annual. First published 1868. Publisher varies

"This is the most comprehensive and well-known of almanacs. . . . Contains a chronology of the year's events, consumer information, historical anniversaries, annual climatological data, and forecasts. Color section has flags and maps. Includes detailed index." N Y Public Libr Book of How & Where to Look It Up

032.02   English books of miscellaneous facts

Guinness book of records 2008. Guinness Media 2008 il $28.95 *   **032.02**

1. Curiosities and wonders
ISSN 1475-7419
ISBN 1-904994-19-9; 978-1-904994-19-0

Also available in paperback from Bantam Bks.

Annual. First published 1955 in the United Kingdom; in the United States 1962. Variant titles: Guinness book of world records; Guinness world records

Editors and publisher vary

"Ready reference for current record holders in all fields, some esoteric. Index provides access to information arranged in broad subject categories. Must be replaced annually." N Y Public Libr. Ref Books for Child Collect

060.25   General organizations— Directories

The **Europa** world of learning. 59th ed. Routledge; distributed by Taylor & Francis 2008 2v set $950 *   **060.25**

1. Societies—Directories
ISSN 0084-2117
ISBN 978-185743-471-2

Also available online

Annual. First published 1947

"The standard international directory for the nations of the world, covering learned societies, research institutes, libraries, museums and art galleries, and universities and colleges. Includes for each institution address, officers, purpose, foundation date, publications, etc." Ref Sources for Small & Medium-sized Libr. 6th edition

060.4   Special topics of general organizations

Robert, Henry Martyn, 1837-1923

Robert's Rules of order newly revised. Perseus Pub. 2000 various paging $37.50 *   **060.4**

1. Parliamentary practice
ISBN 0-7382-0384-X; 978-0-7382-0384-3
            LC 2004-351757

First published 1876 as Pocket manual of rules of order for deliberate assemblies. Title and publisher vary

"A new and enlarged edition by Sarah Corbin Robert, Henry M. Robert III, William J. Evans, Daniel H. Honemann, Thomas J. Balch"

"Long the standard compendium of parliamentary law, explaining methods of organizing and conducting the business of societies, conventions, and other assemblies. Includes convenient charts and tables." Ref Sources for Small & Medium-sized Libr. 6th edition

Sturgis, Alice

The standard code of parliamentary procedure; original edition by Alice Sturgis. 4th ed, revised by the American Institute of Parliamentarians. McGraw-Hill 2001 xxiv, 285p pa $14.95
            060.4

1. Parliamentary practice
ISBN 0-07-136513-3   LC 2001-265929

First published 1950

This guide to the rules of parliamentary procedure includes explanations of their purpose and examples of their use. Also considers ways the Internet and other technologies have rewritten rules of meetings.

Includes bibliographical references

Webster's New World Robert's rules of order; simplified and applied; by Robert McConnell Productions. 2nd ed. Hungry Minds 2001 xx, 409p pa $10.99 *   **060.4**

1. Parliamentary practice
ISBN 0-7645-6399-8   LC 2001-92064

First Webster's New World edition published 1999

This explains the rules of parliamentary procedure, discussing the concepts behind each rule and including examples. This revised edition includes procedures for conducting meetings online, voting by mail and by e-mail, and adopting election procedures

061.025   American organizations— Directories

Encyclopedia of associations. 46th ed. Gale Res. 2008 3v in 5 v1 $835; v2 $650; v3 $660 *
            061.025

Encyclopedia of associations—*Continued*
1. Societies—Directories 2. Trade and professional associations
ISSN 0071-0202
ISBN 978-1-4144-2006-6 (v1); 1-4144-2006-4 (v1); 978-1-4144-2010-3 (v2); 1-4144-2010-2 (v2); 978-1-4144-2011-0 (v3); 1-4144-2011-0 (v3)
Also available online as part of Associations unlimited and as a CD-ROM edition; Also available: International organizations 3v set $960 (ISSN 1041-0023; ISBN 978-1-4144-2012-7, 1-4144-2012-9); Regional, state, and local organizations 5v set $830 (ISBN 978-0-7876-9697-9, 0-7876-9697-8)
Annual. First published 1956 with title: Encyclopedia of American associations
Contents: v1 pt 1-3 National organizations of the U.S.; v2 Geographic and executive indexes; v3 Supplement
This is a guide to more than 23,000 nonprofit American membership organizations of national scope

The **Foundation** directory; compiled by The Foundation Center. 2008 edition. Foundation Center 2008 2730p $215 *   **061.025**
1. Endowments—Directories
ISSN 0071-8092
ISBN 978-1-59542-176-9
Also available CD-ROM version and online
Annual. First published 1960 by Russell Sage. Replaces American foundations and their fields
"Provides detailed information concerning independent, corporate, community, and private foundations with assets of at least $2 million or annual giving of at least $200,000. Geographical arrangement. Entries give date founded; names of officers, contact, and donors; foundation type; financial data; fields of interest; types of support; limitations; application information; and number of staff. Six indexes: Donors, officers, and trustees; Geographic; Types of support; Subject; Foundations new to edition; Foundations name index." Guide to Ref Books. 11th edition

National trade and professional associations of the United States. 43rd ed. Columbia Bks. 2008 1423p pa $299 *   **061.025**
1. Trade and professional associations
ISBN 978-1-88087-356-4; 1-88087-356-7
Annual. First published 1966 with title: Directory of national trade and professional associations of the United States
"Includes nearly 6500 organizations arranged by subject. Indexed by title, key word, geographical location, size of budget, and executive officers. Particularly valuable for its data on the annual budget as well as such general information as date of establishment, address, headquarters staff, size of membership, publications, and telephone number." Ref Sources for Small & Medium-sized Libr. 6th edition

069.025   Museums—Directories

Museums of the world; [editors: Nikolaus Himmler, Ruth Lochar, Hildegard Toma] 15th rev. and enl. ed. K.G. Saur 2008 2v il set $749 *   **069.025**

1. Museums—Directories
ISBN 978-3-598-20695-5; 3-598-20695-X
First published 1973. Periodically revised
This set "covers more than 54,500 museums in 202 countries, listed hierarchically by country and place, and within places alphabetically by name. A separate chapter records some 500 museum associations in 132 countries." Publisher's note

The **Official** museum directory. National Register Pub. 2v set $297 *   **069.025**
1. Museums—Directories
ISSN 0090-6700
ISBN 978-0-87217-756-7
Annual. Supersedes the Museums directory of the United States and Canada, first published 1961 by The American Association of Museums and the Smithsonian Institution
This directory contains "listings on more than 8,100 museums operating in 87 different fields, ranging from science museums to zoos to historic homes to fine arts. It is one of the most trusted and accessible sources for museum professionals to identify vendors, access unique collections and exhibitions, and contact directors and curators. Volume 1 lists institutions by state, and contains a number of indexes: an alphabetic index to institutions, an index to personnel, an index to institutions by category, an index to institutions by collection, and new listings. Volume 2 is a guide to more than 2,100 vendors, their products, and their services, subdivided by category. . . . This product is one of the most useful and up-to-date reference works in the area of museums, especially in relation to current personnel and exhibitions." Recomm Ref Books for Small & Medium-sized Libr & Media Cent, 2003

070.025   Newspapers and journalism—Directories

Gale directory of publications and broadcast media. 143rd ed. Gale Res. 2008 5v maps set $1050 *   **070.025**
1. Newspapers—Directories 2. Periodicals—Directories
ISSN 1048-7972
ISBN 978-0-7876-9669-6; 0-7876-9669-2
Also available online as part of the Gale directory library
Annual. First published 1869. Variant titles: Gale directory of publications and Ayer directory of publications
"An annual guide to publications and broadcasting stations"
Contents: v1 U.S. and Canada: Alabama-New Hampshire; v2 U.S. and Canada: New Jersey-Wyoming; Canada; v3 Networks and syndicates; Indexes and tables; v4 Regional market index; v5 International; International index.
Identifies specific print and broadcast sources of news and advertising for trade, business, labor, and professionals. Arrangement is geographic with a thumbnail description of each local market. Indexes are classified (by format and subject matter) and alphabetical (by name and keyword)

070.1 Documentary media, educational media, news media

Henderson, Harry, 1951-
Power of the news media. Facts on File 2004
316p il (Library in a book) $45   **070.1**
1. Broadcast journalism 2. Press
ISBN 0-8160-4768-5   LC 2003-18900
This book "covers the history of news traced through
newspapers, television, radio, and the Internet; issues related to the media; and information on laws related to
the media and how legislation affects our news coverage.
Important cases are reviewed chronologically from 1735
to 2003." Libr Media Connect
The author's "format—breaking topics into quick-hit
subsections—makes it an ideal source for students researching a particular aspect of news media. . . . Every
American should have a working knowledge of the topic,
and this book is a recommended resource." Voice Youth
Advocates
Includes bibliographical references

070.4 Journalism

Friedlander, Edward Jay
Feature writing for newspapers and magazines;
the pursuit of excellence; {by} Edward Jay
Friedlander, John Lee. 5th ed. Allyn & Bacon
2003 c2004 337p $57.33   **070.4**
1. Journalism
ISBN 0-205-38191-X   LC 2002-43729
First published 1988
Through suggestions and examples this guide for the
novice writer provides tips from Pulitzer Prize-winning
journalists and other magazine and newspaper feature
writers.

Johnson, Marilyn
The dead beat; lost souls, lucky stiffs, and the
perverse pleasures of obituaries. HarperCollins
2006 244p il $24.95 *   **070.4**
1. Obituaries
ISBN 0-06-075875-9   LC 2005-52817
The author "examines the style of obituaries found in
. . . [English and American newspapers], interviews
well-known obituary writers, visits an obituary writers'
conference and provides a sampling of some of the obituaries that have appeared over the years." N Y Times
(Late N Y Ed)
"Johnson handles her offbeat topic with an appropriate
level of humor, while still respecting the gravity of mortality." Publ Wkly
Includes bibliographical references

Reporting America at war; an oral history;
compiled by Michelle Ferrari with commentary
by James Tobin. Hyperion 2003 241p il $23.95
070.4
1. War 2. Reporters and reporting
ISBN 1-401-30072-3   LC 2003-49966

"Beginning with Edward R. Morrow's live reports
during the London blitz and ending with an epilogue on
the second war in Iraq, this oral history contains transcripts of interviews with 11 top correspondents. Murrow
is one of three deceased reporters included (the others
are Martha Gellhorn and Homer Bigart), along with Walter Cronkite, Andy Rooney, Frank Gibney, Malcolm
Browne, David Halberstam, Morley Safer, Ward Just,
Gloria Emerson, Chris Hedges and Christiane Amanpour.
. . . Tobin's introductions and transitional and informational interpolations within the transcripts hold this informative volume together." Publ Wkly
Includes bibliographical references

070.5 Publishing

2009 guide to literary agents. 18th annual ed.
Writer's Digest 2008 362p il pa $27.99
070.5
1. Authors and publishers—Directories
ISSN 1078-6945
ISBN 978-1-58297-548-1; 1-58297-548-5
Annual. Supersedes in part Guide to literary agents &
art/photo reps
"An invaluable tool for writers in search of an agent,
this guide is indexed by agency, agent, format, subject,
and geographic location. Submission procedures, fees,
contracts and what to ask a prospective agent are covered." Libr J

Appelbaum, Judith
How to get happily published. 5th ed.
HarperPerennial 1998 380p pa $15.95 *
070.5
1. Authors and publishers 2. Publishers and publishing
ISBN 0-06-273509-8   LC 97-41128
First published 1978 with co-author Nancy Evans
Covers the mechanics of writing and manuscript preparation, selling the book to a publisher, stages of publication and the self-publishing option, promotional ideas,
and possible markets such as poetry and children's
books.
Includes bibliographical references

The **Columbia** guide to digital publishing; edited
by William E. Kasdorf. Columbia Univ. Press
2003 lxi, 750p $65; pa $34.95 *
070.5
1. Electronic publishing
ISBN 0-231-12498-8; 0-231-12499-6 (pa)
LC 2002-41462
This volume begins with an introductory chapter on
"the role of digital publishing in various facets of the
publishing industry. . . . Other chapters address topics
such as: the technical infrastructure, mark-up, content
management, digital rights management, e-books, archiv-
ing issues, legal issues, accessibility, and international issues." The Indexer
"The editor and contributors . . . have exerted great
effort to include all relevant information for beginners,
yet they offer enough detail to capture the attention of
advanced users without expanding to a multivolume
work or becoming too long. . . . A superb opening ges-

The Columbia guide to digital publishing—*Continued*
ture for creating a dialog on the scholarly communication process." Choice
Includes bibliographical references

Germano, William P., 1950-
Getting it published; a guide for scholars and anyone else serious about serious books; [by] William Germano. University of Chicago Press 2001 197p (Chicago guides to writing, editing, and publishing) $35; pa $15   **070.5**
1. Authors and publishers 2. Publishers and publishing
ISBN 0-226-28843-9; 0-226-28844-7 (pa)
LC 00-46715
The author "deconstructs and demystifies what publishers and editors actually do and what authors should look for in finding the right house for their subject and in putting the right words in their contract. He also does a lot of hand-holding through the review process and the production of the manuscript." Booklist
Includes bibliographical references

Herman, Jeff, 1958-
Jeff Herman's guide to book publishers, editors, & literary agents 2008; who they are! what they want! how to win them over! 18th ed. Three Dog Press; Distributed to the book trade by Watson-Guptill 2008 991p $29.95   **070.5**
1. Authors and publishers 2. Publishers and publishing
ISBN 978-0-9772682-2-1; 0-9772682-2-5
Annual. First published 1992 by Prima Pub. with title: Insider's guide to book editors, publishers, and literary agents. Variant title: Writer's guide to book editors, publishers, and literary agents
Herman provides "portraits of more than 100 agents plus tips on writing query letters and nonfiction book proposals, dealing with rejections, ghostwriting, and self-publishing. With an excellent glossary and sample author-agent and collaboration agreements." Libr J
Includes bibliographical references

Marcus, Leonard S., 1950-
Minders of make-believe; idealists, entrepreneurs, and the shaping of American children's literature. Houghton Mifflin Co. 2008 402p $28   **070.5**
1. Children's literature—History and criticism 2. Children—Books and reading 3. Publishers and publishing
ISBN 978-0-395-67407-9; 0-395-67407-7
LC 2008-00589
"This broad survey distills the history of American children's publishing and librarianship, from colonial times to British interloper Harry Potter, including children's periodicals, major publishers and changes in printing technology." Publ Wkly
"Marcus' approach and tone are always, and irresistibly, well informed, sensible, and intelligent. . . . It is hard to imagine any issue that he has overlooked, and the resulting book is, in word, *indispensable*." Booklist
Includes bibliographical references

Poynter, Dan
The self-publishing manual; how to write, print and sell your own book. 16th ed. Para Pub. 2007 463p pa $19.95 *   **070.5**
1. Publishers and publishing
ISBN 978-1-568601-42-7; 1-568601-42-5
First published 1979. Periodically revised
"Poynter gives the basics for producing a commercially successful manuscript, taking the reader step-by-step through printing a book, determining its value, promoting and advertising, fulfilling orders, and coping with being published. There are appendixes on printers, professional organizations, and fulfillment warehouses." Libr J

The **Publish-it-yourself** handbook; [literary tradition and how to]; edited by Bill Henderson. 25th anniversary ed. Pushcart Press 1998 346p il pa $18   **070.5**
1. Publishers and publishing
ISBN 1-888-88903-9
First published 1973. Periodically revised
An anthology of articles about how to publish without the assistance of commercial or vanity publishers.

Rose, M. J.
How to publish and promote online; {by} M. J. Rose and Angela Adair-Hoy. St. Martin's Griffin 2001 266p pa $13.95   **070.5**
1. Publishers and publishing
ISBN 0-312-27191-3   LC 00-45833
The authors "provide encouragement and tips for aspiring authors hoping to publish their works electronically." Booklist

070.5025   Publishing—Directories

American book trade directory 2008-2009. 54th ed. Information Today 2008 1850p $299.95 *
070.5025
1. Book industry 2. Publishers and publishing—Directories 3. Book collecting
ISSN 0065-759X
ISBN 978-1-57387-317-8; 1-57387-317-9
Annual. First published 1915 by Bowker with title: American book trade manual
"Includes lists of booksellers, wholesalers, and publishers in the United States, with related information on the book trade in Canada, the United Kingdom, and Ireland. Bookstores are arranged under state and city with speciality of each noted. Separate lists include exporters, importers, and dealers in foreign books. Index of retailers and wholesalers in the United States and Canada." Ref Sources for Small & Medium-sized LIbr. 6th edition

International literary market place 2009. Information Today 2008 1800p pa $259
070.5025
1. Publishers and publishing—Directories
ISSN 0074-6827
ISBN 978-1-57387-325-3; 1-57387-325-X
Also available online
Annual. First published 1965 by Bowker

International literary market place 2009—*Continued*

This directory of the international book publishing industry covers over 180 countries worldwide and profiles "more than 15,000 book-related concerns around the globe, including . . . 10,500 publishers and literary agents; 1,100 major booksellers and book clubs; 1,500 major libraries and library associations . . . and thousands of other book-related concerns—including trade organizations, distributors, dealers, literary associations, trade publications, book trade events, and other resources . . . organized in a country-by-country format." Publisher's note

Literary market place 2009. Bowker 2008 2v pa $309　　　　　　**070.5025**
1. Publishers and publishing—Directories
ISSN 0075-9899
ISBN 978-1-57387-329-1; 1-57387-329-2
Also available online

Annual. First published 1940. In 1972 absorbed Names & numbers. Subtitle varies

"Directory of U.S. and Canadian book publishers and related businesses such as book clubs, literary agents, translators, and manufacturers. Gives names of executives and addresses, telephone numbers, and fields of specialization for each publishing company." N Y Public Libr Book of How & Where to Look It Up

Publishers, distributors & wholesalers of the United States 2009. Bowker 2008 2v set $475
　　　　　　070.5025
1. Publishers and publishing—Directories
ISSN 0000-0671
ISBN 978-0-8352-4966-9

Annual. First published 1979 with title: Publishers and distributors of the United States

This directory provides information on "more than 150,000 U.S. publishers, wholesalers, distributors, software firms, audiocassette producers, museum and association imprints, and trade organizations that publish." Publisher's note

071　Journalism and newspapers in North America

Baker, Nicholson

The World on Sunday; graphic art in Joseph Pulitzer's newspaper (1898-1911); [by] Nicholson Baker and Margaret Brentano. Bulfinch Press 2005 131p il $50　　　　　　**071**
1. New York world (Newspaper)
ISBN 0-8212-6193-2　　　　　　LC 2005-00224

This book collects 85 examples of graphic art from the Sunday edition of the New York World

This volume "offers a kaleidoscopic tour through, an ebullient moment in American history when the country was emerging from the shadowy gaslight age and bursting into the glare of the modern. It is a big, lush, coffee-table-size book suffused with gaiety and the optimism of an age blissfully unaware of darknesses soon to come. . . . The World on Sunday is the result of a heroic piece of cultural preservation." N Y Rev Books

Burns, Eric

Infamous scribblers; the founding fathers and the rowdy beginnings of American journalism. Public Affairs 2006 467p $27.50　　　　　　**071**
1. Journalism 2. Newspapers—United States
ISBN 978-1-58648-334-0; 1-58648-334-X
　　　　　　LC 2005-53542

The author "explores the role newspapers played in the founding of the country." Libr J

"From the sniping feuds among Boston's first papers to sex scandals involving Alexander Hamilton and Thomas Jefferson, the snappy patter gives clear indication of how much Burns . . . relishes telling his story." Publ Wkly

Includes bibliographical references

The **New** new journalism; conversations with America's best nonfiction writers on their craft; [edited and with an introduction by] Robert S. Boynton. Vintage Books 2005 xxxiv, 456p pa $13.95　　　　　　**071**
1. Journalism
ISBN 1-400-03356-X　　　　　　LC 2004-57161

The author "offers interviews with 19 writers who detail how and why they produce their work. . . . A fascinating book that makes the reader want to go out and get every book the writers have written as well as those mentioned as sources of inspiration." Booklist

Includes bibliographical references

Ostertag, Bob, 1957-

People's movements, people's press; the journalism of social justice movements. Beacon Press 2006 232p il $23.95　　　　　　**071**
1. Alternative press 2. Social movements
ISBN 0-8070-6164-6; 978-0-8070-6164-0
　　　　　　LC 2005-31735

The author "focuses on five social movements—abolition, women's suffrage, gay and lesbian liberation, veterans against the Vietnam War, and environmentalism—and examines the resulting journalism in the context of each. He argues that the press played an integral part in the development and effectiveness of each movement and explores . . . the interplay among the publications, the movements, and society." Libr J

"Readers interested in the intersection of the media and social movements will appreciate this insightful book." Booklist

Includes bibliographical references

Ritchie, Donald A.

Reporting from Washington; the history of the Washington press corps. Oxford University Press 2005 390p il $30　　　　　　**071**
1. Journalism—Objectivity 2. Press—Government policy 3. Reporters and reporting
ISBN 0-19-517861-0　　　　　　LC 2004-18892

The author "focuses on the period from 1932, when the rising influence of radio and FDR's aggressive politicking broke the dominance of newspapers, until 2001, when the terrorist attacks on the U.S. refocused attention on the government and the press. . . . Ritchie presents a rich perspective on the people who write the first draft

Ritchie, Donald A.—*Continued*
of history, investigating and then breaking the Teapot
Dome and Watergate scandals, among others." Booklist
Includes bibliographical references

Written into history; Pulitzer Prize reporting of
the twentieth century from the New York times;
edited and with an introduction by Anthony
Lewis. Times Bks. 2001 xxv, 355p hardcover
o.p. pa $17   **071**
1. Journalism 2. Pulitzer Prizes
ISBN 0-8050-6849-X; 0-8050-7178-4 (pa)
                                          LC 2001-35555
The award-winning articles "are sorted into the following categories: investigative reporting; dangerous stories that put reporters at risk; international news; public
advocacy; criticism of the arts; science reporting; and
biographical and human-interest stories. Among the topics are Russian slave-labor camps during the 1950s, the
Pentagon Papers, the Vietnam War, and exploitation of
illegal aliens in the U.S." Booklist
"For anyone interested in recent history or journalism
at its best, this book will prove worthwhile." Publ Wkly

080 Quotations

Adler, Mortimer J., 1902-2001
How to think about the great ideas; from the
great books of Western civilization; {by}
Mortimer J. Adler; edited by Max Weismann.
Open Court 2000 xxiv, 530p pa $24.95
                                                       080
1. Great books of the Western world
ISBN 0-8126-9412-0   LC 99-45251
This volume contains the transcripts of 52 half-hour
segments of Adler's 1953-1954 television program The
great ideas
"The book showcases Adler's ideas about all the big
categories—truth, beauty, freedom, love, sex, art, justice,
rationality, humankind's nature, Darwinism, government." Publ Wkly

098 Prohibited works, forgeries, hoaxes

Bosmajian, Haig A.
Burning books; [by] Haig Bosmajian. McFarland
2006 233p $39.95 *   **098**
1. Book burning
ISBN 0-7864-2208-4; 978-0-7864-2208-1
                                          LC 2005-35201
"This work provides a detailed account of book burning worldwide over the past 2000 years. The book burn-
ers are identified, along with the works they deliberately
set aflame." Publisher's note
Includes bibliographical references

100 PHILOSOPHY

Blackburn, Simon
Think: a compelling introduction to philosophy.
Oxford Univ. Press 1999 312p $25 *
                                                       100
1. Philosophy
ISBN 0-19-210024-6   LC 00-265266
The author explores such areas as knowledge, mind,
free will, identity, God, goodness and justice. "His meth-
od is to introduce what other philosophers—primarily
Plato, Descartes, Locke, Berkeley, Leibniz, Hume, and
Kant—have had to say about these themes. . . . Readers
new to the subject could very well be captivated." Libr
J
Includes bibliographical references

The **many** faces of philosophy; reflections from
Plato to Arendt; edited by Amélie Oksenberg
Rorty. Oxford Univ. Press 2003 xxix, 512p $40;
pa $24.95 *   **100**
1. Philosophy
ISBN 0-19-513402-8; 0-19-517655-3 (pa)
                                          LC 2002-30342
This is a collection of "self-reflective musings by canonical Western philosophers, culled from letters, prefaces, memoirs, political tracts, and replies to critics. . . .
No single-volume collection of philosophical autobiographies spans the entire history of philosophy as this one
does." Choice
Includes bibliographical references

Russell, Bertrand, 1872-1970
The problems of philosophy. Hackett Pub. Co
1990 167p (Hackett classics) $27.95; pa $8.95 *
                                                       100
1. Philosophy
ISBN   978-0-87220-099-9;   0-87220-099-X;
978-0-87220-098-2 (pa); 0-87220-098-1 (pa)
                                          LC 90-81389
First published 1912 by Holt
The author discusses: appearance and reality, matter,
idealism, theories of knowledge, universals, intuition, and
truth
"The work is concise, free from technical terms and
perfectly clear to the general reader with no prior knowledge of the subject." Booklist
Includes bibliographical references

103 Dictionaries, encyclopedias, concordances of philosophy

Blackburn, Simon
The Oxford dictionary of philosophy. 2nd ed.
Oxford University Press 2005 407p il $45
                                                       103
1. Philosophy—Dictionaries
ISBN 0-19-861014-9; 978-0-19-861014-4
                                          LC 2006-271895
First published 1994

Blackburn, Simon—*Continued*

This dictionary "contains over 2,500 entries, including biographies of nearly 500 influential philosophers. The dictionary provides . . . coverage of not only Western philosophical traditions, but also themes from Chinese, Indian, Islamic, and Jewish philosophy." Publisher's note

Includes bibliographical references

The **Cambridge** dictionary of philosophy; edited by Robert Audi. 2nd ed. Cambridge Univ. Press 1999 xxxv, 1001p il hardcover o.p. pa $32.99 *
103

1. Philosophy—Dictionaries
ISBN 0-521-63136-X; 0-521-63722-8 (pa)
LC 99-12920

First published 1995

This work contains some 4,400 entries including 50 on major contemporary philosophers. Wide coverage of Western philosophy as well as non-Western and non-European philosophers is included. The rapidly growing fields of philosophy of mind and applied ethics are also covered

Encyclopedia of philosophy; Donald M. Borchert, editor in chief. 2nd ed. Macmillan Reference USA 2005 10v il set $995 *
103

1. Philosophy—Encyclopedias
ISBN 0-02-865780-2
LC 2005-18573

First published 1967 in eight volumes under the editorship of Paul Edwards

"Among the many topics covered are African, Islamic, Jewish, Russian, Chinese, and Buddhist philosophies; bioethics and biomedical ethics; art and aesthetics; epistemology; metaphysics; peace and war; social and political philosophy; the Holocaust; feminist thought; and much more. Additionally, . . . [it] also features 1,000 biographical entries on major figures in philosophical thought throughout history." Publisher's note

For a fuller review, see: Booklist, June 1 & 15, 2006

Includes bibliographical references

The **Oxford** companion to philosophy; edited by Ted Honderich. 2nd ed., new ed. Oxford University Press 2005 1056p il $60 *
103

1. Philosophy—Encyclopedias
ISBN 0-19-926479-1
LC 2005-275452

First published 1995

"Including more than 2200 alphabetically arranged entries from nearly 300 contributors, . . . [this book] provides an encyclopedic view of philosophy's past and present, its ideas, disputes (the editor himself contributes an article on unlikely philosophical propositions), and key figures, living and dead. . . . This title makes an excellent companion for standard multivolume subject encyclopedias." SLJ

For a fuller review, see: Booklist, Nov. 15, 2005

Includes bibliographical references

109   Historical and collected persons treatment of philosophy

A **Companion** to world philosophies; edited by Eliot Deutsch and Ron Bontekoe; advisory editors, Tu Weiming {et al.}. Blackwell 1997 587p (Blackwell companions to philosophy) pa $34.95 hardcover o.p. *
109

1. Philosophy
ISBN 0-631-21327-9 (pa)
LC 96-36179

This volume "focuses on non-Western philosophies. . . . The editors have drawn together leading authors in the fields of Chinese, Indian, Buddhist, Islamic, Polynesian, and African philosophy to produce an excellent single-volume survey. . . . The essays are of a uniformly high quality and are accessible even to those with little background in non-Western philosophies." Libr J

Durant, William James, 1885-1981

The story of philosophy; the lives and opinions of the great philosophers; by Will Durant. [2nd ed] Simon & Schuster 1933 412p hardcover o.p. pa $15 *
109

1. Philosophy—History 2. Philosophers
ISBN 0-671-69500-2; 0-671-20159-X (pa)
First published 1926

A selective account of western thinkers from Socrates and Kant to Schopenhauer and Dewey.

Includes bibliographical references

King, Peter J., 1935-

One hundred philosophers; the life and work of the world's greatest thinkers. Barron's Educ. Ser. 2004 192p il pa $19.95 *
109

1. Philosophers
ISBN 0-7641-2791-8
LC 2003-110643

This is "an overview of 100 important philosophers, from the ancient Greek pre-Socratics to today's analytic philosophers. Each thinker is summarized in an illustrated page . . . with a biographical sketch and summary of major works and ideas." Publisher's note

The author "has done a masterful job in presenting the life and work of what he calls 'the world's greatest thinkers.' . . . The concise and clearly written description of the thinker's life and ideas are just what a student or a layperson needs to gather an overview of the thinker's life and intellectual contributions." Am Ref Books Annu, 2005

Includes bibliographical references

Russell, Bertrand, 1872-1970

A history of Western philosophy; and its connection with political and social circumstances from the earliest times to the present day. Simon & Schuster 1945 xxiii, 895p
109

1. Philosophy—History 2. Philosophers
ISBN 0-671-31400-9; 0-671-20158-1 (pa)

Originally designed and partly delivered as lectures at the Barnes Foundation in Pennsylvania

Contents: Ancient philosophy; Catholic philosophy; Modern philosophy.

Russell, Bertrand, 1872-1970—*Continued*
"My purpose is to exhibit philosophy as an integral part of social and political life; not as the isolated speculations of remarkable individuals." Preface

Solomon, Robert C., 1942-2007
A passion for wisdom; a very brief history of philosophy; {by} Robert C. Solomon, Kathleen M. Higgins. Oxford Univ. Press 1997 137p pa $12.95 hardcover o.p. **109**
1. Philosophy—History
ISBN 0-19-511209-1 (pa)   LC 96-42034
Part one "examines the Greek roots of Western philosophy . . . {and} also looks at philosophical traditions in India, elsewhere in Asia, Africa, and the Americas. Part two covers the period from the origins of Christianity to the rise of Islam to Adam Smith; Part three begins with Kant and ends with a brief look at postmodernism." Libr J
The authors "provide a multicultural account of philosophical thought and developments across nearly 4000 years. The volume is necessarily simplified but not simplistic, and the thoughts themselves are given precedent over the biographies of the thinkers." SLJ
Includes bibliographical references

World philosophers and their works; editor, John K. Roth; managing editor, Christina J. Moose; project editor, Rowena Wildin. Salem Press 2000 3v il set $331   **109**
1. Philosophers
ISBN 0-89356-878-3   LC 99-55143
The editor "presents substantial entries that for 226 philosophers give brief biographies, justify the inclusion of each thinker, list their most important works, analyze their lifework, and locate them within the context of philosophy." Choice
Includes bibliographical references

111 Ontology

Barrow, John D., 1952-
The book of nothing; vacuums, voids, and the latest ideas about the origins of the universe. Pantheon Bks. 2001 361p il pa $15 hardcover o.p. **111**
1. Zero (The number) 2. Science—History
ISBN 0-375-72609-8 (pa)   LC 00-58894
Includes index
This volume traces the concept of nothing "from a Babylonian place holder, a Mayan decoration in the empty space where no number fell and an Indian dot signifying all the current aspects of zero, to one of the most essential elements in mathematics, physics and cosmology." Publ Wkly

The infinite book; a short guide to the boundless, timeless, and endless. Pantheon Books 2005 328p il $26   **111**
1. Infinite
ISBN 0-375-42227-7   LC 2004-60206
First published 2004 in the United Kingdom

The author "approaches the subject [of infinity] from the viewpoints of mathematics, physics, and scientific cosmology and also delves into philosophers' and theologians' reflections concerning infinity. . . . Well suited to a general audience, this book requires no specialized knowledge of mathematics or science." Libr J
Includes bibliographical references

Eco, Umberto
History of beauty; translated by Alastair McEwen. Rizzoli Int. Pubs. 2004 438p il $40
111
1. Aesthetics 2. Arts—Philosophy
ISBN 0-8478-2646-5
Published in the United Kingdom with title: On beauty: a history of a western idea
The editor "traces the protean subject of beauty in art, literature, philosophy, the mass media, and other humanities from ancient times to the present, setting forth various Western cultural aesthetic ideals ranging from ancient Greek to modern American. . . . This is not a quick, one-time coffee-table read but a nearly flawless presentation of the history of a fascinating and elusive idea that will delight and enlighten general readers as well as scholars." Libr J
Includes bibliographical references

Encyclopedia of aesthetics; editor in chief, Michael Kelly. Oxford Univ. Press 1998 4v set $495 *   **111**
ISBN 0-19-511307-1   LC 98-18741
"Drawing from experts in the areas of philosophy, art, history, psychology, feminist theory, legal theory, and many more, the encyclopedia presents 600 signed essays alphabetically arranged. Most entries include a headnote clarifying the topic. Entries range from the philosophical essay on ugliness, to the more reality-based article on the impact of AIDS on the arts. Comprehensive coverage includes key figures, concepts, periods, theories, and movements in the history of aesthetics." Am Libr

Heidegger, Martin, 1889-1976
Being and time; translated by John Macquarrie & Edward Robinson. Harper & Row 1962 589p $29.95 *   **111**
1. Ontology 2. Phenomenology
ISBN 0-06-063850-8
Also available in paperback from State Univ. of New York Press
Original German edition, 1927
"All of Heidegger's work revolves around the essential inquiry: what is the nature of being? In his most important book, . . . he distinguishes between two types of being: human existence (*Dasein*) and nonhuman presence (*Vorhandensein*)." Reader's Ency. 4th edition
Includes bibliographical references

On time and being; translated by Joan Stambaugh. University of Chicago Press 2002 84p pa $12   **111**
1. Ontology 2. Phenomenology
ISBN 0-226-32375-7; 978-0-226-32375-6
This translation first published 1972 by Harper & Row
Original German edition, 1969

Heidegger, Martin, 1889-1976—*Continued*

This volume by the 20th Century philosopher "contains four items: a 1962 lecture, 'Time and Being,' and a seminar report on it by Alfred Guzzoni; a 1964 lecture, 'The End of Philosophy and the Task of Thinking'; and a 1963 Festschrift essay, 'My Way to Phenomenology.'" Libr J

Includes bibliographical references

On ugliness; edited byUmberto Eco; translated by Alastair McEwen. Rizzoli 2007 455p il $45
                                                                 111
1. Aesthetics 2. Arts—Philosophy
ISBN 978-0-8478-2986-6; 0-8478-2986-3
                                              LC 2007-930249
In this "collection of images and written excerpts from ancient times to the present, all woven together with a provocative commentary and translated by Alastair McEwen, . . . [the editor] asks: Is repulsiveness, too, in the eye of the beholder? And what do we learn about that beholder when we delve into his aversions? Selecting stark visual images of gore, deformity, moral turpitude and malice, and quotations from sources ranging from Plato to radical feminists, Eco unfurls a taxonomy of ugliness. As gross-out contests go, it's both absorbing and highbrow." N Y Times Book Rev

Includes bibliographical references

Watson, Lyall

Dark nature; a natural history of evil. HarperCollins Pubs. 1996 c1995 318p pa $19 hardcover o.p.   **111**
1. Good and evil 2. Human beings 3. Biology—Philosophy
ISBN 0-06-092790-9 (pa)   LC 96-1663
First published 1995 in the United Kingdom
The author "ranges through philosophy, psychology, anthropology, history, ecology and especially biology. . . . Watson believes that aggression is in our genes and examines such phenomena as war, rape and murder as manifestations of that aggression. But while he firmly believes that humans are made up of both good and evil and that natural selection is completely amoral, he is sanguine about humans as the world's first ethical animals with the capability of making moral decisions." Publ Wkly

Includes bibliographical references

113   Cosmology (Philosophy of nature)

Teilhard de Chardin, Pierre

The phenomenon of man; with an introduction by Julian Huxley. Harper & Row 1959 318p pa $14.95 hardcover o.p. *   **113**
1. Universe 2. Evolution 3. Human beings
ISBN 0-06-090495-X (pa)
Original French edition, 1955; this translation by Bernard Wall
The author integrates scientific findings with the tenets of Christian faith in this study of human evolution and destiny

Whitehead, Alfred North, 1861-1947

Process and reality; an essay in cosmology. corrected ed, edited by David Ray Griffin, Donald W. Sherburne. Free Press 1978 xxxi, 413p pa $18.95 hardcover o.p. *   **113**
1. Universe 2. Science—Philosophy
ISBN 0-02-934570-7 (pa)   LC 77-90011
First published 1929
Gifford lectures delivered in the University of Edinburgh during the session, 1927-28
This book presents a condensed scheme of cosmological ideas developed by confrontation with various topics of experience. The aesthetic, moral and religious interests are thus brought into relation with those elements of knowledge which have their origin in natural science

Includes bibliographical references

Wilson, Edward O., 1929-

In search of nature. Island Press 1996 214p il $22; pa $15 *   **113**
1. Philosophy of nature 2. Human beings 3. Human ecology
ISBN 1-55963-215-1; 1-55963-216-X (pa)
                                              LC 96-11226
"A Shearwater book".
"A compilation of a dozen journal articles and book chapters published between 1975 and 1993, this collection is grouped into three thematic sections dealing with the importance of the preservation of biodiversity to our physical and emotional well-being, the deep-seated interconnectedness of animal nature and human nature . . . and the underlying genetic basis of human social behavior." Libr J
"Concerned people of all ages should enjoy the reasoning provided by the dedicated scientific writing presented in this attractive book." Sci Books Films

Includes bibliographical references

115   Time

Gorst, Martin, 1960-

Measuring eternity; the search for the beginning of time. Broadway Bks. 2002 338p il $23.95; pa $13.95 *   **115**
1. Time
ISBN 0-7679-0827-9; 0-7679-0844-9 (pa)
                                              LC 2001-37556
Published in the United Kingdom with title: Aeons
The author "discusses how human understanding of time shifted throughout the centuries, as models of the universe became more accurate and instruments for gathering data grew more sophisticated." Publ Wkly
"For the most part Gorst avoids retrospective judgments on what now seem to be spectacular errors of calculation. Instead, he peppers his account with snippets and asides that bring the protagonists to life and make the story of time surprisingly easy to trace." New Sci

Includes bibliographical references

121 Epistemology (Theory of knowledge)

Blackburn, Simon
Truth; a guide; Simon Blackburn. Oxford University Press 2005 xxi, 238p $25 *

121
1. Truth
ISBN 0-19-516824-0   LC 2004-19800
The author "wants to help readers attain a philosophical understanding of the concept of 'truth.' . . . Blackburn reviews what philosophers, writers, novelists, scientists, and disparate thinkers have had to say about it, including Plato, Francis Bacon, Voltaire, Locke, Hume, Wittgenstein, William James, Rorty, and Nietzsche." Libr J

This book "traverses a broad terrain, exploring many points of the map of human knowledge and thinkers of all stripes." N Y Times Book Rev
Includes bibliographical references

Hecht, Jennifer Michael
Doubt: a history; the great doubters and their legacy of innovation, from Socrates and Jesus to Thomas Jefferson and Emily Dickinson. HarperSanFrancisco 2003 xxi, 551p il $27.95; pa $16.95   121
1. Belief and doubt
ISBN 0-06-009772-8; 0-06-009795-7 (pa)
LC 2004-266061
Contents: Doubt is no shadow : a quiz and a guide to the question -- Whatever happened to Zeus and Hera?, 600 BCE-1 CE : Greek doubt -- Smacking the temple, 600 BCE-1 CE : doubt and the ancient Jews -- What the Buddha saw, 600 BCE-1 CE: ancient doubt in Asia -- When in Rome in doubt, 50 BCE-1 CE : empire of reason -- Christian doubt, Zen, Elisha, and Hypatia, 1-800 CE : late-classical mix -- Medieval doubt loops-the-loop, 800-1400 : Muslims to Jews to Christians -- The printing press and the Age of Martyrs, 1400-1600 : Renaissance and inquisition -- Sunspots and White House doubters, 1600-1800 : revolutions in the authority of reason -- Doubt's bid for a better work, 1800-1900 : freethinking in the age of science and reform -- Principles of uncertainty, 1900 : the new cosmopolitan -- The joy of doubt : ethics, logic, mood
The author's "brief but splendid study of the great Renaissance skeptic Montaigne is alone worth the price of the book. Hecht's warm prose, lucid insights, and impeccable research combine for a lively, thoughtful, and first-rate study of a neglected idea." Libr J

Locke, John, 1632-1704
An essay concerning human understanding; edited by Roger Woolhouse. Penguin Books 1997 xxvii, 784p pa $17 *   121
1. Theory of knowledge 2. Thought and thinking
ISBN 0-14-043482-8   LC 98-175907
This essay first published 1690, deals "with the nature and scope of human knowledge. Its basic premise is the empirical origin of ideas, which can be described as the raw material with which the mind works. Locke's essay contributed greatly to the growth of 18th-century empiricism." Reader's Ency. 4th edition
Includes bibliographical references

Sartre, Jean Paul, 1905-1980
Truth and existence; original text established and annotated by Arlette Elkaïm-Sartre; translated by Adrian van den Hoven; edited and with an introduction by Ronald Aronson. University of Chicago Press 1992 xlix, 94p pa $11 hardcover o.p. *   121
1. Theory of knowledge
ISBN 0-226-73523-0 (pa)   LC 92-5889
Written in 1948; original French edition, 1989
This book "presents Sartre's ontology of truth in terms of his characteristic key moral questions of freedom, action, and bad faith. Here is Sartre the existentialist at his most original and most provocative." Univ Press Books for Public and Second Sch Libr
Includes bibliographical references

Wilson, Edward O., 1929-
Consilience; the unity of knowledge. Knopf 1998 332p $27.50; pa $15 *   121
1. Philosophy 2. Theory of knowledge 3. Science—Philosophy
ISBN 0-679-45077-7; 0-679-76867-X (pa)
LC 97-2816
"Wilson argues that there is a genetic and neurological basis for knowledge and that all subjects of human inquiry can be reunited under the umbrella of 'consilience.'" Libr J
The author's "extraordinarily clear, evocative imagery and elegant sentences make us see how a consilient world of knowledge might look. . . . Wilson's book of faith in the dream of reason and objective knowledge is a tour de force." Publ Wkly
Includes bibliographical references

128 Humankind

Abram, David
The spell of the sensuous; perception and language in a more-than-human world. Pantheon Bks. 1996 326p pa $14.95 hardcover o.p.
128
1. Philosophy of nature 2. Mind and body 3. Perception 4. Language and languages
ISBN 0-679-77639-7 (pa)   LC 95-31466
This book grew out of Abram's "explorations of magic and sorcery in indigenous cultures and the relationship between magic and the natural world. Where he leads the reader after this is tough to summarize: Edmund Husserl, Maurice Merleau-Ponty, Balinese sorcerers, origins of the alphabet, Kant, Newton. Word by word this is readable and connected to a fascinating thesis: that our perceptions grew from the natural world around us, and we can 'return to our senses' and be reinvigorated, reformed, by the experience." Libr J
Includes bibliographical references

Bloom, Howard, 1943-
The Lucifer principle; a scientific expedition into the forces of history. Atlantic Monthly Press 1995 466p pa $16 hardcover o.p.   **128**
1. Human beings 2. Evolution 3. History—Philosophy 4. Culture 5. Modern civilization 6. Good and evil
ISBN 0-87113-664-3 (pa)   LC 94-11464
The 'Lucifer principle' is the author's "theory that evil—which manifests in violence, destructiveness and war—is woven into our biological fabric. . . . [In this study] Bloom applies the ideas of sociobiology, ethology and the 'killer ape' school of anthropology to the broad canvas of history." Publ Wkly
"A disturbing book, but its broad generalities wear down the sharp edges of its arguments, leaving something that becomes food for thought rather than reason to despair." Booklist
Includes bibliographical references

Devlin, Keith J.
Goodbye, Descartes; the end of logic and the search for a new cosmology of the mind. Wiley 1997 301p hardcover o.p. pa $14.95   **128**
1. Mind and body 2. Linguistics 3. Logic
ISBN 0-471-14216-6; 0-471-25186-0 (pa)
          LC 96-25493
"Devlin traces the history of logic, particularly mathematical logic, over two-plus millennia and the shorter history of Chomsky's Cartesian linguistics to explain why at least some 'mathematicians and scientists have come to realize that the truly difficult problems of the information age . . . concern *ourselves*—what it is to think, to reason, and to engage in conversation.'" Booklist
"An excellent book that should be read by everyone who has ever wondered how we communicate with one another but find it so frustrating to interact with computers." Libr J
Includes bibliographical references

Frayn, Michael
The human touch; our part in the creation of a universe. Metropolitan Books 2007 505p $32.50   **128**
1. Cosmology 2. Science—Philosophy
ISBN 978-0-8050-8148-0; 0-8050-8148-8
          LC 2006-48204
First published 2006 in the United Kingdom
"Beginning with a description of the continual 'traffic' between humans and the universe, Frayn shapes a cohesive introduction to philosophy that includes elements of science, determinism, physics, mathematics, psychology, linguistics, and epistemology." Libr J
Includes bibliographical references

Irvine, William Braxton, 1952-
On desire; why we want what we want; [by] William B. Irvine. Oxford University Press 2005 322p $24   **128**
1. Desire
ISBN 0-19-518862-4   LC 2005-05938

The author "explains how desire–really a multitude of desires, uninvited and unannounced–manifests itself, how it can be identified and parsed, and how it can be mastered in a way that offers the best chance at self-fulfillment. He uses modern psychology to delineate desire but then shows how the world's great religions–here mainly Christianity and Buddhism, but also Hinduism, Islam, and Judaism–address this phenomenon. He advocates no particular approach, admitting instead that different tacks probably work for different people. And he never lets the reader think that mastering desire will be easy. This is that rare book that should appeal to a wide range of readers without necessarily trying to do so." Booklist

The **Oxford** companion to the mind; edited by Richard L. Gregory. 2nd ed. Oxford University Press 2005 1004p il $75 *   **128**
1. Psychology—Dictionaries
ISBN 0-19-866224-6   LC 2004-275127
First published 1987
This book "contains over 1000 alphabetically arranged entries on all aspects of the mind, including topics in neurophysiology, communication, psychology, and philosophy, as well as people relevant to the field." Libr J
This "is one of those texts one wishes for enough hours in the day to read from cover to cover. . . . For those interested in the mind, this is a wonderful reference and a resource for learning more about themselves." Sci Books Films

Terkel, Studs, 1912-2008
Will the circle be unbroken? reflections on death, rebirth, and a hunger for faith. New Press (NY) 2001 xxiv, 407p $25.95   **128**
1. Death 2. Faith
ISBN 1-56584-692-3
Also available in paperback from Ballantine Bks.
"Terkel talks to 60 people about their encounters with death. His subjects range from emergency room doctors and paramedics to public figures such as author Kurt Vonnegut and guitarist Doc Watson. A stirring celebration of life and exploration of death." Booklist

130 Parapsychology & occultism

Dolnick, Barrie
Luck; understanding luck and improving the odds; [by] Barrie Dolnick and Anthony H. Davidson. Harmony Books 2007 236p $19.95   **130**
1. Chance 2. Superstition
ISBN 978-0-307-34750-3; 0-307-34750-8
          LC 2007-13235
This "mini reference examines the concept of luck throughout history as observed by a variety of religious sects and practiced in many cultures. The authors help readers develop a personal-luck profile and detail how to apply astrology, numerology, and even herbology toward increasing the odds in one's favor. A practical section on gambling advises readers how to play cards, dice, or the roulette wheel with caution." Libr J
Includes bibliographical references

Goodman, Linda, 1925-1995
Linda Goodman's star signs; the secret codes of the universe: forgotten rainbows and forgotten melodies of ancient wisdom. St. Martin's Press 1987 xli, 477p il pa $17.95 hardcover o.p.

130

1. Occultism 2. Parapsychology 3. Astrology 4. New Age movement
ISBN 0-312-19203-7 (pa)   LC 87-28375
Also available in hardcover from Taplinger Pub.
"Goodman explains numerology, lexigrams (secret codes of words, names, and titles), the power of sound, and the power of color. . . . Along with explanations of karma and other modes of spiritual growth, she interweaves her own experiences with avatars and gurus, as well as common folk who are on their own spiritual path." Booklist

133.1   Apparitions

Guiley, Rosemary Ellen
The encyclopedia of ghosts and spirits; foreword by Troy Taylor. 3rd ed. Facts on File 2007 564p il $75 *

133.1

1. Ghosts—Encyclopedias
ISBN 978-0-8160-6737-4; 0-8160-6737-6
LC 2006-103302
First published 1992
This work examines famous hauntings, historical personages and happenings, and various legends and myths about ghosts and spirits throughout the world. Recent events, new findings about old myths and updated information on major figures in the field are covered.
"Believers and skeptics alike seeking information on various phenomena will find this book useful." Booklist
Includes bibliographical references

Norman, Michael, 1947-
Haunted America; {by} Michael Norman and Beth Scott. TOR Bks. 1994 411p maps pa $7.99 hardcover o.p.

133.1

1. Ghosts
ISBN 0-8125-5054-4 (pa)   LC 94-28984
"A Tom Doherty Associates book"
"This collection of chilling tales of the supernatural includes at least one story from each state and from the English-speaking Canadian provinces. The stories recount sightings of ghostly apparitions and mysterious happenings, and their history and evolution is documented." Libr J
Includes bibliographical references

Ramsland, Katherine M., 1953-
Ghost; investigating the other side; {by} Katherine Ramsland. St. Martin's Press 2001 322p il $25.95; pa $6.99

133.1

1. Ghosts
ISBN 0-312-26164-0; 0-312-98373-5 (pa)
LC 2001-41725
"Cast as an adventure in 'participatory journalism,' the book begins with Ramsland's chance acquisition of a

haunted silver ring. Determined to extract its secrets, she sets out on a quest that gradually turns into a full-blown investigation of psychic aberration in America." Publ Wkly
"Although prepared to dismiss many so-called paranormal occurrences in favor of natural explanations, {the author} nevertheless encounters, experiences, and investigates a variety of inexplicable visual, photographic, and verbal manifestations. Both skeptics and believers will be intrigued by this first-person exploration of ghostly visitations." Booklist
Includes bibliographical references

133.4   Demonology and witchcraft

Adler, Margot
Drawing down the moon; witches, Druids, goddess-worshippers, and other pagans in America. [Rev and updated ed] Penguin Books 2006 646p il pa $18

133.4

1. Witchcraft 2. Paganism
ISBN 0-14-303819-2; 978-0-14-303819-1
LC 2006-43786
First published 1979 by Viking
A survey of goddess worship and witchcraft movements discussing their basic philosophies and practices
"Despite its clear anti-Judaic and anti-Christian bias, this book is recommended for general and college audiences interested in religion, the occult, and modern social phenomena." Choice {review of 1979 edition}
Includes bibliographical references

Carlson, Laurie M., 1952-
A fever in Salem; a new interpretation of the New England witch trials. Dee, I.R. 1999 197p hardcover o.p. pa $14.95

133.4

1. Witchcraft 2. Salem (Mass.)—History
ISBN 1-56663-253-6; 1-56663-309-5 (pa)
LC 99-27520
In this reading of the New England witch trials, Carlson argues that "the 'possessed' of Salem, and perhaps of many other places where witchcraft was suspected, were in thrall not to devilry but to a mysterious disease of the brain, encephalitis lethargica, popularly known as sleeping sickness." New Yorker
"Carlson's compelling narrative begs for assessment by medical experts. A valuable purchase for libraries seeking more than a basic summary of the witch trials." Libr J
Includes bibliographical references

Guiley, Rosemary Ellen
The encyclopedia of witches, witchcraft, and Wicca. 3rd ed. Facts On File 2008 448p $85; pa $24.95

133.4

1. Witchcraft—Encyclopedias
ISBN   978-0-8160-7103-6;   0-8160-7103-9;
978-0-8160-7104-3 (pa); 0-8160-7104-7 (pa)
LC 2008-8917
First published 1989 with title: The encyclopedia of witches and witchcraft

Guiley, Rosemary Ellen—*Continued*

This work covers witchcraft practices around the world and throughout history, including entries on magic, the occult, wizardry, Wicca, and shamanism. The entries vary in length from a paragraph to several pages and examine rituals, traditions, and events as well as people and places.

Includes bibliographical references

Hutton, Ronald

The triumph of the moon; a history of modern pagan witchcraft. Oxford Univ. Press 1999 486p $55.50; pa $17.95   **133.4**
1. Witchcraft 2. Neopaganism
ISBN 0-19-820744-1; 0-19-285449-6 (pa)
LC 99-31586

This "history of paganism in 19th- and 20th-century Britain centers on Wicca, the system of witchcraft Gerald B. Gardner introduced to a startled public in the 1950s. . . . Hutton's exceptional work is by far the most scholarly, comprehensive and judicious analysis of the subject yet published." Publ Wkly

Includes bibliographical references

Karlsen, Carol F., 1940-

The devil in the shape of a woman; witchcraft in colonial New England. Norton 1987 360p hardcover o.p. pa $16.95 *   **133.4**
1. Witchcraft 2. New England—History—1600-1775, Colonial period
ISBN 0-393-02478-4; 0-393-31759-5 (pa)
LC 87-16615

Also available in hardcover from P. Smith

The author presents a "social history of witchcraft in Puritan New England (1620-1725). She unearths detailed evidence which demonstrates that prosecuted and accused witches generally were older, married women who had violated the religious and/or economic Puritan social hierarchy. . . . A well-written, provocative addition to the . . . scholarship on New England witchcraft." Libr J

Includes bibliographical references

133.5 Astrology

Goodman, Linda, 1925-1995

Linda Goodman's sun signs. Taplinger 1968 xxiii, 549p $29.95   **133.5**
1. Astrology 2. Zodiac
ISBN 0-8008-4900-0

Also available in paperback from Bantam Bks.

The author tells how to identify and deal with people according to their astrological signs

"This book is part astrology, part psychology, and always entertaining." Libr J

Lewis, James R., 1949-

The astrology book; the encyclopedia of heavenly influences. 2nd ed. Visible Ink Press 2003 928p il pa $24.95 *   **133.5**
1. Astrology—Encyclopedias
ISBN 1-57859-144-9

Also available in hardcover from Omnigraphics

First published 1994 by Gale Res. with title: The astrology encyclopedia

This "defines and explains more than 800 astrological terms and concepts from air signs to Zeus. . . . *The Astrology Book* includes a special section on casting a chart, plus a . . . chapter that explains and interprets every planet in every house and sign. The text also includes a table of astrological glyphs and abbreviations, and a list of organizations, books, periodicals, and Web sites." Publisher's note

"Although aimed at the believer, Lewis' work may be confidently consulted by the skeptic seeking basic information about astrology." Booklist

Miller, Susan

Planets and possibilities; explore the worlds beyond your sun sign. Warner Bks. 2001 418p il $30; pa $15.95   **133.5**
1. Astrology
ISBN 0-446-52434-4; 0-446-67806-6 (pa)

The author provides "character analysis of each sign. The cosmic gifts, relationship trends, financial tendencies, and career tendencies associated with each sign are all described in detail. The mythology of each sign is included as well, nicely rounding out the book." Libr J

Snodgrass, Mary Ellen

Signs of the zodiac; a reference guide to historical, mythological, and cultural associations; illustrated by Raymond Miller Barrett, Jr. Greenwood Press 1997 243p il $46.95
                                                133.5
1. Zodiac 2. Astrology
ISBN 0-313-30276-6   LC 97-5598

"After brief descriptions of zodiacal variants from other parts of the world, plus chapters on the historical foundations of astrology and its pervasiveness in the arts and sciences, Snodgrass treats each sign to a full workover: major stars in each, mythological background and symbology, commonly accepted character traits of those born under its influence, and thumbnail biographies of select prominent people who exemplify those traits." SLJ

Includes bibliographical references

133.6 Palmistry

Reid, Lori

The art of hand reading. DK Pub. 1996 120p il pa $15 hardcover o.p.   **133.6**
1. Palmistry
ISBN 0-7894-4837-8 (pa)   LC 96-15506

This volume uses color photographs of hands and handprints to analyze all the significant lines, mounts, and markings on hands. It shows how the different areas of the palm reveal the balance between instinctive desires and powers of intellect and reason

133.8 Psychic phenomena

Sheldrake, Rupert
Dogs that know when their owners are coming home; and other unexplained powers of animals. Crown 1999 352p il pa $14 hardcover o.p.
        133.8
1. Pets 2. Extrasensory perception
ISBN 0-609-80533-9 (pa)   LC 99-25439
"The author reports the results of five years of extensive research as he followed up on anecdotal accounts from pet owners on the homing abilities of lost pets, animals that show premonitions of earthquakes or epileptic seizures, and the fact that animals anticipate the arrival home of their owners." Booklist
Includes bibliographical references

The sense of being stared at; and other aspects of the extended mind. Crown 2003 369p il pa $13.95 hardcover o.p.   **133.8**
1. Extrasensory perception
ISBN 1-4000-5129-0 (pa)   LC 2002-9943
The author "proposes that the mind extends beyond the conventionally recognized parameters; that 'detectable effects' of this extended mental field can be measured in several phenomena associated with vision; and that there is a biological and evolutionary basis for telepathy." SLJ
"A most unusual book—fascinating, scientifically sound, and fun to read—it posits that ESP and 'other aspects of the extended mind' are not paranormal but natural functions. Every library should make room on its shelves for this one." Libr J
Includes bibliographical references

133.9 Spiritualism

Blum, Deborah
Ghost hunters; William James and the search for scientific proof of life after death. Penguin Press 2006 370p $25.95; pa $15   **133.9**
1. James, William, 1842-1910 2. Parapsychology 3. Spiritualism
ISBN 1-59420-090-4; 978-1-59420-090-8; 0-14-303895-8 (pa); 978-0-14-303895-5 (pa)
      LC 2006-44948
In this book, the author examines the Victorian era conflict between science and religion "by reviewing the history of the British Society for Psychical Research and its U.S. counterpart, the American Society for Psychical Research, both of which aimed to find scientific proof of the existence of the supernatural. . . . Her clearly written presentation of the history, frauds, and personalities involved in this unique slice of Victorian life is recommended for all history of science collections." Libr J
Includes bibliographical references

Moody, Raymond A.
Life after life; the investigation of a phenomenon—survival of bodily death; [by] Raymond A. Moody, Jr.; with a new preface by Melvin Morse and a foreword by Elizabeth Kübler-Ross. HarperSanFrancisco 2001 xxviii, 175p pa $14 *   **133.9**
1. Future life 2. Near-death experiences 3. Death
ISBN 0-06-251739-2   LC 00-46156
First published 1975 by MBB Inc.
The author "investigates more than one hundred case studies of people who experienced 'clinical death' and were subsequently revived." Publisher's note

Roach, Mary
Spook; science tackles the afterlife. Norton 2005 311p il $24.95 *   **133.9**
1. Future life 2. Religion and science
ISBN 0-393-05962-6   LC 2005-14450
The author investigates a range of theories and beliefs about the soul's migration after death.
"Roach perfectly balances her skepticism and her boundless curiosity with a sincere desire to know. . . . She is an original who can enliven any subject with wit, keen reporting and a sly intelligence." Publ Wkly
Includes bibliographical references

141 Idealism and related systems and doctrines

Berlin, Sir Isaiah
The roots of romanticism; edited by Henry Hardy. Princeton Univ. Press 1999 171p (A.W. Mellon lectures in the fine arts, 1965) pa $19.95
      141
1. Romanticism 2. Arts—Philosophy
ISBN 0-691-00713-6; 978-0-691-08662-0 (pa); 0-691-08662-0 (pa)   LC 98-41657
This is an edited transcript of the lectures "and the supporting bibliographic notes from which Berlin worked on his idea of romanticism. . . . Arguing that the concept flows from late 18th-century German thought and society, Berlin addresses romanticism's effect on the Enlightenment, the roles played by Hamann, Herder, and other early Romanticists in the codification of the movement, the more distilled approaches of Kant and Schiller, and romanticism's lingering effects on Western intellectual posture. . . . An excellent resource for both beginning researcher and seasoned scholar." Libr J
Includes bibliographical references

The **essential** transcendentalists; edited and introduced by Richard G. Geldard. J.P. Tarcher/Penguin 2005 265p pa $15.95 *
      141
1. Transcendentalism
ISBN 1-58542-434-X   LC 2005-44016
This study "is divided into three main sections. . . . The first is 'Primary Texts,' with selections from the writings of Sampson Reed, James Marsh, Amos Alcott (father of Louisa May), and Ralph Waldo Emerson. The

The essential transcendentalists—*Continued*
second, 'Individual Voices,' introduces selections from
Frederic Hedge, Margaret Fuller, and Henry David Thoreau. The last is 'The Transcendental Heritage,' which
features the works of Walt Whitman, Emily Dickinson,
Wallace Stevens, Loren Eiseley, and Annie Dillard. This
is a highly informed, elegantly written, fascinating story
told through commentary, historical overview, and selections from classic works. It belongs in all libraries." Libr
J

Includes bibliographical references

142 Critical philosophy

Barrett, William, 1913-1992
Irrational man; a study in existential philosophy.
Doubleday 1958 278p pa $12.95 hardcover o.p. *
142
1. Existentialism
ISBN 0-385-03138-6 (pa)
This discussion of existentialism traces its origins and
analyzes the contributions of chief exponents of existen-
tialist thought—Nietzsche, Kierkegaard, Heidegger and
Sartre

Existentialism from Dostoevsky to Sartre. rev and
expanded. edited, with an introduction, prefaces,
and new translations by Walter Kaufmann. New
Am. Lib. 1975 384p pa $15.95   142
1. Existentialism
ISBN 0-452-00930-8
Also available in hardcover from P. Smith
"A Meridian book"
First published 1956 by World Pub.
This book contains selections from the basic writings
of Dostoevsky, Kierkegaard, Nietzsche, Rilke, Ortega y
Gasset, Jaspers, Heidegger, Sartre and Camus.

Sartre, Jean Paul, 1905-1980
Being and nothingness; an essay on
phenomenological ontology; translated and with an
introduction by Hazel E. Barnes. Philosophical
Lib. 1956 638p *   142
1. Existentialism
Also available in hardcover from P. Smith
Original French edition, 1943
This is "Sartre's major attempt to systematize his the-
oretical analysis of the human condition and human con-
sciousness which underlies 'Existentialism.'" Reader's
Ency. 4th edition

Existentialism and human emotions.
Philosophical Library: Distributed to the Book
trade by Citadel Press 1957 96p pa $9.95 o.p.
142
1. Existentialism
ISBN 0-8065-0902-3 (pa)
"The section on 'Existentialism' is taken from the
book of that name; translated by Bernard Frechtman; all
other selections are from 'Being and nothingness' translated by Hazel E. Barnes"

Contents: Existentialism; Freedom and responsibility;
The desire to be God; Existentialist psychoanalysis; The
hole; Ethical implications

146 Naturalism and related systems and doctrines

Dennett, Daniel Clement
Darwin's dangerous idea; evolution and the
meanings of life; {by} Daniel C. Dennett. Simon
& Schuster 1995 586p il pa $16 hardcover o.p.
146
1. Natural selection 2. Evolution
ISBN 0-684-82471-X (pa)   LC 94-49158
"Current controversies associated with the origin of
life, sociobiology, punctuated equilibrium, the evolution
of culture and language, and evolutionary ethics are investigated rigorously within the context of Darwinian science and philosophy. Dennett challenges the ideas of
several imminent scientists, including Roger Penrose and
Stephen Jay Gould, who, Dennett asserts, tend to limit
the power or implications of Darwin's dangerous ideas."
Libr J
Includes bibliographical references

150 Psychology

Glasser, William, 1925-
Choice theory; a new psychology of personal
freedom. HarperCollins Pubs. 1998 340p il $24; pa
$13.95   150
1. Psychology
ISBN 0-06-019109-0; 0-06-093014-4 (pa)
LC 97-36025
"Choice theory helps its users avoid confrontation and
ask pertinent questions. It sees conscious or unconscious
desire for external control as the main problem in the
four major personal relationships: husband-wife, parent-
child, teacher-student, and manager-worker. . . . Combining choice theory and reality therapy in his practice,
Glasser has been able to shorten the durations of his
treatment programs substantially. As he presents them
here, his theories and approaches can be applied in education and business as well as for self-help." Booklist

150.19 Systems, schools, viewpoints

Bettelheim, Bruno
Freud and man's soul. Knopf 1983 111p pa $9
hardcover o.p. *   150.19
1. Freud, Sigmund, 1856-1939 2. Psychoanalysis
ISBN 0-394-71036-3 (pa)   LC 82-47809
The author argues that Freud was a great humanist
and that mistranslation of his work has lead American
psychoanalysis astray

Blum, Deborah
Love at Goon Park; Harry Harlow and the science of affection. Perseus Bks. 2002 336p $26
150.19
1. Harlow, Harry F., 1905-1981 2. Love 3. Child development
ISBN 0-7382-0278-9   LC 2002-112387
The author "recounts Harlow's work while examining the man himself. Harlow argued that mother-child bonding was crucial for normal development, and his experiments with monkeys showed that social organisms cannot survive isolation. But as Blum reveals, Harlow was an enigma, brilliant but distant from his own children, and his work raised ethical and controversial dilemmas concerning the research treatment of animals." Libr J
Includes bibliographical references

Buhle, Mari Jo, 1943-
Feminism and its discontents; a century of struggle with psychoanalysis. Harvard Univ. Press 1998 432p $39.95; pa $21.50 *   **150.19**
1. Psychoanalysis 2. Feminism 3. Women—Psychology
ISBN 0-674-29868-3; 0-674-00403-5 (pa)
          LC 97-32397
Buhle bases her "historical study on the premise that feminism and psychoanalytic theory, each in its own way concerned with understanding the 'self,' developed in continuous dialogue with each other. The author's captivating, energetic writing style reflects the often spirited, surprisingly tenacious relationship of these two theories." Booklist
Includes bibliographical references

Freud, Sigmund, 1856-1939
The basic writings of Sigmund Freud; translated and edited by A.A. Brill. Modern Lib. 1995 c1938 973p $24.95 *   **150.19**
1. Psychoanalysis
ISBN 0-679-60166-X   LC 95-13411
A reissue of the 1938 edition
Contents: Psychopathology of everyday life; The interpretation of dreams; Three contributions to the theory of sex; Wit and its relations to the unconscious; Totem and taboo; The history of the psychoanalytic movement

The Freud reader; edited by Peter Gay. Norton 1989 832p pa $21.95 hardcover o.p. *
          150.19
1. Psychoanalysis
ISBN 0-393-31403-0 (pa)   LC 89-2949
This "work includes some 50 of Freud's texts, organized chronologically with headnotes. The selections range from case studies and theoretical discussions about dreams, anxiety and anal eroticism to essays on lay analysis and religion as humankind's obsessional neurosis." Libr J
Includes bibliographical references

Freud: conflict and culture; edited by Michael S. Roth. Knopf 1998 173p il pa $14 hardcover o.p.
          150.19
1. Freud, Sigmund, 1856-1939 2. Psychoanalysis
ISBN 0-679-77292-8 (pa)   LC 98-12373

Published in conjunction with an exhibition at the Library of Congress this is a collection of essays by such authors as Oliver Sacks, E. Ann Kaplan, Muriel Dimen, Adolf Grunbaum, Hannah S. Decker, Peter Kramer, and Robert Coles
"Mostly concerned with Freud's large themes and their impact in history, these essays are pitched to a generalized intellectual audience." Libr J
Includes bibliographical references

Fromm, Erich, 1900-1980
On being human; foreword by Rainer Funk. Continuum 1994 180p hardcover o.p. pa $29.95 *
          150.19
1. Humanism 2. Social psychology 3. Psychoanalysis
ISBN 0-8264-0576-2; 0-8264-1005-7 (pa)
          LC 93-9243
This volume includes the author's writings on humanism, social psychology, and psychoanalysis from the 1960s, based on Fromm's lectures, works written for specific occasions, and manuscripts intended as books.
Includes bibliographical references

Gay, Peter, 1923-
A Godless Jew; Freud, atheism, and the making of psychoanalysis. Yale Univ. Press 1987 182p hardcover o.p. pa $17 *   **150.19**
1. Freud, Sigmund, 1856-1939 2. Psychoanalysis 3. Atheism
ISBN 0-300-04008-3; 0-300-04608-1 (pa)
          LC 87-8267
Based on lectures presented at Hebrew Union College, Cincinnati, in 1986
The author "reviews the various claims for the Jewishness of psychoanalysis and finds them to be wholly without merit. Paradoxically, he argues that Freud's position as an outsider—an atheist and Jew—enabled him to pierce the taboo topics of sexuality and the unconscious which led to his momentous discoveries." Publ Wkly
Includes bibliographical references

Horney, Karen, 1885-1952
New ways in psychoanalysis. Norton 1939 313p pa $15.95 hardcover o.p. *   **150.19**
1. Psychoanalysis
ISBN 0-393-31230-5 (pa)
Also available hardcover from Routledge
"A critical re-evaluation of psychoanalysis, accepting Freud's theories as a basis but showing how modern practice is in some ways departing from the limitations set by Freud's viewpoint, particularly in giving more importance to cultural factors." Booklist

Jung, C. G. (Carl Gustav), 1875-1961
The basic writings of C. G. Jung; edited with an introduction by Violet Staub de Laszlo. Modern Lib. 1993 c1959 xxxiii, 691p $21.95 *
          150.19
1. Psychoanalysis
ISBN 0-679-60071-X   LC 93-17801
Also available in paperback from Princeton Univ. Press

Jung, C. G. (Carl Gustav), 1875-1961—*Continued*

This is a reissue of the 1959 edition

This volume contains excerpts from Symbols of transformation, On the nature of the psyche, Relations between the ego and the unconscious, Psychological types, Psychology of the transference, and Psychology and religion. It also includes Archetypes of the collective unconscious, Psychological aspects of the mother archetype, On the nature of dreams, On the psychogenesis of schizophrenia, Introduction to the religious and psychological problems of alchemy, and Marriage as a psychological relationship.

Includes bibliographical references

The essential Jung; selected and introduced by Anthony Storr. Princeton Univ. Press 1983 447p pa $18.95 hardcover o.p.   **150.19**

1. Psychoanalysis

ISBN 0-691-02935-0 (pa)   LC 82-61441

Published in the United Kingdom with title: Jung, selected writings

"This book is an attempt to distill the essential features of Jung's psychology as it developed during the course of his life by means of extracts from his own writings." Preface

Storr's "selections from Jung's writings are lucid and accessible; linked by skillful explanatory passages, they provide both interested laypersons and students with a perspective on Jung." Libr J

Includes bibliographical references

Man and his symbols; {by} Carl G. Jung {et al.}. Doubleday 1964 320p il $30; pa $7.99 *
                150.19

1. Symbolism 2. Psychology 3. Dreams 4. Self 5. Art—Psychology

ISBN 0-385-05221-9; 0-440-35183-9 (pa)

"The basic ideas of Jungian psychology are presented in popular language in six essays by Dr. Jung and {four} of his pupils; these are correlated to dreams and symbols and are shown in their archetypal relationships to ancient myths, present-day thought and art." Libr J

Includes bibliographical references

The portable Jung; edited with an introduction by Joseph Campbell; translated by R. F. C. Hull. Viking 1971 xli, 659p pa $17 hardcover o.p.
                150.19

1. Psychoanalysis

ISBN 0-14-015070-6 (pa)

"The Viking portable library"

A collection of writings spanning the career of the pioneering psychoanalyst. Includes a chronology and bibliography.

May, Rollo

The discovery of being; writings in existential psychology. Norton 1983 192p pa $14.95 **150.19**

1. Existentialism 2. Psychotherapy

ISBN: 0-393-31240-2 (pa)   LC 83-4282

Also available in hardcover from P. Smith

The author "provides the reader with principles of his existential psychotherapy; delineates his view of the cul-

tural-historical context that gave rise to both psychoanalysis and existentialism; and sets forth what he considers to be the contributions to therapy of an existential approach." Choice

Includes bibliographical references

Menninger, Karl A. (Karl Augustus), 1893-1990

Love against hate; {by} Karl Menninger with the collaboration of Jeanetta Lyle Menninger. Harcourt Brace & Co. 1942 311p hardcover op. pa. $17 *   **150.19**

1. Psychoanalysis 2. Sexual behavior 3. Love 4. Instinct

The author "rehearses first the various frustrations which inhibit and misguide human energies, and then, in a series of chapters on Work, Play, Faith, Hope and Love considers how the destructive tendencies may be guided into creative channels." Wis Libr Bull

Includes bibliographical references

Mitchell, Stephen A., 1946-2000

Freud and beyond; a history of modern psychoanalytic thought; {by} Stephen A. Mitchell, Margaret Black. Basic Bks. 1995 293p pa $17.50 hardcover o.p.   **150.19**

1. Freud, Sigmund, 1856-1939 2. Psychoanalysis

ISBN 0-465-01405-4 (pa)   LC 95-8972

The authors "concisely demythologize Sigmund Freud and engage themselves with a score of his key successors (including five women). Brief biographies and succinct theoretical summaries are fleshed out with clinical examples." Libr J

"Mitchell and Black's book establishes itself as the best single treatment of psychoanalytic theories, classical and current. Intended as an introduction, it will be of use to practicing clinicians as well, with virtues of coherent discussion of complex ideas, nonpolemical presentation, and clear, even humorous, writing." Choice

Includes bibliographical references

Rogers, Carl R. (Carl Ransom), 1902-1987

A way of being. Houghton Mifflin 1980 395p pa $15 hardcover o.p. *   **150.19**

1. Psychology 2. Humanism

ISBN 0-395-75530-1 (pa)   LC 80-20275

The author offers a "collection of papers, talks, autobiographical sketches and vignettes of patients' experiences in workshops and therapy." Publ Wkly

"This is a book rich in theoretical insights and experiential sharing, and full of invigorating optimism." Libr J

Includes bibliographical references

Skinner, B. F. (Burrhus Frederic), 1904-1990

About behaviorism. Knopf 1974 256p pa $12 hardcover o.p. *   **150.19**

1. Behaviorism

ISBN 0-394-71618-3 (pa)

The author defines, analyzes and defends the science of behaviorism with chapters exploring the causes of behavior, operant behavior, verbal behavior, thinking, causes and reasons, knowledge, emotion and self

Includes bibliographical references

Thurschwell, Pamela, 1966-
Sigmund Freud. Routledge 2000 158p
(Routledge critical thinkers) $75; pa $16.95
150.19
1. Freud, Sigmund, 1856-1939 2. Psychoanalysis
ISBN 0-415-21520-X; 0-415-21521-8 (pa)
LC 00-32823
"The book contains chapters on early theories, interpretation, sexuality, case histories, maps of the mind, society and religion, and psychoanalysis's aftermath, including feminist criticism and a remarkable summary of Jacques Lacan's role." Booklist
Includes bibliographical references

Watson, John Broadus, 1878-1958
Behaviorism; [by] John B. Watson; with a new introduction by Gregory A. Kimble. Transaction Publishers 1998 251p il pa $24.95 *
150.19
1. Behaviorism
ISBN 1-560-00994-2; 978-1-560-00994-8
LC 97-27084
First published 1925 by Peoples Institute
The author applies the concept of physiological stimuli to the study of human behavior. He rejects conscious and unconscious mental activity as bases of human behavior and believes that man differs from other animals in terms of the types of behavior he displays.
Includes bibliographical references

150.3 Psychology—Encyclopedias and dictionaries

Colman, Andrew M.
A dictionary of psychology. 2nd ed. Oxford University Press 2006 861p il $45; pa $17.95 *
150.3
1. Psychology—Dictionaries
ISBN   978-0-19-280632-1;   0-19-280632-7;
978-0-19-861035-9 (pa); 0-19-861035-1 (pa)
LC 2005-31810
First published 2001
"This work defines the most common as well as the most important issues facing psychology today. . . . [The book features] over 11,000 cross-referenced entries, covering everything from anxiety and cognitive impairment to hypolexia (another name for dyslexia) and postpartum depression. . . . For professionals and students of psychology, this is a good place to start their research." SLJ
Includes bibliographical references

Cordón, Luis A.
Popular   psychology;   an   encyclopedia.
Greenwood Press 2005 274p il $75 *
150.3
1. Psychology—Encyclopedias
ISBN 0-313-32457-3   LC 2004-17426
This "encyclopedia explains the accuracies and fallacies of contemporary popular psychology when compared

to the discipline practiced by professional psychologists. . . . Entries cover pop psychologists (Noam Chomsky, Deepak Chopra, Dr. Phil McGraw) and historical theoreticians (Erikson, Freud, Jung, Skinner). Other entries treat controversial topics and 'pseudoscience'—e.g., aromatherapy, dianetics/scientology, EMDR, facilitated communication, subliminal perception." Choice
This book "provides a concise guide for anyone seeking to understand the true scientific nature of psychology." Libr Media Connect
Includes bibliographical references

The **Corsini** encyclopedia of psychology and behavioral science; co-editors, W. Edward Craighead, Charles B. Nemeroff. 3rd ed. Wiley 2001 4v il set $800
150.3
1. Psychology—Encyclopedias
ISBN 0-471-23949-6   LC 99-58006
Also available in paperback ea $78
First published 1984 under the editorship of Raymond J. Corsini with title: Encyclopedia of psychology
This work presents "more than 2,100 signed articles on topics and persons (living and dead) in all areas of psychology. Full citations for references are provided in a general bibliography. An excellent general resource for beginning and advanced students." Guide to Ref Books. 11th edition {entry for 2nd edition}
"Despite its poor indexing, this edition of *Corsini* is an essential, solid, and important reference work in psychology and behavioral science." Choice
Includes bibliographical references

Encyclopedia of psychology; Alan E. Kazdin, editor in chief. American Psychological Assn. 2000 8v set $750 *
150.3
1. Psychology—Encyclopedias
ISBN 1-55798-187-6   LC 99-55239
The 1500 articles survey behavioral, personal, interpersonal, social, developmental, cultural, pathological, and therapeutic aspects of psychology. Includes nearly 400 biographical entries

The **Gale** encyclopedia of psychology; Bonnie R. Strickland, executive editor. 2nd ed. Gale Group 2001 701p il $191.50 *
150.3
1. Psychology—Encyclopedias
ISBN 0-7876-4786-1   LC 00-34736
First published 1996
Coverage includes noteworthy people, movements, theories, and important case studies and experiments. The articles, ranging from 25 to 1,500 words examine such diverse topics as abnormal psychology, bipolar disorder, Sigmund Freud and insomnia
Includes bibliographical references

Magill's encyclopedia of social science: psychology; editor, Nancy A. Piotrowski; project editor, Tracy Irons-Georges. Salem Press 2003 4v il set $404
150.3
1. Psychology—Encyclopedias
ISBN 1-58765-130-0   LC 2002-151146
First published 1993 with title: Survey of social science, Psychology series

Magill's encyclopedia of social science: psychology—Continued

"Topics include human characteristics, specific disorders, diagnostic and therapeutic methodologies, and individual practitioners. Each entry includes a brief history of the topic, an overview of essential details, and a list of sources for further study." Choice

This "is an attractive, reader-friendly, college-level reference." Libr J

Includes bibliographical references

150.9   Psychology—Historical and geographic treatment

Kagan, Jerome

An argument for mind. Yale University Press 2006 287p $27.50; pa $17   **150.9**

1. Psychology—History
ISBN   978-0-300-11337-2;   0-300-11337-4;
978-0-300-12603-7 (pa); 0-300-12603-4 (pa)
LC 2005-33441

The author "gives an overview of his theories and research on human development as well as the history of the field of psychology in the last half century." Libr J

"Jerome Kagan writes elegantly, with humor . . . and with profound intellectual depth and range." Sci Books Films

Includes bibliographical references

152.1   Sensory perception

Ackerman, Diane

A natural history of the senses. Random House 1990 331p hardcover o.p. pa $14.95

152.1

1. Senses and sensation
ISBN 0-394-57335-8; 978-0-679-73566-3 (pa);
0-679-73566-6 (pa)   LC 89-43416

"Ackerman celebrates the senses by examining their biological bases and the various and bizarre ways we have come to indulge them. Her catalog of the senses is itself a sensuous journey, with prose rich in imagery and rhythm. Ackerman's book is a provocative and entertaining treat whose details will bestir the reader's imagination." Libr J

Includes bibliographic references

Herz, Rachel S., 1963-

The scent of desire; discovering our enigmatic sense of smell; [by] Rachel Herz. William Morrow 2007 xxi, 266p $24.95   **152.1**

1. Smell
ISBN 978-0-06-082537-9; 0-06-082537-5
LC 2007-33563

The author argues that the sense of smell "is vital to our well being—so important to mental and physical health that its loss can drive some people to suicide. Herz explores the relationships between scent, emotion and behavior, emphasizing that scent is an important component of sexual attraction and thus crucial for the survival of our species." Publ Wkly

"This is one of those all-too-rare books that is involving, well written, and solidly grounded in research." Libr J

Includes bibliographical references

152.14   Visual perception

Hoffman, Donald D.

Visual intelligence; how we create what we see. Norton 1998 294p il pa $17.95 hardcover o.p.
152.14

1. Perception 2. Vision
ISBN 0-393-31967-9 (pa)   LC 98-6181

The author "argues that the brain, via the eyes, doesn't see what is 'really' in a scene being viewed but rather constructs one image from 'countless possible interpretations' from the scene gathered at the retina." Booklist

This book offers "wit, insight and charm. . . . An outstanding example of creative popular science." Publ Wkly

Includes bibliographical references

152.4   Emotions

Ackerman, Diane

A natural history of love. Random House 1994 xxiii, 358p pa $14 hardcover o.p.   **152.4**

1. Love 2. Sexual behavior
ISBN 0-679-76183-7 (pa)   LC 94-171385

Companion volume to A natural history of the senses

"Ackerman sets out on her exploration by reviewing the lessons provided across time by such lovers as Antony and Cleopatra, Orpheus and Eurydice, Dido and Aeneas, Abelard and Heloise and Romeo and Juliet. During this journey, she explores the neurophysiology of love. . . . With dazzling poetic charm and insight, she uses history, literature, science, psychology, and personal experience as tools to illuminate the vigor and vehemence of the thrilling, devastating, and comforting phenomenon of love." Libr J

Allport, Gordon, 1897-1967

The nature of prejudice; {by} Gordon W. Allport; introduction by Kenneth Clark, foreword by Thomas Pettigrew. unabridged, 25th anniversary ed. Addison-Wesley 1979 xxxii, 537p il pa $18.50 hardcover o.p. *   **152.4**

1. Prejudices 2. Social psychology
ISBN 0-201-00179-9 (pa)   LC 79-112200

First published 1954

The author examines the roots of prejudice as well as its manifestations. The effects of prejudice on the "in-group" and the "out-group" are discussed, as are the ways in which children form their perceptions of groups

Includes bibliographical references

Damasio, Antonio R.

Looking for Spinoza; joy, sorrow, and the feeling rain; [by] Antonio Damasio. Harcourt 2003 355p il $28; pa $15   **152.4**

1. Spinoza, Benedictus de, 1632-1677 2. Emotions
ISBN 0-15-100557-5; 0-15-602871-9 (pa)
LC 2002-11347

Contents: Enter feelings; Of appetites and emotions; Feelings; Ever since feelings; The body-minded brain; A visit to Spinoza; Who's there?

This is a "discussion of the difference between emotions (of the body) and feelings (of the mind), various sites in the brain that trigger these states, and the . . . synthesis of the homeostatic process, memory, sensory input, imagination, and foresight that links the unconscious to consciousness and feelings to reasoning." Booklist

Includes bibliographical references

Fromm, Erich, 1900-1980

The art of loving. Centennial ed. Continuum 2000 130p $18.95 *   **152.4**

1. Love
ISBN 0-8264-1260-2   LC 00-21030

Also available in paperback from HarperCollins Pubs. A reissue of the title first published 1956

"An astonishingly simple presentation of an abstract subject." Booklist

Gilligan, Carol, 1936-

The birth of pleasure. Knopf 2002 253p $24; pa $13 *   **152.4**

1. Love 2. Interpersonal relations
ISBN 0-679-44037-2; 0-679-75943-3 (pa)
LC 2001-50329

The author examines "why love between a man and a woman is so often burdened by a history of loss and how it can be freed and opened to the pursuit of happiness. Tracing a lineage from Greek mythology to our own most intimate relationships, she asks why we relive tragic stories of loss and betrayal; drawing on her own research, she offers a radical new map of love." Publisher's note

Gilligan's "mastery of literary sources and her intelligent but nonacademic writing style make this an enjoyable, challenging work." Publ Wkly

Includes bibliographical references

Goleman, Daniel

Emotional intelligence. Bantam Bks. 1995 352p $25.95; pa $16.95 *   **152.4**

1. Emotions 2. Intellect
ISBN 0-553-09503-X; 0-553-37506-7 (pa)
LC 95-16685

The author explains "how to develop our emotional intelligence in ways that can improve our relationships, our parenting, our classrooms, and our workplaces. Goleman assures us that our temperaments may be determined by neurochemistry, but they can be altered." Booklist

"Mr. Goleman, with an economy of style that serves his reformer's convictions well, integrates a vast amount of material on issues whose intricacy and problematic character he reveals in an original and persuasive way." N Y Times Book Rev

Includes bibliographical references

Jamison, Kay R.

Exuberance; the passion for life; by Kay Redfield Jamison. Knopf 2004 405p il $24.95   **152.4**

1. Happiness
ISBN 0-375-40144-X   LC 2004-46561

The author "examines the contagious nature of exuberance, which she defines as 'a psychological state characterized by high mood and high energy,' offering diverse examples that range from John Muir and FDR to Mary Poppins and Peter Pan. Having in mind the simply put idea that 'those who are exuberant act,' the author details the energetic efforts of scientists, naturalists, politicians and even her meteorologist father." Publ Wkly

"A major creative contribution to positive psychology, this book belongs in every library." Libr J

Includes bibliographical references

Jampolsky, Gerald G., 1925-

Love is the answer: creating positive relationships; [by] Gerald G. Jampolsky and Diane V. Cirincione. Bantam Bks. 1990 242p il pa $14.95 hardcover o.p.   **152.4**

1. Interpersonal relations 2. Love
ISBN 0-553-35268-7 (pa)   LC 89-18520

The authors suggest "moving past our illusions and perceptions; transforming fear, blame, and guilt into love; communicating with love in all our relationships; transforming relationships of control into relationships of freedom; finding peace, love, and happiness within ourselves; . . . forgiving ourselves and others; and achieving holy relationships. This is a 'New Age' book from which all readers can benefit." Libr J

Jeffers, Susan J.

Feel the fear—and do it anyway; [by] Susan Jeffers. Ballantine Books 2007 214p il pa $13.95   **152.4**

1. Fear
ISBN 978-0-345-48742-1   LC 2007-271292

First published 1987 by Harcourt Brace Jovanovich

On cover: 20th anniversary edition

"By mixing positive thinking with situational exercises that examine basic fear responses, psychologist Jeffers shows that fear is what you make of it and that in most cases it is unfounded." Libr J

Includes bibliographical references

Lerner, Harriet Goldhor

The dance of anger; a woman's guide to changing the patterns of intimate relationships; [by] Harriet Lerner. Perennial Currents 2005 239p il pa $13.95 *   **152.4**

1. Anger 2. Women—Psychology
ISBN 0-06-074104-X   LC 2004-60074

First published 1985

Lerner, Harriet Goldhor—*Continued*

The author examines the ways women express anger, as well as how women's anger is viewed by society and throughout history.

Includes bibliographical references

Lewis, Thomas

A general theory of love; [by] Thomas Lewis, Fari Amini, Richard Lannon. Random House 2000 274p il pa $13 hardcover o.p. *   **152.4**

1. Love

ISBN 0-375-70922-3 (pa)   LC 99-49930

The authors "aim to help physicians treat patients by showing how the many and varied aspects of love, including the lack and the warping of it, affect patients' problems and strengths and by discussing what must, therefore, be involved in treating patients." Booklist

Includes bibliographical references

Lutz, Tom

Crying; the natural and cultural history of tears. Norton 1999 352p il pa $14.95 hardcover o.p.
152.4

1. Crying

ISBN 0-393-320103-7 (pa)   LC 99-21295

"Encompassing history, literature, the arts and the social sciences—Lutz explores how crying has been portrayed and perceived throughout history." Publ Wkly

"An affable, stimulating essay." Booklist

Includes bibliographical references

Nettle, Daniel

Happiness; the science behind your smile. Oxford University Press 2005 216p il $21; pa $13.95   **152.4**

1. Happiness

ISBN   0-19-280558-4;   978-0-19-280558-4; 0-19-280559-2 (pa); 978-0-19-280559-1 (pa)
LC 2004-30585

The author discusses "why the study of happiness is important; how to define happiness from a scientific perspective; why making more money will not make one any happier; why some people seem more adept than others at being happy; and what Prozac and other drugs have to do with happiness." Choice

"With absolute clarity and admirable brevity, Nettle explores the pursuit of happiness and, happily, makes good sense of it all." Publ Wkly

Includes bibliographical references

Tavris, Carol

Anger; the misunderstood emotion. rev ed. Simon & Schuster 1989 383p pa $14
152.4

1. Anger

ISBN 0-671-67523-0   LC 89-33129

"A Touchstone book"

First published 1983

The author contends that anger is a complex, socially learned response that is not necessarily cathartic

Includes bibliographical references

153   Conscious mental processes and intelligence

Arendt, Hannah

The life of the mind. Harcourt Brace Jovanovich 1981 2v in 1 pa $18 *   **153**

1. Intellect 2. Philosophy 3. Free will and determinism

ISBN 0-15-651992-5

First published 1978 as two separate volumes with titles: v1 Thinking and v2 Willing

An exploration of the nature of mind and thought. Among the concepts discussed are: appearance versus reality, free will, determinism, and necessity

Includes bibliographical references

Baars, Bernard J.

In the theater of consciousness; the workspace of the mind. Oxford Univ. Press 1997 193p il $35; pa $14.95   **153**

1. Consciousness 2. Intellect 3. Theory of knowledge

ISBN 0-19-510265-7; 0-19-514703-0 (pa)
LC 96-10379

"Baars offers the theater metaphor—inherited from Aristotle, developed by William James and hotly contested by leading cognitive theorists such as Daniel Dennett—as the best means of unifying the diverse mental phenomena and sensory experiences that make up conscious life." Publ Wkly

The author "does a masterful job of explicating the issues and distinctions related to consciousness providing representative charts, graphs, and figures to relate both theory and data. . . . A most accessible and up-to-date introduction to current ideas about consciousness, and a valuable work for general readers." Choice

Includes bibliographical references

Carter, Rita

Exploring consciousness. University of Calif. Press 2002 320p il $34.95 *   **153**

1. Consciousness

ISBN 0-520-23737-4   LC 2002-25900

This work explores the nature, origins, and purpose of consciousness from philosophical, scientific, and experiential perspectives

"A treasure trove of fact, argument and opinion, doing an excellent job of conveying both research and controversies. The general reader will find it filled with stimulating material." New Sci

Includes bibliographical references

Damasio, Antonio R.

The feeling of what happens; body and emotion in the making of consciousness. Harcourt Brace & Co. 1999 386p il $28; pa $15   **153**

1. Consciousness 2. Emotions

ISBN 0-15-100369-6; 0-15-601075-5 (pa)
LC 99-26357

The author contends "that consciousness arises from our ability to map relations between the self and others through our emotions. This bold attempt to mend the classical breach between emotion and reason is all the more compelling for its poetic expression." Publ Wkly

Includes bibliographical references

Hofstadter, Douglas R., 1945-

I am a strange loop. Basic Books 2007 412p il 26.95 **153**

1. Consciousness 2. Self

ISBN 978-0-465-03078-1; 0-465-03078-5

The author "posits a model of human consciousness as an abstract, self-referential loop—a strange loop: make a decision, take action, observe the consequences, and incorporate this information into your psyche for future decisions. Humans repeat this circular pattern millions of times, resulting in self-awareness. Hofstadter, trying to comprehend his wife's death in 1993, also theorizes that we can replicate the strange loops of others in our minds, thinking with their thoughts and seeing the world through their eyes." Bookmarks

The author's model of self is neither "spiritual—he's not a religious man—nor is it locked into the cold neurological materialism of cellular mechanics. . . . [The book] scales some lofty conceptual heights, but it remains very personal, and it's deeply colored by the facts of Hofstadter's later life." Time

bibliography: p. 377-82

Pinker, Steven, 1954-

How the mind works. Norton 1997 660p il pa $17.95 hardcover o.p. **153**

1. Brain 2. Psychology 3. Evolution

ISBN 0-393-31848-6 (pa)   LC 97-1855

The author "explains what the mind is, how it evolved, and how it allows us to see, think, feel, laugh, interact, enjoy the arts, and ponder the mysteries of life." Publisher's note

Pinker "has a gift for making enormously complicated mechanisms—and human foibles—accessible." Publ Wkly

Includes bibliographical references

Sagan, Carl, 1934-1996

The dragons of Eden; speculations on the evolution of human intelligence. Random House 1977 263p il pa $7.50 hardcover o.p. **153**

1. Intellect 2. Brain 3. Genetics

ISBN 0-345-34629-7 (pa)   LC 76-53472

In this study of human intellect "Sagan is principally preoccupied with the neocortex, with its left hemisphere, responsible for language and logic, a right hemisphere in charge of intuition and spatial dimension, and a corpus callosum that mediates and synthesizes the two." Atl Mon

Includes bibliographical references

153.1 Memory and learning

Goldman, Bob, 1955-

Brain fitness; anti-aging strategies for achieving super mind power; {by} Robert M. Goldman with Ronald Klatz and Lisa Berger. Doubleday 1999 333p il pa $14.95 hardcover o.p. **153.1**

1. Aging 2. Memory 3. Sleep 4. Stress (Physiology)

ISBN 0-385-48869-6 (pa)   LC 98-18785

This is an "exploration of techniques—mental workouts, memory training, physical exercises, and nutrition and dietary supplements—that readers can use to maximize their concentration, memory, imagination, energy, intelligence, and creativity while decreasing fatigue and stress and preventing Alzheimer's disease and other brain diseases." Libr J

Includes bibliographical references

Schacter, Daniel L.

Searching for memory; the brain, the mind, and the past. Basic Bks. 1996 398p il pa $17.50 hardcover o.p. **153.1**

1. Memory 2. Brain

ISBN 0-465-07552-5 (pa)   LC 96-19521

This book "describes how new technologies permit scientists to determine what brain centers control which memories. It also approaches subjects that have been sensationalized—hypnosis, multiple personality, and 'recovered' memories of sexual abuse." New Yorker

"This is an excellent book on an important topic: it is exceptionally well written; its examples of defects in memory are fascinating, as are the theories based on them; and its arguments are illustrated with opposite pictures, reproduced from works by many modern artists, and passages from novels." N Y Times Book Rev

Includes bibliographical references

The seven sins of memory; how the mind forgets and remembers. Houghton Mifflin 2001 272p il $25; pa $14 **153.1**

1. Memory

ISBN 0-618-04019-6; 0-618-21919-6 (pa)

LC 00-53885

The author discusses "the curious processes of memory by classifying its malfunctions into seven categories: transience, absent-mindedness, blocking, misattribution, suggestibility, bias, and persistence. Schacter illustrates each of these 'sins' with examples of routine misfortunes common to all." Libr J

Includes bibliographical references

Turkington, Carol

The encyclopedia of memory and memory disorders; [by] Carol Turkington and Joseph R. Harris. 2nd ed. Facts on File 2001 296p (Facts on File library of health and living) $66 *

153.1

1. Memory—Encyclopedias

ISBN 0-8160-4141-5   LC 00-52806

First published 1995

This volume includes over 70 entries describing: Alzheimer's disease; Football and memory loss; Huffing; Mad cow disease; Memory in infancy; Norepinephrine; "Punch drunk" syndrome; Social memory; Vitamins and memory.

Includes bibliographical references

153.3 Imagination, imagery, creativity

Csikszentmihalyi, Mihaly
Creativity; flow and the psychology of discovery and invention. HarperCollins Pubs. 1996 456p pa $15 hardcover o.p.   **153.3**
1. Creative ability 2. Creative thinking
ISBN 0-06-092820-4 (pa)   LC 96-4116
"Utilizing the interviews garnered from 91 respondents (ranging from philosopher Mortimer Adler to biologist Edward O. Wilson to politician Eugene McCarthy), the author . . . demonstrates the processes that these acknowledged creative thinkers and doers go through and the characteristics that make them stand out. . . . Csikszentmihalyi also deals with creativity and aging and ways to enhance one's own personal creativity." Libr J
Includes bibliographical references

Gardner, Howard
Creating minds; an anatomy of creativity seen through the lives of Freud, Einstein, Picasso, Stravinsky, Eliot, Graham, and Gandhi. Basic Bks. 1993 464p il hardcover o.p. pa $22.50
                                  153.3
1. Creative ability
ISBN 0-465-01455-0; 0-465-01454-2 (pa)
                                 LC 92-56172
In seven "case studies, Gardner focuses on highly creative figures who lived in the same era but who exemplify different human intelligences. He postulates that each of their major innovations involved an intersection of the maturity and confidence of a master with the sensibilities and impulsiveness of a child. This scholarly and insightful study is highly recommended." Libr J
Includes bibliographical references

Gawain, Shakti
Creative visualization; use the power of your imagination to create what you want in your life. 30th anniversary ed. Nataraj Pub./New World Library 2008 175p $25; pa $12.95 *
                                  153.3
1. Self-realization 2. Imagination
ISBN   978-1-577-31636-7;   1-577-31636-3; 978-1-577-31229-1 (pa); 1-577-31229-5 (pa)
                               LC 2008-14400
First published 1978 by Whatever Pub.
Includes CD
"The author asserts that people can achieve an ideal existence simply through mental visualization." Libr J
Includes bibliographical references

May, Rollo
The courage to create. Norton 1975 143p pa $11.95 hardcover o.p. *   **153.3**
1. Creative ability
ISBN 0-393-31106-6 (pa)
Also available in hardcover from P. Smith

The author argues that creativity is an act of encounter and draws on examples from literature, art, and psychoanalysis
Includes bibliographical references

153.4 Thought, thinking, reasoning, intuition, value, judgment

Gladwell, Malcolm
Blink: the power of thinking without thinking. Little, Brown and Co 2005 277p il $25.95
                                  153.4
1. Decision making 2. Intuition
ISBN 0-316-17232-4   LC 2004-13916
The author "decodes the science of rapid cognition, those snap judgments made with only the subtlest clues." Christ Sci Monit
Gladwell "has a dazzling ability to find commonality in disparate fields of study. . . . Each case study is satisfying, and Gladwell imparts his own evident pleasure in delving into a wide range of fields and seeking an underlying truth." Publ Wkly
Includes bibliographical references

153.6 Communication

Deacon, Terrence William
The symbolic species; the coevolution of language and the brain; by Terrence W. Deacon. Norton 1997 527p il pa $16.95 hardcover o.p.
                                  153.6
1. Language and languages 2. Brain
ISBN 0-393-31754-4 (pa)   LC 96-31115
"Deacon proposes a challenging, holistic theory of language that explains, among other things, how children learn to speak and why there are grammatical similarities across languages." Libr J
"Readers who savor the latest scientific research but do not possess the esoteric vocabulary that allows for easy penetration of such lofty thoughts should find Deacon's book both fascinating and accessible." Booklist
Includes bibliographical references

Pease, Allan
The definitive book of body language; [by] Allan & Barbara Pease. Bantam Books 2006 386p il $23   **153.6**
1. Nonverbal communication
ISBN 0-553-80472-3; 978-0-553-80472-0
                               LC 2006-42657
"The authors examine each component of body language." Publisher's note
"The book is amply and wittily illustrated with celebrity photographs. . . . This is a fascinating book." N Y Times Book Rev
Includes bibliographical references

153.7   Perceptual processes

Greenspan, Stanley I.
The first idea; how symbols, language, and intelligence evolved from our early primate ancestors to modern humans; [by] Stanley I. Greenspan, Stuart G. Shanker. 1st Da Capo Press ed. Da Capo Press 2004 504p $25   **153.7**
1. Evolution 2. Theory of knowledge
ISBN 0-7382-0680-6   LC 2004-10658
"A Merloyd Lawrence book"
Contents: Origin of symbols -- Intellectual growth and transformations of emotions during the course of life -- The early stages of emotional regulation, engagement, and signaling: nonhuman primates and the earliest hominids -- Problem-solving collaborations: chimpanzees and early humans -- Symbols, words, and ideas: Archaic H. sapiens and early moderns -- Representation and the beginning of logic Homo sapiens sapiens -- The engine of evolution -- The origins of language -- The role of emotions in language development -- Emotions and the development of intelligence -- How emotional signaling links emotion and cognition and the brain's subsymbolic and symbolic cortical systems: implications for neuroscience and Piaget's cognitive psychology -- Emotional development derailed: pathways to and from autism -- The developmental levels of groups, societies, and cultures -- A new history of history -- Towards a psychology of global interdependency
"This book should appeal most to readers working in psychology and child development, but its revolutionary ideas no doubt will lead to lively and well-publicized debates." Publ Wkly
Includes bibliographical references

Klein, Stefan, 1965-
The secret pulse of time; making sense of life's scarcest commodity; translated by Shelley Frisch. Marlowe & Co. 2007 xxi, 343p il $25
          153.7
1. Time 2. Perception 3. Time management
ISBN 978-1-6009-4017-0; 1-6009-4017-X
Original German edition, 2006
The author "tackles time, approaching the topic from many angles: physiology of circadian rhythms, psychology of memory and perception of time, and physics of relativistic time." Libr J
"Sure to give readers fresh perspective on their everyday lives, Klein's concepts are well illustrated in copious examples from literature and popular culture, and Frisch's fluid, flawless translation makes his text as captivating as it is enlightening." Publ Wkly
Includes bibliographical references

153.8   Will (Volition)

Cialdini, Robert B.
Influence: the psychology of persuasion. Rev. ed.; 1st Collins business essentials ed. Collins 2007 320p il pa $17.95 *   **153.8**
1. Persuasion (Psychology)
ISBN 0-06-124189-X; 978-0-06-124189-5
First published 1984

The author "explains the psychology of why people say 'yes'—and how to apply these understandings." Publisher's note
Includes bibliographical references

Dennett, Daniel Clement
Freedom evolves; [by] Daniel C. Dennett. Viking 2003 347p il $24.95; pa $17
          153.8
1. Free will and determinism 2. Decision making
ISBN 0-670-03186-0; 0-14-200384-0 (pa)
          LC 2002-28085
"Drawing on evolutionary biology, neuroscience, economic game theory, philosophy and Richard Dawkins's meme, the author argues that there is indeed such a thing as free will, but it 'is not a preexisting feature of our existence, like the law of gravity.' . . . This book comprises a kind of toolbox of intellectual exercises favoring cultural evolution, the idea that culture, morality and freedom are as much a result of evolution by natural selection as our physical and genetic attributes. Yet genetic determinism, he argues, does not imply inevitability, as his critics may claim, nor does it cancel out the soul. . . . Dennett clearly relishes pushing other scientists' buttons. Though natural selection itself is still a subject of controversy, the author . . . most certainly is in the vanguard of the philosophy of science." Publ Wkly
Includes bibliographical references

Kohn, Alfie
Punished by rewards; the trouble with gold stars, incentive plans, A's, praise, and other bribes. Houghton Mifflin 1993 398p hardcover o.p. pa $15   **153.8**
1. Awards   2.   Motivation   (Psychology)
3. Behaviorism
ISBN 0-395-65028-3; 978-0-618-00181-1 (pa);
0-618-00181-6 (pa)   LC 93-21897
Also available in hardcover from Replica Bks.
The author "challenges the widely held assumption that incentives lead to improved quality and increased output in the workplace and in schools. . . . Kohn derides rewards as bribes and offers instead the proposition that collaboration (teamwork), content (meaningfulness), and choice (autonomy) will serve to motivate both students and workers. He marshals impressive theoretical support and, at the same time, uses humor disarmingly to argue his case." Booklist
Includes bibliographical references

Levine, Robert
The power of persuasion; how we're bought and sold. Wiley 2003 278p hardcover o.p. pa $14.95
          153.8
1. Persuasion (Psychology) 2. Interpersonal relations
ISBN 0-471-26634-5; 0-471-76317-9 (pa)
          LC 2002-9952
The author "opens by demonstrating that all of us . . . can be persuaded under the right circumstances. He goes on to study financial manipulation and the use of the sense of obligation . . . and then proceeds to a nuts-and-bolts analysis of salesmanship by describing what he learned and did (and had done to him) as an automobile

Levine, Robert—*Continued*

salesman. . . . Inevitably, he moves to cults, the Moonies and the ultimate persuasion horror story, Jonestown." Publ Wkly

Includes bibliographical references

Spence, Gerry

How to argue and win every time; at home, at work, in court, everywhere, every day. St. Martin's Press 1995 307p pa $14.95 hardcover o.p.

153.8

1. Reasoning 2. International relations
ISBN 0-312-14477-6 (pa)   LC 94-43552

The author "distills his bar experience into the secrets of his success and translates that into the plain language of the real world of jobs, romance, and child rearing. Spence exhorts readers to believe that the art of arguing is verily the art of living, and aversion to argumentativeness only hinders people from getting what they want. . . . Though discursive in style, Spence's prose is pointedly sharp in essence and displays unselfconsciously his own flamboyant personality." Booklist

153.9   Intelligence and aptitudes

Bloom, Harold, 1930-

Genius; a mosaic of one hundred exemplary creative minds. Warner Bks. 2002 814p il $35.95; pa $19.95   **153.9**

1. Genius 2. Authors 3. Literature—History and criticism
ISBN 0-446-52717-3; 0-446-69129-1 (pa)
          LC 2002-16808

Bloom conducts an "inquiry into that elusive quality called genius, portraying 100 poets, dramatists, novelists, philosophers, and religious writers whose quests Bloom considers cosmic, their language transcendent, and their lives intriguing." Booklist

"Although the book is a delight to read, its real value lies in the author's ability to provoke the reader into thinking about literature, genius, and related topics. No similar work discusses literary genius in this way or covers this many writers." Libr J

Includes bibliographical references

Calvin, William H., 1939-

How brains think; evolving intelligence, then and now. Basic Bks. 1996 184p il (Science masters series) pa $14 hardcover o.p.

153.9

1. Intellect 2. Thought and thinking 3. Brain 4. Comparative psychology
ISBN 0-465-07278-X (pa)   LC 96-21086

"Before making his argument that competitive processes in the cerebral cortex account for the content of people's thoughts, {Calvin seeks to} build a foundation by describing what intelligence is, how it might have evolved amid the ice ages of the past few million years, and the physiology of the brain's neurons and chemicals." Booklist

Calvin's book "offers an exquisite distillation of his

key ideas. He's a member of that rare breed of scientists who can translate the arcana of their fields into lay language, and he's one of the best." N Y Times Book Rev

Includes bibliographical references

Gould, Stephen Jay, 1941-2002

The mismeasure of man. rev & expanded {ed}. Norton 1996 444p il pa $15.95 hardcover o.p. *

153.9

1. Intelligence tests 2. Ability—Testing
ISBN 0-393-31425-1 (pa)   LC 95-44442

First published 1981

The author examines the history of various scientific methods used to measure intelligence. He demonstrates how the research was used to perpetuate the myth of the intellectual superiority of the white male

Includes bibliographical references

Kurzweil, Raymond, 1948-

The singularity is near; when humans transcend biology; [by] Ray Kurzweil. Viking 2005 652p il $29.95; pa $18 *   **153.9**

1. Evolution 2. Genetics 3. Nanotechnology 4. Robots
ISBN 0-670-03384-7; 0-14-303788-9 (pa)
          LC 2004-61231

The author argues that humankind "is at the threshold of an epoch ('the singularity,' a reference to the theoretical limitlessness of exponential expansion) that will see the merging of our biology with the staggering achievements of 'GNR' (genetics, nanotechnology and robotics) to create a species of unrecognizably high intelligence, durability, comprehension, memory and so on." Publ Wkly

"Anyone can grasp Mr. Kurzweil's main idea: that mankind's technological knowledge has been snowballing, with dizzying prospects for the future. The basics are clearly expressed. But for those more knowledgeable and inquisitive, the author argues his case in fascinating detail." N Y Times (Late N Y Ed)

Includes bibliographical references

Murdoch, Stephen, 1968-

IQ; a smart history of a failed idea. J. Wiley and Sons 2007 269p $24.95   **153.9**

1. Intelligence tests
ISBN 978-0-471-69977-4; 0-471-69977-2
          LC 2006-32488

The author "traces now ubiquitous but still controversial attempts to measure intelligence to its origins in the late 19th and early 20th centuries. . . . This is a thoughtful overview and a welcome reminder of the dangers of relying on such standardized tests." Publ Wkly

Includes bibliographical references

154.2   The subconscious

Tallis, Frank

Hidden minds; a history of the unconscious. Arcade Pub. 2002 194p $25.95   **154.2**

1. Subconsciousness
ISBN 1-55970-643-0   LC 2002-74566

Tallis, Frank—*Continued*

The author "presents the history of the unconscious from Leibniz to Pierre Janet and Freud to current experimentation, and he emphasizes that the unconscious is now at the heart of neuroscience. He describes historic medical and scientific advances and the individuals who made them, and he draws on Coleridge, DeQuincey, Moss Hart, and other writers to show how the literate public viewed the unconscious at various times." Booklist

"Highly readable and possessing a surprising degree of depth, this book manages to be both entertaining and informative." Libr J

Includes bibliographical references

154.6 Sleep phenomena

Alvarez, A. (Alfred), 1929-

Night; night life, night language, sleep, and dreams. Norton 1995 290p pa $13 hardcover o.p.
154.6
1. Dreams 2. Sleep 3. Night 4. Psychoanalysis
ISBN 0-393-31434-0 (pa)   LC 94-35989
This work contains an "account of scientific and scholarly research on sleep and dreaming, . . . {some} chapters, in part autobiographical, about the dark and its attendant fears, and {others} centering on policework in New York and London." Times Lit Suppl

"Alvarez's superb variations on the theme of night enhance our appreciation of the miraculous intricacy and energy of our mind, an energy that produces everything from nightmares to poetry to lightbulbs." Booklist

Freud, Sigmund, 1856-1939

Interpretation of dreams; translated by Joyce Crick; edited with an introduction by Ritchie Robinson. Oxford University Press 2008 514p il (Oxford world's classics) pa $14.95 *
154.6
1. Dreams 2. Psychoanalysis
ISBN 978-0-19-953758-7; 0-19-953758-5
Original German edition, 1900; first English translation published 1913
Groundbreaking analysis of dreams as manifestations of suppressed unconscious desires

Lewis, James R., 1949-

The dream encyclopedia. Gale Res. 1995 xxi, 416p il hardcover o.p. pa $19.95 *
154.6
ISBN 0-7876-0155-1; 0-7876-0156-X (pa)
LC 95-10759
"This work presents brief articles on some 250 topics, from adaptive therapy and astral projections to Zulu and Zuni myths. . . . In addition to the main encyclopedia, a short introductory overview of dream and sleep research and a subject index are included. Also provided is a list of 'dream resources,' with the names and addresses of many of the organizations now focusing on the study of dreams and sleep research." Am Ref Books Annu, 1996

Parker, Julia, 1932-

Parkers' complete book of dreams. Dorling Kindersley 1995 208p il $15 hardcover o.p.
154.6
1. Dreams
ISBN 0-7894-3295-1 (pa)   LC 94-27918
This guide covers the history as well as theories concerning the meaning of dreaming. Advice is given on how to record and improve the ability to recall specific dreams

155.2 Individual psychology

Allport, Gordon, 1897-1967

Becoming; basic considerations for a psychology of personality. Yale Univ. Press 1955 106p pa $14 hardcover o.p.
155.2
1. Personality 2. Psychology
ISBN 0-300-00002-2 (pa)
"The Terry lectures"
In this work Allport attempts "to correlate and interpret psychology's views on human welfare and religion." Booklist

Csikszentmihalyi, Mihaly

Flow: the psychology of optimal experience. Harper Perennial 2008 303p pa $14.95 *
155.2
1. Happiness 2. Attention 3. Applied psychology
ISBN 978-0-06-133920-2; 0-06-133920-2
First published 1990
This book offers a discussion of "'flow,' a field of behavioral science examining connections between satisfaction and daily activities. [According to the author], a flow state ensues when one is engaged in self-controlled, goal-related, meaningful actions. . . . This thoroughly researched study is an intriguing look at the age-old problem of the pursuit of happiness and how, through conscious effort, we may more easily attain it." Libr J

Dimitrius, Jo-Ellan

Reading people; how to understand people and predict their behavior—anytime, anyplace; {by} Jo-Ellan Dimitrius and Mark Mazzarella. Random House 1998 281p pa $14.95 hardcover o.p.
155.2
1. Personality 2. Nonverbal communication
ISBN 0-345-42587-1 (pa)   LC 98-4934
"Dimitrius shares the people-reading techniques she developed over 15 years as a jury consultant. In so doing, she provides a wealth of tips and strategies for ferreting out people's real viewpoints, motives and character traits." Publ Wkly

Hamer, Dean H.

Living with our genes; why they matter more than you think; {by} Dean Hamer and Peter Copeland. Doubleday 1998 355p pa $14.95 hardcover o.p.
155.2
1. Temperament 2. Personality 3. Behavior genetics
ISBN 0-385-48584-0 (pa)   LC 97-29818

Hamer, Dean H.—*Continued*

"The authors devote chapters to the most compelling of human behaviors and conditions: sex, worry, anger, thrill-seeking, addiction, intelligence, eating and aging. They explore the biochemistry underlying the characteristics in question, and ask how much of that biochemistry is under genetic control. . . . This thought-provoking book's explanations of how our genes 'express' themselves is sure to capture the imaginations of readers." Publ Wkly

Includes bibliographical references

Harris, Judith Rich

No two alike; human nature and human individuality. W.W. Norton & Co. 2006 322p il $26.95   **155.2**

1. Individuality 2. Personality
ISBN 0-393-05948-0   LC 2005-25837

The author "tackles a question that has long been a mystery: Why do identical twins who grow up together—same genes, reared by the same parents—differ in personality?" Publisher's note

"Harris makes behavioral genetics and evolutionary psychology enjoyable and accessible to general readers as well as scholars." Libr J

Includes bibliographical references

Lunden, Joan

Wake-up calls; making the most out of every day. McGraw-Hill 2000 230p il $19.95; pa $12   **155.2**

1. Conduct of life 2. Self-realization
ISBN 0-07-136126-X; 0-07-137970-3 (pa)

A collection of aphorisms and life principles the author feels may inspire readers faced with stress, change, and adversity

Includes bibliographical references

Maslow, Abraham Harold

Toward a psychology of being; {by} Abraham H. Maslow. 3rd ed. Wiley 1998 244p $45 *   **155.2**

1. Personality 2. Motivation (Psychology)
ISBN 0-471-29309-1   LC 98-3766
First published 1962
Editor: Richard Lowry

The author presents his theory of psychological health and motivation and explains his belief that human beings can be loving and creative, and capable of pursuing the highest values and aspirations

Includes bibliographical references

Myers, Isabel Briggs

Gifts differing; understanding personality type; [by] Isabel Briggs Myers with Peter B. Myers. Davies-Black Pub 1995 228p il pa $16.95 *   **155.2**

1. Personality
ISBN 0-89106-074-X   LC 95-4184
First published 1980 by Consulting Psychologists Press

This is a guide to the 16 personality types distinguished in the Myers-Briggs Type Indicator.

Includes bibliographical references

Pinker, Steven, 1954-

The blank slate; the denial of human nature in modern intellectual life. Viking 2002 509p $27.95; pa $16   **155.2**

1. Nature and nurture
ISBN 0-670-03151-8; 0-14-2003344 (pa)
    LC 2002-22719

The author "attacks the notion that an infant's mind is a blank slate, arguing instead that human beings have an inherited universal structure shaped by the demands made upon the species for survival, albeit with plenty of room for cultural and individual variation." Publ Wkly

Includes bibliographical references

Seligman, Martin E. P.

Learned optimism; how to change your mind and your life. Vintage Books 2006 319p pa $14.95 *   **155.2**

1. Self-perception 2. Adjustment (Psychology)
ISBN 1-4000-7839-3; 978-1-4000-7839-4
    LC 2006-277713

First published 1991

The author "documents the effects of optimism on the quality of life, provides tests to determine the degree of . . . negative and positive orientation, and offers a program of specific exercises to help . . . break the habit of pessimism and learn the habit of optimism." Publisher's note

Seligman "has written a lively, very accessible book. . . . Presented for lay readers, this book can be highly recommended to professionals as well for its lucid and informative introduction to cognitive therapy and its approach to issues of mood and depression." Libr J

Includes bibliographical references

Steinem, Gloria

Revolution from within; a book of self-esteem. Little, Brown 1992 377p pa $14.95 hardcover o.p.   **155.2**

1. Self-esteem 2. Feminism
ISBN 0-316-81247-1 (pa)   LC 91-11356

The author discusses the importance of self-esteem and offers practical advice on ways of acquiring it.

Steinem's "book unfolds like a flower: it offers literature, art, nature, meditation, and connectedness as ways of finding and exploring the self. . . . Her focus is women, but she is clear that what she has to say is for men, too, and she is neither strident nor dismissive." Libr J

Includes bibliographical references

Weber, Robert J.

The created self; reinventing body, persona, spirit. Norton 2000 350p il pa $14.95 hardcover o.p.   **155.2**

1. Self 2. Psychology
ISBN 0-393-32121-5 (pa)   LC 99-37480

Weber, Robert J.—*Continued*

The author contends that "having a self enables the individual to pursue creative endeavors, which though often adaptive from an evolutionary standpoint, actually extend beyond what can be explained in terms of biological, reproductive aims. Using the model of the self developed by William James . . . Weber attempts to show that the self is a constantly developing, 'unitary system', consisting of bodily awareness, persona and spirit, over which the individual has control." Publ Wkly

Includes bibliographical references

155.3 Sex psychology and psychology of the sexes

Eldredge, Niles

Why we do it; rethinking sex and the selfish gene. Norton 2004 269p il $24.95 *

155.3

1. Sociobiology 2. Sex (Biology)
ISBN 0-393-05082-3   LC 2003-27564
The author "believes that sociobiologists like Richard Dawkins and E.O. Wilson are dead wrong in their explanation of life as a mechanism by which 'selfish genes' try to propagate and ensure their own survival. Explaining that life as we know it combines two drives, one economic and one reproductive, Eldredge writes that 'the drive to eat and simply stay alive' is as fundamental as the drive to reproduce." Publ Wkly

"This book, while written for the lay reader, is appropriate for a scientific audience as well. It could be used as supplementary reading in college courses in animal behavior." Sci Books & Films

Lerner, Harriet Goldhor

The dance of deception; pretending and truth-telling in women's lives. HarperCollins Pubs. 1993 254p hardcover o.p. pa $14   **155.3**
1. Women—Psychology 2. Truthfulness and falsehood
ISBN: 0-06-092463-2 (pa)   LC 92-53376
"Patriarchal culture teaches women to pretend and sometimes deceive, Lerner says, and in her study of the role this dissembling plays in women's lives, she shows how 'pretending reflects deep prohibitions, real and imagined, against a more direct and forthright assertion of self.' . . . She acknowledges that truth telling is not easy, yet her discussion of the many ways women lie and how lying affects them clearly shows the benefits of honesty and makes her prescription appealing." Booklist

Includes bibliographical references

Masters, William H.

Masters and Johnson on sex and human loving; {by} William H. Masters, Virginia E. Johnson, Robert C. Kolodny. Little, Brown 1986 598p il pa $29.99 hardcover o.p. *   **155.3**
1. Sexual behavior 2. Sex (Biology)
ISBN 0-316-50160-3 (pa)   LC 85-23950
"Provides complete coverage of the biological, psychological, and social aspects of human sexuality. Examines both cultural and historical trends and practices." NY Public Libr Book of How & Where to Look It Up

Includes bibliographical references

155.4 Child psychology

Barnet, Ann B.

The youngest minds; parenting and genes in the development of intellect and emotion; {by} Ann B. Barnet and Richard J. Barnet. Simon & Schuster 1998 352p il pa $22.95 hardcover o.p.

155.4

1. Child psychology 2. Child development
ISBN 978-0-684-85440-3; 0-684-85440-6

LC 98-13450

The authors debate "the relative importance of genetics vs. environment in shaping human personality. Explaining recent work in language acquisition and emotional development . . . they provide an accessisble summary of our current state of knowledge of brain development and chemistry while placing significantly greater emphasis on the role played by environmental factors." Publ Wkly

Includes bibliographical references

Brazelton, T. Berry, 1918-

The earliest relationship; parents, infants, and the drama of early attachment; {by} T. Berry Brazelton, Bertrand G. Cramer. Addison-Wesley 1990 252p pa $17 hardcover o.p.   **155.4**

1. Child psychology 2. Parent-child relationship
ISBN 0-201-56764-4 (pa)   LC 89-39839
"A Merloyd Lawrence book"
An examination of "the first bewildering stages of parent-infant interaction and development. Parents are warned about the natural roller coaster of responses they will undergo, from anxiety over the newborn through the resentment often felt when a child displays those first physical signs of independence." Booklist

Includes bibliographical references

The irreducible needs of children; what every child must have to grow, learn, and flourish; {by} T. Berry Brazelton, Stanley I. Greenspan. Perseus Bks. 2000 xx, 228p pa $14 hardcover o.p.

155.4

1. Child development 2. Child psychology 3. Child rearing
ISBN 0-7382-0516-8 (pa)   LC 2001-2290
"Each chapter is devoted to the discussion of an 'irreducible' need, such as the Need for Ongoing Nurturing Relationships, the Need for Physical Protection, Safety and Regulation, the Need for Stable Supportive Communities and Cultural Continuity, and the Need to Protect the Future. After each discussion, the authors recommend ways to meet these needs." Publ Wkly

This is "a practical, well-organized volume, of value to parents, physicians, teachers, sociologists, and others who wish to improve children's lives locally and globally." Booklist

Includes bibliographical references

Brazelton, T. Berry, 1918-—_Continued_

To listen to a child; understanding the normal problems of growing up; photographs by B.A. King. Addison-Wesley 1984 184p il hardcover o.p. pa $16   *   155.4

1. Child development 2. Child psychology 3. Emotionally disturbed children 4. Parent-child relationship

ISBN: 0-201-63270-5 (pa)   LC 84-6174

"A Merloyd Lawrence book"

The author "advises parents on children's transient developmental problems such as fears, thumbsucking, eating and sleeping deviations, enuresis, and stomachaches." Libr J

"Brazelton's sensible, authoritative, clear approach provides parents with the kinds of information they need to relax over the long pull, and to understand and cope with day-to-day difficulties." Publ Wkly

Bruer, John T., 1949-

The myth of the first three years; a new understanding of early brain development and lifelong learning. Free Press 1999 244p il pa $18.95 hardcover o.p.   *   155.4

1. Psychology of learning 2. Child development

ISBN 0-7432-4260-2 (pa)   LC 99-34934

Bruer offers a critique of recent thinking about early childhood development and learning. Specifically, he identifies as myth the notion that "a child's experiences and environment during his first three years play a crucial role in determining the course of his later life." Commentary

Includes bibliographical references

Elkind, David, 1931-

The power of play; how spontaneous, imaginative activities lead to happier, healthier children. Da Capo Lifelong 2007 240p $24 *
                                          155.4

1. Play

ISBN 0-7382-1053-6; 978-0-7382-1053-7
                                   LC 2006-35592

"Prescribing the trinity of play, love, and work, . . . [the author] shows how the integration of these elements at various stages of development, from infancy to adolescence, leads to happier, well-adjusted individuals with a greater potential for academic success. Elkind will connect with parents when he reveals that 'Toys R Not Us' and argues that less is more; that children should use toys for inspiration, not distraction." Libr J

Includes bibliographical references

Gopnik, Alison

The scientist in the crib; minds, brains, and how children learn; [by] Alison Gopnik, Andrew N. Meltzoff, Patricia K. Kuhl. Morrow 1999 279p pa $14 hardcover o.p.   155.4

1. Psychology of learning 2. Child development

ISBN 0-688-17788-3 (pa)   LC 99-24247

The authors examine "how children learn to understand and use language, control their emotions and arouse the emotions of others, and establish relationships. . . . Prospective and actual parents stand to learn much that may be helpful to them and their children from this lively book." Booklist

Includes bibliographical references

Louv, Richard

Last child in the woods; saving our children from nature-deficit disorder. Algonquin Books of Chapel Hill 2005 323p $24.95   155.4

1. Environmental influence on humans 2. Child psychology

ISBN 1-56512-391-3   LC 2004-66034

"Arguing that the alienation of children from nature is detrimental on many levels, the author provides evidence of how exposure to nature can enhance a child's physical, emotional, and spiritual development." Choice

"Louv's book is a call to action, full of warnings—but also full of ideas for change." Publ Wkly

Includes bibliographical references

Montessori, Maria, 1870-1952

The absorbent mind; translated from the Italian by Claude A. Claremont 1967 304p il pa $17 hardcover o.p.   *   155.4

1. Child development 2. Child psychology 3. Educational psychology

ISBN 0-8050-4156-7 (pa)

"In these lectures Dr. Montessori dwells, not so much on the techniques used in her schools, but on her insight into the development of children, physically and psychologically, from birth to adulthood." Publ Wkly

Piaget, Jean, 1896-1980

The moral judgment of the child; {translated by Marjorie Gabain}. Free Press 1948 418p pa $15 hardcover o.p.   *   155.4

1. Child psychology 2. Human behavior 3. Ethics

ISBN 0-684-83330-1 (pa)

Original French edition, 1932

Piaget studies, not the moral behavior of children, but their ideas about right and wrong, the rules of a game, adult authority, and cooperation and justice

Segal, Nancy L., 1951-

Entwined lives; twins and what they tell us about human behavior. Plume 2000 396p il pa $16
                                          155.4

1. Twins

ISBN 0-452-28057-5; 978-0-452-28057-1
                                   LC 99-59376

First published 1999 by Dutton

"Segal describes twin types and elaborates on findings regarding the development of personality and intelligence. She also looks closely at twin relationships (including conjoined twins) to understand grief, competition, bonding, cooperation, and more." Libr J

"This elegantly written study cogently distills and makes available to the general reader a wealth of research from the fields of behavioral genetics, evolutionary psychology and social science." Publ Wkly

Includes bibliographical references

Segal, Nancy L., 1951-—_Continued_

Indivisible by two; lives of extraordinary twins. Harvard University Press 2005 280p il $24.95 *
155.4
1. Twins
ISBN 0-674-01933-4; 978-0-674-01933-1
LC 2005-45979
The author "makes use of a particularly powerful research method for answering . . . vexing questions about why our own and other people's lives turn out the way they do. Segal studies twins—identical, that is, from a single fertilized egg, and fraternal, from two eggs fertilized by different sperm—as well as pseudotwins, children of the same age who are raised together. She does so with a passion that derives in part from the fact that she is a fraternal twin herself." N Y Rev Books

Seligman, Martin E. P.
The optimistic child; {by} Martin E.P. Seligman with Karen Reivich, Lisa Jaycox, and Jane Gillham. Houghton Mifflin 1995 336p il hardcover o.p. pa $14.95
155.4
1. Child psychology
ISBN 0-395-69380-2; 978-0-618-91809-6 (pa); 0-618-91809-4 (pa)
LC 95-12619
The author "discounts prevalent theory that children who are encouraged by others to feel good about themselves will do well. Instead, he proposes that self-esteem comes from mastering challenges, overcoming frustration and experiencing individual achievement. In clear, concise prose peppered with anecdotes, dialogues, cartoons and exercises, Seligman offers a concrete plan of action based on techniques of self-evaluation and social interaction." Publ Wkly
Includes bibliographical references

White, Burton L., 1929-
The new first three years of life. 20th anniversary ed. Fireside Bks. 1995 384p il pa $14 *
155.4
1. Infants—Development 2. Child psychology
ISBN 0-684-80419-0
LC 95-18297
First published 1975 with title: The first three years of life
"White describes the seven developmental phases of the first three years of life. He provides parents with a comprehensive treasury of techniques for enhancing development and establishing discipline that are refreshingly straight-forward and based on real-world experience." Publ Wkly

Wright, Lawrence
Twins; and what they tell us about who we are. Wiley 1997 202p $22.95; pa $14.95
155.4
1. Twins
ISBN 0-471-25220-4; 0-471-29644-9 (pa)
LC 97-38827
Published in the United Kingdom with title: Twins; genes, environment and the mystery of identity

"Wright presents the conflicting, and often confounding results from twin studies done primarily over the last 50 years. . . . The book serves up questions such as: 'Do our genes determine our personality?' 'How much, if any, effect do parents have on the personalities of their children?'." SLJ
"Wright does an admirable job of sorting through the differing research in a well-reasoned, clearheaded manner." Publ Wkly
Includes bibliographical references

155.45 Exceptional children; children distinguished by social and economic levels, by level of cultural development, by ethnic and national origin

Winner, Ellen
Gifted children; myths and realities. Basic Bks. 1996 449p il pa $21 hardcover o.p.
155.45
1. Gifted children
ISBN 0-465-01759-2 (pa)
LC 95-49279
This study considers the following questions "are gifted children gifted in all subject areas? Are artistically gifted children gifted or talented? Does giftedness depend on IQ? What role do environment and biology play in giftedness? Are gifted children psychological and social misfits? In her analyses, Winner cites and explains a broad range of recent research, including extensive notes and references with each chapter. She then offers her recommendations for dealing with gifted children in America's educational systems." Libr J

155.5 Psychology of young people twelve to twenty

Your adolescent; emotional, behavioral and cognitive development from early adolescence through the teen years; David B. Pruitt, editor-in-chief. HarperCollins Pubs. 1999 xxiii, 374p pa $18 hardcover o.p.
155.5
1. Adolescent psychology 2. Parent-child relationship
ISBN 0-06-095676-3 (pa)
LC 98-34587
At head of title: The American Academy of Child and Adolescent Psychiatry
"In addition to discussing the milestones of normal development, common family, behavioral, physical, and emotional disorders are described and treatment options are discussed. . . . This is the most encyclopedic general treatment of the topic to be issued in years and will be a useful starting point for many parents." Libr J

155.6 Psychology of adults

Ackerman, Diane
Deep play; illustrations by Peter Sis. Random House 1999 235p il pa $13 hardcover o.p.
155.6
ISBN 0-679-77135-2 (pa)
LC 98-35067

Ackerman, Diane—*Continued*

The author contends that "deep play, 'ecstatic' play, transcends practical concerns and grants us passage to the sacred and the holy. Art is deep play, so is religion, the contemplation of nature, and playing sports; in short, pursuits that are all-consuming and inspire feelings of awe and a profound sense of connection with the universe. By turns anecdotal and philosophic, Ackerman vividly recounts her own 'deep play' experiences." Booklist

Includes bibliographical references

Estés, Clarissa Pinkola

Women who run with the wolves; myths and stories of the wild woman archetype. Ballantine Bks. 1992 520p pa $15 hardcover o.p. *
                                                     155.6
1. Women—Folklore 2. Women—Psychology
ISBN 0-345-39681-2 (pa)   LC 91-58630
In this "introduction to feminine psychology, a Jungian analyst . . . endeavors to define and describe the wild woman archetype. Arguing that it can be best elucidated through stories and myths, Estés examines traditional tales from various world cultures and explains their symbolism. By studying the meaning of these stories, she claims, a woman gains insight into her inner nature and can tap the wild woman within herself to bring forth new measures of self-determination and fresh expressions of creativity, thus achieving a state of greater empowerment and freedom. Written in a clear, richly evocative style." Libr J

Includes bibliographical references

Friday, Nancy

My mother/my self; the daughter's search for identity. Delta Trade Paperbacks 1997 425p pa $17   **155.6**
1. Women—Psychology 2. Mother-daughter relationship 3. Mothers
ISBN 0-385-32015-9; 978-0-385-32015-3
                              LC 98-115632
First published 1977 by Delacorte Press
The author explores the psychological aspects of the mother-daughter relationship.
Includes bibliographical references

Lerner, Harriet Goldhor

The dance of intimacy; a woman's guide to courageous acts of change in key relationships. Harper & Row 1989 255p pa $14 hardcover o.p.
                                                     155.6
1. Women—Psychology 2. Interpersonal relations
ISBN 0-06-091646-X (pa)   LC 88-45519
The author explains "how to operate more effectively in key relationships—whether it be with a distant or unfaithful spouse, a depressed sister, a difficult mother, an alcoholic father, an uncommitted lover, a dying parent, or a family member that we have written off." Publisher's note

Includes bibliographical references

Levinson, Daniel J., 1920-1994

The seasons of a man's life; by Daniel J. Levinson {et al.}. Knopf 1978 363p pa $15 hardcover o.p.   **155.6**
1. Men—Psychology 2. Middle age
ISBN 0-394-533901-0 (pa)   LC 77-20978
The Levinson theory divides a man's "life cycle into five overlapping eras. . . . Each era is marked by periods of stability during which life structures are built. These stable periods alternate with transition periods during which life structures change." Saturday Rev

Includes bibliographical references

The seasons of a woman's life; in collaboration with Judy D. Levinson. Knopf 1996 438p pa $23 hardcover o.p.   **155.6**
1. Women—Psychology 2. Middle age
ISBN 0-345-31174-4 (pa)   LC 95-20893
"This work asks whether there is a human life cycle and a process of adult growth similar to the process of child development, and how gender affects the lives of individual women and women in general. The Levinson team interviewed 15 homemakers, 15 women with corporate-financial careers, and 15 women with academic careers. Their stories are the core of Levinson's book." Booklist

Includes bibliographical references

155.67   Persons in late adulthood

Hillman, James

The force of character; and the lasting life. Random House 1999 xxx, 236p pa $14 hardcover o.p.   **155.67**
1. Self-realization 2. Character 3. Aging
ISBN 0-345-42405-0 (pa)   LC 99-24097
"According to Hillman, aging is not a process that causes us to decline and become weaker; instead, the aging process strips us of the unimportant, thus exposing and confirming our true character." Libr J
"Perspicacity distinguishes the entire book, as Hillman quotes and cites poets and philosophers more than scientists, and the ancients as much as the moderns." Booklist
Includes bibliographical references

155.7   Evolutional psychology

Clark, William R., 1938-

Are we hardwired? the role of genes in human behavior; by William R. Clark & Michael Grunstein. Oxford Univ. Press 2000 322p il hardcover o.p. pa $24.95   **155.7**
1. Behavior genetics
ISBN 0-19-513826-0; 978-0-19-517800-5 (pa); 0-19-517800-9 (pa)
                              LC 99-54699
The authors offer an "overview of the current evidence supporting genetic causes for general behavioral tendencies, such as aggression, consumption, sexual preferences, and, most controversial, intelligence. Case studies of identical twins separated as infants provide some of the most compelling proofs." Libr J
Includes bibliographical references

Ridley, Matt
Nature via nurture; genes, experience, and what makes us human. HarperCollins Pubs. 2003 326p $25.95 **155.7**
1. Nature and nurture 2. Genetics
ISBN 0-06-000678-1 LC 2003-40687
"In February 2001 it was announced that the human genome contains not 100,000 genes, as originally postulated, but only 30,000. This . . . revision led some scientists to conclude that there are simply not enough human genes to account for all the different ways people behave: we must be made by nurture, not nature. . . . {Ridley argues that} nurture depends on genes, too, and genes need nurture. Genes not only predetermine the broad structure of the brain, they also absorb formative experiences, react to social cues, and even run memory. They are consequences as well as causes of the will." Publisher's note
Includes bibliographical references

155.8 Ethnopsychology and national psychology

Lévi-Strauss, Claude
The savage mind. University of Chicago Press 1966 290p il (Nature of human society series) pa $18 hardcover o.p. * **155.8**
1. Ethnopsychology 2. Anthropology
ISBN 0-226-47484-4 (pa)
Original French edition, 1962
"An anthropological study of the nature of thought, concepts and systems as they occur in various cultures." Chicago Public Libr
Includes bibliographical references

155.9 Environmental psychology

Attig, Thomas, 1945-
The heart of grief; death and the search for lasting love. Oxford Univ. Press 2000 xx, 289p hardcover o.p. pa $15.95 **155.9**
1. Bereavement 2. Death 3. Loss (Psychology)
ISBN 0-19-511873-1; 0-19-515625-0 (pa)
LC 99-49842
"The pain of loss can be overcome, says Attig . . . by survivors who keep alive in their hearts their love for the departed. He repeats his message in each of some 50 brief chapters, using numerous anecdotes gleaned from his experiences as a counselor to explain how he has helped people cope with the loss of loved ones." Publ Wkly
"A reassuring and useful book for those grieving or counseling those who grieve." Libr J

How we grieve; relearning the world. Oxford Univ. Press 1996 201p pa $24.95 hardcover o.p. **155.9**
1. Bereavement 2. Death 3. Loss (Psychology)
ISBN 0-19-507456-4 (pa) LC 95-31907
"For Attig, grieving is a process of learning to live in a world disrupted by death and to accept the changes it

brings. Sensible yet sensitive, this book helps both those who have suffered a loss and those who seek to comfort them." Libr J
Includes bibliographical references

Brehony, Kathleen A.
After the darkest hour; how suffering begins the journey to wisdom; {by} Kathleen Brehony. Holt & Co. 2000 274p il pa $14 hardcover o.p. **155.9**
1. Suffering 2. Adjustment (Psychology)
ISBN 0-8050-6436-2 (pa) LC 00-29577
"Brehony provides stories and anecdotes throughout the book of people both known and unknown who have gotten through traumatic situations and have learned something from them. . . . Peppered throughout with inspirational quotations, this book teeters on the brink of self-help sentiment, but it succeeds where others might fail in its practicality." Booklist
Includes bibliographical references

Buchholz, Ester Schaler
The call of solitude; alonetime in a world of attachment. Simon & Schuster 1997 365p pa $22 hardcover o.p. **155.9**
1. Solitude
ISBN 0-684-87280-3 (pa) LC 97-20698
The author contends "that today's culture overvalues attachment and neglects the importance of time alone. Using case studies, stories, poetry, and other sources, Buchholz shows how alonetime has always been important and that the lack of it in today's frenzied U.S. culture increases stress and depression." Libr J
"Buchholz's wide-ranging discussion, slanted toward professionals but accessible to interested general readers, may overreach on occasion, but she is often convincing in her timely and provocative advocacy of 'alonetime.'" Publ Wkly
Includes bibliographical references

Edelman, Hope
Motherless daughters; the legacy of loss. 2nd ed. Da Capo Press 2006 pa $15.95 **155.9**
1. Loss (Psychology) 2. Mother-daughter relationship 3. Bereavement
ISBN 978-0-7382-1026-1 LC 2005-33840
First published 1994 by Addison-Wesley
"Writing of her own experiences of losing her mother when she was 17, and the grief of hundreds of women she interviewed who lost their mothers through death, abandonment or another form of separation . . . Edelman marshals a wealth of anecdotal evidence, supplemented with psychological research about bereavement, that indicates that one's longing for a mother never disappears." Publ Wkly
Includes bibliographical references

Motherless mothers; how mother loss shapes the parents we become. HarperCollins 2006 xxxiii, 410p pa $14.95 hardcover o.p. **155.9**
1. Loss (Psychology) 2. Mother-daughter relationship 3. Bereavement 4. Parenting
ISBN 0-06-053246-7 (pa); 978-0-06-053246-8 (pa)
LC 2005-52812

Edelman, Hope—*Continued*

In this follow-up to Motherless daughters, the author describes "how the loss of a mother to death or abandonment can affect the ways women raise their own children." Publisher's note

Edelman "presents emotionally charged concepts in clear, memorable terms (e.g., reaching the 'neon number' of a mother's age of death) to encourage frank, cathartic discussion." Publ Wkly

Includes bibliographical references

Emswiler, Mary Ann

Guiding your child through grief; {by} Mary Ann Emswiler and James P. Emswiler. Bantam Bks. 2000 286p il pa $13.95   **155.9**

1. Death 2. Bereavement 3. Child rearing
ISBN 0-553-38025-7   LC 00-23645

"Advice during difficult days to help a child grieve the death of a parent or sibling." Publisher's note

"Thoroughly researched and bolstered with the wisdom of bereavement experts nationwide, this fine guide does those working through the loss of loved ones an enormous service. It should rank amongst the first line of defense and support for those facing a death in the family." Publ Wkly

Includes bibliographical references

Finkbeiner, Ann K., 1943-

After the death of a child; living with loss through the years. Johns Hopkins University Press 1998 273p pa $18.95   **155.9**

1. Bereavement 2. Death 3. Loss (Psychology)
ISBN 0-8018-5914-X; 978-0-8018-5914-4
    LC 97-47017

First published 1996 by Free Press

The author "lost her 18-year-old son and only child in a train wreck in 1987. For her book she interviewed other parents who have lost children, and although she refers to psychological research, their experiences are the heart of the book." N Y Times Book Rev

"Those who have lost a child will find corroboration of many of their feelings in this enlightening and heart-rending study." Publ Wkly

Includes bibliographical references

Gilbert, Sandra M.

Death's door; modern dying and the ways we grieve. Norton 2006 580p il $29.95; pa $17.95 *
    155.9

1. Death 2. Bereavement
ISBN   0-393-05131-5;   978-0-393-05131-5;
0-393-32969-0 (pa); 978-0-393-32969-8 (pa)
    LC 2004-65430

This "mélange of literary criticism, anthropology and memoir looks at death across time and culture: in the Nazi concentration camps, 9/11, and the 21st-century 'hospital spaceship,' as well as through photographs, paintings and poetry." Publ Wkly

"Those who have experienced the death of a loved one will recognize themselves in this meticulously researched, comprehensively organized, and exceptionally caring examination of society's attitudes about mortality and mourning." Booklist

Includes bibliographical references

Kosko, Bart

Noise. Viking 2006 252p il $24.95 *
    155.9

1. Noise
ISBN 0-670-03495-9; 978-0-670-03495-6
    LC 2006-44708

The author "discusses the science and subjectivity of noise, achieving a high 'wow' factor in a highly entertaining disclosure of surprising facts and concepts." Booklist

Includes bibliographical references

Kübler-Ross, Elisabeth

Living with death and dying; how to communicate with the terminally ill. Simon & Schuster 1997 181p il pa $12 *   **155.9**

1. Death 2. Terminal care
ISBN 0-684-83936-9; 978-0-684-83936-3
"A Touchstone book"

First published 1981 by Macmillan

The author argues that caring for, and living with the terminally ill need not be a solely negative experience.

On children and death. Macmillan 1983 279p pa $12 hardcover o.p. *   **155.9**

1. Death 2. Child psychology
ISBN 0-684-83939-3 (pa)   LC 83-11252

A look at how one copes with a child's death by disease, accident or murder

Includes bibliographical references

On death and dying. Scribner Classics 1997 286p il $23; pa $13 *   **155.9**

1. Death 2. Terminal care
ISBN 0-684-84223-8; 0-684-83938-5 (pa)
    LC 97-177294

A reissue of the title first published 1969 by Macmillan

A look at the psychological, sociological and theological issues faced by the terminally ill and their caregivers

Includes bibliographical references

Lazare, Aaron, 1936-

On apology. Oxford University Press 2004 306p $24; pa $13.95   **155.9**

1. Apologizing
ISBN 0-19-517343-0; 0-19-518911-6 (pa)
    LC 2004-43470

"Among the topics covered in this . . . book are the growing importance of apologies (the 'apology phenomenon'), how apologies heal, why people do not apologize, and apology and forgiveness." Sci Books Films

"Everybody on earth could benefit from this small but essential book." Publ Wkly

Includes bibliographical references

Levy, Alexander

The orphaned adult; understanding and coping with grief and change after the death of our parents. Perseus Bks. 1999 190p pa $15.95 hardcover o.p.   **155.9**

1. Death 2. Bereavement 3. Loss (Psychology)
ISBN 0-7382-0361-0 (pa)   LC 99-64773

Levy, Alexander—*Continued*

"Incorporating his own personal experience with the accounts of others who have lost their parents, psychologist Levy examines this profound life-changing event with compassion and understanding." Libr J

Sife, Wallace

The loss of a pet. 3rd ed. Howell Book House 2005 260p il pa $14.99 **155.9**
1. Pets 2. Death 3. Bereavement
ISBN 0-7645-7930-4   LC 2005-12603
First published 1993
The author "addresses the pet owner whose grief at a pet's death is largely misunderstood or even ridiculed by friends, associates and society in general. . . . Sife is to be commended for offering information that is not only compassionate but concise, wide-ranging and, above all, practical." Publ Wkly {review of 1993 edition}

Zimbardo, Philip G.

The Lucifer effect; understanding how good people turn evil; [by] Philip Zimbardo. Random House 2007 xx, 551p il $27.95 **155.9**
1. Good and evil 2. Social psychology
ISBN 978-1-4000-6411-3; 1-4000-6411-2
LC 2006-50388
The author "masterminded the famous Stanford Prison Experiment, in which college students randomly assigned to be guards or inmates found themselves enacting sadistic abuse or abject submissiveness. In this penetrating investigation, he revisits . . . the SPE study and applies it to historical examples of injustice and atrocity, especially the Abu Ghraib outrages by the U.S. military. . . . Combining a dense but readable and often engrossing exposition of social psychology research with an impassioned moral seriousness, Zimbardo challenges readers to look beyond glib denunciations of evil-doers and ponder our collective responsibility for the world's ills." Publ Wkly
Includes bibliographical references

156 Comparative psychology

Fouts, Roger

Next of kin; what chimpanzees have taught me about who we are; {by} Roger Fouts with Stephen Tukel Mills; introduction by Jane Goodall. Morrow 1997 420p il pa $14 hardcover o.p.
156
1. Chimpanzees 2. Animal communication
ISBN 0-380-72822-2 (pa)   LC 97-15144
"A Living planet book"
This is an account of a study known as Project Washoe where a female chimpanzee was taught American Sign Language
"What makes this book an exceptional popularization of scientific research is the authors' ability to charm with a fascinating story while also teaching *why* the story is so fascinating." Booklist
Includes bibliographical references

Waal, Frans de, 1948-

The ape and the sushi master; cultural reflections by a primatologist. Basic Bks. 2001 433p il $26; pa $18 **156**
1. Animal behavior 2. Human behavior 3. Comparative psychology 4. Primates
ISBN 0-465-04175-2; 0-465-04176-0 (pa)
LC 00-57922
The author "argues that, because other animals, particularly other primates, create cultures—that is, add to their behavioral repertoires by nongenetic transmission (learning through innovation, demonstration, and imitation)—they are the same kinds of creatures as humans in all respects." Booklist
This is a "deftly written, deeply reflective work." N Y Times Book Rev
Includes bibliographical references

Our inner ape; a leading primatologist explains why we are who we are; photographs by the author. Riverhead Books 2005 274p il $24.95
156
1. Human behavior 2. Primates—Behavior 3. Comparative psychology
ISBN 1-57322-312-3   LC 2005-42768
This book compares human "social behavior with that of two species of apes: chimpanzees and bonobos." N Y Times Book Rev
"Readers might be surprised at how much these apes and their stories resonate with their own lives, and may well be left with an urge to spend a few hours watching primates themselves at the local zoo." Publ Wkly
Includes bibliographical references

158 Applied psychology

Ban Breathnach, Sarah

A man's journey to simple abundance; [by] Sarah Ban Breathnach and friends; edited by Michael Segell. Scribner 2000 448p $22
158
1. Men 2. Conduct of life
ISBN 0-7432-0061-6   LC 00-45012
"A Simple Abundance Press book"
"A collection of 50-plus pieces on men's experiences. . . . The book's sections cover family, emotional and moral concerns, men's roles and obligations, success and failure, amusements and obsessions, and the deepest values in life. . . . Contributors include respected novelists (Rick Bass, Jim Harrison, Reynolds Price), journalists (Roy Blount, Harold Evans), pop-culture figures (Sting, director Garry Marshall), and representatives of religious and spiritual movements." Booklist
Includes bibliographical references

Bloomfield, Harold H., 1944-

Making peace with your past; the six essential steps to enjoying a great future; {by} Harold H. Bloomfield with Philip Goldberg. HarperCollins Pubs. 2000 269p pa $13 hardcover o.p.
158
1. Self-realization 2. Applied psychology
ISBN 0-06-093314-3 (pa)   LC 99-89719

Bloomfield, Harold H., 1944-—_Continued_

The author "addresses the syndrome Freud called 'repetition compulsion'—humans' tendency to re-create what they have not worked through. . . . With revealing exercises, Bloomfield shows readers how to rediscover 'the passion to live {their} highest destiny.'" Libr J

Includes bibliographical references

Browne, Joy

The nine fantasies that will ruin your life and the eight realities that will save you. Crown 1998 256p pa $13 hardcover o.p.   **158**

1. Conduct of life 2. Happiness

ISBN 0-609-80473-1 (pa)   LC 98-36245

This is a "book of anti-romantic, practical advice about common life problems, cast largely as answers to readers' and listeners' questions. . . . Browne draws on her clinical expertise, her talk-show experience and her store of common sense." Publ Wkly

Burns, David D.

Feeling good; the new mood therapy; preface by Aaron T. Beck. Rev and updated. Avon Bks. 1999 xxxii, 706p il pa $15   **158**

1. Depression (Psychology) 2. Psychotherapy

ISBN 0-380-73176-2   LC 99-461798

First published 1980

"The author reports on results of treating depression (from mild blues to serious cases) with 'cognitive thinking.' . . . The therapy involves fighting automatic responses to disappointments by intelligent thinking that can put one's shortcomings into perspective." Publ Wkly [review of 1980 edition]

"The author . . . writes simply, clearly, and without any jargon; better yet, he has a sense of compassion and a sense of humor, and is aware of his own limitations." Libr J [review of 1980 edition]

Includes bibliographical references

Buscaglia, Leo F.

Loving each other; the challenge of human relationships. Fawcett Columbine 1986 208p pa $13.95   **158**

1. Love 2. Interpersonal relations

ISBN 0-449-90157-2; 978-0-449-90157-1

First published 1984 by Slack

The author offers practical suggestions for improving human relationships.

Includes bibliographical references

Canfield, Jack, 1944-

The success principles; how to get from where you are to where you want to be; by Jack Canfield with Janet Switzer. HarperCollins Publishers 2005 xxxiii, 473p il $24.95   **158**

1. Success

ISBN 0-06-059488-8   LC 2004-54259

A self-improvement guide for business professionals, teachers, students, parents, or anyone interested in promoting themselves within today's success-oriented culture shares sixty-four principles on how to reach desired goals

The author "has an easy style and talks directly to readers, responding to potential 'what ifs' and 'buts' with encouragement and sound advice. The book's layout is superb—small paragraphs are punctuated by italicized quotes, questions for self-study, and several appropriate cartoons." Libr J

Includes bibliographical references

Carnegie, Dale, 1888-1955

How to win friends and influence people; editorial consultant, Dorothy Carnegie, editorial assistance, Arthur R. Pell. Pocket Books 1982 276p pa $6.99 *   **158**

1. Success 2. Applied psychology

ISBN 0-671-72365-0; 978-0-671-72365-1

LC 94-176452

First published 1936 by Simon & Schuster

An examination of the psychology of business and social success.

Includes bibliographical references

Carter, Steve, 1956-

Men like women who like themselves; (and other secrets that the smartest women know about partnership and power); by Steven Carter & Julia Sokol. Delacorte Press 1996 259p pa $13.95 hardcover o.p.   **158**

1. Interpersonal relations 2. Self-confidence 3. Dating (Social customs) 4. Women—Sexual behavior

ISBN 0-440-50615-8 (pa)   LC 95-39450

The authors offer advice on male-female relationships and cover dating, self-esteem, abusive men, counseling, etc.

Covey, Stephen R.

The 7 habits of highly effective people; restoring the character ethic. [Rev. ed.] Free Press 2004 372p il $26; pa $15.95 *   **158**

1. Success 2. Conduct of life

ISBN 0-7432-7245-5; 0-7432-6951-9 (pa)

LC 2004-57494

First published 1989

The author describes seven habits designed to help people solve personal and professional problems.

The 8th habit; from effectiveness to greatness. Free Press 2004 408p il $26   **158**

1. Self-realization 2. Success

ISBN 0-684-84665-9   LC 2004-56371

Includes DVD

"The original seven habits of highly successful people are still relevant, but Covey . . . says that the new Information/Knowledge Worker Age, exemplified by the Internet, calls for an eighth habit to achieve personal and organizational excellence: 'Find your voice and inspire others to find theirs.' . . . The bulk of the book details how, after finding your own voice, you can inspire others and create a workplace where people feel engaged." Publ Wkly

"Though conceived for individuals, Covey's book will be of tremendous importance to organizations and businesses." Libr J

Includes bibliographical references

Covey, Stephen R.—*Continued*

First things first; to live, to love, to learn, to leave a legacy; {by} Stephen R. Covey, A. Roger Merrill, Rebecca R. Merrill. Simon & Schuster 1994 360p il pa $14 hardcover o.p. **158**

1. Conduct of life 2. Time management
ISBN 0-684-80203-1 (pa)   LC 94-2305

The authors "offer a 'principle-centered' approach to time management that emphasizes what 'represents our vision, values, principles, mission, conscience, direction—what we feel is important and how we lead our lives.' The authors argue that central to our lives are 'four needs and capacities—to live, to love, to learn, to leave a legacy.' The ideas here are not only clearly explained but are reinforced by scenarios from the authors' lives and self-directed activities for the reader." Libr J

Includes bibliographical references

Dyer, Wayne W.

The power of intention; learning to co-create your world your way. Hay House 2004 259p $24.95; pa $14.95 * **158**

1. Intentionalism
ISBN 1-401-90215-4; 1-401-90216-2 (pa)
     LC 2003-14622

The author argues that "there are seven faces, or energy fields, of intention: creativity, kindness, love, beauty, expansion, abundance and receptivity. Drawing on a variety of spiritual traditions and gurus, Dyer . . . describes how to surmount the barriers that may get in the way of connecting to this power, such as negative thinking, relying on the opinion of others or retaining a controlling ego." Publ Wkly

Foster, Rick, 1949-

How we choose to be happy; the 9 choices of extremely happy people—their secrets, their stories. Rev. Berkley Publishing Group 2004 xxi, 228p pa $14.95 **158**

1. Happiness
ISBN 978-0-399-52990-0; 0-399-52990-X
"A Perigee book"
First published 1999

The authors "interviewed happy people from all walks of life, from the United States to Eastern Europe. The resulting personal stories, writing exercises, and quotes together inform and instruct the reader in the nine principles discovered by the authors in their travels." Libr J

Gegax, Tom

Winning in the game of life; self-coaching secrets for success. RH Publishing 2003 318p pa $14 **158**

1. Success 2. Self-realization
ISBN 978-0-9740675-0-6; 0-9740675-0-4
First published 1999 by Harmony Bks.

"For Gegax, creating a winning life plan requires defining a mission and taking steps that balances career, friends, community, and family into an integrated whole." Booklist

Gilbert, Daniel T.

Stumbling on happiness; [by] Daniel Gilbert. Alfred A. Knopf 2006 277p il $24.95; pa $14.95 * **158**

1. Happiness
ISBN 1-4000-4266-6; 978-1-4000-4266-1; 1-4000-7742-7 (pa); 978-1-4000-7742-7 (pa)
     LC 2005-44459

This book argues that "events that we anticipate will give us joy make us less happy than we think; things that fill us with dread will make us less unhappy, for less long, than we anticipate." N Y Times Book Rev

"The book is a sly, irresistible romp down, or through, memory lane—past, present, and future. It is not only wildly entertaining but also hilarious . . . and yet full of startling insight, imaginative conclusions, and even bits of wisdom." Booklist

Includes bibliographical references

Goleman, Daniel

Social intelligence; the new science of human relationships. Bantam Books 2006 403p il $28; pa $14 * **158**

1. Emotions 2. Intellect
ISBN 0-553-80352-2; 978-0-553-80352-5; 0-553-38449-X (pa); 978-0-553-38449-9 (pa)
     LC 2006-45971

The author "argues for a new social model of intelligence drawn from the emerging field of social neuroscience. . . . Goleman illuminates new theories about attachment, bonding, and the making and remaking of memory as he examines how our brains are wired for altruism, compassion, concern and rapport." Publ Wkly

Includes bibliographical references

Goodman, Ellen

I know just what you mean; the power of friendship in women's lives; [by] Ellen Goodman, Patricia O'Brien. Simon & Schuster 2000 300p il $25; pa $14 **158**

1. Friendship 2. Women—Psychology
ISBN 0-684-84287-4; 0-7432-0171-X (pa)
     LC 00-24859

Goodman and O'Brien "examine their friendship of more than 25 years and a host of other friendships among women, famous and unknown." Booklist

"Heavy on insight and light on psychological jargon, this book is an intelligent, observant read." Publ Wkly

Hallowell, Edward M.

Connect. Pantheon Bks. 1999 xx, 328p pa $13.95 hardcover o.p. **158**

1. Quality of life 2. Interpersonal relations
ISBN 0-7434-0621-4 (pa)   LC 99-13082

The author "urges readers to 'make time for connectedness,' which he alternately defines as having person-to-person interaction or being involved with something greater than oneself." Libr J

Harris, Thomas Anthony, 1913?-1995

I'm OK, you're OK; a practical guide to transactional analysis. Harper & Row 1969 278p il pa $12.95 o.p. * **158**

Harris, Thomas Anthony, 1913?-1995—*Continued*

1. Transactional analysis

ISBN 0-06-072427-7 (pa)

Also available in paperback by Galahad Bks.

This book describes the method of psychiatric group treatment, and applies the system to problems in marriage and child rearing, violence and revolution, racial prejudice, creativity, and international problems

Includes bibliographical references

Hay, Louise L.

You can heal your life. Hay House 1987 226p pa $14.95 *   **158**

1. Self-realization 2. Holistic medicine 3. Mind and body 4. Health self-care

ISBN 0-937611-01-8   LC 88-200391

First published 1984

The author's "key message in this . . . work is: 'If we are willing to do the mental work, almost anything can be healed.' Louise explains how limiting beliefs and ideas are often the cause of illness." Publisher's note

Includes bibliographical references

Hodgkinson, Tom

How to be idle. HarperCollins Publishers 2005 286p il $18.95   **158**

1. Conduct of life

ISBN 0-06-077968-3   LC 2004-59932

First published 2004 in the United Kingdom

The author "presents 24 essays defending life's idle pleasures, which are, he says, vilified by our modern society. He meditates on sleeping in, fishing, smoking and drinking, and even waxes poetic about the hangover. The whole book is soaked with nostalgia for the turn-of-the-century English gentleman's lifestyle; Hodgkinson defends his arguments by quoting Jerome K. Jerome, G.K. Chesterton and, of course, that icon of British foppery, Oscar Wilde." Publ Wkly

Includes bibliographical references

July, William W., II

Understanding the tin man; why so many men avoid intimacy; [by] William July II. Doubleday 1999 201p $22.95; pa $12.95   **158**

1. Men—Psychology

ISBN 0-385-49663-X; 0-7679-0566-0 (pa)

LC 99-46434

The author addresses "the difficulties many men encounter with commitment—to themselves and others. . . . [He] asserts that men need to acknowledge, understand and learn how to process their emotions in healthy ways." Publ Wkly

Includes bibliographical references

Kephart, Beth

Into the tangle of friendship; a memoir of the things that matter. Houghton Mifflin 2000 204p $23   **158**

1. Friendship

ISBN 0-618-03378-4   LC 00-38915

The author "meditates on circumstances that promote and encourage friends to find each other, stay together, or drift apart." Libr J

"Kephart's writing is luminous, filled with phrases so precise that they are worth committing to memory." Publ Wkly

Klauser, Henriette Anne

Write it down, make it happen; knowing what you want—and getting it! Scribner 2000 250p pa $12 hardcover o.p.   **158**

1. Applied psychology

ISBN 0-684-85002-8 (pa)   LC 99-43551

The author "instructs her readers to write down their most extravagant wishes and, merely by the act of recording them, make them come true. . . . Her technique is intended to clarify goals, increase self-confidence, and dispel self-doubt, and she describes how it has dramatically improved her life and the lives of her friends and acquaintances." Libr J

Includes bibliographical references

May, Rollo

Freedom and destiny. Norton 1981 275p pa $14 hardcover o.p. *   **158**

1. Applied psychology 2. Free will and determinism 3. Fate and fatalism

ISBN 0-393-31842-7 (pa)   LC 81-4009

This book examines "the continuing tension in our lives between the possibilities freedom offers and the various limitations imposed upon us by our particular fate or destiny." America

Includes bibliographical references

McGraw, Phillip C., 1950-

Life strategies; doing what works, doing what matters. Hyperion 1999 282p il $21.95; pa $13.95   **158**

1. Success

ISBN 0-7868-6548-2; 0-7868-8459-2 (pa)

LC 98-46748

"McGraw claims that people in dire situations have serious problems, including denial and choosing initial assumptions without testing them for accuracy. To create a life strategy that works, McGraw lays out his ten 'Life Laws' along with checklists and 18 assignments." Libr J

Peck, M. Scott (Morgan Scott)

Further along the road less traveled; the unending journey toward spiritual growth: the edited lectures. Simon & Schuster 1993 255p pa $14 hardcover o.p.   **158**

1. Self-realization 2. Applied psychology 3. Spiritual life

ISBN 0-684-84723-X (pa)   LC 93-31322

The author "discusses 'growing up'—becoming self-aware, working through cycles of blame and toward wholesale forgiveness—and then the self-examination we each must undergo in order to groom ourselves for the most important step of all: the search for God." Booklist

Peck, M. Scott (Morgan Scott)—*Continued*

The road less traveled; a new psychology of love, traditional values, and spiritual growth. 25th anniversary ed. Simon & Schuster 2002 315p $22.95 * **158**
1. Applied psychology 2. Love
ISBN 0-7432-3825-7 LC 2002-75858
A reissue of the title first published 1978
This book attempts to bring together "psychology and religion. It is divided into four areas—discipline, love, religion and growth, and grace—and within each Peck tackles the . . . struggle between stagnation and progress which goes on in all of us throughout our lives." Libr J

The road less traveled and beyond; spiritual growth in an age of anxiety. Simon & Schuster 1997 314p $23; pa $14 **158**
1. Self-realization 2. Applied psychology
ISBN 0-684-81314-9; 0-684-83561-4 (pa)
LC 96-43391
In this volume Peck "continues his journey through the existential conflicts and baffling paradoxes on the meandering road of personal development. . . . Through copious detailed references from his previous books, he allows readers unfamiliar with them to understand and enjoy the present work, which completes his Road trilogy." Publ Wkly

Prager, Dennis, 1948-
Happiness is a serious problem; a human nature repair manual. ReganBooks 1998 179p pa $13 hardcover o.p. **158**
1. Happiness
ISBN 0-06-098735-1 (pa) LC 97-35404
Includes index
The author "uses the pursuit of happiness as a central motif but generally instructs in the modern art of self-improvement. The 31 short chapters . . . are cogent, complete, and preach a nonreligious yet morally guided moderation that should appeal across a wide range of patron groups." Libr J

Queen Latifah
Ladies first; revelations of a strong woman; {by} Queen Latifah with Karen Hunter; foreword by Rita Owens. Morrow 1999 xxvii, 173p il pa $13 hardcover o.p. **158**
1. Self-esteem 2. Women—Psychology
ISBN 0-688-17583-X (pa) LC 98-41533
"This book attempts to impart the philosophy behind Latifah's image and, in so doing, 'let every woman know that she, too . . . is royalty. She does this by basing the narrative loosely around some of the major events in her life. . . . Also included are Latifah's views on drug use, God, romance and sex." Publ Wkly

Richardson, Brenda Lane, 1948-
What mama couldn't tell us about love; healing the emotional legacy of slavery; celebrating our light; {by} Brenda Lane Richardson and Brenda Wade. HarperCollins Pubs. 1999 xxviii, 241p pa $13.95 hardcover o.p. **158**
1. Love 2. African American women 3. Women—Psychology
ISBN 0-06-09379-9 (pa) LC 99-12127
The authors present a "self-help guide on relationships and intimacy for African American women. What makes this work unique is that it makes the direct connection between slavery and emotional health. . . . The resource sections on assistance for individual or group work, mental health organizations, and sisterly support are valuable additions." Booklist
Includes bibliographical references

Robbins, Tony
Awaken the giant within; how to take immediate control of your mental, emotional, physical & financial destiny! [by] Anthony Robbins. Summit Bks. 1991 539p il hardcover o.p. pa $16 * **158**
1. Success 2. Applied psychology
ISBN 0-671-72734-6; 0-671-79154-0 (pa)
LC 91-27218
The author offers advice and techniques for achieving personal success.
"Robbins' system is somewhat elaborate, but his advice is based on common sense and on psychological and sociocultural reality." Booklist

Unlimited power; the new science of personal achievement; [by] Anthony Robbins. 1st Fireside ed. Simon & Schuster 1997 425p il pa $15 * **158**
1. Success 2. Applied psychology
ISBN 0-684-84577-6 LC 97-35403
First published 1986
The author offers advice and techniques for achieving personal and professional success using neurolinguistic programming (NLP).

Schwartz, David Joseph
The magic of thinking big. 1st Fireside ed. Simon & Schuster 1987 192p pa $14.95 * **158**
1. Success
ISBN 0-671-64678-8 LC 87-8516
"A Fireside book"
First published 1959 by Prentice-Hall
In this motivational book, the author presents a "program for getting the most out of your job, your marriage and family life, and your community." Publisher's note

Siegel, Bernie S.
Prescriptions for living; inspirational lessons for a joyful, loving life. HarperCollins Pubs. 1998 xxiv, 210p pa $14 hardcover o.p. **158**
1. Spiritual life 2. Self-realization
ISBN 0-06-092936-7 (pa) LC 98-39059

Siegel, Bernie S.—*Continued*

"Among the topics Siegel covers are how to find peace of mind; how to love, encourage, and forgive other people as well as yourself; and how to thrive in bad times and survive the good times. For those ready to be uplifted by the soothing repetition of time-tested homilies, Siegel delivers the goods." Booklist

Stone, Douglas

Difficult conversations; how to discuss what matters most; {by} Douglas Stone, Bruce Patton, Sheila Heen. Viking 1999 xxi, 250p il pa $14 hardcover o.p.   **158**

1. Interpersonal relations 2. Communication
ISBN 0-14-028852-X (pa)   LC 98-33346
This is a "guide to the art of handling difficult conversations—e.g., firing an employee, ending a relationship, or discussing marital conflicts." Libr J
The authors "blend a daunting array of disciplines into highly readable and practical advice." Booklist

Tolle, Eckhart, 1948-

A new earth; awakening to your life's purpose. Dutton/Penguin Group 2005 315p $24.95   **158**

1. Spiritual life 2. Self-realization
ISBN 978-0-525-94802-5; 0-525-94802-3   LC 2005-23358
"According to Tolle, . . . humans are on the verge of creating a new world by a personal transformation that shifts our attention away from our ever-expanding egos." Publ Wkly
Includes bibliographical references

The power of now; a guide to spiritual enlightenment. New World Library 1999 193p $22.95; pa $14   **158**

1. Spiritual life 2. Self-realization
ISBN   978-1-57731-152-2;   1-57731-152-3; 978-1-57731-480-6 (pa); 1-57731-480-8 (pa)   LC 99-42366
First published 1997 in Canada
"The author describes his transition from despair to self-realization soon after his 29th birthday. Tolle took another ten years to understand this transformation, during which time he evolved a philosophy that has parallels in Buddhism, relaxation techniques, and meditation theory. . . In The Power of Now he shows readers how to recognize themselves as the creators of their own pain, and how to have a pain-free existence by living fully in the present." Publisher's note

Ury, William

Getting past no; negotiating with difficult people; {by} William L. Ury. Bantam Bks. 1991 161p pa $14.95 hardcover o.p.   **158**

1. Negotiation
ISBN 0-553-37131-2 (pa)   LC 91-10101
"Ury presents a five-step agenda to deal successfully with opponents, be they unruly teenagers, labor leaders, terrorists or international politicians. Strategies focus on self-discipline, or tactics for defusing the adversary's at-

tacks, and suggestions for developing options designed to lead to a mutually satisfactory agreement." Publ Wkly
Includes bibliographical references

Viorst, Judith

Imperfect control; our lifelong struggles with power and surrender. Simon & Schuster 1998 446p pa $14 hardcover o.p. *   **158**

1. Psychology
ISBN 0-684-84814-7 (pa)   LC 97-37302
"Referring to the works of social scientists, psychologists, and philosophers as well as literary examples and personal experiences, Viorst shows how issues of power and surrender confront and affect us throughout our lives. . . . Her book is very readable, with traces of the author's special brand of humor woven throughout." Libr J

Includes bibliographical references

Viscott, David S., 1938-1996

Emotional resilience; simple truths for dealing with the unfinished business of your past; by David Viscott. Harmony Bks. 1996 358p il pa $15 hardcover o.p.   **158**

1. Attitude (Psychology) 2. Human behavior
ISBN 0-517-88825-4 (pa)   LC 96-407
The author outlines his 10 step self help program. "His method, which includes truth telling, acceptance of self and others, letting go of the past and of false expectations, and taking responsibility for one's life, is for those trapped in emotionally confining situations, whether personal relationships, educational impasses, or financial situations." Booklist

160   Logic

Copi, Irving M.

Introduction to logic; [by] Irving M. Copi, Carl Cohen. 13th ed. Pearson/Prentice-Hall 2008 670p il $104 *   **160**

1. Logic
ISBN 978-0-13-614139-6; 0-13-614139-0   LC 2007-41752
First published 1953. Periodically revised
This introduction to logic covers language, fallacies, definitions, categories, arguments, deduction, probability and other areas of logical inquiry such as thought and reasoning
Includes bibliographical references

170   Ethics

Aristotle, 384-322 B.C.

Nicomachean ethics; translation (with historical introduction) by Christopher Rowe; philosophical introduction and commentary by Sarah Broadie. Oxford University Press 2002 468p pa $29.95 *   **170**

1. Ethics
ISBN 978-0-19-875271-4; 0-19-875271-7   LC 2002-283430

Aristotle, 384-322 B.C.—*Continued*

Variant titles: Ethics and Ethica Nichomachea

According to Aristotle's ethical treatises, "happiness is the goal of life. Pleasure, fame, and wealth, however, will not bring one the highest happiness, which is achieved only through the contemplation of philosophic truth, because it exercises man's peculiar virtue, the rational principle." Reader's Ency. 3d edition

Includes bibliographical references

Carter, Stephen L.

Integrity. Basic Bks. 1996 277p pa $14 hardcover o.p. **170**

1. Ethics 2. Conduct of life

ISBN 0-06-092807-7 (pa)   LC 95-44538

The author seeks to define "integrity in both personal and political terms. . . . Mr. Carter divides true integrity into three parts: discernment, steadfastness and forthrightness. Anyone who wants to act with integrity must first think hard about what is right and wrong. . . . Once the right course of action suggests itself, it should be acted upon, even if doing so is risky or unpleasant. . . . People of integrity, finally, are willing to defend what they do in public." N Y Times Book Rev

Includes bibliographical references

Coles, Robert

Lives of moral leadership. Random House 2000 247p pa $13.95 hardcover o.p. * **170**

1. Ethics 2. Conduct of life 3. Leadership

ISBN 0-375-75835-6 (pa)   LC 00-27858

Drawing on interviews he conducted over the past four decades with public and private figures, Coles reflects on the meaning of moral leadership in the United States

Covey, Stephen R.

Everyday greatness; inspiration for a meaningful life; insights and commentary by Steven R. Covey; compiled by David K. Hatch. Rutledge Hill Press 2006 445p $24.99 **170**

1. Conduct of life

ISBN 978-1-4016-0241-3; 1-4016-0241-X
                        LC 2006-19786

"Reader's Digest"

"The stories, which the authors have gleaned from Reader's Digest, illustrate 21 principles such as integrity, gratitude, respect, and perseverance. Covey provides commentary, reflections, and further insights on how readers can apply each principle to their own lives in today's world. Truly inspiring." Libr J

Includes bibliographical references

Edelman, Marian Wright, 1939-

The measure of our success; a letter to my children and yours. HarperPerennial 1993 97p pa $10 **170**

1. Ethics 2. Human behavior 3. Child rearing 4. United States—Moral conditions

ISBN 0-06-097546-6; 978-0-06-097546-3
                        LC 92-54846

First published 1992 by Beacon Press

The author presents her "beliefs on child rearing and moral values. . . . She includes a personal letter to her three sons, who were born into a family with a shared African American and Jewish heritage, and offers 25 lessons, or 'road maps', for life." Libr J

Encyclopedia of applied ethics. Academic Press 1998 4v set $790 **170**

1. Ethics—Encyclopedias

ISBN 0-12-227065-7   LC 97-74395

Editor-in-chief, Ruth Chadwick

"Arranged in an A-Z format, the set describes 282 topics in 5000- to 6000-word articles. Coverage includes most of the 'hot topics' of our day from abortion and adoption to zoos. Typical of the broad coverage, 'Aids in the Developing World' includes a glossary description of clinical research, a discussion of sex education, and comments on resource allocation." Libr J

Encyclopedia of ethics; edited by Lawrence C. Becker and Charlotte B. Becker. 2nd ed. Routledge 2001 3v set $370 * **170**

1. Ethics—Encyclopedias

ISBN 0-415-93672-1   LC 2001-19657

First published 1992 by Garland

"The coverage of ethical theory as pursued among English-speaking philosophers remains the scope of this set. Entries are listed in word-by-word alphabetical order. A list of entries gives a convenient overview of headwords and *see* references. A subject index provides a guide to subjects discussed in the text of the entries, including persons; and a citation index provides an author-by-author listing of writers, and some editors, cited in the bibliographies of all 581 entries." Booklist

Includes bibliographical references and index

Ethics; edited by John K. Roth. Rev. ed. Salem Press 2005 3v set $331 * **170**

1. Ethics—Encyclopedias

ISBN 1-58765-170-X   LC 2004-21797

First published 1994

The aim of this set is "to provide accessible entry points for those grappling with ethical issues and concerns. The 1000-plus articles cover people, events, organizations, trends, and issues. . . . This well-organized, highly useful work will be popular with researchers and general readers." SLJ

For a fuller review, see: Booklist, June 1 & 15, 2005

Includes bibliographical references

Fleming, Thomas, 1945-

The morality of everyday life; rediscovering an ancient alternative to the liberal tradition. University of Missouri Press 2004 270p $44.95 **170**

1. Ethics

ISBN 0-8262-1509-2   LC 2003-23962

The author "restates the communitarian argument that Platonic universal idealism and post-Enlightenment liberalism fail to enlighten in matters of everyday morality, and that one needs to revive moral 'casuistry' (as described by ancient Greek and early Christian philosophy)." Choice

"Writing much more accessibly and knowledgeably

Fleming, Thomas, 1945-—_Continued_
than most modern, professional philosophers, Fleming re-
vivifies the body of thought with which civilization was
created and without which it is disintegrating." Booklist
  Includes bibliographical references

Gaines, Patrice
  Moments of grace; meeting the challenge to
change. Crown 1997 206p pa $15 hardcover o.p.
                        170
  1. Conversion 2. Conduct of life
  ISBN 0-609-80171-6 (pa)   LC 96-25404
  Companion volume to Laughing in the dark (1994)
  The author focuses on the "process of personal
change. . . . She addresses in specific chapters friends,
family, work, dating, love and marriage, 'a higher power,' and perseverance." Libr J
  "Gaines manifests an intelligent and mellow wisdom.
She treats her own insight into her travails as spiritual
awakenings, or gifts from God. Without preaching or
cheerleading, she points out the powerful, life-changing
lessons available in her experiences and in those of others." Publ Wkly

Global values 101; a short course; edited by Kate
  Holbrook . . . [et al.] Beacon Press 2006 c2005
  276p pa $14   **170**
  1. Social values
  ISBN 0-8070-0305-0   LC 2005-13091
  "For Personal Choice and Global Transformation, the
exceedingly popular and controversial Harvard undergraduate religion course that spawned this book, . . .
[the editors] invited about a dozen people—'from janitors
to billionaires, from professors to corporate CEOs to
nuns'—to their class each semester to answer tough,
well-informed questions posed by their students. Transcripts of 16 of those conversations comprise this timely,
thought-provoking volume that opens with historian
Howard Zinn and closes with independent journalist
Amy Goodman." Libr J
  Includes bibliographical references

Gottlieb, Daniel, 1946-
  Learning from the heart; lessons on living,
loving, and listening. Sterling Pub. 2008 170p
$17.95   **170**
  1. Conduct of life
  ISBN 978-1-4027-4999-5; 1-4027-4999-6
                      LC 2007-35100
  "Having rebuilt his life after an accident that left him
a quadriplegic in his thirties, . . . [the author] here
shares his observations on what makes us human. . . .
An uplifting book abounding with encouragement for
daily living; recommended for public libraries." Libr J

Haidt, Jonathan
  The happiness hypothesis; finding modern truth
in ancient wisdom. Basic Books 2005 297p il $26;
pa $15.95   **170**
  1. Happiness
  ISBN   978-0-465-02801-6;   0-465-02801-2;
978-0-465-02802-3 (pa); 0-465-02802-0 (pa)
                      LC 2005-21163

"Using the wisdom culled from the world's greatest
civilizations as a foundation, social psychologist Haidt
comes to terms with 10 Great Ideas, viewing them
through a contemporary filter to learn which of their lessons may still apply to modern lives. . . . Fascinating
stuff, accessibly expressed." Booklist
  Includes bibliographical references

Hauser, Marc D.
  Moral minds; how nature designed our universal
sense of right and wrong. Ecco 2006 489p il
$27.95 *   **170**
  1. Ethics
  ISBN 978-0-06-078070-8; 0-06-078070-3
                      LC 2006-41324
  "Hauser argues that humans have evolved a universal
moral instinct, unconsciously propelling us to deliver
judgments of right and wrong independent of gender, education, and religion. Experience tunes up our moral actions, guiding what we do as opposed to how we deliver
our moral verdicts." Publisher's note
  "Hauser has picked a subject that philosophers have
vented about since philosophy began, and knows it. He
explores Kant and Hume and Rawls in some detail and
uses their insights to characterize different aspects of the
human mental apparatus that can become involved in
moral judgments. But while he pays respects to these
thinkers of the past, he does not kowtow to them." Humanist
  Includes bibliographical references

Kübler-Ross, Elisabeth
  Life lessons; two experts on death and dying
teach us about the mysteries of life and living;
[by] Elisabeth Kübler-Ross and David Kessler.
Scribner 2000 224p $24; pa $13 *   **170**
  1. Conduct of life 2. Death
  ISBN 0-684-87074-6; 0-684-87075-4 (pa)
                      LC 00-57387
  The authors argue that "there is a 'core self,' a real
and eternal 'you,' who is not identified with actions, social roles or history. Happiness is its natural state. This
self is good and pure but always learning; its experience
is to be seen as 'lessons.'" Christ Century
  "As in each of their previous individual works, the authors provide useful and accessible information." Libr J

McMahon, Darrin M.
  Happiness; a history. Atlantic Monthly Press
2005 544p il $27.50 *   **170**
  1. Happiness
  ISBN 0-8711-3886-7   LC 2005-48009
  Published in the United Kingdom with title: The pursuit of happiness
  Utilizing different types of sources including "art and
architecture, music and theology, literature and myth . . .
[the author] traces the transformation of the concept of
happiness through more than 2000 years of Western
thought. . . . Filled with ample and provoking commentary, this work keeps the reader engaged and makes valuable contributions to the concept of happiness with each
successive chapter." Libr J
  Includes bibliographical references

Schoch, Richard W.

The secrets of happiness; three thousand years of searching for the good life. Scribner 2006 243p $23; pa $13.95 **170**

1. Happiness

ISBN 978-0-7432-9292-4; 0-7432-9292-8; 978-0-7432-9293-1 (pa); 0-7432-9293-6 (pa)

LC 2006-44375

"The essence of happiness, Schoch believes, is not simply feeling good—a state some today consider an entitlement. Rather, it lies in one's quest to create a better world. First highlighting the Greek philosopher Epicurus, the Roman Stoic Seneca and medieval Islamic scholar Abu Hamid al-Ghazali, Schoch explains that although these three thinkers had very different experiences, they were united in their search for a more fulfilling life under sometimes adverse conditions. Schoch then explores the ideas found in eight sacred and secular traditions, including Buddhism, Hinduism, Christianity and Epicureanism. . . . Schoch writes in an informed, lively style and his nonjudgmental stance will appeal to many who seek not easy self-help but to wrestle with issues of meaning and values." Publ Wkly

Includes bibliographical references

This I believe; the personal philosophies of remarkable men and women; edited by Jay Allison and Dan Gediman, with John Gregory and Viki Merrick; photographs by Nubar Alexanian. H. Holt 2006 xxi, 281p il $23 **170**

1. Belief and doubt 2. Conduct of life

ISBN 978-0-8050-8087-2; 0-8050-8087-2

LC 2006-43522

This collection of essays from a popular radio series "draws transcripts from both the original series and its newer version, including some remarkable statements from the likes of dancer/choreographer Martha Graham, autistic academic Temple Grandin, writer and physicist Alan Lightman, novelist and social critic Thomas Mann, economic historian Arnold Toynbee, and feminist writer Rebecca West. Astonishing to hear and astonishing to read and reread, this work is a wonderful addition to any library." Libr J

This I believe II; more personal philosophies of remarkable men and women; edited by Jay Allison and Dan Gediman; with John Gregory and Viki Merrick; additional editing by Emily Botein . . . [et al.] Henry Holt 2008 268p $23 **170**

1. Belief and doubt 2. Conduct of life

ISBN 978-0-8050-8768-0; 0-8050-8768-0

LC 2008-10110

"This second collection of This I Believe essays gathers seventy-five essayists, . . . from cellist Yo-Yo Ma to ordinary folks like a diner waitress, an Iraq War veteran, a farmer, [and] a new husband. . . . Included are Sister Helen Prejean writing about learning what she truly believes through watching her own actions, singer Jimmie Dale Gilmore writing about a hard-won wisdom based on being generous to others, and Robert Fulghum writing about dancing all the dances for as long as he can." Publisher's note

"Many [of these essays] will leave you breathless. And those that don't astonish may simply humble you." Christ Sci Monit

Wolfe, Alan

Moral freedom; the impossible idea that defines the way we live now. Norton 2001 256p hardcover o.p. pa $14.95 **170**

1. Ethics 2. Public opinion 3. Values 4. United States—Moral conditions

ISBN 0-393-04843-8; 0-393-32302-1 (pa)

LC 00-51969

"Wolfe here discusses the results of a national public opinion poll he helped design on American beliefs about values, which he supplemented with detailed interviews of people from eight different U.S. communities. These ranged widely, from the Castro district of San Francisco to San Antonio." Libr J

Includes bibliographical references

171 Ethical systems

Rand, Ayn, 1905-1982

The virtue of selfishness; a new concept of egoism; with additional articles by Nathaniel Branden. Centennial ed. Signet/New American Library 2005 173p pa $7.99 * **171**

1. Egoism

ISBN 0-451-16393-1

First published 1964

The author "sets forth the moral principles of Objectivism, the philosophy that holds man's life—the life proper to a rational being—as the standard of moral values and regards altruism as incompatible with man's nature, with the creative requirements of his survival, and with a free society." Publisher's note

172 Political ethics

Ignatieff, Michael

The lesser evil; political ethics in an age of terror. Princeton University Press 2004 212p (The Gifford lectures) $29.95; pa $16.95 **172**

1. Political ethics 2. Terrorism

ISBN 0-691-11751-9; 0-691-12393-4 (pa)

The author "presents an overview of how democracies have dealt with terrorist movements in the past and how they might best approach the terrorist threat today. . . . This should be required reading for all informed citizens as we face an uncertain future." Libr J

Includes bibliographical references

174 Occupational ethics

Barber, Nigel

Encyclopedia of ethics in science and technology. Facts on File 2002 386p il (Facts on File science library) $60 * **174**

1. Science—Ethical aspects

ISBN 0-8160-4314-0   LC 2001-40832

"This work attempts to give a broad overview of the ethical issues surrounding the development of science and the deployment of technology. . . . The more than

Barber, Nigel—*Continued*

400 entries range in length from 25 to more than 1,000 words and fall into five general categories: biography, legal aspects, specific technologies or theories, events, and movements and organizations. . . . The strength of the encyclopedia is its coverage of specific technologies and events and their controversial aspects. The author has done a good job of treating many of the technologies—such as contraception and genetic engineering—that we see in the daily news." Booklist

Includes bibliographical references

Bown, Stephen R.

A most damnable invention; dynamite, nitrates, and the making of the modern world. T. Dunne Books 2005 272p il $23.95   **174**

1. Nobel, Alfred Bernhard, 1833-1896 2. Dynamite 3. Science—Ethical aspects

ISBN 0-312-32913-X   LC 2005-45527

The author writes about "Alfred Nobel and the discovery of dynamite. . . . The new and powerful explosive proved invaluable in the construction of the modern world and also launched a quest for more potent chemical explosives that consisted of seeking out further natural and later synthetic nitrates. Nobel, horror-struck by that reaction to his concoction, compensatorily founded the prizes that bear his name. . . . This excellent addition to the history of science, military history, and the history of human progress as one of accidents and good intentions deserves a much bigger audience than its focus might lead one to expect." Booklist

Callahan, David, 1965-

The cheating culture; why more Americans are doing wrong to get ahead. Harcourt 2004 353p $26; pa $14   **174**

1. Business ethics 2. Social ethics

ISBN 0-15-101018-8; 0-15-603005-5 (pa)
     LC 2003-15529

The author examines "government reports and statistics, studies by social scientists, public opinion polls, and journalistic investigations of scandals and cheating. Callahan also conducted interviews with people who deal with the cheating culture: parents, students, teachers, coaches, athletes, experts in business ethics, stock analysts, lawyers, accountants, doctors, and law enforcement officials." Booklist

"If all business school students could be required to read one book, this should be it." Choice

Includes bibliographical references

Clones and clones; facts and fantasies about human cloning; edited by Martha C. Nussbaum and Cass R. Sunstein. Norton 1998 351p $26.95; pa $15.95   **174**

1. Cloning 2. Reproductive technology 3. Bioethics

ISBN 0-393-04648-6; 0-393-32001-4 (pa)
     LC 97-51781

This is a collection of essays and short stories on cloning. The contributors include Richard Dawkins; Eric A. Posner and Richard A. Posner; Andrea Dworkin; William N. Estridge and Edward Stein; and Richard A. Epstein

"The spectrum of authors and their varying perspec-

tives in fact and fiction are assets to anyone who hopes to understand this broad issue and its vast cultural implications." Publ Wkly

Includes bibliographical references

Encyclopedia of bioethics; Stephen G. Post, editor in chief. 3rd ed. Macmillan Reference USA 2003 5v set $595 *   **174**

1. Bioethics—Encyclopedias 2. Medical ethics—Encyclopedias

ISBN 0-02-865774-8   LC 2003-15694

Contents: v1 Abortion-Death -- v2 Deep-Human -- v3 Immigration-Mormonism -- v4 Nanotechnology-Right -- v5 Science-Xenotransplantation

"This new edition of a classic work, which addresses timely issues such as same-sex marriages and direct advertising of prescription drugs, belongs in all academic libraries and all but the smallest public libraries. It is an outstanding resource for students, professionals, and the interested public." Booklist

Includes bibliographical references

The **Ethics** of organ transplants; the current debate; edited by Arthur L. Caplan and Daniel H. Coelho. Prometheus Bks. 1998 350p il pa $20   **174**

1. Transplantation of organs, tissues, etc. 2. Medical ethics

ISBN 1-57392-224-2   LC 98-31722

The editors "have selected 35 articles that are representative of the ethical issues surrounding organ transplantation. . . . In many cases, the editors have selected companion articles that illustrate contrasting viewpoints on a particular issue." Libr J

Includes bibliographical references

Fox, Michael W., 1937-

Beyond evolution; the genetically altered future of plants, animals, the earth—humans. Lyons Press 1999 256p $24.95   **174**

1. Genetic engineering 2. Bioethics

ISBN 1-55821-901-3   LC 99-12866

The author "argues that biotechnology—coupled with industrial, chemical-based agriculture—will only accelerate the adverse environmental and consumer-health consequences of factory farming." Publ Wkly

Includes bibliographical references

Human cloning and human dignity; the report of the President's Council on bioethics; with a foreword by Leon R. Kass, chairman. PublicAffairs 2002 350p il pa $14 *   **174**

1. Cloning 2. Bioethics

ISBN 1-58648-176-2

This "report focuses on three major issues: cloning to produce children (reproductive uses), cloning for biomedical research (therapeutic uses), and various public policies that could be enacted. The council members were divided on their recommendations regarding human cloning, so both a majority and a minority opinion are presented here." Libr J

Includes bibliographical references

Lutz, Tom

Doing nothing; a history of loafers, loungers, slackers and bums in America. Farrar, Straus and Giroux 2006 384p $25 **174**

1. Conduct of life

ISBN 0-8654-7650-0; 978-0-8654-76

LC 2005-27230

The author traces "the history of society's attitudes toward working and slacking." N Y Times Book Rev

"With layabouts such as Theodore Dreiser, the Beats, and our epoch's own Anna Nicole Simpson on offer, cultural-history mavens won't be able to pass Lutz up." Booklist

Munson, Ronald, 1939-

Raising the dead; organ transplants, ethics, and society. Oxford Univ. Press 2002 288p $55; pa $19.95 * **174**

1. Transplantation of organs, tissues, etc. 2. Medical ethics

ISBN 0-19-513299-8; 0-19-517801-7 (pa)

LC 2001-36119

This examination of the "variety of ethical issues surrounding organ transplantation . . . discusses the definition of death, methods for obtaining organs, recipient selection, xenotransplantation, and stem cell research." Libr J

"Lucid and compelling writing on a much-debated topic." Booklist

Includes bibliographical references

Wilmut, Ian

The second creation; Dolly and the age of biological control; [by] Ian Wilmut, Keith Campbell and Colin Tudge. Harvard University Press 2001 360p il pa $16.95 * **174**

1. Cloning

ISBN 978-0-674-00586-0

First published 2000 by Farrar, Straus & Giroux

The scientists responsible for cloning the ewe Dolly "tell the full story of how they did it. . . . To demystify cloning (now called nuclear transfer by experts), the authors trace the history of cell biology and embryology, the linked sciences that made it possible, explaining in lucid terms the fundamental principles that brought Dolly and her successors to life." Booklist

174.2 Occupational ethics—Medical professions

Caplan, Arthur L.

Smart mice, not-so-smart people; an interesting and amusing guide to bioethics. Rowman & Littlefield 2006 210p $21.95; pa $14.95 **174.2**

1. Medical ethics

ISBN 978-0-7425-4171-9; 0-7425-4171-1; 978-0-7425-4172-6 (pa); 0-7425-4172-X (pa)

LC 2006-14275

The author discusses "issues at the center of the new genetics, cloning in the laboratory and in the media, stem cell research, experiments on human subjects, blood donation and organ transplantation, and healthcare delivery." Publisher's note

Scott, Christopher Thomas

Stem cell now; from the experiment that shook the world to the new politics of life; [by] Christopher Thomas Scott; foreword by Donald Kennedy. Pi Press 2006 243p il $24.95 **174.2**

1. Stem cell research

ISBN 0-13-173798-8; 978-0-13-173798-3

LC 2005-23266

In addition to discussing the political and ethical implications of stem cell research, the author "outlines the many types of stem cells and how they hold promise for biomedical applications, particularly for people with Parkinson's, spinal cord injuries, and other conditions with great unmet medical needs." Libr J

"This book is illuminating reading for everyone who wants to understand a hot-button topic that will dominate the political, medical and religious arenas for years to come." Publ Wkly

Includes bibliographical references

Tucker, Todd, 1968-

The great starvation experiment; the heroic men who starved so that millions could live. Free Press 2006 270p il $26 * **174.2**

1. Keys, Ancel, 1904-2004 2. Starvation 3. Human experimentation in medicine

ISBN 0-7432-7030-4; 978-0-7432-7030-4

LC 2006-278255

Also available in paperback from Univ. Of Minnesota Press

"As WWII neared an end, 36 idealistic conscientious objectors, members of the Civilian Public Service, volunteered to be systematically starved. The project, headed by Dr. Ancel Keys, was designed to develop an understanding of the physiology and psychology of starvation and to provide strategies to manage the mass starvation that might follow the war's end in Europe. Tucker . . . provides a fascinating and moving history of the experiment, centering on the lives and experiences of the volunteers and the formidable obstacles they overcame." Publ Wkly

Includes bibliographical references

Washington, Harriet A.

Medical apartheid; the dark history of medical experimentation on Black Americans from colonial times to the present. Doubleday 2006 501p il $27.95 * **174.2**

1. Human experimentation in medicine 2. African Americans—Health and hygiene

ISBN 0-385-50993-6; 978-0-385-50993-0

LC 2005-51873

The author offers a "history of medical experimentation on and mistreatment of black Americans in this stunning work, which is both broad in scope and well documented." Booklist

Includes bibliographical references

176 Ethics of sex and reproduction

Green, Ronald Michael, 1942-
Babies by design; the ethics of genetic choice.
Yale University Press 2007 279p il $26
176
1. Medical genetics 2. Genetic engineering
3. Reproductive technology
ISBN 978-0-300-12546-7; 0-300-12546-1
LC 2007-19927
"A Caravan book"
The author offers a discussion "of human genetic self-modification and the possibilities it opens up. . . . [He] outlines the new capabilities of genomic science, addresses . . . questions of safety that genetic interventions pose, and explores questions of parenting and justice." Publisher's note
"By providing examples, contextualizing issues within the framework of stories in popular fiction, and presenting a balanced view of the topics, the author allows the reader to fully explore the issues embedded in the scientific transformation created by the genomic revolution." Sci Books Films
Includes bibliographical references

Mundy, Liza, 1960-
Everything conceivable; how assisted reproduction is changing men, women, and the world. Alfred A. Knopf 2007 xx, 406p $26.95
176
1. Reproductive technology
ISBN 978-1-4000-4428-3; 1-4000-4428-6
LC 2006-51432
Mundy provides an "account of the technological innovations that have allowed us to "cure" infertility. She interviews heartbroken would-be parents and those who worry about the social ramifications of generations of children who don't know who their biological parents are. Moreover, she explores the far-reaching effects of such medical technologies as fertility drugs, in vitro fertilization, sperm and egg donation, surrogacy, and genetic testing." Libr J
The author "opens a mind-boggling Pandora's box to issues that surely give us pause. This book is destined to become a bible for those seeking to examine the many ways of making babies and the complex questions that result." Dallas Morning News
Includes bibliographical references

Stock, Gregory
Redesigning humans; our inevitable genetic future. Houghton Mifflin 2002 277p $24; pa $14
176
1. Genetics 2. Reproductive technology 3. Genetic engineering
ISBN 0-618-06026-X; 0-618-34083-1 (pa)
LC 2001-51890
The author gives an "overview of the new biotechnology that will allow scientists to delay aging and to insert genes that enhance physical and cognitive performance, combat disease or improve looks into embryos. Stock thoughtfully weighs the ethical dilemmas such advances

present, arguing that the real threat is not frivolous abuse of technology but the fact that we don't know the long-term effects of these genetic changes." Publ Wkly
Includes bibliographical references

Wilmut, Ian
After Dolly; the uses and misuses of human cloning. Norton 2006 335p il $24.95; pa $15.95 *
176
1. Cloning 2. Reproductive technology
ISBN 0-393-06066-7; 978-0-393-06066-9; 0-393-33026-5 (pa); 978-0-393-33026-7 (pa)
LC 2006-2030
In this "account of the program that eventuated in Dolly, . . . [Wilmut] covers a variety of the social, medical, and scientific implications of cloning. . . . Wilmut, aided by science writer Highfield, well explains potentially confusing issues, in the end making a strong enough case to convince us that Dolly neither lived nor died in vain." Booklist
Includes bibliographical references

177 Ethics of social relations

Campbell, Jeremy, 1931-
The liar's tale; a history of falsehood. Norton 2001 363p $26.95; pa $15.95
177
1. Truthfulness and falsehood
ISBN 0-393-02559-4; 0-393-32361-7 (pa)
LC 2001-30286
Campbell discusses lying in history and in the writings of "philosophers and thinkers from the ancient Greeks to Darwin, Nietzsche, Marx, and Freud, down to . . . [the] postmodern deconstructionists." Christ Sci Monit
"This challenging romp through the underbelly of intellectual history . . . is fascinating and troublesome." NY Times Book Rev
Includes bibliographical references

Stengel, Richard, 1955-
You're too kind; a brief history of flattery. Simon & Schuster 2000 315p $25; pa $14
177
1. Flattery
ISBN 0-684-85491-0; 0-684-85492-9 (pa)
"Charting the uses of flattery and the social contexts in which it is used from biblical times to the present, Stengel . . . illustrates that more than mere praise, flattery is praise with a motive, be it benign or grasping. . . . Enjoyable and informative." Libr J
Includes bibliographical references

Sullivan, Evelin E., 1947-
The concise book of lying; [by] Evelin Sullivan. Farrar, Straus & Giroux 2001 334p il $25; pa $15
177
1. Truthfulness and falsehood
ISBN 0-374-12868-5; 0-312-42047-1 (pa)
LC 2001-18760

Sullivan, Evelin E., 1947-—*Continued*
The author discusses lying in history and literature. She examines what impels people to lie and what the results of lying might be
"Anyone interested in the history and philosophy of human nature will appreciate this compelling and cleverly written volume." Libr J
Includes bibliographical references

179   Other ethical norms

Baur, Gene
Farm Sanctuary; changing hearts and minds about animals and food. Simon & Schuster 2008 286p il $25   **179**
  1. Livestock industry 2. Animal welfare
  ISBN 978-0-7432-9158-3; 0-7432-9158-1
                    LC 2008-297873
"A Touchstone book"
A founder of an organization dedicated to promoting the compassionate treatment of animals and combating factory farming addresses the ethics of breeding animals for food, exposing inhumane practices utilized by typical food-production companies.
"Baur's report is not for the faint of heart, but it is critical reading for anyone willing to ask about the origin of their food, and readers are rewarded with tales of animals who have been saved, and the surprising things that have been learned about farm animals from close observation of their habits. A life-altering read." Booklist
Includes bibliographical references

Beers, Diane L.
For the prevention of cruelty; the history and legacy of animal rights activism in the United States. Swallow Press/Ohio University Press 2006 312p il $34.95; pa $19.95   **179**
  1. Animal rights movement
  ISBN   0-8040-1086-2;   978-0-8040-1086-3; 0-8040-1087-0 (pa); 978-0-8040-1087-0 (pa)
                    LC 2006-4294
This "study of the animal advocacy movement in the U.S. since the ASPCA's founding in 1866 fills a glaring historical gap with exceptional style, accuracy and insight." Publ Wkly
Includes bibliographical references

Blum, Deborah
The monkey wars. Oxford Univ. Press 1994 306p pa $19.95 hardcover o.p.   **179**
  1. Animal experimentation 2. Animal rights
  ISBN 0-19-510109-X (pa)   LC 94-12439
"The 'wars' between scientific researchers and animal-rights activists have several aspects: fanaticism, propaganda, pragmatism, and idealism. Blum has written a beautifully balanced account of the major individuals and organizations involved. She points out the different shades of belief and approaches in the conflict and shows how these have developed over the years." Booklist
Includes bibliographical references

Coetzee, J. M., 1940-
The lives of animals; {by} J.M. Coetzee; {reflections by} Marjorie Garber {et al.}; edited and introduced by Amy Gutmann. Princeton Univ. Press 1999 127p (University Center for Human Values series) $29.95; pa $13.95   **179**
  1. Animal rights 2. Animal welfare
  ISBN 0-691-00443-9; 0-691-07089-X (pa)
                    LC 98-39591
"This hybrid collection of fiction and essays is a provocative version of Socratic philosophy. It begins with a story about a Doris Lessing-like author who visits her conflicted son and his antagonistic wife while lecturing at the university where they teach. The mother's hobby-horse, that Animals R Us, embarrasses the academic couple, and her suggestion that they are like Nazis because they eat meat infuriates them. Other distinguished academics carry on this dialogue in playful fiction and sober commentary, in which the most eloquent part may be the descriptions of communication with animals." New Yorker
Includes bibliographical references

Comte-Sponville, André
A small treatise on the great virtues; the uses of philosophy in everyday life; translated by Catherine Temerson. Metropolitan Bks. 2001 352p $27.50; pa $16   **179**
  1. Ethics
  ISBN 0-8050-4555-4; 0-8050-4556-2 (pa)
                    LC 2001-30299
Original French edition, 1995
"Dividing the book into 18 virtue-based chapters—'Politeness,' 'Fidelity,' 'Prudence,' 'Temperance,' 'Courage,' 'Mercy,' 'Gratitude,' and so on—Comte-Sponville quotes a multitude of philosophers from the ancient Greeks through Spinoza, Hobbes and Nietzsche to modern Frenchmen like Vladimir Jankelevitch." Publ Wkly
"His subject demands a sober seriousness, but Comte-Sponville still manages to avoid taking himself too seriously: humility makes it into his litany of virtues, as does humor. A laudable renewal of the ancient quest for ethical wisdom." Booklist
Includes bibliographical references

Encyclopedia of animal rights and animal welfare; edited by Marc Bekoff with Carron A. Meaney; foreword by Jane Goodall. Greenwood Press 1998 xxi, 446p il $64.95   **179**
  ISBN 0-313-29977-3   LC 97-35098
This "work offers about 170 essays by well-known names in the animal industry who represent many fields. . . . The result is a welcome multidisciplinary approach that shows us the extensive roles nonhuman animals play in virtually all areas of our lives. The essays are well reasoned and often extensive." Libr J
Includes bibliographical references

Fox, Michael W., 1937-
Inhumane society; the American way of exploiting animals; introduction by Cleveland Amory. St. Martin's Press 1990 268p pa $18.95 hardcover o.p.   **179**
  1. Animal welfare
  ISBN 0-312-30213-4 (pa)   LC 89-70299

Fox, Michael W., 1937-—_Continued_

The author "looks at the exploitative and inhumane treatment of domestic, agriculture, and laboratory animals." Booklist

This book "is very readable and takes a strong stance while presenting a creditably balanced treatment of the issues." Libr J

Includes bibliographical references

Greek, C. Ray

Sacred cows and golden geese; the human cost of experiments on animals; [by] C. Ray Greek and Jean Swingle Greek; foreword by Jane Goodall. Continuum 2000 256p $24.95; pa $18.95

179

1. Animal experimentation
ISBN 0-8264-1226-2; 0-8264-1402-8 (pa)

LC 99-57157

This "covers the history of animal experimentation, legislation that promulgates it, the real cost to humans, and alternatives. It is a well-written, if disturbing, book." Libr J

Includes bibliographical references

McCain, John S., 1936-

Why courage matters; the way to a braver life; [by] John McCain with Mark Salter. Random House 2004 209p il $16.95   **179**

1. Courage
ISBN 1-400-06030-3   LC 2003-58626

Senator McCain tells his favorite stories of courage. "In offering anecdotes of individuals whose actions embody the rarity of true courage, his well-drawn examples range from Navajo leaders to Colorado River explorers to Jewish freedom fighter Hannah Senesh and Burmese dissident and Nobel Peace Prize-recipient Aung San Suu Kyi. He reflects on the wellsprings of courage, defining it as conscious self-sacrifice 'for the sake of others or to uphold a virtue,' encompassing actions that may be spurred by honor, outrage, a sense of duty, one's conscience, or moral obligation." SLJ

Miller, William Ian, 1946-

Faking it. Cambridge University Press 2003 290p $42; pa $18.99   **179**

1. Identity (Psychology) 2. Social role
ISBN 0-521-83018-4; 0-521-61370-1 (pa)

LC 2003-43750

"In this refreshing book, Miller . . . considers the human propensity for fraudulence and the correlative fear of being found out. He makes us laugh as he describes trying to wing it in his class on property law or eyeing an attractive woman a few pews up during prayer, and he entertains us with stories of adults who overestimate their sexual prowess and children who find out that saying 'please' doesn't buy them what they were told it would." Libr J

Includes bibliographical references

Rudacille, Deborah

The scalpel and the butterfly; the conflict between animal research and animal protection. University of California Press 2001 389p pa $21.95 *   **179**

1. Animal experimentation 2. Animal welfare
ISBN 978-0-520-23154-2; 0-520-23154-6

LC 2001-27339

First published 2000 by Farrar, Straus & Giroux with subtitle: the war between animal research and animal protection

The author gives a "history of the conflict between anti-vivisectionists and research scientists. She begins with French physician Claude Bernard. . . . Rudacille then documents the rise of the animal welfare movement in Britain and the United States and legislation designed to govern the use of animals in research. . . . The author also discusses the Nazi 'science' of eugenics and explores the ethical implications of such new scientific developments as xenotransplantation." Libr J

Includes bibliographical references

Tillich, Paul, 1886-1965

The courage to be; with an introduction by Peter J. Gomes. 2nd ed. Yale Univ. Press 2000 197p (Yale Nota bene) pa $12.95 *   **179**

1. Courage 2. Ontology 3. Anxiety 4. Existentialism
ISBN 0-300-08471-4   LC 00-102364

First published 1952

Partial contents: Being and courage; Being, nonbeing and anxiety; Pathological anxiety, vitality, and courage; Courage and participation; Courage and individualization; Courage and transcendence

The author offers advice on how to conquer the anxiety caused by the loss of meaning in one's life

Wise, Steven M.

Drawing the line; science and the case for animal rights. Perseus Bks. 2002 322p $26; pa $18 *   **179**

1. Animal rights
ISBN 0-7382-0340-8; 0-7382-0810-8 (pa)

"A Merloyd Lawrence book"

Wise "sets out to determine whether animals ranging from dolphins to his family dog . . . have mental abilities meriting {legal} protection. . . . The key to granting any of them rights, Wise argues, is whether they possess 'practical autonomy'—desires and the ability to act to satisfy them." Christ Sci Monit

Includes bibliographical references

179.7 Respect and disrespect for human life

Durkheim, Émile, 1858-1917

Suicide, a study in sociology; translated by John A. Spaulding and George Simpson; edited with an introduction by George Simpson. Free Press 1951 405p maps pa $18.95 hardcover o.p. *   **179.7**

Durkheim, Émile, 1858-1917—*Continued*
1. Suicide
ISBN 0-684-83632-7 (pa)
Original French edition, 1897
Durkheim's "*Suicide* is a major sociological classic, one that is still read today, not so much for its data, which are limited and out-of-date, but for the brilliance of his analysis of suicide rates and other data that had been initially obtained for administrative rather than scientific purposes." Reader's Adviser
Includes bibliographical references

Filene, Peter G.
In the arms of others; a cultural history of the right-to-die in America. Dee, I.R. 1998 282p il pa $15.95 hardcover o.p. **179.7**
1. Right to die 2. Euthanasia
ISBN 1-56663-268-4 (pa)   LC 97-42583
The author traces the history of euthanasia from the 19th century "through the present-day thicket of healthcare issues, including the use (and removal) of life support, the question of whether a terminally sick person has the right to doctor-assisted suicide and the practical value of living wills." Publ Wkly
"A fine general overview of the right-to-die question." Libr J
Includes bibliographical references

Humphry, Derek, 1930-
Final exit; the practicalities of self-deliverance and assisted sucide for the dying. 3rd ed. Delta Trade Paperbacks 2002 xxviii, 220p pa $13.95 * **179.7**
1. Suicide 2. Right to die
ISBN 0-385-33653-5   LC 2002-19403
First published 1991 by Hemlock Society
This offers information about how to commit suicide for the terminally ill and about the legality and ethics of assisted suicide and euthanasia
Includes bibliographical references

Kiernan, Stephen P.
Last rights; rescuing the end of life from the medical system. St. Martin's Press 2006 301p $25.95 * **179.7**
1. Terminal care 2. Death
ISBN 978-0-312-34224-1; 0-312-34224-1
          LC 2006-47449
The author "argues that most physicians and other healthcare professionals do not know how to deal with death because textbooks and medical schools fail to address the issue adequately. His final chapters present . . . [an] agenda to improve end-of-life care at both the societal and the individual levels." Libr J
"Anyone who has stood helplessly by as physicians insisted that a battery of tests and interventions could prolong the life of a loved one, only to see those expensive efforts fail, is certain to be moved by Kiernan's presentation." Booklist
Includes bibliographical references

Marcus, Eric
Why suicide? answers to 200 of the most frequently asked questions about suicide, attempted suicide, and assisted suicide. HarperSanFrancisco 1996 240p pa $14 **179.7**
1. Suicide
ISBN 0-06-251166-1   LC 95-33431
The author's "questions range from 'Does everyone have thoughts of suicide?' to 'What are the arguments against legalizing doctor-assisted suicide?' His responses reflect not only a knowledgeable and well-informed consideration of suicidology but also empathetic treatment. The typical response aims to educate by giving factual information and/or practical advice as well as to console by providing personal stories from suicide survivors." Libr J
Includes bibliographical references

McKhann, Charles F., 1930-
A time to die; the place for physician assistance. Yale Univ. Press 1999 268p $42; pa $19 **179.7**
1. Euthanasia
ISBN 0-300-07631-2; 0-300-08698-9 (pa)
          LC 98-22193
The author "believes that physician-assisted suicide is not only desirable but inevitable. Humanity is divided in two parts, he says: those who have seen a loved one die a miserable death and those who have not. . . . McKhann argues level-headedly about patients, doctors, and laws." Booklist
Includes bibliographical references

Peck, M. Scott (Morgan Scott)
Denial of the soul; spiritual and medical perspectives on euthanasia and mortality. Harmony Bks. 1997 242p pa $19 hardcover o.p. **179.7**
1. Euthanasia 2. Suicide 3. Right to die 4. Death 5. Medical ethics
ISBN 0-609-80134-1 (pa)   LC 97-157271
The author "argues against, with very few exceptions, euthanasia and physician-assisted suicide on demand." Publ Wkly
"Peck is a wonderful writer, engaging, intelligent, and full of stories from his long psychiatric practice; as usual, he takes on big issues with seriousness, sensitivity, and balance." Libr J

Wanzer, Sidney H.
To die well; your right to comfort, calm, and choice in the last days of life. Da Capo 2007 209p $24; pa $15 * **179.7**
1. Right to die
ISBN   0-7382-1083-8;   978-0-7382-1083-4; 0-7382-1163-X (pa); 978-0-7382-1163-3 (pa)
The authors present "what individuals can do to achieve a peaceful death for themselves and their loved ones. Using a combination of patient stories and their own expert discussions, the authors describe the legal rights of terminally ill patients to end their medical care. They also address the controversial issue of hastening the

Wanzer, Sidney H.—*Continued*

death of terminally ill patients. . . . More useful than the many other recent books on death and dying, this influential volume should be on the shelves of every public and university library." Libr J

Wiesenthal, Simon

The sunflower; on the possibilities and limits of forgiveness; [by] Simon Wiesenthal; with a symposium edited by Harry James Cargas and Bonny V. Fetterman. rev and expanded ed, 2nd pa. ed. Schocken Books 1998 289p pa $14 *

179.7

1. Holocaust, 1933-1945—Personal narratives 2. Forgiveness
ISBN 0-8052-1060-1   LC 99-198049
Original French edition, 1969

In this expanded version of a book first published in the United States in 1976 "Wiesenthal tackles the question of the possibilities and limits of forgiveness. The first part relates the story of how Wiesenthal, as a prisoner in a Nazi concentration camp, was brought before a dying SS trooper, who explained his actions and asked for forgiveness. . . . In the second section, Wiesenthal presents the story to an array of leading intellectuals and asks, 'What would you have done?' This edition contains all the original responses plus additional ones from Primo Levi, Cynthia Ozick, Albert Speer, and others." Libr J

"The responses to the author's question are as varied as their authors. The mystery of evil and atonement remain, and the reader is left challenged on these most basic issues of meaning in human life." Publ Wkly

Yount, Lisa

Right to die and euthanasia. rev ed. Facts on File 2007 312p il (Library in a book) $45 *

179.7

1. Right to die 2. Euthanasia
ISBN 978-0-8160-6275-1   LC 2006-33424
First published 2000 with title: Physician-assisted suicide and euthanasia

This reference source contains an overview of the subjects, a chronology of significant events (including the Terri Schiavo case), biographical information on important figures, a glossary of terms, and an annotated bibliography.

Includes glossary and bibliographical references

180   Ancient, medieval & eastern philosophy

Encyclopedia of classical philosophy; edited by Donald J. Zeyl; associate editors, Daniel T. Devereux and Phillip K. Mitsis. Greenwood Press 1997 614p $119.95 *   **180**
ISBN 0-313-28775-9   LC 96-2562

"Covering Greek and Roman philosophy from the sixth century B.C. to the sixth century A.D., this encyclopedia boasts more than 270 signed articles from more than 90 contributors. . . . Entries range from a single

paragraph *(Apollonius, Hecataeus, Theon)* to nearly 30 pages *(Aristotle)*. While the majority of entries are for philosophers or other individuals, dozen of articles treat subjects such as the Academy, Cyrenaic philosophy, theories of medicine, tragic poets, and rhetoric." Booklist

"This encyclopedia fills a void in philosophical reference works that has existed for too long, and it will likely become a standard in the field." Libr J

Gottlieb, Anthony

The dream of reason; a history of western philosophy from the Greeks to the Renaissance. Norton 2000 468p $27.95; pa $17.95   **180**
1. Philosophy—History
ISBN 0-393-04951-5; 0-393-32365-X (pa)
LC 00-49012

"This book is the first installment of . . . a survey in two volumes of the whole of Western philosophy, from its origins in Greece in the sixth century B.C. to the present day." N Y Times Book Rev

"This eloquent book offers a lively chronicle of the evolution of Western philosophy." Publ Wkly

Includes bibliographical references

181   Eastern philosophy

Buber, Martin, 1878-1965

I and thou; translated by Ronald Gregor Smith. Scribner 2000 c1986 126p $22; pa $11 *

181

1. Jewish philosophy 2. God 3. Ontology
ISBN 0-7432-0133-7; 0-7432-0133-7 (pa)
Original German edition, 1923; first published in English 1958

In this book, the author "conceived the individual as in permanent relationship with all forms of life, finding his fulfillment in the reciprocity of the relationship—the 'Thou' being God." Reader's Adviser

Confucius

The Analects; [by] Confucius; translated by Arthur Waley; with an introduction by Sarah Allan. Knopf 2000 xxxi, 257p $19 *

181

1. Chinese philosophy 2. Chinese ethics
ISBN 0-375-41204-2   LC 00-53460

This translation first published 1938 in the United Kingdom

"One of the Chinese 'Four Books.' A brief, unsystematic collection of fragmentary writings attributed to Confucius and his school. . . . It is one of the most influential works in the history of Chinese thought." Reader's Ency

Includes bibliographical references

183   Sophistic, Socratic, related Greek philosophies

Stone, I. F. (Isidor Feinstein), 1907-1989

The trial of Socrates. Anchor Bks. 1989 282p pa $14.95 *   **183**

Stone, I. F. (Isidor Feinstein), 1907-1989—*Continued*
1. Socrates
ISBN 0-385-26032-6; 978-0-385-26032-9
First published 1988 by Little, Brown
The author attempts "to show that Athens was totally committed to free speech and did not normally place any check on it, and, therefore, that the trial of Socrates was a singular aberration which might be explicable, if finally not justifiable." Commentary
Includes bibliographical references

184 Platonic philosophy

Hare, R. M. (Richard Mervyn)
Plato. Oxford Univ. Press 1982 82p (Past masters series) pa $9.95 hardcover o.p.
184
1. Plato
ISBN 0-19-287585-X (pa)   LC 83-159441
The author examines the chief Platonic concepts in their political and intellectual contexts
Includes bibliographical references

185 Aristotelian philosophy

Adler, Mortimer J., 1902-2001
Aristotle for everybody; difficult thought made easy. Macmillan 1978 206p $13 hardcover o.p.
185
1. Aristotle, 384-322 B.C.
ISBN 0-684-83823-0 (pa)   LC 78-853
Adler traces "in the simplest language and with occasional modern analogues, the logic and growth of Aristotle's basic doctrines." Publ Wkly
Includes bibliographical references

188 Stoic philosophy

Marcus Aurelius, Emperor of Rome, 121-180
Meditations; a new translation, with an introduction, by Gregory Hays. Modern Lib. 2002 lvii, 191p $19.95 *
188
ISBN 0-679-64260-9   LC 2001-57947

"An emperor and Stoic philosopher records his thoughts as he struggles for composure and order in the face of national disaster." Good Read

189 Medieval Western philosophy

The **Renaissance** philosophy of man; {by} Petrarca {and others}; selections in translation, edited by Ernst Cassirer, Paul Oskar Kristeller, John Herman Randall, Jr. University of Chicago Press 1948 405p pa $17.50 hardcover o.p.
189

1. Medieval philosophy
ISBN 0-226-09604-1 (pa)
This book provides English translations from selected writings of six early Italian Renaissance philosophers from about the middle of the fourteenth century to the end of the sixteenth. Francesco Petrarca, Lorenzo Valla, Marsilio Ficino, Giovanni Pico della Mirandola, Pietro Pomponazzi, and Juan Luis Vives are represented. An introduction accompanies each of the translations
Includes bibliographical references

Rubenstein, Richard E.
Aristotle's children; how Christians, Muslims, and Jews rediscovered ancient wisdom and illuminated the Dark Ages. Harcourt 2003 368p $27
189
1. Aristotle, 384-322 B.C. 2. Medieval philosophy
ISBN 0-15-100720-9   LC 2003-6582
"In 12th-century Spain, a group of Muslim scholars, Jewish teachers, and Christian monks discovered Aristotle's De Anima (On the Soul). Until then, Aristotle's writings, like most of Greek culture, had been lost for centuries, following the fall of the Roman Empire around A.D. 480. . . . Aristotle's work, which was embraced enthusiastically by devotees of the three major religions, transformed the Dark Ages, reconciling faith and reason. Indeed, the impact of the Greek philosopher's new ideas (which focused on the material world, rather than the supernatural) was so far reaching that it created a revolution in thought that laid the foundation for the Renaissance and the 18th century's Age of Enlightenment." SLJ
"Although the book purports to trace Aristotle's influence on Christianity, Islam and Judaism, it devotes more attention to Christianity. Even so, Rubenstein's lively prose, his lucid insights and his crystal-clear historical analyses make this a first-rate study in the history of ideas." Publ Wkly
Includes bibliographical references

Thomas, Aquinas, Saint, 1225?-1274
Selected writings; edited and translated with an introduction and notes by Ralph McInerny. Penguin Bks. 1998 xxxviii, 841p pa $14.95 *
189
ISBN 0-14-043632-4
Arranged chronologically, this collection of theological and philosophical writings brings together sermons, commentaries, responses to criticism and lengthy extracts from the Summa theologia.
Includes bibliographical references

190 Modern western philosophy

The **Columbia** history of Western philosophy; edited by Richard H. Popkin. Columbia Univ. Press 1999 xxvi, 836p $64.50 *
190
1. Philosophy—History
ISBN 0-231-10128-7   LC 98-15219
This is an overview "of Western philosophy, from the pre-Socratics to 20th-century philosophy, both analytic and continental." Libr J
"This survey's coverage of medieval Islamic, Jewish, and Christian philosophy is particularly strong." Choice
Includes bibliographical references

Gay, Peter, 1923-
The rise of modern paganism. Norton 1995
xviii, 555, xvp (The Enlightenment: an
interpretation) pa $19.95   **190**
1. Modern philosophy 2. Europe—Intellectual life
3. Enlightenment
ISBN 0-393-31302-6
First published 1966 by Knopf
Voume one of a two volume series examining the
ideas, experiences and impact of leading Enlightenment
figures in 18th century Europe and America.
Includes bibliographical references

The science of freedom. Norton 1996 xx, 705,
xviiip (The Enlightenment: an interpretation) pa
$19.95   **190**
1. Modern philosophy 2. Europe—Intellectual life
3. Enlightenment
ISBN 0-393-31366-2
First published 1969
Volume two of a two-volume series examining the
ideas, experiences and impact of leading Enlightenment
figures in 18th century Europe and America.

Great thinkers of the Western world; edited by
Ian P. McGreal. HarperCollins Pubs. 1992 572p
$47   **190**
1. Philosophy 2. Theology 3. Science
ISBN 0-06-270026-X   LC 91-38362
"The major ideas and classic works of more than 100
outstanding Western philosophers, physical and social
scientists, psychologists, religious writers, and theologians." Title page
"This guide to 116 selected authors . . . spans the ancient Greeks to the first half of the twentieth century.
. . . The guide is arranged chronologically by the
birthdate of the writer. Each entry contains birth and
death dates, a list of the author's major ideas, an essay
of three to five pages, and a short annotated list of secondary sources. . . . Its readable essays . . . are accessible to the layperson." Booklist

Himmelfarb, Gertrude
The moral imagination; from Edmund Burke to
Lionel Trilling. Ivan R. Dee 2006 259p $26
190
1. Modern philosophy 2. Political science
ISBN 1-56663-624-8   LC 2005-19838
The author "specializes in Victorian Britain and profiles some of its leading writers and statesmen, along
with philosophical forerunners and descendants, to probe
the complexities of two centuries of conservative
thought. . . . Himmelfarb's stylish blend of literary criticism and intellectual history yields a stimulating reappraisal of a multifaceted and influential worldview." Publ
Wkly
Includes bibliographical references

The roads to modernity; the British, French, and
American enlightenments. Knopf 2004 284p $25
190
1. Enlightenment 2. Europe—Intellectual life
3. United States—Intellectual life
ISBN 1-400-04236-4   LC 2003-60576

"Analyzing the traditional stalwarts of Enlightenment
thought in America (Jefferson, Paine), France (Tocqueville, Voltaire, Diderot), and Britain (Locke, Smith, and
. . . Burke), Himmelfarb presents a . . . case for the
chronological priority and philosophical primacy of the
British model in shaping the philosophy of reason and
liberty on the cusp of modernity." Booklist
"This is a book with important ideological implications that deserves to be read and debated across the political spectrum." Publ Wkly
Includes bibliographical references

Magee, Bryan
The story of philosophy. DK Pub. 1998 240p il
$29.95; pa $20   **190**
1. Philosophy
ISBN 0-7894-3511-X; 0-7894-7994-X (pa)
LC 98-3780
This "illustrated volume converts two-and-a-half millennia of Western philosophy into a colorful parade of
provocative figures—from Heraclitus to Heidegger—who
have enlarged the boundaries of thought." Booklist
"Writing with a clear and lively style, Magee provides
an excellent introduction to the topic." SLJ
Includes bibliographical references

The **Oxford** history of Western philosophy; edited
by Anthony Kenny. Oxford Univ. Press 1994
407p il maps hardcover o.p. pa $15 *
190
1. Philosophy—History
ISBN 0-19-824278-6; 0-19-289329-7 (pa)
LC 94-9858
Also available illustrated paperback edition with title:
The Oxford illustrated history of Western philosophy
$31.95 (ISBN: 0-19-285440-2)
This volume covers "the ancients, the medievals, continental philosophers like Hegel, Nietzsche, and Sartre,
and the English analyticals (Bentham and Mill), followed
by a survey of political philosophies." Booklist
"The illustrations have been wisely chosen to show
the constant play between art and idea. Some familiarity
with analytic philosophy would be useful to gain the
most from the text, but this is a significant addition to
the literature." Libr J
Includes bibliographical references

Sedgwick, Peter
Descartes to Derrida; an introduction to
European philosophy. Blackwell 2001 310p
$76.95; pa $33.95 *   **190**
1. Modern philosophy
ISBN 0-631-20142-4; 0-631-20143-2 (pa)
LC 00-57917
"This critical survey of issues in European philosophy
offers . . . accounts of crucial texts by important thinkers. Sedgwick draws key ideas from these sources,
analysing the various relationships between them and
linking them to central themes in philosophical enquiry,
such as the nature of subjectivity, reason and experience,
anti-humanism and the nature of language." Publisher's
note
"This book should take a place as one of the key texts

Sedgwick, Peter—*Continued*

in humanities programs throughout the English-speaking world." Choice

Includes bibliographical references

191 United States and Canada

Dewey, John, 1859-1952

The philosophy of John Dewey; edited with an introduction and commentary by John J. McDermott. University of Chicago Press 1981 2v in 1 pa $25 *   191

ISBN 0-226-14401-1   LC 80-39766

"Phoenix edition"

First published 1973 in two volumes by Putnam

Contents: v1 The structure of experience; v2 The lived experience

A digest of extracts from the American philosopher's most important works

Includes bibliographical references

Rand, Ayn, 1905-1982

The voice of reason; essays in objectivist thought; edited and with an introduction by Leonard Peikoff; and with additional essays by Leonard Peikoff and Peter Schwartz. New Am. Lib. 1989 c1988 353p hardcover o.p. pa $18 *
                                       191

1. American philosophy 2. Egoism

ISBN 0-45-300634-5; 0-45-201046-2 (pa)

                                  LC 88-18192

The late author opposed liberalism and championed "capitalism, self-interest, and objective reality against collectivism, altruism, and mysticism. . . . These lectures, newspaper columns, and magazine articles are entirely characteristic of her—surprisingly emotional and dogmatic for a professed rationalist. Additional essays by editor Peikoff and disciple Peter Schwartz are of a piece." Booklist

Includes bibliographical references

192 British Isles

Edmonds, David, 1964-

Wittgenstein's poker; the story of a ten-minute argument between two great philosophers; [by] David Edmonds and John Eidinow. Ecco Press 2001 340p il $24; pa $13.95   192

1. Wittgenstein, Ludwig, 1889-1951 2. Popper, Sir Karl Raimund, 1902-1994

ISBN 0-06-621244-8; 0-06-093664-9 (pa)

                                  LC 2002-276301

"On the Cambridge University campus in 1946, two of the twentieth-century's most notable philosophers, Ludwig Wittgenstein and Karl Popper, squared off in an intense 10-minute clash rumored to have culminated with Wittgenstein brandishing a red-hot poker. The authors explain what the fight was about and how it reflects the development of philosophy. Ivory-tower drama at its crackling best." Booklist

Includes bibliographical references

193 Germany and Austria

Hegel, Georg Wilhelm Friedrich, 1770-1831

The philosophy of Hegel; edited with an introduction by Carl J. Friedrich. Modern Lib. 1954 552p pa $10.75 o.p. *   193

ISBN 0-07-553655-2 (pa)

"Modern Library College editions"

Contents: The philosophy of history; The history of philosophy; The science of logic; Philosophy of right and law, or natural law and political science outlines; Lectures on aesthetics; The phenomenology of the spirit (1807); Political essays; Bibliography

Kant, Immanuel, 1724-1804

Basic writings of Kant; edited and with an introduction by Allen W. Wood. Modern Lib. 2001 xxv, 478p pa $15.95 *   193

1. Philosophy

ISBN 0-375-75733-3   LC 2001-18303

First Modern Library edition published 1949 with title: The philosophy of Kant

This volume presents the essential works of the philosopher including "selected excerpts from his most frequently taught essays and book-length publications, including 'Critique of Pure Reason, Critique of Judgment,' and 'Eternal Peace.'" Publisher's note

Critique of pure reason; translated by Marcus Weigelt. Rev ed. Penguin 2003 lxxvi, 708p (Penguin classics) pa $20 *   193

1. Theory of knowledge 2. Reason

ISBN 978-0-14-044747-7; 0-14-044747-4

Original German edition, 1781

In this philosophical work Kant "attempted to define the possibility and limits of our knowledge. He denied that we can ever know how the world 'really' is. However, he tried to show that science nevertheless has a sort of universal validity, insofar as it consists of sense experience, which comes from the world, coupled with the mind, which orders this sense experience according to the 'categories of the understanding' and the intuitions of space and time." Reader's Ency. 4th edition

Krell, David Farrell

Basic writings; from Being and time (1927) to The task of thinking (1964); edited, with general introduction and introductions to each selection by David Farrell Krell. rev and expanded ed. HarperSanFrancisco 1993 452p pa $17.95
                                       193

ISBN 0-06-063763-3   LC 91-58187

This anthology first published 1977 by Harper & Row

Contents: Being and time: introduction; What is metaphysics?; On the essence of truth; The origin of the work of art; Letter on humanism; Modern science, metaphysics, and mathematics; The question concerning technology; Building dwelling thinking; What calls for thinking?; The way to language; The end of philosophy and the task of thinking

Includes bibliographical references

Nietzsche, Friedrich Wilhelm, 1844-1900

Basic writings of Nietzsche; introduction by Peter Gay; translated and edited, with commentaries, by Walter Kaufmann. Modern Lib. 2000 xxiv, 862p pa $14.95 *   **193**

ISBN 0-679-78339-3   LC 00-64578

First Modern Library edition published 1968

"Gathers the complete texts of five of Nietzsche's most important works, from his first book to his last: The Birth of Tragedy, Beyond Good and Evil; On the Genealogy of Morals; The Case of Wagner; and Ecce Homo. . . . Included also are seventy-five aphorisms, selections from Nietzsche's correspondence, and variants from drafts for Ecce Homo." Publisher's note

The portable Nietzsche; selected and translated, with an introduction, prefaces, and notes, by Walter Kaufmann. Viking 1954 687p pa $17 hardcover o.p.   **193**

ISBN 0-14-015062-5 (pa)

"The Viking portable library"

Includes the complete texts of Thus spake Zarathustra, Twilight of the idols, The antichrist, and Nietzsche contra Wagner. Selections from other works, notes and letters complete the volume

Thus spoke Zarathustra; a book for everyone and nobody; [by] Friedrich Nietzsche; translated with an introduction and notes by Graham Parkes. Oxford University Press 2005 xliii, 335p (Oxford world's classics) pa $14.95 *   **193**

ISBN 0-19-280583-5   LC 2005-19431

Written between 1883-1892

A philosophical narrative in which Nietzsche "transforms the ancient Persian philosopher Zarathustra . . . into a mouthpiece for his own views. Nietzsche develops his doctrine of the 'Ubermensch' in a prophetic, quasi-biblical style. Nietzsche's Zarathustra announces the death of God, and preaches a new 'faithfulness to the earth,' which includes a new respect for the body . . . and attentiveness to this world rather than the next. He also attacks pity and virtue as weapons of weakness." Reader's Ency. 4th edition

Includes bibliographical references

The will to power; a new translation by Walter Kaufmann and R. J. Hollingdale; edited with commentary by Walter Kaufmann; with facsimiles of the original manuscript. Random House 1967 xxxii, 576p $16 hardcover o.p.   **193**

ISBN 0-394-70437-1 (pa)

Partial contents: European nihilism: Critique of morality; The will to power as knowledge; The will to power as art; Discipline and breeding

Solomon, Robert C., 1942-2007

What Nietzsche really said; {by} Robert C. Solomon and Kathleen M. Higgins. Schocken Bks. 2000 263p pa $13 hardcover o.p.   **193**

1. Nietzsche, Friedrich Wilhelm, 1844-1900

ISBN 0-8052-1094-6 (pa)   LC 99-33796

The authors offer an "overview of Friedrich Nietzsche's life, thought, and influence. . . . Particularly help-ful are their brief annotations of Nietzsche's 14 books and short analyses of the thinkers who influenced him." Libr J

Includes bibliographical references

194 France

Descartes, René, 1596-1650

Descartes: selected philosophical writings; translated by John Cottingham, Robert Stoothoff, Dugald Murdoch; with an introduction by John Cottingham. Cambridge University Press 1988 249p il hardcover o.p. pa $26.99 *   **194**

1. French philosophy

ISBN 0-521-35264-9; 0-521-35812-4 (pa)

LC 87-26799

A single-volume edition of the first two volumes of a three-volume set published 1984-1991 with title: The philosophical writings of Descartes

Contents: Rules for the direction of our native intelligence — Discourse on the method — Optics — Meditations on First philosophy — Objections and replies — Principles of philosophy — Comments on a certain broadsheet — The passions of the soul

196 Spain and Portugal

Ortega y Gasset, José, 1883-1955

What is philosophy? translated from the Spanish by Mildred Adams. Norton 1961 c1960 252p pa $10.95 hardcover o.p. *   **196**

1. Philosophy

ISBN 0-393-00126-1 (pa)

This volume by the influential Spanish philosopher, essayist and critic "consists of a series of lectures begun in 1929 at the University of Madrid. Interrupted when the University was closed as a result of political troubles, they were resumed in a Madrid theatre. Part of the lectures had been given earlier in Buenos Aires." N Y Times Book Rev

200 RELIGION

Anderson, Sherry Ruth

The feminine face of God; the unfolding of the sacred in women; [by] Sherry Ruth Anderson and Patricia Hopkins. Bantam Bks. 1991 253p pa $17 hardcover o.p.   **200**

1. Women—Religious life 2. Femininity of God

ISBN 0-553-35266-0 (pa)   LC 91-6657

This book is "an attempt to see the divine face as mirrored on the faces of more than 100 women from all walks of life who were willing to describe their inner lives in open and intimate detail. . . . What these women have in common, the authors tell us, is that they were willing to trust their own essential natures and become their own teachers." N Y Times Book Rev

Includes bibliographical references

Armstrong, Karen

The battle for God; fundamentalism in Judaism, Christianity, and Islam. Knopf 2000 442p $29.95; pa $15.95 *   **200**

1. Religious fundamentalism

ISBN 0-679-43597-2; 0-345-39169-1 (pa)

LC 99-34022

This is a "study of fundamentalism among Jews (in Israel), Christians (American Protestants), and Muslims (Sunni Egyptians and Shiite Iranians). Armstrong argues that all strains of fundamentalism, despite their differences, are fearful defenses against modernity. . . . The author is sympathetic to the human need for spiritual meaning, but she points out that the intellectual flaws of fundamentalist beliefs are customarily accompanied by paranoia, anger, and aggression—which, in turn, frequently betray the message of the faith." New Yorker

Includes bibliographical references

A history of God; the 4000 year quest of Judaism, Christianity, and Islam. Knopf 1993 xxiii, 460p maps pa $15.95 hardcover o.p.   **200**

1. God

ISBN 0-345-38456-3 (pa)   LC 92-38318

This is a study of ideas and experiences of God in Judaism, Christianity and Islam from Abraham to the twentieth century

"Public librarians should be aware that conservative readers may be offended by this book, and even religious scholars may find Armstrong's rather one-sided 'death of God' optimism about humanity a bit passé. Otherwise, this is an excellent and informative book." Libr J

Bowker, John, 1935-

World religions; contributing consultants: David Bowker [et al.] DK Pub. 1997 200p il maps $35; pa $16.95   **200**

1. Religions 2. Religion

ISBN 0-7894-1439-2; 0-7566-1772-3 (pa)

LC 96-38277

Each chapter begins with an "introduction and is followed by one-or-two page sections that explain the basic tenets of the faith, symbols, events, people, buildings, works of art, and the differences and similarities to other religions. Hinduism, Buddhism, Judaism, Christianity, and Islam are included as are Jainism, Sikhism, Chinese and Japanese religions, and Native religions." SLJ

Chittister, Joan

Welcome to the wisdom of the world and its meaning for you. William B. Eerdmans 2007 186p $20   **200**

1. Religions

ISBN 978-0-8028-2894-1; 0-8028-2894-9

LC 2007-9964

"Each chapter tackles a separate existential question such as 'Where is God?' or 'What does it mean to be a spiritual person?' She begins each of the 25 chapters with a description of a particular person's struggle to find meaning amid hardship, moving the narrative toward a wisdom story or parable from one of five religious traditions: Hinduism, Buddhism, Judaism, Christianity and Islam. A concluding meditation rounds out each section.

. . . This refreshing book will be welcomed by Chittister's many admirers and is sure to win new ones as well." Publ Wkly

Controversial new religions; edited by James R. Lewis and Jesper Aagaard Petersen. Oxford Univ. Press 2004 496p $74; pa $29.95 *
          200

1. Cults

ISBN 0-19-515682-X; 0-19-515683-8 (pa)

LC 2003-24374

"This volume collects papers on those specific New Religious Movements (NRMS) that have generated the most scholarly attention. With few exceptions, these organizations are also the controversial groups that have attracted the attention of the mass media, often because they have been involved in, or accused of, violent or anti-social activities. Among the movements . . . profiled are such groups as the Branch Davidians, Heaven's Gate, Aum Shinrikyo, Solar Temple, Scientology, and Falun Gong." Publisher's note

Includes bibliographical references

Dennett, Daniel Clement

Breaking the spell; religion as a natural phenomenon; [by] Daniel C. Dennett. Viking 2006 448p il $25.95   **200**

1. Religion

ISBN 0-670-03472-X   LC 2005-42415

This book examines the "question of why we believe in God and how religion shapes our lives and our future. . . . [Dennett] contends that the 'belief in belief' has fogged any attempt to rationally consider the existence of God and the relationship between divinity and human need." Publisher's note

"A book certain to spark heated controversy." Booklist

Includes bibliographical references

Guiley, Rosemary Ellen

The encyclopedia of angels; foreword by Lisa Schwebel. 2nd ed. Facts on File 2004 398p il $75; pa $24.95   **200**

1. Angels—Dictionaries

ISBN 0-8160-5023-6; 0-8160-5024-4 (pa)

LC 2003-60147

First published 1996

"Guiley's encyclopedia provides researchers with a historical and phenomenological approach to studying angels by examining what folklore, myth, and religion have contributed to research in the field. . . . Brief bibliographies follow most of the alphabetically arranged entries, which cover topics such as encounters with angels and the roles of angels in religion, culture, and art." Choice

Includes bibliographical references

Hitchens, Christopher

God is not great; how religion poisons everything. Twelve 2007 307p $24.99
          200

1. Religion 2. Atheism

ISBN 978-0-44657-980-3; 0-44657-980-7

LC 2006-23039

Published in the United Kingdom with title: God is not great; the case against religion

Hitchens, Christopher—*Continued*

In this work Hitchens catalogs "the major arguments against religion, which he deems a pernicious force. First, he writes, faith misrepresents the origin of the cosmos as well as that of humanity; second, it fosters servility, solipsism, and sexual repression; and, third, it is based on wishful thinking. Hitchens spares no targets in this manifesto, criticizing both Western and Eastern faiths." Libr J

"Hitchens has outfoxed the Hitchens watchers by writing a serious and deeply felt book, totally consistent with his beliefs of a lifetime. And God should be flattered: unlike most of those clamoring for his attention, Hitchens treats him like an adult." N Y Times Book Rev

Includes bibliographical references

Hopfe, Lewis M., Jr.

Religions of the world; revised by Mark R. Woodward. 10th ed. Prentice-Hall 2007 390p il maps pa $82.20   **200**

1. Religions

ISBN 978-0-13-224045-1; 0-13-224045-9

First published 1976 by Glencoe. Periodically revised

Includes CD-ROM. New edition in preparation

In exploring the major religions of the world, the author traces the historical development of each, its founders, teachings, and present status.

Includes bibliographical references

Hutchison, William R.

Religious pluralism in America; the contentious history of a founding ideal. Yale University Press 2003 262p $32.50; pa $18   **200**

1. United States—Religion

ISBN 0-300-09813-8; 0-300-10516-9 (pa)

                LC 2002-151893

The author "illuminates the cultural transformations that enabled twentieth-century Americans to embrace belatedly the religious diversity that emerged in the nineteenth-century influx of Catholic and Jewish immigrants and in the rise of new American-born faiths such as Mormonism and Transcendentalism. . . . Though he acknowledges the concerns of critics worried about the moral balkanization of a society lacking shared religious premises, Hutchison hails America's new religious pluralism as a great achievement. A balanced and informative narrative." Booklist

Includes bibliographical references

The **Illustrated** guide to world religions; general editor, Michael D. Coogan. Oxford Univ. Press 1998 288p il maps hardcover o.p. pa $19.95   **200**

1. Religions

ISBN 0-19-521366-1; 0-19-521997-X (pa)

                LC 98-6784

An introductory survey of seven major world religions: Judaism, Christianity, Islam, Hinduism, Buddhism, and Chinese and Japanese traditions.

The information presented "is accurate and presented in lively prose, and the color photographs and maps greatly enhance reading pleasure." Libr J

Includes bibliographical references

Messadié, Gérald

A history of the devil; translated from the French by Marc Romano. Kodansha Int. 1996 377p pa $16 hardcover o.p. paperback available $16   **200**

1. Devil 2. Demonology

ISBN 1-56836-198-X (pa)   LC 95-4949

"Using a comparative and phenomenological approach, the author traces the idea of the Devil from ancient Greece and India to contemporary Western culture. What emerges from Messadie's explorations is that the Devil is a very recent concept, arising primarily out of Zoroastrianism in Persia in the sixth century B.C." Publ Wkly

"Messadie's highly engaging and provocative cultural history is essential for most libraries." Libr J

Includes bibliographical references

Prothero, Stephen R.

Religious literacy; what every American needs to know—and doesn't; [by] Stephen Prothero. HarperSanFrancisco 2007 296p $24.95

     200

1. Religions

ISBN 978-0-06-084670-1; 0-06-084670-4

                LC 2006-41310

"In this book, the author combines a lively history of the rise and fall of American religious literacy with a set of proposed remedies based on his hope that 'the Fall into religious ignorance is reversible.' He also includes a useful multicultural glossary of religious definitions and allusions, in which religious illiterates can find the prodigal son, the promised land, the Quakers and the Koran." Washington Post Book World

Includes bibliographical references

Turner, Alice K.

The history of hell. Harcourt Brace & Co. 1993 275p il pa $22 hardcover o.p. paperback available $22   **200**

1. Hell

ISBN 0-15-600137-3 (pa)   LC 93-9909

"Belief in a hell or some sort of afterlife has been intrinsic to the religions of the world ever since the first stories were shared aloud and incised in clay tablets. Turner's richly illustrated history surveys the myriad forms hell has taken in the West from Sumer to Rome and beyond." Booklist

Weber, Eugen, 1925-2007

Apocalypses; prophesies, cults, and millennial beliefs through the ages; [by] Eugen Weber. Harvard Univ. Press 1999 294p $27.50; pa $16.95

     200

1. End of the world 2. Millennium

ISBN 0-674-04080-5; 0-674-00395-0 (pa)

                LC 99-18001

"Weber traces millennial beliefs as professed through the ages. From ancient and pre-Christian times to the present day, humankind has had an unshakable belief that the end is at hand. . . . Weber has an excellent grasp of his subject, an accessible style, and an understated sense of humor." Booklist

Includes bibliographical references

Williams, Juan

This far by faith; stories from the African-American religious experience; [by] Juan Williams and Quinton Dixie. Morrow 2003 326p il hardcover o.p. pa $15.95   **200**
    1. African Americans—Religion 2. African Americans—History
    ISBN 0-06-018863-4; 0-06-093424-7 (pa)
                         LC 2002-71884
    This study of African American worship "interweaves stories of individual spiritual journeys and accounts of church leaders and religious movements. The authors . . . [aim to] link blacks' faith to their ongoing fight for equality." Christ Sci Monit
    "Brief topical articles and captioned illustrations supplement the main text, creating a balanced, readable, and nuanced introduction to the power of faith to sustain the African American community." Libr J

Wise women: over two thousand years of spiritual writing by women; edited by Susan Cahill. Norton 1996 xxiii, 395p pa $15.95 hardcover o.p.   **200**
    1. Spiritual life 2. Women—Religious life
    ISBN 0-393-31679-3 (pa)   LC 95-40575
    This anthology includes material "drawn from diverse traditions, genres, and places. . . . Each selection is prefaced by a brief biographical-historical introduction that locates the selection without presuming to tell readers how to interpret it. . . . More than half the book is devoted to material from the twentieth century." Booklist
    "Cahill's collection of poems, stories, and essays is a rich and powerful testimony to the liberating power of divine love and justice in the lives of women." Libr J
    Includes bibliographical references

200.3 Religion—Encyclopedias and dictionaries

The **encyclopedia** of cults, sects, and new religions; {edited by} James R. Lewis. 2nd ed. Prometheus Bks. 2002 951p il $180
                                  200.3
    1. Cults 2. Sects—Encyclopedias 3. United States—Religion—Encyclopedias
    ISBN 1-57392-888-7   LC 2002-19180
    First published 1998
    This reference contains "information on approximately 1,000 religious groups, ranging from small churches with less than a hundred members (Chishti Order of America) to organizations such as the Assemblies of God that number in the millions. Most entries are relatively short. The more controversial religions, as well as religious groups that have had a high profile lately, receive more lengthy treatments. Also included are entries on broader religious movements such as the New Age and the Charismatic Movement. . . . Each article outlines the history of the group, its founders and leaders, its main teachings, and an approximate number of followers or congregations. The explanations are clearly written, interesting and understandable, without too much scholarly jargon." Booklist
    Includes bibliographical references

Encyclopedia of religion; Lindsay Jones, editor in chief. 2nd ed. Macmillan Reference USA 2005 15v il set $1295 *   **200.3**
    1. Religions—Encyclopedias
    ISBN 0-02-865733-0   LC 2004-17052
    Replaces the 1993 edition under the editorship of Mircea Eliade
    First published 1987 in 16 volumes
    "Treats theoretical (e.g., doctrines, myths, theologies, ethics), practical (e.g., cults, sacraments, meditations), and sociological (e.g., religious groups, ecclesiastical forms) aspects of religion; includes extensive coverage of non-Western religions. Signed articles by some 1,400 contributors worldwide end with bibliographies. Many composite entries treat two or more related topics. . . . Has quickly become the standard work." Guide to Ref Books. 11th edition [review of 1993 edition]
    Includes bibliographical references

Encyclopedia of religious and spiritual development; editors, Elizabeth M. Dowling, W. George Scarlett. Sage Publications 2006 xxiv, 528p $150   **200.3**
    1. Youth—Religious life—Encyclopedias
    ISBN 0-7619-2883-9   LC 2005-12704
    "A SAGE reference publication"
    "This work addresses the complexity of factors involved in religious and spiritual development. . . . The work includes over 250 entries written by 125 international scholars on religions and traditions, institutions, and important texts and practices that have had an impact throughout history." Libr J
    "This book deserves a place in every library because it is a rich source of insight and information on topics of growing relevance and interest." Choice
    Includes bibliographical references

Religions of the world; a comprehensive encyclopedia of beliefs and practices; J. Gordon Melton, Martin Baumann, editors; David B. Barrett, world religious statistics; Donald Wiebe, introduction. ABC-CLIO 2002 4v il maps set $385   **200.3**
    1. Religions—Encyclopedias
    ISBN 1-57607-223-1   LC 2002-5617
    This "work details the history, development, organization, current status, and contact information for major organizations associated with various living world faiths. Edited with the requisite authority by Melton . . . and Baumann . . . this unique encyclopedia is not concerned with defining and analyzing the major world religions but rather with presenting the constitutive communities, groups, and associations within each religion. The result is a sort of 'encyclopedia of associations' for world religions with superb commentary." Libr J
    Includes bibliographical references

200.9 Historical, geographic, persons treatment

Almond, Gabriel Abraham, 1911-2002
Strong religion; the rise of fundamentalisms around the world; {by} Gabriel A. Almond, R. Scott Appleby, and Emmanuel Sivan. University of Chicago Press 2003 281p il $49; pa $19 *
200.9
1. Religious fundamentalism
ISBN 0-226-01497-5; 0-226-01498-3 (pa)
LC 2002-13665
This "may be the single most cogent sociohistorical analysis of the modern religious phenomenon called fundamentalism. . . . This foundational work is essential for academic and major public libraries." Libr J
Includes bibliographical references

Armstrong, Karen
The great transformation; the beginning of our religious traditions. Knopf 2006 469p il map $30
*
200.9
1. Religion—History
ISBN 0-375-41317-0
LC 2005-47536
"Taking the Axial Age, which spans roughly 900 B.C.E. to 200 B.C.E., as her focal point, Armstrong examines the ways that specific religious traditions from Buddhism and Confucianism to Taoism and Judaism responded to the various cultural forces they faced during this period." Publ Wkly
"This could very possibly be one of the greatest intellectual histories ever written." Libr J
Includes bibliographical references

Balmer, Randall Herbert
Religion in twentieth century America; {by} Randall Balmer. Oxford Univ. Press 2001 142p il (Religion in American life) $28
200.9
1. United States—Religion
ISBN 0-19-511295-4
LC 00-60674
The author "traces the evolution of various movements, including the Pentecostal, Fundamentalist, Evangelical, and New Age movements, the emergence of the Religious Right, Promise Keepers, and televangelism." Booklist
"This title is accessible and reliable, brief and lively, and makes a fine addition to most libraries." SLJ
Includes bibliographical references

Butler, Jon, 1940-
Religion in American life; a short history; [by] Jon Butler, Grant Wacker, and Randall Balmer. Updated ed. Oxford University Press 2008 496p il pa $19.95
200.9
1. United States—Religion
ISBN 978-0-19-533329-9; 0-19-533329-2
LC 2007-24915
First published 2002
This volume begins by describing the state of religious affairs in the old and new worlds. The survey continues

with a look at the religious landscape of 19th-century America and concludes with an examination of current religious beliefs and practices.
Includes bibliographical references

The **Cambridge** illustrated history of religions; edited by John Bowker. Cambridge Univ. Press 2002 336p il (Cambridge illustrated history) $40
*
200.9
1. Religions
ISBN 0-521-81037-X
LC 2001-37866
"The major religions get thoroughgoing treatment, with short introductions also given to the Zoroastrianism; the religions of Greece, Rome, Egypt, and Mesopotamia; aboriginal religions; and new religious movements. . . . Christianity receives a separate chapter as well as substantial treatment in chapters on Chinese, Korean, and Japanese religions. . . . This volume presents a large amount of information in an engaging way, offering much scholarly insight for the lay reader." Libr J
Includes bibliographical references

Contemporary American religion; Wade Clark Roof, editor in chief. Macmillan Ref. USA 2000 2v set $275
200.9
1. United States—Religion—Encyclopedias
ISBN 0-02-864928-1
LC 99-46712
"This work describes various aspects of religious life in America from 1965 to the present. Each signed entry offers a . . . discussion of the topic followed by see-also references and a bibliography. Major religions and smaller and fringe groups are represented as are individual, symbols, traditions, beliefs, and practices." SLJ

Corrigan, John, 1952-
Religion in America; an historical account of the development of American religious life; {by} John Corrigan, Winthrop S. Hudson. 7th ed. Prentice-Hall 2004 482p il map pa $67.60 *
200.9
1. United States—Religion
ISBN 978-0-13-092389-9; 0-13-092389-3
LC 2003-2297
First published 1965 with authors' names in reverse order. Periodically revised
A survey of American religious life from 1607 to the present
Includes bibliographical references

Eastern religions; origins, beliefs, practices, holy texts, sacred places; general editor, Michael D. Coogan; [contributors] Vasudha Narayanan . . . [et al.] Oxford University Press 2005 552p il $35; pa $19.95 *
200.9
1. South Asia—Religion 2. East Asia—Religion
ISBN   0-19-522190-7;   978-0-19-522190-9; 0-19-522191-5 (pa); 978-0-19-522191-6 (pa)
LC 2004-30376
This is an introduction "to major South Asian and East Asian religious traditions. Four expert authors introduce Hinduism, Buddhism, Taoism, Confucianism, and Shinto. To aid comparison, each article has parallel sections on origins and historical development, aspects of

Eastern religions—*Continued*
the divine, sacred texts, sacred persons, ethical principles, sacred space, sacred time, death and the afterlife, and society and religion. The clear, crisp prose avoids academic jargon without losing the complexity and richness of the traditions being examined." Libr J

Includes bibliographical references

Encyclopedia of fundamentalism; Brenda E. Brasher, editor. Routledge 2001 558p il (Religion and society) $125 * 200.9
1. Religious fundamentalism
ISBN 0-415-92244-5   LC 2001-19951

"A Berkshire Reference work"

This reference covers "fundamentalism, from definition, history, and beliefs to movements and churches, significant individuals, and expressions in various world religions. Creationism, fascism, rock music, and the Taliban are a sample of the topics covered. The contributors provide clear, readable explanations. . . . This beautifully laid-out work is the one to have." Libr J

Includes bibliographical references

Falsani, Cathleen, 1970-
The God factor; inside the spiritual life of public people. Farrar, Straus and Giroux 2006 271p il $24 200.9
1. Faith 2. Celebrities
ISBN 978-0-374-16381-5; 0-374-16381-2
LC 2005-27229

"Sarah Crichton books"

The author presents interviews on religion with public figures, including Senator Barack Obama, Sandra Bernhard, Studs Terkel, Anne Rice, Barry Scheck, David Lynch, Hakeem Olajuwon, Sandra Cisneros, Tom Robbins, John Patrick Shanley, The Reverend Al Sharpton, Annie Lennox, Seamus Heaney, Jonathan Safran Foer, Mark Morris, Jeffrey Sachs, Laura Esquivel, Sherman Alexie, Russell Simmons, Dr. Henry Lee, Melissa Etheridge and Elie Wiesel.

"While those profiled may not be representative of ordinary Americans, this sensitive spiritual portrait of popular culture evokes, in thought-provoking fashion, the vibrant and highly individualized nature of contemporary faith." Christ Sci Monit

Feiler, Bruce S.
Where God was born; a journey by land to the roots of religion; [by] Bruce Feiler. William Morrow 2005 405p $26.95 200.9
1. Bible. O.T. —History of Biblical events 2. Middle East—Description and travel
ISBN 0-06-057487-9; 978-0-06-057487-1
LC 2005-43412

The author "visits biblical sites and rereads the scriptural episodes that took place there." N Y Times Book Rev

This "is at once a riveting journey through contemporary conflict zones in Israel, the West Bank, Iraq, and Iran, and a provocative analysis of the Bible considered in the broader context of its times." Christ Sci Monit

Includes bibliographical references

Gaustad, Edwin Scott
New historical atlas of religion in America; by Edwin Scott Gaustad and Philip L. Barlow; with the special assistance of Richard W. Dishno. Oxford Univ. Press 2001 xxiii, 435p maps $160 * 200.9
1. United States—Church history 2. United States—Religion
ISBN 0-19-509168-X   LC 00-30001

First published 1976 with title: Historical atlas of religion in America

"A completely reorganized, updated, and expanded edition of Gaustad's 1962 original work and the 1976 revision, this beautifully illustrated atlas presents a historical narrative of America's rich and diverse religious past. Lively text along with 260 colorful, detailed maps and 200 other graphics provide the histories, migration, developments, and growths of religious communities in the United States." Am Libr

Jenkins, Philip, 1952-
God's continent; Christianity, Islam, and Europe's religious crisis. Oxford University Press 2007 340p map $28 200.9
1. Europe—Religion 2. Islam—Relations—Christianity 3. Christianity and other religions
ISBN 978-0-19-531395-6; 0-19-531395-X
LC 2006-38654

The third book in a "trilogy that includes The Next Christendom and The New Faces of Christianity, [this volume offers an] appraisal of the future of Christianity in a rapidly changing Europe." Publisher's note

This is a "stimulating, informative, meaty, and judicious book." Commonweal

Includes bibliographical references

Melton, J. Gordon
Encyclopedia of American religions. 7th ed. Gale 2003 xxiv, 1408p $335 * 200.9
1. United States—Religion—Encyclopedias 2. Sects—Encyclopedias
ISBN 0-7876-6384-0

First published 1978 by McGrath Publishing Company

New edition in preparation

"Presents coverage of more than 2,500 North American religious groups in the U.S. and Canada, from Adventists to Zen Buddhists. Entries contain essays and directory listings that describe the historical development of religious families and give . . . information about each group within those families, including, where available, headquarter location, membership figures, a listing of educational facilities and information on periodicals published by the group." Publisher's note

Moore, R. Laurence (Robert Laurence), 1940-
Selling God; American religion in the marketplace of culture. Oxford Univ. Press 1994 317p pa $19.95 hardcover o.p. 200.9
1. United States—Religion
ISBN 0-19-509838-2 (pa)   LC 93-19624

"Moore traces the history of marketing techniques in American religion. The first amendment ban on state re-

Moore, R. Laurence (Robert Laurence), 1940-
Continued
ligion necessitated a competitive approach. Moore asserts
that religion 'had to sell itself not only in the competitive
church market, but also in a general market of other cultural commodities.'" Libr J
The author "is balanced and nonpedantic, treating religion as a cultural element of history." N Y Times Book
Rev
Includes bibliographical references

Queen, Edward L.
The encyclopedia of American religious history;
{by} Edward L. Queen II, Stephen R. Prothero,
and Gardiner H. Shattuck, Jr.; foreword by Martin
E. Marty, editorial advisor. rev ed. Facts on File
2001 2v il set $137.50   **200.9**
1. United States—Religion—Encyclopedias
ISBN 0-8160-4335-3   LC 00-69512
First published 1995
New edition in preparation
This reference source presents over 500 articles, ranging from a few hundred words to approximately 9,000
examining different religions, religious leaders, events,
and other topics that helped shape the history of religion
in America. The coverage extends from Puritan America
to the moral majority
This "is an excellent and readable resource for the
study of the history of religion in the U.S." Booklist
Includes bibliographical references

Religion and American cultures; an encyclopedia
of traditions, diversity, and popular expressions;
Gary Laderman and Luis León, editors;
foreword by Amanda Porterfield. ABC-CLIO
2003 3v set $285   **200.9**
1. United States—Religion—Encyclopedias
ISBN 1-57607-238-X   LC 2003-8644
"This resource explores the various ways Americans
approach religion. Its first volume features chapters on
ethnic groups and sectarian beliefs, the second comprises
essay entries on distinct practices, and the third collects
primary documents. Cotton Mather, Shirley MacLaine,
and Elijah Muhammad are represented, along with such
pivotal documents as *The Maryland Toleration Act* and
the *American Indian Religious Freedom Act*." Libr J
Includes bibliographical references

Religious foundations of western civilization;
Judaism, Christianity, and Islam; Jacob Neusner,
editor. Abingdon Press 2006 686p pa $39
                                                 200.9
1. Western civilization 2. Christianity 3. Judaism
4. Islam
ISBN 0-687-33202-8; 978-0-687-33202-1
                                      LC 2005-19409
The editor "divides the book into six parts that profile
the three faiths; show how they hold common interests
in such areas as philosophy, law, politics, and culture;
and explore their modernization and their places in the
21st century. . . . This work is essential reading for students of comparative religion and, although scholarly, is
also accessible to general readers with an interest in religions." Libr J
Includes bibliographical references

Wolfe, Alan
The transformation of American religion; how
we actually live our faith. Free Press 2003 309p
$26   **200.9**
1. United States—Religion
ISBN 0-7432-2839-1   LC 2003-44870
The author "examines the ways that American religion
has been so transformed over the past five decades that
it is no longer recognizable. He explores every facet of
American religion—worship, fellowship, doctrine, tradition, morality, sin, witness and identity—as he investigates the fading of practices or beliefs that once dominated." Publ Wkly
"This provocative book is a must-read for a wide variety of readers." Choice
Includes bibliographical references

201 Religious mythology, general classes of religion, interreligious relations and attitudes, social theology

Atlas of the world's religions; edited by Ninian
Smart and Frederick W. [i.e. M.] Denny;
[cartographic editor, Ailsa Heritage; cartography,
Advanced Illustration Ltd.] 2nd ed. Oxford
University Press 2007 272p il map $110
                                                 201
1. Religions—Maps
ISBN 978-0-19-533401-2; 0-19-533401-9
First published 1999
"Beginning with a geographic examination of
Palaeolithic religions, the text and maps chart the growth
and development of religions throughout history, including the rise and fall of secular alternatives such as New
Age belief systems and Marxism. Most of the ten sections are organized by major religion, i.e., the Hindu
world, Buddhism, Judaism, Christianity, Islam, and indigenous religions, while the remainder is given to regional
treatments of religion. . . . This is an attractive, informative, and practical reference tool that emphasizes the role
geography plays in shaping culture and religion." Libr J
Includes bibliographical references

Barbour, Ian G.
When science meets religion; enemies, strangers,
or partners? HarperSanFrancisco 2000 205p pa
$16.95   **201**
1. Religion and science
ISBN 0-06-060381-X   LC 99-55579
The author "guides readers through a four-fold typology of the science/religion relationship—Conflict, Independence, Dialogue and Integration. . . . Barbour's own
sympathies are markedly on the side of dialogue and integration, but he makes an unusually sucessful effort to
represent other perspectives in a fair light." Publ Wkly
Includes bibliographical references

Barr, Stephen M., 1953-
Modern physics and ancient faith. University of
Notre Dame Press 2003 312p il hardcover o.p. pa
$18 * **201**
1. Physics 2. Religion and science
ISBN 0-268-03471-0; 978-0-268-02198-6 (pa);
0-268-02198-8 (pa) LC 2002-151565
The author "argues that the great discoveries of modern physics are more compatible with the central teachings of Christianity and Judaism about God, the cosmos,
and the human soul than with the atheistic viewpoint of
scientific materialism." Publ Wkly
"Neither religiously sectarian nor technically daunting,
this is a book that invites the widest range of readers to
ponder the deepest kind of questions." Booklist
Includes bibliographical references

Campbell, Joseph, 1904-1987
Creative mythology. Arkana 1991 c1968 730p
(The masks of God, v4) pa $18 * **201**
1. Mythology in literature
ISBN 978-0-14-019440-1; 0-14-019440-1
First published 1968 by Viking
"This volume explores the whole inner story of mod-
ern culture since the Dark Ages, treating modern man's
unique position as the creator of his own mythology."
Publisher's note
Includes bibliographical references

Occidental mythology. Arkana 1991 c1964 564p
(The masks of God, v3) pa $18 * **201**
1. Mythology
ISBN 978-0-14-019441-8; 0-14-019441-X
First published 1964 by Viking
"A systematic . . . comparison of the themes that un-
derlie the art, worship, and literature of the Western
world." Publisher's note
Includes bibliographical references

Oriental mythology. Arkana 1991 c1962 561p
(The masks of God, v2) pa $18 * **201**
1. Oriental mythology
ISBN 978-0-14-019442-5; 0-14-019442-8
First published 1962 by Viking
"An exploration of Eastern mythology as it developed
into the distinctive religions of Egypt, India, China, and
Japan." Publisher's note
Includes bibliographical references

The power of myth; [by] Joseph Campbell, with
Bill Moyers; Betty Sue Flowers, editor. Doubleday
1988 231p il hardcover o.p. pa $29.95 *
201
1. Mythology 2. Religious art 3. Spiritual life
ISBN 0-385-24773-7; 0-385-24774-5 LC 88-4218
Also available in paperback from Anchor Bks. $14.95
(ISBN 0-385-41886-8)
This companion to a public television series records
conversations between Campbell and Bill Moyers. Campbell reflects on themes and symbols from world religions
and mythologies and explores their relevance for his own
spiritual journey.
"Campbell is the hero on his own voyage of discov-

ery. This well-bound book on lovely paper with helpful
illustrations from art is highly recommended for all libraries." Choice

Primitive mythology. Arkana 1991 c1959 504p
(The masks of God, v1) pa $18 * **201**
1. Mythology
ISBN 978-0-14-019443-2; 0-14-019443-6
First published 1959 by Viking
The author "discusses the primitive roots of mytholo-
gy, examining them in light of . . . discoveries in ar-
chaeology, anthropology, and psychology." Publisher's
note
Includes bibliographical references

Transformations of myth through time. Perennial
Lib. 1990 263p il pa $21.95 hardcover o.p. *
201
1. Mythology
ISBN 0-06-096463-4 (pa) LC 89-45788
"This book consists of 13 chapters, each of which is
a slightly edited version of one of the lectures in the
PBS series of the same title. Drawing on his vast knowledge, Campbell explains in simple language, with copious examples from all times and cultures, how the same
myths occur everywhere in slightly different forms." Libr
J

Coles, Robert
The secular mind. Princeton Univ. Press 1999
189p $45; pa $15.95 **201**
1. Secularism 2. Religion and science
ISBN 0-691-05805-9; 0-691-08862-4 (pa)
LC 98-39388
"In examining the nature of the secular and the sacred,
Coles draws on his interviews with such notables as Paul
Tillich, Dorothy Day, Anna Freud, and Walker Percy, as
well as nuanced readings of the Bible and a range of
great literature." Booklist
"This is a potent and powerful work readers will think
about and return to again and again." Publ Wkly

Consolmagno, Guy, 1952-
God's mechanics; how scientists and engineers
make sense of religion. Jossey-Bass 2007 245p
$24.95 **201**
1. Religion and science
ISBN 978-0-7879-9466-2; 0-7879-9466-9
LC 2007-19067
"Combining personal memoir with conversations within the techie world, Consolmagno describes questions
about the universe and the meaning of life that attract
techies into religious belief and practice, concluding that
'techies are not looking for proof. They're looking for
confidence.'" Publ Wkly

Davis, Kenneth C.

Don't know much about mythology; everything you need to know about the greatest stories in human history but never learned. HarperCollins Publishers 2005 545p $26.95; pa $14.95

                  201

  1. Mythology
    ISBN   0-06-019460-X;   978-0-06-019460-4;
  0-06-093257-0 (pa); 978-0-06-093257-2 (pa)
                        LC 2005-43341

The author "examines the myths created by societies ranging from Egypt, Greece and Rome to Africa, India and the Americas, proceeding . . . by way of question and answer as he surveys each mythmaking culture. . . . His survey provides a superb starting point for entering the world of mythology." Publ Wkly
  Includes bibliographical references

Deloria, Vine

Evolution, creationism, and other modern myths; a critical inquiry; [by] Vine Deloria, Jr. Fulcrum 2002 274p $24.95; pa $18.95   **201**
  1. Religion and science 2. Evolution 3. Creationism
  ISBN 1-55591-159-5; 1-55591-458-6 (pa)
                        LC 2002-8171

Contents: Do we need a beginning?; The nature of science; The primacy of science; The logic of evolution; The nature of the present earth history; The nature of "religion"; The philosophy/science of other "religions"; The nature of history; Efforts at synthesis; The rocky road ahead

The author "argues that both sides in the evolution-versus-creationism debate are wrong. . . . This intellectual duel finds only mistaken orthodoxies in the field, for creationism has no scientific basis, but evolution is far from proven. . . . Certain to be controversial, likely to outrage the faithful of both camps, and a stunning good read." Booklist
  Includes bibliographical references

Frazer, Sir James George, Sir, 1854-1941

The golden bough; a study in magic and religion; a new abridgment from the second and third editions ; edited with an introduction by Robert Fraser. Oxford University Press 1998 xlix, 858p (Oxford world's classics) pa $17.95

                   201

  1. Mythology 2. Religions 3. Superstition
  ISBN 978-0-19-283541-3; 0-19-283541-6
                        LC 2001-522510

A "study of the beliefs and institutions of mankind, and the progress through magic and religion to scientific thought. . . . First published in 1890, The Golden Bough was eventually issued in a twelve-volume edition (1906-15) which was abridged in 1922 by the author and his wife. That abridgment has never been reconsidered for a modern audience. In it some of the more controversial passages were dropped, including Frazer's daring speculations on the Crucifixion of Christ. For the first time this one-volume edition restores Frazer's bolder theories." Publisher's note
  Includes bibliographical references

The **History** of science and religion in the western tradition; an encyclopedia; Gary B. Ferngren, general editor; Edward J. Larson, Darrel W. Amundsen, co-editors; Anne-Marie E. Nakhla, assistant editor. Garland 2000 xxi, 586p (Garland reference library of the humanities) $195   **201**
  1. Religion and science
  ISBN 0-8153-1656-9   LC 00-25153

This is a collection of articles "grouped under ten headings covering everything from the relationship of science and religion to the approaches taken by specific religious traditions, from alchemy to chemistry to materialism to spiritualism. Ferngren . . . and his coeditors take the stand that the historical relationship between science and religion follows a complex model rather than the popularly understood model of unalterable conflict. The result is a work, well worth reading through or browsing, that is filled with respect for the roles and methodologies of both religion and science." Libr J
  Includes bibliographical references and index

Human rights and the world's major religions. Praeger 2005 5v set $399.95   **201**
  1. Human rights 2. Religions
  ISBN 0-275-98425-7   LC 2003-68987

"Using the 1948 UN Universal Declaration of Human Rights as a springboard, these five similarly structured volumes examine human rights within the context of Judaism, Christianity, Islam, Hinduism, and Buddhism. The first part of each volume considers the historical development and analysis of the religion; the second is a selection of excerpts from relevant texts followed by brief biographies of the major thinkers mentioned and an annotated bibliography." Libr J

"This set will be indispensable to those researching human rights in religion, as it pulls together important elements of the topic previously unavailable in a single reference work." Choice
  Includes bibliographical references

Idliby, Ranya, 1965-

The faith club; a Muslim, a Christian, a Jew—three women search for understanding; [by] Ranya Idliby, Suzanne Oliver, Priscilla Warner. Free Press 2006 308p $25   **201**
  1. Interfaith relations 2. Christianity and other religions 3. Islam—Relations—Christianity 4. Islam—Relations—Judaism 5. Judaism—Relations—Christianity 6. Judaism—Relations—Islam
  ISBN 0-7432-9047-X; 978-0-7432-9047-0
                        LC 2006-45408

"In the wake of 9/11, Idliby, an American Muslim of Palestinian descent, sought out fellow mothers of the Jewish and Christian faiths to write a children's book on the commonalities among their respective traditions. In their first meeting, however, the women realized they would have to address their differences first. . . . The ladies come to call their group a 'faith club' and, over time, midwife each other into stronger belief in their own respective religions. More Fight Club than book club, the coauthors pull no punches; their outstanding honesty makes for a page-turning read." Publ Wkly
  Includes bibliographical references

Juergensmeyer, Mark

Terror in the mind of God; the global rise of religious violence. 3rd ed, rev and updated. University of California Press 2003 319p il (Comparative studies in religion and society) pa $16.95 *   **201**

1. Terrorism 2. Religion and politics

ISBN 0-520-24011-1   LC 2003-8770

This book "incorporates the events of September 11, 2001 into Mark Juergensmeyer's . . . study of religious terrorism. Juergensmeyer explores the 1993 World Trade Center explosion, Hamas suicide bombings, the Tokyo subway nerve gas attack, and the killing of abortion clinic doctors in the United States." Publisher's note

The author "is a powerful, skillful writer whose deeply empathic interviewing techniques allow readers to enter the minds of some of the late 20th century's most feared religious terrorists. Yet he is also a sensitive scholar who aptly dissects religious terrorism as a sociological phenomenon." Publ Wkly [review of 2000 edition]

Includes bibliographical references

Karabell, Zachary

Peace be upon you; the story of Muslim, Christian, and Jewish coexistence. Random House 2007 343p map $26.95   **201**

1. Interfaith relations 2. Christianity and other religions 3. Islam—Relations 4. Judaism—Relations

ISBN 978-1-4000-4368-2; 1-4000-4368-9

LC 2006-31501

"Countering the tendency to focus on crusaides, jihads, and pogroms, Karabell highlights epochs of interfaith toleration and cooperation, insisting that such harmony reflects the pacific doctrine central to the Abrahamic faiths." Booklist

"This outstanding book . . . combines in a single volume centuries of interaction among the three great monotheistic religions." Choice

Includes bibliographical references

Lilla, Mark

The stillborn God; religion, politics, and the modern West. Knopf 2007 334p $26   **201**

1. Religion and politics

ISBN 978-1-4000-4367-5; 1-4000-4367-0

LC 2007-02470

"The 'stillborn God' of the title is what Lilla calls the deity of liberal theology, a post-Hegelian movement, active particularly in Germany, that 'wedded romantic soulfulness with the modern conviction that man attains happiness by freely developing his capacities, not by submitting them to God's authority.'" N Y Times Book Rev

This book "will influence discussions of politics and theology for the next generation." Booklist

Includes bibliographical references

Stark, Rodney

For the glory of God; how monotheism led to reformations, science, witch-hunts, and the end of slavery. Princeton Univ. Press 2003 488p il $45; pa $18.95   **201**

1. Monotheism 2. Reformation 3. Religion and science 4. Witchcraft 5. Slavery

ISBN 0-691-11436-6; 0-691-11950-3 (pa)

LC 2002-31746

"In this follow-up volume to . . . [One true God], Stark investigates the role of monotheistic religions in reformations, witch-hunts, slavery and science. Such efforts represent an attempt by monotheistic religions to preserve the idea of the One True God against corrupting influences inside and outside the religions themselves. Stark asserts that, contrary to traditional notions, no single religious reformation can be isolated in any monotheistic religion. Thus, Christianity has experienced not simply the Reformation of Luther but many and various reformations that resulted in a diversity of sectarian movements that practice the worship of the One True God in their own ways." Publ Wkly

A "provocative volume—lucid and tightly reasoned." Booklist

Includes bibliographical references

One true God; historical consequences of monotheism. Princeton Univ. Press 2001 319p il $47.50; pa $19.95   **201**

1. Monotheism 2. God

ISBN 0-691-08923-X; 0-691-11500-1 (pa)

LC 2001-21128

Stark seeks "a theoretical understanding of monothetheism that will be . . . 'sociologically useful.' . . . Stark's theory has monotheism—the belief that there is just one God, just one giver of supernatural blessings and curses—as its object. He wants to explain monotheism's origins and development, to show its main effects upon the behavior and attitudes of social groups, and to account for the fact that monotheists are sometimes aggressively intolerant of those who do not share their beliefs and at other times civilly forebearing." Commonweal

Includes bibliographical references

Woodward, Kenneth L.

The book of miracles; the meaning of the miracle stories in Christianity, Judaism, Buddhism, Hinduism, Islam. Simon & Schuster 2000 429p pa $16 hardcover o.p.   **201**

1. Miracles

ISBN 0-7432-0029-2 (pa)   LC 99-88083

The author "contends that miracles are found in all the major religions, and that one cannot understand or 'fully appreciate' any of the religions without some acquaintance with their miracle traditions." Publ Wkly

"A great resource for studies in comparative religions and interfaith dialog." Libr J

Includes bibliographical references

201.03   Religious mythology—Encyclopedias and dictionaries

Cotterell, Arthur
A dictionary of world mythology. new ed rev & expanded. Oxford Univ. Press 1990 314p il maps pa $14.95   **201.03**
1. Mythology—Dictionaries
ISBN 0-19-217747-8   LC 85-18941
First published 1979 in the United Kingdom; first United States edition, 1980
"Contains some five hundred brief entries for mythic figures and themes, arranged according to the seven 'great traditions of world mythology' (West Asia, South and Central Asia, East Asia, Europe, America, Africa, and Oceania). For each tradition there is an overview article of several pages that discusses the historical background of the area's mythology." Wilson Libr Bull [review of 1980 edition]

Encyclopedia of science and religion; J. Wentzel Vrede van Huyssteen, editor in chief. Macmillan Ref. 2003 2v set $280 *   **201.03**
1. Religion and science—Encyclopedias
ISBN 0-02-865704-7   LC 2002-152471
This reference "addresses the interactions, contradictions and tensions between science and religion, both historically and in contemporary life. The 2-vol. set examines technologies like in vitro fertilization, cloning, and continuing developments in neurophysiology against the backdrop of deeply-held religious beliefs. In addition, phenomena such as the Church of Scientology are also studied, along with more traditional issues, such as the origins of life, the nature of sin, and the philosophy of science and religion." Publisher's note
"Thousands of books have been written about the relationship between science and religion, but few can be characterized as reference resources. This two-volume set helps fill that niche with more than 400 scholarly articles written by experts from around the world." Libr J
Includes bibliographical references

Jordan, Michael
Dictionary of gods and goddesses. 2nd ed. Facts on File 2004 402p il (Facts on File library of religion and mythology) $45   **201.03**
1. Gods and goddesses—Dictionaries
ISBN 0-8160-5923-3   LC 2004-13028
First published 1993
The author's "alphabetical list includes gods and goddesses from a variety of religions. Each entry provides a brief description with cross-references where appropriate; some supply translations of the names. Longer entries include origin, dates of observance, synonyms, geographic location of the cult center, art references by type (e.g., stone carvings), and literary sources. . . . This [is] a usable, well-written resource for short descriptions of cross-cultural deities." Choice
Includes bibliographical references

Leeming, David Adams, 1937-
A dictionary of Asian mythology; [by] David Leeming. Oxford Univ. Press 2001 232p $39.95; pa $29   **201.03**
1. Asian mythology—Dictionaries 2. Asia—Religion—Dictionaries
ISBN 0-19-512052-3; 0-19-512053-1 (pa)
     LC 00-62389
"This concise dictionary references the mythologies of India, China, Tibet, Central and Southeast Asia, and Japan. The authoritative text is clearly written, thorough in coverage, and stylistically distinguished." Libr J
Includes bibliographical references

Mercatante, Anthony S.
The Facts on File encyclopedia of world mythology and legend; revised by James R. Dow. 2nd ed. Facts on File 2003 2v il (Facts on File library of religion and mythology) set $125
     201.03
1. Mythology—Dictionaries
ISBN 0-8160-4708-1   LC 2003-40262
First published 1988
New edition in preparation
"The entries discuss the folktales of both ancient and modern Eastern and Western cultures and clarify the relationship of these tales to the scriptural traditions of Buddhism, Hinduism, Judaism, Christianity, and Islam. Various botanical, zoological, and other references with mythical implications are . . . identified, and brief portraits of gods, heroes, demons, saints, and universal mythic figures are provided. . . . This reliable resource will be used by both students and scholars in public and academic libraries." Libr J
Includes bibliographical references

Shamanism; an encyclopedia of world beliefs, practices, and culture; edited by Mariko Namba Walter and Eva Jane Neumann Fridman. ABC-CLIO 2004 2v xxxi, 1055p il set $185
     201.03
1. Shamanism—Encyclopedias
ISBN 1-576-07645-8   LC 2004-20416
This encyclopedia "covers the earliest indications of shamanism, its historical development (including some of the field's major figures and issues), how it is practiced in particular societies and cultures, and its existence as a universal phenomenon. The volumes are divided into two sections. The first, 'General Themes in World Shamanism,' consists of over 50 entries ranging from 'Animal Symbolism (Africa)' to 'Witchcraft and Sorcery.' The second consists of 10 regional surveys of North, Central and South America, Europe, Africa, Asia and Australasia, and Oceania. . . . This is clearly, interestingly, and authoritatively written." Choice
Includes bibliographical references

203 Public worship and other practices

Davidson, Linda Kay
Pilgrimage: from the Ganges to Graceland: an encyclopedia; [by] Linda Kay Davidson and David M. Gitlitz. ABC-CLIO 2002 2v il maps set $185
203
1. Pilgrims and pilgrimages
ISBN 1-57607-004-2   LC 2002-10119
"Defining a pilgrimage site by 'its ability to attract a transient population of devotees,' this . . . encyclopedia surveys the world's major destinations, from Delphi to Stonewall Inn. Entries are alphabetical and in addition to the sites also profile prominent figures, belief systems, activities, and institutions." Libr J
"This splendid encyclopedia is a delight to read and pleasing to view." Booklist
Includes bibliographical references

Encyclopedia of religious rites, rituals, and festivals; Frank A. Salamone, editor. Routledge 2004 487p il (Routledge encyclopedias of religion and society) $150 *   **203**
1. Religions—Encyclopedias 2. Rites and ceremonies
ISBN 0-415-94180-6   LC 2003-20389
"A Berkshire Reference work"
"Articles describing types of practices common to many cultures treat such topics as death rituals, hunting rituals, puberty rites, and sport and ritual. Specific occasions that involve ceremonies include Divali, Easter, Ramadan, and Yom Kippur. Some practices like cannibalism, haircutting rituals, and snake handling are described in separate articles." SLJ
"The entries can be understood by readers unfamiliar with the topics covered, but the work is suitable for all levels of scholars." Choice
Includes bibliographical references

How to be a perfect stranger; the essential religious etiquette handbook; edited by Stuart M. Matlins & Arthur J. Magida. 4th ed. SkyLight Paths Pub. 2006 403p pa $19.99 *
203
1. Etiquette 2. Rites and ceremonies
ISBN 1-59473-140-3; 978-1-59473-140-2
First published 1996-1997 in two volumes by Jewish Lights Pub.
This guide "provides brief overviews of many religions: services, life-cycle events, home celebrations. It explains rituals so that those unfamiliar with them will know what to expect, how to dress, whether to bring a gift, and so on. It also has a glossary, explains various religious calendars, and lists religious festivals." Booklist [review of 1996-1997 edition]
Includes bibliographical references

Leeming, David Adams, 1937-
The Oxford companion to world mythology. Oxford University Press 2006 xxxvii, 469p $65 *
203
1. Mythology—Dictionaries
ISBN 0-19-515669-2   LC 2005-14216

"This volume presents approximately 2,000 concise entries in dictionary format. Leeming, . . . in an attempt to be 'inclusive and reasonably comprehensive,' ranges far outside the Western tradition to cover figures and folklore from Africa, Asia, and the Americas, as well as from the sacred narratives of religions. . . . Approximately 100 black-and-white illustrations, along with a few color plates, provide examples of artistic renderings of various myths. . . . This work should find a place in any general reference collection." Choice
Includes bibliographical references

Religious holidays and calendars; edited by Karen Bellenir. 3rd ed. Omnigraphics 2004 424p $84
*   **203**
1. Calendars 2. Religious holidays
ISBN 0-7808-0665-4   LC 2004-041500
Replaces the 2nd edition published 1997
First published 1993 under the editorship of Aidan A. Kelly, Peter Dresser, and Linda M. Ross
This "handbook provides an overview of the timekeeping and holiday traditions of the world's religions. Part 1 has four chapters that outline the history of calendars. Part 2 covers 24 religious groups in 17 chapters, each surveying the history of the religion, then listing it chronologically and describing the holidays it celebrates. The 28 contributors provide accurate information in readable, double-columned articles, ranging in length from 66 pages on types of Christianity to one on Scientology." Choice

204 Religious experience, life, practice

Colegate, Isabel
A pelican in the wilderness; hermits and solitaries. Counterpoint 2002 284 p il $25 hardcover o.p. pa $15.95   **204**
1. Hermits 2. Solitude
ISBN 1-58243-121-3; 1-58243-238-4 (pa)
LC 2001-47242
This "is a study of the soul that wants to be alone and knows how to do it; frequently met (so to say) in religion, the urge is also found in celebrities (J.D. Salinger, Howard Hughes)." N Y Times Book Rev

Coles, Robert
The spiritual life of children. Houghton Mifflin 1990 358p il pa $14 hardcover o.p. *
204
1. Children—Religious life
ISBN 0-395-59923-7 (pa)   LC 90-40097
"A Peter Davison book"
In this book the author presents "his research regarding children's understanding of and reflections on spiritual matters." Libr J
"One of the delights of his presentation is the combination of the children's searching comments and the struggle the author makes to hear beyond his own conceptions." J Youth Serv Libr
Includes bibliographical references

Schmidt, Leigh Eric
Restless souls; the making of American spirituality; [by] Leigh E. Schmidt. HarperSanFrancisco 2005 336p il $26.95

204

1. United States—Religion
ISBN 0-06-054566-6   LC 2005-46078
The author "examines the development of spirituality in American culture and explores its links to liberal progressivism and the religious left." Booklist
"This is recommended reading for anyone with an interest in American spirituality, and required reading for anyone who thinks spirituality was born after WWII with the baby boomers." Publ Wkly
Includes bibliographical references

Zaleski, Philip
Prayer; a history; [by] Philip Zaleski & Carol Zaleski. Houghton Mifflin Co. 2005 415p il $29.95 *

204

1. Prayer
ISBN 0-618-15288-1   LC 2005-12990
"From Ramses II's petitions invoking Amun's assistance in battle to Ansel Adams' photographs offered as an opus Dei, this . . . cultural history illumines the abiding influence of prayer in shaping human thought and behavior. . . . A much-needed study of a neglected topic." Booklist
Includes bibliographical references

208 Sources

Peters, F. E. (Francis E.)
The voice, the Word, the books; the sacred scripture of the Jews, Christians, and Muslims. Princeton University Press 2007 292p il $29.95

208

1. Sacred books
ISBN 978-0-691-13112-2; 0-691-13112-0
LC 2006-36912
The author "offers a volume on the history of the Hebrew Bible, the New Testament, and the Qur'an." Choice
"This is undoubtedly one of the best single volumes on the history of sacred text in the Abrahamic faiths, and many readers will find it an invaluable resource." Publ Wkly

209 Sects and reform movements

Belief beyond boundaries; Wicca, Celtic spirituality and the new age; edited by Joanne Pearson. Ashgate 2002 339p il maps (Religion today) $94.95; pa $29.95 *

209

1. Cults
ISBN 0-7546-0744-5; 0-7546-0820-4 (pa)
LC 2001-53654
This volume "explores 'religions' or forms of spirituality that tend to be marginal to the mainstream of British and North American religious expression. The book examines how alternative spiritualities traditionally classed as 'New Age' or new religious movements have grown exponentially in recent years. It progresses to detailed examination of Paganism, Celtic spirituality, Wicca, witchcraft, North American indigenous religion and New Age, considering the impact of the rise of science on religion and the emergence of new categories of spirituality." Publisher's note
"Though somewhat academic in tone, this is a solid overview of several New Age spiritual movements." Libr J
Includes bibliographical references

210 Philosophy & theory of religion

Huxley, Aldous, 1894-1963
The perennial philosophy. Harper & Row 1945 312p pa $14 hardcover o.p. *

210

1. Philosophy and religion 2. Religion—Philosophy
ISBN 0-06-057058-X (pa)
An anthology of and commentary on Chinese, Latin, Greek, Catholic and Protestant mysticism
Includes bibliographical references

James, William, 1842-1910
The varieties of religious experience; a study in human nature; introduction by Reinhold Niebuhr. Simon & Schuster 2004 398p pa $15 *

210

1. Religion—Philosophy 2. Psychology 3. Conversion
ISBN 978-0-7432-5787-9; 0-7432-5787-1
LC 2004-42870
"A Touchstone book"
First published 1902 by Longman
"Based on material James had collected on the psychology and philosophy of religion for lectures at the University of Edinburgh in 1901 and 1902. The varieties of religious experience contains numerous descriptions of religious states of consciousness, which James presented from a pragmatic point of view." HarperCollins Reader's Ency of Am Lit. 2nd edition
Includes bibliographical references

211 Concepts of God

Dawkins, Richard, 1941-
The God delusion. Houghton Mifflin Co. 2006 406p $27 *

211

1. Atheism 2. God 3. Religion
ISBN 978-0-618-68000-9; 0-618-68000-4
LC 2006-15506
The author examines "the major arguments for religion and [aims to] demonstrate the supreme improbability of a supreme being. He . . . [contends that] religion fuels war, foments bigotry, and abuses children. . . . [Dawkins argues that] belief in God is not just irrational, but potentially deadly." Publisher's note
"Both fans of Dawkins and his many opponents will want to read this book." Libr J
Includes bibliographical references

Jacoby, Susan
Freethinkers: a history of American secularism.
Metropolitan Books 2004 417p il $27.50; pa $16
211
1. Secularism
ISBN 0-8050-7442-2; 0-8050-7776-6 (pa)
LC 2003-59294
The author "chronicles 200 years of religious doubt in
the United States, including in her discussion many historical figures overlooked as freethinkers, such as Abraham Lincoln, Elizabeth Cady Stanton, and Robert Green
Ingersol." Libr J
"Enlightening, invigorating, and responsibly yet passionately argued, Jacoby's unparalleled history of American secularism offers a much needed perspective on today's most urgent social issues." Booklist
Includes bibliographical references

Stewart, Matthew
The courtier and the heretic; Leibniz, Spinoza,
and the fate of God in the modern world. Norton
2006 351p $25.95   **211**
1. Leibniz, Gottfried Wilhelm, Freiherr von, 1646-
1716 2. Spinoza, Benedictus de, 1632-1677 3. God
ISBN 0-393-05898-0   LC 2005-19962
In this history of the 1676 meeting between the two
philosophers, the author "chronicles the events and arguments linking the illustrious German polymath to the
controversial Dutch lens grinder. . . . The drama Stewart
recounts will rivet readers skeptical and devout alike."
Booklist
Includes bibliographical references

Turner, James, 1946-
Without God, without creed; the origins of
unbelief in America. Johns Hopkins Univ. Press
1985 316p (New studies in American intellectual
and cultural history) pa $20.95 hardcover o.p.
211
1. Religion 2. Faith
ISBN 0-8018-3407-4 (pa)   LC 84-15397
The author traces the development of agnosticism and
atheism in the United States
"Mr. Turner allows us to see clearly the decline of
transcendental Christianity and its replacement by ever
softer religions and ever harder systems of social metaphysics." N Y Times Book Rev
Includes bibliographical references

215   Science and religion

Campbell, Jeremy, 1931-
The many faces of God; science's 400-year
quest for images of the divine. W.W. Norton &
Co. 2006 314p $26.95   **215**
1. Religion and science 2. God
ISBN 978-0-393-06179-6; 0-393-06179-5
LC 2006-17845
The author "illuminates the ways in which science has
recast the meaning of religious faith. . . . An essential
acquisition." Booklist
Includes bibliographical references

Collins, Francis S.
The language of God; a scientist presents
evidence for belief. Free Press 2006 294p il $26
215
1. Religion and science 2. Apologetics
ISBN 0-7432-8639-1; 978-0-7432-8639-8
LC 2006-45316
The author "entertains propositions both for and
against the existence of God and biblical authority, as
well as the moral implications of bioethics. He personalizes the narrative by recounting his own journey from
atheism to faith, portraying it as much an intellectual
quest as a spiritual one. . . . An essential read, equally
for readers of religious or secular persuasions." Libr J
Includes bibliographical references

Sagan, Carl, 1934-1996
The varieties of scientific experience; a personal
view of the search for God; edited by Ann
Druyan. Penguin Press 2006 284p il $27.95
215
1. Natural theology 2. Religion and science
ISBN 1-59420-107-2; 978-1-59420-107-3
LC 2006-44827
The author's 1985 Gifford lectures
In this collection of lectures, the author discusses "the
relationship between religion and science and his person-
al search for God." Publisher's note
"Even readers who turn elsewhere for a fuller under-
standing of religion will appreciate Sagan's passion for
a science that teaches us to look up." Booklist
Includes bibliographical references

Smith, Huston
Why religion matters; the fate of the human
spirit in an age of disbelief. HarperSanFrancisco
2001 290p pa $14.95 hardcover o.p.   **215**
1. Religion and science
ISBN 0-06-067102-5 (pa)   LC 00-58188
"Smith claims humanity is in the grip of a spiritual
crisis. The cause: scientism, the modern belief, enforced
by education and law, that the scientific method is the
most reliable path to truth and that the material entities
science deals with are the only things that exist. . . .
What {Smith} opposes is the extension of scientific conclusions into areas of human experience about which,
{he believes}, science can tell us nothing." Chirst Sci
Monit

220   Bible

Jacobs, A. J., 1968-
The year of living biblically; one man's humble
quest to follow the Bible as literally as possible.
Simon & Schuster 2007 388p il $25   **220**
1. Bible—Criticism
ISBN 978-0-7432-9147-7; 0-7432-9147-6
LC 2007-09573
For this book, the author turned "himself from a guy
who is 'Jewish in the way the Olive Garden is an Italian
restaurant' into a follower of 'the ultimate biblical life.'

Jacobs, A. J., 1968-—*Continued*

This means spending a year strictly following a typed list of more than 700 biblical rules, including the obscure (don't wear garments of mixed fibers, bind money to your hand, pay the wages of your workers every day) and the potentially awkward (don't touch your wife seven days after her 'discharge of blood,' bathe after sex and don't tell lies, in their many variations)." N Y Times Book Rev

"Throughout his journey, Jacobs comes across as a generous and thoughtful (and, yes, slightly neurotic) participant observer, lacing his story with absurdly funny cultural commentary as well as nuanced insights into the impossible task of biblical literalism." Publ Wkly

Includes bibliographical references

The **Oxford** illustrated history of the Bible; edited by John Rogerson. Oxford Univ. Press 2001 395p il $40 *   **220**

1. Bible—History
ISBN 0-19-860118-2   LC 2001-272513

This volume offers an "overview of the origins of the Bible we know (consisting of the Old and New Testaments and the Apocrypha), the transmission and translation of the texts, and the historical and contemporary interpretation and influence of the Bible. Enhancing this overview are numerous color and black-and-white illustrations." Libr J

Includes bibliographical references

Pelikan, Jaroslav Jan, 1923-2006

Whose Bible is it? a history of the Scriptures through the ages; [by] Jaroslav Pelikan. Viking 2004 274p il $24.95 *   **220**

1. Bible—History
ISBN 0-670-03385-5   LC 2004-58049

"Beginning with the ancient oral traditions surrounding Abraham and Moses, Pelikan recounts how the early Israelites finally recorded their beliefs in a Hebrew text." Booklist

The author "offers a masterly overview of [the] complex development of the Bible over the ages. . . . This engaging, concise, and highly readable work demonstrates that the most influential book in Western civilization has always held different meanings for different peoples." Christ Sci Monit

Includes bibliographical references

220.1 Bible—Origins and authenticity

Sheler, Jeffery L.

Is the Bible true? how modern debates and discoveries affirm the essence of the Scriptures. HarperSanFrancisco 1999 278p pa $15 hardcover o.p.   **220.1**

1. Jesus Christ—Historicity 2. Bible—History of contemporary events
ISBN 0-06-0675420-X (pa)   LC 99-16882

The author explores the "reliability of the Bible as a historical source. Drawing on both the literature and personal interviews with leading scholars he describes the

history of biblical interpretation and research, the evidence of archaeology, the nature and relevance of the Dead Sea Scrolls, and the three 'quests for the historical Jesus.'" Libr J

Includes bibliographical references

220.3 Bible—Encyclopedias and topical dictionaries

The **Anchor** Yale Bible dictionary; David Noel Freedman, editor-in-chief; associate editors, Gary A. Herion, David F. Graf, John David Pleins; managing editor, Astrid B. Beck. Yale University Press 1992 6v il map set $510

                                         220.3

1. Bible—Dictionaries
ISBN 978-0-300-14081-1; 0-300-14081-9

                                    LC 91-8385

First published 1992 by Doubleday with title: The Anchor Bible dictionary

"The 6,000 separate subject entries reflect many of the changes that have taken place in biblical research over the last 30 years. . . . There are individual entries for all the different books of the Bible, major figures, places, names, and biblical terms. Substantial bibliographies and numerous cross references enhance the usefulness of this as a reference source." Am Libr

"With its sound scholarship, good organization, and readable prose, the ABD deserves a place in all academic and public libraries." Libr J

Eerdmans dictionary of the Bible; David Noel Freedman, editor-in-chief; Allen C. Myers, associate editor; Astrid B. Beck, managing editor. Eerdmans 2000 xxxiii, 1425p il maps $45   **220.3**

1. Bible—Dictionaries
ISBN 0-8028-2400-5   LC 00-56124

This "dictionary contains nearly 5,000 alphabetically ordered articles by 600 biblical scholars on the books, persons, places and significant terms found in the Bible." America

"Up-to-date, comprehensive, and well written, the *EDB* is highly recommended." Libr J

Includes bibliographical references

The **HarperCollins** Bible dictionary; general editor, Paul J. Achtemeier; associate editors, Roger S. Boraas [et al.] with the Society of Biblical Literature. HarperSanFrancisco 1996 xxiv, 1256p il $47   **220.3**

1. Bible—Dictionaries
ISBN 0-06-060037-3   LC 96-25424

First published 1985 with title: Harper's Bible dictionary

This volume features a "two-column format, with 16 single-column articles interspersed throughout (including 'Art in the Biblical Period,' 'Jesus Christ,' and 'The temple'), and it is well illustrated. Many of the longer articles include a brief bibliography. . . . Though not a flawless work (e.g., the article 'Manasseh' treats only the 14th king of Judah but neither the patriarch nor the tribe of Israel that also bear the name), it is outstanding in terms of scholarship and writing." Libr J

The **New** Interpreter's dictionary of the Bible; [edited by Katharine Doob Sakenfeld et al.] Abingdon Press 2006-2008 3v il map ea $80

220.3

1. Bible—Encyclopedias
ISBN 0-687-05427-3 (v1); 978-0-687-05427-5 (v1); 978-0-687-33355-4 (v2); 0-687-33355-5 (v2); 978-0-687-33365-3 (v3); 0-687-33365-2 (v3)

LC 2006-025839

First published 1962-1976 under the editorship of George A. Buttrick with title: The Interpreter's dictionary of the Bible

Volumes 1-3 edited by Katharine Doob Sakenfeld. Volumes 4 and 5 in preparation. Supplementary volume published 1976 and edited by Keith Crim, available separately for $45 (ISBN 0-687-19269-2; 978-0-687-19269-4)

"A scholarly encyclopedic dictionary designed for the preacher, scholar, student, teacher, and general reader, referring to both the King James Version and the Revised Standard Version, to the Apocrypha, the Pseudepigrapha, the Dead Sea Scrolls, and other ancient manuscripts. . . . Important for modern biblical study." (Guide to Ref Books. 11th edition) Guide to Ref Books. 11th edition

Includes bibliographical references

The **Oxford** companion to the Bible; edited by Bruce M. Metzger, Michael D. Coogan. Oxford Univ. Press 1993 xxi, 874p il map $70

220.3

1. Bible—Dictionaries 2. Bible (as subject)—Dictionaries
ISBN 0-19-504645-5   LC 93-19315

This volume "contains more than 700 signed entries treating the formation, transmission, circulation, sociohistorical situation, interpretation, theology, uses, and influence of the Bible." Libr J

"The many contributors read as a veritable who's who among biblical scholars. Although this companion is not meant to be an exhaustive reference, it is a highly reliable guide." Booklist

220.5   Bible—Modern versions and translations

Bible.

The Bible: Authorized King James Version; with an introduction and notes by Robert Carroll and Stephen Prickett. Oxford University Press 1998 lxxiv, 1039, 248, 445p il, maps (Oxford world's classics) pa $18.95 *   **220.5**

ISBN 0-19-283525-4; 978-0-19-283525-3

LC 96-28858

"Reissued as an Oxford world's classics paperback 1998" Verso of title page

The authorized or King James Version originally published 1611.

Includes bibliographical references

Good news Bible; today's English version. American Bible Soc. $10.99   **220.5**

ISBN 978-1-58516-154-6; 1-58516-154-3

"Begun in 1964 with the Gospel of Mark, The New Testament was completed in 1966, with rev. eds. in 1971 and 1976. The whole Bible was published in 1976. An extremely popular, inexpensive translation using contemporary American English. . . . Especially useful for youth or lay Bible study as well as for private reading." Bollier. Lit of Theology

The HarperCollins study Bible; New Revised Standard Version, including the Apocraphal/Deuterocanonical books with concordance; general editor, revised edition, Harold W. Attridge; general editor, original edition, Wayne A. Meeks; associate editors, Jouette M. Bassler [et al.] with the Society of Biblical Literature. Fully rev and updated. HarperSanFrancisco 2006 lxvi, 2204p il map $44.95   **220.5**

ISBN 978-0-06-078685-4; 0-06-078685-X

LC 2007-277226

First published 1993

"This edition of the Bible—newly annotated by the Society of Biblical Studies—is definitely for a wide audience. It is interdenominational, incorporates the latest in biblical scholarship, and is sensitive to unnecessary gender specificity." Booklist

The Holy Bible; containing the Old and New Testaments with the Apocryphal/Deuterocanonical books: New Revised Standard Version. Oxford University Press 1989 xxi, 996, 298, 284p map $29.99 *   **220.5**

ISBN 0-19-528330-9; 978-0-19-528330-3

LC 90-222105

"Intended for public reading, congregational worship, private study, instruction, and meditation, it attempts to be as literal as possible while following standard American English usage, avoids colloquialism, and prefers simple, direct terms and phrases." Sheehy. Guide to Ref Books. 10th edition. suppl

The Holy Bible; updated New American Standard Bible: containing the Old Testament and the New Testament. Zondervan Pub. House 1999 1263p map $24.99   **220.5**

ISBN 978-0-310-93127-0; 0-310-93127-4

LC 98-61548

Title on cover: NASB Classic Reference Bible

This translation, completed 1971, is a modernization of the American Standard Version of 1901

The New American Bible; translated from the original languages with critical use of all the ancient sources including the revised Psalms and the revised New Testament; authorized by the Board of Trustees of the Confraternity of Christian Doctrine and approved by the Administrative Committee Board of the National Conference of Catholic Bishops and the United States Catholic Conference. Oxford University Press 2006 c2005 xxiii, 1514p $39.99 *   **220.5**

ISBN 978-0-19-528900-8; 0-19-528900-5

First published 1970 by Kenedy

"Roman Catholic version based on modern English translations; replaces the Douay edition." N Y Public Libr Book of How & Where to Look It Up

Bible.—*Continued*

The new Jerusalem Bible; [general editor: Henry Wansbrough] Doubleday 1985 2108p map $45; pa $29.95 *   **220.5**

    ISBN   0-385-14264-1;   978-0-385-14264-9; 0-385-24833-4 (pa); 978-0-385-24833-4 (pa)

                                   LC 85-16070

    First published in this format 1966 with title: The Jerusalem Bible

    "Derives from the French version edited at the Dominican Ecole Biblique de Jerusalem and known as 'La Bible de Jerusalem.' The introductions and notes are 'a direct translation from the French, though revised and brought up to date in some places' but translation of the Biblical text goes back to the original languages." Guide to Ref Books. 11th edition

The new Oxford annotated Bible; new revised standard version. Oxford Univ. Press 2007 2048p pa $42.99   **220.5**

    ISBN 978-0-19-528875-9; 0-19-528875-0

    Also available with the Apocrypha $45 (ISBN 978-0-19-52880-3)

    This study Bible incorporates the full text of the New revised standard version translation, with cross-referenced annotations, a collection of essays and introductions, and a section of maps

The Oxford study Bible; Revised English Bible with the Apocrypha; edited by M. Jack Suggs, Katharine Doob Sakenfeld, James R. Mueller. Oxford University Press 1992 xxviii, 199, 1597p map hardcover o.p. pa $34.99   **220.5**

    ISBN 0-19-529001-1; 0-19-529000-3 (pa)

                                   LC 92-137886

    A revised edition of The new English Bible, published 1970

    An annotated version of the Revised English Bible. "This volume combines a cultural guide to the biblical world and an annotated Bible. Its notes feature the reflections of Protestant, Roman Catholic, and Jewish scholars." Publisher's note

Cruden, Alexander, 1701-1770

Cruden's Complete concordance; with index to proper names and their meanings; edited by A.D. Adams, C.H. Irwin, S.A. Waters. Zondervan Pub. House 1968 803p (Zondervan classic reference series) $24.99; pa $8.99 *   **220.5**

    1. Bible—Concordances

    ISBN 0-310-22920-0; 0-310-48971-7 (pa)

    Also available in hardcover from Hendrickson Publishers

    "Notes and biblical proper names under one alphabetical arrangement plus a list of proper names with a foreword by Dr. Walter L. Wilson"

    First edition 1737. Frequently revised

    "The special value of this title is that Cruden provides an index to the Apocrypha. Note that some reprints of the work omit the Apocrypha in the concordance." Ref Sources for Small & Medium-sized Libr. 5th edition

Daniell, David

The Bible in English. Yale University Press 2003 xx, 899p $40   **220.5**

    1. Bible—History 2. Bible—Versions

    ISBN 0-300-09930-4   LC 2002-153177

    "This book is a vibrant history of the more than 350 English translations of the Bible and what they meant to their translators, readers, and times. The fascinating story ranges from the translations of William Tyndale (who was martyred in 1536 for his work), to Coverdale's translation, the Geneva Bibles, the King James Bible, and the many American translations in the twentieth century." Univ Press Books for Public and Second Sch Libr, 2004

    Includes bibliographical references

Nicolson, Adam, 1957-

God's secretaries: the making of the King James Bible. HarperCollins Pubs. 2003 280p il $24.95 *   **220.5**

    1. James I, King of Great Britain, 1566-1625 2. Bible—History

    ISBN 0-06-018516-3

    First published in the United Kingdom with title: Power and glory

    "The English Bible that King James I commissioned in 1604 really was committee work. Each of six committees, or companies, as they were called, was charged with translating a different portion of the original Hebrew and Greek texts. . . . Their handiwork was to be the preferred pulpit Bible, so it had to be accessible in vocabulary and tonally. In that respect, the Translators succeeded so brilliantly that their style remains the quintessence of sacred prose to this day. . . . Nicolson tells the KJV's story so well that his book may prove to be the KJV's indispensable companion for years to come." Booklist

    Includes bibliographical references

Seek, find; the Bible for all people: Contemporary English Version. G.P. Putnam's Sons/American Bible Society 2006 1725p $24.95; pa $15.95 *   **220.5**

    ISBN   0-399-15385-3;   978-0-399-15385-3; 0-399-15397-7 (pa); 978-0-399-15397-6 (pa)

    "The CEV was published by the American Bible Society in response to an urgent need for a translation that would reach those many millions who are not reading the Bible. The goal was a serious translation—not a paraphrase—combining historical and scholarly accuracy with contemporary language that everyone can understand." Publisher's note

Strong, James, 1822-1894

The strongest Strong's exhaustive concordance of the Bible. 21st century ed, fully rev and corrected by John R. Kohlenberger III and James A. Swanson. Zondervan 2001 1742p maps $34.99   **220.5**

    1. Bible—Concordances

    ISBN 0-310-23343-7   LC 2001-26577

    A version of Strong's exhaustive concordance of the Bible originally published 1894

Strong, James, 1822-1894—*Continued*

"Kohlenberger has teamed with James A. Swanson to produce a volume that cross-indexes a . . . database with exhaustive Hebrew and Greek dictionaries and adds *Nave's Topical Bible Reference System* (essentially a Bible dictionary with subjects, persons, places, and biblical books in alphabetical order). . . . Charts plot the chronology of events in the Old and New Testament, miracles and parables of Jesus, and messianic prophecies. There is a harmony (parallels) of gospel stories, lists of biblical kings, weights and measures, Old Testament feasts, sacred days, sacrifices, and the major social concerns of the Mosaic Covenant. There is also a chart of the Hebrew Calendar. The work is based on the King James Version of the Bible and is generally conservative." Am Ref Books Annu, 2003

220.6 Bible—Interpretation and criticism (Exegesis)

Bowker, John, 1935-

The complete Bible handbook; an illustrated companion. DK Pub. 1998 544p il maps $39.95; pa $25   **220.6**
 1. Bible—Commentaries
 ISBN 0-7894-3568-3; 0-7894-8154-5 (pa)
                                              LC 98-4478
In this volume "every book of the Bible (including Jewish Apocrypha) has its own entry, and there are supplementary entries on specific stories, theological concerns, history (Routes of the Exodus), or background (Gods and Goddesses of the Ancient Near East). In his introduction, Bowker presents a well-balanced summary of the Bible as a piece of literature and as scripture in our time and in history. . . . One of the book's strengths is its abundance of pictures." Voice Youth Advocates
 Includes bibliographical references

Davis, Kenneth C.

Don't know much about the Bible; everything you need to know about the Good Book but never learned. Avon Books 1999 xxiv, 533p map pa $14.95   **220.6**
 1. Bible—Introductions 2. Bible—Study and teaching
 ISBN 978-0-380-72839-8; 0-380-72839-7
First published 1998 by Eagle Brook/William Morrow
 "David analyzes the Bible book by book, asking and answering a succession of perplexing questions. . . . In addition, he also traces the actual evolution of the Good Book itself, placing many biblical stories more firmly in historical context. Brimming with fascinating facts and fresh interpretations." Booklist
 Includes bibliographical references

220.7 Bible—Commentaries

The **HarperCollins** Bible commentary; general editor, James L. Mays; associate editors, Joseph Blenkinsopp {et al.}; with the Society of Biblical Literature. rev ed. HarperSanFrancisco 2000 xxvi, 1203p il $49.50 *   **220.7**
 1. Bible—Commentaries
 ISBN 0-06-065548-8   LC 00-20818

First published 1988 with title: Harper's Bible commentary

This "covers all of the Hebrew Bible, as well as the books of the Apocrypha and those of the New Testament. . . . [It includes] general essays setting the literary, cultural, and historical context for the entire Bible; articles introducing major sections of the Bible {and} commentaries on the individual books themselves." Publisher's note

This work is "outstanding in terms of scholarship and writing." Libr J

Includes bibliographical references

Oxford Bible commentary; edited by John Barton and John Muddiman. Oxford Univ. Press 2001 xxv, 1386p maps $79.95 *   **220.7**
 1. Bible—Commentaries
 ISBN 0-19-875500-7   LC 2001-21139
A team of scholars "examine the books of the Bible . . . taking a historical-critical approach that attempts to shed light on the scriptures by placing them in the context in which their first audiences would have encountered them, asking how they came to be composed and what were the purposes of their authors." Publisher's note

"An international, interfaith group of scholars is responsible for this rich, far-reaching commentary, which is most profitably studied alongside a copy of the New Revised Standard Version upon which it is based." Choice

Includes bibliographical references

Reader's digest complete guide to the Bible; an illustrated book-by-book companion to the Scriptures. Reader's Digest Assn. 1998 448p il maps $29.95   **220.7**
 1. Bible—Commentaries
 ISBN 0-7621-0073-7   LC 98-6836
This volume describes events, people, and themes of the Bible, and includes approximately 400 color illustrations and 25 maps and charts.

220.8 Nonreligious subjects treated in Bible

Murphy, Cullen

The Word according to Eve; women and the Bible in ancient times and our own. Houghton Mifflin 1998 302p $24; pa $14   **220.8**
 1. Bible—Criticism 2. Women in the Bible 3. Feminism
 ISBN 0-395-70113-9; 0-618-00192-1 (pa)
                                              LC 98-18015
"A Peter Davison book"
This is an examination of feminist Biblical scholarship. Murphy "divides his study into Old Testament scholarship and New Testament and early church history." N Y Times Book Rev
 Includes bibliographical references

220.9   Bible—Geography, history, chronology, persons of Bible lands in Bible times

Calvocoressi, Peter
Who's who in the Bible. New illustrated ed., rev. ed. Penguin Books 1999 xxiii, 200p il map (Penguin reference books) pa $19.95

220.9

1. Bible—Biography
ISBN 0-14-051426-0   LC 00-266958
First published 1987
"This work provides profiles, ranging in length from a sentence to several pages, of some 450 biblical characters. It is unusual in discussing the literature, visual arts, and music associated with many of these characters." Libr J [review of 1987 edition]

Deen, Edith
All of the women of the Bible. Harper & Row 1955 xxii, 410p pa $19 hardcover o.p.

220.9

1. Bible—Biography 2. Women in the Bible
ISBN 0-06-061852-3 (pa)
"Good or bad, they are all here: three hundred and sixteen of them. They are not vague historical personages but living women whom we get to know well. Most of the portraits are preceded by the Bible chapters and verses which are the sources and by an outline sketch that establishes the background." Cincinnati Public Libr

The **HarperCollins** concise atlas of the Bible; edited by James B. Pritchard. HarperSanFrancisco 1997 c1991 151p il maps pa $25 *   220.9
1. Bible—Geography
ISBN 0-06-251499-7
First published 1991 with title: The Harper concise atlas of the Bible
Based upon Harper atlas of the Bible (1987)
This atlas offers "access to the current knowledge of the historical geography of the Bible. . . . The arrangement is chronological, and uses maps, charts, and artwork to visually stimulate its multidisciplinary text." Libr J

Kee, Howard Clark
The Cambridge companion to the Bible; Bruce Chilton, general editor; Howard Clark Kee . . . [et al.] 2nd ed. Cambridge University Press 2008 724p il $100; pa $34.99   220.9
1. Bible—History of Biblical events
ISBN 978-0-521-86997-3; 978-0-521-69140-6 (pa)
       LC 2008-270190
First published 1997
"This work offers materials that are designed to give background to and interpretations of the canonical and apocryphal books of the Old and New Testaments as well as of selected pseudographical books. Four specialists present their ideas in four main subdivisions: intro-

duction, Old Testament world, Jewish responses to Greco-Roman culture, and formation of the Christian community." Libr J [review of 1997 edition]
"This is an excellent, single-volume resource for serious students of the Bible. . . . The text is generally accessible; extensive maps and illustrations add to its popular appeal." Bookist [review of 1997 edition]
Includes bibliographical references

Oxford Bible atlas; edited by Adrian Curtis. 4th ed. Oxford University Press 2007 229p il map $35   220.9
1. Bible—Geography
ISBN 0-19-100158-9; 978-0-19-100158-1
First published 1962
This atlas includes "81 full-color illustrations as well as 27 maps—e.g., of Jerusalem and the Holy Land, the Middle East and the eastern Mediterranean lands—all with terrain modeling. The text is divided into four main sections: 'The Setting,' 'The Hebrew Bible,' 'The New Testament,' and 'Archaeology in Bible Lands.' . . . [This is] a handsome background resource for Bible study." Libr J
Includes bibliographical references

The **Oxford** history of the biblical world; edited by Michael D. Coogan. Oxford Univ. Press 1998 643p il maps $60; pa $19.95
     220.9
1. Bible—History of biblical events 2. Ancient civilization
ISBN 0-19-508707-0; 0-19-513937-2 (pa)
       LC 98-16042
"Organized chronologically, the essays explore the many cultures of ancient Canaan, Israel, Judea, and Palestine from 10,000 B.C.E. to the rise of Islam in the seventh century C.E. Illustrations, maps, charts, chronologies, and bibliographies enhance the uniformly well-written essays. But the strengths of the work are its currency and breadth of coverage and perspective." Libr J
Includes bibliographical references

Tischler, Nancy M., 1931-
Men and women of the Bible; a readers guide. Greenwood Press 2002 267p il $59.95
     220.9
1. Bible—Biography
ISBN 0-313-31714-3   LC 2002-75347
This resource provides "information on 100 biblical characters and their cultural significance in Western civilization. . . . Entries are arranged alphabetically from *Aaron* to *Zephaniah*, concisely written, and adhere to a uniform pattern. Subjects are listed by name with the addition of etymological information. A synopsis of the relevant biblical story follows, utilizing the King James version of the Bible. . . . The author also includes information on each person as a character in later works, including Western literature, legend, and painting." Booklist
Includes bibliographical references

Women in scripture; a dictionary of named and unnamed women in the Hebrew Bible, the Apocryphal\Deuterocanonical books, and the New Testament; Carol Meyers, general editor; Toni Craven and Ross S. Kraemer, associate editors. Eerdmans Pub. 2001 592p il pa $50 *

220.9

1. Bible—Biography 2. Women in the Bible
ISBN 978-0-8028-4962-5; 0-8028-4962-8
First published 2000 by Houghton Mifflin
This "reference describes every woman in Jewish and Christian scripture—with or without names—plus female dieties and personifications. . . . Frequent cross-referencing and bibliographical suggestions enrich the entries. Useful essays on biblical scholarship, biblical literature, and biblical naming enhance the volume." Libr J
Includes bibliographical references

221.5 Bible. Old Testament—Modern versions

Bible. O.T.
The Old Testament: King James Version; with an introduction by George Steiner. Knopf 1996 li, 1382p $35 *

221.5

ISBN 0-679-45102-1   LC 96-22789
"Everyman's library"
An edition of the classic translation of the Old Testament into the language of seventeenth-century England. Steiner's introduction provides a look at the historical, social, political, literary and philosophical impact of the King James version

Tanakh; a new translation of the Holy Scriptures according to the traditional Hebrew text. Jewish Publ. Soc. 1985 xxvi, 1624p $35; pa $22 *

221.5

ISBN 0-8276-0252-9; 0-8276-0366-5 (pa)
LC 85-10006
Also available in other bindings and editions
This volume represents a "collaboration between rabbis from the Orthodox, Conservative, and Reform branches of Judaism, and scholars in Semitic languages and biblical studies. The translators relied on the Hebrew tenth-century Masoretic text that is Judaism's standard. The Torah, Prophets, and Writings are here in a single volume." Publisher's note

221.6 Bible. Old Testament—Interpretation and criticism

Kugel, James L.
How to read the Bible; a guide to scripture, then and now. Free Press 2007 819p il map $35

221.6

1. Bible. O.T. —Criticism
ISBN 978-0-7432-3586-0; 0-7432-3586-X
LC 2007-23466

This book presents a "look at the work of today's scholars, together with a . . . consideration of what the Bible was for most of its history—before the rise of modern scholarship." Publisher's note
"Kugel has written a wonderful book, one that lays bare the worlds both of modem biblical scholarship and of ancient biblical interpretation with wit and erudition." Commentary
Includes bibliographical references

Levin, Christoph, 1950-
The Old testament; a brief introduction; translated by Margaret Kohl. Princeton University Press 2005 191p $22.95

221.6

1. Bible. O.T.
ISBN 0-691-11394-7   LC 2004-58693
The author "begins with the post-exilic writings and reads back into the Old Testament story the insights gained during the important period of Israel's captivity in Babylon, and its subsequent return to Jerusalem. . . . This is a fine introduction to the study of the Old Testament." Publ Wkly
Includes bibliographical references

Telushkin, Joseph, 1948-
Biblical literacy; the most important people, events, and ideas of the Hebrew Bible. Morrow 1997 xxviii, 628p $29.95

221.6

1. Bible. O.T. —Criticism 2. Jewish ethics
ISBN 0-688-14297-4   LC 97-6645
This volume is "intended as a reference work, to be used as an introduction to the weekly readings that are a part of Jewish Sabbath worship services. . . . The book is divided into three parts. . . . The first, titled 'People and Events,' takes up more than half the book. These are . . . chapter by chapter summaries of the Old Testament, in order of their appearance in the Jewish canon. Most of the summaries end with a short section titled 'Reflections.'" Christ Sci Monit
"Biblical truths that many a reader may have glossed over before stand out, thanks to this superb book, and, more important, misunderstandings are cleared up and previously mistranslated words correctly rendered." Booklist
Includes bibliographical references

222 Historical books of Old Testament

Armstrong, Karen
In the beginning; a new interpretation of Genesis. Knopf 1996 195p pa $14 hardcover o.p.

222

1. Bible. O.T. Genesis—Criticism
ISBN 0-345-40604-4 (pa)   LC 96-26170
Armstrong "interprets selected accounts of Genesis using an archetypal approach to literature so as to offer insights into the problematic nature of human religion, especially the problems of separation between humans and God. . . . The text of Genesis (NRSV) makes up a third of the book's volume." Libr J
Includes bibliographical references

Bible. O.T. Pentateuch.

The book of J; translated from the Hebrew by David Rosenberg; interpreted by Harold Bloom. Vintage Books 1991 340p pa $12   **222**

1. Bible. O.T. —Criticism

ISBN 0-679-73624-7; 978-0-679-73624-0

First published 1990 by Grove Weidenfeld

This volume "contains three works: David Rosenberg's translation of those parts of the Pentateuch that have been attributed to the J Writer (most of Genesis and Exodus, parts of Numbers and Deuteronomy), Bloom's introduction, and, following the translation, his [commentary]." Voice Lit Suppl

The five books of Moses; a translation with commentary; {by} Robert Alter. Norton 2004 xlviii, 1064p map $39.95 *   **222**

ISBN 0-393-01955-1   LC 2004-14067

In "this new translation of the first five books of the Bible {Alter} . . . seeks to reproduce as faithfully as possible in standard English the nuances, literary devices, and metaphors of the original Hebrew text. In doing so, he aims to show where many modern translations (including the King James Bible) have failed to represent the original Hebrew's varied nuances. In his commentary, found in the introductions to each book and on many individual verses, Alter expounds the theological meaning of the text's narrative in its larger biblical context." Libr J

Includes bibliographical references

The five books of Moses; Genesis, Exodus, Leviticus, Numbers, Deuteronomy; a new translation with introductions, notes, and commentary by Everett Fox. Schocken Bks. 1995 xxxi, 1024p pa $27.50 hardcover o.p.   **222**

ISBN 0-8052-1119-5 (pa)   LC 95-10143

Fox's "introductions propose and outline a literary structure for each book, his commentary {addresses} . . . thematic and structural characteristics of the text, {and} his . . . notes point out linguistic features and cruxes and the interpretive issues that surround them." N Y Times Book Rev

This translation "captures the beautiful, majestic, and dynamic character of biblical Hebrew. . . . An essential purchase for all libraries." Libr J

The Torah: the five books of Moses; a new translation of the Holy Scriptures according to the Masoretic text; first section. Jewish Publ. Soc. 1963 393p $20; pa $15 *   **222**

ISBN 0-8276-0015-1; 0-8276-0680-X (pa)

This "translation of Genesis, Exodus, Leviticus, Numbers, and Deuteronomy was prepared . . . to present a version of the Bible that takes into account modern insights and knowledge of ancient times. . . . Of chief value to persons of the Jewish religion but of interest to Bible scholars of any religion." Booklist

Dershowitz, Alan M.

The Genesis of justice; ten stories of biblical injustice that led to the Ten Commandments and modern law. Warner Bks. 2000 273p $28; pa $14.95   **222**

1. Bible. O.T. Genesis—Criticism 2. Justice

ISBN 0-446-52479-4; 0-446-67677-2 (pa)

LC 99-50220

"The narratives deal with Adam and Eve, Cain and Abel, Abraham, Lot, Jacob, Dina, Tamar and Joseph. Dershowitz includes a translation of each story, recounts some theological commentaries and offers his own interpretations." Publ Wkly

"For believers of all faiths, as well as nonbelievers, this is an outstanding work." Libr J

Includes bibliographical references

Feiler, Bruce S.

Abraham; a journey to the heart of three faiths; [by] Bruce Feiler. Morrow 2002 224p $23.95; pa $12.95   **222**

1. Abraham (Biblical figure)

ISBN 0-380-97776-1; 0-06-052509-6 (pa)

LC 2002-70309

"Feiler explores how Christian, Judaic, and Islamic understandings of Abraham, a patriarch to all three faiths, express interfaith disagreements. On the way to a passionate, prayerful argument for interfaith peace, Feiler mixes theological meditation, adventurous travelogue, and sly wit." Booklist

Friedman, Richard Elliott

Who wrote the Bible? HarperSanFrancisco 1997 299p il map pa $15.95   **222**

1. Bible. O.T. Pentateuch—Criticism

ISBN 978-0-06-063035-5; 0-06-063035-3

First published 1987 by Prentice Hall

The author describes the documentary hypothesis in Bible exegesis which ascribes the Torah to four sources: "J" (the Yahwist), "E" (the Elohist), "P" (the priestly writer), and "D" (the Deuteronomist). He then attempts to discover the authors of the four documents. Friedman "turns a potentially dry scholarly inquiry into a lively detective story. . . . This book is neither comprehensive nor unduly complex, making it a good introductory text for beginners and nonspecialists." Libr J

Includes bibliographical references

Kass, Leon

The beginning of wisdom; reading Genesis; [by] Leon R. Kass. Free Press 2003 576p $35

222

1. Bible. O.T. Genesis—Criticism

ISBN 0-7432-4299-8   LC 2002-45593

The author "sees Genesis as a text that offers wisdom about the nature of man and how we ought to live, while it also calls for interpretation, reflection, and judgment. . . . Kass presents many enlightening insights, the result of his attempts to understand the text on its own terms and relating it to contemporary concerns, especially tradition and parenthood. While not everyone will agree with his interpretations, which tend to the conservative, Kass

Kass, Leon—*Continued*
offers much to be pondered by thoughtful readers, both academics and, especially, educated laypeople." Libr J
Includes bibliographical references

Klinghoffer, David
The discovery of God; Abraham and the birth of monotheism. Doubleday 2003 348p map $26; pa $14.95 **222**
1. Abraham (Biblical figure) 2. Bible. O.T. —History of Biblical events 3. Monotheism
ISBN 0-385-49973-6; 0-385-49974-4 (pa)
LC 2002-31566
The author "edifies the reader with examples of how Abraham was taught to bring humankind closer to the One God. . . . Klinghoffer concludes that Abraham discovered or invented monotheism and that part of the blessings of Abraham were the development of Christianity and Islam, both of which educated the pagan world in the ways of God." Libr J
This book "makes no attempt to prove the historical accuracy of the stories from Genesis, but rather advances an impassioned argument for their relevance." Natl Rev
Includes bibliographical references

McKenzie, Steven L., 1953-
King David; a biography. Oxford Univ. Press 2000 232p il maps $41.50 **222**
1. David, King of Israel
ISBN 0-19-513273-4 LC 99-44315
McKenzie "views David as a ruthless, brutal usurper who would be well at home among many modern-day rulers. . . . Much of this portrait is inevitably speculation, and it is likely to outrage David's defenders . Still, given the limitations of written sources, McKenzie effectively coats his assertions with a veneer of credibility." Booklist
Includes bibliographical references

Moyers, Bill
Genesis: a living conversation. Doubleday 1996 361p il pa $22.95 hardcover o.p. **222**
1. Bible. O.T. Genesis—Criticism
ISBN 0-385-49043-7 (pa) LC 96-15318
Companion volume to the PBS series led by Bill Moyers in which writers and religious thinkers discussed episodes from the first book of the Bible. Among the participants are Burton Visotzky, a rabbi who initiated the conversations which gave rise to the series, "Elaine Pagels, Karen Armstrong, . . . John Barth, and Oscar Hijuelos. The book is divided by biblical tale (Adam and Eve, Cain and Abel, the blinding of Isaac) with five or six of the participants discussing the moral, literary, and personal meanings of the stories." Booklist

Robinson, George, 1953-
Essential Torah; a complete guide to the five books of Moses. Schocken Books 2006 xxiii, 593p $35 * **222**
1. Bible. O.T. Pentateuch—Criticism
ISBN 0-8052-4186-8; 978-0-8052-4186-0
LC 2005-40174

The author "discusses the basics of Jewish theology and history as they are derived from Torah; explains how the Dead Sea Scrolls shed light on the Bible; chronicles the evolution of the Torah's place in the synagogue liturgy; summarizes the 54 portions punctuating the Jewish year; and distills 2000 years of biblical commentaries." Libr J
"This book is a stellar achievement in which a gifted and diligent author guides readers of all faiths to a source book for religious belief and behavior." Publ Wkly
Includes bibliographical references

Satinover, Jeffrey, 1947-
Cracking the Bible code. Morrow 1997 346p il $23; pa $16.95 **222**
1. Bible. O.T. Pentateuch—Inspiration 2. Ciphers
ISBN 0-688-15463-8; 0-688-15994-X (pa)
LC 97-25280
"Satinover sets out to show how reading the Torah in a strict letter-by-letter sequence, as well as by applying the methods of the science of cryptology to the texts, decodes the Torah to yield startling information about contemporary events." Publ Wkly
This book "is the one to read if you really want to know about the Bible code." Booklist
Includes bibliographical references

223 Poetic books of Old Testament

Bible. O.T.
The Song of songs; the world's first great love poem; translated with an introduction and commentary, by Ariel Bloch and Chana Bloch; foreword by Stephen Mitchell; afterword by Robert Alter. Modern Library 2006 249p pa $16 **223**
ISBN 978-0-8129-7620-5; 0-8129-7620-7
LC 2006-46199
First published 1995
This book begins with an "introduction that establishes the date and date of the poem as well as the history of its incorporation into the canon of Hebrew scripture and its translation and interpretation in Jewish and Christian traditions. The translation and the Hebrew text are printed on facing pages, followed by Robert Alter's afterword and an extensive commentary accessible to laypersons as well as scholars, to readers who know Hebrew as well as those who don't." Booklist
Includes bibliographical references

225 Bible. New Testament

Brown, Raymond Edward
An introduction to the New Testament; by Raymond E. Brown. Yale University Press 1997 xxxviii, 878p map (Anchor Bible reference library) $55 **225**
1. Bible. N.T. —Criticism
ISBN 978-0-300-14016-3; 0-300-14016-9
A reissue of the title first published 1997 by Doubleday

Brown, Raymond Edward—Continued

The author "focuses on the established 27-book New Testament canon. . . . He deemphasizes the prehistory of the documents (sources, editions, and so forth) and emphasizes the documents in their canonical form. He begins most chapters with a 'General Analysis of the Message' and addresses issues such as authorship, date, and composition afterward." Libr J

Brown's book "culminates his life's work and synthesizes the best of his generation's historical-critical scholarship clearly and cogently for beginners and advanced students alike." N Y Times Book Rev

Ehrman, Bart D.

Misquoting Jesus; the story behind who changed the Bible and why. HarperSanFrancisco 2005 242p il $24.95 **225**

1. Bible. N.T. —Criticism

ISBN 0-06-073817-0 LC 2005-46326

The author "tells the story behind the mistakes and changes that ancient scribes made to the New Testament and shows the great impact they had upon the Bible we use today." Publisher's note

"This is a useful overview for biblical history collections." Booklist

Includes bibliographical references

225.9 Bible. New Testament— Geography, history, stories

Crossan, John Dominic

Excavating Jesus; beneath the stones, behind the texts; [by] John Dominic Crossan & Jonathan L. Reed. HarperSanFrancisco 2001 298p il pa $19.95 hardcover o.p. **225.9**

1. Bible. N.T. Gospels—Criticism 2. Excavations (Archeology)—Israel

ISBN 0-06-061634-2 (pa) LC 2001-24960

The authors examine "what clues archaeology can offer about Jesus' life and times. . . . [They focus on] the 10 most significant archaeological digs in the towns of ancient Palestine (Nazareth, Tiberias, and Jerusalem) in context with 10 important textual discoveries, including the Dead Sea Scrolls and writings such as the Gnostic gospels of Thomas." Booklist

This "book provides a fascinating, beautifully illustrated and elegantly written account of the life and times of Jesus, providing readers with one of the richest glimpses into Jesus and his world now available." Publ Wkly

Includes bibliographical references

Ehrman, Bart D.

Peter, Paul, and Mary Magdalene; the followers of Jesus in history and legend. Oxford University Press 2006 285p il $25 * **225.9**

1. Peter, the Apostle, Saint 2. Paul, the Apostle, Saint 3. Mary Magdalene, Saint

ISBN 0-19-530013-0; 978-0-19-530013-0

LC 2005-58996

The author "examines discussions of Simon Peter, the apostle Paul, and Mary Magdalene in Scripture and other writings of the first few centuries." Libr J

Ehrman "presents three of the best known and most important of Jesus' followers and does so in a way that is uncompromising in its scholarship yet utterly engaging for general readers." Booklist

Includes bibliographical references

Wills, Garry, 1934-

What Paul meant. Viking 2006 193p $24.95 **225.9**

1. Bible. N.T. Epistles of Paul—Criticism

ISBN 0-670-03793-1; 978-0-670-03793-3

LC 2006-46101

The author argues that "what Paul meant was not something contrary to what Jesus meant. Rather, the best way to know Jesus is to discover Paul." Publisher's note

"Provocative yet helpful, this book is sure to create a buzz." Publ Wkly

Includes bibliographical references

226 Gospels and Acts

Bible. N.T. Gospels.

The five Gospels; the search for the authentic words of Jesus: new translation and commentary; by Robert W. Funk, Roy W. Hoover, and the Jesus Seminar. Harper San Francisco 1997 xxii, 553p il map pa $28 **226**

1. Jesus Christ—Historicity

ISBN 0-06-063040-X

"A Tree Clause book"

First published 1993 by Macmillan

"Based on the work of the Jesus Seminar, which brought together a group of biblical scholars, this new translation of and commentary on the five Gospels offers an answer to the perennial question, What did Jesus really say? The group not only surveyed all the surviving ancient texts for words attributed to Jesus, but also examined the Gnostic Gospel of Thomas." Booklist

Includes bibliographical references

The three Gospels; [by] Reynolds Price. Scribner 1996 288p $23; pa $13 **226**

1. Jesus Christ

ISBN 0-684-80336-4; 0-684-83281-X (pa)

LC 95-39948

Contents: The good news according to Mark; The good news according to John; An honest account of a memorable life

"Of the four canonical Gospels, Mr. Price has chosen to translate the two that seem to him to express the strongest differing yet complementary perceptions of the life of Jesus—Mark and John. To these he has appended a third text, roughly the same length as each of the other two, which he calls 'An Honest Account of a Memorable Life: An Apocryphal Gospel.' . . . [The author also includes] a general preface, mainly devoted to the problems of translating New Testament Greek, and . . . prefatory interpretative essays for Mark and John and an explanatory introduction to the modern Apocryphal Gospel." N Y Times Book Rev

"Although there is so much to appreciate in these commentaries and in the translated texts, the best part of the book . . . is left to last: Price's own joyously written account of Jesus' life." Booklist

Bonhoeffer, Dietrich, 1906-1945
The cost of discipleship; containing material not previously translated. rev and unabridged ed. Macmillan 1959 pa $12 hardcover o.p. *
226
1. Bible. N.T. Gospels—Criticism 2. Sermon on the mount
ISBN 0-684-81500-1 (pa)
Also available in hardcover from P. Smith
Original German edition, 1937. This edition translated by R. H. Fuller with some revision by Irmgard Booth
The first part of the book "is an exposition of the conception of discipleship that is to be found in the Synoptic Gospels, together with an interpretation of the Sermon on the Mount. The second part consists of Bonhoeffer's attempt to show how the terminology used by the evangelists has been translated into the language of the Church of the Apostle Paul." Magill. Masterpieces of Christ Lit in Summary Form

Chilton, Bruce
Mary Magdalene; a biography. Doubleday 2005 220p map $23.95
226
1. Mary Magdalene, Saint
ISBN 0-385-51317-8
LC 2005-45446
Through an "examination of available texts (canonical gospels, the most important noncanonical gospels, and other early Christian writings) and sober speculation, Chilton traces [Mary Magdalene's] . . . relationship to Jesus and claims that it was she who taught Jesus the power of vision, anointing, and touch and the disciples that Jesus had overcome death; without her, according to Chilton, resurrection might never have become a central Christian teaching. He also traces her later legend, the ambivalence of Gnosticism toward her, her medieval cult and denigration, and 20th-century reassessments." Libr J

Wroe, Ann
Pontius Pilate. Modern Library 2000 412p $26; pa $14.95
226
1. Pilate, Pontius, 1st cent.
ISBN 0-375-50305-6; 0-375-75397-4 (pa)
LC 99-43000
First published 1999 in the United Kingdom with title: Pilate: the biography of an invented man
The author offers "a reconstructed life of the Roman official who, by ordering the execution of Jesus of Nazareth but otherwise serving with little distinction, managed to become simultaneously famous and obscure. Outside the Gospels, which each bring the governor on stage for a brief if highly charged cameo appearance, there are only a few references to Pilate in contemporary sources." Publ Wkly
"As long as readers don't take this as accurate history but enjoy it as a well-written, imaginative, and creative portrait of Pilate and his times, the book serves a useful purpose." Libr J
Includes bibliographical references

229 Apocrypha, pseudepigrapha, intertestamental works

Bible. O.T. Apocrypha.
The Apocrypha; new revised standard version. Cambridge University Press 1993 262p pa $14.99 *
229
ISBN 978-0-521-50776-9; 0-521-50776-6
Also available in an annotated edition from Oxford University Press
On cover: The Apocryphal/Deuterocanonical books of the Old Testament
"These books form part of the sacred literature of the Alexandrian Jews. . . . Some of them form an historical link between the Old and New Testament, others have a linguistic value in connexion with the Hellenistic phraseology of the latter. The narratives of Apocrypha are partly historical records, and partly allegorical." Oxford Univ. Press

Dead Sea scrolls.
The Dead Sea scriptures; in English translation with introduction and notes by Theodor H. Gaster. 3rd ed rev and enl. Anchor Press 1976 580p pa $25 *
229
ISBN 0-385-08859-0
First published 1956
A translation, with commentary and notes, of the scrolls relating the life and faith of the Dead Sea sect
Includes bibliographical references

Pagels, Elaine H., 1943-
Beyond belief; the secret Gospel of Thomas; {by} Elaine Pagels. Random House 2003 241p $26.95 *
229
1. Gospel of Thomas 2. Bible. N.T. John—Criticism 3. Christianity
ISBN 0-375-50156-8
LC 2002-36840
Pagels discusses the early Christian writings known as the Gnostic Gospels that were discovered at Nag Hammadi, Egypt. She focuses particularly on the Gospel of Thomas. Pagels contends "that the Gospel of John is the only one in the New Testament that actually promotes the idea of Jesus as God in human form, and she argues . . . that it was written explicitly to counter the Gospel of Thomas, which said otherwise. Thomas's gospel, she writes, teaches 'that God's light shines not only in Jesus but, potentially at least, in everyone . . . and encourages the hearer . . . to seek to know God through one's own divinely given capacity, since all are created in the image of God.'" Christ Sci Monit
"Even those who possess only a nodding acquaintance with Gnostic writings will find themselves stimulated by the author's arguments and perhaps transformed by her conclusions. A fresh and exciting work of theology and spirituality." Booklist
Includes bibliographical references

Pagels, Elaine H., 1943-—*Continued*
Reading Judas; the Gospel of Judas and the shaping of Christianity; [by] Elaine Pagels and Karen L. King. Penguin 2007 xxiii, 198p diag $24.95   **229**
1. Judas Iscariot 2. Gospel of Judas Iscariot 3. Church history—30-600, Early church
ISBN 978-0-670-03845-9; 0-670-03845-8
                                   LC 2007-296641

"In fall 2006, the National Geographic Society made quite a splash, bringing to light the discovery of a new gospel in the Gnostic tradition told from Judas' point of view. . . . The Gospel of Judas can be a convoluted, even bizarre, reading experience, but the combination of King's translation, which appears at the end of the book, and Pagels' text will help general readers get past the difficulties and into the fascinating message, which emphasizes spiritual rather than physical resurrection for both Jesus and his followers. Pagels also shows why this message was so noxious to church leaders and explains how the gospel fits into the body of noncanonical literature." Booklist

230   Christianity & Christian theology

Bonhoeffer, Dietrich, 1906-1945
A testament to freedom; the essential writings of Dietrich Bonhoeffer; edited by Geffrey B. Kelly and F. Burton Nelson. HarperSanFrancisco 1990 xxii, 579p il pa $23 hardcover o.p. *
                                          230
1. Theology
ISBN 0-06-064214-9 (pa)   LC 89-45514
"This book features previously untranslated writings, sermons, and selections from letters spanning {Bonhoeffer's} entire pastoral-theological career, including his prison letters." Publisher's note
This book will not "subsitute for the individual volumes of Bonhoeffer's best-known works. But as a single volume collection of Bonhoeffer's writings, however, there is none better." Christ Today
Includes bibliographical references

Davies, Brian, 1951-
The thought of Thomas Aquinas. Oxford Univ. Press 1992 391p pa $44.95 hardcover o.p.
                                          230
1. Thomas, Aquinas, Saint, 1225?-1274 2. Doctrinal theology
ISBN 0-19-826753-3 (pa)   LC 91-35671
This book on Aquinas "is arranged topically in 17 chapters with . . . {discussion of} the nature of God and creation, negative and positive theology, perfection, eternity, knowledge, justice, and providence. Chapters 10 through 16 treat the Trinity, human nature, and Christology. The final chapter treats Aquinas on the sacraments, particularly the Eucharist." Choice
"Davies aims to cover the whole programme of the Summa in 370 pages. This necessarily means that, though his writing is admirably clear and never cryptic, much of what he says is extremely concise, and some topics get less airing than others." Times Lit Suppl
Includes bibliographical references

Holifield, E. Brooks
Theology in America; Christian thought from the age of the Puritans to the Civil War. Yale University Press 2003 617p hardcover o.p. pa $23
*   **230**
1. Doctrinal theology
ISBN 0-300-09574-0; 978-0-300-10765-4 (pa); 0-300-10765-X (pa)   LC 2003-42289
The author "examines mainstream Protestant and Catholic traditions as well as those of more marginal groups. . . . The book explores a range of themes, including the strand of Christian thought that sought to demonstrate the reasonableness of Christianity, the place of American theology within the larger European setting, the social location of theology in early America, and the special importance of the Calvinist traditions in the development of American theology." Univ Press Books for Public and Second Sch Libr, 2004
"In this majestic achievement, Holifield . . . provides a first-rate, richly evocative and unrivaled history of theology in America. . . . This masterfully narrated, splendid book will become the definitive study of the development of American theology." Publ Wkly
Includes bibliographical references

Kierkegaard, Søren, 1813-1855
The present age, and Of the difference between a genius and an apostle; translated by Alexander Dru; introduction by Walter Kaufman. Harper & Row 1962 108p pa $12   **230**
1. Theology
ISBN 0-06-130094-2
"Harper torchbooks. The Cloister library"
First published 1846. This translation "originally published, together with a third essay, by Oxford University Press under the title 'The Present Age and Two Minor Ethico-Religious Treatises in 1940'." Verso of title page
"Those who would know Kierkegaard, the intensely religious humorist, the irrepressibly witty critic of his age and ours, can do no better than to begin with this book." Introduction

Küng, Hans, 1928-
Great Christian thinkers. Continuum 1994 235p pa $19.95 hardcover o.p.   **230**
1. Theology
ISBN 0-8264-0848-6 (pa)   LC 94-883
The author "attempts a new approach to the introduction-to-theology genre by critically tracing the developing thought of key, usually 'paradigm-shifting,' theologians (Paul, Origen, Augustine, Aquinas, Luther, Schleiermacher, and Karl Barth) in relation to their social, intellectual, and religious environment. He explores the significance of their life and work for the Christian world in an interesting, quite understandable manner." Libr J
Includes bibliographical references

Lewis, C. S. (Clive Staples), 1898-1963
Mere Christianity; a revised and amplified edition, with a new introduction, of the three books, Broadcast talks, Christian behaviour, and Beyond personality. HarperSanFrancisco 2001 xx, 227p $19.95; pa $10 *   **230**
1. Christian philosophy
ISBN 0-06-065288-8; 0-06-065292-6 (pa)
LC 00-49862
First published 1952
This omnibus edition includes most of C. S. Lewis' writings on Christian theology and moral philosophy
Includes bibliographical references

The world's last night, and other essays. Harcourt Brace & Co. 1960 113p pa $12 hardcover o.p.   **230**
1. Christian philosophy
ISBN 0-15-602771-2 (pa)
These seven essays cover topics such as culture, democracy, education, good works, prayers, the second coming of Christ, and space exploration

Price, Reynolds, 1933-
Letter to a Godchild; concerning faith. Scribner 2006 95p il $15.95   **230**
1. Christianity 2. Faith
ISBN 0-7432-9180-8   LC 2006-42328
"A true godfather sees to the godchild's religious education, and so Price addresses the mildest of hortatory letters on his convictions to his six-year-old godson, to be read much later, 'if ever.' He affirms that he believes in God and that most other people do, too, at least occasionally. Unconvinced by theological proofs, much less by dogma, he rests his assurance on a mystical experience in his childhood and another from just before the surgery for spinal cancer that rendered him paraplegic in his fifties. . . . Price is almost debilitatingly aware of how greatly his own academic and professional circles disdain Christianity, in particular." Booklist
"Although his novels, poetry and essays provide glimpses of Price's vision of religious experience, this marvelous little missive comes closest to being a spiritual autobiography." Publ Wkly

Teilhard de Chardin, Pierre
The divine milieu; an essay on the interior life. Harper & Row 1960 144p pa $14 hardcover o.p.
*   **230**
1. Christian philosophy
ISBN 978-0-06-093725-6 (pa); 0-06-093725-4 (pa)
Original French edition, 1957
In this book Father de Chardin describes his spiritual philosophy

Tillich, Paul, 1886-1965
Theology of culture; edited by Robert C. Kimball. Oxford Univ. Press 1959 213p $13.95 hardcover o.p.   **230**
1. Christian philosophy 2. Culture
ISBN 0-19-500711-5 (pa)
Selected essays by the influential theologian focus on ethics, education, science, aesthetics, psychology, and existential philosophy

230.003   Christianity—Encyclopedias and dictionaries

The **Encyclopedia** of Christianity; editors, Erwin Fahlbusch [et al.]; translator and English-language editor, Geoffrey W. Bromiley; statistical editor, David B. Barrett; foreword, Jaroslav Pelikan. Eerdmans 1999-2008 5v il set $500 *   **230.003**
1. Christianity—Encyclopedias
ISBN 978-0-8028-6350-8   LC 98-45953
The "*Evangelisches Kirchenlexikon* (3d ed.) is being published in a five-volume expanded English translation. . . . The German editors have worked with the editors of the English edition to add significant content for American and British audiences. . . . Essential; this is possibly the best encyclopedic reference on Christianity." Libr J [review of volume 1]

Encyclopedia of Christianity; edited by John Bowden. Oxford University Press 2005 xli, 1364p il $125 *   **230.003**
1. Christianity—Encyclopedias
ISBN 978-0-19-522393-4; 0-19-522393-4
LC 2005-48801
"This single volume contains 33 gateway entries to pivotal subjects; 300 major articles . . . [166] boxed items on various themes; and a who's who of 400 (mainly male) historically influential Christians." Christ Century
"This is probably the most comprehensive single-volume encyclopedia of Christianity." Choice
Includes bibliographical references

Encyclopedia of early Christianity; edited by Everett Ferguson. 2nd ed. Garland 1997 2v il maps (Garland reference library of the humanities) set $245; pa set $55
230.003
1. Christianity—Encyclopedias
ISBN 0-8153-1663-1; 0-8153-3319-6 (pa)
LC 96-36865
First published 1990
"Covers persons, places, doctrines, practices, art, liturgy, heresies, and schisms from the time of Jesus to approximately 600 CE. Articles by . . . specialists include bibliographies and cross-references. Extensive subject index. Intended for general readers, students, and professionals in fields outside religion who want information concerning early Christianity." Guide to Ref Books. 11th edition [entry for 1990 edition]

Oxford companion to Christian thought; edited by Adrian Hastings {et al.}. Oxford Univ. Press 2000 xxviii, 777p $75   **230.003**
ISBN 0-19-860024-0   LC 2001-267818
This volume focuses "on the movement of ideas among Christians. The articles (more than 500) by 268 scholars (mostly British) range in length from half a column . . . to seven pages. . . . They broadly cover the themes . . . persons . . . places . . . and historical periods . . . that characterize Christian thought." Choice
Includes bibliographical references

The **Oxford** dictionary of the Christian Church; edited by F.L. Cross. 3rd ed. rev., edited by E.A. Livingstone. Oxford University Press 2005 xl, 1800p $150 *   **230.003**
1. Christianity—Dictionaries
ISBN 0-19-280290-9; 978-0-19-280290-3
LC 2005-282601
Replaces the edition published 1997
First published 1957
This book "contains more than 6000 cross-referenced A-to-Z entries on theology, churches and denominations, patristic scholarship, the Bible, the Church calendar and its organization, popes, archbishops, saints, and mystics." Libr J

Includes bibliographical references

231   God

Miles, Jack, 1942-
God: a biography. Knopf 1995 446p $32.50; pa $15   **231**
1. Bible. O.T. —Criticism 2. God
ISBN 0-679-41833-4; 0-679-74368-5 (pa)
LC 94-30153
The author discusses "God's nature, character, motives and designs through a close textual analysis of the Hebrew Bible, or Old Testament. He deduces that the God of Judeo-Christian tradition is an amalgam of several ancient, divine personalities. Worshiped as the source of mercy, wisdom, strength and love, God is also at times an abrupt, unpredictable, wrathful being: a destroyer as well as a creator." Publ Wkly
Miles "has produced a well-written, provocative study." Choice
Includes bibliographical references

Price, Reynolds, 1933-
Letter to a man in the fire; does God exist and does He care? Scribner 1999 108p $20; pa $11
231
1. God 2. Suffering
ISBN 0-684-85626-3; 0-684-85627-1 (pa)
LC 98-54197
This book "consists of Price's response to a 1997 letter he received from a medical student stricken with cancer. Price telephoned and then followed up with this long, eloquent letter on the nature of suffering and the justice and righteousness of God." Publ Wkly

231.7   God—Relation to the world

Humes, Edward
Monkey girl; evolution, education, religion, and the battle for America's soul. HarperCollins Publishers 2007 380p $25.95   **231.7**
1. Evolution 2. Creationism
ISBN 978-0-06-088548-9; 0-06-088548-3
LC 2006-50263
This is the "story of the Dover, Pa., school board's attempt in 2004 to 'balance' the well-tested scientific theo-

ry of evolution with a faith-based version of human origins." Newsday
Humes "may be the most successful so far in making a complicated issue accessible and in putting human faces on both sides of the evolution divide. Clearly based on exhaustive reporting that takes the reader from the hard benches of a Harrisburg, Pa., federal district courtroom to the kitchen tables of Dover families whose children were taunted as 'monkey girls,' Humes' fast-moving, richly detailed book reads like a suspense novel." Chicago Tribune

Lewis, C. S. (Clive Staples), 1898-1963
Miracles;   a   preliminary   study. HarperSanFrancisco 2001 294p pa $13.95
231.7
1. Miracles
ISBN 0-06-065301-9; 978-0-06-065301-9
LC 00-49863
First published 1947 by Macmillan
"Mr. Lewis casts his net fairly wide and, under the guise of a book on miracles, offers a rational justification both of theism and of doctrinal Christianity." Times Lit Suppl

Miller, Kenneth R. (Kenneth Raymond), 1948-
Finding Darwin's God; a scientist's search for common ground between God and evolution. Cliff St. Bks. 1999 338p il $25; pa $14   **231.7**
1. Evolution 2. Religion and science
ISBN 0-06-017593-1; 0-06-093049-7 (pa)
LC 99-16754
The author "explains the difference between evolution as validated scientific fact and as an evolving theory. He illustrates his contentions with examples from astronomy, geology, physics and molecular biology, confronting the illogic of creationists with persuasive reasons based on the known physical properties of the universe. . . . Then standing firmly on Darwinian ground, he turns to take on, with equal vigor, his outspoken colleagues in science who espouse a materialistic, agnostic or atheistic vision of reality." Publ Wkly
Includes bibliographical references

Ruse, Michael
The evolution-creation struggle. Harvard University Press 2005 327p $25.95 *
231.7
1. Evolution 2. Religion and science
ISBN 0-674-01687-4   LC 2005-40282
This book features an "explanation of the common origins of evolutionism and creationism in the Enlightenment's crisis of faith and . . . [a] description of the Victorian social forces before and after the publication of Darwin's The Origin of Species. . . . This book takes a nonpolemical approach, which is rare. Highly recommended." Libr J
Includes bibliographical references

Teilhard de Chardin, Pierre
Christianity and evolution; translated by René Hague. Harcourt Brace Jovanovich 1971 255p pa $14 hardcover o.p.   **231.7**

Teilhard de Chardin, Pierre—*Continued*
1. Theology
ISBN 978-0-15-602818-9; 0-15-602818-2
"A Helen and Kurt Wolff book"
Original French edition, 1969
These essays "covering a wide expanse of Teilhard's thought . . . stimulate the reader to reflect seriously on the Christian dogma of creation, the role of Christ in evolution as a cosmic phenomenon, and on the relationship of the church to the modern world." Choice
Includes bibliographical references

232   Jesus Christ and his family. Christology

Charlesworth, James H.
Jesus and the Dead Sea scrolls; {by} James H. Charlesworth, with internationally renowned experts. Doubleday 1992 xxxvii, 370p il maps (Anchor Bible reference library) pa $25 hardcover o.p. **232**
1. Jesus Christ 2. Dead Sea scrolls
ISBN 0-385-47844-5 (pa)   LC 92-2617
These essays "explore the question of Jesus' relationship to those who wrote the scrolls, and whether or not the scrolls' original scholars were hiding something profound or damaging to the Christian faith." Booklist
This book "will inform and challenge both scholars and lay readers." Libr J
Includes bibliographical references

Miles, Jack, 1942-
Christ: a crisis in the life of God. Knopf 2001 352p $26.95; pa $14   **232**
1. Jesus Christ 2. Bible. N.T. —Criticism
ISBN 0-375-40014-1; 0-679-78160-9 (pa)
LC 2001-33808
"Miles continues the literary analysis of the Bible that he began in . . . *God* (1995). Taking up the story of Jesus, he treats it as the record of God's sojourn on earth as a man. That is, unlike the hordes of scholars concerned with the historical Jesus, Miles takes the Gospels at face value, though he argues, with plenty of demonstration and reason, that in them Jesus is an ironist, who turns old messianic understandings, in particular, inside out and upside down." Booklist
"Weaving philosophy and literature into his reflections on the Bible, Miles offers literary perspectives on the life of Christ that are at once provocative and revelatory. After reading this book, one can never look at God, Jesus or the Bible in quite the same way." Publ Wkly
Includes bibliographical references

Vermès, Géza, 1924-
The changing faces of Jesus. Viking 2001 324p map hardcover o.p. pa $15.86   **232**
1. Jesus Christ
ISBN: 0-14-026524-4 (pa)   LC 00-43897
The author examines "how the Jesus of history became the Church's divine figure. . . . Vermes calls his prologue 'From Christ to Jesus.' He traces the process of

divinization backward, . . . according to the degree of 'evolution' of the Christological doctrine that Jesus was both entirely divine and entirely human." N Y Rev Books
"Vermes's vast knowledge of first century Judaism ensures that this work will become one of the most important works in historical Jesus studies, and his readable style makes it useful for both public and academic library patrons." Libr J
Includes bibliographical references

Wills, Garry, 1934-
What Jesus meant; Garry Wills. Viking 2006 143p $24.95   **232**
1. Jesus Christ—Teachings 2. Bible. N.T. Gospels—Criticism
ISBN 0-670-03496-7   LC 2005-42377
The author "tries to understand Jesus as someone who, without the strictures of religion and politics, managed to transcend the powers and faults of the human condition and explicates the individual Jesus Christ through the Gospels." Libr J
"This book invites Christians toward more honest reflection on the life and message of the one they call 'Savior.'" Publ Wkly

232.9   Family and life of Jesus

Benedict XVI, Pope, 1927-
Jesus of Nazareth; [by] Joseph Ratzinger (Pope Benedict XVI); translated from the German by Adrian J. Walker. Doubleday 2007 xxiv, 374p $24.95   **232.9**
1. Jesus Christ
ISBN 978-0-385-52341-7; 0-385-52341-6
LC 2007-22357
Pope Benedict presents his reflections on the Jesus of the Gospels, calling his book "a testimony to his 'personal search for the face of the Lord.'" America
This book "is full of luminous passages that offer a fruitful basis for meditation on the mysterious and gracious figure of Jesus." First Things
Includes bibliographical references

Bloom, Harold, 1930-
Jesus and Yahweh; the names divine. Riverhead Books 2005 238p $24.95   **232.9**
1. Jesus Christ 2. God—Judaism 3. Christianity and other religions
ISBN 1-57322-322-0   LC 2005-46409
The author examines "the character of Jesus. . . . He also examines the character of Yahweh, who he finds has more in common with Mark's Jesus than he does with God the Father of the Christian and later rabbinic Jewish traditions. Bloom further argues that the Hebrew Bible of the Jews and the Christian Old Testament are very different books with very different purposes, political as well as religious." Publisher's note
This "book is, among other things, a powerful complaint against the New Testament, and against the version of Christ that the church has detached from the revolutionary Jewish teacher who roams through the canonical Gospel accounts." New Repub

Borg, Marcus J.

The last week; a day-by-day account of Jesus's final week in Jerusalem; [by] Marcus J. Borg and John Dominic Crossan. HarperSanFrancisco 2006 220p $21.95 * **232.9**

1. Jesus Christ 2. Bible. N.T. Mark—Criticism

ISBN 0-06-084539-2; 978-0-06-084539-1

LC 2005-55148

This is an "account of Jesus's final week, largely focusing on the Gospel of Mark. Writing in clear, readable prose and devoting one chapter to each day of the week in question, . . . [the authors] provide some useful historical and textual information." Libr J

Includes bibliographical references

Chilton, Bruce

Rabbi Jesus; an intimate biography. Doubleday 2000 xxii, 330p il maps pa $14.95 hardcover o.p. **232.9**

1. Jesus Christ—Biography

ISBN 0-385-49793-8 (pa) LC 00-31548

The author presents a "wonderfully fresh presentation of the implications of Jesus's being a Jewish male living in the context of first-century Judaism." Libr J

Includes bibliographical references

Cox, Harvey Gallagher

When Jesus came to Harvard; making moral choices today; [by] Harvey Cox. Houghton Mifflin 2004 338p $26 **232.9**

1. Jesus Christ 2. Conduct of life

ISBN 0-618-06744-2 LC 2004-54069

"After more than 20 years of teaching a course on Jesus and the moral life to Harvard undergraduates, [the author] shares his experience. . . . Cox organizes the book around the New Testament stories told by and about Jesus to demonstrate the ways that each can be used to inform moral choices." Publ Wkly

"Like the course, Cox's book doesn't offer answers so much as pose questions that inspire the moral decision-making process." Booklist

Includes bibliographical references

Crossan, John Dominic

Who killed Jesus? exposing the roots of anti-semitism in the Gospel story of the death of Jesus. HarperSanFrancisco 1995 238p pa $15 hardcover o.p. **232.9**

1. Jesus Christ—Resurrection 2. Bible. N.T. Gospels—Criticism

ISBN 0-06-061480-3 (pa) LC 94-40200

"The two main theses of this . . . book are that the roots of anti-Semitism spring from gospel narratives of the death of Jesus and that the Romans, not the Jews, killed Jesus as a revolutionary agitator inimical to their continued governance of Judea. Crossan . . . pleads for a reevaluation of the passion stories, which have caused such animus toward Jews for the past 2000 years." Libr J

"Well argued and highly readable, Who Killed Jesus? also includes an important epilogue stating Crossan's own faith perspectives on the divinity and resurrection of Christ." Publ Wkly

Includes bibliographical references

Fredriksen, Paula

Jesus of Nazareth, King of the Jews; a Jewish life and the emergence of Christianity. Knopf 1999 327p pa $14 hardcover o.p. **232.9**

1. Jesus Christ

ISBN 0-679-76746-0 (pa) LC 99-31054

"To Fredriksen, Jesus was an observant Jew immersed in a context bounded by Galilee and Jerusalem. He was crucified as an imperial Roman deterrent to unruly inhabitants of a region prone to rebellion, and the emergence of Christianity is a work of creative theological reinterpretation as much as of historical memory." Booklist

Includes bibliographical references

Girzone, Joseph F.

A portrait of Jesus. Doubleday 1998 179p il pa $11.95 hardcover o.p. **232.9**

1. Jesus Christ—Biography 2. Christian life

ISBN 0-385-48477-1 (pa) LC 98-15618

The author "gives a simple narrative account of Jesus' life, envisioning facets of the person reflected in the gospel stories." Libr J

"This is popular liberal Catholic theology, more filled with forgiveness and fellowship than shaming and hierarchy. Many a non-Catholic and even non-Christian may embrace it, too." Booklist

Meier, John P.

A marginal Jew; rethinking the historical Jesus. Doubleday 1991-2001 3v maps (Anchor Bible reference library) v1 $45; v2 $42.50; v3 $45 **232.9**

1. Jesus Christ—Historicity

ISBN 0-385-26425-9 (v1); 0-385-46992-6 (v2); 0-385-46993-4 (v3) LC 91-10538

Contents: v1 The roots of the problem and the person; v2 Mentor, message, and miracles; v3 Companions and competitors

The first three volumes in a projected series of four devoted to an examination of the historical Jesus and his Jewish environment

The author "summarizes the first two volumes of A Marginal Jew and forecasts the next while meticulously documenting his understanding of the relations between the historical Jesus, his historical companions, and his historical competitors—Pharisees, Sadducees, Essenes, and others. . . . The only thing common about Meier's project is fascination with the character of Jesus. Those who share that will find this dense, academic work worth their effort." Booklist [review of volume 3]

Includes bibliographical references

Pelikan, Jaroslav Jan, 1923-2006

The illustrated Jesus through the centuries. Yale Univ. Press 1997 254p il $25 * **232.9**

1. Jesus Christ—Historicity

ISBN 0-300-07268-6 LC 97-7360

Companion volume to Mary through the centuries

In this revision of Jesus through the centuries (1985) the author "has abridged the text and turns to illustrations to convey his interpretations. . . . Very beautiful and very appealing for the general reader, this edition by no

Pelikan, Jaroslav Jan, 1923-2006—*Continued*
means replaces the scholarship and documentation of the first; those notations and references are missing in the illustrated edition. However, the illustrations enhance this interesting and insightful text." Libr J

Sanders, E. P.
The historical figure of Jesus. Allen Lane/The Penguin Press 1994 c1993 337p map pa $14.95 hardcover o.p. **232.9**
1. Jesus Christ—Biography
ISBN 0-14-014499-4 (pa)   LC 94-136152
First published 1993 in the United Kingdom
Sanders gives "an account of Jesus' life and activity. . . . After discussing the context of Jesus in first-century Palestine and facing the problem of sources, he treats Jesus' ministry, miracles, preaching of God's kingdom, self-understanding and passion and death." America
"Highly readable, this is a key addition to literature on the historical Jesus." Libr J
Includes bibliographical references

Wilson, A. N. (Andrew Norman), 1950-
Jesus. Norton 1992 269p $22.95   **232.9**
1. Jesus Christ—Biography
ISBN 0-393-03087-3   LC 92-37046
Also available in paperback from Fawcett Columbine
The author attempts to understand Jesus as a historical figure and ethical teacher within the context of first-century Judaism
Includes bibliographical references

Zahl, Paul F. M.
The first Christian; universal truth in the teachings of Jesus. Eerdmans 2003 138p pa $16   **232.9**
1. Jesus Christ 2. Christianity
ISBN 0-8028-2110-3   LC 2003-59943
The author examines "the Jesus who proclaimed the kingdom of God and announced the good news of salvation but also made clear that each person's salvation depends solely on God, not on anything any human does. Basic Christianity restated with maximal cogency." Booklist
Includes bibliographical references

232.91   Mary, mother of Jesus

Pelikan, Jaroslav Jan, 1923-2006
Mary through the centuries; her place in the history of culture. Yale Univ. Press 1996 267p il $40; pa $14.95 *   **232.91**
1. Mary, Blessed Virgin, Saint
ISBN 0-300-06951-0; 0-300-07661-4 (pa)
      LC 96-24726
Companion volume to The illustrated Jesus through the centuries
Pelikan explores the history of Christian doctrine in regard to the Virgin Mary as well as representations of Mary in art and literature. "Each of Pelikan's 16 chapters

is centered on a Marian title." Christ Century
"Although volumes have been written about the Virgin Mary from a wide variety of perspectives, it is rare to find a scholarly work that is easily accessible to the general, educated reader." Choice
Includes bibliographical references

234   Salvation and grace

Tillich, Paul, 1886-1965
Dynamics of faith. Harper & Row 1957 127p pa $14 hardcover o.p. *   **234**
1. Faith
ISBN 0-06-093713-0 (pa)
"World perspectives"
"The author considers what faith is and is not, the symbols and types of faith and the truth and the life of faith. The discussion treats of history, science, the Bible, the individual and the community and the claims of Judaism, Mohammedanism, Protestantism and Catholicism." N Y Times Book Rev

235   Spiritual beings

Pagels, Elaine H., 1943-
The origin of Satan; {by} Elaine Pagels. Random House 1995 214p pa $12 hardcover o.p. *   **235**
1. Bible. N.T. Gospels—Criticism 2. Devil
ISBN 0-679-73118-0 (pa)   LC 95-7983
The author "traces the development of Satan in the Jewish community from a sort of roving agent acting on God's behalf—always obstructing but not always evil—to an increasingly evil force identified more and more with intimate enemies, members of one's own community with whom one is in conflict. That trend toward demonization of portions of the Jewish community intensified with the emergence of Christianity and became the basis for demonization of heretics and centuries of anti-Semitism." Booklist
Pagels "shows herself to be a masterful guide through the risk-laden complexities of biblical studies." Publ Wkly
Includes bibliographical references

Wray, T. J.
The birth of Satan; tracing the devil's biblical roots; [by] T.J. Wray, Gregory Mobley. Palgrave Macmillan 2005 211p $24.95   **235**
1. Devil
ISBN 1-4039-6933-7   LC 2005-43046
The authors find Satan's "origins in a biblical character and in early Jewish and Christian writings outside of the scriptures. They try to understand why we as a species strive to feel fearful, why being frightened—vicariously, at least—is so appealing. . . . A thoughtful, informative examination." Booklist
Includes bibliographical references

236 Eschatology

Polkinghorne, John, 1930-
The God of hope and the end of the world. Yale
Univ. Press 2002 xxv, 154p $19.95   **236**
1. Eschatology
ISBN 0-300-09211-3   LC 2001-46577
"Theoretical physicist and Anglican priest
Polkinghorne sees in modern cosmology's grim predic-
tions of universal decay the absolute necessity for a theo-
logical affirmation of human hope. That hope, he insists,
depends upon the faithfulness of God, as revealed in the
Resurrection of Jesus Christ. . . . Though the casually
religious will find him too technical, thoughtful Chris-
tians will find much to praise in this modern Aquinas."
Booklist
Includes bibliographical references

Russell, Jeffrey Burton
Paradise mislaid; how we lost heaven—and how
we can regain it. Oxford University Press 2006
210p $28   **236**
1. Heaven
ISBN 978-0-19-516006-2; 0-19-516006-1
LC 2005-32361
The author "traces the history of heaven from the 16th
century through the late 20th, providing . . . [an]
overview of the many philosophical, literary, social, and
even religious forces that have challenged the concept of
heaven. . . . Russell's elegant survey of heaven offers a
first-rate history of a much debated subject." Publ Wkly
Includes bibliographical references

Wright, N. T. (Nicholas Thomas)
Surprised by hope; rethinking heaven, the
resurrection, and the mission of the church.
HarperOne 2008 332p $24.95   **236**
1. Eschatology 2. Hope 3. Future life
ISBN 978-0-06-155182-6; 0-06-155182-1
The author "critiques the views of heaven that have
become regnant in Western culture, especially the assumption of the continuance of the soul after death in a
sort of blissful non-bodily existence." Publ Wkly
"Readers will need a Bible handy to appreciate this
work fully, as Wright prefers to cite rather than print
Scripture. His prose, deep but not murky, is lightened by
glints of humor. For any library serving patrons who are
willing to think a bit about religion." Libr J
Includes bibliographical references

239 Apologetics and polemics

Augustine, Saint, Bishop of Hippo
Concerning the city of God against the pagans;
[by] St. Augustine ; translated by Henry Bettenson
; with a new introduction by G.R. Evans. Penguin
Books 2003 lxxi, 1097p (Penguin classics) pa $16
239
1. Apologetics
ISBN 978-0-14-044894-8; 0-14-044894-2
LC 2004-269353

This translation first published 1972
Cover title: City of God
"Written as an eloquent defence of the faith at a time
when the Roman Empire was on the brink of collapse,
it examines the ancient pagan religions of Rome, the arguments of the Greek philosophers and the revelations of
the Bible. Pointing the way forward to a citizenship that
transcends worldly politics and will last for eternity, City
of God represents a dramatic turning point in the unfolding of Christian doctrine. The new introduction by Gill
Evans examines the text in the light of contemporary
Greek and Roman thought and political change." Publisher's note
Includes bibliographical references

Keller, Timothy J., 1950-
The reason for God; belief in an age of
skepticism. Dutton 2008 293p $24.95   **239**
1. Apologetics 2. Faith 3. Skepticism
ISBN 978-0-525-95049-3; 0-525-95049-4
LC 2007-43745
"Using literature, philosophy, and pop culture, the author gives . . . reasons for a strong belief in God. . . .
[The author] presents a religious view without being
overly critical of the secular side presented in other
books. . . . This book presents a valid, well-written, and
well-researched argument." Libr J

241 Christian ethics

Pagels, Elaine H., 1943-
Adam, Eve, and the serpent. Random House
1988 xxviii, 189p pa $12 hardcover o.p. *
241
1. Bible. O.T. —Criticism 2. Sexual behavior
ISBN 0-679-72232-7 (pa)   LC 87-43227
The author "focuses on six schools of early Christian
opinion concerning sexuality, marriage, family, procre-
ation, celibacy, moral freedom, and human nature, as reflected in various interpretations of Genesis 1-3." Choice
"Pagels writes with a rare combination of formidable
knowledge and easy fluency. The old controversies she
discusses become, in her hands, matters of immediate interest." Economist
Includes bibliographical references

Price, Reynolds, 1933-
A serious way of wondering; the ethics of Jesus
imagined. Scribner 2003 146p hardcover o.p. pa
$14.95   **241**
1. Jesus Christ 2. Christian ethics
ISBN:0-7432-3008-6;   978-0-7432-3009-4(pa)
0-7432-3009-4 (pa)   LC 2003-41506
"In three . . . apocryphal gospel stories, Price's Jesus
engages in conversations about homosexuality, suicide
and the plight of women in male-dominated societies.
. . . Elegant and passionate, Price's provocative parables
provide no simple answers to the saccharine question
'What would Jesus do?' Rather, they compel us to imagine creatively our engagements with Jesus' teachings and
the impact of those teachings on our lives." Publ Wkly
Includes bibliographical references

242 Devotional literature

The **African** prayer book; selected and with an introduction by Desmond Tutu. Doubleday 1995 xx, 139p $21; pa $9.95 *   242
1. Prayers
ISBN 0-385-47730-9; 0-385-51649-5 (pa)
LC 94-43444
Tutu "draws on the breadth and depth of African spirituality to assemble this little treasury of prayer and devotion. He has arranged material from throughout the African continent and the African diaspora into a traditional pattern of adoration, contrition, thanksgiving, and supplication." Booklist

Augustine, Saint, Bishop of Hippo
Confessions; translated with an introduction and notes by Henry Chadwick. Oxford University Press 1998 xxviii, 311p (Oxford world's classics) pa $7.95 *   242
ISBN 978-0-19-283372-3; 0-19-283372-3
"These confessions were written at the end of the fourth century by the most distinguished of the Latin fathers as a revelation of his spiritual experience. They have been a source of religious inspiration through the centuries." Pratt Alcove
Includes bibliographical references

Imitation of Christ.
The imitation of Christ; {by} Thomas à Kempis. Vintage Books 1998 xliii, 242p pa $12.95
242
ISBN 978-0-375-70018-7; 0-375-70018-8
This devotional classic originally written in Latin in the 15th century "traces in four books the gradual progress of the soul to Christian perfection, its detachment from the world, and its union with God." Oxford Companion to Engl Lit. Concise edition

The **little** flowers of St. Francis of Assisi; written by Ugolino di Monte Santa Maria; edited by and adapted from a translation by W. Heywood; with a new preface by Madeleine L'Engle. Vintage Books 1998 xxxviii, 120p (Vintage spiritual classics) pa $13 *   242
1. Francis, of Assisi, Saint, 1182-1226—Legends
ISBN 978-0-375-70020-0; 0-375-70020-X
LC 97-48815
This translation first published 1906 in the United Kingdom
These "simple anecdotes exemplify St. Francis' love of nature, man and of God." Bookman's Manual
Includes bibliographical references

Wills, Garry, 1934-
The rosary: prayer comes round. Viking 2005 190p il $24.95   242
1. Prayer 2. Catholic Church
ISBN 0-670-03449-5   LC 2005-42283

The author "looks at the meaning of the beads and at the mysteries, or events, in the lives of Jesus and Mary that the beads are meant to signify." Publisher's note
This "guide will be helpful to anyone interested in the rosary, but especially to those seeking new insights into its practice." Publ Wkly
Includes bibliographical references

248 Christian experience, practice, life

Girzone, Joseph F.
Never alone; a personal way to God. Doubleday 1994 115p il pa $10.95 hardcover o.p.
248
1. Spiritual life
ISBN 0-3854-7683-3 (pa)   LC 93-38725
Girzone's "empathy for the loneliness and insecurity of being human guides readers toward a more satisfying religious experience than that provided by organized religions, which he continues to criticize for not sufficiently following the living message of Jesus' life." Booklist

Lewis, C. S. (Clive Staples), 1898-1963
Letters to Malcolm: chiefly on prayer 1964 124p pa $13 hardcover o.p.   248
1. Christian life 2. Prayer
ISBN 978-0-15-602766-3
The author's "reflections on prayer are here set down in the form of thoughtful and engaging letters to his friend Malcolm." Cincinnati Public Libr

The Screwtape letters; with, Screwtape proposes a toast. HarperSanFrancisco 2001 209p $22.95; pa $11.95 *   248
1. Christian life 2. Satire
ISBN 0-06-065289-6; 0-06-065293-4 (pa)
LC 00-49860
The Screwtape letters first published 1943 by Macmillan; this combined edition first published 1961 by Macmillan
"A popular work on Christian moral and theological problems. . . . It is in the form of a series of letters in which a devil, Screwtape, advises his nephew, Wormwood, on how to deal with his human 'patients.'" Reader's Ency. 4th edition

Merton, Thomas, 1915-1968
The Asian journal of Thomas Merton; edited from his original notebooks by Naomi Burton, Patrick Hart & James Laughlin; consulting editor: Amiya Chakravarty. New Directions 1973 xxviii, 445p il pa $16.95 hardcover o.p.   248
1. Spiritual life
ISBN 0-8112-0570-3 (pa)
This volume is based on "notes written during {Merton's} last journey which took him to the monasteries of the Orient and ended with his accidental death in Bangkok." Libr J
Includes bibliographical references

Merton, Thomas, 1915-1968—*Continued*

Love and living; [by] Thomas Merton; edited by
Naomi Burton Stone & Patrick Hart. Harcourt
2003 232p pa $14   **248**
1. Spiritual life
ISBN 978-0-15-602799-1; 0-15-602799-2
"A Harvest/HBJ book"
First published 1979 by Farrar Straus Giroux
These essays include "aspects of the perennial themes
of love, death, life and the divine and also demonstrate
the ease with which Merton assimilated the spiritual heritages of East and West." Publ Wkly

New seeds of contemplation; introduction by
Sue Monk Kidd. New Directions 2007 xxi, 297p
pa $15.95   **248**
1. Spiritual life
ISBN 978-0-8112-1724-8
First published 1949 with title: Seeds of contemplation; this is a reissue with a new intoduction of the title
first published 1962
Meditations on integrity, fear, faith, liberty, love and
renunciation

Peale, Norman Vincent
The power of positive living. Fawcett
Columbine 1996 224p pa $13.95 *   **248**
1. Pastoral psychology 2. Applied psychology
3. Success
ISBN 0-449-91166-7; 978-0-449-91166-2
                                          LC 96096721
First published 1952 by Prentice-Hall
In this volume "Peale strings together dozens of personal success stories ('success' is always materialistic)
that make readers feel good. Believing (in yourself, others, values, God) is all-important, and the stories of
wealthy business executives who made it on their own
grab center stage." Libr J

248.2   Religious experience

Armstrong, Karen
Visions of God; four medieval mystics and their
writings. Bantam Bks. 1994 228p pa $19
                                             248.2
1. Rolle, Richard, of Hampole, 1290?-1349 2. Hilton,
Walter, 1340-1396 3. Julian, of Norwich, b. 1343
4. Mysticism
ISBN 0-553-35199-0   LC 94-20217
Contents: Richard Rolle of Hampole; Author of The
cloud of unknowing; Walter Hilton; Dame Julian of Norwich
"The collection is eminently readable and should serve
to make these important sources more accessible to a
general audience. The selections are arranged
chronologically, but Armstrong's reflections also place
them in a 'developmental sequence.'" Booklist
Includes bibliographical references

Downing, David C.
Into the region of awe; mysticism in C. S.
Lewis. InterVarsity Press 2005 207p $17
                                             248.2
1. Lewis, C. S. (Clive Staples), 1898-1963
2. Mysticism
ISBN 0-8308-3284-X; 978-0-8308-3284-2
                                          LC 2004-29844
This is a "book on the writer/thinker's complex attitudes toward mysticism and mystical experience.
Downing is keenly responsible in his approach to Lewis's biography and background and candid about Lewis's
reservations about mysticism in his own theology; the
author's affection for his subject ably informs this sensitive reading of Lewis's life and writings." Libr J
Includes bibliographical references

The **Essential** writings of Christian mysticism;
edited and with an introduction by Bernard
McGinn. Modern Library 2006 559p (Modern
Library classics) pa $19.95 *   **248.2**
1. Mysticism
ISBN 0-8129-7421-2; 978-0-8129-7421-8
                                          LC 2006-44877
"The anthology is organized into three broad parts—
'Foundations of Mystical Practice,' 'Aspects of Mystical
Consciousness,' and 'Implications of the Mystical
Life'—which are further divided into a total of 15 sec-
tions containing some 90 chronologically ordered selec-
tions. . . . McGinn's life of scholarship is evident in his
introduction to each of the sections, which, when read together, comprise an outstanding introduction to Christian
mysticism." Libr J
Includes bibliographical references

Furlong, Monica
Visions & longings; medieval women mystics.
Shambhala Publs. 1996 248p pa $24.95 hardcover
o.p.   **248.2**
1. Mysticism 2. Europe—History—476-1492
3. Women—Religious life
ISBN 1-57062-314-7 (pa)   LC 95-48804
This anthology contains a "range of material—from
Heloise to Julian, from the eleventh century through the
fourteenth. . . . These are not new translations, but readers—particularly those who are coming to some or all of
these writings for the first time—will find it useful to
have them gathered together with Furlong's introductions
and biographical notes. The collection is a window into
a medieval European world that is not widely known or
understood." Booklist

248.4   Christian life and practice

Carter, Jimmy, 1924-
Sources of strength; meditations on scripture for
a living faith. Times Bks. 1997 252p pa $14.99
hardcover o.p.   **248.4**
1. Bible—Meditations 2. Christian life
ISBN 0-8129-3236-6 (pa)   LC 97-27501
Companion volume to Living faith

Carter, Jimmy, 1924- — *Continued*
This "is a collection of 52 brief Bible lessons—one for each week of the year—written by former president Jimmy Carter. All were used in adult Sunday school classes he taught himself. Carter's lessons are open-minded and socially progressive while remaining unapologetically conservative and Christian theologically. . . . The lessons are grouped in nine categories, such as 'What We Believe' and 'Christians in the World,' but each lesson stands well on its own." Libr J

McMinn, Lisa Graham, 1958-
The contented soul; the art of savoring life. InterVarsity Press 2006 184p $17   **248.4**
    1. Christian life
    ISBN 978-0-8308-3335-1; 0-8308-3335-8
                                    LC 2005-33147
The author "explores the nature and practice of contentment from a contemporary Christian vantage point in this excellent guide to spiritual practice. She turns her attention first to what constitutes contentment and then to some ways we can cultivate it in our busy and sometimes unfulfilled lives." Publ Wkly
Includes bibliographical references

252 Texts of sermons

American sermons; the pilgrims to Martin Luther King, Jr. Library of Am. 1999 939p $40 *
                                                252
    1. Sermons
    ISBN 1-88301-165-5   LC 98-34295
This anthology "rounds up in chronological order 58 sermons, from Robert Cushmans address to the colony of Plimmoth in New England in 1621 to Kings 1968 Ive been to the mountaintop speech. Also includes biographical notes and notes on the texts." Libr J
"To peruse this work is to become reacquainted with the literary eloquence of our distant and recent past and to observe what has happened to rhetoric itself over the centuries." N Y Times Book Rev
Includes bibliographical references

King, Martin Luther, Jr., 1929-1968
Strength to love. Fortress 1981 c1963 155p pa $17 *   **252**
    1. Sermons
    ISBN 0-8006-1441-0   LC 80-2374
First published 1963 by Harper & Row
A collection of sermons addressing social injustice and racism.
Includes bibliographical references

255 Religious congregations and orders

Norris, Kathleen, 1947-
The cloister walk. Riverhead Bks. 1996 384p pa $12.95 hardcover o.p.   **255**
    1. Monasticism and religious orders 2. Catholic Church—Liturgy 3. Spiritual life
    ISBN 1-57322-584-3 (pa)   LC 96-863

Companion volume to Dakota: a spiritual geography (1993)
The author relates her experiences as a lay oblate at St. John's Abbey, a Benedictine monastery in Collegeville, Minnesota. The narrative is arranged chronologically according to the rhythm of the Catholic liturgical calendar
"Kathleen Norris knows about faith. She also knows a lot about doubt. . . . As a married Protestant woman, Norris appears to be an improbable candidate to live in a community of celibate men. Yet as she 'walks' with the Benedictine monks, spending days in continual reading, prayer, and singing, she gains new perspectives on their life and her own." Christ Sci Monit

261 Social theology and interreligious relations and attitudes

Benedict XVI, Pope, 1927-
Without roots; Europe, relativism, Christianity and Islam; [by] Pope Benedict XVI and Marcello Pera; foreword by George Weigel; translated by Michael F. Moore. Basic Books 2006 159p $22; $13.95 *   **261**
    1. Europe—Civilization 2. Philosophy and religion
    ISBN 0-465-00634-5; 0-465-00627-2 (pa)
In May of 2004, Marcello Pera "gave a university lecture in Rome, bemoaning the paralyzing effects of relativism and deconstructionism on European self-confidence, in rendering the continent impotent in its response to the threats of militant Islam. By chance, Cardinal Ratzinger, now Pope Benedict XVI, gave a speech the very next day to the Italian Senate, voicing similar concerns about the deleterious effects of Europe's departure from its spiritual roots. This volume offers the speeches and a subsequent exchange of letters between the two speakers. . . . This insightful religious analysis of the contemporary crisis of European culture also provides insight into the current pope's vision of faith and culture." Choice

Niebuhr, H. Richard (Helmut Richard), 1894-1962
Christ and culture. HarperSanFrancisco 2001 lv, 259p pa $15.95   **261**
    1. Christian sociology 2. Christian civilization 3. Culture
    ISBN 0-06-130003-9   LC 2002-284347
First published 1951
"Expanded edition, fiftieth anniversary." On cover
"Important, scholarly study presents five viewpoints of Christ and culture held over the centuries: (1) Christ against culture—and separation from 'the world'; (2) the Christ of culture—the identification of Christianity and civilization; (3) Christ above culture—the Thomist position; (4) Christ and culture in paradox—Luther's position; (5) Christ transforming culture—exemplified by Augustine and Calvin." Cincinnati Public Libr
Includes bibliographical references

261.2 Christianity and other systems of belief

Carroll, James
Constantine's sword; the church and the Jews: a history. Houghton Mifflin 2001 756p $28; pa $16
                                                                                              261.2
1.   Catholic   Church—Relations—Judaism
2. Christianity and other religions 3. Judaism
ISBN 0-395-77927-8; 0-6142-1908-0 (pa)
                                                         LC 00-61329
Carroll's thesis is "that the relationship with the Jews is not merely one issue among many for the modern church. It is the central issue in church history and inextricable from the core of what Christianity is about." NY Times Book Rev
"This magisterial work will satisfy Jewish and Christians readers alike, challenging both to a renewed conversation with one another." Publ Wkly
Includes bibliographical references

Kertzer, David I., 1948-
The Popes against the Jews; the Vatican's role in the rise of modern anti-semitism. Knopf 2001 355p $27.95; pa $15   **261.2**
1.   Catholic   Church—Relations—Judaism
2. Antisemitism
ISBN 0-375-40623-9; 0-375-70605-4 (pa)
                                                        LC 2001-33728
"Kertzer argues that the modern popes and their minions helped create and perpetuate an anti-Semitic Catholic culture that facilitated the eventual extermination of six million European Jews." Libr J
"This is a devastating indictment, and fair-minded critics will find flaws in Kertzer's methodology and sweeping conclusions. Nevertheless, he has opened a window that should be opened." Booklist
Includes bibliographical references

261.5 Christianity and secular disciplines

Grant, Edward, 1926-
Science and religion, 400 B.C. to A.D. 1550; from Aristotle to Copernicus. Greenwood Press 2004 xxvi, 307p il (Greenwood guides to science and religion) $67.95 *   **261.5**
1. Religion and science
ISBN 0-313-32858-7   LC 2004-17429
Contents: Introduction — Aristotle and the beginnings of two thousand years of natural philosophy — Science and natural philosophy in the Roman empire — The first six centuries of Christianity: Christian attitudes toward Greek philosophy and science — The emergence of a New Europe after the Barbarian invasions — The medieval universities and the impact of Aristotle's natural philosophy — The interrelations between natural philosophy and theology in the fourteenth and fifteenth centuries — Relations between science and religion in the Byzantine empire, the world of Islam, and the Latin West
Includes bibliographical references

Noble, David F.
The religion of technology; the divinity of man and the spirit of invention. Knopf 1997 273p pa $14.95 hardcover o.p.   **261.5**
1. Technology and civilization 2. Religion and science 3. God
ISBN 0-14-027916-4 (pa)   LC 96-48019
"Covering a period of a thousand years, Noble traces the evolution of the Western idea of technological development from the ninth century, when, {he argues}, the useful arts became connected to the concept of redemption, up to the twentieth, when humans began to exercise God-like knowledge and powers." Publisher's note
"This is a dense, fascinating study of technology and Christianity." Libr J
Includes bibliographical references

Olson, Richard, 1940-
Science and religion, 1450-1900; from Copernicus to Darwin; [by] Richard G. Olson. Greenwood Press 2004 292p il (Greenwood guides to science and religion) $65 *   **261.5**
1. Religion and science
ISBN 0-313-32694-0   LC 2004-47501
This book "explores the many ways in which religion—its ideas, attitudes, practices, and institutions—interacted with science from the beginnings of the Scientific Revolution to the end of the 19th century." Publisher's note
The issues discussed "should be especially helpful to those who are interested in the historical background to current science-religion issues being debated in the United States." Sci Books Films
Includes bibliographical references

Schroeder, Gerald L.
The science of God; the convergence of scientific and biblical wisdom; [by] Gerald Schroeder. Broadway Books 1998 226p il pa $14.95   **261.5**
1. Bible and science
ISBN 0-7679-0303-X (pa); 0-7679-0303-5 (pa)
                                                        LC 98-25031
First published 1997 by Free Press
The author a physicist, "wants to show that modern study of the physical universe is really telling the same story of life and creation as the Hebrew Bible. To do this, Schroeder draws on . . . Jewish study of the Pentateuch, the first five books of the Bible, and on his understanding of modern physics, cosmology, archeology, and the biology of evolution." Christ Sci Monit
This book contains "many interesting reflections and meaningful insights; and for those who need scientific backing to accept the pronouncements of ancient seers, this book may be highly recommended." Choice
Includes bibliographical references

261.7 Christianity and political affairs

Zagorin, Perez

How the idea of religious toleration came to the West. Princeton University Press 2003 371p il hardcover o.p. pa $24.95 **261.7**

1. Religious tolerance

ISBN 0-691-09270-2; 978-0-691-12142-0; 0-691-12142-7 (pa) LC 2002-42565

The author discusses "a time when both the Catholic Church and the main new Protestant denominations embraced a policy of endorsing religious persecution, coercing unity, and, with the state's help, mercilessly crushing dissent and heresy. This position had its roots in certain intellectual and religious traditions, which Zagorin trace before showing how out of the same traditions came the beginnings of pluralism in the West. . . . His book—which ranges from England through the Netherlands, the post-1685 Huguenot Diaspora, and the American colonies—also exposes a close connection between toleration and religious freedom." Publisher's note

"A deeply scholarly but ultimately engaging argument for the origins of religious toleration in Western culture since the Enlightenment." Libr J

Includes bibliographical references

261.8 Christianity and socioeconomic problems

Albright, Madeleine Korbel, 1937-

The mighty and the Almighty; reflections on America, God, and world affairs; [by] Madeleine Albright with Bill Woodward. HarperCollins 2006 339p $25.95 **261.8**

1. Religion and politics 2. United States—Foreign relations

ISBN 0-06-089257-9; 978-0-06-089257-9 LC 2005-55002

The author discusses "the role of faith in international relations. In a remarkably accessible, even breezy style, she looks at these issues in light of recent history both abroad and at home, from the religious fundamentalism that led to the ouster of the shah of Iran to the invasion of Iraq and American hope that a political culture can emerge there that integrates democracy and Islam." Publ Wkly

Includes bibliographical references

Cone, James H., 1938-

A black theology of liberation. 20th anniversary ed. Orbis Bks. 1990 xx, 214p pa $17

261.8

1. Church and race relations 2. African Americans—Religion

ISBN 0-88344-685-5 LC 90-43041

First published 1970 by Lippincott

The author "takes as his theme the belief that 'Christian theology is a theology of liberation.' He then proceeds to relate the struggle for black liberation to the de-

velopment of black theology in reaction to the indifference of white Christians to the plight of their fellow church members." Libr J

Includes bibliographical references

Martin, William C. (William Curtis), 1937-

With God on our side; the rise of the religious right in America; [by] William Martin. Broadway Bks. 1996 418p il $27.50; pa $15 **261.8**

1. Religion and politics 2. Religious fundamentalism 3. Conservatism 4. Christianity and politics

ISBN 0-553-06745-1; 0-553-06749-4 (pa)

LC 96-2919

"Focusing on the modern era, the author analyzes the significance of church and clergy in the tradition of social action, from the civil rights movement through the growth of the Christian Coalition." Publ Wkly

"Unlike some companion volumes to television documentaries, Martin's well-written, superbly organized work stands on its own. . . . [It] is required reading for anyone seeking to understand the rise of the Religious Right. . . . Nothing has been published that can match Martin's book in sweep and substance." Christ Century

Includes bibliographical references

262 Ecclesiology

Chaves, Mark

Ordaining women; culture and conflict in religious organizations. Harvard Univ. Press 1997 237p pa $18.50 hardcover o.p. **262**

1. Ordination of women 2. Women in Christianity 3. Christian sociology 4. United States—Church history

ISBN 0-674-64146-9 (pa) LC 97-12518

The author provides a "study of the 19th- and 20th-century ordination policies and practices of many Christian groups in the United States, including the Roman Catholic Church." Libr J

Includes bibliographical references

Pham, John-Peter

Heirs of the Fisherman; behind the scenes of papal death and succession. Oxford University Press 2004 368p $28; pa $16.95 **262**

1. Papacy

ISBN 0-19-517834-3; 0-19-530561-2 (pa)

LC 2004-9726

"The author traces, in six chapters, the development of the ritual governing the period following a pope's death and the election of his successor." Choice

"Pham's exhaustive approach and informed view will appeal to anyone interested in more than a cursory treatment of this fascinating subject." Publ Wkly

Includes bibliographical references

Wills, Garry, 1934-

Papal sin; structures of deceit. Doubleday 2000 326p $25; pa $15.95 **262**

1. Papacy 2. Catholic Church

ISBN 0-385-49410-6; 0-385-49411-4 (pa)

LC 99-54851

Wills, Garry, 1934-—*Continued*

The author "argues that the Church is not merely the clergy but the whole body of believers. His examination of papal policies on such topics as the Holocaust, clerical celibacy, and the role of women finds that the Church has often distorted history and Scripture in the attempt to bolster its authority. There's an undertone of grief to this rationally argued book, which ends with a wistful vision of the Church as it might be." New Yorker

Includes bibliographical references

264   Public worship

Episcopal Church

The Book of common prayer and administration of the sacraments and other rites and ceremonies of the church; together with the Psalter or Psalms of David according to the use of the Episcopal Church. Church Hymnal Corp, Seabury Press 1979 1001p pew ed., black $19 *   **264**
   ISBN 0-89869-081-1   LC 81-204603
   Also available red pew edition $19 (ISBN: 0-89869-080-3); other bindings and editions also available
   The official liturgy of the Episcopal Church.

270   History of Christianity

Chadwick, Owen

A history of Christianity. St. Martin's Press 1996 304p il pa $35 hardcover o.p.   **270**
   1. Church history
   ISBN 0-312-18723-8 (pa)   LC 96-2631
   "A Thomas Dunne book"
This overview of Christianity is "illustrated, with the text and pictures working well together to give the reader a clear meaning of basic Christian concepts. . . . The facts are correct, the time lines are accurate, the voice is that of a lover of Christian history rather than a purely academic scholar." Libr J

Chidester, David

Christianity;   a   global   history. HarperSanFrancisco 2000 627p il $32; pa $21
                                        270
   1. Church history 2. Christianity
   ISBN 0-06-251708-2; 0-06-251770-8 (pa)
                                    LC 00-37006
This volume is divided into three parts: "the emergence of Christian doctrine and ritual from the time of Jesus up until the year 600; the practices and personages of both the Roman and the Eastern churches up through the time of the Reformation; and, finally, the spread of Christianity around the globe beginning at the time of Columbus." Christ Sci Monit
   "Highly recommended for religion and history collections looking for a work that anchors modern sensibilities to ancient ideas." Libr J
   Includes bibliographical references

Jenkins, Philip, 1952-

The new faces of Christianity; believing the Bible in the global south. Oxford University Press 2006 252p $26   **270**
   1. Christianity 2. Forecasting
   ISBN 978-0-19-530065-9; 0-19-530065-3
                                    LC 2006-15490
Second volume in the author's trilogy about the future of Christianity, begun with: The next Christendom
   Jenkins explores the growth of Christianity in Africa, Asia and Latin America.
   "Those interested in religious trends across the globe, the Muslim-Christian friction, and world politics will benefit from this resource." Libr J
   Includes bibliographical references

Riley, Gregory J. (Gregory John), 1947-

The river of God; a new history of Christian origins. HarperSanFrancisco 2001 252p $24; pa $14.95   **270**
   1. Church history—30-600, Early church
   ISBN 0-06-066979-9; 0-06-066980-2 (pa)
                                    LC 2001-16888
The author "contends that Christianity originated from the tremendous theological diversity of Near Eastern religions and that its origins cannot be explained or understood adequately by simply emphasizing its roots in Judaism. . . . He proposes instead a threefold model of genealogy, punctuated equilibrium and the 'river of God' to investigate Christian origins." Publ Wkly
   "This volume will become one of the most important books on the subject." Libr J
   Includes bibliographical references

270.6   Christian church— Reformation

MacCulloch, Diarmaid

The Reformation; a house divided. Viking 2004 xxiv, 792p il map $34.95; pa $18   **270.6**
   1. Reformation
   ISBN 0-670-03296-4; 0-14-303538-X (pa)
                                    LC 2003-61607
   First published 2003 in the United Kingdom
   In this "study of the Reformation, MacCulloch challenges traditional interpretations, arguing instead that there were many reformations. Arranging his history in chronological fashion, MacCulloch provides . . . studies of reform movements in central, northern and southern Europe and examines the influences that politics and geography had on such groups." Publ Wkly
   The author "has produced the definitive survey for this generation. . . . This well-written book is a joy to read, with new facts and interpretations on nearly every page." Libr J
   Includes bibliographical references

271 Religious congregations and orders in church history

Lacouture, Jean
Jesuits; a multibiography; translated from the French by Jeremy Leggatt. Counterpoint Bks. 1995 550p il pa $30.95 hardcover o.p.   271
1. Jesuits
ISBN 1-887178-60-0 (pa)   LC 95-34002
"A Cornelia and Michael Bessie book"
Original French edition, 1991
The author "presents a series of biographies of prominent Jesuits from the founder, Ignatius of Loyola, down to such modern disciples as Karl Rahner, Daniel Berrigan, and Robert Drinan." Libr J
This book "will appeal even to audiences that do not have a special interest in Jesuit history. . . . Insofar as particular stories of particular people and places are the best sources of global insight, this is an especially valuable work." Booklist
Includes bibliographical references

272 Persecutions in general church history

Foxe, John, 1516-1587
Fox's book of martyrs; a history of the lives, sufferings and triumphant deaths of the early Christian and the Protestant martyrs; edited by William Byron Forbush. Zondervan 1978 c1926 370p hardcover o.p. pa $12.99 *   272
1. Martyrs 2. Persecution 3. Church history
ISBN 0-310-24390-4; 0-310-24391-2 (pa)
First complete version published 1563 in England under title: Actes and monuments of these latter and perilous days
"The Actes and Monuments was tremendously influential, being used practically as a companion volume to the Bible in English churches and households for many years. The work is of interest historically for its many accounts of the deaths of contemporary Protestant martyrs." Reader's Ency. 4th edition

Kamen, Henry
The Spanish Inquisition; a historical revision. Yale Univ. Press 1998 369p il $45; pa $14.80
272
1. Inquisition 2. Spain—History
ISBN 0-300-07522-7; 0-300-07880-3 (pa)
LC 97-32451
First published 1965 in the United Kingdom; first United States edition 1966 by New Am. Lib.
In this revision of his 1965 study, the author "restates his original argument. . . . He reaffirms his contention that an all-powerful, torture-mad Inquisition is largely a 19th-century myth. In its place he portrays a poor, understaffed institution whose scattered tribunals had only a limited reach and whose methods were more humane than those of most secular courts. . . . As for the Inquisition's much-vaunted role as Big Brother and its

responsibility for intellectual decline, Kamen rejects this hypothesis out of hand. . . . [He] also dismisses the notion that the Inquisition enjoyed widespread popular support." N Y Times Book Rev
Includes bibliographical references

Pérez, Joseph, 1931-
The Spanish Inquisition; a history; trans. by Janet Lloyd. Yale University Press 2005 248p $26; pa $17 *   272
1. Inquisition 2. Spain—History
ISBN 0-300-10790-0; 0-300-11982-8 (pa)
LC 2004-114614
The author "tells the history of the Spanish Inquisition from its medieval beginnings to its nineteenth-century ending. . . . He explores the inner workings of its councils, and shows how its officers, inquisitors, and leaders lived and worked." Univ Press Books for Public and Second Sch Libr, 2006
Includes bibliographical references

277 Christian Church in North America

Yearbook of American & Canadian churches, 2008; edited by Eileen W. Lindner. Seventy-sixth issue. Abingdon Press 2008 440p pa $55 *   277
1. Religious institutions—Directories
ISSN 0084-3644
ISBN 978-0-687-65149-8; 0-687-65149-2
"Prepared and edited for the National Council of Churches of Christ in the U.S.A."
Annual. First published 1916. Title and publisher vary
"Directory, statistical, and historical information on many religious and ecumenical organizations and service agencies, accredited seminaries, colleges and universities, and depositories of church history materials. Also a list of religious periodicals." Ref Sources for Small & Medium-sized Libr. 6th edition
Includes bibliographical references

277.3 Christian Church in the United States

Bawer, Bruce, 1956-
Stealing Jesus; how fundamentalism betrays Christianity. Crown 1997 340p pa $14 hardcover o.p.   277.3
1. Christian fundamentalism 2. Christianity 3. United States—Church history
ISBN 0-609-80222-4 (pa)   LC 97-20111
The author "contends that fundamentalist Christianity, what he calls the 'Church of Law,' has been preaching a message of wrath and judgment to modern American culture that Bawer believes is incompatible with Jesus' message of love. . . . [His] graceful prose and lucid insights make this a must-read book for anyone concerned with the relationship of Christianity to contemporary American culture." Publ Wkly

Callahan, Allen Dwight
The talking book; African Americans and the Bible. Yale University Press 2006 286p $30 *
277.3
1. Bible—Criticism 2. African Americans—Religion
ISBN 9780300109368; 0-300-10936-9
LC 2006-6464
The author "examines how the music and literature of black Americans are shot through with biblical images. His opening chapter rehearses familiar history, explaining how white evangelicals introduced slaves to the Bible, and arguing that the Bible has given black Americans the resources to critique injustice. More innovatively, Callahan examines how black readers have engaged the Bible's 'toxic' passages, like Genesis 9:25, which racists have read to say that dark skin is a curse. Callahan then turns to his central task: teasing out the various biblical themes that have been important to black writers and readers." Publ Wkly
Includes bibliographical references

Lincoln, C. Eric (Charles Eric), 1924-2000
The black church in the African American experience; {by} C. Eric Lincoln and Lawrence H. Mamiya. Duke Univ. Press 1990 519p pa $26.95 hardcover o.p.
277.3
1. African Americans—Religion 2. United States—Church history
ISBN 0-8223-1073-2 (pa)
LC 90-34050
This book was "developed from a ten-year field study that investigated the black church as it relates to the history of African Americans and to contemporary black culture. . . . {It considers} the church's relationships to politics, economics, women (attitudes of clergy as pastors), youth, music, civil rights, and trends for the next century." Libr J
Includes bibliographical references

Marty, Martin E., 1928-
Pilgrims in their own land; 500 years of religion in America. Penguin Books 1985 500p il pa $18
277.3
1. United States—Church history 2. United States—Religion
ISBN 0-14-008268-9; 978-0-14-008268-5
LC 85-3596
First published 1984 by Little, Brown
This book examines "the force of religion in the United States since colonial times. Marty considers not only the religious beliefs and rituals brought to America by the various European settlers, but also those of native Americans. The clashes between Protestant, Catholic, Judaic, and other religious groups are perceived in light of their influence upon the development of this nation up to the present." Booklist
Includes bibliographical references

Wills, Garry, 1934-
Head and heart; American Christianities. Penguin Press 2007 626p il $29.95
277.3
1. United States—Church history
ISBN 978-1-59420-146-2
LC 2007-12631

The author argues that "the history of Christianity in the U.S. is a dialectic of the intellect and the emotions. . . . [This book] ought to be the one volume everyone interested in the subject reads—it is lucid and grandly informative—and reacts to, thus keeping the conversation alive." Booklist
Includes bibliographical references

280 Christian denominations

The **encyclopedia** of Protestantism; Hans Hillerbrand, editor. Routledge 2004 4v set $695 *
280
1. Protestantism—Encyclopedias
ISBN 0-415-92472-3
LC 2003-11582
"Nearly 500 contributors provide descriptions and explanations of matters of theology, culture, eminent lives, material artifacts, and comparative religions; the A-to-Z entries range from 'Apocalypticism' to 'Latin America,' 'Pilgrim's Progress,' and 'Women Clergy.' . . . [This work] is an excellent resource to engage in the exploration of humanities, policy issues, and concerns beyond the specifically religious while also providing deep analyses of theological matters." Libr J
Includes bibliographical references

McGrath, Alister E., 1953-
Christianity's dangerous idea; the Protestant revolution— a history from the sixteenth century to the twenty-first. HarperOne 2007 552p il $29.95
280
1. Protestantism
ISBN 978-0-06-082213-2; 0-06-082213-9
LC 2007-61021
This is an "overview of 'the Protestant revolution' filtered through the 'dangerous idea' that all Christians have the right to interpret the Bible for themselves. . . . [This book is] a readable, informative, and challenging 'grand narrative' that deftly describes the tonalities of Protestantism's varied historical, political, socioeconomic, and religious contexts." Choice
Includes bibliographical references

Mead, Frank Spencer, 1898-1982
Handbook of denominations in the United States; [by] Frank S. Mead, Samuel S. Hill, Craig D. Atwood. 12th ed. Abingdon Press 2005 430p il $20 *
280
1. Sects 2. United States—Religion
ISSN 0072-9787
ISBN 0-687-05784-1; 978-0-687-05784-9
LC 2005-11023
First published 1951. Periodically revised
"History and present structure of Christian religious bodies in the United States. Reports on doctrines of different churches. Includes bibliography and index." NY Public Libr Book of How & Where to Look It Up

282 Roman Catholic Church

Briggs, Kenneth
Double crossed; uncovering the Catholic Church's betrayal of American nuns; [by] Kenneth A. Briggs. Doubleday 2006 258p $24.95
282
1. Catholic Church—United States 2. Nuns
ISBN 0-385-51636-3; 978-0-385-51636-5
LC 2006-282243
The Roman Catholic Church in the United States "has lost nearly 100,000 religious sisters in the last forty years, a much greater loss than the priesthood. While the explanation is partly cultural—contemporary women have more choices in work and life—Kenneth Briggs contends that the rapid disappearance of convents can be traced . . . to the Church's betrayal of the promises of reform made by the Second Vatican Council." Publisher's note
"Readers sympathetic to the cause of sisters who sought greater reform than was achieved will most appreciate Briggs's work on this important topic." Publ Wkly
Includes bibliographical references

Brophy, Donald, 1934-
One hundred great Catholic books; from the early centuries to the present; [by] Don Brophy. BlueBridge 2007 xvii, 222p pa $16
282
1. Catholic literature
ISBN 978-1-933346-08-3; 1-933346-08-6
LC 2007-10195
"Entries are chronologically arranged, beginning with early Christian sayings from the Desert Fathers and ending with biographical considerations of such authors as Thomas Merton, Dorothy Day, Walker Percy, and Flannery O'Connor. Other topics examined in these reflective essays include German theologian Meister Eckhart, the 19th-century encyclical Rerum Novarum (Of New Things), the documents of Vatican II, and Patricia Hampl's Virgin Time. The succinct considerations address the historical or contemporary context of the work, explain the significance of the author, and contain a brief synopsis of the actual title. Many literary genres are covered." Libr J
Includes bibliographical references

Carroll, James
Toward a new Catholic Church; the promise of reform. Houghton Mifflin 2002 130p pa $8.95
282
1. Catholic Church
ISBN 0-618-31337-0
LC 2002-27262
"A Mariner book"
The author "has a reform agenda . . . consisting of five proposals: expand the faithful's biblical literacy in sophistication and depth; purge the church's political pretensions and behavior; reformulate Christology to emphasize Jesus as revelator rather than savior; run the church democratically; and repent of anti-Semitism, sexism, homophobia, and other ills by admitting the church has sinned. . . . An important statement." Booklist
Includes bibliographical references

Catholic Almanac, 2008; Matthew Bunson, D.Min., general editor. Our Sunday Visitor 2008 640p pa $28.95 *
282
1. Catholic Church—Directories 2. Almanacs
ISSN 0069-1208
ISBN 978-1-59276-334-4; 1-59276-334-0
Annual. First published 1904. Title varies
At head of title: Our Sunday Visitor's
"Includes much miscellaneous information, e.g., annual survey of news, ecclesiastical calendar, glossary of terms in Catholic use, the Catholic church in various countries of the world, statistics, directory of information, etc." Guide to Ref Books. 11th edition

Collins, Paul
The modern Inquisition; seven prominent Catholics and their struggles with the Vatican. Overlook Press 2002 260p $29.95
282
1. Catholic Church
ISBN 1-58567-270-X
LC 2002-25223
This work is an "assessment of the Roman Catholic Church's treatment of its theologians who reflect contrary views from those of the Congregation for the Doctrine of the Faith (CDF). . . . In eight passionately written essays, [Collins] considers the lives, work, and trials of several priests and sisters whose ideas were reviewed by the CDF. . . . Among them Hans Kung, Lavinia Byrne, Charles Curran, Jeannine Gramick and Robert Nugent, Tissa Balusaria, and the author himself." Libr J
Includes bibliographical references

Duffy, Eamon
Saints & sinners; a history of the Popes. Yale Univ. Press 1997 326p il maps $30; pa $17.95
282
1. Papacy
ISBN 0-300-07332-1; 0-300-09165-6 (pa)
LC 97-60897
Published "in association with S4C."
This illustrated volume is a companion piece to a six-part television series of the same name. The book offers an overview of the 2,000-year history of the papacy
"Duffy's task is to present a balanced and continuous narrative with as much personal and historical detail as possible. This he does admirably with an eye for lively anecdotes and apt quotations." Commonweal

Flinn, Frank K.
Encyclopedia of Catholicism. Facts on File 2006 xxxi, 670p (Encyclopedia of world religions) $75
282
1. Catholic Church—Encyclopedias
ISBN 0-8160-5455-X; 978-0-8160-5455-8
LC 2006-9645
This encyclopedia "covers the key people, movements, institutions, practices, and doctrines of Roman Catholicism from its earliest origins." Publisher's note
Includes bibliographical references

Gillis, Chester, 1951-
Roman Catholicism in America. Columbia Univ. Press 1999 365p il (Columbia contemporary American religion series) $60; pa $20.50
282
1. Catholic Church—United States 2. United States—Church history
ISBN 0-231-10870-2; 0-231-10871-0 (pa)
LC 99-17945
The author "provides a broad overview of the history and practice of Catholicism in America at the end of the 20th century." Publ Wkly
This is "an excellent survey." Libr J
Includes bibliographical references

The **HarperCollins** encyclopedia of Catholicism; general editor, Richard P. McBrien; associate editors, Harold W. Attridge [et al.] HarperSanFrancisco 1995 xxxviii, 1349p il maps $47.50   **282**
1. Catholic Church—Encyclopedias
ISBN 0-06-065338-8   LC 94-39972
"This encyclopedic dictionary contains 4700 entries by 277 experts. . . . Broad-ranging topics in Catholic theology, history, culture, art, canon law, literature, etc., are replete with cross references, photos, maps, tables, diagrams, and charts." Libr J

Jenkins, Philip, 1952-
The new anti-catholicism; the last acceptable prejudice. Oxford Univ. Press 2003 258p hardcover o.p. pa $18.95   **282**
1. Catholic Church—United States
ISBN 0-19-515480-0; 978-0-19-517604-9 (pa); 0-19-517604-9 (pa)   LC 2002-12488
Contents: Limits of hatred -- The Catholic menace -- Catholics and liberals -- The church hates women -- The church kills gays -- Catholics and the news media -- "The perp walk of sacramental perverts" : the pedophile priest crisis -- Catholics in movies and television -- Black legends : rewriting Catholic history -- The end of prejudice?
Jenkins begins with a survey of the history of anti-Catholicism in the United States from colonial times through the twentieth century. In looking at the present, the author devotes chapters to conflicts between Catholics and liberals, Catholics and feminists, Catholics and gay people, Catholics and the news media, the pedophile priest crisis, and Catholics in movies and television
"Honest, passionate, and convincing, it will cause the reader to reconsider basic assumptions. Some 30 pages of notes and bibliography add heft to this serious work." Libr J

John Paul II, Pope, 1920-2005
Crossing the threshold of hope; edited by Vittorio Messori. Knopf 1994 244p pa $15 hardcover o.p. *   **282**
1. Apologetics 2. Catholic Church 3. Christian life 4. Faith
ISBN 0-679-76561-1 (pa)   LC 94-78675
In this book the Pope responds to written questions by an Italian Catholic journalist originally planned for a television interview which never took place. The questions addressed include: what is the papacy?; when and how should one pray?; is there proof of God's existence?; is Jesus the Son of God?; why is there so much evil in the world?; why does God tolerate suffering?; is only Rome right?; and what are human rights?
"This is a book to be read for insights, perspectives, connections, formulations that spark meditation and enrich our understanding." Commonweal

Küng, Hans, 1928-
The Catholic Church; a short history; translated by John Bowden. Modern Lib. 2001 xxv, 221p (Modern Library chronicles) $19.95; pa $9.95
282
1. Catholic Church
ISBN 0-679-64092-4; 0-8129-6762-3 (pa)
LC 00-67568
Includes index
The author "presents a summary of the major persons and movements that have formed the Catholic Church from its beginnings to the present." Libr J
"About as good a brief presentation of the 'liberal' view of church history as anyone could reasonably expect." Booklist

Maxwell-Stuart, P. G.
Chronicle of the popes; the reign-by-reign record of the papacy from St. Peter to the present. Thames & Hudson 1997 240p il maps $34.95
282
1. Papacy
ISBN 0-500-01798-0   LC 97-60230
This survey examines the lives and deeds of the 264 popes from St. Peter to John Paul II
This history of the papacy "provides a good selection of illustrations with a lightweight text." N Y Times Book Rev
Includes bibliographical references

Neuhaus, Richard John
Catholic matters; confusion, controversy, and the splendor of truth. Basic Books 2006 260p $25
282
1. Catholic Church
ISBN 978-0-465-04935-6; 0-465-04935-4
LC 2005-34569
The author argues that "Catholicism is more vital and important to the cultural and political life of Americans than ever before. . . . [He discusses] the battles over the meaning of the Second Vatican Council, the 'destabilizing' of the liturgy, the declining number of priests, and the sexual abuse scandals. Looking beyond these troubles, . . . he proposes a vibrant, forward-thinking way of being Catholic in America." Publisher's note
Neuhaus "makes an erudite case for the old teachings, while humanizing them in the context of his own biography." N Y Times Book Rev
Includes bibliographical references

New Catholic encyclopedia; prepared by an editorial staff at the Catholic University of America. 2nd ed. Gale Group 2003 15v il maps set $1,728 * **282**
1. Catholic Church—Encyclopedias
ISBN 978-0-7876-4004-0; 0-7876-4004-2
LC 2002-924
First published 1967 as an update to the Catholic encyclopedia
Published "in association with the Catholic University of America."
This encyclopedia "covers the history of the eastern churches, the churches of the Protestant Reformation, and other ecclesial communities as well as the Christian roots based in ancient Israel and Judaism. No comprehensive resource on Catholicism can be complete without touching on other world religions as well, including Islam, Buddhism, and Hinduism. This resource provides entries not only on the doctrine, organization, and history of the church, but also on the people, institutions, and social changes that have affected the church over the years. Arranged alphabetically, the entries run in length from half a page to several pages in length. All entries provide the name of the contributor and a bibliography. Cross-references to related articles are located throughout the work. Adding to the usefulness of the set are more than 3,000 black-and-white photographs, maps, and charts that complement the scholarly articles." Am Ref Books Annu, 2003

The **Official** Catholic directory 2008. National Register Pub. 2008 2109p $335 * **282**
1. Catholic Church—Directories
ISSN 0078-3854
ISBN 978-0-87217-550-1; 0-87217-550-1
Supplementary paperback volume published midyear included in price of subscription
Annual. First published 1886. Title and publisher vary
"Contains a large amount of useful and detailed directory, institutional, and statistical information about the organization, clergy, churches, missions, schools, religious orders, etc., of the Catholic church in the U.S. and its possessions. Coverage varies." Guide to Ref Books. 11th edition

Reese, Thomas J.
Inside the Vatican; the politics and organization of the Catholic Church. Harvard Univ. Press 1996 317p il $30; pa $16.95 **282**
1. Papacy 2. Vatican City 3. Catholic Church
ISBN 0-674-93260-9; 0-679-93261-7 (pa)
LC 96-26641
The author examines "the internal workings of the Vatican both as city-state and the headquarters of the Roman Catholic Church. . . . With its wealth of information, historical background, and analysis, Reese's work should be an important addition for a variety of libraries." Libr J
Includes bibliographical references

Steinfels, Peter
A people adrift; the crisis of the Roman Catholic Church in America. Simon & Schuster 2003 xxi, 392p hardcover o.p. pa $15 **282**
1. Catholic Church—United States
ISBN 0-684-83663-7; 0-7432-6144-5 (pa)
LC 2003-54208
The author "places the sex abuse scandal in a larger context and traces the church's crisis to a vacuum of leadership." N Y Times Book Rev
"Steinfels sounds a call for a reasoned common ground that respects the richness of tradition and also reflects the reality of the practices and needs of more than 60 million American Catholics, rather than the agendas of any number of the small but vocal groups within Catholicism. This book will be hailed by many, and with good reason." Publ Wkly
Includes bibliographical references

Wills, Garry, 1934-
Why I am a Catholic. Houghton Mifflin 2002 390p $26; pa $14 **282**
1. Papacy 2. Catholic Church
ISBN 0-618-13429-8; 0-618-38048-5 (pa)
LC 2002-283644
Sequel to: Papal sin
The author "begins with a very personal, though brief, look at his life as a Catholic, which includes time spent as a Jesuit novice, then proceeds with a detailed defense of his views on the church and its papacy. He concludes with an explanation of the Apostles' Creed, which he regards as the true foundation of his faith." Publ Wkly
This book is "intellectually satisfying, and spiritually moving." Booklist
Includes bibliographical references

Woodward, Kenneth L.
Making saints; how the Catholic Church determines who becomes a saint, who doesn't, and why. Simon & Schuster 1990 461p il pa $21.50 hardcover o.p. **282**
1. Christian saints 2. Catholic Church
ISBN 0-684-81530-3 (pa)
LC 90-10117
A study of the politics and procedures of the modern process of canonization in the Roman Catholic church
This is "the most comprehensive, critical and up-to-date look at saint making so far written." N Y Times Book Rev
Includes bibliographical references

283 Anglican churches

Jenkyns, Richard
Westminster Abbey. Harvard University Press 2005 215p il map $19.95 **283**
1. Westminster Abbey—History
ISBN 0-674-01716-1
LC 2004-54312
First published 2004 in the United Kingdom
"Jenkyns' discussion points incorporate architecture, history, and culture as he defends and details . . . [a]

Jenkyns, Richard—*Continued*
conviction that 'the Abbey exists as an idea as well as a building.' Exploration of the abbey's evolving functions since its origins in the thirteenth century takes the author specifically into such topics as the nature of Gothic architecture (with particular attention paid to Henry VII's chapel), the circumstances by which the abbey became a royal mausoleum and pantheon of the great, its importance as a gallery of sculpture, its physical setting within London's changing cityscape, and its major function as the site of coronations. A mellifluous writing style caps this splendid reading and learning experience." Booklist

Includes bibliographical references

286   Baptist, Disciples of Christ, Adventist churches

Leonard, Bill
Baptists in America; [by] Bill J. Leonard. Columbia University Press 2005 316p il (Columbia contemporary American religion series) $48.50; pa $27 *   286
1. Baptists
ISBN 0-231-12702-2; 0-231-12703-0 (pa)
                                    LC 2005-41363
"In an introduction and ten chapters, Leonard examines the history of the Baptist tradition in America, pointing out the distinctive diversity that characterizes the movement." Choice
"Anyone interested in American religious history or simply American history will find this an enlightening and substantively informative book." Libr J
Includes bibliographical references

287.9   Churches related to Methodism

Winston, Diane H., 1951-
Red-hot and righteous; the urban religion of the Salvation Army; [by] Diane Winston. Harvard Univ. Press 1999 290p il $31; pa $16.95
                                                287.9
1. Salvation Army
ISBN 0-674-86706-8; 0-674-00396-9 (pa)
                                    LC 98-47842
"Winston traces the development of the Salvation Army from 1880, when it first arrived in New York, to 1950. . . . Winston's lively study is a must-read for anyone interested in the Salvation Army as a case study for the interrelationship of religion and culture." Publ Wkly
Includes bibliographical references

289   Other denominations and sects

Stein, Stephen J., 1940-
The Shaker experience in America; a history of the United Society of Believers. Yale Univ. Press 1992 xx, 554p il $65; pa $21   289
1. Shakers
ISBN 0-300-05139-5; 0-300-05933-7 (pa)
                                    LC 91-30836
A historical look at the evolution of Shakerism focusing on the movement's cultural values, religion and artifacts

Includes bibliographical references

289.3   Latter-Day Saints (Mormons)

Abanes, Richard
One nation under gods; a history of the Mormon Church. Four Walls Eight Windows 2002 xxv, 651p il $32; pa $22 *   289.3
1. Church of Jesus Christ of Latter-day Saints
ISBN 1-56858-219-6; 1-56858-283-8 (pa)
                                    LC 2001-40430
The author "explains what Mormons believe, as well as how Mormonism came to be the religion that it is today. . . . {He also discusses the} origins of Mormonism, the socioeconomic factors that contributed to its growth, its ongoing political agenda, and its religious teachings." Publisher's note
"This well-researched and readable history will be of interest to anyone seeking an objective Mormon history." Libr J
Includes bibliographical references

Book of Mormon.
The Book of Mormon; another testament of Jesus Christ; [translated by Joseph Smith, Jr.] Doubleday 2004 586p $24.95 *   289.3
1. Mormons
ISBN 0-385-51316-X   LC 2004-51982
Also available in other bindings and editions
First published 1830
"Based on golden plates which Joseph Smith claimed were revealed to him, and which he unearthed from Cumorah Hill, New York, this book is roughly similar in structure to the Bible. . . . Emphasized are the doctrines of pre-existence, perfection, the afterlife, and Christ's second coming." Haydn. Thesaurus of Book Dig

Bushman, Richard L., 1931-
Joseph Smith and the beginnings of Mormonism. University of Ill. Press 1984 262p maps pa $16.95 hardcover o.p.   289.3
1. Smith, Joseph, 1805-1844 2. Church of Jesus Christ of Latter-day Saints
ISBN 0-252-06012-1 (pa)   LC 84-2451
The author surveys the historical background of the Mormon church with particular emphasis on the spiritual growth of its founder, Joseph Smith

Bushman, Richard L., 1931—*Continued*
"Resulting from many years of careful research and reflections, this book will stand for decades as a major contribution in the field." Choice
Includes bibliographical references

Mormonism; a very short introduction; [by] Richard Lyman Bushman. Oxford University Press 2008 130p il (Very short introductions) pa $11.95
289.3
1. Church of Jesus Christ of Latter-day Saints
ISBN 978-0-19-531030-6   LC 2007-44444
This book "explains who Mormons are: what they believe and how they live their lives . . . [and] ranges from the history of the Church of Jesus Christ of Latter-day Saints to the contentious issues of contemporary Mormonism." Publisher's note
This is an "outstanding, reliable overview of Mormon history and beliefs." Libr J
Includes bibliographical references

Givens, Terryl
By the hand of Mormon; the American scripture that launched a new world religion; [by] Terryl L. Givens. Oxford Univ. Press 2002 230p il maps hardcover o.p. pa $16.95   **289.3**
1. Book of Mormon
ISBN 0-19-513818-X; 0-19-516888-7 (pa)
LC 2001-53118
The author "investigates the history and theology of the Book of Mormon, which he calls 'perhaps the most religiously influential, hotly contested, and, in the secular press at least, intellectually under-investigated book in America.' Givens persuasively demonstrates how the Book of Mormon was trumpeted by early Latter-day Saints more for the fact of its existence . . . than for its content per se." Publ Wkly
Includes bibliographical references

Krakauer, Jon
Under the banner of heaven; a story of violent faith. Doubleday 2003 xxxii, 665p map $26; pa $14.95   **289.3**
1. Church of Jesus Christ of Latter-day Saints
ISBN 0-385-50951-0; 1-4000-3280-6 (pa)
LC 2003-43824
"In 1984, Brenda Lafferty and her baby daughter Erica were found murdered in their Utah home, victims of a 'removal revelation' that her Mormon brother-in-law had supposedly received from God. Krakauer . . . aims to explain why and how this crime happened by recounting the history of Mormonism from its conception by Joseph Smith in the 19th century and tracing the origins of its extremist sects through to the present day." Libr J
Includes bibliographical references

Ostling, Richard N.
Mormon America; the power and the promise; [by] Richard N. Ostling and Joan K. Ostling. Rev. ed. HarperOne 2007 xxvi, 469p il map pa $17.95
289.3
1. Church of Jesus Christ of Latter-day Saints
ISBN 978-0-06-143295-8   LC 2008-275419

First published 1999
"This thorough, thoughtful treatment of LDS beliefs and practices, written by non-Mormons, is a boon to members and interested lay readers alike." Libr J
Includes bibliographical references

Riess, Jana
Mormonism for dummies; by Jana Riess and Christopher Kimball Bigelow. Wiley Pub. 2005 365p il (—For dummies) pa $21.99   **289.3**
1. Church of Jesus Christ of Latter-day Saints
ISBN 0-7645-7195-8   LC 2004-117769
The authors "clearly, cogently answer FAQs about LDS practices and beliefs. Breezy but thorough, accurate." Libr J

289.5   Church of Christ, Scientist (Christian Science)

Eddy, Mary Baker, 1821-1910
Science and health, with key to the Scriptures; Trustees under the will of Mary Baker G. Eddy. Christian Science Pub. Soc. 2000 pa $9.95 *
289.5
1. Christian Science
ISBN 978-0-87952-259-9; 0-87952-259-3
First published 1875
This work is the foundation of the Christian Science religion, setting forth Mrs. Baker's interpretations of the Holy Scriptures and the method of healing. It has not been revised since her death in 1910.

Fraser, Caroline
God's perfect child; living and dying in the Christian Science Church. Metropolitan Bks. 1999 561p il pa $16 hardcover o.p.   **289.5**
1. Eddy, Mary Baker, 1821-1910 2. Christian Science
ISBN 0-8050-4431-0 (pa)   LC 99-17535
This "history traces the roots of the Christian Science church to nineteenth-century Calvinism, Emersonian self-reliance, and the remarkable life of its grandiose, anxiety-ridden founder, Mary Baker Eddy. . . . A work of compelling skepticism and scholarship." New Yorker
Includes bibliographical references

Schoepflin, Rennie B.
Christian Science on trial; religious healing in America. Johns Hopkins Univ. Press 2002 301p il (Medicine, science, and religion in historical context) $39.95   **289.5**
1. Christian Science
ISBN 0-8018-7057-7   LC 2001-8512
"A historical examination of Christian Science's evolution during the late 19th and early 20th centuries and the faith's struggle for existence and respectability in the midst of organized American medicine's efforts to curtail its influence." Libr J
Includes bibliographical references

289.6 Society of Friends (Quakers)

Hamm, Thomas D., 1957-
The Quakers in America. Columbia Univ. Press 2003 293p il (Columbia contemporary American religion series) $48.50; pa $27 * **289.6**
1. Society of Friends
ISBN 0-231-12362-0; 0-231-12363-9 (pa)
LC 2002-41422
The author provides an "introduction to Quaker origins abroad, their influences on American politics and culture, as well as their beliefs and traditions as they are played out on American soil. Though this is a serious history with a glossary, chronology, and 40 pages of notes, cartoons and anecdotes leaven the text. For both public and academic libraries." Libr J
Includes bibliographical references

289.7 Mennonite churches

Amish roots; a treasury of history, wisdom, and lore; [edited by] John A. Hostetler. Johns Hopkins Univ. Press 1989 319p il hardcover o.p. pa $21.95 **289.7**
1. Amish
ISBN 0-8018-3769-3; 0-8018-4402-9 (pa)
LC 88-31688
This is a compilation of "writing by and about the Amish from journals and letters, family and farm records, newspaper stories, poems, songs and stories. Ranging from the observations of the first Anabaptist immigrants in the 1700s to the present, the over 150 entries—commenting on church, family life, work, school and the rich Amish agricultural heritage—form a remarkably complete portrait." Publ Wkly
Includes bibliographical references

Hostetler, John A., 1918-
Amish society. 4th ed. Johns Hopkins Univ. Press 1993 435p il maps hardcover o.p. pa $20 **289.7**
1. Amish
ISBN 0-8018-4441-X; 0-8018-4442-8
LC 92-19304
First published 1963
This book discusses the sectarian origins of the Amish, immigration history, family and community life, population trends, farming practices, technological innovations, education, medicine and the effects of government regulation.
Includes bibliographical references

Kraybill, Donald B.
On the backroad to heaven; Old Order Hutterites, Mennonites, Amish, and Brethren; {by} Donald B. Kraybill, Carl F. Bowman. Johns Hopkins Univ. Press 2001 330p il maps (Center books in Anabaptist studies) $57; pa $16.95 * **289.7**
1. Mennonites 2. Amish 3. Hutterian Brethren
ISBN 0-8018-6565-4; 0-8018-7089-5 (pa)
LC 00-10406

"This look at the history, similarities and differences between four groups of Old Order faithful in North America—Hutterites, Mennonites, Amish and Brethren—is fascinating. . . . A book that, in one volume, tackles history, sociology and future trends—and does it well." Christ Century
Includes bibliographical references

The riddle of Amish culture. rev ed. Johns Hopkins Univ. Press 2001 397p il maps (Center books in Anabaptist studies) $65; pa $16.95 **289.7**
1. Amish
ISBN 0-8018-6771-1; 0-8018-6772-X (pa)
LC 00-13054
First published 1989
"Published in cooperation with the Center for American Places, Santa Fe, New Mexico, and Harrisonburg, Virginia"
The author examines the history and culture of the Amish, discussing such topics as the social structure of Amish society, rites of redemption and purification, recreation and social gatherings, work, technology, public relations, and social change
Includes bibliographical references

289.9 Denominations and sects not provided for elsewhere

Holden, Andrew, 1964-
Jehovah's Witnesses; portrait of a contemporary religious movement. Routledge 2002 206p $80; pa $23.95 * **289.9**
1. Jehovah's Witnesses
ISBN 0-415-26609-2; 0-415-26610-6 (pa)
LC 2001-45726
"This ethnographic study, academic in tone and British in orientation, offers several chapters of general information about the faith and analyzes its relationship to the wider society." Libr J
Includes bibliographical references

292 Classical religion (Greek and Roman religion)

Broad, William, 1951-
The Oracle; the lost secrets and hidden message of ancient Delphi; [by] William J. Broad. Penguin Press 2006 320p il map $25.95 **292**
1. Oracles
ISBN 1-59420-081-5 LC 2005-55515
This is a study of the Oracle in Delphi, Greece. Broad discusses how scientists "uncovered scientific evidence to explain the Oracle's powers. They discovered that the vapors from the ancient accounts were, in fact, petrochemical fumes containing a hallucinogenic gas, rising through natural faults hidden underneath the temple floor." Publisher's note
The author's "lively prose and fast-paced storytelling conduct us on a breathless adventure of religious mystery

Broad, William, 1951-—Continued
and scientific discovery—and ends with a surprising consideration of the meaning of the oracle's powers and the
existence of 'shadowy worlds . . . beyond the ken' of
science." Publ Wkly
Includes bibliographical references

Graves, Robert, 1895-1985
The Greek myths. Combined ed. Penguin Books
1992 782p pa $19.95 *   **292**
1. Classical mythology
ISBN 0-14-017199-1
Also available in an illustrated paperback edition
First published 1955
On cover: Complete edition
A collection of the author's interpretations of Greek
myths based on anthropological and archaeological find-
ings

Grimal, Pierre, 1912-
The dictionary of classical mythology; translated
by A.R. Maxwell-Hyslop. Blackwell 1986 603p il
pa $32.95 hardcover o.p.   **292**
1. Classical mythology—Dictionaries
ISBN 0-631-20102-5 (pa)   LC 85-7387
Original French edition, 1951; this translation first
published 1985 in the United Kingdom
"The dictionary is a comprehensive source dealing
with every mythological creature and character, from
Abas to Zeuxippe, and all the versions of the associated
myths and legends. Articles are clear and readable, explain historical and literary allusions, and are attractively
illustrated. . . . An essential purchase for both school
and public libraries." Am Libr

Hamilton, Edith, 1867-1963
Mythology; illustrated by Steele Savage. Little,
Brown 1942 497p il $27.95; pa $13.95
                                                        292
1. Classical mythology 2. Norse mythology
ISBN 0-316-34114-2; 0-316-34151-7 (pa)
Contents: The gods, the creation and the earliest heroes; Stories of love and adventure; Great heroes before
the Trojan War; Heroes of the Trojan War; Great families of mythology; Less important myths; Mythology of
the Norsemen; Genealogical tables
A retelling of Greek, Roman and Norse myths

The **Oxford** dictionary of classical myth and
religion; edited by Simon Price and Emily
Kearns. Oxford University Press 2003 599p
maps $39.95; pa $17.95 *   **292**
1. Classical mythology—Dictionaries
ISBN 0-19-280288-7; 0-19-280289-5 (pa)
                                        LC 2004-298013
Spine title: Classical myth & religion
"Instead of separating mythology and Judeo-Christian
religion into separate references, this work covers all religious life in the ancient Greco-Roman world. The result
is a generally accessible and academically current compendium of information on gods and holy beings, religious practices, festivals, sacred sites, myths, authors,

and texts of the period. The reader will find not only
Athena and Zeus but also Jesus Christ and St. Augustine,
Mani and Zoroaster." Libr J

294.3   Buddhism

Bernstein, Richard
Ultimate journey; retracing the path of an
ancient Buddhist monk who crossed Asia in search
of enlightenment. Knopf 2001 352p il maps pa
$14 hardcover o.p.   **294.3**
1. Hsüan-tsang, ca. 596-664 2. Buddhism
ISBN 0-679-78157-9 (pa)   LC 2001-267521
"In 629, a Buddhist monk named Hsuan Tsang set out
from China, crossing Asia in search of Buddhist truth.
Bernstein . . . decided to retrace the monk's journey
over the silk road to Pakistan and India and back to China. In this entertaining and well-written account, more
travel literature than religious study, he juxtaposes his
account of Hsuan Tsang's experiences with descriptions
of his own trials." Libr J
Includes bibliographical references

Crane, George
Bones of the master; a Buddhist monk's search
for the lost heart of China. Bantam Bks. 2000
293p il maps pa $14.95 hardcover o.p.
                                                       294.3
1. Tsung-tsai, 1925- 2. Buddhism 3. Mongolia
ISBN 0-553-37908-9 (pa)   LC 99-37868
This is an account of the friendship between Crane
and Tsung Tsai, a Buddhist monk, and their journey to
Mongolia to bury the bones of the monk's teacher
"Crane chronicles their perilous and miraculous adventures, the beauty of Mongolia's wilderness of wind and
sand, and Tsung Tsai's transcendent determination with
uncommon clarity, wit, vitality, and love." Booklist

Dalai Lama XIV, 1935-
Violence and compassion; {by} the Dalai Lama
and Jean-Claude Carrière. Doubleday 1996 248p
pa $11.50 hardcover o.p.   **294.3**
1. Buddhism
ISBN 0-385-50144-7 (pa)   LC 95-30694
"This book records the conversation that screenwriter
Carrière . . . held with the Dalai Lama, the exiled leader of Tibetan Buddhism, in 1993. The topics covered range
from exile and reincarnation to education and science."
Libr J
"This is a rich and invigorating volume, full of pon-
derable wisdom." Booklist

The wisdom of forgiveness; intimate
conversations and journeys; {by} His Holiness the
Dalai Lama and Victor Chan. Riverhead Books
2004 266p $24.95   **294.3**
1. Buddhism
ISBN 1-573-22277-1   LC 2004-46874
"Drawing on Buddhist principles, this book loosely
discusses His Holiness's ideas on forgiveness, though
Chan presents them gently through stories, not didactical-

Dalai Lama XIV, 1935-—*Continued*
ly as a step-by-step how-to manual. For example, one chapter arises in the context of the Dalai Lama's travels in war-torn Belfast, where he spoke about forgiveness to the families of victims of terrorist attacks. . . . Apart from the expected teachings on forgiveness, what comes through most clearly is the personality of the Dalai Lama himself: his humor, playfulness and joy." Publ Wkly

The **Dalai** Lama; a policy of kindness: an anthology of writings by and about the Dalai Lama; foreword by Claiborne Pell; compiled and edited by Sidney Piburn. Snow Lion Publs. 1990 150p pa $10.95   **294.3**
1. Dalai Lama XIV, 1935-
ISBN 1-55939-022-0   LC 90-31752
This collection of writings includes "both biographical essays and the Dalai Lama's discussions of science and religion, human rights, the environment, and spiritual subjects." Antioch Rev
This book is "accessible to those who know nothing of Buddhism or of Tibet." Libr J
Includes bibliographical references

Encyclopedia of Buddhism. Macmillan Ref. USA 2004 2v il map set $265 *   **294.3**
1. Buddhism—Encyclopedias
ISBN 0-02-865718-7   LC 2003-9965
This encyclopedia covers "Buddhist history and doctrines from cultural and national perspectives worldwide. The entries also address sacred texts and significant places, people, and schools." Libr J
"Macmillan sets a new standard of excellence for Western reference works on Buddhism with the most impressive reference title published in the past several years. . . . Every detail about Macmillan's set reflects the care and pride that went into its creation—extensive bibliographies, signed articles by a global roster of contributors, dazzling color plates depicting the warm tones of Buddhist art, and spectacular aerial photographs of remote Buddhist temples. This first-class effort will be most welcome and has been long awaited." Choice

Essential Zen; edited by Kazuaki Tanahashi and Tensho David Schneider; brushwork by Kazuaki Tanahashi. HarperSanFrancisco 1994 174p pa $13 hardcover o.p. *   **294.3**
1. Zen Buddhism
ISBN 0-06-251046-0 (pa)   LC 94-10615
An anthology of Zen writings drawn from classic texts and contemporary masters and practitioners
Includes bibliographical references

Irons, Edward A.
Encyclopedia of Buddhism; J. Gordon Melton, series editor. Facts on File 2007 xxxv, 634p il map (Encyclopedia of world religions) $75
                    294.3
1. Buddhism—Encyclopedias
ISBN 978-0-8160-5459-6   LC 2007-4503
This encyclopedia provides "access to the terms, concepts, personalities, historical events, institutions, and movements that helped shape the history of Buddhism and the way it is practiced today. Although the primary

focus of the encyclopedia is clearly on Buddhism in all its forms, it also provides introductions to Daoism, Shinto, Confucianism, and other religious practices in East and Southeast Asia." Publisher's note
Includes bibliographical references

Keown, Damien, 1951-
A dictionary of Buddhism; contributors, Stephen Hodge, Charles Jones, Paoli Tinti. Oxford Univ. Press 2003 357p il maps hardcover o.p. pa $15.95 *   **294.3**
1. Buddhism
ISBN 0-19-860560-9; 978-0-19-280062-6 (pa); 0-19-280062-0 (pa)   LC 2003-276701
This dictionary covers Buddhist terms, biography, scriptures, important places and includes discussions of ethical issues and other matters
"The entries are short . . . but such accessibility is the very reason why this should be on the bookshelf of every student of Buddhism." Publ Wkly

Kerouac, Jack, 1922-1969
Some of the dharma. Viking 1997 419p pa $20 hardcover o.p.   **294.3**
1. Buddhism
ISBN 0-14-028707-8 (pa)   LC 97-12870
"Begun in December 1951 as a notebook for his Buddhist studies, this work records Kerouac's reactions to a variety of Buddhist texts. Over the course of five years, it grew to include poems, prayers, dialogs, meditations, and notes on his reading, as well as commentary on family, friends, and meaningful concerns in his life. . . . Long anticipated by Kerouac scholars, this major work belongs in all literature collections." Libr J

Mishra, Pankaj
An end to suffering; the Buddha in the world. Farrar, Straus & Giroux 2004 422p map $25
                    294.3
1. Gautama Buddha 2. Buddhism
ISBN 0-314-14836-8   LC 2004-56266
Also available Picador paperback edition
This "book about the Buddha's life and his influence throughout history . . . also considers the impact of Buddhist ideas on such modern politicians as Gandhi and Nelson Mandela." Publisher's note
"Mishra's book is in the best tradition of Buddhism, both dispassionate and deeply engaged, complicated and simple, erudite and profoundly humane." N Y Times Book Rev
Includes bibliographical references

Prebish, Charles S.
Historical dictionary of Buddhism. Scarecrow Press 1993 xxxiii, 387p (Historical dictionaries of religions, philosophies, and movements) $65
                    294.3
1. Buddhism
ISBN 0-8108-2698-4   LC 93-4247
The author "narrows his dictionary topics to significant persons, places, texts, events, doctrines, practices,

Prebish, Charles S.—*Continued*

and movements within the Buddhist tradition. While he focuses on monastic and sectarian traditions, his concise introduction includes Buddha's life, the foothold of Buddhism in India, and its spread via Emperor Asoka's missionaries." Libr J

Ross, Nancy Wilson, 1905?-1986

Buddhism, a way of life and thought. Knopf 1980 208p il hardcover o.p. pa $12.95   **294.3**
1. Buddhism

ISBN: 0-394-74754-2 (pa)   LC 80-7652

The author "presents the basic data of Buddha's life, his teachings, and Buddhist practice. . . . [She] describes Theravada Buddhism (of Southeast Asia), Tantra Buddhism (of Tibet), and Zen Buddhism (of Japan). . . . The book is a clear introduction to Buddhism, enthusiastically written and designed for the general public or beginning student." Choice

Includes bibliographical references

Smith, Huston

Buddhism: a concise introduction; [by] Hurston Smith and Philip Novak. HarperSanFrancisco 2003 242p hardcover o.p. pa $12.95   **294.3**
1. Buddhism

ISBN 0-06-050696-2; 0-06-073067-6 (pa)
    LC 2003-544630

This "book grew out of Smith's *The World's Religions.* . . . The first 12 chapters present his outstanding survey of the life and fundamental teachings of the 'Perfectly Enlightened One,' basic Buddhist concepts, and the major divisions of Buddhism (e.g., Mahayana, Theravada, Zen, and Tibetan). . . . Novak . . . is the primary author of the final six chapters, all-new sections on the migration of Buddhism to the West. Impressively, this informative portion with its emphasis on Buddhism in America lives up to the standards of lucidity so evident in earlier chapters." Libr J

Includes bibliographical references

Sogyal, Rinpoche

The Tibetan book of living and dying; edited by Patrick Gaffney and Andrew Harvey. rev and updated ed. HarperSanFrancisco 2002 441p il $28.95; pa $17.95   **294.3**
1. Buddhism 2. Death

ISBN 0-06-250793-1; 0-06-250834-2 (pa)
    LC 2002-523084

First published 1992

This "modern reinterpretation of the classic *Tibetan Book of the Dead* is a manual on learning to accept death, on caring for the dying, and on spiritual growth. Rinpoche, . . . draws parallels between contemporary Western near-death experiences and the afterlife journey through *bardos*, or intermediate planes between death and rebirth, described in sacred Tibetan texts." Publ Wkly [review of 1992 edition]

The author "is well qualified to pass on his tradition. He does this beautifully, in limpid prose free of the scholastic list making that deadens many Tibetan Buddhist primers." N Y Times Book Rev [review of 1992 edition]

Includes bibliographical references

Sutin, Lawrence, 1951-

All is change; the two-thousand year journey of Buddhism to the West. Little, Brown 2006 403p il $25.99 *   **294.3**
1. Buddhism

ISBN 978-0-316-74156-9; 0-316-74156-6
    LC 2006-40824

"Greeks and Buddhists in India found common metaphysical ground 2,000 years ago, and Sutin also documents parallels between Buddist and Gnostic teachings in this vital study of a remarkable spiritual migration." Booklist

Includes bibliographical references

Suzuki, Daisetz Teitaro, 1870-1966

Manual of Zen Buddhism. Grove Press 1960 192p il pa $13 *   **294.3**
1. Zen Buddhism

ISBN 0-8021-3065-8

"An Evergreen original"

Fisrt published 1950 in the United Kingdom

In this volume, D. T. Suzuki has brought together some of Zen Buddhism's original sources. Included are the sutras or sermons of the Buddha: the gathas or hymns; the philosophical puzzles known as koan; and the dharanis or invocations to expel evil spirits. In addition to the written selections there are reproductions of Buddhist drawings and paintings, including religious statues found in Zen temples

Thondup, Tulku

Enlightened journey; Buddhist practice as daily life; edited by Harold Talbott. Shambhala Publs. 1995 268p pa $16.95   **294.3**
1. Buddhism

ISBN 1-57062-021-0   LC 94-36154

This is an "exposition on one of the more important sects of Tibetan Buddhism. As such, it comprises 15 talks and articles by Thondup, [a] leader and teacher of the Nyingma school of Tibetan Buddhism. His purpose here is to show how daily life can become the basis of Buddhist spiritual training, and each talk is an introduction to various aspects of Buddhism, covering such topics as meditation as a means to arouse compassion and the importance of suffering to reach enlightenment." Libr J

Includes bibliographical references

Tibetan book of the dead.

The Tibetan book of the dead; or, The after-death experiences on the Bardo plane, according to Lāma Kazi Dawa-Samdup's English rendering; compiled and edited by W.Y. Evans-Wentz; with a new foreword and afterword by Donald S. Lopez, jr. Oxford Univ. Press 2000 lxxxiv, 264p il $40; pa $12.95 *   **294.3**
1. Buddhism 2. Death

ISBN 0-19-513311-0; 0-19-513312-9 (pa)
    LC 00-22529

This translation first published 1927

A translation of the Bardo thödol, a Tibetan Buddhist scriptural work describing the mind's projections imme-

Tibetan book of the dead.—*Continued*
diately after death. The accompanying commentary explains the symbolism and outlines applications of the teachings of the Bardo for living
Includes bibliographical references

Watts, Alan, 1915-1973
The way of Zen; by Alan W. Watts. Pantheon Bks. 1957 236p il hardcover o.p. pa $12.95 **294.3**
1. Zen Buddhism   ISBN: 0-375-70510-4 (pa)
This is an historical and cultural survey of Zen, tracing its origins in Indian and Chinese thought. The author describes the Zen way of living and its techniques for overcoming the mind's conflict between symbolic thought and actual experience
Includes bibliographical references

294.5 Hinduism

Basham, Arthur Llewellyn
The origins and development of classical Hinduism; [by] A.L. Basham; edited and completed by Kenneth G. Zysk. Oxford University Press 1991 159p il map pa $18.95 **294.5**
1. Hinduism
ISBN 0-19-507349-5; 978-0-19-507349-2
LC 91-18884
First published 1989 by Beacon Press
This illustrated history "traces the spiritual life of India from the time of the Indus Culture (around 2700 B.C.E) through the crystallization of classical Hinduism in the first centuries of the common era. It chronicles as well the rise of other mystical and ascetic traditions, such as Buddhism and Jainism, and follows Hinduism's later incarnations in the West." Publisher's note
Includes bibliographical references

Jones, Constance, 1961-
Encyclopedia of Hinduism; [by] Constance A. Jones and James D. Ryan; J. Gordon Melton, series editor. Facts on File 2006 xxxvii, 552p il (Facts on File library of religion and mythology) $75 *   **294.5**
1. Hinduism—Encyclopedias
ISBN 0-8160-5458-4; 978-0-8160-5458-9
LC 2006-44419
This encyclopedia "focuses on the most significant groups within this religion, noteworthy teachers and their contributions, the religions and cultural movements that enriched its history, and the diaspora of Hindu thought and practice around the world. Two major religious traditions that sprang from Hindu influence, Jainism and Sikhism, also have many entries." Publisher's note
Includes bibliographical references

Klostermaier, Klaus K., 1933-
Hinduism; a short history. Oneworld Publs. 2000 342p pa $23.95 **294.5**

1. Hinduism
ISBN 1-85168-213-9
The author "addresses 'Hinduism' as a collection of indigenous Indian religions, myths, and modes of worship that have mutually influenced one another for millennia. . . . Klostermaier deals with controversial interpretations of history in a frank and careful manner." Libr J
Includes bibliographical references

Yoga, mind & body; {by} Sivananda Yoga Vedanta Center. DK Pub. 1996 168p il $24.95; pa $15   **294.5**
1. Yoga
ISBN 0-7894-0447-8; 0-7894-3301-X (pa)
LC 95-44387
"Five main principles of yoga based on the tenet of 'simple living and high thinking' are introduced. Each one is explained and illustrated in a separate section of the book. The chapter on proper exercise is the longest section and goes through a complete workout session with full-color photographs and drawings of each position. The mental and physical benefits of each position are listed as well as possible problems, and variations for different skill levels. The chapter on vegetarian diet has 20 pages of recipes." SLJ

295 Zoroastrianism (Mazdaism, Parseeism)

Kriwaczek, Paul
In search of Zarathustra; the first prophet and the ideas that changed the world. Knopf 2003 248p il maps hardcover o.p. pa $15   **295**
1. Zoroaster, fl. 6th cent. B.C. 2. Zoroastrianism
ISBN 0-375-41528-9; 1-4000-3142-7 (pa)
LC 2002-73015
First published 2002 in the United Kingdom
The author contends "that Zoroastrianism, through its prophet Zarathustra, greatly affected the three great monotheistic religions and gave them their common beliefs of light and darkness, good and evil, heaven and hell, angels, and life after death. . . . An enthralling, sober, and (sometimes) humorous exploration into the earliest roots of Judaism, Christianity, and Islam." Libr J
Includes bibliographical references

296 Judaism

American Jewish year book 2007. American Jewish Com. $49.95   **296**
1. Jews—Periodicals 2. Jews—United States
ISSN 0065-8987
ISBN 978-0-87495-142-4; 0-87495-142-9
Annual. First published 1899
"An almanac of Jewish life and culture including population statistics, directories of Jewish organizations and periodicals, a religious calendar, necrology, coverage of international Jewish politics and communities, and periodicals." Ref Sources for Small & Medium-sized Libr.
6th edition

The **Cambridge** history of Judaism; edited by W.D. Davies [and] Louis Finkelstein. v1: Introduction; the Persian period. Cambridge Univ. Press 1984 461p il maps $194 *
296

1. Judaism—History
ISBN 0-521-21880-2   LC 77-85704
"The first of . . . four volumes on the history of the Jews from the destruction of the Temple in 586 BC to the closure of the Mishnah in AD 250, the work deals not solely with Judaism . . . but with the entire material history of the Jews in the Land of Israel as well as in Babylonia and Egypt." Choice
Includes bibliographical references

The **Cambridge** history of Judaism; edited by W.D. Davies [and] Louis Finkelstein; assistant editor, John Sturdy. v2: The Hellenistic age. Cambridge Univ. Press 1990 738p il maps $205 *
296

1. Judaism—History
ISBN 0-521-21929-9
This "second volume in the four-volume Cambridge History of Judaism deals with Judaism's encounter with Hellenism under Alexander the Great and his successors, the efforts of Jews led by the Maccabees to counter this influence and to establish their own state and the resulting Jewish ideologies and literary activities. The 18 chapters treat the archaeology of Hellenistic Palestine, languages, the interpenetration of Judaism and Hellenism in the pre-Maccabean period, the Hasmonean revolt and dynasty, the matrix of apocalyptic and the Samaritans, as well as various writings and historical movements." America
Includes bibliographical references

The **Cambridge** history of Judaism; edited by William Horbury, John Sturdy and W.D. Davies. v3: The early Roman period. Cambridge Univ. Press 1999 1254p il maps $190 *
296

1. Judaism—History
ISBN 0-521-24377-7
This third volume of a four-volume history "contains thirty-two essays on aspects of Judaism in the early Roman period, primarily the period between Pompey and Vespasian but often ranging into the rabbinic period." J Relig
Includes bibliographical references

The **Cambridge** history of Judaism; edited by Steven T. Katz. v4: the late Roman-Rabbinic period. Cambridge University Press 2006 1135p il map $235 *
296

1. Judaism—History
ISBN 978-0-521-77248-8
"The fourth volume of The Cambridge History of Judaism covers the period from 70 CE to 640 CE (the rise of Islam), addressing the major historical, political and cultural developments in Jewish history during this crucial era. The volume [includes] . . . coverage of the growth and development of rabbinic Judaism and the major classical rabbinic sources such as the Mishnah, Jerusalem Talmud, Babylonian Talmud and various Midrash-ic collections. In addition, it surveys the growth of early Jewish mystical literature and the liturgical literature of the developing synagogue." Publisher's note
Includes bibliographical references

Freedman, Samuel G.
Jew vs. Jew; the struggle for the soul of American Jewry. Simon & Schuster 2000 397p $26; pa $14
296
1. Judaism 2. Jews—United States
ISBN 0-684-85944-0; 0-684-85945-9 (pa)
LC 00-33907
The author "describes the paradoxical situation faced by today's American Jews, living in a country where religious freedom has yielded unreconcilable devisiveness. . . . This is a helpful guide for anyone seeking an understanding of intra-Jewish conflicts in contemporary America." Libr J
Includes bibliographical references

Glazer, Nathan
American Judaism. 2nd ed rev, with a new introd. University of Chicago Press 1989 xxix, 214p (Chicago history of American civilization) pa $21
296
1. Judaism 2. Jews—United States—History
ISBN 0-226-29843-4   LC 89-161422
First published 1957
Focusing upon Jews as a people and as a religious group, the author surveys the history of Jews in the United States beginning with the first Jewish settlement in New Amsterdam in 1654. Among the topics considered are the German and East European immigrants, the Sephardic communities, and the Orthodox, Reform and Conservative movements
Includes bibliographical references

Kushner, Harold S., 1935-
To life! a celebration of Jewish being and thinking. Warner Books 1994 304p pa $14.99
296
1. Judaism
ISBN 0-446-67002-2; 978-0-446-67002-9
LC 94-25828
First published 1993 by Little, Brown
The author discusses the meaning of Jewish customs and ceremonies and the purpose of prayer. Antisemitism, Jewish-Christian relations, and the importance of Israel to contemporary Jews are also examined.
"This is a very easy book to read, to discuss, even to argue about, and Kushner's celebration is everything his many readers could have hoped it would be." Booklist

Robinson, George
Essential Judaism; a complete guide to beliefs, customs and rituals. Pocket Bks. 2000 xxi, 644p hardcover o.p. pa $20
296
1. Judaism
ISBN 0-671-03480-4; 0-671-03481-2 (pa)
LC 99-55288

Robinson, George—*Continued*

This book "attempts to provide the essentials of Judaism for novices, outsiders and those who, like Robinson, rediscovered their heritage as adults. It's an excellent introductory resource, vast but accessibly organized." Publ Wkly

Includes bibliographical references

Sarna, Jonathan D.

American Judaism; a history. Yale University Press 2004 xx, 490p il $35 *   **296**

1. Judaism 2. Jews—United States

ISBN 0-300-10197-X   LC 2003-14464

This "work chronicles the 350-year history of the Jewish religion in America. Tracing American Judaism from its origins in the colonial era through the present day, Sarna explores the ways in which Judaism adapted in this new context. How did American culture—predominantly Protestant and overwhelmingly capitalist—affect Jewish religion and culture? And how did American Jews shape their own communities and faith in the new world?" Publisher's note

"This comprehensive and insightful study of the American Jewish experience is much more than just a record of events. It is an account of how people shaped events: establishing and maintaining communities, responding to challenges, and working for change. It is compelling reading for Jews and non-Jews alike." Booklist

Includes bibliographical references

Telushkin, Joseph, 1948-

Jewish wisdom; ethical, spiritual, and historical lessons from the great works and thinkers; [by] Rabbi Joseph Telushkin. Morrow 1994 xxiv, 663p $26   **296**

1. Judaism 2. Jewish ethics

ISBN 0-688-12958-7   LC 94-9186

Companion volume to Jewish literacy (1991)

"Organized by subject, this is a collection of teachings and quotations from the Talmud, the Bible, rabbinical commentaries, and ancient and modern religious and secular writings. Writers include Elie Wiesel, Isaac Bashevis Singer, Hebrew poet Hayim Bialik, Cynthia Ozick, Emile Zola, Albert Einstein, Bruno Bettelheim, Gertrude Stein, Irving Howe, and Maimonides. . . . Jews—and even non-Jews—will find the book a treasure." Booklist

Includes bibliographical references

Wouk, Herman, 1915-

This is my God: the Jewish way of life. Little, Brown 1987 345p pa $16.95 hardcover o.p.
                    296

1. Judaism

ISBN 0-316-95514-0 (pa)   LC 87-3245

First published 1959 by Doubleday

The author, an orthodox Jew, writes a personal declaration of faith. He explains holy days, fasts, and presents the historical background of Judaism.

Includes bibliographical references

The will to live on; this is our heritage. Cliff St. Bks. 2000 308p hardcover o.p. pa $15   **296**

1. Judaism 2. Holocaust, 1933-1945

ISBN 0-06-095562-7 (pa) LC 99-49885

Wouk "explores the mystery of the survival of the Jewish people through the ages. The three main sections of this book cover the Holocaust, surveys of Jewish sacred and historical literature, and contemporary Jewish life in Israel and the United States. . . . Readers seeking an introduction to Judaism will be enlightened by the depth of knowledge here, as Wouk tells a complicated story so simply, and those who have read widely in Jewish literature will be entranced by his deeply felt and articulate sense of the importance of being a committed and believing Jew." Libr J

296.03   Judaism—Encyclopedias and dictionaries

Encyclopaedia Judaica; Fred Skolnik, editor-in-chief; Michael Berenbaum, executive editor. 2nd ed. Macmillan Reference USA in association with the Keter Pub. House 2007 22v il map set $1,995   **296.03**

1. Judaism—Encyclopedias

ISBN 978-0-02-865928-2; 0-02-865928-7
                    LC 2006-20426

Also available online

First published 1972 in 16 volumes

"Included are more than 22,000 signed entries on Jewish life, culture, history and religion, written by Israeli, American and European subject specialists." Publisher's note

This "is a welcome addition to reference collections. By documenting the modern Jewish experience while retaining links with its rich past, it provides users with information about all aspects of Jewish religion and culture." Booklist

Includes bibliographical references

The **encyclopaedia** of Judaism; edited by Jacob Neusner, Alan J. Avery-Peck, William Scott Green. 2nd ed. Brill 2005 4v il map set $399 *
                    296.03

1. Judaism—Encyclopedias

ISBN 90-04-14787-X   LC 2006-273507

First published 1999-2004 as a five-volume set by Continuum with title: The Encyclopedia of Judaism

Published in collaboration with the Museum of Jewish Heritage, New York

For this "encyclopedia, an international set of noted religious studies scholars has produced 115 essays and articles on Judaism. . . . The articles, which run from a few pages to 15 pages, touch on many contemporary issues, e.g., the article on medical ethics discusses the controversy surrounding 'test tube' babies. There is also in-depth discussion of concepts such as monotheism or creeds and modern Jewish movements such as Reform Judaism." Libr J

Karesh, Sara E.

Encyclopedia of Judaism; [by] Sara E. Karesh and Mitchell M. Hurvitz. Facts on File 2006 xxxvi, 602p il (Facts on File library of religion and mythology) $75 *   **296.03**
1. Judaism—Encyclopedias
ISBN 0-8160-5457-6   LC 2004-26537
This encyclopedia "covers individuals, places, events, theologies, ideologies, organizations, movements, and denominations that span Jewish history. . . . This is a very good one-volume resource that is especially accessible to young adults and non-Jews." Libr J
Includes bibliographical references

The **New** encyclopedia of Judaism; editor-in-chief, Geoffrey Wigoder; coeditors, Fred Skolnik & Shmuel Himelstein. New York Univ. Press 2002 856p il $79.95 *   **296.03**
1. Judaism—Dictionaries
ISBN 0-8147-9388-6   LC 2002-16614
First published 1989 with title: The Encyclopedia of Judaism
This reference "seeks to present a balanced picture, offering current thinking among scholars in Reform, Conservative, and Orthodox movements and a roster of contributors hailing from Israel, England, and the United States. While the scholarship is solid, the material is readily accessible to a popular audience, and the work is magnificently illustrated." Libr J
Includes bibliographical references

The **Oxford** dictionary of the Jewish religion; editors in chief, R.J. Zwi Werblowsky, Geoffrey Wigoder. Oxford Univ. Press 1997 764p $110 *   **296.03**
1. Judaism—Dictionaries
ISBN 0-19-508605-8   LC 96-45517
"The 2400 entries in this dictionary include unsigned but revised articles from the editors' Encyclopedia of the Jewish Religion (1966), as well as . . . new signed articles covering {topics} . . . and biographies related to the Jewish religion and interfaith relations." Libr J

Reader's guide to Judaism; editor, Michael Terry. Fitzroy Dearborn Pubs. 2000 718p (Reader's guide) $135   **296.03**
1. Judaism—Encyclopedias
ISBN 1-57958-139-0   LC 2001-274119
This "work covers over 400 topics, including interfaith relations, historical periods, philosophical and mystical movements, important figures, and more. Preceding each essay is a bibliography of five to ten English-language titles. . . . Written by librarians and scholars . . . these 1000 to 2000-word essays include a descriptive and often analytical overview of each book. . . . This is an excellent tool for building Judaica collections in public and academic libraries." Libr J
Includes bibliographical references

296.1 Judaism—Sources

Cohen, A. (Abraham), b. 1887

Everyman's Talmud; the major teachings of the rabbinic sages; by Abraham Cohen; foreword by Jacob Neusner. Schocken Books, Distributed by Pantheon Books 1995 405p pa $18   **296.1**
1. Talmud 2. Judaism
ISBN 0-8052-1032-6; 978-0-8052-1032-3
LC 95-139158
First published 1932 in the United Kingdom
This book's "aim is to provide a summary of the teachings of the Talmud on Religion, Ethics, Folklore, and Jurisprudence. . . . All that is offered is a sufficient number of extracts to give [the] reader a general idea of the Talmudic doctrine." Preface
"A comprehensive and satisfactory summary of Talmudic doctrine . . . prefaced by an excellent introduction." Commonweal
Includes bibliographical references

Dead Sea scrolls.

The complete Dead Sea scrolls in English; [translated and edited with an introduction by] Geza Vermes. Rev ed. Penguin Books 2004 648p (Penguin classics) pa $20   **296.1**
1. Dead Sea scrolls
ISBN 0-14-044952-3 (pa); 978-0-14-044952-5
This translation was first published 1962 with title: The Dead Sea scrolls in English; the 1997 edition included an introduction summarizing the 50-year history of scrolls research
Translated from the Hebrew
This "is an English version of the nonbiblical, sectarian and intertestamental Qumran writings. Vermes's preface explains that he does not offer a translation of every fragment retrieved from the caves,' but of 'all the texts sufficiently well preserved to be understandable in English.'" N Y Times Book Rev [review of 1997 edition]
The "discussion of the Essene community, whom Vermes believes created the scrolls, the scrolls' meanings for early Christianity and other topics will be valuable to anyone looking for accurate summaries of the fascinating history of the discovery, translation and transmission of the scrolls." Publ Wkly [review of 1997 edition]
Includes bibliographical references

The **Encyclopedia** of the Dead Sea scrolls; {edited by} Lawrence H. Schiffman and James C. VanderKam. Oxford Univ. Press 2000 2v set $295   **296.1**
1. Dead Sea scrolls
ISBN 0-19-508450-0   LC 99-55300
"In addition to individual texts, coverage extends to the archeological sites themselves; important historical figures (Moses) and groups (Essenes, Pharisees) as they are represented in the scrolls; scholars important to Dead Sea scroll research . . . and methods employed both to date and to preserve these ancient documents." Booklist

Frankel, Ellen, 1951-
The classic tales; 4,000 years of Jewish lore.
Aronson, J. 1989 659p pa $40 hardcover o.p.
296.1

1. Jewish legends 2. Hasidic legends
ISBN 1-56821-038-8 (pa)   LC 88-35119
"Frankel selects and retells a wide selection of tales
arranged in broadly thematic sections. Biblical, hasidic,
and midrashic sources predominate, but the oral tradition
is also represented. Likewise, the balance between Ash-
kenazi and Sephardic stories aims for a broader geographical representation. Frankel also takes the opportunity to personalize the woman's role in many of these
tales and makes the references to God genderless."
Booklist
Includes bibliographical references

Golb, Norman
Who wrote the Dead Sea scrolls? the search for
the secret of Qumran. Scribner 1995 446p il maps
pa $22 hardcover o.p.   **296.1**
1. Dead Sea scrolls 2. Judaism—History
ISBN 0-684-80692-4 (pa)   LC 94-23295
Golb argues that "the Dead Sea Scrolls were the work
of individuals from many diverse groups and that they
were deposited in the caves near the Dead Sea (among
other locations) by Jews fleeing the Roman army during
the First Revolt (c.70 c.e.). He also claims that the Qumran complex served not as an Essene monastery but as
a fortress for Jews involved in the revolt." Libr J
"This is an archival book that should be considered
for any collection dealing with the Dead Sea Scrolls. It
is well written and can be read by the interested person
as well as by the professional scholar." Choice
Includes bibliographical references

Schiffman, Lawrence H.
Reclaiming the Dead Sea scrolls; the history of
Judaism, the background of Christianity, the lost
library of Qumran; with a foreword by Chaim
Potok. Doubleday 1995 xxvii, 529p il map (The
Anchor Bible reference library) pa $27.50
296.1
1. Dead Sea scrolls 2. Bible—Antiquities
3. Judaism—History
ISBN 0-385-48121-7   LC 95-17280
First published 1994 by Philadelphia Jewish Publiation
Society
Schiffman provides a "description and evaluation of
the scrolls, the archeology of Qumran (the site near the
Dead Sea from which the scrolls originated), the history
and nature of the Jewish community that lived at Qumran and the setting of the scrolls in Jewish history and
thought from the second century B.C. through the first
century A.D." N Y Times Book Rev
Includes bibliographical references

Shanks, Hershel
The mystery and meaning of the Dead Sea
scrolls. Random House 1998 xxi, 246p il maps pa
$14 hardcover o.p.   **296.1**
1. Dead Sea scrolls
ISBN 0-679-78089-0 (pa)   LC 97-29391
"Shanks looks at the key questions surrounding the
Dead Sea Scrolls (who wrote them, what they say, and
what they mean vis-à-vis Judaism and Christianity) and
gives readers the most up-to-date information along with
his own best guesses about what it all means, easily incorporating many divergent theories." Booklist
Includes bibliographical references

Understanding the Dead Sea scrolls; a reader
from the Biblical archaeology review; edited by
Hershel Shanks. Random House 1992 xxxviii,
336p il maps pa $14 hardcover o.p.
296.1

1. Dead Sea scrolls
ISBN 0-679-74445-2 (pa)   LC 91-45727
This is a compilation of "22 articles from the pages
of BAR and *Bible Review* dealing with the discovery of
the Scrolls, the ancient community that stored them
away, and their impact upon the study of the Bible, Rabbinic Judaism, and early Christianity. Three chapters on
the controversy surrounding the publication (and in many
cases non-publication) of the materials round out the volume. . . . The articles included are written by scholars
but are easily accessible to laypersons. Coverage is balanced, including opposing viewpoints." Libr J
Includes bibliographical references

Wise, Michael Owen, 1954-
The Dead Sea scrolls; a new translation; [by]
Michael O. Wise, Martin G. Abegg Jr., and
Edward M. Cook. Rev ed. HarperSanFrancisco
2005 662p pa $24.95   **296.1**
ISBN 0-06-076662-X   LC 2005-46285
First published 1996
On cover: 'Translated and with commentary by Mi-
chael Wise'
This translation captures "the nuances of the Hebrew,
and sometimes the Greek, of the scrolls, many of which
are merely fragments. Also contained here is a thorough
introduction to the history of the discovery of the scrolls
and a theory about the community that produced the
scrolls." Publ Wkly
"An engaging necessity for updating Dead Sea Scrolls
collections." Booklist
Includes bibliographical references

296.3 Judaism—Theology, ethics, views of social issues

Gager, John G.

The origins of anti-Semitism; attitudes toward Judaism in pagan and Christian antiquity. Oxford Univ. Press 1983 312p pa $26 hardcover o.p.

296.3

1. Paul, the Apostle, Saint 2. Antisemitism 3. Christianity and other religions

ISBN 0-19-503607-7 (pa)   LC 82-24523

"Gager attempts to survey Greek and Roman attitudes toward Jews and Judaism, and to examine the bases of early Christian (especially Paul's) thinking about Jewish religion. He aims to show that Greek and Roman opinion about the Jews and their religion was divided." Choice

Includes bibliographical references

Heschel, Abraham Joshua, 1907-1972

Heavenly Torah; as refracted through the generations; [by] Abraham Joshua Heschel; edited and translated from the Hebrew with commentary by Gordon Tucker with Leonard Levin. Continuum 2004 xxxiv, 814p il $95 *   **296.3**

1. Torah 2. Talmud

ISBN 0-8264-0802-8   LC 2004-21088

Original Hebrew edition published in three seperate volumes from 1962 to 1990

The author "offers an introduction to the main lines of rabbinic thought by investigating different rabbinic interpretations of revelation (Torah). He argues that there are two major hermeneutical traditions, one associated with Rabbi Ishmael, the other with Rabbi Akiba." Choice

"This is an ambitious work of tremendous significance, an indispensable guide to understanding the Torah and—consequently—the Jewish religion. Not simply for large religious collections but for any with active borrowers." Booklist

Includes bibliographical references

Kushner, Harold S., 1935-

When bad things happen to good people; with a new preface by the author. 20th anniversary ed. Schocken Bks. 2001 202p $21 *   **296.3**

1. Providence and government of God 2. Suffering

ISBN 0-8052-4193-0   LC 2001-531062

Also available in paperback from Avon Bks.

A reissue of the title first published 1981

"A bright and happy infant, Rabbi Kushner's first-born son gradually succumbed to progeria, 'rapid aging': he never grew beyond three feet tall, looked like a hairless, wizened old man, and died in his teens. This book is his father's attempt to make sense out of his son's fate, his own pain, and the pain of others enduring undeserved misfortunes." Libr J

296.4 Judaism—Traditions, rites, public services

Celebration & renewal; rites of passage in Judaism; edited by Rela M. Geffen. Jewish Publ. Soc. 1993 277p pa $19.95 hardcover o.p.

296.4

1. Judaism—Customs and practices

ISBN 0-8276-0510-2 (pa)   LC 93-12493

Explains such life-cycle events as birth, marriage, midlife, sickness, religious conversion, and mourning as viewed, experienced, and treated from a Jewish perspective

"The book is not only practical to Jews, but useful to students of other religions and ethnic backgrounds who could benefit by comparing this book's portrayal of Jewish traditions with their own heritages." Booklist

Includes bibliographical references

Eisenberg, Ronald L.

The JPS guide to Jewish traditions; [by] Ron Eisenberg. The Jewish Publication Society 2004 xxiii, 806p $40 *   **296.4**

1. Judaism—Encyclopedias

ISBN 0-8276-0760-1   LC 2004-6399

This "work covers the major elements of Jewish life, including life-cycle events (birth, bar and bat mitzvah, marriage, divorce, parenting, and death), the Sabbath and holidays, the synagogue, prayer, and the Bible and Jewish literature. . . . The author has done a masterful job in distilling the major beliefs and practices of a 3,000-year-old religion into lively and informative prose and in creating an accessible, essential reference work." Booklist

Includes bibliographical references

Goldman, Ari L., 1949-

Being Jewish; the spiritual and cultural practice of Judaism today. Simon & Schuster 2000 286p $25   **296.4**

1. Judaism—Customs and practices

ISBN 0-684-82389-6   LC 00-44047

"The book's three sections cover life cycle events, holidays, and daily activities. Specific chapters include coming of age, mourning, Sukkot, Passover, Yom Ha'atzmaut, prayer, and study." Libr J

"An excellent resource." Booklist

Includes bibliographical references

Greenberg, Irving, 1933-

The Jewish way; living the holidays. Summit Bks. 1988 463p pa $15 hardcover o.p.

296.4

1. Jewish holidays 2. Judaism—Customs and practices

ISBN 0-671-87303-2 (pa)   LC 88-20085

The author "explains and interprets each holiday's origin and background, ceremonial rituals, and religious significance. He shows how the holidays relate to one another and to Judaism's central themes and how they offer the individual the capacity to experience the full range of Judaism's and humankind's values." Publisher's note

Includes bibliographical references

Isaacs, Ronald H.

Sacred seasons; a sourcebook for the Jewish holidays. Aronson, J. 1997 163p $25

296.4

1. Jewish holidays 2. Jews—Folklore 3. Jewish legends

ISBN 0-7657-5963-2   LC 96-33635

Isaacs "notes in his introduction that the holidays and fast days in the Jewish calendar form an integral part of the body of ritual and social laws through which Jews relate both to society and to God. . . . Using basic rabbinic texts—the Talmud, Midrashim, the Zohar, etc.—as his source material, Isaacs presents a fascinating collection of folk tales and legends pertaining to these holidays." Libr J

Strassfeld, Michael

The Jewish holidays; a guide and commentary; illustrated by Betsy Platkin Teutsch; commentaries by Arnold Eisen {et al.}. Harper & Row 1985 248p il pa $24 hardcover o.p.   **296.4**

1. Jewish holidays 2. Judaism—Customs and practices

ISBN 0-06-272008-2 (pa)   LC 84-48196

This book examines the history and customs surrounding the major Jewish holidays

Wieseltier, Leon

Kaddish. Knopf 1998 588p $27.50; pa $16

296.4

1. Kaddish 2. Judaism—Customs and practices
3. Funeral rites and ceremonies

ISBN 0-375-40389-2; 0-375-70362-4 (pa)

LC 98-15881

"When his father died in 1996 . . . Wieseltier began to observe the Jewish rituals of the traditional year of mourning. His own mourning led him to an in-depth study of the history and meaning of Kaddish in Judaism. Wieseltier provides a work of history, philosophy and spiritual memoir that demonstrates how the practice of religion meets the needs of a troubled soul." Publ Wkly

296.7 Judaism—Religious experience, life, practice

Diamant, Anita, 1951-

Living a Jewish life; Jewish traditions, customs, and values for today's families; [by] Anita Diamant with Howard Cooper. Updated and rev ed. HarperCollins 2007 308p pa $16.95

296.7

1. Jews—Social life and customs

ISBN 978-0-06-117364-6; 0-06-117364-9

LC 2007-297208

First published 1991

This book "is written as a kind of handbook to help those who are perhaps new to the faith or rebuilding for themselves as adults the traditions with which they were (or were not) brought up. It would also make an excellent introduction for anyone unacquainted with Jewish customs." Booklist

Includes bibliographical references

Pitching my tent; on marriage, motherhood, friendship, and other leaps of faith. Scribner 2003 223p hardcover o.p. pa $15   **296.7**

1. Jewish women

ISBN:0-7432-4616-0;   978-0-7432-4617-0(pa)
0-7432-4617-9 (pa)   LC 2003-45440

"This collection of short essays, culled primarily from the *Boston Globe Sunday Magazine* and then reworked, . . . {are} organized around such themes as love and marriage, child rearing, friendship and living a religious life. . . . The book's strength lies in its woman-to-woman conversational tone, especially in the opening section about married life and its dark side. . . . These morsels will make a tasty snack for Diamant's admirers." Publ Wkly

Isaacs, Ronald H.

Kosher living; it's more than just the food; [by] Ron Isaacs. Jossey-Bass 2005 xlvii, 286p $22.95
*   **296.7**

1. Judaism—Customs and practices

ISBN 0-7879-7642-3   LC 2004-26727

"An Arthur Kurzweil book"

"The book not only covers the expected Jewish topics— circumcision, marriage, prayer, Shabbat, synagogue behavior and more—but also . . . [items] such as employer-employee relations, shopping and even war. . . . This resource offers timeless wisdom through a contemporary lens." Publ Wkly

Includes bibliographical references

Kaplan, Aryeh

Jewish meditation; a practical guide. Schocken Bks. 1985 165p pa $12 hardcover o.p.

296.7

1. Meditation 2. Judaism—Customs and practices

ISBN 0-8052-1037-7 (pa)   LC 84-23589

The author "outlines various forms of meditation based on Jewish writings and practices. He discusses mantra meditation, visualization, and ways to contemplate God. With an eye toward traditional Judaism, Kaplan also explains how following the many commandments of the Bible is also a form of meditation. A profound book that is complex in subject matter yet simple in methodology." Booklist

Kushner, Harold S., 1935-

How good do we have to be? a new understanding of guilt and forgiveness. Little, Brown 1996 181p $11.95 hardcover o.p.

296.7

1. Bible. O.T. Genesis—Criticism 2. Guilt 3. Good and evil

ISBN 0-316-51933-2 (pa)   LC 95-25350

The author "here retells the Genesis story of . . . {Adam and Eve to argue} that the imperfections of humankind do not merit the loss of God's love, nor should they foster the guilt and anxiety that they often do in a society driven by a misguided attachment to perfection. . . . {Kushner sees} acceptance and forgiveness as a means of overcoming the insidious consequences of a preoccupation with perfection." Libr J

"This is one psychological self-help book that deserves the popularity it is likely to achieve." Booklist

Kushner, Harold S., 1935-—*Continued*

Who needs God; [by] Harold Kushner. Fireside
2002 212p pa $14 **296.7**
1. God—Judaism
ISBN 0-7432-3477-4
First published 1989 by Summit Bks.
The author "believes that 'human life has meaning
. . . but only in religious terms.' According to this crucial realization, it is religion that connects us to God and
community." Libr J

Levy, Naomi

To begin again; a journey toward comfort,
strength, and faith in difficult times. Knopf 1998
267p pa $12.95 hardcover o.p. **296.7**
1. Judaism—Customs and practices 2. Bereavement
ISBN 0-345-41383-0 (pa) LC 98-16024
The author "offers a progressive Jewish approach to
coping with life's darker moments. Having faced the
murder of her father when she was 15, Levy joined the
first class of women to study at the Jewish Theological
Seminary. Drawing on her own suffering and her experience as a rabbi, she constructs a map for personal renewal." Publ Wkly
"A wise and practical guide for readers of any religious persuasion." Libr J

296.8 Judaism—Denominations and movements

Wiesel, Elie, 1928-

Souls on fire; portraits and legends of Hasidic
masters; translated from the French by Marion
Wiesel. Summit Bks. 1982 c1972 268p pa $14
hardcover o.p. **296.8**
1. Hasidism 2. Hasidic legends
ISBN 0-671-44171-X (pa) LC 82-5984
A reissue of the title first published 1972 by Random
House
"A collection of legends and portraits of the founder
of the Hasidic movement and his disciples. . . . Wiesel
assumes the role of a storyteller, who simply transmits
tales he heard as faithfully as his personal experience
will allow." Publ Wkly

297 Islam, Babism, Bahai Faith

American jihad; Islam after Malcolm X; {edited
by} Steven Barboza. Doubleday 1994 370p il pa
$19 hardcover o.p. **297**
1. Black Muslims
ISBN 0-385-47694-9 (pa) LC 93-31469
A "collection of more than 50 brief interviews. While
the interviews are not too deep, they do correct certain
tabloid stereotypes of this rapidly growing religion. Some
interviewees are famous: Kareem Abdul-Jabbar talks
about how his conversion gave him credibility but not
marketability, while Jamil Abdullah Al-Amin (the former
H. Rap Brown) observes how Islam has enabled him to
control his anger. A section on the separatist Nation of
Islam fills out interesting history." Publ Wkly

Armstrong, Karen

Islam; a short history. Modern Lib. 2000 xxxiv,
222p maps $19.95; pa $11.95 * **297**
1. Islam
ISBN 0-679-64040-1; 0-8129-6618-X (pa)
LC 00-25285
This history of the Islamic faith focuses on the reli-
gion's attitude toward politics
The author "does an admirable job of presenting Is-
lamic history from an objective, unbiased point of view."
Libr J
Includes bibliographical references

Aslan, Reza

No god but God; the origins, evolution, and
future of Islam. Random House 2005 xxiv, 310p
$25.95; pa $14.95 * **297**
1. Islam
ISBN 1-4000-6213-6; 0-8129-7189-2 (pa)
LC 2004-54053
"Beginning with an exploration of the religious climate in the years before the Prophet's Revelation, Aslan
traces the story of Islam from the Prophet's life and the
so-called golden age of the first four caliphs all the way
through European colonization and subsequent independence. . . . This is an excellent overview that doubles as
an impassioned call to reform." Booklist
Includes bibliographical references

Ben Jelloun, Tahar, 1944-

Islam explained. New Press (NY) 2002 120p
hardcover o.p. pa $13.95 **297**
1. Islam
ISBN 1-56584-781-4; 1-56584-897-7 (pa)
LC 2002-30500
Translated from the French by Franklin Philip
"Cast in the form of an extended conversation between Ben Jelloun and his young daughter. . . . Father
and child discuss the history of Islam, what it means to
be a Muslim today, the challenges facing the Islamic
world, and terrorism. . . . Its openness and emotional
honesty, particularly when discussing the tragedy of 9/11,
make it a valuable addition to a growing public discourse. As an introduction to the religion, it is spotty, but
as a liberal Muslim voice of reconciliation, heartbreak,
and compassion, it is priceless." Booklist

Encyclopedia of Islam in the United States; edited
by Jocelyne Cesari. Greenwood Press 2007 2v
il set $199.95 **297**
1. Islam—Encyclopedias 2. Muslims—United States—
Encyclopedias
ISBN 978-0-313-33625-6; 0-313-33625-3
LC 2007-16142
"The first volume of this . . . work is an A-Z encyclopedia on American Muslim topics. The second volume
offers over 400 pages of primary resources about the social, political, religious, and artistic life of American
Muslims." Choice
This set "takes a refreshing look at Islam and Muslims
from a uniquely Muslim American perspective. Hence, it
is a valuable reference to both Muslims and non-Muslims
alike." Am Ref Books Annu, 2008
Includes bibliographical references

Ernst, Carl W., 1950-
Following Muhammad; rethinking Islam in the
contemporary world. University of North Carolina
Press 2003 244p il (Islamic civilization & Muslim
networks) $24.95; pa $16.95   **297**
  1. Islam
  ISBN 0-8078-2837-8; 0-8078-5577-4 (pa)
                              LC 2003-11162
The author "informs readers of the roles played by co-
lonialism, Christian missionary efforts, and Western con-
ceptions of just what 'religion' is, all in relation to
American conceptions of Islam." Libr J
Includes bibliographical references

The Shambhala guide to Sufism. Shambhala
Publs. 1997 xxi, 264p il pa $18.95   **297**
  1. Sufism
  ISBN 1-57062-180-2   LC 97-10189
This guide to Sufism "covers its beginnings, its basic
philosophies, and its place in Islam." Libr J
Includes bibliographical references

Esposito, John L.
Islam; the straight path. Rev. 3rd ed., updated
with new epilogue. Oxford University Press 2005
304p map pa $39.95   **297**
  1. Islam
  ISBN 0-19-518266-9   LC 2004-61688
  First published 1988
This "survey text introduces the faith, belief, and practice of Islam from its earliest origins up to its contemporary resurgence." Publisher's note
Includes bibliographical references

What everyone needs to know about Islam.
Oxford Univ. Press 2002 204p $18.95
                                  297
  1. Islam
  ISBN 0-19-515713-3   LC 2002-8387
In question-and-answer format the author presents information on a variety of aspects of Islam. The "format
allows readers to skip ahead to areas that interest them,
including hot-button issues such as 'Why are Muslims so
violent?' or 'Why do Muslim women wear veils and
long garments?' In his answers, which are anywhere
from a paragraph to several pages long, Esposito elegantly educates the reader through what the Qur'an says,
how Muslims are influenced by their local cultures, and
how the unique politics of Islamic countries affects Muslims' views." Publ Wkly
Includes bibliographical references

Essential Sufism; edited by James Fadiman and
  Robert Frager. HarperSanFrancisco 1997 265p
  pa $13 hardcover o.p.   **297**
  1. Sufism
  ISBN 0-06-251475-X (pa)   LC 97-2555
This "volume offers sayings, religious quotes, poems,
aphorisms, and prayers from many Sufi masters. . . .
The book {also} includes the . . . discussions of the ma-
jor Sufi teachers, history, culture, and beliefs." Libr J
Includes bibliographical references

Gardell, Mattias
In the name of Elijah Muhammad; Louis
Farrakhan and the Nation of Islam. Duke Univ.
Press 1996 482p (C. Eric Lincoln series on the
black experience) $59.95; pa $23.95   **297**
  1. Farrakhan, Louis, 1933- 2. Elijah Muhammad,
  1897-1975 3. Black Muslims
  ISBN 0-8223-1852-0; 0-8223-1845-8 (pa)
                                LC 96-22666
The author presents a history of the Nation of Islam
and "details the activities of the group and Farrakhan,
covering their position on gangs, hip-hop, drugs, prisons,
African American politics, public health, and black unity." Libr J
"Some will appreciate the author's brief critical airing
of claims of pre-Columbian Africans in America and accounts of Muslims and the slave trade, but he is at his
best when focusing on the leaders and on the changing
theology of the Nation of Islam (NOI) and similar African American groups in the 20th-century US. The book
is balanced and well researched." Choice
Includes bibliographical references

Gordon, Matthew
Islam; origins, practices, holy texts, sacred
persons, sacred places; [by] Matthew S. Gordon.
Oxford Univ. Press 2002 112p il $17.95
                                  297
  1. Islam
  ISBN 0-19-521885-X   LC 2002-70371
  First published 2001 by Facts on File
The author "discusses the rise of Islam; the centrality
of its sacred text, the Qur'an; the importance of the
Prophet Muhammad; the major developments of both
Sunni and Shi'i Islam . . . the ethical principles and
'Five Pillars' of the faith; the role of the mosque and of
sacred sites such as Mecca; the concept of sacred time
and the Islamic lunar calendar; Muslims' beliefs about
death and the afterlife; and Islam in the modern world."
Publ Wkly
Includes bibliographical references

Grieve, Paul
A brief guide to Islam; history, faith and
politics: the complete introduction. Carroll & Graf
2006 433p il map pa $13.95 *   **297**
  1. Islam
  ISBN 0-7867-1804-8; 978-0-7867-1804-7
                               LC 2006-282191
The author "starts his book with a look at the similarities and differences among the three major world religions: Judaism, Christianity, and Islam. From there, he
explores the history of Islam and the foundations of the
culture that grew out of the Islamic faith." Libr J
"If you read only one book about Islam this year, this
should be it." Publ Wkly

Karsh, Efraim
Islamic imperialism; a history. Yale University
Press 2006 276p map $30   **297**
  1. Islam and politics 2. Imperialism 3. Jihad
  ISBN 0-300-10603-3   LC 2005-34836

Karsh, Efraim—*Continued*

The author "surveys for a general audience the region's Islamic political past. Parallel to his narrative, Karsh frequently contrasts the universalistic proclamations of Islam with cycles of imperial consolidation and fragmentation. After recounting the Prophet Muhammad's religio-political establishment of Islam, and the discord about his legacy that continues today, Karsh narrates the battles over Muhammad's caliphate that eventuated in the Umayyad and Abbasid Empires. Karsh's commentary often looks forward to contemporary ideologues of Islam who ransack history to justify grievances. . . . An informative foundation for further exploration of Islamic history." Libr J

Kepel, Gilles

Jihad; the trail of political Islam; translated by Anthony F. Roberts. Harvard Univ. Press 2002 454p $33.95; pa $15.95 **297**

1. Islam and politics
ISBN 0-674-00877-4; 0-674-01090-6 (pa)
LC 2002-17181

Original French edition, 2000

"Kepel argues that the terrorism seen today throughout the world results from the failure of Islamic fundamentalism and not its success. . . . Fascinating despite its copious detail." Booklist

Lewis, Bernard

The crisis of Islam; holy war and unholy terror. Modern Library 2003 xxxii, 184p map $19.95; pa $12.95 * **297**

1. Terrorism 2. Islam and politics 3. Islamic fundamentalism
ISBN 0-679-64281-1; 0-8129-6785-2 (pa)
LC 2002-45219

This is an "overview of the geopolitical events and religious/cultural belief systems that underlie current tensions between the West and Muslim populations around the globe. An amplification of an article Lewis wrote for the *New Yorker*, the book spans more than 13 centuries but primary emphasis is on key happenings from the early 20th century to the present." SLJ

"Written in an easily accessible style, this analysis provides a digestible overview for Westerners still asking why." Booklist

Includes bibliographical references

Lippman, Thomas W.

Understanding Islam; an introduction to the Muslim world. 2nd rev ed. Penguin Bks. 1995 198p pa $14 **297**

1. Islam
ISBN 0-452-01160-4
LC 95-24015

"A Meridian book"

First published 1982

The author explains fundamental Islamic beliefs and practices. The life and work of Mohammed is examined in depth

Includes bibliographical references

The **Many** faces of Islam; perspectives on a resurgent civilization; Nissim Rejwan [editor] University Press of Fla. 2000 282p $55 **297**

1. Islam 2. Islamic countries—Politics and government
ISBN 0-8130-1807-2
LC 00-32587

The editor offers "perspectives on modern Islamic culture and religious practice. Seeking to dispel the perception that Islamic fundmentalism and extremism represent Islam in its entirety, Rejwan surveys the issues and provides numerous excerpts from modern writers and scholars, Muslim and non-Muslim, summarizing the many problems and dilemmas facing contemporary Muslims." Univ. Press Books for Public and Second Sch Libr, 2001

Naipaul, V. S. (Vidiadhar Surajprasad), 1932-

Among the believers; an Islamic journey. Knopf 1981 430p pa $16 hardcover o.p. **297**

1. Islam
ISBN 0-394-71195-5 (pa)
LC 81-47503

"Based on his seven-month journey across the Asian continent, Naipaul explores the life, the culture, the ferment inside the nations of Islam." Publisher's note

Beyond belief; Islamic excursions among the converted peoples. Random House 1998 408p pa $15 hardcover o.p. **297**

1. Islam
ISBN 0-375-70648-8 (pa)
LC 97-37350

"Retracing a voyage he made in 1979, the novelist and essayist journeys through Indonesia, Iran, Pakistan and Malaya, using Islam as a window on the animism, nationalism, capitalism and other isms he encounters there." N Y Times Book Rev

Nasr, Seyyed Hossein

Islam: religion, history, and civilization. HarperSanFrancisco 2002 xx, 198p pa $12.95 **297**

1. Islam 2. Islamic civilization
ISBN 0-06-050714-4
LC 2002-32810

This introduction to the world of Islam explores the following topics: What is Islam?; The doctrines and beliefs of Islam; Islamic practices and institutions; The history of Islam; Schools of Islamic thought; Islam in the contemporary world; Islam and other religions; The spiritual and religious significance of Islam

"Provides compelling analysis of contemporary Islam and its conflicts without overwhelming the reader with information." Booklist

Includes bibliographical references

Nasr, Vali

The Shia revival; how conflicts within Islam will shape the future. Norton 2006 287p map $25.95 * **297**

1. Shi'ah 2. Islam and politics
ISBN 0-393-06211-2; 978-0-393-06211-3
LC 2006-12361

This "is a historical account of sectarian conflicts in the Muslim world, and how the future rests in finding a peaceful solution to the ancient rivalries between the Shi-

Nasr, Vali—*Continued*
as and the Sunnis." Publisher's note
"So enlightening and perspective altering that no one concerned about the Middle East should miss reading it." Booklist
Includes bibliographical references

The **Oxford** dictionary of Islam; John L. Esposito, editor in chief. Oxford Univ. Press 2003 359p hardcover o.p. pa $18.95 *   297
1. Islam—Dictionaries
ISBN 0-19-512558-4; 0-19-512559-2 (pa)
LC 2002-30261
"Aimed at general readers with little knowledge of Islam, the dictionary focuses on 19th- and 20th-century topics, including many social, religious, and political aspects of modern Islam. Entries include hot topics (e.g., al-Qaeda, Osama Bin Laden, Afghanistan), various religious and political sects (Nation of Islam, Sevener Shiis, the Philippines' Moro National Liberation Front), and muslim views on a variety of issues (abortion, suicide, science, the treatment of women). Entries arranged alphabetically, use standard transliterations. Cross-references are listed at the end of entries, and attempts are made to link Arabic and English terms." Choice
"This is an excellent resource for ready-reference collections in any library." Libr J
Includes bibliographical references

The **Oxford** history of Islam; {edited by} John Esposito. Oxford Univ. Press 1999 749p il map $49.95   297
1. Islam
ISBN 0-19-510799-3   LC 99-13219
"Contributors treat, among other things, Muslim history, law, and society; art and architecture; and regional differences. Chapters on the 'Globalization of Islam' and 'Contemporary Islam' are particularly relevant to current events. . . . An ideal one-volume source." Libr J
Includes bibliographical references

Rogerson, Barnaby, 1960-
The heirs of Muhammad; Islam's first century and the origins of the Sunni-Shia split. Overlook 2007 415p $27.95   297
1. Muḥammad, d. 632 2. 'Aïshah, d. 7th cent. 3. 'Alī ibn Abī Tālib, Caliph, ca. 600-661 4. Islam
ISBN 978-1-58567-896-9; 1-58567-896-1
LC 2006-51520
First published 2006 in the United Kingdom with title: The heirs of the prophet Muhammad
This is a "journey back to seventh-century Medina and the various schemes that led to the division of Islam into Shia and Sunni factions. . . . Helpful tables of key characters in the Prophet's life and genealogies of Muhammad and the four caliphs round out Rogerson's charming and captivating chronicle." Publ Wkly
Includes bibliographical references

Smith, Jane Idleman, 1937-
Islam in America; [by] Jane I. Smith. Columbia Univ. Press 1999 251p il (Columbia contemporary American religion series) $60; pa $20.50
297
1. Islam
ISBN 0-231-10966-0; 0-231-10967-9 (pa)
LC 98-31943
The author discusses "the basic tenets of the Muslim faith, surveys the history of Islam in this country, and profiles the lifestyles, religious practices, and worldviews of American Muslims. Sections of the book cover the role of women in American Islam, raising and educating children, the use of products acceptable to Muslims, appropriate dress and behavior, concerns about prejudice and unfair treatment, and other issues related to life in [America]." Univ Press Books for Public and Second Sch Libr, 2001
Includes bibliographical references

297.1   Sources of Islam

Koran.
The meaning of the glorious Koran; an explanatory translation by Marmaduke Pickthall; with an introduction by William Montgomery Watt. A.A. Knopf, Distributed by Random House 1992 xxiv, 693p il $22 *   297.1
ISBN 0-679-41736-2; 978-0-679-41736-1
LC 92-52928
"Everyman's library"
This translation first published 1930
"The sacred scripture of Islam, regarded by Muslims as the Word of God, and except in sura I.—which is a prayer to God—and some few passages in which Muhammad or the angels speak in the first person, the speaker throughout is God." Ency Britannica

The **Qur'an:** an encyclopedia; edited by Oliver Leaman. Taylor & Francis Group 2006 xxvii, 771p $240   297.1
1. Koran—Encyclopedias
ISBN 0-415-32639-7; 978-0-415-32639-1
"The objective of this encyclopedia is to fill a gap between general introductions and more technical works and provide the non-specialist with a resource covering all aspects of the text and its reception." Booklist
Includes bibliographical references

299   Religions not provided for elsewhere

The **Gnostic** Bible; edited by Willis Barnstone and Marvin Meyer. Shambhala 2003 860p $39.95; pa $24.95 *   299
1. Gnosticism
ISBN 1-57062-242-6; 1-59030-199-4 (pa)
LC 2003-7148
"The book provides Gnostic texts from their Jewish origins, into early Christianities, on into the medieval world. Though it concentrates on the early Jewish-

The Gnostic Bible—*Continued*

Christian matrix of early Gnosticism, the collection . . . manifests the breadth and depth of Gnostic variations in neo-Platonist, Manichean, Mandean, Islam, and Cathar movements." Choice

"This book may well be the most comprehensive collection of Gnostic materials ever gathered in one volume." Publ Wkly

Pagels, Elaine H., 1943-

The Gnostic Gospels; by Elaine Pagels. Random House 1979 xxxvi, 182p pa $12 hardcover o.p. *

299

1. Gnosticism
ISBN 0-679-72453-2 (pa)   LC 79-4764

An examination of the origins of early Christianity based on Gnostic texts rediscovered in the 20th century.

Pagels "writes for the layman, which is refreshing, and she does so lucidly, which is a challenge, especially when 'gnosticism' was regarded by its own adherents to be for the initiated only." Christ Sci Monit

Includes bibliographical references

Valantasis, Richard, 1946-

The Beliefnet guide to Gnosticism and other vanished Christianities; preface by Marcus Borg. Three Leaves Press 2006 xxix, 159p (The Beliefnet guides) pa $9.95   299

1. Gnosticism 2. Church history—30-600, Early church
ISBN 0-385-51455-7   LC 2005-50577

This guide "covers Gnostic theology as well as Gnostic sects (e.g., the Sethians, Valentinianas, and Carpocratians) and other gospels and includes a list of recommended reading, a glossary, and two appendixes (the complete text of and an outline of the canon)." Libr J

"This book offers a concise but fact-filled approach to the study of early Christianity in its broad diversity." Publ Wkly

Includes bibliographical references

Wilkinson, Richard H.

The complete gods and goddesses of ancient Egypt. Thames & Hudson 2003 256p il $39.95 *

299

1. Egyptian mythology 2. Egypt—Religion 3. Gods and goddesses
ISBN 0-500-05120-8   LC 2002-110321

A guide to "Egyptian deities—a complete catalogue of gods and goddesses supplemented by examinations of the history of Egyptian religion, the rise and fall of the gods, and the ways in which they were worshipped." Publ Wkly

"Wilkinson's gorgeously illustrated book adds new dimension to popular literature on ancient Egypt. . . . And once readers open the book to look at the pictures, they well may stay to read the well-organized, comprehensive, clearly written text." Booklist

Includes bibliographical references

299.5 Religions of East and Southeast Asian origin

Blofeld, John Eaton Calthorpe, 1913-1987

Taoism: the road to immortality; [by] John Blofeld. Shambhala Publs. 1978 195p il pa $19.95 o.p.   299.5

1. Taoism
ISBN 1-570625-891 (pa)   LC 77-90882

The author seeks to explain the fundamental concepts of Taoism, tells stories of its masters and offers reflections on Taoist verse. In addition, he describes his visits to Taoist monasteries in China and discussions he had with contemporary masters

I ching.

The classic of changes; a new translation of the I Ching as interpreted by Wang Bi; translated by Richard John Lynn. Columbia Univ. Press 1994 602p (Translations from the Asian classics) $27.95; pa $17.95 *   299.5

1. Divination
ISBN 0-231-08294-0; 0-231-08295-9 (pa)
LC 93-43999

"Most available editions of the *I Ching* are based on the James Legge translation, a work produced over 140 years ago and characterized by romanticized and idiomatic Victorian English. Although not more accurate or revealing than the Legge, this new translation is welcome because of its crisp usage of modern-day English." Libr J

Lao-tzu, 6th cent. B.C.

Tao te ching; the new translation from Tao te ching: the definitive edition; translation by Jonathan Star. Jeremy P. Tarcher/Penguin 2008 103p pa $10 *   299.5
ISBN 978-1-58542-618-8   LC 2007-44948

This translation first published 2001 with title: Tao te ching: the definitive edition

"Chinese Taoist text attributed to Lao Tzu, supposedly an elder contemporary of Confucius (551?-479 BC). . . . A brief work in eighty-one-paragraphs in both verse and prose, it probably dates from the 4th or 3rd century BC, although some believe it may be as early as the 6th century BC. Because of its concise, poetic language, its meaning is subject to many interpretations. It is generally agreed that it is both a mystical book about union with the absolute, and a political handbook on how to rule and survive in chaotic times." Reader's Ency. 4th edition

Yang Lihui

Handbook of Chinese mythology; [by] Lihui Yang and Deming An, with Jessica Anderson Turner. ABC-CLIO 2005 293p il (Handbooks of world mythology) $75 *   299.5

1. Asian mythology
ISBN 1-57607-806-X   LC 2005-13851

This is a "work of historical and contemporary Chinese myths, including a . . . collection of historical doc-

Yang Lihui—*Continued*
uments, detailing myths as they live and change in China
today." Publisher's note

"This volume provides useful information to the reader. The authors' credibility and in-depth scholarship offer
a rare opportunity to experience Chinese mythology
through Chinese eyes." Booklist

Includes bibliographical references

299.6 Religions originating among Black Africans and people of Black African descent

Chevannes, Barry
Rastafari: roots and ideology. Syracuse Univ.
Press 1994 298p (Utopianism and
communitarianism) pa $19.95 hardcover o.p.
299.6
1. Rastafari movement 2. Jamaica—Religion
ISBN 0-8156-0296-0 (pa)   LC 94-18608
"Chevannes begins by tracing the cultural roots of the
Rastafari movement to the slave trade in Jamaica from
the sixteenth through the nineteenth century, in reaction
to which a foundation was laid for the spirit of resistance
that was later a major factor in Rastafari's spread on the
island. Chevannes also closely attends to the internal rifts
and doctrinal disputes that caused denominational splits
within the movement." Booklist
"Vital for students of African American religions and
Caribbean religions, but also of interest to anthropologists, sociologists, and historians." Choice
Includes bibliographical references

The **Encyclopedia** of African and
African-American religions; Stephen D. Glazier,
editor. Routledge 2000 xx, 452p il maps $150
*   **299.6**
1. African Americans—Religion—Encyclopedias
2. Blacks—Religion
ISBN 0-415-92245-3   LC 00-59136
"A Berkshire Reference work"
This encyclopedia presents "145 articles that explore
the interaction of religion and culture and portray diversities of religious experience and research methodology.
Religions outside North America, including lesser-known
movements, receive the most coverage, and authors often
present fruits of their own ethnographic studies." Choice
"This encyclopedia is a good starting point for understanding the complex interrelationships among African,
African American, and European religious beliefs, practices, and traditions in a global context." Libr J

Kebra Nagast.
The Kebra Nagast; the last Bible of Rastafarian
wisdom and faith from Ethiopia and Jamaica;
edited by Gerald Hausman; introduction by Ziggy
Marley. St. Martin's Press 1997 203p il $19.95
299.6
1. Rastafari movement
ISBN 0-312-16793-8   LC 97-18817

"The Kebra Nagast supports the claims to black presence in biblical lore through the lineage of King Solomon's Ethiopian children. Hausman augments the main
text with a little compendium of parallel quotations from
the Bible and the most famous Rastafarian . . . the late
Bob Marley." Booklist
Includes bibliographical references

299.7 Religions of North American native origin

Castaneda, Carlos
The teachings of Don Juan; a Yaqui way of
knowledge. University of Calif. Press 1968 196p
$32.50; pa $16.95   **299.7**
1. Juan, Don 2. Yaqui Indians—Religion
ISBN 0-520-21755-1; 0-520-21757-8 (pa)
Available 30th anniversary edition with a new commentary by the author; Also available in paperback from
Washington Square Press
"This book is the record of a young anthropologist's
experiences as the apprentice of a [Yaqui] Indian sorcerer. Over a period of four years, Mr. Castaneda paid
intermittant visits to Don Juan, first in Arizona, then in
Sonora, Mexico." N Y Times Book Rev
Other titles about Don Juan are:
The active side of infinity (1999)
The art of dreaming (1993)
The eagle's gift (1981)
The fire from within (1984)
Journey to Ixtlan (1972)
Magical passes (1998)
The power of silence (1987)
The second ring of power (1977)
A separate reality (1971)
Tales of power (1974)

Hirschfelder, Arlene B.
The encyclopedia of Native American religions;
[by] Arlene Hirschfelder, Paulette Molin; foreword
by Walter R. Echo-Hawk. updated ed. Facts on
File 2000 390p il $75 *   **299.7**
1. Native Americans—Religion—Encyclopedias
ISBN 978-0-8160-3949-4; 0-8160-3949-6
                                         LC 99-21586
First published 1991
"The entries in this encyclopedia provide descriptions
of religious ceremonies and terminology; biographies of
native American religious leaders, missionaries, and others who have influenced the practice of these religions;
summaries of major court cases affecting native religious
practices; healing and other ceremonial practices that are
spiritual rather than religious in nature; and some . . .
mythology." Booklist [review of 1991 edition]
Includes bibliographical references

Hultkrantz, Åke
The religions of the American Indians;
translated by Monica Setterwall. University of
Calif. Press 1979 335p il pa $22.95   **299.7**
1. Native Americans—Religion
ISBN: 0-520-04239-5)pa)   LC 73-90661

Hultkrantz, Åke—*Continued*

Both sections of this book on North and South American Indians "provide fundamental knowledge and point to genetic connections between cultural areas. A well-researched work with a comprehensive bibliography, sure to be of interest to historians of religion and those interested in American culture." Libr J

Miller, Mary Ellen

The gods and symbols of ancient Mexico and the Maya; an illustrated dictionary of Mesoamerican religion; [by] Mary Ellen Miller and Karl Taube. Thames & Hudson 1993 216p il pa $18.95 hardcover o.p. * **299.7**

1. Mayas—Religion 2. Aztecs—Religion
ISBN 0-500-27928-4 (pa)   LC 92-80338
Paperback published with title: An illustrated dictionary of the gods and symbols of ancient Mexico and the Maya

"The authors give a brief history of the different Mesoamerican civilizations, explaining the rise and fall of each, and how one may have influenced the others. . . . The major portion of the work is the alphabetical dictionary section of approximately 300 terms. Most entries are between one-half column and one column in length, but some are more extensive; for example, *Calendar* is six pages with several illustrations and a chart of day names in Mayan and Aztec. The entries give etymologies where available, definitions, and commentary when appropriate." Booklist

Nabokov, Peter

Where the lightning strikes; the lives of American Indian sacred places. Viking 2005 350p $24.95   **299.7**

1. Sacred space 2. Native Americans—Religion
ISBN 0-670-03432-0   LC 2005-42227
The author presents "16 'biographies of place,' each of a habitat illustrating the bond between North American Indian cultures and their environment perpetuated by myths, legends, and rituals. . . . The author's careful documentation of unbroken reverence for these sacred places powerfully illuminates Native American attachment to the earth itself." Booklist
Includes bibliographical references

Popol vuh.

Popol vuh; the Mayan book of the dawn of life; translated by Dennis Tedlock; with commentary based on the ancient knowledge of the modern Quiché Maya. rev ed. Simon & Schuster 1996 388p il maps pa $15 *   **299.7**

1. Mayas—Religion 2. Native Americans—Religion
ISBN 0-684-81845-0   LC 95-46822
A modern translation of the 16th century Mayan holy book

"Tedlock's translation splendidly combines scholarship, imagination, and literary sensitivity. His photographs (derived from field work in Guatemala) vividly illustrate the text, and the notes (based on his collaboration with a contemporary Quiché shaman) fascinate and inform." Libr J
Includes bibliographical references

300 SOCIAL SCIENCES, SOCIOLOGY & ANTHROPOLOGY

300.3 Social sciences— Encyclopedias and dictionaries

Dictionary of the social sciences; edited by Craig Calhoun. Oxford Univ. Press 2002 563p $75 *   **300.3**

1. Social sciences—Dictionaries
ISBN 0-19-512371-9   LC 00-68151
This dictionary provides "definitions of key terms, offering entries that also discuss the intellectual issues behind the terms' usage. The entries cover all the social sciences except for law, education, and public administration. . . . Some 275 biographies are included." Libr J
Includes bibliographical references

The social science encyclopedia; edited by Adam Kuper and Jessica Kuper. 3rd ed. Routledge 2004 2v xxxix, 1119p il set $295 *   **300.3**

1. Social sciences—Encyclopedias
ISBN 0-415-32096-8   LC 2004-46829
First published 1985
The entries cover "the areas of anthropology, business, economics, education, government and politics, law and criminology, linguistics, psychology, social work, sociology, women's studies and beyond." Publisher's note
Includes bibliographical references

301 Sociology and anthropology

Encyclopedia of sociology; Edgar F. Borgatta, editor-in-chief, Rhonda Montgomery, managing editor. 2nd ed. Macmillan Ref. USA 2000 5v set $575   **301**

1. Sociology—Encyclopedias
ISBN 0-02-864853-6   LC 00-28402
First published 1992
This set includes about 400 articles covering all fields and subfields of sociology: social psychology, social demography, social anthropology, social history, social geography, social ecology, certain branches of political science, political economy, and sociolinguistics. More recent studies include affirmative action, alernative lifestyles, genocide, information society, sexually transmitted diseases and terrorism
Includes bibliographical references

Required reading; sociology's most influential books; edited by Dan Clawson. University of Mass. Press 1998 221p pa $17.95 hardcover o.p.   **301**

1. Best books
ISBN 1-55849-153-8 (pa)   LC 98-11944
This volume "identifies and discusses 17 of the 'most influential' books in sociology written during the last 25 years. . . . The power of this book lies in reconsidera-

Required reading—*Continued*

tions by eminent sociologists of important titles in light of a quarter of a century's worth of political, social, and economic change." Libr J

Includes bibliographical references

Whybrow, Peter C.

American mania; when more is not enough. Norton 2005 338p $24.95; pa $15.95   **301**

1. Consumption (Economics) 2. Wealth 3. Social values

ISBN 0-393-05994-4; 0-393-32849-X (pa)

LC 2004-18699

In this "analysis of our prosperous American society, . . . [the author] reveals why as a nation of acquisitive migrants our insatiable quest for more now threatens our health and happiness." Publisher's note

"The indictment of American society offered here . . . is familiar. What's more idiosyncratic and compelling is the author's grounding his treatise in political economy (citing everyone from Adam Smith to Thorstein Veblen) as well as in neuropsychiatry, primatology and genetics." Publ Wkly

Includes bibliographical references

World of sociology; Joseph M. Palmisano, editor. Gale Group 2001 2v il set $160   **301**

1. Sociology—Encyclopedias

ISBN 0-7876-4965-1   LC 00-48399

This is a "subject-specific guide to concepts, theories, discoveries, pioneers, issues and ethical questions associated with sociology. It includes approximately 1,000-1,500 alphabetically arranged topical essays, definitions and biographies." Publisher's note

Includes bibliographical references

302   Social interaction

Fromm, Erich, 1900-1980

To have or to be? [Rev. ed.] Continuum 2005 xx, 182p pa $17.95 *   **302**

1. Human behavior 2. Ontology 3. Civilization

ISBN 0-8264-1738-8   LC 2006-271140

First published 1976 by Harper & Row as part of the World perspectives series

The author maintains "that two modes of existence are struggling for the spirit of humankind: the having mode, which concentrates on material possession, acquisitiveness, power, and aggression . . . and the being mode, which is based in love." Publisher's note

Includes bibliographical references

Heath, Chip

Made to stick; why some ideas survive and others die; [by] Chip Heath & Dan Heath. Random House 2007 291p $24.95 *   **302**

1. Social psychology

ISBN 9781400064281; 1-4000-6428-7

LC 2006-46467

"Based on a class at Stanford taught by one of the authors, this book profiles how some ideas 'stick' in our

minds while the majority fall by the wayside." Booklist

"Fun to read and solidly researched, this book deserves a wide readership." Publ Wkly

Includes bibliographical references

302.2   Communication

Biedermann, Hans, 1930-

Dictionary of symbolism; cultural icons and the meanings behind them; translated by James Hulbert. Meridan Book 1994 465p il pa $25 *   **302.2**

1. Signs and symbols

ISBN 0-452-01118-3   LC 93-30616

Original German edition, 1989

This dictionary "incorporates symbols that originated in Asia, Africa, Europe and the 'New World'. There are almost 600 entries from mythology, fairy tale, psychology, religion, and sociology, plus historical and legendary figures. With 2000 black-and-white illustrations, the book is highly attractive. The symbols are accompanied by thorough interpretations based on various sources." SLJ

Includes bibliographical references

The **Complete** dictionary of symbols; Jack Tresidder, general editor. Chronicle Books 2005 544p il $22.95 *   **302.2**

1. Signs and symbols

ISBN 0-8118-4767-5

First published 2004 in the United Kingdom

"The greater part of the dictionary consists of 2,000 alphabetical entries on figures (many biblical and classical), myths, animals, natural phenomena, ideograms, and artistic and cultural works. Entries include the Slavic Baba Iaga, the Japanese Susano, [and] the Indian Mahabharata. . . . The book is inexpensive and well-constructed." Choice

Gordon, Edward E.

Literacy in America; historic journey and contemporary solutions; [by] Edward E. Gordon and Elaine H. Gordon; foreword by Gerald Gutek. Praeger Pubs. 2003 xxi, 329p il map $83.95; pa $24.95   **302.2**

1. Literacy—United States

ISBN 0-275-95524-9; 0-275-97864-8 (pa)

LC 2002-68609

This "comprehensive history of American literacy from 1620 to the present includes excellent chapters on African American and Native American education." Libr J

Includes bibliographical references

Tannen, Deborah

You just don't understand; women and men in conversation. Quill 2001 342p pa $13.95

302.2

1. Conversation 2. Sex differences (Psychology)

ISBN 978-0-06-095962-3; 0-06-095962-2

First published 1990 by Morrow

Tannen, Deborah—*Continued*

The author "ponders gender-based differences that, she claims, define and distinguish male and female communication. . . . She asserts that for most women conversation is a way of connecting and negotiating. . . . Men, on the other hand, use conversation to achieve or maintain social status." Publ Wkly

"Aside from the vivid examples and lively prose, what makes this book particularly engaging is that the author makes linguistics . . . interesting and usable." N Y Times Book Rev

Includes bibliographical references

302.23   Media (Means of communication)

Alterman, Eric

What liberal media? the truth about bias and the news. Basic Books 2003 322p $25; pa $15

302.23

1. Journalistic ethics

ISBN 0-465-00176-9; 0-465-00177-7 (pa)

LC 2002-152568

The author argues "that the whole idea of a predominantly liberal press is a pernicious myth. Calling for a more open-minded approach to the discussion of media bias, Alterman documents the range of conservative media outlets in all formats, showing that the conservatives far outnumber the small and underfunded liberal media." Libr J

"Whether readers agree with Alterman or not, his writing on the business of opinion making is eye-opening. This book will be required reading for anyone in politics or journalism, or anyone curious about their complicated nexus." Publ Wkly

Includes bibliographical references

Bok, Sissela

Mayhem; violence as public entertainment. Perseus Books 1999 194p pa $16   302.23

1. Violence 2. Mass media

ISBN 978-0-7382-0145-0; 0-7382-0145-6

"A Merloyd Lawrence book"

First published 1998 by Addison-Wesley

The author "examines the shallow debates surrounding violent entertainments, especially on television. She fleshes out both sides of the issue, offering a rigorous discussion of the ill effects of violent shows and of censorship, and then advances nongovernmental solutions to curbing exposure to violent media. . . . Packed with citations and rich in anecdote . . . this may be the best primer for a serious debate." Libr J

Includes bibliographical references

History of the mass media in the United States; an encyclopedia; edited by Margaret A. Blanchard; commissioning editor Carol J. Burwash. Fitzroy Dearborn Pubs. 1998 xxxii, 752p il $150

302.23

1. Mass media 2. United States—Civilization

ISBN 1-57958-012-2   LC 98-233183

This volume examines the ways in which mass media affects and is affected by United States society. From the 1690s to 1990, the alphabetically arranged entries cover subjects ranging from newspaper history to media coverage of wars, court cases, legislation and interest groups.

"Beautifully designed, with a nice clear typeface, this work is also enhanced by superb illustrations and well-chosen photographs. . . . This volume is outstanding." Booklist

Jones, Gerard

Killing monsters; why children need fantasy, super heroes, and make-believe violence; foreword by Lynn Ponton. Basic Bks. 2002 261p $25; pa $15   302.23

1. Mass media 2. Children 3. Fantasy 4. Violence

ISBN 0-465-03695-3; 0-465-03696-1 (pa)

LC 2001-52667

The author "argues that violent video games, movies, music and comics provide a safe fantasy world within which children learn to become familiar with and control the frightening emotions of anger, violence and sexuality." Publ Wkly

"Although not an academic, the author has done his homework. He presents his case convincingly, and the concluding notes provide support." SLJ

Includes bibliographical references

McLuhan, Marshall, 1911-1980

The global village; transformations in world life and media in the 21st century; [by] Marshall McLuhan and Bruce R. Powers. Oxford Univ. Press 1989 220p il (Communication and society) pa $14.95 hardcover o.p. *   302.23

1. Mass media 2. Technology and civilization

ISBN 0-19-507910-8 (pa)   LC 88-22718

This book "was written, according to Powers, between 1974 and 1980 . . . and 'put together' between 1976 and 1984. McLuhan's thesis has always been that electronic technologies have been altering and reconstituting people in ways they don't understand and causing them to lose their private identities. This book probes the same theme from different angles, but with the same McLuhanesque all-over-the-place reasoning." Libr J

Includes bibliographical references

Postman, Neil

Amusing ourselves to death; public discourse in the age of show business. Viking 1985 184p pa $14 hardcover o.p.   302.23

1. Mass media 2. Television broadcasting 3. United States—Civilization

ISBN 0-14-009438-5 (pa)   LC 85-5335

"Elisabeth Sifton books"

The author argues that the constant exposure to television has contributed to a decline in America's intellectual life.

"A sustained, withering and thought-provoking attack on television and what it is doing to us." Publ Wkly

Includes bibliographical references

302.3   Social interaction within groups

Epstein, Joseph, 1937-
Friendship; an exposé. Houghton Mifflin 2006
270p hardcover o.p. pa $14.95   **302.3**
1. Friendship
ISBN   0-618-34149-8;   0-618-87215-9   (pa);
978-0-618-87215-2 (pa)   LC 2005-20059
The author "offers a thoughtful consideration of the
pleasures and obligations of friendship and a learned tour
of the best that has been written on the subject, from Aristotle and Cicero to the touching late-life correspondence between the theologian Karl Barth and the playwright Carl Zuckmayer. Along the way, he examines his
own friendships, weighing their successes and failures,
and judging his own performance as a friend." N Y
Times (Late N Y Ed)

King, Larry, 1933-
How to talk to anyone, anytime, anywhere; the
secrets of good communication; [by] Larry King
with Bill Gilbert. Crown 1994 220p pa $12.95
hardcover o.p.   **302.3**
1. Conversation 2. Communication
ISBN 0-517-88453-4 (pa)   LC 94-31458
King "shows you how to break the ice with strangers,
what to say at a wedding or a funeral, and how to sell
yourself to a prospective employer—or interview a prospective employee. He gives his secrets for how to survive if you have to appear on radio or television, and
how to recover from making a blooper." Publisher's note

Locke, John L.
The de-voicing of society; why we don't talk to
each other anymore. Simon & Schuster 1998 256p
pa $18.95 hardcover o.p.   **302.3**
1. Conversation 2. Communication
ISBN 0-684-85574-7 (pa)   LC 98-14921
"Locke offers a pointed diagnosis of the isolated society created by disembodied interaction. Ever more atom-
ized and shackled to video screens, modern people watch
and type, rather than talk. The loss, argues Locke, can be
discerned in the purposes of talk, specifically gossip, in
creating relationships and social networks. . . . An
insightful lamentation about a palpable social pandemic."
Booklist
Includes bibliographical references

302.4   Social interaction between groups

Maalouf, Amin
In the name of identity; violence and the need
to belong; translated from the French by Barbara
Bray. Arcade Pub. 2001 164p $22.95
                                             302.4
1. Identity (Psychology) 2. Violence
ISBN 1-55970-593-0   LC 2001-24929
Also available in paperback from Penguin Bks.

"This meditation on identity asks why the Arab world
increasingly looks like a stronghold of fanaticism. The
author, a Lebanese-born Christian who is now a resident
of France, points out that Islam is not, historically, any
more violent than Christianity, and looks at the forces
currently acting upon it. While noting the Middle East's
poverty and instability, he also suggests that after the fall
of the Soviet Union those who might once have turned
to Communism as an agency of political change now
turn to fanaticism, and its promise of salvation through
action." New Yorker
"This is an important addition to contemporary literature on diversity, nationalism, race and international politics." Publ Wkly

303.3   Coordination and control

Himmelfarb, Gertrude
The de-moralization of society; from Victorian
virtues to modern values. Knopf 1995 314p pa $19
hardcover o.p. *   **303.3**
1. Social values 2. United States—Moral conditions
3. Great Britain—Moral conditions 4. United States—
Social conditions
ISBN 0-679-76490-9 (pa)   LC 94-12365
The author examines "post-industrial and post-modern
society. Himmelfarb contends that if we can overcome
our prejudices against Victorian society and . . . the so-
called values—or disvalues—they bequeathed us, then
maybe we can learn from the Victorians as we deal with
crime, drug addiction, illiteracy, illegitimacy and welfare
dependency in American society." America
"This is intellectual history and historically based argument as good as they get." Booklist
Includes bibliographical references

Huxley, Aldous, 1894-1963
Brave new world revisited. Harper & Row 1958
147p pa $11.95 hardcover o.p. *   **303.3**
1. Propaganda 2. Totalitarianism 3. Brainwashing
4. Culture
ISBN 0-06-089852-6 (pa)
Also available in hardcover from Amereon
In response to his 1932 novel Brave new world "Huxley reconsiders his prophecies and fears that some of
these may be coming true much sooner than he thought."
Oxford Companion to Engl Lit. 5th edition

Iacocca, Lee A.
Where have all the leaders gone? with Catherine
Whitney. Scribner, a division of Simon &
Schuster, Inc. 2007 274p $25   **303.3**
1. Leadership
ISBN 1-4165-3247-1; 978-1-4165-3247-7
                                 LC 2007-5179
"The former CEO of Chrysler supplies a surprisingly
outspoken take on the pressing need for real leadership
in this country." Booklist

Sowell, Thomas, 1930-
The quest for cosmic justice. Free Press 1999
214p $25; pa $14   **303.3**
1. Justice 2. Equality
ISBN 0-684-86462-2; 0-684-86463-0 (pa)
LC 99-31470
"Thomas Sowell argues that government cannot afford
to remedy, and should therefore ignore, a broad spectrum
of . . . hardships caused by poverty, disability, geography, even race and nationality." N Y Times Book Rev
The author "presents his case in clear, convincing, and
accessible language." Libr J
Includes bibliographical references

Surowiecki, James
The wisdom of crowds; why the many are
smarter than the few and how collective wisdom
shapes business, economies, societies and nations.
Doubleday 2004 xxi, 296p $24.95; pa $14
303.3
1. Crowds 2. Social psychology
ISBN 0-385-50386-5; 0-385-72170-6 (pa)
LC 2003-70095
The author "analyzes the concept of collective wisdom
and applies it to various areas of the social sciences, including economics and politics. . . . This work is an intriguing study of collective intelligence and how it works
in contemporary society." Libr J
Includes bibliographical references

Wills, Garry, 1934-
Certain trumpets; the call of leaders. Simon &
Schuster 1994 336p il hardcover o.p. pa $16
303.3
1. Power (Social sciences)
ISBN 0-671-65702-X; 978-0-684-80138-4 (pa);
0-684-80138-8 (pa)   LC 94-6526
The author "has chosen 16 figures who exemplify a
distinctive leadership type—for example, military (Napoleon), charismatic (King David), saintly (Catholic worker
activist Dorothy Day). Each leader is contrasted with an
'anti-type' who, in Wills's judgment, failed to capitalize
on strengths similar to those of his or her successful
counterpart. . . . Wills pairs Martha Graham with Madonna, Socrates with Ludwig Wittgenstein, Eleanor Roosevelt with Nancy Reagan in a wise, witty, entertaining
look at the psychology of leaders and their followers."
Publ Wkly
Includes bibliographical references

Wuthnow, Robert
American mythos; why our best efforts to be a
better nation fall short. Princeton University Press
2006 288p $29.95   **303.3**
1. Social values 2. Social ethics 3. United States—
Moral conditions 4. Immigrants—United States
ISBN 0-691-12504-X; 978-0-691-12504-6
LC 2005-18789
"America was built on stories: tales of grateful immi-
grants arriving at Ellis Island, Horatio Alger-style trans-
formations, self-made men, and the Protestant work ethic.
. . . [The author] examines these most American of sto-

ries—narratives about individualism, immigration, success, religion, and ethnicity—through the eyes of recent
immigrants." Publisher's note
This book "challenges the reader to confront some
unsettling truths about who we are, what we believe, and
what we must do if we are truly to become a great nation." Libr J
Includes bibliographical references

Young-Bruehl, Elisabeth
The anatomy of prejudices. Harvard Univ. Press
1996 632p pa $18.95 hardcover o.p.
303.3
1. Prejudices
ISBN 0-674-03191-1 (pa)   LC 95-43754
In this book the author "argues that anti-Semitism,
racism, sexism and homophobia differ in their internal
logic (or illogic) and, more important, that they are deeply rooted in character structure and the unconscious." N
Y Times Book Rev
"Clearly written and accessible to general as well as
scholarly readers, this is a major work in personality and
culture that asserts the plurality rather than the unity of
prejudice." Libr J
Includes bibliographical references

303.4   Social change

Anderson, Terry H., 1946-
The movement and the sixties. Oxford Univ.
Press 1995 500p il pa $19.95 hardcover o.p.
303.4
1. Radicalism 2. Demonstrations 3. United States—Social conditions
ISBN 0-19-510457-9 (pa)   LC 94-16344
This "book is a national study of U.S. social activism
from 1960 to 1973, focusing on how 'the Movement'
was experienced by participants and exploring why this
activism arose when it did, how it developed, and what
it accomplished." Booklist
Anderson's "sweeping study is a valuable, refreshingly
unbiased reassessment of the '60s legacy." Publ Wkly
Includes bibliographical references

Baker, Stephen
The numerati. Houghton Mifflin Co. 2008 244p
$26   **303.4**
1. Mathematical models 2. Data processing
ISBN 978-0-618-78460-8; 0-618-78460-8
LC 2008-17830
The author "spotlights a new breed of entrepreneurial
mathematicians (the numerati) engaged in harnessing the
avalanche of private data individuals provide when they
use a credit card, donate to a cause, surf the Internet—or
even make a phone call. . . . An intriguing but disquieting look at a not too distant future when our thoughts
will remain private, but computers will disclose our
tastes, opinions, habits and quirks to curious parties, not
all of whom have our best interests at heart." Publ Wkly
Includes bibliographical references

Diamond, Jared M.

Guns, germs, and steel; the fates of human societies; [by] Jared Diamond. Norton 2005 518p il map $24.95 * **303.4**

1. Technology and civilization 2. Social change 3. Environmental influence on humans

ISBN 0-393-06131-0; 978-0-393-06131-4

LC 2005-284261

First published 1997

"This book poses a simple but profound question about the distribution of wealth and power in the modern world: 'Why weren't Native Americans, Africans, and Aboriginal Australians the ones who decimated, subjugated, or exterminated Europeans and Asians?'. . . To explore the discrepancies in technological and cultural development he looks not at peoples but at places, and at the natural resources available to different indigenous populations since 11,000 B.C. The scope and the explanatory power of this book are astounding." New Yorker [review of 1997 edition]

Includes bibliographical references

Dissent in America; voices that shaped a nation; [edited by] Ralph F. Young. Pearson Education 2006 792p $35 **303.4**

1. United States—Politics and government—Sources 2. United States—Social conditions—Sources

ISBN 0-321-44297-0 LC 2006-15415

"Divided chronologically, the anthology collects essays, speeches, organizational statements, songs, posters, interviews, broadsides and texts in other media. . . . For readers with something on their minds, 400 years of precedent may be just what they need to stimulate some questions of their own." Publ Wkly

Dyson, Freeman J., 1923-

The sun, the genome, & the Internet; tools of scientific revolutions. Oxford Univ. Press 1999 124p hardcover o.p. pa $10.95 **303.4**

1. Forecasting 2. Social change 3. Technology and civilization

ISBN 0-19-512942-3; 0-19-513922-4 (pa)

LC 98-53830

This volume "is based on lectures given at the New York Public Library in 1997. . . . [The author] believes that solar energy, genetic engineering and the Internet have the potential to transform society profoundly in the next century." N Y Times Book Rev

"A wide-ranging, fascinating view of science and society's distant horizon." Booklist

Includes bibliographical references

Goldsmith, Jack L.

Who controls the Internet? illusions of a borderless world; [by] Jack Goldsmith and Tim Wu. Oxford University Press 2006 226p il $28 * **303.4**

1. Internet—Social aspects 2. Internet—Law and legislation

ISBN 978-0-19-515266-1; 0-19-515266-2

LC 2005-27404

The authors "show how different nation-states and international organizations have shaped a local Internet ex-

perience based on their own prevailing societal values." Libr J

"Goldsmith and Wu contribute to Internet scholarship in a format that is accessible to a general readership and relevant to anyone who uses e-mail, surfs the Web, or shops online." Afterimage

Includes bibliographical references

Hoffman, Abbie

The best of Abbie Hoffman; foreword by Norman Mailer; edited by Dan Simon with the author. Four Walls Eight Windows 1989 421p il $21.95; pa $18.95 **303.4**

1. Radicalism 2. United States—Civilization

ISBN 0-941423-27-1; 0-941423-42-5 (pa)

LC 89-23585

This volume contains selections from Revolution for the hell of it, Woodstock Nation, Steal this book, and New writings.

Keen, Andrew

The cult of the amateur; how today's internet is killing our culture. Doubleday/Currency 2007 228p $22.95 **303.4**

1. Internet 2. Social change

ISBN 978-0-385-52080-5 LC 2006-103058

"Blogs, wikis, YouTube: they're all free, but can you really trust their content? A former Silicon Valley entrepreneur worries about the debasement of knowledge." Libr J

"Keen's relentless 'polemic' is on target about how a sea of amateur content threatens to swamp the most vital information and how blogs often reinforce one's own views rather than expand horizons." Publ Wkly

Nye, David E., 1946-

Technology matters; questions to live with. MIT Press 2006 282p $27.95 * **303.4**

1. Technology—Philosophy 2. Technology and civilization

ISBN 0-262-14093-4; 978-0-262-14093-5

LC 2005-52114

In a question-and-answer format, the author "views technology in terms of evolution, society, the known past, and an uncertain future. Chapter titles focus on questions, e.g., 'How Do Historians Understand Technology?' and 'Should 'The Market' Select Technologies?' . . . This is a book that deserves to be read, contemplated, and then read again. It should be discussed in seminars and by just plain folks." Choice

Includes bibliographical references

Postman, Neil

Technopoly; the surrender of culture to technology. Knopf 1992 222p pa $12 hardcover o.p. **303.4**

1. Technology and civilization

ISBN 0-679-74540-8 (pa) LC 91-53121

According to Postman, "the history of the world can be retold from the perspective of technological advances. In 'technopoly,' the present stage in Western culture, our

Postman, Neil—*Continued*

tools, especially the computer, have committed a palace revolt, 'redefining what we mean by religion, by art, by family, by politics, by history, by privacy, by intelligence, so that our definitions fit its new requirements.'" Natl Rev

Postman's "style is comfortable, his exposition incisive, and his reasoning hard to ignore." Christ Sci Monit
Includes bibliographical references

The **Radical** reader; a documentary history of the American radical tradition; edited by Timothy Patrick McCarthy and John McMillian; foreword by Eric Foner. New Press 2003 688p $65; lib bdg $21.95 *   **303.4**
1. Radicalism
ISBN 1-56584-827-6; 1-56584-682-6 (lib bdg)
LC 2002-41051

The editors present "more than 200 declarations, appeals, editorials, and essays by such radical thinkers (each introduced in a brief bio) as Frederick Douglass, Sarah Grimké, Henry David Thoreau, Upton Sinclair, Emma Goldman, Angela Davis, Betty Friedan, Mario Savio, César Chávez, Rachel Carson, Tony Kushner, and Ralph Nader." Booklist

"By bringing many hard-to-find documents under one cover, this anthology will excite readers in discussing why radicals from all walks of life have made progressive ideals meaningful to Americans. Recommended for college, high school, and public libraries." Libr J
Includes bibliographical references

Social change in America; the historical handbook, 2006; edited by Patricia C. Becker. Bernan 2006 xxxiv, 307p map $75   **303.4**
1. United States—Statistics 2. United States—Social conditions
ISSN 1558-9471
ISBN 978-1-59888-012-0; 1-59888-012-8

First published 1998 with title: A Statistical portrait of the United States. Periodically revised

This book offers "commentary about U.S. society and how it has changed—not just in comparison to the past, but also within a global context. The narrative is supported by population data from the 2000 Decennial Census and other . . . surveys. Topics covered in *Social Change in America* include family life; work and employment; housing; wealth and poverty; education; health; crime; volunteer activity; religion and religious affiliation; politics; the impact of the Internet on American society." Publisher's note
Includes bibliographical references

Tenner, Edward

Our own devices; the past and future of body technology. Alfred A. Knopf 2003 336p hardcover o.p. pa $14.95   **303.4**
1. Technology and civilization 2. Technological innovations
ISBN 0-375-40722-7; 0-375-70707-7 (pa)
LC 2002-40694

"Tenner examines the reciprocal relationship between technology (in the broad sense of useful created objects) and technique (the methods we use to employ them) as

they have developed together culturally. . . . A handful of examples provide insight into the history, ergonomics, and symbolism of some of the tools that are figuratively and literally closest to us: shoes (thong sandals and athletic varieties), chairs, eyeglasses, and headgear. Tenner also explores technologies that have influenced medicine (bottle feeding), arts (musical keyboards), and commerce (typing keyboards)." Libr J

"For a work that covers such a broad topic, this book is a page-turner, largely due to its clear prose and the author's approach to the material. While not lavishly illustrated, there seems to be a picture every time one is needed to illustrate the technology being discussed." SLJ
Includes bibliographical references

Toffler, Alvin

Future shock. Bantam Books 1990 561p pa $7.99 *   **303.4**
1. Social change 2. Technology and civilization 3. Modern civilization—1950-
ISBN 978-0-553-27737-1; 0-553-27737-5

First published 1970 by Random House

According to the author, "future shock is 'the dizzying disorientation brought on by the premature arrival of the future.' . . . Toffler outlines some interesting strategies for survival, writing in a clear popular style." Publ Wkly
Includes bibliographical references

Powershift; knowledge, wealth, and violence at the edge of the 21st century. Bantam Bks. 1990 xxii, 585p pa $7.99 hardcover o.p.   **303.4**
1. Social change 2. Power (Social sciences) 3. Modern civilization—1950-
ISBN 0-553-29215-3 (pa)   LC 90-1068

The author "argues that the control of knowledge has become the principal means to create wealth and power. Aided by the widespread use of computers and other communications technologies, this 'powershift,' Toffler predicts, will dramatically alter the world's political balance." Libr J
Includes bibliographical references

The third wave. Bantam Books 1989 537p pa $7.99 *   **303.4**
1. Social change 2. Technology and civilization 3. Modern civilization—1950-
ISBN 0-553-24698-4; 978-0-553-24698-8

First published 1980 by Morrow

Toffler argues that mankind, having already experienced the agricultural age and the industrial age, is on the verge of a new age characterized by "new technical systems, especially those in electronics, genetics and biology." N Y Times Book Rev
Includes bibliographical references

303.49 Social forecasts

Rees, Martin J., 1942-
Our final hour; a scientist's warning: how terror, error, and environmental disaster threaten humankind's future in this century on earth and beyond; [by] Martin Rees. Basic Books 2003 228p $25; pa $15   **303.49**
1. End of the world
ISBN 0-465-06862-6; 0-465-06863-4 (pa)
LC 2003-301
This is an "assessment of the risks associated with myriad scientific advances, from nuclear weapons to genetic engineering. . . . Rees' most arresting futuristic scenarios involve biotechnologies that will change the very essence of human nature, and he also offers some chilling observations regarding bioterror and bioerror, certain that one or the other will kill a million people by 2020. Chilling predictions of doom are interrupted by compelling insights into various scientific discoveries." Booklist
Includes bibliographical references

Zakaria, Fareed
The post-American world. W.W. Norton & Company 2008 292p $25.95   **303.49**
1. Economic forecasting 2. International economic relations 3. United States—Foreign relations 4. Globalization
ISBN 978-0-393-06235-9; 0-393-06235-X
LC 2008-01306
The author argues that "the weakened global economic and political position of the United States results not from the waning of its own powers but from the rapid rise of many other global players." Libr J
"This is a relentlessly intelligent book that eschews simpleminded projections from crisis to collapse." N Y Times Book Rev
Includes bibliographical references

303.6 Conflict and conflict resolution

Anderson, Sean, 1952-
Historical dictionary of terrorism; [by] Sean K. Anderson, Stephen Sloan. 2nd ed. Scarecrow Press 2002 588p (Historical dictionaries of religions, philosophies, and movements) $90   **303.6**
1. Terrorism—Dictionaries
ISBN 0-8108-4101-0   LC 2001-49656
First published 1995
The authors "investigate various underlying causes and motivations, providing insight into organizations, groups, and individuals directly involved or related to terrorism. They supply a typology of terrorists that will be valuable to researchers or others interested in penetrating the murkiness of terrorism." Choice
Includes bibliographical references

Arendt, Hannah
On revolution; introduction by Jonathan Schell. Penguin Books 2006 xxix, 336p pa $16 *   **303.6**
1. Revolutions
ISBN 0-14-303990-3; 978-0-14-303990-7
LC 2006-45397
First published 1963
The author "believes that war and revolution are the central facts of our time. But while war may become obsolete through nuclear terror, revolution seems likely to persist as the order of the day, and those who understand revolution may well be the masters of the future." Atl Mon
Includes bibliographical references

Benjamin, Daniel, 1961-
The age of sacred terror; [by] Daniel Benjamin, Steven Simon. Random House 2002 490p $25.95; pa $15.95   **303.6**
1. Terrorism 2. Islam and politics
ISBN 0-375-50859-7; 0-8129-6984-7 (pa)
LC 2003-265413
"The authors, both staff members of the National Security Council in the Clinton administration, give an account of bureaucratic inertia in antiterrorist efforts before Sept. 11, with the F.B.I., the C.I.A. and the military reluctant to share information or work with one another." N Y Times Book Rev
Includes bibliographical references

Burns, Vincent
Terrorism; a documentary and reference guide; [by] Vincent Burns and Kate Dempsey Peterson; foreword by James K. Kallstrom. Greenwood Press 2005 xxxvii, 293p il $75 *   **303.6**
1. Terrorism
ISBN 0-313-33213-4   LC 2005-3390
This is a "volume of 70 documents, some never before in print, pertaining to terrorism and the US. Readings include speeches, policy statements, letters, reports, and laws. . . . An easy-to-use resource that is full of pertinent information, this volume should be read all the way from the introduction . . . to the resources section." Choice
Includes bibliographical references

Camus, Albert, 1913-1960
The rebel; an essay on man in revolt; with a foreword by Sir Herbert Read; a revised and complete translation of L'homme révolté by Anthony Bower. Vintage Bks. 1991 306p pa $12   **303.6**
1. Revolutions 2. Nihilism
ISBN 0-679-73384-1   LC 91-50022
Original French edition, 1951; this translation first published 1956 by Knopf
The author describes how the theories of philosophers have been used with disastrous effect by political leaders from the French Revolution through the nihilist revolutions of Russia and the governments of Lenin, Hitler and Stalin. The conclusion calls for a return to a political philosophy having as its aim the happiness and development of living human beings

Carr, Caleb, 1955-

The lessons of terror; a history of warfare against civilians: why it has always failed and why it will fail again. Random House 2002 272p pa $12.95 hardcover o.p.   **303.6**
1. Terrorism
ISBN 0-375-76074-1 (pa)   LC 2002-280604
The author argues "that terrorism must be viewed in terms of 'military history, rather than political science or sociology,' and that the refusal to label terrorists as soldiers, rather than criminals, is a mistake. . . . This often fascinating, accessible tome skillfully contends that the terrorizing of civilians has a long and controversial history but, as an inferior method, is prone to failure." Publ Wkly
Includes bibliographical references

Combs, Cindy C.

Encyclopedia of terrorism; [by] Cindy C. Combs and Martin Slann. Rev ed. Facts on File 2007 478p il map (Facts on File library of world history) $95 *   **303.6**
1. Terrorism—Encyclopedias
ISBN 0-8160-6277-3; 978-0-8160-6277-5
LC 2006-15853
First published 2002
This encyclopedia provides articles on "the events, people, organizations, and places that have played a major role in international terrorism. Each entry is placed within its . . . historical context to help readers understand the wide-ranging motivations behind terrorist actions." Publisher's note
Includes bibliographical references

Confronting fear; a documentary history of terrorism; edited by Isaac Cronin. Thunder's Mouth Press 2002 561p pa $18.95
303.6
1. Terrorism
ISBN 1-56025-399-1   LC 2002-18005
Featuring essays by such authors as Simon Schama, Joseph Conrad, and V. S. Naipaul, this is "a compilation of writings on various forms of terrorism—political, religious, and 'fringe,' such as the Unabomber. . . . This is a good volume to have at hand in today's uncertain world as a quick reference to various instant newsmakers who populate our 'Breaking News' mindset." Booklist
"Cronin provides a rare overview for the public to understand this important and disturbing subject." Choice

Dershowitz, Alan M.

Why terrorism works; understanding the threat, responding to the challenge. Yale Univ. Press 2002 271p $24.95; pa $16   **303.6**
1. Terrorism
ISBN 0-300-09766-2; 0-300-10153-8 (pa)
LC 2002-6387
The author "argues forcefully that the attacks of September 11 were largely of our own doing—the international community, Dershowitz says, repeatedly rewards terrorists with appeasement and legitimization, refusing to take the necessary steps to curtail attacks. . . . These penetrating arguments force readers to consider how we got to September 11, how far we are willing to pursue terrorists and how much freedom we are willing to give up for our security." Publ Wkly
Includes bibliographical references

Ferguson, Niall

The war of the world; twentieth-century conflict and the descent of the West. Penguin Press 2006 lxxi, 808p il map $35   **303.6**
1. War 2. World history—20th century
ISBN 1-59420-100-5   LC 2006-50304
In this book, the author seeks to answer the question, "Why was the 20th century one of the most violent and brutal in history? . . . Ferguson comes up with three explanations he considers more plausible—namely, economic volatility, disintegrating empires, and ethnic conflict—which he illustrates with numerous examples in this ambitious, thoroughly researched work." Libr J
Includes bibliographical references

Garbarino, James

See Jane hit; why girls are growing more violent and what we can do about it. Penguin Press 2006 294p $25.95; pa $15   **303.6**
1. Girls—Psychology 2. Violence
ISBN   1-59420-075-0;   978-1-59420-075-5; 0-14-303868-0 (pa); 978-0-14-303868-9 (pa)
LC 2005-49341
This study of the increase of aggressive behavior among girls "includes interviews with female students at Cornell University who relate . . . stories of childhood bullying and abuse that confound the stereotypes of feminine behavior. Garbarino attributes these behavioral shifts to increased participation in sports, escalating media depictions of violence, and general societal shifts toward rewarding aggression." Libr J
This is "fascinating look at girls getting physical—from the assertive physicality expressed by healthy girls to criminal violence on the part of troubled ones." Publ Wkly
Includes bibliographical references

Herbst, Philip

Talking terrorism; a dictionary of the loaded language of political violence. Greenwood Press 2003 220p $49.95   **303.6**
1. Terrorism—Dictionaries
ISBN 0-313-32486-7   LC 2003-44071
"This is a dictionary with a social and political objective: to explore how supposedly civilized people, groups, and governments the world over use language to provide a moral justification for violence. . . .The 150 A-to-Z entries range from one half to several pages in length and include definitions, an examination of the charged use of a term both historically and in the present, and . . . cross references." Libr J
"This work is original, refreshing, and insightful. It attempts to discern the why of terrorism and political violence from the perspective of language." Choice
Includes bibliographical references

Kronenwetter, Michael
Terrorism: a guide to events and documents.
Greenwood Press 2004 298p il $55 *

303.6

1. Terrorism
ISBN 0-313-32578-2   LC 2004-6619
This "book examines the phenomenon of terrorism,
discussing the methods, tactics, and weapons used by terrorists and exploring the attraction that terrorism holds
for many individuals, groups, and movements." Publisher's note
"Kronenwetter's book is seminal to an understanding
of terrorism. Honest, insightful, and easily understood,
his book articulates the core ideals of terrorism and expertly presents its philosophical motivations within a historical context." Choice
Includes bibliographical references

Kushner, Harvey W.
Encyclopedia of terrorism. Sage Publs. 2003
xxvii, 523p il maps $130   **303.6**
1. Terrorism—Encyclopedias
ISBN 0-7619-2408-6   LC 2002-15938
"This guide presents more than 300 article-length entries, arranged alphabetically and covering such topics as
terrorist groups, key terrorists, types of terrorism, and
terrorist events (including 9/11). . . . Kushner (along
with a number of expert contributors) provides a solid
powerful collection of timely data on the who, what,
where, when, and why of international terrorism." Libr J
Includes bibliographical references

The **psychology** of terrorism; edited by Chris E.
Stout; foreword by Klaus Schwab. Praeger 2002
4v il (Psychological dimensions to war and
peace) set $349.95   **303.6**
1. Terrorism
ISBN 0-275-97771-4   LC 2002-72845
"Academics, clinicians, and activists address the roots
and fulmination of terrorism from a variety of perspectives. Child psychologists point out the early role of the
authoritarian family in creating terrorists, whereas
neoconservatives opine that realism—not psychology—is
needed to eliminate terrorists." Voice Youth Advocates
"These volumes offer readers diverse opinions and
perspectives in order to generate further thinking on the
complex subject of terrorism. . . . These contributions
go a long way in expanding readers' general knowledge
of politically motivated violence, as well as elucidating
the causes and consequences of 9/11." Choice
Includes bibliographical references

Sontag, Susan, 1933-2004
Regarding the pain of others. Farrar, Straus &
Giroux 2003 131p pa $12 hardcover o.p.

303.6

1. War photography 2. Photojournalism
3. Documentary photography 4. Atrocities
5. Violence
ISBN 978-0-312-42219-6   LC 2002-192527
Companion volume to On photography (1977)
"In this long reflective essay, which examines photographs of calamities and the moral uses of looking at

them, Sontag follows the trail of photojournalism from
the Crimean War on and refines some of the observations of her 1977 book, 'On Photography.'" N Y Times
Book Rev
"All libraries, regardless of type, size, or demographics, should own this book." Libr J

Stern, Jessica, 1958-
Terror in the name of God; why religious
militants kill; [by] Jessica Stern. Ecco 2003 xxxi,
368p $27.95; pa $15.95   **303.6**
1. Terrorism 2. Violence
ISBN 0-06-050532-X; 0-06-050533-8 (pa)
     LC 2003-48508
"In 'Terror in the Name of God,' Stern recounts her
four-year odyssey into the hearts and minds of religious
terrorists. She talks to Christian, Jewish and Muslim extremists, violent anti-abortion warriors and admirers of
Timothy McVeigh." N Y Times Book Rev
"Recent world events will heighten readers' interest in
the chapters dealing with al-Qaeda and its allies."
Booklist
Includes bibliographical references

Violence in America; an encyclopedia; Ronald
Gottesman, editor; Richard Maxwell Brown,
consulting editor {et al.}. Scribner 1999 3v set
$400   **303.6**
1. Violence—Encyclopedias
ISBN 0-684-80487-5   LC 99-52027
This reference "on the social, historical, biological,
and cultural aspects of violence in the United States offers 600 entries on topics ranging from violence, homicide, and race and ethnicity to women, child abuse, labor
and unions, sociobiology, 'ultimate fighting,' television,
gun violence, and various events and persons." Libr J
Includes bibliographical references

304.2   Human ecology

Diamond, Jared M.
Collapse: how societies choose to fail or
succeed. Viking 2005 575p il $29.95; pa $17 *

304.2

1. Social change 2. Environmental policy
ISBN 0-670-03337-5; 0-14-303655-6 (pa)
     LC 2004-57152
The author "examines storied examples of human economic and social collapse, and even extinction, including
Easter Island, classical Mayan civilization and the Greenland Norse. He explores patterns of population growth,
overfarming, overgrazing and overhunting, often abetted
by drought, cold, rigid social mores and warfare, that
lead inexorably to vicious circles of deforestation, erosion and starvation prompted by the disappearance of
plant and animal food sources. . . . Readers will find his
book an enthralling, and disturbing, reminder of the in-
dissoluble links that bind humans to nature." Publ Wkly
Includes bibliographical references

Encyclopedia of environment and society; Paul Robbins, general editor. Sage Publications 2007 5v xlix, 2105p il map set $695   **304.2**
1. Human ecology—Encyclopedias
ISBN 978-1-4129-2761-1; 1-4129-2761-7
LC 2007-21378
"Sage reference publication"
"This compilation of 1200 entries, authored by a score of international scholars and contributors, reflects the impact that various peoples, their cultures, and other societal features like politics have on the environment." Libr J

This encyclopedia "combines in one place hundreds of interrelated topics with a consistent editing and level of authority. I highly recommend this encyclopedia set to any library with holdings in science and contemporary society, which I hope is any library." Am Ref Books Annu, 2008

Includes bibliographical references

The **Encyclopedia** of human ecology; edited by Julia R. Miller [et al.] ABC-CLIO 2003 2v set $255 *   **304.2**
1. Human ecology—Encyclopedias
ISBN 1-57607-852-3   LC 2003-4178
"This encyclopedia blends disciplines such as biology, nutrition, psychology, sociology, anthropology, family, and environmental science. Readers will gain an understanding of the interdependence of humans with their environment as they research such topics as gambling, parenting, tobacco, elder abuse, clothing design, stress, 'Air Quality,' and 'Catholic Schooling.' Biographies of significant social scientists and psychologists are included in the alphabetical arrangement. The authoritative, scholarly articles provide more in-depth information than a general encyclopedia. . . . This well-documented resource will prove useful in larger libraries for health, life-skills, psychology, and sociology classes." SLJ

Includes bibliographical references

Gore, Al, Jr., 1948-
Earth in the balance; ecology and the human spirit; [by] Al Gore. Houghton Mifflin 2000 xxiv, 407p il maps $26   **304.2**
1. Human ecology 2. Environmental protection
ISBN 0-618-05664-5   LC 00-38311
A reissue of the title first published 1992
In this discussion of the global environment and civilization the author "argues that only a radical rethinking of our relationship with nature can save the earth's ecology for future generations." Publisher's note
"The author exhibits little of the clichéd myopia of his profession and is aware of the political obstacles posed by such an integrated approach. He identifies the root of our current problems as spiritual. If civilization is to persist, he maintains, it must make the rescue of the environment its organizing principle." N Y Times Book Rev
Includes bibliographical references

Leakey, Richard E., 1944-
The sixth extinction; patterns of life and the future of humankind; [by] Richard Leakey and Roger Lewin. Doubleday 1995 271p il pa $11.20 hardcover o.p.   **304.2**
1. Evolution 2. Human influence on nature 3. Mass extinction of species
ISBN 0-385-46809-1 (pa)   LC 95-18286
The authors contend that "human beings, by destroying tropical rain forests and driving tens of thousands of species into extinction, are dangerously reducing biodiversity, damaging ecosystems and possibly precipitating the next major mass extinction." Publ Wkly
Leakey and Lewin "present a powerful message based on years of observation and fieldwork." Libr J
Includes bibliographical references

Mitchell, Alanna
Dancing at the Dead Sea; tracking the world's environmental hotspots. University of Chicago Press 2005 239p $25   **304.2**
1. Human influence on nature 2. Mass extinction of species
ISBN 0-226-53200-3   LC 2004-62123
First published 2004 in Canada
The author "treks to exotic locales as varied as the rain forests of Suriname and the Arctic desert of Banks Island to determine the inevitability of a sixth mass species extinction for humans. . . . This is an entertaining read for both armchair travelers and students of environmental studies." Libr J
Includes bibliographical references

Weisman, Alan
The world without us. Thomas Dunne Books/St. Martin's Press 2007 324p il $24.95   **304.2**
1. Human influence on nature
ISBN 978-0-312-34729-1; 0-312-34729-4
LC 2007-11565
"Teasing out the consequences of a simple thought experiment—what would happen if the human species were suddenly extinguished—Weisman has written a sort of pop-science ghost story, in which the whole earth is the haunted house. Among the highlights: with pumps not working, the New York City subways would fill with water within days. . . . Texas's unattended petrochemical complexes might ignite, scattering hydrogen cyanide to the winds—a 'mini chemical nuclear winter.' After thousands of years, the Chunnel, rubber tires, and more than a billion tons of plastic might remain, but eventually a polymer-eating microbe could evolve, and, with the spectacular return of fish and bird populations, the earth might revert to Eden." New Yorker
Includes bibliographical references

304.5   Genetic factors

Taylor, Shelley E.
The tending instinct; how nurturing is essential for who we are and how we live. Times Bks. 2002 290p $25; pa $16   304.5
1. Sociobiology 2. Sex differences (Psychology) 3. Stress (Psychology)
ISBN 0-8050-6837-6; 0-8050-7289-6 (pa)
LC 2002-19879
The author "launched a series of innovative experiments that led her to believe that humans are biologically wired to nurture. She thus devised no less than a whole new psychology of women, presented in this accessible and well-grounded work." Libr J
Includes bibliographical references

304.6   Population

The **American** people; Census 2000; [edited by] Reynolds Farley and John Haaga. Russell Sage 2005 456p il map $35 *   304.6
1. United States—Population 2. United States—Census
ISBN 0-8715-4273-0   LC 2005-50433
This book "is more than just a compilation of tables and charts of raw census data. It is an interpretative guide to understanding the demographic breakdown of American society. Chapters include: 'Gender Inequalities', 'Cohorts and Socioeconomic Progress' and 'The Lives and Times of the Baby Boomers'. Editors Farley and Haaga show trends in American culture that will not be found anywhere else." Univ Press Books for Public and Second Sch Libr, 2006
Includes bibliographical references

Encyclopedia of genocide and crimes against humanity; Dinah L. Shelton, editor in chief. Macmillan Reference 2004 3v il map set $415 *   304.6
1. Genocide—Encyclopedias 2. Atrocities
ISBN 0-02-865847-7   LC 2004-6587
The scope of this encyclopedia starts "with the Roman persecution of Christians and . . . [continues] to recent Sudanese Arab massacres of Sudanese Africans. Arranged alphabetically by topic, each entry contains a narrative, a bibliography including books, reports, and Web sites, and . . . cross-references." Choice
"The editorial team has cast its net wide to create an outstanding comprehensive sourcebook that will be the standard resource for many years." Booklist
Includes bibliographical references

Encyclopedia of the U.S. Census; Margo J. Anderson, editor. CQ Press 2000 xxiv, 424p il $140   304.6
1. United States—Census
ISBN 1-56802-428-2   LC 00-30522
The alphabetically arranged articles "explain the history, methodology, and results of U.S. censuses since 1790. . . . Maps, tables, and charts show how the composition of the population has changed, where the center of population has moved over time, and how the address lists and census tracts are developed." Booklist
Includes bibliographical references

United Nations. Statistical Office
Demographic yearbook 2003 = Annuaire démographique 2003; [by the] United Nations Department of Economic and Social Affairs. 55th ed. U.N. Publs. 2006 815p $120 *
304.6
1. Population—Statistics
ISBN 978-9210510974; 9210510976
Also available online in .PDF format
Annual. First issue for 1948 published 1949. Text in English and French
"Official compilation of international demographic data in such fields as area and population, natality, mortality, marriage, divorce, and international migration. Each year some aspect of demographic statistics is treated intensively." Ref Sources for Small & Medium-sized Libr. 6th edition

304.8   Movement of people

Keneally, Thomas, 1935-
The great shame; and the triumph of the Irish in the English-speaking world. Talese 1999 712p il maps $35; pa $18   304.8
1. Ireland—Civilization 2. Ireland—Immigration and emigration
ISBN 0-385-47697-3; 0-385-72026-2 (pa)
LC 99-24888
First published 1998 in the United Kingdom
The author "tells the story of the Irish diaspora in the 19th century, especially the thousands of men and women sent in chains to penal colonies in Australia, among them a core of political prisoners who continued to fight for an independent Ireland." N Y Times Book Rev
Includes bibliographical references

Powell, John, 1954-
Encyclopedia of North American immigration. Facts on File 2005 464p il map (Facts on File library of American history) $75 *
304.8
1. United States—Immigration and emigration—Encyclopedias 2. Canada—Immigration and emigration—Encyclopedias
ISBN 0-8160-4658-1   LC 2004-7361
The author "presents an introduction to immigration to English and French-speaking regions over the past 500 years. . . . His intent is to offer 'a convenient one-volume reference full of straightforward and concise information on people, groups, policies, and events that defined the world's greatest migration of peoples to a continent and shaped their reception in North America.'" Booklist
"This valuable reference work on a hot topic belongs in all types of libraries—not only in the US and Canada, which offered shelter to immigrants, but also in libraries worldwide." Choice
Includes bibliographical references

Sowell, Thomas, 1930-
Migrations and cultures; a world view. Basic Bks. 1996 516p pa $23 hardcover o.p.

304.8
1. Immigration and emigration 2. Ethnic groups 3. Ethnic relations
ISBN 0-465-04589-8 (pa)　　　LC 95-44316
In this book the author seeks "to determine how migrations have transformed nations and continents over the course of human history. . . . He believes the habits and beliefs that migrants bring to a new homeland, what he calls their cultural capital, are far more important in determining their fate than the homeland's economy, culture or politics. . . . This is a lively and provocative book that is important reading for anyone who thinks we have too many immigrants or too few, who favors affirmative action and multicultural programs or opposes them." N Y Times Book Rev
Includes bibliographical references

305　Social groups

Bawer, Bruce, 1956-
While Europe slept; how radical Islam is destroying the West from within. Doubleday 2006 247p $23.95　　　**305**
1. Islamic fundamentalism 2. Europe—Immigration and emigration
ISBN 0-385-51472-7; 978-0-385-51472-9
　　　　　　　　　　　　　　LC 2005-51904
This "is the story of one American's experience in Europe before and after 9/11, and of his many arguments with Europeans about the dangers of militant Islam and America's role in combating it." Publisher's note
"A book of the utmost importance, full of deep concern for Europe and almost unbelievable revelations for most Americans." Booklist

Berreby, David
Us and them; understanding your tribal mind. Little, Brown and Company 2005 370p $26.95
　　　　　　　　　　　　　　　　　305
1. Prejudices 2. Social psychology
ISBN 0-316-09030-1　　　LC 2005-3825
The author "attempts to apply the tools of science to an impossibly large question: what is it about the human mind that makes us believe in categories like race, gender and ethnicity?" Publ Wkly
"At a time when everything from high-school initiations to ethnic genocide can trace its root to such segregationist tendencies, Berreby's thought-provoking analysis is essential." Booklist
Includes bibliographical references

Robb, Christina, 1946-
This changes everything; the relational revolution in psychology. Farrar, Straus and Giroux 2006 xxiv, 454p il $30; pa $17
　　　　　　　　　　　　　　　　　305
1. Interpersonal relations 2. Social psychology
ISBN　　0-374-27581-5;　　978-0-374-27581-5;
0-312-42615-1 (pa); 978-0-312-42615-6 (pa)
　　　　　　　　　　　　　　LC 2005-16270

Subtitle on cover: How the work of Carol Gilligan, Jean Baker Miller, Judith Lewis Herman, and their colleagues brought democracy to our personal lives
The author "tells the story of the birth and development of what has come to be called relational psychology. Constructed as a narrative, the book examines the work of Carol Gilligan, Jean Baker Miller, Judith Lewis Herman, Judith Jordan, and others—psychologists, psychiatrists, and psychotherapists whose theories and research ushered in new ways of thinking about the psychology of women. . . . This is an invaluable account of a crucial and continuingly vital movement in psychology." Choice
Includes bibliographical references

305.23　Young people

Canada, Geoffrey
Fist, stick, knife, gun; a personal history of violence in America. Beacon Press 1995 179p pa $13　　　**305.23**
1. Violence 2. Children 3. New York (N.Y.)—Social conditions
ISBN　0-8070-0422-7;　978-0-8070-0423-4　(pa);
0-8070-0423-5 (pa)　　　LC 94-41357
The author explains "what is happening to poor, mostly black and brown youth in this country, as guns have replaced fist, stick, and knife as aggressive and protective weapons of choice. Canada's own battles for survival as a youth in the South Bronx punctuate and shape his argument." Libr J
"A more powerful depiction of the tragic life of urban children and a more compelling plea to end 'America's war against itself' cannot be imagined." Publ Wkly

Reaching up for manhood; transforming the lives of boys in America. Beacon Press 1998 160p pa $12.50 hardcover o.p.　　　**305.23**
1. Boys—Psychology 2. African American children 3. Youth—United States
ISBN 0-8070-2316-7 (pa)　　　LC 97-19919
The author "grew up on tough South Bronx streets, where he witnessed friends dying by the handful. Recounting his childhood at midlife, he powerfully depicts what children face in today's world, especially the crippling problems of African American boys." Libr J

Chudacoff, Howard P.
Children at play; an American history. New York University Press 2007 269p il $27.95
　　　　　　　　　　　　　　　　　305.23
1. Children—United States 2. Play
ISBN 978-0-8147-1664-9; 0-8147-1664-4
　　　　　　　　　　　　　　LC 2007-07865
This book "provides a chronological history of play in the U.S. from the point of view of children themselves." Publisher's note
This "work gives historical depth to debates that continue to rage over what constitutes appropriate child's play." Publ Wkly
Includes bibliographical references

Coles, Robert

Children of crisis; selections from the Pulitzer Prize-winning five-volume Children of crisis series; with a new introduction by the author. Little, Brown 2003 714p il $35; pa $22.45 *

305.23

1. Children—United States 2. Socially handicapped children

ISBN 0-316-15547-0; 0-316-15102-5 (pa)

LC 2003-47522

These are selections of Coles' social study of "African American children caught in the throes of the South's racial integration; the young children of impoverished sharecroppers, migrant workers, and mountaineers in Appalachia; children whose families were transformed by the migration from South to North, from rural to urban communities; Latino, Native American, and Eskimo children in the poorest communities of the American West; the children of America's wealthiest families, wrestling with the burden of their own privilege." Publisher's note

Hine, Thomas, 1947-

The rise and fall of the American teenager. Bard 1999 322p $24; pa $14 **305.23**

1. Teenagers 2. Adolescence

ISBN 0-380-97358-8; 0-380-72853-2 (pa)

LC 99-24381

In this social history Hine "writes about ways the culture has affected what teenage has meant for youth and how youth have been perceived, as in World War II when teenagers readily took on roles supporting the war effort. Interesting, enjoyable, and multifaceted, Hine's work defies pigeonholing by covering anthropology, psychology, communications, and sociology." Libr J

Includes bibliographical references

Kozol, Jonathan

Ordinary resurrections; children in the years of hope. Harper Perennial 2001 388p pa $14

305.23

1. Children 2. Bronx (New York, N.Y.)—Social conditions

ISBN 978-0-06-095645-5; 0-06-095645-3

First published 2000 by Crown

"Kozol tells of his continued visits with the children who attend the afterschool program at St. Ann's Episcopal Church in the racially segregated, impoverished South Bronx." SLJ

Includes bibliographical references

Medved, Michael

Saving childhood; protecting our children from the national assault on innocence; [by] Michael Medved and Diane Medved. HarperCollins Pubs. 1998 324p pa $13 hardcover o.p. **305.23**

1. Children—United States 2. Child rearing

ISBN 0-06-093224-4 (pa) LC 98-11850

The authors "express their concerns about the climate of violence, sexuality, immorality, and activism that children encounter in America today." Libr J

This is a "lively, heartfelt book. . . . An honorable addition to the strain of child-advocacy literature." Booklist

Includes bibliographical references

Mintz, Steven, 1953-

Huck's raft; a history of American childhood. Belknap Press of Harvard University Press 2004 445p il $29.95 * **305.23**

1. Children—United States

ISBN 0-674-01508-8 LC 2004-42220

The author "revisits the treatment of children from the Puritan era up to the edge of the millennium, . . . showing that we have alternately vilified our offspring . . . and glorified them. . . . In addition, the roles children have assumed in the workforce have fluctuated with the needs of the era—economic expansion led to harsh child labor, while its aftermath, prosperity, led to an interest in child welfare. . . . Mintz's thorough yet accessibly written study delves into the external forces that have shaped the lives of our young while also probing the internal developments in their collective consciousness." Libr J

Includes bibliographical references

Nazario, Sonia

Enrique's journey. Random House 2006 291p il $26.95; pa $14.95 * **305.23**

1. Illegal aliens 2. United States—Immigration and emigration

ISBN 1-4000-6205-5; 978-1-4000-6205-8; 0-8129-7178-7 (pa); 978-0-8129-7178-1 (pa)

LC 2005-44347

The author "retraces the travel of immigrants from Central America to El Norte and writes . . . about the trials and tribulations that besiege the journey. Specifically, she focuses on a Honduran boy, Enrique, left behind by his mother, Lourdes, who fled to the United States, like many Central American women before her, to make enough money to give her children a better life back home and ultimately return to them." Libr J

"Descriptions of rapes, beatings, and jailing of immigrant children and accounts of those who suffered loss of limbs falling from freight trains are graphic and disturbing. But no one can doubt the authenticity of this reporting." SLJ

Orme, Nicholas

Medieval children. Yale Univ. Press 2001 387p il $39.95; pa $19.95 **305.23**

1. Middle Ages

ISBN 0-300-08541-9; 0-300-09754-9 (pa)

LC 2001-26172

This is an "examination of the daily lives of medieval children from diverse classes and backgrounds. . . . Orme's exacting research gives the book weight, and his affectionate, eloquent prose carries its immediate manner from history to sociology to philosophy and back again." Booklist

Includes bibliographical references

Pollack, William S.

Real boys; rescuing our sons from the myths of boyhood; [by] William Pollack. Henry Holt & Company 1999 xxvi, 447p pa $16 **305.23**

1. Boys 2. Child rearing

ISBN 0-8050-6183-5 LC 99-10388

"An Owl book"

First published 1998 by Random House

Pollack, William S.—*Continued*

Pollack "dismantles what he terms 'the Boy Code'—society's image of boys as tough, cool, rambunctious and obsessed with sports, cars and sex. These stereotypes, he argues, thwart creativity and originality in boys. Linking clinical insights to practical suggestions, Pollack advises caregivers how to help boys repair their fragile self-esteem, develop empathy and explore their sensitive sides." Publ Wkly

Includes bibliographical references

Real boys' voices; [by] William S. Pollack with Todd Shuster. Penguin Books 2001 xxxv, 392p pa $15   **305.23**
1. Boys
ISBN 978-0-14-100294-1; 0-14-100294-8
First published 2000 by Random House

The author "talked with 11-to-20-year-old boys of all races and economic backgrounds about sex, drugs, parents, religion, violence, emotions, and changes in the social expectations of boys and men. Here he presents the boys not only through his interviews but also through their poems, essays, and journals." Booklist

Robbins, Alexandra, 1976-

The overachievers; the secret lives of driven kids. Hyperion 2006 439p $24.95; pa $13.95
                                                    305.23
1. Workaholism 2. High school students
ISBN   1-4013-0201-7;   978-1-4013-0201-6; 1-4013-0902-2 (pa); 978-1-4013-0902-2 (pa)
                                                    LC 2006-41244

The author "follows the lives of students from a Bethesda, Md., high school as they navigate the SAT and college application process. These students are obsessed with success, contending with illness, physical deterioration (senior Julie is losing hair over the pressure to get into Stanford), cheating (students sell a physics project to one another), obsessed parents (Frank's mother manages his time to the point of abuse) and emotional breakdowns. The portraits of the teens are compelling and make for an easy read." Publ Wkly

Includes bibliographical references

Savage, Jon

Teenage; the creation of youth culture. Viking 2007 xx, 551p il $29.95   **305.23**
1. Teenagers 2. Popular culture
ISBN 978-0-670-03837-4; 0-670-03837-7
                                                    LC 2006-36229

Savage has written a "history of the role of youth in American and European life from 1875 to the end of World War II, when teenage culture may be said to have taken off. He addresses American and European youth cultures separately while covering the American influence on European youth after World War I. For each time period, he uses diaries written by teenagers, media reports of the time, and books and movies to evoke the era." Libr J

This "evocative, exuberant chronicle overflows with ideas it will probably take a dozen writers a decade to work out in more rigorous books. It's safe to say that none of them are likely to be as marvelous or maddening as this one." Washington Post Book World

Shachtman, Tom, 1942-

Rumspringa; to be or not to be Amish. North Point Press 2006 286p $25 *   **305.23**
1. Amish 2. Teenagers—Religious life
ISBN 0-86547-687-X; 978-0-86547-687-5
                                                    LC 2006-4329

"When Amish youth reach the age of about 16, they enter a months to years-long period of 'running around,' or rumspringa, during which there is the tacit acceptance and expectation that they will participate in such activities as drinking, sexual exploration, automobile driving, and living away from the community. The author examines the role rumspringa plays in the life of the community, the teens, and the teens' families." SLJ

"Shachtman is like a maestro, masterfully conducting an orchestra of history, anthropology, psychology, sociology, and journalism together in a harmonious and evocative symphony of all things Amish." Christ Sci Monit

Includes bibliographical references

Simmons, Rachel, 1966-

Odd girl out; the hidden culture of aggression in girls. Harcourt 2002 296p $25; pa $14 *
                                                    305.23
1. Girls 2. Aggressiveness (Psychology)
ISBN 0-15-100604-0; 0-15-602734-8 (pa)
                                                    LC 2001-6864

"Why are girls inclined to relational rather than physical aggression? Simmons contends that girls are socialized into a psychological double bind. They are told that they must be good, nice and quiet and that they should value close and intimate relationships. . . . Trapped in a constraining, stereotypical gender role, some girls craft ways of expressing their anger covertly. . . . Odd Girl Out explores this grim side of girlhood with [stories] . . . about girls hurting other girls." Women Rev Books

The author "does an excellent job of articulating to adults exactly the pain and subtle warfare that many teen girls experience." Booklist

Includes bibliographical references

305.24 Adults

Kiss tomorrow hello; notes from the midlife underground by twenty-five women over forty; edited by Kim Barnes and Claire Davis. Doubleday 2006 334p $24.95   **305.24**
1. Middle age 2. Women
ISBN 0-385-51541-3   LC 2005-48496

A diverse "mixture of midlife stories from urban, suburban, and rural writers who, through the more lucid self-awareness and self-acceptance that comes with growing older, have come to terms with considerable challenges, including poverty, illness, addiction, and sexual abuse. Diana Abu-Jaber, Mary Clearman Blew, Joyce Maynard, Lisa Norris, and the other authors reminisce about their childhoods, happy and otherwise, and consider love, desire, sex, careers, beauty, aging, and death. What unites these new essays is their vivid honesty, capturing universal truths and personal experiences in sparkling prose." Libr J

Sheehy, Gail

New passages; mapping your life across time. Random House 1995 xxv, 498p pa $15.95 hardcover o.p. *   **305.24**

1. Adulthood 2. Aging 3. Socialization 4. Middle age 5. United States—Social conditions

ISBN 0-345-40445-9 (pa)   LC 94-43996

Companion volume to Passages (1976)

The author examines "what she calls 'second adulthood'—the period from what used to be thought of as middle age into an ever-expanding 'age of integrity'—an increasingly enjoyable, even serene old age. . . . Making use of specially configured census data, extensive questionnaires and interviews with dozens of people, from celebrities to participants in middle-and lower-income discussion groups, she offers a broad picture of how they can expect to experience the 'bonus years.'" Publ Wkly

This work is "grounded in the economic and psychological realities that make adult life so complex today. The major themes of this book are accurate and important." N Y Times Book Rev

Includes bibliographical references

Twenge, Jean M., 1971-

Generation me; why today's young Americans are more confident, assertive, entitled—and more miserable than ever before. Free Press 2006 292p il $25; pa $14 *   **305.24**

1. Youth—United States

ISBN   0-7432-7697-3;   978-0-7432-7697-9; 0-7432-7698-1 (pa); 978-0-7432-7698-6 (pa)

LC 2005-58514

"Lumping together Gen-X and Y under the moniker 'GenMe,' Twenge argues that those born after 1970 are more self-centered, more disrespectful of authority and more depressed than ever before." Publ Wkly

"Accessible and a must-read for the generation they address." Booklist

Includes bibliographical references

305.26   Persons in late adulthood

Carter, Jimmy, 1924-

The virtues of aging. Ballantine Pub. Group 1998 140p (Library of contemporary thought) hardcover o.p. pa $11.95   **305.26**

1. Aging

ISBN 0-345-42826-9; 0-345-42592-8 (pa)

LC 98-25298

"Published in conjunction with Times Books"

"At age 56, Jimmy Carter 'involuntarily retired' when he was defeated for a second term as president by Ronald Reagan in 1980. . . . Carter sketches how he and Rosalynn created new careers and new lives for themselves—as authors, educators, and senior family members and as a couple growing old together. He adds statistics about the aging population, makes suggestions for healthy living, and defines successful aging." Libr J

Coles, Robert

Old and on their own; with photographs by Alex Harris, Thomas Roma. Norton 1998 184p pa $19.95 hardcover o.p.   **305.26**

1. Elderly

ISBN 0-393-31912-1 (pa)   LC 97-36922

"A DoubleTake book"

Published by the Center for Documentary Studies in association with W.W. Norton

A series of interviews about aging with 11 men and women from 75 to nearly 100 years of age

Includes bibliographical references

Encyclopedia of aging; David J. Ekerdt, editor in chief. Macmillan Ref. USA 2002 4v set $450 *
                    305.26

1. Gerontology—Encyclopedias 2. Aging—Encyclopedias 3. Elderly—Encyclopedias

ISBN 0-02-865472-2   LC 2002-2596

"Topics represent the range of information in gerontology, covering biological, medical, psychological, and sociological topics as well as social and public policy issues. Articles range from very specific, for example, *Congregate housing* or *Fluid balance,* to more general essays, such as *Bereavement* or *Visual arts and aging.* About one-third to one-half of the articles focus on biological, medical, or psychological aspects of aging." Booklist

This includes "400-plus concise and readable entries that offer excellent introductions to important concepts." Libr J

Includes bibliographical references

Friedan, Betty, 1921-2006

The fountain of age. Simon & Schuster 1993 671p pa $26.95 hardcover o.p.   **305.26**

1. Old age 2. Women—United States

ISBN 0-671-89853-1 (pa)   LC 93-4090

The author "challenges our culture's pessimistic attitude toward aging. Friedan argues that we should view the years after 60 as a new stage of development, rather than as a time of decline and disease." Libr J

"Betty Friedan's metaphorical fountain of age spouts research, observation, conjecture, evangelical fervor, revolutionary rhetoric, and denial. The result is a pool of optimism in which the mother of the woman's movement examines the unlifted face of age and finds it lovable." New Repub

Includes bibliographical references

Kaplan, Lawrence J. (Lawrence Jay), 1915-

Retiring right; planning for a successful retirement. 3rd ed. Square One Publishers 2003 387p il pa $17.95   **305.26**

1. Retirement income

ISBN 0-7570-0132-7; 978-0-7570-0132-1

LC 00-10597

First published 1986. Periodically revised

The author "addresses lifestyle issues like continuing to work and housing; long-term funding vehicles like savings, investments, and pensions; day-to-day financial concerns such as credit, budgeting, and inflation; life, health, and medical insurance; and 'final facts' like es-

Kaplan, Lawrence J. (Lawrence Jay), 1915-—
Continued
tates, probate, and trusts. . . . [Includes] a section on retirement communities. . . . Given the difficulty in choosing among the many guide on retirement, the durability
of Kaplan's manual makes an attractive option." Booklist
Includes bibliographical references

Vaillant, George E.
Aging well; surprising guideposts to a happier
life from the landmark Harvard study of adult
development. Little, Brown 2002 373p $24.95; pa
$14.95   **305.26**
    1. Aging
    ISBN 0-316-98936-3; 0-316-09007-7 (pa)
                                         LC 2001-30651
    "Vaillant posits that successful physical and emotional
aging is most dependent on a lack of tobacco and alcohol abuse by subjects, an adaptive coping style, maintaining healthy weight with some exercise, a sustained loving (in most cases, marital) relationship and years of education." Publ Wkly
    The author "offers much valuable information about
aging, and his judgment calls (his term) are perceptive,
understanding, and often tinged with delightful humor."
Booklist
Includes bibliographical references

305.3   Men and women

Dowd, Maureen
Are men necessary? when sexes collide.
Putnam's 2005 338p $25.95   **305.3**
    1. Sex role 2. Feminism 3. Women—United States
    ISBN 0-399-15332-2   LC 2005-53484
    This book "addresses the confusion of postfeminist
dating, gender conflicts in the workplace, the media's
disparate treatment of men and women, American culture's saturation with sexual imagery, our collective obsession with youth and appearances, the objectification of
women by men and, finally, sex as 'a tripwire in American history.'" N Y Times Book Rev
    This is a "funny, biting, and incisive take on women's
place in American society today." Libr J

305.31   Men

Bly, Robert
Iron John; a book about men. DaCapo Press
2004 268p pa $15 *   **305.31**
    1. Men—Psychology
    ISBN 0-306-81376-9   LC 2004-56137
    First published 1990 by Addison-Wesley
    "Drawing vitally upon such diverse sources as ancient
mythology, classic literature (including his own poetry),
anthropology, psychology, and even the responses of the
real-life men who have participated in his seminars
('gatherings'), Bly staunchly redefines male identity, emphasizing the importance of what he calls 'warrior energy' and all its positive implications." Booklist
Includes bibliographical references.

Bordo, Susan, 1947-
The male body; a new look at men in public
and in private. Farrar, Straus & Giroux 1999 358p
il pa $16 hardcover o.p.   **305.31**
    1. Men
    ISBN 0-374-52732-6 (pa)   LC 99-25386
    "Bordo sets out to map the ambivalent attitudes that
exist in the American cultural imagination toward male
bodies and, in particular, toward the penis and its 'symbolic double,' the phallus. . . . Part memoir, part elegy,
this feminist guided tour of the male body concludes
with real hope for improved relations between the sexes." Publ Wkly
Includes bibliographical references

Faludi, Susan
Stiffed; the betrayal of the American man.
Morrow 1999 662p il pa $16 hardcover o.p.
                                         305.31
    1. Men
    ISBN 0-380-72045-0 (pa)   LC 99-35504
    "Men, Faludi argues, are actually suffering under the
thumb of a cultural oppression similar to the one that in-
spired feminism's second wave." Libr J
Includes bibliographical references

Men and masculinities; a social, cultural, and
    historican encyclopedia; edited by Michael
    Kimmel and Amy Aronson. ABC-CLIO 2004
    2v set $255   **305.31**
    1. Men 2. Sex role
    ISBN 1-57607-774-8   LC 2003-20729
    "Also available on the World Wide Web as an e-
book" Verso of title page
    This reference covers "individuals, creative works and
characters, theories, and events that over centuries have
shaped the notion of American masculinity and its implications for men and women." Booklist

Sheehy, Gail
Understanding men's passages; discovering the
new map of men's lives. Random House 1998
xxvi, 292p pa $14 hardcover o.p.   **305.31**
    1. Men—Psychology 2. Middle age
    ISBN 0-345-40690-7 (pa)   LC 98-9942
    The author discusses the lives of "men over 35. . . .
Sheehy interviewed 100 men . . . and the book is mostly
made up of these 'case studies.' Another major part of
the text is given over to a discussion of male sexual po-
tency and how it affects men and the women in their
lives." Booklist
    "Sheehy's advice, bolstered with demographic re-
search, group interviews, medical commentary and personal testimony, is tough and wise." N Y Times Book
Rev
Includes bibliographical references

Vincent, Norah
Self-made man; one woman's journey into
manhood and back again. Viking 2006 290p
$24.95 *   **305.31**
    1. Men 2. Sex role
    ISBN 0-670-03466-5; 978-0-670-03466-6
                                         LC 2005-54798

Vincent, Norah—Continued

"For more than a year and a half [the author] ventured into the world as Ned, with an ever-present five o'clock shadow, a crew cut, wire-rim glasses, and her own size 11 1/2 shoes—a perfect disguise that enabled her to observe the world of men as an insider. . . . [This book examines the] mysteries of gender identity as well as who men are apart from and in relation to women." Publisher's note

This is "a thoughtful, diligent, entertaining piece of first-person investigative journalism." N Y Times Book Rev

305.4   Women

Adovasio, J. M. (James M.), 1944-

The invisible sex; uncovering the true roles of women in prehistory; by J .M. Adovasio, Olga Soffer & Jake Page. Collins 2007 320p il map $26.95   **305.4**

1. Sex role 2. Prehistoric peoples
ISBN 978-0-06-117091-1; 0-06-117091-7
                        LC 2006-50582

In this study of prehistoric culture, the authors argue "that women invented all kinds of critical materials, including the clothing necessary for life in colder climates, the ropes used to make rafts that enabled long-distance travel by water, and nets used for communal hunting. Even more important, women played a central role in the development of language and social life—in short, in our becoming human." Publisher's note

"What makes the book so readable is its gentle—even tongue-in-cheek—approach to its own iconoclasms. There's no in-your-face dogma here, but rather a chuckling that almost subliminally comes through to the reader. . . . It is a great read and seamlessly written." Sci Books Films

Includes bibliographical references

Baumgardner, Jennifer, 1970-

Grassroots: a field guide for feminist activism; [by] Jennifer Baumgardner and Amy Richards. 1st ed. Farrar, Straus and Giroux 2005 xxv, 306p pa $14 *   **305.4**

1. Feminism 2. Social action
ISBN 0-374-52865-9   LC 2004-10306

The authors "offer anyone interested in improving the world small but significant ways to effect social change. Regardless of one's area of interest—whether it's assuring access to abortion, stopping rape, helping welfare recipients, or legalizing gay marriage—the authors detail ways to formulate campaigns and set tangible goals. . . . Would-be agitators, look no further for the sass, savvy, and skills you'll need to begin." Libr J

Includes bibliographical references

Beauvoir, Simone de, 1908-1986

The second sex; translated and edited by H. M. Parshley; with an introduction by Margaret Crosland. Knopf 1993 lv, 786p $23; pa $17 *   **305.4**

1. Women
ISBN 0-679-42016-9; 0-679-72451-6 (pa)
                        LC 92-54303

"Everyman's library"
Original French edition, 1949; this translation first published 1953

This "thorough analysis of women's secondary status in society, became a classic of feminist literature." Reader's Ency. 3d edition

Bitchfest; ten years of cultural criticism from the pages of Bitch magazine; edited by Lisa Jervis and Andi Zeisler. Farrar, Straus & Giroux 2006 372p pa $16   **305.4**

1. Feminism 2. Popular culture—United States
ISBN 978-0-374-11343-8 (pa); 0-374-11343-2 (pa)
                        LC 2005-36156

"This work represents an alternating mix of the most hilarious, alarming, and unexpected essays from Bitch magazine's first ten years. . . . Readers new to this feminist quarterly will find the articles, almost without exception, original, intelligent, and well written. This compilation has staying power." Libr J

Includes bibliographical references

Brooks, Geraldine

Nine parts of desire; the hidden world of Islamic women. Anchor Bks. (NY) 1995 255p pa $14 hardcover o.p.   **305.4**

1. Muslim women 2. Islamic countries
ISBN 0-385-47577-2 (pa)   LC 94-17496

"Taking on the *hijab* (the Muslim woman's black veil) herself, Brooks talked with women throughout the Islamic world, reexamined the Koran, spent time with fundamentalist and feminist alike, and emerged with a deeper understanding of the religion as one that once empowered but now cripples women." Booklist

"The author's revelations about these women's lives behind the veil are frank, enraging, and captivating." New Yorker

Includes bibliographical references

Brownmiller, Susan

In our time; memoir of a revolution. Dial Press (NY) 1999 360p pa $15.95 hardcover o.p.   **305.4**

1. Women's movement 2. Feminism
ISBN 0-385-31831-6 (pa)   LC 99-39344

This book focuses on the women's movement between 1967 and 1977

"A riveting blend of eyewitness accounts and keen analysis, this is history at its most vital and a stirring testament to our ability to come together to combat social injustice, no matter how deeply entrenched it has become." Booklist

Collins, Gail

America's women; four hundred years of dolls, drudges, helpmates, and heroines. Morrow 2003 556p il $27.95; pa $15.95   **305.4**

1. Women—United States—History
ISBN 0-06-018510-4; 0-06-122722-6 (pa)
                LC 2003-51011

This is a history of American women from colonial times to the present

"Collins elegantly and eruditely celebrates the hard-won victories, overwhelming obstacles, and selfless contributions of a captivating array of influential women." Booklist

Includes bibliographical references

The **Columbia** documentary history of American women since 1941; edited by Harriet Sigerman. Columbia University Press 2003 690p $94; pa $34.50 *   **305.4**

1. Women—United States—History—Sources
ISBN 0-231-11698-5; 0-231-11699-3 (pa)
                LC 2002-41395

This collection of public and private primary sources includes such topics as employment opportunities, "the ideas and changes brought about by the women's movement, the challenges to and defense of reproductive rights, the backlash against feminism in the name of family values, and new visions for women's lives in the twenty-first century." Publisher's note

Includes bibliographical references

Cullen-DuPont, Kathryn

Encyclopedia of women's history in America. 2nd ed. Facts on File 2000 418p il $71.50
    305.4

1. Women—United States—History 2. Feminism
ISBN 0-8160-4100-8   LC 99-87498
First published 1996

This work highlights the lives and contributions of women in American history ranging from Pocahontas to Hillary Clinton and Madeleine Albright. Entries cover individuals, movements, court cases and women's issues from Colonial times to the present

"Well-written and informative . . . . An excellent quick reference source . . . recommended." Choice

Includes bibliographical references

Encyclopedia of women in the American West; Gordon Morris Bakken and Brenda Farrington, editors. Sage 2003 xxiii, 381p il $125
    305.4

1. Women—West (U.S.)
ISBN 0-7619-2356-X   LC 2003-6729

"The encyclopedia covers historical and contemporary women, adding topical articles on such subjects as the club women's movement, education, prostitution, emigrants, homesteaders, rodeo, and literary women. Appendixes provide a chronology of the US and its women, a list of women's organizations, and sections on strategies for research, additional readings, resources, and references." Choice

"There is a clear need for this encyclopedia. . . . Recommended for academic and public libraries and all libraries with a special interest in the western region and women's studies." Libr J

Includes bibliographical references and index

Ensler, Eve

Insecure at last; losing it in our security-obsessed world. Random House 2006 xx, 202p $21.95   **305.4**

1. Women—History 2. Feminism
ISBN 978-1-4000-6334-5; 1-4000-6334-5
                LC 2006-46219

"Focusing on the rage for security on a national level, . . . [the author] draws connections to her own quest for security, engendered amid a chaotic upbringing in a family headed by her abusive, alcoholic father. . . . She presents interviews with women in Afghanistan, Mexico, and Indonesia; antiwar activist Cindy Sheehan; and others." Libr J

"This is an important work by a major American writer." Publ Wkly

The **essential** feminist reader; edited and with an introduction by Estelle B. Freedman. Modern Library 2007 472p pa $17.95   **305.4**

1. Feminism
ISBN 0-8129-7460-3; 978-0-8129-7460-7

This collection of writings by feminist authors "features primary source material from around the globe, including short works of fiction and drama, political manifestos, and the work of less well-known writers." Publisher's note

Includes bibliographical references

Fox-Genovese, Elizabeth, 1941-2007

Within the plantation household; black and white women of the Old South. University of N.C. Press 1988 544p il (Gender & American culture) $49.95; pa $19.95   **305.4**

1. Women—Southern States 2. Plantation life 3. Slavery—United States
ISBN 0-8078-1808-9; 0-8078-4232-X (pa)
                LC 88-40139

"In this study, Fox-Genovese examines class, race, and gender in the antebellum South. . . . In her narrative, Fox-Genovese draws upon the letters, diaries, and journals of white women, and . . . the WPA slave narratives." Choice

"An illuminating and solid book of social history, with appeal to those who take a serious interest in historical research." Booklist

Includes bibliographical references

Freedman, Estelle B., 1947-

No turning back; the history of feminism and the future of women. Ballantine Bks. 2002 446p pa $15.95 hardcover o.p.   **305.4**

1. Feminism 2. Women—Social conditions
ISBN 0-345-45053-1 (pa)   LC 2002-280895
Includes bibliographical references

"Refuting a widespread misconception that feminism is either dead or irrelevant, Freedman presents a reflective history of the divergent roots of this essential yet controversial social movement." Booklist

This "work goes beyond previous studies in being interdisciplinary, international, and a pleasure to read." Libr J

Includes bibliographical references

Friedan, Betty, 1921-2006
The feminine mystique; with a new introduction. Norton 1997 xlviii, 452p pa $15.95 hardcover o.p.
*   **305.4**
1. Feminism 2. Women—United States
ISBN 0-393-32257-2 (pa)   LC 97-8877
A reissue of the title first published 1963
An "analysis of the dilemma facing the educated American woman; the post-war emphasis on the feminine image of the role as wife and mother has caused the American woman to lose her identity, says the author." Cincinnati Public Libr
Includes bibliographical references

Goodwin, Jan
Price of honor; Muslim women lift the veil of silence on the Islamic world. rev ed. Plume Bks. 2003 351p il pa $16   **305.4**
1. Muslim women 2. Islamic countries
ISBN 0-452-28377-9   LC 2002-28257
First published 1994 by Little, Brown
The author "examines the movement that is aggressively spreading a fundamentalist version of Islam throughout much of the world. Her interviews with Muslim women in ten countries both fascinate and disturb, for their candor reveals the movement's profound and often devastating effects on them. . . . A necessary purchase." Libr J [review of 1994 edition]

The **Greenwood** encyclopedia of women's issues worldwide; Lynn Walter, editor-in-chief. Greenwood Press 2003 6v il maps set $550 *
                                        305.4
1. Women—Social conditions—Encyclopedias
ISBN 0-313-32787-4   LC 2004-695024
Volume editors include Manisha Desai; Amy Lind; Aili Mari Tripp; Bahira Sherif-Trask and Cheryl Toronto Kalny
Contents: {v1} Asia and Oceania; {v2} Central and South America; {v3} Europe; {v4} The Middle East and North Africa; {v5} North America and the Caribbean; {v6} Sub-Saharan Africa
This "reference set documents the achievements and current challenges for women in more than 130 countries. . . . Topics covered include education, employment, economy, family and sexuality, health, politics and law, religion, and violence." Libr Media Connect
"Readers looking for information on women's everyday lives around the world will welcome this country-by-country survey." Booklist
Includes bibliographical references

Greer, Germaine, 1939-
The madwoman's underclothes; essays and occasional writings. Atlantic Monthly Press 1987 xxvii, 305p pa $12.95 hardcover o.p.
                                        305.4
1. Feminism 2. Women—Social conditions
ISBN 0-87113-308-3 (pa)   LC 87-11475
First published 1986 in the United Kingdom
A collection of the British feminist's nonfiction writings spanning her career from the 1960s to the 1980s.

The whole woman. Knopf 1999 373p pa $14 hardcover o.p.   **305.4**
1. Women—History 2. Women's rights 3. Women—Social conditions 4. Feminism 5. Sex role
ISBN 0-385-72003-3 (pa)   LC 99-18918
Greer argues that "women have come a long way in the past three decades but that innumerable forms of insidious discrimination and exploitation persist in every area of life." Publisher's note
"This is vintage Greer, profane and highly quotable." Time
Includes bibliographical references

Hirshman, Linda R.
Get to work; a manifesto for women of the world. Viking 2006 101p $19.95   **305.4**
1. Feminism 2. Women—Social conditions
ISBN 0-670-03812-1; 978-0-670-03812-1
                                  LC 2006-45704
"Expanding on a 2005 article in the American Prospect titled 'Homeward Bound,' which drew the interest of conservatives and liberals alike, . . . [the author] asserts that the real glass ceiling is found in women's homes. . . . Hirshman presents a strategic action plan, suggesting that women use education to prepare for a lifetime of work, take their work seriously, bargain relentlessly for a just and equal household, consider a reproductive strike, and elect officials that do not punish women's work. Her manifesto, which is sure to spark controversy and debate, may just lead the way to a new feminism." Libr J
Includes bibliographical references

Imagining ourselves; global voices from a new generation of women; editor, Paula Goldman; associate editor, Hafsat Abiola; foreword by Isabel Allende. New World Library 2006 239p il pa $26.95 *   **305.4**
1. Women—Social conditions
ISBN 1-57731-524-3   LC 2005-22617
"Published in association with the International Museum of Women"
This anthology "samples an outpouring of essays, photographs, paintings, and other visual and textual artwork submitted by women in their twenties and thirties from around the world in response to the question, 'What defines your generation of women?'" Libr J
"This lovely and visually kinetic book is the perfect antidote to the constant barrage of bleak reports about the future." Publ Wkly
Includes bibliographical references

In her place; a documentary history of prejudice against women; edited by S.T. Joshi. Prometheus Books 2006 458p $28
                                        305.4
1. Sexism 2. Sex role
ISBN 1-59102-380-7; 978-1-59102-380-7
                                  LC 2005-32639
This "compilation of articles, excerpts, and treatises traces more than a century of the most vitriolic antifeminist writings from preeminent scholars, clergy, physicians, and politicians. Anyone wishing to understand the overwhelming challenges faced by women's-rights activ-

In her place—*Continued*

ists from the movement's earliest days to the dawn of the Second Wave need look no further than Joshi's illuminating and downright infuriating examples of pervasively misogynistic thinking." Booklist

Includes bibliographical references

Jones, Jacqueline, 1948-

Labor of love, labor of sorrow; black women, work, and the family from slavery to the present. Vintage Bks. 1986 432p il pa $15   **305.4**

1. African American women
ISBN 0-394-74536-1; 978-0-394-74536-7
First published 1985 by Basic Books

"Jones examines the nature of employment and home life for the black woman through such socioeconomic eras as the period of bondage in the South, the so-called freedom that came with Reconstruction, the years between emancipation and the great migration to the North, the northern flight itself, the Depression, and the civil rights and feminist movements." Booklist

"Ambitious in scope, bold in interpretation, and comprehensive in its scholarship, Jones's book is a rare blend of seminal study and synthesis." Libr J

Includes bibliographical references

Levy, Ariel, 1974-

Female chauvinist pigs; women and the rise of raunch culture. Free Press 2005 224p $25; pa $14
*   **305.4**

1. Feminism 2. Sexism
ISBN 0-7432-4989-5; 0-7432-8428-3 (pa)
LC 2005-48811

The author argues that "our popular culture . . . has embraced a model of female sexuality that comes straight from pornography and strip clubs, in which the woman's job is to excite and titillate—to perform for men." N Y Times Book Rev

"A piercing look at how women are sabotaging their own attempts to be seen as equals by going about the quest the wrong way, Levy's engrossing book should be required reading for young women." Booklist

Includes bibliographical references

Makdisi, Jean Said

Teta, mother, and me; three generations of Arab women. W. W. Norton & Co. 2006 404p il $25.95
*   **305.4**

1. Women—Middle East
ISBN 0-393-06156-6   LC 2005-29991
First published 2005 in the United Kingdom

The author "explores the lives of three generations of Palestinian women, deftly illuminating a tumultuous century of modern Middle Eastern history, while raising important questions about the efficacy of ideology, the process of social development and the role of memory. . . . Valuable in its insights, sophisticated in its execution, this book deserves to be widely read." Publ Wkly

Includes bibliographical references

No small courage; a history of women in the United States; edited by Nancy Cott. Oxford Univ. Press 2000 646p il maps hardcover o.p. pa $21.95   **305.4**

1. Women—United States—History
ISBN 0-19-513946-1; 978-0-19-517323-9 (pa); 0-19-517323-6 (pa)   LC 00-21130

This "book examines women's experiences in the New World since Columbus landed. . . . Its 10 chapters . . . look at 'work and leisure, family patterns, political activities, forms of organization and outstanding accomplishments.'" N Y Times Book Rev

"By examining the flow of American history as it has affected women {the authors} illuminate aspects of the past that have often been neglected." Booklist

Includes bibliographical references

Peril, Lynn

College girls; bluestockings, sex kittens, and coeds, then and now. Norton 2006 408p il pa $16.95   **305.4**

1. Women—Education 2. College students
ISBN 978-0-393-32715-1; 0-393-32715-9
LC 2006-18896

This is a "history of the American college girl." N Y Times Book Rev

The author's "witty, irreverent style, her generous use of old advertisements and photos and her careful footnotes make this text unusually user-friendly." Publ Wkly

Includes bibliographical references

Roberts, Cokie

We are our mothers' daughters. Morrow 1998 197p $19.95; pa $11   **305.4**

1. Women—United States—History 2. Sex discrimination 3. Feminism
ISBN 0-688-15198-1; 0-688-16967-8 (pa)
LC 98-14816

"Roberts uses the vantage point of mother, daughter and exasperated observer as she discusses the evolution of women's roles over the past few generations. . . . Although there's no sophisticated analysis or new material here, Roberts is at her best when describing the ambivalences and ambitions of a woman's life." N Y Times Book Rev

Rodriguez, Deborah

Kabul Beauty School; an American woman goes behind the veil. Random House 2007 275p $24.95; pa $14.95   **305.4**

1. Kabul Beauty School (Afghanistan) 2. Women—Afghanistan 3. Beauty shops
ISBN 978-1-4000-6559-2; 1-4000-6559-3; 978-0-8129-7673-1 (pa); 0-8129-7673-8 (pa)
LC 2006-50384

This is an account of the author's "creation of an academy to train Afghan beauticians." N Y Times (Late N Y Ed)

"Rodriguez's experiences will delight readers as she recounts such tales as two friends acting as 'parents' and negotiating a dowry for her marriage to an Afghan man or her students puzzling over a donation of a carton of

Rodriguez, Deborah—*Continued*

thongs. Most of all, they will share her admiration for Afghan women's survival and triumph in chaotic times." SLJ

Rosen, Ruth

The world split open; how the modern women's movement changed America. Viking 2000 446p il hardcover o.p. pa $15 **305.4**
1. Women's movement 2. Feminism
ISBN 0-670-81462-8; 0-14-009719-8 (pa)
LC 99-54439

"Rosen details the rebirth of feminism, from the liberalism of NOW through women's liberation, which grew out of the civil rights movement. Her focus is on the 'hidden injuries of sex' and how what had been construed as 'personal' problems—abortion, compulsory heterosexuality, rape and sexual violence, prostitution and pornography—became political issues." Publ Wkly
Includes bibliographical references

Sommers, Christina Hoff

Who stole feminism? how women have betrayed women. Simon & Schuster 1994 320p il pa $14 hardcover o.p. **305.4**
1. Feminism
ISBN 0-684-80156-6 (pa)
LC 94-4734

The author's "critique of what she calls 'gender feminism' exposes numerous examples of distorted data and totalitarian methodology in the work of such feminist leaders as Susan Faludi, Catherine MacKinnon, and a cabal of like-minded academics. Controversial, to be sure, but objectively presented and impossible to dismiss." Booklist
Includes bibliographical references

Steinem, Gloria

Moving beyond words. Simon & Schuster 1994 319p pa $19.95 hardcover o.p. * **305.4**
1. Feminism
ISBN 0-671-51052-5 (pa)
LC 94-4839

"In these essays—some newly published, some reworked—Steinem surveys the women's movement." Libr J

"Ms. Steinem's enduring contribution to the women's movement has been her ability to popularize feminist issues to a wide and often wary audience." N Y Times Book Rev
Includes bibliographical references

Outrageous acts and everyday rebellions. 2nd ed, with a new preface and notes by the author. Holt & Co. 1995 xxii, 406p pa $17
305.4
1. Feminism
ISBN 0-8050-4202-4
LC 95-31711
First published 1983

In addition to material addressing specific feminist issues, this collection includes personal accounts of political leaders and noted women.
Includes bibliographical references

Ulrich, Laurel

Well-behaved women seldom make history; [by] Laurel Thatcher Ulrich. Alfred A. Knopf 2007 xxxiv, 284p il $24 **305.4**
1. Women—History 2. Women in literature 3. Feminism
ISBN 978-1-4000-4159-6; 1-4000-4159-6
LC 2006-100581

The author "uses 'three classic works in Western feminism' as a springboard for examining the theme of 'bad' behavior. . . . [They are] Christine de Pizan's 'Book of the City of Ladies,' written in 1405; Elizabeth Cady Stanton's 'Eighty Years and More,' published in 1898; and 'A Room of One's Own' [1929], based on two lectures Virginia Woolf gave in 1928." N Y Times Book Rev

This book "is by no means jargon-ridden or academic in tone. Ulrich's style is plain and direct, agreeable but without frills, and she moves efficiently right along. The book is a pleasure to read." Washington Post Book World
Includes bibliographical references

Wolf, Naomi

The beauty myth; how images of beauty are used against women. Perennial 2002 348p pa $14.95 * **305.4**
1. Women 2. Sex role 3. Personal appearance
ISBN 0-06-051218-0
LC 2002-72516
First published 1991 by Morrow

A "book about the ways women enslave themselves—and their bank accounts—to an industry that promises physical perfection." N Y Times Book Rev

The author "presents a provocative and persuasive account of the pervasiveness of the beauty ideal in all facets of Western culture." Libr J
Includes bibliographical references

Women in the Middle Ages; an encyclopedia; edited by Katharina M. Wilson and Nadia Margolis. Greenwood Press 2004 2v il set $199.95 **305.4**
1. Middle Ages—Encyclopedias 2. Women—History—Encyclopedias
ISBN 0-313-33016-6
LC 2004-53042

"In addition to entries on renowned women, there is a . . . number of articles covering topics such as footbinding, clothing, medicine, law, literary motifs, and geography-specific information. Terminology is defined in context, making the work readily accessible to high school students and lay readers." Libr J
Includes bibliographical references

Women's letters; America from the Revolutionary War to the present; edited by Lisa Grunwald & Stephen J. Adler. Dial Press 2005 824p il $35 * **305.4**
1. Women—United States—History—Sources
ISBN 0-385-33553-9
LC 2005-41446

This "book, with over 400 letters, is arranged chronologically, covering 230 years of American history. Each of its sections is preceded by a . . . timeline of events, and each letter is introduced with an explanatory note." N Y Times Book Rev

Women's letters—*Continued*
"This is a delightful collection of belles letters in the most literal sense of the term." Publ Wkly
Includes bibliographical references

Zeitz, Joshua
Flapper; a madcap story of sex, style, celebrity, and the women who made America modern. Crown Publishers 2006 338p il $24.95

305.4

1. Women—United States 2. Popular culture—United States 3. United States—History—1919-1933
ISBN 1-4000-8053-3; 978-1-4000-8053-3

LC 2005-24297
The author "examines the roles played by writer F. Scott Fitzgerald and his wife, Zelda, fashion designer Coco Chanel, various advertising specialists, and film actresses Clara Bow and Louise Brooks in developing and promoting the image of the modern American woman who was embodied by the flapper." Libr J
"An essential exploration of the women Zeitz deems 'the first thoroughly modern American[s].'" Booklist
Includes bibliographical references

305.5 Social classes

All the money in the world; how the Forbes 400 make—and spend—their fortunes; edited by Peter W. Bernstein and Annalyn Swan. Alfred A. Knopf 2007 416p il map $26.95

305.5

1. Millionaires 2. Wealth
ISBN 978-0-307-26612-5; 0-307-26612-5

LC 2007-15676
The editors present a "historical breakdown of the 400 richest Americans according to *Forbes* magazine, examining how the list's members actually make and spend their money." Libr J
This "is an intriguing picture of a varied group of America's richest citizens and the businesses and industries that produced this wealth." Choice
Includes bibliographical references

Chen Guidi, 1943-
Will the boat sink the water? the life of China's peasants; [by] Chen Guidi and Wu Chuntao; translated from Chinese by Zhu Hong. Public Affairs 2006 xxv, 229p $25   **305.5**

1. Peasantry 2. China
ISBN 978-1-58648-358-6; 1-58648-358-7

LC 2005-55344
This is an "expose of the poverty and injustice experienced by China's 900 million peasants, told through a series of . . . personal narratives." Publisher's note
"Readers interested in the unseen and unreported lives of Chinese peasants will appreciate this revealing book." Booklist
Includes bibliographical references

Ehrenreich, Barbara
Nickel and dimed; on (not) getting by in boom-time America. Metropolitan Bks. 2001 221p $23; pa $13 *   **305.5**

1. Minimum wage 2. Labor—United States 3. Poverty
ISBN 0-8050-6388-9; 0-8050-6389-7 (pa)

LC 00-52514
This is an exposé "of such abstractions as 'living wage' and 'affordable housing.' Ehrenreich worked, for a month at a time, at 'unskilled' jobs—as a waitress and chambermaid in Florida, a housecleaner and nursing-home aide in Maine, a Wal-Mart clerk in Minnesota—to report on how people survive on wages of six or seven dollars an hour." New Yorker
"No real answers to the problem but a compelling sketch of its reality and pervasiveness." Libr J

Epstein, Joseph, 1937-
Snobbery: the American version. Houghton Mifflin 2002 274p $25; pa $14   **305.5**

1. Snobs and snobbishness
ISBN 0-395-94417-1; 0-618-34073-4 (pa)

LC 2001-51623
This "work examines the nature and place of snobbery and its various manifestations in America, from the country's founding to the present." Libr J
"Every bracing page is a mirror in which readers can't help but recognize themselves, and each offers a quotable quip . . . and much to think about." Booklist
Includes bibliographical references

Frank, Robert H.
Falling behind; how rising inequality harms the middle class. University of California Press 2007 148p il $50; pa $19.95   **305.5**

1. Middle class 2. Consumption (Economics)
ISBN   978-0-520-25188-5;   0-520-25188-1; 978-0-520-25252-3 (pa); 0-520-25252-7 (pa)

LC 2006-26248
"Although middle-income families don't earn much more than they did several decades ago, they are buying bigger cars, houses, and appliances. To pay for them, they spend more than they earn and carry record levels of debt. . . . Robert Frank explains how increased concentrations of income and wealth at the top of the economic pyramid have set off 'expenditure cascades' that raise the cost of achieving many basic goals for the middle class." Publisher's note
"A compact example of a professional economist brilliantly deploying the tools of social science to illuminate the human condition." N Y Times Book Rev
Includes bibliographical references

Freeman, Joshua Benjamin
Working-class New York; life and labor since World War II; [by] Joshua B. Freeman. New Press (NY) 2000 409p il $35; pa $19.95   **305.5**

1. Working class 2. Labor unions 3. New York (N.Y.)—Social conditions
ISBN 1-56584-575-7; 1-56584-712-1 (pa)

LC 99-87940

Freeman, Joshua Benjamin—*Continued*
In this study the author "describes the social, political, ethnic, racial, and numerical changes in New York's working class over the years; the alterations in the city's landscape that the working class effected; and the change in how the working class itself has been viewed." Booklist
"Freeman charts the postwar rise and eventual fall of Manhattan working-class life and culture. . . . Strong narrative drive, attention to detail and historical insight make this a superb addition to studies of postwar culture, urbanology and labor history." Publ Wkly
Includes bibliographical references

Jadhav, Narendra, 1953-
Untouchables; my family's triumphant journey out of the caste system in modern India. Scribner 2005 307p $26 *   **305.5**
1. Caste 2. India—Social conditions
ISBN 0-7432-7079-7   LC 2005-44166
Original Indian edition, 1993; first published in English 2003 by Viking with title: Outcaste, a memoir
The author "is a member of India's Dalits—or untouchables—a group that numbers 165 million. His . . . memoir is a tribute to his parents, who made it their goal to educate their children, especially his father, Damu, who stood up to the caste system." Booklist
"This moving story of perseverance from a sector of India rarely represented to American readers will be a standard text on Indian and Dalit themes for years to come." Libr J

LeBlanc, Adrian Nicole
Random family; love, drugs, trouble, and coming of age in the Bronx. Scribner 2003 408p $25   **305.5**
1. Poor—New York (N.Y.) 2. Youth—New York (N.Y.) 3. Bronx (New York, N.Y.)—Social conditions
ISBN 0-684-86387-1   LC 2002-26673
"This is a slice-of-life chronicle of black and Puerto Rican teens in the South Bronx during the 1980s. Looking for excitement, prosperity, love, sex, connection, and family, they instead find drugs, abuse, babies, and prison—a continuation of the home life they had hoped to escape." Libr J
"A painstaking feat of reporting and empathy that resulted from 10 years of hanging out with a hard-pressed, loosely defined family in the Bronx." N Y Times Book Rev

Lubrano, Alfred
Limbo: blue-collar roots, white-collar dreams. Wiley 2003 248p $37.95; pa $19.95
                305.5
1. Social classes 2. Working class
ISBN 0-471-26376-1; 0-471-71439-9 (pa)
                LC 2003-273869
The author examines "the challenges that upwardly mobile children of blue-collar families (he calls them Straddlers) face in establishing themselves in white-collar enclaves. . . . Lubrano's interviews with other Straddlers have convinced him that ambition puts many of them in

positions fraught with . . . ambivalence and unexpected culture shock." Publ Wkly
"This is an emotionally charged study of class values, a subject even touchier than race or gender." Booklist

Newman, Katherine S., 1953-
The missing class; portraits of the near poor in America; [by] Katherine S. Newman and Victor Tan Chen. Beacon Press 2007 258p $24.95
                305.5
1. Working class 2. Poor—United States 3. United States—Economic conditions
ISBN 978-0-8070-4139-0; 0-8070-4139-4
                LC 2007-13553
The authors "posit that the middle class gains of the 1990s have been imperiled by the recent rollback of New Deal-style government aid." Publ Wkly
"This revealing exposé gives voice to this growing segment of the population." Booklist
Includes bibliographical references

Phillips, Kevin P.
Wealth and democracy; a political history of the American rich; {by} Kevin Phillips. Broadway Bks. 2002 xxii, 473p $29.95; pa $16.95 *
                305.5
1. Wealth 2. Political corruption 3. Representative government and representation 4. United States—Politics and government
ISBN 0-7679-0533-4; 0-7679-0534-2 (pa)
                LC 2001-52656
The author "relates how the disparity between rich and poor correlates with our propensity for speculative excess and technology manias and the corruption of government throughout this nation's history." Booklist
"Phillips's astute analysis of the effects of wealth and capital upon democracy is both eye-opening and disturbing." Publ Wkly
Includes bibliographical references

Rothkopf, David J. (David Jochanan), 1955-
Superclass; the global power elite and the world they are making; [by] David Rothkopf. Farrar, Straus and Giroux 2008 400p   **305.5**
1. Elite (Social sciences) 2. Power (Social sciences)
ISBN 978-0-374-27210-4; 0-374-27210-7
                LC 2007-36569
"The 6,000 most powerful people in the world occupy Rothkopf's analysis of current global leaders in business and global affairs. Their identities, their routes to the top, and their interactions form his principal areas of inquiry, which he explores in a mixture of personal interviews and anecdotes, . . . monetary statistics, and the main ideas in the 1956 book *The Power Elite*, by C. Wright Mills." Booklist
"Neither hand-wringing nor worshipful, this book delivers an unsettling account of what the immense and growing power of this superclass bodes for the future." Publ Wkly
Includes bibliographical references

Shipler, David K.
The working poor; invisible in America. Knopf 2004 319p $25; pa $14 * **305.5**
1. Poor—United States 2. Working class
ISBN 0-375-40890-8; 0-375-70821-9 (pa)
LC 2003-56191
The author "examines the complex issues behind poverty and changes in policy and ideology regarding the poor. Shipler fleshes out statistics and social policy with compelling portraits of people who struggle to maintain lives for themselves and their families with low-paying jobs and little social support. . . . This is a compelling, insightful book for those interested in issues of poverty and social justice." Booklist
Includes bibliographical references

Veblen, Thorstein, 1857-1929
The theory of the leisure class; edited with an introduction and notes by Martha Banta. Oxford University Press 2007 (Oxford world's classics) pa $15.95 * **305.5**
1. Social classes
ISBN 978-0-19-280684-0; 0-19-280684-X
LC 2007-8544
First published 1899 by Macmillan
In this economic treatise, "Veblen held that the feudal subdivision of classes had continued into modern times, the lords employing themselves uselessly . . . while the lower classes labored at industrial pursuits to support the whole of society. The leisure class, Veblen said, justifies itself solely by practicing 'conspicuous leisure and conspicuous consumption'; he defined waste as any activity not contributing to material productivity." Benet Reader's Ency. 4th edition

305.8 Ethnic and national groups

The **African** American almanac. Gale Res. 2007 il $240 * **305.8**
1. African Americans
ISSN 1071-8710
ISBN 0-7876-4021-2; 978-0-7876-4021-7
First edition under the editorship of Harry A. Ploski published 1967 by Bellwether with title: The Negro almanac. Periodically revised. Editors vary
"Reference covering the cultural and political history of Black Americans. Includes generous amount of statistical information and biographies of Black Americans, both historical and contemporary." N Y Public Libr. Book of How & Where to Look It Up

The **African** American encyclopedia. 2nd ed, managing editor, R. Kent Rasmussen. Marshall Cavendish 2001 10v il maps set $599.93
305.8
1. African Americans—Encyclopedias
ISBN 0-7614-7208-8
LC 00-31526
First published 1993
This source contains some 1,950 essays on many aspects of the African American experience such as religion, music, films, art, literature, dance, food, politics, the military, family life, and sports

American Jewish history; edited by Jeffrey S. Gurock. Routledge 1998 8v in 13 set $1,705
305.8
1. Jews—United States—History
ISBN 0-415-91933-9
Sponsored by the American Jewish Historical Society
Contents: v1 The colonial and early national periods, 1654-1840; v2 Central European Jews in America, 1840-1880; v3 pt 1-3 East European Jews in America, 1880-1920: immigration and adaptation; v4 American Jewish life, 1920-1990; v5 pt 1-3 The history of Judaism in America: transplantations, transformations, and reconciliations; v6 pt 1-2 Anti-semitism in America; v7 America, American Jews, and the Holocaust; v8 American Zionism: mission and politics
"This set is a compilation of 211 articles . . . chosen to relate the history of American Jews to that of other Americans or to that of Jews all over the world. . . . The wide range of issues discussed in the set includes anti-Semitism among the suffragettes, Jewish-black relations, the role of synagogue sisterhoods, and the political and cultural impact of Zionism. *American Jewish History* is a unique source." Booklist

Antisemitism; a historical encyclopedia of prejudice and persecution; Richard S. Levy, editor. ABC-CLIO 2005 2v il set $185 *
305.8
1. Antisemitism—Encyclopedias
ISBN 1-85109-439-3
LC 2005-9480
This encyclopedia provides an "overview and examination of anti-Semitism, with 650 double-column entries by over 200 contributors from 21 countries. . . . The focus of this work is on modern times, particularly the 19th and 20th centuries, but there are also many entries on anti-Jewish expression and actions through the ages." Libr J
This is "a balanced, well-written, exceedingly useful, and often compelling tool. . . . Levy's encyclopedia is crucial for any library serving a thinking public." Choice
Includes bibliographical references

Asante, Molefi K., 1942-
The African-American atlas; black history and culture—an illustrated reference; [by] Molefi K. Asante and Mark T. Mattson. Macmillan 1998 251p il maps $135 **305.8**
1. African Americans—History
ISBN 0-02-864984-2
LC 98-25556
First published 1991 with title: The historical and cultural atlas of African Americans
"The authors introduce African-American history by interweaving information about the people and events that influenced our nation's development with maps, charts, reproductions, and photographs." SLJ
Includes bibliographical references

Avakian, Monique
Atlas of Asian-American history. Facts on File 2002 214p il maps (Facts on File library of American history) $85 * **305.8**
1. Asian Americans—History
ISBN 0-8160-3699-3
LC 00-49509

Avakian, Monique—_Continued_

This "overview of the political, social, and cultural history of Asian Americans opens with a discussion of the Asian heritage and ends with comments on Asian America today. Personal anecdotes throughout range from the Chinese miners in 19th-century California to modern day health-care workers from India. Sixty full-color maps, 100 historical photos, and 34 line drawings and graphs lead the reader through discussions of the people of China, Japan, Korea, India, the Philippines, and Southeast Asia." Libr J

Includes bibliographical references

Bishop, Bill, 1957-

The big sort; why the clustering of like-minded America is tearing us apart; with Robert G. Cushing. Houghton Mifflin 2008 370p il map $25

305.8

1. Minorities 2. Regionalism—United States 3. United States—Politics and government—1989- 4. United States—Social conditions

ISBN 978-0-618-68935-4; 0-618-68935-4

LC 2007-43907

The author "looks at the 'geodemographic segmentation' of America: like-minded people clumping together by age, income, education, religion, ethnicity, occupation, housing types, and family status in communities across the nation." SLJ

"Bishop's argument is meticulously researched—surveys and polls proliferate—and his reach is broad. . . . [The] portrait of our 'post materialistic' society will . . . generate chatter [and] the idea is catchy." Publ Wkly

Includes bibliographical references

Black firsts: 4,000 ground-breaking and pioneering historical events; [edited by] Jessie Carney Smith. 2nd ed rev and expanded. Visible Ink Press 2003 787p il $58; pa $24.95

305.8

1. African Americans—History

ISBN 1-57859-153-8; 1-57859-142-2 (pa)

LC 2002-154346

First published 1994 by Gale Research with title: Black firsts; 2,000 years of extraordinary achievement

"The chapters survey broad fields such as 'Arts and Entertainment,' 'Government: Local,' and 'Science and Medicine' and are broken down into more specific subject headings. 'Arts and Entertainment,' for example, encompasses 'Architecture,' 'Dance,' 'Music,' and 'Television,' among others. Under each of these headings, firsts are arranged chronologically. Each is described in an entry ranging from a line or two to half a page, and sources are always cited. . . . Many of the sidebars highlight achievements by women. . . . _Black firsts_ remains an important part of the reference collection." Booklist

Includes bibliographical references

Carr, Cynthia, 1951-

Our town; a heartland lynching, a haunted town, and the hidden history of white America; Cynthia Carr. Crown Publishers 2005 501p il $25.95

305.8

1. Indiana—Race relations 2. Lynching

ISBN 0-517-70506-0   LC 2005-11697

The author "uses the 1930 lynching of two African-American men in Marion, Ind., where her father and grandfather grew up, as a prism to examine not only the psychology of the lynch mob members but the thousands of bystanders. . . . Carr's discovery that her beloved grandfather belonged to the Ku Klux Klan and may have been involved in the hate crime leads her to return to Marion and ask questions that many on both sides of the racial divide find uncomfortable." Publ Wkly

"This beautifully written, detail-filled work brings together the historical and personal in a powerful and moving fashion and belongs on the shelves of every U.S. library." Libr J

Includes bibliographical references

Chang, Iris, 1968-2004

The Chinese in America; a narrative history. Viking 2003 496p il hardcover o.p. pa $16 *

305.8

1. Chinese Americans—History

ISBN 0-670-03123-2; 0-14-200417-0 (pa)

LC 2002-44858

The author recounts "the immigration of Chinese people to the U.S. from the early nineteenth century to the end of the twentieth. . . . Chang threads personal stories of individuals she came across in her research into her book, making it a much more human account. . . . This is history at its most dramatic and relevant." Booklist

Includes bibliographical references

Chesler, Phyllis

The new anti-semitism; the current crisis and what we must do about it. Jossey-Bass 2003 307p $24.95; pa $15.95   **305.8**

1. Antisemitism

ISBN 0-7879-6851-X; 0-7879-7803-5 (pa)

LC 2003-6448

"A Wiley imprint"

The author "addresses what she sees as a re-emergence of virulent anti-Jewish hatred cloaked in 'political correctness,' closely linked to anti-American attitudes, sustained by many liberal feminists, intellectuals and Jewish leftists, acted upon by Islamic terrorists and jihadists, and fueled by a 'demonization of Jews' in the media. One of the main thrusts of Chesler's argument is that in our contemporary world anti-Zionism is nearly inseparable from anti-Semitism, and that while there are valid criticisms to be made of Israeli policies—for instance, she sees the West Bank settlements as an impediment to peace—many of these critiques are, she contends, rooted in a profound and socially accepted anti-Semitism." Publ Wkly

Includes bibliographical references

Cleaver, Eldridge, 1935-1998

Soul on ice. Delta Trade Paperbacks 1999 242p pa $15   **305.8**

1. African Americans

ISBN 978-0-385-33379-5; 0-385-33379-X

First published 1968 by McGraw-Hill

In a collection of essays and open letters written from California's Folsom State Prison, the author writes about the forces which shaped his life.

Cleaver, Eldridge, 1935-1998—*Continued*
There are sections "on the Watts riots, on Cleaver's religious conversion, on the black man's stake in the Vietnam War, on fellow-writers and white women." Saturday Rev

Cose, Ellis
Color-blind; seeing beyond race in a race-obsessed world. HarperCollins Pubs. 1997 260p pa $13 hardcover o.p.   **305.8**
1. Race discrimination 2. Affirmative action programs 3. United States—Race relations
ISBN 0-06-092887-5 (pa)   LC 96-34433
Issues discussed include racial classification and discrimination, race and genetics, achieving educational parity, affirmative action in colleges and the workplace, and the concept of a color-blind society. The author concludes by proposing twelve steps toward a race-neutral nation
"Bolstered by research data and his own personal experience, Cose convincingly illuminates why race still remains a determining factor of success in America." Libr J
Includes bibliographical references

The envy of the world; on being a Black man in America. Washington Sq. Press 2002 163p $22; pa $13   **305.8**
1. African Americans 2. United States—Race relations 3. United States—Social conditions
ISBN 0-7434-2715-7; 0-7434-2817-x (pa)
                       LC 2001-52073
"Cose's book is a journalist's report on the state of the black male (and black masculinity) at the start of the 21st century." N Y Times Book Rev
The author's "stated objective of opening a discussion on how racism affects individuals makes this book interesting reading for a broad range of readers." Booklist

Cox, Anna-Lisa
A stronger kinship; one town's extraordinary story of hope and faith. Little, Brown and Co. 2006 272p il map $24.95   **305.8**
1. Michigan—Race relations
ISBN 0-316-11018-3   LC 2005-20332
The author "details the founding families—black and white—who established . . . [the town of Covert, Michigan] in 1860 as a mixed-race community that defied the social conventions of the time, electing blacks to powerful political positions and providing a haven for economic development for achievers of all races. . . . This is a revealing look at a small town whose accomplishments have been virtually forgotten." Booklist
Includes bibliographical references

Dash, Leon, 1944-
Rosa Lee; a mother and her family in urban America. Plume 1997 279p il pa $15
                       305.8
1. Cunningham, Rosa Lee 2. African Americans—Social conditions
ISBN 0-452-27896-1; 978-0-452-27896-7
                       LC 97-11543

First published 1996 by Basic Books
"Rosa Lee Cunningham, who died of AIDS in 1994, at the age of fifty-nine, was an illiterate thief, prostitute, and drug addict. She was also the mother of eight children (by assorted fathers), only two of whom escaped her pattern of crime and dependency on drugs and welfare, a pattern passed on to her grandchildren. . . . [This] is an attempt to understand the underclass that has grown up in our ghettos." New Yorker
"What makes Rosa Lee, Leon Dash's report on a particular Washington ghetto family, so convincing and so valuable is [Dash's] intimacy with his subjects, an intimacy that very few writers about the underclass have ever achieved." N Y Rev Books

Dershowitz, Alan M.
The vanishing American Jew; in search of Jewish identity for the next century. Simon & Schuster 1998 395p il pa $15   **305.8**
1. Jews—United States 2. Judaism 3. Antisemitism
ISBN 978-0-684-84898-3; 0-684-84898-8
First published 1997 by Little, Brown
Noting "that since 1988 the intermarriage rate has been over 50 percent, and adding to that figure the low birth rates of non-Orthodox Jews, Mr. Dershowitz . . . [argues] that 'if trends continue apace, American Jewry—indeed, Diaspora Jewry—may virtually vanish by the third quarter of the 21st century.'" N Y Times Book Rev
"Although this title is primarily of interest to Jews, Dershowitz's notoriety and lively writing style broaden its appeal." Booklist
Includes bibliographical references

Diner, Hasia R.
A time for gathering; the second migration, 1820-1880. Johns Hopkins Univ. Press 1992 313p il (Jewish people in America) hardcover o.p. pa $20.95   **305.8**
1. Jews—United States—History
ISBN 0-8018-4344-8; 0-8018-5121-1 (pa)
                       LC 91-45368
This second volume in a five-volume history of American Jewry focuses on the German-speaking Jewish immigrants who came to the United States in the nineteenth century.
Includes bibliographical references

Dodson, Howard, 1939-
Jubilee: the emergence of African-American culture; {by the} Schomburg Center for Research in Black Culture, the New York Public Library; [text] by Howard Dodson; with Amiri Baraka [et al.] National Geographic Soc. 2002 224p il maps $35 *   **305.8**
1. African Americans—History 2. African Americans—Social life and customs
ISBN 0-7922-6982-9   LC 2002-24504
This "book demonstrates in words and pictures the extent to which the colonization of North and South America depended on slave labor, and how black resistance resulted in cultural adaptations that now form the basis of cultures in the Americas." Publ Wkly

Dodson, Howard, 1939——*Continued*
"The cultural legacies displayed here make this exceptional work essential for any collection on the culture or history of the Americas." Libr J
Includes bibliographical references

Du Bois, W. E. B. (William Edward Burghardt), 1868-1963
The Oxford W. E. B. Du Bois reader; edited by Eric J. Sundquist. Oxford Univ. Press 1996 680p pa $34.95 *   **305.8**
1. African Americans 2. United States—Race relations
ISBN 0-19-509178-7   LC 95-21307
This reader covers Du Bois's "writing career, from the 1890s through the early 1960s. The volume selects key essays and longer works that portray the range of Du Bois's thought on such subjects as African American culture, the politics and sociology of American race relations, art and music, black leadership, gender and women's rights, Pan-Africanism and anti-colonialism, and Communism in the U.S. and abroad." Publisher's note
Includes bibliographical references

The souls of Black folk; edited with an introduction and notes by Brent Hayes Edwards. Oxford University Press 2007 xxxvi, 223p il (Oxford world's classics) pa $12.95 *
                                                     305.8
1. African Americans
ISBN 978-0-19-280678-9; 0-19-280678-5
                                            LC 2006-35193
First published 1903 by McClurg
"A collection of fifteen essays and sketches by W.E.B. Du Bois. In it he describes the lives of African American farmers, sketches the role of music in their churches, details the history of the Freedman's Bureau, discusses the career of Booker T. Washington, and advocates a commitment to higher education for the most talented African American youth." Benet's Reader's Ency of Am Lit
Includes bibliographical references

Dyson, Michael Eric, 1958-
Race rules; navigating the color line. Vintage Books 1997 241p pa $13   **305.8**
1. Jackson, Jesse L., 1941- 2. Powell, Colin L., 1937-3. Farrakhan, Louis, 1933- 4. United States—Race relations
ISBN 0-679-78156-0; 978-0-679-78156-1
First published 1996 by Addison-Wesley
"From the aftermath of the O.J. Simpson trial to the posturing of black leaders following the Million Man March, Dyson explores the social issues governed by race. . . . Dyson identifies three African American leaders—Jesse Jackson, Colin Powell, Louis Farrakhan—and how he believes they have aided or hindered justice for African Americans." Libr J
"Mr. Dyson has mapped out some valuable coordinates for the course the nation continues to steer." N Y Times Book Rev

Eberstadt, Fernanda, 1960-
Little Money Street; in search of Gypsies and their music in the south of France. Knopf 2006 242p $24.95   **305.8**
1. Gypsies—France
ISBN 0-375-41116-X; 978-0-375-41116-8
                                            LC 2005-44139
"After moving outside the French town of Perpignan—home to the largest Gypsy population in Western Europe—Eberstadt, a fan of Gypsy music, undertook a quest to interview members of the renowned Gypsy band Tekameli. . . . Personally introduced to the elusive Gypsy culture, she does readers a tremendous service by providing them with an intimate glimpse into the vibrant social life, customs, and music of one of the world's most reviled, misunderstood, and richly textured societies." Booklist

Encyclopedia of African-American culture and history; the Black experience in the Americas; Colin A. Palmer, editor in chief. 2nd ed. Macmillan Reference USA 2006 6v il map set $695 *   **305.8**
1. African Americans—Encyclopedias
ISBN 0-02-865816-7   LC 2005-13029
First published 1996 under the editorship of Jack Salzman, David L. Smith, and Cornel West
"Readers can find comparative analyses of social movements, languages, religions and family structures in the context of an interdisciplinary framework." Publisher's note
For a fuller review, see: Booklist, March 15, 2006
Includes bibliographical references

Encyclopedia of African American history, 1619-1895; from the colonial period to the age of Frederick Douglass; editor in chief, Paul Finkelman. Oxford University Press 2006 3v il set $375   **305.8**
1. African Americans—History—Encyclopedias
ISBN 0-19-516777-5; 978-0-19-516777-1
                                            LC 2005-33701
This encyclopedia, the first of a projected two sets focusing on African-American history, documents "blacks' experiences from the first slave ships to Frederick Douglass's death. The set offers depth, reaching most important persons, events, and developments through 1895 but is written for easy access with multiple cross references, chronologies, topical outlines, and a comprehensive index." Libr J
Includes bibliographical references

Encyclopedia of Black studies; editors Molefi Kete Asante, Ama Mazama. SAGE Publications 2005 xxxii, 531p il $150   **305.8**
1. African Americans—Encyclopedias
ISBN 0-7619-2762-X   LC 2004-10091
This encyclopedia contains an "analysis of the economic, political, sociological, historical, literary, and philosophical issues related to Americans of African descent." Publisher's note
"For students seeking a good grounding in Afrocentricity, this is an excellent place to start. . . . [This encyclopedia] provides a thorough understanding of and easy reference into a growing, dynamic field of

Encyclopedia of Black studies—*Continued*
study." Booklist
Includes bibliographical references

Encyclopedia of Latino popular culture; Cordelia Chávez Candelaria, executive editor . . . [et al.] Greenwood Press 2004 2v il set $175
305.8
1. Hispanic Americans—Encyclopedias 2. Popular culture—United States—Encyclopedias
ISBN 0-313-32215-5   LC 2004-47454
"This encyclopedia describes the key components of daily Latino life in the United States to include art, food, religion, celebrations, fashion, literature, music, media movies, political organizations, people, places, and entertainment. This guide to Latino popular culture focuses primarily on the Mexican-American, Puerto Rican, and Cuban-American experience." Am Ref Books Annu, 2005
"This outstanding, up-to-date resource is a must-buy for all libraries that serve Latino populations." SLJ
Includes bibliographical references

Encyclopedia of modern ethnic conflicts; edited by Joseph R. Rudolph, Jr. Greenwood Press 2003 xxvi, 375p il map $74.95   **305.8**
1. Ethnic relations 2. Culture conflict
ISBN 0-313-31381-4   LC 2002-70025
These "essays explore the history and issues that were the root causes of 38 major ethnic conflicts, the attempts to 'manage' them, and the impact they have had on the politics of the region in question. . . . Organized alphabetically by country or geographic area, the entries include a time line of significant events in the region, followed by a general discussion of the area. . . . Students will find this volume to be a useful tool in understanding the history and causes behind some of the major events in today's world." SLJ
Includes bibliographical references

Encyclopedia of racism in the United States. Greenwood Press 2005 3v il set $249.95 *
305.8
1. Racism—Encyclopedias 2. United States—Race relations—Encyclopedias
ISBN 0-313-32688-6   LC 2005-8523
"The majority of the 450 entries run about a paragraph to a page in length, covering sociological terms, current and historical events, individuals, organizations, books, court cases, government programs, and legislation. Twenty-five of the entries deal with such broad concepts as affirmative action or the Civil Rights Movement." Libr J
"With nearly a hundred pages of primary documents, the Encyclopedia will be a valuable supplement to studies of racism and multiculturalism." Choice
Includes bibliographical references

Encyclopedia of the world's minorities; Carl Skutsch, editor; Martin Ryle, consulting editor. Routledge 2005 3v set $495 *   **305.8**
1. Minorities—Encyclopedias
ISBN 1-57958-392-X   LC 2004-20324
"The 562 alphabetically arranged entries fall into four main categories: minority groups (including coverage of

their history and current situation), topics (e.g., immigration, Diaspora, genocide), biographies (i.e., individuals who have played a significant part in the history of minority communities, such as Nelson Mandela), and countries (including historical background, social conditions, and current situation). Ranging in length from 1000 to 5000 words, the entries provide capsule summaries on location, population, languages spoken, and religious affiliations and include cross references and suggestions for further reading." Libr J
For a fuller review, see: Booklist, Apr. 15, 2005
Includes bibliographical references

Epstein, Lawrence J. (Lawrence Jeffrey)
At the edge of a dream; the story of Jewish immigrants on New York's Lower East Side. Jossey-Bass 2007 299p il $40   **305.8**
1. Jews—New York (N.Y.) 2. United States—Immigration and emigration
ISBN 978-0-7879-8622-3   LC 2007-4000
"An Arthur Kurzweil Book; A Lower East Side Tenement Museum Book"
The author "explores why the immigrants left Eastern Europe, how they came here, and what they found when they arrived. He describes their journey in steerage, their life in tenements, and their search for jobs. Also under discussion are Yiddish theater, journalism, and literature, as well as such famous personalities as Jacob Adler, George Burns, Fanny Brice, Irving Berlin, George Gershwin, Sholom Aleichem, Eddie Cantor, and Jack Benny. . . . Words and pictures combine to make this book a foremost chronicle of Jewish immigration." Booklist
Includes bibliographical references

Faber, Eli, 1943-
A time for planting; the first migration, 1654-1820. Johns Hopkins Univ. Press 1992 188p il (Jewish people in America) hardcover o.p. pa $14.95   **305.8**
1. Jews—United States—History
ISBN 0-8018-4343-X; 0-8018-5120-3 (pa)
LC 91-45341
This is the initial volume in a five-volume series tracing the history of Jews in the United States from the seventeenth century to the period following World War II. It focuses on the Sephardic Jews who settled in New Amsterdam, Newport, Rhode Island, Philadelphia, Charleston and other colonial towns.
Includes bibliographical references

Feingold, Henry L.
A time for searching; entering the mainstream, 1920-1945. Johns Hopkins Univ. Press 1992 338p il (Jewish people in America) hardcover o.p. pa $21.95   **305.8**
1. Jews—United States—History
ISBN 0-8018-4346-4; 0-8018-5123-8 (pa)
LC 91-45367
This fourth volume in The Jewish People in America series addresses the period from the end of World War I to World War II. The author discusses "the emergence of anti-Semitism, second-generation Jewish acculturation

Feingold, Henry L.—*Continued*
and secularization, political behavior, and Zionism, . . .
aiming to explain the disarray of the American Jewish
community during the Holocaust." Libr J
Includes bibliographical references

Franklin, John Hope, 1915-
From slavery to freedom; a history of African
Americans; [by] John Hope Franklin, Alfred A.
Moss, Jr. 8th ed. Alfred A. Knopf 2000 xxiv, 742p
il map $49.95 *   **305.8**
1. African Americans—History 2. Slavery—United
States
ISBN 0-375-40671-9   LC 2005-299886
Also available edition with study guide CD-ROM and
in paperback from McGraw-Hill
First published 1947
A survey of African-Americans history from slavery
to the present.
Includes bibliographical references

Freedom on my mind; the Columbia documentary
history of the African American experience;
Manning Marable, general editor; Nishani
Frazier and John McMillian, assistant editors.
Columbia University Press 2003 734p $80 *
     305.8
1. African Americans—History—Sources
ISBN 0-231-10890-7   LC 2003-51605
This "anthology features the works of noteworthy figures of African American history and culture . . . and
provides a tapestry of personal correspondence, excerpts
from slave narratives and autobiographies, leaflets,
speeches, oral histories and interviews, political manifestos, song lyrics, and important statements of black institutions and organizations. . . . A necessary text of readings for both introductory and advanced African American studies courses." Choice
Includes bibliographical references

Gates, Henry Louis
The future of the race; by Henry Louis Gates,
Jr. and Cornel West. Knopf 1996 196p hardcover
o.p. pa $12.95   **305.8**
1. Du Bois, W. E. B. (William Edward Burghardt),
1868-1963 2. African Americans—Social conditions
3. African Americans—Intellectual life 4. United
States—Race relations
ISBN 0-679-44405-X; 0-679-76378-3 (pa)
     LC 96-14450
"Gates and West explore the challenge of W.E.B. Du-
Bois's famous essay 'The Talented Tenth' and consider
the future of African American society in light of it. . . .
The authors examine the responsibility of the successful
and talented black middle and upper classes to uplift the
impoverished. . . . The text includes DuBois's 'The Talented Tenth' and, reprinted for the first time, his 1948
critique of it." Libr J
Includes bibliographical references

Glazer, Nathan
Beyond the melting pot; the Negroes, Puerto
Ricans, Jews, Italians, and Irish of New York City;
by Nathan Glazer and Daniel Patrick Moynihan.
2nd ed. MIT Press 1970 xcviii, 363p pa $26.95
hardcover o.p.   **305.8**
1. Minorities 2. New York (N.Y.)—Population
ISBN 0-262-57022-X (pa)
First published 1963
A study of the different levels of achievement of the
five major ethnic groups of New York City in education,
business, and politics
Includes bibliographical references

Graham, Lawrence Otis
Our kind of people; inside America's Black
upper class. HarperCollins Pubs. 1999 418p il pa
$14 hardcover o.p.   **305.8**
1. African Americans—Social conditions 2. Elite (Social sciences) 3. United States—Race relations
ISBN 0-06-098438-4 (pa)   LC 98-34046
Graham presents a "study of the customs, social organizations, educational institutions, vacation enclaves and
histories of wealthy African-American communities in a
dozen cities across the country." N Y Times Book Rev
"This book is both a thorough work of social history
and a thoughtful appraisal of [the author's] own place in
the black social hierarchy." Publ Wkly

The **Greenwood** encyclopedia of African
American civil rights; from emancipation to the
twenty-first century; Charles D. Lowery and
John F. Marszalek, editors; Thomas Adams
Upchurch, associate editor; foreword by David
J. Garrow. Greenwood Press 2003 2v il set $175
*   **305.8**
1. African Americans—Civil rights—Encyclopedias
2. United States—Race relations—Encyclopedias
ISBN 0-313-32171-X   LC 2003-40837
First published 1992 with title: Encyclopedia of African-American civil rights
"Entries are alphabetically arranged and cross-
referenced, and each is followed by a selected bibliography. Many of the entries focus on seminal political issues of the 1950s and 1960s—*Black Power, March on
Washington, Voter Education Project*—but also cover
important developments both before and after this time.
Other entries are biographical, ranging from politicians to
writers, artists, actors, musicians, and athletes. Important
literary documents are covered, including not only novels, plays, and political treatises but also journals."
Booklist

Griffin, John Howard, 1920-1980
Black like me; the definitive Griffin estate
edition, corrected from original manuscripts; with
a foreword by Studs Terkel; historic photographs
by Don Rutledge; and an afterword by Robert
Bonazzi. Wings Press 2004 239p il $24.95; lib bdg
$29.95 *   **305.8**
1. African Americans—Southern States 2. Prejudices
ISBN 0-930324-72-2; 0-930324-73-0 (lib bdg)
     LC 2004-1549

Griffin, John Howard, 1920-1980—*Continued*
Also available in hardcover from Buccaneer Bks. and in paperback from New Am. Lib.
First published 1961
The author, "who is white, a Catholic, and a Texan, conceived and carried out the unusual notion of blackening his skin with a newly developed pigment drug and traveling through the Deep South as a Negro. This book, part of which appeared in the Negro magazine Sepia, is a journal account of that experience." New Yorker
Includes bibliographical references

Gross, Jan Tomasz
Fear: anti-semitism in Poland after Auschwitz; an essay in historical interpretation; [by] Jan T. Gross. Random House 2005 303p il $25.95
305.8
1. Antisemitism 2. Jews—Poland 3. Jews—Persecutions 4. Holocaust, 1933-1945
ISBN 0-375-50924-0; 978-0-375-50924-7
LC 2005-52913
The author describes "how surviving Polish Jews, having escaped the fate of 90 percent of their community—three million people—returned to their homeland to be vilified, terrorized and, in some 1,500 instances, murdered, sometimes in ways as bestial as anything the Nazis had devised." N Y Times Book Rev
"This is a masterful work that sheds necessary light on a tragic and often-ignored aspect of postwar history." Booklist
Includes bibliographical references

Hahn, Steven, 1951-
A nation under our feet; Black political struggles in the rural South, from slavery to the great migration; Steven Hahn. Belknap Press of Harvard University Press 2003 610p il $35; pa $18.95
305.8
1. African Americans—Political activity 2. Southern States—Race relations
ISBN 0-674-01169-4; 0-674-01765-X (pa)
LC 2003-45326
The author "examines the development of African American political culture during its formative years in the last half of the 19th century, arguing that African Americans actively shaped their own political identity during this critical time period in an often overlooked comprehensive grassroots movement." Choice
This book "is one of the most important works in American social history to appear in recent years." Nation
Includes bibliographical references

Harley, Sharon
The timetables of African-American history; a chronology of the most important people and events in African-American history. Simon & Schuster 1995 400p il pa $21 hardcover o.p.
305.8
1. African Americans—History
ISBN 0-684-81578-8 (pa)
LC 94-22571

This work "is arranged by year; under each date events are listed across the page under such categories as *Education; Laws and Legal Actions; Religion; Arts; Science, Technology, and Medicine;* and *Sports.*" Booklist
"These timetables would be an excellent addition to any collection of African American studies as a ready reference source or a starting point for further research." Libr J

Hendrickson, Paul
Sons of Mississippi; a story of race and its legacy. Knopf 2003 343p il map $26; pa $15
305.8
1. African Americans—Mississippi 2. Mississippi—Race relations 3. Police brutality
ISBN 0-375-40461-9; 0-375-70425-6 (pa)
LC 2002-29857
"Sons of Mississippi recounts the story of seven white Mississippi lawmen depicted in a . . . 1962 Life magazine photograph. . . . [In this photograph], the lawmen (six sheriffs and a deputy sheriff), . . . [are] preparing for the unrest they anticipate—and to which they clearly intend to contribute—in the wake of James Meredith's planned attempt to integrate the University of Mississippi. . . . [Hendrickson's] ultimate focus is on the part [their] legacy has played in the lives of their children and grandchildren." Publisher's note
"The number of telling quotes, interviews with friends and family, primary and secondary sources, allusions to art and history, and gut reactions Hendrickson offers are what really make the book. . . . He repeatedly comes up with electric interview material, and deftly places these men within the defining events of their times, when 'a 100-year-old way of life was cracking beneath them.'" Publ Wkly
Includes bibliographical references

The **Hispanic** American almanac; a reference work on Hispanics in the United States; edited by Sonia G. Benson. 3rd ed. Gale Group 2003 xxvii, 886p il maps $135 *
305.8
1. Hispanic Americans
ISBN 0-7876-2518-3
LC 2002-10070
First published 1993 under the editorship of Nicolás Kanellos
This is a "resource covering people of the U.S. whose ancestors come from Mexico, Cuba, Puerto Rico, and Central America. The book contains 25 subject chapters (e.g., 'Spanish Explorers and Colonizers'; 'Law, Government, and Military'; 'Art'. . . . A chronology offers a year-by-year outline of the migration of Hispanics to this country. . . . The 'Historical Overview' chapter details the evolution of three major Hispanic groups: Mexicans, Puerto Ricans, and Cubans. The 'Significant Documents' chapter provides the researcher with documents such as the Treaty of Guadalupe Hidalgo (1948), the NAFTA agreement, and California's Proposition 227. . . . The final chapter contains more than 500 biographies highlighting Hispanics. . . . Well organized and written at a reading level that is easily understood, this volume is an excellent resource." Booklist
Includes bibliographical references

Kennedy, Randall

Nigger; the strange career of a troublesome word. Pantheon Bks. 2002 226p hardcover o.p. pa $12   **305.8**

1. African Americans 2. Racism 3. United States—Race relations

ISBN 0-375-42172-6; 0-375-71371-9 (pa)

                         LC 2001-36442

Kennedy examines the history of the use of the racial epithet in American society by both African Americans and whites and its implications for race relations

"An insightful and highly provocative book that raises vital questions about the relationship between language, politics, social norms and how society and culture confront racism." Publ Wkly

Includes bibliographical references

Lasch-Quinn, Elisabeth

Race experts; how racial etiquette, sensitivity training, and New Age therapy hijacked the civil rights revolution. Norton 2001 267p $25.95

                                  305.8

1. African Americans 2. United States—Race relations 3. Multiculturalism 4. Group relations training

ISBN 0-393-04873-X   LC 2001-30913

Also available in paperback from Rowman & Littlefield

The author "probes the intersection of the civil rights struggle and modern social psychology, in particular the human potential movement. She highlights the 'overthrow of the social code of segregation' and the adoption of an etiquette of black assertiveness and white submissiveness that has produced a 'harangueflagellation' ritual that does not advance the goal of racial equality. . . . This is sure to be a controversial book among readers interested in race issues." Booklist

Includes bibliographical references

Lewis, Elliott, 1966-

Fade: my journeys in multiracial America. Carroll & Graf 2006 306p $25   **305.8**

1. Racially mixed people

ISBN 0-7867-1668-1; 978-0-7867-1668-5

                         LC 2006-297756

The author "looks at the ever-shifting landscape of self-identification among individuals of mixed racial heritage, including himself. . . . This is a most interesting read on evolving notions of racial self-identification in America." Booklist

Includes bibliographical references

Loury, Glenn C.

The anatomy of racial inequality. Harvard Univ. Press 2001 226p il (W.E.B. Du Bois lectures) $22.95   **305.8**

1. African Americans—Social conditions 2. African Americans—Economic conditions 3. United States—Race relations

ISBN 0-674-00625-9   LC 2001-39192

"Loury argues that the image white Americans have of black Americans as less than full citizens influences policy far more than who African-Americans actually are.

Although much of Loury's argument is theoretical . . . he grapples eloquently and vigorously with such concrete examples as affirmative action, arguments about racial IQ differences and racial profiling." Publ Wkly

Includes bibliographical references

Lukas, J. Anthony, 1933-1997

Common ground; a turbulent decade in the lives of three American families. Knopf 1985 659p il maps pa $18 hardcover o.p.   **305.8**

1. Boston (Mass.)—Race relations 2. Busing (School integration) 3. School integration

ISBN 0-394-74616-3 (pa)   LC 85-127

"By focusing on three families—one of them welfare black, one upper-middle-class white and one working-class Irish—a veteran journalist recreates the school-busing struggles of Boston in the 1970s, and delineates . . . the moral complexities of caste and class in America." Newsday

Marable, Manning, 1950-

Living Black history; how reimagining the African-American past can remake America's racial future. Basic Civitas 2005 xxii, 266p $26

                                  305.8

1. African Americans—Historiography 2. African Americans—Civil rights 3. United States—Race relations

ISBN 978-0-465-04389-7; 0-465-04389-5

                         LC 2005-21166

"Focusing on the life work of activist scholar W.E.B. Du Bois (1868-1963), black Muslim spokesman Malcolm X (1925-65), and NAACP desegregation strategist and federal judge Robert L. Carter (b. 1917), . . . [the author] reviews differing approaches to overthrowing Jim Crow's physical and psychological oppression. . . . [This is] a moving vision of America's past, present, and future." Libr J

Includes bibliographical references

McWhorter, John H.

Losing the race; self-sabotage in Black America; [with a new afterword by the author] Perennial 2001 299p pa $13.95   **305.8**

1. African Americans—Social conditions 2. African Americans—Education

ISBN 978-0-06-093593-1; 0-06-093593-6

                         LC 2001-24092

First published 2000 by Free Press

McWhorter discusses what he sees as "a cult of anti-intellectualism 'that has infected black America. . . . He concluded [black students] were held back by three defeatist thought patterns': the Cult of Victimology, which leads blacks to blame their problems on racism; the Cult of Separatism, which makes blacks think that whatever whites do, they should do the opposite; and the Cult of Anti-Intellectualism, which holds that scholastic excellence is a white thing." Time

Includes bibliographical references

McWhorter, John H.—*Continued*

Winning the race; beyond the crisis in black America; [by] John McWhorter. Gotham Books 2005 434p $27.50 **305.8**

1. African Americans—Social conditions 2. United States—Race relations

ISBN 1-59240-188-0 LC 2005-23472

The author "claims that racism is not the most daunting barrier to success for African Americans. He states that the social behaviors attributed to some poor, inner-city blacks are rooted in cultural rather than economic causes." Libr J

"McWhorter's provocative, tough-love message is both grounded in history and forward-looking." Publ Wkly

Includes bibliographical references

Meagher, Timothy J.

The Columbia guide to Irish American history. Columbia University Press 2005 398p (Columbia guides to American history and cultures) $47.50 * **305.8**

1. Irish Americans

ISBN 0-231-12070-2 LC 2005-43233

The author "examines Irish American history from the first Irish settlements in the seventeenth century through the famine years in the nineteenth century to the unpredictability of 1960s America and beyond to the twentieth century. Teachers and students interested in the history of Irish America will welcome this book." Univ Press Books for Public and Second Sch Libr, 2006

Includes bibliographical references

Meier, Matt S.

The Mexican American experience; an encyclopedia; [by] Matt S. Meier and Margo Gutiérrez. Greenwood Press 2003 xxix, 456p il $79.95 * **305.8**

1. Mexican Americans—Encyclopedias

ISBN 0-313-31643-0 LC 2003-52845

"Entries treat everything from the arts to religion, political activism to sports, and education to business, all within the context of historical experience. Much of the strength of this work lies in the biographical entries, which create coherent portraits with few words yet put a human face on events and issues. Almost every entry ends with suggested readings or short bibliographies, which are extremely useful and relevant and include books, Web sites, and articles from popular and scholarly journals. The work focuses on the Southwest." Choice

Includes bibliographical references

Morales, Ed

Living in Spanglish; the search for a new Latino identity in America. St. Martin's Press 2002 310p $25.95; pa $14.95 **305.8**

1. Hispanic Americans 2. Racially mixed people 3. United States—Ethnic relations

ISBN 0-312-26232-9; 0-312-31000-5 (pa) LC 2001-48867

"To the author, *Spanglish* isn't just . . . {an} increasingly common linguistic mélange. . . . It is the break-down of the either/or of a black/white worldview through the inevitable mingling of race and culture. . . . The author meditates on his own coming to terms with Latino identity as well as positing the larger point that 'We have spent the last several centuries preparing for our role as the first wholly postmodern culture.'. . . His ideas are provocative and engaging." Booklist

The **New** York Public Library African American desk reference. Wiley 1999 606p il $40 **305.8**

1. African Americans—Encyclopedias

ISBN 0-471-23924-0

"A Stonesong Press book"

This reference is "arranged into 19 chapters covering topics such as slavery, education, health, law, science and technology, the arts, and sports. Chapters include numerous tables, lists, photographs, and sidebars and end with sources for additional information. Quotations are sprinkled throughout." Booklist

Includes bibliographical references

Olmos, Edward James

Americanos; Latino life in the United States; [by] Edward James Olmos, Lea Ybarra, Manuel Monterrey; preface by Edward James Olmos; introduction by Carlos Fuentes. Little, Brown 1999 176p il $39; pa $25 **305.8**

1. Hispanic Americans

ISBN 0-316-64914-7; 0-316-64909-0 (pa) LC 98-51930

This work includes essays, poetry, and commentary in English and Spanish by such authors as Carlos Fuentes and Maya Angelou and over 200 photographs of Latin Americans from many parts of the United States.

"This is a beautiful, vibrant . . . book; it may also be one of the more socially important books to appear in some time." Booklist

The **Oxford** encyclopedia of Latinos and Latinas in the United States; Suzanne Oboler and Deena J. González, editors in chief. Oxford University Press 2005 4v il map set $525 * **305.8**

1. Hispanic Americans—Encyclopedias

ISBN 0-19-515600-5 LC 2005-7764

"Some 900 A-Z essays ranging in length from 500 to 7,500 words and written by 500 experts document the impact of Latinos in all spheres of U.S. history and society, from conquistador to migrant worker and from economic refugee to political exile. More than 400 illustrations, sidebars, maps, and charts accompany the text." Booklist

"This is one of the most thorough sets on the topic to date." Libr J

Includes bibliographical references

Packard, Jerrold M.

American nightmare; the history of Jim Crow. St. Martin's Press 2002 291p $24.95; pa $14.95 **305.8**

1. African Americans—Segregation 2. Southern States—Race relations

ISBN 0-312-26122-5; 0-312-30241-X (pa) LC 2001-41960

Packard, Jerrold M.—*Continued*

The author provides an "overview of the Jim Crow era, from Reconstruction through passage of the Voting Rights Act in 1965." Booklist

"This is a clear, concise, historical narrative of a draconian reality." Publ Wkly

Includes bibliographical references

Pfaelzer, Jean

Driven out; the forgotten war against Chinese Americans. Random House 2007 xxix, 400p il map $27.95   **305.8**
1. Chinese Americans 2. California—Race relations
ISBN 1-4000-6134-2; 978-1-4000-6134-1
LC 2006-51031

The author "reveals one of the most disgraceful chapters in American history—the purging of thousands of Chinese immigrants in the Pacific Northwest and Rocky Mountain region between 1850 and 1906." Booklist

"This work contributes to the understanding of class and racism, legal issues and cases, and international relations with China, and is an important history of the usually neglected West Coast territories and California." Choice

Includes bibliographical references

Reed, Ishmael, 1938-

Another day at the front; dispatches from the race war. Basic Bks. 2002 xliv, 189p $24; pa $14.95   **305.8**
1. Racism 2. African Americans—Civil rights 3. United States—Race relations
ISBN 0-465-06891-X; 0-465-06892-8 (pa)
LC 2002-10563

The author "gathers a series of original and revamped essays from recent years on a variety of topics, from the Confederate flag to NPR, with the underlying theme that African Americans have been living in a police state for the past 300 years. These brief essays, written in Reed's lively hit-and-run style, are certainly provocative, particularly as he jabs at many well-known critics both black and white." Libr J

Remembering Jim Crow; African Americans tell about life in the segregated South; edited by William H. Chafe [et al.] New Press (NY) 2001 xxxv, 346p il $55; pa $16.95 *   **305.8**
1. African Americans—Segregation 2. African Americans—Southern States 3. Southern States—Race relations
ISBN 1-56584-697-4; 1-56584-778-4 (pa)
LC 2001-31224

Companion volume to Remembering slavery

Recollections taken from interviews compiled by the Behind the Veil Project at the Center for Documentary Studies at Duke University

This work offers "views into the thoughts, activities, and anxieties of black Americans. . . . Included are two one-hour CDs of the radio documentary produced by American Radio Works, a transcript of the audio program, 50 rare segregation-era photographs, biographical information, and suggestions for further reading. This [is a] superb primary source." Libr J

Includes bibliographical references

Rodriguez, Gregory

Mongrels, bastards, orphans, and vagabonds; Mexican immigration and the future of race in America. Pantheon Books 2007 317p $26.95
305.8
1. Mexican Americans 2. United States—Immigration and emigration 3. Ethnic relations
ISBN 978-0-375-42158-7; 0-375-42158-0
LC 2007-17464

This book "offers an . . . account of the long-term cultural and political influences that Mexican Americans will have on the collective character of our nation. . . . Rodriguez examines the complexities of its heritage and of the racial and cultural synthesis—*mestizaje*—that has defined the Mexican people since the Spanish conquest in the sixteenth century." Publisher's note

This "volume is required reading for anybody interested in the future of the United States." Foreign Affairs

Includes bibliographical references

Rodriguez, Richard, 1944-

Brown: the last discovery of America. Viking 2002 232p $24.95; pa $14   **305.8**
1. Hispanic Americans 2. Racially mixed people 3. United States—Race relations
ISBN 0-670-03043-0; 0-14-200079-5 (pa)
LC 2001-57919

Rodriguez presents a "meditation on identity, racial and otherwise, in American culture. . . . This book draws upon . . . cultural figures and artifacts—e.g., Milton, James Baldwin, Ralph Waldo Emerson, Ralph Lauren advertisements, Leontyne Price in the opera *Cleopatra*, Edith Sitwell, *Showboat*, Carlos Fuentes, Francis Parkman's *Oregon Trail*—to make his case that our historical and contemporary conceptualization of race is rudimentary and psychologically and culturally damaging." Publ Wkly

Roediger, David R., 1952-

Working toward whiteness; how America's immigrants became white: the strange journey from Ellis Island to the suburbs. Basic Books 2005 339p $26.95; pa $17   **305.8**
1. Americanization 2. United States—Ethnic relations 3. Race discrimination
ISBN 0-465-07073-6; 0-465-07074-4 (pa)

This is an "account of how Ellis Island immigrants became accepted as cultural insiders in America." Publisher's note

"While slow going, Roediger's book tills some major historical ground." Publ Wkly

Includes bibliographical references

Sachar, Howard Morley, 1928-

A history of the Jews in America; by Howard M. Sachar. Knopf 1992 1051p pa $25 hardcover o.p.   **305.8**
1. Jews—United States—History
ISBN 0-679-74530-0 (pa)   LC 91-4261

The author examines "two different subjects. One is the rich, sometimes dark, ultimately triumphant story of Jews in the United States. The other is the relation be-

Sachar, Howard Morley, 1928-—*Continued*
tween American Jews and Israel, a matter of the widest
interest, for probably no other group in this country is so
deeply committed to the success of a foreign state. That
poses problems that Mr. Sachar confronts unflinchingly
and in detail, making his narrative not only good history
but a contribution to the current debate over American-
Israeli relations." N Y Times Book Rev
Includes bibliographical references

Shapiro, Edward S., 1938-
A time for healing; American Jewry since
World War II. Johns Hopkins Univ. Press 1992
313p il (Jewish people in America) hardcover o.p.
pa $14.95 **305.8**
1. Jews—United States—History
ISBN 0-8018-4347-2; 0-8018-5124-6 (pa)
LC 91-38385
This volume is the fifth and last in The Jewish People
in America, a series sponsored by the American Jewish
Historical Society. "This history of American Jewry after
1945 has two broad themes. One is the rapid social and
economic mobility of American Jews. . . . The other
major theme is the adaptation of Jews to unprecedented
conditions of affluence and freedom." Preface
Includes bibliographical references

Sokol, Jason
There goes my everything; white Southerners in
the age of civil rights, 1945-1975. Knopf 2006
433p il $27.95 * **305.8**
1. Southern States—Race relations 2. African Americans—Civil rights
ISBN 0-307-26356-8; 978-0-307-26356-8
LC 2005-44488
This book "explores the complexities of white attitudes in the South during the civil rights era." N Y
Times Book Rev
"This chronicle of the destruction of the white Southern hierarchy belongs in all libraries, public and academic." Libr J
Includes bibliographical references

Sorin, Gerald, 1940-
A time for building; the third migration,
1880-1920. Johns Hopkins Univ. Press 1992 306p
il (Jewish people in America) hardcover o.p. pa
$14.95 **305.8**
1. Jews—United States—History
ISBN 0-8018-4345-6; 0-8018-5122-X (pa)
LC 91-40700
This volume, the third in The Jewish People in Ameri-
ca, a series sponsored by the American Jewish Historical
Society, focuses on Eastern European Jewish immigration
to the United States between 1880 and 1920.
Includes bibliographical references

Sowell, Thomas, 1930-
The economics and politics of race; an
international perspective. Morrow 1983 324p pa
$14 hardcover o.p. **305.8**
1. Race relations
ISBN 0-688-04832-3 (pa)
LC 83-715

"Through a comparative examination of migrants
(Chinese, Germans, Italians, blacks, and others), each
studied in a variety of overseas settings, the author seeks
to discount the factor of race or racism as a lasting, or
seriously disruptive, determinant in socioeconomic and
political development." Choice
This book is "thoroughly, almost dauntingly, researched, yet it is as readable as a novel." Commentary
Includes bibliographical references

Ethnic America; a history. Basic Bks. 1981
353p pa $21 hardcover o.p. **305.8**
1. Minorities 2. Ethnic groups
ISBN 0-465-02075-5 (pa)
LC 80-68957
"Offering concise accounts of the Old World experiences of European groups (Irish, German, Jews, Italians)
and Asians (Chinese, Japanese) as well as blacks, Puerto
Ricans and Mexicans, the author examines the complexities and nuances of their American stories." Publ Wkly
"While bringing together the best of primary and secondary source materials from several vast fields, the
book's extraordinary merit is its application of demographic and economic analysis to historical and social
materials." New Repub

Steele, Shelby
White guilt; how blacks and whites together
destroyed the promise of the civil rights era.
HarperCollins Publishers 2006 181p $24.95
305.8
1. Racism 2. African Americans—Political activity
3. United States—Race relations
ISBN 978-0-06-057862-6; 0-06-057862-9
LC 2005-52784
The author "mixes reminiscences with observations on
race relations since the 1950s to argue that America has
tragically veered from a quest for civil rights to the defining of blacks as victims, an approach that does not
treat them as equals." Libr J
"Steele's writing is a marvel of lapidary elegance."
Natl Rev

Takaki, Ronald T., 1939-
Strangers from a different shore; a history of
Asian Americans; [by] Ronald Takaki. Updated
and rev ed, 1st Back Bay ed. Little, Brown 1998
591p il pa $16.95 **305.8**
1. Asian Americans—History
ISBN 0-316-83130-1
LC 98-218270
First published 1989
This work discusses the Chinese transcontinental railroad workers, the plantation workers in the Hawaii
canefields, the Japanese Americans in the U.S. internment camps during World War II, the Hmong refugees
in Wisconsin and the stereotypical image of Asian American youth as model students
Includes bibliographical references

Tatum, Beverly Daniel, 1954-
"Why are all the Black kids sitting together in
the cafeteria?" and other conversations about race.
Basic Bks. 2003 294p pa $15.95 **305.8**

Tatum, Beverly Daniel, 1954-—*Continued*
1. African Americans—Race identity 2. United
States—Race relations
ISBN 0-465-08361-7
First published 1997
"Tatum explains the development of racial identity. To
illustrate her point she uses anecdotes about her sons, excerpts from research interviews and essays written by her
students." Libr J

Terkel, Studs, 1912-2008
Race; how blacks and whites think and feel
about the American obsession. New Press (NY)
1992 403p pa $16.95 hardcover o.p.

305.8

1. United States—Race relations
ISBN 0-385-46889-X   LC 91-66864
"In this new oral history, Terkel explores Americans'
inner feelings and values pertaining to the subject of
race. . . . His study is primarily centered in Chicago, but
the people chosen to be interviewed represent a broad
spectrum of society. . . . Terkel demonstrates how very
skilled he is at drawing out interviewees' intrinsic feelings pertaining to race." Libr J

Those who forget the past; the question of
anti-Semitism; edited and with an introduction
by Ron Rosenbaum; afterword by Cynthia
Ozick. Random House Trade Paperbacks 2004
lxix, 649p pa $16.95   **305.8**
1. Antisemitism
ISBN 0-8129-7203-1   LC 2003-65542
This "anthology comprises nearly 50 short contemporary essays by sociologists, literary figures, critics, educators, philosophers, and others. . . . This volume not only
provides historical background from which to investigate
the global comeback of 'the oldest hatred' but looks at
artifacts of its resurgence." Libr J
"This is an important and vital contribution to efforts
to comprehend what is new and what is the same in this
ancient virus of ignorance and hatred." Booklist
Includes bibliographical references

West, Cornel, 1953-
Race matters; with a new preface by the author.
Beacon Press 2001 108p $20   **305.8**
1. Malcolm X, 1925-1965 2. Thomas, Clarence
3. United States—Race relations
ISBN 0-8070-0972-5; 978-0-8070-0972-7
                                       LC 2001-025310
Also available in paperback from Vintage Books
First published 1993
In this collection of essays the author "addresses a
number of issues of concern to black Americans: the Los
Angeles riots after the Rodney King verdict; Malcolm X;
Clarence Thomas and Anita Hill, and black street life.
. . . West's essays have the feel of a fine sermon, with
thought-provoking ideas and new ways of looking at the
same old problems." Libr J

Restoring hope; conversations on the future of
Black America; edited by Kelvin Shawn Sealey.
Beacon Press 1997 xx, 226p il pa $13 hardcover
o.p.   **305.8**
1. African Americans—Social conditions 2. United
States—Social conditions
ISBN 0-8070-0943-1 (pa)   LC 97-21797
"A project of the Obsidian Society"
The author addresses "the topic of hope and meaning
in the African American community by conducting a se-
ries of interviews with leading politicians, writers, musi-
cians, journalists, and scholars, including Bill Bradley,
Charlayne Hunter-Gault, Wynton Marsalis, and Maya
Angelou. . . . The interviews—thoughtful, intimate, and
intriguing—make the reader believe that hope in black
America can indeed be restored." Libr J

Wohlforth, Charles, 1963-
The whale and the supercomputer; on the
northern front of climate change. 1st ed. North
Point Press 2004 322p $25; pa $14   **305.8**
1. Climate 2. Arctic regions 3. Inuit
ISBN 0-86547-659-4; 0-86547-714-0 (pa)
                                       LC 2003-19448
"While the book's main focus is on climate change in
the Arctic, . . . [the author includes] discussions of the
worldview of the Inupiat in contrast to that of Western
scientists, the conflict between rural and urban culture,
the philosophy of science, and the machinations surrounding funding for science. Wohlforth writes beautifully, managing to wax philosophical while providing detailed notes for those skeptical of the points he makes."
Sci Books Films
Includes bibliographical references

Woodward, C. Vann (Comer Vann), 1908-1999
The strange career of Jim Crow. 3rd rev ed.
Oxford Univ. Press 1974 233p pa $17.95
hardcover o.p.   **305.8**
1. African Americans—Segregation
ISBN 0-19-514690-5 (pa)
First published 1955
An account of segregation in the South which ana-
lyzes events from 1877 to the Nixon administration.
Includes bibliographical references

305.9 Occupational and miscellaneous groups

Lehrer, Warren
Crossing the blvd; strangers, neighbors, aliens in
a new America; conceived, written, and compiled
by Warren Lehrer & Judith Sloan; photography
and design by Warren Lehrer. Norton 2003 393p
il map $35; pa $19.95 *   **305.9**
1. New York (N.Y.)—Social conditions
ISBN 0-393-05737-2; 0-393-32466-4 (pa)
                                       LC 2002-44353
"Based on interviews with participants in the crossing
the blvd project." Includes CD-ROM

Lehrer, Warren—*Continued*

This is a "look into the stories and lives of those living in the area of Queens BLVD, known as one of the most dangerous intersections in New York City. In the midst of this danger, the authors reveal a neighborhood where over 65 countries and 138 languages are represented, and show the people behind the numbers. With no analysis of the 80 interviews themselves, the authors allow the voices of the residents to resonate throughout the book, drawing readers into their tales of coming to and living in the US." Choice

Martínez, Rubén

The new Americans; photographs by Joseph Rodríguez. New Press 2004 251p il $25 *

305.9

1. United States—Immigration and emigration
ISBN 1-565-84792-X   LC 2003-70621

"This book, a companion to a PBS miniseries, details the lives of seven families who have recently arrived in the United States from the West Bank, Nigeria, the Dominican Republic, Mexico, and India." Libr J

"Masterfully evoking such diverse settings as a Palestinian wedding in Chicago, a raucous ball game in Guatemala City and a torpid migrant trailer camp in California, Martínez's writing is clear-eyed and incisive—and sometimes heartbreaking and hilarious." Publ Wkly

Includes bibliographical references

Moorehead, Caroline

Human cargo; a journey among refugees. H. Holt 2005 330p maps $26; pa $16 *

305.9

1. Refugees
ISBN 0-8050-7443-0; 0-312-42561-9 (pa)
          LC 2004-54239

The author "tours a number of refugee milieus, visiting, among others, Liberian refugees in Cairo, Mexican migrants waiting to cross into the United States, Mideastern refugees detained in Australian internment camps and Palestinian refugees still nursing hopes of returning to a homeland they have never seen. . . . Moorehead draws sympathetic portraits of individual refugees, replete with horror stories of the travails they fled and their precarious but hopeful efforts to build new lives, but also pulls back to examine what she says are the sometimes counterproductive policies of aid organizations and the indifference and callousness of Western governments." Publ Wkly

Includes bibliographical references

Nugent, Benjamin

American nerd; the story of my people. Scribner 2008 224p $20   **305.9**

1. Gifted children 2. Creative ability 3. Popular culture—United States
ISBN 978-0-7432-8801-9; 0-7432-8801-7

A study of the nerd in American popular culture and throughout history discussed in such contexts as the rise of online gaming, the science fiction club, ethnicity, Asperger's syndrome, autism, and high school and college debating.

"In a lighthearted, often laugh-out-loud manner, Nugent challenges us to reexamine our long-held belief of what it means to be a nerd and to reposition the nerd as, if not an American hero, at least an American antihero. Great fun and remarkably insightful between the laughs." Booklist

306 Culture and institutions

Ault, James M., Jr., 1946-

Spirit and flesh; life in a fundamentalist Baptist church. Knopf 2004 435p $27.95   **306**

1. Christian fundamentalism
ISBN 0-375-40242-X   LC 2003-65650

"In an attempt to understand the growing influence of the Christian Right . . . [the author] spent three years inside the world of a Massachusetts fundamentalist church he encountered while studying a variety of new-right groups. He observed—and where possible participated in—the daily lives of the members of a church he calls Shawmut River. His book takes us into worship services, home Bible studies, youth events, men's prayer breakfasts and Saturday work groups, after-Sunday-service family dinners, and bitter conflicts leading to a church split." Publisher's note

This "is a mix of ethnography and spiritual autobiography that deserves a hearing from fundamentalism's cultured despisers." N Y Times Book Rev

Bok, Derek Curtis

The trouble with government; [by] Derek Bok. Harvard Univ. Press 2001 493p $36; pa $20.50
          306

1. United States—Politics and government—1989-
2. Social policy—United States
ISBN 0-674-00448-5; 0-674-00832-4 (pa)
          LC 00-63476

This "volume seeks to explain and propose remedies for government failings that affect the wide range of areas in which America lags. Bok first considers and largely rejects common diagnoses of what ails American government—politicians and parties, the media and special interests—then proposes his own theory of the four basic weaknesses that afflict this country: poorly designed legislation, burdensome regulation, the neglect of working-class interests and failed antipoverty policies." Publ Wkly

Bork, Robert H., 1927-

Slouching towards Gomorrah; modern liberalism and American decline. ReganBooks 1996 382p il hardcover o.p. pa $14.95   **306**

1. Liberalism 2. Social values 3. United States—Social conditions
ISBN 0-06-039163-4; 0-06-057311-2 (pa)
          LC 96-31277

The author claims that "with its emphasis on outcomes vs. opportunity and on personal gratification, liberalism is destroying the cultural fabric of America." Libr J

"Forthright and magisterial, this is a fine summary of 'social conservatism.'" Booklist

Includes bibliographical references

Carter, Jimmy, 1924-
Our endangered values; America's moral crisis.
Simon & Schuster 2005 212p $25   **306**
   1. Social values 2. United States—Moral conditions
3. Christianity and politics 4. Church and state
5. United States—Politics and government—2001-
ISBN 0-7432-8457-7   LC 2005-54051
The author offers a "consideration of 'moral values' as
they relate to the important issues of the day. He puts
forward a . . . defense of separation of church and state,
and a . . . warning of where the country is heading as
the lines between politics and rigid religious fundamentalism are blurred." Publisher's note
"This book is an eloquent personal testament that deserves a wide readership, regardless of political affiliation." Libr J

De Grazia, Victoria
Irresistible empire; America's advance through
twentieth-century Europe. Belknap Press of
Harvard University Press 2005 586p il $29.95
                                306
   1. Consumption (Economics) 2. Europe—Foreign relations—United States 3. United States—Foreign relations—Europe
ISBN 0-674-01672-6   LC 2004-59943
The author "contends that U.S. companies—and
consumerism—have been making inroads in Europe for
the past hundred years. She argues that an early, and major, U.S. innovation treated foreign territories as exten-
sions of domestic markets. . . . De Grazia writes clearly,
giving an uncommon perspective on the ways and means
by which the U.S. and Europe drew close after WWII."
Publ Wkly
Includes bibliographical references

Dionne, E. J., Jr.
Stand up, fight back; Republican toughs,
Democratic wimps, and the politics of revenge.
Simon & Schuster 2004 243p $24   **306**
   1. Democratic Party (U.S.) 2. United States—Politics
and government—2001-
ISBN 0-7432-5858-4   LC 2004-45155
"Using the format of writing a letter to three friends—
a liberal, a moderate, and a conservative—political commentator Dionne analyzes the current American political
scene. . . . Dionne questions how a nation that tries to
keep to the center has gotten so divided." Booklist
The author "proffers perhaps the most cogent analysis
to date of why Democrats have lost the battle to the
right, and how they might regain control of the debate."
Publ Wkly
Includes bibliographical references

Encyclopedia of contemporary Chinese culture;
edited by Edward L. Davis. Routledge 2005
xxxiv, 786p $280; pa $80 *   **306**
   1. China—Civilization—Encyclopedias 2. China—Social life and customs—Encyclopedias
ISBN 0-415-24129-4; 0-415-77716-X (pa)
This "work focuses on the cultural developments in
mainland China over the last quarter century and also
covers aspects of contemporary culture in Hong Kong

and Taiwan. He classifies the 1,200 signed entries written by a team of 215 international specialists into 18 categories: architecture and space, education, ethnicity and
ethnic identity, fashion and design, film, food and drink,
health, language, literature, media, music, performing
arts, political culture, religion, society, sports and recreation, visual arts, and women and gender. . . . Davis's
book is an effective reference source for understanding
contemporary Chinese culture." Choice
Includes bibliographical references

Encyclopedia of social issues; editor, John K.
Roth. Marshall Cavendish 1997 6v il maps set
$459.95   **306**
   1. United States—Social conditions—Encyclopedias
ISBN 0-7614-0568-2   LC 96-38361
"This encyclopedia on current U.S. and Canadian social issues covers topics in government and politics, social policy, information, economics, human rights, health,
law, environment, religion, etc." Libr J

Faludi, Susan
The terror dream; fear and fantasy in post-9/11
America. Metropolitan Books 2007 351p $26 *
                                306
   1. September 11 terrorist attacks, 2001 2. American
national characteristics 3. Women—United States
ISBN 978-0-8050-8692-8; 0-8050-8692-7
                             LC 2007-12028
The author argues "that 9/11 killed off serious dialog
on gender equity in America, fostering instead the
crudest ideals of macho heroism and female acquies-
cence. . . . A book that deserves to be read; enthusiastically recommended for all libraries." Libr J
Includes bibliographical references

Flanders, Judith
Inside the Victorian home; a portrait of
domestic life in Victorian England. W.W. Norton
2004 xxviii, 499p il $34.95   **306**
   1. Great Britain—History—19th century 2. Great Britain—Social life and customs
ISBN 0-393-05209-5   LC 2003-27693
First published 2003 in the United Kingdom with title:
The Victorian house
"Room by room, Flanders walks us through the typical home of upper-middle-class Britain, explaining its
use, its décor, the habits of occupants, and more. The result is a genteel yet absorbing and thoroughly researched
book. . . . Fearsomely entertaining and yet a wonderful
addition to academic literature, this book is sure to become a classic." Libr J
Includes bibliographical references

Freud, Sigmund, 1856-1939
Totem and taboo; some points of agreement
between the mental lives of savages and neurotics;
translated and edited by James Strachey; with a
biographical introduction by Peter Gay. W.W.
Norton 1989 213p pa $13.95   **306**
   1. Totems and totemism 2. Psychoanalysis 3. Taboo
ISBN 978-0-393-00143-3; 0-393-00143-1
                             LC 91-120509

Freud, Sigmund, 1856-1939—*Continued*
Original German edition published 1912-1913 in Vienna; first United States edition, 1918
In the four essays in this volume Freud seeks to bridge the gap between psychoanalysis and such disciplines as social anthropology, philology and folklore
Includes bibliographical references

Johnson, Steven
Everything bad is good for you; how today's pop culture is actually making us smarter. Riverhead Books 2005 238p il $23.95; pa $14 *
306
1. Popular culture 2. Intellect
ISBN 1-57322-307-7; 1-59448-194-6 (pa)
LC 2005-42769
The author "makes the case that popular culture has become more intellectually challenging in the past 30 years. . . . He suggests that increases in IQ scores in the past century could be related to more challenging entertainment." Christ Sci Monit
This "is a brisk, witty read, well versed in the history of literature and bolstered with research." Time
Includes bibliographical references

King, Barbara J., 1956-
Evolving God; a provocative view on the origins of religion. Doubleday 2007 262p il $24.95
306
1. Religion 2. Social change
ISBN 978-0-385-51104-9; 0-385-51104-3
LC 2006-270101
The author "contends that religion, conceived as a system not of beliefs but of actions, not as theology but as worship, is a consequence of primate evolution. . . . In conclusion, she weighs the popular debate over evolution, noting high skepticism about human evolution and high belief in God, and questions the compulsion to choose either evolution or belief. Anyone who recognizes that compulsion, internal or external, may profit from reading this brilliant book." Booklist
Includes bibliographical references

Lasch, Christopher
The revolt of the elites; and the betrayal of democracy. Norton 1995 276p $22; pa $14.95
306
1. Elite (Social sciences) 2. Democracy 3. United States—Social conditions
ISBN 0-393-03699-5; 0-393-31371-9 (pa)
LC 94-37270
Lasch "argues that democracy today is threatened not by the masses, as José Ortega y Gasset (The Revolt of the Masses) had said, but by the elites. These elites—mobile and increasingly global in outlook—refuse to accept limits or ties to nation and place. Lasch contends that, as they isolate themselves in their networks and enclaves, they abandon the middle class, divide the nation, and betray the idea of a democracy for all America's citizens." Publisher's note
Includes bibliographical references

Lindsey, Brink
The age of abundance; how prosperity transformed America's politics and culture. Collins 2007 394p $26.95
306
1. United States—Social conditions 2. United States—Civilization
ISBN 978-0-06-074766-4; 0-06-074766-8
LC 2006-51753
On cover: Why the culture wars made us more libertarian
"With breathtaking analysis, Lindsey offers a dizzying look back at American economics, politics, and culture to examine the complexities of prosperity." Booklist
Includes bibliographical references

McKibben, Bill
Deep economy; the wealth of communities and the durable future. Times Bks. 2007 261p $25 *
306
1. Economic development 2. Community development
ISBN 0-8050-7626-3; 978-0-8050-7626-4
LC 2006-51100
"Challenging the prevailing wisdom that the goal of economies should be unlimited growth, . . . [the author] argues that the world doesn't have enough natural resources to sustain endless economic expansion. . . . McKibben's proposals for new, less growth-centered ways of thinking about economics are intriguing, and offer hope that change is possible." Publ Wkly
Includes bibliographical references

Mead, Margaret, 1901-1978
Coming of age in Samoa; a psychological study of primitive youth for Western civilisation; foreword by Franz Boas. Morrow 1928 297p il pa $14 hardcover o.p. *
306
1. Adolescence 2. Sex differences (Psychology)
ISBN 0-688-05033-6 (pa)
An anthropological study of adolescent Samoan girls

Morgan, Peter W., 1951-
The appearance of impropriety; how ethics wars have undermined American government, business, and society; [by] Peter W. Morgan, Glenn H. Reynolds. Free Press 1997 272p pa $16.95 hardcover o.p.
306
1. Political ethics 2. Business ethics 3. United States—Moral conditions
ISBN 0-7432-4266-1 (pa)   LC 97-19251
"The authors recall how the press and public became . . . aware of lies and cover-ups during Vietnam and Watergate. Since then, . . . [they argue], the entire country has grown obsessed with ethics. Instead of paying attention to real transgressions, however, [they maintain], government agencies and private businesses and institutions have concentrated on appearances." N Y Times Book Rev
"Examples the authors give, concerning plagiarism and election-posturing 'anti-crime' legislation, are so deliciously preposterous that the reader is well primed for the concluding recommendations for reform." Booklist
Includes bibliographical references

Reich, Robert B.
The future of success. Knopf 2001 289p $26; pa
$14   **306**
1. Work 2. Information society 3. Quality of life
ISBN 0-375-41112-7; 0-375-72512-1 (pa)
LC 00-40552
The author provides an "analysis of the new economy
and how it is affecting lives. . . . He argues that the current economic opportunities afforded by new communication, transportation, and information technologies have
produced a workforce that is unable to perform individual, family, and community roles effectively in a job market that is frenzied, economically divergent, and socially
stratified." Libr J
Includes bibliographical references

Underhill, Paco
The call of the mall; a walking tour through the
crossroads of our shopping culture. Simon &
Schuster 2004 227p $25.95; pa $14   **306**
1. Shopping centers and malls 2. Consumption (Economics) 3. Consumers
ISBN 0-7432-3591-6; 0-7432-3592-4 (pa)
LC 2003-64960
The author takes readers on a "tour of a typical Saturday at a large, regional mall. He examines the routes
there, the shopping center itself, the stores, food, entertainment, ambience. and the customers. He shows why
the mall is the way it is and how it could be improved.
He provides insight into how the stores are arranged,
how they display merchandise. and the different ways
that men and women respond to this environment." SLJ

Worldmark encyclopedia of cultures and daily
life. Gale Res. 1997 4v il maps set $375
306
1. Ethnology—Encyclopedias 2. Manners and customs—Encyclopedias
ISBN 0-7876-0552-2   LC 97-3278
Contents: v1 Africa; v2 Americas; v3 Asia & Oceania;
v4 Europe
Provides information on 500 cultures of the world,
covering twenty different areas of daily life including
clothing, food, language, and religion.
Includes bibliographical references

306.4   Specific aspects of culture

Ekirch, A. Roger, 1950-
At day's close; night in times past. Norton 2005
447p il $25.95 *   **306.4**
1. Night
ISBN 0-393-05089-0   LC 2005-2784
"This history finds Ekirch reminding us of how
preindustrial Westerners lived during the nocturnal hours,
when most were plunged into almost total darkness. . . .
A rich weave of citation and archival evidence, Ekirch's
narrative is rooted in the material realities of the past,
evoking a bygone world of extreme physicality and
preindustrial survival stratagems." Publ Wkly
Includes bibliographical references

Elliott, Carl
Better than well; American medicine meets the
American dream; foreword by Peter D. Kramer.
Norton 2003 xxi, 357p $26.95; pa $14.95
306.4
1. Social medicine 2. American national characteristics
3. Self-perception
ISBN 0-393-05201-X; 0-393-32565-2 (pa)
LC 2002-15947
The author "goes beyond cosmetic surgery to examine
enhancements such as antianxiety drugs, steroids, growth
hormones, cochlear implants, gene therapy, and Botox to
analyze why many Americans think that they have an
obligation to drive themselves to be better and better. Elliott argues that as we become obsessed with fitting in,
we are susceptible to peer pressure and marketing campaigns aimed at selling us products and procedures that
will make our lives 'better.'" Libr J
This is an "engaging and provocative book. . . . As
Elliott considers Americans' yearning for self-
improvement and fulfillment, he takes readers on a
refreshingly quirky journey, its twists and turns dotted
with cultural and literary references." Christ Sci Monit
Includes bibliographical references

Gross, Michael, 1952-
Starstruck: when a fan gets close to fame; [by]
Michael Joseph Gross. Bloomsbury 2005 239p
$23.95; pa $14.95   **306.4**
1. Fans 2. Celebrities 3. Popular culture
ISBN 1-58234-316-0; 1-59691-094-1 (pa)
LC 2004-30339
The author "interviews fans, collectors, celebrities and
publicists in an effort to paint a broad portrait of changing celebrity culture. . . . Gross's writing is honest and
humane, and his book is an entertaining look at modern
celebrity culture." Publ Wkly

Science, technology, and society; an encyclopedia;
Sal Restivo, editor in chief. Oxford University
Press 2005 xxiv, 701p $165   **306.4**
1. Science—Encyclopedias 2. Technology—Encyclopedias
ISBN 0-19-514193-8; 978-0-19-514193-1
LC 2004-31121
This work "examines the rise of scientific and technical knowledge such as computers, bioengineering, and
physics, . . . [and] explores the relationships between institutions in articles that address law, government, military, economics, media, religion, and more." Publisher's
note
"This is an excellent source for readers needing an
overview of societal issues raised by science, technology,
and medicine." Choice
Includes bibliographical references

306.43   Education

Kozol, Jonathan
Death at an early age; the destruction of the
hearts and minds of negro children in the Boston
Public schools. Penguin 1985 246p pa $15
306.43

Kozol, Jonathan—*Continued*
1. Discrimination in education 2. Public schools—Boston (Mass.) 3. African Americans—Education
ISBN 978-0-452-26292-8; 0-452-26292-5
"A Plume book"
First published 1967 by Houghton Mifflin
The author relates his experience as a fourth-grade teacher in 1964 at a predominantly black Boston school, emphasizing poorly trained teachers, biased text books, overcrowded conditions, prejudiced school administrators, and their effects upon the students.
Includes bibliographical references

306.44   Language

Lepore, Jill, 1966-
A is for American; letters and other characters in the newly United States. Knopf 2002 241p il $25; pa $13   **306.44**
1. English language—Social aspects 2. Americanisms 3. Sociolinguistics
ISBN 0-375-40449-X; 0-375-70408-6 (pa)
                              LC 2001-38057
The author "explores the significant and occasionally unsettling ways language was used to define national character and boundaries in the early American republic. Focusing on seven men—Noah Webster, Samuel F.B. Morse, William Thornton, Sequoyah, Thomas Gallaudet, Abd al-Rahman Ibrahima and Alexander Graham Bell—Lepore offers a scholarly analysis of how they devised alphabets, syllabaries, codes and signs." Publ Wkly
"Each man's story delivers a wealth of irony along with valuable history. . . . Some familiar accounts, some not well known, but all told with a fresh eye to their national significance." Booklist
Includes bibliographical references

Poole, Steven, 1972-
Unspeak: how words become weapons, how weapons become a message, and how that message becomes reality. Grove Press 2006 282p $23 *
                              306.44
1. Language and languages
ISBN 978-0-8021-1825-7; 0-8021-1825-9
                              LC 2006-40054
"Focusing on the use of specific words, Poole . . . examines how those in power manipulate language to hoodwink the public." Choice
"Thought-provoking analysis of an insidious trend." Booklist
Includes bibliographical references

306.7   Sexual relations

Bader, Michael J.
Arousal, the secret logic of sexual fantasies. Thomas Dunne Bks./St. Martin's Press 2002 293p $23.95; pa $14.95   **306.7**
1. Sexual behavior
ISBN 0-312-26933-1; 0-312-30242-8 (pa)
                              LC 2001-51290

"Bader covers how arousal works, how fantasies assist in arousal, the role of fantasies in therapy, and the social meaning of fantasies. Throughout, he gives numerous case studies, examples, and sensible and compassionate conjectures about particular fantasies and the fantasizing process. Bader is a clear, graceful writer, and he makes his points with rare facility in a way useful to both lay people and therapeutic professionals." Libr J
Includes bibliographical references

Barash, David P.
The myth of monogamy; fidelity and infidelity in animals and people; [by] David P. Barash, Judith Eve Lipton. Freeman, W.H. 2001 227p $24.95; pa $15   **306.7**
1. Sexual behavior 2. Marriage 3. Adultery
ISBN 0-7167-4004-4; 0-8050-7136-9 (pa)
The author offers "evidence that both sexes in supposedly monogamous species cheat, then segues into a . . . study of why faithless behavior is endemic. Ultimately, he concludes that cheating produces offspring of superior genetic quality and that genetic monogamy isn't 'natural,' not even for humans." Booklist
This is "guaranteed to entertain and may even pique thoughtful readers' interests." Sci Books Films
Includes bibliographical references

Brown, Louise, 1978-
The dancing girls of Lahore; selling love and hoarding dreams in Pakistan's ancient pleasure district. Fourth Estate 2005 311p $23.95 *
                              306.7
1. Prostitution 2. Women—Pakistan
ISBN 0-06-074042-6   LC 2004-63596
"Though their trade can be described with accuracy as prostitution, the dancing girls have an illustrious history: Beloved by emperors and nawabs, their sophisticated art encompassed the best of Mughal culture. . . . [The author] spent four years in the . . . study of the family life of a Lahori dancing girl." Publisher's note
The author "has a sociologist's eye and a novelist's appreciation of her surroundings and the human drama that plays out before her." N Y Times (Late N Y Ed)

The **Continuum** complete international encyclopedia of sexuality; edited by Robert T. Francoeur and Raymond J. Noonan; associate editors, Africa: Beldina Opiyo-Omolo . . . [et al.] ; foreword by Robert T. Francoeur; preface by Timothy Perper; introduction by Ira L. Reiss. Continuum 2004 1419p map $225 *
                              306.7
1. Sexual behavior
ISBN 0-8264-1488-5   LC 2003-6391
First published 1997-2001 in four volumes with title: The International encyclopedia of sexuality
"Covered here are the sexual attitudes and behavior of more than 60 countries . . . including most large and influential nations like the United States, China, Russia, South Africa, India, Japan, and Mexico. . . . This unique compilation of specialized knowledge is recommended for research collections in the social sciences, where it could be useful for reference as well as a secondary

The Continuum complete international encyclopedia of sexuality—*Continued*

source for cross-cultural research." Libr J

Includes bibliographical references

Hooks, Bell

Salvation; Black people and love. Morrow 2001
xxiv, 225p pa $12.95 hardcover o.p.

306.7

1. African Americans—Social life and customs
2. Interpersonal relations 3. Love

ISBN 0-06-095949-5 (pa)   LC 00-61648

The author contends "that there is a crisis of 'lovelessness' in the black community. . . . [In this exploration of love]she addresses its meaning in black experience today and offers a plan of action for 'black survival and self-determination.'" Libr J

Levine, Judith

Harmful to minors; the perils of protecting children from sex; foreword by Joycelyn Elders. University of Minn. Press 2002 xxxv, 299p $25.95

306.7

1. Sex education

ISBN 0-8166-4006-8   LC 2001-6553

"Levine argues that sex is not necessarily bad for minors, and that puritanical attitudes often backfire. . . . She notes the disturbing trend toward pathologizing young children's eroticized play and criticizes mainstream America for letting the Christian right steer sex education toward an emphasis on abstinence. Compounding that, she says, the right wing has expunged abortion discussions. . . . It's a good start to confronting some vital questions." Publ Wkly

Includes bibliographical references

Longing to tell; Black women talk about sexuality and intimacy; [compiled by] Tricia Rose. Farrar, Straus & Giroux 2003 415p $25; pa $15

306.7

1. African American women 2. Women—Sexual behavior

ISBN 0-374-19061-5; 0-312-42372-1 (pa)

LC 2002-32541

This "is a collection of 20 first-person narratives from a cross section of black women speaking frankly about a range of topics, such as coming-of-age, sexual abuse, drug addiction, marriage, divorce, AIDS, and interracial dating." Booklist

"By letting the women speak for themselves and following the histories with a passionate afterword, Rose provides a collection that is as compelling as it is sorely needed." Publ Wkly

Includes bibliographical references

Reinisch, June

The Kinsey Institute new report on sex; what you must know to be sexually literate; [by] June M. Reinisch with Ruth Beasley; edited and compiled by Debra Kent. St. Martin's Press 1990 xx, 540p il pa $18.95 hardcover o.p. *

306.7

1. Sexual behavior

ISBN 0-312-06386-5 (pa)   LC 90-41444

This volume offers information about sexual matters, divided into general areas, including "body image and self esteem, problems with sexual functioning, sex and aging, contraception, [and] sexually transmitted diseases." Libr J

Shlain, Leonard

Sex, time, and power; how women's sexuality shaped human evolution. Viking 2003 xx, 420p il $25.95; pa $16   **306.7**

1. Women—Sexual behavior 2. Evolution

ISBN 0-670-03233-6; 0-14-200467-7 (pa)

LC 2002-41186

The author "takes an evolutionary approach to solving the conundrums of misogyny and patriarchy, guiding his . . . readers through . . . speculations about the purpose of such seemingly impractical, even dangerous traits as bipedalism, menstruation, the perils of childbirth, and the helplessness of infants. . . . Lucid and compelling, Shlain asks startling and crucial questions about human nature and presents truly imaginative and mind-stretching answers." Booklist

Includes bibliographical references

Wolf, Naomi

Promiscuities; the secret struggle for womanhood. Random House 1997 xxx, 286p pa $15 hardcover o.p.   **306.7**

1. Girls—Sexual behavior 2. Women—Sexual behavior

ISBN 0-449-90764-3 (pa)   LC 96-46724

This "work centers on the way American culture of the late Sixties and Seventies created a generation of females torn between the need to express their sensuality and the desire to meet society's behavioral expectations. To illustrate her position, Wolf relies . . . on the coming-of-age experiences of herself, her friends, and acquaintances in her hometown, San Francisco." Libr J

"Wolf offers some astute and eminently realizable suggestions for a new approach to sexual education, even healing." Booklist

Includes bibliographical references

306.76   Sexual orientation

Chauncey, George

Why marriage? the history shaping today's debate over gay equality. Basic Bks. 2004 200p $22   **306.76**

1. Same-sex marriage 2. Gay men—Civil rights

ISBN 0-465-00957-3   LC 2004-14747

Chauncey, George—*Continued*
Contents: Introduction: Why marriage? -- The legacy of antigay discrimination -- Gay rights, civil rights -- How marriage changed -- Why marriage became a goal -- The present as history

This is a "wonderfully readable account of how the [same-sex marriage] issue emerged." N Y Times Book Rev

Includes bibliographical references

Encyclopedia of lesbian and gay histories and cultures. Garland 2000 2v il set $315
306.76
1. Homosexuality 2. Lesbianism
ISBN 978-0-8153-4055-3; 0-8153-4055-9
Contents: v1 Lesbian histories and cultures, Bonnie Zimmerman, editor; v2 Gay histories and cultures, George E. Haggerty, editor

"The volumes consist of short, signed entries arranged alphabetically. This set, which should become the standard in its field, will be a useful addition to all public and academic libraries." Am Libr

Encyclopedia of lesbian, gay, bisexual, and transgender history in America; Marc Stein, editor in chief. Thomson Learning 2003 3v set $380 *
306.76
1. Homosexuality 2. Lesbianism
ISBN 0-684-31261-1   LC 2003-17434
This set "includes approximately 545 articles ranging from short biographical entries to longer essays surveying topics such as the Stonewall riots, federal law and policy, same-sex institutions and AIDS. . . . Features include a guide to archival sources, a chronology/timeline, a historical overview essay and a comprehensive index." Publisher's note

"Stein puts together an impressive set. . . . This information is available elsewhere, but this resource gathers it in one easy-to-use source." Voice Youth Advocates

Includes bibliographical references

Faderman, Lillian
Gay L.A.; a history of sexual outlaws, power politics, and lipstick lesbians; [by] Lillian Faderman and Stuart Timmons. Basic Books 2006 431p il $27.50
306.76
1. Homosexuality 2. Los Angeles (Calif.) 3. Gay liberation movement
ISBN 978-0-465-02288-5; 0-465-02288-X
LC 2006-23470
This history of lesbian and gay life in Los Angeles "stretches from the humane tolerance of pre-contact indigenous peoples, through the 20th-century crisis years of homophobia and AIDS and ultimately into the victories and setbacks in this century. . . . Full of fascinating anecdotes (including much on Hollywood), wise and fair analysis, and significant and inspiring examples of courageous resistance recaptured from the unwritten histories of the past, Gay L.A. deserves a prominent place in every library." Libr J

Includes bibliographical references

Kaiser, Charles
The gay metropolis; the landmark history of gay life in America. Grove Press 2007 418p il pa $17
306.76
1. Gay men 2. New York (N.Y.)—History
ISBN 978-0-8021-4317-4; 0-8021-4317-2
First published 1997 by Houghton Mifflin
"Kaiser's history of American gay life and culture in the second half of the twentieth century centers on New York." Booklist
"Though Kaiser does not make a concerted or effective case for the existence of the borderless American gay metropolis that the title is meant to conjure, the decade-by-decade breakdown of people and events provides an excellent portrait of the urban gay community." Publ Wkly

Includes bibliographical references

Marcus, Eric
Is it a choice? answers to the most frequently asked questions about gay and lesbian people. 3rd ed. HarperSanFrancisco 2005 258p pa $14.95
306.76
1. Homosexuality 2. Gay men 3. Lesbians
ISBN 978-0-06-083280-3; 0-06-083280-0
LC 2005-52527
First published 1993
"Straightforward answers for both straight and lesbian/gay readers to fundamental questions about definitions and origins of homosexuality and bisexuality, lesbian and gay life, and lesbians and gay men in American culture. Highly useful." Libr J [review of 1993 edition]

Includes bibliographical references

Mondimore, Francis Mark, 1953-
A natural history of homosexuality. Johns Hopkins Univ. Press 1996 282p il pa $18.95 hardcover o.p.
306.76
1. Homosexuality 2. Sex (Biology)
ISBN 0-8018-5440-7 (pa)   LC 96-16191
This is a "summary of history, biology, psychology, and social issues regarding homosexuality." Libr J
"The information in the book is basic, accurate, wide-ranging, up-to-date, and compassionate." Choice

Includes bibliographical references

Robb, Graham
Strangers: homosexual love in the nineteenth century. W.W. Norton 2004 341p il $26.95; pa $15.95 *
306.76
1. Homosexuality
ISBN 0-393-02038-X; 0-393-32649-7 (pa)
LC 2003-66239
"In contrast to the general view of gay oppression and persecution and the Foucauldian view of the construction of homosexuality, Robb illustrates how gay men and women dealt with their sexuality, loved one another, and learned to live in the dominant cultures of 19th-century Britain, France, and Germany." Choice
The author "has produced a brilliant work of social archaeology. . . . In excavating the long-buried lives of our gay great-great-granduncles and lesbian great-great-

Robb, Graham—*Continued*

grandaunts, Robb has done more than make a major historical contribution. He has, as it were, provided their distant nieces and nephews, gay and straight, with a family tree that we have never had before." N Y Times Book Rev

Rudacille, Deborah

The riddle of gender; science, activism, and transgender rights. Pantheon Books 2005 xxiv, 355p $26; pa $15.95   **306.76**

1. Transsexualism

ISBN 0-375-42162-9; 0-385-72197-8 (pa)

LC 2004-55297

"In her assessment of the state of affairs in the transsexual community, Rudacille builds on the commentary that has accumulated since a Berlin physician (Magnus Hirschfeld) pioneered research on transsexuality in the 1920s, and especially since George Jorgensen Jr. became Christine Jorgensen and a worldwide sensation in the early 1950s. . . . Rudacille's work is uniquely informative, particularly about the history of transsexuality." Booklist

Includes bibliographical references

306.8   Marriage and family

Alter, Robert Mark

It's (mostly) his fault; for women who are fed up and the men who love them; foreword by Jane Alter. Warner Books 2006 359p $22.95; pa $13.99
306.8

1. Marriage counseling

ISBN   978-0-446-57777-9;   0-446-57777-4; 978-0-446-69525-1 (pa); 0-446-69525-4 (pa)

LC 2005-23754

The author argues "that males are (mostly) at the root of their relationship problems. Despite this amusing premise, his book is written for both men and women who want to improve their partnerships. . . . Candid and written in a refreshing, man-to-man, tell-it-like-it-is style, Alter's how-to manual presents the opportunity for men and women to work together to create mutually deep, intimate, and fulfilling connections." Libr J

Includes bibliographical references

Because I said so; 33 mothers write about children, sex, men, aging, faith, race, and themselves; from the editors of Mothers who think Camille, Peri, & Kate Moses. HarperCollins 2005 xxi, 372p $24.95; pa $13.95
306.8

1. Mothers

ISBN 0-06-059878-6; 0-06-059879-4 (pa)

LC 2004-62007

Contributors to this collection of essays on modern motherhood include "writers such as Janet Fitch, Mariane Pearl, Mary Roach, Susan Straight, Margaret Talbot, Rosellen Brown, Beth Kephart, Ariel Gore, and Ana Castillo." Publisher's note

"Women will appreciate the humor and candor, and men will gain insight into the stunning challenges of motherhood." Booklist

Includes bibliographical references

Brodey, Denise

The elephant in the playroom; ordinary parents write intimately and honestly about the extraordinary highs and heartbreaking lows of raising kids with special needs. Hudson Street Press 2007 235p $21.95   **306.8**

1. Handicapped children

ISBN 978-1-59463-035-4; 1-59463-035-6

LC 2006-39393

The author "uses her experiences as the mother of a four-year-old boy diagnosed with sensory integration dysfunction and childhood depression as a springboard to assemble a series of essays from parents of special-needs children across the country. . . . Parents of special-needs kids often feel isolated and criticized; in these pages, they will find a wise and understanding community." Libr J

Celani, David P.

Leaving home; the art of separating from your difficult family. Columbia University Press 2005 156p $24.95   **306.8**

1. Adult child abuse victims

ISBN 0-231-13476-2   LC 2004-51980

The author "explains how children in abusive or neglectful homes develop both wounded and hopeful selves and why they compulsively pick the worst possible mate or make self-destructive decisions. Full of compassion and encouragement, this book will prepare readers to leave home and to live a life free of interpersonal failures." Libr J

Includes bibliographical references

Cusk, Rachel, 1967-

A life's work; on becoming a mother. Picador 2002 c2001 213p $22; pa $13   **306.8**

1. Mothers 2. Parenting

ISBN 0-312-26987-0; 0-312-31130-3 (pa)

LC 2001-54894

First published 2001 in the United Kingdom

"Taking an unsentimental approach to one of the most dramatic changes in a woman's life, British novelist Cusk . . . dissects the process of new motherhood from a psychological and emotional perspective." Publ Wkly

"This is not a happy guide; instead, it is a penetrating, sometimes joyful and amusing, sometimes frightening and disturbing look at pregnancy and motherhood." Booklist

Engber, Andrea

The complete single mother; reassuring answers to your most challenging concerns; by Andrea Engber and Leah Klungness. 3rd ed. Adams Media 2006 xxiv, 439p il pa $14.95 *   **306.8**

1. Single parent family 2. Mother-child relationship 3. Parenting

ISBN 1-59337-490-9; 978-1-59337-490-7

LC 2005-21885

First published 1995

This handbook for single mothers offers "practical advice on meeting the challenges of parenting without partners. In part 1, Engber and Klungness look for the vari-

Engber, Andrea—*Continued*

ous ways women become single mothers . . . and the special demands of each situation. In part 2, the authors focus on how single moms can handle pregnancy and birth, maintaining a household and maintaining their self-esteem alone, and in part 3, they talk . . . about the day-today difficulties of 'raising terrific kids.' They address in part 4 relations outside the family unit." Booklist [review of 1995 edition]

Includes bibliographical references

Garner, Abigail

Families like mine; children of gay parents tell it like it is. HarperCollins 2004 256p hardcover o.p. pa $13.95 * **306.8**

1. Gay parents 2. Parent-child relationship
ISBN 0-06-052757-9; 0-06-052758-7 (pa)

LC 2003-56975

The author "examines growing up in a queer household from every angle, using her own experiences and those of about fifty other adult children of LGBT parents." Voice Youth Advocates

This book "should quickly become a mainstay resource for many family service agencies and public libraries serving LGBT patrons." Booklist

Includes bibliographical references

Gore, Al, Jr., 1948-

Joined at the heart; the transformation of the American family; [by] Al and Tipper Gore. Holt & Co. 2002 417p il $26; pa $16 **306.8**

1. Family
ISBN 0-8050-6893-7; 0-8050-7450-3 (pa)

LC 2002-27252

The authors "examine subjects as diverse as the increased divorce rate, the parent-teen gap, dual-income households and the health problems associated with sleep deprivation. They divide the book into themes, including love, communication, work, play and community, and show how these factors influence one another, taking a holistic approach to the underlying problems affecting today's families." Publ Wkly

Includes bibliographical references

Hite, Shere

The Hite report on the family; growing up under patriarchy. Grove Press 1995 xxiv, 424p pa $14 hardcover o.p. **306.8**

1. Family 2. Parent-child relationship 3. Sexual behavior
ISBN 0-8021-3451-3 (pa) LC 94-42157
First published 1994 in the United Kingdom

This study "based on some 3000 questionnaires completed by children and adults in 16 countries (50% from the U.S.), focuses on the child's developing psychosexual identity and the impact of this process on adulthood. . . . Her respondents' testimonies, organized around specific themes, touch on all manner of taboo subjects." Publ Wkly

Includes bibliographical references

Howey, Noelle

Dress codes of three girlhoods—my mother's, my father's, and mine. Picador 2002 332p $24; pa $14 **306.8**

1. Parent-child relationship 2. Transsexualism
ISBN 0-312-26921-8; 0-312-42220-2 (pa)

LC 2001-59060

This is a "look back at how teenager Howey and her mother struggled with her father's transformation from a bad-tempered dad to a loving transgendered woman." Libr J

"Howey manages to entertain, console, and enlighten readers. The book is impossible to ignore, and impossible to put down." SLJ

International encyclopedia of marriage and family; James J. Ponzetti, Jr., editor in chief. 2nd ed. Macmillan Ref. USA 2003 4v il set $495 * **306.8**

ISBN 0-02-865672-5 LC 2002-14107
First published 1995 with title: Encyclopedia of marriage and the family

This set "surveys the patterns of family life from an interdisciplinary and multicultural perspective. . . . The authoritative, often lengthy essays consider topics such as 'Abortion,' 'Adoption,' 'Asian-American Families,' 'Assisted Reproductive Technologies,' 'Gay Parents,' 'Homeless Families,' 'Intimacy,' 'Surrogacy,' and 'War/Political Violence.'" SLJ

Includes bibliographical references

Isay, Jane

Walking on eggshells; navigating the delicate relationship between adult children and their parents. Doubleday/Flying Dolphin Press 2007 240p $23.95 * **306.8**

1. Parent-child relationship
ISBN 978-0-7679-2084-1; 0-7679-2084-8

LC 2006-25378

This is a "guidebook on communicating with adult children. Using interviews with parents and children from ages 70 to 25, book editor Isay examines the wrenching difficulty of separating and staying close from both sides of the equation. . . . With empathy and support, Isay touches on areas that no other authors on this subject have. Highly recommended for all libraries." Libr J

Maybe baby; 28 writers tell the truth about skepticism, infertility, baby lust, childlessness, ambivalence, and how they made the biggest decisions of their lives; edited by Lori Leibovich; foreword by Anne Lamott. HarperCollins 2006 266p $24.95; pa $13.95 **306.8**

1. Parenting 2. Pregnancy 3. Childlessness
ISBN 0-06-073781-6; 978-0-06-073781-8; 0-06-073782-4 (pa); 978-0-06-073782-5 (pa)

LC 2005-52686

"This work, an outgrowth of a Salon.com series that ran in 2003, considers one of modern life's great issues: parenthood. Divided into three sections ('No,' 'Maybe,' and 'Yes'), the 28 essays personalize the choices found in broader society today. . . . These superbly written essays are recommended for all libraries, especially gender studies and sociology collections." Libr J

Moats, David R.
Civil wars; a battle for gay marriage; [by] David Moats. Harcourt 2004 288p $25; pa $14

306.8

1. Same-sex marriage
ISBN 0-15-101017-X; 0-15-603003-9 (pa)
LC 2003-19811
"Moats offers an insightful account of the fierce battle that led to the legalization of civil unions in Vermont in 2001." Booklist

My father married your mother; writers talk about stepparents, stepchildren, and everyone in between; edited and with an introduction by Anne Burt. W.W. Norton 2006 283p $24.95

306.8

1. Stepfamilies
ISBN 0-393-06088-8; 978-0-393-06088-1
LC 2005-31832
This anthology is a "look at blended families from the perspectives of 27 writers, including Jacquelyn Mitchard, Steve Romagnoli, Susan Cheever, Andrew Solomon, and Barbara Kingsolver, each of whom has experienced some version of blended family life. . . . Certain to stir discussion and deserving of a wide readership, this book reveals the human side of the ever-changing idea of family." Libr J

Pipher, Mary Bray
Another country; navigating the emotional terrain of our elders; [by] Mary Pipher. Riverhead Bks. 1999 xx, 328p pa $13.95 hardcover o.p.

306.8

1. Aging parents 2. Parent-child relationship
ISBN 1-57322-784-6 (pa)   LC 98-31877
The author is interested in studying "the aging process in order to promote meaningful connections between the generations and more cultural support for pursuing them. . . . Pipher describes strategies for dealing with illness, physical decline, the death of a husband or wife and the emotional problems that arise for both the elderly and their families. . . . One of the strengths of this excellent study is that Pipher includes examples of troubled as well as rewarding marital and parent/child relationships." Publ Wkly

Polhemus, Robert M.
Lot's daughters; sex, redemption, and women's quest for authority. Stanford University Press 2005 432p il $29.95 *

306.8

1. Lot (Biblical figure) 2. Oedipus complex 3. Father-daughter relationship
ISBN 0-8047-5051-3   LC 2004-19649
The author, "interested in 'canonized incest' that has created patterns, figures, and imagery of the older male and younger female in familial modeled relationships, here draws on the story of Lot and his women to argue that these relationship patterns live on in social history and popular culture." Choice
"Polhemus has written a sensitive, unsensationalist book which grips the reader's interest throughout. . . . It is a remarkable achievement." Times Lit Suppl
Includes bibliographical references

Roiphe, Anne Richardson, 1935-
Married; a fine predicament; [by] Anne Roiphe. Basic Bks. 2002 285p $25; pa $14.95

306.8

1. Marriage
ISBN 0-465-07066-3; 0-465-07067-1 (pa)
LC 2002-3506
The author writes "about how marriage and women's lives have changed since the 1950s, and about constants in human nature and the beleaguered but not yet improved upon institution of marriage. . . . Roiphe's rumination is a bit indulgent and soft with hearsay, yet it is timely, clever, candid, generous, and free of sentiment or trivialization." Booklist

Smith, Janna Malamud
A potent spell; mother love and the power of fear. Houghton Mifflin 2003 289p $25; pa $14

306.8

1. Child care 2. Mothers
ISBN 0-618-06349-8; 0-618-44673-7 (pa)
LC 2002-27632
This is an "examination of the powerful, visceral anxiety of mothers for their children's lives and welfare, and of its exploitation by experts and authorities interested in keeping mothers scared and in their place." N Y Times Book Rev
"Smith concludes by asserting that what the child needs most is a mother who is free, who believes she is living her own life, and who has adequate food, sleep, wages, education, safety, opportunity, institutional support, health care, child care, and emotional support. To say that the best mother is a free woman is simplistic yet radical when considered in historical context." Choice
Includes bibliographical references

Taffel, Ron
The second family; how adolescent power is challenging the American family; [by] Ron Taffel with Melinda Blau. St. Martin's Press 2001 204p $23.95; pa $12.95   **306.8**
1. Teenagers 2. Parenting 3. Popular culture
ISBN 0-312-26137-3; 0-312-28493-4 (pa)
LC 00-45993
In this work the author "tracks adolescents' defection from the 'first family' (Mom, Dad, and siblings) for the 'second family' (the peer group and pop culture). This is not, he argues, an angry or rebellious culture but a comfort-seeking one—be it with sex, drugs, recreation, body sculpture, and consumer items." Libr J
This book is "required reading for anyone interacting with adolescents today." Voice Youth Advocates

Tannen, Deborah
I only say this because I love you; how the way we talk can make or break family relationships throughout our lives. Random House 2001 xxvii, 336p pa $15.95 hardcover o.p.   **306.8**
1. Family 2. Communication
ISBN 0-345-40752-0 (pa)   LC 00-68851
The author "explores how caring and concern, connection and control are communicated between family mem-

Tannen, Deborah—*Continued*
bers." Booklist
"With lively prose and genuine concern for people, Tannen brings linguistic concepts—metamessage, reframing, indirect request—to bear on dozens of situations to help lay readers strenghten family ties." Libr J
Includes bibliographical references

Waite, Linda J.
The case for marriage; [by] Linda J. Waite and Maggie Gallagher. Doubleday 2000 260p pa $14.95 hardcover o.p.   **306.8**
1. Marriage 2. Married people 3. Single people
ISBN 0-7679-0632-2 (pa)   LC 00-22672
The authors defend marriage and enumerate what they consider the benefits of the institution.
"Waite and Gallagher overstate contemporary attacks on marriage, but they make a valid point that the revered institution has suffered stings lately." Booklist
Includes bibliographical references

Warner, Judith
Perfect madness; motherhood in the age of anxiety. Riverhead Books 2005 327p $23.95; pa $15 *   **306.8**
1. Mothers 2. Dual-career families
ISBN 1-573-22304-2; 1-594-48170-9 (pa)
                                    LC 2004-56615
"Writing from the perspective of her first few years of motherhood spent in France and her subsequent return to the U.S., Warner ponders the cultural factors driving the madness of pursuing perfect motherhood and the toll it is taking on American women." Booklist
Includes bibliographical references

Westheimer, Ruth
The value of family; a blueprint for the 21st century; [by] Ruth Wertheimer and Ben Yagoda. Warner Bks. 1996 211p pa $12.99 hardcover o.p.
                                         306.8
1. Family 2. Social values
ISBN 0-446-67336-6 (pa)   LC 96-15154
Westheimer "and Yagoda examine what constitutes a family, defined in the traditional sense of a household, and then recommend how the family can be helped by individuals, government, and business." Libr J
"A humane, levelheaded, eye-opening look at changing family dynamics." Publ Wkly
Includes bibliographical references

Winik, Marion
The lunch-box chronicles; notes from the parenting underground. Pantheon Bks. 1998 229p pa $15 hardcover o.p.   **306.8**
1. Single parent family 2. Parenting
ISBN 0-375-70170-2 (pa)   LC 97-26753
The author "covers death, bedtime stories, sexuality, God, team sports for geeks and other topics in this collection of personal essays on raising children." N Y Times Book Rev
"Winik brings together in winning fashion her decidedly nonmainstream attitude, laugh-out-loud humor, and refreshing candor." Booklist

Wolfson, Evan, 1957-
Why marriage matters; America, equality, and gay people's right to marry. Simon & Schuster 2004 242p $22 *   **306.8**
1. Same-sex marriage 2. Gay men—Civil rights
ISBN 0-7432-6458-4   LC 2004-302047
The author "presents his legal brief for equal marriage rights for gays. The book is structured like a brief, in that each chapter addresses a different aspect of marriage and dismantles arguments against gay marriage." Libr J
"Framing his argument strictly in terms of civil rights and grounding it in conventional definitions of the public significance of marriage, Wolfson is refreshing, smart, thorough and easy to follow." Publ Wkly
Includes bibliographical references

Yalom, Marilyn
A history of the wife. HarperCollins Pubs. 2001 441p il pa $14.95 hardcover o.p.   **306.8**
1. Marriage 2. Women—History
ISBN 0-06-093156-6 (pa)   LC 00-58153
The author examines the "history of women and marriage in the Western world." Publ Wkly
Yalom "has apparently written the first truly comprehensive history of the Western female spousal experience; indeed, there are precious few long views of either marriage or the family to which this book can be compared." Libr J

306.89   Separation and divorce

Moffett, Kay
Not your mother's divorce; a practical, girlfriend-to-girlfriend guide to surviving the end of an early marriage; [by] Kay Moffett and Sarah Touborg. Broadway Bks. 2003 259p pa $12.95
                                         306.89
1. Divorce
ISBN 0-7679-1350-7   LC 2003-58531
The authors "help young divorcées tackle both legal and emotional problems. . . . Overwhelming issues like mutual photographs, wedding rings, and family, as well as legal console, mediators, and even Internet divorce, are discussed with authority and sensitivity. The authors realize that each person is different and comes out her relationship with a different set of circumstances, so they also provide many personal stories—including their own." Libr J

Wallerstein, Judith S.
Second chances; men, women, and children a decade after divorce; [by] Judith S. Wallerstein and Sandra Blakeslee. Houghton Mifflin 2004 329p il pa $14   **306.89**
1. Divorce 2. Children of divorced parents
ISBN 0-618-44689-3; 978-0-618-44689-6
                                    LC 2004-273131
First published 1989 by Ticknor & Fields
In 1971 the author "began a study of 131 children and adolescents from 60 families and their divorcing parents, in Marin County, California. . . . The researchers

Wallerstein, Judith S.—*Continued*
reinterviewed all family members 18 months later, again
5 years after divorce, and again 10 years after divorce.
. . . 'Second Chances' is Ms. Wallerstein's account of
the course and consequences of divorce for these parents
and children." N Y Times Book Rev
Includes bibliographical references

306.9   Institutions pertaining to death

Encyclopedia of death and dying; edited by
Glennys Howarth and Oliver Leaman. Routledge
2001 xxii, 534p il $140   **306.9**
1. Death—Encyclopedias
ISBN 0-415-18825-3   LC 2001-19234
"In dictionary format, topics in historical, social, cultural, and technical areas are presented. . . . Biographical
entries and information on important associations and
journals are also included." Booklist
"This work will enrich all academic and public library
collections." Libr J
Includes bibliographical references and index

Handbook of death & dying; Clifton D. Bryant,
editor in chief. Sage Publications 2003 2v il set
$350   **306.9**
1. Death
ISBN 0-7619-2514-7   LC 2003-14864
"A Sage reference publication"
Contents: Vol.1 The presence of death - Vol.2 The response to death
This is "a collection of 103 comprehensive essays
clustered in 10 general areas. . . . In the first volume the
section 'Death in the Cultural Context' treats issues in
confronting death, with essays on fear of death, death in
popular culture, spiritualism, and more. The 12 essays
that make up 'Death in the Social Context' consider topics such as trends in mortality, accidental death, and terrorism. Suicide, capital punishment, euthanasia, and the
hospice movement are among other topics in the first
volume. The second volume deals with the response to
death. . . . The substantive essays are generally between
9 to 15 pages, with extensive bibliographies." Booklist

Macmillan encyclopedia of death and dying;
Robert Kastenbaum, editor in chief. Macmillan
Ref. USA 2002 c2003 2v set $250 *
                                                306.9
1. Death—Encyclopedias
ISBN 0-02-865689-X   LC 2002-5809
"The 327 signed entries . . . range in length from a
few paragraphs to several pages. . . . Types of entries
include causes of death . . . practices surrounding death
. . . individuals and events that have influenced the way
we think about death . . . and entries on the nature or
meaning of death from various multidisciplinary and
multicultural perspectives. . . . An appendix profiles and
gives contact information for 75 organizations active in
death-related education, research, advocacy, or other areas." Booklist

307   Communities

Belleville, Bill, 1945-
Losing it all to sprawl; how progress ate my
cracker landscape. University Press of Florida
2006 xx, 199p il (The Florida history and culture
series) $24.95   **307**
1. Urbanization 2. Cities and towns 3. Florida
ISBN 0-8130-2928-7; 978-0-8130-2928-3
                                          LC 2005-42434
The author "describes the gradual destruction of his
Cracker-style rural homestead and neighborhood near Orlando in central Florida. . . . Given that urban sprawl is
pervasive in the United States, this work should attract
a wide readership." Libr J
Includes bibliographical references

The **Encyclopedia** of community; from the village
to the virtual world; Karen Christensen and
David Levinson, editors. Sage Publications 2003
4v set $595   **307**
1. Community life—Encyclopedias
ISBN 0-7619-2598-8   LC 2003-9119
"In 500 entries, this encyclopedia focuses on the hard-
to-define concept of community and works to explore
and position that concept within many disciplines and
contexts. For collections supporting community studies
programs, it is a good choice." Booklist
Includes bibliographical references

Encyclopedia of the great Black migration; edited
by Steven A. Reich. Greenwood Press 2006 3v
il (Greenwood milestones in African American
history) set $325   **307**
1. African Americans—History—Encyclopedias
2. Internal migration—Encyclopedias
ISBN 0-313-32982-6; 978-0-313-32982-1
                                          LC 2005-33783
"This encyclopedia deals with its topic in social, economic, cultural, and political contexts, covering the migrations since the time of the Exodusters of 1879 moving
into Kansas and the Middle West to the return migrations
sparked by deindustrialization at the end of the twentieth
century." Booklist
Includes bibliographical references

Etzioni, Amitai
The spirit of community; the reinvention of
American society. Simon & Schuster 1994 323p il
pa $20.95   **307**
1. Community development 2. Social action
3. United States—Moral conditions
ISBN 0-671-88524-3; 978-0-671-88524-3
                                          LC 94-180840
First published 1993 by Crown
"The book is divided into theoretical chapters, which
come at the beginning and the end, and a series of topical chapters in which social analysis is interspersed with
case studies and examples. The topics progress from the
family to the school, to a view of local institutions, . . .
including religious institutions, as the mainstay of communities, and then to policy issues such as safety and
health." Commonweal
Includes bibliographical references

307.7 Specific kinds of communities

Duany, Andres
Suburban nation; the rise of sprawl and the decline of the American Dream; [by] Andres Duany, Elizabeth Plater-Zyberk, and Jeff Speck. North Point Press 2000 289p il $35; pa $18
307.7
1. Urbanization 2. Cities and towns 3. City planning 4. Urban renewal
ISBN 0-86547-557-1; 0-86547-606-3 (pa)
LC 99-52186
The authors, town planners associated with the New Urbanism movement, argue that American suburbs have failed on ecological, economic, aesthetic, and social levels. Drawing on their experiences with a variety of community development projects, they advocate a return to more traditional planning principles
Includes bibliographical references

Hunt, Tristram, 1974-
Building Jerusalem; the rise and fall of the Victorian city. Metropolitan Books/Henry Holt and Co. 2005 576p il $32.50
307.7
1. Cities and towns 2. Great Britain—History—19th century
ISBN 0-8050-8026-0
LC 2005-53116
First published 2004 in the United Kingdom
The author investigates "the social, cultural, and intellectual aspects of seven British cities that saw spectacular growth during the Victorian period." Libr J
This "is among the best—among the most ambitious, sweeping, original, and significant—books of urban history to be published in the past decade." Atl Mon
Includes bibliographical references

Mumford, Lewis, 1895-1990
The city in history; its origins, its transformation, and its prospects. Harcourt Brace & World 1961 657p il pa $29 hardcover o.p.
307.7
1. City and town life 2. Civilization—History
ISBN 0-15-618035-9 (pa)
More than a history of the forms and functions of the city throughout the ages, this is a portrait of the development of man as a religious, a political, an economic, a cultural, and a sexual being
Includes bibliographical references

The culture of cities. Greenwood Press 1981 586p il lib bdg $57.95
307.7
1. Cities and towns 2. City planning 3. Regional planning
ISBN 0-313-22746-2
LC 80-23130
First published 1938 by Harcourt Brace & Co.
Traces the growth of cities from medieval times to the twentieth century
Includes bibliographical references

Rybczynski, Witold
Last harvest; how a cornfield became New Daleville: real estate development in America from George Washington to the builders of the twenty-first century, and why we live in houses anyway. Scribner 2007 309p il $27
307.7
1. New Daleville (Pa.)—History 2. Real estate 3. Housing
ISBN 978-0-7432-3596-9; 0-7432-3596-7
LC 2006-52136
"The title refers to the final thing a farmer can reap from his land: a sale. Rybczynski . . . begins his tale where a sale leaves off, with 90 acres of land in semirural Chester County, Pa. That it will be developed is a foregone conclusion. . . . How that will happen makes for a gently entertaining and frequently enlightening tale with many players. There are no bad guys here, no rapacious developers or unscrupulous town council members. No one is preyed upon or done in. A lot of good intentions—along with plenty of completely random events—shape the building of the subdivision of New Daleville, a rather atypical 'typical' planned community." N Y Times Book Rev
Includes bibliographical references

Savageau, David
Places rated almanac; the classic guide for finding your best places to live in America. 7th (and 25th Anniversary) ed. Places Rated Books 2007 662p il map pa $24.99 *
307.7
1. Cities and towns—United States 2. Quality of life
ISBN 978-0-97931-990-7; 0-97931-990-0
First published 1981. Periodically revised. Publisher varies
This ranks "metropolitan areas as to factors that affect the quality of life: the arts, economics, education, crime, transportation, environment, housing, climate, and health care. Provides statistical information on American cities and towns. People planning to move will find it useful." Ref Sources for Small & Medium-sized Libr. 6th edition

Retirement places rated; what you need to know to plan the retirement you deserve. 7th ed. Wiley 2007 302p il pa $24.99 *
307.7
1. Retirement communities
ISBN 978-0-470-08959-0; 0-470-08959-8
First published 1983 by Prentice Hall Press with title: Places rated retirement guide. Periodically revised. Publisher varies
On cover: Completely revised and updated
Retirement areas in the U.S. are "ranked and compared for cost of living, climate, health care, economic factors, crime, services, cultural life, and recreation. Included are climate graphs, maps of retirement regions, comparison charts, and demographic profiles of each area." Publisher's note

310.5 General statistics—Serial publications

The **Europa** world year book 2008. 49th ed. Europa 2008 2v $1,295 *
310.5

The Europa world year book 2008—*Continued*
1. Statistics 2. Political science
ISSN 0956-2273
ISBN 978-1-85743-451-4; 1-85743-451-X
Annual. First published 1959 with title: The Europa year book
"The best annual directory of the nations of the world. For each country it includes demographic and economic statistics, and facts about constitution and government, political parties, press, trade and industry, publishers, etc. Also incorporates a substantive section with listings and information about international organizations." Ref Sources for Small & Medium-sized Libr. 6th edition

The **statesman's** yearbook 2009; the politics, cultures and economies of the world; edited by Barry Turner. Palgrave Macmillan 2008 xxxi, 1573p il $265 *   **310.5**
1. Statistics 2. Political science
ISSN 0081-4601
ISBN 978-1-4039-9278-9; 1-4039-9278-9
Also available online
Annual. First published 1864
"Descriptive and statistical information about international organizations and countries of the world-brief history, area, political status, economy, etc." N Y Public Libr. Ref Books for Child Collect. 2d edition
Includes bibliographical references

United Nations. Statistical Office
Statistical yearbook 2006. 51st ed. U.N. Publs. 2008 836p $150 *   **310.5**
1. Statistics
ISBN 978-9-2106-1228-9; 9-2106-1228-0
Also available CD-ROM version and online
First published 1948. Text in English and French
An annual giving statistics under the following headings: Population; Manpower; Production summary; Agriculture; Forestry; Fishing; Mining, quarrying; Manufacturing; Construction; Electricity, gas consumption; Transport; Communications; Internal trade; External trade; Balance of payments; International economic aid; Wages and prices; National income; Public finance; Housing statistics; Education, culture.

317.1   General statistics of Canada

Canadian almanac & directory 2008 = Répertoire et almanach Canadien; editorial director Laura Mars-Proietti. Grey House Pub. 2007 various paging il map $315 *   **317.1**
1. Canada—Directories 2. Almanacs
ISSN 0068-8193
ISBN 978-1-59237-220-1; 1-59237-220-1
Also available online
Annual. First published 1847. Publisher varies
"Contains reliable legal, commercial, governmental, statistical, astronomical, departmental, ecclesiastical, financial, educational, and general information." Guide to Ref Books. 11th edition

317.3   General statistics of the United States

CQ's state fact finder 2007; rankings across America. CQ Press 2007 $100; pa $60 *
                                                            317.3
1. United States—Statistics
ISSN 1079-7149
ISBN   978-0-87289-495-2;   0-87289-495-9;
978-0-87289-496-9 (pa); 0-87289-496-7 (pa)
Annual. First published 1993 under the authorship of Victoria Van Son. Authors vary
"This guide provides data, state by state, under such headings as *Business and Economy, Education, Energy, Health, Population, Recreation, Social Services,* and *Transportation.* . . . A second section of the book rearranges the data by state, so that the user can go directly to a particular state and see where it ranks in each of 325 areas. . . . This is a must purchase for all academic, high-school, and public libraries, where information like this is sure to be in demand." Booklist
Includes bibliographical references

Historical statistics of the United States; earliest times to the present; [by] Susan B. Carter . . . [et al.] Millennial ed. Cambridge University Press 2006 5v il set $990 *   **317.3**
1. United States—Statistics
ISBN 0-521-81791-9; 978-0-521-81791-2
                                            LC 2005-27089
Also available online
First published 1949 by U.S. Govt. Print. Off. with title: Historical statistics of the United States, 1789-1945
"Each of the 39 chapters begins with an essay on the 'quantitative history' of the topic and comments on the reliability of the data and possible limits to interpretation. Included are approximately 1900 tables and 170 maps, graphs, and time lines; the text is fully cross-referenced and indexed. . . . A bargain for all libraries supporting research." Libr J
Includes bibliographical references

United States. Bureau of the Census
County and city data book, 2007; a statistical abstract supplement; [by the] Economics and Statistics Administration, U.S. Census Bureau. Claitor's Publishing Division 2007 various paging map $75; pa $58   **317.3**
1. Cities and towns—United States 2. United States—Statistics
ISBN   978-1-59804-424-9;   1-59804-424-9;
978-1-59804-423-2 (pa); 1-59804-423-0 (pa)
Also available online
First published 1949 by U.S. Govt. Ptg. Office. Periodically revised
"Presents the latest available census figures for each county, and for the larger cities in the United States. Also has summary figures for states, geographical regions, urbanized areas, standard metropolitan areas, and unincorporated places." Guide to Ref Books. 11th edition

United States. Bureau of the Census—*Continued*

Statistical abstract of the United States, 2008; the national data book. 127th ed. U.S. Census Bureau 2007 994p il map $39; pa $35 *

317.3

1. United States—Statistics
ISBN   978-0-16-079584-8;   0-16-079584-2; 978-0-16-079581-7 (pa); 0-16-079581-8 (pa)
Also available online
Annual. First published for the year 1878
"Compendium of statistics on the social, political and economic organization of the U.S. presented in tables. Lists other sources of such information." N Y Public Libr. Ref Books for Child Collect. 2d edition

320   Political science

Aristotle, 384-322 B.C.

Politics. Oxford University Press 1998 480p (Oxford world's classics) pa $12.95 *

320

1. Political science
ISBN 978-0-19-283393-8
"Discussion of public affairs by the most eminent of the Greek philosophers in terms applicable to many of the problems of modern political science." Pratt Alcove

Encyclopedia of politics; the left and the right; Rodney P. Carlisle, general editor. Sage Reference 2005 2v il map set $295 *

320

1. Right and left (Political science)—Encyclopedias 2. Political science—Encyclopedias
ISBN 1-4129-0409-9   LC 2005-2334
"In this two-volume set, movements, ideologies, political parties, and people are split into Left and Right volumes. Thus, affirmative action, environmentalism, and Thomas Jefferson meet in Volume 1: The Left, while capitalism, unilateralism, and George Will appear in Volume 2: The Right. . . . The work is a solid and lasting contribution to the understanding of the issues that divide us politically." Libr J
Includes bibliographical references

Kaplan, Robert D.

Warrior politics; why leadership demands a pagan ethos. Random House 2002 xxii, 198p $22.95; pa $12   **320**
1. International relations 2. Leadership 3. Political ethics
ISBN 0-375-50563-6; 0-375-72627-6 (pa)
                                LC 2001-31862
"Integrating classic and contemporary scholarship, the author argues that the ills of the twentieth century are 'less unique than we think' and draws parallels between the complacency of Rome at its height and that of the U.S." Booklist
"This is a provocative, smart and polemical work that will stimulate lively discussion." Publ Wkly
Includes bibliographical references

Kennedy, Edward Moore, 1932-

America back on track; [by] Edward M. Kennedy. Viking 2006 210p il $24.95

320

1. United States—Politics and government—2001-
ISBN 0-670-03764-8; 978-0-670-03764-3
                                LC 2006-44717
The author "offers his analysis of how and why the nation has gone astray from its values and principles and how it can recover. . . . Whether Kennedy fans or not, readers will appreciate his heartfelt concerns about the nation's direction and the ideals we all share." Booklist
Includes bibliographical references

Machiavelli, Niccolò, 1469-1527

The prince. Knopf 1992 xxxi, 190p (Everyman's library) $16 *   **320**
1. Political science 2. Political ethics
ISBN 0-679-41044-9   LC 91-53225
Also available from the University of Chicago Press and in paperback from Penguin Bks.
Written in 1513
"A handbook of advice on the acquisition, use, and maintenance of political power, dedicated to Lorenzo de Medici." Haydn. Thesaurus of Book Dig

Paine, Thomas, 1737-1809

Rights of man; and, Common sense. Knopf 1994 lii, 306p $19 *   **320**
1. Political science 2. France—History—1789-1799, Revolution 3. United States—Politics and government—1775-1783, Revolution
ISBN 0-679-43314-7   LC 94-5989
"Everyman's library"
This volume combines Rights of man with Common sense which was "published anonymously at Philadelphia (Jan. 10, 1776). . . . Over 100,000 copies were sold by the end of March, and it is generally considered the most important literary influence on the movement for independence." Oxford Companion to Am Lit. 5th edition
Includes bibliographical references

Reich, Robert B.

Supercapitalism; the transformation of business, democracy, and everyday life. Alfred A. Knopf 2007 272p il $25   **320**
1. Democracy 2. Capitalism 3. Lobbying 4. United States—Economic conditions
ISBN 978-0-307-26561-6; 0-307-26561-7
                                LC 2007-02471
The author "urges us to rebalance the roles of business and government. Power, he writes, has shifted away from us in our capacities as citizens and toward us as consumers and investors. While praising the spread of global capitalism, he laments that supercapitalism has brought with it alienation from politics and community. The solution: to separate capitalism from democracy, and guard the border between them. . . . Provocatively argued, this book could help begin a necessary national conversation." Publ Wkly
Includes bibliographical references

320.025   Political science— Directories

Government phone book USA; a comprehensive guide to federal, state, county, and local government offices in the United States; editorial data provided by Carroll Publishing Co. 16th ed. Omnigraphics 2008 2538p map lib bdg $317 *   **320.025**
1. State governments—Directories
ISSN 1091-9643
ISBN 978-0-7808-0696-2; 0-7808-0696-4
Annual. First published 1992 with title: The Government directory of addresses and telephone numbers
This is a "compilation of more than 100,000 listings, giving names, mailing addresses, and telephone numbers for key offices and officials at every level of government. Each of the three sections (federal, state, and city and county) begins with quick reference listings of frequently called numbers, abbreviations, area codes, etc. Keyword indexes facilitate access to federal and states offices." Guide to Ref Books. 11th edition
"Despite ever-increasing access to directory information on the Internet, comprehensive direct contact information for government offices at all levels is still often time-consuming to collate, making this set a useful addition to reference collections." Am Ref Books Annu, 2006

Washington information directory 2008-2009. Congressional Quarterly 2008 1008p $165 *
                                                 320.025
ISSN 0887-8064
ISBN 978-0-872899-46-9; 0-872899-46-2
Annual. First published 1975/76
"Lists names, telephone numbers, addresses, and responsibilities of 5,000 key personnel and agencies, both private and governmental, in the Washington, DC area; includes detailed indexes." N Y Public Libr Book of How & Where to Look It Up

320.03   Political science— Encyclopedias and dictionaries

The **Oxford** guide to the United States Government; edited by John J. Patrick, Richard M. Pious, Donald A. Ritchie. Oxford Univ. Press 2001 802p $35   **320.03**
1. United States—Politics and government—Encyclopedias
ISBN 0-19-514273-X   LC 00-51024
"In this alphabetical encyclopedia on topics relating to both the present activities and history of the U.S. government, entries include biographies of presidents and vice presidents, selected First Ladies and members of congress, and all Supreme Court justices who have ever served. Other types of biographical entries are those of unofficial groups of people who have played important roles in American government and history. . . . There are also articles on the various departments of the federal government; important historical events . . . issues and concepts . . . laws and decisions; and Supreme Court cases." Booklist
"This solid reference work is highly recommended for public, academic, and high school libraries." Libr J
Includes bibliographical references

320.1   The state

Cicero, Marcus Tullius, 106-43 B.C.
The republic; and, The laws; [by] Cicero; translated by Niall Rudd; with an introduction and notes by Jonathan Powell and Niall Rudd. Oxford University Press 1998 xliii, 242p (Oxford world's classics) pa $12.95   **320.1**
1. Political science 2. State, The 3. Rome—History
ISBN 978-0-19-283236-8; 0-19-283236-0
                                          LC 97-23394
"Cicero's The Republic is an impassioned plea for responsible government written just before the civil war that ended the Roman Republic in a dialogue following Plato. Drawing on Greek political theory, the work embodies the mature reflections of a Roman ex-consul on the nature of political organization, on justice in society, and on the qualities needed in a statesman. Its sequel, The Laws, expounds the influential doctrine of Natural Law, which applies to all mankind, and sets out an ideal code for a reformed Roman Republic, already half in the realm of utopia." Publisher's note
Includes bibliographical references

Hobbes, Thomas, 1588-1679
Leviathan; edited with an introduction and notes by J. C. A. Gaskin. Oxford University Press 1998 lv, 508p pa $9.95 *   **320.1**
1. Political science 2. State, The
ISBN 978-0-19-283498-0; 0-19-283498-3
                                          LC 99-178169
First published 1651
"A treatise on the origin and ends of government. . . . This work, a defense of secular monarchy, written while the Puritan Commonwealth ruled England, contains Hobbes's famous theory of the sovereign state." Benet's Reader's Ency. 4th edition

Locke, John, 1632-1704
Two treatises of government; and, A letter concerning toleration; edited and with an introduction by Ian Shapiro; with essays by John Dunn, Ruth Grant, Ian Shapiro. Yale University Press 2004 358p (Rethinking the Western tradition) pa $17 *   **320.1**
1. Political science 2. State, The 3. Toleration
ISBN 0-300-10017-5
Two treatises of government first published 1690; A letter concerning tolerance first published 1689
This book contains the complete texts of Locke's *Two treatises of government* and *A letter concerning toleration*, with essays from several scholars discussing the works. In *Letter*, the author argues that religion and government should be considered separate institutions and that tolerance of multiple religious groups can ensure the stability of a civil society. Locke's *Two treatises*, written in "defense of the Glorious Revolution, revealed his belief in the natural goodness and cooperative spirit of man

Locke, John, 1632-1704—*Continued*
and his theory that the state should operate according to
natural laws of reason and tolerance. He advocated religious tolerance and rights to personal property." Benet's
Reader's Ency. 4th edition
Includes bibliographical references

Rousseau, Jean-Jacques, 1712-1778
The social contract; translated by Maurice
Cranston. Penguin Books 2006 167p pa $10 *
                                                        320.1
1. Political science
ISBN 978-0-14-303749-1; 0-14-303749-8
                                        LC 2006-43772
First published 1762
"A treatise on the origins and organization of govern-
ment and the rights of citizens. Rousseau's thesis states
that, since no man has any natural authority over another,
the social contract, freely entered into, creates natural re-
ciprocal obligations between citizens." Benet's Reader's
Ency. 4th edition
Includes bibliographical references

320.5   Political ideologies

Atkins, Stephen E.
Encyclopedia of modern worldwide extremists
and extremist groups. Greenwood Press 2004
xxviii, 404p il $75 *   **320.5**
1. Radicalism 2. Right and left (Political science)
3. Cults
ISBN 0-313-32485-9   LC 2003-64256
Companion volume to Encyclopedia of modern American extremists and extremist groups (2002)
"Focusing on post-1945, with 85 percent of the information coming from the period since 1980, the 285 entries encompass people and organizations on every continent, many not widely known. . . . The arrangement is
alphabetical, with *see* and *see also* references leading the
reader futher. The information is accurate, clearly written, and relatively current. . . . It is also objective and
balanced." Booklist
Includes bibliographical references

Dean, John W. (John Wesley), 1938-
Conservatives without conscience. Viking 2006
246p $25.95   **320.5**
1. Republican Party (U.S.) 2. Conservatism 3. United
States—Politics and government—2001-
ISBN 0-670-03774-5; 978-0-670-03774-2
                                        LC 2006-45705
The author "argues that some leaders of the Republican Party and of the conservative movement generally
are authoritarian personalities without conscience." Libr
J
Dean offers "a penetrating and highly disturbing portrait of many of the major players in Republican politics
and power. . . . Readers of all political perspectives will
find this book riveting." Booklist
Includes bibliographical references

Halstead, Ted
The radical center; the future of American
politics; [by] Ted Halstead and Michael Lind.
Doubleday 2001 264p $24.95; pa $13
                                                        320.5
1. United States—Politics and government—1989-
ISBN 0-385-50045-9; 0-385-72029-7 (pa)
                                        LC 2001-28285
"According to the authors, the basic problem [in contemporary politics] is that the two dominant parties have
been captured by their extremes. 'Instead of expanding
their voter bases, both parties have allowed themselves to
be taken hostage by narrow pressure groups on certain
defining issues,' Republicans by 'social conservatives
and economic libertarians' and Democrats by 'a constellation of aggrieved minority groups and public employee
unions.' . . . Halstead and Lind propose a new 'center'
that's not halfway between right and left but outside the
standard range of political debate." N Y Times Book
Rev
"Sure to have its detractors across the political spectrum, this book adds many fresh insights to our currently
stale political discourse." Libr J
Includes bibliographical references

Micklethwait, John
The right nation; conservative power in
America; [by] John Micklethwait and Adrian
Wooldridge. Penguin Press 2004 450p il maps
$25.95; pa $16   **320.5**
1. Conservatism 2. Right and left (Political science)
3. United States—Politics and government—20th century
ISBN 1-594-20020-3; 0-14-303539-8 (pa)
                                        LC 2003-70749
The authors' "analysis shows that American conservatives differ from their European counterparts. While both
are nationalistic and suspicious of state power, preferring
liberty over equality, American conservatives are more
liberal in regard to hierarchy, pessimism, and elitism.
. . . Political junkies on both sides of the political spectrum will enjoy and gain from the analysis." Libr J
Includes bibliographical references

The **neocon** reader; edited, with and [sic]
introduction by Irwin Stelzer. Grove Press 2005
328p pa $15 *   **320.5**
1. Conservatism
ISBN 0-8021-4193-5   LC 2004-54063
Published simultaneously in the United Kingdom under the title: Neoconservatism
This is a "collection of essays that reflect the breadth
and depth of neo-conservative thought. Among the contributors are academics James Q. Wilson, Robert Kagan,
and both Kristol (the father of neo-conservatism) and his
son, William Kristol . . . journalists David Brooks,
Charles Krauthammer, and George Will, and former and
current political figures such as Jeane Kirkpatrick and
Condoleeza Rice. The essays are informative and challenging and, taken as a whole, present a reasonably complete portrait of the neo-conservative approach." Libr J
Includes bibliographical references

Pipes, Daniel, 1949-
Militant Islam reaches America. Norton 2002
309p $25.95; pa $15.95 *   **320.5**
1. Islamic fundamentalism 2. Muslims—United States
3. Islam and politics 4. Terrorism
ISBN 0-393-05204-4; 0-393-32531-8 (pa)
LC 2002-6482
"Pipes argues that Islam is not an inherent threat to
Western civilization, but that militant Islam . . . is the
greatest threat since the cold war. He goes on to explore
the threats posed to America by an influx of Muslim immigrants, extol the benefits of racial profiling, and argue
that the only viable form of Islamic belief is 'secularist'
Islam, which embraces Western values and eschews traditional Islamic ones. . . . It's controversial and often interesting stuff." Booklist
Includes bibliographical references

321   Systems of governments and states

More, Sir Thomas, Saint, 1478-1535
Utopia; translated with an introduction and notes
by Paul Turner. Reissued with new and updated
editorial material. Penguin Books 2003 xxviii,
135p (Penguin classics) pa $9 *   **321**
1. Utopias
ISBN 0-14-044910-8; 978-0-14-044910-5
LC 2003-267785
Originally published 1516 in Latin; 1551 in English
In his study of the ideal state, "More assigns the narrative to a Raphael Hythloday 'Hythloday' is Greek for
'talker of nonsense'). . . . Book I treats of the evils of
the world and asserts the need for an ideal commonwealth, which Book II describes." Haydn. Thesaurus of
Book Dig
Includes bibliographical references

321.8   Democratic government

Feldman, Noah, 1970-
After Jihad; America and the struggle for
Islamic democracy. Farrar, Straus and Giroux 2003
260p $24; pa $14   **321.8**
1. Islam and politics 2. United States—Foreign relations—Middle East 3. Middle East—Foreign relations—United States
ISBN 0-374-17769-4; 0-374-52933-7 (pa)
LC 2002-192524
Feldman "wonders if democracy 'can be made to
flourish in the lands where Islam prevails?' The answer,
according to the author, is a resounding yes. Further-
more, he argues . . . that the West in general and the
U.S. in particular must encourage democratic growth
even at the expense of existing relations with autocratic
Islamic regimes viewed as our traditional allies. . . .
Certain to spur debate, this thought-provoking discourse
couldn't be published at a more appropriate time."
Booklist
Includes bibliographical references

Zakaria, Fareed
The future of freedom; illiberal democracy at
home and abroad. Norton 2003 286p $24.95
321.8
1. Democracy 2. Political science
ISBN 0-393-04764-4   LC 2002-153051
Drawing on history, political philosophy, and current
affairs, Zakaria investigates the impact of democratization on politics, economics, and culture. He challenges
the notion that democracy automatically promotes liberty
"In his brave and ambitious book, Fareed Zakaria has
updated Tocqueville. 'The Future of Freedom' is brave
because its central conclusion—that liberty is threatened
by an excess of democracy—is deeply unfashionable and
easily misrepresented." N Y Times Book Rev
Includes bibliographical references

321.9   Authoritarian government

Arendt, Hannah
Origins of totalitarianism. new ed with added
prefaces. Harcourt Brace Jovanovich 1973 xliii,
527p pa $19 *   **321.9**
1. Totalitarianism 2. Imperialism 3. Antisemitism
ISBN 0-15-670153-7
Also published as separate paperbacks with titles:
Antisemitism; Imperialism; Totalitarianism; the first and
third titles are available
"A Harvest book"
First published 1951 in the United Kingdom with title:
The burden of our time
In this book, the author documents her "belief that
Nazism and Communism had their roots in the anti-
Semitism and imperialism of the 19th century." Benet's
Reader's Ency. 4th edition
Includes bibliographical references

Paxton, Robert O.
The anatomy of fascism; [by] Robert Paxton.
Knopf 2004 321p $26; pa $15 *   **321.9**
1. Fascism
ISBN 1-4000-4094-9; 1-4000-3391-8 (pa)
LC 2004-100489
The author "shows . . . why fascists came to power
in some countries and not others, and explores whether
fascism could exist outside the early-twentieth-century
European setting in which it emerged." Publisher's note
"While there are countless studies on fascism, readers
will be hard pressed to find anything more in-depth from
a scholar with Paxton's credentials." Libr J
Includes bibliographical references

322   Relation of the state to organized groups and their members

Balmer, Randall Herbert
Thy kingdom come; how the religious right
distorts the faith and threatens America, an
Evangelical's lament; [by] Randall Balmer. Basic
Books 2006 xxviii, 242p $24   **322**

Balmer, Randall Herbert—*Continued*
1. Evangelicalism 2. Christianity and politics
3. Conservatism
ISBN 0-465-00519-5; 978-0-465-00519-2
"Describing himself as 'a jilted lover' whose evangelical faith 'has been hijacked by right-wing zealots,' Balmer accuses those zealots of distorting the Gospel, ignoring the legacy of nineteenth-century evangelical activism, and failing to appreciate 'the genius' of the First Amendment." Booklist

Carter, Stephen L.
God's name in vain; how religion should and should not be involved in politics. Basic Bks. 2000 248p pa $15 hardcover o.p. **322**
1. Religion and politics 2. Church and state
ISBN 0-465-00887-9 (pa) LC 00-33741
The author "argues that religion mustn't and can't be walled out of politics but that church and clergy involvement in political parties only sullies religion. One of the most important books about freedom of religion of this, or perhaps any, era." Booklist
Includes bibliographical references

Djupe, Paul A.
Encyclopedia of American religion and politics; [by] Paul A. Djupe and Laura R. Olson. Facts on File 2003 512p il (Facts on File library of American history) $85 **322**
1. Religion and politics 2. United States—Religion—Encyclopedias
ISBN 0-8160-4582-8 LC 2002-33921
"An A-to-Z reference covering all facets of American politics and religion, from the early days of the American republic to the rise of the political power of the Christian Right. More than 600 entries cover key religious and political leaders, important historical events, descriptions of court cases, concepts, and religious denominations." Publisher's note
"The encyclopedia is timely and accessible. . . . Recommended for most reference collections in public libraries." Libr J
Includes bibliographical references

Feldman, Noah, 1970-
Divided by God; America's church-state problem—and what we should do about it. Farrar, Straus and Giroux 2005 306p $25 * **322**
1. Church and state
ISBN 0-374-28131-9 LC 2005-07064
The author "traces the evolution of the role of religion in American political life from the Colonial period to the present, paying particular attention to the development of legal doctrines." Libr J
"Intelligently respectful of both secularist and religious camps, this is the ideal book with which to ponder the Supreme Court's recent Ten Commandments decisions and to hope for balance in the future of American church-state relations." Booklist
Includes bibliographical references

Meacham, Jon
American gospel; God, the founding fathers, and the making of a nation. Random House 2006 399p il $23.95; pa $15.95 * **322**
1. Religion and politics 2. United States—Religion
ISBN 1-4000-6555-0; 978-1-4000-6555-4; 0-8129-7666-5 (pa); 978-0-8129-7666-3 (pa)
LC 2006-41161
This book "tells the story of how the Founding Fathers viewed faith, and how they ultimately created a nation in which belief in God is a matter of choice." Publisher's note
"Mr. Meacham's invaluable book serves as a lodestar for original thought on—the American gospel." Natl Rev
Includes bibliographical references

322.4 Political action groups

Alinsky, Saul
Rules for radicals; a practical primer for realistic radicals; by Saul D. Alinsky. Random House 1971 196p pa $12 hardcover o.p. **322.4**
1. Community organization 2. Radicalism
ISBN 0-679-72113-4 (pa)
The author discusses how radicals should organize and work within the system to effect social change
Includes bibliographical references

Atkins, Stephen E.
Encyclopedia of modern American extremists and extremist groups. Greenwood Press 2002 xxiv, 375p $74.95 * **322.4**
1. Radicalism 2. Right and left (Political science)
ISBN 0-313-31502-7 LC 2001-57729
"An Oryx book"
This is "a reference source that lists 275 of the most influential and significant domestic extremists, organized groups, and extreme events. . . . Here they are divided into three categories: political, religious, and economic/social. While the book covers activities since the 1950s, three quarters of the entries focus on the period from 1980 to 2001." Libr J
"This is an excellent reference tool." Recomm Ref Books for Small & Medium-sized Libr & Media Cent, 2003
Includes bibliographical references

Bushart, Howard L.
Soldiers of God; white supremacists and their holy war for America; by Howard L. Bushart, John R. Craig, and Myra Barnes. Kensington Bks. 1998 308p il pa $15 hardcover o.p. **322.4**
1. White supremacy movements 2. Racism 3. United States—Race relations
ISBN 1-57566-659-6 (pa) LC 97-74364
"Through dozens of interviews with members involved in various supremacists organizations such as the Ku Klux Klan and Aryan Nation, the authors look at the motivations that drive individuals to support these extremist associations." Publ Wkly
"The authors should be commended for their even-

Bushart, Howard L.—*Continued*

handed reporting of this inflammatory issue. . . . This book is a clear window into the mind of the white supremacist." Libr J

Includes bibliographical references

Chalmers, David Mark

Hooded Americanism: the history of the Ku Klux Klan. 3rd ed. Duke Univ. Press 1987 c1981 477p il pa $24.95 hardcover o.p.   **322.4**

1. Ku Klux Klan

ISBN 0-8223-0772-3 (pa)   LC 86-29133

First published 1965 by Doubleday; this is a reissue of the 1981 edition published by Watts

This book recounts the history of the Klan. It describes the sociological and psychological forces behind the Klan, and sets forth its dogmas

"The book is written in a breezy, journalistic style. . . . Especially instructive and sobering is Chalmers' account of the role of the Klan in politics." J Am Hist

Includes bibliographical references

Esposito, John L.

Unholy war; terror in the name of Islam. Oxford Univ. Press 2002 196p hardcover o.p. pa $15.95   **322.4**

1. Terrorism 2. Islam and politics 3. United States—Foreign opinion

ISBN 0-19-515435-5; 0-19-516886-0 (pa)

     LC 2001-58009

The author "explains the teachings of Islam—the Qur-an, the example of the Prophet, Islamic law—about jihad or holy war, the use of violence, and terrorism. He chronicles the rise of extremist groups and examines their frightening worldview and tactics." Publisher's note

"Engaging, evenhanded, and highly readable . . . this is essential reading for every concerned citizen and all those who wish to gain a deeper understanding of contemporary Islam and its internal struggles." Libr J

Includes bibliographical references

Ezekiel, Raphael S., 1931-

The racist mind; portraits of American Neo-Nazis and Klansmen. Viking 1995 xxxv, 330p pa $20 hardcover o.p.   **322.4**

1. Ku Klux Klan 2. White Aryan Resistance 3. Racism 4. White supremacy movements 5. United States—Race relations

ISBN 0-14-023449-7 (pa)   LC 94-45177

"White supremacy groups are examined in this brutally honest portrait of hate and fear, based on personal interviews and interactions. A disturbingly provocative look at the frightening ignorance existing in the 1990s." Booklist

Includes bibliographical references

Gandhi, Mahatma, 1869-1948

Gandhi on non-violence; selected texts from Mohandas K. Gandhi's Non-violence in peace and war; edited with an introduction by Thomas Merton; preface by Mark Kurlansky. New Directions 2007 101p pa $13.95 *   **322.4**

1. Passive resistance 2. India—Politics and government

ISBN 978-0-8112-1686-9   LC 2007-32262

"A New Directions Paperbook"

First published 1965

In an introductory essay Merton "considers Gandhi's ideas, not in relation to their Indian context, but in terms of their applicability to all men's lives. Brief quotations from Gandhi's writings make up most of the book." Asia: a Guide to Paperbacks

Includes bibliographical references

Gerges, Fawaz A.

Journey of the Jihadist; inside Muslim militancy. Harcourt 2006 312p $25 *   **322.4**

1. Terrorism 2. Jihad 3. Islamic fundamentalism

ISBN 0-15-101213-X; 978-0-15-101213-8

     LC 2005-37759

In this "account of the development of militant Islamist praxis and ideology in the contemporary Middle East, Gerges . . . explains what the jihadists are about and what they intend to accomplish. . . . The author's ability to explain complex issues in a jargon-free and easy-flowing narrative makes this book one of the best, most useful, and most timely volumes for nonspecialist readers." Libr J

Includes bibliographical references

Hamilton, Neil A., 1949-

Rebels and renegades; a chronology of social and political dissent in the United States. Routledge 2002 361p il $100   **322.4**

1. Radicalism 2. Right and left (Political science)

ISBN 0-415-93639-X   LC 2002-8916

The author "examines the historical role that radicals and reactionaries have played in shaping American society and culture. Arranged in nine chapters, the book features a chronological format that begins in 1620 with the Pilgrims and ends with the September 11, 2001 terrorist attacks. Each chapter opens with an overview of the time period, and individual entries consist of one- or two-page descriptions of radicals, their activities, and their impact." Libr J

Includes bibliographical references

Ronson, Jon, 1967-

Them: adventures with extremists. Simon & Schuster 2002 330p $24; pa $13   **322.4**

1. Radicalism 2. Conspiracies

ISBN 0-7432-2707-7; 0-7432-3321-2 (pa)

     LC 2001-47411

First published 2001 in the United Kingdom

"Ronson spent the last five years with extremists: religious fundamentalists in Great Britain, Texas, and Cameroon; white supremacists in Arkansas, Michigan, and Idaho; and New World Order conspiracy chasers in Por-

Ronson, Jon, 1967-—*Continued*

tugal and California. Despite their differences, all seem to believe that the world is controlled by an elite group known as 'them.'" Libr J

This book "is at times funny, other times unsettling, but always astonishing. So difficult to accept are Ronson's narratives that any conclusions must be left up to the reader." Booklist

Stern, Kenneth S. (Kenneth Saul), 1953-

A force upon the plain; the American militia movement and the politics of hate; [by] Kenneth S. Stern; with a new foreword by the author. University of Oklahoma Press 1997 303p pa $16.95   **322.4**
1. Militia movements 2. Resistance to government 3. Radicalism
ISBN 0-8061-2926-3; 978-0-8061-2926-6
LC 96-41861
First published 1996 by Simon & Schuster
This is a "survey of various right-wing militia groups, selected leaders, and members." Booklist
Stern "links militias to preexisting racist groups such as the Ku Klux Klan, Aryan Nations, and Posse Comitatus. . . . This book provides an excellent introduction to the latest incarnation of racist and paranoid politics." Libr J

323 Civil and political rights

Arsenault, Raymond

Freedom riders; 1961 and the struggle for racial justice. Oxford University Press 2006 690p il map (Pivotal moments in American history) $32.50 *
                                          323
1. African Americans—Civil rights 2. African Americans—Segregation 3. Southern States—Race relations
ISBN 0-19-513674-8; 978-0-19-513674-6
LC 2005-18108
This is a history of the "six months [in 1961] in which black and white volunteers descended on the South to challenge segregated travel." N Y Times (Late N Y Ed)
Includes bibliographical references

Dershowitz, Alan M.

Rights from wrongs; a secular theory of the origins of rights. Basic Books 2004 261p $24 *
                                          323
1. Human rights 2. Civil rights
ISBN 0-465-01713-4   LC 2004-20006
The author "asserts that human rights derive from the world's experience with 'wrongs,' i.e., injustice. Only after seeing genocide, for example, did the notion develop that this was a violation of human rights. Dershowitz . . . has a rare ability to develop complex ideas in readable prose. . . . Whether conservative or liberal, absolutist or relativist, readers will find areas of disagreement, but most will concur that a talented and creative legal mind is at work." Publ Wkly
Includes bibliographical references

Devine, Carol

Human rights; the essential reference; {by} Carol Devine, Carol Rae Hansen, Ralph Wilde {et al.}; edited by Hilary Poole. Oryx Press 1999 311p il $73.95   **323**
1. United Nations. General Assembly. . Universal Declaration of Human Rights 2. Human rights
ISBN 1-57356-205-X   LC 99-24395
"This volume is divided into four sections; the first 'traces the evolution of our modern concept of human rights' beginning with the ancient Greeks and continuing through World War II to the adoption of the Universal Declaration of Human Rights by the United Nations General Assembly in 1948. Part two is a thorough examination of this historical document, article by article. Part three provides a detailed overview of the contemporary human-rights movement. . . . The final section consists of short essays on 33 of the most pressing human-rights issues today." SLJ
Includes bibliographical references

Kotz, Nick

Judgment days; Lyndon Baines Johnson, Martin Luther King, Jr., and the laws that changed America. Houghton Mifflin 2005 522p $26 *
                                          323
1. Johnson, Lyndon B. (Lyndon Baines), 1908-1973 2. King, Martin Luther, Jr., 1929-1968 3. Civil Rights Act of 1964 4. Voting Rights Act of 1965 5. United States—Politics and government—1961-1974 6. United States—Race relations
ISBN 0-618-08825-3   LC 2004-59852
This is a "narrative of how President Johnson and King temporarily overcame their mutual suspicion to battle successfully for the Civil Rights Acts of 1964 and 1968 and the 1965 Voting Rights Act. . . . This book is an informed political investigation of these two civil rights warriors and the cause for which they fought and, in King's case, died." Libr J

Maddex, Robert L., 1942-

International encyclopedia of human rights; freedoms, abuses, and remedies. CQ Press 2000 xxxii, 404p il $156.25   **323**
1. Human rights—Encyclopedias
ISBN 1-56802-490-8   LC 00-42941
"Beginning its coverage with the 1948 Universal Declaration of Human Rights, the volume includes definitions of more than 150 important concepts . . . entries on decisions of national and international bodies; descriptions of well over 100 documents . . . information about agencies and organizations involved in human rights; and biographies of some key individuals." Booklist
Includes bibliographical references

Nader, Ralph

The good fight; declare your independence & close the democracy gap. ReganBooks 2004 294p $25.95   **323**
1. Social movements 2. United States—Politics and government—2001-
ISBN 0-06-075604-7   LC 2005-295013

Nader, Ralph—*Continued*

Activist and presidential candidate Ralph Nader discusses how political engagement benefits society.

"Nader's voice is full of anger and frustration. He rages as much as reasons. This will no doubt please those who already follow him." NY Times Book Rev.

Includes bibliographical references

Schulz, William F., Jr.

In our own best interest; how defending human rights benefits us all; foreword by Mary Robinson. Beacon Press 2001 235p $25; pa $15   **323**

1. Human rights
ISBN 0-8070-0226-7; 0-8070-0227-5 (pa)
LC 2001-392

According to the author, "defending human rights pays off not only in terms of justice, but also in ways that can include greater economic growth, a more protected environment, better public health, and a generally less violent world." America

Includes bibliographical references

323.1   Civil and political rights of nondominant groups

Boyd, Herb, 1938-

We shall overcome; a living history of the civil rights struggle told in words, pictures and the voices of the participants. Sourcebooks 2004 272p il $45 *   **323.1**

1. African Americans—Civil rights
ISBN 1-402-20213-X   LC 2004-12509
Accompanied by 2 CDs

"Through text, images, and actual recordings (found on 2 CDs), Boyd . . . presents some of the major events in the Civil Rights Movement, including the murder of Emmett Till, the march on Washington, and the life and death of Martin Luther King Jr." Libr J

Includes bibliographical references

Civil rights in the United States; Waldo E. Martin, Jr., Patricia Sullivan, editors. Macmillan Ref. USA 2000 2v set $260 *   **323.1**

1. Civil rights 2. African Americans—Civil rights
ISBN 0-02-864765-3   LC 99-57548

"Covering the period from 1865 to the present, the set features more than 700 entries comprised of historical and state surveys, biographies, entries on civil rights and other organizations, political and social movements, legislation and government programs, court cases, overall concepts, cultural and educational institutions, as well as film, literature, music and art." Publisher's note

Egerton, John, 1935-

Speak now against the day; the generation before the civil rights movement in the South. University of North Carolina Press 1995 704p il pa $27.50   **323.1**

1. African Americans—Civil rights 2. Southern States—Race relations
ISBN 0-8078-4557-4; 978-0-8078-4557-8
First published 1994 by Knopf

Egerton presents a "historical narrative of black and white Southerners opposing white supremacy during the 1930s and 1940s. . . . He explains why the South failed to dismantle white supremacy when the possibility existed for voluntary, peaceful social reform." Libr J

This "book is a stunning achievement: a sprawling, engrossing, deeply moving account." N Y Times Book Rev

Includes bibliographical references

The **Eyes** on the prize civil rights reader; documents, speeches, and firsthand accounts from the black freedom struggle, 1954-1990; general editors, Clayborne Carson {et al.}. Penguin Bks. 1991 764p pa $18   **323.1**

1. African Americans—Civil rights 2. United States—Race relations
ISBN 0-14-015403-5   LC 91-9507

First published 1987 with title: Eyes on the prize: America's civil rights years, a reader and guide

"An anthology of primary material important in the historiography of this country's civil rights movement. . . . Not simply for reference use, this compilation makes provocative cover-to-cover reading and is extremely worthy of consideration by every library." Booklist

Includes bibliographical references

Fairclough, Adam

Better day coming; Blacks and equality, 1890-2000. Viking 2001 384p il $26.95; pa $16   **323.1**

1. African Americans—Civil rights 2. United States—Race relations 3. Southern States—Race relations
ISBN 0-670-87592-9; 0-14-200129-5 (pa)
LC 00-51342

This is a "history of black emancipation from 1890 to the present." N Y Times Book Rev

"Although it adds little to what experts in the field already know, this well-written work is a fine general introduction to the topic." Libr J

Includes bibliographical references

Guinier, Lani

The miner's canary; enlisting race, resisting power, transforming democracy; [by] Lani Guinier and Gerald Torres. Harvard Univ. Press 2002 392p $28.95; pa $16.95   **323.1**

1. United States—Politics and government 2. Minorities 3. United States—Race relations
ISBN 0-674-00469-8; 0-674-01084-1 (pa)
LC 2001-39629

"Guinier and Torres call for the building of grassroots, cross-racial coalitions to remake . . . structures of power by fostering public participation in politics and reforming the process of democracy." Publisher's note

The authors "grapple intelligently and with passionate wit with such explosive topics as racial profiling and the elusiveness of racial identification and identity . . . making this one of the most provocative and challenging books on race produced in years." Publ Wkly

Includes bibliographical references

Halberstam, David, 1934-2007
The children. Fawcett Books 1999 783p il pa
$18.95 * 323.1
1. African Americans—Civil rights 2. United States—
Race relations
ISBN 978-0-449-00439-5; 0-449-00439-2
First published 1998 by Random House
This is a "recreation of the early days of the civil
rights movement. . . . The author focuses on a small
group of young African Americans who attended the
Reverend James Lawson's workshop for nonviolent dem-
onstrators in Nashville in 1959, then went on to play ac-
tive roles in the movement. . . . A masterful achieve-
ment in reporting, research and understanding." Publ
Wkly
Includes bibliographical references

Joseph, Peniel E.
Waiting 'til the midnight hour; a narrative
history of Black power in America. Henry Holt
and Co. 2006 399p il $27.50 * 323.1
1. Black power 2. African Americans—Civil rights
ISBN 9780805075397; 0805075399
LC 2005-46765
"Rather than simply detailing the history of radical organizations, Joseph . . . also profiles several famous
leaders and uses their stories to spearhead a discussion
of the intellectual and practical history of Black Power
as a political movement. . . . Enthusiastically recommended for public and academic libraries." Libr J
Includes bibliographical references

Katznelson, Ira
When affirmative action was white; an untold
history of racial inequality in twentieth-century
America. W.W. Norton 2005 238p $25.95 *
323.1
1. Affirmative action programs 2. Race discrimination
3. African Americans—Economic conditions
ISBN 0-393-05213-3 LC 2004-24359
The author "offers history and analysis demonstrating
that the national social welfare programs of 60 and 70
years ago—e.g., Social Security, labor laws that created
collective bargaining for unions, and the GI Bill—in fact
gave affirmative economic opportunities to whites at the
expense of racial minorities, particularly blacks." Libr J
"Katznelson offers a penetrating . . . analysis, supported by vivid examples and statistics." N Y Times
Book Rev
Includes bibliographical references

King, Martin Luther, Jr., 1929-1968
A testament of hope; the essential writings of
Martin Luther King, Jr.; edited by James Melvin
Washington. Harper & Row 1986 xxvi, 676p
hardcover o.p. pa $23.95 * 323.1
1. African Americans—Civil rights 2. United States—
Race relations
ISBN 0-06-250931-4; 0-06-064691-8 (pa)
LC 85-45370
"King's most important writings are gathered together
in one source. The arrangement is topical: philosophy,

sermons and public addresses, essays, interviews and ex-
cerpts of his books. The material within each of these
categories is arranged chronologically. Included are Dr.
King's writings on nonviolence, integration and politics."
SLJ
Includes bibliographical references

Why we can't wait; [by] Martin Luther King, Jr.
Harper & Row 1964 178p il hardcover o.p. pa
$6.95 323.1
1. African Americans—Civil rights 2. Birmingham
(Ala.)—Race relations
ISBN 0-06-012395-8; 0-451-52753-4 (pa)
The author first reviews the background of the 1963
civil rights demands. He then describes the strategy of
the Birmingham campaign and outlines future action

Nguyen, Tram
We are all suspects now; untold stories from
immigrant communities after 9/11. Beacon Press
2005 187p pa $14 * 323.1
1. Immigrants 2. United States—Ethnic relations
3. War on terrorism 4. September 11 terrorist attacks,
2001
ISBN 0-8070-0461-8 (pa) LC 2005-11579
The author "reveals the human cost of the domestic
war on terror and examines the impact of post-9/11 policies on people targeted because of immigration status,
nationality, race, and religion." Publisher's note
"Mesmerizing personal accounts of poor treatment by
the US government, as well as everyday trials and tribulations that immigrants face in the aftermath of September 11th, make this book impossible to put down." Univ
Press Books for Public and Second Sch Libr, 2006
Includes bibliographical references

Olson, Lynne
Freedom's daughters; the unsung heroines of the
civil rights movement from 1830 to 1970. Scribner
2001 460p il $30; pa $16 323.1
1. African American women 2. African Americans—
Civil rights
ISBN 0-684-85012-5; 0-684-85013-3 (pa)
LC 00-41306
Olson discusses the contribution of such women as
Fannie Lou Hamer, Diane Nash, Rosa Parks and Ella Ba-
ker to the civil rights movement
This book "expertly mines oral history collections
housed in Southern universities, biographies and testa-
ments published in the last decade by Southern university
presses and more general works by historians." N Y
Times Book Rev
Includes bibliographical references

Reporting civil rights. Library of Am. 2003 2v ea
$40 * 323.1
1. African Americans—Civil rights 2. Journalism
3. United States—Race relations
ISBN 1-931082-28-6 (v1); 1-931082-29-4 (v2)
LC 2002-27459
Contents: pt1 American journalism, 1941-1963; pt2
American journalism, 1963-1973

Reporting civil rights—*Continued*

These "volumes present newspaper and magazine articles from the popular and African American press. . . . The 151 writers whose works are collected here include Ralph Ellison, Langston Hughes, John Hersey, Robert Penn Warren, David Halberstam, Jimmy Breslin, James Baldwin, Marshall Frady, and Tom Wolfe. . . . Each volume also contains a chronology and biographical sketches of the contributors." Libr J

"An important anthology for readers interested in the history of the civil rights movement." Booklist

Voices in our blood; America's best on the civil rights movement; edited by Jon Meacham. Random House 2001 561p pa $16.95 hardcover o.p.　　　　　　　　　　　　　　　　**323.1**

1. African Americans—Civil rights 2. United States—Race relations

ISBN 0-375-75881-X (pa)　　　　　LC 00-41474

A "collection of acclaimed 'voices' narrating the environment, origin, and progress of the Civil Rights movement, as told by reporters, artists, novelists, historians, and authors such as Maya Angelou, Eudora Welty, James Baldwin, Richard Wright, Willie Morris, Robert Penn Warren, Alice Walker, Murray Kempton, E. B. White, William Faulkner, Ralph Ellison, and Rebecca West." Libr J

Williams, Juan

Eyes on the prize: America's civil rights years, 1954-1965; [by] Juan Williams with the Eyes on the prize production team; introduction by Julian Bond. Viking 1987 300p il hardcover o.p. pa $20　　　　　　　　　　　　　　　　　　　**323.1**

1. African Americans—Civil rights 2. United States—Race relations

ISBN 0-670-81412-1; 0-14-009653-1 (pa)

LC 86-40271

"A Robert Lavelle book"

"This companion volume to the PBS TV series of the same name is an . . . account of black America's struggle for social and political equality, covering the civil rights battle from the landmark Brown v. Board of Education decision in 1954 to the Selma protest marches, and Voting Rights Act of 1965." Libr J

"Highly recommended both as a socio-historical document and as a heartfelt, poignant remembrance of a movement and its activists." Booklist

Includes bibliographical references

323.3　Civil and political rights of other social groups

Pybus, Cassandra

Epic journeys of freedom: runaway slaves of the American Revolution and their global quest for liberty. Beacon Press 2006 281p map $26.95

323.3

1. Slavery 2. United States—History—1775-1783, Revolution

ISBN 0-8070-5514-X　　　　　　　LC 2005-13093

This "book traces the steps of 32 fugitive slaves who fled their American colonial masters at the onset of the American Revolution and sought refuge from the British. . . . Readers will obtain a much greater understanding of an aspect of the American Revolution that finally gets some much-deserved scholarship." Libr J

Includes bibliographical references

323.4　Specific civil rights; limitation and suspension of civil rights

Conroy, John, 1951-

Unspeakable acts, ordinary people; the dynamics of torture. University of California Press 2001 304p pa $19.95　　　　　　　　　　　**323.4**

1. Torture

ISBN 0-520-23039-6　　　　　　　LC 2001-33218

First published 2000 by Knopf

The author "interviews torturers, torture victims, and government officials from such diverse locations as Israel, Northern Ireland, and a Chicago police interrogation room, focusing on how torture is performed and why." Booklist

Includes bibliographical references

McCoy, Alfred W.

A question of torture; CIA interrogation from the Cold War to the War on Terror. Metropolitan Books 2006 290p il (The American empire project) $25; pa $15 *　　　　　　　　**323.4**

1. United States. Central Intelligence Agency 2. Torture 3. Intelligence service—United States

ISBN　978-0-8050-8041-4;　0-8050-8041-4; 978-0-8050-8248-7 (pa); 0-8050-8248-4 (pa)

LC 2005-51124

The author "shows how, since 1950, the CIA and various nations have augmented traditional physical torture with psychological abuse techniques of 'sensory disorientation' and 'self-inflicted pain,' which he documents with some gruesome first-person accounts by victims and with stories of doctors who conducted horrific experiments." Libr J

Includes bibliographical references

Pipes, Richard

Property and freedom. Knopf 1999 328p pa $15 hardcover o.p.　　　　　　　　　　**323.4**

1. Freedom 2. Property

ISBN 0-375-70447-7 (pa)　　　　　LC 98-41728

This is a "survey of the Western philosophical stance toward property, primarily concerning its origins, justification of possession, and wisdom of redistribution. . . . After rendering compact constitutional histories of England and Russia, Pipes usefully provides concrete, rather than theoretical, illustrations of the liberty-property nexus in action. An incisive essay." Booklist

Includes bibliographical references

Razac, Olivier
Barbed wire; a political history; translated from the French by Jonathan Kneight. New Press 2002 132p $22.95; pa $13.95   **323.4**
1. Barbed wire
ISBN 1-56584-735-0; 1-56584-812-8 (pa)
    LC 2002-19536
"First introduced in 1874 as an inexpensive means of fencing off U.S. prairie land, barbed wire quickly became not only a way to manage livestock but a means to contain Native Americans on reservations. . . . Arguing that barbed wire is 'the political management of space,' Razac traces how it radicalized trench warfare during WWI . . . and, electrified, literally defined the space of Nazi concentration camps. . . . The simplicity and clarity of Razac's prose reinforces the enormous power and originality of his ideas, making this a vital work of cultural criticism." Publ Wkly
Includes bibliographical references

323.44   Freedom of action (Liberty)

Dadge, David
Casualty of war; the Bush administration's assault on a free press. Prometheus Books 2004 349p $26   **323.44**
1. Freedom of the press 2. War on terrorism
ISBN 1-59102-147-2   LC 2003-23766
The author "provides an indictment of U.S. media and information policies adopted since 9/11." Libr J
Dadge "has written a disquieting book, useful to anyone concerned with First Amendment freedoms. . . . This well-written, well-researched book should be read by journalism students and interested citizens." Choice
Includes bibliographical references

Etzioni, Amitai
The limits of privacy. Basic Bks. 1999 280p pa $21 hardcover o.p.   **323.44**
1. Right of privacy 2. Public interest
ISBN 0-465-04090-X (pa)   LC 98-47082
The author addresses the right to privacy and the common good. Topics discussed include HIV testing of infants, sex offender laws, deciphering encrypted messages, I.D. cards, and medical records
"Etzioni advocates rethinking privacy and placing it in the context of the common good. This book provides a valuable and informative analysis of a timely and interesting topic." Booklist
Includes bibliographical references

Fischer, David Hackett
Liberty and freedom. Oxford University Press 2004 851p il (America, a cultural history) $50
    323.44
1. American national characteristics 2. Freedom
3. United States—History
ISBN 0-19-516253-6   LC 2004-5197
"This book studies American ideas of liberty and freedom as visions of an open society, through the symbols they have inspired from the Revolutionary era through

9/11." Publisher's note
This "beautifully illustrated book shifts subtly from a rich graphic survey, incorporating painting, flags and sculpture, to a broader chronicle of the many ways Americans have articulated their most cherished ideals." Publ Wkly
Includes bibliographical references

Foner, Eric
The story of American freedom. Norton 1998 422p il pa $16.95 hardcover o.p.   **323.44**
1. Freedom 2. United States—History
ISBN 0-393-31962-8 (pa)   LC 98-3290
Foner offers a "survey of the various meanings—political, economic, personal, moral—that Americans have attached to freedom from the Revolution until today." Commentary
"The book's strongest claim to distinction lies . . . in its succinct, information-packed, wonderfully readable account of the twists and turns in 20th-century American history." N Y Times Book Rev
Includes bibliographical references

Grayling, A. C.
Toward the light of liberty; the struggles for freedom and rights that made the modern western world. Walker & Company 2007 336p il $25.95
    323.44
1. Civil rights 2. Freedom
ISBN 0-8027-1636-9; 978-0-8027-1636-1
This is a "survey that tracks the development of free, democratic societies and institutions over the past five centuries. He begins with the Protestant Reformation. . . . Grayling proceeds to examine the role of Enlightenment figures, early feminists, and the Chartist movement in securing both individual liberty and the expansion of the franchise." Booklist
"This book is, in some respects, an old-fashioned, triumphalist history of the rise of Western liberty since the 16th century (with Martin Luther, John Locke and Elizabeth Cady Stanton playing leading role), but nevertheless serves as a stirring call to arms to defend freedom from its enemies within and without." Publ Wkly
Includes bibliographical references

Henderson, Harry, 1951-
Privacy in the information age. Rev. ed. Facts On File 2006 314p (Library in a book) $45
    323.44
1. Right of privacy
ISBN 0-8160-5697-8; 978-0-8160-5697-2
    LC 2005-37387
First published 1999
This book surveys the topic "by providing an overview of the issues, a survey of the applicable laws and court cases, a chronology, and an extensively annotated bibliography. . . . Librarians will like the section on organizations and agencies that directs users to associations with an interest in privacy rights." Libr J [review of 1999 edition]
Includes bibliographical references

Intellectual freedom manual; compiled by the Office for Intellectual Freedom of the American Library Association. 7th ed. American Library Association 2006 xx, 521p pa $52 *

                        323.44

1. Intellectual freedom 2. Libraries—Censorship

ISBN 0-8389-3561-3; 978-0-8389-3561-3

                      LC 2005-22409

First published 1974

This guide to preserving intellectual freedom includes: ALA interpretations to the Library Bill of Rights; recommendations for special libraries and specific situations; information about legal decisions affecting school and public libraries; a section on the ALA's Intellectual Freedom Action Network.

"This manual details the professional standards to which librarians aspire and offers practical information about how to achieve those goals; it's a must for any librarian's professional library." Book Rep

Includes bibliographical references

Smith, Huston

A seat at the table; Huston Smith in conversation with Native Americans on religious freedom; edited and with preface by Phil Cousineau; with assistance from Gary Rhine. University of California Press 2006 xxi, 232p il $24.95   **323.44**

1. Native Americans—Religion

ISBN 0-520-24439-7   LC 2005-5290

The author "interviewed Native American leaders ranging from the well-known (Vine Deloria Jr., Walter Echo-Hawk and Charlotte Black Elk) to the less widely recognized, such as Lenny Foster and Tonya Gonella Frichner. The . . . conversations trace the common thread that Native Americans follow a spiritual path imbuing all their life, encompassing art, morality and literature. Topics include the fight for prisoners' rights, ceremonial rituals, the role of elders and the genius of oral traditions. . . . The interviews provide a fine introduction to Native American religions." Publ Wkly

Includes bibliographical references

Stone, Geoffrey R.

Perilous times; free speech in wartime from the Sedition Act of 1798 to the war on terrorism. Norton 2004 xx, 730p il $35 *   **323.44**

1. Freedom of speech

ISBN 0-393-05880-8   LC 2004-17871

This "history examines America's tendency in wartime to compromise First Amendment rights in the name of national security." New Yorker

The author "delivers rich material in an engaging, character-based narrative. Stone offers deep insight into rhetorical history and the men and women who made it—resisters like Clement Vallandingham, Emma Goldman, Fred Korematsu and Daniel Ellsberg; presidents faced with wartime dilemmas; and the prosecutors, defenders and Supreme Court justices who shaped our understanding of the First Amendment today." Publ Wkly

Includes bibliographical references

323.6   Citizenship and related topics

Ellis, Richard

To the flag; the unlikely history of the Pledge of Allegiance; [by] Richard J. Ellis. University Press of Kansas 2005 297p il $29.95; pa $15.95

                        323.6

1. Pledge of Allegiance

ISBN 0-7006-1372-2; 0-7006-1521-0 (pa)

                    LC 2004-23110

The author provides an "account not only of the pledge's 19th century beginnings, but also of its recent use as a political tool. A must read for political junkies of any age!" Univ Press Books for Public and Second Sch Libr, 2006

Pass the U.S. citizenship exam. 3rd ed. LearningExpress 2008 151p il map pa $12.95 *

                        323.6

1. Citizenship 2. United States—Politics and government—Study and teaching

ISBN 978-1-57685-619-2   LC 2007-48381

First published 1999

This book covering the civics test and the N-400 "includes bilingual lessons, quizzes, translated civics terms/definitions, sample questions/forms, embassy data, and more." Libr J

United States. Dept. of Homeland Security. U.S. Citizenship and Immigration Services

The citizen's almanac; fundamental documents, symbols, and anthems of the United States. U.S. Citizenship and Immigration Services, [Office of Citizenship] 2007 102p il pa $7.50 *

                        323.6

1. Citizenship 2. United States—Politics and government

ISBN 0-16-078027-6; 978-0-16-078027-1

                    LC 2008-354023

Also available online in PDF format and in packages of 25

Contents: Citizenship in America: rights and responsibilities of U.S. citizens — Patriotic anthems and symbols of the United States — Presidential and historical speeches — Fundamental documents of American democracy — Landmark decisions of the U.S. Supreme Court — Presidential statements on citizenship and immigration — Prominent foreign-born Americans

"Featuring historical speeches, songs, landmark Supreme Court decisions, and more; all public libraries should point patrons here." Libr J

Welcome to the United States; a guide for new immigrants. Rev. ed. U.S. Dept. of Homeland Security, Citizenship and Immigration Services 2007 114p il map (Civics and citizenship toolkit) pa $9.50 *   **323.6**

1. Immigrants—United States 2. United States—Immigration and emigration

ISBN 0-16-078733-5; 978-0-16-078733-1

Also available from the U.S. Citizenship and Immigration Services website in PDF format

First published 2005

United States. Dept. of Homeland Security. U.S. Citizenship and Immigration Services—*Continued*

"A key document available in 12 different languages that lays out the basic path toward and requirements for naturalization." Libr J

324 The political process

American presidential campaigns and elections; William G. Shade, and Ballard C. Campbell, editors; Craig R. Coenen, documents editor. Sharpe Ref. 2002 3v set $325 * **324**
1. Presidents—United States—Election 2. United States—Politics and government
ISBN 0-7656-8042-4   LC 2002-21185
This reference source covers "every presidential election from 1788-89 to 2000. Each election chapter offers a description of the issues, conventions, campaigns, and election results; a chronology; a 'highlight' sidebar focusing on an interesting aspect of the election; a vote analysis in chart and map form; a bibliography; and a collection of between five and seven documents. . . . Also provided are more than 170 fact boxes presenting brief biographical summaries for each candidate, including place and date of birth, political party, parents' names, schooling, marriage, family, military service, career, and death information. . . . Although there are other reference sources that cover various aspects of U.S. presidential elections, none provide this kind of detailed election-by-election history. The text is both readable and informative, enhanced by good organization, well-chosen features, and attractive design." Booklist
Includes bibliographical references

Dershowitz, Alan M.
Supreme injustice; how the high court hijacked election 2000. Oxford Univ. Press 2001 275p il hardcover o.p. pa $14.95   **324**
1. Bush, George W. 2. Gore, Al, 1948- 3. Presidents—United States—Election—2000
ISBN 0-19-514827-4; 0-19-515807-5 (pa)
                        LC 2001-32193
Dershowitz evaluates the Supreme Court's final decision in the presidential election of 2000. He argues that the five majority justices "acted out of personal political preference, and therefore Bush v. Gore 'may be ranked as the single most corrupt decision in Supreme Court history.'" N Y Times Book Rev
"This well-reasoned and controversial book asks central questions about American democracy and the role of citizens and courts in our society." Libr J
Includes bibliographical references

Gumbel, Andrew
Steal this vote; dirty elections and the rotten history of democracy in America. Nation Books 2005 xxi, 362p pa $15.95 *   **324**
1. Elections—United States
ISBN 1-56025-676-1   LC 2004-447878
The author "traces election fraud in America from the 18th century to the present, spotlighting the Hayes-Tilden

election of 1876, vote buying in the Gilded Age and the history of black disenfranchisement in the post-Reconstruction South. The last 100 pages are devoted to the elections of 2000 and 2004." Publ Wkly
"An important book, rich in anecdotal detail and filled with impassioned anger." Libr J
Includes bibliographical references

Historical atlas of U.S. presidential elections 1788-2004; [by] J. Clark Archer . . . [et al.] CQ Press 2006 164p map $150 *   **324**
1. Presidents—United States—Election—Maps 2. Presidents—United States—Election—Statistics 3. Elections—United States—Maps 4. Elections—United States—Statistics
ISBN 1-56802-955-1; 978-1-56802-955-9
                        LC 2006-42406
This "atlas of election data is divided into three sections. Section one is an overview of United States election history and current procedure as well as the methods as sources used in compiling this volume. Next is a series of full-color presidential election maps, while section three contains individual analyses of each election since Washington's first landslide victory." Voice Youth Advocates
"Offering detailed geographic and historical visual evidence of every presidential election held in the US, this book is a required source of reference." Choice
Includes bibliographical references

Karabell, Zachary
The last campaign; how Harry Truman won the 1948 election. Knopf 2000 308p pa $14 hardcover o.p.   **324**
1. Truman, Harry S., 1884-1972 2. Dewey, Thomas E. (Thomas Edmund), 1902-1971 3. Presidents—United States—Election—1948
ISBN 0-375-70077-3 (pa)   LC 99-28567
This is an account of the presidential campaign which pitted Truman against Dewey.
"The author is strongest discussing the impact of the press, polls, and radio and describing the importance of the convention, which was then 'a mix of high politics, low politics and entertainment.'" Libr J
Includes bibliographical references

Larson, Edward J.
A magnificent catastrophe; the tumultuous election of 1800, America's first presidential campaign. Free Press 2007 335p il $27
                        324
1. Jefferson, Thomas, 1743-1826 2. Adams, John, 1735-1826 3. Burr, Aaron, 1756-1836 4. Hamilton, Alexander, 1757-1804 5. Presidents—United States—Election—1800 6. United States—Politics and government—1783-1809
ISBN 978-0-7432-9316-7; 0-7432-9316-9
                        LC 2007-16017
The author "recreates the dramatic presidential race of 1800, which, Larson says, stamped American democracy with its distinctive partisan character as Republicans and Federalists battled for the presidency. . . . [This is] an invaluable study of a crucial chapter in the lives of the founding fathers—and of the nation." Publ Wkly
Includes bibliographical references

Maisel, Louis Sandy, 1945-
American political parties and elections; a very short introduction. Oxford University Press 2007 175p il (Very short introductions) pa $11.95
324
1. Political parties 2. Elections—United States
ISBN 978-0-19-530122-9; 0-19-530122-6
LC 2007-1843
"A brief . . . look at political parties in America." Publisher's note
Includes bibliographical references

Morris, Roy
Fraud of the century; Rutherford B. Hayes, Samuel Tilden, and the stolen election of 1876; {by} Roy Morris, Jr. Simon & Schuster 2003 311p il hardcover o.p. pa $14
324
1. Hayes, Rutherford B., 1822-1893 2. Tilden, Samuel J., 1814-1886 3. Presidents—United States—Election 4. Political corruption
ISBN 0-7432-2386-1; 978-0-7432-5552-3; 0-7432-5552-6 (pa)
LC 2002-36507
This is an account of the "1876 contest between Ohio Republican governor Rutherford B. Hayes and New York governor Samuel J. Tilden." Publisher's note
"Morris has an eye for detail and a lively writing style that make this highly detailed, first-rate work of history read more like a whodunnit than a historical examination." Libr J
Includes bibliographical references

Witcover, Jules
No way to pick a president. Routledge 2001 303p pa $22.95
324
1. Presidents—United States—Election 2. United States—Politics and government—20th century
ISBN 0-415-93031-6; 978-0-415-93031-4
LC 2001-19126
First published 1999 by Farrar, Straus, and Giroux
Witcover contends that "there is too much special-interest money distorting the [election] process. . . . The nominating conventions have become useless affairs. Political consultants, willing to do anything to win, have too much power. The press is at once shallow and relentlessly negative." N Y Times Book Rev
Includes bibliographical references

324.025 The political process— Directories

Political handbook of the world: 2008; edited by Arthur S. Banks, Thomas C. Muller, and William R. Overstreet. CQ Press 2008 1827p map $240 *
324.025
1. Political science—Handbooks, manuals, etc. 2. Political parties
ISSN 0913-175X
ISBN 978-0-87289-528-7; 0-87289-528-9
Annual. First published 1927 with title: A political handbook of Europe

"Provides data for each country on chief officials, government and politics, political parties, and news media. Sections devoted to intergovernmental organizations and to issues concerned with particular regions; e.g., Middle East, Latin America. Index to geographical, organizational, and personal names." Ref Sources for Small & Medium-sized Libr. 6th edition

324.2 Political parties

Gould, Lewis L.
Grand Old Party; a history of the Republicans. Random House 2003 597p il $35 *
324.2
1. Republican Party (U.S.)
ISBN 0-375-50741-8
LC 2003-46604
This is an "account of the Grand Old Party that spans its earliest days under Abraham Lincoln to its conservative bent today. Much of the book documents the shifts of its platform. . . . Gould also discusses the leadership qualities, farsighted policies, conservative federal spending, and willingness to provide social programs at the cost of future generations of four Republican presidents—Lincoln, Theodore Roosevelt, Eisenhower, and Reagan." Libr J
Includes bibliographical references

McGerr, Michael E.
A fierce discontent; the rise and fall of the Progressive movement in America, 1870-1920; [by] Michael McGerr. Oxford University Press 2005 395p pa $19.95
324.2
1. Progressivism (United States politics)
ISBN 978-0-19-518365-8; 0-19-518365-7
LC 2004-30592
First published 2003 by the Free Press
The author "examines the social, cultural and political currents of a movement that, through its early successes and ultimate failure, has defined today's 'disappointing' political climate. . . . In three parts, McGerr illuminates the origins of Progressive thought, the movement's meteoric ascent in American life and its descent into 'the Red scare, race riots, strikes and inflation,' positing that the Progressive vision of remaking America in its own middle-class image eventually sparked a backlash that persists to this day. . . . Simply put, this is history at its best." Publ Wkly
Includes bibliographical references

Tamimi, Azzam
Hamas: a history from within. Olive Branch Press 2007 372p pa $20
324.2
1. Hamas 2. Islam and politics
ISBN 978-1-56656-689-6; 1-56656-689-4
LC 2007-6828
This is a "document-based study of the formation, politics, and actions of Hamas, the Islamist party that recently formed a Palestinian government despite the opposition of the United States and the rival Fatah Party. . . . [The author] has written a sound academic work on a key group that libraries need to have." Libr J
Includes bibliographical references

324.5 Nominating candidates

National party conventions, 1831-2004. CQ Press 2005 325p il pa $40   **324.5**
1. Political conventions 2. Political parties
ISBN 1-56802-982-9
First published 1995 with title: National party conventions, 1831-1992
This volume offers information about Republican and Democratic Party national conventions including sites, delegates, chief officers and keynote speakers, party organization and rules, credential fights, platform fights, ballots, and candidates.
Includes bibliographical references

324.6 Election systems and procedures; suffrage

Benenson, Bob
Elections A to Z. 3rd ed. CQ Press 2008 xxxvi, 704p il (CQ's American government A to Z series) $85   **324.6**
1. Elections—United States—Encyclopedias
ISBN 978-0-87289-366-5   LC 2007-41388
Also available online
First published 1999
"Topics include individuals, current and defunct political parties, and significant events in election history. Landmark court cases on this topic are also discussed. . . . Public libraries and media centers will find this a convenient and useful addition to their collections." Am Ref Books Annu, 2008
Includes bibliographical references

Choosing the president 2008; a citizen's guide to the electoral process; [by] League of Women Voters; edited by Bob Guldin. Lyons Press 2008 178p il pa $14.95   **324.6**
1. Presidents—United States—Election 2. Elections—United States
ISBN 978-1-59921-214-2; 1-59921-214-5
     LC 2007-51852
"An essential text for understanding the process, laws, and issues that impact a U.S. presidential election. . . . Covers political parties, media, money, campaigning, primaries, conventions, and election day processes." Libr J
Includes videography and bibliographical references

Fortier, John C.
Absentee and early voting; trends, promises, and perils. AEI Press 2006 105p il pa $20
     324.6
1. Elections—United States 2. Absentee voting
ISBN 978-0-8447-4247-2; 0-8447-4247-3
     LC 2006-24261
The author "documents the dramatic increase in absentee voting and, more recently the meteoric rise in early voting. He examines the legal and historical reasons for changes in the voting system and the many differences across states." Publisher's note
Includes bibliographical references

Guide to U.S. elections. 5th ed. CQ 2005 2v il map set $335   **324.6**
1. Elections—United States—Statistics
ISBN 1-56802-981-0
First published 1975 with title: Congressional Quarterly's guide to U.S. elections
This is a compilation of data drawn from different sources on gubernatorial, congressional, and presidential elections. "Data on elections is accompanied by historical background and essays on topics such as campaign finance and redistricting." Booklist
Includes bibliographical references

Henderson, Harry, 1951-
Campaign and election reform. Facts on File 2004 316p (Library in a book) $45   **324.6**
1. Elections—United States 2. Campaign funds—United States
ISBN 0-8160-5136-4   LC 2003-6485
Contents: Introduction to campaign and election reform; The law of campaigns and elections; Chronology; Biographical listing; How to research campaign and election reform; Organizations and agencies
"Beginning with the Declaration of Independence and ending with the 2002 Bipartisan Campaign Reform Act, coverage includes the Electoral College and the complicated world of campaign-finance reform as well as the technology used to record individual voter records. Legislation and court cases that have determined the current electoral process in our country are reviewed and explanations of the legal battles waged during the 2000 presidential election between George Bush and Al Gore are included. . . . A solid one-stop resource." SLJ
Includes bibliographical references

Presidential elections, 1789-2004. CQ Press 2005 277p il map pa $43 *   **324.6**
1. Presidents—United States—Election
ISBN 1-56802-983-7; 978-1-56802-983-2
     LC 2006-282339
First published 1995 with title: Presidential elections, 1789-1992
This offers information about the electoral college, electoral votes and popular votes in each presidential election, voter turnout, primary returns, and Democratic and Republican Party conventions.
Includes bibliographical references

Rubin, Aviel D.
Brave new ballot; the battle to safeguard democracy in the age of electronic voting. Morgan Road Books 2006 280p $24.95   **324.6**
1. Voting machines
ISBN 0-7679-2210-7; 978-0-7679-2210-4
     LC 2006-41917
The author "found himself at center stage of the debate surrounding the safety and security of electronic voting when he and his grad students exposed serious failings in the code in electronic voting machines manufactured by Diebold. . . . Rubin thoroughly analyzes the vulnerabilities of electronic voting and offers an absorbing account of how his involvement in the e-voting controversy affected his life and career, in what he describes

Rubin, Aviel D.—*Continued*

as a scenario from a bad Hollywood script. In this highly accessible book, Rubin offers readers a look at the weaknesses of electronic voting systems and the need for paper records." Booklist

Includes bibliographical references

Walters, Ronald W.

Freedom is not enough; black voters, black candidates, and American presidential politics. Rowman & Littlefield 2005 239p (American political challenges) $27.95; pa $24.95

324.6

1. Voting Rights Act of 1965 2. African Americans—Suffrage 3. United States—Politics and government 4. Presidents—United States—Election

ISBN   0-7425-3837-0;   978-0-74253-837-5; 978-0-7425-4806-0 (pa); 0-7425-4806-6 (pa)

LC 2005-8343

The book "examines the impact of the black vote on presidential elections . . . [and] offers useful background information on black voting habits and how the black vote is both obtained and obstructed, with an emphasis on voter turnout rather than the issues blacks should base their votes upon." Libr J

Includes bibliographical references

324.7   Conduct of election campaigns

Grey, Lawrence

How to win a local election; a complete step-by-step guide. 3rd ed. M. Evans; Distributed by National Book Network 2007 259p il pa $17.95 *

324.7

1. Elections—United States 2. Politics 3. Local government

ISBN 978-1-59077-131-0; 1-59077-131-1

LC 2007-11662

First published 1994

Includes CD-ROM

This guide on how to get elected features "chapters that follow the course of a campaign: organizing volunteers, advertising, analyzing your district's demographics, etc. Grey supplies customizable worksheets and forms on a CD-ROM. . . . This is a smart, informed, and practical package. It belongs in every public library, supplemented by official publications on local election requirements." Libr J

Guide to political campaigns in America; Paul S. Herrnson, editor-in-chief; Colton Campbell, Marni Ezra, Stephen K. Medvic, associate editors. CQ Press 2005 457p il $125 *

324.7

1. Politics 2. Elections—United States

ISBN 1-56802-876-8   LC 2005-18123

Also available online

"Organized into seven sections, [this book] contains 27 chapters that discuss every aspect of the American political campaign process—including a historical overview, nomination politics, voter turnout, polling, debates, and campaign reform. The editors examine various political campaigns, e.g., presidential, congressional, gubernatorial, state, and local. They also look at judicial elections and initiatives and referenda. . . . This volume should be found in every reference collection." Choice

Includes bibliographical references

325   International migration and colonization

Chamberlain, Lesley

Lenin's private war; the voyage of the Philosophy Steamer and the exile of the intelligentsia. St. Martin's Press 2007 414p il $27.95

325

1. Lenin, Vladimir Il'ich, 1870-1924 2. Soviet Union—History—1917-1921,   Revolution 3. Intellectuals—Soviet Union

ISBN 978-0-312-36730-5; 0-312-36730-9

LC 2007-17626

"In late 1922, two ships departed Petrograd for Germany. On board were dozens of the finest minds in Russia, expelled from their homeland on the order of Lenin as part of his war against the intelligentsia. In 'Lenin's Private War,' Lesley Chamberlain recounts this little-known episode, one that was to have disastrous consequences for Russia and figure as a dark omen for the country's future. . . . The steamers landed in Stettin on the Baltic Sea, and from there the passengers made for Prague or Berlin and later Paris, all centers of vibrant Russian expatriate communities. In the second half of her book, Chamberlain tells the story of Russia Abroad, that other Russia spawned by the upheavals of revolution and war that became a surrogate homeland for the new émigrés. . . . [This study] is infused with a deep understanding of the rich history of Russian thought." Seattle Times

Includes bibliographical references and index

325.73   Immigration to the United States

Brownstone, David M.

Facts about American immigration; [by] David M. Brownstone and Irene M. Franck. Wilson, H.W. 2001 xxx, 818p il $105 *

325.73

1. United States—Immigration and emigration 2. Immigrants—United States

ISBN 0-8242-0959-1   LC 00-53422

"Coverage begins with the earliest Americans and continues to today's immigrants. An overview places the process of immigration in a wide historical context covering efforts to restrict immigration, a portrait of the immigrant journey over the centuries, and a chronology. The main section of the book covers emigration from Europe, Africa, Asia, the Americas, and Oceania." Publisher's note

Includes bibliographical references

Daniels, Roger

Coming to America; a history of immigration and ethnicity in American life. 2nd ed. Perennial 2002 515p il map pa $17.95   **325.73**

1. Minorities 2. United States—Immigration and emigration

ISBN 0-06-050577-X   LC 2002-72436

First published 1990

"After discussing the topic of immigration in general and sociological theories of why people migrate between countries, Daniel discusses each racial or national group that came to the United States during the various eras of the nation's history." SLJ {review of 1990 edition}

Includes bibliographical references

Handlin, Oscar, 1915-

The uprooted. 2nd ed. Little, Brown 1973 333p pa $18.99 hardcover o.p.   **325.73**

1. United States—Immigration and emigration 2. Acculturation

ISBN 0-316-34313-7 (pa)

"An Atlantic Monthly Press book"

First published 1951

This account of the American immigrant experience and the acculturation process describes employment, religion, ghetto life, benevolent societies, boss politics, family life, and social alienation

Pipher, Mary Bray

The middle of everywhere; the world's refugees come to our town; {by} Mary Pipher. Harcourt 2002 xxv, 390p $25; pa $14   **325.73**

1. Refugees

ISBN 0-15-100600-8; 0-15-602737-2 (pa)

LC 2001-5863

"Pipher explores the changing face of the U.S. as immigrants fan out from the coasts and inhabit more and more of the American heartland, changing the culture." Booklist

The author "writes in rich, empathetic language and with a keen, observant eye for detail and nuance." Publ Wkly

Includes bibliographical references

Yans-McLaughlin, Virginia, 1943-

Ellis Island and the peopling of America; the official guide; [by] Virginia Yans-McLaughlin and Marjorie Lightman, with the Statue of Liberty-Ellis Island Foundation. New Press (NY) 1997 209p il maps pa $19.95   **325.73**

1. Ellis Island Immigration Station 2. United States—Immigration and emigration

ISBN 1-56584-364-9   LC 96-54713

Photographs, time lines, charts and historical documents from the Ellis Island Museum accompany a text that places immigration policy in its historical context.

326 Slavery and emancipation

Berlin, Ira, 1941-

Generations of captivity; a history of African-American slaves. Belknap Press 2003 374p maps $29.95; pa $16.95   **326**

1. Slavery—United States

ISBN 0-674-01061-2; 0-674-01624-6 (pa)

LC 2002-28142

The author "delineates the ways slavery varied according to time and place and compares slavery in the Americas, mapping the migrations of peoples from Africa to America and then across the South in its various incarnations, discovering within slave life the roots of African American religions, family, folkways, foodways, crafts, and more." Libr J

"Berlin has given us a moving, insightful account of slavery in the United States. Readers will not soon forget the story he has told, nor should they." N Y Times Book Rev

Includes bibliographical references

Davis, David Brion

Inhuman bondage; the rise and fall of slavery in the New World. Oxford University Press 2006 440p il maps $30 *   **326**

1. Slavery—History

ISBN 0-19-514073-7; 978-0-19-514073-6

LC 2005-31850

The author "follows the large story of slavery into all corners of the Atlantic world, demonstrating that hardly anyone or anything was untouched by it. . . . [Davis] provides dozens of new insights, large and small, into events as familiar as the revolt on Saint-Domingue (now Haiti) and the American Civil War." N Y Times Book Rev

Includes bibliographical references

Douglass, Frederick, 1817?-1895

Frederick Douglass: selected speeches and writings; edited by Philip S. Foner; abridged and adapted by Yuval Taylor. Hill Bks. 1999 789p pa $32.95 hardcover o.p. *   **326**

ISBN 1-55652-352-1 (pa)   LC 99-23180

Based on Foner's five-volume The life and writings of Frederick Douglass (1950-1975), this volume "covers Douglass' speeches and writings over a 54-year period. The breadth and depth of his focus and concerns reflected in more than 2,000 speeches, editorials, articles, and letters provide a wellspring of knowledge about the man and his intellect." Booklist

Includes bibliographical references

Encyclopedia of slave resistance and rebellion;

edited by Junius P. Rodriguez. Greenwood Press 2006 2v il (Greenwood milestones in African American history) set $199.95   **326**

1. Slavery—United States—Encyclopedias

ISBN 0-313-33271-1; 978-0-313-33271-5

LC 2006-31210

Encyclopedia of slave resistance and rebellion—
Continued

This encyclopedia "focuses solely on the history of resistance in slave societies, most notably in the Americas. The 20-page introduction provides a solid examination of the history of resistance to slavery and begins to examine some of the cultural issues that both maintained slavery and downplayed resistance. . . . The text will serve as a good accompaniment to reference materials on slavery, so that readers understand that with slavery went resistance." Booklist

Includes bibliographical references

Gallay, Alan

The Indian slave trade; the rise of the English empire in the American South, 1670-1717. Yale Univ. Press 2002 444p maps $35; pa $18
                                                          326
1. Native Americans—Southern States 2. Slave trade
ISBN 0-300-08754-3; 0-300-10193-7 (pa)
                                              LC 2001-5270
The author "examines how Europeans and Native Americans together developed a trade in Native American slaves that proved critical in the development of plantation slavery." Libr J

"Powerfully argued and densely detailed. . . . Gallay's stunning and engrossing work, aimed especially at advanced students and scholars, seems to spur a renewed debate on the origins and meaning of racial slavery." Choice

Includes bibliographical references

Hartman, Saidiya V.

Lose your mother; a journey along the Atlantic slave route; [by] Saidiya Hartman. Farrar, Straus and Giroux 2007 270p il $25; pa $14 *
                                                          326
1. Slave trade 2. Ghana—Description and travel
ISBN   978-0-374-27082-7;   0-374-27082-1;
978-0-374-53115-7 (pa); 0-374-53115-3 (pa)
                                              LC 2006-29407
The author "journeys along a slave route in Ghana, following the trail of captives from the hinterland to the Atlantic coast. She retraces the history of the Atlantic slave trade from the fifteenth to the twentieth century and reckons with the blank slate of her own genealogy." Publisher's note

This "is a groundbreaking book for its ability to combine autobiography, history, and politics in an unprecedented style. . . . Hartman's book is not just to be read by historians of slavery or the Atlantic world, but by all of those who desire to write of the past." Rev Am Hist

Includes bibliographical references

Hochschild, Adam, 1942-

Bury the chains; prophets, slaves, and rebels in the first human rights crusade. Houghton Mifflin 2005 468p il $26.95 *
                                                          326
1. Slavery
ISBN 0-618-10469-0   LC 2004-54091
This is an account of the "methods, and motivations behind the cause officially launched in 1787 that culminated by 1838 in the formal end of forced labor in the British Empire." Libr J

The author "brings drama and incredible research to this thrilling look at the little-celebrated abolition movement in Britain and its reverberations throughout modern democracies." Booklist

Includes bibliographical references

Horton, James Oliver

Slavery and the making of America; [by] James Oliver Horton [and] Lois E. Horton. Oxford University Press 2004 254p il maps $35; pa $18.95 *
                                                          326
1. Slavery—United States 2. African Americans—History
ISBN 0-19-517903-X; 0-19-530451-9 (pa)
                                              LC 2004-13617
The authors "explore the economic, social, and cultural implications of the enslavement of Africans in America, from the selection of slaves from certain regions of Africa to harvest the newly introduced rice crops of the Carolinas to the incentive of freedom offered on both sides of the American Revolution and Civil War to induce the assistance of slaves." Booklist

"The oft-told tale is made fresh through up-to-date slavery scholarship, the extensive use of slave narratives and archival photos and, especially, a focus on individual experience." Publ Wkly

Johnson, Charles Richard, 1948-

Africans in America: America's journey through slavery; [by] Charles Johnson, Patricia Smith, WGBH series Research Team. Harcourt Brace & Co. 1998 494p il $30; pa $15   326
1. Slavery—United States 2. African Americans—History
ISBN 0-15-100339-4; 0-15-600854-8 (pa)
                                              LC 98-20829
Based on a television series produced by WGBH Television, in Boston, Massachusetts

This book is a "history of American slavery from the pre-Colonial era to the Civil War." Libr J

"This is an impressively researched book . . . that includes photographs, drawings, and posters." Booklist

Includes bibliographical references

Johnson, Walter

Soul by soul; life inside the antebellum slave market. Harvard Univ. Press 1999 283p il $28.50; pa $15.95   326
1. Slavery—United States 2. Slave trade 3. New Orleans (La.)—Race relations
ISBN 0-674-82148-3; 0-674-00539-2 (pa)
                                              LC 99-46696
This is an examination of the antebellum slave market. "Using slave narratives, court records, planters' letters, and more, Johnson enters the slave pens and showrooms of the New Orleans slave market to observe how slavery turned men and women into merchandise and how slaves resisted such efforts to steal their humanity." Libr J

Includes bibliographical references

Nash, Gary B.

The forgotten fifth; African Americans in the age of revolution. Harvard University Press 2006 235p il $19.95 * **326**
1. United States—History—1775-1783, Revolution 2. Slavery—United States 3. African Americans—History
ISBN 0-674-02193-2 LC 2005-52692
This "book features three provocative essays based on the author's 2004 Nathan Huggins Lectures at Harvard. . . . [The] first essay examines the erroneous assumption that African Americans either supported the war or remained neutral. Instead, evidence shows that the Revolutionary War represented the first great slave revolt, wherein thousands of slaves fought for the British, who offered them freedom. The second essay argues that the period immediately following the war was the opportune time to abolish slavery. Nash convincingly shows that the arguments against abolition were flawed and that blame for the failure to abolish slavery rests squarely on poor leadership by Northern leaders. The final essay looks at the issue of race and citizenship in early America. . . . Well researched, engaging, and thought-provoking." Libr J
Includes bibliographical references

Passages to freedom; the Underground Railroad in history and memory; edited by David W. Blight. Smithsonian Books 2004 337p il map hardcover o.p. pa $19.95 * **326**
1. Underground railroad 2. Abolitionists 3. Slavery—United States
ISBN 1-58834-157-7; 0-06-085118-X (pa)
LC 2003-44289
"Among the contributing scholars are Ira Berlin, David Blight, Eddie S. Glaude, Jr., and Deborah Gray White. This is a scholarly but thoroughly accessible resource." Booklist
Includes bibliographical references

Postma, Johannes

The Atlantic slave trade. Greenwood Press 2003 xxii, 177p map (Greenwood guides to historic events, 1500-1900) $45 **326**
1. Slave trade
ISBN 0-313-31862-X LC 2002-35338
Also available in paperback from University Press of Florida
The author "covers the entire Atlantic slave trade era, from the 1400s to the final abolition of chattel slavery in the New World in 1888. The focus is on Africa and the entire New World. While he describes the many horrors of the Middle Passage, he also examines how the slave trade contributed to the development of the modern international economy. The last chapters discuss the efforts to abolish the slave trade and its legacy." SLJ
Includes bibliographical references

Rediker, Marcus Buford

The slave ship; a human history; [by] Marcus Rediker. Viking 2007 434p il map $27.95
326
1. Slave trade 2. Slavery 3. Sailors
ISBN 978-0-670-01823-9; 0-670-01823-6
LC 2007-18081

The author "considers the relationships between the slave ship captain and his crew, between the sailors and the slaves, and among the captives themselves as they endured the violent, terror-filled and often deadly journey between the coasts of Africa and America." Publ Wkly
"Rediker has made magnificent use of archival data; his probing, compassionate eye turns up numerous finds that other people who've written on this subject . . . have missed." N Y Times Book Rev
Includes bibliographical references

Remembering slavery; African Americans talk about their personal experiences of slavery and emancipation; edited by Ira Berlin, Marc Favreau, and Steven F. Miller. New Press (NY) 1998 355p pa $16.95 hardcover o.p.
326
1. Slavery—United States 2. African Americans—History—Sources
ISBN 1-56584-587-0 (pa)
This "book-and-tapes collection of slave narratives, drawn from slave narratives and audio recordings of former slaves collected by the Federal Writers' Project (FWP) during the 1930s and 1940s (some of which have been remastered and included in two 60-minute cassettes with the book), brings slavery to life as few recent books have done." Libr J
Includes bibliographical references

Schama, Simon

Rough crossings; Britain, the slaves, and the American Revolution. Ecco 2006 478p il map $29.95 * **326**
1. United States—History—1775-1783, Revolution 2. Slavery—United States
ISBN 0-06-053916-X; 978-0-06-053916-0
LC 2005-49504
First published 2005 in the United Kingdom
This book focuses on "the African American slave struggle, during and after the American Revolution, to achieve freedom in Nova Scotia and Sierra Leone and the British citizens who supported them." Libr J
This is "an epic work that gets the reader's blood rushing as it debunks the traditional American view of the Revolution." N Y Times Book Rev
Includes bibliographical references

Schneider, Dorothy

Slavery in America; [by] Dorothy Schneider and Carl J. Schneider. Rev ed. Facts on File 2007 554p il map (American experience) $80; pa $21.95
326
1. Slavery—United States
ISBN 0-8160-6241-2; 978-0-8160-6241-6; 0-8160-6839-9 (pa); 978-0-8160-6839-5 (pa)
LC 2006-24798
First published 2000 as part of the Eyewitness history series
This book recounts the history of slavery, "as well as the Reconstruction period that followed, by examining, chapter by chapter, many of its aspects: the slave catchers and their coffles in Africa, the crowded slave ships, slave auctions, life and labor on plantations, escape at-

Schneider, Dorothy—*Continued*

tempts and insurrections, and the Civil War and eventual emancipation." Publisher's note

Includes bibliographical references

Segal, Ronald, 1932-

Islam's Black slaves; the other Black diaspora. Farrar, Straus & Giroux 2001 273p maps hardcover o.p. pa $14 *   **326**

1. Slavery 2. Slave trade

ISBN 0-374-22774-8; 0-374-52797-0 (pa)

LC 00-62256

This book presents "an overview of black slavery in the Islamic world from its beginnings to modern Sudan and Morocco. . . . {It} explores Islamic slavery in China, India, the Middle East, and Africa and focuses on the differences between Islamic and Western slavery." Libr J

"The strength of this account is the meticulous documentation of what is fact and what is surmise. The dramatic narrative is sure to spark discussion and further research." Booklist

Soodalter, Ron

Hanging Captain Gordon; the life and trial of an American slave trader; Ron Soodalter. Atria Books 2006 318p il hardcover o.p. pa $15   **326**

1. Gordon, Nathaniel, 1826-1862 2. Slavery—United States 3. Slave trade 4. Trials

ISBN 0-7432-6727-3; 978-0-7432-6728-1 (pa); 0-7432-6728-1 (pa)   LC 2005-55897

This is the "story of the 1862 hanging of Nathaniel Gordon, one of many ship captains charged with breaking an 1820 law banning slave-trading, but the only one to ever be executed. Soodalter . . . uses this singular event as a prism to provide an overview of Civil War-era politics, Lincoln's presidency and the maritime economy of slavery." Publ Wkly

"This outstanding work will interest both specialists and general readers." Booklist

Includes bibliographical references

White, Shane

The sounds of slavery; discovering African American history through songs, sermons, and speech; [by] Shane White and Graham White. Beacon Press 2005 xxii, 241p hardcover o.p. pa $17 *   **326**

1. Slavery—United States 2. African Americans—History 3. Plantation life

ISBN 0-8070-5026-1; 0-8070-5027-X (pa)

LC 2004-21447

Includes audio CD

"Drawing on WPA interviews with former slaves, slave narratives, and other historical documents from the 1700s through the 1850s, the authors provide the context for the field calls, work songs, sermons, and other sounds and utterances of slaves on American plantations. The authors also focus on recollections of the wails of slaves being whipped, the barking of hounds hunting down runaways, and the keening of women losing their children to the slave block. The combination of the CD

and the book brings vibrancy and texture to a complex history that has been long neglected." Booklist

Includes discography and bibliographical references

Wills, Garry, 1934-

'Negro president'; Jefferson and the slave power. Houghton Mifflin 2003 274p il $25; pa $14   **326**

1. Jefferson, Thomas, 1743-1826 2. Slavery—United States 3. United States—Politics and government—1783-1865

ISBN 0-618-34398-9; 0-618-48537-6 (pa)

LC 2003-56710

The author "argues that the Constitution's three-fifths clause for slave 'representation' in Congress and the Electoral College gave slaveholders the edge in winning most presidential elections, controlling the federal government, and maintaining slavery by throttling personal liberties. Jefferson, Madison, Jackson, and other slaveholders became 'Negro' Presidents because of the three-fifths clause, claimed their political opponents, including the Federalists." Libr J

"Wills makes a valuable contribution to our understanding of Jefferson and the new American nation." Choice

Includes bibliographical references

327 International relations

Bobbitt, Philip

The shield of Achilles; war, peace, and the course of history. Knopf 2002 xxxii, 919p $40; pa $19.95   **327**

1. State, The 2. International relations 3. Peace 4. War

ISBN 0-375-41292-1; 0-385-72138-2 (pa)

LC 2001-38085

In this volume, Bobbitt presents "a history of diplomacy from 1500 to 1990; a theory of the history of the state; [and] an analysis of globalization. As he moves from the past into our current embrace of free-market ideology, Bobbitt introduces what he calls the 'market-state'—a new kind of government. . . . In the new 'market-state,' citizens transcend terrestrial borders and adhere to economic allegiances, rendered ever more fluid by the Internet." Christ Sci Monit

"This work will be a valuable and intriguing look at where we have been and where we might be going." Booklist

Includes bibliographical references

Nolan, Cathal J.

The Greenwood encyclopedia of international relations. Greenwood Press 2002 4v maps set $475   **327**

1. International relations—Encyclopedias

ISBN 0-313-30743-1   LC 2002-19495

This alphabetically arranged set covers the history of international relations in over 6,000 entries

This "work dwells primarily on the deeds of the great powers since the 1648 Peace of Westphalia. . . . Lively, objective writing characterizes the first-rate historical es-

Nolan, Cathal J.—*Continued*

says. . . . This work belongs in all academic and large public libraries." Libr J

Includes bibliographical references

Wright, Jonathan, 1969-

The ambassadors; from ancient Egypt to Renaissance Europe, the men who introduced the world to itself. Harcourt 2006 xxiv, 374p il $26 *

327

1. Diplomats 2. International relations

ISBN 978-0-15-101111-7; 0-15-101111-7

LC 2005-33185

The author "takes a chronological approach in examining ambassadorial history, covering missions by emissaries to Greece, India, China, and other areas of the world. Interesting vignettes from diplomatic delegations make up the majority of the book. . . . Wright fleshes out how the treatment of ambassadors has varied from outright violence to impressive displays of generosity. He also describes how ambassadors through the lens of their own cultural background have typically analyzed the actions of the rulers with whom they have consulted. Ultimately, his book fulfills its aim of serving as a good primer on ambassadorial pursuits. But more than that, it is the most comprehensive effort to examine the subject in recent years, as most diplomatic histories deal with particular conflicts." Libr J

327.1 Foreign policy and specific topics in international relations

Patten, Chris, 1944-

Cousins and strangers; America, Britain, and Europe in a new century. Times Books 2006 309p $26 *

327.1

1. World politics—1991- 2. United States—Foreign relations—Europe 3. Europe—Foreign relations—United States 4. United States—Foreign relations—Great Britain 5. Great Britain—Foreign relations—United States

ISBN 0-8050-7788-X

LC 2005-53825

First published 2005 in the United Kingdom with title: Not quite the diplomat

In this history of international relations between the United States, Great Britain, and the rest of Europe, the author "scrutinizes the final years of the twentieth century and how the fall of the Berlin Wall in 1989 fundamentally changed the nature of this Western alliance." Publisher's note

"Well-informed and light on its feet, this is the most enjoyable, readable and engaging a political book in recent memory." Publ Wkly

Richelson, Jeffrey

Spying on the bomb; American nuclear intelligence from Nazi Germany to Iran and North Korea; [by] Jeffrey T. Richelson. Norton 2006 702p il maps $34.95 *

327.1

1. American espionage 2. Nuclear weapons

ISBN 0-393-05383-0; 978-0-393-05383-8

LC 2005-14415

This is an account of "Washington's efforts to track the nuclear weapons projects of other countries. [Richelson] examines the nuclear projects of Nazi Germany, the Soviet Union, China, France, Israel, India, South Africa, Taiwan, Libya, Pakistan, Iran and North Korea, as well as Iraq." N Y Times Book Rev

The author "tells the story in exhaustive detail. It is difficult to conceive of a more thorough account, or one more prodigiously researched." Bull Atomic Sci

Includes bibliographical references

Schlesinger, Arthur M., 1917-2007

War and the American presidency; [by] Arthur M. Schlesinger, Jr. W. W. Norton 2004 160p $23.95 *

327.1

1. United States—Foreign relations 2. Iraq War, 2003

ISBN 0-393-06002-0

LC 2004-9872

This book "explores the war in Iraq, the presidency, and the future of democracy." Publisher's note

"This intelligent collection of essays, sketching historical congruities (most conspicuously between the Bush administration and Nixon's original 'imperial presidency') as well as incongruities, includes a compelling discussion of the challenges inherent to history's lens." Booklist

Schram, Martin

Avoiding armageddon; our future, our choice: companion to the PBS series from Ted Turner Documentaries. Basic Bks. 2003 356p il $26

327.1

1. Arms control 2. Terrorism

ISBN 0-465-07255-0

LC 2003-2721

This book "details the threats facing the U.S. today—from nuclear, chemical and biological attack and from terrorism—and outlines possible solutions." Publ Wkly

The author "offers fresh insights into such relevant subtopics as the Al-Qaeda operation and the mind-set of the typical suicide bomber. . . . The book . . . is shocking, discomfiting, and necessary." Booklist

Includes bibliographical references

327.12 Espionage and subversion

Dorril, Stephen

MI6; inside the covert world of Her Majesty's secret intelligence service. Free Press 2000 907p $40; pa $22

327.12

1. Great Britain. MI6 2. Intelligence service—Great Britain

ISBN 0-7432-0379-8; 0-7432-1778-0 (pa)

LC 00-29385

This study of the British secret intelligence service "focuses on the years since World War II, when MI6 was dedicated to winning the cold war. . . . The book is invaluable for readers who want to separate spy fact from spy fiction." Booklist

Garton Ash, Timothy

The file; a personal history. Random House 1997 262p pa $14 hardcover o.p.

327.12

Garton Ash, Timothy—*Continued*
1. Germany (East). Ministerium für Staatssicherheit
2. Intelligence service—Germany (East)
ISBN 0-679-77785-7 (pa)

"The author went to Berlin to study in 1978 and soon came under the scrutiny of the Stasi, the notorious East German secret police. In 1993, Garton Ash had the opportunity to examine the secret file kept on him. Comparing the file reports with his private diary of the time, he finds distortions, fabrications, and surprising omissions in the file. . . . This work makes an important contribution to the literature of the new Europe." Libr J

Grose, Peter, 1934-
Operation Rollback; America's secret war behind the Iron Curtain. Houghton Mifflin 2000 256p il map $25; pa $15 **327.12**
1. Kennan, George Frost, 1904-2005 2. Cold war
3. United States—Foreign relations—Soviet Union
4. Soviet Union—Foreign relations—United States
ISBN 0-395-51606-4; 0-618-15458-2 (pa)
LC 99-89830
"Thorough, thought-provoking and entertaining, this is a work that casts considerable light on a topic that has long lingered in the shadows." Publ Wkly
Includes bibliographical references

Gup, Ted, 1950-
Book of honor; covert lives and classified deaths at the CIA. Doubleday 2000 390p il pa $15 hardcover o.p. **327.12**
1. United States. Central Intelligence Agency 2. Spies
ISBN 0-385-49541-2 (pa) LC 99-89017
This exposé "reveals the names—and personal stories—of some three dozen CIA agents who died in the line of duty and whose identities have been kept secret—sometimes for decades. . . . Gup's sleuthing is a remarkable coup, full of high-level intrigue, cover-ups and drama." Publ Wkly

Hamrick, S. J.
Deceiving the deceivers; Kim Philby, Donald Maclean & Guy Burgess. Yale University Press 2004 297p $29.95 **327.12**
1. Philby, Kim, 1912-1988 2. Maclean, Donald Duart, 1913-1983 3. Burgess, Guy Francis de Moncy, 1911-1963 4. Espionage 5. Spies
ISBN 0-300-10416-2; 978-0-300-10416-5
LC 2004-53695
In this "analysis of one of the most famous Cold War espionage cases, Hamrick . . . asserts that British Intelligence had identified Donald Maclean as a Soviet agent earlier than the accepted date of spring 1951. . . . [Hamilton's] subversive recasting of the Philby-Maclean-Burgess case will fascinate and challenge all those interested in Cold War history." Publ Wkly
Includes bibliographical references

Haynes, John Earl
Venona; decoding Soviet espionage in America; [by] John Earl Haynes and Harvey Klehr. Yale Univ. Press 1999 487p $35; pa $14.95 **327.12**
1. Communist Party (U.S.) 2. Russian espionage
3. Communism—United States
ISBN 0-300-07771-8; 0-300-08462-5 (pa)
LC 98-51464
"The Venona Project, a U.S. secret revealed only in 1995, decrypted Soviet intelligence's wartime cable traffic. . . . The authors systematically recount Venona's references to approximately 350 Soviet spies in U.S. government and industry—some of them highly placed, most notoriously Alger Hiss. . . . *Venona* may open a fundamental revision of U.S. history." Booklist

Herrington, Stuart A., 1941-
Traitors among us; inside the spy catcher's world. Harcourt 2000 409p il pa $14 **327.12**
1. Intelligence service—United States 2. Russian espionage
ISBN 0-15-601117-4 LC 00-38893
First published 1999 by Presidio Press
"Herrington, former head of the U.S. Army Counterintelligence Unit . . . offers a fascinating view of life as a spy catcher in West Berlin during the height of the Cold War. His description of the search for and capture of Clyde Conrad and James Hall . . . (who for 13 years handed over America's secret war plans to the Soviets) surpasses any spy fiction." Libr J

Kessler, Ronald
Inside the CIA; revealing the secrets of the world's most powerful spy agency. Pocket Bks. 1992 xxiii, 283p il pa $7.99 hardcover o.p. **327.12**
1. United States. Central Intelligence Agency
2. Intelligence service—United States
ISBN 0-671-73458-X (pa) LC 92-11084
"Writing with the cooperation of active and retired personnel, Kessler offers a working portrait of the contemporary CIA. His background in journalistic study of intelligence, augmented by an unusual array of other resources, enables him to provide an account unique for balance, perspective, clarity of writing, and the large amount of factual material." Booklist

Laird, Thomas
Into Tibet; the CIA's first atomic spy and his secret expedition to Lhasa. Grove Press 2002 364p il $26; pa $15 **327.12**
1. American espionage 2. United States—Foreign relations—China 3. China—Foreign relations—United States 4. Tibet (China)
ISBN 0-8021-1714-7; 0-8021-3999-X (pa)
LC 2001-58459
The author "traces the story of two CIA agents, Douglas Mackiernan and Frank Bessac, sent on an intelligence expedition to Tibet in 1949-1950. . . . Focusing on the heart-stopping details of the expedition itself, Laird gives

Laird, Thomas—*Continued*

the now familiar story of callous CIA manipulation an absorbing twist." Publ Wkly

Includes bibliographical references

Prados, John

Presidents' secret wars; CIA and Pentagon covert operations from World War II through the Persian Gulf. rev & expanded ed. Dee, I.R. 1996 572p pa $18.95 **327.12**

1. United States. Central Intelligence Agency 2. Intelligence service—United States

ISBN 1-56663-108-4 LC 95-49737

"An Elephant paperback"

First published 1986

The author argues that presidents have too much freedom of action in covert operations, and discusses such operations with regard to the Cold War, Asia, Cuba, Vietnam, Angola, Afghanistan, Nicaragua, and the Persian Gulf

Includes bibliographical references

Richelson, Jeffrey

The wizards of Langley; inside the CIA's Directorate of Science and Technology; {by} Jeffrey T. Richelson. Westview Press 2001 386p il pa $17 hardcover o.p. **327.12**

1. United States. Central Intelligence Agency. Directorate of Science and Technology

ISBN 0-8133-4059-4 (pa)

One of the three main divisions of the CIA, "the Directorate of Science and Technology, was created in 1963, and Richelson offers this chronological narrative of its leaders and known activities. The text is peppered with code names as Richelson tracks the course of projects, such as the U-2 and its successors in the overhead reconnaissance role, spy satellites. Alongside stories of the CIA's fencing with the military over the years for operational control of these expensive spacecraft, Richelson relates specific international incidents in which satellite-gathered intelligence figured, as well as the stories of sundry eavesdropping technologies." Booklist

The author "provides a richly detailed account of the agency's work." Libr J

Smith, W. Thomas

Encyclopedia of the Central Intelligence Agency; [by] W. Thomas Smith Jr. Facts on File 2003 282p il (Facts on File library of American history) $60; pa $19.95 * **327.12**

1. United States. Central Intelligence Agency

ISBN 0-8160-4666-2; 0-8160-4667-0 (pa)

This encyclopedia includes "more than 500 historical, biographical, and general entries about the intelligence-gathering, covert-action agency established in 1947. . . . Current through March 2003, the encyclopedia also covers predecessor organizations such as the World War II-era Office of Strategic Services (OSS). . . . The work covers terrorism extensively, not only in the entry *September 11, 2001, terrorist attacks on the United States,* which is one of the longest in the volume, but also in entries for Osama bin Laden and the Department of Homeland Security, among others." Booklist

Includes bibliographical references

Stafford, David, 1942-

Spies beneath Berlin. Overlook Press 2003 211p il $24.95; pa $15.95 **327.12**

1. United States. Central Intelligence Agency 2. KGB 3. Espionage 4. Cold war

ISBN 1-58567-361-7; 1-58567-549-0 (pa)

LC 2002-34628

This is the "story of the secret tunnel beneath the Russian sector of Berlin that existed for more than a year in the mid-1950s and enabled the British and Americans to tap into all area Russian telephone conversations. But this amazing intelligence achievement was complicated by another development: the KGB knew about the tunnel through the traitorous activities of its undercover agent, George Blake, but could not reveal that they knew for fear that they might compromise the invaluable Blake. . . . What a great story! And Stafford tells it exceedingly well in sprightly prose. This book belongs in all collections that cover Cold War espionage." Libr J

Includes bibliographical references

Taubman, Philip

Secret empire; Eisenhower, the CIA, and the hidden story of America's space espionage. Simon & Schuster 2003 xx, 441p il $27; pa $15 **327.12**

1. United States. Central Intelligence Agency 2. Aerial reconnaissance 3. Cold war

ISBN 0-684-85699-9; 0-684-85700-6 (pa)

LC 2002-42937

The author "chronicles the development of overhead reconnaissance, a technology that made the world safer by providing accurate information about Soviet capacities." N Y Times Book Rev

"This book functions marvelously as a history of science, detailing the research, engineering and policy decisions behind the U2 and Corona, but it's also an excellent social history of the Cold War in the 1950s and early '60s. It's a page-turner as well." Publ Wkly

Includes bibliographical references

Theoharis, Athan G.

Chasing spies; how the FBI failed in counterintelligence but promoted the politics of McCarthyism in the Cold War years; [by] Athan Theoharis. Dee, I.R. 2002 307p $27.50 **327.12**

1. United States. Federal Bureau of Investigation 2. Intelligence service—United States 3. United States—Politics and government—1945-

ISBN 1-56663-420-2 LC 2001-47399

The author "argues that Hoover's FBI was much more interested in promoting an anti-Communist agenda, which would enhance the credibility of the agency and its political influence, than in countering Soviet espionage. . . . Theoharis's book is an outstanding contribution to the growing historical literature on the Cold War and a potent warning to anyone who thinks we have heard the last word on the Cold War." Libr J

Includes bibliographical references

Trulock, Notra

Code name Kindred Spirit; inside the Chinese nuclear espionage scandal. Encounter Bks. 2002 xxi, 385p il $26.95   **327.12**

1. Lee, Wen Ho 2. Los Alamos National Laboratory—Security measures 3. Spies

ISBN 1-89355-451-1   LC 2002-67856

Trulock was the head of the Department of Energy's "intelligence office during the investigation into whether Los Alamos scientist Wen Ho Lee had given nuclear warhead secrets to China. . . . This detailed account reveals that the spy hunt didn't focus solely on Lee, or even on Los Alamos. . . . While he denies knowledge as to whether Lee 'did it,' the author drops hints that Lee and his wife may have been double agents. . . . He provides a unique look into the American intelligence community and an unsettling perspective on the lax attitude toward national security." Publ Wkly

Includes bibliographical references

Vise, David A.

The bureau and the mole; the unmasking of Robert Philip Hanssen, the most dangerous double agent in FBI history. Atlantic Monthly Press 2002 272p il $25; pa $14   **327.12**

1. Hanssen, Robert Philip 2. United States. Federal Bureau of Investigation 3. Espionage

ISBN 0-87113-834-4; 0-8021-3951-5 (pa)

LC 2001-53872

"In February 2001, FBI special agent Bob Hanssen was arrested as a double agent for Russian intelligence in what turned out to be the biggest sellout of U.S. national security secrets in the long history of the bureau. . . . [The author] details how Hanssen did it and how he got caught." Booklist

Includes bibliographical references

Weiner, Tim

Legacy of ashes; the history of the C.I.A. Doubleday 2007 702p il $27.95   **327.12**

1. United States. Central Intelligence Agency 2. Intelligence service—United States

ISBN 978-0-385-51445-3; 0-385-51445-X

LC 2007-04077

This book "takes the CIA from its creation after World War II, through its battles in the cold war and the war on terror, to its . . . [circumstances] after 9/11." Publisher's note

This "is a credible and damning indictment of American intelligence policy." Publ Wkly

Includes bibliographical references

Weinstein, Allen

The haunted wood; Soviet espionage in America—the Stalin era; {by} Allen Weinstein, Alexander Vassiliev. Random House 1999 xxviii, 402p il pa $23 hardcover o.p.   **327.12**

1. Russian espionage 2. Spies 3. United States—History—1933-1945

ISBN 0-375-75536-5 (pa)   LC 98-11801

The authors examine "the espionage networks that Moscow created in the United States, especially after

Franklin Roosevelt's establishment of diplomatic relations with the USSR in 1934. From then until 1945, the Soviets amassed . . . information from agents and sources in a range of U.S. government agencies. . . . The information included diplomatic secrets and planning for the postwar period (particularly policy toward Germany and the USSR), U.S. industrial and military production, and, . . . the atom-bomb project." Natl Rev

"This is a relentlessly powerful book and an eye-opener for all readers." Libr J

Includes bibliographical references

Wise, David, 1930-

Cassidy's run; the secret spy war over nerve gas. Random House 2000 228p il pa $15 hardcover o.p.   **327.12**

1. Cassidy, Joseph Edward 2. United States. Federal Bureau of Investigation 3. Russian espionage

ISBN 0-8129-9263-6 (pa)   LC 99-15802

The "reconstruction of a hitherto unknown counterespionage case. Joseph Cassidy's double life began in August 1959. . . . For 20 years Cassidy, a master sergeant, worked for the United States during the day and pretended to work for the Soviet Union at night. . . . The F.B.I. decided to use this double agent to undermine the Soviet chemical weapons industry." N Y Times Book Rev

Spy: the inside story of how the FBI's Robert Hanssen betrayed America. Random House 2002 309p $24.95; pa $13.95   **327.12**

1. Hanssen, Robert Philip 2. United States. Federal Bureau of Investigation 3. Espionage

ISBN 0-375-50745-0; 0-375-75894-1 (pa)

LC 2002-31867

This book attempts to "unravel the mystery of how and why FBI staffer Robert Hanssen was able to sell secrets to the KGB for almost 22 years. . . . Wise presents a comprehensive portrait of Hanssen's life as a spy and the government's quest to uncover and prosecute him." Publ Wkly

"A relentless reporter and true expert on the world of spying, Wise recounts Hanssen's story and the hunt to catch him in precise, if sometimes overwhelming detail." N Y Times Book Rev

327.73   United States—Foreign relations

Bernstein, Richard

The coming conflict with China; {by} Richard Bernstein and Ross H. Munro. Knopf 1997 245p pa $13 hardcover o.p.   **327.73**

1. United States—Foreign relations—China 2. China—Foreign relations—United States 3. China—Politics and government

ISBN 0-679-77662-1 (pa)   LC 96-44434

"The authors argue that China is no longer a strategic friend of the United States but a formidable enemy. China's intention to play a more active role in Asian affairs is presented here as a threat to U.S. political and economic interests." Libr J

"A controversial but effective critique." Booklist

Includes bibliographical references

Brands, H. W.
What America owes the world; the struggle for the soul of foreign policy. Cambridge Univ. Press 1998 335p $65; pa $23 **327.73**
   1. United States—Foreign relations
   ISBN 0-521-63031-2; 0-521-63968-9 (pa)
                              LC 97-38837
"With the end of the Cold War, a long time debate has been resumed between two schools of thought, the *exemplarists* and the *vindicators*. The former . . . contends that the US owes the world the example of a humane democratic and prosperous society. The vindicators go beyond example and, through active measures, coercion, and force, support what is right in the world. The literature offers examples of the two schools analyzed in Brands's intellectual history. . . . This is a valuable contribution to the intellectual history of American foreign policy." Choice
Includes bibliographical references

Cohen, Stephen F.
Failed crusade; America and the tragedy of post-Communist Russia. Norton 2000 304p pa $14.95 hardcover o.p. **327.73**
   1. United States—Foreign relations—Russia 2. Russia (Federation)—Economic conditions
   ISBN 0-393-32226-2 (pa)   LC 00-35501
"In part 1, Cohen describes the arrogant missionary crusade to impose U.S. political and economic institutions on the former Soviet Union. . . . Part 2 gathers 10 Cohen critiques of this American crusade published between 1992 and 1998. . . . In part 3, Cohen urges that the goal of U.S. policy should be to reduce the risk of nuclear disaster by stabilizing this giant nuclear power." Booklist
Includes bibliographical references

Dreyfuss, Robert
Devil's game; how the United States helped unleash fundamentalist Islam. 1st ed. Metropolitan Books 2005 388p (American empire project) $27.50 **327.73**
   1. Islamic fundamentalism 2. United States—Foreign relations—Middle East 3. Middle East—Foreign relations—United States
   ISBN 0-8050-7652-2   LC 2005-43881
This is the "story of America's misguided efforts, stretching across decades, to dominate the strategically vital Middle East by courting and cultivating Islamic fundamentalism." Publisher's note
This "is a stunning summary of missed opportunities and signals ignored." Libr J
Includes bibliographical references

Fukuyama, Francis
America at the crossroads; democracy, power, and the neoconservative legacy. Yale University Press 2006 226p (The Castle lectures in ethics, politics, and economics) $25 **327.73**
   1. Conservatism 2. United States—Foreign relations
   ISBN 0-300-11399-4; 978-0-300-11399-0
                         LC 2005-29370

The author offers a history and explanation "of the neoconservative movement and its chief ideas, places himself firmly within that movement, and then goes on to register his strong and passionate dissent from the interpretation of the neoconservative approach to foreign policy that characterized George W. Bush's first term." Foreign Affairs
Includes bibliographical references

Gates, Robert M.
From the shadows; the ultimate insider's story of five presidents and how they won the Cold War. Simon & Schuster 1996 604p il pa $16 hardcover o.p. **327.73**
   1. Cold war 2. United States—Foreign relations—Soviet Union 3. Soviet Union—Foreign relations—United States
   ISBN 0-684-83497-9 (pa)   LC 95-51704
"Gates chronicles the demise of Communism in Eastern Europe and the Soviet Union from the . . . perspective of someone who served during the Nixon through Bush administrations." Libr J
This is an "often entertaining, frequently self-serving but always thoughtful account of the United States' long effort to contain the Soviet Union." N Y Times Book Rev
Includes bibliographical references

Grandin, Greg, 1962-
Empire's workshop; Latin America, the United States, and the rise of the new imperialism. Metropolitan Books 2006 286p (The American empire project) $25 **327.73**
   1. United States—Foreign relations—Latin America 2. Latin America—Foreign relations—United States 3. Imperialism
   ISBN 978-0-8050-7738-4; 0-8050-7738-3
                        LC 2005-56125
This book argues that "Latin America has functioned as a laboratory for American extraterritorial rule." Publisher's note
"This timely book offers an analysis of the ideological foundations of today's foreign policy consensus and a cautionary tale about its dark legacy." Publ Wkly
Includes bibliographical references

Halberstam, David, 1934-2007
War in a time of peace; Bush, Clinton, and the generals. Scribner 2001 543p $28; pa $16
                                    327.73
   1. Bush, George, 1924- 2. Clinton, Bill, 1946- 3. United States—Foreign relations 4. United States—Politics and government—1989-
   ISBN 0-7432-0212-0; 0-7432-2323-3 (pa)
                        LC 2001-38416
Halberstam examines "American foreign and military policy in the 1990s—emphasizing the background, experience, and personalities of the key players." Christ Sci Monit
"This is vintage Halberstam, combining sharp portraits of the political players . . . with nuanced reportage of the events they shape and are shaped by." Publ Wkly
Includes bibliographical references

Hart, Gary, 1936-
The fourth power; a grand strategy for the
United States in the 21st Century. Oxford
University Press 2004 187p $22   **327.73**
1. World politics—1991- 2. Military policy—United
States 3. United States—Foreign relations
ISBN 0-19-517683-9   LC 2004-1444
The author "fears that containment of communism has
been supplanted by a blatant strategy of empire as the
basis of American foreign policy. . . . As an alternative,
Hart promotes a foreign policy designed to advance the
'fourth power'—that is, the power of core American values, including representative government and individual
liberty. . . . Hart states his case with eloquence and generally sound reasoning, and his assertions deserve to be
seriously considered." Booklist

Hastedt, Glenn P., 1950-
Encyclopedia of American foreign policy; by
Glenn Hastedt. Facts on File 2003 562p il map
$85 *   **327.73**
1. United States—Foreign relations—Encyclopedias
ISBN 0-8160-4642-5   LC 2003-49186
In this reference, Hastedt "addresses the four major
foreign policy themes: selection of a grand strategy, the
role of the public voice, the policymaking process, and
the influence of the past. The more than 475 entries, all
by Hastedt, are arranged alphabetically and include people, agencies, documents, and events rather than broader
issues and ideological constructs of US foreign policy.
Entries are quite readable and rarely run longer than a
page; most are also cross-referenced and have bibliographies." Choice
Includes bibliographical references

Hirsh, Michael
At war with ourselves; why America is
squandering its chance to build a better world.
Oxford University Press 2003 288p hardcover o.p.
pa $15.95   **327.73**
1. United States—Foreign relations 2. Globalization
3. American national characteristics
ISBN 0-19-515269-7; 0-19-517602-2 (pa)
    LC 2002-193013
The author argues that post-Cold War presidential administrations "have failed to grasp the nation's historic
mandate as orchestrator of the new world order. . . .
Hirsh reports on the discordant policies of Clinton and
Bush, while providing the lay reader with an overview of
the conflicts and personalities that have shaped a lackluster U.S. foreign policy over the past decade." Publ Wkly
"Hirsh outlines a sensible basis for détente between
the warring hegemonists and internationalists, an America that leads without bullying." N Y Times Book Rev
Includes bibliographical references

Kagan, Robert
Dangerous nation. Knopf 2006 527p $30 *
    327.73
1. United States—Foreign relations 2. United States—
Territorial expansion
ISBN 0-375-41105-4   LC 2006-45264
"This is a Borzoi book"

The author argues "that Americans have been increasing their global power and influence steadily for the past
four centuries. . . . He focuses on the Declaration of Independence as the document that firmly established the
American conviction that the inalienable rights of all
mankind transcended territorial borders and blood ties.
American nationalism, he [aims to] show, was always in-
ternationalist at its core." Publisher's note
This "is a first-rate work of history, based on prodigious reading and enlivened by a powerful prose style."
Economist
Includes bibliographical references

Of paradise and power; America and Europe in
the new world order. Knopf 2003 103p $18; pa
$11   **327.73**
1. European Union 2. Europe—Foreign relations—
United States 3. United States—Foreign relations—Europe
ISBN 1-4000-4093-0; 1-4000-3418-3 (pa)
    LC 2002-38549
Published in the United Kingdom with title: Paradise
and power
"Kagan argues that the United States and Europe no
longer inhabit the same universe where power politics is
concerned. Power, then, lies at the heart of the transatlantic culture war. Americans have it—making them a
target and priming them to use it to address foreign
threats. Europeans don't have it, and, judging by their
trifling defense budgets, don't want it. . . . This brilliant
and controversial work belongs in all library collections."
Libr J
Includes bibliographical references

Kinzer, Stephen
All the Shah's men; an American coup and the
roots of Middle East terror. John Wiley & Sons
2003 258p il map hardcover o.p. pa $14.95
    327.73
1. Mosaddeq, Mohammad, 1880-1967 2. Iran—Politics
and government 3. United States—Foreign relations—
Iran
ISBN 0-471-26517-9; 0-471-67878-3 (pa)
    LC 2003-9968
The author "has reconstructed the CIA's 1953 overthrow of the elected leader of Iran, Mohammad
Mossadegh, who was wildly popular at home for having
nationalized his country's oil industry. The coup ushered
in the long and brutal dictatorship of Mohammad Reza
Shah, widely seen as a U.S. puppet and himself overthrown by the Islamic revolution of 1979." Publ Wkly
"This comprehensive . . . account of the nationaliza-
tion of the Anglo-Iranian Oil Company under the leadership of Mohammad Mossadegh in 1951 . . . is a valuable and informative work." Choice
Includes bibliographical references

Overthrow; America's century of regime change
from Hawaii to Iraq. Times Books 2006 384p il
$27.50 *   **327.73**
1. United States—Foreign relations 2. Intervention (International law)
ISBN 0-8050-7861-4; 978-0-8050-7861-9
    LC 2005-54856

Kinzer, Stephen—*Continued*

This "is the history of forcible regime changes by the United States and its local allies over the past 110 years, starting with the undermining of the Hawaiian monarchy in 1893, passing through Cuba (1898), the Philippines (1898), Iran (1953), Guatemala (1954) and elsewhere, and ending with present-day Iraq. . . . It should be essential reading for any Americans who wish to understand both their country's historical record in international affairs, and why that record has provoked anger and distrust in much of the world." N Y Times Book Rev

Includes bibliographical references

Kissinger, Henry, 1923-

Diplomacy. Simon & Schuster 1994 912p il maps pa $22 hardcover o.p. **327.73**
1. Diplomacy 2. United States—Foreign relations
ISBN 0-671-51099-1 (pa) LC 93-44001
Kissinger "draws lessons from the statecraft of Richelieu, Napoleon, Bismarck and Metternich, then . . . reappraises the foreign policy blunders and the failures of moral nerve and vision that led in our century to the mass carnage of two world wars, genocide, Cold War and a nuclear arms race." Publ Wkly

"This is an important contribution to the theoretical literature on foreign affairs and will also serve quite ably as a one-volume synthesis of modern diplomatic history. All libraries should have this impressive book." Libr J

Includes bibliographical references

Does America need a foreign policy? towards a diplomacy for the 21st century. Simon & Schuster 2001 318p maps $30; pa $15 **327.73**
1. United States—Foreign relations
ISBN 0-684-85567-4; 0-684-85568-2 (pa)
LC 2001-20564
Kissinger "surveys Europe, Latin America, Asia, Africa and the Middle East, giving the historical context, raising the issues in each region, and then searching out some ideas on what a wise American policy would do about them." Christ Sci Monit

Includes bibliographical references

LaFeber, Walter

The clash; a history of U.S.-Japan relations. Norton 1997 xxii, 508p il maps pa $16.95 hardcover o.p. **327.73**
1. United States—Foreign relations—Japan 2. Japan—Foreign relations—United States
ISBN 0-393-31837-0 (pa) LC 96-48565
LaFeber presents an overview of U.S.-Japan relations from the 1850s to the present. He argues that "amid all the changes in the American-Japanese relationship, two fundamental continuities persist: . . . different conceptions of capitalism and divergent approaches to China." Booklist

Includes bibliographical references

MacMillan, Margaret

Nixon and Mao; the week that changed the world. Random House 2007 404p il map $27.95 *
327.73
1. Nixon, Richard M. (Richard Milhous), 1913-1994 2. Mao Zedong, 1893-1976 3. United States—Foreign relations—China 4. China—Foreign relations—United States
ISBN 978-1-4000-6127-3; 1-4000-6127-X
LC 2006-48644
Published in Canada with title: Nixon in China
"In February 1972, President Nixon met Chairman Mao in Beijing. The meeting was the result of intensive diplomatic activity that had been ongoing for several months but was itself anticlimactic. . . . [The author] recounts the negotiations in a crisp narrative that utilizes a wide variety of sources." Booklist

Includes bibliographical references

Mahbubani, Kishore

Beyond the age of innocence; a worldly view of America; Kishore Mahbubani. Public Affairs 2005 235p il $26 **327.73**
1. United States—Foreign opinion
ISBN 1-586-48268-8 LC 2004-43182
The author "expresses his anguish over deepening distrust and resentment of the United States. . . . His thesis is that in dominating the world the United States also transformed it, unleashing globalizing forces that Washington is ill equipped to manage." Foriegn Affairs

"Pragmatic tough love for the new century." Booklist

Includes bibliographical references

Mann, Jim, 1946-

About face; a history of America's curious relationship with China, from Nixon to Clinton. Knopf 1999 433p il $30; pa $16 **327.73**
1. United States—Foreign relations—China 2. China—Foreign relations—United States
ISBN 0-679-45053-X; 0-679-76861-0 (pa)
LC 98-6285
The author contends that "the hallmark of the current policy, which was originated by Richard Nixon and reached its apogee under Jimmy Carter, is a preoccupation with the balance of power and . . . [a] lack of concern with China's domestic system or the human rights of the Chinese people." New Repub

"Mann's descriptions of the behind-the-scenes jockeying among U.S. policy makers—the micropolitics behind the geopolitics—are so entertaining that his book will appeal to readers beyond foreign policy junkies." Publ Wkly

Includes bibliographical references

Moynihan, Daniel Patrick, 1927-2003

On the law of nations. Harvard Univ. Press 1990 211p $37; pa $10.95 **327.73**
1. International law 2. United States—Foreign relations
ISBN 0-674-63575-2; 0-674-63576-0 (pa)
LC 90-33227

Moynihan, Daniel Patrick, 1927-2003—_Continued_

"In the seven essays in this volume, Moynihan traces U.S. attitudes toward international law from the American Revolution to the current administration, and he makes a powerful argument for a return to the conventions of international behavior set out by Woodrow Wilson and the United Nations." Libr J

Nye, Joseph S., Jr.

The paradox of American power; why the world's only superpower can't go it alone; [by] Joseph S. Nye, Jr. Oxford Univ. Press 2002 222p hardcover o.p. pa $13.95   **327.73**

1. Power (Social sciences) 2. United States—Foreign relations 3. International cooperation

ISBN 0-19-515088-0; 0-19-516110-6 (pa)

           LC 2001-52369

The author "offers a prescription for America's new role in the world that calls for a broader, more responsible, and cooperative relationship with the rest of the world. . . . A very thoughtful look ahead at American power through this century." Booklist

Oren, Michael

Power, faith and fantasy; America in the Middle East, 1776 to the Present; [by] Michael B. Oren. W.W.Norton & Co. 2007 xxii, 778p il map $35 *   **327.73**

1. Middle East—Foreign relations—United States 2. United States—Foreign relations—Middle East

ISBN 0-393-05826-3; 978-0-393-05826-0

           LC 2006-36571

"For more than 230 years, the United States has intertwined itself with the Middle East. Starting in 1776 with the attacks by Barbary pirates on American ships and ending with a discussion of America's current involvement in the region, especially Iraq, Oren . . . does a fine job of showing the circumstances that link our two cultures." Libr J

Includes bibliographical references

Pillar, Paul R., 1947-

Terrorism and U.S. foreign policy. Brookings Institution Press 2001 272p $26.95   **327.73**

1. Terrorism 2. United States—Foreign relations

ISBN 0-8157-0004-0   LC 00-13070

This is an "analyses of current terrorist threats, the status of terrorism in world politics, counterterrorist tools available to the United States, state sponsors of terrorism, and how best to educate the public about terrorist threats and counterterrorism." Publisher's note

"Pillar is most useful when he shows that the disunity within the Muslim world indicates that any successful struggle against terrorism must include all kinds of deal-making in order to play off groups and states against one another." N Y Times Book Rev

Includes bibliographical references

Pollack, Kenneth M.

The Persian puzzle; the conflict between Iran and America. Random House 2004 xxvi, 539p il map $26.95   **327.73**

1. United States—Foreign relations—Iran 2. Iran—Foreign relations—United States

ISBN 1-400-06315-9   LC 2004-54153

In this discussion of relations between Iran and the United States the author "argues against invading Iran, . . . calls for a flexible approach that would take into account fluctuations in Iranian foreign policy (caused by internal tensions in the country between hard-liners and pragmatists) and discusses the uses of containment and carrot-and-stick incentives." N Y Times (Late N Y Ed)

"For anyone wanting to understand the stark choices the U.S. faces concerning Iran, and how to respond to them, this is the place to start." Publ Wkly

Purdy, Jedediah, 1974-

Being America; liberty, commerce, and violence in an American world. Knopf 2003 337p $24; pa $14   **327.73**

1. United States—Foreign relations 2. International relations

ISBN 0-375-41307-3; 0-375-72755-8 (pa)

           LC 2002-116390

The author's theme is "globalization in its social, economic and, above all, intellectual aspects, his goal an answer to the oft-repeated question 'Why do they hate us?' In 2001 Purdy went to see for himself, traveling through the Middle East and Asia, talking to students, business executives, ethnic nationalists, religious fanatics. This is his report on the bad news." N Y Times Book Rev

"This is an ambitious book, rooted in Western political philosophy and concerned with concepts like modernity, globalization, and fundamentalism. . . . The result is a timely, thoughtful, and important work showing Purdy to be a writer of great promise." Libr J

Includes bibliographical references

Talbott, Strobe

The Russia hand; a memoir of presidential diplomacy. Random House 2002 478p il $29.95; pa $15.95   **327.73**

1. Clinton, Bill, 1946- 2. Yeltsin, Boris 3. United States—Foreign relations—Russia 4. Russia—Foreign relations—United States

ISBN 0-375-50714-0; 0-8129-6846-8 (pa)

           LC 2001-48843

Talbott writes of his experiences as "President Bill Clinton's top adviser and operative for relations with the former Soviet Union. . . . 'The Russia Hand' recounts the major and minor crises over issues like the expansion of NATO, the removal of missiles from Ukraine, Western military action against the Bosnian Serbs, the . . . confrontation over Kosovo, the question of antimissile defense." N Y Times (Late N Y Ed)

Includes bibliographical references

Tuchman, Barbara Wertheim
Stilwell and the American experience in China, 1911-45; [by] Barbara W. Tuchman. Grove Press 2001 621p map pa $20 *   **327.73**
1. United States—Foreign relations—China 2. China—Foreign relations—United States 3. World War, 1939-1945—China
ISBN 0-8021-3852-7; 978-0-8021-3852-1
LC 2001-40154
First published 1970 by Macmillian
Using the career of General "Vinegar Joe" Stilwell as a vehicle, this is a history of America's relations with China from the end of the Manchu Empire to the rise of Mao Tse-tung.
Includes bibliographical references

Unger, Craig
House of Bush, house of Saud; the secret relationship between the world's two most powerful dynasties. Scribner 2004 356p il $26; pa $15   **327.73**
1. Bush family 2. Saudi Arabia—Kings and rulers 3. September 11 terrorist attacks, 2001
ISBN 0-7432-5337-X; 0-7432-5339-6 (pa)
LC 2004-274217
The author "pieces together the highly unusual and close personal and financial relationships between the Bush family and the ruling family of Saudi Arabia—and questions the implications for Bush's preparedness, or possible lack thereof, for September 11. . . . Unger also questions whether the Bush grew so complacent about the Saudis that his administration ignored then White House terrorism czar Richard Clarke's repeated warnings and recommendations about the Saudis and al-Qaeda." Publ Wkly
Includes bibliographical references

328.73   Legislative process in the United States

Barone, Michael
The almanac of American politics 2008; the senators, the representatives and the governors their records and election results, their states and districts; [by] Michael Barone with Richard E. Cohen. National Journal Group 2007 1864p il $94.95; pa $74.95 *   **328.73**
1. United States. Congress 2. United States—Politics and government 3. Almanacs
ISBN   978-0-89234-116-0;   0-89234-116-5; 978-0-89234-117-7 (pa); 0-89234-117-3 (pa)
First published 1972 by Gambit. Periodically revised
"Provides essential data for the assessment of each representative and senator in Congress. Specifics include political background on the state or congressional district, biographies, voting records, group ratings (by such groups as Americans for Democratic Action and Americans for Constitutional Action), and recent election results. Provides information on the governor of each state. Arranged by state. Congressional district maps." Ref Sources for Small & Medium-sized Libr. 6th edition

Biographical directory of the American Congress, 1774-1996; the Continental Congress, September 5, 1774, to October 21, 1788, and the Congress of the United States, from the First through the 104th Congress, March 4, 1789, to January 3, 1997. CQ Staff Directories 1997 2108p il $295   **328.73**
1. United States. Congress 2. United States—Biography—Dictionaries
ISBN 0-87289-124-0
First published 1869 with title: Dictionary of the United States congress
This directory provides brief biographies of members of Congress from the Continental Congress through the 104th Congress. Each entry includes date and place of birth, education and employment, some entries also give additional biographical references
This is "an indispensable reference tool for students and scholars of U.S. history and politics. . . . It is the most comprehensive biographical source on congressional members." Am Ref Books Annu, 1998

Broder, David S.
Democracy derailed; initiative campaigns and the power of money. Harcourt 2000 260p map pa $14 hardcover o.p.   **328.73**
1. Referendum 2. Democracy 3. United States—Politics and government
ISBN 0-15-601410-6 (pa)
LC 99-54190
"A James H. Silberman book"
"The initiative process, available in half the states and hundreds of cities, allows for the placement on election ballots of legislative proposals that emanate directly from sources outside the legislative branch of government. . . . {The author explores how} lawyers, campaign consultants, signature-gathering firms, and other players sell their services to affluent interest groups or wealthy individuals who mask private policy and business agendas under the guise of political reform." Libr J
Includes bibliographical references

Congress A to Z. 5th ed. CQ Press 2008 xxxiv, 704p il map (CQ's American government A to Z series) $85 *   **328.73**
1. United States. Congress
ISBN 978-0-87289-558-4   LC 2008-11284
"CQ Press, a Division of Congressional Quarterly Inc."
First published 1988
This work provides information on the structure and work of Congress in some 340 alphabetical entries.
Includes bibliographical references

CQ's politics in America; 2008, the 110th Congress; by Congressional Quarterly staff; Jackie Koszczuk and Martha Angle, editors. CQ Press 2007 xxviii, 1212p il $125; pa $85 *   **328.73**
1. United States. Congress 2. Elections—United States
ISSN 1527-8913
ISBN   978-0-87289-545-4;   0-87289-545-9; 978-0-87289-547-8 (pa); 0-87289-547-5 (pa)
Biennial. First published 1981

CQ's politics in America—*Continued*
Current editors: David J. Hawkings and Brian Nutting; Hardcover edition includes free access to online versions and updates

Profiles each current member of Congress, providing political background, statistical information, committee assignments, etc.

Dewhirst, Robert E.
Encyclopedia of the United States Congress; [by] Robert E. Dewhirst; John David Rausch, Jr., associate editor. Facts on File 2006 578p il (Facts on File library of American history) $95 *

328.73

1. United States. Congress
ISBN 0-8160-5058-9   LC 2005-28124

This encyclopedia covers "the people, events, and terms involved in the legislative branch of government. It also provides explanations of the relationships between the legislative and other branches of government, court cases, elections, political opponents, congressional leaders, scandals, controversial issues, and the inner workings of Congress." Publisher's note

Includes bibliographical references

Guide to Congress. 6th ed. CQ Press 2008 2v il map set $350 *   328.73
1. United States. Congress
ISBN 978-0-8728-9295-8   LC 2007-33245

First published 1971 with title: Congressional Quarterly's guide to the Congress of the United States

"Covers history and workings of Congress, with biographical data on all members." N Y Public Libr Book of How & Where to Look It Up

"To really understand Congress, there is nothing better than these large volumes." Booklist

Includes bibliographical references

Hamilton, Lee H.
How Congress works and why you should care. Indiana University Press 2004 156p $29.95; pa $14.95   328.73
1. United States. Congress
ISBN 0-253-34425-5; 0-253-21695-8 (pa)
          LC 2003-17926

This "primer details the history of Congress, its importance and some of the critical actions it has taken. . . . Hamilton also describes the 'complicated and untidy' process by which Congress really works and why we 'need more people who know how to practice the art of politics.' . . . Parents should send this primer off with their kids to college." Publ Wkly

Includes bibliographical references

Official Congressional Directory, 110th Congress. U.S. Govt. Ptg. Office 2007 xxiii, 1209p il map $54; pa $44   328.73
1. United States. Congress
ISSN 0160-9890
ISBN 978-0-16-078878-9; 978-0-16-078879-6 (pa)
Biennial

"Covers biographical information, committee assignments of members of Congress, and officers of Congress." N Y Public Libr Book of How & Where to Look It Up

Remini, Robert Vincent, 1921-
The House: the history of the House of Representatives; [by] Robert V. Remini. HarperCollins Publishers 2006 614p il $34.95 *
          328.73
1. United States. Congress. House—History
ISBN 978-0-06-088434-5; 0-06-088434-7
          LC 2006-615801

"The Library of Congress"
The author "traces the development of this quintessential American institution from a struggling, nascent body to the venerable powerhouse it has become since America's rise on the world stage." Publisher's note

"Published under the aegis of the House itself, Remini's work is nonpartisan, civic-minded, and deserving of every library's consideration." Booklist

Includes bibliographical references

Will, George F.
Restoration; Congress, term limits, and the recovery of deliberative democracy. Free Press 1992 260p maps pa $17.95 hardcover o.p.
          328.73
1. United States. Congress 2. Politics 3. United States—Politics and government
ISBN 0-02-934713-0 (pa)   LC 92-26005

In this book Will argues that "the tireless quest to hang on to office has left individual members of both parties dependent on pleasing special interests, which has all but robbed Congress of any larger notion of the public good. . . . Term limits, Will says, can help restore public faith, deliberative democracy, and congressional supremacy." New Repub

Includes bibliographical references

330   Economics

Galbraith, John Kenneth, 1908-2006
The affluent society. 4th ed. Houghton Mifflin 1984 xxxvii, 291p pa $14 hardcover o.p. *
          330
1. Economics 2. United States—Economic conditions
ISBN 0-395-92500-2 (pa)   LC 84-12880
First published 1958

The author surveys the economic upheavals that have changed the economic climate of the world. He also discusses the proper goals and management of a modern society and the question of how the production and distribution of wealth should be organized

Includes bibliographical references

The **Oxford** encyclopedia of economic history; Joel Mokyr, editor in chief. Oxford University Press 2003 5v set $695   330
1. Economic history—Encyclopedias
ISBN 0-19-510507-9   LC 2003-8992

The Oxford encyclopedia of economic history—
Continued

Contents: v. 1. Accounting and bookkeeping - Contract labor and the indenture system — v. 2. Cooperative agriculture and farmer cooperatives - Jonathan Hughes — v. 3. Human capital - Mongolia — v. 4. Monte di Piet - Spain — v. 5. Spices and spice trade - Zoos and other animal parks

This encyclopedia includes "over 900 contributions from 800 scholars to explore key concepts of economics, firms and individuals, institutions, countries, and cities. Although scholarly in tone, this volume is an excellent starting point for those wishing to trace ideas and industries across chronological boundaries." Libr J

Includes bibliographical references and index

Warsh, David
Knowledge and the wealth of nations; a story of economic discovery. Norton 2006 xxii, 426p il $27.95 **330**

1. Economics 2. Economists

ISBN 978-0-393-05996-0; 0-393-05996-0

LC 2005-33677

The author "journeys through the discipline's history en route to an analysis of an influential 1990 technical paper. Written by Paul Romer, 'Endogenous Technological Change' is described by Warsh as mathematically formidable, which is the way modern economists like their fare, begging the question of why its story would be of general interest. First, hundreds of thousands annually enroll in university-level economics courses; second, Romer's paper, pertinent to the information revolution that is our zeitgeist, is clearly explained by Warsh; and third, Warsh reveals the occupation of economics to the benefit of those who aspire to it. After historical exegesis of Adam Smith and his successors, Warsh depicts post-1945 schools of thought, biographically summarizing figures such as monetarist Milton Friedman and Keynesian Robert Solow, and those of Romer's generation now in their career primes. Appraising the intellectual lineage and gestation of Romer's paper, Warsh imparts in a comprehensible way the engagement many have with economic thought." Booklist

Wheelan, Charles J.
Naked economics; undressing the dismal science; {by} Charles Wheelan; foreword by Burton G. Malkiel. Norton 2002 xxii, 260p $25.95; pa $15.95 * **330**

1. Economics

ISBN 0-393-04982-5; 0-393-32486-9 (pa)

LC 2002-23580

The author explains the essentials of economics, defining "terms like GDP and inflation, explaining how they work and what the short- and long-term impact might be. . . . This is a thoughtful, well-written introduction to economics, with the author projecting a genuine excitement for his material." Libr J

Includes bibliographical references

330.1   Systems, schools, theories

Friedman, Milton, 1912-2006
Free to choose; a personal statement; {by} Milton & Rose Friedman. Harcourt Brace Jovanovich 1980 338p pa $15 hardcover o.p. *

330.1

1. Capitalism 2. United States—Economic conditions 3. Public welfare

ISBN 0-15-633460-7 (pa)   LC 79-1821

The authors "paint a picture in which a marketplace sensitive to the people's wants and needs is frustrated by governmental interference, extreme government costs, and governmentally induced inflation. . . . Citing sociological and economic laws, the Friedmans set out to prove that the harder a nation tries to control capitalism, the worse things get." Libr J

Includes bibliographical references

Heilbroner, Robert L., 1919-2005
The worldly philosophers; the lives, times, and ideas of the great economic thinkers. Rev. 7th ed. Simon & Schuster 1999 365p pa $16 *

330.1

1. Economists 2. Economics

ISBN 0-684-86214-X   LC 99-14050

"A Touchstone book"

First published 1953

The author traces the story of economics and the great economists from Adam Smith, Malthus, Ricardo, the Utopians, Marx, Veblen and Keynes to those working with the problems of our contemporary world

Includes bibliographical references

Keynes, John Maynard, 1883-1946
The general theory of employment, interest and money. Harcourt Brace & Co. 1936 403p pa $15 hardcover o.p. * **330.1**

1. Economics 2. Money 3. Interest (Economics)

ISBN 0-15-634711-3 (pa)

Also available in paperback from Prometheus Bks.

This work "revolutionized economic theory by showing how unemployment could occur 'involuntarily'. For 30 years after the Second World War governments of western nations pursued 'Keynesian' full-employment policies." Oxford Companion to Engl Lit. 5th edition

Klein, Naomi
The shock doctrine; the rise of disaster capitalism. Metropolitan Books/Henry Holt 2007 558p $28 **330.1**

1. Capitalism 2. Economic conditions

ISBN 978-0-8050-7983-8; 0-8050-7983-1

LC 2007-18652

The author argues that Milton Friedman and other economists "have exploited the public disorientation associated with catastrophes and political crises to impose an unwanted free-market ideology on much of the world." N Y Times (Late N Y Ed)

"Assiduously researched, energetically expressed,

Klein, Naomi—Continued

Klein's report bears an ideological perspective that won't leave readers neutral about her economic interpretations." Booklist

Includes bibliographical references

Marx, Karl, 1818-1883

Capital: an abridged edition; edited with an introduction and notes by David McLellan. Oxford University Press 2008 xxxii, 499p (Oxford world's classics) pa $16.95 *   330.1

1. Capital 2. Economics

ISBN 978-0-19-953570-5   LC 2008-274361

Abridged edition first published 1995

This abridged edition of Marx's three-volume "denunciation of mid-Victorian capitalist society . . . offers virtually all of Volume 1, which Marx himself published in 1867; excerpts from a . . . translation of 'The Result of the Immediate Process Production'; and a selection of key chapters from Volume 3, which Engels published in 1895." Publisher's note

McMillan, John, 1951-

Reinventing the bazaar; a natural history of markets. Norton 2002 278p $25.95; pa $15.95
                    330.1

1. Capitalism

ISBN 0-393-05021-1; 0-393-32371-4 (pa)
                    LC 2002-521

The author "examines how markets in ancient times evolved and shows how countries experimented with markets, some successfully and some not. . . . He takes a refreshingly commonsense approach to his subject, doesn't talk down to his readers, and refrains from excessive economic jargon." Libr J

Includes bibliographical references

Smith, Adam, 1723-1790

The wealth of nations; introduction by Robert Reich; edited, with notes, marginal summary, and enlarged index by Edwin Cannan. Modern Library 2000 xxvi, 1154p pa $15.95 *   330.1

1. Economics

ISBN 0-679-78336-9; 978-0-679-78336-7
                    LC 00-64573

First published 1776

Variant title: An inquiry into the nature and causes of the wealth of nations

This treatise "is the first comprehensive treatment of the whole subject of political economy, and is remarkable for its breadth of view. . . . In it, the author presents an attack on the mercantile system, and an advocacy of freedom of commerce and industry." Oxford Companion to Engl Lit. 6th edition

Includes bibliographical references

Soto, Hernando de

The mystery of capital; why captitalism triumphs in the West and fails everywhere else. Basic Bks. 2000 276p il $27.50; pa $17
                    330.1

1. Capitalism

ISBN 0-465-01614-6; 0-465-01615-4 (pa)
                    LC 00-34301

The author contends that "the poor do not really 'own' the property they work, because they are not registered as owning it, and because of this, they cannot turn it into capital. . . . The market is restricted and the growth of wealth retarded. His solution is simple: give the poor title to the property they own de facto, and their countries will become capital rich." N Y Times Book Rev

330.9   Economic situation and conditions

Friedman, Thomas L.

The world is flat; a brief history of the twenty-first century. 1st further updated and expanded hardcover ed. Farrar, Straus and Giroux 2007 660p $35 *   330.9

1. Information society 2. Globalization

ISBN 978-0-374-29278-2; 0-374-29278-7
                    LC 2007-21424

Also available in paperback from Picador

First published 2005

The author's "thesis is that connectedness by computer is leveling the playing field, giving individuals the ability to collaborate and compete in real time on a global scale." SLJ

"No matter your stance on the benefits or pitfalls of globalization, *The World Is Flat* is an important, thought-provoking book." Bookmarks Magazine

Fukuyama, Francis

Trust; the social virtues and the creation of prosperity. Free Press 1995 458p pa $16 hardcover o.p.   330.9

1. Economics 2. International economic relations

ISBN 0-684-82525-2 (pa)   LC 95-19320

The author "compares how selected modern economies organize themselves, and he argues that these same societies depend on 'civil society' and the creation and maintenance of 'social capital' for their vitality and economic success. By social capital he means the set of intermediate institutions, such as businesses, unions, and voluntary organizations (churches, charities, clubs) that facilitate trust beyond the more traditional family oriented structures to socialize people into their culture and transmit both knowledge and values. . . . Fukuyama proposes that natural cultural laws are important determinants of a nation's wealth. This stimulating, well-documented volume will be widely read and discussed." Choice

Includes bibliographical references

Harford, Tim, 1973-

The undercover economist; exposing why the rich are rich, the poor are poor—and why you can never buy a decent used car! Oxford University Press 2005 276p il $26 **330.9**

1. Economic conditions 2. Consumer education

ISBN 978-0-19-518977-3; 0-19-518977-9

LC 2005-10297

"This book applies basic economic theory to such modern phenomena as Starbucks' pricing system and Microsoft's stock values. . . . The book is unequaled in its accessibility and ability to show how free market economic forces affect readers' day-to-day." Publ Wkly

Includes bibliographical references

Kynge, James

China shakes the world; a titan's breakneck rise and troubled future—and the challenge for America. Houghton Mifflin 2006 270p $25 * **330.9**

1. China—Economic conditions 2. China—Foreign economic relations

ISBN 978-0-618-70564-1; 0-618-70564-3

LC 2006-12084

The author "uses interviews and on-the-ground reporting first to bring to life the 1980s development strategies of China as a 'hungry nation': constant innovation, piracy, and relentless pursuit of market share. Successful marketing and investment in Europe soon led to a 'great leap' into American markets. But Kynge also portrays the downside for China: drained natural resources, environmental catastrophe, and the collapse of social trust." Libr J

"In a particularly well-written book, Mr Kynge, a former China bureau chief of the Financial Times, brings alive all the complexities and contradictions of China's development. . . . He also weaves in remarkable stories of Chinese entrepreneurs who disobeyed national edicts for a chance at a future, and who in the process are building modern China. . . . Mr Kynge combines a fresh perspective with an eye for arresting detail." Economist

Meadows, Donella H.

The limits to growth; the 30-year update; [by] Donella Meadows, Jørgen Randers, and Dennis Meadows. Chelsea Green Publishing Company 2004 xxii, 338p il hardcover o.p. pa $22.50 **330.9**

1. Economic development 2. Natural resources—Management 3. Environmental degradation

ISBN 1-931498-51-2; 1-931498-58-X (pa)

LC 2004-125

Also available CD-ROM version

First published 1972 by Universe Books

"This book, by a trio of professors and systems analysts, offers a pessimistic view of the natural resources available for the world's population. Using . . . computer models based on population, food production, pollution and other data, the authors demonstrate why the world is in a potentially dangerous 'overshoot' situation. Put simply, overshoot means people have been steadily using up more of the Earth's resources without replenishing its supplies." Publ Wkly

"A good, clear, objective explanation of causes and possible effects, this book fits well with current concerns that not enough has been done to halt environmental degradation." Choice

Includes bibliographical references

Meredith, Robyn

The elephant and the dragon; the rise of India and China and what it means for all of us. W.W. Norton & Company 2007 252p il $25.95 **330.9**

1. India—Economic conditions 2. India—Foreign economic relations 3. China—Economic conditions 4. China—Foreign economic relations

ISBN 978-0-393-06236-6; 0-393-06236-8

LC 2007-09028

The author "provides an objective, comprehensive, balanced presentation of the rapidly growing economies of India and China. She describes how these two countries are being transformed by major economic and political reforms and considers the implications of their stunning emergence for the US and the rest of the world. . . . A timely, fascinating book." Choice

Includes bibliographical references

330.973 United States—Economic conditions

Altman, Daniel

Neoconomy; George Bush's revolutionary gamble with America's future. Public Affairs 2004 290p $26.95; pa $14 **330.973**

1. Bush, George W. 2. Economic policy—United States 3. United States—Economic conditions 4. Economic forecasting

ISBN 1-586-48229-7; 1-586-48351-X (pa)

LC 2004-50398

"According to Altman, Bush's tax cuts, which were billed as a quick fix to overcome recession, serve goals driven by so-called neoconservatives: eliminating taxes on inherited wealth, investments and corporations. Altman offers a critical blow-by-blow of the hows and seeming whys of these 'revolutionary' cuts as they unfolded in 2001 and 2002." Publ Wkly

Includes bibliographical references

Krugman, Paul R.

The great unraveling; losing our way in the new century; {by} Paul Krugman. Norton 2003 xxix, 426p $25.95; pa $14.95 **330.973**

1. Economic forecasting 2. Economic policy—United States 3. United States—Economic conditions

ISBN 0-393-05850-6; 0-393-32605-5 (pa)

LC 2003-12060

This book contains selections from Krugman's "columns along with new commentary, he chronicles how the boom economy unraveled: how exuberance gave way to pessimism, how the age of corporate heroes gave way to corporate scandals, how fiscal responsibility collapsed." Publisher's note

331 Labor economics

Lichtenstein, Nelson
State of the Union: a century of American labor.
Princeton Univ. Press 2002 336p il (Politics and
society in twentieth-century America) pa $18.95
hardcover o.p.   **331**
1. Labor—United States 2. Labor unions
ISBN 0-691-11654-7 (pa)   LC 2001-36863
The author "analyzes the history of the labor movement from the 1930's to the present in the context of
U.S. economics, politics, and democracy and from this
he formulates ideas about where labor may find opportunities in this new century." Libr J
Includes bibliographical references

Murolo, Priscilla, 1949-
From the folks who brought you the weekend;
a short, illustrated history of labor in the United
States; {by} Priscilla Murolo and A.B. Chitty;
illustrations by Joe Sacco. New Press (NY) 2001
xx, 364p pa $17.95 hardcover o.p.   **331**
1. Labor—United States 2. Working class 3. Labor
movement
ISBN 1-56584-776-8 (pa)   LC 2001-30978
This is a "history of labor in America, starting with
the arrival of Columbus in 1492 and ending with the
election of George Walker Bush to be the 43rd President
of the United States." Libr J
"Brandishing little-known facts, the authors reshape
common views of social history." Publ Wkly
Includes bibliographical references

Murray, R. Emmett
The lexicon of labor; a glossary of more than
500 key terms, biographical sketches, and
historical insights concerning labor in America.
New Press (NY) 1998 208p il pa $14.95 *
                                                331
ISBN 1-56584-456-4   LC 98-12783
This is an "encyclopedia of 500 entries for terms, con-
cepts, people, legislation, places, and events in U.S. labor
history." Booklist
Includes bibliographical references

Reef, Catherine
Working in America. Facts On File 2007 xxviii,
484p il map (American experience) $80
                                                331
1. Labor—United States
ISBN 978-0-8160-6239-3; 0-8160-6239-0
                                   LC 2006-31191
First published 2000
"Each chapter begins with a . . . narrative that chronicles the experience of workers in the United States—
from factory workers, cowboys, seamstresses, and news-
boys to truck drivers, migrant farm workers, computer
programmers, and genetic engineers. Chronologies of important events follow, along with eyewitness testimonies
on the experience of working in a wide range of profes-

sions and trades—from Thomas Jefferson, Malcolm X,
Samuel Gompers, Charlotte Perkins Gilman, Jesse Jackson, Cesar Chavez, and Jane Addams, as well as a wide
range of American workers." Publisher's note
Includes bibliographical references

331.1 Labor force and market

Affirmative action; an encyclopedia; edited by
James A. Beckman. Greenwood Press 2004 2v
il set $175 *   **331.1**
1. Affirmative action programs
ISBN 1-573-56519-9   LC 2003-64257
"The entries discuss the development and debate of
government-sponsored and enforced public policies pursuing equal opportunity for members of groups historically subject to discrimination. . . . While focused on
U.S. developments, the work also explores how countries
such as Australia, Brazil, Great Britain, India, Japan, and
South Africa have structured and struggled with affirmative action." Libr J
"This is a comprehensive resource that effectively and
objectively discusses a complex and controversial topic."
Booklist
Includes bibliographical references

Bowe, John
Nobodies; modern American slave labor and the
dark side of the new global economy. Random
House 2007 xxii, 304p $25.95   **331.1**
1. Slavery—United States 2. Globalization
ISBN 978-1-4000-6209-6; 1-4000-6209-8
                                   LC 2007-12063
In this "look at the contemporary American scourge of
labor abuse and outright slavery . . . [the author] visits
locations in Florida, Oklahoma and the U.S. owned Pacific island of Saipan, where slavery cases have been
brought to light as recently as 2006. There, he talks to
affected workers, providing many moving and appalling
firsthand accounts. . . . Bowe's deeply researched, well-
written treatise on the very real problem of modern
American slavery deserves the attention of anyone living,
working and consuming in America." Publ Wkly
Includes bibliographical references

Taylor, Nick, 1945-
American-made: the enduring legacy of the
WPA; when FDR put the nation to work. Bantam
Book 2008 630p il $27 *   **331.1**
1. United States. Works Progress Administration
2. New Deal, 1933-1939
ISBN 978-0-553-80235-1; 0-553-80235-6
                                   LC 2007-34563
The author "paints the full story of the WPA from its
inception to its shutdown by Congress in 1943. . . . Taylor not only chronicles the WPA's numerous triumphs
(including New York's LaGuardia Airport) but also its
failures, most notably graft and other chicanery at the local level." Publ Wkly
"Lavishly illustrated, the book also has a list of New
Deal organizations, a partial list of construction projects,
a New Deal chronology, and endnotes. It will be a boon
to all 20th-century history collections." Libr J
Includes bibliographical references

Uchitelle, Louis

The disposable American; layoffs and their consequences. Knopf 2006 283p $25.95 *

331.1

1. Employees—Dismissal 2. Unemployed
ISBN 1-4000-4117-1   LC 2005-44423
The author "chronicles the rise and impact of the American corporate culture of layoffs. Until the mid-1970s, American companies dominated the world economy and offered employees at all levels lifetime job security. However, with the rise of foreign competition, rising energy costs, and the retreat of the federal government from Keynesian economics, American corporations turned to massive layoffs as the panacea for their problems. Uchitelle talks to corporate leaders and employees to document the bad management and political failures that make huge layoffs seemingly inevitable. Highly skilled aircraft mechanics, production workers, and middle managers share their stories of emotional exhaustion and economic downgrading." Libr J

This is "an engaging, informed and well-documented book. The author's social justice and Gospel values are clear, although implied." America

Includes bibliographical references

331.2   Conditions of employment

Lowenstein, Roger

While America aged; how pension debts ruined General Motors, stopped the NYC subways, bankrupted San Diego, and loom as the next financial crisis. Penguin Press 2008 274p $25.95

331.2

1. Pensions 2. Retirement income
ISBN 978-1-594-20167-7; 1-59420-167-6

LC 2007-42508

This book chronicles three "pension cases: the collapse of the over-obligated General Motors, the pension strike that haulted New York City's subways, . . . [and the bankrupting of] the city of San Diego." Publisher's note

"A chilling anatomy of one bad decision followed by another—and another." Kirkus

Includes bibliographical references

Shulman, Beth

The betrayal of work; how low-wage jobs fail 30 million Americans and their families. New Press (NY) 2003 255p $25.95   **331.2**

1. Minimum wage 2. Labor—United States 3. Work 4. United States—Economic conditions
ISBN 1-56584-733-4   LC 2003-43413
The author "analyzes one of the downsides of the 'new economy': the large number of American jobs that pay poverty-level wages, have few or no benefits, and create childcare nightmares." Libr J

Includes bibliographical references

Terkel, Studs, 1912-2008

Working; people talk about what they do all day and how they feel about what they do. The New Press 1997 589p pa $16.95   **331.2**

1. Labor—United States 2. Work 3. United States—Social conditions
ISBN 978-1-56584-342-4; 1-56584-342-8
First published 1974 by Pantheon Bks.

Based on interviews, this study describes the working lives and feelings of people engaged in occupations ranging from interstate truck driver to stockbroker to bookbinder to corporation president.

This "is not a dry, academic treatise but a sensitive portrayal of the experience of working, with all its pain, tension, frustrations, and occasional satisfactions." Best Sellers

331.3   Workers by age group

Levine, Marvin J., 1930-

Children for hire; the perils of child labor in the United States. Praeger Pubs. 2003 233p $49.95

331.3

1. Child labor 2. Youth—Employment 3. Teenagers—Employment
ISBN 1-56720-433-3   LC 2002-29767
The author defines the problem of child labor and "analyzes the working conditions of people under 18, the legal context for their employment and exploitation, and the impact of such labor upon the education and development of America's young people. An important work about a hidden social problem." Libr J

Includes bibliographical references

331.4   Women workers

America's working women; a documentary history, 1600 to the present; edited by Rosalyn Baxandall and Linda Gordon, with Susan Reverby. rev and updated. Norton 1995 356p il pa $16.95 hardcover o.p.   **331.4**

ISBN 0-393-31262-3 (pa)   LC 94-32194
First published 1976 by Random House

"This chronologically arranged anthology presents an . . . overview of the changing roles and contributions of woman at home, in the fields, and in today's workplace." Booklist

Includes bibliographical references

Featherstone, Liza

Selling women short; the landmark battle for workers' rights at Wal-Mart. Basic Bks. 2004 282p $25   **331.4**

1. Wal-Mart Stores, Inc. 2. Sex discrimination
ISBN 0-465-02315-0   LC 2004-10298
Using an "investigation of the class action suit *Dukes v. Wal-Mart Stores, Inc.* and . . . interviews with female workers, Featherstone indicts Wal-Mart for low wages, discriminatory policies and sexist practices. . . . This is a clearly written and compelling book." Publ Wkly

Includes bibliographical references

Kessler-Harris, Alice
Out to work; a history of wage-earning women in the United States. 20th anniversary ed. Oxford Univ. Press 2003 414p il pa $19.95 *

331.4

ISBN 0-19-515709-5   LC 2003-267644
First published 1982
"This work remains a landmark in the field of analyzing the history of women's work in the United States from Colonial times to the Reagan era." Libr J
Includes bibliographical references

331.7   Labor by industry and occupation

Boldt, Laurence G.
Zen and the art of making a living; a practical guide to creative career design. 2nd rev ed. Penguin Bks. 1999 li, 640p il pa $17.95

331.7

1. Vocational guidance
ISBN 0-14-019599-8   LC 98-55070
First published 1992 by Lightning Press with title: Zen and the art of making a living in the post-modern world
This "career development guide helps the reader identify 'work purpose,' key talents, and objectives. . . . Boldt moves beyond the basics to address unusual practical and psychological issues such as starting a business, freelancing, founding a nonprofit corporation, maintaining a healthy self-esteem, and building marketing strategy." Libr J
Includes bibliographical references

Bolles, Richard Nelson
What color is your parachute? 2008; a practical manual for job-hunters and career changers. Ten Speed/Celestial Arts 2007 432p il $28.95 *

331.7

1. Applications for positions 2. Vocational guidance
ISBN 978-1-58008-868-8; 1-58008-868-6
Annual. First published 1973
"With a supplemental web site (www.job-huntersbible.com), this perennial best seller remains a self-assessment favorite, identifying techniques to determine mission in life, interest, and skills; describing interview questions and answers and salary negotiation strategies; and advising on locating employment. Includes workbook exercises, listings of counseling firms, and tips for choosing a counselor." Libr J

Encyclopedia of careers and vocational guidance. 14th ed. Ferguson 2008 5v il set $249.95 *

331.7

1. Occupations 2. Vocational guidance
ISBN 978-0-8160-7066-4; 0-8160-7066-0

LC 2006-101604

First published 1967
"These five volumes contain more than 700 . . . [articles] on careers in nearly 100 industries. Each three- to five-page entry provides a concise and engaging profile of fields like accounting, animal care, computers, the en-
vironment, publishing, sales, and the visual arts. Included in each job entry are an overview, a history, a description, requirements, employers, advancement, earnings, work environment, outlook, and more." Libr J
Includes bibliographical references

Farr, J. Michael
100 fastest-growing careers; your complete guideboook to major jobs with the most growth and openings; by Michael Farr. 9th ed. Jist Works 2006 390p il (Top careers series) pa $17.95 *

331.7

1. Occupations 2. Vocational guidance
ISSN 1940-2627
ISBN 978-1-5935-7317-1; 1-5935-7317-0
Biennial. First published 1997 to replace America's 50 fastest growing jobs. Previous title: America's fastest-growing jobs. Continues America's 101 fastest growing jobs
New edition in preparation
This guide "provides information about pay, outlook, education, and skills needed to obtain . . . promising careers. . . . Readers explore 100 in-demand jobs, including those with the most growth and the most openings. It provides—in alphabetical order . . . current . . . descriptions of jobs with great opportunity through 2014. . . . [Also included] is an updated special book-within-a-book that cuts job search time in half and a new assessment that matches personal skills to occupations described in the book." Publisher's note
Includes bibliographical references

New guide for occupational exploration; linking interests, learning, and careers; [by] Michael Farr, Laurence Shatkin. 4th ed. JIST Works 2006 552p $49.95; pa $39.95   **331.7**
1. Occupations 2. Vocational guidance
ISBN 1-59357-180-1; 978-1-59357-180-1; 1-59357-179-8 (pa); 978-1-59357-179-5 (pa)

LC 2005-17637

First published 1979 by U.S. Govt. Ptg. Office. Previous edition published 2001 by JIST Works with title: Guide for occupational exploration
This book is "based on the 16 U.S. Department of Education clusters that connect learning to careers. . . . Readers can drill down to their most appealing job groups through questions that provide a feel for the work and whether it will interest them. . . . More than 900 job descriptions from the U.S. Department of Labor's O*NET (Occupational Information Network) database emphasize skills needed, related courses, education required, earnings, growth, and much more." Publisher's note
Includes bibliographical references

Krantz, Les
Jobs rated almanac; the best and worst jobs—250 in all—ranked by more than a dozen vital factors, including salary, stress, benefits, and more. 6th ed. Barricade Bks. 2002 333p il pa $14.95 *

331.7

1. Occupations 2. Vocational guidance
ISBN 978-1-5698-0224-3; 1-5698-0224-6

LC 2002-20051

Krantz, Les—*Continued*

First published 1988 by World Almanac. Periodically revised. Title varies

This "describes and ranks 250 jobs on the basis of current salary and future prospects, stress factors, environmental conditions, career outlook, and safety and security issues." Libr J

Mainiero, Lisa A.

The opt-out revolt; why people are leaving organizations to create kaleidoscope careers; [by] Lisa A. Mainiero and Sherry E. Sullivan. Davies-Black Pub. 2006 xxii, 378p il $28.95

331.7

1. Career changes 2. Quality of life 3. Self-realization 4. Social change

ISBN 978-0-89106-186-1; 0-89106-186-X

LC 2006-14561

Mainiero and Sullivan "present the results of a five-year-long quantitative and qualitative research study examining how and why the career patterns of both men and women have changed from the traditional 'ever upward' model to a path with multiple forks and rest stops. The authors found that several factors, each examined in a separate chapter, contribute to workers' kaleidoscopic approach to careers, among them the search for challenging assignments and personal authenticity, men's changing views of masculinity, and the quest for work-family balance. . . . Quotations and company profiles, along with the authors' concise writing style, leaven what could have been a dry discourse." Libr J

Includes bibliographical references

O*NET; dictionary of occupational titles. 4th ed. JIST Works 2007 672p $49.95; pa $39.95

331.7

1. Occupations

ISBN 978-1-59357-415-4; 1-59357-415-0; 978-1-59357-416-1 (pa); 1-59357-416-9 (pa)

LC 2007-652

First published 1998 to replace Dictionary of occupational titles published by the government Printing Office. Frequently revised

"Based on information obtained from the U.S. Department of Labor, the U.S. Census Bureau, and other reliable sources"; "Developed under the direction of Michael Farr with database work by Laurence Shatkin"

This book "puts the official job descriptions and other important information from the U.S. Department of Labor's . . . Occupational Information Network (O*NET) database into . . . print form. . . . Descriptions and data included for nearly 950 jobs, covering almost 100 percent of the workforce." Publisher's note

United States. Bureau of Labor Statistics

Occupational outlook handbook 2008-2009; U.S. Department of Labor, U.S. Bureau of Labor Statistics. 2008-09 library ed. Claitor's Publishing Division 2008 890p il (Bulletin of the United States Bureau of Labor Statistics) $39 *

331.7

1. Occupations 2. Vocational guidance

ISBN 978-1-59804-410-2; 1-59804-410-9

Also available in paperback from JIST Works and from McGraw-Hill

Biennial. First published 1949. Supplemented by Occupational Outlook Quarterly, subscription $15

"Gives information on employment trends and outlook in more than 800 occupations. Indicates nature of work, qualifications, earnings and working conditions, how to enter, where to go for more information, etc." Guide to Ref Books. 11th edition

331.8 Labor unions, labor-management bargaining and disputes

Dubofsky, Melvyn, 1934-

Labor in America; a history; [by] Melvyn Dubofsky, Foster Rhea Dulles. 7th ed. Harlan Davidson 2005 472p il pa $34.95 *

331.8

1. Labor—United States 2. Working class 3. Labor unions

ISBN 978-0-88295-998-6; 0-88295-998-0

LC 2003-13265

First published 1949 by Crowell under the authorship of Foster Rhea Dulles. Periodically revised

A study of the social and political impact of the American labor movement since colonial times

Includes bibliographical references

Historical encyclopedia of American labor; edited by Robert Weir and James P. Hanlan. Greenwood Press 2003 2v set $175 *

331.8

1. Labor—United States—Encyclopedias 2. Labor movement—Encyclopedias

ISBN 0-313-31840-9

LC 2003-52847

This "encyclopedia includes approximately 400 entries designed for the general researcher, students, and lay readers interested in learning more about such topics as unions, union leaders, union history, important laws and court cases, and labor terminology. An appendix contains excerpts from over 50 primary documents." Libr J

Includes bibliographical references

Honey, Michael K.

Going down Jericho Road; the Memphis strike, Martin Luther King's last campaign. Norton 2007 619p il $35 *

331.8

1. King, Martin Luther, Jr., 1929-1968 2. Strikes—United States 3. Sanitation

ISBN 978-0-393-04339-6; 0-393-04339-8

LC 2006-32217

The author "examines the intersection between issues of race and economics in the U.S. in the 1960s from the perspective of the Memphis garbage workers' strike, Martin Luther King Jr.'s last campaign." Booklist

"Honey's passionate commitment to labor is undisguised, making this effort a worthy and original contribution to the literature." Publ Wkly

Includes bibliographical references

St. James encyclopedia of labor history worldwide; major events in labor history and their impact; with introductions by Willie Thompson and Daniel Nelson; Neil Schlager, editor; produced by Schlager Groups. St. James Press 2003 2v set $260 *   **331.8**

1. Labor movement—Encyclopedias
ISBN 1-558-62542-9   LC 2003-294

This set offers an "analysis of more than 300 key events in labor history over the last 200 years, focusing on the relevance of these events to both the labor movement as a whole and to societal changes around the world. Each entry . . . is three to five pages in length and includes a description of the event, information about the key players involved and discusses the event in historical context." Publisher's note

"This reference promises to fill an important niche for larger public and academic libraries." Libr J

Stepan-Norris, Judith, 1957-
Left out; Reds and America's industrial unions; [by] Judith Stepan-Norris, Maurice Zeitlin. Cambridge Univ. Press 2002 375p $75; pa $27   **331.8**

1. Labor unions—United States 2. Labor—United States
ISBN 0-521-79212-6; 0-521-79840-X (pa)
      LC 2001-37655

"In 1947, ten 'Communist-dominated unions' were expelled from the CIO. The mythology that developed is that these unions sacrificed the interests of the American worker to the foreign policy dictates of the Statlin-era Soviet Union. The authors, both sociologists, use statistical analysis of contracts to argue that these unions actually had the most democracy, the most pro-labor contracts, and the best track record in fighting for gender and racial equality in the labor movement." Libr J

Includes bibliographical references

Zieger, Robert H.
American workers, American unions; the twentieth century; [by] Robert H. Zieger & Gilbert J. Gall. 3rd ed. Johns Hopkins Univ. Press 2002 292p (The American moment) pa $17.95   **331.8**

1. Labor unions 2. Labor—United States
ISBN 0-8018-7078-X   LC 2002-3250
First published 1986

This is a "history of American workers and their unions in twentieth-century America." Publisher's note

"This standard work of American labor history from the Gilded Age onward has been updated to almost the present, with the last paragraph discussing September 11. Zieger's strength lies in his striving for a balanced survey." Libr J

Includes bibliographical references

332.024   Personal finance

Glink, Ilyce R., 1964-
50 simple things you can do to improve your personal finances; how to spend less, save more, and make the most of what you have. Three Rivers Press (NY) 2001 222p pa $14
      332.024

1. Personal finance
ISBN 0-8129-2742-7   LC 00-66675

The author gives advice on such topics as personal budgets and savings, credit and debt, investments, insurance, taxes, marriage, partnerships and children, and retirement planning.

Hanson, Jon
Good debt, bad debt; knowing the difference can save your financial life. Portfolio 2005 xxxiii, 252p il $21.95   **332.024**

1. Personal finance 2. Consumer credit 3. Debtor and creditor
ISBN 1-591-84073-2   LC 2004-53400

"The author offers advice on the pros and cons of debt while helping us develop a philosophy about it as well as one for spending and saving. This is an excellent primer on a very important topic." Booklist

Includes bibliographical references

Pond, Jonathan D.
Grow your money! 101 easy tips to plan, save, and invest. Collins 2008 xlv, 352p $26.95
      332.024

1. Public finance 2. Investments 3. Retirement income
ISBN 978-0-06-112140-1; 0-06-112140-1
      LC 2007-24071

The author offers "investment and financial definitions, debt-management strategies, retirement and home-ownership considerations, tax tips, and more, enabling lay readers to understand these seemingly daunting and complex issues." Libr J

Quinn, Jane Bryant
Making the most of your money. Simon & Schuster 1997 1066p il $30   **332.024**

1. Personal finance 2. Investments
ISBN 0-684-81176-6   LC 97-23183
First published 1991

"Completely revised and updated for the twenty-first century"

This guide includes information about investing, buying a home, life and health insurance, retirement planning, checklists for life changes, finding a financial advisor, and financing college

Schwab-Pomerantz, Carrie

It pays to talk; how to have the essential conversations with your family about money and investing; [by] Carrie Schwab-Pomerantz and Charles R. Schwab. Crown Business 2003 386p il $24.95; pa $14   332.024
1. Personal finance 2. Investments
ISBN 0-609-61028-7; 1-4000-4960-1 (pa)
LC 2002-5994

The authors "share their insights on money, investing and the conversations that need to accompany these. Their focus is on the importance of conducting different lifestage conversations (e.g., how to financially approach being single, getting married, raising children, helping parents), and this . . . primer provides one-stop shopping for the many phases of financial understanding and planning. . . . This educational volume provides a useful framework that a family can refer to when approaching those often difficult but necessary conversations about finances." Publ Wkly
Includes bibliographical references

Tobias, Andrew P.

The only investment guide you'll ever need; [by] Andrew Tobias. 4th ed, expanded and updated throughout. Harcourt, Inc 2005 304p $14 *   332.024
1. Investments 2. Personal finance
ISBN 0-15-602963-4   LC 2004-15705
First published 1978

This offers advice on such topics as personal investments, tax strategies, life insurance, stock market trading, college funds, real estate, and inheritance

332.1 Banks

Greider, William

Secrets of the temple; how the Federal Reserve runs the country. Simon & Schuster 1987 798p pa $19 hardcover o.p.   332.1
1. Federal Reserve System (U.S.). Board of Governors 2. Banks and banking—United States 3. Monetary policy—United States
ISBN 0-671-67556-7 (pa)   LC 87-16712

An investigation of the structure and influence of the Federal Reserve System during the Reagan era.

"This well-researched study, with its lively style, will certainly provide fuel for the conspiracy theorists but also sheds much-needed light on an often-baffling institution." Booklist
Includes bibliographical references

Mayer, Martin, 1928-

The Fed; the inside story of how the world's most powerful financial institution drives the market. Free Press 2001 350p $27.50; pa $15
                                332.1
1. Greenspan, Alan 2. Federal Reserve System (U.S.). Board of Governors 3. Monetary policy—United States
ISBN 0-684-84740-X; 0-452-28341-8 (pa)
LC 2001-23250

The author "traces the evolution of the Federal Reserve from a sleepy regulatory agency to the most powerful economic institution in the world." Publ Wkly

"Mayer's well-written account helps to . . . demystify the Fed and makes us understand how important its role is in our lives." Libr J
Includes bibliographical references

Meltzer, Allan H.

A history of the Federal Reserve; with a foreword by Alan Greenspan. v1: 1913-1951. University of Chicago Press 2002 800p $75; pa $25 *   332.1
1. Federal Reserve System (U.S.). Board of Governors 2. Federal Reserve banks
ISBN 0-226-51999-6; 0-226-52000-5 (pa)
LC 2002-72007

First volume of a projected two volume work

The author "provides a definitive history of the U.S. Federal Reserve from its founding in 1913 to its establishment as a separate, independent entity in 1951. Using meeting minutes, correspondence, and internal Federal Reserve documents, he traces the reasons behind Federal Reserves policy decisions, highlights the impact that individuals and events had on the Fed, and examines the Fed's influence on international affairs. . . . This well-written and thoroughgoing account is recommended for academic, business, and public libraries." Libr J
Includes bibliographical references

Parks, Tim

Medici money; banking, metaphysics, and art in fifteenth-century Florence. W. W. Norton & Co. 2005 273p il map (Enterprise) $22.95
                                332.1
1. House of Medici 2. Banks and banking 3. Florence (Italy)—History
ISBN 0-393-05827-1   LC 2004-30516
"Atlas Books"

This is an "account of the fabled Medici dynasty of Renaissance Florence spanning 1397-1494." Booklist

"The general reader will learn from this book a great deal about the era, and those who bestrode it, without getting bogged down in excessive scholarly detail." Natl Rev
Includes bibliographical references

Woodward, Bob, 1943-

Maestro: Greenspan's Fed and the American boom. Simon & Schuster 2000 270p il $25; pa $14   332.1
1. Greenspan, Alan 2. Federal Reserve System (U.S.). Board of Governors 3. Monetary policy—United States
ISBN 0-7432-0412-3; 0-7432-0562-6 (pa)
LC 00-52627

The author discusses the influence exerted over the American economy by Alan Greenspan, chairman of the Federal Reserve Board

"In a surprisingly short book, Woodward lucidly explains the axes of intellectual and political disagreement over monetary policy, productivity growth, irrational exu-

Woodward, Bob, 1943- —*Continued*
berance and more, shedding new light on major conflicts of the Greenspan era and demystifying this most political of ostensibly technical institutions." N Y Times Book Rev

Includes bibliographical references

332.6   Investment

Bernstein, William
The four pillars of investing; lessons for building a winning portfolio; [by] William J. Bernstein. McGraw-Hill 2002 316p il $27.95

            332.6

1. Investments
ISBN 0-07-138529-0   LC 2002-726560
The author discusses "the four pillars—the theory of investing, the history of investing, the psychology of investing, and the business of investing. . . . Using humor, Bernstein advises readers to employ sound tenets of investing to manage risk while building a foundation of assests for the long term." Libr J
Includes bibliographical references

Carlson, Charles B.
The smart investor's survival guide; the nine laws of successful investing in a volatile market. Currency 2002 xxiii, 325p il $24.95; pa $14.95

            332.6

1. Investments
ISBN 0-385-50387-3; 0-385-50402-0 (pa)
           LC 2001-58289
"Carlson believes volatility or turbulence is here to stay and demonstrates to investors how to make it work to their advantage. . . . The author discusses diversification within asset classes, across asset classes, and across time. A highlight of his work is the 'easy-hold' ratings on stocks and mutual funds." Booklist

Cramer, James J.
Confessions of a street addict. Simon & Schuster 2002 339p $26; pa $14   **332.6**
1. Wall Street (New York, N.Y.) 2. Stocks
ISBN 0-7432-2487-6; 0-7432-2488-4 (pa)
           LC 2002-22902
The author "recounts his turbulent dual career as hedge fund manager and media pundit. . . . This is a lively, informative portrait of the highest levels of finance and media in the last decade." Publ Wkly

Jim Cramer's real money; sane investing in an insane world. Simon & Schuster 2005 300p il $26
*   **332.6**
1. Investments
ISBN 0-7432-2489-2   LC 2005-42499
The author, a "successful trader and former hedge-fund manager . . . reveals how he made his money and distills his methods so that the average reader can understand them." Booklist

Downes, John
Barron's finance & investment handbook; [by] John Downes, Jordan Elliot Goodman. 7th ed. Barron's Educ. Ser. 2006 1230p il $39.99 *

            332.6

1. Personal finance 2. Investments
ISBN 978-0-7641-5992-3   LC 98-36776
First published 1986. Periodically revised
This handbook includes a "financial dictionary, an analysis of . . . key investment opportunities . . . explanations for laymen on how to read corporate reports and interpret financial news, and . . . [a] directory of . . . publicly traded corporations in the United States and Canada. Readers will also find the names and addresses of all brokerage and mutual funds firms, banks, savings and loan companies, insurance companies, federal and state regulations, and major investment publications." Publisher's note
Includes bibliographical references

Fraser, Steven, 1945-
Every man a speculator; a history of Wall Street in American life. HarperCollins 2005 721p $29.95; pa $18.95 *   **332.6**
1. Wall Street (New York, N.Y.) 2. Securities 3. Investments
ISBN 0-06-662048-1; 0-06-662049-X (pa)
           LC 2005-298631
The author's "ambition is to examine 'how Wall Street has entered into the lives of generations long passed and those alive today . . . the way the character of America has changed.'" N Y Times Book Rev
This is "a richly detailed, comprehensive, and convincing account of Wall Street's place in American cultural history." New Repub
Includes bibliographical references

Hagstrom, Robert G., 1956-
The Warren Buffett way. 2nd ed. John Wiley 2005 xxiii, 245p il $24.95; pa $14.95

            332.6

1. Buffett, Warren E. 2. Investments
ISBN 0-471-64811-6; 0-471-74367-4 (pa)
           LC 2004-13841
First published 1994
This edition "encompasses Buffett's numerous investments and accomplishments over the past ten years, as well as the timeless and highly successful investment strategies and techniques he has always used to come out a market winner." Publisher's note
Includes bibliographical references

Knee, Jonathan A.
The accidental investment banker; inside the decade that transformed Wall Street. Oxford University Press 2006 254p $26   **332.6**
1. Goldman Sachs & Co. 2. Morgan Stanley (Firm) 3. Investments 4. Wall Street (New York, N.Y.)
ISBN 978-0-19-530792-4; 0-19-530792-5
           LC 2006-10822
"Knee, an investment banker at Goldman Sachs for four years beginning in 1994 and at Morgan Stanley

Knee, Jonathan A.—*Continued*

from 1998 to 2003, describes the operations of these firms and explains the role of investment bankers and how 'deals' are done. He weaves a fascinating tale of his employers and a multibillion-dollar industry, which was transformed culturally and structurally by extraordinary growth and then devastating retrenchment at the beginning of the twenty-first century. Knee mourns what he contends is the loss of historic integrity in the transition from boom to bust and describes many industry changes, including competition from hedge funds and LBOs (leveraged buyout firms)." Booklist

"This insider's chronicle brims with humor and insight as it depicts a world driven mad by money." Fast Company

Lewis, Michael

Liar's poker; rising through the wreckage on Wall Street. Penguin Bks. 1990 249p pa $15

332.6

1. Salomon Brothers Inc. 2. Wall Street (New York, N.Y.)

ISBN 0-14-014345-9; 978-0-14-014345-4

First published 1989 by Norton

"Lewis describes his four years with the Wall Street firm Salomon Brothers, from his bizarre hiring through the training program to his years as a successful bond trader." Libr J

"This is a story with much irony. Here is one of America's top investment banking and securities trading firms, an adviser to the largest corporations and money managers, unable to run itself. Its management style is one of warring individuals and factions." N Y Times Book Rev

Lutnick, Howard

On top of the world; Cantor Fitzgerald and 9/11: a story of loss and renewal; {by} Howard Lutnick and Tom Barbash. HarperCollins Pubs. 2002 282p il $25.95; pa $14.95   **332.6**

1. Cantor Fitzgerald LP 2. World Trade Center (New York, N.Y.) 3. September 11 terrorist attacks, 2001

ISBN 0-06-051029-3; 0-06-051030-7 (pa)

LC 2002-27550

The bond-trading firm Cantor Fitzgerald lost 658 employees on September 11, 2001. "'On Top of the World' sets out to tell the story of Cantor Fitzgerald's tragedy, and its survival, largely from its chairman's point of view; the book is interspersed with . . . passages in {Howard} Lutnick's own voice." N Y Times Book Rev

Lynch, Peter

One up on Wall Street; how to use what you already know to make money in the market; by Peter Lynch with John Rothchild. Simon & Schuster 1989 318p pa $14 hardcover o.p.

332.6

1. Investments 2. Stocks 3. Speculation

ISBN 0-7432-0040-3 (pa)   LC 88-32741

The authors argue that "average investors can beat Wall Street professionals by using the information that they encounter in their everyday lives. . . . The book is also a primer on how the stock market works and is written in a light, entertaining style." Publ Wkly

Mahar, Maggie

Bull!: a history of the boom, 1982-1999; what drove the breakneck market—and what every investor needs to know about financial cycles. HarperBusiness 2003 xxii, 486p il $27.95; pa $16.95 *   **332.6**

1. Wall Street (New York, N.Y.) 2. Business cycles

ISBN 0-06-056413-X; 0-06-056414-8 (pa)

LC 2003-51131

This is a "history of the 1982-99 bull market in U.S. stocks. {The author} explains that this bull market got its initial impetus from both the undervaluation of equities during the 1970s and the end of the Cold War. . . . Mahar concludes by summarizing how investors who haven't seen a bear market for 17 years might plan their investing strategies. Mahar takes complicated topics and explains them clearly for the average reader. Her exceptional book is most highly recommended to even the smallest public or academic library." Libr J

Includes bibliographical references

Weiner, Eric J., 1967-

What goes up; the uncensored history of modern Wall Street as told by the bankers, brokers, CEOs, and scoundrels who made it happen. Little, Brown and Company 2005 503p il $27.95   **332.6**

1. New York Stock Exchange, Inc. 2. Wall Street (New York, N.Y.)

ISBN 0-316-92966-2   LC 2005-151

The author "provides an insider's perspective on Wall Street through interviews with financial superstars like Charles Schwab, Peter Lynch and dozens of others. . . . Weiner's book is a sharp, informative history from the people who shaped Wall Street's bottom line." Publ Wkly

Includes bibliographical references

332.7   Credit

Leonard, Robin

Credit repair; updated by John Lamb. 8th ed. Nolo Press (Berkeley) 2007 342p pa $24.99 *

332.7

1. Consumer credit

ISBN 978-1-4133-0635-4; 1-4133-0635-7

LC 2006-39247

First published 1996. Periodically revised

Accompanied by CD-ROM

This offers advice on assesssing your debt situation, avoiding overspending, handling existing debts, cleaning your credit file, how credit reports are used, and building and maintaining good credit

Scurlock, James D.

Maxed out; hard times, easy credit, and the era of predatory lenders. Scribner 2007 248p il $24

332.7

1. Consumer credit 2. Debtor and creditor

ISBN 978-1-4165-3251-4; 1-4165-3251-X

LC 2006-51246

Scurlock, James D.—*Continued*

Scurlock presents a critique of the credit industry in the United States.

This is an "astute indictment of the credit industry. . . . Not all financial experts share Scurlock's pessimism about an indebted society. But he builds a persuasive case that deserves serious attention." Christ Sci Monit

Includes bibliographical references

333.7 Land, recreational and wilderness areas, energy

Moul, Francis, 1940-

The national grasslands; a guide to America's undiscovered treasures; photography by Georg Joutras. University of Nebraska Press 2006 153p il map pa $19.95   333.7

1. Grassland ecology 2. Prairie ecology

ISBN 0-8032-8320-2; 978-0-8032-8320-6

LC 2006-3496

The author describes "how government policies of the New Deal led to the setting aside of managed national grasslands. Included are a description and a map of each of the current 20 national grassland, plus one adjoining the United States in Canada. The book describes the flora and fauna found in each National Grassland, some of the grazing and wildlife management issues, mineral rights issues, and tourism opportunities. . . . Most libraries should consider adding the book to their collection." Sci Books Films

Includes bibliographical references

333.72 Conservation and protection

American earth; environmental writing since Thoreau; edited by Bill McKibben; foreword by Al Gore. Literary Classics of the United States 2008 1047p il (Library of America) $40 *
333.72

1. Environmental movement 2. Environmental protection 3. Nature conservation 4. Literature—Collections

ISBN 978-1-59853-020-9; 1-59853-020-8

LC 2007-940683

This anthology "offers over 100 authors' views on various aspects of environmentalism in the United States, such as global warming, defending our natural resources, nuclear nonproliferation, American Indian rights, air and water pollution, and protecting animals in the wild. The authors include poets, novelists, songwriters, politicians, journalists, essayists, scientists, and academics, but the focus is on those who love the land and strive to protect it from interests that want to harm or neglect it." Libr J

This book "can be read as a survey of the literature of American environmentalism, but above all, it should be enjoyed for the sheer beauty of the writing." Publ Wkly

Includes bibliographical references

Hawken, Paul

Blessed unrest; how the largest movement in the world came into being, and why no one saw it coming. Viking 2007 342p $24.95   333.72

1. Environmental movement 2. Environmental protection

ISBN 978-0-670-03852-7; 0-670-03852-0

LC 2006-101145

This is an account of the present-day movement on behalf of social and environmental justice.

"Fresh and informative, Hawken's inspired overview charts much that is right in the world." Booklist

Includes bibliographical references

McDaniel, Carl N., 1942-

Wisdom for a livable planet; the visionary work of Terri Swearingen, Dave Foreman, Wes Jackson, Helena Norberg-Hodge, Werner Fornos, Herman Daly, Stephen Schneider, and David Orr. Trinity University Press 2005 277p hardcover o.p. pa $17.95   333.72

1. Environmental sciences

ISBN 1-595-34008-4; 1-595-34009-2 (pa)

LC 2004-19081

The author personalizes "critical environmental issues via profiles of eight 'visionaries' agitating for a more livable planet. . . . His subjects are prominent in the areas of hazardous waste incineration, biodiversity, sustainable agriculture, appropriate technology, population control, rational economic planning, climate concerns and environmental education. . . . The stories of these eight ecological warriors are profoundly appealing in that they show the diverse ways that people can commit to a common cause." Publ Wkly

Includes bibliographical references

McKibben, Bill

The Bill McKibben reader; pieces from an active life. Henry Holt 2008 442p pa $18 *
333.72

1. Environmental protection

ISBN 978-0-8050-7627-1 (pa); 0-8050-7627-1 (pa)

LC 2007-39609

"A Holt paperback"

This is a "collection of essays gleaned from books and periodicals published between 1982 and 2007. Most of the 44 essays come from a diverse array of magazines, including *The New Yorker, Mother Jones, Outside, Gourmet,* and *Christian Century.* . . . Essays are loosely divided into categories that include consumerism, activism, the changing planet, the meaning of community, and the sufficiency of nature. . . . Readers new to McKibben will be entertained, informed, and perhaps even inspired to make the positive changes that McKibben desires for the world." Libr J

Murphy, Priscilla Coit, 1945-

What a book can do; the publication and reception of Silent spring. University of Massachusetts Press 2005 254p il (Studies in print culture and the history of the book) $34.95

333.72

1. Carson, Rachel, 1907-1964 2. Authors and publishers

ISBN 1-55849-476-6   LC 2004-19704

The author "details the debate that the best selling book, Silent Spring had with the public and chemical industry on the issue of pesticides. It's a fast paced compelling story. This is an excellent book for a new generation of book lovers, journalist, investigators, and historians." Univ Press Books for Public and Second Sch Libr, 2006

Includes bibliographical references

Nelson, Gaylord

Beyond Earth Day; fulfilling the promise; [by] Gaylord Nelson with Susan Campbell and Paul Wozniak; with a foreword by Robert Kennedy, Jr. University of Wisconsin Press 2002 xx, 201p il map $26.95   **333.72**

1. Earth Day 2. Environmental movement

ISBN 0-299-18040-9   LC 2002-2806

The author, "who in 1970 organized the first Earth Day, here revisits that occasion and some of the many environmental challenges that still face the nation and the world." Choice

"The Earth Day founder presents exceptionally lucid explanations of a host of current ecoissues." Booklist

Includes bibliographical references

333.75   Forest lands

London, Mark

The last forest; the Amazon in the age of globalization; [by] Mark London and Brian Kelly. Random House 2007 312p map $25.95

333.75

1. Rain forests 2. Amazon River valley 3. Rain forest ecology

ISBN 978-0-679-64305-0; 0-679-64305-2

LC 2006-46466

The authors "profile environmentalists, politicians, ranchers, and ordinary citizens; shrewdly consider the impact of new roads and wireless technology; and chronicle the ongoing destruction of forests and displacement of forest people to make way for cattle ranches and soybean fields." Booklist

"This is an essential read for environmentalists, historians, economists, and those who are just awestruck by the Amazon's ecosystem." Libr J

Includes bibliographical references

333.79   Energy

Cravens, Gwyneth

Power to save the world; the truth about nuclear energy. Alfred A. Knopf 2007 439p il $27.95

333.79

1. Nuclear energy

ISBN 0-307-26656-7; 978-0-307-26656-9

LC 2007-17611

"Guided by nuclear scientist and environmental enthusiast Richard 'Rip' Anderson, Cravens embarks upon a 'Nuclear America Tour,' wherein she is introduced to the history, science, potential, and facts of nuclear energy. Systematically, she becomes converted to the notions that there is more ambient radioactivity in Denver than in Chernobyl, that well-designed nuclear plants are safer than coal-fired ones, and that probably the surest way to mitigate global warming is by investing in nuclear energy." Libr J

The author's "thorough inquiry dispels myths, clarifies science, and portrays an astonishing and ever more crucial hidden world." Booklist

Includes bibliographical references

Eichenwald, Kurt

Conspiracy of fools; a true story. Broadway Books 2005 742p $26; pa $16.95 *

333.79

1. Enron Corp. 2. Business failures

ISBN 0-7679-1178-4; 0-7679-1179-2 (pa)

LC 2004-58216

The author "details the characters and business shenanigans that led to the demise of Enron, taking with it the respected accounting firm Arthur Andersen and the pensions of hundreds of its workers." Booklist

"Kurt Eichenwald has written a gripping account of Enron's rise and fall." Economist

Includes bibliographical references

Goodell, Jeff

Big coal; the dirty secret behind America's energy future. Houghton Mifflin Co. 2006 xxvii, 324p il $25.95   **333.79**

1. Coal

ISBN 0-618-31940-9; 978-0-618-31940-4

LC 2005-33199

The author "focuses on the United States' increased coal dependency in the last 20 years and the resulting environmental and health impacts. . . . The book opens our eyes to how we can improve our use of coal and figure out other, less destructive ways to create the energy we need." Libr J

Includes bibliographical references

Yount, Lisa

Energy supply. Facts on File 2005 296p il (Library in a book) $45   **333.79**

1. Energy resources 2. Energy consumption

ISBN 0-8160-5577-7   LC 2004-21607

"This title summarizes . . . the many aspects of important energy issues, furnishing a concise overview of

Yount, Lisa—*Continued*
major points needed for doing research on this topic."
Choice
Includes bibliographical references

Zubrin, Robert
Energy victory; winning the war on terror by
breaking free of oil. Prometheus Books 2007 336p
il $25.95   **333.79**
1. Alcohol as fuel 2. Petroleum as fuel 3. Energy policy 4. War on terrorism
ISBN 978-1-59102-591-7   LC 2007-27122
The author "argues that if Congress passed a law requiring that all new cars sold in the USA be flex-
fueled—that is, able to run on any combination of gasoline or alcohol fuels—this one action would destroy the
monopoly that the oil cartel has maintained on the
globe's transportation fuel supply, opening it up to competition from alcohol fuels produced by farmers worldwide. . . . [This book argues that] we could be using
fuel dollars that are now being sent to countries with ties
to terrorism to help farmers here and abroad, boosting
our own economy and funding world development." Publisher's note
Includes bibliographical references

333.8   Subsurface resources

Goodstein, David L., 1939-
Out of gas; the end of the age of oil; [by] David
Goodstein. Norton 2004 140p il $21.95; pa $13.95
                                              333.8
1. Petroleum
ISBN 0-393-05857-3; 0-393-32647-0 (pa)
                                    LC 2003-10376
The author "warns not only that the last drop will be
pumped by 2100 at the latest, but also that peak production, estimated to occur in the current decade, marks the
beginning of a global shortage. . . . He presents the constraints nature will impose on any fuel-technology combination, beginning with explanations of exploitable
sources of energy, continuing with how chemical and nuclear bonds hold and release energy, and arriving at how
any engine, in principle, converts energy to work."
Booklist
"Goodstein's predictions are based on a sophisticated
understanding of physics and thermodynamics, and on a
simple observation about natural resources." N Y Times
Book Rev
Includes bibliographical references

333.9   Other natural resources

Williams, Wendy
Cape wind; money, celebrity, class, politics, and
the battle for our energy future on Nantucket
Sound; [by] Wendy Williams and Robert
Whitcomb. PublicAffairs 2007 xxiv, 326p il map
$26.95   **333.9**
1. Cape Wind Associates (Firm) 2. Wind power
3. Energy policy 4. Nantucket (Mass.)
ISBN 978-1-58648-397-5; 1-58648-397-8
                                    LC 2007-1106

This is a "firsthand report of the political maneuvers
involving Cape Wind, a proposed wind energy project. In
2001, Boston energy entrepreneur Jim Gordon proposed
building America's first offshore wind farm in Nantucket
Sound using 130 wind turbines to produce 420 mega-
watts of renewable energy for the Cape Cod region. . . .
Using the NIMBY (Not In My Backyard) argument,
some of America's most wealthy residents living on the
cape's south shore and others with Nantucket connections, including Sen. Edward Kennedy and former Gov.
Mitt Romney, launched a well-funded opposition." Libr
J
"This true-life tale of a blinding love of place, outra-
geously irresponsible propaganda, shameful congressional
maneuvering, and egregious social injustice is half farce,
half political thriller, and altogether compelling."
Booklist
Includes bibliographical references

333.91   Water and lands adjoining bodies of water

Barlow, Maude
Blue gold: the fight to stop the corporate theft
of the world's water; {by} Maude Barlow, Tony
Clarke. New Press 2002 278p pa $16.95 hardcover
o.p.   **333.91**
1. Water resources development 2. Water supply
3. Globalization
ISBN 1-56584-813-6 (pa)   LC 2003-389510
In this overview of the current water situation, the authors "warn readers that the time for taking water for
granted is over, and that transnational corporations are
privatizing drinking-water supplies, often charging the
poorest citizens the most for this fundamental substance.
Not to mention the bottled water industry, which is also
wreaking havoc." Booklist
"This well-researched book provides a sobering, in-
depth look at the growing scarcity of fresh water and the
increasing privatization and corporate control of this non-
renewable resource. . . . The proposals for corrective
legislation, lobbying, and citizen environmental action
make this book a highly recommended purchase for public and academic libraries." Libr J
Includes bibliographical references

Dean, Cornelia
Against the tide; the battle for America's
beaches. Columbia Univ. Press 1999 279p il $60;
pa $18.95   **333.91**
1. Coasts 2. Beaches 3. Seashore ecology
ISBN 0-231-08418-8; 0-231-08419-6 (pa)
                                    LC 98-50755
Dean discusses the ecology of American beaches and
contends that they are threatened by coastal development
and erosion
"This thoroughly researched and thoughtful book is
destined to become a classic of environmental science
writing." Libr J
Includes bibliographical references

Knapp, Bevil, 1949-
America's wetland; Louisiana's vanishing coast; photographs by Bevil Knapp; text by Mike Dunne. Louisiana State University Press 2005 129p il $39.95 **333.91**
1. Wetlands 2. Coasts
ISBN 0-8071-3115-6; 978-0-8071-3115-2
LC 2005-9329
"In an eerie prophesy of the flooding to come in New Orleans, this book discusses the job of wetlands in keeping storm surges and waves out of the low-lying areas. Superb color photographs detail fishing, the oil industry, and marine life in the wetlands areas of Louisiana." Univ Press Books for Public and Second Sch Libr, 2006

Pearce, Fred, 1951-
When the rivers run dry; water, the defining crisis of the twenty-first century. Beacon Press 2006 324p map hardcover o.p. pa $16 *
333.91
1. Water resources development 2. Water supply
ISBN 0-8070-8572-3; 0-8070-8573-1 (pa)
LC 2005-27495
The author argues "that a worldwide water shortage is the most fearful looming environmental crisis." Publ Wkly
"Pearce's powerful imagery, penetrating analyses, and passionate advocacy make this required reading for environmental proponents and civic leaders everywhere." Booklist

Reisner, Marc P.
Cadillac desert; the American West and its disappearing water; [by] Marc Reisner. rev and updated. Penguin Bks. 1993 582p il maps pa $17
333.91
1. Irrigation—West (U.S.) 2. Water resources development 3. Political corruption
ISBN 0-14-017824-4
LC 93-173272
First published 1986 by Viking
This "study of the economics, politics, and ecology of water covers more than a century of public and private desert reclamation in the American West." Publisher's note
"Reisner's groundbreaking history of water wheeling-and-dealing in the West helped launch the inquiry into water policy that has grown more urgent each year as the development of dry lands continues." Booklist
Includes bibliographical references

Rothfeder, Jeffrey
Every drop for sale; our desperate battle over water in a world about to run out. Tarcher/Putnam 2001 205p hardcover o.p. pa $14.95
333.91
1. Water supply
ISBN 1-58542-114-6; 978-1-58542-367-5 (pa); 1-58542-367-X (pa)
LC 2001-27903
The author "debunks the myth that dams solve water problems, decries the lack of an adequate method for large-scale desalinization, and condemns the commodification and privatization of clean water."

Booklist
"Like the drip of water on stone, Rothfeder's steady exposition of horrors will wear down any reader's doubts that water is the next flashpoint of global politics, human rights and health issues." Publ Wkly
Includes bibliographical references

Ward, Diane Raines
Water wars; drought, flood, folly, and the politics of thirst. Riverhead Bks. 2002 280p $24.95; pa $14
333.91
1. Water supply 2. Hydraulic engineering 3. Water rights
ISBN 1-57322-229-1; 1-57322-995-4 (pa)
LC 2002-21301
The author considers the problems of "droughts, pollution, population growth, and climate change—which threaten to make water . . . the cause of war within our lifetime. . . . [She] tells the stories of those working to solve them: hydrologists, politicians, engineers, and everyday people." Publisher's note
"Ward writes with the sensibilities and concerns of an environmentalist. But unexpectedly, delightfully, she's an environmentalist who loves the scale, ingenuity and power of engineering." N Y Times Book Rev
Includes bibliographical references

333.95　Biological resources

Adams, Jonathan S.
The future of the wild; radical conservation for a crowded world. Beacon Press 2006 xxiii, 267p $27.95 *
333.95
1. Nature conservation 2. Ecology
ISBN 0-8070-8510-3
LC 2005-7688
The author "presents an optimistic approach to conservation based on scientific research on the interdependency of an ecosystem. . . . Adams proposes ways to accommodate preserving everything from 'genes to species,' combining the latest insights on biodiversity with community organizing and economic planning, and he reports on successful collaborations involving former adversaries." Libr J
"This book represents a leap forward in contemporary thinking about how to heal the human-land relationship. It will appeal to anyone with an interest in conservation, land use, protected areas, and the practical application of science to saving the natural heritage of the planet." Choice
Includes bibliographical references

Cousteau, Jacques Yves, 1910-1997
The human, the orchid, and the octopus; exploring and conserving our natural world; [by] Jacques Cousteau and Susan Schiefelbein. Bloomsbury 2007 305p $25.75 **333.95**
1. Oceanography 2. Nature conservation 3. Human influence on nature
ISBN 978-1-59691-417-9; 1-59691-417-3
LC 2007-18824
Original French edition, 1997

Cousteau, Jacques Yves, 1910-1997—*Continued*
"This is a comprehensive presentation of the conservation and preservation philosophy that inspired Cousteau to become an activist for the oceans and the earth during his lifetime." Libr J

"Cousteau's reverence for life's miracles . . . shines through in this eloquent testimony on the importance of pursuing higher ideals, particularly the preservation of the oceans and the natural world for future generations." Publ Wkly

Includes bibliographical references

Encyclopedia of biodiversity; editor-in-chief, Simon Asher Levin. Academic Press 2001 5v il maps set $1,295   **333.95**
ISBN 0-12-226865-2

This resource "consists of 313 signed, alphabetically arranged articles, prepared by international contributors. Each volume features a table of contents for the set plus a list of all articles arranged by 20 subject categories. . . . The final volume includes a subject index, list of authors, and glossary. Each entry follows a standard format consisting of an outline, glossary, statement of definition, the article, cross-references, and a bibliography. Volume 1 includes a 16-page section of color plates. Black-and-white illustrations . . . are integrated throughout the text. Limited online access time is included with purchase of the print set. Impressive in content and organization; highly recommended for all collections." Choice

Glavin, Terry, 1955-
The sixth extinction; journeys among the lost and left behind. Thomas Dunne Books/St. Martin's Press 2007 318p $24.95   **333.95**
1. Endangered species 2. Mass extinction of species 3. Human influence on nature 4. Biological diversity
ISBN 978-0-312-36231-7; 0-312-36231-5
LC 2007-1068

First published 2006 in Canada with title: Waiting for the macaws

"Five major epochs of mass extinction have marked the past 440 million years, but in this striking and original work, Glavin . . . argues that the most devastating is today's 'sixth' extinction—in which the world is losing many of its cultures, languages and local traditions along with its wildlife." Publ Wkly

Includes bibliographical references

Goodall, Jane, 1934-
The ten trusts; what we must do to care for the animals we love; {by} Jane Goodall and Marc Bekoff. HarperSanFrancisco 2002 xx, 200p hardcover o.p. pa $14.95 *   **333.95**
1. Animal rights 2. Animal welfare 3. Wildlife conservation 4. Human influence on nature
ISBN 0-06-251757-0; 0-06-055611-0 (pa)
LC 2002-68717

The authors "offer a prescriptive conservation plan designed to protect animals as well as help educate people about the importance of saving both animals and the environment." Publ Wkly

"An accessible, compelling, and important exposé." Booklist

Includes bibliographical references

Life on earth; an encyclopedia of biodiversity, ecology, and evolution; edited by Niles Eldredge. ABC-CLIO 2002 2v set $185   **333.95**
ISBN 1-57607-286-X   LC 2002-15852

"Four introductory essays outline the definition, importance, and preservation of biodiversity. Many of the 194 articles are about specific phyla or species . . . or important concepts. . . . Others address issues that will appeal to students and general readers. . . . Articles are clearly written, usually define specialized terms, and include bibliographies of books and popular and scholarly periodical articles." Booklist

Includes bibliographical references

Sustaining life; how human health depends on biodiversity; edited by Eric Chivian and Aaron Bernstein; Center for Health and the Global Environment Harvard Medical School; foreword by Edward O. Wilson; prologue by Kofi Annan. Oxford University Press 2008 xxiii, 542p il map $34.95 *   **333.95**
1. Biological diversity 2. Environmental health
ISBN 978-0-19-517509-7; 0-19-517509-3
LC 2007-20609

"Secretariat of the Convention on Biological Diversity; United Nations Development Programme; United Nations Environment Programme; IUCN-The World Conservation Union"

"A collaborative survey of biodiversity issues written and/or reviewed for accuracy by more than 100 scientists, this volume is motivated by its UN sponsors' sense of the world populace's indifference to the consequences of environmental degradation. Conceiving that implicating human health with the health of other species may enlist its concern, the authors collectively warn that present extinction rates are abnormally high. Seven categories of endangered species stand in as portents of the dire effects to ecosystems when extinction occurs. . . . Abundantly illustrated, this is a valuable, urgent resource suited to any general-interest library." Booklist

Includes bibliographical references

Wilson, Edward O., 1929-
The creation; an appeal to save life on earth. Norton 2006 175p il $21.95 *   **333.95**
1. Biology 2. Creation
ISBN 978-0-393-06217-5; 0-393-06217-1
LC 2006-15573

"Written in the form of an open letter to a generic Southern Baptist minister, . . . [this] book seeks a common ground from which both scientists and persons of faith can confront a common threat: the ravages to nature—especially the loss of biodiversity—caused by humanity." Libr J

The author's "eloquent defense of nature, insights into our resistance to environmental preservation, and praise of scientific inquiry coalesce in a blueprint for a renaissance in biology reminiscent of the technological advances engendered by the space race." Booklist

Includes bibliographical references

Wilson, Edward O., 1929-—_Continued_
The future of life. Knopf 2002 xxiv, 229p il
$22; pa $13 *   **333.95**
1. Endangered species 2. Nature conservation
ISBN 0-679-45078-5; 0-679-76811-4 (pa)
LC 2001-38316
Wilson "proposes that there is yet time to avoid a
grand planetary environmental crash provided we get serious, acknowledge a duty of stewardship and recognize
an emotional affiliation . . . with other kinds of life."
NY Times Book Rev

335.4   Marxian systems

Marx, Karl, 1818-1883
The Communist manifesto; [by] Karl Marx and
Friedrich Engels; with an introduction and notes
by Gareth Stedman Jones. Penguin Books 2002
287p pa $7 *   **335.4**
1. Communism
ISBN 0-14-044757-1
Also available as part of the Great ideas series and
from Bantam Bks.
First published 1848
This document "analyzes history in terms of class conflict, predicts the imminent overthrow of the ruling bourgeoisie by the oppressed proletariat, and envisions a resulting classless society in which personal property
would be abolished. The 'Manifesto' calls upon the proletariat of the world to unite and strengthen itself for this
final revolution." Benet's Reader's Ency 4th edition
Includes bibliographical references

Pipes, Richard
Communism: a history. Modern Lib. 2001 175p
hardcover o.p. pa $10.95 *   **335.4**
1. Communism
ISBN 0-679-64050-9; 0-8129-6864-6 (pa)
LC 2001-275458
"This is a short history on the essentials of communism—as an ideal, as a program outlined by Marx, and
as a state established by Lenin to implement the program." Booklist
"As a brief, polemical diatribe . . . this short account
of communism should provoke and instruct." Libr J
Includes bibliographical references

Service, Robert, 1947-
Comrades! a history of world communism.
Harvard University Press 2007 571p il map $35
335.4
1. Communism
ISBN 978-0-674-02530-1; 0-674-02530-X
LC 2006-101585
This history of world communism covers "every communist state, extinct and surviving, as well as major
communist parties and movements around the world. It
is a daunting undertaking that required mastery of vast
amounts of source materials and the skill to make judicious choices among them. Service . . . makes use of archives, memoirs, and large numbers of 'further sources'

in several languages. The book is organized in chrono-
logical order around six topics: Origins, Experiment, De-
velopment, Reproduction and Mutation and Endings. . . .
[This is] a rich repository of information and insight." N
Y Sun
Includes bibliographical references

336.2   Taxes

J.K. Lasser's your income tax 2009; prepared by
the J.K. Lasser Tax Institute. Wiley 2008 xxviii,
816p il pa $18.95 *   **336.2**
1. Income tax
ISSN 0084-4314
ISBN 978-0-470-28002-7; 0-470-28002-6
Annual. First published by Simon & Schuster. Began
publication with 1936 issue. Title varies. Early issues
prepared by J.K. Lasser
A standard aid for filing income tax returns.

336.3   Public debt and expenditures

Macdonald, James
A free nation deep in debt; the financial roots of
democracy. Farrar, Straus & Giroux 2003 564p il
$30 *   **336.3**
1. Public debts
ISBN 0-374-17143-2
The author "examines the historical linkage between
political freedom and public debt, showing why representative governments have been able to borrow more
cheaply from citizen lenders than autocratic heads of
state who do not consider their citizens to be equals."
Booklist
"The book is exceedingly well written and should be
a necessary purchase for any library with more than cursory holdings in public finance." Libr J
Includes bibliographical references

337   International economics

Cohen, Daniel
Globalization and its enemies; translated by
Jessica B. Baker. MIT Press 2006 192p $27.95 *
337
1. Globalization 2. International economic relations
ISBN 978-0-262-03350-3; 0-262-03350-X
LC 2006-41996
"Cohen divides globalization's enemies into two
camps united by a single assumption: 'that globalization
imposes a model that people do not want.' Cohen asserts
that 'the truth . . . is probably the reverse.'" Publ Wkly
This "is one of the most original and incisive inquiries
into the subject that I have seen. No one who reads and
understands it can come away believing that the current
phase of this complex and uneven process is leading to
the peaceful universal market of business utopians, or accept the simple narrative of anti-capitalist movements in
which underdevelopment is a consequence of the wealth
of advanced countries. There is more wisdom in Cohen's
short book than in dozens of weightier tomes." N Y Rev
Books

Friedman, Thomas L.
The Lexus and the olive tree. Updated and expanded ed. Farrar, Straus, Giroux 2000 xxi, 469p $30   **337**
1. International economic relations 2. Free trade 3. United States—Foreign economic relations
ISBN 978-0-374-18552-7; 0-374-18552-2
LC 00-29411
Also available in paperback from Anchor Bks.
First published 1999
Friedman "explains, with anecdotes as well as analyses, what the instant electronic global economy is and what it may take to live there." N Y Times Book Rev

Stiglitz, Joseph E.
Globalization and its discontents. Norton 2002 xxii, 282p $24.95; pa $15.95   **337**
1. International Monetary Fund 2. International economic relations 3. International finance 4. Developing countries—Economic conditions 5. Globalization
ISBN 0-393-05124-2; 0-393-32439-7 (pa)
LC 2002-23148
The author "posits that 'the level of pain in developing countries created in the process of globalization and development as it has been guided by the IMF and the international economic organizations has been far greater than necessary.'" Booklist
"This smart, provocative study contributes significantly to the ongoing globalization debate." Publ Wkly
Includes bibliographical references

338   Production

Belfiore, Michael, 1969-
Rocketeers; how a visionary band of business leaders, engineers, and pilots is boldly privatizing space. Collins 2007 305p il $26.95   **338**
1. SpaceShipOne (Spacecraft) 2. Rocketry 3. Space flight
ISBN 978-0-06-114902-3   LC 2007-14987
"Touring the rapidly changing non-NASA community, Belfiore reports on the technology and business plans behind dreams of privately financed access to space." Booklist
The author's "engaging style and detailed notes make this an involving book." Libr J
Includes bibliographical references

Boettcher, Jennifer C.
Industry research using the economic census; how to find it, how to use it; [by] Jennifer C. Boettcher and Leonard M. Gaines. Greenwood Press 2004 305p il (How to find it, how to use it) $85 *   **338**
1. United States—Census
ISBN 1-57356-351-X   LC 2004-8607
"This handbook explains 'the Census concepts, methods, terminology, and data sources' and also explains how to locate needed census data." Booklist
This "is an outstanding reference work, a must-have for any academic, public, or special library that deals with business or economic questions." Ref & User Services Quarterly
Includes bibliographical references

Clark, Taylor, 1979-
Starbucked; a double tall tale of caffeine, commerce, and culture. Little, Brown 2007 297p $25.99   **338**
1. Starbucks Corporation 2. Coffee industry 3. Coffeehouses
ISBN 978-0-316-01348-2; 0-316-01348-X
LC 2007-13074
The author explores the "rise of the Starbucks Corporation and the . . . culture that fueled its success." Publisher's note
This "is a breezily written business yarn with plenty of big-picture punch." Christ Sci Monit
Includes bibliographical references

Encyclopedia of American business; general editor, W. Davis Folsom; associate editor, Rick Boulware. Facts on File 2004 516p $95 *
338
1. Business—Encyclopedias
ISBN 0-8160-4643-3   LC 2003-48752
"Five general areas of business are covered: accounting, economics, finance, management, and marketing. Terms, concepts, laws, and institutions defined were drawn from two sources, the *Wall Street Journal* and 'principles' texts used in introductory courses." Booklist
"Entries are informative and readable, and average about 500 words each. . . . This encyclopedia offers a nice balance between a short-entry business dictionary and a multivolume encyclopedia." Choice
Includes bibliographical references

338.1   Agriculture

Berry, Wendell, 1934-
Citizenship papers. Shoemaker & Hoard 2003 189p $24; pa $15   **338.1**
1. Agriculture—Government policy 2. Agriculture—Environmental aspects 3. Economic policy—United States
ISBN 1-593-76000-0; 1-593-76037-X (pa)
LC 2003-13811
Previously published articles
"Berry's recent essays may restate what he has said before—that agribusiness and the new globalism are inimical to human thriving—but they say it better, and through different immediate subjects, saliently including sound sheep raising and 9/11, than ever before." Booklist

The **essential** agrarian reader; the future of culture, community, and the land; edited by Norman Wirzba. University Press of Kentucky 2003 276p il $27   **338.1**
1. Agriculture—Economic aspects 2. Agriculture—Environmental aspects 3. Human ecology
ISBN 0-8131-2285-6   LC 2003-8808
Also available in paperback from Shoemaker & Hoard

The essential agrarian reader—*Continued*

"In this collection of . . . essays, farmers, philosophers, scientists, and environmentalists look at the ways in which industrial agriculture, unchecked consumerism, and the squandering of natural resources have caused great harm. . . . The contributors . . . are leaders in their fields, and have lucid, expressive writing styles. Highly recommended." Libr J

Includes bibliographical references

Pyle, George, 1956-

Raising less corn, more hell; the case for the independent farm and against industrial food. PublicAffairs 2005 xxv, 229p $25   **338.1**

1. Family farms 2. Agricultural industry
ISBN 1-58548-115-0   LC 2005-41902

"Organizing his book into three neatly named sections—'Wealth,' 'Health,' and 'Security'—Pyle . . . addresses in turn the economic aspects of farming and feeding the United States and the much larger world beyond; health and environmental problems attributed to our present large-scale industrial food production methods; and issues of food safety and security, including genetically modified corn, soybeans, and other crops." Libr J

The author's "well-researched, lucid and passionate argument explains not only what is wrong with U.S. agricultural policy but why it matters." Publ Wkly

Stewart, Amy, 1969-

Flower confidential. Algonquin Books 2006 306p il $23.95   **338.1**

1. Cut flower industry
ISBN 978-1-56512-438-7; 1-56512-438-3
LC 2006-40092

The author "tackles the global flower industry. Her investigations take her from an eccentric lily breeder to an Australian business with the alchemical mission of creating a blue rose. . . . This book is as lush as the flowers it describes." Publ Wkly

Includes bibliographical references

338.2   Extraction of minerals

Margonelli, Lisa

Oil on the brain; adventures from the pump to the pipeline. Doubleday 2007 324p $26
338.2

1. Petroleum industry
ISBN 0-385-51145-0; 978-0-385-51145-2
LC 2006-20789

Margonelli examines how oil travels from petroleum fields to neighborhood gas stations.

The author "adds something fresh to the discussion by eschewing the popular (but dreary) doomsday angle in favor of an 'adventures in . . .' approach. . . . By giving voice to the people who are the links in the global oil chain, Margonelli invites us to leapfrog all the rhetoric, dry statistics, and dire pronouncements about oil in order to truly understand it." Fast Company

Includes bibliographical references

Simmons, Matthew R.

Twilight in the desert; the coming Saudi oil shock and the world economy. John Wiley & Sons 2005 422p il maps $24.95; pa $16.95
338.2

1. Petroleum industry 2. Saudi Arabia
ISBN 0-471-73876-X; 0-471-79018-4 (pa)
LC 2005-6852

The author offers "description of the relationship between Saudi Arabia and the U.S and our longstanding dependence upon Saudi oil. With a field-by-field assessment of its key oilfields, he highlights many discrepancies between Saudi Arabia's actual production potential and its seemingly extravagant resource claims. . . . A thought-provoking book." Booklist

Includes bibliographical references

Tertzakian, Peter

A thousand barrels a second; the coming oil break point and the challenges facing an energy dependent world. McGraw-Hill 2006 272p il map $27.95 *   **338.2**

1. Energy resources 2. Petroleum industry 3. Energy consumption
ISBN 0-07-146874-9   LC 2005-28419

The author "predicts the US is headed toward an oil 'break point' by 2010. This occurs when a fuel becomes 'disadvantaged' due to high price, utility, security of sources, or military liability, and can lead to an imbalance between supply and demand. He maintains that 'cheap, clean, easy-to-obtain energy' will no longer be available, but that the US will 'adapt' and 'rebalance' just as it managed to do during the early 1980s. . . . This volume is a thoughtful, well-argued study of a major policy issue facing the US." Choice

Includes bibliographical references

Yergin, Daniel

The prize; the epic quest for oil, money, and power. Simon & Schuster 1991 877, xxxiip il maps pa $22 hardcover o.p.   **338.2**

1. Petroleum industry 2. World politics
ISBN 0-671-79932-0 (pa)   LC 90-47575

This is a "history of the oil industry, from the first oil well ever drilled (near Titusville, Pennsylvania, in 1859) to the Iraqi invasion of Kuwait. It recalls advances in technology, innovations in salesmanship, and wars and truces among corporations and nations." New Yorker

"A comprehensive careful book that pulls together reams of information." N Y Times Book Rev

Includes bibliographical references

338.4   Secondary industries and services

Almond, Steve

Candyfreak: a journey through the chocolate underbelly of America. Algonquin Books of Chapel Hill 2004 266p $21.95 *   **338.4**

1. Almond, Steve 2. Candy 3. Chocolate
ISBN 1-56512-421-9   LC 2003-70801

Almond, Steve—*Continued*

Also available in paperback from Harvest Bks.

The author tells how candy "shaped his childhood and continues to define his life in ways large and small. . . . Once hundreds of American confectioners delivered regional favorites to consumers, but now the big three of candy—Hershey, Mars, and Nestlé—control the market. To find out what happened to those candies of yesteryear, Almond talks to candy collectors and historians and visits a few of the remaining independent candy companies. . . . Flavored with the author's amusingly tart sense of humor, *Candyfreak* is an intriguing chronicle of the passions that candy inspires and the pleasures it offers." Libr J

Includes bibliographical references

Angell, Marcia

The truth about the drug companies; how they deceive us and what to do about it. Random House 2004 305p $24.95 * **338.4**

1. Drug industry

ISBN 0-375-50846-5 LC 2004-41212

This is an "exposé of how money is really spent by this gigantic and immensely wealthy industry. Angell looks at the role of academia in drug research, how the FDA is impacted by the industry, and how pharmaceutical companies influence medical education and research. . . . Every registered voter should read this book." Libr J

Includes bibliographical references

Avorn, Jerry

Powerful medicines; the benefits, risks, and costs of prescription drugs. Knopf 2004 448p $27.50 * **338.4**

1. Drugs 2. Drug industry

ISBN 0-375-41483-5 LC 2003-66119

The author explains "the current American prescription-drug debacle, placing it within the larger context of overall medical cost concerns. He . . . discusses what often goes awry when overworked physicians can't keep abreast of voluminous research, when patients are underinformed about generic drug availability, and when profits provide the sole motivation for pharmaceutical research. . . . A comprehensive, interesting read." Booklist

Includes bibliographical references

Brandt, Allan M.

The cigarette century; the rise, fall and deadly persistence of the product that defined America. Basic Books 2007 600p il $36 * **338.4**

1. Tobacco industry 2. Smoking

ISBN 978-0-465-07047-3; 0-465-07047-7
LC 2006-29005

This is an "analysis of how the tobacco industry successfully defined and promoted its markets and products while all along devising strategies and policies to evade public health regulation of those products. . . . Brandt coherently organizes his analysis of cigarettes and their social significance through the themes of culture, science, politics, law, and globalization. This thorough, diligent study examines and explains the actions and influence of the tobacco industry in the context of an emerging and dominant US culture." Choice

Includes bibliographical references

Campbell-Kelly, Martin

From airline reservations to Sonic the Hedgehog; a history of the software industry. MIT Press 2003 372p il (History of computing) $42.50; pa $16.95 * **338.4**

1. Computer software industry

ISBN 0-262-03303-8; 0-262-53262-X (pa)
LC 2002-75351

The author presents a "history of the software industry from the 1950s to 1995. Dividing the business into three sectors (software contracting, corporate software precuts, and mass-market software products), he examines the key products and players in each. . . . The result is a well-rounded look at the software industry from a business perspective." Libr J

Includes bibliographical references

Critser, Greg

Generation Rx; how prescription drugs are altering American lives, minds, and bodies. Houghton Mifflin 2005 308p $24.95; pa $14.95 * **338.4**

1. Drugs 2. Drug industry

ISBN 0-618-39313-7; 0-6187-7356-8 (pa)
LC 2005-09113

This book "explores the overmedication of America, ranging from the extraordinary number of children treated for ADD or psychiatric disorders to the middle aged relying on daily medications for high cholesterol and/or diabetes to senior citizens taking multiple drugs that interact with poorly researched and sometimes fatal effects." Libr J

"This is a page-turner, all right, though hardly a 'good read' for the faint of heart—or liver." Booklist

Includes bibliographical references

Harris, Mark, 1960-

Grave matters; journey through the modern funeral industry to a natural way of burial. Scribner 2007 193p $24 * **338.4**

1. Undertakers and undertaking 2. Burial

ISBN 978-0-7432-7768-6; 0-7432-7768-6
LC 2006-50622

The author "advocates green (i.e., chemical-free) burial, a concept that is gaining momentum among aging baby boomers. His slender tome is chockablock with information on a variety of burial options, the majority of them environmentally friendly. . . . Through his detailed if grisly explanation of the currently popular embalming and interment process, Harris just may open up entirely new discussions among family members whenever the topic of burial is broached." Booklist

Hurley, Dan

Natural causes; death, lies, and politics in America's vitamin and herbal supplement industry. Broadway Books 2006 324p $23.95 *

338.4

1. Dietary supplements 2. Herbs—Therapeutic use
ISBN 0-7679-2042-2; 978-0-7679-2042-1

LC 2006-47576

The author "takes aim at the $21 billion supplement industry and its potentially injurious 'natural' products. He critiques its strong-arming of the 1994 Dietary Supplement Health and Education Act through Congress—a law that rendered the FDA virtually powerless to regulate these remedies—and observes the FDA's 'coziness' with the industry it regulates." Publ Wkly

"Truly a good book that is good for you." Booklist
Includes bibliographical references

Law, Jacky

Big pharma; exposing the global healthcare agenda. Carroll & Graf Publishers 2006 266p pa $15.95 **338.4**

1. Drug industry
ISBN 978-0-7867-1783-5; 0-7867-1783-1

LC 2006-297422

The author "delivers a tour de force evaluation of the pharmaceutical industry, including its political and economic power, manipulation of the public's naive trust in medicine, and corruption of scientific research." Choice
Includes bibliographical references

Mahar, Maggie

Money-driven medicine; the real reason health care costs so much. HarperCollins Publishers 2006 xxi, 451p il map $27.95 * **338.4**

1. Medical economics 2. Medical care—Costs
ISBN 0-06-076533-X; 978-0-06-076533-0

LC 2005-56023

The author argues that "our privately managed yet mainly publicly funded system produces the worst of both worlds—high costs, rampant inefficiencies and intense competition among providers that doesn't benefit patients. She traces how today's market-driven medical system emerged over the past century thanks to trends that gradually stripped power from doctors and gave it to corporations, turning patients into profit centers." Publ Wkly

"Mahar is to be praised for bringing clarity to one of the most complex issues of our times." Booklist
Includes bibliographical references

Petersen, Melody, 1964-

Our daily meds; how the pharmaceutical companies transformed themselves into slick marketing machines and hooked the nation on prescription drugs. Farrar, Straus and Giroux 2008 432p $26 **338.4**

1. Drug industry
ISBN 978-0-374-22827-9; 0-374-22827-2

LC 2008-2097

"Sarah Crichton books"

The author shows how corporate salesmanship has triumphed over science inside the biggest pharmaceutical companies and, in turn, how this promotion driven industry has taken over the practice of medicine and is changing American life.

"Petersen takes readers beyond glossy advertising and celebrity endorsements to glimpse the alarming dark side of the American pharmaceutical industry." Libr J
Includes bibliographical references

338.5 General production economics

Galbraith, John Kenneth, 1908-2006

The Great Crash, 1929; with a new introduction by the author. Houghton Mifflin 1997 206p il pa $14 * **338.5**

1. Great Depression, 1929-1939 2. United States—Economic conditions—1919-1933
ISBN 0-395-85999-9

LC 97-22051

"A Mariner book"
First published 1955

Beginning with the bull market of Coolidge and Hoover and continuing through the stock market crash, the author analyzes its causes and speculates about the chances of another crash
Includes bibliographical references

The **value** of a dollar: colonial era to the Civil War, 1600-1865; [edited by] Scott Derks and Tony Smith. Grey House Pub. 2005 436p il $155 **338.5**

1. Cost and standard of living 2. Prices 3. Salaries, wages, etc.
ISBN 1-59237-094-2; 978-1-59237-094-8

LC 2006-275331

"A Universal Reference Book"
Companion volume to The Value of a Dollar: Prices and Income in the United States, 1860-2004

"This source is an engaging statistical summary that looks at the history of the American people through the eyes of everyday workers and consumers. The 265 years it covers are presented in six chronological chapters: '1600-1749: The Development of the Colonies,' '1750-1774: The Run up to the War of American Independence,' and so on, ending with the close of the Civil War in 1865. . . . [This book] will find a happy audience among students, researchers, and general browsers. It offers a fascinating and detailed look at early American history from the viewpoint of everyday people trying to make ends meet." Booklist
Includes bibliographical references

The **value** of a dollar: prices and income in the United States, 1860-2004; edited by Scott Derks. 3rd ed. Grey House Pub. 2004 664p il $155 **338.5**

1. Cost and standard of living 2. Prices 3. Salaries, wages, etc.
ISBN 1-59237-074-8; 978-1-59237-074-0

LC 2005-270058

First published 1994

The value of a dollar: prices and income in the United States, 1860-2004—*Continued*

This "statistical summary presents the history of the American people through the prices they paid for a wide variety of products and services. . . . [The book] is organized into six chapters covering 20-year periods and then into subchapters covering 5-year spans. Each subchapter presents a chronology of mostly economic events; tables showing typical wages and incomes, expenditures, and investment yields; a representative food basket comparing prices in different cities; prices on items from alcoholic beverages to travel; and more." Booklist

Includes bibliographical references

338.6   Organization of production

Hamilton, Stewart

Greed and corporate failure; the lessons from recent disasters; [by] Stewart Hamilton and Alicia Micklethwait. Palgrave Macmillan 2006 207p $42.50 *   **338.6**

1. Business failures
ISBN 978-1-4039-8636-8; 1-4039-8636-3
LC 2006-40487

The authors "assert that the reasons for corporate failures are common across all types of industries and countries, in turbulent times and calm: poor strategic decisions, overexpansion, dominant CEOs, greed and a desire for power, failure of internal controls, and ineffective boards. They support their arguments by examining in depth seven representative examples of such failures (Barings, Enron, WorldCom, Tyco, Swissair, Royal Ahold, and Parmalat). The cases are clearly and concisely presented." Choice

Includes bibliographical references

338.7   Business enterprises

Arden, Lynie, 1949-

Work-at-home sourcebook. 9th ed. Live Oak Publs. 2005 pa $19.95 *   **338.7**

1. Home-based business
ISBN 978-0-911781-19-9; 0-911781-29-6

First published 1987. Frequently revised

"Arden lists over 1000 companies that either hire or contract with home workers. Categorized by types of work, home-based opportunities, markets for crafts, etc., entries include addresses, requirements, and provisions." Libr J

Brenner, Joël Glenn

The emperors of chocolate; inside the secret world of Hershey and Mars. Random House 1999 366p il pa $14.95 hardcover o.p.   **338.7**

1. Hershey, Milton Snavely, 1857-1945 2. Mars, Forrest, Sr. 3. Hershey Foods Corp. 4. Mars, Inc. 5. Chocolate
ISBN 0-7679-0457-5 (pa)   LC 98-21610

Published in UK with title: The chocolate wars

"Brenner examines the candy industry, focusing on the rivalry between Hershey and Mars. Milton Hersey was and Forrest Mars is highly secretive and eccentric, and they both amassed huge fortunes. A wonderful inside look at successful businessmen." Booklist

Includes bibliographical references

Brinkley, Douglas

Wheels for the world; Henry Ford, his company, and a century of progress, 1903-2003. Viking 2003 xxii, 858p il $34.95; pa $18 *   **338.7**

1. Ford, Henry, 1863-1947 2. Ford Motor Co. 3. Automobile industry
ISBN 0-670-03181-X; 0-14-200439-1 (pa)
LC 2003-33066

This book is "about the people of Ford, including the Ford family, executives, workers, union organizers and others. . . . Brinkley's focus never strays far from Ford plants in Highland Park, River Rouge and Willow Run, Mich., yet he reflects events taking place in the outside world through the actions and feelings of people in nearby Dearborn, Mich." Publ Wkly

"Car lovers will appreciate this amazing account of the birth of the automobile industry, including funny anecdotes about the trusty Model T, the evolution of the V-8 engine, the artistic design of the Thunderbird, sophistication of the Lincoln Continental, and popularity of the Mustang." Booklist

Includes bibliographical references

Burrows, Peter

Backfire: Carly Fiorina's high-stakes battle for the soul of Hewlett-Packard. Wiley 2003 296p il $27.95   **338.7**

1. Fiorina, Carly 2. Hewlett-Packard Co. 3. Compaq Computer Corporation 4. Computer industry
ISBN 0-471-26765-1   LC 2002-156443

This is an account "of the bitter boardroom fight that erupted after Hewlett-Packard announced plans to merge with Compaq in the late summer of 2001 . . . [with a focus on] the charismatic Carleton S. Fiorina, who became one of the highest-ranking women in American business in 1999 when she was tapped as the first outside chief executive of the Hewlett-Packard company. . . . [This] is a riveting, colorful, fast-paced account of the Compaq battle." N Y Times Book Rev

Includes bibliographical references

Gerstner, Louis V., Jr.

Who says elephants can't dance? inside IBM's historic turnaround. HarperBusiness 2002 372p il $27.95   **338.7**

1. International Business Machines Corp. 2. Computer industry
ISBN 0-06-052379-4   LC 2002-27523

Includes index

This is the "tale of the rise, fall and rise of IBM. . . . [The author] became IBM's CEO in 1993, when the gargantuan company was near collapse. The book's opening section snappily reports Gerstner's decisions in his first 18 months on the job. . . . The following sections describe the marathon fight to make IBM once again 'a company that mattered.' . . . The book is a well-

Gerstner, Louis V., Jr.—*Continued*

rendered self-portrait of a CEO who made spectacular change on the strength of personal leadership." Publ Wkly

Micklethwait, John

The company; a short history of a revolutionary idea; {by} John Micklethwait and Adrian Wooldridge. Modern Library 2003 xxiii, 227p (Modern Library chronicles) hardcover o.p. pa $14.5   **338.7**

1. Corporations 2. Business enterprises
ISBN   0-679-64249-8;978-0-8129-7287-0(pa); 0-8129-7287-2 (pa)   LC 2002-26429

In this history of the joint-stock company, Micklethwait and Wooldridge "trace its progress from Assyrian partnership agreements through the 16th- and 17th-century European 'charter companies' that opened trade with distant parts of the world, to today's multinationals. The authors' breadth of knowledge is impressive. They infuse their engaging prose with a wide range of cultural, historical and literary references, with quotes from poets to presidents. . . . Moreover, the authors argue that for all the change companies have engendered over time, their force has been for an aggregate good." Publ Wkly

Includes bibliographical references

Orbanes, Philip

The game makers; the story of Parker Brothers from Tiddledy Winks to Trivial Pursuit; [by] Philip E. Orbanes. Harvard Business School Press 2003 272p il $29.95   **338.7**

1. Parker Brothers (Firm)
ISBN 1-591-39269-1   LC 2003-10768

This is a study of the Parker Brothers, who developed such games as Monopoly, Clue and Risk. The author contends that the games "reflect the American world view of the 20th century. Life is a ruthless struggle in which there are many losers, but it takes place within a framework of unbendable and fairminded rules." Economist

Includes bibliographical references

Rost, Peter

The whistleblower; confessions of a healthcare hitman. Soft Skull Press 2006 224p pa $14.95   **338.7**

1. Pfizer Inc. 2. Pharmacia Corporation 3. Drug industry 4. Whistle blowing
ISBN 978-1-933368-39-9; 1-933368-39-X   LC 2006-19069

A book "from a former Pfizer exec about his decision to expose corporate activities, including takeovers and layoffs, physician payoffs, marketing to juvenile patients, and tax dodging. This blow-by-blow account amply supports his statement that the current U.S. healthcare system is 'certainly the best system for the drug companies.'" Libr J

Rothfeder, Jeffrey

McIlhenny's gold; how a Louisiana family built the Tabasco empire. Collins 2007 251p il $24.95   **338.7**

1. McIlhenny Co. 2. Tabasco sauce
ISBN 978-0-06-072184-8; 0-06-072184-7   LC 2007-22876

This is a "history of the McIlhenny clan, inventors of one of the world's most recognizable condiments, Tabasco. Rothfeder follows the family business from founder, Edmund McIlhenny's planting his first peppers on Avery Island, LA, to the current CEO, Paul McIlhenny, who, in 1999, wrested control of the company away from Vince Pierse, the only non-McIlhenny ever to head the company." Libr J

"Reading this piquant history means you can never again reach for that little bottle without recalling the amazing history fraught within." Booklist

Includes bibliographical references

Spector, Robert

Amazon.com; get big fast. HarperBusiness 2000 xxii, 263p pa $16 hardcover o.p.   **338.7**

1. Amazon.com Inc. 2. Booksellers and bookselling 3. Internet
ISBN 0-06-662042-2 (pa)   LC 99-87599

"Spector looks at a Seattle company that has turned retailing and customer service upside down. Online bookseller Amazon.com almost instantly became a part of America's popular culture, but Amazon.com has yet to turn a profit." Booklist

Includes bibliographical references

Vise, David A.

The Google story; [by] David A. Vise and Mark Malseed. Knopf 2005 326p il $26; pa $14 *   **338.7**

1. Google, Inc.
ISBN 0-553-80457-X; 0-553-38366-3 (pa)   LC 2005-56947

The authors present a business history of the Internet search engine company, focusing particular attention on the story of founders Larry Page and Sergey Brin.

"For anyone unaware of the Google founders' history, this book explains what happened 'when Larry met Sergey' in the spring of 1995." N Y Times (Late N Y Ed)

Zygmont, Jeffrey

Microchip: an idea, its genesis, and the revolution it created. Perseus Bks. 2003 xxii, 245p $25   **338.7**

1. Computer industry 2. Microelectronics
ISBN 0-7382-0561-3   LC 2002-112395

"Comparing the invention of the integrated circuit to that of steel, Zygmont tracks the incredible story of the microchip from the visionaries who conceived of it to the rapid-fire advances that have made this complex technology integral to everyday life." Booklist

Includes bibliographical references

338.8   Combinations

Agtmael, Antoine van
The emerging markets century; how a new breed of world class companies is overtaking the world. Free Press 2007 374p il $28   **338.8**
1. Multinational corporations 2. Developing countries—Economic conditions 3. Globalization
ISBN 0-7432-9457-2; 978-0-7432-9457-7
LC 2007-310212

The author "who coined the phrase *emerging markets*, explores how companies like Lenovo and Haier are in emerging economies already competing with such household-name brands as Ford and Sony, concluding that global competition is here to stay." Libr J

"This is an excellent book, with valuable information not only for investors but also for corporate management, which faces emerging market competition." Booklist

Includes bibliographical references

Buderi, Robert
Guanxi (The art of relationships); Microsoft, China, and Bill Gates's plan to win the road ahead; [by] Robert Buderi and Gregory T. Huang. Simon & Schuster 2006 306p il $26
338.8
1. Microsoft Corporation 2. Computer software industry 3. United States—Commerce—China 4. China—Commerce—United States
ISBN 978-0-7432-7322-0; 0-7432-7322-2
LC 2006-42253

"This is the story of Microsoft's Beijing computing research lab, Microsoft Research Asia (MSRA). Since its inception in 1998, MSRA has generated hundreds of high-tech innovations, increasing Microsoft's bottom line and grooming many Chinese men and women for future leadership positions in the company's global operations. . . . [The authors] show how Microsoft's initial strategy did not involve penetrating Chinese markets. Instead, Microsoft first partnered with the Chinese government to show how the lab would benefit the country." Libr J

The authors "were given unprecedented access to those who created the lab, interviewing the numerous 'players' and living among them in order to present a firsthand story of the creation of Microsoft Research Asia (MSRA) and its success in developing guanxi—or skillfully building mutually beneficial relationships, which is fundamental to business success in China." Booklist

Burrough, Bryan, 1961-
Barbarians at the gate; the fall of RJR Nabisco; [by] Bryan Burrough and John Helyar. HarperBusiness Essentials 2003 xxiii, 531p il pa $16.95 *   **338.8**
1. RJR Nabisco Inc. 2. Conglomerate corporations
ISBN 0-06-053635-7   LC 2002-191927
First published 1990

The author "describe the battle to control RJR Nabisco, providing a behind-the-scenes account of the deal through interviews with Wall Street power brokers and comments on the restructuring of corporations to-

day." Publ Wkly

This book "contains enough individual examples of greed, egoism, conniving and sheer incompetence to stun even more jaundiced observers of the Wall Street madhouse. . . . [The authors] have done a solid job of American reportage; in other words, they tell a good story without getting bogged down in analysis." Economist

338.9   Economic development and growth

Atlas of global development; a visual guide to the world's greatest challenges; [International Bank for Reconstruction and Development/The World Bank] Collins 2007 144p il map pa $19.95
338.9
1. Economic development 2. Globalization 3. Population—Statistics
ISBN 978-0-8213-6856-5; 0-8213-6856-7

"This volume packs vital statistics and interpretive insights on disparities involving global wealth, education, and sociopolitical conditions. . . . Charts, graphs, and color maps elucidate in detail global population trends, educational opportunities, and political engagement." Libr J

Includes bibliographical references

Ehrlich, Paul R.
One with Nineveh; politics, consumption, and the human future; [by] Paul R. Ehrlich and Anne H. Ehrlich. Island Press, Shearwater Books 2004 447p $27   **338.9**
1. Economic development 2. Consumption (Economics) 3. Overpopulation
ISBN 1-55963-879-6   LC 2003-24789

"Relayed in a clarion voice, this powerful argument for saving the environment from disaster links social and economic policies with the empirical evidence of overpopulation and materialistic consumption." Booklist

Includes bibliographical references

Fishman, Ted
China, Inc.; how the rise of the next superpower challenges America and the world. Scribner 2005 342p $26 *   **338.9**
1. China—Economic conditions
ISBN 0-7432-5752-9   LC 2004-65328

An "account of China's spectacular, 30-year transformation from economic shambles following Mao's Cultural Revolution to burgeoning market superpower, this book offers a torrent of statistics, case studies and anecdotes to tell a by now familiar but still worrisome story succinctly." Publ Wkly

Includes bibliographical references

338.91 International development and growth

Easterly, William
The white man's burden; why the West's efforts to aid the rest have done so much ill and so little good. Penguin Press 2006 436p il $27.95 *

338.91

1. Foreign aid
ISBN 1-59420-037-8   LC 2005-55516
The author "argues that the poor record of foreign aid could be improved by narrowing its objectives and radically changing its organization. Easterly derides the current approach of government-to-government funding via national and international bureaucracies, and advocates a shift from 'Planners' who promote comprehensive development strategies to 'Searchers' who experiment to find small, incremental improvements." Choice
"Easterly asks the right questions, combining compassion with clear-eyed empiricism." N Y Times Book Rev
Includes bibliographical references

339 Macroeconomics and related topics

Toffler, Alvin
Revolutionary wealth; [by] Alvin Toffler and Heidi Toffler. Knopf 2006 492p $27.95 *

339

1. Economic forecasting 2. Wealth 3. Social change
ISBN 0-375-40174-1; 978-0-375-40174-9
LC 2005-44493
This book "is about how tomorrow's wealth will be created, and who will get it and how." Publisher's note
"Brilliant, incisive, and seminal, this book will be talked about for years to come." Libr J
Includes bibliographical references

339.2 Distribution of income and wealth

Bernstein, William
The birth of plenty; how the prosperity of the modern world was created; [by] William J. Bernstein. McGraw-Hill 2004 420p il $29.95

339.2

1. Wealth 2. Quality of life 3. Economic conditions
ISBN 0-07-142192-0   LC 2003-26155
The author "examines the four factors that fell into place to create a formula for human progress: property rights, scientific rationalism, capital markets, and transportation and communication. From the rise of common law to the invention of the steam engine, from the creation of currencies to shipbuilding, this is an in-depth history of the rise of prosperity." Booklist
Includes bibliographical references

Krugman, Paul R.
The conscience of a liberal; [by] Paul Krugman. W.W. Norton & Co. 2007 296p $25.95

339.2

1. Liberalism 2. United States—Economic conditions 3. United States—Politics and government 4. Social policy—United States
ISBN 978-0-393-06069-0; 0-393-06069-1
LC 2007-34334
The author argues that there has been a "reemergence of immense economic and political inequality since the 1970s." Publisher's note
"Those who turn to Mr. Krugman to understand what's unjust about the United States economy, and why it doesn't have to be this way, will be amply rewarded." N Y Times Book Rev
Includes bibliographical references

339.4 Factors affecting income and wealth

Cohen, Lizabeth
A consumer's republic; the politics of mass consumption in postwar America. Knopf 2003 567p il $35; pa $16.95   **339.4**

1. Consumption (Economics) 2. Consumers 3. United States—Social conditions
ISBN 0-375-40750-2; 0-375-70737-9 (pa)
LC 2002-141599
Cohen contends that "the pursuit of prosperity {after World War II} defined much more than the nation's economy; it also became a basic component of American citizenship. . . . [Cohen contends that consumption] has reshaped our relationship to government itself, with Americans increasingly judging public services—as if one more purchased good—by the personal benefits they derive from them." Publisher's note
"Without question, this is a difficult, demanding, and dense book—but it is also a greatly significant contribution to business literature. . . . Cohen submits a copiously researched, brilliantly conceived, and ultimately quite instructive study of American economics since the Depression." Booklist
Includes bibliographical references

Sachs, Jeffrey D.
The end of poverty; economic possibilities for our time. Penguin Press 2005 396p il maps $27.95 *   **339.4**

1. Foreign aid 2. Developing countries—Economic conditions
ISBN 1-59420-045-9   LC 2004-65942
The author "argues that if the wealthy countries of the world were to increase their combined foreign aid budgets to between $134 billion and $195 billion for the next decade, and properly allocate that money, extreme global poverty . . . could be eliminated by 2025." N Y Times Book Rev
"If there is any one work to put extreme poverty back onto the global agenda, this is it." Publ Wkly
Includes bibliographical references

340 Law

Feinman, Jay M.
1001 legal words you need to know; [the ultimate guide to the language of law] Oxford University Press 2005 239p pa $10.95 *

340

1. Law—United States—Dictionaries
ISBN 0-19-518133-6; 978-0-19-518133-3
First published 2003
Subtitle from cover
This "guide to the language of the American legal system . . . defines and explains every term with a sample sentence, and many entries have supplementary notes. In addition, the book includes a number of quick miniguides to legal troubleshooting that includes information on understanding wills, trusts, and inheritance, granting someone the power of attorney, understanding contracts, what to do if you're sued, how to choose a lawyer, exploring law school, and enjoying cop and lawyer dramas." Publisher's note
Includes bibliographical references

Law 101; everything you need to know about the American legal system. 2nd ed. Oxford University Press 2006 363p $28 *   **340**
1. Law—United States
ISBN 978-0-19-517957-6; 0-19-517957-9
LC 2005-55481
First published 2000
This is an "introduction to law, covering the main subjects found in the first year of law school, giving us a basic understanding of how it all works. Readers are introduced to every aspect of the legal system, from constitutional law and the litigation process to tort law, contract law, property law, and criminal law." Publisher's note

Nolo's encyclopedia of everyday law; answers to your most frequently asked legal questions; by Shae Irving & Nolo editors. 7th ed. Nolo 2008 446p pa $29.99 *   **340**
1. Law—United States
ISBN 978-1-4133-0560-9; 1-4133-0560-1
LC 2007-31791
Also available as an eBook
First published as a replacement of Nolo's everyday law book. Frequently revised
This offers answers to frequently asked legal questions about such topics as credit and debt, workplace rights, wills, divorce, bankruptcy, social security, tenant's rights, child custody and visitation, patents and trademarks, travel, partnerships, healthcare directives and powers of attorney
Includes bibliographical references

340.03 Law—Encyclopedias and dictionaries

Black's law dictionary; Bryan A. Garner, editor in chief. 8th ed. Thomson/West 2004 xxv, 1810p $66 *   **340.03**
1. Law—Dictionaries
ISBN 0-314-15199-0   LC 2004-616324
Also available in an abridged paperback edition
First published 1891 with title: A dictionary of law, under the authorship of Henry Campbell Black. Periodically revised to bring terms up to date
"Definitions of the terms and phrases of American and English jurisprudence, ancient and modern." Subtitle
"This comprehensive work is the standard U.S. law dictionary. [It] includes more than 5,000 new or revised entries, as well as thousands of archaic or little-used legal terms. Many entries include references to cases or statutes. Appendixes include a table of abbreviations and the text of the U.S. Constitution." Guide to Ref Books. 11th edition [review of the 7th edition]

Legal systems of the world; a political, social, and cultural encyclopedia; edited by Herbert M. Kritzer. ABC-CLIO 2002 4v il maps set $385
340.03
ISBN 1-57607-231-2   LC 2002-2659
"Written by an international team of more than 350 legal scholars, the more than 400 signed entries cover legal systems of countries from around the world, Australia, and the provinces of Canada; transnational systems (International Court of Justice); general systems (Islamlic law, indigenous, and folk legal systems); and key concepts. Each country profile includes a map with an inset of its location on the globe, general information about the country, its history, diagrams of its court structure, the evolution of its legal framework, its current structure, staffing or how judges are appointed, any specialized judicial bodies (i.e. military court), and the impact that the legal system has had on the country. Articles conclude with references and a bibliography. Academic and public libraries will find this source invaluable for comparative studies in legal and judicial systems."—"The Best of the Best Reference Sources." Am Libr
Includes bibliographical references

340.5 Legal systems

Miller, William Ian, 1946-
Eye for an eye. Cambridge University Press 2005 266p $28; pa $19.99   **340.5**
1. Justice
ISBN 978-0-521-85680-5; 0-521-85680-9; 978-0-521-70467-0 (pa); 0-521-70467-7 (pa)
LC 2005-8077
"Analyzing the law of the talion—an eye for an eye, tooth for a tooth—literally, William Ian Miller presents . . . [a] meditation on the concept of 'pay back.'" Publisher's note
The author "offers a discursive, erudite, idiosyncratic but illuminating reappraisal of our urge to settle scores." Publ Wkly
Includes bibliographical references

341.23 United Nations

Fasulo, Linda M.
An insider's guide to the UN. Yale University Press 2003 245p il hardcover o.p. pa $16 *
341.23
1. United Nations
ISBN 0-300-10155-4; 0-300-10762-5 (pa)
LC 2003-10668
The author "describes how the U.N. actually works, surveys its humanitarian, crime-fighting, and peacekeeping programs, and argues that the organization continues to deserve American support." Univ Press Books for Public and Second Sch Libr
Includes bibliographical references

Kennedy, Paul M., 1945-
The parliament of man; the past, present, and future of the United Nations; [by] Paul Kennedy. Random House 2006 361p il $26.95
341.23
1. United Nations 2. International relations
ISBN 0-375-50165-7
LC 2005-44785
The author "examines the evolution of the variegated missions of the organization over the last 60 years, including its charter, the Security Council, the secretary general, peacekeeping and war making, as well as the body's economic and social roles, its involvement in human rights, proposals for reform and its future." N Y Times (Late N Y Ed)

Moore, John Allphin, 1940-
Encyclopedia of the United Nations; [by] John Allphin Moore, Jr., Jerry Pubantz. 2nd ed. Facts On File 2008 2v il (Facts on File library of world history) set $125 *
341.23
1. United Nations 2. International relations—Encyclopedias
ISBN 978-0-8160-6913-2
LC 2007-29559
First published 2002
This set features entries on "the United Nations's institutions, procedures, policies, specialized agencies, historic personalities, initiatives, and involvement in world affairs. . . . The appendixes contain important UN documents, such as the Charter of the United Nations, the Universal Declaration of Human Rights, the Statute of the International Court of Justice, and the recent Security Council Resolution." Publisher's note
Includes bibliographical references

Osmanczyk, Edmund Jan, 1913-1989
Encyclopedia of the United Nations and international agreements; [by] Jan Edmund Osmancyzk; edited and revised by Anthony Mango. 3rd ed. Routledge 2002 4v set $550
341.23
1. United Nations 2. International relations—Encyclopedias
ISBN 0-415-93920-8
LC 2002-10761
Original Polish edition, 1975; first English language edition 1985

"An alphabetically arranged treasure trove of information on the United Nations, its specialized agencies, and many intergovernmental and non-governmental organizations. This especially valuable resource for smaller collections includes the full or partial texts of some 3,000 international agreements, conventions, and treaties as well as definitions of political, economic, military, geographical, and diplomatic terms. Analytical and agreements-conventions-treaties indexes." Ref Sources for Small & Medium-sized Libr. 6th edition [entry for 1990 edition]
Includes bibliographical references and index

341.242 European regional organizations

The **European** Union; edited by Norris Smith; editorial advisor, Lynn M. Messina. H.W. Wilson 2005 177p il map (Reference shelf) $50 *
341.242
1. European Union
ISBN 0-8242-1046-8
LC 2004-62511
This book "examines the EU from its formation, with a discussion of the economic, political, and social impact of the organization upon its own members and the rest of the international community." Publisher's note
Includes bibliographical references

342 Constitutional and administrative law

Amar, Akhil Reed
America's constitution; a biography. Random House 2005 657p il $29.95; pa $16.95 *
342
1. Constitutional history—United States
ISBN 1-400-06262-4; 0-8129-7272-4 (pa)
LC 2004-61464
This is a "guide to the goals and meaning intended by those who drafted and ratified the original 1787 document and its 27 amendments." Economist
"Only rarely do you find a book that embodies scholarship at its most solid and invigorating; this is such a book." Publ Wkly
Includes bibliographical references

Berkin, Carol
A brilliant solution; inventing the American Constitution. Harcourt 2002 310p $26; pa $14
342
1. United States. Constitutional Convention (1787) 2. Constitutional history—United States 3. United States—Politics and government—1783-1809
ISBN 0-15-100948-1; 0-15-602872-7 (pa)
LC 2002-5648
This history of the 1787 Constitutional Convention "emphasizes the importance of the delegates' anxieties, showing how they insinuated themselves into some of the compromises, such as the equality of the states in the Senate. Shrewd at integrating biographical detail on the delegates into their debates, Berkin fares well in comparison with previous historians on the topic." Booklist

Bezanson, Randall P.

How free can the press be? University of Illinois Press 2003 258p (History of communication) $34.95   **342**

1. Freedom of speech

ISBN 0-252-02866-X   LC 2003-2148

The author "ponders the contradictions of a free press in this study of nine historical court cases involving free speech. He critically explores the thorny issues surrounding freedom of the press and the press's use of First Amendment protections. Drawing on selected Supreme Court and lower court cases to illustrate his argument, Bezanson articulates important legal questions pertaining to First Amendment rights." Libr J

Includes bibliographical references

Boland, Mary L.

Sexual harassment in the workplace. Sphinx Pub. 2006 264p pa $18.95 *   **342**

1. Sexual harassment—Law and legislation

ISBN 1-57248-527-2; 978-1-57248-527-3

LC 2005-27970

The author defines sexual harassment "in the two legal ways—quid pro quo and a hostile work environment—then explains the corporate point of view, remedies, and legal resources. . . . A necessary reference." Booklist

Includes bibliographical references

Bray, Ilona M., 1962-

How to get a green card; by Ilona Bray & Loida Nicolas Lewis. 8th ed. Nolo 2008 326p il pa $29.99 *   **342**

1. Aliens—United States 2. United States—Immigration and emigration

ISBN 978-1-4133-0852-5; 1-4133-0852-X

LC 2007-47045

First published 1993. Periodically revised

This guide to getting a green card discusses "how to work with U.S. officials, how to prepare and present the right documents, and what to expect every step of the way. . . . [It also explains ways] to get a green card through: parents, siblings and adult children; spouses and fiancés; green card lotteries; political asylum or refugee status; and other categories." Publisher's note

Breyer, Stephen G., 1938-

Active liberty; interpreting our democratic Constitution; [by] Stephen Breyer. Knopf 2005 161p $21   **342**

1. United States. Supreme Court 2. Constitutional law—United States

ISBN 0-307-26313-4   LC 2005-44242

The Supreme Court Justice presents his view on the Constitution of the United States.

"This will be essential reading at a possibly watershed moment for the Supreme Court." Publ Wkly

Includes bibliographical references

Carter, Stephen L.

Reflections of an affirmative action baby. Basic Bks. 1991 286p pa $20 hardcover o.p.

342

1. Affirmative action programs

ISBN 0-465-06869-3 (pa)   LC 91-70054

The author begins by "discussing the positive and negative effects of affirmative action on his life. He then expands his study to include other topics such as the increase of racial incidents in America, dealing with political correctness and the conflicts between the mainstream liberal black community and the increasingly vocal so-called black conservatives." Libr J

The **Debate** on the Constitution; Federalist and Antifederalist speeches, articles, and letters during the struggle over ratification. Library of Am. 1993 2v ea $35 *   **342**

1. Constitutional history—United States 2. United States—Politics and government—1783-1809

ISBN 0-940450-42-9; 0-940450-64-X

LC 92-25449

Contents: v1. Debates in the press and in private correspondence, September 17, 1787-January 12, 1788; Debates in the state ratifying conventions: Pennsylvania, Connecticut, Massachusetts—v2. Debates in the press and in private correspondence, January 14, 1788-August 9, 1788; Debates in the state ratifying conventions: South Carolina, Virginia, New York, North Carolina

In addition to the documents themselves, these volumes contain "brief biographical notes on the various speakers and writers, a chronology of key events in American independence and the establishment of the new governmental system, notes on contemporary state constitutions, and notes explicating the text of the reprinted documents." Christ Sci Monit

Encyclopedia of the American Constitution; edited by Leonard W. Levy and Kenneth L. Karst. 2nd ed, Adam Winkler, associate editor for the second ed. Macmillan Ref. USA 2000 6v set $595   **342**

1. Constitutional law—United States

ISBN 0-02-864880-3   LC 00-29203

First published 1986 in 4 volumes

This "reference contains approximately 3000 contributions from academics, lawyers, and judges concerning key constitutional law cases and legislative developments relating to constitutional issues (e.g., abortion, welfare rights, and affirmative action)." Libr J

Includes bibliographical references

The **Federalist**; edited, with introduction and notes, by Jacob E. Cooke. Wesleyan Univ. Press 1982 c1961 xxx, 672p pa $27.95 *

342

1. United States. Constitution

ISBN 0-8195-6077-4   LC 82-2815

A reissue of the 1961 edition

"From 27 Oct. 1787 to 2 April 1788, 77 essays were published in the semi-weekly 'Independent Journal' of New York, entitled 'The Federalist,' and signed first 'A Citizen of Nwe York' then 'Publius.' Eight more were added when they were collected in book form {in 1789}.

The Federalist—*Continued*
. . . They were so acute and massively learned in their exposition of the true intent of the Constitution, that even the courts have accepted them as authoritative comments in doubtful cases; and they are held by all the civilized world as among the noblest storehouses of political philosophy in existence. A classic textbook of political science." Ency Americana

Hamilton, Marci, 1957-
God vs. the gavel; religion and the rule of law; [by] Marci A. Hamilton; foreword by Edward R. Becker. Cambridge University Press 2005 414p $28; pa $16.99 *   342
1. Church and state
ISBN 0-521-85304-4; 978-0-521-85304-0; 0-521-70338-7 (pa); 978-0-521-70338-3 (pa)
                 LC 2005-3344
The author "explores the thorny conflicts between religion and society, detailing how some religious groups and institutions misuse laws intended to protect religious freedoms to justify child abuse, employment discrimination and other ills." Publ Wkly
"This book deserves shelf space at every library." Libr J
Includes bibliographical references

Lewis, Anthony, 1927-
Freedom for the thought that we hate; a biography of the First Amendment. Basic Books 2007 221p (Basic ideas) $25   342
1. Freedom of speech 2. Freedom of the press
ISBN 978-0-465-03917-3; 0-465-03917-0
                 LC 2007-40249
This book examines "free speech controversies—from sedition and obscenity to hate speech and secret wiretapping." N Y Times Book Rev
The author "does a remarkable job of presenting the history and scope of freedom of thought. He writes simply without oversimplifying. . . . Mr. Lewis has produced a concise and wise book. His conclusions are well worth pondering." Economist
Includes bibliographical references

Maddex, Robert L., 1942-
The U.S. Constitution A to Z. 2nd ed. CQ Press 2008 xxix, 736p il map (CQ's American government A to Z series) $85   342
1. Constitutional law—United States—Encyclopedias 2. Constitutional history—United States—Encyclopedias
ISBN 978-0-87289-764-9   LC 2008-21902
Also available online
First published 2002
"Maddex offers over 200 articles about issues (abortion, gun control), legal concepts (due process, privacy), landmark cases (Roe v. Wade, Brown v. Board of Education) and people (John Adams, Thurgood Marshall) related to the Constitution. . . . The unique feature of this work is its collection of source materials. . . . It is an excellent, concise reference." Choice [review of 2002 edition]
Includes bibliographical references

Madison, James, 1751-1836
The Constitutional Convention; a narrative history from the notes of James Madison; [edited by] Edward J. Larson and Michael P. Winship. Modern Library 2005 229p pa $13.95 *   342
1. United States. Constitutional Convention (1787) 2. Constitutional history—United States 3. United States—Politics and government—Sources
ISBN 0-8129-7517-0   LC 2005-41649
"This book tells the convention's turbulent story in Madison's own words, drawn from the notes he took at the scene and giving us a daily blow-by-blow. . . . [The editors] steer readers through the fierce debates with helpful explanations and editorial asides, as well as a cogent epilogue, making this primary source far more than a tidy civics lesson." Publ Wkly
Includes bibliographical references

Margulies, Joseph
Guantánamo and the abuse of presidential power. Simon & Schuster 2006 322p $25   342
1. Guantánamo Bay Naval Base (Cuba) 2. Prisoners of war 3. War on terrorism
ISBN 0-7432-8685-5; 978-0-7432-8685-5
                 LC 2006-45633
The author "served as lead counsel in Rasul v. Bush, successfully petitioning the Supreme Court to extend the right of judicial review to all prisoners at Guantánamo Bay. This book . . . chronicles the attempts of the present administration to extend the bounds of presidential authority while limiting official culpability. . . . Margulies's clear explications of intricate legal points move his narrative effortlessly from the signing of the Geneva Conventions through the conflicts in Korea and Vietnam, to the myriad cases of the detainees in Guantánamo." Publ Wkly
Includes bibliographical references

May it please the court: the First Amendment; edited by Peter Irons. New Press (NY) 1997 262p $59.95; pa $14.95   342
ISBN 1-56584-330-4; 1-56584-487-4 (pa)
Also available volume about the most important arguments made before the Supreme Court since 1955 on a range of issues including a volume dealing with reproductive rights and abortion cases
"Transcripts of the oral arguments made before the Supreme Court in sixteen key First Amendment cases." Title page
This book and accompanying 4 tapes cover sixteen cases dealing with issues of free speech, freedom of the press, and the right to assemble
"New Press' tapes-and-text combination offers a fascinating history lesson." Booklist

Noonan, John Thomas, Jr.
Narrowing the nation's power: the Supreme Court sides with the states; [by] John T. Noonan, Jr. University of Calif. Press 2002 203p $34.95; pa $14.95   342
1. United States. Supreme Court 2. State governments
ISBN 0-520-23574-6; 0-520-24068-5 (pa)
                 LC 2002-19473

Noonan, John Thomas, Jr.—*Continued*

The author "dissects an emerging trend in recent Supreme Court decisions bolstering the sovereign immunity of the 50 states—that is, saying the states and their many agencies . . . are immune from lawsuits by individuals for money damages." Publ Wkly

"In this highly recommended work, the author convincingly sounds the alarm." Libr J

Includes bibliographical references

Nussbaum, Martha Craven, 1947-

Liberty of conscience; in defense of America's tradition of religious equality; [by] Martha Nussbaum. Basic Books 2008 406p $28.95

342

1. Freedom of religion
ISBN 978-0-465-05164-9; 0-465-05164-2

LC 2007-38176

The author "plumbs the historical, political, philosophical, and legal debates surrounding religious freedom." Booklist

"Nussbaum writes engagingly and with generosity; her critiques, particularly those of opinions written by Justices Scalia and Thomas, are pointed but respectful, and she demonstrates warm regard for Supreme Court plaintiffs who have braved persecution as they have followed the dictates of conscience." Publ Wkly

The **Oxford** guide to United States Supreme Court decisions; edited by Kermit L. Hall. Oxford Univ. Press 1999 428p $39.95; pa $19.95

342

1. United States. Supreme Court 2. Constitutional law—United States
ISBN 0-19-511883-9; 0-19-513924-0 (pa)

LC 98-8747

This volume is a guide to approximately 400 Supreme Court decisions. "Each case entry typically provides background information on the case, explains the Court's decision, {and} explores any disagreement among the justices about the legal doctrines and societal values at stake. . . . A glossary of terms, a copy of the U.S. Constitution, . . . appendixes charting the nominations and succession of Supreme Court justices, a case index, and a topical index complete the volume." Booklist

"An impressive accomplishment, this guide will be invaluable to all students of United States history and will also appeal to sophisticated readers." Libr J

Pearlstine, Norman

Off the record; the press, the government, and the war over anonymous sources. Farrar, Straus and Giroux 2007 xxi, 282p $25 **342**

1. Plame, Valerie 2. Journalists 3. Press—Government policy
ISBN 978-0-374-22449-3; 0-374-22449-8

LC 2007-2972

"When Norman Pearlstine . . . agreed to give prosecutor Patrick Fitzgerald a reporter's notes of a conversation with a 'confidential source,' he was vilified for betraying the freedom of the press. But in this [book], . . . Pearlstine shows that 'Plamegate' was not the clear case it seemed to be—and that confidentiality has become a

weapon in the White House's war on the press, a war fought with the unwitting complicity of the press itself." Publisher's note

"Regardless of how readers feel about his actions, this is a vital look at press responsibility in monitoring the government and itself." Booklist

Includes bibliographical references

Rabban, David M., 1949-

Free speech in its forgotten years. Cambridge Univ. Press 1997 404p il (Cambridge historical studies in American law and society) $60; pa $22

342

1. Freedom of speech 2. Constitutional law—United States
ISBN 0-521-62013-9; 0-521-65537-4 (pa)

LC 97-15281

The author "focuses on free speech issues between the Civil War and World War I. Through an impressive marshaling of controversies, cases, and litigants, he persuasively argues that libertarian radicalism and the Free Speech League . . . deserve much of the credit for pushing valuable First Amendment issues to the forefront of American social, political, and legal circles. . . . This enlightening work fills a void in First Amendment civil liberties studies." Libr J

Includes bibliographical references

Rehnquist, William H.

All the laws but one; civil liberties in wartime. Knopf 1998 254p il $27.50; pa $14 **342**

1. Civil rights 2. National security—United States
ISBN 0-679-44661-3; 0-679-76732-0 (pa)

LC 98-12641

"A Borzoi Bk."

This is "Supreme Court Chief Justice Rehnquist's narrative of the conflict between civil liberties and military necessity. . . . Fully two-thirds of the book covers Civil War issues. . . . One chapter discusses World War I espionage and draft resistance cases; three, the World War II internment of Japanese Americans and the imposition of martial law in Hawaii. . . . Far from a *complete* survey of wartime civil liberties—reviewing only cases that reached the Supreme Court before 1950—this is nonetheless both enlightening and entertaining." Booklist

Includes bibliographical references

United States. Constitution.

The Constitution of the United States of America; analysis and interpretation: analysis of cases decided by the Supreme Court of the United States to June 28, 2002; prepared by the Congressional Research Service, Library of Congress; Johnny H. Killian, George A. Costello, Kenneth R. Thomas, co-editors; David M. Ackerman, Henry Cohen, Robert Meltz, contributors. U.S. Govt. Ptg. Office 2004 xxii, 2608p $215 * **342**

1. Constitutional law—United States
ISBN 978-0-1607-2379-7; 0-1607-2379-5

LC 2005-414932

First published 1953. Periodically revised and kept up to date by supplements

United States. Constitution.—*Continued*

"Sometimes known by its short title, the Constitution Annotated provides commentary on every article, section, and clause of the basic instrument, as well as the amendments, with citations to selected United States Supreme Court decisions construing these provisions." Introd to U.S. Govt Info Sources. 5th edition

Includes bibliographical references

Vile, John R.

The Constitutional Convention of 1787; a comprehensive encyclopedia of America's founding. ABC-CLIO 2005 2v il set $185

342

1. Constitutional history—United States—Encyclopedias 2. Constitutional law—United States—Encyclopedias

ISBN 1-85109-669-8   LC 2005-24214

This "resource covers the people, events, committees, ideology, and documents related to the drafting of the Constitution." SLJ

For a fuller review, see: Booklist, Dec. 1, 2005

Includes bibliographical references

Waldman, Steven, 1962-

Founding faith; providence, politics, and the birth of religious freedom in America. Random House 2008 277p $26   **342**

1. Freedom of religion 2. United States—Religion

ISBN 978-1-4000-6437-3; 1-4000-6437-6

LC 2007-21710

The author describes the "birth of religious freedom in the founding of our nation by letting five Founding Fathers—Benjamin Franklin, John Adams, George Washington, James Madison, and Thomas Jefferson—highlight . . . their efforts in, disagreements and battles over, and approaches to dealing with the place of religion in daily life." Libr J

This "is an excellent book about an important subject: the inescapable—but manageable—intersection of religious belief and public life. With a grasp of history and an understanding of the exigencies of the moment, Waldman finds a middle ground between those who think of the Founders as apostles in powdered wigs and those who assert, equally inaccurately, that the Founders believed religion had no place in politics." Newsweek

Includes bibliographical references

Weiner, Mark Stuart, 1967-

Black trials; citizenship from the beginnings of slavery to the end of caste; [by] Mark S. Weiner. Alfred A. Knopf 2004 421p $26.95; pa $16.95

342

1. African Americans—Civil rights 2. Trials

ISBN 0-375-40981-5; 0-375-70884-7 (pa)

LC 2004-40860

The author "examines how court proceedings involving black people—and whites trying to assist them—have served as windows onto race relations and the power of whites over blacks in the U.S. from its earliest days. . . . This book is the best of its kind—a serious, deeply felt reflection on the weight of history on contemporary affairs." Publ Wkly

Includes bibliographical references

Wise, Steven M.

Though the heavens may fall; the landmark trial that led to the end of human slavery. Da Capo Press 2005 282p il $25; pa $17.95   **342**

1. Somerset, James, fl. 1769-1772 2. Slavery 3. Trials

ISBN 0-7382-0695-4; 0-306-81450-1 (pa)

LC 2004-25346

"A Merloyd Lawrence book"

This is an account of "1772 London trial of James Somerset [who was] resuced from a ship found for the West Indies slave markets. . . . [Wise argues that Somerset's trial and] the trials that led up to it set the stage for the unexpected decision by the . . . conservative judge, Lord Mansfield, which would lead to the abolition of slavery, both in England and the United States, and the end of the African slave trade." Publisher's note

The author "has an eye for evocative detail and an interest in the trappings and procedures of an 18th-century courtroom that do as much to engage the reader as the drama of the trials themselves." N Y Times Book Rev

Includes bibliographical references

Simon, James F.

What kind of nation; Thomas Jefferson, John Marshall, and the epic struggle to create a United States. Simon & Schuster 2002 348p $27.50; pa $14   **342.73**

1. Jefferson, Thomas, 1743-1826 2. Marshall, John, 1755-1835 3. United States. Supreme Court 4. Constitutional history—United States 5. Executive power 6. United States—Politics and government—1783-1809

ISBN 0-684-84870-8; 0-684-84871-6 (pa)

LC 2001-55027

The author "examines the decades of conflict between the states' rights views of Thomas Jefferson and the federalist beliefs of John Marshall." Publ Wkly

"Simon's enlivening account proves that writing about constitutional law needn't be the dry preserve of academics." Booklist

Includes bibliographical references

343   Military, defense, public property, public finance, tax, commerce (trade), industrial law

American Bar Association

The American Bar Association legal guide for small business; everything a small-business person must know, from start-up employment laws to financing and selling a business. Three Rivers Press (NY) 2000 523p pa $17 *   **343**

1. Small business

ISBN 0-8129-3015-0   LC 99-86498

Topics covered "include legal forms of operating businesses, buying an existing business or a franchise, hiring and firing employees, managing temps and independent contractors, dealing with contracts and scams, taxes of all types, and, finally, closing, selling, or bequeathing the business." Libr J

Brownlee, Shannon

Overtreated; why too much medicine is making us sicker and poorer. Bloomsbury 2007 343p $25.95 *   **343**

1. Medical care

ISBN 978-1-58234-580-2; 1-58234-580-5

LC 2007-21968

"Contrary to Americans' common belief that in health care more is more—that more spending, drugs and technology means better care—this . . . report posits that less is actually better. . . . [The author] acknowledges that state-of-the-art medicine can improve care and save lives. But technology and drugs are misused and overused." Publ Wkly

"Readers who have grieved over the death of a friend from a minor surgical procedure or agonized over the hospital care of their elderly parents will experience the shock of recognition in science journalist Brownlee's book." Libr J

Includes bibliographical references

344   Labor, social service, education, cultural law

American Bar Association

The American Bar Association guide to workplace law; [principle author, Barbara Fick] 2nd ed. Random House Reference 2006 301p pa $16.95 *   **344**

1. Labor—Law and legislation

ISBN 0-375-72140-1; 978-0-375-72140-3

LC 2006-45186

First published 1997

This guide covers laws affecting hiring, sexual harassment, leave time, health insurance, ending an employment relationship, retirement, unions, government employment and workplace rights.

Includes bibliographical references

Hull, N. E. H., 1949-

Roe v. Wade; the abortion rights controversy in American history; {by} N.E.H. Hull and Peter Charles Hoffer. University Press of Kan. 2001 315p (Landmark law cases & American society) hardcover o.p. pa $15.95 *   **344**

1. McCorvey, Norma 2. Wade, Henry, 1914-2001 3. Roe v. Wade 4. Abortion—Law and legislation

ISBN 0-7006-1142-8; 0-7006-1143-6 (pa)

LC 2001-1785

This "study begins with three chapters on U.S. abortion history: its nineteenth-century criminalization; the effect of improving birth-control methods in the twentieth century; and state-level legal changes in the 1960s. The authors then analyze the decision itself and trace the continuing battles of the next three decades." Booklist

This volume "is crammed with information but remains very readable and a good source for student papers." Libr J

Includes bibliographical references

Joel, Lewin G.

Every employee's guide to the law; what you need to know about your rights in the workplace— and what to do if they are violated; {by} Lewin G. Joel III. 3rd ed, rev and updated. Pantheon Bks. 2001 431p pa $16   **344**

1. Labor—Law and legislation

ISBN 0-375-71445-6   LC 2001-21501

First published 1993

The author offers legal advice on such subjects as employee interviews, wages, hours, health and safety, sexual harassment, privacy, discrimination, and benefits.

Perritt, Henry H., Jr.

Americans with Disabilities Act handbook. 4th ed. Aspen Pubs. 2003 2v + 1 computer laser optical disc set $450 *   **344**

1. Handicapped—Civil rights

ISBN 0-7355-3148-X   LC 2003-265473

First published 1992 by Excellent Bks.

"Supplemented twice a year for complete currency, these volumes . . . explore the statutory definition of disability, the concept of being 'otherwise qualified' for a job, and exactly how employers, business owners, and providers of governmental services must make 'reasonable accommodation.'" Publisher's note

345   Criminal law

Blakeslee, Nate

Tulia; race, cocaine, and corruption in a small Texas town. Public Affairs 2005 450p il $26.95   **345**

1. Trials 2. Drug traffic 3. Texas—Race relations

ISBN 1-58648-219-X   LC 2005-49220

The author describes the events surrounding multiple false drug arrests made in Tulia, TX, in 1999.

This is "a devastating critique of Texas' judicial system and the nation's drug laws. But it is foremost a riveting legal thriller about the inspirational men and women—including those in and around Tulia—who refused to let the injustice stand." N Y Times Book Rev

Bogira, Steve

Courtroom 302; a year behind the scenes in an American criminal courthouse. Knopf 2005 404p $25   **345**

1. Administration of criminal justice 2. Courts

ISBN 0-679-43252-3   LC 2004-57636

This is the author's "account of his 1998 sojourn in a single courtroom of the Cook County Criminal Courthouse (Chicago)." Libr J

Bogira provides "a balanced view of the realities of the day-to-day, assembly-line grind that marks so much of the process from arrest to final disposition. . . . The brilliance of Bogira's insights will lead many to hope that he will follow this debut with proposals to cure the many ills he has diagnosed." Publ Wkly

Includes bibliographical references

Boyle, Kevin, 1960-
Arc of justice; a saga of race, rights, and murder in the Jazz Age. Holt & Co. 2004 415p il $26; pa $15   **345**
1. Sweet, Ossian, d. 1960 2. Trials (Homicide) 3. African Americans—Civil rights
ISBN 0-8050-7145-8; 0-8050-7933-5 (pa)
LC 2004-47352
The author "recreates the racial thinking and tensions that produced the politics, prosecution, and personal tragedy of People v. Ossian Sweet. The 1925 Michigan murder case tried a black physician for shooting and killing a white man in a mob trying to run him out of the home he and his wife had just bought in a previously all-white neighborhood just outside Detroit." Libr J
Boyle "has brilliantly rescued from obscurity a fascinating chapter in American history that had profound implications for the rise of the Civil Rights movement." Publ Wkly
Includes bibliographical references

Criminal justice. Salem Press 2005 3v il set $364 *   **345**
1. Criminal law—Encyclopedias 2. Administration of criminal justice—Encyclopedias
ISBN 1-58765-218-8; 978-1-58765-218-9
LC 2005-17803
This "is a three-volume reference work that explores criminal justice topics with an emphasis on how criminals and the administration of justice are portrayed in the media. Information from an American perspective on corrections, courts, legislation, the U.S. Constitution, law enforcement agencies, and other topics is presented in 625 . . . essays." Ref & User Services Quarterly
"An inviting format, well-written articles, and lavish reference tools combine to make this an interesting and valuable resource." SLJ
Includes bibliographical references

Dunne, Dominick
Justice; crimes, trials, and punishments. Crown 2001 337p pa $14 hardcover o.p.   **345**
1. Trials
ISBN 0-609-80963-6 (pa)   LC 2001-28214
"Dunne describes the events surrounding several high-profile murders, including those of Nicole Simpson and Ron Goldman, Edmond Safra, Sunny von Bulow (attempted murder), Kitty and Jose Menendez, Pati Margello, Patricia Burton Lonergan, Martha Moxley, and, in the work's most affecting piece, his own daughter, Dominique Dunne." Libr J
"Fascinating stuff, though less than complimentary about the American system of justice." Booklist

Geis, Gilbert
Crimes of the century; from Leopold & Loeb to O.J. Simpson; {by} Gilbert Geis and Leigh B. Bienen. Northeastern Univ. Press 1998 227p $40; pa $18.95 *   **345**
1. Trials 2. Crime—United States
ISBN 1-55553-360-4; 1-55553-427-9 (pa)
LC 98-23180

The authors discuss "five of the most famous crimes and trials of the 20th century. The cases of Leopold and Loeb, the Scottsboro boys, the Lindbergh kidnapping, Alger Hiss, and O.J. Simpson. . . . Though each case is covered from crime through punishment (or acquittal) in fewer than 50 pages, the depth of historical detail and legal analysis is remarkable. The authors are particularly adept at placing these crimes within both their immediate historical settings and the larger societal issues." Libr J
Includes bibliographical references

Geoghegan, Thomas
In America's court; how a civil lawyer who likes to settle stumbled into a criminal trial. New Press (NY) 2002 206p $23.95; pa $15.95   **345**
1. Administration of criminal justice
ISBN 1-56584-732-6; 1-56584-817-9 (pa)
LC 2002-20065
The author "describes participating in a criminal trial after arranging to assist in the defense of a young man accused of committing a felony murder. As the trial proceeds, he talks about his work as a civil lawyer, what it means to be a lawyer, and the issues lawyers face." Libr J

Hoffer, Peter Charles
The Salem witchcraft trials; a legal history. University Press of Kan. 1997 165p (Landmark law cases & American society) hardcover o.p. pa $12.95   **345**
1. Trials 2. Salem (Mass.)—History
ISBN 0-7006-0858-3; 0-7006-0859-1 (pa)
LC 97-19986
"Hoffer discusses the legal nature of the charges of witchcraft, the evidential and procedural characteristics of the trials of the accused, and the roles and attitudes of the ministers and magistrates who controlled the proceedings. . . . Hoffer offers little that is new in terms of interpretation, but he presents it well and in a manner easily grasped by the general reader." Choice
Includes bibliographical references

Kadri, Sadakat
The trial; a history, from Socrates to O. J. Simpson. Random House 2005 459p il $29.95   **345**
1. Trials
ISBN 0-375-50550-4   LC 2005-42925
This "history of the trial from ancient times to the present provides . . . [a] history of the various forms and purposes of trials throughout Western civilization. . . . The result is a magnificent book suitable for all sorts of people, from inquisitive high school students to blue-chip lawyers." Choice
Includes bibliographical references

Lewis, Anthony, 1927-
Gideon's trumpet. Random House 1964 262p pa $12.95 hardcover o.p. *   **345**

Lewis, Anthony, 1927-—_Continued_
1. Gideon, Clarence Earl 2. United States. Supreme
Court 3. Law—United States
ISBN 0-679-72312-9 (pa)
An account of the case of a Florida man convicted of
burglary which brought about a historic decision of the
Supreme Court decreeing that in all states a defendant is
entitled to counsel.
Includes bibliographical references

Mack, Raneta Lawson, 1963-
A layperson's guide to criminal law. Greenwood
Press 1999 201p $69.95   **345**
1. Criminal law
ISBN 0-313-30556-0   LC 98-53382
This explanation of the basics of criminal law includes
numerous hypothetical situations that place some of the
more difficult concepts in an "everyday" context. An
overview of the criminal trial process, from the arrest to
the final verdict is also provided
Includes bibliographical references

Rabinowitz, Dorothy
No crueler tyrannies; accusation, false witness,
and other terrors of our times. Simon & Schuster
2003 239p (A Wall Street Journal book) $25; pa
$13 *   **345**
1. Child sexual abuse 2. Trials
ISBN 0-7432-2834-0; 0-7432-2840-5 (pa)
                                       LC 2002-44670
"These articles were previously published individually
in The Wall Street journal"-- Verso of title page
This book "reexamines high-profile cases of the 1980s
and 1990s involving mass sexual abuse. Demonstrating
that overzealous prosecutors and indifferent courts led to
the prosecution of many innocents, Rabinowitz provides
. . . analyses of the major cases, especially those that involved child-care workers. . . . This gripping, well-
written book about social injustice and public hysteria is
recommended for social science and law collections."
Libr J

Spence, Gerry
The smoking gun; day by day through a
shocking murder trial with Gerry Spence: a true
story. Scribner 2003 435p hardcover o.p. pa $7.99
                                                 345
1. Jones, Sandy 2. Jones, Michael, Jr. 3. Trials (Homicide)
ISBN   0-7432-4696-9;   978-0-7434-7052-0;
0-7434-7052-4   LC 2003-42722
"A Lisa Drew book"
The author "recounts in chilling detail the case against
a poor mother {Sandy Jones} and her son {Michael
Jones, Jr.}, both accused of murder in Oregon." Booklist
"This disquieting book shows that the facts don't
speak for themselves, innocence is rarely presumed and
justice is far from a first priority in America's courtrooms. Spence is a gifted storyteller and his rhetorical
skills are mesmerizing. The blizzards of argument and
counterargument that would be tedious reading in less
talented hands are neatly incorporated into this thrilling
account of injustice barely averted." Publ Wkly

Turow, Scott
Ultimate punishment; a lawyer's reflections on
dealing with the death penalty. Farrar, Straus and
Giroux 2003 164p $18 *   **345**
1. Capital punishment
ISBN 0-374-12873-1   LC 2003-7873
"In 2000 Governor George Ryan of Illinois declared
a moratorium on executions. . . . Ryan established a
commission to study the state's capital punishment system and propose reforms. In 2002 the commission issued
its report. . . . Among the people Ryan appointed to the
commission was Scott Turow, a . . . novelist and practicing attorney, with experience in death penalty cases.
He was, at the time of his appointment, a self-described
'agnostic' on capital punishment. Ultimate Punishment is
Turow's account of his struggle to resolve for himself
the question, Should we retain the death penalty?" Christ
Century
Includes bibliographical references

Walsh, John Evangelist, 1927-
Moonlight; Abraham Lincoln and the Almanac
trial. St. Martin's Press 2000 166p il $22.95
                                                 345
1. Lincoln, Abraham, 1809-1865 2. Trials
ISBN 0-312-22922-4   LC 99-59606
This is "the story of how Abraham Lincoln secured
the acquittal of murder suspect William 'Duff' Armstrong, the son of an old New Salem friend, by making
use of an almanac to discredit a witness's description of
the position of the moon on the night in question." Libr
J
Includes bibliographical references

Watson, Bruce
Sacco and Vanzetti; the men, the murders and
the judgment of mankind. Viking 2007 433p il
$25.95   **345**
1. Sacco, Nicola, 1891-1927 2. Vanzetti, Bartolomeo,
1888-1927 3. Sacco-Vanzetti case 4. Trials (Homicide)
ISBN 978-0-670-06353-6; 0-670-06353-3
                                      LC 2006-103092
This is an account of the trial and execution of two
Italian immigrants, Nicola Sacco and Bartolomeo
Vanzetti, accused of murdering two payroll guards in a
robbery in Braintree, Mass., in April 1920. Sacco was
"an edge trimmer at the Three-K shoe factory in Stough-
ton, Mass, and Vanzetti, a fish peddler in nearby Plym-
outh. Both men belonged to the Gruppo Autonomo, an
anarchist cell in East Boston." N Y Times (Late N Y Ed)
The author "has written a well-researched page-turner.
Highly recommended." Libr J
Includes bibliographical references

346   Private law

Choate, Pat
Hot property; the stealing of ideas in an age of
globalization. Knopf 2005 352p $26.95 *
                                                 346
1. Copyright 2. Patents 3. Inventions
ISBN 0-375-40212-8   LC 2004-59440

Choate, Pat—*Continued*

The author "examines the roots of conflicts over intellectual property and how the establishment of patent and copyright protections helped propel the American economy. . . . [He also argues] that the general indifference of our government toward the security of American intellectual property is already affecting job security and the economy in general." Publisher's note

"Well researched and evenhanded, this book offers specific solutions to a serious problem." Libr J

Includes bibliographical references

Hughes, Theodore E.

The executor's handbook; a step-by-step guide to settling an estate for executors, administrators, and beneficiaries; [by] Theodore E. Hughes and David Klein. 3rd ed. Facts On File, Inc. 2007 260p $39.50; pa $18.95 *   **346**

1. Executors and administrators
ISBN   0-8160-6667-1;   978-0-8160-6667-4;
0-8160-6668-X (pa); 978-0-8160-6668-1 (pa)
LC 2006-26207

First published 1994

This "is a step-by-step guide to settling an estate for personal representatives, administrators, and beneficiaries. . . . It explains everything from the provisions of a will to key legal terms to liquidating assets." Publisher's note

The handbook to wills, funerals, and probate; how to protect yourself and your survivors; [by] Theodore Hughes and David Klein. 3rd ed. Checkmark Books 2007 354p $39.50; pa $18.95 *   **346**

1. Wills 2. Undertakers and undertaking
ISBN   0-8160-6669-8;   978-0-8160-6669-8;
0-8160-6670-1 (pa); 978-0-8160-6670-4 (pa)
LC 2006-26726

First published 1983 by Scribner with title: A family guide to estate planning, funeral arrangements, and settling an estate after death

This is a "primer for handling the practical issues that surround the sensitive topic of death: wills, probate, trusts, community property, organ donations, estate planning, guardianship, and taxes. With clearly written brief chapters, concrete examples, a nice glossary, and eye-friendly layout, this specialized handbook offers step-by-step guidance." Booklist

Includes bibliographical references

346.01   Persons and domestic relations

American Bar Association

The American Bar Association legal guide for Americans over 50. 2nd ed. Random House Reference 2006 313p pa $16.95   **346.01**

1. Elderly—Law and legislation
ISBN 0-375-72139-8; 978-0-375-72139-7
LC 2006-47362

First published 1998 by Times Books with title: The American Bar Association legal guide for older Americans

This guide covers such topics as age discrimination in employment, disability rights, Medicare benefits, estate planning, retirement, health insurance, and grandparents' visitation rights

Clifford, Denis

A legal guide for lesbian and gay couples; by Denis Clifford, Frederick Hertz, and Emily Doskow. 14th ed. Nolo 2007 330p pa $34.99
346.01

1. Gay couples—Legal status, laws, etc.
ISBN 978-1-4133-0629-3; 1-4133-0629-2
LC 2006-47026

First published 1980 by Addison-Wesley under the authorship of Hayden Curry and Denis Clifford

Includes CD-ROM

This handbook addresses "legal issues with which gay and lesbian couples are certain to contend . . . [including] advice for GLBT parents and prospective parents. Moreover, it addresses other legal considerations such as finanical arrangements. Indispensable for gay and lesbian readers, as well as for attorneys who may lack familiarity in this area." Libr J

Doskow, Emily, 1962-

Nolo's essential guide to divorce. Nolo 2006 400p il pa $24.99 *   **346.01**

1. Divorce—Law and legislation
ISBN 1-4133-0452-4; 978-1-4133-0452-7
LC 2006-43782

The author "covers the before, during, and after of divorce, counseling readers on the types of divorces, how to make decisions about living arrangements and the division of property, and how custody decisions are made. She advocates minimizing conflict but includes sections on domestic violence and kidnapping if the worst happens. Appendixes contain state-to-state grounds for divorce and financial inventory forms." Libr J

The **Rights** of women; the basic ACLU guide to women's rights; [by] Susan Deller Ross [et al.] 3rd ed, completely rev and up-to-date. Southern Ill. Univ. Press 1993 317p (American Civil Liberties Union handbook) $27.50; pa $19.95
346.01

1. Women—Law and legislation 2. Women's rights
ISBN 0-8093-1898-9; 0-8093-1633-1 (pa)
LC 92-34244

First published 1973 by Sunrise Books/Dutton

New edition in preparation

Topics covered "include employment, education, parenting, family law, and reproductive freedom. This handbook also examines criminal proceedings, insurance, the military, credit, and the rights of homeless women." Publisher's note

Includes bibliographical references

Sember, Brette McWhorter, 1968-

Seniors' rights; your legal guide to living life to the fullest. Sphinx Pub 2004 243p pa $19.95 *
346.01

1. Elderly—Law and legislation
ISBN 1-572-48386-5   LC 2004-10704

Sember, Brette McWhorter, 1968-—*Continued*

"The author endeavors to help seniors understand their rights involving medical care, bank accounts, retirement accounts, housing, and discrimination. . . . The first step to protecting your rights, as she indicates, is understanding them, and this book will help seniors achieve that goal." Booklist

Sitarz, Daniel, 1948-

Divorce yourself. 6th ed. Nova Pub. Co. 2005 333p (Legal self-help series) pa $29.95

346.01

1. Divorce—Law and legislation
ISBN 978-1-89294-911-0; 1-89294-911-3

LC 2005-282096

Also available with CD-ROM for $39.95

First published 1990. Periodically revised

"Legally valid in all 50 states and Washington D.C." Cover. Subtitle on cover: The national divorce kit.

This book "includes clear explanations of divorce-related legal issues and terminology, checklists that facilitate discussion of financial and custodial arrangements, and advice regarding tax consequences and name changes. Sample forms are included, along with precise instructions for preparing and filing them, and also a chapter that advises the user on court appearance and procedures. The appendix consists of a summary of the divorce laws of all 50 states with appropriate citations and the advice to check the latest version for possible changes." Booklist

Women's legal guide; editor, Barbara R. Hauser with Julie A. Tigges. Fulcrum 1996 526p pa $22.95 hardcover o.p.   **346.01**
1. Women—Law and legislation
ISBN 1-55591-303-2 (pa)   LC 95-46893

"This is a collection of essays written by women attorneys for women who need legal information. Family- and health- related issues such as divorce, family violence, and reproductive rights are covered, as are business topics of particular concern to women. . . . Estate planning, sexual discrimination, dealing with disabilities, and the rights of lesbian women are considered as well. The writing is consistently clear, objective, and practical." Libr J

Includes bibliographical references

Woodhouse, Violet, 1948-

Divorce and money; how to make the best financial decisions during divorce; by Violet Woodhouse with Dale Fetherling. 8th ed. Nolo Press (Berkeley) 2006 482p il pa $34.99 *

346.01

1. Divorce—Law and legislation
ISBN 1-4133-0522-9; 978-1-4133-0522-7

LC 2006-48312

First published 1991. Periodically revised

A guide to financial problems that arise as a result of divorce proceedings

346.04   Property

Crews, Kenneth D.

Copyright law for librarians and educators; creative strategies and practical solutions; with contributions from Dwayne K. Buttler . . . [et al.] 2nd ed. American Library Association 2006 141p il pa $45 *   **346.04**
1. Copyright
ISBN 0-8389-0906-X   LC 2005-13804

First published 2000 with title: Copyright essentials for librarians and educators

The author "addresses 18 areas of copyright in 5 parts. He begins with the scope of protectable works as well as works without copyright protection. Next, he discusses the rights of ownership, including duration and exceptions. He then explains fair use and its related guidelines. Part 4 focuses on the TEACH Act, Section 108, and responsibilities and liabilities. Lastly, Crews examines special issues such as the Digital Millennium Copyright Act." Booklist

Includes bibliographical references

Elias, Stephen

Trademark; legal care for your business & product name. 8th ed. Nolo 2007 356p il pa $39.99 *   **346.04**
1. Trademarks
ISBN 978-1-4133-0699-6; 1-4133-0699-3

LC 2007-13018

First published 1992. Periodically revised

The authors explain "how to: choose a distinctive name or logo that others can't copy, conduct a trademark search, register the trademark, protect and maintain the trademark, handle disputes out of Court. Contains all the official forms with step-by-step instructions." Publisher's note

Fishman, Stephen

Copyright handbook; what every writer needs to know. 10th ed. Nolo 2008 527p il pa $39.99

346.04

1. Copyright
ISBN 1-4133-0893-7; 978-1-4133-0893-8

LC 2008-7882

First published 1991. Frequently revised

Includes CD-ROM

"Designed as a practical handbook for writers and publishers. Includes a list of legal aid groups and sample forms." Guide to Ref Books. 11th edition

Copyright handbook; what every writer needs to know. 10th ed. Nolo 2008 527p il pa $39.99 *

346.04

1. Copyright
ISBN 978-1-4133-0893-8; 1-4133-0893-7

LC 2008-7882

First published 1991. Frequently revised

Includes CD-ROM

"Designed as a practical handbook for writers and publishers. Includes a list of legal aid groups and sample forms." Guide to Ref Books. 11th edition

Includes bibliographical references

Lessig, Lawrence
The future of ideas; the fate of the commons in a connected world. Random House 2001 352p pa $15 hardcover o.p.   **346.04**
1. Copyright 2. Internet 3. Information society
ISBN 0-375-72644-6 (pa)   LC 2001-31968
The author "argues that as the Internet faces the challenges of intellectual property laws, it should not become so controlled that it discourages innovation and creativity in the digital world." Libr J
"Some of Lessig's sweeping proposals are sure to spark a lively debate, but his well-reasoned, clearly written argument is powerful." Publ Wkly

Stewart, Marcia
Every landlord's legal guide; by Marcia Stewart, Ralph Warner & Janet Portman. 9th ed. Nolo 2008 483p il pa $44.99 *   **346.04**
1. Landlord and tenant
ISBN 978-1-4133-0856-3; 1-4133-0856-2
                                            LC 2007-47037
Also available as an eBook
First published 1996. Frequently revised
Accompanied by CD-ROM
This guide explains how to "screen and choose prospective tenants, write a legal rental agreement or lease, hire a property manager, deal with problem tenants, understand repair, maintenance and security responsibilities, avoid lawsuits, comply with laws regarding security deposits, privacy, discrimination, housing, habitability and . . . more." Publisher's note

Stim, Richard
Patent, copyright & trademark. 9th ed. Nolo 2007 574p il pa $39.99 *   **346.04**
1. Patents 2. Copyright 3. Trademarks
ISBN 978-1-4133-0646-0; 1-4133-0646-2
                                            LC 2007-2191
First published 1996. Periodically revised
The author explains concepts, issues, and terms concerning intellectual property, discusses trade secret, copyright, patent, and trademark law, and provides sample forms.

Strauss, Steven D., 1958-
Landlord and tenant. Norton 1998 155p (Ask a lawyer) $25; pa $14   **346.04**
1. Landlord and tenant
ISBN 0-393-04585-4; 0-393-31730-7 (pa)
                                            LC 97-33617
At head of title: Ask a lawyer
This book covers the legal rights and responsibilities of tenants and landlords including such topics as what to look for in an apartment or lease, how to evict tenants or avoid eviction, and how to break a lease

Wherry, Timothy Lee
Intellectual property; everything the digital-age librarian needs to know. American Library Association 2008 141p il $50 *   **346.04**
1. Copyright 2. Patents 3. Trademarks
ISBN 978-0-8389-0948-5; 0-8389-0948-5
                                            LC 2007-13893

The author "explains the difference between patents, copyrights, and trademarks and when one would want to obtain any one or a combination of the three. He goes on to instruct readers on how technology has simplified the process of both searching and acquiring these three types of intellectual property protection. . . . This informative and necessary volume is a must have for any professional reference collection." Voice Youth Advocates

346.05   Inheritance, succession, fiduciary trusts, trustees

American Bar Association
The American Bar Association guide to wills & estates; everything you need to know about wills, estates, trusts & taxes. 2nd ed. Random House Reference 2004 366p pa $16.95   **346.05**
1. Wills 2. Estate planning
ISBN 0-609-80934-2   LC 2003-8795
First published 1995 by Times Books
This guide includes information about crafting wills, avoiding unnecessary inheritance taxes, minimizing probate, creating living trusts, choosing an executor, transfering property without a will, and protecting property in case of incapacitation

Clifford, Denis
Make your own living trust. 8th ed. Nolo 2007 368p pa $39.99 *   **346.05**
1. Estate planning 2. Inheritance and succession
ISBN 978-1-4133-0569-2; 1-4133-0569-5
                                            LC 2006-47212
Also available as an eBook
First published 1993. Periodically revised
Accompanied by CD-ROM
This explains how to create a living trust, how to transfer property to it, and how to manage it. Includes forms and instructions

Plan your estate. 9th ed. Nolo 2008 548p il pa $44.99 *   **346.05**
1. Estate planning
ISBN 978-1-4133-0761-0; 1-4133-0761-2
First published 1989. Periodically revised
On cover: Protect your loved ones, property & finances
This guide covers basic estate planning, probate avoidance, living wills, federal estate and gift taxes, trusts, durable powers of attorney, and more.

Plotnick, Charles
How to settle an estate; a manual for executors and trustees; [by] Charles K. Plotnick, Stephan R. Leimberg. 3rd rev ed. Plume Bks. 2002 354p pa $16   **346.05**
1. Executors and administrators
ISBN 0-452-28342-6   LC 2002-727766
First published 1986 by Doubleday with title: The executors manual

Plotnick, Charles—*Continued*

This guide offers estate executors and trustees advice on such topics as "How to raise cash for immediate estate expenses; Dealing with insurance claims; Knowing when to hire a lawyer, an accountant, and a stock broker; Managing real estate [and] Distributing assets." Publisher's note

Shotwell, Barbara, 1946-

Pass it on; a practical approach to the fears and facts of planning your estate; [by] Barbara Shotwell and Nancy R. Greenway. Hyperion 2000 286p il $22.95; pa $14.95   **346.05**

1. Estate planning

ISBN 0-7868-6580-6; 0-7868-8494-0 (pa)

LC 99-49481

The authors explain "the essential estate-planning documents, various kinds of trusts, retirement plans, business considerations, and the probate process. . . . The text is replete with cartoons, quotes, illustrative song titles, and anecdotes that add levity and accessibility without oversimplifying the treatment of the subject." Libr J

Sitarz, Daniel, 1948-

Prepare your own will. 6th ed. Nova Pub. Co. 2005 245p (Legal self-help series) pa $29.95
346.05

1. Wills

ISBN 978-1-89294-915-8; 1-89294-915-6

LC 2005-284031

Also available paperback edition without CD-ROM $19.95 (ISBN-13: 978-1-89294-914-1)

First published 1988 with title: Prepare your own last will and testament—without a lawyer. Periodically revised

Subtitle on cover: The national will kit. Includes CD-ROM

This offers instructions and forms for preparing a will, with assessment questionnaires on property and beneficiaries, checklists, and sample wills, an appendix of state laws relating to wills, and forms on CD-ROM.

Strauss, Steven D., 1958-

Wills and trusts. Norton 1998 176p (Ask a lawyer) $25; pa $14   **346.05**

1. Wills 2. Estate planning

ISBN 0-393-04583-8; 0-393-31728-5 (pa)

LC 97-33619

At head of title: Ask a lawyer

This guide describes "The various phases of wills, trusts, and estate planning and provides legal definitions, tips, sample scenarios, and a typical will." Publisher's note

"Strauss specializes in transforming the arcane and obtuse into everyman's lingo and comprehension." Booklist

346.07   Commercial law

Elias, Stephen

How to file for Chapter 7 bankruptcy; by Stephen Elias, Albin Renauer & Robin Leonard. 14th ed. Nolo Press (Berkeley) 2007 531p il pa $29.99 *   **346.07**

1. Bankruptcy

ISBN 978-1-4133-0627-9; 1-4133-0627-6

LC 2006-47025

First published 1989. Periodically revised; variant title: How to file for bankruptcy

This offers advice on such topics as personal debt, property liability, asset protection, rebuilding credit, and filling out and filing forms

347   Civil procedure and courts

BNA's directory of state and federal courts, judges, and clerks 2008. Bureau of Natl. Affairs 2007 730p pa $200 *   **347**

1. Courts—United States—Directories

ISBN 978-1-57018-670-7; 1-57018-670-7

Annual. First published 1986

A state-by-state and federal listing

This directory lists the names, addresses, and telephone numbers of over 14,000 judges and approximately 5,300 clerks and administrators, in more than 2,400 courts at the three highest levels of all US states and territories

Dwyer, Jim, 1957-

Actual innocence; when justice goes wrong and how to make it right; [by] Jim Dwyer, Peter Neufeld, Barry Scheck. New American Library 2003 xxi, 407p il map pa $16   **347**

1. Administration of criminal justice

ISBN 978-0-451-20982-5; 0-451-20982-6

LC 2003-46499

First published 2000 by Doubleday

This book deals with "men wrongly convicted of rape and murder, some of them sentenced to die, who were able to prove that they were innocent. They largely owe their exoneration to the Innocence Project, a program based at Cardozo Law School in New York. . . . The Innocence Project works to reopen old convictions, using DNA evidence." N Y Times Book Rev

Includes bibliographical references

Faigman, David L. (David Laurence)

Laboratory of justice; the Supreme Court's 200-year struggle to integrate science and the law. Times Books, Henry Holt 2004 417p $27.50; pa $17   **347**

1. United States. Supreme Court 2. Constitutional law—United States 3. Science—Governmental policy

ISBN 0-8050-7274-8; 0-8050-7845-2 (pa)

LC 2003-57049

The author "examines how empirical evidence from natural and social sciences has been employed in key

Faigman, David L. (David Laurence)—*Continued*

U.S. Supreme Court cases." Libr J

"This insightful and accessible study throws light on how new ways of understanding the world produce new readings of our Constitution." Publ Wkly

Includes bibliographical references

Finkelman, Paul, 1949-

Landmark decisions of the United States Supreme Court; [by] Paul Finkelman, Melvin I. Urofsky. 2nd ed. CQ Press 2008 791p il $250 * **347**

1. United States. Supreme Court 2. Constitutional law—United States

ISBN 978-0-87289-409-9   LC 2007-42588

First published 2003

This "provides the historical context and constitutional perspective of more than 1,000 of the most important Supreme Court cases." Publisher's note

Includes bibliographical references

Garbus, Martin, 1934-

Courting disaster; the Supreme Court and the dangerous unmaking of American law. Times Bks. 2002 322p $25; pa $15   **347**

1. United States. Supreme Court 2. Constitutional history—United States

ISBN 0-8050-6918-6; 0-8050-7287-X (pa)

LC 2002-20314

"Garbus sees the Rehnquist Court as undermining the ability of both the Federal judiciary and especially Congress to play a prominent role in the progressive evolution of the modern state. . . . Carefully explicating the conflicting Court perceptions of federalism, he paints a vivid picture of internal conflict among the justices." Libr J

Includes bibliographical references

Great American trials; Edward W. Knappman, editor; Stephen G. Christianson and Lisa Paddock, consulting legal editors. 2nd ed. Gale Group 2002 2v il set $170 *   **347**

1. Trials

ISBN 0-7876-4901-5

"A New England Publishing Associates book"

First published 1994

Contents: v1 1637-1949; v2 1950-2001

Featuring approximately 360 trials from the 1800s to the present, entries "cover the principals involved, the crime charged, the verdict and sentence, and the significance and impact of each trial." Publisher's note

Includes bibliographical references

Great world trials; Edward W. Knappman, editor. Gale Res. 1997 xxviii, 536p il $90   **347**

1. Trials

ISBN 0-7876-0805-X   LC 96-38793

Also available in paperback from Visible Ink Press

"A New England Pub. Assocs. Bk."

This is a "narrative of 100 international trials of historical, political, or social significance." Libr J

"From the Alcibiades trial in 415 B.C. to the 1996 trial of Yigal Amir and covering crimes such as murder, treason, fraud, and negligence, this work paints a vivid portrait of international jurisprudence through the ages." Booklist

Includes bibliographical references

Hartman, Gary R.

Landmark Supreme Court cases; the most influential decisions of the Supreme Court of the United States; [by] Gary Hartman, Roy M. Mersky, [and] Cindy Tate Slavinski. Facts on File 2004 594p (Facts on File library of American history) $70; pa $21.95   **347**

1. United States. Supreme Court 2. Law—United States

ISBN 0-8160-2452-9; 0-8160-6923-9 (pa)

LC 2003-57776

"The authors describe some 350 influential US Supreme Court decisions. Arranged by subjects such as abortion and taxation, the . . . entries include an abstract of the decision, . . . the case's history, summary of the arguments, the salient issues involved, its significance, related cases, and recommended readings including law journal articles." Choice

This is "an excellent source for beginning researchers. . . . The discussion of the case's significance and its implications will be useful for students." SLJ

Includes bibliographical references

Irons, Peter H., 1940-

A people's history of the Supreme Court; the men and women whose cases and decisions have shaped our Constitution. Rev. ed. Penguin Books 2006 xx, 588p pa $18   **347**

1. United States. Supreme Court—History

ISBN 0-14-303738-2; 978-0-14-303738-5

LC 2006-44779

First published 1999

The author "chronicles the decisions that have influenced virtually every aspect of our society, from the debates over judicial power to controversial rulings in the past regarding slavery, racial segregation, and abortion, as well as more current cases about school prayer, the Bush/Gore election results, and 'enemy combatants.'" Publisher's note

Includes bibliographical references

Jost, Kenneth

The Supreme Court A to Z. 4th ed. CQ Press 2007 622p il (CQ's American government A to Z series) $85 *   **347**

1. United States. Supreme Court

ISBN 0-87289-335-9; 978-0-87289-335-1

LC 2006-38701

First published 1993

This book "provides biographies of past and present justices, the history of important cases, and explanations of constitutional principles and legal concepts." Publisher's note

Includes bibliographical references

O'Brien, David M.

Storm center; the Supreme Court in American politics. 8th ed. W.W. Norton 2008 xx, 458p il pa $29.85 **347**

1. United States. Supreme Court

ISBN 978-0-393-93218-8; 0-393-93218-4

LC 2008-7373

First published 1986. Periodically revised

The author discusses "the day-to-day workings of the Court justices and their law clerks, how cases are accepted for hearing, what negotiations and compromises go on, how case opinions get written—and what happens to American society when two conservative presidents, Reagan and Bush, appoint the majority of justices." Publisher's note

Includes bibliographical references

The **Oxford** companion to the Supreme Court of the United States; editor in chief, Kermit L. Hall; editors, James W. Ely, Jr., Joel B. Grossman. 2nd ed. Oxford University Press 2005 xxv, 1239p il $65 * **347**

1. United States. Supreme Court

ISBN 0-19-517661-8   LC 2004-29463

First published 1992

This encyclopedia includes over 1200 articles "on all aspects of the court's history, justices, operations, and cases. Over 300 experts contributed the entries, which vary in length; some have bibliographic references. The organization . . . [includes] alphabetical entries, portraits of the justices, cross-references, and indexes by both case name and topic." Choice

For a fuller review, see: Booklist, Oct. 15, 2005

Schultz, David A., 1958-

The encyclopedia of the Supreme Court; [by] David Schultz. Facts on File 2005 562p il (Facts on File library of American history) $85 * **347**

1. United States. Supreme Court

ISBN 0-8160-5086-4   LC 2004-13174

"The purpose of this one-volume resource is to provide 'an overview of the major cases, concepts, and issues and of the personalities who have shaped' the Supreme Court, as well as to provide a sense of its history and impact on American politics." Libr J

"The ease with which one can search this volume, as well as the style of writing and depth of explanation make this a truly valuable resource." Libr Media Connect

Includes bibliographical references

The **Supreme** Court compendium; data, decisions, and developments; [by] Lee Epstein . . . [et al.] 4th ed. CQ Press 2007 xxix, 808p il $137 **347**

1. United States. Supreme Court 2. Judges

ISBN 0-87289-350-2; 978-0-87289-350-4

LC 2006-49189

Also available online

First published 1994

This book "presents historical and statistical information on every important aspect of the U.S. Supreme Court, including its history, development as an institu-

tion, the justices' backgrounds, nominations, and confirmations, and the Court's relationship with the public and other governmental and judicial bodies." Publisher's note

"For serious students of the Supreme Court this superbly crafted source will be enormously useful, if not indispensable." Am Ref Books Annu, 2008

Includes bibliographical references

Toobin, Jeffrey R.

The nine; inside the secret world of the Supreme Court; [by] Jeffrey Toobin. Doubleday 2007 369p il $27.95 * **347**

1. United States. Supreme Court

ISBN 978-0-385-51640-2   LC 2007-20287

The author provides a "narrative history of the Supreme Court's recent history and [a] . . . look at individual court justices." N Y Times (Late NY Ed)

"Beautifully written, this is an essential purchase for all libraries interested in the contemporary Supreme Court." Libr J

Includes bibliographical references

Warner, Ralph E.

Everybody's guide to small claims court; by Ralph Warner and Emily Oskow. 12th ed. Nolo Press (Berkeley) 2008 500p pa $29.99 * **347**

1. Small claims court

ISBN 978-1-4133-0762-7; 1-4133-0762-0

LC 2007-38828

First published 1980 by Addison-Wesley. Periodically revised

The author "discusses filing court papers, paying fees, and using witnesses and examines typical kinds of small claims. The appendixes detail procedures, list monetary thresholds, and reference statutory citations." Libr J

348   Laws, regulations, cases

Howard, Philip

The death of common sense; how law is suffocating America; [by] Philip K. Howard. Warner Books 1996 213p pa $13.95 **348**

1. Law—United States 2. Law reform 3. Bureaucracy

ISBN 0-446-67228-9; 978-0-446-67228-3

First published 1994 by Random House

The author contends "that we need less law, fewer rules and more common sense. He thinks that American law is now endangering both freedom and prosperity precisely because it is so excruciatingly rule-bound." N Y Times Book Rev

This book "is absolutely wonderful to read. It is accessible to general readers, yet it should at the same time serve as a clarion call to the legal profession to clean up its house and to the legislatures to pass functional statutes." Choice

Includes bibliographical references

Major acts of Congress; Brian K. Landsberg, editor in chief. Macmillan Reference USA 2004 3v il set $290 * **348**

1. Law—United States—Encyclopedias

ISBN 0-02-865749-7   LC 2003-18747

Major acts of Congress—*Continued*

The editor "offers historical overviews of the importance and impact of 262 major congressional acts from 1789 to 2002. The signed, alphabetically arranged entries range from one to five pages in length and conclude with bibliographies and occasional Internet resources." SLJ

This "will be a top-tier reference work for students and laypersons researching federal legislation." Booklist

Includes bibliographical references

Stathis, Stephen W.

Landmark legislation, 1774-2002; major U.S. acts and treaties; {by} Stephen Stathis. CQ Press 2003 22, 429p $130   348

1. Legislation
ISBN 1-56802-781-8   LC 2003-3531

"Stathis summarizes major congressional legislation, both laws and treaties, for more than 225 years chronologically by Congress, along with historical settings for the period." Choice

"This well-organized volume will allow users to quickly find a description of important legislation and determine where they can locate the full text. . . . This will be a useful source for academic and public libraries." Booklist

Includes bibliographical references

U.S. laws, acts, and treaties; edited by Timothy L. Hall. Salem Press 2003 3v (Magill's choice) set $188 *   348

1. Law—United States 2. United States—Foreign relations—Treaties
ISBN 1-58765-098-3   LC 2002-156063
Contents: v1 1776-1928; v2 1929-1970; v3 1970-2002

This "is a collection of 433 major U.S. acts of Congress and U.S. treaties covering the time period from 1776 through 2002, beginning with the Declaration of Independence and ending with the Homeland Security Act. . . . The essays, chronically arranged and varying in length from 500 to 2,000 words, cover the historical origins and main provisions of each law or treaty. . . . This set presents a good coverage of landmark laws and treaties in a concise, easy-to-read, and easy-to-use work. It is geared toward high-school and undergraduate students but would also make a useful and functional reference tool for public libraries." Booklist

Includes bibliographical references

349 Law of specific jurisdictions, areas, socioeconomic regions, regional intergovernmental organizations

Encyclopedia of American law; {edited by} David Schultz. Facts on File 2002 542p il $75
349

1. Law—United States—Encyclopedias
ISBN 0-8160-4329-9   LC 2001-40206

"This encyclopedia's entries average a page in length and include contemporary topics such as affirmative action and recent court cases as well as concepts such as entrapment, equity, and insanity. . . . This resource

packs a lot of material and is easy to read and navigate." Book Rep

Includes bibliographical references

Friedman, Lawrence Meir, 1930-

American law in the 20th century; [by] Lawrence M. Friedman. Yale Univ. Press 2002 722p $38   349

1. Law—United States
ISBN 0-300-09137-0   LC 2001-3332

The author "examines the American legal system as an integral part of the larger society, both reflecting and causing changes therein. By adopting such a focus, the author makes his book accessible to readers who are not legal scholars." Booklist

Includes bibliographical references

Gale encyclopedia of everyday law; Jeffrey Wilson, editor. 2nd ed. Thomson Gale 2006 2v set $325 *   349

1. Law—United States
ISBN 1-4144-0353-4   LC 2006-10071
First published 2003

This encyclopedia includes "descriptions of each issue's historical background, covering important statutes and cases; profiles of various U.S. laws and regulations; details of how laws and regulations vary from state to state, and; . . . bibliographies, including print and Web resources and lists of relevant organizations." Publisher's note

Includes bibliographical references

National survey of state laws; Richard A. Leiter, editor. 6th ed. Thomson Gale 2008 808p $140 *   349

1. Law—United States
ISSN 1078-2095
ISBN 978-0-7876-9874-4; 0-7876-9874-1
Irregular. First published 1993

Summarizes state laws on 50 subjects, divided into general legal categories: business and consumer, criminal, education, employment, family, general civil, real estate, and tax.

The **Oxford** companion to American law; editor in chief, Kermit L. Hall; editors, David S. Clark {et al.}. Oxford Univ. Press 2002 xxvi, 912p $75   349

1. Law—United States
ISBN 0-19-508878-6   LC 2002-284010

The alphabetically arranged "entries consider how law, legal institutions, and court decisions are related to social demands and legal responses. . . . The volume also includes standard legal terms and key legal concepts, such as verdicts and venues, as well as biographical statements about leading individuals in the legal profession. . . . With a substantial breadth of information and analysis, this volume is accessible to every reader. All libraries will find it an invaluable reference source." Libr J

Includes bibliographical references

West's encyclopedia of American law; Jeffrey Lehman, editor, Shirelle Phelps, editor. 2nd ed. Thomson/Gale 2004 13v set $1195 *

349

1. Law—United States—Encyclopedias
ISBN 0-7876-6367-0   LC 2004-4918
First published 1983-1985 with title: The Guide to American law

Over 5,000 alphabetically arranged entries explain legal principles and concepts, landmark documents, laws, famous trials, historical movements, and notable persons

351.076   Review and exercise

Civil service arithmetic and vocabulary; [by] Joe Krasowski . . . [et al.] 15th ed. Arco/Thomson Learning 2005 347p pa $14.95   **351.076**
1. Civil service—Examinations
ISBN 0-7689-1697-6; 978-0-7689-1697-3
First published 1951. Periodically revised
Contains basic instructions for working every type of math problem found on the exams. The vocabulary section includes a review of vocabulary words, verbal analogies, and sentence completion problems.

Federal civil service jobs. 14th ed, {by} Dawn Rosenberg McKay, Michele Lipson. Thomson/Arco 2003 194p pa $14.95 *

351.076

1. Civil service—United States
ISSN 1530-0005
ISBN 0-7689-0921-X
11th-13th editions by Hy Hammer
This is a guide on how to search and apply for federal jobs. Information on eligibility requirements and promotional opportunities is included as well as a glossary of civil service hiring terms, sample questions, test strategies, and techniques for various qualifying exams

352   General considerations of public administration

Moynihan, Daniel Patrick, 1927-2003
Secrecy; the American experience; [by] Daniel Patrick Moynihan; introduction by Richard Gid Powers. Yale Univ. Press 1998 262p il $38; pa $16   **352**
1. National security—United States 2. Executive power
ISBN 0-300-07756-4; 0-300-08079-4 (pa)
                                          LC 98-8144
"Using his background as chairman of the bipartisan Commission on Protecting and Reducing Government Secrecy, Moynihan provides a fascinating account of the development of secrecy as a mode of regulation for the U.S. government since World War I: how it was born, how world events shaped it, how it has adversely affected momentous political decisions—dropping the bomb on Hiroshima, the Bay of Pigs fiasco, the Iran-contra affair—and how it has eluded efforts to curtail or end it." America

Includes bibliographical references

352.13   State and provincial administration

The **book** of the states, 2008. 2008 ed. Council of State Governments 2008 618p $125; pa $99 *

352.13

1. State governments
ISSN 0068-0125
ISBN   978-0-87292-849-7;   0-87292-849-7;
978-0-87292-750-6 (pa); 0-87292-750-4 (pa)
Biennial, 1935-2001, Annual from 2002. Began publication 1935
"In addition to general articles on various aspects of state government, this source provides many statistical and directory data, the principal state officials, and such information as the nickname, motto, flower, bird, song, and tree of each state." Ref Sources for Small & Medium-sized Libr. 6th edition

Counties USA; a directory of United States counties; Darren L. Smith, managing editor. Omnigraphics 2006 840p il map $149 *

352.13

1. County government 2. United States—Statistics
ISBN 978-0-7808-0821-8
First published 1997
This book "provides statistical, descriptive, and contact information for the more than 3,100 counties and county equivalents in the United States." Publisher's note
This is "an excellent choice, offering multiple uses as a country directory, demographic source, and gazetteer." Choice [review of 2003 edition]

352.2   Organization of administration

United States government manual 2007-2008; Office of the Federal Register, National Archives and Records Service, General Services Administration. Claitor's Law Bks. 2007 pa $27 *

352.2

1. United States—Politics and government—Handbooks, manuals, etc.
ISBN 1-59804-377-3; 978-1-59804-377-8
Annual. First published 1935. Variant title: United States government organization manual
"Official handbook of the Federal government describing the purposes and programs of most Government agencies and listing the top personnel." N Y Public Libr. Ref Books for Child Collect. 2d edition

352.23   Chief executives

Fellow citizens; the Penguin book of U.S. presidential inaugural addresses; edited with an introduction and commentaries by Robert V. Remini and Terry Golway. Penguin Books 2008 476p $16   **352.23**
1. Presidents—United States—Inaugural addresses 2. American speeches
ISBN 978-0-14-311453-6; 0-14-311453-0
                                          LC 2008-19970

Fellow citizens—*Continued*

"Two distinguished historians round up every presidential inaugural address and preface it with commentary on the rhetoric and historical context of the discourse. . . . Reflecting the major events of American history, as well as a rhetorical evolution from prolixity to brevity, this . . . is a great resource." Booklist

Includes bibliographical references

Guide to the presidency; Michael Nelson, editor. 4th ed. CQ Press 2008 2v il map set $355 *

352.23

1. Presidents—United States
ISBN 978-0-8728-9364-1; 0-8728-9364-2

LC 2007-25322

First published 1989 with title: Congressional Quarterly's guide to the presidency

"The history of the presidency; the powers of the office . . . ; the president as a public figure; relations with other branches of government; life in the White House; and many other topics are covered in 37 chapters authored by academic scholars." Booklist

Includes bibliographical references

My fellow Americans; the most important speeches of America's presidents, from George Washington to George W. Bush; {compiled} by Michael Waldman; CDs narrated by George Stephanopoulos. Sourcebooks 2003 337p il $45 *

352.23

1. Presidents—United States 2. United States—Politics and government 3. American speeches
ISBN 1-402-20027-7

LC 2003-6879

This "resource contains 43 speeches from 17 presidents, nearly all unabridged, each with an introduction explaining its historical context and significance. Two companion CDs allow listeners to hear all 43 speeches, including the actual voices of presidents from Teddy Roosevelt to George W. Bush. . . . Waldman's stated purpose in putting together this volume is to show how the actions, the dreams, and the big ideas presented by these addresses furthered the American democratic spirit. Some early drafts are included, including several versions of the opening paragraph of JFK's Inaugural Address. The most recent entry is President Bush's Address on Iraq given on March 17, 2003, accompanied by the April news photo showing the fall of the Saddam Hussein statue in Baghdad. A fine addition." SLJ

Includes bibliographical references

The **presidency** A to Z; Gerhard Peters, editor; John T. Woolley, editor; Michael Nelson, advisory editor. 4th ed. CQ Press 2008 675p il map (CQ's American government A to Z series) $85 *

352.23

1. Presidents—United States—Encyclopedias
ISBN 978-0-87289-367-2; 0-87289-367-7

LC 2007-31322

First published 1992 with Michael Nelson's name appearing first

"Volume 1 traces the history of the office from the creation of the United States Constitution to present-day duties and responsibilities. . . . Volume 2 examines the interaction between the President and the other branches

of government. It also includes biographies of Presidents, Vice Presidents, and First Ladies and concludes with tables listing the popular and electoral votes in presidential elections, party nominees for President, and cabinet members. . . . Students of history, political science, and public policy will find it useful when looking for background information about the office of the President." Libr J

Includes bibliographical references

State of the union; presidential rhetoric from Woodrow Wilson to George W. Bush. CQ Press 2007 1185p il $140

352.23

1. Presidents—United States—Messages
2. Presidents—United States—Inaugural addresses
3. American speeches 4. United States—Politics and government—Sources
ISBN 978-0-87289-433-4; 0-87289-433-9

LC 2006-35973

"This volume includes over 100 full-text addresses delivered by Presidents from 1913 to 2006 and comes complete with prefatory notes for context." Libr J

Includes bibliographical references

353.9 Administration of safety, sanitation, waste control Safety administration

Hilts, Philip J.

Protecting America's health; the FDA, business, and one hundred years of regulation. University of North Carolina Press 2004 394p pa $19.95 *

353.9

1. United States. Food and Drug Administration
2. Food—Law and legislation 3. Food adulteration and inspection 4. Drug industry
ISBN 978-0-8078-5582-9; 0-8078-5582-0

First published 2003 by Knopf

This is a "history of the first internal federal agency charged with protecting individual citizens, and of numerous efforts to improve it or wreck it since its beginnings." N Y Times Book Rev

"This fascinating look at the inside story reveals how disastrous unfettered capitalism would be without reasonable regulation." Booklist

Includes bibliographical references

355 Military science

Amazons to fighter pilots; a biographical dictionary of military women; Reina Pennington, editor; foreword by Gerhard Weinberg. Greenwood Press 2003 2v il set $175 *

355

1. Women soldiers—Biography—Dictionaries
ISBN 0-313-29197-7

LC 2002-44777

"Entries profile over 300 remarkable women of the military, covering such groups as the Amazons, women in the Spanish Civil War, and Native Americans. . . . Additional tidbits—quotations, statistics, information on women and war—appear in sidebars throughout the text.

Amazons to fighter pilots—*Continued*
Lists grouping entries by geographical regions, time periods, and branch of service serve as finding aids for researchers." Publisher's note
"This peerless work, situated at the nexus of military history and women's studies, is an essential companion to more male-biased biographical resources." Choice
Includes bibliographical references

Axelrod, Alan, 1952-
The encyclopedia of the American armed forces. Facts on File 2005 2v il (Facts on File library of American history) set $175 *   **355**
1. United States—Armed forces—Encyclopedias
ISBN 0-8160-4700-6   LC 2004-20549
"The four sections each document a major branch of the United States military: Army, Navy, Marine Corps, and Air Force. Each branch has an initial list of entries, a list of branch-specific abbreviations and acronyms, and a short bibliography." Choice
For a fuller review, see: Booklist, Jan. 1 & 15, 2006
Includes bibliographical references

Barron's how to prepare for the ASVAB; Armed Services Vocational Aptitude Battery; compiled by the Editorial Department of Barron's Educational Series, Inc; edited by Terry L. Duran. 8th ed. Barron's Educ. Ser. 2006 484p il pa $18.99 *   **355**
1. United States—Armed forces—Examinations
ISBN 0-7641-3281-4; 978-0-7641-3281-0
Also available with CD-ROM $26.99 (ISBN-13: 978-0-7641-7880-1)
First published 1984. Frequently revised
This study guide includes practice examinations and a review of pertinent subject areas.

The **Book** of war; edited by John Keegan. Viking 1999 492p pa $17 hardcover o.p.   **355**
1. Military history
ISBN 0-14-029655-7 (pa)   LC 99-42660
This is an "anthology of eyewitness and participant writing covering 25 centuries, from Thucydides' history of the Peloponnesian War to a small-unit engagement between British and Iraqi infantry in the Persian Gulf war." N Y Times Book Rev
Includes bibliographical references

Boot, Max, 1968-
War made new; technology, warfare, and the course of history, 1500 to today. Gotham Books 2006 624p il map $24.95 *   **355**
1. Military history 2. Military art and science
ISBN 978-1-592-40222-9; 1-592-40222-4
     LC 2006-15518
"A Council on Foreign Relations book"
"Boot argues that innovations in warfare mark crucial turning points in modern history, influencing events well beyond the realm of combat." Publisher's note
"Throughout, Boot provides a vivid and engaging mix of historical narrative and analysis, showing the bloody real-world results of abstract decisionmaking about the

nature and degree of a country's military preparedness. His twelve case studies, stretching from the defeat of the Spanish Armada to the current situation in Iraq, point to a variety of disparate lessons but some themes that are surprisingly constant over time and space." Commentary

Buckley, Gail Lumet, 1937-
American patriots; the story of Blacks in the military from the Revolution to Desert Storm; [by] Gail Buckley. Random House 2001 xxiv, 534p il hardcover o.p. pa $15.95 *   **355**
1. African American soldiers 2. United States—Military history 3. United States—Race relations
ISBN 0-375-50279-3; 0-375-76009-1 (pa)
     LC 00-51825
This is an account "of blacks in the U.S. military, both at home and abroad, from the 1770s to the 1990s. . . . This readable, spirited story deserves a place in every U.S. history collection, as well as in the black or military collections." Libr J
Includes bibliographical references

Carroll, James
House of war; the Pentagon and the disastrous rise of American power. Houghton Mifflin Co. 2006 657p il $30   **355**
1. Pentagon (Arlington, Va.: Building) 2. United States. Dept. of Defense 3. Military policy—United States
ISBN 0-618-18780-4; 978-0-618-18780-5
     LC 2005-24014
"Chronicling the ascent of America's military establishment from 1943 to the aftermath of 9/11, Carroll uses the Pentagon as a metaphor for a U.S. political culture that values military power over human rights and seeks to project U.S. influence and values abroad by force, if necessary, whether invited by other countries or not. . . . Certain to be a widely read and discussed book, this is worthy of space on the shelves of all libraries." Libr J
Includes bibliographical references

Clausewitz, Carl von, 1780-1831
On war; {by} Carl von Clausewitz; edited and translated by Michael Howard and Peter Paret; introductory essays by Peter Paret, Michael Howard and Bernard Brodie; with commentary by Bernard Brodie. Princeton Univ. Press 1976 717p $95; pa $26.95 *   **355**
1. Military art and science 2. War
ISBN 0-691-05657-9; 0-691-01854-5 (pa)
Original German edition, 1833
"Drawing on the experiences of Frederick the Great and Napoleon, Clausewitz tried to analyze the workings of military genius by isolating the factors that decide success in war. His conclusions have remained generally applicable, and since his work contains a minimum of technical discussion, it has retained a wide appeal." Ency Britannica

De Pauw, Linda Grant
Battle cries and lullabies; women in war from prehistory to the present. University of Okla. Press 1998 395p il pa $21.95 hardcover o.p.

355

1. Military history 2. Women—History 3. Women soldiers
ISBN 0-8061-3288-4 (pa)   LC 98-21219
This is a history of women in the military, "from prehistory to the Persian Gulf War and Tailhook." Booklist
"Though the book never directly states its larger claims, the wealth of evidence it provides renders the controversy over women in combat almost quaint—their presence on and near the battlefield is ancient, inescapable and irreversible." Publ Wkly
Includes bibliographical references

Dictionary of military terms; a guide to the language of warfare and military institutions; compiled by Trevor N. Dupuy {et al.}. 2nd ed. Wilson, H.W. 2003 271p il $85 *

355

ISBN 0-8242-1025-5   LC 2002-32960
First published 1986
This book offers "guidance to the language of contemporary warfare and military institutions, from weapons systems, strategies, and tactics to ranks, decorations, and administration." Publisher's note
"This is a very readable book for the general reader and will make a great addition to public, academic, and some high-school libraries as well as being useful for military professionals." Booklist

Dictionary of wars; George Childs Kohn, editor. 3rd ed. Facts on File 2006 692p il (Facts on File library of world history) $85; pa $22.95

355

1. Military history—Dictionaries
ISBN   0-8160-6577-2;   978-0-8160-6577-6;
0-8160-6578-0 (pa); 978-0-8160-6578-3 (pa)
LC 2005-58936
First published 1986
"Entries include the dates of events and a brief summary of their causes, effects, and consequences. The straightforward writing style emphasizes basic facts rather than arguments justifying or opposing each conflict. This, along with the occasional cross-references and helpful and complete general and geographic indexes, makes the encyclopedia accessible to most students." SLJ

Encyclopedia of American military history; Spencer C. Tucker, general editor; associate editors David Coffey, John C. Fredriksen, Justin D. Murphy. Facts on File 2003 3v il maps set $225 *

355

1. United States—Military history—Encyclopedias
ISBN 0-8160-4355-8   LC 2002-29658
"More than 1,200 entries cover military leaders, wars, campaigns, battles, events, famous soldiers, military branches, key technological developments, overviews of weapons systems, and more. It covers the period from the colonial wars to the present, and gives special attention to the minorities and women who have contributed significantly to American military success." Publisher's note
Includes bibliographical references

Facts about the American wars; edited by John S. Bowman. Wilson, H.W. 1998 750p il maps $110 *

355

1. United States—Military history
ISBN 0-8242-0929-X   LC 97-40298
"A New England Publishing Associates book."
"An introduction explains the text's layout and approach to each war. The reader samples every conflict from the Franco-Spanish War of the mid-1500s to the Persian Gulf War of 1991. Most wars covered have maps; illustrations, or photographs; each has a separate bibliography. The details provided for each war are most impressive." Book Rep
Includes bibliographical references

Gaddis, John Lewis
Surprise, security, and the American experience. Harvard University Press 2004 150p (Joanna Jackson Goldman memorial lecture on American civilization and government) $18.95   355
1. National security—United States 2. United States—Foreign relations
ISBN 0-674-01174-0   LC 2003-56935
The author "argues that three salient elements of President Bush's security strategy—pre-emption, unilateralism and hegemony—have deep roots in America's history." N Y Times Book Rev
"This compact, provocative history of an idea-in-action has the potential to alter the U.S.'s collective self-image." Publ Wkly
Includes bibliographical references

Hanson, Victor Davis
The soul of battle; from ancient times to the present day, how three great liberators vanquished tyranny. Anchor Books 2001 480p pa $16.95

355

1. Sherman, William T. (William Tecumseh), 1820-1891 2. Patton, George S. (George Smith), 1885-1945 3. Military history
ISBN 0-385-72059-9; 978-0-385-72059-5
LC 00-63979
First published 1999 by Free Press
"Hanson narrates the success of three military campaigns-Epaminondas defeat of the Spartans in the fourth century B.C., Sherman's march through Georgia and the Carolinas during the Civil War, and Patton's race into Germany at the head of the Third Army in 1944-45. . . . In Hanson's view, the individual traits of spontaneity and creativity that are nourished in a free society are assets, not hindrances, in warfare." Booklist
Includes bibliographical references

Hedges, Chris
War is a force that gives us meaning. PublicAffairs 2002 211p $23   355
1. War
ISBN 1-58648-049-9   LC 2002-68136
Also available in paperback from Anchor Bks.
"War can only be sustained, Hedges affirms, by imbuing events with meanings they do not have. These 'mythic realities' are essential to suspending the normal rules

Hedges, Chris—*Continued*
of human behavior and justifying the mayhem and personal sacrifice war entails. Each side comes to see itself as the embodiment of absolute goodness; each demonizes the other and reduces its enemies to objects. The killing is thus made easy, but communication is impossible." New Leader

"This should be required reading in this post-9/11 world." Libr J

Includes bibliographical references

Karpin, Michael I.
The bomb in the basement; how Israel went nuclear and what that means for the world; [by] Michael Karpin. Simon & Schuster 2006 404p il map $26; pa $15   **355**
1. Nuclear weapons 2. Israel—Military history
ISBN 0-7432-6594-7; 978-0-7432-6594-2; 0-7432-6595-5 (pa); 978-0-7432-6595-9 (pa)
LC 2005-51689
"This book explores how Israel has been able to finesse the buildup of its nuclear capabilities." Booklist

"For all those interested in understanding how Israel's idealistic origins dovetail with its hawkish position in the game of nuclear deterrence and fraught relationship with other countries in the Middle East, this well-researched study is a must-read." Publ Wkly

Includes bibliographical references

Kindsvatter, Peter S.
American soldiers; ground combat in the World Wars, Korea, and Vietnam; foreword by Russell F. Weigley. University Press of Kan. 2003 432p il (Modern war studies) $34.95   **355**
1. United States. Army. Infantry 2. United States. Marine Corps 3. Soldiers—United States 4. United States—Military history
ISBN 0-7006-1229-7   LC 2002-12957
"Mining twentieth-century foot soldiers' memoirs and novels, Kindsvatter integrates this literature of personal experience into a generalized assessment of what combat was like and how men reacted to it. . . . Kindsvatter's illuminating work is about coping with . . . fear at the foxhole level, and it . . . powerfully conveys the psychology and military sociology of combat in the draft-era armies." Booklist

Includes bibliographical references

Langewiesche, William
The atomic bazaar; the rise of the nuclear poor. Farrar, Straus and Giroux 2007 179p map $22
355
1. Nuclear weapons 2. Arms control
ISBN 978-0-374-10678-2; 0-374-10678-9
LC 2006-102539
"This is the story of the inexorable drift of nuclear weapons technology from the hands of the rich into the hands of the poor. As more unstable and undeveloped nations find ways of acquiring the ultimate arms, the stakes of state-sponsored nuclear activity have soared . . . . Even more disturbing is the likelihood of such weapons being manufactured and deployed by guerrilla

non-state terrorists. Langewiesche also recounts the recent history of Abdul Qadeer Khan, the scientist at the forefront of nuclear development and trade in the Middle East." Publisher's note

"Langewiesche's bracing expose of nuclear criminality blasts away the ubiquitous misinformation usually attendant on this alarming subject." Booklist

Lipsky, David, 1965-
Absolutely American; four years at West Point. Houghton Mifflin 2003 317p il $25   **355**
1. United States Military Academy
ISBN 0-618-09542-X   LC 2002-191339
Also available in paperback from Vintage Bks.
This "examination of cadet life explores the history of the academy, the intense physical and intellectual regimen, and the academy as a reflection of our society." Libr J

"The book must have been extremely hard to organize. And yet it reads with a novelistic flow. . . . It turns out that how teenagers get turned into leaders is not a simple story, but it is wonderfully told in this book." N Y Times Book Rev

Magill's guide to military history; editor, John Powell; managing editor, Christina J. Moose; project editor, Rowena Wildin. Salem Press 2001 5v il set $473   **355**
1. Military history—Dictionaries
ISBN 0-89356-014-6   LC 00-66072
This "is a worldwide, illustrated, alphabetical survey of war, weapons, battles, civilizations, people and their place in military history, ancient times to the 21st century. Its 1,518 entries and over 300 thorough essays with keywords in boldface are all indexed by category in volume 5." Choice

Includes bibliographical references

The **Oxford** companion to American military history; editor in chief, John Whiteclay Chambers II; editors, Fred Anderson [et al.] Oxford Univ. Press 1999 xxxiv, 916p il maps $75   **355**
ISBN 0-19-507198-0   LC 99-21181
This reference work covers "battles and soldiers, ships and weapons, services and doctrines—as well as the social and cultural impact of the U.S. military at home and around the world. . . . There are entries on relevant acts of Congress and on diplomatic policies such as the Monroe Doctrine and the Marshall Plan; on peace and antiwar movements; on war in film, literature, music, and photography; and on war viewed through the disciplinary lenses of anthropology, economics, gender studies, and psychology." Publisher's note

Includes bibliographical references

Phillips, Charles, 1948-
Encyclopedia of wars; [by] Charles Phillips and Alan Axelrod. Facts on File 2005 3v map (Facts on File library of world history) set $300 *
355
1. Military history—Encyclopedias
ISBN 0-8160-2851-6   LC 2003-28010

Phillips, Charles, 1948-—*Continued*

The authors "have compiled some 2,000 alphabetically arranged entries detailing wars, conflicts, and rebellions from ancient to modern times. Each entry comes in two parts. A leadoff summary section offers a simple statement on major causes of the conflict, lists major participants, where fighting took place, final outcome, names and dates of relevant treaties, number of combatants on each side, and casualties (if known). A narrative section then elucidates the overall conduct and context of the war and the major battles and events bearing upon the outcome." Choice

Phillips and Axelrod "have produced a very readable and . . . well-researched book that both scholars and history buffs will enjoy." Booklist

Includes bibliographical references

Reader's guide to military history; edited by Charles Messenger. Fitzroy Dearborn Pubs. 2001 xxxvi, 948p $135   **355**

1. Military history

ISBN 1-57958-241-9   LC 2002-275907

Topics covered "include land, sea, and air services; conflicts; types of warfare; military theory; prominent military leaders; and national armed services. . . . {This} is a unique, well-designed reference tool." Booklist

Includes bibliographical references

Rhodes, Richard, 1937-

Arsenals of folly; the making of the nuclear arms race. Alfred A. Knopf 2007 386p il $28.95   **355**

1. Nuclear weapons 2. Arms race

ISBN 978-0-375-41413-8; 0-375-41413-4

    LC 2007-17613

"Drawing on personal interviews with both Soviet and U.S. participants, and on a . . . documentation, memoir literature, and oral history that has become available only in the past ten years, Rhodes recounts what . . . happened in the final years of the Cold War that led to its dramatic end." Publisher's note

"This historical record, drawing upon many firsthand accounts and interviews, details pivotal events in world history and should be necessary reading for anyone interested in 20th-century history." Libr J

Includes bibliographical references

Ruggero, Ed

Duty first; West Point and the making of American leaders. HarperCollins Pubs. 2001 342p il $27.50; pa $14.95   **355**

1. United States Military Academy 2. Leadership

ISBN 0-06-019317-4; 0-06-093133-7 (pa)

    LC 00-59775

In this report about the contemporary West Point experience, the author "tries to explain precisely what makes the United States Military Academy, better known as West Point, a breeding ground for future leaders." Publ Wkly

Sun-tzu, 6th cent. B.C.

The illustrated art of war; [by] Sun Tzu; the definitive English translation by Samuel B. Griffith. Oxford University Press 2005 272p il map $29.95 *   **355**

1. Military art and science

ISBN 0-19-518999-X; 978-0-19-518999-5

    LC 2005-10651

An illustrated version of The art of war, a military treatise written in China during the 6th century BC discussing different military tactics and strategies.

Includes bibliographical references

Sutherland, Jonathan, 1958-

African Americans at war; an encyclopedia; [by] Jonathan D. Sutherland. ABC-CLIO 2004 2v set $185 *   **355**

1. African American soldiers 2. United States—Armed forces

ISBN 1-57607-746-2   LC 2003-21501

"There are more than 250 [alphabetically arranged] entries conveying biographical, thematic, and conceptual information. Well-known leaders (Colin Powell), groups (Buffalo Soldiers), specific units . . . and battles . . . have their own entries. . . . Most entries range from half a page to three pages, and the references range from one to six sources, including Web sites. . . . This is a superb resource for any . . . library looking to enrich its history, military or African American studies collections." Booklist

Voices of war; stories of service from the home front and the front lines; edited by Tom Wiener. National Geographic Society 2004 336p il $30; pa $6.95 *   **355**

1. Veterans 2. United States—Military history 3. United States—Armed forces—Military life

ISBN 0-7922-7838-0; 0-7922-4204-1 (pa)

    LC 2004-49986

"Library of Congress Veterans History Project"

This book showcases "the oral histories collected by the Veteran's History Project, the Library of Congress's nationwide effort to collect and preserve the stories not only of war veterans, but also of those who served in support of the frontline troops. . . . The personal accounts cover the major conflicts of the 20th century, from World War I to the Persian Gulf War, and include letters, diaries, and journals. The chapters are nicely arranged to show the commonalities of military experience, e.g., basic training, daily life, combat, the home front, and returning home." Libr J

355.6 Military administration

Vogel, Steve
The Pentagon; a history: the untold story of the wartime race to build the Pentagon—and to restore it sixty years later. Random House 2007 xxv, 626p il map $32.95   **355.6**
1. Pentagon (Arlington, Va.: Building) 2. United States. Dept. of Defense 3. Public buildings—United States
ISBN 978-1-4000-6303-1; 1-4000-6303-5
LC 2006-50873
Vogel's "work recounts the construction of one of the world's most iconic buildings—the Pentagon. But more compelling by far, he relates the human stories underlying this huge construction effort. . . . All this would of itself be enough to warrant a book but Vogel plunges on to an appropriate second story: the terrorist assault of 9/11 and the Pentagon's subsequent resurrection. This section of the book, due perhaps to the proximity of the event, is all the more compelling." New York Post
Includes bibliographical references

355.8 Military equipment and supplies (Matériel)

Preston, Diana
Before the fallout; from Marie Curie to Hiroshima. Walker 2005 438p il $27
355.8
1. Atomic bomb
ISBN 0-8027-1445-5   LC 2004-61953
Also available in paperback from Berkley Books
This history of the making of the atomic bomb covers "half a century, beginning with Marie and Pierre Curie's 1898 discovery of radium and continuing through other important scientific findings (e.g., Einstein's relativity theory and Heisenberg's quantum mechanics)." Libr J
"Avidly researched and gracefully constructed, Preston's revelatory history is rich in telling moments, powerful personalities, intense confrontations, and indelible images of the devastation delivered by nuclear weapons, our Damoclean sword." Booklist
Includes bibliographical references

356 Foot forces and warfare

Carney, John T.
No room for error; the covert operations of America's special tactics units from Iran to Afghanistan; {by} John T. Carney Jr. and Benjamin F. Schemmer. Ballantine Books 2003 334p il map $25.95   **356**
1. United States. Army. Special Forces 2. Military art and science
ISBN 0-345-45333-6   LC 2002-28158
"Carney recounts the challenging missions: the secret reconnaissance in the desert of north-central Iran during the hostage crisis; the simple rescue operation in Grenada

that turned into a prolonged bloody struggle." Publisher's note
The author's "dramatic tales place special operations history in perspective, particularly as the war in Afghanistan has been led by special forces units." Publ Wkly
Includes bibliographical references

Clancy, Tom, 1947-
Special forces; a guided tour of U.S. Army Special Forces; written with John Gresham. Berkley Bks. 2001 366p il pa $16   **356**
1. United States. Special Operations Command
ISBN 0-425-17268-6   LC 00-65121
"The book covers recruitment and training of personnel . . . equipment, which includes an exotic mixture of high, low, and no tech components; and the variety of missions special forces execute." Booklist
Includes bibliographical references

Haney, Eric L.
Inside Delta Force; the story of America's elite counterterrorist unit. Delacorte Press 2002 324p il hardcover o.p. pa $14 *   **356**
1. United States. Army. Delta Force
ISBN 0-385-33603-9; 0-385-33936-4 (pa)
LC 2001-58408
The author relates his "experiences during the formation and early operations of 1st Special Forces Operational Detachment-Delta. . . . He served three times in Beirut guarding the American ambassador, participated in the invasion of Grenada, served in several Central American countries and narrowly escaped death during the abortive rescue attempt of the American hostages in Iran. . . . Readers of other special forces memoirs will find this one distinctive for Haney's attention to interservice rivalries . . . that he believes compromised several missions, as well as for Haney's nuanced, often disgusted descriptions of the human cost of war." Publ Wkly

357 Mounted forces and warfare

Cotterell, Arthur
Chariot; from chariot to tank, the astounding rise and fall of the world's first war machine. Overlook Press 2005 344p il map $29.95
357
1. Military art and science
ISBN 1-58567-667-5   LC 2004-65980
The author "examines the use of chariots in war, ritual, and sport." Choice
"This work is a welcome addition to a collection specializing in military history or ancient history but will appeal to general readers as well because the writing is accessible despite the plethora of detail." Libr J
Includes bibliographical references

358 Air and other specialized forces and warfare; engineering and related services

Guillemin, Jeanne, 1943-
Biological weapons; from the invention of state-sponsored programs to contemporary bioterrorism. Columbia University Press 2005 258p $75; pa $22.95 *   **358**
1. Biological warfare
ISBN 0-231-12942-4; 0-231-12943-2 (pa)
LC 2004-51911
This is a "history of biological weaponry, beginning with the British, American and Japanese programs that predate WWII. . . . Admirably free of finger-pointing, shrillness and Luddite tendencies, the book ranks high as a historical introduction to the subject and a handbook on contemporary remedies." Publ Wkly
Includes bibliographical references

Miller, Judith, 1948-
Germs; America's secret war against biological weapons; Judith Miller, Stephen Engelberg, William Broad. Simon & Schuster 2001 382p $27; pa $14   **358**
1. Biological warfare
ISBN 0-684-87158-0; 0-684-87159-9 (pa)
LC 2001-42690
Three reporters survey the history of biological weapons and recount incidents of their use by terrorist groups. They explain why advances in biology and the spread of germ weapons poses grave risks as countries such as Iran, Iraq and North Korea continually engage in research
Includes bibliographical references

Tucker, Jonathan B.
War of nerves; chemical warfare from World War I to al-Qaeda. Pantheon Books 2006 479p il $30; pa $17.95 *   **358**
1. Chemical warfare
ISBN   0-375-42229-3;   978-0-375-42229-4; 1-4000-3233-4 (pa); 978-1-4000-3233-4 (pa)
LC 2005-50053
The author "writes about chemical warfare from World War I to the present." Publisher's note
This "book makes a sobering case for a less poisonous world." N Y Times Book Rev
Includes bibliographical references

Weapons of mass destruction; an encyclopedia of worldwide policy, technology, and history; Eric A. Croddy and James J. Wirtz, editors. ABC-CLIO 2004 2v il set $185   **358**
1. Nuclear weapons 2. Chemical warfare 3. Biological warfare
ISBN 1-85109-490-3   LC 2004-24651
This set covers "the history, context, current issues, and key concepts surrounding biological, chemical, and nuclear weapons." Publisher's note
"No other reference source covers such a wide array of topics related to WMD. It will dispel many myths but will also draw attention to the lethal consequences of WMD." Booklist
Includes bibliographical references

Wright, Patrick, 1951-
Tank: the progress of a monstrous war machine. Viking 2002 499p il $29.95; pa $16   **358**
1. Military tanks
ISBN 0-670-03070-8; 0-14-200191-0 (pa)
The author "traces the cultural history of a kill vehicle variously called 'behemoth,' 'landship' and even 'Mother.' Wright's exhaustive research offers a treasure trove of facts usually eclipsed in conventional military or technical histories." Publ Wkly
Includes bibliographical references

358.4 Air forces and warfare

Boyne, Walter J., 1929-
Beyond the wild blue; a history of the United States Air Force, 1947-1997. St. Martin's Press 1997 442p il $29.95; pa $19.95 *   **358.4**
1. United States. Air Force 2. Military aeronautics
ISBN 0-312-15474-7; 0-312-18705-X (pa)
LC 96-53507
"A Thomas Dunne book"
In this "history of the evolution of the air force, from its beginning as a separate arm of the military in 1947 through its many roles and changes since then, Boyne asserts that the air force's effort and sacrifice won us the Cold War. . . . While his slant may be seen as controversial, this is a large, thorough, and valuable history." Libr J
Includes bibliographical references

359 Sea forces and warfare

Bruce, Anthony, 1949-
An encyclopedia of naval history; [by] Anthony Bruce and William Cogar. Fitzroy Dearborn 1998 440p il $100   **359**
1. Naval history—Encyclopedias
ISBN 1-579-58109-9
An "encyclopedia of world naval history from the 15th century to the present. Its 1,000 articles cover all manner of detail from sea battles and great commanders to warship evolution, naval technology and tactics, organizations, and naval-oriented details of specific campaigns. Although international in scope, the work clearly emphasizes the US and Britain." Choice

Love, Robert William, 1944-
History of the U.S. Navy; {by} Robert W. Love, Jr. Stackpole Bks. 1992 2v ea $39.95   **359**
1. United States. Navy 2. United States—Naval history
ISBN 0-8117-1862-X (v1); 0-8117-1863-8 (v2)
LC 91-27510

Love, Robert William, 1944---_Continued_

Contents: v1 1775-1941; v2 1942-1991

"This pragmatic chronicle pays as much attention to the government context out of which naval policy proceeded as to campaigns at sea. The Navy's main business, in Love's view, has always been to serve as a handmaid to diplomacy and at the same time as the clenched fist of foreign policy. . . . A comprehensive, thoroughly researched review." Publ Wkly

Includes bibliographical references

Naval warfare; an international encyclopedia; edited by Spencer C. Tucker; associate editors, John Fredriksen {et al.}; introduction by James C. Bradford. ABC-CLIO 2002 3v il maps set $295 *   **359**

ISBN 1-57607-219-3   LC 2002-4401

This set "explores the history of combat at sea, from ancient Greek galleys to the sophisticated ships of the U.S. Sixth Fleet. More than 1500 signed entries . . . describe the three key eras: Age of Galley Warfare, Age of Sail, and Age of Steam or Modern Era. . . . Each new development is examined in painstaking detail." Libr J

Includes bibliographical references

Toll, Ian W.

Six frigates; the epic history of the founding of the U.S. Navy. Norton 2006 560p il map $27.95 *   **359**

1. United States. Navy

ISBN 978-0-393-05847-5; 0-393-05847-6

LC 2006-20769

The author "recounts the first two decades of the U.S. Navy, beginning with Congress's decision to build six heavy frigates in 1794 and continuing to the end of the War of 1812 (the navy itself takes its founding from the start of the Continental Navy in 1775)." Libr J

This is "a must-read for fans of naval history and the early American Republic." Publ Wkly

Includes bibliographical references

359.9 Specialized combat forces; engineering and related services

Couch, Dick, 1943-

The warrior elite; the forging of Seal Class 228; photographs by Cliff Hollenbeck. Crown 2001 319p il pa $14.95 hardcover o.p.   **359.9**

1. United States. Navy. Sea Air Land Team

ISBN 1-4000-4695-5 (pa)   LC 2001-28368

This is an account of the Basic Underwater Demolition course, (BUD) training for the U.S. Navy Sea Air Land Team (SEALs)

This book "is unique. Couch, a Vietnam-era SEAL and retired naval reserve captain was given the most complete access possible. . . . On view is much serious thought by serious thinkers on the making of warriors at the dawn of the twenty-first century." Booklist

Parrish, Thomas

The submarine; a history. Viking 2004 576p il $29.95; pa $16 *   **359.9**

1. Submarines

ISBN 0-670-03313-8; 0-14-303519-3 (pa)

LC 2003-70515

This is a "history of the submarine, ranging from the 18th century to present-day, nuclear-submarine technology. . . . [The author provides a] background to the importance of subs in naval warfare, the functional aspects of how subs operate, the significant historical events that involved submarines, the influence of subs on sea power, and the political ramifications during the many eras of sub advancements, including the role played by subs during the Cold War." Libr J

"This brilliant, dramatic account of submarines and the men who sailed in them is a required acquisition for every military history collection." Choice

Includes bibliographical references

361 Social problems and social welfare in general

Social issues in America; an encyclopedia; James Ciment, editor. M.E. Sharpe 2006 8v il set $499 *   **361**

1. United States—Social conditions—Encyclopedias

ISBN 0-7656-8061-0; 978-0-7656-8061-7

LC 2005-18778

"More than 150 key social issues confronting the United States today are covered in this . . . eight-volume set: from abortion and adoption to capital punishment and corporate crime; from obesity and organized crime to sweatshops and xenophobia." Libr J

"Anyone who wants to know more about the problems the world faces and, in particular, any student who has an assignment to learn about a particular social issue will find this set useful." Booklist

Includes bibliographical references

361.2 Social action

Rieff, David

A bed for the night; humanitarianism in crisis. Simon & Schuster 2002 367p $26; pa $15

361.2

1. International agencies

ISBN 0-684-80977-X; 0-7432-5211-X (pa)

LC 2002-29432

The author takes a "look at the effectiveness of humanitarian organizations, which have increasingly been drawn into the politics behind some of the disasters for which they provide relief." Booklist

Readers "will come away from this passionate, eloquent argument with a distinctly clearer understanding of the complex moral issues facing humanitarian aid in a world filled with brutality and suffering." Publ Wkly

Includes bibliographical references

361.6 Governmental action

Hancock, LynNell
Hands to work; the stories of three families racing the welfare clock. Morrow 2002 308p $25.95; pa $13.95   **361.6**
   1. Poor—New York (N.Y.) 2. Public welfare
   ISBN 0-688-17388-8; 0-06-051216-X (pa)
                     LC 2001-31730
This "study depicts welfare in America today through the stories of three women from the South Bronx—Alina, Brenda, and Christine—who were affected by the 1996 Personal Responsibility Act . . . which limits lifetime federal financial assistance to five years for families and two years for singles. . . . Attention-holding and articulate, this important book on how America treats residents who are 'down and out' is highly recommended." Libr J
   Includes bibliographical references

Katz, Michael B.
The price of citizenship; redefining America's welfare state. Metropolitan Bks. 2001 469p pa $17 hardcover o.p.   **361.6**
   1. Public welfare 2. Social policy—United States
   ISBN 0-8050-6929-1 (pa)   LC 00-46906
In this "historical and political study of welfare in 20th-century America {the author} . . . focuses on the destructive influence of the market economy on social welfare programs." Libr J
   Katz "has written a defining history of post-Nixon transformations of America's welfare state, including its nonprofit and private sectors (private pensions, health insurance, etc.)." Publ Wkly

362.1 Physical illness

Chase, Marilyn, 1949-
The Barbary plague; the Black Death in Victorian San Francisco. Random House 2003 276p map $25.95; pa $13.95 *   **362.1**
   1. Plague 2. San Francisco (Calif.)
   ISBN 0-375-50496-6; 0-375-75708-2 (pa)
                     LC 2002-68102
The author offers a "portrait of the roles played by Chinese merchant societies, the white press, and Sacramento officials that initially enabled the disease to gain a foothold. She then turns most of her attention to detailing the scientific and personal strengths and weaknesses of the national public health officials who worked to determine efficient ways to diagnose, treat, and eventually halt the spread of the disease." SLJ
   This is "a pleasure to read, full of people, dramatic situations, individual foibles and collective hard work. I closed the book wishing it had been longer." N Y Times Book Rev

Consumers' guide to hospitals; by the editors of Consumers' checkbook magazine. Center for the Study of Services 2002 359p il pa $19.95 *
                     362.1
   1. Hospitals—United States
   ISSN 1070-2644
   ISBN 978-1-88812-412-5; 1-88812-412-1
                 LC 2002-104079
   Irregular. First published 1988
This guide presents statistics about U.S. hospitals with comparisons on death rates, estimated rates of complications, ratings of physicians, and outcome ratings for particular conditions and diseases. It includes advice on choosing a hospital and cutting costs and lists resources

Coste, Joanne Koenig
Learning to speak Alzheimer's; a groundbreaking approach for everyone dealing with the disease. Houghton Mifflin 2003 240p il $24; pa $14   **362.1**
   1. Alzheimer's disease 2. Caregivers
   ISBN 0-618-22125-5; 0-618-48517-1 (pa)
                 LC 2003-51141
"Key elements of Coste's approach include simplifying the environment for the patient, capitalizing on his or her remaining skills, and making an effort to understand what life must be like for the memory impaired. Because such Alzheimer's behaviors as agitation and physical aggression are often rooted in frustration, she also offers caregivers techniques to help patients compensate for cognitive and sensory losses. . . . Directions for simple activities, recipes for nutritious 'finger foods,' and tips for hiring home caregivers are included. . . . A fine addition to Alzheimer's and caregiving collections." Libr J
   Includes bibliographical references

Encyclopedia of AIDS; a social, political, cultural, and scientific record of the HIV epidemic; edited by Raymond A. Smith; forewords by James W. Curran, Peter Piot; photo editor, Jane Rosett. Fitzroy Dearborn Pubs. 1998 xli, 601p il $135   **362.1**
   ISBN 1-57958-007-6   LC 98-200474
This reference covers "aspects of the global HIV/AIDS crisis, primarily for the period 1991-96. The contents are organized into eight broad domains covering basic science and epidemiology; transmission and prevention; pathology and treatment; impacted populations; government and activism; policy and law; culture and society; and the global epidemic." Choice

Encyclopedia of public health; edited by Lester Breslow. Macmillan Ref. USA 2001 4v set $475   **362.1**
   ISBN 0-02-865354-8   LC 2001-31501
"Information on more than 900 programs, services, organizations, health behaviors, and the prevalence, epidemiology, and costs of communicable diseases. Although the work focuses on the United States, there are also references to worldwide problems." Libr J

Epstein, Helen, 1961-
The invisible cure; Africa, the West, and the fight against AIDS. Farrar, Straus and Giroux 2007 326p il $26 **362.1**
1. AIDS (Disease) 2. Africa
ISBN 978-0-374-28152-6; 0-374-28152-1
LC 2006-35679
In this book, the author "avoids both the patronizing and the 'culturally sensitive' demeanors that infect much of the debate on AIDS in Africa. Ms. Epstein, whose essays in the New York Review of Books over the past decade have provided some of the most illuminating reporting on AIDS in Africa, here offers one of the most personal, thorough, and conclusive studies of this human plague that has utterly devastated a continent. 'The Invisible Cure' is largely a comparison between AIDS in Uganda, which has instituted a variety of successful policies thwarting the disease, and South Africa, which has one of the highest HIV incidence rates in the world." N Y Sun

Fisher, Mary, 1948-
Sleep with the angels; a mother challenges AIDS. Moyer Bell 1994 220p il $24.95; pa $12.95 **362.1**
1. AIDS (Disease)
ISBN 1-55921-105-9; 1-55921-103-2 (pa)
LC 93-27216
"Fisher learned she was HIV+ in July 1991 and began telling her story in public in 1992. . . . Presented in chronological order from May 4, 1992 through June 28, 1993, the transcripts of these 24 speeches . . . include her famous address to the 1992 Republican National Convention in Houston. . . . Utilizing her position as a privileged heterosexual non-drug using white woman, she forces her audiences to confront the reality of the epidemic." Libr J

Garrett, Laurie
Betrayal of trust; the collapse of global public health. Hyperion 2000 754p il $30; pa $16.95 **362.1**
1. Public health 2. Medical care
ISBN 0-7868-6522-9; 0-7868-8440-1 (pa)
LC 00-33425
This book examines contemporary "health systems in the former Soviet Union, India, central Africa, and the United States." N Y Times Book Rev

Greenspan, Stanley I.
The child with special needs; encouraging intellectual and emotional growth; [by] Stanley I. Greenspan, Serena Wieder, with Robin Simons. Addison-Wesley 1998 496p $32 **362.1**
1. Handicapped children 2. Child psychology
ISBN 0-201-40726-4 LC 97-32101
"A Merloyd Lawrence book"
This offers advice to parents on helping children with such disabilities as cerebral palsy, autism, retardation, ADD, and language problems.
This "is an important work for libraries." Libr J
Includes bibliographical references

Halpin, Brendan
It takes a worried man; a memoir. Villard Bks. 2002 239p pa $12.95 hardcover o.p.
362.1
1. Breast cancer
ISBN 0-8129-6687-2 (pa) LC 2001-41907
This is "Halpin's memoir of his wife's struggle with breast cancer." Publ Wkly
"A poignant account with no answers and probing look at how one individual copes with dire circumstances." Booklist

Havemann, Joel
A life shaken; my encounter with Parkinson's disease; foreword by Stephen G. Reich. Johns Hopkins Univ. Press 2002 181p il $26; pa $14.95
362.1
1. Parkinson's disease—Personal narratives
ISBN 0-8018-6928-5; 0-8018-7888-8 (pa)
LC 2001-4650
The author "chronicles the physical and emotional effects . . . [Parkinson's] disease has had on his life since his diagnosis in 1990. While he briefly discusses PD's history, possible causes, medical and surgical treatments, and research progress, it is the account of his personal struggle that is the heart of this book." Libr J
Includes bibliographical references

Kaufman, Francine R., 1951-
Diabesity; the obesity-diabetes epidemic that threatens America—and what we must do to stop it; [by] Francine Ratner Kaufman. Bantam Books 2005 326p $27; pa $15 * **362.1**
1. Obesity 2. Diabetes
ISBN 0-553-80384-0; 0-553-38379-5 (pa)
LC 2004-54189
The author "explains how obesity triggers diabetes, the devastating long-term effects on the human body, and what means of prevention and treatment are available. She also relates the history of diabetes as it has evolved with changes in culture and lifestyle and explains what can be done through education and healthcare systems to improve individuals' health. Kaufman's sympathetic, nonjudgmental accounts of her patients highlight the many factors contributing to the problem, and her compassion and dedication shine through." Libr J

Kaufman, Sharon R.
—And a time to die; how American hospitals shape the end of life. Scribner 2005 400p $28 *
362.1
1. Terminal care—Ethical aspects 2. Death
ISBN 0-7432-6476-2 LC 2004-52530
The author "reveals the dilemmas of hospital death in America today: the shift to patients' control of decision making despite the doctors' greater knowledge; the ethics and practical effects of resuscitation versus pain relief; the complexities of assessing 'quality of life' while guessing at the desires of an unconscious patient. . . . This deeply probing study lays bare the cultural and institutional assumptions and rhetoric that frame our search for 'a good death.'" Publ Wkly
Includes bibliographical references

Kessler, Lauren

Dancing with Rose; finding life in the land of Alzheimer's. Viking 2007 260p $24.95

362.1

1. Alzheimer's disease 2. Caregivers

ISBN 0-670-03859-8; 978-0-670-03859-6

LC 2006-35699

This is the author's "account of the months she worked as an unskilled resident assistant in an Alzheimer's facility on the West Coast." Publ Wkly

"Invaluable intelligence, especially for anyone considering a residential facility for a loved one." Booklist

Mittelman, Mary S.

The Alzheimer's health care handbook; how to get the best medical care for your relative with Alzheimer's disease, in and out of the hospital; {by} Mary S. Mittelman and Cynthia Epstein. Marlowe & Co. 2003 196p pa $14.95 *

362.1

1. Alzheimer's disease 2. Caregivers

ISBN 1-56924-445-6   LC 2003-59966

This guide offers "advice for caregivers on such essential topics as choosing a primary-care physician, preparing the individual with memory loss for a doctor's appointment, coping with emergencies and emergency room treatments, making decisions about treatment options and end-of-life care, and acting as an advocate for an ill family member. . . . Much of the excellent information here is not available elsewhere, making this an essential addition to consumer health collections." Libr J

Monette, Paul

Borrowed time; an AIDS memoir. Harcourt Brace Jovanovich 1988 342p $22; pa $13

362.1

1. AIDS (Disease)

ISBN 0-15-113598-3; 0-15-600581-6 (pa)

LC 88-7215

"In March 1985, after a period of intermittent ill-health, Roger Horwitz was diagnosed as having AIDS, he died in October 1986. [This volume] is his lover's memoir." New Statesman Soc

"The memoir transcends the particulars of the AIDS epidemic to stand as an eloquent testimonial to the power of love and the devastation of loss." Publ Wkly

Relman, Arnold, 1923-

A second opinion; rescuing America's healthcare: a plan for universal coverage serving patients over profit; [by] Arnold S. Relman. PublicAffairs 2007 205p $24   362.1

1. Medical care—Government policy

ISBN 978-1-58648-481-1; 1-58648-481-8

LC 2006-103332

"A Century Foundation book"

This book is the author's "call to reform America's profit-driven health-care system, which fails to cover a large segment of the population. His solution is a single-payer network that provides universal coverage and uses salaried community-based physicians. This thought-provoking book is recommended for all who are interested in health care." Libr J

Includes bibliographical references

Rovner, Julie

Health care policy and politics A to Z. 3rd ed. CQ Press 2008 314p il $93.75 *   362.1

1. Medical care—Government policy—Encyclopedias 2. Public health—Encyclopedias

ISBN 978-0-87289-776-2; 0-87289-776-1

LC 2008-31429

First published 2000

This reference explores changes made in the nation's health system by the private sector, Congress, federal and state courts, and state legislatures. Entries cover such topics as prescription drug benefits, key programs and agencies, committees and organizations, statistics, and the history and background shaping major health policies.

Includes bibliographical references

Shah, Sonia

The body hunters; testing new drugs on the world's poorest patients. New Press 2006 242p $24.95 *   362.1

1. Drug industry 2. Developing countries 3. Medical ethics

ISBN 1-56584-912-4; 978-1-56584-912-9

LC 2005-58394

The author "uncovers a series of recent unethical drug trials conducted on impoverished and sick people in the developing world. . . . Meticulously researched and packed with documentary evidence, Shah's tautly argued study will provoke much needed public debate about this disturbing facet of globalization." Publ Wkly

Includes bibliographical references

Shilts, Randy

And the band played on; politics, people, and the AIDS epidemic. St. Martin's Press 1987 xxiii, 630p pa $16.95 hardcover o.p. *   362.1

1. AIDS (Disease)

ISBN 0-312-24135-6 (pa)   LC 87-16528

A "chronicle of the five-year political, scientific, and social battle to force government, the medical and blood-bank establishments, the news media, and gay men to take AIDS seriously." Booklist

"Shilts successfully weaves comprehensive investigative reporting and commercial page-turner pacing, political intrigue and personal tragedy into a landmark work." Publ Wkly

Includes bibliographical references

Silver, Daniel B., 1941-

Refuge in hell; how Berlin's Jewish hospital outlasted the Nazis. Houghton Mifflin 2003 xxii, 311p $24   362.1

1. Jüdisches Krankenhaus (Berlin, Germany) 2. Holocaust, 1933-1945

ISBN 0-618-25144-8   LC 2003-47896

Silver tells the "story of Berlin's Jewish Hospital during WWII. For decades before the Nazis seized power in Germany, the hospital had served Berlin's Jews as their principal medical resource. At the war's end, it was still functioning, delivering what medical care it could and sheltering a large percentage of the city's few remaining Jews. Silver asks how a Jewish institution, located in the

Silver, Daniel B., 1941-—*Continued*

capital city of a regime dedicated above all to obliterating the Jews, could possibly have survived." Publ Wkly

"This enlightening work is essential for public and academic libraries." Libr J

Includes bibliographical references

Sotile, Wayne M., 1951-

Thriving with heart disease; a unique program for you and your family: live happier, healthier, longer; {by} Wayne M. Sotile with Robin Cantor-Cooke. Free Press 2003 303p $25; pa $13

362.1

1. Heart diseases

ISBN 0-7432-4364-1; 0-7432-4365-X (pa)

LC 2002-45587

This book presents "advice on diet, exercise, mental health, sexual function, and spirituality. . . . Besides addressing the emotional consequences of recovering from a heart attack or heart failure, the text also discusses the ramifications of adjusting to implanted devices. . . . Sotile's guide will appeal to patients and family members . . . and is highly recommended for all academic, consumer health, and public libraries." Libr J

Includes bibliographical references

Steinberg, Jonny, 1970-

Sizwe's test; a young man's journey through Africa's AIDS epidemic. Simon & Schuster 2008 349p il $26

362.1

1. AIDS (Disease) 2. South Africa

ISBN 978-1-4165-5269-7; 1-4165-5269-3

LC 2007-29672

This book "focuses on Lusikisiki, a district in [South Africa's] Eastern Cape Province. . . . Almost one out of three pregnant women in Lusikisiki was H.I.V. positive, but the area also had a first-rate AIDS treatment program. . . . Steinberg presents the district largely through the eyes of one man, whom he calls Sizwe Magadla. Sizwe is 30, healthy and literate." N Y Times Book Rev

The author "becomes intertwined with his subject, but balances critical distance and compassion with gleanings from his own psychological barriers to HIV testing that further deepen the concern and understanding he accords to Sizwe's story." Publ Wkly

Includes bibliographical references

Torrey, E. Fuller (Edwin Fuller), 1937-

The insanity offense; how America's failure to treat the seriously mentally ill endangers its citizens. W.W. Norton 2008 265p il $24.95

362.1

1. Mentally ill—Institutional care

ISBN 978-0-393-06658-6; 0-393-06658-4

LC 2008-2697

"Released en masse from institutions beginning in the 1960s, the most severely ill are most likely to become homeless, incarcerated, victimized, and/or violent. Torrey details how civil liberties suits have prevented such people from being involuntarily institutionalized, leaving them a danger both to themselves and to others. . . . Chilling and well documented, this text has many no-

nonsense solutions to protect the mentally ill themselves as well as society as a whole." Publ Wkly

Includes bibliographical references

Warner, Mark L., 1948-

The complete guide to Alzheimer's-proofing your home. rev ed. Purdue Univ. Press 2000 477p il $54.95

362.1

1. Alzheimer's disease 2. Home accidents

ISBN 1-55753-202-8

LC 99-462016

First published 1998

This is a "design guide to help caregivers and family members create a home environment that will enable them and Alzheimer's patients to handle the difficulties associated with the disease." Libr J [review of 1998 edition]

"A generous directory of relevant products and manufacturers and a helpful glossary further distinguish this superlative resource for home caregivers." Booklist [review of 1998 edition]

Includes bibliographical references

362.28 Suicide

Ackerman, Diane

A slender thread. Random House 1997 305p pa $14 hardcover o.p.

362.28

1. Crisis centers 2. Hotlines (Telephone counseling) 3. Suicide

ISBN 0-679-77133-6 (pa)

LC 96-8721

This is an account of the author's work as a volunteer counselor at a suicide-prevention and crisis center in a New York college town

"In a narrative that is lush with her signature gift for metaphor and delight in the senses and taut with the drama of her often frightening negotiations with people in the throes of every imaginable form of crisis, Ackerman illuminates the bewildering workings of the resilient human psyche." Booklist

Evans, Glen

The encyclopedia of suicide; {by} Glen Evans, Norman L. Farberow; foreword by Alan L. Berman. 2nd ed. Facts on File 2003 xxxiii, 329p $65 *

362.28

ISBN 0-8160-4525-9

LC 2002-27166

First published 1988

Arranged in A-Z format, over 500 entries cover such aspects as causes, history and psychology of suicide. Also covered are philosophical and religious issues as well as sociological viewpoints and research and treatment concerns

Includes bibliographical references

362.29 Substance abuse

Black, Claudia
Straight talk from Claudia Black; what recovering parents should tell their kids about drugs and alcohol. Hazelden 2003 131p il pa $12.95   **362.29**
  1. Drug abuse 2. Alcoholism 3. Children of drug addicts 4. Children of alcoholics
  ISBN 1-59285-041-3   LC 2003-50831
  The author discusses "brain chemistry, generational vulnerability, and phenomena such as multiple addictions, tolerance levels, relapse, and blackouts. The emphasis then moves to . . . advice about self-forgiveness, making amends for past behavior, and new ways of relating to loved ones. . . . This candid and hope-filled book merits strong consideration by large public libraries and specialized collections given the prevalence of some form of addictive behavior in families." Libr J
  Includes bibliographical references

Cermak, Timmen L.
Marijuana: what's a parent to believe? Hazelden 2003 253p il (Informed parent) pa $12.95
                                                362.29
  1. Marijuana 2. Youth—Drug use 3. Parenting
  ISBN 1-59285-039-1   LC 2003-50917
  The author "describes the world of difference between experimenting with marijuana at age 12 and age 20. Rejecting the 'just say no' approach, as well as the legalization model, he urges schools to adopt programs that will teach kids social and emotional competence, not just drug education." Libr J
  Includes bibliographical references

Courtwright, David T., 1952-
Forces of habit; drugs and the making of the modern world. Harvard Univ. Press 2001 277p $24.95; pa $16.95   **362.29**
  1. Drug abuse 2. Psychotropic drugs
  ISBN 0-674-00458-2; 0-674-01003-5 (pa)
                                      LC 00-61466
  "In charting the mostly covert impact of drugs on modern civilization, Courtwright . . . contends that governmental, religious and economic institutions have a centuries-old love-hate relationship with psychoactive substances ranging from alcohol and caffeine to cocaine and peyote." Publ Wkly
  "Reasoned and informative, Courtwright's book is a cogent source of dispassionate information on drugs and their role in society." Booklist
  Includes bibliographical references

Drugs and controlled substances; information for students; Stacey Blachford, Kristine Krapp, editors. Gale Group 2003 xxvi, 495p il $115
                                                362.29
  1. Drugs 2. Drug abuse
  ISBN 0-7876-6264-X   LC 2002-10925
  Provides detailed information about the composition, history, effects, uses and abuses of common drugs, including illegal drugs and addictive substances, as well as commonly abused classes of prescription drugs.
  "In addition to the well-written essays, sidebars discussing legal issues, misconceptions, history, and news stories add depth to each topic. . . . Currency, scope, and authority are the hallmarks of this highly recommended reference work." Booklist
  Includes bibliographical references

Ford, Betty
Healing and hope; six women from the Betty Ford Center share their powerful journeys of addiction and recovery. Putnam 2003 275p $24.95; pa $14   **362.29**
  1. Betty Ford Center 2. Drug abuse 3. Alcoholism 4. Drug addicts—Rehabilitation
  ISBN 0-399-15138-9; 0-425-19830-8 (pa)
                                      LC 2003-47041
  The author presents and comments on the recovery stories of six women who have gone through the Betty Ford Center program, including those of a housewife, a schoolteacher, and a former gang member
  "With its six powerful personal stories and Ford's warm, authoritative overview, this is a solid popular introduction to the experience of recovery from addiction." Booklist

Henderson, Elizabeth Connell
Understanding addiction. University Press of Miss. 2000 209p il (Understanding health and sickness series) pa $12 hardcover o.p.
                                                362.29
  1. Compulsive behavior 2. Drug abuse
  ISBN 1-57806-240-3 (pa)   LC 00-42856
  The author writes "on how addictions develop, how the addicted brain works, and what the different effects of the major addictive drugs are, and on genetic, psychological, and behavioral factors involved in addiction." Booklist
  Includes bibliographical references

Pampel, Fred C.
Drugs and sports. Facts on File 2007 284p (Library in a book) $45 *   **362.29**
  1. Athletes—Drug use
  ISBN 0-8160-6575-6; 978-0-8160-6575-2
                                      LC 2006-20536
  This is an overview of the history of drug use among athletes "from the performance-enhancement methods of the ancient Greeks to the recent accusations of drug use among high-profile professional athletes." Publisher's note
  Includes bibliographical references

Streatfeild, Dominic
Cocaine; an unauthorized biography. Thomas Dunne Bks./St. Martin's Press 2002 510p il $27.95; pa $15   **362.29**
  1. Cocaine 2. Drug abuse 3. Drug traffic
  ISBN 0-312-28624-4; 0-312-42226-1 (pa)
  First published 2001 in the United Kingdom

Streatfeild, Dominic—Continued

This study covers "the rise of the Colombian cartels, government collusion with traffickers, the crack phenomenon, media hype, the U.S. war on drugs and the legalization debate." Publ Wkly

"Thorough, engrossing, balanced, and entertaining, it is important social history in palatable form." Booklist

Includes bibliographical references

362.292   Alcohol

Alcohol and temperance in modern history; an international encyclopedia; Jack S. Blocker, Jr., David M. Fahey, and Ian R. Tyrrell, editors. ABC-CLIO 2003 2v il set $185 *

362.292

1. Alcohol 2. Temperance
ISBN 1-576-07833-7   LC 2003-8679

"The editors present the history of beverage alcohol as commercial product, cultural icon, behavioral solvent, medical/social research, and political issue. Their book admirably fits many purposes, covering many eras and having an international focus. The comprehensive entries (with three levels of coverage: international, regional, and country-specific) trace the history of the subject, 18th century to the present. . . . A storehouse of scholarship." Choice

Includes bibliographical references

Dorris, Michael

The broken cord; with a foreword by Louise Erdrich. Harper & Row 1989 300p il hardcover o.p. pa $14 *   **362.292**

1. Alcoholism 2. Father-son relationship 3. Native Americans
ISBN 0-06-016071-3; 0-06-091682-6 (pa)
                                LC 88-45893

This is a memoir about Dorris' "adopted son, Adam, a victim of fetal alcohol syndrome (FAS). Although the book began as an anthropological investigation of FAS and its effect on native American communities, Dorris soon realized that he couldn't separate the theoretical from the personal." Booklist

"The alarming statistics and consequences of fetal alcohol syndrome are skillfully interwoven with the human story of one of its victims in 'The Broken Cord.' Mr. Dorris's prose is clear and affecting." N Y Times Book Rev

Includes bibliographical references

362.4   Problems of and services to people with physical disabilities

The **Encyclopedia** of blindness and vision impairment; [by] Jill Sardegna [et al.] 2nd ed. Facts on File 2002 333p (Facts on File library of health and living) $65 *   **362.4**
ISBN 0-8160-4280-2   LC 2001-55653
First published 1991

"This volume incorporates a history of blindness and vision impairment with an A-to-Z presentation of health issues, types of surgery, medications, medical terminology, social issues, myths and misconceptions, economic issues, and current research trends." Publisher's note

Includes bibliographical references

Encyclopedia of disability; general editor, Gary L. Albrecht. Sage Publications 2006 5v il set $850 *   **362.4**

1. Handicapped—Encyclopedias
ISBN 0-7619-2565-1   LC 2005-18301

"Almost 200 of the entries are biographical, treating individuals from Homer and Socrates to Helen Keller and Franklin Roosevelt. Others treat history . . . types of disability . . . [and] attitudes and conditions affecting daily life. . . . [This encyclopedia draws] in readers from a wide range of studies and interests and helping them to see disability in an entirely new way." Booklist

Includes bibliographical references

Iezzoni, Lisa

When walking fails; mobility problems of adults with chronic conditions. University of California Press 2003 355p il (California/Milbank books on health and the public) $60; pa $19.95

362.4

1. Movement disorders 2. Chronic diseases
ISBN 0-520-23742-0; 0-520-23819-2 (pa)
                                LC 2002-152225

Contents: Mobility limits — Who has mobility difficulties — Sensations of walking — Society: views of walking — How people feel about their difficulty walking — At home: with family and friends — Outside home: at work and in communities — People talking to their physicians — Physicians talking to their patients — Physical and occupational therapy and other approaches — Ambulation aids — Wheeled mobility — Who pays for what — Paying for mobility-related items and services — Final thoughts

"Iezzoni grounds her readable and compelling discussion with case histories and interviews of people who struggle with policy and environmental barriers in addition to their own physical impairments. . . . This is a valuable work for academic and public libraries." Libr J

Includes bibliographical references

Sacks, Oliver W.

Seeing voices; a journey into the world of the deaf; [by] Oliver Sacks. Vintage Books 2000 222p il pa $13.95   **362.4**

1. Gallaudet University 2. Deaf 3. Sign language
ISBN 0-375-70407-8   LC 00-42340
First published 1989 by University of California Press

The author "scrutinizes the history of treatment of the deaf, investigates the expressive capabilities of sign language and gauges the linguistic and social pressures faced by deaf people. The closing section documents a 1988 student revolt at Gallaudet that led to the appointment of the school's first deaf president." Publ Wkly

"With his philosopher's penchant for profound discovery and his neurologist's knowledge of biology and the brain, Sacks offers provocative connections and acute observations about the nature of language and culture." Booklist

Includes bibliographical references

362.5 Problems of and services to poor people

Encyclopedia of homelessness; David Levinson, editor. Sage Publications 2004 2v il $295 *

362.5

1. Homelessness—Encyclopedias
ISBN 0-7619-2751-4   LC 2004-9279
"Entries cover homelessness in 8 major U.S. cities and 30 cities and nations around the world, as well as causes of homelessness; historical aspects; housing, policy, health and lifestyle issues; and service systems." Booklist
Includes bibliographical references

Kozol, Jonathan
Rachel and her children; homeless families in America. Three Rivers Press 2006 303p pa $13.95

362.5

1. Homeless persons
ISBN 0-307-34589-0   LC 2007-281899
A reissue of the title first published 1988
The author introduces us to "the residents of a hotel for the homeless in New York. . . . Kozol faults everyone involved: governments, social agencies, landlords, the courts, and indifferent Americans in general." Libr J
"While the individual stories that Kozol tells so affectingly point out the vivid realities of urban poverty, the book also supplies statistics that detail the more abstract-and inhuman-attitudes that contemporary society assumes when attempting to deal with its victims." Booklist
Includes bibliographical references

Reef, Catherine
Poverty in America. Facts on File 2006 xxix, 386p il map (American experience) $80

362.5

1. Poor—United States
ISBN 978-0-8160-6062-7; 0-8160-6062-2
                                      LC 2006-6896
This book "examines the lives and experiences of the poor throughout the United States from colonial times to the present, covering trends, events, facts, figures, and anything else related to this topic." Publisher's note
Includes bibliographical references

Vollmann, William T.
Poor people. Ecco 2007 314p il $29.95; pa $16.95 *   **362.5**
1. Poor 2. Poverty
ISBN   0-06-087882-7;   978-0-06-087882-5; 0-06-087884-3 (pa); 978-0-06-087884-9 (pa)
                                      LC 2006-48547
This book describes "encounters between the author and the indigent." N Y Times (Late N Y Ed)
The author "brings to bear his keen powers of observation on the world around him and, not incidentally, on himself; he is unabashed about allowing his emotional reactions to inform his thoughts about what it means to be poor. This remarkable book is sui generis and should be in all collections." Libr J

Zucchino, David
Myth of the welfare queen; a Pulitzer Prize-winning journalist's portrait of women on the line. Scribner 1997 366p pa $21.95 hardcover o.p.
                                      362.5
1. Public welfare 2. Poor—United States 3. African American women
ISBN 0-684-85006-5 (pa)   LC 97-9104
"From July to December 1995, David Zucchino . . . became a participant observer in the lives of two . . . women living on welfare. Zucchino wanted to answer two questions: 'What did welfare mothers do all day?' and '(Has) anyone among a class of women so despised by mainstream America attempted to improve their circumstances and to raise their children for lives beyond poverty?'" Women's Rev Books
This book "a harrowing description of daily subsistence living with very little chance of change, is a powerful exposé of the welfare myth." Libr J

362.6 Problems of and services to persons in late adulthood

Carnot, Edward J., 1947-
Is your parent in good hands? protecting your aging parent from financial abuse and neglect. Capital Books 2004 261p pa $18.95
                                      362.6
1. Aging parents 2. Elderly—Care 3. Caregivers
ISBN 1-931868-37-9   LC 2003-12140
The author "offers advice for adult children who may live far from their elderly parents about the importance of planning, how to find reliable caregivers, how to use the legal system when abuse occurs, and how to keep track of a parent's condition from a distance. This cautionary tale belongs in all aging collections." Libr J
Includes bibliographical references

Delehanty, Hugh
Caring for your parents; the complete AARP guide; [by] Hugh Delehanty & Elinor Ginzler; foreword by Mary Pipher. Rev. and expanded ed. Sterling Pub. 2008 xvii, 238p il pa $12.95
                                      362.6
1. Aging parents 2. Elderly—Care
ISBN 1-4027-5857-X; 978-1-4027-5857-7
                                      LC 2008-277441
First published 2005
The authors "provide information on everything from the first difficult conversations with parents about their changing situation to coping with terminal illness and death. The book has a wealth of data on long-distance caregiving, financial matters, community-based and professional case management, Medicare, and age-related physical changes." Libr J
Includes bibliographical references

362.7 Problems of and services to young people

Adamec, Christine A., 1949-
The encyclopedia of adoption; [by] Christine Adamec, Laurie C. Miller, M.D. 3rd ed. Facts on File 2007 xxxvi, 394p (Facts on File library of health and living) $75 *   **362.7**
1. Adoption—Encyclopedias
ISBN 0-8160-6329-X; 978-0-8160-6329-1
                LC 2005-55514
First published 1991
"Beginning with a brief history of adoption as a concept and touching on key issues in past history and recent times, this book looks at the development of adoption and adoption law in the U.S. . . . It includes entries that discuss not just adoption but also the related institutions of foster care, group homes, and orphanages." Booklist [review of 2000 edition]
Includes bibliographical references

Bartholet, Elizabeth
Nobody's children; abuse and neglect, foster drift, and the adoption alternative. Beacon Press 1999 304p pa $17.50 hardcover o.p.
                          362.7
1. Child welfare
ISBN 0-8070-2319-1 (pa)   LC 99-22976
This is a critique "of American child welfare policy. Examining legislation from all parts of the United States, Bartholet questions why 'family preservation ideology still reigns supreme when children rather than adult women are involved.' . . . Clear and consistent." Libr J
Includes bibliographical references

Bernstein, Nina
The lost children of Wilder; the epic struggle to change foster care. Pantheon Bks. 2001 482p pa $15 hardcover o.p.   **362.7**
1. Wilder, Shirley 2. Foster home care 3. Child welfare
ISBN 0-679-75834-8 (pa)   LC 00-57456
"Bernstein explores the genesis and aftermath of the landmark 1973 legal case filed by young ACLU attorney Marcia Lowry against the New York State foster-care system. Known as *Wilder* for its 14-year-old African-American plaintiff, Shirley 'Pinky' Wilder, the suit claimed Jewish and Catholic child welfare services had a lock on foster care funding and placements. . . . This viscerally powerful history of institutionalized child abuse and the criminalization of poverty, of civil rights and social change, is compelling and essential reading." Publ Wkly
Includes bibliographical references

Gammage, Jeff
China ghosts; my daughter's journey to America, my passage to fatherhood. William Morrow 2007 255p il $25.95   **362.7**
1. Adoption
ISBN 978-0-06-124029-4; 0-06-124029-X
                LC 2007-61204

"A father's account of going to China with his wife to adopt their first and second daughters. . . . Gammage, a staff writer for the Philadelphia Inquirer, had been happily married without children for many years, although he knew his wife really wanted children. By the time they discovered they couldn't have biological children, the best option was adopting from China. While there were tensions over their first daughter's medical problems (an infected scalp injury), both adoptions went reasonably smoothly. Back home, Gammage wrestled with his mixed feelings about the birth parents and his burden of good fortune, that guilty knowledge that his own happiness came from someone else's misfortune. Realizing that his own relationship to China was being shaped by the process of raising two Chinese girls, he ends this upbeat memoir by wondering about the impact of this new wave of immigrants on the future of Sino-American relations." Publ Wkly

Gilman, Lois
The adoption resource book. 4th ed. HarperPerennial 1998 576p pa $16.95
                          362.7
1. Adoption
ISBN 0-06-273361-3   LC 98-21174
First published 1984
This offers information about adoption strategies including international adoptions, private and agency adoptions, and financing and lists more than 1,000 agencies and support groups
Includes bibliographical references

Kozol, Jonathan
Amazing grace; the lives of children and the conscience of a nation. HarperPerennial 1996 284p pa $14.95   **362.7**
1. Poor—New York (N.Y.) 2. Socially handicapped children 3. Inner cities
ISBN 0-06-097697-7; 978-0-06-097697-2
First published 1995 by Crown
In this "book, Mr. Kozol travels the Mott Haven section of the Bronx, one of the poorest neighborhoods in the nation, where he visits with children, their parents and ministers, talking with them about their lives and about what they perceive as their place in the world." N Y Time Book Rev
Kozol's "powerfully understated report takes us inside rat-infested homes that are freezing in winter, overcrowded schools, dysfunctional clinics, soup kitchens. . . . While his narrative offers no specific solutions, it forcefully drives home his conviction: a civilized nation cannot allow this situation to continue." Publ Wkly
Includes bibliographical references

Tucker, Neely
Love in the driest season; a family memoir. Crown Publishers 2004 242p il hardcover o.p. pa $14   **362.7**
1. Adoption 2. Zimbabwe
ISBN 0-609-60976-9; 1-4000-8160-2 (pa)
                LC 2002-154095
This is a "narrative of two Mississippians in Africa— a white reporter and his African-American wife—who

Tucker, Neely—*Continued*
struggle against Third World bureaucracy to adopt an abandoned Zimbabwean baby, as the continent is torn by crisis." SLJ

"This story about the adoption of a tiny, critically ill Zimbabwean orphan appeals to the head as much as the heart." Christ Sci Monit

362.82 Problems of and services to families

Dalpiaz, Christina M.
Breaking free, starting over; parenting in the aftermath of family violence. Praeger 2004 232p $39.95 **362.82**
1. Domestic violence 2. Parenting
ISBN 0-275-98167-3   LC 2003-62436
This guide provides "techniques for reparenting children who've been exposed to domestic violence. Lacking a safe haven, many of these children exhibit significant behavior, communication, and self-management problems." Libr J
Includes bibliographical references

Domestic violence sourcebook; edited by Dawn D. Matthews. 2nd ed. Omnigraphics 2004 628p (Health reference series) $87 **362.82**
1. Domestic violence
ISBN 978-0-7808-0669-6; 0-7808-0669-7
     LC 2004-3519
First published 2000 under the editorship of Helene Henderson with title: Domestic violence & child abuse sourcebook

"Basic consumer health information about the causes and consequences of abusive relationships, including physical violence, sexual assault, battery, stalking, and emotional abuse, and facts about the effects of violence on women, men, young adults, and the elderly, with reports about domestic violence in selected populations, and featuring facts about medical care, victim assistance and protection, prevention strategies, mental health services, and legal issues; along with a glossary of related terms and resources for additional help and information." Title page

"Because this book includes a lot of issues within one volume, this work is recommended for all public libraries." Am Ref Books Annu, 2001 [review of 2000 edition]
Includes bibliographical references

Dutton, Donald G., 1943-
The batterer; a psychological profile; {by} Donald G. Dutton with Susan K. Golant. Basic Bks. 1995 209p pa $15 hardcover o.p. **362.82**
1. Wife abuse 2. Domestic violence 3. Men—Psychology
ISBN 0-465-03388-1 (pa)   LC 95-9556
The authors draw on the O. J. Simpson trial "to help elucidate their points regarding wife batterers. . . . Dutton and Golant provide an excellent introduction to the psychology of wife abusers, examining the different

types of abusers: psychopathic, overcontrolled, and cyclical. They then narrow the focus to the cyclical abuser (the Dr. Jekyll/Mr. Hyde type exemplified by Simpson) and examine the different factors that go into making such an abuser." Libr J
Includes bibliographical references

Encyclopedia of domestic violence; [edited by] Nicky Ali Jackson. Routledge 2007 789p $190 **362.82**
1. Domestic violence—Encyclopedias
ISBN 0-415-96968-9; 978-0-415-96968-0
     LC 2006-103335
"The 138 A-Z entries fall into seven categories, including Child Abuse and Elder Abuse, Domestic Violence and the Law, and several others. . . . Each article is several pages long, with cross-references to other articles in the volume and with substantial bibliographies." Booklist
Includes bibliographical references

Fessler, Ann
The girls who went away; the hidden history of women who surrendered children for adoption in the decades before Roe v. Wade. Penguin Press 2006 354p $24.95 * **362.82**
1. Adoption
ISBN 1-59420-094-7   LC 2005-58179
This "book is the culmination of interviews with more than 100 women who had been forced to give up their children for adoption between the end of World War II and Roe v. Wade (1973). The book discusses all facets of the complex issue, including the women's discovery that they were pregnant out of wedlock, going away to maternity homes to deliver the babies, and later searching for their adult children." Libr J
"These knowing oral histories are an emotional boon for birth mothers and adoptees struggling to make sense of troubled pasts." Publ Wkly
Includes bibliographical references

Forward, Susan
Toxic parents: overcoming their hurtful legacy and reclaiming your life; {by} Susan Forward with Craig Buck. Bantam Bks. 1989 326p pa $16 hardcover o.p. **362.82**
1. Child abuse
ISBN 978-0-553-38140-5; 0-553-38140-7
     LC 89-6812
The authors identify types of hurtful parents, including alcoholics, verbal and physical abusers, and those who emotionally neglect their children. They also offer advice to adult child abuse victims on how to overcome the harm done
Includes bibliographical references

Weiss, Elaine
Family & friends' guide to domestic violence; how to listen, talk, and take action, when someone you care about is being abused. Volcano Press 2003 143p pa $17.95 * **362.82**
1. Domestic violence
ISBN 1-88424-422-X   LC 2003-4642

Weiss, Elaine—*Continued*

This is a "guide for family and friends, with practical tips for communicating with a likely victim of abuse, including how to broach the subject." Libr J

Includes bibliographical references

Surviving domestic violence; voices of women who broke free. Volcano Press 2004 214p pa $17.95   **362.82**

1. Domestic violence

ISBN 1-88424-427-0   LC 2003-27829

First published 2000 by Agreka Bks.

The author tells the "stories of 12 survivors, ranging in age and socioeconomic circumstances. She concludes each case study with a reflective commentary that emphasizes the strength and courage of these women." Libr J

Includes bibliographical references

362.83   Problems of and services to women

Bass, Ellen

The courage to heal; a guide for women survivors of child sexual abuse: featuring "Honoring the truth, a response to the backlash"; [by] Ellen Bass and Laura Davis. 3rd ed rev & updated. HarperPerennial 1994 604p pa $22.50
362.83

1. Child sexual abuse 2. Adult child sexual abuse victims 3. Women—Psychology

ISBN 0-06-095066-8   LC 93-48353

First published 1988

New edition in preparation

The authors offer a three part recovery program: taking stock, the healing process, and changing patterns, followed by the personal experiences of survivors, and a response to critics who claim sexual abuse charges are based on "the false memory syndrome"

Includes bibliographical references

362.88   Problems of and services to victims of crimes

Crompton, Vicki

Saving beauty from the beast; how to protect your daughter from an unhealthy relationship; by Vicki Crompton and Ellen Zelda Kessner. Little, Brown 2003 259p il $22.95; pa $13.95
362.88

1. Abused women 2. Parenting

ISBN 0-316-09058-1; 0-316-73552-3 (pa)

LC 2002-19153

This book "illuminates the problems of dangerous relationships by describing their characteristics, mapping out warning signs of abuse and offering sound advice for parents seeking to empower their daughters. The authors interviewed psychologists, counselors and girls who have had violent boyfriends; the girls' stories, as well as first-person accounts from parents and abusive boyfriends, are

woven throughout the text. . . . This book serves as both fervent friend and practical coach to parents whose daughters may be facing abuse." Publ Wkly

Includes bibliographical references

Feinberg, Kenneth R.

What is life worth? the unprecedented effort to compensate the victims of 9/11. Public Affairs 2005 xxv, 213p $24   **362.88**

1. September 11 terrorist attacks, 2001

ISBN 1-58648-323-4   LC 2005-47699

The author writes about his work administering "a special fund to compensate victims of the 9/11 attacks." N Y Times (Late N Y Ed)

"Feinberg's willingness to put himself into the book makes what could have been an alternately dry and self-serving case study crackle with care, frustration, intellectual energy and good writing." Publ Wkly

362.883   Problems of and services to victims of rape

Encyclopedia of rape; edited by Merril D. Smith. Greenwood Press 2004 xxvii, 301p $75 *
362.883

1. Rape—Encyclopedias

ISBN 0-313-32687-8   LC 2004-44213

"The alphabetically arranged entries cover the physiological, political, and psychological aspects of rape, and supply biographical sketches of notorious rapists and their victims from ancient times to the present. The language used is at times graphic, and by its nature the volume is intended for adult readers, but entries are written with an unflinching regard for facts, avoiding sensationalism. . . . Users at all levels will find this volume a useful resource for scholarly information on recent high-profile rape cases, and it will also serve as an entry point for further research on rape and its subtopics." Choice

Includes bibliographical references

Sebold, Alice

Lucky. Back Bay Books 2002 246p pa $11.95
362.883

1. Rape

ISBN 0-316-09619-9

First published 1999 by Scribner

When the author "was a college freshman at Syracuse University, she was attacked and raped on the last night of school. . . . Sebold launches her memoir headlong into the rape itself, laying out its visceral physical as well as mental violence, and from there spins a narrative of her life before and after the incident, weaving memories of parental alcoholism together with her post-rape addiction to heroin. In the midst of each wrenching episode, from the initial attack to the ensuing courtroom drama, Sebold's wit is as powerful as her searing candor." Publ Wkly

363.1   Public safety programs

Cummins, Ronnie

Genetically engineered food; a self-defense guide for consumers; [by] Ronnie Cummins and Ben Lilliston ; foreword by Frances Moore Lappé. [2nd, rev ed] Marlowe & Co 2004 237p pa $14.95 *   363.1

1. Food—Biotechnology 2. Farm produce
ISBN 1-569-24469-3   LC 2004-45565
First published 2000

The authors "discuss genetically engineered or modified food focusing on the scientific, political, economic, and health issues. . . . [They] include information on what consumers can do, from smart shopping to grassroots lobbying, to reduce the threat of genetically engineered food." Booklist [review of 2000 edition]

Includes bibliographical references

Eban, Katherine

Dangerous doses; how counterfeiters are contaminating America's drug supply. Harcourt 2005 462p il $25   363.1

1. Drugs 2. Counterfeits and counterfeiting 3. Consumer education
ISBN 0-15-101050-1   LC 2004-25581

The author "documents the flaws in the U.S. drug-distribution system that too often result in Americans getting diluted and contaminated drugs. . . . She details in particular the dramatic workings of Operation Stone Cold in Florida, a task force informally called the Horsemen of the Apocalypse, assigned to investigate trafficking in counterfeit drugs. This riveting page-turner provides a fascinating behind-the-scenes look at drug sales and distribution." Booklist

Genetically modified foods; debating biotechnology; edited by Michael Ruse, David Castle. Prometheus Bks. 2002 355p il (Contemporary issues series) $20   363.1

1. Food—Biotechnology 2. Farm produce
ISBN 1-57392-996-4   LC 2002-70510

In this collection of essays the first section focuses on "the history and the science of genetically modified foods. The next section focuses on the morality of modifying organisms for human use. . . . Succeeding sections include articles discussing religious attitudes toward genetically modified food, legal issues involving patenting and environmental damage, risk assessment, and possible environmental threats and benefits." Publisher's note

Includes bibliographical references

Lapierre, Dominique

Five past midnight in Bhopal; [by] Dominique Lapierre, Javier Moro; translated from the French by Kathryn Spink. Warner Bks. 2002 403p il map $25.95   363.1

1. Bhopal Union Carbide Plant Disaster, Bhopal, India, 1984 2. Pesticides industry—Accidents
ISBN 0-446-53088-3   LC 2002-100974
Original French edition, 2001

The authors relate "the story of Bhopal, India, where in 1984 16,000 to 30,000 people were killed and half a million maimed as the result of a deadly gas leak of methyl isocyanate from a Union Carbide pesticide manufacturing plant." America

Nestle, Marion

Safe food; bacteria, biotechnology, and bioterrorism. University of Calif. Press 2003 350p il (California studies in food and culture) $27.50 *   363.1

1. Food adulteration and inspection 2. Food—Biotechnology 3. Terrorism
ISBN 0-520-23292-5   LC 2002-27172

The author "argues that ensuring safe food involves more than washing hands or cooking food to higher temperatures. It involves politics. When it comes to food safety, billions of dollars are at stake, and industry, government, and consumers collide over issues of values, economics, and political power—and not always in the public interest." Publisher's note

Includes bibliographical references

Pringle, Peter

Food, inc; Mendel to Monsanto—the promises and perils of the biotech harvest. Simon & Schuster 2003 239p hardcover o.p. pa $13 *   363.1

1. Food—Biotechnology 2. Farm produce
ISBN 0-7432-2611-9; 0-7432-6763-X (pa)
                              LC 2003-42823

The author "believes that there is nothing inherently unsafe about genetically modified (GM) foods and that technology has the potential to relieve hunger and pain for millions of people. However, in this discussion of the aspects of GM foods, he does not hesitate to point out the perils. . . . Especially troubling to the author is the degree to which plant biotechnology gives control to a few international conglomerates that own patents to the products and processes." Libr J

"This is a book to satisfy curiosity and engender concern, and any of its chapters would provide an excellent subject for discussion groups." SLJ

Puleo, Stephen

Dark tide; the great Boston molasses flood of 1919. Beacon Press 2003 263p il $23
                                            363.1

1. Industrial accidents 2. Boston (Mass.)—History
ISBN 0-8070-5020-2   LC 2003-10433

"On January 15, 1919, a fifty-foot tall steel tank filled with 2.3 million gallons of molasses collapsed on Boston's waterfront, disgorging its contents as a fifteen-foot high wave of molasses that briefly traveled at thirty-five miles per hour. The Great Boston Molasses Flood claimed the lives of twenty-one people and scores of animals, injured 150, and caused widespread destruction. Tracing the era from the tank's construction in 1915 through the multiyear lawsuit that followed the tragedy, *Dark Tide* uses the drama of the flood to examine the sweeping changes brought about by World War I, Prohibition, the Anarchist movement, the Red Scare, Immigra-

Puleo, Stephen—*Continued*

tion, and the role of big business in society." Univ Press Books 2004

Includes bibliographical references

363.2 Police services

Bell, Suzanne

Encyclopedia of forensic science; foreword by Barry A.J. Fisher; preface by Robert C. Shaler. Rev ed. Facts On File 2008 402p il (Facts on File science library) $85 * **363.2**

1. Forensic sciences—Encyclopedias

ISBN 978-0-8160-6799-2; 0-8160-6799-6

LC 2008-5862

First published 2003

"In addition to explaining the science of forensics, Bell . . . reviews various disciplines related to forensic science, among them entomology, odontology, and psychology. Other entries cover professional organizations, government agencies, famous names in the field of forensics, evidence, and legal issues. . . . With its clear language and brief entries [this] volume will provide readers with a nuts-and-bolts understanding of the real world of forensic science." Booklist [review of 2003 edition]

Includes bibliographical references

The Facts on File dictionary of forensic science. Facts on File 2004 278p il (Facts on File science library) $45; pa $17.95 * **363.2**

1. Forensic sciences—Dictionaries

ISBN 0-8160-5131-3; 0-8160-5153-4 (pa)

LC 2003-15735

"Definitions range from a few sentences to several paragraphs, provide fundamental knowledge of the key terms and concepts in forensics, and cover a . . . range of forensic knowledge, including blood, pharmacology, decomposition, and court and legal terms." Choice

The author "has created an exceptional forensic reference guide. . . . I recommend this text highly as a handy pocket reference guide for anyone interested in forensic science or working in a related scientific discipline. It will greatly benefit students, teachers, and high school, university, and public libraries." Sci Books Films

Brenner, John C.

Forensic science; an illustrated dictionary. CRC Press 2003 286p $79.95 * **363.2**

1. Forensic sciences—Dictionaries

ISBN 0-8493-1457-7 LC 2003-55804

"In this dictionary of over 2,000 forensic words and terms . . . the terms are drawn from criminal and forensic disciplines and include court and legal terms. Definitions, ranging from a few sentences to a paragraph, are complete but neither so technical nor scientific that novices will have trouble understanding the definition. When a definition incorporates a large number of subdefinitions, all are included under the umbrella term for ease in finding. . . . A quick reference for forensic scientists and a good source of information for armchair enthusiasts." Choice

Includes bibliographical references

Cole, Simon A., 1967-

Suspect identities; a history of criminal identification and fingerprinting. Harvard Univ. Press 2001 369p il $35; pa $17.95 **363.2**

1. Fingerprints 2. Criminals—Identification

ISBN 0-674-00455-8; 0-674-01002-7 (pa)

LC 00-54054

The author discusses the history of fingerprinting and how it emerged as a separate discipline from anthropometry. He questions how reliable it is as a method of identification. "Cole suggests fingerprint examiners never proved two fingerprints can't be alike. Nor did the decentralized American criminal justice system ever develop a uniform standard for how similar a fragment must be to fingerprints on file." Christ Sci Monit

Includes bibliographical references

Conklin, Barbara Gardner

Encyclopedia of forensic science; a compendium of detective fact and fiction; [by] Barbara Gardner Conklin, Robert Gardner, and Dennis Shortelle. Oryx Press 2002 329p il $64.95 **363.2**

1. Forensic sciences—Encyclopedias 2. Criminal investigation

ISBN 1-57356-170-3 LC 2001-36638

This "illustrates the various ways that evidence can be extracted from a crime scene (e.g., ballistics, toxicology). . . . Though events in Great Britain and France are covered, the book's 85 entries focus on 19th-and 20th-century America. . . . Both famous and infamous people are listed, but what makes this book different and interesting is the inclusion of novelists (e.g., Patricia Cornwell, Jeffery Deaver, and Sir Arthur Conan Doyle) and their characters, who use forensics to solve crimes. . . . This is a solid resource." Libr J

Includes bibliographical references

Encyclopedia of law enforcement. Sage Publications 2005 3v set $310 *

363.2

1. Law enforcement—Encyclopedias

ISBN 0-7619-2649-6 LC 2004-21803

"A Sage Reference Publication"

"In A-to-Z format, 550 articles cover topics that range from agencies, people, and legislation to concepts like broken windows, problem areas like police corruption and terrorism, and staples of law enforcement like profiling, Miranda rights, electronic surveillance, and DNA analysis." Libr J

Sullivan "has edited an outstanding set on law enforcement issues." Choice

Includes bibliographical references

The **FBI:** a comprehensive reference guide; edited by Athan G. Theoharis with Tony G. Poveda, Susan Rosenfeld, Richard Gid Powers. Oryx Press 1999 409p $89.95 **363.2**

1. United States. Federal Bureau of Investigation

ISBN 0-89774-991-X LC 98-26642

Also available in paperback from Checkmark Bks.

This work provides a "chronological history of and guide to the FBI that includes information about the facilities, the organizational structure, and biographies of key individuals. This reference source will not only

The FBI: a comprehensive reference guide—
Continued
please FBI enthusiasts, but it also serves as an excellent resource for those interested in U.S. history, criminal justice, and American culture. Also included is an extensive chronology of key events, a subject index, and an authoritative bibliography." Am Libr

From the secret files of J. Edgar Hoover; edited with commentary by Athan Theoharis. Dee, I.R. 1991 370p $24.95; pa $19.90 **363.2**
1. Hoover, J. Edgar (John Edgar), 1895-1972
2. United States. Federal Bureau of Investigation
3. Internal security—United States 4. Anticommunist movements 5. Subversive activities
ISBN 0-929587-67-7; 1-56663-017-7 (pa)
LC 91-3478
After a history of the Federal Bureau of Investigation, the first section of the book "presents selected files examining the alleged and real sexual indiscretions of JFK, Robert Kennedy, Eleanor Roosevelt, and Martin Luther King Jr. . . . Subsequent chapters examine the FBI's 'investigative' techniques, its relationship with Presidents and the McCarthy committee, and the uses of public relations and the role of the director." Libr J

Kessler, Ronald
The FBI; inside the world's most powerful law enforcement agency. Pocket Bks. 1993 492p il pa $6.99 hardcover o.p. **363.2**
1. United States. Federal Bureau of Investigation
ISBN 0-671-78658-X (pa) LC 93-5207
"Kessler details how the bureau solved prominent cases such as Watergate and the World Trade Center bombing; covered up many detrimental internal cases; and introduced and employed ultra-modern forensic technologies for criminal investigations." Libr J
Includes bibliographical references

Theoharis, Athan G.
The FBI & American democracy; a brief critical history. University Press of Kansas 2004 195p il $24.95 * **363.2**
1. United States. Federal Bureau of Investigation
ISBN 0-7006-1345-5 LC 2004-6077
Contents: Introduction — The early years: creation and proscribed growth — World War I and the origins of political surveillance — Abuse of power, retrenchment, and morality — The New Deal and a war on crime — The origins of FBI intelligence, the crisis of World War II — The early Cold War years: anticipating and curbing subversion — Promoting Mccarthyism—and morality (again) — Secrecy and power: the undermining of accountability — From anticommunism to law and order — Scandal and limited reform — A modern bureau and the politics of terrorism
"This clear, thoughtful presentation is strongly recommended for both public libraries and academic institutions." Libr J
Includes bibliographical references

Wagner, E. J.
The science of Sherlock Holmes; from Baskerville Hall to the Valley of Fear, the real forensics behind the great detective's greatest cases. Wiley 2006 244p il $24.95; pa $16.95
363.2
1. Forensic sciences 2. Criminal investigation
ISBN 0-471-64879-5; 978-0-471-64879-6; 0-470-12823-2 (pa); 978-0-470-12823-7 (pa)
LC 2005-22236
The author discusses forensic science in Arthur Conan Doyle's stories of the 'consulting detective' Sherlock Holmes. She compares Holmes's investigative techniques to those used in actual cases such as the killing of Lizzie Borden's parents in 1892, the 1902 murder of Joseph Browne Elwell, and the disappearance of Dr. George Parkman in 1849.
This book "will intrigue readers with incredible stories and amazing tales from the early days of forensic science." Christ Sci Monit
Includes bibliographical references

363.3 Other aspects of public safety

Maclean, John N.
Fire and ashes; on the front lines of American wildfire. Holt & Co. 2003 238p il map $25; pa $14 **363.3**
1. Wildfires
ISBN 0-8050-7212-8; 0-8050-7591-7 (pa)
LC 2002-38704
"A John Macrae book"
"This work tells of two infernos: a 1999 conflagration in Nevada and a 1953 case of arboreal arson in California that took 15 lives when the fire exhibited unexpected behavior. . . . Careful in analysis, Maclean turns visceral when imparting the sudden terror of life-ending flames, or, as for a survivor of the 1949 Mann Gulch disaster whom he visits, a life-searing whirlwind. A solid choice that will be in demand, particularly during the West's summer fire season." Booklist

363.31 Censorship

Censorship; a world encyclopedia; Derek Jones, editor. Fitzroy Dearborn Pubs. 2001 4v set $450
363.31
1. Censorship—Encyclopedias
ISBN 1-57958-135-8
"This work provides a wide-ranging view of censorship, spanning ancient Egypt to present times and covering art, literature, music, newspapers and broadcasting, and the visual arts, among many other topics. In addition, the work provides country surveys and discussions of major controversies for specific movies, books, and television shows. Some 1,550 entries, arranged in alphabetical order by subject, were written by about 600 contributors from 50 countries. Entries are enhanced by occasional illustrations, a name-subject index, and an alphabetical and thematic list of entries at the beginning of each volume." Booklist
Includes bibliographical references

Green, Jonathon
The encyclopedia of censorship; [by] Jonathon
Green, Nicholas J. Karolides. rev ed. Facts on File
2005 xxii, 698p (Facts on File library of world
history) $85 *   **363.31**
1. Censorship—Encyclopedias
ISBN 0-8160-4464-3   LC 2004-53211
First published 1990
"The crowded roster of those who have been affected
by censorship, as well as the books, films, and other
works attacked, are found in these . . . pages. Controversies that have arisen over the years are given historical context; highly valuable national wrap-ups treat the
culture, law, and predominant trends of diverse lands."
Libr J
Includes bibliographical references

363.32   Control of violence and terrorism

Allison, Graham T.
Nuclear terrorism; the ultimate preventable
catastrophe; [by] Graham Allison. Times
Books\Henry Holt 2004 263p il $24
                                                 363.32
1. Terrorism 2. Nuclear warfare
ISBN 0-8050-7651-4   LC 2004-47427
The author "discusses the perilous situation, from the
technology of nuclear weapons to how terrorists could
acquire an atomic bomb and then infiltrate port and border security. . . . He argues that the U.S. government
should buy the world's loose fissile metal, negotiate a
termination of North Korea's and Iran's bomb projects,
and revamp the International Atomic Energy Agency."
Booklist
"Allison's comprehensive but accessible treatment of
this vital subject is a major contribution to public understanding." N Y Times Book Rev
Includes bibliographical references

Bobbitt, Philip
Terror and consent; the wars for the twenty-first
century. Alfred A. Knopf 2008 672p il $35
                                                 363.32
1. Terrorism 2. United States—Foreign relations
ISBN 978-1-4000-4243-2; 1-4000-4243-7
                               LC 2007-34194
"This is a Borzoi book"
The author examines "the relationship between the
emergent constitutional order and the emergence of modern 'market state terrorism,' which, mirroring the market
state and availing itself of the same technological advances, may be lethal enough to pose an existential
threat to the very possibility of government by consent
of the governed." Booklist
"This is quite simply the most profound book to have
been written on the subject of American foreign policy
since the attacks of 9/11—indeed, since the end of the
cold war." N Y Times Book Rev
Includes bibliographical references

Dershowitz, Alan M.
Preemption; a knife that cuts both ways. W.W.
Norton 2006 348p il (Issues of our time) $24.95
*   **363.32**
1. Military art and science 2. Violence—Prevention
ISBN 0-393-06012-8   LC 2005-27728
The author "examines preemptive war, preventative
detention, and restrictions on dangerous speech, and
claims that in the absence of general legal principles (or
even a healthy debate) about preemptive action, society's
current trend away from deterrence and toward prevention (as accelerated by the 'war on terrorism') threatens
longstanding notions of individual liberty and state sovereignty. . . . This book is an academic and accessible
framing of an important debate." Booklist
Includes bibliographical references

Elshtain, Jean Bethke, 1941-
Just war against terror; the burden of American
power in a violent world. Basic Books 2003 240p
$23; pa $14   **363.32**
1. Terrorism 2. War on terrorism
ISBN 0-465-01910-2; 0-465-01911-0 (pa)
                               LC 2002-154549
The author "examines the anti-terrorist campaign
through the lens of the 'just war' theory, administering
a rebuke to both amoral *realpolitiker* and starry-eyed
pacifists. She concludes that the Bush administration has,
by and large, waged the war on terror justly." Libr J
"While this volume is not a radical departure from the
abundance of post-September 11 books, it presents well
the moral case for U.S. military engagement in the world
and gives credence to those who advocate the use of
force as a response to terrorism." Publ Wkly
Includes bibliographical references

Homeland security; edited by Norris Smith and
Lynn M. Messina. H.W. Wilson Co 2004 197p
il (Reference shelf) $50 *   **363.32**
1. National security—United States 2. Terrorism
ISBN 0-8242-1033-6   LC 2003-70366
"This book looks at the Office of Homeland Security,
evaluating its effectiveness and its impact on civil liber-
ties, law enforcement, and Americans' peace of mind."
Publisher's note
Includes bibliographical references

363.33   Control of explosives and firearms

Henderson, Harry, 1951-
Gun control. rev ed. Facts on File 2005 316p il
(Library in a book) $45 *   **363.33**
1. Gun control
ISBN 0-8160-5660-9   LC 2004-50651
First published 2000
This examination of the history and issues of gun control "includes an annotated bibliography, chronology,
glossary, biographical listing, a chapter on how to research the topic, laws and court cases, and a list of applicable organizations and agencies." Publisher's note

363.34 Disasters

Downey, Tom
The last men out; life on the edge at Rescue 2
firehouse. H. Holt 2004 300p il $25; pa $15

363.34
1. New York (N.Y.). Fire Dept. 2. Fire fighters
ISBN 0-8050-7169-5; 0-8050-7844-4 (pa)
LC 2003-67770
The author "chronicles the building of the elite Rescue
2 company, which practices in Brooklyn and was recognized as one of the best in the country. On 9/11, Rescue
2 charged full force into the World Trade Center and
was decimated. While much of the book is concerned
with the camaraderie, bonding, humor, and training of
the men, the last third or so is concerned with their reaction to the tragedy of losing dozens of friends, relatives,
and comrades." Libr J
"Downey's descriptions burn into the pages with searing intensity. Writing with verve and energy in a gritty
style, he explores all extremes of the firemen's world,
from triumphant moments of heroism to bitter tragedies."
Publ Wkly

Halberstam, David, 1934-2007
Firehouse. Hyperion 2002 201p $22.95; pa $14

363.34
1. New York (N.Y.). Fire Dept. 2. Fire fighters
3. World Trade Center terrorist attack, 2001
ISBN 1-4013-0005-7; 0-7868-8851-2 (pa)
"A journalist's homage to firefighters, their values,
their culture and their courage during the martyrdom imposed on the New York Fire Department by the catastrophe of the attack on the World Trade Center." N Y
Times Bk Rev

Hemingway, Lorian, 1951-
A world turned over; a killer tornado and the
lives it changed forever. Simon & Schuster 2002
244p $23; pa $12 363.34
1. Tornadoes 2. Jackson (Miss.)
ISBN 0-684-85634-4; 0-7432-4767-1 (pa)
LC 2002-73346
"On March 3, 1966, a devastating tornado struck the
Candlestick Shopping Center in South Jackson, Miss.,
flattening buildings and killing 14 people. Because her
family had just moved away from their home across the
road from the shopping center, Hemingway . . . missed
the disaster. All her life she has been obsessed with it,
however, and in 2000 she went back to learn about it
from childhood friends who were there. . . . Hemingway
skillfully draws the reader into the nightmare." Publ
Wkly

Smith, Dennis, 1940-
Report from ground zero; the story of the rescue
efforts at the World Trade Center. Viking 2002
366p il maps $24.95; pa $14 363.34
1. New York (N.Y.). Fire Dept. 2. World Trade Center terrorist attack, 2001 3. Fire fighters
ISBN 0-670-03116-X; 0-452-28395-7 (pa)
LC 2002-19840

Based on his personal observations and interviews
with other rescue workers, the author describes the efforts of the New York City Fire Department to rescue
survivors of the September 11 attack on the World Trade
Center

Tougias, Mike, 1955-
Ten hours until dawn; the true story of heroism
and tragedy aboard the Can Do; [by] Michael
Tougias. St. Martins Press 2005 322p il map
$24.95 363.34
1. Blizzards 2. Shipwrecks 3. Rescue work
ISBN 0-312-33435-4
This book is "about the attempt to rescue the original
rescuers as well as the rescued when a tanker ran
aground off Salem, Massachusetts, in the blizzard of
1978." Booklist
The author "delivers a well-researched, vividly written
tale of brave men overwhelmed by the awesome forces
of nature." Publ Wkly

Zebrowski, Ernest, Jr.
Category 5; the story of Camille, lessons
unlearned from America's most violent hurricane;
[by] Ernest Zebrowski & Judith A. Howard.
University of Michigan Press 2005 276p il map
$27.95 * 363.34
1. Hurricanes 2. Gulf Coast (U.S.)
ISBN 0-472-11525-1 LC 2005-28583
"Partly a narrative and partly a pondering of how people and authorities prepare for predictable risk, the work
focuses on the areas devastated by the maelstrom:
Plaquemines Parish, Louisiana; Mississippi's Gulf Coast;
and faraway Nelson County, Virginia. . . . The authors
sound a pessimistic note about society's short-term memory in their sobering, able history of Camille." Booklist
Includes bibliographical references

Zeilinga de Boer, Jelle
Earthquakes in human history; the far-reaching
effects of seismic disruptions; [by] Jelle Zeilinga
de Boer and Donald Theodore Sanders. Princeton
University Press 2005 278p il maps $24.95 *

363.34
1. Earthquakes
ISBN 0-691-05070-8 LC 2004-40122
The authors provide "facts and insights on geologic
processes and the effects of . . . natural disasters on the
course of human history. Narratives on especially
impactful earthquakes include events in the Holy Land,
Ancient Greece, England, Portugal, Missouri, San Francisco, Japan, Peru and Chile, and Nicaragua. The influence of the earthquakes on religion, politics, economy,
wars, and literature is portrayed in fascinating prose, embellished with carefully selected photos, drawings, and
maps." Choice
Includes bibliographical references

363.4   Controversies related to public morals and customs

Behr, Edward, 1926-2007
Prohibition; thirteen years that changed America. Arcade Pub. 1996 262p il pa $13.95 hardcover o.p.   **363.4**
1. Prohibition
ISBN 1-55970-394-6 (pa)   LC 96-24063
In this study Behr "tracks the 13 years of Prohibition primarily through the actions of Wheeler, bootlegger George Remus and Chicago mayor 'Big Bill' Thomson, and in doing so stresses the corruption of politicians and law enforcement officials that made carrying out the 18th Amendment all but impossible." Publ Wkly
"This is an excellent and honest book that does not flinch at unpalatable facts." N Y Times Book Rev
Includes bibliographical references

Lerner, Michael A.
Dry Manhattan; Prohibition in New York City. Harvard University Press 2007 351p $28.95
363.4
1. Prohibition 2. New York (N.Y.)—Social conditions
ISBN 978-0-674-02432-8; 0-674-02432-X
LC 2006-50885
"Nowhere was Prohibition more keenly felt or more hotly contested, Lerner argues, than in the diverse cosmopolis of New York City. The city's immigrant and working-class populations, disproportionately targeted by the dry lobby, resisted in great numbers by distilling their own alcohol and frequenting speakeasies. Meanwhile, liberalized ideas about drinking, sex, and leisure bred cultural rebellion in the middle classes, whose alcohol-filled night life became the subject of magazine reportage. But illegal alcohol also fostered graft, organized crime, and violence, and, as concern over the Eighteenth Amendment became more widespread, the city organized politically." New Yorker
This book is "in all important respects exemplary, a singularly useful and revealing contribution to our understanding of a time from which the nation probably never will recover." Washington Post Book World
Includes bibliographical references

363.46   Abortion

Abortion wars; a half century of struggle, 1950-2000; edited by Rickie Solinger. University of Calif. Press 1998 413p pa $21.95 hardcover o.p.   **363.46**
1. Abortion
ISBN 0-520-20952-4 (pa)   LC 97-12261
"A collection of 18 essays written by abortion providers, journalists, reproductive-rights activists, legal strategists, and philosophers. In the introduction the editor makes it clear that the book is 'unabashedly a pro-rights book.' . . . The time line alone is so valuable that it's practically worth the price of the book." SLJ

Palmer, Louis J.
Encyclopedia of abortion in the United States. McFarland 2002 420p il map $75 *
363.46
1. Abortion—Encyclopedias
ISBN 0-7864-1386-7   LC 2002-6091
New edition in preparation
The author "focuses on legal aspects of abortion, supplying entries that detail the laws for each state pre and post-Roe v. Wade, chart the number of abortions in each state since 1990, list pro-life and pro-choice groups (with see also references to pro-life or pro-choice organizations), provide important legal cases and legal figures, and describe birth defects that may lead to decisions to abort. The encyclopedia's language is balanced and free of rhetoric." Choice
Includes bibliographical references

Press, Eyal
Absolute convictions; my father, a city, and the conflict that divided America. Henry Holt and Co. 2006 292p il map hardcover o.p. pa $15 *
363.46
1. Press, Shalom, 1940- 2. Abortion 3. Pro-life movement
ISBN 0-8050-7731-6; 978-0-312-42657-6 (pa); 0-312-42657-7 (pa)   LC 2005-34064
"In this inside look at a battleground of the abortion debate—Buffalo, N.Y.—the son of an abortion provider examines both sides of the culture clash that envelops his Israeli father's life." Publ Wkly
The author "manages the extraordinary feat of bringing light to a political issue that for far too long has generated nothing but blistering heat." N Y Times Book Rev
Includes bibliographical references

Reagan, Leslie J.
When abortion was a crime; women, medicine, and law in the United States, 1867-1973. University of Calif. Press 1997 387p il pa $19.95 hardcover o.p.   **363.46**
1. Abortion 2. Women—United States
ISBN 0-520-21657-1 (pa)   LC 96-22568
This is a history of abortion in the United States from its criminalization between 1860 and 1880 to Roe v. Wade in 1973
"Important and original, vigorously written even down to the footnotes, {this book} manages with apparent ease to combine serious scholarship . . . and broad appeal." Atl Mon
Includes bibliographical references

Rose, Melody
Abortion; a documentary and reference guide. Greenwood Press 2008 258p il $85 *
363.46
1. Abortion
ISBN 978-0-313-34032-1; 0-313-34032-3
LC 2007-37489
This "reference work explores the evolution of America's abortion debate in a . . . selection of over 40 primary documents by doctors, feminists, religious leaders,

Rose, Melody—*Continued*
politicians, extremists, and judges from the 19th century to the present day." Publisher's note
Includes bibliographical references

Solinger, Rickie, 1947-
Beggars and choosers; how the politics of choice shapes adoption, abortion, and welfare in the United States. Hill & Wang 2001 290p pa $14 hardcover o.p. **363.46**
1. Pro-choice movement 2. Abortion 3. Women's rights
ISBN 0-8090-2860-3 (pa)   LC 2001-16652
"Solinger argues here that framing issues like abortion as a matter of choice is a mistake. . . . In Solinger's view, the word choice has transformed what ought to be considered a universal right into 'a consumer's privilege' that only affluent women enjoy." N Y Times Book Rev
"The juxtaposition of choice and class when considering women's reproductive rights makes for insightful reading." Libr J
Includes bibliographical references

Tribe, Laurence H.
Abortion: the clash of absolutes. new ed. Norton 1992 318p pa $12.95   **363.46**
1. Abortion
ISBN 0-393-30956-8   LC 93-111762
First published 1990
The author examines both pro-life and pro-choice arguments and analyzes major court and legislative decisions
Includes bibliographical references

Weddington, Sarah Ragle, 1945-
A question of choice. Putnam 1992 306p il pa $15 hardcover o.p.   **363.46**
1. Roe v. Wade 2. Abortion
ISBN 0-14-017798-1 (pa)   LC 92-14311
"Starting with her years at the University of Texas Law School at Austin, Weddington, the attorney who won Roe v. Wade, traces the history of her involvement with this . . . Supreme Court case and its aftermath." Libr J
"This description of the background and legal significance of the 1973 Supreme Court decision . . . provides a sense of how Roe happened that is at once more personal and more knowledgeable than most popular summaries. . . . A sound addition to legal history and current affairs collections." Booklist
Includes bibliographical references

363.5   Housing

Loewen, James W.
Sundown towns; a hidden dimension of American racism. New Press 2005 562p il $29.95 *   **363.5**
1. African Americans—Segregation 2. Discrimination in housing 3. United States—Race relations
ISBN 1-56584-887-X   LC 2005-43855

This is an "account of the towns, suburbs, and neighborhoods throughout the United States that enforced the exclusion of minorities within their borders." Libr J
"This book is sure to become a landmark in several fields and a sure bet among Loewen's many fans." Publ Wkly
Includes bibliographical references

363.6   Public utilities and related services

Amery, Colin
Vanishing histories; 100 endangered sites from the World Monuments Watch; by Colin Amery, with Brian Curran; foreword by John Berendt; preface by Bonnie Burnham and Marilyn Perry. Abrams 2001 207p il maps $60 *   **363.6**
1. Historic sites 2. Monuments
ISBN 0-8109-1435-2   LC 2001-22622
"The World Monuments Fund, which has been monitoring the state of precious architectural and artistic sites since 1965, established the World Monuments Watch in 1995 to heighten awareness of endangered cultural sites in the hope of garnering the support necessary for their preservation. Architectural expert Amery and conservator Curran present the histories of 100 such monuments in a volume as notable for the beauty of its photographs as for the urgency of its message." Booklist

Farabee, Charles R., Jr.
National park ranger; an American icon; {by} Charles R. "Butch" Farabee Jr. Roberts Rinehart Publishers 2003 180p il pa $18.95   **363.6**
1. United States. National Park Service 2. National parks and reserves—United States
ISBN 1-570-98392-5   LC 2003-1022
"In this study of the vocation of park ranger since Maryland's park caretakers in 1696 to the present day, former ranger Farabee not only explores a ranger's role but also touches on the establishment of the National Park Service, the introduction of women rangers, and early resource management. Readers will enjoy the abundance of archival photographs, ranger profiles, and numerous other features." Libr J
Includes bibliographical references

Simpson, John W., 1952-
Dam! water, power, politics, and preservation in Hetch Hetchy and Yosemite National Park; [by] John Warfield Simpson. Pantheon Books 2005 356p il maps $28.50   **363.6**
1. Water supply 2. Water resources development 3. Yosemite National Park (Calif.)
ISBN 0-375-42231-5   LC 2004-65016
The author "argues for the restoration of Yosemite's Hetch Hetchy Valley. . . . Simpson's research is exemplary, and he deftly explores this case study of the nexus of politics, business and the environment. And he's lyrical when recounting his trips to Yosemite and describing the transformative beauty of the wilderness area." Publ Wkly

363.7   Environmental problems

Blatt, Harvey
America's environmental report card; are we
making the grade? MIT Press 2004 277p il maps
$27.95; pa $13.95   **363.7**
1. Environmental policy—United States
ISBN 0-262-02572-8; 0-262-52467-8 (pa)
                     LC 2004-40261
The author "breaks down environmental issues into
their components, describing different aspects of the
problem, offering solutions and suggesting a prognosis.
. . . Frank but hopeful, serious but readable, this is an
excellent environmental science primer." Publ Wkly
Includes bibliographical references

Braasch, Gary
Earth under fire; how global warming is
changing the world; with an afterword by Bill
McKibben. University of California Press 2007
296p il map $34.95   **363.7**
1. Climate—Environmental aspects 2. Greenhouse effect
ISBN 978-0-520-24438-2; 0-520-24438-9
                     LC 2007-2259
The author presents the "environmental changes resulting from the warming of our climate." Publisher's note
"What sets *Earth Under Fire* apart from other books
on the same topic are the inspiring photographs. These
images are an effective tool that helps the reader understand what the implications of climate change are—for
people, for other organisms, and for entire ecosystems."
Sci Books Films
Includes bibliographical references

Carson, Rachel, 1907-1964
Silent spring; introduction by Linda Lear;
afterword by Edward O. Wilson. 40th anniversary
ed. Houghton Mifflin 2002 378p il $24; pa $14 *
                          363.7
1. Pesticides—Environmental aspects 2. Pesticides and
wildlife
ISBN 0-618-25305-X; 0-618-24906-0 (pa)
"A Mariner book"
First published 1962
In The silent spring, Carson "contended that the indiscriminate use of weed killers and insecticides constituted
a hazard to wildlife and to human beings. Her provocative work inspired many subsequent environmental
studies." Reader's Ency. 4th edition

Encyclopedia of global change; environmental
change and human society; Andrew S. Goudie,
editor in chief; David J. Cuff, associate editor.
Oxford Univ. Press 2002 2v il maps set $350
                          363.7
1. Environmental sciences—Encyclopedias 2. Human
influence on nature—Encyclopedias
ISBN 0-19-510825-6   LC 00-58918
"This encyclopedia of environmental science and its
impact on human society reflects the global changes that

have taken place during the past century. The selection
of the various topics cuts across many disciplines in the
social, political, and natural sciences. The physical, biological, and chemical changes in the atmosphere, in the
water, and on land are related to health, industry, economics, and human welfare. Some of the topics discuss
climate models, including cyclones and winter storms.
. . . The importance of the world-wide effort to manage
whole ecosystems and its impact on human society are
also explained. . . . Topics that are discussed briefly include dams, deforestation, earth motions, El Niño, extinction of species, fires, fishing, the Gaia hypothesis, the
greenhouse effect, and biological diversity." Sci Books
Films
Includes bibliographical references

Famous first facts about the environment; edited
    by Ronald J. Formica; contributors, Victoria S.
    Chase {et al.}. Wilson, H.W. 2002 573p $150
    *   **363.7**
1. Environmental sciences
ISBN 0-8242-0974-5   LC 2001-17704
"A New England Publishing Associates book"
This "volume lists 4000 entries of international environmental 'firsts'. . . . Entries are first listed under a
major subject category, such as air pollution, climate and
weather, hazardous waste, population growth, and storms,
which are then broken down into various subdivisions.
. . . This unique work should be purchased by any size
library that needs an account of environmental 'firsts.'"
Libr J
Includes bibliographical references

Flannery, Tim F. (Tim Fridjof), 1956-
The weather makers; how man is changing the
climate and what it means for life on Earth; [by]
Tim Flannery. Atlantic Monthly Press 2006 357p
il maps $24; pa $15 *   **363.7**
1. Climate 2. Greenhouse effect
ISBN 0-8711-3935-9; 0-8021-4292-3 (pa)
                     LC 2005-52350
This is a "look at the connection between climate
change and global warming." Publ Wkly
"This work is distinctive in its marriage of science to
an act-now attitude and should energize environmentally
minded readers." Booklist
Includes bibliographical references

Friedman, Thomas L.
Hot, flat, and crowded; why we need a green
revolution—and how it can renew America. Farrar,
Straus & Giroux 2008 438p il $27.95 *
                             363.7
1. Environmental movement 2. Climate—Environmental aspects 3. Energy resources 4. Environmental policy—United States
ISBN 978-0-374-16685-4; 0-374-16685-4
                   LC 2008-930589
The author calls for "the United States [to] . . . take
the lead in a worldwide effort to replace our wasteful, inefficient energy practices with a strategy for clean energy, energy efficiency, and conservation." Publisher's note
"Friedman's big, passionate, and solidly specific eco-

Friedman, Thomas L.—*Continued*
logical primer, social manifesto, and realistic plan for a green revolution aimed at restoring America's greatness and securing a sustainable future should serve as a playbook for innovators and civic leaders." Booklist

George, Rose, 1969-
The big necessity; the unmentionable world of human waste and why it matters. Metropolitan Books 2008 288p il $26 * **363.7**
1. Sanitation 2. Sewage disposal
ISBN 978-0-8050-8271-5; 0-8050-8271-9
LC 2008-29999
The author "breaks the embarrassed silence over the economic, political, social and environmental problems of human waste disposal. . . . From the depths of the world's oldest surviving urban sewers in to Japan's robo-toilet revolution, George leads an intrepid, erudite and entertaining journey through the public consequences of this most private behavior." Publ Wkly
Includes bibliographical references

Gonzalez, Juan
Fallout; the environmental consequences of the World Trade Center collapse. New Press (NY) 2002 150p $20 **363.7**
1. World Trade Center terrorist attack, 2001 2. Environmental health 3. Pollution
ISBN 1-56584-754-7
LC 2002-72404
González discusses the pollution caused when the World Trade Center collapsed after the terrorist attacks on September 11, 2001. He believes that substances such as asbestos, lead, mercury, dioxins, furans, and diesel fuel were released into the surrounding environment
"This book is a tragic indictment of the breakdown of public trust when it was needed most." Libr J

Grossman, Elizabeth, 1957-
High tech trash; digital devices, hidden toxins, and human health. Island Press/Shearwater Books 2006 334p $25.95 * **363.7**
1. Refuse and refuse disposal 2. Electronic apparatus and appliances
ISBN 1-55963-554-1; 978-1-55963-554-7
LC 2006-4549
The author "traces the toxic substances (lead, mercury, phosphorus, brominated flame retardants, and others) used in digital devices, along with their health hazards. Each of the book's nine chapters has notes and references; there is also an appendix on how to recycle computers. . . . [Grossman] has made a valiant effort to consolidate the information that general, nontechnical readers interested in the subject . . . would find very useful." Sci Books Films
Includes bibliographical references

Hosansky, David
The environment A-Z. CQ Press 2000 320p il maps $58 **363.7**
1. Environmental sciences—Encyclopedias
ISBN 1-568-02583-1
LC 00-62163

"Covering mostly the last 30 years, with some treatment of earlier events when essential to provide perspective, the alphabetic entries include general issues and topics, federal agencies and laws, and individual persons . . . who have influenced environmental decisions. A few international bodies are included, and of course issues like global warming are of broader than national scope, but in these cases the emphasis is primarily on how U.S. policies relate to the agencies and issues. Most entries are one or two pages in length, and are clearly and concisely written." Am Ref Books Annu, 2002
Includes bibliographical references

Hunter, Robert, 1941-2005
Thermageddon: countdown to 2030. Arcade Pub. 2003 276p $24.95 **363.7**
1. Greenhouse effect
ISBN 1-55970-667-8
LC 2002-38349
First published 2002 in Canada with title: 2030: confronting thermageddon in our lifetime
The author goes over "the well-debated points of global warming and comes to an even darker conclusion: the stable global weather system of the last 10,000 years will 'tip' under the weight of the greenhouse effect. . . . The Arctic ice cap will nearly disappear during one summer within the next 30 years; then, on accepted geophysical principles around the radiation effect, what follows must be massive one-way dislocations of climate: heat surges, desertification, floods and other large-scale shifts in local geography." Publ Wkly
This book "is a solid achievement by one of Canada's most important environmentalists." Quill & Quire
Includes bibliographical references

Johansen, Bruce E. (Bruce Elliott), 1950-
The dirty dozen: toxic chemicals and the earth's future. Praeger 2003 297p $49.95 **363.7**
1. Pollution 2. Industrial waste 3. Environmental health
ISBN 0-275-97702-1
LC 2002-29872
This study examines the history, industrial uses, and harmful effects of "the 12 most commonly used persistent organic pollutants (POPs). Also called organochlorines, they are pervasive in air, water, food, animals, pesticides, solvents, and numerous household products. They are responsible for cancer, respiratory ailments, birth defects, other illnesses, and death in humans and animals." Libr J
Includes bibliographical references

Kolbert, Elizabeth
Field notes from a catastrophe; man, nature, and climate change. Bloomsbury Pub. 2006 210p il map $22.95 * **363.7**
1. Greenhouse effect 2. Climate
ISBN 1-59691-125-5; 978-1-59691-125-3
LC 2005-30972
This investigation of global warming is an outgrowth of a three-part series (The Climate of Man) that appeared in The New Yorker in 2005. "The book is organized around notes Ms. Kolbert took on 'field trips,' not only to places where climate change is affecting the natural world but also to ones—labs, offices, observatories—

Kolbert, Elizabeth—*Continued*
where humans are trying to understand the phenomenon
of human-induced global warming." N Y Times (Late
NY Ed))

"On the burgeoning shelf of cautionary but occasionally alarmist books warning about the consequences of dramatic climate change, Kolbert's calmly persuasive reporting stands out for its sobering clarity." Publ Wkly
Includes bibliographical references

Lynas, Mark, 1973-
High tide; the truth about our climate crisis.
Picador 2004 xxxiii, 345p il map pa $14
363.7

1. Greenhouse effect
ISBN 0-312-30365-3   LC 2004-44661
"In a series of . . . travel narratives, Lynas shows the
human side of global warming, taking readers to Britain,
North and South America, China, and the South Pacific.
He introduces them to folks whose houses and roads are
falling crazily through melting permafrost, who are going
hungry because fishing lakes have disappeared, and who
are becoming refugees because their grasslands have
turned to desert. . . . The author clearly explains why
these are not isolated incidents, but interrelated parts of
a worldwide set of phenomena that soon will affect us
all." SLJ
Includes bibliographical references

Mongillo, John F.
Encyclopedia of environmental science; by John
Mongillo and Linda Zierdt-Warshaw. Oryx Press
2000 450p il $99.95   **363.7**
1. Environmental sciences—Encyclopedias
ISBN 1-57356-147-9   LC 00-32657
This encyclopedia covers "the major topics of agriculture, atmosphere, biomes, ecology, endangered plant and
wildlife species, energy, law and regulations, water, and
wetlands. . . . The 1000 entries are arranged alphabetically and range from several paragraphs to two pages in
a clear and straightforward style with plenty of cross references." Libr J
Includes bibliographical references

Mooney, Chris
Storm world; hurricanes, politics, and the battle
over global warming. Harcourt 2007 392p il map
$26   **363.7**
1. Hurricanes 2. Greenhouse effect
ISBN 978-0-15-101287-9; 0-15-101287-3
LC 2007-09742
This book examines "whether the increasing ferocity
of hurricanes is connected to global warming." Publisher's note
"This is certainly one of the most thought-provoking
and accessible accounts of climate change to appear
since Katrina." Booklist
Includes bibliographical references

Rogers, Heather
Gone tomorrow; the hidden life of garbage.
New Press 2005 288p il $23.95   **363.7**
1. Refuse and refuse disposal
ISBN 1-56584-879-9   LC 2005-41562

The author "analyzes the contents of America's garbage and its disposal while also revealing the corporate
strategies behind the disposable-goods explosion and assessing the ecological toll of our consumer habits."
Booklist
"The book is an intriguing look into an often misunderstood and overlooked industry." Publ Wkly
Includes bibliographical references

Royte, Elizabeth
Garbage land; on the secret trail of trash. Little,
Brown 2005 311p $24.95; pa $14.99 *
363.7
1. Refuse and refuse disposal
ISBN 0-316-73826-3; 0-316-15401-X (pa)
LC 2004-24732
The author presents "a cultural tour guided and in-
formed by the things she throws away. Structured around
four separate journeys—those of Royte's household trash,
compostable matter, recyclables, and sewage—[this] is a
literary investigation of the . . . dirty side of consump-
tion." Publisher's note
"There's little waste in Royte's winning words. . . .
Seldom has garbage been handled with such care." Christ
Sci Monit
Includes bibliographical references

Speth, James Gustave
Red sky at morning; America and the crisis of
the global environment. Yale University Press
2004 299p $24; pa $16   **363.7**
1. Environmental protection 2. Globalization
3. Environmental policy—United States
ISBN 0-300-10232-1; 0-300-10776-5 (pa)
LC 2003-20223
The author's "thesis is that the world faces some difficult environmental challenges in the years ahead—chief
among them climate change—and that it is ill-equipped
to tackle those challenges. He contrasts such difficulties
with local environmental problems, which the rich world
has successfully tackled, and aims to explain the reasons
why global problems are likely to prove thornier." Economist
Speth "presents an authoritative, trenchant analysis of
the worsening global environmental crisis." Choice
Includes bibliographical references

Walker, Gabrielle
The hot topic; what we can do about global
warming; [by] Gabrielle Walker and Sir David
King. Harcourt 2008 276p il map pa $14
363.7
1. Greenhouse effect
ISBN 978-0-15-603318-3   LC 2007-45080
"A Harvest original"
The authors "explain how fossil fuels produce carbon
dioxide, show how global warming is affecting individual
species and changing entire ecosystems, predict how
much more climate change we can afford before things
become truly catastrophic, and consider economic and
political solutions to the problem." Publ Wkly
"This is the best overview of global warming that this

Walker, Gabrielle—*Continued*
reviewer has read. . . . What is most valuable about this book is that the text clearly explains to lay readers a very complex and highly controversial topic." Libr J
Includes bibliographical references

Woodard, Colin, 1968-
Ocean's end; travels through endangered seas. Basic Bks. 2000 300p pa $15 hardcover o.p.
363.7
1. Marine pollution 2. Marine resources
ISBN 0-465-01571-9 (pa)   LC 99-51771
The author contends "that pollution, harmful fishing practices, ignorance and global warming are destroying the world's oceans. . . . He uncovers a colorful cast of scientists, officials, activists, divers and religious missionaries who attest to the human and economic costs of ecological decline." Publ Wkly
Includes bibliographical references

Wyman, Bruce C.
The Facts on File dictionary of environmental science; [by] Bruce Wyman, L. Harold Stevenson. 3rd ed. Facts on File 2007 498p il (Facts on File science library) $49.50 *   363.7
1. Environmental sciences—Dictionaries
ISBN 0-8160-6437-7; 978-0-8160-6437-3
LC 2006-45697
First published 1991 with authors names in reverse order
This dictionary contains over 5,000 cross-referenced entries reflecting the diversity of subjects that are relevant to the environmental field.

363.9   Population problems

Black, Edwin
War against the weak; eugenics and America's campaign to create a master race. Four Walls Eight Windows 2003 xxviii, 550p il $27; pa $18 *   363.9
1. Eugenics
ISBN 1-568-58258-7; 1-568-58321-4 (pa)
LC 2003-48857
The author reveals that the American eugenics movement "was extensive, systematic, well funded, and supported by major political and intellectual leaders; perhaps most startling, it directly inspired the rise of Nazism in Hitler's Germany. . . . This chilling and well-researched book is highly recommended." Libr J
Includes bibliographical references

Bruinius, Harry
Better for all the world; the secret history of forced sterilization and America's quest for racial purity. Knopf 2006 401p il $30 *   363.9
1. Eugenics 2. Sterilization (Birth control)
ISBN 0-375-41371-5   LC 2005-44150

The author describes how, "in the early years of the 20th century, a fixation on eugenics led several states to approve forced sterilization to keep thousands of Americans from producing 'morally inferior' or 'feeble-minded' offspring." Publ Wkly
"Bruinius' account of one of America's dirty little secrets is . . . a real page-turner." Booklist
Includes bibliographical references

Family planning sourcebook; edited by Amy Marcaccio Keyzer. Omnigraphics 2000 520p (Health reference series) $78 *   363.9
1. Birth control
ISBN 0-7808-0379-5   LC 00-53029
"Basic consumer health information about planning for pregnancy and contraception, including traditional methods, barrier methods, hormonal methods, permanent methods, future methods, emergency contraception, and birth control choices for women at each stage of life." Publisher's note

Tone, Andrea, 1964-
Devices and desires; a history of contraceptives in America. Hill & Wang 2001 366p $30; pa $15
363.9
1. Birth control
ISBN 0-8090-3817-X; 0-8090-3816-1 (pa)
LC 00-50547
"Part 1 examines the 'contraceptive entrepreneurs' who practiced what was for many years an illegal trade, regulated by no one. In part 2, 'From Smut to Science,' Tone considers the development of relatively reliable contraceptive techniques, . . . part 3, 'The Medicalization of Contraceptives,' covers birth control pills, Norplant, and intrauterine devices." Booklist

364   Criminology

Encyclopedia of criminology; Richard A. Wright, J. Mitchell Miller, editors. Fitzroy Dearborn 2005 3v set $495 *   364
1. Crime—Encyclopedias
ISBN 1-579-58387-3   LC 2004-4861
"More than 500 essays contributed by more that 300 international scholars fall into 12 major substantive areas in the discipline, including criminal behavior (124 essays), the justice system (121), criminal law (61), theories of criminal behavior (49), and prominent figures in the field (44). . . . This reference source is destined to become a standard in the field." Choice
Includes bibliographical references

Famous American crimes and trials; edited by Frankie Y. Bailey and Steven Chermak. Praeger 2004 5v il (Praeger perspectives) set $375
364
1. Administration of criminal justice
ISBN 0-275-98333-1   LC 2004-50548
Contents: v. 1. 1607-1859 -- v. 2. 1860-1912 -- v. 3. 1913-1959 -- v. 4. 1960-1980 -- v. 5. 1981-2000
This set "examines 70 cases, beginning in 1607 with the trial of accused heretic Quaker Mary Dyer and ending with the 2001 execution of convicted Oklahoma City

Famous American crimes and trials—*Continued*
bomber Timothy McVeigh. . . . This work has definite multidisciplinary appeal." Choice
Includes bibliographical references

Rosen, Fred
The historical atlas of American crime. Facts on File 2005 xx, 296p il map (Facts on File crime library) $75; pa $24.95 *   **364**
1. Crime—United States
ISBN 0-8160-4841-X; 0-8160-4842-8 (pa)
                                    LC 2004-11346
"Each chapter covers a span of years and begins with an overview that ties the evolution of crime to political, economic, and technological happenings of its era. The chronologically arranged entries describe cases, persons, and events that were either the first of their sort or unique in some way." Booklist
The author "brings a fresh point of view to American crime by placing it within the larger context of American history; at the same time he observes multiple disciplines (e.g., history, economics, literature) through the lens of crime." Choice
Includes bibliographical references

364.03   Criminology—Encyclopedias and dictionaries

Encyclopedia of crime & justice; Joshua Dressler, editor in chief. 2nd ed. Macmillan Ref. USA 2001 c2002 4v set $475 *   **364.03**
1. Crime—Encyclopedias 2. Criminals—Encyclopedias 3. Administration of criminal justice
ISBN 0-02-865319-X
First published 1982
Contents: v1 Abortion to cruel & unusual punishment; v2 Delinquent & criminal subcultures to Juvenile justice: Institutions; v3 Juvenile justice: Juvenile court to Rural crime; v4 Schools & crime to Wiretapping & eavesdropping
"The signed essays are written by respected scholars in the fields of law, sociology, and criminal justice and range in length from 800 to 12,000 words. . . . This set will be in high demand by 'issues' researchers as well as by researchers in the fields of law and criminal justice." Booklist

Encyclopedia of crime and punishment; edited by David Levinson. Sage Publs. 2002 4v set $600
                                    364.03
1. Crime—Encyclopedias 2. Administration of criminal justice
ISBN 0-7619-2258-X   LC 2002-1220
"The 439 signed entries cover 13 major themes: crimes and related behaviors, law and justice, policing, forensics, corrections, victimology, punishment, social and cultural context, international aspects, concepts and theories, research methods and information, organizations and institutions, and special populations. . . . {This is} easy to understand and useful for beginning research in the field of criminal justice." Booklist
Includes bibliographical references

Nash, Jay Robert
The great pictorial history of world crime. History 2004 2v il set $249   **364.03**
1. Crime—Encyclopedias
ISBN 1-928831-20-6   LC 2004-100992
Contents: v. 1. Assassination; Bigamy; Burglary; Cannibalism; Drugs; Fraud; Gangs, gangsters and organized crime; Kidnapping -- v. 2. Murder/celebrity slayings; Murder/mass murder; Murder/serial killers; Murder/unsolved homicides; Piracy; Robbery; Secret criminal societies; Terrorism; Bibliography
"Each of these topical sections opens with a general overview and then explores individual crimes in chronological order. As befits the title, there are thousands of black-and-white photographs and illustrations and although their quality varies they are, by and large, helpful and interesting. . . . [This is] the most comprehensive true crime book available." SLJ

Newton, Michael, 1951-
The encyclopedia of serial killers. 2nd ed. Facts On File 2006 515p il (Facts on File crime library) $85; pa $19.95 *   **364.03**
1. Criminals—Encyclopedias 2. Homicide—Encyclopedias
ISBN 0-8160-6195-5; 0-8160-6196-3 (pa)
                                    LC 2005-3800
First published 2000
The author "covers hundreds of serial murder cases from early history to the present, among them Jack the Ripper, the Green River Killer, Robert Lee Yates, and Aileen Wuornos. A good starting point for those needing basic information." Libr J
Includes bibliographical references

364.1   Criminal offenses

Atwood, Roger
Stealing history; tomb raiders, smugglers, and the looting of the ancient world. St. Martin's Press 2004 337p il map $25.95 *   **364.1**
1. Art thefts 2. Antiquities—Collection and preservation
ISBN 0-312-32406-5   LC 2004-50862
"Many a private collection is filled with artworks that literally have been ripped from gravesites or unsecured archeological excavations. Atwood . . . focuses on the removal of traditional Peruvian cultural assets—not only into private hands but into major museums, New York's Metropolitan Museum of Art not least among the institutional offenders." Libr J
The author's "ability to bring a story dramatically to life and his keen interest in stemming the illegal antiquities trade makes this an important book for anyone interested in archeology, preservation or the potentially tangled provenance of works they love." Publ Wkly
Includes bibliographical references

The **best** American crime reporting, 2008; guest editor, Jonathan Kellerman; series editors, Otto Penzler and Thomas H. Cook. Harper Perennial 2008 329p pa $14.95 *   **364.1**

The best American crime reporting, 2008—*Continued*

1. Crime 2. Criminals

ISBN 978-0-06-149083-5; 0-06-149083-0

Also available eBook version

"An Ecco book"

Annual. First published 2002 by Pantheon with title: The best American crime writing

This collection "features 15 essays, all but two of which appeared previously in periodicals ranging from the Atlantic and The New Yorker to the Cleveland Free Times and ESPN magazine. The essays feature stories of crime and criminal investigations. . . . This book is engaging to read and will definitely be of interest to fans of true-crime books." Libr J

Bonanno, Bill

Bound by honor; a mafioso's story. St. Martin's Press 1999 282p il $24.95; pa $6.99

364.1

1. Mafia

ISBN 0-312-20388-8; 0-312-97147-8 (pa)

LC 99-14049

"Bonanno not only details Mob infighting and the struggles among rival East Coast Mob families; he also offers specifics concerning Mob influence on Presidents Kennedy, Johnson, and Nixon as well as on other important political figures, such as J. Edgar Hoover . . . and Morris Udall. Even the Mob's involvement in JFK's assassination is spelled out. . . . Straightforward rather than chatty, the book paints a revealing picture of Mob family politics and government intervention." Booklist

Breslin, Jimmy

The good rat; a true story. Ecco 2008 270p $24.95

364.1

1. Mafia 2. Organized crime

ISBN 978-0-06-085666-3; 0-06-085666-1

The "main narrative is devoted to the story of Louis Eppolito and Stephen Caracappa, two New York police detectives who were fingered as mob assassins . . . by Burton Kaplan, a drug dealer and friend of the Luchese crime family." N Y Times Book Rev

"Breslin is a delighted tour guide through the underworld. . . . Nobody does it better." Booklist

Brown, Elaine

The condemnation of Little B. Beacon Press 2002 391p pa $19 hardcover o.p. **364.1**

1. Lewis, Michael, 1983 or 4- 2. Homicide 3. Atlanta (Ga.)—Race relations

ISBN 0-8070-0975-X (pa)   LC 2001-37943

"Brown analyzes the social and political context of the high-profile trial and conviction, amidst media blather about 'super predators,' of 13-year-old Little B. (a legal alias) for killing another black youth in Atlanta just before the Olympics opened." Booklist

"Packed with detail, strong arguments and flashes of brilliance, Brown's book is extraordinarily powerful." Publ Wkly

Includes bibliographical references

Bugliosi, Vincent

Helter skelter; the true story of the Manson murders; {by} Vincent Bugliosi with Curt Gentry. 25th anniversary ed. Norton 1994 528p il $25; pa $13.95 *   **364.1**

1. Manson, Charles, 1934- 2. Homicide

ISBN 0-393-08700-X; 0-393-32223-8 (pa)

LC 94-20957

A reissue of the title published 1974

"This book by the prosecutor at the Tate-LaBianca murder trial tells the inside story of the Manson Family murders, the investigations, and the trial." Libr J

Butterfield, Fox

All God's children; the Bosket family and the American tradition of violence. Avon Bks. 1996 389p il map pa $15   **364.1**

1. Bosket family 2. Violence 3. United States—Race relations

ISBN 0-380-72862-1

First published 1995 by Knopf

Willie Bosket is an inmate "in New York's Woodbourne Correction Center. . . . Butterfield, with Willie's encouragement, set out to trace Bosket's family tree. . . . Butterfield focuses on Edgefield Country in Central South Carolina, where Bosket's family served as slaves." Newsweek

Includes bibliographical references

Capote, Truman, 1924-1984

In cold blood; a true account of a multiple murder and its consequences. Random House 2002 343p $22; pa $13 *   **364.1**

1. Hickock, Richard, 1931-1965 2. Smith, Perry, 1928-1965 3. Homicide

ISBN 0-375-50790-6; 0-679-74558-0 (pa)

LC 2002-282920

A reissue of the title first published 1966

"This edition is set from the first American edition of 1966 and commemorates the seventy-fifth anniversary of Random House"—Jacket

"Truman Capote called his account of the 1959 murder of a Kansas farm family a nonfiction novel. Using information he collected through interviews with townspeople and the killers, Capote created a vivid portrait of the criminals and graphically described the crime, the criminals' escape to Mexico, capture, trial, appeals, and hanging." HarperCollins Reader's Ency of Am Lit. 2nd edition

Carrère, Emmanuel, 1957-

The adversary; a true story of monstrous deception; translated by Linda Coverdale. Picador USA 2002 191p pa $13   **364.1**

1. Romand, Jean-Claude, 1954- 2. Homicide

ISBN 0-312-42060-9; 978-0-312-42060-4

LC 2001-50066

First published 2000 by Metropolitan Books

"In 1933, Jean-Claude Romand, a successful French doctor, seemed devastated when his family was killed in a house fire; then police found evidence of blunt trauma on his wife's skull, and dug bullets out of his children.

Carrère, Emmanuel, 1957-—*Continued*
Soon, the truth began to surface: Romand was not a doctor at all, and he had murdered his family to conceal a web of lies that extended across almost two decades." New Yorker

"In telling Romand's story, [the author] also writes of the process of creating this book. By injecting himself into the narrative, Carrere has managed to make this appalling story both fascinating and highly readable." Libr J

De Vito, Carlo
The encyclopedia of international organized crime. Facts on File 2005 386p il $75; pa $24.95
*   **364.1**
1. Organized crime—Encyclopedias
ISBN 0-8160-4848-7; 0-8160-4849-5 (pa)
                         LC 2003-24724
"This alphabetically arranged volume covers organized crime units in a variety of countries including, but not limited to, the US, Mexico, China, England, and Australia. Not only does this reference tool span a wide geographical area, it also covers a lengthy time period, from the mid-19th century to the present. . . . Presented in an interesting, straightforward manner, this easy-to-read book is also enjoyable." Choice
Includes bibliographical references

Dolnick, Edward, 1952-
The rescue artist; a true story of art, thieves, and the hunt for a missing masterpiece. HarperCollins Publishers 2005 270p il $25.95; pa $14.95
                               364.1
1. Munch, Edvard, 1863-1944 2. Art thefts
ISBN   0-06-053117-7;   978-0-06-053117-1; 0-06-053118-5 (pa); 978-0-06053118-8 (pa)
                         LC 2004-62060
This is an "account of the 1994 theft of one of the world's most famous paintings, The Scream. . . . This is a tightly woven, fast-paced story." SLJ
Includes bibliographical references

Douglas, John E.
The cases that haunt us; from Jack the Ripper to JonBenet Ramsey, the FBI's legendary mindhunter sheds light on the mysteries that won't go away; [by] John Douglas, Mark Olshaker. Pocket Books 2001 487p il pa $7.99
                               364.1
1. Homicide 2. Criminal psychology
ISBN 978-0-671-01706-4; 0-671-01706-3
"A Lisa Drew Book"
First published 2000 by Scribner
The authors discuss "eight controversial cases that include the Lindbergh baby kidnapping, the Boston Strangler, the Zodiac Killer, and the JonBenet Ramsey killing." Libr J

Dray, Philip
At the hands of persons unknown; the lynching of Black America. Random House 2002 528p il pa $14.95 hardcover o.p.   **364.1**
1. Lynching 2. African Americans—Southern States 3. Southern States—Race relations
ISBN 0-375-75445-8 (pa)   LC 2001-40366
The author "looks at specific lynchings, the national history of race and politics, and anti-lynching campaigns of black and biracial organizations." Libr J
"Dray balances moral indignation with a sound understanding of history and politics. The result is vital, hard-hitting cultural history." Publ Wkly
Includes bibliographical references

Drew, Elizabeth
The corruption of American politics; what went wrong and why. Overlook Press 2000 286p pa $15.95   **364.1**
1. Political corruption 2. United States—Politics and government—1989-
ISBN 1-585-67049-9; 978-1-585-67049-9
                       LC 00-22068
First published 1999 by Carol Pub. Group
The author argues "that the prevalence of soft money has lowered the quality of leadership in Washington. The most successful politicians are no longer the best executives or the best legislators, she says, but rather the best fund-raisers. . . . One of the most skillfully written, as well as insightful, looks inside the Beltway to appear in a very long time." Publ Wkly

Glenny, Misha
McMafia; a journey through the global criminal underworld. Alfred A. Knopf 2008 375p il map $27.95   **364.1**
1. Organized crime
ISBN 978-1-4000-4411-5; 1-4000-4411-1
                       LC 2007-30522
"A Borzoi book"
The author discusses "the ability of organized crime worldwide to find and service markets driven by a seemingly insatiable demand for illegal wares. . . . [He contends that] organized crime feeds off the poverty of the developing world. . . . Glenny talked to police, victims, politicians, and members of the global underworld in eastern Europe, North and South America, Africa, the Middle East, China, Japan, and India." Publisher's note
"Readers yearning for a deeper understanding of the real-life, international counterparts to *The Sopranos* need look no further than Glenny's engrossing study." Publ Wkly
Includes bibliographical references

Gourevitch, Philip
A cold case. Picador USA 2002 183p il pa $12
                               364.1
1. Koehler, Frank, 1929- 2. Homicide
ISBN 0-312-42002-1; 978-0-312-42002-4
                       LC 2002-66767
First published 2001 by Farrar, Straus & Giroux

Gourevitch, Philip—*Continued*

"In 1970, Frankie Koehler shot and killed two men after a barroom brawl in Hell's Kitchen and then disappeared; twenty-seven years later, Andy Rosenzweig, the chief investigator for the Manhattan D.A., set out to solve one last case before he retired. Gourevitch reconstructs not only the crime but an era of cops and criminals that's fast passing into myth." New Yorker

Innes, Brian, 1928-

Fakes & forgeries; the true crime stories of history's greatest deceptions: the criminals, the scams, and the victims. Reader's Digest 2005 256p il $26.95   364.1

1. Forgery 2. Swindlers and swindling 3. Fraud

ISBN 0-7621-0625-5   LC 2005-46462

"Was a diary found in 1991 truly written by Jack the Ripper? Was a young woman rescued from a Berlin canal actually Anastasia, daughter of Tsar Nicholas II? The answers to these questions and others are explored. . . . [The author] divides his research into seven categories and provides details on how each case was solved. . . . The book is lively and engaging and will satisfy anyone who enjoys solving a good true-crime story." Libr J

Jentz, Terri, 1957-

Strange piece of paradise. Farrar, Straus & Giroux 2006 542p il $27 *   364.1

1. Offenses against the person 2. Criminal investigation

ISBN 0-374-13498-7; 978-0-374-13498-3

LC 2005-27240

"This book opens 15 years after a horrifyingly brutal assault in which Jentz and a Yale classmate, asleep at an Oregonian campground, were first run over and then attacked by a hatchet-wielding stranger. Jentz first returned to Oregon in 1992 to reclaim the self she lost at 19 and conduct her own investigation into the crime, for which no one was ever prosecuted. Her story is simultaneously riveting and disturbing—not an embellished memoir but a straightforward, chronological account based on notes, crime reports, newspaper accounts, hospital records, lab reports, and the author's own memory of events." Libr J

Jones, Ann, 1937-

Women who kill. Beacon Press 1996 448p pa $16   364.1

1. Homicide 2. Criminals

ISBN 0-8070-6775-X   LC 95-46961

First published 1980 by Holt, Rinehart & Winston

The author examines murders committed by women throughout American history, discussing such cases as Lizzie Borden, Alice Crimmins, and Jean Harris. The cases discussed shed light on women's status in American society

Includes bibliographical references

Kelly, Robert J.

Encyclopedia of organized crime in the United States; from Capone's Chicago to the new urban underworld. Greenwood Press 2000 xxx, 358p $64.95   364.1

1. Organized crime

ISBN 0-313-30653-2   LC 99-33801

This reference source "describes and analyzes issues, criminal personalities, and trends throughout the 20th century. Kelly also examines the conditions that produced criminal activities and organizations. More than 250 entries provide in-depth information on major underworld figures, from Al Capone to Lucky Luciano to John Gotti, as well as key criminal events, from rub outs to FBI stings." Libr J

Includes bibliographical references

Kersten, Jason

Journal of the dead; a story of friendship and murder in the New Mexico desert. HarperCollins 2003 236p il map $24.95; pa $12.95

364.1

1. Kodikian, Raffi 2. Coughlin, David, d. 1999 3. Homicide

ISBN 0-06-018470-1; 0-06095-922-3 (pa)

LC 2003-40714

This is an "account of a fatal 1999 cross-country trip by two best friends, Raffi Kodikian and David Coughlin, that ended in the desert near New Mexico's Carlsbad Caverns with Coughlin stabbed to death and Kodikian claiming that he had, in effect, committed a mercy killing." Publ Wkly

The author "tells the story of Coughlin and Kodikian with quiet authority, lending unexpected dignity to the whole affair. The result is a ruminative, wholly absorbing book." N Y Times Book Rev

King, Joyce

Hate crime: the story of a dragging in Jasper, Texas. Pantheon Bks. 2002 225p $24

364.1

1. Byrd, James, Jr. 2. Homicide 3. Hate crimes 4. African Americans—Southern States 5. Southern States—Race relations

ISBN 0-375-42132-7   LC 2001-58074

"On a Texas back road in 1998 . . . three young whites wrapped a chain around an African American man and dragged him to his death behind their truck. . . . King covers each of the three trials that followed the atrocity." Libr J

The author "provides both objective reporting and sensitive insight into the players on both sides of America's racial divide." Booklist

Larson, Erik

The devil in the white city; murder, magic, and madness at the fair that changed America. Crown 2003 447p il map $25.95 *   364.1

1. Mudgett, Herman W., 1861-1896 2. World's Columbian Exposition (1893: Chicago, Ill.) 3. Homicide

ISBN 0-609-60844-4   LC 2002-154046

Larson, Erik—*Continued*

This is an account of how "H.H. Holmes (born Herman Webster Mudgett) dispatched somewhere between 27 and 200 people, mostly single young women, in the churning new metropolis of Chicago; many of the murders occurred during (and exploited) the city's finest moment, the World's Fair of 1893. Larson's breathtaking new history is a novelistic yet wholly factual account of the fair and the mass murderer who lurked within it." Publ Wkly

Includes bibliographical references

Lebsock, Suzanne

A murder in Virginia; Southern justice on trial. Norton 2003 442p il $26.95; pa $15.95

364.1

1. Trials (Homicide) 2. Virginia 3. Southern States—Race relations
ISBN 0-393-04201-4; 0-393-32606-3 (pa)

LC 2002-15946

"On a warm afternoon in June 1895, a 56-year-old white woman was brutally murdered in Lunenburg County, VA. Despite the absence of any truly incriminating eyewitness testimony or physical evidence, four blacks—three women and one man—were arrested and tried for the murder. Lebsock . . . recreates the subsequent trials, introducing the defendants, their prosecutors, and the witnesses and placing the proceedings within the context of the black and white communities and deteriorating conditions for African Americans in the post-Reconstruction South. Here historical narrative is every bit as intriguing as fictional mystery but more edifying for the information it gives its readers concerning race relations and criminal justice in the latter part of the 19th century." Libr J

Includes bibliographical references

Lévy, Bernard Henri, 1948-

Who killed Daniel Pearl? Melville House Pub 2003 454p $25.95; pa $16.95 * **364.1**

1. Pearl, Daniel, 1963-2002—Assassination 2. Homicide 3. Kidnapping
ISBN 0-9718659-4-9; 0-9749609-4-2 (pa)

LC 2003-13576

Levy reports on "the murder of the Wall Street Journal correspondent Daniel Pearl. . . . [He] follows the trail of the kidnappers to the highest reaches of Osama bin Laden's Al Qaeda and Pakistan's Inter-Services Intelligence agency, and to the links he claims exist between them." N Y Times Book Rev

Mallon, Thomas, 1951-

Mrs. Paine's garage and the murder of John F. Kennedy. Pantheon Bks. 2002 211p $22; pa $13
* **364.1**

1. Paine, Ruth 2. Oswald, Lee Harvey, 1939-1963 3. Oswald, Marina 4. Kennedy, John F. (John Fitzgerald), 1917-1963—Assassination
ISBN 0-375-42117-3; 0-15-602755-0 (pa)

LC 2001-36157

"A journalistic inquiry into Ruth Paine, the woman who welcomed Marina Oswald—and sometimes her husband, Lee—into her suburban Dallas home in 1963; it offers a new theory about the antecedents of the assassination." N Y Times Book Rev

McGinniss, Joe

Fatal vision. New American Library 1989 684p il pa $7.99 * **364.1**

1. MacDonald, Jeffrey R. 2. Homicide
ISBN 978-0-451-16566-4; 0-451-16566-7
"A Signet Book"
First published 1983 by Putnam

"The complex story of Jeffrey MacDonald, a Princeton-educated doctor and Green Beret captain who was accused of brutally murdering his wife and their two young daughters on a dreary February night in 1970." Best Sellers

"This is a wisely observant, well-written, and understated book." Harpers

Includes bibliographical references

Murakami, Haruki, 1949-

Underground; translated from the Japanese by Alfred Birnbaum and Philip Gabriel. Vintage Bks. 2001 366p map pa $14 **364.1**

1. Aum Shinrikyō 2. Terrorism
ISBN 0-375-72580-6 LC 00-69310
"The Tokyo gas attack and the Japanese psyche." Subtitle on cover

"On March 20, 1995, followers of the religious cult Aum Shinrikyo unleashed lethal sarin gas into cars of the Tokyo subway system. Many died, many more were injured. This is {Murakami's} . . . account of this episode." Publ Wkly

Newton, Michael, 1951-

The encyclopedia of unsolved crimes. Facts on File 2004 340p il (Facts on File crime library) $75; pa $21.95 **364.1**

1. Crime—Encyclopedias
ISBN 0-8160-4980-7; 0-8160-4981-5 (pa)

LC 2003-64286

"Entries range from the obvious (Jack the Ripper) to the obscure (Jack the Stripper); from political assassinations (Martin Luther King) to countless acts of violence against African Americans, especially those involved in the civil rights struggle; and from killings along American highways to unsolved crimes in other countries (the Butcher of Mons). Each entry is impressively researched and accessible; the JonBenet Ramsey and West Memphis Three entries, in particular, are models of economy and clarity." Choice

Includes bibliographical references

Olsen, Jack

I: the creation of a serial killer. St. Martin's Press 2002 365p il $24.95; pa $6.99

364.1

1. Jesperson, Keith Hunter 2. Homicide
ISBN 0-312-24198-4; 0-312-98384-0 (pa)

LC 2001-58892

Contains several autobiographical writings of serial killer Keith Hunter Jesperson

Olsen, Jack—*Continued*

The author draws "on interviews and his subject's own diaries to . . . reveal the life and inner workings of Keith Hunter Jesperson, currently serving life in prison for the murders of eight women in the 1990s." Publ Wkly

"A truly horrifying account of a serial killer, told with shocking candor." Booklist

Pepper, William F., 1937-

An act of state; the execution of Martin Luther King. Norton 2003 334p il map $25

364.1

1. King, Martin Luther, Jr., 1929-1968—Assassination
2. Conspiracies

ISBN 1-85984-695-5

Companion volume to Orders to kill (1995)

This book continues the author's examination of the life and death of Martin Luther King Jr.

"Forget everything you think you know, Pepper insists. James Earl Ray did not pull the trigger. . . . Pepper gradually introduces the vast cast of characters in a dizzying murder conspiracy that winds from a Memphis bar through the shadows of organized crime to the far reaches of national government. He carefully maps each player's place and role in the tangled web and doggedly tries to stick to a straightforward narrative. . . . Pepper attempts nothing less than a rewrite of history, and a spurring of further investigation." Publ Wkly

Includes bibliographical references

Queen, William

Under and alone; the true story of the undercover agent who infiltrated America's most violent outlaw motorcycle gang. Random House 2005 270p il $24.95

364.1

1. Gangs

ISBN 1-400-06084-2 LC 2004-51176

This is an "account of how Queen, a veteran agent within the Bureau of Alcohol, Tobacco and Firearms, posed as a hard-core biker." N Y Times Book Rev

"The strength and white-hot intensity of the writing make this read like a movie, and Hollywood is certain to take note." Publ Wkly

Raab, Selwyn

Five families; the rise, decline, and resurgence of America's most powerful Mafia empires. Thomas Dunne Books 2005 765p il $29.95 *

364.1

1. Mafia 2. Organized crime

ISBN 0-312-30094-8 LC 2005-48416

This book is divided "into three sections: one on Mafia history to 1970; a second on the F.B.I.'s awakening and the use of new RICO laws that culminated in the so-called Commission trial of 1985; and a final section that charts the subsequent fates of each of the five [crime] families." N Y Times Book Rev

"With vivid characterizations of a cavalcade of thugs, Raab's account is the most lively and informative Mafia history in years." Booklist

Includes bibliographical references

Reppetto, Thomas A.

American Mafia; a history of its rise to power; {by} Thomas Reppetto. H. Holt 2003 318p il $26; pa $15

364.1

1. Mafia

ISBN 0-8050-7210-1; 0-8050-7798-7 (pa)

LC 2003-56736

This is "a history of the rise of the Mafia in the world of crime and in the mainstream American political and economic life." Publisher's note

"Though this book doesn't answer every question about the Mafia in America, it does present a thought-provoking depiction of the Mob devoid of the sensationalism prevalent in many other portrayals." Publ Wkly

Includes bibliographical references

Rule, Ann

—and never let her go; Thomas Capano, the deadly seducer. Pocket Star Books 2000 680p il pa $7.99

364.1

1. Capano, Thomas J., 1949- 2. Fahey, Anne Marie 3. Homicide 4. Trials (Homicide)

ISBN 0-671-86871-3; 978-0-671-86871-0

First published 1999 by Simon & Schuster

"In June 1996, Anne Marie Fahey, a 30-year-old secretary to the governor of Delaware, disappeared and was reported missing by her family. In the weeks that followed, a charming, successful, and well-connected attorney, Tom Capano, was charged with her murder. Rule . . . tells the riveting story of the three-year secret affair between Fahey and Capano and a cruel obsession that led to murder." Booklist

Dead by sunset; perfect husband, perfect killer? Simon & Schuster 1995 429p il pa $7.99 hardcover o.p.

364.1

1. Keeton, Cheryl, 1949-1986 2. Cunningham, Bradly Morris 3. Trials (Homicide)

ISBN 0-671-00113-2 (pa) LC 95-38326

"Eight years after killing his divorced wife in Portland, Oregon, Brad Cunningham was finally convicted of her murder. . . . {Rule} tackles the case of the five-times-married Cunningham, whose loving personality and demeanor changed after each marriage." Booklist

"Rule's writing is crisp and well paced, full of details that give the reader clear insight into circumstances and surroundings, as well as motive." Libr J

Salamon, Julie

Facing the wind; a true story of tragedy and reconciliation. Random House 2001 302p pa $13.95 hardcover o.p.

364.1

1. Homicide

ISBN 0-375-75940-9 (pa) LC 00-42532

"In 1978, Bob Rowe, an out-of-work Brooklyn lawyer, killed his two sons, his daughter and wife by bashing their heads in with a baseball bat. He was found not guilty by reason of insanity, and after several years in a mental institution was released. He later remarried and had another daughter. Although journalist Salamon . . . did not interview Rowe before his death in 1997, this expertly crafted account is informed by diligent research and interviews with his second wife, Colleen, as well as with a women's support group to which Rowe's first wife, Mary, had belonged." Publ Wkly

Saviano, Roberto, 1979-

Gomorrah; translated from the Italian by Virginia Jewiss. Farrar, Straus & Giroux 2007 301p map $25   **364.1**

1. Organized crime 2. Italy

ISBN 978-0-374-16527-7; 0-374-16527-0

LC 2007-31004

Original Italian edition, 2006

This is the "tale of the Camorra, a network of thugs, exploiters and killers who run Naples and the surrounding countryside." Publ Wkly

This "is an eyepopping, hair-raising, stomach-turning book. The mob has never looked so bad—or read so well." Christ Sci Monit

Schiller, Lawrence

Perfect murder, perfect town. HarperCollins Pubs. 1999 621p pa $7.99 hardcover o.p.

364.1

1. Ramsey, JonBenet, d. 1996 2. Ramsey, Patsy 3. Ramsey, John Bennett 4. Boulder (Colo.). Police Dept. 5. Homicide

ISBN 0-06-109696-2 (pa)   LC 99-207248

This is an account of the investigation "of the murder of six-year-old child beauty-pageant winner JonBenét Ramsey in Boulder, Colorado, on the night of Christmas 1996." N Y Rev Books

Schiller argues that the "Boulder Police Department bungled the investigation, in large part out of ego and inexperience." N Y Times Book Rev

Sifakis, Carl

The mafia encyclopedia. 3rd ed. Facts on File 2005 510p il (Facts on File crime library) $65; pa $21.95 *   **364.1**

1. Mafia—Dictionaries

ISBN 0-8160-5694-3; 0-8160-5695-1 (pa)

LC 2004-58487

First published 1987

The author provides a "survey of the mob's most influential perpetrators and personalities, including their hangouts and hideaways, their plays for power, their schemes and crimes, and their unique culture and jargon." Publisher's note

"Sifakis provides detailed, informed, and colorful information." Libr J

Stewart, James B.

Blind eye; how the medical establishment let a doctor get away with murder. Simon & Schuster 1999 334p il pa $14 hardcover o.p.   **364.1**

1. Swango, Michael 2. Homicide

ISBN 0-684-86563-7 (pa)   LC 99-37044

Stewart discusses the "case against Dr. Michael Swango, a . . . physician suspected of poisoning between 35 and 60 patients and co-workers." Time

This is "not only a fascinating look at a psychopath masquerading as a healer but also a disturbing exposé of the system that fails to protect the public." Libr J

Thornhill, Randy

A natural history of rape; biological bases of sexual coercion; [by] Randy Thornhill and Craig T. Palmer. MIT Press 2000 251p $35; pa $16.95

364.1

1. Rape 2. Men—Sexual behavior

ISBN 0-262-20125-9; 0-262-70083-2 (pa)

LC 99-31685

The authors aim "to show that human rape is a 'natural, biological phenomenon that is a product of the human evolutionary heritage.' . . . Rape, they argue, was favored by natural selection to give sexually dispossessed males the chance to have children, or males with mates the chance to have extra children. . . . They further claim that attempts to root out rape will not succeed until one accepts its evolutionary origin and uses this . . . knowledge as a basis for social policy." New Repub

Includes bibliographical references

The Ultimate Jack the Ripper companion; an illustrated encyclopedia; {compiled by} Stewart P. Evans & Keith Skinner. Carroll & Graf Pubs. 2000 692p il $35; pa $16 *   **364.1**

1. Jack the Ripper 2. Homicide

ISBN 0-7867-0768-2; 0-7867-0926-X (pa)

LC 00-711560

Published in the United Kingdom with title: Ultimate Jack the Ripper sourcebook

This is a collection of primary and secondary source material pertaining to the Whitechapel murders

"This volume is undoubtedly the single largest resource on this case ever published." Libr J

Includes bibliographical references

Walsh, John

Public enemies; the host of America's most wanted targets the nation's most notorious criminals; [by] John Walsh with Philip Lerman. Pocket Bks. 2001 310p il $24.95; pa $7.99

364.1

1. America's most wanted (Television program) 2. Criminals 3. Crime

ISBN 0-671-01995-3; 0-671-01996-1 (pa)

LC 2001-34027

"From the media-popular 'Railroad Killer' to a remorseless member of the Symbionese Liberation Army with 25 years on the lam, to '70s iconoclast Ira Einhorn, who murdered his girlfriend and hid her body for 18 months in a steamer trunk, this title captures the television show's highlights." Publ Wkly

Wambaugh, Joseph

Fire lover; a true story. Morrow 2002 338p $25.95; pa $7.99   **364.1**

1. Orr, John 2. Arson

ISBN 0-06-009527-X; 0-06-009528-8 (pa)

LC 2002-20139

"John Orr was a Glendale, Calif., fire investigator who specialized in arson in more ways than one. . . . Mr. Orr has been linked to four deaths and millions of dollars of property damage. . . . Mr. Wambaugh begins by describing the most lethal fire." N Y Times (Late N Y Ed)

"Wambaugh's painstaking research which included interviews with law-enforcement officers, survivors, and victims' families, is astonishing." Booklist

Weisman, Steve, 1949-
50 ways to protect your identity and your credit; everything you need to know about identity theft, credit cards, credit repair, and credit reports. Prentice Hall 2005 xxii, 232p il pa $19.95 *

364.1

1. Identity theft 2. Consumer credit
ISBN 0-13-146759-X   LC 2004-112968
"This book takes a comprehensive look at the phenomenon of identity theft, explaining what it is, how it happens, how to protect yourself from it, and what to do if it does happen to you. . . . Full of good information presented in usable form, Weisman's book is recommended for public libraries." Libr J

Worrall, Simon
The poet and the murderer; a true story of literary crime and the art of forgery. Dutton 2002 270p il $23.95; pa $14   **364.1**
1. Hofmann, Mark 2. Forgery 3. Homicide
ISBN 0-525-94596-2; 0-452-28402-3 (pa)
                              LC 2001-53878
"In 1997, Sotheby's unveiled what experts believed was a newly discovered poem, 'That God Cannot Be Understood,' by Emily Dickinson. A few weeks later, the . . . discovery was revealed a forgery by a man who had already convincingly forged documents by more than 100 literary and historical figures, including Daniel Boone and Betsy Ross. This book examines the psychology of . . . forger and murderer (he killed two people who threatened his unmasking) Mark Hofmann." Booklist

364.152   Homicide

Bryan, Patricia L., 1951-
Midnight assassin; a murder in America's heartland; [by] Patricia L. Bryan & Thomas Wolf. Algonquin Books of Chapel Hill 2005 278p $23.95   **364.152**
1. Hossack, Margaret, 1843-1916 2. Trials (Homicide)
ISBN 1-565-12306-9   LC 2004-59782
Also available in paperback from University of Iowa Press
The authors discuss the circumstances surrounding and the trial following the "events of the night of December 1, 1900, when a well-to-do farmer named John Hossack was fatally attacked with an ax while sleeping in his bed. Suspicions soon focused on his long-suffering wife, Margaret, who claimed to have been asleep by her husband's side when the assault took place." Publ Wkly
Bryan and Wolf offer "not only an interesting trial drama but also a look into social attitudes of rural America at the beginning of the 20th century, especially toward women." Libr J
Includes bibliographical references

Burke, Timothy M.
The Paradiso files; Boston's unknown serial killer. Steerforth Press 2008 346p il $24.95
                              364.152
1. Paradiso, Leonard J., 1942-2008 2. Homicide
ISBN 978-1-58642-140-3; 1-58642-137-9
                              LC 2007-42576

"Nearly 24 years after attorney Timothy M. Burke locked up a Revere shellfish huckster for life for killing an East Boston woman, the former prosecutor is making his case that the portly predator is also a Bay State serial killer. . . . Burke alleges Leonard 'The Quahog' Paradiso is linked to the deaths of at least seven young women, including a Havard coed who vanished in 1981." Boston Herald
"Burke tells a compelling story, with chilling accounts of Paradiso's crimes gleaned from victims' accounts and evidence that never made it to court. . . . The story transcends Boston with an insider's view of the criminal justice system." Boston Globe

Buruma, Ian
Murder in Amsterdam; the death of Theo van Gogh and the limits of tolerance. Penguin Press 2006 278p $24.95 *   **364.152**
1. Gogh, Theo van—Assassination 2. Netherlands 3. Ethnic relations
ISBN 1-59420-108-0; 978-1-59420-108-0
                              LC 2006-43606
"The Netherlands may be the Western country most affected by radical Muslim violence, with two major assassinations since 9/11, those of politician Pym Fortuyn, who had called for restrictions on Muslim immigration . . . and media celebrity Theo Van Gogh, director of a film lambasting the Qur'an on women. Buruma returned to his homeland after Van Gogh's murder to gain understanding from figures in Dutch and Dutch Muslim politics and society who might provide it." Booklist
This is a "shrewd, subtly argued inquiry into the tensions and resentments underlying two of the most shocking events in the recent history of the Netherlands." N Y Times (Late N Y Ed)
Includes bibliographical references

Buss, David M.
The murderer next door; why the mind is designed to kill. Penguin Press 2005 278p $24.95
                              364.152
1. Homicide
ISBN 1-59420-043-2   LC 2005-43105
The author argues "that murder is the product of evolutionary forces and that the homicidal act, in evolutionary terms, conveys advantages to the killer. . . . Well argued and unsettling." Booklist
Includes bibliographical references

Diebel, Linda
Betrayed; the assassination of Digna Ochoa. Carroll & Graf 2006 513p il $27   **364.152**
1. Ochoa y Plácido, Digna, 1964-2001 2. Homicide
ISBN 0-7867-1753-X; 978-0-7867-1753-8
                              LC 2006-275515
First published 2005 in Canada
"Digna Ochoa, a Mexican human rights lawyer, died of a gunshot wound to the back of her head on October 19, 2001. The investigation into her death was reopened in 2005 after initially being ruled a suicide. Diebel . . . writes that there is no doubt that Ochoa was murdered for defending those tortured and harassed by the Mexican army." Libr J
Includes bibliographical references

Junger, Sebastian
A death in Belmont. Norton 2006 266p il
$23.95 *   **364.152**
1. DeSalvo, Albert, 1931-1973 2. Smith, Roy, d. 1976
3. Goldberg, Bessie, d. 1963 4. Homicide
ISBN 0-393-05980-4
In 1963, a murder took place in Belmont, Massachusetts, that resembled those committed by the Boston
Strangler. A black man, Roy Smith, who had worked in
Bessie Goldberg's house that day, was convicted of the
crime. "On the day of the murder, Albert DeSalvo—the
man who would eventually confess . . . to the Strangler's crimes—was also in Belmont, working as a carpenter at the Jungers' home. . . . Sebastian Junger [here]
chronicles three lives that collide." Publisher's note
"In [Albert] DeSalvo's dark world, Junger's clear,
beautifully reasonable writing is the literary equivalent of
night-vision goggles." Time
Includes bibliographical references

Kraybill, Donald B.
Amish grace; how forgiveness transcended
tragedy; [by] Donald B. Kraybill, Steven M. Nolt,
[and] David L. Weaver-Zercher. Jossey-Bass 2007
237p $24.95   **364.152**
1. West Nickel Mines Amish School (Pa.) 2. Amish
3. Forgiveness
ISBN 978-0-7879-9761-8; 0-7879-9761-7
This book explains "Amish reaction to the horrific
Nickel Mines shootings. . . . This anguished and devastating account of a national tragedy and a hopeful, life-
affirming lesson in how to live is itself a marvel of
grace." Booklist
Includes bibliographical references

Larson, Erik
Thunderstruck. Crown Publishers 2006 463p il
map $25.95 *   **364.152**
1. Crippen, Hawley Harvey, 1862-1910 2. Marconi,
Guglielmo, 1874-1937 3. Radio 4. Homicide
ISBN 1-4000-8066-5; 978-1-4000-8066-3
           LC 2006-11908
This book "alternates the story of Marconi's quest for
the first wireless transatlantic communication amid scien-
tific jealousies and controversies with the tale of [Dr.
Hawley Harvey Crippen,] a mild-mannered murderer
caught as a result of the invention. . . . A thrilling read."
SLJ
Includes bibliographical references

Leake, John, 1970-
Entering Hades; the double life of a serial killer.
Farrar, Straus & Giroux 2007 350p il $25
                       364.152
1. Unterweger, Jack, 1950-1994 2. Homicide
3. Criminals
ISBN 978-0-374-14845-4; 0-374-14845-7
           LC 2007-08644
"Sarah Crichton books"
This is a "study of traveling playwright, poet, and
prostitute killer Jack Unterweger. . . . Unterweger started
his dual career as criminal and crime reporter in his na-

tive Austria, where he was convicted at 18 for murdering
a prostitute. While in prison he became something of a
cause célèbre for European literati and their associates
because of his writings, including a revealing autobiography. Eventually, pronounced rehabilitated, he was released. He decamped for the bloody big time in L.A.
when an Austrian magazine engaged him to write about
. . . crime. He resumed his other trade in the U.S., using
the same method he had used from his first known killing: he strangled his victims with articles of their clothing." Booklist
The author "has written the definitive book—dispassionate, superbly detailed—on Jack Unterweger." N Y
Times Book Rev
Includes bibliographical references

May, Gary, 1944-
The informant; the FBI, the Ku Klux Klan, and
the murder of Viola Liuzzo. Yale University Press
2005 431p il $35   **364.152**
1. Liuzzo, Viola, 1925-1965 2. Ku Klux Klan
3. United States. Federal Bureau of Investigation
4. Homicide
ISBN 0-300-10635-1   LC 2005-2067
The author tells the "story of the murder of civil
rights worker Viola Liuzzo, shot to death by members of
the violent Birmingham Ku Klux Klan at the end of
Martin Luther King's historic Voting Rights March in
1965." Publisher's note
"This is popular history at its best and shines a long
overdue light on a dark chapter in the FBI's past." Publ
Wkly
Includes bibliographical references

Maynard, Joyce, 1953-
Internal combustion; the true story of a marriage
and a murder in the Motor City. Jossey-Bass 2006
490p il $24.95 *   **364.152**
1. Seaman, Nancy 2. Homicide
ISBN 978-0-7879-8226-3; 0-7879-8226-1
           LC 2006-17098
The author "serves up an examination of murder
among the middle class. The setting is a gated community in a suburb outside Detroit. On Mother's Day in 2004,
Nancy Seaman, the wife of a successful auto-industry engineer, herself an award-winning fourth-grade teacher,
bought a hatchet at Home Depot. Three days later, her
husband's mutilated body was found in the back of the
family's Ford. There is no mystery as to who committed
the crime. The mystery revolves around Nancy's defense,
which was based on battered-woman syndrome."
Booklist
"Though she was unable to get Nancy or most of her
immediate family to talk to her, Maynard seems to have
formed a surprisingly complete picture of their lives."
Libr J
Includes bibliographical references

Rivard, Robert
Trail of feathers: searching for Philip True; a
reporter's murder in Mexico and his editor's
search for justice. Public Affairs 2005 417p il
$27.50   **364.152**
1. True, Philip, d. 1998 2. Homicide
ISBN 1-58648-222-X   LC 2005-45822

Rivard, Robert—*Continued*
"In December 1998, . . . True set off on a 10-day expedition into the canyons of the Sierra Madre, hoping to write a story on the region's Huichol Indians. Rivard's book follows the agonizing six-year-long process by which he and others worked to find out what happened to True." Publ Wkly
"This is a fascinating look at an intriguing man and an alien culture." Libr J
Includes bibliographical references

Rule, Ann
Too late to say goodbye; a true story of murder and betrayal. Free Press 2007 456p il $26
364.152
1. Corbin, Jennifer, d. 2004 2. Homicide
ISBN 978-0-7432-3852-6; 0-7432-3852-4
LC 2007-9168
In this true crime account "Georgia dentist Barton Corbin kills his wife, Jennifer, and stages it to make it look like a suicide. One of the couple's young sons finds his mom's body. As it turns out, Corbin had disposed of a dental school girlfriend 14 years earlier by staging another 'suicide.' . . . What's particularly sad about Jennifer Corbin's death is the Internet affair she had hoped would rescue her from her miserable marriage: She had begun an online relationship with a man she knew as Christopher. . . . Jenn Corbin found out only weeks before her death that the new life she had been hoping for was no more real than the facade of her happy marriage to Bart Corbin." PopMatters
"Rule's meticulous 2½ years of research provides a cinematically satisfying look into how police in two jurisdictions worked together to prove Corbin was a serial murderer of women who tried to leave him." USA Today

Stashower, Daniel
The beautiful cigar girl; Mary Rogers, Edgar Allan Poe, and the invention of murder. Dutton 2006 326p il $25.95 **364.152**
1. Rogers, Mary, 1820-1841 2. Poe, Edgar Allan, 1809-1849 3. Homicide
ISBN 0-525-94981-X; 978-0-525-94981-7
LC 2006-19335
The author "tells the story of New York City cigar store clerk Mary Rogers, whose violent death in 1841 brought on a frenzy of sensational newspaper stories and prompted the interest of Edgar Allan Poe. . . . [He] details how the mystery surrounding Rogers's murder became the inspiration for Poe's story 'The Mystery of Marie Rogêt.' . . . Well researched and accessible, here is a gripping story that is hard to put down." Libr J
Includes bibliographical references

Summerscale, Kate, 1965-
The suspicions of Mr. Whicher; a shocking murder and the undoing of a great Victorian detective. Walker & Company 2008 360p il map $24.95 **364.152**
1. Whicher, Jonathan, 1814-1881 2. London (England) 3. Homicide
ISBN 978-0-8027-1535-7; 0-8027-1535-4
LC 2008-00247

This is the story of Inspector Jonathan Whicher of Scotland Yard, who investigated the 1860 murder of three-year-old Francis Saville Kent in the village of Road, Wiltshire.
The author's "clean writing makes . . . [this book] so dynamic that she can't be accused of 'freezing' the past—instead, she has done a masterly job of reviving it, with all its curiosities and contradictions. But, most strikingly, she has created an enthralling mystery by overlaying the fictional tools of misdirection and suspense onto a nonfiction narrative." Am Scholar
Includes bibliographical references

Swanson, James L.
Manhunt; the 12-day chase for Lincoln's killer. William Morrow 2006 448p il $26.95 *
364.152
1. Lincoln, Abraham, 1809-1865—Assassination 2. Booth, John Wilkes, 1838-1865
ISBN 0-06-051849-9
LC 2005-44911
This is an "account of the 12 days following Lincoln's assassination at Ford's Theatre on April 14, 1865." Libr J
While this book "belongs in the history section . . . it's as gripping a page-turner as anything you'll find on the mystery shelf." Entertainment Weekly
Includes bibliographical references

364.3 Offenders

Rhodes, Richard, 1937-
Why they kill; the discoveries of a maverick criminologist. Knopf 1999 371p $26.95; pa $14
364.3
1. Athens, Lonnie H. 2. Criminal psychology 3. Violence 4. Criminals
ISBN 0-375-40249-7; 0-375-70248-2 (pa)
LC 99-18920
The author discusses the history of violence and the work of social scientist Lonnie H. Athens. "Athens interviewed prisoners in maximum security prisons in Iowa, California and elsewhere, predominantly men. . . . His hope was to bypass inmates' typical narratives and get to what they actually thought and felt when they assaulted or raped or killed." N Y Times Book Rev
Includes bibliographical references

364.66 Capital punishment

Henderson, Harry, 1951-
Capital punishment. 3rd ed. Facts on File 2006 316p il (Library in a book) $45 *
364.66
1. Capital punishment
ISBN 0-8160-5708-7
LC 2005-13671
First published 1991 under the authorship of Stephen A. Flanders
A look at both sides of this controversial issue from social, political, ethical, and religious perspectives. Includes a glossary, bibliographies, and Internet sources.
Includes bibliographical references

Kurtis, Bill

The death penalty on trial; crisis in American justice. Public Affairs 2004 218p $25; pa $13.95

364.66

1. Capital punishment

ISBN 1-58648-169-X; 1-58648-446-X (pa)

LC 2004-50564

The author "re-examines his lifelong support of the death penalty, arguing eloquently that the risk of executing the wrong person is too great to let capital punishment stand. His reflections are motivated by the 2003 actions of then governor George Ryan of Illinois . . . who commuted the sentences of the state's 164 death row inmates. Ryan's actions followed the exoneration through DNA evidence of 13 death row inmates. Kurtis frames his argument around two trials in which the wrong men were first convicted and then exonerated." Publ Wkly

Prejean, Helen

The death of innocents; an eyewitness account of wrongful executions. Random House 2005 310p $25.95 *

364.66

1. Capital punishment

ISBN 0-679-44056-9

LC 2004-54154

The author "reexamines the cases of two men she fervently believes were executed for crimes they did not commit. . . . In addition to providing a searing indictment of capital punishment, Prejean also exposes the fundamental inadequacies of the American court system. Expect demand for this extremely thought-provoking book." Booklist

Includes bibliographical references

Solotaroff, Ivan

The last face you'll ever see; the private life of the American death penalty. HarperCollins Pubs. 2001 232p pa $12.95 hardcover o.p.

364.66

1. Capital punishment

ISBN 0-06-093103-5 (pa)

LC 2001-16604

In this examination of the death penalty the author "interviews the executioners who carry out the sentences. He concentrates on Parchman State Penitentiary in Mississippi and on two men, Donald Cabana, who quit his job as warden because he could not stomach the death penalty, and Donald Hocutt, who appears to relish his work yet suffers from a list of physical and psychological ailments." Libr J

"Entertainingly written, well researched and documented, this is important reading for death-penalty activists, pro and con, and other concerned citizens." Booklist

Includes bibliographical references

365   Penal and related institutions

Abbott, Jack Henry, 1944-2002

In the belly of the beast; letters from prison; with an introduction by Norman Mailer. Random House 1981 166p pa $12 hardcover o.p.

365

1. Prisoners 2. Prisons—United States

ISBN 0-679-73237-3 (pa)

LC 80-6038

The writer of these letters began them while "chained to the crossbar of his bed in the Butner, North Carolina Federal Correctional Institution. He addressed his letter to Norman Mailer. . . . {In these letters he} wished to convey something about the effect of {prison life on the individual}." Nation

Abbott's "letters belong with the best prison literature, not because of their accounts of atrocity, but for their disturbing picture of daily life behind bars." Time

Applebaum, Anne, 1964-

Gulag; a history. Doubleday 2003 677p il maps $35 *

365

1. Concentration camps 2. Convict labor 3. Soviet Union—Politics and government

ISBN 0-7679-0056-1

LC 2002-41344

This "describes how, largely under Stalin's watch, a regulated, centralized system of prison labor—unprecedented in scope—gradually arose out of the chaos of the Russian Revolution. . . . Applebaum details camp life, including strategies for survival; the experiences of women and children in the camps; sexual relationships and marriages between prisoners; and rebellions, strikes and escapes. . . . Applebaum's lucid prose and painstaking consideration of the competing theories about aspects of camp life and policy are always compelling." Publ Wkly

Includes bibliographical references

Encyclopedia of American prisons; editors, Marilyn D. McShane, Frank P. Williams III. Garland 1996 xxv, 532p il (Garland reference library of the humanities) $160

365

1. Prisons—United States—Encyclopedias

ISBN 0-8153-1350-0

LC 95-41593

This encyclopedia "traces the history and development of the major prisons in the United States and provides an overview of prison issues such as convicts with AIDS, prisoners' rights, and juveniles behind bars." Libr J

Encyclopedia of prisons & correctional facilities; Mary Bosworth, editor. Sage Publications 2005 2v il set $310 *

365

1. Prisons—United States—Encyclopedias

ISBN 0-7619-2731-X

LC 2004-21802

"A Sage Reference Publication"

The entries in this encyclopedia "revolve around 12 themes, among them theories of punishment, prison architecture, prison populations, juvenile justice, prison reform, treatment programs, and race, gender, and class. . . . Those interested in understanding the US's complex system of incarceration will find this encyclopedia a vital reference tool." Choice

Includes bibliographical references

Ferro, Jeffrey

Prisons. Facts on File 2006 314p il (Library in a book) $45 *

365

1. Prisons—United States

ISBN 0-8160-6035-5

LC 2005-3370

The author "gives an overview of American penitentiaries, tracking the history of prisons and punishments and offering thumbnail biographies of notorious criminals and law enforcers. . . . The title's value is that everything is found in one concise unit." Libr J

Includes bibliographical references

Goewey, David
Crash out; the true tale of a Hell's kitchen kid & the bloodiest escape in Sing Sing history. Crown 2005 304p il $24.95 **365**
1. Sing Sing Correctional Facility (N.Y.) 2. Escapes
ISBN 1-4000-5469-9   LC 2005-7531
The author details the "biggest prison break (crash out) in Sing Sing history, on Easter Sunday 1941. The story tracks back to a Hell's Kitchen gang that ran a series of headline-grabbing robberies; the crew, who would lead the crash out, were imprisoned after a 1939 heist from Consolidated Edison. Goewey's research is impressive: he interviewed the surviving guard on duty during the prison break, gained access to a scrapbook of news clips housed in the Ossining Historical Society, and combed the WPA Guide to New York City and case files from New York's Department of Records and Information Services. His writing produces a grim but fascinating snapshot of Depression-era crime." Booklist

Hubner, John
Last chance in Texas; the redemption of criminal youth. Random House 2005 xxv, 277p $25.95 **365**
1. Giddings State School (Tex.) 2. Juvenile delinquency
ISBN 0-375-50809-0   LC 2005-42892
This book is "about the Capital Offenders Group treatment program at Texas's Giddings State School. The institution houses nearly 400 of the most violent juvenile offenders in a program designed to alter the life trajectory of its residents." SLJ
"Readers of this eye-opening account will find themselves reflecting on their own attitudes about juvenile justice as it's administered today." Booklist

Khlevniuk, Oleg V.
The history of the Gulag; from collectivization to the great terror; foreword by Robert Conquest; translated by Vadim A. Staklo. Yale University Press 2004 418p il (Annals of communism) $45 **365**
1. Concentration camps 2. Convict labor 3. Soviet Union—Politics and government
ISBN 0-300-09284-9   LC 2004-10969
The author "uses Soviet-era archives to create a scholarly portrait of the gulag, focusing on the camps created from the 1929 collectivization of the kulaks to the beginning of World War II as essentially different from what went before—a crystallization of the system. Khlevniuk . . . aims to show how in the 1930s the gulag became a part of social policy." Libr J
This "is a fascinatingly detailed depiction of that horrific symbol of the 20th century, the Soviet prison camp system." Publ Wkly
Includes bibliographical references

Kizny, Tomasz, 1958-
Gulag; life and death inside the Soviet concentration camps. Firefly Books 2004 495p il maps $69.95 **365**
1. Concentration camps 2. Convict labor 3. Soviet Union—Politics and government
ISBN 1-55297-964-4   LC 2005-357207

This book "contains 550 black-and-white photographs of life in the Soviet Gulag. . . . The photos gathered here range from official archival snapshots, showing both inmates and their captors, to scenes of enormous construction projects and snowbound ruins. Kizny has added his own photographs of the abandoned camps or work projects and included a brief history of the camps and personal accounts of survivors. These rare and historically significant photographs can only hint at the appalling horrors committed within the camps, and the importance of the book cannot be overstated." Booklist

Oshinsky, David M., 1944-
"Worse than slavery"; Parchman Farm and the ordeal of Jim Crow justice. Free Press 1996 306p il pa $14 hardcover o.p. * **365**
1. Mississippi State Penitentiary 2. Prisons—United States 3. United States—Race relations
ISBN 0-684-83095-7 (pa)   LC 95-52880
This book examines Mississippi's "Parchman prison farm in the context of sharecropping, convict leasing, lynching and the legalized segregation that replaced slavery." N Y Times Book Rev
"Oshinsky's beautifully constructed narrative brings to vivid life one of the most shameful chapters in American history." New Yorker
Includes bibliographical references

Rees, Siân, 1965-
The floating brothel; the extraordinary true story of an eighteenth-century ship and its cargo of female convicts. Hyperion 2002 236p il maps $23.95 **365**
1. Women criminals 2. Prisoners 3. Penal colonies
ISBN 0-7868-6787-6   LC 2001-46338
"This work of nautical history recounts the 1789-90 voyage from England to Australia of a ship full of female convicts." Libr J
"Rees uses every scrap of information she can muster to produce a lively, vibrant sense of these women as they must have lived their lives." Publ Wkly
Includes bibliographical references

Solzhenitsyn, Aleksandr, 1918-2008
The Gulag Archipelago, 1918-1956 v1; an experiment in literary investigation; [by] Aleksandr I. Solzhenitsyn; translated from the Russian by Thomas P. Whitney; foreword by Anne Applebaum. Harper Perennial Modern Classics 2007 xx, 660p pa $21.95 * **365**
1. Political prisoners 2. Soviet Union—Politics and government
ISBN 978-0-06-125371-3; 0-06-125371-5
All three volumes also available in one abridged paperback edition $18.95 (ISBN-13: 978-0-06-125380-5)
First published 1974
The first volume of the author's three-volume "'literary investigation' of the network of Soviet prison camps as they existed between 1918 and 1956. . . . A mixture of autobiography, history, and analysis, the relentlessly grim picture of life inside the camps forms the basis for an attack not only on Stalinism and Leninism but also on

Solzhenitsyn, Aleksandr, 1918-2008—*Continued*
the whole process of substituting Western rational and secular ideas for Russia's traditional mysticism." Benét's Reader's Ency. 4th edition

The Gulag Archipelago, 1918-1956 v2; an experiment in literary investigation; [by] Aleksandr I. Solzhenitsyn; translated from the Russian by Thomas P. Whitney; foreword by Anne Applebaum. Harper Perennial Modern Classics 2007 712p il map pa $21.95 *   **365**
    1. Political prisoners 2. Soviet Union—Politics and government
    ISBN 978-0-06-125372-0; 0-06-125372-3
    First published 1975
    This second volume of a two-volume series describes "the story of Solzhenitsyn's entrance into the Soviet prison camps, where he would remain for nearly a decade." Publisher's note

The Gulag Archipelago, 1918-1956 v3; an experiment in literary investigation; [by] Aleksandr I. Solzhenitsyn; translated from the Russian by Harry Willetts; foreword by Anne Applebaum. Harper Perennial Modern Classics 2007 558p il map pa $21.95 *   **365**
    1. Political prisoners 2. Soviet Union—Politics and government
    ISBN 978-0-06-125373-7; 0-06-125373-1
    First published 1978
    The final volume of a three-volume series, this book contains the author's "account of resistance within the Soviet labor camps and his own release after eight years." Publisher's note

Wynn, Jennifer
Inside Rikers; stories from the world's largest penal colony. St. Martin's Press 2001 223p $24.95; pa $13.95   **365**
    1. Rikers Island Prison (New York, N.Y.) 2. Prisoners
    ISBN 0-312-26179-9; 0-312-29158-2 (pa)
        LC 2001-19261
    The author presents an "exploration of inmates' lives in New York's 'vast penal colony,' Rikers Island." Publ Wkly
    "Wynn's study is ultimately a call for much-needed prison reform, with emphasis on rehabilitation rather than mere incarceration, and she makes her case well." Booklist
    Includes bibliographical references

366 Associations

Ridley, Jasper Godwin
The Freemasons; a history of the world's most powerful secret society; {by} Jasper Ridley. Arcade Pub. 2001 357p $25.95; pa $14.95 *   **366**
    1. Freemasons
    ISBN 1-55970-601-5; 1-55970-654-6 (pa)
        LC 2001-45745

The author "traces the origins of freemasonry back to the craft guilds in medieval Europe, and then he chronicles their growth and evolution through the modern era. . . . This work of popular history sheds light on a frequently obscure subject." Booklist
Includes bibliographical references

368.4 Government-sponsored insurance

Altman, Nancy J., 1950-
The battle for Social Security; from FDR's vision to Bush's gamble. Wiley 2005 362p $24.95 *   **368.4**
    1. Social security
    ISBN 978-0-471-77172-2; 0-471-77172-4
        LC 2005-20700
    The author "traces the history of Social Security from its introduction in 1935, and provides a thoughtful, well-researched case against the . . . [Bush] administration's efforts to reduce Social Security protection." Booklist
    Includes bibliographical references

370 Education

Encyclopedia of education; James W. Guthrie, editor in chief. 2nd ed. Macmillan Ref. USA 2003 8v il set $850 *   **370**
    ISBN 0-02-865594-X   LC 2002-8205
    First published 1971
    This set includes over 850 signed articles covering educational policy and curriculum issues, learning assessment, standards, history and culture, legislation, and profiles of schools, people, and organizations.
    "The writing is well edited and accessible." Booklist
    Includes bibliographical references

Hirsch, E. D. (Eric Donald), 1928-
The schools we need and why we don't have them; {by} E.D. Hirsch, Jr. Doubleday 1996 317p pa $14.95 hardcover o.p.   **370**
    1. Education
    ISBN 0-385-49524-2 (pa)   LC 96-2192
    The author argues that "our current educational system has failed to reduce social inequity or enhance our economic competitiveness. . . . Hirsch pleads for abandoning Progressivism's 'process' methodology in favor of a curriculum based on challenging content, common knowledge acquisition, and rigorous standardized testing." Libr J
    This "book presents a sophisticated, scholarly and often compelling argument and it deserves serious consideration, whatever one's political predilections." N Y Times Book Rev
    Includes bibliographical references

Postman, Neil
The end of education; redefining the value of school. Knopf 1995 209p pa $13.95 hardcover o.p.   **370**
    1. Education—United States
    ISBN 0-679-75031-2 (pa)   LC 94-46605

Postman, Neil—*Continued*

"The volume initially investigates American education in the earlier part of this century. . . . Part 2 shifts focus to contemporary education, describing the underlying conceptions of today's schools and considering economic utility, consumership, technology, and separatism. . . . Postman responds creatively to the problems of 'modernity,' holding out hope for regaining a sense of purpose and respect for learning." Choice

"Beautifully written, breathtakingly high-minded, this is Postman's best book on American education." Booklist

Includes bibliographical references

Unger, Harlow G., 1931-

Encyclopedia of American education. 3rd ed. Facts on File 2007 3v il (Facts on File library of American history) set $250 *   **370**

1. Education—United States—Encyclopedias
ISBN 0-8160-6887-9; 978-0-8160-6887-6
LC 2006-22174

First published 1996

This encyclopedia "contains more than 2,000 entries spanning the colonial period to the present. This . . . [reference provides information on different aspects] of education, from the evolution of school curriculum, education funding, and church-state controversies to . . . debates on multiculturalism, prayer in school, and sex education." Publisher's note

Includes bibliographical references

370.1 Philosophy and theory, education for specific objectives, educational psychology

Dewey, John, 1859-1952

Democracy and education; an introduction to the philosophy of education. Free Press 1997 378p pa $17.95   **370.1**

1. Education—Philosophy
ISBN 0-684-83631-9; 978-0-684-83631-7

First published 1916 by Macmillan

"The author's aim here is to detect and state the ideas implied in a democratic society and to apply those ideas to the problems of education." Boston Transcr

370.15 Educational psychology

Levine, Melvin D.

A mind at a time; [by] Mel Levine. Simon & Schuster 2002 352p $26; pa $14   **370.15**

1. Educational psychology 2. Child development 3. Learning disabilities
ISBN 0-7432-0222-8; 0-7432-0223-6 (pa)
LC 2001-57670

The author discusses "eight areas of learning (the memory system, the language system, the spatial ordering system, the motor system, etc.). He provides chapters describing how each type of learning works and advises parents and teachers on how to help kids struggling in these areas. . . . This is a must-read for parents and edu-

cators who want to understand and improve the school lives of children." Publ Wkly

Includes bibliographical references

370.25 Education—Directories

The **Handbook** of private schools; an annual descriptive survey of independent education. 89th ed. Sargent Pubs. il map $99 *   **370.25**

1. Private schools—Directories 2. Education—United States—Directories
ISSN 0072-9884
ISBN 978-0-87558-165-1; 0-87558-165-X

Annual. First published 1915 with title: Handbook of the best private schools of the United States and Canada

"Describes more than 1,700 boarding and day schools, providing information on age and grade ranges, whether co-educational or for boys or girls, enrollment, faculty size and background, academic orientation and curriculum, and where graduates attend college. 'Features classifield' section lists institutions offering military programs, elementary boarding divisions, programs for students with learning differences, international and bilingual schools, and schools with more than 500 or fewer than 100 students." Guide to Ref Books. 11th edition

Patterson's American education, Volume CIV; editor, Wayne Moody. 2008 ed., 104th ed. Educational Directories 2008 973p $94 *   **370.25**

1. Education—United States—Directories
ISSN 0079-0230
ISBN 978-0-9771602-6-6; 0-9771602-6-2

Annual. First published 1904

"The first part lists public, private, and Catholic junior high school and high school districts, and combined elementary and secondary districts. Arranged by state, beginning with addresses of officials of state departments of education; then by community; then by district, with names of top officials; then by individual schools, giving names, addresses, and phone numbers of principals. . . . The second part consists of a directory of schools classified by specialty." Guide to Ref Books. 11th edition

Private independent schools, 2008; a comprehensive guide to elementary and secondary schools in North America and abroad. 61st ed. Bunting & Lyon 2008 xxxii, 430p il $115 *   **370.25**

1. Private schools—Directories
ISSN 0079-5399
ISBN 978-0-913094-61-7; 0-913094-61-7

Annual. First published 1943 with title: Independent schools, a directory. Title varies

At head of title: The Bunting and Lyon blue book

"Describes some 1,000 American and 100 foreign boarding and day schools, from kindergarten through high school, plus one-year post-high school programs. Roughly a quarter of the entries are descriptive; the remainder give the school's size, age range, application procedures, administrative control, cost, and special programs, plus a brief statement of its philosophy. A classification grid, arranged by state, identifies institutions

Private independent schools, 2008—*Continued*
with specific characteristics, such as military programs,
church affiliation, and restriction to one sex. Separate
section on summer programs emphasizing academics,
recreation, or travel." Guide to Ref Books. 11th edition

370.3   Education—Encyclopedias and dictionaries

The **Greenwood** dictionary of education; edited by
John W. Collins III and Nancy Patricia O'Brien;
foreword by Catherine Snow. Greenwood Press
2003 431p $59.95 *   **370.3**
1. Education—Dictionaries
ISBN 0-89774-860-3   LC 2003-51766
"An Oryx book"
"The editors asked . . . experts in various fields of
education (e.g., early childhood education, curriculum,
adult education, and language acquisition) to write definitions for the volume's 2600 terms, which are used in education research, practice, and theory. . . . It also contains . . . information on how to use the volume, an alphabetical arrangement of entries, cross references, a bibliography of sources, lists of contributing editors and
contributors arranged by field, and a list of contributors
arranged by initials (so that users can identify entry authors). . . . No library, whether public or academic,
should be without this reference source." Libr J

370.9   Education—Historical, geographic, persons treatment

Wood, John
Leaving Microsoft to change the world; an
entrepreneur's odyssey to educate the world's
children. Collins 2006 272p il $25.95; pa $15.95
                                       370.9
1. Room to Read (Organization)
ISBN   0-06-112107-X;   978-0-06-112107-4;
0-06-112108-8 (pa); 978-0-06-112108-1 (pa)
                           LC 2006-41601
The author, "who was a senior executive at Microsoft
in the 1990s, tells how he went on to found and manage
the successful global nonprofit Room to Read, which has
. . . established more than 2000 schools and libraries
and donated over a million books to them throughout
Asia." Libr J
"Marked by sincerity and savvy, this is the kind of
book that business colleagues will discuss with their acquaintances, spouses and friends." Publ Wkly

371   Schools and their activities; special education

Gross, Martin L. (Martin Louis), 1925-
The conspiracy of ignorance; the failure of
American public schools. HarperCollins Pubs.
2000 291p $25; pa $14   **371**
1. Public schools—United States 2. Education—United
States
ISBN 0-06-019458-8; 0-06-093260-0 (pa)
                           LC 99-34783
Gross examines the current state of public schools in
the United States and argues for the need for reform
Includes bibliographical references

371.04   Alternative schools

Rupp, Rebecca
The complete home learning sourcebook; the
essential resource guide for homeschoolers,
parents, and educators covering every subject from
arithmetic to zoology. Three Rivers Press (NY)
1998 865p pa $29.95 *   **371.04**
1. Home schooling
ISBN 0-609-80109-0   LC 98-38440
Arranged by subject, this resource reviews: books,
videos, magazines, catalogs, timelines, kits, hands-on activities, board games, CD-ROMs, and educational web
sites. Icons denote format and intended age group of
each resource
Includes bibliographical references

371.1   Teachers and teaching, and related activities

Barzun, Jacques, 1907-
Begin here; the forgotten conditions of teaching
and learning; editor, Morris Philipson. University
of Chicago Press 1991 222p $24.95; pa $21
                                        371.1
1. Teaching 2. Psychology of learning
ISBN 0-226-03846-7; 0-226-03847-5 (pa)
                           LC 90-25877
"Some of the topics Barzun addresses include the inadequate ways in which reading is taught; the demeaning
methods of teacher training; the counterfeit 'social
studies' programs which are the offshoot of combined
geography and history curriculums; the benefits of reading the classics; and how television affects learning."
Libr J
Includes bibliographical references

Kozol, Jonathan
Letters to a young teacher. Crown Publishers
2007 288p $19.95   **371.1**
1. Teaching
ISBN 978-0-307-39371-5; 0-307-39371-2
                           LC 2007-2689

Kozol, Jonathan—*Continued*

"Through the framing device of actual letters to a first-year grade school teacher at a New England inner-city school, Kozol . . . shares his passions about the education of children, including his opinion that vouchers will benefit the wealthy at the expense of the poor, deep concerns about the privatization of public education, and ongoing disdain for the dishonesty he discerns lying behind the rhetoric about equality in education." Libr J

"The book will delight and encourage first-year (or for that matter, 40th-year) teachers who need Kozol's reminders of the ways that their beautiful profession can bring joy and beauty, mystery and mischievous delight into the hearts of little people in their years of greatest curiosity." Publ Wkly

Includes bibliographical references

Parini, Jay

The art of teaching. Oxford University Press 2005 160p $17.95 **371.1**

1. Teaching 2. Vocational guidance

ISBN 0-19-516969-7   LC 2004-5443

The author offers "musings about teaching's demands and what it takes to not lose one's other, creative self while meeting those demands in this memoir-cum-advice book for novice instructors. . . . This warm guide should inform, entertain, and inspire young teachers as they seek to 'waken a student to his or her potential.'" Publ Wkly

371.2 School administration; administration of student academic activities

Kohn, Alfie

The schools our children deserve; moving beyond traditional classrooms and "tougher standards". Houghton Mifflin 1999 344p $24; pa $14 **371.2**

1. Education—United States 2. Education—Aims and objectives

ISBN 0-395-94039-7; 0-618-08345-6 (pa)

     LC 99-31122

The author challenges the "back-to-basics" approach to education and test-driven "tougher standards," advocating instead the teaching of creative and critical thinking skills

"Parents as well as educators should read this remarkable book." Libr J

Includes bibliographical references

371.3 Methods of instruction and study

Braun, Linda W.

Listen up! podcasting for schools and libraries. Information Today, Inc. 2007 97p il pa $29.50

     371.3

1. Podcasting

ISBN 978-1-57387-304-8   LC 2007-23650

"In six conversational chapters, Braun explains podcasting's technical terms, ongoing development, necessary components such as an RSS feed and a feed reader, creating subscriptions, and methods of distribution." SLJ

"This is a valuable resource for those interested in learning more about podcasting and utilizing the technology to improve their programming and outreach." Booklist

Includes bibliographical references

Britton, Lesley

Montessori play & learn; a parents' guide to purposeful play from two to six; with an introduction by Joy Starrey Turner. Crown 1992 144p il pa $19.95 **371.3**

1. Montessori method of education 2. Parenting

ISBN 0-517-59182-0   LC 92-5446

This describes educational activities for two to six year olds according to the Montessori method which parents can introduce at home

Montessori, Maria, 1870-1952

The Montessori method; introduction by J. McV. Hunt. Schocken Bks. 1964 xxxix, 376p il pa $14 hardcover o.p. * **371.3**

1. Montessori method of education

ISBN 0-8052-0922-0 (pa)

Originally published in Italy; first published 1912 in the United States

This is an introduction to the author's teaching methods. The Montessori system emphasizes the development of individuality in the child and the careful training of the senses. Education is controlled by interpersonal relations between the children rather than between teacher and child

Ravitch, Diane

The language police; how pressure groups restrict what students learn. Knopf 2003 255p $24; pa $13 * **371.3**

1. Books—Censorship

ISBN 0-375-41482-7; 1-4000-3064-1 (pa)

     LC 2002-40622

The author argues that publishers are "succumbing to political interests and thus producing bland, geographically indistinguishable, and historically inaccurate textbooks and test questions for use in American schools. . . . Parents, educators, students, and the general public will find this detailed and highly readable analysis alarming." Libr J

Includes bibliographical references

371.3025 Audiovisual materials— Directories

AV market place 2008. Information Today 1700p il pa $199.95 **371.3025**

1. Audiovisual materials—Directories

ISSN 1044-0445

ISBN 978-1-57387-316-1; 1-57387-316-0

Annual. First published 1969 with title: Audiovisual market place. Subtitle varies

AV market place 2008—*Continued*

"The complete business directory of: audio, audio visual, computer systems, film, video, programming—with industry yellow pages." Title page

371.9   Special education

The **directory** for exceptional children; a comprehensive listing of special-needs schools, programs and facilities, 2007-08. 16th ed. Sargent Pubs. 2007 1151p $75 *

          371.9

1. Exceptional children—Education—Directories

ISSN 0070-5012

ISBN 978-0-87558-160-6; 0-87558-160-9

First published 1954. Periodically revised

"Contains 14 sections on facilities for specific handicaps (residential facilities for mentally retarded persons, speech and hearing clinics, etc.); within each section, entries are arranged geographically. Each entry includes names of directors, medical directors, and admissions officers, as well as information on which handicaps are targeted; grades served; academic orientation and curriculum; therapy offerings; enrollment; staff; fees and financial aid; summer programs; and organizational structure; plus descriptive text. List of associations, foundations, and societies for specific disabilities; directory of state agency personnel." Guide to Ref Books. 11th edition

Hayden, Torey L.

Beautiful child; [by] Torey Hayden. HarperCollins Pubs. 2002 326p $24.95; pa $7.50

          371.9

1. Special education

ISBN 0-380-81339-4; 0-06-050887-6 (pa)

          LC 2001-39928

This is "the story of a scruffy seven-year-old, Venus, who is so unresponsive that Hayden searches for signs of deafness, brain damage or mental retardation. . . . Hayden sets Venus's bittersweet and complex story against the backdrop of other students. . . . In this first-person narrative, Hayden also shares her own thoughts, worries and strained relationship with a mismatched classroom aide, creating a rich tapestry of the dynamics of a group of special needs youngsters and the adults who try to help them." Publ Wkly

Kozol, Jonathan

Savage inequalities; children in America's schools. HarperPerennial 1992 261p pa $14.95

          371.9

1. Public schools 2. Socially handicapped children 3. Segregation in education

ISBN 0-06-097499-0; 978-0-06-097499-2

First published 1991 by Crown

In 1988, Kozol "visited schools in over 30 neighborhoods, including East St. Louis, Harlem, the Bronx, Chicago, Jersey City, and San Antonio. In this account, he concludes that real integration has seriously declined and education for minorities and the poor has moved backwards by at least several decades." Libr J

"Jonathan Kozol has written an impassioned book,

laced with anger and indignation, about how our public education system scorns so many of our children. 'Savage Inequalities' is also an important book, and warrants widespread attention" N Y Times Book Rev

Includes bibliographical references

Shaywitz, Sally E.

Overcoming dyslexia; a new and complete science-based program for reading problems at any level; {by} Sally Shaywitz. Knopf 2003 416p il $25.95; pa $15 *

          371.9

1. Dyslexia 2. Reading disability

ISBN 0-375-40012-5; 0-679-78159-5 (pa)

          LC 2002-40621

The author "explains what causes dyslexia, how to identify it, and how to help children and adults overcome it. . . . In part 1, she explores the early history of diagnosing reading problems, biases that have crept into the evaluations of reading disabilities, and how dyslexic children are treated in schools. Part 2 explores new theories on identifying and treating dyslexia. Part 3 offers practical advice and exercises to help children become better readers year by year, and part 4 focuses on overcoming the disability. . . . Parents and teachers will appreciate this tremendously helpful resource." Booklist

Includes bibliographical references

Siegel, Bryna

Helping children with autism learn; treatment approaches for parents and professionals. Oxford Univ. Press 2003 498p $30; pa $18.95

          371.9

1. Autism 2. Special education

ISBN 0-19-513811-2; 0-19-532506-0 (pa)

          LC 2002-151673

"Siegel explains how to take an inventory of a child's particular disabilities, breaks down the various kinds unique to autism, discusses our current knowledge about each, and reviews the existing strategies for treating them." Publisher's note

"Carefully tailoring her book to multiple audiences, with free use of commentary and introductory notes, Siegel . . . excels at showing what parents and educators need to do to reach autistic children. She includes a valuable section on having successful individualized educational programs (IEPs), the standard for children with special needs." Libr J

Includes bibliographical references

Turkington, Carol

The encyclopedia of learning disabilities; [by] Carol Turkington, Joseph R. Harris, American Bookworks. 2nd ed. Facts on File 2006 304p (Facts on File library of health and living) $75; pa $19.95 *

          371.9

1. Learning disabilities—Encyclopedias

ISBN   0-8160-6399-0;   978-0-8160-6399-4; 0-8160-6400-8 (pa); 978-0-8160-6400-7 (pa)

          LC 2005-53045

First published 2002

This encyclopedia is a "guide to all types of learning disabilities, including how they function, how they can

Turkington, Carol—*Continued*
be diagnosed, and how they can be treated." Publisher's note

This book "offers a wealth of information useful to teachers, health-care providers, and parents as they seek to communicate and learn about particular developmental and learning problems." Booklist

Includes bibliographical references

372   Elementary education

Dewey, John, 1859-1952
The school and society, and The child and the curriculum; introduction by Philip W. Jackson. University of Chicago Press 1990 xli, 209p pa $11 hardcover o.p. *   372
  1. Elementary education
  ISBN 0-226-14396-1 (pa)   LC 90-43528
  A combined edition of two essays first published separately in 1899 and 1902 respectively
  Both of these works stress the functional relationship between classroom learning activities and real life experiences and analyze the social and psychological nature of the learning process. They present and defend the underlying tenets of Dewey's philosophy of education

372.4   Reading

Flesch, Rudolf Franz, 1911-1986
Why Johnny can't read—and what you can do about it. Harper & Row 1955 222p pa $13 hardcover o.p. *   372.4
  1. Reading 2. Phonetics—Study and teaching
  ISBN 0-06-091340-1 (pa)
  Also available in hardcover from Buccaneer Bks.
  Companion volume to Why Johnny still can't read (1981)
  The author advocates the alphabetic-phonetic system of teaching children to read. He includes step-by-step directions and phonetic drills for use by parents

372.6   Language arts (Communication skills)

Maguire, James, 1959-
American bee; the National Spelling Bee and the culture of word nerds: the lives of five top spellers as they compete for glory and fame. Rodale 2006 371p $24.95 *   372.6
  1. Spelling bees 2. English language—Spelling
  ISBN 978-1-59486-214-4; 1-59486-214-1
                                          LC 2005-37443
  "From the nail-biting denouement of the 2004 Bee, Maguire . . . moves on to brief sketches of some past winners and then takes an informative and wryly humorous look at the English language itself and the evolution of the American spelling bee from Puritan pastime to major media event." Libr J
  Includes bibliographical references

Seeger, Pete
Pete Seeger's storytelling book; by Pete Seeger and Paul Du Bois Jacobs. Harcourt 2000 264p $24; pa $14   372.6
  1. Storytelling
  ISBN 0-15-100370-X; 0-15-601311-8 (pa)
                                          LC 00-29599
  "The tales themselves, tape-recorded by Seeger and re-written by Jacobs . . . are grouped roughly by origin. They range from family stories to versions of Bible tales to stories inspired by songs, history, legends, and Seeger's own imagination. In an introduction to each chapter, Seeger explains the source of the tales and offers suggestions for scouting similar ones. Each story, ready to read aloud or tell, concludes with possible variations, themes, morals, and, sometimes, music." Booklist

373.1   Organization and activities in secondary education

GED: high school equivalency exam; [by] Murray Rockowitz [et al.] Barron's Educ. Ser. 2007 931p il map pa $29.99 *   373.1
  1. High school equivalency examination
  ISBN 978-0-7641-9322-4; 0-7641-9322-8
  Also available paperback edition without CD-ROM $18.99 (ISBN: 978-0-7641-3641-2) and CD-ROM edition
  First published 1968. Frequently revised. Previous title: How to prepare for the GED high school equivalency examination
  Accompanied by CD-ROM. Title on cover: GED 2007-2008
  General advice on how to study and specific suggestions on reviewing for and taking the tests are followed by sample questions in the five areas covered—writing, mathematics, social studies, science, and reading.

Master the GED 2009; teacher-tested strategies and techniques for scoring high; [by] Ronald M. Kaprov, Steffi R. Kaprov. 23rd ed. Peterson's 2008 xx, 860p pa $29.95 *   373.1
  1. High school equivalency examination
  ISBN 978-0-7689-2627-9; 0-7689-2627-0
  Also available paperback edition without CD-ROM $18.95 (ISBN 978-0-7689-2626-2)
  First published 1962 with title: High school equivalency diploma test (GED). Periodically revised. Title varies
  At head of title: Arco; Accompanied by CD-ROM
  This guide to preparing for the General Educational Development (GED) battery of tests includes practice in reading, writing, mathematics, science, and social studies

373.2   Secondary schools and programs of specific kinds, levels, curricula, focus

Peterson's private secondary schools 2009. Peterson's 2008 1488p il $30 *   373.2
  1. Private schools—Directories
  ISSN 1066-5366
  ISBN 978-0-7689-2543-2; 0-7689-2543-6
  Annual. First published 1980. Title varies

Peterson's private secondary schools 2009—
Continued

"Describes more than 1,600 American and foreign boarding and day schools including schools that serve children with special needs. Outlines each institution's setting; enrollment by sex, race, grade, and geographic origin; faculty size and educational background; facilities; subjects offered; special programs; graduation requirements; tuition; admissions procedures; and where the graduates go to college." Guide to Ref Books. 11th edition

374   Adult education

John, Lauren Z.

Running book discussion groups; a how-to-do-it manual; [by] Lauren Zina John. Neal-Schuman Publishers 2006 250p (How-to-do-it manual for librarians) pa $55 *   **374**

1. Discussion groups 2. Books and reading
ISBN 1-55570-542-1; 978-1-55570-542-8
LC 2006-704

This is a "step-by-step guide to the tasks and responsibilities librarians are likely to encounter as book-group leaders conducting booktalks both on-site and online. . . . This is essential reading for anyone who may be considering taking on the role of a book-discussion-group leader and a refresher for the more experienced among us." Booklist

Includes bibliographical references

378   Higher education

Steinberg, Jacques

The gatekeepers; inside the admissions process of a premier college. Viking 2002 xxiii, 292p hardcover o.p. pa $15   **378**

1. Wesleyan University (Middletown, Conn.)
2. College applications
ISBN 0-670-03135-6; 0-14-200308-5 (pa)
LC 2002-16884

The author follows "the procedures at Wesleyan University for a year . . . [to] see how the admissions process really looks, to the admitters as well as the applicants." N Y Times Book Rev

"This insightful and readable book should be purchased by all academic and large public libraries." Libr J

Includes bibliographical references

Women in higher education; an encyclopedia; Ana M. Martinez Alemán and Kristen A. Renn, editors. ABC-CLIO 2002 xxiv, 637p il $85 *   **378**

1. Higher education 2. Women—Education
ISBN 1-57607-614-8   LC 2002-11570

This resource "on women and higher education presents multipage essays organized in nine sections covering historical and cultural contexts, gender theory, feminism, curriculum, policy, and women as students, faculty, administrators, and employees. . . . Destined to become a classic." Choice

Includes bibliographical references

378.1   Organization and activities in higher education

Barron's ACT; [by] George Ehrenhaft . . . [et al.] 15th ed. Barron's Educ. Ser. 2008 686p il pa $18.99 *   **378.1**

1. ACT assessment 2. Colleges and universities—Entrance requirements
ISBN 978-0-7641-4000-6; 0-7641-4000-0

Also available with CD-ROM $29.99 (ISBN: 978-0-7641-9488-7)

First published 1972 with title: Barron's how to prepare for the American College Testing Program (ACT). Continues How to prepare for the ACT, American College Testing Assessment Program, Barron's How to prepare for the ACT assessment, and Barron's ACT assessment. Frequently revised. Editors vary

A guide to achieving higher scores on the ACT which includes subject reviews and practice exams with answers.

Doster, William C., 1921-1999

CLEP 2008; William Doster . . . [et al.] 10th ed. Barron's Educational Series 2007 730p pa $16.99 *   **378.1**

1. College Level Examination Program
ISBN 978-0-7641-3639-9; 0-7641-3639-9
LC 2007-7101

Also available book with CD-ROM edition $29.99 (ISBN: 978-0-7641-9320-0)

First published 1973 with title: Barron's how to prepare for the College-Level Examination Program, CLEP

At head of title: Barron's. Title on cover: CLEP 2007-2008

"The CLEP, or College Level Examination Program, is a battery of tests given as a set of college entrance exams to adults returning to the classroom after an absence of several years. . . . [This] manual presents three full-length sample examinations in each of the test areas covered in this book and provides answer keys, a scoring chart, and answer explanations for all exams. It also presents subject reviews in five CLEP test topics with additional practice and review questions. Test topics covered are the English Composition Exam, the Humanities Exam, the College Mathematics Exam, the Natural Sciences Exam, and the Social Sciences—History Exam." Publisher's note

Fiske, Edward B.

Fiske guide to getting into the right college; [by] Edward B. Fiske & Bruce G. Hammond. 3rd ed. Sourcebooks 2007 351p pa $14.95   **378.1**

1. College choice 2. Colleges and universities—Entrance requirements 3. Colleges and universities—Finance
ISBN 978-1-4022-0916-1; 1-4022-0916-9
LC 2007-281907

First published 1997 by Times Bks.

This guide includes advice and information on constructing applications, writing essays, interviews, the application process, using the Internet when applying for college, and finanical aid.

Golden, Daniel, 1957-

The price of admission; how America's ruling class buys its way into elite colleges—and who gets left outside the gates. Crown 2006 323p $25.95 * **378.1**

1. Colleges and universities—Entrance requirements 2. College choice 3. College costs

ISBN 1-4000-9796-7   LC 2006-12059

This book argues "that the admissions process, at least at the 100 top colleges and universities, is not a meritocracy . . . but a marketplace. Every spot is up for bid. Some people bid with intelligence, . . . some with cold cash, . . . and others with the currency of connections and influence and relationships that serve the institution's interests." N Y Times Book Rev

"Golden has fun making trouble in the best journalistic sense. . . . The Price of Admission is a powerful reminder that the public will increasingly require selective colleges to defend their preferences; that not all are prepared to make their complex case well; and that some of their practices, finally, seem indefensible today." Harvard Magazine

Green, Sharon

Barron's SAT 2008-2009; [by] Sharon Weiner Green & Ira K. Wolf. 24th ed. Barron's 2008 920p il pa $18.99 * **378.1**

1. Scholastic Assessment Test 2. Colleges and universities—Entrance requirements

ISSN 1941-6180

ISBN 978-0-7641-3803-4; 0-7641-3803-0

Also available edition with CD-ROM $29.99 (ISBN-13: 978-0-7641-9398-9)

Annual. Continues Barron's how to prepare for the SAT

This manual "presents a diagnostic test and five full-length practice tests that reflect . . . SATs in length, question types, and degree of difficulty. The book also presents an overview of the SAT, explains its scoring method, and offers subject reviews in critical reading, grammar and usage, and math. In addition, it gives advice on preparing and writing the required SAT essay." Publisher's note

Karabel, Jerome

The chosen; the hidden history of admission and exclusion at Harvard, Yale, and Princeton. Houghton Mifflin Co. 2005 711p il $28; pa $16.95 **378.1**

1. Colleges and universities—Entrance requirements 2. Higher education

ISBN 0-618-57458-1; 0-618-77355-X (pa)

LC 2005-11133

This is a "study of the origins of current practices of selective admission at the 'Big Three' and the ways in which definitions of merit, and attendant admissions policies, evolved during the 20th century. . . . [This book is] required reading for those interested in the idea of meritocracy in America and the idea that truly merit-based access to higher education is the engine of social mobility." Libr J

Includes bibliographical references

Nemko, Marty, 1945-

The all-in-one college guide. 2nd ed. Barron's 2004 224p pa $10.95 * **378.1**

1. College choice 2. College students

ISBN 0-7641-2298-3   LC 2003-63897

First published 1999 with title: You're gonna love this college guide

Subtitle on cover: More-results, less-stress plan for choosing, getting into, finding the money for, and making the most of college

This guide offers advice on how to choose, get into, find the money for, and make the most of college. Also included is information on how to choose a major and a career

Raskin, Robin, 1954-

Parents' guide to college life; 181 straight answers on everything you can expect over the next four years. Random House 2006 351p il pa $13.95 * **378.1**

1. College students 2. Parenting 3. Parent-child relationship

ISBN 0-375-76494-1; 978-0-375-76494-3

LC 2006-284854

This is "an accessible and practical Q&A-formatted guidebook for parents about how to navigate their child's college years and what to expect when it comes to their parent-child relationship during that time." Libr J

Includes bibliographic references

Toor, Rachel

Admissions confidential; an insiders account of the elite college selection process. St. Martin's Press 2001 256p $23.95; pa $12.95 **378.1**

1. Duke University 2. College applications

ISBN 0-312-28405-5; 0-312-30235-5 (pa)

LC 2001-34892

"Toor describes her first year as an admissions officer at Duke from the summer campus tours and interviews to the final push in May to persuade the students who were accepted to commit to her university." SLJ

"Toor tells all—and it's not necessarily a pretty picture. It's a funny, often irreverent overview of her work. . . . The students don't leap off the page, but Toor certainly does." Booklist

378.3 Student aid and related topics

College money handbook 2008. Peterson's 2007 816p pa $32 * **378.3**

1. College costs 2. Student loan funds 3. Scholarships

ISSN 1541-1591

ISBN 978-0-7689-2489-3; 0-7689-2489-8

Annual. First published 1983. Variant titles: Paying less for college; Peterson's college money handbook

At head of title: Peterson's

"Arranged alphabetically and covering more than $36 billion in institutional, state, and federal aid, this . . . book includes profiles of more than 1,600 colleges and universities and the need and non-need-based scholar-

College money handbook 2008—*Continued*
ships they offer. It answers commonly asked questions
about financial aid and provides a step-by-step explanation of the financial aid application process." Publishers's
note

Getting financial aid 2009. College Board 2008
991p pa $19.95 *   **378.3**
1. College costs 2. Student loan funds
ISBN 978-0-8744-7825-9; 0-8744-7825-1
Annual. First published with title: The college cost
book. Continues College Board guide to getting financial
aid
This guide covers over 3000 two-and four-year institutions. Provides information on what each college really
costs, describes aid packages and includes tips on application procedures.

Schlachter, Gail A.
Directory of financial aids for women
2007-2009; [by] Gail Ann Schlachter. Reference
Service Press 2007 560p $45 *   **378.3**
1. Scholarships 2. Women—Education
ISSN 0732-5215
ISBN 1-58841-167-2; 978-1-58841-167-9
Biennial. First published 1978
Describes "scholarships, fellowships, loans, grants,
awards, and internships designed primarily or exclusively
for women. . . . Lists state sources of educational benefits and offers an annotated bibliography of directories
that list general financial aid programs. Program title,
sponsoring organization, geographic, subject, and filing
date indexes." Ref Sources for Small & Medium-sized
Libr. 5th edition

Financial aid for the disabled and their families,
2008-2010; [by] Gail Ann Schlacter, [and] R.
David Weber. Reference Service Press 2008 520p
$40 *   **378.3**
1. Scholarships 2. Physically handicapped
ISBN 978-1-58841-183-9
Biennial. First published 1988
"Provides information on a wide range of funding
needs in such areas as education, career development, research, and travel. Includes multiple indexes; cross-
referenced." N Y Public Libr Book of How & Where to
Look It Up

Scholarships, fellowships and loans; a guide to
education-related financial aid programs for
students and professionals. 24th ed. Gale Group
2007 xxv, 1622p $265 *   **378.3**
1. Scholarships 2. Student loan funds 3. Student aid
ISSN 1058-5699
ISBN 978-0-7876-9943-7; 0-7876-9943-8
Annual. First published 1949. Frequency, editors, and
publisher vary
This "resource provides detailed information about financial aid for formal and informal degree and
nondegree programs at all levels beyond secondary
school. Includes information about awards, grants, loans,
and contests sponsored by corporations, foundations, religious groups, professional associations, and a few gov-

ernment sources. The index directs students to sources
identified by vocational goals, level of study, residence
requirements, and sponsoring organizations." Ref Sources
for Small & Medium-sized Libr. 6th edition

378.73   Higher education—United States

American universities and colleges. 18th ed.
Praeger 2008 2v set $350 *   **378.73**
1. Colleges and universities—United States—Directories
ISSN 0066-0922
ISBN 978-0-275-99437-2; 0-275-99437-6
First published 1928 by De Gruyter. Frequently revised
Sponsored by the American Council on Education
This directory "describes more than 1,900 accredited
schools offering baccalaureate or higher degrees. Its main
section, arranged by state, presents narrative data for
each college, covering its history, institutional structure
and control, admissions and degree requirements, enrollment and degrees conferred, fees and financial arrangements, numbers of teachers in specific departments and
degrees they hold, library collections, and student life
(dormitories, intercollegiate athletics, car regulations, surrounding communities). Another section lists institutions
offering professional degrees at baccalaureate, masters,
and doctoral levels, arranged alphabetically by course of
study." Guide to Ref Books. 11th edition
Includes bibliographical references

Barron's guide to law schools 2009. 18th ed.
Barron's Educ. Ser. 2008 608p pa $18.99 *
                                              378.73
1. Colleges and universities—United States—Directories
ISBN 978-0-7641-3989-5; 0-7641-3989-4
First published 1967. 1st-8th editions published under
the authorship of Elliott M. Epstein, Jerome Shostak, and
Lawrence M. Troy. Frequently revised
Information includes profiles of American Bar Association approved law schools, guidelines for preparing for
the LSAT, and prospects for employment

Barron's profiles of American colleges 2009;
compiled and edited by the College Division of
Barron's Educational Series. 28th ed. Barron's
2008 1654p map pa $28.99 *   **378.73**
1. Colleges and universities—United States—Directories
ISBN 978-0-7641-9451-1; 0-7641-9451-8
Annual. First published 1964
Includes CD-ROM
"More than 1,650 schools are profiled with details on
admission requirements, academic programs, tuitions and
other fees, sources of available financial aid, library facilities, computer facilities, descriptions of campus environments, athletic facilities, extracurricular activities, e-
mail addresses, fax numbers, web sites, and more. Each
school receives Barron's . . . academic rating system,
which advises students on its degree of academic
competitiveness." Publisher's note

The **College** blue book; degrees offered by colleges and subjects. 35th ed. Macmillan Reference USA; distributed by Gale 2007 6v maps set $410 * **378.73**
1. Colleges and universities—United States—Directories
ISSN 1082-7048
ISBN 978-0-02-866013-4; 0-02-866013-7
Also available eBook version
Biennial. First published 1923
"A leading directory of American and Canadian colleges. In five volumes. Vol. 1, Narrative descriptions, provides information for some 3,000 institutions, with entries arranged by state or province. Vol. 2, Tabular data, outlines information such as costs, accreditation, enrollment, and faculty characteristics; it also gives the names of college presidents, registrars, and admissions officers. Vol. 3, is in two parts: Degrees offered by college, which lists for each school the majors it offers; Degrees offered by subject provides a list of all majors offered, showing which schools offer each major." Guide to Ref Books. 11th edition

College Entrance Examination Board
The College Board book of majors. 2nd ed. College Board 2006 1314p pa $24.95 * **378.73**
1. Colleges and universities—United States—Directories 2. Colleges and universities—Curricula
ISBN 0-8744-7765-4; 978-0-8744-7765-8
Annual. First published 1977 with title: The college handbook index of majors. Variant titles: The College Board index of majors and graduate degrees; Index of majors and graduate degrees
Features over nine hundred majors at thirty-six hundred accredited colleges and universities in the United States for degree levels from associate to Ph.D.

College Board college handbook 2008. 45th ed. College Bd. Publs. 2007 2151p pa $28.95 * **378.73**
1. Colleges and universities—United States—Directories
ISBN 0-8744-7783-2; 978-0-8744-7783-2
Accompanied by CD-ROM
Annual. First published 1941 by Ginn with title: Annual handbook. Formerly titled The college handbook
This work offers "detailed information for college-bound students on such subjects as freshman admissions requirements and procedures, enrollment, majors, expenses, financial aid, and many other areas of interest." N Y Public Libr. Book of How & Where to Look It Up

Colleges with programs for students with learning disabilities or attention deficit disorders. 8th ed. Peterson's 2006 pa $29.95 * **378.73**
1. Learning disabilities 2. Colleges and universities—United States—Directories
ISBN 0-7689-2506-1; 978-0-7689-2506-7
First published 1985 with title: Peterson's guide to colleges with programs for learning disabled students. Variant title: Peterson's colleges with programs for students with learning disabilities
At head of title: Peterson's

Profiles two-year and four-year colleges offering special programs and services. Includes information on graduate-level options and financial aid.

Fiske, Edward B.
Fiske guide to colleges 2009; [by] Edward B. Fiske; with Robert Logue and the *Fiske guide to colleges* staff. 25th ed. Sourcebooks 2008 xxxv, 782p pa $22.95 * **378.73**
1. Colleges and universities—United States—Directories 2. College choice
ISBN 978-1-4022-0959-8; 1-4022-0959-2
Annual. First published 1982 with title: The New York Times selective guide to colleges
This guide to some 310 of the best colleges and universities nationwide includes information on admissions, costs, financial aid, housing, social life, and academic strengths and weaknesses.

Peterson's four-year colleges 2008. 38th ed. Peterson's 2007 3144p il pa $32 * **378.73**
1. Colleges and universities—United States—Directories
ISBN 0-7689-2400-6; 978-0-7689-2400-8
Accompanied by CD-ROM
Annual. First published 1966 as part of Peterson's annual guide to undergraduate study. Formerly titled Peterson's guide to four-year colleges
"In two major sections: (1) half-page entries for some 2,000 institutions, with details of enrollment, admission requirements, expenses, housing, student aid, and programs offered; (2) two-page in-depth descriptions of more than 800 institutions, prepared by their officials, which emphasize campus environment, student activities, and lifestyle. Indexes: major, entrance difficulty, cost, and name of institution." Guide to Ref Books. 11th edition

Peterson's two-year colleges 2008. 38th ed. Peterson's 2007 720p il pa $27 * **378.73**
1. Colleges and universities—United States—Directories
ISSN 1541-5066
ISBN 0-7689-2401-4; 978-0-7689-2401-5
Annual. First published 1966 as part of Peterson's annual guide to undergradute study. Formerly titled Peterson's guide to two-year colleges
This reference compiles profiles of over 1,500 accredited institutions in the United States with two year associate degree programs.

Williams, Juan
I'll find a way or make one; a tribute to historically Black colleges and universities; by Juan Williams and Dwayne Ashley. Amistad/HarperCollins 2004 xxiv, 453p il $35 * **378.73**
1. African Americans—Education 2. African American universities and colleges
ISBN 0-06-009453-2   LC 2004-46450

Williams, Juan—*Continued*

The authors "explore America's 107 historically black colleges and universities, in existence for 172 years, showing how the schools were created and how black and white abolitionists united to educate newly freed slaves." Libr J

Includes bibliographical references

379 Public policy issues in education

DelFattore, Joan, 1946-

What Johnny shouldn't read; textbook censorship in America. Yale Univ. Press 1992 209p $40; pa $16.95   **379**

1. Censorship

ISBN 0-300-05709-1; 0-300-06050-5 (pa)

LC 92-3585

DelFattore "discusses the process of textbook censorship, the litigation of specific cases, the role of publishers, and the issues that have an impact on censorship. . . . She lists state policies on textbook selection and explores issues of gender, race, and ethnicity, as well as science and religion." Libr J

The author "thoughtfully presents six specific cases and their immediate and long-term effects in order to open the eyes and, hopefully, to raise the voices of those who treasure intellectual freedom." Booklist

Includes bibliographical references

Greenawalt, Kent, 1936-

Does God belong in public schools? Princeton University Press 2005 261p $29.95 *

379

1. Religion in the public schools 2. Church and state

ISBN 0691121117   LC 2004-45779

The author "considers issues ranging from the teaching of evolution to parents' rights that their children not be exposed to offensive curriculum. He grounds his analyses in a review of the history and purposes of schooling. . . . His legal and philosophical lines of scholarship come together to produce a nonpartisan consideration of the crucial issues facing US courts and the country." Choice

Includes bibliographical references

Kozol, Jonathan

The shame of the nation; the restoration of apartheid schooling in America. Crown Publishers 2005 404p $25; pa $14.95 *   **379**

1. Segregation in education

ISBN 1-4000-5244-0; 1-4000-5245-9 (pa)

LC 2005-8626

The author "spent five years interviewing and observing students, teachers, and principals in 60 schools across 11 states, providing further documentation of the growing caste and color segregation in overcrowded and underfunded schools." Choice

"Readers interested in public education will appreciate—and be challenged by—this compelling book." Booklist

Includes bibliographical references

Laird, Bob, 1939-

The case for affirmative action in university admissions; [with a foreword by Jesse Jackson] Bay Tree Pub. 2005 291p $26.95   **379**

1. Affirmative action programs 2. Colleges and universities—United States

ISBN 0-9720021-4-6   LC 2004-26322

The author "examines the events and consequences of court rulings involving affirmative action in university admissions. . . . This fact-packed piece will leave readers leery of the high courts, media, politicians, and 'well-meaning' individuals. . . . This resource guide, manual, and history text should serve as a starting point in applying the basic tenets to other institutions." Choice

Includes bibliographical references

381 Commerce (Trade)

Bond's franchise guide; Robert E. Bond, publisher; Michelle Yang, Jennifer Young, editor[s] 2008 ed., 19th ed. Source Book Publications 2008 447p il pa $34.95 *

381

1. Franchises (Retail trade)

ISBN 978-1887137591; 1887137599

Annual. First published 1985 by Dow Jones-Irwin with title: The source book of franchise opportunities

This guide to over 1000 franchise opportunities in 45 categories gives background, capital requirements, support and training information as well as specifics on expansion in the U.S and Canada.

Cassidy, John

Dot.con; the greatest story ever sold. HarperCollins Pubs. 2002 372p pa $13.95 hardcover o.p.   **381**

1. Electronic commerce 2. Stocks

ISBN 0-06-000881-4 (pa)   LC 2001-51449

"A history of the dot-com bubble by a financial writer for The New Yorker, with insightful observations about the Federal Reserve and severe views on its chairman, Alan Greenspan." N Y Times Book Rev

Consumer sourcebook. 21st ed. Gale Res. 2008 1762p $423 *   **381**

1. Consumer protection

ISSN 0738-0518

ISBN 978-0-7876-9625-2; 0-7876-9625-0

First published 1974. Frequently revised

This directory describes "programs and services available to the American consumer at little or no cost. Lists federal, state, county, and local governmental agencies, nongovernmental consumer organizations and associations, and consumer affairs and customer services departments of corporations. Describes consumer publications and multimedia products and provides consumer tips and recommendations." Ref Sources for Small & Medium-sized Libr. 6th edition

Marcus, James

Amazonia. New Press 2004 261p $24.95

381

1. Amazon.com Inc. 2. Electronic commerce

ISBN 1-565-84870-5   LC 2003-66505

Marcus, James—*Continued*

"The author spent five years at Amazon cranking out thousands of online book reviews, during which time his stock options made him a paper millionaire, only to see most of it evaporate." Booklist

"While the quotidian world of everyday work might have seemed uninteresting, Marcus makes it fun to peek inside company workings to see how Amazon.com invented itself. And the literati name-dropping from interviews, parties, and the like lends a tone of friendly gossip to this tale." Libr J

Mitchell, Stacy

Big-box swindle; the true cost of mega-retailers and the fight for America's independent businesses. Beacon Press 2006 318p $24.95; pa $15 **381**

1. Chain stores 2. Retail trade 3. Small business
ISBN 978-0-8070-3500-9; 0-8070-3500-9; 978-0-8070-3501-6 (pa); 0-8070-3501-7 (pa)
LC 2006-13818

This is an "indictment of Wal-Mart and other 'big box' stores, based on numerous national examples. . . . [The author catalogues the] ways indie-minded consumers can fight back, by campaigning against government subsidies to big-box stores, and advocating for sales tax collection on Internet sales and stronger antitrust enforcement." Publ Wkly

Mitchell's "call to action reveals the hidden costs of those 'low prices' promoted by the big-box bullies and gives hope to local entrepreneurs and concerned citizens alike." Booklist

Includes bibliographical references

Wal-Mart; the face of twenty-first-century capitalism; edited by Nelson Lichtenstein. New Press 2006 349p il $60; pa $21.95 **381**

1. Wal-Mart Stores, Inc. 2. Discount stores
ISBN 1-59558-035-2; 1-59558-021-2 (pa)
LC 2005-49147

This collection of essays discusses the retailer Wal-Mart.

"With numerous charts and graphs that keep the data flowing, this assemblage thoroughly dissects the Wal-Mart global high-tech phenomenon through overarching historical, cultural, and economic perspectives." Booklist

Includes bibliographical references

Whitaker, Jan

Service and style; how the American department store fashioned the middle class. St. Martin's Press 2006 342p il $35 **381**

1. Department stores 2. Middle class
ISBN 978-0-312-32635-7; 0-312-32635-1
LC 2006-40542

"At their peak, department stores were the nation's largest booksellers and many major chains also sold groceries. But it was clothes that made the stores a prime destination for women of all social classes, and Whitaker discusses at significant length the subtle movements through which major chains from one end of the country to the other cultivated their reputations for being up-to-date with the latest Paris fashions, then tapped into addi-

tional markets for young adult and children's wear. More than 100 photographs and illustrations are integrated into the text, aptly demonstrating the lengths to which stores went in order to present themselves as elegant yet modern and convenient." Publ Wkly

Includes bibliographical references

382 International commerce (Foreign trade)

Snyder, Rachel Louise

Fugitive denim; a moving story of people and pants in the borderless world of global trade. W.W. Norton & Company 2008 352p $26.95 **382**

1. Clothing industry 2. Jeans (Clothing) 3. International trade
ISBN 978-0-393-06180-2; 0-393-06180-9
LC 2007-24335

This is a "look at how jeans are designed, sewn, and transported as well as how the cotton for denim is grown, regulated, purchased, and processed." Libr J

"Snyder's investigation is an essential read for those curious about fashion or the globe-spanning business that produces their clothes." Publ Wkly

Includes bibliographical references

383 Postal communication

Bobrow, Jerry

Barron's comprehensive postal exam, 473/473-C; contributing author and consultant, Michele Spence. Barron's Educational Series 2006 327p il pa $16.99 **383**

1. Postal service—Examinations
ISBN 0-7641-3412-4; 978-0-7641-3412-8
LC 2006-40108

First published 1995 with title: How to prepare for the comprehensive postal exam

"Six full-length model exams plus a diagnostic test are presented to prepare applicants for a variety of jobs in the U.S. Postal Service. . . . The author also provides special drills designed to improve test-taking skills in memory, speed, and following oral directions." Publisher's note

National five digit zip code and post office directory. U.S. Postal Service 2v maps pa $45 * **383**

1. Zip code
ISSN 0731-9185
ISBN 978-1-59804-282-5; 1-59804-282-3

Also available CD-ROM edition and online with title: Zip code lookup

Annual. Continuation of National zip code and post office directory

"Besides ZIP codes and post offices, this directory includes information on the organization of the Postal Service, addressing, parcel weights and sizes, delivery statistics, and other matters." Recomm Ref Books in Paperback. 2d edition

384.1   Telegraphy

Gordon, John Steele
A thread across the ocean; the heroic story of
the transatlantic cable. Walker & Co. 2002 240p il
$26   **384.1**
1. Submarine cables 2. Telegraph
ISBN 0-8027-1364-5   LC 2002-66385
Also available in paperback from HarperCollins Pubs
This is an account of "the laying of the first telegraph
cables between Europe and North America, completed in
1866." N Y Times Book Rev
The author "has written a lively, engaging account of
the extraordinary efforts that brought about this remarkable scientific, technological, and business feat." Libr J
Includes bibliographical references

National E-mail and FAX directory. 21st ed. Gale
Res. 2008 2153p pa $215 *   **384.1**
1. Fax transmission—Directories
ISSN 1045-9499
ISBN 978-0-7876-9867-6; 0-7876-9867-9
Annual. First published 1989 with title: National FAX
directory
New edition in preparation
"The Directory provides more than 180,000 fax num-
bers and e-mail addresses for U.S. companies, organiza-
tions and government agencies." Publisher's note

384.5   Wireless communication

Murray, James B., Jr.
Wireless nation; the frenzied launch of the
cellular revolution in America. Perseus Bks. 2001
338p pa $17.95 hardcover o.p.   **384.5**
1. Cellular telephones
ISBN 0-7382-0391-2 (pa)
An account of the development and growth of the
communications industry with speculations about its future

384.54   Radiobroadcasting

Broadcasting & cable yearbook 2009. Reed
Business Information 2008 2v set $275 *
                                                 384.54
1. Radio broadcasting 2. Cable television
ISSN 0000-1511
ISBN 978-1-60030-121-6
Annual. First published 1993
"The most comprehensive directory to the Fifth Estate,
covering the history and continuing growth of every field
in the industry. There are nine major sections: 'The Fifth
Estate,' 'Radio,' 'Television,' 'Cable,' 'Satellites,' 'Programming,' 'Advertising and Marketing,' 'Technology,'
and 'Professional Services.' Includes extensive equipment
listings and a buyer's guide. The standard directory of
AM and FM radio stations in the United States, Canada,
Mexico, and the Caribbean and of U.S. and Canadian
television stations." Ref Sources for Small & Medium-
sized Libr. 6th edition

Fisher, Marc
Something in the air; radio, rock, and the
revolution that shaped a generation. Random
House 2007 374p il $27.95 *   **384.54**
1. Radio broadcasting
ISBN 978-0-375-50907-0; 0-375-50907-0
                                      LC 2006-47353
This book "provides a history of the development of
radio in the postwar era." N Y Times Book Rev
"There's not a bit of dead air in this well-written and
researched history of radio and its pivotal role in the
emergence of American youth culture." Publ Wkly
Includes bibliographical references

Heil, Alan L., Jr.
Voice of America; a history. Columbia
University Press 2003 538p $75; pa $26.50
                                      384.54
1. Voice of America 2. Radio broadcasting
ISBN 0-231-12674-3; 0-231-12675-1 (pa)
                                      LC 2002-41019
This is a "history of America's largest publicly funded
overseas broadcasting network. . . . From the crises in
eastern Europe to the student uprising in Tiananmen
Square, Mr Heil provides countless examples of people
clinging to their shortwave radios to listen to VOA and
other international broadcasters, in spite of intense jam-
ming, to know what was really going on in their own
countries. . . . Readers fascinated by the technical intricacies of radio and the arcana of Washington's broadcasting policies will no doubt be riveted." Economist
Includes bibliographical references

The **Museum** of Broadcast Communications
encyclopedia of radio; editor, Christopher H.
Sterling; consulting editor, Michael Keith.
Fitzroy Dearborn 2004 3v xl, 1650p il set $375
*   **384.54**
1. Radio broadcasting—Encyclopedias
ISBN 1-579-58249-4   LC 2003-15683
"A premise of this unique encyclopedia is that radio
broadcasting is so pervasive that its importance can be
easily overlooked. More than 600 articles provide ample
illustration of the role this medium plays throughout the
world. From radio's invention to radio on the Internet,
the cross-referenced and thoroughly indexed articles analyze over 100 years of topics, programs, issues, people,
and places, and provide leads to further reading. Some
250 photographs 'give visual context to an often unseen
world.' Scholars, old-time-radio admirers, and curious
readers will appreciate the unparalleled comprehensiveness of this source."—"The Top 20 Reference Titles of
the Year." Am Libr, May 2004

385   Railroad transportation

Ambrose, Stephen E.
Nothing like it in the world; the men who built
the transcontinental railroad, 1863-1869. Simon &
Schuster 2000 471p $28; pa $16   **385**
1. Central Pacific Railroad 2. Union Pacific Railroad
Company 3. Railroads—United States
ISBN 0-684-84609-8; 0-7432-0317-8 (pa)
                                      LC 00-41005

Ambrose, Stephen E.—*Continued*

This is an account of the construction of the transcontinental railroad by the Central Pacific and Union Pacific companies

"Ambrose's scholarship seems impeccable. . . . He writes a brisk, colloquial, straightforward prose that not only is easy to read but also bears the reader on shoulders of wonder and excitement." N Y Times Book Rev

Includes bibliographical references

Bain, David Haward

Empire express; building the first transcontinental railroad. Viking 1999 797p il maps $34.95; pa $18   **385**

1. Railroads—United States 2. West (U.S.)—History

ISBN 0-670-80889-X; 0-14-008499-1 (pa)

LC 99-33375

In this account of the history of the transcontinental railroad, Bain focuses on "the visionaries who dreamed of the railroad, the building of the railroad, and, most of all, the capitalists who organized and promoted the railroads and the engineers who surveyed and planned the road." New Repub

"Bain knits together excellent storytelling and exhaustive research in a rich contextual tale of vision, ambition, and, ultimately, political and personal corruption." Libr J

Includes bibliographical references

386   Inland waterway and ferry transportation

Bernstein, Peter L.

Wedding of the waters; the Erie Canal and the making of a great nation. W.W. Norton 2005 448p il map $24.95; pa $15.95   **386**

1. Erie Canal (N.Y.)

ISBN 0-393-05233-8; 0-393-32795-7 (pa)

LC 2004-22792

The author discusses the building of the Erie Canal and how, in his opinion, it changed the course of American history.

This "is an important window into a vital and too often neglected period in the American past." Foreign Affairs

Includes bibliographical references

Clover, Charles

The end of the line; how overfishing is changing the world and what we eat. New Press 2006 386p $26.95   **386**

1. Commercial fishing

ISBN 978-1-59558-109-9; 1-59558-109-X

LC 2006-12058

First published 2004 in the United Kingdom

The author "examines indiscriminate fishing methods like trawling that are depleting the world's oceans of such fish populations as the northern cod, bluefin tuna, North Sea skate, haddock, and plaice." Libr J

"Clover's hard-hitting approach will probably anger some, but his argument that we will soon run out of fish unless we take drastic measures . . . is persuasive." Publ Wkly

Includes bibliographical references

Karabell, Zachary

Parting the desert; the creation of the Suez Canal. Knopf 2003 310p il map $27.50 *

386

1. Lesseps, Ferdinand Marie de, vicomte, 1805-1894 2. Suez Canal (Egypt)

ISBN 0-375-40883-5   LC 2002-34209

This book describes "the work of Ferdinand de Lesseps, who replaced sand with seawater in 1869, allowing great ships and Western prestige to fare expeditiously through the middle of the Muslim heartland." N Y Times Book Rev

Karabell "has written a thorough and entertaining work. . . . The author is quite comfortable discussing any issue, period, or personality in the canal's history, and many of the references in his 150-title bibliography are from primary sources. This is simply an excellent book." Libr J

387.7   Air transportation

Blatner, David

The flying book; everything you've ever wondered about flying on airplanes. Walker & Co. 2003 248p il $22   **387.7**

1. Commercial aeronautics 2. Airplanes

ISBN 0-8027-1378-5

"Concentrating on commercial aviation, [the author] offers a compendium of fascinating facts. Chapters zero in on specific aspects of flight: what keeps planes in the air, for example, or how a jet engine functions, or the workings of air-traffic control, or airplane maintenance, or the often-bewildering universe of ticket prices. In addition to technological facts, he also covers the human side of air travel: fear of flying and how to control it, what the pilots are up to in the cockpit, even the horrors of airline food." Booklist

"Engaging, upbeat, and fact-filled, *The Flying Book* features an open, airy design with lots of charts and sidebars." SLJ

Includes bibliographical references

Walsh, Kenneth T.

Air Force One; a history of the presidents and their planes. Hyperion 2003 261p il $24.95

387.7

1. Air Force One (Airplane) 2. Presidents—United States

ISBN 1-401-30004-9   LC 2002-38751

Walsh "presents a narrative account of life on *Air Force One* that is part history and part journalistic profile. Beginning with Franklin D. Roosevelt, the first President to fly while in office, through George W. Bush, Walsh highlights the decisions made and crises that happened aboard this 'flying White House.' The author's hypothesis is that the plane's close quarters and relaxed atmosphere allow each President to bring his own distinct personality to the activities and decisions." Libr J

Includes bibliographical references

388   Transportation Ground transportation

McPhee, John A.

Uncommon carriers; [by] John McPhee. Farrar, Straus & Giroux 2006 248p $24   **388**

1. Freight 2. Transportation

ISBN 0-374-28039-8; 978-0-374-28039-0

           LC 2006-7953

The author "sums up eight years of riding around with people who haul freight in vehicles ranging from 18-wheelers to towboats." Libr J

"McPhee's eye for idiosyncratic detail keeps the stories . . . lively and frequently moves them in interesting directions." Publ Wkly

390   Customs, etiquette & folklore

The **Greenwood** encyclopedia of daily life; a tour through history from ancient times to the present; Joyce E. Salisbury, general editor. Greenwood Press 2004 6v il map set $599.95 *   **390**

1. Manners and customs—Encyclopedias 2. Civilization—Encyclopedias

ISBN 0-313-32541-3   LC 2003-54724

Contents: v1 The ancient world / Gregory S. Aldrete, volume editor — v2 The medieval world / Joyce E. Salisbury, volume editor — v3 15th and 16th centuries / Lawrence Morris, volume editor — v4 17th and 18th centuries / Peter Seelig, volume editor — v5 19th century / Andrew E. Kersten, volume editor — v6 The modern world / Andrew E. Kersten, volume editor

This "work provides an overview of the material, domestic, recreational, religious, political, intellectual, and economic aspects of daily life in a selection of cultures from six broad historical periods. . . . Each of the six volumes gives a survey of the historical period in each culture covered, which is representative rather than exhaustive, then covers aspects of daily life from broad topics to narrower." Libr J

Includes bibliographical references

391   Costume and personal appearance

Ashenburg, Kathy

The dirt on clean; an unsanitized history; [by] Katherine Ashenburg. North Point Press 2007 358p il $24   **391**

1. Hygiene 2. Personal grooming

ISBN 978-0-86547-690-5; 0-86547-690-X

           LC 2007-32334

This is a study "of attitudes to hygiene through time." Publisher's note

"Brimming with lively anecdotes, this well-researched, smartly paced and endearing history of Western cleanliness holds a welcome mirror up to our intimate selves, revealing deep-seated desires and fears spanning 2000-plus years." Publ Wkly

Includes bibliographical references

Calasibetta, Charlotte Mankey

The Fairchild dictionary of fashion; {by} Charlotte Mankey Calasibetta, Phyllis Tortora; illustrated by Bina Abling. 3rd ed. Fairchild Publs. 2003 522p il $75 *   **391**

   ISBN 1-5636-7235-9   LC 2002-103884

   First published 1975

This work provides definitions of fashion terms, line drawings, and biographical sketches of designers

Contemporary fashion; editor, Taryn Benbow-Pfalzgraf. 2nd ed. St. James Press 2002 xxi, 743p il $185   **391**

1. Fashion design 2. Clothing industry 3. Fashion—History

ISBN 1-55862-348-5   LC 2002-17801

First published 1995 under the editorship of Richard Martin

This volume "includes coverage of more than 450 designers, milliners, footwear designers, fashion companies and textile houses. Entries . . . include a biographical summary; primary and secondary bibliography, including articles and exhibition catalogs; and a signed, critical essay written by an expert in the field." Publisher's note

Includes bibliographical references

Cosgrave, Bronwyn

The complete history of costume and fashion; from ancient Egypt to the present day. Checkmark Bks. 2001 256p il $37.95   **391**

1. Costume—History

ISBN 0-8160-4574-7   LC 00-64401

"This book explores the development of fashion from its simple and practical beginnings to the growth of the multibillion dollar global industry that it is today. . . . Trends in clothing style, fabric, accessories, and footwear {are examined}." Publisher's note

Includes bibliographical references

De Marly, Diana

Dress in North America. v1: The New World, 1492-1800. Holmes & Meier 1990 221p il $59.95 *   **391**

1. Costume—History 2. United States—Social life and customs—1600-1775, Colonial period

ISBN 0-8419-1199-1   LC 90-4905

"Volume 1 of this projected three-volume series is a historical narrative of the development of clothing styles and industries in Colonial America. Beautifully reproduced art works, mostly portrait paintings, are accompanied by excellent fashion commentary." Libr J

Includes bibliographical references

DeJean, Joan E.

The essence of style; how the French invented high fashion, fine food, chic cafés, style, sophistication, and glamour. Free Press 2005 303p il $25; pa $15   **391**

1. Louis XIV, King of France, 1638-1715 2. Fashion—History 3. France—Social life and customs

ISBN 0-7432-6413-4; 0-7432-6414-2 (pa)

           LC 2005-40019

DeJean, Joan E.—*Continued*

A historian of seventeenth-century French culture argues that "the French under Louis XIV set the standards of sophistication, style, and glamour that still rule our lives today." Publisher's note

"An unusual and delightfully educational perspective on snob appeal." Booklist

Includes bibliographical references

Encyclopedia of clothing and fashion; Valerie Steele, editor in chief. Scribner 2005 3v (Scribner library of daily life) set $395 *

391

1. Costume—Encyclopedias 2. Fashion—Encyclopedias

ISBN 0-684-31394-4   LC 2004-10098

Alphabetically arranged entries range "from a half page for some particular items, clothing types, fibers, and techniques . . . to multiple pages for *Cross dressing; Dandyism; Hats, men's* and *Hats, women's; Kimono; Street style* and *Twentieth century fashion,* among others. Articles on designers or people who influenced fashion . . . are a significant part of the content, as are articles with a historical slant. . . . Many of the articles are entertaining as well as enlightening. . . . *Encyclopedia of Clothing and Fashion* is an exciting and unique resource that excels in depth and range of coverage." Booklist

Etcoff, Nancy L., 1955-

Survival of the prettiest; the science of beauty; {by} Nancy Etcoff. Doubleday 1999 325p il pa $14 hardcover o.p.   391

1. Personal appearance 2. Sexual behavior 3. Natural selection

ISBN 0-385-47942-5 (pa)   LC 98-41332

The author "presents the evolution of our conception of beauty as a biological adaptation that seeks healthy, fertile mates and makes us instinctively seek partners whose physical characteristics reflect this likelihood." Libr J

"Topics as wide-ranging as penis- or breast-enlargement surgery and the basics of haute couture are treated with wit and insight. Etcoff's arguments are certain to initiate a great deal of discussion." Publ Wkly

Includes bibliographical references

Hunnisett, Jean

Period costume for stage & screen; patterns for women's dress, 1500-1800; illustrations by Janette Haslam. Players Press 1991 176p il $55 *

391

1. Costume—History 2. Dressmaking

ISBN 0-88734-610-3   LC 90-50385

Also available volume covering years 1800-1909 $55 (ISBN 0-88734-609-X) and volume covering medieval-1500 $55 (ISBN 0-88734-653-7)

First published 1986 in the United Kingdom

Contains patterns, illustrations, and instructions for more than twenty garments

Includes bibliographical references

In an influential fashion; an encyclopedia of nineteenth- and twentieth-century fashion designers and retailers who transformed dress; {by} Ann T. Kellogg {et al.}; with illustrations by Kamila Dominik. Greenwood Press 2002 371p il $49.95   391

1. Fashion design 2. Clothing industry 3. Fashion—History

ISBN 0-313-31220-6   LC 2001-45124

"This volume chronicles the achievements of 164 renowned international designers and retailers who have most influenced American dress and culture from the late 19th century to the present. . . . The alphabetically arranged entries include biographical data, education, influences, awards, additional references, and the contribution the subject made to fashion." Libr J

Includes bibliographical references

Kelly, Clinton, 1969-

Dress your best; the complete guide to finding the style that's right for your body; [by] Clinton Kelly and Stacy London. Three Rivers Press 2005 255p il pa $18.95   391

1. Clothing and dress 2. Fashion

ISBN 0-307-23671-4   LC 2005-13681

This fashion guide describes specific male and female body types, and the kinds of outfits that match well with them. "Each type's section opens with a photo of an average-looking model sporting a basic swimsuit, along with comments from the model and the authors. . . . Ladies and gentlemen, start your shopping engines—and don't leave home without this book!" Publ Wkly

Laver, James, 1899-1975

Costume and fashion; a concise history. 4th ed, concluding chapter by Amy de la Haye and Andrew Tucker. Thames & Hudson 2002 304p il (World of art) pa $16.95   391

1. Costume—History 2. Fashion—History

ISBN 0-500-20348-2   LC 2001-87366

First published 1969 with title: A concise history of costume

This "guide covers the landmarks of costume history, the forms and materials used through the ages, as well as the underlying motives of fashion and the ways in which clothes have been used to protect, to express identity, and to attract or to influence others." Publisher's note

Includes bibliographical references

Nunn, Joan

Fashion in costume, 1200-2000. 2nd ed. New Amsterdam Bks. 2000 280p pa $18.95

391

1. Costume—History

ISBN 1-56663-279-X   LC 99-47516

First published 1984 by Schocken Bks. with title: Fashion in costume, 1200-1980

This history of American and European costume covers men's, women's, and children's dress, accessories and jewelry, fabrics, and color. Discusses how historical, social, economic, and artistic events influence fashion

Includes bibliographical references

Paterek, Josephine

Encyclopedia of American Indian costume.
Norton 1996 516p il pa $24.95 * **391**

1. Native American costume

ISBN 0-393-31382-4

First published 1994 by ABC-CLIO

Paterek describes "the clothing used for everyday, war, rites, and ceremonies for men, women, and children in hundreds of tribes in diverse climates stretching over centuries. Well-organized text and 400 drawings and authentic photos plus the cultural essays prefacing the 10 regional groupings and each tribe put the costumes in historical, social, and geographic context. Appendixes cover terminology and the materials used in clothing. The excellent bibliographies in this classic work both document and encourage further reading." Am Libr

Includes bibliographical references

Peacock, John, 1943-

Men's fashion; the complete sourcebook.
Thames & Hudson 1996 216p il $29.95

391

1. Costume—History 2. Men's clothing 3. Fashion—History

ISBN 0-500-01725-5 LC 96-60141

This is an illustrated survey of "men's fashion and accessories from roughly the French revolutionary era to the present (1789-1995). The 1000 colored line drawings are hand-rendered, showing a variety of front, side, and rear views of day wear, sportswear, evening wear, negligee, and underwear, as well as accessories and hairstyles. Brief biographies of designers, tailors, and outfitters and a bibliography of related books conclude the work." Libr J

"A highly practical and useful volume." Choice

Peiss, Kathy Lee

Hope in a jar; the making of America's beauty culture; {by} Kathy Peiss. Metropolitan Bks. 1998 334p il pa $15.95 hardcover o.p. **391**

1. Personal appearance 2. Cosmetics

ISBN 0-8050-5551-7 (pa) LC 97-42706

This is a "social history of the origin and development of the U.S. cosmetics industry. . . . An engrossing, highly readable book that should be welcomed by scholars and general readers alike." Libr J

Includes bibliographical references

Scott, Georgia

Headwraps; a global journey. Public Affairs 2003 209p il $35 **391**

1. Hats

ISBN 1-586-48109-6 LC 2003-60655

This "book examines headwraps from cultural, fashion and practical standpoints." Publ Wkly

"On any page, readers will find excellent color photos of Scott's many new friends in their headgear, or archival photos and artistic renderings. Illustrations and text mesh seamlessly to reveal an amazing variety of textiles and methods of tying." SLJ

Includes bibliographical references

392 Customs of life cycle and domestic life

Gollaher, David, 1949-

Circumcision; a history of the world's most controversial surgery; [by] David L. Gollaher. Basic Bks. 2000 253p pa $18 hardcover o.p.

392

1. Circumcision

ISBN 0-465-02653-2 (pa) LC 99-40015

This history of circumcision discusses Jewish, Muslim, and tribal rituals, medical procedures and complications, reasons for the procedure, and its social significance in various cultures and eras

Monger, George

Marriage customs of the world; from henna to honeymoons; [by] George P. Monger. ABC-CLIO 2004 327p il $85 * **392**

1. Marriage customs and rites

ISBN 1-576-07987-2 LC 2004-17586

This is "an encyclopedia of marriage rites, traditions, and beliefs from around the world, ranging from ancient practices to contemporary ceremonies." Publisher's note

Includes bibliographical references

393 Death customs

Laderman, Gary, 1962-

Rest in peace; a cultural history of death and the funeral home in twentieth-century America. Oxford Univ. Press 2003 245p il hardcover o.p. pa $21.95

393

1. Undertakers and undertaking

ISBN 0-19-513608-X; 978-0-19-518355-9 (pa); 0-19-518355-X (pa) LC 2002-6682

This book explores "the world of death specialists, the development of their profession in post-Civil War America, and the profession's role in American culture. . . . The topics covered . . . include embalming, the repatriation of wartime remains, the rise of corporate facilities, the AIDS epidemic, and cultural representations such as *The Night of the Living Dead* and *Six Feet Under*. . . . Laderman's respect, even affection, for the profession is clearly evident, but he maintains objectivity throughout. Especially impressive is his treatment of {Jessica} Mitford, whose accusations he challenges politely but thoroughly." Libr J

Includes bibliographical references

Mitford, Jessica, 1917-1996

The American way of death revisited. Knopf 1998 296p pa $14 hardcover o.p. * **393**

1. Undertakers and undertaking 2. Funeral rites and ceremonies

ISBN 0-679-77186-7 (pa) LC 97-49349

First published 1963 by Simon & Schuster with title: The American way of death

Mitford, Jessica, 1917-1996—*Continued*

The author offers a "scathing critique of the U.S. funeral industry. . . . Furthermore, she charges, the Federal Trade Commission's lax enforcement of its 1984 rule banning morticians' deceptive practices has contributed to an upward spiral of prices and profits. Other developments of the 1990s perceptively analyzed here include the refusal of many funeral directors to embalm AIDS victims and the growing popularity of low-cost funeral and memorial service organizations, which are listed in an appendix." Publ Wkly

"Very interesting, informative, and easy to read, this book is written with wit, solid information, and refreshing bluntness." Libr J

Pringle, Heather Anne, 1952-

The mummy congress; science, obsession, and the everlasting dead; {by} Heather Pringle. Hyperion 2001 368p il hardcover o.p. pa $13.95
393

1. Mummies 2. Forensic anthropology
ISBN 0-7868-6551-2; 0-7868-8463-0 (pa)
LC 00-54487

"Besides outstanding members of the scientific association that gathers as the Mummy Congress, Pringle limns the many varieties of mummies, from the world's oldest, preserved by the high-altitude climate of the Andes, to modern Communist dictators, self-mummifying Buddhists, and the subjects of extreme cosmetic surgery. More astounding than all the fright flicks about shambling, gauze-wrapped menaces wound together." Booklist
Includes bibliographical references

Young, Gregory W.

The high cost of dying; a guide to funeral planning. Prometheus Bks. 1994 142p il $32.50; pa $20
393

1. Death 2. Funeral rites and ceremonies
ISBN 0-87975-868-6; 0-87975-874-0 (pa)
LC 93-41859

The author "discusses working with the funeral director, working out a contract, avoiding ripoffs, and planning a prearranged funeral. . . . Young, a former director of a funeral home chain, sensitively and clearly offers practical guidelines and presents an overview of the funeral service industry." Libr J
Includes bibliographical references

394.1 Eating, drinking; using drugs

Burns, Eric

The spirits of America; a social history of alcohol. Temple University Press 2004 352p $29 *
394.1

1. Drinking of alcoholic beverages
ISBN 1-592-13214-6
LC 2003-50790

Burns contends that drinking alcohol "shaped American politics and culture from the earliest colonial days. He details the transformation of alcohol from virtue to vice and back again, how it was thought of as both scourge and medicine. He tells us how 'the great American thirst' developed over the centuries, and how reform movements and laws . . . sprang up to combat it." Publisher's note

Burns "presents an enjoyable and informative examination of the role of alcoholic beverages in American society." Libr J
Includes bibliographical references

Collingham, E. M.

Curry; a tale of cooks and conquerors. Oxford University Press 2006 315p il maps $28 *
394.1

1. Eating customs 2. India—Civilization
ISBN 978-0-19-517241-6; 0-19-517241-8
LC 2005-16641

This is a "history of Indian cuisine, ranging from the imperial kitchen of the Mughal invader Babur to the smoky cookhouse of the British Raj." Publisher's note

The author "with incredibly engrossing detail, unravels the tantalizing mystery of 'curry' in its innumerable forms, which have ravished the taste buds in far-flung kitchens and dining rooms." MultiCult Rev
Includes bibliographical references

Gately, Iain

Tobacco; the story of how tobacco seduced the world. Grove Press 2002 c2001 403p il $25; pa $15
394.1

1. Tobacco
ISBN 0-8021-1705-8; 0-8021-3960-4 (pa)
LC 2001-54493

First published 2001 in the United Kingdom with title: La diva nicotina

This is a "historical survey of humanity's love/hate relationship with tobacco. . . . Gately pays particular attention to the evolving methods of ingesting tobacco, pays respect to the pleasurable ambience of the smoking experience, and even offers a final chapter on how to grow tobacco in your backyard." Libr J

"An entertaining story of humanity's Faustian bargain with tobacco." Booklist
Includes bibliographical references

Holland, Barbara

The joy of drinking. Bloomsbury 2007 150p il $15
394.1

1. Drinking of alcoholic beverages
ISBN 978-1-59691-337-0; 1-59691-337-1
LC 2006-39322

A "romp across the histories and cultures of alcohol down through the ages. While disclosing facts about the drinking habits—and abuses—of characters like Mark Anthony, Samuel Pepys and Pope Leo XIII, Holland includes summaries of how various kinds of fermentations and distillates were developed, often accidentally, in cultures from ancient Arabia to present-day America, and in times from Ptolemy's to Prohibition. She includes several recipes for home-style 'remedies' like elderberry wine and applejack, as well as diagrams and instructions for the construction of your own backyard still." Publ Wkly

"Mixing fact, fable, anecdote, and personal opinion with irresistible panache, cultural historian Barbara Holland's The Joy of Drinking distills thousands of years of humankind's lusty relationship with alcohol . . . into a slim, sparkling history." Elle

Kluger, Richard

Ashes to ashes; America's hundred-year cigarette war, the public health, and the unabashed triumph of Philip Morris. Knopf 1996 807p pa $19.95 hardcover o.p.   **394.1**

1. Philip Morris, Inc. 2. Smoking 3. Tobacco habit 4. Tobacco industry

ISBN 0-375-70036-6 (pa)   LC 95-42103

"From the Native American usage of tobacco through the law-suits of the 1990s, Kluger follows the industry's agricultural and labor practices, technical advances, and marketing campaigns; he also considers research on tobacco's deleterious health effects and the tobacco control movement. Significant personalities and events such as the invention of the cigarette-rolling machine are featured. . . . Suitable for readers of high school age on up, this book belongs in every library." Libr J

Includes bibliographical references

Mayle, Peter

French lessons; adventures with knife, fork, and corkscrew. Knopf 2001 227p il $24; pa $12.95
                                        394.1

1. France—Social life and customs 2. Eating customs

ISBN 0-375-40590-9; 0-375-70561-9 (pa)

Mayle "relives some of his most precious moments reveling in the cuisine of his adopted homeland. . . . {He tells} savory, sensual, positively transporting stories about his encounters with Gallic gustatory delights and about his growing appreciation of the central place food occupies in French life." Booklist

Pollan, Michael

The omnivore's dilemma; a natural history of four meals. Penguin Press 2006 450p $26.95 *
                                        394.1

1. Eating customs

ISBN 1-59420-082-3   LC 2005-56557

The author "defines the Omnivore's Dilemma as the confusing maze of choices facing Americans trying to eat healthfully in a society that he calls 'notably unhealthy.' He seeks answers to this dilemma by taking readers through the industrial, organic, and hunter-gatherer stages of the food chain. . . . This folksy narrative provides a wealth of information about agriculture, the natural world, and human desires." Libr J

Includes bibliographical references

Schlosser, Eric

Fast food nation; the dark side of the all-American meal. Houghton Mifflin 2001 356p il $25 *   **394.1**

1. Food industry 2. Restaurants 3. Convenience foods

ISBN 0-395-97789-4   LC 00-53886

"Schlosser documents the effects of fast food on America's economy, its youth culture, and allied industries. . . . Starting with a young woman who makes minimum wage working at a Colorado fast-food restaurant, Schlosser relates the oft-told story of Ray Kroc's founding of McDonald's. The author also tells about the development of the franchise method of business ownership and the health and nutrition implications of fast-food consumption." Booklist

Includes bibliographical references

Spencer, Colin

British food; an extraordinary thousand years of history. Columbia Univ. Press 2003 400p il (Arts and traditions of the table) $35   **394.1**

1. Food—History 2. Great Britain—Civilization

ISBN 0-231-13110-0   LC 2003-48492

"Spencer traces the country's lamentable decline in cuisine through the Reformation, Puritanism, and the Industrial Revolution, noting that Britons gradually lost a knowledge of wild foodstuffs and the time in their day to gather and cook more than the most convenient foods. . . . Readers may . . . find the glossary and appendixes of British edible flora and traditional dishes to be particularly valuable." Libr J

Includes bibliographical references

Standage, Tom

A history of the world in 6 glasses. Walker & Co. 2005 311p il $25   **394.1**

1. Beverages

ISBN 0-8027-1447-1   LC 2004-61209

The author's "book divides world history into beer, wine, spirits, coffee, tea and Coca-Cola ages. . . . He begins with humanity's shift from hunting and gathering to agriculture. This transition led to the cultivation of grain, which led to storage and fermentation and, eventually, beer." N Y Times (Late N Y Ed)

Standage "has the ability to connect the smallest detail to the big picture and a knack for summarizing vast concepts in a few sentences." Publ Wkly

Includes bibliographical references

Stern, Jane

Two for the road; our love affair with American food; [by] Jane and Michael Stern. Houghton Mifflin 2006 292p $24   **394.1**

1. Cooking

ISBN 0-618-32963-3; 978-0-618-32963-2
                                        LC 2005-31611

"Over the last three decades, Jane and Michael Stern have logged more than three million miles on America's two-lane highways, eating some 72,427 meals. . . . [In this] culinary memoir, the Sterns tell the story behind their lifelong road trip. . . . Each chapter ends with the Sterns' best recipe finds, from white clam pizza to Elvis's favorite pound cake." Publisher's note

This is "a book to be savored while sitting in the Formica and vinyl booth of your favorite diner eating meatloaf and real mashed potatoes." Libr J

Tobacco in history and culture; an encyclopedia; Jordan Goodman, editor in chief. Thomson Gale 2005 2v il (Scribner turning points library) set $275 *   **394.1**

1. Tobacco—Encyclopedias

ISBN 0-684-31405-3   LC 2004-7109

The author "focuses on the cultural aspects of tobacco as a drug, health hazard, social phenomena, and economic force." Ref & User Services Quarterly

"This makes an excellent starting point for readers looking for quick entrance to the vast body of knowledge of the history and diversity of tobacco uses, tobacco health, addiction, social control issues, advertising, production, and distribution, among other topics." Choice

Includes bibliographical references

394.25 Carnival

Danticat, Edwidge, 1969-
After the dance; a walk through carnival in Jacmel, Haiti. Crown 2002 158p (Crown journeys series) $16   **394.25**
1. Carnival
ISBN 0-609-60908-4   LC 2002-24165
The author "journeyed back to her native Haiti to explore what had been forbidden in her childhood: the colorful, raucous, dangerous carnival. . . . She sought out some of the island's more unusual residents while exploring the history, folklore, and meaning of the many images of carnival. Her lively narrative describes a rich and complicated cultural history." Libr J

394.26 Holidays

The **American** book of days; compiled and edited by Stephen G. Christianson. 4th ed. Wilson, H.W. 2000 xxvi, 945p $140 *   **394.26**
1. Holidays 2. Festivals
ISBN 0-8242-0954-0   LC 99-86611
First published 1937 under the authorship of George William Douglas
This work "consists of essays that are a day-to-day recounting of selective American historic events, including those of festivals and celebrations. . . . The topics of these essays vary, with the editor highlighting notable activities from military, scientific, ethnic, political, and cultural occurrences. Not limited strictly to events, essays are also devoted to individuals who played a significant role in American history. . . . A comprehensive index and table of contents provide excellent means for finding specific topics." Am Ref Books Annu, 2001

Chase's calendar of events 2008. 50th anniversary ed. McGraw-Hill 2008 752p il pa $64.95 *
                                       394.26
1. Calendars 2. Holidays 3. Almanacs
ISBN 978-0-07-148903-4
Annual. First published 1958 by Contemporary Bks. under the editorship of William D. and Helen M. Chase with title: Chase's calendar of annual events. Variant title: Chase's annual events
Includes CD-ROM. New edition in preparation
"Day-by-day listing of national and state holidays, religious observances, special events, festivals and fairs, and historical anniversaries and birthdays. Covers U.S. events primarily, but some international occasions and anniversaries are included." N Y Public Libr Book of How & Where to Look It Up

Christianson, Stephen G.
The international book of days; edited by Lynn M. Messina; contributors, Jennifer Peloso, Norris Smith, Laura Ware. H.W. Wilson 2004 xxxi, 889p il map $140 *   **394.26**
1. Holidays 2. Festivals
ISBN 0-8242-0975-3   LC 2004-42285

This "book presents an international tour of holidays and major historical events. Organized by day of the year, the book covers some 1500 key events in world history." Libr J

Encyclopedia of holidays and celebrations; a country-by-country guide; Matthew Dennis, editor. Facts on File 2006 3v il map (Facts on File library of world history) set $275
                                       394.26
1. Holidays 2. Festivals
ISBN 0-8160-6235-8; 978-0-8160-6235-5
                                   LC 2005-27700
This is "a three-volume guide that explores holidays and festivals in 206 countries. Volumes I and II are organized alphabetically by country, and volume III contains overviews of major internationally observed holidays and religions. . . . This welcome addition to multicultural studies is attractively laid out, easy to use, great for browsing as well as fact finding, and is highly recommended for high school, public, and college libraries." Ref & User Services Quarterly
Includes bibliographical references

Gulevich, Tanya
Encyclopedia of Christmas and New Year's celebrations; illustrated by Mary Ann Stavros-Lanning. Omnigraphics 2003 xx, 977p il $68 *   **394.26**
1. Christmas 2. New Year
ISBN 0-7808-0625-5   LC 2003-40580
First published 2000 with title: Encyclopedia of Christmas
"Over 240 alphabetically arranged entries covering Christmas, New Year's, and related days of observance, including folk and religious customs, history, legends, and symbols from around the world; supplemented by a bibliography and lists of Christmas Web sites and associations . . ." Title page
The author "covers a variety of secular and sacred aspects of Christmas and New Year's celebrations. . . . This encyclopedic work is useful for those schools where folklore is covered, or for those interested in origins of the holidays." Libr Media Connect
Includes bibliographical references

Hillstrom, Laurie, 1965-
The Thanksgiving book; [by] Laurie C. Hillstrom. Omnigraphics 2008 328p il $65
                                       394.26
1. Thanksgiving Day
ISBN 978-0-7808-0403-6   LC 2007-25708
"A companion to the holiday covering its history, lore, traditions, foods, and symbols, including primary sources, poems, prayers, songs, hymns, and recipes: supplemented by a chronology, bibliography with web sites, and index." Title Page
"This book is definitely a wonderful tribute to the holiday of Thanksgiving." Am Ref Books Annu, 2008
Includes bibliographical references

Holidays and anniversaries of the world; Beth A. Baker, editor. 3rd ed. Gale Res. 1998 c1999 1184p $130 **394.26**
1. Holidays 2. Festivals 3. Historical chronology
ISBN 0-8103-5477-2 LC 98-38866
First published 1985
"A comprehensive catalogue containing detailed information on every month and day of the year, with coverage of more than 26,000 holidays, anniversaries, fasts and feasts, holy days of the saints, the blesseds, and other days of religious significance, birthdays of the famous, important dates in history, and special events and their sponsors." Title page

Holidays, festivals, and celebrations of the world dictionary. 3rd ed. Omnigraphics 2005 xxxv, 906p $110 * **394.26**
1. Holidays 2. Festivals
ISBN 0-7808-0422-8 LC 2004-25017
First edition published 1994 compiled by Sue Ellen Thompson and Barbara W. Carlson
"Contains information about nearly 2,500 holidays, festivals, holy days, feasts and fasts, and other observances, including popular, secular, and religious celebrations for more than 100 countries and every state of the United States"—Title page. New edition in preparation
"From Labor Day in the United States to Kallemooi in the North Coast Islands of the Netherlands, the work covers a wide range of religious and political festivities." Libr J
Includes bibliographical references

Marling, Karal Ann
Merry Christmas! celebrating America's greatest holiday. Harvard Univ. Press 2000 442p il $29.95; pa $16.95 **394.26**
1. Christmas 2. United States—Social life and customs
ISBN 0-674-00318-7; 0-674-00679-8 (pa)
LC 00-31935
Topics covered include The Christmas tree, Santa, wrapping paper, cards, gifts, decorating, baking cookies, movies and music
"Imaginatively researched and strewn with surprising details, this engaging cultural history traces the rise of the consumerism that has become . . . integral to the celebration of Christmas in the United States." Publ Wkly
Includes bibliographical references

Rajtar, Steve, 1951-
United States holidays and observances; by date, jurisdiction, and subject, fully indexed. McFarland & Co. 2003 165p $45 * **394.26**
1. Holidays 2. Festivals
ISBN 0-7864-1446-4 LC 2002-154293
This "concentrates on observances and holidays established by statute in the U.S. and American Samoa, District of Columbia, Guam, the Northern Mariana Islands, Puerto Rico, and the U.S. Virgin Islands. In addition, UN-designated holidays are included. . . . The text is arranged by month, and chapters for each month are divided into 'Observances with Variable Dates' and 'Observances with Fixed Dates.' Each entry identifies the ob-

servance as federal or specific to a state and offers a description that ranges in length from three or four lines to a quarter page. . . . [This] would be a good addition to ready-reference desks in public libraries and information centers in schools." Booklist

Thompson, Sue Ellen, 1948-
Holiday symbols and customs. 3rd ed. Omnigraphics 2002 895p $68 * **394.26**
1. Holidays 2. Festivals
ISBN 0-7808-0501-1 LC 2002-193028
First published 1998 with title: Holiday symbols. New edition in preparation
"A guide to the legend and lore behind the traditions, rituals, foods, games, animals, and other symbols and activities associated with holidays and holy days, feasts and fasts, and other celebrations, covering calendar, ethnic, religious, historic, cultural, national, promotional, sporting, and ancient events, as observed in the United States and around the world." Title page
Includes bibliographical references

395 Etiquette (Manners)

Baldrige, Letitia
Letitia Baldrige's new complete guide to executive manners. Rawson Assocs. 1993 xxx, 590p il $40 **395**
1. Business etiquette
ISBN 0-89256-362-1 LC 93-14166
First published 1985 with title: Letitia Baldrige's complete guide to executive manners
The author provides advice on such issues in the workplace as sexual harassment; using nonsexist, ethnically correct forms of address and language; romantic involvement among co-workers; dealing with HIV-positive employees and clients; working with the physically-challenged; and international business manners

Letitia Baldrige's new manners for new times; a complete guide to etiquette; illustrations by Denise Cavalieri Fike. Scribner 2003 xxvi, 709p il $35 * **395**
1. Etiquette
ISBN 0-7432-1062-X LC 2003-65666
First published 1990 with title: Letitia Baldrige's complete guide to the new manners for the 90's
"Combining correctness, consideration, and common sense in equal measure, Baldrige advises readers on proper ways to approach intricate situations. She addresses same-sex unions, pregnant brides, blended and extended families, and sexual harassment with aplomb." Libr J

Bride's book of etiquette; by the editors of Bride's magazine. Rev. ed. Perigee 2003 333p il pa $19.95 * **395**
1. Etiquette 2. Weddings 3. Marriage customs and rites
ISBN 0-399-52866-0 LC 2002-35534
First published 1948. Periodically revised. Publisher and title vary
A guide to planning a wedding ceremony and reception, from announcements to honeymoon plans.
Includes bibliographical references

Dresser, Norine
Multicultural manners; essential rules of etiquette for the 21st century. Rev ed. John Wiley & Sons 2005 285p map pa $16.95 **395**
1. Etiquette 2. Manners and customs
ISBN 978-0-471-68428-2; 0-471-68428-7
LC 2004-27079
First published 1996
"From body language and table manners to classroom behavior and gift giving, this guide to etiquette provides fascinating information about relations in our multicultural society." Booklist
Includes bibliographical references

Martin, Judith, 1938-
Miss Manners' guide to domestic tranquility; the authoritative manual for every civilized household, however harried. Crown 1999 372p pa $18 hardcover o.p. **395**
1. Etiquette
ISBN 0-609-80539-8 (pa) LC 99-22824
This guide to etiquette focusing on the home "considers the myriad facets of living with family, friends, guests, and society in general." Libr J

Miss Manners' guide to excruciatingly correct behavior; illustrated by Gloria Kamen. freshly updated. Norton 2005 858p il $35 * **395**
1. Etiquette
ISBN 0-393-05874-3 LC 2005-00264
First published 1982 by Atheneum Pubs.
This book "covers such modern dilemmas as dealing with intrusive cell phones, handling guests who can't commit, and determining when e-mail is socially correct." Libr J
"Miss Manners is always as entertaining as she is civilized." Booklist

Star-spangled manners; in which Miss Manners defends American etiquette (for a change). Norton 2002 319p $24.95 **395**
1. Etiquette 2. United States—Social life and customs
ISBN 0-393-04861-6 LC 2002-8352
The author "engages in . . . reflections about how American manners got to be the way they are, and why they have proved so suitable to the lives of modern people everywhere." N Y Times Book Rev
"Although Martin's pedantic punditry often overshadows the beauty and sly cunning of her arguments, her insights remain peerless." Booklist

McCrum, Mark, 1958-
Going Dutch in Beijing; how to behave properly when far away from home. H. Holt 2008 208p il $22 **395**
1. Etiquette 2. Travel
ISBN 978-0-8050-8676-8; 0-8050-8676-5
LC 2007-37500
First published 2007 in the United Kingdom
The author "looks at the customs of various nations and regions and explains how different greetings, gestures, gifts, toasts, foods, names, clothes, and salutations can have extremely varied meanings from one land to another. . . . McCrum's chronicle is meant to help the traveler avoid embarrassment or miscommunication, but along the way, he tells much about varied cultures and peoples around the world." Libr J
Includes bibliographical references

Mead, Rebecca, 1966-
One perfect day; the selling of the American wedding. Penguin Press 2007 245p $25.95; pa $15 **395**
1. Weddings
ISBN 978-1-59420-088-5; 978-0-14-311384-3 (pa)
LC 2006-52461
This "critique of the contemporary wedding industry in the US looks at the commercialization of the marriage ceremony from a variety of angles—from the retail side to the ubiquitous wedding planner and in between." Choice
"Part investigative journalism, part social commentary, Mead's wry, insightful work offers an illuminating glimpse at the ugly underbelly of our Bridezilla culture." Publ Wkly

Morrison, Terri
Kiss, bow, or shake hands; the bestselling guide to doing business in more than 60 countries; [by] Terri Morrison and Wayne A. Conaway. 2nd ed. Adams Media 2006 593p il pa $24.95 * **395**
1. Business etiquette 2. Business communication 3. Negotiation
ISBN 1-59337-368-6 LC 2006-13587
First published 1994
"Brief information regarding the history of the country, the type of government, languages, religions, and demographics are included. The authors then provide what they call a cultural orientation for each country, identifying 'cognitive styles, negotiation strategies, and value systems.' A summary of business practices (appointment scheduling, negotiating do's and don'ts, business entertaining, and time zone information) follows. Finally, 'protocol' considerations, such as greetings, titles and forms of address, gestures, gift giving, and appropriate dress, are offered." Booklist
"The definitive reference for doing business around the world." Libr J

Post, Peggy, 1945-
Emily Post's Etiquette. 17th ed., [revised by] Peggy Post. HarperCollins Publishers 2004 876p $39.95 * **395**
1. Etiquette
ISBN 0-06-620957-9 LC 2004-40508
First published 1922 under the authorship of Emily Post. Periodically revised and updated. Title varies. 11th-15th editions revised by Elizabeth Post; 16th-17th editions revised by Peggy Post
"The classic reference for which fork to use has been expanded to include such modern situations as dating, living together, second marriages, and co-ed business traveling." N Y Public Libr Book of How & Where to Look It Up

Post, Peggy, 1945-—*Continued*

Emily Post's wedding etiquette. 5th ed. HarperCollins 2006 xxiv, 405p il $27.95 *

395

1. Etiquette 2. Weddings 3. Marriage customs and rites
ISBN 978-0-06-074503-5; 0-06-074503-7

LC 2005-40387

First published 1982 under the authorship of Emily Post with title: Emily Post's complete book of wedding etiquette

This guide to wedding planning covers such topics as multicultural and interfaith marriages, second marriages, engagements, prewedding events, postwedding duties, financial matters, working with consultants, and responsibilities of participants, and includes flow charts and ckecklists.

Truss, Lynne

Talk to the hand; the utter bloody rudeness of the world today, or six good reasons to stay home and bolt the door. Gotham Books 2005 206p $20

395

1. Conduct of life 2. Etiquette
ISBN 1-59240-171-6

The author "examines the death of civil language, the transfer of customer service from those who serve the customers to the customers themselves, the refusal to live by any rules but one's own, the pervasiveness of profanity, the dismissal of criticism, and the universal lack of responsibility. Each examination is not merely an opportunity to rant but a thoughtful and well-researched effort to understand the behavior." Libr J

Includes bibliographical references

Vanderbilt, Amy

The Amy Vanderbilt complete book of etiquette; entirely rewritten and updated by Nancy Tuckerman and Nancy Dunnan; illustrations by Jackie Aher. Doubleday 1995 786p il $32

395

1. Etiquette
ISBN 0-385-41342-4

LC 93-44452

First published 1952 under the authorship of Amy Vanderbilt

This guide includes "discussions of cellular phones, unmarried couples living together, either heterosexual or gay, business travel, especially for women, and many other new topics, as well as the standard information on table settings, weddings, funerals, and tipping. . . . This is a very comprehensive work that belongs in every public library." Libr J

Warner, Diane, 1937-

How to have a big wedding on a small budget; cut your wedding costs in half. 4th ed. Betterway Bks. 2003 185p il pa $12.99

395

1. Weddings
ISBN 1-55870-646-1

LC 2002-26191

First published 1990

The author provides consumer tips on such subjects as invitations, dresses, food, flowers, and pictures

Includes bibliographical references

Weiss, Mindy

The wedding book; the big book for your big day; by Mindy Weiss with Lisbeth Levine. Workman Pub. Company, Inc. 2007 485p il $35; pa $19.95

395

1. Weddings
ISBN 978-0-7611-3960-7; 978-0-7611-5094-7 (pa)

LC 2008-15510

This book offers wedding planning advice on topics such as announcing the wedding, setting up a budget, planning the ceremony, wedding parties, and designing the dress and tuxedo.

398   Folklore

Bernstein, Peter L.

The power of gold; the history of an obsession. Wiley 2000 432p $27.95; pa $16.95

398

1. Gold
ISBN 0-471-25210-7; 0-471-00378-6 (pa)

LC 00-36647

Also available illustrated edition $34.95 (ISBN: 0-470-09100-2)

The author "recounts the magical, religious, and artistic qualities of gold and moves through the invention of coins, the transformation of gold into money, and the history of the gold standard." Libr J

"Bernstein's prose is lucid if not vivid, and he covers a lot of time and territory in relatively few pages." N Y Times Book Rev

Includes bibliographical references

Bunson, Matthew

The vampire encyclopedia. Crown 1993 303p il pa $7.99 hardcover o.p.

398

1. Vampires—Encyclopedias
ISBN 0-517-16206-7 (pa)

LC 92-42005

This "is an A-Z arrangement of more than 2000 entries drawn from folklore, literature, and popular culture. Entries range in length from a line to over a page, with a few tables (film, literature, etc.) running to several pages. *See* and *See also* references are frequent, . . . appendixes list more novels and anthologies, major works consulted, and vampire societies." Libr J

Encyclopedia of American folklife; Simon J. Bronner, editor. M.E. Sharpe 2006 4v il set $399 *

398

1. Folklore—United States—Encyclopedias 2. United States—Social life and customs—Encyclopedias
ISBN 0-7656-8052-1; 978-0-7656-8052-5

LC 2005-32119

This encyclopedia "provides a survey of the cultural patterns and experiences of diverse communities throughout the United States and the territories of Guam, Samoa, and Puerto Rico as well as other countries and ethnic groups that have influenced American social practices. . . . The encyclopedia covers crafts, foods, architecture, remedies, customs, holidays, narratives, speech, and stereotypes, with an emphasis on contemporary practices." Libr J

Includes bibliographical references

The **Greenwood** encyclopedia of African American folklore; edited by Anand Prahlad. Greenwood Press 2005 3v xl, 1557p il set $299.95 * **398**

1. African Americans—Folklore—Encyclopedias 2. African Americans—Social life and customs—Encyclopedias

ISBN 0-313-33035-2 LC 2005-19214

"The three volume set gives special attention to music, art, folktales, spiritual beliefs, foodways, proverbs, and other topics central to African American folklore, and discusses the Caribbean and African roots of traditional African American culture." Libr Media Connect

For a fuller review, see: Booklist, Feb. 1, 2006

Includes bibliographical references

Melton, J. Gordon

The vampire book; the encyclopedia of the undead. Visible Ink Press 1998 c1999 919p il pa $24.95 **398**

1. Vampires

ISBN 1-57859-071-X

First published 1994

This work "has 375 entries ranging in length from 100 to 5,000 words. The work is illustrated with black-and-white photographs. . . . Four appendixes list vampire organizations and fanzines; a filmography of 650 feature films; a section of vampire drama, opera, and ballet; and a bibliography of vampire books beginning with *Dracula* in 1897 up to the present." Booklist [review of 1994 edition]

398.03 Folklore—Encyclopedias and dictionaries

American folklore; an encyclopedia; edited by Jan Harold Brunvand. Garland 1996 794p il (Garland reference library of the humanities) pa $44.95 hardcover o.p. **398.03**

1. Folklore—United States—Encyclopedias

ISBN 0-8153-3350-1 (pa) LC 95-53734

This volume contains "more than 500 articles covering American and Canadian folklore from holidays, festivals, and rituals to crafts, music, dance, and occupations. Well-chosen black-and-white photographs illustrate many aspects of our rich folklife tradition. Twenty-three ethnic groups receive lengthy articles describing their traditional and contemporary folklore—with the exception of Native Americans." Am Libr

Includes bibliographical references

Radford, Edwin, 1891-1973

Encyclopaedia of superstitions; by E. and M. A. Radford; with a foreword by Sir John Hammerton. Philosophical Lib. 1949 269p pa $19 * **398.03**

1. Superstition—Encyclopedias

ISBN 0-8065-2975-X

First published 1948 in the United Kingdom

This volume "contains over two thousand superstitions of Britain ranging over the past six hundred years, with many references to present day beliefs." Wilson Libr Bull

Rose, Carol, 1943-

Giants, monsters, and dragons; an encyclopedia of folklore, legend, and myth. Norton 2001 428p il pa $21.95 * **398.03**

1. Monsters—Encyclopedias

ISBN 978-0-393-32211-8; 0-393-32211-4

First published 2000 by ABC-CLIO

For inclusion in this reference work "the creature cannot be divine, it must be a supernatural being from mythology, legend, folklore, or classic literature, and it may be a cryptozoological or symbolic being, such as a heraldic beast. . . . Entries give basic descriptions of each creature as well as its activities, region, culture, and historical period." Libr J

Includes bibliographical references

Seal, Graham, 1950-

Encyclopedia of folk heroes. ABC-CLIO 2001 xxiii, 347p $85 **398.03**

1. Folklore—Encyclopedias 2. Heroes and heroines

ISBN 1-57607-216-9 LC 2001-4423

"This volume describes folk heroes from all times and cultures, both individually and as groups. . . . There are indexes by heroic type, country/culture, and a chronology of folk heroes by century." SLJ

This "includes a number of figures not easily found elsewhere. Larger public and academic libraries with folklore collections may find it useful." Booklist

Includes bibliographical references

South Asian folklore; an encyclopedia; Margaret A. Mills, Peter J. Claus and Sarah Diamond, editors. Routledge 2002 xxix, 710p il map $175 **398.03**

1. Folklore—South Asia—Encyclopedias

ISBN 0-415-93919-4 LC 2002-23695

This is a "guide to the complex belief systems, folklore, and customs of the diverse societies of South Asia, both ancient and contemporary. . . . The nearly 500 signed articles range widely, from 'animal performances,' 'Bhakti saints,' 'Catholicism, Sri Lanka,' and 'egg fights' to 'proverbs' 'puberty rituals,' 'sacred geography, Afghanistan,' and 'wedding songs.'" Libr J

Includes bibliographical references

Storytelling encyclopedia; historical, cultural, and multiethnic approaches to oral traditions around the world; general editor, David Adams Leeming; project editor, Marion Sader. Oryx Press 1997 543p $69.95 * **398.03**

1. Storytelling—Encyclopedias

ISBN 1-57356-025-1 LC 97-23081

This volume "includes entries on characters from both mythology and folklore as well as authors, storytellers, scholars, tale types, terminology, cultural traditions, and more. A selected bibliography is included, and most entries are followed by references to further reading." Libr J

"A valuable source on various aspects of folklore and storytelling around the world from early times to the present. It should prove of interest to librarians, teachers, students, and others interested in the subject." Booklist

398.2　Folk literature

American Indian myths and legends; selected and edited by Richard Erdoes and Alfonso Ortiz. Pantheon Bks. 1984 527p il pa $18 hardcover o.p.　　　　　　**398.2**
1. Native Americans—Folklore 2. Native Americans—Religion
ISBN 0-394-74018-1　　　　　　LC 84-42669
"This volume comprises 160 tales of native folklore and myth ranging from one geographical end of our continent to the other. The book is organized according to type of myth. . . . Erdoes and Ortiz seek to keep Indian myth intact and pure through their retellings, using, as often as possible, primary sources." Booklist
Includes bibliographical references

Armstrong, Karen
A short history of myth. Canongate 2005 159p $18 *　　　　　　**398.2**
1. Mythology
ISBN 1-84195-716-X
This is an "overview of the ever-evolving partnership betweeh myth and man from Paleolithic times to the present. Succinct and cleanly written, it is hugely readable and, in its journey across the epochs of human experience, often moving. . . . Armstrong's exposition is streamlined and uncluttered without being simplistic." N Y Times Book Rev
Includes bibliographical references

Brunvand, Jan Harold
The choking Doberman and other "new" urban legends. Norton 1984 240p il pa $11.95 hardcover o.p.　　　　　　**398.2**
1. Folklore—United States 2. Legends—United States
ISBN 0-393-30321-7 (pa)　　　　　　LC 83-22031
"These fictitious narratives . . . circulate widely as true incidents. Brunvand details more than 40 . . . anecdotes, ranging from grisly reports of alleged mutilations to comical tales of sexual mishaps." Libr J
"Brunvand is especially adept at tracing apparently fresh stories to ancient roots." Time
Includes bibliographical references

Too good to be true; the colossal book of urban legends. Norton 1999 480p il $29.95; pa $17.95　　　　　　**398.2**
1. Folklore—United States 2. Legends—United States
ISBN 0-393-04734-2; 0-393-32088-X (pa)　　　　　　LC 99-17562
"This anthology embraces over 200 fanciful, amusing, and often exaggerated stories and beliefs that have, through repetition, become part of the American oral heritage. . . . Thoroughly researched and exhaustive, this fascinating work is characterized by impressive scholarship." Libr J

The vanishing hitchhiker; American urban legends and their meaning. Norton 1981 208p pa $13.95 hardcover o.p.　　　　　　**398.2**
1. Folklore—United States 2. Legends—United States
ISBN 0-393-95169-3 (pa)　　　　　　LC 81-4744

A collection of modern urban folktales with an ironic or supernatural twist. The author reports on how such tales are disseminated and discusses their inherent messages for contemporary society
Includes bibliographical references

Bulfinch, Thomas, 1796-1867
Bulfinch's mythology; foreword by Alberto Manguel. Modern Library pbk. ed. Modern Library 2004 862p pa $17.95 *　　　　　　**398.2**
1. Mythology 2. Folklore—Europe 3. Chivalry
ISBN 0-375-75147-5　　　　　　LC 2005-271850
First combined edition published 1913 by Crowell. Originally published in three separate volumes 1855, 1858 and 1862 respectively
Contents: The age of fable — The age of chivalry — Legends of Charlemagne
"The classic work on mythology, Bulfinch's gives brief summations of Greek, Roman, Norse, Arthurian, and other miscellaneous myths and includes notes on the 'Iliad,' the 'Odyssey,' and the 'Aeneid.'" N Y Public Libr Book of How & Where to Look It Up
Includes bibliographical references

Chase, Richard, 1904-1988
American folk tales and songs; and other examples of English-American tradition as preserved in the Appalachian Mountains and elsewhere in the United States. Dover Publications 1971 c1956 239p il pa $9.95　　　　　　**398.2**
1. Folklore—United States 2. Folk music—United States
ISBN 0-48622-692-1; 978-0-48622-692-7
First published 1956 by New Amsterdam Library
"Full of . . . stories, jokes, and games for performance, the book also includes 40 songs with melody and guitar chords. Written by the . . . practicing folk performer." Publisher's note

Favorite folktales from around the world; edited by Jane Yolen. Pantheon Bks. 1986 498p pa $18 hardcover o.p.　　　　　　**398.2**
1. Folklore 2. Fairy tales
ISBN 0-394-75188-4 (pa)　　　　　　LC 86-42644
"Selections include tales from the American Indians, the brothers Grimm, Italo Calvino's Italian folk-tales, as well as stories from Iceland, Afghanistan, Scotland, and many other countries. Yolen provides each section with a relevant introduction, often including historical and literary factors, thus alerting readers as to what to look for." SLJ

Lynch, Patricia Ann
Native American mythology A to Z. Facts on File 2004 130p il map (Mythology A-Z) $40 *　　　　　　**398.2**
1. Native Americans—Folklore
ISBN 0-8160-4891-6　　　　　　LC 2004-47115
This book presents "coverage of the deities, legendary heroes and heroines, important animals, objects, and places that make up the mythic lore of the many peoples of North America from northern Mexico into the Arctic Circle." Publisher's note
Includes bibliographical references

Malory, Sir Thomas, 15th cent.

Le morte Darthur, or, The hoole book of Kyng Arthur and of his noble knyghtes of the Rounde Table; authoritative text, sources and backgrounds, criticism; [by] Sir Thomas Malory; edited by Stephen H.A. Shepherd. Norton 2004 lii, 954p (A Norton critical edition) pa $16.95 *

398.2

1. Arthur, King
ISBN 0-393-97464-2   LC 2002-26534
Originally published 1485
"The work is a skillful selection and blending of materials taken from the mass of Arthurian legends. The central story consists of two main elements: the reign of King Arthur ending in catastrophe and the dissolution of the Round Table; and the quest of the Holy Grail." Oxford Companion to Engl Lit
Includes bibliographical references

Orenstein, Catherine, 1968-

Little Red Riding Hood uncloaked; sex, morality, and the evolution of a fairy tale. Basic Bks. 2002 289p il hardcover o.p. pa $14.95 *

398.2

1. Little Red Riding Hood
ISBN 0-465-04125-6; 0-465-04126-4 (pa)
          LC 2002-4240
"Once upon a time, Red Riding Hood was a good little girl. When she foolishly strayed from the path in the forest and spoke to strangers, she fell prey to the wicked wolf, but fortunately, the heroic woodcutter rescued her just in time. . . . With wit and insight, Orenstein makes us look again at the old childhood story, how it has changed and what that says about us. From Perrault and the Brothers Grimm to Bruno Bettelheim and Andrea Dworkin, the lively informal narrative surveys the stories and the scholarship in terms of folklore, psychology, feminism, and pornography." Booklist
Includes bibliographical references

Petro, Pamela, 1960-

Sitting up with the dead; a storied journey through the American South. Arcade Pub. 2002 414p $25.95   **398.2**
1. Folklore—Southern States
ISBN 1-55970-612-0   LC 2002-18310
The author "embarked on four meandering trips through the South. . . . Folktales and their tellers serve as her maps and guides; her travelogue is peppered with transcribed stories she hears on the way. The resulting chronicle is an impressive piece of cultural conservation, reportage and memoir that subtly mourns the passing of a rural way of life." Publ Wkly

Pickering, David, 1958-

A dictionary of folklore. Facts on File 1999 324p $44   **398.2**
1. Folklore—Dictionaries 2. Mythology—Dictionaries
ISBN 0-8160-4550-0
The author provides entries "on such subjects as herbal remedies, the superstitions connected with various gemstones, the folklore associated with selected trees,

plants, birds, and animals. He also covers the ritual tradition of holidays and festivals and the origins of proverbs and sayings. In addition, the dictionary mentions characters and heroes from selkies to Joe Magarac, fantasy beings such as sprites and pixies, and some urban myths." Libr J

398.8   Rhymes and rhyming games

The **Oxford** dictionary of nursery rhymes; edited by Iona and Peter Opie. 2nd ed. Oxford Univ. Press 1997 xxix, 559p il $55 *   **398.8**
1. Nursery rhymes—Dictionaries
ISBN 0-19-860088-7   LC 98-140995
First published 1951
An anthology of "over 500 rhymes, songs, nonsense jingles, and lullabies. . . . Complementing the rhymes are nearly a hundred illustrations, including reproductions of early art found in ballad sheets and music books, which highlight the development of children's illustrations over the last two centuries. . . . [The editors note] the earliest known publications of the rhyme, describing how it originated, illustrating changes in wording over time, and indicating variations and parallels in other languages." Publisher's note
"The novice as well as the professional will find it an enjoyable read, as well as a learning experience." Am Ref Books Annu, 1999

398.9   Proverbs

Cordry, Harold V., 1943-

The multicultural dictionary of proverbs; over 20,000 adages from more than 120 languages, nationalities and ethnic groups. McFarland & Co. 1997 406p pa $35   **398.9**
1. Proverbs
ISBN 0-7864-0251-2; 0-7864-2262-9 (pa)
          LC 96-33264
"The proverbs are arranged under 1300 headings (e.g., accidents, divided loyalty, marriage, and shame), and each includes the nationality, group or language in which it originated." Publisher's note
"This well-organized multicultural dictionary of proverbs not only illustrates the common insights that different cultures share but also provides a rich resource of wisdom that the casual reader can glean from perusing the proverbs in an entry." Am Ref Books Annu, 1998

A **Dictionary** of American proverbs; Wolfgang Mieder, editor in chief; Stewart A. Kingsbury and Kelsie B. Harder, editors. Oxford Univ. Press 1992 710p $65   **398.9**
1. Proverbs
ISBN 0-19-505399-0   LC 91-15508
"This scholarly work includes 15,000 proverbs with variants currently used in the United States and parts of Canada. Entries are arranged alphabetically under key words and are often followed by variants and cross references. . . . This collection differs from most such compilations because the proverbs were collected by field workers rather than from written sources. The work sets

A Dictionary of American proverbs—*Continued*
new standards for understanding the oral tradition in
America and is an essential purchase for ready-reference
collections." Libr J

Manser, Martin H.
The Facts on File dictionary of proverbs;
associate editors, Rosalind Fergusson, David
Pickering. 2nd ed. Facts On File 2006 499p (Facts
on File library of language and literature) $55; pa
$19.95 *   **398.9**
1. Proverbs
ISBN   0-8160-6673-6;   978-0-8160-6673-5;
0-8160-6674-4 (pa); 978-0-8160-6674-2 (pa)
LC 2006-24535
Original edition published 1983 compiled by Rosalind
Fergusson
This dictionary "includes more than 1,700 English-
language proverbs . . . that are widely recognized today.
Arranged alphabetically, entries provide the meaning of
each proverb, the date it was first recorded, variant forms
of the proverb, other proverbs that are similar and oppo-
site to it in meaning, and examples of the proverb's use."
Publisher's note
Includes bibliographical references

400   LANGUAGE

Crystal, David, 1941-
The Cambridge encyclopedia of language. 2nd
ed. Cambridge Univ. Press 1997 480p il hardcover
o.p. pa $30 *   **400**
1. Language and languages—Encyclopedias
ISBN 0-521-55050-5; 0-521-55967-7 (pa)
LC 96-3104
First published 1987
This encyclopedia "covers all the major themes of language study, including popular ideas about language, language and identity, the structure of language, speaking
and listening, writing, reading, and signing, language acquisition, the neurological basis of language, and languages of the world. . . . [Also includes] advances in areas such as machine translation, speech interaction with
machines, and language teaching." Univ Press Books for
Public and Second Sch Libr, 1997

Kenneally, Christine
The first word; the search for the origins of
language. Viking 2007 357p $26.95   **400**
1. Language and languages 2. Evolution
ISBN 978-0-670-03490-1; 0-670-03490-8
LC 2007-3182
Kenneally "synthesizes linguistic scholarship regarding
the evolution of language, namely, scholarship's development and current conclusions. She shares intriguing accounts of research not just about humans but about primates, dolphins, and parrots as well. She also discusses
genes specifically identified as impacting language and
the computer modeling of language development.
Kenneally organizes the various research projects as they
relate to a specific scholar's work (e.g., that of

primatologist Sue Savage-Rumbaugh) or aspect of language (e.g., sound or gesture), or as they illumine the
earliest linguistic evolution." Libr J
The author "explains difficult ideas concisely and
clearly, and she maintains a firm grip on the steering
wheel, moving the overall argument along in a straight
line. Above all, she is scrupulously fair-minded." N Y
Times (Late N Y Ed)
Includes bibliographical references

Pinker, Steven, 1954-
The language instinct; how the mind creates
language. Harper Perennial 2007 526p il pa $15.95
       400
1. Language and languages
ISBN 978-0-06-133646-1; 0-06-133646-7
First published 1994 by Morrow
The author "argues that an 'innate grammatical machinery of the brain' exists, which allows children to
'reinvent' language on their own. Basing his ideas on
Noam Chomsky's Universal Grammar theory, Pinker describes language as a 'discrete combinatorial system' that
might easily have evolved via natural selection. Pinker
steps on a few toes . . . but his work, while controversial, is well argued, challenging, often humorous, and always fascinating." Libr J
Includes bibliographical references

401   Philosophy and theory

Crystal, David, 1941-
How language works; how babies babble, words
change meaning, and languages live or die.
Overlook Press 2006 500p $32.50 *   **401**
1. Language and languages 2. Linguistics
ISBN 1-58567-848-1
The author "addresses every aspect of language, including how we learn to speak, read, and write; the
physiology behind the formation of speech sounds; how
we choose what to say; how gestures and tone of voice
impact communication; how the brain handles language;
and how language tells us where we are from." Booklist
Crystal "offers an impeccably organized guide to language and communication that brings clarity to a scholarly subject, and is sure to become a standard reference."
Publ Wkly
Includes bibliographical references

Pinker, Steven, 1954-
The stuff of thought; language as a window into
human nature. Viking 2007 499p il $29.95
       401
1. Language and languages 2. Thought and thinking
ISBN 978-0-670-06327-7; 0-670-06327-4
LC 2007-26601
Pinker argues that "the reason language works is that
it reflects the world as we jointly experience it. That
doesn't mean we always use language to convey reality.
Language is a social medium with social purposes.
Sometimes, we use it not to communicate facts about the
world but to filter them." N Y Times Book Rev
The author's "vivid prose and down-to-earth attitude

Pinker, Steven, 1954——*Continued*
will once again attract an enthusiastic audience outside academia." Publ Wkly

Includes bibliographical references

Words and rules; the ingredients of language. Perennial 2000 349p il pa $15   **401**
1. Language and languages 2. Grammar
ISBN 978-0-06-095840-4; 0-06-095840-5

First published 1999 by Basic Books

Pinker "studies how the mind works by examining the nature of language. In 'Words and Rules,' he examines irregularities, especially irregular verbs and plurals, from the points of view of biology, child development, psychology, philology, and linguistics." Christ Sci Monit

This book "with its crisp prose and neat analogies, makes required reading for anyone interested in cognition and language." Publ Wkly

Includes bibliographical references

Yang, Charles
The infinite gift; how children learn and unlearn the languages of the world. Scribner 2006 275p il $25 *   **401**
1. Language and languages
ISBN 978-0-7432-3756-7; 0-7432-3756-0

The author explains the "process by which children acquire language. He discusses everything from the sounds they hear in the womb to how they distinguish between different languages at three months to their mastery of their language by age five. Throughout this learning process, posits Yang, a child has tested the grammar and sounds that exist in many other languages (and would presumably have no trouble acquiring them) but ultimately settles on the relevant one, and soon after, can no longer distinguish between or articulate nonrelevant sounds. . . . Anyone with the slightest interest in the English language should read his book." Libr J

410   Linguistics

Crystal, David, 1941-
A dictionary of language. 2nd ed. University of Chicago Press 2001 390p il pa $17.50 *   **410**
1. Language and languages—Dictionaries
ISBN 0-226-12203-4   LC 00-69076

First published 1992 with title: An encyclopedic dictionary of language and languages; present edition first published in the United Kingdom with title: The Penguin dictionary of language

This dictionary "offers explanations of the most frequently used linguistic terms, particularly those that can occur in texts read by beginners and by interested laypersons. . . . There are also entries concerned with graphology, shorthand writing, and similar peripheral, but interesting, topics. The impression that this dictionary has been written mainly for the general public is enhanced by the humorous jocose caricatures interspersed throughout the text, but the information is still solid. The author has succeeded in creating a handy dictionary that will serve students and laypeople equally well, for both browsing and study." Am Ref Book Annu, 2002

Language and the internet. 2nd ed. Cambridge University Press 2006 304p $29.99 *
          410
1. Language and languages 2. Internet
ISBN 978-0-521-86859-4; 0-521-86859-9
          LC 2006-12916

First published 2001

"Covering a range of Internet genres, including e-mail, chat, and the Web, this is . . . [an] account of how the Internet is radically changing the way we use language." Publisher's note

Includes bibliographical references

Dalby, Andrew
Dictionary of languages; the definitive reference to more than 400 languages. Columbia Univ. Press 1999 734p il maps $73.50; pa $22.95 *
          410
1. Language and languages—Dictionaries
ISBN 0-231-11568-7; 0-231-11569-5 (pa)
          LC 98-87178

This dictionary includes alphabetical entries that "cover all languages with official status as well as those with a written literature and 175 minor languages with significant historical and/or anthropological interest. A preface explains the author's pronunciation scheme. . . . The entries themselves are from two to four pages long. Each one discusses a specific language. . . . With coverage of languages from Abkhaz to Zulu, explanations of Egyptian hieroglyphics and Sumerian script, and a discussion of Chinese dialects and characters, [this] . . . is a welcome addition to public and academic library collections." Booklist

412   Etymology of standard forms of languages

Hayakawa, S. I.
Language in thought and action; {by} S.I. Hayakawa and Alan R. Hayakawa. 5th ed. Harcourt Brace Jovanovich 1990 287p il $49.95; pa $16 *   **412**
1. Semantics 2. Thought and thinking 3. English language
ISBN 0-15-550120-8; 0-15-648240-1 (pa)
          LC 89-84371

First published 1939 with title: Language in action

The author analyzes the nature of language, discusses the processes of thinking and writing, and gives advice on thinking and writing clearly

Includes bibliographical references

419 Sign languages

Chambers, Diane P., 1959-
Communicating in sign; creative ways to learn American Sign Language (ASL); written by Diane P. Chambers, with Lee Ann Chearney; edited by D. Keith Robertson; illustrations by Paul M. Setzer; with an introduction by Bernard Bragg. Fireside 1998 165p il (Flying hands book) pa $12
419

1. Sign language
ISBN 0-684-83520-7　　　　LC 97-51145
"Produced by Amaranth."
"By combining vocabulary, grammar, syntax, expression, and movement with commentary on etiquette and other cultural issues, Chambers . . . has created a general resource intended for the lay public." Libr J
Includes bibliographical references

Costello, Elaine
Random House Webster's American sign language dictionary; illustrated by Lois Lenderman, Paul M. Setzer, Linda C. Tom. Random House 1998 xxxvi, 539p pa $20
419

1. Sign language
ISBN 0-679-78011-4　　　　LC 97-21538
Also available Concise American sign language dictionary pa (ISBN 0-553-58474-X)
First published 1994 with title: Random House American sign language dictionary
This illustrated sign language dictionary includes over 4,500 signs with complete description of each sign, plus full-torso illustrations. Includes alternate signs for the same meaning and different signs for different meanings of the same word

The **Gallaudet** dictionary of American Sign Language; Clayton Valli, editor in chief; illustrated by Peggy Swartzel Lott, Daniel Renner, and Rob Hills. Gallaudet University Press 2005 xli, 558p il $49.95 *　**419**
1. Sign language—Dictionaries
ISBN 1-56368-282-6; 978-1-56368-282-7
　　　　LC 2005-51129
This "reference work is composed of approximately 3000 illustrated entries, each showing the American Sign Language equivalent for an English word. The entries are arranged alphabetically and include synonyms where appropriate." Libr J
"This is a very valuable language resource for parents, students, and teachers learning ASL as a first language and as a second language." Choice
Includes bibliographical references

Grayson, Gabriel
Talking with your hands, listening with your eyes; a complete photographic guide to American Sign Language. Square One Pubs. 2002 373p il pa $26.95
419
1. Sign language
ISBN 0-7570-0007-X　　　　LC 2002-1125

"The book covers more than 900 signs that represent nearly 1,800 words and phrases, with signs grouped by topic. . . . Grayson provides instructions for each word, explaining the hand shape, the position in front of the body where the sign is made and the type of movement involved in expressing the word." Publ Wkly
"An outstanding, user-friendly resource for those interested in learning ASL." SLJ

Proctor, Claude O.
NTC's multilingual dictionary of American sign language. National Textbook 1995 767p il pa $29.95 hardcover o.p.　**419**
1. Sign language
ISBN 0-8442-0732-2 (pa)
This work contains "2,446 entries arranged alphabetically by the English word, followed by an abbreviation denoting the part of speech and a small line drawing showing the American Sign Language (ASL) gesture with arrow(s) indicating direction of motion of the hand(s). There are four entries per page. Following the ASL illustration are equivalents in 12 languages, Arabic through Swedish, including 3 Asian and 8 European languages. For Russian and Asian words, a romanized spelling is given before the native script itself." Recommended Ref Books for Small & Medium-sized Libr & Media Cent, 1997

Sternberg, Martin L. A.
American Sign Language; a comprehensive dictionary; illustrated by Herbert Rogoff. Unabridged. HarperCollins Pubs. 1998 xxi, 983p il $60; pa $24　**419**
1. Sign language
ISBN 0-06-271608-5; 0-06-273634-5 (pa)
　　　　LC 98-26649
Also available American sign language concise dictionary pa $12 (ISBN 0-06-274010-5)
First published 1981
Arranged alphabetically, this dictionary features 7,000 sign entries, with cross-references and more than 12,000 illustrations
Includes bibliographical references

Tennant, Richard A.
The American Sign Language handshape dictionary; {by} Richard A. Tennant, Marianne Gluszak Brown; illustrated by Valerie Nelson-Metlay. Gallaudet Univ. Press 1998 407p il $39.95
419
1. Sign language
ISBN 1-56368-043-2　　　　LC 97-48389
This work organizes "signs by handshape rather than alphabetically by English word order. In so doing, it acts best as a recognition tool for the ASL learner, leading the user quickly to specific signs without having first to refer to an English-equivalent word." Libr J

420 English and Old English (Anglo-Saxon)

Bragg, Melvyn, 1939-
The adventure of English; the biography of a language. Arcade Pub. 2004 c2003 322p il $27.95
420
1. English language—History
ISBN 1-55970-710-0   LC 2003-19583
First published 2003 in the United Kingdom
The author offers a "biography of the English language, highlighting key individuals, places, and literature that advanced it, as well as the political and social trends that influenced it. . . . Bragg discusses its evolution in the English colonies, devoting four chapters to the United States and one each to India, the West Indies, and Australia. . . . Well researched yet more accessible to a wide audience than scholarly treatments by linguists or historians." Libr J

Bryson, Bill
Made in America; an informal history of the English language in the United States. Avon Books 1996 417p pa $14.95   **420**
1. English language—History 2. Americanisms
ISBN 978-0-380-71381-3; 0-380-71381-0
First published 1994 by Morrow
The author "explains the original meanings of words and phrases by establishing the contexts in which they were popularized, describing particular eras in American history as well as major events and institutions, e.g., war, politics, sports, advertising and movies, that have contributed to language usage." Publ Wkly
"For Bryson's wonderfully sane and reasoned discussion of the issues surrounding 'politically correct' language alone, this book is a worthwhile read." Libr J
Includes bibliographical references

Crystal, David, 1941-
The Cambridge encyclopedia of the English language. 2nd ed. Cambridge Univ. Press 2003 499p il hardcover o.p. pa $35 *   **420**
1. English language
ISBN 0-521-82348-X; 0-521-53033-4 (pa)
LC 2003-272259
First published 1995
This "volume is divided into six broad topics that cover the English language's history, vocabulary, grammar, writing and speech systems, usage, and acquisition. Within these major topics, the book is divided into logical subtopics and finally into the basic unit of the text—the two-page spread. . . . The clear and spirited text is stunning, enhanced with over 500 illustrations, making this a particularly rich reference work and a browser's dream." Libr J {review of 1995 edition}

English as a global language. 2nd ed. Cambridge Univ. Press 2003 212p il maps $45; pa $15 *   **420**
1. English language—Social aspects
ISBN 0-521-82347-1; 0-521-53032-6 (pa)
LC 2003-282119

First published 1997
Crystal's "account of the rise of English as a global language explores the history, current status and potential of English as the international language of communication. {Includes} sections on the future of English as a world language, English on the Internet, and the possibility of an English 'family' of languages." Publisher's note
"This is a fascinating and useful book. . . . a fine introduction for a wide variety of potential users." Choice
Includes bibliographical references

McCrum, Robert
The story of English; [by] Robert McCrum, Willam Cran [and] Robert MacNeil. 3rd rev ed. Penguin Bks. 2003 xxi, 468p pa $16 *
420
1. English language—History
ISBN 0-14-200231-3   LC 2002-29818
First published 1986 by Viking
A "companion to the PBS television series of the same name. . . . The text covers the history of our language from its roots in Latin through its transplanting to other shores and its infusions from other cultures and languages. . . . Good for browsing, this book is a must for word and history buffs." SLJ [review of 1986 edition]
Includes bibliographical references

Metcalf, Allan A.
Predicting new words; the secrets of their success; {by} Allan Metcalf. Houghton Mifflin 2002 206p il $22   **420**
1. New words 2. English language—Terms and phrases
ISBN 0-618-13006-3   LC 2002-68593
This book traces the origins of an "array of words and phrases: *Marlboro Man, Frankenfood, blurb, skycap, quark, scofflaw*. It also introduces us to a fascinating array of would-be words, coinages that never quite caught on. . . . The book is jam-packed with treats for word lovers." Booklist

421 Writing system, phonology, phonetics of standard English

Vos Savant, Marilyn Mach
The art of spelling; the madness and the method; by Marilyn vos Savant; illustrations by Joan Reilly. Norton 2000 204p il hardcover o.p. pa $12.95   **421**
1. English language—Spelling
ISBN 0-393-04903-5; 0-393-32208-4 (pa)
LC 00-37228
The author "offers some suggestions for spelling improvement, supplying common roots like anim-, arch-, and spec- and a list of 500 commonly misspelled words. She also includes a few quizzes, with answers in the back of the book. This is not a how-to book, however, for more than half of it examines what spelling ability tells us about intelligence and personality. . . . The bibliography and web site list are nice additions as well." Libr J

421.03 Writing system, phonology, phonetics of standard English—Dictionaries

Acronyms, initialisms, & abbreviations dictionary. 40th ed. Gale Res. 2008 4v set $1,190 *

421.03

1. Acronyms—Dictionaries
ISSN 0270-4404
ISBN 978-1-4144-1902-2; 1-4144-1902-3

Also available eBook version, and Reverse acronyms, initialisms, & abbreviations dictionary $785 (ISBN 978-1-4144-2154-4)

First published 1960 in one volume with title: Acronyms dictionary. Frequently revised

A guide to acronyms, initialisms, abbreviations, contractions, alphabetic symbols, and similar condensed apellations

Stahl, Dean

Abbreviations dictionary; {by} Dean Stahl, Karen Kerchelich; originated by Ralph De Sola. 10th ed. CRC Press 2001 1529p $79.95 *

421.03

1. Abbreviations—Dictionaries 2. Signs and symbols
ISBN 0-8493-9003-6   LC 00-58549

First published 1958 under the authorship of Ralph De Sola

"The classic status of this title endures: abbreviations are again joined by a dazzling array of acronyms, contractions, initials, nicknames, short forms, signs, and symbols. Its 15,000 new terms swell the dictionary to nearly 300,000 entries. Domestic and international terms are harvested from diverse fields, criminology to music. Computing, technology, and government draw special attention due to active abbreviating. Entries are alphabetically and numerically ordered." Choice

422 Etymology of standard English

Korach, Myron

Common phrases and where they come from; [by] Myron Korach in collaboration with John B. Mordock. Lyons Press 2001 200p pa $9.95 hardcover o.p.   **422**

1. English language—Etymology 2. English language—Terms and phrases
ISBN 1-58574-682-7 (pa)   LC 00-69016

Korach and Mordock "show how much our culture relies on idiomatic speech to enliven discourse, a point further demonstrated by the more than 150 well-known phrases whose interesting histories they have provided. The arrangement of phrases is loosely thematic, with one to several paragraphs devoted to each." Libr J

The **Oxford** dictionary of allusions; edited by Andrew Delahunty, Sheila Dignen, and Penny Stock. 2nd ed. Oxford University Press 2005 472p (Oxford paperback reference) pa $16.95 *

422

1. Allusions
ISBN 0-19-860919-1; 978-0-19-860919-3
      LC 2005-44913

First published 2001

The text "categorizes entries under 190 general headings, ranging from fatness, destruction, and illusion to quest and outlaws. . . . Valuable to students are 22 special entries, nine from Greek mythology and an equal number from the Bible. . . . Selection of cited material is refreshingly unpedantic. Bram Stoker, Saki, V.S. Naipaul, Robertson Davies, Kurt Vonnegut, and Martin Amis are quoted alongside The Guardian, New Scientist, The Independent, and Observer and lines from classic English writers like Keats, Hardy, Thackeray, Pope, Wilde, and Richardson." Choice

Quinion, Michael, 1942-

Ballyhoo, buckeroo, and spuds; ingenious tales of words and their origins. Smithsonian Books 2004 288p $19.95 *   **422**

1. English language—Etymology 2. English language—Terms and phrases
ISBN 1-588-34219-0   LC 2004-52235

A look at common English "words and phrases most readers will probably have wondered about. We're all familiar with the phrase 'happy as a clam.' but why a clam? We know what a 10-gallon hat is, but how did it get its name? And what the heck is a ballyhoo, anyway? The book is simply organized—alphabetically, of course—and endlessly illuminating. Quinion's research and documentation are impeccable, and when he needs to make a leap of imagination, he does so gracefully. For word lovers, this book is indispensable." Booklist

Includes bibliographical references

422.03 Etymology of standard English—Dictionaries

The **Barnhart** dictionary of etymology; Robert K. Barnhart, editor; Sol Steinmetz, managing editor. Wilson, H.W. 1988 xxvii, 1284p $105 *

422.03

1. English language—Etymology
ISBN 0-8242-0745-9   LC 87-27994

Also available The Barnhart concise dictionary of etymology (HarperCollins Pubs. 1995)

This dictionary "focuses on words used in contemporary American English and words of American origin and incorporates current American scholarship. Entries give spelling variations, pronunciation for difficult words, part of speech, definition, and information on word origins. Written for a wide audience, this is a very attractive, readable work suited for most library users." Ref Sources for Small & Medium-sized Libr. 6th edition

The **Concise** Oxford dictionary of English etymology; edited by T. F. Hoad. Oxford Univ. Press 1986 pa $16.95 hardcover o.p. *

422.03

1. English language—Etymology—Dictionaries
ISBN 0-19-283098-8 (pa)   LC 85-31970
Based on The Oxford dictionary of English etymology
"Provides concise statements on the origins of words and their development once they became part of the English language." N Y Public Libr Book of How & Where to Look It Up

Guinagh, Kevin, 1897-
Dictionary of foreign phrases and abbreviations; translated and compiled by Kevin Guinagh. 3rd ed. Wilson, H.W. 1983 261p $70   **422.03**

1. Quotations
ISBN 0-8242-0675-4   LC 82-8486
First published 1965
This dictionary "contains more than 5,000 foreign phrases, proverbs, and abbreviations frequently used in written and spoken English. Provides translations and pronunciations, and for some entries brief explanatory notes; includes a list of phrases by languages." Ref Sources for Small & Medium-sized Libr. 6th edition

Hendrickson, Robert, 1933-
The Facts on File encyclopedia of word and phrase origins. 4th ed., [Updated and expanded ed.] Facts On File 2008 948p (Facts on File library of language and literature) $95; pa $27.95 *   **422.03**

1. English language—Etymology—Dictionaries 2. English language—Terms and phrases
ISBN 978-0-8160-6966-8; 978-0-8160-6967-5 (pa)
LC 2007-48223
First published 1987
"This encyclopedia features anecdotes and information on the development of a wide range of words, including slang, proverbs, animal and plant names, place names, nicknames, historical expressions, foreign language expressions, and phrases from literature." Publisher's note

Manser, Martin H.
The Facts on File dictionary of foreign words and phrases; [by] Martin H. Manser; associate editors: Alice Grandison and David H. Pickering. 2nd ed., [New ed.] Facts on File 2008 469p (Facts on File library of language and literature) $55; pa $19.95 *   **422.03**

1. English language—Foreign words and phrases—Dictionaries
ISBN 978-0-8160-7035-0; 978-0-8160-7036-7 (pa)
LC 2007-29711
First published 2002
This dictionary includes more than 4,500 entries for terms that have entered the English lexicon from foreign languages in the fields of language and literature, religion, law, politics, economics, music, entertainment and cuisine. Examples or quotations are provided to illustrate usage.
"This is a captivating title to browse." SLJ
Includes bibliographical references

Morris, William, 1913-1994
Morris dictionary of word and phrase origins; [by] William and Mary Morris; foreword by Isaac Asimov. 2nd ed. Harper & Row 1988 669p $38
422.03

1. English language—Etymology 2. English language—Terms and phrases
ISBN 0-06-015862-X   LC 87-45651
Original three volume edition published 1962-1971; one volume edition first published 1977
"Traces the origins of several thousand words and phrases commonly used in the English language, including slang terms and clichés not usually found in more formal works. Entries are listed alphabetically by the first word in the phrase, with an index at the end." Ref Sources for Small & Medium-sized Libr. 6th edition

The **Oxford** dictionary of foreign words and phrases; edited by Jennifer Speake. Oxford Univ. Press 1997 512p pa $16.95 *
422.03

1. English language—Foreign words and phrases—Dictionaries
ISBN 0-19-861051-3; 978-0-19-861051-9
LC 96-49006
New edition in preparation
This dictionary features "a pronunciation guide for each word based on the International Phonetic Alphabet, and examples of usage. Some entries also feature notes on the historical or etymological background of the word or phrase. Approximately 8,000 words and phrases from more than 40 languages make up the main entries. . . . Included are words and phrases that have meaning in more than one sense or have come into general use in this century." Choice

423 Dictionaries of standard English

Adelson-Goldstein, Jayme
The Oxford picture dictionary; [by] Jayme Adelson-Goldstein and Norma Shapiro: Monolingual. 2nd ed. Oxford University Press 2008 285p il pa $16.95   **423**
1. Picture dictionaries 2. English language—Dictionaries
ISBN 978-0-19-436976-3; 0-19-436976-5
LC 2007-41017
First published 1998
This picture dictionary features "4,000 words and phrases illustrated with . . . artwork." Publisher's note

The **American** Heritage dictionary of the English language. 4th ed., New updated ed. Houghton Mifflin 2006 xxxvii, 2074p il $60 *
423

1. English language—Dictionaries
ISBN 0-618-70172-9; 978-0-617-70172-8
First published 1969
This dictionary provides over 210,000 main entries with over 4,000 full-color illustrations. Word histories, synonym paragraphs and regionalisms are also explored.

The American Heritage dictionary of the English language—*Continued*
The work also examines the influence of social factors such as age and ethnicity on how American English has been shaped by speakers from every social class.

This "eminently useful dictionary features fabulous full-color design that quickly and effectively guides users to the information they seek." Libr J

The **American** Heritage guide to contemporary usage and style. Houghton Mifflin 2005 512p $19.95 *   **423**
1. English language—Usage
ISBN 978-0-618-60499-9; 0-618-60499-5
    LC 2005-16513
"Drawing on the authoritative knowledge of its lexicographers and the considered collective judgment of a panel of noted writers, the book offers guidance on the simple (the pronunciations of bouquet); the perplexingly redundant (free gift); the often imprecisely used (impeach); the no longer distinct (healthful/healthy); the needless but persistent (irregardless); the easily confused (stationary/stationery); the unfortunately conflated (lay/lie); and many more pitfalls. Articles embodying the precision and lucidity of dictionary definitions explain the history of a word's or expression's usage issue, how and why the issue exists, and the preferred usage." Booklist

Bartlett's Roget's thesaurus. Little, Brown 1996 xxxii, 1415p $21.95; pa $16.95 *   **423**
1. English language—Synonyms and antonyms 2. Americanisms
ISBN 0-316-10138-9; 0-316-73587-6 (pa)
    LC 96-18343
This thesaurus "reflects the current state of American English, including terminology from the worlds of composers and television, with such sub-categories as 'Living Things,' 'The Arts,' 'Feelings.' But what really makes the book a joy to use is the tremendously useful lists—everything from phobias to styles and periods of furniture." Am Libr

Choose the right word; a contemporary guide to selecting the precise word for every situation; {edited by} S.I. Hayakawa. 2nd ed, Eugene Ehrlich, revising editor. HarperPerennial 1994 532p pa $21.95 hardcover o.p.   **423**
1. English language—Synonyms and antonyms
ISBN 0-06-273131-9 (pa)   LC 93-34206
First published 1968 with title: Funk & Wagnalls Modern guide to synonyms & related words

This work contains over 1,000 key word entries which define and compare 6,000 commonly used synonyms and related words. Short explanatory essays provide illustrative sentences

Concise Oxford American thesaurus. Oxford University Press 2006 996p $19.95 *   **423**
1. English language—Synonyms and antonyms
ISBN 0-19-530485-3; 978-0-19-530485-5
    LC 2005-35868
First published 1997 in the United Kingdom with title: The concise Oxford thesaurus; Original American edition

published 1999 with title: The Oxford American thesaurus of current English
This "thesaurus contains over 15,000 entries with more than 350,000 synonyms and is . . . arranged with the typical synonyms listed first. . . . This simple arrangement makes this thesaurus particularly user-friendly." Libr J

Corbeil, Jean-Claude
Merriam-Webster's visual dictionary; [by] Jean-Claude Corbeil, Ariane Archambault; [illustrators, Jean-Yves Ahern . . . [et al.] Merriam-Webster 2006 952p il map $39.95 *   **423**
1. English language—Dictionaries 2. Picture dictionaries
ISBN 978-0-8777-9051-8; 0-8777-9051-5
"Logically organized into 17 broad categories (e.g., astronomy, humans, animals, clothing, and society), with numerous subcategories to make finding the needed terms easy, this is the only visual dictionary that includes definitions with the terms. And its price is very reasonable for such a substantial book. Essential." Libr J

Davidson, Mark
Right, wrong, and risky; a dictionary of today's American English usage. Norton 2006 570p $29.95 *   **423**
1. English language—Usage 2. English language—Dictionaries 3. Americanisms
ISBN 0-393-06119-1   LC 2005-17628
The author "offers a dictionary that 'views the real world of today's American English, identifying usage questions that are debatable, citing conflicting answers, and offering risk-free solutions for each conflict.' . . . Browsers will enjoy the colorful, interesting backstories on the origins of terms such as ground zero, on the sudden warming to the phrase girl talk, and on the widely misunderstood use of the word Neanderthal." Booklist
Includes bibliographical references

Dictionary of confusable words; {edited by} Adrian Room. Fitzroy Dearborn Pubs. 2000 251p $35 *   **423**
1. English language—Synonyms and antonyms 2. English language—Usage
ISBN 1-57958-271-0
A "guide to potentially confusing words. . . . The brief entries give definitions of each of the terms. Each word is then used in at least one sample sentence, clarifying the differences between like terms. The definitions and examples are in simple language and are easy to understand." Libr J

Edmonds, David, 1964-
The Oxford reverse dictionary; compiled by David Edmonds. Reissued, with corrections. Oxford University Press 2002 403p pa $17.95   **423**
1. English language—Synonyms and antonyms 2. English language—Dictionaries
ISBN 0-19-280113-9   LC 2002-282928

Edmonds, David, 1964-—*Continued*

A reissue of the title first published 1999

"This book is a collection of words linked by concept that offers a way for readers to look up words they may already know but are unable to recall. . . . The book makes no attempt to be comprehensive, either in its choice of main entries or in the included definitions; it is limited to 31,000 entries, omitting specialist vocabularies and slang. . . . This is a quite useful resource for the curious, students, and the general public." Libr J

Espy, Willard R.

Words to rhyme with; a rhyming dictionary. 3rd ed., updated by Orin Hargraves. Facts On File 2006 683p (Facts on File library of language and literature) $75; pa $19.95   **423**

1. English language—Rhyme
ISBN   0-8160-6303-6;   978-0-8160-6303-1; 0-8160-6304-4 (pa); 978-0-8160-6304-8 (pa)
LC 2005-51122

First published 1986

"Including a primer of prosody, a list of more than 80,000 words that rhyme, a glossary defining 9,000 of the more eccentric rhyming words, and a variety of exemplary verses, one of which does not rhyme at all." Title page

Garner, Bryan A.

Garner's modern American usage. 2nd ed. Oxford Univ. Press 2003 848p $39.95 *
423

1. English language—Usage 2. Americanisms
ISBN 0-19-516191-2

First published 1998 with title: A dictionary of modern American usage

"Containing roughly 7000 main entries and many cross references, the dictionary offers intelligent, sensible, readable advice concerning usage demons involving problems of grammar, spelling, homonyms, variants, clichés, skunked words, redundancies, phrasal adjectives and verbs, and more." Libr J [review of 1998 edition]

Includes bibliographical references

Lees, Gene

The modern rhyming dictionary; how to write lyrics; including a practical guide to lyric writing for songwriters and poets. Cherry Lane Bks. 1981 360p pa $14.95 hardcover o.p.   **423**

1. English language—Rhyme
ISBN 0-89524-317-2 (pa)   LC 81-4832

"Lees' dictionary is arranged in three sections—masculine (one-syllable), feminine (two-syllable), and three-syllable rhymes—with each section subdivided by vowels and then into subgroups by the consonant beginning the final syllable of the word." Ref Sources for Small & Medium-sized Libr. 5th edition

Lutz, William, 1940-

The Cambridge thesaurus of American English; [by] William D. Lutz. Cambridge Univ. Press 1994 515p $25   **423**

1. English language—Synonyms and antonyms
2. Americanisms
ISBN 0-521-41427-X   LC 93-31878

This thesaurus lists "over 200,000 synonyms and antonyms. . . . Lutz concentrates on idioms, verb phrases, and slang. Phrases are listed under the 'main' word in the phrase. 'Play it by ear,' for example, is found under the noun *ear* instead of the verb *play*. . . . The *Cambridge* is a welcome addition to the list of modern thesauruses and highly recommended for users who need a concise work that provides quick and easy access." Libr J

Merriam-Webster's collegiate dictionary. Eleventh ed. Merriam-Webster 2003 1623p il $23.95 *
423

1. English language—Dictionaries
ISBN 0-87779-808-7   LC 2003-3674

Also available online

First published 1898

This edition includes over 165,000 entries, 10,000 new words and meanings, 38,000 etymologies, a handbook of style, an essay on the English language, a special section on signs and symbols, and a free one-year subscription to the Collegiate Web site.

Merriam-Webster's collegiate thesaurus. Merriam-Webster 1993 868p $17.95 *
423

1. English language—Synonyms and antonyms
ISBN 0-87779-169-4   LC 93-3177

Also available online

First published 1976 with title: Webster's collegiate thesaurus

"Employs a conventional dictionary arrangement, and gives synonyms, related terms, idiomatic equivalents, antonyms, and contrasted words as applicable. Cross-references in small capitals." Guide to Ref Books. 11th edition

Metaphors dictionary; [edited by] Elyse Sommer, with Dorrie Weiss. Visible Ink Press 2001 xlvi, 612p $24.95 *
423

1. English language—Terms and phrases
ISBN 1-57859-137-6

First published 1995 by Gale Res.

This is a "collection of 6,500 colorful classic and contemporary comparative phrases (with full annotations and a complete bibliography of sources) . . . organized under 500 timeless and timely themes, ranging from Aloneness to Love to Zeal." Publisher's note

"Any library serving patrons involved in creative writing, composition, public speaking, or literary criticism should add this volume." Am Ref Books Annu, 1996 [entry for 1995 edition]

Mugglestone, Lynda

Lost for words; the hidden history of the Oxford English Dictionary. Yale University Press 2005 xxi, 273p il $30 **423**

1. Oxford English dictionary

ISBN 0-300-10699-8   LC 2004-29344

This is a "history of the making of the OED." Am Sch

"Serious word lovers will appreciate . . . [this book's] fascinating revelations." Booklist

Includes bibliographical references

The **New** Oxford American dictionary. 2nd ed. Oxford University Press 2005 xl, 2051p il map $60 * **423**

1. English language—Dictionaries 2. Americanisms

ISBN 0-19-517077-6

Also available Concise Oxford American dictionary $19.95 (ISBN-10: 0-19-530484-5; ISBN-13: 978-0-19-530484-8)

First published 1980 with title: The Oxford American dictionary

"The entries are organized around core meanings. . . . [Each entry] shows the major meaning or meanings of the word, plus any related senses. . . . Definitions are supplemented by illustrative, in-context examples of actual usage." Publisher's note

The **Oxford** American writer's thesaurus; compiled by Christine A. Lindberg. Oxford University Press 2004 xxiv, 1088p $40 * **423**

1. English language—Synonyms and antonyms

ISBN 0-1951-7076-8

"In addition to the more than 300,000 synonyms and 10,000 antonyms found in the thesaurus, each . . . editorial board member (including David Auburn, Michael Dirda, David Lehman, Stephin Merritt, Francine Prose, Zadie Smith, Jean Strouse, David Foster Wallace, and Simon Winchester) has contributed . . . mini-essays on words that they particularly love, hate, admire, or are just plain puzzled by." Publisher's note

"This work breaks away from the traditional format of simple lists of synonyms and antonyms by offering a number of ingenious and helpful features set within boxes in the text. . . . Although loaded with special features, this thesaurus doesn't undermine its more traditional duties." Libr J

The **Oxford** dictionary of American English. Oxford University Press 2005 828p il map $27.50; pa $19.95 **423**

1. English language—Dictionaries 2. Americanisms—Dictionaries

ISBN   978-0-19-431714-6;   0-19-431714-5; 978-0-19-439949-4 (pa); 0-19-439949-4 (pa)

LC 2005-174

First published 2004 with title: The Oxford ESL dictionary

This dictionary provides "explanations, illustrations, and related information not given in ordinary dictionaries. All entries use carefully worded definitions and provide contextual examples of usage, grammar, and idioms." Publisher's note

Includes bibliographical references

The **Oxford** dictionary of idioms; edited by Judith Siefring. 2nd ed. Oxford University Press 2004 340p $30; pa $15.95 * **423**

1. English language—Idioms

ISBN 0-19-852711-X; 0-19-861055-6 (pa)

LC 2005-271273

First published 1999

This is a dictionary of "more than 5,000 idiomatic words or phrases used in everyday English." Choice

"Anyone who is addicted to the richness of the English language or simply intrigued by the origin and meaning of an idiom like 'teach your grandmother to suck eggs' will . . . relish this work." Libr J

The **Oxford** English dictionary. 2nd ed, prepared by J.A. Simpson and E.S.C. Weiner. Oxford Univ. Press 1989 20v apply to publisher for price * **423**

1. English language—Dictionaries

ISBN 0-19-861186-2   LC 88-5330

Also available online; Compact edition reproduced micrographically from first edition and supplements available for $399.95

First published 1888 with title: New English dictionary on historical principles

"This is an etymological or word-source dictionary. In addition to definitions, this work gives the history of 290,500 words, both current and archaic, in the English language. Slang entries are very limited. Word histories include early forms, variant forms and roots, and first or exemplary usages in English from ancient to modern times. Short explanatory notes are provided for more common words." N Y Public Libr Book of How & Where to Look It Up

Random House Webster's college dictionary. [Rev and updated ed] Random House Reference 2005 xxvi, 1597p il map $26.95 * **423**

1. English language—Dictionaries

ISBN 0-375-42600-0   LC 2005-280097

First published 1991 as a successor to The Random House college dictionary

"Each entry in the dictionary presents spelling, along with alternatives, syllabication, pronunciation used in conversational speech (with alternatives), and part of speech. Entries also include meanings and definitions, with the most common usage listed first; historical, technical, or other usages of the term; date of first usage, including place of origin; and other related words that use the same root or stem. . . . The dictionary includes over 207,000 definitions, many of them so new they are not yet found in competing products. . . . For libraries seeking a wide variety of dictionaries, this work will prove especially useful for its inclusion of recent terms and idioms." Am Ref Books Annu, 2001 [entry for 2001 edition]

Random House Webster's unabridged dictionary. 2nd ed. Random House 2005 xxvi, 2230p il map $59.95 * **423**

1. English language—Dictionaries

ISBN 0-375-42599-3

A reissue of the edition published 2001

First published 1966 with title: The Random House dictionary of the English language

Random House Webster's unabridged dictionary—*Continued*

This dictionary contains over 315,000 entries. A new-words section and an essay on the growth of English are included. 2,400 spot maps and illustrations complement the text

Roget's 21st century thesaurus in dictionary form; the essential reference for home, school, or office; edited by the Princeton Language Institute; Barbara Ann Kipfer, head lexicographer. 3rd ed. Bantam Dell 2005 962p $15; pa $5.99 * **423**

1. English language—Synonyms and antonyms

ISBN 0-385-33895-3; 0-440-24269-X (pa)

"A Delta book"

First published 1992

"Produced by the Philip Lief Group, Inc."

This thesaurus, cross referencing each word with the same concept, provides 500,000 synonyms and antonyms in a dictionary format and includes recently coined and common slang terms and commonly used foreign terms.

Roget's international thesaurus. 6th ed, edited by Barbara Ann Kipfer; Robert L. Chapman, consulting editor. HarperResource 2001 xxv, 1248p $20.95; pa $16.95 * **423**

1. English language—Synonyms and antonyms

ISBN 0-06-273693-0; 0-06-093544-8 (pa)

LC 2002-276277

Also available thumb-indexed edition

First copyright edition published 1911 with title: The standard thesaurus of English words and phrases classified and arranged so as to facilitate the expression of ideas and assist in literary composition

This edition includes 330,000 words and phrases organized into 1,075 categories and a pinpoint reference system that directs the user from a comprehensive index to the numbered category of the right word. Cross-references throughout lead to other categories. Also included are supplemental word lists that supply the names of things which have no synonyms (measurements, wines, state mottoes) as well as quotations that amplify the meanings of selected words

Shorter Oxford English dictionary on historical principles; [editor-in-chief, Lesley Brown] 6th ed., [editor, Angus Stevenson] Oxford University Press 2007 2v il map set $175 *
423

1. English language—Dictionaries

ISBN 978-0-19-923324-3; 0-19-923324-1

LC 2007-37226

Also available deluxe leather-bound edition with one year's access to online version $350 (ISBN: 978-0-19-923325-0)

First published 1933

Includes CD-ROM

This dictionary "has more than half a million definitions drawn from the Oxford English Corpus database of more than 1.5 billion words. . . . It includes 'all words in current English from 1700 to the present day, plus the vocabulary of Shakespeare, the Authorized Version of the Bible and other major works from before 1700.'"

Booklist

Includes bibliographical references

Upton, Clive

Oxford rhyming dictionary; {by} Clive Upton, Eben Upton. Oxford University Press 2004 659p $37.95 * **423**

1. English language—Rhyme

ISBN 0-19-280115-5

LC 2004-53133

In this dictionary "an index of words leads to numbered sections of phonic groupings of end, double, and triple syllable rhymes, with proximate groupings of near rhymes. But the index (95,000 words) . . . provides many word variations." Choice

Visual dictionary. Rev. and updated. DK Pub. 2006 672p il map $40 * **423**

1. Picture dictionaries 2. English language—Dictionaries

ISBN 0-756-62606-4; 978-0-756-62606-8

First published 1994 with title: Dorling Kindersley ultimate visual dictionary. Variant titles: DK ultimate visual dictionary, Ultimate visual dictionary

This dictionary features over 33,000 terms and more than 6,000 color illustrations detailing everything from the prehistoric earth, the physical and biological science, to the visual arts, architecture, music, sports and common, ordinary everyday things.

Webster's third new international dictionary of the English language, unabridged; editor in chief, Philip Babcock Gove and the Merriam-Webster editorial staff. Merriam-Webster 2002 144a, 2662p il $129 * **423**

1. English language—Dictionaries

ISBN 0-87779-201-1

LC 2003-272164

Prices vary according to binding; Also available online

Original edition by Noah Webster published 1828 with title: An American dictionary of the English language. Has also appeared under various other titles. First published with present title 1961

"Clear, accurate definitions are given in historical order. Outstanding for its numerous illustrative quotations, impeccable authority, and etymologies, Webster's third is regarded as the most reliable, comprehensive general unabridged dictionary." Ref Sources for Small & Medium-sized Libr. 6th edition

Winchester, Simon

The professor and the madman; a tale of murder, insanity, and the making of the Oxford English dictionary. HarperCollins Pubs. 1998 242p il $22; pa $13 **423**

1. Murray, Sir James Augustus Henry, 1837-1915 2. Minor, William C., d. 1920 3. Oxford English dictionary

ISBN 0-06-017596-6; 0-06-099486-X (pa)

LC 98-10204

The author relates the "story of the *Oxford English Dictionary's* first editor and the expatriate American murderer who contributed more than 10,000 quotations as examples. Best of all, among the entertaining tangents

Winchester, Simon—*Continued*
one learns a great deal about the making of that grandest
of all reference works." Libr J
Includes bibliographical references

Young, Sue
The new comprehensive American rhyming
dictionary. Morrow 1991 622p pa $14.95
hardcover o.p.   **423**
1. English language—Rhyme 2. Americanisms
ISBN 0-380-71392-6 (pa)   LC 90-19165
This book contains over 65,000 words and phrases
categorized by sound, rather than spelling. It includes
many colloquialisms and slang expressions.

425   Grammar of standard English Syntax of standard English

Huddleston, Rodney D.
The Cambridge grammar of the English
language; {by} Rodney Huddleston, Geoffrey K.
Pullum in collaboration with Laurie Bauer {et al.}.
Cambridge Univ. Press 2002 1842p il $160 *
                                                 425
1. English language—Grammar
ISBN 0-521-43146-8   LC 2001-25630
"Each chapter comprises core definitions, detailed
analyses, notes explaining alternative interpretations of
difficult or controversial points, and brief notes on usage
and history." Publisher's note
This "comprehensive and detailed look at the principles of the English language . . . {is} an authoritative
addition to the fields of both English grammar and linguistics." Libr J
Includes bibliographical references

427   Historical and geographic variations, modern nongeographic variations

Ammer, Christine
The American Heritage dictionary of idioms.
Houghton Mifflin 1997 729p $32; pa $14.95
                                                 427
1. English language—Idioms 2. English language—
Terms and phrases 3. Americanisms
ISBN 0-395-72774-X; 0-618-24953-2 (pa)
                                      LC 97-12390
"In addition to idioms, the dictionary includes common figures of speech, formula phrases such as 'take
care,' emphatic redundancies whose word order cannot
be reversed such as 'cease and desist,' common proverbs,
colloquialisms, and slang phrases. Each expression is defined briefly and then illustrated by a short, simple sentence showing how it is used in context." SLJ
Includes bibliographical references

Ayto, John
The Oxford dictionary of slang. Oxford
University Press 2003 (Oxford paperback
reference) pa $16.95   **427**
ISBN 0-19-860763-6   LC 427
A reissue of the title first published 1998
"The 10,000 slang terms defined here originated main-
ly in the United States, Britain, Australia, or New Zea-
land and include both old and new coinages. The dictio-
nary's arrangement is topical in thesaurus fashion." Libr
J

The **Cassell** dictionary of English idioms; [editor,
Rosalind Fergusson] Cassell 2000 392p
hardcover o.p. pa $14.95 *   **427**
1. English language—Idioms 2. English language—
Terms and phrases
ISBN 0-304-35009-5; 0-304-36384-7 (pa)
                                      LC 00-340364
"Idiomatic expressions are arranged alphabetically by
their 'core' or key terms. . . . Approximately 10,000 idioms have been selected from English as it is used today
in North America, Australia, New Zealand, and the
British Isles. Usage notes identify country of origin of
expressions tied closely to one culture. Notes also label
terms as colloquial or slang as appropriate." Booklist

Crystal, David, 1941-
The stories of English. Overlook Press 2004
584p il map $35   **427**
1. English language—History
ISBN 1-585-67601-2   LC 2004-54727
The author "traces the diverse and unpredictable influences that have shaped English into an unruly family of
dialects, creoles, and patois. . . . Crystal acknowledges
the emergence during the fourteenth and fifteenth centuries of a prestigious standard version of English. Yet he
shows in instance after instance that the tempests of linguistic change have often overwhelmed the custodians of
the King's English, compelling them to accommodate
forces they could not control. And though he never loses
his focus on language, Crystal allows some of its more
colorful users—including Chaucer, Shakespeare, Samuel
Johnson, and Thomas Jefferson—to bring their personalities and voices into the chronicle." Booklist
Includes bibliographical references

Dickson, Paul
Slang! the topical dictionary of Americanisms.
Walker & Co. 2006 418p $24.95 *   **427**
1.   English   language—Slang—Dictionaries
2. Americanisms—Dictionaries
ISBN 0-8027-1531-1; 978-0-8027-1531-9
First published 1990 by Pocket Bks.
On cover: New and completely updated
This American slang dictionary "includes 30 topics,
such as 'Bureaucratese' and 'Real Estate,' and more than
10,000 words." Libr J
"Informative, reliable, entertaining, and modern, this
topical slang dictionary complements the more staid
slang lexicons and more scholarly general dictionaries."
Booklist
Includes bibliographical references

Dictionary of American slang; Barbara Ann Kipfer, editor; Robert L. Chapman, founding editor. 4th ed., fully rev. and updated. Collins 2007 592p $45   **427**
1. English language—Slang—Dictionaries
2. Americanisms
ISBN 978-0-06-117646-3; 0-06-117646-X
First published 1960 by Crowell. Variant title: New dictionary of American slang
This dictionary of American slang terms "features pronunciation guides, word origins, examples of appropriate usage as well as a . . . highlighting system that lets you know which terms should be used with caution, and never in polite company." Publisher's note

Green, Jonathon
Cassell's dictionary of slang. 2nd ed. Weidenfeld & Nicholson 2005 1565p $39.95 *
                                              427
1. English language—Slang—Dictionaries
ISBN 0-304-36636-6
First published 1998 by Cassell with title: The Cassell dictionary of slang
"Green includes words from the seventeenth century to the present with slang from all English-speaking areas: U.S., U.K., Canada, the Caribbean, New Zealand, Australia, and India. Each entry includes the part of speech, date of use, and definition. In a volume of this size it would be impossible to cite each source, so instead Green includes a bibliography of more than 200 books and numerous newspapers, comics, films, television scripts, and even Internet sites." Booklist [review of 1998 edition]

Hendrickson, Robert, 1933-
The Facts on File dictionary of American regionalisms. Facts on File 2000 786p $82.50 *
                                              427
1. English language—Dictionaries 2. Americanisms
ISBN 0-8160-4156-3   LC 00-28808
This "resource covers colorful and ordinary expressions spoken in several geographical regions, samples from the dialects spoken by Hawaiian and Pennsylvania Dutch people, and brief information about the dialects Bawlamerese, Bonac, Conch, Gullah, and Boont. A typical section includes a general discussion of the regional language or dialect (etymology, pronunciation, and grammatical variations) followed by alphabetized words and phrases briefly defined." Libr J

Herman, Lewis
American dialects; a manual for actors, directors, and writers; by Lewis Herman and Marguerite Shalett Herman. Theatre Arts Bks. 1959 328p il pa $23.95 hardcover o.p. *
                                              427
1. English language—Dialects 2. Americanisms
ISBN 0-87830-049-X (pa)
First published 1947 with title: Manual of American dialects, for radio, stage, screen, and television
"An invaluable guide to reproducing the sounds, rhythms, lilts, and stresses of representative dialects of every major section of the continental United States." Libr J

Holder, R. W.
How not to say what you mean; a dictionary of euphemisms. 4th ed. Oxford University Press 2007 410p pa $18.95 *   **427**
1. Euphemism—Dictionaries
ISBN 978-0-19-920839-5; 0-19-920839-5
                              LC 2007-37558
First published 1987 by Bath University Press with title: A dictionary of American and British euphemisms
"Here are almost five thousand euphemistic expressions listed in alphabetical order, ranging from well-known favorites such as 'push up the daisies,' 'fly-by-night,' 'red light district,' 'take to the cleaners,' 'get lucky,' and 'five-fingered discount,' to less amusing expressions from the bureaucratic and military world such as 'restructuring,' 'collateral damage,' and 'extrajudicial killing.' For each word or expression, Holder includes examples from . . . authors, along with . . . explanations of the words' origins and meaning." Publisher's note
Includes bibliographical references

MacNeil, Robert, 1931-
Do you speak American? a companion to the PBS television series; [by] Robert MacNeil and William Cran. 1st ed. Nan A. Talese/Doubleday 2005 228p $23.95   **427**
1. Americanisms 2. English language—Dialects
ISBN 0-385-51198-1   LC 2004-53735
Sequel to The story of English
Also available in paperback from Harcourt
"Whether talking to crab fishermen in Maryland or country-and-western singers in Tennessee, the authors discover that regional dialects are thriving despite the uniformity of our national tastes in clothing, fast-food chains, and movies. . . . The authors show how mobility, immigration, and racial and ethnic mixing are rapidly and profoundly changing the language. . . . This is colorful, witty, and insightful commentary on American speech patterns." Booklist
Includes bibliographical references

McMahon, Sean
Brewer's dictionary of Irish phrase & fable; [by] Sean McMahon and Jo O'Donoghue; foreword by Maeve Binchy. Weidenfeld & Nicholson 2004 867p $34.95 *   **427**
1. Irish literature—Dictionaries 2. Allusions
ISBN 0-304-36334-0   LC 2005-440092
The more than 5000 entries in this dictionary "define and furnish examples of language, phrases, and legends from the Emerald Isle itself as well as from places like the United States, where the Irish have emigrated in large numbers." Libr J
For a fuller review, see: Booklist, Dec. 15, 2005

Metcalf, Allan A.
How we talk; American regional English today; {by} Allan Metcalf. Houghton Mifflin 2000 206p il pa $14 hardcover o.p.   **427**
1. English language—Dictionaries 2. Americanisms
ISBN 0-618-04362-4 (pa)   LC 00-59777

Metcalf, Allan A.—*Continued*

The author "discusses the origins of American regional dialects and explains why different parts of the country use different words to mean the same thing (*carry* versus *tote*, for example) or why the same words are pronounced differently in the South as opposed to the North. For fiction writers hoping to create authentic-sounding dialogue, this book could function as an indispensable guide." Booklist

The **new** Partridge dictionary of slang and unconventional English; Tom Dalzell (senior editor) and Terry Victor (editor). Routledge 2006 2v set $220 *   **427**

1. English language—Slang—Dictionaries
ISBN 0-415-21258-8; 978-0-415-21258-8

First published 1937

"New editorial matter and selection, Tom Dalzell and Terry Victor; material taken from The dictionary of slang and unconventional English, 8th edition (first published 1984), E. Partridge and P. Beale estates" Verso of title page

"Entries list the term, identify its part of speech, explain its meaning, identify the country of origin, and cite sources or provide quotations showing how the term is used. . . . This dictionary informs, but it also entertains." Booklist

Includes bibliographical references

Spears, Richard A.

McGraw-Hill's dictionary of American slang and colloquial expressions. 4th ed. McGraw-Hill 2006 xxix, 546p pa $19.95 *   **427**

1. English language—Slang—Dictionaries
2. Americanisms
ISBN 0-07-146107-8; 978-0-07-146107-8

LC 2005-52220

First published 1989 with title: NTC's dictionary of American slang and colloquial expressions

This book offers "definitions of more than 12,000 slang and informal expressions from various sources, ranging from golden oldies such as . . . golden oldie, to recent coinages like shizzle (gangsta), jonx (Wall Street), and ping (the Internet). Each entry is followed by examples illustrating how an expression is used in everyday conversation and, where necessary, International Phonetic Alphabet pronunciations are given, as well as cautionary notes for crude, inflammatory, or taboo expressions." Publisher's note

Includes bibliographical references

428 Standard English usage (Prescriptive linguistics) Applied linguistics

Chalker, Sylvia

The Oxford dictionary of English grammar; {by} Sylvia Chalker, Edmund Weiner. Oxford Univ. Press 1994 448p il pa $15.95 hardcover o.p. paperback available $15.95 *   **428**

1. English language—Grammar 2. English language—Dictionaries
ISBN 0-19-280087-6 (pa)   LC 94-19818

"Offering 1,000 grammatical terms and their meanings, this title is a comprehensive reference tool and an updated guide to grammatical and linguistic terms, including entries related to phonetics and semantics. Its emphasis is on the terminology of current mainstream grammar, including Chomskyan generative grammar." Choice

Florey, Kitty Burns

Sister Bernadette's barking dog; the quirky history and lost art of diagramming sentences. Melville House 2006 154p $19.95   **428**

1. English language—Grammar
ISBN 978-1-933633-10-7; 1-933633-10-7

LC 2006-24703

"In its heyday, sentence diagramming was wildly popular in grammar schools across the country. . . . Florey explores the sentence-diagramming phenomena, including its humble roots at Brooklyn Polytechnic, its 'balloon diagram' predecessor, and what diagrams of famous writers' sentences reveal about them." Publisher's note

The author "writes with verve about the nuns who taught her to render the English language as a mess of slanted lines, explains how diagrams work, and traces the bizarre history of the men who invented this odd pedagogical tool. And unlike so many of today's microhistorians, who seek to demonstrate how zippers, azaleas, or hopscotch explain the world, Florey is refreshingly content to recount her tale without any suggestion that the diagramming of sentences somehow illuminates the American character. It's a great read." Slate

Fowler, H. W., 1858-1933.

Fowler's modern English usage; first edition by H.W. Fowler. Rev. 3rd ed., by R.W. Burchfield. Oxford University Press 2004 xxi, 873p $35 *   **428**

1. English language—Etymology 2. English language—Idioms 3. English language—Usage
ISBN 0-19-861021-1; 978-0-19-861021-2

LC 2005-271630

First published 1926 with title: A dictionary of modern English usage; 2000 edition published with title: The new Fowler's modern English usage

This alphabetically arranged guide gives "advice on grammar, syntax, style, and choice of words." Publisher's note

Lipton, James

An exaltation of larks; the ultimate edition. Viking 1991 324p il hardcover o.p. pa $16

428

1. English language—Terms and phrases
ISBN 0-670-30044-6; 0-14-017096-0 (pa)

LC 90-50425

This is a collection of "pithy, and often poetic, terms unearthed by Mr. Lipton in the Books of Venery that were the constant study of anyone who aspired to the title of gentleman in the fifteenth century." Publisher's note

Includes bibliographical references

O'Conner, Patricia T.

Woe is I; the grammarphobe's guide to better English in plain English. Riverhead Bks. 2003 240p $19.95; pa $14 * **428**

1. English language—Grammar 2. English language—Usage

ISBN 1-57322-252-6; 1-59448-006-0 (pa)

LC 2003-41416

First published 1996

This guide to good English offers advice on punctuation, usage, style and grammar as well as e-mail.

"The author doesn't take herself or the subject matter too seriously, offering a delightful romp through the intricacies of our language. . . . She knows her subject, can convey her message with wit and ease, and does it all in a compact, easy-to-read format. In short, this is an entertaining and useful grammar reference." Libr J

Includes bibliographical references

Peters, Pam

The Cambridge guide to English usage. Cambridge University Press 2004 608p il $35 * **428**

1. English language—Usage

ISBN 0-521-62181-X LC 2004-301888

"Covering over 3000 points of word meaning, spelling, punctuation, grammar, and style, the alphabetically arranged entries often include references to resources where the information was found." Libr J

"Considering the abundance of peculiarities and challenges in English usage, *Cambridge* will strengthen even a library well stocked with other guides. It is a serious book for those serious about language." Booklist

Strumpf, Michael

The grammar bible; everything you always wanted to know about grammar but didn't know whom to ask; [by] Michael Strumpf and Auriel Douglas. Holt 2004 489p pa $18 **428**

1. English language—Grammar

ISBN 0-8050-7560-7 LC 2003-57129

The authors move "from the parts of speech to the parts of the sentence and then to spelling, vocabulary, and punctuation, even encompassing thorny issues (e.g., sexist language, split infinitives) and complex grammatical terms (e.g., objective complements, gerund phrases). The authors also include a useful list of collocations and intersperse informative and often amusing 'Hot Line' queries throughout. . . This book is thorough, combining practical information not easily found in trade books, and is lively without trying to be too witty, cute, or humorous." Libr J

Includes bibliographical references

Wilson, Kenneth G. (Kenneth George), 1923-

The Columbia guide to standard American English. Columbia Univ. Press 1993 482p hardcover o.p. pa $26 **428**

1. English language—Dictionaries 2. English language—Usage 3. Americanisms

ISBN 0-231-06988-X; 978-0-231-06989-2 (pa); 0-231-06989-8 (pa) LC 92-37887

"The 6,500 entries in this book provide a unique approach to spoken and written English. Wilson diagrams five levels of speech, from intimate to oratorical, and three levels of writing, from informal to formal. His descriptive discussion of usage is intended to assist in making choices. . . . Cross references are numerous, and a helpful guide to pronunciation is included." Am Libr

433 Dictionaries of standard German

Cassell's German dictionary; German-English, English-German; completely revised by Harold Betteridge. Wiley 2002 xx, 1580p thumb-indexed $27 **433**

1. German language—Dictionaries

ISBN 0-02-522930-3

First compiled 1888 by Elizabeth Weir and published by Heath. Previous American editions published by Funk & Wagnalls with title: The New Cassell's German dictionary

This dictionary provides the words and phrases most commonly used in normal speech and contemporary literature and includes a key to German pronunciation as well as a bibliography of technical and specialist dictionaries

"One of the most useful bilingual dictionaries." Guide to Ref Books. 11th edition

Oxford-Duden German dictionary; German-English, English-German; edited by the Dudenredaktion and the German Section of the Oxford University Press Dictionary Department; chief editors, W. Scholze-Stubenrecht, J.B. Sykes. 3rd ed. Oxford University Press 2005 xxxvii, 1751p $55 * **433**

1. German language—Dictionaries

ISBN 0-19-860974-4 LC 2005-50870

Replaces the edition published 1999

Also available concise Oxford-Duden German dictionary $32.95 (ISBN: 0-19-860976-0)

First published 1990

This dictionary includes over 320,000 definitions, some 520,000 translations, thousands of example sentences, intext features covering grammar, usage, and vocabulary building, preferred spellings, and numerous full-page maps.

This book's "currency and readability make it a paragon of modern lexicography." Am Ref Books Annu, 2006

Random House Webster's German-English, English-German dictionary. Rev. ed. Random House Reference 2006 c1998 547p $12.95 * **433**

1. German language—Dictionaries

ISBN 0-375-72194-0; 978-0-375-72194-6

Also available in paperback from Ballantine Bks.

First published 1997 with title: Random House German-English English-German dictionary

In addition to more than 60,000 entries this dictionary also includes notes on pronunciation, lists of abbreviations, tables of irregular verbs and lists of geographical names.

439 Other Germanic languages

Rosten, Leo, 1908-1997
The new joys of Yiddish; revisions and commentary by Lawrence Bush; illustrations by R. O. Blechman. Rev ed. Crown 2001 xxxii, 458p il $35; pa $18 **439**
1. Yiddish language 2. English language—Foreign words and phrases
ISBN 0-609-60785-5; 0-609-80692-0 (pa)
LC 2001-28366
First published 1968 with title: The joys of Yiddish
This "work explores the nuances and complexities of language, clarifying the interrelationship between Yiddish and English (Yinglish, according to Rosten). The lengthy alphabetical listing not only presents multiple spellings, pronunciation guides, definitions, and cross references but also illustrates usage with background information, anecdotes, and jokes, as well as breezy erudition in the form of tidbits of cultural history, Talmudic and biblical references, tips on pronunciation, and thoughtful commentary. . . . The revision incorporates additional material on modern Yiddish literature and culture and updates on changes in American Jewish life and faith. Also included as an appendix is an English-Yiddish dictionary." Libr J
Includes bibliographical references

Weinreich, Uriel
Modern English-Yiddish, Yiddish-English dictionary. Schocken Bks. 1977 xliii, 789, 15p pa $30 * **439**
ISBN 0-8052-0575-6 LC 77-76038
A reissue of the title first published 1968 by Yivo
Added t.p.: Modern English-Yidish, Yidish-English yerterbukh
"This dictionary is designed in the main for persons who have a firm grounding in English and at least a rudimentary command of Yiddish. . . . Accordingly, the Yiddish rather than the English material has been phonetically and grammatically analyzed, and English glosses have been used, wherever appropriate, to specify sermantic detail."—Author's pref. "A scholarly and useful work." Guide to Ref Books. 11th edition

440 Romance languages French

Nadeau, Jean-Benoît
The story of French; [by] Jean-Benoît Nadeau and Julie Barlow. St. Martin's Press 2006 483p map $25.95 * **440**
1. French language
ISBN 978-0-312-34183-1; 0-312-34183-0
LC 2006-49348
This book explores the origins and evolution of the French language.
This is "a well-told, highly accessible history of the French language that leads to a spirited discussion of the prospects for French in an increasingly English-dominated world." N Y Times (Late N Y Ed)
Includes bibliographical references

443 Dictionaries of standard French

Cassell's French dictionary; French-English, English-French; completely revised by Denis Girard with the assistance of Gaston Dulong, Oliver Van Oss, and Charles Guinness. Wiley 2002 762, 655p thumb-indexed $24.95 **443**
1. French language—Dictionaries
ISBN 0-02-522620-7
First published 1920 with title: Cassell's French-English, English-French dictionary. Previous American editions published by Funk & Wagnalls with title: The New Cassell's French dictionary
"New words including colloquialisms, slang, American English and French-Canadian terms [are included]. . . . There are also sections on French verbs and French and English abbreviations. Reliable, standard dictionary. A first choice." N Y Public Libr. Ref Books for Child Collect. 2d edition

Larousse French-English, English-French dictionary; [managing editor, Janice McNeillie; editors, Marie-Hélène Corréard . . . et al.] New ed. Larousse (Paris) 2007 xviii, 1112, 20, 51, 1221p il map $45 * **443**
1. French language—Dictionaries
ISBN 978-2-03-542132-6; 2-03-542132-2;
LC 2007-280218
Previous edition published with title: Grand dictionnaire français-anglais, anglais-français
Cover title: Larousse advanced dictionary French-English, anglais-français; Added title page: Dictionnaire Larousse français-anglais, anglais-français
This dictionary contains over 250,000 entries and 400,000 translations, an updated vocabulary including technical, IT, and Internet terms, coverage of Canadian, Belgian, and Swiss French, models of letters, faxes, and e-mails, and informative sidebars on French life and culture

The **Oxford-Hachette** French dictionary; French-English, English-French; edited by Marie-Hélène Corréard, Valerie Grundy. 4th ed., edited by Jean-Benoit Ormal-Grenon, Nicholas Rollin. Oxford University Press/Hachette Livre 2007 xxxviii, 1945p $55 * **443**
1. French language—Dictionaries
ISBN 978-0-19-861422-7; 0-19-861422-5
LC 2007-14213
First published 1994
This work provides coverage of French and English vocabulary in general as well as scientific and technical areas with over 350,000 words and phrases and over 530,000 translations. Supplementary material includes information on French society and culture, including famous places, people and much practical information for those planning to reside in France.

Random House Webster's French-English, English-French dictionary. Random House Reference 2006 588p pa $12.95 *

443

1. French language—Dictionaries
ISBN 978-0-375-72193-9; 0-375-72193-2
LC 2006-297159

Also available in paperback from Ballantine Bks.

First published 1997 with title: Random House French-English, English-French dictionary

This dictionary of more than 60,000 entries includes thousands of idioms, phrases and common expressions. Tables of irregular verbs are included as is a single A-Z listing of countries and other geographical names. Informal usages are labeled.

453 Dictionaries of standard Italian

Cassell's Italian dictionary; Italian-English, English-Italian; compiled by Piero Rebora, with the assistance of Francis M. Guercio and Arthur L. Hayward. Wiley 2002 xxi, 1128p $24.95 * ISBN 0-02-522540-5 **453**

1. Italian language—Dictionaries

First published 1958 in the United Kingdom with title: Cassell's Italian-English, English-Italian dictionary. Previous United States editions published by Funk & Wagnalls

"A general dictionary of the Italian language as currently written and spoken." Ref Sources for Small & Medium-sized Libr. 5th edition

463 Dictionaries of standard Spanish

Cassell's Spanish-English, English-Spanish dictionary; completely revised by Anthony Gooch, Angel Garcia de Paredes. Wiley 2002 xxv, 1109p $22.95 * **463**

ISBN 0-02-522910-9

Also available in a concise edition for $13 (ISBN 0-02-522660-6)

Previously published in 1978 by Macmillan

This dictionary emphasizes the Spanish of Latin America, and includes both classical and literary Spanish as well as the language of the modern Spanish-speaking world

The **Concise** American Heritage Spanish dictionary. 2nd ed. Houghton Mifflin 2001 xxiv, 616p $14 **463**

1. Spanish language—Dictionaries
ISBN 0-618-11769-5
LC 00-66461

Abridged edition of: The American Heritage Spanish dictionary. 2nd ed.

"This bilingual dictionary includes more than 70,000 words and phrases. The emphasis on American English and Latin American Spanish as well as the informative guides and tables will assist students of either language." Booklist

Larousse diccionario compact: español inglés, inglés español. {New & rev ed}. Larousse (Paris) 2002 various paging il maps $21.95; pa $11.95 * **463**

1. Spanish language—Dictionaries
ISBN 2-03-542018-0; 2-03-542017-2 (pa)
LC 2003-275808

First published 1993 with title: Larousse diccionario manual: español-inglés, inglés-español. Variant title: Larousse concise dictionary, Spanish-English, English-Spanish

This edition includes over 90,000 words and phrases, 120,000 translations, updated vocabulary in all subject areas, idioms, abbreviations, acronyms, and proper nouns. A supplement on life and culture in Latin America is also provided

The **Oxford** Spanish dictionary; Spanish-English/English-Spanish; chief editors, Beatriz Galimberti Jarman, Roy Russell; edited by Carol Styles Carvajal, Jane Horwood. 3rd ed. Oxford Univ. Press 2003 xlviii, 1977p $49.95

463

1. Spanish language—Dictionaries
ISBN 0-19-860475-0
LC 2003-272816

Also available CD-ROM version; print and CD-ROM edition $75 (ISBN: 0-19-860878-0; ISBN: 978-0-19-860878-3)

First published 1994

Title page in English and Spanish

This dictionary contains over 300,000 words and phrases, 500,000 translations and "covers over 24 varieties of Spanish as it is written and spoken throughout the Spanish-speaking world. . . . Special entries on life and culture explain the differences between institutions, administrative systems, educational systems, and general life in the Spanish and English-speaking worlds, offering vital background to the language." Publisher's note

470 Italic languages Latin

Ostler, Nicholas

Ad infinitum; a biography of Latin. Walker & Company 2007 382p il map $27.95 **470**

1. Latin language
ISBN 978-0-8027-1515-9; 0-8027-1515-X

"In four parts, Ostler covers the origins and development of Latin in the Roman world, Latin's "taking over the church," its medieval continuation and fracturing into vernaculars, and a nuanced rebirth in the Renaissance and its legacy in the contemporary world. Incredibly well documented, with examples from antiquity to the modern era." Libr J

473 Dictionaries of classical Latin

Oxford Latin dictionary; edited by P. G. W. Glare. Oxford Univ. Press 1982 xxiii, 2126p $295 * **473**

1. Latin language—Dictionaries
ISBN 0-19-864224-5
LC 82-8162

Oxford Latin dictionary—*Continued*

"Authorized in 1931 and begun two years later, {this dictionary} appeared in eight fascicles published between 1968 and 1982. These have been combined in a single volume." Wilson Libr Bull

This dictionary looks at the meaning and development of more than 40,000 classical Latin words and phrases

Stone, Jon R., 1959-

Latin for the illiterati; exorcizing the ghosts of a dead language. Routledge 1996 201p $80; pa $18.95 *   **473**

1. Latin language—Dictionaries
ISBN 0-415-91774-3; 0-415-91775-1 (pa)
LC 95-47985

"Here are nearly 6,000 words, phrases, and abbreviations culled from the arts, music, law, philosophy, theology, medicine, and the works of ancient writers. Stone has also included a section of handy lists: the Seven Hills of Rome, countries and regions, colors, and, of course, Roman numerals, both cardinal and ordinal. . . . A ready-reference dream come true." Am Libr

More Latin for the illiterati; exorcizing the ghosts of a dead language. Routledge 1999 201p $75; pa $17.95 *   **473**

1. Latin language—Dictionaries
ISBN 0-415-92210-0; 0-415-92211-9 (pa)
LC 98-43820

This dictionary focuses on "three areas: medicine, law, and religion. Translations are brief and literal. The dictionary concludes with some of the same information given in *Latin for the Illiterati* as well as newer miscellaneous information, including Latin selections (with English translations) from the Roman Catholic liturgy." Libr J

Includes bibliographical references

483   Dictionaries of classical Greek

Liddell, Henry George, 1811-1898

A Greek-English lexicon; compiled by Henry George Liddell and Robert Scott; revised and augmented throughout by Sir Henry Stuart Jones, with the assistance of Roderick McKenzie, and with the cooperation of many scholars. Clarendon Press 1996 xlv, 2042, xxxi, 320p $145 *

ISBN 0-19-864226-1   **483**

1. Latin language—Dictionaries   LC 95-32369

First edition 1843; this is a reprint of the 9th edition (1925-1940) with a new supplement edited by P. G. W. Glare

Originally issued in ten parts. Frequently reprinted. Preliminary leaves include: List of authors and works; Epigraphical publications; Papyrological publications; Periodicals; General list of abbreviations. Addenda and corrigenda

"The standard Greek and English lexicon, covering the language to about 600 A.D., omitting Patristic and Byzantine Greek." Ref Sources for Small & Medium-sized Libr. 6th edition

491   East Indo-European and Celtic languages

The **Oxford** Hindi-English dictionary; edited by R.S. McGregor. Oxford Univ. Press 1993 xx, 1083p pa $30. ISBN 0-19-864339-X (pa)   **491**

1. Hindi language—Dictionaries   LC 92-42314

A dictionary of historical Hindi together with current colloquial and literary vocabulary

Includes bibliographical references

491.7   East Slavic languages Russian

Oxford Russian dictionary; Russian-English, edited by Marcus Wheeler and Boris Unbegaun; English-Russian, edited by Paul Falla; revised and updated by Della Thompson. 4th ed. Oxford University Press 2007 xxi, 1322p $65 *
491.7

1. Russian language—Dictionaries
ISBN 978-0-19-861420-3; 0-19-861420-9
LC 2007-9399

First published 1972 with title: The Oxford Russian-English dictionary

This dictionary features over 500,000 words, phrases, and translations and includes a correspondence section and cultural notes as well as special boxes to help with tricky words and terms.

492   Afro-Asiatic languages. Semitic languages

The **Oxford** English-Arabic dictionary of current usage; edited by N. S. Doniach. Oxford Univ. Press 1972 1392p $95   **492**

ISBN 0-19-864312-8 1.Arabic language—Dictionaries

"Intended both for the English-speaking students of Arabic and for Arabic-speaking students of English. Includes formal literary English, colloquial and slang usage, with the closest Arabic equivalent at the same level of usage." Guide to Ref Books. 11th edition

492.4   Hebrew

The **Oxford** English-Hebrew dictionary; [published] in collaboration with the Oxford Centre for Hebrew and Jewish Studies. Oxford Univ. Press 1996 1091p pa $29.95 hardcover o.p.   **492.4**

1. Hebrew language—Dictionaries
ISBN 0-19-860172-7 (pa)   LC 95-21451

In this dictionary, containing more than 50,000 entries, the "goal of the editors was to describe the language as it is actually used, and thus they list only words currently attested to in usage, including non-Semitic loan words. The editors did not intend the work to be fully comprehensive, but rather sought to furnish the most common words that would be most likely needed by an average user—slang, idioms and phrases, and specialized terminology." Recommended Ref Books for Small & Medium-sized Libr & Media Cent, 1997

Zilkha, Avraham
Modern English-Hebrew dictionary. Yale Univ. Press 2002 457p (Yale language series) $55; pa $30 *   **492.4**
1. Hebrew language—Dictionaries
ISBN 0-300-09004-8; 0-300-09005-6 (pa)
LC 2001-26830
This dictionary includes 30,000 entries, with listings for translating words with multiple meanings, newly coined and slang words, common idioms, vocalization of Hebrew words, acronyms, and gender identification and plural forms of irregular nouns

495.1 Chinese

Cheng & Tsui English-Chinese lexicon of business terms with pinyin; compiled by Andrew C. Chang = [Jianqiao Ying Han shang yong ci hui pin ying ci dian / Zhang Jiezhou bian] Cheng & Tsui Co. 2001 442p (C & T Asian dictionary series) $36.95   **495.1**
1. Chinese language—Dictionaries 2. Business—Dictionaries
ISBN 978-0-88727-394-0; 0-88727-394-7
LC 2001-94244
"A book to hand to your patrons who need to know the Chinese expressions for terms such as Chief Executive Officer, market penetration, and stockholder. More than 9,000 English-language words and phrases are listed with their Chinese simplified characters, with pinyin transliteration equivalents." Booklist

Oxford Chinese dictionary; English-Chinese, Chinese-English = [Ying Han, Han Ying]; monolingual English text edited by Martin H. Manser; English-Chinese dictionary edited and translated by Zhu Yuan, Wang Liangbi, Ren Yongchang; Chinese-English dictionary edited by Wu Jingrong . . . [et al.] Oxford University Press 2003 various paging $39.95
495.1
1. Chinese language—Dictionaries
ISBN 978-0-19-596459-2; 0-19-596459-4
LC 2005-295454
This Chinese dictionary contains "88,000 words and phrases,130,000 translations, an index system of radicals, Pinyin romanizations, a CD-ROM, and full audio of Mandarin pronunciations of 22,000 single-character dictionary entries." Publisher's note

495.6 Japanese

Basic Japanese-English dictionary. 2nd ed. Oxford University Press, Bonjinsha 2004 1000p pa $19.95 *   **495.6**
1. Japanese language—Dictionaries
ISBN 0-19-860859-4   LC 2004-54786
First published 1986 in Japan; 1989 by Oxford University Press
This "dictionary contains over 3,000 entries which, along with providing basic meanings and grammatical information, also distinguish between senses, list com-

pounds, and give sample sentences and idiomatic expressions. . . . It presents all the Japanese words and phrases in roman script with standard Japanese script alongside. . . . Cross-references direct the user to words of contrasting or related meaning, and, where necessary, the dictionary provides notes on special usage. It also includes [an] appendix which gives an introduction to Japanese grammar." Publisher's note

495.7 Korean

Berlitz Korean compact dictionary. Berlitz Publishing 2006 672p pa $12.95   **495.7**
1. Korean language—Dictionaries
ISBN 978-981-246-949-6; 981-246-949-4
This book has "45,000 entries that aim to capture the core words of the language. This dictionary features bold, blue headwords [for navigation]." Publisher's note

495.9 Miscellaneous languages of Southeast Asia; Munda languages

Nguyen, Dinh Hoa, 1924-
NTC's Vietnamese-English dictionary. NTC Pub. Group 1995 728p hardcover o.p. pa $17.95 *
495.9
1. Vietnamese language—Dictionaries
ISBN 0-8442-8356-8; 0-8442-8357-6 (pa)
LC 95-18670
First published 1955 with title: Vietnamese-English vocabulary
This work "contains approximately 50,000 Vietnamese words, morphemes, compound words, and phrases. . . . Entries are accompanied by their English equivalents and, where appropriate, synonyms, antonyms, and usage are provided. Also included are a guide to pronunciation and a 50-page supplement of new Vietnamese words." Recommended Ref Books for Small & Medium-sized Libr & Media Cent, 1997

499 Non-Austronesian languages of Oceania, Austronesian languages, miscellaneous languages

Pukui, Mary Kawena, 1895-1986
Hawaiian dictionary; Hawaiian-English, English-Hawaiian; [by] Mary Kawena Pukui, Samuel H. Elbert. rev & enl ed. University of Hawaii Press 1986 xxvi, 572p $32.95   **499**
1. Hawaiian language—Dictionaries
ISBN 0-8248-0703-0   LC 85-24583
Originally published in two separate parts in 1957 and 1964. First combined edition published 1971
"The Hawaiian-English part now comprises 29,000 entries. It is the most comprehensive and up-to-date dictionary for the language." Guide to Ref Books. 11th edition
Includes bibliographical references

500 SCIENCE

Angier, Natalie

The canon; a whirligig tour of the beautiful basics of science. Houghton Mifflin Company 2007 293p $27 **500**

1. Science

ISBN 978-0-618-24295-5; 0-618-24295-3

LC 2006-26871

"Angier sets out to depict the joys of science and to present them as something in which we all can participate. Chapters explore essential principles in the fields of statistics and probabilities, measurements and calibration, evolutionary and molecular biology, physics, chemistry, geology, and astronomy." Libr J

If Angier "reaches for a joke too often instaed of relying on her admirably supple prose, she's still a matchless scientific decathlete, able to perform with equal adroitness whether examining the infinitesimal or the infinite." Fortune

Includes bibliographical references

The **best** American science and nature writing 2007; edited and with an introduction by Richard Preston. Houghton Mifflin 2007 xxii, 300p $28; pa $14 * **500**

1. Science 2. Nature

ISSN 1530-1508

ISBN 0-618-72224-6; 978-0-618-72224-2; 0-618-72231-9 (pa); 978-0-618-72231-0 (pa)

Annual. First published 2000

A collection of 28 essays on science and nature topics from the past year.

The **Best** American science writing 2008; editor, Sylvia Nasar; series editor, Jesse Cohen. Harper Perennial 2008 336p pa $14.95 **500**

1. Science

ISBN 978-0-06-134041-3; 0-06-134041-3

Annual. First published 2000. Editors vary

A "collection of accessible scientific papers, science-related personal essays and journalistic prose about evolutionary biology, medicine, paleoanthropology, particle physics and more." Publ Wkly [review of 2000 annual]

Bronowski, Jacob, 1908-1974

Science and human values; revised edition with a new dialogue, The abacus and the rose. Harper & Row 1965 119p il pa $12 hardcover o.p. **500**

1. Science

ISBN 0-06-097281-5 (pa)

First published 1958 by Messner

Contains the following three essays, which were first given as lectures at the Massachusetts Institute of Technology in 1953: The creative mind; The habit of truth; The sense of human dignity. The abacus and the rose was originally broadcast by the BBC Third Programme in 1962

The dialogue "discusses the theme that 'science is as integral a part of the culture of our age as the arts are.'" Sci Am

Bryson, Bill

A short history of nearly everything. Broadway Bks. 2003 544p $27.50; pa $15.95 * **500**

1. Science

ISBN 0-7679-0817-1; 0-7679-0818-X (pa)

LC 2003-46006

In presenting this history of science, Bryson's "interest is not simply to discover what we know but to find out how we know it. How do we know what is in the center of the earth, thousands of miles beneath the surface? How can we know the extent and the composition of the universe, or what a black hole is? How can we know where the continents were 600 million years ago?" Publisher's note

"Neither oversimplified nor overstuffed, this exceptionally skillful tour of the physical world covers the basic principles and still has room for profiles of some of the more engaging scientists." N Y Times Book Rev

Includes bibliographical references

Cole, K. C.

Mind over matter; conversations with the cosmos. Harcourt 2003 319p $25; pa $14 **500**

1. Science

ISBN 0-15-100816-7; 0-15-602956-1 (pa)

LC 2003-982

The author "gathers 92 short essays that first appeared primarily in her Los Angeles Times science column. The book's four sections are loosely ordered around the subjectivity of inquiry, the physical world, science in practice and the politics of science. Cole's technique is to set her stage with a scientific factoid or news blip and then ruminate on the unexpected insights, inversions or ironies she finds there." Publ Wkly

"These three-page tidbits may not tax your scientific thought processes, but they'll certainly make you think." Libr J

Dawkins, Richard, 1941-

A devil's chaplain; reflections on hope, lies, science, and love. Houghton Mifflin 2003 263p il $24; pa $14 **500**

1. Evolution 2. Science—Philosophy 3. Religion and science

ISBN 0-618-33540-4; 0-618-48539-2 (pa)

LC 2003-50859

This is "a collection of essays that span 25 years of writing on evolution, education and science versus nonsense. . . . Dawkins is creative, articulate and, above all, emotional." N Y Times Book Rev

Includes bibliographical references

Dyson, Freeman J., 1923-

The scientist as rebel; [by] Freeman Dyson. New York Review Books 2006 360p $27.95 **500**

1. Science

ISBN 978-1-59017-216-2; 1-59017-216-7

LC 2006-22081

Dyson, Freeman J., 1923-—_Continued_

This is a "collection of 33 previously published and frequently updated essays and reviews. Organized into sections on contemporary issues in science, war and peace, history of science and scientists, and personal and philosophical ruminations, these works demonstrate Dyson's far-ranging interests and skill in writing for educated and curious generalists, qualities that ensure this volume's wide appeal." Booklist

Includes bibliographical references

Eiseley, Loren C., 1907-1977

The unexpected universe 1969 239p pa $14 hardcover o.p. **500**

1. Natural history 2. Science

ISBN 0-15-692850-7 (pa)

This volume contains personal interpretative meditations on mankind's relationship to nature.

Includes bibliographical references

Feynman, Richard Phillips, 1918-1988

The meaning of it all; thoughts of a citizen scientist. Basic Books 2005 c1998 133p pa $13.95 * **500**

1. Science 2. Religion

ISBN 0-465-02394-0

First published 1998 by Addison-Wesley

"Originally delivered as a three-part lecture series at the University of Washington in 1963, this collection touches on such far-ranging topics as the existence or nonexistence of God; the Constitution; and UFOs. . . . These memorable lectures confirm that Feynman's gift of insight extended from the subatomic world to the cosmic, and to the very human as well." Publ Wkly

The pleasure of finding things out; the best short works of Richard P. Feynman; by Richard P. Feynman; edited by Jeffrey Robbins; foreword by Freeman Dyson. Perseus Bks. 1999 270p pa $15.95 hardcover o.p. **500**

1. Science

ISBN 0-7382-0349-1 (pa)   LC 99-64775

These lectures and interviews are "expositions about [Feynman's] life, about technical topics in computing and physics, and about science's general place in society." Booklist

Flatow, Ira

Present at the future; from evolution to nanotechnology, candid and controversial conversations on science and nature. Collins 2007 354p il $24.95 **500**

1. Science

ISBN 978-0-06-073264-6; 0-06-073264-4

LC 2007-14583

This book describes current thinking "on nanotechnology, space travel, global warming, alternative energies, stem cell research, and using the universe as a super-super computer." Publisher's note

This is "an entertaining and thought-provoking read that leaves you feeling more informed and as though you might have a little more to offer during your next dinner-party conversation." Sci Books Films

Gardner, Martin, 1914-

Did Adam and Eve have navels? discourses on reflexology, numerology, urine therapy and other dubious subjects. Norton 2000 333p il pa $15.95 hardcover o.p. * **500**

1. Science

ISBN 0-393-32238-6 (pa)   LC 00-34870

This is a collection of the author's pieces culled from the *Skeptical Inquirer*. Gardner "gives succinct and amusing critiques of a number of the fallacies that abound in alternative medicine (including the very peculiar urine-therapy treatment) and many other 'dubious subjects.'" Libr J

Includes bibliographical references

Gribbin, John R.

Almost everyone's guide to science; the universe, life and everything; [by] John Gribbin with Mary Gribbin. Yale Univ. Press 1999 232p $30; pa $11.95 * **500**

1. Science

ISBN 0-300-08101-4; 0-300-08460-9 (pa)

LC 99-26755

First published 1998 in the United Kingdom

In this "general guide to science for the layperson . . . Gribbin combines biographies and history, on the one hand, with the major theories in science, on the other. . . . The text is clear, is based on solid research, and clearly reflects a lifetime love for science." Sci Books Films

Includes bibliographical references

The **Handy** science answer book; compiled by the Science and Technology Department of the Carnegie Library of Pittsburgh; edited by James E. Bobick and Naomi E. Balaban. Centennial ed. Visible Ink Press 2003 660p pa $21.95

500

1. Science 2. Technology

ISBN 1-57859-140-6   LC 2002-15562

First published 1994

"The text is divided into various subject areas including physics and chemistry, space, earth, climate and weather, minerals and other materials, energy, technology, and environment, gathering answers to reference questions. . . . A comprehensive index . . . makes the material accessible and easy to find. Pages are full of fascinating tidbits, complemented by illustrations, photos, charts, graphs, and maps. . . . A librarian will want a copy of this book behind the desk for ready reference, but students will want a copy for themselves to peruse time and again just for fun." Voice Youth Advocates

Includes bibliographical references

Hazen, Robert M., 1948-

Science matters: achieving scientific literacy; {by} Robert M. Hazen and James Trefil. Doubleday 1991 294p il pa $12.95 hardcover o.p.

500

1. Science

ISBN 0-385-26108-X (pa)   LC 90-3786

Hazen, Robert M., 1948-—*Continued*
"This book attempts to acquaint the educated (or miseducated) layperson with the major concepts of modern science. . . . Although many concepts are, perforce, oversimplified, offering the reader only a superficial understanding of some of them, this book is a step in the right direction." Libr J
Includes bibliographical references

Highfield, Roger
The science of Harry Potter; how magic really works. Viking 2002 xxii, 322p hardcover o.p. pa $15   **500**
1. Rowling, J. K.—Characters—Harry Potter
2. Science 3. Magic
ISBN 0-670-03153-4; 0-14-200355-7 (pa)
LC 2002-28878
The author "takes on J.K. Rowling's Harry Potter series 'to show how many elements of her books can be found in and explained by modern science.'" Publ Wkly
"Fans of such science popularizers as Gould and Asimov will certainly get a kick out of Highfield's utterly fascinating take on the subject." Booklist
Includes bibliographical references

Ingram, Jay
The barmaid's brain and other strange tales from science. Henry Holt 2001 271p il pa $15
                                                        500
1. Science
ISBN 978-0-7167-4702-4; 0-7167-4702-2
First published 1998 in Canada
A collection of essays about such topics as "the nature of laughter; perpetual-motion machines; optical illusions . . . the phenomenon of simultaneous discovery; and a possible scientific explanation for the curious behavior that provoked the Salem witch trials. Ingram is an accomplished writer . . . and fans of science books that spotlight the offbeat, the unusual, and the colorful will flock to this title." Booklist
Includes bibliographical references

Kipfer, Barbara Ann
How it happens; the extraordinary processes of everyday things. Random House Reference 2005 322p il pa $16.95   **500**
1. Science
ISBN 0-375-72082-0   LC 2005-40453
This "trivia miscellany describes hundreds of processes, from popcorn popping to radio signal transmission to tango dancing." Publisher's note

Maddox, John Royden, 1925-
What remains to be discovered; mapping the secrets of the universe, the origins of life, and the future of the human race; [by] John Maddox. Kessler Bks./Free Press 1998 434p hardcover o.p. pa $22.95   **500**
1. Science
ISBN 0-684-82292-X; 978-0-684-86300-9 (pa);
0-684-86300-6 (pa)   LC 98-29137

The author reflects "on the nature of science, both its successes and its challenges. . . . By focusing on some of the 'big' fields of science—cosmology, quantum mechanics, cell biology, genetics, evolution and neuroscience, for example—he has crafted a primer worthy of study. But this is not an introduction for the uninitiated." Publ Wkly
Includes bibliographical references

Marshall, I. N.
Who's afraid of Schrödinger's cat? all the new science ideas you need to keep up with the new thinking; [by] Ian Marshall & Danah Zohar, with contributions by F. David Peat. Morrow 1997 xxx, 402p map pa $15 hardcover o.p.   **500**
1. Science
ISBN 0-688-16107-3 (pa)   LC 96-20769
This "is an alphabetically organized, heavily cross-listed compendium of brief descriptions of new areas of science, such as 'Artificial Intelligence,' 'The Edge of Chaos,' 'Mesons' and 'Transpersonal Psychology.' While the 201 entries are weighted toward new areas of physics, the book does justice to every area of natural and social science." Sci Books Films

Oxford dictionary of scientific quotations; edited by W.F. Bynum and Roy Porter; assistant editors, Sharon Messenger, Caroline Overy. Oxford University Press 2005 712p $60; pa $18.95 *   **500**
1. Science 2. Quotations
ISBN 0-19-858409-1; 0-19-861443-8 (pa)
LC 2005-277260
"The quotations collected here are not only by scientists but by writers, politicians, and others with something to say about science. . . . Each entry includes the name of the person being quoted, his or her dates, a . . . biographical statement, and several quotes, with their sources." Booklist
"This hefty volume is a great reference but it is also a great read—open it up to any page and expand the mind with a sampling of scientific ideas and philosophy." Choice

Park, Robert L.
Voodoo science; the road from foolishness to fraud. Oxford Univ. Press 2000 230p hardcover o.p. pa $17.95   **500**
1. Science 2. Fraud
ISBN 0-19-513515-6; 978-0-19-514710-0 (pa);
0-19-514710-3 (pa)   LC 99-40911
The author "aims to expose various beliefs and schemes put forth in the popular press and other places as scientifically real and factual. . . . {He} turns a critical eye on cold fusion, magnet therapy, homeopathy, perpetual motion, and other recent examples of fringe science. . . . Park's book should be required reading for all science writers, journalists, and politicians." Libr J

Pohl, Frederik, 1919-

Chasing science; science as a spectator sport. TOR Bks. 2000 251p $23.95; pa $14.95

500

1. Science

ISBN 0-312-86711-5; 0-7653-0829-0 (pa)

LC 00-57768

In order to witness science in action, Pohl traveled to a variety of sites, museums, laboratories, and observatories around the world. This is an account of his experiences and impressions.

Ray, C. Claiborne

The New York Times second book of science questions and answers; 225 new, intriguing, and just plain bizarre inquiries into everyday scientific mysteries; drawings by Victoria Roberts; edited by Henry Fountain. Anchor Bks. (NY) 2003 228p il pa $13

500

1. Science

ISBN 0-385-72258-3

LC 2002-26192

Also available The New York Times book of science questions and answers published 1997 pa $15 (ISBN 0-385-48660-X)

These selections from the author's weekly column in the science section of The New York Times answer such questions as "What would kill you if you fell into a black hole? Once people finally get to Mars, how will they get back? What makes the holes in Swiss cheese?" Publisher's note

"This eclectic volume of 228 questions with 200-word answers entices readers' interest in science. . . . There is no index and not much structure in this volume, but its charm and interest make up for its informality." Sci Books Films

Includes bibliographical references

Sagan, Carl, 1934-1996

Billions and billions; thoughts on life and death at the brink of the millennium. Random House 1997 241p pa $14.95 hardcover o.p.

500

1. Science

ISBN 0-345-37918-7 (pa)

LC 96-52730

This collection of essays covers such topics as: "the invention of chess, life on Mars, global warming, abortion, international affairs, the nature of government, and the meaning of morality. Writing with clarity and an understanding of human nature, Sagan offers hope for humanity's future." Libr J

Includes bibliographical references

Broca's brain; reflections on the romance of science. Random House 1979 347p pa $7.99 hardcover o.p. *

500

1. Science 2. Philosophy

ISBN 0-345-33689-5 (pa)

LC 78-21810

In this volume Sagan considers the following: "the quest for extraterrestrial life, popular science, and religious questions, as well as numerous concerns more immediate to his own specialty, astronomy." Libr J

The author "is a lucid, logical writer with a gift for explaining science to the layman and infecting the reader with his own boundless enthusiasm and curiosity." Natl Rev

Includes bibliographical references

The **Scientific** American science desk reference. Wiley 1999 690p il $39.95 *

500

1. Science

ISBN 0-471-35675-1

LC 99-32007

This reference "covers the physical, biological/health, and applied sciences. Fifteen chapters each provide a definition of scope, then a topical arrangement, with headings and subheadings in boldface type. . . . Each chapter concludes with a highly effective pattern: chronology, biographies, glossary, and brief-entry bibliography." Choice

Includes bibliographical references

Scientific American's ask the experts; answers to the most puzzling and mindblowing science questions; by the editors of Scientific American. HarperCollins Pubs. 2003 267p il pa $14.95

500

1. Science

ISBN 0-06-052336-0

LC 2004-555579

This "is a book that answers questions big, little, and in between. . . . The book uses the familiar question-and-answer format, with a table of contents allowing the reader to flip to a specific question. The questions are answered by a variety of experts. . . . This is one of those books you put on your reference shelf, and pull out whenever the subject turns to matters of scientific interest. Great for trivia buffs, too." Booklist

Wiggins, Arthur W.

The five biggest ideas in science; [by] Charles M. Wynn [and] Arthur W. Wiggins; with cartoon commentary by Sidney Harris. Wiley 1997 200p il maps pa $15.95

500

1. Science

ISBN 0-471-13812-6

LC 96-27469

Presents five basic scientific hypotheses: the atomic model, the periodic law, the big bang theory, plate tectonics, and evolution

"Each 'Big Idea' is thoroughly described. . . . In explaining the thinking that led to each 'Big Idea,' the authors clearly outline the scientific method and demystify the process." Libr J

Includes bibliographical references

The five biggest unsolved problems in science; {by} Arthur W. Wiggins {and} Charles M. Wynn; with cartoon commentary by Sidney Harris. J. Wiley & Sons 2003 234p il pa $14.95 *

500

1. Science

ISBN 0-471-26808-9

LC 2003-284262

"The problems discussed in this volume are the dueling concepts of mass and masslessness (physics), the passage from chemicals to living matter (chemistry), the complete structure of the proteome (biology), long-range weather forecasting (geology), and the expansion of the universe (astronomy)." Sci Books Films

Includes bibliographical references

500.2   Physical sciences

Encyclopedia of earth and physical sciences. 2nd ed. Marshall Cavendish 2005 13v il map set $657.07   **500.2**
1. Earth sciences—Encyclopedias 2. Physical sciences—Encyclopedias
ISBN 0-7614-7583-4   LC 2004-58630
First published 1998
Contents: 1. Absolute zero-Barrier islands -- 2. Base level-Clouds -- 3. Cloud seeding-Earth, structure of -- 4. Earthquakes-Forests -- 5. Fossil record-Humidity -- 6. Hurricanes-Magnetism -- 7. Maps and mapping-Musical acoustics -- 8. Nanotechnology-Paleoclimatology -- 9. Paleontology-Quasars -- 10. Quaternary period-Space -- 11. Space exploration-Tin -- 12. Titanium-Zinc
Includes bibliographical references

500.5   Space sciences

Space sciences; Pat Dasch, editor in chief. Macmillan Ref. USA 2002 4v il set $395   **500.5**
1. Space sciences
ISBN 0-02-865546-X   LC 2002-1707
"The Macmillan science library." On cover
Contents: v1 Space business; v2 Planetary science and astronomy; v3 Humans in space; v4 Our future in space
"The entries in each volume are in alphabetical order and range from a single paragraph to several pages in length, with most being one or two pages long. The front and back matter are the same in each volume and include a few pages of reference tables such as conversion charts, time lines of milestones in space history and human achievements in space, a list of contributors, a table of contents for the set, and a glossary." Booklist
"A comprehensive and usable survey of space exploration, this marvelous encyclopedia works equally well as a multivolume set and as four standalone volumes. . . . The photographs are excellent." Libr J
Includes bibliographical references

501   Philosophy and theory

Dawkins, Richard, 1941-
Unweaving the rainbow; science, delusion, and the appetite for wonder. Houghton Mifflin 1998 336p $26; pa $14   **501**
1. Science—Philosophy
ISBN 0-395-88382-2; 0-618-05673-4 (pa)
LC 98-40879
Dawkins "argues that scientific fact is both intellectually and esthetically more pleasing than pseudoscientific fantasy." N Y Times Book Rev
Dawkins is a "witty popularizer, whether he is offering a crash course in DNA fingerprinting, explaining the origins of 'mad cow disease' in weird proteins that spread like self-replicating viruses or discussing male birdsong as an auditory aphrodisiac for female birds." Publ Wkly
Includes bibliographical references

502   Miscellany

Ochoa, George
The Wilson chronology of science and technology; [by] George Ochoa and Melinda Corey. Wilson, H.W. 1997 440p $105 *
   502
1. Science—History 2. Technology—History
ISBN 0-8242-0933-8   LC 97-22060
This chronology begins in 2,500,000 B.C. and continues into 1997. "Within each year, entries are arranged alphabetically according to one of 13 categories: archaeology; astronomy, space science, and space exploration; biology, biochemistry, agriculture, and ecology; chemistry; earth sciences (geology, oceanography, meteorology) and earth exploration; mathematics; medicine; miscellaneous; paleontology; physics; psychology, neuroscience, and artificial intelligence; social sciences (anthropology, sociology, economics, political science) and linguistics; and technology and engineering." Publisher's note
Includes bibliographical references

502.8   Auxiliary techniques and procedures; apparatus, equipment, materials

Instruments of science; an historical encyclopedia; editors, Robert Bud, Deborah Jean Warner; associate editor, Stephen Johnston; managing editor, Betsy Bahr Peterson; picture editor, Simon Chaplin. Garland 1998 xxv, 709p il (Garland encyclopedias in the history of science) $175   **502.8**
ISBN 0-8153-1561-9   LC 97-15296
"Published in association with the Science Museum, London, and the National Museum of American History, Smithsonian Institution."
This "encyclopedia presents 325 historically significant scientific instruments from antiquity to the present. Instruments used for testing and monitoring in addition to those used for research are studied, including laboratory organisms such as E coli. Each of the signed entries explains how the instrument works and how it is used, as well as tracing its invention, development, and distribution. . . . Beautiful illustrations accompany many of the entries." Am Libr
Includes bibliographical references

503   Dictionaries, encyclopedias, concordances

Academic Press dictionary of science and technology; edited by Christopher Morris. Academic Press 1992 xxxii, 2432p il $99.95
   503
1. Science—Dictionaries 2. Technology—Dictionaries
ISBN 0-12-200400-0   LC 90-29032
"With over 133,000 entries, this title provides current, concise definitions of the specialized vocabulary used in 124 designated fields from acoustical engineering to zo-

Academic Press dictionary of science and technology—*Continued*

ology. . . . This authoritative, attractive dictionary will be useful to anyone seeking to understand the language of science and technology." Am Libr

The **American** Heritage science dictionary. Houghton Mifflin 2005 694p il maps $19.95
503

1. Science—Dictionaries
ISBN 0-618-45504-3   LC 2004-19696

This "science dictionary includes 8500 terms in anthropology, biology, chemistry, earth science, mathematics, medicine, physics, and technology. There are also 320 biographical entries of noted scientists as well as 30 biographical notes that explain how certain researchers found answers to major scientific problems. Written in clear, simple prose that general readers can understand, the entries are often more than simple definitions, offering in-depth discussions of scientific ideas." Libr J

The **Encyclopedia** of science and technology; James S. Trefil, general editor; contributing editors, Harold Morowitz, Paul Ceruzzi. Routledge 2001 554p il maps $50   **503**
1. Science—Encyclopedias 2. Technology—Encyclopedias
ISBN 0-415-93724-8   LC 2001-19983

This reference includes "1000 entries, arranged alphabetically and color-coded to indicate whether the topic is related to life science, physical science, or technology. Accessible to the general reader, the articles range widely. . . . The excellent cross references direct the reader to related articles that cover either more fundamental or more advanced information. . . . A true pleasure to browse and read; highly recommended." Libr J
Includes bibliographical references and index

Encyclopedia of science, technology, and ethics; edited by Carl Mitcham. Macmillan Reference USA 2005 4v il map set $450   **503**
1. Science—Ethical aspects
ISBN 0-02-865831-0   LC 2005-6968

This "set confronts the major ethical issues of our time in a series of 675 articles, 33 of which are overviews of topics like computer ethics, while the remainder deal with such 'hot-button' issues as abortion and animal rights." Libr J
This "multivolume work on ethics provides a superb introduction to the issues presented." Booklist
Includes bibliographical references

The **Facts** on File encyclopedia of science. Facts on File 1999 2v il set $137.50   **503**
1. Science—Dictionaries
ISBN 0-8160-4008-7   LC 98-53201

"Over 10,000 terms are defined from all areas of the sciences, including medicine and the applied sciences. A series of feature essays gives more depth to certain topics, ranging from the millennium bug to miners' safety lamps, though most are items of current news interest. The work is remarkably current, with many up-to-date entries (e.g., 'FAQ' and 'browser'); photographs and diagrams enhance the text." Libr J

Gale encyclopedia of science; K. Lee Lerner & Brenda Wilmoth Lerner, editors. 4th ed. Thomson Gale 2008 6v il set $685   **503**
1. Science—Encyclopedias
ISBN 978-1-4144-2877-2; 1-4144-2877-4
LC 2006-37485
First published 1996

"From algae to zooplankton, assembly lines to Y2K, and from Agent Orange to weapons of mass destruction, this encyclopedia covers every aspect of the scientific world. . . . It is designed to 'instruct, challenge, and excite' a wide range of users and is a good starting point to answer any scientific question." Libr Media Connect
Includes bibliographical references

McGraw-Hill concise encyclopedia of science & technology. 5th ed. McGraw-Hill 2005 2651p il $185   **503**
1. Science—Encyclopedias 2. Technology—Encyclopedias
ISBN 0-07-142957-3; 978-0-07-142957-3
LC 2004-54909
First published 1984

A condensed version of the McGraw-Hill encyclopedia of science & technology
This encyclopedia features over 7300 articles on branches of technology and science ranging from acoustics to zoology.
Includes bibliographical references

McGraw-Hill dictionary of scientific and technical terms. 6th ed. McGraw-Hill 2003 2380p il $150
503
1. Science—Dictionaries 2. Technology—Dictionaries
ISBN 0-07-042313-X   LC 2002-26436
First published 1974

This dictionary provides "over 100,000 succinct definitions ranging through 102 fields of science, from acoustics to zoology. Many of the definitions contain clear-cut illustrations with labels in the margins of the pages. Phonetics for pronunciation appear at the end of the definition." Sci Books Films
"This continues to be the most comprehensive science and technology dictionary for the student, researcher, and layperson." Booklist

McGraw-Hill encyclopedia of science & technology. 10th ed. McGraw-Hill 2007 20v il map set $2,995 *   **503**
1. Science—Encyclopedias 2. Technology—Encyclopedias
ISBN 978-0-07-144143-8; 0-07-144143-3
LC 2007-6137

"An international reference work in twenty volumes including an index"
First published 1960 in fifteen volumes

This encyclopedia "contains approximately 7,100 articles on major topics in all categories of science and technology, written for the non-specialist. Each entry begins with general information on the topic. Detailed information follows under headings so the reader can focus on specific areas of interest. All but general survey articles have a bibliography at the end. There is extensive cross-referencing between articles that leads to related topics. Scientists who have been major contributors to their field

McGraw-Hill encyclopedia of science & technology—*Continued*

wrote many articles. The index volume contains a list of contributors, a guide to scientific notation, study guides, a topical index, and an analytical index." Sci Books Films [review of 2002 edition]

Includes bibliographical references

The **new** encyclopedia of science. 2nd ed. Oxford University Press 2003 9v il set $299

503

1. Science—Encyclopedias
ISBN 0-19-521918-X   LC 2003-41937
First published 1995
Cover title; Set editorial consultant: John Clark

This set "consists of nine volumes, eight of them devoted to a particular field of modern science: 'Matter and Energy,' 'Animals and Plants,' 'Chemistry in Action,' 'Stars and Atoms,' 'Earth and Other Planets,' 'Ecology and Environment,' 'Computing,' and 'Evolution and Genetics.' The set is intended for both general readers with quick questions and students interested in specific scientific topics. . . . The text is written for the less well informed reader and should be accessible to most. The layout is bright and appealing." Booklist

Trefil, James S., 1938-
The nature of science; an A-Z guide to the laws and principles governing our universe; {by} James Trefil. Houghton Mifflin 2003 xxx, 433p il $35

503

1. Science—Encyclopedias
ISBN 0-618-31938-7   LC 2002-27364
First published 2002 in the United Kingdom with title: Cassell's laws of nature

The author presents a "collection of the 200 most important scientific laws and principles governing our universe, from DNA, mimicry, and molecular clocks to the conservation of energy, quantum mechanics, Gödel's incompleteness theorems, and the big bang. . . . Trefil has included a wonderful must-read introduction, biographies, pictures, diagrams, time lines, and anecdotes to provide human stories behind nature's laws. The comprehensive index, small glossary, and cross-disciplinary time-line provide good search help and historical relationships." Choice

Van Nostrand's concise encyclopedia of science; Christopher G. De Pree, Alan Axelrod, editors; with a foreword by Glenn D. Considine. Wiley 2003 821p il $40

503

1. Science—Encyclopedias
ISBN 0-471-36331-6   LC 2002-34327
Based on the ninth edition of Van Nostrand's scientific encyclopedia

"Written at a level accessible to the general reader, the alphabetically arranged entries range in length from about a sentence to a page. The 5,000 entries cover physics, chemistry, earth sciences, space sciences, life sciences, energy, environmental sciences, materials sciences, and information sciences." Booklist

"This encyclopedia is a great resource for quick and short answers to many scientific questions. There are no references, so it is not a good conduit to further information, but if you need a book that will provide concise answers quickly, this is it." Sci Books Films

Includes bibliographical references

Van Nostrand's scientific encyclopedia. 10th ed., Glenn D. Considine, editor-in-chief; Peter H. Kulik, associate editor. Wiley 2008 3v il map set $450 *

503

1. Science—Encyclopedias
ISBN 978-0-471-74338-5   LC 2007-46658
Also available online
First published 1938

This encyclopedia contains articles contains over 10,000 entries on topics such as biology, chemistry, earth science, mathematics and engineering, anatomy and physiology, physics, botany, and space science.

Includes bibliographical references

Volti, Rudi
The Facts on File encyclopedia of science, technology, and society. Facts on File 1999 3v il set $247.50

503

1. Science—Encyclopedias 2. Technology—Encyclopedias
ISBN 0-8160-3123-1   LC 98-39014

"In 900 alphabetically arranged entries, this title aims to be 'a presentation of the social settings in which science and technology have emerged, been developed, and put to use.' . . . It includes articles on a wide range of topics, such as the origin and chemistry of cheese, the historical development of software, and the rise and fall of drive-in movies." Booklist

507.8 Use of apparatus and equipment in study and teaching

Experiment central; understanding scientific principles through projects; John T. Tanacredi & John Loret, general editors. U.X.L 2000-2004 6v il set $347

507.8

1. Science—Experiments
ISBN 1-4144-0522-7   LC 99-54142
Vols. 1-4 and vols. 5-6 also available as separate sets
Vols. 5-6 by M. Rae Nelson; Allison McNeill, project editor

Demonstrates scientific concepts by means of experiments, including step-by-step instructions, lists of materials, troubleshooter's guide, and interpretation and explanation of the results.

Johnson, George, 1952-
The ten most beautiful experiments. Alfred A. Knopf 2008 192p il $22.95

507.8

1. Science—Experiments
ISBN 978-1-4000-4101-5; 1-4000-4101-5
LC 2007-27839

The author describes "10 historic experiments whose elegant simplicity revealed key features of our bodies and our world." Publ Wkly

"Writing up Luigi Galvani's study of frog's legs, James Joule's of heat, Albert Michelson's of light's

Johnson, George, 1952-—*Continued*
speed, and Robert Millikan's of the electron's charge,
Johnson exerts classic appeal to science readers: presenting the lone genius making a great discovery. Good to
go in any library." Booklist
Includes bibliographical references

Sheldrake, Rupert
Seven experiments that could change the world;
a do-it-yourself guide to revolutionary science.
[2nd ed] Park St. Press 2002 303p pa $16.95

507.8

1. Science—Experiments
ISBN 0-89281-989-8　　　　　　LC 2002-728157
First published 1995 by Riverhead Bks.
"Sheldrake questions many tenets of the mechanistic-
materialistic orthodoxy governing most science today and
proposes certain practical experiments to raise further
doubts about it. He presents experiments by which we
can determine how some pets know when their owners
are coming home, how homing pigeons find their way,
how insect colonies operate, how people know that they
are being stared at from behind and how phantom limbs
sometimes seem to amputees to be still attached. . . . Finally, he offers details of experiments by which even
those who are not trained scientists can measure some of
these possibly paranormal phenomena. A well-reasoned,
accessible and provocative book." Publ Wkly
Includes bibliographical references

508　Natural history

Ackerman, Diane
Cultivating delight; a natural history of my
garden. HarperCollins Pubs. 2001 261p pa $13.95
hardcover o.p.　　　　　　　　　　　**508**
1. Natural history 2. Gardens
ISBN 0-06-050536-2 (pa)　　　　　LC 2001-16607
Although Ackerman's "book is presented as a gardening journal, with sections on the four seasons, her musings know no bounds and verge on stream-of-
consciousness. One typical chapter ranges over topics
that include landscape architecture, lawns, fences, autumn
colors, childhood memories, the difference between laby-
rinths and mazes, the history and definition of gardens,
and compost, all peppered with quotations from a dozen
authors." Libr J

Asma, Stephen T.
Stuffed animals & pickled heads; the culture
and evolution of natural history museums. Oxford
Univ. Press 2001 302p il hardcover o.p. pa $16.95

508

1. Natural history 2. Museums
ISBN 0-19-513050-2; 0-19-516336-2 (pa)
　　　　　　　　　　　　　　LC 00-40674
The author discusses the development of natural history museums, beginning with the "'cabinets of curiosities', put together in the 17th century. . . . The cabinets
changed when Darwin's theory of evolution became
widely accepted in the late 19th century, with less em-

phasis on the exceptional, more on showing how each
species fitted into the supposed scheme of things." Economist
Includes bibliographical references

Darwin, Charles, 1809-1882
The voyage of the Beagle; journal of researches
into the natural history and geology of the
countries visited during the voyage of H.M.S.
Beagle round the world; introduction by Steve
Jones. Modern Lib. 2001 468p il pa $12.95 ＊

508

1. Beagle Expedition (1831-1836) 2. Natural history
3. South America—Description and travel
ISBN 0-375-75680-9　　　　　　　LC 00-46294
Also available in paperback from Penguin Bks.
First published 1839 with title: Journal of researches
into the geology and natural history of the various countries visited by H.M.S. Beagle
This journal records the author's five year voyage
around the world as a naturalist aboard H.M.S. Beagle.
The trip was influential in the formulation of Darwin's
theories of evolution. During the journey he collected
data on wildlife, geological formations, weather, and local customs.

De Villiers, Marq
Sahara: a natural history; [by] Marq de Villiers
and Sheila Hirtle. Walker & Co. 2002 326p il
maps $28; pa $13　　　　　　　　　**508**
1. Sahara Desert 2. Natural history—Africa
ISBN 0-8027-1372-6; 0-8027-7678-7 (pa)
　　　　　　　　　　　　　　LC 2002-71391
This volume includes the Sahara's "history (both natural and human), as well as a look at the complicated ethnology and present-day life of the various tribes
(Tauregs, Berbers, Moors, and Tubu) that have adapted
to this incredibly harsh climate." Libr J
"Insightful and intelligent, this fascinating book will
appeal to anyone with a curiosity about the world's largest desert and the people who inhabit it." Booklist
Includes bibliographical references

Flannery, Tim F. (Tim Fridjof), 1956-
The eternal frontier; an ecological history of
North America and its peoples; [by] Tim Flannery.
Atlantic Monthly Press 2001 404p il maps $27.50;
pa $16　　　　　　　　　　　　　　**508**
1. Natural history—North America
ISBN 0-87113-789-5; 0-8021-3888-8 (pa)
　　　　　　　　　　　　　　LC 2001-18841
First published by Text Publishing, Melbourne Austra-
lia in 2001
This "book explores approximately 65 million years of
the ecology of the entire North American continent."
Libr J
"This book weaves ecological, cultural, and social his-
tory together in a marvelous way." Sci Books Films

Fothergill, Alastair

Planet Earth; as you've never seen it before; [by] Alastair Fothergill [et al.]; foreword by David Attenborough. University of California Press 2007 309p il map $39.95 **508**

   1. Habitat (Ecology) 2. Earth

   ISBN 978-0-520-25054-3; 0-520-25054-0

                  LC 2006-50073

   In this collection of over 400 photographs of natural landscapes and wildlife, the author "takes readers on a kaleidoscopic tour of the flora, fauna and natural history of the Earth's poles, forests, plains, deserts, mountains and oceans." Publ Wkly

Gould, Stephen Jay, 1941-2002

Bully for brontosaurus; reflections in natural history. Norton 1991 540p il pa $15.95 hardcover o.p. * **508**

   1. Natural history 2. Evolution

   ISBN 0-393-30857-X (pa)   LC 91-6916

   A collection of essays from the author's monthly columns in Natural History magazine

   "These pithy essays focus on evolution and the workings of science. Gould's fans . . . will find these works fascinating, literate, and often challenging—vintage Gould." Libr J

Dinosaur in a haystack; reflections in natural history. Harmony Bks. 1995 480p il pa $15.95 hardcover o.p. **508**

   1. Natural history

   ISBN 0-517-88824-6 (pa)   LC 95-51333

   In this collection the author "relates anecdotes from the history of science and demonstrates their relevance to contemporary scientific disputes and social trends." Libr J

   "A discovery awaits in every essay—in every haystack—which solidifies Gould as one of the most eloquent science popularizers writing today." Booklist

   Includes bibliographical references

The flamingo's smile; reflections in natural history. Norton 1985 476p il pa $15.95 hardcover o.p. **508**

   1. Natural history

   ISBN 0-393-30375-6 (pa)   LC 85-4916

   In this collection "the theme is history, both natural and human. . . . The essays are marked by Gould's usual careful scholarship and erudition and clear and non-technical language." Sci Books Films

   Includes bibliographical references

Leonardo's mountain of clams and the Diet of Worms; essays on natural history. Harmony Bks. 1998 422p il pa $15 hardcover o.p. **508**

   1. Natural history 2. Evolution

   ISBN 0-609-80475-8 (pa)   LC 98-11500

   In this collection of essays, Gould "peers less at nature than at scientists' attempts to understand and explain its wonders. Ranging far and wide through the history of science, Gould's sketches in 'humanistic natural history' examine the 'grand false starts in the history of natural science.'" Publ Wkly

   "Gould's incomparable style, by turns colloquial, hu-morous, ironic and insightful, allows readers to revel in his unabashed and contagious enthusiasm." N Y Times Book Rev

   Includes bibliographical references

The lying stones of Marrakesh; penultimate reflections to natural history. Harmony Bks. 2000 372p il pa $15 hardcover o.p. **508**

   1. Natural history 2. Evolution

   ISBN 0-609-80755-2 (pa)   LC 99-36148

   In this collection of essays Gould "chronicles the history of paleontology through a biographical lens, then trains his scientific acumen and keen humor on such subjects as Mozart's *Requiem* and the tragic 1911 Triangle Shirt Factory fire." Booklist

The richness of life; the essential Stephen Jay Gould; edited by Paul McGarr and Steven Rose; with an introduction by Steven Rose and a foreword by Oliver Sacks. 1st American ed. Norton 2007 654p il $35 * **508**

   1. Natural history 2. Evolution

   ISBN 978-0-393-06498-8; 0-393-06498-0

               LC 2006-29208

   Frist published 2006 in the United Kingdom

   "These 44 essays represent . . . [the author's] best-known pieces from his books and from essays for Natural History magazine, as well as never before published speeches." Publ Wkly

   "For collections that have room for only one volume of his writing, this is the essential one." SLJ

   Includes bibliographical references

Keynes, R. D.

Fossils, finches, and Fuegians; Darwin's adventures and discoveries on the Beagle; by Richard Keynes. Oxford Univ. Press 2003 428p il maps $35 **508**

   1. Darwin, Charles, 1809-1882 2. Beagle Expedition (1831-1836) 3. Natural history

   ISBN 0-19-516649-3   LC 2002-154176

   First published 2002 in the United Kingdom

   The author "tracks Darwin's storied 1831-36 voyage of science and surveying on the *Beagle,* quoting unexpurgated tracts not only from Darwin's letters and journals but also from those of the *Beagle's* captain, . . . Robert FitzRoy." Booklist

   "Keynes shows readers how his great-grandfather's belief in the immutability of species slowly began to change during his travels. Handsomely illustrated with sketches and paintings made by Darwin and others associated with the *Beagle,* this is an excellent introduction to the events that led 20 years later to *On the Origin of Species.*" Publ Wkly

   Includes bibliographical references

Leopold, Aldo, 1886-1948

A Sand County almanac; and sketches here and there; illustrated by Charles W. Schwartz; introduction by Robert Finch. Oxford Univ. Press 1987 c1949 xxviii, 228p il hardcover o.p. pa $9.95 **508**

1. Natural history—United States 2. Nature conservation

ISBN 0-19-505305-2; 0-19-505928-X (pa)

LC 87-22015

A reissue of the title first published 1949

The essays in the first section of the book record natural changes observed by the author on his Wisconsin farm during the course of a year. In the other two sections are personal experiences ranging over a wide expanse of country and forty years in time.

This "collection of poetic vignettes about run-down farmland and wilderness trips, seasoned with erudite historical reflections . . . has added a significant ethical concept to the prophecies of Thoreau, John Muir and other voices in the wilderness." N Y Times Book Rev

Lincoln, Roger J.

The Cambridge illustrated dictionary of natural history; {by} R. J. Lincoln and G. A. Boxshall; illustrations by Roberta Smith. Cambridge Univ. Press 1987 413p il pa $29 hardcover o.p. * **508**

ISBN 0-521-39941-6 (pa)   LC 87-8018

This "is principally a dictionary of taxonomic groups down to the level of family, with common names cross-referenced to Latin ones, and frequent illustrations. Technical terms are few, and paleontology is given less attention than current classes of plants, animals, and microorganisms." Recomm Ref Books in Paperback. 2d edition

Matthiessen, Peter

End of the earth; voyaging to Antarctica. National Geographic Soc. 2003 242p il maps $26 **508**

1. Antarctica—Exploration 2. Animals—Antarctica

ISBN 0-7922-5059-1   LC 2003-51254

This account of the author's voyage describes the wildlife he encountered in the region

"Vivid and empathic accounts of the high drama and petty rivalries of Antarctic exploration alternate with Matthiessen's own adventures as he shares his indelible impressions of this cold, white wonderland in the hope that they will inspire readers to appreciate the beauty and bounty of the earth's 'shimmering web of biodiversity' enough to defend and preserve it." Booklist

Includes bibliographical references

Nature writing; the tradition in English; edited by Robert Finch and John Elder. Norton 2002 1152p $39.95 **508**

1. Natural history

ISBN 0-393-04966-3   LC 2001-55825

First published 1990 with title: The Norton book of nature writing

This anthology of nature writings from 1789 to 1987 includes such authors as Henry David Thoreau, John Muir, Annie Dillard, and Barry Lopez

Includes bibliographical references

Quammen, David, 1948-

The boilerplate rhino; nature in the eye of the beholder. Scribner 2000 287p pa $13 hardcover o.p. **508**

1. Natural history 2. Nature

ISBN 0-7432-0032-2 (pa)   LC 99-56894

In this "collection of David Quammen's columns for Outside magazine, the focus is on man's interaction with nature. Sometimes Quammen interacts with the nature he's writing about; at other times he just thinks about it, reads up and summarizes what he's read." N Y Times Book Rev

Includes bibliographical references

Schaller, George B.

A naturalist and other beasts; tales from a life in the field; with photographs by the author. Sierra Club Books 2007 272p il $24.95 **508**

1. Wildlife

ISBN 978-1-57805-129-8; 1-57805-129-0

LC 2006-51153

The author "presents 19 short pieces culled from the dozens of articles and books he has published during half a century spent observing animals around the world. The selections include studies of the daily lives of such exotic beasts as jaguars in Brazil; tigers in central India; lions, wildebeest and cheetahs in Tanzania's Serengeti Plain; giant pandas in China; snow leopards in Pakistan; and chiru (antelope) in the uplands of the Tibetan Plateau." Publ Wkly

"Schaller presents exciting animal lore that will inspire readers to learn more about these precious creatures." Booklist

Includes bibliographical references

Sterling, Eleanor J.

Vietnam; a natural history; [by] Eleanor Jane Sterling, Martha Maud Hurley, Le Duc Minh; with illustrations by Joyce A. Powzyk. Yale University Press 2006 423p il map $40 **508**

1. Natural history—Vietnam

ISBN 978-0-300-10608-4; 0-300-10608-4

LC 2005-29254

"For many, the name Vietnam connotes war and loss. Yet the country itself harbors an incredibly rich natural history, and despite the assault on its landscape and wildlife during its years of war, this complex and diverse land is revealing newly found species or rediscovering presumed extinct species at an exciting rate. . . . This volume fills a major gap by collecting and collating, in English, widely scattered information about Vietnam's natural history. Well organized into chapters that cover humans, biogeography, flora, and fauna; northern, central, and southern Vietnam; and conservation efforts, the text is written in a highly accessible style that will attract interested amateur naturalists and travelers as well as scientists." Libr J

Includes bibliographical references

Wallace, Joseph, 1957-
A gathering of wonders; behind the scenes at the American Museum of Natural History. St. Martin's Press 2000 288p il $24.95; pa $14.95
508
1. American Museum of Natural History 2. Natural history
ISBN 0-312-25221-8; 0-312-28039-4 (pa)
LC 00-25481
This describes the American Museum of Natural History "through its most famous, colorful or important scientists and administrators, from the 1880s to the 1970s." Publ Wkly

509 Historical, geographic, persons treatment

Adler, Robert E., 1946-
Science firsts: from the creation of science to the science of creation; [by] Robert Adler. Wiley 2002 232p il $24.95 *
509
1. Science—History 2. Scientists
ISBN 0-471-40174-9
LC 2002-727233
The author tells the engaging and inspiring stories of thirty-five landmark scientific discoveries from the first accurate prediction of an eclipse in 585 B.C. to the cloning of Dolly the sheep.
Includes bibliographical references

The **Chronology** of science; from Stonehenge to the human genome project; consulting editor, Lisa Rosner. ABC-CLIO 2002 566p $85
509
1. Science—History 2. Scientists
ISBN 1-57607-954-6
LC 2001-7692
The chronologies are "divided into subject areas, including astronomy, biology, chemistry, ecology, mathematics, and physics; 16 feature essays on critical scientific discoveries . . . [are included as well as] biographies of key scientists." Publisher's note
Includes bibliographical references

Crease, Robert P.
The prism and the pendulum; the ten most beautiful experiments in science. Random House 2003 xxii, 244p il hardcover o.p. pa $14.95
509
1. Science—History 2. Science—Experiments
ISBN 1-400-06131-8; 0-8129-7062-4 (pa)
LC 2003-54765
Each scientific experiment discussed here "is followed by an 'interlude,' or commentary, on how the experiment qualifies as most beautiful and how art and science both give meaning to the term 'beauty.'" Sci Books Films

Encyclopedia of the scientific revolution; from Copernicus to Newton; editor Wilbur Applebaum. Garland 2000 xxxv, 758p il (Garland reference library of the humanities) $160
509
1. Science—History—Encyclopedias
ISBN 0-8153-1503-1
LC 00-25149

A "collection of articles on the progress of scientific discovery in the 16th and 17th centuries. . . . The 437 entries vary in length from just half a page to five pages, and each has a short bibliography directing the reader to recent articles and monographs as well as primary sources." Libr J
Includes bibliographical references

Flowers, Charles
Instability rules; the ten most amazing ideas of modern science. Wiley 2002 228p $24.95 *
509
1. Science—History
ISBN 0-471-38042-3
LC 2001-6729
Contents: Hubble and the expanding universe; Einstein and the wonder of light; Bohr and the puzzles of the quantum world; Wegener and the dance of the continents; Big bang; Fermat, Godel, and fuzzy math; Mendel, Watson, Crick, and the human genome; Hominids to humans, and continuing; Turing, the brain as computer, and vice versa; Freud, the unconscious, and other views

Gribbin, John R.
The scientists; a history of science told through the lives of its greatest inventors; [by] John Gribbin. Random House 2003 xxii, 646p il hardcover o.p. pa $16.95
509
1. Scientists 2. Science—History
ISBN 1-4000-6013-3; 0-8129-6788-7 (pa)
LC 2003-46607
First published 2002 in the United Kingdom with title: Science: a history, 1543-2001
"Starting with the Renaissance, Gribbin traces the development of science over the past 500 years through the lives of the people who made it. From Copernicus and Galileo to Albert Einstein and Linus Pauling, Gribbin carefully places the individual in the time in which he or she lived. . . . He also . . . shows the development of science to be the result of the interplay among three factors: the person, the historical time, and the available technology." Libr J
"Replete with scientific clarity, Gribbin's work is the epitome of what a general-interest history of science should be." Booklist
Includes bibliographical references

History of modern science and mathematics; Brian S. Baigrie, editor. Scribner 2002 4v il set $395
509
1. Science—History 2. Mathematics—History
ISBN 0-684-80636-3
LC 2002-4042
This "set attempts to synthesize the history of scientific developments in anthropology, astronomy, biology, chemistry, mathematics, physics, psychology, and the earth sciences. . . . This work ranges from the 17th century to the present without trying to include the most recent developments." Libr J
Includes bibliographical references

The **History** of science in the United States; an encyclopedia; edited by Marc Rothenberg. Garland 2000 xx, 615p (Garland reference library of social science, Special-reference) $160

509

1. Science—History—Encyclopedias

ISBN 0-8153-0762-4   LC 99-43757

This "encyclopedia comprises 500 short- to medium-length articles . . . on the development of science and medicine in the United States. The typical article runs a page, though broad topics . . . receive longer treatments." Libr J

"This book will become a standard reference and belongs in every high school, college, and public library." Sci Books Films

Includes bibliographical references

Horvitz, Leslie Alan

Eureka!: scientific breakthroughs that changed the world. Wiley 2002 246p il $24.95

509

1. Science—History

ISBN 0-471-40276-1   LC 2001-46890

This examines twelve scientific discoveries and their discoverers, including Joseph Priestley and oxygen, Friedrich Kekulé and the structure of carbon compounds, Dmitri Mendeleev and the periodic table, Isaac Newton and gravity, Einstein and the theory of relativity, Philo Farnsworth and television, Alexander Fleming and penicillin, Charles Townes and the laser, Alfred Wegener and continental drift, Darwin and the origin of species, Watson and Crick and the double helix, and Benoit Mandelbrot and fractal geometry.

Includes bibliographical references

Jardine, Lisa, 1944-

Ingenious pursuits; building the scientific revolution. Talese 1999 444p il pa $16 hardcover o.p.   **509**

1. Science—History

ISBN 0-385-72001-7 (pa)   LC 99-41985

In this history of science in the 17th and early 18th centuries the author "chronicles improvements in the tools of observation (telescopes, microscopes) and measurement (clocks) that were used by a pungent cast of characters who collaborated and squabbled with one another as they sorted out comets and discovered microbes." New Yorker

Includes bibliographical references

Lightman, Alan P., 1948-

The discoveries; great breakthroughs in 20th century science; [by] Alan Lightman. Pantheon Books 2005 553p il $32.50; pa $16.95 *

509

1. Science—History

ISBN 0-375-42168-8; 0-375-71345-X (pa)

LC 2005-40854

This book "chronicles 25 landmark findings in astronomy, physics, chemistry, and biology in the 20th century. Beginning with Max Planck's quantum theory and ending with Paul Berg's recombinant DNA, these break-throughs are academically and playfully explored via the nature of the unknown, the circumstances and influences of discovery, and, most originally, the actual words of the scientists." Libr J

Includes bibliographical references

The **Oxford** companion to the history of modern science; editor in chief, J.L. Heilbron; editors, James Bartholomew {et al.}. Oxford Univ. Press 2003 xxviii, 941p il $110 *   **509**

1. Science—History

ISBN 0-19-511229-6   LC 2002-153783

This reference on the history of science from the Renaissance through the 20th century includes some 600 articles covering "a broad spectrum of topics in all scientific disciplines (e.g., biotechnology, geology) as well as disciplines that influenced science, such as religion and politics. Also included are the biographies of 100 leading figures (e.g., Isaac Newton, Marie Curie) and coverage of scientific instruments (e.g., microscopes, Geiger counters). Organized alphabetically, the well-written articles include plenty of cross references. Over 100 black-and-white illustrations appear within their appropriate articles, but the eight pages of color illustrations in the middle of the volume are not associated with any article." Libr J

Includes bibliographical references

Piel, Gerard, 1915-2004

The age of science; what scientists learned in the 20th century; with illustrations by Peter Bradford. Basic Bks. 2001 xx, 460p il maps $40

509

1. Science—History

ISBN 0-465-05755-1   LC 2001-43178

"A Cornelia and Michael Bessie book"

This "survey explores quantum mechanics, subatomic particles, astrophysics, genetics, cell biology, planetary geology, and evolution. . . . While it generally succeeds in making science intelligible to the lay reader, this book is still challenging if rewarding." Libr J

Includes bibliographical references

Reader's guide to the history of science; edited by Arne Hessenbruch. Fitzroy Dearborn Pubs. 2000 xxix, 934p $135   **509**

1. Science—History—Encyclopedias

ISBN 1-884964-29-X   LC 2001-270888

"This volume contains about 600 entries on various aspects of the history of science, including individuals (e.g., Galileo), disciplines (e.g., astronomy), and broad topics (e.g., religion)." Libr J

Includes bibliographical references

Science and its times; understanding the social significance of scientific discovery; Neil Schlager, editor; Josh Lauer, associate editor. Gale Group 2000-2001 8v set $625

509

1. Science—History

ISBN 0-7876-3932-X   LC 00-37542

Contents: v1 2000 B.C.-700 A.D.; v2 700-1450; v3 1450-1699; v4 1700-1799; v5 19th century; v6 1900-1950; v7 1950-present; v8 Cumulative index

Science and its times—*Continued*

This set addresses "a wide variety of scientific developments with explanations of underlying factors and their effects on politics, economics, culture and daily life. [It includes] more than 20 topical essays, 25 full biographies and 85 sketches of notable people in each volume." Publisher's note

Silver, Brian L.

The ascent of science. Oxford Univ. Press 1998 534p il pa $53 hardcover o.p.   **509**
1. Science—History   2. Science—Philosophy 3. Thought and thinking
ISBN 0-19-513427-3   LC 97-15430
"A Solomon Press book"

The author discusses a "variety of topics, from Pythagorean musings and lodestones to quantum mechanical puzzles and DNA structures. Yes, chaos theory and cosmology are included too. All this is sandwiched between interesting references to historical matters, philosophical positions, some controversies, and to Shakespeare, Shelley, and Shaw also. A book commendable for its breadth, depth, and vision." Choice
Includes bibliographical references

Teresi, Dick

Lost discoveries; the ancient roots of modern science, from the Babylonians to the Maya. Simon & Schuster 2002 453p il $27; pa $15
    509
1. Science—History 2. Ancient civilization
ISBN 0-684-83718-8; 0-7432-4379-X (pa)
     LC 2002-75457
"This is a compendium of premodern knowledge of the natural world. Teresi structures his exploration into the science of Sumerian, Babylonian, Mayan, Chinese, and other non-European, premodern cultures around the thesis that classical Greece is not the sole fount of Western science." Booklist
"Teresi offers a great deal of fascinating material largely ignored by many histories of science." Publ Wkly
Includes bibliographical references

Walker, Mark

Nazi science; myth, truth, and the German atomic bomb. Perseus 2001 325p il pa $22.50
    509
1. Science—Germany 2. Atomic bomb 3. National socialism
ISBN 0-7382-0585-0; 978-0-7382-0585-4
First published 1995 by Plenum Press
"Walker examines the effect of the Nazi years on German science. Focusing primarily on physics and such . . . individuals as Einstein, Heisenberg, Gerlach, von Weizsacher, Stark, von Laue, and Planck, the author devotes the first seven of 11 chapters to an . . . analysis of how the German physics community evolved during the growth of the Third Reich. In chapters 8-10, the German work on nuclear fission is discussed." Choice
"Although scholarly, this will be accessible to general readers." Libr J
Includes bibliographical references

Webster, Raymond B.

African American firsts in science and technology; foreword by Wesley L. Harris. Gale Group 1999 462p $80 *   **509**
1. Scientists 2. African American inventors
ISBN 0-7876-3876-5   LC 99-27346
Presents capsule accounts of notable first achievements by African Americans, arranged in the categories "Agriculture and Everyday Life," "Dentistry and Nursing," "Life Science," "Math and Engineering," "Medicine," "Physical Science," and "Transportation."
Includes bibliographical references

Whitfield, Peter

Landmarks in western science; from prehistory to the atomic age. Routledge 1999 256p il $65
    509
1. Science—History
ISBN 0-415-92533-9   LC 99-24976
This survey "highlights significant discoveries and turning points in mathematics, astronomy, physics, medicine, geology, and many other fields." Publisher's note
Includes bibliographical references

510   Mathematics

Acheson, D. J.

1089 and all that; a journey into mathematics; [by] David Acheson. Oxford Univ. Press 2002 178p il $19.95   **510**
1. Mathematics
ISBN 0-19-851623-1   LC 2002-71547
"This book aims to make mathematics accessible to non-experts and the lay reader. Providing an . . . overview of the subject, the text includes several . . . mathematical conundrums. . . . The book contains several cartoons, sketches and photos." Publisher's note
"Not a page passes without at least one intriguing insight. . . . Anyone who is baffled by mathematics should buy it." New Sci

Aczel, Amir D.

The artist and the mathematician; the story of Nicolas Bourbaki, the genius mathematician who never existed. Thunder's Mouth Press 2006 239p il $23.95   **510**
1. Bourbaki, Nicolas 2. Mathematicians
ISBN 978-1-56025-931-2; 1-56025-931-0
"In 1934, a small group of mostly French mathematicians met to reinvent a new math based on a pedagogy of rigorous proofs, clarity, and logical thinking. The group invented a fictitious persona, 'Nicolas Bourbaki,' as a pseudonym under which to author their collective work. Presenting the fascinating story behind the publication of over 40 tomes . . ., Aczel describes the group's cultural context, eccentricities, informal rules, and practices of engagement and offers biographical sketches of such influential members as Andr Weil and Alexandre Grothendieck. Writing in an accessible, conversational style that excludes mathematical proofs, Aczel paints a clear picture of the Bourbaki movement and how it has influenced the way mathematics should be discussed and learned." Libr J

Boyer, Carl B. (Carl Benjamin), 1906-
A history of mathematics; revised by Uta C. Merzbach. 2nd ed. Wiley 1989 762p il hardcover o.p. pa $39.95 **510**
1. Mathematics—History
ISBN 0-471-09763-2; 0-471-54397-7 (pa)
LC 89-5325
First published 1969
"This good general history of mathematics is understandable to the student as well as authoritative for the mathematician." Malinowsky. Best Sci & Technol Ref Books for Young People
Includes bibliographical references

Cole, K. C.
The universe and the teacup; the mathematics of truth and beauty. Harcourt Brace & Co. 1998 214p pa $13 hardcover o.p. **510**
1. Mathematics 2. Truth
ISBN 0-15-600656-1 (pa)
LC 97-22338
The author "leads readers through the mathematical concepts that apply equally well to the behavior of planetary bodies and our own. . . . Cole's arguments occasionally meander, but that doesn't detract from the book's overall clarity and balance, including a well-chosen, succinct list of suggested readings. From the symmetry of spheres to altruism, Cole shows that truth does indeed add up to beauty, and beauty to truth." Publ Wkly

CRC standard mathematical tables and formulae; [editor-in-chief,] Daniel Zwillinger. 31st ed. CRC Press 2003 910p il $59.95 *
510
1. Mathematics—Tables
ISBN 1-58488-291-3
First published 1929 with title: Math tables from the Handbook of Chemistry and Physics. Periodically revised
"This standard mathematical handbook contains both textual and tabular material. The contents include constants and conversion factors; algebra; combinatorial analysis; geometry; trigonometry; logarithmic, exponential, and hyberbolic functions; analytical geometry; calculus; differential equations; special functions; numerical methods; probability and statistics; and financial tables." Malinowsky. Best Sci & Technol Ref Books for Young People
Includes bibliographical references

Cusick, Thomas W., 1943-
Mathematics made simple. 6th ed. Broadway Books 2003 281p il pa $12.95 **510**
1. Mathematics
ISBN 978-0-7679-1538-0; 0-7679-1538-0
LC 2003-41923
"A Made simple book"
First published 1943 by Kenmore Pub. Co.
"This book serves as a review of arithmetic, and an introduction to algebra, geometry, and trigonometry. Combinations and permutations are covered . . . in the Probability chapter. The exercises and answers in this book provide readers with opportunities to test their mastery of each step in these common branches of mathematics." Introduction

Devlin, Keith J.
The math gene; how mathematical thinking evolved and why numbers are like gossip; {by} Keith Devlin. Basic Bks. 2000 328p il pa $17 hardcover o.p. **510**
1. Number concept 2. Mathematics
ISBN 0-465-01619-7 (pa)
LC 2001-520984
"Is the human brain hardwired for mathematical thinking? Just as we have an instinct for language acquisition, Devlin argues that we also possess an innate ability for logical and algorithmic reasoning. This book is an eye-opener for all math phobics." Libr J
Includes bibliographical references

Dewdney, A. K.
200% of nothing; an eye-opening tour through the twists and turns of math abuse and innumeracy. Wiley 1993 182p il hardcover o.p. pa $15.95 **510**
1. Mathematics
ISBN 0-471-57776-6; 0-471-14574-2 (pa)
LC 92-42173
The author discusses the media abuse of numbers "as well as 'percentage pumping,' 'irrational ratios,' 'compound blindness,' 'filtering,' and 'dimensional dementia.'" Libr J
Includes bibliographical references

A mathematical mystery tour; discovering the truth and beauty of the cosmos. Wiley 1999 218p il $22.95; pa $15.95 **510**
1. Mathematics
ISBN 0-471-23847-3; 0-471-40734-8 (pa)
LC 98-36470
Dewdney "addresses two closely related, long-pondered questions. Why is mathematics so uncannily effective in describing the physical universe? Is 'new' mathematics invented, or is it a preexisting something that is discovered?. . . He explores these fundamental questions via discussions of the mathematical work of Pythagoras, the medieval Arab mathematicians, modern theoretical physicists, and modern mathematicians." Libr J

A **Dictionary** of quotations in mathematics; compiled and edited by Robert A. Nowlan. McFarland & Co. 2002 314p pa $45 *
510
1. Mathematics—Quotations 2. Quotations
ISBN 0-7864-1284-4
LC 2002-5268
"This work contains almost 3,000 quotations in mathematics. It is divided into thirty-eight chapters and 389 sections that present quotations over a spectrum from God and religion to the nature of infinity. . . . Areas covered [include] historical origins, linguistics, the arts, mathematicians themselves, logic, real and idealized space, number theory, algebra, computers, probability theory, and statistics." Publisher's note
"For anyone writing a term paper, professional paper, or giving a presentation, whether in mathematics, science, or a related discipline, this reference will be a useful resource. For the rest of us, this book is a delightful read all by itself." Am Ref Books Annu, 2003
Includes bibliographical references

Dunham, William, 1947-

The mathematical universe; an alphabetical journey through the great proofs, problems, and personalities. Wiley 1994 314p il pa $19.95 hardcover o.p.   **510**

1. Mathematics 2. Mathematicians

ISBN 0-471-17661-3 (pa)   LC 93-46702

In this history of mathematics, "Dunham sheds light not only on the personalities—eccentric, vain, brilliant—of major mathematicians, but also on contemporary social issues, such as multiculturalism and gender equity. Readers who want to understand the cultural significance of mathematics would do well to begin with this book." Booklist

Includes bibliographical references

Glazer, Evan, 1971-

Real-life math; everyday use of mathematical concepts; [by] Evan M. Glazer and John W. McConnell. Greenwood Press 2002 165p il $49.95 *   **510**

1. Mathematics

ISBN 0-313-31998-7   LC 2001-58635

The authors "have written this book as a reply to students' complaints that they'll never use the mathematical concepts they're being taught. They look at dozens of mathematical concepts and . . . show how these math ideas relate to the world in which students live. . . . The book is thorough and accurate." Libr Media Connect

Includes bibliographical references

God created the integers; the mathematical breakthroughs that changed history; edited and with commentary by Stephen Hawking. Running Pr. 2005 1160p il $29.95; pa $21.95

    510

1. Mathematicians

ISBN   0-7624-1922-9;   978-0-7624-1922-7; 0-7624-3004-4 (pa); 978-0-7624-3004-8 (pa)

    LC 2005-924493

Follow-up to On the shoulders of giants

This book "features biographies of 17 great figures in the world of mathematics and 31 excerpts of their landmark literature." Libr J

This "is a wonderful resource providing insight into both the mathematics and the personalities involved." Sci Books Films

Includes bibliographical references

Pasles, Paul C., 1968-

Benjamin Franklin's numbers; an unsung mathematical odyssey. Princeton University Press 2008 254p il $26.95   **510**

1. Franklin, Benjamin, 1706-1790 2. Mathematics

ISBN 978-0-691-12956-3; 0-691-12956-8

    LC 2006-102508

The author "documents the famous scientist-statesman's lively interest in numerical enigmas, most particularly those known as Magic Squares. . . . An unexpected but welcome perspective on the genial genius of Philadelphia." Booklist

Includes bibliographical references

Paulos, John Allen

Beyond numeracy; ruminations of a numbers man. Knopf 1991 285p il pa $14 hardcover o.p.

    510

1. Mathematics

ISBN 0-679-73807-X (pa)   LC 90-44999

These seventy short essays "range from summaries of whole disciplines (calculus, trigonometry, topology) to biographical and historical asides (Gödel, Pythagoras, non-Euclidean geometry) to bits of mathematical or quasi-mathematical folklore (infinite sets, Platonic solids, QED)." Introduction

"This well-written and easy-to-follow book gently guides readers through many interesting mathematical topics." SLJ

Includes bibliographical references

A mathematician reads the newspaper. Anchor Books 1996 212p il pa $13.95   **510**

1. Mathematics

ISBN 0-385-48254-X   LC 95-46049

First published 1995 by Basic Books

The author uses newspaper features "as vehicles for explaining mathematical concepts and how they figure in the business of being a well-informed citizen. For instance, he uses stories on the economy to illustrate prediction, regression analysis, statistics, and game theory and how those tools are used to both illuminate and obfuscate underlying truth." Booklist

Includes bibliographical references

Rudman, Peter Strom, 1929-

How mathematics happened; the first 50,000 years; [by] Peter S. Rudman. Prometheus Books 2007 314p il $26 *   **510**

1. Mathematics—History

ISBN 1-59102-477-3; 978-1-59102-477-4

    LC 2006-20255

The author presents a "history of how numbers evolved beyond the finger and stone-counting of hunter-gatherer societies. It all started with the Babylonians, who fit very old body-part measurements into a powerful new arithmetic of squares and square roots. Rudman also probes the physiological logic that equipped the Mayans with base-20 numbers for mapping the heavens, and he scrutinizes the brilliance of Egyptian mathematicians who calculated complex volumes without calculus. Readers can deepen their understanding of ancient feats by working out the numerous 'Fun Questions' Rudman has embedded in his text to provide practical experience with key concepts." Booklist

Includes bibliographical references

Sherlock Holmes in Babylon; and other tales of mathematical history; edited by Marlow Anderson, Victor Katz, Robin Wilson. Mathematical Association of America 2004 387p il maps (Spectrum series) $51.95

    510

1. Mathematics—History

ISBN 0-88385-546-1   LC 2003-113541

This "is a compilation of journal articles written by various mathematical historians and published by the Mathematical Association of America over the past 100

Sherlock Holmes in Babylon—*Continued*
years. The stories deal with many important and fundamental topics from ancient up through 18th-century mathematics. The papers are all self-contained, so the reader with some degree of mathematical maturity can jump around in the book." Sci Books Films
Includes bibliographical references

Szpiro, George G., 1950-
Poincaré's prize; the hundred-year quest to solve one of math's greatest puzzles. Dutton 2007 309p $24.95 **510**
1. Poincaré, Henri, 1854-1912 2. Perelman, Grigori 3. Mathematics
ISBN 978-0-525-95024-0; 0-525-95024-9
LC 2007-12792
The author "recounts the story of how a geometrical puzzle worthy of the most voracious sphinx finally yielded to an eccentric Russian genius who has since refused the honors and million-dollar prize proffered by an astonished world. The mathematical puzzle, readers learn, originated with the French polymath Henri Poincaré, whose revolutionary topology generated a tantalizing conjecture about how multidimensional bodies might all be transformed into spheres. . . . Never has mathematics provided more fascinating human drama!" Booklist
Includes bibliographical references

Tobias, Sheila
Overcoming math anxiety. rev and expanded. Norton 1993 260p il $23; pa $14.95 **510**
1. Mathematics
ISBN 0-393-03577-8; 0-393-31307-7 (pa)
LC 93-3648
First published 1978
The author explains common misconceptions about mathematical concepts, analyzes what makes math seem difficult, discusses alleged sex differences in brain function in relation to math, and describes math programs aimed at women
Includes bibliographical references

510.3 Encyclopedias and dictionaries

Darling, David J.
The universal book of mathematics; from Abracadabra to Zeno's paradoxes; [by] David Darling. Wiley 2004 383p il $40 **510.3**
1. Mathematics—Encyclopedias
ISBN 0-471-27047-4 LC 2003-24670
"The book's entries include numerous mathematical terms, brief biographies of mathematicians from ancient times to the present, and famous mathematical problems (both solved and unsolved), as well as problems and puzzles of a more recreational nature. It is a spirit of whimsy, the fanciful, and the outrageous that makes this book much more than a dry encyclopedia of mathematical terms, however. Darling's writing style and choice of entries make this an easy book to pick up and page through." Choice
Includes bibliographical references

Tanton, James S., 1966-
Encyclopedia of mathematics; [by] James Tanton. Facts on File 2005 568p il (Facts on File science library) $75 * **510.3**
1. Mathematics—Encyclopedias
ISBN 0-8160-5124-0 LC 2004-16785
This encyclopedia "offers more than 800 entries from abacus and compound interest to Bertrand Russell and vector along with essays on the history and evolution of equations and algebra, calculus, functions, geometry, probability and statistics, and trigonometry." SLJ
For a fuller review, see: Booklist, Dec. 1, 2005
Includes bibliographical references

511 General principles of mathematics

Berlinski, David, 1942-
The advent of the algorithm; the idea that rules the world. Harcourt 2000 345p $28; pa $14 **511**
1. Algorithms
ISBN 0-15-100338-6; 0-15-601391-6 (pa)
LC 98-43755
Berlinski "chronicles the discovery of algorithms, the codes that control computers, vividly profiling the key thinkers involved. He also identifies the hidden sources of the algorithm's power as a calculating tool, and exposes its defects as a scientific metaphor for explaining the human intellect." Booklist
Includes bibliographical references

Kaplan, Robert
The nothing that is; a natural history of zero; illustrations by Ellen Kaplan. Oxford Univ. Press 2000 225p $40; pa $11.95 **511**
1. Zero (The number)
ISBN 0-19-512842-7; 0-19-514237-3 (pa)
LC 99-29000
"Kaplan presents cultural, philosophical, historical, and mathematical developments that either encouraged or discouraged the recognition of the role of zero in counting and computation." Sci Books Films

Seife, Charles
Zero; the biography of a dangerous idea. Viking 2000 248p il hardcover o.p. pa $15 **511**
1. Zero (The number)
ISBN 0-670-88457-X; 0-14-029647-6 (pa)
LC 99-36693
"The zero emerges as a daunting intellectual riddle in this . . . chronicle of a once controversial concept as Seife deftly traces the gradual acceptance of the zero and its role as catalyst for the evolution of everything from business to physics to moral thought." Booklist
Includes bibliographical references

512   Algebra

Livio, Mario, 1945-
The equation that couldn't be solved; how mathematical genius discovered the language of symmetry. Simon & Schuster 2005 353p il $26.95
512
1. Abel, Niels Henrik, 1802-1829 2. Galois, Évariste, 1811-1832 3. Symmetry
ISBN 0-7432-5820-7   LC 2005-44123
This "summary of the origins of group theory and symmetry . . . [covers] biographical information on Niels Henrik Abel and Evariste Galois, introductory concepts and problems in group theory, and applications of group theory to broader disciplines." Libr J
"Even the mathematically fainthearted can learn a great deal about symmetry from this book." Sci Books Films
Includes bibliographical references

Singh, Simon
Fermat's enigma; the epic quest to solve the world's greatest mathematical problem; foreword by John Lynch. Anchor Books 1998 315p il pa $13.95
512
1. Wiles, Andrew 2. Number theory
ISBN 0-385-49362-2
First published 1997 in the United Kingdom with title: Fermat's last theorem
"For 350 years, mathematicians staked whole careers—even lives—on solving Fermat's Last Theorem. The story of this immensely difficult problem involves failure, despair, obsession, and, ultimately triumph." Libr J
"This vivid account is fascinating reading for anyone interested in mathematics, its history, and the passionate quest for solutions to unsolved riddles." SLJ
Includes bibliographical references

512.7   Number theory

Clawson, Calvin C.
Mathematical mysteries; the beauty and magic of numbers. Perseus Bks. 1999 313p il pa $18.95
512.7
1. Number theory
ISBN 0-7382-0259-2; 978-0-7382-0259-4
LC 99-66854
First published 1996 by Plenum Press
Topics discussed include "numeric origins, Greek achievements, famous sequences and series, different infinities, prime numbers and secret codes, Goldbach's conjectures, [and] Ramanujan's equations. . . . Various philosophical bases of mathematics are . . . presented at the end of the book." Choice
"A writer in love with his subject, Clawson offers the perfect antidote to the phobias and misconceptions surrounding mathematics." Booklist
Includes bibliographical references

Derbyshire, John
Prime obsession; Bernhard Riemann and the greatest unsolved problem in mathematics. Joseph Henry Press 2003 422p il $27.95
512.7
1. Riemann, Georg Friedrich Bernhard, 1826-1866 2. Number theory
ISBN 0-309-08549-7   LC 2002-156310
Also available in paperback from Plume Bks.
The author "first takes readers through . . . mathematical fundamentals in order to give them a good understanding of Riemann's discovery and its consequences. Interspersed with the hardcore math, other chapters profile Riemann the man and trace the history of mathematics in relation to his still-unproven hypothesis. Derbyshire shows how after 150 years, the world's greatest minds still haven't found a solution." Libr J

Reid, Constance
From zero to infinity; what makes numbers interesting. 5th ed, 50th anniversary ed. A K Peters 2006 188p il pa $19.95
512.7
1. Number theory
ISBN 978-1-568812-73-1; 1-568812-73-6
LC 2005-27860
First published 1955 by Crowell
"This book covers selected topics in number theory. Partly expository, it nonetheless challenges the reader's mind in clever and nonthreatening ways." Sci Books Films

Sabbagh, Karl
The Riemann hypothesis; the greatest unsolved problem in mathematics. Farrar, Straus & Giroux 2002 340p il $25; pa $14 *
512.7
1. Riemann, Georg Friedrich Bernhard, 1826-1866 2. Number theory
ISBN 0-374-25007-3; 0-374-52935-3 (pa)
LC 2003-101178
First published 2002 in the United Kingdom with title: Dr. Riemann's zeroes
"Sabbagh introduces contemporary mathematicians who are working on the problem, one of whom claims, to professional skepticism, to be on the verge of vindicating the hypothesis. Another is working away in search of a single counterexample that would refute it. Such pursuits, which often consume mathematicians' entire lives, may seem incomprehensible or even pointless to the innumerate—but that's a prejudice brilliantly dispelled through Sabbagh's interviews, which are interwoven with his not overly numerical tour of the hypothesis. The drive and competitiveness of mathematicians clearly emerge from Sabbagh's narrative." Booklist

513   Arithmetic

Bunch, Bryan H.
The kingdom of infinite number; a field guide; [by] Bryan Bunch. Freeman, W.H. 2000 388p il hardcover o.p. pa $13.95
513
1. Numbers 2. Number concept
ISBN 0-7167-3388-9; 0-7167-4447-3 (pa)
LC 99-53641

Bunch, Bryan H.—*Continued*
"Bunch limns the personalities, the species linkages, and the field marks of all kinds of numbers—from simple odds and evens to intricate logarithms and transcendentals." Booklist
"The reader will inevitably get caught up in the book's spellbinding mixture of history, language, mathematics, and science." Sci Books Films
Includes bibliographical references

Kogelman, Stanley
The only math book you'll ever need; [by] Stanley Kogelman and Barbara R. Heller. rev ed. HarperPerennial 1995 xx, 268p il pa $15

513
1. Mathematics
ISBN 978-0-06-272507-3; 0-06-272507-6
First published 1986 by Facts on File
Step-by-step operations are reviewed in problems encountered on a daily basis such as comparing credit cards, evaluating investments, estimating interest rates, and converting area measurements.

515 Analysis

Berlinski, David, 1942-
A tour of the calculus. Pantheon Bks. 1995 331p il pa $14.95 hardcover o.p.　　　**515**
1. Calculus
ISBN 0-679-74788-5 (pa)　　　　LC 95-4042
This is an introduction to "the foundations of calculus. It is in part an informal history of the subject; the author interweaves the historical fragments with expository sections that [seek to] explain the concepts from a modern viewpoint." Libr J
"Berlinski tangibly grounds the abstract notions, so that attentive readers can ease into and grasp the several full-blown proofs he sets forth." Booklist

516 Geometry

Gorini, Catherine A.
The Facts on File geometry handbook. Facts on File 2003 280p il (Facts on File science library) $35; pa $17.95　　　　**516**
1. Geometry
ISBN 0-8160-4875-4; 0-8160-6230-7 (pa)
　　　　　　　　LC 2002-12343
This includes a glossary of 3,000 entries with labeled diagrams, biographies of 300 scientists and mathematicians from ancient times to the present, a chronology of geometry history, charts, tables, recommended reading and websites.
Includes bibliographical references

Mlodinow, Leonard
Euclid's window; the story of geometry from parallel lines to hyperspace. Free Press 2001 306p il pa $15 hardcover o.p.　　　　**516**
1. Geometry
ISBN 0-684-86524-6 (pa)　　　　LC 00-54351

Mlodinow's monograph "takes the form of five biographical stories, each about a key figure in the development of geometry: Euclid, Descartes, Gauss, Einstein and Witten." New Sci
"This engaging history does an excellent job of explaining the importance of the study of geometry without making the reader learn any geometry." Libr J
Includes bibliographical references

516.2 Euclidean geometry

Blatner, David
The joy of π. Walker & Co. 1997 129p il hardcover o.p. pa $12　　　　**516.2**
1. Pi
ISBN 0-8027-1332-7; 0-8027-7562-4 (pa)
　　　　　　　　LC 97-23705
The author discusses the history of the number π, as well as the process of "calculating the ratio of a circle's circumference to its diameter, which has advanced from measuring lengths of string and the 'brute force' of measuring polygons to feeding supercomputers sophisticated algorithms. Sidebars . . . abound, containing a factoid, joke, or doggerel inspired by π." Booklist
Includes bibliographical references

Livio, Mario, 1945-
The golden ratio; the story of phi, the world's most astonishing number. Broadway Bks. 2002 294p hardcover o.p. pa $14.95　　　　**516.2**
1. Geometry
ISBN 0-7679-0815-5; 0-7679-0816-3 (pa)
　　　　　　　　LC 2002-23084
The author examines the history and myths of phi, the "golden ratio" of 1.6180339887 that has been related to phenomena as diverse as the arrangements of petals on roses and the breeding patterns of rabbits.
"Overall, an enjoyable work, amply supported by index, extensive references, and ten appendixes presenting mathematical elaborations of text material." Choice
Includes bibliographical references

519.2 Probabilities

Aczel, Amir D.
Chance: a guide to gambling, love, the stock market & just about everything else. Thunder's Mouth Press 2004 161p il $23　　　　**519.2**
1. Chance 2. Probabilities
ISBN 1-56858-316-8　　　　LC 2004-304723
The author "explains the elements of probability theory for lay readers. . . . [He] points out that some of the results of probabilistic calculations can seem contrary to common sense and can even surprise experienced mathematicians and scientists such as himself; nevertheless, the results are mathematically sound and must be accepted. . . . It is not often that one can recommend a mathematics book as good-quality 'light' reading, but this work fits the bill." Libr J
Includes bibliographical references

Rosenthal, Jeffrey, 1967-
Struck by lightning; the curious world of probabilities; [by] Jeffrey S. Rosenthal. HarperCollins Canada 2005 263p il pa $19.95
519.2
1. Probabilities 2. Chance
ISBN 0-309-09734-7; 978-0-309-09734-5
LC 2005-37021
Rosenthal discusses ways in which probability theory affects such areas of everyday life as crime, travel, gambling, politics, and disease.
"The lighthearted presentation ensures that readers will not feel burdened by all the knowledge they are gaining and the concluding summary—disguised as a final exam—is sure to deliver an A to everyone, which is what Rosenthal deserves for this clever book." Publ Wkly

519.5   Statistical mathematics

Cohen, I. Bernard, 1914-2003
The triumph of numbers; how counting shaped modern life. W. W. Norton 2005 209p il $24.95; pa $14.95
519.5
1. Statistics
ISBN   0-393-05769-0;   978-0-393-05769-0; 0-393-32870-8 (pa); 978-0-393-32870-7 (pa)
LC 2004-27322
This is a "history of numbers and the birth of statistics." Publisher's note
"This book presents a persuasive narrative on how numbers have maintained a prominent role not only in science and government throughout time, but in the daily operations of life." Sci Books Films
Includes bibliographical references

Everitt, Brian
The Cambridge dictionary of statistics; [by] B.S. Everitt. 3rd ed. Cambridge University Press 2006 432p il hardcover o.p. pa $35.99 *
519.5
1. Statistics—Dictionaries
ISBN   978-0-521-86039-0;   0-521-86039-3; 978-0-521-69027-0 (pa); 0-52169-027-7 (pa)
LC 2006-283485
First published 1998
"Over 3600 terms are defined, covering medical, survey, theoretical, and applied statistics, including computational aspects. Entries are provided for standard and specialized statistical software. In addition, short biographies of over 100 important statisticians are given." Publisher's note

520   Astronomy

The **Amateur** astronomer; edited by Shawn Carlson. Wiley 2001 271p il pa $16.95
520
1. Astronomy
ISBN 0-471-38282-5   LC 00-47773
At head of title: Scientific American

A collection of articles on the subject of astronomy published in Scientific American magazine from the 1950s to the 1990s
"Carlson provides fascinating assessments of both how much and how little was known 50 years ago, and he charts the evolution of theories and the rise and resolution of controversies, thus offering invaluable insights into the history of scientific thought and methodology. Technically precise yet always clear, these popular science columns remain vital and exciting." Booklist
Includes bibliographical references

Angelo, Joseph A.
The Facts on File space and astronomy handbook; [by] Joseph A. Angelo, Jr. Facts on File 2002 278p il $35; pa $17.95   **520**
1. Astronomy 2. Space sciences
ISBN 0-8160-4542-9; 0-8160-4960-2 (pa)
LC 2001-54323
"Facts on File science library"
This handbook "is organized into four sections: a 1,200-entry glossary, 400 short (one sentence to one paragraph in length) biographies, a 45-page chronology of 8,000 years of discoveries in astronomy and space science, and 17 pages of charts and tables. The glossary provides brief descriptions or definitions for terms such as *Blastoff, Extraterrestrial catastrophe theory, Gemini Project, Galactic cannibalism, Habitable payload, Orion Nebula, Planck's radiation law*, and *Zenith*. Biographies include well-known people such as Galileo Galilei, John Glenn, and Sally Ride as well as some that one would not expect to find in an astronomy resource." Booklist
Includes bibliographical references

Ferris, Timothy
Seeing in the dark; how backyard stargazers are probing deep space and guarding earth from interplanetary peril. Simon & Schuster 2002 379p il hardcover o.p. pa $14   **520**
1. Astronomy 2. Astronomers
ISBN 0-684-86579-3; 0-684-86580-7 (pa)
LC 2002-20693
Ferris examines "the 20th-century in spectroscopic analysis of very distant light from celestial bodies through the personal experiences of . . . astronomers, mostly amateurs." Christ Sci Monit
"This book should turn many novices on to astronomy and captivate those already fascinated by the heavens." Publ Wkly

Miller, Arthur I.
Empire of the stars; obsession, friendship, and betrayal in the quest for black holes. Houghton Mifflin 2005 364p il $26   **520**
1. Chandrasekhar, Subrahmanyan, 1910-1995 2. Eddington, Sir Arthur Stanley, 1882-1944 3. Black holes (Astronomy)
ISBN 0-618-34151-X   LC 2004-60909
This history of the discovery of black holes focuses on the bitter rivalry between Indian astrophysicist Subrahmanyan Chandrasekhar and Cambridge astrophysicist Sir Arthur Eddington.

Miller, Arthur I.—*Continued*
"Astronomy buffs and readers fascinated by the history of science will find this a compelling read." Publ Wkly
Includes bibliographical references

Raymo, Chet
An intimate look at the night sky. Walker & Co. 2001 242p il $25; pa $16 **520**
1. Astronomy
ISBN 0-8027-1369-6; 0-8027-7670-1 (pa)
Raymo discusses astronomy and cosmology. "The narrative follows earth's path through the four seasons [around the sun]." Christ Sci Monit
"A delightful, inspiring introduction to astronomy." Booklist
Includes bibliographical references

Ridpath, Ian
Stars and planets; the most complete guide to the stars, planets, galaxies, and the solar system; illustrated by Wil Tirion. Fully rev. and expanded ed. Princeton University Press 2007 400p il (Princeton field guides) pa $19.95 * **520**
1. Astronomy 2. Stars 3. Planets
ISBN 978-0-691-13556-4; 0-691-13556-8
First published 1998 by DK Pub.
This book features "charts covering all 88 constellations in the Northern and Southern hemispheres; data and notes on all bright stars and other objects of interest; . . . Moon maps and descriptions of the main lunar features; [and] tips on choosing and using binoculars and telescopes." Publisher's note

Sagan, Carl, 1934-1996
Pale blue dot; a vision of the human future in space. Ballantine Books 1997 360p pa $14.95 **520**
1. Outer space—Exploration
ISBN 978-0-345-37659-6; 0-345-37659-5
First published 1994 by Random House
"In a tour of our solar system, galaxy and beyond . . . Sagan meshes a history of astronomical discovery, a cogent brief for space exploration and an overview of life. . . . His exploration of our place in the universe is illustrated with photographs, relief maps and paintings, including high-resolution images made by Voyager 1 and 2, as well as photos taken by the Galileo spacecraft, the Hubble Space Telescope and satellites orbiting Earth." Publ Wkly
Includes bibliographical references

Schaaf, Fred
The 50 best sights in astronomy and how to see them; observing eclipses, bright comets, meteor showers, and other celestial wonders. John Wiley 2007 280p il pa $19.95 **520**
1. Astronomy
ISBN 978-0-471-69657-5; 0-471-69657-9
LC 2006-36221

The author "begins with some basic information and terminology (altazimuth system, for example, or right ascension) and then plunges right in with the most easily accessible astronomical sight, the starry sky above our heads. For each sight, he not only explains what it is and the best conditions under which to observe it, he also tells us about its historical, mythological, or scientific importance and explores how these far-off wonders can have a very real effect on our humble home world. This could so easily have been a dry-as-dust tome, but Schaaf's enthusiasm overflows every page." Booklist
Includes bibliographical references

520.3   Astronomy—Encyclopedias and dictionaries

Angelo, Joseph A.
Encyclopedia of space and astronomy; [by] Joseph A. Angelo, Jr. Facts on File 2006 740p il (Facts on File science library) $75 **520.3**
1. Astronomy—Encyclopedias 2. Space sciences—Encyclopedias
ISBN 0-8160-5330-8 LC 2004-30800
This encyclopedia presents "the main concepts, terms, facilities, and people in astronomy. . . . Coverage includes terms such as astrophysics, planetary science, and cosmology, as well as both American and international astronomy and space technology." Publisher's note
Includes bibliographical references

Bakich, Michael E.
The Cambridge encyclopedia of amateur astronomy. Cambridge Univ. Press 2003 342p il $69 * **520.3**
1. Astronomy—Encyclopedias
ISBN 0-521-81298-4 LC 2002-31551
"The book is arranged in two parts. Part one presents planetary data, such as atmospheric pressure, composition, and future conjunctions and transits. Part two contains a summary on each planet, including its moons. These summaries cover cloud and atmospheric conditions, surface features, historical early ideas about each planet, and recent discoveries from the Hubble Space Telescope and other data collected in the 'late 1990s.'" Booklist
"Any amateur astronomer, or anyone with an interest in seeing what nonprofessionals can do if they are dedicated, would enjoy this book." Sci Books Films
Includes bibliographical references

Darling, David J.
The universal book of astronomy from the Andromeda Galaxy to the zone of avoidance; [by] David Darling. Wiley 2003 570p il $40 * **520.3**
1. Astronomy—Dictionaries
ISBN 0-471-26569-1 LC 2003-13941
This book features "over 3000 alphabetically arranged entries covering history, biography, celestial objects, cosmological phenomena, and more." Libr J
"Designed for nonspecialists, Darling's volume fills a

Darling, David J.—*Continued*

niche in astronomy ready reference. . . . The volume is . . . highly readable and provides bonuses in 22 star charts outlining all 88 constellations in both north and south celestial hemispheres, instructional aids throughout the text, and charts that accompany entries for many stars, galaxies, and clusters and show size, position, etc." Choice

Includes bibliographical references

Firefly astronomy dictionary; [an illustrated A-Z guide to the universe] Firefly Books 2003 256p il pa $14.95   **520.3**
1. Astronomy—Dictionaries
ISBN 1-55297-837-0   LC 2004-271068
First published 1995 in the United Kingdom under the editorship of Ian Ridpath and John Woodruff with title: Philip's astronomy dictionary

"As well as defining scientific terms and explaining theories, the dictionary provides brief biographies of over 100 famous astronomers including Ptolemy, Galileo, Johann Kepler, Copernicus and Edwin Hubble. An appendix provides tables of symbols and mathematical units and calculations used in astronomy." Publisher's note

"Attractively produced, . . . [this book] offers numerous small but sharp and attractive illustrations. Its more than 1,000 entries range from one to several paragraphs, with numerous cross-references in boldface. . . . Recommended." Choice

The **Firefly** encyclopedia of astronomy; edited by Paul Murdin & Margaret Penston. Firefly Books 2004 472p il $59.95 *   **520.3**
1. Astronomy—Encyclopedias
ISBN 1-55297-797-8
"This book covers astronomical objects and phenomena, space missions, observatories, and astronomers and their organizations, among other topics." Libr J

This encyclopedia "provides an engaging trove of information for lay people. Articles on topics in astrophysics and cosmology convey several decades worth of findings in these fields without trying to explain the science to non-experts." Publ Wkly

History of astronomy; an encyclopedia; edited by John Lankford. Garland 1997 594p il (Garland encyclopedias in the history of science) $155
                                                                520.3
ISBN 0-8153-0322-X   LC 96-28558
"Focusing on developments since the Scientific Revolution, the signed articles . . . fall into five broad categories: an historical overview of astronomy, astronomy in national contexts (e.g., Chinese astronomy), the history of observatories, the social history of astronomy (e.g., Women in Astronomy), and biographies. . . . Recommendations for further reading are well chosen and current. An excellent and much-needed work." Libr J

Mitton, Jacqueline

Cambridge illustrated dictionary of astronomy. Cambridge University Press 2007 397p il map $35
                                                                520.3
1. Astronomy—Dictionaries
ISBN 978-0-521-82364-7; 0-521-82364-1
                                            LC 2008-295878

First published 1993 in the United Kingdom with title: The Penguin dictionary of astronomy

"Coverage encompasses named astronomical objects, terms and abbreviations most frequently encountered in astronomy, constellations, principal observatories, space missions, and biographical sketches for 70 well-known individuals in the history of the field." Booklist

"With this dictionary Mitton . . . offers a welcome addition to the reference collection." Choice

Oxford dictionary of astronomy; edited by Ian Ridpath. 2nd ed. Oxford University Press 2007 561p il (Oxford paperback reference) pa $18.95
                                                                520.3
1. Astronomy—Dictionaries
ISBN 978-0-19-921493-8   LC 2007-40707
First published 1997

This dictionary presents "4200 paragraph-sized definitions, along with illuminating technical graphs and charts. Included is an exhaustive, A-to-Z compilation of eminent figures and significant, if sometimes obscure, scientific phenomena, mission names, and project monikers." Libr J

521   Celestial mechanics

Goodstein, David L., 1939-

Feynman's lost lecture; the motion of planets around the sun; [by] David L. Goodstein and Judith R. Goodstein. Norton 1996 191p il $35; pa $19.95   **521**
1. Feynman, Richard Phillips, 1918-1988 2. Universe 3. Astrophysics 4. Solar system
ISBN 0-393-03918-8; 0-393-31995-4 (pa)
                                            LC 95-38719
Includes audio CD

This "book consists of four chapters. The first and largest is a brief history of the establishment of the Copernican cosmology, which Feynman gave as a lecture to the freshman class at Caltech. Feynman then revisits the work of Isaac Newton and the watershed proof of the Scientific Revolution that separated the ancient world from the modern. There is also a chapter with some wonderful reminiscences of Feynman." Libr J

Includes bibliographical references

Rubin, Alan E.

Disturbing the solar system; impacts, close encounters, and coming attractions. Princeton Univ. Press 2002 361p il $29.95   **521**
1. Gravitation 2. Catastrophes (Geology) 3. Life on other planets
ISBN 0-691-07474-7   LC 2001-55197
"After relating a brief history of the solar system, Alan Rubin describes how astronomers determined our location in the Milky Way. He provides . . . accounts of the energetic interactions among planetary bodies, the generation of the Earth's magnetic field, the effects of other solar-system objects on our climate, the moon's genesis, the heating of asteroids, and the origin of the mysterious tektites. . . . He chronicles the history of the search for life on Mars and describes cutting-edge lines of astrobiological inquiry." Publisher's note

Includes bibliographical references

522 Techniques, procedures, apparatus, equipment, materials

Chaisson, Eric

The Hubble wars; astrophysics meets astropolitics in the two-billion-dollar struggle over the Hubble Space Telescope; [by] Eric J. Chaisson. Harvard University Press 1998 xxi, 386p il map pa $17.95 **522**
1. Hubble Space Telescope (Spacecraft) 2. Hubble Space Telescope
ISBN 0-674-41255-9; 978-0-674-41255-2
LC 98-156757
First published 1994 by HarperCollins
The author "recounts the launching and initial experiments of the Hubble Space Telescope, the largest, most complex, and most powerful observatory ever launched into space." Booklist
Includes bibliographical references

Dickinson, Terence

The backyard astronomer's guide; [by] Terence Dickinson & Alan Dyer. 3rd ed. Firefly Books 2008 368p il $49.95 * **522**
1. Astronomy
ISBN 978-1-55407-344-3; 1-55407-344-8
"Revised and expanded"
First published 1991 by Camden House
The authors provide guidance "on the right types of telescopes and other equipment; photographing the stars through a telescope; and star charts, software and other references. They cover daytime and twilight observing, planetary and deep-sky observing, and . . . more." Publisher's note
Includes bibliographical references

Harrington, Philip S.

Star ware; the amateur astronomer's guide to choosing, buying, and using telescopes and accessories. 4th ed. Wiley 2007 417p il pa $21.95 **522**
1. Telescopes
ISBN 978-0-471-75063-5; 0-471-75063-8
LC 2006-25134
First published 1994
This guidebook on choosing and caring for telescopes and related equipment also features advice on practical issues such as keeping dew off a corrector plate, warding off mosquitoes, and staying warm outside.
Includes bibliographical references

Katz, Jonathan I.

The biggest bangs; the mystery of gamma-ray bursts, the most violent explosions in the universe. Oxford Univ. Press 2002 218p il $28 **522**
1. Gamma ray bursts
ISBN 0-19-514570-4
LC 2001-36545
"Discovered in the 1960s, gamma-ray bursts were not as easily measured or explained as quasars and pulsars. Besides recounting the journey to our current understanding of these bursts—which are thought to be explosions from neutron stars either hitting each other or being dragged into a black hole—physicist Katz also elucidates the scientific thinking process." Booklist
Includes bibliographical references

Kerrod, Robin, 1938-

Hubble: the mirror on the universe; [by] Robin Kerrod and Carole Stott. Rev. ed. Firefly Books 2007 192p il $35 * **522**
1. Hubble Space Telescope 2. Outer space—Exploration
ISBN 978-1-55407-316-0; 1-55407-316-2
First published 2003
This book is an "introduction to the objects found in our solar system and universe and to the techniques used to study them. In addition, there is a brief history of telescopes and the HST Hubble Space Telescope." Sci Books Films [review of 2003 edition]

Panek, Richard

Seeing and believing; how the telescope opened our eyes and minds to the heavens. Viking 1998 198p pa $11.94 hardcover o.p. **522**
1. Telescopes 2. Astronomy
ISBN 0-14-028061-8 (pa)
LC 98-18766
"From Galileo's observations of the moon and planets to . . . the 1996 discovery, thanks to the Hubble space telescope, that the universe contains 40 billion more galaxies than we had thought, Panek describes how the technology of telescopes has changed and how our ideas of nature and science and of the universe and our place in it have slowly adjusted to that improving technology. A gracefully written and useful blending of science, biography, and analysis of philosophical consequences." Booklist
Includes bibliographical references

Schilling, Govert

Flash! the hunt for the biggest explosions in the universe; translated by Naomi Greenberg-Slovin. Cambridge Univ. Press 2002 291p il $28 **522**
1. Gamma ray bursts 2. Black holes (Astronomy)
ISBN 0-521-80053-6
LC 2002-283188
Translated from the Dutch
This book "describes the fast moving field of gamma ray burst research. . . . [It] provides an inside view of the scientific challenges involved in unravelling the mystery of gamma-ray bursts." Publisher's note
"Everday examples are frequently used to illustrate the more difficult concepts. Those who want more details will appreciate the glossary and references to the scientific literature. Almost without realizing it, readers will also get a good introduction to elementary astronomy as a bonus. A must-read for anyone interested in GRBs!" Choice
Includes bibliographical references

523   Specific celestial bodies and phenomena

Chartrand, Mark R.
The Audubon Society field guide to the night sky; astronomical charts by Wil Tirion. Knopf 1991 714p il maps $19.95   **523**
1. Astronomy
ISBN 0-679-40852-5   LC 91-52708
"A Chanticleer Press edition. The Audubon Society field guide series"
This guide "begins with monthly star charts and constellation star charts . . . then gives photographs of the constellations; and finally, provides detailed information on each constellation including stars, galaxies, and nebulae. . . . Other information includes hints on observing ther sky; dates of solar and lunar eclipses, meteor showers, and comets, and the Messier catalog. . . . Students interested in astronomy will find lots of observing tips and information." Voice Youth Advocates
Includes bibliographical references

Firefly atlas of the universe; foreword by Arnold Wolfendale. 3rd ed. Firefly Books 2005 288p il $49.95 *   **523**
1. Astronomy
ISBN 1-55407-071-6   LC 2006-275758
First published 1970 by Rand McNally; this edition first published 2003 in Canada. Variant title: Philip's atlas of the universe
This work begins with a "general historical overview, followed by individual sections on the solar system, the sun, the stars, the structure of the universe and our galaxy's place in it, and over 20 useful star maps, all incorporating the newest scientific data." Libr J [review of 2003 edition]

Gribbin, John R.
Stardust; supernovae and life: the cosmic connection; [by] John Gribbin with Mary Gribbin. Yale Univ. Press 2000 238p $35; pa $13.95
                    523
1. Supernovas 2. Universe 3. Life (Biology)
ISBN 0-300-08419-6; 0-300-09097-8 (pa)
                    LC 00-35944
"All the carbon, hydrogen, oxygen and nitrogen (CHON) in our DNA was once floating around in a planetary nebula, to which it had been expelled violently from a red giant star. So how did it get here? Most likely via comets, says Gribbin. . . . The author also argues that we shouldn't necessarily look for life on other planets, but rather on the large moons revolving around the giant planets that orbit distant stars. . . . In a short appendix . . . Gribbin discusses current theories about the evolution of multiple universes." Publ Wkly
"A fine summary of the origin of our elemental constitution." Booklist
Includes bibliographical references

The **Universe** revealed; general editor, Pam Spence. Cambridge Univ. Press 1999 192p il $40   **523**
1. Astronomy 2. Universe
ISBN 0-521-64239-6   LC 99-163022

"Sections on the solar system, cosmology, and observational techniques cover everything from global warming to the size of the universe. Informative facts and figures are provided in side entries, and innovative cross-indexing eases usage and leads the reader to related topics." Libr J

523.1   The universe, galaxies, quasars

Aczel, Amir D.
God's equation; Einstein, relativity, and the expanding universe. Delta Trade Paperbacks 2000 236p il pa $12   **523.1**
1. Einstein, Albert, 1879-1955 2. Cosmology 3. Relativity (Physics)
ISBN 978-0-385-33485-3; 0-385-33485-0
First published 1999 by Four Walls Eight Windows
"Conventional wisdom has it that Einstein made an embarrassing error in introducing a 'cosmological constant' into his formula for the dynamics of the universe, but, as Aczel's . . . scientific detective story reveals, Einstein's infamous mistake was in fact a brilliant discovery." Booklist
"Though Aczel's analysis of Einstein's work requires familiarity with advanced mathematics, that analysis makes up only a minor portion of his book, and most readers will appreciate the author's inclusion of the great physicist's letters to astronomer Erwin Freundlich." Publ Wkly
Includes bibliographical references

Chaisson, Eric
Epic of evolution; seven ages of the cosmos; illustrated by Lola Judith Chaisson. Columbia University Press 2005 478p il $34.50; pa $22.95
                    523.1
1. Cosmology 2. Life—Origin
ISBN   0-231-13560-2;   978-0-231-13560-3; 0-231-13561-0 (pa); 978-0-231-13561-0 (pa)
                    LC 2005-45452
This is "a tour of the seven ages of the cosmos, from the formless era of radiation through the origins of human culture." Publisher's note
The author "has crafted a wonderful vehicle for exploring our universe." Sci Books Films
Includes bibliographical references

Croswell, Ken
The alchemy of the heavens; searching for meaning in the Milky Way; illustrations by Philippe Van. Anchor Bks. (NY) 1995 340p il pa $14.95 hardcover o.p.   **523.1**
1. Milky Way 2. Universe
ISBN 0-385-47214-5 (pa)   LC 94-30452
This is an "overview of our present knowledge concerning the Milky Way. . . . Examples of the numerous topics considered are stellar populations, conflicting models of galactic birth and the origin of the elements." Publ Wkly
A "well-written, crystal-clear presentation. . . . This work will snare all general reading interests." Booklist
Includes bibliographical references

Dauber, Philip M.

The three big bangs; comet crashes, exploding stars, and the creation of the universe; [by] Philip M. Dauber, Richard A. Muller. Perseus Books 1997 207p il pa $15 **523.1**

    1. Cosmology 2. Catastrophes (Geology) 3. Supernovas

    ISBN 978-0-201-15495-5; 0-201-15495-1

First published 1996 by Addison-Wesley

The authors discuss the origins of the universe and of life on Earth.

"Dauber and Muller have not only chosen three 'hot topics' in . . . astronomy but also have masterfully woven the underlying scientific strands together. They paint a colorful picture of the theories and techniques of modern astronomy." Choice

Includes bibliographical references

Davies, P. C. W., 1946-

The last three minutes; conjectures about the ultimate fate of the universe; {by} Paul Davies. Basic Bks. 1994 162p il (Science masters series) pa $14 hardcover o.p. **523.1**

    1. Cosmology

    ISBN 0-465-03851-4 (pa)   LC 94-6345

In this volume, Davies addresses the question of the ultimate demise of the universe. Topics covered include "the big bang theory, the expansion of the universe, the nature of black holes, and the life cycle of stars." Sci Books Films

"The reader will discover that science can sometimes be more creative than art, more stimulating than philosophy, more revelatory than any religion, and more frightening than any fiction thriller." Choice

Includes bibliographical references

Ferguson, Kitty

Measuring the universe; our historic quest to chart the horizons of space and time. Walker & Co. 1999 342p il $27; pa $16.95 **523.1**

    1. Cosmology 2. Measurement

    ISBN 0-8027-1351-3; 0-8027-7592-6 (pa)

    LC 99-19476

"Starting with Eratosthenes and his calculation of the earth's circumference using the shadows cast in a well, and moving through Stephen Hawking's work on black holes, Ferguson tells the tale of our search for our place in the universe. This book is nicely illustrated with photos, tables, and diagrams." Libr J

Includes bibliographical references

Ferris, Timothy

The whole shebang; a state-of-the-universe(s) report. Simon & Schuster 1997 393p hardcover o.p. pa $16 **523.1**

    1. Cosmology

    ISBN 0-684-81020-4; 0-684-83861-3 (pa)

    LC 96-49768

The author "reviews the current state of scientific cosmology, including the now-considerable overlap between astronomical findings and the theories of elementary particle physicists. . . . Ferris adheres to the orthodox Big Bang theory, giving little attention to its critics, but he is candid about the many uncertainties in modern cosmology. He writes clearly, often with considerable eloquence." Libr J

Includes bibliographical references

Gleiser, Marcelo

The prophet and the astronomer; a scientific journey to the end of time. Norton 2002 256p il $26.95; pa $15.95 **523.1**

    1. Cosmology 2. Religion and science 3. End of the world

    ISBN 0-393-04987-6; 0-393-32431-1 (pa)

    LC 2002-538

"Gleiser ponders the dark parallels between the apocalyptic visions of ancient seers and the cosmic predictions of modern scientists. . . . Gleiser's musings . . . occasionally will baffle the nonspecialist, but most readers will consider a few moments of perplexity a small price to pay for the opportunity to probe humanity's oldest nightmares and newest aspirations." Booklist

Includes bibliographical references

Greene, Brian R., 1963-

The fabric of the cosmos; space, time, and the texture of reality. Knopf 2004 569p il $28.95; pa $15.95 * **523.1**

    1. Cosmology

    ISBN 0-375-41288-3; 0-375-72720-5 (pa)

    LC 2003-58918

This is "a discussion of the irreconcilable differences between the cornerstones of theoretical physics—the general theory of relativity and quantum mechanics." N Y Times Book Rev

"Frogs in bowls, falling eggs, loaves of bread, pennies on balloons, ping pong balls in molasses, and babushka dolls are just some of the analogies used to explain complex concepts cleverly. After reading this book, you will never look at a starry night sky the same way again." Libr J

Includes bibliographical references

Gribbin, John R.

The birth of time; how astronomers measured the age of the universe; [by] John Gribbin. Yale Univ. Press 2000 237p $40; pa $11.95 **523.1**

    1. Cosmology

    ISBN 0-300-08346-7; 0-300-08914-7 (pa)

    LC 99-52835

First published 1999 in the United Kingdom

The author "recounts the history of the problem and describes the people who have worked on it. Since the age of the universe is inextricably linked to its size, he devotes most of his work to dealing with methods that have been used, are being used, and are proposed as future means to determine cosmic distances." Libr J

Includes bibliographical references

Gribbin, John R.—*Continued*

The origins of the future; ten questions for the next ten years; [by] John Gribbin. Yale University Press 2006 292p $27.50   **523.1**

1. Cosmology 2. Evolution 3. Life—Origin
ISBN 978-0-300-11998-5; 0-300-11998-4

LC 2006-11062

"In each of this book's 10 chapters, . . . [the author] describes different eras in the evolution of our universe. Each chapter opens with a question setting forth that chapter's theme. . . . Gribbin lays out the history of the universe and takes care to show its intricate workings for us to admire." Sci Books Films

Includes bibliographical references

Guth, Alan H.

The inflationary universe; the quest for a new theory of cosmic origins; with a foreword by Alan Lightman. Perseus Books 1997 358p il pa $18.50
                523.1

1. Cosmology
ISBN 0-201-32840-2
First published 1997 by Addison-Wesley

"In the 1970s as scientists struggled to reconcile several discrepancies in the Big Bang theory, Guth, a young, unknown astrophysicist, put forward his model of an inflationary universe. This is his firsthand account of one of the most astonishing theories of the 20th century." Libr J

This "is a user-friendly guide to getting one's mind round the big bang and . . . the events that preceded it. . . . A significant document in the history of science." NY Times Book Rev

Includes bibliographical references

Hawking, Stephen W., 1942-

Black holes and baby universes and other essays; [by] Stephen Hawking. Bantam Bks. 1993 182p pa $18 hardcover o.p.   **523.1**

1. Cosmology 2. Science—Philosophy
ISBN 0-553-37411-7 (pa)   LC 93-8269

A collection of essays and speeches ranging from autobiographical sketches to theoretical discussions of black holes, relativity and quantum mechanics.

The author "sprinkles his explanations with a wry sense of humor and a keen awareness that the sciences today delve not only into the far reaches of the cosmos, but into the inner philosophical world as well." N Y Times Book Rev

A briefer history of time; [by] Stephen Hawking and Leonard Mlodinow. Bantam Dell 2005 162p il $25 *   **523.1**

1. Cosmology
ISBN 0-553-80436-7   LC 2005-42949
First published 1988 with title: A brief history of time

The authors describe concepts about space and time, black holes, the origin and nature of the universe, the uncertainty principle, and the unification of physics. It also discusses string theory, dark matter, and dark energy.

"Hawking and Mlodinow provide one of the most lucid discussions of this complex topic ever written for a general audience. Readers will come away with an excellent understanding of the apparent contradictions and conundrums at the forefront of contemporary physics." Publ Wkly

Includes bibliographical references

Hooper, Dan, 1976-

Dark cosmos; in search of our universe's missing mass and energy. HarperCollins Publishers 2006 240p il $24.95   **523.1**

1. Cosmology 2. Astrophysics
ISBN 978-0-06-113032-8; 0-06-113032-X

LC 2006-44333

This book discusses "dark matter" and "dark energy," invisible substances which scientists speculate may make up over 95% of the universe.

"Hooper's clear presentation in very simple, jargon-free prose should appeal especially to young people just starting to get excited about the mysteries that still await them in science." Publ Wkly

Jastrow, Robert, 1925-2008

God and the astronomers. 2nd ed. Norton 1992 149p il pa $12.95 hardcover o.p. *
                523.1

1. Cosmology 2. Astronomy 3. Religion and science
ISBN 0-393-85006-4 (pa)   LC 92-32186
First published 1978

The author considers the theological implications of the big bang theory of creation, and summarizes the evidence for the theory including the relativity theory, the life story of stars, and the discovery of the retreat of the galaxies. Includes chapters by a Catholic astronomer and a Jewish theologian with their viewpoints on the origin and destiny of the universe

Includes bibliographical references

Kaku, Michio

Parallel worlds; a journey through creation, higher dimensions, and the future of the cosmos. Doubleday 2005 428p il hardcover o.p. pa $15.95
                523.1

1. Cosmology 2. Big bang theory 3. String theory
ISBN 0-385-50986-3; 1-4000-3372-1 (pa)

LC 2004-56039

The author "begins by describing the extraordinary advances that have transformed cosmology over the last century, and particularly over the last decade, forcing scientists around the world to rethink our understanding of the birth of the universe, and its ultimate fate. . . . As astronomers wade through the avalanche of data from the WMAP satellite, a new cosmological picture is emerging. So far, the leading theory about the birth of the universe is the 'inflationary universe theory,' a major refinement on the big bang theory." Publisher's note

"This is a riveting popular treatment of the string revolution in physics written by a pioneering theorist in the field. Kaku expounds comprehensibly on why astrophysicists love strings and branes and the way they resolve various vexatious cosmological paradoxes." Booklist

Kanipe, Jeff, 1953-
Chasing Hubble's shadows; the search for galaxies at the edge of time. Hill and Wang 2006 205p il $24; pa $15 **523.1**
1. Hubble Space Telescope 2. Outer space—Exploration
ISBN 0-8090-3406-9; 0-8090-3407-7 (pa)
LC 2005-9652
This "is an account of the continuing efforts of astronomers to probe the outermost limits of the observable universe." Publisher's note
The author's "breathless writing conveys his own excitement over the revelations that new advances in astronomy can tell us about our planet and our place in the universe." Publ Wkly

Lightman, Alan P., 1948-
Ancient light; our changing view of the universe; {by} Alan Lightman. Harvard Univ. Press 1991 170p il pa $14.95 hardcover o.p.
523.1
1. Cosmology 2. Astronomers
ISBN 0-674-03363-9 (pa) LC 91-12459
"Adapted from Origins: the lives and worlds of modern cosmologists, by Alan Lightman and Roberta Brawer, published by Harvard University Press, 1990"
The author discusses the development of modern cosmology, the big bang model, and recent challenges to that model
"Lightman's book is a short and simple introduction to modern cosmology, with a strong emphasis upon observation and its interaction with theory. . . . Its merits are that it is accurate and does not go further than current observations warrant." Nat Hist
Includes bibliographical references

O'Dell, C. Robert, 1937-
The Orion Nebula; where stars are born. Belknap Press of Harvard University Press 2003 170p il $27.95 **523.1**
1. Orion Nebula
ISBN 0-674-01183-X LC 2003-50332
"Explains what the Nebula is, how it shines, its role in giving birth to stars, and the insights it affords into how common (or rare) planet formation might be." Publisher's note
"An excellent book for collections of any library serving general readers." Choice

Primack, Joel R., 1945-
The view from the center of the universe; discovering our extraordinary place in the cosmos; [by] Joel R. Primack and Nancy Ellen Abrams. Riverhead Books 2006 386p il $26.95
523.1
1. Cosmology 2. Physics—Philosophy
ISBN 1-5944-8914-9; 978-1-5944-8914-3
LC 2005-55262
The authors "argue that, for the first time in human history, a scientific theory of the universe as a whole is emerging—a theory that explains how the universe operates, what it's made of, where it came from and how it's evolving." Publisher's note
"This very important and fascinating book powerfully describes the scope and depth of human connections to our universe." Sci Books Films
Includes bibliographical references

Rees, Martin J., 1942-
Just six numbers; the deep forces that shape the universe; {by} Martin Rees. Basic Bks. 2000 173p il pa $14.95 hardcover o.p. **523.1**
1. Cosmology 2. Big bang theory
ISBN 0-465-03673-2 (pa) LC 00-268248
First published 1999 in the United Kingdom
"Rees summarizes the history of the universe, pointing out that six numbers related to basic physical constants (for example, the relative strengths of the gravitational and electromagnetic attraction) determine how the universe developed." Libr J
"A brief, readable, and profoundly instructive account of where cosmological knowledge stands at this moment." New Yorker
Includes bibliographical references

Our cosmic habitat; [by] Martin Rees. Princeton Univ. Press 2001 205p il $35; pa $14.95
523.1
1. Cosmology
ISBN 0-691-08926-4; 0-691-11477-3 (pa)
LC 2001-27835
"Rees explores the notion that our universe is just a part of a vast 'multiverse,' or ensemble of universes, in which most of the other universes are lifeless. . . . In this scenario, our cosmic habitat would be a special, possibly unique universe where the prevailing laws of physics allowed life to emerge." Publisher's note
"In the crowded field of popular writing about the universe, Rees is genuinely in the forefront—an accomplished scientist with the superior writing skills that enable him to connect with nonspecialists." Booklist
Includes bibliographical references

Seife, Charles
Alpha and omega; the search for the beginning and end of the universe. Viking 2003 294p il hardcover o.p. pa $15 **523.1**
1. Cosmology 2. Astronomy
ISBN 0-670-03179-8; 978-0-14-200446-3; 0-14-200446-4 (pa) LC 2002-44853
The author "describes the history of cosmology in terms of three 'revolutions.' The first, he says, was the development and gradual acceptance of the Copernican theory of the solar system. The second was the discovery and exposition throughout much of the 20th century of the Big Bang cosmology and the galactic red shifts that demonstrated the continuing expansion of the universe. Seife's 'third revolution' began in 1997 and is still very much a work in progress. It includes research into the composition of so-called dark matter and dark energy." Libr J
"Seife provides lucid explanations of very complicated topics for the science buff or well-rounded general reader." Publ Wkly
Includes bibliographical references

Singh, Simon

Big bang: the origins of the universe. Fourth Estate 2005 532p il $27.95 **523.1**

1. Big bang theory 2. Cosmology

ISBN 0-00716-220-0

The author "presents a brief history of the origins of the universe. . . . He begins with a historical overview of how scientific thought changed from mythology to cosmology, then moves to the debate between the steady state model of an eternal universe and the Big Bang theory, which saw the universe as beginning at a unique moment that was followed by rapid extension. . . . This readable book provides an accessible overview of this complex scientific theory." Libr J

Steinhardt, P. J.

Endless universe; beyond the Big Bang; [by] Paul J. Steinhardt and Neil Turok. Doubleday 2007 284p il $24.95 **523.1**

1. Cosmology

ISBN 0-385-50964-2; 978-0-385-50964-0

LC 2006-25256

The authors recount "developments in astronomy, particle physics, and superstring theory that together form the basis of their . . . 'Cyclic Universe' theory. According to this picture, the Big Bang was not the beginning of time, but the bridge to a past filled with endlessly repeating cycles, each accompanied by the creation of new matter and the formation of new galaxies, stars, and planets." Publisher's note

"This volume is not light reading, but the authors lighten the load with stories of how they met and collaborated on an M-theory (a string theory derivative) based cyclical model of the universe. . . . The illustrations, which play a key role in the book, introduce the reader to difficult material through simplified analogies." Sci Books Films

Includes bibliographical references

Susskind, Leonard

Cosmic landscape; string theory and the illusion of intelligent design. Little, Brown and Co. 2005 403p il hardcover o.p. pa $15.99 **523.1**

1. Cosmology 2. Astrophysics 3. String theory

ISBN 0-316-15579-9; 978-0-316-01333-8 (pa); 0-316-01333-1 (pa) LC 2005-18796

The author, one of the founders of string theory, discusses his theory as to "why the laws of physics are what they are and so finely poised to permit life. . . . Deeming unscientific any proposition of a supernatural agency in setting the physical dials so exactly, Susskind advances a radical concept he calls the 'landscape.'" Booklist

"This is the cutting edge of physics as described by one of the sharpest scientific minds around." Publ Wkly

Includes bibliographical references

Tyson, Neil De Grasse

Origins: fourteen billion years of cosmic evolution; {by} Neil deGrasse Tyson, Donald Goldsmith. W.W. Norton 2004 345p il $27.95 **523.1**

1. Cosmology 2. Evolution 3. Life—Origin

ISBN 0-393-05992-8 LC 2004-12201

The authors investigate "the connections between subatomic physics and the structure of the universe. With that as background, the authors then flit between the epoch of infinite density and temperature and the contemporary eon of galaxies, and they sign off with ruminations on extraterrestrial life." Booklist

"Amateur astronomers—in fact, any reader who enjoys popular science—will find fascinating information presented in clear but never patronizing language." Libr J

Includes bibliographical references

Universe down to Earth. Columbia Univ. Press 1994 277p il $60; pa $19 **523.1**

1. Cosmology

ISBN 0-231-07560-X; 0-231-07561-8 (pa)

LC 93-32259

The author "guides readers through the methods, history, and jargon of cosmology." Booklist

"This book is a genuine joy to read. . . . It is at once witty and profound in its treatment of some of the most 'far-out' concepts of the universe." Sci Books Films

Includes bibliographical references

Universe; written by Robert Dinwiddie . . . [et al.] DK 2005 512p il $50 * **523.1**

1. Cosmology

ISBN 0-7566-1364-7 LC 2005-4794

"The volume is divided into three sections. The first, called 'Introduction,' presents an overview of basic concepts, organized under the broad topics 'What Is the Universe?' 'The Beginning and End of the Universe,' 'The View from Earth,' and 'Exploring Space.' The next section, 'Guide to the Universe,' focuses on the features of the solar system, the Milky Way, and the regions beyond. Among the topics that are covered here are the planets; asteroids, comets, and meteors; the stars; and galaxy clusters. . . . Finally, the book has a section called 'The Night Sky,' with entries on each of the 88 constellations, including maps." Booklist

This is "a visually stunning reference that makes browsing irresistible. Every page of this oversized volume is full color, with an eye-pleasing balance of text and graphics." Libr J

Vilenkin, Alexander

Many worlds in one; the search for other universes; [by] Alex Vilenkin. Hill and Wang 2006 235p il $24 **523.1**

1. Cosmology

ISBN 978-0-8090-9523-0; 0-8090-9523-8

LC 2005-27057

The author discusses the "creation of the universe, its likely demise and the growing belief among cosmologists that there are an infinite number of universes. Vilenkin does an impressive job of presenting the background information necessary for lay readers to understand the ideas behind the big bang and related phenomena. . . . Drawing on the work of Stephen Hawking and recent advances in string theory, Vilenkin gives us a great deal to ponder." Publ Wkly

Includes bibliographical references

523.2 Planetary systems

Greeley, Ronald
The compact NASA atlas of the solar system; [by] Ronald Greeley, Raymond Batson. Cambridge Univ. Press 2002 408p il maps $65 *
                                                        523.2
1. Solar system
ISBN 0-521-80633-X   LC 2001-18259
"Derived from The NASA atlas of the solar system . . . first published 1997." Verso of title page
"Featuring over 150 maps, 214 color illustrations and a gazetteer that lists the names of all features officially approved by the International Astronomical Union, The Compact NASA Atlas of the Solar System includes the full range of information gathered from NASA missions throughout the Solar System." Publisher's note
"An excellent collection of systematic maps, photographs, and overviews of planets and major satellites. . . . It is unique in scope and its use of uniform formats and consistent scales . . . highly recommended." Libr J

Lang, Kenneth R.
The Cambridge guide to the solar system; Kenneth R. Lang. Cambridge University Press 2003 452p il $60   **523.2**
1. Solar system
ISBN 0-521-81306-9   LC 2002-31562
The author "provides an overall view of the solar system, the planets and their moons, comets, asteroids, and meteorites and . . . describes the results of the unmanned space probes responsible for the revolution in knowledge about the sun and its companions in space." Choice
"The photographs are stunning, the numerous charts and graphs are exemplary, and the narrative is bulging with all the important information about the solar system that is available to date. The author has done a wonderful job of making many of the complicated scientific concepts accessible to the layperson." Booklist
Includes bibliographical references

Sobel, Dava
The planets. Viking 2005 270p il $24.95; pa $13   **523.2**
1. Planets 2. Solar system
ISBN 0-670-03446-0; 0-14-200116-3 (pa)
The author turns her attention to "the planets of our solar system. . . . Sobel explores the planets' origins and oddities through the lens of popular culture, from astrology, mythology, and science fiction to art, music, poetry, biography, and history." Publisher's note
"For newcomers to planetary astronomy, 'The Planets' offers a nimble summary of the latest findings on each planet's features and geology. For those who avidly followed the journeys of the Mariners, Voyagers and Vikings through interplanetary space, it lets us fall in love with the heavens all over again." N Y Times Book Rev
Includes bibliographical references

523.3 Moon

Legault, Thierry
New atlas of the moon; [by] Thierry Legault, Serge Brunier. Firefly Books 2006 127p il $55
                                                        523.3
1. Moon—Maps
ISBN 978-1-55407-173-9; 1-55407-173-9
This lunar atlas features a day to day photographic record of the moon in its different phases with clear overlays over the lunar photos to identify major craters. It also features a section on lunar cartography that describes the location and details of different craters.
Includes bibliographical references

Mackenzie, Dana
The big splat; or, How our moon came to be. Wiley 2003 232p il $24.95   **523.3**
1. Moon
ISBN 0-471-15057-6   LC 2003-535402
"Mackenzie's account of humanity's long relationship with Earth's only natural satellite, from a probable lunar calendar found in the Lascaux caves to the new 'giant impact' theory of the moon's origin, is magnetically readable, preternaturally clear, and amazingly concise." Booklist
Includes bibliographical references

523.4 Planets

Beebe, Reta F.
Jupiter; the giant planet; {by} Reta Beebe. 2nd ed. Smithsonian Institution Press 1997 261p il (Smithsonian library of the solar system) pa $17.95 hardcover o.p.   **523.4**
1. Jupiter (Planet)
ISBN 1-56098-685-9 (pa)   LC 96-38604
First published 1994
The author describes the history of discoveries about Jupiter, its atmosphere and interior composition. Includes findings from the 1994 collision of Comet Shoemaker-Levy/9 and observations of the Galileo probe
Includes bibliographical references

Grinspoon, David Harry
Venus revealed; a new look below the clouds of our mysterious twin planet. Addison-Wesley 1997 355p il pa $20 hardcover o.p.   **523.4**
1. Venus (Planet)
ISBN 0-201-32839-9 (pa)   LC 96-38448
The author discusses "the orbital, geological, and atmospheric processes of Venus gathered through Earth-based observations and various U.S. and Soviet probes." Libr J
The author "makes science fun, not forbidding." Booklist

Leutwyler, Kristin

The moons of Jupiter; afterword by John Casani. Norton 2003 240p il $39.95

523.4

1. Jupiter (Planet) 2. Satellites

ISBN 0-393-05060-2   LC 2003-53974

"A Peter N. Nevraumont book"

The author presents an "exploration of Jupiter and its 40 satellites, the largest planet and satellite system within our solar system. . . . The bulk of the book is devoted to the four largest satellites—Io, Europa, Ganymede, and Callisto—with an average of 45-plus pages of images for each. The minor satellites, ring system, and, of course, Jupiter itself complete the rest of this beautiful book. . . . While the book is aimed at the informed lay reader, those without much scientific knowledge will still be able to appreciate the discussions and corresponding breathtaking images." Libr J

Morton, Oliver

Mapping Mars; science, imagination, and the birth of a world. Picador 2002 357p il maps $30; pa $16

523.4

1. Mars (Planet)

ISBN 0-312-24551-3; 0-312-42261-X (pa)

The author "traces scientists' efforts to map and understand the surface of Mars. . . . Morton writes eloquently and displays a breadth of knowledge not often found in science writing." Publ Wkly

Includes bibliographical references

Peebles, Curtis

Asteroids; a history. Smithsonian Institution Press 2000 280p il $29.95; pa $17.95

523.4

1. Asteroids

ISBN 1-56098-389-2; 1-56098-982-3 (pa)

LC 00-20733

Surveys the equipment, techniques, and controversies of 200 years of asteroid research. Prominent theorists are profiled. Impact threats and the mystery of the dinosaurs' extinction are discussed

"For a book aimed at general audiences, Peeble's excellent review of asteroids is unusually well documented. . . . {His} book clearly has a place on the bookshelves of specialists, students, and advanced amateurs." Choice

Includes bibliographical references

Sheehan, William, 1954-

Mars; the lure of the red planet; {by} William Sheehan & Stephen James O'Meara. Prometheus Bks. 2001 406p il $28

523.4

1. Mars (Planet)

ISBN 1-57392-900-X   LC 00-67358

The authors look "at the personalities of the great astronomers who gazed at Mars and, in particular, the aspects of or mysteries about Mars that captivated them. . . . An informative overview of sky watchers' enduring fascination with Mars." Booklist

Includes bibliographical references

Squyres, Steve, 1956-

Roving Mars; spirit, opportunity, and the exploration of the red planet. Hyperion 2005 422p il $25.95

523.4

1. Mars (Planet)—Exploration

ISBN 1-4013-0149-5   LC 2005-928417

This is an account of the ongoing "mission of the Mars Exploration Rovers, for which [the author] serves as principal investigator." Sci Am

"Couched in conversational prose, Squyres' enthusiasm for exploring Mars shines brightly." Booklist

Weintraub, David A., 1958-

Is Pluto a planet? a historical journey through the solar system. Princeton University Press 2007 254p il $27.95

523.4

1. Planets 2. Solar system 3. Pluto (Planet)

ISBN 0-691-12348-9; 978-0-691-12348-6

LC 2006-929630

The author "places the Pluto controversy in context in his . . . account of the development of our solar system and the evolution of the meaning of the word planet, from Aristotle's theories to recent decrees by the International Astronomical Union." Publ Wkly

Weintraub "provides a very interesting and thought-provoking history concerning the whole idea of planets, and I recommend the book highly to anyone interested in the solar system." Sci Books Films

Includes bibliographical references

523.5   Meteors, solar wind, zodiacal light

Bevan, A. W. R.

Meteorites: a journey through space and time; [by] Alex Bevan and John de Laeter. Smithsonian Institution Press 2002 215p il maps $35.95

523.5

ISBN 1-58834-021-X   LC 2001-49551

"The authors trace the formation and breakup of the planets, asteroids, and comets where meteorites originated, their long journey through space, their fall to Earth, their recovery, and what scientists are learning from them. The book contains a great deal of material about the '84001 Martian meteorite, which has raised provocative new questions about life on the red planet." Publisher's note

"Informative and visually appealing, this title meets any library's need for a basic source on meteorites." Booklist

Includes bibliographical references

523.6   Comets

Levy, David H., 1948-

David H. Levy's guide to observing and discovering comets. Cambridge University Press 2003 177p il $70; pa $22.99

523.6

1. Comets

ISBN 0-521-82656-X; 0-521-52051-7 (pa)

LC 2002-31547

Levy, David H., 1948-—*Continued*

The author "describes the observing techniques that have been developed over the years—from visual observations and searching, to photography, through to electronic charge-coupled devices (CCDs). He combines the history of comet hunting with the latest techniques, showing how our understanding of comets has evolved over time." Publisher's note

Includes bibliographical references

Sagan, Carl, 1934-1996

Comet; [by] Carl Sagan and Ann Druyan. Random House 1985 398p il pa $23 hardcover o.p.   **523.6**

1. Comets 2. Halley's comet

ISBN 0-345-41222-2   LC 85-8308

"The authors explore the myth and science of comets in a lavishly illustrated, slightly oversize volume that is both fascinating and authoritative." Booklist

Includes bibliographical references

523.7 Sun

Clark, Stuart

The sun kings; the unexpected tragedy of Richard Carrington and the tale of how modern astronomy began. Princeton Univ. Press 2007 211p il $24.95   **523.7**

1. Carrington, Richard Christopher, 1826-1875 2. Sun 3. Astronomy—History

ISBN 978-0-691-12660-9; 0-691-12660-7

LC 2006-940123

This is a "summary of how our understanding of the sun and its impact on the science of astronomy came to pass." Sci Books Films

"Clark's parade of historical characters dramatize the narrative nicely, and Clark conveys the significance of their scientific observations with plenty of context and thorough references, making this a fascinating work for both casual stargazers and serious astronomy buffs." Publ Wkly

Includes bibliographical references

Golub, Leon

Nearest star; the surprising science of our sun; {by} Leon Golub & Jay M. Pasachoff. Harvard Univ. Press 2001 267p il $29.95; pa $16.95 *
                                                          523.7

1. Sun

ISBN 0-674-00467-1; 0-674-01006-X (pa)

LC 00-63213

The authors "describe for a nonspecialist audience what is currently known of the structure of the sun, the source of its enormous energy, its history and future, its various effects on Earth and its atmosphere." Libr J

This is "a brilliant, richly illustrated survey." Booklist

Includes bibliographical references

523.8 Stars

Bakich, Michael E.

The Cambridge guide to the constellations. Cambridge Univ. Press 1995 320p il maps pa $29 hardcover o.p. *   **523.8**

1. Constellations

ISBN 0-521-44921-9 (pa)   LC 94-4678

"This book is the ultimate constellation reference book that brings together a variety of information about constellations, including: the size, visibility and relative brightness of all eighty-eight constellations; former location of extinct constellations; the number of visible stars in each constellation, and more." Univ Press Books for Public and Second Sch Libr

Includes bibliographical references

Ferguson, Kitty

Prisons of light; black holes. Cambridge Univ. Press 1996 214p il hardcover o.p. pa $17
                                                          523.8

1. Black holes (Astronomy)

ISBN 0-521-49518-0; 0-521-62571-8 (pa)

LC 96-11729

The author discusses the origin, properties, and behavior of black holes and reviews the scientific evidence for their existence.

"The typical reader will find this book an easily understood overview of an interesting subject. . . . A clear and accurate introduction to black holes for the general science reader." Sci Books Films

Includes bibliographical references

Hirshfeld, Alan

Parallax; the race to measure the cosmos; [by] Alan W. Hirshfeld. Freeman, W.H. 2001 314p il $23.95; pa $16   **523.8**

1. Stars

ISBN 0-7167-3711-6; 0-8050-7133-4 (pa)

LC 00-68147

This book chronicles the efforts to secure the first distance to a star through detection of stellar parallax. Scientists involved in the challenge included Tycho Brahe, Robert Hooke, James Bradley and William Herschel

This "is a lively gallery of colorful and, of course, calculating characters. . . . A delightful history of a crucial advance in knowledge." Booklist

Includes bibliographical references

Kaler, James B.

Extreme stars; at the edge of creation. Cambridge Univ. Press 2001 236p il maps $40
                                                          523.8

1. Stars

ISBN 0-521-40262-X   LC 00-58522

"Each chapter covers extreme stars of a different kind, including the faintest, the coolest, the brightest, the largest, the smallest, the youngest, the oldest, and the strangest. . . . {Kaler} piques the curiosity of the novice, while encouraging knowledgeable readers to think about stars from a different perspective. There is a wealth of information, much of it not available elsewhere at this semipopular level." Choice

Kerrod, Robin, 1938-
The star guide; learn how to read the night sky star by star. 2nd ed. Wiley 2005 160p il $29.95
   523.8

1. Stars—Atlases
ISBN 0-471-70617-5   LC 2004-22953
First published 1993
The presentation for this instructional guide to stargazing "is structured around monthly star maps (for midlatitude observers) in two-page spreads, with a follow-up feature on that month's outstanding constellation. . . . Photos featuring Hubble Space Telescope spectaculars, supplemented by tips for viewing the sun, moon, and planets, round out this attractive book on basic astronomy." Booklist

Tirion, Wil
The Cambridge star atlas. 3rd ed. Cambridge Univ. Press 2001 90p il maps $25 *
   523.8

1. Stars—Atlases
ISBN 0-521-80084-6   LC 2001-622030
First published 1991 with title: Cambridge star atlas 2000.0
This star atlas "includes a series of twenty-four monthly sky maps, designed to be of use for almost anywhere on Earth and a series of twenty . . . star charts, covering the whole heavens, with all stars visible to the naked eye under good circumstances." Publisher's note
"Recommended for anyone who plans to observe with the naked eye, binoculars, or small telescope... The printing is excellent, and the pages easily lie flat." Choice
Includes bibliographical references

Tyson, Neil De Grasse
Death by black hole; and other cosmic quandaries. Norton 2007 384p $24.95
   523.8

1. Cosmology 2. Black holes (Astronomy) 3. Space biology 4. Solar system 5. Religion and science
ISBN 978-0-393-06224-3; 0-393-06224-4
    LC 2006-22058
In this collection of essays that were originally published in Natural History magazine, the author takes readers on a "journey from Earth's hot springs, where extremophiles flourish in hellish conditions, to the frozen, desolate stretches of the Oort Cloud and the universe's farthest reaches, in both space and time. Tyson doesn't restrict his musings to astrophysics, but wanders into related fields like relativity and particle physics. . . . He tackles popular myths (is the sun yellow?) and takes movie directors—most notably James Cameron—to task for spectacular goofs. In the last section the author gives his take on the hot subject of intelligent design." Publ Wkly
"A wonderfully informed viewpoint on the slowly expanding boundaries of human knowledge." Boston Globe
Includes bibliographical references

523.9   Satellites and rings; eclipses, transits, occultations

Sheehan, William, 1954-
The transits of Venus; by William Sheehan, John Westfall. Prometheus Books 2004 407p il $28
   523.9
1. Venus (Planet)
ISBN 1-59102-175-8   LC 2003-22420
Sheehan and Westfall "chronicle the explorations of scientists and adventurers who studied the transits of Venus in the quest for scientific understanding." Publisher's note
"This volume is a tour de force not only of the history of observing Venus, but of much of astronomy itself." Sci Books Films
Includes bibliographical references

526   Mathematical geography

100 maps; the science, art and politics of cartography throughout history; edited by John O. E. Clark; introduction by Jeremy Black. Sterling 2006 256p il map $24.95 *
   526

1. Maps
ISBN 1-4027-2885-9
"This atlas contains 100 attractively presented maps, each with a story appended explaining its qualities: scientific, imaginative, propagandistic, etc. . . . The maps range across history from an ancient clay tablet map drawn more than 4,000 years ago in a country now known as Iraq to maps of the tsunami of 2004. . . . This well-wrought production will appeal to both advanced readers and neophytes." Choice
Includes bibliographical references

Alder, Ken
The measure of all things; the seven-year odyssey and hidden error that transformed the world. Free Press 2002 422p $27; pa $15
   526

1. Delambre, J. B. J., 1749-1822 2. Méchain, Pierre-François-André, 1744-1804 3. Metric system 4. Geography
ISBN 0-7432-1675-X; 0-7432-1676-8 (pa)
    LC 2002-70267
"In 1792, two astronomers set out from Paris in opposite directions to measure the meridian and thereby define the length of the meter. Alder's marvelous account of their quest is a dramatic tale of revolution, science, and human error." Libr J
Includes bibliographical references

Danson, Edwin, 1948-
Weighing the world; the quest to measure the Earth. Oxford University Press 2005 289p il $29.95
   526
1. Science—History 2. Surveying 3. Earth
ISBN 978-0-19-518169-2; 0-19-518169-7
    LC 2004-66284

Danson, Edwin, 1948-—_Continued_

This is a "behind-the-scenes look at the scientific events leading to modern map making. . . . Danson presents the stories of the scientists and scholars that had to scale the Andes, cut through tropical forests and how they handled the hardships they faced in the attempt to revolutionize our understanding of the planet." Publisher's note

The author "enlivens data about geodetic surveying, transforming them into greatly interesting dramas of science." Booklist

Includes bibliographical references

Raymo, Chet

Walking zero; discovering cosmic space and time along the Prime Meridian. Walker & Co. 2006 194p il maps $22.95   **526**

1. Longitude 2. Great Britain—Description and travel
ISBN 0-8027-1494-3; 978-0-8027-1494-7
                    LC 2006-282372

This is the author's "expression of his personal exploration of space, time, and scientific history, inspired partly by his walking the footpaths of southeast England in close proximity to the 0 degrees longitude line. . . . . This work is a thought-provoking, highly enlightening discussion of some of the most fascinating concepts in physics, astronomy, and geology, among other subjects." Sci Books Films

Includes bibliographical references

Sobel, Dava

Longitude; the true story of a lone genius who solved the greatest scientific problem of his time; with a new foreword by Neil Armstrong. Hardcover anniversary ed., [10th anniversary ed., 2005 anniversary ed.] Walker & Co. 2005 184p il $19 *   **526**

1. Harrison, John, 1693-1776 2. Longitude
ISBN 0-8027-1462-5; 978-0-8027-1462-6
First published 1995

"In 1714, Britain's Parliament offered the modern equivalent of $12 to anybody who could develop a means of determining longitude at sea. While the likes of Isaac Newton and Edmund Halley sought to calculate longitude by celestial measurement, John Harrison, an uneducated clockmaker, solved the problem with his invention of the chronometer. Science writer Sobel tells this story in a way that enables readers 'to see the globe anew.'" Libr J

Includes bibliographical references

528   Ephemerides

Astronomical almanac for the year 2008; issued by the Nautical Almanac Office, United States Naval Observatory. . . . U.S. Govt. Ptg. Office 2007 il $40 *   **528**

1. Nautical almanacs
ISSN 0737-6421
ISBN 0-16-077396-2; 978-0-16-077396-9
Also available online

Annual. Formed by the union in 1981 of The American ephemeris and nautical almanac and The Astronomical ephemeris published by Her Majesty's Nautical Almanac Office. Spine title: Astronomical almanac

"With basic information contributed by the ephemeris offices of a number of countries, this collection of tables is the authoritative source for annual astronomical data from the movement of heavenly bodies to the calculation of calendars." Ref Sources for Small & Medium-sized Libr. 6th edition

529   Chronology

Aveni, Anthony F.

Empires of time; calendars, clocks, and cultures; [by] Anthony Aveni. rev ed. University Press of Colo. 2002 332p il pa $22.95   **529**

1. Time
ISBN 0-87081-672-1   LC 2002-7120
First published 1989 by Basic Bks.

The author "traces the modern calendar's roots back to Greek pastoral poetry and prehistoric African bone markings, then compares Western, Chinese, Maya, Inca and tribal time systems. He also fathoms our division of time into days, weeks, months, seasons and years for clues to our psychology and worldview." Publ Wkly

Includes bibliographical references

Barnett, Jo Ellen

Time's pendulum; from sundials to atomic clocks, the fascinating history of timekeeping and how our discoveries changed the world. Harcourt Brace 1999 334p il map pa $15   **529**

1. Time
ISBN 0-15-600649-9   LC 98-49612
First published 1998 by Plenum Press

The author "shows how our notion of time is relative on a very human level. Time has undergone a long process of standardization over the centuries, she explains. . . . Barnett's book is a triumph of interdisciplinary scholarship that could appeal to a wide variety of readers." Publ Wkly

Includes bibliographical references

Galison, Peter Louis

Einstein's clocks and Poincaré's maps; empires of time; by Peter Galison. Norton 2003 389p il $23.95 *   **529**

1. Einstein, Albert, 1879-1955 2. Poincaré, Henri, 1854-1912 3. Time 4. Relativity (Physics)
ISBN 0-393-02001-0   LC 2002-155114

"Gallison shows how Einstein's work was influenced by French cartographer Henri Poincaré and by the physicist's own experience working in a Bern patent office, where the numerous patent requests for devices designed to coordinate distant clocks may have prompted further inquiry into the problem of simultaneity, which lies at the heart of relativity. Few books have ever made Einstein's theories more accessible—or more engrossing—for general readers." Booklist

Includes bibliographical references

Gleick, James
Faster; the acceleration of just about everything. Pantheon Bks. 1999 324p il pa $14 hardcover o.p.
529
1. Time
ISBN 0-679-77548-X (pa)   LC 99-21640
Gleick focuses on time and argues that the pace of life has grown faster. He discusses technologies such as "the watch, the typewriter, the phone, the TV, and [the computer, and] . . . the ways these 'time-saving' devices have influenced our world." Christ Sci Monit
The author's "shrewd dissection of the 'psychology of hurriedness' leads to many provocative observations." Booklist

Richards, E. G. (Edward Graham)
Mapping time; the calendar and its history. Oxford Univ. Press 1999 xxi, 438p il pa $43.50 hardcover o.p.
529
1. Calendars 2. Time
ISBN 0-19-286205-7 (pa)   LC 98-24957
"An overview of astronomy, time, clocks, writing, arithmetic, and other theoretical issues lays the groundwork for a description of calendar systems from prehistory to the present. Illustrations, charts, and diagrams, including algorithms for the conversion of calendar systems, are also provided." Libr J
Includes bibliographical references

Sims, Michael, 1958-
Apollo's fire; a day on Earth in nature and imagination. Viking 2007 xxiv, 296p $24.95
529
1. Time 2. Days 3. Astronomy
ISBN 978-0-670-06328-4; 0-670-06328-2
LC 2007-6024
The author "takes a single day and guides readers through the history of what we know, and what we've imagined, about sunrises, clouds and other natural phenomena. . . . His delightful tour of day and night skies will inspire many readers to look up with a marveling new perspective." Publ Wkly
Includes bibliographical references

530   Physics

Bloomfield, Louis
How things work; the physics of everyday life. 3rd ed. Wiley 2006 561p il pa $70.95 *
530
1. Physics
ISBN 978-0-471-46886-8; 0-471-46886-X
LC 2006-271695
First published 1997
This book is an "introduction to physics and science that starts with whole objects and looks inside them to see what makes them work. It's written for students who seek a connection between science and the world in which they live." Publisher's note

Buchanan, Mark
Nexus: small worlds and the groundbreaking science of networks. Norton 2002 235p $25.95; pa $14.95
530
1. Patterns (Mathematics) 2. System analysis
ISBN 0-393-04153-0; 0-393-32442-7 (pa)
LC 2002-518
The author "introduces readers to the dynamics of networks and shows how these networks affect behaviors in both the natural and the social world. . . . [Buchanan] finds the same patterns taking shape in food chains, in the neuronal networks of insects, in the architecture of the Internet and in the cultural backgrounds of elite CEOs. . . . Buchanan's ability as an affable, easygoing storyteller makes up for myriad digressions, and the narrative is, at times, spellbinding." Publ Wkly
Includes bibliographical references

The **Cambridge** companion to Newton; edited by I. Bernard Cohen and George E. Smith. Cambridge Univ. Press 2002 500p il $65; pa $23
530
1. Newton, Sir Isaac, 1642-1727
ISBN 0-521-65177-8; 0-521-65696-6 (pa)
LC 2001-37836
"A team of . . . contributors examines the principal aspects of Newton's thought. They include not only his approach to space, time, mechanics, and universal gravity in Principia and his research in optics and mathematics, but also his lesser known clandestine investigations into alchemy, theology, and prophecy." Publisher's note
This is "the best available brief overview of Newton's contributions to mechanics, cosmology, optics, mathematics, alchemy, and theology. The contributors have produced 16 well-written and admirably focused chapters. Some will be challenging for nonspecialist readers, but even those that discuss mechanics in detail are so well organized and clearly written that they amply repay close attention." Choice
Includes bibliographical references

Cole, K. C.
First you build a cloud; and other reflections on physics as a way of life. Harcourt Brace & Co. 1999 231p il pa $14
530
1. Physics
ISBN 0-15-600646-4   LC 98-47050
"A Harvest book"
First published 1985 by Morrow with title: Sympathetic vibrations
"Cole offers reflections on the place of physics in modern life. . . . Especially compelling are the essays on the aesthetic force behind scientific endeavors—the beauties of theory. For readers without scientific background, Cole gracefully introduces relativity, quantum theory, optics, astrophysics, and other significant disciplines, never getting bogged down in unnecessary explanation." Booklist
Includes bibliographical references

The hole in the universe; how scientists peered over the edge of emptiness and found everything. Harcourt 2001 274p il pa $14 hardcover o.p.
530
1. Physics
ISBN 0-15-601317-7 (pa)   LC 00-44947

Cole, K. C.—*Continued*

Cole discusses the history of nothing, "combining the history of zero (a mathematical nothing) with that of the vacuum (a physical nothing). . . . Until Einstein showed that light needed no tangible medium through which to travel, theorists filled the vacuum with 'ether'—the 'enfant terrible' of substances, as Einstein put it. It was subsequently banished." Atl Mon

Includes bibliographical references

Davies, P. C. W., 1946-

The matter myth; dramatic discoveries that challenge our understanding of physical reality; {by} Paul Davies and John Gribbin. Simon & Schuster 1992 320p il pa $14 hardcover o.p.
530

1. Reality 2. Physics
ISBN 0-671-72841-5 (pa)   LC 91-39522
Topics discussed include "chaos, solitons, the topology of space, quantum field theory, antimatter, magnetic monopoles, special and general relativity, the big bang, inflationary cosmology, the omega point, dark matter, cosmic strings and superstrings, wormholes, and the many-universe model." Sci Books Films

Includes bibliographical references

Deutsch, David

The fabric of reality; the science of parallel universes—and its implications. Allen Lane/The Penguin Press 1997 390p il pa $16 hardcover o.p.
530

1. Reality 2. Physics—Philosophy 3. Life 4. Cosmology
ISBN 0-14-027541-X   LC 97-6171
"Deutsch describes a reality where parallel universes are 'stacked like a pack of playing cards' to comprise a 'multiverse,' with computers communicating between them, where the mechanics and likelihood of time travel exist and where the universe comes to an end. . . . An intellectually stimulating read for the science-literate and motivated lay person." Publ Wkly

"A thoroughly mesmerizing scientific/philosophical view of reality." Libr J

Includes bibliographical references

Einstein, Albert, 1879-1955

The evolution of physics; the growth of ideas from early concepts to relativity and quanta; by Albert Einstein and Leopold Infeld. Simon & Schuster 1938 320p il pa $13 hardcover o.p. *
530

1. Relativity (Physics) 2. Quantum theory
ISBN 0-671-20156-5 (pa)
An "exposition for the layman of the growth of ideas in physical science." Publ Wkly

Feynman, Richard Phillips, 1918-1988

Six easy pieces; essentials of physics, explained by its most brilliant teacher; [by] Richard P. Feynman; originally prepared for publication by Robert B. Leighton and Matthew Sands; new introduction by Paul Davies. Helix Bks. (Reading) 1995 xxix, 145p il hardcover o.p. pa $15 *
530

1. Physics
ISBN 0-201-40955-0; 0-201-40825-2 (pa)
LC 94-30894
Also available in paperback with audio CD from Basic Bks.

This book reprints six chapters from Feynman's Lectures on Physics, which the "scientist delivered from 1961 to 1963 at the California Institute of Technology. . . . They discuss atoms, basic physics, the relation of physics to other sciences, the conservation of energy, gravitation, and quantum behavior." Libr J

"These 'easy pieces' cover key topics with a minimum of mathematics and a wealth of excellent analogies and vivid descriptions." Booklist

Kaku, Michio

Physics of the impossible; a scientific exploration into the world of phasers, force fields, teleportation, and time travel. Doubleday 2008 xxi, 329p $26.95   **530**

1. Physics
ISBN 978-0-385-52069-0; 0-385-52069-7
LC 2007-30290
"From teleportation to telekinesis, Kaku uses the world of science fiction to explore the fundamentals—and the limits—of the laws of physics as we know them today." Publisher's note

"There is a surprising amount of heavyweight, cutting-edge science woven into the fabric of the book. String theory, dark energy, metamaterials and quantum theory are just a few topics—*Physics of the Impossible* is, in fact, an easy-to-read physics primer in disguise." New Sci

Includes bibliographical references

Kragh, Helge, 1944-

Quantum generations; a history of physics in the twentieth century. Princeton Univ. Press 1999 494p $65; pa $22.95   **530**

ISBN 0-691-01206-7; 0-691-09552-3 (pa)
LC 99-17903
The author "details the explosive course physics has taken from the introduction of X rays in the mid-1890's to superstring theory in the present day. . . . [He] explains not only how the groundbreaking ideas of physics progressed but also how they are actively applied." Publisher's note

Includes bibliographical references

Krauss, Lawrence Maxwell

Fear of physics; a guide for the perplexed; [by] Lawrence M. Krauss. Rev ed. Basic Books 2007 257p il pa $29.95 *   **530**

1. Physics
ISBN 978-0-465-00218-4; 0-465-00218-8
LC 2007-04700

Krauss, Lawrence Maxwell—*Continued*
First published 1993
This overview describes what physics is and the work of physicists.

"The writing style genuinely keeps the reader interested. . . . This book is a great resource if you want insight into what physics really is and what physicists do." Sci Books Films

Includes bibliographical references

Rosen, Joe
Encyclopedia of physics. Facts on File 2004 386p il (Facts on File science library) $75 *
530
1. Physics—Encyclopedias
ISBN 0-8160-4974-2   LC 2003-14963
The entries "cover physical concepts, prominent physicists (modern and historical), and physics laboratories, societies, and organizations. The alphabetically arranged entries are supplemented with 11 topical essays that aim to shed some light on physics in a philosophical or practical way. These essays cover such topics as beauty, the nature of the relationship between physics and philosophy, and the desire among some physicists to find the unifying laws governing all physical concepts. . . . The entries are well written, accurate, and include equations where appropriate." Booklist
Includes bibliographical references

Suplee, Curt
Physics in the 20th century; edited by Judith R. Franz and John S. Rigden. Abrams 1999 223p il $49.50; pa $19.95
530
1. Physics
ISBN 0-8109-4364-6; 0-8109-9084-9 (pa)
LC 98-41306
Published "in association with the American Physical Society and the American Institute of Physics."
In this overview of physics Suplee "leads us through the structure and function of atoms, the astonishing intimacy of light and matter, the often amusing improbabilities of quantum mechanics, the architecture of exotic materials, the elusive lives of subatomic particles that are the stuff of all creation, and chaos and order in nature—until we arrive at a vision of the entire universe. He does it without equations or misleading analogies, and often with humor." N Y Times Book Rev

Teller, Edward, 1908-2003
Conversations on the dark secrets of physics; [by] Edward Teller, Wendy Teller and Talley Wilson. Perseus 2002 247p il pa $17.50
530
1. Physics
ISBN 0-7382-0765-9; 978-0-7382-0765-0
First published 1991 by Plenum Press
The authors discuss the work of major physicists starting with Pythagoras and the ancient Greeks and including Einstein, Galileo, Johann Kepler, Isaac Newton, Niels Bohr, and Louis de Broglie, and explain such topics as quantum theory, superconductivity, and lasers.

"Each chapter starts at a low level of understanding, but often ends up at a dramatically high one. Questions at the end of each chapter have answers that are both expansive and illuminating." New Sci

Includes bibliographical references

530.1 Theories and mathematical physics

Barbour, Julian B.
The end of time; the next revolution in physics; [by] Julian Barbour. Oxford Univ. Press 2000 371p il hardcover o.p. pa $17.95
530.1
1. Space and time 2. Relativity (Physics) 3. Quantum theory
ISBN 0-19-511729-8; 0-19-514592-5 (pa)
LC 99-44319
This "book is about time and its history—how it is treated in various physical theories. . . . Barbour asks what time really is. His answer, in light of all we know of the physics involved: nothing; time does not exist." NY Times Book Rev
Includes bibliographical references

Bodanis, David
E=mc2; a biography of the world's most famous equation. Walker & Company 2005 337p il $25
530.1
1. Einstein, Albert, 1879-1955 2. Force and energy 3. Space and time
ISBN 0-8027-1463-3
Also available in paperback from Berkley Pub. Group
First published 2000
The author relates the story of "Einstein's formulation of the equation in 1905 and its association ever after with relativity and nuclear energy. Parallel with the science, Bodanis populates his tale with dramatic lives." Booklist [review of 2000 edition]

Bolles, Edmund Blair, 1942-
Einstein defiant; genius versus genius in the quantum revolution. Joseph Henry Press 2004 348p il $27.95
530.1
1. Einstein, Albert, 1879-1955 2. Bohr, Niels Henrik David, 1885-1962 3. Quantum theory
ISBN 0-309-08998-0   LC 2003-23735
The author "retells the story of modern physicists' struggle to reach a full understanding of quantum physics. His account centers on the debate between two scientific giants, Albert Einstein and Niels Bohr, who famously took opposing sides on the quantum issue." Libr J

"This carefully researched book achieves a nice balance between science and history. The author provides enough scientific information to illuminate the unfolding drama for nonscientists and constructs a marvelously choreographed tale of how just about every physicist of note in the last century contributed to the debate." Sci Books Films

Includes bibliographical references

Davies, P. C. W., 1946-
About time; Einstein's unfinished revolution; {by} Paul Davies. Simon & Schuster 1995 316p il pa $14 hardcover o.p. **530.1**
1. Einstein, Albert, 1879-1955 2. Space and time 3. Relativity (Physics) 4. Astrophysics
ISBN 0-684-81822-1 (pa) LC 94-40281
This book examines scientific "theories about the origin, direction, and end of time." Booklist
This "is intelligent, fascinating, and eminently readable." Sci Books Films
Includes bibliographical references

Einstein, Albert, 1879-1955
The meaning of relativity. 5th ed, Expanded Princeton science library ed. with a new introduction by Brian Greene. Princeton University Press 2005 xxiv, 166p il pa $16.95 **530.1**
1. Relativity (Physics)
ISBN 0-691-12027-7 LC 2004-111082
First published 1922. Translated by Edwin Plimpton Adams, Ernst G. Straus and Bruria Kaufman
The Stafford Little lectures of Princeton University, May 1921
"Though few can understand it, most readers in physics and librarians in charge of science collections know this book as one of the landmarks of modern knowledge. . . . The book is not intended for general reading. Instead it is addressed to . . . those whose training enables them to understand the mathematical expressions of relativity." N Y Public Libr. New Tech Books

Fritzsch, Harald, 1943-
An equation that changed the world; Newton, Einstein, and the theory of relativity; translated by Karin Heusch. University of Chicago Press 1994 279p il $32.50; pa $16 **530.1**
1. Einstein, Albert, 1879-1955 2. Newton, Sir Isaac, 1642-1727 3. Relativity (Physics)
ISBN 0-226-26557-9; 0-226-26558-7 (pa)
LC 94-3876
"Bridging the gap between classical and relativistic concepts, the author describes a variety of phenomena of modern physics. . . . Fritzsch accomplishes his goal by introducing three characters: Sir Isaac Newton and Albert Einstein return from the dead and meet Professor Adrian Haller [a fictitious] . . . American physicist from the present." Sci Books Films
"Many readers will applaud Fritzsch for this lively but profoundly insightful book." Booklist
Includes bibliographical references

Gell-Mann, Murray, 1929-
The quark and the jaguar; adventures in the simple and the complex. Holt & Co. 1995 392p il pa $17 **530.1**
1. Particles (Nuclear physics) 2. Science—Philosophy
ISBN 0-8050-7253-5
First published 1994 by W.H. Freeman
The author "ponders the universe's mix of simplicity and complexity, regularity and randomness, as he ranges from quarks (the fundamental subatomic particles which he discovered) to complex adaptive systems like bacteria developing resistance to antibiotics, mobile robots, jaguars, and people interacting with and learning from their environment." Publ Wkly
"While the topics are technical in nature, Gell-Mann's presentation is clear and will be readily understood by scholars and informed lay readers." Libr J

Gott, J. Richard, 1947-
Time travel in Einstein's universe; the physical possibilities of travel through time; {by} J. Richard Gott, III. Houghton Mifflin 2001 291p il hardcover o.p. pa $14 **530.1**
1. Space and time 2. Fourth dimension
ISBN 0-395-95563-7; 0-618-25735-7 (pa)
LC 00-54243
"Gott tackles the complexities of attempting to turn the fantasy of time travel into a theoretical possibility in a lively and lucid discussion." Booklist
Includes bibliographical references

Gribbin, John R.
In search of Schrödinger's cat; quantum physics and reality. Bantam Bks. 1984 302p il pa $15.95 **530.1**
1. Quantum theory 2. Reality
ISBN 0-553-34253-3 LC 84-2975
This history of quantum mechanics discusses the work of Huygens, Einstein, Schrödinger, Bohr, Planck and Everett
This book "contains many vignettes from the history of science and many insights into the researchers and the work that has led to our current understanding of the quantum theory. Excellent analogies and graphic illustrations are used to present difficult ideas." Sci Books Films
Includes bibliographical references

Schrödinger's kittens and the search for reality; solving the quantum mysteries; {by} John Gribbin. Little, Brown 1995 261p il pa $14.95 hardcover o.p. **530.1**
1. Schrödinger, Erwin, 1887-1961 2. Quantum theory 3. Reality
ISBN 0-316-32819-7 (pa) LC 95-75652
In this sequel to In search of Schrödinger's cat, Gribbin attempts to "explain recent experimental and theoretical findings about the . . . nature of the submicroscopic world of the atom. The 'Copenhagen interpretation' of quantum mechanics offered by Niels Bohr and his colleagues has prevailed for almost 70 years, but there {are} now . . . competing interpretations. Gribbin reviews this . . . {field and} indicates his personal preference for one of the new theoretical models." Libr J
Includes bibliographical references

Guillen, Michael
Five equations that changed the world; the power and poetry of mathematics. Hyperion 1995 277p hardcover o.p. pa $14.95 **530.1**
1. Physics 2. Mathematics
ISBN 0-7868-6103-7; 0-7868-8187-9 (pa)
LC 95-15199

Guillen, Michael—*Continued*

The author discusses "five significant equations in physics and the individuals who developed them. The individuals are Isaac Newton (Universal gravitation), Daniel Bernoulli (hydrodynamic pressure), Michael Faraday (thermodynamics), Rudolf Clausius (thermodynamics), and Albert Einstein (special relativity)." Libr J

"A seamless blend of dramatic biography and mathematical documentary that links the personal with the scientific." Publ Wkly

Hawking, Stephen W., 1942-

The nature of space and time; [by] Stephen Hawking and Roger Penrose. Princeton Univ. Press 1996 141p il (Isaac Newton Institute series of lectures) hardcover o.p. pa $18.95

530.1

1. Space and time 2. Quantum theory 3. Astrophysics
ISBN 0-691-03791-4; 0-691-05084-8 (pa)

LC 95-35582

This volume "takes the form of a debate between Hawking and Penrose at Cambridge in 1994. At the center of the discussion is a pair of powerful theories: the quantum theory of fields and the general theory of relativity. The issue is how—if at all—one can merge the two into a quantum theory of gravity. . . . A substantial background in theoretical physics is needed for full comprehension." Libr J

Includes bibliographical references

The universe in a nutshell; [by] Stephen Hawking. Bantam Bks. 2001 216p il $35 *

530.1

1. Quantum theory
ISBN 0-553-80202-X

LC 2001-35757

Companion volume to A brief history of time

Hawking "explains the basic laws of physics that govern the universe, beginning with a brief history of the concept of relativity, and then he is off and running to explore time, space, the future, and the possibility of time travel, among other fundamental rules of the universe's road. Admirers of Hawking's previous book will continue to appreciate his ability not only to air fresh, provocative ideas but also to say what he means clearly and without watering down his material or condescending to his audience—he even injects humor into his narrative. The profuse, beautifully rendered illustrations contribute greatly to the reader's understanding of his points." Booklist

Kaku, Michio

Hyperspace; a scientific odyssey through parallel universes, time warps, and the tenth dimension; illustrations by Robert O'Keefe. Oxford Univ. Press 1994 359p il $35

530.1

1. Relativity (Physics) 2. Space and time
ISBN 0-19-508514-0

LC 93-7910

Also available in paperback from Anchor Bks.

This is an "overview of the major scientists, discoveries, and ideas involved in an ongoing quest for synthesizing quantum mechanics and relativity physics into a superstring theory of our entire universe." Libr J

Includes bibliographical references

Lloyd, Seth

Programming the universe; a quantum computer scientist takes on the cosmos. Knopf 2006 221p il $25.95 *

530.1

1. Quantum theory 2. Microcomputers
ISBN 1-4000-4092-2; 978-1-4000-4092-6

LC 2005-50408

The author argues that "the universe is a computer that feeds on information and generates complexity." N Y Times Book Rev

"Exploring big questions in accessible, comprehensive fashion, Lloyd's work is of vital importance to the general-science audience." Booklist

Includes bibliographical references

Parker, Barry R.

Albert Einstein's vision; remarkable discoveries that shaped modern science; [by] Barry Parker. Prometheus Books 2004 286p il $28

530.1

1. Einstein, Albert, 1879-1955 2. Relativity (Physics) 3. Quantum theory
ISBN 1-59102-186-3

LC 2004-3990

"The book takes the ideas generated by Einstein, before his death in 1955, and follows the work of other scientists as they continued to build modern physics and cosmology." Sci Books Films

Includes bibliographical references

Quantum legacy; the discovery that changed our universe; [by] Barry Parker. Prometheus Bks. 2002 282p il $29

530.1

1. Quantum theory
ISBN 1-57392-993-X

LC 2002-67966

The author describes the theory of quantum mechanics, its practical applications, and the work of such scientists as Max Planck, Albert Einstein, Niels Bohr, Werner Heisenberg, Erwin Schrodinger, and Richard Feynman

Includes bibliographical references

Rigden, John S.

Einstein 1905; the standard of greatness. Harvard University Press 2005 173p il $21.95; pa $14.95 *

530.1

1. Einstein, Albert, 1879-1955 2. Quantum theory
ISBN 0-674-01544-4; 0-674-02104-5 (pa)

LC 2004-54049

The author "chronicles the . . . theories that Einstein put forth beginning in March 1905: his particle theory of light, rejected for decades but now a staple of physics; his overlooked dissertation on molecular dimensions; his theory of Brownian motion; his theory of special relativity; and the work in which his famous equation, . . . [energy equals mass times the speed of light squared], first appeared." Publisher's note

"The book is a delight to read, with a lot of interesting, useful information." Choice

Includes bibliographical references

Smolin, Lee, 1955-
The trouble with physics; the rise of string theory, the fall of a science, and what comes next. Houghton Mifflin Co. 2006 392p il $26

530.1

1. String theory 2. Science—Methodology
ISBN 978-0-618-55105-7; 0-618-55105-0

LC 2006-07235

The author "argues that physics—the basis for all other sciences—has lost its way. . . . One of the major problems, according to Smolin, is string theory: an ambitious attempt to formulate a 'theory of everything' that explains all the particles and forces of nature and how the universe came to be. . . . [Smolin contends that] there's a deep flaw in the theory: no part of it has been tested, and no one knows how to test it." Publisher's note

"This is a well-written, critical profile of the theoretical physics community, free of equations, from the perspective of a member." Libr J
Includes bibliographical references

Thorne, Kip S.
Black holes and time warps; Einstein's outrageous legacy. Norton 1994 619p il pa $18.95 hardcover o.p.

530.1

1. Physics 2. Relativity (Physics) 3. Astrophysics 4. Black holes (Astronomy)
ISBN 0-393-31276-3 (pa)

LC 93-2014

This book is "about black holes, white holes, wormholes, parallel universes, time travel, 10-dimensional space-time, the origin and fate of the universe and a lot of other subjects dear to science fiction fans." N Y Times Book Rev
Includes bibliographical references

Toomey, David M.
The new time travelers; a journey to the frontiers of physics; [by] David Toomey. W. W. Norton 2007 391p il $28

530.1

1. Space and time
ISBN 978-0-393-06013-3; 0-393-06013-6

LC 2007-11307

This book on the physics of time travel "illustrates dimension-bending concepts with space-time diagrams, M. C. Escher drawings, and the plot of H.G. Wells' Time Machine. Toomey gets a grip on bending the fourth dimension by historically chronicling physicists who have theorized about time travel . . . . If you dream of getting outside your personal light cone, Toomey shows how it might be imagined." Booklist
Includes bibliographical references

Wolfson, Richard, 1947-
Simply Einstein; relativity demystified. Norton 2003 261p il $24.95

530.1

1. Relativity (Physics)
ISBN 0-393-05154-4

LC 2002-2984

"Wolfson's economical and vivid tutorial should open doors for lay readers encountering Einstein's principles for the first time. His popular style, with a minimum of math, should make this a must-have book for Einstein buffs as well." Publ Wkly
Includes bibliographical references

530.8   Measurement

Barrow, John D., 1952-
The constants of nature; from Alpha to Omega—the numbers that encode the deepest secrets of the universe. Pantheon Books 2002 352p il $26; pa $15

530.8

1. Measurement
ISBN 0-375-42221-8; 1-4000-3225-3 (pa)

LC 2002-75975

"Barrow traces scientists' evolving understanding of natural constants, like the speed of light, in this erudite and enthralling work of popular science." Publ Wkly
Includes bibliographical references

531   Classical mechanics. Solid mechanics

Darling, David J.
Gravity's arc; the story of gravity, from Aristotle to Einstein and beyond; [by] David Darling. J. Wiley 2006 278p $24.95

531

1. Gravity
ISBN 0-471-71989-7; 978-0-471-71989-2

LC 2005-30772

This is a "historical review of the human understanding of gravity from the ancient Greeks to the 21st century. Included are examinations of Greek philosophers and their debates, medieval and Arabic developments, Galileo, Tycho, Kepler, Newton, Eotvos, [and] Einstein. . . . The writing style is clear and reader friendly. . . . Read this book to learn about gravity and experience a model scientific exposition for the scientist and general reader alike." Sci Books Films
Includes bibliographical references

535   Light and infrared and ultraviolet phenomena

Magueijo, João
Faster than the speed of light; the story of a scientific speculation. Perseus Bks. 2003 279p il $26

535

1. Light 2. Physics
ISBN 0-7382-0525-7

LC 2002-112394

In this study theoretical physicist Magueijo presents the idea that light traveled faster in the early universe than it does today. He also documents the reactions other scientists are having to this theory, which contradicts Einstein's theory of relativity.

"Breaking the old speed limit posted by . . . Albert Einstein in his 20s, this book deploys a racy and provocative text to convey its popularized content of a new cosmology. Jocular, ironic, witty, self-centered, even indignant, Magueijo is all too ready to castigate his adversaries." Sci Am

Park, David
The fire within the eye; a historical essay on the nature and meaning of light. Princeton Univ. Press 1997 377p il pa $19.95 hardcover o.p.

535

1. Light 2. Optics
ISBN 0-691-05051-1 (pa)   LC 96-45573
A history of the concept and science of light from classical times to the present. Cultural, philosophical, intellectual and theological perspectives are explored and works by Aristotle, Grosseteste, Plotinus and Bohr are among those discussed

"Whether it is Fermat and Huygens on optics or Faraday and Maxwell on electromagnetism, the writing is lively and informed. . . . The very readable style and helpful glossary, along with an excellent bibliography and references, make this work suitable for . . . general readers." Choice

Pendergrast, Mark
Mirror mirror; a history of the human love affair with reflection. Basic Books 2003 404p il $27.50; pa $17   **535**
1. Mirrors
ISBN 0-465-05470-6; 0-465-05471-4 (pa)
    LC 2003-2544
The author "traces the significance of reflective surfaces from ancient cultures to contemporary times. He provides a cursory treatment of the religious, literary, and artistic uses of mirrors throughout history, instead focusing on the scientific and technological achievements resulting from the applications of mirrors." Libr J

"Those with a historical and scientific bent may profitably read this book for insight into the manufacture of mirrors—along with descendents the telescope and microscope—down through the ages. . . . Whether for pleasure or profit, this well-written, entertaining book, packed with historical information, should be read!" Choice

Includes bibliographical references

Perkowitz, S., 1939-
Empire of light; a history of discovery in science and art; [by] Sidney Perkowitz. Joseph Henry Press 1996 229p il pa $16.95 *

535

1. Light
ISBN 0-309-06556-9; 978-0-309-06556-6
    LC 98-43181
First published 1996 by Holt & Co.
The author traces "humanity's understanding of light from both scientific and artistic viewpoints. Later portions of his text deal with light in contemporary physics research and in astronomy and cosmology." Libr J

"This is a wonderful, well-written book that not only enlightens, but also entertains the reader." Sci Books Films

Includes bibliographical references

536   Heat

Segrè, Gino
A matter of degrees; what temperature reveals about the past and future of our species, planet, and universe. Viking 2002 300p il $24.95; pa $15

536

1. Temperature
ISBN 0-670-03101-1; 0-14-200278-X (pa)
    LC 2001-46942
The author "first gives background on the inventors of the thermometer, which prepares the way for the major discoveries in the 1800s about the nature of heat. . . . Segre recounts heat's role in the earth's formation, climate history, and thermophilic life on the ocean bottom, and . . . the temperature of stellar interiors." Booklist

Segre "brings humor and passion to his subject and excels in showing its relevance to both current policy and future research." Publ Wkly

Includes bibliographical references

Shachtman, Tom, 1942-
Absolute zero and the conquest of cold. Houghton Mifflin 1999 261p $25; pa $14

536

1. Low temperatures—Research
ISBN 0-395-93888-0; 0-618-08239-5 (pa)
    LC 99-33305
The author "analyzes the social impact of the chill factor, explains the science of cold and tells the curious tales behind inventions like the thermometer, the fridge and the thermos flask." N Y Times Book Rev

Includes bibliographical references

Von Baeyer, Hans Christian
Maxwell's demon; why warmth disperses and time passes. Random House 1998 xxi, 207p pa $15 hardcover o.p.   **536**
1. Thermodynamics 2. Time
ISBN 0-375-75372-9 (pa)   LC 97-41543
The author "traces the development of the laws of thermodynamics in a narrative spanning a period from 13th-century perpetual motion machines to contemporary thinking about laser technology, information theory, and algorithmic randomness. . . . The star of the story is James Clerk Maxwell's molecule-manipulating demon, who conceivably could challenge the Second Law of Thermodynamics." Choice

Includes bibliographical references

537   Electricity and electronics

Bodanis, David
Electric universe; the shocking true story of electricity. Crown Publishers 2004 308p $24

537

1. Electricity 2. Force and energy
ISBN 1-400-04550-9   LC 2004-11275
The author "examines electricity's theoretical development and how 19th- and 20th-century entrepreneurs har-

Bodanis, David—_Continued_

nessed it to transform everyday existence. Going from 'Wires' to 'Waves' to computers and even the human body, Bodanis pairs electrical innovations with minibiographies of their developers, among them Thomas Edison, Alexander Graham Bell, Guglielmo Marconi, Heinrich Herz and Alan Turing." Publ Wkly

"As a storyteller, author David Bodanis is wonderful. . . . This book is directed at a general audience, but it should be required reading for all scientific professionals." Sci Books Films

Includes bibliographical references

538 Magnetism

Livingston, James D., 1930-

Driving force; the natural magic of magnets. Harvard Univ. Press 1996 311p il maps pa $16.95 hardcover o.p. **538**

1. Magnets

ISBN 0-674-21645-8 (pa) LC 95-39595

The author "explains the uses of magnets, the properties of magnetism, and how modern materials science uses both." Libr J

"A stimulating variety of science, history, and technology delivered enthusiastically." Booklist

Includes bibliographical references

539.7 Atomic and nuclear physics

Cathcart, Brian

The fly in the cathedral; how a small group of Cambridge scientists won the race to split the atom. Farrar, Straus & Giroux 2005 308p il hardcover o.p. pa $15 **539.7**

1. Cockcroft, Sir John, 1897-1967 2. Walton, Ernest T. S., 1903-1995 3. Nuclear physics

ISBN 0-374-15716-2; 0-374-53026-2 (pa)

LC 2004-56348

First published 2004 in the United Kingdom

This is an "account of the genesis of nuclear physics in the first third of the 20th century. Although the centerpiece of his story is the experiment performed on April 14, 1932, by John Cockcroft and Ernest Walton . . . Cathcart fully describes the experiment's scientific and social context. Through crisp prose, interesting analogies and ample insight, he makes the basics of nuclear physics accessible while demonstrating the passion scientists have for their work." Publ Wkly

Includes bibliographical references

The **Facts** on File dictionary of atomic and nuclear physics; edited by Richard Rennie. Facts on File 2002 250p il hardcover o.p. pa $19.95

1. Nuclear physics—Dictionaries **539.7**

ISBN 0-8160-4916-5; 0-8160-4917-3 (pa)

LC 2002-32545

This dictionary "covers areas such as atomic theory, the structure of matter, spectroscopy, quantum theory, nuclear physics, particle physics, and cosmology. Examples of specific entries are _Bohr model; Carbon dating;_

Grand unified theories (GUTs); _Hadron; Hawking, Stephen William; Rydberg constant;_ and _Self-organization._ Appendixes provide tables of fundamental constants, elementary particles, chemical elements, and a selected list of organizational Web pages." Booklist

Includes bibliographical references

Feynman, Richard Phillips, 1918-1988

QED; the strange theory of light and matter; [by] Richard Feynman. Princeton Univ. Press 1985 158p (Alix G. Mautner memorial lectures) $55; pa $15.95 **539.7**

1. Electrons 2. Light 3. Quantum theory

ISBN 0-691-08388-6; 0-691-02417-0 (pa)

LC 85-42685

The author attempts to describe the interaction between light and electrons

"Feynman describes with accuracy, insight, self-deprecating humor, and clarity the centerpiece of modern elementary particle theory—quantum electrodynamics. . . . 'QED' will challenge the mind." Christ Sci Monit

Greene, Brian R., 1963-

The elegant universe; superstrings, hidden dimensions, and the quest for the ultimate theory; [by] Brian Greene. Vintage Books 2000 448p il pa $15.95 * **539.7**

1. String theory 2. Cosmology

ISBN 0-375-70811-1; 978-0-375-70811-4

LC 99-42018

First published 1999 by Norton

"Greene aims to acquaint lay readers with string theory, a hypothesis concerning strings of subatomic particles that could help scientists explain all of nature's forces in one Unified Field Theory." Libr J

The author "makes the terribly complex theory of strings accessible to all. He possesses a remarkable gift for using the everyday to illustrate what may be going on in dimensions beyond our feeble human perception." Publ Wkly

Includes bibliographical references

Gribbin, John R.

Q is for quantum; an encyclopedia of particle physics; [by] John Gribbin; edited by Mary Gribbin; illustrations by Jonathan Gribbin; timelines by Benjamin Gribbin. Free Press 1998 545p il $35; pa $20 **539.7**

ISBN 0-684-85578-X; 0-684-86315-4 (pa)

1. Particles (Nuclear physics)—Dictionaries LC 98-9918

"There are entries for people (Feynman, Richard Phillips; Huygens, Christiaan; Oppenheimer, Robert), places (Brookhaven National Laboratory, Fermilab), and historical highlights (Manhattan Project). . . . Following the entries is a bibliography that lists the books referred to in the text, together with others; the more technical titles are indicated with an asterisk. The volume concludes with time lines of birth dates of famous scientists, key dates in physical sciences, and key dates in history." Booklist

Includes bibliographical references

Gribbin, John R.—*Continued*

The search for superstrings, symmetry, and the theory of everything; {by} John Gribbin. Little, Brown 1999 c1998 212p $23; pa $14.95

539.7

1. Nuclear physics
ISBN 0-316-32975-4; 0-316-32614-3 (pa)
LC 98-34711

First published 1998 in the United Kingdom with title: In search of Susy

This introduction to the world of high-energy physics traces "research from the foundation work done in the 19th century to the latest concepts of superstrings." Libr J

"Diligent readers without any specialized knowledge of physics or mathematics will come away with a flavor of the latest ideas theorists are grappling with." Publ Wkly

Includes bibliographical references

Kane, Gordon, 1937-

The particle garden; our universe as understood by particle physicists. Addison-Wesley 1995 224p il pa $15 hardcover o.p.   **539.7**

1. Particles (Nuclear physics) 2. Nuclear physics
ISBN 0-201-40826-0 (pa)   LC 94-25804

The author explains "the physics of subatomic particles: electrons, quarks, photons, bosons and company. . . . Topics covered include a history of particle physics, the Standard Theory, 'grand unification' and beyond and the relation of particle physics to cosmology and astrophysics." Publ Wkly

"This is an accurate, well-written, up-to-date account of particle physics by an expert in the field." Sci Books Films

Lederman, Leon M.

The God particle; if the universe is the answer, what is the question? [by] Leon Lederman with Dick Teresi. Houghton Mifflin 1993 434p hardcover o.p. pa $15.95   **539.7**

1. Particles (Nuclear physics) 2. Science—Philosophy 3. Universe
ISBN 0-395-55849-2; 978-0-618-71168-0 (pa); 0-618-71168-6 (pa)   LC 92-43583

Lederman examines "the course of experimental physics from 430 B.C. to the planned opening of the Superconducting Supercollider (SSC), of which he is one of the principal architects." Libr J

The author "pokes fun at the theorists and dazzles us with descriptions of the seemingly impossible experiments he and his fellow genius tinkerers executed to prove the existence of those massless, charmed, and strange entities, quarks and leptons." Booklist

Includes bibliographical references

Lindley, David

The end of physics; the myth of a unified theory. Basic Bks. 1993 275p pa $18 hardcover o.p.   **539.7**

1. Nuclear physics 2. Physics
ISBN 0-465-01976-5 (pa)   LC 92-54524

The author has written an "account of the transition made by physicists from the physical world to a theoretical one. . . . As a primer for a history of physical science and experimentation, this book is an invaluable tonic, written in a gentle and pleasing way and with a critical eye. The early chapters on pre-20th century theory and experimentation are especially fine: clear, precise, and highly accessible." Libr J

Includes bibliographical references

Stewart, Ian, 1945-

Why beauty is truth; a history of symmetry. Basic Books 2007 290p il $26.95   **539.7**

1. Symmetry
ISBN 978-0-465-08236-0; 0-465-08236-X
LC 2006-38274

"Beginning with the early struggles of the Babylonians to solve quadratics, Stewart guides his readers through the often-tangled history of symmetry, illuminating for nonspecialists how a concept easily recognized in geometry acquired new meanings in algebra. . . . An exciting foray for any armchair physicist!" Booklist

Includes bibliographical references

540   Chemistry

Cobb, Cathy

The joy of chemistry; the amazing science of familiar things; [by] Cathy Cobb & Monty L. Fetterolf. Prometheus Books 2005 393p il $26

540

1. Chemistry
ISBN 1-591-02231-2   LC 2004-20144

The authors cover "the material of a general chemistry course along with organic, inorganic and analytical chemistry and biochemistry; there's even a chapter on forensic chemistry. . . . They explain everything from flatulence (the chemical composition of intestinal gas) to pizza cheese (why mozzarella rather than, say, parmesan?)." Publ Wkly

Includes bibliographical references

CRC handbook of chemistry and physics; a ready-reference book of chemical and physical data. 88th ed. CRC Press 2007 $139.95

540

1. Chemistry—Tables 2. Physics—Tables
ISBN 0-8493-0488-1; 978-0-8493-0488-0

Also available CD-ROM version and online

First published 1913. Periodically revised

A "reference book containing much-used information on mathematics, chemistry, and physics, including tables, physical constants of chemical elements and compounds, definitions, formulae, etc." AAAS Sci Book List for Young Adults

Includes bibliographical references

Lange's handbook of chemistry. 16th ed. McGraw-Hill 2005 various paging il $150 *

540

1. Chemistry—Tables
ISBN 0-07-143220-5; 978-0-07-143220-7

First published 1934. Periodically revised

Lange's handbook of chemistry—*Continued*
Originally compiled and edited by Norbert Adolph Lange. Editors vary

"A standard reference source for both students and professional chemists. Sections for: organic compounds; general information, conversion tables, and mathematics; inorganic chemistry; properties of atoms, radicals, and bonds; physical properties; thermodynamic properties; spectroscopy; electrolytes, electromotive force, and chemical equilibrium; physiochemical relationships; polymers, rubbers, fats, oils, and waxes; and practical laboratory information." Guide to Ref Books. 11th edition

Le Couteur, Penny, 1943-
Napoleon's buttons; how 17 molecules changed history; {by} Penny Le Couteur, Jay Burreson. Jeremy P. Tarcher/Penguin Books 2003 375p il hardcover o.p. pa $14.95   **540**
1. Chemistry
ISBN 1-58542-220-7; 1-58542-331-9 (pa)
LC 2002-032247
The authors "explore how chemical properties of compounds have altered history. The impacts run the gamut from medicine (e.g., penicillin, vitamin C) to social change (e.g., the contraceptive pill and slavery perpetuated by the farming of glucose, or sugar cane, and cellulose, or cotton) to more direct historical incidents such as the Opium Wars or the spice trade spurring New World exploration." Libr J
"Napoleon's Buttons is a fascinating attempt at recognizing the role of chemistry in the wider world. With its many structural diagrams, the book can resemble a course in organic chemistry, but the chemist-authors are good guides. . . . The best chapter is the one on dyes." Quill & Quire
Includes bibliographical references

540.3   Chemistry—Encyclopedias and dictionaries

Rittner, Don
Encyclopedia of chemistry; [by] Don Rittner and Ronald A. Bailey. Facts on File 2005 342p il (Facts on File science library) $75 *
540.3
1. Chemistry—Encyclopedias
ISBN 0-8160-4894-0   LC 2004-11242
This encyclopedia "offers more than 2000 articles on topics from ABO blood groups to zwitterionic compound." SLJ
For a fuller review, see: Booklist, Dec. 1, 2005
Includes bibliographical references

540.9   Chemistry—Historical and geographic treatment

Cobb, Cathy
Creations of fire; chemistry's lively history from alchemy to the atomic age; [by] Cathy Cobb and Harold Goldwhite. Perseus Pub. 2001 475p il pa $20.95   **540.9**
1. Chemistry—History
ISBN 0-7382-0594-X; 978-0-7382-0594-6
LC 2001-99001
First published 1995 by Plenum Press
This history "begins with chemistry in the Stone Age and ends with current areas of interest such as superheavy elements and the polymerase chain reaction. Along the way, the coverage includes alchemy, cold fusion, and . . . topics like the contributions of Lise Meitner and Marie Lavoisier. . . . This book's light and often humorous style makes it especially appealing to the general reader." Libr J
Includes bibliographical references

Greenberg, Arthur
The art of chemistry; myths, medicines, and materials. Wiley 2003 357p $59.95   **540.9**
1. Chemistry—History 2. Alchemy 3. Medicine—History
ISBN 0-471-07180-3   LC 2002-9950
This book "tracks chemistry's incremental progress from myth to modern science, featuring the figures and diagrams that early chemists used to explain their craft." Publisher's note
"A very interesting mix of information. Although it is not something that a reader would sit down and read through in one sitting, each of the eight sections was interesting by itself." Sci Books Films
Includes bibliographical references

From alchemy to chemistry in picture and story. Wiley-Interscience 2007 xxiii, 637p il $69.95
540.9
1. Chemistry—History
ISBN 978-0-471-75154-0; 0-471-75154-5
LC 2006-33564
According to the author, this "is a combination of his two previous books, A Chemical History Tour and The Art of Chemistry, with some additions and revisions. . . . One could open the book at almost any page to learn something about the remarkable history of the chemical sciences." Sci Books Films
Includes bibliographical references

541   Physical chemistry

Atkins, Peter William, 1940-
The periodic kingdom; a journey into the land of the chemical elements. Basic Bks. 1995 161p il (Science masters series) pa $14 hardcover o.p.
541
1. Chemical elements 2. Periodic law
ISBN 0-465-07266-6 (pa)   LC 95-7362

Atkins, Peter William, 1940-—_Continued_

"Depicting the periodic table of elements as a map, Atkins explores the territories that it represents, from metallic 'deserts' to the hydrogen 'island.' Basic chemistry has never been presented in a more creative and readily comprehensible manner." Libr J

Includes bibliographical references

Ball, Philip, 1962-

Stories of the invisible; a guided tour of molecules. Oxford Univ. Press 2001 204p il hardcover o.p. pa $14.95   **541**

1. Molecules 2. Chemistry

ISBN 0-19-280214-3; 0-19-280317-4 (pa)

LC 2001-36601

This "outlines the advances in the molecular sciences from the discovery of molecules to the present-day widespread use of chemical compounds and chemical processes. . . . This volume presents topics that are exact, instructive, and interesting while providing a unique insight into the molecular nature of living systems." Sci Books Films

Includes bibliographical references

546   Inorganic chemistry

Bernstein, Jeremy, 1929-

Plutonium; a history of the world's most dangerous element. National Academies Press 2007 194p il map $27.95   **546**

1. Plutonium

ISBN 978-0-309-10296-4; 0-309-10296-0

LC 2006-38466

This book "relates the 'life story' of the chemical element plutonium." Sci Books Films

"Bernstein's book should play a useful role by helping to demystify plutonium and by encouraging interested members of the public and Congress to start constructing a more rational policy to deal with the dangers posed by this manmade element." Am Sci

Includes bibliographical references

Rigden, John S.

Hydrogen; the essential element. Harvard Univ. Press 2002 280p il $28; pa $15.95   **546**

1. Hydrogen 2. Science—History

ISBN 0-674-00738-7; 0-674-01252-6 (pa)

LC 2001-51708

The author chronicles "how one enduring conundrum—that of explaining the element hydrogen—has challenged two centuries of brilliant scientists. . . . In the process, he clarifies for general readers the nature of the scientific enterprise, in which elegant theories must meet the test of empirical verification." Booklist

Includes bibliographical references

548   Crystallography

Holden, Alan

Crystals and crystal growing; [by] Alan Holden and Phylis Morrison; introduction by Philip Morrison. MIT Press 1982 318p il pa $19.95   **548**

1. Crystals

ISBN 0-262-58050-0   LC 81-23639

First published 1960 by Anchor Bks.

This book "sets for itself three major goals: 1. Describing the atomistic character of crystallinity; 2. Describing some techniques for preparing large single crystals; and 3. Describing some experiments that display the unexpected properties which flow from crystallinity." Preface

"An excellent introduction to crystallography (and, incidentally, to much basic physics) written in plain language." Libr J

549   Mineralogy

Chesterman, Charles W.

The Audubon Society field guide to North American rocks and minerals; scientific consultant, Kurt E. Lowe. Knopf 1979 c1978 850p il $19.95 *   **549**

1. Minerals 2. Rocks

ISBN 0-394-50269-8   LC 78-54893

"Pocket guide providing color photos and descriptions of some 232 mineral species and forty types of rocks. Includes guide to mineral environments, glossary, bibliography, and indexes by name and locality." Ref Sources for Small & Medium-sized Libr. 5th edition

Johnsen, Ole

Minerals of the world. Princeton Univ. Press 2002 439p il (Princeton field guides) pa $24.95   **549**

1. Minerals 2. Crystals

ISBN 0-691-09537-X   LC 2001-97695

Originally published in hardcover with title: Photographic guide to minerals of the world

The author "provides descriptive information for the identification of more than 500 minerals. . . . This book follows the standard mineralogy textbook approach in which the mineral sections are arranged according to mineral composition and structure. . . . The book's suitability as a field guide is completed by the addition of hundreds of excellent color photographs and drawings. . . . The content material is solid, and superb illustrations on high-quality paper make for an attractive volume." Choice

Pellant, Chris

Rocks and minerals; Helen Pellant, editorial consultant; photography by Harry Taylor. 2nd American ed. Dorling Kindersley 2002 256p il (Smithsonian handbooks) pa $20   **549**

1. Rocks 2. Minerals

ISBN 0-7894-9106-0; 978-0-7894-9106-0

First published 1992 as part of the Eyewitness handbooks series

Pellant, Chris—*Continued*

This field guide to identification of rocks and minerals includes techniques for collection and classification, and facts about physical and chemical composition and formation.

Pough, Frederick H., 1906-2006

A field guide to rocks and minerals; photographs by Jeff Scovil. 5th ed. Houghton Mifflin 1996 396p il hardcover o.p. pa $20 *
549

1. Minerals 2. Rocks
ISBN 0-395-72778-2; 0-395-91096-X (pa)
LC 94-49005
"The Peterson field guide series"
First published 1953
"Sponsored by the National Audubon Society, the National Wildlife Federation, and the Roger Tory Peterson Institute"
This illustrated guide utilizes traditional identification methods and includes discussions of crystallography, mineralogy and home laboratory techniques.
Includes bibliographical references

Simon and Schuster's guide to rocks and minerals; edited by Martin Prinz, George Harlow, and Joseph Peters. Simon & Schuster 1978 607p il pa $17 hardcover o.p. 549

1. Minerals 2. Rocks
ISBN 0-671-24417-5 (pa)
LC 78-8610
Original Italian edition, 1977
"Half of this book consists of color plates; the other half is an authoritative text which describes the elements of mineralogy and petrology. Crystal system or family, physical and chemical properties, occurrence, uses, and rarity are included for each species." Libr J

550 Earth sciences & geology

Earth; editor-in-chief, James F. Luhr. DK Pub. 2003 520p il map $50 * 550

1. Earth
ISBN 0-7894-9643-7
LC 2003-51573
At head of title: Smithsonian Institution
This guide to Earth's physical dynamics is "divided into five major sections—Planet Earth, Land, Ocean, Atmosphere and Tectonic Earth—the book explores the planet's environment, weather systems and general physical makeup." Publ Wkly
"The writing is clear, animated, and engrossing. . . . This superb and stunning volume should be kept handy along with atlases and dictionaries." Booklist

Morton, R. L. (Ronald Lee)

Music of the earth; volcanoes, earthquakes, and other geological wonders; [by] Ron L. Morton. Perseus Pub. 2002 312p il pa $26 550

1. Earth sciences
ISBN 978-0-7382-0870-1; 0-7382-0870-1
First published 1996 by Plenum Press
"Using music as an overall metaphor for the various geologic processes described, Morton . . . [discusses]

tectonics, volcanoes, earthquakes, mass wasting, thermal waters, ore deposits, glaciers, coastal processes, deserts, and mass extinctions." Choice
"An entertaining and readable account of the earth that is full of humor and anecdotes." Sci Books Films
Includes bibliographical references

550.3 Earth sciences— Encyclopedias and dictionaries

The **Facts** on File dictionary of earth science. Rev. ed., edited by Jacqueline Smith. Facts on File 2006 388p il map $55 * 550.3

1. Earth sciences—Dictionaries
ISBN 0-8160-6000-2
LC 2006-42340
First published 1976 in the United Kingdom with title: A dictionary of earth sciences.
In this reference work more than 3700 "cross-referenced entries . . . cover all aspects of Earth science: geomorphology, stratigraphy, mineralogy, petrology, climatology, oceanography, paleontology, hydrology, geophysics, cartography, surveying, and soil science. Key concepts in physics, chemistry, biology, and mathematics are also defined." Publisher's note
Includes bibliographical references

Kusky, Timothy M.

Encyclopedia of earth science; [by] Timothy Kusky. Facts on File 2005 510p il map (Facts on File science library) $75 550.3

1. Earth sciences—Encyclopedias
ISBN 0-8160-4973-4
LC 2004-4389
This encyclopedia covers "earth science subdisciplines (hydrology, oceanography, and so on) as well as concepts, theories and hypotheses, places, events, geological time periods, history, technology, and key individuals." Booklist
"Kusky's encyclopedia will appeal to a broad audience, from high school students to researchers." Choice
Includes bibliographical references

551 Geology, hydrology, meteorology

Interdisciplinary encyclopedia of marine sciences; edited by James W. Nybakken, William W. Broenkow, Tracy L. Vallier. Grolier 2002 3v set $349 551

1. Marine sciences—Encyclopedias 2. Oceanography
ISBN 0-7172-5946-3
LC 2002-192707
"More than 800 alphabetical enries vary in length from 250 to 2500 words and discuss topics ranging from 'Abyssal Gigantism' to 'Zooxanthellae'. The . . . articles cover the subdiscipline of oceanography (biological, chemical, geological, and physical) in addition to economics, marine life, and ecology of the oceans. Technologies used to explore this environment and biographies of important individuals are also included. Each accessible, signed entry concludes with a list of related articles and suggestions for further reading that will be useful for students." SLJ
Includes bibliographical references

Kovach, Robert L. (Robert Louis)

Firefly guide to global hazards; {by} Robert Kovach and Bill McGuire. Firefly Books 2004 256p il pa $14.95 *   **551**

1. Natural disasters

ISBN 1-55297-815-X   LC 2004-300692

An illustrated guide to the many large-scale natural disasters that affect life on Earth, both globally and locally

This title "includes hazards not always easily found in resources: droughts, landslides, avalanches, extinctions, and diseases, to name a few. Various aspects of pollution are included so that students may see what humans are doing to the environment." SLJ

Lamb, Simon

Devil in the mountain; a search for the origin of the Andes. Princeton University Press 2004 335p il $29.95   **551**

1. Andes

ISBN 0-691-11596-6   LC 2003-64124

"Since 1989 {Lamb} and his coworkers have driven 100,000 miles inspecting the mountains, mostly in Bolivia, home to the highest peaks. . . . In 'Devil in the Mountain,' he describes some of these trips and his research." N Y Times Book Rev

The author gives "a clear, solid lecture on geological theory and practice with a few personal snapshots of the unseen hazards of fieldwork and occasional local color. . . . Those interested in geology will find it informative and its conclusion satisfying." Publ Wkly

Includes bibliographical references

Lambert, David, 1932-

The field guide to geology; [by] David Lambert and the Diagram Group. New ed. Checkmark Books 2006 304p il map $39.95; pa $16.95

          551

1. Geology

ISBN   0-8160-6509-8;   978-0-8160-6509-7; 0-8160-6510-1 (pa); 978-0-8160-6510-3 (pa)

          LC 2006-48533

First published 1988

This is an "overview of the processes that forged the planet and the technologies that have revolutionized the way that scientists investigate Earth's systems." Publisher's note

Includes bibliographical references

Newton, David E.

Encyclopedia of air. Greenwood Press 2003 252p il $79.95   **551**

1. Air 2. Meteorology

ISBN 1-57356-564-4   LC 2003-44076

"An Oryx book"

"Entries discuss the science of air (biology, chemistry, meteorology, physics), its technology (air bag, airbrush, air conditioner), and even its social, mythological, and cultural aspects. Newton also includes biographical entries and descriptions of related organizations and associations." Choice

Includes bibliographical references

Oldroyd, D. R. (David Roger)

Thinking about the earth; a history of ideas in geology. Harvard Univ. Press 1996 xxx, 410p il maps (Studies in the history and philosophy of the earth sciences) $55.50   **551**

1. Geology

ISBN 0-674-88382-9   LC 95-48234

"Oldroyd surveys Greek and Islamic philosophers on stones, seventeenth-century theologians on the origins of the world, Enlightenment philosophers on the workings of the earth machine, . . . {and modern} ideas about plate tectonics and the chemical formation of life." Times Lit Suppl

"The sections on mountain-building, seismology, and, especially, the Gaia hypothesis . . . are new to the history of geology. Because of this book, these subjects will now be added to the standard lists of topics that are required reading for the 'complete' geologist." Choice

Includes bibliographical references

551.2   Volcanoes, earthquakes, thermal waters and gases

Calderazzo, John

Rising fire: volcanoes and our inner lives. Lyons Press 2004 268p $22.95   **551.2**

1. Volcanoes

ISBN 1-59228-389-6

"Calderazzo climbs volcanoes, presents dramatic accounts of major eruptions, portrays people who live within a volcano's reach, and muses on the impact volcanoes have had on humankind's sense of the sacred." Booklist

Carson, Rob, 1950-

Mount St. Helens: the eruption and recovery of a volcano; with selected photographs by Geff Hinds, Cheryl Haselhorst and Gary Braasch. Sasquatch Bks. 1990 160p il pa $19.95 hardcover o.p.   **551.2**

1. Mount Saint Helens (Wash.)

ISBN 1-57061-248-X (pa)   LC 90-31009

The author "describes the eruption of Mount St. Helens in 1980, and goes on to report what has happened in the devastated area since then. . . . Mr. Carson has a lively story to tell and does it well. The photographs . . . provide beauty as well as information." Atl Mon

Feldman, Jay

When the Mississippi ran backwards; empire, intrigue, murder, and the new Madrid earthquakes. Free Press 2005 307p il maps $27 *

          551.2

1. Earthquakes—United States 2. Mississippi River valley

ISBN 0-7432-4278-5   LC 2004-57537

"Through four historical figures, Feldman recreates the frontier world of 1811-12, when the New Madrid earthquakes devastated the lower Ohio and mid-Mississippi valleys. . . . Synthesizing lives and times, Feldman composes a fluent, coherent narrative that culminates in the War of 1812." Booklist

Includes bibliographical references

Gates, Alexander E.

Encyclopedia of earthquakes and volcanoes; [by] Alexander E. Gates, PH.D and David Ritchie. 3rd ed. Facts on File 2007 346p il map (Facts on File science library) $75 * **551.2**

1. Earthquakes—Encyclopedias 2. Volcanoes—Encyclopedias

ISBN 0-8160-6302-8   LC 2005-46619

First published 1994

"The book's entries cover information on key environmental issues, economic dilemmas, ethical concerns, advances in research and technology, organizations, and individuals who have left their mark on the fields of volcanology and seismology." Publisher's note

Includes bibliographical references

Thompson, Dick

Volcano cowboys; the rocky evolution of a dangerous science. St. Martin's Press 2000 326p il map $26.95; pa $14.95 **551.2**

1. Volcanoes

ISBN 0-312-20881-2; 0-312-28668-6 (pa)

LC 00-26158

This describes the work of U.S. Geological Survey scientists in predicting volcanic eruptions, focusing on the eruptions of Mount St. Helens in 1980 and Mount Pinatubo in 1991

"An informative book about science's communication with the lay public." Booklist

Includes bibliographical references

Winchester, Simon

Krakatoa: the day the world exploded, August 27, 1883. HarperCollins Pubs. 2003 416p il maps $25.95; pa $13.95 **551.2**

1. Volcanoes

ISBN 0-06-621285-5; 0-06-083859-0 (pa)

"This book chronicles the underlying causes, utter devastation and lasting effects of the cataclysmic 1883 eruption of the volcano island Krakatoa in what is now Indonesia. . . . [The author] demonstrates a keen knack for balancing rich and often rigorous historical detail with dramatic tension and storytelling." Publ Wkly

"As a rich blend of science and history, this book is highly recommended for most public and academic libraries." Libr J

551.3   Surface and exogenous processes and their agents

Fredston, Jill A.

Snowstruck; in the grip of avalanches; [by] Jill Fredston. Harcourt 2005 342p il $24; pa $14 **551.3**

1. Avalanches 2. Survival skills

ISBN   978-0-15-101249-7;   0-15-101249-0; 978-0-15-603254-4 (pa); 0-15-603254-6 (pa)

LC 2005-20454

"As avalanche experts, . . . [the author and her husband] are often called upon to forecast, trigger, and teach about avalanches as well as rescue survivors—or, sadly,

more often to recover remains. Fredston's decades of experience distilled into this instructive and personal narrative will leave readers with a newfound appreciation for the force, the fury, and the cold sorrow of avalanches." Libr J

Gosnell, Mariana

Ice; the nature, the history, and the uses of an astonishing substance. Knopf 2005 560p il $30 **551.3**

1. Ice

ISBN 0-679-42608-6   LC 2005-45126

The author "opens with a description of the sound and sight of a small lake freezing, expanding from there to discuss the seasonal advance and retreat of ice, as on the Great Lakes or Lake Baikal. Taking the next natural step, the persistence of ice through the summer, brings Gosnell to the 1800s origin of glaciology in Louis Agassiz's study of Mont Blanc's Mer de Glace, and subsequently into the contemporary specialty of ice cores in ice-age research. En route through the science, which Gosnell condenses from the technical literature, the author imparts eclectic information through excerpts from poems, adventure and disaster stories, and discussions of ice sports and diversions." Booklist

551.46   Hydrosphere and submarine geology. Oceanography

Ballard, Robert D., 1942-

The eternal darkness; a personal history of deep-sea exploration; [by] Robert D. Ballard with Will Hively. Princeton Univ. Press 2000 388p il maps $55; pa $18.95 **551.46**

1. Underwater exploration

ISBN 0-691-02740-4; 0-691-09554-X (pa)

LC 99-43072

Ballard "blends his personal experiences exploring hydrothermal vents and shipwrecks with stories of earlier deep-sea pioneers, focusing especially on the technology. . . . Ballard's volume is easy to read and will be an excellent addition to collections at all levels on oceanography, history of science, and exploration." Libr J

Includes bibliographical references

Broad, William, 1951-

The universe below; discovering the secrets of the deep sea; {by} William J. Broad; illustrations by Dimitry Schidlovsky. Simon & Schuster 1997 432p il maps pa $15 hardcover o.p.

551.46

1. Oceanography 2. Underwater exploration

ISBN 0-684-83852-4 (pa)   LC 96-50337

This work focuses "on the ships, subs, divers, underwater vehicles both manned and robotic, and satellites used in a variety of applications, from discovering the *Titanic* to observing unusual or new marine species." Libr J

"Intensively researched and crisply told, this is an illuminating, stimulating portrait of one of Earth's last frontiers." Publ Wkly

Includes bibliographical references

Carson, Rachel, 1907-1964
The sea around us. Oxford Univ. Press 2003
274p il maps $45   **551.46**
1. Ocean
ISBN 0-19-514701-4   LC 2002-29299
This is a reissue of the title first published 1951
Beginning with a description of how the earth acquired its oceans, the book covers such topics as how
life began in the primeval sea, the hidden lands, the life
discovered in the abyss by highly delicate sounding apparatus, currents and tides, the formation of volcanic islands, and mineral resources

Day, Trevor, 1955-
Oceans; illustrations by Richard Garratt. Rev ed.
Facts on File 2008 318p il map (Ecosystem) $70
                                                   551.46
1. Ocean 2. Oceanography
ISBN 0-8160-5932-2; 978-0-8160-5932-4
                                         LC 2006-100769
First published 1999
This volume describes the oceans of the world with
regard to their geography, geology, history, chemistry,
biology, ecology, exploration, relationship to the atmo-
sphere, economic resources, and management.
Includes glossary and bibliographical references

Ellis, Richard, 1938-
Encyclopedia of the sea; written and illustrated
by Richard Ellis. Knopf 2000 380p il $35 *
                                                   551.46
1. Oceanography—Encyclopedias
ISBN 0-375-40374-4   LC 99-42401
"The alphabetically arranged text consists of short
paragraphs on topics in marine biology, oceanography,
fisheries, geography, and maritime and naval history.
. . . Eight pages of Ellis's color paintings . . . and hundreds of his own illustrations enhance the text. . . . The
handy format makes the book useful as a ready-reference
source for public and college libraries." Libr J

Kunzig, Robert
The restless sea; exploring the world beneath
the waves. Norton 1999 336p il maps $24.95
                                                   551.46
1. Ocean
ISBN 0-393-04562-5   LC 98-38704
Published in the United Kingdom with title: Mapping
the deep
The author "chronicles the history of oceans from the
Big Bang to the present. Although some of the material
Kunzig sets down as fact is still hotly debated, his writ-
ing is clear and easy to understand. His descriptions of
the ocean are visual, almost poetic." Libr J

Matsen, Bradford
Descent; the heroic discovery of the abyss.
Pantheon Books 2005 286p il $25   **551.46**
1. Beebe, William, 1877-1962 2. Barton, Otis
3. Underwater exploration
ISBN 0-375-42258-7   LC 2004-53530

The author "depicts the story of William Beebe and
Otis Barton and their quest to explore the deep ocean.
. . . Matsen presents an exciting tale of discovery
weaved alongside a complex web of human relations."
Sci Books Films
Includes bibliographical references

McCutcheon, Scott
The Facts on File marine science handbook;
{by} Scott McCutcheon and Bobbi McCutcheon.
Facts on File 2003 266p il maps (The Facts on
File science and math handbooks) $35; pa $17.95
                                                   551.46
1. Marine sciences
ISBN 0-8160-4812-6; 0-8160-4883-5 (pa)
                                           LC 2003-275
This volume "covers everything having to do with the
sea, including navigation, exploration, weather, geology,
and creatures." Booklist
"The information given in the entries is for the most
part general in nature and not too full of scientific jargon, which makes it easy to understand . . . The charts
and tables area is quite interesting and useful with its
miscellaneous information about ocean currents, size of
the oceans, fish catches, and so on." Am Ref Books
Annu, 2004
Includes bibliographical references

Smith, Craig B.
Extreme waves; illustrations by Kurt Mueller.
Joseph Henry 2006 xx, 291p il map $27.95
                                                   551.46
1. Ocean waves
ISBN 0-309-10062-3; 978-0-309-10062-5
                                         LC 2006-19554
This title discusses "damaging waves and their effects
on shipping and coastlines." Sci Books Films
"Written in an engaging format, the chapters are filled
with documented real-world incidents that should con-
vince readers of the power, immensity, and still unre-
vealed mysteries of the world's oceans." Choice
Includes bibliographical references

Stow, Dorrik A. V.
Oceans: an illustrated reference; [by] Dorrik
Stow. University of Chicago Press 2006 c2005
256p il map $55 *   **551.46**
1. Oceanography 2. Ocean 3. Marine biology
ISBN 0-226-77664-6   LC 2004-55333
"An Andromeda book"
This "reference work presents a thorough overview of
the physical, geological, chemical, and biological properties of the world's oceans. . . . [The author's] up-to-date
and well-organized volume would make a valuable introduction to a huge field of knowledge." Libr J
Includes bibliographical references

551.5 Meteorology

551.51 Composition, regions, dynamics of atmosphere

Buckley, Bruce
Weather: a visual guide; [by] Bruce Buckley, Edward J. Hopkins [and] Richard Whitaker. Firefly Books 2004 303p il maps $29.95; pa $27.95 *
551.5
1. Weather 2. Meteorology
ISBN   1-55297-957-1;   978-1-55297-957-0;
1-55407-430-4 (pa); 978-1-55407-430-3 (pa)
LC 2004-303909
The authors "set the local and seasonal conditions that every person experiences within the context of the global forces that generate weather. Each force, such as giant atmospheric convection cells, is illustrated with a combination of a diagram, satellite photographs, ground-level photographs (often depicting the destruction wrought by violent storms), and . . . captions." Booklist
This is "a comprehensive academic resource with information and glorious color photographs on virtually every aspect of weather." SLJ

Encyclopedia of atmospheric sciences; editor-in-chief, James R. Holton; editors, Judith A. Curry, John A. Pyle. Academic Press 2003 6v il set $1,400   1. Atmosphere   **551.5**
ISBN 0-12-227090-8   LC 2002-114120
This reference set "includes the work of 400 scientists worldwide. The 330 authoritative and concise articles review such complex subjects as weather prediction, climate change and variability, and atmospheric chemistry. Beautifully illustrated with maps, charts, photos and illustrations." Libr J
Includes bibliographical references

Walker, Gabrielle
An ocean of air; why the wind blows and other mysteries of the atmosphere. Harcourt 2007 272p il map $25   **551.5**
1. Atmosphere
ISBN 978-0-15-101124-7; 0-15-101124-9
LC 2006-32359
Walker sets out "to unite stories of human research into air pressure, the gases that make up air, the movement of the wind, the ozone layer, ionosphere and outer space, in a history of our atmospheric discovery." New Statesman (Engl)
The author "brings a new perspective to centuries-old stories of wonder and discovery and sheds light on the personalities of the 19th and 20th centuries who have also contributed to the world's body of knowledge. Witty and full of fascinating information, this is a captivating book." Libr J
Includes bibliographical references

Bowen, Mark
Thin ice; unlocking the secrets of climate in the world's highest mountains. Henry Holt 2005 463p il $30; pa $17   **551.51**
1. Upper atmosphere 2. Climate—Research
ISBN 0-8050-6443-5; 0-8050-8135-6 (pa)
LC 2005-40426
"A John Macrae book"
The author "documents the specialized techniques that Thompson used to extract and preserve ice cores from the highest mountains around the world's equator while also examining Thompson's research, which is based on the provocative premise that equatorial mountain glaciers, rather than polar ice, provide the clues to understanding global warming." Libr J
"This book will appeal to mountaineering and climatology buffs, but should be read by everyone concerned about the future of our planet." Publ Wkly

De Villiers, Marq
Windswept; the story of wind and weather. Walker & Co. 2006 344p il $25   **551.51**
1. Winds 2. Weather
ISBN 0-8027-1469-2   LC 2005-23115
This "is the story of humankind's long struggle to understand wind and weather—from the wind gods of ancient times to early discoveries of the dynamics of air movement to high-tech schemes to control hurricanes." Publ Wkly
The author "explains the science clearly, and he describes the workings of wind, weather and the natural world with enormous gusto. He is a greedy observer, with plenty of wind and storms to watch from his seaside home in Eagle Head, Nova Scotia. Simply as a catalog of statistics, [the book] is a grabber." N Y Times (Late N Y Ed)

DeBlieu, Jan
Wind; how the flow of air has shaped life, myth, and the land. Houghton Mifflin 1998 294p $24; pa $14   **551.51**
1. Winds
ISBN 0-395-78033-0; 0-395-95794-X (pa)
LC 98-16851
The author discusses "ancient myths that attest to the enormous influence wind has had on our cosmologies, and lucidly explains the physics of wind. One facet of this wide-ranging discussion involves how wind determines the distribution of moisture on the planet, thus playing an integral role in the rise and fall of civilizations. . . . This is nature writing at its most expansive and rewarding." Booklist
Includes bibliographical references

551.55 Atmospheric disturbances and formations

Davies, Pete, 1959-
Inside the hurricane; face to face with nature's deadliest storms. Holt & Co. 2000 264p pa $14 hardcover o.p.   **551.55**
1. Hurricanes
ISBN 0-8050-6611-X (pa)   LC 00-29562
The author "surveys the 1999 Atlantic hurricane season, focusing on the experiences of a small group of hurricane researchers and forecasters. . . . Vivid and engrossing; recommended for both public and academic libraries." Libr J
Includes bibliographical references

Emanuel, Kerry A., 1955-
Divine wind; the history and science of hurricanes; [by] Kerry Emanuel. Oxford Univ. Press 2005 285p il $45 *   **551.55**
1. Hurricanes
ISBN 0-19-514941-6   LC 2004-13078
This is a study of hurricanes.
"A gripping popular treatment of peril, that will have great resonance in light of recent disasters." Booklist
Includes bibliographical references

Longshore, David
Encyclopedia of hurricanes, typhoons, and cyclones. New ed. Facts on File 2008 468p il map (Facts on File science library) $75   **551.55**
1. Hurricanes—Encyclopedias 2. Typhoons—Encyclopedias 3. Cyclones—Encyclopedias
ISBN 978-0-8160-6295-9; 0-8160-6295-1
                            LC 2007-32336
First published 1998
This encyclopedia describes named hurricanes, typhoons and cyclones, explains meteorological terms and instruments, and includes biographical data, a chronology, and a list of hurricane safety procedures.
"This is an excellent basic reference work that belongs in all school, public, and academic libraries." Sci Books Films
Includes bibliographical references

551.57 Hydrometeorology

Hamblyn, Richard, 1965-
The invention of clouds; how an amateur meteorologist forged the language of the skies. Picador 2002 292p il pa $15   **551.57**
1. Howard, Luke, 1772-1864   2. Clouds 3. Meteorology
ISBN 0-312-42001-3; 978-0-312-42001-7
                            LC 2002-25152
First published 2001 by Farrar, Straus and Giroux
This is a study of Luke Howard, an unknown amateur scientist who in 1802 "gave a lecture in which he named and defined the different types of clouds-cirrus, cumulus,

stratus and their various hybrid forms. . . . [His taxonomy] gave scientists a standardised way to record and compare observations and begin to form theories." Economist
"A remarkable, remarkably pleasing story." Booklist
Includes bibliographical references

Mergen, Bernard
Snow in America. Smithsonian Institution Press 1997 xxi, 321p il $24.95; pa $16.95
                            551.57
1. Snow
ISBN 1-56098-780-4; 1-56098-381-7 (pa)
                            LC 97-12247
This study traces the development of snow technology, explains the importance of snow surveys for climate regulation, and looks at the ski industry, water usage, winter fashions and street cleaning. The author also explores snow in popular culture and its role in the emotional development of the American character
Includes bibliographical references

551.6 Climatology and weather

Allaby, Michael, 1933-
The Facts on File weather and climate handbook. Facts on File 2002 290p il (Facts on File science library) $35; pa $17.95 *
                            551.6
1. Climate 2. Weather
ISBN 0-8160-4517-8; 0-8160-4961-0 (pa)
                            LC 2001-50114
This book covers weather-related issues such as "Area forecast; Bioclimatology; Dust bowl; Greenhouse gas; La Niña; Severe-storm observation {and} Veil of cloud." Publisher's note
"This work is a comprehensive, handy reference tool for weather and climate. The glossary is especially comprehensive . . . {and} is recommended for all reference collections." Am Ref Books Annu, 2003
Includes bibliographical references

Collier, Michael, 1950-
Floods, droughts, and climate change; [by] Michael Collier and Robert H. Webb. University of Arizona Press 2002 153p il map pa $17.95
                            551.6
1. Climate
ISBN 0-8165-2250-2   LC 2002-5314
The authors suggest "that floods and droughts don't always signal climate change. Instead, climatology looks at weather over the long term, and individual weather events are part of the natural process of the earth's redistributing the energy it receives from the sun. Moreover, climate change is also a natural phenomenon and not necessarily caused by humans." Libr J
"Packed with illustrations and balanced between general and specific information, Collier and Webb's work superbly outlines and makes accessible a subject that is complex even for experts in the field." Booklist
Includes bibliographical references

Cox, John D., 1945-
Climate crash; abrupt climate change and what it means for our future. Joseph Henry Press 2005 215p il maps $27.95 **551.6**
1. Climate—Environmental aspects
ISBN 0-309-09312-0   LC 2005-2387
"The author stresses the speed with which climate has changed in the past 100,000 years and the potential for climate to change radically over a span of decades or even less. . . . I recommend Climate Crash highly as an introduction to one of the most exciting developing sciences of the present time." Sci Books Films
Includes bibliographical references

Dow, Kirstin, 1963-
The atlas of climate change; mapping the world's greatest challenge; [by] Kirstin Dow and Thomas E. Downing. University of California Press 2006 112p il map pa $19.95 **551.6**
1. Climate—Environmental aspects—Maps
ISBN 978-0-52025-023-9; 0-52025-023-0
                         LC 2006-50098
This atlas "examines the signs of climate change—glacial and polar melting, rising sea levels, erratic weather patterns—and explains how global warming is being driven by the emission of greenhouse gases. It looks at the serious implications of these changes for food and water supplies, human health, sensitive ecologies, vulnerable cities, and cultural treasures—especially in those countries lacking the resources to adapt." Publisher's note
Includes bibliographical references

Fagan, Brian M., 1936-
The long summer: how climate changed civilization. Basic Books 2003 284p il hardcover o.p. pa $16 **551.6**
1. Climate 2. Civilization—History
ISBN 0-465-02281-2; 0-465-02282-0 (pa)
                         LC 2003-13917
Fagan discusses global climate change and its relation to human society. He "argues that as humans have organized themselves in increasingly complex ways, their susceptibility to large-scale devastation wrought by climate change has also risen. Ice Age hunter-gatherers were vulnerable to the vagaries of their harsh world, but they had a 'flexibility, mobility, and opportunism' that allowed them to move on if their immediate environment became too difficult. As people formed villages, cities, and empires, they became rooted to environments that inevitably changed." Archaeology
"This book is highly recommended for general audiences considering the implications and the challenges posed by human-induced global climate change." Sci Books Films
Includes bibliographical references

Linden, Eugene
The winds of change; climate, weather, and the destruction of civilizations. Simon & Schuster 2006 302p il map $26 **551.6**
1. Climate 2. Weather 3. Social change
ISBN 0-684-86352-9; 978-0-684-86352-8
                         LC 2005-54434

The author argues that there is "a recurring pattern in which civilizations become prosperous and complacent during good weather, only to collapse when climate changes—either through its direct effects, such as floods or drought, or indirect consequences, such as disease, blight, and civil disorder." Publisher's note
"Relatively restrained in tone, and consequently more persuasive by its sobriety, Linden's presentation of scientists' theories on historical climate change will provoke readers concerned about the implications of global warming for modern civilization." Booklist

Ludlum, David M., 1910-1997
The Audubon Society field guide to North American weather. Knopf 1991 656p il maps $19.95 **551.6**
1. Weather forecasting
ISBN 0-679-40851-7   LC 91-52707
"A Chanticleer Press edition"
"The opening essays provide in-depth information on topics such as clouds, snowstorms, floods, etc. About half of the book is comprised of labelled, high-quality photographs. The third section gives description, environment, season, range, and significance of each type of weather. Clear diagrams, simple definitions, and a readable text make this an excellent selection." SLJ

Lynas, Mark, 1973-
Six degrees; our future on a hotter planet. National Geographic 2008 335p $26 * **551.6**
1. Greenhouse effect 2. Environmental influence on humans 3. Climate—Environmental aspects
ISBN 978-1-4262-0213-1   LC 2007-30864
First published 2007 in the United Kingdom
"In 2001, the Intergovernmental Panel on Climate Change released a landmark report projecting average global surface temperatures to rise between 1.4 degrees and 5.8 degrees Celsius (roughly 2 to 10 degrees Fahrenheit) by the end of this century. Based on this forecast, author Mark Lynas outlines what to expect from a warming world, degree by degree." Publisher's note
Includes bibliographical references

Lyons, Walter A. (Walter Andrew), 1943-
The handy weather answer book. Visible Ink Press 1997 397p il pa $19.95 **551.6**
1. Weather
ISBN 0-7876-1034-8   LC 96-30555
This book provides "answers to more than 1,000 frequently asked questions about the weather. It also provides information on such . . . topics as hurricanes, droughts, flash floods, volcanoes . . . the greenhouse effect, Aurora Borealis and St. Elmo's fire." Publisher's note
Includes bibliographical references

Monmonier, Mark S. (Mark Stephen), 1943-
Air apparent; how meteorologists learned to map, predict, and dramatize weather; [by] Mark Monmonier. University of Chicago Press 1999 309p il $27.50; pa $17   **551.6**
1. Meteorology 2. Weather forecasting
ISBN 0-226-53422-7; 0-226-53423-5 (pa)
LC 98-25797
The author presents a "history of more than 200 years of weather maps, an account that embraces technological advances from the telegraph and mercury barometer to the satellite and Doppler radar." Booklist
Includes bibliographical references

Philander, S. George, 1942-
Our affair with El Niño; how we transformed an enchanting Peruvian current into a global climate hazard. Princeton University Press 2004 275p il maps hardcover o.p. pa $17.95   **551.6**
1. El Niño Current 2. Climate
ISBN 0-691-11335-1; 0-691-12622-4 (pa)
LC 2003-44235
"The book begins by outlining the history of El Niño, an innocuous current that appears off the coast of Peru around Christmastime—its name refers to the Child Jesus—and originally was welcomed as a blessing. It goes on to explore how our perceptions of El Niño were transformed." Publisher's note
"This is an exceptional book, enjoyable to read and educational at several levels. El Niño is the springboard for a book that thoroughly explains the phenomenon and even goes far beyond it." Sci Books Films
Includes bibliographical references

Weart, Spencer R., 1942-
The discovery of global warming. Harvard University Press 2003 228p il (New histories of science, technology, and medicine) $24.95; pa $14.95 *   **551.6**
1. Greenhouse effect
ISBN 0-674-01157-0; 0-674-01637-8 (pa)
LC 2003-40703
The author "reports the history of global warming theory, including the internal conflicts plaguing the research community and the role government has had in promoting climate studies. . . . Without resorting to fear-mongering, Weart gives an informed history and offers his readers solutions to consider." Publ Wkly
Includes bibliographical references

551.7   Historical geology

Alvarez, Walter, 1940-
T. rex and the Crater of Doom. Princeton Univ. Press 1997 185p il $35   **551.7**
1. Catastrophes (Geology) 2. Dinosaurs
ISBN 0-691-01630-5   LC 96-49208
The author relates the story of how he "along with four other Berkeley scientists, found the geologic evidence that implicated a cosmic collision in the extinction of the dinosaurs. . . . {Their research involved} the eval-

uation of a thin iridium-rich layer of clay found in Italy and the search for an impact crater." Booklist
This book "gets the facts across in a lighthearted, almost playful manner. But it's also solid science, a clear and efficient exposition." N Y Times Book Rev
Includes bibliographical references

Bjornerud, Marcia
Reading the rocks; the autobiography of the earth. Basic Books 2005 237p $26   **551.7**
1. Geology
ISBN 0-8133-4249-X   LC 2004-22738
In this "volume of pop-geology, . . . Bjornerud chronicles the watersheds in Earth's history from the primordial supernova that seeded the nascent solar nebula to the manmade cataclysms of global warming and habitat destruction." Publ Wkly
"This wonderful book should be examined by anyone with a curiosity about the natural history of our planet and how one science in particular has done such an impressive job of deciphering key mysteries of its origin and evolution." Sci Books Films
Includes bibliographical references

Fortey, Richard A.
Earth; an intimate history; by Richard Fortey. Knopf 2004 429p il hardcover o.p. pa $19 *
          551.7
1. Stratigraphic geology
ISBN 0-375-40626-3; 0-375-70620-8 (pa)
LC 2004-46470
The author "relates his walks in places that visually reveal the deep earth (Vesuvius, Hawaii, the Grand Canyon) as well as sites, which, if not so spectacular, contain puzzling elements that provoked great interpretive controversies. . . . The Alps, the Scottish Highlands, Newfoundland, the Deccan Traps of India—these are among Fortey's destinations as he explains the theory of plate tectonics, showing how the theory came to be, as well as the continents and oceans whose skein of connections it explains. This is a marvelously inviting presentation." Booklist
Includes bibliographical references

Hancock, Graham
Underworld: the mysterious origins of civilization; photographs by Santha Faiia. Crown 2002 769p il maps $27.50; pa $16.95
          551.7
1. Stratigraphic geology 2. Ancient civilization
3. Prehistoric peoples
ISBN 1-4000-4612-2; 1-4000-4951-2 (pa)
The author presents theories on how "civilization rose about 17,000 years ago (rather than about 6,000) and vanished beneath a rising sea level, leaving its traces in flood myths in Sumerian and Vedic texts, in early maps of the Age of Discovery, and more plausibly, in submerged ruins. Hancock throws up a fantastic amount of data on these points in this work, ranging from his personal textual interpretations to his dives at coastal sites in Malta, India, Japan, and the Bahamas." Booklist
Includes bibliographical references

Macdougall, J. D., 1944-
Frozen earth; the once and future story of ice ages; [by] Doug Macdougall. University of California Press 2004 256p il $24.95; pa $15.95
551.7
1. Ice Age
ISBN 0-520-23922-9; 0-520-24824-4 (pa)
LC 2004-8502
The author "presents the scientific history behind ice ages, emphasizing the roles of four great scientists in the field: Louis Agassiz, James Croll, Milutin Milankovitch, and Harlan Bretz. . . . Macdougall's account promotes a welcome reasoning attitude toward ice-age research and its relevance to global warming." Booklist
Includes bibliographical references

A short history of planet earth; mountains, mammals, fire, and ice. Wiley 1996 266p il maps (Wiley popular science) pa $16.95 hardcover o.p.
551.7
1. Stratigraphic geology 2. Life—Origin
ISBN 0-471-19703-3 (pa)
LC 95-46399
In "this survey of four-and-a-half billion years of Earth's past . . . MacDougall traces the rise of continents and the origins of life in each era. He discusses tectonic plates, the major extinctions and their probable causes, climate and the Ice Ages, and he speculates on the future of our planet. To compress Earth's history into a single, lucidly written volume is a major achievement." Publ Wkly
Includes bibliographical references

Richet, Pascal
A natural history of time; translated by John Venerella. University of Chicago Press 2007 471p il $29
551.7
1. Geological time 2. Earth—Age
ISBN 978-0-226-71287-1; 0-226-71287-7
LC 2006-33992
Original French edition, 1999
"How old is the Earth? Mr. Richet sets out to explore humanity's attempts to answer this most perplexing of questions, which acted as a spur and a baffle to human ingenuity for 2,500 years. . . . The book is translated from the French—capably, considering how much scientific terminology it contains, but not gracefully—and . . . can be rough going. Still, 'A Natural History of Time' more that repays the effort it requires. Not only does it shed light on key advances in the history of science, from the ancient Greeks to the X-ray, it reminds us of the real heroism and nobility of the scientific enterprise." N Y Sun

552 Petrology

Coenraads, Robert Raymond, 1956-
Rocks and fossils; a visual guide; [by] Robert R. Coenraads. Firefly Books 2005 304p il $29.95
552
1. Rocks 2. Fossils 3. Minerals
ISBN 1-55407-068-6
In this "introduction to geology and paleontology . . . [the author presents the] facts of how fossils are formed,

how rocks are formed, and how plate tectonics work. . . . A science work perfectly suited for general use." Booklist

553.6 Other economic materials

Kurlansky, Mark
Salt: a world history. Penguin Books 2003 484p il map pa $16 *
553.6
1. Salt
ISBN 0-14-200161-9
LC 2004-270006
First published 2002 by Walker & Co.
The author shows how salt "has influenced and affected wars, cultures, governments, religions, societies, economies, cooking (there are a few recipes), and foods. In addition, he provides information on the chemistry, geology, mining, refining, and production of salt." Libr J
"Throughout his engaging, well-researched history, Kurlansky sprinkles witty asides and amusing anecdotes. A piquant blend of the historic, political, commercial, scientific and culinary, the book is sure to entertain as well as educate." Publ Wkly
Includes bibliographical references

553.7 Water

Kandel, Robert S.
Water from heaven; the story of water from the big bang to the rise of civilization, and beyond; [by] Robert Kandel. Columbia Univ. Press 2003 311p il maps $29.95; pa $24 *
553.7
1. Water
ISBN 0-231-12244-6; 0-231-12245-4 (pa)
LC 2002-31229
Original French edition, 1998
The author "explains the earth's elaborate and essential-to-life water cycle . . . beginning cosmologically with the birth of the solar system and an analysis of various theories as to where the earth's water . . . originated." Booklist
"While dense with facts and figures, Kandel's aquatic history is riveting, an exhaustive and complex examination of our most precious chemical compound." Publ Wkly
Includes bibliographical references

Newton, David E.
Encyclopedia of water. Greenwood Press 2002 401p il $75
553.7
1. Water—Encyclopedias
ISBN 1-57356-304-8
LC 2002-70031
"The 236 entries in this book comprise an A-Z overview of water's manifold roles in human society and the natural world throughout history." Publisher's note
Includes bibliographical references

Pielou, E. C., 1924-
Fresh water. University of Chicago Press 1998 275p il maps $24; pa $14
553.7
1. Water
ISBN 0-226-66815-0; 0-226-66816-9 (pa)
LC 97-51562

Pielou, E. C., 1924-—*Continued*

Pielou provides an "introduction to hydrology as she conducts a guided tour to freshwater's gathering places underground and in streams, rivers, wetlands, lakes, and clouds, then turns to a discussion of how civilization has used this limited resource, and why water conservation must be established as a permanent aspect of life on earth." Booklist

This "is a wonderful natural history of one of life's necessities, a refreshing break from grand theory and special pleading of many a science book. . . . Sometimes Pielou gets political. . . . But the mind-boggling details always hold the attention best." New Scientist

Includes bibliographical references

Water: science and issues; E. Julius Dasch, editor in chief. Macmillan Ref. USA 2003 4v il maps set $395   **553.7**

1. Water—Encyclopedias

ISBN 0-02-865611-3

Contents: v1 Acid-Drought; v2 Earle-Lakes; v3 Land-Pricing; v4 Prior-Women

"This reference contains more than 300 topical entries . . . about a wide array of topics surrounding the nature, sources, use, desecration, and protection of this most valuable resource. *Acid rain, Bottled water, Careers in oceanography, Hoover Dam, Leonardo da Vinci, Plankton, Salmon decline and recovery* and *Wetlands* are examples of entries and help illustrate the set's range. . . . At the beginning of each volume are several tables: metric conversions; symbols, abbreviations, and acronyms; and geologic eras, periods and epochs. Entries range in length from 500 to 2,500 words and include short bibliographies of print and electronic sources. Pages have wide margins, which contain picture captions, definitions of key terms, and boxes of important facts and explanations . . . Photographs, illustrations, and tables are attractive and add meaning to the text. Each volume concludes with the 36-page, detailed cumulative index and the 60-page glossary. . . . The scientific and social aspects of water are well introduced in this set, which is recommended for high-school, public, and undergraduate libraries." Booklist

Includes bibliographical references

553.8 Gems

Hart, Matthew, 1945-

Diamond: a journey to the heart of an obsession. Walker & Co. 2001 276p il maps $26

553.8

1. Diamonds

ISBN 0-8027-1368-8   LC 2001-26348

Also available in paperback from Plume Bks.

Hart's "account of the glittering business of mining and marketing diamonds is also a story of avarice, theft, aesthetics, monopoly, and war. A thoroughly entrancing book." Booklist

Includes bibliographical references

Levy, Adrian, 1965-

The stone of heaven; unearthing the secret history of imperial green jade; [by] Adrian Levy and Cathy Scott-Clark. Little, Brown 2002 xxii, 408p il map $24.95; pa $15.96   **553.8**

1. Jadeite

ISBN 0-316-52596-0; 0-316-09558-3 (pa)

LC 2001-37742

This "chronicle interweaves legend, mythology, and history with a shocking contemporary exposé of the Burmese jadeite mines. . . . An engrossing combination of narrative history and undercover journalism." Booklist

Includes bibliographical references

Oldershaw, Cally

Firefly guide to gems. Firefly Bks. 2004 224p il map $14.95 *   **553.8**

1. Precious stones 2. Gems

ISBN 1-55297-814-1

This book "opens with extensive introductory material including history, various properties, and lore. Then, each gem is presented with text and charts of specific chemical properties. While most gems are discussed on a single page, some that are well known have longer articles." SLJ

Zoellner, Tom

The heartless stone; a journey through the world of diamonds, deceit, and desire. St. Martins Press 2006 293p map $24.95   **553.8**

1. Diamonds

ISBN 0-312-33969-0; 978-0-312-33969-2

LC 2005-33037

The author "probes how 'blood diamonds' are used to fund vicious civil wars in Africa; how De Beers, seeing new markets to exploit, linked diamonds to the ancient yuino ceremony in Japan and played on caste obsession in India; and how India is pushing Belgium and Israel out of the gem trade. . . . This is a superior piece of reportage." Publ Wkly

Includes bibliographical references

557 Earth sciences of North America

McPhee, John A.

Annals of the former world; [by] John McPhee. Farrar, Straus & Giroux 1998 695p maps $35; pa $20   **557**

1. Geology—United States

ISBN 0-374-10520-0; 0-374-51873-4 (pa)

LC 97-39660

This volume combines edited and revised sections from Basin and range (1981), In suspect terrain (1983), Rising from the plains (1986), and Assembling California (1993), with two new essays

McPhee provides a "portrait of the continent—a . . . narrative that not only tracks the drama of North American geological history but also chronicles the rapid evolution of the theories and practice of geology itself and tells the intriguing stories of people for whom love of

McPhee, John A.—*Continued*

rocks has meant love of life." Booklist

"As in any McPhee work, there are gemlike sentences, richly rhythmic paragraphs, nicely burnished synecdoches, metaphors as pungent as wasabi and, behind those felicities, vast amounts of painstaking research." N Y Times Book Rev

560   Fossils & prehistoric life

Eldredge, Niles

Fossils; the evolution and extinction of species; photography by Murray Alcosser; introduction by Stephen Jay Gould. Princeton Univ. Press 1997 xx, 220p pa $45   **560**
1. Fossils 2. Evolution
ISBN 0-691-02695-5   LC 96-26969

A reissue of the title first published 1991 by Abrams

The author "examines what the fossilized remains of earth's ancient flora and fauna reveal about mass extinction and the origin of species." Publisher's note

"Full-page photographs adorn about half the pages of this beautiful book. . . . These essays are not intended as detailed academic treatments; rather, they provide a touch of the history of discovery, and the excitement of delving into the unknown—doing paleontology. The anatomical descriptions are easy to understand. This is a 'coffee table book' of the highest quality." Sci Book Films

Includes bibliographical references

The miner's canary; unraveling the mysteries of extinction. Princeton University Press 1994 246p (Princeton science library) pa $29.95   **560**
1. Extinct animals 2. Fossils
ISBN 978-0-691-03655-7; 0-691-03655-1
                                       LC 93-50185

First published 1991 by Prentice Hall Press

The author "reviews the evidence for extinction and its causes, primarily using fossil evidence and focusing on climatic change and loss of habitat." Libr J

The book "rings with integrity. The author seems almost apologetic about offering views of his own that stray somewhat from his self-imposed syllabus, and he takes care to present opposing views." N Y Times Book Rev

Includes bibliographical references

Encyclopedia of paleontology; editor, Ronald Singer. Fitzroy Dearborn Pubs. 1999 2v il set $295   1. Fossils—Encyclopedias   **560**
ISBN 1-88496-496-6   LC 00-271769

This work has "328 articles that cover all areas of paleontology, including 79 biographies for individuals such as Jean Agassiz, Charles Darwin, and Louis Leakey. The articles are extremely well written, with line drawings, photographs, charts, and other illustrative matter, plus a list of works cited and a further reading list." Booklist

Includes bibliographical references

Fortey, Richard A.

Fossils; the key to the past; [by] Richard Fortey. 3rd ed. Smithsonian Institution Press 2002 232p il maps $55; pa $27.50 *   **560**
1. Fossils
ISBN 1-58834-023-6; 1-58834-048-1 (pa)
                                      LC 2001-49439

First published 1982 by Van Nostrand Reinhold

In this volume, fossils "from earliest Precambrian forms onward are discussed, emphasizing evolutionary trends and extinctions, and relationships with habitat environments and geologic processes, such as volcanism and meteorite impacts, are evaluated. . . . Aspects of preservation, discovery, collection, and identification are discussed." Choice {review of 1991 edition}

Includes bibliographical references

Trilobite! eyewitness to evolution; by Richard Fortey. Knopf 2000 284p il $26; pa $14
                                                 560
1. Fossils 2. Evolution
ISBN 0-375-40625-5; 0-375-70621-6 (pa)
                                      LC 00-34908

The author's "unabashed trilobite-centric view of the evolution of life on Earth is full of personal anecdotes and asides, but it's also full of excellent science." Libr J

Includes bibliographical references

Gould, Stephen Jay, 1941-2002

Wonderful life: the Burgess Shale and the nature of history. Norton 1989 347p il pa $15.95 hardcover o.p.   **560**
1. Fossils 2. Evolution
ISBN 0-393-30700-X (pa)   LC 88-37469

"The Burgess Shale is a rock formation containing the fossilized remains of a large number of marine creatures that no longer exist, and also the remains of some that do. The nonsurvivors appear to have been as well equipped to flourish as their contemporaries. Why did they not? . . . {This is an} account of the studies, the misinterpretations, and the revisions of opinion arising from the Burgess Shale material." Atlantic

"With his usual grace and wit Gould guides readers through the technical terminology and explains the significance of these fossils that exploded past assumptions about the history of life." Libr J

Includes bibliographical references

Poinar, George O.

The quest for life in amber; {by} George and Roberta Poinar. Addison-Wesley 1994 219p il pa $18 hardcover o.p.   **560**
1. Fossils 2. Amber
ISBN 0-201-48928-7   LC 94-3043

This is an account of the authors' search for and work with amber, a fossilized resin. The Poinars also include details of their scientific analyses of the insects trapped within this host material

This is "one of those books that educates the general reader about a scientific topic without requiring very much scientific background. Although educational, it is also highly entertaining and should be read for pleasure as much as for knowledge." Choice

Includes bibliographical references

Raup, David M.
Extinction; bad genes or bad luck? Norton 1991
210p pa $12.95 hardcover o.p.   **560**
1. Mass extinction of species
ISBN 0-393-30927-4 (pa)   LC 90-27192
In this study of extinction, the author challenges the
view that internal factors are critical in explaining the
death of a species. Surveying past extinctions, Raup
seeks to locate their cause in external factors, specifically
the impact of meteorites
"Neither {Raup's} readers nor his scientific colleagues
are likely to endorse everything he says, but his book is
an eminently entertaining and informative read." N Y
Times Book Rev
Includes bibliographical references

Rea, Tom, 1950-
Bone wars; the excavation and celebrity of
Andrew Carnegie's dinosaur. University of
Pittsburgh Press 2001 276p il $25   **560**
1. Carnegie, Andrew, 1835-1919 2. Fossils
3. Dinosaurs
ISBN 0-8229-4173-2   LC 2001-3336
This describes the history of the excavation of the di-
nosaur fossil Diplodocus carnegii in 1899 which was fi-
nanced by Andrew Carnegie
"Rea pieces together countless bits of information to
construct an overall picture of this period of scientific
discovery." Booklist
Includes bibliographical references

Thompson, Ida
The Audubon Society field guide to North
American fossils; with photographs by Townsend
P. Dickinson; visual key by Carol Nehring. Knopf
1982 846p il maps flexible bdg $19.95 *
                                          560
1. Fossils
ISBN 0-394-52412-8   LC 81-84772
"A Chanticleer Press edition. The Audubon Society
field guide series"
"This softbound field guide to fossils is divided into
a section of color photographs followed by a section of
detailed descriptions. It covers 420 fossils of marine and
freshwater invertebrates, insects, plants, and vertebrates
that are likely to be found by the amateur." Malinowsky.
Best Sci & Technol Ref Books for Young People

Travels with the fossil hunters; edited by Peter
Whybrow. Cambridge Univ. Press 2000 211p il
$40   **560**
1. Fossils 2. Scientists
ISBN 0-521-66301-6   LC 99-30134
A collection of essays by paleontologists from London's Natural History Museum describing their work in
such places as China, India, the Sahara, Latvia, and Antarctica
"The essayists give enough details of their quests to
explain their presence in these places and keep science
buffs entertained. . . . Heightening the impact of the stories is an abundance of beautiful, colorful photos of the
places, the people, and the fossils." SLJ

Wallace, David Rains, 1945-
The bonehunters' revenge; dinosaurs, greed, and
the greatest scientific feud of the gilded age.
Houghton Mifflin 1999 366p il $25; pa $14
                                          560
1. Cope, E. D. (Edward Drinker), 1840-1897
2. Marsh, Othniel Charles, 1831-1899 3. Fossils
ISBN 0-395-85089-4; 0-618-08240-9 (pa)
                                    LC 99-31904
This is an account of the rivalry between 19th century
paleontologists Edward Drinker Cope and Othniel
Charles Marsh.
"This curious century-old feud comes alive with mo-
mentum and understanding in Wallace's skillful hands."
Booklist
Includes bibliographical references

567.9 Reptilia

Encyclopedia of dinosaurs; edited by Philip J.
Currie, Kevin Padian. Academic Press 1997
xxx, 869p il $110.95   **567.9**
1. Dinosaurs—Encyclopedias
ISBN 0-12-226810-5   LC 97-23430
"Organized alphabetically by subject, the signed articles cover kinds of dinosaurs, biology, geology, research,
and museums where dinosaurs are on display, including
a worldwide list of museums and sites." Libr J

Fiffer, Steve
Tyrannosaurus Sue; the extraordinary saga of
the largest, most fought over T. rex ever found;
foreword by Robert T. Bakker. Freeman, W.H.
2000 248p pa $14.95 hardcover o.p.
                                          567.9
1. Larson, Peter L. 2. Dinosaurs
ISBN 0-7167-9462-4 (pa)   LC 00-21596
In 1990 "South Dakota fossil-hunters Sue Hendrickson
and Peter Larson dug up an exceptional T. rex—only the
12th tyrannosaur ever found, and the biggest and best-
preserved to date. . . . The ensuing legal, political and
scientific imbroglio set Native Americans against the federal government, the government against itself, the feds
against established scientists and the world's great research universities against independent operators like
Larson. Fiffer's thorough account should prove irresistible to readers with even a marginal interest in the legendary lizards." Publ Wkly

Gillette, David D.
Seismosaurus; the earth shaker; with illustrations
by Mark Hallett. Columbia Univ. Press 1994 205p
il maps $60; pa $21.95   **567.9**
1. Dinosaurs
ISBN 0-231-07874-9; 0-231-07875-7 (pa)
                                    LC 93-40318
"Seismosaurus (Sam, for short) is a new dinosaur discovered by hikers in New Mexico and excavated by the
author. . . . Gillette's step-by-step story of the discovery
of the first bones of the Seismosaurus details how it was
named, unearthed, funded, and shared with the scientific
community. He discusses how Sam fits in among the

Gillette, David D.—*Continued*

better-known Jurassic specimens as well as the potential uses for some exciting new field sensing techniques." Booklist

Includes bibliographical references

Lambert, David, 1932-

Dinosaur encyclopedia; from dinosaurs to the dawn of man; [by David Lambert, Darren Naish, Elizabeth Wyse] Dorling Kindersley 2001 376p il maps $29.95 **567.9**

1. Dinosaurs—Encyclopedias

ISBN 0-7894-7935-4   LC 2001-28433

In association with the American Museum of Natural History

"After a brief discussion of how paleontologists reconstruct the details of prehistory, this comprehensive volume breaks the animal kingdom into four major sections, 'Fish and Invertebrates,' 'Amphibians and Reptiles,' 'Dinosaurs and Birds' and 'Mammals and Their Ancestors.'" Publ Wkly

"This book is an excellent volume for both the uninitiated and the person who wishes to expand his or her knowledge from the basics. The book is logically laid out by groups of animals, and evolutionary connections between the animals are explained clearly. . . . As an encyclopedia, this one accomplishes its mission of providing a good basic foundation for each animal group it presents." Sci Books Films

Larson, Peter L.

Rex appeal; the amazing story of Sue, the dinosaur that changed science, the law, and my life; {by} Peter Larson, Kristin Donnan. Invisible Cities Press 2002 404p il $26.95 **567.9**

1. Dinosaurs 2. Fossils

ISBN 1-931229-07-4   LC 2002-24207

Larson's "team discovered the largest and most complete Tyrannosaurus rex skeleton that the world had seen. Almost immediately, however, the team . . . became embroiled in a dispute with the U.S. government about who owns the fossil, during which the skeleton was seized by the National Guard. . . . The book recounts the heated legal battles but focuses primarily on Larson's adventures in South Dakota, where his group eventually found six more T. rex fossils." Publ Wkly

Includes bibliographical references

Nothdurft, William E.

The lost dinosaurs of Egypt; [by] William Nothdurft with Josh Smith [et al.] Random House 2002 242p il maps $24.95; pa $13.95 **567.9**

1. Stromer, Ernst 2. Dinosaurs 3. Fossils

ISBN 0-375-50795-7; 0-375-75979-4 (pa)

LC 2002-75172

"Between 1910 and 1914, Ernst Stromer . . . unearthed a wealth of dinosaur fossils in Egypt's Bahariya Oasis. Thirty years later, Stromer's discoveries were destroyed in a WWII Allied bombing raid, and the oasis lay neglected for decades until Josh Smith, a Penn State doctoral candidate in paleontology, decided to retrace

Stromer's footsteps in 1999. . . . [This] account highlights Stromer's discoveries . . . and chronicles recent findings by Smith and his colleagues. . . . An engaging mix of history and desert drama, this . . . is first-rate popular science." Publ Wkly

The **Scientific** American book of dinosaurs; Gregory S. Paul, editor. St. Martin's Press 2000 424p il maps $32.95; pa $19.95 * **567.9**

1. Dinosaurs

ISBN 0-312-26226-4; 0-312-31008-0 (pa)

LC 2001-269051

"A Byron Preiss book"

This book features information on "how dinosaurs evolved, how they looked, where they lived, how they behaved, and why they died . . . {as well as} stories about the first discoveries of dinosaur fossils, the beginnings of dinosaur paleontology, how the field has changed with modern technology, the most sensational finds, and the latest theories." Publisher's note

Includes bibliographical references

568   Fossil Aves (birds)

Shipman, Pat

Taking wing; Archaeopteryx and the evolution of bird flight. Simon & Schuster 1998 336p il pa $22.95 hardcover o.p. **568**

1. Archaeopteryx 2. Birds—Flight

ISBN 0-684-84965-8 (pa)   LC 97-27527

The author focuses on "how adaptations needed for animal flight came about. Using the well-known *Archaeopteryx* fossils as a keystone, she discusses historical and current hypotheses about bird evolution, along with the provocative debates they spurred." Libr J

"Shipman brings to her excellent book the authority of a paleontologist and the talent of an accomplished writer on science for popular audiences." N Y Times Book Rev

Includes bibliographical references

569   Fossil mammalia

Lister, Adrian

Mammoths; giants of the ice age; [by] Adrian Lister and Paul Bahn; foreword by Jean M. Auel. Rev ed. University of California Press 2007 192p il $29.95 * **569**

1. Mammoths

ISBN 978-0-520-25319-3; 0-520-25319-1

LC 2007-26369

First published 1994 by Macmillan

This book integrates "research to piece together the story of mammoths, mastodons, and their relatives, icons of the Ice Age." Publisher's note

Includes glossary and bibliographical references

569.9   Hominidae

Sarmiento, Esteban

The last human; a guide to twenty-two species of extinct humans; created by G.J. Sawyer and Viktor Deak; text by Esteban Sarmiento, G.J. Sawyer, Richard Milner; with contributions by Donald C. Johanson, Meave Leakey, and Ian Tattersall. Yale University Press 2006 256p il map $45 *   **569.9**

    1. Fossil hominids 2. Evolution 3. Human beings
    ISBN 978-0-300-10047-1; 0-300-10047-7

    "A Peter N. Nèvraumont book"

    This book "covers 22 species of extinct humans, concluding with the only surviving one, Homo sapiens. . . . Provided for each is information on its emergence, chronology, geographic range, classification, physiology, environment, habitat, cultural achievements, coexisting species, and possible reasons for extinction. Summaries of fossil discoveries for each species are also provided, along with historical notes mentioning publications and controversies." Libr J

    "This is fascinating stuff, not least because it drives home just how much of our knowledge about the past is based on inference." New Sci

    Includes bibliographical references

570   Life sciences; biology

Carson, Rachel, 1907-1964

Lost woods; the discovered writing of Rachel Carson; edited and with an introduction by Linda Lear. Beacon Press 1998 267p pa $16 hardcover o.p.   **570**

    1. Nature 2. Wildlife conservation
    ISBN 0-8070-8547-2 (pa)   LC 98-20058

    This is a collection of previously unpublished essays, speeches, field notes, letters, and other writings by the pioneering environmentalist

    These excerpts provide readers "with samples of some of the most lyrical, clear scientific writing available in the fields of biology, ecology, and wildlife and wilderness conservation." SLJ

    Includes bibliographical references

Gould, Stephen Jay, 1941-2002

An urchin in the storm; essays about books and ideas. Norton 1987 255p il pa $11.95 hardcover o.p.   **570**

    1. Biology
    ISBN 0-393-30537-6 (pa)   LC 87-21718

    This collection of Gould's book reviews is arranged in broad subject areas: evolutionary theory, biological determinism, time and geology.

Hoagland, Mahlon B., 1921-

The way life works; [by] Mahlon Hoagland, Bert Dodson. Times Bks. 1995 xxi, 233p il pa $27 hardcover o.p.   **570**

    1. Life (Biology)
    ISBN 0-8129-2888-1 (pa)   LC 94-48780

Hoagland's text and Dodson's illustrations "present the mechanics of everything from DNA to neural circuits and evolution. As they move from discussion of 16 key patterns in life to chapters titled 'Energy,' 'Information,' 'Feedback,' 'Community,' and 'Evolution' Hoagland and Dodson link the mechanics of the invisible world of molecules to the observable working world of plants and animals, water and light, and human beings and even machines. There is a lively sense of discovery here." Booklist

    Includes bibliographical references

Mayr, Ernst, 1904-2005

This is biology; the science of the living world. Harvard Univ. Press 1997 327p il pa $17.95 hardcover o.p. *   **570**

    1. Biology
    ISBN 0-674-88469-8 (pa)   LC 96-42192

    This is an overview of the major concepts and issues surrounding biology from Aristotle to the present. Topics discussed include genetics, cytology, evolution, development, and biodiversity

    "This is an extremely well-thought-out and eminently scholarly work. . . . Mayr is definitely a grand old man of biology, and this book demonstrates his grasp of the development of the field." Sci Books Films

    Includes bibliographical references

Serafini, Anthony

The epic history of biology 1993 395p il pa $25 hardcover o.p.   **570**

    1. Biology
    ISBN 0-7382-0577-X (pa)   LC 93-27895

    This volume traces the origins and evolution of the discipline "of biology from prehistoric times through the modern revolution in molecular biology." Sci Books Films

    Includes bibliographical references

Whitfield, John, 1970-

In the beat of a heart; life, energy, and the unity of nature. Joseph Henry Press 2006 il $27.95   **570**

    1. Life (Biology) 2. Nature
    ISBN 978-0-309-09681-2; 0-309-09681-2
                            LC 2006-12277

    "Why are there 700 species of North American birds instead of seven? Why do the tropics have more species than the polar regions? If different species—whether tree, bear, or bacterium—are subject to the same physical laws, is there a general unified theory of biology? . . . Whitfield tackles these questions by exploring the role of energy and metabolism as the unifying force in nature. Writing in an engaging style, he describes the work and lives of key scientists whose often controversial ideas also help contribute answers." Libr J

570.1 Philosophy and theory

Capra, Fritjof
The web of life; a new scientific understanding of living systems. Anchor Bks. (NY) 1996 347p il pa $14.95 hardcover o.p. **570.1**
1. Life (Biology) 2. System theory
ISBN 0-385-47676-0 (pa) LC 96-12576
This discourse on the life sciences incorporates "elements from such contemporary schools of thought as the Gaia hypothesis, deep ecology, complexity theory, systems theory, and . . . eco-feminism." Libr J
This is "a rewarding synthesis that will challenge serious readers." Publ Wkly
Includes bibliographical references

Duve, Christian de, 1917-
Vital dust; life as a cosmic imperative. Basic Bks. 1994 362p il pa $24 hardcover o.p.
570.1
1. Life—Origin 2. Life (Biology) 3. Evolution
ISBN 0-465-09045-1 (pa) LC 94-12964
"De Duve begins with hypotheses about the origin of life and ends with speculations about the future and meaning of life and the abundance of life in the universe. He argues . . . for the view that life—including intelligent life—is probably found liberally scattered throughout the universe. In the intervening pages, he reviews the major stages, or innovations, in the history of life on planet Earth. . . . Not always easy reading at times, this book is guaranteed to make the patient reader think and question." Sci Books Films
Includes bibliographical references

Keller, Evelyn Fox, 1936-
Making sense of life; explaining biological development with models, metaphors, and machines. Harvard Univ. Press 2002 388p il $29.95 **570.1**
1. Biology—Philosophy 2. Life (Biology)
ISBN 0-674-00746-8 LC 2001-51559
The author "analyzes the history of developmental biology. She explains the type of information scientists have accepted, why changes in acceptance may occur and, on a broader scale, what it means to understand the natural world. . . . While Keller's prose is graceful and informed, her thesis is complex and unlikely to be fully appreciated by those without significant grounding in philosophy and biology." Publ Wkly
Includes bibliographical references

Lovelock, James
The ages of Gaia; a biography of our living earth. Norton 1988 xx, 252p il pa $13.95 hardcover o.p. * **570.1**
1. Biology—Philosophy 2. Gaia hypothesis 3. Biosphere 4. Life (Biology)
ISBN 0-393-31239-9 (pa) LC 87-36567
"A volume of the Commonwealth Fund Book Program, under the editorship of Lewis Thomas"

"Gaia is the Greek goddess of the earth. For James Lovelock she is the embodiment of a hypothesis: the earth is not merely the abode of life but is a single living organism. He proposes that all living species are components of that organism, as cells are components of the human body." N Y Times Book Rev
Includes bibliographical references

Margulis, Lynn, 1938-
What is life? foreword by Niles Eldredge. University of California Press 2000 288p il pa $24.95 **570.1**
1. Life (Biology) 2. Biology—Philosophy 3. Biological diversity 4. Life—Origin
ISBN 0-520-22021-8 LC 00-25833
"A Peter N. Nevraumont book"
First published 1995 by Simon & Schuster
"Continuing Margulis's contention that organelles within cells, such as mitochondria, were originally free-living organisms that fused with others to form complex cells and bodies, the authors extend this concept to the Earth as a superorganism. Although following traditional evolutionary pathways, the authors argue that life has played a role in its own evolution." Choice
Includes bibliographical references

Sagan, Carl, 1934-1996
Shadows of forgotten ancestors; a search for who we are; {by} Carl Sagan, Ann Druyan. Random House 1992 505p pa $15.95 hardcover o.p. **570.1**
1. Life—Origin 2. Evolution
ISBN 0-345-38472-5 (pa) LC 92-50155
The authors "trace the roots of the *Homo sapiens* family tree down to life at its tiniest. . . . As Sagan and Druyan move up the evolutionary ladder from microorganisms to more complex creatures including insects, snakes, fish, birds, and primates, they track the emergence of sexuality, survival tactics, instinct, and thinking, all sparked by the basic interplay between heredity and environment." Booklist
"Despite a preference for the overly dramatic phrase at the expense of scientific clarity, the argument is coherent throughout." Libr J
Includes bibliographical references

Thomas, Lewis, 1913-1993
The lives of a cell; notes of a biology watcher. Viking 1974 153p pa $13 hardcover o.p.
570.1
1. Biology—Philosophy
ISBN 0-14-004743-3 (pa)
Also available in paperback from Bantam Bks.
In this collection of twenty-nine short essays "the author does not confine his scientist's eye to a microscope. He takes a much wider view of the world, looking at insect behavior and the possibility of intelligent life in outer space or bird songs and the evolution of language. He also offers a modest proposal for saving ourselves from nuclear self-destruction." Time
Includes bibliographical references

571 Physiology and related subjects

Widmaier, Eric P.
Why geese don't get obese (and we do); how evolution's strategies for survival affect our everyday lives. Freeman, W.H. 1998 213p il pa $14.95 hardcover o.p. **571**
1. Comparative physiology
ISBN 0-7167-3649-7 (pa)   LC 98-2698
This book examines "the evolution of normal human and animal physiology, why we work the way we do, and a few conditions where adaptations from our ancestors are not so useful in modern life, for example, diabetes, stress, and the obesity mentioned in the title. What really makes this book stand out are the lucid explanations of how scientific method . . . is used to learn about human and animal physiology." Libr J
Includes bibliographical references

571.4 Biophysics

Vogel, Steven, 1940-
Cats' paws and catapults; mechanical worlds of nature and people; illustrated by Kathryn K. Davis with the author. Norton 1998 382p il $27.50; pa $15.95   **571.4**
1. Human engineering 2. Mechanics
ISBN 0-393-04641-9; 0-393-31990-3 (pa)
LC 97-44807
"This work is a comparison of natural mechanical devices, the cats' paws of the title, and human inventions, the catapults and dozens more of the components of modern life." N Y Times Book Rev
"Composed of curiosity and counter-intuition, this amply illustrated work should attract anyone interested in biology." Booklist
Includes bibliographical references

571.6 Cell biology

The **Facts** on File dictionary of cell and molecular biology; edited by Robert Hine. Facts on File 2002 248p il $49.50   **571.6**
1. Cells—Dictionaries 2. Molecular biology—Dictionaries
ISBN 0-8160-4912-2   LC 2002-32540
"There are 2,000 entries for terms in all major areas of biochemistry, molecular biology, molecular genetics, and cell biology. . . . Brief biographies of significant scientists are included. The appendixes include a chronology of the major discoveries in biochemistry and molecular biology. Also provided are molecular diagrams of 20 amino acids, a chart of the genetic code, a brief list of Web pages, and a bibliography. . . . Each entry is well written and clear. The illustrations are good, and there appear to be all the major terms needed for the purpose of this dictionary." Am Ref Books Annu, 2003
Includes bibliographical references

Harold, Franklin M.
The way of the cell; molecules, organisms, and the order of life. Oxford Univ. Press 2001 305p il hardcover o.p. pa $17.95   **571.6**
1. Cells 2. Life (Biology)
ISBN 0-19-513512-1; 0-19-516338-9 (pa)
LC 00-56670
"Harold tackles the largest of questions (What is life?) within the smallest of settings (the cell) in order to consider where and why a strictly genetic approach to life leads us astray." Booklist
Includes bibliographical references

Loewenstein, Werner R.
The touchstone of life; molecular information, cell communication, and the foundations of life. Oxford Univ. Press 1999 366p il $45; pa $17.95
571.6
1. Cells 2. Evolution
ISBN 0-19-511828-6; 0-19-514057-5 (pa)
LC 97-43408
This work "focuses on the role information transfer has played in the evolution of life over the past four million years. By merging principles of biology and physics, Loewenstein explains the workings of cell biology and biochemistry." Publ Wkly
"Loewenstein writes engagingly, and he provides the background material a nonspecialist needs to follow the intricate story." N Y Times Book Rev
Includes bibliographical references

Panno, Joseph
The cell; evolution of the first organism. Facts on File 2004 186p il (New biology) $35 *
571.6
1. Cells
ISBN 0-8160-4946-7   LC 2003-25841
"From the origins of the first cell to the diseases that attack different types of cells, this . . . volume tells the full story of this organism." Publisher's note
Includes bibliographical references

Rensberger, Boyce
Life itself; exploring the realm of the living cell; illustrations by Nigel Orme. Oxford Univ. Press 1996 290p il pa $16.95 hardcover o.p.
571.6
1. Cells 2. Molecular biology
ISBN 0-19-512500-2 (pa)   LC 96-33679
This is an overview of what is "currently known about the mechanisms by which living cells perform their myriad tasks." N Y Times Book Rev
This is "an elegant, authoritative, yet felicitously written book that will appeal to anyone who is interested in how cells work." New Sci
Includes bibliographical references

571.7 Biological control and secretions

Foster, Russell G.
Rhythms of life; the biological clocks that control the daily lives of every living thing. Yale University Press 2004 276p il $30; pa $18

571.7

1. Biological rhythms
ISBN   0-300-10574-6;   978-0-300-10574-2;
0-300-10969-5 (pa); 978-0-300-10969-6 (pa)

LC 2004-105609

The authors "survey the biological clocks that dictate circadian rhythms, the daily cycles that affect creatures from cockroaches to humans. . . . Biology buffs will marvel at the fascinating material." Publ Wkly
Includes bibliographical references

571.8 Reproduction, development, growth

Carroll, Sean B.
Endless forms most beautiful; the new science of evo devo and the making of the animal kingdom; with illustrations by Jamie W. Carroll, Josh P. Klaiss, Leanne M. Olds. W.W. Norton & Co. 2005 350p il $25.95

571.8

1. Evolution
ISBN 0-393-06016-0   LC 2004-29388

This book explains "the emerging field of evolutionary developmental biology, a.k.a. 'evo devo,' the study of how the shapes and forms of animals and humans have developed and evolved." Libr J
The author's "highly detailed and well-illustrated technical discussions are enriched by his appreciation for the philosophical, aesthetic, and ethical implications of the biological wonders he decodes, adding up to a vital and enjoyable introduction to a field with profound implications." Booklist
Includes bibliographical references

572 Biochemistry

The **Facts** on File dictionary of biochemistry; edited by John Daintith. Facts on File 2002 247p il $49.50; pa $19.95

572

1. Biochemistry—Dictionaries
ISBN 0-8160-4914-9; 0-8160-4915-7 (pa)

LC 2002-35203

"Facts on File science library"
"General areas included in the *Dictionary of Biochemistry* are basic organic and physical chemistry, classes of compounds, cytology and histology, nutrition and metabolism, and natural-product chemistry. Examples of specific entries are *Beta-pleated sheet; cyano-bacteria; Enzyme; G protein; Guanine; Isomerase; McClintock, Barbara; Pollution; Sex determination; Sugar; Vector*; and *Zeolite*. Appendixes provide a chronology of major events in the development of biochemistry and molecular biology, a table of the genetic code, amino acid struc-

tures, the periodic table, chemical elements, the Greek alphabet, and suggested Web pages." Booklist
Includes bibliographical references

572.8 Biochemical genetics

Bodmer, W. F. (Walter Fred), 1936-
The book of man; the Human Genome Project and the quest to discover our genetic heritage; [by] Walter Bodmer, Robin McKie. Oxford University Press 1997 259p il map pa $42 *

572.8

1. Human Genome Project 2. Gene mapping
ISBN 0-19-511487-6; 978-0-19-511487-4

LC 96-37423

First published 1994 in the United Kingdom with subtitle: The quest to discover our genetic heritage
This book discusses the Human Genome Project and contains "information on how human genes are mapped and why this mapping is important in medical, evolutionary, and sociological terms." Libr J
This "is highly readable, clear and accurate." New Sci

Carroll, Sean B.
The making of the fittest; DNA and the ultimate forensic record of evolution; with illustrations by Jamie W. Carroll and Leanne M. Olds. W.W. Norton & Co. 2006 301p il map $25.95 *

572.8

1. DNA 2. Evolution
ISBN 978-0-393-06163-5; 0-393-06163-9

LC 2006-17197

The author presents "discoveries gathered from DNA evidence that confirm Charles Darwin's theory of evolution 'beyond any reasonable doubt.' . . . Readers will gain insight into the evolutionary process and expand their knowledge of how the 'fittest' species were made, from fish that live in subfreezing water to birds that communicate via ultraviolet colors." Libr J
Includes bibliographical references

Cook-Deegan, Robert M.
The gene wars; science, politics, and the human genome. Norton 1994 416p il $25; pa $14.95

572.8

1. Human Genome Project 2. Gene mapping
ISBN 0-393-03572-7; 0-393-31399-9 (pa)

LC 93-10762

This "account of the Human Genome Project is as much about the politics, economics, and personalities as it is about the science of this . . . project to map the 100,000 chromosome sequences of the human genome." Libr J
Includes bibliographical references

Danchin, Antoine
The Delphic boat; what genomes tell us; translated by Alison Quayle. Harvard Univ. Press 2002 368p $35

572.8

1. Genomes
ISBN 0-674-00930-4   LC 2002-27273

Danchin, Antoine—*Continued*

Original French edition, 1998

"The book explores how researchers identify the roles of genes and the proteins they produce, and how understanding genomes leads us to a reconsideration of the very idea of life." Publ Wkly

"Danchin conducts intelligent amateurs surprisingly far into the {book's} central issues. This timely book offers hope that the rhetoric and hype of the antagonists fighting over the genome agenda will not drown out rational dialogue." Booklist

Includes bibliographical references

Lewontin, Richard C., 1929-

The triple helix; gene, organism, and environment; [by] Richard Lewontin. Harvard Univ. Press 2000 136p il $25; pa $15

572.8

1. Molecular biology 2. Genetic code

ISBN 0-674-00159-1; 0-674-00677-1 (pa)

LC 99-53879

In this book the author "demonstrates how all organisms, including humans, are the product of intricate interactions between their genes and the environment in which they live. . . . Although the issues Lewontin addresses are huge, he writes about them in a manner fully accessible to the nonspecialist." Publ Wkly

Includes bibliographical references

Morange, Michel

A history of molecular biology; translated by Matthew Cobb. Harvard Univ. Press 1998 336p $39.95; pa $22.50 **572.8**

1. Molecular biology

ISBN 0-674-39855-6; 0-674-00169-9 (pa)

LC 97-47158

"Molecular biology is responsible for the recent high-profile developments in cloning, genetic engineering, DNA fingerprinting, etc. Morange . . . covers the birth of the field at the beginning of this century, the discovery of DNA and the deciphering of the genetic code, and the practical applications resulting from the revelations of the last 50 years." Libr J

Includes bibliographical references

Rabinow, Paul

Making PCR; a story of biotechnology. University of Chicago Press 1996 190p il $22.50; pa $14 **572.8**

1. Polymers 2. Chemical reactions

ISBN 0-226-70146-8; 0-226-70147-6 (pa)

LC 95-49103

The author provides "an 'ethnographic account' of the Cetus Corporation during the invention of PCR, the polymerase chain reaction, a method for increasing the DNA in samples to usable levels and one of the most important techniques in biotechnology." Publ Wkly

"An intriguing read that raises many questions about our understanding of the twisting process of discovery itself." New Sci

Includes bibliographical references

Sulston, John, 1942-

The common thread; a story of science, politics, ethics, and the human genome; [by] John Sulston, Georgina Ferry. Joseph Henry Press 2002 310p il $24.95 **572.8**

1. Human Genome Project

ISBN 0-309-08409-1 LC 2002-14007

The author gives an "account of the excitement, hard work, vision, and daring needed to move from worm biology to recommending sequencing of the human genome, while senior and influential colleagues argued vigorously against it. He speaks forcefully of the necessity of keeping the sequence public and freely available. . . . {This title is} recommended for almost any library, particularly those with readers willing to go beyond sound bites and media hype." Libr J

Includes bibliographical references

Watson, James D., 1928-

The double helix; a personal account of the discovery of the structure of DNA. Scribner 1998 226p il $25; pa $14 * **572.8**

1. DNA 2. Biochemistry—Research

ISBN 0-684-85279-9; 0-7432-1630-X (pa)

LC 98-136787

A reissue of the title first published 1968 by Atheneum Pubs.

Portions of this book were first published in The Atlantic Monthly

This book is a "personal, day-by-day account of how Watson, [Francis] Crick and their collaborators in the years between 1951 and 1963 hit upon the famous 'double helix' model of the 'DNA' [deoxyribonucleic acid] molecule, the fundamental genetical material." America

573.6 Reproductive system

Friedman, David M., 1949-

A mind of its own; a cultural history of the penis. Penguin Books 2003 358p il pa $16

573.6

1. Penis

ISBN 978-0-14-200259-9; 0-14-200259-3

First published 2001 by Free Press

This is a social and medical history of the male organ. Topics discussed include religious teachings about sex, efforts to overcome male impotence throughout history, attitudes toward masturbation, and racial stereotypes relating to phallus size.

"This valuable analysis of the origins of male sexuality and how the conception of maleness has shaped understanding of female sexuality isn't just educational . . . it's entertaining." Booklist

Includes bibliographical references

573.8 Nervous and sensory systems

Hughes, Howard C.
Sensory exotica; a world beyond human experience. MIT Press 1999 345p $40; pa $18.95
573.8
1. Senses and sensation 2. Comparative physiology
ISBN 0-262-08279-9; 0-262-58204-X (pa)
LC 98-51875
This is a compendium of stories and information regarding the vast array of sensory systems that are utilized by different species, ranging from insects to aquatic mammals to humans. . . . Hughes does an excellent job of presenting the facts and the science behind the vast array of sensory systems." Sci Books Films
Includes bibliographical references

Iacoboni, Marco, 1960-
Mirroring people; the new science of how we connect with others. Farrar, Straus and Giroux 2008 308p il $25
573.8
1. Nervous system
ISBN 978-0-374-21017-5; 0-374-21017-9
LC 2007-47322
The author introduces "readers to the world of mirror neurons and what they imply about human empathy, which, the author says, underlies morality. . . . Iacoboni's expansive style and clear descriptions make for a solid introduction to cutting-edge neurobiology." Publ Wkly
Includes bibliographical references

576 Genetics and evolution

Dawkins, Richard, 1941-
Climbing Mount Improbable; original drawings by Lalla Ward. Norton 1996 340p il pa $15.95 hardcover o.p.
576
1. Natural selection 2. Evolution 3. Genetics
ISBN 0-393-31682-3 (pa)
LC 96-19138
"Dawkins discusses genetics, natural selection, and embryology for hundreds of species spanning millions of years. . . . An invigorating trip through the history of life led by one of Darwin's most articulate disciples." Libr J
Includes bibliographical references

River out of Eden; a Darwinian view of life; illustrations by Lalla Ward. Basic Bks. 1995 172p il (Science masters series) pa $14 hardcover o.p.
576
1. Genetics 2. Evolution
ISBN 0-465-06990-8 (pa)
LC 94-37146
The author "explores the evolution of humans from a single ancestor; evolutions of specific organs (e.g., eyes) and coadaptation of species (e.g., wasps and orchids); nature's physical and behavioral mechanisms to maximize survival of DNA; and, finally, the ultimate results when our DNA reaches out in space. His arguments and examples are clear, compelling, and often amusing." Libr J
Includes bibliographical references

The selfish gene. 30th anniversary ed. Oxford University Press 2006 xxiii, 360p il pa $15.95 *
576
1. Genetics 2. Evolution
ISBN 978-0-19-929115-1; 0-19-929115-2 (pa)
LC 2007-271478
First published 1976
The author examines evolution and contends that genes that benefit individual members of a species will be passed on to future generations, rather than those which may benefit the entire group
Includes bibliographical references

576.5 Genetics

Encyclopedia of genetics; editor, revised edition, Bryan D. Ness; editor, first edition, Jeffrey A. Knight. rev ed. Salem Press 2004 2v il set $210 *
576.5
1. Genetics—Encyclopedias
ISBN 1-587-65149-1
LC 2003-26056
First published 1999
"Each volume starts with an alphabetical list of contents. The essays all follow a similar format. Each begins with top matter that lists 'Field of Study' offering one or more subdisciplines under which the topic falls. This is followed by 'Significance', which provides a definition of the topic and a summary of its importance. Next are definitions of 'Key Terms'. Headings break the main body of each essay into clearly defined subtopics. . . . About half of the essays include 'Web Sites of Interest' directing users to Web sites of government agencies, professional or academic societies, support organizations, and a few relevant personal URLs." Booklist
Includes bibliographical references

Genetics; Richard Robinson [editor in chief] Macmillan Ref. USA 2003 4v set $395
576.5
1. Genetics—Encyclopedias
ISBN 0-02-865606-7
LC 2002-3560
This set contains "approximately 250 signed entries from *Accelerated aging: Progeria* to *Zebrafish*. Articles range from a few paragraphs to a few pages in length and focus on a variety of topics, including inheritance, genes and chromosomes, genetic diseases, biotechnology, history, careers, and the ethical, legal, and social issues associated with genetically modified foods and cloning. The entries appear in alphabetical order and include cross-references to related entries. Most have a list of suggested readings and Internet resources. . . . The clear and well-written articles are informative and should meet the needs of most students." Booklist
Includes bibliographical references

Keller, Evelyn Fox, 1936-
The century of the gene. Harvard Univ. Press 2000 186p il $25; pa $15.95
576.5
1. Genetics
ISBN 0-674-00372-1; 0-674-99825-1 (pa)
LC 00-38319

Keller, Evelyn Fox, 1936-—*Continued*

The author "traces the evolution of genetic science over the course of the twentieth century, during which Gregor Mendel's theories of inheritance were rediscovered, the structure of DNA revealed, and the human genome mapped." Booklist

"In this tight, clearly written survey, Keller does a wonderful job of explaining and demonstrating how our knowledge of genetics has accumulated to the extent that we can fathom what we don't understand." Publ Wkly

Includes bibliographical references

Tudge, Colin

The impact of the gene; from Mendel's peas to designer babies. Hill & Wang 2001 375p $27; pa $15   **576.5**

1. Genetics

ISBN 0-374-17523-3; 0-8090-5743-3 (pa)

LC 00-67306

This is a "narrative on the development of genetics from Gregor Mendel's 19th-century pea experiments to the present. . . . Tudge manages to weave the contributions of hundreds of scientists into a story that is coherent, logical, and readable. He also tackles the social implications of genetics . . . and offers thoughtful and persuasive discussions of difficult topics such as evolutionary psychology." Libr J

Includes bibliographical references

Watson, James D., 1928-

DNA: the secret of life; [by] James D. Watson, with Andrew Berry. Knopf 2003 446p il hardcover o.p. pa $25.95   **576.5**

1. Genetics 2. DNA

ISBN 0-375-41546-7; 0-375-71007-8 (pa)

LC 2002-190725

"Watson begins by describing the history of molecular genetics, pausing at times to introduce the scientific players and to describe the . . . experiments showing how DNA is replicated, how its code is translated into the proteins that compose our bodies and how genes are turned on and off as needed. The remaining two-thirds of the book treats the implications of the new genetics: biotechnology, genetically modified food, the forensic use of DNA, the sequencing of the human genome, the development of genetically based medicine and the search for human behavior." N Y Times Book Rev

"Watson sensitively and sensibly treats the controversies aroused by genetically modified foods and organisms, patenting genes, and playing with the 'stuff of life.' Written for the educated and biologically aware reader, this is recommended for most public and academic libraries." Libr J

Includes bibliographical references

576.8 Evolution

Ayala, Francisco J., 1934-

Darwin's gift to science and religion. Joseph Henry Press 2007 237p il map $24.95

576.8

1. Darwin, Charles, 1809-1882 2. Natural selection 3. Evolution 4. Creationism

ISBN 978-0-309-10231-5; 0-309-10231-6

LC 2007-05821

"With the publication in 1859 of On the Origin of Species by Means of Natural Selection, Charles Darwin established evolution. . . . [Francisco Ayala offers] explanations of the science [and] reviews the history that led us to ratify Darwin's theories." Publisher's note

"This elegant book provides the single best introduction to Darwin and the development of evolutionary biology now available." Publ Wkly

Includes bibliographical references

Boulter, Michael Charles

Extinction: evolution and the end of man; [by] Michael Boulter. Columbia Univ. Press 2002 210p il maps $75.70; pa $24   **576.8**

1. Mass extinction of species 2. Evolution 3. Human influence on nature

ISBN 0-231-12836-3; 0-231-12837-1 (pa)

LC 2002-34783

"This book is . . . [an] introduction to the new developments in the science of life and [an] . . . account of the effects that humans have had on the planet." Publisher's note

Browne, Janet, 1950-

Darwin's Origin of species; a biography. Atlantic Monthly Press 2007 174p (Books that changed the world) $20.95 *   **576.8**

1. Darwin, Charles, 1809-1882

ISBN 0-87113-953-7; 978-0-87113-953-5

LC 2007-275116

In this "biography" of Darwin's book, the author "describes the long genesis of Darwin's theories, from his early readings as a university student and his five-year voyage on the Beagle, to his debates with contemporaries and experiments in his garden." Publisher's note

"This excellent introduction is highly recommended for all readers who want to better understand the heated debates that this book still causes today." Publ Wkly

Includes bibliographical references

Darwin, Charles, 1809-1882

The Darwin reader; edited by Mark Ridley. 2nd ed. Norton 1996 315p il pa $21.30 *

576.8

1. Evolution 2. Natural selection

ISBN 0-393-96967-3   LC 95-50297

First published in the United Kingdom with title: The essential Darwin; first Norton edition published 1987

This collection presents excerpts from Darwin's most important works including Origin of the species, The descent of man and Coral reef. Illustrations are taken from the original editions

Includes bibliographical references

Darwin, Charles, 1809-1882—*Continued*

The origin of species by means of natural selection, or, The preservation of favored races in the struggle for life. Modern Library 1993 689p $21.95 * **576.8**
1. Evolution 2. Natural selection 3. Human origins 4. Heredity
ISBN 0-679-60070-1 LC 93-3598
Also available in paperback from Penguin Classics
First published 1859. Variant title: The origin of species by means of natural selection
The classic exposition of the "theory of evolution by natural selection. Darwin argues that every species develops or evolves from a previous one and that all life is a continuing pattern. His objects of study were the variations from generation to generation in domestic plants and animals. . . . While subsequent investigation has superseded some of Darwin's arguments, Origin of Species remains one of the most influential books ever published." Reader's Ency. 4th edition

Davies, P. C. W., 1946-
The fifth miracle; the search for the origin and meaning of life; {by} Paul Davies. Simon & Schuster 1999 304p il pa $14 hardcover o.p.
576.8
1. Life—Origin
ISBN 0-684-86309-X (pa) LC 98-33421
"Life on earth—God's fifth miracle according to Genesis—may have begun with rock-eating microbes far below the surface of Mars. So suggests Davies in this provocative investigation into the origins of life. . . . In his remarkably lucid style, Davies lays out the evidence for a universe inherently friendly to life. A ground-breaking book." Booklist
Includes bibliographical references

Dawkins, Richard, 1941-
The ancestor's tale; a pilgrimage to the dawn of evolution; with additional research by Yan Wong. Houghton Mifflin 2004 673p il $28 *
576.8
1. Evolution
ISBN 0-618-00583-8 LC 2004-59864
The author "sets out on a pilgrimage tracing the history of the human species back to the very origins of life, marking along the way 39 rendezvous points where the human genealogical path crosses that of other terrestrial species. . . . Lively and daring, a book certain to draw even casual readers deep into the adventure—and controversy—of science." Booklist
Includes bibliographical references

Duve, Christian de, 1917-
Life evolving; molecules, mind, and meaning. Oxford Univ. Press 2002 341p il $30
576.8
1. Life—Origin 2. Evolution 3. Life (Biology)
ISBN 0-19-515605-6 LC 2002-75407

The author "surveys the scientific approach to understanding how life began, crucial bottlenecks in its increasing complexity, and the question of the contingency versus the inevitability of the entire process. . . . Beneath the philosophizing, de Duve delineates biology excellently and authoritatively, introducing it with wonder and curiosity that are bound to excite the next generation." Booklist
"A masterful work of synthesis recommended for all collections." Choice
Includes bibliographical references

Eiseley, Loren C., 1907-1977
The immense journey; [by] Loren Eisley. Random House 1957 210p pa $10 hardcover o.p. * **576.8**
1. Evolution 2. Human origins
ISBN 0-394-70157-7 (pa)
"Essays on biology and paleontology by an anthropologist speculating on the origin of man and the theory of evolution." Publ Wkly
Dr Eiseley's "style is beautiful, compelling in impact and poetic in its imagery. His subject is one of the epics of natural science—the 'immense journey' of life as known on this planet." Christ Sci Monit

Encyclopedia of evolution; Mark Pagel, editor in chief. Oxford Univ. Press 2002 2v il set $325
576.8
1. Evolution—Encyclopedias
ISBN 0-19-512200-3 LC 2001-21588
This reference covers topics in evolutionary theory "including developmental biology, social behavior, consciousness, evolution of disease, systematics, population biology, complexity theory, and even art in prehistory. Some biographical articles are also included. . . . [Contributors include] Stephen Jay Gould, Jane Goodall, Sarah Blaffer Hrdy, and John Maynard Smith." Libr J

Fortey, Richard A.
Life; a natural history of the first four billion years of life on earth; [by] Richard Fortey. Knopf 1998 346p il $32.59; pa $15 * **576.8**
1. Evolution 2. Life—Origin
ISBN 0-375-40119-9; 0-375-70261-X (pa)
LC 97-49466
First published 1997 in the United Kingdom with subtitle: an unauthorized biography
In this survey Fortey summarizes "what we know about the history of life on the planet. Because not all life forms left fossil evidence and because interpretations are subject to change, he offers a provisional, personal, and sometimes speculative picture. Fortey points out how discoveries in such areas as historical geology, molecular biology, and genetics have changed past assumptions about the evolution of life forms." Libr J
This work is "written for readers with no science. It will help them understand the specialized and often technical books on evolution that make headlines but leave most people wondering why." N Y Times Book Rev
Includes bibliographical references

Goodwin, Brian C.

How the leopard changed its spots; the evolution of complextiy. Princeton Univ. Press 2001 252p il pa $25.95   **576.8**

1. Evolution 2. Biology 3. System theory 4. Genetics
ISBN 0-691-08809-8; 978-0-691-08809-9

         LC 00-51652

First published 1994 by Scribner

"Arguing that Darwin's theory of natural selection cannot explain the emergence of distinctive species, British biologist Goodwin proposes an alternative theory of evolution. He views organisms as dynamic systems, themselves the primary agents of creative evolutionary adaptation and change that occurs in a matrix of relationships with other members of the same species." Publ Wkly

"Although light on data, this is a serious presentation for the informed lay reader of the philosophical direction some avant-garde biological thought is taking." Libr J

Includes bibliographical references

Gould, Stephen Jay, 1941-2002

Ever since Darwin; reflections in natural history. Norton 1977 285p il pa $14.95 hardcover o.p.

         576.8

1. Darwin, Charles, 1809-1882 2. Evolution 3. Natural selection
ISBN 0-393-30818-9 (pa)   LC 77-22504

"In a series of essays written originally for Natural History magazine Gould explores the impact of Darwin's evolutionary theory on the study of man and other organisms." Libr J

Gould "not only explains scientific theory but comments on science itself, with clarity and wit, simultaneously entertaining and teaching." N Y Times Book Rev

Includes bibliographical references

Hen's teeth and horse's toes. Norton 1983 413p il pa $15.95 hardcover o.p. *   **576.8**

1. Evolution
ISBN 0-393-31103-1 (pa)   LC 82-22259

The theme of this collection is "biological evolution. {The author} has grouped the 30 essays into seven categories: Sensible Oddities, Personalities, Adaptation and Development, Teilhard and Piltdown, Science and Politics, Extinction and a Zebra Trilogy." America

Includes bibliographical references

The panda's thumb; more reflections in natural history; Stephen Jay Gould. Norton 1980 343p il pa $15.95 hardcover o.p.   **576.8**

1. Evolution 2. Natural selection
ISBN 0-393-30819-7 (pa)   LC 80-15952

In these essays "a variety of creatures, including humans, dinosaurs, pandas, turtles, and microscopic organisms, are considered in light of their reflection of Darwin's theory. One intriguing theme which runs throughout the selections is how imperfectly designed anatomy or haphazardly applied anatomical evolution best supports Darwinism." Booklist

Includes bibliographical references

The structure of evolutionary theory. Belknap Press 2002 xxii, 1433p il $39.95   **576.8**

1. Evolution
ISBN 0-674-00613-5   LC 2001-43556

This is a "history and analysis of classical and twentieth-century evolutionary theory." Booklist

Includes bibliographical references

Hooper, Judith

Of moths and men; an evolutionary tale: the untold story of science and the peppered moth. Norton 2002 xx, 377p il $26.95; pa $15.95

         576.8

1. Kettlewell, Henry Bernard David, 1907-1979 2. Majerus, M. E. N., 1954- 3. Natural selection 4. Evolution 5. Moths 6. Fraud
ISBN 0-393-05121-8; 0-393-32525-3 (pa)

         LC 2002-26315

This is an "account of H.B.D. Kettlewell's famous field experiments on the peppered moth, which were widely known as 'Darwin's missing evidence,' proof of natural selection in action—until 1998, that is, when biologist Michael Majerus showed Kettlewell's findings to be falsified and wrong." Publ Wkly

"A fascinating look at the people behind scientific theories." Booklist

Includes bibliographical references

Impey, Chris

The living cosmos; humankind's search for life in the universe. Random House 2007 393p il map $27.95   **576.8**

1. Life—Origin 2. Space biology 3. Life on other planets
ISBN 978-1-4000-6506-6; 1-4000-6506-2

         LC 2007-10363

This book is a "discussion of three fundamental astrobiological questions: (1) How many habitable worlds might exist in the universe? (2) Is life on Earth unique? (3) If there is extraterrestrial life, are [there] any intelligent civilizations with whom we might be able to communicate?" Sci Books Films

"Aimed squarely at newcomers to general-interest science books, Impey's survey of exobiology will pique curiosity about whether life beyond Earth exists." Booklist

Includes bibliographical references

Jakosky, Bruce M.

The search for life on other planets; by Bruce Jakosky. Cambridge Univ. Press 1998 326p il pa $19.95 hardcover o.p.   **576.8**

1. Life on other planets
ISBN 0-521-59837-0 (pa)   LC 97-51549

"After opening with a look at the development of and requirements for terrestrial life, Jakosky conducts a tour of the universe, steadily progressing toward more speculative venues. The first stop is Mars and the controversial evidence of bacterial life there in ancient epochs. Then it's onward to Venus, the satellites of Jupiter and Saturn and then to possible terrestrial planets in orbit around other stars." Publ Wkly

Includes bibliographical references

Jones, Steve, 1944-
Darwin's ghost; the origin of species updated. Random House 2000 xxix, 377p il pa $15.95 hardcover o.p. **576.8**

1. Natural selection 2. Evolution
ISBN 0-345-42277-5 (pa)   LC 99-53246
First published 1999 in the United Kingdom with title: Almost like a whale

Jones "has updated Charles Darwin's *On the origin of species* (1859) so that the fact of organic evolution is both understandable and relevant to today's general reader. . . . Very informative and cogently argued, this book is an important addition to the natural history literature." Libr J

Includes bibliographical references

Koerner, David
Here be dragons; the scientific quest for extraterrestrial life; [by] David Koerner, Simon LeVay. Oxford Univ. Press 2000 264p il pa $24.95 hardcover o.p. **576.8**

1. Life on other planets 2. Life—Origin
ISBN 0-19-514600-X (pa)   LC 99-38170
In this book the authors explore "the origin of life and its occurrence outside Earth. . . . They offer a broad overview of up-to-date research and thought on topics ranging from the chemistry of life's origins to the search for extra-solar planets, the process of evolution, and the nature of life and the cosmos." Booklist

Includes bibliographical references

Larson, Edward J.
Evolution: the remarkable history of a scientific theory. Modern Library 2004 337p il (Modern Library chronicles) $21.95; pa $14.95
576.8

1. Evolution
ISBN 0-679-64288-9; 0-8129-6849-2 (pa)
LC 2003-64888
This is an "overview of evolutionary thought from ancient speculations to the emergence of a neo-Darwinian synthesis. It focuses on those essential facts, events, and ideas that have contributed to the successes of scientific evolutionism. . . . Larson is to be commended for stressing the value of both scientific inquiry and the evolutionary framework. This outstanding book is highly recommended for all academic and public libraries." Libr J

Includes bibliographical references

Margulis, Lynn, 1938-
Symbiotic planet; a new look at evolution. Basic Bks. 1998 147p il (Science masters series) pa $14 hardcover o.p. **576.8**

1. Symbiosis 2. Evolution 3. Gaia hypothesis
ISBN 0-465-07272-0 (pa)   LC 98-38921
"From the origin of life to the classification and phylogeny of living organisms, from a discussion of Gaia—the belief that Earth operates like a living being—to a discussion of the underlying reasons for sex, iconoclastic biologist Margulis . . . takes on many of the big questions in biology. . . . In a book that is part autobiography and part biological primer, Margulis . . . advances

the idea that a large part of organic evolution can be explained by symbiosis." Publ Wkly

Includes bibliographical references

Mayr, Ernst, 1904-2005
What evolution is. Basic Bks. 2001 318p il maps pa $16 hardcover o.p. **576.8**

1. Evolution
ISBN 0-465-04426-3 (pa)   LC 2001-36562
This introduction to the theory of evolution offers "insights into taxonomy, adaptation, common descent, biodiversity, and those mechanisms of organic evolution that result in the process of speciation." Libr J

"A wise and illuminating examination, by an illustrious evolutionary biologist, that sorts out the complexities of evolution." N Y Times Book Rev

Includes bibliographical references

Novacek, Michael J.
Terra; our 100-million-year-old ecosystem—and the threats that now put it at risk; [by] Michael Novacek. Farrar, Straus and Giroux 2007 xxiv, 451p il map $27 **576.8**

1. Human influence on nature 2. Ecology 3. Evolution 4. Environmental degradation
ISBN 978-0-374-27325-5; 0-374-27325-1
LC 2007-9126
The author takes a "look at what humans have done over time and in more recent years. Combining paleontology, evolutionary biology, and environmental science, he shows how these three perspectives can bring us to a better understanding of the 'mass extinction event' that threatens this planet if changes aren't implemented now." Libr J

"Novacek writes vividly of emptying oceans, vanishing forests, and threatened freshwater sources, and definitively compares past episodes of climate change and mass extinction with today's unique crisis, creating an essential earth-now report." Booklist

Includes bibliographical references

Palumbi, Stephen R.
The evolution explosion; how humans cause rapid evolutionary change. Norton 2001 277p il $24.95; pa $14.95 **576.8**

1. Evolution 2. Human influence on nature
ISBN 0-393-02011-8; 0-393-32338-2 (pa)
LC 00-67004
This describes human causes of rapid evolutionary change, focusing on bacteria which have evolved strains resistant to antibiotics and insects resistant to pesticides

"Palumbi's writing is lively and lucid, and his analogies are felicitous." Booklist

Includes bibliographical references

Parker, Andrew, 1967-
In the blink of an eye. Perseus Pub 2003 316p il hardcover o.p. pa $15 **576.8**

1. Evolution 2. Fossils
ISBN 0-7382-0607-5; 0-465-05438-2 (pa)
LC 2003-282077

Parker, Andrew, 1967-—*Continued*

The author "provides a relatively simple explanation for the sudden explosion of life forms that defines the boundary between the pre-Cambrian and Cambrian eras approximately 543 million years ago: 'The Cambrian explosion was triggered by the sudden evolution of vision' in simple organisms. . . . In readable prose, Parker provides detailed information on the fossil record as well as a wealth of interesting material on the role light plays in environments and how vision operates across a host of species. Although at times his tangents are a bit distracting, Parker's book will bring his controversial ideas to the general public." Publ Wkly

Pennock, Robert T.

Tower of Babel; the evidence against the new creationism. MIT Press 1999 429p $55; pa $21.95
576.8
1. Evolution 2. Creationism 3. Religion and science
ISBN 0-262-16180-X; 0-262-66165-9 (pa)
LC 98-27286
"A Bradford book"

The author "catalogues the wide range of creationist beliefs, dissects their main arguments and highlights what he sees as their internal inconsistencies." Publ Wkly

By "disentangling the scientific issues from the religious and philosophic ones, Pennock has made a valuable contribution to a too-often-overheated debate." Booklist

Includes bibliographical references

Powell, James Lawrence, 1936-

Night comes to the Cretaceous; dinosaur extinction and the transformation of modern geology; [by] James L. Powell. Freeman, W.H. 1998 250p il map $22.95
576.8
1. Catastrophes (Geology) 2. Mass extinction of species 3. Dinosaurs
ISBN 0-7167-3117-7
LC 98-13192

The author "summarizes arguments for and against the controversial 'impact theory' of the extinction of the dinosaurs first proposed by Nobel physicist Luis Alvarez and his geologist son Walter and others in 1980. . . . Powell's book is written for a broad audience. It is slow reading in places, but explanations added in parentheses clarify technical materials." Sci Books Films

Includes bibliographical references

Rice, Stanley Arthur, 1957-

Encyclopedia of evolution; [by] Stanley A. Rice; foreword by Massimo Pigliucci. Facts on File 2007 468p il (Facts on File science library) $75
576.8
1. Evolution—Encyclopedias
ISBN 0-8160-5515-7; 978-0-8160-5515-9
LC 2005-31646

This encyclopedia "contains more than 200 entries that span modern evolutionary science and the history of its development. . . . Five essays that explore . . . questions resulting from studies in evolutionary science are included as well. The appendix consists of a summary of Charles Darwin's Origin of Species." Publisher's note

Includes bibliographical references

Rose, Michael R. (Michael Robertson), 1955-

Darwin's spectre; evolutionary biology in the modern world. Princeton Univ. Press 1998 233p pa $20.95 hardcover o.p.
576.8
1. Evolution 2. Natural selection
ISBN 0-691-05008-2 (pa)
LC 98-11494

Rose "outlines the elements of evolutionary theory and then examines its contemporary applications in agriculture, where it is manifested in genetically engineered crops and animals, and in the new and developed field of 'Darwinian medicine,' which is transforming our understanding of pathogens and how to treat certain diseases." Libr J

Includes bibliographical references

Sawyer, Kathy

The rock from Mars; a detective story on two planets. Random House 2006 394p il $25.95
576.8
1. Life on other planets 2. Meteorites 3. Mars (Planet)
ISBN 1-4000-6010-9
LC 2005-46560

"The titular 'rock' (actually a meteorite) was found in the Antarctic in 1984. . . . [The author] introduces us to the scientists who became obsessed with the rock and takes us through the . . . discovery process that led them to the controversial conclusion that this fractured lump contained evidence that life had existed on Mars in the distant past." Libr J

"This book is an engrossing read for science buffs and general readers alike." Publ Wkly

Includes bibliographical references

Schopf, J. William, 1941-

Cradle of life; the discovery of earth's earliest fossils. Princeton Univ. Press 1999 367p il $55; pa $20.95
576.8
1. Life—Origin 2. Fossils
ISBN 0-691-00230-4; 0-691-08864-0 (pa)
LC 98-42443

An "exploration of how Precambrian fossils came to light and what they've taught us. The author covers the history of evolutionary thought and the exploits of field paleontologists, as well as the trajectory of his own career." Publ Wkly

"Schopf's chapter on the evolution of biochemical pathways is a fascinating and wonderfully clear exposition of a difficult topic." Libr J

Includes bibliographical references

Small, Meredith F.

What's love got to do with it? the evolution of human mating. Anchor Bks. (NY) 1995 xx, 249p pa $14.95 hardcover o.p.
576.8
1. Evolution 2. Sex (Biology) 3. Sexual behavior
ISBN 0-385-47702-3 (pa)
LC 95-1359

The author reviews various "experimental and observational studies on male and female sexuality, choosing a mate, homosexuality, and the impact of technology on sexual behavior, among other topics." Sci Books Films

"Extensively documented and indexed, Small's text is . . . highly readable." Libr J

Includes bibliographical references

Ward, Peter Douglas, 1949-
Life as we do not know it; the NASA search for (and synthesis of) alien life. Viking 2005 292p il $25.95 **576.8**
1. Life on other planets 2. Life—Origin
ISBN 0-670-03458-4 LC 2005-56299
The author "believes researchers might be taking the wrong approach by looking only for earthly DNA-based life forms. Truly alien life, he argues, might have completely different origins. . . . The science is neatly laid out, and readers willing to follow his daring, scientifically based speculations will find their imaginations spurred." Publ Wkly

Rare earth; why complex life is uncommon in the universe; [by] Peter Ward, Don Brownlee. Copernicus 1999 xxviii, 333p il $27.50; pa $16.95 **576.8**
1. Life on other planets
ISBN 0-387-98701-0; 0-387-95289-6 (pa)
LC 99-20532
Partial contents: Why life might be widespread in the universe; Habitable zones of the universe; Life's first appearance on Earth; The enigma of the Cambrian explosion; Mass extinctions and the Rare Earth Hypothesis; The surprising importance of plate tectonics; Assessing the odds
"Arguing that complex life is a rare event in the universe, this compelling book magnifies the significance—and tragedy—of species extinction." Libr J
Includes bibliographical references

Wilson, David Sloan
Evolution for everyone; how Darwin's theory can change the way we think about our lives. Delacorte Press 2007 390p $24 * **576.8**
1. Evolution
ISBN 978-0-385-34021-2; 0-385-34021-4
LC 2006-23685
"Building on diverse examples, Wilson demonstrates that evolution is completely relevant to modern human affairs, including how we use language, create culture and define morality." Publ Wkly
"Rather than catalog its successes, denounce its detractors or in any way present evolutionary theory as the province of expert tacticians like himself, Wilson invites readers inside and shows them how Darwinism is done, and at lesson's end urges us to go ahead, feel free to try it at home. The result is a sprightly, absorbing and charmingly earnest book that manages a minor miracle, the near-complete emulsifying of science and the 'real world,' ingredients too often kept stubbornly, senselessly apart." N Y Times Book Rev
Includes bibliographical references

Young, Christian C., 1968-
Evolution and creationism; a documentary and reference guide; [by] Christian C. Young and Mark A. Largent. Greenwood Press 2007 298p il $85 * **576.8**
1. Evolution 2. Creationism
ISBN 978-0-313-33953-0; 0-313-33953-8
LC 2007-10682

"This reference work provides over 40 of the most important documents to help readers understand the [evolution versus creationism] debate in the eyes of the people of the time. Each document is from a major participant in the debates from the predecessors of Darwin to the judges of the influential court cases of the present day." Publisher's note
Includes bibliographical references

577 Ecology

Baskin, Yvonne
A plague of rats and rubbervines; the growing threat of species invasions. Island Press (Washington, D.C.) 2002 377p il hardcover o.p. pa $16 * **577**
1. Biological invasions 2. Nature conservation
ISBN 1-55963-876-1; 1-55963-051-5 (pa)
LC 2002-4029
"A SCOPE-GISP project"
The author "describes her visits to several environments where alien species have run amok, such as Hawaii, the Galapagos Islands, South Africa, and New Zealand, skillfully revealing her zoological and botanical knowledge. . . . Her survey—with historical perspective on biological interchange since the time of Columbus—of an extinction threat second only to habitat destruction will appeal to ecologically minded readers." Booklist
Includes bibliographical references

Bright, Chris
Life out of bounds; bioinvasion in a borderless world. Norton 1998 287p il (Worldwatch environmental alert series) pa $13.95 **577**
1. Biological invasions 2. Ecology
ISBN 0-393-31814-1 LC 99-163011
"Bright discusses the increasingly urgent issue of invasive exotic plants and animals and their ecological impact worldwide on native species. An excellent introduction to the field, loaded with historical examples and heavily referenced." Libr J
Includes bibliographical references

Buchmann, Stephen
The forgotten pollinators; [by] Stephen L. Buchmann and Gary Paul Nabhan; with a foreword by Edward O. Wilson; illustrations by Paul Mirocha. Island Press (Covelo) 1996 xx, 292p il $30; pa $18 **577**
1. Fertilization of plants 2. Biological diversity 3. Ecology
ISBN 1-55963-352-2; 1-55963-353-0 (pa)
LC 96-802
The authors explore the "link between plants and their pollinators. It is a disturbing story of disappearing insects and diminishing plant reproduction, owing to overuse of pesticide and fragmented habitat. The authors combine anecdotes from the field with discussions of ecology, entomology, botany, crop science and the economics of pollination." Publ Wkly
Includes bibliographical references

Burdick, Alan

Out of Eden; an odyssey of ecological invasion. Farrar, Straus & Giroux 2005 324p il $25; pa $14
*   **577**

    1. Biological invasions 2. Ecology
    ISBN 0-374-21973-7; 0-374-53043-2 (pa)
                            LC 2005-922517
This book argues that "exotic animals and plants are crossing the globe, borne on the . . . tide of human traffic to places where nature never intended them to be. . . . [These species] increasingly crowd native and endangered species out of existence." Publisher's note
"A sober report, Burdick's work still sounds an alarm for readers concerned with the way humans alter nature." Booklist

Preston, Richard

The wild trees; a story of passion and daring. Random House 2007 294p il map $25.95; pa $16
                                    577

    1. Sillett, Steve 2. Redwood
    ISBN   978-1-4000-6489-2;   1-4000-6489-9; 978-0-8129-7559-8 (pa); 0-8129-7559-6 (pa)
                            LC 2006-48646
The author tells the story of Steve Sillett, Marie Antoine and other naturalists and researchers who climb and explore giant redwoods in northern California
"There is something so elementally boyish in searching out the biggest and tallest, poring over maps and measurements, dubbing these trees with names lifted from J.R.R. Tolkien's Middle Earth. . . . Preston knows how to fold the science into the seams of his narrative, and his dry humor crops up, pleasurably, at the edges of his observations." Cleveland Plain Dealer

Roston, Eric

The carbon age; how life's core element has become civilization's greatest threat. Distributed to the trade by Macmillan 2008 309p il $25.99
                                    577

    1. Carbon
    ISBN 978-0-8027-1557-9; 0-8027-1557-5
                            LC 2008-2754
"The first half traces carbon's history from the beginning of the universe, the Big Bang, and the nucleosynthesis (the formation of the elements) through the life cycle of stars, and then covers the development of life and dynamics of the 'natural' carbon cycle of Earth. The second section spans the last 150 years and delves into the impact of humans on the climate in creating what Roston calls the 'industrial carbon cycle.' Without using a great deal of scientific jargon, Roston leads us patiently and clearly through this complex issue." Libr J
Includes bibliographical references

Slobodkin, Lawrence B.

A citizen's guide to ecology. Oxford University Press 2003 245p $40; pa $14.95   **577**
    1. Ecology 2. Human influence on nature
    ISBN 0-19-516286-2; 0-19-516287-0 (pa)
                            LC 2002-72826

This book attempts to explain "the ecological world, and how individual citizens can participate in practical decisions on ecological issues. It tackles such issues as global warming, ecology and health, organic farming, species extinction and adaptation, and endangered species." Publisher's note
"Slobodkin's sober examination of [the issues] . . . offers the empowerment that arises from genuine knowledge about problems." Booklist
Includes bibliographical references

Smil, Vaclav

The earth's biosphere; evolution, dynamics, and change. MIT Press 2002 346p il maps $32.95; pa $19.95   **577**
    1. Biosphere
    ISBN 0-262-19472-4; 0-262-69298-8 (pa)
                            LC 2001-58705
This study of the Earth's biosphere "examines the biosphere's physics, chemistry, biology, geology, oceanography, energy, climatology, and ecology, as well as the changes caused by human activity." Publisher's note
"A presentation marked by balance and clarity. . . . A superior, comprehensive survey." Booklist
Includes bibliographical references

Wilson, Edward O., 1929-

The diversity of life. Harvard Univ. Press 1992 424p il maps (Questions of science) $31.50
                                    577

    1. Ecology 2. Nature conservation
    ISBN 0-674-21298-3   LC 92-9018
    Also available in paperback from Norton
"Identifying five natural events that have disrupted evolution and global diversity (climatic changes, meteorite strikes), Wilson maintains that the present sixth great extinction is being caused by human neglect and ignorance. This important book is highly recommended." Libr J
Includes bibliographical references

577.2   Specific factors affecting ecology

Winston, Mark L.

Nature wars; people vs. pests. Harvard Univ. Press 1997 210p $27.50; pa $15.95   **577.2**
    1. Pesticides—Environmental aspects 2. Pest control 3. Human influence on nature
    ISBN 0-674-60541-1; 0-674-60542-X (pa)
                            LC 97-17302
"Winston provides case studies demonstrating alternative methods of pest control, explaining how political, social, economic, and biologic interactions behind pest-management decisions have contributed to our failure to replace toxic chemicals as our first method of choice. . . . Winston has written a convincing and necessary book." Libr J
Includes bibliographical references

577.3 Forest ecology

Royte, Elizabeth
The Tapir's morning bath; mysteries of the tropical rain forest and the scientists who are trying to solve them. Houghton Mifflin 2001 328p maps $25; pa $14   **577.3**
1. Rain forest ecology
ISBN 0-395-97997-8; 0-618-25758-6 (pa)
    LC 2001-24989
Royte discusses time spent with scientists studying the ecology of Barro Colorado, an island in the Panama Canal.
This is "a superb introduction to tropical ecology and theoretical biology, as well as original and thoroughly engaging travel writing." Publ Wkly
Includes bibliographical references

577.4 Grassland ecology

Manning, Richard, 1951-
Grassland; the history, biology, politics, and promise of the American prairie. Viking 1995 306p pa $15 hardcover o.p.   **577.4**
1. Grassland ecology 2. Human influence on nature
ISBN 0-14-023388-1 (pa)   LC 95-10073
"Our culture's disrespect for grasslands has produced an environmental catastrophe, charges the author. By allowing overgrazing on public lands, our government is wiping out an ecosystem as vital as the Brazilian rain forests. In this sweeping exploration of the prairie, Manning . . . makes an eloquent plea to restore it." Publ Wkly
Includes bibliographical references

577.6 Aquatic ecology Freshwater ecology

Douglas, Marjory Stoneman
The Everglades; river of grass; illustrated by Robert Fink; [update by Michael Grunwald] 60th anniversary ed. Pineapple Press 2007 447p $19.95
    577.6
1. Everglades (Fla.)
ISBN 978-1-56164-394-3   LC 2007-28384
First published 1947 by Rinehart
A natural history of South Florida focusing on the unique ecosystem of the Everglades. Discusses environmental changes, scientific research, and political responses to conservation efforts.
Includes bibliographical references

577.7 Marine ecology

Carson, Rachel, 1907-1964
The edge of the sea; with illustrations by Bob Hines. Houghton Mifflin 1955 276p il pa $14 hardcover o.p.   **577.7**

1. Marine biology 2. Seashore
ISBN 0-395-92496-0 (pa)
Also available in hardcover from P. Smith
"The seashores of the world may be divided into three basic types: the rugged shores of rock, the sand beaches, and the coral reefs and all their associated features. Each has its typical community of plants and animals. The Atlantic coast of the United States [provides] clear examples of each of these types. I have chosen it as the setting for my pictures of shore life." Preface

Ellis, Richard, 1938-
The empty ocean; plundering the world's marine life; written and illustrated by Richard Ellis. Island Press 2003 367p il hardcover o.p. pa $25 *
    577.7
1. Marine ecology 2. Endangered species
ISBN 1-55963-974-1; 1-55963-637-8 (pa)
The author "explains the economic, political, historical, and biological reasons for declining fisheries, the plight of sea turtles, disappearance of marine birds, slaughter of marine mammals, and destruction of coral reefs." Libr J
"Rather than writing the 'Silent Spring' of the oceans, [Ellis] has produced a book that is likely to provide the inspiration and source materials for such a badly needed work . . . It is also a splendid example of history illuminating ecology, with well-chosen facts that enable us to picture a largely invisible catastrophe." N Y Times Book Rev
Includes bibliographical references

578 Natural history of organisms and related subjects

Weidensaul, Scott
Return to wild America; a yearlong journey in search of the continent's natural soul. North Point Press 2005 xx, 394p il map $26; pa $15 *
    578
1. Peterson, Roger Tory, 1908-1996 2. Fisher, James Maxwell McConnell, 1912-1970 3. Natural history—North America
ISBN 0-8654-7688-8; 0-8654-7731-0 (pa)
    LC 2005-47720
Fifty years after the publishing of Roger Tory Peterson's and James Fisher's *Wild America*, the author retraces Peterson and Fisher's steps "from Newfoundland's craggy coastline, down the East Coast, into Mexico and up the West Coast to Alaska. . . . This engrossing state-of-nature memoir, making a vibrant case for preserving America's wild past for future Americans, promises to become a classic in its own right." Publ Wkly
Includes bibliographical references

Wolfe, David W.
Tales from the underground; a natural history of subterranean life. Perseus Bks. 2001 221p il pa $18 hardcover o.p.   **578**

Wolfe, David W.—*Continued*
1. Soil microbiology
ISBN 0-7382-0679-2 (pa)
The author discusses the ecology of life in the soil and the earth's rocky crust, including Darwin's experiments with earthworms, Lewis and Clark's first encounter with prairie dogs, the use of genetic tools, and the possible role of primitive underground microbes in evolution.

Wolfe "explains in a straightforward, readable style that there is probably as much biodiversity and even as much biomass below ground as above." New Sci
Includes bibliographical references

578.4   Adaptation

Bonner, John Tyler
Why size matters; from bacteria to blue whales. Princeton University Press 2006 161p il $16.95
578.4
1. Size
ISBN 978-0-691-12850-4; 0-691-12850-2
LC 2006-04945
"The strength, surface area, complexity, rates of living processes such as metabolism and longevity, and abundance of organisms [are related to body size]." Sci Books Films
The author's "tone is warm and engaging, his illustrative examples are simple to grasp, while his prose is precise, clear and highly readable." Times Lit Suppl
Includes bibliographical references

578.68   Rare and endangered species

Ackerman, Diane
The rarest of the rare; vanishing animals, timeless worlds. Random House 1995 xxi, 184p pa $12 hardcover o.p.   **578.68**
1. Endangered species 2. Rare animals
ISBN 0-679-77623-0 (pa)   LC 95-8499
In these essays the author "tells of her adventures in several relatively isolated habitats of several endangered animal species: monk seals in Hawaii, golden lion tamarins in the Brazilian rain forest, short-tailed albatrosses on a Japanese volcanic island, and monarch butterflies in southern California. For each of the habitats Ackerman has recruited the company of one or more biologically sophisticated guides." Choice
"Every species that is endangered or becomes extinct deserves so poetic a chronicler as Ackerman." Libr J

578.7   Organisms characteristic of specific kinds of environments

Burt, William, 1948-
Marshes; the disappearing Edens. Yale University Press 2007 179p il $35   **578.7**
1. Marshes
ISBN 978-0-300-12229-9; 0-300-12229-2
LC 2006-26961

This book combines photographs of marsh life with information about wetland habitat in North America.
"This well-structured, readable book will be valuable for students, teachers, researchers, and sundry readers interested in a unique kind of wetland. Reading this book is an excellent way to understand marshes as wild places." Choice
Includes bibliographical references

Carson, Rachel, 1907-1964
Under the sea wind; introduction by Linda Lear, illustrations by Howard Frech. Penguin Books 2007 xx, 184p il (Penguin classics) pa $15
578.7
1. Marine biology
ISBN 978-0-14-310496-4   LC 2006-50707
First published 1941 by Simon & Schuster
A series of narratives describe the birds and sea creatures that inhabit the Eastern coasts of North America.
Includes bibliographical references

Jukofsky, Diane
Encyclopedia of rainforests; by Diane Jukofsky for the Rainforest Alliance. Oryx Press 2001 xxxi, 328p il $84.95   **578.7**
1. Rain forests—Encyclopedias
ISBN 1-57356-259-9   LC 2001-32154
This "encyclopedia surveys the flora, fauna, and native peoples of the tropical rainforest, including 261 families of plants and 818 taxonomic groups of animals. The work has five parts: tropical forest wildlife, tropical forest plants, people and tropical forests, saving tropical forests, and rainforests resources. Topics are arranged alphabetically; within the plant and animal sections, related articles are arranged taxonomically." Choice
"The text as a whole, which . . . includes sections on peoples, noted naturalists, and conservation efforts, . . . provides a fine introduction to the world of the rainforest and would be appreciated by any high school/undergraduate library." Libr J
Includes bibliographical references

Kaplan, Eugene H. (Eugene Herbert), 1932-
Sensuous seas; tales of a marine biologist; drawings by Sandy Chichester Rivkin and Susan L. Kaplan. Princeton University Press 2006 271p il $24.95   **578.7**
1. Marine biology 2. Sexual behavior in animals
ISBN 978-0-691-12560-2; 0-691-12560-0
LC 2005-54517
"The feeding and mating habits of some of the ocean's strangest creatures are the subject of these 31 entertaining essays by Hofstra ecologist Kaplan. . . . Kaplan's lively essays, accompanied by 150 exquisite line drawings, are a wonderful introduction to the mysteries of the ocean." Publ Wkly
Includes bibliographical references

Koslow, J. Anthony, 1947-
The silent deep; the discovery, ecology, and conservation of the deep sea; [by] Tony Koslow. University of Chicago Press 2007 270p il map $35 *
578.7
1. Marine ecology 2. Marine resources 3. Conservation of natural resources
ISBN 978-0-226-45125-1; 0-226-45125-9
LC 2006-22282
This is an "overview of 200 years' worth of oceanographic discoveries, research and resource exploitation. Organized chronologically, part one begins with ancient thinkers like Aristotle before profiling the work of pioneering oceanic naturalists of the early 19th century like Forbes, Milne-Edwards, Sars and (of course) Darwin. Part two explores 20th-century methods for tackling the mysteries of the deep sea, including spectacular discoveries of unknown species, hydrothermal hotsprings, methane seeps and whale falls. The third section considers the deep-reaching impact of humanity—not only through fishing, mining and dumping, but also global climate change—whose effects touch every region of the sea." Publ Wkly
"This important book should be read by everyone who cares about Earth's future." Choice
Includes bibliographical references

Marent, Thomas, 1966-
Rainforest; [by] Thomas Marent with Ben Morgan. DK Pub. 2006 360p il map $40 *
578.7
1. Rain forests—Pictorial works
ISBN 0-7566-1940-8; 978-0-7566-1940-4
LC 2006-6774
Includes audio CD
This "book is the product of Swiss photographer Marent's passion for exploring rainforests on five continents and over 16 years. His spectacularly beautiful photographs show much about the nature of rainforests and their curious inhabitants, and the accompanying text explains what you are seeing and what it can tell you about these ecosystems. . . . An accompanying CD provides rainforest sounds from various locations. This book . . . is not only beautiful but an excellent source of information. It also shows the amazing diversity of species that makes rainforests unique and valuable." Libr J

579 Microorganisms, fungi, algae

Sankaran, Neeraja
Microbes and people: an A-Z of microorganisms in our lives. Oryx Press 2000 297p il $62.95 *
579
ISBN 1-57356-217-3
LC 00-10117
"Entries cover environmental, industrial, and food microbiology, in addition to the microbiology of health and disease. Scientific techniques used for studying microorganisms are discussed, and biographies of key individuals are provided. A chronology of infections and disease epidemics from 430 BC to the present is included as an appendix." Publisher's note
"Because it provides very readable coverage of topics

so much in the news lately, this dictionary will be much used in high school, undergraduate, and public libraries." Booklist
Includes bibliographical references

579.3 Prokaryotes

Karlen, Arno
Biography of a germ. Pantheon Bks. 2000 178p pa $12 hardcover o.p.
579.3
1. Microorganisms 2. Lyme disease
ISBN 0-385-72066-1 (pa)
LC 99-57304
This "book examines *Borrelia burgdorferi*, the elusive spirochete that causes Lyme disease." New Yorker
"Karlen has created a vigorous, compact account of Bb's life and times." Publ Wkly

579.5 Fungi Eumycophyta (True fungi)

Hudler, George W.
Magical mushrooms, mischievous molds. Princeton Univ. Press 1998 248p il pa $18.95 hardcover o.p.
579.5
1. Fungi
ISBN 0-691-07016-4 (pa)
LC 98-10163
The author shows how fungi "have dramatically influenced the course of human history. With chapters on yeasts used to make bread and to brew alcoholic beverages, on the medicinal uses of fungi from penicillin to possible treatments for AIDS, on edible mushrooms like the common button mushroom and the more exotic truffle, and on hallucinogenic mushrooms, Hudler takes readers on an enthralling and informative tour of this much maligned kingdom." Publ Wkly
Includes bibliographical references

579.6 Mushrooms

Lincoff, Gary
The Audubon Society field guide to North American mushrooms; [by] Gary H. Lincoff; visual key by Carol Nehring. Knopf 1981 926p il flexible bdg $19.95 *
579.6
1. Mushrooms
ISBN 0-394-51992-2
LC 81-80827
"A Chanticleer Press edition. The Audubon Society field guide series"
This guide to 703 species of common mushrooms provides 762 color photographs and descriptions as keys to identifying these plants.
"The author is an expert on mushroom toxins and instills responsible cautions. The photos are uncommonly beautiful." SLJ

McKnight, Kent H.

A field guide to mushrooms, North America; [by] Kent H. McKnight and Vera B. McKnight; illustrations by Vera B. McKnight. Houghton Mifflin 1987 429p il pa $21 hardcover o.p.

579.6

1. Mushrooms
ISBN 0-395-91090-0 (pa)   LC 86-27799
"The Peterson field guide series"
"Sponsored by the National Audubon Society and the National Wildlife Federation"
"More than 500 species [of mushrooms] are described and depicted. . . . Edibility of each species is noted and signified by marginal pictograms both in the text and on the colorplates. . . . Appended: a genial chapter of recipes by Anne Dow, glossary, selected references, and index." Booklist

Smith, Alexander Hanchett, 1904-1988

The mushroom hunter's field guide; [by] Alexander H. Smith and Nancy Smith Weber. all color & enlarged. University of Mich. Press 1980 316p il $24.95   **579.6**
1. Mushrooms
ISBN 0-472-85610-3   LC 80-10514
First published 1958
This is a "field guide for both novices and experts alike. The introductory chapter explains basic terminology and what to look for when identifying fungi. More than 280 mushrooms are described, including identifying marks, edibility, habitat, native range, and type of spore. A color photograph . . . of each mushroom is most valuable for accurate information." Booklist
Includes bibliographical references

580   Plants (Botany)

The **Facts** on File dictionary of botany; edited by Jill Bailey. Facts on File 2002 250p il $49.50
580
ISBN 0-8160-4910-6   LC 2002-35202
"Facts on File science library"
This dictionary covers "pure and applied plant science, including the taxonomy and classification of plants, with entries for the higher-ranking taxa. Techniques of nucleic acid technology are included, with references made to applications in horticulture and agriculture." Publisher's note
Includes bibliographical references

Magill's encyclopedia of science; plant life; editor, Bryan D. Ness. Salem Press 2002 4v il map set $457 *   **580**
1. Botany—Encyclopedias
ISBN 1-58765-084-3   LC 2002-13319
This encyclopedia provides "information for any study related to plants, archaea, bacteria, algae, or fungi, from molecular-level processes to planet-wide economic or environmental issues. The 379 signed articles, about half of which are published with revisions and updated bibliographies from several of the publisher's earlier reference books, are arranged into a single alphabet." SLJ
Includes bibliographical references

581.6   Miscellaneous nontaxonomic kinds of plants

Angier, Bradford

Field guide to edible wild plants; jacket and book illustrated by Arthur J. Anderson. Stackpole Bks. 1974 256p il pa $16.95 hardcover o.p.
581.6
1. Edible plants
ISBN 0-8117-2018-7 (pa)
"Plants are arranged alphabetically by one of their common names. Each entry includes genus, family affiliation, other common names, a lengthy plant description (including many interesting facts about the plant), notes on distribution, and a statement concerning edibility and preparation of the plant parts." Libr J

Davis, Wade

One river; explorations and discoveries in the Amazon rain forest. Simon & Schuster 1996 537p il pa $16 hardcover o.p.   **581.6**
1. Schultes, Richard Evans, 1915-2001 2. Plowman, Timothy Charles, 1944-1989 3. Ethnobotany 4. Hallucinogens 5. Medical botany
ISBN 0-684-83496-0 (pa)   LC 96-21516
"This is the story of Timothy Plowman, a young ethnobotanist who died while looking for medicinal plants in the South American rain forests. . . . Plowman was the brilliant protégé of Richard Evans Schultes, one of the world's leading authorities on hallucinogenic plants and the Amazon rain forest. The author mixes the backgrounds and travels of the two men with sociology of South American tribes and their sacred plants." Libr J
Davis "writes magnificently, with verve when describing his many adventurous field trips, accurately and efficiently when telling science or history, and with vivid fantasy when portraying hallucinogenic trances." N Y Times Book Rev
Includes bibliographical references

Gibbons, Euell

Stalking the wild asparagus; with illustrations by Margaret F. Schroeder; including a remembrance of the author by John McPhee. 25th anniversary ed. Hood, A.C. 1987 c1962 303p il pa $17.50 hardcover o.p.   **581.6**
1. Edible plants 2. Cooking
ISBN 0-911469-036 (pa)   LC 87-16933
A reprint of the title first published 1962 by McKay
In this series of brief anecdotal essays the naturalist discourses on the identification and preparation of roots, flowers and plants, old Indian legends, and wilderness survival.

Pollan, Michael

The botany of desire; a plant's eye view of the world. Random House 2001 xxv, 271p $24.95; pa $13.95   **581.6**
1. Economic botany
ISBN 0-375-50129-0; 0-375-76039-3 (pa)
LC 00-66479

Pollan, Michael—*Continued*

"Pollan intertwines history, anecdote, and revelation as he investigates the connection between four plants that have thrived under human care—apples, tulips, marijuana, and potatoes—and the four human desires they satisfy in return: sweetness, beauty, intoxication, and control. . . . Pollan's dynamic, intelligent, and intrepid parsing of the wondrous dialogue between plants and humans is positively paradigm-altering." Booklist

Includes bibliographical references

Sumner, Judith

The natural history of medicinal plants; foreword by Mark Plotkin. Timber Press 2000 235p il hardcover o.p. pa $24.95   **581.6**
1. Medical botany
ISBN 0-88192-483-0; 978-0-88192-957-7 (pa); 0-88192-957-3 (pa)   LC 99-76555

In this "introduction to the botanical compounds used medicinally, Dr. Sumner describes their biological and ecological importance as toxins and deterrents in protecting plants." Publisher's note

Sumner presents an "accessible introduction to the world of medicinal plants. . . . Some of her most interesting revelations are about the relationships that animals have with plants." Booklist

Includes bibliographical references

Turner, Nancy J.

Common poisonous plants and mushrooms of North America; [by] Nancy J. Turner and Adam F. Szczawinski. Timber Press 1991 311p il $55; pa $24.95 *   **581.6**
1. Poisonous plants 2. Mushrooms
ISBN 0-88192-179-3; 0-88192-312-5 (pa)
          LC 90-37574

This "presents over 150 of the most common and dangerous poisonous plants, describing not only those of wild areas of temperate North America but also garden and crop plants, house plants, and plant products. Information about each plant includes a description, occurrence, toxicity, symptoms, and treatment for poisoning." Am Libr

Includes bibliographical references

Van Wyk, Ben-Erik

Food plants of the world; an illustrated guide. Timber Press 2005 480p il $39.95 *
          581.6
1. Edible plants
ISBN 0-88192-743-0; 978-0-88192-743-6
          LC 2005-44048

This is an "illustrated guide to more than 350 commercially important plants that are sources of cereals, nuts, fruits, vegetables, drinks, herbs, and spices." Choice

For a fuller review, see: Booklist, Feb. 15, 2005

Includes bibliographical references

582.1 Herbaceous and woody plants, plants noted for their flowers

Symonds, George W. D.

The shrub identification book; the visual method for the practical identification of shrubs, including woody vines and ground covers; photos by A. W. Merwin. William Morrow & Company 1963 379p il pa $22   **582.1**
1. Shrubs
ISBN 978-0-688-05040-5; 0-688-05040-9
First published 1963 by Barrow

"Part I gives pictorial keys for thorns, leaves, flowers, fruit, twigs and bark of broad-leaved upright shrubs. Part II contains 200 master pages arranged under four categories, with data on habitat, blooming period, etc., accompanying the photographs." Wilson Libr Bull

Includes bibliographical references

582.13 Plants noted for their flowers

Burger, William C., 1932-

Flowers: how they changed the world. Prometheus Books 2006 337p il $23
          582.13
1. Flowers
ISBN 1-59102-407-2; 978-1-59102-407-1
          LC 2006-2739

This book "begins with basic facts about the morphology and physiology of plant growth and concludes by explaining how plants have played a major role in creating the modern world." Sci Books Films

This is "an engaging and beautifully written look at how flowering plants, over more than 100 million years, have 'transformed terrestrial ecosystems, supported the origin of primates, and helped us humans become the masters of our planet.'" Publ Wkly

Includes bibliographical references

Flowering plant families of the world; [by] V.H. Heywood . . . [et al.] Updated & rev. Firefly Books 2007 424p il map $59.95
          582.13
1. Flowers
ISBN 978-1-55407-206-4; 1-55407-206-9
          LC 2007-272849

First published 1978 in the United Kingdom with title: Flowering plants of the world

"At the core of the book are . . . entries on 504 flowering plant families. Each entry describes distribution, anatomy, habitat, classification and commercial uses." Publisher's note

Includes bibliographical references

Spellenberg, Richard

National Audubon Society field guide to North American wildflowers, western region. 2nd ed rev. Knopf 2001 862p il map $19.95   **582.13**
1. Wild flowers
ISBN 0-375-40233-0   LC 2001-269242

Spellenberg, Richard—*Continued*
"A Chanticleer Press edition"
First published 1979
"More than 940 . . . full-color images show the
wildflowers of western North America close-up and in
their natural habitats. . . . Images are grouped by flower
color and shape and keyed to . . . descriptions that reflect current taxonomy." Publisher's note

Thieret, John W., 1926-2005
National Audubon Society field guide to North
American wildflowers: eastern region; revising
author, John W. Thieret; original authors, William
A. Niering and Nancy C. Olmstead. Knopf 2001
879p il map (National Audubon Society field
guide series) $19.95   **582.13**
1. Wild flowers
ISBN 0-375-40232-2   LC 2001-269241
"A Chanticleer Press edition"
First published 1979 under the authorship of William
A. Niering and Nancy C. Olmstead
Spine title: Field guide to wildflowers, eastern region
"Covers the area east of the Rockies and east of the
Big Bend area of Texas to the Atlantic. Color photo-
graphs together with family and species descriptions
make this a most useful field guide." Sci News {review
of 1979 edition}

Wells, Diana
100 flowers and how they got their names;
illustrated by Ippy Patterson. Algonquin Bks. 1997
257p il $17.95   **582.13**
1. Flowers 2. Popular plant names
ISBN 1-56512-138-4   LC 96-22296
The author "describes the mythology and history behind 100 favorite garden plants, emphasizing the exploits
of botanists and plant explorers who brought them out of
their native habitats." Libr J
"This is a delightful book for browsing." Booklist
Includes bibliographical references

582.16   Trees

Firefly Encyclopedia of trees; edited by Stephen
Cafferty. Firefly Books 2005 288p il map
$49.95   **582.16**
1. Trees
ISBN 1-55407-051-1
"Delineating the principle genera of trees, from primeval cycads to ancient conifers, deciduous broadleaves to
tropical tree ferns, the compendium augments its . . .
background on the horticultural, ornamental, and economic significance of each species with . . . sidebars
and distribution maps, as well as . . . [color photographs
and] illustrations." Booklist
Includes bibliographical references

Little, Elbert Luther, 1907-
The Audubon Society field guide to North
American trees; [by] Elbert L. Little; photographs
by Sonja Bullaty and Angelo Lomeo [et. al.];
visual key by Susan Rayfield and Olivia Buehl.
Knopf 1980 2v il v1 $19.95; v2 $19.95 *
                                        582.16
1. Trees—North America
ISBN 0-394-50760-6 (v1); 0-394-50761-4 (v2)
                                    LC 79-3474
"A Chanticleer Press edition. The Audubon Society
field guide series"
Contents: [v1] Eastern region; [v2] Western region
These "guides are unusual in that they contain many
color photographs of parts of a living tree. The identification keys are easy to use, being based on an arrangement by leaf shapes, flowers, fruit, and fall leaves, and
giving drawings of winter silhouettes. The eastern guide
covers 364 species, the western guide describes 314 species; they divide the country at central Texas and the
Rockies." Libr J

Pakenham, Thomas, 1933-
Remarkable trees of the world; text and
photographs by Thomas Pakenham. Norton 2002
191p il $49.95; pa $27.95   **582.16**
1. Trees
ISBN 0-393-04911-6; 0-393-32529-6 (pa)
                                    LC 2002-21934
The author presents descriptions and photographs of
sixty exceptional trees from around the world
"This beautiful and unique book is sure to be appreciated by nature lovers. And though it is a highly personal
work and not a scientific text, it demonstrates keen and
accurate observation; it could also serve as an excellent
supplement to studies in science, history, and geography." SLJ
Includes bibliographical references

Tudge, Colin
The tree; a natural history of what trees are,
how they live, and why they matter. Crown
Publishers 2006 459p il map $27.95; pa $14.95 *
                                        582.16
1. Trees
ISBN   1-4000-5036-7;   978-1-4000-5036-9;
0-307-39539-1 (pa); 978-0-307-39539-9 (pa)
                                    LC 2006-6261
The author "explains how biologists identify the different kinds of trees; how trees have evolved over millions of years; how they adapt to their habitats, survive
and reproduce. Describing a multitude of species, Tudge
emphasizes the distinctive characteristics of each." Publ
Wkly
"Attentive readers will not look at trees in quite the
same way." Libr J
Includes bibliographical references

583 Magnoliopsida (Dicotyledons)

Anderson, Edward F., 1932-2001
The cactus family; with a foreword by Wilhelm Barthlott; and a chapter on cactus cultivation by Roger Brown. Timber Press 2001 776p il maps $99.95 * **583**
1. Cactus
ISBN 0-88192-498-9; 978-0-88192-498-5
LC 00-60700
This reference work on cactaceae covers 125 genera and 1810 species
"While more than 1,000 photographs overall illustrate the extraordinary diversity and beautiful flowers of cacti, the main section—an alphabetically arranged reference—will arguably rank as the definitive work readers will use to examine and identify cactus genera, species, and subspecies." Booklist
Includes bibliographical references

587 Pteridophyta

Sacks, Oliver W.
Oaxaca journal; {by} Oliver Sacks. National Geographic Soc. 2002 159p il (National Geographic directions) $20 **587**
1. Ferns
ISBN 0-7922-6521-1 LC 2001-57920
Sacks "joined fellow members of the American Fern Society on a 10-day foray to Oaxaca. . . . {This book} is the story of his search for the fern—and his discovery of Mexico." N Y Times Book Rev

590 Animals (Zoology)

Lavers, Chris
Why elephants have big ears; understanding patterns of life on Earth. St. Martin's Press 2001 269p il $24.95; pa $13.95 **590**
1. Animals 2. Evolution
ISBN 0-312-26902-1; 0-312-30333-5 (pa)
LC 00-45997
"Lavers analyzes why animals look the way they do, why they live where they live, and why their physiology is either warm or cold-blooded. . . . He then examines the evolution of animal life and the corollary evolution of warmbloodedness." Booklist
Includes bibliographical references

590.73 Collections and exhibits of living animals

Anthony, Lawrence
Babylon's ark; the incredible wartime rescue of the Baghdad Zoo; [by] Lawrence Anthony with Graham Spence. Thomas Dunne Books 2007 248p il $23.95 **590.73**
1. Baghdad Zoo (Iraq) 2. Zoos 3. Wildlife conservation 4. Iraq War, 2003-
ISBN 978-0-312-35832-7; 0-312-35832-6
LC 2006-50573
"This remarkable story recounts the recent wartime rescue of the once-world-renowned Baghdad Zoo through the experiences of a South African conservationist and heroic Iraqi zookeepers." Booklist

Baratay, Eric, 1960-
Zoo: a history of zoological gardens in the West; [by] Eric Baratay, Elisabeth Hardouin-Fugier. Reaktion Bks.; distributed by Consortium Bk. Sales & Distr. 2002 400p il $40 * **590.73**
1. Zoos
ISBN 1-86189-111-3
In this history of zoos the authors "take a social history focus, examining how people view wild animals and how that has changed over time. . . . One can read the text or spend hours simply enjoying the images. Libraries that have other titles on zoos will still want to purchase this." Libr J
Includes bibliographical references

Bonner, Jeffrey P., 1953-
Sailing with Noah; stories from the world of zoos. University of Missouri Press 2006 309p il $39.95; pa $19.95 **590.73**
1. Zoos
ISBN 978-0-8262-1636-6; 0-8262-1636-6; 978-0-8262-1637-3 (pa); 0-8262-1637-4 (pa)
LC 2005-31401
The author "explores the role of zoos in today's society and their future as institutions of education, conservation, and research. Along the way, Bonner relates a variety of true stories about animals and those who care for them (or abuse them)." Publisher's note
"This is simply the best book about zoos written in recent memory." Booklist
Includes bibliographical references

Hanson, Elizabeth, 1962-
Animal attractions; nature on display in American zoos. Princeton Univ. Press 2002 243p il $29.95 **590.73**
1. Zoos
ISBN 0-691-05992-6 LC 2001-55198
This book "examines the meaning of nature in the city by looking at the ways zoos have assembled and displayed their animal collections." Publisher's note
"If ever a book lived up to its title and subtitle, this

Hanson, Elizabeth, 1962-—*Continued*
one, an interesting and readable history of zoos and influences on their development in the US, certainly does." Choice

Includes bibliographical references

Robinson, Phillip T.
Life at the zoo: behind the scenes with the animal doctors. Columbia University Press 2004 293p il $27.95; pa $17.95 *   **590.73**
1. Zoos
ISBN 0-231-13248-4; 0-231-13249-2 (pa)
LC 2004-43893
A "look at how animal exhibits are designed, how the animals are cared for, and how illness is detected in animals that want to hide any weakness." Booklist
"It would be difficult to cover even one aspect, such as animal health, that might affect the overall management of a zoo, but Dr. Philip Robinson manages to provide an excellent coverage of just about everything that might be involved in the operation of a zoo." Sci Books Films

Includes bibliographical references

591.3   Genetics, evolution, young animals

Arthur, Wallace
Creatures of accident; the rise of the animal kingdom. Hill & Wang 2006 255p $25
591.3
1. Natural selection 2. Evolution
ISBN 0-8090-4321-1; 978-0-8090-4321-7
LC 2005-33540
The author "advances the argument that the process [of the evolution of life] tends toward greater complexity over time. . . . Arthur sketches out the main structural attributes of complexity in animals, from the cell to organs to embryology to body forms, and when they appeared. . . . Championing naturalistic clarity, Arthur's precision about the processes of evolution will benefit serious students of the topic." Booklist

Includes bibliographical references

Avise, John C.
Genetics in the wild; illustration by Trudy Nicholson. Smithsonian Institution Press 2002 248p il $27.95   **591.3**
1. Genetics 2. Animal behavior 3. Evolution
ISBN 1-58834-069-4   LC 2002-17576
Partial contents: Some evolutionary oddities, Clones and chimeras, Hermaphroditism, Unusual mating practices, Dispersal and migration, Some genetic world records, Fossil DNA
The author "demonstrates how scientists directly examine DNA to address long-standing questions about wild animals, plants, and microbes." Publisher's note

Includes bibliographical references

591.5   Behavior

Balcombe, Jonathan, 1959-
Pleasurable kingdom; animals and the nature of feeling good. Macmillan 2006 274p il $24.95; pa $14.95   **591.5**
1. Animal behavior 2. Pleasure
ISBN 1-4039-8601-0;   978-1-4039-8601-6;
1-4039-8602-9 (pa); 978-1-4039-8602-3 (pa)
LC 2006-41734
This is an "examination of positive feelings in animals. . . . [The author] first defines what is meant by pleasure and why it is worthy of study, then looks at several potentially pleasure-causing activities: play, eating, sex, touching, and love. Full of examples both anecdotal and from refereed journals . . . this book not only makes a case for animal pleasure but calls for more research on the science of pleasure in animals, allowing humans to view them in a new way." Booklist

Includes bibliographical references

Bekoff, Marc
Minding animals; awareness, emotions, and heart; [by] Marc Bekoff; with a foreword by Jane Goodall. Oxford Univ. Press 2002 xxiv, 230p il $27.50; pa $15.95   **591.5**
1. Animal behavior
ISBN 0-19-515077-5; 0-19-516337-0 (pa)
LC 2001-51341
"Chapters cover such broad topics as the richness of behavioral diversity, animal emotions, play and cooperation, and human intrusion into animals' lives. . . . The conversational writing style makes for a highly accessible book." Booklist

Includes bibliographical references

Encyclopedia of animal behavior; edited by Marc Bekoff; foreword by Jane Goodall. Greenwood Press 2004 3v il set $349.95 *   **591.5**
1. Animal behavior
ISBN 0-313-32745-9   LC 2004-56073
This encyclopedia describes "what makes animals tick using techniques that range from molecular approaches to analysis of species. The 300 entries, some stretching to 7000 words, discuss topics as diverse as concept learning in pigeons and stress in dolphins." Libr J

Includes bibliographical references

Griffin, Donald Redfield, 1915-2003
Animal minds; beyond cognition to consciousness; [by] Donald R. Griffin. [Rev and expanded] University of Chicago Press 2001 355p $27.50   **591.5**
1. Animal behavior
ISBN 0-226-30865-0   LC 00-10006
First published 1992
The author "moves beyond considerations of animal cognition to argue that scientists can and should investigate questions of animal consciousness. Using examples from studies of species ranging from chimpanzees and dolphins to birds and honeybees, he demonstrates how

Griffin, Donald Redfield, 1915-2003—*Continued*
communication among animals can serve as a 'window' into what animals think and feel, just as human speech and nonverbal communication tell us most of what we know about the thoughts and feelings of other people." Publisher's note

"Griffin's book will enlighten, delight and even ruffle some feathers." Publ Wkly

Includes bibliographical references

Hauser, Marc D.
Wild minds; what animals really think; illustrations by Ted Dewen. Holt & Co. 2000 xx, 315p il pa $15 hardcover o.p.   **591.5**
1. Animal intelligence 2. Animal behavior
ISBN 0-8050-5670-X (pa)   LC 99-36204

"The first section explores how animals view material objects, their ability to count, and their navigational skills. . . . The second section covers mental abilities, such as self-knowledge, how animals learn, and deception. The final section discusses skills necessary for living in groups—communication and a sense of morals. This entertaining yet highly scientific work is a terrific antidote to all the badly researched popular writing on animal emotions and intelligence." Booklist

Includes bibliographical references

Linden, Eugene
The octopus and the orangutan; more true tales of animal intrigue, intelligence, and ingenuity. Dutton 2002 242p $23.95; pa $14   **591.5**
1. Animal intelligence 2. Animal behavior
ISBN 0-525-94661-6; 0-452-28411-2 (pa)
LC 2002-67434

The author "presents anecdotes that illustrate the workings of the minds of both domestic and wild creatures—how they use tools, play games and adapt to change." Publ Wkly

"Linden's chatty writing style, along with the science behind the stories that he occasionally slips in, makes for entertaining and enlightening reading." Booklist

Includes bibliographical references

Masson, J. Moussaieff (Jeffrey Moussaieff), 1941-
The pig who sang to the moon; the emotional world of farm animals; {by} Jeffrey Moussaieff Masson. Ballantine Books 2003 277p il $25.95; pa $13.95   **591.5**
1. Domestic animals 2. Animal intelligence
ISBN 0-345-45281-X; 0-345-45282-8 (pa)
LC 2003-61773

The author "makes the case that the animals humans eat on a regular basis—pigs, chickens, sheep, cows and ducks—feel, think and suffer. Each animal gets a chapter, in which Masson interweaves folklore, science and literature (he quotes Darwin, Gandhi and the Bible) with his observations of the animals' behaviors." Publ Wkly

"Masson is passionate in his beliefs, and a strong thread of animal rights runs through his entire narrative. Readers not convinced by his philosophy will learn quite a bit about the animals we mostly take for granted." Booklist

Includes bibliographical references

When elephants weep; the emotional lives of animals; {by} Jeffrey Moussaieff Masson and Susan McCarthy. Delacorte Press 1995 xxiii, 291p il pa $15.95 hardcover o.p. *   **591.5**
1. Animal intelligence 2. Animal behavior
ISBN 0-385-31428-0 (pa)   LC 94-23819

The authors gather "the evidence to date for the existence of emotions and, hence, something approaching human consciousness in animals. . . . Masson and McCarthy do a commendable job of synthesizing the material they tackle . . . making it efficiently readable." Booklist

Includes bibliographical references

McCarthy, Susan
Becoming a tiger; how baby animals learn to live in the wild. HarperCollins 2004 418p hardcover o.p. pa $13.95 *   **591.5**
1. Animal intelligence
ISBN 0-06-620924-2; 0-06-093484-0 (pa)
LC 2003-67553

The author examines "the ways that animals figure out how to function in their worlds. . . . One of the basic things a baby animal must learn is how to get from one place to another in a manner appropriate to its species. Other basics involve learning to recognize your own species, to communicate, to find food, and *not* to become some other species' food. McCarthy discusses species as various as horses, bonobos, zebra finches, and fruit-fly maggots to illustrate the learning process." Booklist

"McCarthy writes clearly and her penchant for humor . . . makes the book an easy read, both for students of learning and those who can't get enough of television's *Animal Planet*." Publ Wkly

Includes bibliographical references

Weiner, Jonathan, 1953-
Time, love, memory; a great biologist and his quest for the origins of behavior. Knopf 1999 300p il $27.50; pa $14   **591.5**
1. Benzer, Seymour, 1921-2007 2. Behavior genetics
ISBN 0-679-44435-1; 0-679-76390-2 (pa)
LC 98-43128

"A Borzoi book"

An exploration of the work of "one of the unsung pioneers of molecular biology: brash, eccentric physicist-turned-biologist Seymour Benzer. By studying tiny genetic mutations in the fruit fly, Benzer seeks to shed light on the question of whether genes determine behavior. Weiner . . . presents an elegant scientific detective story." Publ Wkly

Includes bibliographical references

Wynne, Clive D. L.
Do animals think? Princeton University Press 2004 268p il $26.95   **591.5**
1. Animal intelligence
ISBN 0-691-11311-4   LC 2003-60019

The author "shows how bats, bees, pigeons, and dolphins perceive their worlds quite differently from the way humans do. . . . Readers will delight in this insightful, well-referenced book." Choice

Includes bibliographical references

591.56   Behavior relating to life cycle

Bagemihl, Bruce

Biological exuberance; animal homosexuality and natural diversity; illustrated by John Megahan. St. Martin's Press 1999 751p il map $40; pa $21.95   **591.56**

1. Animal behavior 2. Homosexuality

ISBN 0-312-19239-8; 0-312-25377-X (pa)

LC 98-28528

The author "challenges the belief that homosexuality is an aberration in nature by revealing the documented homosexual or transgendered behavior of 450 animal species. Contesting the idea that scarcity and functionality are the primary agents of biological change, biologist Bagemihl persuasively argues that abundance and extravagance are just as crucial to the mosaic of life." Publ Wkly

Includes bibliographical references

Dugatkin, Lee Alan, 1962-

Cheating monkeys and citizen bees; the nature of cooperation in animals and humans; [by] Lee Dugatkin. Harvard University Press 2000 208p pa $14.95   **591.56**

1. Animal behavior

ISBN 978-0-674-00167-1; 0-674-00167-2

First published 1999 by Free Press

The author contends "that animal cooperation could provide a new perspective on human cooperation, as we look at the animal world without the human strictures of morality and free will. He also acknowledges the potential weaknesses of this research. . . . He supports his arguments with many examples from animal behavior studies." Libr J

Wilcove, David S.

No way home; the decline of the world's great animal migrations; with illustrations by Louise Zemaitis. Island Press/Shearwater Books 2008 253p il map $24.95   **591.56**

1. Animals—Migration 2. Environmental degradation

ISBN 978-1-55963-985-9; 1-55963-985-7

LC 2007-26205

The author presents a "report on the status of the world's great migratory species: songbirds, butterflies, locusts, bison, wildebeest, whales, sea turtles, and salmon. Citing both anecdotal and scientific evidence, he describes what these spectacular migrations were like at their peak, what they have dwindled to today, and what they are likely to become in the future." Libr J

"Absorbing and thought provoking, [this work] deserves to be widely read and used to promote conservation action." Science

Includes bibliographical references

Zuk, M. (Marlene), 1956-

Sexual selections; what we can and can't learn about sex from animals; [by] Marlene Zuk. University of Calif. Press 2002 239p il $40; pa $16.95   **591.56**

1. Sexual behavior in animals

ISBN 0-520-21974-0; 0-520-24075-8 (pa)

LC 2001-5771

This book "exposes the anthropomorphism and gender politics that have colored our understanding of the natural world and shows how feminism can help move us away from our ideological biases." Publisher's note

"Fascinating and persuasive. Zuk is not an idealogue, just an unusually clear-eyed scholar." N Y Times Book Rev

Includes bibliographical references

591.59   Communication

Friend, Tim

Animal talk; breaking the codes of animal language. Free Press 2004 274p il $25; pa $15
                                                        591.59

1. Animal communication

ISBN 0-7432-0157-4; 0-7432-0158-2 (pa)

LC 2003-63107

"The author describes the methods of, and reasons behind, animal communication and demonstrates that human and animal communication are not so widely disparate as once believed. Friend also gives background details on the basics of communication theory, genetics, evolution, and the progression of scientific thought regarding animal communication. . . . His humorous and engaging prose style makes this a captivating read." Libr J

Includes bibliographical references

591.6   Miscellaneous nontaxonomic kinds of animals

Quammen, David, 1948-

Monster of God; the man-eating predator in the jungles of history and the mind. Norton 2003 513p maps $26.95; pa $15.95 *   **591.6**

1. Dangerous animals 2. Predatory animals 3. Endangered species

ISBN 0-393-05140-4; 0-393-32609-8 (pa)

LC 2003-7812

This is an "account of efforts to preserve large top-of-the-food-chain carnivores like tigers and crocodiles, and a meditation on what life would be like without them." N Y Times Book Rev

"Rich with personal stories that clarify humanity's true place in the universe, this book will leave the reader eager for more. . . . This has all the makings of a science book of the year. Highly recommended." Libr J

Includes bibliographical references

Todd, Kim, 1970-
Tinkering with Eden; a natural history of exotics in America; illustrations by Claire Emery. Norton 2001 302p il pa $15.95 hardcover o.p.

591.6

1. Animal introduction
ISBN 0-393-32324-2 (pa)   LC 00-58740
"Exotics include such now prosaic, nonnative bird species as starlings, pigeons, and house sparrows. Todd's intriguing history of their introduction in the U.S., some deliberate . . . others accidental, develops into an essential look at the unexpected and, all too often, unwelcome impact exotics have on the ecosystem in which they thrive." Booklist
Includes bibliographical references

591.68   Rare and endangered animals

Chadwick, Douglas H.
The company we keep; America's endangered species; {by} Douglas H. Chadwick and Joel Sartore. National Geographic Soc. 1996 157p il pa $16 hardcover o.p.   **591.68**
1. Endangered species 2. Wildlife conservation 3. Environmental policy—United States
ISBN 0-7922-7132-7 (pa)   LC 96-18874
Topics covered "include a history of the conservation effort (including a description of the Endangered Species Act), accounts of representative species, . . . and the human activities that threaten the Pacific Northwest, desert Southwest, and southern Florida ecosystems." Choice
"The book is not built solely around the photographs. But the pictures are collectively a good storyteller. They're well-edited, and accompanied by maps and charts that help explain how man is threatening many species." Christ Sci Monit
Includes bibliographical references

Weidensaul, Scott
The ghost with trembling wings; science, wishful thinking, and the search for lost species. North Point Press 2002 341p il maps $26; pa $15

591.68

1. Rare animals 2. Extinct animals
ISBN 0-374-24664-5; 0-86547-668-3 (pa)
LC 2001-54605
"Weidensaul's narrative concerns those rare occurrences when a supposedly extinct animal makes a surprise reappearance, and the much more frequent occasions when scientists or civilians only think they've sighted a vanished creature." Publ Wkly
"Weidensaul is a graceful writer who works an amazing amount of scientific theory into his narrative." Booklist
Includes bibliographical references

591.7   Animal ecology, animals characteristic of specific environments

Naskrecki, Piotr
The smaller majority; the hidden world of the animals that dominate the tropics. Belknap Press of Harvard University Press 2005 278p il $35

591.7

1. Invertebrates 2. Animals—Pictorial works 3. Tropics
ISBN 0-674-01915-6; 978-0-674-01915-7
LC 2005-46060
In this book the author "includes over 400 . . . full-color photographs of animals that are generally smaller than the human finger. The author . . . [has] collected images of animals from Costa Rica, Guinea, the Dominical Republic, the Solomon Islands, Australia, South Africa, Botswana, and Namibia." Choice
"Naskrecki's exuberant, expert knowledge of this microscopic world has been distilled down to the most arresting details. Crisp, enjoyable prose, clearly explains complex biological processes." Publ Wkly
Includes bibliographical references

Zimmer, Carl
Parasite rex; inside the bizarre world of nature's most dangerous creatures. Free Press 2000 xxii, 298p il pa $14 hardcover o.p. *   **591.7**
1. Parasites
ISBN 0-7432-0011-X (pa)   LC 00-37593
This is a chronicle of the effects of parasites on plants and animals
"The importance of Zimmer's book lies not only in its accessible presentation of the new science of evolutionary parasitology but in its thoughtful treatment of the global strategies and policies that scientists, health workers and governments will have to consider in order to manage parasites in the future." N Y Times Book Rev
Includes bibliographical references

592   Invertebrates

Attenborough, David, 1926-
Life in the undergrowth. Princeton University Press 2006 288p il $29.95   **592**
1. Invertebrates
ISBN 0-691-12703-4   LC 2005-934727
The author "explores the lives of the planet's land-based invertebrates. Concentrating mainly on insects and spiders, the author investigates all aspects of the animals' life cycles." Booklist
"This wonderful exploration of invertebrates exceeds the requirements for a great nature book through the strength of its photographs and the quality of its prose." Publ Wkly

Hubbell, Sue
Waiting for Aphrodite; journeys into the time before bones; with illustrations by Liddy Hubbell. Houghton Mifflin 1999 242p il $24; pa $13

592

1. Invertebrates
ISBN 0-395-83703-0; 0-618-05684-X (pa)

LC 98-49811

"These essays on natural history discuss everything from the orange-humped crickets that are unique to Missouri and the iridescent butterflies of Costa Rica to the furry sea mice that live in the coastal waters near the writer's new house, in Maine. Hubbell is both a delighted home scientist and a glinting memoirist, and her observations are interspersed with accounts of her fresh life in the East." New Yorker
Includes bibliographical references

Stewart, Amy, 1969-
The earth moved; on the remarkable achievements of earthworms. Algonquin Bks. 2004 223p $23.95; pa $12.95

592

1. Worms
ISBN 1-56512-337-9; 1-56512-468-5 (pa)

LC 2003-52379

The author explores "the impact worms have on humans and on our planet. . . . {She} educates on the vital roles these creatures play in growing crops, how they can neutralize the effects of nuclear waste on soil, and their ability to regenerate new body parts. . . . A book that's as enlightening as it is entertaining." SLJ
Includes bibliographical references

594 Mollusca and Molluscoidea

Ellis, Richard, 1938-
The search for the giant squid. Penguin Bks. 1999 322p il pa $14.95

594

1. Squids
ISBN 0-14-028676-4; 978-0-14-028676-2

LC 98-10436

First published 1998 by Lyons Press
The giant squid (Architeuthis) "has never positively been seen by human eyes in its living, active form. . . . With everything about the giant squid's life, behavior, and geographical range as a mysterious background, Ellis roams through speculative tracts, dating back to Pliny the Elder, about Architeuthis." Booklist
"Some of the appeal of this book is visual, as it presents 30 b&w photographs and 35 line drawings, many historical, several of the drawings by Ellis himself." Publ Wkly
Includes bibliographical references

595.7 Insecta (Insects)

Alcock, John, 1942-
In a desert garden; love and death among the insects; with illustrations by Turid Forsyth. Norton 1997 186p il $27.50 **595.7**

1. Insects 2. Desert ecology
ISBN 0-393-04118-2 LC 97-589

Also available in paperback from University of Ariz. Press
The focus of this "work is the author's own front yard in Tempe, Arizona, and its insect inhabitants. . . . Readers will gain insights into how science is practiced as the author's lively, often humorous observations of assorted beetles, bugs, wasps, bees, caterpillars, and butterflies are related to broad concepts of animal behavior, ecology, and survival." Libr J
Includes bibliographical references

Brock, James P.
Kaufman field guide to butterflies of North America; [by] Jim P. Brock and Kenn Kaufman; with the collaboration of Rick and Nora Bowers and Lynn Hassler. Houghton Mifflin 2006 c2003 391p il map pa $19.95 * **595.7**

1. Butterflies
ISBN 0-618-76826-2; 978-0-618-76826-4

LC 2006-287515

First published 2003 with title: Butterflies of North America
"Each species is listed by common name and scientific name and receives a several-sentence description, including flight time and larval food plants. All except very local or accidental species also are shown on range maps. The illustrations are opposite the written description, with most species pictured in multiple images. . . . The illustrations are created by digital enhancement of photographs. . . . An essential purchase for all libraries." Booklist [review of 2003 edition]

Capinera, John L.
Field guide to grasshoppers, crickets, and katydids of the United States; [by] John L. Capinera, Ralph D. Scott, and Thomas J. Walker. Cornell University Press 2004 249p il maps hardcover o.p. pa $29.95 **595.7**

1. Grasshoppers 2. Crickets
ISBN 0-8014-4260-5; 0-8014-8948-2 (pa)

LC 2004-10727

This "field guide to U.S. and Canadian orthoptera introduces 206 of the most common species. . . . It explains classification, morphology (illustrated), biology, sound production, and collection and preservation, and presents pictorial keys to families and subfamilies." Libr J
"The highlight is certainly the 50 pages of Scott's color illustrations. . . . For those who want to know what's plaguing them when locusts descend, this is the book." Publ Wkly
Includes bibliographical references

Eisner, Thomas
For love of insects. Belknap Press of Harvard University Press 2003 448p il $35; pa $19.95

595.7

1. Insects
ISBN 0-674-01181-3; 0-674-01827-3 (pa)

LC 2003-44399

"Ranging from a caterpillar who feeds on flowers while disguising as one by affixing petals to his back, to

Eisner, Thomas—*Continued*

a beetle who can resist a pull 200 times his own weight, the book is full of little known information about how insects feed, fight, and reproduce." Univ Press Books for Public and Second Sch Libr, 2006

Includes bibliographical references

Secret weapons; defenses of insects, spiders, scorpions, and other many-legged creatures; [by] Thomas Eisner, Maria Eisner, Melody V.S. Siegler. Belknap Press of Harvard University Press 2005 372p il $29.95; pa $18.95 * **595.7**

1. Animal defenses 2. Insects 3. Spiders

ISBN 0-674-01882-6; 0-674-02403-6 (pa)

LC 2005-41042

"This volume presents 69 case studies of organisms from 4 orders of spiders, 2 of centipedes, 5 of millipedes, and 10 of insects. Most of the studies address defensive chemistry and identify the chemical(s) involved, how each is acquired, stored, and deployed." Sci Books Films

"This very readable and well-illustrated book will appeal to all those interested in disciplines like biology, entomology, and ecology." Choice

Includes bibliographical references

Ellis, Hattie, 1967-

Sweetness & light; the mysterious history of the honeybee. Harmony Books 2004 243p il hardcover o.p. pa $13.95 **595.7**

1. Bees 2. Beekeeping

ISBN 1-4000-5405-2; 1-4000-5406-0 (pa)

LC 2004-4116

The author tells the story of the bee in human history, "from Stone Age honey hunters to modern-day hives on the rooftops of New York City." Publisher's note

"What a delightful volume on the honeybee this is: Not only is the reader treated to a wealth of information on the biology, ecology, and economic importance of that insect, but the interrelationship of the honeybee and humanity throughout history is very nicely presented." Sci Books Films

Includes bibliographical references

Encyclopedia of insects; editors, Vincent H. Resh, Ring T. Cardé. Academic Press 2003 xxviii, 1266p il map $99.95 **595.7**

1. Insects—Encyclopedias

ISBN 0-12-586990-8 LC 2002-106355

This encyclopedia provides "descriptions of the ways in which insects interact with their environment and with other organisms, in areas such as ecology, agriculture, public health, human folklore and culture." Publisher's note

"Written by an international team of experts, the 271 articles cover the full spectrum of entomology, providing specialists as well as generalists with data far more thorough than those in identification guides. The awareness of the pivotal role insects play in the survival of all life forms make this an essential acquisition." Libr J

Includes bibliographical references

Evans, Arthur V.

An inordinate fondness for beetles; [by] Arthur V. Evans, Charles L. Bellamy; photography by Lisa Charles Watson; illustrations by Patricia Wynne. University of California Press 2000 208p il pa $31.95 **595.7**

1. Beetles

ISBN 0-520-22323-3; 978-0-520-22323-3

LC 99-46118

"A Peter N. Nevraumont book"

First published 1996 by Henry Holt and Company

"The six chapters cover beetle numbers and diversity, their body plan and functions, their life histories, habits, and defenses, their evolution, their interactions with humans, and their aesthetic importance and conservation." Libr J

"The incredible full-color photographs bring readers up close without a magnifying lens at hand, and the seemingly infinite variations within the species due to size, structure, and color are easily seen. . . . While the text is scientific, it is very readable." SLJ

Includes bibliographical references

The **Firefly** encyclopedia of insects and spiders; edited by Christopher O'Toole. Firefly Bks. 2002 240p il $40 * **595.7**

1. Insects 2. Spiders

ISBN 1-55297-612-2

First published 1986 by Facts on File with title: The Encyclopedia of insects

This work "treats all the major taxonomic groups of arthropods except for the marine groups. The 28 orders of insects are all given separate treatment, as well as millipedes, centipedes, and arachnids. The work focuses in fascinating detail on behavior, morphology, ecology, life cycles, and economic or medical importance. Strikingly beautiful photographs of arthropods around the world supplement drawings that illustrate specific features. Separate essays discuss topics such as flight, pheromones and mating, mimicry, and social life. . . . There is no rival encyclopedia." Choice

Halpern, Sue M.

Four wings and a prayer; caught in the mystery of the monarch butterflies; [by] Sue Halpern. Pantheon Bks. 2001 212p il maps pa $13 hardcover o.p. **595.7**

1. Monarch butterflies

ISBN 0-375-70194-X (pa) LC 00-51055

Halpern discusses her experiences studying the migration of monarch butterflies. "She spends much of her time assisting Bill Calvert, a . . . field biologist, as they drive through rural Mexico tagging, weighing, and counting butterflies." Christ Sci Monit

Hölldobler, Bert, 1936-

The ants; [by] Bert Hölldobler and Edward O. Wilson. Belknap Press 1990 732p il $95

595.7

1. Ants

ISBN 0-674-04075-9 LC 89-30653

This volume includes coverage of ant "evolution, taxonomy, life history, chemical ecology, kin recognition,

Hölldobler, Bert, 1936-—*Continued*
community organization, {and} symbiosis. . . . Army
ants, fungus growers, harvesting ants and weaver ants
. . . are each given a chapter of their own. . . . The
book's last chapter tells the reader how to collect, culture
and observe live ants." Sci Am
"Science is rarely good literature. 'The Ants' is an ex-
alting exception." N Y Times Book Rev
Includes bibliographical references

Journey to the ants; a story of scientific
exploration; [by] Bert Hölldobler and Edward O.
Wilson. Belknap Press 1994 228p il $27.50; pa
$16.95   **595.7**
1. Ants
ISBN 0-674-48525-4; 0-674-48526-2 (pa)
     LC 94-13386
"Based on their field studies ranging from the Arctic
Circle and Finland to rain forests in Brazil, the authors
relate various aspects of ant natural history including foraging behavior, colony structure and organization, and
chemical communication." Choice
"A skillful blend of natural lore, autobiography, and
history." Libr J

Insect lives; stories of mystery and romance from
a hidden world; edited by Erich Hoyt and Ted
Schultz. Harvard University Press 2002 360p il
pa $23   **595.7**
1. Insects
ISBN 978-0-674-00952-3; 0-674-00952-5
First published 1999 by Wiley
"The selections for this volume come from Aristotle,
Charles Darwin, William Wordsworth, the Bible, contemporary entomologists such as Edward O. Wilson, and
dozens of other sources. The editors have arranged the
material into ten chapters on themes dealing with insects
both praised and reviled, insect societies, mating, metamorphosis, behavior, and more. The book is well suited
for browsing, with many illustrations, relatively short entries, and a wide variety of topics and writing styles."
Libr J
Includes bibliographical references

Marshall, Stephen A.
Insects: their natural history and diversity; with
a photographic guide to insects of eastern North
America. Firefly Books 2006 718p il $95 *
     595.7
1. Insects
ISBN 978-1-55297-900-6; 1-55297-900-8
     LC 2006-389462
This "offers more than 4000 excellent color photographs and concise, accurate information about every major insect family worldwide. . . . This book is simply
bigger, prettier, and more comprehensive than any previous publication on insects and will be useful to amateur
and professional alike." Libr J
Includes bibliographical references

Milne, Lorus Johnson, 1912-
The Audubon Society field guide to North
American insects and spiders; {by} Lorus and
Margery Milne; visual key by Susan Rayfield.
Knopf 1980 989p il $19.95   **595.7**
1. Insects 2. Spiders
ISBN 0-394-50763-0   LC 80-7620
"A Chanticleer Press edition. The Audubon Society
field guide series"
The authors "have based their field guide on 702 ex-
cellent color photographs (75 of which are of spiders and
other arachnids). In addition to some general information,
the text (two thirds of the book) is made up of brief
comments on each kind of arthropod pictured." Choice
Includes glossary

The **monarch** butterfly; biology & conservation;
edited by Karen S. Oberhauser & Michelle J.
Solensky. Cornell University Press 2004 248p il
maps (A Comstock book) $39.95   **595.7**
1. Monarch butterflies 2. Wildlife conservation
ISBN 0-8014-4188-9   LC 2004-884
"Covered is every facet of monarch breeding, migration, and overwintering, as well as population modeling
and management. . . . The text is clearly written, and
the mathematical formulas included in certain chapters
are not essential to understanding the main ideas. The
most up-to-date and comprehensive publication on monarch butterfly biology, this will be an important reference
tool." Libr J
Includes bibliographical references

Pyle, Robert Michael
The Audubon Society field guide to North
American butterflies; visual key by Carol Nehring
and Jane Opper. Knopf 1981 916p il $19.95 *
     595.7
1. Butterflies
ISBN 0-394-51914-0   LC 80-84240
"A Chanticleer Press edition. The Audubon Society
field guide series"
This guide "introduces more than 600 species of North
American butterfly, including those native to the Hawaiian Islands. A section of brilliant color plates (more than
1,000 of them) featuring butterflies in their natural habitats, follows a general introduction and notes on text organization and use." Booklist

Schappert, Phil, 1956-
The last Monarch butterfly; conserving the
Monarch butterfly in a brave new world. Firefly
Books 2004 113p il pa $19.95   **595.7**
1. Monarch butterflies 2. Wildlife conservation
ISBN 1-55297-969-5 (pa)   LC 2005-357220
Overview of both eastern and western monarch butterflies, including their life cycle and migratory patterns.
The impact of natural disasters and increasing residential
and industrial development on monarch butterfly populations is also discussed.
"The narrative is enhanced by beautiful photographs
and backed up by some 180 references to the scientific
literature. . . . Let's hear it for the monarch, an amazing
insect; if the reader has any doubts about that, this book
will put them to rest." Sci Books Films

Spielman, A. (Andrew), 1930-2006
Mosquito; a natural history of man's most persistent and deadly foe; {by} Andrew Spielman and Michael D'Antonio. Hyperion 2001 247p il maps pa $12 hardcover o.p.   **595.7**
1. Mosquitoes
ISBN 0-7868-8667-6 (pa)   LC 2001-16815
The authors tell us about the mosquito's "life cycle, its natural enemies and predators, and, of course, its monumental impact on human history. . . . This is truly an unexpected delight, an informative, entertaining, and sometimes skin-crawly book that should appeal to anyone with a taste for popular science." Booklist

Stokes, Donald W.
The butterfly book; an easy guide to butterfly gardening, identification, and behavior; [by] Donald and Lillian Stokes and Ernest Williams. Little, Brown 1991 95p il maps pa $12.95
595.7
1. Butterflies
ISBN 0-316-81780-5   LC 91-15323
This book discusses plants which will attract butterflies, explains butterfly life cycles and behavior, and provides information for identification of over 140 species

Waldbauer, Gilbert
Insects through the seasons. Harvard Univ. Press 1996 289p il $27.50; pa $14.95   **595.7**
1. Moths
ISBN 0-674-45488-X; 0-674-45489-8 (pa)
LC 95-35171
"Waldbauer uses the yearly cycle of the cecropia moth as a base to which he periodically returns while presenting an impressive array of the tactics the moth's fellow insects and arthropod relatives use to live and thrive." Booklist
"The scientific information is excellent and the writing is fascinating." Sci Books Films
Includes bibliographical references

Millions of monarchs, bunches of beetles; how bugs find strength in numbers. Harvard Univ. Press 2000 264p il $27.50; pa $16.95
595.7
1. Insects
ISBN 0-674-00090-0; 0-674-00686-0 (pa)
LC 99-42453
The author "examines many of the reasons that insects form groups. . . . Insects come together for a host of reasons, Waldbauer explains: to find mates, to avoid predators, to enhance their food-gathering abilities, to manipulate their environment and to subdue prey. In each case, Waldbauer provides evocative descriptions of particular species' behaviors while discussing the underlying evolutionary reasons for that behavior." Publ Wkly
Includes bibliographical references

What good are bugs? insects in the web of life. Harvard University Press 2003 384p il $29.95; pa $17.50 *   **595.7**
1. Insects
ISBN 0-674-01027-2; 0-674-01632-7 (pa)
LC 2002-27335

The author "instructs readers on the major roles insects play. He provides . . . examples for every aspect of insect ecology he discusses, sprinkling reports from the scientific literature with personal anecdotes from his many years of research." Booklist
This "is an excellent work about the beneficial insects, that vast majority of insect species of which we are generally unaware. . . . The author is an excellent writer and provides many interesting examples." Choice
Includes bibliographical references

Wilson, Edward O., 1929-
Insect societies. Belknap Press 1971 548p il pa $33.95 hardcover o.p.   **595.7**
1. Insects
ISBN 0-674-45495-2 (pa)
In addition to "descriptions of specific groups of organisms, Wilson attempts to bring much diverse information, including fundamental concepts of evolution and ecology, into a conceptual format he terms unified sociobiology. He devotes several chapters to detailed descriptions of various activities necessary to maintenance of the societies, including a chapter on genetic theories relating to social behavior." Libr J
Includes bibliographical references

597 Cold-blooded vertebrates Pisces (Fishes)

Behnke, Robert J.
Trout and salmon of North America; illustrated by Joseph R. Tomelleri; foreword by Thomas McGuane; introduction by Donald S. Proebstel; edited by George Scott. Free Press 2002 359p il maps $40 *   **597**
1. Trout 2. Salmon
ISBN 0-7432-2220-2   LC 2002-69256
This is a "guide to the more than 70 types of trout and salmon of North America." Libr J
"Along with full and clearly written scientific explanations, statistics and analysis, the author provides anecdotal and historical details that make this not just a field guide, but a fascinating read for those interested in the natural world." Publ Wkly
Includes bibliographical references

Benchley, Peter, 1940-2006
Shark trouble; true stories about sharks and the sea. Random House 2002 186p il hardcover o.p. pa $12.95   **597**
1. Sharks 2. Marine animals
ISBN 0-375-50824-4; 0-8129-6633-3 (pa)
LC 2002-283533
"Benchley describes the many types of sharks (including the ones that pose a genuine threat to man), what is and isn't known about shark behavior, the odds against an attack and how to reduce them even further—all reinforced with the lessons he has learned, the mistakes he has made, and the personal perils he has encountered." Publisher's note
"Handy with statistics and quick to crack a joke with

Benchley, Peter, 1940-2006—*Continued*
himself as the target, Benchley offers riveting accounts
of his and his family's up close and personal encounters
with sharks, a gigantic manta ray, a friendly killer whale,
barracuda, and sundry other wild creatures." Booklist

Capuzzo, Mike
Close to shore; a true story of terror in an age
of innocence. Broadway Bks. 2001 317p map pa
$14.95 hardcover o.p.   **597**
1. Sharks 2. Animal attacks
ISBN 0-7679-0414-1 (pa)   LC 2001-25750
This describes a series of shark attacks in 1916 off the
coast of New Jersey.
"A book full of adventure, mounting tension, some
gore and excitement, and lots of history." SLJ
Includes bibliographical references

Compagno, Leonard J. V.
Sharks of the world; [by] Leonard Compagno,
Marc Dando, Sarah Fowler. Princeton University
Press 2005 368p il map (Princeton field guides)
hardcover o.p. pa $29.95   **597**
1. Sharks
ISBN 0-691-12071-4; 0-691-12072-2 (pa)
                                     LC 2004-111901
First published in the United Kingdom with title: Field
guide to the sharks of the world
The authors cover "over 450 species, including many
as-yet-unnamed species and some that are only known
from a single specimen. Each is illustrated with both a
line drawing and a beautifully rendered color painting; in
most cases a ventral view of the head and illustrations of
the teeth are included. . . . Packed with information, this
is an invaluable guide for anyone interested in this fascinating group." Choice
Includes bibliographical references

Ellis, Richard, 1938-
Great white shark; [by] Richard Ellis and John
E. McCosker; with photographs by Al Giddings
and others, and paintings by Richard Ellis.
HarperCollins 1991 270p il map pa $37.95
hardcover o.p.   **597**
1. Sharks
ISBN 0-8047-2529-2 (pa)   LC 89-46528
"In collaboration with Stanford University Press"
The authors discuss the great white shark's "unique
biology (it's warm blooded), size, distribution, and evolution. They also describe the sport of shark fishing and
the efforts . . . [to save] the white from threats of extinction. Handsomely illustrated with Ellis's paintings
and many simply awesome photographs, . . . the text
has enough scientific fact for armchair icthyologists but
not enough to confuse the casual reader." Libr J
Includes bibliographical references

Gilbert, Carter Rowell, 1930-
National Audubon Society field guide to fishes,
North America; [by] Carter R. Gilbert, James D.
Williams. rev ed, 2nd ed, fully rev. Alfred A.
Knopf 2002 607p il maps pa $19.95 *
                                                  597
1. Fishes—North America
ISBN 0-375-41224-7   LC 2002-20773
"A Chanticleer Press edition"
First published 1983 with title: The Audubon Society
field guide to North American fishes, whales, and dol-
phins
This guide covers over 600 freshwater and saltwater
species in detail, with notes on 771 more species.

McPhee, John A.
The founding fish; [by] John McPhee. Farrar,
Straus & Giroux 2002 358p $25; pa $14
                                                  597
1. Shad
ISBN 0-374-10444-1; 0-374-52883-7 (pa)
                                     LC 2002-25012
The author considers the shad's "role in nature and
American history." Libr J
"McPhee is in great form here, as informative as al-
ways but also funny, unusually self-revealing, and quite
passionate." Booklist

Page, Lawrence M.
A field guide to freshwater fishes: North
America north of Mexico; [by] Lawrence M. Page,
Brooks M. Burr; illustrations by Eugene C.
Beckham III, John Parker Sherrod, Craig W.
Ronto. Houghton Mifflin 1991 432p il maps pa
$19 hardcover o.p. *   **597**
1. Fishes—North America
ISBN 0-395-91091-9 (pa)   LC 90-42049
"The Peterson field guide series"
"Sponsored by the National Audubon Society, the Na-
tional Wildlife Federation, and the Roger Tory Peterson
Institute"
This guide "covers all 790 species known in North
America north of Mexico. Over 700 illustrations, most in
color, show identifying marks. Also includes 377 distri-
bution maps and additional line drawings of key details."
Publisher's note
Includes bibliographical references

Schultz, Ken
Ken Schultz's field guide to saltwater fish.
Wiley 2004 274p il pa $17.95   **597**
1. Fishes
ISBN 0-471-44995-4   LC 2003-15773
"Arranged alphabetically by species, each entry covers
the identification, size/age, distribution, habitat, life histo-
ry/behavior, and feeding habits of each fish." Publisher's
note

Schweid, Richard, 1946-
Consider the eel. University of North Carolina
Press 2002 181p il map $24.95   **597**
1. Eels
ISBN 0-8078-2693-6   LC 2001-48067

Schweid, Richard, 1946--—*Continued*

Also available De Capo paperback edition

The author "tries to fill in the gaps in the eel's astonishing natural history and tie that to sketches of fishery traditions, folklore, literary excerpts and reportage. . . . Anyone with a curiosity about the sea will find Schweid's taste of the eel strangely appealing." Publ Wkly

Includes bibliographical references

Smith, C. Lavett, 1927-

National Audubon Society field guide to tropical marine fishes of the Caribbean, the Gulf of Mexico, Florida, the Bahamas, and Bermuda. Knopf 1997 720p il maps $19.95   **597**

1. Tropical fish

ISBN 0-679-44601-X   LC 97-7690

"A Chanticleer Press edition"

This illustrated guide to tropical fishes describes nearly 1,200 species and includes color photographs, classification and identification information.

Springer, Victor Gruschka, 1928-

Sharks in question; the Smithsonian answer book; {by} Victor G. Springer and Joy P. Gold. Smithsonian Institution Press 1989 187p il pa $24.95 hardcover o.p.   **597**

1. Sharks

ISBN 0-87474-877-1 (pa)   LC 88-18185

"At first, the book deals with the general life history of these fish and presents detailed answers to the most commonly asked questions. The remainder of the book discusses the biology of some spectacular shark species and presents a balanced picture of the question of shark attack on humans. Several appendices with information on shark classification, taxonomy, and sizes of selected sharks are also included." Sci Books Films

Includes bibliographical references

Steel, Rodney

Sharks of the world. Facts on File 2003 192p il $35   **597**

1. Sharks

ISBN 0-8160-5212-3   LC 2002-35228

First published 1985

This volume covers shark classification, anatomy, evolution, behavior, and reproduction

Includes bibliographical references

Thomson, Keith Stewart

Living fossil; the story of the coelacanth. Norton 1991 252p il maps pa $9.95 hardcover o.p.   **597**

1. Coelacanth

ISBN 0-393-30868-5 (pa)   LC 90-43053

This study of the coelacanth discusses "the 1938 discovery of a fish thought to be extinct for 70 million years and the subsequent collection and examination of this {species}." Libr J

"Brisk and engrossing, this is a winning mix of science and adventure." Booklist

Weinberg, Samantha, 1966-

A fish caught in time; the search for the coelacanth. HarperCollins Pubs. 2000 xx, 220p il map pa $13 hardcover o.p.   **597**

1. Coelacanth

ISBN 0-06-093285-6 (pa)   LC 99-44800

First published 1999 in the United Kingdom

"In 1938, a fish believed to be extinct for 70 million years was caught off the South African coast, triggering the 'greatest scientific find of the century.' The search for the coelacanth . . . is a fascinating story, and Weinberg . . . tells it well." Libr J

Includes bibliographical references

597.8   Amphibia (Amphibians)

Beltz, Ellin

Frogs: inside their remarkable world. Firefly Books 2005 175p il $34.95   **597.8**

1. Frogs 2. Toads

ISBN 1-55297-869-9   LC 2006-365517

The author "picture of the history of the frog, its anatomical makeup, its place in the natural world and the threats that are seriously reducing its numbers around the world." Publisher's note

"Beltz presents an entertaining and comprehensive introduction to the order Anura (frogs and toads)." Booklist

Includes bibliographical references

Souder, William E.

A plague of frogs; unraveling an environmental mystery; [by] William Souder. University of Minnesota Press 2002 309p pa $18.95   **597.8**

1. Frogs

ISBN 0-8166-4178-1

First published 2000 by Hyperion

The author examines "the disturbing increase in deformed frogs found in Minnesota in 1995. . . . So far, the biologists have not reached a consensus, but Souder's deep-drilling reportage of their work informs readers how these sentinels of science track 'indicator' species such as frogs." Booklist

Includes bibliographical references

597.9   Reptilia (Reptiles)

Conant, Roger, 1909-

A field guide to reptiles & amphibians; eastern and central North America; {by} Roger Conant and Joseph T. Collins; illustrated by Isabelle Hunt Conant and Tom R. Johnson. 3rd ed, expanded. Houghton Mifflin 1998 616p il maps (Peterson field guide series) $21 *   **597.9**

1. Reptiles 2. Amphibians

ISBN 0-395-90452-8   LC 98-13622

First published 1958 with title: A field guide to reptiles and amphibians of the United States and Canada east of the 100th meridian

Conant, Roger, 1909-—*Continued*

"Sponsored by the National Audubon Society, the National Wildlife Federation, and the Roger Tory Peterson Institute"

This guide describes 595 species and subspecies, featuring color photos, black and white drawings, and color distribution maps of reptiles and amphibians of the region. Also includes information on transporting live reptiles and amphibians

Includes bibliographical references

Stebbins, Robert C. (Robert Cyril), 1915-

A field guide to Western reptiles and amphibians; text and illustrations by Robert C. Stebbins. 3rd ed newly rev. Houghton Mifflin 2003 533p il maps $22   **597.9**

1. Reptiles 2. Amphibians
ISBN 0-395-98272-3   LC 2002-27561
"The Peterson field guide series"
First published 1966
"Sponsored by The National Wildlife Federation and the Roger Tory Peterson Institute"

This "covers all the species of reptiles and amphibians found in western North America. More than 650 full-color paintings and photographs show key details for making accurate identifications. . . . Color range maps give species' distributions. . . . {Includes} information on conservation efforts and survival status." Publisher's note

Includes bibliographical references

Tyning, Thomas F.

A guide to amphibians and reptiles; edited by Donald W. Stokes and Lillian Q. Stokes; illustrations by Andrew Finch Magee; range maps by Thomas F. Tyning and Timothy J. Flanagan. Little, Brown 1990 400p il pa $14.95 hardcover o.p.   **597.9**

1. Amphibians 2. Reptiles
ISBN 0-316-81713-9 (pa)   LC 89-28444
This guide covers common frogs, salamanders, alligators, snakes, turtles, and lizards

Includes bibliographical references

597.92   Chelonia

Ferri, Vincenzo

Tortoises and turtles. Firefly Bks. 2002 c1999 255p il pa $24.95   **597.92**

1. Turtles
ISBN 1-55209-631-9
Original Italian edition, 1999
Cover title: Turtles & tortoises

An "illustrated guide to 190 land, marine and freshwater turtles and tortoises . . . describing the physical and biological characteristics of the majority of species." Publisher's note

Includes bibliographical references

Safina, Carl, 1955-

Voyage of the turtle; in pursuit of the Earth's last dinosaur. Holt 2006 383p il map $27.50; pa $17   **597.92**

1. Turtles
ISBN   978-0-8050-7891-6;   0-8050-7891-6;
978-0-8050-8318-7 (pa); 0-8050-8318-9 (pa)
                    LC 2005-55023
"A John Macrae book"

The author's "main subject is the leatherback, Dermochelys coriacea, largest of all living turtles, which grows to 800 pounds as an average adult." N Y Times Book Rev

"This is a well-written natural history/conservation narrative. General readers will enjoy the book and hopefully will become excited to learn more about critical environmental issues." Sci Books Films

Includes bibliographical references

Spotila, James R., 1944-

Sea turtles; a complete guide to their biology, behavior, and conservation. Johns Hopkins University Press 2004 227p il $24.95
                    597.92

1. Sea turtles
ISBN 0-8018-8007-6   LC 2004-8935
"The volume covers various aspects of sea turtle biology, such as their life history, diving physiology, sense organs, and magnetic orientation. Following the general chapters, individual chapters are devoted to each of the seven species of extant sea turtles." Sci Books Films

"The author is eloquent in his appeal for the conservation of sea turtles. The best single book on the subject." Booklist

Includes bibliographical references

597.96   Serpentes (Snakes)

Badger, David

Snakes; text by David Badger; photography by John Netherton. Voyageur Press 1999 144p $35
                    597.96

1. Snakes
ISBN 0-89658-408-9   LC 98-52379
"The first chapter is a general overview of humans and snakes. . . . The second chapter presents a primer on snake biology and behavior, and the very long third chapter is an overview of various families and species of snakes (mostly native to North America). The photographs are breathtaking in their composition, clarity, and sheer beauty." Booklist

Includes bibliographical references

Campbell, Jonathan, 1961-

The venomous reptiles of the Western Hemisphere; by Jonathan A. Campbell and William W. Lamar, with contributions by Edmund D. Brodie III [et al.] Comstock Pub. Associates 2004 2v il maps (Comstock books in herpetology) set $149.95   **597.96**

1. Poisonous animals 2. Reptiles
ISBN 0-8014-4141-2   LC 2003-7834

Campbell, Jonathan, 1961-—*Continued*

The authors "describe two species of lizards (the Gila monster and the beaded lizard) and 190 species of dangerously venomous snakes of North, Central and South America. Provided are . . . accounts of each species— from the smallest to the largest—complete with descriptions, habitats, and geographic distribution." Libr J

Includes bibliographical references

Ernst, Carl H.

Snakes in question; the Smithsonian answer book; [by] Carl H. Ernst and George R. Zug; illustrations by Molly Dwyer Griffin. Smithsonian Institution Press 1996 203p il pa $24.95 hardcover o.p.   **597.96**

1. Snakes

ISBN 1-56098-649-2 (pa)   LC 96-9367

"The book is organized into five sections: 'Snake Facts,' 'Folk Tales,' 'Giant Snakes: Big and Biggest,' 'Snakebite,' and 'Snakes and Us.' Appendices, a glossary, and general and subject bibliographies are included." Sci Books Films

"The questions and answer format is effective, and readers with no background and others more familiar with snake biology but seeking some biological information or specific data will find the text and tables useful. The careful answers are based on long-term observations as well as current research." Choice

Snakes of the United States and Canada; [by] Carl H. Ernst, Evelyn M. Ernst. Smithsonian Books 2003 668p il map $70   **597.96**

1. Snakes

ISBN 1-58834-019-8   LC 2002-26924

This "reference begins with an introduction to snake biology and evolution, which is followed by an identification guide and key to the North American species. The heart of the book is the species accounts which . . . [provide] information on identifying features, geographic variation, known fossils, current distribution, habitat type, behavior, reproduction, growth, diet, and predators. Completing the book is a glossary of terms and a . . . reference section." Publisher's note

"This current and comprehensive volume contains all the information currently available on the 131 species of snakes living in North America." Libr J

Includes bibliographical references

Greene, Harry W.

Snakes; the evolution of mystery in nature; with photographs by Michael and Patricia Fodgen. University of Calif. Press 1997 351p il $55; pa $29.95   **597.96**

1. Snakes

ISBN 0-520-20014-4; 0-520-22487-6 (pa)

LC 96-21928

The author examines the "biology and ecology of snakes. Throughout, facts on the form, function, habitat, and evolution of these reptiles are mixed with the author's experiences, and the over 200 natural-setting color photographs that complement the text are commendable in their own right." Libr J

Includes bibliographical references

Mattison, Christopher

The new encyclopedia of snakes. Princeton University Press 2007 272p il map $35
                                      597.96

1. Snakes—Encyclopedias

ISBN 0-691-13295-X; 978-0-691-13295-2

LC 2007-922951

First published 1995 by Facts on File with title: The encyclopedia of snakes

This encyclopedia "covers all aspects of snake biology and habitat. This is not a field guide aimed at snake identification. . . . But the work contains a wealth of information about our scaled friends, including patterns of distribution and matters relating to evolution and morphology, feeding, reproduction, and defensive strategies. . . . This captivating work will appeal to students and snake lovers everywhere." Libr J

Includes bibliographical references

Snakes of the world; [by] Chris Mattison. Facts on File 2003 190p il map $35 *   **597.96**

1. Snakes

ISBN 0-8160-5213-1   LC 2002-34737

A reissue of the title first published 1986

Snake morphology, reproduction, diet, self-defense, ecology and behavior are discussed

"Mattison provides an enjoyable introduction to snake biology and snake diversity for the interested general reader. . . . Many of the numerous color photographs are spectacular." Choice [review of 1986 edition]

Includes bibliographical references

Murphy, John C., 1947-

Tales of giant snakes; a historical natural history of anacondas and pythons; [by] John C. Murphy and Robert W. Henderson. Krieger 1997 221p il map $32.50   **597.96**

1. Anacondas 2. Pythons

ISBN 0-89464-995-7   LC 96-54033

Accounts of encounters between large snakes and humans include newspaper articles, adventure writings, and reports of explorers

Includes bibliographical references

O'Shea, Mark

Boas and pythons of the world. Princeton University Press 2007 160p il map $29.95
                                      597.96

1. Boa constrictors 2. Pythons

ISBN 978-0-691-13100-9; 0-691-13100-7

LC 2006-932790

The author examines boas and pythons "in a geographic format, covering the Americas, Europe and Asia, Africa and Indian Ocean islands, and Australian and Pacific Coast islands. An introductory section discusses general snake biology, including evolution and anatomy, and also examines constriction, the myths and realities of giant snakes, and conservation. . . . This excellent book is highly recommended." Booklist

Venomous snakes of the world. Princeton University Press 2005 160p il map $29.95
                                      597.96

1. Snakes 2. Poisonous animals

ISBN 0-691-12436-1   LC 2005-920576

O'Shea, Mark—*Continued*

The author "has produced a compendium of more than 170 venomous snakes, along with their markings, geographical distribution, maximum length, venom, prey, and similar species. But instead of opting for the traditional taxonomic arrangement, he lists these snakes geographically by continent (a final chapter on sea snakes is also included)." Libr J

"Fascinating photographs and descriptions will make this title a favorite." Univ Press Books for Public and Second Sch Libr, 2006

Includes bibliographical references

Rubio, Manny

Rattlesnake; portrait of a predator. Smithsonian Institution Press 1998 xxvii, 239p il $49.95

597.96

1. Rattlesnakes
ISBN 1-56098-808-8   LC 98-22935

This book contains "more than 120 color photographs of various North American rattlesnakes. . . . The text discusses many aspects of rattlesnake evolution, anatomy and physiology, and ecology, including several chapters on interactions between snakes and people." Sci Books Films

Includes bibliographical references

598   Aves (Birds)

Alderfer, Jonathan

National Geographic birding essentials; all the tools, techniques, and tips you need to begin and become a better birder; [by] Jonathan Alderfer and Jon L. Dunn. National Geographic 2007 224p il pa $15.95 *   **598**

1. Bird watching
ISBN 978-1-4262-0135-6; 1-4262-0135-4
LC 2007-30960

This "book offers data on how to begin and how to improve your bird-watching skills. Chapters deal with the pleasures of birding, getting started, where and when birds are found, how common or rare they are at different seasons, parts of a bird, how to identify them, and variations in birds. . . . With a helpful glossary, this is an essential volume for all bird-watchers." Booklist

Includes bibliographical references

Arctic wings; birds of the Arctic National Wildlife Refuge; edited by Stephen Brown; foreword by Jimmy Carter; introduction by David Allen Sibley. Mountaineers Books 2006 192p il map $39.95; pa $27.95   **598**

1. Birds
ISBN   0-89886-975-7;   978-0-89886-975-0; 0-89886-976-5 (pa); 978-0-8988-6976-7 (pa)
LC 2006-865

This "is the story of the birds that return each summer to the Arctic National Wildlife Refuge. About 190 species gather from six continents and all 50 states to nest and rear their young. Included here are essays by biologists and conservationists recounting the life histories of loons and waterfowl; hawks, eagles, and falcons; shore-

birds; gulls, terns, and jaegers; owls; land birds; and a few species that remain within the refuge in significant numbers year-round." Booklist

"The unique aspect of this book is the vivid photographs of bird behavior and the birds in their habitats, showing the importance of the habitats to the birds' continued existence. A great addition is a CD with 60 bird calls recorded on the refuge." Sci Books Films

Includes bibliographical references

The **atlas** of bird migration; tracing the great journeys of the world's birds; general editor Jonathan Elphick; foreword by Thomas E. Lovejoy. Firefly Books 2007 176p il map $35
*   **598**

1. Birds—Migration
ISBN 9781554072484; 1-55407-248-4

First published 1995 by Random House

"The first section is a primer on bird migration and habitat usage patterns, consisting of short, illustrated essays on topics like the evolution of migration, the mechanics of flight, birds' navigational methods and how human development affects migration patterns. Succeeding sections examine different families of migrating birds according to geographical distribution, and each has carefully designed maps that show birds' seasonal ranges and migratory routes. The use of color to describe, clarify, distinguish and compare migration patterns is exceptional, and clear explanations of complicated topics (e.g., how birds fly) make it an excellent text for middle and high school students as well as adults." Publ Wkly

Attenborough, David, 1926-

The life of birds. Princeton Univ. Press 1998 320p il $29.95   **598**

1. Birds
ISBN 0-691-01633-X   LC 98-30705

This survey of bird behavior describes "eating habits, flight, communication, mating, parenthood and environmental adaptability." Publ Wkly

"Well   illustrated   with   color   photographs, Attenborough's latest goes a long way to converting all readers into bird lovers." Booklist

Includes bibliographical references

Beans, Bruce E.

Eagle's plume; the struggle to preserve the life and haunts of America's bald eagle. University of Nebraska Press 1997 318p il pa $17.95

598

1. Bald eagle 2. Birds—Protection
ISBN 0-8032-6142-X; 978-0-8032-6142-6
LC 97-15433

First published 1996 by Scribner

This book "deals with the conservation of eagles and their habitat. [It] also contains details on the biology, behavior, and ecology of eagles." Sci Books Films

Includes bibliographical references

The **Bedside** book of birds; an avian miscellany. Nan A. Talese 2005 369p il $29.95

598

1. Birds
ISBN 0-385-51483-2   LC 2005-47068

The Bedside book of birds—*Continued*

The compiler "employs poems, folk tales, parables, legends, and extracts from the works of naturalists and others to explore humans' relationship with birds through the centuries." Publ Wkly

"This is a book to dip into during those spare minutes, and the reader will be well rewarded by these glimpses into avian-human relations." Booklist

Includes bibliographical references

Book of North American birds. Reader's Digest Assn. 1990 576p il maps hardcover o.p. pa $19.95   **598**
1. Birds—North America
ISBN 0-89577-351-1; 978-0-7621-0576-2 (pa); 0-7621-0576-3 (pa)   LC 89-70261
This book "consists of over 450 page-length species accounts which feature a . . . color painting, a half-page anecdotal narrative essay, a range map, a drawing, plus small sections detailing the bird's identification, habitat, and food. Smaller accounts (three per page) for 117 scarcer birds follow the full-page ones. Appended is a 40-page section with thumbnail sketches of the best birding areas in the United States and Canada." Libr J

Includes bibliographical references

Bull, John L.

The National Audubon Society field guide to North American birds, Eastern region; {by} John Bull and John Farrand, Jr.; revised by John Farrand, Jr.; visual key by Amanda Wilson and Lori Hogan. rev ed. Knopf 1994 797p il maps pa $19.95 *   **598**
1. Birds—North America
ISBN 0-679-42852-6   LC 94-7768
Companion volume to National Audubon Society field guide to North American birds, Western region, by Miklos D. F. Udvardy

"A Chanticleer Press edition"
First published 1977
This pictorial guide to 508 eastern species arranges birds by color and shape to simplify identification. It also includes information on bird-watching and conservation status

Includes bibliographical references

Burger, Joanna

Birds: a visual guide. Firefly Books 2006 304p il map $29.95   **598**
1. Birds
ISBN 978-1-55407-177-7; 1-55407-177-1
"Divided into six sections, the text considers all aspects of birds' lives. Basic anatomy, evolution, physiology, and intelligence are all touched on in the first section, while bird behavior . . . is covered in the second. A large section examines the taxonomy of birds . . . accompanied by a world map showing its distribution. Habitat, migration, and how birds fill their space are discussed in the fourth section, followed by a look at avian adaptations and lifestyles. The final section, on birds and humans, covers such disparate topics as birds in legend, bird-watching, captive birds, and habitat loss. Beautifully illustrated." Booklist

Chu, Miyoko

Songbird journeys; four seasons in the lives of migratory birds. Walker & Co. 2006 312p il map $23   **598**
1. Birds—Migration
ISBN 0-8027-1468-4; 978-0-8027-1468-8
LC 2006-278075
The author describes the "seasonal migrations of American songbirds. . . . In addition to descriptions of the birds' migrations, habits, and life histories for each season, there are details on hotspots for observing the birds, including web sites, addresses, when to go, and special activities. . . . An excellent overview of a compelling subject; highly recommended." Libr J

Includes bibliographical references

Clark, William S., 1937-

A field guide to hawks of North America; {by} William S. Clark and Brian K. Wheeler; illustrations by Brian K. Wheeler. 2nd ed. Houghton Mifflin 2001 316p il maps $30; pa $22 *   **598**
1. Hawks
ISBN 0-395-67068-3; 0-395-67067-5 (pa)
LC 2001-2477
"The Peterson field guide series"
First published 1987
"Accounts are presented for all 39 of North America's diurnal raptors, including eagles, falcons, and vultures. Each species account reviews details of plumages and molts, useful identification features, patterns of flight, and general behavior. . . . The guide also provides size data (weight, length, and wingspread) for all species, as well as the etymology of common and scientific names. Basically, the reference is essential for any student of raptors and useful for serious birders in general." Am Ref Books Annu, 2002

Includes bibliographical references

Cocker, Mark

Birders; tales of a tribe. Atlantic Monthly Press 2002 c2001 229p $24; pa $13   **598**
1. Bird watching
ISBN 0-87113-844-1; 0-8021-3996-5 (pa)
LC 2001-56490
First published 2001 in the United Kingdom
In a "memoir cum essay collection, the author brings the reader into the sometimes obsessive world of bird-watching. . . . Stories of the author and friends going to great lengths and distances to see rare birds, of birding in exotic locales, or of unmasking a fellow birder's claims to finding a rare species are both thought-provoking and amusing." Booklist

Includes bibliographical references

Dunn, Erica H.

Birds at your feeder; a guide to the feeding habits, behavior, distribution, and abundance; [by] Erica H. Dunn and Diane L. Tessaglia-Hymes; illustrations by Peter Burke; abundance maps by Jeffrey Price; sponsored by Cornell Laboratory of Ornithology [et al.] Norton 1999 418p il maps pa $15.95 hardcover o.p. **598**

1. Birds—North America

ISBN 0-393-32231-9 (pa)   LC 98-35661

"For the 93 most widespread feeder species, the authors present several pages of excellent commentary plus two range maps and four bar graphs. For each bird, there is textual and graphic information on its abundance . . . food preferences, behavior, habits, a drawing of the bird, and more." Libr J

Includes bibliographical references

Dunne, Pete, 1951-

Pete Dunne on bird watching; the how-to, where-to, and when-to of birding. Houghton Mifflin 2003 334p il pa $12   **598**

1. Bird watching

ISBN 0-395-90686-5   LC 2002-27558

The author "describes how to attract more birds to the yard by feeding, landscaping, and providing water, then he moves on to the tools needed to see and identify the new additions to the yard, discussing binoculars and field guides and how to choose the best ones. The next chapters cover the fundamentals of birding. Birding ethics and the responsibilities of birders are covered in the final chapter." Booklist

This "book is a superlative introduction to bird watching." Libr J

Includes bibliographical references

Pete Dunne's essential field guide companion. Houghton Mifflin Co. 2006 710p $29.95

598

1. Birds—North America

ISBN 978-0-618-23648-0; 0-618-23648-1

LC 2005-21110

The author provides "information on status, distribution, habitat, cohabitants, movement and migration, behavior, flight, and vocalizations for all species of North American birds." Sci Books Films

This "title should appeal . . . to the serious birder striving to become more accomplished. No serious bird collection should be without it." Libr J

Ehrlich, Paul R.

The birder's handbook; a field guide to the natural history of North American birds: including all species that regularly breed north of Mexico; [by] Paul R. Ehrlich, David S. Dobkin, Daryl Wheye. Simon & Schuster 1988 xxx, 785p il pa $21.95 hardcover o.p.   **598**

1. Birds—North America

ISBN 0-671-65989-8 (pa)   LC 87-32404

This volume contains "basic information on each of the 646 species of birds in North America, enriched by 250 short essays on all aspects of avian behavior and biology. This book is a companion volume to any illustrat-

ed field guide." Am Libr

Includes bibliographical references

Firefly encyclopedia of birds; edited by Christopher Perrins. Firefly Bks. 2003 655p il maps $59.95 *   **598**

1. Birds

ISBN 1-55297-777-3

"An Andromeda book"

First published 1985 by Facts on File with title: The encyclopedia of birds

"Organized in phylogenetic order, the volume covers almost 10,000 bird species; for each bird family (owls, woodpeckers, thrushes, et al.) there is a map, a general text, and sidebars with paragraphs on nesting, voice, size, diet, plumage, habitat, etc. There are also random essays on appropriate related subjects, such as conservation, courtship, and many family-specific topics of interest as well as a helpful glossary. . . . This excellent reference title in an attractive format is highly recommended for most public and academic libraries." Libr J

Gallagher, Tim

The grail bird; hot on the trail of the Ivory-billed woodpecker. Houghton Mifflin 2005 272p il map $25; pa $14.95   **598**

1. Woodpeckers

ISBN 0-618-45693-7; 0-618-70941-X (pa)

LC 2005-42792

The author "was one of the first to rediscover the ivory-billed woodpecker, a fabled bird long believed extinct." Booklist

"An engaging story of the triumph of conservation, this book is highly recommended for most collections." Libr J

Includes bibliographical references

Gessner, David, 1961-

Return of the osprey; a season of flight and wonder. Algonquin Bks. 2001 286p map $23.95

598

1. Ospreys

ISBN 1-56512-254-2   LC 00-68230

Also available in paperback from Ballantine Bks.

"Over 90 percent of the osprey population in New England was wiped out between 1950 and 1975, and then DDT was banned. Gessner writes of the return of nesting ospreys to Cape Cod. . . . This beautifully written story of a season with birds of prey makes for engrossing reading as we learn about osprey life from a master essayist." Booklist

Includes bibliographical references

Heinrich, Bernd, 1940-

Mind of the raven; investigations and adventures with wolf-birds. Cliff St. Bks. 1999 380p il $25; pa $13   **598**

1. Ravens

ISBN 0-06-017447-1; 0-06-093063-2 (pa)

LC 99-18129

Heinrich "describes his field experiments in the feeding habits, play, intelligence, social structure, territoriali-

Heinrich, Bernd, 1940-—*Continued*

ty, and hunting methods of ravens as well as an array of topics from their skill as mimics to their suspected emotional natures. He brings alive the romance of field research, where the discipline of science is often harder to achieve than in the lab but is at least as rewarding. A splendid book." Libr J

Includes bibliographical references

Kaufman, Kenn

Kaufman field guide to birds of North America; with the collaboration of Rick and Nora Bowers and Lynn Hassler Kaufman. Houghton Mifflin 2005 c2000 392p il map pa $18.95   **598**

1. Birds—North America

ISBN 0-618-57423-9; 978-0-618-57423-0

First published 2000 with title: Birds of North America

For this identification guide "Kaufman selected over 2000 digitally edited photographs, enhanced to improve contrast, color, and the like. The excellent result will appeal to beginning birders perhaps intimidated by illustrations. . . . Kaufman's text is simple and uncluttered, a plus for novices." Libr J

Kroodsma, Donald E.

The singing life of birds; the art and science of listening to birdsong; drawings by Nancy Haver. Houghton Mifflin 2005 482p il $28   **598**

1. Birdsongs

ISBN 0-618-40568-2   LC 2004-65130

Includes audio CD

This is an "introduction to the functional and aesthetic aspects of birdsong, dealing with the broader context of how songs develop and their role in communication, courtship, and the defense of territory. The text is integrated with an accompanying CD containing 98 recordings in audio format." Sci Books Films

"Kroodsma is a warm, encouraging guide to the world of birdsong, and his enthusiasm is contagious." Publ Wkly

Includes bibliographical references

Leahy, Christopher W.

The birdwatcher's companion to North American birdlife; illustrations by Gordon Morrison. Princeton University Press 2004 1039p il hardcover o.p. pa $19.95   **598**

1. Birds—North America

ISBN 0-691-09297-4; 0-691-11388-2 (pa)

LC 2003-66383

First published 1982 by Hill & Wang

"This alphabetical compendium of ornithology offers entries ranging from single-line definitions of avian terminology ('Erne') to 12-page essay-style articles ('Systemics') that concentrate primarily on the US and Canada. Entries include a substantial number of biographies and black-and-white drawings. . . . Comprehensive entries on conservation, evolution of birdlife, optical equipment, and human threats to birdlife provide welcome up-to-date information. . . . Leahy's style is by turns serious and scholarly or personal and whimsical, appropriate

to a comprehensive reference for both novice and expert birders. There is no recent comparable work." Choice

Includes bibliographical references

Lynch, Wayne

Penguins of the world; text and photographs by Wayne Lynch. 2nd ed. Firefly Books 2007 175p il map $34.95; pa $24.95   **598**

1. Penguins

ISBN 978-1-55407-334-4; 1-55407-334-0; 978-1-55407-274-3 (pa); 1-55407-274-3 (pa)

LC 2007-299218

First published 1997

This is a "look at Lynch's discoveries about these flightless seabirds in the field and in scientific journals, during day-to-day as well as birth-to-death observations, and from the smallest to the largest type. While Lynch presents detailed descriptions of everything from mating rituals to eating habits, the best parts of his book are the photographs. Lynch's gorgeous and gorgeously printed images . . . display such a refined visual sensibility that even without accompanying text, the images would still achieve Lynch's goal of presenting the scientific and aesthetic appeal of this unique family of birds." Publ Wkly

Includes bibliographical references

Matthiessen, Peter

The birds of heaven; travels with cranes; paintings and drawings by Robert Bateman. North Point Press 2001 349p il $27.50; pa $16

598

1. Cranes (Birds) 2. Endangered species

ISBN 0-374-19944-2; 0-86547-657-8 (pa)

LC 2001-32986

The author writes "of his journeys in search of all the crane species and of his conversations with the scientists working to understand and preserve them." Booklist

"Eloquent and graceful, this lovely, moving narrative will inspire and delight readers with or without ornithological background or interests." Publ Wkly

National Audubon Society

Bird; the definitive visual guide; Audubon; [senior editor, Peter Frances; contributors, BirdLife International, David Burnie] DK Pub. 2007 512p il map $50   **598**

1. Birds

ISBN 978-0-7566-3153-6; 0-7566-3153-X

LC 2007-282186

Includes CD-ROM

"More than 10 percent of the world's 10,000 bird species are featured here, often in their natural habitat. Introductory sections discuss bird anatomy, physiology, behavior, evolution, flight, migration, classification, conservation, and geographic distribution. The main section of the book, arranged taxonomically, begins with general features and behavior of bird families. This is followed by photographs of each species and brief physical descriptions, habitat and behavior notes, and a distribution map." Choice

"From flyleaf to fore edge, the visuals are astounding. . . . An enclosed CD with bird calls and songs adds yet another dimension to a glorious work." Libr J

National Geographic complete birds of North America; edited by Jonathan Alderfer. National Geographic 2006 664p il map $35 * **598**

1. Birds—North America
ISBN 0-7922-4175-4   LC 2005-54495

Companion volume to Field guide to the birds of North America

This guide includes "chapters for the more than 80 avian families, with an overview of plumage, behavior, distribution, taxonomy, and conservation. This is followed by descriptions of all 962 species (covering identification, similar species, voice, status, and distribution) and sidebars that address such topics as difficult identifications." Libr J

"The book pulls together a remarkable amount of information into what can only be described as one of the finest one-volume reference works ever published on North American birds." Booklist

Includes bibliographical references

National Geographic field guide to the birds of North America; edited by Jon L. Dunn and Jonathan Alderfer. 5th ed. National Geographic 2006 503p il map pa $24 * **598**

1. Birds—North America
ISBN 0-7922-5314-0; 978-0-7922-5314-3
LC 2006-49420

First published 1983 with title: Field guide to the birds of North America

An identification guide to more than 800 species of North American birds. Arranged in family groups, the information for each species includes a full-color illustration, a range map, common and scientific names, measurement, and a description of plumage, distinctive songs and calls, behavior, abundance, and habitat.

Includes bibliographical references

Nielsen, John T.

Condor; to the brink and back—the life and times of one giant bird; [by] John Nielsen. HarperCollins Publishers 2006 257p il map $25.95 **598**

1. Condors
ISBN 0-06-008862-1; 978-0-06-008862-0
LC 2004-54336

The author "focuses on the process and players in the $20-million California Condor Recovery program, describing the infighting in the scientific and environmental communities, at war about whether a 'hands on' or a 'hands off' approach will work best." Publ Wkly

"This is popular science writing at its peak." Booklist
Includes bibliographical references

Peterson, Roger Tory, 1908-1996

A field guide to the birds of Britain and Europe; [by] Roger Tory Peterson, Guy Mountfort, P.A.D. Hollom. 5th ed, in collaboration with D.I.M. Wallace. Houghton Mifflin 1993 261p il hardcover o.p. pa $22 **598**

1. Birds—Great Britain 2. Birds—Europe
ISBN 0-395-66931-6; 0-618-16675-0 (pa)
LC 93-22426

"The Peterson field guide series"
First published 1954

"Sponsored by the National Audubon Society, the National Wildlife Federation, and the Roger Tory Peterson Institute"

Covers the British Isles, Iceland, continental Europe and the islands of the Mediterranean. Includes identification, voice and habitat, and names in the foreign language pertinent to location.

Robbins, Chandler S., 1918-

Birds of North America; a guide to field identification; by Chandler S. Robbins, Bertel Bruun, and Herbert S. Zim; revised by Jonathan P. Latimer and Karen Stray Nolting and James Coe; illustrated by Arthur Singer. rev and updated. St. Martin's Press 2001 359p il maps $19.95; pa $15.95 **598**

1. Birds—North America
ISBN 1-58238-091-0; 1-58238-090-2 (pa)
LC 2001-271739

"A Golden field guide"
First published 1966

This resource includes over 800 species and 600 range maps; illustrations featuring male, female, and juvenile plumage; and sonograms picturing sound for song recognition. Feeding habits, migration routes, and characteristic flight patterns as well as American Ornithologists' classifications are also provided.

Rosen, Jonathan, 1963-

The life of the skies. Farrar, Straus and Giroux 2008 324p il $24 **598**

1. Bird watching
ISBN 978-0-374-18630-2; 0-374-18630-8
LC 2007-25668

The author describes "how bird-watching in its broadest sense influences and fits into the fabric of Western and Judeo-Christian heritage. . . . A sort of book-length essay, this is a most thoughtful, literate, and entertaining work." Libr J

Includes bibliographical references

Roth, Sally

The backyard bird feeder's bible; the A-to-Z guide to feeders, seed mixes, projects, and treats. Rodale 2000 268p il $29.95; pa $18.95 **598**

1. Birds
ISBN 0-87596-834-1; 0-87596-918-6 (pa)
LC 00-9063

Conveying "information on attracting, feeding, and observing birds, the entries vary in length from half a page to multiple pages for broad or complex topics such as the benefits of fruiting plants . . . as a source of both food and shelter." Libr J

This "truly is a comprehensive guide for bird enthusiasts." Booklist
Includes bibliographical references

Safina, Carl

Eye of the albatross; visions of hope and survival. Holt & Co. 2002 377p il maps pa $16 hardcover o.p.   **598**

1. Albatrosses

ISBN 0-8050-6229-7 (pa)   LC 2001-51644

"A John Macrae book"

The author "recounts his travels to remote portions of the northwest Hawaiian Islands to witness albatross breeding season, during which parent birds fly across entire oceans—as much as 25,000 miles—to hunt sufficient food to nourish their single chicks. . . . Safina's encyclopedic knowledge and spirited prose provide a stunningly intimate portrait of an environment." Publ Wkly

Includes bibliographical references

Sibley, David

The Sibley field guide to birds of eastern North America; written and illustrated by David Allen Sibley. Knopf 2003 431p il pa $19.95

                                          598

1. Birds—North America

ISBN 0-679-45120-X   LC 2002-114931

Companion volume to The Sibley field guide to birds of western North America

This portable "guide features 650 bird species, plus regional populations found east of the Rocky Mountains. Accounts include . . . illustrations . . . with descriptive caption text pointing out the most important field marks. Each entry contains . . . text concerning frequency, nesting, behavior, food and feeding, voice description, and key identification features." Publisher's note

"All the qualities to be expected in a field guide are here. . . . Image reproduction is crisp, colors are distinct, shading shows well, and despite the very small size, range map colors are clear. . . . Sibley has accomplished the difficult task of condensing . . . [The Sibley guide to birds] to practical field size." Libr J

The Sibley field guide to birds of western North America; written and illustrated by David Allen Sibley. Knopf 2003 473p il pa $19.95 *

                                          598

1. Birds—North America

ISBN 0-679-45121-8   LC 2002-114930

Companion volume to The Sibley field guide to birds of eastern North America

This portable "guide features 703 bird species, plus regional populations found west of the Rocky Mountains. Accounts include . . . illustrations . . . with descriptive caption text pointing out the most important field marks. Each entry contains . . . text concerning frequency, nesting, behavior, food and feeding, voice decription, and key identification features." Publisher's note

"All the qualities to be expected in a field guide are here. . . . Image reproduction is crisp, colors are distinct, shading shows well, and despite the very small size, range map colors are clear. . . . Sibley has accomplished the difficult task of condensing . . . [The Sibley guide to birds] to practical field size." Libr J

The Sibley guide to bird life & behavior; illustrated by David Allen Sibley; edited by Chris Elphick, John B. Dunning, Jr., David Allen Sibley. Knopf 2001 588p il maps $45 *   **598**

1. Birds—North America

ISBN 0-679-45123-4   LC 2001-33903

At head of title: National Audubon Society

This companion volume to The Sibley guide to birds provides "information about birds' lives and behavior. . . . Part 1 ('The World of Birds') discusses basic avian biology, including form, distribution, population, and conservation, in about 100 pages. Part 2 ('Bird Families of North America'), to which over 40 ornithologists contributed, uses a standard format to describe taxonomy, foraging, breeding, range, nests, eggs, longevity, conservation, and more." Libr J

The Sibley guide to birds; written and illustrated by David Sibley. Knopf 2000 544p il maps pa $35

                                          598

1. Birds—North America

ISBN 0-679-45122-6   LC 00-41239

"A Chanticleer Press edition"

At head of title: National Audubon Society

"The treatments of each of the 810 species have detailed paintings to show the natural variations in plumage (e.g., juveniles, male/female adults, seasonal and geographic changes). In all, there are more than 6,600 full-color illustrations. . . . The text for each species has a short summary of identification key points, description of vocalizations, and an up-to-date range map." Choice

"This stunning volume stands out as a must have for even casual birders." SLJ

Sibley's birding basics; written and illustrated by David Allen Sibley. Knopf 2002 154p il pa $15.95   **598**

1. Bird watching 2. Birds

ISBN 0-375-70966-5   LC 2002-20768

Sibley "explores general aspects of birding such as getting started, misidentification, voice, understanding feathers, age variation, ethics and conservation, taxonomy, and finding birds. If being a field naturalist is a craft, then this book is essential in helping to develop and understand the required skills." Libr J

Stokes, Donald W.

The bird feeder book; an easy guide to attracting, identifying, and understanding your feeder birds; [by] Donald and Lillian Stokes; illustrations of feeders by Gordon Morrison; range maps by Leslie Cowperthwaite. Little, Brown 1987 90p il maps pa $12.95   **598**

1. Bird watching

ISBN 0-316-81733-3   LC 87-3016

"This guide for beginners features 72 dramatic color photographs of the most common backyard birds. The text offers chapters on attracting and identifying birds (which types of feeders to use, etc.), dealing with squirrels and other yard pests, and planting shrubbery layouts that offer food and nest sites. A nicely illustrated, logically organized handbook." Booklist

Includes bibliographical references

Tennant, Alan, 1943-

On the wing; to the edge of the earth with the peregrine falcon. Alfred A. Knopf 2004 304p il $26.95; pa $14.95   **598**

1. Falcons

ISBN 0-375-41551-3; 1-4000-3182-6 (pa)

LC 2003-69496

The author "describes his efforts to trail peregrine falcons on their epic migratory flights from the Caribbean to the Arctic. . . . After radio-tagging a young peregrine off the coast of Texas, Tennant teams up with George Vose, a former WWII combat flight instructor, to follow the bird on its spring migration north." Publ Wkly

"An exhilarating and illuminating storyteller, Tennant offers exquisitely poetic descriptions of peregrine falcons—magnificently aerodynamic, keen-sighted, and fearless birds of prey—a galvanizing history of falconry, and a sobering accounting of the consequences of rampant chemical pollution and environmental destruction." Booklist

Udvardy, Miklos D. F., 1919-1998

National Audubon Society field guide to North American birds, Western region; revised by John Farrand, Jr.; visual key by Amanda Wilson and Lori Hogan. rev ed. Knopf 1994 822p il maps pa $19.95 *   **598**

1. Birds—North America

ISBN 0-679-42851-8   LC 94-7415

Companion volume to National Audubon Society field guide to North American birds, Eastern region by John L. Bull

"A Chanticleer Press edition"

First published 1977

This pictorial guide to 544 western species arranges birds by color and shape to simplify identification. It also includes information on bird-watching and conservation status

Includes bibliographical references

Weidensaul, Scott

Living on the wind; across the hemisphere with migratory birds. North Point Press 1999 420p il pa $15 hardcover o.p.   **598**

1. Birds—Migration

ISBN 0-86547-591-1 (pa)   LC 99-11693

"Starting at a wildlife refuge in Alaska, the author follows birds on their southward migration; watches them on their wintering grounds in Central America, Jamaica, Argentina, and the U.S. . . . and then follows them north again. Along the way he discovers how birds navigate on their journeys, using the sun during the day, the stars to orient by night, or even the Earth's magnetic field as a compass." Booklist

"The book will be of interest to biologists and amateur naturalists; birders will particularly appreciate the discussion of key 'fallout' areas." Libr J

Includes bibliographical references

Of a feather; a brief history of American birding. Harcourt, Inc. 2007 358p il $25   **598**

1. Bird watching

ISBN 978-0-15-101247-3; 0-15-101247-4

LC 2007-07364

This narrative history of birding in America "begins in colonial America, where new arrivals from Europe 'made awed note of the continent's teeming skies and waterways.'" N Y Times Book Rev

The author's "vivid descriptions of his own experiences should send many a reader out of doors to look for the small, contained miracle that is a bird." Publ Wkly

Includes bibliographical references

Weiner, Jonathan, 1953-

The beak of the finch; a story of evolution in our time. Knopf 1994 332p il pa $14 hardcover o.p.   **598**

1. Grant, Peter R., 1936- 2. Grant, B. Rosemary 3. Finches 4. Evolution

ISBN 0-698-73337-X (pa)   LC 93-36755

"This is an account of Peter and Rosemary Grant's research on the microevolutionary modifications that occur in finch beaks as they adapt to environmental changes. Analysis of data collected from 18,000 birds on a Galápagos island over 21 years conclusively demonstrates that the pressures of natural selection are currently altering wild populations." Libr J

Includes bibliographical references

Williamson, Sheri L.

A field guide to hummingbirds of North America; [by] Sheri L. Williamson. Houghton Mifflin 2001 263p il maps $30; pa $22   **598**

1. Hummingbirds

ISBN 0-618-02495-6; 0-618-02496-4 (pa)

LC 2001-24473

"The Peterson field guide series"

"The habits, habitats, migratory patterns, physical traits, diet, mating practices, where to find them in short, all the information that a good wildlife guide offers are the stuff of Williamson's book. Clear, engaging prose and 180 full color photographs make this a natural for birdwatchers everywhere." Publ Wkly

599   Mammalia (Mammals)

Attenborough, David, 1926-

The life of mammals. Princeton University Press 2002 320p il $35   **599**

1. Mammals

ISBN 0-691-11324-6   LC 2002-106846

The author "treks across every continent and kind of terrain to introduce us to such unusual and evolutionarily successful creatures as the Patagonian opossum, the Canadian pygmy shrew, the Alpine marmot, and the Malaysian sun bear." Publisher's note

"Heavily illustrated with beautiful photographs and enlivened by Attenborough's friendly, informative writing style, this is a terrific introduction to the wonders of our hairy, milk-producing relatives." Booklist

Elbroch, Mark
Mammal tracks & sign; a guide to North American species. Stackpole Bks. 2003 779p il maps $44.95 **599**
1. Animal tracks
ISBN 0-8117-2626-6   LC 2002-10549
This guide provides "track and trail illustrations, range maps, and full-color photographs showing feeding signs, scat, tunnels, burrows, bedding areas, remains, and more. . . . [It explains] how to find, identify, measure, and interpret the clues mammals leave behind. . . . Includes essays that contextualize tracking as a developing science." Publisher's note
The author "brings an ideal combination of practical experience and careful research to this work. . . . A definitive treatment, Elbroch's book will set the standard for years to come and is essential to anyone interested in tracking this continent's mammals." Libr J
Includes bibliographical references

The Peterson field guide to animal tracks; [by] Mark Elbroch and Olaus J. Murie. 3rd ed. Houghton Mifflin Company 2005 (The Peterson field guide series) hardcover o.p. pa $19.95 *
599
1. Animal tracks
ISBN 978-0-618-51742-8; 978-0-618-51743-5 (pa)
LC 2005-13108
First published 1954
"Murie's handbook is recognized as the classic work on the subject. . . . The illustrated guide describes the tracks, droppings, and marks left on bones and leaves by an army of wild animals-bats, bears, rabbits, reptiles, moles, weasels, and others. A fascinating collection of miscellaneous information about the habits of these creatures is part of the descriptive text." Wynar. Ref Books in Paperback. 2d edition

Mares, Michael A.
A desert calling; life in a forbidding landscape. Harvard Univ. Press 2002 318p il maps $29.95
599
1. Mammals 2. Desert animals
ISBN 0-674-00747-6   LC 2001-51786
The author describes his studies of "small mammals in the deserts of North America, South America, Egypt, and Iran. . . . The wonder of field research and of the discoveries that result shines through his matter-of-fact tone." Booklist
Includes bibliographical references

Nowak, Ronald M.
Walker's mammals of the world. 6th ed. Johns Hopkins Univ. Press 1999 2v il set $135
599
1. Mammals
ISBN 0-8018-5789-9   LC 98-23686
Also available online
First published 1964
"A goal of the work . . . [is] to provide a quality photograph of a living representative of every genus of mammal. . . . Each genus entry contains information on the number of species known, key literature references,

physical description, comparison of characteristics of representative species, description of habitat, general behavior, breeding and care of young, and information on the species' endangered status." Am Ref Books Annu, 2000
Includes bibliographical references

Whitaker, John O., Jr.
National Audubon Society field guide to North American mammals. rev ed. Knopf 1996 937p il maps pa $19.95 *
599
1. Mammals
ISBN 0-679-44631-1   LC 95-81456
First published 1980
This field guide describes 390 species of mammals of North America and includes keys for identification, range maps, information on tracks and anatomy, and 375 color photos

599.2 Marsupialia and monotremata

Flannery, Tim F. (Tim Fridjof), 1956-
Chasing kangaroos; a continent, a scientist, and a search for the world's most extraordinary creature. Grove Press 2007 258p il map $24
599.2
1. Kangaroos 2. Australia—Description and travel
ISBN 978-0-8021-1852-3; 0-8021-1852-6
LC 2006-52628
First published 2004 in Australia with title: Country
"There are 70-odd species of kangaroo: some drink salt water; others live in trees. But as a paleontologist, Flannery is obsessed with finding out when and where the first kangaroos lived. Much of the book is about his searches for the fossils of extinct species in remote areas of the Australian outback." Publ Wkly
"In a time where pride in one's country is a rarity, Flannery has written a love letter to his. . . . Just as much as Chasing Kangaroos is about the evolution of a creature, it's also Flannery's acknowledgement of Australia's inherent uniqueness, a uniqueness he begs is not casually lost in the growing conformity of the global landscape." Paste

599.5 Cetacea and Sirenia

Montgomery, Sy
Journey of the pink dolphins; an Amazon quest. Simon & Schuster 2000 317p il maps pa $16 hardcover o.p. **599.5**
1. Dolphins 2. Amazon River valley
ISBN 0-7432-0026-8 (pa)   LC 99-45840
The author "recounts her Amazonian adventures in search of the *botos,* the famously elusive freshwater pink dolphins, a quest that yields not only invaluable scientific observations but profound insights into the significance of myth." Booklist
Includes bibliographical references

National Audubon Society guide to marine mammals of the world; illustrated by Pieter A. Folkens; written by Randall R. Reeves [et al.] Knopf 2002 527p il maps $26.95   **599.5**

1. Marine mammals

ISBN 0-375-41141-0   LC 2001-38103

"A Chanticleer Press edition"

This describes "120 species of the world's whales, dolphins, porpoises, seals and sea lions, manatees, Marine and Sea Otters, and [Polar Bears]." Publisher's note

"Just about everything one could hope for in a guide can be found in this info-packed yet extremely user-friendly tome. . . . A liberal dose of superb, high-quality action color photographs shows the creatures in their natural surroundings." SLJ

Includes bibliographical references

Rothenberg, David, 1962-

Thousand mile song; whale music in a sea of sound. Basic Books 2008 287p il $27.50

599.5

1. Whales

ISBN 978-0-465-07128-9; 0-465-07128-7

LC 2007-48161

"Biologists know that whale songs, which may carry for hundreds of miles, change over time and are passed on from one generation to the next, but they don't fully understand what these complex sounds are for. . . . [The author] proposes that music played by humans can help us find answers. He tested this theory by playing his clarinet into an underwater speaker and recording the whales' responses on an underwater hydrophone. His intriguing book includes sonograms and a CD demonstrating that the orcas, belugas and humpbacks he played for seemed to interact with his music. . . . His paean to the beautiful music these great mammals make should lend further support to attempts to save the whales at a time when they are increasingly threatened." Publ Wkly

Includes bibliographical references

599.75   Felidae (Cat family)

Adamson, Joy, 1910-1980

Born free; a lioness of two worlds. Pantheon Bks. 1987 220p il pa $14.95 hardcover o.p. *

599.75

1. Lions 2. Kenya—Description and travel

ISBN 0-375-71438-3 (pa)   LC 86-42972

A reissue of the title first published 1960

This is the "story of a lioness who bridged the gulf between two worlds, that of the jungle and of man. The author and her husband, a Kenya game warden, reared a cub to kill and fend for herself when she was returned to the jungle. At the same time they were able to preserve the bond of confidence and affection established with her as a pet." Cincinnati Public Libr

Caputo, Philip

Ghosts of Tsavo; stalking the mystery lions of East Africa. National Geographic Soc. 2002 275p il $27; pa $15   **599.75**

1. Lions 2. Tsavo National Park (Kenya)

ISBN 0-7922-6362-6; 0-7922-4100-2 (pa)

LC 2002-22642

This is a study of the Tsavo lions of Kenya. Philip Caputo discusses "why they are bigger than their counterparts of the Serengeti plains, why the males do not normally grow manes, and why Tsavo lions are more prone than Serengeti lions to make humans a part of their diet. The observable differences between Tsavo lions and Serengeti lions have led some behavioral scientists whom Mr. Caputo interviews to believe that the Tsavo lions are actually a different species." N Y Times (Late N Y Ed)

Kitchener, Andrew

The natural history of the wild cats. Comstock 1991 xxi, 280p il maps (Natural history of mammals series) pa $23.95 hardcover o.p.

599.75

1. Wild cats

ISBN 0-8014-8498-7 (pa)   LC 90-45833

The author provides a "synthesis of what we know about cats, his account always strengthened by the comparative point of view. There are eight vivid chapters packed with graphs, maps and feline parameters. He includes a cat Who's Who in fine color photographs; it shows us most of the small cat species, plus three big cats that, unlike lions and tigers and leopards, are not in the public eye." Sci Am

Includes bibliographical references

Matthiessen, Peter

Tigers in the snow; introduction and photographs by Maurice Hornocker. Farrar, Straus & Giroux 1999 169p il pa $15 hardcover o.p.

599.75

1. Tigers 2. Endangered species

ISBN 0-86547-596-2 (pa)   LC 99-44866

Matthiessen's book focuses on "the Siberian tiger. His account also touches on the fate of other tiger populations that once ranged from Eastern Turkey to the Sea of Japan." Nat Hist

"Mixing information about the lives of all the races of wild tigers with firsthand tales of his visits to Russia, the author brings an immediacy to his narrative that stirs the reader to awe of these great cats. . . . [An] evocative look at one of our rarest animals." Booklist

Includes bibliographical references

Padel, Ruth, 1946-

Tigers in red weather; a quest for the last wild tigers. Walker & Co. 2006 432p il map $26.95

599.75

1. Tigers 2. Asia—Description and travel

ISBN 978-0-8027-1544-9; 0-8027-1544-3

LC 2007-386423

Padel discusses her travels in India, China, Indonesia, Burma, Nepal, Bhutan, Russia, and Korea where she in-

Padel, Ruth, 1946-—*Continued*
terviews scientists, forest guards, trackers, photographers, veterinarians, and conservationists about the state of tigers in the wild.

The author "gives way to neither emotionalism nor despair. Rather, she struggles for glimpses of workable solutions, conservation plans far-reaching enough to take the needs of humans into account as well as those of animals. . . . Her descriptions of travel in exotic locales are delightful and evocative." Christ Sci Monit

Thomas, Elizabeth Marshall, 1931-
The tribe of tiger; cats and their culture; illustrated by Jared Taylor Williams. Simon & Schuster 1994 240p il pa $13.95 hardcover o.p.

599.75

1. Cats 2. Tigers 3. Lions
ISBN 0-7434-2689-4 (pa)   LC 94-20195
The author offers a "look into the lives of various members of the cat family—small and large, domestic and wild, Old World and New. She begins with the evolution and spread of different feline species, explaining the physiology and behavior of cats, including house cats, as meat eaters, that is, in the light of their hunting instincts. She then examines the changes over a period of more than 30 years in the culture . . . of different lion communities in several parts of Africa. In conclusion, she discusses the need for tiger conservation." Booklist
Includes bibliographical references

599.77 Canidae (Dog family)

Busch, Robert
The wolf almanac; a celebration of wolves and their world; by Robert H. Busch. New & rev ed. Lyons Press 2007 274p il map pa $19.95

599.77

1. Wolves
ISBN 978-1-59921-069-8; 1-59921-069-X
First published 1995
This offers information about "the evolution and history of wolves; their biology and physiology; their behavior and sociology; and their influence in ancient cultures and mythology. . . . The author also discusses the conservation politics of all wolf species." Publisher's note
Includes bibliographical references

Lopez, Barry Holstun, 1945-
Of wolves and men; with photographs by John Bauguess; including a new afterword by the author and expanded bibliography. 1st Scribner Classics ed. Scribner Classics 2004 323p il $45 *

599.77

1. Wolves
ISBN 0-7432-4936-4   LC 2004-45429
First published 1978
The author "infuses his natural history of the long relationship between wolves and humankind with both myth and science, then revisits the controversial subject of wolf reintroduction." Booklist
Includes bibliographical references

McNamee, Thomas, 1947-
The return of the wolf to Yellowstone. Holt & Co. 1997 354p il maps pa $15 hardcover o.p.

599.77

1. Wolves 2. Endangered species 3. Yellowstone National Park
ISBN 0-8050-5792-7 (pa)   LC 96-39702
"An advocate for the reintroduction of the gray wolf to Yellowstone National Park, McNamee kept careful watch over the legal wrangling that accompanied this controversial endeavor, the challenges of its execution, and the complex questions it has raised, then recorded the entire story in this vivid day-by-day chronicle." Booklist
Includes bibliographical references

Mowat, Farley
Never cry wolf. Back Bay Books 2001 246p pa $12.99

599.77

1. Wolves
ISBN 978-0-316-88179-1; 0-316-88179-1
First published 1963 by Little, Brown
"A biologist for the Canadian government describes his experiences in the Arctic watching and tracking the activities of a wolf family." Publ Wkly

Smith, Douglas W.
Decade of the wolf; returning the wild to Yellowstone; [by] Douglas W. Smith & Gary Ferguson. Lyons Press 2005 212p il maps $23.95; pa $16.95 *

599.77

1. Wolves 2. Endangered species 3. Yellowstone National Park
ISBN 1-59228-700-X; 1-59228-886-3 (pa)
          LC 2005-40767
This is an "inside look at the Yellowstone Wolf Recovery Project, covering the 10 years that have passed since the U.S. Fish and Wildlife Service made the controversial decision to reintroduce wolves into the national park." Publ Wkly
"Well illustrated with black-and-white and color photographs, this intimate history of the return of the top predator to Yellowstone will find an eager audience." Booklist
Includes bibliographical references

599.78 Ursidae (Bears)

Busch, Robert
The grizzly almanac; [by] Robert H. Busch. Lyons Press 2000 229p il maps hardcover o.p. pa $19.95

599.78

1. Grizzly bear
ISBN 1-58574-143-4; 1-59228-320-9 (pa)
          LC 00-58587
The author "traces the evolution of the 'big bear' from its earliest days, describes its habitat and behavior, and recounts grizzly folklore and tales of grizzly attacks. Maintaining that the grizzly's reputation as a vicious killer is undeserved, he makes recommendations for a more peaceful coexistence with humans." Libr J
Includes bibliographical references

Croke, Vicki

The lady and the panda; the true adventures of the first American explorer to bring back China's most exotic animal; [by] Vicki Constantine Croke. Random House 2005 372p il $25.95; pa $14.95 *
599.78

1. Harkness, Ruth 2. Giant panda
ISBN 0-375-50783-3; 0-375-75970-0 (pa)
LC 2004-51356

The author tells the "story of Ruth Harkness, the Manhattan bohemian socialite who, against all but impossible odds, trekked to Tibet in 1936 to capture the most mysterious animal of the day: a bear that had for countless centuries lived in secret in the labyrinth of lonely cold mountains." Publisher's note

"This well-written, exhaustively researched and documented book should be on every library's shelves." Libr J

Includes bibliographical references

Jans, Nick, 1955-

Grizzly maze; Timothy Treadwell's fatal obsession with Alaskan bears. Penguin Group 2005 274p il $24.95; pa $15 **599.78**
1. Treadwell, Timothy 2. Grizzly bear 3. Animal attacks
ISBN 0-525-94886-4; 978-0-525-94886-5; 0-452-28735-9 (pa); 978-0-452-28735-8 (pa)
LC 2004-30920

This is an "account of the life and death of self-appointed bear guardian Timothy Treadwell, who, along with a girlfriend, was killed and eaten by grizzlies in Alaska's Katmai National Park in 2003." Publ Wkly

The author "presents a fair and exacting account of the events that led up to the tragedy, and, in doing so, shows readers the different sides of a complex and controversial man." SLJ

Includes bibliographical references

Rosing, Norbert

The world of the polar bear. Firefly Books 2006 203p il $45 **599.78**
1. Polar bear
ISBN 978-1-55407-155-5; 1-55407-155-0

This book contains "a season-by-season account of the life of the polar bear, including feeding, mating, rearing of cubs and journeying from the ice; an intimate look at the animals that share the polar bear's environment, including seals, arctic foxes, walruses and muskoxen; a section on such northern sky phenomena as sun dogs and the northern lights; [and] many anecdotes and insights about the polar bear." Publisher's note

Includes bibliographical references

Schooler, Lynn

The blue bear; a true story of friendship, tragedy, and survival in the Alaskan wilderness. Ecco Press 2002 272p il $25.95; pa $13.95
599.78

1. Bears 2. Alaska—Description and travel
ISBN 0-06-621085-2; 0-06-093573-1 (pa)
LC 2001-51079

The author describes his experiences as a wilderness guide in Alaska. "The story centers on the renowned nature photographer Michio Hoshino, a client who became a friend, and the two men's ongoing search for the elusive glacier bear, a blue variant of the North American black bear. . . . [Schooler's] writing reveals an abundance of wilderness savvy, and a mind scrupulous about getting the world down as accurately as possible." New Yorker

Treadwell, Timothy

Among grizzlies; living with wild bears in Alaska; by Timothy Treadwell and Jewel Palovak. Ballantine Bks. 1999 199p il pa $14
599.78

1. Grizzly bear 2. Alaska
ISBN 0-345-42605-3
First published 1997 by HarperCollins

"This firsthand account of living among grizzly bears in a place Treadwell calls the Grizzly Sanctuary, just south of the Arctic Circle, reveals intimate details of the summer lives of these great bears. Fleeing a life of drug and alcohol addiction, Treadwell made an initial foray to Alaska. . . . He returned to Alaska in subsequent summers to live among the bears and observe them close at hand. . . . Full of anecdotal stories about the details of the daily routine of grizzly life, this story of salvation through grizzly bears will help engender concern for their future in the wild." Booklist

Includes bibliographical references

599.8 Primates

Fossey, Dian

Gorillas in the mist. Houghton Mifflin 1983 326p il pa $14 hardcover o.p. * **599.8**
1. Gorillas
ISBN 0-618-08360-X (pa)
LC 82-23332

This book "recounts some of the events of the thirteen years that I have spent with the mountain gorillas in their natural habitat and includes data from the fifteen years of continuing field study." Preface

Includes bibliographical references

Galdikas, Biruté

Reflections of Eden; my years with the orangutans of Borneo; {by} Biruté M.F. Galdikas. Little, Brown 1995 408p il maps pa $19.99 hardcover o.p. **599.8**
1. Orangutan
ISBN 0-316-30186-8 (pa)
LC 94-22948

The author discusses her life in Borneo and her research into the lives of the orangutans of Borneo's rain forest

"Highly recommended for all libraries, this book will inspire young scientists and enthrall anyone interested in orangutans and the rigors of modern field research." Libr J

Goodall, Jane, 1934-

In the shadow of man; photographs by Hugo van Lawick. rev ed. Houghton Mifflin 1988 297p il map pa $15 *   **599.8**

1. Chimpanzees

ISBN 0-618-05679-9   LC 87-36965

First published 1971

The author describes the chimpanzee group she studied during ten years of field observation in the Gombe Stream Chimpanzee Reserve in Tanzania.

Includes bibliographical references

Through a window; my thirty years with the chimpanzees of Gombe. Houghton Mifflin 1990 268p il map pa $16 hardcover o.p.   **599.8**

1. Chimpanzees

ISBN 0-618-05677-7 (pa)   LC 90-36974

This continuation of In the shadow of man "tells two stories: first of how the chimps of Gombe in Tanzania have grown, changed and died, and second, how Goodall and her dedicated group of Tanzanian observers have survived the rigours of the past thirty years. It is beautifully written, and evokes both sympathy and understanding of these animals." Times Lit Suppl

Sapolsky, Robert M.

A primate's memoir. Scribner 2001 304p $25; pa $14   **599.8**

1. Baboons

ISBN 0-7432-0247-3; 0-7432-0241-4 (pa)

LC 00-63522

This is an account of the author's experiences observing baboons in Kenya

"One closes Sapolsky's book a lot more knowledgeable about plenty of baboon-related matters. But mostly one has already begun to miss the company of this sometimes cranky but always impassioned, learned and winningly irreverent man." N Y Times Book Rev

Waal, Frans de, 1948-

Bonobo; the forgotten ape; photographs, Frans Lanting. University of Calif. Press 1997 210p il maps $50; pa $29.95   **599.8**

1. Apes

ISBN 0-520-20535-9; 0-520-21651-2 (pa)

LC 96-41095

The subject of this monograph is the bonobo, a species of ape. "In six chapters, de Waal describes the history of the discovery of bonobos as a separate species; he compares them with common chimps; he describes their natural habitat and their . . . use of sex as social currency, particularly in moderating aggression; he examines bonobo social structure in relation to that of common chimps and humans; and he finishes with an exploration of bonobos' highly developed sense of empathy." New Sci

Includes bibliographical references

World atlas of great apes and their conservation; edited by Julian Caldecott and Lera Miles; foreword by Kofi A. Annan. University of California Press, in association with UNEP-WCMC 2005 456p il map $45 *   **599.8**

1. Apes 2. Biogeography 3. Atlases 4. Wildlife conservation

ISBN 0-520-24633-0; 978-0-520-24633-1

LC 2006-272653

Images, maps and 130-page bibliography available electronically via the World Wide Web

"Each great ape specie is given a separate chapter that contains information on behavior and ecology, communication and tool use, threats and conservation, and exceptionally detailed distribution maps. What sets this book apart is the section that details each country in which apes are found and exactly what conservation efforts are underway." Univ Press Books for Public and Second Sch Libr, 2006

Includes bibliographical references

599.9   Hominidae Homo sapiens

Olson, Steve, 1956-

Mapping human history; discovering the past through our genes. Houghton Mifflin 2002 292p il $25; pa $14   **599.9**

1. Human beings 2. Physical anthropology

ISBN 0-618-09157-2; 0-618-35210-4 (pa)

LC 2001-51880

The author "traces the history of human civilization in five regions of the world—Africa, the Middle East, Asia, Australia, and Europe and the Americas, plus a final chapter on Hawaii—to explain how physical differences originated and to provide evidence of our essential sameness." Publ Wkly

Includes bibliographical references

599.93   Genetics, sex and age characteristics, evolution

The **Cambridge** encyclopedia of human evolution; edited by Steve Jones, Robert Martin and David Pilbeam; executive editor, Sarah Bunney; foreword by Richard Dawkins. Cambridge Univ. Press 1993 506p il maps $120; pa $42

599.93

1. Human origins 2. Evolution

ISBN 0-521-32370-3; 0-521-46786-1 (pa)

LC 92-18037

"This encyclopedia of the human species places modern man in evolutionary perspective, showing the descent of humankind from Mitochondrial Eve and its relationship to other living primates. Genetics, fossils, biology, brain function, disease, the biology, evolution, and ecology of humans and other modern primates are the major themes arranged topically in this encyclopedia. Excellent black-and-white photos, drawings, tables, and maps complement a work with over 70 contributors." Am Libr

Diamond, Jared M.

The third chimpanzee; the evolution and future of the human animal; {by} Jared Diamond. HarperCollins Pubs. 1992 407p il maps hardcover o.p. pa $14.95   **599.93**

1. Human origins 2. Evolution

ISBN 0-06-018307-1; 978-0-06-084550-6 (pa); 0-06-084550-3 (pa)   LC 91-50455

First published 1991 in the United Kingdom with title: The rise and fall of the third chimpanzee

Engl. title: The rise and fall of the third chimpanzee

The author "argues that the human being is just a third species of chimpanzee but nevertheless a unique animal essentially due to its capacity for innovation, which caused a great leap forward in hominoid evolution. After stressing the significance of spoken language, along with art and technology, Diamond focuses on the self-destructive propensities of our species." Libr J

Includes bibliographical references

The **Double-edged** helix; social implications of genetics in a diverse society; edited by Joseph S. Alper [et al.] Johns Hopkins Univ. Press 2002 293p hardcover o.p. pa $26.95 *
            599.93

1. Genetic engineering 2. Bioethics 3. Genetics 4. Medical genetics

ISBN 0-8018-6964-1; 0-8018-7926-4 (pa)
            LC 2001-6618

This "explores the impact of recent genetic discoveries on both different population segments and society as a whole. The authors address the medical and ethical implications of the new technologies, outlining potential positive and negative effects of genetic research on minorities, individuals with disabilities, and those of diverse sexual orientations." Publisher's note

"Bringing the concerns of different communities together in a single volume makes it possible to appreciate the mosaic of human issues fully and forces us to anticipate the challenges that may arise—and that will require our attention—as the genetic revolution proceeds. . . . A much needed antidote to the current genetic hoopla." JAMA

Includes bibliographical references

Dunbar, R. I. M. (Robin Ian MacDonald), 1947-

Grooming, gossip, and the evolution of language; [by] Robin Dunbar. Harvard Univ. Press 1996 230p $25; pa $17.95   **599.93**

1. Human origins 2. Language and languages 3. Gossip 4. Human behavior

ISBN 0-674-36334-5; 0-674-36336-1 (pa)
            LC 96-15934

"Dunbar, a psychologist, thinks that gossip has the same social function in humans as does grooming in other primates and that language evolved to enable humans to chat about their friends and families." Libr J

"Concisely and clearly written for lay readers, Dunbar exhibits a gift for argument and explanation." Publ Wkly

Includes bibliographical references

Gee, Henry

Jacob's ladder; the history of the human genome. Norton 2004 272p $25.95   **599.93**

1. Genetics 2. Genomes

ISBN 0-393-05083-1   LC 2004-49504

This "is an abbreviated history of biology from Aristotle through the sequencing of the human genome. The narrative includes a general description of the major discoveries in cell, developmental, evolutionary, and genetic biology. . . . This book provides a good summary of the discoveries that are the basis of modern-day biology." Sci Books Films

Includes bibliographical references

The **Genomic** revolution; unveiling the unity of life; Michael Yudell and Robert DeSalle, editors. Joseph Henry Press 2002 272p $27.95
            599.93

1. Human Genome Project 2. Genomes

ISBN 0-309-07436-3   LC 2002-4016

Published with the American Museum of Natural History

This book looks at genomics "from the basic presentation of ideas about heredity through the essential principles of molecular biology, including an exploration of the ethical implications of the genome project for individuals and society." Publisher's note

"The essays are well written and accessible to almost anyone interested in the areas represented. . . . All in all, a unique snapshot of a pivotal period in science and a valuable addition to most libraries. Summing up: Highly recommended." Choice

Includes bibliographical references

Gibbons, Ann

The first human; the race to discover our earliest ancestors. Doubleday 2006 306p il map hardcover o.p. pa $14.95   **599.93**

1. Fossil hominids 2. Evolution

ISBN 0-385-51226-0; 978-0-385-51226-8; 978-1-4000-7696-3 (pa); 1-4000-7696-X (pa)
            LC 2005-53780

The author "explains what paleoanthropologists have been doing over the past 15 years: competing, feuding, and making dramatic discoveries. Anchoring her narrative to the anatomy that is the foundation of physical anthropology, Gibbons intentionally emphasizes the personalities involved." Booklist

This "is a near insider's account that still has the critical distance a nonpartisan can offer." Libr J

Includes bibliographical references

Johanson, Donald C.

From Lucy to language; [by] Donald Johanson & Blake Edgar; principal photography, David L. Brill. Rev., updated, and expanded. Simon and Schuster 2006 288p il map $65 *
            599.93

1. Human origins 2. Fossil hominids

ISBN 0-7432-8064-4; 978-0-7432-8064-8
            LC 2007-270098

"A Peter N. Nèvraumont book"

First published 1996

Johanson, Donald C.—*Continued*

This is a "photographic showcase of the essential physical evidence of human origins. . . . Permitting a face-to-face encounter with human ancestors, this work furnishes essential information, [and] an incomparable visual experience." Booklist

Includes bibliographical references

Lucy: the beginnings of humankind; [by] Donald C. Johanson and Maitland A. Edey. Simon & Schuster 1981 409p il pa $16 hardcover o.p.

599.93

1. Human origins 2. Fossil mammals
ISBN 0-671-72499-1 (pa)   LC 80-21759

In November 1974 at a place called Hadar in Ethiopia Donald Johanson "discovered the partial skeleton of an extremely primitive female, erect-walking primate or hominid. . . . The skeleton received the name 'Lucy.' Much later, Lucy received the scientific name, Australopithecus afarensis, and it was determined she was some 3.5 million years old. . . . This book is Johanson's own story of the events leading up to and subsequent to Lucy's discovery." Best Sellers

Includes bibliographical references

Jolly, Alison

Lucy's legacy; sex and intelligence in human evolution. Harvard Univ. Press 1999 518p il hardcover o.p. pa $18.95   **599.93**

1. Evolution 2. Intellect
ISBN 0-674-00069-2; 0-674-00540-6 (pa)
LC 99-32252

"Lucy is the name given to the fossil skeleton of an Australopithecine, a human ancestor, discovered in Ethiopia. The name may be a misnomer, since there's no way yet of telling whether Lucy was female. No matter. Primatologist Jolly's interest is not so much in Lucy as in the crucial role that females in general have played in human evolution. . . . In clear and clever prose, Jolly shows us how we got so smart, what sex had to do with it, and how our brains have become the central force in evolution." Booklist

Includes bibliographical references

Jones, Steve, 1944-

Y: the descent of men. Houghton Mifflin 2003 252p $25   **599.93**

1. Human origins 2. Evolution 3. Genetics 4. Chromosomes
ISBN 0-618-13930-3   LC 2002-27631

The author offers information on such issues as "our evolutionary links with apes, the ties between human and animal behavior, the relations between the sexes, and specifically male characteristics." Libr J

"Jones' sardonic wit enlivens the molecular foundations of maleness, explaining hormones, baldness, sperm count, and even lineages of bastardy in language that is both educational and entertaining. Great general-interest science material." Booklist

Includes bibliographical references

Klein, Richard G.

The dawn of human culture; {by} Richard G. Klein with Blake Edgar. Wiley 2002 288p il maps $27.95   **599.93**

1. Human origins 2. Culture
ISBN 0-471-25252-2   LC 2002-277680

"A Peter N. Nevraumont book"

This book "traces the origin of modern humans from their five-million-year-old roots in East Africa up through the replacement of Neanderthals in Europe some 40,000 years ago. . . . The clarity and information conveyed by the illustrations are superb, adding substantially to the book's value as a reference guide. The index is excellent. The book will appeal to all readers interested in human evolution, regardless of how much paleoanthropological background they have, and will serve admirably for courses on human evolution at any level." Choice

Includes bibliographical references

Leakey, Richard E., 1944-

The origin of humankind; [by] Richard Leakey. Basic Bks. 1994 171p il maps (Science masters series) pa $14.95 hardcover o.p.   **599.93**

1. Human origins
ISBN 0-465-05313-0 (pa)   LC 94-3617

"Leakey summarizes the evolution of theories, from Darwin's to his own, in the process demonstrating the scientific method in action. . . . Covering the taxonomy of skeletons and craniums, shapes of tools, and the first sprouts of art and culture, Leakey knowledgeably points the enthralled neophyte to the wide avenues of future discoveries." Booklist

This "is a worthwhile addition to many kinds of libraries—public, general, science, biological, and psychological." Sci Books Films

Includes bibliographical references

Origins reconsidered; in search of what makes us human; [by] Richard Leakey and Roger Lewin. Doubleday 1992 375p il pa $16.95 hardcover o.p.

599.93

1. Human origins
ISBN 0-385-46792-3 (pa)   LC 92-6661

"Leakey and Lewin discuss how conceptions of human anatomical and behavioral development have been radically altered within the last 12 years by new discoveries and research in other fields. They review the developments and assert Leakey's own hypotheses based on these discoveries. . . . This is an engrossing book written for the layperson, fully explaining anthropological terms and theories when necessary. It's a solid introduction to current theory concerning human development." SLJ

Marks, Jonathan

What it means to be 98% chimpanzee; apes, people, and their genes. University of Calif. Press 2002 312p $27.50 *   **599.93**

1. Human beings 2. Genetics 3. Evolution
ISBN 0-520-22615-1   LC 2001-7085

Contents: Introduction; Molecular anthropology; The ape in you; How people differ from one another; The

Marks, Jonathan—*Continued*

meaning of human variation; Behavioral genetics; Folk heredity; Human nature; Human rights . . . for apes?; A human gene museum; Identity and descent; Is blood really so damn thick?

"With plenty of entertaining sarcasm as well as scientific argument and moral indignation, Marks blasts the pretensions of grandiose geneticists pretty thoroughly out of the water. This may be *the* science book to read this year." Booklist

Includes bibliographical references

Ridley, Matt

Genome; the autobiography of a species in 23 chapters. HarperCollins Pubs. 2000 344p hardcover o.p. pa $14.95   **599.93**

1. Genomes 2. Genetics
ISBN 0-06-019497-9; 978-0-06-089408-5 (pa); 0-06-089408-3 (pa)   LC 99-40933

Ridley presents a "summation of our ever increasing understanding of the roles that genes play in disease, behavior, sexual differences, and even intelligence. More important, though, he addresses not only the ethical quandaries faced by contemporary scientists but the reductionist danger in equating inheritability with inevitability." New Yorker

Includes bibliographical references

Rothman, Barbara Katz

Genetic maps and human imaginations; the limits of science in understanding who we are. Norton 1998 272p $24.95   **599.93**

1. Genetics 2. Genomes 3. Human beings
ISBN 0-393-04703-2   LC 98-18800

A discussion of "the bioethics and consequences of mapping the human genome. . . . Rothman has concentrated on how 'genetic thinking' affects the way we see race, illness and cancer, and reproduction. Scientists may not like a couple of phrases Rothman has coined . . . but most other readers will probably find that the terms make sense as they read." Libr J

Includes bibliographical references

Schwartz, Jeffrey H.

What the bones tell us. University of Arizona Press 1998 292p pa $18.95   **599.93**

1. Physical anthropology
ISBN 0-8165-1855-6   LC 97-34147
"A John Macrae book"
First published in 1993 by Holt & Co.

This volume discusses "the nature and limits of osteology and paleontology and the scientific knowledge the two sciences provide. Part one describes the kinds of fossils and artifacts archaeologists find. [Part two addresses] . . . the places of Darwin, Huxley, and Raymond Dart in human evolutionary theory." Booklist

Includes bibliographical references

Stringer, Christopher B., 1947-

African exodus; the origins of modern humanity; {by} Christopher Stringer and Robin McKie. Holt & Co. 1997 xx, 282p il map pa $17 hardcover o.p. paperback available $17   **599.93**

1. Human origins
ISBN 0-8050-5814-1 (pa)   LC 96-37718
First published 1996 in the United Kingdom
"A John Macrae book."

The authors "argue for a single-origin theory for the recent emergence and essential unity of our species. The authors maintain that the *erectus-sapiens* transition happened only once, with *Homo sapiens sapiens* migrating out of Africa about 100,000 years ago and subsequently spreading worldwide." Libr J

"This intellectually potent yet eminently accessible volume . . . stands tall. It provides broad insight into a complex field." Publ Wkly

Includes bibliographical references

Swisher, Carl C.

Java Man; how two geologists changed our understanding of human evolution; [by] Carl C. Swisher III, Garniss H. Curtis, Roger Lewin. University of Chicago Press 2001 256p il pa $16   **599.93**

1. Fossil hominids 2. Human origins
ISBN 978-0-226-78734-3; 0-226-78734-6   LC 2001-37337
First published 2000 by Scribner

"In the early 1990s, geologists Garniss H. Curtis and Carl C. Swisher III . . . used radiometric rock dating to pin more accurate dates on some Asian 'missinglink' fossils and prove that our close evolutionary relative Homo erectus coexisted with Homo sapiens and was probably not a precursor after all." Libr J

The authors "offer a lively writeup of the technicalities of geochronology, bio-sketches of the discoverers of the erectus fossils, travelogues of their travel in Java, and their side of a spat with paleoanthropology celebrity Don Johansen. An engrossing contribution to the general-interest literature about human origins." Booklist

Includes bibliographical references

Sykes, Bryan

Adam's curse; a future without men. Norton 2004 318p il $25.95; pa $15.95   **599.93**

1. Genetics 2. Sex (Biology) 3. Chromosomes
ISBN 0-393-05896-4; 0-393-32680-2 (pa)   LC 2004-3628
First published 2003 in the United Kingdom

The author argues that "all human existence . . . stems from the battle between the X and Y chromosomes to further their own reproduction at the expense of the other." Publ Wkly

"This book incorporates many genres—scientific protocol, biography, harlequin romance, and historical fiction—all expertly executed by Sykes." Sci Books Films

The seven daughters of Eve. Norton 2001 306p il map pa $15.95 hardcover o.p.   **599.93**

Sykes, Bryan—*Continued*
1. Genetics 2. Human origins
ISBN 0-393-32314-5 (pa)

The author "contends that most Europeans can trace their roots back to seven women—seven daughters of Eve. One of them lived about 10,000 years ago, around the time farmers first cultivated European soil; the six others go back much farther, to Europe's early hunter-gatherers." N Y Times Book Rev

Tattersall, Ian
Extinct humans; by Ian Tattersall and Jeffrey H. Schwartz. Westview Press 2000 256p il pa $35 hardcover o.p. **599.93**
1. Human origins 2. Fossil hominids 3. Evolution
ISBN 0-8133-3918-9 (pa)   LC 00-22088

The authors explain "why the idea of the one-track, lineal descent of human beings is obsolete and the notion of a 'bushy' evolutionary history, like that of other genera, fits the fossil evidence better." Booklist
Includes bibliographical references

The fossil trail; how we know what we think we know about human evolution. Oxford Univ. Press 1995 276p il maps hardcover o.p. pa $17.95
599.93
1. Evolution 2. Human origins 3. Fossils
ISBN 0-19-506101-2; 0-19-510981-3 (pa)
LC 94-31633

New edition in preparation

"As much concerned with the dialectic of scientific advancement as with the specific, though fragmentary, fossil evidence, Tattersall courses through the interpretations of excavated discoveries since the days of Darwin." Booklist

"The task of organising such complex material into a narrative account would have defeated most writers, but Tattersall has mastered it with remarkable skill." New Sci
Includes bibliographical references

The monkey in the mirror; essays on science and what makes us human. Harcourt 2002 203p pa $13 hardcover o.p. **599.93**
1. Evolution 2. Human origins
ISBN 0-15-602706-2 (pa)   LC 2001-24122

The author "explores the current understanding of organic evolution in terms of science and reason." Libr J
"A perceptive and persuasive introduction to human origins." Booklist

Tudge, Colin
The time before history; 5 million years of human impact. Scribner 1996 366p il maps pa $17.95 hardcover o.p. **599.93**
1. Human origins 2. Evolution 3. Mammals
ISBN 0-684-83052-3 (pa)   LC 95-42026

Tudge "begins by putting time into perspective so that we can understand how vast is our past; he helps us see that all evolution is part of a bigger whole—an unfolding process affected by shifting continents, climactic changes, and our own impact on the planet and its ecosystems. . . . He defines our origins in a biological, as well as

historical context and applies the lessons that we should learn from our mistakes as well as our achievements to provide a blueprint for the future." Libr J

"With majestic sweep and subtle wit, . . . Tudge brings an astonishing perspective to the story of humanity." Publ Wkly
Includes bibliographical references

Wade, Nicholas
Before the dawn; recovering the lost history of our ancestors. Penguin Press 2006 312p il map $24.95 **599.93**
1. Evolution 2. Social change
ISBN 1-59420-079-3; 978-1-59420-079-3
LC 2005-55293

This is a "survey of human evolution for lay readers which considers the emergence of man in his entirety: physical, psychological, and social. . . . Wade's book concentrates on the recent evolutionary past: our last 50,000 years. . . . [It] emphasizes genetic over paleontological evidence." N Y Rev Books

"This is highly recommended for readers interested in how DNA analysis is rewriting the history of mankind." Publ Wkly
Includes bibliographical references

Walker, Alan
The wisdom of the bones; in search of human origins; [by] Alan Walker and Pat Shipman. Knopf 1996 338p il maps pa $14 hardcover o.p.
599.93
1. Human origins 2. Evolution 3. Fossil hominids
ISBN 0-679-74783-4 (pa)   LC 95-37525

"In 1984 Walker, along with colleague Richard Leakey and their 'hominidgang' of experienced Kenyan excavators, discovered a near-intact fossil of *Homo erectus*. The find was a veritable trove of theory-busting information, which the authors take up after recounting the scientists who preceded Walker in investigating the species. . . . A fluidly presented portrait of the people and process of paleoanthropology." Booklist
Includes bibliographical references

Wells, Spencer, 1969-
The journey of man; a genetic odyssey; photographs by Mark Read. Princeton University Press 2003 224p il map $29.95 **599.93**
1. Evolution 2. Genetics 3. Human origins
ISBN 0-691-11532-X

Also available in paperback from Random House

The author "chronicles the history of genetic population studies, starting with Darwin's puzzlement over the diversity of humanity he saw first-hand from the deck of the Beagle, and ending with the various attempts to classify human variation on the basis of different political and social agendas." Nature

"Fortunately for the lay reader, Wells has a knack for clear descriptions and clever analogies to help explain the intricacies of the science involved." Libr J
Includes bibliographical references

599.97   Human ethnic groups

Wolpoff, Milford H., 1942-

Race and human evolution; [by] Milford Wolpoff and Rachel Caspari. Simon & Schuster 1997 462p il maps hardcover o.p. pa $21.95

599.97

1. Human origins 2. Fossil hominids 3. Race

ISBN 0-684-81013-1; 978-1-4165-7796-6 (pa); 1-4165-7796-3 (pa)   LC 96-33466

The authors present an "intellectual history behind two primary, diametrically opposed hypotheses: the Eve theory, which states that all races have a single origin, and the multiregional hypothesis, which posits 'multiple origins, different and separate developments, and fundamental and essential racial differences.' The authors support the second theory but present both viewpoints with equal attention in their invaluable, even dramatic chronicle of more than two centuries of evolutionary science." Booklist

Includes bibliographical references

600   TECHNOLOGY

Brain, Marshall

Marshall Brain's more how stuff works; [by] Marshall Brain and the staff at HowStuffWorks.com. Wiley 2003 309p il $24.99

600

1. Technology 2. Inventions

ISBN 0-7645-6711-X   LC 2003-268792

Also available Marshall Brain's how stuff works (2001)

The author "travels inside your computer, to the depths of diamond mines, across the African plains, and on board an Apache helicopter to explain the magic behind how stuff works." Publisher's note

Cool stuff and how it works; written by Chris Woodford [et al.] Dorling Kindersley Pub. 2005 256p il $24.99   **600**

1. Inventions

ISBN 0-7566-1465-1   LC 2005-13587

This book "uses advanced imaging technology such as X rays, scanning electron micrographs, and infrared thermograms, along with traditional graphics, to reveal the workings of . . . [high-tech gadgets and appliances] from the Internet and computers to advanced textiles, space-age materials, and medical marvels. . . . This will rate high on the 'cool' factor, whether at home, school, or library." Booklist

Forbes, Peter, 1947-

The gecko's foot; bio-inspiration: engineering new materials from nature. Norton 2006 272p il $24.95   **600**

1. Technological innovations 2. Nature

ISBN 0-393-06223-6; 978-0-393-06223-6

LC 2006-06731

First published 2005 in the United Kingdom

This is an introduction to the "field of bio-inspiration and its use of life's microscopic features to engineer novel technologies. The volume overviews the history and current status of this field's major research areas and includes material on new adhesives based on the little lizard of the title, on self-cleaning paints modeled on the lotus leaf, and on photonic cells fashioned after butterfly wings." Sci Books Films

"Readers interested in how invention imitates nature, and vice versa, will find much to savor." Publ Wkly

Includes bibliographical references

Gershenfeld, Neil A.

Fab; the coming revolution on your desktop— from personal computers to personal fabrication; [by] Neil Gershenfeld. Basic Books 2005 278p il $26   **600**

1. Computer-aided design 2. Computers and civilization

ISBN 0-465-02745-8   LC 2005-988

The author argues "that the next phase beyond personal laser and ink-jet printers is personal fabrication, where devices will be able to output three-dimensional materials, such as plastics, glass, and metals, in precise tolerances, so that you will literally be able to make anything you can dream of. . . . [This book is] an interesting mix of technical computer theory and fun real-world examples." Booklist

Langone, John, 1929-

The new how things work; everyday technology explained; art by Pete Samek, Andy Christie, and Bryan Christie. National Geographic Society 2004 272p il $35 *   **600**

1. Technology 2. Inventions

ISBN 0-7922-6956-X   LC 2004-50438

First published 1999 with title: National Geographic's how things work

"With eleven chapters, including 'At Home,' 'Building and Buildings,' 'Transportation,' 'At Play,' and 'Tools of Medicine,' the book covers . . . familiar items such as refrigerators and washing machines, planes and trains, elevators and escalators, as well as the not-so-familiar, such as laser surgery and DNA manipulation. . . . {Coverage of recent innovations range} from DVDs and MP3s to plasma screen TVs and wireless Internet technology." Publisher's note

Macaulay, David, 1946-

The new way things work; [by] David Macaulay with Neil Ardley. Houghton Mifflin 1998 400p il $35   **600**

1. Technology 2. Machinery 3. Inventions

ISBN 0-395-93847-3   LC 98-14224

First published 1988 with title: The way things work

Arranged in five sections this volume provides information on "the workings of hundreds of machines and devices—holograms, helicopters, airplanes, mobile phones, compact disks, hard disks, bits and bytes, cash machines. . . . Explanations [are also given] of the scientific principles behind each machine—how gears make work easier, why jumbo jets are able to fly, how computers actually compute." Publisher's note

609 Historical, geographic, persons treatment

Brown, David E.

Inventing modern America; from the microwave to the mouse; text by David E. Brown; foreword by Lester C. Thurow; introductions by James Burke. MIT Press 2001 c2002 209p il hardcover o.p. pa $19.95 **609**

1. Inventions 2. Inventors
ISBN 0-262-02508-6; 0-262-52349-3 (pa)
LC 2001-44768

"A publication of the Lemelson-MIT program for invention and innovation"

This "profiles thirty-five inventors . . . {including} such well-known figures as George Washington Carver, Henry Ford, and Steve Wozniak, as well as . . . Stephanie Kwolek, inventor of Kevlar, and Wilson Greatbatch, inventor of the first implantable cardiac pacemaker." Publisher's note

"Brown simplifies technical data and uses an enthusiastic, almost proselytizing tone. . . . Full color photographs, diagrams and intriguing tidbits . . . make this a good book for most to browse." Publ Wkly

Includes bibliographical references

Burke, James, 1936-

Circles: 50 round trips through history, technology, science, culture. Simon & Schuster 2000 286p $24; pa $13 **609**

1. Technology—History 2. Science—History
ISBN 0-7432-0008-X; 0-7432-4976-3 (pa)
LC 00-57335

"The 50 essays collected here, which concern the history of technology, first appeared in Burke's *Scientific American* column between 1995 and 1999." Libr J

"Readers will be fascinated by Burke's route through the labyrinthine corridors of history. This book is ideal for dipping into, a few essays at a time." Publ Wkly

Includes bibliographical references

The knowledge web; from electronic agents to Stonehenge and back—and other journeys through knowledge. Simon & Schuster 1999 285p il $25; pa $14 **609**

1. Technology—History
ISBN 0-684-85934-3; 0-684-85935-1 (pa)
LC 99-24539

This work "is Burke's effort to replicate, in linear form, the sort of 'webbed' knowledge available to Internet surfers. Its 20 chapters trace often serendipitous developments of particular products or scientific discoveries." Booklist

Burke's "style matches his subject as he skips from one topic to another, moving at the speed of hypertext. . . . This manic, associative tour of the cultural underpinnings of technological advancement is fast, sexy and packed with information." Publ Wkly

Includes bibliographical references

Edgerton, David, 1959-

The shock of the old; technology and global history since 1900. Oxford University Press 2007 270p il $26 **609**

1. Technology—History
ISBN 978-0-19-532283-5; 0-19-532283-5
LC 2006-26435

Edgerton "challenges us to view the history of technology in terms of what everyday people have actually used—and continue to use around the world—rather than just what was invented." Publisher's note

This book "is a necessary reminder of just how important things are in our lives, and how important we are in the life of things." New Yorker

Includes bibliographical references

Flatow, Ira

They all laughed; from lightbulbs to lasers, the fascinating stories behind the great inventions that have changed our lives. HarperCollins Pubs. 1992 238p il pa $13 hardcover o.p. **609**

1. Inventions
ISBN 0-06-092415-2 (pa)
LC 91-58336

The author has put together an "overview of how some of our more interesting scientific discoveries and inventions have come to be. From teflon to lasers, from xerography to velcro, the author humorously describes the often serendipitous events leading to the particular breakthrough. The treatment is enthusiastic and lighthearted and not organized in any thematic or chronological fashion. It's a quick read and informative." Libr J

Includes bibliographical references

Karwatka, Dennis

Technology's past, vol 1; America's industrial revolution and the people who delivered the goods. Prakken Publications 1996 262p il pa $29.95 **609**

1. Inventions—History 2. Inventors 3. Technology—History
ISBN 0-911168-91-5

"This volume profiles 76 Americans who influenced technology in the United States from the Industrial Revolution through the beginning years of World War II. . . . Biographies are three pages long and are arranged chronologically by the birth date of the inventor." Book Rep

"This is a readable, well-documented selection." SLJ

Includes bibliographical references

Technology's past vol. 2; more heroes of invention and innovation. Prakken Publications 1999 264p il pa $29.95 **609**

1. Inventions—History 2. Inventors 3. Technology—History
ISBN 0-911168-96-6

This "book features profiles of 81 inventors and technologists whose creativity, hard work, and persistence changed the way people live. . . . The book also presents . . . details on the day-to-day lives of people in earlier times and discusses how the innovators' work impacted them." Publisher's note

"A sheer delight for everyone, these 81 profiles . . .

Karwatka, Dennis—*Continued*

bring out the symbiotic relationships between technology and science during the course of several centuries." Choice

Includes bibliographical references

Lindsay, David, 1957-

House of invention; the secret life of everyday products. Lyons Press 1999 179p il pa $9.95 hardcover o.p. **609**

1. Inventions

ISBN 1-58574-625-8 (pa) LC 99-53253

"Lindsay not only recounts the improbable origins of many most-used gadgets but also expounds on the occasionally wacky, always interesting individuals who came up with inventions so marvelous that they became ubiquitous." Booklist

Macdonald, Anne L., 1920-

Feminine ingenuity; women and invention in America; {by} Anne Macdonald. Ballantine Bks. 1992 xxiv, 514p il pa $25 hardcover o.p.

609

1. Women inventors 2. Inventions

ISBN 0-345-38314-1 (pa) LC 91-55502

This is a "study of American women's contribution to science, engineering, and technology as represented in the issuance of U.S. patents. From the first patent issued to a woman in 1809, Macdonald traces the uphill struggle women have faced in their efforts to obtain equal rights—in the area of patent awards as well as in the broader educational, economic, and social arenas." Libr J

Includes bibliographical references

Petroski, Henry

The evolution of useful things. Knopf 1992 288p il pa $13.95 hardcover o.p. **609**

1. Inventions 2. Patents

ISBN 0-679-74039-2 (pa) LC 91-39524

The author "provides an intricate look, in lay reader's terms, at the technology and basic rationale behind a number of items we often take for granted. The list is comprehensive: kitchen utensils, zippers, tools, paper clips, fast-food packaging, and more. The text is far from a recital of mere facts. Petroski's anecdotes and stories about individual designers and inventors are told with warm regard. He also provides illuminating thoughts on the theoretical, historical, and cultural frameworks that influenced these creations." Libr J

Includes bibliographical references

Technology & American history; a historical anthology from Technology & culture; edited by Stephen H. Cutcliffe and Terry S. Reynolds. University of Chicago Press 1997 448p il maps $37.50; pa $18.95 **609**

1. Technology—History

ISBN 0-226-71027-0; 0-226-71028-9 (pa)

LC 97-5925

This is a collection of 15 articles reprinted from Technology and Culture magazine from 1963 to 1996, which trace the impact of technology throughout the history of the United States

Includes bibliographical references

Van Dulken, Stephen, 1952-

Inventing the 19th century; 100 inventions that shaped the Victorian Age from aspirin to the Zeppelin. New York Univ. Press 2001 218p il $30 **609**

1. Inventions

ISBN 0-8147-8810-6 LC 2001-30831

This briefly describes the inventions of the 19th century with text and diagrams from the patent applications

Includes bibliographical references

Inventing the 20th century; 100 inventions that shaped the world: from the airplane to the zipper; {by} Stephen Van Dulken; with an introduction by Andrew Phillips. New York Univ. Press 2000 246p il hardcover o.p. pa $17.95 **609**

1. Inventions

ISBN 0-8147-8808-4; 0-8147-8812-2 (pa)

LC 00-41141

This briefly describes inventions of the 20th century, arranged by decade, with text and diagrams from the patent applications

"A fascinating compendium for trivia seekers." Publ Wkly

Includes bibliographical references

610   Medicine & health

Bortolotti, Dan

Hope in hell; inside the world of Doctors Without Borders. Firefly Bks. 2004 303p il $29.95; pa $19.95 **610**

1. Médecins Sans Frontières (Organization)

ISBN 1-55297-865-6; 1-55407-142-9 (pa)

LC 2005-357206

This "portrait of Doctors Without Borders/*Médecins Sans Frontières* (aka MSF), the nonprofit that won the Nobel Peace Prize in 1999, emphasizes the inner workings of the organization and is animated by interviews with mid-level staffers and by site visits to MSF projects in Angola, Afghanistan and Pakistan. In between, . . . Bortolotti traces the history of the world's largest independent medical humanitarian organization, whose genesis was the Biafran horrors of the late '60s." Publ Wkly

"Much of what Bortolotti reports is noticeably absent from the daily headlines, so this eye-opening account is all the more chilling, and MSF's efforts achingly more compelling." Booklist

Includes bibliographical references

Groopman, Jerome E., 1952-

How doctors think; [by] Jerome Groopman. Houghton Mifflin Co. 2007 307p il $26

610

1. Medicine 2. Physicians 3. Diagnosis

ISBN 978-0-618-61003-7; 0-618-61003-0

LC 2006-35718

Groopman, Jerome E., 1952-—*Continued*

This book is comprised of a series of "essays that explore the rational and irrational factors that influence medical decision-making. By turns inspired and dismaying, it explains how even the best doctor can draw the wrong conclusion, and why that same doctor might also come up with a brilliant diagnosis that has eluded his peers. Uncertainty hovers over the practice of medicine, which Dr. Groopman, a clear writer and a humane thinker, presents as an art as well as a science, despite the spectacular advances in medical technology." N Y Times (Late N Y Ed)

Includes bibliographical references

Second opinions; stories of intuition and choice in a changing world of medicine; {by} Jerome Groopman. Viking 2000 243p pa $14 hardcover o.p. **610**

1. Medicine 2. Diagnosis
ISBN 0-14-029862-2 (pa)   LC 99-36692

Groopman "focuses on medical decision-making; in eight dramatic case studies, he reveals the importance of honoring intuition in the evaluation and treatment of illness." Libr J

"Through vivid accounts of the dilemmas he has faced—not only as a doctor but as a patient, a parent, a grandson and a friend—the author illuminates the art, and the perils, of interpreting other people's symptoms." Newsweek

The **Harvard** Medical School family health guide; edited by Anthony L. Komaroff. Simon & Schuster 1999 1288p il hardcover o.p. pa $25 * **610**

1. Medicine 2. Health
ISBN 0-684-84703-5; 0-684-86373-1 (pa)
LC 99-27223

"Divided into ten parts, the text begins with a discussion on how to navigate current healthcare systems; the major areas then covered include health maintenance, how diseases are diagnosed, symptom management illustrated by numerous decision trees, and diseases and disorders." Libr J

Lown, Bernard

The lost art of healing. Ballantine Bks. 1999 xx, 344p pa $14.95   **610**

1. Holistic medicine 2. Physicians 3. Sick
ISBN 0-345-42597-9   LC 98-96703

First published 1996 by Houghton Mifflin

"Cardiologist Lown combines autobiography with a plea for thoughtful and individual medical care of each patient. . . . Healing, he asserts, has been replaced in time by treating, caring by managing, and the art of listening by technological procedures." Booklist

The author's "stimulating inquiry is sound medicine for doctors and patients alike." Publ Wkly

Includes bibliographical references

Pollack, Robert, 1940-

The missing moment; how the unconscious shapes modern science. Houghton Mifflin 1999 240p $25   **610**

1. Medicine—Philosophy 2. Psychology
ISBN 0-395-70985-7   LC 99-26241

"The collective myth of science and of biomedicine, in Pollack's diagnosis, involves misplaced beliefs in the omnipotence of rational thought, absolute control over nature and triumph over death. With eloquence and wit, he contends that biomedicine's heroic goals of beating infectious microbes into total submission, of eradicating cancer and of dramatically extended life expectancy should give way to emphasis on disease prevention and methods to slow the aging process." Publ Wkly

Includes bibliographical references

610.28 Auxiliary techniques and procedures; apparatus, equipment, materials

Friedman, David M., 1949-

The immortalists; Charles Lindbergh, Dr. Alexis Carrel, and their daring quest to live forever. HarperCollins Ecco 2007 337p il $26.95   **610.28**

1. Lindbergh, Charles, 1902-1974 2. Carrel, Alexis, 1873-1944 3. Immortality 4. Longevity 5. Preservation of organs, tissues, etc.
ISBN 978-0-06-052815-7; 0-06-052815-X
LC 2007-299304

This book discusses "the relationship between famed aviator Charles Lindbergh and the Noble Prizewinning French surgeon Alexis Carrel. Driven by a desire to cure his ailing sister-in-law, Elizabeth Morrow, Lindbergh contacted Carrel in 1930 for the purpose of developing an artificial heart." Libr J

The author "makes complex science accessible and serves as an absorbing cautionary tale on how two heroic reputations were marred by fascism and anti-Semitism." Publ Wkly

610.3 Medical sciences— Encyclopedias and dictionaries

American Medical Association complete medical encyclopedia; medical editors, Jerrold B. Leikin, Martin S. Lipsky. Crown 2003 1408p il $45 * **610.3**

1. Medicine—Encyclopedias
ISBN 0-8129-9100-1   LC 2002-67340

This "medical compendium contains over 5000 alphabetically arranged entries (with 2000 on illnesses) and 1750 illustrations (mostly line drawings, as well as photographs). . . . Definitions include parts of the body (e.g., the spinal cord, with a line drawing of the 'Communication Highway,' as the book calls it), procedures (e.g., in vitro fertilization, with four detailed line drawings of the steps involved), disorders (e.g., ectropion, with a line drawing of a sagging lower eyelid), and specialties (e.g., oncologist). . . . Owing to its relatively modest price, reliability of source, and coverage of popular areas in medicine, it is recommended not only for public libraries and consumer health collections but also for high school libraries." Libr J

Dorland's illustrated medical dictionary. 31st ed. Saunders Elsevier 2007 xxvii, 2175p il $49.95
610.3

Dorland's illustrated medical dictionary—*Continued*

1. Medicine—Dictionaries

ISBN 978-1-4160-2364-7; 1-4160-2364-X

Also available deluxe edition with CD-ROM $99.95 and online

First published 1900. Periodically revised

This standard reference includes terms used in medicine, surgery, dentistry, pharmacy, chemistry, nursing, veterinary science, biology, and medical biology. Pronunciation, derivation, and definitions are given.

"This is considered one of the most comprehensive medical dictionaries in print." N Y Public Libr Book of How & Where to Look It Up

The **Gale** encyclopedia of medicine; Jacqueline L. Longe, project editor. 3rd ed. Thomson Gale 2005 5v il set $625 *   **610.3**

1. Medicine—Encyclopedias

ISBN 1-4144-0368-2   LC 2005-11418

First published 1999

New edition in preparation

This encyclopedia "covers more than 1750 disorders, medications, tests, and treatments. . . . Articles incorporate a definition and related key terms and detail causes and symptoms of the disorder, how diagnoses are made, possible treatments (including alternative treatment methods), and the general prognosis. Articles addressing medical tests discuss preparations, aftercare, risks, and normal/abnormal results." Libr J

Includes bibliographical references

The **Merck** manual of diagnosis and therapy; [edited by] Mark H. Beers . . . [et al.] 18th ed. Merck Research Laboratories 2006 xxxii, 2991p il $65 *   **610.3**

1. Medicine—Handbooks, manuals, etc.

ISSN 0076-6526

ISBN 0-911910-18-2; 978-0-911910-18-6

Also available online

First published 1899

"A one-volume reference that attempts to cover all but the most obscure diseases. Sections are organized by type of disease or medical specialty." N Y Public Libr Book of How & Where to Look It Up

Mosby's medical dictionary; [managing editor, Tamara Myers] 7th ed. Mosby/Elsevier 2006 2019p il $37.95   **610.3**

1. Medicine—Dictionaries

ISBN 978-0-3230-3942-0; 0-3230-3942-1

LC 2006-273435

First published 1983 with title: Mosby's medical & nursing dictionary; published 2002 with title: Mosby's medical, nursing, and allied health dictionary. Periodically revised

New edition in preparation

"Many definitions are discursive. Emphasizes allied health professions, with . . . categories of entries in physical therapy, occupational therapy, and respiratory care." Guide to Ref Books. 11th edition

Sloane, Sheila B.

Medical abbreviations & eponyms. 2nd ed. Saunders 1997 905p pa $41   **610.3**

1. Medicine—Dictionaries

ISBN 0-7216-7088-1   LC 96-28595

First published 1985

This dictionary provides a list of medical abbreviations, acronyms, symbols, and eponyms. Also included are definitions for common diseases, syndromes, and operations. An appendix which lists over 400 anticancer drug combinations is provided

Stedman, Thomas Lathrop, 1853-1938

Stedman's medical dictionary. Lippincott Williams & Wilkins 2006 various paging $49.95   **610.3**

1. Medicine—Dictionaries

ISBN 0-7817-3390-1   LC 2005-21544

First published 1911. Periodically revised

Accompanied by CD-ROM

Provides definitions, pronunciation and derivations for terms used in general medicine, veterinary medicine, biochemistry and other related fields

Taber's cyclopedic medical dictionary; Donald Venes, editor. 20th ed. F.A. Davis Co. 2005 xxxv, 2788p il $39.95 *   **610.3**

1. Medicine—Dictionaries

ISBN 0-8036-1207-9

Also available CD-ROM, deluxe, and non-thumb indexed versions

First published 1940. Periodically revised

This work gives "definitions of medical terms and words. Pronunciation is given for all but very common terms and the etymology of most words is included. Appendixes include such information as emergency treatment, dietetic charts, Latin and Greek nomenclature, and normal reference laboratory values." Guide to Ref Books. 11th edition

Includes bibliographical references

610.69 Medical personnel and relationships

America's top doctors. Castle Connolly Medical $79.95; pa $29.95 *   **610.69**

1. Physicians—Directories

ISBN 1-883769-38-8; 1-883769-36-1 (pa)

LC 2003-100260

"A Castle Connolly guide"

First published 2001

This guide identifies and provides information about more than 4,000 top specialists for care and treatment of more than 2,000 diseases and medical conditions, provides information about accessing and using clinical trials, and explains services provided at the National Institutes of Health and how to get the most from your specialist's appointment

Directory of physicians in the United States. 40th ed. American Medical Assn. 2007 4v set $750   **610.69**

Directory of physicians in the United States—
Continued

1. Physicians—Directories

ISBN 978-1-57947-784-4; 1-57947-784-4

Also available CD-ROM version

First published 1906 with title: American medical directory. Periodically revised. New edition in preparation

This directory lists names, addresses, and zip codes; includes information on medical school of graduation; year first licensed in state; primary and secondary practice specialties; type of practice; American Board of Medical Specialties Certification; and Physician's Recognition Award status.

The **Official** ABMS directory of board certified medical specialists. 39th ed. Saunders 2007 4v set $749 **610.69**

1. Physicians—Directories

ISBN 978-1-4160-5146-6; 1-4160-5146-5

Also available CD-ROM version

Formed by the merger of Directory of medical specialists and ABMS compendium of certified medical specialists. Started publication 1994 retaining volume numbering of the Directory. Periodically revised

New edition in preparation

"For each physician, lists name, certification(s), type of practice, birth date and place, education, career history, teaching positions, military record, professional memberships, office address and phone number. Includes an outline of certification requirements for each specialty." Guide to Ref Books. 11th edition

Pikula, Donna L.

After the diagnosis; how to look out for yourself or a loved one. Books 2 Help You 2006 xx, 275p pa $16.95 * **610.69**

1. Patients 2. Medical care

ISBN 0-9768970-0-8; 978-0-9768970-0-2

LC 2006-274957

The author "is clear, thorough, and practical, providing step-by-step forms and checklists that can be used by patients in their own proactive healthcare journey." Libr J

Includes bibliographical references

Wischnitzer, Saul

Barron's guide to medical & dental schools; [by] Saul Wischnitzer with Edith Wischnitzer. 11th ed. Barron's Educ. Ser. 2006 695p il maps pa $18.99 * **610.69**

1. Medicine—Vocational guidance

ISBN 978-0-7641-3372-5; 0-7641-3372-1

LC 2005-57070

First published 1982. Periodically revised

This guide profiles "AMA-accredited American and Canadian schools, ADA-accredited dental schools, as well as osteopathic schools, accredited by the American Osteopathic Association. Advice is also given on applying to schools, with specific recommended courses and procedures for maximizing chances of acceptance." Publisher's note

610.9 Medical sciences—Historical and geographic treatment

Adler, Robert E., 1946-

Medical firsts; from Hippocrates to the human genome. Wiley 2004 232p il $24.95

610.9

1. Medicine—History

ISBN 0-471-40175-7 LC 2003-14212

"The contributors to the annals of medical knowledge [the author] cites include the most famous names—Hippocrates, Pasteur, Freud, Alexander Fleming—and some not so commonly known, such as pioneering gynecologist Soranus (first century C.E.); Ibn al-Nafis (ca. 1210-88), credited as the first to understand and describe pulmonary circulation; and John Snow, an important figure in the war on cholera. . . . Adler discusses each figure's personal, social, and political history as it affected his or her contribution." Booklist

"Adler ably combines good storytelling, clear and cogent scientific explanations [and] a respect for science over superstition." Publ Wkly

Includes bibliographical references

The **Cambridge** illustrated history of medicine; edited by Roy Porter. Cambridge Univ. Press 1996 400p il maps hardcover o.p. pa $35

610.9

1. Medicine—History

ISBN 0-521-44211-7; 0-521-00252-4 (pa)

LC 95-38000

This is a history of medicine from antiquity to the present. In ten "chapters, Roy Porter and his collaborators examine the changing form of medicine and . . . {the} technical successes that it has achieved." Sci Am

Includes bibliographical references

Cassedy, James H.

Medicine in America: a short history. Johns Hopkins Univ. Press 1991 187p (American moment) pa $18.95 hardcover o.p. **610.9**

ISBN 0-8018-4208-5 (pa) LC 91-7058

This history of American medicine traces medical and health-related matters from colonial times to the present

This book "is scholarly, well written, very useful, and fills a void." Choice

Includes bibliographical references

Finger, Stanley

Doctor Franklin's medicine. University of Pennsylvania Press 2006 379p il $39.95

610.9

1. Franklin, Benjamin, 1706-1790 2. Medicine—History

ISBN 978-0-8122-3913-3; 0-8122-3913-X

LC 2005-45659

The author presents the "story of Benjamin Franklin's contributions to modern medicine and hygiene. The book is an important tribute to America's quintessential Enlightenment scholar and statesman." Choice

Includes bibliographical references

Friedman, Meyer, 1910-2001
Medicine's 10 greatest discoveries; [by] Meyer
Friedman, Gerald W. Friedland. Yale Univ. Press
1998 363p il hardcover o.p. pa $14.95
610.9
1. Medicine—History 2. Scientists
ISBN 0-300-07598-7; 0-300-08278-9 (pa)
LC 98-19921
This describes such medical discoveries as the circulation of blood by William Harvey, the X-ray by Roent-
gen, Penicillin by Alexander Fleming, and DNA by Watson, Crick and Maurice Hugh Frederick Wilkins.
Includes bibliographical references

Meyers, Morton A.
Happy accidents; serendipity in modern medical
breakthroughs; [by] Morton Meyers. Arcade Pub.
2007 390p il $29.95; pa $16.99   **610.9**
1. Medicine—Research
ISBN 978-1-55970-819-7; 978-1-55970-845-6 (pa)
LC 2006-100551
The author "details dozens of medicines currently saving millions of lives that are the results of serendipity,
which he defines as 'chance plus judgment'—medicines
discovered while researchers were looking in quite another, often the opposite, direction. . . . Meyers' accounts
of such happy accidents as the discoveries of the lifesav-
ing anticoagulant Coumadin, the manic-depression therapeutic lithium, and others is a significant brief on creativity's critical role in medical research." Booklist
Includes bibliographical references

Porter, Roy, 1946-2002
The greatest benefit to mankind; a medical
history of humanity. Norton 1998 831p il $35; pa
$18.95   **610.9**
1. Medicine—History
ISBN 0-393-04634-6; 0-393-31980-6 (pa)
LC 98-10219
First published 1997 in the United Kingdom
Engl. subtitle: A medical history of humanity from antiquity to the present
Porter's "study traces Western medical thought and
practices from their origins in classical Greece to today's
biomedical developments. Although scholarly, the text is
elegantly written, accessible to the general reader, and
filled with fascinating details." Libr J
Includes bibliographical references

Western medicine: an illustrated history; edited by
Irvine Loudon. Oxford Univ. Press 1997 347p il
$65; pa $27.50   **610.9**
1. Medicine—History
ISBN 0-19-820509-0; 0-19-924813-3 (pa)
LC 97-218848
Spine title: The Oxford illustrated history of Western
medicine
This history "extends from ancient Greece to the present. . . . The book consists of chapters by 20 historians
from England, Germany, and the United States. An introductory chapter describes the long historical relationship
between medicine and the visual arts. Seven subsequent
chapters offer a chronological history of medicine, including a discussion of the influence of Islamic medicine
on medieval and Renaissance physicians. The 11 final
chapters deal with medicine in its social context, such as
histories of childbirth, nursing, and mental illness." Libr
J
Includes bibliographical references

611   Human anatomy, cytology,
histology

Bainbridge, David
Beyond the zonules of Zinn; a fantastic journey
through your brain. Harvard University Press 2008
338p il $25.95   **611**
1. Brain 2. Nervous system
ISBN 978-0-674-02610-0; 0-674-02610-1
LC 2007-21595
"In this 'geographical tour' of the nervous system,
readers will find an entertaining and enlightening history
of neuroscience and a look at the anatomy of the brain.
. . . The book's relaxed pace, interesting tangents and
broad coverage make this book eminently suitable for
anyone curious about the brain." Publ Wkly
Includes bibliographical references

Gray's anatomy; the anatomical basis of clinical
practice; editor-in-chief, Susan Standring; lead
editors, Harold Ellis . . . [et al.]; editors, Barry
K.B. Berkovitz . . . [et al.] 39th ed. Elsevier
Churchill Livingstone 2005 xx, 1627p il $190 *
611
1. Human anatomy
ISBN 0-44307-168-3; 978-0-44307-168-3
LC 2004-63458
First published 1858. Periodically revised. Publisher
varies
Variant title: Gray's anatomy of the human body
A comprehensive standard reference work with illus-
trations, descriptions and definitions.
"Holds its place as a major and authoritative text on
systematic anatomy. Recommended." Annals of Internal
Medicine
Includes bibliographical references

Netter, Frank H., 1906-1991
Atlas   of   human   anatomy.   4th   ed.
Saunders/Elsevier 2006 548, 47p il $76.95 *
611
1. Human anatomy
ISBN 1-4160-3699-7; 978-1-4160-3385-1
LC 2006-47497
First published 1989 by CIBA-GEIGY Corp.
This human anatomy atlas features over 540 illustra-
tions of the human body and its systems and organs.
Includes bibliographical references

Roach, Mary
Stiff; the curious lives of human cadavers. Norton 2003 303p il $23.95; pa $13.95 *
611
1. Human experimentation in medicine 2. Dead 3. Dissection
ISBN 0-393-05093-9; 0-393-32482-6 (pa)
LC 2002-152908
The author "explains how surgeons and doctors use cadavers donated for research purposes to help the living, and also examines potential new variations on how we bury the dead." Libr J
"For those who are interested in the fields of medicine or forensics and are aware of some of the procedures, this book makes excellent reading." SLJ
Includes bibliographical references

Shubin, Neil
Your inner fish; a journey into the 3.5-billion-year history of the human body. Pantheon Books 2008 229p il map $24
611
1. Human anatomy 2. Evolution
ISBN 978-0-375-42447-2; 0-375-42447-4
LC 2007-24699
This is a "look at how the human body evolved into its present state. . . . Shubin excels at explaining the science, making each discovery an adventure, whether it's a Pennsylvania roadcut or a stony outcrop beset by polar bears and howling Arctic winds." Publ Wkly
Includes bibliographical references

612 Human physiology

The **Human** body; an illustrated guide to its structure, function, and disorders; editor-in-chief, Charles Clayman. Dorling Kindersley 1995 240p il $30
612
1. Physiology 2. Human anatomy
ISBN 1-56458-992-7
LC 94-37165
"This body atlas uses current medical illustration techniques to provide unique views of human anatomical features. Color-enhanced microscope photographs and computer-generated images accompany detailed drawings to illustrate various organs, demonstrate body functions, and depict problems or complications. The introduction explains various types of medical illustration such as computerized tomography, ultrasound, and magnetic resonance imaging." Booklist
"This absolutely stunning book succeeds immeasurably as a guide to the human body." Sci Books Films

Mai, Larry L.
The Cambridge Dictionary of human biology and evolution; [by] Larry L. Mai, Marcus Young Owl, M. Patricia Kersting. Cambridge University Press 2005 648p il pa $60
612
1. Biology—Dictionaries 2. Evolution—Dictionaries
ISBN 0-521-66486-1; 978-0-521-66486-8
LC 2004-43553
"This dictionary covers many aspects of human biology: anatomy, growth, physiology, genetics, paleontology,

physical anthropology, primatology, and zoology." Am Ref Books Annu, 2006
"This is one of those dictionaries that will keep even casual browsers intrigued." Choice

McCredie, Scott
Balance: in search of the lost sense. Little, Brown and Company 2007 296p il $24.99
612
1. Balance
ISBN 978-0-316-01135-8; 0-316-01135-5
LC 2006-38089
"After the shock of seeing his fit father fall for no apparent reason, . . . McCredie became curious about the physiology of equilibrium. His extensive and creative research has led him to conclude that balance is the overlooked sixth sense and crucial to our survival. . . . McCredie offers practical advice for maintaining one's equilibrium and acuity and rekindles deep appreciation for life's incredible exactitude and grace." Booklist
Includes bibliographical references

McMillan, Beverly
Human body; a visual guide. Firefly Books 2006 304p il $29.95
612
1. Physiology 2. Human anatomy
ISBN 978-1-55407-188-3; 1-55407-188-7
This book provides "scientific information on the human body, using microphotography, advanced medical imaging and annotated illustrations. The book reveals all the intricacy and beauty of the human body and shows the structure and functions of all the systems that make up a human being." Publisher's note
Includes bibliographical references

Wilson, Frank R.
The hand; how its use shapes the brain, language, and human culture. Pantheon Bks. 1998 397p il $30; pa $16
612
1. Hand
ISBN 0-679-41249-2; 0-679-74047-3 (pa)
LC 97-46427
The author "explores anatomy, anthropology, and evolution to show how the hand shapes human language and thought. He aruges convincingly that a less rigid, more individualized approach to education will yield a student with a unified body and mind. His most inspiring evidence is blessedly anecdotal: interviews with people whose vocations involve the skilled use of their hands." New Yorker
Includes bibliographical references

World of anatomy and physiology; K. Lee Lerner and Brenda Wilmoth Lerner, editors. Gale Group 2002 2v set $160 *
612
1. Physiology—Encyclopedias 2. Anatomy—Encyclopedias
ISBN 0-7876-5684-4
LC 2002-5517
"This reference provides basic information on human anatomy and physiology. The 650 alphabetically arranged entries, ranging in length from several paragraphs to several pages, are written at a level accessible to high

World of anatomy and physiology—*Continued*
school students and the general reader. Topics covered range from classical human anatomy and physiology to developmental and reproductive biology. . . . Lengthy biographies of about 200 famous as well as lesser-known scientists, among them Francis Crick, Herophilus, Rita Levi-Montalcini, Susumu Tonegawa, and Otto Heinrich Warburg, are also included. . . . Although primarily aimed at high-school students and general readers, this reference source could also be of use to undergraduate students in introductory courses." Booklist

Includes bibliographical references

612.1   Blood and circulation

Randall, Otelio Sye, 1937-
The encyclopedia of the heart and heart disease; [by] Otelio S. Randall and Deborah S. Romaine. Facts on File 2005 382p il (Facts on File library of health and living) $75   **612.1**
1. Heart—Encyclopedias
ISBN 0-8160-5087-2   LC 2003-64265
"An Amaranth book"
"This volume, with over 600 entries, covers a multitude of topics related to the heart and blood; they include professional organizations, medications (e.g., nadolol), medical conditions (e.g., cyanosis), and technical terms and procedures (e.g., endarterectomy)." Choice
"This work is an easy-to-use, quick reference for those seeking concise explanations regarding cardiac health." Am Ref Books Annu, 2005

Includes bibliographical references

612.4   Hematopoietic, lymphatic, glandular, urinary systems

Arikha, Noga
Passions and tempers; a history of the humours. Ecco 2007 xxi, 376p il $27.95   **612.4**
1. Body fluids 2. Medicine—History
ISBN 978-0-06-073116-8; 0-06-073116-8
"Leading medical minds were once convinced that health and sickness resulted from the interplay of the four 'humors': blood, phlegm, black bile and yellow bile, each associated with a certain personality trait (e.g., black bile signifies melancholic) and with one of the basic elements of the universe (e.g., yellow bile is linked to fire). The rational mindset naturally recoils at the crudity and superstition of this ancient medical framework, but . . . [the author's] historical survey usefully reminds us that our modern theories of the relationship between mind, mood and body rest on gains made by humoral analogy. To investigate the humors is to probe all of Western medicine." Publ Wkly
This is "an erudite book, drawing on historical and scientific sources in several languages, but a gracefully written one. There are many superb illustrations [and] informative notes. . . . One of the best things about Ms. Arikha's study, in addition to its wealth of intriguing detail, is that it is thoughtful." N Y Sun

612.6   Reproduction, development, maturation

Angier, Natalie
Woman; an intimate geography. Houghton Mifflin 1999 398p $25   **612.6**
1. Physiology 2. Women—Psychology 3. Sex role
ISBN 0-395-69130-3   LC 98-47634
Also available in paperback from Anchor Bks.
"A Peter Davison book"
The author "presents new theories on the evolution of women's anatomy, physiology and social behaviors. . . . Angier discusses such topics as ovulation, conception and birth; the social and physiological functions of breasts; orgasm, mate selection and child-rearing behavior; the complex workings of estrogen; hysterectomy; muscle strength; and female aggression and bonding." Publ Wkly
"Angier proves a knowledgeable, witty guide on our illustrative journey through hordes of cultures and species." Ms

Includes bibliographical references

Benecke, Mark
The dream of eternal life; biomedicine, aging, and immortality; translated by Rachel Rubenstein. Columbia Univ. Press 2002 196p il $29.95
                612.6
1. Longevity 2. Death 3. Life 4. Immortality
ISBN 0-231-11672-1   LC 2001-47366
"The first section of the book discusses the biological fundamentals of why death exists and what modern biology, especially the biology of genetics, tells us about aging and death. . . . In the second part Benecke assesses the various ways that we humans cope with a finite life span and the looming certainty of death. . . . The third part looks at the possibility for extending our lives through cloning, organ and brain transplants, live cell therapy . . . and deep freezing of humans for reawakening in a future age." Publisher's note
An "informative and engaging examination of aging and the meaning of death." Booklist

Includes bibliographical references

Blum, Deborah
Sex on the brain; the biological differences between men and women. Viking 1997 xxii, 329p pa $13.95 hardcover o.p.   **612.6**
1. Sex differences (Psychology) 2. Sex (Biology)
ISBN 0-14-026348-9 (pa)   LC 96-52034
The author examines "the origins of sex, differences in male and female brains, hormones and emotions, monogamy, sexual orientation, love, rape, and power." Libr J
Blum "has a skilled journalist's ability to take abstract and confusing genetic, hormonal, endocrinological and neuroscientific findings and make them intelligible." Publ Wkly

Includes bibliographical references

Chopra, Deepak
Ageless body, timeless mind; the quantum alternative to growing old. Harmony Bks. 1993 342p pa $14 hardcover o.p. **612.6**
1. Longevity 2. Mind and body 3. Aging 4. Holistic medicine
ISBN 0-517-88212-4 (pa) LC 93-16766
Chopra argues that "the mind-body connection is a major player in all facets of health. . . . {He advises} readers to realize that the body is a product of awareness, that beliefs, thoughts, and emotions cause chemical reactions in cells, and that if you change your perception, you can change the experience of your body and the world." Booklist

Hall, Stephen S.
Size matters; how height affects the health, happiness, and success of boys—and the men they become. Houghton Mifflin Co. 2006 388p $26 *
612.6
1. Growth 2. Personal appearance 3. Men—Psychology
ISBN 978-0-618-47040-2; 0-618-47040-9
LC 2006-07304
This book examines what the author sees as "the causes and effects of society's bias against shortness and reveals how short people can and do thrive." Publisher's note
The author's "interpretations of complicated science are readily accessible, and his journalistic style will suit both popular and academic readers." Publ Wkly
Includes bibliographical references

Kirkwood, Tom
Time of our lives; the science of human aging. Oxford Univ. Press 1999 277p $49.95; pa $32.50
612.6
1. Aging
ISBN 0-19-512824-9; 0-19-513926-7 (pa)
LC 98-46932
Among the topics Kirkwood "addresses are the evolutionary advantage of aging, the relationship of aging and cancer, why women live longer then men, Alzheimer's, and the future of gene therapy. He also addresses how to prolong life or at least improve the quality of it in later years." Libr J
Kirkwood "conveys scientific matters lucidly and thought provokingly, posing good questions to show what is definitely known, disposing of myths, and pointing out where more information needs to be ascertained." Booklist
Includes bibliographical references

Medina, John, 1956-
The clock of ages; why we age—how we age—winding back the clock; {by} John J. Medina. Cambridge Univ. Press 1996 332p il pa $25 hardcover o.p. **612.6**
1. Aging
ISBN 0-521-59456-1 (pa) LC 95-40712
This "biological explanation of the aging process explores the changes that occur in the human body as it ap-

proaches death." Book Rep
"This is the best biology book written for the lay public to appear in many years." Libr J
Includes bibliographical references

Nilsson, Lennart, 1922-
A child is born; [photography], Lennart Nilsson; text, Lars Hamberger; translated from the Swedish by Linda Schenck. 4th ed, completely rev and updated. Delacorte Press 2003 239p il $35; pa $21
612.6
1. Pregnancy 2. Embryology 3. Childbirth
ISBN 0-385-33754-X; 0-385-33755-8 (pa)
LC 2003-43854
"A Merloyd Lawrence book"
Original Swedish edition, 1965; first United States edition, 1966
An illustrated look at male and female reproductive anatomy and physiology, the processes of ovulation and fertilization, fetal development, and labor and delivery.

Roach, Mary
Bonk; the curious coupling of science and sex. Norton 2008 319p il $24.95 **612.6**
1. Sex (Biology)
ISBN 978-0-393-06464-3; 0-393-06464-6
LC 2007-51990
"Working from the early 1900s to the present, . . . [the author] surveys sex research and its findings, examining what was scientific about these studies. She also investigates the sometimes bizarre equipment and conditions devised for the research." Libr J
"Tucked between the jokes and anecdotes, you will find lessons on impotence, orgasm, unusual and unusually brave scientists, and the sexual behaviour of other species, including a hilarious description of porcupine sex." New Sci
Includes bibliographical references

Rowe, John W. (John Wallis), 1944-
Successful aging; {by} John W. Rowe and Robert L. Kahn. Pantheon Bks. 1998 265p pa $13.95 hardcover o.p. **612.6**
1. Longevity 2. Aging
ISBN 0-440-50863-0 (pa) LC 97-36900
The authors "report on a 10-year, MacArthur Foundation-funded inquiry into 'successful aging'—that is, remaining healthy, vigorous, mentally acute, and independent well into the ninth and tenth decades of life. . . . Separate chapters illustrate, with the experience of the study's elderly subjects, that good diet and exercise, maintaining and enhancing mental functions, positive social connections, and productive work are essential to living well while living longer." Booklist
Includes bibliographical references

Weil, Andrew
Healthy aging; a lifelong guide to your physical and spiritual well-being. Alfred A. Knopf 2005 293p $27.95 **612.6**
1. Aging
ISBN 0-375-40755-3 LC 2005-45183

Weil, Andrew—*Continued*

The author "explores common Western beliefs and attitudes about aging and urges readers to develop healthier perspectives. The 60-year-old author assesses the growing and lucrative field of anti-aging medicine, takes the position that aging is not reversible, and offers many ways for readers to prevent conditions and illnesses that limit mortality and ensure well-being into the later years. . . . The real value is Weil's courageous stand, one likely to meet resistance in a culture devoted to external indicators of eternal youth." Publ Wkly

Includes bibliographical references

612.8   Nervous system. Sensory functions

Aamodt, Sandra

Welcome to your brain; why you lose your car keys but never forget how to drive and other puzzles of everyday life; [by] Sandra Aamodt and Sam Wang. Bloomsbury USA 2008 220p il $24.95
                                                    612.8
1. Brain
ISBN 978-1-59691-283-0; 1-59691-283-9
                              LC 2007-26739

This is a "'user's guide' to our brains. . . . The text is divided into six main parts, covering the brain's basic structure and function, the senses, the brain's development, emotions, rational processes, and altered states. . . . Rather than didactically lecturing, the authors very effectively engage the reader in a comfortable, interesting, and informative dialog." Sci Books Films

Best of the brain from Scientific American; edited by Floyd E. Bloom. Dana Press 2007 270p il $25   **612.8**
1. Brain 2. Nervous system
ISBN 978-1-93259-422-5; 1-93259-422-1
                              LC 2007-15128

"This collection of essays drawn from Scientific American and Scientific American Mind offers an excellent, readable overview of . . . brain research since 1999." Libr J

Includes bibliographical references

Dement, William C., 1928-

The promise of sleep; a pioneer in sleep medicine explores the vital connection between health, happiness, and a good night's sleep; by William C. Dement with Christopher Vaughan. Delacorte Press 1999 524p il pa $15.95 hardcover o.p.   **612.8**
1. Sleep
ISBN 0-440-50901-7 (pa)   LC 98-23527
"A Living Planet Press book"

This work "offers scientific data on sleep, advice on sleep hygiene and a scenario for a restorative 'sleep camp'. Dement's outstanding book also includes helpful appendixes listing sleep-disorder clinics and Web sites." Libr J

Doidge, Norman

The brain that changes itself; stories of personal triumph from the frontiers of brain science. Viking 2007 427p $24.95   **612.8**
1. Neuroplasticity 2. Brain
ISBN 978-0-670-03830-5; 0-670-03830-X
                              LC 2006-49224

"A woman who perpetually feels like she's falling, a man addicted to hard-core pornography, an amputee with excruciating pain in his phantom elbow: all cured thanks to neuroplasticity, the brain's ability to rewire itself. Doidge provides a history of the research in this growing field, highlighting scientists at the edge of groundbreaking discoveries and telling fascinating stories of people who have benefited. An engaging read for anyone interested in the science behind how our surprisingly moldable brains are changed by our experiences." Psychology Today

Dowling, John E.

Creating mind; how the brain works. Norton 1998 212p il pa $17.50 hardcover o.p.
                                                    612.8
1. Brain
ISBN 0-393-97446-4 (pa)   LC 98-9365
"In this guide to the 'nuts and bolts' of the human brain, neurobiologist Dowling explains how basic brain functions work and are interconnected. He then explores in clear, concise prose the brain's major functions: vision, language, memory, emotion, perception, and consciousness. A good jumping off point for learning about neuroscience and its fascinating discoveries." Libr J

Includes bibliographical references

Eliot, Lise

What's going on in there? how the brain and mind develop in the first five years of life. Bantam Bks. 1999 533p pa $18 hardcover o.p.
                                                    612.8
1. Brain 2. Developmental psychology
ISBN 0-553-37825-2 (pa)   LC 99-35423
"This book is both theoretical and practical, combining scientific reportage with 'how-to' advice for new parents. . . . With clear, mostly simple language, {Eliot} guides readers through a fascinating array of new research—on infant balance, the development of language and memory, and the relationship between the birthing process and the brain." Libr J

Gazzaniga, Michael S.

Human: the science behind what makes us unique. Ecco 2008 447p $27.50   **612.8**
1. Brain 2. Human beings 3. Consciousness
ISBN 978-0-06-089288-3; 0-06-089288-9
                              LC 2008-297703
The author's "main premise is that human brains are not only proportionally larger than those of other primates but have a number of distinct structures, which he explores along with evolutionary explanations for their existence. . . . Throughout, Gazzaniga addresses the nature of consciousness." Publ Wkly

"A savvy, witty guide to neuroscience today." Kirkus

Includes bibliographical references

Glynn, Ian, 1928-

An anatomy of thought; the origin and machinery of mind. Oxford Univ. Press 2000 456p hardcover o.p. pa $17.95 **612.8**
1. Brain 2. Consciousness
ISBN 0-19-513696-9; 0-19-515803-2 (pa)
LC 99-41218

Glynn offers a "summary of what we know about the brain—both its evolution and its mechanisms. Among the topics he covers are natural selection, molecular evolution, nerves and the nervous system, sensory perception, and the specific structures responsible for our intellect." Libr J

Includes bibliographical references

Greenfield, Susan

The private life of the brain; emotions, consciousness, and the secret of the self. Wiley 2000 258p $27.95; pa $16.95 **612.8**
1. Brain
ISBN 0-471-18343-1; 0-471-39975-2 (pa)
LC 99-46191

The author "explores how consciousness and various brain functions differ in a child, a drug user, someone experiencing a nightmare, and a depressive. Examining how emotions affect all states of consciousness, she attempts to make sense of how brain activities constituting the mind and consciousness are interrelated." Libr J

"Greenfield presents a subtle model in everyday language, introducing her readers skillfully to her precedents and rivals in neurobiology and cognitive science." Publ Wkly

Johnson, Steven

Mind wide open; your brain and the neuroscience of everyday life. Scribner 2004 274p il $25; pa $15 **612.8**
1. Brain
ISBN 0-7432-4165-7; 0-7432-4166-5 (pa)
LC 2003-63308

"The author explores the new technologies that can plumb the workings of the mind." N Y Times Book Rev

"Johnson fills this book with important, big-picture ideas, including enough description of the details to give the reader a sense of the science without becoming overwhelmed. His knowledgeable and thoughtful approach makes neuroscience accessible to all." Choice

Includes bibliographical references

Lavie, P. (Peretz), 1949-

The enchanted world of sleep; {by} Peretz Lavie; translated by Anthony Berris. Yale Univ. Press 1996 270p il hardcover o.p. pa $14.35 **612.8**
1. Sleep
ISBN 0-300-06602-3; 0-300-07436-0 (pa)
LC 95-41304

The author "describes our historical fascination with sleep and reviews notable research in the field. Among the topics he covers are the physiological changes that occur during a normal period of sleep, sleep disorders, the purpose of dreams, and the 'evolution' of the sleep cycle from birth to old age." Libr J

Includes bibliographical references

LeDoux, Joseph E.

Synaptic self; how our brains become who we are; [by] Joseph LeDoux. Viking 2002 406p il $29.95; pa $16 **612.8**
1. Personality 2. Self
ISBN 0-670-03028-7; 0-14-200178-3 (pa)
LC 2001-45356

The author puts forth the theory that "it's the neural pathways—the synaptic relationships—in our brains that make us who we are. . . . Writing for a general audience, he succeeds in making his subject accessible to the dedicated nonspecialist. He offers absorbing descriptions of some of the most fascinating case studies in his field, provides insight into the shortcomings of psychopharmacology and suggests new directions for research on the biology of mental illness." Publ Wkly

Linden, David J., 1961-

The accidental mind. Belknap Press of Harvard University Press 2007 276p il $25.95 **612.8**
1. Brain
ISBN 978-0-674-02478-6; 0-674-02478-8
LC 2006-47905

The author "argues that the brain is not an optimized machine, but rather a pieced together mess that gives humans some of their most cherished traits like the ability to love." Libr J

This is an "important counterpoint to breathless paeans to brain design." Choice

Includes bibliographical references

Pert, Candace, 1946-

Molecules of emotion; why you feel the way you feel; [by] Candace B. Pert; with a foreword by Deepak Chopra. Scribner 1997 368p $25; pa $14 **612.8**
1. Emotions 2. Psychosomatic medicine 3. Mind and body
ISBN 0-684-83187-2; 0-684-84634-9 (pa)
LC 97-17463

The author "has been at the forefront of key discoveries in the fields of neuroscience and AIDS therapy, and was intimately involved in the discovery of the brain's opiate receptors in 1972. Her memoir describes some of her breakthroughs while providing very real insight into the processes and politics at the core of modern science. . . . This is an important look at what really goes on inside the human body—and inside the scientific elite." Publ Wkly

Includes bibliographical references

Ratey, John J., 1948-

A user's guide to the brain; perception, attention, and the four theaters of the brain. Pantheon Bks. 2001 404p il pa $14.95 hardcover o.p. **612.8**
1. Brain
ISBN 0-375-70107-9 (pa)
LC 98-27796

The author explains the intricacies of the brain and its functions; he "organizes his material by functional category—development, perception, attention, memory, emo-

Ratey, John J., 1948-—*Continued*
tion, language, and socialization." Libr J
"Far more than a map of the brain's exotic jungles,
this study can serve as a life-enriching guide for keeping
the richest mental fields in cultivation." Booklist
Includes bibliographical references

Restak, Richard M., 1942-
Mozart's brain and the fighter pilot; unleashing
your brain's potential; by Richard Restak.
Harmony Bks. 2001 220p il pa $12 hardcover o.p.
612.8
1. Brain 2. Mental health
ISBN 0-609-81005-7 (pa)   LC 2001-24779
The author "offers 28 ways to improve mental fitness,
including exercises to enhance memory, concentration,
creativity, and analytical ability. . . . Restak's upbeat
and enlightening guide will certainly be a popular addition to public libraries." Libr J

The **Scientific** American book of the brain; from
the editors of Scientific American; introduction
by Antonio Damasio. Lyons Press 1999 340p il
pa $19.95 hardcover o.p.   **612.8**
1. Brain
ISBN 1-58574-285-6 (pa)   LC 99-39387
The articles in this anthology "include overviews of
research and clinical medicine and focused discussions of
such specific diseases as Parkinson's, Alzheimer's, and
depression. They not only present recent accomplishments and research but also show, most intriguingly, how
brain scientists think about a problem and develop its solution." Booklist

Thorpy, Michael J., 1948-
The encyclopedia of sleep and sleep disorders;
{by} Michael J. Thorpy and Jan Yager. 2nd ed,
updated and rev. Facts on File 2001 xxxvii, 314p
$65 *   **612.8**
ISBN 0-8160-4089-3   LC 00-64028
First published 1990 with authors' names in reverse
order
"Terms covered include those for syndromes, medications, disorders, individuals, organizations, treatments,
symptoms, and conditions. The readable and informative
material is useful to the layperson as well as the professional. Extensive appendixes include a state-by-state listing of sleep centers and laboratory members of the
AASM, Websites, and international and diagnostic classifications of sleep disorders." Am Ref Books Annu, 2002
Includes bibliographical references

Turkington, Carol
The encyclopedia of the brain and brain
disorders; foreword by Joseph R. Harris. 2nd ed.
Facts on File 2002 369p $65   **612.8**
1. Brain—Encyclopedias
ISBN 0-8160-4774-X   LC 2002-66512
"Library of health and living series"
First published 1996 with title: The brain encyclopedia
Rev. ed. of: The brain encyclopedia. c1996

This volume "includes more than 600 clear, concise
entries about the brain and treatments for neurological
disorders. Articles, alphabetically arranged, are followed
by directories of self-help organizations and of professional and government organizations in the fields of neurology, chronic pain, and mental illness. The list of references is extensive, the subject index is well organized."
Choice
Includes bibliographical references and index

Victoroff, Jeffrey Ivan
Saving your brain; the revolutionary plan to
boost brain power, improve memory, and protect
yourself against aging and Alzheimer's; [by] Jeff
Victoroff. Bantam Bks. 2002 450p il $25.95; pa
$14.95   **612.8**
1. Brain 2. Aging 3. Memory 4. Alzheimer's disease
ISBN 0-553-10944-8; 0-553-37980-1 (pa)
                          LC 2001-56732
"Contradicting popular scientific opinion, the author
argues memory loss may be a natural part of the aging
process. Using his own clinical experiences and reviews
of 14,000 research studies, [he] explores the many ways
the human brain can be damaged and offers tips for improving brain function and preventing memory loss, from
avoiding exposure to chemicals to not watching television." Libr J
Includes bibliographical references

Watson, Lyall
Jacobson's organ and the remarkable nature of
smell. Norton 2000 255p il hardcover o.p. pa
$19.95   **612.8**
1. Nose 2. Smell
ISBN 0-393-04908-6; 978-0-393-33291-9 (pa);
0-393-33291-8 (pa)   LC 99-56864
First published 1999 in the United Kingdom
"Drawing on both biology and cultural history, Watson employs intriguing and instructive examples as he
describes how humans, animals, and plants secrete and
decode odors; and explains how smell is essential to sexuality, and underlies emotions and many other forms of
subconscious knowledge." Booklist
Includes bibliographical references

Wolf, Maryanne
Proust and the squid; the story and science of
the reading brain. HarperCollins 2007 308p il
$25.95   **612.8**
1. Reading 2. Brain
ISBN 0-06-018639-9; 9780060186395
The author "examines reading's extraordinary evolution. Beginning with an exploration of how the human
brain evolved and adapted itself to become able to read,
she then offers a history of linguistic development that
concludes with the progress of alphabet-based languages." Libr J
This book "is an eye-opening winner, and deserves a
wide readership." Publ Wkly
Includes bibliographical references

Zimmer, Carl

Soul made flesh; the discovery of the brain—and how it changed the world. Free Press 2004 367p il $26 **612.8**

1. Brain

ISBN 0-7432-3038-8   LC 2003-63144

Zimmer tells "the story of the 'discovery' of the human brain by physician Thomas Willis. Exploring the effects of this breakthrough on 17th-century Oxford, the author traces and investigates the subsequent discoveries and theories in neurology and medicine that flowed from Willis and others (e.g., Harvey, Hobbes, Descartes, Boyle, and Locke) in Oxford and on the continent. . . . Zimmer's elegant writing combines these multiple perspectives to produce a fascinating tour-de-force of a man, a time, and a place that readers will greatly enjoy." Libr J

Includes bibliographical references

613 Personal health and safety

Atkins, Robert C.

Dr. Atkins' age-defying diet revolution. St. Martin's Press 2000 335p pa $7.99 hardcover o.p. **613**

1. Nutrition 2. Aging 3. Health

ISBN 0-312-97701-8 (pa)   LC 99-55690

Includes index

The author "argues here that the use of supplements and a change in diet can eliminate many health problems, including cardiovascular disease, diabetes and stroke." Publ Wkly

The **Black** women's health book; speaking for ourselves; edited by Evelyn C. White. new expanded ed. Seal Press 1994 375p pa $16.95 **613**

1. African American women—Health and hygiene

ISBN 1-878067-40-0   LC 93-28901

First published 1990

Contributors to this collection include Zora Neale Hurston, Lucille Clifton, Marian Wright Edelman, bell hooks, and Toni Morrison. Topics covered include: suicide, midwives, the politics of black women's health, sexual abuse, domestic violence, skin color, HIV infection, menopause, etc.

Includes bibliographical references

Carlson, Karen J.

The new Harvard guide to women's health; {by} Karen J. Carlson, Stephanie A. Eisenstat, Terra Ziporyn. Belknap Press of Harvard University Press 2004 688p il (Harvard University Press reference library) $55; pa $24.95 * **613**

1. Women—Health and hygiene 2. Women—Diseases

ISBN 0-674-01282-8; 0-674-01343-3 (pa)

LC 2003-63680

First published 1996 with title: Harvard guide to women's health

"In addition to the expected articles on contraception, pregnancy, sexuality, and sexually transmitted diseases, the 300 alphabetically arranged entries cover such general medical topics as colon and rectal cancer, asthma, cosmetic safety, and pesticides and organic food. There are also discussions of domestic violence, cosmetic surgery, obesity, and nutrition." Libr J

"The guide is an outstanding source for public and professional libraries." Booklist

Davis, Robert J., 1963-

The healthy skeptic; cutting through the hype about your health. University of California Press 2008 243p il $21.95 **613**

1. Consumer education 2. Quacks and quackery 3. Health—Information services

ISBN 978-0-520-24918-9; 0-520-24918-6

LC 2007-37341

The author "shares his experience of researching current health trends. From exploring ancient health 'wisdom' to uncovering the real agendas of modern-day health promoters, Davis guides the reader in analyzing and thinking critically about health-related information. Readers are treated to ten chapters tackling topics like the effectiveness of sunscreens and the failure of diets. . . . This reviewer highly recommends Davis's book for all libraries wishing to promote healthy skepticism." Libr J

Includes bibliographical references

Fitness over fifty; an exercise guide from the National Institute on Aging; with a foreword by John Glenn. Special illustrated ed. Healthy Living Bks. 2003 134p il pa $15.95 **613**

1. Exercise 2. Physical fitness 3. Aging

ISBN 1-57826-136-8

First published 2001 with title: Exercise: a guide from the National Institute on Aging

"Strenght flexibility, vitality, balance. 25 easy exercises for better health." Cover

"A panel of experts in exercise for older adults explain the benefits of physical activity and present basic fitness routines (with illustrated step-by-step instructions) to improve endurance, strength, balance, and flexibility. There are also useful tips for finding a fitness professional, incorporating exercise into daily routines, computing target heart rates, and creating exercise plans and progress charts. Excellent for beginners." Libr J

Gay, Kathlyn, 1930-

Encyclopedia of women's health issues. Oryx Press 2001 300p $74.95 **613**

1. Women—Health and hygiene 2. Women—Diseases

ISBN 1-57356-303-X   LC 2001-37342

This encyclopedia covers "the issues and history surrounding diseases and medical procedures faced by women; health concerns of different ethnic groups of women; information on organizations and programs that deal with women's health; profiles on the people who have pioneered women's health services and information; and legal decisions related to women's health." Publisher's note

Includes bibliographical references

The **"Go** ask Alice" book of answers; a guide to good physical, sexual, and emotional health; [by] Columbia University's Health Education Program. Holt & Co. 1998 345p pa $15.95
   613
1. Youth—Health and hygiene 2. Adolescence 3. Sex education
ISBN 0-8050-5570-3   LC 98-3318
"An Owl book"
"The title within the title refers to a Web site maintained by Columbia University Health Services. Set up to answer questions about relationships, sex, physical and mental health, nutrition, and related matters, the site eventually was opened to the general public as a quick-reference forum. The book's seven chapters round up queries the site has received and responses to them from Columbia-associated health educators." Booklist

Includes bibliographical references

Hall, Stephen S.
Merchants of immortality; chasing the dream of human life extension. Houghton Mifflin 2003 439p $25; pa $14   **613**
1. Medicine—Research
ISBN 0-618-09524-1; 0-618-49221-6 (pa)
       LC 2002-192155
This study discusses "the social and bioethical consequences of expanding the human life span beyond the biblically mandated threescore and ten, or 70, years." Libr J
"A lucid, thorough report on the developments in biology—cloning, stem cells, 'longevity genes'—that may not bring about immortality but appear to carry hope of making life a little longer and a great deal nicer toward the end." N Y Times Book Rev

Includes bibliographical references

Healthy women, healthy lives; a guide to preventing disease from the landmark Nurses' Health Study; senior editors, Susan E. Hankinson {et al.}. Simon & Schuster 2001 xxviii, 546p il $26; pa $16   **613**
1. Women—Diseases 2. Women—Health and hygiene
ISBN 0-684-85519-4; 0-7432-1774-8 (pa)
       LC 2001-34154
"A Harvard Medical School book"
"In 'Lowering the Risk of Disease', the risks of coronary heart disease, breast cancer, lung cancer, stroke, diabetes, colon cancer, osteoporosis, endometrial cancer, ovarian cancer, and skin cancer are discussed. Another chapter covers asthma, arthritis, age-related eye disease, and Alzheimer's disease. . . . The final chapters look at changing behaviors and making decisions that can affect women's health." Libr J

Includes bibliographical references

The **Johns** Hopkins medical guide to health after 50; the latest recommendations from the Hopkins specialists; medical editor, Simeon Margolis; prepared by the editors of The John Hopkins medical letter health after 50. Rebus 2002 704p il $39.95 *   **613**
1. Elderly—Health and hygiene 2. Elderly—Diseases
ISBN 0-929661-73-7   LC 2002-69670

This handbook "explains which measures you can take to increase longevity and protect yourself from the avoidable ailments of aging—and how to deal effectively with those ailments you can't avoid." Publisher's note

Kandel, Joseph
The encyclopedia of senior health and well being; {by} Joseph Kandel, Christine Adamec. Facts on File 2003 xxvi, 324p il (Facts on File library of health and living) $71.50   **613**
1. Elderly—Health and hygiene 2. Elderly—Diseases
ISBN 0-8160-4691-3   LC 2002-10485
This reference covers "health issues, diseases, global and ethnic factors concerning aging, common illnesses, and social issues that affect the daily lives of mature adults." Publisher's note

Includes bibliographical references

Mayo Clinic family health book; Scott C. Litin, editor-in-chief. 3rd ed. HarperResource 2003 1448p il $49.95   **613**
1. Medicine
ISBN 0-06-000250-6   LC 2002-27349
First published 1990 by Morrow
This edition covers over 1,000 illnesses and includes information on immunizations, breast health, genetics, sleep disorders, complementary and alternative medicine, pain management, and end-of-life issues. A medications guide covering more than 500 prescription and over-the-counter drugs is also included.

Men's health concerns sourcebook; edited by Robert Aquinas McNally. 2nd ed. Omnigraphics 2004 644p il (Health reference series) $84
   613
1. Men—Health and hygiene
ISBN 0-7808-0671-9   LC 2004-41520
First published 1998 under the editorship of Allan R. Cook
"Basic consumer health information about the medical and mental concerns of men, including theories about the shorter male lifespan, the leading causes of death and disability, physical concerns of special significance to men, reproductive and sexual concerns, sexually transmitted diseases, men's mental and emotional health, and lifestyle choices that affect wellness, such as nutrition, fitness, and substance use." Title page
Among the topics discussed are: prostate enlargement, impotence, vasectomies, snoring, sleep apnea, urological disorders, hair loss and pulmonary diseases.

Includes bibliographical references

Null, Gary
For women only! your guide to health empowerment; [by] Gary Null and Barbara Seaman. Seven Stories Press 1999 xxiv, 1571p il $49.95; pa $29.95   **613**
1. Women—Health and hygiene 2. Alternative medicine
ISBN 1-58322-015-1; 1-58322-278-2 (pa)
      LC 99-39822
"The first 600 pages of this . . . [book] offer alternative practitioner Null's thoughts on the causes, symp-

Null, Gary—*Continued*

toms, prevention, and treatment of conditions and illnesses, from addiction and arthritis to violence and varicose veins. The remainder is Seaman's history of the women's health movement, featuring selections from . . . feminist writers." Booklist

Includes bibliographical references

Our bodies, ourselves; a new edition for a new era; [by] The Boston Women's Health Book Collective. 35th anniversary ed. Simon & Schuster 2005 832p il pa $24.95 *

613

1. Women—Health and hygiene 2. Women—Psychology

ISBN 0-7432-5611-5 (pa)   LC 2004-65374

"A Touchstone book"

First published 1971

This encyclopedia of women's health covers such topics as body image, food, alcohol and drugs, holistic healing, psychotherapy, occupational health, violence, relationships and sexuality, sexual health and controlling fertility, childbearing, aging and politics of women and health.

This book "is exceedingly readable, strikingly comprehensive, and thoroughly documented." Libr J

Includes bibliographical references

Peck, Brian

The baby boomer body book; the complete health reference for our generation. Sourcebooks 2001 447p il pa $21.94   **613**

1. Middle age 2. Health 3. Aging

ISBN 1-57071-715-X   LC 00-66169

The author "draws on case histories from his practice to discuss age-related physical changes, memory problems, depression, dietary supplements, medical tests, and weight loss. Separate sections on men's and women's health issues cover sexual dysfunction and osteoporosis in men—an often unrecognized condition. Peck also addresses recreational drug use and midlife self-image. His breezy, approachable style will appeal to midlifers (especially men not attracted by conventional resources)." Libr J

Includes bibliographical references

Weil, Andrew

Eight weeks to optimum health; a proven program for taking full advantage of your body's natural healing power. Knopf 1997 276p $25; pa $13.95   **613**

1. Health self-care 2. Alternative medicine

ISBN 0-679-44715-6; 0-449-00026-5 (pa)

LC 96-51918

The program consists of "a schedule of incremental changes in diet (recipes are included), dietary supplements, exercise, and such mental-spiritual practices as breath work, art and music appreciation, and spending some time in a sauna." Booklist

The book's "strength lies in its design, which uses small easy steps to achieve big changes. . . . As a physician, Weil is careful to substantiate every claim, and he debunks some of today's more extreme alternative health theories." Libr J

Includes bibliographical references

613.2   Dietetics

Agatston, Arthur, 1947-

The South Beach diet; the delicious, doctor-designed, foolproof plan for fast and healthy weight loss. Rodale 2003 310p $24.95

613.2

1. Weight loss 2. Low-carbohydrate diet

ISBN 1-57954-646-3   LC 2002-154529

"The South Beach diet begins with a somewhat restrictive two-week program, generally producing a weight loss of from eight to 13 pounds. . . . Complete meal plans along with simple recipes comprise roughly half the book. Of course, there's no perfect diet that works for everyone but the enthusiasm of the conversational tone and the inviting manner make the book more appealing than many other diet tomes." Publ Wkly

Atkins, Robert C.

Dr. Atkins' new diet revolution. Avon Bks. 2002 540p il pa $7.99   **613.2**

1. Weight loss 2. Low-carbohydrate diet

ISBN 0-06-001203-X   LC 2002-278407

First published 1972 by D. McKay with title: Dr. Atkins' diet revolution: the high calorie way to stay thin forever

Completely updated

In this "holistic approach to health and well-being . . . Atkins promotes a diet of protein and fat in four stages: induction, ongoing weight loss, premaintenance, and maintenance. Case histories document his achievements. . . . Useful appendixes include menus, recipes, and a carbohydrate gram counter." Libr J

Includes bibliographical references

Bijlefeld, Marjolijn, 1960-

Encyclopedia of diet fads; {by} Marjolijn Bijlefeld and Sharon K. Zoumbaris. Greenwood Press 2003 242p il $55 *   **613.2**

1. Weight loss

ISBN 0-313-32223-6   LC 2002-192821

This volume "covers vitamins, calcium, cholesterol, dietary guidelines, and medical disorders (diabetes, anorexia). It includes just about every fad diet, diet creators (Beverly Hills, Atkins, Weight-Watchers), and specialized diets (macrobiotic, vegetarian, high protein). . . . Entries are well-written and give factual analysis along with criticism of diet claims." Choice

Includes bibliographical references

Cox, Peter, 1955-

You don't need meat. Thomas Dunne Bks. 2002 xxii, 378p il $24.95; pa $14.95   **613.2**

1. Vegetarianism 2. Vegetarian cooking

ISBN 0-312-27761-X; 0-312-30338-6 (pa)

LC 2001-54814

"Cox's defense of vegetarianism rests largely on health and nutritional issues, but he uses plenty of anthropomorphic imagery to discourage eating animals. He cites low rates of heart disease among Seventh-Day Adventists as empirical evidence for the better health of

Cox, Peter, 1955-—*Continued*

those who refuse to eat meat. . . . A few recipes illustrate general principles of vegetarian cooking." Booklist

Includes bibliographical references

Critser, Greg

Fat land; how Americans became the fattest people in the world. Houghton Mifflin 2003 232p il $24; pa $13   **613.2**

1. Obesity

ISBN 0-618-16472-3; 0-618-38060-4 (pa)

LC 2002-32282

The author "presents a critical analysis of the many social and economic factors that make Americans, contrary to the book's subtitle, the second-fattest people in the world. . . . He blames parents' reluctance to monitor their children's eating habits; the marketing tactics of fast-food companies, which influence us to overeat; the preponderance of fad diets; the phasing out of physical education programs in schools; and the sale of fast foods at schools to save money on dining facilities." Libr J

The author "succeeds in letting laypersons grasp agricultural policy, astute marketing ploys, lipid chemistry, human physioloy, and the follies of institutional feeding schemes and weight-loss quackery." Choice

Diet and nutrition sourcebook; edited by Joyce Brennfleck Shannon. 3rd ed. Omnigraphics 2006 633p il (Health reference series) $87

613.2

1. Diet 2. Nutrition

ISBN 0-7808-0800-2; 978-0-7808-0800-3

LC 2005-31842

First published 1996 under the editorship of Dan R. Harris

"Basic consumer health information about dietary guidelines and the food guidance system, recommended daily nutrient intakes, serving proportions, weight control, vitamins and supplements, nutrition issues for different life stages and lifestyles, and the needs of people with specific medical concerns, including cancer, celiac disease, diabetes, eating disorders, food allergies, and cardiovascular disease: along with facts about federal nutrition support programs, a glossary of nutrition and dietary terms, and directories of additional resources for more information about nutrition." Title page

Includes bibliographical references

Duyff, Roberta Larson

American Dietetic Association complete food and nutrition guide. 2nd ed. Wiley 2002 658p il $45; pa $24.95 *   **613.2**

1. Nutrition

ISBN 0-471-22924-5; 0-471-44144-9 (pa)

First published 1996 by Chronimed Pub.

This book "covers safe weight control; nutritional needs of women, children, teens, and seniors; shopping, eating out, reading labels, and food safety." Booklist {review of 1996 edition}

"Duyff gives sound advice." Libr J {review of 1996 edition}

The **Encyclopedia** of vitamins, minerals, and supplements; [compiled by] Tova Navarra; foreword by Wendy Shankin-Cohen. 2nd ed. Facts on File 2004 xxiii, 353p (Facts on File library of health and living) $65   **613.2**

1. Vitamins 2. Nutrition 3. Dietary supplements—Encyclopedias

ISBN 0-8160-4998-X   LC 2003-61662

First published 1996

Over 900 entries in A-Z format focus on how to use vitamins, minerals, and food supplements "safely, their effects on nutrition, their uses as treatment for assorted health concerns, and common misconceptions about them. Articles on individual vitamins and minerals are detailed." Booklist

Includes bibliographical references

Guiliano, Mireille

French women don't get fat; secrets for enjoying food, having fun, and being thin; Mireille Guiliano. Knopf 2004 272p $22   **613.2**

1. Diet 2. Women—France 3. Eating habits

ISBN 1-400-04212-7   LC 2004-48424

In her strategies and recipes "Mireille reveals the ingredients for a lifetime of weight control—from emergency weekend remedy of Magical Leek Soup to everyday tricks like fool yourself into contentment and painless new physical exertions to save you from the StairMaster. Emphasizing the virtues of freshness, variety, balance, and *always* pleasure, Mireille shows how virtually anyone can learn to eat, drink, and move like a French woman." Publisher's note

Guiliano's "book, with its amusing asides about her life and work, occasional lapses into French and inspiring recipes . . . is a stirring reminder of the importance of joie de vivre." Publ Wkly

Kolata, Gina

Rethinking thin; the new science of weight loss—and the myths and realities of dieting. Farrar, Straus, and Giroux 2007 257p $24

613.2

1. Weight loss

ISBN 978-0-374-10398-9; 0-374-10398-4

LC 2006-33816

The author "traces the history of dieting fads back to the 19th century; discusses our changing ideas about the ideal body (thinner and thinner); and, most importantly, explains how genetic and biochemical understanding has (at least among researchers) replaced the view of obesity as a lack of self-control. . . . This book will change your thinking about weight, whether you struggle with it or not." Publ Wkly

Includes bibliographical references

Kraus, Barbara

Barbara Kraus' calories and carbohydrates. 16th ed, rev. by Marie Reilly-Pardo. Signet Bks. 2005 490p pa $6.99   **613.2**

1. Food—Composition

ISBN 978-0-451-21384-6; 0-451-21384-X

First published 1971 by Grosset & Dunlap. Title varies

Kraus, Barbara—*Continued*

This lists the calorie and carbohydrate count of more than 8,500 brand-name and natural foods, according to portion size, with cross references

Mayo Clinic on healthy weight; Donald D. Hensrud, editor in chief. Mason Crest 2002 208p il $29.95 *   613.2

1. Weight loss 2. Nutrition

ISBN 1-59084-225-1

Also available in paperback from Kensington Bks. and in a Spanish language edition

"Answers to help you achieve and maintain the weight that's right for you." On cover

This guide "begins with Getting Motivated. This portion defines obesity, covers the causes and health risks, and assists in setting goals and analyzing the fundamentals of healthy eating. How To Lose Weight . . . investigates physical activity, helps with changing attitudes and actions, and provides support for when the going gets tough. A chapter also covers the better-known eating plans, such as the Atkins Diet, the Zone, Blood-Type diet, Jenny Craig, and Weight Watchers. The third section, When You Need More Help, explains medications and surgery for weight loss." Voice Youth Advocates

Mindell, Earl, 1940-

Dr. Earl Mindell's unsafe at any meal; how to avoid hidden toxins in your food; [by] Earl Mindell with Hester Mundis. rev and updated. Contemporary Bks. 2002 274p pa $14.95

613.2

1. Nutrition 2. Food—Composition 3. Natural foods

ISBN 0-658-02115-X   LC 2001-58223

First published 1987

The author discusses the food industry's chemical cover-ups and looks at "labelese", pros and cons of new products, genetically modified foods and natural foods fortified with vitamins, minerals, and antioxidants

Includes bibliographical references

Murray, Michael T.

Encyclopedia of nutritional supplements; the essential guide for improving your health naturally. Prima Pub. 1996 564p pa $22.95   613.2

1. Vitamins 2. Nutrition

ISBN 0-7615-0410-9   LC 96-3804

"Written to help users make sense of the voluminous information available on nutritional supplements, this book includes detailed profiles of all the major ones—vitamins, minerals, essential fatty acids, accessory nutrients, and glandular extracts—and tells how they can help one live longer, feel better, and fight the effects of aging. A concluding section counsels which nutritional supplements to take for a host of conditions, including high cholesterol, depression, and fatigue." Am Ref Books Annu, 1997

Includes bibliographical references

Nelson, Miriam E.

Strong women eat well; nutritional strategies for a healthy body and mind; [by] Miriam E. Nelson with Judy Knipe. Putnam 2001 268p il $24.95; pa $13.95   613.2

1. Nutrition 2. Women—Health and hygiene

ISBN 0-399-14740-3; 0-399-52782-6 (pa)

LC 00-69677

"The main body of the work discusses each level of the Food Guide Pyramid—grains; fruits and vegetables; milk and meat products; and fats, oils, and sugars—as well as the importance of water. . . . A large number of recipes . . . provide ways to increase the use and intake of some foods that most of us may be hesitant to try." Libr J

Includes bibliographical references

Nestle, Marion

What to eat. North Point Press 2006 611p $30 *   613.2

1. Nutrition 2. Diet 3. Health

ISBN 0-8654-7704-3; 978-0-8654-7704-9

LC 2006-07886

This book presents "a guided tour of the supermarket, . . . section by section: produce, dairy, meat, fish, packaged foods, breads, juices, bottled waters, and more. . . . [The author] tells us how to make sensible choices based on freshness, taste, nutrition, health, effects on the environment, and . . . price." N Y Times Book Rev

The author's "intelligent and reassuring approach will likely make readers venture more confidently through the jungle of today's super-sized stores." Publ Wkly

Includes bibliographical references

Nichter, Mimi

Fat talk; what girls and their parents say about dieting. Harvard Univ. Press 2000 263p $25; pa $16.95   613.2

1. Obesity 2. Weight loss 3. Girls—Health and hygiene

ISBN 0-674-00229-6; 0-674-00681-X (pa)

LC 99-59521

The author "spent three years studying and interviewing teenage girls about their attitudes toward appearance, eating habits, and dieting. . . . Over two hundred girls were followed over a three-year period so that changing attitudes could be measured. The reader gains a better understanding of teenage girls through the readable narrative that describes the results of the study." Voice Youth Advocates

Includes bibliographical references

Nutrition and well-being A to Z; Delores C.S. James, editor in chief. Macmillan Reference USA 2004 2v il set $175   613.2

1. Nutrition—Encyclopedias

ISBN 0-02-865707-1   LC 2004-6088

Topics covered "include dietary habits, eating diseases and disorders, health risks and food safety, the eating habits of various ethnic groups, weight loss issues as well as professional matters, and health programs and organizations." Libr J

This is "a no-nonsense, comprehensive encyclopedia

Nutrition and well-being A to Z—*Continued*
that will be of use to students researching health and
food-science topics." SLJ

Includes bibliographical references

Reader's Digest Association, Inc.
Foods that harm, foods that heal; an A-Z guide
to safe and healthy eating; chief consultants, Joe
Schwarcz and Fran Berkoff. Reader's Digest
Association 2004 416p il pa $15.95   **613.2**
1. Nutrition
ISBN 0-7621-0505-4; 978-0-7621-0605-9 (pa);
0-7621-0605-0 (pa)   LC 2003-27879
First published 1997

"Alphabetical listings in this . . . resource span general categories of illnesses, food groups, additives, and normal life passages, such as aging. Other entries refer to
specific medical conditions or individual dietary elements. . . . Each medical entry recommends helpful
foods, followed by those that should be avoided."
Booklist

"Over 300 medical and nutrition experts collaborated
to ensure that the information presented in this book is
not only up-to-date but also supported by scientific evidence." Libr J

Ronzio, Robert A.
The encyclopedia of nutrition and good health;
{by} Robert Ronzio. 2nd ed. Facts on File 2003
726p $71.50 *   **613.2**
1. Nutrition—Encyclopedias
ISBN 0-8160-4966-1   LC 2002-35221
First published 1997

"The alphabetical entries cover a broad range of topics. Foods, their ingredients, and nutritional values are
described. Specific diets (Atkins, Mediterranean) are discussed objectively, with the basic premise of the diet explained along with its pros and cons. Entries on foods
and the components implicated in diseases and disorders
explain how and why the problem occurs and offer dietary recommendations. Some articles reflect new health
concerns. For example, the *Transfatty acids* entry gives
a clear explanation of the health risks and offers alternative food options. There is useful information on the
food pyramid and food labels. Medical terms, tests, and
current research are also covered." Booklist

Includes bibliographical references

Sears, William
The family nutrition book; everything you need
to know about feeding your children from birth
through adolescence. Little, Brown 1999 416p il
pa $19 hardcover o.p.   **613.2**
1. Children—Nutrition 2. Infants—Nutrition
ISBN 0-316-77715-3 (pa)   LC 98-51879

"The book progresses from an overview of nutrients
(water and fiber among them) to an extensive evaluation
of food groups, including discussions of vegetarianism,
organic foods and decoding packaging labels. Additional
sections address weight control and the specific roles
various foods play in disease prevention, stamina building, etc. Reference tables and an updated food pyramid
will prove indispensable to the reader." Publ Wkly

Includes bibliographical references

Shintani, Terry
The good carbohydrate revolution. Pocket Bks.
2002 432p il $23; pa $14   **613.2**
1. High-carbohydrate diet 2. Diet
ISBN 0-7434-0598-6; 0-7434-0599-4 (pa)
          LC 2001-55416

The author introduces a "way to control weight and
blood sugar levels by eating more of the right kinds of
carbohydrates. . . . Designed to maximize your health
and keep you lean for life, Dr. Shintani's . . . program
centers on 'good' carbohydrates such as whole-grain pasta, pita bread, corn, sweet potatoes, and brown rice, as
well as an array of vitamin-rich fruits and vegetables."
Publisher's note

Includes bibliographical references

Singh Khalsa, Dharma
Food as medicine; how to use diet, vitamins,
juices, and herbs for a healthier, happier, and
longer life. Atria Books 2003 358p $26; pa $14
          613.2
1. Nutrition 2. Health
ISBN 0-7434-4226-1; 0-7434-4228-8 (pa)
          LC 2003-266194

This guide to nutritional therapy is based "on the sev-
en principles of yoga nutritional therapy: body detoxification; the use of organic products; elimination of genetically engineered foods; eating only clean protein . . .
fresh juices and supplements; cooking consciously and
eating mindfully; and a complete transition to a yoga nutrition therapy diet." Publ Wkly

Includes bibliographical references

Spencer, Colin
Vegetarianism; a history. Four Walls Eight
Windows 2002 384p $28   **613.2**
1. Vegetarianism
ISBN 1-56858-238-2   LC 2002-69298
First published 1996 by University Press of New En-
gland with title: The heretic's feast (available pa $24.95
ISBN 0-87451-760-5)

Originally published under title: The heretic's feast.
Hanover, NH : University Press of New England, 1996

The author "chronicles meat abstinence throughout
history, describing its ancient origins and the myriad
struggles of this growing movement." Publisher's note

Includes bibliographical references

Steward, H. Leighton
The new sugar busters! cut sugar to trim fat;
[by] H. Leighton Steward . . . [et al.] [rev and
updated] 2003 367p il $24.95   **613.2**
1. Carbohydrates 2. Insulin 3. Sugar-free diet
4. Weight loss
ISBN 0-345-45537-1   LC 2003-272004
First published 1998 with title: Sugar busters!

In this guide to reducing sugar in your diet "the authors consider childhood obesity and diabetes, discuss artificial sweeteners and alcohol, offer recipes from restaurants around the country and answer FAQs from Sugar
Busters everywhere. For those with the willpower to cut
out the convenience foods, this will be a helpful guide
to eating better." Publ Wkly

Includes bibliographical references

Vegetarian sourcebook; basic consumer health information about vegetarian diets, lifestyle, and philosophy . . .; edited by Chad T. Kimball. Omnigraphics 2002 360p il (Health reference series) $78 * **613.2**
1. Vegetarianism
ISBN 0-7808-0439-2   LC 2002-70236
"This work answers questions that people might have about the healthfulness of a vegetarian diet as well as how to incorporate it into one's everyday life. . . . The articles in this volume are easy to read and come from authoritative sources." Am Ref Books Annu, 2003
Includes bibliographical references

Vegetarian Times vegetarian beginner's guide; by the editors of Vegetarian Times. Macmillan 1996 181p il pa $13.95 **613.2**
1. Vegetarianism
ISBN 0-02-860386-9   LC 96-4120
The authors "describe the various types of vegetarianism. Stressing the health value of the vegetarian lifestyle, especially in the treatment of various diseases, they point out the possible dangers of dairy foods, discuss whether to use vitamin supplements, and encourage the use of low-fat ingredients. Tips on the basic vegetarian pantry, along with two-weeks' worth of easy recipes and menus, are given for the beginner." Libr J

Weil, Andrew
Eating well for optimum health; the essential guide to food, diet, and nutrition. Knopf 2000 307p $25 **613.2**
1. Nutrition 2. Food 3. Health
ISBN 0-375-40754-5   LC 99-52730
Also available in paperback from Guill
"Weil illuminates the often confusing and conflicting ideas circulating about good nutrition, addressing specific health issues and offering nutritional guidance to help heal and prevent major illnesses. Of particular value is his examination of recent fads, such as low-carbohydrate, vegan and 'Asian' diets, with an eye toward debunking the myths about them while highlighting their valuable aspects." Publ Wkly
Includes bibliographical references

Wenner, Paul F.
Garden cuisine; heal yourself and the planet through low-fat meatless eating; {by} Paul Wenner. Simon & Schuster 1997 367p il pa $21.95 hardcover o.p. **613.2**
1. Low-fat diet 2. Vegetarian cooking
ISBN 0-684-83882-6 (pa)   LC 96-53990
The author "begins by outlining the ethical, health, and environmental benefits of reducing the amount of meat in our diets. He then proposes what is called the Garden Plan for a healthier lifestyle, including three weeks worth of menu plans, a shopping list, and an eight-page list of educational and organizational resources. Wenner's recommendations are easy to follow and commonsensical. . . . The recipes are, for the most part, light and easy to prepare." Libr J
Includes bibliographical references

Willett, Walter, 1945-
Eat, drink and be healthy; the Harvard Medical School guide to healthy eating; [by] Walter C. Willett with P. J. Skerrett; contributions by Edward L. Giovannucci; recipes by Maureen Callahan. Simon & Schuster 2001 299p il $25; pa $13 **613.2**
1. Nutrition
ISBN 0-684-86337-5; 0-7432-2322-5 (pa)
    LC 2001-20565
The author contends that the USDA Food Pyramid, which recommends 6 to 11 servings of carbohydrate-rich foods per day, is wrong and dangerous, and he offers an alternate nutritional plan emphasizing fruits, vegetables, fish, chicken, legumes, and whole grains
Includes bibliographical references

The **Yale** guide to children's nutrition; William V. Tamborlane, editor-in-chief; Janet Z. Weiswasser, managing editor; editors, Teresa Fung, Nancy A. Held, Tara Prather Liskov; foreword by Jane E. Brody; recipes compiled with cooperation from the James Beard Foundation. Yale Univ. Press 1997 415p il hardcover o.p. pa $19.95 **613.2**
1. Children—Nutrition
ISBN 0-300-06965-0; 0-300-07169-8 (pa)
    LC 96-44774
Divided as follows: "From Infancy to Adolescence, which treats developmental nutrition; Common Concerns, which tackles such issues as proper weight gain and dealing with picky eaters; Beyond the Basics, which addresses special problems, such as feeding children with diabetes, cystic fibrosis or food allergies; Building Blocks for Good Nutrition; Eating in, Eating Out, which proffers practical advice on school lunches and fast foods; and Recipes." Publ Wkly
"Comprehensive in its coverage, well organized, and easily understood, this book is highly recommended for any consumer health collection." Libr J
Includes bibliographical references

613.6 Personal safety and special topics of health

Bocij, Paul
Cyberstalking; harassment in the Internet age and how to protect your family. Praeger Publishers 2004 268p $39.95 **613.6**
1. Computer crimes
ISBN 0-275-98118-5; 978-0-275-98118-1
    LC 2003-68988
This book is devoted "to an examination of cyberstalking, providing an overview of the problem, its causes and consequences, and practical advice for protecting yourself and your loved ones." Publisher's note
"This is an extremely alarming book that focuses on the dark side of the Internet and makes it clear that we are all potential victims of cyberstalkers. . . . It's certain to be popular in libraries." Booklist
Includes bibliographical references

Drago, Dorothy A., 1946-

From crib to kindergarten; the essential child safety guide. Johns Hopkins University Press 2007 195p il $45; pa $15 *　　　　　　　**613.6**

1. Parenting 2. Accidents—Prevention

ISBN 978-0-8018-8569-3; 0-8018-8569-8; 978-0-8018-8570-9 (pa); 0-8018-8570-1 (pa)

LC 2006-20809

"In an effort to help readers 'recognize and reduce hazards so . . . children can be as safe from injury as possible,' Drago offers hundreds of tips on how to provide a safe environment for daily activities, concentrating on small children in the home setting. . . . This book is packed with indispensable advice and is an essential resource and reference guide for parents and caregivers." Libr J

Includes bibliographical references

Frist, Bill

When every moment counts; what you need to know about bioterrorism from the Senate's only doctor; [by] Bill Frist. Rowman & Littlefield 2002 181p il pa $14.95　　　　　　　**613.6**

1. Biological warfare 2. Terrorism 3. Anthrax 4. Ebola virus 5. Smallpox 6. Plague 7. Chemical warfare

ISBN 0-7425-2245-8　　　　　LC 2001-8752

Contents: Anthrax in the capitol; Safe at home; Anthrax; Plague; Small pox; Botulism; Tularemia; Ebola and viral hemorrhagic fevers; Chemical weapons; The threat to our food and water supply; A nation prepared

Stilwell, Alexander

Encyclopedia of survival techniques; [illustrations, Tony Randall and Anne Cakebread] Lyons Press 2000 192p il maps pa $19.95 *
　　　　　　　613.6

1. Wilderness survival

ISBN 1-58574-062-4　　　　　LC 2001-271839

This guide covers preparation, basic skills, equipment, various terrains, natural disasters, and first aid.

"Campers, scouts, hikers, or anyone interested in outdoor-survival techniques will find easy to use information here." SLJ

Survival wisdom & know-how; everything you need to know to subsist in the wilderness; from the editors of Stackpole Books; compiled by Amy Rost. Black Dog & Leventhal Publishers 2007 480p il pa $19.95　　　　　　**613.6**

1. Survival skills 2. Wilderness survival

ISBN 978-1-57912-753-4　　　　LC 2007-25379

This oversized guide covers "every aspect of outdoor adventure and survival . . . Topics include Building Outdoor Shelter, Tracking Animals, Winter Camping, Tying Knots, Orienteering, Reading the Weather, Identifying Edible Plants and Berries, Surviving in the Desert, Bird Watching, Fishing and Ice Fishing, Hunting and Trapping, Canoeing, Kayaking, and White Water Rafting, First Aid, Wild Animals, Cookery, and . . . more." Publisher's note

Includes bibliographical references

Wiseman, John, 1940-

SAS survival handbook; how to survive in the wild, in any climate, on land or at sea; [by] John "Lofty" Wiseman. New ed. HarperResource 2004 576p il pa $19.95　　　　　　　**613.6**

1. Wilderness survival 2. Survival after airplane accidents, shipwrecks, etc.

ISBN 0-06-057879-3　　　　LC 2004-302194

First published 1986 in the United Kingdom

This book "is the Special Air Service's complete course in being prepared for any type of emergency. John 'Lofty' Wiseman presents real strategies for surviving in any type of situation, from accidents and escape procedures, including chemical and nuclear to successfully adapting to various climates (polar, tropical, desert), to identifying edible plants and creating fire." Publisher's note

613.7　Physical fitness

Active living every day; [by] Steven N. Blair [et al.] Human Kinetics 2001 194p il pa $22.95
　　　　　　　613.7

1. Exercise 2. Physical fitness 3. Health

ISBN 0-7360-3701-2　　　　　LC 00-47238

The authors "present a week-by-week, self-paced plan for couch potatoes to incorporate physical activity gradually into their daily lives. . . . There is also sensible advice on proper nutrition and additional interactive exercises on the net." Libr J

Includes bibliographical references

Bailey, Covert

Smart exercise; burning fat, getting fit. Houghton Mifflin 1994 292p pa $12 hardcover o.p.　　　　　　　**613.7**

1. Exercise 2. Physical fitness

ISBN 0-395-66114-5 (pa)　　　　LC 94-1667

This fitness guide discusses metabolism, dieting, muscle tone, aerobics, exercise machines, swimming, walking and the benefits and drawbacks of various sports

Bonifonte, Philip, 1958-

T'ai chi for seniors; how to gain flexibility, strength, and inner peace. New Page Bks. 2004 213p il pa $16.99　　　　　　**613.7**

1. Tai chi

ISBN 1-564-14697-9　　　　LC 2003-60207

Includes index

The author describes the ancient Chinese exercise that focuses "on easy, gentle movements that increase aerobic capacity, decrease blood pressure and stress, and improve balance and joint function. Along with a short history of various tai chi styles philosophies, the text features breathing techniques, warm-up exercises, movement forms, and meditation exercises with modifications for those with limited mobility." Libr J

Callahan, Lisa

The fitness factor; every woman's key to a lifetime of health and wellbeing. Lyons Press 2002 xxi, 314p il $24.95 **613.7**

1. Exercise 2. Physical fitness 3. Women—Health and hygiene

ISBN 1-58574-501-4 LC 2001-50729

In this guide the author stresses the importance of exercise in "preventing heart disease; beating osteoporosis; lowering cholesterol; decreasing cancer risk; losing weight; increasing energy; reducing stress; having better sex and much more." Publisher's note

Includes bibliographical references

Decker, Joe

The world's fittest you; four weeks to total fitness; [by] Joe Decker with Eric Neuhaus. Dutton 2004 286p il $24.95; pa $13.95 **613.7**

1. Exercise 2. Physical fitness

ISBN 0-525-94759-0; 0-451-21401-3 (pa)

LC 2004-299995

The author "challenges readers to 'shock' themselves fit through 'positive eating,' hard work and commitment. A former fat kid farm-fed on whole milk and fried chicken, Decker turned flab into fitness before dedicating his life to helping others do the same." Publ Wkly

This is "a scientifically sound fitness guide that reads as if the author had taken exercise principles from a college exercise physiology textbook and condensed and repacked them into a program geared to the working adult." Libr J

Fahey, Thomas D., 1947-

Basic weight training for men and women. 6th ed. McGraw-Hill 2007 248p il pa $30.63

613.7

1. Weight lifting

ISBN 0-07-304688-4; 978-0-07-304688-4

LC 2005-53132

First published 1989 by Mayfield Pub. Co. with title: Basic weight training

This is a "guide to developing a personalized weight-training program with both free weights and machines. Weight training concepts and specific exercises are grouped by body region, and many photographs, illustrations, diagrams, and figures demonstrate proper technique and form." Publisher's note

Includes bibliographical references

Fitness and exercise sourcebook; edited by Amy L. Sutton. 3rd ed. Omnigraphics 2007 663p il (Health reference series) $87 **613.7**

1. Physical fitness 2. Exercise

ISBN 978-0-7808-0946-8; 0-7808-0946-7

LC 2006-36852

First published 1996

"Basic consumer health information about the physical and mental benefits of fitness, including cardiorespiratory endurance, muscular strength, muscular endurance, and flexibility, with facts about sports nutrition and exercise-related injuries and tips about physical activity and exercises for people of all ages and for people with health concerns; along with advice on selecting and using exercise equipment, maintaining exercise motivation, a glossary of related terms, and a directory of resources for more help and information." Title page

Includes bibliographical references

Hesson, James L.

Weight training for life. 8th ed. Thomson Wadsworth 2006 165p il pa $30.95 *

613.7

1. Weight lifting

ISBN 0-495-01275-0; 978-0-495-01275-7

LC 2005-937607

First published 1985 by Morton

This weight training guide features "photos demonstrating exercises and proper techniques, forms for writing goals, for planning a personal weight-training program, and for recording circumference measurements, strength measurements, and muscle endurance measurements." Publisher's note

Includes bibliographical references

Isacowitz, Rael, 1955-

Pilates. Human Kinetics 2006 343p il pa $19.95

613.7

1. Pilates method

ISBN 0-7360-5623-8; 978-0-7360-5623-6

LC 2006-7911

Contents: Enhancing the mind and body — Alignment, posture, and movement — Powerful pilates practice — Mat work — Universal reformer — Cadillac — Wunda chair — Barrels — Ped-a-pul — Arm chair — Magic circle — Sample exercise routines

This guide to Pilates exercises includes information on mat work, breathing, and equipment.

Includes bibliographical references

Iyengar, B. K. S., 1918-

Light on life; the yoga journey to wholeness, inner peace, and ultimate freedom; [by] B.K.S. Iyengar, with John J. Evans and Douglas Abrams. Rodale 2005 xxii, 282p il $24.95; pa $15.95

613.7

1. Yoga

ISBN 1-59486-248-6; 978-1-59486-248-9; 1-59486-524-8 (pa) LC 2005-15700

The author "expounds the philosophy of yoga—its metaphysics, of which yoga poses, or asanas, represent the physical component. . . . Not the book with which to begin the yoga journey, it is highly recommended for those advanced on the path and interested in learning from a master of flexibility and wisdom." Publ Wkly

Kolata, Gina

Ultimate fitness; the quest for truth about exercise and health. Farrar, Straus & Giroux 2003 292p il $24; pa $14 **613.7**

1. Physical fitness 2. Exercise

ISBN 0-374-20477-2; 0-312-42322-5 (pa)

LC 2002-192523

The author " investigates 30 years of the American physical fitness craze, looking at issues like athlete's

Kolata, Gina—Continued

heart, maximum heart rates, fat-burning zones, training, runner's high, weightlifting, walking, food, water, [and] the fitness business. . . . Fascinating historical information about fitness, understandable facts and figures, and a conversational writing style make this an enormously readable book." Libr J

Includes bibliographical references

McFarlane, Stewart

The complete book of t'ai chi. DK Pub. 1997 120p il pa $15 hardcover o.p.   **613.7**

1. Tai chi

ISBN 0-7894-4259-0 (pa)   LC 96-33596

This is an illustrated guide to the Chinese art of t'ai chi, which is aimed at promoting physical and mental well-being.

"The gentle movements are diagrammed in detail with full-color step-by-step photographs and precise explanations. A good how-to book for beginners." BAYA Book Rev

Pagano, Joan

Strength training for women; tone up, burn calories, stay strong. Dorling Kindersley 2005 160p il pa $15 *   **613.7**

1. Weight lifting 2. Physical fitness 3. Women—Health and hygiene

ISBN 0-7566-0595-4; 978-0-7566-0595-7

LC 2005-295208

The author "begins with a three-part fitness test and questionnaire to assess whether the reader should consult a doctor before beginning her program. For true beginners, she provides an anatomy chart that depicts the major muscle groups and the exercises that are best suited to them. She dispels fitness myths like 'lifting weights will bulk you up' and 'you can spot reduce,' and talks about the risk factors, exercise guidelines and restrictions of osteoporosis. . . . This book may be one of the best substitutes for pricey gym memberships and personal trainers." Publ Wkly

Reichmann, Rosie, 1917-

Ageless yoga; yoga exercises for improving your life at any age! Astrolog; distributed by Independent Pubs. Group 2001 192p il pa $18.95
613.7

1. Yoga

ISBN 9-6549-4124-4

The author discusses how her "program of gentle stretching and breathing techniques can be used to create specific workouts to relieve tension, increase flexibility, and reduce age-related functional losses in various parts of the body. Her readable text is illustrated with photos of the author demonstrating the poses, with modifications for those who must use a chair or mattress." Libr J

613.9   Birth control, reproductive technology, sex hygiene

Block, Joel D.

Sex over 50; [by] Joel D. Block with Susan Crain Bakos. Parker Pub. 1999 302p $34; pa $15
613.9

1. Sexual behavior

ISBN 0-13-080968-3; 0-7352-0058-0 (pa)

LC 98-42503

"Highlighting the 'potent sexual benefits' that come with midlife, this light-hearted but informative guide by a psychotherapist and journalist presents exercises to reenergize a routine sex life, suggests how to create moods and fantasies, describes alternative forms of lovemaking (bondage, etc.), and covers the more mundane aspects of midlife sexuality (health issues, impotence, hormonal changes)." Libr J

Comfort, Alex, 1920-2000

The joy of sex; foreword by Claire Rayner. Crown 2002 240p il $29.95; pa $10 *
613.9

1. Sexual behavior

ISBN 1-400-04614-9; 0-7434-7774-X (pa)

LC 2002-67455

"30th anniversary edition of original 1972 publication." Verso of title page; Variant title: The new joy of sex

Describes with illustrations a variety of sexual behaviors, addresses causes and risks of sexually transmitted diseases, and emphasizes the importance of love.

614   Forensic medicine; incidence of injuries, wounds, disease; public preventive medicine

Bass, William M., 1928-

Death's acre; inside the legendary forensic lab the Body Farm where the dead do tell tales; [by] Bill Bass and Jon Jefferson; foreword by Patricia Cornwell. Putnam 2003 304p il $24.95; pa $15
614

1. Forensic anthropology

ISBN 0-399-15134-6; 0-425-19832-4 (pa)

LC 2003-46908

"The author explains the process of decomposition and how bones give clues to identify: approximate age, sex, height, and race, all of which are needed to bring the forensic scientist one step closer to putting a name to a corpse. He describes some of the cases he has been involved with and laughs at himself when he shares stories of mistakes and assumptions. Young adults will gain insight into the forensic process and appreciate Bass's dedication to the truth and his work." SLJ

Evans, Colin

The casebook of forensic detection; how science solved 100 of history's most baffling crimes. Wiley 1996 310p il pa $17.95 hardcover o.p.

614

1. Forensic sciences 2. Medical jurisprudence 3. Criminal investigation

ISBN 0-471-28369-X (pa)   LC 95-26002

Also available in paperback from Berkley Trade

"Covers cases from 1751 to 1991, arranged according to the methodology by which they were solved. Fifteen areas are listed alphabetically, ranging from ballistics through DNA typing, fingerprinting, odontology, serology and toxicology to the still-disputed voiceprint analysis." Publ Wkly

"Written in a popular style as clear as it is brief, this book is suitable for general true-crime collections." Libr J

Lee, Henry C.

Blood evidence; how DNA is revolutionizing the way we solve crimes; [by] Henry C. Lee, Frank Tirnady. Perseus Bks. 2003 xxx, 418p $26

614

1. DNA fingerprinting 2. Forensic sciences

ISBN 0-7382-0602-4   LC 2002-105970

This book "explains the principles and science behind DNA testing and shows how it has both helped solve some of the most puzzling criminal cases in recent history and been used to discredit eyewitness accounts and physical evidence found at the crime scene." Publisher's note

"This volume is an excellent introduction to the science and use of DNA analysis." Publ Wkly

Includes bibliographical references

Maples, William R., 1937-1997

Dead men do tell tales; [by] William R. Maples and Michael Browning. Doubleday 1994 292p il pa $15.95 hardcover o.p.   **614**

1. Forensic anthropology

ISBN 0-385-47968-9 (pa)   LC 94-12290

Maples, a forensic anthropologist, "describes the remains (or, when burnt, cremains) presented to him, describes what he looks for, and guides us through his thinking and the search for additional clues and information. His most difficult, fascinating, and perplexing case dealt with a 1985 apparent double murder and burning, while among historic bodies, Maples dealt with those of Francisco Pizarro, Zachary Taylor, Czar Nicholas II, and Joseph Merrick, 'the Elephant Man.'" Booklist

Wecht, Cyril H., 1931-

Tales from the morgue; forensic answers to nine famous cases including the Scott Peterson & Chandra Levy cases; [by] Cyril Wecht and Mark Curriden with Angela Powell. Prometheus Books 2005 314p il $26 *   **614**

1. Forensic sciences 2. Criminal investigation

ISBN 1-59102-353-X   LC 2005-17805

Pathologist Wecht "sorts out the evidence, or lack thereof, in the scandalous circumstances of Scott Peterson and Chandra Levy, explains why he thinks the JFK assassination was a conspiracy and agrees with the original Marilyn Monroe autopsy that found no signs of foul play. . . . What makes Wecht's arguments so persuasive is that he lets scientific facts—or at least his expert interpretation of them—do the talking." Publ Wkly

Includes bibliographical references

Zugibe, Frederick T.

Dissecting death; secrets of a medical examiner; [by] Frederick Zugibe and David L. Carroll. Broadway Books 2005 240p il $24.95; pa $14

614

1. Forensic sciences 2. Medical jurisprudence 3. Criminal investigation

ISBN 0-7679-1879-7; 0-7679-1880-0 (pa)

LC 2004-62889

Zugibe "presents 10 challenging cases he encountered, as well as his insights as a self-described Monday-morning quarterback on two of the most notorious crimes of the 1990s: the brutal slaying of JonBenét Ramsey and the murders of Nicole Brown Simpson and Ronald Goldman." Publ Wkly

The authors' "straightforward style makes for clear and fascinating reading, and the cases chosen are intriguing." Booklist

614.4 Incidence of and public measures to prevent disease

Allen, Arthur

Vaccine; the controversial story of medicine's greatest lifesaver. Norton 2007 523p il $27.95

614.4

1. Vaccination

ISBN 0-393-05911-1; 978-0-393-05911-3

LC 2006-19480

The author "records the miracles, controversies, and tragedies that have accompanied the development of vaccines since Edward Jenner first combated smallpox in the 18th century. . . . This compelling narrative of the vaccine's undoubted triumphs and troubling challenges is highly recommended to serious readers interested in medicine and public health." Libr J

Includes bibliographical references

Drexler, Madeline, 1954-

Secret agents; the menace of emerging infections. Joseph Henry Press 2002 316p il $24.95   **614.4**

1. Epidemiology 2. Communicable diseases

ISBN 0-309-07638-2   LC 2001-7832

Also available in paperback from Penguin Bks.

This discusses such topics as food-borne pathogens, antibiotic resistance, animals and insect-borne pathogens, pandemic influenza, infectious causes of chronic disease, and bioterrorism, including the threats of anthrax and smallpox

This is a "fascinating thought-provoking book. . . . A substantial contribution to public information about infectious diseases." Booklist

Includes bibliographical references

Encyclopedia of plague and pestilence; from ancient times to the present; George Childs Kohn, editor. 3rd ed. Facts On File 2008 529p il map (Facts on File library of world history) $85 *   **614.4**

1. Epidemics—Encyclopedias

ISBN 978-0-8160-6935-4; 0-8160-6935-2

LC 2006-41296

Replaces the edition published 2001

First published 1995

This encyclopedia provides "descriptions of more than 700 epidemics, listed alphabetically by location of the outbreak. Each . . . entry includes when and where a particular epidemic began, how and why it happened, whom it affected, how it spread and ran its course, and its outcome and significance." Publisher's note

Includes bibliographical references

Garrett, Laurie

The coming plague; newly emerging diseases in a world out of balance. Penguin 1995 750p maps pa $20   **614.4**

1. Communicable diseases 2. Epidemics 3. Ebola virus 4. AIDS (Disease) 5. Viruses

ISBN 0-14-025091-3; 978-0-14-025091-6

First published 1994 by Farrar, Straus & Giroux

"The author demonstrates that the emerging global village means not only superior communication and trade among nations but also the deadly swap of microbes. Analyzing the spread of both familiar diseases like cholera and new viruses like Ebola, this is 'a meticulously researched, genuinely disturbing' account." N Y Times Book Rev

Includes bibliographical references

Karlen, Arno

Man and microbes; disease and plagues in history and modern times. Simon & Schuster 1996 266p pa $14   **614.4**

ISBN 0-684-82270-9   LC 96-1705

First Published 1995 by Putnam

Karlen presents a "report on the current global crisis of new and resurgent diseases. Covering cholera, leprosy, cancer, AIDS, viral encephalitis, lethal Ebola fever, streptococcal 'flesheating' infections and a host of other killers, he shows how the present wave of diseases arose with drastic environmental change, wars, acceleration of travel, the breakdown of public health measures, and microbial adaptation." Publ Wkly

Includes bibliographical references

Kirby, David

Evidence of harm; mercury in vaccines and the autism epidemic: a medical controversy; David Kirby. St. Martin's Press 2005 460p $26.95; pa $14.95   **614.4**

1. Autism 2. Vaccination

ISBN 0-312-32644-0; 0-312-32645-9 (pa)

LC 2004-51492

This book "addresses the front-page question: has a mercury-containing preservative called thimerosal, commonly used in children's vaccines, caused a national epidemic of juvenile autism? . . . . This is the book for medical professionals and concerned parents to read. It's accessible in its handling of medical topics and compelling in its recounting of the parents' fight to advance their agenda in the face of both political and scientific roadblocks." Publ Wkly

Includes bibliographical references

McKenna, Maryn

Beating back the devil; on the front lines with the disease detectives of the Epidemic Intelligence Service. Free Press 2004 303p $26 *   **614.4**

1. Centers for Disease Control and Prevention (U.S.). Epidemic Intelligence Service Program

ISBN 0-7432-5132-6   LC 2004-53214

"This book celebrates a group of unsung heroes, the Epidemic Intelligence Service (EIS) of the U.S. Centers for Disease Control. Since its inception in 1951, the EIS has sent officers around the world to investigate outbreaks of diseases from polio, smallpox, tuberculosis, SARS, and West Nile Virus to the bioterrorist anthrax attacks." Libr J

"This book should serve as an effective antidote for anyone suffering from the misconception that epidemiologists must lead boring lives." Sci Books Films

Includes bibliographical references

Morris, Robert D.

The blue death; disease, disaster and the water we drink. HarperCollins Publishers 2007 310p il $24.95   **614.4**

1. Water supply 2. Water purification 3. Communicable diseases

ISBN 978-0-06-073089-5; 0-06-073089-7

LC 2006-49674

The author recounts "some of history's epic drinking water disasters, from the 1853 London cholera outbreak to the 1993 cryptosporidiosis outbreak that sickened some 4,000 Milwaukee residents, and how thousands were saved by improved water treatment." Booklist

"A clear and convincing argument; recommended for public libraries." Libr J

Includes bibliographical references

Oldstone, Michael B. A.

Viruses, plagues, and history. Oxford Univ. Press 1998 211p il maps hardcover o.p. pa $15.95   **614.4**

1. Communicable diseases 2. Viruses 3. Epidemics

ISBN 0-19-511723-9; 0-19-513422-2 (pa)

LC 97-9545

The author "starts with accounts of smallpox, yellow fever, measles, and polio, providing lively, well-documented stories about those diseases and their investigators. He well understands historical contexts and developments, and he has interviewed scientists involved in pertinent clinical and research work when that was possible. . . . He moves on to Ebola and other terrifying fevers, mad cow disease, and influenza, thoughtfully exploring the problems mutation poses for prevention and treatment." Booklist

Includes bibliographical references

Ryan, Frank, 1944-

Virus-X; tracking the new killer plagues: out of the present and into the future. Little, Brown 1997 430p il maps pa $15 hardcover o.p.   **614.4**

1. Communicable diseases 2. Epidemics 3. Viruses

ISBN 0-316-76306-3 (pa)   LC 96-30495

Ryan discusses "emerging viruses and potential global crises. He defines the issue by reviewing the political, medical, and social history of past and recent epidemics . . . {and presents} his hypothesis for the rise of an emerging virus and the potential global risks." Choice

"Of the many recent books about emerging diseases, this is one of the most interesting and disquieting, not only because of its gripping accounts of recent disease outbreaks such as hantavirus and AIDS but because of what it says about the nature of viruses." Libr J

Includes bibliographical references

Sears, Robert, M.D.

The vaccine book; making the right decision for your child; [by] Robert W. Sears. Little, Brown 2007 278p pa $13.99   **614.4**

1. Vaccination

ISBN 978-0-316-01750-3; 0-316-01750-7

LC 2007-22994

"The first 12 chapters discuss each vaccination in the childhood series, providing explanation of the relative disease, how the vaccine is made and points to assess a child's at-risk level when considering if the vaccine is necessary. . . . Additional chapters illuminate more controversial aspects of the debate, such as how vaccine safety is researched and what the findings are, side effects and how to minimize them, common myths and questions. . . . Sears' tone puts readers at ease as he clearly explains medical terms and elucidates debates." Publ Wkly

Includes bibliographical references

Walters, Mark Jerome

Six modern plagues and how we are causing them. Island Press 2003 206p $22; pa $14

614.4

1. Epidemiology 2. Communicable diseases 3. Environmental health 4. Human ecology

ISBN   1-55963-992-X;   978-1-55963-992-7; 1-55963-714-5 (pa); 978-1-55963-714-5 (pa)

LC 2003-15137

The author "examines six modern diseases: mad cow disease, HIV/AIDS, salmonella DT104, Lyme disease, hantavirus, and West Nile virus. Highlighting the main features of the history and impact of each of these diseases, he presents them as 'parables of the unintended consequences of the careless human disruption of the natural systems that are our home.'" Choice

"A quick read and a great introduction to the topic." Libr J

Includes bibliographical references

Wills, Christopher

Yellow fever, black goddess; the coevolution of people and plagues. Addison-Wesley 1996 324p il pa $16.50 hardcover o.p.   **614.4**

1. Epidemics 2. Communicable diseases

ISBN 0-201-32818-6 (pa)   LC 96-23934

Published in the United Kingdom with title: Plagues: their origins, history, and future

The book's contents range "from the history of particular diseases such as cholera and AIDS (but not yellow fever) to accounts of the author's travels in disease-ridden places to explanations of the genetic mechanisms of evolutionary change." Libr J

The author manages "to provide a good read while weaving seamlessly between historical accounts, scientific detective stories, and personal (or family) anecdotes." New Sci

Includes bibliographical references

614.5 Incidence of and public measures to prevent specific diseases and kinds of diseases

Barry, John M.

The great influenza; the epic story of the deadliest plague in history. Viking 2004 546p il $29.95; pa $16   **614.5**

1. Influenza

ISBN 0-670-89473-7; 0-14-303649-1 (pa)

LC 2003-57646

In this account of the 1918 influenza pandemic, the author "explores how the deadly confluence of biology (a swiftly mutating flu virus that can pass between animals and humans) and politics (President Wilson's all-out war effort in WWI) created conditions in which the virus thrived, killing more than 50 million worldwide and perhaps as many as 100 million in just a year." Publ Wkly

Includes bibliographical references

Cantor, Norman F., 1929-2004

In the wake of the plague; the Black death and the world it made. 1st Perennial ed. Perennial/HarperCollins 2002 245p il map pa $13.95   **614.5**

1. Plague

ISBN 0-06-001434-2   LC 2001-51819

First published 2001 by Free Press

The author "looks at the effects of the Black Death on 14th-century Europe." Libr J

"By animating history and demonstrating our times' connections to even as remote an event as the Black Death, Cantor's erudite excursion proves most engrossing." Booklist

Includes bibliographical references

Carrell, Jennifer Lee

The speckled monster; a historical tale of battling smallpox. Dutton 2003 474p il $24.95; pa $16 *   **614.5**

1. Montagu, Lady Mary Pierrepont Wortley, 1689-1762 2. Boylston, Zabdiel, 1679-1766 3. Smallpox

ISBN 0-525-94736-1; 0-452-28507-0 (pa)

LC 2003-137

The author focuses "on two early pioneers in the practice of smallpox inoculation: Lady Mary Wortley Montagu of London . . . and Dr. Zabdiel Boylston of Boston. Basing much of her reconstructed dialog on Montagu's

Carrell, Jennifer Lee—*Continued*

letters from Turkey, where she observed the local practice of inoculation, and Boylston's medical case studies of African practices, Carrell makes these historical figures come alive." Libr J

Includes bibliographical references

Crosby, Molly Caldwell

The American plague; the untold story of yellow fever, the epidemic that shaped our history. Berkley Books 2006 308p il $24.95   **614.5**

1. Yellow fever

ISBN 0-425-21202-5; 978-0-425-21202-8

LC 2006-50497

This book tells the "story of yellow fever, recounting Memphis Tennessee's near-destruction and resurrection from the epidemic—and the four men who changed medical history with their battle against an invisible foe that remains a threat to this very day." Publisher's note

The author "offers a forceful narrative of a disease's ravages and the quest to find its cause and cure." Publ Wkly

Includes bibliographical references

Fenn, Elizabeth A. (Elizabeth Anne), 1959-

Pox Americana; the great smallpox epidemic of 1775-82. Hill & Wang 2001 370p $25; pa $15
          614.5

1. Smallpox 2. United States—History—1775-1783, Revolution

ISBN 0-8090-7820-1; 0-8090-7821-X (pa)

LC 2001-16886

The author describes the effects of smallpox during the American Revolution, including the disease's toll on Native Americans, the greater vulnerability of Americans as compared to the British, and the conditions which transmitted the disease.

"Noteworthy as scholarship, Fenn's insightful, readable narrative is a welcome addition to literature about the revolutionary period." Booklist

Includes bibliographical references

Greenfeld, Karl Taro, 1964-

China syndrome; the true story of the 21st century's first great epidemic. HarperCollins 2006 442p map $25.95 *   **614.5**

1. SARS (Disease)

ISBN 0-06-058722-9; 978-0-06-058722-2

LC 2005-52684

In this book about the 2002 SARS outbreak in China, the author "traces the origins and spread of the disease in a chronological drumbeat that sometimes follows the events by day." Libr J

"The story unfolds like a whodunnit, with a large cast of rogues, victims and heroes. . . . This book is a parable for our times." New Statesman

Includes bibliographical references

Johnson, Steven

The ghost map; the story of London's most terrifying epidemic—and how it changed science, cities, and the modern world. Riverhead 2006 299p il map $26.95   **614.5**

1. Snow, John, 1813-1858 2. Cholera

ISBN 1-59448-925-4; 978-1-59448-925-9

LC 2006-23114

This book "takes place in the summer of 1854. A devastating cholera outbreak seizes London just as it is emerging as a modern city. . . . Dr. John Snow—whose ideas about contagion had been dismissed by the scientific community—is spurred to intense action when the people in his neighborhood begin dying. . . . Johnson chronicles Snow's day-by-day efforts, as he risks his own life to prove how the epidemic is being spread." Publisher's note

"From Snow's discovery of patient zero to Johnson's compelling argument for and celebration of cities, this makes for an illuminating and satisfying read." Publ Wkly

Includes bibliographical references

Kelly, John, 1945-

The great mortality; an intimate history of the Black Death, the most devastating plague of all time. HarperCollins Publishers 2005 364p $25.95; pa $14.95   **614.5**

1. Plague

ISBN 0-06-000692-7; 0-06-000693-5 (pa)

LC 2004-54213

"Western Europe is the primary focus of Kelly's compact history, which is 'intimate' in that it highlights many particular persons' passages through the crucible years, 1348-49. . . . Kelly proceeds chronologically, beginning with the plague's prehistory in north central Asia and its spread through China before empire-building Mongols brought it west. . . . This sweeping, viscerally exciting book contributes to a literature of perpetual fascination: the chronicles of pestilence." Booklist

Includes bibliographical references

Kolata, Gina

Flu; the story of the great influenza pandemic of 1918 and the search for the virus that caused it. Simon & Schuster 2001 330p il pa $15 *
          614.5

1. Influenza 2. Epidemiology

ISBN 0-7432-0398-4; 978-0-7432-0398-2

LC 00-64861

"A Touchstone book"

First published 1999 by Farrar, Straus & Giroux

Kolata focuses on the influenza epidemic of 1918, during which "at least 20 million people and possibly more than 40 million people throughout the world took sick and died." Time

"Clearly explaining both the science and the social toll of the pandemic, Kolata writes an admirable history and soberly spells out how the U.S. government is prepared—or unprepared—for a similar public health threat today." Publ Wkly

Includes bibliographical references

Marriott, Edward, 1966-
Plague: a story of science, rivalry, and the scourge that won't go away. Metropolitan Bks. 2003 302p il $25 hardcover o.p.   **614.5**
1. Plague
ISBN 0-8050-6680-2   LC 2002-26325
This is "a contemporary history of the plague, from 1894, when top scientists Alexandre Yersin and Shibasaburo Kitasato vied to discover the source of a Hong Kong outbreak, to contemporary New York, which has as many rats as people." Libr J
"The scientists' competition is the stuff of movies, gripping even though Marriott reveals the ending early." Booklist
Includes bibliographical references

Nolen, Stephanie
28: stories of AIDS in Africa. Walker 2007 375p map $25.95   **614.5**
1. AIDS (Disease)—Personal narratives 2. Africa
ISBN 0-8027-1598-2; 978-0-8027-1598-2
Twenty-eight anecdotal stories that chronicle men, women, and children involved in every aspect of the African AIDS crisis.
This "is both an informative and a powerful read, which will help Western readers connect personally with a crisis that too often seems remote." Libr J
Includes bibliographical references

Oshinsky, David M., 1944-
Polio; an American story. Oxford University Press 2005 342p il $30; pa $16.95 *
                    614.5
1. Poliomyelitis vaccine
ISBN 0-19-515294-8; 0-19-530714-3 (pa)
                    LC 2004-25249
This is an account of the "effort to find a cure [for polio], from the March of Dimes to the discovery of the Salk and Sabin vaccines." Publisher's note
This book "is a rich and illuminating analysis that convincingly grounds the ways and means of modern American research in the response to polio." N Y Times Book Rev
Includes bibliographical references

Peters, C. J., 1940-
Virus hunter; thirty years of battling hot viruses around the world; {by} C.J. Peters, with Mark Olshaker. Anchor Bks. (NY) 1997 323p il pa $14.95 hardcover o.p.   **614.5**
1. Medicine—Research
ISBN 0-385-48558-1 (pa)   LC 97-977
Peters describes his career battling deadly diseases in the lab and in the field. He presents "details about generally ignored medical struggles in less-industrialized nations and warnings about the myriad human factors— from crowded slums, agricultural monocultures, and bureaucratic infighting to reduced science funding and managed health care—that make a future viral disaster possible, perhaps probable." Booklist
This book is "smoothly written and provides an interesting overview of its author's career and education in the workings of medical bureaucracies." Libr J

Preston, Richard
The hot zone. Random House 1994 300p pa $14 hardcover o.p.   **614.5**
1. Ebola virus 2. Animal experimentation
ISBN 0-385-49522-6 (pa)   LC 94-13415
"Ebola, a lethal virus that slumbers in an unknown host somewhere in the rain forest, sneaked into the United States in 1989 in a shipment of primates that ended up in a monkey house in Reston, Virginia. This virus jumps between species easily, and takes only weeks to kill its victim, with gory hemorrhaging from various orifices. Preston tells the suspenseful tale of its detection, and gives vivid life to the members of the SWAT team that, for eighteen bio-hazardous days, combatted the strain now known as Ebola Reston." New Yorker

Rhodes, Richard, 1937-
Deadly feasts; tracking the secrets of a terrifying new plague. Simon & Schuster 1997 259p il pa $13 hardcover o.p.   **614.5**
1. Prion diseases
ISBN 0-684-84425-7 (pa)   LC 97-320
This is an "account of how scientists have tracked the emergence of a new group of fatal brain diseases—transmissible spongiform encephalopathies (TSEs)—that affect humans (Creutzfeldt-Jakob disease) and animals (mad cow disease). . . . These diseases are spread via 'industrial cannibalism' (e.g., infected animal remains fed to animals, humans eating contaminated meat)." Libr J
"Rhodes offers the first popular documentation of a disaster with profound implications." Booklist

Siegel, Marc, 1956-
Bird flu; everything you need to know about the next pandemic. Wiley 2006 202p pa $12.95
                    614.5
1. Avian influenza
ISBN 978-0-470-03864-2; 0-470-03864-0
                    LC 2005-36110
The author "cites evidence that the death rate from avian flu could be much lower than the reported estimate of 50% and it will probably not mutate to be readily transmissible between humans. . . . Revisiting the West Nile virus, anthrax, SARS and bioterrorism panics, Siegel sees bird flu as the latest 'bug du jour' hyped by government and media alarmism. . . . Siegel's exemplary bedside manner makes this dose of common sense go down easy." Publ Wkly
Includes bibliographical references

Spurlock, Morgan, 1970-
Don't eat this book; fast food and the supersizing of America. G. P. Putnam's Sons 2005 308p $21.95; pa $14   **614.5**
1. Convenience foods 2. Food industry 3. Restaurants
ISBN 0-399-15260-1; 0-425-21023-5 (pa)
                    LC 2005-43196
The author "describes America's obesity epidemic, its relation to the fast food industry, the industry's cozy relations to U.S. government agencies and how the problem is spreading worldwide. . . . His book is a powerful tool in his rip-roaring campaign to turn around America's love-hate relationship with fast food." Publ Wkly
Includes bibliographical references

Tayman, John

The Colony; John Tayman. Scribner 2006 421p il maps $27.50 *   **614.5**

1. Leprosy 2. Hawaii—History

ISBN 0-7432-3300-X   LC 2005-47767

"A Lisa Drew book."

This is a "history of the leper colony at the Hawaiian island Molokai. . . . Tayman's crisp, flowing writing and inclusion of personal stories and details make this an utterly engrossing look at a heartbreaking chapter in Hawaiian history." Booklist

Waldman, Murray

Dying for a hamburger; modern meat processing and the epidemic of Alzheimer's disease; [by] Murray Waldman & Marjorie Lamb. Thomas Dunne Books/St. Martin's Press 2005 304p il $24.95   **614.5**

1. Alzheimer's disease 2. Meat industry

ISBN 0-312-34015-X   LC 2005-41367

First published 2004 in Canada

The authors "believe the increased incidence of Alzheimer's is due to mass consumption, and the resulting mass production, of meat over the last century, which would explain its rarity in places like India. . . . This isn't a jeremiad against eating meat. Waldman and Lamb lay out their case in a measured fashion that many will find convincing and disturbing." Publ Wkly

Includes bibliographical references

615   Pharmacology and therapeutics

The **AARP** guide to pills; essential information on more than 1,200 prescription and nonprescription medicines, including generics; editor in chief, Maryanne Hochadel. Sterling Pub. 2005 xxxvii, 981p il $24.95   **615**

1. Materia medica 2. Drugs

ISBN 1-4027-1740-7   LC 2005-54444

The content found in this drug reference handbook is based on the "Clinical Pharmacology database [http://www.clinicalpharmacology.com],produced by Gold Standard. . . . Each entry is accompanied by one or two photographs showing such things as the pill size, shape, color, markings, or packaging for common brands. Information is . . . laid out in the form of eight questions covering what each drug is for; what to tell health-care providers before taking the drug; how to take the drug; what to do if a dose is missed; how the drug interacts with other prescription, nonprescription, and illicit drugs as well as foods, beverages, and dietary supplements; what to watch for when taking the drug; what side effects are possible; and how the drug should be stored. . . . This volume is highly recommended and should be available in every public library branch in all communities across the country." Booklist

Booth, Martin, 1944-2004

Opium; a history. St. Martin's Press 1998 381p pa $14.95 hardcover o.p.   **615**

1. Opium

ISBN 0-312-20667-4 (pa)   LC 98-14951

First published 1997 in the United Kingdom

"The first six chapters set the historical scene over time, explore the scientific dimensions and consider the uses and preparations of opium in different cultures, from the medicinal to the escapist and the allegedly creative. The next three chapters focus largely on China. . . . The last seven chapters explore the international criminal distribution of opium in the recent era." N Y Times Book Rev

"An excellent historical treatment of the development, use, and misuse of the drug, as well as of society's efforts to control it." Libr J

Includes bibliographical references

Chevallier, Andrew

Encyclopedia of herbal medicine. 2nd ed. DK Pub. 2000 336p il $40   **615**

1. Materia medica 2. Medical botany

ISBN 0-7894-6783-6   LC 2001-268250

First published 1996 with title: The encyclopedia of medicinal plants

This provides information about the current uses, cultivation, habitat, and folklore of over 550 herbs.

This "volume remains a top choice for a library reference on the medicinal use of herbs for the public." Libr J

Consumer drug reference 2008. Consumer Repts. Bks. 2008 1752p il $44.95 *   **615**

1. Drugs

ISBN 978-1-933524-11-5; 1-933524-11-1

Annual. First published 1980 with title: United States Pharmacopeia drug information for the consumer. Variant title: Complete drug reference

At head of title on cover: Consumer reports; Published in conjunction with the American Society of Health-System Pharmacists

Including more than 12,000 medicines, "this work presents drug information to the patient in clear and easy-to-read language. The drugs are listed by their generic names. The drug monographs make up the greatest portion of the source. Information provided for each drug includes brand names, general description, risks to be considered before taking the medicine (e.g., allergies, pregnancy, breastfeeding), proper use, precautions to be taken while using the medicine, and side effects." Am Ref Books Annu, 1993

Gorman, Jack M.

The essential guide to psychiatric drugs. Rev. and updated 4th ed. St. Martin's Press 2007 xxiv, 424p pa $19.95 *   **615**

1. Psychotropic drugs

ISBN 978-0-312-36879-1; 0-312-36879-8

LC 2007-32207

First published 1990

This guide covers psychotropic prescription medications, including information such as side effects and withdrawal symptoms.

"Since most psychiatric drugs are prescribed by nonpsychiatric physicians, this work will be useful for them and for nurse practitioners as well as for patients and families. Essential for all general libraries." Libr J

Includes bibliographical references

Graedon, Joe

The people's pharmacy guide to home and herbal remedies; [by] Joe Graedon and Teresa Graedon. St. Martin's Press 1999 428p $27.95; pa $17.95 **615**

1. Herbs—Therapeutic use 2. Vitamins

ISBN 0-312-20779-4; 0-312-26764-9 (pa)

LC 99-26613

"The first section combines tested scientific research and accumulated folk wisdom to provide the health consumer with treatment suggestions for common ailments. Also included are possible causes and symptoms for selected conditions, as well as contact information for product manufacturers. The second section lists the 50 most commonly used herbs, including their ingredients and information on usage, dose, adverse effects, and drug interactions." Libr J

Hager, Thomas

The demon under the microscope; from battlefield hospitals to Nazi labs, one doctor's heroic search for the world's first miracle drug. Harmony Books 2006 340p $24.95 **615**

1. Domagk, Gerhard, 1895-1964 2. Sulfonamides

ISBN 1-4000-8213-7; 978-1-4000-8213-1

LC 2006-4510

The author "narrates the story of the race [by doctors such as Gerhard Domagk] to find the 'magic bullet' to eliminate diseases such as pneumonia, childbed fever, and gonorrhea. . . . Hager connects early innovations in medicine to the fortuitous and intuitive leaps that allowed early 20th-century researchers to create sulfa, the first antibiotic. . . . One is left with a sense of gratitude for the relative safety of modern medical practices." Libr J

Includes bibliographical references

Karch, Steven B.

The consumer's guide to herbal medicine. Advanced Res. Press 1999 240p il $29.95

615

1. Herbs—Therapeutic use 2. Materia medica

ISBN 1-889462-06-3

This "guide reviews 67 of the most popular medicinal herbs, including chamomile, echinacea, garlic, ginseng, and St. John's wort. . . . Each two- to three-page entry contains an illustration of the plant. Full botanical and common names are given as well as the plant's geographic origin and the documented and legendary history of its use. Proven effects (based on recent research data), potential problems, warnings, and safe dosage amounts are included." Booklist

Kuhn, Cynthia

Buzzed; the straight facts about the most used and abused drugs from alcohol to ecstasy; {by} Cynthia Kuhn, Scott Swartzwelder, Wilkie Wilson; with Leigh Heather Wilson and Jeremy Foster. 2nd ed. Norton 2003 345p il pa $16.95 **615**

1. Drugs 2. Drug abuse

ISBN 0-393-32493-1

LC 2003-11411

First published 1998

This guide discusses "drugs, from alcohol, caffeine, and nicotine to heroin, ecstasy, and Special K. In both quick-reference summaries and in-depth analysis, it reports on how these drugs enter the body, how they manipulate the brain, their short-term and long-term effects, the kinds of 'high' they produce, and the circumstances in which they can be deadly." Publisher's note

"The book adopts a straight, neutral tone that reflects its commitment to providing unbiased, scientific fact. . . . Best of all, the descriptions are jargon-free, making this book a great choice for anyone looking for clear, reliable information about any kind of drug." Publ Wkly

Includes bibliographical references

Lax, Eric

The mold in Dr. Florey's coat; the story of the penicillin miracle. Henry Holt and Co. 2004 307p il $25; pa $15 **615**

1. Penicillin

ISBN 0-8050-6790-6; 0-8050-7778-2 (pa)

LC 2003-56685

"A John Macrae book"

Penicillin was discovered in 1928. "But it took a team of Oxford scientists headed by Howard Florey and Ernest Chain four more years to develop it as the first antibiotic. . . . Lax tells the story behind the discovery and why it took so long to develop the drug." Publisher's note

"In this fluent, entertaining report on the history of the arguably most significant medical discovery of the twentieth century, Lax delves into the lives of the colorful scientists who played significant roles in developing the antibiotic." Booklist

Includes bibliographical references

The **Merck** index; an encyclopedia of chemicals, drugs, and biologicals; Maryadele J. O'Neil, editor; Patricia E. Heckelman, senior associate editor; Cherie B. Koch, associate editor; Kristin J. Roman, assistant editor; Catherine M. Kenny, editorial assistant; Maryann R. D'Arecca, administrative assistant. 14th ed. Merck 2006 various paging il $125 * **615**

1. Materia medica 2. Drugs

ISBN 0-911910-00-X; 978-0-911910-00-1

Also available CD-ROM version and online

First published 1889. Periodically revised

Includes CD-ROM

"Technical descriptions of the preparation, properties, uses, commercial names, and toxicity of drugs and medicines." N Y Public Libr Book of How & Where to Look It Up

Miller, Richard Lawrence

The encyclopedia of addictive drugs. Greenwood Press 2002 491p $75 **615**

ISBN 0-313-31807-7 LC 2002-75332

"The more than 130 substances included are both natural and pharmaceutical products, all associated with misuse and addiction. Listed by common name, the initial citation includes pronunciation, Chemical Abstracts Service Registry Number, formal and informal names, drug type, U.S. availability, and more. The accompanying article discusses uses, drawbacks, abuse factors, drug interactions, cancer risks, and effects on pregnancy, and concludes with a bibliography." SLJ

Physician's desk reference 2008. 62nd ed. Medical Economics 2007 3482p $94.95　　**615**

1. Materia medica

ISSN 0093-4461

ISBN 978-1-56363-660-8; 1-56363-660-3

Annual. First published 1947. Title varies

"Latest available information intended for physicians on over 2,000 products. Covers dosage, contraindications, precautions, side effects, and undesirable interactions. The information is furnished by the manufacturers of the various products. Product identification in color." N Y Public Libr Book of How & Where to Look It Up

Physicians desk reference for nonprescription drugs, dietary supplements, and herbs 2008. 29th ed. Thomson Healthcare 2008 400p il $59.95 *　　**615**

1. Nonprescription drugs

ISSN 1044-1395

ISBN 978-1-5636-3662-2; 1-5636-3662-X

Also available CD-ROM version and online

Annual. First published 1980 by Medical Economics with title: Physicians desk reference for nonprescription drugs

"A companion to the Physician's Desk Reference. Provides essential information on nonprescription drugs. Indexed by manufacturer, product name, product category, and active ingredients." N Y Public Libr Book of How & Where to Look It Up

Seaman, Barbara

The greatest experiment ever performed on women; exploding the estrogen myth. Hyperion 2003 332p $24.95　　**615**

1. Estrogen 2. Menopause

ISBN 0-7868-6853-8　　LC 2004-271241

The author "demonstrates that the pandemic abuse of the trust women place in their doctors begins with medical practitioners, abetted by drug manufacturers and the Food and Drug Administration, from synthetic estrogen's 1938 debut onward." Booklist

"Seaman passionately and convincingly argues that women have been unneccessarily put at risk by doctors treating menopause as a disease." Publ Wkly

Talbott, Shawn

A guide to understanding dietary supplements; magic bullets or modern snake oil? [by] Shawn M. Talbott. Haworth Press 2003 xxv, 713p il $119.95; pa $59.95　　**615**

1. Dietary supplements 2. Drug industry

ISBN 0-7890-1455-6; 0-7890-1456-4 (pa)

LC 2002-68770

This overview of the dietary supplement industry and its products "examines more than 140 supplements arranged under broad categories such as weight loss and joint health." Booklist

Includes bibliographical references

Taylor, Leslie

The healing power of rainforest herbs; a guide to understanding and using herbal medicinals; Leslie Taylor. Square One Publishers 2005 519p il pa $23.95　　**615**

1. Herbs—Therapeutic use 2. Tropical plants

ISBN 0-7570-0144-0　　LC 2004-22843

The author "introduces readers to the rain forest environment, methods of plant preparation, and herbal recipes for treating common ailments. She describes approximately 75 plants in detail, providing scientific and common names, dosage, preparation, chemical composition, traditional and modern usage, clinical research, and contraindications and interactions." Libr J

Includes bibliographical references

615.5　Therapeutics

Bausell, R. Barker, 1942-

Snake oil science; the truth about complementary and alternative medicine. Oxford University Press 2007 324p il $24.95

615.5

1. Alternative medicine

ISBN 978-0-19-531368-0; 0-19-531368-2

LC 2007-10217

The author builds a "case against CAM, beginning with a look at the history of CAMs and placebos, then the 'poorly trained scientists' and flawed studies (among more than 300 analyzed for this book) that have historically supported CAM's efficacy. . . . Entertaining and informative, with plenty of diverting anecdotal examples, Bausell offers non-professionals and pros a thorough look at the science on CAM, along with a complementary lesson in the methods of good medical research." Publ Wkly

Includes bibliographical references

Bruce, Debra Fulghum, 1951-

Miracle touch; a complete guide to hands-on therapies that have the amazing ability to heal; {by} Debra Fulghum Bruce; foreword by Dolores Krieger. Three Rivers Press 2003 xxi, 216p pa $12.95　　**615.5**

1. Alternative medicine 2. Touch

ISBN 0-609-80734-X　　LC 2002-7443

The author covers "the various types of TT {Therapeutic Touch}, including acupuncture and acupressure, massage, reflexology, and Reiki. For each therapy, they include how it originated, how it works, what it can treat, how therapists are trained and/or certified, and research or case studies. . . . This practical, well-written guide is recommended for most alternative health and consumer health collections." Libr J

Includes bibliographical references

The **Gale** encyclopedia of alternative medicine; Jacqueline L. Longe, project editor. 2nd ed. Thomson Gale 2005 4v il set $445 *

615.5

1. Alternative medicine—Encyclopedias

ISBN 0-7876-7424-9　　LC 2004-22502

First published 2001

The Gale encyclopedia of alternative medicine—
Continued

New edition in preparation

This encyclopedia "identifies 150 types of alternative medicine being practiced today, including reflexology, acupressure, acupuncture, chelation therapy, kinesiology, yoga, chiropractic, Feldenkrais, polarity therapy, detoxification, naturopathy, Chinese medicine, biofeedback, Ayurveda and osteopathy." Publisher's note

For a fuller review, see: Booklist, May 1, 2005

Includes bibliographical references

The **Illustrated** encyclopedia of body-mind disciplines; Nancy Allison, editor. Rosen Pub. Group 1999 xxxii, 448p il $105.95

615.5

1. Alternative medicine

ISBN 0-8239-2546-3   LC 98-24969

This "text is divided into 16 sections, each of which begins with an introductory essay discussing the disciplines included in that section. Each discipline is described by a certified practitioner in terms of history, basic principles, and potential benefits and risks. Short resources/reading lists follow each discipline description." Libr J

Includes bibliographical references and index

Maleskey, Gale

Nature's medicines; from asthma to weight gain, from colds to high cholesterol: the most powerful all-natural cures; by Gale Maleskey, and the editors of Prevention Health Books. Rodale Press 1999 688p $31.95   **615.5**

1. Naturopathy 2. Alternative medicine

ISBN 1-57954-028-7   LC 99-15694

The first three sections of this health guide cover "vitamins, minerals, herbs, and emerging supplements. The major portion of {the book} follows, with an . . . A-Z listing of 61 substances, from Acidophilus to Zinc. Sidebars provide botanical names and highlight special instructions and cautions. Following this section is an A-Z listing of more than 75 health concerns." Booklist

Mayo Clinic book of alternative medicine. Time Inc. Home Entertainment 2007 192p il $24.95

615.5

1. Alternative medicine

ISBN 978-1-93340-592-6; 1-93340-592-9

LC 2006-906801

Subtitle on jacket: The new approach to using the best of natural therapies and conventional medicine

This book features "dozens of natural therapies that have worked safely for many patients in treating 20 top health issues." Publisher's note

McTaggart, Lynne

The field: the quest for the secret force of the universe. HarperCollins Pubs. 2002 288p pa $12.95 hardcover o.p.   **615.5**

1. Alternative medicine 2. Mind and body

ISBN 0-06-093117-5 (pa)   LC 2002-17348

The author "describes scientific discoveries that she believes point to a unifying concept of the universe, one that reconciles mind with matter, classic Newtonian science with quantum physics and, most importantly, science with religion." Publ Wkly

Includes bibliographical references

Murray, Michael T.

Encyclopedia of natural medicine; {by} Michael T. Murray, Joseph Pizzorno. rev 2nd ed. Prima Pub. 1998 946p il pa $24.95   **615.5**

ISBN 0-7615-1157-1   LC 97-50569

First published 1991

This volume is divided into three parts. Part I explains the philosophy and principles of natural medicine; Part II covers body systems, and specific health problems are dealt with in Part III

Includes bibliographical references

Navarra, Tova

The encyclopedia of complementary and alternative medicine; foreword by Adam Perelman. Facts on File 2004 xxiii, 276p $75; pa $18.95

615.5

1. Alternative medicine—Encyclopedias

ISBN 0-8160-4997-1; 0-8160-6226-9 (pa)

LC 2003-43415

"The topics in this book . . . range from yoga, chiropractic, and homeopathy to herbal remedies, imagery and visualization, massage, medication, and naturopathy. . . . Besides the entries, this important resource offers appendixes that list professional and lay organizations and herbs used in varieties of medical disciplines, and a time line of the various therapies." Choice

Includes bibliographical references

Pelletier, Kenneth R.

The best alternative medicine; What works? What does not? introduction by Andrew Weil. Simon & Schuster 2000 448p hardcover o.p. pa $15   **615.5**

1. Alternative medicine

ISBN 0-684-84207-6; 978-0-7432-0027-1 (pa); 0-7432-0027-6 (pa)   LC 99-26629

Pelletier "explains alternative and complementary medicine including commonly used treatment modalities and 75 medical conditions and correlating therapies. What sets Pelletier's work apart in this genre are cited studies and references. The selected bibliography alone is more than 50 pages long." Libr J

Includes bibliographical references

Schneider, Edward L.

What your doctor hasn't told you and the health store clerk doesn't know; the truth about alternative treatment and what works; [by] Edward L. Schneider, M.D., & Leigh Ann Hirschman. Avery 2006 267p pa $19.95   **615.5**

1. Alternative medicine

ISBN 1-58333-252-9; 978-1-58333-252-8

LC 2006-42811

Schneider, Edward L.—*Continued*

"Evaluating the latest medical research on topics ranging from arthritis, depression, menopause and male libido to heart disease, brain function and cancer, . . . [the author] outlines his recommendations for a combination of conventional and alternative treatments. . . . Schneider's balanced view of integrative therapies and his great fund of practical and medical advice are both reassuring and invigorating." Publ Wkly

615.8 Specific therapies and kinds of therapies

Campbell, Don G.

The Mozart effect; tapping the power of music to heal the body, strengthen the mind, and unlock the creative spirit; {by} Don Campbell. Avon Bks. 1997 332p il pa $14 hardcover o.p.   **615.8**
1. Music therapy 2. Music—Psychological aspects
ISBN 0-06-093720-3 (pa)   LC 97-27570
The author "uses case histories to show how music can enhance memory, learning, and creativity. Properly chosen and presented, music can also alleviate and in some cases apparently cure medical problems, he says." Booklist
Includes bibliographical references

Hugo, Lynne

Where the trail grows faint; a year in the life of a therapy dog team. University of Nebraska Press 2005 142p (River teeth literary nonfiction prize) $22   **615.8**
1. Dogs 2. Pet therapy 3. Elderly—Care
ISBN 0-8032-2432-X   LC 2004-24174
The author "shares insights she gained through the nursing home visits she made with her therapy dog, Hannah, a chocolate Labrador Retriever obtained from a rescue organization. . . . Recommended not only for dog lovers interested in learning more about the training and accomplishments of a therapy dog but also for nurses, social workers, gerontologists, and anyone facing the prospect of long-term care for aging parents." Libr J

Mitchell, Deborah R.

The Botox miracle; [by] Deborah Mitchell; consulting medical editor, Roberta D. Sengelmann. Pocket Bks. 2002 212p il pa $11   **615.8**
1. Botulinum toxin 2. Skin—Care
ISBN 0-7434-6463-X   LC 2003-544572
"A Lynn Sonberg book"
The author "describes how wrinkles develop and how Botox works to reduce or eliminate them. Covered are how to find a doctor, what to expect during treatment, the frequency of treatments, side effects, and possible complications. Also describes other wrinkle remedies for Botox-resistant areas. Simply written, this is a good introduction to the subject." Libr J

Panno, Joseph

Gene therapy; treating disease by repairing genes. Facts on File 2004 172p il (New biology) $35   **615.8**
1. Gene therapy
ISBN 0-8160-4948-3   LC 2003-25851
"This book provides an account of the research leading to the first successful gene therapy trial and discusses the worldwide attention and subsequent controversy caused by the tragic death of a patient receiving gene therapy, as well as the future prospects and general ethics of gene therapy." Publisher's note
Includes bibliographical references

Wise, Anna

Awakening the mind; a guide to mastering the power of your brain waves. Tarcher/Putnam 2002 255p il pa $16.95   **615.8**
1. Mental healing 2. Spiritual healing 3. Brain
ISBN 1-58542-145-6   LC 2001-53501
"This work aims to help readers improve their mental powers by optimizing brain-wave patterns. . . . [Wise discusses] the four types of brain-wave patterns, or EEGs, giving readers 'subjective landmarks' to help them gauge their own patterns without an EEG biofeedback machine." Libr J

615.9 Toxicology

Barker, Rodney, 1946-

And the waters turned to blood; the ultimate biological threat. Simon & Schuster 1997 346p il pa $14 hardcover o.p.   **615.9**
1. Burkholder, JoAnn M., 1953- 2. Algae 3. Poisons and poisoning
ISBN 0-684-83845-1 (pa)   LC 97-86
"Barker follows the work of Dr. JoAnn Burkholder, a scientist from North Carolina State University, as she attempts to obtain academic respect and funding for her research on a new species of dinoflagellate that is responsible for a number of major fish kills. . . . He presents a detailed discussion of Burkholder's struggles with state officials as she becomes convinced that the organism is toxic, not only to fish but also to humans. Written in a clear, non-technical style." Libr J

Callahan, Joan R.

Biological hazards; an Oryx sourcebook. Oryx Press 2002 385p il (Oryx sourcebooks on hazards and disasters) $64.95 *   **615.9**
1. Communicable diseases 2. Poisons and poisoning 3. Environmental health
ISBN 1-57356-385-4   LC 2001-55184
This sourcebook provides "introductory information on a wide range of biological hazards. . . . Chapters divide hazards into categories: human pathogens in water, food, and air; those transmitted by contact; plant and animal pathogens and pests; venoms, toxins, and allergens; and animals that are a threat for predatory or other behavior. Another chapter provides information on controversial topics such as immunization and biological warfare. . . .

Callahan, Joan R.—*Continued*
The chapters that deal with different kinds of hazards offer extensive references and recommended readings. Lists of additional resources, including statistics and documents, print resources, nonprint resources, and organizations, comprise the final chapters." Booklist
Includes bibliographical references

Emsley, John
The elements of murder; [a history of poison] Oxford University Press 2005 421p il $30; pa $19.95   **615.9**
1. Poisons and poisoning
ISBN 0-19-280599-1; 0-19-280600-9 (pa)
LC 2005-299328
The author "traces the evolution of alchemy and explains the central role that the quest to turn metal into gold plays in the history of poison. . . . Later chapters discuss the history, uses, and murderous abuses of mercury, arsenic, antimony, lead, and thallium." Booklist
Reading this book "is like watching a hundred episodes of 'CSI,' but without having to sit through the tedious personal relationships of the characters. . . . Emsley mines what he calls 'the darker side of the periodic table' with consummate skill." N Y Times Book Rev
Includes bibliographical references

Fagin, Dan
Toxic deception; how the chemical industry manipulates science, bends the law, and endangers your health; [by] Dan Fagin, Marianne Lavelle, and the Center for Public Integrity. Common Courage Press 1999 xxv, 271p pa $17.95
615.9
1. Chemicals 2. Chemical industry
ISBN 1-56751-162-7   LC 99-13742
First published 1996 by Carol Pub. Group
This work examines "the regulatory foundations of four suspect chemicals—atrazine, alachor, formaldehyde, and perchloroethylene—and the chemical industry's role in the design and calculation of risk assessments. . . . This well-researched expose is recommended." Libr J
Includes bibliographical references

Markowitz, Gerald E.
Deceit and denial; the deadly politics of industrial pollution; [by] Gerald Markowitz and David Rosner. University of Calif. Press 2002 xx, 408p il $45; pa $19.95   **615.9**
1. Environmental health 2. Industrial waste 3. Pollution
ISBN 0-520-21749-7; 0-520-24063-4 (pa)
LC 2001-58515
"This is a historical acccount of corporate control of the lead, plastics, and petroleum industries and the campaign of denial regarding the toxic effects on workers, consumers, and the general public of chemicals used in the manufacture of paint, toys, furniture, plastics, and other products. . . . This is not another diatribe about industrial pollution. Instead, it is a well-researched work that analyzes the conflict between industry's need to pro-

vide products that make life easier for consumers and the public's demand for legislation and standards to protect them from toxic pollution caused by the manufacture of these products. Recommended for health, environment, and law collections." Libr J
Includes bibliographical references

Turkington, Carol
The poisons and antidotes sourcebook; foreword by Shirley K. Osterhout. 2nd ed. Facts on File 1999 408p $38.50; pa $16.95   **615.9**
1. Poisons and poisoning
ISBN 0-8160-3959-3; 0-8160-3960-7 (pa)
LC 98-55190
First published 1994 with title: Poisons and antidotes
This book "describes more than 600 toxins and their sources, including: common household poisons; insecticides and fertilizers; poisonous spiders, snakes, and other venomous creatures; addictive drugs, such as nicotine and cocaine; poison ivy, sumac, and other toxic shrubs." Publisher's note
Includes bibliographical references

616   Diseases

Bacci, Ingrid
Effortless pain relief; a guide to self-healing from chronic pain. Free Press 2005 255p $24
616
1. Chronic pain
ISBN 0-7432-6075-9   LC 2005-295415
This book presents an "explanation of how stress creates chronic pain, along with . . . self-help techniques for reducing and even eliminating pain." Publisher's note

Bakalar, Nick
Where the germs are; a scientific safari; {by} Nicholas Bakalar. Wiley 2003 262p il $24.95 *
616
1. Microbiology 2. Germ theory of disease 3. Bacteria
ISBN 0-471-15589-6   LC 2003-271569
This book is "about our everyday interactions with microbes. . . . It reveals some of the extraordinary things scientists now know about these most ordinary companions." Publisher's note
The author's "excellent chapter on childhood diseases and vaccines should be required reading for parents, and teenagers should be plunked down in a chair with the chapter on sexually transmitted diseases. . . . His writing is witty, and he gives all the details of germs and illnesses without medical school jargon." Publ Wkly

Biddle, Wayne
A field guide to germs. 2nd Anchor Books ed. Anchor Bks. (NY) 2002 209p il pa $13.95
616
1. Microbiology 2. Germ theory of disease
ISBN 1-400-03051-X   LC 2002-511927
First published 1995 by Holt & Co.

Biddle, Wayne—*Continued*

"Relaying essential information about the 100 most prevalent, powerful, or literarily famous microbiological malefactors in dictionary-encyclopedia style, Biddle injects social and political history into the exposition to provide fuller understanding of germs, their roles in society, their histories, and their current statuses. . . . Eminently entertaining, the book yet has the serious purpose of showing how concerns other than science and the relief of human suffering have affected the course of medical history." Booklist {review of 1995 edition}

Includes bibliographical references

Crawford, Dorothy H.

The invisible enemy; a natural history of viruses. Oxford Univ. Press 2000 275p il hardcover o.p. pa $14.95   **616**

1. Viruses

ISBN 0-19-850332-6; 0-19-856481-3 (pa)

LC 00-36756

The author begins by explaining how viruses "subvert the internal machinery of living cells to reproduce and spread. . . . Ms. Crawford examines the threats posed by the Lassa and Hanta viruses—as well as Ebola, . . . and assesses the prospects for a flu pandemic like that of 1918, which infected half the world's population." Economist

"Crawford offers new knowledge and insights for any reader, regardless of the depth of their science education." New Sci

Includes bibliographical references

Dillard, James

The chronic pain solution; your personal path to pain relief; [by] James N. Dillard with Leigh Ann Hirschman. Bantam Bks. 2002 xxiii, 439p il $24.95; pa $13.95   **616**

1. Chronic pain

ISBN 0-553-80183-X; 0-553-38111-3 (pa)

LC 2002-23225

The author discusses how pain affects your body and mind. He outlines treatment methods, from state-of-the-art microsurgery and pharmaceuticals to acupuncture, yoga and feedback. He provides chapters on various forms of pain, from arthritis and back pain to migraines and fibromyalgia and includes a pain-control diet.

Includes bibliographical references

Disease management sourcebook; edited by Joyce Brennfleck Shannon. Omnigraphics 2008 649p il map (Health reference series) $84   **616**

1. Chronic diseases 2. Consumer education

ISBN 978-0-7808-1002-0   LC 2008-4554

"Basic consumer health information about coping with chronic and serious illnesses, navigating the health care system, communicating with health care providers, assessing health care quality, and making informed health care decisions, including facts about second opinions, hospitalization, surgery, and medications along with a section about children with chronic conditions, information about legal, financial, and insurance issues, a glossary of related terms, and directories of additional resources." Title page

"An essential guide to navigating the health care rapids." Libr J

Includes bibliographical references

Gawande, Atul

Better; a surgeon's notes on performance. Metropolitan 2007 273p $24   **616**

1. Medicine 2. Medical ethics

ISBN 978-0-8050-8211-1; 0-8050-8211-5

LC 2006-46962

A collection of "essays on topics as varied as hospital hand washing, polio in India, surgical tents in the Iraq war, physicians' salaries, malpractice insurance, and doctors' roles in lethal injections." Libr J

"Mostly, and repeatedly, the question Gawande pose at the heart of each of his essays is deceptively straightforward and can-do: How do we get it right, or barring that, just an ioat better? . . . Gawande is unassuming in every way, and yet his prose is infused with steadfast determination and hope." Boston Globe

Groopman, Jerome E., 1952-

The anatomy of hope; how people prevail in the face of illness; [by] Jerome Groopman. Random House 2004 248p $24.95   **616**

1. Patients 2. Hope

ISBN 0-375-50638-1   LC 2003-46692

The author "discovered that hope could actually cause physiological change, blocking pain and improving respiratory, circulatory, and motor function. He shares personal experiences from his own life and his patients' case histories that illustrate the power and importance of hope. . . . An excellent narrative for public libraries." Libr J

Includes bibliographical references

Harrington, Anne, 1960-

The cure within; a history of mind-body medicine. W.W. Norton 2008 336p il $25.95

616

1. Psychosomatic medicine 2. Mind and body 3. Mental healing

ISBN 978-0-393-06563-3; 0-393-06563-4

LC 2007-30906

This is a history of alternative and complementary medicine.

The author "has produced a book that desperately needed to be written." N Y Times Book Rev

Includes bibliographical references

Koestler, Angela J.

Understanding chronic pain; [by] Angela J. Koestler, Ann Myers. University Press of Miss. 2002 162p il (Understanding health and sickness series) $28; pa $12 *   **616**

1. Pain

ISBN 1-57806-439-2; 1-57806-440-6 (pa)

LC 2002-1017

The authors "provide basic information about cultural history, definitions, theories, and causes of pain. They describe treatment specialists and the usual and varied

Koestler, Angela J.—*Continued*
approaches to pain relief and the responsibility of self-care. . . . This is a compact and readable self-help handbook for patients and their families." Choice

Moalem, Sharon, 1973-
Survival of the sickest; a medical maverick discovers why we need disease; [by] Sharon Moalem, with Jonathan Prince. William Morrow 267p $25.95   **616**
1. Diseases 2. Evolution 3. Natural selection 4. Genetics
ISBN 978-0-06-088965-4; 0-06-088965-9
                                        LC 2006-50128
The author "uses numerous examples to show how analyzing history might help explain why a certain genetic trait that seems useless—even harmful—to us now made perfect sense in our ancestors' environment. He also introduces such recent research topics as host manipulation, noncoding DNA, and epigenetics. The particularly coherent writing style makes complex ideas accessible to people without a science background. With the book's emphasis on evolution's goals of survival and reproduction, readers will gain insights into why evolution may have selected for certain traits and why having that insight may better our lives." Libr J

Moyers, Bill
Healing and the mind; {by} Bill Moyers; Betty Sue Flowers, editor; David Grubin, executive editor; Elizabeth Meryman-Brunner, art research. Doubleday 1993 369p il pa $21.95 hardcover o.p.
                                        616
1. Medicine 2. Mind and body 3. Psychophysiology
ISBN 0-385-47687-6 (pa)   LC 92-31074
In this "companion volume to a PBS TV series, Moyers explores the roles of thoughts and emotions in illness and health through interviews with 16 doctors and scientists." Publ Wkly

Newton, David E.
Stem cell research. Facts on File 2007 284p il (Library in a book) $45   **616**
1. Stem cell research
ISBN 978-0-8160-6576-9; 0-8160-6576-4
                                        LC 2005-32803
"Covering court cases, legislation, and relevant policies, this volume also includes a chronology; a glossary; a guide to further research; an annotated bibliography . . . ; appendixes; as well as an index." Publisher's note
Includes bibliographical references

Panno, Joseph
Stem cell research; medical applications and ethical controversy. Facts on File 2005 178p il (New biology) $35; pa $18.95   **616**
1. Stem cell research
ISBN 0-8160-4949-1; 0-8160-6931-X (pa)
                                        LC 2003-25975
The author "explains how stem cells can be used to treat, and possibly cure, a wide variety of diseases, and

he predicts that the use of adult stem cells will soon be routine. . . . In addition, there is a chapter summarizing cell biology and recombinant DNA technology. A carefully done, in-depth . . . [book] that will work well for researchers and debaters, adults as well as teens." Booklist
Includes bibliographical references

Rosenfeld, Arthur
The truth about chronic pain; patients and professionals on how to face it, understand it, overcome it. Basic Bks. 2003 299p hardcover o.p. pa $14.95 *   **616**
1. Chronic pain
ISBN 0-465-07138-4; 978-0-465-07139-5 (pa); 0-465-07139-2 (pa)   LC 2002-151003
The author "interviews patients, healthcare professionals, ethicists, policymakers, and clergy to learn about pain from many viewpoints. The excellent result is an inspirational and moving book that sheds light on the issue and pleads for compassion." Libr J

Stephenson, Frank H.
DNA; how the biotech revolution is changing the way we fight disease; foreword by Herbert Boyer. Prometheus Books 2007 333p il $26
                                        616
1. Biotechnology 2. Medical genetics 3. Genetic engineering
ISBN 1-59102-482-X; 978-1-59102-482-8
                                        LC 2006-28339
"From heart disease to AIDS and cancer, . . . [the author describes] how the tools of biotechnology are being used to combat our most common afflictions. Stephenson examines a . . . variety of health threats and illnesses: HIV infection, the many forms of cancer, asthma, diabetes, Alzheimer's, obesity, and even erectile dysfunction." Publisher's note
Includes bibliographical references

Van Tilburg, Christopher
Mountain rescue doctor; wilderness medicine in the extremes of nature. St. Martin's Press 2007 293p il $24.95   **616**
1. Mountaineering 2. Rescue work
ISBN 978-0-312-35887-7; 0-312-35887-3
                                        LC 2007-28304
The author "is a member of the Hood River Crag Rats, the oldest search-and-rescue (S&R) team in the United States. Both adults and teens will relish his vivid recountings of efforts to rescue sports enthusiasts who got lost or injured in the mountains." Libr J

Wynbrandt, James
The encyclopedia of genetic disorders and birth defects; [by] James Wynbrandt and Mark D. Ludman. 3rd ed. Facts On File 2007 682p (Facts on File library of health and living) $75
                                        616
1. Birth defects—Encyclopedias
ISBN 978-0-8160-6396-3   LC 2006-100640
First published 1991

Wynbrandt, James—*Continued*

This book is a "single-volume reference to genetic disorders and birth defects. Topics are arranged in an . . . A-to-Z format covering everything from . . . basic genetic concepts to . . . screening and diagnostic techniques." Publisher's note

This "is an excellent resource for public and consumer-health libraries with limited budgets. It is a good starting point for research, too." Booklist

Includes bibliographical references

616.02   Special topics of diseases

American College of Physicians complete home medical guide; editor-in-chief David R. Goldmann; associate editor David A. Horowitz. 2nd American ed. DK Pub. 2003 1104p il $50

616.02

1. Medicine 2. Health self-care

ISBN 0-7894-9673-9

First published 1999

"Completely revised and updated." Cover

This guide discusses genetics, health, and health care; lifestyle issues such as diet, exercise, and substance abuse, medical examinations, lab tests and imaging techniques; drug treatment, surgery, and therapies. Illustrated with diagrams, anatomical artworks, and over 2000 photographs. A select listing of online medical sites is also included

American Medical Association family medical guide. 4th ed., completely rev. and updated. John Wiley & Sons 2004 1184p il $45 *

616.02

1. Medicine 2. Health self-care

ISBN 0-471-26911-5   LC 2004-5764

Replaces the third edition published 1994

First published 1982

Contents: What you should know: information to keep you healthy -- Staying healthy -- Diet and health -- Exercise, fitness, and health -- A healthy weight -- Reducing stress -- Staying safe -- Preventing violence -- Preventive health care -- Complementary and alternative medicine -- First aid and caregiving -- First aid -- Home caregiving -- What are your symptoms? -- Symptoms charts -- Health issues throughout life -- Children's health -- Adolescent health -- Sexuality -- Infertility -- Pregnancy and childbirth -- Dying and death -- Diseases, disorders, and other problems -- Disorders of the heart and circulation -- Blood disorders -- Disorders of the respiratory system -- Disorders of the brain and nervous system -- Behavioral, emotional, and mental disorders -- Disorders of the digestive system -- Disorders of the urinary tract -- Disorders of the male reproductive system -- Disorders of the female reproductive system and urinary tract -- Hormonal disorders -- Disorders of the immune system -- Infections and infestations -- Genetic disorders -- Disorders of the bones, muscles, and joints -- Disorders of the ear -- Eye disorders -- Disorders of the skin, hair, and nails -- Cosmetic surgery -- Teeth and gums

"This is a well-organized volume, considering the amount of information it covers." Publ Wkly

The **American** Red Cross first aid and safety handbook; [prepared by] American Red Cross and Kathleen A. Handal; foreword by Elizabeth Dole. Little, Brown 1992 321p il hardcover o.p. pa $18.95   **616.02**

1. First aid

ISBN 0-316-73645-7; 0-316-73646-5 (pa)

LC 91-24847

This first aid guidebook is based on course materials used by the Red Cross and covers how to handle such emergencies as allergic reactions, bleeding, choking, and heart attacks.

The **Merck** manual of medical information; Mark H. Beers, editor-in-chief; Andrew J. Fletcher, Thomas V. Jones, and Robert Porter, senior assistant editors; Michael Berkwits, and Justin L. Kaplan, assistant editors. 2nd home ed. Merck Res. Labs. 2003 xxxviii, 1907p il $37.50; pa $19.95   **616.02**

1. Medicine

ISBN 0-9119-1035-2; 0-7434-7733-2 (pa)

LC 2002-115250

Also available online

First published 1997

"A detailed table of contents lists 25 sections divided into chapters. The first, 'Fundamentals,' explains basic anatomy and physiology, the aging process, fitness, communicating with health professionals, and legal and ethical issues. The others cover specific organs, systems, diseases and disorders, drugs, and first aid. The sections dealing with organs and systems begin with the biology of the system and then explain the symptoms, diagnosis, prognosis, and treatment of diseases that may affect it. There are color diagrams of relevant anatomy as well as an eight-page insert of anatomical charts." Booklist

"Written for the layperson, articles are clear, comprehensive and detailed. There are excellent charts and illustrations to further make the material more understandable. Almost every conceivable medical condition is covered." Publ Wkly

616.07   Pathology

The **Johns** Hopkins consumer guide to medical tests; what you can expect, how you should prepare, what your results mean; Simeon Margolis, medical editor. Rebus 2001 400p il $39.95   **616.07**

1. Diagnosis

ISBN 0-929661-63-X   LC 2001-19980

"A John Hopkins health after 50 book"

This is a "guide to over 170 medical tests. . . . The entries, generally about two pages long, list the test's purpose and special concerns, what the results may mean, pretest preparations, risks and complications, and estimated cost." Libr J

Nuland, Sherwin B.

How we die; reflections on life's final chapter. Knopf 1994 278p pa $14 hardcover o.p.

616.07

1. Death

ISBN 0-679-74244-1 (pa)   LC 93-24590

Nuland, Sherwin B.—*Continued*

The author provides "information on the clinical, biological and emotional details of deaths resulting from heart disease, stroke, cancer, AIDS, Alzheimer's disease, old age, accidents, suicide, euthanasia and murder or violent physical assault." Publ Wkly

"Nuland is one of those rare physicians who know a great deal about a great deal, not only medicine but also its history and, beyond that, literature and the humanities." Commentary

Pagana, Kathleen Deska, 1952-

Mosby's diagnostic and laboratory test reference; [by] Kathleen Deska Pagana, Timothy James Pagana. 8th ed. Mosby Elsevier 2007 xxiii, 1095p il pa $44.95 *   **616.07**

1. Diagnosis 2. Nursing

ISBN 0-323-04634-7; 978-0-323-04634-3

         LC 2006-46759

First published 1992. Frequently revised

New edition in preparation

This handbook features alphabetically organized laboratory and diagnostic tests which "are presented in a consistent format. . . . Each test entry includes, where relevant, alternate or abbreviated test names; type of test; normal findings; possible critical values; test explanation and related physiology; contraindications; potential complications; interfering factors; procedure and patient care (before, during, and after); and abnormal findings." Publisher's note

Includes bibliographical references

Segen, J. C.

The patient's guide to medical tests; everything you need to know about the tests your doctor orders; [by] Joseph C. Segen and Josie Wade. 2nd ed. Facts on File 2002 418p (Facts on File library of health and living) $44   **616.07**

1. Diagnosis

ISBN 0-8160-4651-4   LC 2002-18824

First published 1997 with Joseph Stauffer as joint author

This "guide presents information on more than 1,000 commonly prescribed tests and procedures. Each entry includes a description of the test, patient preparation required, a description of the procedure itself, the reference range, what abnormal values may signify, and the approximate cost of each test." Publisher's note

Zuk, M. (Marlene), 1956-

Riddled with life; friendly worms, ladybug sex, and the parasites that make us who we are. Harcourt 2007 328p il $25   **616.07**

1. Pathology 2. Human ecology 3. Diseases 4. Adaptation (Biology) 5. Parasites

ISBN 978-0-15-101225-1; 0-15-101225-3

         LC 2006-28642

"Since the earliest days of life on earth, disease has evolved alongside us. Drawing on the latest research and studies, Zuk explains the role of disease in answering a fascinating range of questions such as: Why do men die younger than women? Why does the average male bird not have a penis? Why do we—and lots of other animals—get STDs? How is our obsession with cleanliness making us sicker? And how can parasites sometimes make us well?" Publisher's note

"Zuk has an amazing gift for turning experiments and facts into stories. . . . She is urging the public to take a new look at disease, though it's one that's well supported by the research. There are moments where she's speculating ahead of the science a bit, but those moments are clearly marked. Riddled with Life will change the way you look at public and private health." PopMatters

Includes bibliographical references

616.1   Diseases of cardiovascular system

Bloom, Miriam, 1934-

Understanding sickle cell disease. University Press of Miss. 1995 126p il map (Understanding health and sickness series) pa $11.95 hardcover o.p.   **616.1**

1. Sickle cell anemia

ISBN 0-87805-745-5 (pa)   LC 94-44275

Topics covered "include a discussion of who gets the disease (which includes not only people of African descent but of Mediterranean ancestry as well), the red blood cell, effects of the disease, care of sickle cell patients, family planning, and the search for a cure. An extensive list of organizations and support groups is included." Libr J

"Although it imparts much technical information, the book is very much for the lay reader." Booklist

Includes bibliographical references

Gould, K. Lance

Heal your heart; how you can prevent or reverse heart disease. Rutgers Univ. Press 1998 xxxi, 274p il pa $20 hardcover o.p.   **616.1**

1. Heart diseases

ISBN 0-8135-2896-8 (pa)   LC 97-39172

The author "advocates early diagnosis to minimize risk {of heart disease}, a very low-fat diet, moderate exercise, and the use of cholesterol-lowering drugs." Libr J

"Although Gould's lucid style . . . makes things easy for the reader, the uncluttered, well-labeled illustrations help substantially, too." Booklist

Includes bibliographical references

Heart attack! advice for patients by patients; [by] Kathleen Berra [et al.] Yale Univ. Press 2002 232p $32.50; pa $14.95   **616.1**

1. Heart diseases

ISBN 0-300-08980-5; 0-300-09190-7 (pa)

         LC 2001-33256

This "book on the current state of the diagnosis and treatment of heart attacks includes 11 personal accounts by patients and 5 chapters by health professionals. . . . Succinct yet detailed, this collection should prove valuable to both health professionals and the general public." Booklist

Includes bibliographical references

McGowan, Mary P., 1959-
Heart fitness for life; the essential guide to preventing and reversing heart disease; by Mary P. McGowan, with Jo McGowan Chopra. Oxford Univ. Press 1997 322p il pa $16.95 hardcover o.p.
616.1
1. Heart diseases—Prevention
ISBN 0-19-512909-1 (pa)   LC 97-29834
The author "seeks to cover all the bases of a heart-healthy lifestyle, particularly for those recovering from heart disease, by discussing diet, exercise, stress relief, smoking, and medications. The information is current, and much is drawn from the work of other experts in the field." Libr J
Includes bibliographical references

The **New** living heart diet; [by] Michael E. DeBakey [et al.] [Completely rev and updated] Simon & Schuster 1996 414p pa $16
616.1
1. Heart diseases—Diet therapy
ISBN 0-684-81188-X   LC 95-40787
"A Fireside book"
First published 1984 with title: The living heart diet
This book includes "information about risk factors for coronary heart disease and . . . dietary recommendations for preventing it. The first half relates such health considerations as cholesterol, diabetes and blood pressure to diet; menus and 300-plus recipes with complete nutritional analyses constitute the second half." Publ Wkly

Ornish, Dean
Love & survival; the scientific basis for the healing power of intimacy. HarperCollins Pubs. 1998 284p il pa $14 hardcover o.p.   **616.1**
1. Heart diseases 2. Health
ISBN 0-06-093020-9 (pa)   LC 98-141279
"Ornish argues that affection is crucial to health with research findings as well as clinical-anecdotal evidence. The second of six . . . chapters presents studies demonstrating that those who give and receive love are healthier than those who don't; this is intriguing and persuasive testimony that many may find squares with common sense. Succeeding chapters present the anecdotal evidence." Booklist

616.2   Diseases of respiratory system

Adams, Francis V.
The asthma sourcebook. 3rd ed. McGraw-Hill 2007 254p il pa $16.95   **616.2**
1. Asthma
ISBN 978-0-07-147652-2; 0-07-147652-0
LC 2006-22980
First published 1995 by Lowell House
Contains a wide variety of information about asthma, providing a description of the disease, and discussing medications, treatments, and self-management.
Includes bibliographical references

Brody, Jane E.
Jane Brody's allergy fighter. Norton 1997 127p il pa $10 hardcover o.p.   **616.2**
1. Allergy
ISBN 0-393-31635-1 (pa)   LC 96-34499
"Discussing the elements that cause allergies, the various OTC and prescription medications that may relieve symptoms, and special strategies for dealing with allergies in children, Brody also supplies a glossary and an information and product guide." Publ Wkly

Fanta, Christopher H.
The Harvard Medical School guide to taking control of asthma; a comprehensive prevention and treatment plan for you and your family; [by] Christopher H. Fanta, Lynda M. Cristiano, Kenan E. Haver, with Nancy Waring. Free Press 2003 331p il pa $14 *   **616.2**
1. Asthma
ISBN 0-7432-2478-7   LC 2003-63145
"The authors explain how asthma is diagnosed and how the various symptoms, such as shortness of breath, wheezing and tightness in the chest, manifest themselves in different individuals. A large portion of the book is devoted to a lengthy and highly useful discussion of the current therapies available, as well as the pros and cons of specific medications." Publ Wkly
Includes bibliographical references

Freedman, Michael R.
Living well with asthma; [by] Michael R. Freedman, Samuel J. Rosenberg, Cynthia L. Divino. Guilford Press 1998 213p pa $15.95
616.2
1. Asthma
ISBN 1-57230-051-5   LC 97-48747
The authors consider the "potentially serious psychological aspects of having a chronic disease. Aimed directly at the asthma sufferer, it includes case studies of commonly encountered problems and discusses family and broader issues that can constrain one's life." Libr J
Includes bibliographical references

Lung disorders sourcebook; edited by Dawn D. Matthews. Omnigraphics 2002 678p il (Health reference series) $78   **616.2**
1. Lungs—Diseases
ISBN 0-7808-0339-6   LC 2002-16976
"Basic consumer health information about emphysema, pneumonia, tuberculosis, asthma, cystic fibrosis, and other lung disorders. Including facts about diagnostic procedures, treatment strategies, disease prevention efforts, and such risk factors as smoking, air pollution, and exposure to asbestos, radon, and other agents: along with a glossary and resources for additional help and information." Title page
"This title is a great addition for public and school libraries because it provides concise health information on the lungs. Readers can start with this reference source and get satisfactory answers before proceeding to other medical reference tools for more in-depth information." Am Ref Books Annu, 2003

Silber, Sherman J.
How to get pregnant. Rev. ed. Little, Brown and Co. 2005 xl, 470p il $27.95; pa $18.99 *
616.2
1. Infertility 2. Reproductive technology
ISBN   0-316-01136-3;   978-0-316-01136-5;
0-316-06650-8 (pa); 978-0-316-06650-1 (pa)
LC 2005-2585
First published 1980 by Scribner
The author "begins with a review of the female anatomy and the physiology of conception before progressing to mechanisms for 'beating your biological clock'; following is coverage of male reproductive physiology and detailed discussions of procedures currently available to help overcome previously unmanageable fertility problems." Libr J
Includes bibliographical references

616.3 Diseases of digestive system

Achord, James L.
Understanding hepatitis. University Press of Miss. 2002 132p il (Understanding health and sickness series) $28; pa $12   **616.3**
1. Liver—Diseases
ISBN 1-57806-435-X; 1-57806-436-8 (pa)
LC 2001-49243
"The book is divided into seven sections: the liver and hepatitis; symptoms and complications of acute and chronic viral hepatitis; hepatitis A; hepatitis B; hepatitis C; other viruses and nonviral causes of hepatitis; and current research. . . . The book's all-encompassing and easy-to-read format helps readers better understand the scope of the disease." Choice
Includes bibliographical references

Chow, James H., 1948-
The encyclopedia of hepatitis and other liver diseases; [by] James H. Chow, Cheryl Chow. Facts on File 2005 372p (Facts on File library of health and living) $75 *   **616.3**
1. Liver—Diseases—Encyclopedias
ISBN 0-8160-5710-9; 978-0-8160-5710-8
LC 2005-18489
"With more than 150 entries, coverage ranges from symptoms, treatments, and research to tests, social issues, and much more. Appendixes list . . . relevant organizations, transplantation and Internet resources, and support groups for those with liver-related issues." Publisher's note
For a fuller review, see: Booklist, Dec. 1, 2006
Includes bibliographical references

Green, Peter H. R.
Celiac disease; a hidden epidemic; [by] Peter H. R. Green and Rory Jones. HarperCollins 2006 2006 334p il $22.95   **616.3**
1. Intestines—Diseases
ISBN 0-06-076693-X; 978-0-06-076693-1
LC 2006-295906

"Because the only treatment is removing gluten from the diet, seven of the 24 chapters are devoted to diet (e.g., foods that contain gluten, eliminating gluten, reading labels, cooking, and eating out). There are also appendixes on print and web resources and a list of gluten-free product manufacturers. This book is important for consumer health libraries and consumer health collections in public libraries." Libr J

Minocha, Anil, 1957-
The encyclopedia of the digestive system and digestive disorders; {by} Anil Minocha, Christine Adamec. Facts on File 2004 xxviii, 350p il (Facts on File library of health and living) $65 *
616.3
1.   Gastrointestinal   system—Encyclopedias
2. Digestive organs—Encyclopedias
ISBN 0-8160-4993-9   LC 2003-21432
This reference addresses "the gastrointestinal system, normal digestive functions, diseases, and preventive measures in more than 300 alphabetically arranged entries. . . . Entries on specific disorders (e.g., acid reflux, gallstones, and ulcers) include definitions, risk factors, symptoms, diagnosis, and treatment, when applicable. Extensive appendixes identify U.S. and Canadian organizations, associations, support groups, and poison control; they also list helpful web sites and suggested readings." Libr J

Palmer, Melissa
Dr. Melissa Palmer's guide to hepatitis & liver disease. Avery 2004 470p il pa $16.95
616.3
1. Liver—Diseases
ISBN 1-58333-188-3   LC 2003-63905
First published 1999
The author "discusses all facets of liver disease, from symptoms and tests to treatment options and lifestyle changes." Publisher's note

Pool, Robert, 1955-
Fat; fighting the obesity epidemic. Oxford Univ. Press 2000 292p $27.50   **616.3**
1. Obesity
ISBN 0-19-511853-7   LC 00-36731
The author "traces the history of obesity in Western society and the ups and downs of medical science's ability to determine what causes some people to gain a considerable amount of weight." Publ Wkly
"This fascinating investigative journey into the history of obesity will go a long way toward removing the stigma attached to being overweight and will increase our understanding of the complex issues that contribute to the obesity epidemic." Libr J

Zonderman, Jon

Understanding Crohn disease and ulcerative colitis; [by] Jon Zonderman and Ronald Vender. University Press of Miss. 2000 116p il (Understanding health and sickness series) $28; pa $12   **616.3**

1. Inflammatory bowel diseases
ISBN 1-57806-202-0; 1-57806-203-9 (pa)
LC 99-52483

"After describing how the digestive system functions, [the authors] show how it can go wrong. They deal with related medical conditions and how Crohn disease and ulcerative colitis can affect persons of different ages differently. Treatment can involve careful dieting . . . and medical and surgical procedures." Booklist

Includes bibliographical references

616.4   Diseases of hematopoietic, lymphatic, glandular systems Diseases of endocrine system

American Diabetes Association complete guide to diabetes. 4th ed. American Diabetes Association 2005 554p il pa $29.95 *   **616.4**

1. Diabetes
ISBN 1-58040-237-2   LC 2005-2996
First published 1996
Includes CD-ROM

This book describes types of insulin and the best ways to use them, insulin pumps and injection-free insulin techniques in research, new oral diabetes medications and therapies, the use of carbohydrate counting techniques as a meal planning tool as well as information on diabetes in the workplace, school, and day care.

Includes bibliographical references

Beaser, Richard S.

The Joslin guide to diabetes; a program for managing your treatment; [by] Richard S. Beaser and Amy P. Campbell. Simon & Schuster 2005 431p il pa $16.95   **616.4**

1. Diabetes
ISBN 0-7432-5784-7   LC 2005-51021
"A Fireside book"
First published 1918 by Lea & Febiger under the authorship of Elliott Proctor Joslin with title: A diabetic manual for the mutual use of doctor and patient

The authors offer "information on diabetes management: insulin pumps, current diet plans, weight management and exercise, foot care, and long-term complications. The authors target children and adult diabetics and offer specific advice for pregnant women." Libr J

Diabetes sourcebook; edited by Karen Bellenir. 4th ed. Omnigraphics 2008 655p il (Health reference series) $93   **616.4**

1. Diabetes
ISBN 978-0-7808-1005-1; 0-7808-1005-8
LC 2008-18819
First published 1994

"Basic consumer health information about type 1 and type 2 diabetes mellitus, gestational diabetes, monogenic forms of diabetes, and insulin resistance, with guidelines for lifestyle modifications and the medical management of diabetes, including facts about insulin, insulin delivery devices, oral diabetes medications, self-monitoring of blood glucose, meal planning, physical activity recommendations, foot care, and treatment options for people with kidney failure; along with a section about diabetes complications and co-occurring conditions, a glossary of related terms, and directories of resources for additional help and information." Title page

Includes bibliographical references

Ditkoff, Beth Ann

The thyroid guide; [by] Beth Ann Ditkoff, and Paul LoGerfo. HarperPerennial 2000 xx, 171p il pa $13.95 *   **616.4**

ISBN 0-06-095260-1   LC 99-34742

A guide to the detection, diagnosis and treatment of thyroid diseases.

Eisenstat, Stephanie A.

Every woman's guide to diabetes; what you need to know to lower your risk and beat the odds; [by] Stephanie A. Eisenstat, Ellen Barlow; David M. Nathan (consulting editor). Harvard University Press 2006 305p il $24.95
616.4

1. Diabetes 2. Women—Diseases 3. Women—Health and hygiene
ISBN 978-0-674-02304-8; 0-674-02304-8
LC 2006-49463

The authors "begin by explaining the differences between Type 1 and Type 2 diabetes, the risk factors and diagnosis of the disease, and treatment options. They also discuss complications that occur if the disease is not well controlled. They then address issues particular to women, e.g., gestational diabetes, the influence of hormonal cycles on the disease, birth control, and pregnancy." Libr J

Includes bibliographical references

Hirsch, James S.

Cheating destiny; living with diabetes, America's biggest epidemic. Houghton Mifflin Co. 2006 307p il $25 *   **616.4**

1. Diabetes
ISBN 978-0-618-51461-8; 0-618-51461-9
LC 2006-11239

The author, a Type 1 diabetic, demonstrates "the impact—personal, economic, scientific—of a disease that many say is the fastest-spreading epidemic of the century. . . . Hirsch has an insider's candor speaking about life with diabetes, the sensitivity of the parent of a child with a chronic illness, and the skill of a good journalist reporting on the medical, social, economic, and scientific details of what was once called 'the wasting disease.'" Booklist

Includes bibliographical references

Kaplan-Mayer, Gabrielle

Insulin pump therapy demystified; an essential guide for everyone pumping insulin; foreword by Gary Scheiner. Marlowe & Co. 2003 192p il pa $15.95 **616.4**

1. Insulin pumps 2. Diabetes

ISBN 0-56924-508-8   LC 2002-113886

"The author, a diabetic who uses the pump, explains how it works, how to decide if it is the right therapy, and how to live with it. Drawing on interviews with 75 pump users and diabetes experts, she discusses blood sugar monitoring, carbohydrate counting, record keeping, financial issues, and support. With practical information about sleeping and having sex while wearing a pump, this outstanding manual covers material not found in most diabetes books." Libr J

Includes bibliographical references

Petit, William, 1956-

The encyclopedia of endocrine diseases and disorders; [by] William Petit Jr., Christine Adamec. Facts on File 2005 xxiv, 326p (Facts on File library of health and living) $75 * **616.4**

1. Endocrine glands—Encyclopedias

ISBN 0-8160-5135-6   LC 2004-4916

"An introduction covers the function of the glands throughout life and discusses the role of each. More than 250 A-to-Z entries, ranging in length from one paragraph to two pages, provide details about specific conditions (acromegaly, myxedema coma), hormones (estrogen, lutenizing hormone), glands (pancreas, adrenal gland), procedures (ultrasound, gastric surgery for weight loss), and organizations (American Thyroid Association, Canadian Diabetes Association)." Libr J

For a fuller review, see: Booklist, Aug. 1, 2005

Includes bibliographical references

Walker, Rosemary A.

Diabetes: a practical guide to managing your health; [by] Rosemary Walker & Jill Rodgers; US medical editor, David S. Schade. DK 2005 224p il $25 **616.4**

1. Diabetes

ISBN 0-7566-0359-5

First published 2004 in the United Kingdom

This guide to living with diabetes covers such issues as medication, diet, and exercise.

Warshaw, Hope S., 1954-

The diabetes food & nutrition bible; a complete guide to planning, shopping, cooking, and eating; with foreword by Graham Kerr. American Diabetes Association 2001 324p il pa $18.95 **616.4**

1. Diabetes—Diet therapy

ISBN 1-58040-037-X   LC 2001-22343

This book features information on counting carbohydrates, planning meals, vitamins, minerals, and methods of meal preparation. It includes more than 100 recipes.

616.5   Diseases of integument

Cram, David L. (David Lee), 1934-

Coping with psoriasis; a patient's guide to treatment. Addicus Bks. 2000 132p pa $14.95 **616.5**

1. Psoriasis

ISBN 1-886039-47-X   LC 0000-8220

This book "covers how the disease starts, choosing the right doctor, treatment options, the importance of treating the emotional symptoms, the role of special diets, alternative therapies, and advances in treatment." Publisher's note

Includes bibliographical references

Greenwood-Robinson, Maggie

Hair savers for women; a complete guide to preventing and treating hair loss. Three Rivers Press (NY) 2000 261p pa $14 **616.5**

1. Hair—Diseases 2. Women—Health and hygiene

ISBN 0-609-80445-6   LC 99-39185

The author discusses "solutions and advances in treating female hair loss, from medicine to natural remedies, and introduces women to . . . safe, clinically proven baldness remedies. For women whose hair loss persists, the book discusses surgical alternatives such as hair transplants and scalp reductions, as well as the pros and cons of hair weaves and wigs." Publisher's note

Includes bibliographical references

Mayes, Maureen D.

The scleroderma book; a guide for patients and families. Rev ed. Oxford University Press 2005 211p il $28 **616.5**

1. Scleroderma (Disease)

ISBN 0-19-516940-9   LC 2004-10878

First published 1999

"Neither the cause nor the cure of the autoimmune connective tissue disease is known. Mayes describes the two main types of scleroderma; discusses who is likely to get the malady, which affects the whole body, as well as sexuality and pregnancy; and zeroes in on such organs as the kidneys, GI tract, lungs, heart, joints, tendons, muscles, and nerves." Booklist [review of 1999 edition]

Includes bibliographical referneces

Panagotacos, Peter J.

The complete book of hair loss answers; your comprehensive guide to the latest and best techniques; [by] Peter Panagotacos. 2nd ed. Midpoint Trade 2006 240p il pa $15 **616.5**

1. Hair—Diseases

ISBN 0-9720028-7-1; 978-0-9720028-7-5

First published 2003 by Card Pub. with title: Hair loss answers by the Hairdoc

This book provides "coverage of normal hair growth, causes of hair loss, bogus treatments, cosmetic treatments, drugs that cause hair loss and promote hair growth, surgical restoration, and questions and answers from concerned men and women experiencing hair loss.

Panagotacos, Peter J.—*Continued*

. . . This straightforward, plainspoken, all-inclusive book is highly recommended for all libraries where patrons are looking for complete, truthful answers to their hair-loss problems." Libr J

Includes bibliographical references

Skin disorders sourcebook; edited by Allan R. Cook. Omnigraphics 1997 647p il (Health reference series) $78   **616.5**

1. Skin—Diseases

ISBN 0-7808-0080-X   LC 97-6570

"Basic information about common skin and scalp conditions caused by aging, allergies, immune reactions, sun exposure, infectious organisms, parasites, cosmetics, and skin traumas including abrasions, cuts, and pressure sores along with information on prevention and treatment." Title page

Includes bibliographical references

Turkington, Carol

The encyclopedia of skin and skin disorders; [by] Carol Turkington, Jeffrey S. Dover; medical illustrations, Birck Cox. 3rd ed. Facts on File 2007 459p (Facts on File library of health and living) $75; pa $17.95 *   **616.5**

1. Skin—Encyclopedias

ISBN   0-8160-6403-2;   978-0-8160-6403-8; 0-8160-6404-0 (pa); 978-0-8160-6404-5 (pa)

LC 2005-57402

First published 1996 with title: Skin deep

Paperback published with title: Skin deep

"More than 1,100 entries cover everything from the sun, skin, and acne to skin cancer, cosmetics, and skin lotions." Publisher's note

Includes bibliographical references

616.6   Diseases of urogenital system. Diseases of urinary system

Genadry, Rene, 1947-

A woman's guide to urinary incontinence; [by] Rene Genadry and Jacek L. Mostwin. Johns Hopkins University Press 2008 184p il $39.95; pa $15.95   **616.6**

1. Urinary incontinence 2. Women—Diseases

ISBN   978-0-8018-8732-1;   0-8018-8732-1; 978-0-8018-8733-8 (pa); 0-8018-8733-X (pa)

LC 2007-14818

"A Johns Hopkins Press health book"

The authors "have written an excellent resource for women with urinary incontinence and their caretakers. Wide in scope and thorough in coverage, the book describes the stages and types of incontinence, kinds of exams and tests, current drugs and methods of treatment, anticipated outcomes, and possible complications." Libr J

Loe, Meika, 1973-

The rise of Viagra; how the little blue pill changed sex in America. New York University Press 2004 289p il $27.95   **616.6**

1. Sildenafil 2. Impotence 3. Sex (Biology)

ISBN 0-8147-5200-4   LC 2004-5125

This book contains "discourse relating to Viagra and the medicalization of sexual dysfunctions, first men's and later women's. Drawing heavily on academic theories, Loe . . . tells a fascinating and sometimes disturbing tale of products discovered before science understood why they worked, diseases expanded to the worried well, and experts keeping cozy and often covert company with pharmaceutical companies." Libr J

Includes bibliographical references

Marrs, Richard P.

Dr. Richard Marrs' fertility book; America's leading fertility expert tells you everything you need to know about getting pregnant; [by] Richard Marrs, and Lisa Friedman Bloch and Kathy Kirtland Silverman. Dell 1998 510p il pa $19

616.6

1. Infertility

ISBN 978-0-440-50803-8; 0-440-50803-7

First published 1997 by Delacorte Press

This guide to infertility discusses causes and treatments, outlines assisted reproductive technologies, considers immunological problems as well as emotional and financial issues.

"A necessary primer for any couple faced with infertility, this is essential for public libraries." Libr J

Includes bibliographical references

616.7   Diseases of musculoskeletal system

Arnot, Bob

Wear and tear; stop the pain and put back the spring in your body. Simon & Schuster 2003 xxvii, 259p il $25; pa $13   **616.7**

1. Arthritis 2. Physical fitness

ISBN 0-7432-2555-4; 0-7432-2556-2 (pa)

LC 2002-30871

The author "shows how good nutrition and cartilage-building supplements, combined with proper biomechanics (the way your body moves) and an awareness of one's skeletal predispositions, can virtually eliminate cartilage damage, the primary cause of joint pain." Libr J

"The information will be useful to those who currently have joint problems and to younger people who want to prevent future damage." Publ Wkly

Includes bibliographical references

Lahita, Robert G. (Robert George), 1945-

Lupus Q&A; everything you need to know; [by] Robert G. Lahita and Robert H. Phillips. Rev ed. Avery 2004 240p pa $14.95   **616.7**

1. Systemic lupus erythematosus

ISBN 1-58333-196-4; 978-1-58333-196-5

LC 2004-40974

Lahita, Robert G. (Robert George), 1945-—Continued

First published 1998 with title: Lupus: everything you need to know

This book "discusses the different types of the disease. Because lupus can be so confusing, Lahita and Phillips also discuss medical disorders similar to it. They subsequently turn to the immune system, which is the body system most likely to be involved in lupus, to tests and diagnosis, and to descriptions of symptoms and complications, usefully conveyed in question-and-answer format." Booklist

Lane, Nancy E.

The osteoporosis book. Oxford Univ. Press 1998 206p il pa $13.95 hardcover o.p. **616.7**

1. Osteoporosis
ISBN 0-19-514238-1 (pa) LC 98-19650

This work is "organized in two parts, with early chapters devoted to educating the lay reader on the life cycle of bone and reasons for its loss. Risk factors and different types of fractures are identified, and diagnostic tests are explained. Later chapters discuss the many types of estrogen replacement therapy and medications other than hormones to prevent and treat osteoporosis." Libr J

Includes bibliographical references

Marek, Claudia

The first year—fibromyalgia; an essential guide for the newly diagnosed; {by} Claudia Craig Marek; foreword by R. Paul St. Amand. Marlowe & Co. 2002 xxii, 369p pa $15.95 **616.7**

1. Fibromyalgia
ISBN 1-56924-521-5 LC 2002-141445

The author "aims to help newly diagnosed patients learn about fibromyalgia and develop coping skills over a one-year time frame. Typical questions a new patient might have (e.g., how to prepare for travel, how to communicate with health professionals and employers) are addressed in a highly readable and understandable style and presented in manageable learning bites. . . . What is especially good about this guide is that the authors' tone is not alarmist but calm and evenhanded in articulating important precautions." Libr J

Includes bibliographical references

Nelson, Miriam E.

Strong women, strong bones; everything you need to know to prevent, treat, and beat osteoporosis; [by] Miriam E. Nelson with Sarah Wernick. Rev ed. Perigee 2006 320p il pa $14.95 **616.7**

1. Osteoporosis
ISBN 978-0-399-53249-8; 0-399-53249-8 LC 2007-274321

First published 2000 by Putnam

The authors explain "how bones grow; osteoporosis risk factors; how to adjust the diet to include calcium, vitamin D, and other bone-essential nutrients; the types of weight-bearing exercises that should be performed to promote maximum bone health; and the latest osteoporosis treatment options." Libr J

Includes bibliographical references

Patarca, Roberto

The concise encyclopedia of fibromyalgia and myofascial pain. Haworth Medical Press 2002 201p $49.95; pa $24.95 * **616.7**

ISBN 0-7890-1527-7; 0-7890-1528-5 (pa) LC 2001-51687

This source of information on fibromyalgia and myofascial pain is in dictionary form and includes entries on symptoms, medication, condition, and findings on related disorders. Also covered are "advances in rheumatology, cardiovascular medicine, endocrinology, epidemiology, immunology, infectious diseases, neurology, psychiatry, and psychology that form the basis for new lines of research and therapeutic intervention." Publisher's note

Includes bibliographical references

Sayler, Mary Harwell

The encyclopedia of the muscle and skeletal systems and disorders; foreword by Lori Siegel. Facts on File 2005 xx, 389p (Facts on File library of health and living) $75 **616.7**

1. Musculoskeletal system—Encyclopedias
ISBN 0-8160-5447-9 LC 2003-26606

"The encyclopedia explores and explains why, by midlife, the body visibly complains of overuse and abuse through its aches, pains, stiffness, muscle weakness, and other symptoms of aging. Approximately 500 entries relating to muscle and skeletal disorders, arranged alphabetically, are presented." Booklist

The author "writes each entry with wit and skill—amazing among health science encyclopedias. It will be useful to health care consumers and students for years to come." Choice

Includes bibliographical references

Starlanyl, Devin

Fibromyalgia & chronic myofascial pain syndrome; a survival manual; [by] Devin Starlanyl, Mary Ellen Copeland; foreword by Christopher R. Brown. 2nd ed. New Harbinger Publs. 2001 398p il $19.95 **616.7**

1. Fibromyalgia
ISBN 1-57224-238-8 LC 2001-132299

First published 1996

In this overview of fibromyalgia syndrome (FMS) and myofascial pain syndrome (MPS) the authors "offer information on the latest medications, tips for bodywork, and suggestions for coping with family and work, getting support, and dealing with the healthcare system." Libr J [review of 1996 edition]

Includes bibliographical references

Wallace, Daniel J. (Daniel Jeffrey), 1949-

Fibromyalgia: an essential guide for patients and their families; {by} Daniel J. Wallace, Janice Brock Wallace. Oxford Univ. Press 2003 196p il pa $12.95 **616.7**

1. Fibromyalgia
ISBN 0-19-514931-9 LC 2002-17096

This guide to fibromyalgia, a form of chronic neuromuscular pain, provides an explanation of the syndrome

Wallace, Daniel J. (Daniel Jeffrey), 1949-—Continued

and its symptoms and also outlines recent advances in treatment and new drugs available.

Includes bibliographical references

616.8 Diseases of nervous system and mental disorders

B., David, 1959-
Epileptic. Pantheon Books 2005 361p il $25; pa $17.95 *   616.8
1. Epilepsy—Graphic novels 2. Graphic novels 3. Autobiographical graphic novels
ISBN 0-375-42318-4; 0-375-71408-5 (pa)
LC 2004-53419
Original French edition, 2002
"Growing up in the 1960s and 1970s in France's Loire Valley, Jean-Christophe developed grand mal epilepsy around the age of 11. Pierre-Francois, nine, observes his brother's battle with the physical and social implications of the disease; their parents' efforts to find management of it through medical, macrobiotic, and even psychic interventions; and the author's own development in this milieu as a boy obsessed with history and warfare and as a dedicated artist." SLJ

The author's "artwork is magnificent—gorgeously bold, impressionistic representations of the world not as it is but as he's taught himself to perceive it. . . . B.'s illustrations constantly underscore his writing's wrenching psychological depth; readers can literally see how the chaos of his childhood shaped his vision and mind." Publ Wkly

Bruno, Richard L.
The polio paradox; uncovering the hidden history of polio to understand and treat "post-polio syndrome" and chronic fatigue. Warner Bks. 2002 350p il $25.95; pa $15.95   616.8
1. Poliomyelitis
ISBN 0-446-52907-9; 0-446-69069-4 (pa)
The author "discusses the history and care of polio patients, the identification of and research into PPS [post-polio syndrome], and the approach to treating the symptoms. . . . [He] also addresses chronic fatigue (CF), multiple sclerosis, fibromyalgia, Gulf War syndrome, and spina bifida disorders that share symptoms, brain changes, and stress links similar to PPS." Libr J
Includes bibliographical references

Chase, Victor D., 1942-
Shattered nerves; how science is solving modern medicine's most perplexing problem. Johns Hopkins University Press 2007 289p $27.50
616.8
1. Nervous system
ISBN 978-0-8018-8514-3; 0-8018-8514-0
LC 2006-9626
"Neural prostheses might be capable of treating or curing some of the most difficult problems afflicting humans today. Devices that simulate, replace, or bypass nerves have the potential to help those disabled with nervous system and sensory disorders. . . . Chase explores the world of these up-and-coming technologies, starting with an explanation of how electrical impulses run our bodies, then moving on to a discussion of the first cochlear implants. Chase profiles the scientists and patients who have contributed to the research that, in addition to helping the neurologically disabled, may have application for Parkinson's disease, bladder disorders, arthritis, and any other condition for which muscle or nerve stimulation could be beneficial." Libr J

"Chase achieves his formidable aim, enabling the reader to make connections between scientific endeavor and its application to the lives of the vivid individuals to whom he introduces us." Cerebrum

Includes bibliographical references

Cram, David L. (David Lee), 1934-
Answers to frequently asked questions in Parkinson's disease; a resource book for patients and families; [by] David L. Cram, M.D. Acorn Pub. 2002 170p pa $19.95   616.8
1. Parkinson's disease
ISBN 0-9710988-8-3   LC 2002-1074
Contents: Financial considerations — Diagnosing early disease and tremor — Parkinson's disease and heredity — Medications in Parkinson's disease — Stress and exercise — Preparing for hospital — Problems with vision, sleep, and restless legs — Fear of falling, freezing, and low blood pressure — Undesirable side effects — Surgery in Parkinson's disease — New discoveries — So, you have just been diagnosed with PD
Includes bibliographical references

Duvoisin, Roger C., 1927-
Parkinson's disease; a guide for patient and family; [by] Roger C. Duvoisin, Jacob Sage. 5th ed. Lippincott Williams & Wilkins 2001 195p il pa $32.95   616.8
1. Parkinson's disease
ISBN 0-7817-2977-7   LC 2001-29689
First published 1978 by Raven Press
The authors "explain the pathology, symptoms, and course of Parkinson's Disease, discuss current drug therapies and surgical procedures, and examine the latest research on the genetics of parkinsonism." Publisher's note
"The complications of advancing disease are particularly well described. While the reading level is high, the determined reader can find a great deal of detailed information not found in other guides." Libr J

Freed, Curt
Healing the brain; [by] Curt Freed and Simon LeVay. Times Bks. 2002 269p $26   616.8
1. Parkinson's disease 2. Transplantation of organs, tissues, etc.
ISBN 0-8050-7091-5   LC 2002-19671
"Freed gives a brief background on the biology of the disease and the history of Parkinson's treatments, but most of the book is devoted to his own surgical experiment, which involved 40 volunteer Parkinson's patients, half of whom received transplanted cells while the other group underwent sham surgeries." Publ Wkly
"Parkinson's patients and others interested in the issue will find this an absorbing account." Libr J

Greene, Gayle, 1943-
Insomniac. University of California Press 2008
503p $29.95 **616.8**
1. Insomnia 2. Sleep disorders
ISBN 978-0-520-24630-0; 0-520-24630-6
LC 2007-8838
The author "has lived with insomnia for as long as
she can remember, and in this . . . [treatise,] she takes
readers into the world of sleep research, sleep clinics,
pharmaceuticals, sleeping potions, alternative medicine,
and sleep physiology and psychology." Libr J
"Greene offers an enjoyable and informative account
that will provoke even readers who get their full eight
hours a night." Publ Wkly
Includes bibliographical references

Halpern, Sue M.
Can't remember what I forgot; the good news
from the front lines of memory research. Harmony
Books 2008 256p $24 * **616.8**
1. Memory 2. Alzheimer's disease
ISBN 978-0-307-40674-3; 0-307-40674-1
LC 2007-33895
In this book about scientific research on memory, the
author "gets to know a prominent neuroscientist, subjects
herself to multiple tests (from paper-and-pencil tests to
nuclear brain imaging), visits businesses involved in the
quixotic race for memory-fixing drugs, and attends the
Memory Olympics. She explains in plain English what
science has discovered about learning and memory, what
is currently agreed to improve memory, and what remains to be seen." Libr J
This "timely book offers a vivid, often amusing introduction to a science that touches us all." Publ Wkly
Includes bibliographical references

Hauser, Robert A.
Parkinson's disease: questions and answers. 4th
ed. Merit Pub. Int. 2003 204p $34.95
616.8
1. Parkinson's disease
ISBN 1-873413-68-8
First published 1996
"Although primarily aimed at general clinicians, this
manual may be useful for patients wishing more in-depth
knowledge than what the consumer guides offer. Hauser
. . . covers test, clinical characteristics, staging and classifications, medical management, and issues frequently
missed in the lay literature." Libr J [review of 2000 edi-
tion]

Kuhn, Daniel
Alzheimer's early stages; first steps for families,
friends and caregivers. 2nd ed. Hunter House 2003
306p $27.95; pa $15.95 **616.8**
1. Alzheimer's disease
ISBN 0-89793-398-2; 0-89793-397-4 (pa)
LC 2002-151932
First published 1999
This book covers "the importance of getting a diagnosis, risk factors (including the role of depression), early
symptoms, treatment and prevention, and information on

physical health, safety concerns, caring for the caregiver,
and financial and end-of-life planning—all illustrated
with brief, first-person narratives. Of special interest are
chapters on relationships, including telling others about
the diagnosis, and the . . . section on current available
treatments. . . . Intelligently written with numerous references to professional and consumer literature, this book
is an excellent choice for Alzheimer's and consumer
health collections." Libr J
Includes bibliographical references

Kushner, Howard I.
A cursing brain? the histories of Tourette
syndrome. Harvard Univ. Press 1999 303p il
$32.50; pa $16,95 * **616.8**
1. Tourette syndrome
ISBN 0-674-18022-4; 0-674-00386-1 (pa)
LC 98-38733
The author presents a "narrative of the development of
knowledge about, treatments of, and medical and lay atti-
tudes toward Tourette's syndrome (TS) patients."
Booklist
"A compassionate and absorbing work of medical his-
tory." Libr J
Includes bibliographical references

Lieberman, A. (Abraham), 1938-
100 questions & answers about Parkinson [sic]
disease; [by] Abraham Lieberman, with Marcia
McCall. Jones & Bartlett 2003 238p il pa $16.95
616.8
1. Parkinson's disease
ISBN 0-7637-0433-4 LC 2002-152130
A patient-oriented guide to the symptoms, diagnosis,
and treatment of Parkinson's disease
"Lieberman is particularly good at telling patients
what they should expect from their physicians, how they
can select a competent movement disorders specialist,
how they can make the most of living with PD, and
what they should know about the new advances in medical, alternative, and surgical therapies. An optimistic resource that should be much in demand." Libr J

Shaking-up Parkinson disease; fighting like a
tiger, thinking like a fox: a book for the puzzled,
the hopeful, the willing and the prepared; by
Abraham Lieberman. Jones & Bartlett 2002 250p
il pa $18.95 **616.8**
1. Parkinson's disease
ISBN 0-7637-1866-1 LC 2001-25721
This book "explains PD and its symptoms (with steps
to alleviate them) and extensively covers treatment options such as drugs and surgery. A plus is the author's
discussion of anxiety and depression as a biological rather than a psychological symptom of the disease. . . . Although nonreligious readers may be put off by the biblical quotes, this is still an outstanding text." Libr J

Managing stroke; a guide to living well after
stroke; edited by Paul R. Rao, Mark N. Ozer,
John E. Toerge; foreword by Don A. Olson.
ABI Professional Publs. 2000 299p il $27
616.8

Managing stroke—*Continued*

1. Stroke

ISBN 1-886236-24-0

"With information on physical therapy, occupational therapy, and daily living skills, this is primarily a guide to rehabilitation for stroke patients or their families rather than a quick reference book or a guide to prevention." Libr J

Marks, David R.

The headache prevention cookbook; eating right to prevent migraines and other headaches; [by] David R. Marks, with Laura Marks. Houghton Mifflin 2000 208p pa $16   **616.8**

1. Headache 2. Diet therapy

ISBN 0-395-96716-3   LC 00-33435

The authors explain how ordinary foods may serve as triggers for headache pain. To help readers with undiagnosed food sensitivities they include more than 100 easy-to-prepare recipes.

Max, D. T.

The family that couldn't sleep; a medical mystery. Random House 2006 xxxi, 299p hardcover o.p. pa $15.95   **616.8**

1. Prion diseases 2. Sleep disorders 3. Insomnia

ISBN 1-4000-6245-4; 978-1-4000-6245-4; 978-0-8129-7252-8 (pa); 0-8129-7252-X (pa)

LC 2006-43885

This book discusses fatal familial insomnia and the history of one family in the Veneto region of Italy that has suffered from this disease for more than two centuries.

This is a "gracefully written medical detective story." N Y Times (Late N Y Ed)

Includes bibliographical references

Moore, Elaine A., 1948-

Encyclopedia of Alzheimer's disease; with directories of research, treatment, and care facilities; [by] Elaine A. Moore; with Lisa Moore; illustrations by Marvin G. Miller. McFarland & Co. 2003 401p il $75 *   **616.8**

ISBN 0-7864-1438-3   LC 2002-12202

"The first section of this encyclopedia explains terms (e.g., scientific, health plans, organizations) relating directly or indirectly to the disease. . . . The next section has three directories (treatment centers listed by state and city, research facilities by state, and resources) followed by an index. . . . For a comprehensive reference on Alzheimer's, the Moores' resource would be an excellent choice." Choice

Includes bibliographical references

Mosley, Anthony D.

The encyclopedia of Parkinson's disease; [by] Anthony D. Mosley and Deborah S. Romaine. Facts on File 2004 406p (Facts on File library of health and living) $65   **616.8**

1. Parkinson's disease—Encyclopedias

ISBN 0-8160-5032-5   LC 2003-52491

"An Amaranth book"

This encyclopedia covers "issues and topics related to the disease, including etiology, symptoms, treatments, medications, surgeries, research, medical terms, coping and caregiving, [and] living with Parkinson's disease." Publisher's note

"The wide range of information about the disease, current research, support, and useful therapeutic techniques and a bibliography with clinical information as well as sources for patients and caregivers make this a valuable addition to all public, health sciences, and consumer health libraries." Booklist

Sacks, Oliver W.

An anthropologist on Mars; seven paradoxical tales; [by] Oliver Sacks. Knopf 1995 327p il pa $14 hardcover o.p.   **616.8**

1. Nervous system—Diseases

ISBN 0-679-75697-3 (pa)   LC 94-26733

In this "collection of previously published essays, the noted neurologist describes his meetings with seven people whose 'abnormalities' in brain function generate new perspectives on the workings of that organ, the nature of experience and concepts of personality and consciousness. . . . Writing with eloquent particularity and compassionate respect, Sacks enlarges our view of the nature of human experience." Publ Wkly

Includes bibliographical references

The man who mistook his wife for a hat and other clinical tales; [by] Oliver Sacks. Simon & Schuster 1998 243p il pa $14 *   **616.8**

1. Nervous system—Diseases

ISBN 0-684-85394-9   LC 98-4723

"A Touchstone book"

First published 1985 by Summit Bks.

"Sacks introduces the reader to real people who suffer from a variety of neurological syndromes which includes symptoms such as amnesia, uncontrolled movements, and musical hallucinations. Sacks recounts their stories in a riveting, compassionate, and thoughtful manner." Libr J

Includes bibliographical references

Schwartz, Maxime, 1940-

How the cows turned mad; translated by Edward Schneider. University of Calif. Press 2003 238p $24.95; pa $15.95   **616.8**

1. Prion diseases

ISBN 0-520-23531-2; 0-520-24337-4 (pa)

LC 2002-75514

The author discusses the spread of "mad-cow disease and its human counterpart, variant Creutzfeldt-Jakob disease (vCJD). . . . His book maps out . . . the scientific investigation into how scrapie—a disease that has long been known to afflict sheep—came to cross the species barrier to cows, and then from cows to humans." Economist

"Writing with immense concentration and clarity, French molecular biologist Schwartz makes the long hunt for the unexpected culprit gene utterly engrossing." Booklist

Includes bibliographical references

Shenk, David, 1966-
The forgetting: Alzheimer's, portrait of an epidemic. Doubleday 2001 290p $24.95; pa $13.95
616.8

1. Alzheimer's disease
ISBN 0-385-49837-3; 0-385-49838-1 (pa)
LC 2001-28012

The author "traces the development of knowledge about Alzheimer's in the work of individuals and such groups as the National Institute of Aging; describes various tests that help in identifying possible sufferers; and discusses the early, middle, and end stages of the malady. . . . Lucid and well organized, this is one of the best books on this increasingly prevalent illness." Booklist
Includes bibliographical references

Sleep disorders sourcebook; edited by Amy L. Sutton. 2nd ed. Omnigraphics 2005 567p (Health reference series) $87 *
616.8

1. Sleep 2. Consumer education
ISBN 0-7808-0743-X; 978-0-7808-0743-3
LC 2004-28389

First published 1999 under the editorship of Jenifer Swanson

"Basic consumer health information about sleep and sleep disorders, including insomnia, sleep apnea, restless legs syndrome, narcolepsy, parasomnias, and other health problems that affect sleep, plus facts about diagnostic procedures, treatment strategies, sleep medications, and tips for improving sleep quality; along with a glossary of related terms and resources for additional help and information." Title page
Includes bibliographical references

Spence, J. David
How to prevent your stroke. Vanderbilt University Press 2006 218p il $39.95; pa $19.95
616.8

1. Stroke
ISBN   0-8265-1536-0;   978-0-8265-1536-0;
0-8265-1537-7 (pa); 978-0-8265-1537-7 (pa)
LC 2005-35450

The author "aims to provide all the information that at-risk patients need to understand the underlying causes of strokes, risk factors and remedies, from diet and exercise to drugs and surgery. He discusses well-known risks (smoking, alcohol, a diet high in saturated fat, diabetes, high blood pressure and cholesterol levels) and those that have more recently come to light (genetics, vitamin deficiencies, infections, stress)." Publ Wkly

Spence "offers a well-organized and engaging narrative with just the right amount of information to help readers make informed decisions regarding cardiovascular disease prevention." Libr J
Includes bibliographical references

Tanzi, Rudolph E.
Decoding darkness; the search for the genetic causes of Alzheimer's disease; {by} Rudolph E. Tanzi & Ann B. Parson. Perseus Bks. 2000 281p il pa $16 hardcover o.p.
616.8

1. Alzheimer's disease
ISBN 0-7382-0526-5 (pa)

This is an "account of the race to uncover the genetics behind Alzheimer's disease. . . . {The author discusses} his research and the work of others that led to recent genetic discoveries associated with early-onset and late-onset Alzheimer's disease." Libr J
"This is a gripping book with a vast amount of fascinating information." Booklist

Turkington, Carol
The encyclopedia of Alzheimer's disease; foreword by James E. Galvin. Facts on File 2003 286p $71.50
616.8

ISBN 0-8160-4818-5
LC 2002-11981

This encyclopedia provides "coverage of the disease and its causes and symptoms, as well as related health conditions and terms . . . advances in treatment, drugs and research; social issues related to Alzheimer's; and . . . organizations." Publisher's note

This is "a useful addition to most consumer health collections." Libr J
Includes bibliographical references

The encyclopedia of multiple sclerosis; [by] Carol Turkington and Kaye D. Hooper in collaboration with Rosalind C. Kalb and Nancy Holland. Facts On File 2005 336p $75
616.8

1. Multiple sclerosis—Encyclopedias
ISBN 0-8160-5623-4; 978-0-8160-5623-1
LC 2004-22858

"Entries range in length from a brief paragraph to several pages. They include events, such as the MS Walk, and celebrities, such as Joan Didion and Lena Horne, who are living with MS. Five appendixes list 'Organizations,' 'National MS Society-Affiliated Clinical Facilities,' 'Clinical Trials in Multiple Sclerosis,' 'State Chapters of the National Multiple Sclerosis Society,' and 'International Multiple Sclerosis Societies.' . . . This is a very good, reasonably priced source for public and consumer health collections." Booklist
Includes bibliographical references

Weiner, Jonathan, 1953-
His brother's keeper; a story from the edge of medicine. HarperCollins 2004 356p $26.95
616.8

1. Heywood, Stephen 2. Heywood, Jamie 3. Nervous system—Diseases
ISBN 0-06-00100-7-X
LC 2004-302468

"When Stephen Heywood, a 29-year-old carpenter, was diagnosed with amyotrophic lateral sclerosis (also known as Lou Gehrig's disease), his older brother, Jamie, launched his own research project to search for a cure. . . . The story's power derives from attention to small, human details, like Stephen's first symptoms of losing strength in his fingers. . . . Weiner can't give readers a happy ending for Stephen, but he can—and does—offer a powerful account of equal parts ambition and hope." Publ Wkly

Weiner, William J.
Parkinson's disease; a complete guide for patients and families; [by] William J. Weiner, Lisa M. Shulman, Anthony E. Lang. 2nd ed. Johns Hopkins University Press 2007 278p il $55; pa $17.95 *   **616.8**
    1. Parkinson's disease
    ISBN   0-8018-8545-0;   978-0-8018-8545-7; 0-8018-8546-9 (pa); 978-0-8018-8546-4 (pa)
                                 LC 2006-18814
"A Johns Hopkins Press health book"
First published 2001
This book contains "information for managing this complex condition, including details on the use of medications, diet, exercise, complementary therapies, and surgery." Publisher's note

When Parkinson's strikes early; voices, choices, resources, and treatment; [edited by] Blake-Krebs & Linda Herman. Hunter House 2001 270p il pa $15.95   **616.8**
    1. Parkinson's disease
    ISBN 0-89793-340-0   LC 2001-16619
This "guide incorporates e-mailings from the members of the Parkinson's Information Exchange Network (PIEN), with detailed advice on diagnosis, treatment, and self-help options. The vivid essays, poetry, and stories personalize the disease's impact; the resources section is outstanding." Libr J
Includes bibliographical references

Wilson, Daniel J., 1949-
Living with polio; the epidemic and its survivors; Daniel J. Wilson. University of Chicago Press 2005 299p il $29 *   **616.8**
    1. Poliomyelitis
    ISBN 0-226-90103-3   LC 2004-24170
The author "has drawn on 150 personal narratives, published and unpublished, weaving quotes from those accounts with historical information on polio treatment and rehabilitation. The result is a vivid portrait of a devastating disease and its repercussions, as well as a glimpse into the physical, social, and psychological challenges of being physically disabled in mid-20th century America." Libr J
Includes bibliographical references

616.85 Miscellaneous diseases of nervous system and mental disorders

Ainsworth, Patricia, 1932-
Understanding mental retardation; [by] Patricia Ainsworth, Pamela Baker. University Press of Mississippi 2004 200p (Understanding health and sickness series) $30; pa $12   **616.85**
    1. Mental retardation
    ISBN 1-578-06646-8; 1-578-06647-6 (pa)
                                 LC 2003-25098
Contents: What is mental retardation and who is affected? -- Normal development -- Evolving concepts of mental retardation -- The first six years: infants, toddlers, and preschool children -- School-aged children, adolescents, and teenagers -- The adult years -- The elderly -- Psychiatric illness and mental retardation -- Research on the future of prevention and treatment of mental retardation
"The value of this work hinges on its accessible presentation: parents and caregivers are given up-to-date information that should enable them to anticipate hurdles, to advocate, and to access necessary support services. Precious few books address the history and needs of people with mental retardation so thoroughly for parents and caregivers." Libr J
Includes bibliographical references

Attwood, Tony, 1952-
The complete guide to Asperger's syndrome. Jessica Kingsley Publishers 2006 c2007 397p il $29.95   **616.85**
    1. Asperger's syndrome
    ISBN 978-1-84310-495-7; 1-84310-495-4
                                 LC 2006-20065
The author covers "topics such as friendship, bullying, special interests, and theory of mind. Each chapter begins with a quote from Hans Asperger himself and includes firsthand experiences from individuals with Asperger's, including Temple Grandin, Liane Holliday Willey, and Stephen Shore. . . . His work skillfully brings together the current information on this fascinating condition." Libr J
Includes bibliographical references

Claude-Pierre, Peggy
The secret language of eating disorders; the revolutionary new approach to understanding and curing anorexia and bulimia. Vintage Books 1999 288p il pa $14.95   **616.85**
    1. Eating disorders
    ISBN 978-0-375-75018-2; 0-375-75018-5
    First published 1997 by Times Bks.
According to the author, "the primary cause of an eating disorder is rooted in confirmed negativity condition, or CNC. . . . She discusses how CNC manifests itself and the stages of recovery from it, with appropriate intervention strategies. . . . Her message and tone are supportive and should comfort those, including desperate parents, dealing with these complex, puzzling afflictions." Booklist
Includes bibliographical references

Coleman, Penny
Flashback; posttraumatic stress disorder, suicide, and the lessons of war. Beacon Press 2006 223p $23.95 *   **616.85**
    1. Post-traumatic stress disorder 2. Veterans
    ISBN 0-8070-5040-7   LC 2005-30606
For this book, the author, the former wife of a Vietnam veteran who committed suicide, "interviewed women whose husbands survived battles but succumbed to the effects of war, researched instances of PTSD dating back to the Civil War, and compiled statistical information pertaining to American soldiers serving in the Middle East. . . . An essential part of any public library collection." Libr J
Includes bibliographical references

Dalton, Katharina, 1916-2004
Depression after childbirth; how to recognize, treat, and prevent postnatal depression; [by] Katharina Dalton, with Wendy Holton. 4th ed. Oxford Univ. Press 2001 240p il pa $19.95
616.85
1. Postpartum depression
ISBN 0-19-263277-9   LC 00-53754
First published 1980
This guide for women and their partners for recognizing, treating and preventing postpartum depression discusses such topics as the role of hormones, symptoms such as exhaustion and irritability, and careers and motherhood
Includes bibliographical references

DePaulo, J. Raymond
Understanding depression; what we know and what you can do about it; [by] J. Raymond DePaulo, Leslie Alan Horvitz. Wiley 2002 296p il $24.95; pa $14.95   **616.85**
1. Depression (Psychology)
ISBN 0-471-39552-8; 0-471-43030-7 (pa)
LC 2001-45449
This describes the nature, causes, effects, and treatment of depression and manic-depressive illness
"The chapters on finding the right treatment and how doctors make diagnoses will be extremely useful for those suffering from the disease. . . . Readers will find this an invaluable resource." Publ Wkly
Includes bibliographical references

Glenmullen, Joseph, 1950-
Prozac backlash; overcoming the dangers of prozac, zoloft, paxil, and other antidepressants with safe, effective alternatives. Simon & Schuster 2000 383p pa $14 hardcover o.p.   **616.85**
1. Antidepressants 2. Depression (Psychology)
ISBN 0-7432-0062-4 (pa)   LC 99-59911
The author presents a "survey of recent studies on the negative effects of antidepressants and their less-publicized alternatives. His title refers not to the growing skepticism toward psychiatric medications but to the brain's compensatory reactions to the artificial elevation of serotonin, including potentially permanent tics, dependence, sexual dysfunction, memory problems, sudden suicidal feelings and violence." Publ Wkly
Includes bibliographical references

Grinker, Roy Richard, 1961-
Unstrange minds; remapping the world of autism. Basic Books 2006 340p $26.95
616.85
1. Autism
ISBN 978-0-465-02763-7; 0-465-02763-6
LC 2006-23003
"The first part of the book is an expanded essay on the history of the classification of psychiatric disorders and how these definitions continue to evolve. . . . The second part of the book explores the cultural issues related to autism in societies as diverse as those of India, South Korea, and South Africa and how the place of the autistic child is changing in those countries. Grinker's experiences as a father of an autistic child are woven throughout the volume. . . . The text is scholarly, but easily read, and is useful not only for providing an understanding of autism, but also for understanding the issues associated with changing diagnoses of psychiatric disorders." Sci Books Films
Includes bibliographical references

Hallowell, Edward M.
Delivered from distraction; getting the most out of life with attention deficit disorder; [by] Edward M. Hallowell, John J. Ratey. Ballantine Books 2004 xxxiii, 380p $25.95; pa $14.95
616.85
1. Attention deficit disorder
ISBN 0-345-44230-X; 0-345-44231-8 (pa)
LC 2004-52815
"Defining ADD as a collection of traits, some positive, some negative, the authors intend to encourage those who have this condition or are raising children with it and advise on how to maximize their abilities and minimize characteristics, such as procrastination, that may hinder them at school or work. . . . Overall, this is an excellent resource." Publ Wkly
Includes bibliographical references

Driven to distraction; recognizing and coping with attention deficit disorder from childhood through adulthood; [by] Edward M. Hallowell and John J. Ratey. Simon & Schuster 1995 319p il pa $14   **616.85**
1. Attention deficit disorder
ISBN 0-684-80128-0   LC 94-40712
"A Touchstone book"
First published 1994 by Pantheon Bks.
This study of Attention Deficit Disorder in children as well as in adults covers biology, neurology, pharmacology, clinical findings and personal and professional experiences.
"This is an absorbing look at efforts to understand troubling and exasperating behaviors." Booklist
Includes bibliographical references

Worry; controlling it and using it wisely. Pantheon Bks. 1997 331p pa $16.95 hardcover o.p.
616.85
1. Anxiety 2. Worry
ISBN 0-345-42458-1 (pa)   LC 97-8609
The author explains "the difference between worry rooted in in-born predispositions and worry that signals other, deeper problems." Libr J
"The book offers useful advice and entertaining stories, and readers can find something here to help them worry less." Booklist
Includes bibliographical references

Hornbacher, Marya, 1974-
Wasted: a memoir of anorexia and bulimia. HarperCollins Pubs. 1998 268p hardcover o.p. pa $13.95   **616.85**
1. Anorexia nervosa 2. Bulimia
ISBN 0-06-018739-5; 978-0-06-085879-7 (pa); 0-06-085879-6 (pa)   LC 97-21375

Hornbacher, Marya, 1974-—*Continued*

This is the author's "account of her bout with anorexia and bulimia, a decade-long struggle that brought her to the brink of death at age 18 and left her with chronic physical ailments." Publ Wkly

This "is a gritty, unflinching look at eating disorders. . . . Hornbacher is at her best when she zeroes in on the specifics of eating disorders and their origins." N Y Times Book Rev

Includes bibliographical references

Kramer, Peter D.

Against depression. Viking 2005 353p $25.95 *
616.85

1. Depression (Psychology)
ISBN 0-670-03405-3   LC 2004-61228

The author "examines the cultural roots of notions about depression and underscores the gap between what we know scientifically and what we feel about the illness. Kramer traces depression from Hippocrates through the Renaissance and Romantic 'cult of melancholy' to advances in medicine, psychiatry and psychotherapy, and at last to the disease we now know it to be. . . . Resolute but not preachy, this book is an important addition to the growing public health campaign against depression." Publ Wkly

Includes bibliographical references

Listening to Prozac; a psychiatrist explores mood-altering drugs and the new meaning of the self. Viking 1993 409p pa $15 hardcover o.p.
616.85

1. Psychotropic drugs 2. Psychiatry 3. Personality disorders 4. Psychotherapy
ISBN 0-14-026671-2 (pa)   LC 92-50733

"Kramer's thesis is that Prozac, in addition to its antidepressant effects, can also act upon aspects of the personality that were previously conceptualized as enduring individual traits (i.e., sensitivity to rejection, social inhibition, and reactivity to stressors). Medication with Prozac appears to have beneficial effects on self-esteem, the ability to experience pleasure, and mental acuity. Kramer is favorable to Prozac, although he documents its side effects, unknown long-term affects, and controversial publicity." Choice

Machoian, Lisa

The disappearing girl; learning the language of teenage depression. Dutton 2005 xxiv, 244p $24.95; pa $15   **616.85**

1. Depression (Psychology) 2. Teenagers
ISBN 0-525-94866-X; 0-452-28710-3 (pa)
     LC 2004-25777

The author "sets out to determine why so many young women seem to emotionally withdraw and to explain how parents and others can help them." Publ Wkly

Includes bibliographical references

Matsakis, Aphrodite

Vietnam wives; facing the challenges of life with veterans suffering post-traumatic stress. 2nd ed. Sidran Press 1996 440p pa $24.95
616.85

1. Post-traumatic stress disorder 2. Veterans 3. Vietnam War, 1961-1975
ISBN 1-88696-800-4   LC 96-15876

First published 1988 by Woodbine House

The author describes post-traumatic stress disorder (PTSD) as it effects Vietnam War veterans and their wives, often resulting in psychic numbness, sexual impotence, alcohol and drug addiction, family violence and depression. The book outlines therapy and coping techniques and includes a resource guide

Includes bibliographical references

Mondimore, Francis Mark, 1953-

Adolescent depression; a guide for parents. Johns Hopkins Univ. Press 2002 287p il (Johns Hopkins Press health book) $45; pa $17.95
616.85

1. Depression (Psychology) 2. Adolescent psychology
ISBN 0-8018-7058-5; 0-8018-7065-9 (pa)
     LC 2001-7992

Mondimore contends "that serious depression in adolescents is an illness. . . . He describes the many forms of depression and the many way it can appear in young people—from intensely sad feelings to irritability, anger, and destructive rages." Publisher's note

"The author provides a solid reference tool for anyone who works with adolescents. It is highly recommended for education professionals as well as public libraries." Voice Youth Advocates

Includes bibliographical references

Osborn, Ian

Tormenting thoughts and secret rituals; the hidden epidemic of obsessive-compulsive disorder. Pantheon Bks. 1998 325p pa $14.95 hardcover o.p.
616.85

ISBN 0-440-50847-9 (pa)   LC 97-31226

"Osborn shows that OCD is caused by a chemical imbalance in the brain and that behavior therapy and drugs, preferably together, can take care of it for most patients; Osborn personalizes this part of the discussion with case histories of individuals. . . . He concludes with a long list of OCD support groups and other helpful information." Booklist

Includes bibliographical references

Penzel, Fred

Obsessive-compulsive disorders; a complete guide to getting well and staying well. Oxford Univ. Press 2000 428p il $35   **616.85**

ISBN 0-19-514092-3   LC 00-32419

This study of OCD (obssessive-compulsive disorder) outlines behavior patterns, discusses new antidepressants and behavior therapy techniques, and includes a do-it-yourself guide for a self-administered program of behavior therapy

"New antidepressants and behavioral therapy tech-

Penzel, Fred—*Continued*

niques have led to great improvements in the condition of sufferers of this biologically based illness. Psychologist Penzel has written a do-it-yourself guide that outlines in great detail procedures for a self-administered program of behavioral therapy. . . . This title is the most useful of the recent books on OCD and is highly recommended to all public libraries." Libr J

Roesch, Roberta

The encyclopedia of depression. 2nd ed. Facts on File 2001 278p il $65   **616.85**
    ISBN 0-8160-4047-8   LC 00-39353
    First published 1991
    "More than 570 A-to-Z entries include . . . information on the history of the disease, current research, treatment options, and the role of various mental health professional and government programs in addressing depression." Publisher's note

Root, Benjamin A., Jr.

Understanding panic and other anxiety disorders; [by] Benjamin A. Root, Jr. University Press of Miss. 2000 109p il (Understanding health and sickness series) pa $12 hardcover o.p. *
    616.85
    1. Panic disorders 2. Anxiety
    ISBN 1-57806-245-4 (pa)   LC 00-21977
    "Root explains physical and mental problems that can mimic panic disorders and that the differentiating diagnosis in emergency room or clinic is often a major hurdle. The unpredictable nature of attacks in panic disorders and their frequent accompaniment, agoraphobia . . . add to the anxiety involved. Root describes those likely to suffer from panic attacks, discusses drug and psychotherapy treatments, and includes a chapter on pertinent research projects." Booklist

Schreiber, Flora Rheta

Sybil. Warner Books 1995 460p il pa $7.99
    616.85
    1. Multiple personality
    ISBN 978-0-446-35940-5; 0-446-35940-8
    First published 1973 by Regnery Pub.
    This is the "true story of Sybil I. Dorsett, a battered child possessed by 16 different personalities. . . . The author skillfully evokes Sybil's patient work during 11 years of psychoanalysis and her eventual success in integrating these selves into a unified personality." Libr J

Solden, Sari

Journeys through ADDulthood; discover a new sense of identity and meaning while living with attention deficit disorder. Walker & Co. 2002 300p il $24; pa $13   **616.85**
    1. Attention deficit disorder
    ISBN 0-8027-1376-9; 0-8027-7679-5 (pa)
    LC 2003-268751
    "The material is organized into three stages: understanding the brain and primary symptoms of ADD, discovering one's true identity and accepting one's unique-

ness, and learning to share one's self with others. . . . This important work stands out among the growing number of books on ADD for its focus on adults and the author's emphasis on learning how to come to terms with and live comfortably with the disease. Highly recommended for all public libraries." Libr J
    Includes bibliographical references

Solomon, Andrew, 1963-

The noonday demon; an atlas of depression. Scribner 2001 569p $28; pa $16   **616.85**
    1. Depression (Psychology)
    ISBN 0-684-85466-X; 0-684-85467-8 (pa)
    LC 2001-18884
    "The author draws on his own life story and other sources for a deeply moving and provocative exploration of depression." Booklist
    Includes bibliographical references

Styron, William, 1925-2006

Darkness visible; a memoir of madness. Random House 1990 84p pa $11 hardcover o.p.
    616.85
    1. Depression (Psychology)
    ISBN 0-679-73639-5 (pa)   LC 90-53141
    This is an account of the author's experience of suicidal depression and his recovery
    "The book's virtues—considerable—are twofold. First, it is a pitiless and chastened record of a nearly fatal human trial far commoner than assumed—and then a literary discourse on the ways and means of our cultural discontents." Publ Wkly

Turkington, Carol

The encyclopedia of autism spectrum disorders; [by] Carol Turkington, Ruth Anan. Facts On File 2007 324p $75 *   **616.85**
    1. Autism—Encyclopedias
    ISBN 0-8160-6002-9; 978-0-8160-6002-3
    LC 2005-27227
    "More than 300 entries address the different types of autism, causes and treatments, institutions, associations, leading scientists, research, social impact, and much more." Publisher's note
    Includes bibliographical references

Wansink, Brian, 1960-

Mindless eating; why we eat more than we think. Bantam Books 2006 276p il $25
    616.85
    1. Eating habits
    ISBN 978-0-553-80434-8; 0-553-80434-0
    LC 2006-47532
    The author "explores some of the psychological aspects of overeating to explain why we in fact consume more than we believe we do. . . . Wansink's dual approach emphasizing food knowledge and self-knowledge offers a sensible route to permanent weight loss." Booklist
    Includes bibliographical references

616.86   Substance abuse (Drug abuse)

Beattie, Melody

Beyond codependency; and getting better all the time. Hazelden Foundation 1989 252p pa $15.95
       616.86

1. Drug abuse 2. Applied psychology
ISBN 0-89486-583-8

The author discusses "the process of recovering from the self-defeating behaviors adopted as survival tactics by adult children of families rendered dysfunctional by parental alcoholism or similar traumas." Publ Wkly

Includes bibliographical references

Codependent no more; how to stop controlling others and start caring for yourself. 2nd ed. Hazelden 1992 250p pa $15.95 *
       616.86

1. Codependency 2. Health self-care
ISBN 0-89486-402-5   LC 2004-351623
First published 1987

This guide offers advice on how to overcome codependency, aimed at the spouses and other caretakers of people who abuse drugs or alcohol.

Includes bibliographical references

Codependents' guide to the twelve steps. Simon & Schuster 1998 273p pa $14   **616.86**
1. Drug abuse
ISBN 0-671-76227-3; 978-0-671-76227-8
           LC 2004-270580

"A Fireside/Parkside recovery book"
First published 1990 by Prentice Hall Press

"Beattie offers an interpretation of the 12 steps based on her own experience as a recovering addict, codependent, and practicing therapist. This includes an excellent annotated bibliography of recovery titles." Libr J

Chopra, Deepak

Overcoming addictions; the spiritual solution. Harmony Bks. 1997 136p il pa $12 hardcover o.p.
       616.86

1. Drug abuse 2. Mind and body
ISBN 0-609-80195-3 (pa)

The author "addresses the topic of dependencies on psychoactive and mood-altering substances and guides the reader to replace addictive behavior with deeper sources of joy and spiritual fulfillment." Publisher's note

Fisher, Edwin B., 1946-

American Lung Association 7 steps to a smoke-free life; [by] Edwin B. Fisher, Jr. with Toni L. Goldfarb. Wiley 1998 226p pa $14.95
       616.86

1. Smoking cessation programs 2. Tobacco habit
ISBN 0-471-24700-6   LC 97-38826

"Based on the American Lung Association's smoking cessation program, this book coaches smokers through discovering their own personal motivations and obstacles to quitting, planning effective strategies to meet and conquer the temptation to pick up a cigarette, and tailoring a cessation program to individual lifestyles." Libr J

Peele, Stanton

7 tools to beat addiction. Three Rivers Press 2004 275p pa $14   **616.86**
1. Alcoholism 2. Drug abuse
ISBN 1-400-04873-7   LC 2003-23765

Contents: Values: building on your values foundation -- Motivation: activating your desire to quit -- Rewards: weighing the costs and benefits of addiction -- Resources: identifying strengths and weaknesses, developing skills to fill the gaps -- Support: getting help from those nearest you -- A mature identity: growing into self-respect and responsibility -- Higher goals: pursuing and accomplishing things of value

"Well written and well researched, this is sure to be an essential text in the addiction field." Libr J

Includes bibliographical references

Weil, Andrew

From chocolate to morphine; everything you need to know about mind-altering drugs; [by] Andrew Weil and Winifred Rosen. Rev ed. Houghton Mifflin 2004 291p pa 14.95
       616.86

1. Psychotropic drugs
ISBN 0-618-48379-9   LC 2004-57677

First published 1983 with title: Chocolate to morphine: understanding mind-active drugs

"Neither condoning nor condemning drug use, the authors cover a wide range of available substances, from coffee to marijuana, from antihistamines to psychedelics, from steroids to the new 'smart drugs.' Besides describing the likely effects of each drug, the authors discuss precautions and alternatives." Publisher's note

"Because drug use (legal or illegal) is not condemned, this volume may be considered unorthodox by some. . . . Aimed at young people, their parents and teachers, this book offers an alternative way of looking at drug Libr J

Includes bibliographical references

West, James W.

The Betty Ford Center book of answers; help for those struggling with substance abuse and for the people who love them; foreword by Betty Ford. Pocket Bks. 1997 206p pa $16.95
       616.86

1. Drug abuse 2. Alcoholism
ISBN 0-671-00182-5   LC 96-41485

"Chapters include straighforward information on how to identify an alcoholic, intervention, effects of substance abuse on the brain and other parts of the body, treatment, prevention, and relapse." Libr J

616.89 Mental disorders

Amen, Daniel
Change your brain, change your life; the breakthrough program for conquering anxiety, depression, obsessiveness, anger, and impulsiveness. Times Bks. 1998 337p il pa $15 hardcover o.p. **616.89**
1. Mental illness 2. Brain
ISBN 0-8129-2998-5 (pa) LC 98-15043
Using brain imaging technology the author identifies which brain systems are associated with specific problems. In addition to changes in diet the author advocates the use of fragrances, music, lighting, and cognitive exercises in combating certain negative behaviors
Includes bibliographical references

Carter, Rosalynn
Helping someone with mental illness; a compassionate guide for families, friends, and caregivers; {by} Rosalynn Carter, with Susan K. Golant. Times Bks. 1998 348p pa $15 hardcover o.p. **616.89**
1. Mental illness
ISBN 0-8129-2898-9 (pa) LC 97-39218
"The chapters of part 1 relate what spurred Carter's involvement with mental-health issues and profile families dealing with mental illness. . . . Part 2 sketches scientific and technological advances that are empowering treatment and homes in on understanding schizophrenia, depression, manic-depression, and anxiety disorders—the four basic kinds of mental illness. The third part discusses intervention, prevention, caregiving, and advocating in respect to mental illness." Booklist
Includes bibliographical references

The **Complete** guide to mental health for women; edited by Lauren Slater, Jessica Henderson Daniel, and Amy Banks. Beacon Press 2003 403p $45; pa $24.95 * **616.89**
1. Mental health 2. Women—Health and hygiene
ISBN 0-8070-2924-6; 0-8070-2925-4 (pa)
  LC 2003-10436
This guide addresses issues ranging "from aging and depression to pregnancy and trauma." Libr J
"Drawing on the latest thinking in psychiatry and psychology, and written for women of diverse backgrounds, this . . . guide to women's mental health provides a comprehensive and readable overview to the psychological issues that concern women most." Univ Press Books 2004
Includes bibliographical references

Duke, Patty
A brilliant madness; living with manic-depressive illness; {by} Patty Duke and Gloria Hochman. Bantam Bks. 1992 285p pa $7.99 hardcover o.p. **616.89**
1. Manic-depressive illness
ISBN 0-553-56072-7 (pa) LC 92-5878

This work "alternates between the actress's first-person description of her experiences as a manic-depressive and Ms. Hochman's informative narrative about this sickness. . . . Ms. Duke is a comforting guide through the terror of mental illness, and Ms. Hochman lightens a weighty topic with interesting, animated writing." N Y Times Book Rev
Includes bibliographical references

The **Gale** encyclopedia of mental health; [by] Laurie J. Fundukian and Jeffrey Wilson, editors. 2nd ed. Thomson Gale 2008 2v il set $389 **616.89**
1. Mental health—Encyclopedias 2. Mental illness—Encyclopedias 3. Psychiatry—Encyclopedias
ISBN 978-1-4144-2987-8 LC 2007-26137
First published 2003 with title: The Gale encyclopedia of mental disorders
This encyclopedia "offers accessible information on mental health for consumers and high school or undergraduate students. . . . The set contains over 400 entries and over 200 color photographs, tables, and illustrations. . . . The disorders covered are mostly recognized by the American Psychiatric Association, with entries for conditions and disorders usually including symptoms and demographics—a great asset for those needing statistics quickly." Libr J
Includes bibliographical references

Hewetson, Ann
The stolen child; aspects of autism and Asperger syndrome; foreword by Susan J. Moreno. Bergin & Garvey Pubs. 2002 240p $26.95 **616.89**
1. Autism 2. Asperger's syndrome
ISBN 0-89789-844-3 LC 2001-43015
"A compendium of historical facts along with the latest thinking about the puzzling field of autism-spectrum disorders, this volume covers theories about what might cause autism and current treatments. Hewetson uses many levels of evidence—including case history, anecdotal observations, correlational studies, controlled research findings—and critiques." Choice
"A strong introductory text. . . . Hewetson, the mother of a son with high-ability autism, carefully balances the different approaches and does not promote one treatment over another as the cure for all people with ASD." Libr J
Includes bibliographical references

Hicks, James Whitney, 1964-
Fifty signs of mental illness; a guide to understanding mental health. Yale University Press 2005 389p (Yale University Press health & wellness) hardcover o.p. pa $17 * **616.89**
1. Mental illness 2. Abnormal psychology
ISBN 0-300-10657-2; 0-300-11694-2 (pa)
  LC 2004-21535
Contents: Anger -- Antisocial behavior -- Anxiety -- Appetite disturbances -- Avoidance -- Body image problems -- Compulsions -- Confusion -- Cravings -- Deceitfulness -- Delusions -- Denial -- Depression -- Dissocia-

Hicks, James Whitney, 1964-—*Continued*
tion -- Euphoria -- Fatigue -- Fears -- Flashbacks -- Grandiosity -- Grief -- Hallucinations -- Histrionics -- Hyperactivity -- Identity confusion -- Impulsiveness -- Intoxication -- Jealousy -- Learning difficulties -- Mania -- Memory loss -- Mood swings -- Movement problems -- Nonsense -- Obsessions -- Oddness -- Panic -- Paranoia -- Physical complaints and pain -- Psychosis -- Religious preoccupations -- Self-esteem problems -- Self-mutilation -- Sexual performance problems -- Sexual preoccupations -- Sleep problems -- Sloppiness -- Speech difficulties -- Stress -- Suicidal thoughts -- Trauma

"A reservoir of useful knowledge, this belongs in almost every library serving real people." Libr J

Kahn, Ada P.
The encyclopedia of mental health; [by] Ada P. Kahn, Jan Fawcett. 3rd ed. Facts On File 2008 520p (Facts on File library of health and living) $75 *   **616.89**
1. Mental health—Encyclopedias 2. Psychiatry—Encyclopedias
ISBN 978-0-8160-6454-0; 0-8160-6454-7
      LC 2006-102540
First published 1993
This encyclopedia "all aspects of general mental health topics . . . [and includes] definitions of theories, syndromes, symptoms, treatments, and contemporary issues." Publisher's note
Includes bibliographical references

Morey, Bodie
The family intervention guide to mental illness; recognizing symptoms & getting treatment; [by] Bodie Morey, Kim T. Mueser. New Harbinger Publications 2007 227p pa $17.95   **616.89**
1. Mental illness
ISBN 978-1-57224-506-8; 1-5722-4506-9
      LC 2007-13002
The authors "guide readers through a step-by-step process for helping a mentally afflicted loved one. Chapters begin with a 'fundamental step' ('Discuss the situation openly,' 'Get a correct diagnosis'), and end with a list of 'good steps' ('Familiarize yourself with the symptoms') and 'missteps' ('Thinking that it's none of your business') which give readers extra guidance. . . . Comprehensive, compassionate and rooted in solid research, this easy-to-read guidebook is suitable for any family in search of answers." Publ Wkly
Includes bibliographical references

Neugeboren, Jay, 1938-
Transforming madness; new lives for people living with mental illness. University of California Press 2001 390p pa $16.95   **616.89**
1. Mentally ill 2. Mental illness
ISBN 0-520-22875-8
First published 1999 by Morrow
"A quiet revolution is taking place in the care and treatment of the mentally ill, observes Neugeboren in this . . . report. Within the last five to 10 years, antipsychotic medications have become much more effec-

tive and their side effects less debilitating. Just as important, he notes, is the emergence of recovery programs, peer support centers and community treatment facilities that make it possible for the severely mentally ill to go to college, hold down jobs, marry and raise children-even without being fully cured." Publ Wkly
The author "provides a literate, lively guide, rich in history, biography, and economics as well as psychology and neurochemistry." Libr J
Includes bibliographical references

Noll, Richard, 1959-
The encyclopedia of schizophrenia and other psychotic disorders; foreword by Leonard George. 3rd ed. Facts on File 2007 xx, 409p (Facts on File library of health and living) $75   **616.89**
1. Schizophrenia—Encyclopedias
ISBN 0-8160-6405-9; 978-0-8160-6405-2
      LC 2005-56749
First published 1992
"Biologically related schizophrenic disorders, genetics, antipsychotic drug treatments, and pathophysiology are a few of the topics explored in the more than 600 entries. . . . The language is clear, making this volume equally suitable for use by patients, scholars, and general readers. A solid addition for health collections." Booklist
Includes bibliographical references

Osborne, Lawrence
American normal; the hidden world of Asperger syndrome. Copernicus 2002 224p $27.50
      616.89
1. Asperger's syndrome
ISBN 0-387-95307-8   LC 2002-73782
"Basing his report on memoirs, clinical histories, poems and stories, and visits with dozens of individuals afflicted with the disorder, journalist and essayist Lawrence Osborne shows us what life with Asperger's is really like." Publisher's note
"Osborne uses his considerable journalistic talents to interview a number of well-known and not so well-known people diagnosed with an enigmatic disorder known as Asperger's Syndrome. . . . Recommended for readers at all levels." Choice
Includes bibliographical references

Park, Clara Claiborne
Exiting nirvana; a daughter's life with autism; foreword by Oliver Sacks. Little, Brown 2001 225p il $23.95; pa $14.95   **616.89**
1. Park, Jessy, 1958- 2. Autism
ISBN 0-316-69117-8; 0-316-69124-0 (pa)
      LC 00-33554
The author "covers the past 40 years of her daughter Jessy's life and . . . describes what Jessy has been able to accomplish, as well as setbacks along the way. Also included are color illustrations of Jessy's . . . artwork." Libr J
"A perceptive, detailed, and empathetic account not of autism but of the experience of autism. . . . A warm, levelheaded, neither overly optimistic nor overly glorified book that proves very rewarding." Booklist
Includes bibliographical references

Phillips, Adam

Going sane; maps of happiness. Fourth Estate 2005 xxi, 199p $24.95 **616.89**

1. Mental health 2. Psychoanalysis

ISBN 0-00-715539-5　　　　LC 2005-40063

The author's "interdisciplinary research, which relies on imaginative writings (e.g., Shakespeare) and traditional psychological theory, makes clear that a viable definition of sanity is surprisingly elusive. This concept is further developed through his exploration of how madness and 'badness' coexist in contemporary society; Freudian issues are raised in the context of sexual and money madness, and modern mental illnesses and disorders (autism, schizophrenia, and depression) are also examined. Phillips concludes with an original blueprint on how a 'sane' life might be constructed, including commentaries on sane parenting and dealing with conflict and personal desires. Though stronger on description and analysis than on prescriptive advice, this book is well argued and stunningly thought-provoking." Libr J

Porter, Roy, 1946-2002

Madness; a brief history. Oxford Univ. Press 2002 241p il pa $12.95 hardcover o.p. *

616.89

1. Mental illness 2. Psychiatry

ISBN 0-19-280267-4 (pa)　　　　LC 2001-52329

This is a study on the many ways madness has been perceived and misperceived from antiquity to modern times. The author "also discusses topical issues, including the relationship between lunacy and creativity, the drive to institutionalize, which peaked in the mid-20th century; the rise and demise of psychoanalysis; and the development of the antipsychiatry movement. This book combines the appeal of history as narrative with the intellectual stimulation derived from cogent analysis." Libr J

Includes bibliographical references

Rogers, Carl R. (Carl Ransom), 1902-1987

On becoming a person; a therapist's view of psychotherapy. Houghton Mifflin 1961 420p pa $16 hardcover o.p. **616.89**

1. Psychotherapy

ISBN 0-395-75531-X (pa)

This collection begins with "two talks in which Dr. Rogers gives some biographical data and outlines his progress toward his concept of client-centered therapy; succeeding chapters express his views on helping others toward personal growth, the therapeutic process, his philosophy of the fully functioning person, the place of research in psychotherapy, its implications for living and the new discipline of behavioral sciences." Booklist

Includes bibliographical references

Scull, Andrew T.

Madhouse; a tragic tale of megalomania and modern medicine; [by] Andrew Scull. Yale University Press 2005 360p il $30 **616.89**

1. Cotton, Henry Aloysius, 1836-1933 2. Psychiatry

ISBN 0-300-10729-3　　　　LC 2004-28567

This book describes the once well-received psychiatric treatments of Dr. Henry Cotton, who, in the early 20th century, promoted the use of invasive surgery, including the removal of internal organs, as a treatment for mental illness.

"The shameful episodes described in these histories deserve our attention. The well-documented stories offer dramatic pictures of the cavalier attitudes adopted toward the mentally ill by professional psychiatry." Sci Books Films

Includes bibliographical references

Shorter, Edward

A history of psychiatry; from the era of the asylum to the age of Prozac. Wiley 1997 436p il pa $30 hardcover o.p. **616.89**

1. Psychiatry

ISBN 0-471-24531-3 (pa)　　　　LC 96-15292

Shorter traces "the development of modern psychiatry from the asylum era of the late 18th and 19th centuries . . . to the recent advent of mind-altering pharmaceuticals (i.e., Thorazine, Valium, Prozac, etc.)." Choice

This "social history of 200 years of psychiatry in the U.S., Great Britain, France, and Germany is informative and at times lively. . . . Dealing ably with the major trends, Shorter does not fail to also illuminate such engaging and horrifying byways as the 'fever cure' and ice pick lobotomy." Booklist

Includes bibliographical references

Sichel, Deborah

Women's moods; what every woman must know about hormones, the brain, and emotional health; {by} Deborah Sichel and Jeanne Watson Driscoll. Morrow 1999 352p pa $14 hardcover o.p.

616.89

1. Women—Health and hygiene 2. Women—Psychology

ISBN 0-380-72852-4 (pa)　　　　LC 99-25412

"Drawing on their own personal experiences, the experiences of their patients, and their own research as well as that of others, the authors discuss why the unique brain chemistry of women and the sensitivity of the brain to female hormones make women more susceptible to mood disorders and anxiety problems. They outline the program they use with their patients, which includes some medications and a great deal of self-care." Libr J

Includes bibliographical references

Slater, Lauren

Prozac diary. Penguin Bks. 1999 203p pa $15

616.89

1. Psychotropic drugs 2. Mental illness

ISBN 0-14-026394-2; 978-0-14-026394-7

LC 97-35727

First published 1998 by Random House

The author "was among the first patients to be given Prozac, and she has now been on it, almost without interruption, for ten years. She credits the drug with enabling her, after an incapacitating adolescence, not only to taste and see but to complete a doctorate; marry; and, as director of a clinic, be useful. But she also ponders what it means to one's sense of self to be more or less permanently under the influence of a personality (and libido) altering drug." New Yorker

Stone, Michael H., 1933-

Healing the mind; a history of psychiatry from antiquity to the present. Norton 1997 516p il $49

616.89

1. Psychiatry

ISBN 0-393-70222-7   LC 96-28209

The author "chronicles the persons, movements, and events that have contributed to modern psychiatry. Starting with accounts of aberrant behavior in religious texts, he traces the diagnosis and treatment of mental illness from ancient Greece to present times." Libr J

Includes bibliographical references

Whitaker, Robert

Mad in America; bad science, bad medicine, and the enduring mistreatment of the mentally ill. Perseus Bks. 2002 334p $27; pa $17.50 *

616.89

1. Mental illness 2. Schizophrenia 3. Psychiatric hospitals

ISBN 0-7382-0385-8; 0-7382-0799-3 (pa)

LC 2001-98251

The author "argues that mental asylums in the U.S. have been run largely as 'places of confinement—facilities that served to segregate the misfits from society—rather than as hospitals that provided medical care.' . . . Whitaker's . . . book will appeal to those interested in medical history, as well as anyone fascinated by Western culture's obsessive need to define and subdue the mentally ill." Publ Wkly

Includes bibliographical references

Whybrow, Peter C.

A mood apart; the thinker's guide to emotion and its disorders. Perennial Bks 1998 xx, 363p il map pa $15   **616.89**

1. Personality disorders 2. Self 3. Personality

ISBN 978-0-06-097740-5

Originally published 1997 by Basic Books

"Whybrow examines mania and depression, . . . describing several individual cases. . . . The author guides us through the evolutionary growth of both the so-called lizard, ancient mammal and the new mammal brains within the human brain, then examines areas of behavior, types of diseases, precipitating causes of disease, and treatments." Booklist

"Seldom has the inner emotional landscape of melancholic depression, mania and manic-depressive illness been mapped with so much clarity, empathy and sensitivity." Publ Wkly

Yalom, Irvin D., 1931-

The gift of therapy; an open letter to a new generation of therapists and their patients. HarperCollins Pubs. 2002 xxi, 263p $23.95; pa $12.95   **616.89**

1. Psychotherapy

ISBN 0-06-621440-8; 0-06-093811-0 (pa)

LC 2001-39319

"Yalom offers what he calls a series of tips for therapists, emphasizing process rather than content. . . . His 85 brief advices, while certainly helpful to therapists and patients, may also help any thoughtful person seeking to improve relationships with others and self-understanding." Booklist

Includes bibliographical references

616.9   Other diseases

Edlow, Jonathan A., 1952-

Bull's-eye: unraveling the medical mystery of Lyme disease. Yale University Press 2003 285p il $35; pa $17   **616.9**

1. Lyme disease

ISBN 0-300-09867-7; 0-300-10370-0 (pa)

LC 2002-154119

This account of the discovery of Lyme disease relates how connections were "established between symptoms and tick bites, leading to the discovery of the stages of the disease, its specific microbial cause, and its treatment." Publisher's note

"This well-documented book is . . . as important for the light it sheds on the nature of scientific inquiry within the contemporary social and political context as it is for its information about Lyme disease." Booklist

Includes bibliographical references

Glynn, Ian, 1928-

The life and death of smallpox; [by] Ian and Jenifer Glynn. Cambridge Univ. Press 2004 278p il $25   **616.9**

1. Smallpox

ISBN 0-521-84542-4; 978-0-521-84542-7

LC 2005-297126

The authors "describe the history of the disease from the time of the ancient Egyptian pharaohs to the last natural case, which occurred in Somalia in 1977. . . . This book is thoroughly researched and eminently readable. Although several books have been written on the history of smallpox, this is the definitive work on the subject." Choice

Includes bibliographical references

Kahn, Ada P.

The encyclopedia of stress and stress-related diseases; foreword by Delbert H. Meyer. 2nd ed. Facts on File 2005 438p il (Facts on File library of health and living) $75   **616.9**

1. Stress (Psychology) 2. Stress (Physiology)

ISBN 0-8160-5937-3; 978-0-8160-5937-9

LC 2005-43668

First published 1998 with title: Stress A-Z

In addition to describing how to identify and manage stress this work explores causes and a variety of traditional and alternative methods of treatment.

This book "includes authoritative, up-to-date, and practical encyclopedic information on more than 800 entries . . . related to stress, mental health, and coping in a world in which as many as '80 percent of visits to physicians' offices may result from stress in patients' lives.'" Libr J

Includes bibliographical references

Koplow, David A., 1951-
Smallpox: the fight to eradicate a global scourge. University of Calif. Press 2003 265p $30; pa $14.95   **616.9**
1. Smallpox
ISBN 0-520-23732-3; 0-520-24220-3 (pa)
LC 2002-5539
The author "provides a brief overview of the disease's history, its basic biology, biodiversity concerns, and the role of the World Health Organization in the virus's eradication. He concludes his timely book with a lengthy consideration of the pros and cons of eliminating the smallpox stockpiles." Libr J
Includes bibliographical references

Preston, Richard
The demon in the freezer; a true story. Random House 2002 240p hardcover o.p. pa $7.99
616.9
1. Smallpox 2. Biological warfare
ISBN 0-375-50856-2; 0-345-46663-2 (pa)
Also available in paperback from Fawcett Bks.
The author explains "the chemical properties of the smallpox virus; how a single infected person . . . can set off an epidemic; and what this horrendous disease can be like. . . . We learn how the disease was eliminated by an international vaccination campaign in the 1970's; why there are reasons to believe that the Soviet Union grew staggering quantities of the virus, allegedly in part to arm intercontinental missiles; and how the virus might now be used by others as a 'strategic weapon.'" N Y Times Book Rev

Rocco, Fiammetta
The miraculous fever tree; malaria and the quest for a cure that changed the world. HarperCollins Pubs. 2003 348p il maps $24.95; pa $13.95 *
616.9
1. Malaria 2. Quinine
ISBN 0-06-019951-2; 0-06-095900-2 (pa)
LC 2003-51128
Rocco presents a history of malaria and the drug that eventually cured it, quinine. The tree of the title is the cinchona, whose bark is the source of the drug.
The author's "clear prose and personal investment—having grown up in Africa, she knows malaria and quinine all too personally—ensure that every episode of her narrative enthralls." Booklist
Includes bibliographical references

Turkington, Carol
The encyclopedia of infectious diseases; [by] Carol Turkington, Bonnie Lee Ashby. 3rd ed. Facts On File 2007 412p (Facts on File library of health and living) $75 *   **616.9**
1. Communicable diseases—Encyclopedias
ISBN 0-8160-6397-4; 978-0-8160-6397-0
LC 2006-13795
First published 1998
"The alphabetically arranged volume covers diseases, treatment options, and relevant organizations. . . . Information is provided for each disease and includes its cause, symptoms, treatment, and prevention. Major diseases that have had an impact on the world's population (tuberculosis, AIDS) are covered . . . and include a history. This feature makes the volume useful to researchers and students." Booklist [review of 2003 edition]
Includes bibliographical references

Vanderhoof-Forschner, Karen
Everything you need to know about Lyme disease and other tick-borne disorders; foreword by Willy Burgdorfer. 2nd ed. Wiley 2003 270p il pa $15.95   **616.9**
1. Lyme disease 2. Ticks
ISBN 0-471-40793-3   LC 2003-45066
First published 1997
The author "discusses the status of Lyme disease as a public health threat; the nature and characteristics of ticks; the history of Lyme disease; its symptoms, diagnosis, and treatment; and the search for vaccines. . . . The author's writing is conversational and clear even when discussing complex topics, and her appendixes are outstanding." Libr J
Includes bibliographical references

616.95   Sexually transmitted diseases

Hayden, Deborah
Pox: genius, madness, and the mysteries of syphilis. Basic Bks. 2003 xx, 379p il pa $19.95 hardcover o.p.   **616.95**
1. Syphilis
ISBN 0-465-02881-0 (pa)   LC 2002-15847
The author "presents case studies of various nineteenth- and twentieth-century luminaries rumored to have been syphilitic. The . . . accounts allow readers to draw their own conclusions about men as diverse as Beethoven, Flaubert, Lincoln, and Hitler." Booklist
"A fascinating account . . . any book that combines genius, madness, sex, and disease is bound to find an audience." Libr J
Includes bibliographical references

Marr, Lisa
Sexually transmitted diseases; a physician tells you what you need to know. 2nd ed. Johns Hopkins Univ. Press 2007 371p il $45; pa $18.95 *   **616.95**
1. Sexually transmitted diseases
ISBN   978-0-8018-8658-4;   0-8018-8658-9;
978-0-8018-8659-1 (pa); 0-8018-8659-7 (pa)
LC 2006-100443
"A Johns Hopkins Press health book"
First published 1998
The author "begins with basic anatomy, symptoms, and the components of a medical examination for men and women. She then offers important advice about communications with sex partners and safe sex. The second part of her book discusses specific diseases and their symptoms, diagnosis, and treatment." Libr J
Includes bibliographical references

616.97   Diseases of immune system

Baron-Faust, Rita

The autoimmune connection; essential information for women on diagnosis, treatment and getting on with your life; [by] Rita Baron-Faust, Jill M. Buyon. McGraw-Hill 2004 411p il pa $16.95   **616.97**

1. Immune system
ISBN 0-07-143315-5; 978-0-07-143315-0
First published 2002 by Contemporary Bks.

This volume "covers some 20 diseases, including autoimmune hepatitis, myasthenia gravis, antiphospholipid antibody syndrome, vasculitis, and premature ovarian failure. It also addresses in a single chapter some disorders that often 'travel' with autoimmune diseases (e.g., chronic fatigue syndrome, fibromyalgia, and endometriosis), which can further downgrade a patient's quality of life. . . . The up-to-date information provided here will be welcome in most women's health collections." Libr J
Includes bibliographical references

Cassell, Dana K.

The encyclopedia of autoimmune diseases; {by} Dana Cassell, Noel Rose. Facts on File 2002 364p il (The Facts on File library of health and living) $71.50   **616.97**

1. Autoimmune diseases—Encyclopedias
ISBN 0-8160-4340-X   LC 2002-2029

This encyclopedia "includes more than 300 cross-referenced entries on immunity and autoimmunity. It provides information on autoimmune diseases, their prevalence, levels of severity, demographics, suspected causes, clinical features, possible complications, and treatments." Am Ref Books Annu, 2004
Includes bibliographical references

Gallo, Robert C.

Virus hunting; AIDS, cancer, and the human retrovirus: a story of scientific discovery. Basic Bks. 1991 352p pa $17.50 hardcover o.p.
                               616.97

1. AIDS (Disease) 2. Medicine—Research
ISBN 0-465-09815-0 (pa)   LC 90-55600
"A New Republic book"
The author describes his biomedical research of the cancer-causing retrovirus, how it led to the discovery of the AIDS virus, and the political and ethical controversies surrounding AIDS research

Grmek, Mirko D., 1924-2000

History of AIDS; emergence and origin of a modern pandemic; translated by Russell C. Maulitz and Jacalyn Duffin. Princeton Univ. Press 1990 279p pa $30 hardcover o.p. *   **616.97**

1. AIDS (Disease)
ISBN 0-691-02477-4 (pa)   LC 90-32514
Original French edition, 1989

In this "medical and social history of the disease, Dr. Grmek . . . speculates about the prehistory of AIDS, before its seemingly sudden appearance from nowhere in 1981. He argues that while today's runaway epidemic is a new phenomenon, the viruses that cause AIDS have infected people for many decades, if not for centuries." NY Times Book Rev
Includes bibliographical references

Lipkowitz, Myron

Encyclopedia of allergies; [by] Myron A. Lipkowitz, Tova Navarra. 2nd ed. Facts on File 2001 340p (Library of health and living) $65; pa $19.95   **616.97**

ISBN 0-8160-4404-X; 0-8160-4405-8 (pa)
1. Allergies—Encyclopedias   LC 00-49490
First published 1994 with title: Allergies A-Z

This guide to the symptoms and treatments of a variety of allergies includes over 1,000 entries that provide information on medications, occupational and environmental allergies, inherited allergies, and antihistamines, etc.
Includes bibliographical references

Nakazawa, Donna Jackson

The autoimmune epidemic; bodies gone haywire in a world out of balance and the cutting edge science that promises hope. Simon & Schuster 2008 328p $25   **616.97**

1. Autoimmune diseases
ISBN 978-0-7432-7775-4; 0-7432-7775-9
                        LC 2007-48306
"A Touchstone book"

The author provides information on autoimmune diseases "drawing on personal experience, extensive research, and interviews with medical personnel to look at what autoimmune diseases are, why they happen, and what may trigger them. Special attention is paid to the overwhelming number of seemingly harmless triggers that surround all of us every day. . . . Nakazawa articulates highly complicated medical processes in extremely comprehensible language." Libr J
Includes bibliographical references

Null, Gary

AIDS: a second opinion. Seven Stories Press 2001 750p $34.95   **616.97**

1. AIDS (Disease)
ISBN 1-58322-062-3   LC 00-51013
The author "argues that the AIDS drama has exposed problematic issues having to do with the functioning of U.S. medical institutions. . . . The book dissects the claims of the AZT and drug-cocktail approach to treating AIDS and offers a trilogy of treatment strategies based on wide views of how to enhance the immune system and improve overall functioning." Publisher's note
Includes bibliographical references

Pescatore, Fred, 1961-
The allergy and asthma cure; a complete 8-step nutritional program. Wiley 2003 251p $24.95; pa $15.95 **616.97**
1. Allergy 2. Asthma 3. Food allergy 4. Diet therapy
ISBN 0-471-21468-X; 0-470-27541-3 (pa)
LC 2002-14024
Contents: Understanding and diagnosing allergies; Understanding and diagnosing asthma; Conventional therapies for the treatment of allergies; Conventional therapies for the treatment of asthma; Understanding food sensitivities: the allergy and asthma cure step one; Understanding candida and yeast: the allergy and asthma cure step two; Setting the stage: the allergy and asthma cure step three; The healing phase diet: the allergy and asthma cure step four; The healing phase diet—weight loss: the allergy and asthma cure step five; Breathing better: the allergy and asthma cure step six; Nutritional supplements to treat allergies: the allergy and asthma cure step seven; Nutritional supplements to treat asthma: the allergy and asthma cure step eight; Meal plans; Recipes; A resource guide
Includes bibliographical references

Rumpf, Teri P.
The Sjogren's syndrome survival guide; [by] Teri P. Rumpf, Katherine Morland Hammitt. New Harbinger Publs. 2003 234p pa $15.95
1. Immune system—Diseases **616.97**
ISBN 1-57224-356-2
This discusses Sjogren's syndrome, the most prevalent autoimmune disorder in the U.S. and includes medical information, methods of treatment, and advice on how to cope with the disorder

Walsh, William E.
Food allergies; the complete guide to understanding and relieving your food allergies. Wiley 2000 286p pa $16.95 * **616.97**
1. Allergy
ISBN 0-471-38268-X
LC 00-24608
"While providing an overview of the physiology and types of food allergies, Walsh concentrates on what he terms 'MALS' (monosodium glutamate, acidic foods, low-calorie sweeteners, and refined sugar), the most common allergens identified in his patients. He lists MALS foods, provides a sample elimination diet, and includes information on common fast-food restaurant choices." Libr J
Includes bibliographical references

Watstein, Sarah B.
The encyclopedia of HIV and AIDS; [by] Sarah Barbara Watstein, Stephen E. Stratton; foreword by Evelyn J. Fisher. 2nd ed. Facts on File 2003 660p $71.50 **616.97**
1. AIDS (Disease)—Dictionaries
ISBN 0-8160-4808-8
LC 2002-35220
"Facts on File library of health and living"
First published 1998 with title: The AIDS dictionary
This volume includes "entries covering the basic biological, medical, financial, legal, political, and social issues and terms associated with HIV and AIDS. Entries explain symptoms and treatments, opportunistic infections, prevention strategies, and much more. Appendixes include HIV/AIDS associations, education centers, clinical trials, hotlines, publications, and additional material." Publisher's note
"The coverage is . . . broad and the language is pitched for the intended audience of nonspecialists . . . vastly expanded and brought up to date. . . . Recommended." Choice
Includes bibliographical references

616.99   Tumors and miscellaneous communicable diseases

Adrouny, A. Richard, 1952-
Understanding colon cancer. University Press of Miss. 2002 146p il (Understanding health and sickness series) pa $12 hardcover o.p. **616.99**
1. Colon (Anatomy) 2. Cancer
ISBN 1-57806-473-2 (pa)
LC 2002-788
Contents: Who gets colon cancer and why; The colon; How colon cancer develops; The "look" of colon cancer; The "feel" of colon cancer; Stages and prognosis of colon cancer; Surgical treatment of colon cancer; Treatment of later stages of colon cancer; Prevention; The future
The author "describes the anatomy and physiology of the colon. A detailed chapter makes clear the stages of the disease and how they affect the prognosis. Adrouny describes various surgical procedures, their results, and possible complications. . . . The understandable, thorough book concludes with a resources list and a glossary." Booklist
Includes bibliographical references

American Cancer Society's complete guide to prostate cancer; edited by David G. Bostwick ... [et al.] American Cancer Society, Health Promotions 2005 xxii, 394p il pa $19.95 * **616.99**
1. Prostate 2. Cancer
ISBN 0-944235-54-9
LC 2004-15407
This guide to prostate cancer includes information on "advances in prevention, early detection, and treatment; the range of treatment options available and their advantages, expected outcomes, and potential side effects; how to cope with emotional stresses and potential physical side effects such as incontinence and erectile dysfunction; how to maintain quality of life, sexuality, and relationships after treatment; and practical issues like managing medical information, work, insurance, and money." Publisher's note
This "is an accessible and comprehensive survey that describes PCa and explains who is at risk, backing up its discussions with statistics." Libr J
Includes bibliographical references

American Cancer Society's Guide to complementary and alternative cancer methods. American Cancer Soc. 2000 438p $32.95; pa $24.95 **616.99**
1. Cancer 2. Alternative medicine
ISBN 0-944235-29-8; 0-944235-24-7 (pa)
LC 00-40596

American Cancer Society's Guide to complementary and alternative cancer methods—*Continued*

"The first part of the book defines complementary and alternative methods and commonly used terms; it also explains how to evaluate treatment and discusses types of research, safety, and usage guidelines. The second section covers a wide range of treatment methodologies, arranged into five categories: Mind, Body, and Spirit; Manual Healing and Physical Touch; Herb, Vitamin, and Mineral; Diet and Nutrition; and Pharmacological and Biological Treatment." Libr J

Includes bibliographical references

Arnot, Bob

The breast health cookbook; fast and simple recipes to reduce the risk of cancer; recipes and menus by Barbara Sutherland and Rita Mitchell. Little, Brown 2001 262p hardcover o.p. pa $14.95
616.99

1. Breast cancer 2. Cancer—Diet therapy
ISBN 0-316-05133-0; 0-316-09528-1 (pa)
LC 00-046942

"In this companion volume to . . . The Breast Cancer Prevention Diet, Arnot offers an array of recipes featuring the foods most likely to help people avoid breast cancer (and prostate cancer as well). With more than 150 recipes from nutritionists Rita Mitchell and Barbara Sutherland, the book is structured around ethnic categories of diet Asian, New American, Mediterranean along with suggested meals. Recipes are provided for main courses, sandwiches, soups, desserts and more. The recipes frequently involve soy products, which Arnot believes are key for preventing cancer." Publ Wkly

Breast cancer; beyond convention: the world's foremost authorities on complementary and alternative medicine offer advice on healing; edited by Mary Tagliaferri, Isaac Cohen, and Debu Tripathy. Atria Bks. 2002 478p il hardcover o.p. pa $16   **616.99**

1. Breast cancer 2. Alternative medicine
ISBN 0-7434-1011-4; 0-7434-1012-2 (pa)
LC 2002-16930

This collection of essays "is intended to serve as a guide to the alternative therapies most often used by women with breast cancer. The book includes . . . chapters on approaches such as Chinese Medicine, vitamin and mineral supplementation, meditation and prayer. . . . Women with breast cancer looking for alternative therapies might find this book to be a good start in their own research." Publ Wkly

Includes bibliographical references

Breast cancer sourcebook; edited by Sandra J. Judd. 2nd ed. Omnigraphics, Inc 2004 595p (Health reference series) $78 *
616.99

1. Breast cancer
ISBN 0-7808-0668-9   LC 2004-15399
First published 2001

"Basic consumer health information about breast cancer, including facts about risk factors, prevention, screening and diagnostic methods, treatment options, complementary and alternative therapies, post-treatment concerns, clinical trials, special risk populations, and new developments in breast cancer research along with breast cancer statistics, a glossary of related terms, and a directory of resources for additional help and information." Title page

This is a "thoroughgoing, very readable reference." Libr J [review of 2001 edition]

Cancer sourcebook; edited by Karen Bellenir. 5th ed. Omnigraphics 2007 1133p (Health reference series) $87   **616.99**

1. Cancer
ISBN 978-0-7808-0947-5   LC 2007-3054
First published 1991

"Basic consumer health information about major forms and stages of cancer, featuring facts about head and neck cancers, lung cancers, gastrointestinal cancers, genitourinary cancers, lymphomas, blood cell cancers, endocrine cancers, skin cancers, bone cancers, metastatic cancers, and more; along with facts about cancer treatments, cancer risks and prevention, a glossary of related terms, statistical data, and a directory of resources for additional information." Title page

Includes bibliographical references

Davis, Devra Lee

The secret history of the war on cancer; [by] Devra Davis. Basic Books 2007 505p il $27.95
616.99

1. Cancer 2. Environmental health 3. Public health
ISBN 978-0-465-01566-5; 0-465-01566-2

The author "reveals the serious risks posed by the many environmental carcinogens we're exposed to and the huge effort to suppress this crucial information." Booklist

Includes bibliographical references

Everyone's guide to cancer therapy; how cancer is diagnosed, treated, and managed day to day; {by} Malin Dollinger {et al.}. 4th ed. Andrews McMeel Pub. 2003 xxxiv, 925p il $29.95 *
616.99

1. Cancer
ISBN 0-7407-1856-8   LC 2002-28289
First published 1991

This offers information on cancer diagnosis and treatment options and includes chapters on cryotherapy, radio frequency treatment, genetic risk assessment, and managed care

Goodwin, Scott C.

What your doctor may not tell you about fibroids; new techniques and therapies—including breakthrough alternatives to hysterectomy; {by} Scott C. Goodwin, Michael Broder, and David Drum; foreword by Carla Dionne. Warner Books 2003 xxiv, 320p pa $14.95   **616.99**

1. Uterine fibroids
ISBN 0-446-67853-8

This book "discusses how fibroids grow, the diagnostic tests used to distinguish them from other conditions,

Goodwin, Scott C.—*Continued*

and major symptoms. The roles of diet, exercise, stress reduction, and alternative treatments such as homeopathy and acupuncture are also covered. The book's greatest strength lies in the final chapters, which explain uterine fibroid embolization, myomectomy, and new alternative treatments, both invasive and drug-based." Libr J

Includes bibliographical references

Gordon, James Samuel, 1941-

Comprehensive cancer care; integrating alternative, complementary and conventional therapies; the complete guide; {by} James Gordon and Sharon Curtin. Perseus Bks. 2000 pa $18.50 hardcover o.p. **616.99**

1. Cancer

ISBN 0-7382-0486-2 (pa)

"Based on a series of medical conferences exploring new approaches to cancer, this guide discusses a wide variety of cancer-fighting modalities. Throughout . . . {the authors} encourage readers to consider unfamiliar ideas, form effective patient/doctor partnerships and adopt empowered, informed patient attitudes." Publ Wkly

Harpham, Wendy Schlessel

Diagnosis, cancer; your guide to the first months of healthy survivorship; illustrations by Ann Bliss Pilcher. Expanded and updated ed. W.W. Norton 2003 xxiii, 262p il pa $14.95 **616.99**

1. Cancer

ISBN 0-393-32460-5; 978-0-393-32460-0

LC 2002-156597

First published 1992 with subtitle: Your guide through the first few months

The author discusses current developments in cancer diagnosis and treatments for the newly diagnosed patient, with advice on decision making and emotional and practical problems

Includes bibliographical references

Henschke, Claudia I.

Lung cancer; myths, facts, choices—and hope; {by} Claudia I. Henschke, and Peggy McCarthy, with Sarah Wernick. Norton 2002 389p il $27.95; pa $16.95 **616.99**

1. Lung cancer

ISBN 0-393-04154-9; 0-393-32498-2 (pa)

LC 2002-513

The authors present a "guide to the basics of how lung cancer develops, risk factors, diagnosis, treatment options, and living well with lung cancer. . . . Treatment modalities detailed here include surgery, chemotherapy, and radiation, with additional chapters on alternative therapies such as acupuncture for pain and getting access to the latest treatment through clinical trials." Libr J

Informed decisions; the complete book of cancer diagnosis, treatment, and recovery; [edited by] Harmon Eyre, Dianne Partie Lange; Lois B. Morris, consulting editor. 2nd ed. American Cancer Soc. 2001 768p il pa $29.95 *

616.99

1. Cancer

ISBN 0-944235-27-1 LC 2001-1880

First published 1997 by Viking

"Covering all types of cancer in general terms, this tome from the American Cancer Society discusses detection, diagnosis, and treatment in five parts, subdivided into 31 chapters. Throughout, the information is presented logically, clearly, and in a visually accessible manner, with copious subheads, sidebars (case histories, checklists, dos and don'ts, etc.), headnotes (Tips and Advice, Cancer Basics), and questions to ask the doctor." Libr J

Lerner, Barron H.

The breast cancer wars; hope, fear, and the pursuit of a cure in twentieth century America. Oxford Univ. Press 2001 383p il hardcover o.p. pa $16.95 **616.99**

1. Breast cancer

ISBN 0-19-514261-6; 0-19-516106-8 (pa)

LC 00-63691

This is an account of the development of breast cancer treatments in the United States from the nineteenth-century to the present.

"Lerner's book is essential for women's studies and history of medicine collections, but no public or academic library could go wrong in adding it to its collection." Libr J

Includes bibliographical references

Link, John

The breast cancer survival manual; a step-by-step guide for the woman with newly diagnosed breast cancer. 4th ed. H. Holt 2007 237p il pa $16 **616.99**

1. Breast cancer

ISBN 978-0-8050-8234-0; 0-8050-8234-4

LC 2006-51596

"An Owl book"

First published 1998

This book offers advice on how to get a second opinion, how to work with doctors, exploring different treatment options, and considering genetic testing.

Includes bibliographical references

Montz, Fredrick J.

A guide to survivorship for women with ovarian cancer; [by] F.J. Montz, Robert E. Bristow with assistance from Paula J. Anastasia. Johns Hopkins University Press 2005 209p (Johns Hopkins Press Health Book) $39.95; pa $15.95 **616.99**

1. Ovaries—Cancer

ISBN 0-8018-8090-4; 0-8018-8091-2 (pa)

LC 2004-19610

The authors offer "information on diagnosis and treatment, including chemotherapy, surgery, radiation therapy, pain management, and alternative/complementary options. . . . This important book should be included in all consumer health collections, as well as purchased by women affected by the disease." Libr J

Olson, James Stuart, 1946-

Bathsheba's breast; women, cancer, and history; by James S. Olson. Johns Hopkins Univ. Press 2002 302p $24.95; pa $16.95   **616.99**

1. Breast cancer

ISBN 0-8018-6936-6; 0-8018-8064-5 (pa)

LC 2001-6265

"Olson examines the evolution of cancer research, the politics and economics of the disease, the gender dynamics of female patients and male physicians, and the rise of patient activism. The book chronicles advances in breast-cancer diagnosis and treatment and the uncertainty that women must face while making difficult choices." Libr J

Includes bibliographical references

Panno, Joseph

Cancer: the role of genes, lifestyle, and environment. Facts on File 2004 162p il (New biology) $35   **616.99**

1. Cancer

ISBN 0-8160-4950-5   LC 2003-25840

This book "begins with a . . . summary of cell biology and continues with an overview of the way cancer cells work and how researchers have discovered the nature of these cells. The book looks . . . at the successes and failures of treatments using high doses of chemo- or radiation therapy; the plight of cancer survivors; recent advances in the use of light-activated compounds, monoclonal antibodies, gene therapy, and stem cells . . . as well as the extensive research that has been done to determine the causes of different types of cancer." Publisher's note

Includes bibliographical references

Patt, Richard B.

The complete guide to relieving cancer pain and suffering; {by} Richard B. Patt, Susan S. Lang. rev and expanded ed. Oxford University Press 2004 446p il $30 *   **616.99**

1. Cancer 2. Pain

ISBN 0-19-513501-6   LC 2003-17317

First published 1994 with title: You don't have to suffer with authors' names in reverse order

The authors cover "cancer pain management, from pain undermanagement and the quality-of-life benefits of properly managed pain to types and causes of cancer pain, pain assessment, and medications. Also addressed are high-tech interventions, such as implantable pumps and nerve blocks; nondrug approaches, including relaxation and biofeedback; the special problems of pain in children, teens, and the elderly; psychological aspects; and comfort to the dying." Libr J

Includes bibliographical references

Schwartz, Anna

Cancer fitness; exercise programs for cancer patients and survivors; {by} Anna L. Schwartz. Simon & Schuster 2004 283p il pa $13

616.99

1. Cancer 2. Exercise

ISBN 0-7432-3801-X   LC 2004-45340

"A Fireside book"

This guide "details the physical and mental benefits of exercise before, during, and after cancer. Following a review of the science behind her book (including selected references), . . . {the author} explains how and when to start exercising and presents examples of safe and effective aerobic and strength-building exercises designed for both men and women, young and old. . . . This unique guide is highly recommended for all public, consumer health, and nursing collections." Libr J

Scott, Walter J., 1954-

Lung cancer; a guide to diagnosis and treatment. Addicus Bks. 2000 156p il pa $14.95

616.99

1. Lung cancer

ISBN 1-886039-43-7   LC 00-8028

Scott "explains how the lungs work, the different types of lung cancer, diagnosis, treatment, and end-of-life care. An appendix contains a list of chemotherapy agents, a resource list, and a glossary." Libr J

Silver, Julie K., 1965-

After cancer treatment; heal faster, better, stronger. Johns Hopkins University Press 2006 269p (Johns Hopkins Press health book) $45; pa $16.95   **616.99**

1. Cancer

ISBN 0-8018-8437-3; 978-0-8018-8437-5; 0-8018-8438-1 (pa); 978-0-8018-8438-2 (pa)

LC 2005-33971

This book is "a hands-on guide to survival issues: exercise, diet, fatigue, mental health, spirituality, and how to seek assistance from both Western and alternative medicine. Helpful lists (e.g., symptoms of grief vs. symptoms of depression, problems that cancer survivors may encounter with exercise) and bibliographies at the end of each chapter will assist readers in exploring their own survivorship issues." Libr J

Includes bibliographical references

Silver, Marc, 1951-

Breast cancer husband; how to help your wife (and yourself) through diagnosis, treatment, and beyond; foreword by Frederick P. Smith. Rodale 2004 319p pa $14.95   **616.99**

1. Breast cancer 2. Caregivers

ISBN 1-579-54833-4   LC 2004-7914

The author, "who consulted with surgeons and oncologists for this book, first helps readers deal with the diagnosis, addressing men's stereotypical reactions (usually saying little, followed by overbearing urges to fix the problem), then advising them how to behave (ask questions and, more importantly, listen)." Publ Wkly

"Silver's prose is funny, tender, and filled with rock-solid advice." Libr J

Torrey, E. Fuller (Edwin Fuller)

Surviving prostate cancer; what you need to know to make informed decisions; illustrations by Carlton Stoiber. Yale University Press 2006 280p il (Yale University Press health & wellness) $25

616.99

Torrey, E. Fuller (Edwin Fuller)—*Continued*
1. Prostate 2. Cancer
ISBN 0-300-11640-3
In this guide, the author "describes his own medical and personal experiences while offering detailed explanations of diagnostic and staging procedures, treatment options, potential complications, recurrence, risk factors, possible causes, and other essential topics backed with numerous references to the professional literature." Libr J
Includes bibliographical references

Turkington, Carol
The encyclopedia of breast cancer; [by] Carol Turkington, Karen Krag. Facts on File 2004 308p (Facts on File library of health and living) $75 *
616.99
1. Breast cancer—Encyclopedias
ISBN 0-8160-5028-7   LC 2003-49533
In this reference over 500 "entries discuss breast cancer in men and women, including statistics, prevention, symptoms, causes, treatments, and much more." Publisher's note
"Few libraries will want to be without this all-in-one volume for the layperson. . . . Information is current, with several 2004 studies cited in the text and hundreds of journal articles from 1993 to 2003 listed in the bibliography." Booklist

The encyclopedia of cancer; [by] Carol Turkington, William LiPera. Facts on File 2005 448p (Facts on File library of health and living) $75
616.99
1. Cancer—Encyclopedias
ISBN 0-8160-5029-5   LC 2004-43444
"The encyclopedia covers subjects ranging from adenocarcinoma to melanoma to Wilms' tumor. It includes such cancer-related subjects as laetrile and lasers. . . . It also includes current national and global statistics, gender differences, and promising research. . . . This jargon-free, comprehensive encyclopedia provides essential information to help patients and their families better understand the disease and deal with the various shocks associated with cancer." Choice
Includes bibliographical references

The encyclopedia of men's reproductive cancer; [by] Carol Turkington, Charles R. Pound. Facts on File 2004 304p $75   **616.99**
1. Cancer—Encyclopedias 2. Reproductive system 3. Men—Health and hygiene
ISBN 0-8160-5030-9   LC 2004-10241
"More than 400 entries cover prostate, testicular, and penile cancers (among the most dangerous forms of cancer in men) and explain statistics, prevention, symptoms, causes, treatments, and much more." Publisher's note
"This book is well organized and provides reliable general information." Booklist
Includes bibliographical references

The encyclopedia of women's reproductive cancer; [by] Carol Turkington, Mitchell Edelson. Facts on File 2005 306p $75   **616.99**
1. Cancer—Encyclopedias 2. Reproductive system 3. Women—Health and hygiene
ISBN 0-8160-5031-7   LC 2004-43253

"More than 400 . . . entries discuss ovarian cancer, fallopian tube cancer, uterine cancer, and endometrial cancer, among others, as well as statistics, prevention, symptoms, causes, treatments, and much more." Publisher's note
Includes bibliographical references

617 Miscellaneous branches of medicine. Surgery

Alpert, Michelle J., 1966-
Spinal cord injury and the family; a new guide; [by] Michelle J. Alpert, Saul Wisnia. Harvard University Press 2008 338p il (The Harvard University Press family health guides) $35; pa $16.95   **617**
1. Spinal cord
ISBN   978-0-674-02714-5;   0-674-02714-0; 978-0-674-02715-2 (pa); 0-674-02715-9 (pa)
LC 2007-50307
This is a "basic guide for SCI patients and their families, covering a multitude of important issues from basic spine anatomy, how injuries occur, and the impact of the injury's location to the first days after an injury, the emotional turmoil of the patient and family, and adjusting to work or school. . . . This excellent overview with an emphasis on the physical effects of SCI will be invaluable to a growing, currently underserved audience." Libr J
Includes bibliographical references

Current surgical diagnosis & treatment; edited by Gerard M. Doherty, Lawrence W. Way. 12th ed. Lange Medical Books/McGraw-Hill 2006 1453p il pa $66.95   **617**
1. Surgery
ISSN 0894-2277
ISBN 978-0-07-142315-1; 0-07-142315-X
LC 2006-278501
First published 1977. Periodically revised
This book "covers over 1,000 diseases and disorders managed by surgeons . . . {and} emphasizes quick recall of major diagnostic features and succinct descriptions of disease processes, followed by procedures for definitive diagnosis and treatment, epidemiology, pathophysiology, and pathology." Publisher's note
Includes bibliographical references

Mailhot, Claire B.
Surgery: a patient's guide from diagnosis to recovery; [by] Claire Mailhot, Melinda Brubaker, Linda Garratt Slezak. University of Calif. Press 1999 253p il $20   **617**
1. Surgery
ISBN 0-943671-19-1
"Starting from the moment of diagnosis, the authors walk readers through general topics common to all inpatient treatment, including getting a second opinion; decoding insurance policies; understanding surgical procedures, anesthesia, and medications; preadmission testing (e.g., blood work, chest X-rays); discharge; and home care." Libr J
Includes bibliographical references

Mason, Michael Paul, 1971-

Head cases; stories of brain injury and its aftermath. Farrar, Straus and Giroux 2008 310p $25   **617**

1. Brain—Wounds and injuries
ISBN 978-0-374-13452-5; 0-374-13452-9
                                    LC 2007-32335

This book "deals primarily with patients struggling with the long-term effects of brain injury, the problems that start after the brain has been operated on and the skull put back together." N Y Times (Late N Y Ed)

"The strange effects of neurological damage will draw fans of Oliver Sacks, but Mason's poignant and caring accounts of his clients' lives are sure to touch the hearts of a wide range of readers." Publ Wkly

Includes bibliographical references

McLanahan, Sandra A.

Surgery and its alternatives; how to make the right choices for your health; by Sandra A. McLanahan, David J. McLanahan; preface by Bernie S. Siegel. Twin Streams 2002 814p $35; pa $22   **617**

1. Surgery
ISBN 0-7582-0201-6; 1-57566-739-8 (pa)
                                    LC 2001-92972

The authors discuss "the surgical perspective for conditions that include many types of cancer, coronary artery disease, varicose veins, gallstones and hernias . . . [describing] the surgical techniques available, various anesthetics and preoperative tests. [Also outlined are] alternative methods to surgery as well as ways to utilize complementary medical strategies that improve both body and mind when an operation is necessary." Publ Wkly

Includes bibliographical references

Palmer, Sara

Spinal cord injury; a guide for living; [by] Sara Palmer, Kay Harris Kriegsman, Jeffrey B. Palmer; with contributions by John W. McDonald and Cristina L. Sadowsky. 2nd ed. Johns Hopkins University Press 2008 xx, 352p il (Johns Hopkins Press health book) $45; pa $19.95 *

                                    617

1. Spinal cord
ISBN   978-0-8018-8777-2;   0-8018-8777-1;
978-0-8018-8778-9 (pa); 0-8018-8778-X (pa)
                                    LC 200735741

First published 2000

"Combining first-person accounts with up-to-date medical information, the book addresses all aspects of spinal cord injury—recovery and coping, sex and family matters, transportation and housing, employment and leisure—and reviews the challenges encountered by people with spinal cord injury throughout their lives." Publisher's note

Includes bibliographical references

Sayler, Mary Harwell

The encyclopedia of the back and spine systems and disorders; [by] Mary Harwell Sayler with Arya Nick Shamie. Facts On File 2007 354p (Facts on File library of health and living) $75
                                    617

1. Back—Encyclopedias 2. Spine—Encyclopedias
ISBN 978-0-8160-6678-0   LC 2006-35678

"More than 250 . . . entries provide information on all aspects of the back and spine, including anatomy, metabolic processes, neurological systems, injuries, diseases and disorders, treatments, medicines, nutrition, exercise and lifestyle issues, current research, and . . . more." Publisher's note

Includes bibliographical references

617.1   Injuries and wounds

Burns sourcebook . . .; edited by Allan R. Cook. Omnigraphics 1999 604p il (Health reference series) $78 *   **617.1**

1. Burns and scalds
ISBN 0-7808-0204-7   LC 99-24510

"Basic consumer health information about various types of burns and scalds, including flame, heat, cold, electrical, chemical, and sun burns; along with information on short-term and long-term treatments, tissue reconstruction, plastic surgery, prevention suggestions, and first aid." Title page

Kuhn, Cynthia

Pumped; straight facts for athletes about drugs, supplements, and training; by Cynthia Kuhn, Scott Swartzwelder, and Wilkie Wilson. Norton 2000 190p il pa $14.95   **617.1**

1. Athletes—Drug use 2. Dietary supplements
ISBN 0-393-32129-0   LC 00-30455

The authors offer "advice regarding drugs and supplements. Some of them work but are dangerous; some are dangerous and don't work; many are harmless and have little effect other than to fill the coffers of the sellers. . . . This is an excellent book that provides a realistic overview on the topic of drugs, dietary supplements, and athletics." Booklist

Includes bibliographical references

Micheli, Lyle J., 1940-

The sports medicine bible for young athletes; {by} Lyle J. Micheli, with Mark Jenkins; foreword by T. Barry Brazelton. Sourcebooks 2001 252p il pa $19.95 hardcover o.p.   **617.1**

1. Sports medicine 2. Children—Health and hygiene
ISBN 1-57071-710-9 (pa)   LC 2001-31322

The author provides "advice for parents about choosing a good coach, proper nutrition, stress, and the concerns of young athletes. He then discusses each body system, specific injuries that can occur, and their treatment." Libr J

Oakes, Elizabeth H., 1951-

The encyclopedia of sports medicine; [by] Elizabeth Oakes; foreword by Connie Lebrun. Facts on File 2005 322p il (Facts on File library of health and living) $75   **617.1**

1. Sports medicine—Encyclopedias

ISBN 0-8160-5334-0   LC 2003-24720

"More than 150 entries . . . describe causes, diagnosis, prevention, and treatment of sports injuries for amateur and professional athletes." Booklist

"This is an excellent resource for weekend, varsity high school and college, and professional athletes, and for trainers." Choice

Includes bibliographical references

617.6 Dentistry

Dental care and oral health sourcebook; edited by Amy L. Sutton. 2nd ed. Omnigraphics 2003 609p (Health reference series) $78 *

617.6

1. Dentistry 2. Mouth—Diseases

ISBN 0-7808-0634-4   LC 2003-58485

First published 1997 with title: Oral health sourcebook

"Basic consumer health information about dental care, including oral hygiene, dental visits, pain management, cavities, crowns, bridges, dental implants, and fillings, and other oral health concerns, such as gum disease, bad breath, dry mouth, genetic and developmental abnormalities, oral cancers, orthodontics, and temporomandibular disorders; along with updates on current research in oral health, a glossary, a directory of dental and oral health organizations, and resources for people with dental and oral health disorders." Title page. New edition in preparation

Includes bibliographical references

Wynbrandt, James

The excruciating history of dentistry; toothsome tales & oral oddities from Babylon to braces. St. Martin's Press 1998 248p il pa $14.95 hardcover o.p.   **617.6**

1. Dentistry—History

ISBN 0-312-26319-8 (pa)   LC 98-9794

The author "discusses the development of dentistry as a profession, the use of different anesthetics, and the evolution of dentures and dental prosthetics, among other topics. Much of the book is devoted to anecdotes illustrating discontinued dental practices." Libr J

Includes bibliographical references

617.7 Ophthalmology

Cassel, Gary H., 1953-

The eye book; a complete guide to eye disorders and health; [by] Gary H. Cassel, Michael D. Billig, Harry G. Randall. Johns Hopkins Univ. Press 1998 367p il (Johns Hopkins Press health book) hardcover o.p. pa $19.95   **617.7**

1. Eye—Diseases

ISBN 0-8018-5835-6; 0-8018-5847-X (pa)

LC 97-35348

This "guide covers routine eye care and the more common eye diseases, providing up-to-date facts on refractive surgery, treatment for optical neuritis, and possible nutritional therapies for cataracts and macular degeneration." Libr J

Includes bibliographical references

Kornmehl, Ernest W., 1959-

LASIK: a guide to laser vision correction; [by] Ernest W. Kornmehl, Robert K. Maloney, Jonathan M. Davidorf. 2nd ed. Addicus Books 2006 121p il pa $14.95 *   **617.7**

1. Eye—Surgery

ISBN 1-886039-79-8; 978-1-886039-79-7

LC 2005-35027

First published 2001

"Among the topics the authors cover: how laser surgery works, who is a good candidate for surgery, finding a qualified surgeon, what to expect from the procedure, and post-procedure care." Publisher's note

"The color illustrations are clear and instructive, and the risks and complications associated with the procedure are well delineated." Libr J

Sacks, Oliver W.

The island of the colorblind; and, Cycad island; {by} Oliver Sacks. Knopf 1997 c1996 298p il maps pa $13 hardcover o.p.   **617.7**

1. Color blindness 2. Parkinson's disease 3. Islands of the Pacific

ISBN 0-375-70073-0 (pa)   LC 96-34252

First published 1996 in the United Kingdom

In this "travelogue, the neurologist Oliver Sacks investigates Pingelap, a Pacific atoll where the incidence of total congenital color blindness is an astonishing one in twelve; he also visits Guam, where a mysterious neurodegenerative disorder has had tragic consequences for the native population. Sacks's empathy has always been uncanny, but equally remarkable is his contagious fascination with just about everything." New Yorker

"As a travel writer, Sacks ranks with Paul Theroux and Bruce Chatwin. As an investigator of the mind's mysteries, he is in a class by himself." Publ Wkly

Includes bibliographical references

617.8 Otology and audiology

Burkey, John M., 1959-

Overcoming hearing aid fears; the road to better hearing. Rutgers Univ. Press 2003 175p il $44.95; pa $17.95   **617.8**

1. Hearing aids

ISBN 0-8135-3309-0; 0-8135-3310-4 (pa)

LC 2003-432

The author "explains how the ear works and addresses the most common misconceptions and fears that people have about using hearing aids. He demonstrates the devices' advantages for both the wearers and those with whom they interact. He also discusses the various types of hearing aids, their cost, and the process of diagnosing hearing loss and obtaining the proper hearing aid. A practical guide, with advice to which readers should listen." Libr J

Includes bibliographical references

Myers, David G.

A quiet world; living with hearing loss. Yale Univ. Press 2000 211p $23   **617.8**

1. Deafness 2. Hearing aids

ISBN 0-300-08439-0   LC 00-38153

The author "explores the problems faced by the hard of hearing at home and at work and provides information on the new technology and groundbreaking surgical procedures that are available." Publisher's note

617.9 Operative surgery and special fields of surgery

Cheney, Annie

Body brokers; inside America's underground trade in human remains. Broadway Books 2006 205p $23.95; pa $14 *   **617.9**

1. Procurement of organs, tissues, etc.

ISBN   0-7679-1733-2;   978-0-7679-1733-9; 0-7679-1734-0 (pa); 978-0-7679-1734-6 (pa)

LC 2005-54278

This is an exposé of "the lucrative business of procuring, buying, and selling human cadavers and body parts." Publisher's note

This book "speeds along like a circular saw through a thigh joint. It's a zippy, entertaining read, and more formal, scholarly works on the topic are not." N Y Times Book Rev

Includes bibliographical references

Cosmetic and reconstructive surgery sourcebook; edited by Karen Bellenir. 2nd ed. Omnigraphics 2007 512p il (Health reference series) $78   **617.9**

1. Plastic surgery 2. Consumer education

ISBN 978-0-7808-0951-2; 0-7808-0951-3

LC 2007-18893

First published 2001 with title: Reconstructive and cosmetic surgery sourcebook

"Basic consumer information about plastic surgery and non-surgical appearance-enhancing procedures, including facts about botulinum toxin, collagen replacement, dermabrasion, chemical peels, eyelid surgery, nose reshaping, lip augmentation, liposuction, breast enlargement and reduction, tummy tucking, and other skin, hair, facial, and body shaping procedures." Title page

Includes bibliographical references

Finn, Robert

Organ transplants; making the most of your gift of life. O'Reilly & Assocs. 2000 311p (Patient-centered guides) pa $19.95   **617.9**

1. Transplantation of organs, tissues, etc.

ISBN 1-56592-634-X   LC 00-29837

This guide is "sprinkled with comments from actual recipients, their families, and members of the transplant teams. . . . Appendixes include Internet discussion groups, mailing lists and other web sites, pharmaceutical and financial assistance programs, and contact information for scores of transplant-related organizations." Libr J

Includes bibliographical references

Gilman, Sander L.

Making the body beautiful; a cultural history of aesthetic surgery. Princeton Univ. Press 1999 396p il pa $20.95 hardcover o.p.   **617.9**

1. Plastic surgery

ISBN 0-691-07053-9 (pa)   LC 98-48423

An "inquiry into how aesthetic surgery has evolved into a major area of modern medicine, this book combines cultural perspectives on the body beautiful with a medical chronology." Publ Wkly

Gilman's "book shows a dazzling European erudition. . . . He tells a strange, macabre, and often richly comic story of shifting desires." N Y Rev Books

Includes bibliographical references

Perry, Arthur W.

Straight talk about cosmetic surgery; with a foreword by Michael F. Roizen. Yale University Press 2007 360p il $45; pa $18 *   **617.9**

1. Plastic surgery 2. Consumer education

ISBN 978-0-300-11999-2; 978-0-300-12104-9 (pa)

LC 2007-1333

First published 1997 by Avon Books with title: Are you considering cosmetic surgery?

In this guide to cosmetic surgery, the author "examines the latest innovations, provides sound advice for those considering any cosmetic procedure, and offers an overview of the field. . . . The author also advises on choosing a practitioner, cautioning patients to opt only for a board-certified plastic surgeon, and then discusses the consultation. . . . The rest of the book covers specific procedures (e.g., Botox injections, facial surgery, body contouring) and techniques that do not work (e.g., enderomologie, 'antiaging' medicine). There are also chapters about cosmetic dentistry, hair restoration, and tattoo removal." Libr J

Includes bibliographical references

Transplantation sourcebook; edited by Joyce Brennfleck Shannon. Omnigraphics 2002 628p il (Health reference series) $78 *   **617.9**

1. Transplantation of organs, tissues, etc.

ISBN 0-7808-0322-1   LC 2002-16975

"Basic consumer health information about organ and tissue transplantation, including physical and financial preparations, procedures and issues relating to specific solid organ and tissue transplants, rehabilitation, pediatric transplant information, the future of transplantation, and organ and tissue donation." Publisher's note

Includes bibliographical references and index

618.1 Gynecology

Greer, Germaine, 1939-

The change; women, aging and the menopause. Ballantine 1993 422p pa $23   **618.1**

1. Menopause 2. Women—Psychology 3. Self-realization 4. Aging

ISBN 0-449-90853-4; 978-0-449-90853-2

"A Fawcett Columbine book"

First published 1991 in the United Kingdom

Greer, Germaine, 1939-—*Continued*

This is a discussion of menopause in Western society. Greer looks at medical, psychological and social aspects of the cessation of menstruation and the aging process. She views the climateric as an important turning-point in a woman's life.

"In a wise, witty and inspiring book, Greer rebukes doctors, psychiatrists—and women themselves—who blame the aging female for her menopausal distress. . . . Greer dispels all manner of myths and misconceptions about menopause." Publ Wkly

Includes bibliographical references

Henig, Robin Marantz

Pandora's baby; how the first test tube babies sparked the reproductive revolution. Houghton Mifflin 2004 326p $25   **618.1**
1. Fertilization in vitro 2. Reproductive technology
ISBN 0-618-22415-7   LC 2003-61372
The author "presents the history of in vitro fertilization and the moral, ethical, and political controversies of reproductive technologies." Booklist
Includes bibliographical references

Love, Susan M.

Dr. Susan Love's breast book; [by] Susan M. Love with Karen Lindsey; illustrations by Marcia Williams. 4th ed fully rev. Da Capo Press 2005 620p il pa $22 *   **618.1**
1. Breast
ISBN 978-0-7382-0973-9; 0-7382-0973-2
First published 1990 by Addison-Wesley
A Merloyd Lawrence book
This offers "information on breast health and care, with advice on self-examination, anatomy, cancer, cosmetic surgery, benign tisssue changes, and breast feeding." Booklist [review of 1995 edition]
"A highly readable book that educates, supports and encourages women to become their own advocates of breast health." Publ Wkly [review of 1995 edition]

Dr. Susan Love's menopause and hormone book; making informed choices; {by} Susan M. Love with Karen Lindsey. Rev. pbk. ed. Three Rivers Press (NY) 2003 420p il pa $15.95
            618.1
1. Menopause 2. Hormones 3. Women—Health and hygiene
ISBN 0-609-80996-2   LC 2002-15811
First published 1997 with title: Dr. Susan Love's hormone book
Contents: What is menopause?; The medicalization of menopause; What does it feel like?; Prevention and risk: understanding research; Osteoporosis: are we all going to crumble?; Heart disease: what's your real risk?; Breast cancer: every women's fear?; Endometrial cancer: the first problem with estrogen; For better or worse: hormone therapy and other diseases; Approaches to symptom relief; From flashes to fuzzy thinking: what you can do right now?; For prevention: first, look to your lifestyle!; Alternatives: from acupuncture to herbs; Drugs: other means of prevention; Hormones: the menu of options; Decisions: what should I do?
Includes bibliographical references

Minkin, Mary Jane

The Yale guide to women's reproductive health; {by} Mary Jane Minkin, Carol V. Wright. Yale Univ. Press 2003 448p il $29.95   **618.1**
1. Women—Health and hygiene
ISBN 0-300-09820-0   LC 2002-35738
"Aiming to provide readers with information needed to make choices that may be presented in a gynecologist's office, the text covers menstruation, contraceptives, infections and sexually transmitted diseases, breast and genital tract cancer, pregnancy and infertility, and abortion and miscarriage." Libr J
Includes bibliographical references

Moore, Michele

The only menopause guide you'll need. 2nd ed. Johns Hopkins University Press 2004 164p hardcover o.p. pa $15.95 *   **618.1**
1. Menopause
ISBN 0-8018-8012-2; 0-8018-8013-0 (pa)
            LC 2004-43483
"A Johns Hopkins Press Health Book"
First published 2000
In this guide the author "includes specific recommendations for coping with symptoms ranging from night sweats to low libido, and outlines menopausal women's 'major health concerns,' namely, osteoporosis, cancer and heart disease. . . . Women looking for a comforting guide to menopause, with practical information as well as a sense of spirituality, will find it here." Publ Wkly
Includes bibliographical references

Our bodies, ourselves: menopause; [by] the Boston Women's Health Book Collective; with a preface by Vivian Pinn. Simon & Schuster 2006 350p il pa $15 *   **618.1**
1. Menopause 2. Women—Health and hygiene
ISBN 978-0-7432-7487-6; 0-7432-7487-3
            LC 2006-44362
"The authors consider menopause within the totality of women's health and as a natural process, not a medical problem. They detail typical menopausal symptoms, mainstream and alternative treatments, and risk factors for such conditions as osteoporosis, heart disease, cancer and diabetes as women age. . . . As a general reference on menopause, this volume will be embraced by a wide female audience." Publ Wkly
Includes bibliographical references

Sheehy, Gail

The silent passage: menopause. Rev and updated with four brand-new chapters. Pocket Bks. 1998 xxvi, 293p pa $7.50   **618.1**
1. Menopause
ISBN 0-671-56777-2   LC 98-65873
First published 1992
The author examines the medical, psychological, and social aspects of menopause and includes interviews with women in various stages of menopause and with experts. Discussions of herbal remedies, exercise and diet, menopause in the workplace, estrogen and brainpower, and new frontiers in treatment are included

Wallach, Edward E.

Hysterectomy: exploring your options; [by] Edward E. Wallach & Esther Eisenberg. Johns Hopkins University Press 2004 204p il $45; pa $16.95   **618.1**

1. Hysterectomy 2. Consumer education

ISBN 0-8018-7622-2; 0-8018-7623-0 (pa)

       LC 2003-6239

"A Johns Hopkins Press health book"

This is a "guide to provide the information women need to determine whether a hysterectomy is the best alternative in their specific medical situation. Part 1 reviews the anatomy and physiology of the uterus and related structures, Part 2 discusses the specific conditions that may indicate the need for a hysterectomy, Part 3 addresses the surgery itself, and Part 4 details post-hysterectomy issues. The authors stress two important points: hysterectomy is often performed unnecessarily, and the surgery is almost always done as an elective. This important decision-making tool for women should be included in most consumer health and public library collections." Libr J

West, Stanley

The hysterectomy hoax; the truth about why many hysterectomies are unnecessary and how to avoid them; by Stanley West with Paula Dranov. 3rd ed. Next Decade 2002 243p il pa $19.95

       618.1

1. Hysterectomy 2. Consumer education

ISBN 0-9700908-1-1   LC 2001-55868

First published 1994 by Doubleday

"West, an infertility specialist, makes a strong case against hysterectomy unless a woman has cancer. Providing clear, illustrated explanations of female anatomy and physiology, he also thoroughly discusses fibroids, endometriosis, uterine prolapse, ovarian cysts, and precancerous conditions. West offers effective treatments that enable women to preserve their ovaries and uterus as these organs are important for sexuality and hormone production, even after menopause." Libr J {review of 1994 edition}

Wingert, Pat

Is it hot in here? Or is it me? the complete guide to menopause; [by] Pat Wingert & Barbara Kantrowitz. Workman Pub. 2006 532p il $29.95; pa $17.95   **618.1**

1. Menopause

ISBN   0-7611-4370-X;   978-0-7611-4370-3; 0-7611-3808-0 (pa); 978-0-7611-3808-2 (pa)

This is a "guide to major menopausal complaints: hot flashes, sleep disorders, sexual dysfunction, bleeding, and mood and memory changes. There is also information on midlife health issues like osteoporosis, heart disease, and cancer, as well as evidence-based discussions of available treatment options. Q&A sections, case studies, material on what to tell your daughter, memory tests, and 'Looking Good' beauty tips, combined with the writers' reader-friendly, authoritative tone, make this book an outstanding addition to menopause and midlife health collections." Libr J

618.2   Obstetrics

Alcañiz, Lourdes

Waiting for bebé; a pregnancy guide for Latinas. Ballantine Books 2003 xxiii, 390p il pa $14.95

       618.2

1. Pregnancy 2. Hispanic American women—Health and hygiene 3. Childbirth

ISBN 0-345-45211-9

Also available Spanish language edition

The author "includes Spanish terminology and specifically addresses herbs, foods, beverages, customs, and social beliefs indigenous to Latino culture. Her comprehensive text spans from preconception to post-labor and includes sections for the father-to-be, checklists, questions to ask the doctor, a section describing insurance options, and a really well-written portion on gestational diabetes and other pregnancy-related conditions that affect Hispanic women in particular. Practical but not preachy, this is sure to be of enormous help to mothers-to-be, especially first-time mothers." Libr J

Includes bibliographical references

Bruce, Debra Fulghum, 1951-

Making a baby; everything you need to know to get pregnant; {by} Debra Fulghum Bruce and Samuel Thatcher. Ballantine Bks. 2000 379p pa $14.95 *   **618.2**

1. Pregnancy 2. Infertility

ISBN 0-345-43543-5

The authors offer a guide to "babyboosting medicines, IVF, sperm injection, and egg donation. They explain how the male and female reproductive systems work and detail the many common, and sometimes hidden, threats to fertility. They offer practical, low-tech-solutions, such as lifestyle changes, as well as the more advanced therapies." Libr J

Includes bibliographical references

Curtis, Glade B.

Your pregnancy week by week; [by] Glade B. Curtis, Judith Schuler. 6th ed., fully rev. and updated. Da Capo/Lifelong Books 2008 648p il (Lifelong books) $23; pa $15.95 *

       618.2

1. Pregnancy 2. Prenatal care

ISBN 978-0-7382-1108-4; 978-0-7382-1109-1 (pa)

"A Lifelong original"

First published 1989 by Fisher Books

This pregnancy guide includes information on fetal development, medical procedures and tests, nutrition, and exercise during pregnancy, and advice for fathers.

Includes bibliographical references

Greene, Alan R., 1959-

Raising baby green; the earth-friendly guide to pregnancy, childbirth, and baby care; [by] Alan Greene; with Jeanette Pavini and Theresa Foy DiGeronimo; illustrations by Val Lawton. Jossey-Bass 2007 306p il pa $16.95

618.2

1. Pregnancy 2. Infants—Care 3. Environmental protection

ISBN 978-0-7879-9622-2; 0-7879-9622-X

LC 2007-23342

The author "discusses everything from what to take with you to the delivery room to questions to ask hospitals/birth centers about how green they are. 'Buying Green' text boxes give contact info for recommended retailers of products of all types." Libr J

This "informative guide for raising children in the most environmentally friendly way possible makes for some fascinating (and surprising) reading. . . . An excellent choice for those who don't know where to begin when it comes to environmental parenting." Booklist

Includes bibliographical references

Kitzinger, Sheila, 1929-

The complete book of pregnancy and childbirth; black-and-white photography by Marcia May. rev ed. Knopf 2003 448p $35; pa $19.95

618.2

1. Pregnancy 2. Childbirth 3. Infants—Care

ISBN 1-400-04108-2; 0-375-71047-7 (pa)

LC 2002-43433

First published 1980

After an overview of basic embryology the author covers health, nutrition and emotional well-being during pregnancy. Hospital facilities, home birthing rooms, drugs and exercise are discussed

Includes bibliographical references

Murkoff, Heidi Eisenberg

What to expect when you're expecting; by Heidi Murkoff and Sharon Mazel; foreword by Charles J. Lockwood. 4th ed. Workman 2008 xxiii, 614p il pa $14.95 *

618.2

1. Pregnancy 2. Childbirth

ISBN 978-0-7611-4857-9; 0-7611-4857-4

First published 1984 under the authorship of Arlene Eisenberg, Heidi E. Murkoff, and Sandee E. Hathaway.

"The book is arranged by month, from pregnancy test through labor and delivery. Each section offers answers to frequently asked questions, along with features such as 'What You May Be Feeling' . . . This book remains an indispensable guide for pregnant women and their partners." Publ Wkly [review of 2002 edition]

Our bodies, ourselves: pregnancy and birth; [by] the Boston Women's Health Book Collective. Simon & Schuster 2008 370p il pa $15 *

618.2

1. Pregnancy 2. Childbirth

ISBN 978-0-7432-7486-9; 0-7432-7486-5

LC 2007-49498

This book includes "information on making health-care decisions (e.g., choosing a provider and a birth setting), nutrition, labor and delivery, Cesarean birth, recovery, feeding an infant, and life as a new mother. It also addresses special situations such as prenatal testing and pregnancy loss. . . . This is an excellent book for public and consumer health library collections; highly recommended." Libr J

Includes bibliographical references

Port, David

The caveman's pregnancy companion; a survival guide for expectant fathers; [by] David Port and John Ralston; Brian M. Ralston, consultant; Gideon Kendall, illustrator. Sterling 2006 227p il pa $12.95

618.2

1. Pregnancy 2. Childbirth 3. Fathers

ISBN 1-4027-3526-X; 978-1-4027-3526-4

This "pregnancy guide is based on the conceit that most men are 'twenty-first-century Cro-Magnons' at those times when an expectant father 'stops, scratches his head, and mutters to his woman, "I don't get it."'" What is immediately obvious about the book, however, is that it is actually a superb overview of the birthing experience. . . . [It also covers] prenatal massages, amniocentesis and a wonderful range of easy meals to prepare for a tired spouse." Publ Wkly

Includes bibliographical references

Puryear, Lucy J.

Understanding your moods when you're expecting; emotions, mental health, and happiness—before, during, and after pregnancy. Houghton Mifflin Co. 2007 240p $24

618.2

1. Pregnancy 2. Women—Psychology 3. Childbirth 4. Child care

ISBN 978-0-618-34107-8; 0-618-34107-2

LC 2006-35606

Puryear "reassures readers with her authoritative, sensitive, and calming tone as she discusses what to expect during and after pregnancy. Medical facts are effectively interspersed with real-life scenarios. Tips offer down-to-earth coping advice in bite-sized chunks." Libr J

Riley, Laura

You & your baby: pregnancy; the ultimate week-by-week pregnancy guide. Meredith Books 2006 455p il (You & your baby) pa $14.95

618.2

1. Pregnancy 2. Prenatal care

ISBN 0-696-22221-3; 978-0-696-22221-4

Subtitle on cover: Your ultimate week-by-week pregnancy guide; "Full-color fetal development photos inside" Cover

This "guide begins with the first clues that one might be pregnant and progresses week by week until the baby reaches three months. Major sections cover first, second, and third trimesters; labor and delivery; feeding your baby; and postpartum and baby care. The trimester sections are further broken down into weeks, with each week addressing baby, body, self, diet and exercise, and common questions. . . . This easy-to-read guide is excellent for any library." Libr J

Sember, Brette McWhorter, 1968-

The everything guide to pregnancy over 35; from conquering your fears to assessing health risks—all you need to have a happy, healthy nine months; technical review by Bruce D. Rodgers and Diane E. Rodgers. Adams Media 2007 289p pa $14.95   **618.2**

1. Pregnancy 2. Childbirth 3. Middle age
ISBN 978-1-59869-245-7; 1-59869-245-3
LC 2007-15890

"An everything series book"

This guide to pregnancy over the age of thirty-five includes information on fertility treatments, prenatal care options, nutrition and exercise, prenatal testing, preparing for labor and delivery, and financial issues.

This "upbeat book gives a clear and honest overview of issues facing pregnant women over 35." Libr J

Van der Ziel, Cornelia

Big, beautiful & pregnant; expert advice and comforting wisdom for the expecting plus-size woman. Marlowe & Co. 2006 273p il pa $15.95   **618.2**

1. Pregnancy 2. Prenatal care 3. Obesity
ISBN 1-56924-319-0; 978-1-56924-319-0
LC 2006-7832

Contents: Accept yourself: key steps to a healthy pregnancy — Fertility and weight — The Sisterhood's guide to prenatal health care — Trimester by trimester: your medical concerns addressed — Prenatal nutrition — Prenatal exercise — Gestational diabetes — Celebrate your pregnancy — Labor and delivery — Beautiful beginnings: postpartum life

"This belongs in every library's pregnancy collection." Libr J

Includes bibliographical references

Vincent, Peggy, 1942-

Baby catcher; chronicles of a modern midwife. Scribner 2002 336p $26; pa $13 *   **618.2**

1. Midwives
ISBN 0-7432-1933-3; 0-7432-1934-1 (pa)
LC 2001-54988

This is an account of a midwife specializing in home births who "over the course of 40 years, brought some 2,000 babies into the world. . . . A solid writer, Vincent doesn't preach the virtues of unmedicated birthing; she just lays consistent stories of women doing it—Christian Science moms, Muslim moms, spiritualist moms, lesbian moms, teen moms and just plain ordinary moms." Publ Wkly

618.3 Diseases and complications of pregnancy

Kohn, Ingrid

A silent sorrow; pregnancy loss: guidance and support for you and your family; [by] Ingrid Kohn and Perry-Lynn Moffitt, with Isabelle A. Wilkins. 2nd ed. Routledge 2000 xx, 299p pa $16.95   **618.3**

1. Miscarriage 2. Bereavement
ISBN 0-415-92481-2   LC 99-25720

First published 1993 by Delacorte Press

The authors provide "suggestions to validate parents' grief; cope with the unique concerns of early loss, crisis pregnancies, stillbirth, and newborn death; find medical, religious, and family support; and manage their lives afterwards. The writing is insightful and the tone respectful and supportive." Libr J [review of 1993 edition]

Includes bibliographical references

Lerner, Henry M.

Miscarriage: a doctor's guide to the facts; why it happens and how best to reduce your risks; with contributions by Alice Domar; introduction by Robert Barbieri. Perseus Bks. 2003 291p pa $16.95 *   **618.3**

1. Miscarriage
ISBN 0-7382-0634-2   LC 2002-114586

This book provides "explanations to questions concerning the etiology, diagnosis, prevention, and treatment of miscarriage. His medical and scientific discussion, while exceedingly thorough, is easy to understand. . . . Especially helpful are the concluding chapters, which focus on dealing with the emotional trauma of miscarriage." Libr J

618.4 Childbirth. Labor

Block, Jennifer

Pushed; the painful truth about childbirth and modern maternity care. Da Capo Press 2007 316p il $26; pa $16   **618.4**

1. Medical ethics 2. Childbirth 3. Prenatal care
ISBN   978-0-7382-1073-5;   0-7382-1073-0;
978-0-7382-1166-4 (pa); 0-7382-1166-4 (pa)

The author "examines childbirth in the United States today. A normal physiological process, she argues, has become a medical procedure, often depriving women of the right to choose how they give birth. . . . Readers get objective analysis of informed consent, reproductive rights, and the rights of the fetus vs. the rights of the mother in this thought-provoking text." Libr J

Includes bibliographical references

Gaskin, Ina May, 1940-

Ina May's guide to childbirth. Bantam Books 2003 348p il pa $14.95   **618.4**

1. Natural childbirth
ISBN 0-553-38115-6   LC 2002-29901

Gaskin, Ina May, 1940-—*Continued*

Gaskin "explains that the female body is well designed for normal birth and provides techniques for dealing with the discomforts of labor. A whole chapter devoted to women's birthing experiences supports her stance. More than a childbirth guide, this comprehensive book provides insight into the sociological and historical aspects of the natural childbirth movement." Libr J

Includes bibliographical references

Leboyer, Frédérick

Birth without violence; new translation by Yvonne Fitzgerald. rev ed. Healing Arts Press 2002 131p il pa $16.95   **618.4**

1. Natural childbirth

ISBN 0-89281-983-9   LC 2002-3503

Original French edition, 1974; first English translation published 1975 by Knopf

"The work's stylistic qualities, in addition to the beautiful photographs, jar the reader into thinking about childbirth in a unique and revolutionary way." Choice [review of 1975 edition]

Moore, Michele

Cesarean section; understanding and celebrating your baby's birth; [by] Michele Moore, Caroline de Costa. Johns Hopkins University Press 2003 149p il $49.95; pa $14.95   **618.4**

1. Cesarean section 2. Childbirth

ISBN 0-8018-7336-3; 0-8018-7337-1 (pa)

LC 2002-13625

The authors "explain why C-sections are sometimes the best method of delivery and discuss the anesthesia, surgical procedure, recovery, and care of the mother and child when they return home. They also cover postpartum depression, planning for future births, and the possibility of vaginal birth after Cesarean section (VBAC). They provide a list of questions for women to ask their doctors, nutritional information, an Apgar score chart, a glossary, and a bibliography." Libr J

Includes bibliographical references

Murphy, Magnus, 1963-

Pelvic health and childbirth; what every woman needs to know; by Magnus Murphy, and Carol L. Wasson; foreword by Linda Brubaker. Prometheus Books 2003 312p il pa $21 *   **618.4**

1. Childbirth 2. Pelvic floor disorders

ISBN 1-59102-078-6   LC 2003-5896

The author "has written a unique book about a neglected subject. It explains the symptoms and treatment as well as the advances in labor and delivery and the politics of childbirth, including the option of elective Cesarean birth. An excellent presentation of childbirth options." Libr J

Includes bibliographical references

618.92   Pediatrics

Autism and pervasive developmental disorders sourcebook; edited by Sandra J. Judd. Omnigraphics 2007 631p il (Health reference series) $87   **618.92**

1. Autism

ISBN 978-0-7808-0953-6; 0-7808-0953-X

LC 2007-28714

"Basic consumer health information about autism spectrum and pervasive developmental disorders, such as classical autism, asperger syndrome, rett syndrome, and childhood disintegrative disorder, including information about related genetic disorders and medical problems and facts about causes, screening methods, diagnostic criteria, treatments and interventions, and family and education issues." Title page

Includes bibliographical references

Baby and child health; Jennifer Shu, editor-in-chief. DK Pub 2004 352p il $30

618.92

1. Infants—Health and hygiene 2. Children—Health and hygiene

ISBN 0-7566-0454-0   LC 2004-768

"Published in association with the American Academy of Pediatrics (AAP), this guide provides information for parents of children up to the age of 11 years. It includes all aspects of physical growth and health as well as emotional and intellectual developments. . . . The book starts out with sections for infants and young children. Each includes information about growth and development and diagnosis charts for common symptoms. There are also sections on diseases and disorders by organ system and on first aid. . . . {This} is a useful addition to public and consumer-health library collections." Booklist

Barkley, Russell A., 1949-

Taking charge of ADHD; the complete, authoritative guide for parents. rev ed. Guilford Press 2000 321p $42; pa $19.95   **618.92**

1. Attention deficit disorder 2. Child rearing

ISBN 1-57230-600-9; 1-57230-560-6 (pa)

LC 00-34130

First published 1995

The author "reports on his own theory, recent research, and strategies for parents in the challenge of raising children with attention problems. His view is that attention-deficit hyperactivity disorder (ADHD) is a 'disorder of self-regulation' and that the problems of inattention, overactivity, and lack of inhibition become a developmental disability when extreme. ADHD is described as a neurologically based disorder with a probable genetic base." Sci Books Films

Includes bibliographical references

Bashe, Patricia Romanowski

The oasis guide to Asperger syndrome; advice, support, insight, and inspiration; [by] Patricia Romanowski Bashe and Barbara L. Kirby; forewords by Simon Baron-Cohen and Tony Attwood. 1st rev. ed., completely rev. and updated. Crown Publishers 2005 497p $27.50

618.92

1. Asperger's syndrome 2. Autism
ISBN 1-4000-8152-1   LC 2005-274486
First published 2001

"In addition to discussing what AS looks like and how parents can guide their unique child through the social, emotional, and intellectual challenges of growing up, this edition includes new developments made in AS research over the past four years, new thinking on diagnosis and evaluation, the latest approaches to medication and social skills development, and tips on navigating the maze of interventions, therapies, and special education." Publisher's note

"Bashe and Kirby acknowledge that every AS child is different, but with the help of numerous anecdotes from parents of AS children, they manage to provide a wide-ranging, indispensable guide." Publ Wkly

Includes bibliographical references

Carlton, Pamela

Take charge of your child's eating disorder; a physician's step-by-step guide to defeating anorexia and bulimia; [by] Pamela Carlton and Deborah Ashin. Marlowe & Co. 2007 226p pa $15.95   **618.92**

1. Eating disorders
ISBN 978-1-56924-263-6; 1-56924-263-1
    LC 2006-25836
Carlton "presents practical support for parents of children with anorexia and bulimia. Underscoring the importance of a multidisciplinary treatment team, she provides useful advice on finding appropriate programs and getting insurance companies to pay for treatment. Quotes from teens and family members offer a reality check." Libr J

Includes bibliographical references

Children with autism; a parent's guide; edited by Michael D. Powers; foreword by Temple Grandin. 2nd ed. Woodbine House 2000 xxvii, 427p il pa $17.95   **618.92**
1. Autism
ISBN 1-89062-704-6   LC 00-35165
First published 1989

Coverage includes "daily and family life, early intervention, educational programs, legal rights, advocacy, and a look at the years ahead with a chapter on adults with autism. . . . [Information is also provided] on current diagnostic criteria, Applied Behavior Analysis, the Individuals with Disabilities Education Act (IDEA), autism advocacy via the Internet, and much more." Publisher's note

Includes bibliographical references

Children with spina bifida; a parents' guide; edited by Marlene Lutkenhoff. 2nd ed. Woodbine House 2008 395p il pa $21.95

618.92

1. Spina bifida
ISBN 978-1-890627-77-5   LC 2007-39480
First published 1999 by Woodbine House

"The chapters deal with issues parents will face, from prenatal diagnosis to adulthood—legal issues, education, health concerns, treatments, therapies, and causes. The extensive Resource Guide at the back of the book is remarkable." Libr J [review of 1999 edition]

Includes bibliographical references

The **Children's** Hospital guide to your child's health and development; with a foreword by T. Berry Brazelton. Perseus Bks. 2001 xx, 796p il pa $20 hardcover o.p.   **618.92**
1. Children—Health and hygiene 2. Children—Diseases 3. Child development
ISBN 0-7382-0743-8 (pa)
"A Merloyd Lawrence book"

This is a "parental guide to a child's physical, behavioral, and psychological health and development. The book is divided into five sections: prenatal preparation and birth of the newborn; norms at one month, one year, toddler, preschooler, and school age; choosing a doctor and childcare; sickness and emergencies and . . . an alphabetical list of common childhood illnesses and injuries." Libr J

"Presented in a friendly, matter-of-fact style with simple but helpful illustrations, it is a veritable encyclopedia on current developmental theory, medical recommendations, and diverse parenting ideas." Publ Wkly

DeGrandpre, Richard J.

Ritalin nation; rapid-fire culture and the transformation of human consciousness. Norton 1999 284p pa $13.95 hardcover o.p.

618.92

1. Attention deficit disorder 2. Ritalin
ISBN 0-393-32025-1 (pa)   LC 98-20687
The author questions "psychiatry's identification of ADHD as a biologically based brain disease. He argues that societal adjustments and a change in human consciousness are the real antidotes for this development disorder. Viewing hyperactivity in a multidisciplinary context, *Ritalin Nation* is richly referenced and offers a critical perspective suited to academic and specialized collections." Libr J

Includes bibliographical references

Diller, Lawrence H.

Running on Ritalin; a physician reflects on children, society, and performance in a pill. Bantam Bks. 1998 386p $12.95 hardcover o.p.

618.92

1. Attention deficit disorder 2. Ritalin 3. Children—Health and hygiene
ISBN 0-553-37906-2 (pa)   LC 98-232695
The author discusses Attention deficit disorder (ADD), "the effects of Ritalin and behavior therapy, societal and parental expectations, ADD in adults, and treatment op-

Diller, Lawrence H.—*Continued*

tions." Libr J

Includes bibliographical references

Ferber, Richard

Solve your child's sleep problems. Completely rev. and updated ed. Fireside 2006 440p pa $15.95
618.92

1. Sleep 2. Children—Health and hygiene

ISBN 0-7432-0163-9   LC 2006-41406

First published 1985

The author argues "that most sleep disruptions in one to six-year-olds are caused by improper sleep association (e.g., being rocked instead of lying still). Suggested corrections, often backed with specific case studies, are considerate of children; ditto for advice on prebedtime routines. . . . Interruptions in sleep (e.g., bedwetting, nightmares), establishing schedules, and children's natural sleep rhythms are all explored." Libr J

Foa, Edna B.

If your adolescent has an anxiety disorder; an essential resource for parents; [by] Edna B. Foa and Linda Wasmer Andrews. Oxford University Press 2006 227p il (The Annenberg Foundation Trust at Sunnylands' adolescent mental health initiative) $30; pa $9.95   **618.92**

1. Anxiety

ISBN   0-19-518150-6;   978-0-19-518150-0; 0-19-518151-4 (pa); 978-0-19-518151-7 (pa)

LC 2005-23770

"The Annenberg Public Policy Center of the University of Pennsylvania"

"This text covers seven different conditions—social anxiety disorder, generalized anxiety disorder, obsessive-compulsive disorder, posttraumatic stress disorder, separation anxiety disorder, panic disorder, and specific phobias—emphasizing the first four. . . . Each disorder is accompanied by a definition, contributing factors, treatment information, and case studies." Libr J

Includes bibliographical references

Frith, Uta, 1941-

Autism: explaining the enigma. 2nd ed. Blackwell 2003 249p il $59.95; pa $26.95
618.92

1. Autism

ISBN 0-631-22900-0; 0-631-22901-9 (pa)

LC 2002-12932

First published 1989

Contents: What is autism?; The enchantment of autism; Lessons from history; Is there an autism epidemic?; Mind-reading and mind-blindness; Autism aloneness; The difficulty of talking to others; Intelligence and special talent; A fragmented world; Sensations and repetitions; Seeing the brain through a scanner

This "book is valuable for educated parents interested in learning about autism in a larger historical context. Frith writes a great deal on the problem that autistic people have with 'mind blindness,' the inability to look at and see other people." Libr J

Includes bibliographical references

The **Gale** encyclopedia of children's health; infancy through adolescence; Kristine Krapp and Jeffrey Wilson, editors. Thomson Gale 2005 4v 2178p il set $550   **618.92**

1. Children—Health and hygiene—Encyclopedias
2. Children—Diseases—Encyclopedias

ISBN 0-7876-9241-7   LC 2005-3478

The encyclopedia "covers the prenatal stages to age 18. It contains approximately 600 articles that range from 500 to 4000 words each and address medical conditions such as hernias, ringworm, and strep throat as well as topics like acting out, bullies, single-parent homes, and even allowances and money management. . . . This clearly written encyclopedia will be useful for students conducting research and for parents wanting to learn more about their children's conditions." Libr J

Includes bibliographical references

Hayden, Torey L.

Twilight children; three voices no one heard until a therapist listened; [by] Torey Hayden. William Morrow 2005 331p $24.95
618.92

1. Child abuse 2. Psychotherapy

ISBN 0-06-056088-6   LC 2004-47376

"The author documents the particulars of her approach to treating a volatile, manipulative nine-year-old abuse victim; a mute but sociable and atypically charismatic four-year-old; and, in a change of pace, an 82-year-old stroke victim. The dysfunctional family dynamics impacting each patient are explored, as are impediments to the therapist's interfacing with relatives." SLJ

Hilden, Joanne M.

Shelter from the storm; caring for a child with a life-threatening condition; {by} Joanne M. Hilden and Daniel R. Tobin, with Karen Lindsey. Perseus 2003 224p pa $15.95 *   **618.92**

1. Terminally ill children

ISBN 0-7382-0534-6

This guide "empowers parents to ask the right questions so that they can get necessary information and make the best decisions about their child's care. It also supports them through death and the grieving process if treatment fails. Using a combination of medical advice and quotes from parents who have been there, the authors have created a sensitive and useful resource." Libr J

Includes bibliographical references

Ives, Martine, 1975-

Caring for a child with autism; a practical guide for parents; [by] Martine Ives and Nell Munro; illustrations by Fiona Bleach. Kingsley, J. 2002 304p il pa $18.95   **618.92**

1. Autism

ISBN 1-85302-996-3   LC 2001-38436

Published with the National Autistic Society

This "guide answers the questions commonly asked by parents and carers following a diagnosis of autism, and discusses the challenges that can arise in home life, education and socializing." Publisher's note

Includes bibliographical references

Jackson, Luke

Freaks, geeks and asperger syndrome; a user guide to adolescence; foreword by Tony Attwood. Kingsley, J. 2002 217p il pa $17.95

618.92

1. Asperger's syndrome 2. Autism 3. Adolescent psychology

ISBN 1-8431-0098-3 LC 2002-70930

"In this terrific book that is sure to inspire other adolescents with the same condition, 13-year-old Jackson offers a teenager's perspective on what it's like to live with Asperger's. He also writes about his younger brother, who has a more severe condition on the ASD spectrum." Libr J

Includes bibliographical references

Janes-Hodder, Honna, 1966-

Childhood cancer; a parent's guide to solid tumor cancers; [by] Honna Janes-Hodder, Nancy Keene. 2nd ed. O'Reilly & Assocs. 2002 xx, 537p il (Patient-centered guides) pa $29.95 *

618.92

1. Cancer 2. Children—Diseases

ISBN 0-59650-014-9 LC 2002-72284

First published 1999

One booklet attached to inside back cover

This guide provides information on solid tumor childhood cancers, including neuroblastoma, Wilms tumor, liver tumors, soft tissue sarcomas, bone sarcomas and retinoblastoma. Medical terminology, diagnosis, treatment and hospitalization are discussed

Includes bibliographical references

Johnson, Christopher M., 1952-

Your critically ill child; life and death choices parents must face; by Christopher Johnson. New Horizon Press 2007 212p pa $15.95

618.92

1. Children—Medical care 2. Terminally ill children

ISBN 978-0-88282-284-6; 0-88282-284-5

LC 2006-923968

The author explains how pediatric intensive care units "operate and tells parents what to expect while their child is a patient. Case histories illustrate what may happen, while suggestions for self-care and lists of questions coach parents to play an active role. Johnson tackles issues such as ethics and medical expenses with sensitivity. A unique and much-needed resource for parents." Libr J

Lederman, Judith

The ups and downs of raising a bipolar child; a survival guide for parents; {by} Judith Lederman, Candida Fink. Fireside Books 2003 320p $14

618.92

1. Manic-depressive illness 2. Depression (Psychology) 3. Child rearing

ISBN 0-7432-2940-1 LC 2003-50696

"A Fireside book"

This book offers parents advice on coping "with this challenging diagnosis, and shows how to provide essential care and support for a bipolar child as well as for the rest of the family." Publisher's note

"This guide's main strength lies in its suggestions for handling everyday issues between parent and child—how to minimize the misery of frequent blood tests, what to tell siblings, and coping with teens who get into legal trouble." Libr J

Includes bibliographical references

Linden, Dana Wechsler

Preemies; the essential guide for parents of premature babies; [by] Dana Wechsler Linden, Emma Trenti Paroli, and Mia Wechsler Doron. Pocket Bks. 2000 578p il pa $24.95

618.92

1. Premature infants

ISBN 0-671-03491-X LC 00-28554

This guide "covers risk factors, the first day, the first week, surgery, taking the baby home and many other topics. Each section contains personal observations from parents of preemies, insightful comments from 'the doctor's perspective' and information on procedures, equipment, common problems and other issues." Publ Wkly

Martin, Katherine L., 1960-

Does my child have a speech problem? Chicago Review Press 1997 160p il pa $16.95

618.92

1. Speech disorders 2. Children—Health and hygiene

ISBN 1-55652-315-7 LC 96-35302

The author addresses stuttering, fluency and articulation issues. Listening and auditory processing skills are discussed

"Martin's writing style is clear and engaging, making this slim volume a quick, easy read." Libr J

Includes bibliographical references

Ozonoff, Sally

A parent's guide to asperger syndrome and high-functioning autism; how to meet the challenges and help your child thrive; [by] Sally Ozonoff, Geraldine Dawson, James McPartland. Guilford Press 2002 278p il $38; pa $17.95

618.92

1. Autism 2. Parenting

ISBN 1-57230-767-6; 1-57230-531-2 (pa)

LC 2002-5507

Partial contents: Part I: Understanding asperger syndrome and high-functioning autism; What are asperger syndrome and high-functioning autism?; The diagnostic process; Causes of autism spectrum disorders; Treatments for asperger syndrome and high-functioning autism?; Part II: Living with asperger syndrome and high-functioning autism; Channeling your child's strengths: a guiding principle; Asperger syndrome and high-functioning autism at home; Asperger syndrome and high-functioning autism at school; The social world of children and adolescents with asperger syndrome and high-functioning autism; Looking ahead: asperger syndrome and high-functioning autism in late adolescence and adulthood

"This is an excellent resource for parents of children of the higher end of the autistic spectrum. All educators, the authors provide the basics on diagnosis, causes, and

Ozonoff, Sally—*Continued*

treatment. What makes their title essential is their positive emphasis on finding and channeling a child's strengths, as well as a sensitive discussion of home life, school, and the social world and life as an adult." Libr J

Includes bibliographical references

Papolos, Demitri F.

The bipolar child; the definitive and reassuring guide to childhood's most misunderstood disorder; [by] Demitri F. Papolos and Janice Papolos. 3rd ed. Broadway Books 2006 xxii, 474p il $27.95 *

618.92

1. Manic-depressive illness 2. Depression (Psychology) 3. Child psychology

ISBN 0-7679-2297-2   LC 2005-55312

First published 2000

The authors "detail the diagnosis, explain how to find good treatment and medications, and advise parents about ways to advocate effectively for their children in school." Publisher's note

Includes bibliographical references

Richman, Shira, 1972-

Raising a child with autism; a guide to applied behavior analysis for parents. Kingsley, J. 2000 173p pa $19.95   **618.92**

1. Autism 2. Parent-child relationship

ISBN 1-85302-910-6   LC 00-47818

"Behavior therapy consultant Richman clearly outlines the applied behavior analysis (ABA) activities that parents can use with ASD children. Included is helpful guidance for toilet training, daily living, and increasing communication and sibling interaction. Since ABA consultants may be out of the financial or geographic reach of many parents, having a strong resource like this is invaluable." Libr J

Includes bibliographical references

Ryder, Christopher S., 1947-

Take your pediatrician with you; keeping your child healthy at home and on the road. Johns Hopkins University Press 2007 xxiii, 621p il (Johns Hopkins Press health book) pa $16

618.92

1. Children—Travel 2. Health self-care 3. First aid

ISBN 978-0-8018-8601-0; 0-8018-8601-5

LC 2006-23120

First published 2004 by C. Ryder with title: Handbook for pediatric health problems at home and on the road

This book "covers common pediatric illnesses and conditions, first aid, and travel-associated illnesses, clearly telling parents when to treat at home and when to seek medical attention. He also supplies a chapter on bringing a child adopted abroad back to the United States. This is an excellent choice and a bargain for both libraries and parents." Libr J

Sandler, Adrian

Living with spina bifida; a guide for families and professionals; illustrations by Peter Bedick. University of N.C. Press 1997 xxvii, 262p il pa $19.95 hardcover o.p.   **618.92**

1. Spina bifida

ISBN 0-8078-4657-0 (pa)   LC 96-47697

This guide covers "issues of clinical management, habilitation, and early intervention from an interdisciplinary, holistic, and family-based perspective. In a series of chapters arranged according to the developmental stages of childhood—from birth through infancy, school age, adolescence, and young adulthood—Sandler discusses relevant medical, health, and psychosocial aspects of spina bifida. He addresses such concerns as education, daily living, and family relationships." Publisher's note

Selikowitz, Mark

Down syndrome; the facts. 3rd ed. Oxford University Press 2008 211p il (The facts) pa $19.95 *   **618.92**

1. Down syndrome

ISBN 978-0-19-923277-2   LC 2008-3360

First published 1990

Discusses possible causes of Down's syndrome, development of the child with the disease, medical problems and educational strategies, and includes advice for parents about future pregnancies.

Includes bibliographical references

Seroussi, Karyn, 1965-

Unraveling the mystery of autism and pervasive developmental disorder; a mother's story of research and recovery. Broadway Books 2002 289p pa $14.95   **618.92**

1. Autism

ISBN 0-7679-0798-1   LC 2001-35575

First published 2000 by Simon & Schuster

This is an account of the author's experiences with her son, who was diagnosed with autism at 19 months. She discusses various therapies and the possible connections between autism and diet

Includes bibliographical references

Sicherer, Scott H.

Understanding and managing your child's food allergies. Johns Hopkins University Press 2006 312p il $45; pa $18.95 *   **618.92**

1. Food allergy

ISBN   0-8018-8491-8;   978-0-8018-8491-7; 0-8018-8492-6 (pa); 978-0-8018-8492-4 (pa)

LC 2006-5261

"A Johns Hopkins Press health book"

This "book provides parents with practical advice for managing a child's environment at home, at school, or out in the world at large. In Part 2, 'Diagnosing a Food Allergy,' the practice of taking a detailed medical history is espoused and case studies serve to bring the issue home. An action plan for anaphylaxis, a life-threatening type of allergic reaction, as well as a chapter on food allergy resources are included." Libr J

Includes bibliographical references

Terr, Lenore, 1936-

Magical moments of change; how psychotherapy
turns kids around. W. W. Norton 2008 304p
$27.95   **618.92**

1. Psychotherapy 2. Child psychiatry
ISBN 978-0-393-70530-0; 0-393-70530-7
LC 2007-16745

The author "has compiled 48 vignettes offered by 33
psychiatrists dealing with myriad cases, from mild development problems to juvenile delinquency to schizophrenia, recounting the almost magical moments of breakthrough." Booklist

Includes bibliographical references

Thompson, Charlotte E.

Raising a child with a neuromuscular disorder;
a guide for parents, grandparents, friends, and
professionals. Oxford Univ. Press 1999 275p $25
                                                618.92

1. Children—Diseases
ISBN 0-19-512843-5   LC 99-30834

Thompson "suggests ways parents can be strong advocates for their children. . . . In addition to a chapter with
descriptions and treatments of various neuromuscular disorders, there is a brief overview on genetics, a table
summarizing the characteristics of various neuromuscular
diseases, and a glossary of medical terms." Libr J

Includes bibliographical references

Wing, Lorna

The autistic spectrum; a parents' guide to
understanding and helping your child. Ulysses
Press 2001 240p pa $14.95   **618.92**

1. Autism
ISBN 1-56975-257-5

Includes bibliographical references

This guide "shows parents how to understand their
child and teach basic skills, improve communication, develop potential abilities, and expand social interaction
skills." Publisher's note

"While the depth of information here may be overwhelming to the parents of a newly diagnosed child . . .
it is an excellent choice for those who require a text with
more substance." Libr J

Includes bibliographical references

620 Engineering

Berlow, Lawrence H., 1945-

The reference guide to famous engineering
landmarks of the world; bridges, tunnels, dams,
roads, and other structures. Oryx Press 1997 c1998
250p il $73.95   **620**

ISBN 0-89774-966-9   LC 97-36051

"The main section is an alphabetically arranged, double-column compendium of facts and histories of 600
structures. The format of each entry begins with the
structure's location and date of construction. Size is often
given, including metric, and the basic facts of the construction are provided. . . . A biography section provides
background on 52 significant engineers or designers. A

chronology section begins with the oldest surviving dam
in the world (in Egypt) and continues to 2010, when a
monster skyscraper, Millennium Tower, will be completed in Tokyo." Booklist

Frenay, Robert, 1946-

Pulse; the coming age of systems and machines
inspired by living things. Farrar, Straus and Giroux
2006 545p $30   **620**

1. Bionics
ISBN 9780374113278; 0-374-11327-0
LC 2005-22285

The author "shows how ideas that have shaped Western science, industry, and culture for centuries are being
displaced by the rapid and dramatic rise of a 'new biology'—by human systems and machines that work like living things." Publisher's note

"A smorgasbord de luxe, Frenay's reportage is sustaining fare for environmentalists." Booklist

Includes bibliographical references

Hall, J. Storrs

Nanofuture; what's next for nanotechnology;
foreword by K. Eric Drexler. Prometheus Books
2005 333p il $29 *   **620**

1. Nanotechnology
ISBN 1-59102-287-8   LC 2005-1789

The author covers "the physical principles of engineering at the atomic scale, possible applications of
nanomachines, and their potential alteration of human society." Booklist

"This book fills a niche as a brief, inspirational introduction to nanotechnology for budding nanoscientists as
well as the general public." Choice

Molotch, Harvey Luskin

Where stuff comes from; how toasters, toilets,
cars, computers, and many other things come to be
as they are; [by] Harvey Molotch. Routledge 2003
324p il $35; pa $29.95   **620**

1. Engineering
ISBN 0-415-94400-7; 0-415-95042-2 (pa)
LC 2003-1191

The author examines "the complicated, dynamic relationships between inventor, society, corporation, regula-
tor, shopkeeper, community, family and customer. . . .
Myriad links, he argues, ultimately produce and constantly change what we want, buy, keep and throw away;
thus, neither consumers nor producers are to be blamed
for our numerous possessions. . . . Molotch's description
of systemic person-product complexes could work to end
blame-the-consumer guilt-mongering in the popular discourse." Publ Wkly

Includes bibliographical references

Petroski, Henry

Invention by design; how engineers get from
thought to thing. Harvard Univ. Press 1996 242p
il map pa $14.95 hardcover o.p.   **620**

1. Engineering 2. Inventions
ISBN 0-674-46368-4 (pa)   LC 96-19227

Petroski, Henry—*Continued*

"By examining the relationship between the invention of devices and their refinement over time by others, Petroski identifies design principles that engineers use to make things work. Written as a series of case studies ranging from the paper clip to the zipper to the FAX machine to the Boeing 777." Libr J

"Every case study includes well-chosen pictures and schematic drawings to clarify how inventors resolve technical difficulties, and the carefully research text explains how they make their new creations economically feasible and socially acceptable." Booklist

Includes bibliographical references

Remaking the world; adventures in engineering. Knopf 1997 239p il pa $13 hardcover o.p.

620

1. Engineering
ISBN 0-375-70024-2 (pa)   LC 97-29328

A collection of the author's essays originally written for American Scientist. "Several pieces are about particular engineers . . . or engineering projects (the Channel Tunnel, the Ferris Wheel); others are provocative (the flaws of engineering software, the creep of technology)." Libr J

Includes bibliographical references

Success through failure; the paradox of design. Princeton University Press 2006 235p il $22.95

620

1. Engineering 2. Design
ISBN 978-0-691-12225-0; 0-691-12225-3

LC 2005-34126

The author explores the "relationship between success and failure in engineering design. Ingenuity is explored as a pendulum that swings between success and failure, driven by design philosophy and practices in a given place and time. Case studies and examples include bridges, spacecrafts, airports, buildings with architectural celebrity, New Coke, U-Locks, and notable structures that have suffered from performance issues." Libr J

An "engaging and readable book. . . . Petroski uses countless interesting case histories to show how failure motivates technological advancement." IEEE Spectrum

Includes bibliographical references

Sargent, Ted

The dance of molecules; how nanotechnology is changing our lives. Thunder's Mouth Press 2006 234p il $25; pa $15.95   **620**

1. Nanotechnology
ISBN   1-56025-809-8;   978-1-56025-809-4;
1-56025-895-0 (pa); 978-1-56025-895-7 (pa)

LC 2006-275492

The author "gives an overview of recent advances in nanotechnology, the science of engineering materials at the atomic and molecular levels." Libr J

"This book is an enjoyable way to obtain a basic understanding of nanotechnology." Sci Books Films

Includes bibliographical references

Tobin, James, 1956-

Great projects; the epic story of the building of America: from the taming of the Mississippi to the invention of the Internet. Free Press 2001 322p il maps $40   **620**
ISBN 0-7432-1064-6   LC 2001-33016

This describes eight construction projects and innovations including "the flood-control works of the lower Mississippi, Hoover Dam, Edison's lighting system, the spread of electricity across the nation, the great Croton Aqueduct, the bridges of New York City, Boston's revamped street system, known as the Big Dig, and the [Internet]." Publisher's note

"The clearly written, nontechnical narratives are lively and comprehensive." Libr J

Includes bibliographical references

620.1   Engineering mechanics and materials

Brady, George S. (George Stuart)

Materials handbook; an encyclopedia for managers, technical professionals, purchasing and production managers, technicians and supervisors. 15th ed, [by] George S. Brady, Henry R. Clauser, John A. Vaccari. McGraw-Hill 2002 1244p (McGraw-Hill handbooks) $99.95 *

620.1

1. Materials—Encyclopedias
ISBN 978-0-07-136076-0; 0-07-136076-X

First published 1929. Periodically revised. Subtitle varies

"Covers more than 15,000 minerals, animal and plant substances, and commercial and engineering materials. Uses, production methods, and trade names are included for common items. Most entries are shorter than half a page. The special chapter on structure and properties of materials includes charts, tables, and a glossary of terms. Uses both SI and U.S. customary units. Subject index is very important because the main text has no cross-references." Guide to Ref Books. 11th edition

621   Applied physics

Landmarks in mechanical engineering; [by] ASME International History and Heritage. Purdue Univ. Press 1997 364p il $62.95; pa $24.95   **621**
1. Mechanical engineering
ISBN 1-55753-093-9; 1-55753-094-7 (pa)

LC 96-31573

This collection of essays on "American 'industrial archaeology' discusses still-existing artifacts ranging from the Saugus Ironworks (1640s) to the Saturn V rocket. . . . [Areas considered] include pumping, mechanical and electrical power, power tranmission, minerals extraction and refining, manufacturing, food processing, materials handling, environmental control, water transportation through space transportation, research, communications and processing, and biomedical engineering." Choice

Includes bibliographical references

Marks' standard handbook for mechanical engineers; [edited by] Eugene A. Avallone, Theodore Baumeister, Ali Sadegh. 11th ed. McGraw-Hill 2006 1800p il $199.95

621

1. Mechanical engineering—Handbooks, manuals, etc.
ISBN 978-0-07-142867-5; 0-07-142867-4

Also available ebook version

First published 1916 under the editorship of Lionel S. Marks with title: Mechanical engineers' handbook. Periodically revised. Editors vary

Known as Standard handbook for mechanical engineers

This volume presents concisely the basic scientific and technical data of mechanical engineering, covering theory, basic mechanism, standard practice, often-needed mathematical formulae and technical data

Includes bibliographical references

621.3   Electrical, magnetic, optical, communications, computer engineering; electronics, lighting

American electricians' handbook; [by] Terrell Croft, Wilford I. Summers, [and] Frederic P Hartwell. 15th ed. McGraw-Hill 2008 various pagingp il $89.95 *   **621.3**

1. Electrical engineering—Handbooks, manuals, etc.
ISBN 978-0-07-149462-5

First published 1913. Periodically revised

"A Standard handbook, written to be in accordance with the latest ed. of the National Electrical code." Guide to Ref Books. 11th edition

Kaplan, Steven M.

Wiley electrical and electronics engineering dictionary. John Wiley & Sons 2004 885p pa $73.50   **621.3**

1. Electronics—Dictionaries 2. Electrical engineering—Dictionaries
ISBN 0-471-40224-9   LC 2003-66068

This dictionary "defines over 35,000 {terms} and includes electronics as well as electrical engineering. It also includes three appendixes: Greek letters, symbols, and numbers (which includes IEEE standards numbers)." Libr J

This "will be an asset to any university library that supports an electrical and electronics engineering curriculum, or to any professional engineering library. . . . A superb resource." Choice

Includes bibliographical references

McGraw-Hill's National Electrical Code handbook. 25th ed, 1360. McGraw-Hill 2005 $75   **621.3**

1. Electrical engineering—Handbooks, manuals, etc.
ISBN 978-0-07-144340-1; 0-07-144340-1

Also available eBook version

First published 1932 with title: National Electrical Code handbook. Periodically revised to reflect changes in the code. Title varies

New edition in preparation

This handbook presents analysis and commentary on the National Electrical Code, as it pertains to wiring of appliances, buildings, emergency systems, and other types of electrical construction.

National Electrical Code handbook. 11th ed. National Fire Protection Assn. 2008 1440p $130

621.3

1. Electrical engineering—Handbooks, manuals, etc.
ISBN 978-0-87765-793-4; 0-87765-793-9

Also available CD-ROM version

First published 1978. Periodically revised

This "is a nationally accepted guide to the safe installation of electrical conductors and equipment, and is, in fact, the basis for all electrical codes used in the United States." Ref Sources for Small & Medium-sized Libr. 5th edition

Shulman, Seth

The telephone gambit; chasing Alexander Graham Bell's secret. W. W. Norton & Co. 2008 256p il $24.95 *   **621.3**

1. Bell, Alexander Graham, 1847-1922 2. Gray, Elisha, 1835-1901 3. Telephone
ISBN 978-0-393-06206-9; 0-393-06206-6

LC 2007-30904

The author argues that Alexander Graham Bell is not the true inventor of the telephone.

This book "does a neat job of painting, in rapid brush strokes, a portrait of the thrilling era of innovation in which Bell lived and also of the interesting circumstances of his life. . . . [He] also manages to lace his work with just enough technology to tell his story without losing the interest of any low-tech readers." Christ Sci Monit

Includes bibliographical references

Standard handbook for electrical engineers. 15th ed., H. Wayne Beaty, editor, Donald G. Fink, late editor. McGraw-Hill 2007 various pagings il $195   **621.3**

1. Electrical engineering—Handbooks, manuals, etc.
ISBN 978-0-07-144146-9; 0-07-144146-8

First published 1908. Periodically revised

Contains data on all branches of electrical engineering including material in the field of nuclear physics, plastics and resins, transistors and television.

621.319   Transmission

Cauldwell, Rex

Safe home wiring projects. Taunton Press 1997 151p il pa $19.95   **621.319**

1. Electric wiring
ISBN 1-56158-164-X   LC 97-5789

"A Fine woodworking book"

The author "starts by explaining basic electrical principles and shows which tools to use. A section on inspecting your home's electrical system is particularly helpful, describing various hazards and pitfalls. Other sections cover repairing wiring switches and receptacles and installing light fixtures, ceiling and bathroom fans and home entertainment systems. . . . This is an excellent title for beginners." Libr J

621.381 Electronics

Goodman, Robert L.
How electronic things work—and what to do when they don't. 2nd ed. TAB Electronics 2003 xx, 426p il $24.95   **621.381**
1. Electronic apparatus and appliances—Maintenance and repair
ISBN 0-07-138745-5   LC 2003-265249
First published 1999
"Explains the practical side of electronics—troubleshooting problems, testing, repair, and servicing. Although the reader may not learn all the basics of electronics here, there is certainly a lot to be learned about resolving typical problems with common household items." Libr J

The **illustrated** dictionary of electronics; Stan Gibilisco, editor-in-chief. 8th ed. McGraw-Hill 2001 791, [11]p il pa $44.95   **621.381**
1. Electronics—Dictionaries
ISBN 0-07-137236-9   LC 2001-272029
First published 1980 under the authorship of Rufus P. Turner. Periodically revised
Includes CD-ROM
This illustrated dictionary contains nearly 28,000 entries—definitions, abbreviations, and acronyms—including terms in the fields of robotics, artificial intelligence, and personal computing as they relate to electronics. Also included is terminology in: lasers; television; radio; IC technology; digital and analog electronics; audio and video; power supplies; fiber optic communications, etc.
Includes bibliographical references

Schultz, Mitchel E.
Grob's basic electronics. McGraw-Hill 2006 c2007 various paging il $130 *   **621.381**
1. Electricity 2. Electronics
ISBN 0-07-322276-3
First published 1959 under the authorship of Bernard Grob. Periodically revised
Accompanied by computer laser optical disc
An introductory text on the fundamentals of electricity and electronics for technicians in radio, television, and industrial electronics.
Includes bibliographical references

Standard handbook of electronic engineering; Donald Christiansen, editor, Charles K. Alexander, editor, Ronald K. Jurgen, associate editor. 5th ed. McGraw-Hill 2005 various pagingsp il (McGraw-Hill standard handbooks) $157.50 *   **621.381**
1. Electronics—Handbooks, manuals, etc.
ISBN 978-0-07-138421-6; 0-07-138421-9
LC 2005-47880
First published 1975 with title: Electronics engineers' handbook. Periodically revised
Includes CD-ROM
Covers essential principles, data, and design information on the components, circuits, equipment, and systems of electronics engineering. Emphasizes practical use of basic principles. Includes computer-aided design and electronic data processing.

621.382 Communications engineering

Weems, David B.
Designing, building, and testing your own speaker system with projects. 4th ed. McGraw-Hill hardcover o.p. pa $19.95   **621.382**
1. Intercommunication systems
ISBN 0-07-069428-1; 978-0-07-069429-3 (pa); 0-07-069429-X (pa)   LC 96-30967
First published 1981. Periodically revised
This manual offers instructions on building low cost high quality loudspeaker systems using the latest audio technology

621.384 Radio and radar

Carr, Joseph J.
Old time radios! restoration and repair. TAB Bks. 1991 256p il pa $19.95 hardcover o.p.
621.384
1. Radio—Repairing
ISBN 0-8306-3342-1 (pa)   LC 90-44411
This guide includes the history, theory and practical operation of old-time radio sets and detailed instructions and schematics for repairing and rebuilding them

621.3841 Specific topics in general radio

The **ARRL** handbook for radio communications. 2009 ed. American Radio Relay League 2008 $59; pa $44.95 *   **621.3841**
1. Radio—Handbooks, manuals, etc.
ISSN 0890-3565
ISBN   978-0-87259-140-0;   0-87259-140-9; 978-0-87259-139-4 (pa); 0-87259-139-5 (pa)
Also available CD-ROM edition
Annual. Began publication 1926. Editions 1 through 61 published with title: The Radio amateur's handbook. Editions 62 through 79 published with title: The ARRL handbook for radio amateurs
Includes CD-ROM
"Chapters cover fundamentals and changing technology in the field and include many tables, circuit diagrams, photographs, and occasional references." Guide to Ref Books. 11th edition

621.388 Television

Abramson, Albert
The history of television, 1942 to 2000; foreword by Christopher H. Sterling. McFarland & Co. 2003 309p il hardcover o.p. pa $75 *
621.388
1. Television—History
ISBN 0-7864-1220-8; 978-0-7864-3243-1 (pa); 0-7864-3243-8 (pa)   LC 2002-326

Abramson, Albert—*Continued*

Also available The history of television, 1880 to 1941, published 1987

"Chapters are devoted to television and World War II and the postwar era, the development of color television, Ampex Corporation's contributions, television in Europe, the change from helical to high band technology, solid state cameras, the television coverage of Apollo II, the rise of electronic journalism, television entering the studios, the introduction of the camcorder, the demise of RCA at the hands of GE, the domination of Sony and Matsushita, and the future of television in e-cinema and the 1080 P24 format." Publisher's note

"No reference work available in print right now matches the attention to detail that is obvious here. A significant work on how the machinery of television has evolved, this . . . should stand as the authority for years to come." Libr J

Includes bibliographical references

Capelo, Gregory R.

VCR troubleshooting & repair; [by] Gregory R. Capelo, Robert C. Brenner. 3rd ed. Newnes 1998 434p il $34.95   **621.388**

1. Home video systems—Maintenance and repair
ISBN 0-7506-9940-X   LC 97-27610

First published 1987 by Sams with authors in reverse order

This is a guide to caring for VCRs including preventative maintenance, diagnosing problems and making repairs

Davidson, Homer L.

TV repair for beginners. rev and expanded ed. McGraw-Hill 1998 376p il $44.95; pa $29.95
                                       621.388

1. Television—Repairing
ISBN 0-07-015805-3; 0-07-015806-1 (pa)
                                       LC 97-25446

First published under the authorship of George Zwick with title: Beginner's guide to TV repair. Periodically revised

This is a guide to the operation and repair of standard TV components as well as universal remote transmitters, stereo TV, digital controls, new color circuits and picture tube sizes, and digital satellite receivers.

621.39   Computer engineering

Mueller, Scott

Upgrading and repairing PCs. 18th ed. Que Pub. 2007 1556p il $59.99 *   **621.39**

1. Microcomputers—Maintenance and repair
2. Microcomputers—Upgrading
ISBN 978-0-7897-3697-0; 0-7897-3697-7
                                       LC 2007-34956

Accompanied by 1 DVD-ROM

First published 1988. Periodically revised

At head of title: Scott Mueller's

This guide to maintaining, upgrading, and repairing personal computers explains physical disassembly and reassembly, primary system components, input/output

hardware, mass storage systems, maintenance, troubleshooting and diagnostics. It includes a technical reference, a glossary, and lists vendors of replacement parts

621.43   Internal-combustion engines

Weil, Elizabeth

They all laughed at Christopher Columbus; an incurable dreamer builds the first civilian spaceship. Bantam Bks. 2002 230p il pa $13.95 hardcover o.p.   **621.43**

1. Hudson, Gary 2. Rotary Rocket Company 3. Rocketry 4. Space flight 5. Outer space
ISBN 0-553-38236-5 (pa)   LC 2002-18665

"Gary Hudson, the subject of the book, was a space enthusiast of the 1950s. He believed that NASA engineers were wrong in their approach to space travel. He was convinced that private industry could build a vehicle to deliver humans into space more cheaply and more effectively than the government. . . . He sketched a rough drawing of his idea for a space vehicle he called the Roton. It looked like a 60-foot nose cone with a helicopter blade." Sci Books Films

621.8   Machine engineering

Gurstelle, William

Adventures from the technology underground; catapults, pulsejets, rail guns, flamethrowers, tesla coils, air cannons, and the garage warriors who love them. Clarkson Potter 2006 224p $25; pa $13.95   **621.8**

1. Machine design
ISBN 1-4000-5082-0; 0-307-35125-4 (pa)
                                       LC 2005-20412

The author takes "readers into the hidden communities of people involved in developing hurling machines (catapults and trebuchets), pulse jet engines, flamethrowers, tesla coil-powered electric current theater, air cannons, robots, high-powered rockets, and magnetic linear accelerator guns. . . . Gurstelle balances scientific explanations of the technologies with profiles of the people who built them and descriptions of the events at which they were showcased." Libr J

Includes bibliographical references

621.9   Tools

Hack, Garrett

Classic hand tools; photographs by John S. Sheldon. Taunton Press 1999 218p il $34.95; pa $24.95   **621.9**

1. Tools
ISBN 1-56158-273-5; 1-56158-507-6 (pa)
                                       LC 99-23719

In this look at old, muscle-powered tools Hack discusses "how to maintain them; and, for some of the obscurer ones, what exactly their purposes are. The result-

Hack, Garrett—_Continued_
ing book is surprisingly comprehensive, covering just about everything from scrapers to saws and including a most interesting chapter on antique-tool collecting." Booklist
Includes bibliographical references

Nagyszalanczy, Sandor
Power tools; an electrifying celebration and grounded guide; written and photographed by Sandor Nagyszalanczy. Taunton Press 2001 266p il $40; pa $24.95 *   **621.9**
1. Power tools
ISBN 1-56158-427-4; 1-56158-576-9 (pa)
LC 2001-33097
This work covers the history, design, accessories and recent developments of portable and stationary power tools
"Tool collectors and those considering tool purchases will find this title invaluable." Libr J

622   Mining and related operations

Reece, Erik
Lost mountain; a year in the vanishing wilderness: radical strip mining, and the devastation of Appalachia; foreword by Wendell Berry; photographs by John J. Cox. Riverhead Books 2006 250p il $24.95; pa $14   **622**
1. Coal mines and mining 2. Human influence on nature 3. Appalachian region
ISBN 1-59448-908-4; 1-59448-236-5 (pa)
LC 2005-52921
The author explores the effects of strip mining on the landscape of Eastern Kentucky.
Reece "has written an impassioned account of a business rife with industrial greed, devious corporate ownership and unenforced environmental laws. It's also a heartrending account of the rural residents whose lives are being ruined by strip-mining's relentless, almost unfettered, encroachment." Publ Wkly
Includes bibliographical references

623.4   Ordnance

Conant, Jennet
109 East Palace; Robert Oppenheimer and the secret city of Los Alamos. Simon & Schuster 2005 425p map hardcover o.p. pa $14 *
623.4
1. McKibbin, Dorothy Scarritt, 1897-1985 2. Oppenheimer, J. Robert, 1904-1967 3. Los Alamos Scientific Laboratory 4. Manhattan Project 5. Atomic bomb
ISBN 0-7432-5007-9; 0-7432-5008-7 (pa)
LC 2005-42497
In this history of the creation of the atomic bomb, the author focuses "on daily life in Los Alamos. She tells the story largely through the eyes of Dorothy McKibben, who was in charge of the project's Santa Fe office, at

109 East Palace Street. This unassuming storefront was the portal to Los Alamos for all the physicists and military personnel who arrived in New Mexico." Booklist
"Anyone interested in the history of atomic weapons will find this book totally engrossing." Sci Books Films
Includes bibliographical references

De Groot, Gerard J.
The bomb; a life; Gerard J. DeGroot. Harvard 2005 397p il $27.95   **623.4**
1. Nuclear weapons
ISBN 0-674-01724-2   LC 2004-57657
First published 2004 in the United Kingdom
This history of the nuclear age "begins with the bomb's development during WW II and ends with the aftermath of 9/11. . . . Ideal for both scholars and general readers, this promises to be a standard work for years to come." Choice
Includes bibliographical references

Light, Michael
100 suns, 1945-1962. Knopf 2003 208p il $49.95   **623.4**
1. Nuclear weapons—Pictorial works
ISBN 1-4000-4113-9   LC 2003-106275
"The 'suns' Light presents to readers in this . . . photography collection are manmade: aboveground atomic detonations captured on film both in the Nevada desert and at sea, terrifyingly beautiful images that remind readers of the apocalyptic might of nuclear weapons." Booklist
Includes bibliographical references

Rhodes, Richard, 1937-
Dark sun; the making of the hydrogen bomb. Simon & Schuster 1995 731p il pa $18 hardcover o.p. *   **623.4**
1. Hydrogen bomb
ISBN 0-684-82414-0   LC 95-11070
This is a "chronicle of the rivalry between the U.S. and the U.S.S.R. to invent, build, test and stockpile hydrogen bombs. . . . Rhodes places the story of the bomb's development in the context of politics, science, technical hurdles and espionage. . . . He also brings in the case of convicted atomic spies Julius and Ethel Rosenberg." Publ Wkly
"This meticulously documented treatise presents a gripping story." Libr J

The making of the atomic bomb. Simon & Schuster 1986 886p il pa $20 hardcover o.p.
623.4
1. Atomic bomb
ISBN 0-684-81378-5 (pa)   LC 86-15445
This book chronicles the development of the bomb "from the birth of modern physics in the late 19th century to the first tests of hydrogen bombs, by the United States in 1954 and the Soviet Union in 1955." Science
"The book provides portraits of the many players from Szilard and Einstein to Oppenheimer. . . . The book is heavily documented and includes a 13-page bibliography. This is a definitive work, well written, with a gripping story. It is not an easy book to read, but is well worth the effort." Libr J

Shooter's bible; Keith Sutton, editor. 99th ed.
Stoeger 2007 576p il pa $24.95   **623.4**
1. Firearms—Catalogs
ISBN 978-0-8831-7343-5; 0-8831-7343-3
Annual. First published 1925 by Follett
Contains specifications and manufacturers' current
prices for a variety of firearms and accessories. Also includes articles on related subjects, gun finder index, and
caliber finder index

Weapons & warfare; editor, John Powell;
managing editor, Christina J. Moose. Salem
Press 2001 2v il maps $194 *   **623.4**
1. Military weapons 2. Military art and science
ISBN 1-58765-000-2   LC 2001-34150
"Each of the volumes is arranged with the same
scheme. Discussions of major weapon groups are followed by sections that survey historical periods and are
further divided by geographic region. The total number
of topics covered in the two volumes exceeds 100, ranging from 2,000 to 7,000 words." Booklist
Includes bibliographical references

623.74   Vehicles

Fredriksen, John C.
Warbirds; an illustrated guide to U.S. military
aircraft, 1915-2000. ABC-CLIO 1999 363p il $75
    623.74
1. Military airplanes
ISBN 1-57607-131-6   LC 99-16624
This guide "covers all fighters, bombers, trainers, pa-
trol craft, transports, and helicopters manufactured and
deployed by military or naval units. . . . There are 325
entries, each with a black-and-white photograph of the
aircraft and a listing of performance, power plant, arma-
ment, and service dates and a brief narrative detailing the
development, deployment, and eventual retirement of the
machines." Booklist

623.8   Nautical engineering and seamanship

Jane's fighting ships 2008-2009; edited by
Stephen Saunders. Jane's Information Group
2008 il $915   **623.8**
1. Warships 2. Navies
ISBN 978-0-7106-2845-9
Also available CD-ROM version and online
Annual. First published 1898. Title and publisher vary
"Arranged alphabetically by country, subdivided by
class of ship. Gives numbers and names of ships in each
class; builders; dates of laying down, launching, and
completion; a photograph of a ship in the class; and
specifications for the class." Guide to Ref Books. 11th
edition

Stewart, Matthew
Monturiol's dream; the extraordinary story of
the submarine inventor who wanted to save the
world. Pantheon Books 2004 338p il map $25
    623.8
1. Monturiol, Narciso, 1819-1885 2. Submarines
ISBN 0-375-41439-8   LC 2003-62368
"Utopian revolutionary Monturiol had a vision of a
submarine to free coral divers from hardship and then
free the world from the tumult of the atmosphere. Stewart . . . comes admirably close to capturing the transcendent weirdness of Monturiol's quest." Publ Wkly
Includes bibliographical references

623.82   Nautical craft

Green, Rod
Building the Titanic; an epic tale of the creation
of history's most famous ocean liner. Reader's
Digest 2005 160p il $27.95   **623.82**
1. Titanic (Steamship) 2. Shipbuilding
ISBN 0-7621-0689-1; 978-0-7621-0689-9
    LC 2005-44307
The author "presents the intricate details of the design
and construction of the ship—from hull dimensions to
Grand Staircase—with four double-page diagrams of
decks and boiler room plans." Libr J
"The book, with more than 100 photographs and illustrations, is a meticulous account of the ship's construction." Booklist

623.88   Seamanship

Pawson, Des
The handbook of knots. Expanded ed. DK 2004
176p il pa $17   **623.88**
1. Knots and splices
ISBN 0-7566-0374-9; 978-0-7566-0374-8
    LC 2004-274491
First published 1998
"This is a step-by-step guide to tying and using more
than 100 knots. . . . There's a chapter on rope construction, rope materials, and properties of ropes and their
main uses. It's very informative and put together concisely." BAYA Book Rev [review of 1998 edition]

623.89   Navigation

Dutton's nautical navigation; [by] Thomas J.
Cutler; with the U.S. Naval Institute Navigation
Board. 15th ed. Naval Inst. Press 2004 447p il
map $55   **623.89**
1. Navigation
ISBN 1-557502-48-X   LC 2003-11183
First published 1926 under the authorship of Benjamin
Dutton with title: Navigation and nautical astronomy.
Variant title: Dutton's navigation & piloting
This guide for the coastal and seagoing mariner focus-
es on piloting, celestial navigation, radio navigation and
dead reckoning

624.2   Bridges

Brown, David J., 1946-
Bridges: three thousand years of defying nature. Firefly Books 2005 208p il pa $29.95 *
624.2
1. Bridges
ISBN 1-55407-099-6 (pa)
The author "offers a history of more than 100 of the world's greatest bridges, organized chronologically. He explains their origins and structure principle, beginning with the ancient world (Rome and China) and the medieval period (France, Italy, and the Czech Republic). . . . There are more than 300 color and black-and-white illustrations in this very informative account." Booklist

Petroski, Henry
Engineers of dreams; great bridge builders and the spanning of America. Knopf 1995 479p il pa $16 hardcover o.p.
624.2
1. Eads, James Buchanan, 1820-1887 2. Ammann, Othmar Hermann, 1879-1965 3. Lindenthal, Gustav, 1850-1935 4. Steinman, David Barnard, 1886-1960 5. Strauss, Joseph Baermann, 1870-1938 6. Bridges 7. Civil engineering
ISBN 0-679-76021-0 (pa)
LC 94-48893
Focusing on the men who designed them, "Petroski depicts the building of several famous American bridges—New York's George Washington, St. Louis's Eads, and Michigan's Mackinaw, among others." Libr J
"An exhilarating saga of ingenuity and sheer determination." Publ Wkly
Includes bibliographical references

625.7   Roads

Sobey, Ed
A field guide to roadside technology. Chicago Review Press 2006 204p il pa $14.95
625.7
1. Roads 2. Traffic signs and signals 3. Electronic apparatus and appliances
ISBN 1-55652-609-1
LC 2006002979
"For those travelers who have ever wondered what certain poles, signs, wires, markings, pipes, and other devices that line our streets, highways, and interstates are called and what functions they serve, this is the perfect book. More than 150 individual items, grouped in categories, are identified and concisely and understandably explained, often citing their unique characteristics and interesting facts. A small black-and-white photo of each device is included. The text is sufficiently detailed without being overly technical." SLJ
Includes bibliographical references

627   Hydraulic engineering

Matson, Tim, 1943-
Earth ponds A to Z; an illustrated encyclopedia; illustrated by Frank Fretz. Countryman Press 2003 225p il pa $18.95
627
1. Water supply engineering 2. Ponds
ISBN 0-88150-494-7
LC 2002-67672
"From Acid Rain to Zooplankton . . . Tim Matson defines and explains . . . {over} two hundred terms associated with pond building and maintenance. . . . The reader will find descriptions and definitions of . . . pond elements, including: structural features; construction materials; water conditions and treatments; aquacultural topics and crops; environmental concerns; government support and regulatory agencies {and} landscaping." Publisher's note
Includes bibliographical references

628.9   Other branches of sanitary and municipal engineering

Golway, Terry, 1955-
So others might live; a history of New York's bravest; the FDNY from 1700 to the present. Basic Bks. 2002 368p $27.50; pa $17
628.9
1. New York (N.Y.). Fire Dept. 2. Fire fighting
ISBN 0-465-02740-7; 0-465-02741-5 (pa)
The author describes the New York City Fire Department's "emergence from amateur bucket brigades into the beginnings of a specialized force and up to the present, never letting a memorable figure or vivid moment escape his narrative." Libr J
Includes bibliographical references

National Fire Protection Association
Fire protection handbook. National Fire Protection Assn. il $149.95
628.9
1. Fire prevention
First published 1896. (19th edition 2003) Periodically revised. Title varies
"A handbook of approved practice in the fields of fire prevention and fire protection. Will be useful to owners and superintendents of buildings, and to architects and engineers interested in designing safe buildings and planning for their protection against fire." Carnegie Libr of Pittsburgh

629   Other branches of engineering

Space exploration; edited by Christopher Mari. Wilson, H.W. 1999 157p (Reference shelf) pa $50
629
1. United States. National Aeronautics and Space Administration 2. Astronautics—United States 3. Outer space—Exploration
ISBN 0-8242-0963-X
LC 99-25424
Contents: John Glenn's return to space; Exploration of Mars; The international space station; Private enterprise and space exploration; New technologies and discoveries
Includes bibliographical references

629.13 Aeronautics

Chaikin, Andrew, 1956-
Air and space; the National Air and Space Museum's story of flight. Little, Brown 1997 317p il $50; pa $29.95   **629.13**
1. National Air and Space Museum (U.S.)
ISBN 0-8212-2082-9; 0-8212-2670-3 (pa)
           LC 96-31929
"National Air and Space Museum, Smithsonian Institution in association with Bulfinch Press."
This illustrated work connects artifacts on display at the Smithsonian's aeronautics museum with a brief history of air and space flight
"A few photos, as of the DC-3, show the vehicle in its exhibit hall, but most pictures depict planes or rockets in action, right up through the latest images of the space age—Mars as viewed from Pathfinder. An enthusiast's delight." Booklist

Demetz, Peter, 1922-
The air show at Brescia, 1909. Farrar, Straus & Giroux 2002 254p $24   **629.13**
1. Aeronautics—History
ISBN 0-374-10259-7   LC 2002-23259
This is an "account of a flying competition that took place in northern Italy during the early days of aviation. Attending the event, among other notables, were Franz Kafka and Italian poet Gabriele d'Annunzio. Kafka, who traveled to Brescia with several friends, including novelist and editor Max Brod, published a journalistic article about the show. . . . Those interested in aviation history as well as a glimpse of the young Kafka will greatly enjoy this serendipitous account." Publ Wkly
Includes bibliographical references

Gorn, Michael H.
Expanding the envelope; flight research at NACA and NASA. University Press of Ky. 2001 472p il $35   **629.13**
1. United States. National Aeronautics and Space Administration 2. United States. National Advisory Committee for Aeronautics 3. Aeronautics
ISBN 0-8131-2205-8   LC 00-12287
"A history of government-sponsored flight research, from the testing of kites and gliders in the 19th century through the Wright brothers, the creation of the National Advisory Committee on Aeronautics, and NASA in the 20th century." Choice
Includes bibliographical references

Grant, R. G. (Reg G.)
Flight: 100 years of aviation. DK Pub. 2002 440p il $50; pa $24.95   **629.13**
1. Aeronautics—History
ISBN 0-7894-8910-4; 0-7566-1902-5 (pa)
           LC 2002-73935
Grant "divides this book into sections that include a prehistory of flight and the Wright brothers; accounts of air combat in World War I, and a focus on the 'golden age' that recounts the flights of Charles Lindbergh, Ame-

lia Earhart, Jimmy Doolittle, and the great airships and flying boats. He also presents a history of aircraft's role in World War II (the Battle of Britain, the air war at sea, and the Allied bombing raids on Axis cities); the cold war and Vietnam; space travel; and jet passenger travel." Booklist
"The impressive illustrations include over 300 gorgeous, full-color profiles of the world's major military and civilian aircraft and space vehicles." Libr J

Haynsworth, Leslie
Amelia Earhart's daughters; the wild and glorious story of American women aviators from World War II to the dawn of the space age; {by} Leslie Haynsworth and David Toomey. Morrow 1998 322p il pa $14 hardcover o.p.
           629.13
1. Women air pilots 2. Women astronauts
ISBN 0-380-72984-9 (pa)   LC 98-8727
This "study of American women aviators concentrates almost exclusively on the WASPs of World War II and the would-be female astronauts of the early 1960s." Booklist
Includes bibliographical references

Lindbergh, Charles, 1902-1974
The spirit of St. Louis; [by] Charles A. Lindbergh. Scribner 1998 562p il $35
           629.13
1. Aeronautics—Flights 2. Spirit of St. Louis (Airplane)
ISBN 0-684-85277-2   LC 98-33556
Also available in paperback from Minnesota Historical Society
First published 1953
This is an account of the first solo transatlantic flight from New York to Paris, as well as a detailed description of the preparation for the flight which in turn mirrors aviation of the 1920's.

Tobin, James, 1956-
To conquer the air; the Wright Brothers and the great race for flight. Free Press 2003 433p il hardcover o.p. pa $16 *   **629.13**
1. Wright, Orville, 1871-1948 2. Wright, Wilbur, 1867-1912 3. Aeronautics—History
ISBN 0-684-85688-3; 0-7432-5536-4 (pa)
           LC 2002-44778
"In this centenary of the airplane, Tobin recreates the course, in its technological and biographical dimensions, of the Wright brothers' claim to its invention." Booklist
"This book represents the most forceful argument to date for the brothers' monumental legacy to the history of flight. . . . This lucidly written and exhaustively researched study is recommended for all aviation collections and all libraries." Libr J
Includes bibliographical references

629.133 Aircraft types

Botting, Douglas
Dr. Eckener's dream machine; the great Zeppelin and the dawn of air travel. Holt & Co. 2001 331p il maps $27.50; pa $16

629.133

1. Eckener, Hugo, 1868-1954 2. Graf Zeppelin (Airship) 3. Airships 4. Aeronautics—Flights
ISBN 0-8050-6458-3; 0-8050-6459-1 (pa)
LC 2001-24770
Botting discusses the history of the Zeppelin, a rigid airship designed by a Prussian army officer, Ferdinand Count von Zeppelin, and the career of Hugo Eckener, who promoted and flew the dirigible
"A truly exciting book, filled with colorful characters and plenty of derring-do and laced with just the right amount of sadness and tragedy." Booklist
Includes bibliographical references

Chiles, James R.
The god machine; from boomerangs to black hawks, the story of the helicopter. Bantam Dell 2007 354p il $25

629.133

1. Helicopters
ISBN 978-0-553-80447-8
LC 2007-28575
The author "chronicles helicopter development from ancient observations of birds and boomerangs in flight to Leonardo da Vinci's aerodynamic ideas to modern police, fire, and medical response helicopters." Libr J
This "is an engaging blend of pop science and pop culture." Publ Wkly
Includes bibliographical references

Jane's all the world's aircraft 2008-2009. Jane's Information Group 2008 973p il $915

629.133

1. Aeronautics
ISSN 0075-3017
ISBN 978-0-7106-2837-4; 0-7106-2837-4
Also available CD-ROM version and online
Annual. First published 1909
"Offers illustrations, descriptions, and specifications of aircraft of various countries of the world including: airplanes, drones, sailplanes, airships, military missiles, research rockets, space vehicles, aero-engines. Arranged in sections by: Aircraft; Lighter than air; Aero engines, then alphabetically by country of manufacture." Guide to Ref Books. 11th edition

629.2 Motor land vehicles, cycles

Bradsher, Keith
High and mighty; SUVs—the world's most dangerous vehicles and how they got that way. PublicAffairs 2002 468p il $28; pa $14

629.2

1. Sport utility vehicles 2. Consumer protection 3. Automobile industry
ISBN 1-58648-123-1; 1-58648-203-3 (pa)
LC 2002-28722

The author discusses sport utility vehicles (S.U.V.'s), which are classified as light trucks and therefore exempt from the environmental and safety rules that apply to cars. Bradsher examines their marketing, environmental impact, safety record, and user psychology
"This fascinating history and troubling analysis of both the politics and the design of the SUV should appeal to readers on both sides of the debate." Booklist
Includes bibliographical references

629.222 Passenger automobiles

Adler, Dennis, 1948-
The art of the sports car; the greatest designs of the 20th century; written and with photographs by Dennis Adler. HarperCollins Pubs. 2002 236p il $44.95

629.222

1. Sports cars
ISBN 0-06-018885-5
LC 2001-51810
In this illustrated history of the sports car the author provides an "account of the evolution of small cars with big engines, recounting the travails of famous auto designers, the engineering and styling innovations they pioneered and the races and road rallies at which cars proved (and advertised) themselves. His narrative dwells mostly on European makes such as Jaguar, Porsche and Ferrari, but also discusses the American Corvette and muscle cars like the Ford Thunderbird and the Dodge Challenger. . . . Hard-core aficionados will derive much gratification from the detailed descriptions of mechanical design and performance. . . . But just about anyone will be entranced at the pictures of classic cars meticulously restored, polished to a sheen and photographed on opulent country estates." Publ Wkly

The **Beaulieu** encyclopedia of the automobile; editor in chief, Nick Georgano; foreword by Lord Montagu of Beaulieu. Fitzroy Dearborn Pubs. 2000 2v il set $325

629.222

1. Automobiles—Encyclopedias
ISBN 1-57958-293-1
LC 2001-316285
This encyclopedia "provides A-Z coverage of almost every make of car that was intended to be manufactured and sold. . . . Most entries are brief descriptions of individual makes, although major names (Chrysler, Citroën, Toyota, etc.) are accorded long entries within which their models are discussed." Booklist
"The most comprehensive automobile encyclopedia available today." Am Libr

629.223 Light trucks

Perry, Michael, 1964-
Truck: a love story. HarperCollins Publishers 2006 281p $24.95

629.223

1. Trucks
ISBN 978-0-06-057117-7; 0-06-057117-9
LC 2006-43394
The author delivers an "account of his somewhat idiosyncratic life and times in a small Wisconsin town. . . Here, he focuses on two main events over the course of a year: fixing up a 1951 International Harvester pickup

Perry, Michael, 1964-—*Continued*
truck and developing a romance with a local woman after a long stretch of failed relationships." Publ Wkly

Perry "propels the story forward as if he were writing a novel, helped by a cast of characters who range from the lightly offbeat to the totally bizarre." Booklist

629.227   Cycles

Herlihy, David
Bicycle: the history; [by] David V. Herlihy. Yale University Press 2004 470p il $40 *
                                                629.227
1. Bicycles
ISBN 0-300-10418-9   LC 2004-12992
Herlihy "takes us from the mathematician Jacques Ozanam's 1696 challenge to develop a 'human-powered carriage' to the creation of the draisine and the velocipede and eventually to the development of the bicycle. . . . The author demonstrates how the development and success of the bicycle were contingent on engineering, marketing, patents, the culture of various regions, and changing views of recreation and health; therefore, this book will also appeal to anyone interested in the history of those fields." Libr J
Includes bibliographical references

Sidwells, Chris, 1956-
Complete bike book. DK Pub. 2003 240p il hardcover o.p. pa $17.95   **629.227**
1. Cycling 2. Bicycles—Maintenance and repair
ISBN 0-7894-9337-3; 0-7566-1427-9 (pa)
                                  LC 2003-40985
"The author begins with a short history of the bicycle, charting its evolution from a simple two-wheeled machine propelled by foot power . . . to today's ultramodern, high-tech vehicle. Individual chapters discuss such matters as proper cycling attire, how to teach a child to ride, how to tailor your diet to maximize its effectiveness, and how to maintain and repair your bike. . . . The book is perfect for newbies, for someone who cycles to work, and for the off-roader, the racer, and the person who sees cycling as a healthy workout." Booklist
Includes bibliographical references

Sloane, Eugene A.
Sloane's complete book of bicycling. 25th anniversary ed. Simon & Schuster 1995 429p il pa $21.95   **629.227**
1. Cycling 2. Bicycles
ISBN 0-671-87075-0   LC 94-46788
"A Fireside book"
First published 1970 by Trident Press with title: The complete book of bicycling. Variant titles: The new Complete book of bicycling; The all new Complete book of bicycling
Covers choosing a bicycle, repair and tools, preventive maintenance, safety tips for commuters, new technologies, bike touring, all-terrain and mountain bikes, and facts on health
Includes bibliographical references

629.28   Tests, driving, maintenance, repairs

Bennett, James S.
The complete motorcycle book; a consumer's guide. 2nd ed. Facts on File 1999 258p il $30.75; pa $14.95   **629.28**
1. Motorcycles
ISBN 0-8160-3853-8; 0-8160-3854-6 (pa)
                                  LC 98-30311
First published 1995
This book covers "motorcycle mechanics, road skills, buying, riding, and caring for motorcycles. Information about factors to consider in buying a motorcycle are covered as well as advice about how to find a new or used bike to meet the rider's needs. Thorough evaluations of many top brands such as BMW, Harley-Davidson, Honda, Suzuki, Yamaha, and others are included. This book offers the most information for the widest variety of motorcyle enthusiasts." Libr J

Christensen, Lisa
Clueless about cars; an easy guide to car maintenance and repair; [by] Lisa Christensen, with Dan Laxter. Rev. and updated ed. Firefly Books 2007 174p il pa $16.95   **629.28**
1. Automobiles—Maintenance and repair
ISBN 978-1-55407-333-7; 1-55407-333-2
First published 2004
On cover: With a new chapter on hybrid cars
This book describes "each major system of the automobile, what can go wrong and how to prevent breakdowns. Step-by-step do-it-yourself instructions are provided for the most important engine maintenance routines and basic automotive repairs." Publisher's note

Downs, Todd
The bicycling guide to complete bicycle maintenance & repair; for road & mountain bikes. Rodale 2005 378p il pa $19.95   **629.28**
1. Bicycles—Maintenance and repair
ISBN 1-57954-883-0   LC 2004-24331
Replaces the edition published 1999 under the authorship of Jim Langley with title: Bicycling magazine's complete guide to bicycle maintenance and repair for road and mountain bikes
First published 1986 with title: Bicycling magazine's Complete guide to bicycle maintenance and repair
This illustrated guide includes step-by-step instructions for major and minor repairs and maintenance for many types of bicycles.

Kachur, Bridget
Every woman's quick & easy car care; a worry-free guide to car troubles, trials & travels. Storey Bks. 2002 262p il pa $14.95
                                                629.28
1. Automobiles—Maintenance and repair
ISBN 1-58017-451-5   LC 2002-1117

Kachur, Bridget—*Continued*

This "guide presents a complete lesson in Auto Mechanics 101, from identifying the different parts of the engine to improving gas mileage to checking the air pressure in tires. . . . {It features} illustrated tutorials on changing a tire, jumpstarting a car, installing a car seat, replacing belts and hoses, changing the oil, detailing, winterizing, performing seasonal maintenance, and much more." Publisher's note

Plas, Rob van der, 1938-

Bicycle repair step by step; how to maintain and repair your bicycle. Van der Plas Publs. 2002 144p il pa $18.95   **629.28**

1. Bicycles—Maintenance and repair
ISBN 1-89249-539-2   LC 2002-104475
First published 1994

This illustrated volume covers the proper maintenance and repair of a bicycle's mechanical systems from changing tires to complex overhauls

Includes bibliographical references

Wilson, Hugo

Motorcycle owner's manual. DK Pub. 1997 112p il pa $10   **629.28**

1. Motorcycles—Maintenance and repair
ISBN 0-7894-1615-8   LC 96-35925

This guide to motorcycle maintenance starts with simple procedures and routines then goes on to basic servicing and complex jobs

"Handy, attractive, and easy to follow." Booklist

629.4   Astronautics

Angelo, Joseph A.

Encyclopedia of space exploration; {by} Joseph A. Angelo, Jr. Facts on File 2000 305p il (Facts on File science library) $55; pa $21.95 *   **629.4**

ISBN 0-8160-3942-9; 0-8160-4902-5 (pa)
LC 99-59659

In an A to Z format, this reference "presents the most recent lunar missions, the exploration of Mars, the latest images and discoveries via the *Hubble Space Telescope*, a special focus on Mission to planet Earth and the use of space to monitor and protect the biosphere, an update on the *International Space Station*, a focus on asteroid detection and negation systems, and the role of robotics and virtual reality in exploring the solar system." Publisher's note

Includes bibliographical references

The Facts on File dictionary of space technology; [by] Joseph A. Angelo, Jr. rev ed. Facts on File 2004 474p $49.95; pa $19.95
629.4

1. Astronautics—Dictionaries
ISBN 0-8160-5222-0; 0-8160-5223-9 (pa)
LC 2003-49148

"Facts on File science library"

First published 1982 with title: The dictionary of space technology

This dictionary contains approximately 1,500 cross-referenced entries that present the basic concepts and phrases in the science of space, spaceflight, and space technology. Among the topics covered are: abort modes; ballistic missile defense; launch vehicles; Milstar; ocean remote sensing; robotics and space stations

Brzezinski, Matthew, 1965-

Red moon rising; Sputnik and the hidden rivalries that ignited the Space Age. Times Books 2007 322p il $26   **629.4**

1. Outer space—Exploration 2. Cold war
3. Astronautics—United States 4. Astronautics—Soviet Union 5. Artificial satellites
ISBN 978-0-8050-8147-3; 0-8050-8147-X
LC 2007-08227

This is a "narrative of the superpower space race in the months surrounding the Sputnik shot." N Y Times Book Rev

"Matthew Brzezinski's history of 1957 is not a potted retelling of the space race highlights we have perhaps encountered once too often in television documentaries and Sunday supplements, but a vivid and anecdotal account of the nerve-wracking delays, tormented decisions and agonizing uncertainties that unquestionably lent a human, and even heroic, aspect to his subject." Times Lit Suppl

Includes bibliographical references

Burrows, William E.

The survival imperative; using space to protect Earth. Forge Books 2006 317p $24.95
629.4

1. United States. National Aeronautics and Space Administration 2. Astronautics 3. Outer space
4. Asteroids
ISBN 978-0-765-31114-6; 0-765-31114-3
LC 2005-33803

"A Tom Doherty Associates book"

"Presenting a case for establishing a new direction and vision for our space program, longtime science technology reporter Burrows . . . proposes that NASA undertake a program to detect and protect Earth from asteroids and comets, provide advance notice of hurricanes and other natural disasters, pinpoint environmental pollution, furnish replacement power sources, and even detect and deter nuclear attacks. One of the best things about the book is the historical background Burrows includes—on the space program, nuclear proliferation, and environmental concerns—as he builds his argument for creating an overall defense strategy using space." Libr J

This new ocean; the story of the first space age. Random House 1998 723p il pa $18.95 hardcover o.p.   **629.4**

1. Astronautics 2. Outer space—Exploration
ISBN 0-375-75485-7 (pa)   LC 98-3252

This is a "history of space exploration, from its ancient roots in mythology and literature to the theoreticians and pioneering engineers who made it a reality in this century." Libr J

"'This New Ocean' is most distinguished by the successful integration of three different story lines: manned space flight, the militarization of space and space science." N Y Times Book Rev

Includes bibliographical references

Cadbury, Deborah

Space race; the epic battle between America and the Soviet Union for dominion of space. HarperCollins 2006 370p il $24.95   **629.4**

1. Outer space—Exploration 2. Cold war 3. Astronautics—United States 4. Astronautics—Soviet Union

ISBN 0-06-084553-8   LC 2005-52693

First published 2005 in the United Kingdom

This book "reveals how two brilliant scientists, former Gulag inmate Sergei Korolev and V-2 rocket program designer Wernher von Braun, were cynically controlled by the USSR and America, respectively, as indispensable tools during the Cold War." Libr J

"From the opening account of Washington and Moscow's race to grab the models, machines, drawings, and personnel from Hitler's V-2 missile program at the end of World War II to Sputnik and then to Neil Armstrong's moonwalk, this is an utterly engrossing book—largely because of the two characters around whom the story unfolds, and because Cadbury has the material to tell it from the inside." Foreign Affairs

Includes bibliographical references

Hardesty, Von, 1939-

Epic rivalry; the inside story of the Soviet and American space race; [by] Von Hardesty and Gene Eisman; foreword by Sergei Khrushchev. National Geographic Society 2007 275p il map $28

     629.4

1. Outer space—Exploration 2. Cold war 3. Astronautics—United States 4. Astronautics—Soviet Union

ISBN 978-1-4262-0119-6   LC 2007-17393

"The authors compare the U.S. and Soviet space exploration programs during the cold war." Libr J

"This is a true saga, full of daring, danger, death, ego conflicts, and triumphs. . . . All readers should love this fabulous and profusely illustrated combined story." Sci Books Films

Includes bibliographical references

National Geographic encyclopedia of space; [compiled by] Linda K. Glover; with Andrew Chaikin . . . [et al.]; foreword by Buzz Aldrin. National Geographic Society 2004 400p il map $40 *   **629.4**

1. Astronautics 2. Astronomy—Encyclopedias 3. Outer space—Exploration

ISBN 0-7922-7319-2   LC 2004-55229

The essays in this encyclopedia "discuss deep space, our solar system and space travel. There are also sections on using space to study Earth and on the military and intelligence uses of space. The essays in general are readable and show the implications of astronomy for life on Earth, such as the impact of solar flares on the weather. . . . This volume will suit astronomy enthusiasts better than total novices. Everyone, however, can enjoy the gorgeous photos." Publ Wkly

Walsh, Patrick J.

Echoes among the stars; a short history of the U.S. space program. Sharpe, M.E. 2000 204p $35.95; pa $29.95   **629.4**

1. Astronautics—United States

ISBN 0-7656-0537-6; 0-7656-0538-4 (pa)

      LC 99-38899

Walsh "recounts the early successes of the Mercury and Gemini missions that paved the way for the Apollo moon landings as well as the Skylab and Apollo-Soyuz mission that marked the end of the first era of U.S. manned space flight." Libr J

Includes bibliographical references

Williamson, Mark

The Cambridge dictionary of space technology. Cambridge Univ. Press 2001 464p il maps $50

     629.4

1. Astronautics—Dictionaries 2. Astronomy—Dictionaries

ISBN 0-521-66077-7   LC 00-59884

First published 1990 by Hilger with title: Dictionary of space technology

"This dictionary is a comprehensive reference on the words and phrases related to many aspects of the evolving field of space technology. The work contains material ranging from basic concepts to advanced applications and includes over 2,000 entries. The extraordinary breadth of coverage ensures that there are entries on all major space technology subject areas. While the emphasis on each entry is on defining the meaning of the word or phrase, entries have been written with the intention of enhancing the understanding of the subject for a variety of users, ranging from the practicing specialist to the layperson to the student." Sci Books & Films

Zimmerman, Robert

The chronological encyclopedia of discoveries in space. Oryx Press 2000 410p il maps $95

     629.4

1. Outer space—Exploration 2. Astronautics

ISBN 1-57356-196-7

"Over 1,000 entries record the date of launch, name of the spacecraft(s), summary of the mission, names of the crew members, experiments, problems, and discoveries in a clear and concise fashion. Seemingly every single space mission is included, encompassing spaceflight with and without human crews, military and civilian ventures, public and commercial ventures, planetary probes, and communications satellites. . . . An excellent, cross-referencing system within the text, as well as extensive subject indices by satellite, mission, and nation or consortia, helps the reader follow particular interests in detail. . . . There is no comparable source to this volume for its comprehensiveness and conciseness." Sci Books Films

Includes bibliographical references

629.45 Manned space flight

Barbree, Jay
Live from Cape Canaveral; covering the space race, from Sputnik to today. Smithsonian Books/Collins 2007 321p il $26.95
629.45
1. Astronautics—United States
ISBN 978-0-06-123392-0; 0-06-123392-7
LC 2007-15247
The author "retraces the politics—domestic and international—as well as the science and technology behind the U.S. space program." Booklist
"Barbree writes with infectious enthusiasm about the glory days of space exploration, and his book will be an enjoyable introduction for a new generation and a fond remembrance for boomers." Publ Wkly

Chaikin, Andrew, 1956-
A man on the moon; the voyages of the Apollo astronauts. Viking 1994 670p il hardcover o.p. pa $18
629.45
1. Apollo project 2. Space flight to the moon
ISBN 0-670-81446-6; 978-0-14-311235-8 (pa); 0-14-311235-X (pa)
LC 93-48680
In this chronicle of NASA's Apollo program "diary-like reports mix with first- and third-person accounts as Chaikin . . . delivers a chronological view of the missions and those who planned and flew them. Focusing closely on the Apollo astronauts, including Buzz Aldrin, Pete Conrad and Neil Armstrong, Chaikin gives his topic a sense of immediacy." Publ Wkly
Includes bibliographical references

French, Francis
In the shadow of the moon; a challenging journey to Tranquility, 1965-1969; [by] Francis French and Colin Burgess; with a foreword by Walter Cunningham. University of Nebraska Press 2007 425p il (Outward odyssey) $29.95
629.45
1. Space flight to the moon 2. Astronautics—United States 3. Astronautics—Soviet Union 4. Apollo project
ISBN 978-0-8032-1128-5; 0-8032-1128-7
LC 2006-103047
The authors "chronicle the missions on which American astronauts learned how to live in space for more than a few hours; steer a spacecraft around the Earth at almost 20,000 miles an hour; rendezvous with a companion ship; and navigate to another world and return safely." Publ Wkly
"This book will have an important place in the recorded history of space exploration." Sci Books Films
Includes bibliographical references

Kevles, Bettyann
Almost heaven; the story of women in space; [by] Bettyann Holtzmann Kevles. Basic Books 2003 274p il $25.95 *
629.45
1. Women astronauts
ISBN 0-7382-0209-6
LC 2003-13801

Also available in paperback from MIT Press
This is a "history of the U.S. space program, with special emphasis on, and stories about, the women who have had the courage to venture into space. Each one is special, the book reveals; yet they all share a spirit of adventure and a willingness to put up with hardship in order to fulfill their dream." Sci Books Films
Includes bibliographical references

Kranz, Eugene F., 1933-
Failure is not an option; mission control from Mercury to Apollo 13 and beyond; {by} Gene Kranz. Simon & Schuster 2000 415p il $26
629.45
1. United States. National Aeronautics and Space Administration 2. Space flight 3. Astronautics—United States
ISBN 0-7432-0079-9
LC 00-27720
Also available in paperback from Berkley Pub. Group
This memoir by the NASA flight director "follows his and NASA's careers from the start of the space race through 'the last lunar strike,' Apollo 17 (1972-1973)." Publ Wkly
"A welcome contribution to the history of space flight. More than any previous book, it gives the view of that history as lived by the brotherhood of Mission Control. The writing, like Kranz himself, is brisk, unadorned and informative, but warmed from time to time by characteristic expressions of irony and humor." N Y Times Book Rev

Launius, Roger D.
Frontiers of space exploration. 2nd ed. Greenwood Press 2004 245p il $45
629.45
1. Astronautics—International cooperation 2. Outer space—Exploration
ISBN 0-313-32524-3
LC 2003-60402
First published 1998
"The text includes a chronology, a general historical overview of space flight, 3 lengthy essays on space exploration, and 21 biographical essays. In addition, 26 primary documents trace U.S. space flight history, and there is an up-to-date listing of all U.S. space flights up to and including the Columbia disaster of January 2003. A fine annotated bibliography rounds out the volume." Booklist

Pyle, Rod
Destination moon; the Apollo missions in the astronauts' own words. HarperCollins Publishers 2005 192p il $24.95; pa $14.95
629.45
1. Project Apollo 2. Space flight to the moon
ISBN 0-06-087349-3; 0-06-087350-7 (pa)
LC 2005-51350
This "survey of the Apollo moon program includes a brief summary of each flight and attempted flight of the great effort, from the fatal fire on Pad 34 in 1967 to the landing of a scientist on the moon in Apollo 17 in 1972. . . . Space collections of all sizes should welcome Pyle's book, and smaller ones will find it invaluable." Booklist

Schefter, James L.

The race; the uncensored story of how America beat Russia to the moon; by James Schefter. Doubleday 1999 303p il pa $14 hardcover o.p.

629.45

1. Astronautics 2. Space flight to the moon 3. Apollo project

ISBN 0-385-49254-5 (pa)   LC 98-54430

Schefter chronicles the early days of space flight competition describing "the subtle infighting among the astronauts, the complex nature of lesser-known people like manned-flight champion Bob Gilruth, and the American leaders struggling with military, scientific and public relations concerns." Publ Wkly

Wolfe, Tom

The right stuff. Picador 2008 352p pa $16 *

629.45

1. Astronauts 2. Astronautics—United States

ISBN 0-312-42756-5; 978-0-312-42756-6

First published 1979 by Farrar, Straus & Giroux

This volume chronicles "the handful of adrenaline-junkie military test pilots who became the Mercury astronauts. Their story is juxtaposed against that of Chuck Yeager, the ace of aces pilot who broke the sound barrier but couldn't apply to the space program because he lacked a college degree. . . . A terrific read from beginning to end." Libr J

Zimmerman, Robert

Genesis: the story of Apollo 8; the first manned flight to another world. Dell 1999 350p il pa $7.99

629.45

1. Apollo project 2. Space flight to the moon

ISBN 978-0-440-23556-9; 0-440-23556-1

First published 1998 by Four Walls Eight Windows

The author tells the story of "Apollo 8 from the time it blasted into space on December 21, 1968, until it splashed down in the Pacific nearly a week later. He focuses on three brave men—Frank Borman, Jim Lovell, and Bill Anders—who volunteered to ride an inadequately tested space vehicle equipped with a primitive computer on a journey of some quarter-million miles to orbit the Moon and return. He also focuses on the astronauts' wives." Choice

Includes bibliographical references

629.46 Engineering of unmanned spacecraft

Dickson, Paul

Sputnik: the shock of the century. Walker & Co. 2001 310p il $28   **629.46**

1. Artificial satellites 2. Astronautics 3. United States—Politics and government—20th century

ISBN 0-8027-1365-3   LC 2001-26156

Also available in paperback from Berkley Pub. Group

This is an "analysis of the impact of the Soviet space program on American politics, as well as on the military, public opinion, education, science, and research." Sci Books Films

"Paul Dickson skillfully puts the story of Sputnik and its aftermath into . . . perspective in his informative and readable book." Christ Sci Monit

Includes bibliographical references

629.47 Astronautical engineering

Dyson, George, 1953-

Project Orion; the true story of the atomic spaceship. Holt & Co. 2002 345p il $26; pa $16

629.47

1. Nuclear rockets 2. Astronautics

ISBN 0-8050-5985-7; 0-8050-7284-5 (pa)

LC 2001-46500

The author "charts the history of the failed Project Orion, which called for a massive rocket to be built atop a nuclear-powered piston. . . . Dyson's explanations of the nuclear science behind the system are lucid. A great strength of Dyson's project is the interviews he conducted with surviving Orion team members." Publ Wkly

Includes bibliographical references

Stine, G. Harry (George Harry), 1928-1997

Handbook of model rocketry; [by] G. Harry Stine and Bill Stine. 7th ed. Wiley 2004 363p il pa $22.95   **629.47**

1. Rockets (Aeronautics)—Models

ISBN 978-0-471-47242-1; 0-471-47242-5

LC 2004-2230

First published 1965 by Follett. Periodically revised. Publisher varies

"Stine, an authority on model rocketry, describes all aspects of the subject from basics to international competition." Ref Sources for Small & Medium-sized Libr. 4th edition

Includes bibliographical references

629.8 Automatic control engineering

Brooks, Rodney Allen

Flesh and machines; how robots will change us. Pantheon Bks. 2002 260p il $26; pa $14

629.8

1. Robots 2. Artificial intelligence

ISBN 0-375-42079-7; 0-375-72527-X (pa)

LC 2001-36636

"A scientist at MIT's famous artificial intelligence lab, Brooks here splits his book in two: the first part describes various robots he and his group have built; the second part philosophizes on the nature of artificial intelligence." Booklist

A "stimulating book written by one of the major players in the field . . . about the state of robotics and its short-term future. It also offers surprisingly deep glimpses into what it is to be human. Brooks appears to have gained a boundless appreciation for human beings by attempting to copy them." N Y Times Book Rev

Cook, David

Robot building for beginners. APress 2002 568p il (Technology in action) pa $29.95 **629.8**

1. Robots—Design and construction

ISBN 1-893115-44-5

This book contains instructions on how to build a robot. "General sources for tools and parts are provided in a consolidated list, and specific parts are recommended throughout the book. . . . {The book also features information on} basic safety precautions and essential numbering and measuring systems." Publisher's note

Gutkind, Lee

Almost human; making robots think. Norton 2007 284p il $25.95 * **629.8**

1. Robots 2. Artificial intelligence

ISBN 978-0-393-05867-3; 0-393-05867-0

LC 2006-101046

"Drawing on years of observational curiosity at Carnegie Mellon's Robotics Institute, both in the lab and in the field, Gutkind explores the people and ideas behind machines developed to do the impossible: operate autonomously. This so-called bleeding-edge robotics is illuminated through stories of success and failure, tension between engineers developing bodies and the coders programming their artificial intelligence, motivational cross-pollination between seasoned veterans and young grad students, and performance tests chock-full of moments of elation and depression. Readers are given a strong sense of the drama inherent in the discipline, whether advancing incrementally or by leaps and bounds." Libr J

Includes bibliographical references

McComb, Gordon

Robot builder's sourcebook. McGraw-Hill 2002 711p il pa $24.95 **629.8**

1. Robots

ISBN 0-07-140685-9

LC 2002-31999

A "listing (with address, phone numbers, web sites) of over 2500 suppliers and manufacturers of robot components, materials, tools, and much more. There are even sources for tracking down older and hard-to-find parts. Also listed are books, journals, magazines, professional societies, and Internet resources, including education sites, competition information, and web sites where hobbyists can find examples of program code. Dozens of sidebars and articles on various robotics topics break up the directory feel. The author also indicates recommended sources based on his own experiences and identifies 'premium' sources that are dedicated to robot hobbyists." Libr J

Menzel, Peter

Robo sapiens: evolution of a new species; [by] Peter Menzel and Faith D'Aluisio. MIT Press 2000 239p il $29.95; pa $19.95 **629.8**

1. Robots 2. Artificial intelligence

ISBN 0-262-13382-2; 0-262-63245-4 (pa)

LC 00-33946

"A Material world book"

This book is a collection of "interviews, essays, illustrations, and numerous photographs of all aspects of cur-

rent research and actual production locations using robots, some of which approach the 'intelligent' level. The coverage includes more than 100 different researchers and developers with their robots. . . . The interviews are interesting, and the range of applications areas is fascinating; from medicine to housecleaning, from game playing to dancing robots, there is something for everyone in this collection." Libr J

Includes bibliographical references

Rosheim, Mark E.

Robot evolution; the development of anthrobotics. Wiley 1994 423p il $140

629.8

1. Robots

ISBN 0-471-02622-0

LC 94-13687

This book "offers a blend of robotic history, technology, ideas, and trends. It surveys robotics history from the days of Greeks up to Joseph Engelberger, the father of modern robotics." Choice

This "book is highly recommended because of its content, organization, completeness, quality of illustrations, and value." Sci Books Films

Wood, Gaby

Edison's Eve; a magical history of the quest for mechanical life. Knopf 2002 xxviii, 304p il $24; pa $14 **629.8**

1. Robots 2. Artificial intelligence

ISBN 0-679-45112-9; 1-4000-3158-3 (pa)

LC 2002-25467

Published in the United Kingdom with title: Living dolls

The author discusses "the thinking, hoaxes, and inventions that presage contemporary robotics and the current experiments with artificial intelligence." Publisher's note

This is "a lively, elegant and surprising book, packed with curious details and enticing anecdotes." N Y Times Book Rev

630 Agriculture

Fatal harvest; the tragedy of industrial agriculture; edited by Andrew Kimbrell. Island Press (Washington, D.C.) 2002 384p il $75; pa $45

630

1. Agriculture—Environmental aspects

ISBN 1-55963-940-7; 1-55963-941-5 (pa)

LC 2001-5800

The contributors to this "volume trace the shift from agrarian to industrial agriculture, assess how and why the latter is now wreaking environmental havoc, and analyze alternative practices." Booklist

Includes bibliographical references

Hurt, R. Douglas

Problems of plenty; the American farmer in the twentieth century. Dee, I.R. 2002 192p (American ways series) $24.95; pa $13.95 **630**

1. Agriculture—United States 2. Agriculture—Government policy 3. Agriculture—Economic aspects

ISBN 1-56663-463-6; 1-56663-462-8 (pa)

LC 2002-67431

Hurt, R. Douglas—*Continued*

The author argues "that farmers face the same fundamental issues they did a century ago: overproduction,
low commodity prices coupled with high production
costs, and ineffective government intervention that often
encourages rather than discourages overproduction. . . .
He focuses chiefly on macroeconomic threads into which
he incorporates the influence of farm organizations, technological developments (especially the gasoline tractor
and later biotechnology), and federal farm programs. . . .
Hurt has produced a very solid, readable history which
should be useful for collections in general agriculture,
agricultural economics and history, or rural sociology."
Choice

Includes bibliographical references

631.4   Soil science

Stoll, Steven

Larding the lean Earth; soil and society in
nineteenth-century America. Hill & Wang 2002
287p il maps $30; pa $15   **631.4**
1. Soil conservation 2. Agriculture—Environmental aspects 3. Land settlement—United States
ISBN 0-8090-6431-6; 0-8090-6430-8 (pa)
                                  LC 2002-23279
"Stoll blends biology and history in this . . . study of
soil, which performs more ecological functions than most
people realize and which is being lost at an alarming
rate." Booklist

Includes bibliographical references

631.5   Cultivation and harvesting

Cummings, Claire Hope, 1943-

Uncertain peril; genetic engineering and the
future of seeds. Beacon Press 2008 232p $24.95 *
                                          631.5
1. Biotechnology 2. Seeds
ISBN 978-0-8070-8580-6   LC 2007-26298
The author "argues that, thanks to the patenting and
high-pressure global marketing of genetically modified
seeds by multinational corporations, there is now a seed
crisis." Booklist
This "authoritative portrait of another way in which
our planet is at peril provides stark food for thought."
Publ Wkly

Includes bibliographical references

631.8   Fertilizers, soil conditioners, growth regulators

Pleasant, Barbara

The complete compost gardening guide; banner
batches, grow heaps, comforter compost, and other
amazing techniques for saving time and money,
and producing the most flavorful, nutritious
vegetables ever; [by] Barbara Pleasant & Deborah
L. Martin. Storey Pub. 2008 319p il map $29.95;
pa $19.95 *   **631.8**
1. Compost 2. Gardening
ISBN 978-1-58017-703-0; 978-1-58017-702-3 (pa)
                                  LC 2007-49729
The authors "provide both a reference guide and an
introduction to composting. The first section . . . includes a number of interesting facts, definitions, and
even recipes (e.g., for Miracle Leaf Mold). The second
section, on compost gardening techniques, examines easy
methods of composting with piles, bins, and cans as well
as more elaborate approaches involving pits and trenches.
It also discusses the use of earthworms in composting.
Finally, the third section treats in detail the kinds of
plants that will do well in a composter's garden. . . . Essential reading for any gardener interested in composting,
this should find its way into many public libraries with
active gardening communities and academic and special
libraries with an interest in horticulture and gardening."
Libr J

632   Plant injuries, diseases, pests

Lockwood, Jeffrey A., 1960-

Locust; the devastating rise and mysterious
disappearance of the insect that shaped the
American frontier; Jeffrey A. Lockwood. 1st ed.
Basic Books 2004 xxiii, 294p il $25; pa $14.95 *
                                            632
1. Locusts 2. West (U.S.)—History
ISBN 0-7382-0894-9; 0-465-04167-1 (pa)
                                  LC 2003-25538
The author "tells the fascinating story of how the
Rocky Mountain locust invasions shaped American life
in the 1870s. . . . This book is great for natural-history
lovers, American history lovers, mystery lovers, and all
who love a well-told real-life tale." Sci Books Films

Waldbauer, Gilbert

Insights from insects; what bad bugs can teach
us. Prometheus Books 2005 311p il $18
                                            632
1. Insect pests
ISBN 1-59102-277-0   LC 2004-26928
The author "profiles a rogue's gallery of unhealthful,
unprofitable and unsavory creatures from the mosquito
and house fly to an array of agricultural scourges. From
their ingenious strategies for wreaking havoc and evading
retribution from predators, toxic plant chemicals, insecticides and eradication programs, he gleans lessons about
the Darwinian struggle for survival and the complex, eas-

Waldbauer, Gilbert—*Continued*
ily upset balance of ecosystems. Waldbauer's lucid, engaging style, informed by accessible discussions of his and other scientists' research, maintains a lab-coated tone of interested objectivity." Publ Wkly
Includes bibliographical references

634.9　Forestry

Brown, Daniel, 1951-
Under a flaming sky; the great Hinckley firestorm of 1894; [by] Daniel James Brown. Lyons Press 2006 256p il map $22.95
634.9
1. Forest fires 2. Minnesota
ISBN 1-59228-863-4; 978-1-59228-863-2
"On September 1, 1894, a firestorm consumed timber-boomtown Hinckley, Minnesota, and three nearby hamlets. Brown, grandson of an 11-year-old survivor, makes riveting, affecting, white-knuckle reading of that horrifying, internationally reported day's lethal passage." Booklist
Includes bibliographical references

Maclean, John N.
The Thirtymile fire; a chronicle of bravery and betrayal. Henry Holt 2007 241p il map $25
634.9
1. Fire fighters 2. Wildfires 3. Cascade Range region
ISBN 978-0-8050-7578-6; 0-8050-7578-X
LC 2006-45846
"A John Macrae book"
"The 'Thirtymile Fire' snuck up on firefighters who were cleaning up after an earlier blaze in Washington State, near the Canadian border. Sparked by an untended campfire, the fire (which was named for is closest geographical landmark, Thirtymile Peak) didn't appear to be much of a threat. But fire is unpredictable, and soon firefighters were in the midst of a raging and deadly inferno. Maclean takes us inside the fire and puts us beside the men and women trying to tame it. Ultimately, it's a tragic story—some members of the firefighting crew died." Booklist
Maclean "interviewed families, survivors, investigators and fire experts, and the result is an evenhanded, lucid recreation of catastrophe and its aftermath. The author gives a human face to national headlines, capturing the dignity and sense of mission of the lost firefighters." Publ Wkly

Taylor, Murry A.
Jumping fire; a smokejumper's memoir of fighting wildfire. Harcourt 2000 445p il pa $14 hardcover o.p.
634.9
1. Forest fires 2. Fire fighting
ISBN 0-15-601397-5 (pa)
LC 99-87608
"The oldest smoke jumper in the 60-year history of Alaskan firefighting, Taylor gives a detailed and exciting account of his adventures parachuting into the wilderness to combat wildfires during the summer of 1991." Publ Wkly

635　Garden crops (Horticulture) Vegetables

Adam, Judith
Landscape planning; practical techniques for the home gardener. 2nd ed., rev. and expanded. Firefly 2008 247p il $39.95; pa $29.95
635
1. Landscape gardening
ISBN 978-1-55407-381-8; 1-55407-381-2; 978-1-55407-258-3 (pa); 1-55407-258-1 (pa)
First published 2002
The author provides steps "in designing and implementing a landscape plan: from assessing specific needs and planning a budget and timeline, to making the best choices for a successful garden." Publisher's note
"Adam's language is both practical and reflective of a love of gardening. A sound resource for any size collection." Libr J [review of 2002 edition]

American Horticultural Society encyclopedia of gardening; editor-in-chief, Christopher Brickell. Rev. US ed., Rev. & expanded ed. DK Pub. 2003 752p il map $60
635
1. Gardening—Encyclopedias
ISBN 0-7894-9653-4
LC 2003-279089
First published 1992 in the United Kingdom with title: The Royal Horticultural Society encyclopedia of gardening
"Originally a British publication, this beautifully illustrated encyclopedia . . . has been thoroughly revised for the American gardener. The book covers all aspects of gardening including techniques, plants, and maintenance for indoor and outdoor plants. It also discusses equipping the garden, the garden environment, and plant problems. An outstanding feature of the book is the 3,000-plus color photos that illustrate clearly written instructions and make gardening procedures easy to follow. While extremely valuable as a reference, some patrons will want more time to explore the book so a circulating copy is also recommended." Am Libr [review of 1993 edition]
An "essential purchase for all public libraries." Libr J [review of 1993 edition]

The **American** Horticultural Society gardening manual. Dorling Kindersley 2000 420p il map $40 *
635
1. Gardening
ISBN 0-7894-5952-3
LC 00-22644
Published simultaneously under title: The Royal Horticultural Society gardening manual
"The book is divided into four parts, the first of which covers garden planning, illustrating various garden styles, hardscape choices, and advice on designing the space. . . Part 2, which is arranged by plant type . . . covers the care and maintenance of the plants. . . . Part 3 offers thumbnail descriptions, including hardiness zones and the mature size of reliable, recommended plants arranged by the season they are at their best. The final part summarizes the routine but essential tasks the gardener should do each month." Libr J

Beginner's guide to gardening; creating a beautiful yard from the ground up. Reader's Digest 2005 256p il $32.95   **635**

1. Landscape gardening

ISBN 0-7621-0498-8   LC 2004-45350

Such "topics as plant selection, pest and disease diagnosis and control, lawn care, soil composition, chores, and equipment are covered, as are container gardening, greenhouses, vegetables, and fruits. A discussion of the seasonal aspects of gardening is also included, along with a glossary of terms and FAQs." Libr J

"Color photographs and line drawings illustrate step-by-step methods that help take the mystery out of plant propagation methods like sowing seeds and dividing perennials, so that beginners can acquire necessary skills. . . . [Beginners] will find adequate information on how to mulch and prune, plant a container, maintain a lawn, or equip a greenhouse." Booklist

Borchardt, Rudolf, 1877-1945

The passionate gardener; English translation by Henry Martin. McPherson & Company 2006 340p $30   **635**

1. Gardening

ISBN 978-0-92970-173-8; 0-92970-173-9

LC 2006-04312

Original German edition, 1968

"A poet and philosopher who was 'both famous and obscure' during his lifetime (1877-1945), Borchardt was also a gardening enthusiast. He was intimately involved with the contemporary German literary scene, but 19th-century ideas and ideals continued to dominate his outlook when he wrote this series of essays from self-imposed exile in Italy in 1938. . . . Borchardt begins with a discourse on 'The Flower and the Human Being,' exploring the ancient origins of that relationship through mythology, legend and language. He goes on to philosophize about the different natures of wild and cultivated plants and about the relationship between plants and their native landscapes. Martin's translation captures the Germanic density and impassioned, freewheeling inquiry behind this difficult but rewarding addition to the garden reader's bookshelf." Publ Wkly

Burpee complete gardener; a comprehensive, up-to-date, fully illustrated reference for gardeners at all levels; [by] Maureen Heffernan [et al.]; edited by Barbara W. Ellis. Macmillan 1995 422p il $29.95   **635**

1. Gardening

ISBN 0-02-860378-8   LC 95-13141

This volume presents "information on 420 annuals, biennials, perennials, bulbs, roses, vegetables, herbs, ground covers, and vines. There's a description of each plant, along with growing instructions and its uses. Other chapters cover designing, starting, planting, and caring for a garden; tools and equipment; and pests and diseases." Booklist

Includes bibliographical references

Cuthbertson, Yvonne, 1944-

Beginners' guide to herb gardening. Guild of Master Craftsman Publs.; distributed by Sterling 2001 168p il pa $17.95   **635**

1. Herb gardening

ISBN 1-86108-198-7

This covers such topics as designing and planning an herb garden, choosing and planting herbs, propagation and pruning, culinary herbs and herbs for fragrance and color, growing herbs in containers or indoors, and harvesting and drying.

This "guide provides a thorough overview of the subject. . . . All the basics are presented in an informative, attractively illustrated format." Booklist

Damrosch, Barbara

The garden primer; illustrations by Linda Heppes Funk, Ray Maher, and Carol Bolt. 2nd ed. Workman Pub. 2008 820p il map $28.95; pa $18.95   **635**

1. Gardening

ISBN 978-0-7611-4856-2; 978-0-7611-2275-3 (pa)

LC 2007-51425

First published 1988

This is a "book for the new gardener that clearly explains the basics of garden planning, plant care, and equipment. Detailed chapters on the different categories of plants—annuals, perennials, vegetables, fruits, lawns, shrubs, roses, vines, trees, wildflowers, and even house plants—give general advice on how to use and care for these varieties. A valuable book for public libraries." Libr J

Includes bibliographical references

Denckla, Tanya

The organic gardener's home reference; a plant-by-plant guide to growing fresh, healthy food. Storey Communications 1994 273p il pa $21.95 hardcover o.p.   **635**

1. Organic gardening

ISBN 0-88266-839-0 (pa)   LC 93-22835

"A Garden Way Publishing book"

First published 1991 with title: Gardening at a glance

This work "covers vegetables, herbs, fruits and nuts, and pest and disease control. The book has a good introduction on garden stewardship, followed by chapters on vegetables, fruits and nuts, herbs, macro- and microdestructive agents with organic remedies, and allies and companions. For those who want to know about an edible plant, the book describes growth conditions, harvesting, storage requirements, growing tips, and selected varieties." Recomm Ref Books for Small & Medium-sized Libr & Media Cent, 1996

Includes bibliographical references

Encyclopedia of gardens; history and design; editor, by Candice A. Shoemaker. Fitzroy Dearborn Pubs. 2001 3v set $385   **635**

ISBN 1-57958-173-0

At head of title: Chicago Botanic Garden

"Produced under the auspices of the Chicago Botanic Garden . . . this comprehensive resource provides information on garden history and design. The contributors . . . describe and provide analysis of garden-related individuals, places, and topics. The entries are alphabetically arranged and vary in length from a page to more than 10 pages for the entry *United States*. Depending on whether

Encyclopedia of gardens—*Continued*

the entry deals with an individual, a place, or a topic, it includes an essay, a biography, a list of works, a chronology, and a bibliography." Booklist

Gardening basics; a complete guide to designing, planting, and maintaining gardens; {by Ken Beckett et al.; consulting editor, John E. Elsley}. Sterling 1999 276p pa $19.95 hardcover o.p.

635

1. Gardening

ISBN 0-8069-2429-2 (pa)   LC 99-20247

This is "a comprehensive introduction to gardening, with basic information on designing and creating family gardens, patio gardens, large gardens, and low-maintenance gardens. From fences to hedges to soil types to fundamental plants for most gardens, the contributors bring great expertise and detail." Booklist

Great garden formulas; the ultimate book of mix-it-yourself concoctions for your garden; Joan Benjamin and Deborah L. Martin, editors; contributing writers, Erin Hynes {et al.}. Rodale Press 1998 342p il map pa $17.95 hardcover o.p.

635

1. Organic gardening

ISBN 0-87596-848-1 (pa)   LC 98-8915

Organic recipes and techniques for gardeners to "improve their soil, fertilize their plants, reduce weeds and pests, and even concoct a soothing hand cream to use when the work is done. Grouped thematically by chapter, these formulas employ either natural ingredients or simple chemicals such as Epsom salts, and most are easy to make and use." Libr J

Includes bibliographical references

Land, Leslie

The New York times 1000 gardening questions & answers; based on the column "Gardeners Q & A"; with additional material by Leslie Land; botanical illustrations by Bobbi Angell; how-to illustrations by Elayne Sears. Workman 2003 852p il $34.95; pa $19.95

635

1. Gardening

ISBN 0-7611-2886-7; 0-7611-1997-3 (pa)

LC 2002-34206

"The text uses a Q&A format to address a gamut of gardening topics. The result is a substantial reference work useful to novice and experienced gardeners alike, with the Q&As organized into five sections: 'Flowering Plants,' 'Landscaping,' 'Edible Plants,' 'Container Gardening,' and 'Maintenance.' The subtopics within each section are many and diverse, including historically appropriate plantings, houseplants, over-wintering, and organic vegetable growing, as well as standard topics such as deer damage, roses, pruning, soil types and amendment, and recommended plant lists for specific situations." Libr J

Rodale's all-new encyclopedia of organic gardening; the indispensable resource for every gardener; edited by Fern Marshall Bradley and Barbara W. Ellis. Rodale Press 1992 690p il $29.95; pa $19.95

635

1. Organic gardening

ISBN 0-87857-999-0; 0-87596-599-7 (pa)

LC 91-32088

First published 1959 with title: Rodale's encyclopedia of organic gardening

"Entries are cross referenced and include further reading lists, related organizations, and key words. Common and botanical names are listed, and while food plants are entered under their common names, ornamentals and herbs are entered under their botanical names. This is an important, complete, well-arranged, and attractive reference tool." Libr J

Rodale's illustrated encyclopedia of herbs; Claire Kowalchik & William H. Hylton, editors; writers: Anna Carr {et al.}. Rodale Press 1987 545p il pa $17.95 hardcover o.p.

635

1. Herbs—Encyclopedias 2. Medical botany

ISBN 0-87696-964-X (pa)   LC 87-16019

Provides "the history, uses, and cultivation of over 100 herbs, plus information on making teas, lotions, scents, and dyes. Other sections include herbs as houseplants, the history and botany of herbs, and a particularly valuable chapter on the dangers of herbs. The book is attractive and well illustrated." Libr J

Includes bibliographical references

Silber, Mark

Growing herbs and vegetables; from seeds to harvest; [by] Mark and Terry Silber. Knopf 1999 274p il $35

635

1. Herb gardening 2. Vegetable gardening

ISBN 0-394-57346-3   LC 98-38189

The authors offer "advice on how to start vegetables and herbs from seed—both indoors and planting seeds directly into garden beds. They discuss the entire process from choosing varieties of seed to starting the seed to planting the beds. Next the authors discuss individual species of vegetables and herbs. . . . A final chapter covers preparing and storing seeds. Useful, easy-to-read charts summarize seeding specifics." Libr J

Includes bibliographical references

Smith, Edward C., 1941-

The vegetable gardener's bible; discover Ed's high-yield W-O-R-D system for growing your best garden ever! for all North American gardening regions; foreword by John Storey. Storey Bks. 2000 309p il maps $35; pa $24.95

635

1. Vegetable gardening 2. Organic gardening

ISBN 1-58017-213-X; 1-58017-212-1 (pa)

LC 99-52610

Smith "recommends a method of gardening that calls for wide, raised, deep beds, resulting in more vegetables with less work. In part 1 Smith explains how this is achieved. . . . Part 2 deals with soil requirements, making and using compost, and pest and disease control. Part 3 is an A-to-Z listing of vegetables and herbs, with details on growing, harvesting, and storing." Booklist

Speichert, C. Greg

Encyclopedia of water garden plants; [by] Greg Speichert & Sue Speichert; foreword by Ann Lovejoy. Timber Press 2004 386p il $49.95

635

1. Freshwater plants 2. Landscape gardening
ISBN 0-88192-625-6   LC 2003-16619

"The authors devote separate chapters to hardy waterlilies, tropicals, lotus, marginal plants, irises, waterlily-like plants (such as water snowflakes), floaters, and submerged plants. . . . This is the most comprehensive guide to all types of water plants and would make an excellent addition to gardening collections." Libr J

Springer, Lauren

Passionate gardening; good advice for challenging climates; essays and photography by Lauren Springer & Rob Proctor. Fulcrum 2000 336p il $34.95   **635**

1. Gardening
ISBN 1-55591-348-2   LC 99-49511

The "authors dispense practical advice to gardeners facing difficult growing conditions, such as poor soil, dry shade, etc. . . . [They also] discuss what plants to select—whether working with bulbs or ornamental grasses—and how to use them in conjunction with other plants." Libr J

Includes bibliographical references

Step-by-step yard & garden basics. Better Homes & Gardens Bks. 2000 323p il pa $24.95 *
635

1. Gardening 2. Lawns 3. Landscape architecture
ISBN 0-6962-1288-9; 978-0-6962-1288-8
LC 0013-4297

At head of title: Better Homes and Gardens; "Writer, Liz Ball." Verso of title page

This guidebook covers "starting a lawn and growing roses . . . pruning trees and creating a front yard garden. It provides 200 . . . weather-related tips for lawns and lawn alternatives—flowers, vines, edibles, trees, shrubs and ornaments. [It features] more than 750 photos . . . plus a . . . list of tools and supplies needed for each project. Each chapter closes with a seasonal checklist of related chores for yards and gardens in both northern and southern climates." Publisher's note

Warren, Susan, 1959-

Backyard giants; the passionate, heartbreaking, and glorious quest to grow the biggest pumpkin ever. Bloomsbury USA 2007 245p il $24.95

635

1. Pumpkin
ISBN 978-1-59691-278-6; 1-59691-278-2

This book focuses on the competition to grow the world's largest pumpkin. "Although Warren probes the fortunes of growers all over the country, especially in New England, she centers her story on the father-and-son growing team of Dick and Ron Johnson in Rhode Island and their very special relationship." Libr J

The author's "hilarious yet enlightening exposé reveals why and how these passionate, peculiar, and painstaking pumpkin growers are willing to put it all on the line for one big—one very big—payoff." Booklist

Includes bibliographical references

Wyman, Donald, 1903-1993

Wyman's gardening encyclopedia. new expanded 2nd ed. Macmillan 1986 xxvi, 1221p il $65   **635**

1. Gardening—Encyclopedias 2. Ornamental plants—Encyclopedias
ISBN 0-02-632070-3   LC 86-12509
First published 1961

Contains information on major horticultural practices, including use of pesticides and herbicides, and on ornamental and agricultural plant species. Includes scientific names according to Hortus third, with cross-references for common names

635.9   Flowers and ornamental plants

The **American** Horticultural Society A-Z encyclopedia of garden plants; Christopher Brickell, H. Marc Cathey, editors-in-chief. Rev. US ed. DK Pub. 2004 1099p il map $80
635.9

1. Ornamental plants—Encyclopedias
ISBN 0-7566-0616-0   LC 2004-559196
First published 1997

This volume "covers over 2000 genera with more than 15,000 individual entries of annuals, perennials, trees, shrubs, climbers, rock plants, biennials, bulbs, orchids, and much more. . . . Arranged by genus, each entry includes family name, a description of the genus, native habitat, garden uses, cultivation, propagation, and pests and diseases. The entries contain a description, height, width, USDA hardiness zones, heat zones, and cultivars." Libr J

"Equal parts gem and tool, this book is like a diamond. Clear, concise, and thoroughly useful, it fits the needs of all gardeners." Am Ref Books Annu, 2005

American Horticultural Society encyclopedia of plants and flowers; editors in chief, Christopher Brickell & Trevor Cole. Rev and updated ed. DK Pub. 2002 720p il $60 *   **635.9**

1. Ornamental plants
ISBN 0-7894-8993-7   LC 2002-73553

First published 1989 in the United Kingdom with title: The Royal Horticultural Society gardeners' encyclopedia of plants and flowers

This "volume features design information, an illustrated catalog of plants arranged by color as well as kind, and a plant dictionary. With over 8000 trees, shrubs, water plants, cacti, succulents, and more profiled here, there is something for nearly every kind of garden." Libr J

Armitage, Allan M.

Armitage's manual of annuals, biennials, and half-hardy perennials; illustrations by Asha Kays and Chris Johnson. Timber Press 2001 539p il $39.95   **635.9**

1. Annuals (Plants) 2. Perennials
ISBN 0-88192-505-5   LC 00-66789

"Armitage has compiled descriptions and assessments of 245 genera of true annuals as well as plants that be-

Armitage, Allan M.—*Continued*
have like annuals in USDA zones 1-7. Focusing on plant identification, successful culture, and garden uses, he discusses 279 species." Publisher's note

"A wonderfully written resource chockablock with gardening information." Booklist

Includes bibliographical references

Armitage's native plants for North American gardens. Timber Press 2006 451p il $49.95

635.9

1. Ornamental plants
ISBN 0-88192-760-0; 978-0-88192-760-3

LC 2005-22495

This book provides "information on more than 630 native species and cultivars of perennials, biennials, and annuals that are readily available to mainstream gardeners. . . . With more than 400 color photos, this is an essential reference book for nursery people and horticulturalists, home gardeners, and all libraries." Libr J

Includes bibliographical references

Cave, Yvonne
Succulents for the contemporary garden. Timber Press 2003 176p il $29.95 *
635.9
1. Succulent plants
ISBN 0-88192-573-X

LC 2003-271441

"After defining succulents or xerophytes, Cave presents short discussions of succulent's cultivation, pests and diseases, and propagation. The real core of this work is the A-Z of genera, which lists 60 genera and hundreds of their species. Each entry contains a detailed description, with shape, size, color, and country of origin for each plant, often with a beautiful close-up photograph and cultivation and propagation information. . . . This first-rate reference belongs in . . . libraries everywhere." Am Ref Books Annu, 2003

Courtier, Jane
Indoor plants; the essential guide to choosing and caring for houseplants; {by} Jane Courtier & Graham Clarke; consultant, Anne Halpin. Reader's Digest Assn. 1997 240p il $30
635.9
1. House plants 2. Indoor gardening
ISBN 0-89577-921-8

LC 96-42046

At head of title: Reader's Digest

This discussion of houseplants includes information on care, feeding, temperature control, propagation, and pests and diseases. Display ideas are also provided

Cox, Jeff, 1940-
Perennial all-stars; the 150 best perennials for great-looking, trouble-free gardens. Rodale Press 1998 344p il map $29.95; pa $16.95

635.9

1. Perennials
ISBN 0-87596-780-9; 0-87596-889-9 (pa)

LC 97-33811

Each perennial "is highlighted in a two-page spread that includes information on how to grow, propagation, picking the right site, and the best companion plants. In addition to the individual entries, there is a chapter on 'ten steps to starting a perennial garden' and lists of the perennials categorized by color, size, bloom time, specific conditions, and those that will attract butterflies and hummingbirds." Libr J

Includes bibliographical references

Darke, Rick
The American woodland garden; capturing the spirit of the deciduous forest; text and photography by Rick Darke. Timber Press 2002 377p il $49.95
635.9
1. Gardening 2. Forest plants
ISBN 0-88192-545-4

LC 2002-20474

This "is both a pictorial and narrative account of a wooded locale in Pennsylvania that the author spent years studying, as well as a design and planting guide. . . . He explains the different elements of a woodland garden and thoroughly describes the plants (features, zones, and growth ranges) that will perform well. The author's photographs illustrate both the overall effect and the beauty of individual plants." Libr J

Includes bibliographical references

Dash, Mike
Tulipomania; the story of the world's most coveted flower and the extraordinary passions it aroused. Crown 2000 273p pa $13.95 hardcover o.p.
635.9
1. Tulips 2. Netherlands—History
ISBN 0-609-80765-X (pa)

LC 99-39186

"The centerpiece of this story is a stunning two months, December 1636 and January 1637, when fortunes were made and lost in the Netherlands—in tulip bulb futures trading. Stripped to its basics, this would be a dry case study in an economics textbook. But Dash adds depth to the tale by including relevant bits of botany, sociology and history, as well as glimpses of the personalities involved in the creation of the tulip market." Publ Wkly

Includes bibliographical references

Dirr, Michael
Dirr's Hardy trees and shrubs; an illustrated encyclopedia; by Michael A. Dirr. Timber Press 1997 493p il $69.95
635.9
1. Trees 2. Shrubs 3. Landscape gardening
ISBN 0-88192-404-0

LC 96-54032

"Depicting both character and traits (fruit, flower, bark, or autumn color), the volume covers over 500 species and some additional varieties and cultivars. Each entry enumerates scientific name, common name, detailed plant description, environmental conditions, place in the landscape, i.e., woodlawn tree or lawn tree, and hardiness zones." Libr J

Dirr's trees and shrubs for warm climates; an illustrated encyclopedia; by Michael A. Dirr. Timber Press 2002 446p il map $69.95

635.9

1. Ornamental plants 2. Trees 3. Shrubs 4. Landscape gardening
ISBN 0-88192-525-X

LC 2001-35810

Dirr, Michael—_Continued_

"This volume, in conjunction with _Dirr's Hardy Trees and Shrubs_, completes [the author's] coverage of the woody ornamentals cultivated in North America. In a witty and informative style, Dirr presents botanic, cultural, and landscaping details on over 400 species. Entries are accompanied by magnificent color photos." Libr J

DiSabato-Aust, Tracy

The well-tended perennial garden; planting & pruning techniques. Expanded ed. Timber Press 2006 383p il map $34.95　　　　635.9

1. Perennials
ISBN 978-0-88192-803-7; 0-88192-803-8
　　　　　　　　　　　　　　　LC 2006-10388
First published 1998
In addition to details on pruning and maintenance this work contains an A-Z encyclopedia of perennials
Includes bibliographical references

Duffield, Mary Rose

Plants for dry climates; how to select, grow, and enjoy; [by] Mary Rose Duffield and Warren D. Jones. rev ed. Perseus Pub. 2001 216p il pa $27.50
　　　　　　　　　　　　　　　635.9

1. Desert plants 2. Gardening
ISBN 1-55561-251-2　　　　LC 2001-280011
First published 1981
The authors "explore strategies for gardening in dry or arid climates. . . . They cover climate conditions and predesign concerns such as possible planting restrictions by neighborhood covenants, the use of professional landscaping services, costs, and maintenance. A detailed plant guide identifies more than 300 species best suited to arid gardens, explaining conditions in which they thrive or are compromised." Libr J
Includes bibliographical references

Ellis, Barbara W.

Covering ground; unexpected ideas for landscaping with colorful, low-maintenance ground covers. Storey Pub. 2007 224p il map $29.95; pa $19.95　　　　635.9

1. Ornamental plants 2. Climbing plants 3. Grasses
ISBN　1-58017-664-X;　978-1-58017-664-4;
1-58017-665-8 (pa); 978-1-58017-664-4 (pa)
　　　　　　　　　　　　　　　LC 2007-335
"Divided into three main sections, the book addresses why one should consider using ground covers, types of plants for different areas, and planting, growing, and propagating. . . . Suitable for all gardening collections, this easy and fun read is essential for the home gardener looking for low-maintenance or problem-area ground covers." Libr J

Taylor's guide to annuals; how to select and grow more than 400 annuals, biennials, and tender perennials. Houghton Mifflin 1999 441p il (Taylor's guides to gardening) pa $23　*
　　　　　　　　　　　　　　　635.9

1. Annuals (Plants) 2. Flower gardening
ISBN 0-395-94352-3　　　　LC 99-33188
First published 1986

This guide features information on over five hundred popular plants and cultivars for landscaping and gardening

Taylor's guide to perennials; more than 600 flowering and foliage plants, including ferns and ornamental grasses. Houghton Mifflin 2001 490p il map (Taylor's guide to gardening) pa $23
　　　　　　　　　　　　　　　635.9

1. Perennials 2. Flower gardening
ISBN 0-395-98363-0　　　　LC 00-33436
First published 1986
Text and numerous illustrations cover popular perennials, their cultivars, ornamental grasses, and ferns

Fell, Derek

Encyclopedia of hardy plants; annuals, bulbs, herbs, perennials, shrubs, trees, vegetables, fruits & nuts; Derek Fell. Firefly Books 2007 224p il map $29.95　*　　　　635.9

1. Plants—Encyclopedias
ISBN 978-1-55407-240-8; 1-55407-240-9
　　　　　　　　　　　　　　　LC 2007-296324
This reference features descriptions of more than 700 hardy plants, each with color photos and hardiness zone ranges. Also contains indexes of both common plant names and botanical names.

Fisher, Kathleen, 1948-2005

Taylor's guide to shrubs; how to select and grow more than 500 ornamental and useful shrubs for privacy, ground covers, and specimen plantings. Houghton Mifflin 2001 441p il map (Taylor's guides to gardening) pa $23　*
　　　　　　　　　　　　　　　635.9

1. Shrubs
ISBN 0-618-00437-8　　　　LC 00-36941
First published 1987
This guide covers information on popular shrubs and their cultivars and includes growing instructions

Flora: a gardener's encyclopedia; over 20,000 plants; chief consultant, Sean Hogan. Timber Press 2003 2v il map set $99.95　　　　635.9

1. Ornamental plants—Encyclopedias 2. Flowers
ISBN 0-88192-538-1　　　　LC 2003-59663
Accompanied by CD-ROM
"_Flora_ treats more than 20,000 plants, selected for their significance in horticulture and forestry, including use as food, fiber, drugs, and dyes. Cultivated plants found in gardens and parks in the temperate zones are covered most completely, but many plants are included solely for their beauty, fame, and unique evolution to adaptation. . . . The volumes are beautifully illustrated, and most plant entries include a color photograph with the botanical name as caption." Choice
"Although gardening books abound, none matches this work's range of detail." Libr J

Freeman, Mark, 1927-
Gardening in your greenhouse; illustrations by
Heather Bellanca. Stackpole Bks. 1998 200p il pa
$19.95   **635.9**
    1. Greenhouses 2. Gardening
    ISBN 0-8117-2776-9   LC 98-4842
Companion volume to Building your own greenhouse
(1997)
    This work "begins with chapters on types of green-
houses, equipment, soil, air, water, heat, light, pests, and
diseases. The rest of the book covers growing seedlings
for transplanting into the outdoor garden and raising vegetables and herbs in the greenhouse. Freeman lists vegetable, flower, and herb species suitable for growing to
maturity in a greenhouse." Libr J

Hansen, Eric
Orchid fever; a horticultural tale of love, lust,
and lunacy. Pantheon Bks. 2000 288p pa $13
hardcover o.p.   **635.9**
    1. Orchids
    ISBN 0-679-77183-2 (pa)   LC 99-44582
    This book focuses on "the failure of the 1973 Conven-
tion on International Trade in Endangered Species of
Wild Fauna and Flora (CITES) to protect orchids." Nat
Hist
    "Most of Hansen's sketches are fundamentally vehi-
cles for illustrating his serious and provocative argument
against CITES (the Convention on International Trade in
Endangered Species of Wild Fauna and Flora). According to the author, CITES thwarts orchid conservation and
perversely legitimizes plant smuggling by botanical institutions." Libr J

Heffernan, Cecelia
Flowers A to Z; buying, growing, cutting,
arranging; photography T.K. Hill. Abrams 2001
160p $49.50; pa $17.95 *   **635.9**
    1. Flowers 2. Flower gardening 3. Flower arrangement
    ISBN 0-8109-3348-9; 0-8109-2122-7 (pa)
                        LC 00-64282
    "Recommendations for the best tools and containers
are followed by in-depth profiles of 55 of the most popular garden and hothouse flowers, in which Heffernan
shares such trade secrets as the flower's vase life and its
cost at different seasons. . . .Straightforward directions
are supported by close-up photographs." Booklist

Hewitt, Terry
The complete book of cacti & succulents.
Dorling Kindersley 1993 176p il hardcover o.p. pa
$20   **635.9**
    1. Cactus 2. Succulent plants
    ISBN 1-56458-337-6; 0-7894-1657-3 (pa)
                        LC 93-22107
    An illustrated look at the history and cultivation of
more than 300 plants. Ideas for containers and display
are included.

Hill, Lewis, 1924-
Bulbs; four seasons of beautiful blooms; {by}
Lewis & Nancy Hill. Storey Communications 1994
218p il pa $19.95 hardcover o.p.   **635.9**
    1. Bulbs
    ISBN 0-88266-877-3 (pa)   LC 94-14240
    "A Garden Way Publishing book"
    The authors "examine bulbs that will bloom in each
of four seasons, as well as give guidance on such subjects as forcing bulbs successfully, pests and disease, and
naturalizing bulbs. They go into the 'big four' (crocuses,
hyacinths, narcissus and tulips) in wonderful detail and
pique our interest in lesser-known bulbs." Publ Wkly
    Includes bibliographical references

Hillier, Malcolm
Container gardening through the year;
photography by Matthew Ward. Dorling
Kindersley 1995 160p il pa $13.95 hardcover o.p.
                                        635.9
    1. Container gardening
    ISBN 0-7894-3296-X (pa)   LC 94-26717
    "Hillier advises on how to match surprising plant
combinations with an array of containers. Various themes
(shape and proportion, texture, and harmonizing or contrasting colors) are represented in lovely color plates that
provide a pleasing supplement to Hillier's reassuring
guidance." Booklist

The **Hillier** gardener's guide to trees & shrubs;
editor, John Kelly; consultant editor, John
Hillier. Reader's Digest Assn. 1997 640p il
maps $50   **635.9**
    1. Trees 2. Shrubs
    ISBN 0-89577-973-0   LC 97-4282
    First published 1995 in the United Kingdom
    "Alphabetically arranged plant directory covering more
than 4000 plants with over 400 genres represented. . . .
[It discusses] basic biology, theory and practice, selection
and purchase, care and maintenance, pest and diseases,
plant propagation, plant names, and plant selection." Libr
J

Hodgson, Larry
Perennials for every purpose; choose the plants
you need for your conditions, your garden, and
your taste. Rodale 2000 502p il $29.95; pa $19.95
                                        635.9
    1. Perennials
    ISBN 0-87596-823-6; 0-87596-893-7 (pa)
                        LC 99-6968
    "Preliminary chapters cover the basics such as getting
started, creating a design, and keeping plants healthy.
The highlight, however, is the 14 chapters that profile
perennials that can be used in unique situations (e.g., dry,
wet, sunny, shade, easy-care). Each plant profile includes
a photograph, a sidebar listing plant characteristics, and
informative paragraphs detailing good companion plants,
problems and solutions, and the top performers and recommended varieties for each plant." Libr J
    Includes bibliographical references

Joyce, David
Topiary and the art of training plants; illustrated by Laura Stoddart. Firefly Bks. 2000 160p il $40; pa $24.95   **635.9**
1. Ornamental plants 2. Landscape gardening
ISBN 1-55209-420-0; 1-55209-442-7 (pa)
The author "explains the technical steps necessary to achieve an array of plant forms that will function in the garden as living sculptures. . . . Joyce's handbook offers an instructive tour that will surely fire up the imagination of keen gardeners. A directory of recommended plants and suppliers is included." Booklist

Kelaidis, Gwen Moore
Hardy succulents; tough plants for every climate; photography by Saxon Holt. Storey Pub. 2008 159p il map $29.95; pa $19.95
                                                          635.9
1. Succulent plants
ISBN 978-1-58017-701-6; 978-1-58017-700-9 (pa)
                                          LC 2007-39890
The author "offers practical tips on siting, planting, soil requirements, and care of succulents for every hardiness zone in a clear and confident voice. Advice on pairing succulents with perennials, using them as focal points in the garden, and protecting them from the cold of winter is dispensed in lively prose. . . . This delightful book will be practical and inspiring for both novice and experienced gardeners." Libr J

King, Michael, 1952-
Gardening with grasses; [by] Michael King and Piet Oudolf; foreword by Beth Chatto. Timber Press 1998 152p il $34.95   **635.9**
1. Grasses 2. Landscape gardening
ISBN 0-88192-411-3   LC 97-24467
The authors discuss the application of grasses "in comtemporary settings from lawns to urban landscaping projects. . . . Plant lists for particular situations augment the text, and the many color photographs illustrate the roles grasses can play in a natural garden design." Libr J
Includes bibliographical references

Michener, David
Taylor's guide to ground covers; more than 400 flowering and foliage ground covers for every garden situation; [by] David Michener and Nan Sinton. completely rev and updated. Houghton Mifflin 2001 375p il maps (Taylor's guides to gardening) pa $23   **635.9**
1. Ornamental plants 2. Climbing plants 3. Grasses
ISBN 0-618-03010-7   LC 2001-39566
First published 1987 with title: Taylor's guide to ground covers, vines & grasses
This guide features instructions on how "to stabilize banks and control erosion; to substitute for turf where grass won't grow or is hard to mow; to line curbs and driveways, where salt will damage ordinary plants [and] to enhance a landscape with broad, dramatic sweeps." Publisher's note
"In this guide luscious photographs of 400 ground

covers are paired with information about gardening zones and sun tolerance. . . . The splendor of the photography aside, the no-nonsense approaches are recommended." Am Ref Books Annu, 2003

Ondra, Nancy J.
Taylor's guide to roses; how to select, grow, and enjoy more than 380 roses. Houghton Mifflin 2001 474p il maps (Taylor's guides to gardening) pa $23   **635.9**
1. Roses
ISBN 0-618-06888-0   LC 00-68248
First published 1986
Text and numerous full color illustrations describe classes of roses including floribundas, grandifloras, miniatures, and climbers. Suggestions are provided for carefree border and ground cover roses. Entries are given for each plant, noting its uses and limitations

O'Sullivan, Penelope
The homeowner's complete tree & shrub handbook; the essential guide to choosing, planting and maintaining perfect landscape plants; photography by Karen Bussolini. Storey Pub. 2007 408p il map $39.95; pa $29.95   **635.9**
1. Trees 2. Shrubs 3. Ornamental plants
ISBN 978-1-58017-571-5; 978-1-58017-570-8 (pa)
                                          LC 2007-10718
This guide to planting trees and shrubs discusses planning the landscape and buying, planting and caring for trees and shrubs. Includes descriptions of 348 trees and shrubs.
Includes bibliographical references

The homeowner's complete tree & shrub handbook; the essential guide to choosing, planting, and maintaining perfect landscape plants; photography by Karen Bussolini. Storey Pub. 2007 408p il map $39.95; pa $29.95   **635.9**
1. Trees 2. Shrubs
ISBN 978-1-58017-571-5; 978-1-58017-570-8 (pa)
                                          LC 2007-10718
"The real jewel of this volume is the extensive A-Z directory of nearly 350 trees and shrubs, many offering more than one season of interest. There is even a handy pronounciation guide for every plant name." Libr J
Includes webliography and bibliographical references

Phillips, Ellen
Rodale's illustrated encyclopedia of perennials; {by} Ellen Phillips & C. Colston Burrell. Rodale Press 1993 533p il pa $19.95 hardcover o.p.
                                                          635.9
1. Perennials
ISBN 0-8759-6999-2 (pa)   LC 92-30109
"The book is divided into three major sections, focusing on designing gardens, growing perennials, and an A-Z dictionary of plant types. . . . The last half of the book is devoted to the individual perennials. One hundred sixty-one flowers, foliage plants, and ground covers are described. Besides descriptions, pointers are given on how to grow them and on their landscape uses. . . . The volume closes with a glossary, lists of sources and organizations, and suggested reading." Booklist

The **plant** finder; the right plants for every garden; senior consultants, Tony Rodd and Geoff Bryant. Firefly Books 2007 992p il map $49.95
*   635.9
1. Ornamental plants 2. Gardening 3. Landscape gardening
ISBN 978-1-55407-265-1; 1-55407-265-4
                              LC 2007-298960
On cover: Over 5,000 plants
This book "gives basic descriptions and growing conditions for more than 5,000 plants, with a focus on the temperate zones. . . . Beginning gardeners as well as plant fanatics may find this comprehensive volume an indispensable midwinter reference for yearly garden planning, as well as a useful outdoor planting companion come spring." Publ Wkly

Pleasant, Barbara
The complete houseplant survival manual; essential know-how for keeping (not killing) more than 160 indoor plants; photography by Rosemary Kautzky. Storey Pub. 2005 365p il pa $24.95 *
                                                     635.9
1. House plants
ISBN 1-58017-569-4   LC 2005-14205
"Following an enlightening introduction that discusses the history, uses, and benefits that houseplants bestow, the manual is divided into three main sections. The first two are plant directories offering in-depth plant profiles of first flowering, then foliage, houseplants. The third is an extensive compilation of houseplant-care topics, from acclimatization to watering. With vivid color photographs, precise illustrations, appendixes listing helpful resources, definitions, and a cross-reference chart of botanical and common names, this is a must-have manual for anyone who shares home or office space with potted plants." Booklist

Pruning & training; Christopher Brickell, editor in chief. DK Pub. 1996 336p il $35   635.9
1. Pruning
ISBN 1-56458-331-7   LC 96-10836
At head of title: American Horticultural Society
"The authors begin by explaining how plants grow and offer general information on the principles of pruning and training and on tools and equipment. They follow this with chapters on ornamental trees, fruit trees, ornamental shrubs, soft fruits . . . climbing plants, and roses. In each category are instructions on basic techniques, initial training, and renovation. Also included is a dictionary of ornamental trees and shrubs. This comprehensive and practical guide lists more than 800 plants and contains more than 1,500 color photographs and illustrations." Booklist

Rodale's illustrated encyclopedia of organic gardening; Henry Doubleday Research Association; editor-in-chief, Pauline Pears. DK Pub. 2002 416p il hardcover o.p. pa $25
                                                     635.9
1. Organic gardening
ISBN 0-7894-8908-2; 0-7566-0932-1 (pa)
                              LC 2002-73477
First published 2001 in the United Kingdom with title: HDRA encyclopedia of organic gardening

This "encyclopedia offers guidance on growing flowers, herbs, and fruits and vegetables the organic, chemical-free way." Booklist
Includes bibliographical references

Scott, Aurelia C.
Otherwise normal people; inside the thorny world of competitive rose gardening. Algonquin Books of Chapel Hill 2007 235p $22.95
                                                     635.9
1. Roses 2. Flower shows
ISBN 978-1-56512-464-6; 1-56512-464-2
                              LC 2006-27489
The author "spent a year of her life being seduced by a bunch of truly obsessed people—a small but ardent fraternity of folks who grow roses in great abundance not necessarily for their beauty or scent but to nurture elusive prizewinning blooms. . . . Not content to sit back and smell the roses, these gardeners then clip their most promising blossoms and carefully tote them by car or plane to the National Rose Show, held twice a year. There, more hours are spent huddled over these fragile creatures, fussing with elaborate grooming rituals designed to nudge a bud to its proper degree of openness at the perfect moment." San Jose Mercury News
"Among the stories of the rose maniacs she encounters, Scott interweaves intruiging pieces of rose history and other fascinating bits of trivia." American Gardener
Includes bibliographical references

Swindells, Philip
The water garden encyclopedia. Firefly Bks. 2003 256p il $45; pa $29.95   635.9
1. Hydroponics
ISBN 1-55297-715-3; 1-55297-717-X (pa)
                              LC 2003-271624
This book "offers a host of ideas for creating and maintaining many types of water gardens, from small containers with fountains to re-creations of natural landscape settings. . . . Instructions for making each type of garden are given through a combination of text and photographs that . . . illustrate each step in the process, from choosing and marking out the site to finishing the project with suitable aquatic plants. Accompanying each design idea are lists of water-loving plants suitable for that type of garden—including water lilies, reeds and rushes, bog plants, and floating and submerged aquatics—and there are chapters on how to buy, plant, fertilize, divide, propagate and care for these plants." Publ Wkly

Taylor's encyclopedia of garden plants; edited by Frances Tenenbaum. Houghton Mifflin 2003 464p il map (Taylor's guides to gardening) $45
*   635.9
1. Ornamental plants—Encyclopedias
ISBN 0-618-22644-3   LC 2002-27630
"A Frances Tenenbaum book"
"The text includes over 1000 species (with myriad cultivars) of trees, shrubs, roses, perennials, annuals, bulbs, and ground covers. The book is arranged by scientific name, with each entry including genus name, pronunciation, plant family, where the plant is native, num-

Taylor's encyclopedia of garden plants—*Continued*

ber of species, a general description, cultivation, uses in the landscape, where the plant grows best (from area of the country to garden site), and any pests or diseases." Libr J

"This beautifully illustrated encyclopedia offers North American gardeners a definitive resource for all their questions, from flowers to trees to shrubs." Publ Wkly

Taylor's master guide to gardening; editor-in-chief: Frances Tenenbaum; editors: Rita Buchanan, Roger Holmes; designer: Deborah Fillion; illustrator: Steve Buchanan; copy editor: Nancy J. Stabile. Houghton Mifflin 1994 612p il $60   **635.9**
1. Landscape gardening 2. Gardening
ISBN 0-618-15907-X   LC 93-48865

The first part of this book consists of a discussion of "30 topics (annuals, perennials, trees, design, color, containers, shade, water, etc.) . . . Next, a 200-page 'Gallery' of recommended plants is arranged alphabetically by Latin name, with photographs and climate zone numbers. The third section, a 300-page encyclopedia, list 3000 unillustrated species and cultivars with a short paragraph about each." Libr J

Includes bibliographical references

636   Animal husbandry

Belozerskaya, Marina, 1966-
The Medici giraffe; and other tales of exotic animals and power. Little, Brown and Co. 2006 414p il $24.99 *   **636**
1. Exotic animals
ISBN 0-316-52565-0; 978-0-316-52565-7
                                      LC 2006-09659
This book explores the role of exotic animals "in history as among the most advantageous diplomatic gifts, the most cherished royal treasures, and the most impressive symbols of power and learning." Publisher's note

"This is a sumptuous read—smart, funny and utterly compelling." Publ Wkly

Includes bibliographical references

Katz, Jon
Dog days; dispatches from Bedlam Farm. Villard Books 2007 273p il $23.95   **636**
1. Domestic animals 2. Farm life—New York (State)
ISBN 978-1-4000-6404-5; 1-4000-6404-X
                                      LC 2006-52804
This is a "collection of stories from upstate New York's Bedlam Farm. . . . Bedlam Farm, a cross between a working and a hobby farm, is the home of the animals that are . . . [the author's] inspiration. . . . A must-read for all animal lovers." Booklist

636.088   Animals for specific purposes

Sutherland, Amy
Kicked, bitten, and scratched; life and lessons at the world's premier school for exotic animal trainers. Viking 2006 320p $25.95
                                      636.088
1. Moorpark College. Exotic Animal Training and Management Program 2. Animals—Training
ISBN 0-670-03768-0; 978-0-670-03768-1
                                   LC 2005-57474
This is an account "of the Exotic Animal Training and Management Program (EATM) at Moorpark College in Ventura County, Calif. EATM produces specialists who train animals for television and film and hold jobs at aquariums and zoos." N Y Times Book Rev

"Readers will acquire new and enhanced respect for a little-studied profession." Booklist

636.089   Veterinary sciences
Veterinary medicine

Black's veterinary dictionary; [edited by] Edward Boden. Rowman & Littlefield 1998 il $156
                                      636.089
1. Veterinary medicine—Dictionaries
ISBN 978-0-389-21017-7; 0-389-21017-X

First published 1928 by Macmillan with title: Black's veterinary cyclopedia. Title and publisher vary

"Gives comprehensive coverage of terms in veterinary medicine and animal husbandry, as well as the anatomy and physiology of domesticated animals. Includes 'information on accidents, worldwide disease eradication campaigns, health promotion, the housing of animals, and pest control.'—Pref. Includes references and cross-references." Guide to Ref Books. 11th edition

Goldstein, Martin, 1947-
The nature of animal healing; the path to your pet's health, happiness, and longevity. Knopf 1999 357p pa $16 hardcover o.p.   **636.089**
1. Pets 2. Veterinary medicine
ISBN 0-345-43919-8 (pa)   LC 98-38193
"Goldstein outlines an approach to healing that revolves around strengthening the immune system through diet and such holistic healing techniques as acupuncture and homeopathy, so that an animal can heal itself. . . . This is a life-affirming book that should interest any pet owner." Publ Wkly

The **Merck** veterinary manual; editor, Susan E. Aiello. 9th ed. Merck 2005 xxxix, 2712p $45
                                      636.089
1. Veterinary medicine—Handbooks, manuals, etc.
ISBN 0-911910-50-6
Also available online
First published 1955. Periodically revised
"Technical manual for use by veterinarians in the diagnosis and treatment of animal diseases. Authoritative, up-to-date information presented in a brief, convenient format; includes recommended prescriptions." Ref Sources for Small & Medium-sized Libr. 6th edition

Petspeak; you're closer than you think to a great relationship with your dog or cat! by the editors of Pets, part of the family books. Rodale 2000 485p il $29.95; pa $16.95 **636.089**
1. Dogs 2. Cats
ISBN 1-57954-077-5; 1-57954-337-5 (pa)
LC 00-9290
This volume "attempts to explain pet behavior to improve pet-owner relationships. Addressing the habits of both cats and dogs, this book helps make sense out of pet peculiarities and offers practical solutions and advice." Booklist

Pinney, Chris C.
The complete home veterinary guide. McGraw-Hill 2004 736p il $29.95 * **636.089**
1. Veterinary medicine
ISBN 0-07-141272-7 LC 2003-52668
First published 1992 by Tab Bks. with title: The illustrated veterinary guide for dogs, cats, birds & exotic pets
This guide covers "preventive health care, diet, grooming, training, diseases, traveling with pets, selection, first aid, anatomy, {and} holistic pet care." Publisher's note

Schoen, Allen M.
Kindred spirits; how the remarkable bond between humans and animals can change the way we live. Broadway Bks. 2001 280p pa $14 hardcover o.p. **636.089**
1. Veterinary medicine 2. Pets
ISBN 0-7679-0431-1 (pa) LC 00-57891
This book "covers the benefits of the human-animal bond; seven ways to foster a spiritual bond with your animal; wellness approaches, such as diet therapy and preventing and treating cancer the natural way; finding veterinary support; and how to let go when there is nothing further that can be done." Libr J
Includes bibliographical references

636.1 Equines. Horses

Edwards, Elwyn Hartley
The new encyclopedia of the horse; photography by Bob Langrish, Kit Houghton; foreword by Sharon Ralls Lemon. [rev ed] DK Pub. 2000 464p il maps $40 **636.1**
1. Horses—Encyclopedias
ISBN 0-7894-7181-7 LC 2001-271665
"A Dorling Kindersley book"
First published 1994 with title: The encyclopedia of the horse
The author "traces the evolution of the horse, covering every major breed of horse and pony as well as the contribution the horse has made to civilization—in the wild, at work, at war, and in sport and recreation. . . . The origin, history, and uses of each breed are explained. . . . Specimens of familiar as well as obscure breeds are featured, including Dutch Warmbloods and Camargues, Icelandic and Timor Ponies, Morgans and Shetlands,

Andalucian and Lusitano, and the Cutting Horse. . . . Sections on horse management, training, and equipment explain the basics of the proper care of the horse. Information is also included on farriers, feeding, grooming, horse behavior, training techniques, and which equipment to use, including saddles, bridles, and bits." Publisher's note
"A beautiful reference work for the true horse enthusiast." Libr J

Ultimate horse. Rev ed. DK Pub. 2002 272p il $35 **636.1**
1. Horses
ISBN 0-7894-8928-7 LC 2002-71493
First published 1991 with title: The ultimate horse book
The author "delves into the origins of the equine species, the 6,000-year relationship between horse and human, and equine anatomy and behavior. More than 80 breeds of horse and pony are described in . . . two-page spreads highlighting each breed's history and distinctive physical traits and temperaments. Owning and caring for a horse are covered in . . . illustrated discussions of equipment, health, and stable management." Booklist [review of 1991 edition]
"A brilliantly conceived and executed work, this book has captured in color photos what other horse books have previously illustrated in drawings or descriptive text. . . . Recommended for all equine collections. This will be a classic." Libr J

Faurie, Bernadette
The horse riding & care handbook. Lyons Press 2000 160p il hardcover o.p. pa $19.95 **636.1**
1. Horses 2. Horsemanship
ISBN 1-58574-058-6; 1-58574-517-0 (pa)
"Each section contains pictures or diagrams to clarify the explanations, from horse evolution and history with humans to markings, colors, and breeds. Topics such as tack, how to mount, a first riding lesson, and techniques of western riding are all simply described with wonderful graphics." Libr J

Richards, Susan, 1949-
Chosen by a horse; a memoir. Soho Press 2006 248p $20 **636.1**
1. Horses
ISBN 1-56947-419-2 LC 2005-52337
"Richards adopts an emaciated mare and her foal, overriding the small voice telling her that she already has three horses to care for and a herniated disk. Her experience with her new charges proves profoundly instructive in terms of how love can foster growth of the human spirit and help in overcoming pain and loss. The abused mare, Lay Me Down, proves to be one of those rare creatures that remain gentle despite years of mistreatment, responding profoundly to the kind treatment that is part of everyday life for Richards' animals. Fascinated by the affection this animal accords a stranger, Richards notes the mare's courage and slowly begins to emulate it in her own life, opening up to a love affair and its aftermath." Booklist

Storey's horse-lover's encyclopedia; an English and Western A-to-Z guide; edited by Deborah Burns. Storey Bks. 2001 471p il $37.50; pa $24.95 *   **636.1**
1. Horses
ISBN 1-58017-336-5; 1-58017-317-9 (pa)
LC 00-46329
"The alphabetically arranged entries vary in length from a few sentences to a few pages, with the most thorough coverage going to extensive topics like breeding, foot care, and feeding. Most entries consist of one or two paragraphs and provide a good definition of the term at hand." Libr J

636.4   Swine

Montgomery, Sy
The good good pig; the extraordinary life of Christopher Hogwood. Ballantine Books 2006 228p il $21.95; pa $13.95   **636.4**
1. Pigs
ISBN   0-345-48137-2;   978-0-345-48137-5;
0-345-49609-4 (pa); 978-0-345-49609-6 (pa)
LC 2005-57094
This is a "description of the 14-year life of a 750-pound pet pig who was named after the conductor [Christopher Hogwood]. Anyone who has ever loved a pet can enjoy reading about the relationship between Montgomery and her Christopher." Sci Books Films

Rath, Sara
The complete pig. Voyageur Press 2000 144p $29.95   **636.4**
1. Pigs
ISBN 0-89658-435-6   LC 99-45618
"A Town Square book"
This book contains "accounts of pigs in history, art and literature." N Y Times Book Rev
This book is "liberally illustrated with color photographs, lithographs, advertisements, and vintage photographs. A good bibliography rounds out a book that is not only fun but informative." Booklist
Includes bibliographical references

636.6   Birds other than poultry

Lantermann, Werner, 1956-
The new parrot handbook; everything about purchase, acclimation, care, diet, disease, and behavior of parrots, with a special chapter on raising parrots; 50 color photographs by outstanding animal photographers, 30 drawings by Fritz W. Köhler, and 35 maps indicating distribution; translated from the German by Rita and Robert Kimber; American advisory editor, Matthew M. Vriends. Barron's Educ. Ser. 1986 144p il maps pa $11.95   **636.6**
1. Parrots
ISBN 0-8120-3729-4   LC 86-17289

This book "is divided into two parts, the first about selecting, housing, and caring for a bird; the other devoted to breeding and behavior and including a large section of descriptions of individual species." Booklist
Includes bibliographical references

636.7   Dogs

American Kennel Club
The complete dog book; American Kennel Club. 20th ed. Ballantine Books 2006 xxi, 858p il $35 *   **636.7**
1. Dogs
ISBN 0-345-47626-3; 978-0-345-47626-5
LC 2005-48263
"Official publication of the American Kennel Club"
First published 1935. Periodically revised
"The official guide to 124 AKC registered breeds and their history, appearance, selection, training, care and feeding, and first aid. Some color plates." N Y Public Libr. Ref Books for Child Collect. 2d edition

Budiansky, Stephen
The truth about dogs; an inquiry into the ancestry, social conventions, mental habits, and moral fiber of Canis familiaris. Viking 2000 263p il pa $13 hardcover o.p.   **636.7**
1. Dogs
ISBN 0-14-100228-X (pa)   LC 00-34966
The author "uses scientific and genetic research to explain why dogs do what they do and are the way they are. In a conversational and entertaining way, the author shows how dog behavior is much more complex and interesting than we have previously thought, and how that behavior is firmly grounded in the breed's successful evolution." Booklist
Includes bibliographical references

Coile, D. Caroline
Encyclopedia of dog breeds. Barron's Educational Series 2005 352p il $29.95
636.7
1. Dogs—Encyclopedias
ISBN 0-7641-5700-0   LC 2004-52977
First published 1998
At head of title: Barron's
"More than 150 breed descriptions are grouped along American Kennel Club divisions: the sporting group, the hound group, the working group, and so on. . . . Breed descriptions are organized into subsections entitled 'History,' 'Temperament,' 'Upkeep,' 'Health,' and 'Form and Function.'" Booklist

Coppinger, Raymond
Dogs; a startling new understanding of canine origin, behavior, and evolution; [by] Raymond Coppinger and Lorna Coppinger. Scribner 2001 352p il $26   **636.7**
1. Dogs
ISBN 0-684-85530-5   LC 00-54137

Coppinger, Raymond—*Continued*

"Taking a biological approach to the study of canine behavior and intelligence, the authors promulgate a theory of how the dog evolved. They explain in depth how the interplay of nature and nurture and critical periods of development produced an animal that has more shapes and sizes and uses than any other. . . . They define what constitutes a breed and criticize today's purebred breeding programs." Libr J

"This important book belongs in all libraries." Booklist

Includes bibliographical references

Coren, Stanley

Why we love the dogs we do; how to find the dog that matches your personality. Free Press 1998 308p il pa $13 hardcover o.p. **636.7**

1. Dogs

ISBN 0-684-85502-X (pa) LC 97-50333

"Coren offers insight into dog-and-owner personality conflicts and shows prospective owners how to choose the dog that is right for them. His book shows why some breeds of dogs turn out to be disasters for certain people, provides personality tests for readers to determine their own distinctive personality types, and includes amusing 'famous pet' anecdotes. Humanitarian, witty, and full of common sense, this is a perfect primer for novice dog owners." Booklist

Includes bibliographical references

Dibra, Bashkim

Dogspeak; how to learn it, speak it, and use it to have a happy, healthy, well-behaved dog; {by} Bash Dibra; with Mary Ann Crenshaw; illustrations by José Dennis. Simon & Schuster 1999 270p il pa $13 hardcover o.p. **636.7**

1. Dogs

ISBN 0-684-86548-3 (pa) LC 99-30194

"Discusses the social, or pack, nature of dogs and explains eight factors important to pack dynamics: the dominance hierarchy aggression, territorial behavior, food guarding, flight behavior, chase behavior, socialization, and vocalization. Throughout, Dibra provides examples of how these factors come into play when training the family dog." Libr J

The **Doctor's** book of home remedies for dogs and cats; over 1,000 solutions to your pet's problems—from top vets, trainers, breeders, and other animal experts; by the editors of Prevention Magazine Health Books; edited by Matthew Hoffman. Rodale Press 1996 403p il pa $16.95 hardcover o.p. **636.7**

1. Dogs 2. Cats

ISBN 0-87596-010-4 (pa) LC 95-46481

This volume "provides hints for everyday pet healthcare. Each section includes descriptions and suggestions for coping with or curing ailments ranging from arthritis to shedding. Almost 100 different symptoms and problems are covered." Libr J

Dodman, Nicholas H.

Dogs behaving badly; an A to Z guide to understanding and curing behavioral problems in dogs. Bantam Bks. 1999 284p pa $13.95 hardcover o.p. **636.7**

1. Dogs

ISBN 0-553-37968-2 (pa) LC 98-46042

The author covers "behavioral traits and problems from A (aggression) to Z (zoonosis) . . . he describes canine foibles such as chewing, barking, and eating everything they can find, he shows how these little problems can mutate into major behavioral abnormalities. Many of the definitions are illustrated with tales from the author's practice treating behavioral problems, making the book extremely user-friendly." Booklist

Dogs: the ultimate care guide; good health, loving care, maximum longevity; edited by Matthew Hoffman; medical advisor, Lowell Ackerman. Rodale Press 1998 450p il pa $19.95 hardcover o.p. **636.7**

1. Dogs

ISBN 1-57954-244-1 (pa) LC 97-46600

Subjects covered range "from bringing up puppy, basic training, and emergency first aid, to easing common complaints." Booklist

Fogle, Bruce

ASPCA complete dog care manual; foreword by Roger Caras. Dorling Kindersley 1993 192p il pa $14.95 **636.7**

1. Dogs

ISBN 1-56458-168-3; 978-0-7566-1743-X (pa); 0-7566-1743-1 (pa) LC 92-53474

This book "presents the history, grooming, training, and showing of canines while emphasizing basic nursing, first aid, and breeding. The author gives commonsense tips, answers myriad questions, promotes owners' responsibility for pets, and discourages buying puppies from pet shops and the cruel practice of docking tails. The . . . text is supplemented by detailed diagrams and clear instructions." SLJ

Dog owner's manual. DK Pub. 2003 288p il pa $25 **636.7**

1. Dogs

ISBN 0-7894-9321-7 LC 2002-41146

This is a "guide to dog care, including first aid, training, and behavior." Publisher's note

"Fogle's succinct writing style packs a tremendous amount of information into each sentence. Heavily illustrated with beautiful photographs." Booklist

New complete dog training manual; {by} Bruce Fogle and Patricia Holden White. Dorling Kindersley 2002 176p il $25 * **636.7**

1. Dogs—Training

ISBN 0-7894-8398-X LC 2001-47931

First published 1994 with title: ASPCA complete dog training manual

This book "shows you how to establish routines, implement commands, break bad habits, and learn how to train various breeds." Publisher's note

Fogle, Bruce—*Continued*

The new encyclopedia of the dog; photography by Tracy Morgan. 2nd American ed. Dorling Kindersley 2000 416p il $40   **636.7**

1. Dogs—Encyclopedias

ISBN 0-7894-6130-7   LC 00-22642

First published 1995 with title: The encyclopedia of the dog

This describes over 420 breeds and varieties of dogs, including their histories, tempers, and physical features.

Geeson, Eileen

Ultimate dog grooming; additional material by Barbara Vetter & Lia Whitmore. Firefly Books 2004 288p il $29.95; pa $27.95   **636.7**

1. Dogs

ISBN 1-55297-873-7; 1-55407-328-6 (pa)

The author "offers a three-part introduction to grooming for both owners and professionals. In Part 1, she briefly addresses what an owner needs to know about grooming as well as how to choose the right groomer. Part 2 is geared toward those who want to become professional groomers. . . . The bulk of the book offers well-done profiles of 170 dog breeds—arranged by coat type—that include worthwhile tips and hints. Supplementing the text are more than 500 color illustrations, ranging from detailed drawings to photographs." Libr J

Healy, Thomas, 1944-

I have heard you calling in the night. Harcourt 2006 204p $22   **636.7**

1. Dogs 2. Alcoholism

ISBN 978-0-15-10125-6; 0-15-101259-8

LC 2006-6363

"Novelist Healy was a raging, brawling drunk until, on a whim, he adopted a Doberman pinscher puppy he named Martin. He nursed Martin through illness and wounds; Martin in turn stood guard over him while he lay passed out in fields. Their bond, and the slight but persistent duty of caring for Martin enabled Healy to very fitfully begin to recover from his alcoholism and propensity to violence and gently nudged him toward an understanding of himself and God. Healy embeds the story in a memoir of his life in the slums of Glasgow, his relationship with his parents, his conflicted attitude toward the church and his many loves. . . . In Healy's heartfelt prose, this eccentric friendship becomes the core of a moving meditation on the mysterious nature of redemption." Publ Wkly

Herriot, James

James Herriot's dog stories. St. Martin's Press 1986 xxxiii, 426p il $23.95; pa $7.99

636.7

1. Dogs

ISBN 0-312-43968-7; 0-312-92558-1 (pa)

LC 86-6637

Herriot "has gathered 50 recollections of canines, some of them sentimental, a few tragic and at least one—the story of a terrier male who abruptly becomes attractive to other males—as odd as anything in the De-

cameron. Herriot recalls that in his student days domestic animals were customarily listed in descending order of importance: horse, ox, sheep, pig, dog. In the latest work, he has brought his favorites to the front and given them a new leash on life." Time

Katz, Jon

Katz on dogs; a commonsense guide to training and living with dogs. Villard 2005 xxviii, 240p il $24.95 *   **636.7**

1. Dogs—Training

ISBN 1-4000-6403-1   LC 2005-46209

In this dog training guide, the author "covers the basics—choosing a dog, why training matters, and basic training—as well as the more esoteric aspects of the dog-human relationship, including multiple-dog households, setting boundaries, and loving and losing dogs." Booklist

Katz's "commonsense approach and skill as a story-teller make this an appealing, informative book." Libr J

Includes bibliographical references

The new work of dogs; tending to life, love, and family. Villard Bks. 2003 xxiii, 225p $19.95; pa $13.95   **636.7**

1. Dogs

ISBN 0-375-50814-7; 0-375-76055-5 (pa)

LC 2002-44915

The author "explores the bond between dogs and their owners. Focusing on 12 people-dog relationships in Montclair, N.J., and drawing on current research into attachment theory, interviews with animal workers and psychiatrists, as well as conversations with dog owners, Katz offers nuanced portraits of what happens when humans depend on dogs to satisfy their emotional needs. . . . In this well-written and thoughtful account, Katz makes a convincing case that dog owners must be more self-aware and responsible when they use their pets as human substitutes." Publ Wkly

Kerasote, Ted

Merle's door; lessons from a freethinking dog. Harcourt, Inc. 2007 398p $25   **636.7**

1. Dogs

ISBN 978-0-15-101270-1   LC 2006-38041

"A Labrador mix, Merle first appeared while the author was on a camping trip. Kerasote . . . decided to take his canine friend home to rural Wyoming. This chronicle of their 13 years together is interspersed with studies by animal behaviorists that strengthened Kerasote's desire to see Merle as a responsible individual rather than a submissive pet." Publ Wkly

"In telling Merle's story, Kerasote also explores the science behind canine behavior and evolution, weaving in research on the human-canine bond and musing on the way dogs see the world. Merle is a true character, yet Merle is also Everydog. An absolute treasure of a book." Booklist

Includes bibliographical references

Lane, Marion

The Humane Society of the United States complete guide to dog care; {by} Marion S. Lane and the staff of the Humane Society of the United States. Little, Brown 1998 390p il $24.95; pa $16.95   **636.7**

1. Dogs

ISBN 0-316-51305-9; 0-316-59547-0 (pa)

         LC 97-44392

"Emphasizing the importance of companionship between dogs and owners, this guide offers activities and ideas for including your dog in your lifestyle as much as possible." Booklist

McConnell, Patricia

For the love of a dog; understanding emotion in you and your best friend. Ballantine Books 2006 332p il $24.95   **636.7**

1. Dogs

ISBN 0-345-47714-6; 978-0-345-47714-9

         LC 2006-45200

This "book focuses on the signals that humans can 'read' ('talking' eyebrows, wrinkles, body shape, tongue flicks) in order to understand their dog's internal state." Libr J

"This is not a book on how to train dogs, but McConnell's examination of cases from her veterinary practice, backed up by her scientific study of animal behavior, will help readers better understand their closest companions." Booklist

McGinnis, Terri

The well dog book; the classic, comprehensive handbook of dog care; illustrated by Pat Stewart. rev ed. Random House 1991 287p il pa $19   **636.7**

1. Dogs

ISBN 0-679-77001-1 (pa)   LC 91-52680

First published 1974

This illustrated manual introduces canine anatomy and offers training, grooming and nutrition guidelines. Diagnostic and preventive information is included

Monks of New Skete

How to be your dog's best friend; the classic training manual for dog owners; [by] the Monks of New Skete. completely rev and updated, 2nd ed. Little, Brown 2002 336p il $25.95   **636.7**

1. Dogs—Training

ISBN 0-316-61000-3   LC 2002-102894

First published 1978

This guide to dog training focuses on important aspects of the canine-human relationship, including discipline and choosing a breed that fits the owner's personality and lifestyle

This book's "unique value lies in the monks' insights and thoughts about the human-canine bond. . . . Without devolving into New Age psychobabble, the monks make philosophical and spiritual observations that no dog lover could resist." Publ Wkly

Includes bibliographical references

The **Original** dog bible; the definitive new source for all things dog; edited by Kristin Mehus-Roe. Bowtie Press 2005 750p il pa $24.95

     636.7

1. Dogs

ISBN 1-931993-34-3   LC 2004-9985

This "volume covers every aspect of responsible dog ownership and includes additional details on evolution, genetics, history, folklore, competitive events, careers, and rescue groups. Appendixes include explanations of performance titles, lists of record holders, a glossary, and a 54-page listing of resources." Libr J

Palika, Liz, 1954-

K.I.S.S. guide to raising a puppy; foreword by Alan Gomberg. DK Pub. 2002 288p il (Keep it simple series) pa $20   **636.7**

1. Dogs

ISBN 0-7894-8947-3   LC 2001-58418

This guide provides instructions on feeding, grooming, exercising, trips to the vet, and other important aspects of caring for a puppy.

Includes bibliographical references

Taylor, David, 1934-

Old dog, new tricks; understanding and retraining older and rescued dogs. Firefly Books 2006 176p il pa $19.95 *   **636.7**

1. Dogs—Training

ISBN 1-55407-197-6; 978-1-55407-197-5

         LC 2006-286105

"Chapters cover basic commands, dealing with aggressive and destructive behaviors, housebreaking problems, fears and phobias, excitable and unruly dogs, and feeding problems. With full-color photos throughout, this book should be readable and understandable to even the first-time dog owner." Libr J

Thomas, Elizabeth Marshall, 1931-

The social lives of dogs; the grace of canine company; illustrated by Jared Taylor Williams. Simon & Schuster 2000 253p pa $13.95 hardcover o.p.   **636.7**

1. Dogs

ISBN 0-7434-2236-8 (pa)   LC 99-87357

Thomas discusses how dogs interact with various members of the household, including other dogs and pets of other species

The author "draws upon her extensive knowledge of the behavior and treatment of feral dogs in East Africa to explain the domestication of the dog. Appendixes containing advice on controlling dogs' behavior and on keeping parrots as pets conclude this entertaining and informative book." Libr J

636.8   Cats

Christensen, Wendy
The Humane Society of the United States complete guide to cat care; [by] Wendy Christensen and the staff of the Humane Society of the United States. St. Martin's Press 2002 322p il hardcover o.p. pa $16.95   **636.8**
  1. Cats
  ISBN 0-312-26929-3; 0-312-32608-4 (pa)
                        LC 2001-57892
  This "guide includes sections on choosing a healthy cat, feeding and nutrition, training, grooming, disease, vet visits, caring for an aging cat, feline first-aid kits and emergency care." Publisher's note

Edney, A. T. B.
ASPCA complete cat care manual; [by] Andrew Edney; foreword by Roger Caras. Dorling Kindersley 1992 192p il hardcover o.p. pa $14.95
                             636.8
  1. Cats
  ISBN 1-56458-064-4; 0-7566-1742-1 (pa)
                        LC 92-52783
  Subtitle on cover: The ultimate illustrated guide to caring for your cat
  "Cat care is made easy through step-by-step photographs that illustrate grooming, handling, detecting illness, first aid, and other concerns. Difficult-to-explain procedures, such as how to administer medication or transport an injured cat, are clearly understandable." Libr J
  Includes bibliographical references

Fogle, Bruce
The new encyclopedia of the cat. DK Pub. 2001 288p il maps $35 *   **636.8**
  1. Cats—Encyclopedias
  ISBN 0-7894-8021-2   LC 2001-275714
  First published 1997 with title: The encyclopedia of the cat
  "Opening sections cover the cat family, cats and people, and feline design and behavior. Entries on more than 60 longhair and shorthair breeds include discussions on the ancestry of each breed, shape and form, colors and patterns, and standards and temperament. Over 1300 beautiful color illustrations make this an essential purchase for both circulating and reference collections." Libr J [review of 1997 edition]
  Includes bibliographical references

Herriot, James
James Herriot's cat stories; with illustrations by Lesley Holmes. St. Martin's Press 1994 161p $17.95   **636.8**
  1. Cats
  ISBN 0-312-11342-0   LC 94-20131
  A "collection of favorite cat tales from Herriot's veterinary practice. Retired after over 50 years in practice, Herriot continues to entertain young and old alike with his storytelling ability. His current collection includes 'Alfred, the Sweet-Shop Cat,' 'Boris and Mrs. Bond's Cat Establishment,' 'Moses Found Among the Rushes,' and others." Libr J

McGinnis, Terri
The well cat book; the classic comprehensive handbook of cat care; illustrated by Pat Stewart. 2nd ed. Random House 1993 325p il pa $19 hardcover o.p.   **636.8**
  1. Cats
  ISBN 0-679-77000-3 (pa)   LC 92-56834
  First published 1975
  The author provides "professional advice on nutrition, diagnosing illnesses, treating injuries, and preventing health problems. . . . {She also includes} information on new illnesses such as feline infectious peritonitis and feline immunodeficiency virus, and she clearly explains their symptoms. Among her work's other useful features is the chapter on emergency first aid. . . . Highly recommended for all pet care collections." Libr J

Morris, Desmond
Cat watching. Crown 1987 c1986 136p pa $8.95 hardcover o.p.   **636.8**
  1. Cats
  ISBN 0-517-88053-9 (pa)   LC 86-23938
  First published 1986 in the United Kingdom
  Spine title: Catwatching
  In question-and-answer format, the author examines mating, hunting behavior and physical characteristics of cats

Richards, James R., 1960-
ASPCA complete guide to cats. Chronicle Bks. 1999 368p il pa $24.95   **636.8**
  1. Cats
  ISBN 0-8118-1929-9   LC 99-12354
  This guide offers advice on feeding, grooming, veterinary care, litterbox training, and the special needs of kittens, old cats, and cats from shelters. The text is accompanied by over 450 illustrations and photos
  Includes bibliographical references

Wilbourn, Carole, 1940-
The total cat; understanding your cat's physical and emotional behavior from kitten to old age. HarperCollins Pubs. 2000 xxxvii, 233p il pa $14
                             636.8
  1. Cats
  ISBN 0-380-79051-3   LC 00-40846
  Wilbourn presents "general information about the care, feeding, and medical needs of cats. . . . From the selection of a cat by its age and personality type, along with suggestions for finding a good match for the character and lifestyle of the potential owner, to fitting a cat into a household that may include other pets to causes and cures of less desirable feline behavioral traits, the author covers all aspects of cat behavior." Booklist

638   Insect culture

Hubbell, Sue
A book of bees; and how to keep them; drawings by Sam Potthoff. Houghton Mifflin 1998 193p il pa $13 *   **638**
1. Bees
ISBN 0-395-88324-5   LC 98-10191
"A Mariner book"
First published 1988 by Random House
"Following the seasons of the beekeeper's year the author imparts practical hints along with literary, mythological, entomological, and anecdotal commentary." Booklist

639   Hunting, fishing, conservation, related technologies

Greenlaw, Linda, 1960-
The lobster chronicles; life on a very small island. Hyperion 2002 238p $22.95; pa $13.95
                                            639
1. Lobster fisheries 2. Isle au Haut (Maine)
ISBN 0-7868-6677-2; 0-7868-8591-2 (pa)
In this companion to The hungry ocean, the author gives "up swordfishing to return to her parents' home on Isle Au Haut off the coast of Maine and fish for lobster. . . . She intersperses her narrative with plenty of eccentrics who live on her tiny island. . . . Self-speculation and uncertainties . . . nicely balance her delightfully cocky essays of island life." Publ Wkly

639.2   Commercial fishing, whaling, sealing

Dolin, Eric Jay
Leviathan; the history of whaling in America. W.W. Norton & Company 2007 479p il $27.95
                                            639.2
1. Whaling—History
ISBN 978-0-393-06057-7; 0-393-06057-8
                                    LC 2007-06113
The author "chronicles the long history of whaling in North America, from the voyages of Capt. John Smith, who, like many after him, 'found this Whale-fishing a costly conclusion,' to the last voyage of the Wanderer, a whaler that set sail from the once-teeming port of New Bedford, Mass., in 1924 and promptly wrecked in the shallows before a crowd of curious onlookers. . . . Anyone whose knowledge of whaling begins and ends with 'MobyDick' will get a solid education from Mr. Dolin, who fills in the historical record and sets the stage for the glory years when men like Melville set out from Nantucket, New Bedford, Sag Harbor and dozens of other ports on voyages lasting as long as four years." N Y Times (Late N Y Ed)
Includes bibliographical references

Fagan, Brian M., 1936-
Fish on Friday; feasting, fasting, and the discovery of the New World; [by] Brian Fagan. Basic Books 2006 338p il maps $26.95
                                            639.2
1. Commercial fishing 2. Fish as food
ISBN 0-465-02284-7   LC 2005-21322
The author "traces the rise of the European fishing industry. He posits the root of popular demand for fish in the early church's cycle of fasts and feasts. . . . Fagan intersperses his account with delightfully rendered, updated versions of ancient and modern fish-based recipes from Roman, British, and Jamaican traditions." Booklist

Greenlaw, Linda, 1960-
The hungry ocean; a swordboat captain's journey. Hyperion 1999 265p map $22.95; pa $14
                                            639.2
1. Fishing
ISBN 0-7868-6451-6; 0-7868-8541-6 (pa)
                                    LC 98-51985
The author "details a 30-day swordfishing trip from Gloucester to the Grand Banks. Greenlaw describes her boat, equipment, and various electronic gear, including the 'temperature bird' that is lowered to measure the temperature at the fishing depth, as well as her technique for finding just the right area to fish. . . . An exciting and detailed look inside the commercial fishing industry." Libr J

Kurlansky, Mark
Cod; a biography of the fish that changed the world. Penguin Bks. 1998 294p il pa $14
                                            639.2
1. Codfish 2. Commercial fishing 3. Cooking—Fish
ISBN 0-14-027501-0   LC 97-12165
First published 1997 by Walker & Co.
Kurlansky discusses the history of commercial cod fishing and the plight of the Atlantic fish and fisheries today as the cod faces extinction.
This book offers "maximum readability, plenty of handsome illustrations, and a 40-page appendix of superlatively annotated recipes." Booklist
Includes bibliographical references

The last fish tale; the fate of the Atlantic and survival in Gloucester, America's oldest fishing port and most original town. Ballantine Books 2008 269p il map $25 *   **639.2**
1. Commercial fishing 2. Gloucester (Mass.)
ISBN 978-0-345-48727-8; 0-345-48727-3
                                    LC 2007-51116
The author "provides a delightful, intimate history and contemporary portrait of the quintessential northeastern coastal fishing town: Gloucester, Mass., on Cape Anne. Illustrated with his own beautifully executed drawings, Kurlansky's book vividly depicts the contemporary tension between the traditional fishing trade and modern commerce, which in Gloucester means beach-going tourists." Publ Wkly
Includes bibliographical references

639.3   Culture of cold-blooded vertebrates. Of fishes

Alderton, David

Firefly encyclopedia of the vivarium. Firefly Books 2007 224p il $39.95   **639.3**

1. Terrariums 2. Reptiles 3. Amphibians 4. Insects 5. Invertebrates

ISBN 978-1-55407-300-9; 1-55407-300-6

A "reference for those starting out with a terrarium or vivarium, it covers . . . [a range] of suitable animals, from invertebrates to large snakes and lizards. David Alderton explains how to design setups that re-create natural habitats, as well as more clinical environments for closely monitoring difficult or delicate species. A brief account of some of the more suitable vivarium plants and their requirements is also included. The book is divided into three main sections—Reptiles, Amphibians and Invertebrates." Publisher's note

"With its vibrant photographs and easy reading level, this text is suggested for school and public libraries that are in need of a basic guide." Booklist

Includes bibliographical references

639.34   Fish culture in aquariums

Alderton, David

Encyclopedia of aquarium & pond fish. Dorling Kindersley 2005 400p il $35   **639.34**

1. Fishes—Encyclopedias

ISBN 0-7566-0941-0

This reference provides care and identification information on over 800 freshwater, saltwater, coldwater and tropical fish, showing "what each fish looks like, what food they eat, which species they can cohabit with and how big they grow." Publisher's note

The author "has created the definitive work on the subject, with photos to match." Libr J

Jennings, Greg

The new encyclopedia of the saltwater aquarium. Firefly Books 2007 304p il $49.95
                                                    639.34

1. Marine aquariums 2. Fishes—Encyclopedias

ISBN 978-1-55407-182-1; 1-55407-182-8
                                       LC 2007-296089

First published 2003 under the authorship of Nick Dakin with title: Complete encyclopedia of the saltwater aquarium

"Over 150 species of reef fish, invertebrates and algae are described: their distribution in the wild, size, behavior, diet, aquarium requirements and compatibility. A large, full color photograph appears for each featured species, with personal recommendations on the fish considered best for the beginner." Publisher's note

Includes bibliographical references

Maître-Allain, Thierry

Aquariums; the complete guide to freshwater and saltwater aquariums; [by] Thierry Maitre-Allain and Christian Piednoir; [English translation by Matthew Clarke] Firefly Books 2006 281p il $39.95 *   **639.34**

1. Aquariums 2. Marine aquariums

ISBN 1-55407-085-6

The authors "walk the novice through all aspects of setting up and maintaining an underwater habitat. . . . Beautiful photos clearly illustrate this good all-in-one handbook that will fill the needs of beginning aquarists." Booklist

Includes bibliographical references

Mills, Dick

Aquarium fish; photography by Jerry Young. Dorling Kindersley 1993 304p il (Eyewitness handbooks) pa $20 hardcover o.p.   **639.34**

1. Fishes 2. Aquariums

ISBN 1-56458-293-0 (pa)   LC 93-3155

This illustrated "guide provides general information on the choice and care of fish, natural habitats, required aquarium conditions, and specific details on freshwater and marine tropical and coldwater fishes. Data for each species include family, common name, maximum adult size, physical characteristics of species, habitat, range, geographical distribution, peculiarites of species, alternative names, and a small, attractive photograph showing the male of the species." Libr J

Sandford, Gina

Aquarium owner's manual. DK Publishing 2003 256p il pa $25   **639.34**

1. Aquariums

ISBN 0-7894-9677-1

First published 1999

Full color pictures accompany information on creating, stocking, and maintaining a home aquarium. Types of fish, water, and aquarium environments are discussed.

639.9   Conservation of biological resources

Owens, Delia

The eye of the elephant; an epic adventure in the African wilderness; [by] Delia and Mark Owens. Houghton Mifflin 1992 305p il hardcover o.p. pa $16   **639.9**

1. Elephants 2. Wildlife conservation

ISBN 0-395-42381-3; 0-395-68090-5 (pa)
                                       LC 92-17691

This is an account of the authors' efforts to save elephants in the Luangwa Valley of Zambia from poachers by involving and educating the local people.

This "is a provocative, disturbing, and eminently readable work." Nat Hist

Includes bibliographic references

Followed by Secrets of the savanna

Owens, Mark

Secrets of the savanna; twenty-three years in the African wilderness unraveling the mysteries of elephants and people; [by] Mark and Delia Owens. Houghton Mifflin 2006 230p il map $26; pa $14.95 **639.9**

1. Elephants 2. Wildlife conservation
ISBN   978-0-395-89310-4;   0-395-89310-0; 978-0-618-87250-3 (pa); 0-618-87250-7 (pa)
LC 2005-23842

Sequel to The eye of the elephant
The authors "describe traveling to the 'remote and ruggedly beautiful' Luangwa Valley, in northeastern Zambia, to help save the North Luangwa National Park, where the elephant population had been decimated by poachers." Publ Wkly

"This book, full of adventure and a few hair-raising moments, deserves a wide readership." Libr J
Includes bibliographical references

640   Home & family management

Heloise

All-new hints from Heloise; a household guide for the '90s. Putnam 1989 416p il pa $13.95 **640**

1. Home economics
ISBN 0-399-51510-0   LC 88-33651
Also available Hints from Heloise (1980) from Avon Bks. $12 (ISBN 0-380-53066-X)
"A Perigee book"
The author "offers a mother lode of salient tips on cleaning, child-care, pet care, traveling and much more. . . . She is at her most ingenious and credible in the kitchen and on household maintenance." Publ Wkly

Huff, Darrell

The complete how to figure it; {by} Darrell Huff with Kristy Maria Huff; illustrated by Carolyn R. Kinsey; designed by Kristy Maria Huff. Norton 1996 470p il pa $17.95 hardcover o.p. **640**

1. Mathematics 2. Personal finance
ISBN 0-393-31924-5 (pa)   LC 95-46480
The author presents "solutions (with and without a pocket calculator) to the . . . calculations we need to make day by day, from budgeting current expenses to planning for retirement, from purchasing a home to travel, sports, and entertainment." Publisher's note
"This makes an ideal browser on a rainy afternoon, and it is especially friendly to those who can't quite cope with calculators." Booklist

Mendelson, Cheryl

Home comforts; the art and science of keeping house; illustrations by Harry Bates. Scribner 1999 884p il $35 **640**

1. Home economics
ISBN 0-684-81465-X   LC 99-37555
Mendelson includes "sections on food, clothing, cleanliness, daily life, and safety, with information on negligence, domestic employment laws, insurance, and even the impact of clothing label laws on our laundry. Preferred methods are explained in detail, and some alternatives are offered for those who need to compromise. This is a valuable tool." Libr J
Includes bibliographical references

Nakone, Lanna

Organizing for your brain type; finding your own solution to managing time, paper, and stuff. St. Martin's Griffin 2005 xlvii, 222p pa $13.95 **640**

1. Home economics 2. Time management
ISBN 0-312-33977-1   LC 2004-60159
"A quiz at the beginning assigns readers to the maintaining, harmonizing, innovating, or prioritizing style. Nakone then describes the strengths and weaknesses of each type and matches a prescription for how that type can best manage time. . . . This book should do well in most libraries." Libr J
Includes bibliographical references

Walsh, Peter

How to organize just about everything; more than 500 step-by-step instructions for everything from organizing your closets to planning a wedding to creating a flawless filing system. Free Press 2005 501p $25 **640**

1. Home economics
ISBN 0-7432-5494-5   LC 2004-56277

"Inside the 16 sections are 501 activities, both the usual and out-of-the-ordinary tasks, from getting organized and planning a remodeling project to joining the Peace Corps or becoming an astronaut. Each features the step-by-step procedures, tips, a warning (if necessary), and 'who knew?'—additional advice designed to make the activity a success. . . . A great humane reference anytime, anywhere, for any occasion." Booklist

640.73   Evaluation and purchasing guides

Levine, Judith

Not buying it; my year without shopping. Simon & Schuster 2006 274p $25 **640.73**

1. Consumer education 2. Shopping
ISBN 0-7432-6935-7   LC 2005-55517
The author discusses her experiences when she decided not to buy any nonessential items for a year.
"This honest and humorous tale of a nonspending year is well worth putting aside a few hours to read." Christ Sci Monit

641 Food and drink

Allen, Stewart Lee
In the devil's garden; a sinful history of forbidden food. Ballantine Bks. 2002 315p hardcover o.p. pa $13.95 *   **641**
1. Food 2. Eating customs 3. Cooking 4. Menus
ISBN 0-345-44015-3; 0-345-44016-1 (pa)
LC 2001-43882
"Different cultures and religions have defined certain foods as taboo over the centuries. Allen examines these taboos and looks for possible explanations for forbidding some otherwise edible foodstuffs from human consumption." Booklist
"The historical and cultural links between food, sex and religion make for fascinating reading." Publ Wkly
Includes bibliographical references

Bourdain, Anthony
A cook's tour; in search of a perfect meal. Bloomsbury Press 2001 274p $25.95   **641**
1. Cooking 2. Food
ISBN 1-58234-140-0   LC 0001-52428
Also available in paperback from Ecco Press
This is an "account of the author's global search for the 'perfect mix of food and context' that takes the reader to the culinary corners of the earth: from Vietnam (a live cobra heart) and Japan (poisonous blowfish) to England (roasted bone marrow) and Scotland (deep-fried Mars bar)." N Y Times Book Rev

David, Elizabeth, 1913-1992
An omelette and a glass of wine. Lyons & Burford 1997 320p il (The cook's classic library) pa $14.95   **641**
1. Cooking
ISBN 978-1-55821-571-9; 1-55821-571-9
LC 96-37821
First published 1984 in the United Kingdom
A collection of book reviews, restaurant reviews, articles and recipes that originally appeared in The Spectator, Gourmet magazine, Vogue, and The (London) Sunday Times, among others.
David's "fine-tuned sense of good taste pervades the book. The writing is elegant; the thought behind the writing subtle. . . . A civilized and learned book to sip, not gulp." Libr J
Includes bibliographical references

Fisher, M. F. K. (Mary Frances Kennedy), 1908-1992
A stew or a story; an assortment of short works by M.F.K. Fisher; gathered and introduced by Joan Reardon. Shoemaker & Hoard 2006 364p $28; pa $15.95   **641**
1. Food 2. Cooking
ISBN   978-1-59376-115-8;   1-59376-115-5; 978-1-59376-165-3 (pa); 1-59376-165-1 (pa)
LC 2006-08708
"Fisher's food writing was ahead of its time; a frequent contributor to Gourmet, Bon App tit, and other publications, Fisher had lived in both France and the California wine country and offered cooking tips that predate the American culinary 'revolution' of the 1960s. As these enjoyable pieces show, she was also a witty writer who offered astute observations along with the occasional recipe. The topics chosen for this collection include coffee making, borscht, olives, picnics, holidays, and places." Libr J
Includes bibliographical references

Kamp, David
The United States of Arugula; how we became a gourmet nation. Broadway Books 2006 392p il $26   **641**
1. Dining
ISBN 0-7679-1579-8   LC 2006-42599
The author "details the development of fine dining in the U.S. and proves healthy, even exotic food movements are having an effect on our diet. . . . This cultural history makes for an engrossing read, documenting the dramas and rivalries of the food industry." Publ Wkly
Includes bibliographical references

Kingsolver, Barbara
Animal, vegetable, miracle; a year of food life; [by] Barbara Kingsolver, with Steven L. Hopp and Camille Kingsolver; original drawings by Richard A. Houser. HarperCollins Publishers 2007 370p il $26.95   **641**
1. Farm life 2. Appalachian region 3. Eating customs
ISBN 978-0-06-085255-9; 0-06-085255-0
LC 2006-53516
"When Kingsolver and her family move from suburban Arizona to rural Appalachia, they take on a new challenge: to spend a year on a locally produced diet, paying close attention to the provenance of all they consume. . . . [This book] follows the family through the first year of their experiment." Publisher's note
"This is a serious book about important problems. Its concerns are real and urgent. It is clear, thoughtful, often amusing, passionate and appealing. It may give you a serious case of supermarket guilt, thinking of the energy footprint left by each out-of-season tomato, but you'll also find unexpected knowledge and gain the ability to make informed choices about what — and how — you're willing to eat." Washington Post Book World

Secret ingredients; the New Yorker book of food and drink; edited by David Remnick. Random House 2007 xv, 582p il $29.95   **641**
1. Cooking 2. Food 3. Eating customs
ISBN 978-1-4000-6547-9   LC 2007-14490
"A wide range of authors are represented, from the familiar A.J. Liebling and M.F.K. Fisher to the piquant Anthony Bourdain and the delightful Calvin Trillin. Those seeking an introduction to fiction and nonfiction food writing would do well to graze this work; seasoned readers will enjoy the nostalgic places and tastes depicted, and the quintessential New Yorker cartoons are a delightful addition." Libr J

Wright, Clifford A., 1951-

A Mediterranean feast; the story of the birth of the celebrated cuisines of the Mediterranean, from the Merchants of Venice to the Barbary Corsairs: with more than 500 recipes. Morrow 1999 xxiv, 815p il $35   **641**

1. Food 2. Eating customs

ISBN 0-688-15305-4   LC 98-49155

Wright "traces the influences and interconnections among the food and cooking of the diverse cultures that ring the Mediterranean Sea. . . . A unique work, this is recommended for history as well as cookery collections." Libr J

Includes bibliographical references

641.03   Food and drink— Encyclopedias and dictionaries

Davidson, Alan, 1924-2003

The Oxford companion to food; edited by Tom Jaine; illustrations by Soun Vannithone. 2nd ed. Oxford University Press 2006 907p il map $65   **641.03**

1. Food—Encyclopedias

ISBN 0-19-280681-5; 978-0-19-280681-9

                 LC 2006-48602

First published 1999

"Covering everything from individual ingredients and cooking techniques to food celebrities and national cuisines, the authoritative and engaging The Oxford Companion to Food is one of the best basic culinary reference books available." Libr J

Includes bibliographical references

International dictionary of food & cooking; compiled by Charles G. Sinclair. Fitzroy Dearborn Pubs. 1998 594p $60   **641.03**

1. Food—Dictionaries

ISBN 1-57958-057-2

This work contains over "24,000 words and terms that professional chefs and amateur cooks encounter in their kitchens. The entries, varying in length from a few words to a paragraph at most, are arranged alphabetically, with the country of origin for foreign words and phrases indicated within those entries." Libr J

Larousse gastronomique; with the assistance of the Gastronomic Committee, president Joël Robuchon. [rev ed] Potter 2001 1350p il $75 *   **641.03**

1. Cooking—Encyclopedias 2. Food—Encyclopedias 3. French cooking

ISBN 0-609-60971-8   LC 2001-32863

Original French edition published 1938 under the authorship of Prosper Montagné; first United States edition 1961

Based on the work of Prosper Montagné

This book "presents the history of foods, eating, and restaurants; cooking terms; techniques from elementary to advanced; a review of basic ingredients with advice on recognizing, buying, storing, and using them; biographies of important culinary figures; and recommendations for

cooking nearly everything." Publisher's note

This "will probably be the first choice of cooks who need information on culinary terms and cooking techniques, and . . . it contains more than 3500 recipes and an array of gorgeous color photographs. An indispensable part of any culinary reference collection, this is highly recommended for all libraries." Libr J

Rolland, Jacques L., 1945-

The food encyclopedia; over 8,000 ingredients, tools, techniques and people; [by] Jacques L. Rolland and Carol Sherman with other contributors. Robert Rose 2006 701p il $49.95   **641.03**

1. Food—Encyclopedias 2. Cooking—Encyclopedias

ISBN 978-0-7788-0150-4; 0-7788-0150-0

This encyclopedia "has 8,000 entries, with cross-reference on foods, wines, beverages, cooking methods and techniques, and biographies of prominent people." Publisher's note

Includes bibliographical references

641.2   Beverages (Drinks)

Kolpan, Steven

Exploring wine; the Culinary Institute of America's complete guide to wines of the world; {by} Steven Kolpan, Brian H. Smith, Michael A. Weiss. 2nd ed. Wiley 2001 820p il maps $65   **641.2**

1. Wine and wine making

ISBN 0-471-35295-0   LC 2001-24345

First published 1996 by Van Nostrand Reinhold

Accompanied by: Instructor's manual to accompany Exploring wine ... second edition. 174 p. ; 28 cm. c2002

The authors "cover wine tasting, wine making, and the wines of the world. They provide information about health and pairing wine with food and offer detailed coverage of service, storage, and purchasing, including buying wine at auctions." Booklist

Includes bibliographical references

Larousse encyclopedia of wine; general editor, Christopher Foulkes. Ed fully updated in 2001 by Larousse. Larousse 2001 624p il maps $45   **641.2**

1. Wine and wine making

ISBN 2-03-585013-4   LC 2003-269288

First published 1994

This book is a "reference to the world's vineyards and to the enjoyment of wine. . . . Full-color photographs, maps and drawings illustrate the country-by-country, vineyard-by-vineyard descriptions of all the world's wine regions from the United States and Europe to New Zealand and the Orient. . . . The book also details the intricacies of pairing wine with food, wine selection and etiquette, as well as historical and technical information about how wine is made." Publisher's note

The **Oxford** companion to wine; edited by Jancis
Robinson. 3rd ed. Oxford University Press 2006
840p il map $65   **641.2**
1. Wine and wine making
ISBN 978-0-19-860990-2; 0-19-860990-6
                                   LC 2006-50303
First published 1994
This book offers over 4000 entries on topics ranging
"from regions and grape varieties to the owners, connois-
seurs, growers, and tasters in wine through the ages;
from viticulture and oenology to the history of wine."
Publisher's note
The contributors "write with zesty enthusiasm about
everything from the different varieties of grapes to the
world's greatest wineries and geographic areas of production." Libr J

Peynaud, Emile, 1912-2004
The taste of wine; the art and science of wine
appreciation; [by] Emile Peynaud; with the
assistance of Jacques Blouin; translated from the
French by Michael Schuster; with a foreword by
Michael Broadbent. 2nd ed. Wiley 1996 xxi, 346p
il $95   **641.2**
1. Wine and wine making
ISBN 0-471-11376-X   LC 96-24181
Original French edition 1980; first English translation
published 1987 in the United Kingdom
This volume "covers the visual aspects of wine, sense
of smell, taste and tasters, and errors in perception. It in-
cludes a wine tasting vocabulary and other elements es-
sential to evaluating a wine's quality." Publisher's note
"Long considered the definitive tome on winetasting."
Libr J
Includes bibliographical references

641.3   Food

The **Cambridge** world history of food; editors,
Kenneth F. Kiple, Kriemhild Coneè Ornelas.
Cambridge Univ. Press 2000 2v set $190 *
                                              641.3
1. Food—History
ISBN 0-521-40216-6   LC 00-57181
In slipcase
"The two volumes are arranged in eight parts covering
the diet of early man, staple foods, dietary liquids, nutri-
ents and food-related disorders, food and drink around
the world, nutrition and health, current food-related is-
sues and concluding with a dictionary of plant foods.
. . . *The Cambridge World History of Food* is a thorough study of a topic that is eternally popular. It should
become a standard source in reference collections."
Booklist
Includes bibliographical references

Chilies to chocolate; food the Americas gave the
world; edited by Nelson Foster & Linda S.
Cordell. University of Ariz. Press 1992 191p pa
$15.95 hardcover o.p.   **641.3**
1. Edible plants
ISBN 0-8165-1324-4 (pa)   LC 92-5243

Essays explore the biological and cultural history of
crops cultivated by indigenous peoples of the Americas
and trace their dispersion into the fields and kitchens of
the Old World.
Includes bibliographical references

Colquhoun, Kate
Taste: the story of Britain through its cooking.
Bloomsbury 2007 460p il $34.95   **641.3**
1. British cooking 2. Eating customs
ISBN 978-1-59691-410-0; 1-59691-410-6
The author offers a culinary history of Great Britain.
"Colquhoun's enthusiasm for her subject leaps from
every page." Economist
Includes bibliographical references

Fernández-Armesto, Felipe
Near a thousand tables; a history of food. Free
Press 2002 258p $25; pa $14   **641.3**
1. Food—History
ISBN 0-7432-2644-5; 0-7432-2740-9 (pa)
                                   LC 2002-23318
Engl. title: Food; a history
The author "charts how the evolution of human culture is directly connected to the way food is obtained.
The logistics of agriculture and hunting have shaped notions of gender and community; food is often integral to
concepts of the sacred in a society; and the 'loneliness
of the fast food eater'—aided by such inventions as the
microwave—has become emblematic of contemporary
society's fragmentation." Publ Wkly
This is a "well-written, thought-provoking overview of
food history." Libr J
Includes bibliographical references

Hill, Tony, 1966-
The contemporary encyclopedia of herbs and
spices; seasonings for the global kitchen. J. Wiley
2004 432p il $40   **641.3**
1. Spices—Encyclopedias 2. Herbs—Encyclopedias
ISBN 0-471-21423-X   LC 2003-007733
The author provides information on some 350 herbs,
spices and spice blends and includes history and countries of origin as well as cooking and use guidelines
Includes bibliographical references

Norman, Jill
Herbs & spices; photography, Dave King. DK
Pub. 2002 336p il $30   **641.3**
1. Herbs 2. Spices
ISBN 0-7894-8939-2   LC 2003-544667
First published in the United Kingdom with title: Herb
& spice
On cover: The cook's reference
"Ranging from one to four pages each, the entries for
60 different herbs and 60 different spices include an
overview, tasting notes, the parts of the herb or spice
used in cooking, buying and storage information, culinary uses, and some details on cultivation. Separate
chapters on preparation, recipes for blending herbs and
spices (as in sauces and pastes), recipes that draw on cui-

Norman, Jill—*Continued*

sines around the world, and purchasing sources are also included . . . Norman's volume excels at giving the practical details and clear illustrations cooks need when it comes to using these ingredients in the kitchen." Libr J

Includes bibliographical references

The **Oxford** encyclopedia of food and drink in America; Andrew F. Smith, editor in chief. Oxford University Press 2004 2v il set $250 *

641.3

1. Food—Encyclopedias 2. Beverages
ISBN 0-19-515437-1; 978-0-19-515437-5

LC 2003-24873

This reference covers "the regions, people, ingredients, foods, drinks, publications, advertising, companies, historical periods, and political and economic aspects pertinent to American cuisine." Publisher's note

"Whether readers make a living studying culinary traditions or just enjoy eating, they'll find this book a marvel. . . . For food lovers of all stripes, this work inspires, enlightens and entertains." Publ Wkly

Parsons, Russ

How to pick a peach; the search for flavor from farm to table. Houghton Mifflin 2007 412p $27

641.3

1. Cooking—Fruit 2. Cooking—Vegetables
ISBN 978-0-618-46348-0; 0-618-46348-8

LC 2006-35462

"Equal parts cookbook, agricultural history, chemistry lesson and produce buying guide. . . . [Parsons begins with a] tale of agribusiness trumping our taste buds en route to supplying year-round on-demand produce, and how farmer's markets are bringing back both appreciation of, and access to, local and seasonal foods. He then takes readers on a delectable season-by-season produce tour, from springtime Artichokes Stuffed with Ham and Pine Nuts to midwinter Candied Citrus Peel, and provides readers with the lowdown on where each fruit or vegetable is grown and how to choose, store and prepare it." Publ Wkly

Rosenblum, Mort

Chocolate: a bittersweet saga of dark and light. North Point Press 2005 290p il $24; pa $14

641.3

1. Chocolate
ISBN 0-86547-635-7; 0-86547-730-2 (pa)

LC 2004-54734

The author "unveils chocolate's history and its various incarnations, including in his fresh and insightful discussions the origins of mole; the differences between, say, Hershey's kisses and Valrhona's products; the invention of Nutella; and the small boutique chocolate artisans found nearly everywhere. . . . A compelling and tasty read." Booklist

641.4 Food preservation and storage

Costenbader, Carol W.

The big book of preserving the harvest; {foreword by Joanne Lamb Hayes}. {rev ed}. Storey Bks. 2002 347p il pa $18.95 *

641.4

1. Canning and preserving
ISBN 1-58017-458-2

LC 2002-21172

First published 1997

In addition to recipes this book provides instructions for food preservation techniques, including canning, drying, freezing, the preparation of jams and jellies, pickles, relishes and chutneys, vinegars and seasonings, and cold storage. Includes a section on gift giving, directions on building a food dehydrator, a table of equivalents, and a conversion chart to metric measures

Includes bibliographical references

The **Good** Housekeeping step-by-step cookbook; edited by Susan Westmoreland with the assistance of Susan Deborah Goldsmith and Elizabeth Brainerd Burge. Hearst Books 2008 576p il $29.95

641.4

1. Cooking
ISBN 978-1-58816-760-6; 1-58816-760-7

First published 1997

This offers over 1,000 basic recipes illustrated by 1,800 color photographs divided into sections such as appetizers, soups, eggs and cheese, shellfish, poultry, meat, vegetables, pasta, grains and beans, breads, and desserts.

Ziedrich, Linda

The joy of pickling; 200 flavor-packed recipes for all kinds of produce from garden or market. Harvard Common Press 1998 382p il pa $19.95 hardcover o.p.

641.4

1. Canning and preserving
ISBN 1-55832-133-0 (pa)

LC 98-22880

This is a "guide to pickles of all sorts, including kimchi and others from Asia, chutneys and salsas, and 'freezer pickles,' along with traditional favorites like Half-Sours by the Quart." Libr J

Includes bibliographical references

641.5 Cooking

The **150** best American recipes; edited by Fran McCullough and Molly Stevens; foreword by Rick Bayless; photography by Ben Fink; [selected by the editors of The best American recipes] Houghton Mifflin 2006 352p il $30

641.5

1. Cooking
ISBN 978-0-618-71865-8; 0-618-71865-6

LC 2006-5604

Subtitle on cover: Indispensable dishes from legendary chefs & undiscovered cooks

The 150 best American recipes—*Continued*

The editors "have selected the 'best of the best' recipes from . . . [The Best American Recipes series], choosing from more than 1000 contenders. The recipes come from a variety of sources, from cookbooks to web sites to cooking schools, and the result is a mouthwatering array: Charred Tomatillo Guacamole; Tuscan Pork Roast with Herbed Salt; Mussels with Smoky Bacon, Lime, and Cilantro; and Mocha Fudge Pudding." Libr J

Algar, Ayla Esen

Classical Turkish cooking; traditional Turkish food for the American kitchen; [by] Ayla Algar. HarperCollins Pubs. 1991 306p $35; pa $17
641.5

1. Turkish cooking
ISBN 0-06-016317-8; 0-06-093163-9 (pa)
LC 91-55096

"A cuisine that melds the fragrances and flavors of the Far East, Central Asia, Iran, Anatolia, and the Mediterranean is enriched by Algar as she goes well beyond the standard recipes (160 of them) to explain Turkey's historical, cultural, and culinary traditions—and, along the way, to include a glimpse of her personal family heritage." Booklist
Includes bibliographical references

American food writing; an anthology with classic recipes; edited by Molly O'Neill. Library of America 2007 753p il $40 *   **641.5**
1. Cooking
ISBN 978-1-59853-005-6; 1-59853-005-4

This "collection of essays, anecdotes, and recipes spans three centuries of American food writing, from Meriwether Lewis's account of killing 'two bucks and two buffaloe' during his famous trek across the continent, to Michael Pollan's up-to-the-minute account of the politics of organic food. . . . With so many wonderful ingredients, this rich, delectable treat is a must-have for American foodies." Publ Wkly
Includes bibliographical references

The **America's** test kitchen family cookbook; the editors at America's test kitchen; photography, Daniel J. Van Ackere & Carl Tremblay. Revised ed. America's Test Kitchen 2006 726p il $34.95
641.5

1. Cooking
ISBN 978-1-933615-01-1; 1-933615-01-X
LC 2007-296245

First published 2005

This volume "offers over 1,200 approachable recipes for a very wide range of dishes-from 'weekday' fare like Creamy Rice Casserole, Cheesy Nachos with Spicy Beef, and Skillet Lasagna, to dressier recipes, including Pan-Seared Lamb Chops with Red Wine Rosemary Sauce, Roasted Trout Stuffed with Bacon and Spinach, and Chocolate Marshmallow Mousse. There are 'specialty' chapters devoted to sandwiches, drinks, and slow cooker and pressure cooker dishes; a grilling section is a tutorial in itself. . . . The book delivers solid, family-friendly dishes with enough fully orchestrated 'how to' to make even novice cooks feel secure when tackling the basics or more ambitious fare." Amazon.com

Anderson, Jean, 1929-

The food of Portugal; color photography by the author. Morrow 1986 304p il map pa $19.95 hardcover o.p.   **641.5**
1. Portuguese cooking
ISBN 0-688-13415-7 (pa)   LC 86-2510

The author "first covers Portugal's geography and touches on distinctive regional cooking styles. The following glossary delineates Portuguese food, drink, and dining terminology. . . . Part 2, . . . is a guide to the country's best food." Booklist
Includes bibliographical references

The new German cookbook; more than 230 contemporary and traditional recipes; [by] Jean Anderson and Hedy Würz. HarperCollins Pubs. 1993 416p $30   **641.5**
1. German cooking
ISBN 0-06-016202-3   LC 92-56211

"This book should give many cooks a new perspective on German cooking. All of the ingredients traditionally associated with this cuisine appear, but veal, for example, shows up in a Riesling wine sauce as well as in Wiener schnitzel, and dumplings are scented with tarragon and tossed into a clear asparagus soup." Libr J
Includes bibliographical references

Anderson, Pam

How to cook without a book; recipes and techniques every cook should know by heart. Broadway Bks. 2000 290p $25   **641.5**
1. Cooking
ISBN 0-7679-0279-3   LC 99-43776

"In chapters organized mostly by course or by technique, Anderson provides basic templates for tossed salads, pasta dishes with vegetables, simple stir-fries, and so forth, with easy suggestions for variations on the theme." Libr J

Perfect recipes for having people over; photographs by Rita Maas. Houghton Mifflin 2005 304p il $35   **641.5**
1. Cooking 2. Entertaining
ISBN 0-618-32972-2   LC 2005-46370

Anderson "offers 200 recipes from entrées to desserts. Most are easy to make; some require guest participation, such as shish kebabs, with a variety of ingredients for all tastes. The book begins with main courses since they will dictate the accompaniments. Each recipe has a question section–e.g., 'Any Shortcuts?' 'What Should I Serve with It?' 'How Far Ahead Can I Make It?' There are many familiar dishes like macaroni and cheese and deviled eggs, but readers will also encounter innovative recipes." Libr J

Barrenechea, Teresa, 1956-

The Basque table; passionate home cooking from one of Europe's great regional cuisines; {by} Teresa Barrenechea, with Mary Goodbody. Harvard Common Press 1998 232p il hardcover o.p. pa $16.95   **641.5**
1. Basque cooking
ISBN 1-55832-140-3; 978-1-55832-327-8 (pa); 1-55832-327-9 (pa)   LC 98-29295

Barrenechea, Teresa, 1956——*Continued*

The author's "Basque dishes are characterized by fresh, lively flavors; garlic, hot chilis, and roasted sweet peppers, fish of all types, and beef and lamb are favorite ingredients. While home-style dishes are her emphasis here, there are some entries from *nueva cocina* as well. A chapter on pinchos, the Basque version of tapas, is a highlight, and there are sidebars on Basque ingredients and traditions throughout." Libr J

Bastianich, Lidia

Lidia's family table; [by] Lidia Matticchio Bastianich, with David Nussbaum; photographs by Christopher Hirsheimer. Knopf 2004 xxiv, 419p il $35   **641.5**

1. Italian cooking
ISBN 1-4000-4035-3   LC 2004-22411

This cookbook "presents the food Bastianich prepares at home for her large family. . . . The range is impressive, the flavors strong. It's enough to make readers clamor to be adopted into the Bastianich clan." Publ Wkly

Lidia's Italian-American kitchen; by Lidia Matticchio Bastianich; photographs by Christopher Hirsheimer. Knopf 2001 xxvi, 432p il $35
                    641.5

1. Italian cooking
ISBN 0-375-41150-X   LC 2001-45009

In this cookbook "recipes are divided into antipasto, soups, pasta and risotto, pizza, entrees, side dishes and desserts." Publ Wkly

"Bastianich has a warm, engaging style, and she's a teacher as well as a chef: throughout, she provides thoughtful head-notes and sidebars along with useful boxes on cooking with wine, 'resting' soup, and other such practicalities." Libr J

Lidia's Italian table; edited by Christopher Styler; photography by Christopher Hirscheimer. Morrow 1998 390p il $30   **641.5**

1. Italian cooking
ISBN 0-688-15410-7   LC 98-2949

This companion to the PBS series centers on Istrian cuisine which "represents a transition zone, Italian cooking gradually merging with Slavic traditions to create some unique flavor pairings." Booklist

This book contains recipes that "are unusual, not to be found in the average Italian cookbook, and Bastianich's considerable knowledge and experience, as well as her enthusiasm, are evident throughout." Libr J

Bayless, Rick

Rick Bayless's Mexican kitchen; capturing the vibrant flavors of a world-class cuisine; [by] Rick Bayless with Deann Groen Bayless and JeanMarie Brownson; photographs by Maria Robledo; illustrations by John Sandford. Scribner 1996 448p il $35   **641.5**

1. Mexican cooking
ISBN 0-684-80006-3   LC 96-218444

This cookbook "includes more than 200 tantalizing recipes and is packed with information on Mexican in-

gredients and cooking techniques, regional cuisine, and history. . . . A serious guide to an often underestimated cuisine, this is important as both a reference and a cookbook." Libr J

Includes bibliographical references

Beard, James, 1903-1985

The armchair James Beard; edited by John Ferrone; foreword by Barbara Kafka. Lyons Press 1999 346p $24.95   **641.5**

1. Cooking
ISBN 1-55821-737-1   LC 98-29728

Articles previously published in various journals

This collection assembles "essays on everything from main courses to condiments; dining in restaurants, hospitals, and al fresco; libations and desserts; and broader philosophical concerns on gastronomy. Each chapter has captured Beard's feeling for food, his wicked sense of humor, his consummate excellence as a writer, and even his love of controversy. . . . The 150 recipes cover the globe and honor the palate." Libr J

The fireside cook book; a complete guide to fine cooking for beginner and expert; [by] James A. Beard; Illustrated by Alice Provensen and Martin Provensen Foreword by Mark Bittman. Simon & Schuster 2008 336p il $30
                    641.5

1. Cooking
ISBN 978-1-4165-8967-9; 1-4165-8967-8
                    LC 2008-25094

First published 1949

This volume "includes more than 12,000 recipes and variations, with chapters on every course of a meal, as well as 'Outdoor Cookery,' 'Frozen Foods and PickUp Meals,' and more. This 60th-anniversary edition includes the original watercolor illustrations and a brief new foreword by cookbook author Mark Bittman. While some of the information and language is dated, of course, it's amazing how ahead of his time Beard often was. . . . The amount of information the book provides is equally impressive, and Beard's straightforward, opinionated prose remains a delight to read." Libr J

James Beard's American cookery. Little, Brown 1972 877p pa $24.95 hardcover o.p. *
                    641.5

1. Cooking
ISBN 0-316-08566-9 (pa)

"Comprehensive in scope the cookbook gives eighteen-and nineteenth-century recipes as well as modern directions for preparation of a full range of U.S. cookery. . . . The format is attractive and the historical data add to the value of an authoritative guide." Booklist

Includes bibliographical references

Berley, Peter

The modern vegetarian kitchen; [by] Peter Berley with Melissa Clark. ReganBooks 2000 450p il $35   **641.5**

1. Vegetarian cooking
ISBN 0-06-039295-9   LC 00-42524

Berley, Peter—Continued

The author "organizes his recipes first by type (e.g., soups, salads, pasta, and beans) and then by season. . . . He also provides lots of background information and recommendations on ingredients, necessary utensils and appliances, and techniques." Libr J

Includes bibliographical references

Bernstein, Richard K.

The diabetes diet; Dr. Bernstein's low-carbohydrate solution; recipes by Marcia Miele. Little, Brown and Co 2005 291p $24.95

641.5

1. Diabetes—Diet therapy 2. Low-carbohydrate diet

ISBN 0-316-73784-4   LC 2004-11739

The author offers low-carbohydrate recipes designed "to interrupt the cycle of obesity and insulin resistance and maintain a healthy weight." Publisher's note

The **best** American recipes 2005-2006; the year's top picks from books, magazines, newspapers, and the Internet; Fran McCullough and Molly Stevens, series editors; with a foreword by Mario Batali. Houghton Mifflin 2004 303p il (The Best American series) $26   **641.5**

1. Cooking

ISSN 1525-1101

ISBN 978-0-0618-57478-0; 0-618-57478-6

Annual. First published 1999

Editors vary

This is a compilation of popular recipes taken from cookbooks, newspapers, magazines, and other sources

The **best** International recipe; a home cook's guide to the best recipes in the world; by the editors of Cook's Illustrated. America's Test Kitchen 2007 579p il $35   **641.5**

1. Cooking

ISBN 978-1-933615-17-2; 1-933615-17-6

This volume contains more than 300 recipes from around the world. Each has been tested to ensure success. Includes explanations of ingredients and what to look for, and in some cases, what you can substitute without compromising flavor. Specialty equipment is also discussed. Core techniques are highlighted throughout the book.

Better homes and gardens new cook book. 14th ed. Meredith Books 2006 656p il $29.95; pa $19.95   **641.5**

1. Cooking

ISBN 0-696-22403-8; 978-0-696-22403-4; 0-696-22565-4 (pa); 978-0-696-22565-9 (pa)

LC 2006-921302

First published 1930 with title: My Better Homes and Gardens cook book. Periodically revised

"A standard cookbook . . . with staple recipes and types of cooking." N Y Public Libr. Book of How & Where to Look It Up

Betty Crocker cookbook; everything you need to know to cook today. 10th ed. Wiley 2005 575p il $29.95; pa $17.95 *   **641.5**

1. Cooking

ISBN 0-7645-6877-9; 978-0-7645-6877-0; 0-7645-8374-3 (pa); 978-0-7645-8374-2 (pa)

LC 2006-281166

First published with this title 1969 by Golden Press. Periodically revised. Publisher varies. Variant title: Betty Crocker's new cookbook

"This book gives easily readable and understandable recipes. Also has a glossary of cooking terms in back, as well as nutritional guidelines and 'special helps.'" N Y Public Libr. Book of How & Where to Look It Up

Betty Crocker's cooking basics; learning to cook with confidence. Macmillan 1998 280p il $19.95

641.5

1. Cooking

ISBN 0-02-862451-3   LC 98-20522

In addition to recipes, this illustrated volume contains tips on food selection, grocery shopping, thawing, and nutrition. Cooking equipment is discussed

Bittman, Mark

How to cook everything; 2,000 simple recipes for great food; illustrations by Alan Witschonke. 2nd ed. J. Wiley 2008 1044p il $35

641.5

1. Cooking

ISBN 978-0-76-457865-6; 0-76-457865-0

LC 2008-18984

First published 1998 by Macmilllan

The author presents "more than 1000 basic recipes and simple and inventive variations. The enormous breadth of recipes along with Bittman's engaging, straightforward prose will appeal to cooks looking for reliable help with kitchen fundamentals." Publ Wkly

Includes bibliographical references

How to cook everything vegetarian; simple meatless recipes for great food; illustrations by Alan Witschonke. Wiley 2007 996p il $35 *

641.5

1. Vegetarian cooking

ISBN 978-0-7645-2483-7; 0-7645-2483-6

LC 2006-36937

This vegetarian cookbook "presents more than 2000 recipes and variations. Most of the recipes are quick and easy; prep times are given for each one, and icons indicate those that are especially fast, can be made ahead, and/or are vegan. . . . An essential purchase for all cookery collections." Libr J

Buford, Bill

Heat; an amateur's adventures as kitchen slave, line cook, pasta-maker, and apprentice to a Dante-quoting butcher in Tuscany. Knopf 2006 318p $25.95   **641.5**

1. Batali, Mario 2. Italian cooking

ISBN 1-4000-4120-1; 978-1-4000-4120-6

LC 2005-57868

Buford, Bill—*Continued*

In this account of how the author learned to be a cook, Buford presents a "chronicle of his experience as 'slave' to Mario Batali in the kitchen of Batali's three-star New York restaurant, Babbo." Publisher's note

"Mr Buford also has a biographer's gift of bringing characters to life. . . . [He] fills his book with people as pungent and spicy as the food." Economist

Burke, David, 1962-

David Burke's new American classics; [by] David Burke and Judith Choate. Knopf 2006 300p il $35 **641.5**
1. Cooking
ISBN 0-375-41231-X LC 2005-44960

"Burke presents each dish in three separate and distinctive guises: classic, contemporary, and second day (leftovers). This tripartite approach allows him to address cooks possessing different levels of expertise and sophistication. . . . A large number of these recipes require advanced kitchen techniques so that only the most experienced cooks will have the skills to reproduce Burke's results. Color photographs help guide when the instructions alone fail to communicate the chef's intent." Booklist

Child, Julia

From Julia Child's kitchen; photographs and drawings by Paul Child; additional technical photographs by Albie Walton. Knopf 1975 687, xxvip il $13.99 * **641.5**
1. French cooking
ISBN 0-517-20712-5

The author "has taken many of the recipes she demonstrated in her 72 'French Chef' TV shows; grouped them by subject {soups, appetizers, egg dishes, fish, poultry, meat, vegetables, salads, bread} added variations and additional recipes; and introduced each section and most recipes with commentaries." Libr J

Includes bibliographical references

Julia and Jacques cooking at home; by Julia Child and Jacques Pepin, with David Nussbaum. Knopf 1999 430p il $40 **641.5**
1. French cooking
ISBN 0-375-40431-7 LC 98-32418

A companion volume to the PBS series. "For each show, the two chefs started out with ideas and ingredients but no set recipes, so they improvised as they went along, cooking a lot of their favorite traditional dishes and coming up with new ones as well. . . . Dozens of boxes throughout the text provide information on a wide variety of topics." Libr J

Mastering the art of French cooking; by Julia Child, Louisette Bertholle, Simone Beck. updated ed. Knopf 1983 2v il v1 $40; v1 pa $30; v2 $60; v2 pa $30 * **641.5**
1. French cooking
ISBN 0-375-41340-5 (v1); 0-394-72178-0 (v1 pa); 0-394-40152-2 (v2); 0-394-72177-2 (v2 pa)
LC 83-48113

Volume 1 first published 1961 with Beck's name first; volume 2 by Julia Child and Simone Beck

Volume one includes, in addition to usual categories, a chapter dealing with entrees and luncheon dishes, including quiches, pâtés, and crepes, and other cold buffet items. Volume two emphasizes French bread and pastries, with chapters also devoted to soups, meats, chickens, vegetables, and desserts. Appendices discuss stuffings and kitchen equipment.

The way to cook; photographs by Brian Leatart and Jim Scherer; food designer, Rosemary Manell. Knopf 1989 511p il $65; pa $39.95 **641.5**
1. Cooking
ISBN 0-394-53264-3; 0-679-74765-6 (pa)
LC 88-45838

"With her sensible-as-always approach to food, Child has produced a comprehensive cooking bible, filled with stunning photographs and practical illustrations, that will aid the novice {and} inspire the gourmet. . . . A masterwork from a master chef." Libr J

David, Elizabeth, 1913-1992

A book of Mediterranean food; decorated by John Minton. 2nd rev. ed. New York Review Books 2002 203p il (New York Review Books classics) pa $14.95 **641.5**
1. Mediterranean cooking
ISBN 978-1-59017-003-8; 1-59017-003-2
LC 2002-749

First published 1950 in the United Kingdom

This is a "mixture of recipes, culinary lore, and frank talk. In bleak postwar Great Britain, when basics were rationed and fresh food a fantasy, David set about to cheer herself—and her audience—up with dishes from the south of France, Italy, Spain, Portugal, Greece, and the Middle East." Publisher's note

French provincial cooking. Grub Street 2008 c2007 519p il $34.95 **641.5**
1. French cooking
ISBN 978-1-904943-71-6; 1-904943-71-3
LC 2008-411778

First published 1960 in the United Kingdom

This book "should be approached and read as a series of short stories, as well as written and evocative as the best literature. The voice is highly personal and opinionated, sometimes sharp but always true and always entertaining. This book is a long essay on French cuisine, offering background stories and sketches of recipes very different from the prescriptive type of recipes that most modern readers might be used to today." Living France

Is there a nutmeg in the house? compiled by Jill Norman. Viking 2001 318p il pa $15 hardcover o.p. * **641.5**
1. Cooking 2. Food
ISBN 0-14-200166-X (pa) LC 2001-26185

Companion volume to An omelette and a glass of wine (1985)

Consists of previously unpublished material and published articles; Continues: An omelette and a glass of wine

This "collection of essays and more than 150 recipes, compiled by David's long-time associate Jill Norman, brings some new work to light. There are 12 sections,

David, Elizabeth, 1913-1992—*Continued*
from 'Stocks and Soups' to 'Ice Creams and Sorbets."
Libr J
An "evocative and entertaining exploration of cooking
and the time, place and personalities that shaped it.'"
Publ Wkly
Includes bibliographical references

Italian food. rev ed. Penguin Books 1999 xxxiii,
376p pa $16   **641.5**
  1. Italian cooking
  ISBN 978-0-14-118155-4; 0-14-118155-9
                                          LC 99-200031
First published 1958 in the United Kingdom
This "was one of the first books to demonstrate the
enormous range of Italy's regional cooking. For the
foods of Italy, explained David, expanded far beyond
minestrone and ravioli, to the complex traditions of Tuscany, Sicily, Lombardy, Umbria, and many other regions.
David imparts her knowledge from her many years in Italy, exploring, researching, tasting and testing dishes."
Publisher's note
"David studies and analyzes cooking the way a scholar analyzes literature, and, as a result, her titles are far
more than just cookbooks. Along with the recipes, of
which there are many, she explains at length the histories
of the dishes and offers splendid advice on serving wine
with the meals." Libr J
Includes bibliographical references

Summer cooking; illustrated by Adrian Daintrey.
New York Review Books 2002 234p il (New York
Review Books classics) pa $12.95   **641.5**
  1. British cooking
  ISBN 978-1-59017-004-5; 1-59017-004-0
                                          LC 2002-744
First published 1955 in the United Kingdom
"Don't let the unsophisticated subject fool you into
expecting only cheese sandwiches and potato salads. For
all its simplicity, 'Summer Cooking' is a wonderfully
subversive volume — every bit as unexpected and enchanting to read today as it must have been 50 years
ago, when England was just stirring from its wartime fast
and garlic was an ingredient still capable of provoking
controversy. . . . David earned her place in gastronomic
history by being one of the first writers to suggest that
thoughtful food and cooking itself could be a means of
escape. Now, 15 years after her death, that voice remains
a singular note in the chorus of her contemporaries and
acolytes, neither frankly amiable like Julia Child, nor seductively literate like M.F.K. Fisher, nor playfully mod
like Nigella Lawson. No matter how trivial the point,
David speaks her mind." Salon.com

Dojny, Brooke
The New England cookbook; 350 recipes from
town and country, land and sea, hearth and home;
illustrations by John MacDonald. Harvard
Common Press 1999 652p il $29.95; pa $21.95
                                          641.5
  1. Cooking
  ISBN 1-55832-138-1; 1-55832-139-X (pa)
                                          LC 99-14393

This volume includes traditional dishes as well as
"dozens of ethnic specialties from the various immigrant
groups who have helped populate New England: Orega-
no-Scented Greek Lamb Shanks, Portuguese Tuna
Escabeche, and Garlicky Mussels, Italian-style, to name
a few." Libr J
Includes bibliographical references

Fairchild, Barbara
The Bon appétit cookbook. Wiley 2006 xxiv,
792p il $34.95   **641.5**
  1. Cooking
  ISBN 0-7645-9686-1; 978-0-7645-9686-5
                                          LC 2005-5181
"Mirroring the magazine on which it is based, this
collection of 1,200 recipes is accessible, applicable to
most home cooks' lives and a pleasure to cook from."
Publ Wkly

The Bon appétit fast easy fresh cookbook. J.
Wiley 2008 xxix, 770p il $34.95   **641.5**
  1. Cooking
  ISBN 978-0-470-22630-8   LC 2007-44562
This cookbook "presents hundreds of quick and simple
recipes from the magazine's popular 'Fast Easy Fresh'
feature. An introductory 'Shopping Guide' covers buying
and storing produce, meat, and fish, and dozens of
sidebars and boxes provide more information on ingredients and techniques. . . . Sure to appeal to any busy
cook as well as the magazine's numerous fans, this is
highly recommended." Libr J

Fant, Maureen B.
Rome; authentic recipes celebrating the foods of
the world; recipes and text Maureen B. Fant;
photographs Jean-Blaise Hall; general editor Chuck
Williams. Oxmoor House 2005 192p il map
(Williams-Sonoma foods of the world) $24.95
                                          641.5
  1. Italian cooking
  ISBN 978-0-8487-3006-2
Full-color photographs accompany 45 classic and contemporary recipes, from tonnarelli cacio e pepe and spa-
ghetti alla carbonara to saltimbocca alla Romano and
abbacchio alla cacciatora. Seasonal side dishes, wines,
and covered. Includes glossary and ingredient sources.

Fearnley-Whittingstall, Hugh
The River Cottage cookbook; photography by
Simon Wheeler. Ten Speed Press 2008 447p il $35
                                          641.5
  1. Cooking—Natural foods 2. English cooking
  ISBN 978-1-58008-909-8; 1-58008-909-7
                                          LC 2007-43795
First published 2001 in the United Kingdom
"There are 95 healthy recipes, everything from Straw-
berry Sandwiches to Nettle Soup, Crispy Pig's Ears to
Pigeon Pitas (yes, real pigeons), but the work is primari-
ly . . . [an] almanac of raising and eating organic plants
and animals without the intrusive use of slaughterhouses,
packaging plants or grocery stores." Publ Wkly
"The author writes with passion and humor, and his

Fearnley-Whittingstall, Hugh—_Continued_
unusual book will be useful as both a reference and a
cookbook." Libr J
Includes bibliographical references

Flay, Bobby, 1964-
Bobby Flay's grilling for life; 75 healthier ideas
for big flavor from the fire; [by] Bobby Flay with
Stephanie Banyas and Sally Jackson; foreword by
Joy Bauer; color photographs by Gentl & Hyers;
black-and-white photographs by John Dolan.
Scribner 2005 210p il $22 *   **641.5**
    1. Barbecue cooking
    ISBN 0-7432-7272-2   LC 2005-45053
    This is "a healthy-eating cookbook, complete with nu-
tritional analysis for each recipe. . . . [The author] offers
mostly simple recipes (including some based on 'good
carbs,' as he refers to complex carbohydrates), from Zucchini Succotash to Beef Filet with Arugula and Parmesan
to Grilled Apricots with Bittersweet Chocolate." Libr J
    The author's "trademark use of bold flavors in dishes
like Grilled Red Snapper with Grapefruit-Thyme Mojo,
and (skinless) Grilled Duck Breast with Black Pepper-
Sweet Mustard Sauce bring out appealing contrasts and
result in food that's satisfying even if it's reduced in calories, carbs or fat." Publ Wkly

Garten, Ina
Barefoot Contessa family style; easy ideas and
recipes that make everyone feel like family;
photographs by Maura McEvoy; food styling by
Rori Trovato. Potter 2002 240p il $35
                        641.5
    1. Cooking
    ISBN 0-609-61066-X   LC 2002-74979
    "Garten's 'family style' cooking includes dishes like
Chicken Noodle Soup and Parker's Fish & Chips (separate chapters are devoted to breakfast and kids' foods),
but there are also elegant dishes like Tuna Tartare, Saf-
fron Risotto, and Lobster Cobb Salad." Libr J
    This is "simple, elegant home cooking with good in-
gredients and a minimum of fuss. It takes a certain
amount of chutzpah to include ordinary chicken noodle
soup and mashed potatoes and gravy in a cookbook, but
Garten pulls it off with heart and style." Publ Wkly

Gentry, Ann, 1954-
The Real Food Daily cookbook; really fresh,
really good, really vegetarian; [by] Ann Gentry
with Anthony Head. Ten Speed Press 2005 232p
$24.95   **641.5**
    1. Vegetarian cooking
    ISBN 1-58008-618-7   LC 2005-16245
    The author presents "what she has learned about sea-
sonal, organic, macrobiotic and vegan cooking. Gentry
doesn't break new ground—sandwiches made with
tempeh instead of meat, and nut cheeses like cashew
cheddar will be familiar to most vegans—but she provides clear and comprehensive directions on how to
make them more interesting and flavorful. . . . Gentry
explains the basics without preaching or condescending
to readers, and discusses nutritional benefits without unnecessary jargon." Publ Wkly

Giedt, Frances Towner
The Joslin Diabetes great chefs cook healthy
cookbook; [by] Frances Towner Giedt and Bonnie
Sanders Polin, with the nutrition services staff at
Joslin Diabetes Center; foreword by Alan C.
Moses. Simon & Schuster 2002 308p il hardcover
o.p. pa $15   **641.5**
    1. Diabetes—Diet therapy 2. Cooking
    ISBN 0-7432-1586-9; 0-7432-1588-5 (pa)
                           LC 2002-70745
    This book features "recipes from well-known chefs,
each designed to fit the special dietary requirements of
diabetics." Publ Wkly
    "The recipes are sophisticated and elegant—perfect
dinner-party fare—but many of them are quite easy to
prepare. The authors have grouped main course recipes
under 'Small Plates' and 'Large Plates,' along with starters, soups, salads, vegetables and other sides, and desserts. Each recipe, of course, includes nutrition information, and there are many suggested menus scattered
throughout." Libr J

Good Housekeeping great American classics
    cookbook; edited by Susan Westmoreland.
    Hearst Communications 2004 336p il $24.95 *
                                641.5
    1. Cooking
    ISBN 1-588-16280-X   LC 2004-933
    "This volume of American standards offers a . . .
snapshot of the state of cooking in the nation's homes at
the beginning of the second millennium. . . . Most startling is the European-influenced casual use of wines and
spirits in all kinds of appetizers, entrees, and desserts.
Current emphasis on food's nutritional value manifests itself in tables enumerating calories, proteins, carbohydrates, and fats appended to each recipe. . . . Brilliant
color photos throughout." Booklist

The **gourmet** cookbook; more than 1000 recipes;
    edited by Ruth Reichl. Houghton Mifflin 2004
    1040p $40   **641.5**
    1. Cooking
    ISBN 0-618-37408-6   LC 2004-47873
    Recipes culled from issues of Gourmet magazine in-
clude "concoctions like Coq au Vin, Beef Wellington,
Coulibiac, Chop Suey, Bananas Foster, and Black Forest
Cake. . . . Every chapter begins with an overview of its
subject; each recipe has an introduction; and many dishes
feature helpful 'cook's notes,' which give tips for food
preparation, technique and storage." Publ Wkly

Green, Aliza
Starting with ingredients; quintessential recipes
for the way we really cook. Running Press 2006
1055p il $39.95   **641.5**
    1. Cooking
    ISBN 0-7624-2747-7; 978-0-7624-2747-5
                              LC 2006-921032
    This is a "compendium of ingredients from A to Z
(with a special chapter on 'X-tras' basic recipes and information). Each chapter opens with an informative and
very readable introduction to the featured ingredient,
touching on everything from its history to culinary lore
. . . to its uses in various cultures around the world.

Green, Aliza—*Continued*
. . . This is an invaluable reference with hundreds of fresh, lively recipes. Essential." Libr J

Greene, Gloria Kaufer, 1950-
The new Jewish holiday cookbook; an international collection of recipes and customs. Completely rev and updated with more than 80 new recipes! Times Bks. 1999 539p $29.95
        641.5
1. Jewish cooking 2. Jewish holidays
ISBN 0-8129-2977-2   LC 98-55721
First published 1985 with title: The Jewish holiday cookbook
"Starting with the chief and weekly holiday, Sabbath, Greene offers tasty recipes that occasionally draw on ingredients outside traditional ones. . . . Greene labels each recipe as 'meat,' 'dairy,' or 'pareve' so that readers may determine instantly how the recipe correlates with dietary laws." Booklist

Hagman, Bette
The gluten-free gourmet; living well without wheat. rev ed. Holt & Co. 2000 xx, 330p pa $18
*   **641.5**
1. Gluten-free diet 2. Diet in disease
ISBN 0-8050-6484-2   LC 00-22448
First published 1990
This book features over 200 "recipes using special flours for pizza, pasta, breads, pies, cakes, and cookies. . . . A complete sourcebook on how to live healthily with celiac disease or wheat intolerance, it features . . . information on developing a celiac diet, raising a celiac child, avoiding hidden glutens, eating well while traveling or in the hospital, and locating and ordering from suppliers of gluten-free food and flour." Publisher's note
The recipes "are easy to prepare. Mail-order sources for gluten-free flours will be especially helpful. The . . . accurate information in this makes it a useful purchase for large cookbook collections." Booklist [review of 1990 edition]
Includes bibliographical references

Harris, Jessica B.
The Africa cookbook; tastes of a continent. Simon & Schuster 1998 382p il $27
        641.5
1. African cooking
ISBN 0-684-80275-9   LC 98-38882
The author begins with an "introductory section that provides history, . . . background on the four general divisions of the continent, and a very good glossary of ingredients and equipment. Recipes are organized by course, with country of origin listed for each, and headnotes offer context as well as useful tips. Harris writes well, and her accounts of various visits and encounters are particularly readable. With few other cookbooks available even on specific African cuisines, her ambitious new book is unique." Libr J
Includes bibliographical references

Hazan, Marcella
Essentials of classic Italian cooking; illustrated by Karin Kretschmann. Knopf 1992 688p il $30
        641.5
1. Italian cooking
ISBN 0-394-58404-X   LC 92-52954
Revised and updated edition of the author's The classic Italian cookbook (1973) and More classic Italian cooking (1978)
A guide to the products, techniques and dishes of classic Italian cooking. Regional specialities are dealt with at length
This "could readily assume the mantle of *the* definitive resource for Italian cuisine." Booklist

Marcella cucina; photography by Alison Harris, design by Joel Avirom. HarperCollins Pubs. 1997 471p il $35   **641.5**
1. Italian cooking
ISBN 0-06-017103-0   LC 97-1253
This book includes both the author's "old favorites and recent creations, along with her versions of regional dishes from chefs and home cooks throughout Italy. . . . She offers an intimate, at times nostalgic glimpse at her life with cooking." Libr J

Marcella says . . .; Italian cooking wisdom from the legendary teacher's master classes, with more than 120 of her irresistible new recipes. HarperCollins Publishers 2004 390p il $29.95
        641.5
1. Italian cooking
ISBN 0-06-620967-6   LC 2004-42892
The author shares lessons in Italian cooking, discussing techniques, ingredients and planning and preparing Italian dishes

Iyer, Raghavan, 1961-
660 curries; the gateway to the world of Indian cooking; by Raghavan Iyer. Workman Pub. 2008 809p il $32.50; pa $22.95   **641.5**
1. Cooking—Curry
ISBN   978-0-7611-4855-5;   0-7611-4855-8; 978-0-7611-3787-0 (pa); 0-7611-3787-4 (pa)
                       LC 2008-1288
"A wide-ranging guide to the curries of the Indian subcontinent, including Pakistan, Nepal, and Sri Lanka. Iyer explains that Indian curries are not based on a can of curry powder and that the term 'curry' refers to any dish simmered in or covered with a fragrant, spicy (though not necessarily hot) sauce or gravy. The hundreds of recipes include appetizer curries such as Skewered Chicken with Creamy Fenugreek Sauce, main-course curries like Yogurt-Marinated Lamb with Ginger and Garlic, and 'contemporary curries' such as Wild Salmon with Chiles, Scallions, and Tomato; there are also recipes for 'curry cohorts'—rice, bread, and other accompaniments." Libr J

Jaffrey, Madhur
Madhur Jaffrey's ultimate curry bible; India, Singapore, Malaysia, Indonesia, Thailand, South Africa, Kenya, Great Britain, Trinidad, Guyana, Japan, USA. Ebury 2003 352p il $51.65
        641.5

Jaffrey, Madhur—*Continued*
1. Cooking—Curry
ISBN 978-0-09-187415-5; 0-09-187415-7
With over 150 recipes, "Madhur starts with the best curry recipes in India today, moves on to Asian curries, and even includes European curry ideas such as French curry sauces. Some recipes have never before appeared in print, such as fish seasoned with tamarind and coconut and lamb braised with oranges. Also included are Madhur's tips for the best accompanying foods — she gives us ideas for rice, bread, chutneys, relishes and sweets — the perfect complement for any curry." Publisher's note

Jamison, Cheryl Alters
The big book of outdoor cooking and entertaining; spirited recipes and expert tips for barbecuing, charcoal and gas grilling, rotisserie roasting, smoking, deep-frying, and making merry; [by] Cheryl and Bill Jamison. Morrow 2006 548p $24.95   641.5
1. Barbecue cooking 2. Entertaining
ISBN 0-06-073784-0; 978-0-06-073784-9
LC 2006-41918
This book features "more than 850 recipes and information on every aspect of backyard cooking. There are dozens of 'Party-Time Tips' and other helpful hints, menu suggestions, and sidebars and boxes on techniques, ingredients, and more. . . . New grilling books appear as the season approaches every year, but this one is an essential purchase." Libr J

Jenkins, Nancy Harmon
The essential Mediterranean; how regional cooks transform key ingredients into the world's favorite cuisines. HarperCollins Pubs. 2003 436p $29.95
641.5
1. Mediterranean cooking
ISBN 0-06-019651-3   LC 2002-69054
The author begins each chapter "with an introduction, providing both historical and cultural context, including interviews with, for example, an artisan cheese maker in eastern Provence, an olive oil producer in Tunisia, and other such experts. Then come a dozen or more recipes that both showcase the specific ingredient and display the diversity of the cuisines that rely on it. . . . Jenkins concludes with a section of basic recipes and a source guide for the featured ingredients." Libr J
"Jenkins's writing experience stands her in good stead in this innovative exploration of this sunny region." Publ Wkly
Includes bibliographical references

Kasper, Lynne Rossetto
The Splendid table's how to eat supper; recipes, stories, and opinions from public radio's award-winning food show; [by] Lynne Rossetto Kasper and Sally Swift. Clarkson Potter/Publishers 2008 338p il $35   641.5
1. Dining 2. Cooking
ISBN 978-0-307-34671-1   LC 2007-24749

"The recipes gathered here, ranging from Thai Cantaloupe Salad with Chile to Filipino-Style Chicken Adobo, were inspired by a variety of cuisines. Many of them include variations, and sidebars titled 'Cook to Cook' provide . . . information on all sorts of topics. There are also . . . digressions on various culinary matters and recommendations for favorite cookbooks." Libr J
"This superb book should grace the shelves of even the most infrequent of cooks." Publ Wkly

Kennedy, Diana
The essential cuisines of Mexico. Potter 2000 526p $35   641.5
1. Mexican cooking
ISBN 0-609-60355-8   LC 00-23156
The author has gathered "the recipes from her first cookbook, the groundbreaking *Cuisines of Mexico* (1972), as well its two successors, *The Tortilla Book* (1975) and *Mexican Regional Cooking* (1978) . . . in this new collection. She's revised the recipes and simplified some, and there are also 30 or so new recipes. Kennedy's books became classics long ago; this compilation of her early works is an essential purchase." Libr J
Includes bibliographical references

From my Mexican kitchen; techniques and ingredients; photographs by Michael Calderwood; and styled by the author. Clarkson Potter 2003 320p il $40   641.5
1. Mexican cooking
ISBN 0-609-60700-6   LC 2002-70405
The author "explains how to produce authentic enchiladas, tacos, tamales, *sopes*, *panuchos*, and other Mexican classics. Kennedy also provides a guide to wild greens, items rarely seen outside provincial markets. Her advice on freezing excess quantities of *cuitlacoche* (corn fungus) will reward fans of that uncommon mushroom. This is an indispensable addition to any library cookbook collection." Booklist

Kochilas, Diane
The glorious foods of Greece. Morrow 2000 496p map $40   641.5
1. Greek cooking
ISBN 0-688-15457-3   LC 00-28158
This cookbook includes over 400 recipes from various "regions, starting with the Peloponnesus and the Ionian Islands, moving on to Macedonia, the islands of the Aegean, and Crete, and finishing up in the city of Athens. . . . Kochilas also provides extensive historical background, cultural as well as culinary, along with detailed descriptions and explanations of ingredients." Libr J
Includes bibliographical references

Lagasse, Emeril
From Emeril's kitchens; favorite recipes from Emeril's restaurants. William Morrow/HarperCollins 2003 342p il $27.50
641.5
1. Cooking
ISBN 978-0-06-018535-0; 0-06-01853-5
LC 2002-27568

Lagasse, Emeril—*Continued*

"Spreading his philosophy and history in the introduction, [Emeril] entreats the user not to be put off by the complexity of many of the recipes, but to use the components and mix and match the dishes. The first chapter, 'Basics,' contains the building blocks of many of the dishes, ranging from the customary stocks to Hard Boiled Eggs and Roast Duck. Subsequent chapters are structured in the usual manner ranging from appetizers and first courses through desserts. Each dish is attributed to its restaurant or chef and results in a range of styles and inspirations." Publ Wkly

Lawson, Nigella, 1960-

Feast: food that celebrates life; photographs by James Merrell. Hyperion 2004 472p il $35

641.5

1. Cooking
ISBN 1-4013-0136-3
The author offers "recipes for Thanksgiving, Christmas, Hanukah, Eid, New Year's, Passover, Easter gatherings, and any time you want to celebrate food and life." Publisher's note
This cookbook "makes the preparation of Thanksgiving, Christmas and other feasts seem so approachable and richly rewarding that it may coax even hardcore cynics or cowards to give roast turkey with all the trimmings a try." Publ Wkly
Includes bibliographical references

Nigella express; good food, fast; photographs by Lis Parsons. Hyperion 2007 390p il $35

641.5

1. Cooking
ISBN 978-1-4013-2243-4; 1-4013-2243-3
"Recipes in this book run the gamut from retro crepe suzettes to modern favorites like quesadillas and smoothies; and from orange French toast for breakfast to cocktail nibbles for a party. In the interest of speed Lawson uses prepared ingredients, but they're the ones many of us use already, like mayonnaise from a jar or frozen puff pastry. And if her tastes are sometimes nostalgically British (Eton mess, roly poly pudding) she also has a whole chapter on quick Tex-Mex food." WeightWatchers.com

Lee, Jennifer 8., 1976-

The fortune cookie chronicles; adventures in the world of Chinese food. Twelve 2008 307p $24.99

641.5

1. Chinese cooking 2. Restaurants 3. Eating customs
ISBN 978-0-446-58007-6; 0-446-58007-4
LC 2007-33432
"When a large number of Powerball winners in a 2005 drawing revealed that mass-printed paper fortunes were to blame, the author . . . went in search of the backstory. She tracked the winners down to Chinese restaurants all over America, and the paper slips the fortunes are written on back to a Brooklyn company. This travellike narrative serves as the spine of her cultural history—not a book on Chinese cuisine, but the Chinese food of takeout-and-delivery—and permits her to frequently but safely wander off into various tangents related to the cookie. . . . Like the numbers on those lottery

fortunes, the book's a winner." Publ Wkly
Includes bibliographical references

Lee, Matthew

The Lee Bros. southern cookbook; stories and recipes for southerners and would-be southerners; [by] Matt Lee and Ted Lee; color photography by Gentl & Hyers. W.W. Norton 2006 589p il $35

641.5

1. Southern cooking
ISBN 978-0-393-05781-2; 0-393-05781-X
LC 2006-22745
This "cookbook begins with a collection of drink recipes, from sweet tea to potent planters' punch. To accompany these beverages, the Lee brothers array a long series of snack and party foods. A section on preserves and pickles documents some rarely seen regional treats, such as Jerusalem artichoke relish. Meats, seafood, sweets, and breads round out the book. Every recipe has a story attached, and the large format makes for easy reading." Booklist

Lewis, Edna, 1916-2006

The gift of Southern cooking; recipes and revelations from two great Southern cooks; by Edna Lewis and Scott Peacock. Knopf 2003 352p il $29.95 **641.5**

1. Southern cooking
ISBN 0-375-40035-4
LC 2002-73153
The authors provide "recipes, from pan-fried chicken, creamy grits, and Southern biscuits to cakes and hand-cranked ice cream, sharing as well the culinary discoveries that resulted from their collaboration in the kitchen." Libr J
"If you care—and I mean really care—about coleslaw, pan-fried chicken, trout, . . . greens simmered in pork stock and Southern-style ketchups, relishes and vinegars, this is a book you shouldn't be without." N Y Times Book Rev

The taste of country cooking; [with a foreword by Alice Waters] 30th anniversary ed. Knopf 2006 xxi, 268p il $22.95 * **641.5**

1. Southern cooking
ISBN 0-307-26560-9; 978-0-307-26560-9
"This is a Borzoi book"
First published 1976
"Recipes are categorized by the four seasons and are ones . . . [the author] grew up with in a small Virginia farming community (personal reminiscences about her family life appear throughout the text)." Booklist

Madison, Deborah

Vegetarian cooking for everyone. 10th anniversary ed, with a new introduction. Broadway Books 2007 742p il $40 **641.5**

1. Vegetarian cooking
ISBN 978-0-7679-2747-5; 0-7679-2747-8
LC 2007-10075
First published 1997
Following information on ingredients and techniques, the recipes focus "mainly on vegetables and grains, aiming at flavor and variety, both often arrived at via assorted ethnic approaches." Publ Wkly

Marks, Gil

The world of Jewish cooking; more than 500 traditional recipes from Alsace to Yemen. Simon & Schuster 1996 406p il pa $17 hardcover o.p.

641.5

1. Jewish cooking
ISBN 0-684-83559-2 (pa)   LC 96-2848

This cookbook is "loosely arranged by food category, with chapters on appetizers, soups, and main dishes, as well as side items, breads, and desserts. . . . You'll find recipes from India, Africa, even China, here, alongside many dishes that originated in one of the two major Jewish cultural communities, Ashkenazic and Sephardic." Booklist

Nathan, Joan

Jewish cooking in America. expanded ed. Knopf 1998 518p il $35   **641.5**

1. Jewish cooking
ISBN 0-375-40276-4   LC 98-27952
First published 1994

This companion volume to the PBS television series contains nearly 300 recipes. It "is also a history of the Jewish people through their food. Nathan introduces both people and food in a preface that discusses dietary laws, Jewish holidays, Jewish immigration to the U.S., and the impact of Jews—and their food—on American culture. With every recipe comes an original story or a reprint of an article or a personal vignette that intrigues and/or edifies." Booklist

Includes bibliographical references

Negrin, Micol

Rustico: regional Italian country cooking. Potter 2002 384p il $35   **641.5**

1. Italian cooking
ISBN 0-609-60944-0   LC 2001-57793

This "cookbook/guidebook offers a tour of Italy's 20 regions, with ten . . . recipes for each. Some are 'signature' dishes intimately associated with a particular region, but more are what she describes as lesser-known 'regional gems.' Each chapter opens with a brief, scene-setting introduction and a list of favorite restaurants and shops." Libr J

"Recipes are lucid and easy to follow, and chapter introductions stylishly and accurately convey a sense of place, while sidebars offer bits of folklore." Publ Wkly

Includes bibliographical references

The **new** American Heart Association cookbook. 7th ed. Clarkson Potter 2004 xx, 700p il $30; pa $19.95   **641.5**

1. Cooking 2. Low-cholesterol diet
ISBN 1-4000-4826-5; 0-307-35205-6 (pa)
LC 2004-11239

Also available in paperback 25th anniversary edition

First published 1973 with title: American Heart Association cookbook

"Each recipe comes with a breakdown of calories, protein content, carbohydrates, cholesterol, fats (broken down by saturated, polyunsaturated and monounsaturated) and sodium content, along with a table of dietary exchange. . . . This book remains a basic in many heart-conscious kitchens." Publ Wkly

The **new** American plate cookbook; recipes for a healthy weight and a healthy life; American Institute for Cancer Research. University of California Press 2005 306p il $24.95 *

641.5

1. Cooking
ISBN 0-520-24234-3   LC 2004-17993

The recipes in this book are "built around vegetables and whole grains, with an emphasis on brown rice, wheat pasta, and other healthful foods, rather than protein. . . . Recipes are appealing and easy to make and cover every course of a meal. Well-known dishes are reworked, e.g., New England Clam Chowder, to help with the transition to healthier eating." Libr J

The **new** best recipe; by the editors of Cook's illustrated; photography, Carl Tremblay, Daniel J. Van Ackere; illustrations, John Burgoyne. 2nd ed. America's Test Kitchen 2004 1028p il $35

641.5

1. Cooking
ISBN 978-0-936184-74-6; 0-936184-74-4
First published 1999 by Boston Common Press

A compendium of more than 1,000 recipes. "Twenty-two chapters cover appetizers to desserts. Even the simplest tasks, such as blanching vegetables or peeling an egg, are explained and illustrated in detail. More involved techniques include brining poultry and roasting a turkey. . . . Well organized and extremely clear." Publ Wkly

The **New** York Times Jewish cookbook; more than 825 traditional and contemporary recipes from around the world; edited by Linda Amster; introduction by Mimi Sheraton. St. Martin's Press 2003 xxvi, 614p $35   **641.5**

1. Jewish cooking
ISBN 978-0-312-29093-1; 0-312-29093-4
LC 2002-68358

"Included here are hundreds of recipes from Jewish communities all over the world, reflecting Mimi Sheraton's introductory comment that Jewish food is 'the world's oldest fusion cuisine.' Recipes range from Persian Chicken Soup with Chickpea Dumplings to Alain Ducasse's Rib-Eye Steaks with Peppered Cranberry Marmalade to Fresh Corn and Red Pepper Blini. All the classics are here, too, and there's a separate chapter on 'Trimmings,' including an array of condiments and garnishes. . . . This is an essential purchase." Libr J

The **New** York Times Passover cookbook; more than 200 holiday recipes from top chefs and writers; edited by Linda Amster. Morrow 1999 xxii, 328p il $25   **641.5**

1. Jewish cooking 2. Passover
ISBN 0-688-15590-1   LC 98-41282

This book's recipes "range from the traditional to the innovative and are drawn from European, Mediterranean and Middle Eastern traditions. . . . Amster has produced what may be the definitive word in Passover cookbooks, from recipes to the feelings evoked by sitting at a beautifully set, bountifully laden table." Publ Wkly

Includes bibliographical references

Newgent, Jackie

The all-natural diabetes cookbook; the whole food approach to great taste and healthy eating. American Diabetes Association 2007 337p il pa $18.95 **641.5**

1. Cooking—Natural foods 2. Diabetes—Diet therapy

ISBN 978-1-58040-275-0   LC 2007-11961

The author presents a "cookbook designed to provide diabetes-friendly recipes that emphasize fresh and organically grown produce. . . . A wide variety of food styles are presented, ranging from Southern Black-Eyed Pea Salad to Vietnamese-Style Beef and Soba Noodle Soup. Even desserts are here, with such enticing options as Fudgy Brownies and New Fashioned Oatmeal Cookies. Highly recommended for all cooking collections." Libr J

Oliver, Jamie

Cook with Jamie; my guide to making you a better cook; photography: David Loftus and Chris Terry. Hyperion 2007 447p il $37.50

641.5

1. Cooking

ISBN 978-1-4013-2233-5; 1-4013-2233-6

"Aiming to educate readers on cooking basics, Oliver offers more than 175 recipes, which emphasize flavor and freshness over labor-intensive preparation. With a conversational style that favors general guidelines over strict instructions—recipes often call for a 'knob of butter,' a 'handful of shelled peas' or 'a big handful of freshly grated Parmesan'—Oliver's friendly and enthusiastic approach handily deflates new-cook anxiety. Loaded with photos that cover common skills like cleaning and preparing fresh lobster, discerning degrees of doneness in meat and crafting homemade pasta, Oliver's patient explanations leave little room for confusion. His dishes, many of which are updated versions of classics, are impressive and accessible." Publ Wkly

Ortega, Simone

1080 recipes; [by] Simone and Ines Ortega; illustrations, Javier Mariscal. Phaidon 2007 975p il $39.95 * **641.5**

1. Spanish cooking

ISBN 978-0-7148-4836-5; 0-7148-4836-0

First published 1977 in Spain

On cover: The bible of authentic Spanish cooking

"Something like the Joy of Cooking for the Spanish home cook, . . . [this book] includes recipes for both traditional regional fare and dishes inspired by a variety of other cuisines. . . . An essential purchase." Libr J

Pépin, Jacques

Jacques Pépin celebrates; by Jacques Pépin with Claudine Pépin; photographs by Christopher Hirsheimer; illustrations by Jacques Pépin. Knopf 2001 458p il $40 **641.5**

1. Cooking 2. Entertaining

ISBN 0-375-41209-3   LC 2001-29929

"In this companion to a new PBS series, Pépin builds on a broad definition of celebrations—encompassing holidays, special occasions, and simply nice weather—to present a collection of typically solid French recipes and

numerous useful tips and techniques. . . . More valuable than the recipes . . . are the many notes on chopping, garnishing, carving and so forth." Publ Wkly

Peterson, James

Cooking. Ten Speed Press 2007 534p il $40

641.5

1. Cooking

ISBN 978-1-580-08789-6; 1-580-08789-2

LC 2007-21065

Subtitle on cover: 600 recipes, 1500 photographs, one kitchen education

This book "opens with a fairly brief description of ten basic cooking techniques and then moves on to Recipes To Learn By, organized by course or main ingredient. Many of the recipes are traditional French standbys, from Celeriac Rémoulade to Beef à la Mode, although there are dishes inspired by Thai, Mexican, and other cuisines as well. . . . Essentially an intensive course for home cooks in the classic techniques that underlie good cooking, this is recommended for all cookery collections." Libr J

Glorious French food; a fresh approach to the classics. Wiley 2002 xxv, 742p il map $45 *

641.5

1. French cooking

ISBN 0-471-44276-3   LC 2001-46972

The author presents "50 classic recipes as the starting point for his wide-ranging exploration of French food and techniques; each recipe serves both to demonstrate a variety of techniques and as the inspiration for a diverse collection of other recipes related to it in one way or another. . . . Each chapter includes boxes and charts on improvising with different ingredients and flavors. The suggested variations for individual recipes, often mini-essays in themselves, open up dozens of other possibilities. Peterson is both passionate and knowledgeable about his subject, and his . . . book is an essential purchase." Libr J

Includes bibliographical references

Poses, Steven

The Frog Commissary cookbook; by Steven Poses, Anne Clark, and Becky Roller ; illustrated by Becky Roller. Camino Books 2002 272p pa $19.95 **641.5**

1. Cooking

ISBN 978-0-940159-73-0; 0-940159-73-2

LC 2001-43691

First published 1985 by Doubleday

This is a "cookbook that brings together hundreds of kitchen-tested recipes, tips, and information about [the authors'] personal approach to food preparation. Organized by meal course, the book contains a multitude of creative recipes, adapted for serving at home and reflecting a quixotic, multiethnic blend of foods and ingredients. Full of insider tips on food preparation and service and . . . anecdotes." Publisher's note

"Lighthearted, full of ideas. . . . Could inject new life into your dining and entertaining style." Bon Appetit

The **professional** chef; the Culinary Institute of America. 8th ed. Wiley 2006 1215p il map $70

641.5

1. Cooking 2. Restaurants
ISBN 978-0-7645-5734-7; 0-7645-5734-3

LC 2004-27110

First published 1962

"The nation's most prestigious training school for food careerists concentrates the essence of its course work within a comprehensive volume that competent students must master. Every aspect of the restaurant business is addressed, from nutrition and portion sizing to fiscal and human resource management. Sections on equipment, from major appliances to handheld tools, show the bond between chef and technology. Chapters on world cooking identify the most typical cooking processes and give examples of commonly appearing ingredients in each style. Recipes record classic preparations that form the foundation for myriad elaborations and personalization to move cooking from mere technique to high art. Although beyond the need of most home cooks, this massive tome is a necessary reference-collection purchase for any library whose community includes food-service-training programs." Booklist

Prudhomme, Paul

Chef Paul Prudhomme's Louisiana tastes; exciting flavors from the state that cooks. Morrow 2000 347p il $25

641.5

1. Cooking—Louisiana
ISBN 0-688-12224-8

LC 99-35611

"Chronicling dishes from his native state, Prudhomme acknowledges that Louisiana home cooks don't normally serve anything so fancy as appetizers, so he offers dozens of ideas for starters that may readily serve as entrees by simply increasing portion size. . . . Each recipe now has its own unique seasoning mix varying from a few to a dozen spices and herbs." Booklist

Puck, Wolfgang

Live, love, eat! the best of Wolfgang Puck. Gramercy Books 2006 243p il $14.99

641.5

1. Cooking
ISBN 978-0-517-22868-5; 0-517-22868-8

LC 2006-41232

First published 2002 by Random House

This volume contains more than 125 recipes for appetizers, a variety of seasonal soups and salads, and, along with pasta and risotto recipes, the California-style pizzas that first made Puck and his original Spago Hollywood a favorite of international celebrities. Puck also serves up all manner of main courses, including seafood recipes, poultry dishes, and meat recipes. To round out the collection, he offers a variety of vegetable and other side-dish recipes, plus desserts. A section covering basics, sauces, and techniques provides guidance for beginning and experienced cooks alike. Illustrated throughout with more than 150 color images of finished dishes and closeup how-to shots demonstrating key techniques and tips.

Roberts, Michael, 1949-2005

Parisian home cooking; conversations, recipes, and tips from the cooks and food merchants of Paris; photographs by Perre-Gilles Vidoli. Morrow 1999 335p il $28

641.5

1. French cooking
ISBN 0-688-13868-3

LC 98-41750

Roberts re-examines "a cuisine that can intimidate with its sometimes exacting procedures. He shows that Parisian home cooks are as hampered by small kitchens and time shortages as the rest of us, and that, as a result, their daily recipes are far less complicated than traditional French cookbooks suggest. Roberts proves that techniques are within the reach of anyone." Publ Wkly

Robertson, Robin

Vegan planet; 400 irresistible recipes with fantastic flavors from home and around the world. Harvard Common Press 2003 576p hardcover o.p. pa $21.95

641.5

1. Vegetarian cooking
ISBN 1-55832-210-8; 1-55832-211-6 (pa)

LC 2002-7435

The author "offers dozens of imaginative vegan recipes inspired by a wide range of cuisines, from Five-Spiced Portobello Satays and Lebanese Fattoush (bread salad) to Cajun-Style Collards and Moroccan Fava Bean Stew." Libr J

Roden, Claudia

Arabesque: a taste of Morocco, Turkey, and Lebanon. Knopf 2006 341p il $35

641.5

1. Moroccan cooking 2. Turkish cooking 3. Lebanese cooking
ISBN 0-307-26498-X; 978-0-307-26498-5

LC 2006-45258

First published 2005 in the United Kingdom

The author "has chosen more than 150 recipes from Morocco, Turkey, and Lebanon, some newly discovered, some variations on more familiar dishes, and a selection of favorite classic dishes. Each section opens with a fascinating insider's guide, providing both cultural and culinary history as well as information on specific ingredients and techniques. . . . An essential purchase." Libr J

Rombauer, Irma von Starkloff, 1877-1962

Joy of cooking; [by] Irma S. Rombauer, Marion Rombauer Becker, Ethan Becker; illustrated by John Norton. 75th anniversary ed. Scribner 2006 1132p il $30

641.5

1. Cooking
ISBN 978-0-7432-4626-2; 0-7432-4626-8

LC 2006-51231

First published 1931

"All-purpose cookbook for informal and formal use with American and foreign recipes. Includes menu planning suggestions, nutrition, basic information on foods, basic cooking terminology, and methods of preparation." N Y Public Libr Book of How & Where to Look It Up

This is the "backbone for any library's cookery reference collection, its nearly 4,000 recipes defining essential American home cooking." Booklist

Samuelsson, Marcus

The soul of a new cuisine; a discovery of the foods and flavors of Africa; foreword by Desmond Tutu. Wiley 2006 xxii, 344p il map $40

641.5

1. African cooking

ISBN 0-7645-6911-2

For this African cookbook, the author "traveled to Africa and even took cooking lessons in Ethiopia, the country of his birth. Samuelsson emphasizes that this is not the definitive cookbook of an area with over 800 languages and dialects, but an overview of what he saw and ate in his travels. . . . This is a unique cookbook about a little-known cuisine, including travel essays and enhanced by beautiful color photographs that depict the food and the people of Africa. A necessary acquisition for international cookery collections." Libr J

Includes bibliographical references

Shimbo, Hiroko

The Japanese kitchen; 250 recipes in a traditional spirit; illustrations by Rodica Prato. Harvard Common Press; distributed by National Bk. Network 2000 512p il hardcover o.p. pa $21.95　　**641.5**

1. Japanese cooking

ISBN 1-55832-176-4; 1-55832-177-2 (pa)

LC 00-33505

The author provides a "guide to equipment, techniques, and ingredients, followed by a wide-ranging selection of recipes of all sorts. There are both the home-style dishes she grew up on and more elaborate ones for special occasions, as well as the traditional Japanese classics, with her own touches, of course, and innovative new recipes. . . . An essential purchase." Libr J

The **silver** spoon. Phaidon Press 2005 1263p il $39.95　　**641.5**

1. Italian cooking

ISBN 978-0-7148-4531-9; 0-7148-4531-0

Original Italian edition, 1950

"Newly updated and translated into English for the first time, the book contains recipes for everything from basic sauces and marinades to salads, game, fish and baked goods, with each section color-coded for easy browsing. Recipes emphasize fresh ingredients and are to-the-point, typically summed up in a paragraph sans photo illustrations. Those who know their way around a kitchen will appreciate the brevity. . . . Almost all of the ingredients called for can be found in a typical supermarket. . . . Globe-trotting gourmands will appreciate the menu and 'signature dish' contributions by famous Italian chefs that round out the book. The most exhaustive Italian cookbook in recent memory, this volume offers something for every cook, regardless of their skill level, and deserves to be a fixture in American kitchens." Publ Wkly

Silverton, Nancy

A twist of the wrist; quick flavorful meals with ingredients from jars, cans, bags, and boxes; [by] Nancy Silverton with Carolynn Carreño; photographs by Amy Neunsinger. Knopf 2007 262p il $29.95　　**641.5**

1. Quick and easy cooking 2. Convenience foods

ISBN 978-1-4000-4407-8; 1-4000-4407-3

LC 2006-49557

The author offers recipes requiring "premium prepared ingredients as shortcuts to ease the home cooking time crunch. Most recipes are timed at 30 minutes or less, but the elegance and seeming difficulty of the dishes set them apart from the usual quick-fix crowd pleasers. . . . Cooks looking for upscale yet quick meal ideas, and who will pay extra for pricey exotic items, are sure to appreciate this stylish cheat sheet." Publ Wkly

Includes bibliographical references

Spieler, Marlena

Paris; authentic recipes celebrating the foods of the world; recipes and text Marlena Spieler; photographs Jean-Blaise Hall; general editor Chuck Williams. Oxmoor House 2004 191p il map (Williams-Sonoma foods of the world) $24.95

641.5

1. French cooking

ISBN 978-0-8487-2854-8

Illustrated with full-color photographs. "Dozens of stories reveal the secrets of making long-cherished foods and profile people, places, and influences that have shaped the Parisian food scene. More than 45 recipes allow you to sample traditional dishes, such as Boeuf en Daube, Steak withe Shallot Sauce, or Raspberry Charlotte, as well as such innovations as Duck Breasts with Port and Figs or Strawberry Soup." Publisher's note

Stow, Josie

The African kitchen; a day in the life of a safari chef; {by} Josie Stow and Jan Baldwin. Interlink Bks. 1999 144p il hardcover o.p. pa $20

641.5

1. African cooking

ISBN 1-56656-354-2; 978-1-56656-580-6 (pa); 1-56656-580-4 (pa)　　LC 99-52120

"When Stow first took over the kitchen at a game preserve in South Africa, she found that most such establishments were serving European-style food. Drawing on the knowledge and experience of the cooks working with her, she developed a repertoire of traditional and modern African dishes. . . . Beautiful photographs of African nightcapes, people, and Stow's food illustrate the text." Libr J

Tausend, Marilyn

Cocina de la familia; more than 200 authentic recipes from Mexican-American home kitchens; {by} Marilyn Tausend with Miguel Ravago. Simon & Schuster 1997 415p pa $20 hardcover o.p.　　**641.5**

1. Mexican American cooking

ISBN 0-684-85259-4 (pa)　　LC 97-26979

Tausend, Marilyn—*Continued*

This cookbook includes recipes for "Green Enchiladas with Spinach and Tofu, Chicken with Spicy Prune Sauce made with Coca-Cola, and Mexican Beef Chow Mein, {as well as} more traditional Mexican fare like Guacamole and Braised Chicken with Rice and Vegetables." Publ Wkly

Includes bibliographical references

Thompson, David, 1960-

Thai food = Arharn Thai; with photography by Earl Carter. Ten Speed Press 2002 673p $40

641.5

1. Thai cooking

ISBN 978-1-580-08462-8; 1-580-08462-1

LC 2002-18117

"The first section of the book provides detailed cultural and social history and a guide to the regions and regional cuisines of Thailand. Then a detailed glossary of ingredients and a guide to techniques introduce the hundreds of recipes. These are grouped into chapters on relishes, soups, curries, salads, and sides, followed by one of menus with recipes. . . . [This] culinary history/cookbook is unique and will be an important purchase for any Asian cookery collection." Libr J

Includes bibliographical references

Trang, Corinne

Essentials of Asian cuisine; fundamentals and favorite recipes; black-and-white photographs by Corinne Trang; color photographs by Christopher Hirscheimer. Simon & Schuster 2003 592p il $40

641.5

1. Asian cooking

ISBN 0-7432-0312-7   LC 2002-30490

This volume covers "the cooking of the Southeast Asian peninsula's nations, China, Japan, and Korea. . . . Trang opens with a discussion of the cuisines' shared cooking techniques and the importance of using all one's senses when preparing a meal. . . . The exhaustive inventory of recipes methodically treats soups, starches, meats, fish, vegetables, and sweet dishes." Booklist

"Authoritative and thoroughly researched, this will be invaluable as both a reference and a cookbook." Libr J

Includes bibliographical references

Tsai, Ming, 1964-

Blue Ginger; East-meets-West cooking with Ming Tsai; by Ming Tsai and Arthur Boehm. Potter 1999 275p $32.50   641.5

1. Cooking

ISBN 0-609-60530-5   LC 99-36393

Includes index

"Chapters divide the 125-plus recipes into soups, dim sum, rice and noodles, poultry, meat, seafood, elaborate side dishes and desserts, with mail-order sources. . . . Instructions are clearly written and often include tips for wine and food pairings and advice on ingredient substitutions and techniques." Publ Wkly

Waters, Alice

The art of simple food; notes, lessons, and recipes from a delicious revolution; [by] Alice Waters, with Patricia Curtan, Kelsie Kerr & Fritz Streiff ; illustrations by Patricia Curtan. Clarkson Potter 2007 405p il $35   641.5

1. Quick and easy cooking

ISBN 978-0-307-33679-8; 0-307-33679-4

LC 2007-300393

"After a useful discussion of ingredients and equipment come chapters on techniques, such as making broth and soup. Each of these includes three or four recipes that rely on the technique described. . . . The final third of the book divides many more recipes traditionally into salads, pasta and so forth. Waters taps an almost endless supply of ideas for appealing and fresh yet low-stress dishes." Publ Wkly

Weil, Andrew

The healthy kitchen; recipes for a better body, life, and spirit; {by} Andrew Weil and Rosie Daley; photographs by Sang An, Amy Haskell, and Eric Studer. Knopf 2002 xxxvii, 325p il $24.95; pa $16.95   641.5

1. Cooking 2. Natural foods

ISBN 0-375-41306-5; 0-375-71031-0 (pa)

LC 2001-50391

This volume features "healthful recipes and information on topics ranging from growing herbs to wine to the Mediterranean diet. Recipes contain nutrition information, but this is not 'diet food': recipes include Smoked Fish with Horseradish Sauce, Roasted Cornish Hens with Roasted Garlic, and Thai Shrimp and Papaya Salad." Libr J

This is "a stimulating invitation to healthy, pleasurable eating." Publ Wkly

Wells, Patricia

Patricia Wells' trattoria; simple and robust fare inspired by the small family restaurants of Italy. William Morrow 2003 338p il pa $18.95

641.5

1. Italian cooking

ISBN 978-0-06-093652-5

First published 1993

This "collection of informal, robust recipes, gathered from Italy's small family-run restaurants, should appeal to anyone who appreciates the unmasked flavors of high-quality fresh ingredients, simply but lovingly prepared. Wells's often lengthy headnotes are full of personal reminiscences but also paint a colorful picture of the country's relaxed, generous lifestyle. Wine suggestions follow each recipe, and there are sensible cooking tips throughout." Libr J

The Provence cookbook; 175 recipes and a select guide to the markets, shops, & restaurants of France's sunny south. HarperCollins 2004 338p il $29.95   641.5

1. French cooking

ISBN 978-0-06-050782-4; 0-06-050782-9

LC 2003-56977

Wells, Patricia—*Continued*

Wells offers "her own recipes, along with some from her butcher, fishmonger, other merchants, neighborhood restaurants, and other sources slightly farther afield. Most of the dishes are simple, allowing the flavors of Provence's wonderfully fresh produce and other ingredients to come through. . . . Wine suggestions are included throughout—sometimes for Wells's own label, since her vineyard is now productive—and she provides addresses and other relevant details about her favorite restaurants and purveyors." Libr J

Wolfert, Paula

The slow Mediterranean kitchen; recipes for the passionate cook. Wiley 2003 350p il $34.95

641.5

1. Mediterranean cooking
ISBN 0-471-26288-9   LC 2002-153265

The author offers "dishes from all the countries of the region: *brodetto Pasquale* (Italian Easter Lamb Soup), Expatriate Roast Chicken with Lemon and Olives from Morocco, and Catalonian Fall-Apart Lamb Shanks. Although many recipes call for braising, stewing, and other techniques of long cooking, others are not limited to those techniques, for Wolfert's definition of slow cooking also encompasses marinating and similar techniques." Libr J

Zanger, Mark H.

The American history cookbook. Greenwood Press 2003 xxiii, 459p il (Cookbooks for students) pa $29.95   641.5

1. Cooking
ISBN 1-57356-376-5   LC 2002-69608

"An Oryx book"

"This book uses historical commentary and recipes to trace the history of American cooking from the first European contact with Native Americans to the 1970s. Each of 50 chronologically arranged topical chapters contain 500-1,000 words of general commentary followed by descriptions and . . . step-by-step instructions for 3-4 recipes. The recipes are drawn from a wide variety of historical cookbooks and other historical sources." Publisher's note

Includes bibliographical references

641.6 Cooking specific materials

Aidells, Bruce

The complete meat cookbook; a juicy and authorative guide to selecting, seasoning, and cooking today's beef, pork, lamb, and veal; {by} Bruce Aidelle and Denis Kelly; photographs by Beatriz Da Costa; illustrations by Mary De Palma. Houghton Mifflin 1998 604p il $35   641.6

1. Cooking—Meat
ISBN 0-618-13512-X   LC 98-28216

"More than 230 recipes, many with several variations, are presented along with charts and illustrations to help the reader understand different types of meat." Libr J

The **best** chicken recipes; by the editors of Cook's illustrated; photography, Keller + Keller, Carl Tremblay, and Daniel J. Van Ackere; illustrations, John Burgoyne. America's Test Kitchen 2008 422p il $35   641.6

1. Cooking—Poultry
ISBN 978-1-933615-23-3; 1-933615-23-0

This volume "offers more than 300 recipes for chicken, along with a primer called 'Chicken 101,' information on techniques (including step-by-step illustrations), and ratings of equipment and ingredients." Libr J

Brody, Jane E.

Jane Brody's good seafood book; by Jane E. Brody with Richard Flaste; illustrations by Pat Stewart. Norton 1994 577p il $27.50 *

641.6

1. Cooking—Seafood 2. Seafood
ISBN 0-393-03687-1   LC 94-16482

Part One of this book is an "overview of seafood lore that includes chapters on how to select fish; how to clean, fillet, and store it. . . . Part Two is a collection of some 250 recipes for hors d'oeuvres and appetizers, soups, salads, and main courses, including special sections on grilling and microwaving." Publisher's note

"This is a more than usually comprehensive, conscientious and trustworthy cookbook." Publ Wkly

Cameron, Angus

The L.L. Bean game and fish cookbook; by Angus Cameron and Judith Jones; illustrations by Bill Elliott. Random House 1983 475p il $25.95

641.6

1. Cooking—Game 2. Cooking—Fish
ISBN 0-394-51191-3   LC 82-15089

This book "explains how to dress, hang, smoke, age and clean fish and game. It . . . covers field dressing of deer, moose, elk and bear. There are also directions for smoking, grilling, barbecuing, poaching, marinating and larding." N Y Times Book Rev

"With handsome wildlife and botanical drawings by Bill Elliott, the book was written by two experts and is complete and comprehensive." Christ Sci Monit

Corson, Trevor, 1969-

The zen of fish; the story of sushi, from Samurai to supermarket. HarperCollins Publishers 2007 372p $24.95   641.6

1. Cooking—Fish 2. Sushi
ISBN 978-0-06-088350-8; 0-06-088350-2
LC 2006-52964

"The book details sushi's origins as a means of preserving old fish, its transformation into a kind of Japanese fast food in the 19th century, and its journey to the U.S. in the mid-20th century. It provides rich details into the science behind everything from the process of making sushi rice to what makes salmon taste so good. It's also a character study of the chefs and chefs-in-training at the California Sushi Academy, the first culinary school in the country devoted solely to sushi. 'Zen' focuses on Kate Murray, a young apprentice learning the traditionally male-dominated trade from some tough teachers.

Corson, Trevor, 1969-—*Continued*
Readers learn the art of sushi right alongside Murray and her fellow students; it's a lot more than just raw fish and rice." Bangor Daily News
Includes bibliographical references

Desaulniers, Marcel
Celebrate with chocolate; totally over-the-top recipes; recipes with Ganache Hill test kitchen chef Brett Bailey; photographs by Ron Manville. Morrow 2002 175p il $24.95   **641.6**
  1. Cooking—Chocolate 2. Desserts
  ISBN 0-688-16298-3   LC 2002-71777
This cookbook features "recipes ranging from Dancing Gingerbread Men Peppermint Fudge Cake to Chocolate-Peanut Butter Fusion Brownies. Many of the recipes are complicated, but the instructions are detailed and clear, and there are mouth-watering color photographs of selected showstoppers. For all baking collections." Libr J
Includes bibliographical references

Issenberg, Sasha
The sushi economy; globalization and the making of a modern delicacy. Gotham 2007 xxiv, 323p $26   **641.6**
  1. Sushi 2. Cooking—Fish
  ISBN 978-1-59240-294-6; 1-59240-294-1
                LC 2007-3927
This "book reveals the complex web of commerce, culture, and culinary expertise that hauls fish from the sea, ships it around the world, and delivers it artfully to the plate. Sprinkled throughout with fascinating character studies of the many buyers, importers, sushi chefs, restaurateurs, critics, and diners who make the wheels turn, this work is solidly rooted in place—allowing one to tour four continents slowly. It makes enjoying sushi not only a delight for the palate but also a thought-provoking repast for the mind." Libr J
Includes bibliographical references

Kafka, Barbara
Vegetable love; a book for cooks; [by] Barbara Kafka with Christopher Styler; photographs by Christina Cornish. Artisan 2005 708p il $35
      641.6
  1. Cooking—Vegetables 2. Vegetables
  ISBN 1-57965-168-2   LC 2005-47818
"The first section contains 750 recipes arranged by vegetable origin, e.g., 'New World' and 'Mediterranean Basin.' . . . [Though the author's] emphasis is on vegetables, many of the recipes . . . call for meat, fowl, or fish." Libr J
The author "has triumphed with an outstanding, indispensable cookbook that not only summons the reader to get into the kitchen and cook but also constitutes a valuable and comprehensive reference tool." Booklist
Includes bibliographical references

Moonen, Rick
Fish without a doubt; the cook's essential companion; [by] Rick Moonen and Roy Finamore; photographs by Ben Fink. Houghton Mifflin Co. 2008 496p il $35   **641.6**
  1. Cooking—Seafood 2. Cooking—Fish
  ISBN 978-0-618-53119-6; 0-618-53119-X
                LC 2007-52084
In this cookbook that covers the preparing of sustainable fish, the authors "show how to clean, bone, and portion both finfish and shellfish. Recipes are organized by cooking method—broiling, poaching, roasting, grilling, steaming, [and] frying. . . . Succeeding chapters cover such fish basics as chowders, fish cakes, and salads. . . . Both the book's organization and its comprehensive coverage make this a necessary addition to any cookbook collections." Booklist

Schlesinger, Chris
How to cook meat; [by]Chris Schlesinger and John Willoughby. Morrow 2000 466p il pa $24.95 hardcover o.p.   **641.6**
  1. Cooking—Meat
  ISBN 0-06-050771-3 (pa)   LC 00-62482
This cookbook includes 200 recipes for beef, veal, lamb and pork dishes. "Most every recipe is accompanied by useful sidebars that detail the cut of meat to use, offer alternative cuts and even tell you how the dish holds up as a leftover. With humor, clarity and expertise, these two renowned food writers have created a requisite text for any serious meat lover." Publ Wkly

Schneider, Elizabeth, 1943-
Vegetables from amaranth to zucchini; the essential reference: 500 recipes and 275 photographs; photographs by Amos Chan. Morrow 2001 xxiv, 777p il $60 *   **641.6**
  1. Cooking—Vegetables 2. Vegetables
  ISBN 0-688-15260-0   LC 2001-30423
This is a reference to more than 350 vegetables with information on availability, selection, storage, preparation, use, and recipes
"Schneider treats each vegetable with poetic directness, consulting authorities from around the world. . . . {This is a} landmark volume, a tribute to one writer's passion and patience." N Y Times Book Rev
Includes bibliographical references

Vegetables; recipes and techniques from the world's premier culinary college; the Culinary Institute of America; photography by Ben Fink. Lebhar-Friedman Books 2007 293p il $40
      641.6
  1. Cooking—Vegetables
  ISBN 978-0-86730-918-8; 0-8673-0918-0
                LC 2007-298057
At head of title: The Culinary Institute of America
Includes "over 150 recipes for soups, appetizers, salads, entrees, side dishes, and a chapter devoted to sauces and relishes made from vegetables or perfect to serve with vegetables. Accompanied by 75 full-color photos." Publisher's note

Waters, Alice

Chez Panisse vegetables; [by] Alice Waters and the cooks of Chez Panisse; illustrations by Patricia Curtan. HarperCollins Pubs. 1996 344p il $35

641.6

1. Chez Panisse (Berkeley, Calif.: Restaurant)
2. Cooking—Vegetables
ISBN 0-06-017147-2   LC 96-11305

The author "includes more than 40 vegetables in this beautifully illustrated book, describing them and how to prepare them in detail and offering more than 250 recipes. . . . An invaluable resource." Libr J

Includes bibliographical references

Wells, Patricia

Vegetable harvest; vegetables at the center of the plate. William Morrow 2007 324p il $34.95

641.6

1. Cooking—Vegetables
ISBN 978-0-06-075244-6; 0-06-075244-0
LC 2006-43723

"After surveying the bounty of her backyard garden, Wells became inspired to build meals around vegetables rather than starting with meat, fish or poultry. She tripled the number she served at each meal and tried different cooking methods, looking for the best-tasting, most wholesome ways of cooking each type. She includes nutritional information and an equipment list for each recipe, and selectively offers wine suggestions, translations of French food idioms, and nuggets of folklore connected to the dish or main ingredient. . . . This collection is highly recommended for cooks and gardeners alike." Publ Wkly

Werlin, Laura

Laura Werlin's cheese essentials; an insider's guide to buying and serving cheese: with 50 recipes; photographs by Maren Caruso. Stewart, Tabori & Chang 2007 272p il $24.95

641.6

1. Cheese
ISBN 978-1-58479-627-5   LC 2007-15459

This is an "introduction to cheese—tasting it, buying it, storing it, and cooking with it. An introductory section describes the basics of cheese making, offers empowering tips for navigating the cheese counter, and lists the basic vocabulary for cheese tasting. The majority of the volume is divided into sections for each of the eight styles of cheese, from mild, fresh cheeses to strong-flavored washed-rind varieties. . . . This well-organized, stylish, timely, and indispensable guide belongs in every cook's library." Booklist

Wright, Clifford A., 1951-

Some like it hot; spicy favorites from the world's hot zones. Harvard Common Press 2005 xxv, 453p $32.95; pa $18.95   **641.6**

1. Cooking 2. Spices
ISBN 1-55832-268-X; 1-55832-269-8 (pa)
LC 2005-4953

The author's "assembly of recipes calling for hot peppers originates from tropical countries, but there are

some exceptions to that rule. He inventories Oaxacan mole, Korean kimchi, Thai curries, Louisiana gumbo, Jamaican jerk, Texan chili con carne, African piripiri, and Bengali fish stew. . . . Devotees of spicy cooking will enjoy every fiery mouthful." Booklist

641.7 Specific cooking processes and techniques

Schlesinger, Chris

The thrill of the grill; techniques, recipes & down-home barbecue; [by] Chris Schlesinger & John Willoughby, line drawings by Laura Hartman Maestro; photography by Vincent Lee. Morrow 1990 395p il $30; pa $17.95   **641.7**

1. Barbecue cooking
ISBN 0-688-08832-5; 0-06-008449-9 (pa)
LC 89-77522

The authors present a collection of recipes as well as advice about grilling and barbecuing food

Schlesinger "favors what he calls 'equatorial cuisine,' and Caribbean, Mexican, and Southeast Asian influences are evident in his recipes. His grilled dishes are full-flavored and often hot and spicy." Libr J

641.8 Cooking specific kinds of dishes, preparing beverages

The **America's** test kitchen family baking book; [by] the editors at America's Test Kitchen; photography, Daniel J. Van Ackere, Carl Tremblay, Keller + Keller. America's Test Kitchen 2008 544p il $34.95   **641.8**

1. America's test kitchen (Television program)
2. Baking
ISBN 978-1-933615-22-6; 1-933615-22-2

This "book includes more than 700 recipes and 1000 color photographs. The recipes encompass both traditional favorites and more contemporary treats, and there are separate chapters on light baking and 'shortcut baking' (using packaged mixes), as well as one devoted to how to make a wedding cake." Libr J

"Expert bakers and novices scared of baking's requisite exactitude can all learn something from this hefty, all-purpose home baking volume." Publ Wkly

Andrés, José

Tapas; a taste of Spain in America; [by] José Andrés with Richard Wolffe. Clarkson Potter 2005 256p il $35   **641.8**

1. Spanish cooking 2. Appetizers
ISBN 1-4000-5359-5   LC 2004-27466

The author presents some of the small-plate dishes "he serves at his tapas restaurants, including traditional favorites recreated with American ingredients. . . . Recipes are organized by ingredient, from olives and olive oil to citrus to fish, shellfish, and meat, and they are mouthwatering: Oven-Roasted Potatoes and Oyster Mushrooms, for example, or Lobster with Pimentón and Olive Oil." Libr J

Includes bibliographical references

Baking illustrated; a best recipe classic; by the editors of Cook's illustrated; illustrations, John Burgoyne; photography, Carl Tremblay, Keller + Keller, Daniel Van Ackere. America's Test Kitchen 2004 515p il $35 *   **641.8**
1. Baking
ISBN 0-936184-75-2
"Test kitchen cooks analyzed brand-name baking ingredients and equipment and . . . make 'best buy' recommendations. . . . The test summaries preceding each recipe include both successes and failures; the resulting recipes (more than 350) cover everything from the simplest quick breads to more complex yeast breads and cookies and pastries. . . . This is the best instructional book on baking this reviewer has seen." Libr J

Beard, James, 1903-1985
Beard on bread; drawings by Karl Stuecklen. Knopf 1973 230p il pa $15 hardcover o.p.
    641.8
1. Bread
ISBN 0-679-75504-7 (pa)
"An inclusive guide to the preparation of a variety of breads with recipes for coffee cakes, rolls, flat breads, fried cakes. . . . The recipes included are those Beard considers the best from around the world which can be made in a U.S. kitchen." Booklist

Beranbaum, Rose Levy
The cake bible; edited by Maria D. Guarnaschelli; photographs by Vincent Lee; foreword by Maida Heatter. Morrow 1988 555p il $35   **641.8**
1. Cake
ISBN 978-0-688-04402-2; 0-688-04402-6
    LC 88-1369
A collection of recipes for classic cakes, buttercreams, icings, fillings and toppings. Ingredients are listed in tabular form with weights given in both ounces and grams. Assembly and storage instructions are included
Includes bibliographical references

Child, Julia
Baking with Julia; based on the PBS series hosted by Julia Child; written by Dorie Greenspan; photographs by Gentl & Hyers. Morrow 1996 480p il $40   **641.8**
1. Baking
ISBN 0-688-14657-0   LC 96-23061
"The 200 recipes are organized as a course in baking, with an early, energetic section on the basic batters and doughs for cakes and pastries. The book moves on to recipes of varying degrees of complexity. . . . But the book's success is due to more than organization: the text never misses a chance to explain, expand and entertain." N Y Times Book Rev
Includes bibliographical references

The **Complete** book of pasta and noodles; by the editors of Cook's illustrated; preface by Christopher Kimball; illustrations by Judy Love; photographs by Daniel J. van Ackere. Potter 2000 483p il pa $19.95 hardcover o.p.
    641.8
1. Cooking—Pasta products
ISBN 0-609-80930-X (pa)   LC 99-40076
This work brings "together information and recipes covering pasta's worldwide range from North America's beloved macaroni and cheese through Italy's sophisticated sauces, across China's exotic rice noodles, and up to Japan's modest Zen noodles in broth. . . . Content and organization combine to make this a superior cooking reference book for libraries." Booklist

Corriher, Shirley
BakeWise; the hows and whys of successful baking with over 200 magnificent recipes; [by] Shirley O. Corriher. Scribner 2008 532p $40
    641.8
1. Baking
ISBN 978-1-4165-6078-4; 1-4165-6078-5
    LC 2008-32681
This "collection of more than 200 recipes offers amateur and expert bakers alike clear, numbered steps and a plethora of information on ingredients, equipment and method. Invaluable troubleshooting sections solve pesky problems on everything from pale and crumbly cookies to fallen soufflés. . . . Astute references to a variety of chefs, cookbook authors and restaurants add a knowing punch to this solid collection that's sure to please bakers of all skill levels." Publ Wkly

Crocker, Betty
Betty Crocker cookie book. rev ed. Wiley 2003 xxix, 322p il $22.95 *   **641.8**
ISBN 0-7645-3940-X   LC 2003-270127
First published 1963 by Golden Press with title: Cooky book
This book features "over 240 cookie favorites, from heirloom showstoppers to contemporary treats . . . {including} everything from chocolate chip cookies to brownies, oatmeal cookies to date bars and more." Publisher's note

Desaulniers, Marcel
Death by chocolate cakes; an astonishing array of chocolate enchantment; recipes with Brett Bailey and Kelly Bailey; photography by Duane Winfield. Morrow 2000 216p il $35
    641.8
1. Cake 2. Cooking—Chocolate
ISBN 0-688-16297-5   LC 00-56247
This "cookbook features indulgent showstoppers, from Happy All the Time Cakes to Excessively Expressive Espresso Ecstasy, each one shown in a full-page color photograph. Although many of the recipes are complicated, instructions are detailed and clear; there are no headnotes per se to introduce these creations, but 'The Chef's Touch' section at the end of each recipe provides tips and some background." Libr J
Includes bibliographical references

Farmer, Fannie Merritt, 1857-1915

The Fannie Farmer baking book; illustrated by Lauren Jarrett. Knopf 1984 624p il pa $12.99 hardcover o.p.   **641.8**

1. Baking

ISBN 0-517-14829-3   LC 84-47862

"Separate chapters cover pies and tarts, cookies, cakes, yeast breads, quick breads, and crackers in encyclopedic detail with brisk but reassuring professionalism. Many of the 800 recipes are standard favorites." Libr J

Fowler, Damon Lee

Damon Lee Fowler's new southern baking; classic flavors for today's cook; photographs by Ann Stratton. Simon & Schuster 2005 360p il $26   **641.8**

1. Southern cooking 2. Baking

ISBN 0-7432-5058-3   LC 2005-51591

The author presents an "overview of Southern baking from historical, cultural and social perspectives. . . . Damon traces the influences of Southern mamas; African-American domestic workers and cooks; English, German and French settlers; and Native Americans in his introduction, while his chapter openers delve deeper into specifics, distinguishing between, say, soft winter wheat and red summer wheat and the different flours derived from them. . . . This cookbook is a treat, equally satisfying to cook from or to read." Publ Wkly

Includes bibliographical references

Haedrich, Ken, 1954-

Pie: 300 tried-and-true recipes for delicious homemade pie. The Harvard Common Press 2004 639p il $37.95; pa $24.95 *   **641.8**

1. Baking

ISBN 1-558-32253-1; 1-558-32254-X (pa)

     LC 2004-3635

This book "features 25 new recipes for . . . {apple pie} alone, along with dozens for summer fruit and berry pies, pecan and other nut pies, 'personal pies,' and icebox and freezer pies." Libr J

Haedrich's "zeal and solid expertise make this book a worthy addition to the baker's bookshelf." Publ Wkly

Heatter, Maida

Maida Heatter's book of great desserts; drawings by Toni Evins. Andrew McMeel 1999 xxxii, 528p il $26.95   **641.8**

1. Desserts

ISBN 0-8362-7861-5   LC 98-45993

First published 1974 by Knopf

This cookbook features nearly 300 dessert recipes for both light and rich desserts including Queen Mother's Cake, Mushroom Meringues, and East 62nd Street Lemon Cake

Maida Heatter's brand-new book of great cookies; illustrations by the author. Random House 1995 244p il pa $19 hardcover o.p.   **641.8**

1. Cookies

ISBN 0-8129-9175-3 (pa)   LC 95-5250

First published 1977 with title: Book of great cookies

This volume contains "recipes for biscotti, drop cookies, icebox cookies, bar cookies, zwieback, . . . crackers, and some desserts." Libr J

"The instructions here are true to a long line of Heatter recipes: foolproof. Ms. Heatter's instructions are famously meticulous. They are also lengthy and chatty, full of learned asides." N Y Times Book Rev

Hensperger, Beth

The best quick breads; 150 recipes for muffins, scones, shortcakes, gingerbreads, cornbreads, coffeecakes, and more; Beth Hensperger. Harvard Common Press; distributed by National Bk. Network 2000 256p pa $22.95   **641.8**

1. Bread

ISBN 1-55832-171-3   LC 00-36962

First published 1994 by Chronicle Books with title: The art of quick breads

Orig. pub. under title: The art of quick breads. San Francisco : Chronicle Books, 1994

This book includes about 150 recipes. "In addition to quick loaves, both sweet and savory, there are waffles, dumplings, biscuits, popovers, and a variety of other easy baked goods, along with some tasty accompaniments, such as the Fruit Salsa for her Hopi Blue Corn Hotcakes." Libr J

Patent, Greg, 1939-

Baking in America; traditional and contemporary favorites from the past 200 years. Houghton Mifflin 2002 552p il $35   **641.8**

1. Baking

ISBN 0-618-04831-6

In this "collection of baking recipes, Patent . . . takes classics from old American cookbooks and makes them work with modern-day ingredients, encompassing all aspects of baking from Savory Yeast Breads through Pound Cakes to Pies and Tarts. After explaining the ingredients and equipment, he moves on to the recipes, which include timeless treasures of America's baking tradition such as Parker House Rolls, Lindy's Cheesecake and Lady Baltimore Cake." Publ Wkly

"Patent's cookbook will be irresistible to anyone interested in the rich traditions and history of American baking." Libr J

Peters, Colette

Colette's cakes; the art of cake decorating. Little, Brown 1991 163p il $35   **641.8**

1. Cake decorating

ISBN 0-316-70205-6   LC 90-24676

"This is not intended as a cookbook, although recipes for a white as well as a chocolate cake precede instructions for basic cake decorating. The bulk of the guide contains step-by-step directions for assembling four fabulous cake designs that range from an impressive seashell cake to multitiered wedding cakes." Booklist

Includes bibliographical references

Pillsbury best cookies cookbook; favorite recipes from America's most-trusted kitchens; [by] the Pillsbury Company. Wiley Pub 2003 255p il $22.95 *   **641.8**

Pillsbury best cookies cookbook—*Continued*

1. Cookies

ISBN 0-7645-8854-0; 978-0-7645-8854-9

First published 1997 by Potter

This "cookbook includes more than 175 recipes for cookies, brownies, and other bars, from old favorites like Chocolate Chips to new ones like Cherry Poppy Seed Twinks. . . . There are also lots of tips and hints, suggestions to 'Make It Special,' and variations, as well as 'real-time' prep times and nutrition analyses for each recipe." Libr J [review of 1997 edition]

Tornabene, Wanda

100 ways to be pasta; perfect pasta recipes from Gangivecchio; [by] Wanda and Giovanna Tornabene with Carolynn Carreño. Knopf 2005 182p il $24.95   **641.8**

1. Cooking—Pasta products

ISBN 1-400-04104-X   LC 2004-48522

The authors "focus on both traditional and contemporary Sicilian ways of dealing with pasta. . . . Cooks everywhere will find inspiring ideas here to feed both families and guests." Booklist

Vollstedt, Maryana

The big book of soups & stews; 262 recipes for serious comfort food. Chronicle Bks. 2001 334p pa $19.95   **641.8**

1. Soups 2. Stews

ISBN 0-8118-3056-X   LC 2001-28034

These recipes range "from a hearty Beef and Chile Stew with Cornmeal Dumplings to a more sophisticated Shrimp and Scallop Chowder; there are many kid-friendly recipes as well, including several hamburger soups. Some of the recipes are staples (such as a classic Irish Stew), but many busy cooks will find it handy to have such favorites gathered in one place." Libr J

Walter, Carole

Great pies & tarts; over 150 recipes to bake, share, and enjoy; foreword by Arthur Schwartz. Gramercy Books 2006 512p $12.99   **641.8**

1. Baking

ISBN 978-0-517-22807-4; 0-517-22807-6

LC 2006-41104

First published 1998 by Clarkson Potter

"Walter begins with an extensive inventorying and analysis of the ingredients that make up today's pies, from crusts' shortening and flour to the various fruits (and vegetables) that fill them. Detailed instructions for preparing piecrust, that touchstone of home kitchen expertise, follow. . . . A glossary, a listing of mail-order sources, and a comprehensive bibliography ensure that no pie-related topic goes unaddressed." Booklist

Includes bibliographical references

642   Meals and table service

Stewart, Martha

Great parties; recipes, menus, and ideas for perfect gatherings: the best of Martha Stewart living. Potter 1997 144p il pa $20   **642**

1. Entertaining

ISBN 0-609-80099-X   LC 97-30271

This describes such parties as a Louisiana lunch, a Polynesian fantasy picnic, an East Hampton garden harvest party, a Vietnamese-Thai feast, and a Harlem soul food brunch, including menus, recipes, and table decorations

Martha Stewart's menus for entertaining; photographs by Dana Gallagher; design by Robert Valentine Incorporated. Potter 1994 224p il $30; pa $20 *   **642**

1. Cooking 2. Entertaining 3. Menus

ISBN 0-517-59099-9; 1-4000-4660-2 (pa)

LC 94-12930

Full-color photographs accompany step-by-step instructions for preparing 20 complete menus for a variety of gatherings. Over 150 recipes are included as well as tips on table settings and flower arrangements

643   Housing and household equipment

Becker, Norman

The complete book of home inspection. 3rd ed. McGraw-Hill 2002 289p il pa $19.95   **643**

1. Houses—Inspection

ISBN 0-07-139125-8   LC 2002-27892

First published 1980

The author "provides the novice homebuilder and buyer with inspection information for roofs, exterior landscaping, plumbing, and electrical, as well as tips on searching for insects and rotting materials. Helpful checklists guide readers in inspecting all parts of a home from the exterior walkway to the interior basement." Libr J

Better Homes and Gardens new complete guide to home repair & improvement. 2nd ed. Meredith Corp. 1997 600p il pa $24.95 hardcover o.p.   **643**

1. Houses—Maintenance and repair

ISBN 0-696-21189-0 (pa)   LC 97-71323

First published 1980 with title: Better homes and gardens complete guide to home repair, maintenance and improvement

This manual "includes 500 projects and more than 3,000 full-color illustrations. Organized in four large sections that cover basics as well as a homes' inside, outside, and systems. Projects list skills, time, and tools necessary for completion." Publisher's note

"This all-in-one, do-it-yourself guide offers exceptionally good tool coverage—an entire 60-pages are devoted to tools and their use, including uncommon information such as threading with taps and dies." Libr J

Bouknight, Joanne Kellar

The kitchen idea book. Taunton Press 1999
201p il $29.95; pa $24.95   **643**
1. Kitchens
ISBN 1-56158-161-5; 1-56158-393-6 (pa)
LC 98-41873
The author covers "cabinets, shelves, countertops, appliances, flooring, and light. Information on the choices with the advantages and disadvantages of each is provided. What makes this book especially useful are the numerous photographs that illustrate how all these materials have been used in actual kitchens." Libr J
Includes bibliographical references

Bray, Ilona M., 1962-

Nolo's essential guide to buying your first home; by Ilona Bray, Alayna Schroeder, & Marcia Stewart. Nolo 2007 380p il pa $24.99 *
643
1. Houses—Buying and selling
ISBN 978-1-4133-0628-6; 1-4133-0628-4
LC 2006-34216
Includes CD-ROM
This guide to buying a home features "chapter outlines highlighting key topics in each section, as well as the personal anecdotes and tips from real estate experts. . . . Packaged with a CD-ROM that includes essential forms (e.g., a Final Walk-Through Checklist, a sample inspection report, and a Questions for the Sellers Worksheet) and MP3-formatted audio files of extended insight from the real estate experts, this is highly recommended for most public libraries." Libr J

Complete do-it-yourself manual; with the editors of Family handyman. rev and updated. Reader's Digest 2005 528p il $35 *   **643**
1. Houses—Maintenance and repair
ISBN 0-7621-0579-8   LC 2004-50945
Replaces the 1991 edition with title: New complete do-it-yourself manual
First published 1973 with title: Reader's Digest complete do-it-yourself manual
At head of title: Reader's Digest
This manual for homeowners covers topics such as power tools, plumbing, landscaping, and storage projects with photos, diagrams and illustrations
"Intriguing sidebars on wood refinishers (the fastest drying versus the safest), the financial benefits of renting specialty tools for a large drywall project and other subjects round out this must-have guide." Publ Wkly

Fields, Alan

Your new house; the alert consumer's guide to buying and building a quality home; [by] Alan & Denise Fields. 4th ed. Windsor Peak Press 2002 356p il pa $15.95   **643**
1. Houses—Buying and selling 2. Mortgages
ISBN 978-1-88939-211-0; 1-88939-211-1
First published 1993. Periodically revised
This "volume addresses working with real estate agents, planning a budget, designing a home, assembling a building team, and understanding home inspections." Libr J
Includes bibliographical references

Home improvement 1-2-3. 2nd ed {New ed. completely rev. and expanded}. Meredith Bks. 2003 560p il $34.95 *   **643**
1. Houses—Maintenance and repair 2. Houses—Remodeling 3. Interior design
ISBN 0-696-21327-3   LC 2002-109107
First published 1995
"Easy step-by-step instructions; expert advice from the Home Depot." Cover
This offers illustrated instructions for home remodeling, decorating, and repair
"This well-illustrated all-in-one guide . . . is great for novices: it tells the skill level for each task and how long it should take. Boxes in the text indicate helpful hints, required tools, and how to avoid common problems." Libr J {review of 1995 edition}

Jackson, Albert, 1943-

Popular mechanics complete home how-to; [by] Albert Jackson and David Day. Hearst Books 2004 514p il $24.95   **643**
1. Houses—Maintenance and repair
ISBN 1-58816-302-4   LC 2003-56853
"Interior and exterior repairs are included, from simple tasks like replacing an electrical switch to difficult ones like constructing a wall or building a pond, as well as common upgrades. Everything is explained in detail, with a wealth of clear photos and illustrations. A section on skills and tools shows the use of woodworking, building, decorating, plumbing, and electrical equipment, and a reference section describes hardware/materials and defines commonly used terminology. A great general guide to home repairs of all types, this book will see heavy use in most collections." Libr J

Litchfield, Michael W.

Renovation; [by] Michael Litchfield; Chip Harley, technical editor. 3rd ed, completely rev and updated. Taunton Press 2005 534p il $39.95
643
1. Houses—Remodeling
ISBN 978-1-5615-8588-5; 1-5615-8588-2
LC 2005-110
First published 1982 by Wiley
This "guide covers all aspects of home renovation, including how to assess a house's structure, tools, materials, wiring, plumbing, painting, flooring, etc. Instructions are to the point—there is less hand-holding here than in other titles because some remodeling experience is assumed. A classic." Libr J

Nagyszalanczy, Sandor

The homeowner's ultimate tool guide; choosing the right tool for every home improvement job. Taunton Press 2003 282p il pa $19.95
643
1. Tools 2. Houses—Remodeling 3. Houses—Maintenance and repair
ISBN 1-561-58582-3   LC 2003-5648
"The tools are organized by function (e.g., 'Tools That Saw,' 'Tools That Pound and Pry'), including both hand and electric models, with information on which tool will

Nagyszalanczy, Sandor—*Continued*
work best in every situation." Libr J

"Large, detailed color photos accompany each clearly explained entry. . . . With a 'pros and cons' explanation for each tool, as well as 'pro tip' boxes, this book is essential for any homeowner wanting to make the most of his or her toolbox." Publ Wkly

New fix-it-yourself manual. Reader's Digest Assn. 1996 448p il $35　　　　　**643**
1. Repairing 2. Household equipment and supplies—Maintenance and repair
ISBN 0-89577-871-8　　　　　LC 96-15189
First published 1977 with title: Reader's Digest fix-it-yourself manual
This illustrated book offers instructions for repairing, buying, cleaning and maintaining a wide variety of household items including appliances, furniture, plumbing fixtures, air conditioners, electronic and sports equipment

Papolos, Janice
The virgin homeowner; the essential guide to owning, maintaining, and surviving your first home. Norton 1997 444p il pa $24.95
　　　　　643
1. Houses
ISBN 0-393-04035-6; 978-0-393-33496-8 (pa); 0-393-33496-1 (pa)　　　　　LC 96-31304
Also available in paperback from Penguin Bks.

"Beginning with how to get the most out of the initial home inspection, Papolos takes the reader through a house, describing each system, its quirks, and its potential problems. Later, she covers pest control, security, and safety. This highly readable book will prove useful to both new homeowners and those just thinking of making a purchase, and veteran homeowners will undoubtedly learn something, too." Libr J
Includes bibliographical references

Sussman, Julie
Dare to repair; a do-it-herself guide to fixing (almost) anything in the home; {by} Julie Sussman and Stephanie Glakas-Tenet; illustrations by Yeorgos Lampathakis. HarperCollins Pubs. 2002 253p il pa $14.95 *　　　　　**643**
1. Houses—Maintenance and repair
ISBN 0-06-095984-3　　　　　LC 2002-27625
The authors "show women how to perform a number of the most common repairs, including unclogging drains and toilets, replacing electrical switches and outlets, leveling appliances, lighting pilot lights, unsticking windows, and installing a door peephole. . . . This is a wonderful book that should be purchased by every public library." Libr J

Vila, Bob
Bob Vila's complete guide to remodeling your home; everything you need to know about home renovation from the #1 home improvement expert; by Bob Vila and Hugh Howard; principal photography by Michael Fredericks; line drawings by Nancy Hull. Avon Bks. 1999 335p il pa $23.95 hardcover o.p.　　　　　**643**
1. Houses—Remodeling
ISBN 0-380-79955-3 (pa)　　　　　LC 99-25410
In this book, Vila "details the remodeling of his own family dwelling, explaining his choices along the way. In nine chapters, he details house examination, planning, and implementation. His prose is lively, encouraging, and well written." Libr J

Wing, Charlie, 1939-
The big book of small household repairs; your goof-proof guide to fixing over 200 annoying breakdowns. Rodale Press 1995 308p il pa $15.95 hardcover o.p.　　　　　**643**
1. Houses—Maintenance and repair 2. Household equipment and supplies—Maintenance and repair
ISBN 0-7621-0162-8 (pa)　　　　　LC 95-7408
Illustrations accompany step-by-step instructions for 243 home repair projects that are considered 'too small' to involve professionals. Lists of recommended tools and materials are provided for each job

How your house works; a visual guide to understanding & maintaining your home. RSMeans 2007 152p il pa $21.95　　　　　**643**
1. Houses—Maintenance and repair
ISBN 978-0-87629-015-6; 0-87629-015-2
This book "teaches the basics of home systems and appliances. Providing clean and detailed diagrams, Wing describes the purpose and function of that system or fixture. Also accompanying each is a list of tips to use before you call in a professional. This book is more a 'how' than a 'how-to' and fills its role quite nicely." Libr J

645　Household furnishings

Cone, Steve, 1948-
Singer upholstery basics plus; complete step-by-step photo guide. Creative Pub. International 2007 155p il pa $19.95　　　　　**645**
1. Upholstery
ISBN 978-1-58923-329-4; 1-58923-329-8
　　　　　LC 2007-7252
First published 1997 with title: Upholstery basics
"Projects include all styles of chairs or couches, stools, different styles of ottomans, a bench, and a headboard. Some projects are built-from-scratch items that require only simple carpentry skills for building the frames. Others show the complete process of stripping, repairing, and reupholstering old furniture pieces to like-new condition." Publisher's note
"If there ever was an upholstery bible, this is it." Libr J

Engelbreit, Mary

Mary Engelbreit's children's companion; the Mary Engelbreit look and how to get it; illustrations by Mary Engelbreit; written by Charlotte Lyons; photographs by Barbara Elliott Martin. Andrews & McMeel 1997 144p il $24.95

645

1. Interior design 2. Handicraft

ISBN 0-8362-3675-0   LC 97-7261

This book offers ideas for designing and decorating children's rooms, parties, and backyard and garden play areas

646.2   Sewing and related operations

Bednar, Nancy

The encyclopedia of sewing machine techniques; [by] Nancy Bednar, JoAnn Pugh-Gannon. Sterling Pub. 2007 336p il pa $24.95   **646.2**

1. Sewing

ISBN 1-4027-4293-2; 978-1-4027-4293-4

First published 1999

Among the techniques covered in this illustrated step-by-step guide are beading, fringing, pintucks, and puffing.

Betzina, Sandra

Fabric savvy; essential advice for every sewer. Taunton Press 1999 203p il $24.95; pa $17.95

646.2

1. Fabrics 2. Dressmaking

ISBN 1-56158-267-0; 1-56158-573-4 (pa)

LC 98-44107

"A guidebook to 85 different fabrics available to the home sewer, from African mudcloth to wool melton. Each fabric is given a two-page spread that includes information on recommended thread and needles, stitch length, presser foot, finishing, seams, marking, interfacing, cutting, types of hems, topstitching, and closures as well as basic information about the fabric and the types of garments for which it is suitable." Libr J

Sandra Betzina sews for your home; [by] Sandra Betzina and Debbie Valentine. Taunton Press 2002 202p il $29.95   **646.2**

1. Sewing

ISBN 1-56158-446-0   LC 2002-3395

The authors offer ideas and instructions for "sewing accessories for the home. In addition to complete, richly illustrated instructions for dozens of pillows, window treatments, table coverings, bed linens, and gifts for children and pets, there are solid sewing instructions that the reader can use in myriad future sewing projects." Libr J

Colgrove, Debbie

Teach yourself visually sewing. Wiley 2006 283p il (Visual read less, learn more) pa $24.99

646.2

1. Sewing

ISBN 0-471-74991-5; 978-0-471-74991-2

LC 2005-939196

This visual guide explains the "basics of hand sewing and sewing with a machine. . . . [It includes] information about tools and fabrics." Publisher's note

The **complete** book of sewing. Rev ed. DK Pub. 2003 320p il $40   **646.2**

1. Sewing 2. Dressmaking

ISBN 0-7894-9658-5   LC 2002-41761

First published 1996

Subtitle on cover: A practical step-by-step guide to every technique

This "sewing guide provides a detailed reference for both novices and experts. . . . Chapters explain how to pick and use patterns; select fabrics and notions; sew basic stitches and seams; attach interfacings and interlinings; form darts, tucks, pleats, and gathers; sew necklines, collars, waistlines, sleeves, and cuffs; hem; and add edges, fastenings, and pockets." SLJ [review of 1996 edition]

The **complete** photo guide to window treatments; do-it-yourself draperies, curtains, valances, swags, and shades; edited by Linda Neubauer. Creative Pub. International 2007 304p il pa $24.95   **646.2**

1. Draperies

ISBN 978-1-58923-294-5; 1-58923-294-1

LC 2006-34243

This book features "instructions for 50 projects, including valances, swags, cornices, draperies, and shades. Skills taught include measuring the window, cutting the fabric, sewing, and installing. More than 500 photos and diagrams." Publisher's note

James, Chris

The complete serger handbook. Sterling 1997 159p il pa $17.95 hardcover o.p.   **646.2**

1. Sewing 2. Sewing machines

ISBN 0-8069-9807-5 (pa)   LC 96-39316

"A Sterling/Sewing Information Resources book"

This "is a concise guide to the serger and serger techniques. Major sections of the book include identifying the parts of a serger (with photos of each part), serger accessories, types of threads, threading and testing the threading, learning to regulate tension, and techniques." Libr J

Lee, Linda, 1948-

Sewing edges and corners. Taunton Press 2000 134p il pa $19.95   **646.2**

1. Sewing

ISBN 1-56158-418-5   LC 00-29919

"An embellishment idea book"

The author offers about 40 corner and edge techniques for garments and home decorating projects

"Readers appreciate the clarity of Lee's instructions, since each step is numbered, photographs and other illustrations ease difficult tasks, and sidebars ensure the comfortableness of the sewing." Booklist

New complete guide to sewing; step-by-step techniques for making clothes and home accessories; from the editors at Reader's digest. Reader's Digest Assn. 2002 384p il $35

646.2

1. Sewing
ISBN 0-7621-0420-1   LC 2002-69944
First published 1976 with title: Complete guide to sewing

This illustrated guide begins with an overview of basic equipment and techniques. A discussion of patterns and fabrics is included. The bulk of the book provides step-by-step instructions for making clothes and home furnishings.

Step-by-step sewing course; essential techniques for making over 150 creative home projects. Reader's Digest 2006 208p il $26.95

646.2

1. Sewing
ISBN 0-7621-0630-1   LC 2005-44331
"The more than 150 projects . . . stick closely to mass market when it comes to project type and design. Expect a variety of different shades and curtains (even paint-it-yourself plastic for the shower), pillows, and furniture covers. Projects and techniques have been divided into beginner, intermediate, and more experienced categories, making any reader's selection far easier to digest." Booklist

646.4   Clothing and accessories construction

Armstrong, Helen Joseph
Patternmaking for fashion design; technical illustrator, Vincent James Maruzzi; fashion illustrator, Kathryn Hagen. 4th ed. Pearson Prentice Hall 2006 xxi, 805p il $104.40

646.4

1. Dressmaking—Patterns
ISBN 978-0-13-194893-9; 0-13-194893-8
                                LC 2005-283500
First published 1987 by Harper & Row
Includes DVD
"Covers the three steps in the development of design patterns—dart manipulation, added fullness, and contouring—with a central theme that all designs are based on one, or more of these three major patternmaking and design principles." Publisher's note
Includes bibliographical references

Betzina, Sandra
Power sewing step-by-step. Taunton Press 2000 231p il $34.95; pa $24.95   **646.4**
1. Sewing 2. Dressmaking
ISBN 1-56158-363-4; 1-56158-572-6 (pa)
                                LC 00-23431
"Vests, pants, shirts, dresses, and jackets for women are the focus of this book, with Betzina guiding the reader step by step through her thinking process in planning, constructing, fitting, customizing, and finishing each type

of garments. More than 500 color photos illustrate many tricks of the trade, shortcuts, and tips. This will be a core title in any sewing collection." Libr J

646.7   Management of personal and family life

Begoun, Paula, 1953-
Don't go to the cosmetics counter without me; a unique guide to thousands of skin-care and cosmetic products, plus the latest research on keeping skin beautiful at every age; [by] Paula Begoun with Bryan Barron. 7th ed. Beginning Press 2008 1167p pa $29.95 *   **646.7**
1. Cosmetics 2. Consumer education 3. Skin—Care
ISBN 1-877988-32-4; 978-1-877988-32-5
First published 1992
The authors review "thousands of products from cleansers and moisturizers through foundations, lip and eye colors, blushers, and mascaras while inspecting their ingredients. Arranging the book by product type, she notes possible irritants, carcinogens, companies against animal testing, and products that make unsubstantiated claims. Separates the hype from the reality." Libr J [review of 2003 edition]

Berg, Rona
Beauty: the new basics; illustrations by Anja Kroencke; photography by Deborah Jaffe. Workman 2001 404p il pa $19.95   **646.7**
1. Personal appearance
ISBN 0-7611-0186-1   LC 00-43631
The author discusses "hair and skin care, bath and body, aging, skin cancer, makeup, home spa treatments, aromatherapy, and cosmetic surgery. She includes a directory of day and destination spas and recommended salons. Amusing time lines give thumbnail histories of style and popular products. Essential for small collections in particular." Libr J

Bonner, Lonnice Brittenum
Good hair; for colored girls who've considered weaves when the chemicals became too ruff. Crown Trade Paperbacks 1994 98p il pa $9.95

646.7

1. Hair
ISBN 0-517-88151-9   LC 93-42027
Reprint. First published 1991 by Sapphire Bks.
The author explains hair "structure and texture while exploring the damaging effects of hot combs and chemical relaxants, in addition to hair care essentials and how to style crimps and corkscrews. Although she doesn't cover a wide range of natural 'dos, her overarching message—that black women should embrace rather than tame their hair—makes this essential." Libr J
Includes bibliographical references

Brown, Bobbi

Bobbi Brown beauty evolution; a guide to a lifetime of beauty; [by] Bobbi Brown, with Sally Wadyka. HarperCollins Pubs. 2002 211p il $29.95

646.7

1. Personal appearance 2. Women—Health and hygiene

ISBN 0-06-008881-8   LC 2002-22988

The author suggests "that readers look beyond the retouched images in magazines to see the possibilities of individual features. Addressing all ages and races, she recommends products that enhance your assets, even during pregnancy and illness. With a chapter on men." Libr J

Cullinane, Jan

The new retirement; the ultimate guide to the rest of your life; {by} Jan Cullinane and Cathy Fitzgerald. Rodale 2004 486p pa $19.95

646.7

1. Retirement

ISBN 1-579-54796-6   LC 2004-5600

Contents: What makes retirement successful? -- How do you reprogram your time? -- What are the opportunities for travel? -- What and where is home? -- Where should you move: recommended locations within the U.S. -- Niche retirement lifestyles -- Where should you move: recommended locations outside the U.S. -- Forever young? -- How do you make your money last as long as you do? -- What are the tax issues?

"Readers just starting to consider what changes they want to make when they 'retire' and those contemplating relocation or lifestyle changes will find the bulk of the book quite helpful." Publ Wkly

Includes bibliographical references

DuPriest, Laura

Natural beauty; pamper yourself with salon secrets at home. Prima Pub. 2002 230p il pa $10.95   **646.7**

1. Personal appearance 2. Cosmetics 3. Skin—Care

ISBN 0-7615-2099-6   LC 2002-72554

"This provides recipes for at-home beauty treatments, including facials, manicures, and waxing. Warns against the hyped claims of cosmetic-counter products and emphasizes useful kitchen ingredients that produce the same results at a fraction of the cost." Libr J

The author's "obvious knowledge about everything from waxing to massaging to not being taken in at the cosmetics counter, as well as her inventive concoctions . . . make this a solid beauty resource." Publ Wkly

Essence total makeover; body, beauty, spirit; [by the editors of Essence]; Patricia Mignon Hinds, editor; introduction by Susan L. Taylor. Crown 2000 216p il pa $18 hardcover o.p.

646.7

1. Personal appearance 2. African American women—Health and hygiene

ISBN 0-609-80527-4 (pa)   LC 99-14442

"Hinds provides practical tips on caring for skin, hair, body, and spirit. Glossy and attractive, this comprehensive volume is aimed at African American women." Libr J

Includes bibliographical references

Fornay, Alfred

The African American woman's guide to successful makeup and skincare. rev ed. Wiley 2002 184p il pa $16.95   **646.7**

1. Skin—Care 2. Personal appearance 3. African American women—Health and hygiene

ISBN 0-471-40278-8   LC 2001-56781

"An Amber book"

First published 1998 by Amber Bks.

The author "covers basic skin care and types, aging, and special problems such as acne and facial hair. He also provides guidance in selecting colors to complement skin tone and applying makeup to downplay flaws and accentuate good points. With a chapter on skin care for men." Libr J

Gross, Kim Johnson

Woman's face; skin care and makeup; [by Kim Johnson Gross, Jeff Stone; written by Rachel Urquhart] Knopf 1997 190p il (Chic simple) $30   **646.7**

1. Personal grooming 2. Face—Care 3. Cosmetics

ISBN 0-679-44578-1   LC 97-5164

This answers nearly 100 frequently asked questions about make-up and skin care, including advice on the best products, and describing how to accentuate a woman's best features

Kashuk, Sonia

Real beauty; concept by Sonia Kashuk; written with Amie Valentine. Potter 2003 137p il + 1 DVD ROM $27.50   **646.7**

1. Personal appearance 2. Women—Health and hygiene

ISBN 1-4000-4774-2   LC 2003-535298

The author "showcases women of all ages and ethnic types, covering nutrition and fitness in addition to the usual hair and skin care. The accompanying DVD shows the suggested makeup techniques being performed." Libr J

Kirsch, Melissa

The girl's guide to absolutely everything. Workman Pub. 2006 477p il $26.95; pa $15.95

646.7

1. Young women 2. Conduct of life

ISBN 978-0-7611-4213-3;   0-7611-4213-4;
978-0-7611-3579-1 (pa); 0-7611-3579-0 (pa)

LC 2006-41840

The author provides "advice for women in their twenties and thirties on everything from body image and friendship to first jobs and money. . . . Her well-designed book is pleasurable to read and encourages healthy, responsible behavior." Libr J

Includes bibliographical references

Massey, Lorraine

Curly girl; more than just hair—it's an attitude: a celebration of curls: how to cut them, care for them, love them & set them free. Workman 2001 148p il pa $9.95   **646.7**

1. Hair

ISBN 0-7611-2300-8   LC 2001-26842

Massey, Lorraine—*Continued*

This book features "tips on shampoo . . . conditioners . . . drying, combing . . . styling, getting the right cut, and how to Heal Thy Hair after years of strong detergents and damaging blow-dryers. There are before-and-after photographs . . . self-help tests, confessions from curly girls {and} advice." Publisher's note

Pedersen, Stephanie

K-I-S-S beauty; foreword by Victoria Moran. DK Pub. 2001 352p il (Keep it simple series) pa $19.95   **646.7**
1. Personal appearance
ISBN 0-7894-8146-4   LC 2001-2551
"A Dorling Kindersley book"
Spine title: KISS guide to beauty
This guide features advice on hair, nail, and skin care and discusses issues such as cosmetic surgery, the effects of sleep, nutrition, stress, and UV rays on your appearance

"Clearly written, it will appeal to people who are intimidated by the higher-end guides." Libr J

Scott, Susan Craig

The hair bible; the ultimate guide to healthy, beautiful hair forever; {by} Susan Craig Scott with Karen W. Bressler. Atria Bks. 2003 270p il pa $15
*   **646.7**
ISBN 0-7434-4260-1   LC 2003-271695
This guide begins with a short history of hair care and treatments and goes on to discuss "the basics of hair care, how to choose the best cut, color and styling products and how to cope with hair treatments, enhancements and problems. . . . The authors {also} offer home remedies for scalp troubles, discuss female pattern baldness and explore the emotional effects of hair loss. They even cover surgical procedures, such as hair grafts or scalp reductions, that can mitigate hair loss." Publ Wkly
Includes bibliographical references

Worthington, Charles

The complete book of hairstyling. Firefly Bks. 2002 304p il pa $19.95   **646.7**
1. Hair
ISBN 1-55297-576-2   LC 2002-277803
This describes over 100 hairstyles and offers advice on coloring and cutting hair, maintenance of hair style and health, and hair products.

648 Housekeeping

Consumer Reports how to clean and care for practically anything; [by] the editors of Consumer reports. Consumer Reports Special Publications 2002 280p il pa $16.95
                                                   648
1. House cleaning 2. Cleaning
ISBN 978-0-89043-965-4; 0-89043-965-4
                                     LC 2004-297314
First published 1986 with title: How to clean practically anything. Periodically revised. Variant title: How to clean and care for practically anything

On cover: Hundreds of timesaving solutions for all around the house plus super stain-removal guide
This volume offers advice on buying and using cleaning products and appliances and includes a stain removal chart for fabrics

Friedman, Virginia M.

Field guide to stains; how to identify and remove virtually every stain known to man; by Virginia M. Friedman, Melissa Wagner, and Nancy Armstrong. Quirk Bks. 2003 280p il pa $14.95   **648**
1. Cleaning
ISBN 1-931686-07-6   LC 2002-104065
This guide to identifying and removing over 100 stains features sections on sauces, fruits and vegetables, office products, and yard and garage stains. It also includes information on when and where certain stains are most likely to occur

649 Child rearing; home care of persons with disabilities and illnesses

Agnew, Connie L., 1957-

Twins! pregnancy, birth, and the first year of life; [by] Connie L. Agnew, Alan H. Klein, and Jill Alison Ganon; illustrations by Victor Robert. 2nd ed. Collins 2005 360p il pa $18.95
                                                   649
1. Twins
ISBN 0-06-074219-4; 978-0-06-074219-5
                                     LC 2005-45585
First published 1997
An overview of the physical, medical, emotional, and psychological issues involved in having twins. Fetal and embryonic development, nutrition, and exercise are among the topics covered. Includes interviews with parents of twins.
Includes bibliographical references

Ames, Louise Bates

Your eight-year-old; lively and outgoing; by Louise Bates Ames and Carol Chase Haber; illustrated with photographs by Betty David. Delacorte Press 1989 147p il pa $12.95 hardcover o.p.   **649**
1. Child rearing
ISBN 0-440-50681-6 (pa)   LC 88-31150
A discussion of the basic personality and typical physical and mental development of the eight-year-old
Includes bibliographical references

Your five-year-old; sunny and serene; by Louise Bates Ames and Frances L. Ilg, Gesell Institute of Child Development; illustrated with photographs by Betty David. Delacorte Press 1979 123p il pa $12.95 hardcover o.p.   **649**
1. Child rearing
ISBN 0-440-50673-5 (pa)   LC 78-11622

Ames, Louise Bates—*Continued*

Beginning with a description of the general characteristics of the five-year-old, the authors go on to discuss how the child relates to parents and others

Includes bibliographical references

Your four-year-old; wild and wonderful; by Louise Bates Ames and Frances L. Ilg, Gesell Institute of Child Development. Delacorte Press 1976 152p il pa $12.95 hardcover o.p.

649

1. Child rearing

ISBN 0-440-50675-1 (pa)

A discussion of the basic personality and typical physical and mental development of the four-year-old

Includes bibliographical references

Your one-year-old; the fun-loving, fussy 12-to-24-month-old; by Louise Bates Ames, Frances L. Ilg, and Carol Chase Haber (Gesell Institute of Child Development); illustrated with photographs by Betty David. Delacorte Press 1982 178p il pa $12.95 hardcover o.p. **649**

1. Child rearing

ISBN 0-440-50672-7 (pa)   LC 81-17275

A discussion of the basic personality and typical physical and mental development of the one-year-old

Includes bibliographical references

Your seven-year-old; life in a minor key; by Louise Bates Ames and Carol Chase Haber; illustrated with photographs by Betty David. Delacorte Press 1985 165p il pa $12.95 hardcover o.p. **649**

1. Child rearing

ISBN 0-440-50650-6 (pa)   LC 84-15627

A discussion of the basic personality and typical physical and mental development of the seven-year-old

Includes bibliographical references

Your six-year-old; defiant but loving; by Louise Bates Ames and Frances L. Ilg, Gesell Institute of Child Development. Delacorte Press 1976 132p il pa $12.95 hardcover o.p. **649**

1. Child rearing

ISBN 0-440-50674-3 (pa)

A discussion of the basic personality and typical physical and mental development of the six-year-old

Includes bibliographical references

Your three-year-old; friend or enemy; by Louise Bates Ames, and Frances L. Ilg, Gesell Institute of Child Development. Delacorte Press 1976 168p il pa $12.95 hardcover o.p. **649**

1. Child rearing

ISBN 0-440-50649-2 (pa)

A discussion of the basic personality and typical physical and mental development of the three-year-old

Includes bibliographical references

Your two-year-old; terrible or tender; by Louise Bates Ames, and Frances L. Ilg, Gesell Institute of Child Development. Delacorte Press 1976 149p il pa $12.94 hardcover o.p. **649**

1. Child rearing

ISBN 0-440-50638-7 (pa)

A discussion of the basic personality and typical physical and mental development of the two-year-old

Includes bibliographical references

The **Baby** book; everything you need to know about your baby—from birth to age two; [by] William Sears [et al.] 2nd ed. [rev. and updated] Little, Brown 2003 769p il pa $21.95

649

1. Infants—Care 2. Infants—Development

ISBN 0-316-77800-1   LC 2002-016142

First published 1993

"The authors teach new parents how to bond with their babies through seven fundamental behaviors, including breastfeeding, 'babywearing' and setting proper boundaries. . . . From tips for a healthy birth, getting your baby to sleep and feeding him the 'right fats,' to information about early health concerns, the major steps in infant development and troublesome but typical toddler behavior, the authors of this comprehensive volume . . . are assured and reassuring experts." Publ Wkly

Bailey, Rebecca Anne, 1952-

Easy to love, difficult to discipline; the 7 basic skills for turning conflict into cooperation; {by} Becky A. Bailey. Morrow 2000 285p pa $12.95 hardcover o.p. **649**

1. Child rearing 2. Parenting

ISBN 0-06-000775-3 (pa)   LC 99-44313

"Bailey contends that the difficult but rewarding task of guiding children's behavior starts only when parents are able to discipline themselves and become models of self-control. . . . Bailey's underlying message is positive and hopeful, supported with humorous anecdotes and helpful solutions." Publ Wkly

Includes bibliographical references

Brazelton, T. Berry, 1918-

Touchpoints three to six; your child's emotional and behavioral development; [by] T. Berry Brazelton, Joshua D. Sparrow. Perseus Bks. 2001 xxiii, 502p il $27; pa $18   **649**

1. Child development 2. Child rearing

ISBN 0-7382-0199-5; 0-7382-0678-4 (pa)

LC 2001-92010

Companion volume to Touchpoints

"A Merloyd Lawrence book"

"This book follows children from early language development to entry into first grade, charting temperament, learning, moral development, relationships, independence, and separation at each stage. The second part is arranged alphabetically by topics from adoption to parents working and caring for children in a range of family situations and backgrounds." Booklist

"Destined to become required reading for parents and early childhood educators, this is a valuable addition to any public library." Libr J

Includes bibliographical references

Brooks, Robert B.

Raising resilient children; fostering strength, hope, and optimism in your child; {by} Robert Brooks, Sam Goldstein. Contemporary Bks. 2001 317p $14.95 hardcover o.p.   **649**

1. Child rearing 2. Parent-child relationship

ISBN 0-8092-9765-5 (pa)   LC 00-60316

The authors "synthesize research on children's coping skills; define and describe resilience (the capacity to cope and feel competent); and offer specific strategies for nurturing resilience in children." Booklist

Includes bibliographical references

Bullard, Sara

Teaching tolerance; raising open-minded empathetic children. Doubleday 1996 235p pa $19 hardcover o.p.   **649**

1. Prejudices 2. Children 3. Toleration 4. Parenting

ISBN 0-385-47265-X (pa)   LC 95-36045

Bullard "states the principles of tolerance adults need to impart to children and provides guidelines for modeling the behavior we want to encourage." Libr J

"Also included is an extensive list of books, toys, games and music that explore ethnicity and promote tolerance. More thought-provoking than prescriptive, Bullard's reasoned and persuasive essay offers convincing inspiration for parents to serve as open-minded models for their children." Publ Wkly

Caring for your school-age child; ages 5 to 12; editor-in-chief, Edward L. Schor. rev trade pa. ed. Bantam Bks. 1999 xxviii, 624p il pa $19.95   **649**

1. Child care 2. Child rearing

ISBN 0-553-37992-5   LC 99-12639

Also available Caring for your baby and young child (1998)

First published 1995

On cover: The American Academy of Pediatrics

This book "offers comprehensive information about the growth, development, and behavior of children from five to 12 years of age. . . . Bicycle safety, latchkey children, dealing with violence and crime, guns in the home, prejudice, gender identity and sexual orientation, and physical and sexual abuse appear along with the usual information about immunization, diet, school problems, illness, and first aid. The text also offers sound, practical advice about how parents in traditional and nontraditional families can handle a wide variety of situations, stating clearly when they should seek professional help. . . . This book belongs in all parenting and consumer health collections." Libr J [review of 1995 edition]

Cohen, Lawrence J.

Playful parenting; a bold new way to use play in raising your children. Ballantine Bks. 2001 307p $23.95; pa $14   **649**

1. Parenting 2. Play 3. Games

ISBN 0-345-43897-3; 0-345-44286-5 (pa)

LC 00-66809

"A Living Planet book"

"According to Cohen, children of all ages have an ongoing need for connectedness, security and attachment;

playful interaction with parents is an important way to develop such bonds. Through play, parents can help their kids develop greater confidence, express bottled up or difficult feelings, recover from daily emotional upheavals, negotiate agreements, express love and—not least— have fun." Publ Wkly

Deak, JoAnn

Girls will be girls; a parent's guide to cultivating confident, competent and connected daughters; by JoAnn Deak with Teresa Barker. Hyperion 2002 287p $23.95; pa $14.95   **649**

1. Girls 2. Child rearing 3. Teenagers

ISBN 0-7868-6768-X; 0-7868-8657-9 (pa)

LC 2001-39247

"Deak discusses the differences between fathers and daughters and mothers and daughters and also some of the more common problems faced by teens, such as body image and peer pressure." Publ Wkly

"This no-nonsense book offers a wealth of practical advice for parents and teachers." Booklist

Delmolino, Lara

Incentives for change; motivating people with autism spectrum disorders to learn and gain independence; [by] Lara Delmolino and Sandra L. Harris. Woodbine House 2004 145p il (Topics in autism) pa $17.95 *   **649**

1. Autism 2. Motivation (Psychology)

ISBN 1-89062-760-7   LC 2004-19940

"Easy to follow, this first-rate introduction to ABA [Applied Behavioral Analysis] is accessible to a wide range of audiences." Libr J

Includes bibliographical references

Deutsch, Francine, 1948-

Halving it all; how equally shared parenting works. Harvard Univ. Press 1999 327p $27.50; pa $14.95   **649**

1. Parenting 2. Sex role 3. Dual-career families 4. Child rearing

ISBN 0-674-36800-2; 0-674-00209-1 (pa)

LC 98-30738

Based on interviews, Deutsch "describes four groups of working parents: those who share responsibilities and duties equally; those in which one parent, usually the mother, does somewhat more; those in which the mother provides most of the childcare; and parents, primarily blue collar workers, who choose alternate work shifts to share duties." Libr J

Includes bibliographical references

Donovan, Denis M.

What did I just say!?! how new insights into childhood thinking can help you communicate more effectively with your child; {by Denis M. Donovan, Deborah McIntyre}. Holt & Co. 1999 230p il pa $14 hardcover o.p.   **649**

1. Parent-child relationship 2. Communication

ISBN 0-8050-6502-4 (pa)   LC 99-11987

Donovan, Denis M.—*Continued*

"Unless parents state what they want of a child explicitly, literally, logically, and in simple, commonsense terms, what they say and what the child hears and does will rarely be in sync. Donovan and McIntyre scrutinize many phrases . . . through the lens of logic to demonstrate embarrassingly ineffective ways for parents to communicate." Booklist

Includes bibliographical references

Dosick, Wayne D., 1947-

Golden rules; the ten ethical values parents need to teach their children; {by} Wayne Dosick. HarperSanFrancisco 1995 221p pa $13 hardcover o.p. **649**

1. Child rearing 2. Moral education

ISBN 0-06-251249-8 (pa) LC 94-37098

The author "has chosen 10 values that he feels parents must teach their children if they are to have any hope of becoming 'good, decent, honorable human beings, with strength of character and depth of moral commitment.' Each chapter of 'Golden Rules' embodies one of these ethical values—respect, honesty, fairness, responsibility, compassion, gratitude, friendship, peace, maturity and faith. The value is amplified by admonitions to parents, and by stories, poems, prayers, activities to share and discussion questions for various age levels." N Y Times Book Rev

Includes bibliographical references

Douglas, Ann, 1963-

The mother of all baby books. Hungry Minds 2002 c2001 604p pa $15.99 **649**

1. Infants—Care 2. Childbirth 3. Parenting

ISBN 0-7645-6616-4

First published 2001 in Canada

Baby care basics covered in this guide include "basic childcare, nutrition, health, and physical, emotional, and social development. [Also discussed are] facts about sleeping patterns, breastfeeding, circumcision, and immunization issues." Publisher's note

Includes bibliographical references

Eisenberg, Arlene

What to expect the toddler years; [by] Arlene Eisenberg, Heidi E. Murkoff, and Sandee E. Hathaway. Workman 1994 xx, 904p il pa $16.95 **649**

1. Child rearing

ISBN 0-89480-994-6 LC 93-8932

This guide for parents of two- and three-year-olds covers such topics as pediatric checkups, toilet training, sibling rivalry, and working parents

"This is an outstanding source written by and for parents. Easy to use, affordable and reassuring, it encourages parents to enjoy their children." Libr J

Elias, Maurice J.

Emotionally intelligent parenting; how to raise a self-disciplined, responsible, socially skilled child; {by} Maurice J. Elias, Steven E. Tobias, and Brian S. Friedlander; foreword by Daniel Goleman. Harmony Bks. 1999 246p pa $13 hardcover o.p. **649**

1. Child rearing 2. Parenting

ISBN 0-609-80483-9 (pa) LC 98-20835

The authors encourage parents to "try to see things from the child's perspective; stop nagging, threatening and yelling to get your point across; foster positive, and discourage negative, behaviors." Publ Wkly

Elman, Natalie Madorsky

The unwritten rules of friendship; simple strategies to help your child make friends; by Natalie Madorsky Elman and Eileen Kennedy-Moore. Little, Brown 2003 340p il pa $14.95 **649**

1. Socialization 2. Friendship 3. Child rearing

ISBN 0-316-91730-3 LC 2002-40611

The authors "formulate nine prototypes of children with friendship problems. These range from passive (e.g., 'sensitive soul') to more aggressive (e.g., 'intimidating' children, 'short-fused' children, and born leaders) personalities. Chapters provide checklists for evaluation, social rules such children need to know, learning activities, and case studies. . . . Colorfully written and practical, *Unwritten Rules* offers many tips for anxious parents." Libr J

Includes bibliographical references

Faber, Adele

How to talk so kids will listen & listen so kids will talk; [by] Adele Faber and Elaine Mazlish; illustrations by Kimberly Ann Coe. 1st Avon Books rev (20th anniversary) print., 20th anniversary ed updated. Avon Books 1999 286p il pa $13.95 **649**

1. Parenting 2. Communication

ISBN 0-380-81196-0 LC 99-94868

First published 1980 by Rawson, Wade Publishers

This book designed to facilitate communication between parents and their children discuss how to cope with an unhappy child, resolving family conflicts, and how to set boundaries for a child without damaging goodwill.

Includes bibliographical references

Füredi, Frank

Paranoid parenting; why ignoring the experts may be best for your child. Chicago Review Press 2002 233p pa $14.95 **649**

1. Parenting 2. Child rearing 3. Parent-child relationship

ISBN 1-55652-464-1 LC 2002-4121

"Previously published in a substantially different form in the U.K. in 2001." Verso of title page

The author contends "that parents are not just worried but downright paranoid, due, in part, to a glut of much-

Füredi, Frank—*Continued*

publicized expert advice. . . . Claiming that society had become 'child-obsessed rather than child-centered' Furedi calls for a return to reliance on parents' own instincts, and for the re-establishment of adult trust and collaboration in caring for children." Publ Wkly

"This book is provocative, well argued, and clearly written, though the rhetoric can be stinging." Libr J

Includes bibliographical references

Garbarino, James

Parents under siege; why you are the solution, not the problem in your child's life; {by} James Garbarino, Claire Bedard. Free Press 2001 246p $24; pa $13   **649**

1. Parent-child relationship 2. Child rearing

ISBN 0-7432-0134-5; 0-7432-2383-7 (pa)

LC 2001-23692

Includes bibliographical references

"In Part 1, the toxic cultural environment of the last decade is described; in Part 2, parents are offered some usable tools to help them become more in control." Libr J

"This book offers a sound theoretical starting point for parents grappling with a difficult child. It also lists many helpful resources, Web sites and groups, along with suggested further reading." Publ Wkly

Garber, Stephen W., 1946-

Monsters under the bed and other childhood fears; helping your child overcome anxieties, fears, and phobias; {by} Stephen W. Garber, Marianne Daniels Garber, and Robyn Freedman Spizman. Villard Bks. 1993 378p pa $23 hardcover o.p.

649

1. Child rearing 2. Fear

ISBN 0-8129-9222-9 (pa)   LC 92-56812

"Following opening chapters on understanding and identifying a child's fear and some overall guidelines on teaching basic relaxation techniques, the authors introduce their basic plan for overcoming fear through imagination, information, observation, and exposure. Subsequent chapters apply these four techniques to specific fears." Libr J

Includes bibliographical references

Harris, Sandra L.

Siblings of children with autism; a guide for families; [by] Sandra L. Harris and Beth A. Glasberg. 2nd ed. Woodbine House 2003 180p il pa $16.95   **649**

1. Autism 2. Siblings

ISBN 1-89062-729-1   LC 2003-1239

First published 1994

This "resource for families with autistic children and nonautistic siblings examines the perceptions, needs, compromises, and inevitable stresses that brothers and sisters face." Libr J

Includes bibliographical references

Hewlett, Sylvia Ann, 1946-

The war against parents; what we can do for America's beleaguered moms and dads; {by} Sylvia Ann Hewlett and Cornel West. Houghton Mifflin 1998 302p il pa $14 hardcover o.p.

649

1. Parenting 2. Family

ISBN 0-395-95797-4 (pa)   LC 98-5779

The authors contend that "current American political and economic policy, as well as the popular media, discriminate severely against people trying to bring up children. . . . This salutary jeremiad should be required reading in Washington and Hollywood." Publ Wkly

Includes bibliographical references

Huggins, Kathleen

The nursing mother's companion; foreword by Ruth A. Lawrence; photographs by Harriette Hartigan. 4th ed. Harvard Common Press 1999 284p il $24.95; pa $13.95 *   **649**

1. Breast feeding

ISBN 1-55832-151-9; 1-55832-152-7 (pa)

LC 98-51793

First published 1986

This offers advice on preventing and solving breast feeding problems and includes sections on premature babies, babies at risk for underfeeding, and breast pumps, as well as an appendix on drug safety

Includes bibliographical references

Hulbert, Ann

Raising America; experts, parents, and a century of advice about children. Knopf 2003 450p il $27.50; pa $15   **649**

1. Child rearing 2. Parenting

ISBN 0-375-40120-2; 0-375-70122-2 (pa)

LC 2002-73152

This is "an intellectual history of how children and parents have been studied in modern America. Here is the story of how Drs. Hall and Holt begat Drs. Gesell and Watson, who begat Dr. Spock and even Dr. Seuss, and how they in turn spawned an entire mini-industry of parenting experts. . . . This provocative and informative study is a model of lay scholarship." Publ Wkly

Includes bibliographical references

Is it a big problem or a little problem? when to worry, when not to worry, and what to do; [by] Amy Egan . . . [et al.] St. Martin's Press 2007 335p il pa $15.95   **649**

1. Child psychology 2. Child development

ISBN 978-0-312-35412-1   LC 2007-17218

The authors "divide the book into three sections, 'The Basics,' 'Understanding Development,' and 'Where Children Struggle.' Within these, they illustrate specific concerns (e.g., 'She can hear, why doesn't she understand?'), explore the range of normal, and examine signals that indicate a need for professional intervention. . . . Never using an alarmist tone, the authors strike a perfect balance between advocating for early intervention and appreciating the ups and downs of typical childhood behavior." Libr J

Includes bibliographical references

Karp, Harvey

The happiest baby on the block; the new way to calm crying and help your baby sleep longer. Bantam Bks. 2002 267p il $21.95; pa $13.95

649

1. Infants—Care 2. Parent-child relationship 3. Child rearing

ISBN 0-553-80255-0; 0-553-38146-6 (pa)

LC 2001-56734

To calm a crying baby the author "recommends a series of five steps designed to imitate the uterus. These steps include swaddling, side/stomach position, shhh sounds, swinging and sucking. The book includes detailed advice on the proper way to swaddle a child, the difference between a gentle rocking versus shaking and more." Publ Wkly

Leach, Penelope

Your baby & child; from birth to age five; photographs by Jenny Matthews. 3rd ed completely rev. Knopf 1997 559p il $35; pa $20

649

1. Infants—Care 2. Child care 3. Child development

ISBN 0-375-40007-9; 0-375-70000-5 (pa)

LC 97-29325

First published 1977 in the United Kingdom with title: Baby and child; first United States edition 1978

The author explores the psychosocial needs of children along with their physical growth and progress. Parental concerns are addressed

"Public and academic libraries would do well to stock . . . this primer on children and their development for circulation as well as for the reference shelf." Libr J

Lev, Arlene Istar

The complete lesbian & gay parenting guide. Berkeley trade pbk. ed. Berkley Books 2004 379p pa $17

649

1. Gay parents 2. Parenting

ISBN 0-425-19197-4; 978-0-425-19197-2

LC 2004-57080

"This book addresses the concerns of transgendered parents, as well as those of lesbian and gay parents. . . . [The author] knows how to tackle relevant issues, e.g., dealing with the homophobia that children of GLBT parents will inevitably encounter. Humorous and replete with valuable narratives." Libr J

Includes bibliographical references

Lippincott, Jenifer Marshall

7 things your teenager won't tell you; and how to talk about them anyway; [by] Jenifer Marshall Lippincott and Robin M. Deutsch. Ballantine Books 2005 223p pa $14.95

649

1. Teenagers 2. Parent-child relationship 3. Parenting 4. Adolescent psychology

ISBN 0-8129-6959-6

LC 2005-297256

"The first section of the book reviews psychological and physiological research on brain development in adolescents. The authors then identify seven important facts to keep in mind, among them: truth is a malleable concept for teens, they suffer from distorted self-images, and

they are attracted to risks. . . . Parents of teens will recognize the us-and-them dialogues and will find encouragement and guidance." Booklist

Includes bibliographical references

Marzollo, Jean

Fathers & babies; how babies grow and what they need from you from birth to 18 months; illustrated by Irene Trivas. HarperPerennial 1993 235p il pa $13.95

649

1. Infants—Care 2. Father-child relationship

ISBN 0-06-096908-3

LC 92-53386

Marzollo covers "infant development from the physical and social to the intellectual, psychological and creative. . . . Her book provides step-by-step instructions on fixing bottles, bathing and feeding, changing a diaper, toilet training, helping a child develop langauge skills, and disciplining the older baby." Libr J

Mayes, Linda C.

The Yale Child Study Center guide to understanding your child; healthy development from birth to adolescence; {by} Linda C. Mayes and Donald J. Cohen with John E. Schowalter and Richard H. Granger; J. L. Bell, editorial consultant; W. Rodney Torbert, illustrator. Little, Brown 2002 548p $40; pa $21.95

649

1. Child rearing 2. Child development 3. Parent-child relationship

ISBN 0-316-95432-2; 0-316-79432-5 (pa)

LC 00-39116

"The book offers three perspectives: the scientific, with basic information about meeting a growing child's needs; the emotional, with attention to understanding a child's feelings; and the parental, with emphasis on the feelings and expectations the parent brings to the relationship. . . . The objective is to help parents balance the three perspectives. . . . This approach lends the guide a broad and deep perspective on parenting even as it covers typical issues such as imaginary friends and sibling rivalry." Booklist

Murkoff, Heidi Eisenberg

What to expect the first year; [by] Heidi Murkoff, Arlene Eisenberg & Sandee Hathaway. 2nd ed, rev and updated. Workman 2003 704p $25.95; pa $15.95 *

649

1. Infants—Care 2. Child rearing

ISBN 0-7611-3184-1; 0-7611-2958-8 (pa)

LC 2003-57578

First published 1996 with Eisenberg's name appearing first

This guide to "taking care of a newborn through the milestone of his or her first birthday . . . [covers] issues such as newborn screening, home births and the resulting at-home newborn care, vitamins and vaccines, milk allergies, causes of colic, sleep problems, SIDS, returning to work, dealing with siblings, weaning, sippy cups, . . . [and] the expanded role of the father." Publisher's note

Nachman, Patricia Ann

You and your only child; the joys, myths, and challenges of raising an only child; {by} Patricia Nachman with Andrea Thompson. HarperCollins Pubs. 1997 244p pa $12 hardcover o.p.

649

1. Only child 2. Parenting
ISBN 0-06-092896-4 (pa) LC 96-32531
"A Skylight Press book"
The authors discuss social attitudes about only children and offer advice on issues ranging from friendships and stereotyping to the only child and divorce
Includes bibliographical references

The **Nursing** mother's problem solver; Claire Martin {with Nancy Funnemark Krebs, editor; foreword by William Sears and Martha Sears}. Fireside 2000 336p il pa $13 **649**
1. Breast feeding
ISBN 0-684-85784-7 LC 00-37198
"Based on questions that were asked on the lactation consultant hot-line at the Children's Hospital of Denver, this book addresses common issues of new mothers (e.g., 'latching on', sore nipples, night feedings) as well as less common situations, such as breastfeeding babies with special needs. The scope of the Q&A is wide, providing a wealth of detailed information from a modern-day perspective." Libr J

Overcoming the odds; raising academically successful African American young women; [by] Freeman A. Hrabowski III [et al.] Oxford Univ. Press 2002 272p $25 **649**
1. African American women 2. African Americans—Education
ISBN 0-19-512642-4 LC 2001-32152
Companion volume to Beating the odds; raising academically successful African American males (1998)
This volume "focuses on young black women overcoming the stereotypical image: high-school dropout, unwed mother, welfare recipient. Based on interviews with students and parents, the book answers the question, What does it take to succeed academically?" Booklist
Includes bibliographical references

Pryor, Gale

Nursing mother, working mother; the essential guide to breastfeeding your baby before and after you return to work; [by] Gale Pryor and Kathleen Huggins. 2nd ed. Harvard Common Press 2006 237p pa $12.95 * **649**
1. Breast feeding 2. Mothers
ISBN 1-55832-331-7; 978-1-55832-331-5
LC 2006-26173
First published 1997
This book provides "information on legal rights in the workplace, breast pumps, and the basics of expressing, storing, and feeding breast milk. Women planning on returning to paid work will find excellent advice to make breastfeeding a long-term reality even if mother and baby are separated for many hours of the day." Libr J
Includes bibliographical references

Rosenfeld, Alvin A.

Hyper-parenting; are you hurting your child by trying too hard? {by} Alvin Rosenfeld and Nicole Wise; foreword by Robert Coles. St. Martin's Press 2000 xxix, 257p $13.95 hardcover o.p.

649

1. Parenting 2. Child rearing
ISBN 0-312-26339-2 (pa) LC 99-56670
The author "advocates 'just playing' and just spending time with one's children rather than living the overbooked family life of a stereotypical soccer mom. He notes that family schedules are at a breaking point and that parents face a great deal of guilt and anxiety because they cannot give their children everything. He promotes the need for more balance and suggests that parents take to heart Dr. Spock's advice for parents to trust themselves." Libr J
Includes bibliographical references

Sears, William

Parenting the fussy baby and high-need child; everything you need to know—from birth to age five; {by} William Sears and Martha Sears. Little, Brown 1996 237p il pa $12.95 hardcover o.p.

649

1. Parenting 2. Child psychology
ISBN 0-316-77916-4 (pa) LC 95-48381
To cope with a high-need child the authors "recommend the approach they label *attachment parenting*; it includes such techniques as on-demand feeding and weaning; nighttime parenting; sharing sleep; soothing through motion, sound, visual distraction, and physical contact; and learning via close study how to anticipate the baby's needs." Booklist
Includes bibliographical references

Shapiro, Lawrence E.

How to raise a child with a high EQ; a parent's guide to emotional intelligence. HarperCollins Pubs. 1997 256p pa $13 hardcover o.p.

649

1. Parenting 2. Emotions 3. Child psychology
ISBN 0-06-092891-3 (pa) LC 97-5533
"Through games, activities, tricks, skills, and habits, {this book} guides parents in developing the moral emotions of empathy, honesty, shame, and guilt; thinking skills such as realism and optimism; resourcefulness; social skills including conversation, humor, manners, and friendliness; persistence and motivation; and emotional control." Booklist
Includes bibliographical references

Small, Meredith F.

Our babies, ourselves; how biology and culture shape the way we parent. Anchor Bks. (NY) 1998 xxii, 292p il pa $14.95 hardcover o.p.

649

1. Infants—Care 2. Infants—Development 3. Parent-child relationship
ISBN 0-385-48362-7 (pa) LC 97-44348
The author "explores ethnopediatrics, an interdisciplinary science that combines anthropology, pediatrics, and

Small, Meredith F.—*Continued*

child development research in order to examine how child-rearing styles across cultures affect the health and survival of infants. Small describes the different parenting styles of several cultures, including . . . the nomadic Ache tribe of Paraguay, the agrarian !Kung San society of the Kalahari Desert in Africa, and the American industrialized society." Libr J

Includes bibliographical references

Spock, Benjamin, 1903-1998

Dr. Spock on parenting; sensible advice from America's most trusted child care expert. Simon & Schuster 1988 318p pa $16.95 hardcover o.p.

649

1. Parenting
ISBN 0-7434-2683-5 (pa)   LC 88-15792

"The author presents a personal critique on parenting, often bordering on the autobiographical. . . . He discusses in depth and with great conviction contemporary and traditional parent concerns, such as divorce, discipline, sex education, and the father's role." Libr J

Dr. Spock's the first two years; the emotional and physical needs of children from birth to age two; edited by Martin T. Stein. Pocket Bks. 2001 153p pa $13.95   **649**

1. Child development 2. Child care 3. Child rearing
ISBN 0-7434-1122-6

In these articles culled from *Redbook* and *Parenting* Spock's advice to parents is that they should "trust themselves" and "expands on this idea in his reply to the question, 'What has eroded so many parents' self-asssurance in asking for reasonably good behavior?'" Libr J

Dr. Spock's the school years; the emotional and social development of children; edited by Martin T. Stein. Pocket Bks. 2001 283p pa $15.95

649

1. Child development 2. Child care 3. Child rearing
ISBN 0-7434-1123-4

This volume collects Spock's essays published in *Redbook* and *Parenting*. They address "our contemporary culture's tendency to overschedule children." Libr J

Stoppard, Miriam

Complete baby & child care. Rev. ed. Dorling Kindersley 2006 352p il $27.50 *   **649**

1. Child care 2. Infants—Care 3. Child development 4. Child rearing
ISBN 0-7566-1707-3   LC 2006-274086

First published 1995 in the United Kingdom

The author offers advice on behavior, clothing, choosing nursery equipment and supplies, and traveling with children.

White, Burton L., 1929-

Raising a happy, unspoiled child. Simon & Schuster 1994 253p il pa $13 hardcover o.p.

649

1. Child rearing 2. Parenting
ISBN 0-684-80134-5 (pa)   LC 94-7838

The author argues "that many difficulties—testing parental authority, refusal to share toys with playmates, etc.—can virtually be eliminated if parents are not overly permissive with children of more than five months old." Publ Wkly

Includes bibliographical references

The **Womanly** art of breastfeeding. 7th rev ed, [revised and edited by Judy Torgus and Gwen Gotsch] Plume 463p il pa $18   **649**

1. Breast feeding
ISBN 978-0-452-28580-4; 0-452-28580-1
LC 2004-557599

First published 1956. Periodically revised

Simultaneously published by La Leche League International

This guide explains the benefits of breastfeeding and offers advice on avoiding problems, breastfeeding and working mothers, family life, and weaning

Includes bibliographical references

649.8   Home care of sick and infirm

Caregiving: a step-by-step resource for caring for the person with cancer at home; editors, Peter S. Houts, Julia A. Bucher. rev ed. American Cancer Soc. 2003 288p il pa $18.95 *

649.8

1. Cancer 2. Caregivers
ISBN 0-944235-45-X   LC 2003-1115

First published 1994 by The American College of Physicians with title: American College of Physicians home care guide for cancer

Contents: How to use this book; Cancer treatments; Surgery; Chemotherapy; Radiation therapy; Biological therapies; Hormone therapy; Bone marrow and peripheral blood stem cell transplants; Clinical trials; Paying for treatments; Managing care; Understanding caregiving; Helping children understand; Coordinating care from one treatment setting to another; Getting help from community agencies and volunteer groups; Getting information from medical staff; Emotional conditions; Anxiety; Depression; Physical conditions; Appetite; Bleeding; Confusion and seizures; Constipation; Diarrhea; Fever and infections; Mouth conditions; Nausea and vomiting; Pain; Skin conditions; Vein conditions; Living with cancer and cancer treatments; Hair loss; Lymphedema; Mobility (moving around the house); Ostomies and prostheses; Tiredness and fatigue; Sexual conditions

This book "explains each major kind of cancer treatment, obstacles to recovery, when it is time to call in professional help, plentiful examples of how individuals can help their loved ones, and how to adjust your plan of action as needed. Also addressed are topics such as managing care by involving other family members and using available community resources, emotional conditions such as anxiety or depression, and the most common physical side effects of cancer treatments such as nausea, pain, and fatigue and how to cope with them. A six-step plan successfully solving problems forms the backbone of each chapter. Chockfull of sensible and reassuring information, this guide is easily accessible to the average reader." Libr J [review of 2000 edition]

Carter, Rosalynn

Helping yourself help others; a book for caregivers; {by} Rosalynn Carter with Susan K. Golant. Times Bks. 1994 278p pa $14 hardcover o.p. **649.8**

1. Home care services 2. Caregivers

ISBN 0-8129-2591-2 (pa) LC 94-11924

The authors "describe the stages the caregiver progresses through, from first facing the illness or declining health of a loved one to the 'long-term, hard-work phase of caregiving.' Questions regarding in-home professional care and nursing homes are addressed, and the authors provide information on strategies, support groups, program recommendations, helpful organizations, and books." Booklist

McFarlane, Rodger

The complete bedside companion; no-nonsense advice on caring for the seriously ill; {by} Rodger McFarlane, Philip Bashe. Simon & Schuster 1998 544p pa $25.95 hardcover o.p. **649.8**

1. Home nursing 2. Caregivers 3. Terminal care

ISBN 0-684-84319-6 (pa) LC 97-43746

"This primer provides information on general illness and specific diseases, questions to ask the physician, basic nursing skills, making hospital visits, dealing with insurance companies, sources of additional information, and support groups. The authors . . . supplement this material with case studies and personal experiences." Libr J

Includes bibliographical references

650 Management & public relations

Encyclopedia of business information sources; Linda D. Hall, [project editor] 23rd ed. Gale Res. 2008 xli, 1314p $500 **650**

1. Business—Information services

ISSN 0071-0210

ISBN 978-0-7876-9703-7; 0-7876-9703-6

First published 1970. Frequently revised

This is a comprehensive listing of business related finding aids including abstracting and indexing services, almanacs and yearbooks, bibliographies, biographical sources, directories, encyclopedias and dictionaries, financial ratios, handbooks and manuals, online databases, periodicals and newsletters, price sources, research centers and institutes, statistical sources, trade associations and professional societies, and other related sources of information on each topic.

Folsom, W. Davis

Understanding American business jargon; a dictionary; W. Davis Folsom. 2nd ed. Greenwood Press 2005 364p $79.95 **650**

1. Business—Dictionaries

ISBN 0-313-33450-1 LC 2005-16817

First published 1997

"From 'AAA' to 'Zombie Bonds,' Folsom takes us on a tour of over 2500 concepts that cover the spectrum of business-speak." Publisher's note

This book "will help businesspeople, researchers, and students gain understanding of not only the buzzword-laden business-speak but business culture." Am Ref Books Annu, 2006

Includes bibliographical references

Moss, Rita Warwick

Strauss's handbook of business information; a guide for librarians, students, and researchers. 2nd ed. Libraries Unlimited 2003 455p il pa $85 * **650**

1. Business—Bibliography 2. Business—Information services 3. Government publications—United States

ISBN 1-56308-520-8 LC 2003-54569

First edition by Diane Wheeler Strauss published 1988 with title: Handbook of business information

This edition "first covers 'formats': directories, periodicals, loose-leaf services, government information services, and electronic sources. References are then organized by 'fields': banking, marketing, accounting, stocks and bonds, etc. Graphics include screen shots of e-sources." Libr J

Includes bibliographical references

650.1 Personal success in business

Adams, Scott

The Dilbert principle; a cubicle's-eye view of bosses, meetings, management fads & other workplace afflictions. HarperBusiness 1996 336p il pa $14.95 hardcover o.p. **650.1**

1. Dilbert (Comic strip) 2. Business

ISBN 0-88730-858-9 (pa) LC 96-388

"Dilbert, Scott Adams' cartoon character, has become the workplace hero for the 1990s. . . . More than a compilation of past strips—though over 100 do appear—this book includes new essays on all aspects of corporate life and culture, and each one is on target and deliciously sardonic!" Booklist

Comaford, Christine

Rules for renegades; how to make more money, rock your career, and revel in your individuality; [by] Christine Comaford-Lynch. McGraw-Hill 2007 268p $24.95 **650.1**

1. Business 2. Success

ISBN 978-0-07-148975-1; 0-07-148975-4

The author presents "step-by-step advice for starting a company, making it in a cutthroat environment and reaching life goals in record time, while recounting her entertaining, often hilarious life story. . . . Entrepreneurs and leaders at all levels of their careers will find this inspiring, rags-to-riches story as pleasurable to read as it is thought provoking." Publ Wkly

Decker, Diane C., 1952-

First-job survival guide; how to thrive and advance in your new career; [by] Diane C. Decker, Victoria A. Hoevemeyer, and Marianne Rowe-Dimas. JIST Works 2006 214p pa $12.95

650.1

1. Vocational guidance
ISBN 1-59357-253-0   LC 2005-24684

"This first-job survival guide begins with tips on surviving the first day on the job. . . . Part 1 deals with one's professional image (including grooming and vocal impression), business-writing basics, and business etiquette. Part 2, concentrating on working with people, gives advice on handling difficult coworkers, developing a positive relationship with the boss, and being an effective team member. Part 3, focused on skills for getting ahead, is a guide to tapping into the positive side of conflict situations, influencing others, and maximizing the results. Concludes with checklists and self-tests." Booklist

Graham, Stedman

You can make it happen; a nine-step plan for success. Simon & Schuster 1997 270p il pa $13 hardcover o.p.

650.1

1. Success
ISBN 0-684-83866-4 (pa)   LC 96-45457

Graham's "nine-step plan involves increasing self-awareness, creating a vision, developing a plan, understanding and following personal values, taking risks, managing responses to those risks, building a support team, making wise decisions, and forming a total commitment. Although his plan may be most applicable to people focusing on business and career goals, Graham notes that this plan can also be applied to other aspects of life." Libr J

Hill, Napoleon, 1883-1970.

Think and grow rich; the landmark bestseller—now revised and updated for the 21st century; rev. and expanded by Arthur R. Pell. 1st Jeremy P. Tarcher/Penguin ed. Jeremy P. Tarcher/Penguin 2005 302p pa $10 *

650.1

1. Success 2. Entrepreneurship
ISBN 1-585-42433-1   LC 2005-44133

First published 1937 by The Ralston Society

A motivational guide to achieving wealth and success, drawing upon stories of successful millionaires as examples.

McCormack, Mark H.

What they don't teach you at Harvard Business School. Bantam Bks. 1984 256p pa $16.95 hardcover o.p.

650.1

1. Success 2. Management
ISBN 0-553-34583-4 (pa)   LC 84-45172

"A John Boswell Associates book"

McCormack's firm, the International Management Group, merchandises professional sports figures and markets the international television rights to sporting events. In this book, McCormack offers advice on business management.

Popcorn, Faith

Clicking; 16 trends to future fit your life, your work, and your business; {by} Faith Popcorn and Lys Marigold; illustrated by Gerti Bierenbroodsot. HarperCollins Pubs. 1996 498p il pa $14 hardcover o.p.

650.1

1. Success
ISBN 0-88730-857-0 (pa)   LC 96-379

The authors provide tips on how to find one's proper slot in a rapidly changing world. Recognizing and adapting to new trends is discussed. Includes tips on finding a new career

Includes bibliographical references

650.14 Success in obtaining jobs and promotions

The **Adams** resume almanac. Adams Media Corp. 1996 768p pa $19.95   **650.14**

1. Résumés (Employment) 2. Applications for positions
ISBN 1-55850-618-7   LC 96-15500

This "guide reviews résumé layouts and various formats and strategies, along with 600 samples and 25 cover letters. With the disk, the job seeker can actually generate a résumé." Libr J

Beatty, Richard H., 1939-

175 high-impact cover letters. 3rd ed. Wiley 2002 244p pa $14.95   **650.14**

1. Applications for positions 2. Job hunting
ISBN 0-471-21084-6   LC 2001-46963

First published 1992

Contents: Importance of cover letters; Letters to employers; Letters to search firms; Advertising response cover letters; Networking cover letters; The resume letter; Thank-you letters; Cover letters "Do's" and "Don'ts"

The interview kit. 3rd ed. Wiley 2003 248p pa $14.95   **650.14**

1. Interviewing 2. Applications for positions
ISBN 0-471-44925-3   LC 2003-45071

First published 1995

This offers advice for success in job interviews, with answers to 500 questions, strategies for making a good impression, and negotiating salaries and benefits.

Cohen, Carol Fishman

Back on the career track; a guide for stay-at-home moms who want to return to work; [by] Carol Fishman Cohen and Vivian Steir Rabin. Warner Books 2007 297p il $24.99 *

650.14

1. Vocational guidance 2. Women—Employment
ISBN 978-0-446-57820-2; 0-446-57820-7
LC 2006-20986

The authors present a "step-by-step relaunch guide for stay-at-home moms. Both Harvard MBA relaunchers themselves, they explore the role career plays in the quality of life for professional women. . . . A listing of resources, recommended reading, and sample résumés are

Cohen, Carol Fishman—*Continued*

provided. One of only a few books for the millions of professional women/mothers who are not working for pay; highly recommended for public libraries." Libr J

Includes bibliographical references

Enelow, Wendy S.

Cover letter magic; [by] Wendy S. Enelow [and] Louise Kursmark. 2nd ed. JIST Works 2004 412p pa $16.95 * **650.14**

1. Applications for positions 2. Résumés (Employment)

ISBN 1-563-70986-4 LC 2003-23186

First published 2000

This guide to writing cover letters includes "more than 150 . . . cover letters for every profession and situation. Before-and-after transformations . . . tips on resumes, e-mail and scannable cover letters, thank-you letters [and] . . . dozens of sample opening paragraphs [are included.]" Publisher's note

Fry, Ronald W.

Your first resume; for students and anyone preparing to enter today's job market; by Ron Fry. 5th ed. Career Press 2001 188p pa $11.99 **650.14**

1. Résumés (Employment)

ISBN 1-56414-583-2 LC 2001-35875

First published 1988

A step-by-step guide for preparing a successful résumé. Numerous examples accompany the text.

Gardella, Robert

The Harvard Business School guide to finding your next job; [by] Robert S. Gardella. Harvard Business School Press 2000 143p pa $16.95 **650.14**

1. Job hunting

ISBN 1-57851-223-9 LC 99-58454

"Gardella covers references, résumés, letters, interviews, and negotiation. He also details a strategy for planning and executing a job search campaign, and discusses the emotional aspects of looking for work. Special topics include the 'long-distance' job search, job fairs, and overcoming age discrimination." Booklist

Includes bibliographical references

Jackson, Tom

The perfect resume; today's ultimate job search tool. Broadway Books 2004 223p pa $12.95 **650.14**

1. Résumés (Employment) 2. Applications for positions

ISBN 0-7679-1623-9 LC 2003-62972

First published 1980; Previous edition published with title: The new perfect resume

This guide to resumes and job applications emphasizes temporary, freelance, and consulting positions, and offers advice on preparing a capabilities portfolio, on using e-mail, talents banks on the Internet, and electronic job searches.

McGraw-Hill's big red book of resumes; [compiled by Luisa Gerasimo] McGraw-Hill 2002 473p pa $16.95 **650.14**

1. Résumés (Employment)

ISBN 0-07-140195-4 LC 2002-25523

"Some 300 résumés target a wide variety of jobs, experience, and styles that will prove useful as models." Libr J

Mornell, Pierre

Games companies play; the job hunter's guide to playing smart & winning big in the high-stakes hiring game; designed by Kit Hinrichs; illustrations by Regan Dunnick. Ten Speed Press 2000 208p il pa $17.95 hardcover o.p. **650.14**

1. Job hunting

ISBN 1-58008-408-7 (pa) LC 00-26736

The author "offers advice on how to ready résumés and recommendations, write eye-catching cover letters, shine in the most difficult interview situation, and finalize job offers. He includes more than 40 sample interview questions and answers, legal considerations, and a list of important web and print resources." Libr J

Includes bibliographical references

Parker, Yana

The damn good resume guide; a crash course in resume writing. 4th ed. Ten Speed Press 2002 73p il pa $9.95 **650.14**

1. Résumés (Employment)

ISBN 1-58008-444-3 LC 2002-9177

First published 1983

This guide offers a ten-step approach to resume writing, providing creative solutions and strategies to various resume problems. Also included are sections on formatting resumes and submitting resumes over the Internet

Resumes and cover letters that have worked; [edited by Anne McKinney] PREP Pub. 1996 270p pa $25 **650.14**

1. Résumés (Employment) 2. Applications for positions

ISBN 1-88528-804-2 LC 95-19458

"The superior, readable samples, customized to professionals, college graduates, and career changers, distinguish this work from others." Libr J

Richardson, Bradley G.

Career comeback; 8 steps to getting back on your feet when you're fired, laid off, or your business venture has failed—and finding more job satisfaction than ever. Broadway Bks. 2004 319p pa $14.95 **650.14**

1. Job hunting 2. Employees—Dismissal 3. Vocational guidance

ISBN 0-767-91557-7 LC 2003-56271

"In addition to providing detailed suggestions for sharpening skills—such as resume writing, interviewing, working with recruiters and networking—{the author} addresses the psychological and emotional problems that often accompany the loss of a job. . . . Upbeat and clearly written, Richardson's comeback program will be welcomed by many." Publ Wkly

Includes bibliographical references

Wendleton, Kate

Building a great résumé; for job hunters, career changers, consultants, and freelancers; with hints for new grads by Mark Gonska. 2nd ed. Career Press 1999 195p il pa $13.99   **650.14**
1. Résumés (Employment) 2. Job hunting 3. Career changes
ISBN 1-56414-433-X   LC 99-38052
First published 1997 by Five O'Clock Books
"Creator of the career-counseling network The Five O'Clock Club, Wendleton uses the club's case study approach with before-and-after examples (over 80 industries are featured) to address the entire process of résumé writing for career changers, consultants, freelancers, and job-hunters." Libr J

Yate, Martin John

Knock 'em dead 2008; the ultimate job search guide; [by] Martin Yate. Adams Media Corp. 341p il pa $14.95   **650.14**
1. Interviewing 2. Applications for positions 3. Job hunting
ISBN 1-59869-165-1; 978-1-59869-165-8
Annual. First published 1985
"Great answers to over 200 tough interview questions—plus the latest electronic job search strategies." Cover
"Updated regularly since 1987, Yate's comprehensive how-to covers the entire job search process from résumé writing and interviewing to salary negotiation and psychological and drug testing, with information on recent developments in the job market. Three appendixes address online searching with valuable listings of web sites and resources arranged by subject." Libr J

651   Office services

The **New** York Public Library business desk reference. Wiley 1998 494p il map hardcover o.p. pa $24.95   **651**
1. Office practice—Handbooks, manuals, etc.
ISBN 0-471-14442-8; 0-471-32835-9 (pa)
LC 97-7408
"A Stonesong Press book"
This work "has sections focusing on information delivery, communications, the office environment, equipment, supplies and systems, human resources, finances, law, public relations, marketing, travel, and information resources. The lists of further information that end each section include organizations, service providers, books, and online resources." Booklist

651.3   Office management

Burton, Sharon

Office procedures for the 21st century; [by] Sharon Burton, Nelda Shelton. 7th ed. Pearson/Prentice-Hall 2008 xxvii, 534p il pa $88   **651.3**

1. Office practice—Handbooks, manuals, etc.
2. Secretaries—Handbooks, manuals, etc.
ISBN 978-0-13-234343-5; 0-13-234343-6
First published 1981 under the authorship of Lucy Mae Jennings with title: Secretarial and general office procedures. Previous title: Procedures for the automated office. Periodically revised
Accompanied by student workbook
This covers business math and language arts skills, the role of office support staff, interpersonal communication, records management, telecommunications, computers and job search skills. Includes application exercises, projects, sample forms and documents
Includes bibliographical references

Stroman, James

Administrative assistant's & secretary's handbook; [by] James Stroman, Kevin Wilson, Jennifer Wauson. 2nd ed. AMACOM 2004 556p il $34.95 *   **651.3**
1. Secretaries—Handbooks, manuals, etc. 2. Office practice—Handbooks, manuals, etc.
ISBN 0-8144-0784-6   LC 2003-10063
First published 1995
This handbook provides information on general procedures and techniques covering such topics as telephone usage and mailing, office equipment and computers, language usage, financial activities, banking, etc.
Includes bibliographical references

651.7   Communication Creation and transmission of records

Lindsell-Roberts, Sheryl

Strategic business letters and e-mail; Sheryl Lindsell-Roberts. Houghton Mifflin 2004 374p il pa $19.95   **651.7**
1. Business letters 2. Electronic mail systems
ISBN 0-618-44833-0   LC 2004-14030
Contents: Making your mark in the business world -- Catapulting your career -- The A, B, Cs of letters -- Crafting your own letters -- Jump start your writing process -- Fine-tuning your message -- Writing results-oriented letters -- Sales and marketing with pizzazz -- Successful job search and employment issues -- Customer relations -- Credit and collections -- Invitations you are cordially invited -- Placing orders and acknowledging orders -- Personal business notes -- Media relations -- Professional potpourri -- Applying e-mail and e-marketing know-how -- E-mail messages that shout read me! -- E-mail etiquette -- E-marketing for results
"This is a book that is not only easy to comprehend but also easy to adapt to one's own business needs." Booklist

Phillips, Ellen Haygood, 1947-

Shocked, appalled, and dismayed! How to write letters of complaint that get results. Vintage Bks. 1999 333p pa $12   **651.7**
1. Business letters 2. Customer relations
ISBN 0-375-70120-6   LC 98-13819

Phillips, Ellen Haygood, 1947-—*Continued*
A guide to writing effective letters of complaint. Legal advice, illustrative anecdotes, and sample letters are provided. An appendix lists the names and addresses of over 600 major companies, government agencies, and consumer organizations

651.8 Data processing. Computer applications

Jaderstrom, Susan
Complete office handbook; the definitive reference for today's electronic office; {by} Susan Jaderstrom, Leonard Kruk, and Joanne Miller; general editor, Susan W. Fenner. 3rd ed. Random House Ref. 2002 596p il maps pa $21.95
651.8
1. Office practice—Handbooks, manuals, etc.
ISBN 0-375-70929-0   LC 2002-727980
First published 1992 with title: Professional Secretaries International complete office handbook
This book "is designed to assist the individual who serves as an administrative assistant, executive assistant, or project manager. . . . It covers, in detail, every facet of office operations, from office supplies and financial record keeping to complex operations, including computers, dictation equipment, and telecommunications equipment. . . . This handbook is just as useful for the entry-level office worker as it is for the professional advancing to the level of executive assistant." Recomm Ref Books for Small & Medium-sized Libr & Media Cent, 2003

652 Processes of written communication

Singh, Simon
The code book; the evolution of secrecy from Mary, Queen of Scots, to quantum cryptography. Doubleday 1999 402p il map hardcover o.p. pa $15
652
1. Cryptography
ISBN 0-385-49531-5; 0-385-49532-3 (pa)
LC 99-35261
This survey explores the evolution of cryptography. "Along the way, we encounter Charles Babbage, the nineteenth-century British polymath who conceived of a steam-powered computer; archeologists who used cryptographic methods to translate Egyptian hieroglyphics; and Navajo code-talkers employed by the U.S. military in the Second World War." New Yorker
Includes bibliographical references

657 Accounting

Siegel, Joel G.
Accounting handbook; [by] Joel G. Siegel, Jae K. Shim. 4th ed. Barron's 2006 993p il $35
657
1. Accounting
ISBN 0-7641-5776-0   LC 2005-45279

First published 1990
Includes bibliographical references
This reference includes sections on financial accounting, tax preparation, auditing, personal financial planning, and governmental and nonprofit accounting and includes a dictionary of accounting terms

658 General management

Barajas, Louis, 1961-
Small business, big life; five steps to creating a great life with your own small business. Thomas Nelson 2007 xx, 199p il $22.99
658
1. Small business 2. Management 3. Success
ISBN 978-1-4016-0336-6; 1-4016-0336-X
LC 2007-1070
The author "describes his and his father's entrepreneurial paths and suggests an inspirational approach to business that relies on four personal greatness cornerstones—truth, responsibility, awareness, and courage—and on keeping in mind your vision and your team's needs. A new take on how to achieve work/life balance." Libr J
Includes bibliographical references

Baskin, Elizabeth Cogswell
How to run your business like a girl; successful strategies from entrepreneurial women who made it happen. Adams Media 2005 210p pa $14.95
658
1. Businesswomen 2. Self-employed women 3. Entrepreneurship
ISBN 1-59337-455-0   LC 2005-7451
The author "examines the state of female entrepreneurship today, not so much from a philosophical or psychological perspective but rather from a very pragmatic point of view: the pros and cons of partnerships, guiding principles to consider, people management 101, weathering economic vicissitudes, among other topics. In the center, acting as exemplars, are three different businesswomen–owners of a public relations agency, a kid-friendly direct mail retailer, and a financial workshop presenter-speaker–accompanied by 'instant wisdom' sidebars." Booklist

Bredin, Alice, 1962-
The virtual office survival handbook; what telecommuters and entrepreneurs need to succeed in today's nontraditional workplace. Wiley 1996 259p pa $16.95 hardcover o.p.
658
1. Home-based business 2. Telecommuting
ISBN 0-471-12059-6 (pa)   LC 96-1327
The author "starts by describing the professions and industries most suited to virtual or home offices and the employee personality and temperament that will thrive in the situation. Then she offers first-rate nitty-gritty advice on setting up an office, from choosing computer systems, legal and tax requirements for home business, time management and more." Publ Wkly
Includes bibliographical references

Business: the ultimate resource. 2nd ed. Basic Books 2006 liii, 1973p il $59.95
658

Business: the ultimate resource—*Continued*
1. Management 2. Entrepreneurship
ISBN 0-465-00830-5; 978-0-465-00830-8
First published 2002
This book offers "information and insights from experts in the business field and covers a wide array of topics, among them telecommuting, leadership, finance, and biographies of business and management notables. . . . This unique resource offers a huge selection of articles and provides a first step for students and scholars gathering information." Libr J
Includes bibliographical references

Collins, James C.
Good to great; why some companies make the leap, and others don't; [by] Jim Collins. HarperBusiness 2001 300p il $27.50   **658**
1. Leadership 2. Management
ISBN 0-06-662099-6   LC 2001-24818
"Starting with every company that ever appeared in the Fortune 500, Collins identifies 11 great ones and looks for similarities among them, and what he finds will both surprise and fascinate anyone involved in management." Booklist
Includes bibliographical references

Drucker, Peter F., 1909-2005
Management challenges for the 21st century; {by} Peter F. Drucker. HarperBusiness 1999 207p $27.50; pa $18   **658**
1. Management
ISBN 0-88730-998-4; 0-88730-999-2 (pa)
                                     LC 99-17087
"Drucker outlines the changing role of management, the new realities of strategy, how to lead in times of great change, how to develop new information sources for effective decision-making, and how individual workers must assume responsibility for managing their own careers." Libr J

Encyclopedia of small business; Arsen J. Darnay, Monique D. Magee, editors. 3rd ed. Thomson Gale 2007 2v set $550   **658**
1. Small business—Encyclopedias
ISBN 0-7876-9112-7; 978-0-7876-9112-7
                                     LC 2006-22623
First published 1998 under the editorship of Kevin Hillstrom and Laurie Collier Hillstrom
This reference arranged in A-Z format contains articles and overviews on areas "including financing; financial planning; business plan creation; market analysis; sales strategy; tax planning and more." Publisher's note
Includes bibliographical references

Fenn, Donna
Alpha dogs; how your small business can become a leader of the pack. Collins 2005 224p il $24.95   **658**
1. Businesspeople 2. Small business 3. Entrepreneurship 4. Success
ISBN 0-06-075867-8; 978-0-06-075867-7
                                     LC 2006-275386

The author "takes us inside the reality of small businesses by showcasing eight successful entrepreneurs who share their stories and strategies. . . . This book offers valuable insight for current and aspiring entrepreneurs." Booklist
Includes bibliographical references

Giuliani, Rudolph W.
Leadership; by Rudolph W. Giuliani with Ken Kurson. Miramax Bks. 2002 407p $25.95
                                                    658
1. Management
ISBN 0-7868-6841-4
This is a "book of guidelines about exemplary management skills {by} New York City's former mayor. . . . {He includes} opening and closing segments about the destruction of the World Trade Center." N Y Times (Late N Y Ed)

Kelley, Robert Earl
How to be a star at work; nine breakthrough strategies you need to succeed. Times Business 1998 xxi, 312p il pa $13 hardcover o.p.
                                                    658
1. Office workers 2. Success
ISBN 0-8129-3169-6 (pa)   LC 97-28117
Kelley's "program is commonsense advice to workers: take initiatives, network for useful information, self-manage, know whom you're trying to please, be a biddable follower when necessary, be a reliable leader when that's called for, work effectively in teams, know your organization and how to present your ideas." Publ Wkly
Includes bibliographical references

Kurtzman, Joel
MBA in a box; the practical guide to the big ideas of business; [by] Joel Kurtzman with Glenn Rifkin & Victoria Griffith. Crown Business 2004 437p $34.95 *   **658**
1. Management
ISBN 0-609-61088-0   LC 2003-19647
"This practical guidebook to business concepts is appropriately straightforward in its approach. . . . The book makes for a refreshing and often humorous read." Publ Wkly
Includes bibliographical references

Lonier, Terri
Working solo; the real guide to freedom & financial success with your own business. 2nd ed. Wiley 1998 xxiv, 354p il pa $14.95   **658**
1. Self-employed 2. Small business
ISBN 0-471-24713-8   LC 98-10660
Also available companion volume The working solo sourcebook (1998)
First published 1994 by Portico Press
This offers advice on starting a small business covering such topics as time management, buying a computer, setting up an office, business planning, low-cost marketing techniques, using technology and the Internet. Includes a resource section on books, on-line services, and software'
Includes bibliographical references

Michelli, Joseph A., 1960-
The Starbucks experience; 5 principles for turning ordinary into extraordinary. McGraw-Hill 2006 208p $21.95 **658**
1. Starbucks Corporation 2. Management 3. Success
ISBN 978-0-07-147784-0; 0-07-147784-5
LC 2006-16788
The author "takes an in-depth look at Starbucks's proven and practical strategies for building a successful, multinational corporation. His chapters illustrate the company's five basic success principles: make it your own, everything matters, surprise and delight, embrace resistance, and leave your mark. Readers will discover a rich mix of ideas and techniques that will help them apply the Starbucks vision, creativity, and leadership to their own careers, workplaces, and companies." Libr J
Includes bibliographical references

O'Reilly, Charles A., III
Hidden value; how great companies achieve extraordinary results with ordinary people; {by} Charles A. O'Reilly III, Jeffrey Pfeffer. Harvard Business School Press 2000 286p il $29.95 **658**
1. Management 2. Human capital
ISBN 0-87584-898-2
LC 00-25016
"Through eight case studies, *Hidden Value* shows how a firm can use existing talent rather than how firms can attract talent. Smart organizations make it possible for ordinary people to perform as stars by engaging their emotional and intellectual resources." Libr J
Includes bibliographical references

Shipley, David
Send; the essential guide to email for office and home; [by] David Shipley and Will Schwalbe. Alfred A. Knopf 2007 247p $19.95 **658**
1. Electronic mail systems 2. Business communication
ISBN 978-0-307-26364-3
LC 2006-35235
The authors discuss the dos and don'ts of composing the body of the [e-mail] text—figuring out what your message really is, then deciding how to begin, how to end, what tone to take, what to say and what not to say. N Y Times Book Rev
A "humorous, pithy, and much-needed guide to the art and science of e-mail. . . . These tutorials are peppered with true tales of e-mail misuse that are both illustrative and amusing. For the more technically inclined, sidebars spell out e-mail's history, . . . briefly explain how it works, and define great moments in e-mail history." Christ Sci Monit

658.1 Organization and finance

Judson, Bruce
Go it alone; the secret to building a successful business on your own; Bruce Judson. HarperBusiness 2004 229p $23.95; pa $14.95 **658.1**
1. Entrepreneurship 2. Small business 3. Management
ISBN 0-06-073113-3; 0-06-073114-1 (pa)
LC 2004-52391

This primer for starting one's own business features "case studies of successful businesses, from which readers can glean . . . tips on marketing, fee structures and customer management." Publ Wkly
The author "offers sound, cogent advice for budding entrepreneurs in a book that will be of value to all readers thinking about going into business." Booklist
Includes bibliographical references

McGuckin, Frances
Business for beginners; from research and business plans to money, marketing and the law. Sourcebooks, Inc. 2005 318p il pa $16.95 * **658.1**
1. Entrepreneurship 2. Small business 3. Management
ISBN 1-4022-0392-6
LC 2005-3351
First published 1997 in Canada
This "is the ultimate of primers, starting with a good self-assessment—do you have the skills for success?—and concluding with real-life tales of seven entrepreneurs." Booklist

Small business sourcebook. 23rd ed. Gale 2007 2v $535 **658.1**
1. Small business
ISSN 0883-3397
ISBN 978-0-7876-9950-5; 0-7876-9950-0
Annual. First published 1983
This "is a standard reference work for identifying information resources for starting, developing, and growing 341 specific small businesses as well as for finding information on general small business topics and sources of assistance at the state and federal levels and by Canadian province. . . . The strength of the reference work lies in its catalog of resources for specific kinds of small businesses as well as the variety of sources covered and the copious annotations. It will aid entrepreneurs who need both general and specific information to help them solve problems." Am Ref Books Annu, 2003

Sullivan, Robert, 1940-
The small business start-up guide. Rev 3rd ed. Information Int. 2000 xx, 339p il pa $17.95 **658.1**
1. Small business
ISBN 1-882480-19-8
LC 99-73135
Also available online
First published 1996
"Sullivan suggests how one can evaluate his or her 'entrepreneurial aptitude' and advises how to get started, obtain financing, select partners, prepare a business plan, establish banking relationships, set up home-based operations, and market effectively. He also considers legal, tax, and personnel issues. Each chapter includes useful checklists and recommends additional sources of information." Booklist [review of 1998 edition]

658.3   Personnel management (Human resource management)

Hewlett, Sylvia Ann, 1946-
Off-ramps and on-ramps; keeping talented women on the road to success. Harvard Business School Press 2007 299p il $29.95   **658.3**
1. Women—Employment
ISBN 978-1-422-10102-5; 1-422-10102-9
           LC 2006-38271
The author "examines why many women exit their careers—taking 'off-ramps' (leaving altogether) or 'scenic routes' (opting to work part-time), often during critical, competitive times. She also provides valuable suggestions for companies hoping to retain talented employees of any gender." Libr J
Includes bibliographical references

Kelly, Matthew, 1973-
The dream manager. Hyperion 2007 158p $19.95   **658.3**
1. Personnel management 2. Motivation (Psychology)
ISBN 978-1-4013-0370-9; 1-4013-0370-6
           LC 2007-13597
This "business fable extols the virtues of helping those working for and with you to achieve their dreams. In this way . . . managers can boost morale and control turnover. . . . This one's sure to appeal to business readers." Libr J

Lancaster, Lynne C.
When generations collide; who they are, why they clash, how to solve the generational puzzle at work; by Lynne C. Lancaster and David Stillman. HarperCollins Pubs. 2002 xxv, 352p $25.95; pa $15.95   **658.3**
1. Personnel management 2. Conflict of generations
ISBN 0-06-662106-2; 0-06-662107-0 (pa)
           LC 2001-39221
At head of title: Traditionalists, baby boomers, generation Xers, millennials
The authors address the "ways of attracting and retaining individuals from the four generations that make up the American workforce. . . . Their book is a guide for employers and employees on how to take advantage of generational differences rather than allowing those differences to drain productivity. As with all outstanding business books, this wise and personable one will appeal to a wide range of readers." Booklist
Includes bibliographical references

658.4   Executive management

Batstone, David B., 1958-
Saving the corporate soul & (who knows?) maybe your own; eight principles for creating and preserving integrity and profitability without selling out; {by} David Batstone. Jossey-Bass 2003 270p $26.95   **658.4**
1. Leadership 2. Business ethics
ISBN 0-7879-6480-8   LC 2002-154858

The author sends a "message to business leaders that conscience and profit go hand in hand. He believes principled companies excel financially over the long haul, are respected more by the public, and are rated as better places to work." Booklist
Includes bibliographical references

Bossidy, Lawrence A.
Execution: the discipline of getting things done; [by] Larry Bossidy & Ram Charan; with Charles Burck. Crown Business 2002 278p $27.50
                            658.4
1. Executive ability 2. Management
ISBN 0-609-61057-0   LC 2002-18743
The authors "present the viewpoint that execution (that is, linking a company's people, strategy, and operations) is what will determine success in today's business world. . . . Details of both successful and unsuccessful executions at corporations such as Dell, Johnson & Johnson, and Xerox, to name a few, support not only their how-to method for bringing execution to the forefront but also the need for it." Libr J
"This is a terrific book that will make smart managers rethink how business gets done within every level of their organization or department." Publ Wkly

Byron, Christopher
Testosterone inc.; tales of CEOs gone wild. Wiley 2004 402p il $27.95; pa $16.95
                            658.4
1. Executives
ISBN 0-471-42005-0; 0-471-70623-X (pa)
           LC 2004-3667
"This self-described tale of 'CEOs Gone Wild' chronicles four of the best-known businessmen of the 1980s and 1990s, mixing stories of their personal and professional lives with an emphasis on their marital infidelities and career power plays. General Electric CEO Jack Welch takes center stage." Booklist
Includes bibliographical references

Camp, Jim
Start with no; the negotiating tools that the pros don't want you to know. Crown Business 2002 271p $22.95   **658.4**
1. Negotiation 2. Business 3. Management
ISBN 0-609-60800-2   LC 2001-47742
"Camp has developed a system of negotiating that reflects the common concept of 'win-win,' and the result is an excellent book with valuable insights." Booklist

Daniels, Cora
Black Power Inc.; the new voice of success. John Wiley & Sons, Inc 2004 xxi, 218p $24.95
                            658.4
1. African American businesspeople 2. African Americans—Social conditions
ISBN 0-471-47090-2   LC 2003-25143
The author "focuses on black professionals in their mid-30s and younger, including both entrepreneurs and those working in the upper ranks of corporate America, showing how they see themselves working the system to benefit the race." Booklist

Encyclopedia of leadership; editors, George R. Goethals, Georgia J. Sorenson, James MacGregor Burns. Sage Publications 2004 4v il map set $595 **658.4**
1. Leadership—Encyclopedias
ISBN 0-7619-2597-X LC 2004-1252
"What is leadership? What is a great leader? What is a great follower? What are the types of leadership? And how does someone become a leader? This set was designed with the needs of several user communities in mind, including students, scholars, and professionals who want to explore such questions." Booklist
Includes bibliographical references

Goleman, Daniel
Primal leadership; realizing the power of emotional intelligence; [by] Daniel Goleman, Richard Boyatzis, Annie McKee. Harvard Business School Press 2002 306p $26.95 **658.4**
1. Leadership 2. Management 3. Executive ability
ISBN 1-57851-486-X LC 2001-41207
This title focuses "on the relationship between Emotional Intelligence (EI) and successful leadership. . . . The book is arranged in three sections, with the first section describing the characteristics of resonant and dissonant leadership as well as the four dimensions of EI, which are self-awareness, self-management, social awareness, and relationship management. This section also describes the different types of leadership styles, such as visionary, coaching, and commanding. The second section outlines the steps one needs to take to become a more positive leader, and the third section discusses how to use these newfound skills to build a better organization." Libr J
This "book is well written, intelligent, approachable, and stimulating." Booklist
Includes bibliographical references

Heller, Robert, 1932-
Essential manager's manual; {by} Robert Heller & Tim Hindle. DK Pub. 1998 864p il $40 **658.4**
1. Management 2. Time management 3. Decision making
ISBN 0-7894-3519-5 LC 98-6507
The authors "focus on time management, decision making, and communication, but subjects also include successful delegation, interviewing, stress reduction, and managing change. This sturdy manual is well organized and well written, and it has an excellent index." Booklist

Krames, Jeffrey A.
The Rumsfeld way; leadership wisdom of a battle-hardened maverick. McGraw-Hill 2002 244p il $18.95; pa $12.95 **658.4**
1. Rumsfeld, Donald H. 2. Leadership
ISBN 0-07-140641-7; 0-07-141516-5 (pa)
LC 2002-523119
This book looks "at the leadership skills, methods, and strategies that have made Secretary of Defense Donald Rumsfeld an accomplished public figure." Libr J
Includes bibliographical references

Peters, Thomas J.
The circle of innovation; you can't shrink your way to greatness; by Tom Peters. Knopf 1997 xxi, 518p il $35; pa $16 **658.4**
1. Success 2. Executive ability 3. Management
ISBN 0-375-40157-1; 0-679-75765-1 (pa)
LC 97-74755
The author argues for constant innovation as a survival strategy for both the individual and the organization. Topics discussed include company decentralization, product design, empowering customers, system building, and corporate willingness to experiment

Rubinfeld, Arthur
Built for growth; expanding your business around the corner or across the globe; [by] Arthur Rubinfeld, Collins Hemingway. Wharton School Pub. 2005 xxiv, 343p il map $25.95 *
658.4
1. Retail trade 2. Management
ISBN 0-13-146574-0 LC 20040114697
"The authors intend the book to be 'a valuable primer on all aspects of retail: brand, location, people, finance, property management, expansion strategy and long-term thinking.' . . . An informative read for both beginners and seasoned retailers, this outstanding book abounds with insightful case studies and expert advice that should enhance the success of any retail brand." Libr J

Sawyer, R. Keith (Robert Keith)
Group genius; the creative power of collaboration; [by] Keith Sawyer. Basic Books 2007 274p il $26.95; pa $16.95 **658.4**
1. Group problem solving 2. Creative thinking
ISBN 978-0-465-07192-0; 0-465-07192-9; 978-0-465-07193-7 (pa); 0-465-07193-7 (pa)
LC 2007-8007
The author "reveals how organizations can foster a spirit of collaboration to encourage creativity and innovation among their constituents. . . . Sawyer demonstrates how breakthroughs frequently grow from discussion, argumentation, and group activities." Libr J
Includes bibliographical references

Tatum, Doug
No man's land; what to do when your company is too big to be small but too small to be big. Portfolio 2007 245p il $24.95 **658.4**
1. Small business 2. Management
ISBN 978-1-59184-172-2; 1-59184-172-0
LC 2007-9388
The aim of this guide is to help "companies navigate the fatal trap of 'no man's land,' a perilous zone where they have outgrown the habits and practices that fueled their early growth but have not yet adopted new practices and resources to cope with their new situation and challenges. . . . Tatum's potent guide communicates the key ideas vividly with engaging stories and evocative writing, and will help leaders identify and survive a key phase in a company's growth." Publ Wkly
Includes bibliographical references

Welch, John F.
Winning; [by] Jack Welch with Suzy Welch.
HarperBusiness 2005 384p $27.95   **658.4**
1. Business 2. Success
ISBN 0-06-075394-3   LC 2005-40337
The author offers business advice "from practices he
employed at GE (e.g., the much-debated differentiation,
which includes winnowing 10% of the workforce at regular intervals), to the personal qualities that lead to success (to Welch, candor is essential), to advice on job
hunting and how to work with a bad boss, to ways to
maximize the budget process. . . . It's difficult to think
of anyone in business who wouldn't benefit from reading
this savvy, engaging cubicle-to-boardroom guide to success." Publ Wkly

658.8   Management of marketing

Anderson, Christopher
The long tail; why the future of business is
selling less of more; [by] Chris Anderson.
Hyperion 2006 238p il $24.95   **658.8**
1. Internet marketing
ISBN 1-4013-0237-8; 978-1-4013-0237-5
LC 2006-43378
"Citing statistical curves called 'long-tailed distributions' because the tails are very long relative to the
heads, Anderson . . . focuses on the tail, or the development in the new digital world of an infinite number of
niche markets of any size that are economically viable
due to falling distribution costs and in the aggregate represent significant sales." Booklist
This "book does an excellent job of spotting trends
and fitting them into an easily accessible theoretical
framework that helps explain the changing culture around
us." N Y Times (Late N Y Ed)
Includes bibliographical references

Gerhards, Paul
How to sell what you make; the business of
marketing crafts. rev & updated ed. Stackpole Bks.
1996 151p il pa $12.95   **658.8**
1. Selling 2. Handicraft
ISBN 0-8117-2436-0   LC 95-37330
First published 1990
This offers advice on how to market crafts through
fairs, trade shows, and galleries, and includes information
on small business management
Includes bibliographical references

Underhill, Paco
Why we buy; the science of shopping. Simon &
Schuster 1999 255p hardcover o.p. pa $15
          658.8
1. Marketing 2. Consumers
ISBN 0-684-84913-5; 0-684-84914-3 (pa)
LC 99-12125
"Each chapter delves into a particular aspect of a store
environment and its interface with customers: the importance of signage and why less is more, how men shop,
. . . the need to cater to boomers, and clues about waiting time. Throughout, insights are peppered with one or
several examples." Booklist

659.1   Advertising

The **Advertising** age encyclopedia of advertising;
editors, John McDonough and the Museum of
Broadcast Communications, Karen Egolf;
illustration editor, Jacqueline V. Reid. Fitzroy
Dearborn Pubs. 2003 3v il set $385
          659.1
ISBN 1-57958-172-2   LC 2003-270744
This encyclopedia provides "historic surveys of the
world's leading agencies and major advertisers, as well
as brand and market histories; it also profiles the influential men and women in advertising, overviews advertising
in the major countries of the world, covers important issues affecting the field, and discusses the key aspects of
methodology, practice, strategy, and theory." Publisher's
note
"Well-researched, thorough, and fascinating, it belongs
in all business collections and most academic and large
public libraries." Booklist

Tungate, Mark, 1967-
Adland; a global history of advertising. Kogan
Page Ltd 2007 278p il $39.95   **659.1**
1. Advertising—History
ISBN 978-0-7494-4837-0; 0-7494-4837-7
LC 2007-16432
The author "illustrates the history and globalization of
the $400-billion-a-year advertising industry." Publ Wkly
"As a definitive record of what happened and why,
there is none finer. Whether you're a novice in the in-
dustry or . . . a veteran of 25 years, there is much to
learn." Management Today
Includes bibliographical references

660.6   Biotechnology

Hubbell, Sue
Shrinking the cat; genetic engineering before we
knew about genes; with illustrations by Liddy
Hubbell. Houghton Mifflin 2001 175p il $25; pa
$13   **660.6**
1. Breeding 2. Genetic engineering
ISBN 0-618-04027-7; 0-618-25748-9 (pa)
LC 2001-24547
This is a "history of how genetic engineering began,
how it has been used, and how humankind has benefited
from a combination of natural selection and scientific
manipulation of genes. Hubbell . . . shows that genetic
engineering has always been with us, illustrating by way
of silkworm breeding from its origins in China to the
New World, where it spawned an industry that depends
on genetics to thrive; the domestication of corn from its
wild state to the product we eat today; [and] how we
turned wildcats into house cats by selective breeding that
changed size, color, and demeanor." Libr J
"An engaging synthesis of material that will appeal to
Hubbell's well-established audience." Booklist
Includes bibliographical references

Steinberg, Mark L.
The Facts on File dictionary of biotechnology and genetic engineering; authors, Mark L. Steinberg and Sharon D. Cosloy. 3rd ed. Facts on File 2006 275p il (Facts on File science library) $49.50   **660.6**
1. Biotechnology—Dictionaries 2. Genetic engineering—Dictionaries
ISBN 0-8160-6351-6; 978-0-8160-6351-2
LC 2005-56751
First published 1994
"Among the topics covered [in this dictionary] are: Medicine, agriculture, and biochemistry, including fields related to biochemical research; cancer treatments and genetically engineered growth hormones; vaccines; the scientists responsible for major research breakthroughs and the products they've helped to create." Publisher's note

664   Food technology

Charles, Daniel
Lords of the harvest; biotech, big money, and the future of food. Perseus Bks. 2001 348p il pa $17.50 hardcover o.p.   **664**
1. Food—Biotechnology 2. Genetic engineering 3. Agricultural industry 4. Farm produce
ISBN 0-7382-0773-X (pa)
The author "covers the history of genetic engineering in plant crops from the early 1980s to the present. . . . What makes this book particularly interesting are the author's tales of the key individuals and groups involved in the biotechnology controversy. . . . This carefully researched and balanced account is intended to help the reader understand the how and the why of genetic engineering rather than make an argument for or against it." Libr J
Includes bibliographical references

Winston, Mark L.
Travels in the genetically modified zone. Harvard Univ. Press 2002 280p hardcover o.p. pa $19.50   **664**
1. Food—Biotechnology 2. Food—Biotechnology 3. Farm produce
ISBN 0-674-00867-7; 978-0-674-01529-6 (pa); 0-674-01529-0 (pa)   LC 2002-17192
The author "first describes the development of hybrid corn, then delves into the use of genetic modifications to combat weeds and diseases. The facets of genetic modification he takes into account include research, industrial processes, growing modified crops, protecting nearby crops, the safety of consumers, and the profits of agribusiness. . . . Winston also fields practical ideas for solving the major problems involved in the rapidly growing field of genetically modified crops. Throughout, however, he maintains a moderate stance on his controversial subject." Booklist
Includes bibliographical references

Winter, Ruth, 1930-
A consumer's dictionary of food additives; descriptions in plain English of more than 12,000 ingredients both harmful and desirable found in foods. Completely rev. and updated 6th ed. Three Rivers Press 2004 579p pa $16.95   **664**
1. Food additives—Dictionaries
ISBN 1-4000-5232-7   LC 2004-5062
First published 1972. Periodically revised
This book provides "facts about the relative safety and side effects of more than 12,000 ingredients that end up in your food as a result of processing and curing, such as preservatives, food-tainting pesticides, and animal drugs." Publisher's note

666   Ceramic and allied technologies

Macfarlane, Alan
Glass: a world history; {by} Alan Macfarlane and Gerry Martin. University of Chicago Press 2002 255p il $27.50 *   **666**
1. Glass
ISBN 0-226-50028-4   LC 2002-20493
The authors "make the case for the centrality of glass in the artistic renaissance and scientific revolution that took place in Western Europe from the 14th to 17th centuries. They discuss the origins of glass making and trace its development and usage across centuries and multiple cultures (Europe, the Middle East, China, India, and Japan). Their discussion combines cultural, artistic, and aesthetic viewpoints of glass within these cultures with history and developments in science. The result is a thoroughly readable, carefully argued work, filled with delightful surprises. . . . An excellent example of microhistory . . . this is required for history of science collections and recommended for large public and academic collections." Libr J
Includes bibliographical references

667   Cleaning, color, coating, related technologies

Garfield, Simon
Mauve; how one man invented a color that changed the world. Norton 2001 222p il pa $13.95 hardcover o.p.   **667**
1. Perkin, William Henry, 1838-1907 2. Dyes and dyeing
ISBN 0-393-32313-7 (pa)   LC 00-69533
This volume discusses how a British student, William Henry Perkin, while trying to synthesize quinine from coal tar, developed mauve, "the first mass-produced artificial dye. . . . By the turn of the 20th century, because of Perkin's novel idea, dye makers had 2,000 synthesized colors at their disposal." N Y Times Book Rev
"The text is understandable by the average layman and is enjoyable reading for the scientist and non-scientist alike." Sci Books Films
Includes bibliographical references

Greenfield, Amy Butler, 1968-
A perfect red; empire, espionage, and the quest for the color of desire; Amy Butler Greenfield. 1st ed. HarperCollins 2005 338p il $26.95

667

1. Dyes and dyeing
ISBN 0-06-052275-5   LC 2004-42376
This is a "history of Europe's centuries-long clamor for cochineal, a dye capable of producing the 'brightest, strongest red the Old World had ever seen.'" Publ Wkly
The author "combines the investigative prowess of a detective with the intellectual reasoning of an academician to create an eminently entertaining and educational read." Booklist
Includes bibliographical references

668   Technology of other organic products

Turin, Luca
The secret of scent; adventures in perfume and the science of smell. Ecco 2006 207p il $23.95; pa $13.95

668

1. Perfumes
ISBN   0-06-113383-3;   978-0-06-113383-1; 0-06-113384-1 (pa); 978-0-06-113384-8 (pa)
LC 2006-46273
The author "investigates the reason things smell they way they do." N Y Times Book Rev
"This volume is a triumph of popular science writing. . . . Readers to whom scents and odorants were not at the top of their reading list will find that this volume propels a narrative they will hardly want to put down." Sci Books Films
Includes bibliographical references

Winter, Ruth, 1930-
A consumer's dictionary of cosmetic ingredients. 6th ed., completely rev. and updated. Three Rivers Press 2005 563p pa $16.95

668

1. Cosmetics—Dictionaries
ISBN 1-4000-5233-5; 978-1-4000-5233-2
LC 2005-273775
First published 1974. Periodically revised
This volume describes over 6,000 ingredients used in cosmetics including preservatives, coloring agents, flavorings, fragrances, and preserving agents, their effectiveness and possible toxic and allergic effects.
Includes bibliographical references

671.5   Joining and cutting of metals

Geary, Don
Welding. McGraw-Hill 2000 264p il pa $34.95

*   **671.5**

1. Welding
ISBN 0-07-134245-1   LC 99-35501
"Starting with the basics of setting up a welding outfit and with a focus on oxyacetylene welding, this book discusses . . . processes, fuels, equipment, supplies and welding techniques. . . . It even covers safety issues and how to set up your own welding workshop. It also provides welding projects for beginners to try out what they've learned." Publisher's note

674   Lumber processing, wood products, cork

The **Encyclopedia** of wood; a tree-by-tree guide to the world's most versatile resource; general editor, Aidan Walker. Facts on File 2005 192p il map $35   **674**
1. Wood
ISBN 0-8160-6181-5   LC 2004-60849
First published 1989
This book "provides an A-to-Z directory featuring more than 150 of the world's most popular woods, with information on growth rate, distribution, key characteristics, working properties, and commercial uses." Publisher's note
"A nice addition to libraries with strong interior design or DIY collections." Libr J
Includes bibliographical references

Petroski, Henry
The pencil; a history of design and circumstance. Knopf 1990 434p il hardcover o.p. pa $20   **674**
1. Pencils
ISBN 0-394-57422-2; 0-679-73415-5 (pa)
LC 89-45362
The author discusses the manufacture, design, history, and sociological significance of the pencil.
"An incredibly rich and complex history of this entirely unremarkable instrument of communication." SLJ
Includes bibliographical references

676   Pulp and paper technology

Asunción, Josep
The complete book of papermaking. Lark Books 2003 160p il $24.95   **676**
1. Papermaking
ISBN 1-57990-456-4   LC 2002-155637
The author "covers the history and present-day techniques of the craft in a well-illustrated book that includes paper samples. . . . This excellent guide is highly recommended for all arts and crafts collections." Libr J
Includes bibliographical references

677   Textiles

Fairchild's dictionary of textiles; Phyllis G. Tortora, editor; Robert S. Merkel, consulting editor. 7th ed. Fairchild Publications 1995 c1996 xx, 662p il $50   **677**
1. Textile industry—Dictionaries
ISBN 978-0-87005-707-6; 0-87005-707-3
LC 94-61457
First published 1959. Periodically revised

Fairchild's dictionary of textiles—*Continued*
"Reference source for all branches of the industry. Includes entries on fibers, yarns, fabric construction, finishing and sale, inventors and developers, and government standards and regulations. Includes appendix of organizations involved with the textile industry." N Y Public Libr Book of How & Where to Look It Up
Includes bibliographical references

Schoeser, Mary, 1950-
World textiles: a concise history. Thames & Hudson 2003 224p il (World of art) pa $14.95 *
677
1. Fabrics 2. Textile industry
ISBN 0-500-20369-5   LC 2002-110919
"Arranged roughly into chronological periods, the book . . . details technique, materials, and designs and puts them in historical and cultural context. This is truly a fantastic history of textile arts. . . . The text itself is a delight to read and more comprehensive than in other comparable works." Libr J
Includes bibliographical references

681 Precision instruments and other devices

Angel, Solly
The tale of the scale; an odyssey of invention. Oxford University Press 2003 304p il $28
681
1. Inventions 2. Industrial design
ISBN 0-19-515868-7   LC 2003-48699
This is the "story of one man's attempt to design a novel personal (bathroom) scale. . . . The book is more than simply a narrative of the author's successes and failures; it also contains his musings on topics that should be of interest to scientists and engineers: the . . . scientific method, the relationship between form and function, design theory, and creativity, among others. . . . I highly recommend this very interesting, very entertaining account of how one person went through the product design and development process." Sci Books Films
Includes bibliographical references

682 Small forge work (Blacksmithing)

Parkinson, Peter, 1942-
The artist blacksmith; design and techniques. Crowood Press; distributed by Trafalgar Sq. Pub. 2002 160p il $40
682
1. Blacksmithing
ISBN 1-86126-428-3
"Parkinson explains the tools, materials, and equipment needed by blacksmiths as well as the most commonly used techniques. Numerous illustrations of beautiful creations (such as gates, sculptures, household items, and furniture) appear throughout this fascinating title." Libr J

684 Furnishings and home workshops

Abram, Norm
Measure twice, cut once; lessons from a master carpenter. Little, Brown 1996 196p il $18.95
684
1. Woodwork 2. Carpentry
ISBN 0-316-00494-4   LC 96-7584
In this book about woodwork and carpentry the author "deals mainly with hand tools. Abram covers items such as levels, chalk lines, and plumb-bobs, detailing his experiences with them and his preferences. . . . Even experienced woodworkers will pick up a tip or two from this book." Libr J

Bird, Lonnie
The complete illustrated guide to shaping wood. Taunton Press 2001 294p il $39.95   684
1. Woodwork
ISBN 1-56158-400-2   LC 2001-27430
This guide shows "the many ways of shaping wood (cutting, edge treatments, decorative techniques, turning, and carving). Techniques of all types and complexity are covered, usually including several means to accomplish each task, such as using hand or power tools. Profusely illustrated with drawings and photos, this book offers something for every woodworker." Libr J
Includes bibliographical references

Hoadley, R. Bruce, 1933-
Understanding wood; a craftsman's guide to wood technology. 2nd ed. Taunton Press 2000 280p il $39.95   684
1. Woodwork 2. Wood
ISBN 1-56158-358-8   LC 00-44322
First published 1980
This guide "covers the nature of wood and its properties, the basics of wood technology, and the woodworker's raw materials." Publisher's note
Includes bibliographical references

Horwood, Roger
The woodworker's handbook. Lyons Press 2003 160p il pa $19.95   684
1. Woodwork
ISBN 1-58574-839-0
First published 1999 in the United Kingdom
This book "features sections on: the most popular natural and manmade woods; use, care and maintenance of tools and equipment; techniques and basic woodworking skills; a . . . range of step-by-step projects; repairs and restoration of old wood." Publisher's note

Peters, Rick
Popular mechanics router fundamentals; the complete guide. Hearst Books 2004 192p il pa $17.95   684
1. Woodworking machinery 2. Woodwork
ISBN 1-588-16365-2   LC 2004-47572

Peters, Rick—*Continued*

"Readers are first told what to look for when selecting a router—the numerous types are outlined in table format—and then given an overview of the huge variety of bits and accessories. Instructions are provided for handheld and table-mounted routing operations, as well as tool maintenance, troubleshooting, and the creation and use of numerous shop-made jigs and fixtures; four projects (a clock, box, picture frame, and trivet) illustrate important techniques. Router books are published so frequently that libraries hardly need all of them, but this is one of the best to date." Libr J

Woodworker's guide to wood; softwoods, hardwoods, plywoods, composites, veneers. Sterling 2000 192p il pa $24.95   **684**

1. Wood 2. Lumber and lumbering
ISBN 0-8069-3687-8   LC 99-86641

Peters' book is "geared toward hobbyist woodworkers. He covers the process of making lumber from start to finish, including how trees grow, their structure, common ways of milling and drying lumber, grading, and possible defects found in wood. One section shows wood samples (both finished and plain) and describes their basic working characteristics." Libr J

Reed, Carol

Router joinery workshop; common joints, simple setups & clever jigs. Lark Bks. 2003 160p il pa $19.95   **684**

1. Woodworking machinery 2. Woodwork
ISBN 1-57990-328-2   LC 2002-30169

"Part 1 covers router features and tool selection, bits, maintenance, the creation of a number of utilitarian (but effective) jigs from common materials, and basic tool use. Part 2 shows how to make several popular joints: rabbets, dadoes, dovetails, box joints, and mortise and tenons. . . . Reed does a thorough job of explaining a somewhat complicated tool and its numerous accessories. Routers are very popular because they are so versatile; this title is among the best on the subject and should be considered by all public libraries." Libr J

Taunton's complete illustrated guide to woodworking; [by] Lonnie Bird . . . [et al.] Taunton Press 2005 311p il $29.95 *   **684**

1. Woodwork
ISBN 1-56158-769-9   LC 2004-28678

This "guide covers a wide array of woodworking topics. . . . The arrangement is consistent and well thought out, with illustrated referencing at the beginning of each chapter." Libr J

Underhill, Roy

The woodwright's apprentice; twenty favorite projects from the Woodwright's shop; with drawings & photographs by the author. University of N.C. Press 1996 196p il $34.95; pa $22.50   **684**

1. Woodwork
ISBN 0-8078-2304-X; 0-8078-4612-0 (pa)
LC 96-14911

Photographs and measured drawings accompany step-by-step directions for 20 projects, among them: a workbench, a music stand, a fireplace bellows and a revolving Windsor chair. Skills covered include dovetailing, turning, steam-bending, and carving. An illustrated glossary of tools and terms is included

Warner, Pat

The router book. Taunton Press 2001 185p pa $19.95   **684**

1. Power tools 2. Woodwork
ISBN 1-56158-423-1   LC 2001-27149

"Warner shows readers how to get the most from their router, covering tools, accessories, and its use. Fixed-base, plunge routers, and laminate trimmers are introduced with excellent evaluations of specific models of each type." Libr J

684.1   Furniture

Storage & shelving solutions; over 70 projects and ideas that fit your budget, space, and lifestyle; with the editors of The Family Handyman. Reader's Digest Association 2006 255p il $26.95   **684.1**

1. Cabinetwork 2. Storage in the home
ISBN 0-7621-0636-0; 978-0-7621-0636-3
LC 2005-50772

Spine title: Family handyman storage and shelving solutions

"These home storage projects are neatly packaged, each accompanied by a box listing skill level, tools needed, and approximate cost (a nice feature) as well as a box with a shopping and cutting list. . . . This polished book on a great topic is recommended for public libraries." Libr J

686   Printing and related activities

Lee, Marshall, 1921-

Bookmaking: editing, design, production; technical consultant Joseph Gannon. 3rd ed. Norton 2004 494p il $49.95   **686**

1. Books 2. Book industry
ISBN 0-393-73018-2   LC 2003-59672

"A Balance House book"

First published 1965 by Bowker

This book describes "the business and art of transmitting an author's manuscript to readers by means of a book. The process includes editing, physical and visual design, costing, production planning, scheduling, procurement, and distribution. . . . This timeless classic should be acquired while it is still available." Choice

Includes bibliographical references

687 Clothing and accessories

Sullivan, James, 1965-
Jeans: a cultural history of an American icon.
Gotham Books 2006 303p il $26   **687**
1. Jeans (Clothing)
ISBN 1-59240-214-3; 978-1-59240-214-4
LC 2005-35698
This book "traces the itinerary of denim pants from
their 19th-century origins as a workingman's wardrobe
staple to their present status as 'the best-selling garment
of all time.'" N Y Times Book Rev
The author "keeps the writing brisk and the major
players . . . distinct while ranging across continents and
decades, giving devotees the definitive account of the development of the denim that decorates their derrieres."
Publ Wkly
Includes bibliographical references

690 Building & construction

The **Art** of natural building; design, construction,
resources; editors: Joseph F. Kennedy, Michael
Smith, Catherine Wanek; illustrated by Joseph
F. Kennedy. New Soc. Pubs. 2002 291p il pa
$26.95   **690**
1. Building 2. Building materials 3. House construction
ISBN 0-86571-433-9
"The authors, who are practitioners in the natural
building movement, introduce a variety of nontraditional
construction options, including underground building and
building with alternative materials such as adobe,
recycled agricultural materials, rammed earth, and straw
bale. They also address energy efficiency, design, and
the desire to create a healthy environment. The final
chapters include case studies." Libr J
Includes bibliographical references

Bukowski, Steven J.
Flooring instant answers. McGraw-Hill 2003
xxv, 285p il pa $49.95   **690**
1. Floors
ISBN 0-07-140204-7   LC 2003-266285
"This ready-reference covers flooring materials (mar-
ble, hardwood, carpet, and vinyl), installing procedures,
layout, and more. For each material there is a discussion
of the varying qualities of products as well as information on installation, maintenance, and repair." Libr J

Gonzalez, Steve, 1959-
Before you hire a contractor; a construction
guidebook for consumers. Consumer's Press 1994
180p il pa $12.95   **690**
1. House construction 2. Consumer education
ISBN 1-8912-6465-6   LC 94-37497
The author "discusses the essentials of selecting a contractor, negotiating contracts, and avoiding scams and
provides rudimentary information about liens, insurance,
bonding, and consumer rights. . . . The numbers and addresses of consumer protection agencies are listed state
by state, as are construction regulatory offices." Libr J

Inwood, Robert
Creative country construction; building & living
in harmony with nature; {by} Robert Inwood &
Christian Bruyere. Sterling 2000 288p il pa $19.95
    690
1. House construction
ISBN 0-8069-7115-0   LC 99-86650
A combined and revised edition of In harmony with
nature and Country comforts, first published 1975 and
1976 respectively by Drake Pub.
This is "a general resource with illustrations depicting
various construction practices derived from the building
techniques of early American homesteaders. Chapters focus on stone masonry, wood-frame construction, log
homes, and post-and-beam construction." Libr J

Kidder, Tracy
House. Houghton Mifflin 1985 341p il pa $14
hardcover o.p.   **690**
1. House construction
ISBN 0-618-00191-3 (pa)   LC 85-7630
"A Richard Todd book"
"The saga of a couple who supervised the building of
their house in Massachusetts, this report interweaves the
personal lives of those involved in the project with New
England history, the sociology of building, popular lore
and practical tips for would-be homebuilders." Publ
Wkly
Includes bibliographical references

Levy, Matthys
Why buildings fall down; how structures fail;
{by} Matthys Levy and Mario Salvadori;
illustrations by Kevin Woest. Norton 1992 334p il
pa $14.95 hardcover o.p.   **690**
1. Building failures 2. Structural failures
ISBN 0-3933-1152-X (pa)   LC 91-34954
"Two structural engineers examine puzzling structural
failures and collapses and the destruction of ancient and
modern buildings, bridges, dams, and other constructions.
Plenty of illustrations accent the lively text." Booklist

Means illustrated construction dictionary. 3rd ed,
unabridged. Means 2000 790p il + 1 computer
optical disc $99.95 *   **690**
1. Building—Dictionaries
ISBN 0-87629-538-3   LC 2001-266365
Also available paperback condensed edition $59.95
(ISBN 0-87629-697-5)
First published 1985
Over 19,000 definitions of words, terms, and concepts
related to the construction industry. Tables of weights,
measures, conversions, size determinations, and symbols
are included
"This is an indispensable resource for large do-it-
yourself, homeowner, or construction collections. Highly
recommended." Libr J

Nash, George, 1949-
Do-it-yourself housebuilding; the complete
handbook; illustrations by Roland Dahlquist.
Sterling 1995 704p il pa $24.95   **690**
1. House construction
ISBN 0-8069-0424-0   LC 94-2371

Nash, George, 1949--—*Continued*

This "book covers every step of house construction from site selection to finishing touches. The authors discuss both rough and finish carpentry and show how to install plumbing, and electrical, heating, and air-conditioning systems. The text is supplemented by numerous excellent photographs and illustrations." Libr J

Includes bibliographical references

Peters, Rick

Popular mechanics garage makeovers; adding space without adding on. Hearst Books 2006 192p il pa $17.95   **690**

1. Garages

ISBN 978-1-58816-513-8; 1-58816-513-2

LC 2006-7912

"The book is divided into three main parts: planning, which covers basic construction methods and styles; real-life examples of different projects (including budget estimates); and plans for implementing any or all of the features shown. . . . Peters covers everything from basic construction techniques such as drywalling a ceiling and building walls to installing garage door openers and wall-mounted storage systems. . . . Those considering tackling a garage renovation will find the book's common-sense approach and practical advice invaluable." Publ Wkly

Schoenherr, Matthew

House transformed; getting the home you want—with the house you have; [by] Matthew Schoenherr with Linda Hunter and Wendy Jordan. Taunton Press 2005 186p il $32   **690**

1. Houses—Remodeling

ISBN 1-56158-711-7   LC 2004-26818

This book outlining projects for home renovation describes "seven keys to a successful remodel, whether you are redoing a kitchen, building an addition, or making over the whole house." Publisher's note

Schuttner, Scott

Building and designing decks. Taunton Press 1993 153p il $19.95   **690**

1. Patios

ISBN 1-56158-320-0   LC 92-30687

"A Fine Homebuilding book"

"With step-by-step instructions, this book shows how to build a deck from design to completion, including finishing touches such as seats and planters. A 'gallery of deck designs' portrays a number of beautiful decks." Libr J

Scutella, Richard M.

How to plan, contract, and build your own home; [by] Richard M. Scutella, Dave Heberle; illustrations by Jay Marcinowski. 4th ed. McGraw-Hill 2005 xxi, 793p il pa $34.95   **690**

1. House construction 2. Building

ISBN 0-07-144885-3   LC 2005-49607

First published 1987 by Tab Bks.

"Full of basic technical information for the owner who wants to gain building knowledge for a home project, this book goes beyond floor plans and appearances to focus on construction details and considerations, from building a foundation to planning a bathroom or kitchen. Every chapter ends with a 'Points to Ponder' section that summarizes what to consider when choosing building methods and addresses details that should be discussed with builders and contractors." Libr J

Woodson, R. Dodge (Roger Dodge), 1955-

Build your dream home for less. Betterway Bks. 1995 185p pa $18.99   **690**

1. House construction 2. Building

ISBN 1-55870-383-7   LC 95-9087

This "explains the unknown elements of general contracting to the novice homebuilder. The author organizes the building process, proposes ways to save money, and suggests valuable DIY projects for the homeowner." Libr J

692   Auxiliary construction practices

Architectural graphic standards; authored by the American Institute of Architects; Andrew Pressman, editor-in-chief; Smith Maran Architecture and Interiors, graphics editor; with additional illustrations from the Magnum Group. 11th ed. Wiley 2007 xxxvi, 1080p il map $250   **692**

1. Architecture—Details

ISBN 978-0-471-70091-3; 0-471-70091-6

LC 2006-102175

Also available CD-ROM version and student edition $110 (ISBN: 978-0-470-08546-2)

First published 1932 under the authorship of Charles G. Ramsey and Harold R. Sleeper. Periodically revised

A guide to structural elements and details, types and dimensions of modern building materials, hardware and furniture.

Includes bibliographical references

694   Wood construction Carpentry

Bollinger, Don

Hardwood floors; laying, sanding and finishing. Taunton Press 1990 137p il pa $19.95   **694**

1. Floors

ISBN 0-942391-62-4   LC 90-11065

The author "addresses the three types of flooring: strip, plank, and parquet—covering such topics as estimating costs; selecting wood types and grades; preparing the underlayment; planning the layout; sanding; and applying various finishes." Libr J

Includes bibliographical references

Burch, Monte, 1943-
Complete guide to building log homes; drawings by Richard J. Meyer and Lloyd P. Birmingham. Sterling 1990 406p il pa $19.95   **694**
1. Log cabins and houses
ISBN 0-8069-7486-9   LC 90-39505
This offers instruction in building log cabins including purchasing the land, making floor plans, shaping the logs, and construction techniques

695   Roof covering

Kennedy, Terry
Roofing instant answers. McGraw-Hill 2002 500p il pa $49.95 *   **695**
1. Roofs
ISBN 0-07-138712-9   LC 2002-284416
This companion volume to Steven Bukowski's Flooring instant answers provides answers to questions about roofing, including more than 300 photos, drawings, tables and checklists
Includes bibliographical references

696   Utilities

Henkenius, Merle, 1950-
Plumbing: complete projects for the home. New expanded ed. Creative Homeowner 2006 287p il pa $19.95 *   **696**
1. Plumbing
ISBN 1-58011-311-7; 978-1-58011-311-3
          LC 2006-924699
First published 2002 with title: Plumbing: basic, intermediate & advanced projects
Variant title: Ultimate guide to plumbing: complete projects for the home
The author "shows homeowners how to tackle expensive plumbing repairs (e.g., replacing a washer in a leaky faucet). . . . The skill level of each project is rated, and photos walk users step by step through the instructions. . . . Strongly recommended for all collections." Libr J

697   Heating, ventilating, air-conditioning engineering

Kittle, James L., 1913-
Home heating and air conditioning systems; line drawings by Gary McKinney. TAB Bks. 1990 230p il pa $19.95 hardcover o.p.   **697**
1. Houses—Heating and ventilation 2. Air conditioning
ISBN 0-8306-3257-3 (pa)   LC 89-29159
A guide to the examination and repair of gas- and oil-fired furnaces, boilers, air-conditioning systems, and heat pumps. A troubleshooting chart is appended

698   Detail finishing

Donegan, Francis
Paint your home; skills, techniques, and tricks of the trade for professional looking interior painting. Reader's Digest Assn. 1997 135p il $18.95   **698**
1. House painting
ISBN 0-89577-838-6   LC 96-46950
"Preparation, application, and clean-up are detailed, with drawings to illustrate the directions given; photographs show how color can make various elements in a room look different. Donegan intersperses professional tips throughout the text and offers safety advice, information on different paint products, and solutions to commonplace problems. This is the best book currently available to the do-it-yourselfer on home painting." Libr J

Lord, Gary, 1952-
It's faux easy by Gary Lord. North Light Books 2005 144p il pa $24.99   **698**
1. House painting
ISBN 1-58180-554-3   LC 2004-49282
On cover: Paint 30 fabulous finishes for your home
The author's "20 projects, graduated in difficulty from simple texturizing to complicated stencil work, take handy home owners from gathering supplies and wall prep to application techniques. . . . A first-rate addition to the do-it-yourself shelf." Booklist

Skinner, Kerry
The paint effects bible; 100 recipes for faux finishes. Firefly Bks. 2003 256p il spiral bdg $29.95   **698**
1. House painting 2. Decoration and ornament
ISBN 1-55297-718-8   LC 2003-271574
The author "demonstrates how to create a multitude of paint effects, from faux parquet floors to freehand murals. The book begins with an overview of color, paint, equipment, basic techniques, and safety measures, followed by a handy guide consisting of thumbnail photos of the various techniques. Each effect is described in two pages, with a list of materials and equipment needed, a photograph of the finished product, and a page of well-illustrated instructions. . . . Amateur painters may require more detailed instructions for some of the complex techniques, but for the amount of techniques covered, this book is highly recommended for any size public library." Libr J

Travis, Debbie
Debbie Travis' painted house; quick and easy painted finishes for walls, floors, and furniture using water-based paints; {by} Debbie Travis with Barbara Dingle. Potter 1997 184p il pa $19.95 hardcover o.p.   **698**
1. House painting 2. Furniture finishing 3. Interior design
ISBN 0-609-80816-8 (pa)   LC 96-37440
This offers instructions for water-based paint finishes for walls and floors, including textured, patterned, and

Travis, Debbie—*Continued*

stone types, and for furniture, including antique, metallic, and stencilling methods, and techniques such as colorwashing, ragging, sponging, and dragging

700 ARTS

Arts and humanities through the eras. Gale 2004
5v il set $450 *   **700**
1. Arts—History 2. Civilization—History
ISBN 0-7876-5695-X   LC 2004-10243
Also available as separate volumes ea $105
Contents: v1 Ancient Egypt (2675 B.C.E.-332 B.C.E.) -- v2 Ancient Greece and Rome (1200 B.C.E.-476 C.E.) -- v3 Medieval Europe (814-1450) -- v4 Renaissance Europe (1300-1600) -- v5 The age of Baroque and Enlightenment (1600-1800)
"Each volume consists of nine chapters covering the major branches of the humanities: architecture and design, dance, fashion, literature, music, philosophy, religion, theater, and visual arts. . . . This outstanding series offers a wealth of information; the chapters on architecture, dance, and theater alone are worth the price of each volume." Libr J
Includes bibliographical references

Impelluso, Lucia

Gods and heroes in art; edited by Stefano Zuffi; translated by Thomas Michael Hartmann. Getty Mus. 2003 383p il pa $19.95   **700**
1. Art and mythology—Dictionaries 2. Classical mythology—Dictionaries
ISBN 0-89236-702-4   LC 2002-13422
Translated from the Italian
The characters of ancient Greek and Roman mythology "are each described in entries summarizing their distinctive stories, their special attributes, and the ways in which artists have depicted them. Each entry is . . . illustrated with reproductions of works of art in which the god or hero is pictured. . . . The book concludes with . . . indexes, including a list of iconographic symbols associated with the subjects, and a bibliography." Publisher's note
Includes bibliographical references

Murray, Albert

The blue devils of Nada; a contemporary American approach to aesthetic statement. Pantheon Bks. 1996 238p $23; pa $12
    700
1. African American arts 2. Blues music
ISBN 0-679-44213-8; 0-679-75859-3 (pa)
    LC 95-23331
In these essays Murray "presents Louis Armstrong, Count Basie, Duke Ellington, painter Romare Bearden and Ernest Hemingway as embodying, in their work and their lives, a peculiarly American strain of existential improvisation and epic storytelling. His theme, variously elaborated, is the effort of the engaged artist to document and give shape to the rootlessness and chaos underlying contemporary life in general—and African American life, in particular—in a way that transcends 'agitprop journalism.'" Publ Wkly

Ochoa, George

The Wilson chronology of the arts; [by] George Ochoa and Melinda Corey. Wilson, H.W. 1998 476p $115   **700**
1. Arts—History
ISBN 0-8242-0934-6   LC 97-23541
First published 1995 by Ballantine Books with title: The timeline book of the arts
"The authors provide a timeline detailing human creativity that progresses from ca. 43,000 B.C.E. to 1997, with 4,000 entries spread over 13 categories of artistic endeavor. . . . The chronology is global in scope and comprehensive in coverage, emphasizing well-established art forms without neglecting the oral traditions and decorative art forms of nonliterate societies and currently emerging art forms. . . . The straightforward organization of this work makes it suitable for many different uses." Recomm Ref Books for Small & Medium-sized Libr & Media Cent, 1999

Peterson's college guide for visual arts majors 2008. Peterson's 2007 398p il $24   **700**
1. Art—Study and teaching 2. Colleges and universities—United States—Directories
ISBN 978-0-7689-2423-7; 0-7689-2423-5
Annual. First published 2003
"Describes undergraduate and graduate programs in art, dance, music, and theater, providing information on tuition expenses, financial aid, scolarships, enrollment, and portfolio presentation." Publisher's note

Reid, Jane Davidson, 1918-

The Oxford guide to classical mythology in the arts, 1300-1990s; {by} Jane Davidson Reid; with the assistance of Chris Rohmann. Oxford Univ. Press 1993 2v set $195 *   **700**
1. Classical mythology—Catalogs 2. Arts
ISBN 0-19-504998-5   LC 92-35374

Contents: v1 Auchelous-Leander; v2 Leda-Zeus
This work catalogs "more than 205 mythological characters and themes as they are represented in the arts from the early Renaissance to the present. More than 30,000 representations, including those from literature, music, dance, and art, are listed. Arranged alphabetically by character or theme, each entry briefly describes the subject and its place in classical mythology, and concludes with a comprehensive bibliography. . . . This is an impressive piece of scholarship that will quickly become a standard reference source." Am Libr

701 Philosophy and theory of fine and decorative arts

Leland, Nita

Exploring color. 2nd ed. North Light Books 1998 144p il pa $24.99   **701**
1. Color in art
ISBN 0-89134-846-8; 978-0-89134-846-7
    LC 98-16932
First published 1985

Leland, Nita—*Continued*
"This guide to color covers the history, science and theory of color, the 'split color-mixing system', and techniques for controlling color." Publisher's note
Includes bibliographical references

702 Miscellany of fine and decorative arts

Michels, Caroll
How to survive and prosper as an artist; selling yourself without selling your soul. 5th ed. H. Holt 2001 369p pa $18 **702**
    1. Vocational guidance 2. Art—Marketing
    ISBN 978-0-8050-6800-9; 0-8050-6800-7
        LC 2001-039307
"An Owl book"
First published 1983
A "guide to taking control of your career and making a good living in the art world . . . [that includes] strategies for using the Web." Publisher's note
Includes bibliographical references

702.5 Art—Directories

2008 artist's & graphic designer's market; Erika O'Connell, editor; Michael Schweer, assistant editor. 33rd ed. Writer's Digest Bks. 2007 602p il pa $26.99 * **702.5**
    1. Art—Marketing—Directories
    ISSN 1075-0894
    ISBN 978-1-58297-500-9; 1-58297-500-0
Annual. First published 1974 with title: Artist's market
"Listings of places where art can be sold and exhibited include brokers, studios, agencies, magazines, galleries, and art fairs. Each listing covers who to contact and where, how much they pay, and additional information such as shipping requirements, preparing a portfolio, etc." Ref Sources for Small & Medium-sized Libr. 5th edition

American art directory 2005-2006. 60th ed. National Register Pub. 2004 1004p il $299 *
        702.5
    1. Art—Directories 2. American art—Directories
    3. Canadian art—Directories
    ISSN 0065-6968
    ISBN 978-0-87217-846-5; 0-87217-846-3
Biennial. First published 1898 by Bowker with title: American art annual
New edition in preparation
"Now in three main sections: (1) Art organizations (national and regional associations, museums, and libraries of the U.S. and Canada); (2) Art schools and college and university departments of art and architecture (U.S. and Canada); (3) Art information (major museums and art schools abroad, state arts councils, art magazines, newspapers carrying art notes and their critics, scholarships and fellowships, open exhibitions and traveling exhibitions, etc.) Indexes of organizations, personnel, and subjects." Guide to Ref Books. 11th edition

702.8 Techniques, procedures, apparatus, equipment, materials

Hoving, Thomas, 1931-
False impressions; the hunt for big-time art fakes. Simon & Schuster 1996 366p il pa $22 hardcover o.p. **702.8**
    1. Art—Forgeries
    ISBN 0-684-83148-1 (pa)   LC 95-53800
In this book the author discloses "details of major art forgeries and the intricate chicanery of con artists who have duped the world's most prestigious art institutions, art experts, and collectors." Libr J
Hoving "is a magnetic storyteller, achieving just the right blend of humor and mettle." Booklist
Includes bibliographical references

Smith, Ray, 1949-
The artist's handbook. Rev ed. DK Pub. 2003 384p il $30; pa $21.95 **702.8**
    1. Art—Technique 2. Artists' materials
    ISBN 0-7894-9336-5; 0-7566-2621-8 (pa)
        LC 2002-41583
First published 1987 by Knopf
Cover title: New artist's handbook; equipment, materials, procedures, techniques
The author presents "information on established materials that he organizes first by function—pigments, resins, solvents, and the like—then by media categorized according to discipline. . . . This excellent overall guide to the visual arts boasts multiple appendixes on color, perspective, health, and safety. With glossary and index, this far-ranging overview is hard to beat." Booklist

703 Dictionaries, encyclopedias, concordances of fine and decorative arts

The **Concise** Oxford dictionary of art and artists; edited by Ian Chilvers. 3rd ed. Oxford University Press 2003 653p pa $14.95
        703
    1. Art—Dictionaries 2. Artists—Dictionaries
    ISBN 0-19-860477-7   LC 2003-278290
First published 1990
This "is an abbreviated lexicon based on 'The Oxford Dictionary of Art'.... It includes western art from the fifth century B.C.E., but has been expanded to include more recent artists born prior to 1965 instead of 1945. Entries include biographies of artists, sculptors, writers, leading collectors and dealers, materials and techniques, and galleries and museums." Am Ref Books Annu, 2004

Facts on File encyclopedia of art; Sir Lawrence Gowing, general editor. Facts on File 2005 5v il map set $325 * **703**
    1. Art—Encyclopedias
    ISBN 0-8160-5797-4   LC 2005-40505
First published 1983 by Prentice-Hall as volume one of Encyclopedia of visual art

Facts on File encyclopedia of art—*Continued*

"The chapters cover not only aesthetics but social and cultural context as well and not only Western arts (which do seem to dominate) but arts from other parts of the world. The most striking feature is the vivid, full-color photography on nearly every page, with three-dimensional objects ranging from Aegean armor to a Japanese Zen temple particularly well treated." Libr J

For a fuller review, see: Booklist, Jan. 1 & 15, 2006

Includes bibliographical references

Frazier, Nancy

The Penguin concise dictionary of art history. Penguin Ref. 1999 774p pa $20 hardcover o.p.
           703

1. Art—Dictionaries
ISBN 0-14-051420-1 (pa)   LC 98-56089

"This volume seeks to present an interdisciplinary approach to art history. It uses information from a number of fields, such as literature, psychology, history, geography, and economics, to give a cultural context to the changes in art. There are more than 1,500 alphabetically arranged entries. . . . Each biographical entry includes birth and death dates when known, nationality, medium used, and style of work or school of art." Booklist

"An easy-to-read, scholarly yet not lofty, fascinating, and very well-organized book." Libr J

Includes bibliographical references (p. {731}-736) and index

Langmuir, Erika

Yale dictionary of art and artists; [by] Erika Langmuir and Norbert Lynton. Yale Univ. Press 2000 753p $30; pa $12.95   **703**

1. Art—Dictionaries 2. Artists—Dictionaries
ISBN 0-300-08702-0; 0-300-06458-6 (pa)
                       LC 00-25800

"Varying in length from a few lines to several pages for artists such as Leonardo da Vinci, Pablo Picasso, or John Constable, the 3000 entries cover Western art from 1300 until the present. The work covers painters, sculptors, graphic artists, patrons, technical processes, movements, and terminology." Libr J

Lucie-Smith, Edward, 1933-

The Thames & Hudson dictionary of art terms. 2nd ed. Thames & Hudson 2004 240p il (World of art) pa $16.95 *   **703**

1. Art—Dictionaries
ISBN 0-500-20365-2   LC 2003100802

First published 1984; this edition first published 2003 in the United Kingdom

"More than 2,000 entries define and explain terms used to describe painting, sculpture, architecture, graphic arts, decorative and applied arts, and photography, including the terminology of non-Western art. Several entries contain cross-references, and the book's 400 illustrations and diagrams, although reproduced in black and white, help explain the concepts defined. The thorough and clear entries make this volume appropriate for any beginning art history student." Choice

704   Special topics in fine and decorative arts

Farrington, Lisa E.

Creating their own image; the history of African-American women artists. Oxford University Press 2005 354p il $55 *
           704

1. African American women 2. African American artists 3. Women artists
ISBN 0-19-516721-X   LC 2003-66171

This is a "study of women of color and their works, starting with slavery, moving through the Harlem Renaissance, and continuing to the new millennium." Libr J

"A richly detailed yet fluent work of trailblazing research, fresh interpretations, and cogent argument, Farrington's treatise discusses vital aesthetic as well as social and cultural issues and creates a vibrant context for such seminal artists as Augusta Savage, Faith Ringgold, Barbara Chase-Riboud, Kara Walker, and many more." Booklist

Patton, Sharon F.

African-American art. Oxford Univ. Press 1998 319p il maps (Oxford history of art) pa $18.95 hardcover o.p.   **704**

1. African American art
ISBN 0-19-284213-7 (pa)   LC 98-190459

This "book provides a chronological examination of the development of African American art from its earliest manifestations to the present day." Libr J

"Comprehensively and with sharp, scholarly accuracy, Patton has closed gaps between the chronological and thematic directions of Black American art and complexities of Euro-American art history." Choice

704.9   Iconography

Bussagli, Marco, 1957-

Angels. Abrams 2007 780p il $19.95
           704.9

1. Art and religion 2. Angels
ISBN 978-0-8109-9436-2; 0-8109-9436-4
                     LC 2007-010749

"Art historian Marco Bussagli has organized the book by significant Biblical events. . . . Each work of art is accompanied by the Biblical passage it illustrates, along with a commentary exploring its form and meaning." Publisher's note

Includes bibliographical references

Fantasy art now; the very best in contemporary fantasy art & illustration; General editor, Martin McKenna; foreword by Boris Vallejo. Collins Design 2007 192p il $29.95   **704.9**

1. Fantasy in art
ISBN 978-0-06-137097-7; 0-06-137097-5
                     LC 2007-021737

This book on fantasy art covers "images from . . . fantasy artists, . . . fantasy art, and artwork from graphic novels, book coves, card games, and role-playing games." Publisher's note

708 Galleries, museums, private collections of fine and decorative arts

Grant, Daniel
Selling art without galleries; toward making a living from your art. Allworth Press 2006 277p pa $19.95 **708**
1. Art—Marketing
ISBN 1-58115-460-7; 978-1-58115-460-3
LC 2006-26630
This "resource shows artists how to make a living from their art—without relying on galleries. . . . Artists will also find . . . information for marketing their work, including photographing and framing, selling at art fairs, getting into juried shows, and selling over the Internet." Publisher's note

The **J.** Paul Getty Museum and its collections; a museum for the new century; {by} John Walsh, Deborah Gribbon. Getty Mus. 1997 288p pa $40 hardcover o.p. **708**
1. Getty, J. Paul, 1892-1976 2. J. Paul Getty Museum
ISBN 0-89236-476-9 (pa)   LC 97-12170
This volume is a history of the J. Paul Getty Museum and a guide to its collections
This is "a lavish visual compendium of J. Paul Getty's amazing art collection; in addition, the text reveals important background details surrounding Getty's life and his passion for art. Walsh and Gribbon communicate just how the magnate's fortunes were put to the test as planned acquisitions of artwork flourished." Booklist

Loebl, Suzanne
America's art museums; a traveler's guide to great collections large and small. Norton 2002 426p il pa $18.95 **708**
1. Art museums
ISBN 0-393-32006-5   LC 2001-44208
This is a "guide to some of America's finest art museums. Not only does it focus on the major and more familiar art museums, it also supplies some much-needed information and marketing for some of the small and little-known, yet important, art galleries in the United States. The book is alphabetically arranged by state and then by city, and provides information on times open, strengths of the museum's collection, activities for children, the museum's history, and Websites." Am Ref Books Annu, 2003
Includes bibliographical references

Meier, Richard, 1934-
Building the Getty. University of California Press 1999 204p il pa $25.95 **708**
1. Getty Center (Los Angeles, Calif.)
ISBN 0-520-21730-6; 978-0-520-21730-0
LC 99-20219
First published 1997 by Knopf
"Charting his involvement in the Getty's construction, Meier recounts in an intriguingly candid, eminently personal style the formidable bureaucratic process entailed upon undertaking to realize this grandiose endeavor. Beginning with the competition itself, Meier's detailed reminiscences offer fascinating insights into the design process and the extraordinarily intricate procedures and systems, as well as endless setbacks, associated with executing a modern-day megalithic structure." Booklist

National Gallery of Art; [foreword by Earl A. Powell III] 2nd ed. Thames and Hudson 2006 332p il (World of art) pa $18.95 *
708
1. National Gallery of Art (U.S.)
ISBN 0-500-20390-3; 978-0-500-20390-3
LC 2005-904459
First published 2004 by National Gallery of Art; Based on John Walker's National Gallery of Art, published 1984
"The collection of the National Gallery of Art in Washington includes works by the greatest masters of Western art from the twelfth century to the present. . . . [In this] look at the National Gallery's masterpieces . . . the works are illustrated in full color, and the curators have written the texts." Publisher's note

709 Art—Historical, geographic, persons treatment of fine and decorative arts

Atlas of world art; edited by John Onians. Oxford University Press 2004 352p il maps $150 *
709
1. Art—History—Maps
ISBN 0-19-521583-4   LC 2003-55029
This atlas offers a "framework for coverage of art activity around the world from prehistoric times to 2000. . . . Each of the book's seven parts (each covers a period in art history) includes a brief illustrated introduction followed by a standardized sequence of sections on World, American, European, African, Asian and Pacific Art." Choice
"Groundbreaking and handsomely produced, this is a welcome addition to any reference collection." Libr J
For a fuller review see: Booklist, Nov. 1, 2004
Includes bibliographical references

Barnitz, Jacqueline
Twentieth-century art of Latin America. University of Tex. Press 2001 400p il $70; pa $34.95 **709**
1. Latin American art 2. Art—20th century
ISBN 0-292-70857-2; 0-292-70858-0 (pa)
LC 99-50871
A survey of 20th century Latin American art which includes coverage of regional movements, and discussion of historical, political, and cultural influences
"Latin American art, the fruit of violent collisions among diverse indigenous, European, and African cultures, is revealed as provocative and vibrant in Barnitz's well-illustrated and groundbreaking overview of its dazzling twentieth-century flowering." Booklist
Includes bibliographical references

Beckett, Wendy

Sister Wendy's American collection; {by} Sister Wendy Beckett. HarperCollins Pubs. 2000 288p il $40 **709**

ISBN 0-06-019556-8 LC 00-40953

Includes index

The author provides a "discussion of works in six of America's renowned art museums. . . . {She} includes a variety of media-- paintings, sculpture, decorative arts, armor, and other art objects-- and the individual works originate from a dizzying array of time periods and several countries." Libr J

Fenton, James, 1949-

Leonardo's nephew; essays on art and artists. University of Chicago Press 2000 283p il pa $15 **709**

1. Art—History

ISBN 0-226-24147-5; 978-0-226-24147-0 LC 99-55666

First published 1998 by Farrar, Straus, and Giroux

Fenton presents a collection of fifteen essays on various aspects of art history. Subjects "include Freud's collection of antique statuettes, Egyptian funerary portraits and Joseph Cornell. These essays educate, enlighten, surprise and thrill, unfailingly." N Y Time Book Rev

Includes bibliographical references

Gardner, Helen, d. 1946

Gardner's art through the ages; [revised by] Fred S. Kleiner, Christin J. Mamiya. 12th ed. Thomson/Wadsworth 2005 2v il map set $133.95 * **709**

1. Art—History

ISBN 0-15-505090-7; 978-0-15-505090-7 LC 2003-111627

First published 1926 by Harcourt Brace & Co.

This book surveys world art from prehistoric times to the present day. Painting, sculpture, architecture and some decorative arts are considered. Although the focus is on European art, there are also chapters on ancient Near Eastern, Asian, pre-Columbian, American Indian, African and Oceanic art.

Includes bibliographical references

Gombrich, E. H. (Ernst Hans), 1909-2001

The story of art. 16th ed rev and expanded. Phaidon Press 1995 688p il $49.95; pa $29.95 * **709**

1. Art—History

ISBN 0-7148-3355-X; 0-7148-3247-2 (pa) LC 96-140698

First published 1950

This survey of art examines artistic achievements in historical context to consider how prevailing social, political, and economic factors may have influenced the succession and popularity of certain artistic styles.

Includes bibliographical references

Harclerode, Peter, 1947-

The lost masters; World War II and the looting of Europe's treasurehouses; [by] Peter Harclerode & Brendan Pittaway. Welcome Rain 2000 402p il hardcover o.p. pa $18.95 **709**

1. Art thefts 2. World War, 1939-1945—Destruction and pillage

ISBN 1-56649-165-7; 1-56649-253-X (pa) LC 00-42867

The authors "trace the elusive web of collaborators, opportunists and dealers who exploited the Third Reich's lust for prestigious trophies. Gripping vignettes and revelatory anecdotes illuminate the fates of specific works of art, including the outstanding story of four paratroopers who contrived to rescue the largest cache of stolen art sequestered by the Nazis." Publ Wkly

Includes bibliographical references

Hoving, Thomas, 1931-

Art for dummies; foreword by Andrew Wyeth. IDG Books Worldwide, Inc 1999 382p il (--For dummies) $24.99 **709**

1. Art appreciation 2. Art—History

ISBN 978-0-7645-5104-8; 0-7645-5104-3 LC 99-65838

"In this delightful book, Hoving . . . leads readers gently through thousands of years of art history. . . . His breathless enthusiasm is avuncular, scholarly, and quite infectious—an attitude that happily precludes condescension. . . . A terrific book for students, travelers, tyros, and old hands alike." Libr J

Includes bibliographical references

Janson, H. W. (Horst Woldemar), 1913-1982

Janson's history of art; the western tradition; Penelope J.E. Davies . . . [et al.] 7th ed. Pearson Prentice-Hall 2007 various paging il map $120.20 * **709**

1. Art—History

ISBN 0-13-193455-4; 978-0-13-193455-9 LC 2005-54647

Also available in a two-volume paperback edition ea $101.20

First published 1962 by Abrams with title: History of art

A history of art from prehistoric cave paintings to video art. While the focus is primarily on Western art, brief discussions of Oriental, Near Eastern, Islamic, African and Latin American arts are included.

Includes bibliographical references

Johnson, Paul, 1928-

Art: a new history. HarperCollins Pubs. 2003 777p il $39.95 * **709**

1. Art—History

ISBN 0-06-053075-8

"This book reconsiders the conventional art historical canon and the traditional Eurocentric view of history. . . . He devotes entire chapters to African, Russian, and Scandinavian art and to the significance of landscapes and watercolors, and he presents the work of many underrecognized artists." Libr J

Johnson, Paul, 1928-—*Continued*

"While {Johnson's} narrative is for the most part a conventional journey through the canon, his headlong pace, quirky views and pungent prose make it anything but dull." Publ Wkly

Kampen O'Riley, Michael

Art beyond the west; the arts of Africa, India and Southeast Asia, China, Japan and Korea, the Pacific, and the Americas; afterword by Anne D'Alleva. Abrams 2002 c2001 344p il maps $75

709

1. Art

ISBN 0-8109-1433-6   LC 2001-27923

Also available from Prentice-Hall

First published 2001 in the United Kingdom

The author "has attempted to encapsulate the entirety of non-Western art in one volume. . . . {Chapters} range over Africa, India, Southeast Asia, China, Japan and Korea, the Americas, and the Pacific and consider such issues as post- and intercolonialism and postmodernism." Libr J

The author "succeeds in defining the essence of each distinct artistic tradition. Add to that impressive feat a clear, relaxed, and engaging prose style and superb illustrations, and the sum is a prime introductory guide to much of the world's art." Booklist

Includes bibliographical references

Little, Stephen, 1954-

. . . isms: understanding art. Universe 2004 159p il pa $16.95   **709**

1. Art—History

ISBN 0-7893-1209-3   LC 2004-94996

The author "identifies four types of isms: trends specific to the visual arts (perspectivism), broad cultural trends (romanticism), artist-defined movements (cubism), and retrospectively named movements (mannerism). He then moves forward chronologically, deftly defining more than 50 isms, naming key artists, and showcasing splendid examples." Booklist

North American women artists of the twentieth century; a biographical dictionary; edited by Jules Heller and Nancy G. Heller. Garland 1995 xxii, 612p il (Garland reference library of the humanities) pa $41.95 hardcover o.p.

709

1. Women artists—Dictionaries

ISBN 0-8153-2584-3 (pa)   LC 94-49710

This is a "guide to more than 1500 Canadian, Mexican, and United States women artists born between 1850 and 1960. Artists are listed alphabetically, and each artist . . . is briefly treated in several paragraphs that end with bibliographical citations, often to important journal articles. More than 100 illustrations provide a small sampling of their work. . . . An essential acquisition for all art reference libraries." Libr J

Petropoulos, Jonathan

The Faustian bargain; the art world in Nazi Germany. Oxford Univ. Press 2000 395p il $42.50

709

ISBN 0-19-512964-4   LC 99-33372

"Spotlighting five groups--art museum directors, art dealers, art journalists, art historians, and artists--Petropoulos . . . details how each of these groups either directly or indirectly facilitated the theft of countless works of art and legitimized the Nazi regime." Libr J

Includes bibliographical references

Schama, Simon

The power of art. Ecco 2006 448p il $50

709

1. Art—History

ISBN 0-06-117610-9; 978-0-06-117610-4

LC 2007-270937

"This book is published to accompany the television series Simon Schama's Power of Art, created by BBC Arts and first broadcast on BBC2 in 2006" Verso of title page

The author "presents eight remarkable artists who created their masterworks against a backdrop of personal and professional distress. From politically charged commentaries (David, Picasso, Turner and Rembrandt) to intensely personal visions of the world (van Gogh and Rothko) and the reinvention of the divine (Bernini and Caravaggio), Schama takes these masters' hallowed works off the museum wall and drags them through the mud and muck that went into their creation." Publ Wkly

Includes bibliographical references

709.01 Arts of nonliterate peoples, and earliest times to 499

Bahn, Paul G.

The Cambridge illustrated history of prehistoric art. Cambridge Univ. Press 1998 xxxii, 302p il $45   **709.01**

1. Prehistoric art

ISBN 0-521-45473-5   LC 96-51099

The author "discovers the initial 'discoveries' of this art form, then weaves an excellent accounting of research, from the earliest to the recent. This discourse encompasses mobiliary art, art on rocks and walls, the application of scientific scrutiny, literal and symbolic interpretations, and the press of time. Bahn also describes current threats and future prospects. The writing is lucid and descriptive, satisfying to the advanced anthropologist or artist while quite comprehensible to uninitiated readers." Choice

Berlo, Janet Catherine

Native North American art; by Janet Catherine Berlo and Ruth B. Phillips. Oxford Univ. Press 1999 c1998 291p il map (Oxford history of art) pa $24.95 hardcover o.p.   **709.01**

1. Native American art

ISBN 0-19-284218-8 (pa)   LC 99-177938

This survey covers the "artistic output of most Native American tribes across the northern hemisphere over a period of more than eight centuries. . . . In an introduction that stresses the commonality of themes—cosmology, vision quests, love of ornament, reverence of materials—[the authors] emphasize the importance of today's

Berlo, Janet Catherine—*Continued*
Native art as a natural extension. Five regional chapters then incorporate history, outstanding crafts and arts, some prominent figures, and social, religious, and cultural aspects." Libr J

709.02   Art—6th-15th centuries, 500-1499

Adams, Laurie, 1941-
Italian Renaissance art. Westview Press 2001 420p il map $75; pa $65   **709.02**
1. Italian art 2. Art—15th and 16th centuries
ISBN   978-0-8133-3690-9;   0-8133-3690-2; 978-0-8133-3691-6 (pa); 0-8133-3691-0 (pa)
                                        LC 2001-269582
"Adams has produced a near-perfect introduction to the people, places, and events of the Italian Renaissance. . . . The text follows Italian art as it transforms from a highly religious activity into a very human one, and culminates with a focus on the multitalented genius of da Vinci, Raphael, and Michelangelo. . . .The side boxes are helpful and provide further information about the religious figures, ideas, and historical events that directly influenced the era, such as Dante and the black death. . . . This, along with numerous superb photographs, adds incalculable value to the understanding of the Italian Renaissance." Booklist
Includes bibliographical references

Campbell, Gordon
Renaissance art and architecture. Oxford University Press 2004 278p il $55 *
                                        709.02
1. Art—15th and 16th centuries 2. Architecture—15th and 16th centuries
ISBN 0-19-860985-X   LC 2004-275931
"Campbell's introductory, geographically arranged overview covers the art, architecture, and gardens in Europe from 1415 to 1618. . . . The numerous cross-references, the time line of key artistic and world events, and the bibliography of traditional, 20th-century surveys and early sources make this a valuable reference work." SLJ
Includes bibliographical references

Graham-Dixon, Andrew
Renaissance. University of Calif. Press 1999 336p il $29.95   **709.02**
1. Art—15th and 16th centuries 2. Renaissance
ISBN 0-520-22375-6   LC 00-698469
This companion to a BBC television series is an "introduction to Renaissance art and the cultural milieu that spawned it. . . . The bulk of the text is given over to canonic figures ranging from Giotto to Michelangelo. . . . In addition, the author discusses religion, humanistic thought, the changing social status of the artist, and the larger historic ebb and flow." Libr J

Lowden, John
Early Christian & Byzantine art. Chronicle Bks. 1997 447p il (Art & ideas) pa $24.95
                                        709.02
ISBN 0-7148-3168-9
In this illustrated history of the origins and growth of Christian art Lowden works "deftly through fascinatingly complex and epoch-defining artistic and theological debates, including the so-called Iconoclast Controversy." Booklist
Includes bibliographical references

Snyder, James
Art of the Middle Ages; [by] James Snyder, Henry Luttikhuizen, Dorothy Verkerk. 2nd ed. Prentice Hall 2006 530p il map $90 *
                                        709.02
1. Medieval art 2. Christian art 3. Medieval architecture
ISBN 0-13-193825-8   LC 2004-60135
First published 1989 with title Medieval art
"Church architecture and decoration receive the bulk of Snyder's attention, with manuscript illumination and sumptuary and secular arts presented rather briefly. The volume is well illustrated, though chiefly in black-and-white photographs." Libr J [review of 1989 edition]
Includes bibliographical references

709.03   Art—Modern period, 1500-

Craske, Matthew
Art in Europe, 1700-1830; a history of the visual arts in an era of unprecedented urban economic growth. Oxford Univ. Press 1997 320p il (Oxford history of art) pa $21.50 hardcover o.p.
                                        709.03
1. Art—19th century 2. World history—18th century
ISBN 0-19-284206-4 (pa)   LC 96-37917
At head of title: Oxford history of art
This study analyzes "the fundamental historical causes of change that took place from the early 1700s to 1839. . . . Craske . . . provides a series of four stimulating chapters devoted respectively to the function of the artist, art worlds, the appreciation of the visual arts, and evolving ideas of history and civilization. The text is enhanced by 129 high-quality illustrations." Choice

Escritt, Stephen
Art Nouveau. Phaidon 2000 447p il map (Art & ideas) $24.95   **709.03**
1. Art nouveau
ISBN 0-7148-3822-5; 978-0-7148-3822-9
                                        LC 00-344423
In this book "Stephen Escritt defines Art Nouveau broadly, analyzing the work of such diverse designers as Victor Horta in Belgium, Emile Galle in France, Charles Rennie Mackintosh in Glasgow and Antoni Gaudi in Barcelona." Publisher's note
Includes bibliographical references

Rosenblum, Robert

19th century art; painting, Robert Rosenblum ; sculpture, H.W. Janson. rev and updated ed. Prentice Hall 2005 544p il $85; pa $112 *

709.03

1. Art—19th century
ISBN 0-13-189614-8; 0-13-189562-1 (pa)
LC 2004-46660

This "survey of 19th-century Western art views the period as a heterogeneous one, marked by reciprocal influences of art, technology, politics, economics, and literature. Coauthored by two distinguished scholars, it is a comprehensive international history that upholds recent interpretations of the period and takes a non-Francocentric approach towards major and minor artists. . . . Over 500 reproductions . . . reinforce the text." Libr J {review of 1984 edition}
Includes bibliographical references

709.04 Art—20th century, 1900-1999

Art deco 1910-1939; edited by Charlotte Benton, Tim Benton, and Ghislaine Wood. Bulfinch Press 2003 464p il $65 *

709.04

1. Art deco
ISBN 0-8212-2834-X
LC 2002-113762

Catalog of an exhibition held at the Victorian and Albert Museum, London, March 27-July 20, 2003

This exhibition catalog includes 40 essays about the Art Deco movement and its sources and expression throughout the world in such fields as architecture, ceramics, fashion, jewelry, graphic design, metalwork, glasswork, and film
Includes bibliographical references

Balken, Debra Bricker

Abstract expressionism. Distributed in North America by Harry N. Abrams 2005 80p il (Movements in modern art) $16.50

709.04

1. Abstract expressionism 2. American art
ISBN 1-85437-306-4; 978-1-85437-306-9
LC 2004-111326

This book has "60 color illustrations of works created by the artists of the movement . . . [and] examines the critical response to Abstract Expressionism from the time of its heyday up until the present day." Publisher's note
Includes bibliographical references

Brandon, Ruth

Surreal lives; the surrealists, 1917-1945. Grove Press 1999 527p il pa $16 hardcover o.p.

709.04

1. Surrealism
ISBN 0-8021-3727-X (pa)
LC 99-25492

This study of surrealism "gives an account of the school's major practitioners, from Apollinaire to Dali; their flamboyant eccentricities and unconventional sexual entanglements prove a lively and absorbing complement to their work." New Yorker
Includes bibliographical references

Dempsey, Amy

Art in the modern era; a guide to styles, schools & movements 1860 to the present. Abrams 2002 304p il $55

709.04

1. Art—20th century—Encyclopedias
ISBN 0-8109-4172-4
LC 2001-46261

This guide to art from 1860 to the present describes 300 schools and movements and includes a fold-out timeline

"All major and minor movements are mentioned in this very comprehensive guide, which could easily become a standard for modern art survey courses, making it a sensible purchase for most libraries." Libr J
Includes bibliographical references

Dickerman, Leah, 1964-

Dada; Zurich, Berlin, Hannover, Cologne, New York, Paris; with essays by Brigid Doherty [et al.] National Gallery of Art in association with Distributed Art Publishers 2005 519p il $65 *

709.04

1. Dadaism
ISBN 1-933045-20-5
LC 2005-17984

Catalog of an exhibition held at the Musée national d'art moderne, Centre Pompidou, Paris, Oct. 5, 2005-Jan. 9, 2006; at the National Gallery of Art, Washington, Feb. 19-May 14, 2006; and at the Museum of Modern Art, New York, June 16-Sept. 11, 2006

"Seven scholars and curators contribute essays that examine each of the various Dada centers in turn. . . . Each essay examines key locations (e.g., the Cabaret Voltaire), individuals, publications (including Merz magazine), and inventions (such as ready-mades and photomontage.) . . . Its comprehensive scholarship and color illustrations of many rarely seen works make this book essential for all art collections." Choice
Includes bibliographical references

Fineberg, Jonathan David

Art since 1940; strategies of being; [by] Jonathan Fineberg. 2nd ed. Abrams 2000 528p il $65

709.04

1. Art—20th century 2. Modern art
ISBN 0-18-094209-7
LC 99-51584

Also available from Prentice-Hall
First published 1995

This surveys American and European art from 1940 to 2000 through a series of biographical profiles of individual artists linked by discussions of the cultural influences on their work

"Fineberg surveys the visual arts in Europe, England, and North America from 1940 to the present, focusing on the avant-garde artist in the major Western capitals. . . . The text is arranged in 15 chapters in chronological order. Within each chapter the individual artist is discussed, as are the ideas and events relevant to understanding how cultural and social situations influenced the artist." Choice [review of 1995 edition]
Includes bibliographical references

Hughes, Robert
The shock of the new. 2nd ed. McGraw-Hill 1991 444p il pa $55 *   **709.04**
1. Modern art
ISBN 0-07-031127-7   LC 90-61591
First published 1980 in the United Kingdom
Originally based on a BBC television series, this survey of vanguard art covers the last one hundred years and concludes with a chapter on the 1980s
Includes bibliographical references

Hunter, Sam, 1923-
Modern art; painting, sculpture, architecture, photography; [by] Sam Hunter, John Jacobus, Daniel Wheeler. 3rd ed, rev and expanded. Prentice Hall 2005 472p il $90   **709.04**
1. Modern art
ISBN 978-0-13-150519-3; 0-13-150519-X
                    LC 2004-46659
First published 1985
This book explains "how European and American vanguard culture created modernist art by heeding the call 'to make it new.'. . . . Coverage ranges across a broad spectrum of visual arts, from painting, sculpture, and photography to conceptual forms, installation and video art, and architecture." Publisher's note
Includes bibliographical references

Livingstone, Marco
Pop art; a continuing history; 2nd ed. Thames & Hudson 2000 272p il $29.95   **709.04**
1. Pop art
ISBN 978-0-500-28240-3; 0-500-28240-4
                    LC 00-100788
First published 1991 in the United Kingdom
With 300 color plates this volume chronicles the work of 130 artists of the Pop Art movement, including Jasper Johns, Robert Rauschenberg, Andy Warhol, and Roy Lichtenstein.
"Recommended as the best single historical survey on Pop Art." Libr J

Lucie-Smith, Edward, 1933-
Art today. Phaidon Press 1995 511p il pa $45 hardcover o.p.   **709.04**
1. Art—20th century
ISBN 0-7148-3888-8 (pa)
This "survey attempts to essay the scope and aims of the art of the world over the past 30 years. . . . As well as such . . . ground as Pop Art, Lucie-Smith covers Conceptual Art, Installation Art, and Neo-Expressionism. He also covers . . . artists and works from the former Soviet Union, Africa, the Far East, and Latin America. Chapters are also included on 'Racial Minorities' and 'Feminist and Gay' art. . . . The book offers brief biographies of all artists mentioned, a chronology, and bibliography." Libr J

Surrealism; edited by Mary Ann Caws. Phaidon 2004 304p il (Themes and movements) $75   **709.04**

1. Surrealism
ISBN 978-0-7148-4259-2; 0-7148-4259-1
"In this well-organized and nicely illustrated survey of Surrealism, Caws . . . discusses many of the basic ideas and tenets of the movement, emphasizing chance and freedom as the central surrealist concepts." Libr J
Includes bibliographical references

709.1   Art—Treatment by areas, regions, places in general

Khalili, Nasser D., 1945-
Islamic art and culture; a visual history. Overlook Press 2006 186p il $60   **709.1**
1. Islamic art 2. Islamic civilization
ISBN 1-58567-839-2; 978-1-58567-839-6
This "visual history of Islamic art introduces readers to the diverse peoples, cultures, and styles making up Islam today. Spanning 12 centuries and covering everything from miniature painting to architecture, it shows, e.g., various Qur'ans, coins, armor, and scientific instruments. . . . This is an excellent introduction to the subject that combines aptly chosen and beautifully reproduced photographs with a concise and informative text." Libr J
Includes bibliographical references

O'Kane, Bernard
Treasures of Islam; artistic glories of the Muslim world. Duncan Baird; Distributed in the USA by Sterling Pub. 2007 224p il map $35 *
                    709.1
1. Islamic art 2. Islamic civilization
ISBN 978-1-84483-483-9; 1-84483-483-2
The author "combines an overview of Islamic art and architecture with a cursory history of Islam's empires and dynasties. Beginning with a brief discussion of the earliest mosque from the seventh century, and showing how Islamic architects created a distinctive artistic tradition, O'Kane . . . follows architectural and artistic ideas to the 19th century. . . . The wealth of glorious full-color illustrations make this beautifully designed book an excellent introduction to the art of Islam." Publ Wkly
Includes bibliographical references

Claridge, Laura P.
Norman Rockwell; a life; {by} Laura Claridge. Random House 2001 546p il pa $16.95 hardcover o.p.   **709.2**
ISBN 0-8129-6723-2 (pa)   LC 2001-19784
"Claridge peers beyond the idyllic public image that Rockwell himself helped to perpetuate to find the insecure, impulsive artist underneath." Libr J
The author "isn't overwhelmed by the complexities and contradictions of Rockwell's temperament, relationship, and oeuvre but rather is invigorated by them, and her insightful portrait matches Rockwell's paintings in its judicious detail, layers of perception, delight in discovery, and reflections on 'the slippery nature of truth in art' and life." Booklist
Includes bibliographical references

709.32   Ancient Egyptian art

Egyptian treasures from the Egyptian Museum in Cairo; edited by Francesco Tiradritti; photographs by Araldo De Luca. Abrams 1999 416p il $75   **709.32**
1. Egyptian Museum 2. Egyptian art 3. Egypt—Antiquities
ISBN 0-8109-3276-8   LC 99-72419
Also published in the United Kingdom with title: The Cairo Museum
This is a "descriptive guide to the ancient history exhibit at the Egyptian Museum in Cairo. . . . Following the introduction are educational essays by Egyptologists from around the world, on topics ranging from the early dynastic eras through to the later periods of invasion by the Greeks. Throughout the book, there are vivid photographs of artifacts with a narration explaining the historical and artistic significance of each piece." Booklist
Includes bibliographical references

Robins, Gay
The art of ancient Egypt. Harvard Univ. Press 1997 271p il $42; pa $24.95   **709.32**
1. Egyptian art 2. Egypt—Antiquities
ISBN 0-674-04660-9; 0-674-00376-4 (pa)
                                      LC 97-19458
"The first chapter orients the reader in the cultural, technical, and iconographic contexts needed to explore the evolution of the Egyptian artistic tradition in subsequent chapters. Beginning with the predynastic origins (5000 BCE) and concluding in the Ptolemaic Period (304-30 BCE), Robins traces the development of sculpture, painting, funerary and religious art, and architecture with over 300 illustrations, many in color." Libr J
Includes bibliographical references

Smith, William Stevenson, 1907-1969
The art and architecture of ancient Egypt; [by] W. Stevenson Smith. rev with additions, by William Kelly Simpson. Yale Univ. Press 1998 296p il map (Pelican history of art) hardcover o.p. pa $35 *   **709.32**
1. Egyptian art 2. Egypt—Antiquities
ISBN 0-300-07715-7; 0-300-07747-5 (pa)
                                      LC 98-24893
First published 1958 by Penguin Bks.
"This book shows the tombs at Thebes, including the treasure-filled burial place of Tutankhamen, the temples of Luxor and Karnak, and the palaces of Akhenaten at Tell el Amarna and of Amenhotep III at Thebes. It also presents many revealing portraits depicting a range of subjects from the kings and queens who built the pyramids at Giza and Saqqara to their own civil servants." Publisher's note
Includes bibliographical references

709.38   Ancient Greek art

Boardman, John, 1927-
Greek art. 4th ed, rev and expanded. Thames & Hudson 1996 304p il map (World of art) pa $16.95   **709.38**
1. Greek art
ISBN 0-500-20292-3   LC 96-60184
First published 1964 by Praeger Pubs.
Partial contents: The beginnings and geometric Greece; Greece and the arts of the East and Egypt; Archaic Greek art; Classical sculpture and architecture; Hellenistic art; Selected bibliography
"This is a classic in the field made even more readable and useful than before. Highly recommended for all collections." Libr J

709.39   Art of other parts of ancient world

Frankfort, Henri, 1897-1954
The art and architecture of the ancient Orient. 5th ed, with supplementary notes and additional bibliography and abbreviations by Michael Roaf and Donald Matthews. Yale Univ. Press 1996 483p il maps (Pelican history of art) pa $35 *
                                      709.39
1. Ancient art 2. Middle East—Antiquities
ISBN 0-300-06470-5   LC 97-224901
First published 1954 in the United Kingdom, 1955 in the United States
This traces the development of art in the Near East from 3500 B.C. to 539 B.C., covering the Sumerians, Assyrians, Babylonians, Hittites, Aramaeans, Levants, and Phoenicians
Includes bibliographical references

709.45   Italian art

Wittkower, Rudolf, 1901-1971
Art and architecture in Italy, 1600-1750; revised by Joseph Connors and Jennifer Montagu. 6th ed. Yale Univ. Press 1999 3v il maps (Pelican history of art) set $160; pa set $80   **709.45**
1. Italian art 2. Baroque art
ISBN 0-300-07890-0; 0-300-07889-7 (pa)
                                      LC 98-49066
Also available as separate volumes ea pa $28; v2 also available in hardcover $65
First published 1958 by Penguin Bks.
Contents: v1 The early Baroque, 1600-1625; v2 The high Baroque, 1625-1675; v3 Late Baroque and Rococo, 1675-1750
The author examines works produced during the Early, High, and Late Baroque periods of Italian art, covering such artists as Caravaggio, Bernini, Borromini and Cortona.
Includes bibliographical references

709.47   Russian art

Hamilton, George Heard
The art and architecture of Russia. Yale University Press 1983 482p il map (Pelican history of art) pa $32   **709.47**
1. Russian art 2. Christian art 3. Church architecture
ISBN 978-0-300-05327-2; 0-300-05327-4
First published 1954 by Penguin Bks.
Hamilton traces the development of Russian art from the height of the Byzantine Empire, through its flowering under Peter the Great, to contemporary work and the influence of Western European culture.
Includes bibliographical references

McPhee, John A.
The ransom of Russian art; {by} John McPhee. Farrar, Straus & Giroux 1994 181p il $20; pa $12   **709.47**
1. Dodge, Norton T., 1927-
ISBN 0-374-24682-3; 0-374-52450-5 (pa)
                                   LC 94-14723
The author "recounts the surreptitious activities of U.S. economist Norton Dodge, who during the 1960s and 1970s, slipped by the KGB and smuggled out of the Soviet Union 8000 artworks by 600 dissident artists." Libr J
"McPhee's engaging narrative sheds light on this suppressed creative milieu." Publ Wkly

709.51   Chinese art

Hearn, Maxwell K.
Splendors of Imperial China; treasures from the National Palace Museum, Taipei. Metropolitan Mus. of Art 1996 144p il pa $29.95 hardcover o.p.   **709.51**
1. National Palace Museum (Taipei, Taiwan) 2. Chinese art
ISBN 0-87099-766-1 (pa)   LC 95-46590
Hearn "selected more than 100 works to present here, drawn from an extensive traveling exhibition featuring Neolithic and Bronze Age works, as well as Sung, Ming, and other dynasty masterpieces. This beautifully produced book contains fine quality reproductions that illuminate a splendid collection of rare artwork. . . . The text describes in accessible terms important background information, including cultural climate, historical events, and artistic elements." Booklist

Tregear, Mary
Chinese art. rev ed. Thames & Hudson 1997 216p il maps (World of art) pa $14.95
                                   709.51
1. Chinese art
ISBN 0-500-20299-0
First published 1980 by Oxford Univ. Press
An introduction to major decorative, ceremonial, figurative and narrative aspects of Chinese art. Coverage ranges from works of Neolithic groups and the bronzes of the Shang dynasty to Buddhist sculpture, ceramics, garden design and architecture. Emphasis is also placed on the interaction of poetry, painting and calligraphy.
Includes bibliographical references

709.6   African art

Visonà, Monica Blackmun, 1953-
A history of art in Africa; [by] Monica Blackmun Visona, Robin Poynor, Herbert M. Cole; with contributions by Suzanne Preston Blier (introduction), Rowland Abiodun (preface) and Michael D. Harris (chapter 16). 2nd ed. Pearson/Prentice Hall 2007 c2008 560p il pa $111
                                   709.6
1. African art
ISBN 978-0-13-612872-4; 0-13-612872-6
                                   LC 2007-15831
First published 2000
"Treating the subject from an art historical rather than an anthropological perspective, this groundbreaking book is organized geographically to cover the entire continent. Each of the five regional sections focuses on selected major art traditions. . . . Accompanying the text are over 700 photos and scores of maps, plans, drawings, etc." Libr J [review of 2000 edition]
Includes bibliographical references

709.73   American art

Craven, Wayne
American art; history and culture. McGraw-Hill 2003 687p il pa $69   **709.73**
1. American art
ISBN 978-0-07-282329-5; 0-07-282329-1
                                   LC 2002-035777
First published 1994
The author "establishes seven main stylistic periods—colonial, Federal, romantic, the American Renaissance, early modern, postwar modern, and postmodern—and then goes into great detail within each section, profiling individual artists and discussing the effects of various social, political, and technological changes on aesthetics and the role of art in daily life. . . . Coverage of American photography and twentieth-century art are particularly dynamic, but his examples and emphases prove to be insightful and creative throughout." Booklist
Includes bibliographical references

FitzGerald, Michael C.
Picasso and American art; [by] Michael FitzGerald; with a chronology by Julia May Boddewyn. Whitney Museum of American Art; in association with Yale University Press 2006 400p il $65 *   **709.73**
1. Picasso, Pablo, 1881-1973—Influence 2. American art
ISBN 9780300114522; 0-300-11452-4
                                   LC 2006-1402

FitzGerald, Michael C.—*Continued*
A "study of Picasso's influence on some of the most significant American artists of the 20th century. Fitzgerald moves chronologically, from the earliest Americans who engaged cubism in the teens (Max Weber, Mardsen Hartley, Man Ray, Stuart Davis), through the modernist investigations of Arshile Gorky, Willem De Kooning and Jackson Pollack, and winds up with Roy Lichtenstien's pop-art and Jasper Johns' postmodern responses to Picasso. Fitzgerald takes great pains to triangulate exhibition specifics with the work and words of each artist to document the precise nature and extent of the influence in each case. . . . There is a generous supply of images presented with the text, and they are as successful as Fitzgerald's prose in illuminating the complexities of Picasso's influence on these artists." Publ Wkly
Includes bibliographical references

Harlem Renaissance; art of Black America; introduction by Mary Schmidt Campbell; essays by David Driskell, David Levering Lewis, and Deborah Willis Ryan. Studio Museum in Harlem; Abradale Press 1994 200p il $17.98
709.73
1. Harlem Renaissance 2. African American artists 3. American art
ISBN 0-8109-8128-9   LC 93-20814
A reissue of the title first published 1987
This book "features four black artists: the sculptor Meta Warrick Fuller and the painters Aaron Douglas, Palmer Hayden and William H. Johnson. Also included are photographs . . . by James Van Der Zee." N Y Times Book Rev [review of 1987 edition]
"An eye-catching and eye-opening introduction to the black intelligensia who created the Harlem Renaissance of 1919-1930. . . . Black-and-white figures and color plates are plentiful and of fine quality." Choice [review of 1987 edition]
Includes bibliographical references

Haskell, Barbara, 1946-
The American century; art and culture. Norton 2000 2v il boxed set $120
709.73
1. American art 2. Arts—United States
ISBN 978-0-393-04859-9; 0-393-04859-4
A reissue of the title first published 1999
Contents: v1 1900-1950; v2 1950-2000 by Lisa Phillips
Based on exhibitions at the Whitney Museum, these illustrated volumes cover 20th century American painting, sculpture, printmaking, and photography through political, historical, social, economic, and culture contexts

Hughes, Robert
American visions; the epic history of art in America. Knopf 1997 635p il $65; pa $39.95
709.73
ISBN 0-679-42627-2; 0-375-70365-9 (pa)
LC 96-45111
The author examines "art and architecture in America from the earliest Spanish works in New Mexico to contemporary art done in the late 1990s." Libr J
"Hughes has orchestrated a spectacular integration of

facts, observations, and insights in this ambitious, lively, and gloriously illustrated volume." Booklist
Includes bibliographical references

Marin, Cheech, 1946-
Chicano visions; American painters on the verge; essays by Max Benavidez, Constance Cortez, Tere Tomo. Little, Brown 2002 160p il $35; pa $19.95
709.73
1. American painting 2. Mexican Americans
ISBN 0-8212-2805-6; 0-8212-2806-4 (pa)
LC 2002-104645
Published on the occasion of an exhibition that will travel to fiteen U.S. cities over a five-year period-Jkt
This "presents the work of 30 Chicano artists whose paintings will be exhibited at the Smithsonian and tour the country." Publ Wkly
"Marin's extraordinary collection forms the foundation for this exciting and invaluable showcase . . . [which includes works by] John Valadez, Gronk, Diane Gamboa, Patssi Valdez, Adan Hernandez, and Carlos Almaraz." Booklist
Includes bibliographical references

Smithsonian American Art Museum
America's art, Smithsonian American Art Museum; [project manager] Theresa J. Slowik; foreword by Eleanor Harvey; introduction by Elizabeth Broun. H.N. Abrams 2005 322p il $65
*
709.73
1. American art
ISBN 0-8109-5532-6; 978-0-8109-5532-5
LC 2005-17164
This catalog, created to commemorate the reopening of the Smithsonian American Art Museum after six years of renovation, features 225 works of American art from its collection.
"Here is American art in all its glory and innovation as a quest for understanding and connection, and a public collection that constitutes a genuine national treasure." Booklist
Includes bibliographical references

Updike, John
Still looking; essays on American art. Knopf 2005 222p il $40
709.73
1. American art 2. Art criticism 3. Aesthetics
ISBN 1-4000-4418-9   LC 2004-61568
The author presents eighteen "essays on American art and artists that present the reader with historical, biographical, and . . . technical information about the works he analyzes. The artists discussed range from late 19th-century masters Winslow Homer and Thomas Eakins to avant-garde figures Alfred Stieglitz and Elie Nadelman." Libr J
"The essays are uniformly thoughtful, focused, original, and provocative. . . . This small volume educates, informs, and engages. It's hard to ask for more." Christ Sci Monit

709.8   Latin American art

Encyclopedia of Latin American & Caribbean art; edited by Jane Turner. Oxford University Press 2006 803p il (Grove library of world art) $250

709.8

1. Latin American art
ISBN 978-0-19-531075-7; 0-19-531075-6
First published 1999 by Grove's Dictionaries
"This work covers the art of every country in Central and South America and the Caribbean, from the colonial period to the present. The entries, expanded and updated from the publisher's mammoth Dictionary of Art, cover countries, artists, and artistic styles, with cross-referencing where appropriate." Libr J [review of 1999 edition]
Includes bibliographical references

Scott, John F., 1936-
Latin American art; ancient to modern. University Press of Fla. 1999 xxiv, 240p il $49.95; pa $29.95

709.8

1. Latin American art
ISBN 0-8130-1645-2; 0-8130-1826-9 (pa)

LC 98-46535
A study "of Latin American art from pre-Columbian times to the present, encompassing media ranging from sculpture, pottery, and painting to architecture. Scott . . . addresses the major styles and artists that define each period." Libr J
Includes bibliographical references

711   Area planning (Civic art)

McGregor, James H. (James Harvey), 1946-
Rome from the ground up; [by] James H.S. McGregor. Belknap Press of Harvard University Press 2005 344p il map $29.95; pa $18.95 *

711

1. City planning—Rome 2. Rome—History
ISBN 0-674-01911-3; 0-674-02263-7 (pa)

LC 2005-48213
The author "chronologically traces the successive periods of intense architecture and planning that helped Rome achieve strategic greatness, from the Etruscan management of the Tiber Island ford 3,000 years ago, to the city's unparalleled artistic stamp by Bramante and Michelangelo during the Renaissance, to Mussolini's monumental Fascist vision, to the precarious repairs heralding the Jubilee Year of 2000. . . . Here is a walking tour in stately, inviting prose that renders wonderfully manageable a massive history lesson for the intellectually curious and adept." Publ Wkly
Includes bibliographical references

712   Landscape architecture (Landscape design)

Buchanan, Rita
Taylor's master guide to landscaping. Houghton Mifflin 2000 384p il $40   **712**
1. Landscape gardening
ISBN 0-618-05590-8   LC 99-54110
Companion volume to Taylor's master guide to gardening
"A Frances Tenenbaum book"
"Buchanan offers a comprehensive treatment of landscape design, emphasizing designing with plants and including extensive information about choosing and caring for plants, trees, shrubs, vines, and ground covers. . . . A landmark work destined to become a classic." Libr J

Clausen, Ruth Rogers, 1938-
Dreamscaping; 25 easy designs for home gardens. Hearst Bks. 2002 127p il $30

712

1. Garden design
ISBN 1-58816-067-X   LC 2001-16928
The author provides "plans, plant lists, and well-illustrated planting directions for all sorts of situations in sun or shade, outdoors and in the home. Tips and reminders are used to address design issues and maintenance, and to point out poisonous species. . . . The book's pretty layout and colorful photographs should entice novices to try something new in the garden." Booklist

DiSabato-Aust, Tracy
The well-designed mixed garden; building beds and borders with trees, shrubs, perennials, annuals, and bulbs. Timber Press 2003 460p il map $39.95

712

1. Landscape gardening
ISBN 0-88192-559-4   LC 2002-23191
The author focuses on "the mixed border, which incorporates permanent woody plants as well as perennials, annuals, and other plants that die back to the ground every year. . . . Particularly impressive are the author's designs for using the mixed-garden approach in small properties, such as townhouse gardens and around foundations. . . . The motivated gardener will find a wealth of information and ideas in this book." Libr J
Includes bibliographical references

Gertley, Jan
The art of the kitchen garden; [by] Jan and Michael Gertley. Taunton Press 1999 151p il $29.95   **712**
1. Gardens 2. Vegetable gardening
ISBN 1-56158-180-1   LC 97-23710
The authors "accentuate a formal approach to line, shape, color, and texture, arriving at patterned garden plans distinguished by detailed combinations of flowers, herbs, and vegetables." Booklist
"If the prose is somewhat utilitarian, the book is commendably complete, enlivened by vivid photographs that effectively illustrate the title." Publ Wkly
Includes bibliographical references

Goodwin, Nancy

Montrose; life in a garden; with illustrations by Ippy Patterson; foreword by Maureen Quilligan. Duke University Press 2005 292p il $34.95

712

1. Gardening
ISBN 0-8223-3604-9   LC 2005-11387
"Goodwin and her husband, Craufurd, searched for 10 years for a larger piece of property before buying Montrose, a nineteenth-century estate in historic Hillsborough, North Carolina. . . . Godwin taught piano and ran a mail-order nursery before she settled into the full-time gardening . . . that has shaped the rhythm of her life since 1994. This lovely little book, exquisitely illustrated with a friend's penciled and watercolored botanical drawings, chronicles a year in her garden. It's a story of the seasons, the weather, hard work, triumphs, and disappointments. Goodwin's voice, precise and detailed when discussing the differences between various hellebores and snowdrops, remains fondly appreciative of the treasures she grows so lovingly and well." Horticulture

Griswold, Mac K.

The golden age of American gardens; proud owners, private estates, 1890-1940; {by} Mac Griswold, Eleanor Weller; with research assistance by Helen E. Rollins. Abrams 1991 408p il $75; pa $34.95

712

ISBN 0-8109-3358-6; 0-8109-2737-3 (pa)
LC 91-8283
Published in association with the Garden Club of America
A "history of owners, designers, and the ultimate country retreats resulting from their collaborations. . . . Weller's compilation of rare, hand-colored lantern slides and hundreds of black-and-white historical photographs of the era are particularly noteworthy." Booklist
Includes bibliographical references

Hayward, Gordon

Stone in the garden; inspiring designs and practical projects. Norton 2001 224p il $39.95

712

ISBN 0-393-04779-2   LC 00-69945
"The book's first half focuses on the philosophical and design considerations of stone forms as varied as walls, paths, terraces, and even benches. The second half is more practical, covering topics such as estimating the amount of stone needed for a wall, the methods of cutting and laying stone, and building pools and fountains." Libr J
Includes bibliographical references

Newbury, Tim

20 best garden designs. Cassell 2002 96p il pa $20

712

1. Garden design
ISBN 1-8418-8208-9; 978-1-8418-8208-6
First published 1995 with title: The ultimate garden designer
This book "offers a range of designs for varied settings, from rooftop and urban gardens to family gardens and natural gardens. Plans include plant keys, photographs, and a discussion of aims and effects. Variations for yards of different sizes or shapes complete each plan. A useful, affordable resource." Libr J

The **Oxford** companion to the garden; edited by Patrick Taylor. Oxford University Press 2006 xxx, 554p il $65 *

712

1. Landscape architecture 2. Gardens 3. Landscape gardening
ISBN 978-0-19-866255-6; 0-19-866255-6
LC 2006-1269
First published 1986 with title: The Oxford companion to gardens
"All sizes, shapes, and types of gardens throughout the world are showcased here, from the Chelsea Physic Garden in London to the Chinampas of Xochimilco, Mexico City. The 1,750 alphabetically arranged entries range in size from just a few lines to several pages. Descriptions of the history of gardening within selected countries, including the styles and movements, are the longest entries. Greatest emphasis is on Great Britain, the U.S., France, Germany, and Italy. Garden descriptions are usually brief and outline histories, designers, size, type, and whether the garden is open to visitors. Biographical entries cover architects, artists, designers, gardeners, scientists, sculptors, writers, and others who influenced garden design. Other entries treat garden styles, features, and terms and various aspects of gardening history and gardening-related activities." Booklist
"An exciting and innovative volume. . . . A monumental achievement." Antiques Magazine

Van Sweden, James A.

Architecture in the garden; {by} James van Sweden with Thomas Christopher; foreword by Penelope Hobhouse. Random House 2002 264p il $39.95 *

712

1. Landscape architecture 2. Garden design
ISBN 0-375-50154-1   LC 2002-69702
The author attempts "to show that architectural elements are essential in developing a successful garden design. Van Sweden focuses on such components as paths, edgings, fences, walls, water, and artwork, explaining that a garden is not a garden without a sound structural organization that uses these elements. . . . A well-illustrated glossary is included. Recommended for most gardening and landscape architecture collections." Libr J
Includes bibliographical references

720 Architecture

De Botton, Alain

The architecture of happiness. Pantheon Books 2006 280p il $25 *

720

1. Architecture—Social aspects 2. Aesthetics
ISBN 0-375-42443-1   LC 2006-44797
This book "traces how human needs and desires have been served by styles of architecture, from stately Classical to minimalist Modern, arguing that the stylistic choices of a society can represent both its cherished ideals and the qualities it desperately lacks." Publisher's

De Botton, Alain—*Continued*

note

The author "is a lively guide, and his eclectic choices of buildings and locations evince his conclusion, that 'we should be as unintimidated by architectural mediocrity as we are by unjust laws.'" New Yorker

O'Gorman, James F.

ABC of architecture; drawings by Dennis E. McGrath. University of Pa. Press 1997 127p il $35; pa $13.45   **720**

ISBN 0-8122-3423-5; 0-8122-1631-8 (pa)

LC 97-22616

The author discusses the history of architecture, types of buildings, advances in technology, and architectural analysis

This book, "a model of brevity and clarity, may be the best-written work on the subject in English for lay people." N Y Times Book Rev

Includes bibliographical references

Palladio, Andrea, 1508-1580

The four books on architecture; translated by Robert Tavernor and Richard Schofield. MIT Press 1997 xxxv, 436p il $69.95; pa $24.95

720

ISBN 0-262-16162-1; 0-262-66133-0 (pa)

LC 96-36406

This is a translation of a Renaissance architectural treatise that was first published in Venice in 1570. "The new translation includes thirty-one pages of notes and forty pages of glossary." Times Lit Suppl

"Drawing on the monuments of ancient Rome as well as the author's own villas and public works, this philosophical treatise and practical guide served as the pattern book for countless Palladian buildings by other architects around the world. Elegantly translated (in the first new English translation since 1738) and illustrated with the lyrical, rarely seen woodcuts of Palladio's original." N Y Times Book Rev

Includes bibliographical references

720.3 Architecture—Encyclopedias and dictionaries

Ching, Frank, 1943-

A visual dictionary of architecture; {by} Francis D. K. Ching. Van Nostrand Reinhold 1995 319p il $44.95; pa $39.95   **720.3**

1. Architecture—Dictionaries

ISBN 0-471-28451-3; 0-471-28821-7 (pa)

LC 95-1476

This volume arranges some "5,000 entries thematically under 68 concepts covering architectural design, history, and technology. The topics, which are treated alphabetically, include building types (church, house, theater), sections (door, roof, stair), features (arch, column, vault), and materials (brick, paint, wood). Terms are logically clustered on oversize pages and defined with both line drawings and text, usually 20 to 100 words." Booklist

Curl, James Stevens, 1937-

A dictionary of architecture and landscape architecture; with line-drawings by the author. 2nd ed. Oxford University Press 2006 xxv, 880p il $45 *   **720.3**

1. Architecture—Dictionaries 2. Landscape architecture—Dictionaries

ISBN 978-0-19-280630-7; 0-19-280630-0

LC 2006-40248

First published 1999 with title: Oxford dictionary of architecture

This is a dictionary of the "many stylistic and technical terms used in architecture today. The work covers all periods of Western architectural history in more than 5000 articles." Libr J

For a fuller review, see: Booklist, Nov. 15, 2006

Includes bibliographical references

Dictionary of architecture & construction; edited by Cyril M. Harris. 4th ed. McGraw-Hill 2005 1089p il $74.95 *   **720.3**

1. Architecture—Dictionaries 2. Building—Dictionaries

ISBN 0-07-145237-0   LC 2005-42340

First published 1975

This dictionary features "definitions of more than 27,000 important architecture and construction terms . . . [including] terms in legal areas, technologies, techniques, materials, organizations, historic architectural styles, and architectural trends." Publisher's note

"The handy one-volume format, the reasonable cost, the clarity and accuracy of entries, the legible type and drawings, and the inclusive approach to current developments in the design, building, and scholarly professions related to architecture make this publication a crucial tool." Choice

The **Penguin** dictionary of architecture and landscape architecture; edited by John Fleming, Hugh Honour and Nikolaus Pevsner. 5th ed. Penguin Bks. 1998 643p il pa $16.95 hardcover o.p.   **720.3**

1. Architecture—Dictionaries

ISBN 0-14-051323-X (pa)

First published 1966 with title: The Penguin dictionary of architecture

This reference covers "architecture from ancient times to the present. Major entries on key individuals, styles, movements, materials, and terms range up to several pages in length and include cross references and bibliographies for further reading." Publisher's note

"A magnificent panorama of world architecture, scholarly conciseness at its best." Art Review

720.9 Architecture—Historical, geographic, persons treatment

Boucher, Bruce

Andrea Palladio; the architect in his time; principal photography by Paolo Marton. 2nd ed. Abbeville Press 2007 324p il pa $39.95

720.9

Boucher, Bruce—*Continued*
1. Palladio, Andrea, 1508-1580
ISBN 978-0-7892-0940-5; 0-7892-0940-3
First published 1994
"In this careful, comprehensive, stunningly illustrated survey, Boucher . . . capably illuminates Palladio's stylistic evolution. . . . Among the 300 plates are more than 100 newly commissioned photographs of building interiors and exteriors, which superbly capture Palladio's distincitve blend of simplicity and grandeur." Publ Wkly
Includes bibliographical references

Ching, Frank, 1943-
A global history of architecture; [by] Francis D.K. Ching, Mark Jarzombek, Vikramaditya Prakash. J. Wiley & Sons 2006 800p il map $75 **720.9**
1. Architecture—History
ISBN 978-0-471-26892-5; 0-471-26892-5
LC 2005-34527
"Ching and colleagues comprehensively look at the history of architecture worldwide from 3500 BCE to CE 1950. . . . The book includes most of the major monuments found in other architectural surveys, plus many more, especially from the non Western world. . . . The book's most informative and attractive feature is its illustrations, hundreds of drawings by Ching, a noted author and architectural illustrator. . . . Includes a portfolio of color photographs, companion Web site, and list of coordinates for Google Earth to provide satellite images of the major monuments." Choice
Includes bibliographical references

Fletcher, Sir Banister Flight, 1866-1953
Sir Banister Fletcher's A history of architecture. 20th ed, edited by Dan Cruickshank; consultant eds., Andrew Saint, Peter Blundell Jones, Kenneth Frampton; asst. ed., Fleur Richards. Architectural Press 1996 xxxviii, 1794p il $145 **720.9**
1. Architecture—History
ISBN 0-7506-2267-9
LC 96-35511
First published 1896 with title: A history of architecture on the comparative method
"Overarching view of architectural history, newly rewritten and expanded to include worldwide coverage. Extensively illustrated, with glossary, index, and bibliographies appended to each chapter. Includes general introductions and background for each chapter." N Y Public Libr Book of How & Where to Look It Up [1987 edition]
Includes bibliographical references

Frank Lloyd Wright; master builder; text by Bruce Brooks Pfeiffer; edited by David Larkin and Bruce Brooks Pfeiffer. Rev. ed. Universe 1997 240p il pa $29.95 **720.9**
1. Wright, Frank Lloyd, 1867-1959
ISBN 978-0-7893-0098-0; 0-7893-0098-2
LC 97-61188
First published 1993 by Rizzoli
"Published in association with the Frank Lloyd Wright Foundation, this . . . volume features previously unpublished photographs . . . of Wright's masterworks. . . .

The works featured here are . . . documented by one of Wright's former apprentices, with text that details the development and execution of each commission. Also included throughout is a selection of Wright's extensive writings, unpublished talks, and private letters." Publisher's note
Includes bibliographical references

Glancey, Jonathan
Architecture. DK Pub. 2006 512p il (Eyewitness companions) pa $30 **720.9**
1. Architecture—History
ISBN 0-7566-1732-4
LC 2005-36013
First published 2000 with title: The story of architecture
The author "examines 5000 years of architecture throughout the world. In well-executed and consistent writing, he briefly introduces each era and region, then touches on significant buildings and complexes (e.g., the Parthenon, the Sydney Opera House)." Libr J

Ruan Xing 1965-
New China architecture; by Xing Ruan; photography by Patrick Bingham-Hall. Periplus Editions 2006 239p il $49.95 **720.9**
1. Asian architecture
ISBN 978-0-7946-0389-2; 0-7946-0389-0
"China's remarkable economic boom is generating prodigious architectural and building activity. Ruan . . . offers a sampling by presenting 43 recent and projected buildings or complexes. . . . A diverse parade of designs is featured throughout, including airports, offices, stores, theaters, libraries, museums, villas, and sport showcases for the 2008 Olympic Games. Each rates a brief description and several excellent photographs or artist renderings. Floor plans or sections are often included." Libr J

The **Seventy** wonders of the modern world; 1500 years of extraordinary feats of engineering and construction; edited by Neil Parkyn. Thames & Hudson 2002 304p il $40 **720.9**
1. Architecture 2. Curiosities and wonders
ISBN 0-500-51047-4
LC 2002-100549
Published in the United Kingdom with title: The seventy architectural wonders of our world
"Most of the featured 'wonders' date from the second half of the 20th century. The selections are divided into seven categories: churches, palaces, public buildings, towers and skyscrapers, bridges and railways, canals and dams, and statues. Each entry includes basic information on history, structural and engineering details, innovations, aesthetics, and a sidebar 'fact-file.'" Libr J
Includes bibliographical references

Watkin, David, 1941-
A history of Western architecture. 4th ed. Watson-Guptill Publications 2005 720p il $50 **720.9**
1. Architecture—History
ISBN 978-0-8230-2277-9; 0-8230-2277-3
LC 2005-921992
First published 1986

Watkin, David, 1941-—*Continued*

This study focuses on the development of architecture in Europe and the United States and includes chapters on Mesopotamian and Egyptian architecture.

"The book is persuasively written, its illustrations are numerous and well chosen, and readers are often introduced to buildings known only to specialists." Choice

Includes bibliographical references

720.973   Architecture—United States

LeBlanc, Sydney

The architecture traveler; a guide to 262 key American buildings. Rev ed. W.W. Norton 2005 291p il pa $24.95   **720.973**

1. Architecture—United States

ISBN 978-0-393-73174-3; 0-393-73174-X

         LC 2004-65971

First published 1993 by Whitney Library of Design with title: 20th century American architecture

This guide "'examines [over] 250 important American buildings' and provides the information needed to visit them. . . . This book should be of use to travelers and architecture buffs alike." Libr J

Mathewson, Casey C. M.

Frank O. Gehry: selected works; 1969 to today. Firefly Books 2007 599p il $69.95

         720.973

1. Gehry, Frank

ISBN 978-1-55407-276-7; 1-55407-276-X

         LC 2008-271852

First published 2006 in Germany

"Mathewson reviews Gehry's windows, furniture, and his use of natural light, as well as highlights specific buildings and includes hundreds of artfully composed color photographs of Gehry's interior and exterior projects." Libr J

Storrer, William Allin

The Frank Lloyd Wright companion. Rev ed. University of Chicago Press 2006 492p il $99

         720.973

1. Wright, Frank Lloyd, 1867-1959

ISBN 0-226-77621-2   LC 2006-44502

First published 1993

This "volume covers more than 450 buildings designed by master architect Wright between 1886 and 1959. Storrer documents each structure with plans, drawings, photographs, and commentary. Each presentation is both complete and concise, following each stage of Wright's aesthetic development, each leap of his imagination, and each instance of technical innovation." Booklist

Wiseman, Carter

Shaping a nation; twentieth-century American architecture and its makers. Norton 1998 412p il $45   **720.973**

1. Architecture—20th century 2. Architecture—United States 3. Architects

ISBN 0-393-04564-1   LC 97-9896

In this survey the author is "concerned to trace the ways in which buildings express an American identity. Though his subject is twentieth-century architecture, his search for roots extends back to the colonial vernacular and Thomas Jefferson. . . . Wiseman has written a solid mainstream history in which the look of buildings is seen as important. More significantly, he argues the case for social relevance alongside beauty." Archit J

Includes bibliographical references

Wolfe, Tom

From Bauhaus to our house. Bantam Books 1999 111p il pa $15   **720.973**

1. Bauhaus—Influence 2. Architecture—United States 3. Architecture—20th century

ISBN 978-0-553-38063-7; 0-553-38063-X

First published 1981 by Farrar, Straus & Giroux

A humorous history of American architecture in the 20th century.

721   Architectural structure

The **elements** of style; an encyclopedia of architectural detail; general editor, Stephen Calloway; consultant editor, Elizabeth Cromley. New ed., rev. and updated by Alan Powers. Firefly Books 2005 502p il $75 *

         721

1. Domestic architecture 2. Architecture—Details

ISBN 1-55407-079-1

First published 1991 by Simon & Schuster

This book "focuses on styles and design elements of British and North American vernacular domestic architecture from 1485 (Tudor) to the present. About half of the book deals with periods and styles before the 20th century. . . . It is an outstanding and economical single-volume resource" Choice

Includes bibliographical references

Maliszewski-Pickart, Margaret, 1963-

Architecture and ornament; an illustrated dictionary. McFarland & Co. 1998 198p il $35

         721

1. Architecture—Details

ISBN 0-7864-0383-7   LC 97-33112

This source pairs a traditional dictionary of architectural elements with a series of illustrations of the same elements. The names located in the numbered illustrations may be found alphabetically in the dictionary; and cross-references in the dictionary refer to specific illustrations. The illustrations are grouped by category: windows and doors; walls; roofs; columns; stairs; ornament and moldings; arches, vaults, and domes

Rybczynski, Witold

The look of architecture. Oxford Univ. Press 2001 130p il hardcover o.p. pa $9.95   **721**

1. Architecture 2. Design

ISBN 0-19-513443-5; 0-19-515633-1 (pa)

         LC 00-53077

Rybczynski, Witold—*Continued*

This book provides "commentary on the significance of style and fashion in architecture. Using anecdote, historical data, and descriptive prose to comment on Western architecture during the modern era, Rybczynski shows how the often dismissed discipline of apparel design finds its correlative in architectural fashion." Libr J

"The author's deeply informed enthusiasm is infectious, and his removal of architectural writing from an airily theoretical discourse to the realm of practical experience is empowering for the lay reader." Publ Wkly

Includes bibliographical references

722 Architecture from earliest times to ca. 300

The **Grove** encyclopedia of classical art and architecture; edited by Gordon Campbell. Oxford University Press 2007 2v il map set $250 * **722**

1. Greek art—Encyclopedias 2. Roman art—Encyclopedias 3. Greek architecture—Encyclopedias 4. Roman architecture—Encyclopedias
ISBN 978-0-19-530082-6; 0-19-530082-3

LC 2007-487

"The two-volume encyclopedia begins with a section on abbreviations, a thematic index, and continues with the A-Z entries, a list of contributors, and an index. . . . Each entry includes the name or term followed by dates and an article ranging from a few hundred words to several pages." Am Ref Books Annu, 2008

"One cannot speak too highly of this publication; it should grace the library of every scholar and library interested in the subject. It is a fundamental resource— from the most basic entry to the most in-depth reading and research." Choice

Includes bibliographical references

724 Architecture from 1400

Curtis, William J. R.

Modern architecture since 1900. 3rd ed [rev, expanded, and redesigned] Phaidon 1996 736p il $59.95; pa $39.95 **724**

1. Architecture—20th century
ISBN 978-0-7148-3524-2; 0-7148-3524-2; 978-0-7148-3356-9 (pa); 0-7148-3356-8 (pa)

LC 97-112837

First published 1982

An "analysis of the modern architectural tradition and its origins." Publisher's note

"The volume's well-detailed text is buttressed with 650 color and black-and-white illustrations. This should be a standard volume in all architecture collections." Lib J

Includes bibliographical references

Gropius, Walter, 1883-1969

The new architecture and the Bauhaus; translated from the German by P. Morton Shand; with an introduction by Frank Pick. MIT Press 1965 112p il pa $14.95 * **724**

1. Bauhaus 2. Architecture—20th century
ISBN 0-262-57006-8

LC 65-10279

"The MIT paperback series"

Original German edition, 1925; this is a reissue of the translation first published 1935 in the United Kingdom

The founder of the Dessau Bauhaus describes the work of that institution, and his own architectural theories

Rybczynski, Witold

The perfect house: a journey with the Renaissance architect Andrea Palladio. Scribner 2002 266p il $25; pa $15 **724**

1. Palladio, Andrea, 1508-1580 2. Architecture—15th and 16th centuries
ISBN 0-7432-0586-3; 0-7432-0587-1 (pa)

LC 2002-66838

The author offers a historical and architectural analysis of ten villas attributed to 16th century Italian architect Andrea Palladio

"With its intriguing biographical detail, precise descriptions of design elements, and engaging insights into daily life in the 16th century, Rybczynski's book is a small but lasting gift to the reader." Libr J

Includes bibliographical references

726 Buildings for religious and related purposes

Adams, Henry, 1838-1918

Mont-Saint-Michel and Chartres; with an introduction by Ralph Adams Cram. Princeton Univ. Press 1981 401p il pa $40 hardcover o.p. *
726

1. Mont-Saint-Michel (France). Abbey 2. Notre-Dame (Cathedral: Chartres, France) 3. Middle Ages
ISBN 0-691-00335-1 (pa)

LC 81-47279

Also available in paperback from Penguin Bks.

"This classic study of medieval civilization is written as the commentary of Henry Adams to an imaginary niece as they tour the Abbey Church at Mont-Saint-Michel and the Chartres Cathedral." Benet's Reader's Ency of Am Lit

King, Ross, 1962-

Brunelleschi's dome; how a Renaissance genius reinvented architecture. Penguin Books 2001 194p il pa $14 **726**

1. Brunelleschi, Filippo, 1377-1446 2. Santa Maria del Fiore (Cathedral: Florence, Italy) 3. Church buildings
ISBN 0-14-200015-9

LC 2001-280068

First published 2000 by Walker & Co.

"King illuminates the mysterious sources of inspiration and the secretive methods of architectural genius Filippo Brunelleschi in a fascinating chronicle of the building of

King, Ross, 1962--—*Continued*

his masterwork, the dome of Santa Maria del Fiore in Florence. A remarkable saga of how one incandescent mind performed the one matchless feat that would forever transform architecture from a mechanical craft into a creative art." Booklist

Includes bibliographical references

728 Residential and related buildings

Altman, Adelaide, 1925-

Elderhouse: planning your best home ever. Chelsea Green 2002 232p il pa $19.95
728

1. Elderly—Housing 2. Domestic architecture—Designs and plans

ISBN 1-931498-11-3   LC 2002-31481

"The first section is full of ideas for creating a safe and comfortable home for wheelchair access or for a time in our lives when we are less nimble. The second section addresses the psychology of moving to a new smaller space in the later years of life." Libr J

Includes bibliographical references

Eck, Jeremiah

The distinctive home; a vision of timeless design. Taunton Press 2003 234p il $40 *
728

1. Domestic architecture—Designs and plans 2. Building

ISBN 1-561-58528-9   LC 2002-151820

"Eck firmly believes it is possible to build creative houses without a large budget. He discusses a home's site placement, examines the flow of activity within a modern home, and encourages the reader to think of rooms beyond their traditional uses. Eck's book encourages creativity and provides a series of color photographs for developing sound ideas." Libr J

Friedman, Avi

The adaptable house; designing homes for change. McGraw-Hill 2002 271p il $45
728

1. Domestic architecture—Designs and plans 2. Prefabricated houses

ISBN 0-07-137746-8   LC 2002-141433

"Friedman urges the reader to reimagine the traditional static home as dynamic space that changes as the needs of the occupants change. A single house, according to the author, should be able to accommodate an individual and/or family throughout their lives. Friedman examines how space functions within a house and the ways a house can be expanded and contracted based on the needs of its owners." Libr J

Includes bibliographical references

The **house** plans bible. Creative Homeowner 2006 559p il pa $14.95   **728**

1. Domestic architecture—Designs and plans

ISBN 978-1-58011-300-7; 1-58011-300-1

LC 2005-909003

This book "offers readers over 650 [home designs]. . . . Tips supplement the designs, with advice on everything from hiring a contractor to adding finishing touches such as window treatments and landscaping." Publisher's note

Jordan, Wendy Adler, 1946-

Universal design for the home; great looking, great living design for all ages, abilities, and circumstances. Quarry Books 2008 207p il pa $24.99   **728**

1. Domestic architecture—Designs and plans

ISBN 978-1-59253-381-7; 1-59253-381-7

LC 2007-32663

This book "shows how a home that is accommodating to all can also have a stylish decor. . . . Color photographs and some before-and-after floor plans show how accessibility standards have been incorporated. A list of resources is provided." Libr J

Lind, Carla

The Wright style. Simon & Schuster 1992 224p il $50   **728**

1. Wright, Frank Lloyd, 1867-1959 2. Domestic architecture

ISBN 0-671-74959-5   LC 91-44553

"An Archetype Press book"

This book "takes us inside dozens of Frank Lloyd Wright's 'organic' houses, including his home and studio in Oak Park, Illinois, and the two Taliesins. . . . Carla Lind's text traces the development and components of Wright's unique, revolutionary aesthetic while 250 color photographs allow readers to appreciate the harmony of Wright's light-filled, graciously rectilinear rooms." Booklist

Includes bibliographical references

Maddex, Diane

Wright-sized houses; Frank Lloyd Wright's solutions for making small houses feel big; photography by Alan Weintraub. Abrams 2003 159p il $30   **728**

1. Wright, Frank Lloyd, 1867-1959 2. Domestic architecture 3. Architects

ISBN 978-0-8109-4626-2; 0-8109-4626-2

LC 2003-6958

The author "takes the reader inside a selection of . . . small houses from across the country . . . turning the spotlight on Wright's . . . solutions to make these homes look and feel large." Publisher's note

Includes bibliographical references

McAlester, Virginia, 1943-

A field guide to American houses; by Virginia and Lee McAlester; with drawings by Lauren Jarrett, and model house drawings by John Rodriquez-Arnaiz. Knopf 1984 525p il $40; pa $24.95   **728**

1. Domestic architecture

ISBN 0-394-51032-1; 0-394-73969-8 (pa)

LC 82-48740

McAlester, Virginia, 1943-—*Continued*

A guide to the "numerous architectural styles of American single-family houses. Houses featured range from 17th-century Georgians to Neoeclectics of the late 1970s, with more than 1200 drawings and photographs and brief histories and notable architects of each style." Libr J

Includes bibliographical references

Nettleton, Sarah

The simple home; the luxury of enough; [by] Sarah Nettleton and Frank Edgerton Martin; photographs by Randy O'Rourke. Taunton Press 2007 249p il map (American Institute Architects) $40 **728**

1. Domestic architecture

ISBN 1-56158-831-8; 978-1-56158-831-2

LC 2006-19645

This book "explores the inspiration and philosophy behind 21 simple . . . homes built in diverse areas of the country. All designed, built or renovated around the simple needs of each owner. . . . The 21 featured homes are organized according to six different pathways, each owner arriving at his own concept of simple with an emphasis on slightly different priorities." Publisher's note

Includes bibliographical references

Roberts, Jennifer, 1962-

Good green homes; creating better homes for a healthier planet. Gibbs Smith 2003 160p il $39.95 **728**

1. Housing—Environmental aspects 2. Domestic architecture

ISBN 978-1-58685-179-8; 1-58685-179-9

LC 2003-7570

A "guide for people who want to live in . . . environmentally conscious homes. . . . This book lays out seven fundamental principles of green building, illustrated with more than 150 color and 20 black and white photographs of more than twenty-five homes." Publisher's note

Includes bibliographical references

Small house designs; edited by Kenneth R. Tremblay, Jr. & Lawrence von Bamford. Storey Communications 1997 201p il pa $19.95 hardcover o.p. **728**

1. Domestic architecture—Designs and plans

ISBN 0-88266-966-4 (pa) LC 96-47252

"A Storey Publishing book"

"This compilation of small house designs by architects participating in the American Institute of Architects design competition features 34 floor plans and exterior sketches or photographs for each design. Also included are the square footage, estimated cost to build, and a short description of special or hidden elements. While not a book of ready-to-use designs, it is a good idea book for individuals looking for creative suggestions for small city lots." Libr J

Stewart, Martha

Martha Stewart's new old house; restoration, renovation, decoration, landscaping; photographs by Mathieu Roberts; illustrations by Rodica Prato. Potter 1992 288p il $45 **728**

1. Architecture—Conservation and restoration

ISBN 0-517-57701-1 LC 92-15900

This work follows the step-by-step renovation, restoration, decoration and landscaping of a 19th-century Federal farmhouse in Connecticut

"Lots of atmospheric photography show workers at their labors." Publ Wkly

Susanka, Sarah

Creating the not so big house; insights and ideas for the new American home; photographs by Grey Crawford. Taunton Press 2000 258p il $34.95; pa $24.95 **728**

1. Domestic architecture 2. Interior design

ISBN 1-56158-377-4; 1-56158-605-6 (pa)

LC 00-44323

Susanka provides photographs and plans of houses that are designed to look bigger than their actual size

"Architect Susanka has big ideas about small design. . . . {This book promotes} well-designed, efficient, interesting modest-size homes. . . . {She} includes 25 delightful examples of houses designed by architects from around the country." Booklist

Not so big solutions for your home. Taunton Press 2002 155p il pa $22.95 **728**

1. Domestic architecture—Designs and plans 2. Interior design

ISBN 1-56158-613-7 LC 2002-7101

The author presents a compilation of 31 essays from her "Drawing Board" column in Fine Homebuilding magazine "that offer a number of solutions to household design problems both big and small. . . . Susanka offers an eclectic mix: tips on site selection, mud room design, planning to fit specific furniture, creating a family room that works, personalizing with tile, and planning window seats, pantries, TV placement, and floor plan changes." Libr J

Vassallo, Marc

The barefoot home; dressed-down design for casual living; [photographs by Ken Gutmaker] Taunton Press 2006 218p il $30 **728**

1. Domestic architecture 2. Interior design

ISBN 978-1-56158-807-7; 1-56158-807-5

LC 2006-2623

"A barefoot home, as described by Vassallo . . . is an 'open house' suited to casual living. Over 20 homes are shown here that in some way exemplify the type, providing an informality, openness, use of light and texture, and indoor/outdoor connection suited to a 21st-century lifestyle. The residences are depicted in color photographs and are either newly constructed or remodeled." Libr J

728.8   Large and elaborate private dwellings

Wiencek, Henry

National Geographic guide to America's great houses; more than 150 outstanding mansions open to the public; by Henry Wiencek and Donna M. Lucey. National Geographic Soc. 1999 320p il pa $25   **728.8**

1. Domestic architecture 2. Architecture—United States

ISBN 0-7922-7424-5   LC 98-53013

Arranged by state, this guide includes information on past owners, furnishings, renovations, room descriptions, and excursion plans for other nearby houses of note. The text is accompanied by 170 full-color photos

729   Design and decoration of structures and accessories

Martin, Sam, 1968-

Manspace; a primal guide to marking your territory. Taunton Press 2006 218p il $24.95

729

1. Interior design 2. Personal space 3. Men—Attitudes

ISBN 978-1-56158-820-6; 1-56158-820-2

LC 2006-6545

The author "shows how various men have etched out a stylish locale in a home to pursue their passion, whether for fishing or lawn bowling or motorcycles. . . . Even women will get plenty of ideas for creating their own space." Libr J

730.9   Historical, geographic, persons treatment of sculpture

Manca, Joseph, 1956-

1000 sculptures of genius; [by] Joseph Manca, Patrick Bade and Sarah Costello. English version. Sirrocco 2007 543p il $24.95   **730.9**

1. Sculpture

ISBN 978-1-84484-215-5; 1-84484-215-0

Translated by: Sofoya Hundt, Nick Cowling and Marie-Noëllle Dumaz

"This sculpture collection offers a vision of western art. . . . It also includes references, comments on masterworks and biographies." Publisher's note

Nevelson, Louise, 1900-1988

The sculpture of Louise Nevelson; constructing a legend; edited by Brooke Kamin Rapaport; essays by Arthur C. Danto . . . [et al.]; chronology by Gabriel de Guzman. Yale University Press 2007 238p il $55   **730.9**

ISBN 978-0-300-12172-8; 0-300-12172-5

LC 2006-31684

Catalog of an exhibition held at the Jewish Museum, New York

"Nevelson and her black-wood sculptures were major art-world attractions in the 1970s and 1980s, only to be forgotten after her death. This dazzling book resurrects both the artist and her work in all their magical glory." Booklist

Includes bibliographical references

731.4   Sculpture—Techniques and procedures

Belcher, Judy

Polymer clay creative traditions; techniques and projects inspired by the fine and decorative arts; principal photography by Steve Payne. Watson-Guptill 2006 144p il $21.95

731.4

1. Clay 2. Modeling

ISBN 0-8230-4065-8; 978-0-8230-4065-0

LC 2005-927912

"Addressing novices to the medium of polymer clay as well as more advanced crafters in the field, Belcher prepares an attractive handbook on making clay items." Booklist

Bütz, Richard

How to carve wood; a book of projects and techniques. Taunton Press 1984 215p il pa $19.95

731.4

1. Wood carving

ISBN 0-918804-20-5   LC 83-50680

"A Fine Woodworking Book"

The author introduces "the most common types of carving, whittling, chip carving, relief carving, lettering, and architectural carving. The information on tools and their care is very helpful. This is the best book available on the subject." Libr J

Includes bibliographical references

Hessenberg, Karin

Sculpting basics; everything you need to know to create fantastic three-dimensional artwork. Barron's 2005 128p il $23.99   **731.4**

1. Sculpture—Technique

ISBN 978-0-7641-5843-8; 0-7641-5843-0

"A Quarto book"

The author "presents a fine overview for beginning sculptors. . . . [The book] touches on a wide range of sculptural forms and styles, including the traditional figure, symbolic compositions, and abstract reliefs. . . .For such a slight book, [it] bundles a surprising amount of information." Libr J

Includes bibliographical references

Plowman, John

The encyclopedia of sculpting techniques; a comprehensive visual guide to traditional and contemporary techniques. Sterling 2003 176p il pa $16.95   **731.4**

1. Sculpture—Technique

ISBN 978-1-4027-0394-2; 1-4027-0394-5

First published 1995 in the United Kingdom

Plowman, John—*Continued*

This book on sculpting covers "more than 30 techniques . . . [including] clay, plaster, wood, stone, and papier mâché, as well as . . . aerated concrete block, rubber, and found objects." Publisher's note

736   Carving and carvings

Stern, Joel, 1953-

Jewish holiday origami; photographs by David Greenfield. Dover Publications 2006 64p il pa $5.95   **736**

1. Origami 2. Jewish holidays
ISBN 0-486-45076-7; 978-0-486-45076-6
LC 2005-56934

This book contains a "year's worth of holiday projects — from Chanukah dreidels and a menorah with candles, to Passover pyramids and an image of the Red Sea parting." Publisher's note

Van Sicklen, Margaret

The joy of origami. Workman 2005 152p il pa $16.95   **736**

1. Origami
ISBN 0-7611-3988-5; 978-0-7611-3988-1
LC 2005-43687

"Includes 100 sheets of origami paper"

"The 57 [origami] models [included] range in difficulty from a simple Elephant in Pajamas to a more challenging Tyrannosaurus Rex." Publisher's note

737.4   Coins

Coins 2007. 63rd ed., 2007 ed. Frederick Fell Publishers 2006 272p il (Numismatic library series) pa $18.95   **737.4**

1. Coins
ISSN 1541-8022
ISBN 978-0-88391-156-3; 0-88391-156-6

Annual. Replaced Fell's United States coin book in 2000

Cover on title: Coins 2007-2008.

This guide contains complete tables showing today's value of every coin minted in the United States. Along with illustrations are information on the history of coins, speculation and investment, how to start a collection, how to sell coins and recognize worthless coins.

Includes bibliographical references

A **Guide** book of United States coins, 2008; by R. S. Yeoman; edited by Kenneth Bressett. Western 2007 il $16.95 *   **737.4**

1. Coins
ISSN 0072-8829
ISBN 0-7948-2267-3; 978-0-7948-2267-5

Also available in spiral-binding format

Annual. First published 1946 by Whitman

At head of title: The official red book

This guide "known as the 'Red Book' is an outstanding reference on U.S. coins designed for use in identifying and grading coins. All issues from 1616 to the present are covered. The guide provides historical data, statistics, values, and detailed photographs for each coin. Additional sections deal with specialties such as Civil War and Hard Times tokens, misstruck coins, and uncirculated and proof sets." Nichols. Guide to Ref Books for Sch Media Cent. 4th edition

Handbook of United States coins 2009; by R. S. Yeoman; edited by Kenneth Bressett. 66th ed. Whitman Publishing 2008 256p il $12.95; pa $9.95 *   **737.4**

1. Coins
ISSN 0072-9949
ISBN   978-0-7948-2539-3;   0-7948-2539-7; 978-0-7948-2540-9 (pa); 0-7948-2540-0 (pa)

Annual. First published 1942

At head of title: The official blue book

This companion volume to A Guide book of United States coins gives the wholesale values of U.S. coins from colonial times to the present

Krause, Chester L.

Standard catalog of world coins; by Chester L. Krause and Clifford Mishler. Krause Publs. il pa $55 *   **737.4**

1. Coins
ISSN 1556-2263
ISBN 0-8968-9365-0; 978-0-8968-9365-8

Also available volumes covering the 17th, 19th and 21st centuries

First published 1972. Periodically revised

This illustrated volume currently covers coins from throughout the world minted 1901-2000. Prices are provided for each coin in up to four grades of preservation. Includes commemorative issues.

738   Ceramic arts

Kovel, Ralph M.

Kovels' dictionary of marks: pottery and porcelain; by Ralph M. and Terry H. Kovel. 2nd ed. Crown 1995 278p il $17   **738**

1. Pottery—Marks 2. Porcelain—Marks
ISBN 0-517-70137-5   LC 95-3361

First published 1953 with title: Dictionary of marks—pottery and porcelain

On cover: Pottery and porcelain,1650-1850

This is a guide to identification of American, English, and European pottery and porcelain including an "index of 5,000 marks, listed by prominent features and with a complete cross-reference {showing} at a glance (a) geographical location of mark, (b) factory or family name of manufacturer, (c) type of ware, (d) method of producing the mark on the object, (e) color of the mark, and (f) date when the mark was used. The authors have included a foreword, bibliography, index of manufacturers and a . . . guide to the often misunderstood marks of Delft, Sevres, and England 1842-1883." Publisher's note

Kovel, Ralph M.—*Continued*

Kovels' new dictionary of marks; {by} Ralph and Terry Kovel. Crown 1986 290p il $19

738

1. Pottery—Marks 2. Porcelain—Marks
ISBN 0-517-55914-5   LC 85-15146

Covering pottery and porcelain from 1850 to the present this volume is regarded as a complimentary volume to the one covering 1650 to 1850

738.1 Ceramic arts—Techniques, procedures, apparatus, equipment, materials

Burleson, Mark

The ceramic glaze handbook; materials, techniques, formulas. Lark Bks. 2001 144p il pa $24.95 hardcover o.p.   **738.1**

1. Pottery 2. Glazes
ISBN 1-57990-439-4 (pa)   LC 00-63486

"Burleson covers glaze chemistry, application techniques, firing, and problem solving. Color photographs comparing fired samples are particularly good. A collection of formulas by other artists is categorized by type of clay body and firing temperature. Useful for studio potters and hobbyists." Libr J

Hamer, Frank

The potter's dictionary of materials and techniques; Frank and Janet Hamer. 5th ed. University of Pa. Press 2004 L 45.00 : CIP entry (Jun.)   **738.1**

1. Pottery—Dictionaries 2. Ceramics—Dictionaries
ISBN 0-8122-3810-9

First published 1975 by Watson-Guptill

Articles in this "potter's reference include soda firing, paper clay, computer glaze calculations, and fuming. . . . Alphabetically arranged entries range in length from a brief paragraph or half-page . . . to longer essays on subjects such as formulas, health hazards, and cones. Subject matter ranges widely, covering all the processes and materials involved in pottery formation, decoration, and firing." Am Ref Books Annu, 1998 {entry for 4th edition}

Kenny, John B., d. 1988

The complete book of pottery making; drawings by Carla Kenny. 2nd ed. Chilton 1976 310p il (Chilton's creative crafts series) pa $29.95 hardcover o.p.   **738.1**

1. Pottery
ISBN 0-8019-5933-0 (pa)   LC 76-302

First published 1949 by Greenberg

The whole process of pottery making is covered in a series of step-by-step photographs which explain the wheel, modeling, mold work, glaze, coil-building a teapot, etc.

Includes bibliographical references

Nelson, Glenn C.

Ceramics: a potter's handbook; [by] Glenn C. Nelson, Richard Burkett. 6th ed. Wadsworth/Thomson Learning 2002 439p il pa $90.95 *   **738.1**

1. Ceramics 2. Pottery
ISBN 0-03-028937-8   LC 2001-96329

First published 1960. Periodically revised

This manual for beginner to advanced potters presents forming and decorating techniques, body and glaze recipes, and sources for raw materials and equipment.

Includes bibliographical references

738.4 Enamels

Darty, Linda

The art of enameling; techniques, projects, inspiration. Lark Books 2004 176p il $24.95

738.4

1. Enamel and enameling
ISBN 1-579-90507-2   LC 2004-5540

This is an "introduction to enameling fundamentals with practice exercises for techniques such as cloisonné and champlevé. There are also a dozen jewelry projects by other artists. This is an excellent and beautifully illustrated summary of a difficult craft." Libr J

Includes bibliographical references

738.5 Mosaics

Biggs, Emma, 1956-

The encyclopedia of mosaic techniques. Running Press 1999 160p il $24.95   **738.5**

1. Mosaics
ISBN 0-7624-0444-2

This is a "guide to the materials and techniques of designing and laying mosaic tiles in both indoor and outdoor settings. Well illustrated with color photographs throughout, the 'A to Z of Techniques' section has step-by-step instructions. Finished mosaics are pictured in the 'Gallery' section. Workshop set-up and safety tips are included." Libr J

739.27 Jewelry

Codina, Carles

The complete book of jewelry making. Lark Bks. 2000 160p il hardcover o.p. pa $19.95

739.27

1. Jewelry
ISBN 1-57990-188-3; 1-57990-304-5 (pa)
          LC 00-42809

This book covers "the basics, from the ABCs of metallurgy to such complicated techniques as enameling and lacquering. . . . Most of the examples are contemporary, taken from European designers, and all blessed with great color photographs." Booklist

Codina, Carles—*Continued*

The new jewelry; contemporary materials & techniques. Sterling/Lark Books 2006 160p il (Arts and crafts series) $29.95   **739.27**
1. Jewelry 2. Nature craft
ISBN 1-57990-734-2; 978-1-57990-734-1
LC 2005-16029

The author reviews jewelry-making "processes step-by-step in color photographs, a variety of techniques (e.g., twister in glassmaking), and galleries of samples. A shorter section is devoted to the use of high-tech methods, followed by six specific designs to emulate or to employ as a foundation. Amazing the forms that simple colored cardboard can take." Booklist

Includes bibliographical references

Gollberg, Joanna

The art & craft of making jewelry; a complete guide to essential techniques. Lark Books 2006 176p il (A Lark jewelry book) $27.95 *
   739.27
1. Jewelry
ISBN 978-1-57990-570-5; 1-57990-570-6
LC 2005-34040

"This is an overview of contemporary jewelry-making techniques for studio artists. Individual chapters cover various aspects of metalworking, color addition, and the use of findings, with project instructions and color photographs of finished works by multiple artists supplementing the technical information and practice exercises. This beautifully illustrated book should find a place in public library collections needing additional material on jewelry making." Libr J

741.2 Drawing and drawings— Techniques, procedures, apparatus, equipment, materials

Edwards, Betty

The new drawing on the right side of the brain. 2nd ed. Jeremy P. Tarcher\Putnam 1999 291p il $27.95; pa $16.95   **741.2**
1. Drawing—Technique 2. Creative ability
ISBN   978-0-87477-419-1;   0-87477-419-5; 978-0-87477-424-5 (pa); 0-87477-424-1 (pa)
LC 99-35809

First published 1979 with title: Drawing on the right side of the brain

This book describes the author's technique for teaching people how to draw more accurately and creatively by developing the capabilities of the brain's right side, which, according to "split-brain" research, controls the visual and perceptual functions.

Includes bibliographical references

Hammond, Lee

Lifelike drawing with Lee Hammond; Lee Hammond. North Light Books 2005 159p il pa $19.99 *   **741.2**
1. Drawing—Technique
ISBN 1-581-80587-X   LC 2004-56093

This book "encompasses techniques for rendering still lifes, portraiture, landscapes, and a variety of surfaces including fabric and transparent glass. . . . Filled with useful suggestions such as how to use statues and photo albums for ready reference and practice, Hammond's drawing how-to should satisfy a wide audience with a broad range of abilities." Booklist

Micklewright, Keith, 1933-

Drawing: mastering the language of visual expression. Harry N. Abrams 2005 168p il (Abrams studio) pa $29.95 *   **741.2**
1. Drawing—Technique
ISBN 0-8109-9238-8   LC 2005-5862

"Using examples of master artists such as Ingres and Michelangelo as well as more contemporary work of Cezanne, Hockney, and others, different aspects of drawing are examined. Each chapter ends with 'Ideas to Explore,' in which the reader is given suggestions for practice. . . . This book is valuable for those learning the theory behind the elements of drawing and for those looking for practical instruction." Voice Youth Advocates

Includes bibliographical references

Nicolaides, Kimon

The natural way to draw; a working plan for art study. Houghton Mifflin 1990 221p il pa $16
   741.2
1. Drawing—Technique
ISBN 0-395-53007-5
First published 1941

"After the author's death, the manuscript was prepared for publication . . . by Mamie Harmon." Publisher's note

Among the topics discussed by the author are contour and gesture; drapery; the use of black and white crayon; studies of structure; study from reproductions; and the use of color

Price, Maggie, 1947-

Painting with pastels; easy techniques to master the medium. North Light Books 2007 128p il pa $24.99   **741.2**
1. Pastel drawing
ISBN 978-1-58180-819-3; 1-58180-819-4
LC 2006-029048

"This book shows the reader . . . [how] to paint with pastels, from materials and techniques to painting from photographs. . . . Hand-in photos show how to hold and apply the pastel, and the twenty-two step-by-step demonstrations cover . . . preparing your surface, underpainting, figure drawing and more." Publisher's note

741.5 Cartoons, caricatures, comics

An **anthology** of graphic fiction, cartoons & true stories, vol. 2; edited by Ivan Brunetti. Yale University Press 2008 400p il $28 *
   741.5

An anthology of graphic fiction, cartoons & true stories, vol. 2—*Continued*

1. Comic books, strips, etc. 2. American wit and humor

ISBN 978-0-300-12671-6; 0-300-12671-9

"Brunetti's second collection of his favorite cartoonists' work is even better than the first—more far-ranging, more personal and eccentric. Clearly a tour of one person's singular tastes, it's arranged in a stream-of-consciousness 'oh, and you have to see this one' sort of way: work by 80-odd cartoonists, mostly from the past few decades, but also incorporating some early-1900s comic strips, a 1940s-vintage Fletcher Hanks story and several circa 1950 Harvey Kurtzman pieces as well as a smattering of previously unpublished gems." Publ Wkly

An **Anthology** of graphic fiction, cartoons, and true stories; edited by Ivan Brunetti. Yale University Press 2006 400p il $28 *
741.5

1. Comic books, strips, etc. 2. American wit and humor

ISBN 978-0-300-11170-5; 0-300-11170-3

LC 2006-14095

Brunetti presents "an overview of the art-comics movement, complete with a handful of the classic newspaper strips that informed today's creators. He finds room for such established veterans as R. Crumb, Lynda Barry, Gilbert and Jaime Hernandez, Daniel Clowes, Gary Panter, and Chester Brown as well as many less-familiar creators. . . . Brunetti admits that his selection criteria are highly personal, but as a cartoonist himself, whose work combines a socially transgressive spirit and impressive formal capability, his idiosyncratic approach is based in professional expertise. If his choices are sometimes arguable, his iconoclasm makes the book livelier and less predictable than such anthologies are wont to be." Booklist

Batman unauthorized; vigilantes, jokers, and heroes in Gotham City; edited by Dennis O'Neil. Benbella Books, Inc. 2008 219p il (Smart pop series) $17.95
741.5

1. Batman (Fictional character) 2. Comic books, strips, etc.—History and criticism 3. Graphic novels

ISBN 978-1-93377130-4; 1-933771-30-5

LC 2007-46504

Former Batman comics editor and comic book writer O'Neil edits this collection of essays about Batman and his world, written by comics writers, magazine editors, and others. Topics include the cost of being Batman, calculated to the last dollar; why Batman is the most American of superheroes; whether Bruce Wayne might be mentally ill; why Batman needs Robin more than Robin needs Batman; why Arkham Asylum is doing more harm than good for Gotham City; why Batman works better when his world remains closer to reality; and more.

Includes bibliographical references

Chinn, Mike, 1954-

Writing and illustrating the graphic novel; everything you need to know to create great graphic works. Barron's Educ. Ser. 2004 128p il pa $21.95 *
741.5

1. Comic books, strips, etc.—Authorship 2. Graphic novels—Authorship

ISBN 0-7641-2788-8

LC 2003-110234

"A Quarto book"

The author "helps intermediate writers and illustrators marry narrative to visuals and create lively characters in dynamic locations. He also offers advice on establishing one's own style, building a portfolio, and making a professional presentation. Whether for creating new varieties of superheroes or adapting the classics, this will be the standard resource for most collections." Libr J

Includes bibliographical references

The **complete** cartoons of the New Yorker; edited by Robert Mankoff; foreword by David Remnick. Black Dog & Leventhal 2004 655p il $60 *
741.5

1. New Yorker Magazine, Inc. 2. New Yorker (Periodical) 3. Cartoons and caricatures

ISBN 1-579-12322-8

LC 2004-46371

"Issued as part of the *New Yorker's* eightieth anniversary celebration, this . . . volume collects, in two formats, the cartoons that have appeared in the pages of that magazine over the course of its distinguished publishing history. . . . The book itself gathers 2,500 of the most representative cartoons for display, but two accompanying CDs contain all the cartoons (68,647, to be exact) ever published in the magazine. Arrangement is by chapter, with each covering a decade of the *New Yorker's* existence. . . . A testament—a tribute—to the great magazine but also an absolutely special way to spend quality time." Booklist

Daniels, Les, 1943-

Marvel; five fabulous decades of the world's greatest comics; introduction by Stan Lee. Abrams 1991 287p il pa $26.95 hardcover o.p.
741.5

1. Marvel comics (New York, N.Y.) 2. Comic books, strips, etc.

ISBN 0-8109-2566-4

LC 91-8783

"Daniels' behind-the-scenes look at the development of Marvel, his profiles of the line's foremost heroes and villains, and biographies of leading writers and artists will entice . . . young fans. . . . But the book's strongest appeal lies in the generous samplings of artwork spread throughout." Booklist

The **DC** Comics encyclopedia; the definitive guide to the characters of the DC universe; written by Phil Jimenez . . . [et al.] DK Publishing 2004 351p il $40 *
741.5

1. DC Comics Group 2. Comic books, strips, etc.

ISBN 0-7566-0592-X

LC 2004-3379

This is a "one-volume encyclopedia of more than 1,000 characters created by DC Comics . . . featuring some of DC's most creative artists and heroes and villains from the world famous to lesser known one-offs." Publisher's note

The DC Comics encyclopedia—*Continued*

"The colorful design makes this book a pleasure to browse." Libr J

Gorman, Michele

Getting graphic!: comics for kids; with a foreword by Jeff Smith; and original comic art by Jimmy Gownley. Linworth Books 2007 84p il $24.95   **741.5**

1. Graphic novels—Administration 2. Graphic novels—History and criticism

ISBN 978-1-58683-327-5   LC 2007-35033

Gorman presents annotated bibliographies of recommended graphic novels for children ages 6-12 to help librarians develop a quality, age-appropriate graphic novel collection that includes fiction, nonfiction, and manga. Amelia Rules! creator Jimmy Gownley created a comic story featuring his characters, just for this book. The book entries include the title, author, year of publication, publisher, ISBNs (both 10-digit and 13-digit), an annotation, and an age range recommendation. Gorman provides series annotations for series published by Capstone, Stone Arch, Rosen, Lerner, and other educational publishers.

Hajdu, David

The ten-cent plague; the great comic-book scare and how it changed America. Farrar, Straus and Giroux 2008 434p $26   **741.5**

1. Comic books, strips, etc.

ISBN 978-0-374-18767-5; 0-374-18767-3

LC 2007-25024

"In the years after World War II, American society was in flux, and its kids were rebelling full-speed ahead. The older generation, looking for something to blame for juvenile delinquency other than, say, bad parenting and schools, zeroed in on an easy target: Crime Does Not Pay, Shock Suspense Stories, Young Love, and their kind — the vivid, gaudy, low-class comic books their children were reading. . . . After a few chapters describing the dawn of the American comics industry, [Hajdu] turns his attention to the parallel evolution of the publishers who tried to churn out stuff kids would flock to, the creators who balanced 'art' against 'product,' and the bluenoses who played on public fear for children's wellbeing to make themselves known as defenders of virtue." Boston Phoenix

"Hajdu offers captivating insights into America's early bluestocking-versus-blue-collar culture wars, and the later tensions between wary parents and the first generation of kids with the buying power to mold mass entertainment." Village Voice

Includes bibliographical references

Hart, Christopher

Cartooning for the beginner. Watson-Guptill 2000 144p il pa $19.95   **741.5**

1. Cartoons and caricatures

ISBN 0-8230-0586-0   LC 00-101905

This guide to cartooning techniques "covers the world of cartoon animals, animation, and 'edgy 'toons.'" Libr J

Hirschfeld, Al, 1903-2003

Hirschfeld on line. Applause Theatre Bk. Pubs. 1998 343p $59.95   **741.5**

1. Cartoons and caricatures 2. Entertainers

ISBN 1-55783-356-7

Hirschfeld "is the irreplaceable M.V.P. of the New York theatre world, and this compendium of his drawings amounts to a historic work of droll, generous-minded theatre criticism. The artist himself has annotated the drawings, which cover a range of the performing arts . . . and his comments are as swooping and witty as his lines." New Yorker

Jones, Gerard

Men of tomorrow; geeks, gangsters and the birth of the comic book. Basic Books 2004 320p il $26; pa $15   **741.5**

1. Comic books, strips, etc. 2. Cartoonists

ISBN 0-465-03656-2; 0-465-03657-0 (pa)

LC 2004-9031

This book tells "the surprising story of the young Jewish misfits, hustlers and nerds who invented the superhero and the comic book industry. . . . Springing unheralded out of working-class Jewish immigrant neighborhoods in the depths of the Depression, these young men transformed an odd mix of geekdom, science fiction, and outsider yearnings into blue-eyed chisel-nosed crime-fighters and adventurers who quickly captured the mainstream imagination. . . . He chronicles how the comics sparked a frightened counterattack that nearly destroyed the industry in the 1950's and how later they surged back at an underground level, to inspire a new generation to transmute those long-ago fantasies into art, literature, blockbuster movies and graphic novels." Publisher's note

Kanfer, Stefan

Serious business; the art and commerce of animation in America from Betty Boop to Toy story. Da Capo Press 2000 256p il pa $17.50
    741.5

1. Animated films

ISBN 0-306-80918-4; 978-0-306-80918-7

LC 98-50687

First published 1997 by Scribner

"As an art form, animation is magically irresistible; as a reflection of broader American popular culture, it is amazingly on target. . . . Kanfer here shows how the people, politics, prejudices, trends, and technologies of various eras have been so aptly reflected in each set of frames. . . . While Kanfer's humbly stated intention is to augment previous writings on the subject, his work should certainly join the ranks of important literature in the field." Libr J

Lin, Selena

Manga school; draw your own Manga. Tokyopop 2008 128p il $14.99   **741.5**

1. Graphic novels 2. Manga 3. Drawing—Technique

ISBN 978-1-4278-1023-6

Global manga artist Lin provides five basic lessons on drawing shojo manga (girls' comics), from the nitty grit-

Lin, Selena—*Continued*

ty basics of art supplies and how to use dip pens, using screentone sheets, to creating one's own story with characters, how to draw characters, costuming one's characters, how to use the computer for graphics, panel composition, drawing backgrounds, and coloring one's work. Throughout the book photographs and Lin's art provide examples and guidance.

Masters of American comics; essay by John Carlin; with contributions by Stanley Crouch . . . [et al.]; edited by John Carlin, Paul Karasik, and Brian Walker. Yale University Press 2005 316p il $45 *   **741.5**
1. Comic books, strips, etc. 2. Cartoonists
ISBN 0-300-11317-X   LC 2005-19449

"This catalogue was published in conjunction with Masters of American Comics, an exhibition jointly organized by The Hammer Museum and The Museum of Contemporary Art, Los Angeles"—Verso of title page

This book focuses "on the 15 'Masters' of American comics, including George Herriman, Jack Kirby and R. Crumb. . . . Jules Feiffer, Pete Hamill and Matt Groening, among others, contribute essays on each of the artists." Publ Wkly

"Hundreds of color reproductions allow the ingenuity of the artists' work to speak for itself." New Yorker

Includes bibliographical references

McCloud, Scott

Making comics; storytelling secrets of comics, manga, and graphic novels. HarperCollins 2006 264p il pa $22.95 *   **741.5**
1. Comic books, strips, etc.—Authorship 2. Graphic novels—Drawing
ISBN 0-06-078094-0; 978-0-06-078094-4

The author "explores practical matters, including comics devices such as panels, word balloons, and sound effects; facial expressions and body language; the creation of convincing and evocative settings; and the different tools artists can use for the job, from pencils to computers. He also delves into the framing of images in panels, the flow of panels on a page, and the relationships between words and pictures in comics. . . . This is thoughtful, fascinating, stimulating, potentially controversial, and inspiring." Libr J

Includes bibliographical references

Reinventing comics; how imagination and technology are revolutionizing an art form. Paradox Press 2000 237p il pa $22.95
    741.5
1. Comic books, strips, etc. 2. Cartoons and caricatures
ISBN 0-06-095350-0   LC 00-710457

The author maps out "'12 revolutions', which, he believes, need to take place for comics to survive and finally be recognized as a legitimate art form. The topics progress from the oldest of comic-related arguments (seeking respect) to the use of computer technology to renew and expand its audience. These brilliantly presented discussions concern comics as literature, comics as art, creators' rights, industry innovation, and public perception, among other topics." Libr J

O'Neil, Dennis, 1939-

The DC comics guide to writing comics; introduction by Stan Lee. Watson-Guptill 2001 128p il $19.95   **741.5**
1. Comic books, strips, etc.—Authorship
ISBN 0-8230-1027-9   LC 2001-26101

The author "discusses story structure, characterization, script preparation, and other general writing topics. He also covers those more specific to comics writing such as miniseries, maxiseries, and continuity. O'Neil addresses the visual component of the art, the importance of page layout, and the relationship between the writer and the artist." SLJ

"O'Neil addresses the universals of writing in a way that makes the book useful to all aspiring scripters, regardless of their knowledge of comics." Booklist

Pilcher, Tim

The essential guide to world comics; [by] Tim Pilcher, Brad Brooks. Collins & Brown, Distributed in the U.S. by Sterling 2005 319p il pa $19.95 *   **741.5**
1. Comic books, strips, etc.
ISBN 1-84340-300-5

The authors "examine the cultural impact of comics in over 20 countries, from Japan—where popular titles sell 6.5 million copies per week—to France, where comics are considered an art from on par with music and poetry." Publisher's note

"A stunning eye-opener to the comics medium's variety." Booklist

The **Psychology** of superheroes; an unauthorized exploration; edited by Robin S. Rosenberg; with Jennifer Canzoneri. Benbella Books, Inc. 2008 259p il (BenBella Books psychology of popular culture series) pa $17.95   **741.5**
1. Conduct of life 2. Superheroes (Fictional characters)—Psychology
ISBN 1-933771-31-3; 978-1-933771-31-1
    LC 2007-41418

This book collects essays about superheroes from several psychological viewpoints, ranging from the positive moral aspects of superheroes to gender stereotypes, prejudice, anti-heroes, the place of Arkham Asylum (the notorious place where DC super villains get locked up), the role of rage in The Incredible Hulk, and more. Editor Rosenberg is a clinical psychologist, and many of the contributors hold degrees in psychology and have faculty positions at various universities.

Includes bibliographical references

Rhoades, Shirrel

A complete history of American comic books; afterword by Steve Geppi. Peter Lang Publishing Inc. 2008 353p il $119.95; pa $39.95   **741.5**
1. Comic books, strips, etc.—History and criticism 2. Graphic novels
ISBN978-1-4331-0107-6(pa);1-4331-0107-6(pa);
978-1-4331-0110-6; 1-4331-0110-6
    LC 2007-43460

Rhoades, former publisher of Marvel Comics (after Stan Lee stepped down to move to Hollywood and focus

Rhoades, Shirrel—*Continued*

on Marvel Comics in the movies), dates the beginning of the American comic book to the 1930s, when the format was first used. He covers the history of comics from that time to the present, covering all the big names (Will Eisner, Jack Kirby, Stan Lee, etc.). The book is peppered with fun sidebars with such labels as "flashback," "comics trivia," "looking back," "true facts," and so one. These help to make the book fun to read. Rhoades doesn't employ a straight narrative, but includes interviews, the side bars, comics milestones, a list of fanboys who have and had careers in comics, and a comic book quiz.

Includes bibliographical references

Rosenkranz, Patrick

Rebel visions: the underground comix revolution, 1963-1975. Fantagraphics Books 2008 292p il pa $34.99   **741.5**

1. Graphic novels 2. Cartoonists 3. Comic books, strips, etc.—History and criticism
ISBN 978-1-56097-706-3

"The most lasting artistic legacy of the 1960s hippie movement, other than its music, is its eye-poppingly transgressive underground comics—black-and-white pamphlets that spread the counterculture message of sex, drugs, and rebellion to freak and straight alike. Rosencranz thoroughly documents the phenomenon, providing a year-by-year account of the underground scene, from 1968's Zap #1, which artist R. Crumb sold from a baby carriage on the streets of Haight Ashbury, to its crash in 1973 in the wake of obscenity rulings and a crackdown on head shops. . . . Rosencranz's writing may lack flair, but with personalities this colorful (the artists themselves provide fly-on-the-wall reminiscences) and art this outrageous (reprinted on nearly every page) to write about, who needs it?" Booklist

Steinberg, Saul, 1914-1999

Steinberg at the New Yorker; introduction by Ian Frazier. H.N. Abrams 2005 239p il $50
                                      741.5

1. Steinberg, Saul, 1914-1999 2. New Yorker Magazine, Inc. 3. Cartoons and caricatures
ISBN 0-8109-5901-1   LC 2004-19498

The author "surveys six decades of Steinberg's pieces, including all 89 New Yorker covers (in full color), cartoons, wartime sketches from overseas, evocative (but never literal-minded) illustrations for articles, and unpublished items from the artist's portfolio. The material is arranged thematically, examining such recurring motifs as cats, pedestals and rubber-stamped figures and documenting the turn to visual metaphor in Steinberg's later work. . . . Steinberg's cartoons usually made readers think before they laughed, and so will this splendid memorial to a 20th-century artistic landmark." Publ Wkly

Includes bibliographical references

Studio space; the world's greatest comic illustrators at work. Image Comics 2008 318p il $49.99; pa $29.99   **741.5**

1. Graphic novels 2. Cartoonists 3. Comic books, strips, etc.
ISBN 978-1-58240-909-2; 978-1-58240-908-5 (pa)

Twenty modern comics artists talk about their careers, their work, and their working methods. Each of them is photographed in his studio, and samples of their artwork are included. The artists are: Brian Bolland, Tim Bradstreet, Howard Chaykin, Steve Dillon, Tommy Lee Edwards, Duncan Fegredo, Dave Gibbons, Adam Hughes, Joe Kubert, Jim Lee, Mike Mignola, Frank Miller, Sean Phillips, George Pratt, Alex Ross, Tim Sale, Walt Simonson, Bryan Talbot, Dave Taylor, and Sergio Toppi.

The **Superhero** book; the ultimate encyclopedia of comic-book icons and Hollywood heroes; edited by Gina Misiroglu with David A. Roach. Visible Ink Press 2004 xxi, 725p il $29.95
                                      741.5

1. Cartoons and caricatures 2. Motion pictures
ISBN 0-7808-0772-3   LC 2004-19059

This is an "encyclopedic reference work that profiles superheroes from all companies and in all media. . . . Its 300 full entries provide information on more than 1,000 mythic overachievers, covering . . . comic book, movie, television, and novel superheroes." Publisher's note

This "is a must-buy for comic readers interested in knowing the early roots and conceptions of comic-book heroes." SLJ

Thompson, Jason, 1974-

Manga: the complete guide. Ballantine Books/Del Rey Manga 2007 592p il pa $19.95
                                      741.5

1. Graphic novels—History and criticism 2. Manga—Bibliography
ISBN 978-0-345-48590-8

"A Del Rey Trade Paperback Original"

Former manga editor at Viz, Thompson reviews more than 900 manga titles that have been translated and published in the U.S. This book includes only original manga series published in Japan and then translated into English for U.S. publication. Titles include series that are no longer in print. The book also includes sidebar discussions on the many genres included in manga, including the age and genre divisions and such topics as otaku (hard-core fans), underground manga, and more. Separate sections cover yaoi and gay manga, and adult manga (often called hentai). It also includes an artist index. Each review includes a description of the series, how many volumes it has, an age rating, and content indicators.

"This volume—highly useful for reference, readers' advisory, and collection development—is strongly recommended for all libraries." Libr J

Includes bibliographical references

Watterson, Bill

The complete Calvin and Hobbes. Andrews McMeel Pub. 2005 3v il set $150   **741.5**

1. Comic books, strips, etc.
ISBN 0-7407-4847-5; 978-0-7407-4847-9
                            LC 2004-62709

This is a collection of the entire run of the comic strip Calvin and Hobbes, which ran from 1985 to 1995.

"This is one of the all-time great comic strips, absolutely essential for every library." Libr J

741.6   Graphic design, illustration, commercial art

Heller, Steven
Becoming a graphic designer; a guide to careers in design; Steven Heller & Teresa Fernandes. 3rd ed. J. Wiley & Sons 2006 368p il pa $35

741.6

1. Commercial art 2. Graphic arts 3. Vocational guidance
ISBN 0-471-71506-9; 978-0-471-71506-1

LC 2005-47493

First published 1999
This book provides a "survey of the graphic design market, including . . . coverage of print and electronic media and the evolving digital design disciplines. . . . This visual guide has more than 600 illustrations and covers everything from education and training, design specialties, and work settings to preparing an effective portfolio and finding a job." Publisher's note
Includes bibliographical references

Salisbury, Martin
Illustrating children's books; creating pictures for publication. Barron's Educational Series 2004 144p il pa $22.95   **741.6**

1. Illustration of books 2. Illustrators 3. Picture books for children
ISBN 0-76412-717-9
"A Quarto book"
The author "surveys the genre's distinguished history with examples from Caldecott, Greenaway, N. C. Wyeth, Maxfield Parrish, and Howard Pyle. . . . Through sketches and annotations, Salisbury explains how to create fantasy, fairy tale, realism, and nature drawing. Written for advanced students, the book covers storyboards and layouts, contracts, copyrights, and how to present one's work professionally. Highly recommended for all collections." Libr J
Includes bibliographical references

743   Drawing and drawings by subject

Hart, Christopher
Human anatomy made amazingly easy. Watson-Guptill 2000 114p il pa $19.95

743

1. Artistic anatomy 2. Figure drawing
ISBN 0-8230-2497-0   LC 00-43514
In this work for the beginning artist "Hart simplifies the process in an accessible manual that concentrates on line and forgoes the complexity of color." Libr J

Robins, Clem, 1955-
The art of figure drawing. North Light Bks. 2003 143p il pa $22.99   **743**

1. Figure drawing
ISBN 1-58180-204-8   LC 2002-69598
Includes index

"Robins' guide considers the elements—line, light and shade, mass, texture, foreshortening, and more—using basic geometric shapes to achieve accurate renderings of the nude human figure. His explanation of equilibrium and center of gravity as applied to figure drawing is particularly helpful to the novice exploring this essential foundational skill, and the index makes for user-friendliness." Booklist

Watson, Lucy, 1968-
Life drawing class. Watson-Guptill Publications 2003 125p il pa $24.95   **743**

1. Figure drawing
ISBN 0-8230-2767-8   LC 2003-102105
"A Quarto book"
"Watson presents each chapter as a class in which she introduces basic concepts such as measuring angles, plotting positions, perspective light and tone, and so on. Also included in each section are suggestions for pose lengths, lists of materials, and clearly explained, illustrated step-by-step instructions. Throughout Watson includes examples of her and other professionals' work in a wide range of styles and media." Booklist

745   Decorative arts

Encyclopedia of American folk art; Gerard C. Wertkin, editor; Lee Kogan, associate editor; in association with the American Folk Art Museum. Routledge 2004 xxxiii, 612p il $125

*   **745**

1. American folk art
ISBN 0-415-92986-5   LC 2003-18051
This volume "covers more than three centuries of folk artists and provides information about museum collections, institutions that collect and sponsor folk art, and subjects related to the various forms of folk art. Entries tend to be detailed, and in some cases, extensive. . . . The work is heavily and usefully cross-referenced. Most entries end with brief bibliographies. Although not heavily illustrated, the work offers a number of interesting color and black-and-white illustrations keyed to specific entries." Choice
Includes bibliographical references

The **Grove** encyclopedia of decorative arts; edited by Gordon Campbell. Oxford University Press 2006 2v il set $195 *   **745**

1. Decorative arts—Encyclopedias
ISBN 978-0-19-518948-3; 0-19-518948-5

LC 2006-9866

This encyclopedia "covers all aspects of the decorative arts from ancient times to the present day and throughout Western and non-Western cultures. . . . [The editor has] culled hundreds of entries from the 34-volume Dictionary of Art (1996) and added more than 1000 new entries. Topics include artists and crafters, decorative arts production, the qualities and historical uses of materials, furniture styles, and jewelry." Libr J
Includes bibliographical references

Kilby, Janice Eaton, 1955-

By hand; 25 beautiful objects to make in the American folk art tradition; [by] Janice Eaton Kilby with the assistance of Veronika Alice Gunter. Lark Bks. 2001 144p il pa $17.95 hardcover o.p.   **745**

1. Handicraft

ISBN 1-57990-376-2 (pa)   LC 00-54974

This is a "survey collection of two dozen projects for familiar items, such as samplers, decoys, and copper weathervanes, that have been designed by professional artists. Each type of craft has a historic introduction and is illustrated by photographs of museum and gallery pieces. . . . A handy all-in-one source for public libraries." Libr J

Includes bibliographical references

Lauria, Jo

Craft in America; celebrating two centuries of artists and objects; [by] Jo Lauria and Stephen Fenton; prologue by Jimmy Carter. Clarkson Potter 2007 320p il $60   **745**

1. Decorative arts—United States

ISBN 978-0-307-34647-6; 0-307-34647-1

LC 2006-34839

This collection of photographs and "prose pays homage to two centuries' worth of baskets, textiles, furniture, pottery, and jewelry from U.S. artisans. . . . Famous artisans, from Revolutionary War silversmith Paul Revere to modern-day jewelers Denise and Sam Wallace, and their works are featured, as are the numerous schools and workshops inspiring those creations and today's student crafts movement. . . . A wondrous companion to read over and over and over again." Booklist

Includes bibliographical references

Miller, Judith, 1948-

Arts & crafts; [by] Judith Miller with Jill Bace; photography by Graham Rae . . . [et al.] DK Publishing 2005 240p il (DK collector's guides) $30   **745**

1. Arts and crafts movement

ISBN 0-7566-0963-1   LC 2005-299490

Includes the most important arts and crafts designers and factories from Great Britain, continental Europe, and the United States, with examples of their work and current prices.

This is "a well-organized, carefully captioned picture catalog of Arts and Crafts guilds and designers, with highlights of their styles and photos of their furniture, jewelry, textiles, ceramics, metalware, and glass, wallpaper, and paper creations." Booklist

745.1 Antiques

Kovel, Ralph M.

Kovels' antiques & collectibles price list 2008; [by Ralph and Terry Kovel] 40th anniversary ed. Black Dog & Leventhal 2007 750p il pa $27.95 *
                                        745.1

1. Antiques 2. Collectors and collecting

ISBN 978-1-57912-745-9; 1-57912-745-2

First published 1968 with title: The complete antiques price list. Revised annually to reflect current prices. Title varies

Current American market prices for 45,000 entries for antiquities and collectibles. Included are photographs, factory marks and logos, catalogs, reports of sales, auctions, and tips on buying, collecting, restoring, and preserving.

Kovel's know your collectibles; {by} Ralph and Terry Kovel. Crown 1992 c1981 404p il pa $17 hardcover o.p.   **745.1**

1. Antiques 2. Collectors and collecting

ISBN 0-517-58840-4 (pa)   LC 81-5515

"Advises on what collectible objects are likely to increase in value and how to preserve, protect, and sell them. Covers ceramics, pottery, furniture, glass, toys, print advertisements, and many other items. Has bibliographies for each major specialty." N Y Public Libr Book of How & Where to Look It Up

Prisant, Carol

Antiques roadshow primer; the introductory guide to antiques and collectibles from the most-watched show on PBS. Workman 1999 366p il pa $19.95 hardcover o.p.   **745.1**

1. Antiques roadshow (Television program) 2. Antiques

ISBN 0-7611-1624-9 (pa)   LC 99-29960

"The goal of this volume is to educate collectors about antiques and to help them evaluate pieces they find. . . . It highlights American antiques, focusing primarily on the types of antiques frequently seen on Roadshow." Libr J

Includes bibliographical references

745.4 Pure and applied design and decoration

Fiell, Charlotte

Design now! [by] Charlotte & Peter Fiell. Taschen 2007 560p il $39.99
                                        745.4

ISBN 978-3-8228-5267-5; 3-8228-5267-8

LC 2008-384048

Text in English, French, and German.

"What's perhaps most striking about this chunky trilanguage volume is the sheer variety of design talent included. . . . As ever with a design compendium of this nature, there are countless additional designers who could and arguably should also have been included. However that subjective observation should not be allowed to detract too heavily from what in all other respects can be considered an important point of reference for anyone studying or working in design."Designer magazine (London)

The **Work** of Charles and Ray Eames; a legacy of invention; essays by Donald Albrecht . . . {et al.}. Abrams 1997 205p il hardcover o.p. pa $24.95 **745.4**
1. Eames, Charles 2. Eames, Ray 3. Design
ISBN 0-8109-1799-8; 978-0-8109-9232-0 (pa); 0-8109-9232-9 (pa)   LC 97-4086
Published "in association with the Library of Congress and the Vitra Design Museum"

This overview of the work of two prominent American postwar designers features "pictures of famous furniture, toys, exhibitions, promotional material, informal snapshots, stills from films, comics, advertisements, exhibitions for the federal government, and much more. The work features six major essays, each with extensive notes, by scholars, designers, academics, and architecture/design writers." Choice

Includes bibliographical references

745.5 Handicrafts

Arendt, Madeline
Altered art for the first time. Sterling Pub. 2005 112p il $19.95   **745.5**
1. Handicraft
ISBN 1-4027-1655-9   LC 2005-10344
"A Sterling/Chapelle Book"
"This guide concentrates on altering books. Beginning with complete coverage of needed and suggested materials and supplies, and taking the reader/crafter step-by-step through a series of specific projects, Arendt shows how to take a book and make, among other things, an attractive journal, a display for souvenirs of a special occasion, or, using a book's covers, a box for holding commemorative items. Her encouraging tone will inspire even new crafters to venture into this rewarding activity." Booklist
Includes bibliographical references

Banker, Susan M.
1001 full-size patterns, projects & ideas; [writer: Susan M. Banker] Better Homes and Gardens Books 2003 288p il $29.95   **745.5**
1. Handicraft
ISBN 0-696-21624-8; 978-0-696-21624-4
"More than 1,000 ideas will keep crafters busy year-round. Full-size patterns . . . [and] detailed instructions [are included]." Publisher's note

Taylor, Terry
Altered art; techniques for creating altered books, boxes, cards & more. Lark Books 2004 144p il $19.95   **745.5**
1. Handicraft
ISBN 1-57990-550-1   LC 2004-5313
Taylor "begins with a brief history of altered art (Joseph Cornell was an early practitioner), discusses copyright issues with regard to borrowed images, then moves straight into techniques, tools, and a . . . gallery of a variety of artists' works. The author includes a few projects with step-by-step instructions. . . . [This book] is without a doubt one of the finest craft books available." SLJ

Ultimate Christmas book; editors of Reader's Digest. Reader's Digest 2006 288p il $24.95   **745.5**
1. Christmas decorations 2. Handicraft
ISBN 978-0-88850-799-0; 0-88850-799-2
"This book contains over 120 projects, crafts, decorating tips, recipes, photos and illustrations." Publisher's note

745.54 Paper handicrafts

Bartkowski, Alli
Paper quilling for the first time. Sterling 2006 112p il $19.95   **745.54**
1. Paper crafts
ISBN 978-1-4027-2216-5; 1-4027-2216-8
LC 2005-27791
"A Sterling/Chapelle book"
In this book, the "author uses a question-and-answer format, introducing the needed tools and supplies at the outset, then following the basics with techniques (including combing, crimping, and boondoggling, or a form of braiding), and patterns. Among the illustrated choices are a minirose gift tag, scrolled border frames for all kinds of mementos, and Christmas ornaments. A four-artist gallery at the end demonstrates possible results from a 3-D imagination." Booklist

The **Michaels** book of paper crafts; edited by Dawn Cusick & Megan Kirby; [photography, Steve Mann, Evan Bracken; contributing writers, Kelly Banner . . . et al.] Lark Books 2005 319p il $24.95 *   **745.54**
1. Paper crafts
ISBN 1-57990-638-9   LC 2004-25211
The authors discuss "the basics of nine different paper-based crafts—from decoupage to scrapbooking to quilling . . . Once it's discovered, this won't sit on the craft shelf for long." Booklist

Roehm, Carolyne
Presentations; a passion for gift wrapping; photographed by Sylvie Becquet and Antonis Achilleos. Broadway Books 2005 207p il $29.95   **745.54**
1. Gift wrapping
ISBN 0-7679-2112-7; 978-0-7679-2112-1
LC 2005-46958
The author "offers her ideas for creating . . . gift wrappings using readily available paper, tags, rubber stamps, ribbons, artificial flowers, and other inexpensive materials. Arranged seasonally, . . . the book focuses on holidays as well as on ways to make children's gifts look unique and adorable." Publisher's note
"An instant classic that emphasizes the author's definition of gift-wrapping as a wondrous form of self-expression." Booklist

Sowell, Sharyn
Paper cutting techniques for scrapbooks &
cards. Sterling Pub. 2005 128p il $19.95
745.54
1. Paper crafts 2. Scrapbooks 3. Greeting cards
ISBN 1-4027-1921-3   LC 2005-15043
"A Sterling/Chapelle book"
The author shows how to "fashion delicate borders, alphabets, flowery frames, and 3D embellishments. How to
use vintage papers, cut with patterns or freehand, and understand positive and negative space, are also here." Publisher's note
"Both experienced and novice paper users will learn
something from this beautifully illustrated book, which is
pretty enough to be an art book in and of itself."
Booklist

745.55   Shell handicrafts

Marshall, Marlene Hurley
Shell chic; the ultimate guide to decorating your
home with seashells; photographs by Sabine
Vollmer von Falken. Storey Bks. 2002 152p il $35
745.55
1. Handicraft 2. Shells
ISBN 1-58017-440-X   LC 2002-1140
Includes index
This "contains step-by-step projects for traditional
items of shell art such as flower arrangements and shell-
encrusted boxes, all interspersed with a colorful running
narrative describing decorative uses of shells by contemporary designers." Libr J

745.56   Metal handicrafts

Browning, Marie
Metal crafting workshop. Sterling Pub. 2006
128p il $24.95 *   **745.56**
1. Metalwork
ISBN 978-1-4027-2450-3; 1-4027-2450-0
LC 2006-2927
The author shows "how working with metal can enhance practically every area of crafting—scrapbooking,
collage, altered art, jewelry. . . . The funky colorful
projects on the cover will draw readers in, while the basic explanations of equipment, materials, and techniques
will excite and inspire crafters." Booklist

745.58   Handicrafts from beads, found and other objects

Barry, Bethany, 1953-
Bead crochet. Interweave Press 2004 124p il
(Beadwork how-to-book) $21.95   **745.58**
1. Beadwork 2. Crocheting
ISBN 1-931499-42-X   LC 2003-23190
The author explains how to combine a "selection of
seed and accent beads with simple crochet techniques to
create an enticing cache of jewelry, accessories, and
sculptural pieces." Publisher's note
"One look at Barry's snazzy bracelets, necklaces, and
doodads, and handicrafters will rush out for supplies. Experience in both beading and crochet is a must here, but
readers skilled in both crafts will have a wonderful time
with this beautiful book." Booklist
Includes bibliographical references

Benson, Ann
Beading for the first time. Sterling 2000 112p il
$19.95   **745.58**
1. Beadwork
ISBN 0-8069-6098-1   LC 00-48265
"Step-by-step instructions for jewelry and accessories
are accompanied by large color photographs and line
drawings. There are sections on materials and equipment
with a gallery of the work of several bead artists." Libr
J

Boyd, Heidi, 1966-
Simply beautiful beading; 53 quick and easy
projects. North Light Books 2004 127p il $19.99
745.58
1. Beadwork
ISBN 1-581-80563-2   LC 2004-40625
The author presents earrings, chokers, bracelets, necklaces, hair combs, ponytail holders, picture frames, journals, cards and gift boxes

Geary, Theresa Flores
Creative native American beading. Sterling Pub.
2005 128p il $24.95   **745.58**
1. Native American beadwork
ISBN 978-1-4027-1077-3; 1-4027-1077-1
LC 2004-20304
"This follow-up book to Geary's Native American
Beadwork: Projects & Techniques from the Southwest
includes more of her original projects based on Native
American designs. These include beadwork bags, covered
bowls, and freeform jewelry. As in her previous title, the
well-illustrated, step-by-step projects call for easily obtained materials." Libr J

Native American beadwork; projects &
techniques from the Southwest. Sterling Pub. 2003
128p il $19.95   **745.58**
1. Native American beadwork
ISBN 978-1-4027-0330-0; 1-4027-0330-9
The author "has built on her family traditions of beadwork and expanded them into step-by-step projects for
popular jewelry and decorations using motifs such as
corn and chili peppers as well as more traditional medicine bags and fetishes. . . . Providing fun projects for all
beaders." Libr J

Wells, Carol Wilcox
The art & elegance of beadweaving; new
jewelry designs with classic stitches. Lark Bks.
2002 160p il $27.95; pa $14.95   **745.58**
1. Beadwork 2. Jewelry
ISBN 1-57990-200-6; 1-57990-533-1 (pa)
LC 2001-38958

Wells, Carol Wilcox—*Continued*
Includes instructions for craft projects using beads and five types of weaving stitches.

What the author "conjures up in more than 30 bracelets, earrings, and necklaces is nothing short of breathtaking." Booklist

745.59 Making specific objects

Banes, Helen
Fiber & bead jewelry; beautiful designs to make & wear; [by] Helen Banes with Sally Banes. Sterling 2000 128p il $27.95; pa $14.95
745.59

1. Beadwork 2. Jewelry
ISBN 0-8069-6082-9; 1-4027-0073-3 (pa)
LC 00-58316
"A Sterling/Chapelle book"
This "book has photos of many of {the author's} bead and fiber necklaces, with diagrammed patterns for the woven fiber parts. This off-loom needle weaving is worked over pins on a foam board in a technique similar to pillow lacemaking. . . . This unique approach to jewelry design belongs in art as well as advanced crafts collections." Libr J

Michaels, Chris Franchetti
Teach yourself visually jewelry making & beading. Wiley Publishing 2007 290p il (Visual read less, learn more) pa $24.99   **745.59**
1. Jewelry 2. Beadwork 3. Beads
ISBN 978-0-470-10150-6; 0-470-10150-4
This book explains how "to craft designs that are chic but inexpensive. With hundreds of detailed photos, this book covers tools and supplies, bead stringing and weaving, wire wrapping, and more." Publisher's note

Oppenheimer, Betty, 1957-
Candlemaker's companion; a complete guide to rolling, pouring, dipping, and decorating your own candles. Completely rev and updated. Storey Bks. 2001 199p il pa $18.95   **745.59**
1. Candles
ISBN 1-58017-366-7   LC 00-53802
First published 1997
This offers a brief history of candles followed by information about wicks, waxes and additives, color and scent, and equipment. Step-by-step instructions on candlemaking techniques and decoration, and a list of suppliers
Includes bibliographical references

Wire, CeCe
Creative metal clay jewelry; techniques, projects, inspiration. Lark Bks. 2003 144p il $27.95   **745.59**
1. Jewelry 2. Precious metal clay
ISBN 1-57990-301-0   LC 2002-34398
Metal clay "consists of precious metal particles combined with an organic binder and water to make a sub-stance that looks and feels like potters clay. It is worked, dried, and fired like clay. Firing burns off the organic material leaving a fused piece of pure gold or silver. The piece can then be finished like any other metal. Wire . . . gives detailed instructions for using it as a jewelry medium, with step-by-step projects for earrings, bracelets, and other pieces. Contemporary in style, these items tend to resemble cast pieces. This book on an interesting new craft belongs in every crafts collection." Libr J

745.593 Useful objects

Ludens, Rebecca
Teach yourself visually scrapbooking; by Rebecca Ludens and Jennifer Schmidt. Wiley Pub. 2006 287p il (Visual read less, learn more) pa $24.99   **745.593**
1. Photograph albums 2. Scrapbooks 3. Handicraft
ISBN 0-7645-9945-3; 978-0-7645-9945-3
LC 2005-939195
"This visual guide walks you through choosing albums and papers, organizing and cropping photos, and more, and explains step-by-step . . . techniques like journaling, designing appealing pages, and using embellishments to add pizzazz." Publisher's note

Pickering Rothamel, Susan
The encyclopedia of scrapbooking tools & techniques. Sterling Pub. 2005 320p il $24.95 *
745.593
1. Scrapbooks
ISBN 1-4027-1031-3   LC 2004-12512
"Scrapbooking incorporates so many paper-related crafts–e.g., collage, calligraphy, photocraft, and rubber stamping–that a comprehensive reference book of tools and materials on the subject is quite welcome. Collage artist Rothamel has compiled a history of scrapbooking from the 17th century onward, along with an alphabetical encyclopedia defining tools, techniques, and projects. Well-illustrated sidebars share tips and examples from papercraft experts." Libr J

The **scrapbook** in American life; edited by Susan Tucker, Katherine Ott, and Patricia P. Buckler. Temple University Press 2005 332p il $69.50; pa $25.95   **745.593**
1. Photograph albums 2. Scrapbooks
ISBN   1-59213-477-7;   978-1-59213-477-9;
1-59213-478-5 (pa); 978-1-59213-478-6 (pa)
LC 2005-52875
This "volume explores the myriad ways 19th- and 20th-century Americans scrapbooked, turning photographs, magazine ads, love notes and recipes into albums that fashioned identities and preserved memories. . . . Scholars and scrapbookers alike will enjoy these slices of social history." Publ Wkly
Includes bibliographical references

Ure, Susan
The altered book scrapbook. Sterling Pub. 2006
128p il $24.95   **745.593**
1. Handicraft 2. Scrapbooks
ISBN 978-1-4027-1327-9; 1-4027-1327-4
LC 2005-34083
"A Sterling/Chapelle Book"
"This author reinvents the book by turning it into a
memory scrapbook, showing that the most innovative and
magical side of recycling is one that pays homage to the
original form while crafting an entirely new item."
Booklist

Scrapbooking your vacations; 200 page designs.
Sterling Pub 2004 127p il $24.95   **745.593**
1. Photograph albums 2. Scrapbooks
ISBN 1-402-70819-X   LC 2003-23619
"A Sterling/Chapelle book"
This is a "collection of more than 200 page plans,
which brings together designs inspired by choice vacation spots across the globe. Crafters will find great-
looking, full-color pages motivated by trips to Asia, Africa, Europe, and more to copy or adapt as they choose.
For each sample scrapbook page, Ure provides a list of
the materials used to create it and commentary about the
design itself, often including hints that can be applied to
other scrapbook projects." Booklist

745.594   Decorative objects

Beaman, Sarah
Ultimate cardmaking; a collection of over 100
techniques and 50 inspirational projects. Collins &
Brown; Distributed in the U.S. by Sterling Pub.
2008 192p il $24.95   **745.594**
1. Greeting cards 2. Paper crafts
ISBN 978-1-84340-438-5; 1-84340-438-9
This collection of cardmaking techniques with pictures
and instructions covers a "range of occasions from anniversaries and seasonal highlights to children's cards and
invitations." Publisher's note

Creative beading; compiled by Julia Gerlach.
Kalmbach Pub. 2006 256p il $29.95
745.594
1. Beads 2. Beadwork
ISBN 0-87116-228-8; 978-0-87116-228-1
LC 2006-278804
This book about beading "showcases more than 80
. . . projects and . . . ideas selected from the pages of
Bead&Button magazine." Publishor's note

Eakin, Jamie Cloud
Beading with cabochons; simple techniques for
beautiful jewelry. Lark Books 2005 127p il (A
Lark jewelry book) $24.95   **745.594**
1. Beadwork 2. Jewelry
ISBN 1-57990-718-0   LC 2005-14242
This book contains "step-by-step jewelry projects
based exclusively on the many variations of cabochon
work. . . . The designs are all beautiful and have a dramatic neo-Victorian look." Libr J

Geary, Theresa Flores
The illustrated bead bible; terms, tips &
techniques; photographs by Debra Whalen. Sterling
Pub. 2008 406p il $29.95   **745.594**
1. Beadwork 2. Beads
ISBN 978-1-4027-2353-7; 1-4027-2353-9
LC 2007-026120
"This may be the ultimate bead reference book. The
majority of the text is made up of an illustrated alphabetical encyclopedia of beads, broadly defined, and beading
terms. Additional chapters include tips and techniques,
charts illustrating bead characteristics, and stitch diagrams." Libr J
Includes glossary and bibliographical references

Mann, Elise
The bead directory; the complete guide to
choosing and using more than 600 beautiful beads.
Interweave Press 2006 256p il $24.95 *
745.594
1. Beadwork 2. Beads
ISBN 1-59668-002-4; 978-1-59668-002-9
LC 2005-24503
"A Quarto book"
This is a "handbook of currently available beads made
of metal, wood, and plastic as well as of the more usual
glass, stone, and clay. Entries for each bead include
name, description, suggested use, relative cost, and country of origin and are accompanied by color photos. . . .
This resource will prove crucial for public library patrons." Libr J

Michaels book of wedding crafts. Lark Books
2006 200p il $24.95   **745.594**
1. Handicraft 2. Wedding decorations
ISBN 1-57990-639-7; 978-1-57990-639-9
LC 2006-15067
"Never have the to-be bride and groom had so many
options for personalizing their wedding day—and for
saving bucks. . . . Fifty-plus projects, ranging from decorated cakes to scrapbook pages, will fill the days between the announcement and 'I do.'" Libr J

745.6   Calligraphy, heraldic design, illumination

Child, Heather
Calligraphy today; twentieth century tradition &
practice. [rev ed] Taplinger 1988 128p il $22.95
745.6
1. Calligraphy
ISBN 0-8008-1206-9
Original edition first published 1963 in the United
Kingdom; first United States edition published 1964 by
Watson-Guptill
"This largely pictorial survey embraces the develop-
ment and practice of Western calligraphy. . . . Illustra-
tions include examples of historical scripts and the work
of some 100 calligraphers." Publisher's note
Includes bibliographical references

Cicale, Annie, 1950-
The art & craft of hand lettering; techniques, projects, inspiration. Lark Books 2004 192p il $24.95   **745.6**

1. Calligraphy 2. Lettering

ISBN 1-579-90403-3   LC 2004-659

The author "presents what is essentially a course in lettering with historical examples, explanations of tools and techniques, and practice exercises. Step-by-step projects include greeting cards, maps, and T-shirts. There is a strong emphasis on design and layout throughout." Libr J

Harris, David, 1929-
The art of calligraphy. Dorling Kindersley 1995 128p il hardcover o.p. pa $17.95   **745.6**

1. Calligraphy

ISBN 1-56458-849-1; 0-75661-304-3 (pa)
          LC 94-26722

An "introduction to a wide variety of written scripts used from Roman times to modern days. The detailed, practical instructions for 26 styles focus on step-by-step, clear visuals, as well as on the proper equipment-- brushes, pens, pencils, paper, and ink. A brief history with examples from calligraphic masters introduces each style." SLJ

Shepherd, Margaret
Learn calligraphy; the complete book of lettering and design. Broadway Bks. 2001 167p il pa $16.95   **745.6**

ISBN 0-7679-0732-9   LC 00-53016

This guide presents historical background, and advice on materials, technique, and workspace organization. Also included are recommended usages for the various alphabets. Step-by-step illustrations are provided

745.7   Decorative coloring

Fresh & fabulous painted furniture. Sterling 2000 128p il pa $14.95 hardcover o.p.   **745.7**

1. Furniture 2. Stencil work

ISBN 0-8069-7797-3 (pa)   LC 99-55370

"A Sterling/Chapelle book"

This describes 25 projects for painting furniture employing techniques such as stenciling, stamping, block-printing, and découpaging.

Ganderton, Lucinda
The complete practical guide to stencilling and stamping; 160 inspirational and stylish projects with easy-to-follow instructions and illustrated with 1500 stunning step-by-step photographs and templates; [by] Lucinda Ganderton, Stewart Walton & Sally Walton. Lorenz Books 2007 512p il $29.99   **745.7**

1. Stencil work 2. Rubber stamp printing

ISBN 978-0-7548-1777-2; 0-7548-1777-6

On cover: How to decorate and personalize your home with beautiful stencil and stamp techniques for interiors, furniture, fabrics, china and accessories

This book has "projects with . . . instructions and [is] illustrated with 1500 . . . photographs and templates." Publisher's note

Haupert, Debba
The new book of image transfer; how to add any image to almost anything with fabulous results. Lark Books 2004 128p il $24.95
          745.7

1. Decalcomania 2. Transfer printing

ISBN 1-579-90529-3   LC 2003-22165

This is a "beginner's book on decorative image transfer. {The author} explains how to give every kind of surface, from pillows to glassware to candles, a smooth, fun, new look." Booklist

745.92   Floral arts

Hillier, Malcolm
Flowers. Dorling Kindersley 2000 516p il $40
          745.92

ISBN 0-7894-5954-X   LC 00-29485

This book "features 150 floral display ideas using fresh and dried flowers. . . . {The author explains} elements of design (color, shape, and texture) and how to create displays for use in the home, for Thanksgiving and Christmas, at weddings, and in churches." Booklist

Pryke, Paula
Flowers, flowers! inspired arrangements for all occasions; photography by Kevin Summers. Rizzoli Int. Publs. 1993 191p il $39.95
          745.92

ISBN 0-8478-1679-6   LC 93-862

This volume contains "sequences of photographs providing step-by-step instructions for creating arrangements. Separate sections deal with containers, the use of a single color range, and themes and period styles, while a 'Gazetteer' supplies the plant names, common and Latin, brief descriptions and necessary care instructions." Libr J

Stewart, Martha
Great American wreaths; created by Martha Stewart and Hannah Milman; directed by Gael Towey; photographs by William Abranowicz. Potter 1996 144p il maps pa $20   **745.92**

1. Handicraft

ISBN 0-517-88776-2   LC 96-70330

This offers instructions in creating 51 wreaths honoring the 50 states and the District of Columbia made from natural materials inspired by their locations, such as cranberries for Massachusetts and golden wheat for Oklahoma

746 Textile arts

White, Christine, 1962-
Uniquely felt; dozens of techniques from fulling and shaping to nuno and cobweb: includes 46 creative projects. Storey Pub. 2007 311p il pa $24.95 **746**
  1. Fabrics 2. Handicraft
  ISBN 978-1-58017-673-6; 1-58017-673-9
                        LC 2007-23531
  The author covers "basic feltmaking techniques as well as needle, nuno, cobweb, 3-D, and carved techniques and featuring 46 projects. . . . What makes this a title of lasting value for libraries is the depth of solid information it offers on the craft and its history, on various artists, and on related topics like setting up a feltmaking studio, teaching felt making, and leading community feltmaking projects." Libr J
  Includes bibliographical references

746.1 Yarn preparation and weaving

Blumenthal, Betsy, 1943-
Hands on dyeing; {by} Betsy Blumenthal & Kathryn Kreider; illustrations by Ann Sabin. Interweave Press 1988 111p il pa $16.95
                              746.1
  ISBN 0-934026-36-X   LC 88-12260
  The authors provide techniques and tips on a variety of hand-dyeing projects. Equipment, yarns, dyes, pots, and finishing are covered
  Includes bibliographical references

Brown, Rachel
The weaving, spinning, and dyeing book; illustrated by Rachel Brown and Cheryl McGowen. 2nd ed, rev and expanded. Knopf 1983 430p il pa $40 **746.1**
  1. Weaving 2. Spinning 3. Dyes and dyeing
  ISBN 0-394-71595-0   LC 83-176576
  First published 1978
  Following a chapter of general information about weaving the author discusses Navajo weaving, Hopi sash weaving, counterbalanced looms, inkle looms, card weaving, spinning and natural dyeing. Directions are provided for 50 projects. Over 400 line drawings and color illustrations accompany the text

Dixon, Anne, 1939-
The handweaver's pattern directory; over 600 weaves for 4-shaft looms. Interweave Press 2007 254p il $34.95 **746.1**
  1. Weaving
  ISBN 978-1-59668-040-1   LC 2007-26351
  This "guide to more than 600 different weaving patterns for four-shaft looms divides weaves into basic groups by structure (e.g., basic threadings, block drafts). Each weave is accompanied by warp threading and weaving drafts (the latter, explained in a handy extended flap), a tieup grid, closeup photos of the weave, and color photos of the actual woven fabric. Beginning weavers will appreciate the sections on weaving basics and finishing techniques as well as the glossary of common weaving terms." Libr J

746.43 Knitting, crocheting, tatting

Brant, Sharon
Finishing techniques for hand knitters; give your knitting that professional look. Trafalgar Square Pub. 2006 112p il $24.95 **746.43**
  1. Knitting
  ISBN 978-1-57076-336-6; 1-57076-336-4
                        LC 2005-902663
  "Starting with reading patters and instructions, this . . . guide then explains the different ways of casting on and binding off and the importance of shaping and sizing." Publisher's note
  "Sure to become a well-worn, frequently referenced book." Booklist

Breiter, Barbara
Complete idiot's guide to knitting and crocheting illustrated; by Barbara Breiter and Gail Diven. 3rd ed. Alpha 2006 xxii, 234p il pa $19.95
                              746.43
  1. Knitting 2. Crocheting
  ISBN 978-1-59257-491-9; 1-59257-491-2
                        LC 2006-924210
  First published 1999 under the authorship of Gail Diven and Cindy Kitchel
  This offers instruction for beginners in knitting and crocheting and includes projects and illustrations
  Includes bibliographical references

Budd, Ann, 1956-
The knitter's handy book of patterns; basic designs in multiple sizes and gauges. Interweave Press 2002 112p pa $24.95 * **746.43**
  1. Knitting
  ISBN 1-931499-04-7   LC 2001-59208
  The patterns in this book "allow the knitter to create garments in any size from toddler to extra-large adult in any weight of yarn, from fingering to bulky. The knitter has only to knit a generous swatch with yarn and needles of her/his choice and plug the resulting gauge information into the charted instructions and schematics provided. Highly recommended for all knitting collections." Libr J

Buss, Katharina
Big book of knitting. Sterling 1999 239p il pa $19.95 hardcover o.p. **746.43**
  1. Knitting
  ISBN 0-8069-6317-4 (pa)   LC 99-20386
  Original German edition, 1996
  Translation from the German

Buss, Katharina—*Continued*

This is an "illustrated knitting reference particularly strong in its coverage of both basic techniques like increasing and decreasing and more advanced techniques like knitting cables without a cable needle, working with charts, and placing sleeve increases in openwork patterns." Libr J

Del Vecchio, Michael

Knitting with balls; a hands-on guide to knitting for the modern man. DK Pubs. 2006 160p il pa $20   **746.43**

1. Knitting 2. Men's clothing
ISBN 0-7566-2289-1; 978-0-7566-2289-3
LC 2006-286354

After an "introduction to knitting basics, including cast-ons, how to read yarn labels and how to tie a slip knot, del Vecchio offers . . . instructions for everything from a business card holder and iPod case to sweaters, throws and a knee-length coat." Publ Wkly

"An essential addition to any knitting library, not just because it challenges our ideas of his-and-her crafts but also because of the stunning, modern patterns inside." Booklist

Eckman, Edie, 1960-

The crochet answer book. Storey Pub. 2005 320p il pa $12.95   **746.43**

1. Crocheting
ISBN 1-58017-598-8   LC 2005-16484

This book features "chapters on topics ranging from equipment needs to resources for more information. . . . Appended are standard crochet abbreviations, common crochet terms and phrases, standard body measurements and sizing, suggested sizes for accessories and household items, and yarn care symbols." Booklist

Includes bibliographical references

Ham, Catherine

25 gorgeous sweaters for the brand new knitter. Lark Bks. 2000 127p il $24.95; pa $17.95   **746.43**

ISBN 1-57990-172-7; 1-57990-437-8 (pa)
LC 00-30953

This volume features "cardigans, jackets, vests, tunics, cropped tops, kid wear, and more. {Included are} tips and ideas for embellishments that transform a plain-knit sweater into a statement—specialty buttons and closures, easy embroidery, and more." Publisher's note

Includes bibliographical references

Kagan, Sasha

Sasha Kagan's country inspiration; knitwear for all seasons; photographs by Jack Deutsch. Taunton Press 2000 170p il $27.95   **746.43**

ISBN 1-56158-338-3   LC 99-52956

This book features 45 knitting patterns. "Most of the patterns are for sweaters, but there are also throws, caps, and coats. Kagan takes her inspiration from the Welsh countryside where she lives. The knitwear is grouped by topics such as roses, autumn leaves, meadow flowers, and forest fruits." Booklist

Kimmelstiel, Laurie

Exquisite little knits; hand-knitting with luxurious specialty yarns; [by] Laurie Kimmelstiel, Iris Schreier. 1st ed. Lark Books 2004 144p il $19.95   **746.43**

1. Knitting
ISBN 1-579-90536-6   LC 2004-5314

"The book is divided by both project and type of yarn. Much information is given about each yarn and how it knits up, and several projects are offered for each. There is nothing very complicated among the projects: lots of scarves, shawls, and caps. But by using yarns as varied as lattice, mohair, eyelash, and fur, everything ends up looking great." Booklist

KnitLit: sweaters and their stories and other writing about knitting; Linda Roghaar & Molly Wolf, editors. Three Rivers Press (NY) 2002 270p pa $13   **746.43**

1. Knitting
ISBN 0-609-80824-9   LC 2002-5962

This book "is really about what it means to create something. Sometimes, as many knitters know, there is only the dream of what could be, as unused yarn gathers dust. But that's what's so nice about this book of knitters' personal remembrances. . . . People who love to knit will love this book." Booklist

Includes bibliographical references

Morse, Linda

Luxury knitting; the ultimate guide to exquisite yarns—cashmere, merino, silk; with the assistance of Lidia Karabinech, Lina Perl, Colby Brin. Sixth&Spring Books 2006 168p il $24.95   **746.43**

1. Knitting 2. Yarn
ISBN 1-931543-86-0; 978-1-931543-86-6
LC 2005-929982

This collection is "focused on luxury (and, yes, expensive) fibers for needling. . . . Although the more than 20 patterns are, for the most part, classically styled, the distinction Morse makes is the background information on cashmere, merino, silk, and blends. Every subject from history and manufacturing to 'watch outs' at retail is featured, often with ready-to-drool-on photographs of faraway places in Australia, China, Italy, and Tibet." Booklist

Newton, Deborah

Designing knitwear. Taunton Press 1992 263p il pa $24.95 hardcover o.p.   **746.43**

1. Knitting
ISBN 1-56158-265-4 (pa)   LC 91-36451

"A Threads book"

In this book for experienced knitters the author "lets out all the stops, revealing working methods, knitwear design tips, and techniques that have taken her years to perfect." Libr J

Includes bibliographical references

Radcliffe, Margaret

The knitting answer book. Storey Pub. 2005
400p il pa $14.95   **746.43**
  1. Knitting
  ISBN 1-58017-599-6   LC 2005-16466

Framed as a series of questions that might be asked
by knitters, this manual covers knitting "materials, techniques, and resources. . . . Radcliffe answers such specific queries as 'What is the best cast-on when you're
planning to add fringe to a piece?' and 'Is there a more
durable cast-on I can use for children's clothes?'" Libr
J

Silverman, Sharon Hernes

Basic crocheting; all the skills and tools you
need to get started; Annie Modesitt, consultant;
photographs by Alan Wycheck; illustrations by
Marjorie Leggitt. Stackpole Books 2006 112p il pa
$19.95 *   **746.43**
  1. Crocheting
  ISBN 978-0-8117-3316-8; 0-8117-3316-5
                         LC 2005-37862

This book begins with a look at the yarn, hooks, and
other tools one needs to get started, and then moves on
to cover the fundamental techniques and stitches.
Instuctions are provided for creating a wide variety of
home accessories and wearables. Skill workshops accompany each project. Instructions for every step of each
project are supplemented with photographs and illustrations.

Stafford, Jennifer

Domiknitrix; whip your knitting into shape.
North Light Books 2007 256p il pa $19.99
                                  746.43
  1. Knitting
  ISBN 978-1-58180-853-7   LC 2006-20117

"Mastering knitting skills requires discipline, attitude,
and wit to transform a ho-hum stitcher into a badass
knitter—a domiknitrix. Stafford uses the dominatrix language well and with humor in this entertaining, beautifully designed, and instructive book." Booklist

Includes bibliographical references

Stoller, Debbie

Son of stitch 'n bitch; 45 projects to knit &
crochet for men; fashion photography by Anna
Wolf; illustrations by Adrienne Yan. Workman
Pub. 2007 215p il pa $15.95   **746.43**
  1. Knitting 2. Men's clothing
  ISBN 978-0-7611-4617-9; 0-7611-4617-2
                         LC 2007-38085

"While the book is aimed largely at the women who
knit for them, men will be happy to know that Stoller's
first concern is for their particular tastes: many interesting elements—fancy stitches, unusual yarn, unique designs—are anathema to most males, who prefer simple
pieces in a darker palate. Part two includes a wide array
of (not too) colorful, occasionally edgy projects. . . .
Stoller's directions are clear, terms are well explained, illustrations are easy-to-follow and accompanying photos
are stylish and sexy." Publ Wkly

Stitch 'n bitch; the knitter's handbook;
illustrations by Adrienne Yan; fashion photography
by John Dolan. Workman 2003 248p il $23.95; pa
$13.95 *   **746.43**
  1. Knitting
  ISBN 0-7611-3258-9; 0-7611-2818-2 (pa)
                         LC 2003-53543

"An introduction chronicles the history of knitting
from the female perspective, while subsequent chapters
cover topics such as yarn type, instruments, stitches, and
patterns. Perhaps the most exciting bit is Stoller's 'knit
as you learn' technique: with every new stitch, she presents a new pattern, thereby allowing knitters to build on
their knowledge. . . . Essential for all crafts collections
and perfect for a display." Libr J

Tracy, Gloria

Crochet your way; a learn to crochet afghan,
over 40 projects for home and family,
easy-to-understand text and symbols, special
instructions for left-handers; [by] Gloria Tracy and
Susan Levin. Taunton Press 2000 218p il pa
$22.95   **746.43**
  1. Crocheting
  ISBN 1-56158-310-3   LC 99-58398

An explanation of basics "including simple and complex stitches, alternative chain techniques, color tips, and
felting instructions." Booklist

Turner, Pauline

How to crochet; the definitive crochet course,
complete with step-by-step techniques, stitch
libraries, and projects for your home and family.
Collins & Brown; distributed by Sterling 2001
160p il $29.95 *   **746.43**
  1. Crocheting
  ISBN 1-85585-827-4

"This is a complete crochet course presented as a series of workshops that cover not only standard crochet
but also those varieties of crochet that do not employ a
standard crochet hook, such as Tunisian, broomstick, and
hairpin crochet. Each workshop features an illustrative
project, full-color illustrations of techniques, and step-by-
step instructions. . . . Public libraries will want to add
this title to their short list of essential crochet books."
Libr J

Turner, Sharon, 1962-

Teach yourself visually knitting. Wiley Pub.
2006 285p il (Visual read less, learn more) pa
$24.99   **746.43**
  1. Knitting
  ISBN 0-7645-9640-3; 978-0-7645-9640-7
                         LC 2005-24428

This guide to knitting contains techniques, color photos, step-by-step instructions and tips for additional guidance. Publisher's note

Vogue knitting; the ultimate knitting book; by the
editors of Vogue Knitting Magazine. Sixth &
Spring 2003 280p il $38.95   **746.43**
  1. Knitting
  ISBN 1-931543-16-X   LC 2002-17571

Vogue knitting—*Continued*

Reissue of the title first published 1989 by Pantheon Bks.

"Following an introductory chapter on the history of knitting, the editors offer tips on how to understand knitting instructions and advice on the whole range of basic and advanced techniques. A stitch dictionary containing instructions and a photo for over 120 stitches is a real bonus. The book also contains patterns for what are referred to as 'classic sweaters.'" Booklist [review of 1989 edition]

Vogue knitting American collection; edited by Trisha Malcolm. Butterick Pub. Co 2000 160p il $29.95; pa $19.95   **746.43**
1. Knitting
ISBN 1-573-89020-0; 1-931543-10-0 (pa)
LC 00-40365

This book features patterns from the top 10 American designers featured in the magazine. . . . Except for 2 patterns, all of the more than 50 of them are targeted to the intermediate or experienced knitter."Booklist

Vogue knitting stitchionary: cables; the ultimate stitch dictionary; from the editors of Vogue knitting magazine. Sixth & Spring Books 2006 200p il $29.95   **746.43**
1. Knitting
ISBN 978-1-931543-89-7; 1-931543-89-5

This book presents a "collection of cable stitches. . . . The options range from simple to expert level . . . and all the stitches . . . are organized thematically and shown in large, closeup images." Publisher's note

Vogue knitting stitchionary: color knitting; the ultimate stitch dictionary; from the editors of Vogue knitting magazine. Sixth & Spring Books 2006 188p il $29.95   **746.43**
1. Knitting
ISBN 978-1-933027-02-9; 1-933027-02-9

This book "features more than 200 . . . colorwork patterns culled from the pages of Vogue Knitting magazine. . . . Chapters arranged thematically—TwoColor Knitting, Intarsia and Motifs, Fair Isle/Multicolor Knitting, Adding Texture, and Slip Stitches—each pattern accompanied by a . . . chart, clear photo of a sample swatch, and . . . instructions." Publisher's note

Vogue knitting stitchionary: crochet; the ultimate stitch dictionary; from the editors of Vogue knitting magazine. Sixth & Spring Books 2007 172p il $29.95   **746.43**
1. Knitting 2. Crocheting
ISBN 978-1-933027-20-3; 1-933027-20-7

This book about crocheting "includes chapters on the most important crochet techniques: basics, geometrics, color, lace, edgings, and embellishments." Publisher's note

Vogue knitting stitchionary: knit & purl; the ultimate stitch dictionary; from the editors of Vogue knitting magazine; [foreword by Carla Scott] Sixth & Spring Books 2005 184p il $29.95   **746.43**

1. Knitting
ISBN 978-1-931543-77-4; 1-931543-77-1

"Some 300 stitches are detailed, and hundreds of charts, photographs, and illustrations . . . [show] how to construct each stitch, as well as the ways they can be used in projects." Publisher's note

Werker, Kim P.

Teach yourself visually crocheting; by Kim P. Werker and Cecily Keim. Wiley Pub. 2006 280p il (Visual read less, learn more) pa $24.99   **746.43**

1. Crocheting
ISBN 0-7645-9641-1; 978-0-7645-9641-4
LC 2005-923413

"This book about crocheting contains an introduction, techniques, stitches, patterns, color photos and step-by-step instructions." Publisher's note

746.44   Embroidery

2001 cross stitch designs; the essential reference book. Better Homes and Gardens Books 1999 335p il hardcover o.p. pa $19.95   **746.44**

1. Cross-stitch 2. Needlework—Patterns
ISBN   978-0-696-20780-8;   0-696-20780-X; 978-0-696-22153-8 (pa); 0-696-22153-5 (pa)
LC 98-066924

This book contains "2001 cross-stitch designs, project ideas, and tips." Publisher's note

The **big** book of cross-stitch designs; over 900 simple-to-stitch decorative motifs. Reader's Digest Association 2007 320p il $29.95   **746.44**

1. Cross-stitch 2. Needlework—Patterns
ISBN 0-7621-0673-5; 978-0-7621-0673-8
LC 2006-044634

"When editors at Reader's Digest identify a subject to publish, they explore its history, plumb the most popular techniques, then apply those learnings pragmatically. Here, cross-stitching takes on a more artistic bent, starting with the book's layout-big type fonts, step-by-step illustrations with full-color photographs of the projects—and ending with more than 900 designs." Booklist

Campbell, Jennifer, 1950-

The complete guide to embroidery stitches; photographs, diagrams, and instructions for over 260 illustrated stitches; embroidery by Jennifer Campbell and Ann-Marie Bakewell. Reader's Digest Association 2006 il $22.95   **746.44**

1. Embroidery
ISBN 978-0-7621-0658-5; 0-7621-0658-1
LC 2005-50773

First published 2004 in France

This work "includes 263 stitches on fabric (surface and counted-thread embroidery), smocking stitches, and stitches on canvas (needlepoint). Each stitch is allotted a full or half-page spread and is illustrated with a color photo, a stitch diagram, and step-by-step instructions.

Campbell, Jennifer, 1950-—_Continued_

Working direction—often omitted from other stitch dictionaries—is specified, and useful information on how and when to use each stitch as well as instructions for left-handed modifications are included." Libr J

The **encyclopedia** of stitches; with 245 stitches illustrated and 24 exquisite projects; edited by Karen Hemingway. New Holland; distributed by Sterling 2005 176p il pa $19.95 *

746.44

1. Embroidery
ISBN 1-84537-203-4; 978-1-84537-203-3

"Each technique is prefaced with history, fabrics, threads, needles, and uses and then segues into the practice. Plus, each is accompanied by, for the most part, a sampler of stitches with occasional real-life items—like a shisha bag and a Hardanger table mat—to try." Booklist

Greenoff, Jane

The cross stitcher's bible. David & Charles 2000 176p il pa $18.99 hardcover o.p.

746.44

1. Cross-stitch
ISBN 0-7153-1470-X (pa)

The author explains the needlecraft and its techniques. He provides instructions on working with charts, tips on threads and wools as well as creative options from charms to blackwork. "A 39-stitch and 59-motif library will give sewers a wide spread of available projects, whether a single-object Victorian posy or complex winter sampler." Booklist
Includes bibliographical references

Hasler, Julie S.

Native American cross stitch. David & Charles 2001 128p il pa $19.99

746.44

1. Cross-stitch 2. Native American art
ISBN 0-7153-1240-5; 978-0-7153-1240-7
First published 1999

The author "has adapted traditional Native American designs into 40-plus projects that include complex pictures based on motifs from many tribes. Projects are chartered in full color, with symbols and DMC thread keys. Many of the motifs are suitable for clothing decoration." Libr J
Includes bibliographical references

Marsh, Gail

18th century embroidery techniques. Guild of Master Craftsman 2006 192p il por $24.95

746.44

1. Embroidery 2. Clothing and dress—History
ISBN 1-86108-476-5; 978-1-86108-476-7

LC 2006-389320

Featuring "drawings, color photos of museum-held pieces, and excerpts from 18th-century writings, this . . . book explains how embroiderers embellished the bewitching, sumptuous clothing of the day." Publisher's note
Includes bibliographical references

746.46 Patchwork and quilting

Beyer, Jinny

Quiltmaking by hand; simple stitches, exquisite quilts. Breckling Press 2003 262p il pa $29.95

746.46

1. Quilting
ISBN 0-9721218-2-X

LC 2003-15827

In this guide to the "traditional methods of quilt assembly—all by hand, the author begins with threading the needle and progresses to perfecting hand quilting stitches." Libr J
Includes bibliographical references

Brackman, Barbara

Facts & fabrications: unraveling the history of quilts and slavery; 8 projects - 20 blocks - first-person accounts. C & T Pub. 2006 110p il $27.95

746.46

1. Quilting 2. Slavery—United States
ISBN 978-1-57120-364-9; 1-57120-364-8

LC 2006-13689

"Enslaved peoples in the American South preserved their memories with quilts. . . . Quilt historian and artist Barbara Brackman guides readers through the stories they told—and lets crafters create quilts and samplers that capture their own memories." Publisher's note
Includes bibliographical references

Burns, Eleanor

Underground railroad sampler; [by] Eleanor Burns & Sue Bouchard. Quilt in a Day 2003 168p il (Quilt in a day) $24.95

746.46

1. Quilting
ISBN 978-1-891776-13-7; 1-891776-13-4

The book explains "how fifteen quilt blocks may have played a significant role in communication between the slaves and how it helped them on their way to freedom. . . . The book has 168 full color pages with step by step instructions for each of the 15 blocks. There are also directions to make a miniature Underground Railroad quilt." Publisher's note
Includes bibliographical references

Causee, Linda

Quilts A to Z; 26 techniques every quilter should know. Sterling 2006 192p il $24.95 *

746.46

1. Quilting
ISBN 978-1-4027-2318-6; 1-4027-2318-0

LC 2006-42345

"Deciding to arrange techniques and patterns according to the 26 letters of the alphabet, . . . Causee treats readers to some unusual information in her presentation. . . . In addition to the incorporated instructions for 14 techniques, Causee also delights with examples of new-fashioned quilting-stained glass, or a pictorial representation outlined by mini black fabric strips; and watercolor, in which print fabrics are treated as color gradations. For new and experienced stitchers." Booklist

Fassett, Kaffe

Glorious patchwork; more than 25 glorious quilt designs; {by} Kaffe Fassett with Liza Prior Lucy; special photography by Debbie Patterson. Potter 1997 160p il $35; pa $25 **746.46**

1. Quilting

ISBN 0-517-70853-1; 978-0-307-45150-7 (pa); 0-307-45150-X (pa) LC 97-24317

The author offers instructions and diagrams for patchwork projects for curtains, cushions, and table covers as well as quilts. The projects are divided into five color themes: soft pastels, circus, leafy gardens, antique stone, and Renaissance

Gaudynski, Diane

Guide to machine quilting. American Quilter's Soc. 2002 143p il pa $24.95 **746.46**

1. Quilting

ISBN 1-57432-796-8 LC 2002-9502

The author "covers every aspect of quilting with a sewing machine, from choosing equipment and supplies to marking and quilting the design and finishing the quilt. Of special note are the sections on free-motion quilting and dealing with the bulk of a quilt in the machine. The text is rounded out by three machine-quilting projects designed to illustrate techniques taught in the book." Libr J

Includes bibliographical references

Hakala, Sonja

Teach yourself visually quilting. Wiley Pub. 2007 285p il (Read less, learn more) pa $24.99 **746.46**

1. Quilting

ISBN 978-0-470-10149-0; 0-470-10149-0 LC 2007-30203

This reference guides readers through the quilting process, from selecting fabrics to assembling blocks to finishing seams, covering both hand-stitching and machine-quilting techniques.

Hargrave, Harriet

Heirloom machine quilting; comprehensive guide to hand-quilting effects using your sewing machine. 4th ed. C&T Pub 2004 176p il spiral bdg $29.95 **746.46**

1. Quilting

ISBN 1-571-20236-6 LC 2004-781

First published 1987 by Burdett Publications

The author "addresses everything from choosing a chair to selecting thread and batting to marking, basting, and sewing. Exquisite examples of finished quilts will inspire." Libr J

Includes bibliographical references

Kavaya, Karol

Community quilts; how to organize, design, and make a group quilt; by Karol Kavaya and Vicki Skemp. Lark Bks. 2001 136p il $27.95; pa $17.95 **746.46**

1. Quilts 2. Quilting

ISBN 1-57990-181-6; 1-57990-377-0 (pa) LC 00-46378

This work presents three beginners projects and "a gallery of community quilts that includes background information, full-color photos, and working notes as well as a practical, step-by-step method for planning, organizing, and making a group quilt." Libr J

Includes bibliographical references

Michler, J. Marsha

Crazy quilting; the complete guide. Krause Publications 2008 255p il $29.99 **746.46**

1. Quilting 2. Needlework—Patterns

ISBN 978-0-89689-520-1; 0-89689-520-3 LC 2007-940515

This book contains "methods of patching a crazy quilt, more than 100 embroidery stitches, step-by-step illustrations and how-to directions for finishing a crazy quilt." Publisher's note

The magic of crazy quilting; a complete resource for embellished quilting. 2nd ed. Krause Publs. 2004 160p il pa $24.99 **746.46**

1. Quilting 2. Needlework

ISBN 0-87349-724-4

First published 1998

"Michler takes the reader step by step through the creation of a crazy quilt and in the process teaches four different piecing methods, 15 embellishments, and more than 1000 embroidery stitch variations. Stitches are divided into broad groups and include stitch diagrams, color photos, and suggestions for use." Libr J

Includes bibliographical references

746.6 Printing, painting, dyeing

Wells, Kate, 1959-

Fabric dyeing & printing. Interweave Press 1997 192p il $39.95 **746.6**

ISBN 1-88301-035-7 LC 97-16366

This describes more than 30 fabric dyeing and printing techniques including block, screen, and resist dyeing, devore, and others

The techniques espoused by "Wells, and the resulting fabrics, are brilliant enough to inspire any and all attempts at dyeing and printing textiles." Booklist

Includes bibliographical references

746.9 Textile products and fashion design

Houtte, Alison

Alligators, old mink, & new money; one woman's adventures in vintage clothing; [by] Alison Houtte & Melissa Houtte. William Morrow 2005 243p il hardcover o.p. pa $14.95 **746.9**

1. Clothing industry 2. Women's clothing

ISBN 0-06-078667-1; 978-0-06-078668-7 (pa); 0-06-078668-X (pa) LC 2005-43416

The author, along with her sister, recalls "her family's obsession with fashion, her early days as a model and

Houtte, Alison—*Continued*

her second career as owner of Hooti Couture, a Brooklyn boutique specializing in vintage clothing. . . . Throughout, she weaves in shopping tips for amateurs and admits mistakes she's made through the years. . . . Houtte's emphasis on personal style and emotional ties to clothing make this a book that many women—and men—will enjoy." Publ Wkly

747 Interior decoration

Butler, Amy

Amy Butler's midwest modern; a fresh midwest spirit for the modern lifestyle; text & style by Amy Butler; photography & design by David Butler. Stewart, Tabori & Chang 2007 223p il $35
747

1. Fashion 2. Interior design 3. Gardening
ISBN 978-1-58479-581-0; 1-58479-581-6
LC 2006-100282

This is a "complete lifestyle book, encompassing fashion, interiors, and gardens . . . with information on budgeting money and time, a shopping resources list, and 'how-to' projects in every chapter." Publisher's note

Campbell, Nina

Nina Campbell's decorating notebook; insider secrets and decorating ideas for your home; text by Alexandra Campbell; photography by Jan Baldwin. Clarkson Potter 2004 171p il $40
747

1. Interior design
ISBN 1-4000-5172-X
LC 2004-303467

The author "reveals the trademark touches, the secret sources and techniques, and the methods she uses to create her . . . interiors." Publisher's note

"For readers tasked with redecorating their penthouse apartments or country homes, this is a 'must have' volume. Decorating enthusiasts will enjoy reading the text as well as studying the luxurious pictures, and anyone with a flair for decorating will find this volume fascinating midnight reading." Publ Wkly

Conran, Terence

The ultimate house book; general editor and contributor, Elizabeth Wilhide. Conran Octopus 2003 272p il $39.95 *
747

1. Interior design
ISBN 1-8409-1352-5
LC 2004-401850

On cover: For home design in the twenty-first century

"What homeowners want from a home is flexibility to suit changing lifestyles. At least that is Conran's premise in this update of The Essential House Book. He begins with examples of home design, each with a case study to illustrate the ideas, advocating an open layout rather than individual rooms and considering various lifestyles from first homers to empty nesters, with information on such concerns as child safety and universal design. The next section discusses purchasing, remodeling, and decorating a home, including practical information on budgeting and planning. The compendium contains information on the material choices for the entire home, such as floor coverings, appliances, and furniture." Libr J

"A book that should be in any collection on home design." Booklist

Crochet, Treena

Bungalow style; creating classic interiors in your arts and crafts home. Taunton Press 2005 186p il $29.95
747

1. Houses—Remodeling 2. Domestic architecture 3. Interior design
ISBN 978-1-56158-623-3; 1-56158-623-4
LC 2004-9748

This book pictures a "variety of interior details and describes how to add or restore elements that suggest a historic flair while keeping the home comfortable and functional. Common problems such as integrating modern conveniences or gaining needed space are also addressed." Publisher's note

Gilliatt, Mary

Mary Gilliatt's great renovations and restorations; a new life for older homes. Watson-Guptill 2003 192p il $35
747

1. Interior design 2. Houses—Remodeling
ISBN 978-0-8230-2166-6; 0-8230-2166-1

"An educational and photographically intriguing guide for wannabe renovators. . . . Gilliatt thoroughly grounds potential remodelers in the advantages and disadvantages of different options, teaching them to ask the right questions about architectural quality, materials, setting, and atmosphere." Booklist

Jordan, Wendy Adler, 1946-

The kidspace idea book; [by] Wendy A. Jordan. Taunton Press 2001 168p il $29.95; pa $24.95
747

1. Interior design
ISBN 1-56158-352-9; 1-56158-617-X (pa)
LC 00-51026

"Jordan believes that functional space should be designed for children and adults throughout the house. Large and colorful photographs illustrate details described in the text. Ideas include creating fun yet safe bathrooms, dynamic and playful bedrooms, and built-in storage space." Libr J

Includes bibliographical references

Ledoux, Jeanée

Abode à la mode; 44 projects for hip home decor. Sterling 2006 176p il pa $14.95
747

1. Handicraft 2. Interior design
ISBN 1-4027-1343-6
LC 2005-12392

"Aimed at hip, young renters on a budget, this craft title combines an overview of basic interior-design principles with cheap, high-style home-decor projects. . . . Ledoux's instructions are clear and easy to follow, her materials inexpensive, and the finished projects—the kitchen backsplash made of dominoes; a light sconce made of blueprints—are unique and inspired." Booklist

Michael, Michele

The new apartment book; {by} Michele Michael; text with Wendy S. Israel; photographs by Jeff McNamara. Potter 1996 207p il pa $30

747

1. Apartment houses 2. Interior design
ISBN 0-517-88759-2   LC 96-296
First published 1979 with title: The apartment book
This offers ideas for apartment decoration discussing principals of function, style, and color in terms of time, space, and budget constraints
"More than 250 color photos and some valuable tips, such as buying the best sofa that one can afford, make this a handsome guide." Publ Wkly

The **New** decorating book; [editor, Paula Marshall] 9th ed. Better Homes & Gardens Bks. 2007 431p il pa $24.95   **747**
1. Interior design
ISBN 978-0-6962-3299-2; 0-6962-3299-5
    LC 2007-921762
First published 1956 with title: Better Homes and Gardens decorating book. Periodically revised
This guide to home decorating discusses style, budgeting, color schemes, furniture, fabrics and patterns, window treatments, and accessories and includes floor plans, and furniture templates

Paper, Heather J.

Decorating idea book; [by] Heather Paper. Taunton Press 2005 313p il (Taunton's idea books) $24.95   **747**
1. Interior design
ISBN 978-1-56158-762-9; 1-56158-762-1
    LC 2005-8440
This guide to decorating a home covers choosing colors and furniture, room arrangements, window treatments, wall and floor coverings, storage, lighting, and accessories.

Sheridan, Judy

How to work with an interior designer. Gibbs Smith, Publisher 2008 134p il pa $24.95

747

1. Interior design
ISBN 978-1-4236-0195-1; 1-4236-0195-5
    LC 2007-48220
The author "discusses how to find and work with a decorator, including developing a budget and what to do if things go wrong." Libr J

Spier, Carol

The apartment book; smart decorating for spaces large and small. Hearst Books 2007 271p il (House Beautiful) $19.95   **747**
1. Apartment houses 2. Interior design
ISBN 978-1-58816-598-5; 1-58816-598-1
    LC 2006-29559
This book explains how "anyone can turn an apartment—whether dorm room or duplex—into a lovely home. . . . Featuring almost 300 photos, a dozen floor plans, countless tips, and numerous sidebars, this . . .

handbook covers a wide variety of styles." Publisher's note
Includes bibliographical references

Starmer, Anna

The color scheme bible; inspirational palettes for designing home interiors. Firefly Books 2005 255p il $29.95   **747**
1. Color 2. Interior design
ISBN 978-1-55407-032-9; 1-55407-032-5
    LC 2005-280569
This book provides "information on how to choose colors and what types to use in the home. . . . The main colors are given in a table-of-contents format where one can select a color and then turn to its page to find suggested room use, different tones of the main color, and accent and highlight colors, as well as the type of mood or look conveyed by each choice." Libr J

747.2   Interior decoration— Historical and geographic treatment

Lowell, Christopher

Christopher Lowell's one-of-a-kind decorating projects; fast & flexible ways to personalize your home. Clarkson Potter/Publishers 2007 175p il $29.95   **747.2**
1. Handicraft 2. Interior design
ISBN 978-0-307-34171-6; 0-307-34171-2
    LC 2006-15191
"Television personality and interior decorator Lowell . . . decorates a room from top to bottom and shows readers, in the process, how each piece in the room is constructed or repurposed. . . . Lowell's instructions are clear and easy to follow, and he offers plenty of encouragement along the way." Publ Wkly

748.5   Stained, painted, leaded, mosaic glass

Zaccaria, Donatella

Stained glass crafting. Sterling 1998 159p il pa $19.95 hardcover o.p.   **748.5**
1. Glass painting and staining
ISBN 0-8069-4329-7 (pa)   LC 98-3575
Translated from the Italian
The author "gears her explanations to both beginners and experienced crafters through step-by-step projects illustrated with photographs. Five patterns . . . become the basis for learning two stained-glass techniques: copper foil with lead and 'straight' lead soldering. Each technique includes excellent closeup photographs of the cutting, trimming, welding, and sealing processes, with enough text to guide unsteady hands." Booklist

749   Furniture and accessories

Logan, M. David
Mat, mount and frame it yourself. Watson-Guptill 2002 160p il pa $24.95
749
1. Picture frames and framing 2. Decoration and ornament
ISBN 0-8230-3038-5   LC 2001-93246
This describes how to mat, mount, and frame art on paper or cloth, how to determine measurements and proportions, select colors, and glaze, install, and hang framed art
"Logan does a great job of explaining everything and supplements the text with attractive photos. . . . There is something here for framers of all skill levels." Libr J

Miller, Judith, 1948-
Furniture; [world styles from classical to contemporary]; [foreword by David Linley] DK Publishing 2005 560p il $60   **749**
1. Furniture
ISBN 0-7566-1340-X   LC 2005-296398
This "work examines the evolution of furniture styles up through the 20th century." Libr J
The author "presents a lavish four-color and highly educational book, and the result will never lose its library-patron appeal." Booklist
Includes bibliographical references

751   Techniques, procedures, apparatus, equipment, materials, forms

Ganz, Nicholas
Graffiti world; street art from five continents; edited by Tristan Manco. H.N. Abrams 2004 376p il $35 *   **751**
1. Street art 2. Graffiti
ISBN 0-8109-4979-2   LC 2004-4248
Ganz's survey of graffiti art includes "upward of 2,000 full-color photographs. . . . An ephemeral, often despised, yet irrefutably powerful mode of expression, graffiti has always been political, and although many of the street artists Ganz succinctly profiles have moved away from illegal spray painting, they have not compromised the inherent subversiveness of their work. . . . Ganz's global array captures the power and synergy of this vibrant alternative art world in which artists form crews and collectiveness to ensure that their art is seen." Booklist
Includes bibliographical references

751.2   Painting—Materials

Mayer, Ralph, 1895-1979
The artist's handbook of materials and techniques. 5th ed, revised and updated by Steven Sheehan. Viking 1991 761p il $45   **751.2**
1. Artists' materials 2. Pigments 3. Painting—Technique
ISBN 0-670-83701-6   LC 90-50357
First published 1940
Partial contents: Pigments; Oil painting; Acrylics; Tempera painting; Watercolor and gouache; Pastel; Solvents and thinners; Conservation of pictures
Includes bibliographical references

751.4   Painting—Techniques and procedures

All about techniques in acrylics; {an indispensable manual for artists}; {author, Parramón's Editorial Team}. Barron's 2004 143p il (All about techniques) $26.95 *   **751.4**
1. Acrylic painting—Technique
ISBN 0-7641-5710-8   LC 2003-68843
Originally published in Spain
"A brief history of the use of acrylics by people such as Jackson Pollack is followed by sections on the varieties of acrylics available, tools for their use, and techniques for skies, vegetation, landscapes, still lifes, interiors, animals, and the nude. The demonstrations of color mixing, sgraffito, texturing, transparent impastos, and layering with glazes are especially well done." Libr J
"The book is a delight for anyone interested in acrylics." Voice Youth Advocates

Weber, Mark Christopher, 1949-
Brushwork essentials; how to render expressive form and texture with every stroke. North Light Bks. 2002 143p il $28.99   **751.4**
1. Painting—Technique
ISBN 1-58180-168-8   LC 2001-52162
This "book deals exclusively with oil brushwork. Painters learn how to render expressive form and texture using the myriad shapes and types of brushes available. Mixing and loading paint, cleaning and shaping brushes for maximum control, and picking the right paint for specific types of strokes are all covered." Libr J
"Weber writes with humor and confidence, keeping things lighthearted whether he is teaching the mechanics of holding a brush or a wet-into-wet application of paint on canvas." Booklist

751.42   Watercolor painting

Crawshaw, Alwyn
You can paint watercolors; a step-by-step guide for absolute beginners. Watson-Guptill 2000 96p il pa $9.95   **751.42**
ISBN 0-8230-5989-8   LC 00-104483

Crawshaw, Alwyn—*Continued*

This introduction to watercolors covers basic washes, color mixing, light and shadow, a variety of still life subjects, and composition

Kunz, Jan, 1942-

Painting beautiful watercolors from photographs. North Light Bks. 1998 128p il pa $22.99 hardcover o.p.   **751.42**

1. Watercolor painting—Technique

ISBN 1-581-80431-8 (pa)   LC 97-27742

The author makes a "case for painting from photographs. While this method is often maligned, Kunz points out that it allows one to paint in a situation where weather doesn't change, children don't wiggle, flowers don't wilt, and reflections stay in place. To keep such paintings from seeming static, she suggests doing outdoor sketches and keeping notes at the time of each photo session. Kunz includes instruction on shooting photographs and transferring them to sketches, along with nine nicely done demonstrations." Libr J

MacKenzie, Gordon, 1939-

The watercolorist's essential notebook. North Light Books 1999 144p il $24.99   **751.42**

1. Watercolor painting—Technique

ISBN 978-0-89134-946-4; 0-89134-946-4

LC 99-40862

A reprint of the title first published 1999

This "guide to watercolor materials and processes . . . includes observations, tips, and methods for designing strong compositions, achieving different textures, utilizing masking materials, setting up a palette, and working with transparent as well as deeply hued colors." Booklist

Taylor, Jo, 1927-

Watercolor wisdom; lessons from a lifetime of painting and teaching. North Light Bks. 2003 175p il $29.99   **751.42**

1. Watercolor painting—Technique

ISBN 1-58180-240-4   LC 2002-29529

"Based on 30 years of studying with some of America's best watercolor artists and teaching thousands in her classes and workshops, [the author] offers a comprehensive yet still low-stress volume for the beginner. The sections on developing one's own style are especially good." Libr J

751.7   Paintings—Specific forms

Seligman, Patricia, 1950-

Painting murals; images, ideas, and techniques. North Light Bks. 1988 c1987 168p il pa $22.99
                                              751.7

1. Mural painting and decoration

ISBN 1-5818-0470-9; 978-1-5818-0470-6

LC 88-9963

"A Macdonald Orbis book"

First published 1987 in the United Kingdom

A "do-it-yourself course in mural painting. . . . Seligman covers all the procedures and processes involved, providing clear and thorough instructions. Materials, equipment, techniques, designs, and procedures are all examined as the author shows how to create trompe l'oeil effects ranging from small designs to huge wall-sized murals." Booklist

Includes bibliographical references

752   Color in painting

Edwards, Betty, 1926-

Color; a course in mastering the art of mixing colors. Jeremy P. Tarcher/Penguin 2004 206p il $27.95; pa $17.95   **752**

1. Color in art

ISBN   978-1-58542-199-2;   1-58542-199-5; 978-1-58542-219-7 (pa); 1-58542-219-3 (pa)

LC 2003-67215

"This new guide distills the . . . existing knowledge about color theory into a practical method of working with color to produce harmonious combinations. . . . Using techniques tested and honed in her five-day intensive color workshops, Edwards provides a basic understanding of how to see color, how to use it, and—for those involved in art, painting, or design—how to mix and combine hues." Publisher's note

Includes bibliographical references

759   Painting—Historical, geographic, persons, treatment

Beckett, Wendy

The story of painting; contributing consultant, Patricia Wright. 2nd American ed, enhanced & expanded ed. Dorling Kindersley 2000 736p il $40
                                              759

1. Painting

ISBN 0-7894-6805-0   LC 2001-266885

First published 1994

"In association with the National Gallery of Art, Washington, D.C."

This history of painting over the past 800 years chronicles movements such as Romanticism, Impressionism, Post-Impressionism and Modernism, focusing on 450 masterpieces and including timelines

759.05   Painting—1800-1899

Impressionism and post-impressionism in the Art Institute of Chicago; selected by James N. Wood. The Institute 2000 168p il $50
                                           759.05

1. Impressionism (Art)

ISBN 978-0-86559-176-9; 0-86559-176-8

LC 99-067929

"The 147 paintings, drawings, prints, and sculptures are presented chronologically and in full color. Brief descriptions by art historians, accompanying each illustration, point out details that may not be obvious to a casu-

Impressionism and post-impressionism in the Art Institute of Chicago—*Continued*
al viewer and also concentrate on the influences of other artists as well as interactions among artists. . . . This volume is international in scope, especially with its inclusion of American impressionists, and does provide a good overview." Libr J

759.13   American painting

Biel, Steven, 1960-
American Gothic; a life of America's most famous painting. W.W. Norton & Co. 2005 215p il $21.95; pa $13.95   **759.13**
1. Wood, Grant, 1891-1942
ISBN 0-393-05912-X; 0-393-32855-4 (pa)
LC 2005-4726
This is a study of Grant Wood's "portrait of two people, a woman and a man holding a rake. He recruited his sister to be the woman and the local dentist to play the man." N Y Times Book Rev
"In this ingenious gem of a book, Stephen Biel . . . weaves together a rich cultural history of this unforgettable picture and asks why it has become, for better or for worse, America's most popular painting." Economist
Includes bibliographical references

Carter, Alice A.
The Red Rose girls; an uncommon story of art and love. Abrams 2000 216p il pa $19.95 hardcover o.p.   **759.13**
1. Smith, Jessie Willcox, 1863-1935 2. Green, Elizabeth Shippen, 1871-1954 3. Oakley, Violet, 1874-1961
ISBN 0-8109-9068-7 (pa)   LC 99-39866
"Three of the first American women artists to achieve fame and fortune in the Victorian era—Jessie Willcox Smith, Elizabeth Shippen Green and Violet Oakley—lived unconventional lives marked by a remarkable degree of collaboration. In this . . . study, Carter explores the trio's internecine artistic and romantic relations." Publ Wkly
Includes bibliographical references

Cikovsky, Nicolai, Jr.
Winslow Homer; {by} Nicolai Cikovsky, Jr., Franklin Kelly; with contributions by Judith Walsh and Charles Brock. National Gallery of Art 1995 420p il $80   **759.13**
1. Homer, Winslow, 1836-1910
ISBN 0-300-06555-8 (Yale Univ. Press)
LC 95-19025
In this catalog of the American artist's retrospective exhibition, the contributors "present a contextually rich and vibrant analysis of Homer's life and groundbreaking work." Booklist
Includes bibliographical references

Cohen-Solal, Annie
Painting American; the rise of American artists, Paris 1867-New York 1948; translated from the French with Laurie Hurwitz-Attias. Knopf 2001 436p il $30 *   **759.13**
1. American painting
ISBN 0-679-45093-9   LC 2001-32669
Original French edition, 2000
The author "offers a broad overview of the shift of artistic center from Paris to New York throughout the late 19th and early 20th centuries." Libr J
"When writing about the founders, trustees, directors and staffs of museums, {the author} is consistently rewarding. . . . Ms Cohen-Solal is at her best when mining the private history of the art trade." Economist
Includes bibliographical references

Gerdts, William H.
American impressionism; William H. Gerdts. 2nd ed. Abbeville Press 2001 368p il $85   **759.13**
1. American art 2. Impressionism (Art)
ISBN 978-0-7892-0737-1; 0-7892-0737-0
LC 2001-22419
First published 1984
"The best general source available on American Impressionism. . . . [The] book covers the major artists in the movement, including expatriates working in Europe and regional schools throughout the United States during the late 19th and early 20th centuries. . . .The well-chosen illustrations include many full-page color reproductions as well as photographs of many of the artists." Libr J
Includes bibliographical references

Hennessey, Maureen Hart
Norman Rockwell; pictures for the American people; [by] Maureen Hart Hennessey and Ann Knutson. Abrams 1999 199p il $35   **759.13**
1. Rockwell, Norman, 1894-1978
ISBN 0-8109-6392-2   LC 99-73071
A catalogue of a traveling exhibition of Rockwell's work. "Colorplates reproduce Rockwell's paintings in . . . detail, and the essays set them in fresh contexts, discussing such themes as Rockwell's urban scenes; the reaction by both black and white Southerners to Rockwell's historic civil rights painting *The Problem We All Live With*; and Rockwell's role in the development of American illustration." Publisher's note
Includes bibliographical references

Hopper, Edward, 1882-1967
Edward Hopper: the art and the artist; [by] Gail Levin. Norton 1982 299p il $50; pa $39.95
759.13
ISBN 0-393-01374-X; 0-393-31577-0 (pa)
Published in association with the Whitney Museum of American Art
This "introduction to the paintings and drawings of the American realist stems from a {1981} exhibition at New York City's Whitney Museum. Curator Levin traces

Hopper, Edward, 1882-1967—*Continued*
Hopper's development as an artist and illustrates the painter's characteristic themes in a lengthy introductory essay. Following this text is a large section of plates, in color and black and white." Booklist
Includes bibliographical references

Livingston, Jane, 1944-
The paintings of Joan Mitchell; with essays by Linda Nochlin, Yvette Lee. University of Calif. Press 2002 237p il $65; pa $35   **759.13**
1. Mitchell, Joan
ISBN 0-520-23568-1; 0-520-23570-3 (pa)
LC 2001-58514
Catalog of an exhibition held at the Whitney Museum of American Art, New York, June-Oct. 2002
"Using Mitchell's journals and correspondence, Livingston . . . follows the evolution of Mitchell's painting and discusses her technique. . . . Linda Nochlin demonstrates that Mitchell's rage at being viewed as a 'feminine other' was transformed into a positive energy that brought emotional intensity to her paintings. . . . Yvette Lee discusses the 'Grand Vall,e' series of 16 paintings (1983-84) as some of Mitchell's most luminous and lyrical." Libr J
This is a "vivid portrait of the artist. . . . Mitchell's compositions [are] gorgeously reproduced here in vibrant color." Booklist
Includes bibliographical references

Marsden Hartley; general editor, Elizabeth Mankin Kornhauser; with Ulrich Birkmaier . . . {et al.}. Wadsworth Atheneum Museum of Art in Association with Yale Univ. Press 2003 334p il $55   **759.13**
1. Hartley, Marsden, 1877-1943
ISBN 0-300-09767-0   LC 2002-8215
"The book contains essays, full catalog entries, a chronology, and over 100 full-color plates. Particularly refreshing are Wanda Corn's look at Hartley's 'Native Amerika' paintings and Carol Troyen's examination of his primitive late work. There have been many excellent publications in the past ten years . . . devoted to certain aspects of Hartley's life and art, but a major exhibition and catalog is long overdue." Libr J
Includes bibliographical references

Thomas Eakins; organized by Darrel Sewell with essays by Kathleen A. Foster [et al.]; chronology by Kathleen Brown. Yale Univ. Press 2001 xli, 446p il $75   **759.13**
1. Eakins, Thomas, 1844-1916
ISBN 0-300-09111-7   LC 2001-53142
This is a catalog of an exhibition held at the Philadelphia Museum of Art, Musée d'Orsay, Paris, and the Metropolitan Museum of Art, New York
"This enormous volume accompanies the largest retrospective of [Eakins' work]. . . . [It] includes some 120 photographs as well as examples of his work in watercolor, drawing, and sculpture. . . . Several lengthy and interesting biocritical essays, themselves making up 175 pages of text, separate four sections of color plates. This is clearly the definitive monograph on one of the most significant artists America has produced." Libr J
Includes bibliographical references

Wilton, Andrew
American sublime; landscape painting in the United States, 1820-1880; [by] Andrew Wilton & Tim Barringer. Princeton Univ. Press 2002 284p il $49.95; pa $35   **759.13**
1. American painting 2. Landscape painting
ISBN 0-691-09670-8; 0-691-11556-7 (pa)
Published to accompany an exhibition at Tate Britain, London 21 February- 19 May 2002
"Wilton, of the Tate Gallery, considers the influence of Edmund Burke's theory of sublimity and the surge in scientific development on American painters, while Barringer . . . discusses the profound effect on the painters' imaginations of a pristine land free of Western religious, literary, and historical associations. . . . Wilton and Barringer's commentary is stimulating and important, and the exceptional plates are bliss unadulterated." Booklist
Includes bibliographical references

759.2   British painting

Asleson, Robyn, 1961-
Albert Moore. Phaidon Press 2000 240p il hardcover o.p. pa $29.95   **759.2**
1. Moore, Albert Joseph, 1841-1893
ISBN 0-7148-3846-2; 978-0-7148-4392-6 (pa); 0-7148-4392-X (pa)   LC 00-421386
"This book focuses on the artist's interaction with the Victorian art world as well as his formal pictorial concerns. . . . In addition, the author looks at the politics of Victorian art institutions. This is an excellent book filled with gorgeous color reproductions. Recommended for general collections as well as libraries that support art programs." Libr J
Includes bibliographical references

759.36   Austrian painting

Fliedl, Gottfried, 1948-
Klimt. Taschen 2006 239p il $14.99
          759.36
1. Klimt, Gustav, 1862-1918
ISBN 978-3-8228-5016-9; 3-8228-5016-0
First published 1998
This book "discusses the Secession movement and Klimt's role within this important group of artists." Publisher's note

759.4   French painting

Cézanne, Paul, 1839-1906
Cézanne; [by] Françoise Cachin, [et al.] Abrams 1996 600p il $70; pa $45   **759.4**
1. Cézanne, Paul, 1839-1906
ISBN 0-8109-4039-6; 0-876-33100-2 (pa)
LC 95-51493
This "exhibition catalogue, published in conjunction with a major international Cézanne retrospective, is a

Cézanne, Paul, 1839-1906—*Continued*
handsome tribute to the artist who revolutionized modern painting. The 258 color and 350 black-and-white reproductions of Cézanne's (1839-1906) oil paintings, watercolors, drawings and sketchbook pages are splendid, and they are accompanied by lucid, insightful commentaries." Publ Wkly
Includes bibliographical references

Edouard Vuillard; [by] Guy Cogeval with Kimberly Jones [et al.] National Gallery of Art, in association with Yale University Press 2003 501p il $70   **759.4**
  1. Vuillard, Édouard, 1868-1940
  ISBN 0-300-09737-9   LC 2002-151120
"National Gallery of Art, Washington, 19 January-20 April 2003, Montreal Museum of Fine Arts, 15 May-24 August 2003, Galeries nationales du Grand Palais, Paris, 23 September 2003-4 January 2004, Royal Academy of Arts, London, 27 January-27 April 2004"
"In a series of illustrated essays, the authors explore Vuillard's . . . career, which began with his academic training in Paris in the late 1880s. . . . The book concludes with an examination of Vuillard's sumptuous large-scale decorations, luminous landscapes, and elegant portraits from the last decades of his career as well as a substantial selection of his pastels and prints, in addition to his photographs." Publisher's note
"A superb display of the surprising colors, forceful textures, and mysterious atmosphere of Vuillard's paintings, accompanied by commentaries in which aesthetics, art history, and biography are perfectly balanced." Booklist
Includes bibliographical references

Kelder, Diane
  The great book of French impressionism. 2nd Abbeville ed. Abbeville Press 2001 400p il $85
                                                            759.4
  1. Impressionism (Art) 2. French painting
  ISBN 978-0-7892-0688-6; 0-7892-0688-9
                                        LC 2001-266313
  First published 1980
This book "traces the development of Impressionism from its roots in landscape and Realist painting through its focus on modern urban life. . . . The works of the major Impressionists and Post Impressionists, Manet, Monet, Renoir, Degas, Toulouse-Lautrec, Seurat, and Cezanne, are featured." Publisher's note
Includes bibliographical references

King, Ross, 1962-
  The judgment of Paris; the revolutionary decade that gave the world impressionism. Walker 2006 448p il $28   **759.4**
  1. Manet, Édouard, 1832-1883 2. Meissonier, Jean-Louis-Ernest, 1815-1891 3. Impressionism (Art) 4. French art
  ISBN 0-8027-1466-8   LC 2005-31089
This is an "account of the years from 1863—when paintings denied entry into the French Academy's yearly Salon were shown at the Salon des Refusés—to 1874, the date of the first Impressionist exhibition. . . . [The

author] follows the careers of two formidable, and very different, artists: Jean-Louis-Ernest Meissonier, a conservative painter celebrated for detailed historical subjects, and Édouard Manet, whose painting Le Déjeuner sur l'herbe caused an uproar at the Salon des Refusés." Publ Wkly
"The book serves as an entertaining if broad account of a revolutionary transformation in vision—not least of all through art." Libr J
Includes bibliographical references

Silverman, Debora, 1954-
  Van Gogh and Gauguin; the search for sacred art. Farrar, Straus & Giroux 2000 494p il $60; pa $25   **759.4**
  1. Gogh, Vincent van, 1853-1890 2. Gauguin, Paul, 1848-1903
  ISBN 0-374-28243-9; 0-374-52932-9 (pa)
                                        LC 00-37146
By delving "into the religious legacies of Van Gogh and Gauguin, and forging new connections between their disparate spirituality and revolutionary artistic techniques, subject matter, and styles, Silverman casts new light on these two seminal figures and their timeless masterpieces." Booklist
"Silverman's scholarship and lucid writing makes this one of the most refreshing and insightful texts on these two artists in years." Libr J
Includes bibliographical references

Tucker, Paul Hayes, 1950-
  Monet in the 20th century; [by] Paul Hayes Tucker with George T.M. Shackelford and MaryAnne Stevens; essays by Romi Golan, John House, and Michael Leja. Yale Univ. Press 1998 300p il $70; pa $35   **759.4**
  1. Monet, Claude, 1840-1926
  ISBN 0-300-07749-1; 0-300-07944-3 (pa)
                                        LC 98-86163
"This catalog for a show at Boston's Museum of Fine Arts, . . . is the first to consider Monet as a 20th-century artist. In four focused, critical essays by specialists, it chronicles the still-powerful older painter, who was not involved with formulae but with seeing and redefining 19th-century art with experience, color, feeling, refraction, and multiplicity while freeing painting from perspective and spatial observation. His work later influenced American abstract expressionists and color field artists of the mid-20th century. The second part of the book contains resplendent full-color reproductions." Libr J

759.5 Italian painting

Brown, David Alan, 1942-
  Leonardo da Vinci; origins of a genius. Yale Univ. Press 1998 240p il $65   **759.5**
  1. Leonardo, da Vinci, 1452-1519
  ISBN 0-300-07246-5   LC 98-15164
The author traces the "early influences and the emergence of da Vinci's intense curiosity about nature and ability to re-create it in drawing and painting. The chap-

Brown, David Alan, 1942-—*Continued*
ter on 'Ginevra de'Benci' is a splendid example of how art history and contemporary scientific techniques can be combined in the examination and attribution of a painting. The excellent full page reproductions and small detail examples are carefully placed within the text for ease of reference." Libr J
Includes bibliographical references

De Vecchi, Pierluigi
Raphael. Abbeville Press 2002 380p il $125
759.5
1. Raphael, 1483-1520
ISBN 0-7892-0770-2   LC 2002-23206
In slip case
This is a survey of the life and work of the Italian Renaissance painter including some 300 illustrations
Includes bibliographical references

King, Ross, 1962-
Michelangelo & the Pope's ceiling. Walker & Co. 2002 371p il hardcover o.p. pa $15
759.5
1. Michelangelo Buonarroti, 1475-1564 2. Vatican. Cappella Sistina 3. Mural painting and decoration 4. Italy—History—0-1559
ISBN 0-8027-1395-5; 0-14-200369-7 (pa)
LC 2002-38074
The author "recounts the creation, despite the demanding patronage of irascible Pope Julius II and myriad other adversities, of the most famous painted ceiling in the world." Booklist
"This engaging narrative sets the record straight on a few points and is highly recommended for most public library collections." Libr J
Includes bibliographical references

Marani, Pietro C.
Leonardo da Vinci—the complete paintings; appendices edited by Pietro C. Marani and Edoardo Villata. Abrams 2000 384p il $85
759.5
1. Leonardo, da Vinci, 1452-1519
ISBN 0-8109-3581-3   LC 00-27556
Original Italian edition, 1999
This guide covers Leonardo's 31 paintings "intensively, recording possible precedents for design and technique in the work of other artists, calling attention to significant details, offering preparatory drawings and cartoons for comparison with the finished, which is not to say completed, works, and presenting X rays to elucidate the gestation of the *Mona Lisa* and other paintings Leonardo spent years striving to perfect. Such scrupulous attention to Leonardo's total creative process boosts the number of illustrations, mostly colorplates, to 295." Booklist
Includes bibliographical references

Sassoon, Donald
Becoming Mona Lisa; the making of a global icon. Harcourt 2001 337p il $30; pa $16
759.5
1. Leonardo, da Vinci, 1452-1519. Mona Lisa
ISBN 0-15-100828-0; 0-15-602711-9 (pa)
LC 2001-24956
This is a history of Leonardo's most famous portrait and its meanings and popularization in the centuries since it was painted
"Sassoon's knowledge of the minutiae of history and his respect for the image drive the narrative. . . . [This work is] thoroughly researched and highly readable." Libr J
Includes bibliographical references

759.6 Spanish painting

Dali; curated by Dawn Ades and Michael R. Taylor with the assistance of Montse Aguer. Rizzoli 2004 607p il $75   **759.6**
1. Dalí, Salvador, 1904-1989
ISBN 978-0-8478-2673-5; 0-8478-2673-2
Original Italian edition, 2004
"Published on the occasion of the exhibition Dali" Verso of title page
This "retrospective of the artist's work from his early years. . . . [includes] comparative illustrations and photographs." Publisher's note
Includes bibliographic references

Hensbergen, Gijs van
Guernica: the biography of a twentieth-century icon. Bloomsbury 2004 373p il $35; pa $16.95
759.6
1. Picasso, Pablo, 1881-1973
ISBN 1-582-34124-9; 1-582-34606-2 (pa)
LC 2004-55054
This is a "study of Picasso's antiwar masterpiece, which folds the disciplines of art criticism, political history and biography into a passionate, detailed and well-argued narrative." Publ Wkly
Includes bibliographical references

Wach, Kenneth
Salvador Dali; masterpieces from the collection of the Salvador Dali Museum. Harry N. Abrams, Publishers in association with the Salvador Dali Museum, St. Petersburg, Fla 1996 128p il $35
759.6
1. Dalí, Salvador, 1904-1989
ISBN 978-0-8109-3235-7; 0-8109-3235-0
LC 96-3544
"In this slim volume, 40 of the museum's paintings are exquisitely reproduced in full color and accompanied by brief commentaries. . . . A number of Dalís drawings are included in the introduction, and there is an extensive chronology of the artist's life and a bibliography." Publ Wkly
Includes bibliographical references

759.9492 Dutch painting

Bosch, Hieronymus, d. 1516
Hieronymus Bosch; the complete paintings and drawings; {by} Jos Koldeweij, Paul Vandenbroeck, Bernard Vermet. Nai Pubs. 2001 207p il $60

759.9492
ISBN 0-8109-6735-9   LC 2001-092544
Published on the occasion of an exhibition held at the Museum Boijmans Van Beuningen, Rotterdam, Sept. 1-Nov 11, 2001

This volume includes all of the paintings attributed to Bosch by current scholarly consensus, as well as all surviving drawings linked to Bosch and his workshop. An overview and one or two details from each painting are reproduced, along with a generous selection of related artwork by contemporaries and artists who have been influenced by Bosch including Salvador Dali, Robert Gober, Bill Viola, and others. The essays by European art scholars discuss what is known about Bosch and his cultural milieu, along with the likely meanings of his paintings and the residual interpretive mystery that has intrigued scholars and the public for centuries. Libr J

"As keen as the book's historical and technical sections are, its most enthralling passages contain the authors' insights into Bosch's original and satiric worldview and cosmic iconography." Booklist
Includes bibliographical references

Liedtke, Walter A.
Vermeer and the Delft school; by Walter Liedtke in collaboration with Michiel C. Plomp and Axel Rüger; with contributions by Reinier Baarsen {et al.}. Metropolitan Mus. of Art; distributed by Yale Univ. Press 2001 626p il $85

759.9492
1. Vermeer, Johannes, 1632-1675 2. Dutch painting
ISBN 0-300-08848-5   LC 00-49550
"This is the catalog of an exhibition held at the Metropolitan Museum of Art, New York, N.Y., Mar. 8-May 27, 2001 and at the National Gallery, London, June 20-Sept. 16, 2001. It includes fifteen works by Vermeer and paintings, tapestries and drawings by other Delft artists, including Gerard Houckgeest, Emanuel de Witte, Carel Fabritius, Paulus Potter, Leonaert Bramer, Jan de Bisschop and Pieter de Hooch. . . . Liedtke believes that Vermeer was nurtured and goaded exclusively by Dutch art of his time and by the traditions of his hometown." N Y Rev Books
Includes bibliographical references

Saltzman, Cynthia
Portrait of Dr. Gachet; the story of a van Gogh masterpiece, modernism, money, politics, collectors, dealers, taste, greed, and loss. Viking 1998 xxii, 406p il pa $14.95 hardcover o.p.

759.9492
1. Gogh, Vincent van, 1853-1890. Dr. Gachet 2. Gachet, Paul, 1828-1909
ISBN 0-14-025487-0 (pa)   LC 97-37006
"In van Gogh's portrait of his physician, the painter sought to convey the 'heartbroken expression' of his time; Saltzman has taken up where he left off, charting the portrait's progress through our century. From the Nazis who confiscated it as an example of 'degenerate art,' to the Japanese tycoon who bought it for over eighty million dollars, only to keep it hidden in a Tokyo warehouse, the list of the painting's owners is a who's who of modernity, and touches upon the rise and fall of empires and individuals alike." New Yorker
Includes bibliographical references

Schwartz, Gary, 1940-
The Rembrandt book. Abrams 2006 384p il $65
*
759.9492
1. Rembrandt Harmenszoon van Rijn, 1606-1669
ISBN 0-8109-4317-4; 978-0-8109-4317-9
LC 2006-11006
"In addition to a brief biography, . . . [the author] provides a complete thematic overview of key issues, materials, techniques, and people encompassing Rembrandt's world, including family members and patrons, and he treats the artist's drawings, etchings, landscape paintings, portraits, and allegorical as well as genre paintings within the context of 17th-century Holland." Libr J

"This masterful presentation of Rembrandt fulfills the diverse and divergent goals of making Rembrandt accessible to general readers and providing fresh interpretations for scholars." Choice
Includes bibliographical references

Thomson, Belinda
Van Gogh paintings; the materpieces. Thames & Hudson 2007 190p il $45   **759.9492**
1. Gogh, Vincent van, 1853-1890
ISBN 978-0-500-23838-7; 0-500-23838-3
This book "offers a general survey of Van Gogh's paintings. . . . [and] discusses Van Gogh's paintings in terms of a chronological and biographical progression . . . . Filled with beautifully written descriptive passages of the works and careful analysis of the artist's style. . . . This book is a solid introduction to Van Gogh's paintings." Choice
Includes bibliographical references

759.9493 Belgian painting

Magritte, René, 1898-1967
The portable Magritte; with an essay by Robert Hughes. Universe 2002 438p il $29.95
759.9493
ISBN 978-0-7893-0665-4; 0-7893-0665-4
LC 2001-095170
"A glossy, compact collection of 400 works spanning the career of the phlegmatic Belgian painter. . . . [This book is] supplemented by lesser known experiments in cubism, impressionism and expressionism." Publ Wkly
Includes bibliographical references

759.972   Mexican painting

Frida Kahlo. Bulfinch Press 2001 c2000 245p il
$85   **759.972**
1. Kahlo, Frida, 1907-1954
ISBN 0-8212-2766-1   LC 2001-89093
Original Mexican edition, 2000
Jacket title: Frida; Contributions by Luis-Martin
Lozano and others

In this "illustrated survey of Frida Kahlo's work
Lozano . . . explores her life and paintings in a series of
essays that range from a poetic study by noted Mexican
cultural critic Carlos Monsiváis to a short, prosaic piece
written in 1943 by her husband, Diego Rivera, to an academic essay by Lozano himself. . . . Lozano uses
Kahlo's own stunning images, offering high-quality reproductions of some of Kahlo's most famous works as
well as some of her lesser-known pieces. Previously unseen photos of Kahlo at work in her studio are also included. The detail and clarity of the images is incredible." Libr J

760   Graphic arts

Eskilson, Stephen, 1964-
Graphic design; a new history; [by] Stephen J.
Eskilson. Yale University Press 2007 464p il $65
                                                          760
1. Graphic arts—History
ISBN 978-0-300-12011-0; 0-300-12011-7
                                    LC 2006-39466
The author focuses "on the evolution of graphic design since the 19th century as well as on what recent developments in the field of information technology mean
for today's designers. . . . The result is an effective description of the political effects of design (e.g., strategies
used by illustrators of war posters) and countercultural
influences (e.g., drugs and graffiti) supported beautifully
by 400-plus large color reproductions." Libr J
Includes bibliographical references

Riley, Charles A.
The art of Peter Max; by Charles Riley II.
Abrams 2002 240p il $49.95   **760**
1. Max, Peter, 1937-
ISBN 0-8109-3270-9   LC 2002-18229
"Peter Max's gorgeous, technically innovative 1960s
rock-music posters and album covers made him an instant success and celebrity. Amid a gallery of brilliant reproductions, Riley charts his life before and after as well
as during his star turn." Booklist

770   Photography & computer art

The **Abrams** encyclopedia of photography; edited
by Brigitte Govignon; translated from the
French by Graham Edwards . . . [et al.] Harry
N. Abrams 2004 287p il $36 *   **770**
1. Photography—Encyclopedias
ISBN 0-8109-5609-8   LC 2004-7710

This "encyclopedia traces the . . . journey of photography, from the invention of the daguerreotype in 1829
to the digital photograph of today. In outlining nearly
two centuries of this innovative art form, the book touches on some of the medium's key themes, from portraits,
nudes, and still lifes, to sports and fashion photography,
photojournalism, news coverage, and NASA images."
Publisher's note

Dyer, Geoff, 1958-
The ongoing moment. Pantheon Books 2005
285p il $28.50 *   **770**
1. Photography
ISBN 0-375-42215-3   LC 2005-47586
Cultural critic Dyer turns his "eye to photography. Essentially a fast-moving series of highly focused 'close
readings,' his volume zeros in on the way 'certain photographs serve as nodes, places where subjects initially
considered distinct converge and merge.' Thus Paul
Strand's 'Blind Woman, New York, 1916' leads Dyer
not only to other photographs of the blind by Lewis Hine
and Gary Winogrand, but also to a survey of different
portraits of blind author Jorge Luis Borges and to a consideration of Walker Evans's SX-70 photographs." Publ
Wkly

The book is a "curious encyclopedia, purposefully
eclectic and incomplete. . . . He imagines William Eg-
gleston's pictures to be the work of a Martian, stranded
in Middle America, who keeps looking for his lost ticket
home, 'with a haphazard thoroughness that confounds established methods of investigation.' The Martian is an
apt stand-in for Dyer, a flâneur in the world of photography, who bypasses the famous sights in favor of back al-
leys and side streets." New Yorker

Willis, Deborah, 1952-
Reflections in Black; a history of Black
photographers, 1840-1999. Norton 2000 348p il
$50; pa $35   **770**
ISBN 0-393-04880-2; 0-393-32280-7 (pa)
                                    LC 99-55185
Companion volume to A Smithsonian traveling exhibition
"Willis sketches important figures and traces both developments in photographic techniques and the practice
of photography by African Americans. . . . A beautiful
and informative album." Booklist
Includes bibliographical references

770.2   Photography—Miscellany

Drager, Kerry
Scenic photography 101; a crash course in
shooting better pictures outdoors. AMPHOTO
1999 144p il $24.95   **770.2**
1. Outdoor photography
ISBN 0-8174-5819-0   LC 99-29592
This guide discusses equipment, light and color, composition, and how to capture specific details.

Grimm, Tom

The basic book of photography; Tom Grimm and Michele Grimm ; photographs by Michele Grimm and Tom Grimm ; drawings by Ezelda Garcia and Cindy King. 2004 ed. Plume Book 2003 *   **770.2**

1. Photography—Handbooks, manuals, etc.
ISBN 0-452-28425-2 (pbk.)   LC 2003-49789
First published 1974

"In addition to equipment and materials, the two most important elements of good photography-lighting and composition are considered. Although the emphasis is upon 35mm photography, other types of cameras, including point and shoot, Polaroid, and digital cameras, are also discussed in detail. The final chapter and appendixes offer an abundance of useful information, including recommended books, photography schools, workshops, competitions, and an extensive glossary of photographic terms." Libr J {review of 1997 edition}

McDarrah, Gloria S.

The photography encyclopedia; [by] Gloria S. McDarrah, Fred W. McDarrah, and Timothy S. McDarrah. Schirmer Bks. 1999 689p il $125
                                                           770.2

1. Photography—Encyclopedias
ISBN 0-02-865025-5   LC 98-46084

This work "covers all angles of photographers and the tools of their craft. . . . It is filled with carefully selected photographs portraying the irony and beauty of life seen through the camera lens. As a reference work, the photographs are the glue between biographies and terminology. Additional sections list book reviews, films about photographers, and a time line of photography. Additional appendixes include lists of US museums, galleries, manufacturers, booksellers, etc." Choice

770.9 Photography—Historical, geographic, persons, treatment

Encyclopedia of twentieth-century photography; Lynne Warren, editor. Routledge 2005 set $525 *   **770.9**

1. Artistic photography
ISBN 1-57958-393-8   LC 2005-46287

"International in scope, most of the entries in this work cover people, primarily photographers. The remaining articles cover equipment, institutions and collections, geographical regions, and other topics." Booklist

Newman, Cathy

Women photographers at National Geographic. National Geographic Soc. 2000 271p il $40; pa $25   **770.9**

1. Women photographers
ISBN 0-7922-7689-2; 0-7922-6934-9 (pa)
                                    LC 00-41575

This look at the life and careers of the photographers "describes their conflicted lives as they balance assignments that took them away from families, homes, and communities for long periods of time. . . . But it is the 144 photographs that attest to the place these women deserve in the history of photography." Libr J
Includes bibliographical references

Photography past forward: Aperture at 50; with a history by R. H. Cravens; and excerpts from Aperture issues 1952-2002; [Melissa Harris, editor] Farrar, Straus & Giroux 2002 239p il $50   **770.9**

1. Aperture (Periodical) 2. Photography—History 3. Artistic photography
ISBN 0-89381-996-4   LC 2002-107716

"Aperture celebrates 50 years as the premier venue for art photography in the United States with a book worthy of its founders' ideals. An anecdotal history lovingly details its transformation from a bright idea for a magazine—conceived by the likes of Minor White and Ansel Adams—to the publisher of hundreds of books, sampled in the accompanying photos, themselves a dizzying display of artistic variety." Libr J

775 Digital photography

Ang, Tom

Advanced digital photography. Rev. ed. Amphoto Books 2007 144p il pa $24.95
                                                           775

1. Digital photography 2. Photography—Processing
ISBN 978-0-8174-3272-0; 0-8174-3272-8
First published 2003
Subtitle on cover: Techniques & tips for creating professional quality images

The author "explains the capture of photographs, processing of data, printing, and much more, complete with full-color illustrations." Publisher's note

"Technically detailed yet clearly written, . . . [this book is] for the serious photographer or professional and . . .[is] a rich source for mastering the manipulation of digital images." Libr J
Includes bibliographical references

Digital photographer's handbook. Fully updated 3rd ed. Dorling Kindersley 2006 407p il pa $25 *
                                                           775

1. Digital photography 2. Digital cameras
ISBN 0-7566-2355-3; 978-0-7566-2355-5
                                    LC 2006-285530
First published 2002

The author "discusses digital technology, including cameras, lenses, scanners, and printers, along with computers, accessories, and software. He then goes on to explore the unique challenges and advantages of composition and exposure with digital cameras. . . . This is certainly one of the best and most comprehensive books available about digital photography." Libr J [review of 2002 edition]
Includes bibliographical references

KISS guide to digital photography. DK Pub 2004 288p il (Keep it simple series) pa $20
                                                           775

1. Digital photography
ISBN 0-7894-9696-8   LC 2003-55522

Ang, Tom—*Continued*
This guide aims to help readers "find the right camera and accessories, master digital tricks, lighting and composition, while demystifying buzzwords, from pixels and jpegs to cropping and cloning." Publisher's note

Cope, Peter
Secrets of the digital darkroom; {by} Peter Cope and Simon Joinson. AMPHOTO 2003 192p il pa $29.95   **775**
1. Digital photography
ISBN 0-8174-5824-7
"The introductory chapters deal with digital photography in general and basic techniques of working with these images. Separate chapters discuss professional techniques, classic techniques, and creating a 'digital darkroom,' followed by a useful glossary, index, and bibliography. Generously illustrated, this is one of the best books published to date on this subject." Libr J

Freeman, Michael, 1945-
The complete guide to digital photography; [by] Michael H. Freeman. 4th ed. Lark Books 2008 224p il pa $29.95 *   **775**
1. Digital photography 2. Digital cameras
ISBN 978-1-60059-301-7; 1-60059-301-1
LC 2007-42160
First published 2001
This book covers digital technologies including cameras, lenses, printers, inks, Photoshop and other image-processing software, and workflow managers. It also offers advice on shooting and processing digital photos.
Includes bibliographical references

Johnson, Dave, 1964-
How to do everything: digital camera. 5th ed. McGraw-Hill 2008 xx, 428p il pa $24.99 *
775
1. Digital cameras 2. Digital photography
ISBN 978-0-07-149580-6   LC 2008-4602
First published 2001
This book teaches "the fundamentals of photography, composition, lighting, and exposure, and . . . techniques for different subjects and situations. The book also explains how to use a variety of photo-editing tools and offers . . . tips for storing, sharing, and printing your photographs." Publisher's note

Sheppard, Rob
Kodak guide to digital photography. Lark Books 2008 368p il pa $19.95   **775**
1. Digital photography
ISBN 978-1-57990-969-7; 1-57990-969-8
LC 2007-4832
"Kodak books"
"The best widely available book on every technical aspect of the digital camera is this encyclopedic new guide. . . . [The author] helps readers choose the right camera, understand the workings of the camera's sensor, master exposure measuring techniques, and determine the best shutter speed and aperture combinations for shooting various subjects. Highly recommended for all collections." Libr J

776   Computer art (Digital art)

Caplin, Steve
The complete guide to digital illustration; [by] Steve Caplin and Adam Banks; Nigel Holmes, consultant editor. Watson-Guptill 2003 192p il pa $35   **776**
1. Computer graphics 2. Computer art
ISBN 0-8230-0784-7   LC 2002-33190
This guide examines "the key areas where digital illustration is utilized—covering the traditional arenas such as print, corporate identity, and advertising as well as multimedia presentations and the new media of the Internet." Publisher's note
"This picture-rich resource boasts a glossary, bibliography, and listing of further readings, ensuring that digital designers who are manipulating photos, doing 3D modeling, and exploring the complexities of stacking and layers in illustration will have a wealth of useful instruction and information at hand." Booklist
Includes bibliographical references

778.5   Cinematography, video production, related activities

Harryhausen, Ray
The art of Ray Harryhausen; [by] Ray Harryhausen & Tony Dalton; with a foreword by Peter Jackson. Billboard Books 2006 230p il $50
778.5
1. Cinematography 2. Animated films
ISBN 0-8230-8400-0   LC 2005-930364
First published 2005 in the United Kingdom
This "book chronicles the oft-forgotten work of the master of stop-motion animation, Ray Harryhausen. It discusses his techniques from rough sketches to final filming and explores his creations in broze sculpture." Choice
"The text is fun and informative, but the main feast here is the art, and the reproductions of the concept drawings and photos of the models are superb." Libr J

Netzley, Patricia D.
The encyclopedia of movie special effects. Oryx Press 2000 291p il $73.95   **778.5**
1. Cinematography
ISBN 1-57356-167-3   LC 99-47733
"This volume provides 366 entries on visual, mechanical, and makeup effects and techniques used in film and includes discussions of every movie to win an Oscar for special effects." Libr J
Includes bibliographical references

Weishar, Peter
Blue Sky; the art of computer animation: featuring Ice Age and Bunny. Abrams 2002 86p il pa $24.95   **778.5**
1. Computer animation
ISBN 0-8109-9069-5   LC 2001-58988

Weishar, Peter—*Continued*

This goes behind the scenes at "Blue Sky Studios and uses their . . . film Ice Age to illustrate computer modeling, rigging, texture mapping, and special effects. Weishar entertainingly details the technological wizardry used to create 3-D animation of everything from storms and smoke to fully realized film sets and woolly mammoths." Libr J

779 Photographs

Brandow, Todd

Edward Steichen; lives in photography; [by] Todd Brandow and William A. Ewing. W. W. Norton & Company 2008 355p il $100
779
1. Steichen, Edward, 1879-1973 2. Artistic photography
ISBN 978-0-393-06626-5   LC 2007-20128

"Wending through Steichen's 70-year career, the book presents his early, impressionistic black-and-white nudes and portraits of luminaries such as Rodin as well as atmospheric still lives and editorial fashion shots for *Vogue* and *Vanity Fair*." Publ Wkly

"One of the finest photography books published in many years; highly recommended for all libraries." Libr J

Includes bibliographical references

Christenberry, William, 1936-

William Christenberry; foreword by Elizabeth Broun; essays by Walter Hopps, Andy Grundberg, and Howard N. Fox. Aperture; Smithsonian American Art Museum 2006 203p il $50 *
779
1. Artistic photography
ISBN 1-9317-8889-8   LC 2005-25408

"Trained as a painter in the late 50's, Christenberry demonstrates in many of his photographs from the 60's and 70's an eye for the commercial semiotics that delighted pop artists at the time. He can't resist battered or fading road signs and crooked hand-lettered messages. His serial images of isolated buildings, viewed year after year in various seasonal lights and states of decay, also have affinities with minimalism. He presents many of these structures as though they were inscrutable, functionless pieces of sculpture. They stand with doors and windows shut, uninviting, even a little hostile to outsiders. By now he is one himself, and that status helps him resist the lure of sentimentality." N Y Times Book Rev

Coles, Robert

When they were young; a photographic retrospective of childhood from the Library of Congress; preface by James H. Billington. Kales Press 2002 160p il $39.95 *   **779**
1. Library of Congress 2. Artistic photography 3. Children—Pictorial works
ISBN 0-9670076-5-8   LC 2002-7177

"Published in conjunction with the Library of Congress exhibition." Verso of title page

This is an "illustrated portrayal of early life and the legacies that live on from coming of age. . . . Spanning the history of photography from the daguerreotype to the documentary, each tritone image in this volume is illustrated on a full page. Works by internationally renowned photographers such as Edward Curtis and Dorothea Lange are included." Publisher's note

Elkins, Ken

Picture taker. Univ. of Alabama 2005 120p il $35   **779**
1. Photojournalism
ISBN 0-8173-1478-4   LC 2004-25921

A collection of 100 black-and-white photographs taken by the chief photographer of the Anniston Star.

"Elkins is very good at the perfect image caught on the fly. See the picture of a man in a boat who has just paddled it one stroke forward . . . ; a curled ribbon of water is caught leaping from the misted, glassy surface. See the baby crawling on pavement in the driving rain . . . . See the dogs wading in floodwater while fog swallows the whole scene. . . . Perhaps even more than the many exquisitely casual portraits of housedress- and overalls-clad farmers, such visions become engraved in one's memory instantaneously, ineradicably." Booklist

Evans, Walker, 1903-1975

Many are called; introduction by James Agee; foreword by Luc Sante; afterword by Jeff L. Rosenheim. Yale University Press, Metropolitan Museum of Art 2004 207p il $40 *   **779**
1. Portrait photography 2. Subways—Pictorial works
ISBN 0-300-10617-3   LC 2004-13851
First published 1966 by Houghton Mifflin

"Between 1938 and 1941, Evans rode New York City subways with a 35mm Contax camera strapped to his chest. With the lens poking through a button hole, he snapped more than 600 clandestine photos of fellow riders. . . . Like many of Evans's projects, the purpose of his art was to celebrate the common man/woman in everyday activities. . . . Stunning." Libr J
Includes bibliographical references

Face to face; the art of portrait photography; [edited by] Paul Ardenne; photo research, Élisabeth Nora; [translated from the French by Michael Taylor] Flammarion 2004 299p il $65
779
1. Portrait photography
ISBN 2-0803-0462-3

"What is the role of a portrait? To capture? Tell a story? Inform? This . . . book explores such questions through the work of dozens of photographers (e.g., Annie Liebovitz, Cecil Beaton), whose subjects include such icons as Marilyn Monroe and Fidel Castro." Libr J
Includes bibliographical references

Greenough, Sarah, 1951-

Alfred Stieglitz: the key set; the Alfred Stieglitz collection of photographs; {text by} Sarah Greenough. Abrams 2002 2v il set $150 *
779

ISBN 0-8109-3533-3   LC 2002-5066

Greenough, Sarah, 1951—*Continued*
Contents: v1 1886-1922; v2 1923-1937
This is a "captioned catalog of 1,642 Stieglitz photographs. . . . It contains 'the finest print of every mounted photograph in Stieglitz's possession at the time of his death.' . . . Greenough's essay examines 'what is and is not in the key set in order to clarify the evolution of Stieglitz's understanding of modernist photography....' The set contains very useful, dense chronologies of Stieglitz's process and techniques (1882-1944) and of exhibitions (1888-1944), a bibliography (1875-2001), and an essay on Stieglitz's concern with reproduction printing and publishing." Choice
Includes bibliographical references

Icons of photography; the 20th century; edited by Peter Stepan. 2nd ed. Prestel 2005 199p il pa $19.95   **779**
1. Artistic photography
ISBN 3-7913-3336-4   LC 2005-280157
First published 1999
A "chronological assembly of 90 photographers, from Berenice Abbott to Heinrich Zille. . . . Each artist is given a two-page spread, including a portrait shot and an example of a key image; there are 165 images in all, representing the artists' best and most challenging work." Libr J

In focus; National Geographic greatest portraits. National Geographic Society 2004 504p il $30 *   **779**
1. Portrait photography
ISBN 0-7922-7363-X   LC 2004-44953
Companion volume to Through the lens
"Comprising 280 portraits by 150 of National Geographic's celebrated photographers . . . the book spans over 100 years and covers the entire globe. Organized chronologically as well as thematically and enriched with essays on the development of photographic styles through decades, it is a tasteful celebration of the medium but even more so of human diversity." Libr J

Lee, Russell, 1903-1986
Russell Lee photographs; images from the Russell Lee photograph collection at the Center for American History; foreword by John Szarkowski; introduction by J. B. Colson; photographs selected and arranged by Linda Peterson. University of Texas Press 2007 236p il (Focus on American history series) $50   **779**
1. Documentary photography
ISBN 978-0-292-71499-1; 0-292-71499-8
      LC 2006-15020
Documentary photographer Russell is widely acclaimed for "his images of American life during the Great Depression, created for the Farm Security Administration between 1936 and 1942. . . . [This] is the first book to show the full range and quality of Lee's entire oeuvre beyond the FSA work. . . . The book contains over 140 images, 101 of which have never appeared in book publication. The photographs are grouped into suites of images that represent all of Lee's important, non-FSA subjects: early work from New York City and Woodstock; the Spanish-speaking people of Texas; the

mentally and physically disabled; political campaigns, including the Kennedy-Johnson campaign of 1960; commercial work for chemical and other companies; a portfolio of images of Italy; and quintessential scenes of small-town life." Publisher's note
"Lee's quietly passionate images are masterful works. They set a high standard for a kind of reflective journalism that reminds us that a fine artist may tell you most about himself when first he focuses on others." Texas Observer

Leibovitz, Annie
A photographer's life, 1990-2005. Random House 2006 unp il $75   **779**
1. Portrait photography
ISBN 978-0-375-50509-6; 0-375-50509-1
      LC 2006-45765
This is a collection of Leibovitz's "work from 1990-2005. . . . [Portraits of] Johnny Cash, Nicole Kidman, Mikhail Baryshnikov, Keith Richards, Michael Jordan, Joan Didion, R2-D2, Patti Smith, Nelson Mandela, Jack Nicholson, William Burroughs, [and] George W. Bush with members of his Cabinet appear alongside pictures of Leibovitz's family and friends, reportage from the siege of Sarajevo in the early Nineties, and landscapes." Publisher's note

Women; {photographs by} Annie Leibovitz; {essay by} Susan Sontag. Random House 1999 239p il $75; pa $49.95   **779**
1. Women—Portraits
ISBN 0-375-50020-0; 0-375-75646-9 (pa)
      LC 99-24968
"Leibovitz greatly increases our lexicon of womanhood with her brilliant photographs of musicians, doctors, teachers, trapeze artists, gangbangers, nude women, a woman in chador, women soldiers, and girls with their Barbies, all commanding attention and respect." Booklist

Photos that changed the world; the 20th century; edited by Peter Stepan; with contributions by Claus Biegerd {et al.}. Prestel-Verlag 2000 183p il hardcover o.p. pa $19.95   **779**
1. Photojournalism
ISBN 3-7913-2395-4; 3-7913-3628-2 (pa)

Translated from the German
Stepan provides "105 images that had the lasting visual power to capture a moment that could be the image of an era held in the instant of a shutter's click for distribution to a generation. . . . The photos are well reproduced and gain from the explanations of time, place, and context included in the excellent short essays that accompany each." Libr J

Platinum anniversary collection; 70 years of extraordinary photography. Time-Life Books 2006 304p il $29.95 *   **779**
1. United States—History—20th century—Pictorial works 2. Photojournalism 3. Documentary photography
ISBN 1-933405-17-1; 978-1-933405-17-9
      LC 2006-900123
At head of title: Life

Platinum anniversary collection—*Continued*

This book, "illustrated with nearly 300 remarkable color and black-and-white photographs, provides an overview of 70 years of the most influential photography magazine on the planet. . . . With an interesting section featuring all the magazine's covers, this book clearly succeeds in demonstrating the immense and enduring power of photography." Libr J

Plowden, David

David Plowden: vanishing point; fifty years of photography; foreword by Richard Snow; introduction by Steve Edwards. W.W. Norton 2007 340p il $100   **779**

1. Photography
ISBN 978-0-393-06254-0; 0-393-06254-6
LC 2007-5992

This "book chronicles the American photographer's finest work over a 50-year career that has included some 20 books and numerous exhibits. . . . The breadth, depth, and sheer abundance of Plowden's work over the years are just amazing. Destined to be a classic, this is one of the finest photography books to come along in quite a while." Libr J

Renaldi, Richard

Richard Renaldi; figure and ground; photographs by Richard Renaldi; essay by Roger Hargreaves. Aperture 2006 156p il $45   **779**

1. Artistic photography
ISBN 978-1-597110-29-7; 1-5-97110-29-9

"Renaldi has traveled cross-country and photographed men and women he's encountered on the street, at their minimum-wage jobs, and in the bus terminals punctuating the major routes between the East and West Coasts. This book of his work is largely without explanation, presenting posed photographs that carry brief captions made up of only the subject's name, location, and a glimpse of his or her individual route. . . . A definitive essay by independent curator Hargreaves . . . at the collection's conclusion does not interfere with independent consideration of the works themselves, but it does guide readers to a deeper understanding of Renaldi's intention and process." Libr J

Smith, Joel

Edward Steichen: the early years. Princeton Univ. Press 1999 167p il $65   **779**

1. Steichen, Edward, 1879-1973 2. Artistic photography
ISBN 0-691-04873-8   LC 99-26617

Smith examines the photography of Edward Steichen. Alfred Stieglitz was a patron of Steichen's, and Smith discusses "the interrelationship between Steichen's work and Stieglitz's shifting aesthetic interests, as well as the influence of Paris on Steichen's development." N Y Times Book Rev

Includes bibliographical references

Sommer, Frederick, 1905-1999

The art of Frederick Sommer; photography, drawing, collage; [essay by Keith F. Davis; interview by Michael Torosian; chronology by April M. Watson] Yale University Press 2005 251p il $65 *   **779**

1. Artistic photography
ISBN 0-300-10783-8   LC 2004-118000

This book "chronicles the extraordinary life and work of Frederick Sommer (1905-1999)." Publisher's note

"The book's sequencing of images wholly succeeds in creating a powerful contemplative experience, and the enticing arguments Davis offers in his introductory remarks incite a hunger for fresh, detailed scholarship about each of Sommer's works." Publ Wkly

Spirit capture; photographs from the National Museum of the American Indian; edited by Tim Johnson. Smithsonian Institution Press 1998 205p il $60; pa $34.95   **779**

1. National Museum of the American Indian (U.S.)
2. Native Americans—Pictorial works
ISBN 1-56098-924-6; 1-56098-765-0 (pa)
LC 98-4173

The more than 200 reproductions included in this volume range from daguerrotypes to color slides. Essays by Native American authors explore how Indians of the Western hemisphere were documented and depicted

Includes bibliographical references

Testino, Mario, 1954-

Let me in! [photographs by] Mario Testino ; [foreword by Nicole Kidman ; essays by Michael Roberts, Mario Testino and Patrick Kinmoth ; German translation, Clara Drechsler ; French translation, Philippe Safavi] Taschen 2007 il $39.99   **779**

1. Portrait photography
ISBN 978-3-8228-4418-2; 3-8228-4418-7

"It's tough to tell where fashion photography ends and celebrity photography begins but both are getting some respect from the world of high art these days, and nothing proclaims that fact more eloquently than this . . . book of Mario Testino's behind-the-scenes photographs of celebrities in fashionable garb." Miami Herald

Through the lens; National Geographic greatest photographs. National Geographic Soc. 2003 504p il $30   **779**

1. Documentary photography
ISBN 0-7922-6164-X   LC 2003-52757

This is a "collection of 250 photos, mostly in color and drawn from the National Geographic Society's archive. . . . The society's signature blend of dramatic, rigorously composed natural shots and 'family of nations'-style culture peeps are backed by broad captions and text. . . . The six sections ('Europe'; 'Asia'; 'Africa & the Middle East'; 'The Americas'; 'Oceans and Isles'; 'The Universe') include the first color underwater photographs, as well as collaborative work with NASA, and prominently credit the 84 photographers whose work is featured." Publ Wkly

780 Music

Day, Timothy
A century of recorded music; listening to musical history. Yale Univ. Press 2000 306p il $40; pa $19 *   **780**
1. Sound recordings—History 2. Music—History and criticism 3. Sound—Recording and Reproducing—History
ISBN 0-300-08442-0; 0-300-09401-9 (pa)
LC 00-43490
This work provides a "narrative of the evolution of recording from cylinders (1887), shellac discs, and acoustic rerecording through the reproducing piano, electrical amplifications (1925), and magnetic tape to the long-playing record (1948) and compact disc of the 1980s. Day also discusses studio practices and the emergence of influential record producers, the role of radio and recordings in creating a mass audience, the expansion of recorded repertoire, and new ways to experience music. Recommended for all music collections." Choice
Includes bibliographical references

Krasilovsky, M. William
This business of music; the definitive guide to the music industry; [by] M. William Krasilovsky and Sidney Shemel; contributions by John M. Gross, Jonathan Feinstein. 10th ed. Billboard Bks. 2007 il $29.95   **780**
1. Music industry 2. Music—Economic aspects 3. Copyright—Music 4. Popular music—Writing and publishing
ISBN 978-0-8230-7723-6; 0-8230-7723-3
First published 1964
"A compendium of useful information on contracts, copyrights, record production, music videos, agents and managers, performing-rights organizations, and other business practices specific to music." Guide to Ref Books. 11th edition

780.3 Music—Encyclopedias and dictionaries

The **Harvard** concise dictionary of music and musicians; edited by Don Michael Randel. Belknap Press 1999 757p il $35; pa $18.95   **780.3**
1. Music—Dictionaries 2. Music—Bio-bibliography
ISBN 0-674-00084-6; 0-674-00978-9 (pa)
LC 99-40644
Based on the New Harvard dictionary of music and The Harvard biographical dictionary of music (1996)
"Entries are arranged alphabetically and encompass terms, musical forms and styles, individual works, and instruments, as well as composers, performers, and theorists." Booklist

The **Harvard** dictionary of music; edited by Don Michael Randel. 4th ed. Belknap Press 2003 978p il (Harvard University Press reference library) $39.95 *   **780.3**
1. Music—Dictionaries
ISBN 0-674-01163-5
LC 2003-58262

First published 1944 under the authorship of Willi Apel
This reference "includes entries on all the styles and forms in Western music; . . . articles on the music of Africa, Asia, Latin America, and the Near East; descriptions of instruments . . . {with} historical background, and articles that reflect today's best, including popular music, jazz, and rock." Publisher's note

Hoffman, Miles
The NPR classical music companion; an essential guide for enlightened listening. Houghton Mifflin 2005 306p pa $15   **780.3**
1. Music—Dictionaries
ISBN 978-0-618-61945-0; 0-618-61945-3
LC 2006-273343
First published 1997 with title: The NPR classical music companion: terms and concepts from A to Z
"Hoffman, host of National Public Radio's Coming to Terms, attempts to make classical music terminology more accessible to the lay reader {in this book}." Libr J
This musical guide includes This musical guide includes "entries that are at least a good-size paragraph in length and liable to include, besides technical information, historical and listener's advisory material." Booklist

Kennedy, Michael, 1926-
The Oxford dictionary of music; associate editor, Joyce Bourne. 2nd ed., rev. Oxford University Press 2006 985p il $60   **780.3**
1. Music—Dictionaries 2. Musicians—Dictionaries
ISBN 978-0-19-861459-3   LC 2006-50238
First published 1985
Includes over 12,000 entries on composers, performers, conductors, musical terms and forms, instruments, works, venues, and other topics.

The **New** Grove dictionary of music and musicians; edited by Stanley Sadie; executive editor, John Tyrrell. 2nd ed. Oxford University Press 2004 c2000 29v set $1, 500 *   **780.3**
1. Music—Dictionaries
ISBN 978-0-19-517067-2
Also available online
First published 1980 in twenty volumes to supersede Grove's dictionary of music and musicians; this edition first published 2000
This dictionary includes "29,000 signed articles written by 5,700 contributors from 98 countries. The articles include 20,000 biographies; 2,200 entries for instruments and their makers; 1,400 entries on styles, terms, and genres; 1,300 entries on world music; 1,200 entries on popular music; plus entries on other topics, such as acoustics (89 articles)." Booklist
"Grove is not fat, it is limitless. Whether Grove is on the reference shelf or online, teachers, students, researchers, and the common reader will find it an abiding source of satisfaction." Commonweal
Includes bibliographical references

The **Oxford** companion to music; edited by Alison Latham. Oxford Univ. Press 2002 1434p il $65
* **780.3**
1. Music—Dictionaries 2. Musicians—Dictionaries
ISBN 0-19-866212-2 LC 2002-537302
"New edition of two quite different earlier companions . . . Oxford companion to music . . . The new Oxford companion to music." Preface
"Among the 8000 entries are articles on composers, theorists, and some performers; instruments, forms, and terms; subjects like electronic music, individual countries, and politics and music; and some pieces (and even some famous arias). Each entry is presented in a dictionary format, with a select index of names appended and sometimes with bibliographic references. . . . The bias is still English, but the book provides cross references to American terms and includes plenty of American composers and musical subjects. A solid reference with a grand pedigree, usefully improved for home and general library use, this is highly recommended for all public libraries." Libr J
Includes bibliographical references

780.9 Music—Historical, geographic, persons, treatment

The **Garland** encyclopedia of world music; advisory editors, Bruno Nettl and Ruth M. Stone; founding editors, James Porter and Timothy Rice. Garland; distributed by Routledge 1998-2002 10v il maps (Garland reference library of the humanities) set $2,500
780.9
ISBN 0-8153-1865-0 LC 97-9671
Volumes also available separately $250 each
Volumes 6-7, 10 published by Routledge
Contents: v1 Africa, by R. M. Stone, editor; v2 South America, Mexico, Central America, and the Caribbean, by D. A. Olsen and D. E. Sheehy, editors; v3 The United States and Canada, by E. Koskoff, editor; v4 Southeast Asia, by T. E. Miller and S. Williams, editors; v5 South Asia: the Indian subcontinent, by A. Arnold, editor; v6 The Middle East, by V. Danielson, S. Marcus, and D. Reynolds, editors; v7 East Asia: China, Japan, and Korea, by R. C. Provine, Y. Tokumaru, and J. L. Witzleben, editors; v8 Europe, by T. Rice, J. Porter, and C. Goertzen, editors; v9 Australia and the Pacific Islands, by A. L. Kaeppler and J. W. Love, editors; v10 The world's music: general perspectives and reference tools, by R. M. Stone, editor
This is an "encyclopedia dedicated to exploring the social and cultural context of music around the world. Individual volumes are devoted to specific regions of the world . . . and each has an accompanying audio compact disc of representative examples keyed to the text. Articles are authoritative, well illustrated, and provide cultural and historical perspectives on the musical styles, genres, and performances of each of the nine regions covered." Ref Sources for Small & Medium-sized Libr. 6th edition

Grout, Donald Jay, 1902-1987
A history of western music; [by] J. Peter Burkholder, Donald Jay Grout, Claude V. Palisca. 7th ed. W.W. Norton 2006 xxviii, 965, 128p il map $71.25 **780.9**
1. Music—History and criticism
ISBN 0-393-97991-1; 978-0-393-97991-6
LC 2005-48797
First published 1960
The authors survey the course of Western music from the ancient world to modern atonalism and dodecaphony. They cover vocal and instrumental forms, notation, performance, music-printing, the development of instruments, and biographical information on composers.
Includes bibliographical references

Hart, Mickey
Songcatchers; in search of the world's music; [by] Mickey Hart with K.M. Kostyal. National Geographic Society 2003 172p il $30
780.9
1. Folk music 2. Music—History and criticism
ISBN 0-7922-4107-X LC 2003-45901
"For some time now, Grateful Dead drummer Hart has been a songcatcher, a collector of the originally noncommercial music popularly called traditional music. Many anthropologists, musicians, political and labor organizers, composers, social workers, and others were songcatchers before him, and it is their collective story that he and professional writer Kostyal tell in this engaging book. . . . A book for every popular library." Booklist
Includes bibliographical references

Lang, Paul Henry, 1901-1991
Music in Western civilization; with a new foreword by Leon Botstein. Norton 1997 xxii, 1107p il maps $45 **780.9**
1. Music—History and criticism
ISBN 0-393-04074-7 LC 97-5883
First published 1941
This is a history of Western music from Ancient Greece to the 1920s
"Lang's volume has long been hailed as a benchmark in the field." Libr J
Includes bibliographical references

Mithen, Steven J.
The singing neanderthals; the origins of music, language, mind, and body; [by] Steven Mithen. Harvard University Press 2006 374p il map $25.95; pa $16.95 **780.9**
1. Music 2. Evolution
ISBN 0-674-02192-4; 978-0-674-02192-1; 978-0-674-02559-2 (pa); 0-674-02559-8 (pa)
LC 2005-30187
First published 2005 in the United Kingdom
The author argues "that as a species, humans most likely made musical noises that led to language, not the other way around. . . . This book is a rich resource." Choice
Includes bibliographical references

New Oxford history of music. Oxford Univ. Press 1954-1990 10v il music * **780.9**

New Oxford history of music—*Continued*

1. Music—History and criticism

Apply to publisher for price and availability

Supersedes The Oxford history of music, first published 1901-1905

Contents: v1 Ancient and Oriental music, edited by Egon Wellesz; v2 2nd ed. The Early Middle Ages to 1300, edited by Richard Crocker and David Hiley; v3 Ars nova and the Renaissance, 1300-1540, edited by Dom Anselm Hughes and Gerald Abraham; v4 The Age of humanism, 1540-1630, edited by Gerald Abraham; v5 Opera and church music, 1630-1750, edited by Nigel Fortune and Anthony Lewis; v6 Concert music, 1630-1750, edited by Gerald Abraham; v7 The age of enlightenment, 1745-1790, edited by Egon Wellesz and Frederick Sternfeld; v8 The age of Beethoven, 1790-1830, edited by Gerald Abraham; v9 Romanticism, 1830-1890, edited by Gerald Abraham; v10 The modern age, 1890-1960, edited by Martin Cooper

"It would be difficult to find a scholarly multi-volume history of music of comparable stature. . . . {This work is marked by} comprehensiveness, consistency, evenness, and sheer readability." Choice

Norton anthology of western music; edited by Claude V. Palisca. 4th ed. Norton 2001 2v music pa ea $42.50   **780.9**

1. Music—History and criticism

LC 2001-545308

Also available The Norton recorded anthology of western music, consisting of 2 sets of 6 CDs each, and a concise edition consisting of 4 CDs

First published 1980

Contents: v1 Ancient to Baroque (ISBN 0-393-97690-4); v2 Classic to Modern (ISBN 0-393-97691-2)

This is a collection of musical scores designed to accompany the sixth editon of A history of western music by Donald J. Grout and Claude V. Palisca

Perlis, Vivian

Composer's voices from Ives to Ellington; an oral history of American music; [by] Vivian Perlis and Libby Van Cleve. Yale University Press 2005 477p il $50   **780.9**

1. Composers—United States 2. Jazz musicians

ISBN 0-300-10673-4; 9780300106732

LC 2005-361

"In the first of four planned volumes, the authors cover the early 20th century, tapping reminiscences from the OH archives by and about such luminaries as Charles Ives, Edgard Varèse, Carl Ruggles, Charles Seeger, Henry Cowell, George Gershwin, Duke Ellington, and three of Nadia Boulanger's most illustrious students: Aaron Copland, Roy Harris, and Virgil Thompson." Libr J

"This volume offers the reader a unique perspective on the composers who created ragtime, 'new' music, and early jazz. A very enjoyable read supplemented by 2 compact discs that contain excerpts of interviews." Univ Press Books for Public and Second Sch Libr, 2006

Includes bibliographical references

Rosen, Charles, 1927-

The classical style; Haydn, Mozart, Beethoven. expanded ed. Norton 1997 xxx, 533p il $35; pa $19.95   **780.9**

1. Haydn, Joseph, 1732-1809 2. Mozart, Wolfgang Amadeus, 1756-1791 3. Beethoven, Ludwig van, 1770-1827 4. Music—History and criticism

ISBN 0-393-04020-8; 0-393-31712-9 (pa)

LC 96-27335

First published 1971 by Viking

"This remains simply the most important book on the classical style in music." Choice

Includes bibliographical references

The romantic generation. Harvard Univ. Press 1995 723p il pa $18.95 hardcover o.p.

     780.9

1. Music—History and criticism

ISBN 0-674-77934-7 (pa)   LC 94-46239

"Based on the Charles Eliot Norton lectures"

The author "explains and describes the first half of the 19th century in conjunction with literature, art, and social changes. . . . Rosen also examines the lives of the composers and pursues some detailed analysis of numerous compositions to make his points. The result is a fresh, challenging, and stimulating view of the society in which Chopin, Liszt, Berlioz, and Schumann flourished." Libr J

Ross, Alex

The rest is noise; listening to the twentieth century. Farrar, Straus and Giroux 2007 624p il $30 *   **780.9**

1. Music—History and criticism

ISBN 978-0-374-24939-7; 0-374-24939-3

LC 2007-4504

This is a "history of music and culture from 1900 to 2000. Ross . . . details—in 15 chapters organized into three large chronological sections (i.e., 1900-33, 1933-45, and 1945-2000)—the personalities, the ideological battles, and, of course, the musical works that helped to define their era." Libr J

This book "is a work of immense scope and ambition. . . . 'The Rest Is Noise' is a great achievement." N Y Times Book Rev

Includes discography and bibliographical references

Taruskin, Richard

The Oxford history of western music. Oxford University Press 2004 6v 6vp il map set $699 *   **780.9**

1. Music—History and criticism

ISBN 0-19-516979-4   LC 2004-17897

This set covers "the Western classical tradition from medieval Gregorian chant to the contemporary avant-garde, with two . . . chapters on 20th-century jazz and pop. . . . The result is a judicious but richly stimulating history, valuable both to scholars and to ordinary readers who want to listen with new ears to the music they love." Publ Wkly

Includes bibliographical references

Terkel, Studs, 1912-2008
And they all sang; adventures of an eclectic disc jockey. New Press 2005 xxii, 301p $25.95; pa $16.95
780.9
1. Musicians
ISBN 1-59558-003-4; 978-1-59558-118-1; 1-59558-118-9 (pa)
LC 2005-43866
In this "collection of 40 interviews, . . . Terkel recalls his venerable radio program, The Wax Museum, which premiered shortly after the end of WWII in 1945, profiling composers, entertainers and impresarios of nearly every type of music. . . . Insightful and daring, Terkel always asks the right questions, whether culturally or musically." Publ Wkly

Women and music in America since 1900; an encyclopedia; edited by Kristine H. Burns. Oryx Press 2002 2v il set $150
780.9
1. Women musicians 2. American music—Encyclopedias
ISBN 1-57356-267-X
LC 2001-54570
This is an "alphabetically arranged reference set on women composers, performers, teachers, and scholars from all genres of music since 1900, as well as issues, organizations, and broad topics." Libr J
"This set will become an essential reference tool." Choice

780.973 Music—United States

Crawford, Richard, 1935-
America's musical life; a history. Norton 2000 976p il hardcover o.p. pa $23.95
780.973
ISBN 0-393-04810-1; 978-0-393-32726-7 (pa); 0-393-32726-4 (pa)
LC 99-47565
This survey of music in America covers "blues, jazz, swing, pop, rock, hip hop . . . with economics and history as cultural backdrops. Well researched and sensitively constructed, this is highly recommended." Libr J
Includes bibliographical references

781.1 Music—Aesthetics, appreciation, taste

Copland, Aaron, 1900-1990
Music and imagination. Harvard Univ. Press 1952 116p pa $12.95 hardcover o.p.
781.1
1. Music appreciation 2. Music—History and criticism
ISBN 0-674-58915-7 (pa)
Charles Eliot Norton lectures, 1951-1952
The author "considers many of the problems of the contemporary composer . . . the qualities of the sensitive listener, the meaning of music, 'the sonorous image,' the creative mind and the interpretive mind, the pull of tradition and the attraction of innovation upon European composers of our day, the twelve-tone procedure, and distinctive contributions of American composers." Libr J

Forney, Kristine
The enjoyment of music; an introduction to perceptive listening; [by] Kristine Forney, Joseph Machlis. 10th ed. Norton 2007 xxxvii, 677p il $82.50 *
781.1
1. Music appreciation 2. Music—History and criticism
ISBN 978-0-393-17410-6; 0-393-17410-7
LC 2006-27598
First published 1955
Includes DVD
This guide to music appreciation brings together biographical, historical, and analytical material, from the music of the Middle Ages to contemporary music
Includes bibliographical references

Levitin, Daniel J.
This is your brain on music; the science of a human obsession. Dutton 2006 314p il $24.95
781.1
1. Music—Psychological aspects
ISBN 0-525-94969-0
LC 2006-9055
"How the brain processes all aspects of music is the subject of this book rooted in cognitive psychology, neuroscience, and the evolution of the brain." Booklist
The author's "snappy prose and relaxed style . . . will leave readers thinking about the contents of their iPods in an entirely new way." Publ Wkly
Includes bibliographical references

Sacks, Oliver W.
Musicophilia; tales of music and the brain; [by] Oliver Sacks. Knopf 2007 381p $26; pa $14.95
781.1
1. Music—Psychological aspects
ISBN 978-1-4000-4081-0; 1-400-04081-7; 978-1-4000-3353-9 (pa); 1-4000-3353-5 (pa)
LC 2007-6810
Sacks "examines the powers of music through the individual experiences of patients, musicians, and everyday people." Publisher's note
"With the sensibilities of the most caring professor, Sacks leads the reader through summer camps, concert halls, the odd hospital ward—even a Grateful Dead concert—in search of illumination. Using case studies in his trademark style, with the utmost compassion and empathy, and many personal details . . . Sacks lays out some of the intricate and highly complex neural 'machinery' of music that, he notes, is a uniquely human trait. Although many of the questions about the brain and musicality remain unanswered, and the fabric holding the stories together is loosely woven, the result is brilliant, stimulating, and enlightening." Lancet (North American Edition)
Includes bibliographical references

781.2 Elements of music

Piston, Walter, 1894-1976
Counterpoint. Norton 1947 235p music $41.75
781.2

Piston, Walter, 1894-1976—*Continued*

1. Counterpoint
ISBN 978-0-393-09728-3; 0-393-09728-5
This work covers the principles and techniques of counterpoint as represented in the works of 18th and 19th century composers

Harmony. 5th ed, revised and expanded by Mark DeVoto. Norton 1987 575p $59.95

781.2

1. Harmony
ISBN 0-393-95480-3   LC 86-23901
First published 1941
A presentation of the harmonic structures utilized by composers of the 18th and 19th centuries. Includes examples and exercises

781.6   Traditions of music

All music guide to classical music; the definitive guide to classical music; edited by Chris Woodstra, Gerald Brennan, Allen Schrott. Backbeat Books 2005 1607p $34.95

781.6

1. Music—Discography
ISBN 0-87930-865-6   LC 2005-23988
Also available online
Includes discographies
"The 1500 A-to-Z entries include established composers, performers, and ensembles of every style and era. . . . The final 25 pages are devoted to one-page discussions of form in classical music, historical periods (ten divisions), and genres such as ballet, film music, and opera. . . . This is an excellent resource for both classical novices and aficionados. There is simply no other single volume on the market as inclusive." Libr J

Classical music: the listener's companion; edited by Alexander Morin; foreword by Harold C. Schonberg. Backbeat Bks. 2002 1201p pa $29.95 *

781.6

1. Music—Discography 2. Music
ISBN 0-87930-638-6   LC 2001-52702
This "guide to classical music examines historical and contemporary works by American, British, German and other composers, some dating back to the 1500s. It focuses on the very finest recordings of symphonies, operas, choral pieces, chamber music, and more. . . Historical essays explore the classical repertory from medieval to electronic, Broadway to Hollywood, and more. . . . {This} guide also profiles conductors, artists, and instruments." Publisher's note
Includes discographies and bibliographical references

Horowitz, Joseph, 1948-
Classical music in America; a history of its rise and fall. W. W. Norton & Company 2005 606p il $39.95 *

781.6

1. Music—United States
ISBN 0-393-05717-8   LC 2004-27754
The author "argues that classical music in the United States is peculiarly performance-driven, and he traces a musical trajectory rising to its peak at the close of the nineteenth century and receding after World War I." Publisher's note
"As a comprehensive, convincing analysis of the contemporary dilemma, and a riveting portrait of the century and a half of events and personalities which brought it about, Mr Horowitz's account would be hard to beat." Economist
Includes bibliographical references

Plotkin, Fred
Classical music 101; a complete guide to learning and loving classical music. Hyperion 2002 673p pa $18.95

781.6

1. Music appreciation
ISBN 0-7868-8627-7   LC 2002-69075
This introduction to classical music "revolves almost entirely around the orchestra's instruments and the listening experience. [The author] presents material as coursework, and his strictures about really listening (as opposed to mere 'hearing') are well taken and certainly apply to all kinds of music. A valuable feature are the interviews with classical musicians interspersed throughout. . . . Recommended for libraries desiring an up-to-date and informative general introduction to classical music." Libr J
Includes discography and bibliographical references

The **rough** guide to classical music; edited by Joe Staines & Duncan Clark; written by Joe Staines . . . [et al.] 4th ed, rev & expanded. Rough Guides 2005 642p il pa $25.99

781.6

1. Music 2. Composers 3. Music appreciation 4. Sound recordings—Reviews
ISBN 978-1-8435-3247-7; 1-8435-3247-6

LC 2005-282348

First published 1998 with title: Classical music: the rough guide
This is an A-Z guide to composers, key works and top recordings. "Articles on such topics as sonata form, the concerto, atonality, and film music are also included." Publisher's note

781.62   Folk music

Allen, William Francis
Slave songs of the United States; the complete 1867 collection of slave songs; [collected and compiled] by William Francis Allen, Charles Pickard Ware, and Lucy McKim Garrison ; piano accompaniments by Irving Schlein; Peter Schlein, editor. Hal Leonard 2007 183p pa $15.95

781.62

1. African American music 2. Folk music—United States 3. Spirituals (Songs) 4. Slavery—United States—Songs
ISBN 978-1-42342-262-4 (pa); 1-42342-262-7 (pa)
"One of the first documentary collections of Negro folk songs was compiled in 1867 by William Francis Allen, Charles Pickard Ware and Lucy McKim Garrison. . . . This collection of 136 authentic folk songs of the Negro people revolutionized America's understanding of

Allen, William Francis—*Continued*
this music. The book, which contains spirituals, work songs, field hollers, soldier songs of Civil War days, and freedom songs, has become a classic of its kind. . . . In 1965, composer Irving Schlein created . . . piano settings for every song from the original edition. Chords for guitar have also been added to the musical notation." Publisher's note

American ballads and folk songs; [compiled by] John A. Lomax and Alan Lomax; with a foreword by George Lyman Kittredge. Dover Publications 1994 xxxix, 625p pa $21.95 *
                                                          781.62
  1. Ballads 2. Folk music—United States
  ISBN 0-486-28276-7 (pa); 978-0-486-28276-3 (pa)
  First published 1934 by MacMillan
  Treasury of authentic songs, many recorded on location by noted father-and-son folklorists. Music and lyrics for over 200 ballads about the railroads, mountain songs, chain gang songs, creole songs, songs about cocaine and whisky, reels, minstrel songs, songs of childhood and much more. Includes such time-honored favorites as John Henry, Goin Home, Frankie and Albert, Down in the Valley, Little Brown Jug, Alabama-Bound, Shortenin Bread, Skip to My Lou, Frog Went a-Courtin and a host of others. Notes about the origin of each melody, a bibliography and an index are included.

Courlander, Harold, 1908-1996
  Negro folk music U.S.A; [by] Harold Courlander. New ed. Dover Pub. 1992 324p il pa $11.95
                                                          781.62
  1. African American music 2. Folk music—United States
  ISBN 0-486-27350-4 (pa); 978-0-486-27350-1 (pa)
  First published 1963 by Columbia University Press
  The author "explores the essence and development of Negro folk music, both vocal and instrumental; examines it in terms of its historical and organic development; and relates it to its social setting and to the traditions out of which it took shape. . . . There is an appended section of forty-three songs. . . There is also a comparative discography of United States, West Indian, and African musical recordings." Publisher's note
  "An authoritative book. . . . Mr. Courlander's study is outstanding in that it has brought the material together in a well-organized, lucid volume that is well written." Libr J

Murdock, Lee
  Lake rhymes; folk songs of the Great Lakes region, a songbook and study guide with an 18-song companion CD; by Lee and Joann Murdock. Depot Recordings Publications 2004 146p il map $30   **781.62**
  1. Folk music—United States 2. Great Lakes region—Songs
  ISBN 978-0-97586-690-0; 0-97586-690-7
  An updated and expanded edition of Folk songs of the Great Lakes region, published 1989
  CD contents: The Erie Canal — The Illinois and Michigan Canal — Haul Away Joe — Rolling Home —

The Sailor's Alphabet — The Lumberman's Alphabet — Deep Blue Horizon — The Great Lakes Song — Follow the Drinkin' Gourd — Shenandoah-Shenandore — The Persia's Crew — Lost on the Lady Elgin — Yankee Brown — The Housewife's Lament — The Red Iron Ore — The Christmas Ship — The Bigler's Crew — The Crack Schooner Moonlight
  This "book, with an accompanying CD . . . covers songs of North America's Great Lakes and inland waterways. . . . The Murdocks explain the uses that songs were put to in and around the lakes. Each chapter includes vocabulary, maps, illustrations and photographs. . . . The accompanying CD includes all 18 songs covered in the text. . . . *Lake Rhymes* is a beautiful book, an easy-to-use book, and a book that will become a classic, both in the classroom and in the hands of folksingers." Sing Out! Magazine

Music of the sea; [compiled by] David Proctor; edited by Richard Baker. Rev. and updated ed. National Maritime Museum 2005 143p il pa $34.95   **781.62**
  1. Sea songs 2. Seafaring life
  ISBN 0-94806-561-3 (pa); 978-0-94806-561-3 (pa)
                                      LC 2006560588
  This book "explores the wide range of musical experience in the story of man's relationship with ships and the sea. . . . Researched with the help of major maritime museums in both Europe and America, *Music of the Sea* looks . . . at the weave of cultures how seafarers exchanged musical skills and knowledge with peoples of other lands, bringing new ideas and sounds back home." Publisher's note
  Includes bibliographical references

Our singing country; folk songs and ballads; collected and compiled by John A. Lomax and Alan Lomax; music editor, Ruth Crawford Seeger; introduction to the Dover edition by Judith Tick; includes bibliography by Harold W. Thompson. Dover 2000 pa $16.95 *
                                                          781.62
  1. Folk music—United States 2. Ballads
  ISBN 978-0-486-41089-0 (pa); 0-486-41089-7 (pa)
  First published 1941 by MacMillan
  Contents: Religious songs: Negro spirituals; White religious songs; The Holiness people — Social songs: White dance tunes; Negro game songs; Bahaman Negro songs; Lullabies; Whoppers; Courting songs; Old-time love songs; French songs and ballads from southwestern Louisiana — Men at work: Soldiers and sailors; Lumberjacks and teamsters; Cowboy songs; Railroaders and hobos; Miners' songs; Farmers of the South; Outlaws; Hollers and blues; Negro gang songs
  This includes melodies and words for tunes from all parts of the United States. Songs include spirituals, hollers, game songs, lullabies, courting songs, chain-gang work songs, Cajun airs, breakdowns, and many more. Includes over 200 authentic folk songs and ballads.

Sandburg, Carl, 1878-1967
  The American songbag; [compiled by] Carl Sandburg; introduction by Garrison Keillor. Harcourt Brace Jovanovich 1990 xxix, 495p pa $35   **781.62**

Sandburg, Carl, 1878-1967—*Continued*
1. Folk music—United States
ISBN 978-0-15-605650-2 (pa); 0-15-605650-X (pa)
A reissue of the title first published 1927
"Sandburg was not only a poet but also a noted collector and performer of American folk music. This anthology contains words and music to 290 songs that people have sung in the making of Americanca." Publisher's note

Sharp, Cecil James, 1859-1924
One hundred English folksongs; for medium voice. Dover Publications 1975 c1916 235p (The musician's library) pa $18.95 *   **781.62**
1. Ballads 2. Folk music—Great Britain
ISBN 978-0-48623-192-1 ; 0-48623-192-5
First published 1916
"Border ballads, folksongs, collected from all over Great Britain. Lord Bateman, Henry Martin, The Green Wedding, many others. Text, music, and piano accompaniment." Publisher's note

Strom, Yale
The book of Klezmer; the history, the music, the folklore. A Cappella Bks. 2002 381p il music $28   **781.62**
1. Klezmer music
ISBN 1-55652-445-5   LC 2002-2701
This history of Klezmer music is divided into "four chapters: 'From King David to Duvid the Klezmer,' 'From the Enlightenment to the Holocaust,' 'Klezmer in the New World, 1880-1960,' and 'From Zev to Zorn: The Masters of the Culture.' The first appendix, 'Klezmer Memories in the Memorial Books,' is one of the most moving sections, featuring a collection of commentaries on klezmer music and musicians from hundreds of memorial books written by Holocaust survivors." Libr J
Includes discography and bibliographical references

781.64   Western popular music

Best music writing 2008; Nelson George, guest editor; Daphne Carr, series editor. Da Capo Press 2008 337p pa $15.95 *   **781.64**
1. Popular music—History and criticism
ISBN 978-0-306-81734-2; 0-306-81734-9
Annual. First published 2000
A collection of writings on rock, hip-hop, jazz, pop, country and other genres.
Includes bibliographical references

Chang, Jeff
Can't stop, won't stop; a history of the hip-hop generation; introduction by D.J. Kool Herc. St. Martin's Press 2005 546p il hardcover o.p. pa $16   **781.64**
1. Rap music
ISBN 0-312-30143-X; 0-312-42579-1 (pa)
LC 2004-56656

This is "a history of hip-hop and the cultural movement the music inspired." N Y Times Book Rev
"A fascinating, far-reaching must for pop-music and pop-culture collections." Booklist
Includes bibliographical references, discography, and filmography

The **encyclopedia** of popular music; edited by Colin Larkin. 4th ed. Oxford University Press 2006 10v set $1,295   **781.64**
1. Popular music—Encyclopedias
ISBN 978-0-19-531373-4; 0-19-531373-9
LC 2006-18335
First published 1992 in four volumes by New England Pub. Assoc. with title: The Guinness encyclopedia of music
This set contains over 27,000 entries about persons, places and things associated with popular music. A song and album title index is included. Blues, country, R&B, soul, indie, new wave, techno, hip-hop and reggae are among the musical forms covered.
"This title will be invaluable for research." SLJ
Includes discographies and bibliographical references

George, Nelson
Hip hop America. Viking 1998 226p hardcover o.p. pa $15   **781.64**
1. Rap music 2. Popular culture—United States
ISBN 0-670-87153-2; 978-0-14-303515-2 (pa); 0-14-303515-0 (pa)   LC 98-23414
A social and economic history of the rap music industry and hip-hop culture
"This is an invaluable, entertaining and well written account from one who has not only witnessed the evolution of hip-hop but who, through his own passion and devotion to it as a critic, has had a hand in shaping it as well." N Y Times Book Rev
Includes bibliographical references

Hawkins, Martin
A shot in the dark; making records in Nashville 1945-1955. Vanderbilt University Press 2006 416p $65   **781.64**
1. Popular music 2. Music industry 3. Nashville (Tenn.)
ISBN 0-8265-1532-0   LC 2006003517
In this look at the early Nashville music industry, Hawkins "profiles the pioneering producers and entrepreneurs who took a vibrant local music scene and presented it to the world for the first time. His focus is on the years before rock'n'roll took off (1945-55), when the music that was recorded and promoted ranged from dance band to gospel, from rhythm and blues to country; promoter-producers like Bill Beasley, Jim Bulleit, and Owen Bradley get their due." Libr J
"Only deep-dyed, history-minded pop fans will fully appreciate Hawkins' achievement, but the book is so handsome and so full of entrancing period photos that casual readers will find lots of good browsing in it." Booklist
Includes bibliographical references

Myers, Mitch

The boy who cried freebird; rock-and-roll fables and sonic storytelling. HarperEntertainment 2007 321p $25.95 **781.64**

1. Popular music 2. Popular culture—United States
ISBN 978-0-06-113901-7; 0-06-113901-7

LC 2006-49774

A "collection of essays, short stories, artist profiles, and rock fables. Myers' pieces run the gamut from the serious, such as an examination of the legendary recording Art Blakely's Jazz Messengers with Thelonious Monk, to the entertaining, including a fictionalized account of traveling back in time to attend a historic Grateful Dead concert in the story 'Back to the Fillmore.' Myers covers blues, gospel, jazz, psychedelia, and ambient sound, all in prose that keeps a fervent tempo and pulses with electricity." Booklist

Schoemer, Karen

Great pretenders; my strange love affair with '50s pop music. Free Press 2006 241p $25

781.64

1. Popular music
ISBN 978-0-7432-7246-9; 0-7432-7246-3

LC 2005-58002

The author profiles "seven former pop idols of the late 1950s and early 1960s: Connie Francis, Fabian, Pat Boone, Patti Page, Tommy Sands, Georgia Gibbs, and Frankie Laine." Publisher's note

This book "offers a truly unique background to a grossly underappreciated era in American music." N Y Times Book Rev

Includes bibliographical references

Watkins, S. Craig (Samuel Craig)

Hip hop matters; politics, pop culture, and the struggle for the soul of a movement. Beacon Press 2005 295p $24.95; pa $16 * **781.64**

1. Rap music
ISBN 0-8070-0982-2; 0-8070-0986-5 (pa)

LC 2004-24187

This book "focuses on the . . . battles being waged in politics, pop culture, and academe to assert greater control over the [hip hop] movement." Publisher's note

The author "presents a concise, clear history of the hip-hop movement in the US and uses it as a springboard for discussion of contemporary issues of politics, pop culture, and struggle." Choice

Includes bibliographical references

Whitburn, Joel

The Billboard book of top 40 hits; [compiled by] Joel Whitburn. Rev. and expanded 8th ed. Billboard Bks. 2004 852p il pa $27.95

781.64

ISBN 978-0-8230-7499-0; 0-8230-7499-4

LC 2004-104967

First published 1983

A guide to all single recordings that have made Billboard's Top 40 lists since 1955. Entries are alphabetical by artist and give such information as date the record made the charts, number of weeks on the charts, highest position, etc. Biographical data and trivia on most of the artists are also included

781.642 Country music

All music guide to country; the definitive guide to country music; edited by Vladimir Bogdanov, Chris Woodstra, and Stephen Thomas Erlewine. 2nd ed. Backbeat Bks. 2003 700p pa $27.95

781.642

ISBN 0-8793-0760-0

LC 2003-62827

Also available online

First published 1997 by Miller Freeman

"Featuring concise career biographies of more than 1,000 performers, both individuals and groups, the guide covers the entire range of country music from the early trailblazers like Jimmie Rodgers and the Sons of the Pioneers to the newest stars like LeAnn Rimes. It also covers a broad array of subgenres, ranging from traditional country to contemporary alternative country. . . . Albums considered to be essential recordings for any good country collection and those recommended as a first purchase for the particular performer are separately labeled. More than 5,500 recordings are included, making this an excellent resource for collectors." Am Ref Books Annu, 1998 {entry for 1997 edition}

The **Encyclopedia** of country music; the ultimate guide to the music; compiled by the staff of the Country Music Hall of Fame and Museum; edited by Paul Kingsbury with the assistance of Laura Garrard, Daniel Cooper, and John Rumble. Oxford Univ. Press 1998 634p il hardcover o.p. pa $39.95 **781.642**

1. Country music—Encyclopedias
ISBN 0-19-511671-2; 978-0-19-517608-7 (pa); 0-19-517608-1 (pa)

LC 97-51362

"Interspersed with the biographical entries are historical and sociological essays on the literature of country music, country songwriting, gospel, folk and popular music connections, and even touring and costuming. Thirteen appendixes cover the Country Music Hall of Fame, radio stations, and best-selling country albums." Libr J

Includes bibliographical references

Escott, Colin

The Grand ole opry; the making of an American icon; Brenda Colladay, photo editor. Center Street 2006 250p il $24.99 **781.642**

1. Grand ole opry (Radio program) 2. Country music
ISBN 978-1-931722-86-5; 1-931722-86-2

LC 2006-7796

"Escott's overview of the long-running Saturday-night performance showcase takes the form of oral history. The preponderance of the text consists of statements by Grand Ole Opry producers, sponsors, and stars, with the older comments drawn from old books and newspaper stories and the newer from Escott's interviews. . . . With decade-by-decade lists of the Opry's members and scads of performance photos, it's a honey of a book for every American library." Booklist

Harris, Steve, 1960-

Texas troubadours; Texas singer songwriters; foreword by Kinky Friedman. University of Texas Press 2007 127p il (Jack and Doris Smothers series in Texas history, life, and culture) $39.95
781.642

1. Country music 2. Musicians—Portraits

ISBN 978-0-292-71324-6; 0-292-71324-X

LC 2006-17296

"Over six years, Harris travelled the Lone Star State with his 4x5 camera and made dozens of evocative portraits of singers, also gathering handwritten quotes from each of them (printed in the book along with a typeset version of each quote to help decipher the scribbles). The quotes range from pithy—'Simplicity don't need to be greased,' writes Billy Joe Shaver; 'I'd rather be a dead Gram Parsons than a live Garth Brooks,' Kinky Friedman opines—to mysterious: 'Up on the ridge, there's a fire about to burn,' says Joe Ely. It seems that only one artist, the notoriously cranky Steve Earle, failed to submit any words, instead offering a steely, let'sfinishthisthing gaze at the camera. But most of these pictures are warm and atmospheric, reflecting lots of wizened faces that still show a passion for their work and a love of their homeland." PopPhoto.com

Jennings, Dana Andrew

Sing me back home; love, death, and country music; [by] Dana Jennings. Faber and Faber 2008 257p $24
781.642

1. Country music—History and criticism

ISBN 978-0-86547-960-9; 0-86547-960-7

LC 2007-47955

The author "relates the cruel and bitter desperation, depression, alcoholism, infidelity, physical abuse, and poverty of his youth to the country music of the period (1950-70) by Johnny Cash, Patsy Cline, Merle Haggard, Loretta Lynn, Little Jimmy Dickens, Faron Young, Lefty Frizzell, Dolly Parton, and others." Libr J

This "quirky, endearing combination memoir, family history, music criticism, and love-of-place offering, made up of short, punchy chapters and sharp observations about country's appeal and how country has expressed the inchoate emotions of its largely rural following, essentiallypresents the music as the portrayal of a way of life and a way of being." Booklist

Includes discography and bibliographical references

Russell, Tony

Country music originals; the legends & the lost. Oxford University Press 2007 258p il $29.95
781.642

1. Country musicians 2. Country music

ISBN 978-0-19-532509-6   LC 2007-8471

This "book contains biographical sketches and selected CD discographies for a host of mostly pre-1950 country artists, some famous (e.g., Jimmie Rodgers, the Carter Family) and some considerably more obscure (e.g., Chris Bouchillon, Narmour & Smith). What ties all of these artists together is their originality, either as often-imitated innovators or as one-of-a-kind curiosities." Libr J

"Russell has accomplished a spectacular feat in that he has written a thorough reference book that is as pleasing to read as the best of narrative nonfiction." Publ Wkly

Includes bibliographical references

781.643   Blues

Encyclopedia of the blues; Edward Komara, editor. Routledge 2006 2v il set $295 *
781.643

1. Blues music—Encyclopedias

ISBN 0-415-92699-8   LC 2005-44346

In addition to "biographical entries, this encyclopedia also includes entries for important record labels, instruments, styles, geographic regions, aspects of the business, and additional topics." Choice

"Essential for any library collecting the history of the blues." Libr J

Includes bibliographical references

Gioia, Ted

Delta blues; the life and times of the Mississippi Masters who revolutionized American music; artwork by Neil Harpe. W. W. Norton 2008 449p il $27.95
781.643

1. Blues music

ISBN 978-0-393-06258-8; 0-393-06258-9

LC 2008-9412

Gioia describes the "beginnings of the Delta sound with Charley Patton and former Parchman inmates Son House and Bukka White. He relates the stories of such obscure Delta artists as Tommy Johnson and Big Joe Williams before delivering the bulk of the book, which describes the lives and influences of Delta blues icons Robert Johnson, Muddy Waters, Howlin' Wolf, B.B. King, and John Lee Hooker. Gioia ends with a chapter about the rediscovery of Delta legends by rabid blues collectors during the 1960s and then oddly leaps to 1990s performers such as Chris Thomas King and Junior Kimbrough in the last few pages. . . . Though presenting little new information and not geared for the blues fanatic, this is an excellent introduction to Delta blues for the novice and the general reader." Libr J

Includes bibliographical references

Lomax, Alan, 1915-2002

The land where the blues began. New Press 2002 539p il pa $21.95 *
781.643

1. Blues music 2. African American music 3. African Americans—Mississippi

ISBN 1-56584-739-3; 978-1-56584-739-2

LC 2004-268632

First published 1993 by Pantheon

Includes audio CD

This is an account of the folklorist and musicologist's travels in the Mississippi Delta in the 1940s as he recorded the work of African American blues musicians.

"If it were a novel, Alan Lomax's long-awaited account of his adventures in the Mississippi Delta would be called 'sprawling' and a 'must read.' . . . It is as delightful and hard to put down as any fictional epic." Booklist

Includes bibliographical references, discography and filmography

Nothing but the blues; the music and the musicians; {edited by} Lawrence Cohn. Abbeville Press 1993 432p il pa $39.95 hardcover o.p. **781.643**
1. Blues music
ISBN 0-7892-0607-2 (pa)   LC 93-2791
This "illustrated compilation of articles by 10 notable writers examines the origins of blues and the music's various styles and artists, including women." Booklist
Includes discography and bibliographical references

Russell, Tony
The Penguin guide to blues recordings; [by] Tony Russell and Chris Smith, with Neil Slaven, Ricky Russell and Joe Faulkner. Penguin 2006 923p pa $30   **781.643**
1. Blues music—Discography 2. Sound recordings—Reviews
ISBN 978-0-14-051384-4; 0-14-051384-1
"Listing more than 1000 blues artists in alphabetical order with a final section for compilations, the editors start each entry with a brief but adequate biography, following with the name and date of a recording, the label, and the musicians on the session. They . . . concentrate on artists who play primarily acoustic and electric blues, among them Charley Patton, Bessie Smith, B.B. King, and Buddy Guy. They critically and carefully rate nearly 6000 CDs on a one to four-star scale (with a special indicator for essential recordings), applying tongue-in-cheek wit and assigning ratings in a meaningful way to help the discriminating blues listener make a decision about his or her next purchase." Libr J

781.644   Soul music

Danielsen, Anne
Presence and pleasure; the funk grooves of James Brown and Parliament. Wesleyan University Press 2006 262p il (Music/culture) $65; pa $24.95
        781.644
1. Brown, James 2. Parliament (Musical group) 3. Funk (Music)
ISBN   978-0-8195-6822-9;   0-8195-6822-8; 978-0-8195-6823-6 (pa); 0-8195-6823-6 (pa)
        LC 2006-10987
"Danielson concentrates on the golden age of funk in the late 1960s and the 1970s, focusing on two of the era's artists who made a substantial impact on the landscape of popular music: James Brown and George Clinton/Parliament." Publisher's note
The author "brings a unique perspective to this book. . . . Her discussion of funk comes from the dual angles of musicologist and longtime performer." Choice
Includes bibliographical references

781.646   Reggae

Bradley, Lloyd
This is reggae music; the story of Jamaica's music. Grove Press 2001 c2000 572p il pa $17
        781.646
1. Reggae music
ISBN 0-8021-3828-4   LC 2001-33462
First published 2000 in the United Kingdom with title: Brass culture: when reggae was king
This "account identifies and traces the genealogy of reggae. . . . Focusing on reggae as a commerical entity rather than as a means of proselytizing Rastafarianism, Bradley nevertheless describes Rasta influences on it and how it affected Jamaican culture." Booklist
Presented "in a witty and engaging manner. . . . For enthusiasts, this book is fabulous." Libr J
Includes bibliographical references

781.65   Jazz

The **Billboard** illustrated encyclopedia of jazz & blues; [contributors,] Ted Drozdowski . . . [et al.]; general editor, Howard Mandel; foreword by John Scofield. Watson Guptill 2005 352p il $45   **781.65**
1. Jazz music—Encyclopedias 2. Blues music—Encyclopedias
ISBN 0-8230-8266-0   LC 2005-924576
This book "chronicles the history of jazz and blues from their roots to the present day." Booklist
"This volume will serve as a quick introduction to blues or jazz for the uninitiated or for those wishing to learn about musicians unfamiliar to them." Choice
Includes bibliographical references

Cook, Richard, 1957-2007
The Penguin guide to jazz recordings; [by] Richard Cook and Brian Morton. 9th ed. Penguin 2008 pa $37.50   **781.65**
1. Jazz music—Discography
ISBN 978-0-14-102327-4; 0-14-102327-9
Biannual. First published 1992
"Entries include very brief descriptions of the artists and a list of their recordings, with reviews and ratings by the authors. The lengths of the CD entries vary from very short (label, catalog number, issue date, and performers) to extensive, multiparagraph descriptions of the album's history, reception, and individual songs. The authors are clearly devout jazz historians, and the character of the entries is as much admiring as it is strictly factual. Their detailed descriptions of albums, songs, and even artists' tone colors and interpretations within specific songs are testament to their expertise." Booklist

Crouch, Stanley
Considering genius; writings on jazz. Basic Civitas Books 2006 359p $27.50 *
        781.65
1. Jazz music—History and criticism
ISBN 0-465-01517-4   LC 2006-2225

Crouch, Stanley—*Continued*

"This collection brings together a healthy sampling of [Crouch's] jazz writings dating from 1977 to the present. A long and spirited prologue, 'Jazz Me Blues,' lays out Crouch's jazz aesthetic, but he really shows his stuff in the essays on particular musicians, combining trenchant analysis of the artist with fascinating biographical material and feeling free to speculate at will about the psychology and inner lives of such jazz greats as Miles Davis, Thelonious Monk, and John Coltrane. . . . Essential reading for jazz fans." Booklist

Friedwald, Will, 1961-

Jazz singing; America's great voices from Bessie Smith to bebop and beyond. Da Capo Press 1996 505p il pa $18.50   **781.65**

1. Jazz music 2. Singers 3. Jazz vocals—History and criticism

ISBN 0-306-80712-2   LC 96-23837

First published 1990 by Scribner, this edition has a new discography

"Starting with blues singers who laid the foundations for jazz-oriented popular singing, the author follows the development of this vocal style from Bing Crosby and Louis Armstrong through a host of performers to the present day." Publ Wkly

"This is an absolutely essential book for anybody who cares in the slightest about adult popular music." Booklist

Includes discography

Gennari, John

Blowin' hot and cool; jazz and its critics. University of Chicago Press 2006 480p $35

       781.65

1. Jazz music—History and criticism

ISBN 0-226-28922-2   LC 2005-30539

This is a "history of jazz criticism from the 1920s to the present." Publisher's note

"Gennari's book does for jazz critics what most of them were unable to do for themselves, but with a postmodern twist: The scholar demystifies and historicizes the journalists. The first sustained scholarly book exclusively about jazz criticism—and, not least, about the passions that have driven and surrounded it—Blowin' Hot and Cool is thorough, absorbing and original, an obsessive study of professional obsessives that will circumvent the need for any other." Nation

Includes bibliographical references

Giddins, Gary

Visions of jazz; the first century. Oxford Univ. Press 1998 690p pa $18.95 hardcover o.p.

       781.65

1. Jazz musicians 2. Jazz music—History and criticism

ISBN 0-19-513241-6 (pa)   LC 98-12199

"Alongside his virtuoso considerations of Ellington, Monk, Mingus, and the predictable greats, Giddins illuminates the contributions to be found in the likes of Al Jolson's minstrel posing and Stan Kenton's florid kitsch. His writing, like the music he loves, is joyously polyphonic, with history, legend, musicology, biography, and performance all rising out of the mix." New Yorker

Weather bird; jazz at the dawn of its second century; Gary Giddins. Oxford University Press 2004 xxiv, 632p $35   **781.65**

1. Jazz music—History and criticism

ISBN 0-19-515607-2   LC 2004-654

"This book collects more than 140 essays, articles, and reviews that Giddins wrote from 1990 to November 2003. . . . The breadth and depth of his knowledge is extremely impressive, his ear is astounding, and his masterly style routinely achieves the near impossible in writing engagingly about something that inherently eludes description." Libr J

Kahn, Ashley

The house that Trane built; the story of Impulse Records. Norton 2006 338p il $29.95

       781.65

1. Coltrane, John, 1926-1967 2. Impulse Records (Firm) 3. Jazz music

ISBN 0-393-05879-4   LC 2005-037218

"Following the path of its star musician John Coltrane, Impulse Records cut a creative swath through the 1960s and 1970s with the politically charged avant-garde jazz that defined the label's musical and spiritual identity. The House That Trane Built tells the story of the label, balancing tales of individual passion, artistic vision, and commercial motivation." Publisher's note

The author "offers a fascinating insider's view of the sessions that produced not only Coltrane's classics but also top-grade albums by both fiery radicals and such timeless stars as Duke Ellington, Coleman Hawkins and Benny Carter." Economist

Morgenstern, Dan

Living with jazz; a reader; edited by Sheldon Meyer. Pantheon Books 2004 712p $35

       781.65

1. Jazz music—History and criticism

ISBN 0-375-42072-X   LC 2004-43432

This is a compilation of "nearly half a century of Morgenstern's profiles, liner notes, record and show reviews and other musings. . . . Morgenstern reminisces about his introduction to jazz in a brief opening memoir, then segues into lengthy sections on his greatest heroes, Louis Armstrong and Duke Ellington. . . . His exuberant characterizations make this monumental volume a stimulating guide to jazz in the second half of the 20th century." Publ Wkly

The **New** Grove dictionary of jazz; edited by Barry Kernfeld. 2nd ed. Grove's Dictionaries Inc. 2002 3v set $295 *   **781.65**

1. Jazz music

ISBN 1-56159-284-6   LC 2001-40794

First published 1988 in two volumes

This reference to jazz and jazz musicians includes "more than 7750 entries. . . . [It covers] jazz styles, instruments, record labels, nicknames, guilds and associations, jazz language, libraries and archives, false fingering techniques for horns, festivals, titles of films containing jazz scenes, a list of contrafacts . . . and even biographies of a few jazz writers and critics." Libr J

Includes bibliographical references and discographies

Ratliff, Ben

Jazz: a critic's guide to the 100 most important recordings. Times Bks. 2002 xx, 250p il (New York Times essential library) pa $16

781.65

ISBN 0-8050-7068-0   LC 2002-69551

The author "presents essays on what he considers the 100 most important jazz recordings. In each, he discusses a recording's merits and shortcomings and includes a list of its performers. . . . As a guide for the uninitiated it is essential for academic music libraries and public libraries large and small. It would also be most useful for collection development librarians building a well-rounded jazz CD collection." Libr J

Ward, Geoffrey C.

Jazz; a history of America's music; based on a documentary film by Ken Burns written by Geoffrey C. Ward; with a preface by Ken Burns. Knopf 2000 489p il $65; pa $29.95

781.65

1. Jazz music
ISBN 0-679-44551-X; 0-679-76539-5 (pa)

LC 00-22604

Companion volume to PBS series of the same title

The authors "have assembled a comprehensive history with a focus on the musicians and the sociology of jazz. . . . The short articles by Wynton Marsalis, Dan Morgenstern, Gerald Early, Stanley Crouch, and Gary Giddins, which are woven into the text, provide a . . . specific focus on a number of jazz's aspects." Libr J

"The illustrations are copious, including about 500 pieces and running from cover to cover; the text, picture captions, and sidebars reflect the research that went into the six-year project. A very competent and lovingly rendered history." Booklist

Includes bibliographical references

781.66   Rock (Rock 'n' roll)

Bangs, Lester, 1948-1982

Mainlines, blood feasts and bad taste; a Lester Bangs reader; edited by John Morthland. Anchor Books 2003 409p pa $15.95   **781.66**

1. Rock music—History and criticism
ISBN 978-0375-71367-5; 0-375-71367-0

LC 2003-40392

"Here are excerpts from an autobiographical piece Bangs wrote as a teenager, travel essays, and, of course, the music pieces, essays, and criticism covering everything from titans like Miles Davis, Lou Reed, and the Rolling Stones to esoteric musicians like Brian Eno and Captain Beefheart." Publisher's note

Mothland includes includes Bangs's "riffs on jazz, heretofore not seen by many eyes. Readers will be reminded of what Bangs . . . should really be famous for: his lust for life and 'soul' music, any tune that hits a nerve and the heart at the same time. Truly, this is a time capsule of when pop music still crackled and people held the stuff to an emotional standard." Libr J

Psychotic reactions and carburetor dung; edited by Greil Marcus. Knopf 1987 386p hardcover o.p. pa $16   **781.66**

1. Rock music—History and criticism
ISBN 0-394-53896-X; 0-679-72045-6 (pa)

LC 87-45122

This is a collection of "essays, record reviews and rock star profiles that [Bangs] wrote for publications such as Rolling Stone, The Village Voice and the Detroit rock magazine Creem, which [he] edited between 1970 and 1976." N Y Times Book Rev

"For rockers whose tastes demand more than Madonna and who remember back before Bruce, this is a gem." Libr J

The **Beatles** anthology. Chronicle Bks. 2000 367p il $60; pa $35   **781.66**

1. Beatles
ISBN 0-8118-2684-8; 0-8118-3636-3 (pa)

LC 00-23685

The story of the Beatles as "told through quotes from John, Paul, George, and Ringo, as well as the group's closest aides: George Martin, Neil Aspinall, and Derek Taylor. . . . The density of the text is daunting, but the book's browsability makes it as appealing to casual readers as it is indispensable to Beatlemaniacs." Libr J

Includes bibliographical references

Beaujon, Andrew

Body piercing saved my life; inside the phenomenon of Christian rock. Da Capo Press 2006 291p il $16.95   **781.66**

1. Christian rock music
ISBN 0-306-81457-9; 978-0-306-81457-0

LC 2006-6254

The author "chronicles the Christian rock subculture, beginning with the 'Jesus People' of the early 1970s to its substantial popularity today. . . . This important, well-written study of the Christian rock phenomenon brings the personalities to life." Libr J

Includes bibliographical references

Christgau, Robert

Grown up all wrong; 75 great rock and pop artists from vaudeville to techno. Harvard Univ. Press 1998 495p $32.50; pa $18.95

781.66

1. Rock music—History and criticism
ISBN   978-0-674-44318-1;   0-674-44318-7; 978-0-674-00382-8 (pa); 0-674-00382-9 (pa)

LC 98-25779

Christgau's subjects "include Elvis Presley, the punk girl band Sleater-Kinney, the rap artist KRS-One, the country singer Geroge Jones and the minstrel singer Emmett Miller, among many, many others. He writes on each with equal erudition, examining the artists and their music as both cultural products and influences." N Y Times Book Rev

Crampton, Luke

Rock & roll year by year; {by} Luke Crampton & Dafydd Rees. DK Publishing 2003 599p il hardcover o.p. pa $30   **781.66**

     1. Rock music

     ISBN 0-7894-9649-6; 0-7566-1334-5 (pa)

                       LC 2003-51655

Contents: 1950s: the birth of rock 'n' roll; 1960s: from Mersey beat to flower power; 1970s: a blend of glam rock, glitter, and punk; 1980s: the decade of MTV and Live Aid; 1990s: from Seattle grunge to girl power; 2000s: the new breed

"Beginning with January 1950 . . . rock history is chronicled month by month through December 2002 . . . In addition to the facts, figures, and personalities highlighted within each month, lively essays summarize significant developments of each decade, charts compare No. 1 hits in the U.S. and U.K. during identical periods, and entertaining sidebars provide expanded commentary and quotations. Every page includes fascinating historical photographs and color images of artifacts from the {Rock and Roll Hall of Fame Museum}." SLJ

Epting, Chris, 1961-

Led Zeppelin crashed here; the rock and roll landmarks of North America. Santa Monica Press 2007 327p il map pa $16.95   **781.66**

     1. Rock music 2. United States—Description and travel

     ISBN 978-1-59580-018-3; 1-59580-018-2

                       LC 2007-6246

"Discover where Bob Dylan's motorcycle crashed, where Elvis Presley first performed, where Ozzy Osbourne bit the head off a bat and the real location of Bruce Springsteen's E Street. The book includes nearly 600 landmarks along with historical information, trivia, photos and backstage lore. Chapters cover topics such as sex and drugs, live performance locations, recording sites, blues and jazz shrines, places where homicides and suicides occurred, and rock and roll museums. There's also a list of 100 classic road trip songs, 100 road trip albums and 30 great North American music stores. An appendix lists rock and roll landmarks by state." Salt Lake Tribune

Klosterman, Chuck, 1972-

Killing yourself to live; 85% of a true story. Scribner 2005 245p $23; pa $14   **781.66**

     1. Rock musicians 2. Death

     ISBN   0-7432-6445-2;   978-0-7432-6445-7; 0-7432-6446-0 (pa); 978-0-7432-6446-4 (pa)

                       LC 2005-42498

The author describes his journey "across the United States visiting the places where famous rock-related deaths occurred." N Y Times (Late N Y Ed)

"Klosterman's keen eye for American pop-cultural themes and undercurrents facilitates thoughtful observation, and his prose brings those themes and undercurrents together in strange, fresh ways. A treat for the adventurous." Booklist

Miller, Jim, 1947-

Flowers in the dustbin; the rise of rock and roll, 1947-1977. Simon & Schuster 1999 415p il hardcover o.p. pa $26.95   **781.66**

     1. Rock music

     ISBN 978-0-684-86560-7; 0-684-86560-2 (pa)

                       LC 99-21077

Miller "explores the cultural underpinnings of Fifties and Sixties rock'n'roll. In dozens of brief chapters, he identifies turning points in rock history: the rise of jump blues, the introduction of Top 40 radio, Alan Freed's rock'n'roll dances, Dick Clark's *American Bandstand*, and the payola scandal. Miller pays special attention to Elvis Presley and the Beatles." Libr J

Includes discography

The **Rolling** Stone illustrated history of rock & roll; the definitive history of the most important artists and their music; edited by Anthony DeCurtis and James Henke with Holly George-Warren; original editor: Jim Miller. {new ed}. Random House 1992 710p il pa $36.95   **781.66**

     1. Rock music

     ISBN 0-679-73728-6   LC 92-6339

     First published 1976

This history of four decades of rock music includes essays and photographs covering individual artists, groups, trends and styles

Spicer, Al, 1950-

The rough guide to punk. Penguin 2006 378p il (Rough guides reference) $24.99   **781.66**

     1. Punk rock music

     ISBN 1-84353-473-8; 978-1-84353-473-0

                       LC 2006-299066

This book is divided "into three main sections: a time line (1965-85) of the movement, 250-plus A-to-Z entries (which make up the bulk of the book), and a brief 'Punkology' media guide of further resources. . . . Perfect for the Hot Topic-haunting preteen, the crusty with the thinning mohawk, and all serious enthusiasts of the seedy underbelly of popular music." Libr J

Includes bibliographical references, discography, and filmography

Strong, M. C. (Martin Charles), 1960-

The great rock discography. 6th ed. Canongate 2002 1185p $50; pa $30   **781.66**

     ISBN 1-8419-5311-3; 1-8419-5312-1 (pa)

     First published 1994

This work contains: discographies listing every track by more than 1,000 groups; band histories, lineup changes, career milestones; catalog numbers for ordering recordings and evaluating collections; top U.S. and U.K. chart positions; name changes, breakups, solo albums

782 Vocal music

The **Cambridge** companion to singing; edited by John Potter. Cambridge Univ. Press 2000 286p il (Cambridge companions to music) hardcover o.p. pa $24   **782**
1. Singing 2. Vocal music
ISBN 0-521-62225-5; 0-521-62709-5 (pa)
                                        LC 99-32948
"Articles on popular traditions, including world music, rock, rap, and jazz, describe the major singers and song-writers in each. Then come histories of theatrical singing encompassing twentieth-century stage and screen artists, the beginnings of opera, and grand opera. The growth of choral music and art songs is traced next. . . . The last and largest section concerns performance practices in choral and ensemble singing, medieval singing techniques, singing in the pre-romantic and contemporary periods, teaching singing, children's singing, and vocal production. . . . The guide covers its wide range of topics accessibly as well as thoroughly for a one-volume work." Booklist
Includes bibliographical references

782.25 Sacred songs

Encyclopedia of American gospel music; W.K. McNeil, editor. Routledge 2005 489p il $150 *
                                        782.25
1. Gospel music—Encyclopedias
ISBN 0-415-94179-2   LC 2005-44994
The editor "goes beyond his core subject—American gospel music—to cover awakenings and revivals from the 18th to the 20th century, contemporary Christian artists, record labels, religious organizations, major song collections like The Sacred Harp, and musical styles (e.g., spirituals). . . . McNeil's title will likely become the definitive work on the subject and fills a gap in a field that has had only sporadic reference documentation." Libr J
Includes discography and bibliographical references

782.27 Hymns

American hymns old and new; [compiled by] Albert Christ-Janer, Charles W. Hughes, Charles Sprague Smith. Columbia Univ. Press 1980 838p music $104   **782.27**
1. Hymns
ISBN 0-231-03458-X
Also published as a two-volume set, with v2 consisting of notes on the hymns and biographies, compiled by Charles W. Hughes (o.p.)
This is an interdenominational compilation of 625 hymns sung in America since 1615

782.28 Carols

The **New** Oxford book of carols; edited by Hugh Keyte and Andrew Parrott; associate editor, Clifford Bartlett. Oxford Univ. Press 1992 xxxiv, 702p music pa $34.95 hardcover o.p.
                                        782.28
1. Carols
ISBN 0-19-353322-7 (pa)   LC 92-756468
First published 1928 with title: The Oxford book of carols
This book contains over 300 settings of sacred and secular carols spanning the Catholic and Protestant traditions. The selections are drawn from: folk carols, medieval Latin songs, English medieval carols, Lutheran hymnody, and English "gallery" and American "primitive" carols

782.42 Songs

The **Books** of the American Negro spirituals; edited by James Weldon Johnson and J. Rosamond Johnson. Da Capo Press 2002 pa $25
                                        782.42
1. Spirituals (Songs) 2. African American music
ISBN 0-306-81202-9
A reprint of the volumes first published separately in 1925 and 1926 by Viking and reissued in the present format 1940
Includes "The book of American Negro spirituals" (1925) and "The second book of Negro spirituals" (1926). Contains words and music of 120 spirituals

The **Children's** song index, 1978-1993; compiled by Kay Laughlin, Pollyanne Frantz, Ann Branton. Libraries Unlimited 1996 153p $40
                                        782.42
1. Songs—Indexes
ISBN 1-56308-332-9   LC 95-40236
"This book indexes more than 2,500 songs from 77 song books listed in *Cumulative Book Index*, 1977-1994. . . . [Songs are indexed] by song title, first line, or subject. . . . A quick-reference tool for those who need to locate in which songbook a particular song can be found, this index encompasses songs appealing to children pre-kindergarten through middle school." Booklist
Includes bibliographical references

Ferguson, Gary Lynn
Song finder; a title index to 32,000 popular songs in collections, 1854-1992; compiled by Gary Lynn Ferguson under the auspices of the State Library of Louisiana. Greenwood Press 1995 344p (Music reference collection) $88.95
                                        782.42
1. Songs—Indexes
ISBN 0-313-29470-4   LC 95-9936
Comp. from coll. held by State Lib. of La.
In this index "the song collections include theater, folk, children's, African American, military, patriotic, pop, rock, and country music. Movie and TV themes ('M*A*S*H Theme Song') and advertising jingles

Ferguson, Gary Lynn—*Continued*

('Chiquita Banana') are also covered. . . . It provides indexing to so many songs and books not covered elsewhere that it is a useful and necessary addition to the reference collection." Booklist

Includes bibliographical references

Gioia, Ted

Work songs; [by] Theodore Gioia. Duke University Press 2006 352p $27.95

782.42

1. Labor—Songs 2. Folk music
ISBN 0-8223-3726-6; 978-0-8223-3726-3

LC 2005026241

Gioia "poignantly tells the story of work songs sung by everyone from prehistoric hunters to today's consumers. His task involved drawing on multilayered and diverse resources that include travel literature, slave narratives, historical accounts and personal journals, myths and legends, biographies, and labor union writings; the focus is on the rhythms, melodies, and lyrics of music that has accompanied such tasks as raising and lowering sails, felling trees, and weaving and sewing garments. . . . This book provides an opportunity to re-experience the history and dignity of our human toils. Highly recommended for public and academic libraries." Libr J

Includes bibliographical references

Gray, Michael, 1946-

The Bob Dylan encyclopedia. Continuum 2006 832p il $40

782.42

1. Dylan, Bob, 1941-
ISBN 0-82646-933-7; 978-0-82646-933-5

LC 2006-12728

This book "covers many of his songs, albums, and film work, as well as just about every personality associated with the folk singer/rock star. . . . Overall, this is an amazingly well-researched and surprisingly readable work." Libr J

Includes bibliographical references

Guthrie, Woody, 1912-1967

The Woody Guthrie songbook. Hal Leonard Corporation 2000 61p il pa $10.95

782.42

1. Songs 2. Folk music
ISBN 978-0-63402-405-4 (pa); 0-63402-405-1 (pa)

This features 48 of Guthrie's songs along with a bio, introduction, complete lyrics, a discography, photos and sketches. Songs include: Jig Along Home, Roll On, Columbia, Sinking of the Reuben James, This Land Is Your Land, Tom Joad and more.

Havlice, Patricia Pate

Popular song index. Scarecrow Press 1975 933p

782.42

1. Songs—Indexes
First supplement (1978) $60 (ISBN 0-8108-1099-9);
Second supplement (1984) $65 (ISBN 0-8108-1642-3);
Third supplement (1989) $72 (ISBN 0-8108-2202-4);
Fourth supplement 2v $210 (ISBN 0-8108-5260-8)

"Indexes 301 song collections published between 1940 and 1972 in the original volume and adds 253 collections in the supplements, mainly from the 1970-87 period, but with some published earlier. 'Popular' includes folk songs, hymns, children's songs, etc. The index is by title, first line of verse, and first line of chorus, all coded to the numbered anthologies." Ref Sources for Small & Medium-sized Libr. 5th edition

Hischak, Thomas

The American musical film song encyclopedia; {by} Thomas S. Hischak. Greenwood Press 1999 521p $83.95

782.42

ISBN 0-313-30737-7

LC 98-34723

"Coverage is restricted to songs actually written for film. . . . Entries, arranged by song title, include vocalist, composer, lyricist, and information on the place of the song in the film, as well as recordings by artists other than those in the film. The concise entries combine a wealth of information not found in other sources." Libr J

Includes bibliographical references

The Tin Pan Alley song encyclopedia; [by] Thomas S. Hischak. Greenwood Press 2002 530p $74.95

782.42

1. Popular music—Encyclopedias
ISBN 0-313-31992-8

LC 2002-23250

Companion volume to The American musical film song encyclopedia and The American musical theatre song encyclopedia (1995)

"*Tin Pan Alley* refers to the American popular music business from the mid-nineteenth through the mid-twentieth centuries, and the songs written for parlor pianos, sing-alongs, dance orchestras, radio broadcasts, etc. This book is an A-Z listing of more than 1,200 popular songs. . . . Each entry includes the year the song was published and highly readable information about its composition and performance history." Booklist

Includes bibliographical references

Leadbelly, 1885-1949

The Leadbelly songbook; the ballads, blues, and folksongs of Huddie Ledbetter. Oak Publications 1962 96p il pa $17.95

782.42

1. African American music 2. Folk music—United States 3. Songs
ISBN 978-0-82560-042-5 (pa); 0-82560-042-1 (pa)

More than 70 songs by Huddie Ledbetter, with chord names, musical transcriptions, and biographical notes. Includes: Midnite Special, Backwater Blues, John Henry, and House Of The Rising Sun.

National anthems of the world. 11th ed. Weidenfeld & Nicolson 2006 629p $90 *

782.42

1. National songs
ISBN 0-304-36826-1

First published 1943 in the United Kingdom with title: National anthems of the United Nations and France

This volume contains national anthems of about 198 nations, including melody and accompaniment. Words are presented in the native language with transliteration

National anthems of the world—*Continued*
provided where necessary. English translations follow. Brief historical notes on the adoption of each anthem are included.

"An essential reference resource for all libraries." Libr J

Peterson, Carolyn Sue, 1938-
Index to children's songs; a title, first line, and subject index; compiled by Carolyn Sue Peterson and Ann D. Fenton. Wilson, H.W. 1979 318p $80

782.42
1. Songs—Indexes
ISBN 0-8242-0638-X; 978-0-8242-0638-3
LC 79-14265
"A numbered indexed list of 298 children's song books published between 1909 and 1977, identifying more than 5000 songs (both American and foreign) and variations, arranged alphabetically by author. There are also a title and first line index and a subject index using more than 1000 subject headings. The titles are likely to be held in schools and public libraries." Ref Sources for Small & Medium-sized Libr. 5th edition

Porter, Cole, 1891-1964
Selected lyrics; Robert Kimball, editor. Library of America 2006 178p (American poets project, 21) $20 **782.42**
1. American songs
ISBN 978-1-93108-294-5; 1-93108-294-4
LC 2006-40809
"For those hankering after a happy medium between American poetry and American Idolatry, Kimball's reading edition affords a golden opportunity to brush up on your Porter—just be sure to listen up, too, if you really want to be wowed." N Y Times Book Rev

Sheed, Wilfrid
The house that George built; with a little help from Irving, Cole, and a crew of about fifty. Random House 2007 xxvi, 335p il $29.95 *
782.42
1. Composers—United States 2. Lyricists 3. Popular music
ISBN 978-1-4000-6105-1; 1-4000-6105-9
LC 2006-51030
This is a "look at the classic era of American popular song from the 'piano era' of Irving Berlin and George Gershwin to the post-World War II era." Libr J
This book "is a big rich stew of an homage that makes you want to listen to Gershwin and Berlin and Porter and Arlen all over again. Wilfrid Sheed's jazzy prose is a joy to read" N Y Times Book Rev

Songwriter's market 2007. Writer's Digest Bks. 2006 pa $26.99 * **782.42**
1. Popular music—Writing and publishing
ISSN 0161-5971
ISBN 1-58297-431-4; 978-1-58297-431-6
Annual. First published 1978
The main section of this guide consists of listings of music publishers, record companies, producers, managers, booking agents, and firms interested in original music. Also included are articles which present an overview of the songwriting field, and listings of resources such as organizations, workshops, and contests.

782.5   Choral music

Steinberg, Michael
Choral masterworks; a listener's guide; Michael Steinberg. Oxford University Press 2005 321p $30
782.5
1. Choral music
ISBN 0-19-512644-0
LC 2004-13619
"The book covers music from Bach's Passions and the B-Minor Mass to John Adams's Harmonium and Charles Wuorinen's Genesis." N Y Rev Books
"Well-written, concise introductions that record collectors, concertgoers, and chorus members alike should enjoy." Booklist

784   Instruments and instrumental ensembles and their music

Piston, Walter, 1894-1976
Orchestration. Norton 1955 477p il music $56.75 **784**
1. Instrumentation and orchestration 2. Musical instruments
ISBN 978-0-393-09740-5; 0-393-09740-4
This text on writing for the orchestra begins with a discussion of individual instruments and their playing techniques. The last two sections cover analysis and specific problems of orchestration

784.19   Musical instruments

Stein, Stephanie
Music lessons; guide your child to play a musical instrument (and enjoy it!); [by] Stephanie Stein Crease. Chicago Review Press 2006 192p il pa $14.95 **784.19**
1. Music—Study and teaching
ISBN 978-1-55652-604-6; 1-55652-604-0
LC 2006-6752
The author "guides parents through the potentially overwhelming process of choosing a musical instrument for their child, and nurturing musical development throughout childhood. . . . This clear-cut guide will help parents find the right musical fit for their child—and introduce them to what might be a fun and engaging hobby." Publ Wkly
Includes bibliographical references

784.2 Full orchestra (Symphony orchestra)

Steinberg, Michael
The symphony; a listener's guide. Oxford Univ. Press 1995 678p music $42.50; pa $25
784.2
1. Symphony 2. Music appreciation 3. Composers
ISBN 0-19-506177-2; 0-19-512665-3 (pa)
LC 95-5568
"Steinberg describes 36 composers and, movement by movement, 118 symphonies, including all the standard repertory . . . as well as a few by less well known composers such as Gorecki, Harbison, Martinu, and Sessions. The writing varies from formal and factual to chatty, with candid asides and stories relevant to the composer, the composition, or an important performance." Libr J
Includes bibliographical references

786.2 Pianos

Piano: an encyclopedia; Robert Palmieri, editor; Margaret W. Palmieri, associate editor. 2nd ed. Routledge 2003 534p il (Encyclopedia of keyboard instruments) $150
786.2
1. Pianos
ISBN 0-415-93796-5
LC 2003-2696
This guide to the history of the piano covers topics ranging "from the acoustics and construction of the piano to the history of the companies that have built them." Publisher's note
This edition "is most impressive in its expanded size, improved layout, substantial amount of new material, and beautiful illustrations including a larger selection of photographs. Articles are more readable in outline form with headings in boldface, and with better cross-references. . . . An outstanding reference source, thoroughly indexed." Choice
Includes bibliographical references

786.5 Keyboard wind instruments. Organs

Whitney, Craig R., 1943-
All the stops; the glorious pipe organ and its American masters. Public Affairs 2003 xxv, 323p il $30; pa $17.95
786.5
1. Organs (Musical instruments)
ISBN 1-586-48173-8; 1-586-48262-9 (pa)
LC 2002-37025
"In examining the lives of master organists and organ builders, the author . . . reveals what it's like to command an instrument the size of a minor principality, and investigates the effect over time on the human ego." NY Times Book Rev
"Whitney extolls the organ's eclectic heritage at a time when the instrument seems poised for a return to the mainstream, and his glossary of its colorful terminology will help novices tell a windchest from a bombarde." New Yorker
Includes bibliographical references

787.8 Plectral lute family

Seeger, Pete
How to play the 5-string banjo; a manual for beginners. 3rd ed. Oak Publications 1962 72p il pa $16.95
787.8
1. Banjos
ISBN 0-8256-0024-3 (pa); 978-0-8256-0024-1 (pa)
First published 1948 by People's Songs
A basic manual for banjo players, with melody line, lyrics, and banjo accompaniment and solos notated in standard form of tablature. Appendix includes material on where to buy a banjo, books on the banjo, books of songs to sing and phonograph records

787.87 Guitars

Bacon, Tony
The ultimate guitar book; {by} Tony Bacon & Paul Day. Knopf 1991 192p il pa $27.50 hardcover o.p.
787.87
1. Guitars
ISBN 0-375-70090-0
LC 91-52714
This is a "chronological history of the guitar, beginning with an example from 1552 and continuing through current times. Covering acoustic, electrical, and bass guitars, including all the big-name manufacturers such as Fender, Gibson, Martin, and Stratocaster, this informative and beautifully illustrated work will have wide appeal." SLJ

Chapman, Richard
The complete guitarist. Dorling Kindersley 1993 192p il pa $20 hardcover o.p.
787.87
1. Guitars
ISBN 1-56458-711-8 (pa)
LC 92-56493
This work ranges "from fundamentals such as tuning, scales, chords, picking, and strumming, to advanced techniques of various styles such as rock, blues, and jazz. . . . {It also} includes discussions on such topics as sound and amplification, choosing a guitar, studio and home recording, plus care and maintenance of the instrument. An appealing book in the style of the 'Eyewitness' series." SLJ

787.9 Harps and musical bows

Ritchie, Jean, 1922-
The dulcimer book; by Jean Ritchie. Oak Publications 1974 45p il pa $12.95
787.9
1. Dulcimers 2. Appalachian region 3. Folk music—United States
ISBN 978-0-82560-016-6 (pa); 0-82560-016-2 (pa)
Including some ways of tuning and playing; some recollections in its local history in Perry and Knott Counties, Kentucky; some observations on the probable origins of the instrument in the old countries of Europe; with plentiful photographic illustrations and drawings; and with words and music for some sixteen songs from the Ritchie Family of Kentucky.
Includes discography and bibliographical references

790 Sports, games & entertainment

Encyclopedia of leisure and outdoor recreation; edited by John M. Jenkins and John J. Pigram. Routledge 2003 595p il $210 *   **790**
1. Leisure—Encyclopedias 2. Outdoor recreation—Encyclopedias
ISBN 0-415-25226-1   LC 2003-58529
"International in scope and including concepts from economics, geography, sociology, history, ecology, anthropology, politics, and marketing, the entries explore 'a broad range of issues, concepts, practices, and methods related to people researching, learning, and working in the field of leisure and outdoor recreation.' . . . [This] will be a key reference tool and complement other specialized encyclopedias, such as those on sports and tourism." Am Ref Books Annu, 2005
Includes bibliographical references

Encyclopedia of recreation and leisure in America; Gary S. Cross, editor in chief. Charles Scribner's Sons 2004 2v il (Scribner American civilization series) set $270 *   **790**
1. Recreation—Encyclopedias
ISBN 0-684-31265-4   LC 2004-4617
"This work provides information on all aspects of leisure in America, including historical influences, cultural changes, economic effects, and more. . . . This is a fascinating look at data useful for research papers, sociological studies, and historical evaluations or simply to satisfy curiosity." Libr J
Includes bibliographical references

790.1 General kinds of recreational activities

Conner, Bobbi
Unplugged play; no batteries, no plugs, pure fun; illustrations by Amy Patacchiola. Workman Pub. 2007 xxv, 401p il $27.95; pa $16.95
790.1
1. Games 2. Play
ISBN 978-0-7611-4114-3; 978-0-7611-4390-1 (pa)
LC 2007-23999
"Conner has compiled more than 710 games and activities sorted by age level. Good old-fashioned play and fun are the motto here with simple props from around the house or just an imagination. The book is separated into three major parts: 'Toddler Play,' 'Preschool Play,' and 'Grade School Play.' Each has a section on solo play, ideas for parent and child, playing with others, and birthday-party activities. Each chapter and section is loaded with ideas and suggestions for simple crafts. There is such a wealth of information in this book." SLJ

791 Public performances

Rockwell, John
Outsider; John Rockwell on the arts, 1967-2006. Limelight Editions 2006 544p $34.95   **791**

1. Performing arts
ISBN 978-0-87910-333-0; 0-87910-333-7
This collection of the journalist's arts criticism and commentary over the past 40 years includes pieces "about classical music, rock, dance, performance art, sculpture, movies, theater and literature. . . . [This book] provides a valuable record of the cultural period through which we have just passed: an enthusiastic verbal snapshot album of everyone from Bob Dylan and Bruce Springsteen to Shostakovich and Mark Morris. Finally, it offers invaluable insights into the evolution and career of a working critic, one who has survived the many fashion shifts in pop and high culture by remaining optimistic and young at heart." N Y Times Book Rev

Terkel, Studs, 1912-2008
The spectator. New Press 1999 364p $26.95; pa $16.95   **791**
1. Entertainers 2. Dramatists
ISBN 1-56584-553-6; 1-56584-633-8 (pa)
LC 99-17129
This is "a compendium of forty-five years of [Terkel's] conversations with film and theater people." Nation
"Telling portraits of a wide range of artists in conversation with a passionately involved, prodigiously well prepared interlocutor." Booklist

791.3 Circuses

McVicar, Wes
Clown act omnibus; everything you need to know about clowning plus over 200 clown stunts. 2nd ed. Meriwether 1987 184p il pa $14.95
791.3
1. Clowns
ISBN 0-916260-41-0   LC 87-42958
First published 1960
This volume covers "the basics of being a clown; clown equipment; walk-ons and walk-arounds; clown acts with special equipment [and includes] over 200 skit ideas, classified." Publisher's note
Includes bibliographical references

Wilkins, Charles (Charles Everett)
The circus at the edge of the earth; travels with the Great Wallenda Circus. McClelland & Stewart 1998 270p il $22.95; pa $15.95   **791.3**
1. Great Wallenda Circus
ISBN 0-7710-8847-7; 0-7710-8842-6 (pa)
LC 99-161790
"Wilkins chronicles a month on the road in his native Canada with the Great Wallenda Circus in the spring of 1997 and, in the process, offers remarkable insight into a subculture—the diverse assortment of gymnasts, animal trainers, daredevils and wanderers who identify themselves as circus folk—that is slowly disappearing from public consciousness." Publ Wkly

791.43   Motion pictures

The New York times guide to the best 1,000 movies ever made; [by] the film critics of the New York times; edited by Peter M. Nichols; introduction by A.O. Scott. St. Martin's Griffin 2004 xxiv, 1174p pa $24.95   **791.43**
1. Motion pictures—Reviews
ISBN 0-312-32611-4   LC 2004-274390
First published 1999
This updated edition includes "full cast and production credits for every movie; the '10 Best' lists for every year from 1931 to the present; an index of films by genre, and an index of foreign films by country of origin." Publisher's note
"This volume compiles alphabetically the original reviews of the 1000 'best' films as selected by New York Times critics from 1927 to 1998. . . . The result is fascinating in two respects. First, the book provides easy access to historical criticism. . . . Second, it encourages reflection on the politics of taste." Libr J [review of 1999 edition]

The **Actor's** book of movie monologues; edited by Marisa Smith and Amy Schewel. Penguin Bks. 1986 xxx, 240p pa $14   **791.43**
1. Motion pictures 2. Monologues
ISBN 0-14-009475-X   LC 86-8093
"Although designed as a sourcebook for aspiring thespians who need material for auditions, this collection of famous movie monologues makes great browsing for all film buffs. . . . Featuring memorable speeches from more than 80 films, the text is arranged chronologically." Booklist

Allen, Woody
Woody Allen on Woody Allen; in conversation with Stig Björkman. Grove Press 1995 288p il pa $14 hardcover o.p.   **791.43**
ISBN 0-8021-3425-4 (pa)   LC 94-26866
"Swedish filmmaker Björkman compiled this volume from several weeks of interviews, conducted over a six-month period, in which he led Allen through a film-by-film discussion of his quarter century as director, actor, and writer." Booklist
"This is the most comprehensive discussion so far by Allen of his films. . . . The Woody Allen that emerges is a craftsman whose real obsession is his work." Sight Sound
Includes filmography

American movie critics; an anthology from the silents until now; edited by Phillip Lopate. Library of America 2006 720p $40 *   **791.43**
1. Motion pictures—Reviews
ISBN 1-93108-292-8   LC 2005-55164
This is an anthology of reviews by American film critics, from the silent movie era to the present. The contributors include Vachel Lindsay, Hugo Munsterberg, Carl Sandburg, Robert E. Sherwood, Edmund Wilson, H. L. Mencken, Gilbert Seldes, H. D., Cecilia Ager, James Agee, Ralph Ellison, Barbara Deming, Manny Farber, Stanley Kauffmann, Andrew Sarris, Susan Sontag, Pauline Kael, Dwight Macdonald, Renata Adler, Vincent Canby, Molly Haskell, Walter Kerr, Richard Schickel, David Denby, Libby Gelman-Waxner, David Thomson, bell hooks, Roger Ebert, Gilberto Perez, A. O. Scott and Manohla Dargis
In this collection Lopate has "admirably championed critics who have long gone underappreciated. And, most important, he's highlighted writings of extraordinary literary merit by several movie critics, a few of whom are long forgotten except by the cognoscenti. With a few glaring exceptions (nearly all of which can be attributed to that lamentable, dogged pursuit of inclusiveness and diversity), Lopate displays highly cultivated taste." Atlantic Monthly
Includes bibliographical references

Auiler, Dan
Vertigo; the making of a Hitchcock classic; foreword by Martin Scorsese. St. Martin's Press 1998 220p il pa $17.95 hardcover o.p.
    791.43
1. Hitchcock, Alfred, 1899-1980 2. Vertigo (Motion picture)
ISBN 0-312-26409-7 (pa)   LC 97-31654
In this account of the film's production Auiler "reconstructs the sometimes uneasy give-and-take between Hitchcock and his players—actors Jimmy Stewart, Kim Novak and Barbara Bel Geddes; screenwriters Samuel Taylor and Alec Coppel; Robert Burks and his second-unit cameraman who created the now-famous Vertigo effect . . . and Bernard Hermann, who composed the mesmerizing score. Interesting factoids abound." Publ Wkly
Includes bibliographical references

Biskind, Peter
Easy riders, raging bulls; how the sex-drugs-and-rock-'n'-roll generation saved Hollywood. Simon & Schuster 1998 506p il pa $15 hardcover o.p.   **791.43**
1. Motion picture producers and directors 2. Motion pictures
ISBN 0-684-85708-1 (pa)   LC 98-2919
This is an account "of 'New Hollywood' filmmakers like Francis Ford Coppola, Martin Scorsese, Steven Spielberg, George Lucas, William Friedkin, Peter Bogdanovich, Hal Ashby, Robert Towne, Paul Schrader, Dennis Hopper and the producer Bert Schneider." N Y Times Book Rev
"Biskind does relish the tales of outlandish behaviour. . . . But in kicking over the traces of survivors' more or less reliable memories, he shows that libidinal and pharmaceutical urges were intrinsic to the film-makers' ferocious need to outdo each other as auteurs along the lines of the European greats they studied and worshipped." Sight Sound
Includes filmography and bibliographical references

Bogle, Donald
Bright boulevards, bold dreams; the story of Black Hollywood. One World Ballantine Books 2005 411p il $26.95; pa $15.95 **791.43**
1. African American actors 2. African Americans in motion pictures
ISBN 0345454189; 0345454197 (pa)
LC 2004-54781
"Starting with Madame Sul-Te-Wan's work in D.W. Griffith's 1915 The Birth of a Nation and ending with the 1960s deaths of Louise Beavers, Nat 'King' Cole and Dorothy Dandridge, Bogle tells the stories of the stars of Black Hollywood: their outfits, their love affairs and their struggles for better roles. . . . Bogle's lively style . . . and his many anecdotes will entertain and inform film students and black history buffs alike." Publ Wkly
Includes bibliographical references

Chadwick, Bruce
The reel Civil War; mythmaking in American film. Knopf 2001 366p il pa $15 hardcover o.p.
791.43
1. Motion pictures 2. United States—History—1861-1865, Civil War—Motion pictures and the war
ISBN 0-375-70832-4 (pa)   LC 2001-91008
The author "charts the resiliency of myths about the Civil War in films dating from the silent era to the post-Civil Rights 1970s." Libr J
"One-third of 'The Reel Civil War' concentrates on {'The Birth of a Nation' and 'Gone With the Wind'}. Given their prominence, that seems a reasonable balance, and Chadwick's dissection of the myths they helped to foster is superb." N Y Times Book Rev
Includes bibliographical references

Cook, David A.
A history of narrative film. 4th ed. W.W. Norton 2004 xxviii, 1120p il pa $78.75
791.43
1. Motion pictures—History and criticism
ISBN 0-393-97868-0; 978-0-393-97868-1
LC 2003-61090
First published 1981
This volume provides discussion and analysis of major films, directors, and national cinemas. In addition to historical and aesthetic concerns, the author explores the technological, social, and economic context of world cinema. Includes in-depth coverage of contemporary filmmaking in Hollywood, the Third World, and the former Soviet Union, as well as an entire chapter on computer-generated imaging
Includes bibliographical references

Dunne, John Gregory, 1932-2003
Monster; living off the big screen. Random House 1997 203p pa $12 hardcover o.p.
791.43
1. Up close & personal (Motion picture) 2. Motion pictures—Production and direction
ISBN 0-375-75024-X (pa)   LC 96-26212
The author "traces the life of a screenplay from the first draft to the final wrap. The work in question . . .

Up Close & Personal, is the story of two newscasters and was originally intended to follow the life of Jessica Savitch. By the end of the eight years that Dunne and his wife, author Joan Didion, worked on it, however, very little of that germinal plan remained. . . . The account is forthright and written with the wry detachment of true experience." Libr J

Ebert, Roger
Roger Ebert's movie yearbook 2007. Andrews McMeel Publishing 2006 1008p pa $24.95 *
791.43
1. Motion pictures 2. Videotapes
ISSN 1532-8147
ISBN 978-0-7407-6157-7; 0-7407-6157-9
Annual. First published 1985 with title: Roger Ebert's movie home companion. Later title: Roger Ebert's video companion
New edition in preparation
In addition to reviews this volume contains interviews and essays, questions and answers, film festival information, and a rated list of previously reviewed films

Fagen, Herb
The encyclopedia of westerns; foreword by Tom Selleck; preface by Dale Robertson. Checkmark Bks. 2003 xx, 618p il $75; pa $24.95
791.43
1. Western films
ISBN 0-8160-4456-2; 0-8160-4457-0 (pa)
LC 2002-26355
The author "traces the history of the genre, . . . defining purpose, methodology, and organization. The bulk of the book is made up of more than 3500 film entries, ranging from *The Great Train Robbery* (1902) to *The Quick and the Dead* (1995). Typically, entries include title, studio, year, running time, VHS/DVD availability, credits, and annotation. . . . Fagen's knowledge of, and love for, his subject shine through every page of this unique and valuable work." Libr J
Includes bibliographical references

Frayling, Christopher
Once upon a time in Italy; the westerns of Sergio Leone. Harry N. Abrams, in association with the Autry National Center 2005 240p il $40
791.43
1. Leone, Sergio, 1929-1989 2. Western films
ISBN 0-8109-5884-8   LC 2004-26343
"Conceived as a catalog to accompany an exhibition on Leone at the Autry National Center in Los Angeles, this book includes essays on Leone's career and legacy, short pieces on each of his films, and 11 interviews with the director, his actors, and collaborators." Choice
"This is a work of scholarship and depth on the Italian western and the man who pioneered it." Publ Wkly
Includes filmography

Gallagher, Tag

John Ford; the man and his films. University of Calif. Press 1986 572p il $42.50; pa $17.95

791.43

1. Ford, John, 1894-1973 2. Motion pictures
ISBN 0-520-05097-5; 0-520-06334-1 (pa)

LC 83-18047

"Gallagher's reassessment of John Ford's life and career revels in the complexity of the film director's personality while reconsidering his cinematic achievement. . . . Ford's philosophical and intellectual character is also sketched in this honest yet sympathetic account." Booklist

Includes bibliographical references

Giddins, Gary

Natural selection; Gary Giddins on comedy, film, music, and books. Oxford University Press 2006 410p $35 *

791.43

1. Motion pictures 2. Jazz music—History and criticism 3. Popular music 4. Books—Reviews
ISBN 978-0-19-517951-4; 0-19-517951-X

LC 2005-32469

In this collection of uncollected essays, including two written expressly for this volume, journalist Giddins offers "perspectives on such diverse subjects as Federico Fellini and Jean Renoir, Norman Mailer and Ralph Ellison, Marlon Brando and Groucho Marx, Duke Ellington and Bob Dylan, horror and noir, the cartoon version of Animal Farm and the comic book series Classics Illustrated." Publisher's note

"In an age of blogs and the everyman critic, it's reassuring to know people as brilliant as Giddins are still ready to offer insights only a true critic can provide. This is an exceptional addition to a remarkable career. . . . Nowhere else in his works do we find such a wide range of subjects, which proves his perceptive talents and in-depth knowledge of the mediums of which he writes are unequalled." Libr J

Halliwell's film guide 2008; [edited by] David Gritten. 23rd ed. HarperCollins Pubs. 2007 1396p pa $39.95 *

791.43

1. Motion pictures
ISBN 978-0-00-726080-5; 0-00-726080-6

Annual. First published 1977 by Scribner. Variant titles: Halliwell's film and video guide; Halliwell's film, video & DVD guide

"Arranged alphabetically by film title, entries include a critical rating of one to four stars; country of origin; year of release; running time; color or black and white; special film techniques . . . availability of videotape, laser disc, and sound-track on CD; producer and distributor; alternative titles; synopsis of plot; short critical assessment; writing, directing, photography, music, and other credits; principal actors; comments from professional critics; and Academy Award nominations and wins." Ref Sources for Small & Medium-sized Libr. 6th edition

Harris, Mark

Pictures at a revolution; five movies and the birth of the new Hollywood. Penguin Press 2008 490p il $27.95 *

791.43

1. Motion pictures
ISBN 978-1-59420-152-3; 1-59420-152-8

LC 2007-32633

The author examines the five films nominated for the Academy Award for Best Picture in 1967: Bonnie and Clyde, The Graduate, Guess Who's Coming To Dinner, In the Heat of the Night, and Dr. Dolittle.

"Harris gives us a juicy, multilayered chronicle of a turning point in American culture. This is page-turning social history; someone reading this book who didn't live through those days would understand why 'the '60s' had to happen." Newsweek

Includes bibliographical references

Harvey, James, 1929-1965

Movie love in the 50's. Da Capo Press 2002 448p il pa $18.95

791.43

1. Motion pictures
ISBN 978-0-306-81177-7; 0-306-81177-4

First published 2001 by Knopf

"For every 'sanitized' movie that came out of the Fifties, there were others that shook up old formulas. Critic and essayist Harvey explores—and ultimately eulogizes—Hollywood films of this era, a time of transition when the Production Code was being scrapped and the studio system abandoned. . . . His movie love is inspired and infectious." Libr J

Includes bibliographical references

Howard, Jean

Jean Howard's Hollywood; a photo memoir; photographs by Jean Howard; text by Jim Watters. Abrams 1989 248p il pa $24.95 hardcover o.p.

791.43

1. Motion picture industry—Pictorial works
ISBN 978-0-8109-2679-0; 0-8109-2679-2

LC 89-264

"Miss Howard has recorded the rarefied behind-the-gates lives of some of the most famous personalities in the history of the motion picture business. No outsider was she, hired for the occasion to 'snap' the swells. Miss Howard is very much one of the swells herself; her pictures are shot from the intimate perspective of the insider, either as a guest at the party or, frequently, as the hostess." N Y Times Book Rev

International motion picture almanac. 79th ed. Quigley 1225p $195

791.43

1. Motion pictures
ISSN 1043-8122
ISBN 978-0-900610-82-0; 0-900610-82-4

Annual. First published 1929 with title: Motion picture almanac. Variant title: Motion picture and television almanac

"Includes biographical sketches of movie personalities, lists of services, distributors, film corporations, companies, theaters, suppliers, organizations, markets, and government agencies, primarily in the United States. Lists of films of the previous decade and a review of the previous year in film: awards, polls, and festivals." Ref Sources for Small & Medium-sized Libr. 6th edition

Jones, G. William

Black cinema treasures; lost and found; foreword by Ossie Davis. University of N. Tex. Press 1991 242p il pa $17.95 hardcover o.p.

791.43

1. Motion pictures 2. African Americans in motion pictures
ISBN 1-57441-028-8 (pa)   LC 91-10882

This book "documents black independent filmmaking from the 1920s to the 1950s, spotlighting sixteen films salvaged from a warehouse in Tyler, Texas, by the author. . . . There are also brief biographies of pioneers such as Oscar Micheaux and Spencer Williams. . . . For anyone with an interest in the social history of the movie industry, this book helps bring to light a much-neglected body of work." San Francisco Rev Books

Includes filmography

Kashner, Sam

The bad & the beautiful; Hollywood in the fifties; {by} Sam Kashner and Jennifer MacNair. Norton 2002 380p il $26.95; pa $15.95

791.43

1. Motion pictures
ISBN 0-393-04321-5; 0-393-32436-2 (pa)
LC 2002-317

This "is a series of vignettes capturing a Hollywood in transition, pressured by television, the studio system's decline, and the postwar emerging permissiveness. Topics include the influence of the short-lived but much-feared Confidential; the clout of aging gossip queens Louella Parsons, Hedda Hopper, and Sheila Graham; and the uproar over an interracial romance between Sammy Davis and Kim Novak." Libr J

"These accounts, often dipped in acid, will keep readers flipping pages." Publ Wkly

Includes bibliographical references

Keaton, Eleanor, 1918-1998

Buster Keaton remembered; [by] Eleanor Keaton and Jeffrey Vance; afterword by Kevin Brownlow; Manoah Bowman, photographic editor; photographs from the collection of the Academy of Motion Picture Arts and Sciences. Abrams 2001 238p il $45   **791.43**

1. Keaton, Buster, 1895-1966
ISBN 0-8109-4227-5   LC 00-61853

This is an account of "Keaton's career, from the shorts he made with Fatty Arbuckle during the years 1917-20 to his final cameo appearances in feature films." Booklist

A "photographic tribute . . . comprising formal and behind-the-scenes stills, staged publicity shots, and previously unpublished personal photos, this book is the most comprehensive pictorial retrospective on Keaton to date." Libr J

Includes filmography and bibliographical references

Lane, Anthony

Nobody's perfect; writings from the New Yorker. Knopf 2002 xx, 752p $30; pa $16.95
791.43

1. Motion pictures—Reviews
ISBN 0-375-41448-7; 0-375-71434-0 (pa)
LC 2002-20809

This is a "compilation of movie reviews, which also includes several book reviews and other critical pieces about art and other aspects of culture." Booklist

"One of the best aspects of Lane's column, and of this anthology, is that it wanders across cultural and intellectual borders." Libr J

Lax, Eric

Conversations with Woody Allen; his films, the movies, and moviemaking. A.A. Knopf 2007 390p il $30 *   **791.43**

1. Allen, Woody 2. Motion picture producers and directors
ISBN 978-0-375-41533-3; 0-375-41533-5
LC 2007-06350

This book contains interviews with Woody Allen from 1971 to the present.

"A fine, never-disappointing achievement, this book is in competition with no other." Choice

Levy, Edmond, 1929-1998

Making a winning short; how to write, direct, edit, and produce a short film. Holt & Co. 1994 290p pa $17   **791.43**

1. Motion pictures—Production and direction
ISBN 0-8050-2680-0   LC 94-6621

"An Owl book"

"Using examples from his own career, Levy . . . explains all aspects of creating a short film, from the development of the idea to what food and drink to provide for actors and crew. After Levy's easy-to-follow lessons are finished, he offers a list of film festivals that accept short films, titles of short films that he believes to be some of the finest examples of the genre, and a reading list. . . . A worthy addition to all performing arts collections." Libr J

Lumet, Sidney

Making movies. Knopf 1995 220p pa $12 hardcover o.p.   **791.43**

1. Motion pictures—Production and direction
ISBN 0-679-75660-4 (pa)   LC 94-34449

This is a "book about the job of being a movie director. From the creation of the screenplay to the final previews, Mr. Lumet explains every step in the process, drawing examples from his own career." N Y Times Book Rev

"A fascinating look at the artist at work." Libr J

Magill's cinema annual. 2008 edition. Gale Group 2008 604p $165 *   **791.43**

1. Motion pictures
ISSN 0739-2141
ISBN 978-1-5586-2611-9; 1-5586-2611-5
Annual. First published 1982 by Salem Press

Magill's cinema annual—*Continued*

"Each entry includes the movie's tagline (promotional catch phrases), year-end domestic box office gross, a signed review and comments on the film's reception, cast/production credits, a bibliography of reviews from major newspapers and industry trade papers, memorable dialogue quotes, a trivia section, and awards and nominations. Reviews average about two pages in length and strive to be both entertaining and analytical. In addition to numerous specialized indexes (directors, screenwriters, editors, cinematographers, performers, and subject), the annual also features an obituaries section and a selected list of film books." Am Ref Books Annu, 2003

Maltin, Leonard

Leonard Maltin's 2009 movie guide. Plume/Penguin 2008 1644p pa $20

                   791.43

1. Motion pictures 2. Videotapes

ISSN 1555-7235

ISBN 978-0-452-28978-9; 0-452-28978-5

Also available in paperback from Signet Bks.

Annual. First published 1969 with title: TV movies. Title varies

This contains summaries and capsule reviews of thousands of films, videos, DVDs, and laserdisc releases, a list of recommended family films, filmographies of famous actors, and a list of specialty video mail-order companies.

Mamet, David

Bambi vs. Godzilla; on the nature, purpose, and practice of the movie business. Pantheon Books 2007 250p $22   **791.43**

1. Motion pictures 2. Authorship

ISBN 978-0-375-42253-9; 0-375-42253-6

                 LC 2006-20018

Mamet's "essay collection focuses on the movie industry, and his stance is that of someone who has seen Hollywood's facelift scars and whose advice to eager novices just off the bus can be summarized thusly: 'Go back.' . . . . He outlines the Hollywood caste system with a precision that reflects the bitter experience of the person at the bottom—the screenwriter. Scorn, betrayal, and subjugation—this is the lot of the writer, who, according to Mamet, is resented by nearly everyone in the business. Miraculously, though, great drama is occasionally realized on the screen, and Mamet offers writers some guidelines on how to approach it." Booklist

Includes filmography

On directing film. Viking 1991 107p pa $14 hardcover o.p.   **791.43**

1. Motion pictures—Production and direction

ISBN 0-14-012722-4 (pa)   LC 90-50428

"Noted playwright, screenwriter, and director Mamet offers his views on film directing taken, some in transcript form, from lectures and classes at Columbia. . . . Refreshingly untheoretical, particularly regarding acting technique, this is fitfully interesting stuff." Libr J

Mann, William J.

Behind the screen; how gays and lesbians shaped Hollywood, 1910-1969. Viking 2001 xxiv, 422p il $29.95; pa $16   **791.43**

1. Homosexuality in motion pictures 2. Motion picture industry

ISBN 0-670-03017-1; 0-14-200114-7 (pa)

                 LC 2001-17984

In this study "Mann examines how the movie capital of the world was transformed by a host of writers, directors, designers, actors, and producers often at odds with the official codes, and mores of the times. . . . Mann's book is important reading for anyone interested in the history of American film. Essential for all film and gay studies collections." Libr J

Mast, Gerald, 1940-1988

A short history of the movies; [by] Gerald Mast, Bruce F. Kawin. 10th ed. Pearson/Longman 2007 772p il pa $88   **791.43**

1. Motion pictures—History and criticism 2. Motion pictures—History and criticism

ISBN 978-0-2055-3755-6; 0-2055-3755-3

First published 1971 by Pegasus Press. Periodically revised

The author traces the history of motion pictures from their birth to the present day. Among the topics discussed are the coming of sound, the studio system and the cinemas of various countries including Russia, France and Germany. D. W. Griffith, Mack Sennet and Charlie Chaplin are among the personalities covered

Includes bibliographical references

Mayer, Geoff

Guide to British cinema. Greenwood Press 2003 440p (Reference guides to the world's cinema) $99.95   **791.43**

1. Motion pictures—Great Britain

ISBN 0-313-30307-X   LC 2002-75325

This guide "focuses on the best films, award winners, and on films that were socially or politically significant at the time of their release. . . . For films, [the author] supplies year of release, studio, production staff, cast, plot summary, and running commentary to provide insight into the creation and significance of each film. For actors and actresses, he gives relevant biographical information and filmographies." Choice

"Neither a comprehensive guide nor a 'best of' compendium, Mayer's work is nevertheless useful as an introduction to the country's film history." Libr J

Includes bibliographical references

Muller, Eddie

Dark city; the lost world of film noir. St. Martin's Griffin 1998 206p il pa $22.95

                   791.43

1. Motion pictures

ISBN 0-312-18076-4   LC 98-5677

"The book is organized around the city motif, with chapters devoted to various thematic neighborhoods, for example, 'The Precinct' (cop flicks) and 'Vixenville' (femme fatales)." Booklist

Muller, Eddie—*Continued*

"There are few fresh insights because the book is essentially a retro trip--and it does succeed in conveying the patina of 40s and 50s crime films pretty magnificently." Sight Sound

Includes bibliographical references

Neupert, Richard John

A history of the French new wave cinema; [by] Richard Neupert. University of Wis. Press 2002 368p il (Wisconsin studies in film) $50; pa $24.95
791.43

1. Motion pictures—France

ISBN 0-299-18160-X; 0-299-18164-2 (pa)

LC 2002-2305

The author "argues that the new wave was not just a film movement but a cultural phenomenon. He explores the critical and commercial, social and technological climate that enabled 120 first-time directors to make features between 1958 and 1964, Chabrol to premiere four in 15 months, and Godard to make eight in four years." Choice

"Refreshingly jargon-free and full of interesting details and anecdotes, this book is a pleasure to read." Libr J

Includes bibliographical references

Osborne, Robert A.

75 years of the Oscar; the official history of the Academy Awards; {by} Robert Osborne. Abbeville Press 2003 416p il $75
791.43

1. Academy Awards (Motion pictures)

ISBN 0-7892-0787-7

LC 2003-45311

First published 1989 with title: 60 years of the Oscar

This includes a history of the Academy of Motion Picture Arts and Sciences, overviews of Academy Award nominees and winners, award ceremonies, and a complete listing of nominees and winners in every category

Includes bibliographical references

The **Rough** Guide to film; [by] Richard Armstrong . . . [et al.] Distributed by Penguin Putnam 2007 649p il pa $27.99
791.43

1. Motion picture producers and directors—Biography—Dictionaries

ISBN 978-1-84353-408-2; 1-84353-408-8

LC 2007-300132

Subtitle on cover: An A-Z of directors and their movies: the essential guide to a world of cinema

"This volume looks beyond the Hollywood mainstream to provide assistance to anyone who is browsing rental-store shelves or online DVD catalogs in search of something new. More than 800 directors from around the globe are profiled, and more than 2,000 of their most important films are briefly reviewed. . . . If you're in a hurry, you can turn to the various categorized lists of five great directors, five classic films, and five 'lesser-known gems.'" Booklist

Siegel, Scott

The encyclopedia of Hollywood; [by] Scott Siegel and Barbara Siegel; revised and updated by Tom Erskine and James Welsh. Facts on File 2004 548p il $75; pa $24.95 *
791.43

1. Motion picture industry

ISBN 0-8160-4622-0; 0-8160-4623-9 (pa)

LC 2003-14967

"This encyclopedia offers representative entries on the American film industry, from the early, pre-Hollywood days to the present. Entries cover people, including actors, directors, producers, editors, cinematographers, and more; films; studios; genres . . . [jobs] and terms. . . . [This book] is easy to use and could be a welcome addition to the circulating as well as the reference collection." Booklist

Includes bibliographical references

Sklar, Robert

A world history of film. rev & expanded ed. Abrams 2002 600p il $75
791.43

1. Motion pictures

ISBN 0-8109-0606-6

LC 2001-22853

First published 1993 with title: Film: an international history of the medium

"Beginning with such precursors of cinema as the magic lantern and such pioneer filmmakers as the Lumières and Griffith, Sklar thereafter chronicles the rise of Hollywood, the development of genres, the advent of sound, and modern developments, right up to Pixar and the Farrelly brothers. . . . Well-selected photos profusely enhance the incisive text." Booklist

Includes filmography and bibliographical references

Taub, Eric

Gaffers, grips, and best boys. rev ed. St. Martin's Press 1994 276p il pa $14.95
791.43

1. Motion pictures—Production and direction

ISBN 0-312-11276-9

LC 94-28113

First published 1987

The author "draws on interviews with contemporary filmmakers—from director to camera operator and sound mixer—to give an insider's look at who does what in the making of a motion picture." Booklist

Thomas, Tony, 1927-1997

A wonderful life: the films and career of James Stewart. Citadel Press 1988 255p il pa $19.95
791.43

1. Stewart, James

ISBN 0-8065-1953-3

LC 87-37493

Black-and-white photographs of Stewart's professional and private life illustrate this look at his 77 films

Thomson, David, 1941-

The whole equation; a history of Hollywood. 1st ed. Knopf 2005 402p il $27.95 *
791.43

1. Motion picture industry—History 2. Motion pictures—History and criticism

ISBN 0-375-40016-8

LC 2004-48358

Thomson, David, 1941-—*Continued*

The author "examines the films of Capra, Wilder, Hitchcock, Spielberg; of Gable, Cagney, Monroe, Crawford, Brando, Bogart, Nicholson, Kidman; of Irving Thalberg, Lew Wasserman, Harvey Weinstein—and scores more." Publisher's note

"Peeling back the layers, goring sacred cows, correcting misconceptions, and revealing truth rather than reprinting legends, Thomson offers history, yes, but also a philosophical meditation on how the movie industry has inspired and influenced L.A. and America, and vice versa." Booklist

Includes bibliographical references

Welsch, Janice R.

Multicultural films; a reference guide; [by] Janice R. Welsch and J. Q. Adams. Greenwood Press 2005 231p il $49.95   **791.43**

1. Minorities in motion pictures
ISBN 0-313-31975-8   LC 2004-22529

This book "is a collection of synopses and brief analyses of selected American films. . . . It is divided into six sections, each of which covers a particular racial or ethnic group. The groups covered are African Americans, Arab and Middle Eastern Americans, Asian Americans, European Americans, Latino/a Americans, and Native Americans. . . . Each entry examines the way race or ethnicity functions in the film." Ref & User Services Quarterly

Includes bibliographical references

791.4303   Motion pictures— Encyclopedias and dictionaries

Davenport, Robert

The encyclopedia of war movies; the authoritative guide to movies about wars of the twentieth century. Facts on File 2004 452p il $75; pa $24.95 *   **791.4303**

1. War films
ISBN 0-8160-4478-3; 0-8160-4479-1 (pa)
LC 2002-45201

"Entries list cast, producers, director, writers, production company, color or black and white, year of release, and running time. Added information includes interesting facts, glaring mistakes, historical inaccuracies, quotes from the film, major awards, and any military service performed by the cast." Choice

"The volume is a worthwhile addition to war movie literature." Booklist

Includes bibliographical references

Encyclopedia of the documentary film; Ian Aitken, editor. Routledge 2005 3v il set $565 *
791.4303

1. Documentary films
ISBN 1-57958-445-4   LC 2005-46519

"The essay entries cover individual films, filmmakers, geographic areas, and themes (activist filmmaking, Third Cinema), and contain bibliographies, filmographies, and, for individuals, brief biographical summaries." Choice

For a fuller review, see: Booklist, Feb. 15, 2006

Includes bibliographical references

Grant, Barry Keith, 1947-

Schirmer encyclopedia of film. Schirmer Reference 2007 4v il set $425   **791.4303**

1. Motion pictures—Encyclopedias
ISBN 978-0-02-865791-2; 0-02-865791-8
LC 2006-13419

This encyclopedia's "articles include theory (Queer theory, Reception theory); genres (Road movies, Westerns); national cinema (Cuba, India); artistic and technical topics (Cinematography, Makeup); actor categories (Animal actors, Child actors); writing (Adaptation, Screenwriting); historical contexts (Cold war, Vietnam War); and studios (United Artists, Walt Disney Company). Each article concludes with suggestions for further reading, mostly recent or classic books plus the occasional Web site." Booklist

"The set provides an easy entrée into film scholarship across a wide arc of the field." Libr J

Includes bibliographical references

Slide, Anthony

The new historical dictionary of the American film industry. Scarecrow Press 1998 266p pa $19.95 hardcover o.p.   **791.4303**

1. Motion pictures—Dictionaries
ISBN 1-57886-015-6 (pa)   LC 97-35737

First published 1986 with title: The American film industry

This reference "covers studios, companies, clubs and associations, and related concepts. Lots here that is not found elsewhere." Booklist

Includes bibliographical references

Tibbetts, John C., 1946-

The encyclopedia of novels into film; [by] John C. Tibbetts, James M. Welsh; additional research by Rodney Hill . . . [et al.]; foreword by Robert Wise. 2nd ed. Facts on File 2005 xxii, 586p il (The Facts on File film reference library) $75; pa $24.95 *   **791.4303**

1. Film adaptations—Encyclopedias
ISBN 0-8160-5449-5; 0-8160-6381-8 (pa)
LC 2004-3317

First published 1998

This encyclopedia provides over 300 "essays about novels that were sources for one or more films. Each essay supplies production information, a synopsis of the source novel, an assessment of its literary importance, a description of challenges faced by filmmakers adapting the novel, and an assessment of the choices they made." Choice

Includes bibliographical references

791.44   Radio

Dunning, John, 1942-

On the air; the encyclopedia of old-time radio. Oxford Univ. Press 1998 822p $60 *
791.44

1. Radio programs
ISBN 0-19-507678-8   LC 96-41959

First published 1976 with title: Tune in yesterday

Dunning, John, 1942-—*Continued*

Dunning has "compiled and organized a massive amount of research data on hundreds of radio shows aired from the 1920s through the 1960s. The entries, listed alphabetically by show title, each contain a treasure trove of information—broadcast dates, casts and personnel, anecdotes, special analyses, and a detailed overview of each show's background, format, and content." Libr J

Includes bibliographical references

Ely, Melvin Patrick

The adventures of Amos 'n' Andy; a social history of an American phenomenon. University Press of Va. 2001 xxi, 322p il pa $18.50

791.44

1. Amos 'n' Andy (Radio program) 2. Amos 'n' Andy (Television program) 3. African Americans on television

ISBN 0-8139-2092-2   LC 2001-45538

First published 1991 by Free Press

A "historian examines one of America's greatest cultural enigmas—the amazing popularity, among blacks as well as whites, of 'Amos 'n' Andy' on radio for more than 30 years." N Y Times Book Rev

Includes bibliographical references

Neer, Richard

FM: the rise and fall of free-form rock radio. Villard Bks. 2001 367p pa $19 hardcover o.p.

791.44

1. WNEW (Radio station: New York, N.Y.) 2. Radio broadcasting

ISBN 0-8129-9265-2 (pa)   LC 2001-33251

Neer "recalls the brief moment when FM radio, in its infancy, coincided with the extraordinary vitality of sixties rock, and FM stations became important countercultural institutions. Free to play (and say) what they wanted, disk jockeys concocted a heady, often unpredictable brew of extended album tracks, shaggy-dog stories, and political commentary." New Yorker

This is "a nice little snapshot of cultural history." Booklist

Sies, Luther F.

Encyclopedia of American radio, 1920-1960. 2nd ed. McFarland & Co. 2008 2v set $195 *

791.44

1. Radio broadcasting—Encyclopedias 2. Radio programs—Encyclopedias

ISBN 978-0-7864-2942-4; 0-7864-2942-9

LC 2007-36686

First published 2000

The author "attempts to identify as many broadcasters and their programs as possible. Programs from the early days of radio reflect the work mainly of individual performers and are entered that way in the encyclopedia. After 1929, entries are primarily for programs, with individual entries only for performers whose programs bear their names or for newscasters, commentators, home economists, DJs, singers, and vocal and instrumental groups. There are . . . entries on special topics such as Black radio, Networks, Sports, and Wartime radio." Booklist

Includes bibliographical references

791.45   Television

Brooks, Tim

The complete directory to prime time network and cable TV shows, 1946-present; [by] Tim Brooks and Earle Marsh. 9th ed, completely rev and updated. Ballantine Books 2007 xxi, 1832p il pa $29.95 *   **791.45**

1. Television programs

ISBN 978-0-345-49773-4; 0-345-49773-2

First published 1979. Periodically revised

"Provides coverage of more than 5,000 nighttime series on commerical networks, with information on the type of show, broadcast history, cast, spin-offs, and plot or format. Index to actors and actresses. Appendixes list each season's prime time schedules, Emmy award winners, long-running and highly rated programs, and spin-offs. Coverage of original cable series began with the sixth edition." Ref Sources for Small & Medium-sized Libr. 6th edition

Encyclopedia of television; Museum of Broadcast Communications; Horace Newcomb, editor. 2nd ed. Fitzroy Dearborn 2005 4v set $595 *

791.45

1. Television broadcasting

ISBN 1-579-58394-6   LC 2004-3947

"The work chronicles the development of television through 1000 essays by more than 250 contributors. . . . Although the focus is on the development of U.S. television, a healthy number of entries relate to British and Canadian television, and country-specific entries give a nod to international issues. The first volume features an alphabetical listing of subjects, mostly shows or personalities." Libr J

"This excellent encyclopedia is the most comprehensive and up-to-date compendium on television broadcasting. . . . It is essential for any library that supports a journalism program." Booklist

Includes bibliographical references

Harris, Bob

Prisoner of Trebekistan; a decade in Jeopardy! Crown Publishers 2006 339p $23.95

791.45

1. Jeopardy (Television program)

ISBN 0-307-33956-4; 978-0-307-33956-0

LC 2006-06267

This book details Harris's experiences on the Jeopardy television show. Harris "won five straight games in 1997 (the maximum allowed at the time) and has played in several tournaments of champions since." N Y Times Book Rev

"Harris' account is a personal story and manages to cram in enough fun facts to keep any trivia nut happy." Booklist

Includes bibliographical references

Morris, Bruce B.

Prime time network serials; episode guides, casts, and credits for 37 continuing television dramas, 1964-1993; with a foreword by Michele Lee. McFarland & Co. 1997 841p il $95

791.45

1. Television programs

ISBN 0-7864-0164-8   LC 96-31166

This volume provides information of thirty-seven serials that aired on the major networks from the 1964 season through 1992-93

This "work belongs in any library collection that serves a devoted television viewing public." Booklist

Morris, Holly, 1965-

Adventure divas; searching the globe for a new kind of heroine. Villard 2005 xx, 283p il $23.95; pa $14.95   **791.45**

1. Adventure divas (Television program)

ISBN 0-375-50827-9; 0-375-76063-6 (pa)
                                LC 2005-45171

The author describes the "people and places she's encountered on the road while filming her PBS series Adventure Divas and other programs." Publisher's note

This "is a delightful triangulation of adventure travel, telecommuting and self-reinvention that proves it does not, in fact, take a rocket scientist to achieve personal flight." N Y Times Book Rev

Includes bibliographical references

Richards, Thomas, 1956-

The meaning of Star Trek. Doubleday 1997 194p pa $15 hardcover o.p.   **791.45**

1. Star trek: the next generation (Television program)

ISBN 0-385-48439-9 (pa)   LC 97-6845

The author "presents his own literary examination of Gene Roddenberry's creation . . . in four sections: conflict, character, story, and sense of wonder. While he draws on themes that span the canon of celluloid Trek, the examples he cites are mainly from *Star Trek: The Next Generation* televison series." Publ Wkly

"One of the best recent *Star Trek* books and also one of the most cogent, exciting recent literary analyses." Booklist

Stashower, Daniel

The boy genius and the mogul; the untold story of television. Broadway Bks. 2002 xx, 277p il $24.95   **791.45**

1. Farnsworth, Philo T., 1906-1971 2. Sarnoff, David, 1891-1971 3. Television—History

ISBN 0-7679-0759-0   LC 2002-283169

Stashower chronicles the life of the "farm boy who came up with the revolutionary idea that would ultimately make television possible as we know it today. Yet young Philo Farnsworth, with limited funding and a handful of friends to help build the apparatus, could not compete with the powerful David Sarnoff, president of RCA, who was determined to become the leader in the television effort. This book intermingles biographies of both men with the broader story of television's early years. . . . The amount of technical detail [Stashower]

provides . . . is enough to give the reader an idea of what the inventors had to work with, yet simplified enough to be accessible to a general audience." Booklist

Includes bibliographical references

Terrace, Vincent, 1948-

Television sitcom factbook; over 8700 details from 130 shows, 1985-2000. McFarland & Co. 2000 164p pa $25   **791.45**

1. Television programs

ISBN 0-7864-0900-2   LC 00-57865

This volume includes "over 8,700 facts concerning 130 television sitcoms broadcast from 1985 to those still current in 2000 by ABC, CBS, NBC, Fox, UPN, WB and in syndication." Publisher's note

791.5   Puppetry and toy theaters

Blumenthal, Eileen, 1948-

Puppetry; a world history. Abrams 2005 272p il $65 *   **791.5**

1. Puppets and puppet plays

ISBN 0-8109-5587-3   LC 2004-29349

This is a "history of the puppet world, from prehistoric times to Tony-winning Broadway hit Avenue Q. . . . This would be a welcome addition to the libraries of performing arts buffs who want to learn more about a lesser known form." Publ Wkly

Includes bibliographical references

791.8   Animal performances

Hemingway, Ernest, 1899-1961

The dangerous summer; introduction by James A. Michener. Scribner 1985 228p il pa $13 hardcover o.p.   **791.8**

1. Bullfights

ISBN 0-684-83789-7 (pa)   LC 84-27578

Originally written as a series of articles for Life magazine

A look at the "personal and professional rivalry of the two greatest bullfighters since the death of Manolete in 1947: Luis Miguel Dominguín and Antonio Ordóñez. The Dangerous Summer provides an insider's view based on extensive experience, mingles memory and desire, and is essential reading for anyone interested in the subject or the author." Natl Rev

Death in the afternoon. Scribner 1999 397p il $35 *   **791.8**

1. Bullfights

ISBN 0-684-85922-X   LC 99-231717

First published 1932

"A loosely organized book on bullfighting in Spain. . . . Hemingway depicts the bullfight as an emblematic tragedy, a test of courage, with a bloody and not entirely predictable end. Throughout, he digresses to philosophize on life and death in exchanges with a character he calls the Old Lady." HarperCollins Reader's Ency of Am Lit. 2nd edition

Lewine, Edward

Death and the sun; a matador's season in the heart of Spain. Houghton Mifflin 2005 258p map $24 **791.8**

1. Bullfights

ISBN 0-618-26325-X   LC 2005-40424

This is an account of a year spent observing the Spanish matador Francisco Rivera Ordonez.

"What Lewine has created may be the most in-depth, incisively written literary guide to bullfighting available in English. Every drunken sophomore riding the rails to Pamplona this summer ought to keep a volume in his backpack." N Y Times Book Rev

Includes bibliographical references

Peter, Josh

Fried twinkies, buckle bunnies & bull riders; a year inside the professional bull riders tour. Rodale 2005 246p il $24.95 **791.8**

1. Professional Bull Riders, Inc. 2. Bull riding

ISBN 1-59486-119-6   LC 2005-17297

"The argument can be made that the Professional Bull Riders Tour may be the most dangerous, least financially rewarding of all sporting endeavors. Skull fractures, punctured lungs, and destroyed knees are all relatively routine injuries. At least now there is a million-dollar payout for the overall champion each season, but even that is in deferred dollars. Peter, a sportswriter for the New Orleans Times-Picayune, spent the 2004 season with the PBR tour and offers a penetrating portrait of a sport that stands at that awkward stage between minor league and national acceptance. . . . Fried Twinkies are a genuine but rare concession delicacy, and buckle bunnies are the young ladies who curry the favor of the young macho men who ride the bulls. This is a tough book to walk away from." Booklist

792   Stage presentations

Adler, Stella, 1901-1992

Stella Adler: the art of acting; compiled and edited by Howard Kissel. Applause Theatre Bk. Pubs. 2000 271p il $25.95 * **792**

1. Acting

ISBN 1-55783-373-7

In this collection of Adler's papers Kissel "has taken tapes, transcriptions, notebooks, and other sources to reconstruct an acting course in 22 lessons. . . . The lessons are graduated from very basic matters to quite complex issues of textual analysis and decorum. Though mostly monologs, they include enough exercises and student responses to get the flavor of Adler's work. . . . This is required reading for anyone interested in theater practice." Libr J

Brestoff, Richard

The actor's wheel of connection; how to integrate your skills and refine your performance. Smith and Kraus 2005 160p (Career development series) $16.95 **792**

1. Acting

ISBN 1-57525-391-7   LC 2005-44120

This "acting manual likens the craft to six spokes in a wheel, in which one spoke represents the actor's connection to himself, the second a connection to the other, the third an actor's connection to circumstances, the fourth a connection to the text, the fifth a connection to character and the last a connection to the audience." Publ Wkly

"Brestoff draws on the teachings of the great acting teachers–such as Strasberg, Adler, Meisner, Grotowski, and Stanislavsky–in shaping and explaining his methods. Although probably not appropriate for beginners, his wheel will appeal to actors grappling with disparate techniques." BackStage

Briggs, Jody, 1945-

Encyclopedia of stage lighting; foreword by Scott Nolte. McFarland & Co. 2003 334p il $95; pa $49.95 * **792**

ISBN 0-7864-1512-6; 0-7864-4043-0 (pa)

LC 2003-7619

"Peppered with some 300 simple line drawings and diagrams to illustrate basic concepts, this work emphasizes the principles and practices of the founding fathers of theatrical lighting, among whom are Stanley McCandless, Ariel Davis, Adolphe Appia, and Gordan Craig. . . . This book often goes beyond most encyclopedias, addressing standard lighting procedures and practices, briefly outlining the historical development of theatrical lighting, and providing strategies for dealing with theater directors and other theatrical personalities." Choice

Includes bibliographical references

Brook, Peter, 1925-

The empty space. Atheneum 1968 141p pa $11 hardcover o.p. **792**

1. Theater 2. Drama

ISBN 0-684-82957-6 (pa)   LC 68-12531

The author "distinguishes four types of theater: the Deadly Theatre (conventional), the Holy Theatre (ritualistic), the Rough Theatre (combative), and the Immediate Theatre (mutative and organic). An impassioned treatise that is also very accessible and direct." Libr J

Chekhov, Michael, 1891-1955

To the actor. [rev and expanded ed. by Mala Powers] Routledge 2002 lii, 222p il $75; pa $19.95 **792**

1. Acting

ISBN 0-415-25875-8; 0-415-25876-6 (pa)

First published 1953 by Harper & Row

"Chekhov is among a handful of master acting teachers who have profoundly influenced not only a constellation of famous stars but also shaped an acting style and sensibility. . . . This new edition contains all of Chekhov's brilliant insights, techniques, and exercises, as well as a previously unpublished chapter on the 'Psychological Gesture,' a central precept of his system." Libr J

Includes bibliographical references

Corson, Richard

Stage makeup; [by] Richard Corson, James Glavan. 9th ed. Allyn and Bacon 2001 xix, 428p il $130 **792**

1. Theatrical makeup

ISBN 0-13-606153-2 LC 00-46879

First published 1942 by Appleton. Periodically revised

The authors discuss the art and technique of theatrical makeup, covering such topics as facial anatomy, various methods for applying greasepaint and other makeup, and the use of beards, wigs, and prosthetic pieces

Gillette, J. Michael

Designing with light; an introduction to stage lighting. 4th ed. McGraw-Hill 2003 various paging il pa $55.45 **792**

1. Stage lighting

ISBN 0-7674-2733-5 LC 2002-19777

First published 1978 by Mayfield Pub.

The author "divides his standard text for undergraduate lighting design students into the two constituent elements of his craft—technology and design. He clearly and completely presents both technical and aesthetic design aspects." Libr J

Theatrical design and production; an introduction to scene design and construction, lighting, sound, costume, and makeup. 6th ed. McGraw-Hill Higher Education 2008 613p il $78.20 **792**

1. Theaters—Stage setting and scenery

ISBN 978-0-07-351419-2; 0-07-351419-5

LC 2007-35218

First published 1987 by Mayfield

This is a "survey of the technical and design aspects of play production, including scene design and construction, lighting, sound, costume, and makeup. Health and safety precautions for the backstage crew appear throughout in boxes labeled 'Safety Tips,' and 'Design Inspiration' boxes show how professional designers create the desired look." Publisher's note

Includes bibliographical references

Hagen, Uta, 1919-2004

Respect for acting; by Uta Hagen with Haskel Frankel. Macmillan 1973 227p $19.95 **792**

1. Acting

ISBN 0-02-547390-5

This "classic treatise on the process and craft of acting has significantly benefited actors for three decades. Juxtaposed with Hagen's aesthetic is a wealth of practical information, creative ideas, and her uniquely useful object exercises." Libr J

Harold, Madd, 1973-

An actor's guide to performing Shakespeare; for film, television, and theatre. Lone Eagle 2002 288p pa $18.95 **792**

1. Shakespeare, William, 1564-1616—Dramatic production 2. Acting

ISBN 1-58065-046-5 LC 2002-34213

"Harold is the anti-academic incarnate, who, through his own considerable Shakespearean experience as both an actor and a director, has accrued some useful ideas, collected in this breezy vernacular guide." Libr J

Hodge, Francis

Play directing; analysis, communication, and style; [by] Francis Hodge, Michael McLain. 6th ed. Pearson/Allyn & Bacon 2005 400p il $116.40 **792**

1. Theater—Production and direction

ISBN 0-205-41923-2 LC 2004-57261

First published 1971 by Prentice-Hall

This presents a "methodology for textual analysis, communicative relationships with actors, and understanding and cultivating a sense of interpretive style. All production areas are considered and illustrated with diagrams and photographs. Numerous exercises assist in the explanation of each area." Libr J

Includes bibliographical references

Lipton, James

Inside Inside. Dutton 2007 492p il $27.95

792

1. Actors Studio 2. Inside the Actors Studio (Television program)

ISBN 978-0-525-95035-6; 0-525-95035-4

LC 2007-12790

This book from the host of the television program *Inside The Actors Studio* interweaves anecdotal stories from the author's own life with excerpts from interviews with actors given on that program.

"The anecdotes from the fine actors who have appeared on *Inside the Actors Studio* and the manifold insights into the craftsmanship of acting together justify the purchase of this exemplary book. An unqualified hit among this season's theatrical offerings and a necessary purchase for all performing arts collections." Libr J

Mamet, David

True and false; heresy and common sense for the actor. Pantheon Bks. 1997 127p pa $11 hardcover o.p. **792**

1. Acting

ISBN 0-679-77264-2 (pa) LC 97-19336

"Mamet exhorts actors to show up early, have their lines down cold, and have a single objective for each scene. He contends that overthinking and too much emotional interpretation is not the actor's role. Essential reading for theater collections." Libr J

Marasco, Ron

Notes to an actor. Ivan R. Dee 2007 214p $24.95 **792**

1. Acting

ISBN 978-1-56663-757-2; 1-56663-757-0

LC 2007-11653

This is "a compendium of suggestions, inspirations, warnings, and musings about the art of acting. Marasco speaks to actors who already possess at least a basic knowledge of their craft, seeking to heighten their abili-

Marasco, Ron—*Continued*

ties, clarify their artistic choices, eliminate blocks, and make their work more exciting and enriching. . . . This book is truly unique among acting resources. Useful both to those seeking to further their development as actors and to those for whom acting has long been a profession, this is an insightful, invaluable, and definitive work." Choice

Includes bibliographical references

Moore, Sonia, d. 1995

The Stanislavski system; the professional training of an actor; digested from the teachings of Konstantin S. Stanislavski. 2nd rev ed. Penguin Bks. 1984 96p pa $12.95 *   **792**

1. Stanislavsky, Konstantin, 1863-1938 2. Acting
ISBN 0-14-046660-6   LC 84-2855
First published 1960 with title: The Stanislavski method

This is a concise, simplified guide to the teachings of the great master of the Moscow Art Theater

Stanislavsky, Konstantin, 1863-1938

An actor's work; a student's diary; [by] Konstantin Stanislavski; translated and edited by Jean Benedetti. Routledge 2008 xxviii, 693p $35 *   **792**

1. Acting
ISBN 978-0-415-42223-9; 0-415-42223-X
     LC 2007-45357
A combined translation of Stanislavsky's *An actor prepares* and *Building a character*, which describe and illustrate the principles of method acting.

This "translation by Benedetti of Stanislavski's famous works . . . will be greeted with excitement by actors everywhere." Libr J

Includes bibliographical references

Creating a role; [by] Constantin Stanislavski; translated by Elizabeth Reynolds Hapgood; edited by Hermine I. Popper; foreword by Robert Lewis. Routledge 2003 c1989 271p pa $19.95
     792

1. Acting
ISBN 0-87830-981-0   LC 91-228412
"A Theatre Arts book"

"Stanislavski unifies his conceptual canon and applies it to detailed preparatory work for the roles of Othello and Gogol's Inspector General." Libr J

Troubridge, Emma

Scenic art and construction; [by] Emma Troubridge and Tim Blaikie. Crowood Press; distributed by Trafalgar Sq. 2002 192p il pa $29.95   **792**

1. Theaters—Stage setting and scenery
ISBN 1-86126-499-2
A "guide for upper-level theater students, scenic artists, and technical directors, this details the nuts and bolts of the production process, beginning with a design and culminating in a full-blown set." Libr J

Includes bibliographical references

792.03 Stage presentations—Encyclopedias and dictionaries

Bordman, Gerald Martin

The Oxford companion to American theatre; [by] Gerald Bordman, Thomas S. Hischak. 3rd ed. Oxford University Press 2004 681p $75 *
     792.03

1. Theater—United States—Dictionaries 2. American drama—Dictionaries
ISBN 0-19-516986-7   LC 2003-21367
First published 1984

"The volume includes playwrights, plays, actors, directors, producers, songwriters, famous playhouses, {and} dramatic movements. . . . The book covers not only classic works (such as *Death of a Salesman*) but also many commercially successful plays (such as *Getting Gertie's Garter*), plus entries on foreign figures that have influenced our dramatic development (from Shakespeare to Beckett and Pinter)." Publisher's note

"Individual entries are packed with detail. . . . Hischak provides ample material for researchers, and should be a mainstay of any performing arts reference collection." Choice

The **Cambridge** guide to American theatre; edited by Don B. Wilmeth; assistant to the editor, Leonard Jacobs. 2nd hardcover ed. Cambridge University Press 2007 757p il $150
     792.03

1. Theater—United States—Dictionaries
ISBN 978-0-521-83538-1; 0-521-83538-0
     LC 2008-270062
First published 1993

This guide covers different "aspects of the American theatre from its earliest history to the present. Entries include people, venues and companies scattered through the USA, plays and musicals, and theatrical phenomena." Publisher's note

Includes bibliographical references

The **Cambridge** guide to theatre; [edited by] Martin Banham; editorial advisory board, James Brandon [et al.] new ed. Cambridge Univ. Press 1995 1233p il $50   **792.03**

1. Theater—Dictionaries
ISBN 0-521-43437-8   LC 95-1011
First published 1988 with title: The Cambridge guide to world theatre

"A broad-ranging source of information on individuals, organizations, theatrical forms and movements, individual countries, and a variety of specific topics. Articles are signed; some longer articles have bibliographies. Covers popular theater and entertainments, as well as the legitimate stage. Because of global perspective, especially useful for country surveys of cultures outside the U.S. and Western Europe and entries for forms and individuals associated with those cultures." Guide to Ref Books. 11th edition [1988 edition]

Includes bibliographical references

The **Oxford** encyclopedia of theatre & performance; edited by Dennis Kennedy. Oxford Univ. Press 2003 2v il set $275 *

792.03

ISBN 0-19-860174-3   LC 2003-266308

This encyclopedia "encompasses opera and film, dance and radio, and para-theatrical, non-dramatic performances including circuses and carnivals, and parades and public executions—providing . . . coverage from ancient Greek theatre to developments in London, Paris, New York, and around the globe. The Encyclopedia pays special attention to non-Western styles." Publisher's note

This "work on theater and performance will set the standard for decades and become the reference of choice in these areas. . . . It is thorough, carefully thought out, and easy to use." Libr J

Includes bibliographical references

792.09   Theater—Historical, geographic, persons treatment

Brockett, Oscar Gross, 1923-

History of the theatre; [by] Oscar G. Brockett, Franklin J. Hildy. 9th ed. Allyn and Bacon 2003 692p il map $116   **792.09**

1. Theater—History 2. Drama—History and criticism
ISBN 0-205-35878-0   LC 2002-25352
First published 1968

This work traces the development of the theater from primitive times to the present, with an emphasis on European theater.

Includes bibliographical references

The **Oxford** illustrated history of theatre; edited by John Russell Brown. Oxford Univ. Press 1995 582p il pa $27.50 hardcover o.p.

792.09

1. Theater—History
ISBN 0-19-285442-9   LC 95-231683

Covering theatre history from the ancient Greeks to the 1990s, this "resource provides a wide variety of information from basic theatre chronology to detailed analyses of several well-known and important plays and playwrights. . . . The emphasis is on European and Western theatre, but a chapter provides a concise summary on Southern and Eastern Asian theatre." SLJ

Includes bibliographical references

Sova, Dawn B.

Banned plays; censorship histories of 125 stage dramas. Facts on File 2003 400p (Facts on File library of world literature) $55; pa $16.95 *

792.09

1. Drama—History and criticism 2. Censorship
ISBN 0-8160-4018-4; 0-8160-5070-8 (pa)
LC 2003-63113

This book "details the censorship of plays throughout 2,500 years of theater history. Each entry begins with a . . . list of the play's author or authors, date and place of original production, characters, and filmed versions. A . . . plot summary is followed by . . . [an] account of the play's censorship history." Choice

The author "has chosen a fine, representative selection of suppressed plays throughout the centuries. . . . This meticulously researched title offers valuable information for both scholars and casual readers." SLJ

Includes bibliographical references

792.5   Opera

Fiedler, Johanna

Molto agitato; the mayhem behind the music at the Metropolitan Opera. Doubleday 2001 393p il $30; pa $15.95   **792.5**

1. Metropolitan Opera (New York, N.Y.)
ISBN 0-385-48187-X; 1-4000-3231-8 (pa)
LC 2001-27158

This book is about "the business of New York City's Metropolitan Opera and the personalities who have shaped it from its beginnings in the late 19th century to the present day. . . . [The author] spins a fascinating account of strong egos, clashing personalities, power plays, and frequent major disasters. There are enough heroes, villains, and side plots to fill a dozen adventure novels. . . . For those interested in the dirt behind the golden curtain, this will be a feast." Libr J

Grout, Donald Jay, 1902-1987

A short history of opera; {by} Donald Jay Grout and Hermine Weigel Williams. 4th ed. Columbia University Press 2003 1030p $65 *

792.5

1. Opera
ISBN 0-231-11958-5   LC 2002-41470
First published 1947

"After surveying anticipations of the operatic form in the lyric theater of the Greeks, medieval dramatic music, and other forerunners, the book reveals the genre's beginnings in the seventeenth century and follows its progress to the present day. . . . The section on twentieth-century opera {is organized} around national operatic traditions, including a chapter devoted solely to opera in the United States that incorporates material on the American musical and ties between classical opera and popular musical theater. A separate section on Chinese opera is also included." Publisher's note

Includes bibliographical references

The **New** Grove dictionary of opera; edited by Stanley Sadie. Grove's Dictionaries of Music 1992 4v il pa set $275 hardcover o.p.

792.5

ISBN 1-56159-228-5 (pa)   LC 92-36276

This set "developed from The New Grove Dictionary of Music and Musicians, covers all aspects of the modern Western opera tradition, including composers, performers, directors, companies, stagecraft, theaters, cities, terms, and individual works." Libr J

Includes bibliographical references

Osborne, Charles, 1927-

The complete operas of Mozart; a critical guide. Da Capo Press 1986 349p il pa $17.95

792.5

Osborne, Charles, 1927-—_Continued_
1. Mozart, Wolfgang Amadeus, 1756-1791 2. Opera—Stories, plots, etc.
ISBN 978-0-306-80190-7; 0-306-80190-6
First published 1978 by Atheneum
In this introduction to Mozart's operas, "each opera is treated as a separate chapter. . . . Each chapter begins with a separate page containing the dramatis personae and their voice range . . . the date, place, and cast for the first performance . . . the name of the librettist, and the Kochel number." Choice

The complete operas of Puccini; a critical guide. Da Capo Press 1983 279p il pa $9.95
792.5
1. Puccini, Giacomo, 1858-1924 2. Opera—Stories, plots, etc.
ISBN 0-306-80200-7; 978-0-306-80200-3
LC 83-10142
First published 1982 by Atheneum
The author "provides general background information on all 13 Puccini operas. . . . Unencumbered by technical language, this enjoyably written book is accessible to all admirers of one of the most popular opera composers of all time." Choice
Includes bibliographical references

The complete operas of Richard Wagner. Da Capo Press 1993 288p il pa $16.95 **792.5**
1. Wagner, Richard, 1813-1883 2. Opera—Stories, plots, etc.
ISBN 0-306-80522-7; 978-0-306-80522-6
LC 92-34417
First published 1990 in the United Kingdom
In this book, "biography—often in Wagner's own words—combined with criticism by Wagner's contemporaries, literary background, Wagner's librettos, plot summaries, descriptions of musical elements illustrated with musical examples, and Osborne's own insights form a clear picture of Wagner, his world, and the operas." Libr J
Includes bibliographical references

Plotkin, Fred
Opera 101; a complete guide to learning and loving opera. Hyperion 1994 494p pa $16.95
792.5
1. Opera
ISBN 0-7868-8025-2
LC 94-9477
The author introduces the reader to the "basic components of an opera, including how to understand the partnership of words and music, to make oneself aware of opera plots, to be sensitive to vocal techniques and types, and to know something about staging. Plotkin even instructs the reader on purchasing a ticket and on behavioral rules at a performance (including the issue of applause). But all this is preliminary to the real meat of the book: excellent, even exciting, studies of 11 operas." Booklist
Includes discographies, videography and bibliographical references

Pogue, David
Opera for dummies; by David Pogue and Scott Speck; foreword by Roger Pines. IDG Bks. Worldwide 1997 xxiv, 356p il (—For dummies) pa $24.99 **792.5**
1. Opera
ISBN 0-7645-5010-1
LC 97-80116
A guide to appreciation of opera for beginners, accompanied by a CD
"Icons throughout pinpoint tips, advanced information, listening guides, when to use the accompanying CD, and stories to use in conversation. . . . Recommended for public libraries." Libr J

792.6   Musical plays

Bloom, Ken
Broadway musicals; the 101 greatest shows of all time; [by] Ken Bloom & Frank Vlastnik; new preface by Broadway's leading ladies; foreword by Jerry Orbach. Revised and updated ed. Black Dog & Leventhal 2008 336p il pa $22.95
792.6
1. Musicals
ISBN 978-1-57912-313-0; 1-57912-313-9
First published 2004
This is a history of Broadway musicals from the past 100 years. Each entry features commentary, photos and brief features on performers and creators.

Boland, Robert, 1925-
Musicals! directing school and community theatre; {by} Robert Boland and Paul Argentini. Scarecrow Press 1997 xxv, 202p il pa $35
792.6
1. Musicals—Production and direction
ISBN 0-8108-3323-9
LC 97-11996
This is "a handbook for novice directors of the musical. This illustrated nuts-and-bolts compendium includes 22 chapters divided among three major sections addressing preparation, production, and performance. Through accessible prose and a you-can-do-it tone, the authors provide an overview of preproduction planning, auditioning and casting, blocking, stage composition, rehearsals, and choreography, as well as the more technical layers of set design, costumes, and lights." Libr J
Includes bibliographical references

Bordman, Gerald Martin
American musical theatre; a chronicle; {by} Gerald Bordman. 3rd ed. Oxford Univ. Press 2001 917p $75 * **792.6**
1. Musicals
ISBN 0-19-513074-X
LC 00-59812
First published 1978
This book offers "show-by-show, season-by-season descriptions—from the first musical to the 1999/2000 Broadway season. . . . {It} encompasses all musical entertainment from plays, revues, opera bouffe and operettas to one-man and one-woman shows. {It} includes mini-biographies and . . . song, show and people indexes." Publisher's note

Gänzl, Kurt
The musical; a concise history. Northeastern Univ. Press 1997 432p il $50 **792.6**
1. Musicals
ISBN 1-555-53311-6 LC 97-3008
This is a "guidebook to 300 years of musicals, both romantic and comedic, which spans the early 18th to the late 20th centuries, and covers the theatrical scenes in America, Europe and Australia." Publ Wkly
Includes discography

Kantor, Michael, 1961-
Broadway: the American musical; [by] Michael Kantor; Laurence Maslon. Bulfinch Press 2004 480p il $60 * **792.6**
1. Musicals
ISBN 0-8212-2905-2 LC 2003-69715
Contents: A real live nephew of my Uncle Sam (1893-1919) -- Syncopated city (1920-1929) -- I got plenty o' nuttin' (1930-1941) -- Oh, what a beautiful mornin' (1942-1960) -- Tradition (1960-1980) -- Lullaby of Broadway (1980-present)
This companion volume to a PBS documentary includes interviews and photographs of Broadway musicals from 1893 to 2004
"With its beguiling blend of entertainment and history, this splendid work is a must-have." Publ Wkly
Includes bibliographical references

Mordden, Ethan, 1947-
Rodgers & Hammerstein. Abrams 1992 224p il hardcover o.p. pa $24.95 **792.6**
1. Rodgers, Richard, 1902-1979 2. Hammerstein, Oscar, 1895-1960 3. Musicals
ISBN: 0-8109-8144-0 (pa) LC 91-46586
The author "devotes one chapter each to the Rodgers and Hammerstein musicals—nine for the stage (Oklahoma! through The Sound of Music), one for film (State Fair), and one for television (Cinderella). He describes the genesis of the show, changes occurring during production, and subsequent history (e.g., film versions, revivals)." Choice
"Lovers of the American musical theater will find a treat in . . . [this] lavishly illustrated sort of glorified scrapbook. . . . Mordden's text provides a diverting, informal, and informative backstage tour." Christ Sci Monit
Includes bibliographical references

Norton, Richard C., 1953-
A Chronology of American musical theater. Oxford Univ. Press 2002 3v set $466.50 * **792.6**
1. Musicals—Chronology
ISBN 0-19-508888-3 LC 2001-55710
Contents: v1 1750-1912; v2 1912-1952; v3 1952-2001
"The gorgeous illustrations in this season-by-season chronology of every musical comedy, operetta, comic opera, burlesque, and revue performed on a major New York City stage from 1851 through May 2001 might be enticement enough to acquire this set. Entries for more than 3,000 plays include details such as the full cast, crew, production staff, venues, number of performances, creative personnel, and songs, which are listed as they occur within acts when this information is known. Three indexes cover song titles, show names, and names of principal players and famous chorus menbers. Leaving appraisal and plot summaries to other classic references, these volumes are the most in-depth documentary source on the New York musical stage available, with a chapter that carries the timeline for selected plays back to 1750." Am Libr
Includes bibliographical references

792.7 Variety shows and theatrical dancing

Trav S. D., 1965-
No applause, just throw money; or, The book that made vaudeville famous; a high-class, refined entertainment. Faber and Faber 2005 328p il $25 **792.7**
1. Vaudeville
ISBN 0-571-21192-5 LC 20050-9787
This book documents the history and legacy of vaudeville in the United States.
"One of the year's best historical performing arts texts; a wonderful story wonderfully told." Libr J
Includes bibliographical references

792.8 Ballet and modern dance

Craine, Debra
The Oxford dictionary of dance; by Debra Craine, Judith Mackrell. Oxford Univ. Press 2000 527p hardcover o.p. pa $16.95 * **792.8**
1. Dance—Dictionaries
ISBN 0-19-860106-9; 0-19-860400-9 (pa)
LC 2001-274422
Based on The concise Oxford dictionary of ballet by Horst Kroegler
"The styles covered range from the Brazilian martial art form of *capoeria* to American hip-hop. . . . Most entries are brief, except for those on major individuals, institutions, and works. Some themes are treated (shoes, film, dance notation). Work lists are provided, as well as an extensive bibliography." Choice
Includes bibliographical references

International dictionary of ballet; editor, Martha Bremser; assistant editor, Larraine Nicholas; picture editor, Leanda Shrimpton. St. James Press 1993 2v il set $295 **792.8**
ISBN 1-55862-084-2 LC 93-25051
"With more than 750 entries, this source covers the major figures in ballet (dancers, choreographers, composers, etc.). Individual ballets, and internationally known ballet companies from the Renaissance to the present. Entries are arranged alphabetically and each includes items such as a list of major roles, premiere performances, a critical essay, biographical or historical information, and a lengthy bibliography. The two-volume work is well-researched and comprehensive." Am Libr

International encyclopedia of dance; a project of Dance Perspectives Foundation, Inc; founding editor, Selma Jeanne Cohen; area editors, George Dorris {et al.}. Oxford Univ. Press 1998 6v hardcover o.p. pa set $450   **792.8**
ISBN 0-19-509462-X; 978-0-19-517369-7 (pa); 0-19-517369-4 (pa)   LC 97-36562
This work presents entries on "dances, dancers, and dance topics. . . . Aspects of dance in more than 100 countries are written about by more than 600 writers. . . . Dance as ceremony and ritual in religious as well as social and cultural traditions is covered here, as are the related topics of music, scenic design, dance notation, costumes, aesthetics, and training." Booklist
"In the emerging field of dance scholarship, this set is a milestone." Libr J

Reynolds, Nancy, 1938-
No fixed points; dance in the twentieth century; {by} Nancy Reynolds and Malcolm McCormick. Yale Univ. Press 2003 907p il $50   **792.8**
1. Dance 2. Ballet 3. Modern dance
ISBN 0-300-09366-7   LC 2003-10754

This is a "narrative of the development of ballet, modern dance, and postmodern choreography. Synthesizing a century's worth of observation and opinion, Reynolds and McCormick chart the pendulum swing of styles and isolate individual contributions. . . . They highlight the significance of factors as large as government funding and as small as the depth of Baryshnikov's demi-plié." New Yorker
"Although everyone will be using the book for reference, Reynolds and McCormick have produced a work that is completely unlike a standard reference book; you don't just look things up in it—you read it. Here is a coherent, reasoned and entertaining chronicle of dance performance in the West over the hundred years that are unquestionably the fullest and most complicated in the long history of this fragmented and elusive art." N Y Times
Includes bibliographical references

793   Indoor games and amusements

Lithgow, John, 1945-
A Lithgow palooza! 101 ways to entertain and inspire your kids. Simon & Schuster 2004 351p il pa $15   **793**
1. Amusements 2. Games 3. Recreation
ISBN 0-7432-6124-0   LC 2004-42820
Also available Lithgow party paloozas
"This book contains 101 ideas for creating paloozas for children ages 3 to 12 wherever you are. Grouped according to interests and themes like art, drama, music, vacations, and birthdays and incorporating lots of extrapaloozas, fun facts for parent and child, and suggested additional reading for all ages, John's paloozas range from adopting your own soup can for a day to inventing your own secret language to establishing left-handed day or creating a self-portrait." Publisher's note
"One dictionary defines a lollapalooza as 'something outstanding of its kind,' which adequately describes Lithgow's latest book. . . . Essential for all child-rearing collections." Libr J

793.2   Parties and entertainments

Sedaris, Amy
I like you; hospitality under the influence. Warner Books 2006 303p il $27.99   **793.2**
1. Entertaining 2. Cooking
ISBN 978-0-446-57884-4; 0-446-57884-3   LC 2006-07521
"Novice party-planners will actually find some helpful hints along the way as Sedaris offers instructions and real recipes. . . . [This book] is an outrageous and deadpan delight, greatly enhanced by her deliriously kitschy illustrations and photos." Publ Wkly

Tutera, David, 1966-
The party planner; David Tutera. Bulfinch Press 2005 196p il $29.95   **793.2**
1. Parties
ISBN 0-8212-6165-7   LC 2004-21614
This book "covers cocktail parties, dinner parties, holiday entertaining and special occasions, showing two examples of each that Tutera has thrown for his clients." Publ Wkly
"A beautiful and helpful book to consult and be encouraged by time and again." Booklist

793.3   Social, folk, national dancing

Soffee, Anne Thomas
Snake hips; belly dancing and how I found true love. Chicago Review Press 2002 xxii, 262p $22.95   **793.3**
1. Belly dancing
ISBN 1-55652-458-7   LC 2002-572
This is the author's story of how she cured a broken heart and changed her life for the better through belly-dancing
"Soffee's witty, flowing prose draws readers into this unlikely but captivating story." Booklist
Includes bibliographical references

793.73   Puzzles and puzzle games

Merriam-Webster's crossword puzzle dictionary. 2nd ed. Merriam-Webster 1996 775p $18.95; pa $5.99   **793.73**
1. Crossword puzzles—Dictionaries
ISBN 0-87779-121-X; 0-87779-919-9 (pa)   LC 96-24796
First published 1992
This "dictionary is structured in accordance with the way crossword puzzles are constructed and solved. Main entries are in alphabetic order letter-by-letter. If the main entry is a large category, the list of answer words is broken down into alphabetically arranged subcategories. When more than one answer is possible to a clue representing a main entry, the answer words are grouped together according to the number of letters they contain. . . . This dictionary has a broad range of the most current words used in crossword puzzles. The format is easy to use." Am Ref Books Annu, 1997

The **Official** Scrabble players dictionary. 4th ed. Merriam-Webster 2005 704p $24.95; pa $7.50
*　　　　　　　　　　　　　　　**793.73**
　1. Scrabble (Game)—Dictionaries
　ISBN　978-0-87779-420-2;　0-87779-420-0;
　0-87779-929-6 (pa)　　　　　LC 2005-5110
　Replaces the 3rd edition published 1995

　First published 1978
　This is a dictionary of words which can be used in the game of Scrabble including 100,000 2 to 8 letter words.

Pulliam, Tom
　The New York times crossword puzzle dictionary; by Tom Pulliam and Clare Grundman. 3rd ed. Times Bks. 1995 656p $27.50; pa $18.95
*　　　　　　　　　　　　　　　**793.73**
　1. Crossword puzzles—Dictionaries
　ISBN 0-8129-2373-1; 0-8129-2823-7 (pa)
　　　　　　　　　　　　　　　LC 95-11416
　"A Hudson Group book"
　First published 1977
　This dictionary of synonyms for crossword puzzles includes more than 50,000 entries.
　"One of the more useful works of its kind." Ref Sources for Small & Medium-sized Libr. 6th edition

Random House Webster's crossword puzzle dictionary. 3rd ed. Random House 1998 854p $27.95; pa $18.95　　　　　　**793.73**
　1. Crossword puzzles—Dictionaries
　ISBN 0-679-45856-5; 0-375-70624-0 (pa)
　　　　　　　　　　　　　　　LC 98-67266
　First published 1989 with title: The Random House crossword puzzle dictionary
　Each entry lists a variety of terms that may be substituted for the entry term. The arrangement within each term listing is alphabetical and by number of letters
　"A useful and entertaining companion for both crossword puzzle and trivia buffs." Ref Sources for Small & Medium-sized Libr. 6th edition

793.74　Mathematical games and recreations

Stewart, Ian, 1945-
　The magical maze; seeing the world through mathematical eyes. Wiley 1998 268p il $24.95; pa $16.95　　　　　　　　　　　　**793.74**
　1. Mathematics 2. Mathematical recreations
　ISBN 0-471-19297-X; 0-471-35065-6 (pa)
　　　　　　　　　　　　　　　LC 98-13185
　Stewart presents various mathematical puzzles and problems through the metaphorical structure of a maze.
　Chapters "contain good discussions of such topics as modular arithmetic, Marilyn vos Savant's Monty-Hall problem, depth-first and other search strategies, static and dynamic symmetry, Turing machines, optimization, fractals, and chaos. This is an excellent mix of topics and the material is very much up-to-date." Choice

Tahan, Malba, 1895-
　The man who counted; a collection of mathematical adventures; illustrated by Patricia Reid Baquero & translated by Leslie Clark and Alastair Reid. Norton 1993 244p il pa $15.95 hardcover o.p.　　　　　　　　　**793.74**
　1. Mathematical recreations
　ISBN 0-393-30934-7 (pa)　　　LC 92-18822
　"First published in Brazil in 1949 by the mathematician Julio de Melo e Sousa (Tahan is the imaginary Arab author he claimed to have translated), [this book] is a series of . . . 'Arabian Nights'-style tales, with each story built around a classic mathematical puzzle." Libr J
　"This small book is a joy. . . . These are beautifully expressive tales that find mathematical puzzles and numerical intrigue in human situations and speak not just of solving the problems but of the needs we all have for friendship, love, and beauty." Booklist

793.8　Magic and related activities

Gardner, Martin, 1914-
　The colossal book of short puzzles and problems; combinatorics, probability, algebra, geometry, topology, chess, logic, cryptarithms, wordplay, physics and other topics of recreational mathematics; edited by Dana Richards. Norton 2006 494p il $35　　　　　　　**793.8**
　1. Mathematical recreations 2. Scientific recreations
　ISBN 0-393-06114-0; 978-0-393-06114-7
　　　　　　　　　　　　　　　LC 2005-24080
　This is a compilation of puzzles from Martin Gardner's "column, 'Mathematical Games,' which appeared for over 25 years in Scientific American. . . . [The topics] include combinatorics, probability, algebra, plane and solid geometry, topology, games, chess, logic, wordplay, and physics, among others. . . . Anyone interested in recreational mathematics should like this book. The puzzles are fascinating and the book is easily browsed. It can also serve as a good reference for (high school and college) teachers seeking interesting problems to complement routine ones in mathematics texts." Sci Books Films

794　Indoor games of skill

Botermans, Jack
　The book of games; strategy, tactics & history; [by] Jack Botermans; [translated from the Spanish by Edgar Loy Fankbonner] Sterling 2008 736p il $29.95　　　　　　　　　　　**794**
　1. Indoor games 2. Board games
　ISBN 978-1-4027-4221-7; 1-4027-4221-5
　　　　　　　　　　　　　　　LC 2007-10173
　"Some 65 international games are described and demonstrated in this colorful book. Ranging from dominoes to mancala and shogi to Yut, each entry highlights the game's origins, versions, and playing rules. . . . Color illustrations and diagrams are used liberally to illustrate strategic moves and the variations of game boards and pieces, while photographs show the games being played. . . . Libraries should consider this for their circulating collections." Booklist

794.1   Chess

Capablanca, José Raúl, 1888-1942
Chess fundamentals. McKay Co. 1988 246p il (McKay chess library) pa $14.95   **794.1**
1. Chess
ISBN 978-0-679-14004-7; 0-679-14004-2
First published 1921 by Harcourt Brace & Co.
Explains the general principles of chess through eighteen illustrative games, so that, when grounded in these, the novice may understand the whole elementary science of the game.

Fischer, Bobby, 1943-2008
Bobby Fischer teaches chess; by Bobby Fisher, Stuart Margulies, Donn Mosenfelder. Bantam 1972 334p il pa $7.99   **794.1**
1. Chess
ISBN 0-553-26315-3; 978-0-553-26315-2
First published 1966 by Basic Systems, Inc.
In this book the authors give specific advice and hints aimed at both the beginning and advanced player. Each step-by-step lesson is fully illustrated.

Hallman, J. C.
The chess artist. Thomas Dunne Bks. 2003 334p il map $25.95; pa $13.95   **794.1**
1. Chess
ISBN 0-312-27293-6; 0-312-33396-X (pa)
LC 2003-46872
"During a postcollege stint as a blackjack dealer in Atlantic City . . . Hallman discovered the chess community that thrives in dealer lounges. There he met 39-year-old chess master Glenn Umstead, who performed exhibitions while blindfolded and had 'hoped to become the world's first black grandmaster.' The two became friends and embarked on an exploration of the chess subculture, a grand tour that took them from Princeton to prisons, from windowless rooms to the 'giant electronic chess room' of the Internet Chess Club." Publ Wkly
"Educational, fanciful, entertaining, this is a book that will make every reader see the game of chess in an entirely new—if slightly weird—light." Booklist
Includes bibliographical references

United States Chess Federation
U.S. Chess Federation's official rules of chess; compiled and sanctioned by the U.S. Chess Federation; Tim Just, chief editor; Daniel B. Burg, editor. 5th ed. Random House Puzzles & Games 2003 xxxvii, 370p il (McKay chess library) pa $18.95 *   **794.1**
1. Chess
ISBN 0-8129-3559-4   LC 2003-278349
First published 1974
This "edition features the latest rules, including guidelines for the popular game of speed chess, an updated quick rating system, and the latest conventions of governing tournaments. It also contains explanations of every legal move, a guide to calculating lifetime rankings, guidelines for sponsoring and running a tournament, and a lesson on how to read and write chess notation." Publisher's note

794.7   Indoor ball games

Byrne, Robert, 1930-
Byrne's new standard book of pool and billiards. Harcourt Brace & Co. 1998 xxv, 406p il hardcover o.p. pa $20   **794.7**
1. Pool (Game) 2. Billiards
ISBN 0-15-100325-4; 0-15-600554-9 (pa)
LC 98-14656
First published 1978 with title: Byrne's standard book of pool and billiards
The author explains the rules of pool and billiards and offers advice on strategy with diagrams of various shots.
Includes bibliographical references

McCumber, David
Playing off the rail; a pool hustler's journey. Avon Books 1997 384p pa $14.95   **794.7**
1. Annigoni, Tony 2. Pool (Game)
ISBN 0-380-72923-7
First published 1996 by Random House
A "look at the game of pool, which is a gambling sport not yet sanitized by what McCumber calls the 'Fellowship of Christian Athletes types.' He plays financial backer to a sharp-tongued player named Tony Annigoni, and takes him on the road across North America in search of highstakes games. . . . This is a terrific book." New Yorker

794.8   Electronic games. Computer games

Neiburger, Eli
Gamers . . . in the library?! the why, what, and how of videogame tournaments for all ages. American Library Association 2007 178p pa $42 *   **794.8**
1. Video games 2. Computer games 3. Young adults' libraries
ISBN 978-0-8389-0944-7; 0-8389-0944-2
LC 2007-10512
This is a "guide to setting up video-gaming tournaments in public libraries. The author . . . [shares] advice on every aspect of this crowd-pleasing lure for kids, tweens, and teens: promotion, hardware and software, rules and regulations, scoring, prizes, snacks, feedback, and follow-up activities." Booklist
"With the writing as vibrant as its topic, . . . [this book] is a must-have professional tool." Voice Youth Advocates
Includes bibliographical references

Wark, McKenzie, 1961-
Gamer theory. Harvard University Press 2007 unp il $19.95   **794.8**
1. Computer games
ISBN 978-0-674-02519-6; 0-674-02519-9
LC 2006-102852

Wark, McKenzie, 1961-—*Continued*

"For Wark, video games are worth studying because they offer insights into contemporary society and culture. For example, Katamari Damacy exemplifies the way digital technology has altered the experience of space and time; Rez demonstrates how individual identity is now a matter of action not essence, doing not being; Vice City maps out the territory of the new world order of seemingly unending risk and reward. Gamer Theory devotes complete chapters to particular games and the key concepts they clarify. . . . Gamer Theory concerns itself with more than just the interpretation of video games; it's about gaming ambience—that is, gamespace—as the kinetic field within which game players exist." PopMatters

Includes bibliographical references

795.4   Card games

Bellin, Andy, 1968-

Poker nation; a high stakes, low-life adventure into the heart of a gambling country. HarperCollins Pubs. 2001 258p il pa $12.95 hardcover o.p.   **795.4**

1. Card games

ISBN 0-06-095847-2 (pa)   LC 2001-42409

The author "a lapsed astrophysics student who left science for his true calling of professional poker, introduces us to the world of legal and illegal poker games and the cast of strange characters who can be found therein." Libr J

"Bellin offers the best of both worlds, combining detailed advice on how to play the game with engagingly written, humorous stories about those who play it with passion." Booklist

Includes bibliographical references

Hoyle, Edmond, 1672-1769

Hoyle's rules of games; descriptions of indoor games of skill and chance, with advice on skillful play: based on the foundations laid down by Edmond Hoyle, 1672-1769; edited by Albert H. Morehead and Geoffrey Mott-Smith. 3rd rev. & updated ed., revised and updated by Philip D. Morehead. Plume 2001 362p il pa $14 *   **795.4**

1. Card games

ISBN 0-452-28313-2   LC 2002-278550

Also available in paperback from Signet Bks.

This guide "includes rules, strategies, and playing odds for more than 250 games." Publisher's note

Includes bibliographical references

McManus, James

Positively Fifth Street; murderers, cheetahs, and Binion's World Series of Poker. Farrar, Straus & Giroux 2003 422p il $26   **795.4**

1. Poker

ISBN 0-374-23648-8   LC 2002-33882

"McManus went to Las Vegas in May 2000 on assignment for *Harper's* to cover the World Series of Pok-

er. . . . He was to throw in coverage of the trial of Sandy Murphy, an ex-stripper, and her boyfriend, Rick Tabish, accused of murdering Ted Binion, the tournament's host. . . . To satisfy his own gambling urge, McManus enter the poker competition and spends 10 days immersed in the culture of Vegas and gambling, rendering a fast-paced, riveting account of his progress through the tournament. . . . A delicious inside look." Booklist

Includes bibliographical references

Scarne, John, 1903-1985

Scarne's encyclopedia of card games. Quill 2001 c1983 475p il pa $18   **795.4**

1. Card games

ISBN 0-06-273155-6; 978-0-06-273155-5

A reissue of the title first published 1983 by Harper & Row

The material in this book has been excerpted, with alterations and additions, from Scarne's encyclopedia of games (1973)

796   Athletic and outdoor sports and games

Berkow, Ira

The minority quarterback, and other lives in sports. Dee, I.R. 2002 307p $26; pa $16.95   **796**

1. Sports

ISBN 1-56663-422-9; 1-56663-502-0 (pa)   LC 2001-47578

Reprints of columns and feature stories originally published in The New York Times between 1981 and 2000

"Berkow brings together essays on a theme: athletes overcoming hardships. Whether his subject is minority football players struggling to win recognition as quarterbacks—a position once restricted to whites—or baseball pitcher Jim Abbott working past the handicap of having only one arm, he writes with skill, empathy, and insight." Booklist

The **best** American sports writing 2008; edited with an introduction by William Nack; Glen Stout, series editor. Houghton Mifflin 2008 407p (The best American series) $28; pa $14   **796**

1. Sports

ISBN   978-0-618-75117-4;   0-618-75117-3; 978-0-618-75118-1 (pa); 0-618-75118-1 (pa)

Annual. First published 1991. Editors vary

With selections culled from 350 American and Canadian newspapers, this series covers a wide range of sports and sports figures of interest to both the general reader and the diehard sports fan.

The **Best** American sports writing of the century; edited by David Halberstam. Houghton Mifflin 1999 776p $30; pa $18 *   **796**

1. Sports

ISBN 0-395-94513-5; 0-395-94514-3 (pa)

"Although there are pieces about mountain climbing, tennis and chess, fully half of the selections are about

The Best American sports writing of the century—*Continued*

two sports: baseball and boxing. The book begins with a Best of the Best section led by Gay Talese's 1966 profile of Joe DiMaggio, 'The Silent Season of a Hero.'. . . The final section is a special six-piece tribute to a man who himself claimed to be the best of the best—Muhammad Ali." Publ Wkly

Franck, Irene M.

Famous first facts about sports; {by} Irene M. Franck & David M. Brownstone. Wilson, H.W. 2001 903p $160 *   **796**
1. Sports
ISBN 0-8242-0973-7   LC 00-43883
"Franck and Brownstone have compiled 5,415 'firsts' covering more than 110 sports. . . . Arranged alphabetically by sport, the concisely described events are listed in chronological order, with headers for time periods. Entries are given consecutive four-digit numbers, which are cited in the five indexes (subjects, years, days, personal names, and geographical locations). . . . The indexes provide essential access and are easy to use. . . . The depth of coverage is impressive." Choice
Includes bibliographical references

Guttmann, Allen

Women's sports; a history. Columbia Univ. Press 1991 339p il pa $24 hardcover o.p.
                                              796
1. Sports 2. Women athletes
ISBN 0-231-06957-X (pa)   LC 90-28692
The author explores "the social and cultural contexts of women's athletics in ancient civilizations, the Middle Ages, and the Renaissance. This lays the groundwork for a subsequent discussion of the subject's current state, in which he . . . exposes controversial issues which threaten the development of women's sports." Libr J
Includes bibliographical references

Krantz, Les

Not till the fat lady sings; the most dramatic sports finishes of all time; foreword by Doug Flutie. Triumph Books 2003 148p il $29.95
                                              796
1. Sports
ISBN 1-57243-558-5   LC 2003-47331
Includes DVD
"This compendium of the 50 most dramatic endings to sports events divides the great plays into first, second and third place rankings, along with honorable mentions. . . . Many of the book's finishes concern football, baseball and basketball, with just a smattering of other sports (such as golf, tennis and hockey) thrown in. Photos accompany each entry. . . . The supplementary DVD, narrated by Jim McKay, adds a dramatic edge to the package, with commentators relating moments with wild excitement and fans roaring." Publ Wkly
This is "an excellent addition to any sports collection." Booklist

Levine, Peter

Ellis Island to Ebbet's Field; sport and the American-Jewish experience. Oxford Univ. Press 1992 328p il (Sports history and society) hardcover o.p. pa $38   **796**
1. Jews—United States—History 2. Sports
ISBN 0-19-505128-9; 0-19-508555-8 (pa)
                                              LC 91-42016
The author "explores the importance of sport in transforming Jewish immigrants into American Jews. Drawing on interviews with celebrities as well as lesser-known neighborhood stars, Levine vividly recounts the stories of Red Auerbach, Hank Greenberg, Moe Berg, and many others who became Jewish heroes and symbols of the difficult struggle for American success." Univ Press Books for Public and Second Sch Libr
Includes bibliographical references

Nike is a goddess; the history of women in sports; edited by Lissa Smith; introduction by Mariah Burton Nelson. Atlantic Monthly Press 1998 331p il pa $14 hardcover o.p.   **796**
1. Sports 2. Women athletes
ISBN 0-87113-761-5   LC 98-27049
This "anthology documents the athletic achievements of female athletes during the late-nineteenth and twentieth centuries. Separate chapters written by noted sports journalists (Grace Lichtenstein, Michelle Kaufman, Karen Karbo) cover such disciplines as basketball, soccer, baseball, swimming, horseback riding, tennis, golf, and hockey, among others." Booklist
"The quality of writing in the different sections varies but each writer is well connected with her field and all give a good background history as well as an assessment of current developments in the sport. Controversial issues are not ignored, and lesbianism is addressed." SLJ

Rhoden, William C.

$40 million slaves; the rise, fall, and redemption of the Black athlete. Crown Publishers 2006 286p il $23.95   **796**
1. African American athletes 2. Race discrimination 3. Sports
ISBN 0-609-60120-2; 978-0-609-60120-4
                                              LC 2005-34952
Cover title: Forty million dollar slaves
The author offers an "assessment of the state of black athletes in America, using the pervasive metaphor of the plantation to describe a modern sports industry defined by white ownership and black labor." Publ Wkly
"In his provocative, passionate, important and disturbing book—part memoir, part history, part journalism—William Rhoden . . . builds a historic framework that both accounts for the varieties of African-American athletic experience in the past and continues to explain them today." N Y Times Book Rev
Includes bibliographical references

Sports: the complete visual reference; François Fortin {general editor}. Firefly Bks. 2000 372p il $39.95; pa $24.95   **796**
1. Sports
ISBN 1-55209-540-1; 1-55297-807-9 (pa)
This is a "reference source on 120 contemporary sports . . . pulling together the history, physical environ-

Sports: the complete visual reference—*Continued*

ment for competitions, roles of the players and officials, specific terms and expressions, and dynamics of each. All of this is done with an emphasis on visual presentation, and each entry includes copious illustrations." Booklist

"A sure winner for any sports reference collection." Am Libr

The **unlevel** playing field; a documentary history of the African American experience in sport; [edited by] David K. Wiggins and Patrick B. Miller. University of Ill. Press 2003 xxi, 493p il (Sport and society) $39.95   **796**

1. African American athletes
ISBN 0-252-02820-1   LC 2002-14269

"This collection contains several of the most significant primary documents tracing the sports experiences of African Americans. Athletes, sports historians, and some of the nation's foremost intellectuals deliver commentaries on a wide range of subjects and athletic events." Libr J

Includes bibliographical references

796.03   Sports—Encyclopedias and dictionaries

Berkshire encyclopedia of world sport; David Levinson and Karen Christensen, editors. Berkshire Pub. Group 2005 4v il set $475   **796.03**

1. Sports—Encyclopedias
ISBN 0-9743091-1-7   LC 2005-13050

"This encyclopedia covers a range of topics from professional and amateur sports and sporting events to national sports and issues and influences affecting athletics. . . . A broad, well-written resource." SLJ

For a fuller review, see: Booklist, Sept. 1, 2005

Includes bibliographical references

796.09   Sports—Historical and geographic treatment

Miller, Stephen G. (Stephen Gaylord), 1942-
Ancient Greek athletics. Yale University Press 2004 288p il map $35 *   **796.09**

1. Athletics 2. Greece—Civilization 3. Olympic games
ISBN 0-300-10083-3   LC 2003-16875

"Five chapters discuss the origins and history of the [Olympic] games and their sociopolitical significance, but at the core of the book are the 11 chapters that use archaeological and textual evidence . . . to reconstruct the physical reality of Greek athletics. Particularly valuable are the vivid reconstruction of the ancient Olympic program and the lucid discussion of the evidence for female athletic contests in ancient Greece." Choice

Includes bibliographical references

796.323   Basketball

Araton, Harvey
Crashing the borders; how basketball won the world and lost its soul at home. Free Press 2005 207p $25   **796.323**

1. Basketball
ISBN 0-74328-069-5   LC 2005-44906

"The catalyst for this book . . . was the November 2004 Detroit brawl in which Indiana Pacer basketball players went into the stands in pursuit of cup-tossing fans, and the fans spilled onto the court in search of arrogant, multimillionaire players. Araton sees the brawl as symptomatic of the racial and economic divide that currently characterizes professional basketball. Mostly black, multimillionaire players perform in all their cornrowed, tattooed glory before emissaries of corporate America, in attendance because their companies provided tickets. The spectators often aren't real fans but are increasingly antagonistic in berating the players." Booklist

"Mr. Araton has several superb chapters on the global growth of the N.B.A. and the influence of basketball in poverty-stricken areas of Eastern Europe. He explains why foreign players have superior fundamentals and are becoming stars in what is supposed to be 'our' game." N Y Times Book Rev

Blais, Madeleine, 1949-
In these girls, hope is a muscle. Warner Bks. 1996 266p pa $13.95   **796.323**

1. Cathedral High School (Springfield, Mass.)
2. Basketball
ISBN 0-446-67210-6; 978-0-446-67210-8

First published 1995 by Atlantic Monthly Press

"Weaving accounts of players' personal histories with reportage on their on-court performances, Madeleine Blais recounts the dramatic 1992-93 season of the Lady Hurricanes of Amherst (Mass.) Regional High School." N Y Times Book Rev

"Alternately funny, exciting and moving, the book should be enjoyed not only by girls and women who have played sports but also those who wanted to but let themselves be discouraged." Publ Wkly

Bradley, Bill
Values of the game. Artisan 1998 160p il $30   **796.323**

1. National Basketball Association 2. Basketball
ISBN 1-57965-116-X   LC 98-7280

Also available in paperback from Bantam Bks.

In this book, the former senator and New York Knick presents a "blend of sports memoir and inspirational advice interspersed with more than 100 dramatic photos of basketball players past and present. . . . While some may dismiss much of his volume as a collection of copybook maxims, the whole is larger than the sum of its parts, not only because it is so personal but because Bradley moves so deftly from the specific to the general." Publ Wkly

D'Orso, Michael

Eagle blue; a team, a tribe, and a high school basketball season in Arctic Alaska. Bloomsbury Pub. 2006 323p il map $23.95   **796.323**

1. Basketball 2. School sports 3. Fort Yukon (Alaska)

ISBN 978-1-58234-623-6; 1-58234-623-2

LC 2005-25430

The author "follows the Fort Yukon Eagles through their 2005 season to the state championship, shifting between a mesmerizing narrative and the thoughts of the players, their coach and their fans. What emerges is more than a sports story; it's a striking portrait of a community consisting of a traditional culture bombarded with modernity, where alcoholism, domestic violence and school dropout rates run wild." Publ Wkly

Feinstein, John

Last dance; behind the scenes at the Final Four; John Feinstein. Little, Brown 2006 369p il $25.95 *   **796.323**

1. Basketball

ISBN 0-316-16030-X   LC 2005-28478

The author "employs the 2005 [Final Four] weekend as the catalyst to discuss the history of the event, the key people, and, most significantly, the effect that involvement in the Final Four has had on participants' lives. . . . The anecdotes are entertaining, and the insights into the tournament's logistics fascinating, but what will linger most are the remembrances of players, especially those who ended up on the losing side." Booklist

A march to madness; the view from the floor in the Atlantic Coast Conference. Little, Brown 1997 464p il hardcover o.p. pa $14   **796.323**

1. Atlantic Coast Conference 2. Basketball

ISBN 0-316-27740-1; 0-316-27712-6 (pa)

LC 97-31060

Feinstein "covers one year with all of the teams in the perennially powerful Atlantic Coast Conference. After introducing each of the schools, their teams, their coaches, and their expectations for the 1996/97 basketball season, the book describes their progress week by week, culminating with Dean Smith's run to the NCAA Final Four. Such a detailed accounting of a sports season could seem interminable to readers, but Feinstein has again produced a narrative that is not only interesting but often exciting." Libr J

Kent, Richard G.

Inside women's college basketball; anatomy of a season; {by} Richard Kent. Taylor, W.T. 2000 222p il hardcover o.p. pa $16.95   **796.323**

1. Basketball

ISBN 0-87833-188-3; 978-0-87833-278-6 (pa); 0-87833-278-2 (pa)   LC 00-42589

"Kent chronicles the 1999-2000 season as experienced by four top women's programs: Tennessee, Connecticut, Rutgers, and Sacred Heart. . . . This is a fine overview for those looking for insights into the women's game." Booklist

Lazenby, Roland

The show; the inside story of the spectacular Los Angeles Lakers in the words of those who lived it. McGraw-Hill 2006 468p il $27.95

796.323

1. Los Angeles Lakers (Basketball team) 2. Basketball

ISBN 0-07-143034-2   LC 2005-18571

This is the "behind-the-scenes story of the basketball franchise as told by the Lakers and by opposing players, announcers, administrators, and fans who have worked for or followed the team since its start in Detroit almost 60 years ago." Libr J

"The book is must reading for NBA fans both young and old." Booklist

Includes bibliographical references

Swidey, Neil

The assist; hoops, hope, and the game of their lives. PublicAffairs 2008 358p il $26

796.323

1. O'Brien, Jack 2. Charlestown High School (Boston, Mass.) 3. Basketball 4. School sports

ISBN 978-1-58648-469-9; 1-58648-469-9

LC 2007-35826

At the center of this book about Boston's Charlestown High School basketball team "are the interwoven lives of [coach Jack] O'Brien and two of his stars, easygoing Ridley Johnson and fierce Jason 'Hood' White. The book follows Ridley and Hood on their hunt for a state title. But it also stays with them, to see how young men who seldom get second chances survive without their coach hovering over them—and how he survives without them." Publisher's note

"This is a prodigiously reported, compulsively readable book that readers (sport fans or not) will savor." Publ Wkly

Wolff, Alexander

Big game, small world; a basketball adventure. Warner Bks. 2002 xxiv, 424p il $24.95; pa $15.95

796.323

1. Basketball

ISBN 0-446-52601-0; 0-446-67989-5 (pa)

"Wolff traveled to 16 countries and 10 states to assess basketball's impact as a global phenomenon. He profiles a cloistered nun who was once a talented hoopster and investigates the origins of the crossover dribble. Wolff's passion for the game burns feverishly throughout." Booklist

796.332   American football

Anderson, Lars

Carlisle vs. Army; Jim Thorpe, Dwight Eisenhower, Pop Warner, and the forgotten story of football's greatest battle. Random House 2007 349p il $24.95   **796.332**

    1. Thorpe, Jim, 1888-1953 2. Eisenhower, Dwight D. (Dwight David), 1890-1969 3. Warner, Pop, 1871-1954 4. United States Indian School (Carlisle, Pa.) 5. Football

    ISBN 978-1-4000-6600-1; 1-4000-6600-X

                        LC 2007-8410

"A forgotten football game in 1912, between Carlisle, led by Jim Thorpe and coached by the legendary Pop Warner, and Army, led by Dwight Eisenhower, becomes the launching point for a fascinating look at multiple levels of American popular culture." Booklist

Includes bibliographical references

Bissinger, H. G.

Friday night lights; a town, a team, and a dream. Da Capo Press 2000 367p il pa $15.95 *   **796.332**

    1. Permian High School (Odessa, Tex.) 2. Football

    ISBN 0-306-80990-7   LC 00-40510

    First published 1990 by Addison-Wesley

In 1988, the author, a "Philadelphia Inquirer editor, left his job to spend a year with a high school sports team. The sport he picked was football, the location, the . . . West Texas oil town of Odessa. . . . Here 20,000 fans turn out regularly to watch their Permian Panthers win." Libr J

"It is a tricky balancing act, but Mr. Bissinger carries it off: 'Friday Night Lights' offers a biting indictment of the sports craziness that grips not only Odessa but most of American society, while at the same time providing a moving evocation of its powerful allure." N Y Times Book Rev

Curtis, Brian, 1971-

Every week a season; a journey inside big-time college football. Ballantine Books 2004 299p il $24.95; pa $14.95   **796.332**

    1. Football 2. College sports

    ISBN 0-345-47014-1; 0-345-48337-5 (pa)

                   LC 2004-303037

The author "describes the 10 weeks he spent with 10 teams, including Louisiana State, Florida State and Boston College." N Y Times Book Rev

Curtis provides "an appreciation for the preparation and emotional investment at the foundation of every college football game. Legions of fans will savor every word." Booklist

Dent, Jim

The Junction boys; how ten days in hell with Bear Bryant forged a champion team. St. Martin's Press 1999 290p il $24.95; pa $13.95

                          796.332

    1. Bryant, Bear 2. Football

    ISBN 0-312-19293-2; 0-312-26755-X (pa)

                   LC 99-22179

"In February 1954, Paul 'Bear' Bryant took the head football coaching position at Texas A & M. The story of his first Aggie team, vividly recounted here by journalist Dent, is a little-known but memorable chapter in the legendary coach's career." Booklist

The undefeated; the Oklahoma Sooners and the greatest winning streak in college football history. St. Martin's Press 2001 288p il $24.95; pa $14.95

                          796.332

    1. Oklahoma Sooners (Football team) 2. Football

    ISBN 0-312-26656-1; 0-312-30326-2 (pa)

                   LC 2001-34896

The author recounts how "Oklahoma Sooner football coach Bud Wilkinson won an all-time record 47 straight games over five seasons, which included three undefeated years, from 1954 through 1956. . . . [This] is a fascinating account of an extraordinary athletic achievement that is unlikely to be approached, let alone equaled." Booklist

Includes bibliographical references

Feinstein, John

Next man up; a year behind the lines in today's NFL. Little, Brown 2005 502p il $25.95

                          796.332

    1. Baltimore Ravens (Football team) 2. Football

    ISBN 0-316-00964-4

Feinstein's look at the current state of the National Football League (NFL) focuses on the 2004 Baltimore Ravens' season.

"Even those who are not fanatical football fans will find that, beyond the information provided on players and coaches, there are two other engaging topics in the book: Feinstein's ruminations on how reporting and writing about football are different from reporting and writing about other sports, and his portrayal of the business side of the game through conversations with Ravens owner Steve Bisciotti. . . . Professional football fans cannot lose by reading this book. As for the rest of us, [it] provides interesting glimpses into a strange but popular cultural realm." Christ Sci Monit

Green, Tim

The dark side of the game; my life in the NFL. Warner Bks. 1996 272p pa $7.50 hardcover o.p.

                          796.332

    1. National Football League 2. Football

    ISBN 0-446-60520-4 (pa)   LC 95-51000

The author "offers a collection of approximately 70 brief, engagingly written essays on such dark topics as drug use, sex, violence, injuries, cheating, gambling, and money in professional football." Libr J

MacCambridge, Michael, 1963-

America's game; the epic story of how pro football captured a nation. Random House 2004 552p il hardcover o.p. pa $15   **796.332**

    1. National Football League 2. Football

    ISBN 0-375-50454-0; 0-375-72506-7 (pa)

                   LC 2004-52003

MacCambridge, Michael, 1963-—*Continued*
The author traces pro football's history "with particular attention paid to six key franchises—the Rams, Browns, Colts, Cowboys, Chiefs, and Raiders—and how their fortunes reflected the larger growth of the game itself." Publisher's note

"This magisterial history is a fitting acknowledgment of the sport's legacy." Publ Wkly
Includes bibliographical references

St. John, Warren
Rammer jammer yellow hammer; a journey into the heart of fan mania. Crown Publishers 2004 275p $24   **796.332**
1. Alabama Crimson Tide (Football team) 2. Football
ISBN 0-609-60708-1   LC 2003-24718
"Wearing a thin veneer of journalistic detachment, St. John followed his beloved Alabama Crimson Tide football team during the 1999 season. The result is a sharp, sneaky-funny, but loving portrait of the team and its incredibly loyal fans." Booklist

796.334 Soccer

Bellos, Alex
Futebol: the Brazilian way of life. Bloomsbury Pub. 2002 407p il maps $25.95; pa $16.95
                                               796.334
1. Soccer 2. Brazil—Social life and customs
ISBN 1-58234-250-4; 1-58234-287-3 (pa)
The author aims "to paint a 'portrait of {Brazil}, Latin America's largest country, seen through its passion for {soccer}'." Economist
"Compelling. . . . Alternately funny and dark. . . . Bellos offers a cast of characters as colorful as a Carnival parade." Publ Wkly

Hamm, Mia, 1972-
Go for the goal; a champion's guide to winning in soccer and life; {by} Mia Hamm with Aaron Heifetz. HarperCollins Pubs. 1999 222p il pa $12.95 hardcover o.p.   **796.334**
1. Soccer
ISBN 0-06-093159-0 (pa)   LC 99-19592
Personal anecdotes and both action and instructional photos illustrate soccer skills and techniques

Haner, Jim, 1957-
Soccerhead; an accidental journey into the heart of the American game. North Point Press 2006 275p $24   **796.334**
1. Soccer
ISBN 0-86547-694-2; 978-0-86547-694-3
                              LC 2005-6798
The author "delves into the subject of youth soccer in suburban Washington, DC, and relates his own experiences coaching a team of nine-year-olds. He explores soccer's history, mixing bits of unmatched soccer wit and wisdom into a lively narrative as fast-paced as the game itself and inserts social commentary on the topics of soccer parents, young players, and winning and losing." Libr J

796.35 Games with ball driven by club, mallet, bat

Will, George F.
Men at work; the craft of baseball. HarperPerennial 1991 353p il pa $9.95
                                               796.35
1. LaRussa, Tony 2. Hershiser, Orel 3. Gwynn, Tony, 1960- 4. Ripken, Cal, Jr. 5. Baseball
ISBN 0-06-097372-2   LC 90-55518
First published 1990 by Macmillan
This book's four chapters cover these "aspects of baseball: The Manager (Tony LaRussa of Oakland), The Pitcher (Orel Hershiser of Los Angeles), The Batter (Tony Gwynn of San Diego), and The Defense (Cal Ripken, Jr., of Baltimore)." Natnl Rev
"The author's own devotion to detail in defining the components of the game is sure to instill in readers a greater appreciation of what is required to master the sport at the major league level, thereby providing a deeper understanding of the foundation of the game. Altogether, this is hardcore baseball presented in fluent style" Libr J

796.352 Golf

Andrisani, John
The Tiger Woods way; secrets of Tiger Woods's power swing technique. Crown 1997 153p il pa $12 hardcover o.p.   **796.352**
1. Woods, Tiger, 1975- 2. Golf
ISBN 0-609-80139-2 (pa)   LC 97-6083
The author "shares his discovery of the secrets of Tiger's flawless swing technique to help golfers of all levels learn how to increase their driving distance and improve their game." Publisher's note

Chopra, Deepak
Golf for enlightenment; seven lessons for the game of life. Harmony Bks. 2003 200p $21
                                               796.352
1. Golf 2. Spiritual life
ISBN 0-609-60390-6   LC 2002-27636
The author tells a story about "Adam, who, on a day particularly productive of shanks and slices, is accosted by an apparition who adjures the despairing soul to consult golf pro Wendy, likewise an ethereal being. In a seven-part 'fable,' Wendy heightens Adams' awareness of 'now,' relieves him of his control compulsions, and restores his golfing life to balance and harmony. The authorial brand and publicity ensure that Chopra's confection will be highly, if transiently, popular." Booklist

Feinstein, John
A good walk spoiled; days and nights on the PGA tour. Little, Brown 1995 xx, 475p il pa $14.95 hardcover o.p.   **796.352**
1. PGA Tour Inc. 2. Golf
ISBN 0-316-27737-1 (pa)   LC 94-49552

Feinstein, John—*Continued*

Along with "profiles of the game's big names—Norman, Price, Watson—Feinstein's sojourn through the 1994 PGA tour also offers remarkable glimpses of the marginal players who struggle to first qualify for the tour and then maintain their tenuous places on it. . . . Golfers of all ages simply won't be able to put this book down." Booklist

The majors: in pursuit of golf's Holy Grail. Little, Brown 1999 480p $25; pa $14.95

796.352

1. Golf

ISBN 0-316-27971-4; 0-316-27795-9 (pa)

LC 99-11390

"Feinstein tackles the sport's four major championships: the Masters, the U.S. Open, the British Open and the PGA, as they were played in 1998." Publ Wkly

"If you want to know how touring pros think, on and off the course but particularly on the courses that are the crucibles of the majors, this is the book. It also tells how golf officials, especially those at the Masters and at the United States Golf Association, think in setting up their courses." N Y Times Book Rev

Frost, Mark

The greatest game ever played; Harry Vardon, Francis Ouimet, and the birth of modern golf. Hyperion 2002 488p il $30   **796.352**
1. Vardon, Harry, 1870-1937 2. Ouimet, Francis, 1893-1967 3. Golf

ISBN 0-7868-6920-8   LC 2002-68930

The author "tells the story behind the legendary 1913 U.S. Open, in which Francis Ouimet, a 20-year-old golf amateur from Massachusetts, shocked the genteel golf world by defeating British champion Harry Vardon." Publ Wkly

"The climax of the narrative . . . is genuinely exciting, a marvelous re-creation of a signature moment in golf history." Booklist

Nicklaus, Jack

Golf my way; by Jack Nicklaus with Ken Bowden; illustrated by Jim McQueen. Simon & Schuster 1974 264p il pa $15 hardcover o.p.

796.352

1. Golf

ISBN 0-684-85211-X (pa)

"This is the only book written by {Jack Nicklaus} that covers in depth his entire technique of the game as he plays it, from top to bottom. The intellectual and scholarly dedication that Nicklaus brings to his game is explained fully." Choice

Player, Gary

The complete golfer's handbook; [by Gary Player, with Chris Whales & Duncan Cruickshank; foreword by Ernie Els] Lyons Press 2000 160p il $24.95; pa $19.95   **796.352**
1. Golf

ISBN 1-58574-029-2; 1-58574-765-3 (pa)

This guide covers "etiquette, equipment, course design, and strategy, in addition to how to swing the club.

The material is introductory only, but even experienced golfers will enjoy the graphics and profit from reviewing the concise, clearly presented swing advice." Booklist

Rubenstein, Lorne

A season in Dornoch; golf and life in the Scottish Highlands. Citadel 2003 242p il pa $14.95

796.352

1. Golf 2. Scotland

ISBN 978-0-8065-2457-3; 0-8065-2457-X

First published 2001 by Simon & Schuster

This is "Rubenstein's account of spending an entire summer in the village of Dornoch, living above a bookshop, immersing himself in the rhythms of the community, and playing golf both casually . . . and seriously. . . . Whether Rubenstein is recounting fascinating bits of Highlands history or offering vivid character sketches of Dornoch natives, the prose breathes a kind of atmospheric calm that works on the reader like a mild summer breeze." Booklist

Sampson, Curt

Masters; golf, money, and power in Augusta, Georgia. Villard Bks. 1998 xxxiv, 263p il pa $14.95 hardcover o.p.   **796.352**
1. Augusta National Golf Club 2. Golf

ISBN 0-375-75337-0 (pa)   LC 97-49143

This history of one of the PGA's most prestigious events "traces the tournament's history since 1933, revealing both the dramatic moments and the controversial secrets, most notably racism—certainly a book to raise eyebrows at the Augusta National Golf Club." Libr J

796.357 Baseball

Angell, Roger

Game time: a baseball companion; edited by Steve Kettmann. Harcourt 2003 398p $25; pa $15
*   **796.357**
1. Baseball

ISBN 0-15-100824-8; 0-15-601387-8 (pa)

LC 2002-152611

"A Harvest original"

"Half of the essays in this compilation of highlights from Angell's 40 years of covering baseball for the *New Yorker* have not previously appeared in book form, and even those that have are well worth revisiting. Angell . . . remains the dean of baseball writers." Booklist

Once more around the park; a baseball reader. Ivan R. Dee 2001 351p pa $16.95

796.357

1. Baseball

ISBN 1-566-63371-0; 978-1-566-63371-0

LC 00-50436

First published 1991 by Ballantine Books

A collection of 21 pieces, some from Angell's earlier books and others previously uncollected.

"Outstanding among the choices . . . are visits with Hall of Famer Bob Gibson and then-91-year-old Smoky Joe Wood." Libr J

Barra, Allen

Clearing the bases; the greatest baseball debates of the last century; foreword by Bob Costas. St. Martin's Press 2002 xxi, 261p $23.95; pa $13.95
796.357

1. Baseball

ISBN 0-312-26556-5; 0-312-30253-3 (pa)

LC 2001-48992

The author "provides considerable insight into many of the most hotly debated topics of baseball's last 100 years." Booklist

Baseball register 2007. Sporting News 712p pa $22.95 * **796.357**

1. Baseball—Statistics

ISSN 0162-542X

ISBN 978-0-89204-866-3; 0-89204-866-2

Annual. First published 1940. Variant title: Official baseball register

At head of title: The Sporting News

This book gives information, mostly in tabular form, about active players, managers, coaches and recently retired players in major league baseball. Included are place and date of birth; nicknames; whether right or left-handed; height and weight; hobbies; colleges attended; records and awards; yearly statistics for batting, fielding and pitching in the major and minor leagues and major league career totals; and team records of managers. Includes statistics for play in World Series and All-Star games

Bissinger, H. G.

Three nights in August; strategy, heartbreak, and joy, inside the mind of a manager; [foreword by Tony La Russa] Houghton Mifflin 2005 xxi, 280p $25; pa $13.95 **796.357**

1. LaRussa, Tony 2. St. Louis Cardinals (Baseball team)

ISBN 0-618-40544-5; 0-618-71053-1 (pa)

LC 2004-65134

For this book, the author "was given complete access to Tony La Russa and his St. Louis Cardinals. . . . La Russa collaborated fully, hid nothing, freely divulged his thoughts, notes, fears. The result is a fascinating look inside the day-to-day, game-by-game, inning by inning managing of a professional baseball team." N Y Times Book Rev

Includes bibliographical references

Block, David, 1944-

Baseball before we knew it; a search for the roots of the game; with a foreword by Tim Wiles. University of Nebraska Press 2005 340p il $29.95; pa $16.95 * **796.357**

1. Baseball

ISBN 0-8032-1339-5; 0-8032-6255-8 (pa)

LC 2004-16099

"Baseball always attracts impassioned amateur writers pleading a cause. Here, baseball collector Block beats his way back through the mists of baseball time. He dismisses the English game of rounders as the primary foreign borrowing, arguing that baseball's origins lie in the many sports that have used a ball since the Middle Ages. This book is made memorable by the numerous quaint but fascinating illustrations of these early games, which Block uses to make his rather controversial point." Libr J

Boston, Talmage, 1953-

1939, baseball's tipping point; foreword by John Grisham. Bright Sky Press 2005 288p il $24.95
796.357

1. Baseball

ISBN 1-931721-53-X

LC 2004-65046

This is a "terrific collection of stories and profiles of some of the baseball figures that made 1939 one of the most extraordinary years that any sport has ever enjoyed." Newberg Report

Includes bibliographical references

Bouton, Jim

Ball four; edited by Leonard Shecter. Twentieth-anniversary ed. Collier Bks. 1990 472p il pa $15.95 hardcover o.p. **796.357**

1. Baseball

ISBN 0-02-030665-2 (pa)

LC 89-49151

Also available in hardcover from Midpoint Trade Bks.

First published 1970 by World

The author offers a behind-the-scenes look at major league baseball, its players and management

Bradley, Richard, 1964-

The greatest game; the Yankees, the Red Sox, and the playoff of '78. Free Press 2008 286p il $25 **796.357**

1. New York Yankees (Baseball team) 2. Boston Red Sox (Baseball team)

ISBN 978-1-4165-3438-9; 1-4165-3438-5

LC 2007-45382

"In 1978, the American League East division champion was determined by a one-game playoff, a taut battle between the Yankees and the Red Sox at Fenway Park. Bradley gives a pitch-by-pitch breakdown of the Boston loss (a three-run homer by Bucky Dent in the top of the seventh cemented the Yankees' lead), and an account of the volatile season preceding it. At a time when pro baseball was making the transition from homegrown pastime to big business, emotions ran high and outsized personalities clashed; New York's pugnacious manager, Billy Martin, resigned in tears midseason. Bradley's prosaic style and his penchant for statistics sometimes test the reader's patience, but his portraits of the coaches and players who converged that day in October lend an intimacy and richness to the book." New Yorker

Includes bibliographical references

Bryant, Howard, 1968-

Juicing the game; drugs, money, and the fight for the soul of Major League Baseball. Viking 2005 439p $24.95; pa $15 **796.357**

1. Athletes—Drug use 2. Steroids 3. Baseball

ISBN 0-670-03445-2; 0-452-28741-3 (pa)

LC 2005-42411

Bryant, Howard, 1968-—_Continued_

Bryant evaluates the current state of baseball in America, focusing particular attention on the implications of steroid use for the game.

This "is a remarkable book: well reported, compellingly written, a narrative breathtaking in scope. . . . Bryant treats all his real-life characters with empathy, admirably refusing to stereotype." Christ Sci Monit

Includes bibliographical references

Shut out; a story of race and baseball in Boston. Routledge 2002 278p il $27.50   **796.357**

1. Boston Red Sox (Baseball team) 2. Baseball 3. Race discrimination 4. Boston (Mass.)—Race relations

ISBN 0-415-92779-X   LC 2002-69950

Also available in paperback from Beacon Press

The author "examines the race relations of one of baseball's most storied teams, the Boston Red Sox, from the early 1930s to the present." Libr J

"Bryant looks at both sides of the race issue, and backs his conclusions with exhaustive research from a variety of sources." Publ Wkly

Includes bibliographical references

Costas, Bob

Fair ball; a fan's case for baseball. Broadway Bks. 2000 179p pa $12.95 hardcover o.p.

    796.357

1. Baseball

ISBN 0-7679-0466-4 (pa)   LC 99-87992

"The root of baseball's ills, the sports broadcaster Bob Costas argues, lies in how teams like the Yankees and Atlanta Braves, by virtue of vastly higher revenues than franchises like the Montreal Expos or Kansas City Royals, threaten the game's legitimacy by having 'a monopoly on sustained success.' Costas's solution is for team owners to start meaningful revenue sharing and force a salary cap on the intransigent players union, even if it takes another strike or lockout to do it." N Y Times Book Rev

Deford, Frank

The old ball game; how John McGraw, Christy Mathewson, and the New York Giants created modern baseball. Atlantic Monthly Press 2005 241p il $24; pa $13   **796.357**

1. McGraw, John Joseph, 1873-1934 2. Mathewson, Christy, 1880-1925 3. New York Giants (Baseball team) 4. Baseball

ISBN 0-87113-885-9; 0-8021-4247-8 (pa)

       LC 2004-62313

This is a portrait of the manager of the New York Giants, John McGraw, and the team's ace pitcher, Christy Mathewson. "Mathewson and McGraw led the Giants to five pennants between 1904 and 1913." N Y Times Book Rev

"A fine baseball book but just as fine a study of American popular culture." Booklist

Dickson, Paul

The hidden language of baseball; how signs and sign-stealing have influenced the course of our national pastime. Walker & Co 2003 230p il $22

    796.357

1. Baseball

ISBN 0-8027-1392-0   LC 2003-41125

The author "explores the intricacies of baseball's 'hidden language,' the rapid-fire signs that are delivered in a manner that can escape even well-tutored fans." Libr J

"Anyone who has ever played or coached youth baseball or paid close attention to the third-base coach at a big-league game will appreciate the author's guided tour through the history of diamond sign language. Dickson is a fine storyteller, and his latest book is a welcome addition to the rich canon of baseball literature." Booklist

Includes bibliographical references

Geist, Bill

Little League confidential; one coach's completely unauthorized tale of survival. Dell Pub 1999 217p pa $15   **796.357**

1. Little League Baseball, Inc. 2. Baseball

ISBN 0-440-50877-0

"A Dell trade paperback"

First published 1992 by Macmillan

The author "relates his decade of service as a little-league baseball coach. He admittedly distills his experiences—and those of others—into a season-long 'docudrama' journal. He tells of pompous coaches lecturing their miniplayers on the subtleties of the infield fly rule; he addresses the question of positioning a player with a personal-injury lawyer for a dad. The book is a wonderful effort filled with empathy for kids, impatience for pushy parents, and a good sense of humor." Booklist

Giamatti, A. Bartlett, 1938-1989

A great and glorious game; baseball writings of A. Bartlett Giamatti; edited by Kenneth S. Robson; foreword by David Halberstam. Algonquin Bks. 1998 121p $15.95   **796.357**

1. Baseball

ISBN 1-56512-192-9   LC 97-32803

Giamatti's "writings make baseball a metaphor for America and Americans. His imagery, in the nine essays in this . . . book, elevates the game from ordinary to beautiful and sometimes humorous." N Y Times Book Rev

Golenbock, Peter, 1946-

Amazin'; the miraculous history of New York's most beloved baseball team. St. Martin's Press 2002 654p il $27.95; pa $18.95   **796.357**

1. New York Mets (Baseball team)

ISBN 0-312-27452-1; 0-312-30992-9 (pa)

       LC 2001-48870

This is a history of the New York Mets baseball team

"Golenbock combines his own well-researched commentary with the recollections of eyewitnesses. . . . This is a delightful and painstakingly detailed trip down memory lane that Mets fans will cherish." Publ Wkly

Includes bibliographical references

Gould, Stephen Jay, 1941-2002
Triumph and tragedy in Mudville; a lifelong passion for baseball; foreword by David Halberstam. Norton 2003 342p il hardcover o.p. pa $14.95 **796.357**
    1. Baseball
    ISBN 0-393-05755-0; 978-0-393-32557-7 (pa); 0-393-32557-1 (pa)   LC 2002-155523
This is a collection of Gould's "essays about baseball, written over 20 years and published in venues as divergent as the *New York Times* and *Vanity Fair*. . . . The essays are uniformly wonderful. . . . Scientific analysis intersects gently with flat-out fandom. Gould could think, he could write, he was funny, and he loved, loved baseball." Booklist

Halberstam, David, 1934-2007
Summer of '49. Morrow 1989 304p il pa $14.95 hardcover o.p. * **796.357**
    1. New York Yankees (Baseball team) 2. Boston Red Sox (Baseball team)
    ISBN 978-0-06-088426-0; 0-06-088426-6
    LC 89-2886
"This book is ostensibly about the pennant race between the Yankees and Red Sox {in 1949} and the 'rivalry' between Joe DiMaggio and Ted Williams. . . . It is a study of all the elements and personalities that influenced baseball that year and beyond. Halberstam brings them together in such an enjoyable, interesting, and informative manner that a reader needn't be a baseball fan to appreciate the book." Libr J

Hample, Zack
Watching baseball smarter; a professional fan's guide for beginners, semi-experts, and deeply serious geeks. Vintage 2007 254p il pa $13.95 **796.357**
    1. Baseball
    ISBN 978-0-307-28032-9; 0-307-28032-2
    LC 2007-296737
The author "covers basics such as what to watch for in pitchers, catchers, hitters, fielders and base runners; he also provides answers to such nagging questions as why spectators stretch in the seventh inning and why most ballplayers grab their crotches. . . . Hample hits the equivalent of a reference book home run with his witty and loose style—taking a friendly for-a-fan-by-a-fan approach that doesn't hide his enormous depth of knowledge." Publ Wkly

Hogan, Lawrence D., 1944-
Shades of glory; the Negro Leagues and the story of African-American baseball; with a foreword by Jules Tygiel. National Geographic 2006 422p il $26 * **796.357**
    1. Negro leagues 2. Baseball 3. African American athletes
    ISBN 0-7922-5306-X; 978-0-7922-5306-8
    LC 2006-273216
Published in association with the National Baseball Hall of Fame and Museum

This book "traces the history of black baseball from the 19th century to the first great teams, such as the Cuban Giants, and on to the era of the vibrant barnstorming teams from the East Coast, Chicago, and Cuba." Publisher's note
"This is an important, informative, and entertaining contribution to sports history." Booklist

Joy in Mudville; the big book of baseball humor; edited by Dick Schaap and Mort Gerberg. Doubleday 1992 xx, 424p il pa $15.95 hardcover o.p. **796.357**
    1. Baseball
    ISBN 0-385-46953-5 (pa)   LC 91-42417
"Including articles, book excerpts, and comic strips, this humorous baseball anthology ranges from the familiar 'Casey at the Bat' and Abbott and Costello's hilarious 'Who's on First' routine to selections penned by Garrison Keillor, George Plimpton, and W. P. Kinsella. Suggested for both personal and reference use." Booklist

Kahn, Roger, 1927-
Beyond the boys of summer; the very best of Roger Kahn; edited by Rob Miraldi. McGraw-Hill 2005 xxxvi, 364p $24.95 **796.357**
    1. Baseball
    ISBN 0-07-144727-X   LC 2004-24851
This book "presents a showcase of 50 years worth of Kahn's . . . work." Publisher's note
"Kahn is a giant among sports journalists, and this is a fine sampling of his most memorable work." Booklist
Includes bibliographical references

The boys of summer. Harper & Row 1972 xxii, 442p il pa $14.95 hardcover o.p. * **796.357**
    1. Brooklyn Dodgers (Baseball team) 2. Baseball
    ISBN 978-0-06-088396-6; 0-06-088396-0
The author describes attending Brooklyn Dodger games as a boy, covering Dodger games as a reporter for the Herald Tribune, and traveling throughout the country to speak with former Dodgers after the team left New York

The head game; baseball seen from the pitcher's mound. Harcourt 2000 xxii, 310p il $25; pa $14 **796.357**
    1. Baseball
    ISBN 0-15-100441-2; 0-15-601304-5 (pa)
    LC 00-32014
"The title refers to the battle of wits between pitcher and batter, which is the essence of baseball. Kahn sides with pitching, and in a narrative that is both analytical and anecdotal, he rewards the reader with what amounts to a scholarly treatise on the craft. He does so through engrossing portraits of pitching masters, from Candy Cummings, the reputed inventor of the curveball, to Bruce Sutter, the popularizer of the split-finger fastball. Kahn also presents us with Christy Mathewson on the fadeaway, Warren Spahn on the changeup and Don Drysdale on the duster." Sports Illustrated
Includes bibliographical references

Kahn, Roger, 1927-—*Continued*

October men; Reggie Jackson, George Steinbrenner, Billy Martin, and the Yankees' miraculous finish in 1978. Harcourt 2003 382p il $25 **796.357**

1. Jackson, Reggie, 1946- 2. Steinbrenner, George M. (George Michael), 1930- 3. Martin, Billy, 1928-1989 4. New York Yankees (Baseball team)

ISBN 0-15-100628-8 LC 2003-536

This is an "account of the 1978 Yankees. . . . The core of the book is Kahn's portrayal of . . . the principal owner, George Steinbrenner; the right fielder, Reggie Jackson; and the manager, Billy Martin." N Y Times Book Rev

"When it comes to writing about baseball, especially New York City baseball, Kahn is king of the hill." Publ Wkly

Kelly, Jerry, 1953-

Bushville; life and time in amateur baseball. McFarland & Co. 2001 202p il pa $21 **796.357**

1. Baseball

ISBN 0-7864-0979-7 LC 01-31264

Kelly's "reflections on what the game has meant to him—from fascination with baseball's special geometry to the sensual pleasure he takes in its textures of leather and wood—make the perfect antidote to most fans' disgust with the big money and big egos of today's major leaguers." Booklist

Includes bibliographical references

Lewis, Michael

Moneyball; the art of winning an unfair game. Norton 2003 288p $23.95 **796.357**

1. Beane, Billy, 1962- 2. Baseball

ISBN 0-393-05765-8 LC 2003-5089

The author "examines the proceedings of Billy Beane, general manager of the Oakland Athletics, who finished first in the American League West . . . [in 2002] with as many victories as the Yankees despite the third-smallest payroll in the major leagues." N Y Times Book Rev

"With so many baseball books to choose from, it is difficult to single out a few as must-haves, but this one comes pretty close." Booklist

Light, Jonathan Fraser, 1957-

The cultural encyclopedia of baseball. 2nd ed. McFarland & Co. 2005 1105p il $75 * **796.357**

1. Baseball—Encyclopedias

ISBN 0-7864-2087-1 LC 2005-1718

First published 1997

This encyclopedia "profiles every Hall of Fame player, as well as every National and American League club (and predecessors). . . . Statistics play a large role in this resource, which includes facts and figures on just about every conceivable event in the game. Cultural references to baseball are noted throughout in numerous quotations. Some of the more fascinating sections include 'Nicknames,' 'Presidents,' and 'Salaries.' Other entries

that make for offbeat perusal include 'Freak Accidents,' 'Sex,' and 'Injuries and Illnesses.'" Choice

Includes bibliographical references

Madden, Bill

Pride of October; what it was to be young and a Yankee. Warner Books 2003 453p il $24.95; pa $14.95 **796.357**

1. New York Yankees (Baseball team) 2. Baseball

ISBN 0-446-52932-X; 0-446-69269-7 (pa)

LC 2002-191063

Includes index

The author "profiles 18 former Yankees, offering insider looks at the most successful franchise in professional sports." Libr J

Madden "has pieced together a loving appreciation of what it means to wear pinstripes. Some of the better profiles are those of lesser lights, like the backup catcher Charlie Silvera and the pitchers Marius Russo and Tommy Byrne." N Y Times Book Rev

McCarver, Tim

Tim McCarver's Baseball for brain surgeons and other fans; understanding and interpreting the game so you can watch it like a pro; {by} Tim McCarver with Danny Peary. Villard Bks. 1998 xxi, 344p pa $12.95 hardcover o.p.

796.357

1. Baseball

ISBN 0-375-75340-0 (pa) LC 97-49301

"This book on the strategy of the diamond sport, covering managing, pitching, catching, batting, fielding and base running, is a discourse that all players could study profitably, from Little Leaguers to major league regulars. It offers well-thought-out positions backed by careful reasoning and broad experience." Publ Wkly

Murphy, Cait, 1961-

Crazy '08; how a cast of cranks, rogues, boneheads, and magnates created the greatest year in baseball history. Smithsonian/Collins 2007 368p il $24.95 * **796.357**

1. Baseball

ISBN 978-0-06-088937-1; 0-06-088937-3

LC 2006-50646

This is an account of the 1908 major league baseball season.

"A book that will long claim the attention of serious sports enthusiasts." Booklist

Includes bibliographical references

Pearlman, Jeff

The bad guys won; a season of brawling, boozing, bimbo-chasing, and championship baseball with Straw, Doc, Mookie, Nails, the Kid, and the rest of the 1986 Mets, the rowdiest team to put on a New York uniform, and maybe the best. HarperCollins 2004 287p il $24.95; pa $13.95 **796.357**

1. New York Mets (Baseball team) 2. Baseball

ISBN 0-06-050732-2; 0-06-050733-0 (pa)

LC 2003-56991

Pearlman, Jeff—*Continued*

The author "tracks the ascendancy of the 1986 New York Mets while foreshadowing the team's inability to resemble anything approximating a dynasty." Libr J

"Baseball aficionados, especially Mets fans, will enjoy this affectionate but critical look at this exciting season." Publ Wkly

Posnanski, Joe

The soul of baseball; a road trip through Buck O'Neil's America. Morrow 2007 276p $24.95

796.357

1. O'Neil, Buck, 1911-2006 2. Baseball 3. United States—Description and travel

ISBN 978-0-06-085403-4; 0-06-085403-0

An account of how the author "spent a year on the road with the iconic Negro Leagues player and manager Buck O'Neil (1911-2006), recording the magnanimous 94-year-old's encounters with scores of fans and his vast repertoire of entertaining stories." Publ Wkly

Prager, Joshua

The echoing green; the untold story of Bobby Thomson, Ralph Branca, and the shot heard round the world. Pantheon Books 2006 498p il $26.95 *

796.357

1. Thomson, Bobby, 1923- 2. Branca, Ralph 3. New York Giants (Baseball team) 4. Baseball

ISBN 0-375-42154-8; 978-0-375-42154-9

LC 2006-43157

This book "is about a long-rumored but never before substantiated plot by the 1951 New York Giants to steal the signs of opposing catchers in games played at their home park, the Polo Grounds, during the last 10 weeks of the season." N Y Times Book Rev

The author exposes "multiple layers of fascinating backstory to the drama within a drama, and his psychobiographies of Thomson and especially Branca are unfailingly compelling." Booklist

Includes bibliographical references

Ripken, Cal, Jr.

Play baseball the Ripken way; the complete illustrated guide to the fundamentals; [by] Cal Ripken, Jr. and Bill Ripken with Larry Burke. Random House 2004 236p il $24.95; pa $15.95

796.357

1. Baseball

ISBN 1-4000-6122-9; 0-8129-7050-0 (pa)

LC 2003-66725

"Chapters written by Cal cover batting, base running, infield play, and catching; Bill's chapters outline pitching and outfield play. The text is interspersed with . . . photographs as well as sidebars on special tips, and each chapter closes with a review checklist." Libr J

"This book is the next best thing to a personal lesson with the man who broke Lou Gehrig's record of playing in 2,632 consecutive games; it's a comprehensive look at all aspects of how to play baseball that will benefit young players and adult weekend warriors." Publ Wkly

Robinson, Ray, 1920-

Yankee Stadium; 75 years of drama, glamor, and glory; by Ray Robinson and Christopher Jennison. Penguin Studio 1998 182p il pa $19.95

796.357

1. Yankee Stadium (New York, N.Y.)

ISBN 0-670-87093-5; 978-0-670-03301-0 (pa); 0-670-03301-0 (pa)

LC 97-48496

"This book is about all the great sporting events—including great boxing matches such as Joe Louis's 1938 demolition of Max Schmeling—and some nonsporting events (such as papal visits and religious revivals) that have occurred at Yankee Stadium over its three-quarters of a century. Baseball does predominate, however, in this tale of 'The House That Ruth Built.' . . . Reminiscences by journalist Pete Hamill, broadcaster Bob Costas, and a few Yankee greats add an extra dimension." Libr J

Shapiro, Michael, 1952-

The last good season; Brooklyn, the Dodgers, and their final pennant race together. Doubleday 2003 356p il $24.95; pa $14.95

796.357

1. Brooklyn Dodgers (Baseball team) 2. Baseball

ISBN 0-385-50152-8; 0-767-90688-8 (pa)

LC 2002-71410

This is a "chronicle of the Dodger's 1956 season, their next-to-last in Brooklyn, and a . . . defense of the team's owner, Walter O'Malley, whose unsuccessful quest for a new stadium ended with the team's departure for Los Angeles." N Y Times Book Rev

"Equal parts sports, history, politics and sociology, Shapiro's book is reminiscent of the works of Caro, Halberstam and Kahn, and belongs in every sports fan's library." Publ Wkly

Includes bibliographical references

Smith, Red, 1905-1982

Red Smith on baseball; the game's greatest writer on the game's greatest years; with a foreword by Ira Berkow. Dee, I.R. 2000 363p il $24.95; pa $18.95 *

796.357

1. Baseball

ISBN 1-56663-289-7; 1-56663-415-6 (pa)

LC 99-53675

This volume contains columns written from the 1940s to the early 1980s. "Smith's essays on Bobby Thomson's 'shot heard 'round the world,' Mickey Mantle's first game and Don Larsen's no-hit pitching in the 1956 World Series are all worthy of memorization, and his trenchant views on the reserve clause and the night World Series games are strikes down the middle. As a bonus, the collection offers readers a fascinating look at how baseball writing has changed over the years, as have American attitudes." Publ Wkly

Snyder, Brad

Beyond the shadow of the Senators; the untold story of the Homestead Grays and the integration of baseball. Contemporary Books 2003 418p il $24.95; pa $14.95   **796.357**

1. Homestead Grays (Baseball team) 2. Washington Senators (Baseball team) 3. Baseball 4. United States—Race relations

ISBN 0-07-140820-7; 0-07-143197-7 (pa)

LC 2002-31335

This is the "story of the Homestead Grays, the Negro League's most successful franchise." Publisher's note

The author "gives a rich panorama of Washington as it evolved from a Southern provincial town to a large city with a black majority. . . . Snyder's book is not just the history of a team but the tale of one city in all its social complexity." N Y Times Book Rev

Includes bibliographical references

Sokolove, Michael Y.

The ticket out: Darryl Strawberry and the boys of Crenshaw; [by] Michael Sokolove. Simon & Schuster 2004 291p hardcover o.p. pa $14   **796.357**

1. Strawberry, Darryl 2. Crenshaw High School (Los Angeles, Calif.) 3. Baseball

ISBN 0-7432-2673-9; 0-7432-7885-2 (pa)

LC 2004-41745

"The individual stories of a vastly talented 1979 L.A. high-school baseball team come to life in this heartbreaking account of the players' last season and the difficulties they faced in the years that followed." Booklist

Includes bibliographical references

Tofel, Richard J., 1957-

A legend in the making; the New York Yankees in 1939. Dee, I.R. 2002 269p $24.95   **796.357**

1. New York Yankees (Baseball team) 2. Baseball

ISBN 1-56663-411-3   LC 2001-40824

This is the "story of the Yankees' 1939 winning season. . . . The casual racism against Italians and the utter dismissal of black baseball are not ignored, and Tofel grounds the year in events outside of baseball: the *Wizard of Oz* opens, Freud dies, Germany invades Poland. A fine gift for fans." Booklist

Includes bibliographical references

Tygiel, Jules

Baseball's great experiment; Jackie Robinson and his legacy; [with a new afterword] 25th anniversary ed, expanded ed. Oxford University Press 2008 415p il pa $19.95   **796.357**

1. Robinson, Jackie, 1919-1972 2. Baseball 3. United States—Race relations

ISBN 978-0-19-533928-4; 0-19-533928-2

LC 2008-273059

First published 1983

A history of the segregation and gradual integration of Afro-American athletes into major league baseball. In addition to Jackie Robinson, the author explores the careers of Larry Doby, Luke Easter, Satchel Paige, and others.

Tygiel also notes the vast social and demographic changes wrought by WWII that made integration inevitable

Includes bibliographical references

Vecsey, George

Baseball: a history of America's favorite game. Modern Library 2006 252p il (Modern Library chronicles) $21.95   **796.357**

1. Baseball

ISBN 0-679-64338-9; 978-0-679-64338-8

LC 2006-45033

This history of baseball "unfolds much like a highlights tape, with a breezy background narrative of the game from its pre-Civil War roots to its current drug scandals, structured around set pieces spotlighting the outsized deeds of luminaries like Babe Ruth, Jackie Robinson, Branch Rickey and George Steinbrenner. . . . Vivid, affectionate and clear-eyed, Vecsey's account makes for an engaging sports history." Publ Wkly

Includes bibliographical references

Ward, Geoffrey C.

Baseball: an illustrated history; narrative by Geoffrey C. Ward; based on a documentary filmscript by Geoffrey C. Ward and Ken Burns; preface by Ken Burns and Lynn Novick; with an introduction by Roger Angell; contributions by John Thorn [et al.] Knopf 1994 xxv, 486p il $65; pa $39.95   **796.357**

1. Baseball

ISBN 0-679-40459-7; 0-679-76541-7 (pa)

LC 93-39809

This "book is the companion to a nine-part PBS television documentary. . . . Each chapter, or 'inning,' proceeds chronologically with a dominant theme and dramatis personae." Libr J

"This lavishly produced, gorgeously illustrated history of the game rises far above the often dreary 'companion volume' genre." Booklist

Wendel, Tim

The new face of baseball; the one-hundred year rise and triumph of Latinos in America's favorite sport; foreword by Bob Costas; color photographs by Victor Baldizon. Rayo 2003 266p il hardcover o.p. pa $13.95   **796.357**

1. Baseball 2. Hispanic Americans

ISBN 0-06-053631-4; 0-06-053632-2 (pa)

LC 2004-300834

"Going as far back as the mid-nineteenth century, to the early days of Cuban baseball, Wendel traces the spread of American baseball fever in the Caribbean and Mexico." Publisher's note

"Fans will recognize names like Minoso, Clemente, Cepeda, or Sosa, but it is enlightening to see them presented as part of a single accomplished group . . . This is an excellent overview." Libr J

Includes bibliographical references

Will, George F.
Bunts: Curt Flood, Camden Yards, Pete Rose, and other reflections on baseball. Scribner 1998 352p il $25; pa $14   **796.357**
1. Baseball
ISBN 0-684-83820-6; 0-684-85374-4 (pa)
               LC 98-23500
A gathering of the author's "uncollected essays on the national pastime. Will holds forth on everything from Pete Rose's ban to the politics of team allegiance (Cubs or White Sox) in Chicago." Libr J
"Will has a passion for the game that he never allows to degenerate into intellectual prattlings or gooey rhapsodies. Indeed, his view of baseball is refreshingly unromantic." Christ Sci Monit

796.42   Track and field

Burfoot, Amby
Runner's world complete book of beginning running. Distributed to the trade by Holtzbrinck Publishers 2005 320p il pa $17.95   **796.42**
1. Running
ISBN 1-59486-022-X   LC 2004-17559
This book offers training advice to beginning runners and covers topics including stretching, cross-training, strength exercises, nutrition, and special issues for women runners.
Includes bibliographical references

Complete book of running; everything you need to know to run for fun, fitness and competition; edited by Amby Burfoot. Rodale 2004 312p il pa $17.95   **796.42**
1. Running
ISBN 1-57954-929-2
First published 1997 with title: Runner's world complete book of running
Among this volume's contributors are Liz Applegate, Hal Higdon, Joe Henderson and Joan Benoit Samuelson. Topics covered include: nutrition, injury prevention and treatment, shoe selection, mental readiness, and marathon preparation.

Higdon, Hal
Marathon: the ultimate training guide. 3rd ed. Rodale 2005 369p pa $17.95   **796.42**
1. Marathon running
ISBN 978-1-59486-199-4; 1-59486-199-4
             LC 2005-14083
First published 1993
This "manual includes training schedules designed for busy runners, nutritional information, motivational tips, and race-day guidance to help runners of all experience levels reach the 26.2-mile mark with speed, safety, and great satisfaction." Publisher's note

Scott, Dagny
Runner's world complete book of women's running; the best advice to get started, stay motivated, lose weight, run injury-free, be safe, and train for any distance; [by] Dagny Scott Barrios. Rev. and updated ed. Distributed to the trade by Holtzbrinck Publishers 2007 324p il pa $16.95   **796.42**
1. Running
ISBN 978-1-59486-758-3; 1-59486-758-5
             LC 2007-30645
First published 2000
Topics covered include racing, nutrition, running during pregnancy, weight loss, and proper clothing.

796.48   Olympic games

Guttmann, Allen
The Olympics, a history of the modern games. 2nd ed. University of Ill. Press 2002 214p il (Illinois history of sports) $39.95; pa $16.95   **796.48**
1. Olympic games
ISBN 0-252-02725-6; 0-252-07046-1 (pa)
             LC 2001-41383
First published 1992
"The author's premise is that politics have been at the foundation of modern Olympics from its inception in Athens (1896) to Seoul (1988). Gold, silver, and bronze medals have shared the victory stand with nationalism, and have even been tarnished by arrogance, protests, terrorists, and boycotts. Although the text emphasizes the political and socioeconomic climate of the Olympics, it also contains memorable accounts of athletic competition." Libr J {review of 1992 edition}
"Guttmann discusses the intended and actual meaning of the modern Olympic Games, from 1896 to 2000. Recounting the memorable and significant athletic events of the Olympics in terms of their social and political impact, Guttmann . . . {attempts to demonstrate} that the modern games were revived to propagate a political message and continue to serve political purposes." Publisher's note
Includes bibliographical references

Spivey, Nigel Jonathan
The ancient Olympics; [by] Nigel Spivey. Oxford University Press 2004 xxi, 273p il $28; pa $14.95 *   **796.48**
1. Olympic games
ISBN 0-19-280433-2; 0-19-280604-1 (pa)
             LC 2004-46147
In this study of the Olympics in the ancient world, "the author explores what the events were, the rules for competitors, training and diet, the pervasiveness of cheating and bribery, the prizes on offer, the exclusion of 'barbarians,' and protocols on pederasty." Publisher's note
This book "lets us imagine both the strangeness and the glory that surrounded sports in its infancy." Christ Sci Monit
Includes bibliographical references

796.51   Walking

Hart, John, 1948-
Walking softly in the wilderness; the Sierra
Club guide to backpacking. 4th ed, complete rev
and updated. Sierra Club Books 2005 508p il map
(Sierra Club outdoor adventure guide) pa $16.95
*   **796.51**
> 1. Backpacking 2. Wilderness areas
> ISBN 1-578-05123-1   LC 2004-56554
> First published 1977

This guide for both the novice and experienced hiker
reflects the environmental concerns of the Sierra Club.
Among topics covered are: clothing and equipment; making and breaking camp; problem animals and plants; hik-
ing and camping with kids. Listings of conservation and
wilderness travel organizations, map and equipment
sources, land management agencies, and Internet contacts
are appended.
Includes bibliographical references

Kemsley, William, Jr.
Backpacker and hiker's handbook. Stackpole
Books 2008 290p il map pa $24.95
                                       796.51
> 1. Backpacking 2. Hiking
> ISBN 978-0-8117-3462-2; 0-8117-3462-5
>   LC 2007-21147

This book "tells how to plan and prepare for a
backpacking trip and discusses equipment, safety, and the
essential trail skills of using a compass, purifying water,
cooking, and where and how to set up camp." Publisher's note
Includes bibliographical references

Solnit, Rebecca
Wanderlust; a history of walking. Viking 2000
326p il pa $15 hardcover o.p.   **796.51**
> 1. Walking 2. Hiking 3. Voyages and travels
> ISBN 0-14-028601-2 (pa)   LC 99-41153

The author presents a "look at how the act of walking
. . . has influenced our history, our science, our literature, and the very way that we see ourselves as human
beings. Drawing on a multitude of diverse disciplines,
Solnit illustrates that walking has led to some of the best,
and worst, incidents in all of history." Booklist
Includes bibliographical references

796.52   Walking and exploring by kind of terrain

Hurd, Barbara
Entering the stone; on caves and feeling through
the dark. Houghton Mifflin 2003 170p $23 *
                                       796.52
> 1. Caves
> ISBN 0-618-19138-0   LC 2003-47839

The author "uses the sport of caving Maryland's Devil's Hole cave and Oregon's Siskiyous Mountains . . . as

the launching point for observations about the ways we
'use landscape and the people in our lives to orient ourselves.' Hurd often weaves resonant parallels between
what she sees in the nature of caves and her own life,
such as her moving recollections of her father and of a
friend dying of cancer." Publ Wkly

Taylor, Michael Ray, 1959-
Caves; exploring hidden realms. National
Geographic Soc. 2001 216p il maps $35
                                       796.52
> 1. Caves
> ISBN 0-7922-7904-2   LC 00-52710

This book was produced in conjunction with an IMAX
project filming two caver's explorations in the Yucatan,
Greenland, and the South-Central United States
"The photographs and the story of the explorations
would be sufficient to recommend this work, but it also
includes fascinating background material on the history
of the caves, their biological diversity, {and} the tools
used by spelunkers." Booklist
Includes bibliographical references

796.522   Mountaineering

Blum, Arlene, 1945-
Breaking trail; a climbing life. Scribner 2005
313p il map $27.50   **796.522**
> 1. Mountaineering
> ISBN 0-7432-5846-0   LC 2005-44053

"In hiker's parlance, the person who 'breaks trail' is
one who leads others across difficult terrain, creating a
path as they go. This aptly describes Blum's role, not
only in her experiences as a climber, but also as a scientist doing innovative, groundbreaking work. Blum . . .
covers a cross section of her life as a climber, from her
first experience, as a college student in 1964, to 1993,
when she semiretired. Through climbing, she experiences
a wide range of emotions, from exhilaration at success to
grief over the death of friends. Interspersed between the
climbing stories are scenes from her childhood that do
much to explain the person she became. This is an engaging, well-written adventure that also serves as a social
history of women's roles." Booklist

Boukreev, Anatoli, d. 1997
The climb; tragic ambitions on Everest; [by]
Anatoli Boukreev and G. Weston Dewalt. St.
Martin's Press 1997 255p il pa $14.95 hardcover
o.p.   **796.522**
> 1.   Mount   Everest   Expedition   (1996)
> 2. Mountaineering
> ISBN 0-312-20637-2 (pa)   LC 97-23194

"This is a first-person account of the tragic climbing
experience in May 1996 on Mount Everest that left eight
hikers dead and several others struggling to stay alive.
. . . Fast-paced and easy to read, Boukreev's story of
adventure and survival will remain in the reader's memory long after the book is finished." Libr J

Coburn, Broughton, 1951-

Everest: mountain without mercy; introduction by Tim Cahill, afterword by David Breashears. National Geographic Soc. 1997 256p il maps $35; pa $24   **796.522**

1. Mount Everest Expedition (1996)
2. Mountaineering
ISBN 0-7922-7014-2; 0-7922-6984-5 (pa)

LC 97-10765

"Bringing an understated yet powerful Buddhist/Sherpa ethical perspective to the tragedy on Everest chronicled in Jon Krakauer's Into Thin Air, Coburn reports on the IMAX film crew who participated in the rescue effort when the May 1996 expeditions led by guides Rob Hall and Scott Fischer ended in death and crippling injury." Publ Wkly

Jamling Tenzing Norgay

Touching my father's soul; a Sherpa's journey to the top of Everest; [by] Jamling Tenzing Norgay with Broughton Coburn. HarperSanFrancisco 2001 316p il map pa $15.95 hardcover o.p.   **796.522**

1. Tenzing Norgay, 1914-1986 2. Mount Everest Expedition (1996) 3. Mountaineering
ISBN 0-06-251688-4 (pa)   LC 00-68723

"Norgay, who led the IMAX *Everest* expedition, is the son of legendary mountaineer Tenzing Norgay, the first Sherpa to conquer Everest with Sir Edmund Hillary in 1953. In this blend of autobiography, family history, and adventure, Norgay describes how he summited Mount Everest in 1996 by following in his father's footsteps." Libr J

This "work has considerably more depth than an exposition of the climb. . . . The son's climb is a pilgrimage exploring his relationship to his father, his Sherpa culture, and Buddhism. It is also a fascinating look into the world of climbers and their relationship to the Sherpas who risk their lives to assist them." Booklist

Krakauer, Jon

Into thin air; a personal account of the Mount Everest disaster. Villard Bks. 1997 xx, 293p il $25.95; pa $14.95 *   **796.522**

1. Mount Everest Expedition (1996)
2. Mountaineering
ISBN 0-679-45752-6; 0-385-49478-5 (pa)

LC 96-30031

This is an account of the author's May 1996 Mount Everest climbing expedition in which twelve fellow climbers died during a snow storm

"This tense, harrowing story is as mesmerizing and hard to put down as any well-written adventure novel." SLJ

Includes bibliographical references

796.54   Camping

Guide to summer camps and summer schools 2008/2009; an objective, comparative reference source for residential summer programs. 31st ed. Porter Sargent Pub. 2008 862p il (Porter Sargent Handbook series) $45; pa $27 *

796.54

1. Camps—Directories
ISSN 0072-8705
ISBN   978-0-87558-163-7;   0-87558-163-3;
978-0-87558-164-4 (pa); 0-87558-164-1 (pa)

First published 1936. Periodically revised. Title varies

"This reliable comprehensive source of summer academic and tutorial programs, travel programs, specialized study programs, and recreational camps lists about 1,300 such programs in the U.S. and Canada. An extensive table of contents and an index make it possible to access all of this information." Safford. Guide to Ref Materials For Sch Media Cent. 5th edition

796.6   Cycling and related activities

Bicycling magazine's 1,000 all-time best tips; top riders share their secrets to maximize fun, safety, and performance; edited by Ben Hewitt. Fully rev and updated. Rodale 2005 168p il pa $10.95   **796.6**

1. Cycling
ISBN 978-1-59486-051-5; 1-59486-051-3

LC 2005-638

Replaces Bicyling magazine's 900 all-time best tips

A collection of information on such topics as bicycle models, accessories, riding styles, and repair techniques

Carmichael, Chris

The ultimate ride; get fit, get fast, and start winning with the world's top cycling coach; [by] Chris Carmichael with Jim Rutberg. G.P. Putnam's Sons 2003 325p il hardcover o.p. pa $15

796.6

1. Cycling 2. Physical fitness
ISBN 0-399-15071-4; 0-425-19601-1 (pa)

LC 2003-43214

The author offers advice to "serious cyclists wanting to improve their abilities, compete more successfully and train without incurring injuries." Publ Wkly

"This is an excellent guide to obtaining peak performance in cycling competition, but the wealth of training tips and intelligent discussion of nutrition will be almost as valuable to noncompetitive cyclists and even to other athletes serious about conditioning." Booklist

796.63   Mountain biking

Bicycling magazine's mountain biking skills; skills and techniques to master any terrain. Rodale 2005 122p pa $9.95   **796.63**

1. Mountain biking
ISBN 978-1-59486-299-1; 1-59486-299-0

LC 2005-23045

First published 1990

This guide to mountain biking covers basic and intermediate skills and techniques including "ways to handle tough terrain, steer clear of hazardous obstacles, and even crash properly to avoid injury." Publisher's note

796.72   Automobile racing

Menzer, Joe
The wildest ride; a history of NASCAR (or, How a bunch of good ol' boys built a billion-dollar industry out of wrecking cars). Simon & Schuster 2001 311p il hardcover o.p. pa $14   **796.72**
1. National Association for Stock Car Auto Racing
2. Automobile racing
ISBN 0-7432-0507-3; 0-7432-2625-9 (pa)
LC 2001-031088
This history focuses on the "legacy of the founding France family, the evolution of the cars from modified stock cars to purpose-built racers, and the fan-base expansion of the 1980s and 1990s. . . . Highly entertaining and full of facts." Libr J
Includes bibliographical references

Wright, James D., 1947-
Fixin' to git; one fan's love affair with NASCAR's Winston Cup; [by] Jim Wright. Duke Univ. Press 2002 305p il $26.95; pa $18.95
796.72
1. National Association for Stock Car Auto Racing
2. Automobile racing
ISBN 0-8223-2926-3; 0-8223-3220-5 (pa)
LC 2002-485
The author offers his perspectives on NASCAR Winston Cup auto racing "and its significance in modern American culture. . . . {He discusses} a variety of issues, such as fan allegiance, the growth and popularity of NASCAR racing, and the difficulty of setting up a car for the unique conditions of each race track." Libr J
"This is the very best book to surface on auto racing in many years. Informative, entertaining, and eye-opening." Booklist

796.8   Combat sports

Anasi, Robert, 1966-
The gloves; a boxing chronicle. North Point Press 2002 331p $24; pa $14 *   **796.8**
1. Boxing
ISBN 0-86547-599-7; 0-86547-652-7 (pa)
LC 2001-44111
In this "look at the world of amateur boxing, freelance writer Anasi chronicles how jabbing and jump-roping at a grubby gym in San Francisco's Tenderloin district developed into a life-altering quest to compete, in his early 30s, in New York's storied amateur boxing tournament, the Golden Gloves." Publ Wkly

Beekman, Scott
Ringside; a history of professional wrestling in America; [by] Scott M. Beekman. Praeger 2006 188p il $39.95 *   **796.8**
1. Wrestling
ISBN 0-275-98401-X; 978-0-275-98401-4
LC 2006-8230

"This chronological work begins with a brief account of wrestling's global history, and then proceeds to investigate the sport's growth as a specifically American institution." Publisher's note
"An eye-opening reappraisal of a much-maligned sport, and (for wrestling fans) perhaps a much-needed vindication." Booklist
Includes bibliographical references

Cohen, Richard
By the sword; a history of gladiators, musketeers, samurai, swashbucklers, and Olympic champions. Random House 2002 xxiv, 519p il $29.95; pa $15.95   **796.8**
1. Fencing
ISBN 0-375-50417-6; 0-8129-6966-9 (pa)
LC 2002-21309
This is a worldwide history of sword fighting from Ancient Egypt to the present which considers its role in combat and sports, word origins and customs, and the fencing skills of politicians and actors
"A fascinating story told with literary verve and the pride of a longtime practitioner; highly recommended." Libr J
Includes bibliographical references

Kram, Mark
The ghosts of Manila; the fateful, brutal blood feud between Muhammad Ali and Joe Frazier. HarperCollins Pubs. 2001 232p pa $12.95 hardcover o.p.   **796.8**
1. Ali, Muhammad, 1942- 2. Frazier, Joe, 1944-
3. Boxing
ISBN 0-06-095480-9 (pa)   LC 00-53934
The author "tells the story of Joe Frazier and Muhammad Ali's epic 1975 Manila fight, and the bitter and complex rivalry between the two men that preceded it." Publ Wkly
This is "a fascinating blend of history and biography." Booklist

Kreidler, Mark
Four days to glory; wrestling with the soul of the American heartland. HarperCollins Publishers 2007 262p il $24.95 *   **796.8**
1. Wrestling 2. School sports
ISBN 978-0-06-082318-4; 0-06-082318-6
LC 2007-272997
Jay Borschel and Dan LeClere aspire to be four-time high school wrestling champions in Iowa.
The author's "deftness in 'Four Days' is in turning a niche sport into one as accessible as baseball or basketball." N Y Times Book Rev

Margolick, David
Beyond glory; Joe Louis vs. Max Schmeling, and a world on the brink. Knopf 2005 423p il $26.95 *   **796.8**
1. Louis, Joe, 1914-1981 2. Schmeling, Max, 1905-2005 3. Boxing
ISBN 0-375-41192-5   LC 2005-45141

Margolick, David—*Continued*

The author discusses the historical significance of the fights between Joe Louis and German boxer Max Schmeling in 1936 and 1938.

This book "will be the definitive account of Louis versus Schmeling. And it's a hell of a good read besides." Booklist

Includes bibliographical references

Park, Yeon Hwan

Black belt tae kwon do; the ultimate reference guide to the world's most popular martial art; by Y.H. Park & Jon Gerrard. Facts on File 2000 272p il hardcover o.p. pa $16.95   **796.8**

1. Tae kwon do

ISBN 0-8160-4240-3; 0-8160-4241-1 (pa)

LC 99-57876

Coverage includes practice, warm-up, and advanced techniques and forms, sparring strategies, self-defense, and breaking. Over 700 photographs accompany the text. Appendixes cover official competition rules, weight classes, governing bodies, and international organizations and associations. Includes two glossaries, English to Korean and Korean to English

Schulberg, Budd

Ringside; a treasury of boxing reportage; with an introduction by Hugh McIlvanney. I. R. Dee 2006 364p il $27.50 *   **796.8**

1. Boxing

ISBN 978-1-56663-707-7; 1-56663-707-4

LC 2006-11639

"In more than five decades of writing about boxing, Schulberg has distinguished himself by knowing as much about the sport as he does about writing. The likes of Oates and Plimpton and even Remnick may turn a phrase, but only Schulberg has seen most every important fight since Louis-Schmeling. This collection gathers together reviews, biographical sketches, and boxing reportage from throughout his life. . . . With relatively few punch-by-punch recounts of fights and quite a lot of strategy analysis, this collection will appeal most to seasoned boxing fans. But most anyone can enjoy the wonderful 80-page piece that closes the book, a stirring eulogy for the famously greedy and self-involved fight promoter Mike Jacobs." Booklist

Includes bibliographical references

Sparring with Hemingway and other legends of the fight game. Dee, I.R. 1995 256p $25   **796.8**

1. Boxing

ISBN 1-56663-080-0

LC 94-49153

This is a collection of the author's articles about boxing, originally published between 1954 and 1994

"Included are beautifully crafted portraits of legends such as Benny Leonard, Muhammad Ali, and ageless wonder George Foreman. . . . This literate, entertaining collection represents some of the best writing on any sport." Libr J

796.9 Ice and snow sports

Bennett, Jeff

The complete snowboarder; {by} Jeff Bennett, Scott Downey and Charles Arnell. 2nd ed. Ragged Mountain Press 2000 148p il pa $14.95   **796.9**

1. Snowboarding

ISBN 0-07-135787-4   LC 00-39059

First published 1994

This offers advice on getting started in snowboarding, equipment, techniques, snowboarding areas and trails, tricks, competitions, safety, and equipment maintenance.

796.962 Ice hockey

A **basic** guide to ice hockey; the U.S. Olympic Committee. Griffin Pub, Distributed by G. Stevens Pub 2002 152p il (Olympic guides) lib bdg $23.93; pa $9.95   **796.962**

1. Hockey

ISBN 0-8368-3103-9 (lib bdg); 1-58000-085-1 (pa)

LC 2001-55096

Provides information on such aspects of ice hockey as the history of Olympic competition, game rules and strategies, relevant nutrition, safety and first aid, and more. Describes Olympic and ice hockey organizations.

Duplacey, James

The official rules of hockey; edited by Dan Diamond. Lyons Press 2001 208p il pa $19.95 *   **796.962**

1. National Hockey League 2. Hockey

ISBN 1-58574-052-7   LC 00-67176

First published 1996 with title The annotated rules of hockey

"The Official Rules of Hockey is a historical, anecdotal, and illustrated guide to the rules of the world's fastest game. . . . {It includes} rink diagrams, illustrations of officials' signals, and a compendium of milestone moments chronicling the sport's evolving rules of play." Publisher's note

McKinley, Michael, 1961-

Hockey: a people's history. McClelland & Stewart 2006 346p il $45 *   **796.962**

1. Hockey

ISBN 0-7710-5769-5; 978-0-7710-5769-4

This history "chronicles hockey from its genesis as a winter substitute for lacrosse. A companion to a similarly titled CBC TV series, the lavishly illustrated book combines punchy boxed features celebrating individuals and hockey oddments and a detailed tracing of the game's development. . . . Essential for general sports as well as hockey-intensive collections." Booklist

Includes bibliographical references

796.98   Winter Olympic games

Wallechinsky, David, 1948-
The complete book of the Winter Olympics.
2002 ed. Overlook Press 2001 xxxviii, 353p il
$25.95; pa $15.95   **796.98**
  1. Olympic games
  ISBN 1-58567-195-9; 1-58567-185-1 (pa)
                     LC 2001-36018
  First published 1984
  This compendium of Olympic history provides "backgrounds, stories, and statistics from every Winter Olympics since the Chamonix games of 1924." Publisher's
note

797.1   Boating

Fredston, Jill A.
Rowing to latitude; journeys along the Arctic's
edge; [by] Jill Fredston. North Point Press 2001
289p il $24; pa $14   **797.1**
  1. Canoes and canoeing
  ISBN 0-374-28180-7; 0-86547-655-1 (pa)
                     LC 2001-30049
  The author and her husband, Doug Fesler "canoe the
Arctic and sub-Arctic coastlines of Alaska, Canada,
Greenland, Norway and Sweden for three months out of
each year. . . . Fredston ably describes both the big picture—the coastline, encounters with polar bears, the
high-stakes game of second-guessing storms and tides—
and the details of their travels. . . . A must-read for
armchair travelers, as well as a close and loving look at
an intimate relationship." Publ Wkly

Mason, Bill, 1929-
Path of the paddle; [an illustrated guide to the
art of canoeing] Rev. and updated. Firefly Books
1999 200p il pa $19.95   **797.1**
  1. Canoes and canoeing
  ISBN 1-55209-328-X; 978-1-55209-328-3
  First published 1980 by Van Nostrand Reinhold
  Illustrated with photographs of Canadian rivers, this
instructional guide demonstrates that "canoeing isn't just
a mellow flatwater pursuit but can be an extremely risky
and challenging way to explore some of the world's most
rugged back-country." Libr J
  Includes bibliographical references

Rousmaniere, John
The illustrated dictionary of boating terms; 2000
essential terms for sailors & powerboaters. [rev ed]
Norton 1998 168p il $23.95   **797.1**
  ISBN 0-393-04649-4   LC 97-45938
  First published 1976 with title: A glossary of modern
sailing terms
  "Much of the newer terminology is derived from current boating and sailing magazines and from the author's
active participation in boating. The illustrations help clarify definitions. . . . The work is aimed at two audiences,
powerboaters and sailors, who do not always speak the

same language; variations in terminology are noted. This,
and the dictionary's currency, will make it useful for all
boat lovers and landlubbers." Choice

797.2   Swimming and diving

Busch, Akiko
Nine ways to cross a river; midstream
reflections on swimming and getting there from
here. Bloomsbury USA 2007 208p map $19.95
                               797.2
  1. Swimming 2. Rivers
  ISBN 978-1-59691-045-4; 1-59691-045-3
                     LC 2006-30270
  The author chronicles "her intimate involvement with
rivers. Busch swam across the river she loves best, the
Hudson, in August 2001, and somehow the tragic events
that followed made it seem 'essential to mark each summer after that with a river crossing.' . . . Her immer-
sions literally and figuratively in the Delaware, Connecticut, Susquehanna, Monongahela, Mississippi, and other
rivers involve pondering each one's complex and telling
history, particularly its 'industrial archaeology.' . . . In
all, a beautiful and gracefully enlightening book of river-
ine reflections." Booklist

Graver, Dennis
Scuba diving; [by] Dennis K. Graver. 3rd ed.
Human Kinetics 2003 209p il pa $23.95
                               797.2
  1. Scuba diving
  ISBN 0-7360-4539-2   LC 2002-152325
  First published 1993
  On cover: Official scuba instructional manual of the
YMCA of the USA
  "This colorful beginner's guide is used by many div-
ing classes, including the YMCA Scuba Diving program.
All the basics are covered: why dive, equipment, diving
science, and what you might see on a dive." Libr J
  Includes bibliographical references

Katz, Jane
Swimming for total fitness; a progressive
aerobic program; by Jane Katz with Nancy P.
Bruning; illustrations by Phillip Jones. updated ed.
Doubleday 1992 400p il pa $18.95   **797.2**
  1. Swimming 2. Physical fitness
  ISBN 0-385-46821-0   LC 92-31877
  First published 1981
  This introduction to swimming covers basic strokes,
kicks, turns, starts, and dives. Progressive training regi-
mens for beginning to advanced swimmers are then presented, followed by a chapter on equipment. A question
and answer section concludes the book

Mullen, P. H., Jr.

Gold in the water; the true story of ordinary men and their extraordinary dream of Olympic glory. Thomas Dunne Bks. 2001 326p il hardcover o.p. pa $14.95 **797.2**

1. Swimming 2. Olympic games, 2000 (Sydney, Australia)

ISBN 0-312-26595-6; 0-312-31116-8 (pa)

LC 2001-31955

"Mullen chronicles the U.S. Olympic swimming team on its journey to the 2000 Summer Games in Sydney. The text moves back and forth in time, giving a sense of the athletes as people and showing what motivates someone to structure his or her whole life toward a single goal." Booklist

797.3   Other aquatic sports

Grannis, LeRoy, 1917-

Surf photography of the 1960s and 1970s; [photographs by] LeRoy Grannis ; edited by Jim Heimann ; essay by Steve Barilotti. Taschen 2006 276p il $39.99 **797.3**

1. Surfing—Pictorial works 2. Artistic photography

ISBN 978-3-8228-4859-3

"In LeRoy Grannis: Surf Photography of the 1960s and 1970s, the myth of sun-soaked California is spun out in elegiac Technicolor: A hot-dogging Miki Dora, one of the sport's great pioneers, catches a tube; a stack of amber-hued boards at Greg Noll's surf shop in Hermosa glows like honey; the dewy-fresh surf model Marsha Bainer poses next to a longboard twice her height; and the towering green wall of Hawaii's Pipeline tumbles with apocalyptic fury. Grannis's motto was 'Shoot it now or you'll never get it back.' In this dappled monograph, the period that Grannis documented—California at maximum stokage, surfing evolving from fad to ethos—appears much like a wave itself, as evanescent as it was indelible." Men's Vogue

Martin, Andrew, 1952-

Stealing the wave; the epic struggle between Ken Bradshaw and Mark Foo; [by] Andy Martin. Bloomsbury 2007 244p $24.95 **797.3**

1. Foo, Mark, d. 1994 2. Bradshaw, Ken 3. Surfing

ISBN 978-1-59691-380-6; 1-59691-380-0

First published 2006 in the United Kingdom

"A couple of days before Christmas 1994, two of big-wave surfing's biggest names and fiercest competitors, Ken Bradshaw and Mark Foo, met near San Francisco for what would prove to be a turning point for both men. At a new reef, appropriately called Maverick's, they challenged each other, pushing themselves to the limit. Foo, a competitor who never knew when to hold back, drowned that day. . . . [The author] celebrates the lives of both men: Foo, the attention-grabbing, headline-seeking self-promoter, and his rival, Bradshaw, a handful of years older and considered to be a more solid, down-to-earth fellow. . . . A story not just about surfing but also about friendship, perseverance, and passion." Booklist

798.4   Horse racing

Barich, Bill

A fine place to daydream; racehorses, romance, and the Irish. Knopf 2006 228p $23

798.4

1. Horse racing 2. Ireland

ISBN 1-4000-4279-8; 978-1-4000-4279-1

LC 2005-44545

First published 2005 in the United Kingdom

The author "moves to Dublin after falling in love with an Irish woman, but shortly after his arrival he develops an (arguably) even stronger passion for gambling on Irish horse races. . . . Barich follows a steeplechase season from October to March, culminating in a weeklong series of races at Cheltenham, England, and consults as many horse trainers, jockeys, bookies and fellow fans as he can find to get the inside dope on how he should place his bets." Publ Wkly

This "is an enjoyable, freewheeling book in itself, but implicit herein is a smart disapprobation of our racing culture, and with that, the book gains weight." N Y Times Book Rev

Includes bibliographical references

Drape, Joe

The race for the Triple Crown; horses, high stakes, and eternal hope. Atlantic Monthly Press 2001 261p pa $14 hardcover o.p. **798.4**

1. Horse racing

ISBN 0-8021-3885-3 (pa) LC 2001-16044

In this "look at the highest level of horse racing, the author traces the lives of a handful of preeminent horse owners, trainers and jockeys in their preparations for the Kentucky Derby, the Preakness and the Belmont." Publ Wkly

Eisenberg, John, 1956-

The great match race; when North met South in America's first sports spectacle. Houghton Mifflin Co. 2006 258p il $25 * **798.4**

1. Horse racing

ISBN 978-0-618-55612-0; 0-618-55612-5

LC 2005-31540

In 1823 "sixty thousand people gathered on Long Island to watch two thoroughbreds battle it out in three grueling heats. . . . Eclipse was the . . . champion representing the North's evolving industrial machine, and Henry was an equine arriviste embodying Southern perceptions of superiority." Publisher's note

The author "succeeds in creating a gripping yarn of sporting contest, portrayal of a historical moment and smart analysis of a country headed eventually for civil war." Publ Wkly

Includes bibliographical references

Hillenbrand, Laura

Seabiscuit; an American legend. Random House 2001 399p il $25.95; pa $15.95 * **798.4**

1. Horse racing 2. Seabiscuit (Race horse)

ISBN 0-375-50291-2; 0-449-00561-5 (pa)

LC 2001-267852

Hillenbrand, Laura—*Continued*

Hillenbrand tells the story of the race horse who defeated "Triple Crown Winner War Admiral in what [has been] called the greatest horse race of all time [Pimlico, Nov. 1, 1938]." Newsweek

"This is a remarkable tale well told by a writer who deftly blends history and sport." Economist

Includes bibliographical references

Mitchell, Elizabeth, 1966-

Three strides before the wire; the dark and beautiful world of horse racing. Hyperion 2002 403p $24.95; pa $14.95 *　　**798.4**

1. Horse racing

ISBN 0-7868-6723-X; 0-7868-8622-6 (pa)

　　　　　　　　　　　　　　LC 2002-68817

The author "tells the story of Charismatic, who exploded out of the proletarian ranks of claiming horses to come within a stone's throw of sweeping the Triple Crown in 1999 before suffering a career-ending injury in the Belmont Stakes. . . . Mitchell's book possesses an appeal that extends well beyond its subject." Booklist

Ours, Dorothy

Man o' War; a legend like lightning. St Martin's Press 2006 342p il $24.95　　**798.4**

1. Man o' War (Race horse) 2. Horse racing

ISBN 0-312-34099-0; 978-0-312-34099-5

　　　　　　　　　　　　　　LC 2006-41631

This is an account of the thoroughbred racehorse Man o' War, also known as Big Red.

This book "is clearly a labor of love, and it certifies Big Red's claim to immortality." N Y Times Book Rev

Includes bibliographical references

Smiley, Jane, 1949-

A year at the races; reflections on horses, humans, love, money, and luck. Knopf 2004 287p $22　　**798.4**

1. Horse racing

ISBN 1-4000-4058-2　　　　LC 2003-65655

This is an "exploration of the . . . bond between humans and horses." Publisher's note

"The very qualities of mind that make Smiley such a compelling novelist—her keen attentiveness to the sensuous world, her deep sensitivity to psychological states, and her fascination with life's entwinement of chance and inevitability—enable her to write about horses, both their interior and exterior selves, with extraordinary avidity, empathy, wonder, and gratitude." Booklist

Includes bibliographical references

Squires, James D.

Horse of a different color; a tale of breeding geniuses, dominant females, and the fastest Derby winner since Secretariat; [by] Jim Squires. PublicAffairs 2002 300p il $26; pa $14

　　　　　　　　　　　　　　798.4

1. Horse racing 2. Kentucky Derby

ISBN 1-58648-117-7; 1-58648-180-0 (pa)

　　　　　　　　　　　　　　LC 2001-59602

This is the story of how the author, a former editor of the Chicago Tribune, became a breeder of thoroughbred race horses, including a horse named Monarchos, the champion of the 2001 Kentucky Derby

This "is fast paced and fun to read. It will appeal not only to horseracing fans but also to people making midlife career changes." Libr J

798.401　Horse race betting

Ainslie, Tom

Ainslie's complete guide to thoroughbred racing. 3rd ed. Simon & Schuster 1986 349p il pa $14 hardcover o.p.　　**798.401**

1. Horse racing 2. Gambling

ISBN 0-671-65655-4 (pa)　　LC 86-3879

First published 1968

A guide to the fundamentals of handicapping races including such topics as breeding, judging condition of the horses, calculating speed, track ratings and other tips for successful betting

798.8　Dog racing

Paulsen, Gary

Winterdance; the fine madness of running the Iditarod. Harcourt Brace & Co. 1994 256p il $26; pa $15　　**798.8**

1. Iditarod Trail Sled Dog Race, Alaska 2. Sled dog racing

ISBN 0-15-126227-6; 0-15-600145-4 (pa)

　　　　　　　　　　　　　　LC 93-42096

"This book is primarily an account of Paulsen's first Iditarod and its frequent life-threatening disasters. . . . However, the book is more than a tabulation of tribulations; it is a meditation on the extraordinary attraction this race holds for some men and women." Libr J

799.1　Fishing

Frazier, Ian

The fish's eye; essays about angling and the outdoors. Farrar, Straus & Giroux 2002 163p $20; pa $12　　**799.1**

1. Fishing

ISBN 0-374-15520-8; 0-312-42169-9 (pa)

　　　　　　　　　　　　　　LC 2001-54451

A compendium of the author's essays written for The New Yorker over the last two decades

"It's almost impossible to read these heartfelt and lovingly rendered essays without sharing the author's fascination with woods and water and fish." Booklist

Fulsher, Keith, 1922-

Thunder Creek flies; tying and fishing the classic baitfish imitations; [by] Keith Fulsher with David Klausmeyer. Stackpole Books 2006 109p il $34.95　　**799.1**

1. Artificial flies 2. Fishing

ISBN 978-0-8117-0171-6; 0-8117-0171-9

　　　　　　　　　　　　　　LC 2005-29043

Fulsher, Keith, 1922-—_Continued_

An expanded edition of Flying and fishing the Thunder Creek series, published 1973

Provides details on constructing twenty-two freshwater flies and six saltwater designs, descriptions of specific baitfish they imitate, and large photographs of each pattern. Includes step-by-step instructions for tying and tips for fishing the flies throughout the year in all water conditions.

Includes bibliographical references

Hafele, Rick

Nymph-fishing rivers and streams; a biologist's view of taking trout below the surface. Stackpole Books 2006 178p il $49.95 *   **799.1**

1. Fly casting 2. Trout fishing

ISBN 978-0-8117-0169-3; 0-8117-0169-7

LC 2005-27278

The author begins by "feeding patterns-where trout feed, when they feed, and what's available for them to eat. Sections on tackle and pattern selection help anglers sort through equipment and imitations to find the best outfit for their needs. The DVD complements the photos in the book that show various methods for nymph fishing. Also included is an angler's field guide to nymphs with details on their habitat, importance to trout, and the most effective patterns and fishing tactics to imitate them." Publisher's note

Includes bibliographical references

Hersey, John, 1914-1993

Blues; with drawings by James Baker. Knopf 1987 205p il pa $13 hardcover o.p. *   **799.1**

1. Fishing

ISBN 0-394-75702-5 (pa)   LC 86-46008

"This book about fishing for bluefish off the coast of Cape Cod features a wide array of information about that one group of fish, but not in straightforward fashion. It is written in the form of fictional conversations between the 'fisherman' and 'the stranger,' who discuss everything from the blues' mating habits to recipes for preparing them. They also cover sea lore, fishing, and ecology, with frequent references to literature and poetry." Libr J

"People who love and care about nature and their place in it, be they fishermen or not, should thoroughly enjoy 'Blues.'" Wilson Libr Bull

L.L. Bean ultimate book of fly fishing. Lyons Press 2002 344p il hardcover o.p. pa $24.95   **799.1**

1. Fishing 2. Fly casting

ISBN 1-58574-632-0; 1-59228-891-X (pa)

LC 2002-73191

Each chapter also published separately

Contents: L.L. Bean fly-fishing handbook / Dave Whitlock — L.L. Bean fly-casting handbook / Macauley Lord — L.L. Bean fly-tying handbook / Dick Talleur

The topics discussed in this book include "assembly of fly tackle; the biology of fish; natural fish foods and how to imitate them; safety techniques; bass flies; where to find bass; the eleven habits of highly effective fly casters; the basic four-part cast; the roll cast; the basics of fly tying; types of flies; the top ten most popular and successful fly patterns; and . . . more." Publisher's note

Pollizotto, Martin

Saltwater fishing made easy. International Marine/McGraw-Hill 2006 350p il pa $22.95   **799.1**

1. Fishing

ISBN 0-07-146722-X; 978-0-07-146722-3

LC 2006-751

This book covers saltwater fishing basics, equipment, techniques and methods, and how to prepare the fish.

Schullery, Paul

The rise; streamside observations on trout, flies, and fly fishing; photographs by the author; illustrations by Marsha Karle; with additional illustrations from angling literature. Stackpole Books 2006 194p il $26.95 *   **799.1**

1. Trout fishing 2. Artificial flies

ISBN 978-0-8117-0182-2; 0-8117-0182-4

LC 2005-37913

This work "distills five centuries' worth of angling lore and wisdom about trout feeding behavior and includes a photographic sequence that shows in detail how trout take a fly. . . . [An] examination of flies includes the importance of wings and what they are made of, hooks, soft-hackled flies, and skipping, dapping, and dry-fly techniques." Publisher's note

Includes bibliographical references

799.2   Hunting

Jones, Robert F., 1934-

The hunter in my heart; a sportsman's salmagundi. Lyons Press 2002 268p $24.95   **799.2**

1. Game and game birds 2. Hunting

ISBN 1-58574-465-4

This "is a collection of 30 essays and two short stories. . . . Jones not only tells great outdoor stories but also explores his thoughts on hunting and friendship." Libr J

Shilling, Jane

The fox in the cupboard; a memoir. Simon & Schuster 2005 c2004 328p $24   **799.2**

1. Fox hunting

ISBN 0-7432-7681-7   LC 2005-49793

First published 2004 in the United Kingdom

"When the author, a British single mother looking for a new hobby, took up the sport of foxhunting, she had no idea she would wind up in the middle of an international controversy. A sport with a long and venerable history (it dates back at least to 1327, when the rules were first codified), foxhunting came under criticism a few years ago from animal-rights activists who claimed that the hunt was not only cruel to the animals but also a barbaric and uncivilized activity, demeaning to humanity. Eventually, early in 2005, the sport was outlawed in Britain. She may have come in at the end, but Shilling quickly grew to know and love foxhunting and its quirky, eccentric subculture. Her book is an eye-opening introduction to the sport–not a defense of foxhunting but a thought-provoking acknowledgment of a vanishing part of British history." Booklist

800 LITERATURE, RHETORIC & CRITICISM

801 Literature—Philosophy and theory

Gardner, John, 1933-1982
On moral fiction. Basic Bks. 1978 214p pa $18
hardcover o.p. **801**
1. Literature—Philosophy
ISBN 0-465-05226-6 (pa) LC 77-20409
Gardner "submits that contemporary U.S. art, primarily that of fiction, is generally not of high quality because it is not moral, in that it strives to devalue rather than improve life. Furthermore, Gardner charges that critics have lost track of true, moral art and have failed to denounce that which is false or immoral." Booklist

Kermode, Frank, 1919-
An appetite for poetry. Harvard Univ. Press
1989 242p $32 **801**
1. Poetry—History and criticism 2. Literature—History and criticism 3. Criticism
ISBN 0-674-04093-7 LC 89-31725
This collection contains critical and textual readings of Milton, T. S. Eliot, Wallace Stevens, William Empson and the Bible
"Kermode is not simply a critic but also an artist. . . . In An Appetite for Poetry we encounter writing of balance and decorum, and reading of unflinching audacity." Commonweal
Includes bibliographical references

Kundera, Milan
The curtain; an essay in seven parts; translated from the French by Linda Asher. HarperCollins Publishers 2007 168p $22.95 * **801**
1. Literature—Philosophy 2. Fiction—History and criticism
ISBN 978-0-06-084186-7; 0-06-084186-9 LC 2006-43420
The author "investigates the history of the novel, beginning with the moment in which Cervantes denied Don Quixote's desire for elevation to knight-errant and instead 'cast a legendary figure down: into the world of prose.'" Publ Wkly
"The immediacy of Kundera's evocative prose and the rich tapestry he weaves compel us to pick up and read, or reread, the bountiful literary treasures of Western literature. This could be a book from which to draw a summer reading list." Libr J

Weinstein, Arnold
A scream goes through the house; what literature teaches us about life. Random House 2003 xxxvii, 423p il $29.95; pa $14.95 **801**
1. Literature—Philosophy
ISBN 0-375-50624-1; 0-8129-7243-0 (pa) LC 2002-31719

"In the process of showing that literature concerns not merely thoughts about life but also life itself as it is embodied, lived, and felt, {the author} discusses a wide variety of feelings, from love to depression." Libr J
"Blending the literary passion of Harold Bloom with the physiological insights of Antonio Damasio, Weinstein offers splendid readings of the creations of James Baldwin, Ingmar Bergman, Edvard Munch, Kafka, Faulkner, William Burroughs, and Toni Morrison." Booklist
Includes bibliographical references

803 Literature—Encyclopedias and dictionaries

Abrams, M. H. (Meyer Howard), 1912-
A glossary of literary terms; with contributions by Geoffrey Galt Harpham. 8th ed. Thomson, Wadsworth 2005 370p pa $34.95 * **803**
1. Literature—Dictionaries
ISBN 1-4130-0218-8; 978-1-4130-0218-8 LC 2004-111345
First published 1957
In a series of essays, the author discusses literary terms and definitions ranging from the traditional to the avant-garde. Subsidiary terms are included under major or generic terms.

Benét's reader's encyclopedia; edited by Bruce Murphy. 4th ed. HarperCollins Pubs. 1996 1144p $50 * **803**
1. Literature—Dictionaries
ISBN 0-06-270110-X LC 96-217151
First published 1948 under the editorship of William Rose Benet
This encyclopedia contains over 10,000 entries and covers world literature from early times to the present. Includes entries on authors, literary movements, principal characters, plot synopses, terms, awards, myths and legends, etc.

Brewer's dictionary of modern phrase & fable; edited by John Ayto & Ian Crofton. 2nd ed. Weidenfeld & Nicolson 2006 853p $34.95 * **803**
1. Literature—Dictionaries 2. Allusions
ISBN 0-304-36809-1; 978-0-304-36809-9
First published 2000 by Cassell
This modern version of Brewer's dictionary of phrase and fable "focuses on material from the 20th and 21st centuries. More than 800 entries, arranged alphabetically with cross-references and accompanying quotations, contain insightful and informative descriptions and etymologies. . . . The contemporary phrases contain slang usage as well as technical terms." Choice [review of 2000 edition]

Brewer's dictionary of phrase & fable. 17th ed., revised by John Ayto. Collins 2005 xxvii, 1523p il $55 * **803**
1. Literature—Dictionaries 2. Allusions
ISBN 0-06-112120-7; 978-0-06-112120-3
First published 1870 under the editorship of Ebenezer Cobham Brewer

Brewer's dictionary of phrase & fable—*Continued*

"Over 15,000 brief entries give the meanings and origins of a broad range of terms, expressions, and names of real, fictitious and mythical characters from world history, science, the arts and literature." N Y Public Libr. Ref Books for Child Collect. 2d edition

"This classic for the ages is immensely browseable; one can get lost in it for hours." Libr J

Cuddon, J. A. (John Anthony), 1928-
The Penguin dictionary of literary terms and literary theory. 4th ed. Penguin 1999 1024p (Penguin reference) pa $29   **803**
1. Literature—Dictionaries
ISBN 0-14-051363-9; 978-0-14-051363-9
First published 1977 in the United Kingdom with title: A dictionary of literary terms; first United States edition published 1977 by Doubleday; this edition first published 1998 by Blackwell Publishers
"Comprehensive dictionary covering all literatures and time periods with basic definitions as currently used. Categories include technical terms, forms, genres, groups, movements, -isms, character types, phrases, motifs or themes, concepts, objects, and styles. Entries often indicate origin and cite examples. Numerous see and see also references." Guide to Ref Books. 11th edition

Cyclopedia of literary characters. rev ed, edited by A. J. Sobczak; original eds edited by Frank N. Magill; associate editor, Janet Alice Long. Salem Press 1998 5v set $368   **803**
1. Literature—Dictionaries 2. Characters and characteristics in literature
ISBN 0-89356-438-9   LC 97-45813
This "edition combines the characters profiled in Cyclopedias of Literary Characters (1963) and Literary Characters II (1990). It also includes all characters that appeared in more recent works of Masterplots II published through 1995." Publisher's note
"Entries are arranged alphabetically by the title of the work. . . . {They} begin with the book's title, foreign title if originally published in a language other than English, author's name with birth and death years, date of first publication, genre, locale, time of action, and plot type. Characters are arranged in order of importance; major characters have 100- to 150-word write-ups. Volume 5 contains three indexes: title, author, and character." Booklist

Oxford dictionary of phrase and fable; edited by Elizabeth Knowles. 2nd ed. Oxford University Press 2005 805p $40; pa $18.95 *
          803
1. Literature—Dictionaries 2. Allusions
ISBN 978-0-19-860981-0; 978-0-19-920246-1 (pa)
First published 2000
This work seeks to define words and phrases of British cultural history.
This "is a highly useful tool to help understand what phrases mean and where they come from and should definitely be added to all reference collections." Booklist

808 Rhetoric

2008 writer's market; [where & how to sell what you write]; Robert Lee Brewer, editor; Chuck Sambuchino, assistant editor. 87th annual ed. Writer's Digest 2007 1170p pa $29.95 *
          808
1. Authorship—Handbooks, manuals, etc. 2. Publishers and publishing
ISSN 0084-2729
ISBN 978-1-58297-496-5; 1-58297-496-9
Also available deluxe edition with access to Writer's Market online database $49.99
Guide to Ref Books. 11th edition
Subtitle from cover; On cover: 3,500 listings for book publishers, consumer magazines, trade journals, literary agents and more
"A guide for freelance writers, covering the practical side of writing for publication, including information about book publishers; consumer magazines; trade, technical and a few professional journals; scriptwriting; syndicates; greeting card and gift markets. Provides extensive lists of contests and awards and of relevant organizations and publications. Subject index of book publishers." Guide to Ref Books. 11th edition
Includes bibliographical references

2009 children's writer's & illustrator's market; edited by Alice Pope. Writer's Digest Books 2008 442p il pa $27.99 *   **808**
1. Authorship—Handbooks, manuals, etc. 2. Publishers and publishing
ISSN 0897-9790
ISBN 978-1-58297-549-8; 1-58297-549-3
Annual. First published 1998
This reference includes listings of children's book publishers, magazines, agents, art reps, contests, clubs, conferences, awards, and grants with contact information, along with articles and interviews on a variety of subjects relating to children's writing, illustrating, and publishing.
Includes bibliographical references

The **Chicago** manual of style. 15th ed. University of Chicago Press 2003 956p il $55 *
          808
1. Authorship—Handbooks, manuals, etc. 2. Publishers and publishing—Handbooks, manuals, etc. 3. English language—Usage
ISBN 0-226-10403-6   LC 2003-1860
First published 1906 with title: A manual of style
Updated to reflect current style, technology, and professional practice, this style manual includes journals and electronic publications, descriptive headings on all numbered paragraphs, and reorganized chapters on grammar, usage, and documentation, including guidance on citing electronic sources
Includes bibliographical references

Conway, Jill K., 1934-
When memory speaks; reflections on autobiography; [by] Jill Ker Conway. Knopf 1998 205p pa $13 hardcover o.p.   **808**
1. Autobiography 2. Biography as a literary form
ISBN 0-679-76645-6 (pa)   LC 97-49452
In this work Conway "turns her attention to the form of autobiography in general—to 'why readers like to read autobiography, and why individuals are moved to write their life stories'—and to the ways that cultural assumptions, especially those about gender, influence that writing and reading." Libr J
"Conway's small gem is a landmark in eliciting fresh contemplation of the inchoate complexity of memory's manifold voices." Publ Wkly
Includes bibliographical references

Gibaldi, Joseph, 1942-
MLA handbook for writers of research papers. 6th ed. Modern Lang. Assn. of Am. 2003 361p il pa $17 *   **808**
1. Report writing
ISBN 0-87352-986-3   LC 2002-156363
First published 1977 with title: MLA handbook for writers of research papers, theses, and dissertations
This manual discusses research strategies, formatting, documenting sources, writing basics and utilizing electronic sources.
Includes bibliographical references

Hodges' Harbrace handbook; [by] Cheryl Glenn . . . [et al.] 16th ed. Thomson Wadsworth 2007 xxxi, 793p il $81.95   **808**
1. English language—Composition and exercises 2. English language—Grammar
ISBN 1-4130-1031-8   LC 2005-937964
First published 1941 under the authorship of John C. Hodges with title: Harbrace handbook of English. Frequently revised
Variant title: Harbrace college handbook
A guide to the fundamentals of grammar, composition, and usage

Hooks, Bell
Remembered rapture; the writer at work. Holt & Co. 1999 237p pa $13 hardcover o.p.   **808**
1. Authorship 2. American literature—African American authors
ISBN 0-8050-5910-5 (pa)   LC 98-7998
"The redoubtable Hooks offers a series of essays on writing, focusing on women, black writers (e.g., why there are so many black women novelists and so few in nonfiction), and what it was like to move to writer-saturated New York." Libr J

LaRocque, Paula
The book on writing; the ultimate guide to writing well. Marion Street Press 2003 240p pa $18.95   **808**
1. Authorship
ISBN 0-9665176-9-5   LC 2003-13308

The author "organizes her book into three sections: mechanical and structural guidelines (i.e. sharpening accuracy and brevity), creative elements of storytelling (e.g., 'Let the Reader Do Some Work'), and style (grammar, usage and punctuation). LaRocque's advice is sane and sound: avoid pretension and over-complication, and stay away from jargon and clichés. . . . Beginning writers should find clear, useful advice here." Publ Wkly

McMahan, Elizabeth
The writer's handbook; [by] Elizabeth McMahan, Susan Day. 2nd ed. McGraw-Hill 1988 400p pa $40.31   **808**
1. English language—Grammar 2. Rhetoric
ISBN 0-07-045432-9   LC 87-24160
First published 1980
This guide for acquiring the skills to develop writing proficiency covers grammar, punctuation, style, usage and spelling. A chapter is devoted to business writing

MLA style manual and guide to scholarly publishing. 3rd ed. Modern Language Association of America 2008 xxiv, 336p $32.50 *   **808**
1. Authorship—Handbooks, manuals, etc.
ISBN 978-0-87352-297-7; 0-87352-297-4
    LC 2008-2894
First published 1985 under authorship of Walter S. Achtert and Joseph Gibaldi
This book offers "guidance on writing scholarly texts, documenting research sources, submitting manuscripts to publishers, and dealing with legal issues surrounding publication." Publisher's note
Includes bibliographical references

Plotnik, Arthur, 1937-
Spunk & bite; a writer's guide to punchier, more engaging language & style. Random House 2005 263p $16.95; pa $12.95   **808**
1. Rhetoric
ISBN 0-375-72115-0; 0-375-72227-0 (pa)
    LC 2005-44934
The author "demonstrates how . . . unexpected humor, loquaciousness, and apt description can jolt a writer into engaged authorship. This primer is dotted with illustrative examples that range from Shakespeare and J.K. Rowling to Dave Barry and Maeve Binchy. . . . This is an entertaining and engaging choice for writers." Libr J

Prose, Francine, 1947-
Reading like a writer; a guide for people who love books and for those who want to write them. HarperCollins Publishers 2006 273p $23.95; pa $13.95 *   **808**
1. Rhetoric 2. Creative writing 3. Books and reading
ISBN   978-0-06-077704-3;   0-06-077704-4; 978-0-06-077705-0; 0-06-077705-2 (pa)
    LC 2005-58457
The author "devotes a chapter each to eight elements of writing: words, sentences, paragraphs, narration, character, dialog, details, and gesture. These chapters are framed by an opening piece that urges close reading as

Prose, Francine, 1947-—*Continued*
most productive for writers; a chapter devoted to Chekhov, particularly his short stories, as translated by Constance Garnett; and a closing chapter, 'Reading for Courage.'" Libr J

This book "should be greatly appreciated in and out of the classroom. Like the great works of fiction, it's a wise and voluble companion." N Y Times Book Rev

Rabiner, Susan
Thinking like your editor; how to write serious nonfiction—and get it published; by Susan Rabiner and Alfred Fortunato. Norton 2002 284p $26.95; pa $14 **808**
1. Authorship
ISBN 0-393-03892-0; 0-393-32461-3 (pa)
LC 2001-44551
"In part one, on submissions, the authors discuss how to put together a book proposal and, . . . whether to work through an agent or go solo. In part two, they move to the writing process. . . . Part three discusses how authors and editors (both in-house and freelance) can work together well." Publ Wkly

Salzman, Mark
True notebooks. Alfred A. Knopf 2003 330p hardcover o.p. pa $13.95 **808**
1. Creative writing 2. Juvenile delinquency
ISBN 0-375-41308-1; 0-375-72761-2 (pa)
LC 2002-43435
"While teaching writing to 17-year-olds detained in Los Angeles Central Juvenile Hall, Salzman found himself surprised by the boys' talent. The teens' heartwarming, funny voices are included in his irresistible, provocative memoir." Booklist

Siegal, Allan, 1940-
The New York times manual of style and usage; [by] Allan M. Siegal and William G. Connolly. rev and expanded ed. Times Bks. 1999 364p pa $15 hardcover o.p. **808**
1. Authorship—Handbooks, manuals, etc.
ISBN 0-8129-6389-X (pa) LC 99-10630
First published 1962 by McGraw-Hill under the editorship of Lewis Jordan with title: Style book for writers and editors
Rules and guidelines observed by The New York Times for consistency of spelling, capitalization, punctuation, abbreviation, and preferred usage
This work "contends with the AP stylebook in authority and usefulness." Columbia J Rev

Stein, Sol
Stein on writing; a master editor of some of the most successful writers of our century shares his craft techniques and strategies. St. Martin's Press 1995 308p $24.95; pa $14.95 **808**
1. Authorship
ISBN 0-312-13608-0; 0-312-25421-0 (pa)
LC 95-31793

The author discusses the process of writing "fiction and nonfiction in terms of characterization, pacing, revision, evoking emotion, and 'liposuctioning flab.' Stein's own writing demonstrates the 'resonance' and 'particularities' he discusses, and his original checklists, writing exercises, and numerous examples encourage the reader/writer to see and do the same. A chapter of help sources and a glossary of terms provide the finishing touch." Libr J

Strunk, William, 1869-1946
The elements of style; with revisions, an introduction, and a chapter on writing by E.B. White. 4th ed. Allyn & Bacon 1999 105p $14.95; pa $7.95 * **808**
1. Rhetoric
ISBN 0-205-31342-6; 0-205-30902-X (pa)
LC 99-16419
First privately printed in 1918
This work provides guidelines for proper usage and composition. Misused expressions and commonly misspelled words are discussed. Includes examples.
This work is "prescriptive, conservative, and humorous; in sum, it is the best book available on how to write English prose." Nichols. Guide to Ref Books for Sch Media Cent. 4th edition

Turabian, Kate L., 1893-1987
A manual for writers of research papers, theses, and dissertations; Chicago style for students and researchers; revised by Wayne C. Booth, Gregory G. Colomb, Joseph M. Williams, and University of Chicago Press editorial staff. 7th ed. University of Chicago Press 2007 466p il (Chicago guides to writing, editing, and publishing) $35; pa $17 * **808**
1. Report writing 2. Dissertations
ISBN 978-0-226-82336-2; 0-226-82336-9; 978-0-226-82337-9 (pa); 0-226-82337-7 (pa)
LC 2006-25443
First published 1937 with title: A manual for writers of dissertations
Designed to serve as a guide to suitable style in the presentation of formal papers—term papers, reports, articles, theses, dissertations—both in scientific and in non-scientific fields.

Student's guide for writing college papers. 3rd ed. University of Chicago Press 1977 c1976 256p pa $10 hardcover o.p. **808**
1. Report writing 2. Dissertations
ISBN 0-226-81623-0 LC 76-435
First published 1963
This guide covers selecting a topic, collecting material, planning and writing the paper, and preparing footnotes and bibliographies.

United States. Government Printing Office
Style manual. [29th ed.] U.S. Govt. Ptg. Office 2000 326p $29 * **808**

United States. Government Printing Office—
Continued
1. Authorship—Handbooks, manuals, etc.
2. Publishers and publishing—Handbooks, manuals,
etc. 3. Printing—Style manuals
ISBN 0-16-050083-4
Also available CD-ROM version and online
First published 1908 with title: Manual of style. Frequently revised
"A useful and extensive manual giving the practices of
the Government Printing Office on copy preparation,
with rules for capitalization, punctuation, abbreviations,
etc., and information on foreign languages, including alphabets, with pronunciation, special rules, lists of numbers, etc." Guide to Ref Books. 11th edition

Van Wicklen, Janet
The tech writer's survival guide; a
comprehensive handbook for aspiring technical
writers. Facts on File 2001 269p $35; pa $15.95
808
1. Technical writing
ISBN 0-8160-4038-9; 0-8160-4039-7 (pa)
LC 00-62231
First published 1992 with title: The tech writing game
"This guide offers some basic principles of document
structure and design for both printed and online media
and is full of practical advice on how to glean information from product developers and determine the needs of
a document's audience. Van Wicklen draws from her
own experience as well as giving testimony from colleagues, demonstrating the wide variability of technical
writing jobs. It will be a helpful resource for anyone
considering or beginning a career in technical writing."
Booklist
Includes bibliographical references

Walker, Janice R.
The Columbia guide to online style; [by] Janice
R. Walker and Todd Taylor. 2nd ed. Columbia
University Press 2006 xxi, 288p il $45; pa $19.50
808
1. Authorship—Data processing—Handbooks, manuals, etc. 2. Bibliographical citations
ISBN 0-231-13210-7; 978-0-231-13210-7;
0-231-13211-5 (pa); 978-0-231-13211-4 (pa)
LC 2006-24383
First published 1998
This is a "resource for citing electronic and electronically accessed sources. It is also a . . . style guide for
creating documents electronically for submission for print
or electronic publication." Publisher's note
Includes bibliographical references

The **Writer's** digest guide to good writing; edited
by Thomas Clark {et al.}. Writer's Digest Bks.
1994 338p pa $14.99 hardcover o.p.
808
1. Authorship—Handbooks, manuals, etc.
ISBN 1-58297-138-2 (pa) LC 93-43554
This collection of articles culled from issues of Writer's Digest magazine contains "essays on how to write
with simplicity, plot and pace a story, build suspense,

create characters, and tackle certain genres, including
mysteries, horror, romance, and various forms of nonfiction. The selections are organized by decades and include
essays by Erle Stanley Gardner, Irving Wallace, Louis
L'Amour {and} Allen Ginsberg." Booklist

Zinsser, William Knowlton
Writing to learn. Harper & Row 1988 256p pa
$145 hardcover o.p. **808**
1. Rhetoric—Study and teaching
ISBN 0-06-272040-6 (pa) LC 87-45825
"Eschewing theory and philosophical breast-beating,
Zinsser uses his own experience to reinforce the fact that
clear, eloquent writing can be taught for every subject
across the curriculum. A practical manual for teachers
and a powerful reminder for everyone that good writing
makes possible good thinking." Am Libr
Includes bibliographical referneces

808.06 Writing children's literature

Aiken, Joan, 1924-2004
The way to write for children. St. Martin's
Griffin 1999 97p pa $9.95 **808.06**
1. Authorship 2. Children's literature—Technique
ISBN 0-312-20048-X LC 99-166931
First published 1982 in the United Kingdom
This book is directed to authors who seek to write for
children. Aiken's suggestions are intended to aid them
"in directing their writing toward specific audiences, beginning with the organization of initial ideas and progressing to the choice of voice, plot, and characters." Publisher's note
"In this crisp, informative and often witty survey of
'the market' Aiken is also giving the customers—teachers, librarians, parents, every one concerned with children's literature of quality-a good general idea of what
is available already and of what authors are trying to
do." Times Lit Suppl

Seuling, Barbara
How to write a children's book and get it
published. 3rd ed. Wiley 2005 233p il pa $15.95
808.06
1. Children's literature—Technique 2. Authorship
ISBN 0-471-67619-5 LC 2004-4691
First published 1984
Presents "five essential steps (from researching the
current marketplace to submitting your manuscript) to
publishing works for children." Libr J
Includes bibliographical references

Shulevitz, Uri, 1935-
Writing with pictures; how to write and
illustrate children's books. Watson-Guptill 1985
271p il pa $29.95 hardcover o.p. **808.06**
1. Children's literature—Technique 2. Picture books
for children
ISBN 0-8230-5935-9 (pa) LC 85-15604

Shulevitz, Uri, 1935-—*Continued*

"With heavy emphasis on illustration, this detailed book guides aspiring authors/illustrators through telling the story and drawing the pictures to preparing artwork for the printer." Libr J

Includes bibliographical references

808.1   Rhetoric of poetry

2009 poet's market; Nancy Breen, editor. Writer's Digest Bks. 2008 572p pa $27.99 *

808.1

1. Poetry—Marketing
ISSN 0883-5470
ISBN 978-1-58297-544-3; 1-58297-544-2
Annual. First published 1989

"Useful for those aspiring to publish their poems in literary journals and magazines. . . . Entries include a brief journal profile, submission requirements, and contact information. Offers advice to beginning poets on getting published, brief articles by working poets/editors, grant information, contests and awards, poetry readings, writing colonies, organizations and publications useful to poets. Indexes for chapbook publishers, publishers by subject, publishers by state, and a general index." Guide to Ref Books. 11th edition

Includes bibliographical references

Addonizio, Kim, 1954-

The poet's companion; a guide to the pleasures of writing poetry; [by] Kim Addonizio and Dorianne Laux. Norton 1997 284p pa $14.95

808.1

1. Poetics
ISBN 0-393-31654-8   LC 96-40451

This work contains "three main sections: 'Subjects for Writing' (e.g. death, the erotic), 'The Poet's Craft' (metaphor, rhyme), and 'The Writing Life' (self-doubt, writer's block); four separate appendixes list other writing texts, anthologies, marketing tips, and electronic resources. . . . Both knowledgeable and practical in their approach, the authors offer everything a poet needs, including . . . a gentle yet insistent lesson on grammar." Libr J

Includes bibliographical references

Deutsch, Babette, 1895-1982

Poetry handbook: a dictionary of terms. 4th ed. HarperResource 2002 203p pa $14   **808.1**

1. Poetics—Dictionaries 2. Poetry—Terminology
ISBN 0-06-463548-1
First published 1957 by Funk & Wagnalls

"The craft of verse described in dictionary form. Terms and techniques are defined and illustrated." N Y Public Libr. Ref Books for Child Collect. 2d edition

Higginson, William J., 1938-

The haiku handbook; how to write, share, and teach haiku; [by] William J. Higginson with Penny Harter. Kodansha International 1989 c1985 331p pa $14   **808.1**

1. Haiku
ISBN 4-770-01430-9
First published 1985 by McGraw-Hill

The author "surveys the original and related forms (renga, haibun, senryu), inventors and developers (Basho, Buson, Issa, Shiki), and the numerous variations that later authors, especially in other languages, have wrought on haiku's simple principles. He discusses the many uses—artistic, personal, psychological—that the mode can serve, encouraging the reader all along the way to use the form, to experiment, and thus to express thoughts and feelings. . . . An extensive reference section gives word lists, a glossary, and good bibliographies." Booklist

Hirsch, Edward

How to read a poem; and fall in love with poetry. Harcourt Brace & Co. 1999 352p $23; pa $15   **808.1**

1. Poetics 2. Poetry—History and criticism
ISBN 0-15-100419-6; 0-15-600566-2 (pa)
                                    LC 98-50065

"A DoubleTake book"

The author "has gathered an eclectic group of poems from many times and places, with selections as varied as postwar Polish poetry, works by Keats and Christopher Smart, and lyrics from African American work songs. A prolific, award-winning poet in his own right, Hirsch suggests helpful strategies for understanding and appreciating each poem. The book is scholarly but very readable and incorporates interesting anecdotes from the lives of the poets." Libr J

Includes bibliographical references

Kooser, Ted

The poetry home repair manual; practical advice for beginning poets. University of Nebraska Press 2005 163p $19.95; pa $13.95 *   **808.1**

1. Poetics
ISBN 0-8032-2769-8; 0-8032-5978-6 (pa)
                                    LC 2004-24700

The author's advice "includes both broad and specific ideas on revising, and . . . discussion of matters ranging from the often-underestimated power of simile to employing narrative effectively." Booklist

"Among the many books offering advice on writing poetry, . . . [this book] stands out for its usefulness and, at the same time, for its inspiring view of the purposes of poetry." Midwest Quarterly

Includes bibliographical references

Oliver, Mary, 1935-

A poetry handbook. Harcourt Brace & Co. 1994 130p pa $13   **808.1**

1. Poetics
ISBN 0-15-672400-6   LC 93-49676

"A Harvest original"

A "handbook for young poets on the formal aspects and structure of poetry. Oliver excels at explaining the sound and sense of poetry—from scansion to imagery, diction to voice. She stresses the importance of reading poetry, since, in order to write well, 'it is entirely necessary to read widely and deeply.' Sage advice is given in an entire chapter dedicated to revision, wherein Oliver

Oliver, Mary, 1935-—*Continued*

urges poets to consider their first draft 'an unfinished piece of work' that can be polished and improved later. Written in a pleasant and lucid style, this book is a wonderful resource." Libr J

808.2   Rhetoric of drama

Field, Syd

Screenplay; the foundations of screenwriting. Rev. ed. Delta Trade Paperbacks 2005 320p il pa $16 *   **808.2**
1. Motion picture plays—Technique
ISBN 0-385-33903-8   LC 2005-48491
First published 1979
This book covers the basics of writing a screenplay, including how to build a character, set up a scene, and what to do after the screenplay is written.

Hauge, Michael

Writing screenplays that sell. HarperPerennial 1991 325p pa $12   **808.2**
1. Motion picture plays—Technique
ISBN 0-06-272500-9; 978-0-06-272500-4
          LC 91-55005
First published 1988 by McGraw-Hill
This book provides a "discussion of the craft—characters, story development, etc.—and industry; lays out the all-important details of format; then tells how to market the finished product. Hauge's volume is a detailed manual offering a step-by-step methodology, a scriptual analysis of a hit film, 'The Karate Kid,' and handy chapter summaries." Libr J
Includes bibliographical references

Straczynski, J. Michael, 1954-

The complete book of scriptwriting. rev and expanded [ed] Writer's Digest Bks. 1996 424p il pa $19.99 hardcover o.p.   **808.2**
1. Drama—Technique 2. Television authorship 3. Motion picture plays—Technique 4. Radio authorship
ISBN 1-58297-158-7 (pa)   LC 96-30630
First published 1982
This "encyclopedic exploration of writing scripts for TV, motion pictures, animation, radio, and the stage includes examples of actual scripts formatted for each medium." Libr J

808.3   Rhetoric of fiction

Butler, Robert Olen

From where you dream; the process of writing fiction; edited, with an introduction by Janet Burroway. Grove Press 2005 269p $24; pa $13
      808.3
1. Authorship 2. Fiction—Technique
ISBN 0-8021-1795-3; 0-8021-4257-5 (pa)
          LC 2005-40251

This is a collection of lectures the author has given for his creative writing course at Florida State University.

This "is a remarkably candid, clarifying, and profoundly demanding how-to. . . . Incisive and provocative, Butler's tutorials are a must for anyone even thinking about writing fiction, and readers, too, will benefit from his passionate exhortations." Booklist

Gardner, John, 1933-1982

The art of fiction; notes on craft for young writers. Knopf 1984 224p pa $12.95 hardcover o.p.   **808.3**
1. Fiction—Technique
ISBN 0-679-73403-1   LC 83-47850
"This essay distills the late Gardner's ripest thoughts about what fiction is and how to go about learning to write it. The initial section deals with 'literary-aesthetic theory,' the second with 'the fictional process.' . . . The book concludes with two sets of exercises, one for class use and one for individual use. Recommended for any young writer or writing class, and for all readers who care about the craft of fiction." Booklist

On becoming a novelist; foreword by Raymond Carver. W.W. Norton 1999 xxv, 150p pa $14.95
      808.3
1. Authorship 2. Fiction—Technique
ISBN 0-393-32003-0
Also available in hardcover from P. Smith
First published 1983 by Harper & Row
The author "explores the dynamic chemistry at the heart of the writer's creative process. Gardner's book is a superbly written, thoroughly original, eminently useful volume." Choice

Koch, Stephen

The modern library writer's workshop; a guide to the craft of fiction. Modern Library 2003 246p pa $12.95 *   **808.3**
1. Fiction—Technique 2. Authorship
ISBN 0-375-75558-6   LC 2002-32593
The author "takes the beginning fiction writer through the entire writing process, from conceptualizing a story to making characters come alive. Seeing writing as a vocation, he persuasively argues that it is hard work and craft (and not always talent) that enables writers to succeed." Libr J
"Koch's tone is both encouraging and forthright, and his accessible, friendly guide will be essential for aspiring writers." Booklist
Includes bibliographical references

Lukeman, Noah

The plot thickens; 8 ways to bring fiction to life. St. Martin's Press 2002 221p $19.95; pa $12.95   **808.3**
1. Fiction—Technique
ISBN 0-312-28467-5; 0-312-30928-7 (pa)
          LC 2001-58564
"Lukeman focuses on the mechanics of storytelling. He introduces budding writers to the techniques of char-

Lukeman, Noah—*Continued*

acterization (ask yourself questions about the people you've created), the various ways of generating suspense (danger, a ticking clock), and the importance of conflict." Booklist

Maass, Donald

Writing the breakout novel; winning advice from a top agent and his bestselling client; foreword by Anne Perry. Writer's Digest Bks. 2001 264p pa $16.99 hardcover o.p.

808.3

1. Fiction—Technique
ISBN 1-58297-182-X (pa)   LC 2001-22036

"Using his own clients as case studies, Maass defines the most crucial elements of a breakout novel—a powerful sense of time and place, larger-than-life characters, a high degree of tension, good subplots, and universal themes—and shows the reader how to use these elements efficiently to write a novel that will generate interest and have the potential to hit the best sellers lists. Each section ends with checklists for review." Libr J

Nabokov, Vladimir Vladimirovich, 1899-1977

Lectures on literature; {by} Vladimir Nabokov; edited by Fredson Bowers; introduction by John Updike. Harcourt Brace Jovanovich 1980 xxviii, 385p il pa $18 hardcover o.p.   **808.3**

1. Fiction—History and criticism
ISBN 978-0-15-602775-5; 0-15-602775-5
LC 79-3690

Companion volume to Lectures on Russian literature
"A Bruccoli-Clark book"

In the early 1950s, before Nabokov became a famous writer, he taught literature at Wellesley and Cornell. The editor, with the help of Nabokov's wife and son, has collected seven lectures on "Mansfield Park," "Bleak House," "Madame Bovary," "The Strange Case of Dr. Jekyll and Mr. Hyde," "The Walk by Swann's Place," "The Metamorphosis" and "Ulysses." There are two additional lectures on other topics related to literature. The volume includes a sample examination for the course and pages of original manuscripts with maps and diagrams which the author used to illustrate his lectures

Piercy, Marge

So you want to write; how to master the craft of writing fiction and memoir; [by] Marge Piercy and Ira Wood. 2nd ed. Leapfrog Press 2005 324p pa $16.95   **808.3**

1. Fiction—Technique 2. Biography as a literary form
ISBN 0-9728984-5-X
First published 2001

This book "uses talks, exercises, anecdotes and examples proven in the classroom, to address: How to begin a piece by seducing your reader, How to create characters that embody the infinite contradictions of human behavior, How to master the elements of plotting fiction, How to create a strategy for telling the story of your life, How to learn to read critically, like a professional writer, How to write about painful personal material without coming off as a victim, [and] How to proceed if your

work is continually rejected by publishers." Publisher's note
Includes bibliographical references

Roberts, Gillian

You can write a mystery. Writer's Digest Bks. 1999 124p il pa $12.99   **808.3**

1. Mystery fiction—Technique
ISBN 0-89879-863-9   LC 99-19316

"Along with analysis of the literary aspects of mystery writing, Roberts also surveys such practical matters as grammar, punctuation, and how to submit the manuscript. If character and setting are what distinguish the best mysteries, failed plot mechanics are invariably what derail the worst. Roberts' basic but too-often-overlooked advice will help keep your story on track." Booklist
Includes bibliographical references

Stein, Sol

How to grow a novel; the most common mistakes writers make and how to overcome them. St. Martin's Press 1999 240p $25.95; pa $14.95

808.3

1. Fiction—Technique
ISBN 0-312-20949-5; 0-312-26749-5 (pa)
LC 99-36922

"Stein states bluntly right from the beginning that 'liars say they write only for themselves' and that a 'lack of courtesy' toward the reader is one of the chief faults of unsuccessful writing. While this is perhaps a controversial notion, prospective writers will nonetheless be well rewarded by reading this collection of tips, methods, and numerous anecdotes." Libr J

Swain, Dwight V.

Creating characters; how to build story people. Writer's Digest Bks. 1990 195p pa $14.99 hardcover o.p.   **808.3**

1. Fiction—Technique 2. Characters and characteristics in literature
ISBN 0-89879-662-8 (pa)   LC 90-39640

"Swain talks to his readers in a conversational tone, suggesting techniques, giving examples to illuminate his points, and offering activities for sharpening character development skills. This is a book for those already committed to writing fiction and who want to think about the craft of writing." SLJ
Includes bibliographical references

Techniques of the selling writer. University of Okla. Press 1981 330p $24.95   **808.3**

1. Fiction—Technique
ISBN 0-8061-1191-7

First published 1965 with title: Tricks & techniques of the selling writer

The author offers practical advice for creating and marketing publishable fiction

"Often called 'the bible of fiction writing,' this classic is dated slightly by references to such things as 'carbon copies.' But Swain's tried-and-true scene-and-sequel approach has generated many books and workshops." Libr J

Wheat, Carolyn

How to write killer fiction; the funhouse of mystery & the roller coaster of suspense. Perseverance Press 2003 191p il pa $13.95

808.3

1. Mystery fiction—Technique 2. Suspense fiction—Technique

ISBN 1-88028-462-6   LC 2002-15588

Wheat begins with a "discussion of the distinction between mystery and suspense . . . and then devotes a section to each genre. She offers up plenty of useful tips, such as how to dispense vital information in subtle ways and how to plant clues without being too obvious about it." Booklist

Includes bibliographical references

Wood, James

How fiction works. Farrar, Straus and Giroux 2008 265p $24 *   **808.3**

1. Fiction

ISBN 0-374-17340-0; 978-0-374-17340-1

LC 2008-10290

The author addresses such questions as "What is character, point of view, the value of metaphor and simile, and detail? Is it all artifice or realism, or could it be labeled imaginative truth? His engaging discussion covers narration in all its forms, the impersonal author, the tension that exists between an author's and a character's style, flat vs. round characters, irony, and more. Wood uses excerpts from works by notable authors, from Miguel Cervantes and Jane Austen to Saul Bellow and John Updike, to illustrate his statements with pinpoint precision. Whether he is commenting on a work's weakness or strength, he supports his opinion with reasoned scholarship." Libr J

Includes bibliographical references

808.5   Rhetoric of speech

Detz, Joan

How to write and give a speech; a practical guide for executives, PR people, the military, fund-raisers, politicians, educators, and anyone who has to make every word count. 2nd rev ed. St. Martin's Press 2002 xx, 202p pa $12.95 *

808.5

1. Public speaking

ISBN 0-312-30273-8   LC 2002-67975

First published 1984

Among the various aspects of public speaking discussed are: tips on topic focus, audience assessment, humor, delivery techniques and media coverage.

Karpf, Anne

The human voice; how this extraordinary instrument reveals essential clues about who we are. Bloomsbury 2006 399p $24.95   **808.5**

ISBN 1-58234-299-7; 978-1-58234-299-3

LC 2006-9698

"Beginning with a description of how the voice actually works, [the author argues for] . . . its vital role in the bonding of mothers and children, and eventually in all social interaction." Publisher's note

This "book is packed with information . . . backed up by prolific references to relevant research." Times Lit Suppl

Includes bibliographical references

Linklater, Kristin, 1936-

Freeing the natural voice; drawings by Douglas Florian. Drama Bk. Specialists 1976 210p il pa $19.95 hardcover o.p.   **808.5**

1. Voice

ISBN 0-89676-071-5 (pa)

"Predicated on the basic assumptions that everyone has a voice capable of expressing a full range of emotions within a normal two- to four-octave scale and that daily stress compromises the voice's natural abilities and power {the author} presents a simple and clear narrative, as well as a full set of exercises to cultivate and strengthen the voice." Libr J

Pinsky, Robert

The sounds of poetry; a brief guide. Farrar, Straus & Giroux 1998 129p pa $13 hardcover o.p.

808.5

1. Poetry

ISBN 0-374-52617-6   LC 98-18873

Pinsky presents "a manual of proposals on how to read poems—or, more accurately, how to 'hear more of what is going on in poems.' That distinction, in Pinsky's view is vital." Atl Mon

"By bringing his passion for the sound of language—so evident in his own poems—to his expert interpretations of the work of others, Pinsky cracks open the glass case that seems to separate poetry from everyday language, allowing the song of each poem to ring bright and clear." Booklist

Includes bibliographical references

808.8   Literature—Collections

The **Book** of eulogies; a collection of memorial tributes, poetry, essays, and letters of condolence; edited with commentary by Phyllis Theroux. Scribner 1997 400p $26

808.8

1. Eulogies 2. Bereavement

ISBN 0-684-82251-2   LC 97-2197

"Theroux has gathered over 100 eulogies delivered in the form of spoken tributes, editorials, letters of condolence, essays, and poetry. Many of these testimonials are eloquently penned by the well known to commemorate the well known (e.g., Thomas Merton on Flannery O'Connor, Robert F. Kennedy on Martin Luther King). Others are equally compelling memorials to unknown souls by everyday people. There are helpful commentaries by the author." Libr J

Into the garden; a wedding anthology: poetry and prose on love and marriage; edited by Robert Hass and Stephen Mitchell. HarperCollins Pubs. 1993 193p pa $13.95 hardcover o.p.

808.8

1. Poetry—Collections 2. Weddings
ISBN 0-06-092469-1 (pa)   LC 92-53339

This anthology of readings suitable for wedding ceremonies contains "American Indian, aboriginal Australian, ancient Egyptian, Buddhist, Hindu, and Sufi poetry and prose in addition to . . . biblical, classical Greek and Roman, European, and American passages. . . . {Also included are} traditional or tradition-respecting ceremonies." Booklist

Journalistas; 100 years of the best writing and reporting by women journalists; edited by Eleanor Mills with Kira Cochrane. Carroll & Graf 2005 xx, 364p pa $14.95   **808.8**
1. Women journalists 2. Literature—Collections
ISBN 0-7867-1667-3

Published in the United Kingdom with title: Cupcakes and kalashnikovs

This anthology contains work by such authors as "Martha Gellhorn, Rebecca West, Susan Sontag and Mary McCarthy. . . . The book is divided into subject areas." N Y Times Book Rev

"From Djuna Barnes' 1914 account of being force-fed to end her hunger strike, to Eleanor Roosevelt's 1938 'My Day' column, to Rose George's 2004 article about gang rapes in France, this collection provides a broad and deep look at reporting by women in the past century." Booklist

The **Norton** book of modern war; edited by Paul Fussell. Norton 1991 830p $24.95

808.8

1. Literature—Collections 2. War in literature
ISBN 0-393-02909-3   LC 90-36495

This anthology of 20th century prose and poetry about war covers World War I, the Spanish Civil War, World War II, the Korean War and Vietnam. Authors represented include Heinrich Böll, Marguerite Duras, Ernest Hemingway, Ron Kovic, Norman Mailer, Wilfred Owen and Siegfried Sassoon.

Nothing makes you free; writings by descendants of Jewish Holocaust survivors; edited by Melvin Jules Bukiet. Norton 2002 394p $27.95; pa $15.95   **808.8**
1. Holocaust survivors 2. Holocaust, 1933-1945, in literature 3. Literature—Collections
ISBN 0-393-05046-7; 0-393-32425-7 (pa)
LC 2001-55863

"Excerpts from the works of 30 writers whose parents survived the Holocaust make up this anthology of fiction and memoirs. . . . In these remarkable pieces issues such as guilt, anger, faith, and accountability are explored. They capture not only the experience of the concentration camps but also its powerful legacy, passed down to a new generation through the bond of love that ties parent and child." Booklist

The **Paris** review book of heartbreak, madness, sex, love, betrayal, outsiders, intoxication, war, whimsy, horrors, God, death, dinner, baseball, travels, the art of writing, and everything else in the world since 1953; by the editors of the Paris review; with an introduction by George Plimpton. Picador 2003 751p $30; pa $19

808.8

1. Literature—Collections
ISBN 0-312-42238-5; 0-312-42239-3 (pa)
LC 2003-45971

This anthology includes works by "W.H. Auden, Ernest Hemingway, William Faulkner, Jack Kerouac, Elizabeth Bishop, Truman Capote, William Burroughs, Susan Sontag, Joyce Carol Oates, Toni Morrison, Jonathan Franzen, Ian McEwan and Alice Munro." Publ Wkly

Remembrances and celebrations; a book of eulogies, elegies, letters, and epitaphs; edited by Jill Werman Harris. Pantheon Bks. 1999 xxiii, 308p $25; pa $14   **808.8**
1. Eulogies 2. Bereavement
ISBN 0-375-40123-7; 0-375-70125-7 (pa)
LC 98-32149

"Comprised of eulogies from the 20th century, as well as, poetic elegies, condolence letters and tombstone epitaphs spanning from the 17th century to the present, this eclectic sourcebook offers inspiration for anyone seeking to memorialize a loved one. Since the mourners and the dead in each instance are well-known writers (Lillian Hellman eulogizes Dashiell Hammett) and public figures (Reverend Jesse Jackson lays Jackie Robinson to rest), the collection is a bonanza for the morbidly minded browser as well." Publ Wkly

808.81 Poetry—Collections

Americans' favorite poems; the Favorite Poem Project anthology; edited by Robert Pinsky and Maggie Dietz. Norton 1999 327p $27.50

808.81

1. Poetry—Collections
ISBN 0-393-04820-9   LC 99-31979

"People across America, including many teens, share the poetry they love, and talk about what it means in their lives. Their choices—from John Keats to Lucille Clifton—defy stereotypes, and their comments are heartfelt." Booklist

A **Book** of love poetry; edited and with an introduction by Jon Stallworthy. Oxford Univ. Press 1974 c1973 393p pa $18.95 hardcover o.p.

808.81

1. Love poetry
ISBN 0-19-504232-8

First published 1973 in the United Kingdom with title: The Penguin book of love poetry

A collection of poems written during the past 2000 years arranged thematically from young love to the "long look back" of the aged

Includes indexes of poets, translators, titles and first lines

A **Book** of lumininous things; an international anthology of poetry; edited and with an introduction by Czeslaw Milosz. Harcourt Brace & Co. 1996 xx, 320p pa $15 hardcover o.p.

808.81

1. Poetry—Collections
ISBN 0-15-600574-3 LC 95-38060
"Nobel laureate Milosz states in his introduction that the purpose of this personal and eclectic collection is to present poetry that is 'short, clear, readable, and . . . realistic, that is, loyal toward reality and attempting to describe it as concisely as possible.' . . . Most of the selections are from classical Chinese and 20th-century American and European (primarily Eastern European, Scandinavian, and French) poets." Libr J

City lights pocket poets anthology; edited by Lawrence Ferlinghetti. City Lights Bks. 1995 259p $18.95 **808.81**
1. Poetry—Collections
ISBN 0-87286-311-5 LC 95-31608
"Drawing from the 52 volumes published in the Pocket Poets series since 1956, this selection provides a handy sampler of many of the prominent avant-garde and leftist poets of the post-WW II era. . . . The series' extensive international scope is highlighted in poems culled from German, Russian, Italian, Dutch, Nicaraguan and Spanish poets." Publ Wkly

The **Columbia** Granger's index to poetry in anthologies; edited by Tessa Kale. 13th ed., completely rev., indexing anthologies published through May 31, 2006. Columbia University Press 2007 xxviii, 2376p $295 *

808.81

1. Poetry—Indexes
ISBN 0-231-13988-8; 978-0-231-13988-5
LC 2006-14853
Also available as part of Columbia Granger's world of poetry online
First edition, edited by Edith Granger, published 1904 by A. C. McClurg with title: Index to poetry and recitations. Fifth through eighth editions have title Granger's index to poetry
"The 400 total entries are organized alphabetically into three sections: 'Title, First Line, Last Line,' 'Author,' and 'Subject.' The anthologies referenced appear as abbreviations explained in a 14-page introductory list. An essential purchase for literature and poetry collections." Libr J
Includes bibliographical references

The **Columbia** Granger's Index to poetry in collected and selected works; edited by Keith Newton. 2nd ed, completely rev. Columbia Univ. Press 2004 xxi, 1847p $225 *

808.81

1. Poetry—Indexes
ISBN 0-231-12528-3 LC 2003-51469
Also available as part of Columbia Granger's world of poetry online
First published 1996
"Indexing works published through March 31, 2003."

This "edition includes 315 works, by 266 different poets, locating more than 65,000 poems by title, first line, author, and subject. Included . . . are the works of many of the major American and British poets of the last thirty years, such as Robert Pinsky, Seamus Heaney, and Paul Muldoon; important twentieth-century American poets such as Langston Hughes, Dorothy Parker, and Robert Penn Warren; twentieth-century foreign poets in new translations, such as Eugenio Montale and Paul Celan; and diverse poets from all times and places, collected in new editions, such as Cold Mountain, Jones Very, and Guido Cavalcanti." Publisher's note

Holocaust poetry; compiled and introduced by Hilda Schiff. St. Martin's Press 1995 xxiv, 234p $22; pa $14.95 **808.81**
1. Poetry—Collections
ISBN 0-312-13086-4; 0-312-14357-5 (pa)
LC 95-2708
"In English and in translation from many languages, more than 80 poets—including Wiesel, Fink, Brecht, Yevtushenko, Auden, and Sachs—give voice to what seems unspeakable. Schiff points out that compelling historical accounts document the facts and numbers, but a poem, like a story, makes us imagine how it felt for one person. These poems are stark and deceptively simple." Booklist
Includes bibliographical references

Index to children's poetry; a title, subject, author, and first line index to poetry in collections for children and youth; compiled by John E. and Sara W. Brewton. Wilson, H.W. 1942-1965 3v $115 **808.81**
1. Poetry—Indexes
ISBN 0-8242-0021-7
Basic volume published 1942; first supplement published 1954 $85 (ISBN 0-8242-0022-5); second supplement published 1965 $85 (ISBN 0-8242-0023-3)
The main volume indexes 15,000 poems by 2,500 authors in 130 collections. The two supplements analyze another 15,000 poems by 2700 authors in 151 collections.
"This tool is an invaluable reference source." Peterson. Ref Books for Child

Index to poetry for children and young people; a title, subject, author, and first line index to poetry in collections for children and young people. Wilson, H.W. 1972-1998 6v $105

808.81

1. Poetry—Indexes
ISBN 0-8242-0435-2
A continuation of Index to children's poetry
The volume covering 1964-1969 published 1972 and compiled by John E. and Sara W. Brewton and G. Meredith Blackburn III; 1970-1975 published 1978 compiled by John E. Brewton, G. Meredith Blackburn III and Lorraine A. Blackburn $105 (ISBN 0-8242-0621-5); 1976-1981 published 1984 compiled by John E. Brewton, G. Meredith Blackburn III and Lorraine A. Blackburn $105 (ISBN 0-8242-0681-9); 1982-1987 published 1989 compiled by G. Meredith Blackburn III and Lorraine A. Blackburn $111 (ISBN 0-8242-0773-4); 1988-1992 published 1994 compiled by G. Meredith Blackburn III $110

Index to poetry for children and young people—*Continued*
(ISBN 0-8242-0861-7); 1993-1997 published 1998 compiled by G. Meredith Blackburn III $115 (ISBN 0-8242-0939-7)

Each volume analyzes approximately 10,000 poems by some 2,000 authors in more than 110 collections. Over 2,000 subject headings are used in each volume.

Language for a new century; contemporary poetry from the Middle East, Asia, and beyond; edited by Tina Chang, Nathalie Handal, and Ravi Shankar. W.W. Norton 2008 l, 734p il pa $27.95   **808.81**
1. Poetry—Collections
ISBN 978-0-393-33238-4; 0-393-33238-1
LC 2007-49424
This is an anthology of poems of "hundreds of poets from various parts of Asia, the Middle East, Africa, Europe, America and elsewhere." Publ Wkly
"Even a diligent reader of contemporary poetry will leave this gathering feeling humbled by ignorance of the immense poetic energy of what used to be called the East." Booklist
Includes bibliographical references

Music of a distant drum; classical Arabic, Persian, Turkish, and Hebrew poems; translated and introduced by Bernard Lewis. Princeton Univ. Press 2001 222p il $22.95   **808.81**
1. Arabic poetry—Collections 2. Hebrew poetry—Collections 3. Persian poetry—Collections 4. Turkish poetry—Collections
ISBN 0-691-08928-0   LC 2001-19858
"Lewis, one of the foremost scholars of the Middle East, has devoted much of his career to the history of Islam; this volume collects his translations of poems—nearly all appearing in English for the first time—that span eleven centuries and four major Middle Eastern traditions. Many of the most striking works address, in spare, stirring lines, the twin demands of serving the self and serving God." New Yorker
Includes bibliographical references

The **Oxford** book of war poetry; chosen and edited by John Stallworthy. Oxford Univ. Press 1984 xxxi, 358p $31.95; pa $16.95
808.81
1. War poetry 2. Poetry—Collections
ISBN 0-19-214125-2; 0-19-280454-5 (pa)
LC 83-19303
New edition in preparation
"This comprehensive anthology focuses on poetic treatment of warfare ranging from the battlefields of ancient history to the conflicts in Vietnam, Northern Ireland, and El Salvador." Univ Press Books for Second Sch Libr
This collection "reminds one of the large numbers and great variety of war poems from many centuries that are very good poems. Mr. Stallworthy's selections include most of the best, at least the best in English." N Y Times Book Rev
Includes bibliographical references

Poems for the millennium; the University of California book of modern and postmodern poetry; edited by Jerome Rothenberg and Pierre Joris. University of Calif. Press 1995-1998 2v il v1 $70; v1 pa $29.95; v2 pa $29.95 *
808.81
1. Poetry—Collections
ISBN 0-520-07225-1 (v1); 0-520-07227-8 (v1 pa);
0-520-20864-1 (v2 pa)   LC 93-49839
"A Centennial book"
Contents: v1 From fin de siécle to negritude; v2 From postwar to millennium
The poetry in this anthology is "often self-referential, certainly aware of its own artistry, embedded in political consciousness, and transgressive. It is the work of more than 100 poets, many little known in the U.S. Rothenberg and Joris see twentieth-century poetics as international and have postwar Japanese poet Fujii Sadakazu rubbing shoulders with Amiri Baraka and Andrei Voznesensky, Tomas Tranströmer and Diane di Prima." Booklist {review of v2}

Poems to read; a new favorite poem project anthology; edited by Robert Pinsky and Maggie Dietz. Norton 2002 xxv, 352p $27.95
808.81
1. Poetry—Collections
ISBN 0-393-01074-0   LC 2002-321
This anthology "features works by a wide selection of well-known, mostly American and European writers from throughout the ages: Henry King, Rabindranath Tagore, Gwendolyn Brooks, J.W. von Goethe, Issa, Jorie Graham, Robert Herrick, Dionisio Martinez and Frank O'Hara are just a few of them." Publ Wkly
"A graceful, sometimes jubilant, sometimes lyrical, sometimes brooding, but always welcoming and stirring collection." Booklist
Includes bibliographical references

The **Poetry** of our world; an international anthology of contemporary poetry; edited by Jeffrey Paine. HarperCollins Pubs. 2000 xxviii, 511p hardcover o.p. pa $18.95   **808.81**
1. Poetry—Collections
ISBN 0-06-055369-3; 0-06-095193-1 (pa)
LC 99-34921
In this global anthology "each section is preceded by a thoughtful introduction of several pages by the selector in that area. . . . A stunning and highly readable anthology." Libr J

The **Vintage** book of contemporary world poetry; edited and with an introduction by J.D. McClatchy. Vintage Bks. 1996 xxviii, 654p pa $16   **808.81**
1. Poetry—Collections
ISBN 0-679-74115-1   LC 95-50628
A "varied collection of contemporary poetry from Europe, the Middle East, Africa, Asia, Latin America, and the Caribbean. Here readers will find Nobel laureates and other luminaries, such as Joseph Brodsky, Derek Walcott, Czeslaw Milosz, Octavio Paz, Wole Soyinka, Breyten Breytenbach, and Nguyen Chi Thien, as well as less well known poets. Editor McClatchy has chosen well, select-

The Vintage book of contemporary world poetry—*Continued*
ing poems that illuminate the personal as well as the universal." Booklist

Includes bibliographical references

World poetry; an anthology of verse from antiquity to our time; Katharine Washburn and John S. Major, editors; Clifton Fadiman, general editor. Norton 1998 xxii, 1338p $45
808.81

1. Poetry—Collections
ISBN 0-393-04130-1   LC 97-10879

This volume presents poetry "arranged chronologically in eight sections, from the Bronze and Iron Ages to the 20th century, with each time period subdivided by region and language." Christ Sci Monit

The anthology's "stated aim—'to surprise and delight the common reader'—may seem rather quaint; yet it is a worthy one, and is, on the whole, impressively fulfilled." Times Lit Suppl

Includes bibliographical references

808.82   Drama—Collections

The best men's stage monologues of 2007; edited by Lawrence Harbison; foreword by D.L. Lepidus. Smith and Kraus 2008 100p (Monologue audition series) pa $11.95 *
808.82

1. Monologues 2. Acting
ISSN 1067-134X
ISBN 978-1-57525-586-6; 1-57525-586-3

Annual. First published 1991 for the 1990 theater season under the editorship of Jocelyn Beard

This title and The Best women's stage monologues provide monologues "from contemporary dramatic luminaries. . . . Both volumes offer scenic descriptions and brief leads into the speechs and indicate the tone (dramatic, comic, or seriocomic). In the volume for women, there are no strictly comedic pieces." Libr J [review of 2000 edition]

The best plays of 2006-2007; edited by Jeffrey Eric Jenkins; illustrated with production photographs. Limelight Eds. 2008 560p il (Best plays theater yearbook) $49.95 *
808.82

1. Drama—Collections 2. Theater—United States
ISSN 1071-6971
ISBN 978-0-8791-0352-1

Annual. First published 1920. Variant titles: The Burns Mantle theater yearbook; The Applause/best plays theater yearbook

Some back volumes published by Dodd, Mead available from Applause Theatre Bk. Pubs.; reprints of older annuals available from Ayer; for full information on availability and price contact publishers.

The yearbook gives listings of casts and technical personnel for on- and off-Broadway productions, a summary of the season, synopses and lengthy extracts of dialogue from the best plays, and facts and figures on the New York and regional theater.

The best stage scenes of 2007; edited by Lawrence Harbison; with a foreword by D.L. Lepidus. Smith & Kraus 2007 202p (Scene study series) pa $14.95
808.82

1. Drama 2. Acting
ISSN 1067-3253
ISBN 978-1-57525-588-0; 1-57525-588-X

Annual. First published 1992 under the editorship of Jocelyn Beard

This title culls "selections from recent plays, divided among scenic groupings for men and women, men, and women. . . . The scenes vary in length and intensity, with each scene providing a setting, description, and the number of needed characters." Libr J

The best women's stage monologues of 2007; edited by Lawrence Harbison; foreword by D.L. Lepidus. Smith and Kraus 2008 104p (Monologue audition series) pa $11.95 *
808.82

1. Monologues 2. Acting
ISBN 978-1-57525-587-3; 1-57525-587-1

Annual. First published 1991 for the 1990 theater season under the editorship of Jocelyn Beard

This title, along with The Best men's stage monologues, provide monologues "from contemporary dramatic luminaries. . . . Both volumes offer scenic descriptions and brief leads into the speeches and indicate the tone (dramatic, comic, or seriocomic). In the volume for women, there are no strictly comedic pieces." Libr J [review of 2000 edition]

Nine plays of the modern theater; with an introduction by Harold Clurman. Grove Press 1981 896p pa $21
808.82

1. Drama—Collections
ISBN 0-8021-5032-2   LC 79-52121

Contents: Waiting for Godot, by S. Beckett; The birthday party, by H. Pinter; The caucasion chalk circle, by B. Brecht; Rhinoceros, by E. Ionesco; Rosencrantz and Guildenstern are dead, by T. Stoppard; Tango, by S. Mrozek; American buffalo, by D. Mamet; The visit, by F. Durrenmatt; The balcony, by J. Genet

Ottemiller's index to plays in collections; an author and title index to plays appearing in collections published between 1900 and 1985. 7th ed, revised & enlarged by Billie M. Connor and Helene G. Mochedlover. Scarecrow Press 1988 564p $80
808.82

1. Drama—Indexes
ISBN 0-8108-2081-1   LC 87-34160

First edition compiled by John H. Ottemiller, published 1943 by H.W. Wilson

This index analyzes 1,350 collections and "covers plays by 2,555 authors. The arrangement is by playwright, with lists of plays and collections in which each is designated by symbols. A list of collections analyzed and key to symbols and a title index complete the volume." Nichols. Guide to Ref Books for Sch Media Cent. 4th edition

Play index. Wilson, H.W. 1953-2003 10v v10 $255 *
808.82

Play index—*Continued*

1. Drama—Indexes

ISSN 0554-3037

ISBN 999083-4164 (v10); 978-999083-4161 (v10)

Also available on-line version

First volume published 1953 covering the years 1949-1952, and edited by Dorothy Herbert West and Dorothy Margaret Peake $80. Additional volumes: 1953-1960 $80 edited by Estelle A. Fidell and Dorothy Margaret Peake; 1961-1967 $70 edited by Estelle A. Fidell; 1968-1972 $80 edited by Estelle A. Fidell; 1973-1977 $80 edited by Estelle A. Fidell; 1978-1982 $80 edited by Juliette Yaakov; 1983-1987 $240 edited by Juliette Yaakov and John Greenfieldt; 1988-1992 $240 edited by Juliette Yaakov and John Greenfieldt; 1993-1997 edited by Juliette Yaakov and John Greenfieldt $240; 1998-2002 edited by John Greenfieldt $240

Play index indexes plays in collections and single plays; one-act and full-length plays; radio, television, and Broadway plays; plays for amateur production; plays for children, young adults, and adults. It is divided into four parts. Part I is an author, title, and subject index; the author or main entry includes the title of the play, brief synopsis of the plot, number of acts and scenes, size of cast, number of sets, and bibliographic information. Part II is a list of collections indexed, and Part III, a cast analysis, lists plays by the type of cast and number of players required.

"This index is an excellent source for locating published plays." Safford. Guide to Ref Materials for Sch Media Cent. 5th edition

The **Ultimate** audition book; 222 monologues, 2 minutes & under; edited by Jocelyn A. Beard. Smith & Kraus 1997-2005 2v + v4 (Monologue audition series) ea pa $19.95 **808.82**

1. Monologues 2. Acting

ISBN 1-57525-066-7 (v1); 1-57525-270-8 (v2); 1-57525-420-4 (v4) LC 97-10471

Volume 2 edited by John Capecci, Laurie Walker, and Irene Ziegler; Variant title: 222 monologues, 2 minutes & under from literature. Volume 4 edited by Irene Ziegleraston and John Capecci; variant title for v4: 222 comedy monologues, 2 minutes & under

This collection draws "upon lesser-known works from significant writers and those of contemporary favorites and reflects a wide range of tone, age, time period, and voice. Divided among female, male, and unisex categories, all meet the obligatory two minutes or less time limit imposed by most directors and auditions." Libr J [review of volume 2]

Includes bibliographical references

808.84   Essays—Collections

The **Art** of the personal essay; an anthology from the classical era to the present; selected and with an introduction by Phillip Lopate. Anchor Bks. (NY) 1994 liv, 777p pa $17.95 hardcover o.p. **808.84**

1. Essays

ISBN 0-385-42339-X (pa) LC 93-29708

"A Teachers & Writers Collaborative book"

Lopate "has selected and introduced some 75 personal essays, covering over 400 years, from East as well as the West, in an attempt to show the development of the genre." Libr J

"Not only are the selections a veritable feast, but Lopate's genre-defining introduction is not to be missed." Booklist

Includes bibliographical references

The **Norton** book of personal essays; edited by Joseph Epstein. Norton 1997 477p $30 * **808.84**

1. Essays

ISBN 0-393-03654-5 LC 96-26975

George Orwell, James Baldwin, Joan Didion, M. F. K. Fisher, Barbara Tuchman and Cynthia Ozick are among the authors chosen by Epstein for inclusion in this collection of "53 personal essays written in English by well-known authors during the past century. They were chosen because he 'found them interesting, touching, pleasing, amusing, delightful—above all, entertaining.' The result is a potpourri of selections that vary widely in subject and style. Topics range from music, racism, and traveling to fathers, children, and childhood." Libr J

808.85   Speeches—Collections

Sutton, Roberta Briggs

Speech index; an index to 259 collections of world famous orations and speeches for various occasions. 4th ed rev & enl. Scarecrow Press 1966 947p $85 **808.85**

ISBN 0-8108-0138-8

Supplement, 1966-1980, by Charity Mitchell, published 1982 $82.50 (ISBN 0-8108-1518-4)

First published 1935 by the H.W. Wilson Company

"Speeches are indexed by orator, type of speech, and by subject, with a selected list of titles given in the appendix. Particularly useful for amateur speakers in locating examples to use in preparing a speech and models they can adapt to their needs." Ref Sources for Small & Medium-sized Libr. 6th edition

The **World's** great speeches; edited by Lewis Copeland, Lawrence W. Lamm, and Stephen J. McKenna. 4th enl 1999 ed. Dover Publs. 1999 xxii, 920p pa $17.95 **808.85**

1. Speeches

ISBN 0-486-40903-1 LC 99-32880

First published 1942 by Garden City Pub. Co.

An international collection of approximately 300 speeches by over 200 speakers arranged chronologically

Includes a topical index, index by nations and index of speakers

808.88   Collections of miscellaneous writings

Andrews, Robert, 1957-
The Columbia dictionary of quotations.
Columbia Univ. Press 1993 1092p $50.95
                                       808.88
1. Quotations
ISBN 0-231-07194-9   LC 93-27305
This work "offers 18,000 quotes arranged alphabetically by speaker under 1500 well-selected topics. Brief citations to original sources are noted, and *See references* guide one to related quotes under other topics. For those who feel most comfortable quoting contemporaries, this sourcebook supplies an ample serving. . . . This should prove a popular general quotation sourcebook for academic, public, and school libraries." Libr J

Famous lines; a Columbia dictionary of familiar quotations. Columbia Univ. Press 1997 xxiii, 625p $38.95   **808.88**
1. Quotations
ISBN 0-231-10218-6   LC 96-43879
This work "contains more than 6,000 witticisms, enduring observations, and incendiary statements from all kinds of people from antiquity to yesterday. Besides identifying the source, Andrews . . . provides details of the first publication, specific chapter and scene, and even the character speaking. Besides quotes from Shakespeare and Oscar Wilde, readers will find fascinating quotes from Monty Python, Gloria Steinem, and maybe your favorite author, for example, Agatha Christie. The more than 500 subject headings include homelessness, AIDS, sexual harassment, murder, and war." Booklist
Includes bibliographical references

Bartlett, John, 1820-1905
Bartlett's familiar quotations; a collection of passages, phrases, and proverbs traced to their sources in ancient and modern literature. Little, Brown 2002 1431p $50 *   **808.88**
1. Quotations
ISBN 0-316-08460-3   LC 2003-269668
First published 1855. Periodically revised. Editors vary
"Arranged chronologically by author, with exact references. Includes many interesting footnotes, tracing history or usage of analogous thoughts, the circumstances under which a particular remark was made, etc. Author and keyword indexes. One of the best books of quotations with a long history." Guide to Ref Books. 11th edition
Includes bibliographical references

Boller, Paul F.
They never said it; a book of fake quotes, misquotes, and misleading attributions; [by] Paul F. Boller, Jr., and John George. Oxford Univ. Press 1989 xxv, 159p pa $15.95 hardcover o.p.
                                         808.88
1. Quotations 2. Errors 3. Literary forgeries
ISBN 0-19-506469-0 (pa)   LC 88-22115
In an alphabetical list of attributees' names or titles the authors expose the truth behind more than 200 phony quotations

The **Columbia** Granger's dictionary of poetry quotations; edited by Edith P. Hazen. Columbia Univ. Press 1992 1132p $131   **808.88**
1. Quotations
ISBN 0-231-07546-4   LC 91-42240
This work contains the "most memorable lines written by the greatest poets of English. Quotations are organized alphabetically by poet, and coded so one can find full text in hundreds of current anthologies. With keyword and subject indexing." Univ Press Books for Public and Second Sch Libr

Nowlan, Robert A.
Born this day; a book of birthdays and quotations of prominent people through the centuries. 2nd ed. McFarland & Co. 2007 511p $55   **808.88**
1. Birthdays 2. Quotations
ISBN 978-0-7864-2935-6; 0-7864-2935-6
                                LC 2007-3809
First published 1996
"Arranged chronologically by date of the month, the volume offers lists of 12 'significant' people born on each day, with a very brief biography and a representative or telling quotation uttered by the individual. In addition, each date lists the birthdays of a dozen or more lesser-known individuals, noting only name and year. . . . [This is] a fine ready-reference volume offering unique information." Booklist

The **Oxford** book of aphorisms; chosen by John Gross. Oxford University Press 2003 383p pa $19.95   **808.88**
1. Quotations
ISBN 0-19-280456-1   LC 2003-269712
First published 1983
"Contains a well-chosen collection of aphorisms, maxims, quotations, and pensees from ancient times to the present. Entries, arranged under 58 subject sections, are identified with name of aphorist, source, publication date, or approximate date of original statement. Headings include 'nature,' 'good and evil,' 'illusion and reality,' and 'secrets.' An introduction gives definitions of aphorisms and their use throughout history." Wynar. Guide to Ref Books for Sch Media Cent. 3d edition
Includes bibliographical references

The **Oxford** book of death; chosen and edited by D.J. Enright. Oxford Univ. Press 1987 351p $30; pa $16.95   **808.88**
ISBN 0-19-214129-5; 0-19-280380-8 (pa)
                                LC 82-14341
This is a collection of quotations. Enright divides his "subject into 14 parts, beginning with 'Definitons' and ending with 'Epitaphs, Requiems and Last Words.' He introduces each section . . . [and] then presents his selections." Newsweek
"Much work has gone into this compilation, and the individual introductions to the component sections are, as we would expect, elegant, modest and very wise." Times Lit Suppl
Includes bibliographical references

Oxford dictionary of humorous quotations; edited by Ned Sherrin. 3rd ed. Oxford University Press 2005 xxxii, 525p $40 *   **808.88**
1. Quotations 2. Wit and humor
ISBN 0-19-861004-1; 978-0-19-861004-5
LC 2005-541489
First published 1995 with title: The Oxford book of humorous quotations

A compilation of nearly 6,000 quotations arranged in themes. Shakespeare, Austen, Groucho Marx, Monty Python and Roseanne are among humorists and pundits represented. Includes author and key word indexes.

"Readers will benefit from this reference work cover to cover, soaking in the insights while smiling and chuckling to themselves along the way." Am Ref Books Annu, 2006

The **Oxford** dictionary of quotations; edited by Elizabeth Knowles. 6th ed. Oxford University Press 2004 1140p $50 *   **808.88**
1. Quotations
ISBN 0-19-860720-2   LC 2004-558811
First published 1941

This edition "has over 17,000 quotations. . . . The quotations are arranged alphabetically by author of the quotation. . . . An individual quotation entry includes, besides the quotation itself: the author; dates of birth and death; brief descriptions of the author; cross-references to other quotations about the author in the book and to references to him or her; the context (if necessary); and published source." Am Ref Books Annu, 2005

Quotations for all occasions; compiled by Catherine Frank. Columbia Univ. Press 2000 260p $55; pa $18.95   **808.88**
1. Quotations
ISBN 0-231-11290-4; 0-231-11291-2 (pa)
LC 00-24048
This title "organizes its 1500-plus quotes into three sections that cover 150 different occasions. 'Every Year' contains quotes for such annual events as holidays, birthdays, days of the week, and seasons, while 'Occasionally' encompasses quotes for less frequent events, like going back to school, breaking up, quitting smoking, and school reunions. The final section is for 'Once in a Lifetime' experiences, such as turning 16, getting a first car, menopause, and retirement." Libr J
Includes bibliographical references

Toasts; over 1,500 of the best toasts, sentiments, blessings, and graces; {compiled by} Paul Dickson; illustrated by Rollin McGrail. Crown 1991 256p il $19   **808.88**
1. Toasts 2. Wit and humor
ISBN 0-517-58412-3   LC 91-6967
"Covering traditional occasions such as anniversaries and weddings as well as a variety of other 'toastable' events, this book organizes 1,500 toasts under 75 alphabetically arranged subject headings. Included are ethnic, military, birthday, and holiday toasts. There are also toasts related to sports, aging, food, parents, and even cheese and champagne! The toasts have been gathered from a variety of toast books, many of which date from the late nineteenth and early twentieth centuries. An interesting history of toasting is included." Booklist
Includes bibliographical references

The **Yale** book of quotations; edited by Fred R. Shapiro; foreword by Joseph Epstein. Yale University Press 2006 1104p $50 *
808.88
1. Quotations
ISBN 978-0-300-10798-2; 0-300-10798-6
LC 2006-12317
The more than 12,000 "range over literature, history, popular culture, sports, computers, science, politics, law, and the social sciences, and although American quotations are emphasized, the book's scope is global. The authors represented are as diverse as William Shakespeare, John Lennon, Jack Dempsey, both Presidents Bush, J.K. Rowling, Rita Mae Brown, Confucius, Warren Buffet, and Deng Xiaoping. The entries are arranged by author, then chronologically and alphabetically by source title within the same year. A significant effort was made to trace the first published occurrence of a quotation, and whenever possible the wording is taken from the original source. . . . Electronic products such as the Times Digital Archive, JSTOR, Proquest Historical Newspapers and American Periodical Series, LexisNexis, Newspaperarchive.com, Questia, Eighteenth Century Collections Online, and Literature Online were all used." Libr J

809   Literary history and criticism

Bloom, Harold, 1930-
The Western canon; the books and school of the ages. Riverhead Bks. 1995 546p   **809**
1. Shakespeare, William, 1564-1616 2. Literature—History and criticism
ISBN 1-57322-514-2; 978-1-57322-514-4
First published 1994 by Harcourt Brace & Co.
Bloom examines the "question of which books constitute the core of Western literature and are thus the proper object of serious literary study. . . . The twenty-six authors to whom the bulk of 'The Western Canon' is devoted . . . [are] Shakespeare, Dante, Chaucer, Cervantes, Montaigne, Moliere, Milton, Johnson, Goethe, Wordsworth, Austen, Whitman, Dickinson, Dickens, George Eliot, Tolstoy, Ibsen, Freud, Proust, Joyce, Woolf, Kafka, Borges, Neruda, Pessoa, and Beckett." New Yorker
The "book succeeds not as a polemic but as a passionate, erudite and highly idiosyncratic series of essays about the literature dearest to one of America's most influential academics." Publ Wkly

Calvino, Italo
Why read the classics? translated from the Italian by Martin McLaughlin. Pantheon Bks. 1999 277p pa $13 hardcover o.p.   **809**
1. Literature—History and criticism
ISBN 0-679-74349-9 (pa)   LC 99-21535
Original Italian edition, 1991
This is a collection of literary criticism by the Italian author. "Apart from the title essay, all the pieces treat individual authors or works—almost always works." N Y Rev Books
"Calvino celebrates a wide range of great thinkers in these provocative essays. Here are writers from the ancient world, the Renaissance and recent times, and from

Calvino, Italo—*Continued*

the old and new worlds. . . . [These essays] are a reminder to us that 'rereading' the classics can amuse as well as reward." New Sci

Includes bibliographical references

Cyclopedia of literary places; consulting editor, R. Baird Shuman; editor, R. Kent Rasmussen; introduction by Brian Stableford. Salem Press 2003 3v set $305 *   **809**

1. Literary landmarks

ISBN 1-58766-094-0   LC 2002-156159

"This three-volume set completes Salem's trilogy of reference works analyzing stories (*Masterplots*), characters (*Cyclopedia of Literary Characters*), and now settings in classic works of literature (mostly novels, though a few plays and poems are included). . . . *Literary Places* provides details of both real and imaginary geographic places that serve as settings for approximately 1300 titles covered in the previous works. . . . The entries are alphabetized by title, range in length from 300 to 1000 words, and feature author, type of work, type of plot, time of plot, and a brief synopsis. . . . Well written, easy to use, and fun to read, this set . . . is a valuable addition to all libraries." Libr J

Includes bibliographical references

Damrosch, David

The buried book; the loss and rediscovery of the great Epic of Gilgamesh. H. Holt 2007 315p il map $26   **809**

1. Gilgamesh

ISBN 978-0-8050-8029-2; 0-8050-8029-5

LC 2006-49523

This is a "look at the history behind the world's oldest known literary epic." Libr J

"Combining acuity about cultural contexts with wide-ranging knowledge, Damrosch's account is a superb and engrossing popular presentation." Booklist

Includes bibliographical references

The **Facts** on File dictionary of classical and biblical allusions; [edited by] Martin H. Manser; associate editor, David H. Pickering. Facts on File 2003 448p (Facts on File writer's library) $45 *   **809**

1. Allusions 2. Literature—Dictionaries

ISBN 0-8160-4868-1   LC 2002-192752

"This companion volume to The Facts On File Dictionary of Cultural and Historical Allusions (2000) focuses on literary references from Greek, Roman, Norse, Egyptian, and Celtic mythology, as well as the Bible. The book contains approximately 2000 alphabetically arranged entries with pronunciations, definitions examples, origins, and quotes. . . .This is a valuable book for students and for casual readers to find word or phrase origins." SLJ

Includes bibliographical references

James, Henry, 1843-1916

Literary criticism. Library of Am. 1984 2v v1 ea $50; v2 *   **809**

1. Literature—History and criticism

ISBN 0-94050-023-2 (v1); 0-94050-22-4 (v2)

LC 84-11241

Edited by Leon Edel and Mark Wilson

Contents: v1 Essays on literature, American writers, English writers; v2 French writers, other European writers. The prefaces to the New York edition

"Grouped by nationality, alphabetically by author, and chronologically, the essays provide a kind of critical book within a book on such writers as Balzac, George Eliot, and Hawthorne. These groupings enable the reader to see how James approached a writer and to follow the development of his thinking about particular writers over the years." Publisher's note

Includes bibliographical references

Jarrell, Randall, 1914-1965

No other book; selected essays; edited and introduced by Brad Leithauser. HarperCollins Pubs. 1999 xx, 376p pa $15 hardcover o.p.

809

1. Stead, Christina, 1902-1983. The man who loved children 2. American poetry—History and criticism 3. Literature—History and criticism

ISBN 0-06-095638-0 (pa)   LC 98-55353

"Michael di Capua books"

"Jarrell taught his peers to appreciate first the young Robert Lowell and W. H. Auden, then Marianne Moore, William Carlos Williams, Elizabeth Bishop, Walt Whitman and Robert Frost. . . . The later Jarrell divided his prose between appreciations of poets, digressions on idiosyncratic passions, and funny or sad indictments of 1950s-style popular culture. . . . As a convincing, above all personal, guide to modern poets, and as a captivating writer of criticism Jarrell has no obvious 20th century equal." Publ Wkly

Kurian, George Thomas

Timetables of world literature. Facts on File 2003 457p $65 *   **809**

1. Literature—Chronology

ISBN 0-8160-4197-0   LC 2002-3891

Chronicles world literature from the Classical Age through the twentieth century, discussing literary developments and the relationship between literature and the political and social climate of each historical period

"This comprehensive reference . . . helps academic researchers place major works of literature from 58 countries in historical and cultural context." Libr J

Includes bibliographical references

Literary movements for students; presenting analysis, context, and criticism on literary movements; David Galens, project editor. Gale Group 2002 2v il set $185   **809**

1. Literature—History and criticism

ISBN 0-7876-6517-7   LC 2002-10928

Entries provide "historical background information on each movement as well as modern critical interpretation of each movement's characteristic styles and themes. Ap-

Literary movements for students—*Continued*
proximately 25 movements are covered, including
absurdism, Greek drama, modernism, science fic-
tion/fantasy, surrealism and many others." Publisher's
note

Includes bibliographical references

Literature and its times; profiles of 300 notable
literary works and the historical events that
influenced them. Gale Res. 1997 5v set $570
809
1. Literature—History and criticism
ISBN 0-7876-0606-5   LC 97-34339
Also available supplement $199 (ISBN 0-7876-
6550-9)
Edited by Joyce Moss and George Wilson
"The editors chose the selections (fiction, poetry, short
stories, plays, biographies, and speeches) with the input
of public libraries and secondary-school teachers. . . .
Each volume covers a time range subdivided by dates
and a general description . . . and begins with a brief
overview of the historical events of the era, with a timeline providing a synopsis of each period." Libr J

Masterpieces of world literature; edited by Frank
N. Magill. Harper & Row 1989 957p $55
809
1. Literature—History and criticism
ISBN 0-06-270050-2   LC 89-45052
"The work, arranged alphabetically by title, contains
plot summaries, character portrayals, and critical evaluations of 270 classics of world literature (novels, plays,
stories, poems, and essays), all reprints from other Magill
guides." Nichols. Guide to Ref Books for Sch Media
Cent. 4th edition

Reference guide to world literature; editors, Sara
Pendergast, Tom Pendergast. 3rd ed. St. James
Press 2003 2v set $350 *   **809**
1. Literature—History and criticism 2. Literature—
Bio-bibliography
ISBN 1-55862-490-2   LC 2002-15410
First published 1984 by St. Martin's Press with title:
Great foreign language writers
Contents: v1 Authors; v2 Works, index
This work "contains 1,100 entries, about equally divided between entries on authors and on literary works.
Each author entry in volume 1 includes a short biography, a signed critical essay, and selected lists of works
by and about the author. Each literary work entry in volume 2 includes the author and date of publication (if
known), a signed critical essay, and a selected list of
critical studies. The scope of coverage is major works in
languages other than English from the earliest known
manuscripts to present day writers. . . . Because of its
comprehensiveness and authority, this sturdily bound set
is recommended for ready reference in libraries with
large world literature sections and for smaller libraries
needing more information in this area." Am Ref Books
Annu, 2003
Includes bibliographical references

Roth, Philip
Shop talk; a writer and his colleagues and their
work. Houghton Mifflin 2001 160p $23
809
1. Authors 2. Literature—History and criticism
ISBN 0-618-15314-4   LC 2001-24523
"In this collection of encounters with distinguished
minds—unguarded interviews with Primo Levi and
Aharon Appelfeld, among others; an odd exchange of
letters with Mary McCarthy; fondly contentious portraits
of Bernard Malamud and the painter Philip Guston—
Roth manages to tease from his subjects the convictions
that fuel their work and the vulnerabilities that make
them human." N Y Times Book Rev

809.1   Poetry—History and criticism

Borges, Jorge Luis, 1899-1986
This craft of verse; edited by Calin-Andrei
Mihailescu. Harvard Univ. Press 2000 154p il
(Charles Eliot Norton lectures) $25; pa $14.95
809.1
1. Poetry—History and criticism
ISBN 0-674-00290-3; 0-674-00820-0 (pa)
LC 00-33541
Also available CD-ROM version
This volume is based on the Argentine writer's
"Charles Eliot Norton lectures [delivered] at Harvard in
1967-68. . . . [Borges] discusses some of his favorite
texts, conducting a literary journey that began in his fa-
ther's library in Buenos Aires." N Y Times Book Rev
Includes bibliographical references

Classic writings on poetry; edited by William
Harmon. Columbia University Press 2003 538p
$79; pa $27.50 *   **809.1**
1. Poetry—History and criticism
ISBN 0-231-12370-1; 0-231-12371-X (pa)
LC 2003-40917
This anthology contains "writing on poetry by such
philosophical royalty as Plato, Aristotle, Milton, Sir Philip Sidney, Wordsworth, and Emily Dickinson. Readers
are given a peek through the hole of history's fence into
the lives and worlds of our poetic geniuses and reminded
of the poem's matchless role in conveying reverence, remembering wars, recording history, entertaining, expressing deep emotion, and above all, allowing the finite
mind, for one moment, to contain infinity." Libr J
Includes bibliographical references

Gioia, Dana
Can poetry matter? essays on poetry and
American culture; Dana Gioia. 10th Anniversary
ed. Graywolf Press 2002 231p pa $16
809.1
1. Poetry—History and criticism 2. Criticism
ISBN 1-55597-370-1   LC 2002-102971
First published 1992
In addition to addressing the business of being a poet
and the new formalism, the author offers readings of
Robinson Jeffers, Weldon Kees, Robert Bly and others.
"Gioia makes his case with erudition and skill, and the
best essays bring attention to underappreciated poets like
Ted Kooser." Libr J

Hirsch, Edward

Poet's choice; Edward Hirsch. Harcourt 2006
432p $25   **809.1**
1. Poetry—History and criticism
ISBN 0-15-101356-X; 978-0-15-101356-2
     LC 2005-26890

The author "began writing a column in the Washington Post Book World called 'Poet's Choice' in 2002. This book brings together those . . . [columns] to present a minicourse in world poetry; Poet's Choice includes the work of more than 130 poets—from Asia and the Middle East to Europe and America, from ancient times to the present." Publisher's note

"Hirsch's aesthetic is unerring, and his interpretations are profound as he considers our 'collective destiny' and takes measure of poetry's encompassing vision." Booklist

Koch, Kenneth, 1925-2002

Making your own days; the pleasures of reading and writing poetry. Simon & Schuster 1999 317p
pa $15   **809.1**
1. Poetry—Collections 2. Poetry—History and criticism
ISBN 0-684-82438-8   LC 98-115810
"A Touchstone book"
First published 1998 by Scribner

"This book is divided into two parts: a series of essays on subjects such as meter, rhyme, and personification and an anthology of favorite poems. Most remarkably, non-English poems often appear with several translations, underscoring the flexibility of poetic language. Making Your Own Days will be most useful to writers already familiar with the basics." Libr J

Masterplots II, poetry series. rev ed, editor, Philip K. Jason; project editor, Tracy Iron-Georges. Salem Press 2002 8v set $499   **809.1**
1. Poetry—History and criticism
ISBN 1-58765-037-1   LC 2001-55059

"This set supersedes the six-volume *Masterplots 2: Poetry Series* (1992) and the three-volume *Masterplots 2: Poetry Series Supplement* (1998). It contains 1,385 signed entries written by scholars on individual poems, arranged alphabetically by poem title and ranging in length from three to five pages apiece." Booklist

Includes bibliographical references

The **New** Princeton encyclopedia of poetry and poetics; Alex Preminger and T.V.F. Brogan, co-editors; Frank Warnke, O.B. Hardison, Jr., and Earl Miner, associate editors. Princeton Univ. Press 1993 xlvi, 1383p pa $45 hardcover o.p.   **809.1**
1. Poetry—History and criticism 2. Poetry—Dictionaries
ISBN 0-691-02123-6 (pa)   LC 92-41887
First published 1965 with title: Encyclopedia of poetry and poetics

This work deals with the history, forms, genres, movements and critical approaches to oral and written verse. It examines issues in such areas as: hermenuetics, feminist poetics, Chicano poetry, deconstruction, poststructuralism and cultural criticism. Non-Western and emergent poetries are featured and 106 national poetries are covered

Paglia, Camille, 1947-

Break, blow, burn; Camille Paglia. Pantheon Books 2005 247p $20; pa $12.95 *   **809.1**
1. English poetry—History and criticism 2. American poetry—History and criticism
ISBN 0-375-42084-3; 0-375-72539-3 (pa)
     LC 2004-56573

This "book anthologizes 43 short works in verse from Shakespeare through to Joni Mitchell, with an essay about each." N Y Times Book Rev

This work "is vintage Paglia: bracing, opinionated, and deliciously enjoyable." Natl Rev

Includes bibliographical references

809.2   Drama—History and criticism

Bentley, Eric, 1916-

The life of the drama. Applause Theatre Bk. Pubs. 1991 371p pa $12.95   **809.2**
1. Drama—History and criticism
ISBN 1-55783-110-6   LC 91-28774
First published 1964 by Atheneum

The author discusses plot, character, dialogue, and action in various theatrical genres. Among the dramatists discussed are Aeschylus, Beckett, Brecht, Chekhov, Corneille, Goethe, Ibsen, Ben Jonson, Molière, Pirandello, Racine, Shakespeare, Shaw, and Sophocles

Includes bibliographical references

Critical survey of drama; edited by Carl Rollyson. 2nd rev ed. Salem Press 2003 8v set $499 *   **809.2**
1. Drama—Dictionaries 2. English drama—Dictionaries 3. American drama—Dictionaries
ISBN 1-58765-102-5   LC 2003-2190

"Combines, updates, and expands two earlier Salem Press reference sets: Critical survey of drama, revised edition, English language series, published in 1994, and Critical survey of drama, foreign language series, published in 1986." Preface

This set contains "about 630 essays, of which 570 discuss individual dramatists and 60 cover overview topics. . . . Each essay on a dramatist provides . . . material as birth and death dates, lists of the author's major dramatic works (with dates of first production and publication). Each essay opens with a brief survey of the author's publications in literary forms other than drama, a summary of the writer's professional achievements and awards, an extended biographical sketch that centers on the writer's development as a dramatist, and an extensive critical analysis of the writer's major dramatic works. Following this discussion is a list of major publications in fields other than drama and an annotated bibliography of critical works about the author." Publisher's note

Includes bibliographical references

Masterplots II, drama series; editor, Christian H. Moe. rev ed. Salem Press 2003 4v set $404 *   **809.2**
1. Drama—Stories, plots, etc. 2. Drama—History and criticism
ISBN 1-58765-116-5   LC 2003-12651

Masterplots II, drama series—*Continued*

First published 1990

The titles included "represent a diverse range of themes, issues, cultures, minority playwrights, and international locales. While the majority of the plays covered in the set are English-language works, plays from such countries as Italy, France, Germany, the Czech Republic, Nigeria, Poland, South Africa, and Sweden are also covered. The vast majority of the plays were first produced during the twentieth century, while a handful were produced earlier." Publisher's note

"This newest addition to a reference standard belongs in most public, academic, and secondary libraries." Booklist

809.3 Fiction—History and criticism

Beacham's encyclopedia of popular fiction; edited by Kirk H. Beetz. Beacham Pub. 1996-2002 19v
809.3
1. Fiction—Bio-bibliography
ISSN 1530-1028
ISBN 0-93383-338-5   LC 96-20771
This reference work consists of a three volume set of Biography series and sixteen volumes of Analyses series. Available separately or in sets. Apply to publisher for price

Critical survey of mystery and detective fiction; editor, Carl Rollyson. Rev ed. Salem Press 2008 5v il set $399 **809.3**
1. Mystery fiction—History and criticism
ISBN 978-1-58765-397-1; 1-58765-397-4
  LC 2007-40208
First published 1988 in four volumes under the editorship of Frank Northen Magill

"This set features an international scope of authors of modern and historical thrillers, horror, espionage, cozies, police procedurals, and metaphysical parodies. An entire volume is devoted to topical essays, awards, genre terms, a crime and detective fiction time line, a character index, and more (the other volumes are alphabetical by author)." SLJ

This "is the most exhaustive and best-documented account of this genre available." Choice

Includes bibliographical references

Critical survey of short fiction; editor, Charles E. May. 2nd rev ed. Salem Press 2001 7v il set $473 **809.3**
1. Short stories—History and criticism
ISBN 0-89356-006-5   LC 00-46384
First published 1981 under the editorship of Frank Magill

"The first six volumes contain 515 author entries arranged alphabetically. . . . They vary in length but have the same items included, beginning with birth and death dates, and a portrait if available, followed by a list of principle works of short fiction. . . . Volume 7 consists of 29 survey essays on history, theory, and genre as well as world cultures. These vary in length from 3,000 to 10,000 words. A new feature, 'Research Tools,' provides lists of award winners as well as a chronology, glossary,

and bibliography." Booklist
Includes bibliographical references

Hooper, Brad
The short story readers' advisory; a guide for librarians. American Lib. Assn. 2000 135p pa $32
809.3
1. Short stories—History and criticism
ISBN 0-8389-0782-2   LC 99-85751
This work contains over 200 critical essays covering short story authors past and present. A step-by-step guide on how to interview readers in order to match their tastes with appropriate stories is included.
Includes bibliographical references

Manguel, Alberto
The dictionary of imaginary places; [by] Alberto Manguel & Gianni Guadalupi; illustrated by Graham Greenfield; with additional illustrations by Eric Beddows; maps and charts by James Cook. Newly updated and expanded. Harcourt Brace & Co. 1999 755p il maps $40; pa $24
809.3
ISBN 0-15-100541-9; 0-15-600872-6 (pa)
  LC 99-46994
First published 1980 by Macmillan
This resource "contains entries for more than 1,200 imaginary places from literature and folklore. Each entry describes the place, its locale, and history and provides citations to the source work or tale. More than 220 maps and illustrations are included." Booklist
Includes bibliographical references

Mystery and suspense writers; the literature of crime, detection, and espionage; Robin W. Winks, editor in chief; Maureen Corrigan, associate editor. Scribner 1998 2v set $250
809.3
1. Spies in literature
ISBN 0-684-80521-9   LC 98-36812
"Articles on 68 mystery writers ranging from Edgar Allen Poe to Sarah Paretsky run from ten to 20 pages and include information on the life and works as well as solid bibliographies for each author." Libr J

Niebuhr, Gary Warren
Make mine a mystery; a reader's guide to mystery and detective fiction. Libraries Unlimited 2003 605p $65 **809.3**
1. Mystery fiction—Bibliography 2. Mystery fiction—History and criticism
ISBN 1-56308-784-7   LC 2003-271056
"The book is divided into two parts. In part 1, 'Introduction to Mystery Fiction,' Niebuhr devotes considerable space to background material: discussion of readers'-advisory service in general and the appeal of mystery fiction in particular and how to build and manage a mystery collection, followed by a history of the genre beginning in 1845. Part 2, 'The Literature,' annotates more than 2,500 titles by more than 200 authors. . . . Among guides to mystery fiction, this one stands out as being thorough and current. Essential for public libraries." Booklist

A **Reader's** companion to the short story in English; edited by Erin Fallon [et al.]; under the auspices of the Society for the Study of the Short Story. Greenwood Press 2001 xxxiv, 432p $105   **809.3**

1. Short stories—History and criticism

ISBN 0-313-29104-7   LC 00-25113

"Although most of the stories covered by Fallon's compilation were written in the later half of the 20th century, the scope is international. . . . Each chapter concisely profiles a writer and contains a biography, a brief review of criticism, a lengthier analysis of specific works, and a bibliography. A section covers the short story genre. This work is extremely important because of the popularity of the genre." Choice

Includes bibliographical references

Short story writers; edited by Charles E. May. Rev. ed. Salem Press 2008 3v il (Magill's choice) set $217   **809.3**

1. Short stories—History and criticism

ISBN 978-1-58765-389-6   LC 2007-32789

First published 1997

This set "covers writers from Giovanni Boccaccio and Geoffrey Chaucer to Anton Chekhov and Sandra Cisneros. . . . Readers, whether in need of a brief critical overview or in search of what to read next, will find this set extremely useful. Each entry includes a brief biography, a list of principal works, a note on other literary forms the author explored, and a concise list of achievements as well as brief essays . . . on particular stories." SLJ

Includes bibliographical references

Supernatural fiction writers; contemporary fantasy and horror; Richard Bleiler, editor. 2nd ed. Scribner 2003 2v 1048p (Scribner writers series) set $250 *   **809.3**

1. Fantasy fiction—History and criticism

ISBN 0-684-31250-6   LC 2002-11128

First published 1985

Contents: v1 Peter Ackroyd to Graham Joyce; v2 Guy Gavriel Kay to Roger Zelazny

This edition "is organized alphabetically by writer. Articles range in length from 5 to 12 pages. There is some biographical information but emphasis is on the works, with analysis of important themes, types of work, and, in many cases, individual series and titles. Each article concludes with a selected bibliography of works by the author under discussion, critical and biographical studies, and Web sites if they are available." Booklist

Includes bibliographical references

Symons, Julian, 1912-1994

Bloody murder; from the detective story to the crime novel. 3rd rev ed. Mysterious Press 1993 c1992 349p pa $30   **809.3**

1. Mystery fiction—History and criticism

ISBN 0-89296-496-0   LC 92-54127

First published 1972 in the United Kingdom. Present edition first published 1992 in the United Kingdom

A critical survey of crime fiction, including detective stories, psychological crime stories, thrillers, and espionage, covering authors from Poe to the 1990s

810.3   American literature— Encyclopedias and dictionaries

The **Cambridge** handbook of American literature; edited by Jack Salzman. Cambridge Univ. Press 1986 286p $60   **810.3**

1. American literature—Dictionaries

ISBN 0-521-30703-1   LC 86-2587

This handbook's "750 entries, two thirds of them about authors, briefly describe the contents and contribution of key works, assess the careers of writers, and explain the tenets and characteristics of literary movements." Wilson Libr Bull

The **Companion** to southern literature; themes, genres, places, people, movements, and motifs; edited by Joseph M. Flora and Lucinda H. MacKethan; associate editor, Todd Taylor. Louisiana State Univ. Press 2001 xxvi, 1054p $69.95 *   **810.3**

1. Southern States—Intellectual life

ISBN 0-8071-2692-6   LC 2001-29959

This sourcebook "explores the multifaceted aspects of the 'southern experience as it is depicted in literature.' Focusing on common threads that run through southern writing and set it apart from the literature of other regions, the more than 500 alphabetical entries cover a wide range of topics." Booklist

"This unique compilation [is] . . . an excellent addition to libraries that support studies of Southern literature." Libr J

Includes bibliographical references

Encyclopedia of American literature. 2nd ed. Facts On File 2008 4v il (Facts on File library of American literature) set $375 *   **810.3**

1. American literature—Encyclopedias

ISBN 978-0-8160-6476-2   LC 2007-25662

First published 2002

Contents: vol. I. Settlement to the New Republic, 1607-1815 / revised and augmented by Susan Clair Imbarrato — vol. II. The age of Romanticism and realism, 1816-1895 / revised and augmented by Brett Barney — vol. III. Into the modern, 1896-1945 / revised and augmented by George Parker Anderson, Judith S. Baughman, Matthew J. Bruccoli — vol. IV. The contemporary world, 1946 to the present / revised and augmented by Marshall Boswell

Entries in this encyclopedia cover works, writers, movements and other American literature-related topics from colonial times to the present. Each volume includes a chronology.

Includes bibliographical references

The **Greenwood** encyclopedia of multiethnic American literature. Greenwood Press 2005 5v il set $499.95 *   **810.3**

1. American literature—Encyclopedias 2. Minorities—Encyclopedias

ISBN 0-313-33059-X   LC 2005-18960

This encyclopedia contains "more than 1100 entries, approximately 1000 of them devoted to individual au-

The Greenwood encyclopedia of multiethnic American literature—*Continued*

thors. The remaining entries describe relevant literary topics (e.g., The Blues, Tricksters), key literary works (e.g., The Bluest Eye, Tracks), and other relevant topics (e.g., Holocaust narratives)." Libr J

"A comprehensive set unique in its scope, this encyclopedia is an excellent foundational resource that adds much to the growing field of ethnic American literature." Choice

Includes bibliographical references

Hart, James David, 1911-1990

The Oxford companion to American literature; [by] James D. Hart; with revisions and additions by Phillip W. Leininger. 6th ed. Oxford Univ. Press 1995 779p $49.95 * **810.3**

1. American literature—Dictionaries
ISBN 0-19-506548-4 LC 94-45727
First published 1941

In addition to over 2000 entries for individual authors and more than 1,100 for important works this reference includes entries for literary movements, awards, magazines, printers, book collectors and newspapers. A chronological index of literary and social history is appended.

The **Oxford** companion to Canadian literature; general editors, Eugene Benson & William Toye. 2nd ed. Oxford Univ. Press 1997 1199p $75 * **810.3**

ISBN 0-19-541167-6 LC 98-162071
First published 1983

More than 1100 signed entries cover Québéçois, Acadian, and English-Canadian literature

"The scope of this volume is impressive. It includes not only information about writers and poets but also publishers, publishing houses, themes and symbols in Canadian literature, and essays on individual works that stand out as landmarks in the field. It is the kind of reference work one can 'dip into' for interest or use as a quick reference tool." Booklist

The **Oxford** encyclopedia of American literature; Jay Parini, editor-in-chief. Oxford University Press 2004 4v il set $495 * **810.3**

1. American literature—Encyclopedias
ISBN 0-19-515653-6 LC 2002-156325

Contents: v. 1. Academic novels-The essay in America—v. 2. William Faulkner -Mina Loy—v. 3. Norman Mailer-Sentimental literature—v. 4. Anne Sexton-Writing as a woman in the twentieth century

This set "provides a wealth of reliable information on standard bearers of American literature in an easy-on-the eyes format for students and general readers." SLJ

810.8 American literature—Collections

Baseball: a literary anthology; edited by Nicholas Dawidoff. Library of Am. 2002 721p $35 * **810.8**

1. Baseball 2. American literature—Collections
ISBN 1-931082-09-X LC 2001-38654

"Beginning with Thayer's *Casey at the Bat* and ending with Buster Olney, there are more than 700 pages of prose and poetry, fiction and sportswriting, writers and players. Scanning the table of contents, it almost seems like *everybody* wrote about baseball: Damon Runyon, Ring Lardner, James Weldon Johnson, William Carlos Williams, James Thurber. But so did Paul Gallico, Nelson Algren, Tallulah Bankhead, and Jacques Barzun. . . . Ineffable, indispensable, inimitable—just like baseball." Booklist

The **Chronology** of American literature; America's literary achievements from the colonial era to modern times; edited by Daniel S. Burt. Houghton Mifflin 2004 805p il $40 * **810.8**

1. American literature—Collections
ISBN 0-618-16821-4 LC 2003-51142

"This chronology includes more than 8,400 literary works by more than 5,000 writers. Sections for each year are grouped in five chapters by period, from 1582 to 1999. Within each year, entries are grouped by genre, such as diaries and other personal writings, fiction, essays, literary criticism and scholarship, nonfiction, poetry, and drama. Within each genre, authors are listed alphabetically, generally with birth and death dates and short descriptions of named works for the year. . . . The *Chronology of American Literature* is easy to browse and, for book lovers, difficult to put down." Booklist

Includes bibliographical references

Crossing the danger water; three hundred years of African-American writing; edited and with an introduction by Deirdre Mullane. Anchor Bks. (NY) 1993 xxii, 769p pa $20 **810.8**

1. American literature—African American authors—Collections
ISBN 0-385-42243-1 LC 93-17194

This anthology "includes fiction, autobiography, poetry, songs, and letters by such writers as Frederick Douglass, Sojourner Truth, W.E.B. Du Bois, Zora Neale Hurston, and Richard Wright. Many topics are covered, from slavery, education, the Civil War, Reconstruction, and political issues to spirituals, songs of the Civil Rights movement, and rap music." Libr J

Includes bibliographical references

I thought my father was God and other true tales from the National Story Project; edited and introduced by Paul Auster; Nelly Reifler, assistant editor. Holt & Co. 2001 xxi, 383p il hardcover o.p. pa $15 **810.8**

1. American literature—Collections
ISBN 0-8050-6714-0; 0-312-42100-1 (pa)
LC 00-54397

"In 1999, novelist Paul Auster . . . and the hosts of National Public Radio's All Things Considered asked listeners to send in true stories to be read on-air as part of the National Story Project. Auster received more than 4,000 submissions; the 180 best are published here." Publ Wkly

"These are stop-you-in-your-tracks stories about hair-raising coincidences, miracles, tragedies, redemption, and moments of pure hilarity." Booklist

Jewish American literature; a Norton anthology; [compiled and edited by] Jules Chametzky [et al.] Norton 2000 xxiv, 1221p il $39.95
810.8
1. American literature—Jewish authors 2. American literature—Collections
ISBN 0-393-04809-8 LC 00-55393
The editors have attempted "to encompass Jewish literature from 1654 to the present in this collection of poems, cartoons, sermons, diaries, letters, stories, speeches, plays, prayers, novel excerpts, and critical writings either translated from Hebrew or Yiddish or written in English. Major sections group the literature chronologically to help identify large movements. . . . This great anthology is essential for Jewish studies and American literature collections." Libr J
Includes bibliographical references

Modern American memoirs; selected and edited by Annie Dillard and Cort Conley. HarperCollins Pubs. 1995 449p pa $16 hardcover o.p. **810.8**
1. American literature—Collections 2. Authors, American
ISBN 0-06-092763-1 (pa) LC 95-30755
The editors "have collected excerpts from the memoirs of 35 20th-century American authors. The selections represent the best in autobiographical writing published between 1917 and 1992. Included are nine women and 26 men, both black and white, some better known than others, all distinguished writers and wonderful storytellers. . . . The editors precede each entry with a biographical and contextual note. There's an opening essay on the art of the memoirist and an afterword listing additional classics in the genre." Libr J

The **Norton** anthology of African American literature; Henry Louis Gates, Jr., general editor, Nellie Y. McKay, general editor. 2nd ed. Norton 2003 2800p 2 computer laser optical discs pa $70.30 * **810.8**
1. American literature—African American authors—Collections
ISBN 0-393-97778-1 LC 2003-66176
First published 1996
"The anthology is divided into seven sections, each with a separate introduction giving the sociopolitical factors that impacted on the material included therein. Featured are 120 writers, 52 of whom are women, richly representing African American vernacular literature, poetry, drama, short stories, novels, slave narratives, and autobiographies." Libr J [review of 1996 edition]
Includes bibliographical references

The **Norton** anthology of American literature; Nina Baym, general editor. Norton 5v maps * apply to publisher for price and availability
810.8
1. American literature—Collections
First published 1979. (6th edition, 2003) Periodically revised
An anthology of American prose, poetry and drama dating from 1620 to the late 20th century. Includes essays and introductions to authors and works

The **Oxford** book of the American South; testimony, memory, and fiction; edited by Edward L. Ayers, Bradley C. Mittendorf. Oxford Univ. Press 1997 597p pa $22 hardcover o.p. **810.8**
ISBN 0-19-512493-6 (pa) LC 96-45135
"Not limiting themselves to fiction (short stories and novels, either in full or in extract), the editors also gather memoirs, diaries, and essays. From both genders and races, from opposite poles on the economic scale, from an eighteenth-century naturalist to a former slave, from Thomas Jefferson to Eudora Welty, these writings give ringing voice to the experiences that have engendered a distinctive southern culture." Booklist

The **Oxford** book of women's writing in the United States; edited by Linda Wagner-Martin, Cathy N. Davidson. Oxford Univ. Press 1995 596p pa $27.50 hardcover o.p. **810.8**
ISBN 0-19-513245-9 (pa) LC 95-1499
This anthology provides "samples of the public and private work of 99 women of diverse racial and ethnic backgrounds who write in English and were born in or have lived in the United States over the past four centuries. They include short fiction (almost half of the book), poems, essays, plays, and speeches but have also gone beyond traditional genre categories to include performance pieces, erotica, diaries, letters, and recipes." Libr J

The **Portable** beat reader; edited by Ann Charters. Viking 1992 xxxvi, 642p pa $17 hardcover o.p.
810.8
1. American literature—Collections 2. Bohemianism
ISBN 0-14-243753-0 (pa) LC 91-16155
"Viking portable library"
"The collection proceeds chronologically and from east to west, in effect tracking Kerouac's cross-country journey and linking the East Coast Beats with San Francisco poets such as Kenneth Rexroth, Lawrence Ferlinghetti, Gary Snyder, and Michael McClure. The works of 'second wave' Beat writers Amiri Baraka (LeRoi Jones), Diana DiPrima, Frank O'Hara, Bob Dylan, even Norman Mailer, to name a few, are included, with the connections to the original group discussed." Booklist
"Cutting through bohemian posturing and excess, Charters here reprints much of the most vital, readable and relevant material produced by the Beat generation." Publ Wkly
Includes bibliographical references

The **Portable** Harlem Renaissance reader; edited and with an introduction by David Levering Lewis. Viking 1994 xlvii, 766p pa $18 hardcover o.p. **810.8**
1. American literature—African American authors—Collections 2. Harlem Renaissance
ISBN 0-14-017036-7 LC 93-30233
"General categories include essay, memoir, fiction, poetry, and drama; specific writers include such expected names as Langston Hughes, Zora Neale Hurston, and Claude McKay, but lesser-known names are also represented. There is anger in these pages and also frustration, pride, pain, and elation, but above all there is incredible

The Portable Harlem Renaissance reader—*Continued*

talent. Reading the collection straight through would be a wonderful education, but most readers will dip in here and there, and that is edifying, too." Booklist

The **Portable** sixties reader; edited by Ann Charters. Penguin Bks. 2003 xli, 628p il pa $16
810.8
1. United States—History—1961-1974 2. American literature—Collections
ISBN 0-14-200194-5   LC 2002-32266
This reader includes "essays, poetry, and fiction under thematic subjects, such as civil rights; women's rights; the sexual revolution; environmental issues; the antiwar, free-speech, and black-arts movements; and the use of drugs in pursuit of enlightenment. . . . [Includes works by] James Baldwin, Thomas Merton, Susan Sontag, Gary Snyder, Allen Ginsburg, Rachel Carson, Kate Millett, Nikki Giovanni, and many more." Booklist
Includes bibliographical references

The **Portable** Western reader; edited and with an introduction by William Kittredge. Penguin Bks. 1997 xxi, 600p pa $14.95   **810.8**
ISBN 0-14-023026-2   LC 96-47243
"Viking portable library"
"Part 1, 'Ancient Stories,' shows the evolution of Native American storytelling from the early legends to contemporary stories and includes writings by Catherine McClellan, John Graves, and Louise Erdrich. Parts 2 and 3 contrast the mythology of the 19th-century 'Western' with the actual experience of living in the West. Most of these authors, from Walt Whitman to Larry McMurtry, will be familiar to readers. Part 4, 'Brilliant Possibilities,' showcases the new generation of Western writers, including Gretel Ehrlich, Jimmy Santiago Baca, and Sherman Alexie." Libr J

Pushcart prize XXXII: best of the small presses 2008; edited by Bill Henderson with the Pushcart Prize editors. Pushcart Press 2008 619p $35; pa $16.95 *   **810.8**
1. American literature—Collections
ISBN 978-1-888889-48-2; 978-1-888889-46-8 (pa)
Some back numbers available in hardcover and paperback from Pushcart Press and Norton
Annual. First published 1976
New edition in preparation
Each volume in the Pushcart Prize series "consists of short stories, poems and essays; includes the work of established and beginning writers, and has a faintly subversive character. Its audience would seem to be primarily the young, yet among its contributors are many of the best writers in America. . . . Like all interesting literary journals, 'The Pushcart Prize' is eclectic and uneven. . . . The number and diversity of journals represented and the sheer length of it are impressive." Books of the Times
Includes bibliographical references and author index to the series since 1976

"The **Real** war will never get in the books"; selections from writers during the Civil War; edited by Louis P. Masur. Oxford Univ. Press 1993 301p il pa $18.95 hardcover o.p.
810.8
1. American literature—Collections 2. United States—History—1861-1865, Civil War
ISBN 0-19-509837-4 (pa)   LC 92-24446
This is a collection of excerpts from letters, journal entries, articles, and speeches written during the American Civil War. The fourteen contributors include such writers as Henry Adams, Louisa May Alcott, Frederick Douglass, Nathaniel Hawthorne, Herman Melville, William Gilmore Simms, Harriet Beecher Stowe, and Walt Whitman.
"This collection makes available to a wide audience some of the best contemporary writing about the conflict." Libr J
Includes bibliographical references

Transcendentalism; a reader; [edited by] Joel Myerson. Oxford Univ. Press 2001 xxxvii, 712p hardcover o.p. pa $32   **810.8**
1. New England—Intellectual life
ISBN 0-19-512212-7; 0-19-512213-5 (pa)
LC 00-21484
This reader "draws together in their entirety the essential writings of the Transcendentalist group during its most active period, 1836-1844. It includes the major publications of the *Dial*, the writings on democratic and social reform, the early poetry, nature writings, and all of Emerson's major essays, as well as an . . . introduction and annotations by Myerson." Publisher's note
Includes bibliographical references

810.9   American literature—History and criticism

The **Beat** generation; a Gale critical companion; Lynn M. Zott, project editor. Gale 2003 3v (Gale critical companion collection) set $350 *
810.9
1. American literature—History and criticism 2. Beat generation
ISBN 0-7876-7569-5   LC 2002-155786
"Volume 1 gathers a variety of sources that place the movement in cultural context. . . . Volumes 2-3 supply entries for 28 Beat authors. . . . Author entries include a brief biography, notes on major works and critical reception, a list of principal works, a selection of primary sources and secondary criticism, and further readings. . . . The selections include contributions by major Beat Generation scholars and provide a well-balanced, representative view of the Beats." Choice
Includes bibliographical references

Black women writers (1950-1980); a critical evaluation; edited by Mari Evans. Anchor Press 1984 xxviii, 543p pa $25 hardcover o.p.
810.9
1. American literature—African American authors 2. American literature—Women authors 3. American literature—History and criticism
ISBN 0-385-17125-0 (pa)   LC 81-43914

Black women writers (1950-1980)—*Continued*

Critical essays on Maya Angelou, Alice Childress, Toni Morisson, Lucille Clifton, and 11 other post World War II Afro-American women writers

"This important work, a tribute to the corpus of literature produced by black women, is an indispensable resource for any serious student, scholar or teacher desiring to probe the depths of the Afro-American literary tradition." Freedomways

Includes bibliographical references

The **Cambridge** history of American literature; general editor, Sacvan Bercovitch; associate editor, Cyrus R.K. Patell. Cambridge Univ. Press 1994-2003 8v set $1,050　　　**810.9**
1. American literature—History and criticism
ISBN 0-521-85760-0　　　　　　LC 92-42479
Contents: v1 1590-1820 $165 (ISBN 0-521-30105-X); v2 Prose writing 1820-1865 $165 (ISBN 0-521-30106-8); v3 Prose writing, 1860-1920 $165 (ISBN 0-521-30107-6); v4 Nineteenth-century poetry, 1800-1910 $165 (ISBN 0-521-30108-4); v5 Poetry and criticism, 1900-1950 $165 (ISBN 0-521-30109-2); v6 Prose writing, 1910-1950 $165 (ISBN 0-521-49731-0); v7 Prose writing, 1940-1990 $165 (ISBN 0-521-49732-9); v8 Poetry and criticism, 1940-1995 $165 (ISBN 0-521-49733-7)

Scholars contribute essays assessing major authors, movements and trends in the development of American literature

Cheever, Susan

American Bloomsbury; Louisa May Alcott, Ralph Waldo Emerson, Margaret Fuller, Nathaniel Hawthorne, and Henry David Thoreau: their lives, their loves, their work. Simon & Schuster 2006 223p il $26　　　　　　　　　**810.9**
1. Authors, American 2. American literature—History and criticism
ISBN 0-7432-6461-4; 978-0-7432-6461-7
　　　　　　　　　　　　　　LC 2006-45015
This book offers a "glimpse into life in Concord, MA, from about 1840 to the mid-1860s, when such luminaries as Louisa May Alcott, Ralph Waldo Emerson, Margaret Fuller, Nathaniel Hawthorne, and Henry David Thoreau lived, worked, and loved. . . . [This] volume examines the dynamic relationships among these remarkable men and women, who constituted what may be considered the first American literary community. . . . Essential reading for anyone with an interest in American letters." Libr J
Includes bibliographical references

Columbia literary history of the United States; Emory Elliott, general editor; associate editors, Martha Banta [et al.]; advisory editors, Houston A. Baker [et al.] Columbia Univ. Press 1988 xxviii, 1263p $119　　　　　　**810.9**
1. American literature—History and criticism
ISBN 0-231-05812-8　　　　　　LC 87-14672
This anthology "expands the traditional subjects of literary history by incorporating current theoretical ideas and newly discovered writers. Includes treatment of recently explored subjects, such as the role of women and minorities in U.S. literature. No separate bibliography other than what is found in the text." N Y Public Libr Book of How & Where to Look it Up

Elie, Paul

The life you save may be your own; an American pilgrimage. Farrar, Straus and Giroux 2003 554p il hardcover o.p. pa $16　　**810.9**
1. Merton, Thomas, 1915-1968 2. Day, Dorothy, 1897-1980 3. Percy, Walker, 1916-1990 4. O'Connor, Flannery 5. American literature—History and criticism 6. American literature—Bio-bibliography
ISBN 0-374-25680-2; 978-0-374-52921-5 (pa); 0-374-52921-3 (pa)　　　　　　LC 2002-192522
This "is a study of the religious imagination at work in four American writers—Flannery O'Connor, Walker Percy, Thomas Merton and Dorothy Day." N Y Times Book Rev
"This thoroughly researched and well-sourced work deserves attention from students of history, literature and religion, but it will be of special significance to Catholic readers interested in the expression of faith in the modern world." Publ Wkly

Encyclopedia of American Indian literature; [edited by] Jennifer McClinton-Temple, Alan Velie. Facts on File 2007 466p (Encyclopedia of American ethnic literature) $75　　**810.9**
1. Native American literature—Encyclopedias 2. Native Americans in literature—Encyclopedias
ISBN 0-8160-5656-0; 978-0-8160-5656-9
　　　　　　　　　　　　　　LC 2006-23762
This "reference work presents information about American Indian literature, including authors from the contiguous 48 states, Alaska, and Canada. . . . The body of the text includes A-Z entries on specific native works and authors, as well as important issues such as 'Reservation Life,' 'Alcoholism,' 'Gaming,' and more. . . . Authors of poetry, plays, nonfiction, and novels are featured." Libr Media Connect
"This book brings together solid information from scattered sources, facilitating research on an esoteric subject." Libr J
Includes bibliographical references

The **Greenwood** encyclopedia of African American literature; edited by Hans Ostrom and J. David Macey, Jr. Greenwood Press 2005 5v il set $499.95 *　　　　　　**810.9**
1. American literature—African American authors—Encyclopedias
ISBN 0-313-32972-9　　　　　　LC 2005-13679
This "set provides coverage of the foundations, development, and proliferation of African American literature, from Colonial times to the present. . . . The depth and breadth of the 1,029 entries make this an invaluable resource." Choice
Includes bibliographical references

Kazin, Alfred, 1915-1998

An American procession. Harvard University Press 1996 408p pa $15.95 *　　　　**810.9**
1. American literature—History and criticism
ISBN 0-674-03143-1　　　　　　LC 97-220259
First published 1984 by Knopf
This book "starts with Ralph Waldo Emerson in the 1830's and ends a century later with Eliot, Ezra Pound, John Dos Passos, William Faulkner, Ernest Hemingway,

Kazin, Alfred, 1915-1998—*Continued*

and F. Scott Fitzgerald. . . . Between Emerson and the moderns the critical authors . . . are Thoreau, Hawthorne, Poe, Whitman, Melville, Emily Dickinson, Mark Twain, Henry James, Stephen Crane, Theodore Dreiser, and Henry Adams." N Y Times Book Rev

"'An American Procession' is a refresher in the best sense: without any fundamental revision of our understanding of our classics, it vivaciously refreshes our awareness of them, and our gratitude for them." New Yorker

Latino and Latina writers; Alan West-Durán, editor. Charles Scribner's Sons 2004 2v 1072p (Scribner writers series) set $265 *

810.9

1. American literature—Hispanic American authors
ISBN 0-684-31293-X   LC 2003-15728
Contents: v. 1. Introductory essays. Chicano and Chicana authors.—v. 2. Cuban and Cuban-American authors. Dominican and other authors. Puerto Rican authors

This set "begins with five essays of social and historical commentary that focus on key elements of Latino culture in this country. What follows is a series of ten to 20-page biocritical essays on nearly 60 authors (e.g., Gary Soto, Pat Mora, Sandra Cisneros, Victor Villaseñor, Julia Alvarez, Richard Rodriguez, and Lorna Dee Cervantes). . . . One of the most comprehensive anthologies available of Latino writing in the United States." Libr J

Includes bibliographical references

Magill's survey of American literature; edited by Steven G. Kellman. Rev. ed. Salem Press 2007 6v il set $499 *   **810.9**

1. Literature—History and criticism 2. Literature—Bio-bibliography
ISBN 978-1-58765-285-1; 1-58765-285-4
LC 2006-16503
First published 1992 with two volume supplement published 1996 under the editorship of Frank Northen Magill

"Examining selected works of 339 U.S. and Canadian writers, from Anne Bradstreet and Benjamin Franklin to Edward Bloor and Octavia E. Butler, this clearly written resource provides sturdy support for assignments, and will also be popular with discussion groups and with general readers of literature." SLJ

Includes bibliographical references

Matthiessen, F. O. (Francis Otto), 1902-1950

American renaissance; art and expression in the age of Emerson and Whitman. Oxford Univ. Press 1941 xxiv, 678p il pa $53 hardcover o.p. *

810.9

1. American literature—History and criticism
ISBN 0-19-500759-X (pa)
A critical study of works by Emerson, Thoreau, Melville, Hawthorne and Whitman and their impact on American intellectual history.

Modern American literature. 5th ed. St. James Press 1999 3v set $594 *   **810.9**

1. American literature—History and criticism
ISBN 1-55862-379-5   LC 98-38952

First published 1960 by Ungar and edited by Dorothy Nyren. The 5th edition incorporates the 3 volumes of the 4th edition and its 3 supplements and adds 70 new entries.

"This work consists of short excerpts of criticism of 20th-century American authors by important critics writing in newspapers, magazines, scholarly journals, and books. The excerpts (ranging in length from one or two paragraphs to two columns) are allowed to stand on their own without separate plot synopses, summaries, or background information on the authors. The original words of the critics . . . are arranged chronologically to paint a picture of the critical reception of an author over time." Libr J

Includes bibliographical references

Pierpont, Claudia Roth

Passionate minds; women rewriting the world. Knopf 2000 298p il hardcover o.p. pa $13

810.9

1. American literature—Women authors—History and criticism 2. English literature—Women authors—History and criticism 3. Women authors
ISBN 0-679-43106-3; 0-679-75113-0 (pa)
LC 99-33349
"A scintillating collection of brief lives of women writers, a book that sparkles with intelligence, wit and human interest. . . . Unfolding with the dramatic élan of a novella, each one is exhaustively researched, sharply focused, convincingly opinionated." N Y Times Book Rev

Samet, Elizabeth D.

Soldier's heart; reading literature through peace and war at West Point. Farrar, Straus and Giroux 2007 259p $23 *   **810.9**

1. United States Military Academy 2. Literature—Study and teaching 3. Soldiers—United States
ISBN 978-0-374-18063-8; 0-374-18063-6
LC 2007-9159
"In the late 1990s, Samet left graduate school at Yale to become a literature instructor at West Point, where she has for the last decade taught the humanities to young men and women preparing to lead others into combat. Here, she illustrates how literature can transform raw cadets into reflective, conscientious leaders. She and her students struggle with the relationship between art and life as well as the true meaning of sacrifice and honor and their place in a world of peace and a world at war. Samet also reflects on the dramatic changes to the academy, its cadets, and herself over the past ten years. She focuses on the post-9/11 change in attitudes and the juxtaposition between leadership and obedience in the lives of military officers." Libr J

"Like the best professors, Samet asks tough questions and offers no easy answers. Her book is filled with lively classroom discussions and poignant e-mails from former students now in Iraq, often writing about the books they're reading there. . . . I know of no other new book that's a better choice for any reading group that loves to debate literature and politics." USA Today

Wall, Cheryl A.

Women of the Harlem Renaissance. Indiana Univ. Press 1995 246p il (Women of letters) pa $14.95 hardcover o.p.   **810.9**

1. American literature—African American authors
2. Harlem Renaissance

ISBN 0-253-20980-3 (pa)   LC 95-3132

This study of women writers of the Harlem Renaissance begins with an overview: On being young—a woman—and colored, followed by critical and biographical studies of Jessie Redmond Fauset, Nella Larsen, and Zora Neale Hurston

"Wall offers strong critiques of these women's work, uncovering certain similarities, including, most importantly, the travel motif as not only a reflection of the mass migrations of the day but also a larger dislocation." Publ Wkly

Includes bibliographical references

Wilson, Edmund, 1895-1972

Patriotic gore; studies in the literature of the American Civil War. Norton 1994 816p pa $19.95   **810.9**

1. American literature—History and criticism
2. United States—History—1861-1865, Civil War

ISBN 978-0-393-31256-0; 0-393-31256-9

First published 1962 by Oxford University Press

"A collection of sixteen essays on writing related to the war including the memoirs of Union generals Grant and Sherman and Confederates Mosby and Lee, diaries, political writing, and fiction by writers such as Ambrose Bierce and John De Forest." Benet's Reader's Ency of Am Lit

811 American poetry

Ackerman, Diane

Origami bridges; poems of psychoanalysis and fire. HarperCollins Pubs. 2002 147p $22.95; pa $11.95   **811**

1. Poetry—By individual authors

ISBN 0-06-019988-1; 0-06-055529-7 (pa)
    LC 2002-24685

"Sometimes addressed to herself and her personal history, at least as often addressed to 'Dr. B—,' Ackerman's passionate free verse (short, fluent and adorned by irregular rhyme) describes with nearly unmixed awe the relationship she created with her analyst, and the personal transformation she achieved." Publ Wkly

Adair, Virginia Hamilton, 1913-2004

Ants on the melon; a collection of poems. Random House 1996 158p pa $15 hardcover o.p.   **811**

1. Poetry—By individual authors

ISBN 0-375-75229-3 (pa)   LC 95-25977

"The appearance of a first collection by a poet now blind and in her 83rd year must be accounted a triumph . . . {Adair} works with equal daring in free verse and more traditional forms; her subjects include social and religious commentary, but her principal theme is ordinary experience and its resistance to facile interpretation." Libr J

Beliefs and blasphemies; a collection of poems. Random House 1998 109p pa $15 hardcover o.p.   **811**

1. Poetry—By individual authors

ISBN 0-8129-9245-8 (pa)   LC 97-47403

The author presents poems "on God, Jesus, the church, the world as divine creation, experiences of divine immanence, sin, and the afterlife." Booklist

"Adair's searching verses may not always have the ring of the contemporary, and they often stop short here of fully unfurling their insights. But at its best, this collection points the way back to an American tradition of religious poetry understood and cherished by the likes of Elizabeth Bishop and Louise Bogan." Publ Wkly

Adam, Helen, 1909-1993

A Helen Adam reader; edited, with notes and an introduction by Kristin Prevallet. National Poetry Foundation 2007 492p il $59.95; $29.95   **811**

1. Poetry—By individual authors

ISBN 978-0-943373-74-4;   0-943373-74-3; 978-0-943373-73-7 (pa); 0-943373-73-5 (pa)
    LC 2007-34740

Includes DVD

In the Bay Area of the late 1940s Adam "found herself a member—some said godmother, witch or Nurse of Enchantment—of the interlocking Robert Duncan and Jack Spicer poetry circles, which, with the Beats, formed the avant-garde San Francisco Renaissance. . . . Adam combined the narrative economy of ballads—where each line is a discrete unit of information—with the lush sonic tapestry we associate with older Anglo-Saxon and Celtic strains of British verse. . . . On the page, Adam's intricate soundscapes compare with anything by Gerard Manley Hopkins and Dylan Thomas. But to see her sing her ballads—she chants 'Kiltory' on the Reader's accompanying DVD—is to appreciate how the language, trilling and seething by turns, possessed its acolyte." Nation

Includes bibliographical references

Alvarez, Julia, 1950-

The woman I kept to myself; poems. Algonquin Books of Chapel Hill 2004 155p $17.95   **811**

1. Poetry—By individual authors

ISBN 1-56512-406-5   LC 2003-70807

This "collection of 75 poems is divided into three sections, and each poem has three stanzas, exactly . . . The poet, who is from the Dominican Republic, writes about being raised with her sisters in New York. The subjects are personal—love, marriage, rejection, divorce, death, religion—but also universal." SLJ

Ammons, A. R., 1926-2001

Selected poems; David Lehman, editor. Library of America 2006 130p (American poets project) $20 **811**

1. Poetry—By individual authors

ISBN 978-1-931082-93-8; 1-931082-93-6

LC 2006-40807

Ammons "was a difficult figure to pin down. While unassociated with any particular poetic school or group, he picked up threads from Whitman, Williams, Frost and Stevens, weaving them into poetry all his own: equal parts pastoral meditation, philosophical speculation and homespun resignation. In the process, he won nearly every honor a major American poet can. Now, in the first selection to present samplings from the whole of his oeuvre (which ranges from two-line lyrics to book-length sequences), we can survey the extent is his poetic powers." Publ Wkly

Angelou, Maya

The complete collected poems of Maya Angelou. Random House 1994 273p $24.95 * **811**

1. Poetry—By individual authors

ISBN 0-679-42895-X LC 94-14501

This volume contains all of Angelou's published poems including her inaugural poem On the pulse of morning

I shall not be moved. Random House 1997 48p $15; pa $9.95 **811**

1. Poetry—By individual authors

ISBN 0-679-45708-9; 0-553-35458-3 (pa)

First published 1990

"Angelou's themes include loss of love and youth, human oneness in diversity, the strength of blacks in the face of racism and adversity." Publ Wkly

The author "speaks eloquently of black life, unfolding a significant history in poems that are highly controlled and yet powerful." Libr J

Ashbery, John

Collected poems 1956-1987. Library of America 2008 1042p $40 **811**

1. Poetry—By individual authors

ISBN 978-1-59853-028-5

Edited by Mark Ford

"This first volume of the collected Ashbery includes the texts of his first twelve books: Some Trees (1956), selected by W. H. Auden for the Yale Younger Poets; The Tennis Court Oath (1962); Rivers and Mountains (1966); The Double Dream of Spring (1970); Three Poems (1972) . . . ; The Vermont Notebook (1975), presented with the original art by Joe Brainard; Self-Portrait in a Convex Mirror (which won the Pulitzer Prize, the National Book Award, and the National Book Critics Circle Award in 1976); Houseboat Days (1977); As We Know (1979); Shadow Train (1981); A Wave (1984); and April Galleons (1987). In addition it presents an unprecedented gathering of more than 60 previously uncollected poems written over a period of four decades." Publisher's note

"This major book, the first collection from Library of America by a living poet, offers a view of Ashbery's artistic development over many decades. . . . Watching Ashbery's art grow from the slippery romanticism and verbal hijinks of the early poems through the philosophical, if sideways, inquiry of the '70s, to the chattier, colloquial period inaugurated in the early '80s, is arresting. Though Ashbery has confounded and inspired in seemingly equal measure, he is, according to both his admirers and critics, the towering figure in contemporary American poetry." Publ Wkly

Notes from the air; selected later poems. Ecco 2007 364p $34.95 **811**

1. Poetry—By individual authors

ISBN 978-0-06-136717-5; 0-06-136717-6

LC 2008-270813

This "volume—beginning with poems from April Galleons (1987) and ending with Where Shall I Wander (2005)—presents . . . [a] panoramic view of Ashbery's second phase, in which he explores, celebrates, sends up and revels in the American vernacular. . . . This is an essential book." Publ Wkly

Selected poems. Viking 1985 349p pa $17.95 hardcover o.p. **811**

1. Poetry—By individual authors

ISBN 0-14-058553-2 (pa) LC 85-40549

"Elisabeth Sifton books"

"Ashbery's work is seductive precisely because it alludes to shared traditions and assumptions about poetry. His poems attract us with their gestures of 'meaningful' discourse, the meditative pace of their syntax and the memories and expectations of meaningfulness that it evokes, the careful use of qualifiers, and the precisions and surprises of his diction." Benet's Reader's Ency of Am Lit

Where shall I wander; new poems; J. Ecco 2005 81p $22.95 * **811**

1. Poetry—By individual authors

ISBN 0-06-076529-1 LC 2004-53267

This collection of poetry features the poems "Ignorance of the Law Is No Excuse" and "A Visit to the House of Fools."

"Ashbery expresses a sly playfulness, a tender theatricality, a surreal sensibility, and an urbane wit. . . . Mercurial, elegant, funny, and magical, these mind-bending and beautifully haunting poems are the knowing work of a virtuoso." Booklist

A worldly country; new poems. Ecco Press 2007 76p $23.95 * **811**

1. Poetry—By individual authors

ISBN 0-06-117383-5; 978-0-06-117383-7

LC 2006-50279

This is a volume of poems by the author of Some Trees (1956); The Tennis Court Oath (1957); Rivers and Mountains (1966); Sunrise in Suburbia (1968); The Double Dream of Spring (1970); Self-portrait in a Convex Mirror (1975); Houseboat Days (1977); As We Know (1979); Shadow Trains (1981); Your Name Here (2000); and Where Shall I Wander (2006).

"Ashbery's syncopated lyrics are sheer pleasure in their music, collaged images, stabbing perceptions. Mysterious and truth-bearing poems that inspire us to 'flame on, flame on.'" Booklist

Baca, Jimmy Santiago, 1952-
Spring poems along the Rio Grande. New
Directions Pub. 2007 75p pa $12.95 **811**
1. Poetry—By individual authors
ISBN 978-0-8112-1685-2; 0-8112-1685-3
LC 2006-101678
"The Rio Grande, as both setting and symbol of freedom and life, meanders through the poems, evoking a
natural progression of time and the natural ebb and flow
of feelings such as love, hope, and connection. The
bosque along the river is home to birds both resident and
migratory, trees, fish, bushes, insects, and encroaching
urban life represented by power lines and interstate traffic noise. Jogging here, Baca evinces a love of his
hometown of Albuquerque but, even more, reveals his
well of poetic inspiration: Chicano, Catholic religiosity,
Native American symbolism, and universal milestones.
. . . With its highly accessible language and thoughtful
reflections on the natural world, readers will find Baca's
poetry extremely inviting." Booklist

Bang, Mary Jo
Elegy; poems. Graywolf 2007 92p $20
811
1. Poetry—By individual authors
ISBN 978-1-55597-483-1; 1-55597-483-X
LC 2007-924768
The author "captures the complexity and courage of
surviving the death of a child, an adult child, an imperfect child. The grief is multilayered, palpable. In this rendition of living in pain, in absence, in an altered reality,
the reader never questions the authenticity of the work.
. . . This is a book of exceptional grace and strength; it
belongs in every library." Libr J

Berrigan, Ted, 1934-1983
The collected poems of Ted Berrigan; edited by
Alice Notley, with Anselm Berrigan and Edmund
Berrigan; introduction and notes by Alice Notley.
University of California Press 2005 749p $60; pa
$24.95 * **811**
1. Poetry—By individual authors
ISBN 978-0-520-23986-9; 0-520-23986-5;
978-0-520-25155-7 (pa); 0-520-25155-5 (pa)
LC 2005-42259
This volume collects the published and unpublished
works of a leading figure of the second-generation New
York School. Includes the first presentation of the Easter
Monday sequence in the order authorized by Berrigan
shortly before his death.
"More than 20 years in preparation, this is a major
volume of 20th-century American poetry. . . . Berrigan
was a notoriously charismatic reader, teacher and participant in the community that developed around the Poetry
Project at St. Mark's Church; his persona has been cited
as often as his poems. This book closes the gap once and
for all." Publ Wkly

Berry, Wendell, 1934-
Collected poems, 1957-1982. North Point Press
1985 268p pa $17 hardcover o.p. **811**
1. Poetry—By individual authors
ISBN 978-0-86547-197-9
LC 84-62305

"What must a man do to be at home in the world?
This is the overriding concern in Wendell Berry's poems,
gathered here from eight books from the past 25 years.
Though rooted in the rugged rural landscape of Kentucky, the poems ultimately grow from the landscape of
the human heart. The interplay of the natural world and
the human spirit is the informing principle." Libr J
"As a nature poet Berry has a grass-roots, homespun
quality that reminds one of Frost. He moves easily from
witty lyrics and graceful elegies to moving love poems,
philosophical odes and confessionals." Publ Wkly

Given; new poems. Shoemaker & Hoard 2005
152p $22 **811**
1. Poetry—By individual authors
ISBN 1-59376-061-2
LC 2005-3762
"The latter half, 'Sabbaths 1998-2004,' . . . [contains]
the meditational poems Berry conceives on Sundays
alone in the woods on his farm. The other half's three
parts contain, respectively, short poems of observation,
hortatory poems varying in length from epigram to six-
page public epistle, and a brief verse play. . . . For those
who believe that life and the world are gifts, this is an
invaluable book." Booklist

A timbered choir; the sabbath poems,
1979-1997. Counterpoint 1998 216p pa $14.95
hardcover o.p. **811**
1. Poetry—By individual authors
ISBN 978-15823-006-5
LC 98-4925
"Berry has continued periodically to write poems out-
of-doors on days of little other work. This book reprints
Sabbaths, a collection of that writing, adding to it about
one and a half times as much new work. . . . Few other
poets have such chaste and precise diction or manage
line and stanza with such unaffected serenity." Booklist

Berryman, John, 1914-1972
Collected poems, 1937-1971; edited and
introduced by Charles Thornbury. Farrar, Straus &
Giroux 1989 347p hardcover o.p. pa $25 *
811
1. Poetry—By individual authors
ISBN 978-0-374-52281-0; 0-374-52281-2
LC 89-30944
"Brings together in chronological order for the first
time the seven collections of short poems Berryman himself arranged and published. 'Homage to Mistress Bradstreet' is included, though 'The Dream Songs,' as a self-
contained work, is excluded." N Y Times Book Rev
"Berryman's poetry, sometimes mannered, elliptical,
and convoluted, is distinguished by precise technical control and continued experiments with style." Reader's
Ency. 4th edition

The dream songs. Farrar, Straus & Giroux 1969
xx, 427p hardcover o.p. pa $18 * **811**
1. Poetry—By individual authors
ISBN 978-0-374-53066-2; 0-374-53066-1
This book contains the author's 385 'dream songs'
that originally appeared in various magazines, the Pulitzer Prize winning 77 dream songs (1964) and His toy,
his dream, his rest (1968). The poet also provides a brief
note about Henry, the poems' central character

Berryman, John, 1914-1972—*Continued*

"Berryman makes brilliant use of his speaker's indiscriminately retentive perception—the patter of jukeboxes, of cocktail parties, of the gutter and the cathedral—to drop us dizzily into an original world where life is lived naked and unashamed." Va Q Rev

Bidart, Frank, 1939-

Star dust. Farrar, Straus and Giroux 2005 84p $20   **811**
1. Poetry—By individual authors
ISBN 0-374-26973-4   LC 2004-56293
This is a collection of poetry by the author of *Desire*.
"The poems in this collection range from terribly lame confections questioning the appellation of 'poem' itself—to gracefully and powerfully moving lyrics. . . . The more formal Bidart gets, the stronger his work, like a living example of Richard Wilbur's dictum that the genie gains his strength from confinement in the bottle." Am Book Rev

Bishop, Elizabeth, 1911-1979

Edgar Allan Poe & the juke-box; uncollected poems, drafts, and fragments; edited and annotated by Alice Quinn. Farrar, Straus, and Giroux 2006 367p $30   **811**
1. Poetry—By individual authors
ISBN 0-374-14645-4   LC 2005-11511
"The publication of 'Edgar Allan Poe & the Juke-Box,' which gathers for the first time Bishop's unpublished material, isn't just a significant event in our poetry; it's part of a continuing alteration in the scale of American life." N Y Times Book Rev
Includes bibliographical references

Poems, prose, and letters; [selected and edited by Robert Giroux and Lloyd Schwartz] Library of America 2008 979p $40   **811**
1. Poetry—By individual authors
ISBN 978-1-59853-017-9; 1-59853-017-8
                                       LC 2007-935885
"From the quietly riveting photograph on the dust jacket through the thorough index, the book is an elegant achievement that one imagines even the scrupulous and discriminating Elizabeth Bishop would approve. . . . This generous new collection lets us make connections across boundaries among many genres: poems, some hitherto uncollected and some mighty rough; translations over many years from ancient Greek, French, Spanish, and Portuguese; 'Personal Essays, Reminiscences, and Reporting'; 'Literary Statements and Reviews'; . . . and letters." Yale Rev

Blackburn, Paul, 1926-1971

The collected poems of Paul Blackburn; edited, with an introduction, by Edith Jarolim. Persea Bks. 1985 xxxv, 667p il $55   **811**
1. Poetry—By individual authors
ISBN 978-0-89255-086-9; 0-89255-086-4
                                       LC 85-9309
"Blackburn wrote over 1200 poems, and Jarolim has rescued 523 of them, working mainly with out-of-print

editions. She includes poems from 1945 to 1971, a period when Blackburn became associated with the Black Mountain poets and gained fame as a translator of Spanish and Provencal poetry." Libr J
"Much of Blackburn's poetry is an engaging mix of sharp, allusive adventuring, humor and wordplay, annotated fragments of musical speech, and a moderate but distinctive use of metaphor. Edith Jarolim's introduction provides a concise view of Blackburn's art and life." Choice

Bly, Robert

Eating the honey of words; new and selected poems. HarperFlamingo 1999 270p pa $14.95 hardcover o.p.   **811**
1. Poetry—By individual authors
ISBN 0-06-093069-1 (pa)   LC 98-51152
"Collecting over 200 poems from 1950 to 1998, this volume is an appealing poetic sampler, although the ten new poems are unexciting. The poems celebrating discoveries Bly makes when alone and silent are always striking, and his imaginative prose poems radiate witty delight." Libr J

The night Abraham called to the stars; poems. HarperCollins Pubs. 2001 95p pa $12.95 hardcover o.p.   **811**
1. Poetry—By individual authors
ISBN 0-06-093444-1 (pa)   LC 00-66360
"The book's 48 lyrics are written in a single (here terceted) form, the ghazal, used by such great Islamic poets as Ghalib, and harness high points of Western art and literature to draw general, biblically backed conclusions about the human condition out of the mire." Publ Wkly

Booth, Philip, 1925-2007

Selves; new poems; by Philip Booth. Viking 1990 75p pa $9.95 hardcover o.p.   **811**
1. Poetry—By individual authors
ISBN 0-14-058646-6 (pa)   LC 89-40317
This collection "features contemplative poems born of the observant patience of North country life. The best are based on concrete observation. . . . Booth's strength is that he speaks of significant issues like the ultimate privacy of suffering, the painful hidden destruction of relationships, the coming of aging and death." Libr J

Bowers, Edgar

Collected poems. Knopf 1997 168p pa $15 hardcover o.p.   **811**
1. Poetry—By individual authors
ISBN 0-679-76607-3 (pa)   LC 96-38580
"Surety of rhythm, swiftness of thought, and deftness of phrase animate Bowers' triumphant poems about loss and the struggle to be whole. He is, above all, a delineator—vital, ironic, capable of panoramic sweep—of his transfiguring experiences in Germany during and after the Second World War. His roots are deep in Horace and Pindar, but amid all the eloquent austerity there are blessed moments of unexpected Mozartian lilt and wit." New Yorker

Bronk, William
Selected poems; selected by Henry Weinfield. New Directions 1995 80p pa $8.95 **811**
1. Poetry—By individual authors
ISBN 978-0-8112-1314-1; 0-8112-1314-5
LC 95-290
"Bronk's poems are almost entirely abstract and disembodied . . . his language desiccated but also conversationally halting and embedded. There is no flesh, no world, precious little metaphor—as though every human attachment is cheating. If anything seems to work—such as cause and effect—it never adds up to anything. . . . Bronk is thinking and thinking, as purely as possible, about how we want—want not to be alone, want things to matter, want to feel that we are connected to reality. His poems are all about wanting and how there is no end to it." Poetry Foundation

Brooks, Gwendolyn
The essential Gwendolyn Brooks; Elizabeth Alexander, editor. Library of America 2005 148p il (American poets project) $20 **811**
1. Poetry—By individual authors
ISBN 978-1-931082-87-7; 1-931082-87-1
LC 2005-44162
"A book like [this] can't make the statement that needs to be made: Gwendolyn Brooks is as important to twentieth-century American poetry as Robert Lowell. . . . Her best poems offer a curative, not only to the narcissistic gloom that we've inherited from the Confessionals, but to Eliot's overaestheticized visions of social life. That Brooks's purposes were so different from Eliot's only strengthens the connection. It shows the vitality of true poetic inspiration, how it can cut across time, temperament, race, and even the motives of its own practitioners." Poetry (Modern Poetry Association)

In Montgomery, and other poems. Third World Press 2003 146p $22.95 **811**
ISBN 0-88378-232-4
LC 2003-50749
This is a "posthumous collection consisting primarily of dramatic monologues in a stunning variety of voices, from those of urban children to Winnie Mandela's. Reading the title sequence resembles randomly tuning a radio dial to listen to the diverse voices of Montgomery, Alabama, a city of 'leaning and lostness, glazed paralysis.' . . . Especially moving are the children's monologues. . . . Brooks captures the fierce purity of these children's needs and desires. Her loving witness never sounded more clearly than in these late poems." Booklist

Bukowski, Charles
The pleasures of the damned; poems, 1951-1993; edited by John Martin. Ecco 2007 556p $29.95 * **811**
1. Poetry—By individual authors
ISBN 978-0-06-122843-8; 0-06-122843-5
LC 2007-282394
This is a selection of work from Bukowski's "poetic career, including the last of his never-before-collected poems." Publisher's note
This book is "an insightful walk through the work of a poet by the man who knew him best, and it reveals Bukowski in the many, often conflicting dimensions that make him such a popular, accessible, and, yes, great artist. . . . This extraordinary collection establishes Bukowski as much more than just another West Coast Beat poet." Washington Post

Burnshaw, Stanley, 1906-2005
The collected poems and selected prose; foreword by Thomas F Stanley. University of Texas Press 2002 487p il (Harry Ransom Humanities Research Center) $50 **811**
1. Poetry—By individual authors
ISBN 978-0-292-70909-6; 0-292-70909-9
LC 2001-52226
"Stanley Burnshaw is one of those men of letters who are so variously productive, and for so long, that they can too easily be taken for granted as merely part of the climate. . . . Since any poet considers himself—and deserves to be considered—a poet first of all, it is wonderful news that Burnshaw's work has now been made available for a new generation of readers. The Collected Poems and Selected Prose . . . allows us to see Burnshaw as a genuine and very American heir of the Romantic tradition in poetry, who has pursued the highest themes over his long career." New Republic
Includes bibliographical references

Carruth, Hayden, 1921-2008
Toward the distant islands; new & selected poems; edited and with an introduction by Sam Hamill. Copper Canyon Press 2006 181p pa $17 * **811**
1. Poetry—By individual authors
ISBN 1-55659-236-1 (pa)
LC 2005-28705
Carruth's "books encompass Frostian tales of farm life with New England eccentrics, compilations of haiku, long and unguarded poems of erotic devotion, autobiographical laments, and sensitive odes to jazz greats. . . . All sides of Carruth's oeuvre find a place in this welcome volume. . . . The selection here gives just enough of everything Carruth has learned, and he has learned a lot, especially about the ways and landscapes of New England." Publ Wkly

Carson, Anne, 1950-
Autobiography of red; a novel in verse. Knopf 1998 149p pa $12 hardcover o.p. **811**
1. Poetry—By individual authors
ISBN 0-375-70129-X (pa)
LC 97-49472
The core of the book is the author's re-interpretation of a lost poem by the Greek poet Stesichoros entitled 'Tale of Geryon'. In the author's recasting, Geryon, "the red giant of myth, has become a small red-winged person of present day life. . . . Geryon is picked on by his schoolmates . . . and bullied by his big brother. His mother seems to be his only refuge. Falling in love at last with the beautiful Herakles . . . their love becomes the centre of Geryon's life until Herakles suddenly leaves him." Quill Quire
"Is it poetry? Is it a novel in verse? A fable? A myth? However you define Carson's distinctive and wildly inventive new work, it is riveting reading. . . . Wistful yet whimsical, offhand yet intense, funky yet erudite . . . this is a reading experience like no other." Libr J

Carson, Anne, 1950-—*Continued*

The beauty of the husband; a fictional essay in 29 tangos. Knopf 2001 147p $24; pa $12
811

1. Poetry—By individual authors
ISBN 0-375-40804-5; 0-375-70757-3 (pa)
LC 00-62002

This poem is "at once the story of a failed marriage and an exploration of Romantic notions of beauty and truth. But Carson's idiosyncratic voice and her punchy declarative style—'You want a clean life I live a dirty one'—quickly make it clear that hers is a thoroughly modern take on the intimate cruelties of married life. And this is the primary pleasure of her writing: it is both entirely new and strangely familiar, like remembering a private language we thought we'd forgotten." New Yorker

Men in the off hours. Knopf 2000 166p il pa $12 hardcover o.p.
811

1. Poetry—By individual authors
ISBN 0-375-70756-5 (pa)
LC 00-267850

The author "makes bold references to everyone from Oedipus to Akhamatova, but the effect of these astute, gemlike little poems is less a history lesson than a challenging conversation in a sunlit garden." Libr J

Carver, Raymond

All of us; the collected poems. Knopf 1998 xxx, 386p hardcover o.p. pa $15
811

1. Poetry—By individual authors
ISBN 978-0-375-70380-5; 0-375-70380-2
LC 98-15880

"The great short story writer's poems are dark and funny, like the stories, and tell of domestic discord, crazy adventures and sweet intimacies, sometimes with sorrow but more often with thankfulness and affection." Booklist
Includes bibliographical references

A new path to the waterfall; poems; introduction by Tess Gallagher. Atlantic Monthly Press 1989 xxxi, 126p pa $14 hardcover o.p.
811

1. Poetry—By individual authors
ISBN 978-0-87113-374-8 (pa); 0-87113-374-1 (pa)
LC 88-34989

"In her moving introduction, Carver's widow, writer Tess Gallagher, notes how often a particular poem calls to mind a corresponding story, and the reverse is also true. Indeed, to know Carver by his prose is to know him only partially. Master at illuminating those often mundane moments that starkly dramatize entire lives, Carver was also master at creating mood, and many of those poems have a striking lyrical intensity, especially when Carver unflinchingly faces death while celebrating life. A coda to a remarkable literary career." Libr J

Ciardi, John, 1916-1986

The collected poems of John Ciardi; compiled and edited by Edward M. Cifelli. University of Ark. Press 1997 xxxii, 618p hardcover o.p. pa $34.95
811

1. Poetry—By individual authors
ISBN 978-1-55728-449-5; 1-55728-449-0
LC 96-46331

"This volume supersedes the earlier *Selected Poems* (1984) providing a vastly more comprehensive sampling of Ciardi's work: 450 poems culled from over 20 individual volumes published between 1940 and 1993. In it we find testimony to Ciardi's desire to achieve not 'a voice,' a style formed to forward an author's individuality, but 'voice'—one that is determined by the externals the poet addresses." Libr J

Clark, Tom, 1941-

Light & shade; new and selected poems; introduction by Amy Gerstler. Coffee House Press 2006 338p pa $20 *
811

1. Poetry—By individual authors
ISBN 1-56689-183-3
LC 2005-35810

"Disarmingly casual yet saturated with loss, Clark's body of work revels in simplicities: lovers, friends, cities and landscapes (New York, Southern California, the Southwest), baseball, basketball, modern painters, sad weather, brief visions and ethereal promises. All make repeat appearances in a poetry rooted at once in spontaneity and in High Romantic aspiration." Publ Wkly

Clifton, Lucille, 1936-

Mercy; poems. 1st ed. BOA Editions 2004 79p (American poets continuum series) $22; pa $14.95
811

1. Poetry—By individual authors
ISBN 1-929918-54-2; 1-929918-55-0 (pa)
LC 2004-10396

The themes explored within the poems in this book include "the tenuous relationship between mothers and daughters, the open wounds of terrorism and racial prejudice, and the redemptive gifts of faith and art." Publisher's note

"These are poems where great restraint mingles with disarming primal imagery to convey poems which hold tremendous emotional weight." Va Q Rev

Cole, Henri

Middle earth; poems. Farrar, Straus & Giroux 2003 55p $23; pa $11
811

1. Poetry—By individual authors
ISBN 0-374-20881-6; 0-374-52928-0 (pa)
LC 2002-29776

The author "examines the dichotomies between life and death, animal and human, and the lover and the beloved. Many of the poems, including, 'My Tea Ceremony' and 'Self-Portrait at the Red Princess,' show a marked Japanese influence; others record a grown son's grief over the death of his father. . . . Cole writes with clarity and an emotive resonance. These poems succeed as the best poems do: they transport the reader to other worlds, no less beautiful or complicated than our own. Highly recommended." Libr J

Collins, Billy

Nine horses; poems. Random House 2002 120p $21.95; pa $12.95
811

1. Poetry—By individual authors
ISBN 1-4000-6177-6; 0-375-75520-9 (pa)
LC 2002-24868

Collins, Billy—*Continued*

Collins is "often able to proceed unburdened by many of the tools—assonance, alliteration, wordplay, complex metrics—that hang from the poet's belt; he makes his way in the world by being funny." N Y Times Book Rev

Sailing alone around the room; new and selected poems. Random House 2001 171p $21.95; pa $13.95 *   **811**

1. Poetry—By individual authors
ISBN 0-375-50380-3; 0-375-75519-5 (pa)

                                LC 99-52861

"Collins will tackle any topic: his subject matter varies from snow days to Aristotle to forgetfulness. The results are accessible but not trite, comical but not laughable, and well crafted but not overly flamboyant. Collins relies heavily on imagery, which becomes the cornerstone of the entire volume." Libr J

The trouble with poetry and other poems; Billy Collins. Random House 2005 88p $22.95

                                   811

1. Poetry—By individual authors
ISBN 0-375-50382-X   LC 2005-46562

The themes explored in this collection include "boyhood, jazz, love, [and] the passage of time." Publisher's note

"Skeptical of love and scornful of pretension, Collins is breathtaking in his appreciation of the earth's beauty and the precious daily routines that define life." Booklist

Corso, Gregory, 1930-2001

Mindfield; with foreword by William S. Burroughs & Allan Ginsberg; and drawings by the author. Thunder's Mouth Press 1989 268p il pa $13.95 hardcover o.p. *   **811**

1. Poetry—By individual authors
ISBN 0-938410-86-5 (pa)   LC 89-5152

"This volume includes substantial selections from each of {the author's} six volumes of published poetry and 23 previously unpublished poems. Corso has written a number of the most memorable American poems since WW II. His poetry combines a lyrical directness of speech with a unique blend of surrealism and aphoristic statement." Choice

Crane, Hart, 1899-1932

Complete poems and selected letters. Library of America 2006 849p $40 *   **811**

1. Poetry—By individual authors
ISBN 1-93108-299-5   LC 2006-40922

This volume "gathers all of the author's poetry and collected prose with a large sampling of his letters, some appearing in print for the first time. The correspondents include top writers William Carlos Williams, Marianne Moore, e.e. cummings, and Katherine Anne Porter. A good one-stop resource for Crane." Libr J

Creeley, Robert, 1926-2005

The collected poems of Robert Creeley. University of California Press 1982-2006 2v v1 o.p.; v1 pa $27.50; v2 $60; v2 pa $24.95 *   **811**

1. Poetry—By individual authors
ISBN 0-520-04243-3 (v1); 978-0-520-24158-9 (v1 pa); 978-0-520-24159-6 (v2); 978-0-520-25620-0 (v2 pa)
Contents: v1, 1945-1975; v2, 1975-2005

Creeley's style is "notably spare and laconic; his primary subject is love and the infinite incongruities that characterize love relationships. There is a distinct dearth of imagery in his poetry; the themes are rendered in a cerebral rather than sensual manner. For Creeley, the intent of the poem is definition, not description." Reader's Ency. 4th edition

Cummings, E. E. (Edward Estlin), 1894-1962

Complete poems, 1904-1962; containing all the published poetry; edited by George J. Firmage. rev corr & expanded ed. Norton 1994 xxxii, 1102p $50 *   **811**

1. Poetry—By individual authors
ISBN 978-0-87140-152-6; 0-87140-152-5

                          LC 91-29158

Expanded version of Complete poems, 1913-1962 (1972)

"This volume has been prepared directly from the poet's original manuscripts, preserving the original typography and format. It includes all the previously published works, from *Tulips* (1922) to *Etcetera* (1983), as well as 36 uncollected poems that originally appeared in little magazines or anthologies." Libr J

Cunningham, J. V. (James Vincent), 1911-1985

The poems of J.V. Cunningham; edited with an introduction & commentary by Timothy Steele. Swallow Press 1997 xxxviii, 215p $32.95; pa $19.95 *   **811**

1. Poetry—By individual authors
ISBN 0-8040-0997-X; 0-8040-0998-8 (pa)

                          LC 97-355

"Cunningham is an austere poet with a passion for exact statement in tightly controlled forms, whose ideal poetic models were those of Roman satire and the conceits of the most formal sixteenth- and seventeenth-century poetry. . . . His chosen form is the classical epigram, his elected idiom the satiric and self-parodic, which allows for the play of wit and irony in his commentary on the absurdity of human life." Oxford Companion to 20th Cent Lit in Engl

Dickinson, Emily, 1830-1886

The poems of Emily Dickinson; edited by R.W. Franklin. Reading ed. Belknap Press 1999 692p $34.50; pa $18.50 *   **811**

1. Poetry—By individual authors
ISBN 978-0-674-67624-4; 0-674-67624-6; 978-0-674-01824-2 (pa); 0-674-01824-9 (pa)

                          LC 99-11821

This work includes a single version of each poem included in the 1998 Variorum. In this one-volume edition, Franklin selects the latest 'manifestation' of a poem in those not uncommon instances when Dickinson herself produced multiple copies. Am Lit

"Within the guidelines Franklin has set himself, his choices of versions and of alternatives within versions

Dickinson, Emily, 1830-1886—*Continued*
are extremely sensible-and they are efficiently recorded
at the end of the volume, making this the first time any
volume of Dickinson's poems aimed at a general audience has offered information about the derivation of its
texts." Raritan

Dorn, Edward, 1929-1999
Way more West; new and selected poems;
introduction by Dale Smith; edited by Michael
Rothenberg. Penguin Books 2007 321p (Penguin
poets) $20 *   **811**
  1. Poetry—By individual authors
  ISBN 978-0-14-303869-6   LC 2006-50727
"Best known for his chatty, satirical mock-western
long poem 'Gunslinger,' Dorn (1929–1999) came to poetic maturity alongside Creeley and Olson, with whom
he studied at the now legendary experimental Black
Mountain College, though his fast-paced, angry poetry
sometimes suggests the beats. Included in this volume
are Dorn's poetic travelogues about the U.S. and Britain;
a poetic history of the Apache nation; epigrams and commentaries against war, capitalism and environmental degradation; and a memorable verse journal of his chemotherapy." Publ Wkly
"Throughout his career, he was the least endearing,
domesticated or predictable of poets, always determined
to go his own way, no matter what anyone thought. And
if he hadn't been that way, American poetry would be a
lot less vital and interesting." N Y Times Book Rev
  Includes bibliographical references

Doty, Mark
Fire to fire; new and selected poems. Harper
2008 336p $22.95; pa $15.95   **811**
  1. Poetry—By individual authors
  ISBN   978-0-06-075247-7;   0-06-075247-5;
978-0-06-075251-4 (pa); 0-06-075251-3 (pa)
                      LC 2007-44646
The author "combines new poems with the best of his
previous volumes. His narrative style is expansive, filled
with what has been described as a 'lyric glitter' that
creates radiance around the ordinary." Libr J
  Includes bibliographical references

Dove, Rita
American smooth; poems. W.W. Norton 2004
143p $22.95; pa $13.95   **811**
  1. Poetry—By individual authors
  ISBN 0-393-05987-1; 0-393-32744-2 (pa)
                      LC 2004-11793
"In these free-verse poems, Dove speaks from her
own perspective—as well as from that of biblical characters, black soldiers from World War I, a ten-year-old girl
from Harlem, several musicians, and a pair of dancers.
The selections work by lists, line breaks where ideas collide, and a juxtaposition of voices. Then using razor-
sharp metaphors, Dove goes for the jugular and usually
finds it. Although the book's sense of audience seems inconsistent, with some poems suitable for *A Child's Garden of Verses* and others for *The Kama Sutra*, the poems
are evocative." Libr J

On the bus with Rosa Parks; poems. Norton
1999 95p pa $12.95 hardcover o.p.   **811**
  1. Poetry—By individual authors
  ISBN 0-393-32026-X   LC 98-45057
Dove's "poems effortlessly suggest grand narratives
and American myths, yet ground themselves tersely in
localities, characters, practicalities and particulars. This
seventh collection leads off with a Dove specialty, the
historical sequence: her 'Cameos' lend broad, social relevance to an intermittently abandoned Depression-era wife
and her family." Publ Wkly

Selected poems. Vintage Bks. 1993 xxvi, 210p
pa $13   **811**
  1. Poetry—By individual authors
  ISBN 0-679-75080-0   LC 93-26112
"This volume places three previous collections under
one cover. . . . The selection begins with *The Yellow
House on the Corner,* Dove's first book, most notable for
its poems derived from slave narratives. *Museum,* her
second book, offers a potpourri of work that ranges over
several continents and many millenia; Dove's tirelessly
exact language illuminates the lives of saints, contemporary lifestyles, and Greek myths." Booklist

Dugan, Alan, 1923-2003
Poems seven; new and complete poetry. Seven
Stories Press 2001 422p $35; pa $18.95 *
                             811
  1. Poetry—By individual authors
  ISBN 1-58322-265-0; 1-58322-512-9 (pa)
                      LC 2001-41089
This collection documents "Dugan's project of comic,
bleak and formally varied commentary on a dirty, terminally frayed and yet attractive America. . . . This carefully constructed, funny and sometimes unvarying volume combines all six of Dugan's previous books with a
decade's worth of new verse." Publ Wkly

Duncan, Robert Edward, 1919-1988
Selected poems; [by] Robert Duncan; edited by
Robert J. Bertholf. New Directions 1993 147p
hardcover o.p. pa $12.95   **811**
  1. Poetry—By individual authors
  ISBN 978-0-8112-1227-4; 0-8112-1227-0
                      LC 92-35812
Duncan "was one of the true masters of contemporary
American poetry. His oeuvre is by turns lyrical, experi-
mental, archaic, visionary and political. . . . In
Bertholf's brief, insightful introduction, he makes neces-
sary connections between the often-neglected early work
and the later masterpieces." Publ Wkly

Dunn, Stephen, 1939-
Different hours; poems. Norton 2000 121p $22;
pa $12.95   **811**
  1. Poetry—By individual authors
  ISBN 0-393-04986-8; 0-393-32232-7 (pa)
                      LC 00-30556
"Stephen Dunn's poetry is strangely easy to like:
philosophical but not arid, lyrical but rarely glib, his storytelling balanced effortlessly between the casual and the
vivid. But don't mistake that ease for lack of staying
power." N Y Times Book Rev

Dunn, Stephen, 1939-—*Continued*

Local visitations; poems. Norton 2003 96p
$21.95 **811**
1. Poetry—By individual authors
ISBN 0-393-05200-1 LC 2002-14204
"The opening section of poems recasts Dunn's average
American as the mythic Sisyphus, imprisoned by repetitive work ('a repetition/which would never mean more/at
the end than at the start') and yet bereft without it ('But
more often he finds himself dreaming/of his rock, wishing it back, the better/to defend himself against so many
hours'). Nearly half the collection transports 19th-century
literary figures to contemporary New Jersey towns
('Mary Shelley in Brigantine,' 'Hawthorne in
Tuckerton'), a series of poems more attractive in concept
than in practice, where the subjects often fail to transcend the contrivance they inhabit." Libr J

Loosestrife. Norton 1996 96p $19; pa $12
811
1. Poetry—By individual authors
ISBN 0-393-03982-X; 0-393-31683-1 (pa)
LC 96-1238
"Dunn understands that there is sorrow in beauty and
a 'strange loneliness' even in pleasure, and he examines
these dichotomies in language and form as clear and
chilling as ice. We feel knocked off balance by the end
of one line, then steadied by the beginning of the next."
Booklist

New & selected poems, 1974-1994. Norton
1994 296p hardcover o.p. pa $16.95 **811**
1. Poetry—By individual authors
ISBN 978-0-393-31300-0; 0-393-31300-X
LC 93-33212
"Dunn might be called a Neo-Horatian poet. He is
level-headed, witty, conversational in his diction, and
willing to see in domestic life his means for attaining
and imparting wisdom. Yet Dunn's variations on Horatian odes and epodes are rarely the drab reportorial missives from the daily grind which are found in so much
contemporary poetry. He knows that his first duty is to
keep the quotidian life interesting, and this is no mean
feat. . . . This is to say that Dunn's a gifted talker, a
kind of querulous raconteur, and even his less successful
poems are highly readable." Poetry (Modern Poetry Association)

Eady, Cornelius, 1954-
Brutal imagination; poems. Putnam 2001 108p
$24; pa $13 **811**
1. Poetry—By individual authors
ISBN 0-399-14718-7; 0-399-14720-9 (pa)
LC 00-62674
"A Marian Wood book"
In this "collection of poetry, Eady invokes a chorus of
fictional black characters, from Uncle Tom to the invented criminal whom Susan Smith blamed for the kidnapping of her children. A white woman's 'stray thought,'
this man haunts the best of these spare, stirring poems.
If the poet's premise—the personification of a black fig-
ment of the white imagination—is complex, his verse is
unsettlingly direct." New Yorker

Edson, Russell, 1935-
The rooster's wife; poems. BOA Editions 2005
91p hardcover o.p. pa $14.95 **811**
1. Poetry—By individual authors
ISBN 978-1-929918-63-8; 1-929918-63-1
LC 2004-24831
"Edson's prose poems are directly and indirectly concerned with feelings customarily suppressed during wake-
fulness, whose content is violent, scatological, and, especially, sexual. An Edson prose poem, however amusing
and ridiculous—however jokelike—it may be, is disturbing. . . . Laughter never blunts the edges of Edson's elegantly maculate conceptions." Booklist

Eliot, T. S. (Thomas Stearns), 1888-1965
Collected poems, 1909-1962. Harcourt Brace
Jovanovich 1963 221p $23 * **811**
1. Poetry—By individual authors
ISBN 0-15-118978-1
This volume contains the complete text of 'Collected
poems, 1909-1935,' the 'Four quartets,' and several other
poems accompanied by brief prefatory notes

The complete poems and plays, 1909-1950.
Harcourt Brace & Co. 1952 392p $35 *
811
1. Poetry—By individual authors
ISBN 0-15-121185-X
This book is made up of six individual titles formerly
published separately: Collected poems (1909-1935); Four
quartets; Old Possum's book of practical cats; Murder in
the cathedral; Family reunion; Cocktail party

Inventions of the March Hare; poems
1909-1917; edited by Christopher Ricks. Harcourt
Brace & Co. 1997 xlii, 428p $30; pa $15
811
1. Poetry—By individual authors
ISBN 0-15-100274-6; 0-15-600587-5 (pa)
LC 96-45399
"Though available in manuscript to scholars since
1968, this is the first appearance—for all but five poems—of Eliot's 'lost' notebook of drafts and fragments.
Eliot never intended this unfinished work to see publication, but in page after page his autumnal sensibility, his
signature aura of languid urban malaise—however tentative—surfaces unmistakably. . . . For scholars and devotees, Eliot's rehearsals for immortality will yield a cornu-
copia of delights." Libr J

Emerson, Ralph Waldo, 1803-1882
Collected poems & translations. Library of Am.
1994 637p $35 * **811**
1. Poetry—By individual authors
ISBN 0-940450-28-3 LC 93-40245
Contains Emerson's published poetry, plus selections
of his unpublished poetry from journals and notebooks,
and some of his translations of poetry from other languages, notably Dante's La vita nuova

Erdrich, Louise

Original fire; selected and new poems. HarperCollins Pubs. 2003 158p $23.95; pa $13.95

811

1. Poetry—By individual authors
ISBN 0-06-620986-2; 0-06-093534-0 (pa)

LC 2003-40700

"With this volume, drawn from two previous collections and including 100 pages of new poems, [the author] presents her first collection in over a decade. . . . Poems from the first collection chronicle her Native American childhood and early schooling, while those from the second rework or invent Native American mythology. The new poems are more rooted in Catholicism and life as a middle-class American. . . . Essential reading for fans of Erdrich's fiction, this volume can be expected to draw poetry readers into the fold." Libr J

Everson, Landis, 1926-

Everything preserved: poems, 1955-2005; edited by Ben Mazer. Graywolf Press 2006 106p pa $15

811

1. Poetry—By individual authors
ISBN 978-1-55597-453-4; 1-55597-453-8

LC 2006-924341

"Everson, who makes his book-length debut in his 70's as winner of the Poetry Foundation's Emily Dickinson first book award, swapped poems with a young Jack Spicer and John Ashbery, then stopped writing for 43 years until a recent creative outburst. This volume—divided into two sections, one for nine poems written between 1955 and 1960, and the other comprising the remaining 66, written since 2003—quickly establishes the charms of the playful early work. . . . The recent work is much more uneven—though much of it has been published in major literary magazines—and there are still plenty of pleasures to be found. Everson evokes the ordinary with a continually surprising touch." Publ Wkly

Fearing, Kenneth, 1902-1961

Selected poems; Robert Polito, editor. Library of America 2004 xxi, 183p (American poets project) $20

811

1. Poetry—By individual authors
ISBN 978-1-931082-57-0; 1-932082-57-X

LC 2003-60482

"Kenneth Fearing writes noir poetry, which is no surprise, considering that he also wrote several noir novels. . . . His poems flirt with narrative (but rarely commit), and they're written in a jittery free verse that sounds like the byproduct of a paranoid, slightly strung-out Whitman. . . . There are plenty of people currently writing variations on Fearing (possibly without being aware of it), but it's tough to beat the stylish chill of the original. These poems may be leaves the wind blows from one gutter to another, but sometimes the gutter's the only place to be." Poetry (Modern Poetry Association)

Fenton, James, 1949-

Selected poems. Farrar, Straus & Giroux 2006 196p pa $14

811

1. Poetry—By individual authors
ISBN 978-0-374-26065-1; 0-374-26065-6

LC 2006-2691

This "collection offers an introduction to the work of a leading British poet and former professor of poetry at Oxford. Love and menace are the principal muses for Fenton's dark wit. Whether describing how an ex is safe because she's no longer loved . . . or narrating war's awful arithmetic . . . the control behind these lines is often terrifying." Publ Wkly

Ferlinghetti, Lawrence

These are my rivers; new & selected poems, 1955-1993. New Directions 1993 308p il pa $13.95 hardcover o.p. *

811

1. Poetry—By individual authors
ISBN 0-8112-1273-4

LC 93-10383

"Reading this hefty selection from 12 previous volumes, plus 50 pages of new poems, we realize how accurately the poet described himself in 1979: a man who 'thinks he's Dylan Thomas and Bob Dylan rolled together with Charlie Chaplin thrown in.' . . . His style is recognizable throughout—phlegmatic poems running several pages, often lacking stanza breaks, with short lines at the left margin or moving across the page as hand follows eye." Libr J

Forché, Carolyn

Blue hour. HarperCollins Pubs. 2003 73p hardcover o.p. pa $13.95

811

1. Poetry—By individual authors
ISBN 0-06-009912-7; 978-0-06-009913-8 (pa); 0-06-009013-5 (pa)

LC 2002-27270

This "gathering of elegiac meditations calls up ghostly memories both personal and universal as the poet mourns the terrible death of her grandmother, gives thanks for the blessing of her son's birth, and alludes with few words and deep feelings to the anguish of war and exile." Booklist

Gallagher, Tess

Dear ghosts,; poems. Graywolf Press 2006 140p $20

811

1. Poetry—By individual authors
ISBN 1-55597-443-0

LC 2005-938149

"Moving beyond the elegy to a kind of love letter, she addresses both the living and the dead, invoking her Pacific Northwest childhood in a lumber worker's family, her Irish roots, and Japanese and Eastern European friends and colleagues." Libr J

"So compelling are Gallagher's graceful poems, they leave the reader feeling 'rearranged from the cells out.'" Booklist

Galvin, Brendan

Habitat; new and selected poems, 1965-2005; Brendan Galvin. Louisiana State University Press 2005 250p $49.95; pa $26.95 *

811

1. Poetry—By individual authors
ISBN 0-8071-3046-X; 0-8071-3047-8 (pa)

LC 2004-22441

This voulume "combines eighteen new works with lyric pieces from the past forty years—including two book-length narratives, Wampanoag Traveler and Saints in

Galvin, Brendan—*Continued*
Their OxHide Boat." Publisher's note
"Galvin's work is not only accessible, it turns the commonplace over into something new. A dory, a cormorant, a pack of dogs, a chickadee—all served up with the eye of someone who can take you on a trip of rediscovery into your own backyard." Cape Cod Voice

Gander, Forrest, 1956-
Eye against eye; with ten photographs by Sally Mann. New Directions 2005 80p il pa $14.95 *
        811
1. Poetry—By individual authors
ISBN 0-8112-1635-7   LC 2005-14907
The "opener, 'Burning Towers, Standing Wall,' compares the building of a Mayan wall and its destruction–both from political and natural forces–to the collapse of the Twin Towers. In three long poems, linked with pieces that contrast a couple's relationship with a boy's budding adolescence, the reader is asked to regard the relationships between words and subjects. . . . Owing to the poems' placement and the near absence of punctuation, the reader is propelled through the verse, left with a sense of urgency and awe." Libr J

Torn awake. New Directions 2001 95p pa $13.95   **811**
1. Poetry—By individual authors
ISBN 0-8112-1486-9   LC 2001-32657
"There is no solid ground in the world Forrest Gander conjures in his new book of poems, yet his tentativeness is one of this book's essential qualities. . . . The voices vary throughout this book's six highly speculative sequences, . . . yet again and again they call from their spectral airiness a single recurring image, an elemental configuration of man, woman and child." N Y Times Book Rev

Getty, Sarah, 1943-
Bring me her heart; poems. Higganum Hill Books 2006 98p pa $12.95   **811**
1. Poetry—By individual authors
ISBN 978-0-9741158-8-6; 0-9741158-8-6
         LC 2005-23805
These "poems focus on the pain and joy of creating art, the endurance of love, and the prospect of old age and mortality." Publisher's note
The author "makes meter, rhyme, and formal stanzas the vehicles of winning, natural expression." Booklist

Gibbons, Reginald, 1947-
It's time: poems. Louisiana State Univ. Press 2002 64p $22.95; pa $15.95   **811**
1. Poetry—By individual authors
ISBN 0-8071-2814-7; 0-8071-2815-5 (pa)
         LC 2002-73076
This collection of poems considers "all manner of things: the migration of birds, the vast variety of hats, and, in a nearly 200-line work called 'Poem Including History' that serves as the volume's centerpiece, Europe itself." Libr J
"If the thoughtful poems in Gibbons' elegant seventh collection were pieces of music, they would be measured piano sonatas, each note, each word, carefully struck, precisely enunciated." Booklist

Gibran, Kahlil, 1883-1931
The Prophet. Knopf 1923 107p il $15 *
        811
1. Poetry—By individual authors
ISBN 0-394-40428-9
Also available pocket library editions
A collection of poems by the mystical writer/artist, who was born in Lebanon and died in the United States, in which the prophet Almustafa deals with fundamental aspects of human life such as love, friendship, good and evil, self-knowledge, passion and reason, joy and sorrow, freedom, work, marriage and children, prayer and death

Gilbert, Jack, 1925-
Refusing heaven; poems. Knopf 2005 92p $25 *
        811
1. Poetry—By individual authors
ISBN 1-4000-4365-4   LC 2004-48844
"Jack Gilbert is a poet of reckless charisma and its aftermaths: a catch-as-catch-can Castiglione, consigned by the waywardness of his imagination to write his canon of manners and gestures in lyric poetry. The poems have the quality of brilliant, searching, addled talk after a wild night out. There's a sort of strung-out sprezzatura to this poet, as he bobs and weaves among the memories of old loves in old, European cities. . . . These poems are the stream-of-consciousness work of a consciousness radically narrowed over time, practically armored against new experience. At their best, shuttling associatively between a few old obsessions, they attain claustrophobic beauty that sounds like nobody else." Poetry (Modern Poetry Association)

Ginsberg, Allen, 1926-1997
Collected poems, 1947-1997. HarperCollins Publishers 2006 xx, 1189p il $39.95 *
        811
1. Poetry—By individual authors
ISBN 978-0-06-113974-1; 0-06-113974-2
         LC 2006-41191
First published 1984 with title: Collected poems, 1947-1980
This books "reprints the complete text of 1984's Collected Poems 1947-1980, along with the collections that followed: White Shroud, Cosmopolitan Greetings, and Death and Fame, including the original book attributes of each collection. A poet of extremes at times too trusting of his instincts, Ginsberg could be playful, angry, strident, obscene, graceful, and hilarious in the space of a page, and by now his readers know they are likely to encounter as many embarrassing poems as enlightening ones. Still, this compendium provides the most complete edition of Ginsberg available." Libr J

Gioia, Dana
Disappearing ink; poetry at the end of print culture. Graywolf Press 2004 271p pa $16
        811
1. American poetry—History and criticism
ISBN 1-55597-410-4   LC 2004-104190
In this collection of essays, the author discusses the current relevance of poetry and the ways in which it is

Gioia, Dana—*Continued*
evolving with the times.

The author "offers accessible, necessary criticism for lay and academic readers of serious poetry." Am Book Rev

Giovanni, Nikki
The collected poetry of Nikki Giovanni, 1968-1998; chronology and notes by Virginia C. Fowler. William Morrow 2003 xliii, 452p $24.95
811

1. Poetry—By individual authors
ISBN 0-06-054133-4   LC 2004-302269
Contents: Black feeling Black talk— Black judgement—Re: Creation—My house—The Women and the men— Cotton candy on a rainy day—Those who ride the night winds—Occasional poems
"Giovanni observes and embraces the world like few other poets; seize on these poems spanning three decades, and listen to her sing." Booklist
Includes bibliographical references

Glück, Louise, 1943-
Averno. Farrar, Straus and Giroux 2006 79p $22
811

1. Poetry—By individual authors
ISBN 0-374-10742-4; 978-0-374-10742-0
LC 2005-42658
"In eighteen linked poems, . . . [the author] rewrites the legend of Persephone." Booklist
"Empathic and unforgiving, the voice that unifies Persephone's despondent homelessness, Demeter's rageful mothering and Hades's smitten jealousy is unique in recent poetry, and reveals the flawed humanity of the divine." Publ Wkly

Goldbarth, Albert
The kitchen sink; new and selected poems, 1972-2007. Graywolf Press 2007 345p $26 *
811

1. Poetry—By individual authors
ISBN 978-1-55597-462-6; 1-55597-462-7
LC 2006-929502
"Albert Goldbarth just may be the American poet of his generation for the ages. Often humorous but always serious, Goldbarth combines erudite research, pop-culture fanaticism, and personal anecdote in ways that make his writings among the most stylistically recognizable in the literary world." Georgia Rev

Graham, Jorie, 1951-
The dream of the unified field; selected poems, 1974-1994. Ecco Press 1995 199p pa $15 hardcover o.p.
811

1. Poetry—By individual authors
ISBN 0-88001-476-8 (pa)   LC 95-16572
"Combining great vision like Blake's, a Dickinsonian philosophical introspection, and a richly modern sensuality, this selection demonstrates the full range of Graham's poetic gifts." Booklist

Overlord; poems. Ecco 2005 93p $22.95
811

1. Poetry—By individual authors
ISBN 0-06-074565-7   LC 2004-53681
This poetry collection "is largely a meditation on the current political atmosphere as filtered through World War II; the poet's general sense is that we're in big trouble." N Y Times Book Rev
"In a distinctly forthright and empathic collection, Graham has constructed poems of lyrical steeliness and cauterizing beauty." Booklist

Grossman, Allen R., 1932-
Descartes' loneliness. New Directions 2007 64p il pa $16.95
811

1. Poetry—By individual authors
ISBN 978-0-8112-1711-8; 0-8112-1711-6
LC 2007-26896
"Grossman once claimed poetry to be the historical enemy of human forgetfulness. This interest—or better, faith—in poetry's capacity to perform distinctly human acts of preservation has informed Grossman's writing from the beginning. This most recent book showcases some of Grossman's most affecting and memorable lyrics to date." Publ Wkly

H. D. (Hilda Doolittle), 1886-1961
Collected poems, 1912-1944; edited by Louis L. Martz. New Directions 1983 xxxvi, 629p hardcover o.p. pa $24.95 *
811

1. Poetry—By individual authors
ISBN 978-0-8112-0971-7; 0-8112-0971-7
LC 83-6380
This volume includes "H.D.'s poetry, published and unpublished, through her *Trilogy* completed in 1944, excepting her verse dramas and poems in prose works. Also excluded is the late verse in *By Avon River* and *Helen in Egypt*." Libr J
The editor's textual notes "offer valuable and illuminating scholarly commentary and present the most important of the textual variants. An informative and sensitively written introduction discusses aspects of the interpenetration of H.D.'s biography with her poetic sensibility. This volume is an impressive scholarly work." Choice

Hacker, Marilyn, 1942-
Selected poems; 1965-1990. Norton 1994 250p $22; pa $13.95
811

1. Poetry—By individual authors
ISBN 0-393-03675-8; 0-393-31349-2 (pa)
LC 94-27507
"Few poets have been as successful as Hacker in negotiating the boundary of the feminist and lesbian canon while generating a buzz around their early work. Iambic and readable, the pieces in *Selected Poems*—taken from five previous volumes—use unique inversions to explore self and other through changing situations between friends, lovers, family, and one's surroundings. . . . Often, these are poems of loss, of desire delayed, of pleasure deferred." Libr J

Hacker, Marilyn, 1942-—_Continued_
Squares and courtyards. Norton 2000 107p $21;
pa $12   **811**
1. Poetry—By individual authors
ISBN 0-393-04830-6; 0-393-32095-2 (pa)
LC 99-39110
"With customary fortitude and intelligence, Hacker
confronts such sobering subjects as the trauma of her
own chemotherapy and the loss of friends, in poems that
are at once clear-sighted and emotionally full." New
Yorker

Hall, Donald, 1928-
White apples and the taste of stone; poems,
1946-2006. Houghton Mifflin Co. 2006 431p $30;
pa $16.95   **811**
1. Poetry—By individual authors
ISBN   978-0-618-53721-1;   0-618-53721-X;
978-0-618-91999-4 (pa); 0-618-91999-6 (pa)
LC 2005-20047
Includes a CD of Hall reading from his own work
"Given to formal short work in the '50s, to lengthy
verse essays and verse memoirs later on, Hall shows
consistent topics and moods: adult life among New
Hampshire's farms and mountains, childhood in the Connecticut suburbs, equanimity and nostalgia, satire and
self-satire, middle age and old age, regret and reserve.
Most original in his long poems from the '80s and '90s,
Hall achieved popular success in recent years,. . . col-
lecting elegies and laments for his late wife, the poet
Jane Kenyon." Publ Wkly

Harjo, Joy, 1951-
A map to the next world; poetry and tales.
Norton 2000 138p hardcover o.p. pa $13.95
     811
1. Poetry—By individual authors
ISBN 978-0-393-32096-1; 0-393-32096-0
LC 99-41099
"One of the most significant American Indian poets
here expands her poetic practice to include what she calls
tales but might as easily be considered prose poems.
Harjo's verse has lately taken on a flowing, narrative
quality; these tales, by contrast, take an imagistic,
stream-of-consciousness form. . . . Written with authority and Harjo's trademark exploratory verve, this is fine,
mature work." Booklist

Harrington, Janice N.
Even the hollow my body made is gone; poems;
foreword by Elizabeth Spires. BOA Editions, Ltd.
2007 85p (A. Poulin Jr. new poets of America
series) pa $15.50   **811**
1. Poetry—By individual authors
ISBN 978-1-929918-89-8; 1-929918-89-5
LC 2006-30823
The author "sets her first poetry collection mainly in
Alabama during the civil-rights era. Her rich, colloquial
poems, drawing on both folklore and science, are paeans
to a weary but tenacious black family and their journey
north through 'a night as wide as the River Jordan.' . . .
When the poems themselves seem less pioneering than
the spirit they evoke, their scope and empathy largely
compensate." New Yorker

Harrison, Jim, 1937-
The shape of the journey; new & collected
poems. Copper Canyon Press 1998 463p $30; pa
$20 *   **811**
1. Poetry—By individual authors
ISBN 1-55659-095-4; 1-55659-149-7 (pa)
LC 98-25501
"This large collection, which also includes a new grab
bag of nature verse and prose poems called 'Geo-
Bestiary,' has a meandering feel, although Harrison's
concerns—aging, women, eating and drinking, hunting,
the craft of writing and above all the spirit and rhythms
of the natural world—are remarkably constant. . . . Harrison's writing is graceful, direct and muscular, even in
those occasional places where the poems feel like
dashed-off diary entries or, rarer still, when they hit a
mawkish note." N Y Times Book Rev

Hass, Robert, 1941-
Time and materials; poems, 1997-2005. Ecco
2007 88p $22.95   **811**
1. Poetry—By individual authors
ISBN 978-0-06-134960-7; 0-06-134960-7
LC 2007-30294
This collection of poetry by the former U.S. poet laureate "show a rare internal variety, even as they reflect
his constant concerns. One is human impact on the planet at the century's end. . . . Another concern is biography and memory, not so much Hass's own life as the
lives of family and friends. . . . Through it all runs a
rare skill with long sentences, a light touch, a wish to
make claims not just on our ears but on our hearts, and
a willingness to wait—few poets wait longer, it seems—
for just the right word." Publ Wkly
Includes bibliographical references

Hayden, Robert Earl, 1913-1980
Collected poems; edited by Frederick Glaysher.
Liveright 1985 205p hardcover o.p. pa $15 *   **811**
1. Poetry—By individual authors
ISBN 978-0-87140-159-5; 0-87140-159-2
LC 84-28880
"Hayden's poetry is a blend of unrivaled craftsmanship with a sharp, unrestrained vision. His subjects encompass the whole of human experience, from the extremely personal but never obscure ('Approximations') to
the historical but never pedantic ('Belsen, Day of Liberation'). His technique is similarly varied. Hayden is as adept with haiku, imitations of Eskimo song-poems, or sonnets as he is with free verse. A particularly important addition to libraries with black literature collections."
Booklist

Hecht, Anthony, 1923-2004
Collected later poems. Knopf 2003 255p
hardcover o.p. pa $16.95   **811**
1. Poetry—By individual authors
ISBN 978-0-375-71030-8; 0-375-71030-2
LC 2003-44601
This volume contains: The transparent man (1990),
Flight among the tombs (1996), and The darkness and

Hecht, Anthony, 1923-2004—*Continued*

the light (2001)

"From the outset a fastidious craftsman, Hecht developed out of the legacy of modernism a stately, intricate, rigorously formal poetry that slowly expanded in its range of tones and subject matter." Times Lit Suppl

Hillman, Brenda

Cascadia. Wesleyan Univ. Press 2001 77p (Wesleyan poetry) $26; pa $13.95 **811**

1. Poetry—By individual authors

ISBN 0-8195-6491-5; 0-8195-6492-3 (pa)

LC 2001-35504

"Geologists know 'Cascadia' as the name for the landmass that became the American West Coast: Hillman's serial mix of long and short poems links Californian geology, geography, history (a Gold Rush-era diarist named Shirley), continental philosophy, and personal experience. . . . Some poems are content with their lyrical verbal effects; others play with typography for effects that are energetic, familiar to readers of Susan Howe and Jorie Graham." Publ Wkly

Pieces of air in the epic. Wesleyan Univ. Press 2005 87p $22.95; pa $14.95 **811**

1. Poetry—By individual authors

ISBN 978-0-8195-6787-1; 0-8195-6787-6; 978-0-8195-6788-8 (pa); 0-8195-6788-4 (pa)

LC 2005-18749

"The second in a tetralogy exploring the four elements, Hillman's expansive new work examines air not just as 'gusts & siroccos, chinooks, hamskin, whooshes' but as voice, song, and spirit. Were it not such a pun, one would be tempted to call this collection literally breathtaking; Hillman has pursued an ambitious program with remarkably fine-tuned language." Libr J

Hirsch, Edward

Earthly measures; poems. Knopf 1994 93p hardcover o.p. pa $18 **811**

1. Poetry—By individual authors

ISBN 978-0-679-76566-0; 0-679-76566-2

LC 93-26410

"Hirsch contemplates manifestations of the divine in this set of ravishing poems infused with a deeply felt sense of place and history, seeking insights into how instances of spiritual revelation occur in the frequently brutal everyday world." Booklist

On love; poems. Knopf 1998 86p hardcover o.p. pa $15 **811**

1. Poetry—By individual authors

ISBN 978-0-375-70260-0; 0-375-70260-1

LC 97-49460

"The affirmation of On Love is its language, and the sense it gives that the language of love is inexhaustible. However conversant with the abyss, however true to the devastating logic of desire, the poems ultimately feel triumphant. They are held aloft by nothing but their own joyous artistry." Yale Rev

Special orders; poems. Alfred A. Knopf 2008 64p $25 **811**

1. Poetry—By individual authors

ISBN 978-0-307-26681-1; 0-307-26681-8

LC 2007-40336

This collection "brings its demotic, heartfelt, autobiographical pieces together to form a picture of Hirsch's whole life, with sadness always visible, but joy in the foreground. He begins with his immigrant 'grandfather,/ an old man from the Old World'; remembers 'the second-story warehouse' where the young poet 'filled orders for the factory downstairs'; and moves on to his own life as a struggling, and then a successful, writer, teacher and father. Jewish and Yiddish heritage, in memory and on canvas (Chaim Soutine, Marc Chagall) pervades the first half of the volume. . . . The second half follows Hirsch as an adult, to Houston (where he taught for many years) and back to New York City, where he now heads the Guggenheim Foundation." Publ Wkly

Hirshfield, Jane

After; poems. HarperCollins 2006 97p $23.95 **811**

1. Poetry—By individual authors

ISBN 0-06-077916-0 LC 2005-50260

"These poems' topics range from global warming to insomnia, passion, cheese making, and sneezing. . . . [The author] engages historical figures from Rembrandt, Poe, and Tu Fu to Linnaeus, Roget, and Darwin. The beauty of these historically engaging poems, though, is that they remain firmly tied to our contemporary world." Va Q Rev

Hoagland, Tony

What narcissism means to me. Graywolf Press 2003 78p pa $14 **811**

1. Poetry—By individual authors

ISBN 1-55597-386-8 (pa) LC 2003-101172

The author's "speaker devotes considerable energy to unmasking . . . [his] vulnerable self, revealing its ugliness, hatred and social sensitivity. . . . In milder poems, which often revolve around eating dinner, drinking wine and hanging out with friends (typically other creative writing professors), he explores a more social self, slipping into a 'he said, she said' mode, and reporting at great length on friends' witticisms." Publ Wkly

Hoffman, Daniel, 1923-

Beyond silence; selected shorter poems, 1948-2003. Louisiana State Univ. Press 2003 226p $49.95; pa $26.95 **811**

1. Poetry—By individual authors

ISBN 0-8071-2860-0; 0-8071-2861-9 (pa)

LC 2002-34090

The author "presents his favorites among his short poems thematically in eight sections." Booklist

The collection's "organization by theme brings poems from remote parts of his *oeuvre* into illuminating conversation with one another. And substantial recent poems such as 'Scott Nearing's Ninety-Eighth Year' and 'The Cape Racer' are as strong as anything he's written." NY Times Book Rev

Hollander, John

A draft of light; poems. Alfred A. Knopf 2008 109p $26 **811**

1. Poetry—By individual authors

ISBN 978-0-307-26911-9; 0-307-26911-6

LC 2008-4751

Hollander, John—*Continued*

"As one would expect of a poet whose work has been set to music, Hollander sees poetry as an oral art even though it is first written on paper. What one might not expect from this 78-year-old poet is the wordplay, lighthearted tone, and general mischievousness that seems to come trippingly from his pen. . . . This volume's title poem, for example, ends with a paraphrase of T.S. Eliot's 'Little Gidding.' Other poems paraphrase Percy Bysshe Shelley, Wallace Stevens, and Joyce Kilmer, to say nothing of William Shakespeare. Like Shakespeare, Hollander fuses a somber tone with comic conventions, resulting in the poetic equivalent of the problem play." Libr J

Includes bibliographical references

Figurehead & other poems. Knopf 1999 89p
hardcover o.p. pa $15   **811**
  1. Poetry—By individual authors
  ISBN 978-0-375-70433-8; 0-375-70433-7
                                  LC 98-14208
Hollander's "justifiably confident in his skills, the solid grace of his constructions, and his ability to make both the light and dark sides of words, thoughts, and even life itself simultaneously visible. It's no wonder that among nimbly philosophic poems about Arachne, Cain, and a painting by Velázquez he disarms, charms, and intrigues his readers with a witty and imaginative tribute to the tabletop sculptures of Saul Steinberg and a bittersweet remembrance of George Moran, an old vaudevillian." Booklist

Howard, Richard, 1929-

Inner voices; selected poems, 1963-2003. Farrar,
Straus and Giroux 2004 428p $35 *   **811**
  1. Poetry—By individual authors
  ISBN 0-374-25862-7   LC 2004-40464
The author "chooses artists and art as the personae and subjects of many of his poems. . . . Besides artists, Howard often chooses writers as personae, including prominent Victorians (Whitman, Ruskin and Browning); correspondents with other writers and artists; and increasingly, himself as traveler, museumgoer, and engaged reader." Booklist

The silent treatment; new poems. Turtle Point
Press 2005 114p pa $16.95 *   **811**
  1. Poetry—By individual authors
  ISBN 1-885586-38-3   LC 2004-113837
Hannah Arendt, George Eliot, Cosima Wagner, and a boy in a photograph by Arkansas photographer Mike Disfarmer are among the speakers in this collection.
"In characterizing the poems of Richard Howard's latest collection, one is tempted to bypass 'golden' as a description and head straight on to platinum. Now in his eighth decade, Howard has long been–along with the late James Merrill, who jokingly coined the phrase–one of American poetry's 'Great Fancies.'" Wkly Stand

Howe, Susan, 1937-

Souls of the Labadie tract. New Directions
Books 2007 127p pa $16.95   **811**
  1. Poetry—By individual authors
  ISBN 978-0-8112-1718-7; 0-8112-1718-3
                                  LC 2007-34255

"In her newest book, Howe stands in thrall to a 17th-century history of Deerfield, Mass., and then chases down an obscure reference to 'Labadist' in Wallace Stevens's family tree, which brings her to the story of a short-lived Utopian 'quietest sect,' followers of Jean de Labadie who established a community in Maryland in 1684 that vanished within 40 years. It is in these vast tracts of time made intimate by texts, by language, that Howe operates. . . . Beginning with a quote from Jonathan Edwards equating the silkworm to 'a type of Christ' and ending with a photograph of a fragment of the silk wedding dress of Edwards's wife, onto which Howe projects a text ('I have already shown that space is God'), this is intense stuff." Publ Wkly

Howes, Barbara, 1914-1996

Collected poems, 1945-1990. University of Ark.
Press 1995 134p pa $16 hardcover o.p. *
                                         811
  1. Poetry—By individual authors
  ISBN 0-679-76592-1 (pa)   LC 94-32343
"How often has a forgotten writer been resurrected, heralded as an important voice, only to end up a disappointment? All too often, alas. Luckily, this is not the case with Barbara Howes, who . . . is as obscure a worthy poet as I can think of. Her book not only exceeds expectations, but exceeds them in ways I never would have guessed. . . . Certainly there is much in this book for lovers of poetic forms: villanelles, sestinas and a 'Near-Pantoum,' as the poet calls it." N Y Times Book Rev

Hughes, Langston, 1902-1967

The collected poems of Langston Hughes;
Arnold Rampersad, editor; David Roessel,
associate editor. Knopf 1994 708p $39.95; pa $18
*   **811**
  1. Poetry—By individual authors
  ISBN 0-679-42631-0; 0-679-76408-9 (pa)
                                  LC 94-14509
"The editors have attempted to collect every poem (860 in all) published by the writer in his lifetime, and have also provided a brief but informative introduction, a detailed chronology and extensive textual notes that include the original date and place of publication for each poem. . . . Although Hughes is best known for his poems celebrating African American life, he was also a passionately political poet." Publ Wkly

Selected poems of Langston Hughes; drawings
by E. McKnight Kauffer. Knopf 1959 297p il
hardcover o.p. pa $13.95   **811**
  1. Poetry—By individual authors
  ISBN 978-0-679-72818-4; 0-679-72818-X
This collection represents Langston Hughes' own decisions as to which of his poems he wanted to preserve and reprint

Hugo, Richard F.

Making certain it goes on; the collected poems of Richard Hugo. Norton 1983 xxi, 456p hardcover o.p. pa $19.95 *   **811**

1. Poetry—By individual authors
ISBN 978-0-393-30784-9; 0-393-30784-0
    LC 83-8016

"Though he would never be a serene poet, his collected poems show Hugo turning toward a calm peace that would mark his best work in 'White Center' (1980) and 'The Right Madness On Skye' (1981), and in the 22 new poems in this volume. . . . Among the new poems included [here] Hugo was still driving, looking, and naming. If we had not noticed before that his great gift was the elegy, we see it now." N Y Times Book Rev

Ignatow, David, 1914-1997

I have a name. University Press of New England 1996 75p (Wesleyan poetry) hardcover o.p. pa $13.95   **811**

1. Poetry—By individual authors
ISBN 978-0-8195-2240-5; 0-8195-2240-6
    LC 96-19350

"Ignatow's words are spare and apparently casual, holding us riveted by the force of what is articulated but not spoken. . . . The subjects are timeless: loss, age, death, the joy of fleeting moments." Booklist

Shadowing the ground. Wesleyan Univ. Press 1991 68p (Wesleyan poetry) hardcover o.p. pa $13.95   **811**

1. Poetry—By individual authors
ISBN 978-0-8195-1197-3; 0-8195-1197-8
    LC 90-20872

"Here are sixty-five short, spare, untitled poems, their uniformity of appearance (two-thirds of them ten lines or fewer) belying the plural perspectives that David Ignatow brings to his considerations of age and death's imminence. . . . Shadowing the Ground celebrates contrary responses to unplanned obsolescence." World Lit Today

Jackson, Major, 1968-

Hoops; poems. Norton 2006 125p $23.95
    811

1. Poetry—By individual authors
ISBN 0-393-05937-5; 978-0-393-05937-3
    LC 2005-33320

"Set mostly in an urban landscape, the poems range over a variety of addresses: one envisions neighborhood basketball as a metaphor for life . . . ; others recall the trials and travails of adolescence or pay homage to writers like Shirley Jackson, Robert Frost, Langston Hughes and Gwendolyn Brooks." Publ Wkly

The author's "poems are witty, musical, and intelligent; he is equally happy discussing the war on terror . . . or describing early crushes." New Yorker

Jacobsen, Josephine

In the crevice of time; new and collected poems. Johns Hopkins Univ. Press 1995 258p (Johns Hopkins, poetry and fiction) hardcover o.p. pa $25
    811

1. Poetry—By individual authors
ISBN 978-0-8018-6339-4; 0-8018-6339-2
    LC 95-2798

"In this retrospective spanning nearly six decades of distinguished poetry, the best work comes at the beginning and the end. A contemporary of Robert Penn Warren and Elizabeth Bishop, Jacobsen continues to write stately poems informed by irony, fatalism, and an eloquent appreciation of strength in all its guises, physical and moral. An unabashed formalist, she carefully composes poems that are aggressively metrical . . . and whose surfaces are dense with metaphor, rhyme, assonance, alliteration, and omniscient authority." Libr J

Jarrell, Randall, 1914-1965

The complete poems. Farrar, Straus & Giroux 1969 507p pa $22 hardcover o.p. *   **811**

1. Poetry—By individual authors
ISBN 0-374-51305-8 (pa)

Collected here are the entire contents of three published volumes Selected poems (1955), The woman at the Washington Zoo (1960), and The Lost World (1965) plus poems published from 1934 to 1964 but never collected and some never before published

Jeffers, Robinson, 1887-1962

The collected poetry of Robinson Jeffers; edited by Tim Hunt. Stanford Univ. Press 1988-2001 5v set $300 *   **811**

1. Poetry—By individual authors
ISBN 0-8047-4418-1   LC 87-18083

Individual volumes also available ea $75

Contents: v1 1920-1928; v2 1928-1938; v3 1938-1962; v4 Poetry 1903-1920, prose, and unpublished writings; v5 Textual evidence and commentary

"Jeffers' strengths and weaknesses as a poet are inextricable, but he wrote nothing trivial. His narratives owe much to the example of Edward Arlington Robinson, but they surpass the model and have not been equaled since. Their plots and characterizations are repetitive and even obsessive, but the narrative pulse of the ten and five stressed lines is both supple and controlled, while the interspersed authorial commentary varies the cadence and lends shrewd perspective. No reevaluation can ignore them. The shorter poems share the same rhythm of lyric thrust checked by terse observation and dicta." Benet's Reader's Ency of Am Lit

The selected poetry of Robinson Jeffers; edited by Tim Hunt. Stanford Univ. Press 2001 758p pa $34.95   **811**

1. Poetry—By individual authors
ISBN 978-0-8047-4108-8; 0-8047-4108-5
    LC 00-48490

"Hunt's edition strips the punctuation added by contemporary printers (which 'often obscures the rhythm and pacing of what Jeffers actually wrote, and at points even obscures meaning and nuance') and includes a carefully

Jeffers, Robinson, 1887-1962—*Continued*
weighed choice of long and short works, as well as un-published work. . . . This new selection will get readers closer than ever to the poems as Jeffers himself saw them." Publ Wkly

Johnson, James Weldon, 1871-1938
Complete poems; edited with an introduction by Sondra Kathryn Wilson. Penguin Bks. 2000 xxxiii, 202p pa $14 **811**
1. Poetry—By individual authors
ISBN 0-14-118545-7   LC 00-39969
This volume contains Fifty years and other poems (1917), God's trombones (1927), Saint Peter relates an incident of the resurrection day (1935), and a number of previously unpublished poems. The editor's introduction considers Johnson's achievements and influence
Includes bibliographical references

Johnson, Ronald, 1935-1998
The shrubberies; edited by Peter O'Leary. Flood Editions 2001 136p pa $14 **811**
1. Poetry—By individual authors
ISBN 0-9710059-0-7   LC 2002-279220
This "book consists of a loosely linked sequence writ-ten in the last years of the poet's life. With their brevity and almost microscopic wordplay, the poems resemble epigrams. But where epigrams click into place, these po-ems leave implications floating. . . . The pleasure and insight of these poems come from more than prosodic specifics. Unlike so many 'experimental poets,' Johnson writes from necessity. As Peter O'Leary explains in his eloquent afterword, Johnson had a 'sense that these po-ems completed his work as a poet.' Several of the poems address mortality with starkness and force." Poetry (Modern Poetry Association)

Jordan, June, 1936-2002
Directed by desire; the collected poems of June Jordan; edited by Jan Heller Levi and Sara Miles. Copper Canyon Press 2005 649p $40 *
                                                    811
1. Poetry—By individual authors
ISBN 1-55659-228-0   LC 2005-11701
This collection "gathers the finest work from Jordan's ten volumes, as well as seventy new, never-before-published poems that she wrote while dying of breast cancer." Publisher's note
Jordan's poems "consistently display a loving devotion to black English and pride in her femininity, race, and individuality. Directed by Desire is an important addition to African American or feminist poetry collections." Booklist

Justice, Donald Rodney, 1925-2004
Collected poems. Knopf 2004 288p $25 *
                                                    811
1. Poetry—By individual authors
ISBN 1-4000-4239-9   LC 2003-65735
This volume reprints work from Justice's first collec-tion written in 1960 "through six subsequent volumes

and includes some pieces done since his previous selec-tion, published in 1995." New Leader
"Though its primary subject is the past, his work as a whole is more extraordinarily present—more thrillingly contemporary—than most of the styles that have adver-tised their commitment to 'making it new' over the past half-century." N Y Times Book Rev

Kelly, Robert, 1935-
Lapis; poems. Godine 2005 221p pa $18.95
                                                    811
1. Poetry—By individual authors
ISBN 1-57423-186-3   LC 2004-16724
"A Black Sparrow book"
This collection "offers dream narratives, elegies, prayers, anecdotes, parables, dialogues, and folktales from a land that may not exist. . . . Kelly has done something remarkable. He has given magic back its dig-nity, finding it in human warmth." Bookforum

Red actions; selected poems, 1960-1993. Black Sparrow Press 1995 398p hardcover o.p. pa $18.95
                                                    811
1. Poetry—By individual authors
ISBN 978-0-87685-977-3; 0-87685-977-5
                                                    LC 95-35351
"In more than 35 collections of poetry, Kelly has utterly failed at one thing: to pigeonhole himself into predictability. This rich selection from more than a quar-ter-century of work contains imagistic bits that seem like fragments of poetic tapestry, long surreal narratives, se-ries poems, and sonorous chants. Whatever the form, they are marked by Kelly's erudition, which covers Greek archaeology as readily as twentieth-century music, Sumerian gods as well as contemporary painting. Yet his work is never merely academic, inspired as it is by a passionate intellect reminiscent of Wallace Stevens. This survey may draw him more of the readers he well de-serves." Booklist

Kenyon, Jane, 1947-1995
Collected poems. Graywolf Press 2005 357p $26 * **811**
1. Poetry—By individual authors
ISBN 1-55597-428-7
"This collected edition reproduces verbatim the four books Kenyon saw through to press; the poems from two posthumous collections, Otherwise and A Hundred White Daffodils; Kenyon's translations of Akhmatova; and four previously uncollected poems. . . . Taken as a whole, Kenyon's poems remain a sustaining record of a life staked out in very difficult terrain." Publ Wkly

Kerouac, Jack, 1922-1969
Book of blues. Penguin Bks. 1995 273p (Penguin poets) pa $13.95 **811**
1. Poetry—By individual authors
ISBN 0-14-058700-4   LC 94-45902
A "set of eight previously unpublished 'blues' poems written between 1954 and 1961. These long poems, se-ries of 'choruses' or sketches, resemble, in form and avidity, Kerouac's amazing verse creation *Mexico City Blues* (1959). They are strongly tied to place and are, as the allusion to music implies, boldly improvisational." Booklist

Kerouac, Jack, 1922-1969—*Continued*

Book of sketches, 1952-53; introduction by George Condo. Penguin Books 2006 413p (Penguin poets) pa $18 * **811**
1. Poetry—By individual authors
ISBN 978-0-14-200215-5; 0-14-200215-1
LC 2005-44535
"Somewhere between diary, verbal sketchbook and play-by-play account of whatever passed before his eyes, this collection of poems transcribed from notebooks Kerouac kept in his pocket between 1952 and 1954 turns out to rank with his most interesting work. . . . Kerouac hits all the notes for which he and his fellow beats are known. While not everything here is golden, the immediacy and unpretentiousness of this off-the-cuff writing makes it an intimate glimpse into the consciousness of a man who simply couldn't stop observing." Publ Wkly

Pomes all sizes; introduction by Allen Ginsberg. City Lights Bks. 1992 175p pa $13.95
811
1. Poetry—By individual authors
ISBN 0-87286-269-0 LC 92-1204
"This book, which Kerouac prepared for publication before his death in 1969, collects poems written between 1954 and 1965. Most are playful—comments about friends, variations on the sounds of words. Yet a few extremely sensitive longer pieces appear, including 'Caritas,' in which the poet runs after a barefoot beggar boy to give him money for shoes and then begins to doubt the boy's veracity. Other intriguing poems reflect the poet's religious concerns of the moment, running the gamut of Eastern and Western religions." Libr J

Scattered poems. City Lights Bks. 1971 76p pa $7.95 **811**
1. Poetry—By individual authors
ISBN 0-87286-064-7
"The Pocket poets series"
This collection "contains poems that either have previously appeared in periodicals or have not appeared in print at all. The poems are delightfully representative of Kerouac: that free and easy style of writing from the music of the imagination, without a score to follow. Those familiar with the San Francisco school of poetry will readily see Kerouac's affinity in style and content with such writers as Rexroth, Everson, Snyder, Ferlinghetti, Ginsberg, et al. . . . Kerouac sings in the American language to an American tune." Libr J

Kinnell, Galway, 1927-
A new selected poems. Houghton Mifflin 2000 173p hardcover o.p. pa $14 **811**
1. Poetry—By individual authors
ISBN 978-0-618-15445-6; 0-618-15445-0
LC 99-48904
"New England resides in these pages. Kinnell is a native of America's first literary region. Cold snow and clear nights work their way into his poems. The sounds of the woods are everywhere. But these sounds do not echo Emerson. Like any good transcendentalist, Kinnell sees the spiritual in material things." Christ Sci Monit

Strong is your hold. Houghton Mifflin 2006 69p $25; pa $14.95 **811**
1. Poetry—By individual authors
ISBN 978-0-618-22497-5; 0-618-22497-1; 978-0-547-05366-0 (pa); 0-547-05366-5 (pa)
LC 2006-11292
"To many readers, the most appealing of these poems will be the half dozen in which the aging poet writes about his wife: cuddling with her in sleep, making love with startling ferocity, waking to find they are holding hands, preparing to say goodbye if one dies before the other. Getting old, as we've heard, is not for sissies. The poet who once chased bears may have slowed a step, but here he's still making like Johnny Cash as he walks the line between sex and death, the odd and the normal, domesticity and wildness, this world and the next. . . . 'Strong Is Your Hold' comes with a CD of Kinnell reading his work in a steady, pleasant voice." N Y Times Book Rev

Kizer, Carolyn
Cool, calm & collected; poems 1960-2000. Copper Canyon Press 2000 509p $30; pa $20
811
1. Poetry—By individual authors
ISBN 1-55659-146-2; 1-55659-181-0 (pa)
LC 00-10243
Kizer "covers civil rights, women's rights and almost everything in between, but even when she's writing about more intimate matters, her underlying concern is freedom. . . . Despite her constant railing against the machine, however, Kizer's poetry remains fundamentally optimistic, perhaps because she seems to love existence almost in spite of herself." N Y Times Book Rev

Kleinzahler, August
Sleeping it off in Rapid City; poems, new and selected. Farrar, Straus and Giroux 2008 234p $26
811
1. Poetry—By individual authors
ISBN 978-0-374-26583-0; 0-374-26583-6
LC 2007-41926
This is a collection of poetry by the author of Earthquake Weather (1989), Red Sauce, Whiskey, and Snow (1996), and Live from the Hong Kong Nile Club (2000).
The author "writes most often in a strongly accented free verse that is among the most articulate and alive sounds American poetry is currently making. He plays effortlessly with forms, voices, registers. And his range of cultural reference—from Catullus to Custer, from Lorca to Eric Dolphy—is wide and artfully deployed. Rarely does high, learned poetic art sound this casual." N Y Times (Late N Y Ed)

Knott, Bill, 1940-
The unsubscriber. Farrar, Straus and Giroux 2004 122p $20; pa $13 **811**
1. Poetry—By individual authors
ISBN 978-0-374-26415-4; 0-374-26415-5; 978-0-374-53014-3 (pa); 0-374-53014-9 (pa)
LC 2004-41160

Knott, Bill, 1940-—*Continued*

"Knott's talent for compression—his awareness of the physicality of language—has remained undiminished since his youth, surfacing in one poem after another. . . . Like a gifted composer also capable of brilliantly playing every instrument in the orchestra, Knott possesses talent beyond the average allotment. In all fairness, you are not likely to find a more imaginative and provocative book of poetry published in the last year than The Unsubscriber, but neither will you find one that can be more at odds with itself." Am Book Rev

Koch, Kenneth, 1925-2002

The collected poems of Kenneth Koch. Knopf 2005 761p $40 * **811**

1. Poetry—By individual authors
ISBN 1-4000-4499-5   LC 2004-63827

"All of the poems in [Koch's] ten collections—from Sun Out, poems of the 1950s, to Thank You, published in 1962, to A Possible World, published in 2002, the year of the poet's death—are gathered in [this] volume." Publisher's note

"The products of a lifetime of continual inventing are beautifully on display in this awe-inspiring banquet of a book." Publ Wkly

On the edge; collected long poems. Alfred A. Knopf 2007 411p $35   **811**

1. Poetry—By individual authors
ISBN 978-0-307-26284-4; 0-307-26284-7
LC 2007-24041

"A principal force behind the New York School of poets that flourished at mid-century, Kenneth Koch never quite won the pride of place occupied by the likes of Frank O'Hara and John Ashbery. This volume compiles Koch's long poems, making an eloquent argument for his unique stature." New York

Komunyakaa, Yusef

Talking dirty to the gods; poems. Farrar, Straus & Giroux 2000 134p pa $13 hardcover o.p.
811

1. Poetry—By individual authors
ISBN 0-374-52793-8 (pa)   LC 00-21277

"Komunyakaa's mournful surrealism seems to have found a perfect mathematical embodiment in this . . . collection, which comprises a hundred and thirty-two poems of four four-line stanzas. These are poems about the uncontrollable human and natural mysteries, and they are made sharper and more mysterious by the eternal recurrence of the stanzaic structure." New Yorker

Thieves of paradise. University Press of New England 1998 128p (Wesleyan poetry) $26; pa $14.95   **811**

1. Poetry—By individual authors
ISBN 0-8195-6330-7; 0-8195-6422-2 (pa)
LC 97-40294

"The central subjects of Komunyakaa's poetry—his experiences in the Vietnam War and as an African-American male—have always been made compelling in his hands, and equally compelling has been the moodily energetic, jazz-inspired improvisatory technique that he employs with increasing mastery. But what is most gratifying about Komunyakaa's surrealist riffs, with their almost hallucinatory lushness, is their power to convince us that the individual imagination is more than equal to the most excruciating historical burden." New Yorker

Kooser, Ted

Delights & shadows; poems. Copper Canyon Press 2004 87p pa $15   **811**

1. Poetry—By individual authors
ISBN 1-55659-201-9   LC 2003-18447

These "poems reflect a joy for life through powerful human images and intimate observations of everyday things." Booklist

Flying at night; poems, 1965-1985. University of Pittsburgh Press 2005 142p (Pitt poetry series) $24.95; pa $14.95   **811**

1. Poetry—By individual authors
ISBN 0-8229-4258-5; 0-8229-5877-5 (pa)
LC 2004-28397

In this book, "Kooser has selected poems from two of his earlier works, Sure Signs (1980) and One World at a Time (1985)." Publisher's note

"There is a simplicity to these poems, a healthy, peaceful spirit. . . . Kooser is a skilled craftsman, with a sharp eye and fine ear." Libr J

Kumin, Maxine, 1925-

Connecting the dots; poems. Norton 1996 86p $18.95; pa $11.95   **811**

1. Poetry—By individual authors
ISBN 0-393-03962-5; 0-393-31695-5 (pa)
LC 95-44441

"Kumin's is a poetry of wide sympathy and tact in which the ecumenical flavor is dominant, starting with the author's description of herself as a 'Jewish agnostic' educated at a convent school. Here both the odd and the even are at home: New Hampshire farm country as well as cosmopolitan Boston, Heidegger and Berlioz interwoven among depictions of spring training, Bosnia, and a New Year's Eve party. This collection is full of generational severance and renewal." New Yorker

Jack and other new poems. W.W. Norton & Co 2005 112p hardcover o.p. pa $13.95   **811**

1. Poetry—By individual authors
ISBN 978-0-393-32852-3; 0-393-32852-X
LC 2004-21762

This collection of poetry "focuses on three subjects the poet knows well: first, the fauna (wild and domestic) in and around her New Hampshire farm; second, the troubles and lessons of advancing age; third, large-scale political history, 'this century born in blood and bombs' as this Jewish-American poet has known it. . . . Most of her strongest work (the title poem included) concerns elderly or deceased animals, obvious analogues for Kumin's ill, deceased or grieving human beings." Publ Wkly

The long marriage; poems. Norton 2001 118p $21; pa $12   **811**

1. Poetry—By individual authors
ISBN 0-393-04351-7; 0-393-32437-0 (pa)
LC 2001-34553

Kumin, Maxine, 1925-—_Continued_

"Although several of the poems treat Kumin's 50-plus year marriage, one feels that the book's title may refer to 'marriage' as a kind of covenant between the poet and her environment. . . . Divided into seven sections, this collection also includes poems about sociopolitical situations (capital punishment, extinct wildlife, revolutions), considerations of aging and rehabilitation, and tributes to Hopkins, Wordsworth, Rukeyser, and Rilke." Libr J

Selected poems, 1960-1990. Norton 1997 294p $27.50; pa $17.95   **811**
1. Poetry—By individual authors
ISBN 0-393-04073-9; 0-393-31836-2 (pa)
    LC 96-42433
"A pastoral poet who was strongly influenced by friend and mentor Anne Sexton, Kumin is quite simply one of the very best poets writing today. The present collection represents a lifetime . . . of Kumin's work and includes selections from all her published volumes." Libr J

Kunitz, Stanley, 1905-2006
The collected poems. Norton 2000 285p $27.95; pa $15.95 *   **811**
1. Poetry—By individual authors
ISBN 0-393-05030-0; 0-393-32294-7 (pa)
    LC 00-41130
In this volume "Kunitz brings together his entire oeuvre, including many unavailable early works and poems from the recent _Passing Through_." Libr J
"What makes this collection of a lifetime's work so valuable is the way it allows us to perceive the interconnectedness of all Kunitz has written. Each poem stands alone, but each also enriches the others." N Y Times Book Rev
Includes bibliographical references

Kyger, Joanne
About now; collected poems. National Poetry Foundation 2007 798p il $49.95; pa $34.95
    811
1. Poetry—By individual authors
ISBN 978-0-943373-72-0; 0-943373-72-7; 978-0-943373-71-3 (pa); 0-943373-71-9 (pa)
    LC 2006-48192
This volume "begins with poems of the 1950's, written when Kyger first came to San Francisco and joined the circle of poets around Robert Duncan and Jack Spicer, and ends with Night Palace, poems written in 2003 to 2004. . . . What is exciting about Kyger's poetry is the way she highlights moments which might seem mundane, but under her perceptive eye connect the individual with a greater reality, opening readers' awareness in the process. That immersion in the details of everyday life, quail crossing a yard, a phone call from a friend, or a retelling of last night's dream, is plumbed by Kyger to great depth and is epitomized by the collection's title." Jacket
Includes bibliographical references

Laughlin, James, 1914-1997
The collected poems of James Laughlin; with an introduction by Hayden Carruth. Moyer Bell 1994 xxxi, 574p il $34.95; pa $19.95   **811**
1. Poetry—By individual authors
ISBN 978-1-559-21067-6; 1-559-21067-2; 978-1-559-21128-4 (pa); 1-559-21128-8 (pa)
    LC 91-32232
This collection of Laughlin's poems is "gathered from material written over a span of sixty years." Poetry
"These poems are the work of a man of keen intellectual and moral sophistication, who has read, thought, and lived deeply." Libr J

The secret room; poems. New Directions 1997 184p $22.95; pa $14.95   **811**
1. Poetry—By individual authors
ISBN 0-8112-1343-9; 0-8112-1344-7 (pa)
    LC 96-26188
Laughlin "shares his thoughts with humor and tenderness as he wades in the waters of his golden years. The speaker in many of these poems admires young women and thinks, 'I could see I was entirely out of/my depth.' He realizes he is not as strong as he once was, but he can still 'make old, sick words sound new.'" Libr J

Lax, Robert, 1915-2000
Love had a compass; journals and poetry; edited by James J. Uebbing. Grove Press 1996 253p $22
    811
1. Poetry—By individual authors
ISBN 978-0-8021-1587-4; 0-8021-1587-X
    LC 96-1255
"Lax is a somewhat legendary poet known primarily for two reasons: he traveled in a circle in the 1930s that included Thomas Merton, John Berryman, Robert Giroux and Ad Reinhardt; and he has lived and written on the Greek island of Patmos since the early 1960s." Publ Wkly
The author has produced "some of the sparest imagist poetry in English with no thought about publishing where the literary high and mighty would read him. Lax dispenses with metaphor and largely with ego . . . to present what he sees with elemental forcefulness, as if in strong Mediterranean sunlight." Booklist

A thing that is; new poems; edited by Paul Spaeth. Overlook Press 1997 77p $25; pa $14.95
    811
1. Poetry—By individual authors
ISBN 978-0-87951-699-4; 0-8795-1699-2; 978-0-87951-885-1 (pa); 0-87951-885-5 (pa)
    LC 96-29264
"Given to short lines arranged in long columns, Lax's poems link the natural and personal in simple, direct, deadpan narration. The simplicity can be misleading, not in its initially unnoticed depth or metaphor but in its very purity, its almost ascetic singleness of purpose. . . . Lax has been working at the margins for a long time and has found a crisp and comfortable way of ordering and exploring his contemplations. This collection is not for everyone, but it is a essential for that special audience for truly avante-garde work." Libr J

Lazarus, Emma, 1849-1887

Emma Lazarus; selected poems; John Hollander, editor. Library of America 2005 151p (American poets project) $20 **811**

1. Poetry—By individual authors

ISBN 978-1-931082-77-8; 1-931082-77-4

LC 2004-61551

"At the age of eighteen [Lazarus] had written an impressive poem titled 'In the Jewish Synagogue at Newport,' which all readers recognized as a response to Longfellow's dignified and respectful poem about the Jewish cemetery there. . . . Lazarus became perhaps the most accomplished American writer of sonnets between the generations of Longfellow and Robert Frost. . . . [Her] remarkable 'Little Poems in Prose,' the title borrowed from Baudelaire, ranged with visionary power across centuries of Jewish experience." N Y Rev Books

Lee, Li-Young, 1957-

Behind my eyes. W.W. Norton 2008 106p $24.95 **811**

1. Poetry—By individual authors

ISBN 978-0-393-06542-8; 0-393-06542-1

"In this fourth collection by [the author], timely immigration issues drive such poems as 'Self-Help for Fellow Refugees,' but Lee swiftly folds them into broader inquiries about inheritance, memory and loss. . . . Lee's ringing clarity and his compelling life story have brought him uncommonly loyal readers: this volume should swell their ranks. A CD of Lee reading many of the poems is included." Publ Wkly

Lerner, Ben, 1979-

Angle of yaw. Copper Canyon Press 2006 127p pa $15 **811**

1. Poetry—By individual authors

ISBN 1-55659-246-9   LC 2006-14260

"Employing the language of aphorism, advertising, parable, personal essay, political tirade, journalism and journal, the collage-like poems of Lerner's . . . collection express the ennui of American life in an era when even war feels like a television event." Publ Wkly

Levertov, Denise, 1923-1997

Selected poems; with a preface by Robert Creeley; edited and with an afterword by Paul Lacey. New Directions 2002 220p hardcover o.p. pa $14.95 **811**

1. Poetry—By individual authors

ISBN 978-0-8112-1554-1; 0-8112-1520-2

LC 2002-11891

This volume "endeavors to do what all 'selecteds' do: give readers a chance to see for themselves the development of a poetic sensibility. Editor Paul A. Lacey has brought together poems from nearly every collection of Levertov's oeuvre, producing a catalogue of the wildly diverse subjects that engaged her throughout her long career. Here are poems about love and war, about religion and art, about sorrow and joy, about political resistance and familial intimacy and, perhaps most significantly for Levertov's legacy, numerous poems about the practice of poetry itself." Harvard Rev

Levine, Philip, 1928-

Breath; poems. Knopf 2004 82p $23

811

1. Poetry—By individual authors

ISBN 1-400-04291-7   LC 2004-40839

The author writes "free verse about American manliness, physical labor, simple pleasures and profound grief, often set in working-class Detroit (where Levine grew up) or in central California (where he now resides), sometimes tinged with reference to his Jewish heritage or to the Spanish poets of rapt simplicity (Machado, Lorca) who remain his most visible influence. Levine's 18th book will neither disappoint his devotees nor silence the doubters." Publ Wkly

The mercy; poems. Knopf 1999 81p hardcover o.p. pa $16 **811**

1. Poetry—By individual authors

ISBN 978-0-375-70135-1; 0-375-70135-4

LC 98-43353

"Levine's poetry has been steadily moving to the front rank of American poetry for three decades. . . . If Walt Whitman's vision contained multitudes, and if Emerson's vision of nature transcended what it saw with its own eyes, Levine's poetic vision, nearly religious, transcends class, transcends natural boundaries, and transcends time." Atl Mon

New selected poems. Knopf 1991 292p hardcover o.p. pa $20 **811**

1. Poetry—By individual authors

ISBN 978-0-679-74056-8; 0-679-74056-2

LC 90-53422

This selection contains poems Levine chose for his earlier Selected poems (1984), plus 15 new works

"This is a monumental work that somehow remains wonderfully accessible, largely because Levine has chosen pieces carefully, favoring shorter works and poems that address his staple themes of family (like 'Uncle' and 'My Son and I') and childhood ('Coming Home'). Many of the poems are powerfully imagistic." Libr J

The simple truth; poems. Knopf 1994 69p hardcover o.p. pa $16 **811**

1. Poetry—By individual authors

ISBN 978-0-679-76584-4; 0-679-76584-0

LC 94-14508

This "collection of poetry is largely about the past: friends lost, fates assigned, potatoes eaten, decisions made. . . . Levine's mingling of realism and romanticism, involving many near-meetings between them, produces fascinating, emotionally persuasive shifts and tonal modulations that closely approach a lived truth." Publ Wkly

What work is; poems. Knopf 1991 77p hardcover o.p. pa $15 **811**

1. Poetry—By individual authors

ISBN 978-0-679-74058-2; 0-679-74058-9

LC 90-53421

"This collection amounts to a hymn of praise for all the workers of America. These proletarian heroes, with names like Lonnie, Loo, Sweet Pea, and Packy, work the furnaces, forges, slag heaps, assembly lines, and loading docks at places with unglamorous names like Brass Craft or Feinberg and Breslin's First-Rate Plumbing and Plat-

Levine, Philip, 1928-—*Continued*

ing. . . . But Levine's characters are also significant for their inner lives, not merely their jobs." Libr J

Longfellow, Henry Wadsworth, 1807-1882

Poems and other writings. Library of Am. 2000 854p $35 * **811**

1. Poetry—By individual authors

ISBN 1-88301-185-X LC 00-26678

Edited by J. D. McClatchy

This volume includes "*Hiawatha, Evangeline, The Courtship of Miles Standish* and 'The Midnight Ride of Paul Revere.' Here, too, are some surprisingly powerful lyric and meditative poems—well made, deeply felt, and not much like the schoolhouse favorites." Publ Wkly

Includes bibliographical references

Lorde, Audre

The collected poems of Audre Lorde. Norton 1997 489p $35; pa $17.95 **811**

1. Poetry—By individual authors

ISBN 0-393-04090-9; 0-393-31972-5 (pa)

LC 97-10878

"Since her death in 1992, Lorde's reputation has continued to grow. In life a tough, eloquent crusader who demanded that we honor the varieties of human experience, she retained her hold on readers despite the unavailability of much of her work. This edition, then, should be welcomed wherever there is interest in women's, minority, and lesbian literature. It includes Lorde's passionately private early work as well as her later, more obviously political work." Booklist

Lowell, Amy, 1874-1925

Selected poems; Honor Moore, editor. Library of America 2004 xxxi, 156p (American poets project) $20 **811**

1. Poetry—By individual authors

ISBN 978-1-93108-270-9; 1-93108-270-7

LC 2004-48505

This volume contains "the 'cadenced verse' of [Lowell's] Imagist . . . works, her experiments in 'polyphonic prose,' her narrative poetry, and her adaptations from the classical Chinese." Publisher's note

Lowell, Robert, 1917-1977

Collected poems; edited by Frank Bidart and David Gewanter, with the editorial assistance of DeSales Harrison. Farrar, Straus & Giroux 2003 1186p il $45 * **811**

1. Poetry—By individual authors

ISBN 0-374-12617-8

This collection includes "Lowell's first book, *Land of Unlikeness* (1944); and poems from his 11 ensuing collections, including *Life Studies* (1959) and *The Dolphin* (1973). . . . Substantial notes, a chronology, glossary, and critical essays make this an essential title. Readers who think they know Lowell's work will discover new facets, and readers just venturing into Lowell's potently rendered and ceaselessly evocative poetic universe will find much to contemplate." Booklist

Includes bibliographical references

Mackey, Nathaniel, 1947-

Splay anthem. New Directions Book 2006 126p pa $15.95 **811**

1. Poetry—By individual authors

ISBN 0-8112-1652-7 LC 2005-35051

"Divided into three sections 'Braid,' 'Fray,' and 'Nub,' . . . Splay Anthem weaves together two ongoing serial poems Mackey has been writing for over twenty years, Song of the Andoumboulou and 'Mu.'" Publisher's note

"Often turning adversity to their advantage, the poems sing not of resurrection but repair, and Splay Anthem is the most delicate and delirious installment of Mackey's epic song of salvage. Its poems speak with a torn voice, a rasp punctuated by gasps of anguish and rumbling with the desire for rejuvenation." Nation

MacLeish, Archibald, 1892-1982

Collected poems, 1917-1982; with a prefatory note to the newly collected poems by Richard B. McAdoo. Houghton Mifflin 1985 524p pa $19 hardcover o.p. **811**

1. Poetry—By individual authors

ISBN 0-395-39569-0 (pa) LC 85-14392

Collects all the known poetry of the author/public servant. As an expatriate in Paris his early work was heavily influenced by Pound and Eliot. After returning to the States his verse concerned itself more with America's political, social, and cultural heritage

Matthews, William, 1942-1997

After all; last poems. Houghton Mifflin 1998 55p pa $13 hardcover o.p. **811**

1. Poetry—By individual authors

ISBN 0-618-05685-8 (pa) LC 98-22909

"Since Matthews was one of the few contemporary poets who really knew how to make the vernacular sing, it's sad to think that these are his last poems. Fittingly, some of them are autumnal, but they range widely and brightly from Prague in 1419 to a Caribbean island in 1967 to Martha Mitchell, Finn sheep, and a poetry reading at West Point. A lovely finale." Libr J

Selected poems and translations, 1969-1991. Houghton Mifflin 1992 200p hardcover o.p. pa $22.95 **811**

1. Poetry—By individual authors

ISBN 978-0-395-66993-8; 0-395-66993-6

LC 91-45716

"This collection brings together more than 100 poems, chosen from eight previously published volumes, and 40 translations from the French, Latin and Bulgarian." Publ Wkly

"Matthews has been widely praised for the solid grounding of his poems, and rightly so. His clear-cut metaphors illuminate the everyday world with the magic of semantic revelation and the grace of othermindedness." Booklist

Mayer, Bernadette, 1945-

Scarlet tanager. New Directions 2005 117p pa $14.95 **811**

1. Poetry—By individual authors

ISBN 0-8112-1582-2 LC 2005-5539

Mayer, Bernadette, 1945-—*Continued*

This collection demonstrates Mayer's "ease in many poetic forms, her attraction to New York City and to the Berkshires (where she now lives), her recovery from a recent stroke and her continued enthusiastic enmeshment with writing itself." Publ Wkly

McGrath, Thomas, 1916-1990

Letter to an imaginary friend. Copper Canyon Press 1997 413p pa $20   **811**

1. Poetry—By individual authors
ISBN 978-1-55659-078-8; 1-55659-078-4
    LC 97-33929

"Although McGrath, who died in 1990 at 74, published the poem's four parts separately, it appears here complete for the first time. . . . A surprisingly accessible long poem in the Pound tradition of personal epics, *Letter* arrives 'helved, greaved, and garlanded' and compels our intimate attention." Publ Wkly

McMichael, James, 1939-

Capacity. Farrar, Straus and Giroux 2006 74p $22   **811**

1. Poetry—By individual authors
ISBN 978-0-374-11890-7; 0-374-11890-6
    LC 2005-51628

"Better known for the infrastructural sweep of his work, McMichael is also a poet of the kind of centripetal force and barely contained emotional heat that we more often associate with the short lyric. What makes him unique in American poetry right now is the strength and subtlety with which he blends conceptual ambition with emotional power. It's very common these days to hear poets talking about their 'projects.' But in James McMichael we actually have a poet whose sustained investigation of a small set of obsessions has produced the most integral and surprising structures." Yale Rev

Melville, Herman, 1819-1891

The poems of Herman Melville; edited by Douglas Robillard. rev ed. Kent State Univ. Press 2000 349p pa $29 *   **811**

1. Poetry—By individual authors
ISBN 0-87338-660-4   LC 99-52872

First published 1976 by College and University Press Service

This volume "presents the complete texts of 'Battle-Pieces,' 'John Marr and Other Sailors,' and 'Timoleon,' as well as additional manuscript poems. Also presented are excerpts from the long narrative poem *Clarel* to give the reader a taste of the style and content of this work. The editor's introduction, as well as his notes at the end of each section, are informative as well as appreciative of Melville's status as a poet." Libr J

Includes bibliographical references

Menashe, Samuel

New and selected poems; Christopher Ricks, editor. Library of America 2005 191p (American poets project) $20 *   **811**

1. Poetry—By individual authors
ISBN 1-931082-85-5   LC 2005-44161

"Samuel Menashe is the first recipient of the Neglected Masters Prize established by The Poetry Foundation, and this volume is published in conjunction with that award." Publisher's note

"Menashe is a curious and meticulous writer, whose brief, sparsely punctuated poems depend on difficult rhyme and assonance schemes to relay his observations. A wry but basically optimistic poet, his best writing shows that the stylistic restrictions one selects rapidly cease to be restrictions, even when one identifies them as such." N Y Times Book Rev

Meredith, William, 1919-2007

Effort at speech; new and selected poems. TriQuarterly Bks. 1997 231p $46; pa $17.95   **811**

1. Poetry—By individual authors
ISBN 0-8101-5070-0; 0-8101-5071-9 (pa)
    LC 97-9679

Meredith's early poems "are as subtle as aspirin. So easily digestible in their precise meter and perfectly tuned end-rhyme, their power goes virtually unnoticed until the reader lifts his eyes from the page to find himself moved, affected. In work inspired by the poet's service at sea during WWII, devastation comes on the hushed waves of sonnets. . . . The poems in the book's latter half (1970-1987) find formalism surrendering some ground to free verse as Meredith attempts to salve not the sharp pains of war but the blunted ache of aging." Publ Wkly

Merrill, James

The changing light at Sandover; with the stage adaptation Voices from Sandover; edited by J.D. McClatchy and Stephen Yenser. 2nd Knopf hardcover ed. Knopf 2006 627p il $40   **811**

1. Poetry—By individual authors
ISBN 978-0-307-26321-6; 0-307-26321-5
    LC 2006-273431

First published 1982 by Atheneum; 1992 by Knopf, without Voices from Sandover

Contents: Book of Ephraim; Mirabell's book of number; Scripts for the pageant; Coda: The higher keys; Appendix: Voices from Sandover

This "is an arduous poem, steep and lofty, more than a little difficult to climb, explore, and comprehend, its intricate faceting of the serious and unserious, sacred and profane, vexing to many a reader; but it has, I believe, one controlling stratagem, Merrill's persistent use of doubling or 'entwinning.'. . . The trilogy (though it goes on far too long, gets periodically dizzy, has too much felix culpa and not enough mea culpa) is, surely, an astonishing performance." N Y Rev Books

The collected poems of James Merrill; edited by J.D. McClatchy and Stephen Yenser. Knopf 2001 xx, 885p $40; pa $27.50 *   **811**

1. Poetry—By individual authors
ISBN 0-375-41139-9; 0-375-70941-X (pa)
    LC 00-40542

"Excluded are some juvenilia and light verse, as well as Merrill's book-length poem *The Changing Light at*

Merrill, James—*Continued*

Sandover, in print as a separate volume. Merrill's sonnets, sapphics, longer sequences and sinuous sentences encompass lyric pathos, ebullient comedy, rapt romance and acrid satire. Their formal sophistication can belie their depth of feeling, which is exactly what some readers love best about Merrill's work." Publ Wkly

Merton, Thomas, 1915-1968

In the dark before dawn; new selected poems of Thomas Merton; edited with an introduction and notes by Lynn R. Szabo; preface by Kathleen Norris. New Directions 2005 253p pa $16.95

811

1. Poetry—By individual authors
ISBN 978-0-8112-1613-5; 0-8112-1613-6
LC 2004-30957

"Szabo has drawn widely from the furious poetic writing of Merton's final years. This new spectrum of poems helps us tap into the complexity and mystery of Thomas Merton. Readers of Merton's journals will be aware of his shifting attitude to all sorts of things—being an American, being a monk at Gethsemani, being a writer, in particular a poet. Szabo helps us here by assembling the poems in eight thematic sections, so as to display the multiple Mertons. There was the contemplative, drawn to the silent beauties of Gethsemani Abbey, especially at night. There was the stinging and at times declamatory social critic, the admiring and painstaking translator, the avant garde experimentalist and, toward the end, the lovelorn monk." America

Merwin, W. S. (William Stanley), 1927-

Migration; new & selected poems. Copper Canyon Press 2005 545p $40 *   811
1. Poetry—By individual authors
ISBN 1-55659-218-3   LC 2004-17473

This volume contains poetry from sixteen of Merwin's collections.

"Complex, spiritual, and evocative, Merwin is a major poet, and this is a sublime measure of his achievements." Booklist

Present company. Copper Canyon Press 2005 137p $22   811
1. Poetry—By individual authors
ISBN 1-55659-227-2   LC 2005-08867

"Nearing 80, the Pulitzer Prize winner seems especially mindful of age and mortality, and these poems–like a series of heartfelt thank-you notes–offer homage to the things of this world. In a manner that recalls the cool, spare diction of H.D., Merwin addresses the local and the nondescript . . . as well as the abstract and the universal. . . . The emotional timber rarely rises above muted melancholy, and Merwin's thoughtful, measured pace never quickens, but the poems are suffused with a warmth and clarity achieved over six decades of disciplined dedication to his art." Libr J

Millay, Edna St. Vincent, 1892-1950

Collected poems; edited by Norma Millay. Harper & Row 1956 xxi, 738p pa $22.95 hardcover o.p.   811

1. Poetry—By individual authors
ISBN 0-06-090889-0 (pa)

Also available in hardcover from Buccaneer Books

The poems in this collection "are divided into two separate sections of lyrics and sonnets, arranged chronologically and printed in groups under the titles of the original volumes, ranging from 'Renascence' of 1917 to 'Mine the harvest,' published in 1954, four years after the poet's death." Booklist

Selected poems; J.D. McClatchy, editor. Library of Am. 2003 xxxiii, 231p (American poets project) $20 *   811
1. Poetry—By individual authors
ISBN 1-931082-35-9   LC 2002-32126

This collection draws from all Millay's "verse books to display her career-long adroitness in her favorite form, the sonnet, and her variety by including even excerpts from an opera libretto. . . . Read occasionally and mixed with her saucy lyrics about erotic love, . . . [her sonnets] reveal their strengths—not of imagery, but of surprising attitudes expressed within strictly observed poetic conventions." Booklist

Moore, Marianne, 1887-1972

The poems of Marianne Moore; edited by Grace Schulman. Viking 2003 449p pa $18 hardcover o.p. *   811
1. Poetry—By individual authors
ISBN 0-14-303908-3 (pa)   LC 2003-50159

This collection "contains all of Moore's poems, including 120 previously uncollected and unpublished ones. Organized chronologically to allow readers to follow Moore's development as a poet, the volume includes an introduction, all of Moore's original notes to the poems, along with Schulman's notes, attributions, and some variants." Publisher's note

"The great modernist poet finally gets her due with this outstanding compilation." Libr J

Includes bibliographical references

Nemerov, Howard

The selected poems of Howard Nemerov; edited by Daniel Anderson; foreword by Wyatt Prunty. Swallow Press, Ohio University Press 2003 xxi, 154p $24.95; pa $16.95 *   811
1. Poetry—By individual authors
ISBN 0-8040-1059-5; 0-8040-1060-9 (pa)
LC 2003-42380

The selections in this volume span Nemerov's entire poetic output

This volume "represents the broad spectrum of Nemerov's virtues as a poet—his intelligence, his wit, his compassion, and his irreverence. It stands as the retrospective collection of the best of what Nemerov left behind." Publisher's note

Niedecker, Lorine, 1903-1970
Collected works; edited by Jenny Penberthy.
University of Calif. Press 2002 xxiii, 471p $55; pa
$25.95   **811**
  1. Poetry—By individual authors
  ISBN   978-0-520-22433-9;   0-520-22433-7;
  978-0-520-22434-6 (pa); 0-520-22434-5 (pa)
                    LC 2001-5376
Niedecker "is often likened to Emily Dickinson. She,
too, remained in the backwater where she was born.
Large-scale interest in her work came only years after
her death. Her characteristic poems are, like Dickinson's,
short or in short stanzas, short-lined, and elliptical. But
she wasn't reclusive; she connected with the Objectivists,
New York poets 'led' by Louis Zukofsky. . . . Whereas
Dickinson's poetry is metaphysical, Niedecker's mature
work is profoundly physical, sparked by wry, class-
conscious humor and usually rooted in her Black Lake
Island, Wisconsin, neighborhood." Booklist
Includes bibliographical references

Nims, John Frederick, 1913-1999
The powers of heaven and earth; new and
selected poems. Louisiana State Univ. Press 2002
247p $36.95; pa $19.95 *   **811**
  1. Poetry—By individual authors
  ISBN 0-8071-2826-0; 0-8071-2827-9 (pa)
                   LC 2002-30055
This is a "collection of the work of one of the foremost formalists and classicists among twentieth-century
American poets: epigrams, odes, sonnets, shaped verse,
and other kinds of poems on life, nature, culture, literature, but first and foremost, on love." Booklist

Norris, Kathleen, 1947-
Journey: new and selected poems, 1969-1999.
University of Pa. 2001 131p pa $16.95 hardcover
o.p.   **811**
  1. Poetry—By individual authors
  ISBN 0-8229-5761-2 (pa)
A collection of Norris' "poetry spanning 30 years.
Here are poems, arranged chronologically in four sections each beginning with a verse from the *Song of Solomon,* that tenderly describe an event or scene, examine
it, and conclude with a flash of seemingly unrelated insight, leaving profound questions in the reader's heart.
. . . Carrying her readers along on her deeply Christian
journey, Norris avoids spiritual certainty and preachiness,
remaining ever the seeker. Her poems are lyrical, accessible, and hauntingly touching to read and to reread."
Libr J

Notley, Alice, 1945-
Grave of light; new and selected poems,
1970-2005. Wesleyan University Press 2006 364p
$29.95 *   **811**
  1. Poetry—By individual authors
  ISBN 0-8195-6772-8   LC 2006-15712
"Experimental in every sense of the word, Alice
Notley has produced an extensive body of work over 30
years in print. This new collection unites previously unpublished poems as well as those from both small-press

chapbooks and more widely distributed volumes. Arranged in chronological order while maintaining poetic
sequences, Notley's poems tell the story of her artistic
development and bear witness to the multitude of styles
and influences that Notley has explored. . . . Diversity
is Notley's most consistent quality, and this makes her
not only somewhat of an enigma aesthetically but also
appealing to varying poetic tastes." Booklist

In the pines. Penguin Books 2007 131p
(Penguin poets) pa $18   **811**
  1. Poetry—By individual authors
  ISBN 978-0-14-311254-9; 0-14-311254-6
                  LC 2007-12076
"Notley takes the title of her 30-somethingth collection from a notorious American folk song: a man tries to
get his lover to admit she's been unfaithful, asking her
where she's slept, and her ambiguous answer—in the
pines—only makes things worse. That menacing rhetorical moment informs the whole of this searing collection,
which is part autobiography, part riposte to literary culture, and part lyrical reclamation of feminist territory.
. . . This master poet continues to inspire and challenge." Publ Wkly

Nye, Naomi Shihab, 1952-
You & yours: poems. BOA Editions 2005 87p
(American poets continuum series) hardcover o.p.
pa $15.50   **811**
  1. Poetry—By individual authors
  ISBN 1-929918-68-2; 1-929918-69-0 (pa)
                  LC 2005-11360
"Part one covers Nye's personal experience, at home
with her child in San Antonio or as a 'Frequent Frequent
Flyer' enjoying the sights of Scotland. . . . Part two covers the Middle East." Publ Wkly
"Tender yet forceful, funny and commonsensical, reflective and empathic, Nye writes radiant poems of nature and piercing poems of war, always touching base
with homey details and radiant portraits of family and
neighbors." Booklist

O'Brien, Michael, 1939-
Sleeping and waking. Flood Editions 2007 63p
pa $12.95   **811**
  1. Poetry—By individual authors
  ISBN 978-0-9787467-2-8 (pa); 0-9787467-2-4
"O'Brien is primarily an observer rather than a debat-
er, and the poems here are heavy on isolated images,
dream logic, bits of overheard conversation (typically urban conversation) and memories, with larger themes
emerging through juxtapositions and repetitions. . . .
While O'Brien's technical skills should be crisp enough
to please the iciest avant-gardist, he has one virtue more
cerebral poets often lack: he isn't afraid to make a plain
statement. In other hands, that virtue can become a self-
satisfied vice, but here it lends a necessary sharpness to
an otherwise fluid and dreamlike collection." N Y Times
Book Rev

O'Hara, Frank, 1926-1966

The collected poems of Frank O'Hara; edited by
Donald Allen; with an introduction by John
Ashbery. University of Calif. Press 1995 xxix,
586p pa $24.95 *   **811**
   1. Poetry—By individual authors
   ISBN 0-520-20166-3   LC 94-24660
A reissue of the title first published 1971 by Knopf
The subjects of this collection "are lunch-time strolls
past construction workers and bargains in wrist watches,
the lives of artists (whether distant heroes or close
friends), the distractions of city life, . . . homosexuality,
. . . headlines glimpsed on newstands. . . . Some {are}
. . . about friendships, occasional pieces written for a
marriage or a departure." Newsweek
   Includes bibliographical references

Frank O'Hara: selected poems; edited by Mark
Ford. Alfred A. Knopf 2008 288p $30
                     811
   1. Poetry—By individual authors
   ISBN 978-0-307-26815-0; 0-307-26815-2
                        LC 2007-42865
"At his strongest O'Hara profoundly affected the development of American poetry. . . . His acute eye and
finely tuned ear combined with his breezy idiolect and
thoughtful intelligence to create a style expressive of a
generation that returned from a brutal war intent on
throwing off old conventions and seeking new sensations.
If O'Hara's work lacks the gravitas ultimately achieved
by Koch and Ashbery, his clear, youthful voice will
nonetheless continue to evoke a heady, hopeful time in
our cultural history—before optimism turned to ashes."
New Leader

Olds, Sharon

Blood, tin, straw. Knopf 1999 125p hardcover
o.p. pa $16   **811**
   1. Poetry—By individual authors
   ISBN 978-0-375-70735-3; 0-375-70735-2
                        LC 99-15602
"Olds has always been a frank and transcendent poet
of the body, and now . . . she expands her profoundly
tactile sensibility to embrace the entire cosmos in poems
of powerful female eroticism and emotional acuity that
celebrate love both earthly and spiritual." Booklist

The unswept room. Knopf 2002 96p $25; pa
$15   **811**
   1. Poetry—By individual authors
   ISBN 0-375-41489-4; 0-375-70998-3 (pa)
                        LC 2002-18444
"Organized like her previous works, this work begins
with poems about her early life and then moves on to
grade school, her marriage, and up to the present day.
Throughout, Olds re-creates her life, building a scrapbook through words. Although many of her subjects
(family, love, sex) stay the same, her tone has shifted
from an angry questioning of fate to a passionate acceptance of her own mortality and the experiences she has
had." Libr J

The wellspring. Knopf 1996 88p hardcover o.p.
pa $16   **811**
   1. Poetry—By individual authors
   ISBN 978-0-679-76560-8; 0-679-76560-3
                        LC 95-15835
This collection "takes the form of an intimate family
portrait. Olds begins by imagining her parents making
love for the first time. This explicitness informs the entire cycle, from poems about her own birth to snapshots
of her youth and early sexual experiences, poems remarkable for their integrity, eroticism, tough humor, and
unceasing wonder. . . . Olds continues with a series of
strikingly original and profoundly moving poems about
her children." Booklist

Oliver, Mary, 1935-

The leaf and the cloud; a poem. Da Capo Press
2000 55p pa $15 hardcover o.p.   **811**
   1. Poetry—By individual authors
   ISBN 0-306-81073-5 (pa)   LC 00-57008
A "book-length poem by a poet devoted to close scrutiny of the natural world and exact, sensuous, and ecstatic description. Lyrical and philosophical in the American
transcendental tradition, Oliver addresses her readers directly to ravishing effect." Booklist

New and selected poems. Beacon Press 2005
c1992 2v v1 $28.50; v1 pa $16; v2 $24.95; v2 pa
$16 *   **811**
   1. Poetry—By individual authors
   ISBN 0-8070-6878-0 (v1); 0-8070-6877-2 (v1 pa);
   0-8070-6886-1 (v2); 0-8070-6887-X (v2 pa)
   Vol. 1 first published 1992; redesigned ed. to accompany the publication of vol. 2
   Volume one contains poems written from 1965 to
1992. Volume two contains poems written from 1994 to
2005.

West wind. Houghton Mifflin 1997 63p pa $14
hardcover o.p.   **811**
   1. Poetry—By individual authors
   ISBN 0-395-85085-1 (pa)   LC 97-2986
"Although her papers may scatter as the west wind
sweeps through her room, Oliver's house is in order.
From the chaos of the world, her poems distill what it
means to be human and what is worthwhile about life.
Echoing the Romantics and Whitman, she affirms the
value of aloneness with nature, of watching and listening—not just to get it down as art but simply to live it."
Libr J

Olson, Charles, 1910-1970

The collected poems of Charles Olson;
excluding the Maximus poems; edited by George
F. Butterick. University of Calif. Press 1987 xxxvi,
675p pa $45 hardcover o.p. *   **811**
   1. Poetry—By individual authors
   ISBN 0-520-21231-2   LC 86-14652
"Perhaps the most important American postmodernist
poet, Olson was little published during his life. This
work, . . . should solidify his reputation. Olson burst
into poetry in his maturity, sure of his instincts. Though
his debt to Pound is evident, he went further in exploring

Olson, Charles, 1910-1970—*Continued*
both American language and experience. What amazes us
now is not just the profundity and erudition of his
themes but the variety of ways he expresses his humanity. Ceaselessly experimental, his poems do not lose their
intelligence or intelligibility." Libr J

The Maximus poems; edited by George F.
Butterick. University of Calif. Press 1985 652p
hardcover o.p. pa $42   **811**
1. Poetry—By individual authors
ISBN 978-520-05595-7; 0-520-05595-0
LC 79-65759
This edition contains the entire sequence of poems set
in Gloucester, Massachusetts, whose protagonist is the
mythical figure, Maximus
"It is impossible to describe in this small space the
immensity of Charles Olson's achievement—as poet, the-
oretician and explorer of the 'human universe.' Just as
Ezra Pound's writing energized Western poetry in the
first half of this century, Olson in the 1950s redefined its
direction and inspired the next generation of writers. . . .
'The Maximus Poems' are a complex far-ranging attempt
to grasp the history of human thought." Christ Sci Monit

Oppen, George, 1908-1984
New collected poems; edited with an
introduction and notes by Michael Davidson;
preface by Eliot Weinberger. New Directions 2002
xlv, 433p il $37.95 *   **811**
1. Poetry—By individual authors
ISBN 0-8112-1488-5   LC 2001-44048
Replaces The collected poems of George Oppen
(1975)
"Oppen, a Communist and an objectivist poet deeply
influenced by Pound and Williams, believed that there
were no ideas except in things, but he also believed,
fiercely, that our relationship to things was inherently
moral. . . . In 1934, he published a book of stunning, elliptical lyrics about 'big-Business' and American capitalism; he then fell silent for the next twenty-five years,
during which he struggled to reconcile his fealty to social
causes with the demands of aesthetic originality. The culmination of this struggle was his Pulitzer Prize-winning
collection 'Of Being Numerous,' published in 1968,
which, to a degree unmatched by any book of American
poetry since, movingly portrays the individual in a collective world." New Yorker
Includes bibliographical references

Orr, Gregory
The caged owl; new and selected poems.
Copper Canyon Press 2002 235p pa $16
811
1. Poetry—By individual authors
ISBN 1-55659-177-2   LC 2001-6504
"The constraints of personal narrative are stretched to
their limits in this summation from Orr, . . . as his poems are often based on tragic experiences occurring to
those close to him. Orr's archetypal subject in the new
poems and selections from six previous collections . . .
is fratricide. As a child, Orr accidentally shot and killed
his young brother in a hunting accident." Publ Wkly

Ostriker, Alicia
No heaven; [by] Alicia Suskin Ostriker.
University of Pittsburgh Press 2005 136p (Pitt
poetry series) pa $12.95   **811**
1. Poetry—By individual authors
ISBN 0-8229-5875-9
The author focuses on such subjects as "sectarian violence, urban geography, family history, easel painting
and Jewish identity." Publ Wkly
In this "collection of clarion poems intimate and
worldly, Ostriker writes about her life as a wife, mother,
and grandmother with tenderness, but she is also edgy,
erotic, funny, and ornery." Booklist

Padgett, Ron
How to be perfect. Coffee House Press 2007
114p pa $15   **811**
1. Poetry—By individual authors
ISBN 978-1-56689-203-2; 1-56689-203-1
LC 2007-17772
"Padgett's plainspoken, wry poems deliver their wis-
dom through a kind of connoisseurship of absurdity. . . .
Yet these observational, reminiscent, and prescriptive
verses are also informed by a sense of loss—not just for
his late mother and for departed comrades like Kenneth
Koch but for the bohemian ideal that drew him to New
York to begin with. . . . Even so, Padgett's cockeyed
humor is ultimately optimistic." New Yorker

You never know; poems. Coffee House Press
2001 84p pa $14.95   **811**
1. Poetry—By individual authors
ISBN 978-1-56689-128-8; 1-56689-128-0
LC 2001-52945
"Padgett is the undisputed Zen master of the chicane,
maintaining a perfectly readable and casual tone while
turning meanings on a dime, or several dimes, on his
way to a reliably radiant and melancholy conclusion.
. . . These poems make a go at the epistemological concerns of the title, but like his collaborator Ted Berrigan
or his predecessors James Schuyler and Kenneth Koch,
Padgett shines brightest when he interrupts his crazy
word combinations to be serious about love and death."
Publ Wkly

Page, P. K. (Patricia Kathleen), 1916-
The hidden room; collected poems; {by}
Patricia Kathleen Page. Porcupine's Quill 1997 2v
ea $18.95   **811**
1. Poetry—By individual authors
ISBN 0-88984-190-X (v1); 0-88984-193-4 (v2)
LC 98-113870
These two volumes incude the majority of all of the
poet's works published in volume form, from Unit of
five to Hologram, along with some unpublished poems
and poems hitherto published only in magazines

Palmer, Michael, 1943-
Company of moths. New Directions Books 2005
70p pa $16.95   **811**
1. Poetry—By individual authors
ISBN 0-8112-1623-3   LC 2005-994

Palmer, Michael, 1943-—*Continued*

Palmer "combines spare lyricism and nocturnal visions ('This writing inside/ the lids of the eyes') in poems that resemble dream notes or lost translations from the French symbolists. They derive their tropes from an evocative if limited palette (owl, star, stone, book, moth) and create a sense of metaphysical unease through rhetorical questioning . . ., repetition, and paradox. . . . Whether or not one is absorbed by Palmer's deep image aesthetic and metanarrative stance, his enigmatic voice continues to fascinate." Libr J

Phillips, Carl, 1959-

The rest of love. Farrar, Straus and Giroux 2003 70p $20   **811**
1. Poetry—By individual authors
ISBN 0-374-24953-9   LC 2003-45213
The author presents a "set of poems on love, sex, masculinity and their classical contours. . . . The result will not only please fans, but will send new readers back to recent books, which may be accumulating more quickly than they can be absorbed." Publ Wkly

Rock Harbor. Farrar, Straus & Giroux 2002 110p $20; pa $12   **811**
1. Poetry—By individual authors
ISBN 0-374-25140-1; 0-374-52885-3 (pa)
                            LC 2002-20588
"Phillips reduces lyric poetry to its bare minimum, translating complex states of being into spare and clever syllogisms. His landscapes are stark, singular, and still. The living entities present, be they bird, tree, horse, or man, stand alone in wind and shifting light. Monumental in their carved perfection and deep mystery, they are embodiments of transcendence, objects of desire, instruments of pleasure and pain." Booklist

Piercy, Marge

Colors passing through us; poems. Knopf 2003 157p $23; pa $15   **811**
1. Poetry—By individual authors
ISBN 0-375-41537-8; 0-375-71005-1 (pa)
                            LC 2002-66145
The author "tempers 1960s politics and 1970s feminism with nostalgia for the world of her childhood. . . . Piercy celebrates daily life on Cape Cod, where she and her husband live, with poems about gardening, cats, cooking, canning, and sex after 60. While all of these poems are eminently readable, the best are angry and funny. . . . Piercy fans, of which there are many, will relish this collection." Libr J

Pinsky, Robert

The figured wheel; new and collected poems, 1966-1996. Farrar, Straus & Giroux 1996 303p pa $17 hardcover o.p.   **811**
1. Poetry—By individual authors
ISBN 0-374-52506-4   LC 95-47617
"Brought together here are 16 new poems, the work of Pinsky's four original collections and a sampling of his fine translations, including a canto from his well-received version of the *Inferno*. Taken as a whole, this is the record of a poet who grows from highly competent to near-transcendent." Publ Wkly

Gulf music. Farrar, Straus and Giroux 2007 83p $22 *   **811**
1. Poetry—By individual authors
ISBN 978-0-374-16749-3; 0-374-16749-4
                            LC 2007-4325
This collection "presents a carefully tuned yet impassioned vision of a past-haunted present where lessons of history remain unlearned and individuals struggle for comprehension amid atrocities ('In Africa/ The raiders with machetes to cut off hands/ Might make the victim choose, "long sleeve or short"') and contradictions ('Culture the penalty. Culture the escape'). . . . This anthology contains some of Pinsky's most invigorating work." Libr J

Jersey rain. Farrar, Straus & Giroux 2000 52p hardcover o.p. pa $12   **811**
1. Poetry—By individual authors
ISBN 978-0-374-52772-3; 0-374-52772-5
                            LC 99-44209
"The discursive mode suits Pinsky because it allows his mind to range, to consider, to try out images and ideas. The pleasure comes less from the poem's perfection as an artifact than from our sense of the poet's sensitive, inquisitive mind at work." N Y Times Book Rev

Plath, Sylvia

Ariel; the restored edition; foreword by Frieda Hughes. HarperCollins Publishers 2004 xxi, 211p $24.95   **811**
1. Poetry—By individual authors
ISBN 0-06-073259-8   LC 2004-47703
Also available Perennial Classics edition pa $12 (ISBN 0-06-093172-8)
First published 1955 in the United Kingdom
A collection of forty of Plath's poems written between 1960 and her death in 1963, in their original order along with facsimile drafts of the poems included
"Readers can see Plath's actual manuscript in this handsome facsimile, which provides a missing piece in the Plath annals and proves that there's nothing like going to the source." Booklist

The collected poems; edited by Ted Hughes. Harper & Row 1981 351p pa $17.95 hardcover o.p. *   **811**
1. Poetry—By individual authors
ISBN 0-06-155889-3 (pa)
Also available in hardcover from Buccaneer Bks.
The collection contains "all the poems Plath wrote, published and unpublished, from 1956 to 1963, as well as a sample of her early work." Publ Wkly
"Although her best poems deal with suffering and death, others are exhilarating and affectionate, and her tone is frequently witty as well as disturbing." Concise Oxford Companion to Engl Lit

Poe, Edgar Allan, 1809-1849

Complete poems; edited by Thomas Ollive Mabbott. University of Ill. Press 2000 xxx, 627p il pa $25   **811**
1. Poetry—By individual authors
ISBN 0-252-06921-8   LC 00-38639

Poe, Edgar Allan, 1809-1849—_Continued_
First published 1969 as volume 1 of: Collected works
of Edgar Allan Poe by Belknap Press of Harvard University Press
This book contains 101 poems and their variants. In
addition to classic poems such as The raven, The bells,
and Annabel Lee, this volume contains previously uncollected poems, fragments, verses published in reviews,
and poems attributed to Poe
Includes bibliographical references

Poems and poetics; Richard Wilbur, editor.
Library of Am. 2003 xxv, 179p (American poets
project) $20 *   **811**
1. Poetry—By individual authors
ISBN 1-931082-51-0   LC 2003-46637
"Wilbur wants Poe to be appreciated as a transcendental cosmic theorist and 'the most difficult of the symbolist writers of his century,' and he appends selections
from Poe's writings about poetics to help understanding
of his cosmology and discusses some of Poe's most intense stories to exemplify his symbolism. The poems,
presented chronologically, show again what a young
prodigy Poe was, formulating his poetic thought while
still in his teens, and what a sonorous Romantic musician
he became." Booklist
Includes bibliographical references

Ponsot, Marie
Springing; new and selected poems. Knopf 2002
233p $25; pa $16.95   **811**
1. Poetry—By individual authors
ISBN 0-375-41389-8; 0-375-70987-8 (pa)
                                          LC 2001-38432
"Ponsot's poems are built around . . . unflinching observations of intimate interactions and misfires, whether
of familial relations ventriloquized through updated
Greek dramatis personae, a French woman's accommodation of her mother's married lover or the self's castings
about the natural world." Publ Wkly

Porter, Anne, 1911-
Living things; collected poems; foreword by
David Shapiro. Zoland Books 2006 176p pa $15
*   **811**
1. Poetry—By individual authors
ISBN 1-58195-216-3   LC 2005-029944
Porter "deserves to be called a religious poet, for she
sees the world, in all its aspects, as whole within a providential design. In her verse there pulsates a probing,
praying spiritual intelligence as well as a poet's sensibility and graceful generosity. . . . Living Things offers
over 100 of Porter's poems, all 76 that appeared in An
Altogether Different Language (1994) . . . and 39 new
poems. The new poems come first. Reading this collection from beginning to end lets the newer work enrich
and deepen the older, enhancing the reader's appreciation
not for Porter's 'development,' but for discerning and
valuing this poet's integrity and vision. The cumulative
impact is dazzling." America

Pound, Ezra, 1885-1972
The cantos of Ezra Pound. New Directions 1970
802p $42; pa $22.95 *   **811**

1. Poetry—By individual authors
ISBN 0-8112-0350-6; 0-8112-1326-9 (pa)
"The first sections of the 'Cantos' were published in
magazine form as early as 1917. Pound's conception of
his epic changed several times during different phases of
his life. Originally intended as a didactic treatise for
'philistine' Americans, it combined elements from classical myth, ancient Oriental poetry, Provençal ballads, and
modern economic theory, to create a vast disjointed panorama of the growth of civilization. A monumental work
of poetic enterprise." Reader's Ency. 4th edition

Poems and translations. Library of America
2003 1363p $45 *   **811**
1. Poetry—By individual authors
ISBN 978-1-931082-41-9; 1-931082-41-3
                                          LC 2003-40142
This volume "offers, in addition to the convenience of
having Pound's shorter works compacted into a single
volume, a useful chronology of his life and some very
helpful, if at times overly terse, annotations to the poems' myriad foreign phrases and proper nouns. Richard
Sieburth, an award-winning translator and the author of
a previous book on Pound, is clearly at home with the
material. . . . More important than all of this, however,
what emerges from Poems and Translations is a personality, one of the strongest and strangest in modern poetry." Parnassus: Poetry in Review

Price, Reynolds, 1933-
The collected poems. Scribner 1997 xxiv, 471p
$37.50; pa $20 *   **811**
1. Poetry—By individual authors
ISBN 0-684-83203-8; 0-684-86002-3 (pa)
                                          LC 96-53117
"Price has always stood apart from contemporary
movements in poetry, and although it is true that he is
not a technical innovator, it would be perilous to ignore
him: he has a rare facility for making the strange familiar, and the familiar fresh. Compassionate and candid,
Price seems likely to reach an audience unusually wide
for contemporary poetry with this generous collection."
Libr J

Reed, Ishmael, 1938-
New and collected poems, 1966-2006. Carroll &
Graf 2006 xxi, 482p $25.95; pa $17.95
                                                  811
1. Poetry—By individual authors
ISBN 978-0-7867-1788-0; 978-1-56858-341-9 (pa)
                                          LC 2006-299409
"The mixture of humor and anger is . . . a hallmark
of Ishmael Reed, whose strength as an editor, essayist,
and novelist (and whose reputation as provocateur) has
overshadowed his achievement as a poet. That achievement . . . is based in the vernacular, as well as in his
use of folk materials, his fearlessness with form, and his
'irrational' tendency toward the spiritual, which stands as
an indictment of the impoverished soul of a bottom-line
age." Harvard Review

Revell, Donald

Pennyweight windows; new & selected poems.
Alice James 2005 220p $26.95; pa $18.95 *

811

1. Poetry—By individual authors
ISBN 1-882295-51-X; 1-882295-52-8 (pa)

LC 2004-26191

"Using history, mythology, and contemporary events
as a backdrop . . . [the author] tries to balance a public,
nearly didactic voice with a personal and revealing one.
. . . This readable and well-edited collection—mostly
culled from eight previous collections, with some new
poems added—is a good representation of Revell's
work." Libr J

A thief of strings. Alice James Books 2007 68p
pa $14.95

811

1. Poetry—By individual authors
ISBN 978-1-882295-61-6; 1-882295-61-7

LC 2007-1116

"Revell is a post-Romantic, his natural imagery clear
and immediate, his feelings never very far from his
sleeve, his tone approaching a prayerful devotion that
evinces an unshakable love of the real world despite
its—or our—compromised state." Libr J

Rexroth, Kenneth, 1905-1982

The complete poems of Kenneth Rexroth; edited
by Sam Hamill & Bradford Morrow. Copper
Canyon Press 2003 xxxvi, 764p pa $24 hardcover
o.p. *

811

1. Poetry—By individual authors
ISBN 1-55659-217-5 (pa)

LC 2002-1706

This collection "includes, in sequence, all of Rexroth's
individual collections, as well as several long-out-of-print
older poems and previously unavaliable works." N Y
Times Book Rev

"If you love looking things up and taking reading
side-trips, Rexroth is one of the most readable and rewarding twentieth-century American poets." Booklist

Reznikoff, Charles, 1894-1976

Holocaust. David R. Godine 2007 93p pa
$15.95

811

1. Poetry—By individual authors
ISBN 978-1-57423-208-0; 1-57423-208-8

LC 2006-33803

"Black Sparrow books"
First published 1975 by Black Sparrow Press
"A book-length poem about the Shoah as recounted by
witnesses at the Nuremberg Military Tribunal and the trial of Adolf Eichmann, architect of Hitler's 'Final Solution,' held in Jerusalem. From U.S. government transcripts of these trials, [the author] selected and spliced
together witness testimonies. . . . Reznikoff's historicism
and objectivism are brought together in an ethical and
spiritual climax. By using the language of others he attends to the 'object' of genocide without imaginative or
philosophical flourish, and by reciting it again in his own
rhythm he becomes a second witness to its truth. Ultimately, the reader responds not to the poet but to the testimony itself. . . . It presents a story already told and a
story never to be finished. It is neither novel nor revela-

tory, only horrific; as a piece of art it does not seduce
us. But this is precisely its moral power as a document."
Boston Rev

The poems of Charles Reznikoff; 1918-1975;
edited by Seamus Cooney. David R. Godine 2005
445p $45; pa $21.95 *

811

1. Poetry—By individual authors
ISBN 1-57423-204-5; 1-57423-203-7 (pa)

LC 2005-21218

First published 1989 with title: Poems 1918-1975

This volume contains the author's "complete shorter
poems—all of his poetry except the book-length works
Testimony and Holocaust." Publisher's note

This collection "of his poems . . . will be welcomed
both by old and new readers of his work." Publ Wkly

Includes bibliographical references

Rich, Adrienne

Collected early poems, 1950-1970. Norton 1993
xxi, 435p pa $15 hardcover o.p.

811

1. Poetry—By individual authors
ISBN 0-393-31385-9 (pa)

LC 92-13150

This collection "contains all of the work included in
Rich's first six books, and a few previously uncollected
pieces as well. Her poetry of the 1950s stems from a
strong, mostly male tradition, obviously and intentionally
echoing the work of Frost, Williams, Dickinson and Stevens. . . . The poems written in the 1960s are pervaded
by the poet's consciousness of the subversive nature of
creativity, especially for women, a gift at risk of being
suppressed or curtailed at any moment by the self, family
or the male-dominated society. In the last poems of the
period, Rich's voice is firm and brave, her language still
searingly beautiful and individual. This important volume
charts the radical transformation of one of America's
most significant poets." Publ Wkly

Fox; poems, 1998-2000. Norton 2001 64p $21;
pa $12

811

1. Poetry—By individual authors
ISBN 0-393-04166-2; 0-393-32377-3 (pa)

LC 2001-31240

"Rich's recent style—developed slowly throughout the
1990s—comes to full fruition here, conveying her familiar attentions to social injustice and intense introspection
with and a sometimes harsh, fragmented, versatile line
whose sources include George Oppen and Anglo-Saxon
accentual verse." Publ Wkly

Midnight salvage; poems, 1995-1998. Norton
1999 75p $22; pa $11

811

1. Poetry—By individual authors
ISBN 0-393-04682-6; 0-393-31984-9 (pa)

LC 98-19293

Rich's "well-known, fiercely held political ideals—her
commitments to economic justice, feminism and gay liberation—manifest themselves, now, in her sense of passing the torch, of trying to show the readers and writers
who will come after her what she has learned and how
she learned it. Her juxtaposed fragments, self-
questionings and self-interruptions, and taut, Anglo-
Saxonate verse lines, let her sound accessible, democratic, inspiring, while making us work to discover her poems' formal secrets." Publ Wkly

Rich, Adrienne—*Continued*

The school among the ruins: poems, 2000-2004.
W.W. Norton 2004 113p $22.95   **811**
1. Poetry—By individual authors
ISBN 0-393-05983-9   LC 2004-8370
In this collection the poet "confronts dislocations and
upheavals at the beginning of the twenty-first century."
Publisher's note
"Rich, a clarion poet of conscience, gets the fractured
timbre of our times just right in a collection of vigorous
lyric poems about cell phones and television, terror and
war, commercialization and 'social impotence.'" Booklist

Roethke, Theodore, 1908-1963
The collected poems of Theodore Roethke.
Doubleday 1966 279p pa $14.95 hardcover o.p. *
811
1. Poetry—By individual authors
ISBN 0-385-08601-6 (pa)
Roethke's "refreshingly original rhythms are keenly
articulated and often hypnotic. Although his work is uneven and he sometimes gives way to self-indulgence or
to surprising naiveté, many of his best poems recreate
disconcertingly intense psychic or mystical experience.
He also had a flair for the seductively lyrical and the
brashly irreverent. He ranks as one of the best poets of
the first postmodern generation." Benet's Reader's Ency
of Am Lit

Rukeyser, Muriel, 1913-1980
Selected poems; Adrienne Rich, editor. Library
of America 2004 xxv, 180p (American poets
project) $20   **811**
1. Poetry—By individual authors
ISBN 978-1-931082-58-7; 1-931082-58-8
LC 2003-60484
"Rukeyser was born in 1913, which puts her in the
generation of Bishop, Berryman, Lowell, and Jarrell. Her
poems range from the sprawling to the epigrammatic;
they often have a flat, documentary feel ('The tunnel is
part of a huge water power project/begun, latter part of
1929'), and they're formally various (excerpted sections
from a single long poem, 'Letter to the Front,' contain
both a sonnet and a sestina). . . . At its best, Rukeyser's
work can be open, energetic, and well constructed, if a
little enamored of its own goody-goodness." Poetry
(Modern Poetry Association)

Ryan, Kay, 1945-
Elephant rocks. Grove Press 1996 84p $18; pa
$14   **811**
1. Poetry—By individual authors
ISBN   978-0-8021-1586-7;   0-8021-1586-1;
978-0-8021-3525-4 (pa); 0-8021-3525-0 (pa)
LC 95-42668
This volume is comprised of "miniature five-paragraph
essays, something like those little books the Brontes
wrote for their dolls. They're epigrams or digestifs or,
better, aphorisms if we remember the source of such
things: Hippocrates making little pills of pithiness, haiku
with punch lines, prescriptions not meant for the pharma-

cist. . . . If John Skelton had been Emily Dickinson's tu-
tor instead of Jane Scrope's, these poems would not surprise us. But they do." Antioch Review

The Niagara River; poems. Grove Press 2005
72p (Grove Press poetry series) pa $13
811
1. Poetry—By individual authors
ISBN 0-8021-4222-2   LC 2005-40423
"In two or three shifty sentences per short-lined poem,
Ryan brazenly questions the extent to which we are in
control of, and thus responsible for, our own and others'
suffering. Her work . . . operates in an American tradition stretching from Dickinson through Stevens and Frost
to Ammons and Bronk, where fidelity to the natural
world works as a scrim for staging such self-exploration.
. . . Empathic and wryly unforgiving of the human condition, the poems are equal parts pith and punch. The effect is bracing." Publ Wkly

Say uncle; poems. Grove Press 2000 76p pa $14
811
1. Poetry—By individual authors
ISBN 978-0-8021-3717-3; 0-8021-3717-2
LC 00-26454
"These precise, epigrammatic poems, which come
with hook-and-eye rhymes that click sweetly into place,
move deftly and economically. . . . Though they dispose
of their subjects wittily and ingeniously, they cannot always suppress a smile of self-satisfaction at having mastered their material; and, like macaroons, they should be
taken a few at a time. They are cleverly made. . . . Like
cat's cradles, they may be taken in or let out, but at their
best they alter the fit of the mind." Atl Mon

Sandburg, Carl, 1878-1967
The complete poems of Carl Sandburg. rev and
expanded ed. Harcourt Brace Jovanovich 1970
xxxi, 797p $40 *   **811**
1. Poetry—By individual authors
ISBN 0-15-100996-1
First published 1950
Introduction by Archibald MacLeish
A collection of seven of the author's books: Chicago
poems, 1916; Cornhuskers, 1918; Smoke and steel, 1920;
Slabs of the sunburnt West, 1922; Good morning, America, 1925; The people, yes, 1936; Honey and salt, 1963
"Known for his free verse, written under the influence
of Walt Whitman and celebrating industrial and agricultural America, American geography and landscape, figures in American history, and the American common
people, {Sandburg} frequently makes use of contemporary American slang and colloquialisms." Herzberg.
Reader's Ency of Am Lit

Sarton, May, 1912-1995
Selected poems of May Sarton; edited and with
an introduction by Serena Sue Hilsinger and Lois
Brynes. Norton 1978 206p hardcover o.p. pa $25
811
1. Poetry—By individual authors
ISBN 978-0-393-04512-3; 0-393-04512-9
LC 78-14850

Sarton, May, 1912-1995—*Continued*

"What May Sarton does is to follow the round of a woman's life. Her verse is traditional, warm, ripe with the wisdom of her years as a poet, novelist, autobiographer. She draws on the artifacts of the past for images to live by in the here and now." Christ Sci Monit

Scalapino, Leslie

It's go in horizontal; selected poems, 1974-2006. University of California Press 2008 241p il (New California poetry) $45; pa $16.95　　**811**
　　ISBN　978-0-520-25461-9;　0-520-25461-9; 978-0-520-25462-6 (pa); 0-520-25462-7 (pa)
　　　　　　　　　　　　　　　　　LC 2007-50133

"Most often classified with the language poets, Scalapino is shown in this welcome overview to have developed a distinctive idiom, as fresh and powerful here as when first published in 14 mostly small press editions. Scalapino fuses a richly detached Buddhist mindfulness with an algorithmically precise disjunctive syntax to explore sex, gender and violence—their politics and their moment-to-moment embodiedness. The longish, serial form that she favors works well in the selected format when the poems are presented in full." Publ Wkly

Schulman, Grace

Days of wonder; new and selected poems. Houghton Mifflin 2002 189p $25; pa $14

　　　　　　　　　　　　　　　　　811
　　1. Poetry—By individual authors
　　ISBN 0-618-08623-4; 0-618-34082-3 (pa)
　　　　　　　　　　　　　　　　　LC 2001-39531

"In a characteristic Schulman poem, large, difficult questions resonate in the small, singular moments of appreciation. . . . There are allusions to canonical painters and canonical poems, and a variety of religious references, which engender equal portions of reverence and lament. Many of the poems' small pleasures are found amid sometimes difficult sometimes serene backdrops." Publ Wkly

Schuyler, James

Collected poems. Farrar, Straus & Giroux 1993 429p hardcover o.p. pa $32 *　　**811**
　　1. Poetry—By individual authors
　　ISBN 978-0-374-52403-6; 0-374-52403-3
　　　　　　　　　　　　　　　　　LC 92-40977

"Schuyler's subject is his life, and his poems often read like elegant journal entries. The book presents intimate and conversational accounts of life in the Eastern literary landscape—New York City, New England, Long Island. In urbane free verse, the poet recalls and meditates on music and painting, homosexuality, weekends with friends—John Ashbery and Fairfield Porter among them—deaths, a drive to the Hamptons. . . . Rarely has a poet imparted so much of his experience as honestly and engagingly as Schuyler does here." Publ Wkly

Sexton, Anne

The complete poems; with a foreword by Maxine Kumin. Houghton Mifflin 1981 xxiv, 622p pa $19 hardcover o.p.　　**811**
　　1. Poetry—By individual authors
　　ISBN 0-395-95776-1 (pa)　　　　LC 81-2482
"This collection contains all the poems in the eight volumes published in Sexton's lifetime, the two published after her death, and seven poems never before in print." Libr J

"Even before her death in 1974, Sexton's work was the subject of critical controversy, often dismissed as mere confessionalism. But, as Maxine Kumin observes in an insightful introductory essay, Sexton 'delineated the problematic position of women—the neurotic reality of the time' and in so doing 'earned her place in the canon.'" Choice

Shapiro, David, 1947-

New and selected poems (1965-2006). Overlook Press 2007 267p $21.95　　**811**
　　1. Poetry—By individual authors
　　ISBN 978-1-58567-877-8; 1-58567-877-5
　　　　　　　　　　　　　　　　　LC 2006-52718

"Shapiro is usually thought of as a New York School poet, but from the evidence of this selection it would probably be more accurate to call him a Greater New York School poet. His metropolis radiates outward to comprehend Weequahic Park and the Palisades, and his aleatory, portent-free sophistication seems confident enough to accommodate primitive, endearing, and frankly tender tropes and situations, as when a poet faces an ailing mother or a growing son. A perennial drama in this volume is that of an erudite and restlessly modernizing mind confronting pains and peculiarities that no amount of urbanity can assuage. . . . The effect is of unforeseen intimacy at the heart of abstraction." New Yorker

Shapiro, Karl Jay, 1913-2000

Selected poems; [by] Karl Shapiro; John Updike, editor. Library of Am. 2003 xxxi, 197p il (American poets project) $20 *　　**811**
　　1. Poetry—By individual authors
　　ISBN 1-931082-34-0　　　　LC 2002-32123

"Karl Shapiro, one of the more influential voices of the late 20th century, displayed complex and contrary tendencies in both his life and his poetry. Editor Updike notes that Shapiro's experimentation with voices and forms alienated those who admired the metrical dexterity of his early poems." Libr J

Includes bibliographical references

Shaughnessy, Brenda, 1970-

Human dark with sugar. Copper Canyon Press 2008 77p pa $15　　**811**
　　1. Poetry—By individual authors
　　ISBN 978-1-55659-276-8; 1-55659-276-0
　　　　　　　　　　　　　　　　　LC 2007-52225

On cover: Winner of the James Laughlin Award of the Academy of American Poets

"The book's three sections contain nine, 11 and 10 poems, respectively, and that off-kilter triangulation . . .

Shaughnessy, Brenda, 1970-—*Continued*
proves the right three-cornered lens for looking into the
darkest corners of human relationships, including their
embodiment. . . . This is a brilliant, beautiful and essential continuation of the metaphysical verse tradition."
Publ Wkly

Simic, Charles, 1938-
Selected early poems. Braziller 1999 255p $22;
pa $14.95   **811**
1. Poetry—By individual authors
ISBN 0-8076-1456-4; 0-8076-1483-1 (pa)
                                        LC 99-34872
First published 1985 with title: Selected poems, 1963-
1983
"Charles Simic shows that he is among the very few
poets for whom surrealism is a genuine vision, a tool of
discovery, rather than a collection of abitrary shocks.
. . . His skewed vision manages both to capture the
alien concreteness of things and to make them reflect his
own consciousness. . . . His skill and sure instinct make
this book one of the important poetic achievements of
our time." N Y Times Book Rev

That little something; poems. Harcourt 2008 73p
$23   **811**
1. Poetry—By individual authors
ISBN 978-0-15-101359-3; 0-15-101359-4
                                        LC 2007-32812
"Among contemporary poets, Simic, now 70, is not
only one of the most prolific but also one of the most
distinctive, accessible and enjoyable—the commonplace
critique of contemporary poetry as dull, obscure and
lacking in individuality definitely does not apply. . . .
Just about the only thing critics complain of is that his
style has shown relatively little development over the
years. That's true, although in the last decade or so his
poems seem to me to have become shorter, simpler, less
manic." N Y Times Book Rev

The voice at 3:00 a.m; selected late & new
poems. Harcourt 2003 177p $25 *   **811**
1. Poetry—By individual authors
ISBN 0-15-100842-6   LC 2002-38715
This "volume collects outstanding poems from six previous books, beginning with *Unending Blues* (1986) and
ending with *Jackstraws* (1999), and presents a sterling
set of new poems, each moody, surprising, and tonic."
Booklist
"An important purchase for all libraries." Libr J

Simpson, Louis Aston Marantz, 1923-
The owner of the house; new collected poems,
1940-2001; [by] Louis Simpson. BOA 2003 407p
(American poets continuum series) $30.95; pa
$19.95 *   **811**
1. Poetry—By individual authors
ISBN 1-929918-38-0; 1-929918-39-9 (pa)
                                        LC 2003-45241
The author "opens with 42 new poems and continues
with selections from his 11 previous books, ending with
There You Are. This work is filled with evocations of
places like Jamaica, Manhattan, Paris, and Venice and

range over time from tsarist Russia to World War II to
the 1960s. Simpson's obsessive theme is the stultifying
effect of middle-class suburban life. . . . The result is a
collection both timely and accessible. . . . Highly recommended for all poetry collections." Libr J

Smith, William Jay, 1918-
The world below the window; poems,
1937-1997. Johns Hopkins Univ. Press 1998 240p
il (Johns Hopkins, poetry and fiction) pa $25
hardcover o.p. *   **811**
1. Poetry—By individual authors
ISBN 978-0-8018-6783-5   LC 97-40731
"Excluding Smith's translations, longer poems, poetry
for children and much of his light verse, this . . . volume both slims down and augments 1990's *Collected
Poems*. Appearing for the first time, the original, absorbing seven-part series 'Indian Removal' searchingly explores the poet's Choctaw heritage by dramatizing America's shameful past on a hot, tear-laden, swampy Southern stage." Publ Wkly

Snodgrass, W. D. (William De Witt), 1926-
Not for specialists; new and selected poems.
BOA Editions 2006 251p (American poets
continuum series) $27.95; pa $21.95 *
                                                    811
1. Poetry—By individual authors
ISBN 1-92991-877-1; 1-92991-876-3 (pa)
                                        LC 2005-54846
"If you think that writing primarily in rhyme and meter bespeaks equanimity, or sweetness of character, read
Snodgrass. Oh, he mellows out in the face of nature, but
he's prickly. . . . His many profoundly bemused and
persuasive poems of love's tougher moments, his marvelous angry and denunciatory poems, and the chilling
Fuehrer Bunker poems in the voices of the major Nazis
during the war's last month—all these might have been
impossible if Snodgrass was a nice, easygoing guy. He's
not that sort, and his best work seems permanent because
he isn't." Booklist

Snyder, Gary
Danger on peaks; poems. Shoemaker & Hoard,
Distributed by Publishers Group West 2004 112p
il $22; pa $14   **811**
1. Poetry—By individual authors
ISBN 1-59376-041-8; 1-59376-080-9 (pa)
                                        LC 2004-11649
This is a collection of poetry by the author of *Turtle
Island* (1975), *Axe Handles* (1984), *No Nature* (1992),
and *The Practice of the Wild* (1990).
"From the opening prose-and-verse section on several
climbs of Mount St. Helens, through short poems of observation and longer ones on daily life, to more prose-
and-verse pieces on journeys near and far, Snyder seems
more accepting than ever before. His 1960s eco-Marxist
scolding is gone, and he's the wiser for it." Booklist
Includes bibliographical references

Mountains and rivers without end. Counterpoint
1996 165p pa $14.50 hardcover o.p.   **811**
1. Poetry—By individual authors
ISBN 1-887178-57-0 (pa)   LC 96-26064

Snyder, Gary—*Continued*

"Woven of poems written from 1956 to 1996, this vigorous epic, spanning the landscapes of cities and un-sullied nature and covering a period that includes the Beats and their survivors, is rooted in both the American geography and an Eastern spiritual orientation." Publ Wkly

No nature; new and selected poems. Pantheon Bks. 1992 390p pa $16 hardcover o.p. *

811

1. Poetry—By individual authors
ISBN 978-0-679-74252-4   LC 92-54110

This is a "selection of the best of Snyder's career, spanning from *Riprap* (1959), published at the time of his involvement with the Beatniks and the San Francisco Renaissance, to a previously unpublished group of sixteen poems entitled 'No Nature.'" Libr J

"There is an understated majesty about the ease with which Mr. Snyder puts the present into perspective." N Y Times Book Rev

Sobin, Gustaf

The places as preludes. Talisman House 2005 76p pa $14.95   811

1. Poetry—By individual authors
ISBN 1-58498-040-0

"One of the most significant poets of his generation, the late Gustaf Sobin's verse was enigmatic, unique, thought-provoking, and memorable." Midwest Book Rev

Soto, Gary

New and selected poems. Chronicle Bks. 1995 177p hardcover o.p. pa $14.95   811

1. Poetry—By individual authors
ISBN 0-8118-0761-4; 0-8118-0758-4 (pa)
LC 94-27081

"In one of his more striking poems, Soto stares longingly at the unkempt lot in the California slum where his family's house used to be. Elsewhere, a Mexican American simply jogs and laughs after he has been ushered out the back door when immigration officials show up at his workplace. With rare lyricism, gentleness, and a touch of humor, Soto covers the ground that leads many highly touted poets to erupt in pulsating anger. Soto has it all—the learned craft, the intrinsic abilities with language, a fascinating autobiography, and the storyteller's ability to manipulate memories into folklore." Libr J

Stafford, William Edgar, 1914-1993

The way it is; new & selected poems. Graywolf Press 1998 xx, 268p $24.95; pa $16   811

1. Poetry—By individual authors
ISBN 1-55597-269-1; 1-55597-284-5 (pa)
LC 97-80082

This volume presents "some 400 of Stafford's poems, work gathered from 67 books published between 1960 and 1996, as well as from journals and the poet's Daily Writings." Indep Publ

"Including 71 previously unpublished new poems, among them the poem Stafford wrote the day he died, this collection fully reacquaints us with a quiet, generous presence on the American poetic landscape." Publ Wkly

Stern, Gerald

This time; new and selected poems. Norton 1998 288p pa $15.95 hardcover o.p.   811

1. Poetry—By individual authors
ISBN 0-393-31909-1 (pa)   LC 97-43670

"At once self-involved and sympathetic, Stern catalogues with wry dexterity a vast range of sensory data and cultural detritus, always united by 'women and men of all sizes and all ages/living together, without satire.' This healthy collection of new poems and selections from his seven previous volumes . . . is remarkable for its generosity of spirit, manifested in a warm surrealism that is often turned with humor toward his own past." Publ Wkly

Stevens, Wallace, 1879-1955

Collected poetry and prose. Library of Am. 1997 xxii, 1032p $35 *   811

1. Poetry—By individual authors
ISBN 1-88301-145-0   LC 97-7023

Having all of Stevens' "poems—especially all the late poems—in one volume is a great thing (previously, one had to seek them out in three different books); the 'Adagia' and his replies to questionnaires are marvelous; and even in the somewhat turgid prose pieces, he sometimes expresses himself with exemplary force and concision." N Y Times Book Rev

Stone, Ruth, 1915-

In the dark. Copper Canyon Press 2004 113p $22   811

1. Poetry—By individual authors
ISBN 1-55659-210-8   LC 2004-6039

In this book, the author focuses on "issues of memory, aging, and loss." Publisher's note

"Stone appeals to the mind's eye and the physical ear, each word tested for ripeness like fruit, each a perfectly held note. Wry animal parables, spare and intense dramas, gorgeous nature lyrics, and bracing metaphysical musings constitute a clarion collection." Booklist

In the next galaxy. Copper Canyon Press 2002 99p $20   811

1. Poetry—By individual authors
ISBN 1-55659-178-0   LC 2001-7424

"Stone writes conversationally, with lyricism, honesty, wit, and plenty of focus on the passage of time. The suicide of her much-loved husband 40 years ago is a frequent theme, as are observations about aging (which she has achieved with great wisdom), the lives of her young students and neighbors, and ecological and political concerns." Libr J

Strand, Mark, 1934-

Blizzard of one; poems. Knopf 1998 55p $21; pa $15   811

1. Poetry—By individual authors
ISBN 0-375-40139-3; 0-375-70137-0 (pa)
LC 97-49172

"Strand doesn't approach the universal through the particular. He approaches the universal through the universal. In his masterly new collection, 'Blizzard of One,'

Strand, Mark, 1934——*Continued*
even the single snowflake that gives the volume its title
. . . is a kind of Platonic essence, linked to a continuum
of snowflakes out there in the weather and inside, in the
reader's consciousness." N Y Times Book Rev

Chicken, shadow, moon and more. Turtle Point
Press 2000 91p il $21.95   **811**
1. Poetry—By individual authors
ISBN 1-885586-45-X
This volume "is a book of lists that at times sounds
like a collection of one-line poems and at other times
like a collection of epigrams. Each list is constructed by
a repeated use of a single word." N Y Rev Books
"Startling visions, unexpected truths, an aura of wist-
fulness, and trills of playful humor waft from every page,
and always the language is exact, musical, and transcendent." Booklist

Man and camel; poems. Knopf 2006 51p $24
                                             811
1. Poetry—By individual authors
ISBN 0-307-26296-0; 978-0-307-26296-7
                                  LC 2006-40986
This collection "begins with a group of light but
haunting fables, populated by figures like the King, a
tiny creature in ermine who has lost his desire to rule,
and by the poet's own alter ego. . . . The poet has Arctic adventures and encounters with the bearded figure of
Death." Publisher's note
The author "writes spare, melancholy, and haunting
poems." Booklist

Swenson, May, 1919-1989
Nature; poems old and new. Houghton Mifflin
1994 xxiii, 240p pa $15 hardcover o.p.
                                             811
1. Poetry—By individual authors
ISBN 0-618-06408-7 (pa)   LC 93-45642
This collection of Swenson's poetry "brings together
poems from several earlier books, as well as poems published only in magazines, and introduces us to nine
splendid poems published here for the first time. This
collection . . . is brought together with special attention
to poems describing the environment; poems of tides and
the sea, of birds and gardens, of moods and seasons, of
self and others. . . . This is a collection to be treasured;
it belongs in all libraries with even a modest selection of
poetry." Libr J

Taggart, John, 1942-
Pastorelles. Flood Editions 2004 104p pa $13.95
*   **811**
1. Poetry—By individual authors
ISBN 0-974690-21-X   LC 2004-303826
"Among the small number of poets who have followed the difficult path of Zukofsky, George Oppen,
Lorraine Niedecker, and William Bronk, John Taggart
has kept more closely to the Objectivist trail than most,
while at the same time developing his own signature
style and deepening his explorations into the strata where
vision, music, and language converge. Pastorelles may be
his most consistent and fully realized collection, one that

maintains and enlivens a literary movement that, even after decades, has still not been granted the degree of attention and critical analysis it deserves." Am Book Rev

Tarn, Nathaniel
Selected poems; 1950-2000. Wesleyan
University Press 2002 335p (Wesleyan poetry)
$45; pa $19.95   **811**
1. Poetry—By individual authors
ISBN   978-0-8195-6541-9;   0-8195-6541-5;
978-0-8195-6542-6 (pa); 0-8195-6542-3 (pa)
                                  LC 2002-1701
"Arranged chronologically, [this volume] has reprints
from nineteen of Tarn's thirty-five books. Here the literary reader can find reality hybrids and can experience the
camaraderie of whole image systems from the twentieth
century. No syllable is lonely or aloof. One is often reminded, by Tarn's references, his subjects, and his dedi-
cations, not only of Blake but of Yeats, Vallejo, Charles
Olson, and Robert Duncan. Like those writers, his work
brings together mythology, Western and Eastern philosophy (including Gnostic thought), political commentary,
scientific investigations, naturalist descriptions and very
personal love poetry." Jacket

Tate, James, 1943-
The ghost soldiers; poems. Ecco 2008 217p
$22.95   **811**
1. Poetry—By individual authors
ISBN 978-0-06-143694-9; 0-06-143694-1
                                  LC 2007-29856
"These poems engage everything from war to police-
state oppression to romance to small-town family life.
Aliens make appearances, as do mythical creatures, talking animals, shadowy government agencies and malevo-
lent corporations. Tate is clearly responding to contemporary issues. . . . By locating humor in tragedy, by highlighting the false connections by which we mortals construct daily life, Tate distills the sad little details of existence into a potent elixir, at once pathetic and noble."
PopMatters

Selected poems. Wesleyan Univ. Press 1991
239p hardcover o.p. pa $18.95   **811**
1. Poetry—By individual authors
ISBN 978-0-8195-1192-8; 0-8195-1192-7
                                  LC 90-50918
Tate has "created a voice and a kind of poem that no
one else could have written. His comedy works not only
to entertain, which it does marvelously—he has the rare
ability to be very, very funny on the page—but partly to
cover and partly to reveal underlying disorientation and
angst." N Y Times Book Rev

Shroud of the gnome; poems. Ecco Press 1997
72p pa $15 hardcover o.p.   **811**
1. Poetry—By individual authors
ISBN 0-880015-62-4 (pa)   LC 97-16224
"The master of our idioms takes us on another dizzy,
dangerous career through absurd and disintegrating
Americana, with his speakers looking on bemusedly as
their folk narratives spin out of control. Tate . . . continues to draw on small-town kitsch, haywire nature documentaries and 'a giantess by the name of Anna Swan' to
fuel his often hilarious antistories. The joke has not
tired." Publ Wkly

Tate, James, 1943-—*Continued*

Worshipful Company of Fletchers; poems. Ecco Press 1994 82p pa $13 hardcover o.p.

811

1. Poetry—By individual authors
ISBN 0-880014-31-8 (pa)   LC 94-9821
The author "offers a collection full of confused narrative voices, prosaic images made startlingly fresh, and landscapes that curve at the sides like hallucinations. . . . Tate is at his best when he weaves into his shimmering language such ordinary objects as toy poodles, crayons, Camp Fire Girls, and gum wrappers. In so doing, he solicits the reader with the familiar, then proceeds to act as trail guide to other worlds." Booklist

Toomer, Jean, 1894-1967

The collected poems of Jean Toomer; edited by Robert B. Jones and Margery Toomer Latimer; with an introduction and textual notes by Robert B. Jones. University of N.C. Press 1988 xxxv, 111p hardcover o.p. pa $17.95 *

811

1. Poetry—By individual authors
ISBN 978-0-8078-4209-6; 0-8078-4209-5

LC 87-19203
"This is the only collected edition of poems by Jean Toomer, the enigmatic Afro-American writer, Gurdjieffian guru, and Quaker convert who is perhaps best known for his 1923 lyrical narrative, Cane. The fifty-five poems here—most of them previously unpublished—chart a fascinating evolution of artistic consciousness." Univ Press Books for Public Libr

Troupe, Quincy

Transcircularities; new and selected poems. Coffee House Press 2002 368p $30; pa $17 *

811

1. Poetry—By individual authors
ISBN 1-56689-137-X; 1-56689-135-3 (pa)

LC 2002-71277
Troupe's "verse returns continually to swing, bebop and free-jazz giants, imitating, commemorating or praising Coltrane, Duke, Bud Powell and others in a series of musicianly poems culminating in the recent 'Back to the Dream Time: Miles Speaks from the Dead.' Troupe's forms, driven by performability, range from ecstatic odes to overtly political expostulations." Publ Wkly

Updike, John

Americana and other poems. Knopf 2001 95p $23

811

1. Poetry—By individual authors
ISBN 0-375-41254-9   LC 2001-88571
This volume "ranges from a number of brilliant, expositional epics that converse as they describe, to shorter works with their quicksilver epiphanies." Christ Sci Monit

Collected poems, 1953-1993. Knopf 1993 xxiv, 387p il hardcover o.p. pa $25

811

1. Poetry—By individual authors
ISBN 978-0-679-76204-1; 0-679-76204-3

LC 92-28957

"From the outset Updike's poems are crisp and exact. There is a mock humbleness, ready wit, and divine concreteness to his subjects, an unrelenting curiosity behind his descriptions, and a prodding tension between the tactile and the abstract. . . . From the cocky exuberance of 'Midpoint,' a 1968 autobiographical cycle, to the wry, tender mischief of poems about domesticity, marriage, and aging, Updike's thrill over the unending discovery of poetry inspires images and metaphors of time-stopping perfection as well as humor rich in grace and knowingness." Booklist

Includes bibliographical references

Valentine, Jean

Door in the mountain; new and collected poems, 1965-2003. Wesleyan University Press 2004 285p (Wesleyan poetry) $29.95

811

1. Poetry—By individual authors
ISBN 0-8195-6712-4   LC 2004-16019
"This volume gathers together all of Valentine's published poems and includes a new collection, 'Door in the Mountain.'" Publisher's note
"The defiant, angular, yet propulsively emotional recent poems that occupy the first and last parts of the book should please both fans of Valentine's earliest poetry and fans of her strongly feminist middle period." Publ Wkly

Includes bibliographical references

Van Duyn, Mona

Selected poems. Knopf 2002 218p $27.50; pa $16 *

811

1. Poetry—By individual authors
ISBN 0-375-41369-3; 0-375-70980-0 (pa)

LC 2001-50672
"Characterized by candor and compassion, Van Duyn's poetry depicts the pleasures and drudgeries of middle-class American life, an approach that at its best becomes an exploration of the spiritual and psychological dimensions of that life. . . . The casually formal surfaces of Van Duyn's poems often resemble those of her model, Elizabeth Bishop, and like Bishop she excels at both formal and free verse." N Y Times Book Rev

Walcott, Derek

Collected poems, 1948-1984. Farrar, Straus & Giroux 1986 515p pa $20 hardcover o.p. *

811

1. Poetry—By individual authors
ISBN 0-374-52025-9 (pa)   LC 85-20688
"It is difficult to think of a poet in our century who—without ever betraying his native sources—has so organically assimilated the evolution of English literature from the Renaissance to the present, who has absorbed the Classical and Judeo-Christian past, and who has mined the history of Western painting as Walcott has. Throughout his entire body of work he has managed to hold in balance his passionate moral concerns with the ideal of art." Poetry

Includes bibliographical references

Walcott, Derek—*Continued*

Omeros. Farrar, Straus & Giroux 1990 325p pa
$16 hardcover o.p. *   **811**
1. Poetry—By individual authors
ISBN 0-374-52350-9 (pa)   LC 90-33592

This epic poem "follows the wanderings of a present-
day Odysseus and the inconsolable sufferings of those
who are displaced and traveling with trepidation toward
their homes. Written in seven circling books and . . .
tercets, the poem illuminates the classical past and its
motifs through an extraordinary cast of contemporary
characters from the island of Santa Lucia." Publ Wkly

"No poet rivals Mr. Walcott in humor, emotional
depth, lavish inventiveness in language or in the ability
to express the thoughts of his characters and compel the
reader to follow the swift mutations of ideas and images
in their minds. This wonderful story moves in a spiral,
replicating human thought." N Y Times Book Rev

The prodigal. Farrar, Straus and Giroux 2004
112p $20   **811**
1. Poetry—By individual authors
ISBN 0-374-23743-3   LC 2004-5147

"Styling himself as a 'prodigal son' (prodigal, too, in
the richness of his appetite and his verse), [Walcott]
presents a continuous narrative of his travels from his native St. Lucia through New York, Italy, Germany, the
Alps, and Cartegena, on Colombia's coast. This is at
once a journey through vividly rendered landscape and
cultural history." Libr J

"The constants in Nobel laureate Walcott's work are
the ravishing beauty of his language, his attunement to
the sensuous, his feel for the pulse of history in landscape and seascape, and his despair over the contrast between the glory of European art and the prejudice and
brutality that stoked the European conquest of the New
World." Booklist

Waldman, Anne, 1945-

In the room of never grieve; new and selected
poems, 1985-2003. Coffee House Press 2003 494p
il $30   **811**
1. Poetry—By individual authors
ISBN 978-1-566-89145-5; 1-566-89145-0
     LC 2003-55096

"If early work found [Waldman] most engaged with
the New York School, these later poems integrate her
passions for Buddhism and ethnopoetics into a unique
style of vocal, unabashedly current-event-laden,
collagistic, wide-ranging work. Waldman's quest to find
forms appropriate to her shamanistic, didactic content is
particularly compelling in Marriage: A Sentence, with its
liquefied gender roles and synthesis of influences ranging
from Stein to Corso. . . . Waldman's untiring efforts to
link language, ritual and political action come through
clearly, urgently and often beautifully." Publ Wkly

Includes bibliographical references and indexes

Warren, Robert Penn, 1905-1989

The collected poems of Robert Penn Warren;
edited by John Burt; with a foreword by Harold
Bloom. Louisiana State Univ. Press 1998 xxvi,
830p $44.95 *   **811**
1. Poetry—By individual authors
ISBN 0-8071-2333-1   LC 98-26104

"This immense volume gathers 15 books of poetry—
as well as uncollected verse from the beginning and end
of his writing life—from a formidable American man of
letters and our first poet laureate. . . . Scholars will especially cherish the careful, copious textual and explanatory notes provided by Warren's literary executor Burt
. . . and fans of American poetry and literary history
alike should welcome this opportunity to explore the prodigious oeuvre of one of the New Criticism's most forceful, convincing proponents." Publ Wkly

Whalen, Philip, 1923-2002

The collected poems of Philip Whalen; edited
by Michael Rothenberg. Weseleyan University
Press 2007 871p $49.95 *   **811**
1. Poetry—By individual authors
ISBN 978-0-8195-6859-5; 0-8195-6859-7
     LC 2007-16905

"Whalen was a Beat writer who read at the famous
Six Gallery event at which Ginsberg debuted 'Howl.' He
adored Jane Austen and Gertrude Stein, had more than
a passing knowledge of several realms of science, read
widely in ancient and modern history, and was a thoroughly cultivated gent, 'a Fat and Silly poet' who rarely
took himself seriously. He committed the last 35 years of
his life to Zen Buddhism. . . . The distinguishing features of Whalen's poetry are its playful freedom, . . . its
whizzing momentum, its offhand erudition, its quick eye,
its radar ear. But what stands out is his voice. No other
American poet sounds like Whalen, though Ginsberg in
his less vatic moments and Kerouac in his novels come
close." Phoenix

Includes bibliographical references

Wharton, Edith, 1862-1937

Selected poems; Louis Auchincloss, editor.
Library of America 2005 183p (American poets
project) $20   **811**
1. Poetry—By individual authors
ISBN 978-1-931082-86-0; 1-931082-86-3
     LC 2005-44163

"From first to last, poetry was part of Edith Wharton's
writing life. . . . Her first models were Romantic, but in
the course of her life she absorbed the influences of
Symbolism and Modernism; and throughout her poetic
career she showed a care for form even in her most private utterances, as in the erotic ode 'Terminus,' never
published in her lifetime. This volume collects the bulk
of Wharton's significant poetry, including much work
previously uncollected or unpublished." Publisher's note

Wheatley, Phillis, 1753-1784

The poems of Phillis Wheatley; edited with an
introduction by Julian D. Mason, Jr. rev & enl ed.
University of N.C. Press 1989 235p pa $22.95
hardcover o.p. *   **811**
1. Poetry—By individual authors
ISBN 0-8078-4245-1 (pa)   LC 88-23280
First published 1966

This volume contains all of the poems and letters
known to have been written by Wheatley, America's first
significant black woman writer

Whitman, Walt, 1819-1892
Complete poetry and collected prose. Library of
Am. 1982 1380p $35; pa $17.95 *   **811**
1. Poetry—By individual authors
ISBN 0-940450-02-X; 1-883011-35-3 (pa)
                              LC 81-20768
Edited by Justin Kaplan
Contents: Leaves of grass (1855); Leaves of grass
(1891-92); Complete prose works (1892); Supplementary
prose

Leaves of grass; edited and with a new
afterword by David S. Reynolds. 150th anniversary
ed. Oxford University Press 2005 167p $23 *
                                        811
1. Poetry—By individual authors
ISBN 0-19-518342-8   LC 2004-26509
Also available in paperback from Penguin Classics
and Bantam Books
First published 1855
"The book, radical in form and content, takes its title
from the themes of fertility, universality, and cyclical
life. . . . As he revised and added to the original edition,
Whitman arranged the poems in a significant autobiographical order." Reader's Ency. 4th edition

Selected poems; Harold Bloom, editor. Library
of Am. 2003 xxxi, 221p (American poets project)
$20 *   **811**
1. Poetry—By individual authors
ISBN 1-931082-32-4   LC 2002-32124
The editor "is concerned with Whitman's construction
of his all-encompassing persona, and he selects with that
in mind. . . . Bloom connects Whitman's project to the
thesis of his *The American Religion* (1992) that the tendency of religion in America is to replace God with man,
and with the fragments, Bloom presents explicit evidence
of the attempt." Booklist
Includes bibliographical references

Whittier, John Greenleaf, 1807-1892
Selected poems; Brenda Wineapple, editor.
Library of America 2004 xxvii, 187p $20
                                        811
1. Poetry—By individual authors
ISBN 978-1-931082-59-4; 1-931082-59-6
                              LC 2003-60483
"Touching and effective as [many of] these poems are,
there is a longer one that ensures Whittier's place in our
canon. Of course I have 'SnowBound' in mind. This
poem of over nine hundred lines evokes a rural way of
life, already past when it was written, in its memories of
a family isolated in their farmhouse for a week by a blizzard. . . . This new selection may not restore Whittier to
the schoolroom wall, but surely it will help readers
reassess the author of one major long poem and a score
of attractive lyrics and narratives that deserve their place
in our poetic tradition." Sewanee Rev

Wilbur, Richard, 1921-
Collected poems, 1943-2004. Harcourt 2004
608p il $35 *   **811**
1. Poetry—By individual authors
ISBN 0-15-101105-2   LC 2004-9228

A comprehensive collection of works written throughout the course of the poet's more than sixty-year career
includes "In Trackless Woods" and several new and previously unpublished pieces
"Technically, Wilbur remains assured and impressive;
he is the premier American master of formal verse. His
knowledge has expanded with his life, and his wit has
grown in humor while mellowing linguistically. . . .
He's indispensable." Booklist

Williams, C. K. (Charles Kenneth), 1936-
Collected poems. Farrar, Straus and Giroux
2006 682p $40 *   **811**
1. Poetry—By individual authors
ISBN 978-0-374-12652-0; 0-374-12652-6
                              LC 2005-51867
"This weighty, even daunting, tome shows new and
old readers the long arc of this Pulitzer Prize and National Book Award winner's career, from the morbid
sanguinities of his apprentice work to the careful, moving, stanzaic focus evident in 21 new poems." Publ Wkly

Williams, Jonathan, 1929-2008
Jubilant thicket; new & selected poems;
Jonathan Williams. Copper Canyon Press 2005 pa
$20 *   **811**
1. Poetry—By individual authors
ISBN 1-55659-202-7   LC 2004-20436
"Pared down from 1,450 works over 55 years, this selection features jaunty dances through naughty woods
. . ., jokes to and about Ezra Pound, selected listings
from the Western Carolina Telephone Company phone
book, limericks, 'meta-fours' (poems in which each line
has four words), a poem for each Mahler symphony and
acrostics using the names of friends like Guy Davenport.
. . . By the end of the book, it becomes clear that Williams can make a verse out of whatever's at hand; the
result is a kind of commonplace book for a life lived,
with wry but inextinguishable enthusiasm, in the company of artists and arts." Publ Wkly

Williams, Tennessee, 1911-1983
The collected poems of Tennessee Williams;
edited by David Roessel and Nicholas
Moschovakis. New Directions Pub 2002 xxxi,
304p il hardcover o.p. pa $18.95   **811**
1. Poetry—By individual authors
ISBN 978-0-8112-1691-3; 0-8112-1691-8
                              LC 2001-55760
Includes a CD of the author reading from his work
"In the Winter of Cities and Androgyne, Mon Amour,
the two collections Williams published in his lifetime,
are here, as are uncollected pieces, verse from his plays
and fiction, early works from the 1930s indebted to his
hero Hart Crane, and even juvenilia by 'Thos. Williams,
9th gr.'" Publ Wkly
"The painful longing and sense of loss that inhabit
Williams's plays and stories are no less present in the
poems." Oyster Boy Rev

Williams, William Carlos, 1883-1963

The collected poems of William Carlos Williams. New Directions 1986-1988 2v v1 $40; v1 pa $23.95; v2 $38; v2 pa $22.95 *

811

1. Poetry—By individual authors
ISBN 0-8112-0999-7 (v1); 0-8112-1187-8 (v1 pa); 0-8112-1063-4 (v2); 0-8112-1188-6 (v2 pa)
Contents: v1 1909-1939; edited by A. Walton Litz and Christopher MacGowan; v2 1939-1962; edited by Christopher MacGowan

"Williams's poetry is firmly rooted in the commonplace detail of everyday American life. He conceived of the poem as an object: a record of direct experience that deals with the local and the particular. He abandoned conventional rhyme and meter in an effort to reduce the barrier between the reader and his consciousness of his immediate surroundings. . . . Williams's original approach to poetry, his insistence on the importance of the ordinary, and his successful attempts at making his verse as 'tactile' as the spoken word had a far-reaching effect on American poetry." Reader's Ency. 4th edition

Paterson; prepared by Christopher MacGowan. rev ed. New Directions 1992 311p hardcover o.p. pa $15.95 *

811

1. Poetry—By individual authors
ISBN 978-0-8112-1298-4; 0-8112-1298-X

LC 92-22956

First published 1963

"Set in Paterson, N.J., the poem is a statement on contemporary civilization. Williams uses one dominant metaphor throughout: the city is the human mind beside the river of time; the language of contemporary events (the waterfall) gives the only kind of meaning possible in the flux of time. The poem is composed of lyrics, narrative episodes, prose interludes, bits of letters, etc., to comprise an ecstatic statement on human life." Herzberg. Reader's Ency of Am Lit

Winters, Yvor, 1900-1968

Selected poems; Thom Gunn, editor. Library of America 2003 xxviii, 171p (American poets project) $20

811

1. Poetry—By individual authors
ISBN 978-1-93108-250-1; 1-93108-250-2

LC 2003-46638

A volume of verse by "one of the most famous critics and teachers of his lifetime, whose poetry was then more respected than discussed. Now it seems to be some of the best from his generation of American poets. His early work . . . exemplifies imagism at its best, and it is based in the American West rather than the classical Greece that predominates in the work of H. D., the best imagist, Winters' later, formally precise poetry is elegant, allusive, profound, and rather dour, demanding careful reading and rereading and always repaying the effort. Adding immense value to this edition is the inclusion of an autobiographical story with an eerie account of self-confrontation in which Gunn sees the pivot between Winters' early and late poetic styles." Booklist

Wright, C. D.

Steal away; selected and new poems. Copper Canyon Press 2002 235p $25; pa $17 *

811

1. Poetry—By individual authors
ISBN 1-55659-172-1; 1-55659-194-2 (pa)

LC 2001-7423

Wright's "poems are crazy quilts constructed out of bits of conversation, a to-do list, dreams, a treatment for a harrowing silent film, and a saxophone solo, but Wright also offers sophisticated readings of the routines and cycle of ordinary life, and ponders the amazing persistence of the ever-hungry body and the tricky mind. It's a boon to have such a wealth of her crackling, intelligent, erotic, 'painfully beautiful,' keep-you-on-your-toes poems in one place. New works accompany selections from nine previous, mostly out of print collections, and all are electrifying in their clear-eyed reports on desire, determination, and survival." Booklist

Wright, Charles, 1935-

Appalachia. Farrar, Straus & Giroux 1998 67p hardcover o.p. pa $12

811

1. Poetry—By individual authors
ISBN 978-0-374-52624-5; 0-374-52624-9

LC 98-16803

Wright's "inquisitive poems reside at the crux of faith and art: the realization that no matter how sincerely one prays, or how devotedly one writes, the universe and the divine force that animates it remain out of reach of language, reason, and imagination. . . . Wright tries to connect with the spiritual by conjuring the ancient beaming of stars, winter's starkness, and the valor of flowers. Finally, in sweet, bemused surrender, he acknowledges both the impossibility of certainty, and our insatiable hunger for it." Booklist

Negative blue; selected later poems. Farrar, Straus & Giroux 2000 206p $23; pa $15 *

811

1. Poetry—By individual authors
ISBN 0-374-22020-4; 0-374-52773-3 (pa)

LC 99-36987

The author "collects a decade's worth of striking description and laid-back meditation in this sample of work from his last three books. . . . Wright's power lies less in whole poems than in lines within them: those linear strenghts owe something to Ezra Pound, and something more to the antiphonal balances of the Psalms. Wright ends the volume with seven new short poems." Publ Wkly

Wright, James Arlington, 1927-1980

Above the river; the complete poems; [by] James Wright; with an introduction by Donald Hall. Farrar, Straus & Giroux 1990 xxxvii, 387p hardcover o.p. pa $20 *

811

1. Poetry—By individual authors
ISBN 978-0-374-52282-7; 0-374-52282-0

LC 89-16538

"A Wesleyan University Press edition"

"The narrowed range of Wright's characteristic subjects and format, the very delicacy of his instincts, con-

Wright, James Arlington, 1927-1980—*Continued*
fine him. But his best poems, with their grace and intelligence, not only stand as a rebuke to most of the glib work of his time, but remain among the finest examples of the midcentury American lyric." N Y Times Book Rev

Wright, Jay

Transfigurations; collected poems. Louisiana State Univ. Press 2000 619p $59.95; pa $24.95 *

811

1. Poetry—By individual authors
ISBN 0-8071-2629-2; 0-8071-2630-6 (pa)

LC 00-40560

"Lyric poetry is a way of compressing experience into a heightened moment, but what happens when the experience is one of wanting not to be contained? Wright is an African-American poet who has contended with this dilemma for the last thirty years, and the result is a substantial collection of work. His forcefully musical rhythms drive even poems of everyday experience to a pleasingly contradictory transport. And the later, meditative poems are bound to the world by their attention to the sensual within the spiritual." New Yorker

Zukofsky, Louis, 1904-1978

Selected poems; Charles Bernstein, editor. Library of America 2006 xxvii, 172p $20

811

1. Poetry—By individual authors
ISBN 978-1-93108-295-2   LC 2006-40808
"Louis Zukofsky was preeminent among the radical Objectivist poets of the 1930s. This is the first collection to draw on the full range of Zukofsky's poetry—containing short lyrics, versions of Catullus, and generous selections from 'A', his 24-part 'poem of a life.'" Publisher's note
"Contemporary poet Charles Bernstein uses these pages skillfully to present a compact but diverse selection of Zukofsky's writing, and he supplies a cogent introduction to both the biography and the poetics." Tikkun

811.008   American poetry— Collections

180 more; extraordinary poems for every day; selected and with an introduction by Billy Collins. Random House 2005 xxiii, 373p pa $14.95   **811.008**
1. American poetry—Collections
ISBN 0-8129-7296-1   LC 2005-42798
Sequel to: Poetry 180
This is a second collection of 180 poems for each day of the school year, designed to expose high school students to poetry.

African-American poetry of the nineteenth century; an anthology; edited by Joan R. Sherman. University of Ill. Press 1992 506p pa $26.95 hardcover o.p.   **811.008**
1. American poetry—African American authors—Collections
ISBN 0-252-06246-9 (pa)   LC 91-41709

Companion to Sherman's Invisible poets (1989)
"The introduction surveys the historical and cultural values of African American poetry. The poems themselves have historical as well as lyric value; unfamiliar as well as familiar poets are included. Though the poems are formal, the rhymes are generally unforced. . . . This anthology also includes an extensive bibliography to help researchers find other resources." Libr J

American poetry: the nineteenth century; edited by John Hollander. Library of Am. 1993 2v ea $35 *   **811.008**
1. American poetry—Collections
ISBN 0-940450-60-7 (v1); 0-940450-78-X (v2)

LC 93-10702

Volume 1 also available in paperback $14.95 (ISBN 1-88301-136-1)
Contents: v1 Freneau to Whitman; v2 Melville to Stickney; American Indian poetry; Folk songs and spirituals
An anthology of more than 1,000 poems by nearly 150 poets. Arrangement is chronological by poet's date of birth. Biographical sketches of the poets, a chronology of significant events from 1800 to 1900, and an essay on textual selection are included
Hollander has compiled "a selection of nineteenth-century American verse so wonderfully catholic that it not just augments but supersedes every other similar collection." Booklist

American poetry, the twentieth century. Library of Am. 2000 2v ea $35 *   **811.008**
1. American poetry—Collections
ISBN 1-88301-177-9 (v1); 1-88301-178-7 (v2)

LC 99-43721

The first two volumes of a projected four volume set
Contents: v1 Henry Adams to Dorothy Parker; v2 E.E. Cummings to May Swenson
"Over 200 poets are represented, all born before 1914, and presented in birth-date order." Publ Wkly
These volumes represent a "remarkable feat of assemblage, with excellent capsule biographies and explanatory notes at the end of each volume—the biographies, especially, are well worth reading." N Y Times Book Rev
Includes bibliographical references

American religious poems; an anthology by Harold Bloom; Harold Bloom and Jesse Zuba, editors. Library of America 2006 685p $40   **811.008**
1. American poetry—Collections 2. Religious poetry
ISBN 1-931082-74-X   LC 2006-41031
An anthology of "verse on Christian, Jewish, Islamic, Buddhist, Native American spiritual, Transcendentalist and even agnostic themes, from 17th-century European colonists (one poet is Roger Williams, who founded Rhode Island) to up-and-comers in contemporary verse. Pious readers will have no trouble finding high-quality poetry that confirms their beliefs—from the monk Thomas Merton, the Anglican T.S. Eliot, the Jewish liturgical poet Esther Schor and the Louisiana-based Christian poet Martha Serpas. Yet from the 19th century to the present, from the decidedly heterodox Emily Dickinson forwards, the anthology often highlights the ways in which American spirituality has challenged all doctrines about who

American religious poems—*Continued*
God is and what God does. . . . More than half of the
book is taken up by 20th-century poets, who offer varied
takes on what religion has come to mean in America."
Publ Wkly

American war poetry; an anthology; edited by
Lorrie Goldensohn. Columbia University Press
2006 413p $27.95 *   **811.008**
1. War poetry 2. American poetry—Collections
ISBN 0-231-13310-3   LC 2005-54762
"Arranged by war, the book begins with the Colonial
period and proceeds through Whitman admiring Civil
War soldiers crossing a river to end with Brian Turner,
who published his first book in 2005, beckoning a bullet
in contemporary Iraq. Many voices, by turns elegiac, out-
raged, rhetorical and ecstatic are represented." Publ Wkly
Includes bibliographical references

American wits; an anthology of light verse; John
Hollander, editor. Library of America 2003 xxv,
194p (American poets project) $20
                                       811.008
1. American poetry—Collections 2. Humorous poetry—Collections
ISBN 978-1-931082-49-5; 1-931082-49-9
                                       LC 2003-46636
This anthology "offers some exceptionally clever writing, much of which will be unfamiliar to many readers
(and therefore all the more amusing). Hollander sensibly
allots the most space to Ogden Nash and Dorothy Parker;
the selections from both are solid. But Hollander's good
judgment is best demonstrated by the third most represented poet here, the screenwriter Samuel Hoffenstein
(1890-1947). . . . The poetry world currently has a sur-
plus of writers who are eager, sometimes even desperate,
to be funny, but we're suffering from a shortage of genuine wit." Poetry (Modern Poetry Association)

Beat poets; selected and edited by Carmela
Ciuraru. Knopf 2002 250p (Everyman's library
pocket poets) $12.50   **811.008**
1. Beat generation 2. American poetry—Collections
ISBN 978-0-375-41332-2; 0-375-41332-4
                                       LC 2002-510236
"The defining work of Allen Ginsberg and Jack
Kerouac provides the foundation for this collection,
which also features statements on Beat poetics, selections
from the alternately ardent, incendiary, and earnest correspondence of Beat Generation writers, and the improvisational verse of such Beat legends as Robert Creeley, Diane Di Prima, Gregory Corso, Denise Levertov, Lawrence Ferlinghetti, Philip Whalen, Bob Kaufman, and Peter Orlovsky, along with the work of other women writers and the lesser-known poets of this school." Publisher's note

The **best** American poetry 2008; Charles Wright,
editor; David Lehman, series editor. Scribner
2008 224p $35; pa $16   **811.008**
1. American poetry—Collections
ISSN 1040-5763
ISBN 978-0-7432-9974-9; 978-0-7432-9975-6 (pa)
An annual collection of American verse culled from
large-circulation magazines and smaller literary reviews.

"This is a fun, varied, and generous collection of poems by 75 poets at various stages in their writing lives,
all of whom will inspire a wide spectrum of poetry lovers." Booklist
Includes bibliographical references

Blues poems; selected and edited by Kevin Young.
Knopf 2003 256p (Everyman's library pocket
poets) $12.50   **811.008**
1. Blues music—Poetry 2. American poetry—Collections
ISBN 978-0-375-41458-9; 0-375-41458-4
                                       LC 2003-53149
A collection of "blues-influenced and blues-inflected
poems from, among others, Gwendolyn Brooks, Allen
Ginsberg, June Jordan, Richard Wright, Nikki Giovanni,
Charles Wright, Yusef Komunyakaa, and Cornelius Eady.
And here, too, are classic song lyrics—poems in their
own right—from Bessie Smith, Robert Johnson, Ma Rainey, and Muddy Waters." Publisher's note

Every shut eye ain't asleep; an anthology of
poetry by African Americans since 1945; edited
by Michael Harper and Anthony Walton. Little,
Brown 1994 327p pa $19 hardcover o.p.
                                       811.008
1. American poetry—African American authors—Collections
ISBN 0-316-34710-8 (pa)   LC 93-10788
"Using Robert Hayden and Gwendolyn Brooks's poetry as 'emblematic' successes, this anthology selects 35
African American poets (spanning three generations) who
were born between 1913 and 1962 and came of age after
1945. Besides the well-known Imamu Baraka, Lucille
Clifton, Rita Dove, and Etheridge Knight, the editors feature little-known or younger poets like Elizabeth Alexander, Gerald Barrax, Jayne Cortex, and Dolores
Kendrick." Libr J

From totems to hip-hop; edited by Ishmael Reed.
Thunder's Mouth Press 2003 xxx, 523p $34.95;
pa $17.95   **811.008**
1. American poetry—Collections
ISBN 1-56025-500-5; 1-56025-458-0 (pa)
                                       LC 2002-75691
"Reed's selections range from classic poems like Carl
Sandburg's 'Chicago' to contemporary texts like Tupac
Shakur's 'Why Must U Be Unfaithful (4 women).'
Along the way, readers will encounter familiar names
like Marianne Moore, Claude McKay, Robert Frost, and
T.S. Eliot but will also find less anthologized writers like
Agha Shahid Ali, Bessie Smith, Speckled Red, Lorna
Dee Cervantes, Haki Madhubuti, and the rock'n'roll
composers Jerry Leiber and Mike Stoller." Libr J
This is "a dynamic and original anthology, an unprec-
edented amalgam of poets representing many facets of
American culture and society." Booklist

Good poems; selected and introduced by Garrison
Keillor. Viking 2002 xxvi, 476p $25.95; pa $15
                                       811.008
1. American poetry—Collections 2. English poetry—
Collections
ISBN 0-670-03126-7; 0-14-200344-1 (pa)
                                       LC 2002-16881

Good poems—*Continued*

Keillor "has put together a collection of close to 300 poems he has read during . . . [the] PBS broadcast, The Writer's Almanac. . . . Poems are arranged by 19 general themes, such as 'Snow,' 'Failure,' and 'A Good Life.' Authors range from well-known oldies like Emily Dickinson and Robert Frost to unknowns like C.K. Williams. . . . An outstanding feature of this collection is that the selections are all so accessible—even folks who say they don't like poetry can find something here to enjoy." SLJ

Harper's anthology of 20th century Native American poetry; edited by Duane Niatum. Harper & Row 1988 xxxii, 396p pa $24.95 hardcover o.p. **811.008**

1. American poetry—Native American authors
ISBN 0-06-250666-8 (pa)   LC 86-45023

This collection "contains the work of 36 native American poets, with hearty selections from each. Among the 36 are poets near the mainstream (Scott Momaday, James Welch, Louise Erdrich); those in academe (Gerald Vizenor, Linda Hogan, Jim Barnes); those writing in the tribal oral tradition (Barney Bush, Peter Blue Cloud, Wendy Rose); and those working in a modernist voice (Gladys Cardiff, Paula Gunn Allen). This book belongs in every collection that claims to represent the multiple voices of American literature today." Booklist

Includes bibliographical references

Jazz poems. Alfred A. Knopf 2006 256p (Everyman's library pocket poets) $12.50 **811.008**

1. Jazz music—Poetry 2. American poetry—Collections
ISBN 978-1-4000-4251-7; 1-4000-4251-8

A collection of poetry inspired by jazz music. Includes poems by Langston Hughes, E. E. Cummings, William Carlos Williams, Frank O'Hara, Gwendolyn Brooks, Yusef Komunyakaa, Charles Simic, Rita Dove, Ntozake Shange, Mark Doty, William Matthews, and C. D. Wright, among others.

The **Oxford** anthology of African-American poetry; edited by Arnold Rampersad; associate editor, Hilary Herbold. Oxford University Press 2006 432p $32.50 * **811.008**

1. American poetry—African American authors—Collections
ISBN 0-19-512563-0; 978-0-19-512563-4
                                          LC 2005-15242

"Predicated on the fact that there is a vast body of poetry written by gifted black poets, this . . . anthology tells the story of African American culture and explicates its crucial role within the larger literary tradition. . . . There is much to admire about the artistry of the poems, and even more to discover about the African American experience." Booklist

The **Oxford** book of American poetry; chosen and edited by David Lehman; associate editor, John Brehm. Oxford University Press 2006 lvii, 1132p $35 * **811.008**

1. American poetry—Collections
ISBN 0-19-516251-X; 978-0-19-516251-6
                                          LC 2005-36590

First published 1950 with title: The Oxford book of American verse

This is an anthology of "American poetry from its origins in the 17th century right up to the present." Publisher's note

"The book is not only a sound historical survey, but also gives the reader a powerful taste of poetry's impact upon the wider world." Economist

Includes bibliographical references

Poetry 180; a turning back to poetry; selected and with an introduction by Billy Collins. Random House Trade Paperbacks 2003 xxiv, 323p pa $13.95   **811.008**

1. American poetry—Collections
ISBN 0-8129-6887-5   LC 2002-36949
Also available online

The editor "has collected 180 accessible modern poems: one for each day of the school year and together signifying a 180° turning back to poetry. These are poems, he says, you can 'get' the first time around, and he hopes that high schools will expose students to a poem a day via public address system or assemblies. A fine gathering of contemporary poets." Libr J

Includes bibliographical references

The **Poetry** anthology, 1912-2002; ninety years of America's most distinguished verse magazine; edited by Joseph Parisi & Stephen Young; with an introduction by Joseph Parisi. Ivan R. Dee 2002 lv, 509p $29.95; pa $16.95
                                          811.008

1. American poetry—Collections
ISBN 1-56663-468-7; 1-56663-604-3 (pa)
                                          LC 2002-31178

A collection of 600 poems previously published in Poetry magazine, written by such poets as W.H. Auden, Elizabeth Bishop, Sylvia Plath, James Merrill, and Susan Hahn

This is a "comprehensive and thrilling anthology, a veritable history of twentieth-century poetry in English." Booklist

The **Poetry** of black America; anthology of the 20th century; introduction by Gwendolyn Brooks. Harper & Row 1973 xxxi, 552p $25.95
                                          811.008

1. American poetry—African American authors—Collections
ISBN 0-06-020089-8   LC 72-76518

A collection of over 600 poems by 145 authors. James Weldon Johnson, Paul Laurence Dunbar, Langston Hughes, Gwendolyn Brooks, Sonia Sanchez, Don Lee and Nikki Giovanni are among the poets represented. Biographical sketches are provided

Poetry speaks expanded; hear poets from Tennyson to Plath read their own work; Elise Paschen & Rebekah Presson Mosby, editors; Charles Osgood, narrator. [2nd ed.] Sourcebooks 2007 384p il $49.95   **811.008**

1. American poetry—Collections 2. English poetry—Collections
ISBN 978-1-4022-1062-4; 1-4022-1062-0
                                          LC 2007-37080

Poetry speaks expanded—*Continued*

First published 2001 with title: Poetry speaks

Includes 3 audio CDs

"Each of the 47 poets, all deceased, is introduced through a biographical sketch, an essay by a contemporary poet, the text of a few representative poems and . . . select recordings." SLJ

"Reluctant poetry readers may find themselves drawn to the printed page by the spoken work, and poetry fans are likely to find much to love here." Publ Wkly

Poets of the Civil War; J.D. McClatchy, editor. Library of America 2005 211p il (American poets project, 14) $20   **811.008**

1. United States—History—1861-1865, Civil War—Poetry 2. American poetry—Collections

ISBN 978-1-93108-276-1; 1-93208-276-6

LC 2004-61552

"The poems wisely selected represent not only the main kinds of responses to the war but also the radically conflicting sympathies of the poets—with the Union cause or with the Confederacy—and the important postwar theme of reconciliation of North and South. McClatchy's selection has not only breadth of representation but fine choices within forms, causes, and poets." Sewanee Rev

Poets of World War II; Harvey Shapiro, editor. Library of Am. 2003 xxxii, 262p (American poets project) $20 *   **811.008**

1. World War, 1939-1945—Poetry

ISBN 1-931082-33-2   LC 2002-32125

The editor's "objective is to show that the American *poets* of the Second *World War* were as significant as their English counterparts in the first one, if different in tone. Even at their most biting, Siegfried Sassoon and Wilfred Owen struck a heroic note, penning anthems for 'doomed youth' and the destruction of innocence. . . . But those who survived battles of the second conflict to become important *poets* avoided the attempt to sound noble, or to celebrate fallen comrades. . . . Shapiro, a B-17 gunner, takes pains to show the spectrum of opinion that actually existed and how it evolved." New Leader

Includes bibliographical references

Twentieth-century American poetry; edited by Dana Gioia, David Mason, Meg Schoerke. McGraw Hill 2004 xlvi, 1143p il pa $79.69   **811.008**

1. American poetry—Collections

ISBN 0-07-240019-6   LC 2003-61449

"The text is divided into sections like 'Realism and Naturalism' and 'The Harlem Renaissance,' with each section prefaced by a penetrating overview and each poet introduced by a biographical essay. Included are poets as diverse as Sherman Alexie, Ezra Pound, and Lucille Clifton, along with Nuyorican poets, New Formalists, Beats, imagists, and surrealists. Make room for this affordable, remarkable volume." Libr J

Includes bibliographical references

The **Vintage** book of African American poetry; edited and with an introduction by Michael S. Harper and Anthony Walton. Vintage Bks. 2000 xxxiii, 403p pa $14.95   **811.008**

1. American poetry—African American authors—Collections

ISBN 0-375-70300-4   LC 99-39428

"A Vintage original"

"Included in chronological order here are over two centuries of poets, from Jupiter Hammon (1720-1800) to Reginald Shepherd (b.1963). . . . The editors' eloquent, outspoken vision provides a springboard for further examination of what constitutes the mainstream of American poetry." Libr J

Includes bibliographical references

"**Words** for the hour"; a new anthology of American Civil War poetry; edited by Faith Barrett and Cristanne Miller. University of Massachusetts Press 2005 xxx, 401p il lib bdg $80; pa $27.95   **811.008**

1. American poetry—Collections 2. War poetry 3. United States—History—1861-1865, Civil War—Poetry

ISBN 1-55849-510-X (lib bdg); 1-55849-509-6 (pa)

LC 2005-18477

For this collection, the editors "limit their selection to work written between 1834 and 1891 by poets who lived through and often actively participated in antebellum, wartime, and aftermath events. . . . An interpretational, literary, and documentary monument." Booklist

Includes bibliographical references

811.009   American poetry—History and criticism

The **Columbia** history of American poetry; Jay Parini, editor; Brett C. Millier, associate editor. Columbia Univ. Press 1993 xxxi, 894p $86.50   **811.009**

1. American poetry—History and criticism

ISBN 0-231-07836-6   LC 92-29399

"These 31 essays by various experts in the field interrogate, dismantle, and ultimately reassemble the history of poetry in the United States, from the work of the slave George Moses Horton . . . to the writings of Beat, Black Arts, and Marxist-oriented Language Poets of today. The great figures of the past—Whitman, Poe, Eliot, and so on—still loom, yet each time we are made to see them in some new way. . . . An essential volume that shows how poetry intersects with our lives and vice versa." Libr J

Includes bibliographical references

Encyclopedia of American poetry, the twentieth century; edited by Eric L. Haralson. Fitzroy Dearborn Pubs. 2001 846p $125   **811.009**

1. American poetry—Bio-bibliography 2. Poets, American—Dictionaries

ISBN 1-57958-240-0

"The volume features more than 400 entries written by academic contributors on individual poets, landmark po-

Encyclopedia of American poetry, the twentieth century—*Continued*

ems, and major topics. The poet entries are usually 1,000 to 2,000 words long and offer critical treatment of the poet's career and major achievements along with a capsule biography. . . . Approximately one-third of the poet entries include subentries for one or more landmark poems. The 'major topics' entries are longer (around 3,000 words) and include periods or movements (*Black Arts movement, Dada*), verse traditions (often ethnic, such as *Asian American poetry*), and styles and themes (*Confessional poetry, War and antiwar poetry*)." Booklist

Fagan, Deirdre

Critical companion to Robert Frost; a literary reference to his life and work. Facts on File 2007 454p il $75 **811.009**
   1. Frost, Robert, 1874-1963
   ISBN 0-8160-6182-3; 978-0-8160-6182-2
   LC 2006-13269
"This encyclopedic guide offers critical entries on each of Frost's published poems, including such classics as 'The Road Not Taken,' 'Stopping By Woods on a Snowy Evening,' and 'The Death of the Hired Man.'" Publisher's note
Includes bibliographical references

Kenner, Hugh

The Pound era. University of Calif. Press 1971 606p il hardcover o.p. pa $26.95 *
811.009
   1. Pound, Ezra, 1885-1972
   ISBN 978-0-520-02427-4; 0-520-02427-3
"A detailed account of Pound's career from the viewpoint of ideas, movements, and personalities of his age. A main theme of the book is that to Pound and his era, ages and cultures share in a basic continuity. . . . Vorticism, imagism, social credit, China—all receive detailed new treatment as the author probes their impact on Pound's work." Libr J
"As a reader of Pound, Kenner is superb. He moves with ease and authority through the most tangled passages of allusion, ideogram and fragments of Greek and Latin." N Y Times Book Rev
Includes bibliographical references

Leiter, Sharon

Critical companion to Emily Dickinson; a literary reference to her life and work. Facts on File 2006 448p il $75 **811.009**
   1. Dickinson, Emily, 1830-1886
   ISBN 0-8160-5448-7; 978-0-8160-5448-0
   LC 2005-28123
This book "opens with a foreword by poet and Dickinson scholar Gregory Orr and includes an introduction; an approximately 20-page biography of Dickinson; explications of 150 of her best-known poems (e.g., 'Because I Could Not Stop for Death'); an A-to-Z dictionary of relevant persons, places, and ideas illustrated with black-and-white photos; a chronology; bibliographies; and a comprehensive index." Libr J
Includes bibliographical references

MacGowan, Christopher J. (Christopher John)

Twentieth-century American poetry; [by] Christopher MacGowan. Blackwell Pub 2004 331p (Blackwell guides to literature) $66.95; pa $27.95
811.009
   1. American poetry—History and criticism
   ISBN 0-631-22025-9; 0-631-22026-7 (pa)
   LC 2003-12196
This guide explores the historical and cultural contexts within which twentieth-century American poetry was created and includes a biographical dictionary of such key writers as Robert Frost, Ezra Pound, T. S. Eliot, Langston Hughes, James Dickey, Adrienne Rich, and Rita Dove
Includes bibliographical references

Murphy, Russell E.

Critical companion to T.S. Eliot; a literary reference to his life and work; [by] Russell Elliott Murphy. Facts On File 2007 614p il (Facts on File library of American literature) $75
811.009
   1. Eliot, T. S. (Thomas Stearns), 1888-1965
   ISBN 978-0-8160-6183-9; 0-8160-6183-1
   LC 2006-34076
This book "explores the life and works of this Nobel Prize-winning writer, with . . . analyses of Eliot's writing, as well as entries on related topics and relevant people, places, and influences." Publisher's note
"This is an excellent and exhaustive resource and a good buy for most libraries." Booklist
Includes bibliographical references

Oliver, Charles M.

Critical companion to Walt Whitman; a literary reference to his life and work. Facts on File 2005 408p il (Facts on File library of American literature) $65 **811.009**
   1. Whitman, Walt, 1819-1892
   ISBN 0-8160-5768-0 LC 2005-4172
The author "begins this work with a biographical essay that includes several illustrations. A large portion of this book addresses Whitman's works, with entries for the individual poems and for the complete volumes. Each entry describes when and where the book was published and includes a brief account of the poem and its context. The third section of the volume covers people, places, publications, and topics related to Whitman's life and work." Choice
Includes bibliographical references

Pinsky, Robert

Democracy, culture, and the voice of poetry. Princeton Univ. Press 2002 96p (University Center for Human Values series) $29.95; pa $12.95
811.009
   1. American poetry—History and criticism
   ISBN 0-691-09617-1; 0-691-12263-6 (pa)
   LC 2002-25288
This is an "analysis of the way the intimate rhythms of American poetry invoke a social presence. Pinsky, a former poet laureate, passionately argues that American

Pinsky, Robert—*Continued*
poetry is driven by the anxiety of being forgotten; the
solitary poet makes us aware of the presence of others
as he yearns for their approval while striving to preserve
his uniqueness." N Y Times Book Rev

812   American drama

Albee, Edward, 1928-
Who's afraid of Virginia Woolf? Scribner
Classics 2003 243p $24 *   **812**
   ISBN 0-7432-5525-9   LC 2003-54206
Also available in paperback from Dramatists Play Ser-
vice and Signet Bks.
A reissue of the title first published 1962 by
Atheneum Pubs.
Characters: 2 men, 2 women. 3 acts. First produced at
the Billy Rose Theatre, New York City, October 13,
1962
"The play is a virulent unveiling of the relationship
between George, a history professor, and his wife, Martha, the college president's daughter. Another couple,
Nick and Honey, get caught in the crossfire of George
and Martha's verbal and emotional lacerations, and it becomes clear that each character is engaged in an isolated
struggle through a personal hell." Reader's Ency. 4th edition

Auburn, David
Proof; a play. Faber & Faber 2001 83p pa $13
                                                 812
   ISBN 0-571-19997-6   LC 00-50284
Also available in paperback from Dramatists Play Service
Characters: 2 men, 2 women. 2 acts, 9 scenes. First
produced by the Manhattan Theatre Club, New York
City, May 23, 2000
"Twenty-five-year-old Catherine, who sacrificed college to care for her mentally ill father (once a brilliant,
much-admired mathematician), is left in a kind of limbo
after his death. Socially awkward and a bit of a shut-in,
she is gruff with Hal, a former student who shows up
even before the funeral wanting to root through the
countless notebooks her father kept in the years of his
decline, hoping to find mathematical gold. On the heels
of his arrival comes Claire, Catherine's cosmopolitan,
blandly successful, and pushy sister, with plans to sell
their father's house and take Catherine . . . with her
back to New York." SLJ
Includes bibliographical references and index

Baraka, Imamu Amiri, 1934-
Dutchman, and The slave; two plays; [by]
LeRoi Jones. Morrow 1964 88p hardcover o.p. pa
$9.95   **812**
   ISBN 978-0-688-21084-7; 0-688-21084-8
In Dutchman Baraka "explores the revolutionary po-
tential of the educated black middle-class intellectual,
represented by the protagonist, Clay, a would-be poet.
When Clay is exposed as dangerous—that is, as a latent
killer—by white society, seductively imaged as a beauti-
ful white woman named Lula, he is summarily executed

by that society. *The Slave* (1964), a fable set in a future
of war between the races, continues the theme of black
revolutionary militancy." Benet's Reader's Ency of Am
Lit

Cruz, Nilo
Anna in the tropics. Theatre Communications
Group 2003 84p pa $12.95   **812**
   ISBN 1-55936-232-4   LC 2003-15859
Characters: 5 men, 3 women. 2 acts, 10 scenes. First
produced at the New Theatre, Coral Gables, Florida, October 12, 2002
"Set in a cigar factory in Tampa, Florida, in 1929,
where the Cuban-American employees have just hired a
new 'lector' to read novels to them while they work,
Anna and the Tropics is written in the lyrical, somewhat
formalized parlance of a folktale. The play is both a
piece of cultural history and a warm-spirited tribute to
the transformative power of art." Time

Edson, Margaret
Wit; a play. Faber & Faber 1999 85p pa $13
                                                 812
   ISBN 0-571-19877-5   LC 99-11921
Also available in paperback from Dramatists Play Ser-
vice
Characters: 3 men, 3 women, extras. First produced at
Long Wharf Theatre, New Haven, Connecticut, October
31, 1997
Drama about English literature professor and Donne
scholar hospitalized with advanced ovarian cancer.

Foote, Horton
Collected plays. v2. Smith & Kraus 1996 216p
hardcover o.p. pa $19.95   **812**
   ISBN 978-1-57525-019-9; 1-57525-019-5
Also available volume I: 4 new plays and volume III:
Getting Frankie married—and afterwards, and other plays
"Contemporary playwrights series"
Contents: The trip to Bountiful; The chase; The travel-
ing lady; The roads to home
"Foote's ear for naturalistic dialogue never fails him,
and even in the midst of telling an exciting story . . . he
never lets the potential for melodrama overwhelm
things." Booklist

Gardner, Herb, 1934-2003
Herb Gardner: the collected plays and the
screenplay Who is Harry Kellerman and why is he
saying those terrible things about me? Applause
Theatre Bk. Pubs. 2000 489p il $27.95; pa $16.95
                                                 812
   ISBN 1-55783-394-X; 1-55783-466-0 (pa)
Contents: Thousand clowns; Goodbye people; Thieves;
I'm not Rappaport; Conversations with my father; Who
is Harry Kellerman and why is he saying those terrible
things about me?
These works "have furnished star actors with some of
their most memorable roles and star directors with some
of their biggest successes. Those favors are returned by
the likes of Jason Robards, Judd Hirsch, Elaine May,
Charles Grodin, and Dustin Hoffman, who introduce the
plays that brightened their reputations." Booklist

Gibson, William, 1914-

The miracle worker. Pocket Books 2002 120p
pa $5.99 *   **812**
  1. Keller, Helen, 1880-1968—Drama 2. Sullivan,
Anne, 1866-1936—Drama
  ISBN 0-7434-5758-7; 978-0-7434-5758-3
  First published 1957
  Dramatic portrayal of relationship between Helen Keller and her teacher Anne Sullivan.
  "The present text is meant for reading, and differs
from the telecast version in that I have restored some
passages that read better than they play and others omitted in performance for simple lack of time." Author's
note

Goodrich, Frances, 1891-1984

The diary of Anne Frank; by Frances Goodrich
and Albert Hackett; newly adapted by Wendy
Kesselman. Dramatists Play Service 2000 70p il pa
$7.50   **812**
  1. Netherlands—History—1940-1945, German occupation—Drama 2. World War, 1939-1945—Jews—Drama
  ISBN 0-8222-1718-X   LC 2006-455205
  First published 1956 by Random House
  Characters: 5 men, 5 women. 2 acts. First produced at
the Cort Theatre, New York City, October 5, 1955.
  Dramatization of Anne Frank: diary of a young girl.
Portrays ultimately unsuccessful attempt of Jewish family
to remain hidden during the German occupation of Holland.

Guare, John

Six degrees of separation; a play. Random
House 1990 120p pa $12.95 hardcover o.p.
                                                   812
  ISBN 0-679-73481-3 (pa)   LC 90-53449
  Also available in paperback from Dramatists Play Ser-
vice
  Characters: 13 men, 4 women. First produced at the
Mitzi Newhouse Theater, New York City, June 1990
  Satirical look at contemporary urban America.
Upscale, liberal New York City couple is manipulated by
young black man.

Gurney, A. R., 1930-

Love letters and two other plays: The golden
age and What I did last summer; with an
introduction by the playwright. Penguin Bks. 1990
209p pa $14   **812**
  ISBN 978-0-452-26501-1; 0-452-16501-0
                        LC 90-34177
  "A Plume book"
  Love letters dramatizes the 30-year epistolary "exchange between an upper-class man and an upper-upper-
class woman. . . . The Golden Age is an updated, ro-
mantic-comic variation upon Henry James' Aspern Papers in which a young academic locates an old woman
who may possess a missing chapter of The Great Gatsby
and schemes to get it from her. What I did Last Summer
is about 14-year-old Charlie's bohemian season with
Anna, the Pig Woman, who fosters his creativity as she
once did his mother's." Booklist

Hansberry, Lorraine, 1930-1965

A raisin in the sun. Modern Lib. 1995 xxvi,
135p $14.95; pa $6.50 *   **812**
  ISBN 0-679-60172-4; 0-679-75533-0 (pa)
                        LC 95-16074
  Also available in paperback from Plume Bks.
  First published 1959
  Characters: 8 men, 3 women. 6 scenes in 3 acts. First
produced at the Ethel Barrymore Theatre, New York
City, March 11, 1959
  "Hansberry's drama focuses on the Youngers, a 1950s
African-American working-class family in Chicago striv-
ing to realize their individual dreams of prosperity and
education, and their collective dream of a better life. It
was the first play by an African-American woman to be
produced on Broadway." Reader's Ency. 4th edition

Hughes, Langston, 1902-1967

Five plays; edited with an introduction by
Webster Smalley. Indiana Univ. Press 1963 258p
hardcover o.p. pa $14.95   **812**
  ISBN 0-253-32230-8; 0-253-20121-7 (pa)
  Contents: Mulatto; Soul gone home; Little Ham; Sim-
ply heavenly; Tambourines to glory

Inge, William, 1913-1973

4 plays. Grove Press 1979 c1958 304p pa $16
                                                   812
  ISBN 0-8021-3209-X   LC 78-73032
  "A Black cat book"
  First published 1958 by Random House
  Contents: Come back, Little Sheba; Picnic; Bus stop;
The dark at the top of the stairs

Kaufman, George S., 1889-1961

Kaufman & Co.; Broadway comedies; [by]
George S. Kaufman with Edna Ferber [et al.]
Library of America 2004 911p (Library of
America) $35 *   **812**
  ISBN 1-931082-67-7   LC 2004044200
  Contents: The royal family, by George S. Kaufman
and Edna Ferber — Animal crackers, by George S.
Kaufman and Morrie Ryskind; music and lyrics by Bert
Kalmar and Harry Ruby — June moon, by Ring Lardner
and George S. Kaufman — Once in a lifetime, by Moss
Hart and George S. Kaufman — Of thee I sing, by
George S. Kaufman and Morrie Ryskind; music and lyr-
ics by George and Ira Gershwin — Dinner at Eight, by
George S. Kaufman and Edna Ferber — Stage Door, by
Edna Ferber and George S. Kaufman — You can't take
it with you, by Moss Hart and George S. Kaufman —
The man who came to dinner, by Moss Hart and George
S. Kaufman
  This compilation includes "Animal Crackers . . . a lit-
tle-known version that was found among Groucho
Marx's personal papers and published here for the first
time." Libr J

Kushner, Tony

Angels in America; a gay fantasia on national themes. 1st combined pbk. ed. Theatre Communications Group 2003 289p pa $15.95

812

1. Cohn, Roy, 1927-1986—Drama
ISBN 1-55936-231-6   LC 2003-17904
Contents: pt. 1. Millennium approaches — pt. 2. Perestroika

Millennium approaches first presented at the Eureka Theatre Company, San Francisco, May 1991. Perestroika first presented at the Mark Taper Forum, Los Angeles, November 1992.

A look at the political, sexual and religious aspects of contemporary American life set against the AIDS epidemic and the life of Roy Cohn.

Lawrence, Jerome, 1915-2004

Inherit the wind; [by] Jerome Lawrence and Robert E. Lee. Ballantine Books trade pbk. ed. Ballantine Books 2007 129p pa $9.95

812

1. Evolution—Study and teaching—Drama
ISBN 978-0-345-50103-5; 0-345-50103-9
LC 2007-281039
Characters: 23 men, 7 women. 3 acts 5 scenes. First produced at the National Theater, New York City, April 21, 1955

A drama based on the Scopes Monkey Trial of 1925, in which a Tennessee teacher was tried for teaching evolution

Mamet, David

Glengarry Glen Ross; a play. Grove Press 1984 108p pa $14   **812**
ISBN 978-0-8021-3091-4; 0-8021-3091-7
LC 83-49380
Characters: 7 men. 2 acts, 4 scenes. First produced at The Cottlesoe Theatre, London, England, September 21, 1983

A "comedy is about smalltime, cutthroat real esate salesmen trying to grind out a living by pushing plots of land on reluctant buyers in a never-ending scramble for their fair share of the American dream." Publisher's note

Speed-the-plow. Grove Press 1988 82p (An Evergreen bk) pa $13   **812**
ISBN 978-0-8021-3046-4; 0-8021-3046-1
LC 87-7252
Characters: 2 men 1 woman. 3 acts. First produced on Broadway at the Royale Theater, May 3, 1988

"A brilliant black comedy, a dazzling dissection of Hollywood cupidity and another tone poem by our foremost master of the language of moral epilepsy. . . . On its deepest level it belongs with the darker disclosures of movie-biz pathology like Nathanael West's The Day of the Locust and F. Scott Fitzgerald's The Last Tycoon. In a sense Speed-the-Plow distills all of these to a stark quintessence: there's hardly a line in it that isn't somehow insanely funny or scarily insane." Newsweek

McCullers, Carson, 1917-1967

The member of the wedding; a play; an introduction by Dorothy Allison. New Directions 2006 118p pa $11.95 *   **812**
ISBN 0-8112-1655-1; 978-0-8112-1655-5
LC 2005-36493
First published 1951
Characters: 6 men, 7 women. 3 acts with 3 scenes in the last act. First produced at the Empire Theatre, New York City, January 3, 1950

Based on the author's book of the same title, this is "a study of the loneliness of an overimaginative young Georgian girl." Saturday Rev

Miller, Arthur, 1915-2005

Collected plays, 1944-1961. Library of America 2006 774p $35 *   **812**
ISBN 978-1-931082-91-4; 1-931082-91-X
LC 2005-49442
Contents: Man who had all the luck; All my sons; Death of a salesman; Enemy of the people; Crucible; Memory of two Mondays; View from the bridge (one act version); View from the bridge (two act version); Misfits (screenplay)

Norman, Marsha

Collected plays. v1. Smith & Kraus 1998 412p (Contemporary playwrights series) pa $19.95

812

ISBN 1-57525-029-2   LC 97-7665
Spine title: Collected works, volume 1
Contents: Getting out; Third and Oak; Circus Valentine; The holdup; Traveler in the dark; Sarah and Abraham; Loving Daniel Boone; Three speeches

Norman's "characters, whether they be performers in a struggling two-bit circus, women in an all-night laundromat, or a Western outlaw, are ones we can easily identify with and understand." Libr J

O'Neil, Eugene, 1888-1953

Complete plays; edited by Travis Bogard. Literary Classics of the United States 1988 3v (Library of America) v1 $40; v2 $40; v3 $35

812

ISBN 978-0-940450-48-6 (v1); 978-0-940450-49-3 (v2); 978-0-940450-50-9 (v3)
Contents: [v 1] 1913-1920: A wife for life; The web; Thirst; Recklessness; Warnings; Fog; Bread and butter; Bound east for Cardiff; Abortion; The movie man; Servitude; The sniper; The personal equation; Before breakfast; Now I ask you; In the zone; Ile; The long voyage home; The moon of the Caribbees; The rope; Beyond the horizon; Shell shock; The dreamy kid; Where the cross is made; The straw; Chris Christophersen; Gold; Anna Christie; The Emperor Jones

[v2] 1920-1931: Diff'rent; The first man; The hairy ape; The fountain; Welded; All God's chillun got wings; Desire under the elms; Marco Millions; The great god Brown; Lazarus laughed; Strange interlude; Dynamo; Mourning becomes Electra

[v3] 1932-1943: Ah, wilderness; Days without end; A touch of the poet; More stately mansions; The iceman cometh; Long day's journey into night; Hughie; A moon for the misbegotten. Appendix: Tomorrow (short story)

Parks, Suzan-Lori

Topdog/underdog. Theatre Communications Group 2001 110p pa $12.95 **812**

ISBN 1-55936-201-4 LC 2001-27316

"Underdog" in the title appears reversed and upside down on the title page

Characters: 2 men. 6 scenes. First produced at The Joseph Papp Public Theater/New York Shakespeare Festival, New York City, July 22, 2001

This is "the story of Lincoln and Booth, two brothers whose names were given to them as a joke foretelling a lifetime of sibling rivalry and resentment. Haunted by the past, the brothers are forced to confront the shattering reality of their future." Publisher's note

Rose, Reginald, 1920-2002

Twelve angry men; introduction by David Mamet. Penguin Books 2006 73p (Penguin classics) pa $11 **812**

ISBN 0-14-310440-3; 978-0-14-310440-7

LC 2006-46006

First published 1955 by Dramatic Pub.

Characters: 12 men. 3 acts. Original television broadcast on CBS program Studio One, September 20, 1954.

Television play in which one man in a jury tries to convince the other eleven jurors that the defendant in a murder trial is not guilty.

Shepard, Sam, 1943-

Fool for love, and other plays; introduction by Ross Wetzsteon. Bantam Bks. 1984 307p pa $15 **812**

ISBN 978-0-553-34590-2; 0-553-34129-4

LC 84-45182

Contents: Fool for love; Angel city; Melodrama play; Cowboy mouth; Action; Suicide in B-flat; Seduced; Geography of a horse dreamer

"Sam Shepard fills the role of professional playwright as a good ballet dancer or acrobat fulfills his role in performance. That is, he always delivers, he executes feats of dexterity and technical difficulty that an untrained person could not, and makes them seem easy." Village Voice

Sam Shepard; seven plays; introduction by Richard Gilman. Bantam Bks. 1981 337p pa $16 **812**

ISBN 978-0-553-34611-4; 0-553-34611-3

LC 83-100533

Contents: True West; Buried child; Curse of the starving class; The tooth of crime; La turista; Tongues; Savage/Love

The unseen hand and other plays. Vintage Bks. 1996 383p pa $14.95 **812**

ISBN 978-0-679-76789-3; 0-679-76789-4

LC 95-47723

Contents: The unseen hand; The rock garden; Chicago; Icarus's mother; 4H Club; Fourteen hundred thousand; Red cross; Cowboys #2; Forensic & the navigators; The holy ghostly; Operation sidewinder; The mad dog blues; Back bog beast bait; Killer's head

Simon, Neil

Brighton Beach memoirs. Plume 1995 130p pa $12 **812**

ISBN 0-452-27528-8 LC 95-21788

First published 1984 by Random House

"Sex and baseball are the primary preoccupations of 15-year-old Eugene Jerome, narrator of a seriocomic slice of lower-middle-class Jewish family life in Depression-era New York City. The several adolescent characters in the extended family add to the teenage appeal of Simon's . . . play." Booklist

The collected plays of Neil Simon; with an introduction by Neil Simon. Random House 1979-1998 4v hardcover o.p. v1-2 each pa $25, v3 o.p., v4 pa $17 * **812**

ISBN 978-0-452-25870-9 (v1); 978-0-452-26358-1 (v2); 978-0-679-40889-5 (v3); 978-0-684-84785-6 (v4)

Contents v1: Come blow your horn; Barefoot in the park; The odd couple; The star-spangled girl; Promises, promises; Plaza suite; Last of the red hot lovers; v2: Little me; The gingerbread lady; The prisoner of Second Avenue; The Sunshine Boys; The good doctor; God's favorite; California suite; Chaper two; v3: Sweet Charity; They're playing our song; I ought to be in pictures; Fools; The odd couple (female version); Brighton Beach memoirs; Biloxi blues; Broadway bound; v4: Rumors; Lost in Yonker's; Jake's women; Laughter on the 23rd floor; London suite

Lost in Yonkers. Plume 1993 120p (Plume drama) pa $12 **812**

ISBN 0-452-26883-4 LC 92-29111

First published 1991 by Random House

Characters: 4 men, 3 women. 2 acts. First presented at the Stevens Center for the Performing Arts, Winston-Salem, December 31, 1990.

This play, "set in 1940s New York, is a sad-funny portrait of a dysfunctional family, headed by a woman who provided for her children but never showed them love." Booklist

Wasserman, Dale, 1917-

Man of La Mancha; a musical play; lyrics by Joe Darion; music by Mitch Leigh. Random House 1966 82p il hardcover o.p. pa $9.95 **812**

ISBN 0-394-40621-4; 0-394-40619-2 (pa)

Characters: 14 men, 5 women, extras. First produced at the ANTA Washington Square Theatre, New York City, November 22, 1965

This musical play-adaption of Don Quixote is built around Cervantes' defense, when imprisoned and held for inquisition. He arranges a mock trial performance to present his case.

Wasserstein, Wendy, 1950-2006

An American daughter. Harcourt Brace & Co. 1998 105p il pa $14 hardcover o.p. **812**

ISBN 0-15-600645-6 (pa) LC 97-36079

Characters: 6 men, 4 women. 2 acts, 8 scenes. First produced by the Lincoln Center Theater, New York City, April 13, 1997

Satirical drama about intense media scrutiny that woman is subjected to after she is nominated for Surgeon General.

Wasserstein, Wendy, 1950-2006—*Continued*

The Heidi chronicles and other plays. Vintage
Bks. 1991 249p pa $13.95 **812**
   ISBN 0-679-73499-6   LC 90-55681
   First published 1990 by Harcourt Brace Jovanovich
   Contents: Uncommon women and others; Isn't it ro-
mantic; The Heidi chronicles
   This collection traces "three decades of changing
styles, mores, life objectives, and intellectual challenges.
Wasserstein examines her characters and their times with
great good humor, complexity, depth of feeling, and a
firm refusal to accept trite and easy images." Libr J

The sisters Rosensweig 1993 109p il pa $11
hardcover o.p. **812**
   ISBN 0-15-600013-X (pa)   LC 93-224
   Also available in paperback from Dramatists Play Service
   Characters: 4 men, 4 women. 2 acts 7 scenes. First
produced at the Mitzi E. Newhouse Theater, New York
City, October 22, 1992
   This is "a domestic, romantic comedy partly about the
three middle-aged sisters of the title and their relations
with men and careers and partly about how the eldest
sister, international banker Sara, in whose London home
the play is set, meets a man who comes to dinner and,
through not much effort on her part . . . sweeps him off
his feet. Wasserstein's filled the play with the sharp but
poignantly revealing developments and dialogue that she
writes so well." Booklist

Wilder, Thornton, 1897-1975
Collected plays & writings on theater. Library
of America 2007 871p $40 **812**
   1. Poetry—By individual authors
   ISBN 978-1-59853-003-2; 1-59853-003-8
                      LC 2006-48620
   Contents: Nascuntur Poetae; Proserpina and the devil;
Fanny Otcott; Brother fire; The penny that beauty spent;
The angel on the ship; The message and Jehanne; Childe
Roland to the dark tower came; Centaurs; Leviathan;
And the sea shall give up it dead; Now the servant's
name was Malchus; Mozart and the gray steward; Hast
thou considered my servant Job?; The flight in Egypt;
The angel that troubled the waters; The long Christmas
dinner; Queens of France; Pullman car Hiawatha; Love
and how to cure it; Such things only happen in books;
The happy journey to Trenton and Camden; Our town;
The skin of our teeth; The matchmaker; The Alcestiad;
The drunken sisters; The marriage we deplore; The unerring instinct; Scenes from the Emporium; Bernice; The
wreck on the five-twenty-five; A ringing of doorbells; In
Shakespeare and the Bible; Someone from Assisi; Cement hands; Infancy; Childhood; Youth; The rivers under
the earth; Shadow of doubt (screenplay)
   "Complementing the selection of plays is [a] . . .
group of essays that captures Wilder's reflections on his
plays and contains a revealing epistolary account of the
film adaptation of Our Town, as well as evaluations of
dramatists such as Sophocles, George Bernard Shaw, and
the Austrian satirist Johann Nestroy (whose farce Einen
Jux will er sich machen Wilder . . . transformed into
The Matchmaker)." Publisher's note

Our town; a play in three acts; foreword by
Donald Margulies. HarperCollins Pubs. 2003 xx,
181p $19.95; pa $9.95 * **812**
   ISBN 0-06-053525-3; 0-06-051263-6 (pa)
   A reissue with a new foreword of the title first published 1938 by Coward-McCann
   Large mixed cast. First produced at McCarter's Theatre, Princeton, N.J., January 22, 1938.
   "Presented without scenery of any kind, utilizing a
narrator and loose episodic form, adventurous and imaginative in style, this unique play . . . is one of the most
distinguished in the modern repertoire. It deals with the
simplest and most touching aspects of life in a small
town." HarperCollins Reader's Ency of Am Lit

Williams, Tennessee, 1911-1983
Plays, 1937-1955. Library of America 2000
1054p $40 * **812**
   ISBN 978-1-883011-86-4; 1-883011-86-4
   Contents: Spring storm; Not about nightingales; Battle
of angels; I rise in flame, cried the phoenix; 27 wagons
full of cotton; The lady of Larkspur Lotion; The last of
my solid gold watches; Portrait of a madonna; Auto-
da-fé; Lord Byron's love letter; This property is condemned; The glass menagerie; A streetcar named Desire;
Summer and smoke; The rose tattoo; Camino Real;
"Something wild"; Talk to me like the rain and let me
listen; Something unspoken; Cat on a hot tin roof

Plays, 1957-1980. Library of America 2000
999p $40 * **812**
   ISBN 978-1-883011-87-1; 1-883011-87-6
   Contents: Orpheus descending; Suddenly last summer;
Sweet bird of youth; Period of adjustment; The night of
the iguana; The eccentricities of a nightingale; The milk
train doesn't stop here anymore; The mutilated; Kingdom
of earth (The seven descents of Myrtle); Small craft
warnings; Out cry; Vieux Carre; A lovely Sunday for
Creve Coeur

Wilson, August
Fences; a play; introduction by Lloyd Richards.
New Am. Lib. 1986 101p pa $12 * **812**
   ISBN 978-0-452-26401-4   LC 86-5264
   Also available in hardcover from Theatre Communica-
tions Group
   "A Plume book"
   Characters: 5 men, 1 woman, 1 girl. 2 acts, 9 scenes.
First produced at the Yale Repertory Theatre, New Ha-
ven, Connecticut, April 30, 1985
   Family drama about black experience in America.
1960's spirit of liberation alienates hard-working father
from wife and son.

Gem of the ocean. Theatre Communications
Group 2006 85p $25; pa $13.95 **812**
   ISBN   978-1-55936-281-8;   1-55936-281-2;
   978-1-55936-280-1 (pa); 1-55936-280-4 (pa)
                      LC 2006-7812
   Characters: 5 men, 2 women. First produced at the
Eugene O'Neill Theater Center, Waterford, Ct., 2002
   Set in 1904 Pittsburgh, this is chronologically the first
work in August Wilson's Century cycle. "Aunt Esther,

Wilson, August—*Continued*

the drama's 287-year-old fiery matriarch, welcomes into her Hill District home Solly Two Kings, who was born into slavery and scouted for the Union Army, and Citizen Barlow, a young man from Alabama searching for a new life." Publisher's note

"A swelling battle hymn of transporting beauty. Theatergoers who have followed August Wilson's career will find in Gem a touchstone for everything else he has written." N Y Times

Jitney. Overlook Press 2001 96p hardcover o.p. pa $14.95   812
ISBN 978-158567-370-4; 1-58567-370-6
LC 2001-33962
Also available in hardcover from Theatre Communications Group
Characters: 8 men, 1 woman. 2 acts, 8 scenes. This is a revised version of a play written 1979
Drama set in 1977 about gypsy cabdrivers who service Pittsburgh's black Hill District.

Joe Turner's come and gone; a play in two acts. New Am. Lib. 1988 94p pa $12   812
ISBN 978-0-452-26009-2; 0-452-26009-4
LC 88-1660
Also available in hardcover from Theatre Communications Group
"A Plume book"
Characters: 6 men, 5 women. 2 acts, 10 scenes. 1 setting. First produced at the Yale Repertory Theatre, New Haven, Connecticut, April 29, 1986
This drama looks at life in a Pittsburgh boarding house for blacks in 1911.

King Hedley II. Theatre Communications Group 2005 103p $27.95; pa $13.95   812
ISBN   978-1-55936-261-0;   1-55936-261-8;
978-1-55936-260-3 (pa); 1-55936-260-X (pa)
LC 2005-12535
Characters: 4 men, 2 women. First produced at the Seattle Repertory Theatre, Seattle, Wa., 1999
"King Hedley II is the eighth work in playwright August Wilson's 10-play cycle chronicling the history of the African American experience in each decade of the twentieth century. It's set in 1985 and tells the story of an ex-con in post-Reagan Pittsburgh trying to rebuild his life." Publisher's note
This is a "big play, filled with big emotions and big speeches. These aria-like monologues are rich in humor, heartbreak and the astonishing details that go into creating real people." Associated Press

Ma Rainey's black bottom; a play in two acts. New Am. Lib. 1985 111p pa $12   812
ISBN 978-0-452-26113-6; 0-452-26113-9
LC 84-27156
Also available in hardcover from Theatre Communications Group
"A Plume book"
Characters: 8 men, 2 women. 2 acts. First produced at the Yale Repertory Theatre, New Haven, Connecticut, April 6, 1984
Recording session by Black blues great Ma Rainey for white-owned studio, is setting for exploration of racial relations and conflicts.

The piano lesson. New Am. Lib. 1990 108p hardcover o.p. pa $12 *   812
ISBN 978-0-452-26534-9; 0-452-26534-7
LC 90-38734
Also available in hardcover from Theatre Communications Group
Characters: 5 men, 3 women. 2 acts, 7 scenes. First presented at the Yale Repertory Theatre, New Haven, November 26, 1987
Drama set in 1936 Pittsburgh chronicles black experience in America. Family conflict arises over heirloom piano.

Radio golf. Theatre Communications Group 2007 81p $25; pa $13.95   812
ISBN   978-1-55936-306-8;   1-55936-306-1;
978-1-55936-308-2 (pa); 1-55936-308-8 (pa)
LC 2007-32541
Characters: 4 men, 1 woman. First produced at the Cort Theatre, New Haven Connecticut, May 8, 2007
"Set in 1997 in a storefront redevelopment office in Pittsburgh's Hill District, Radio Golf is the concluding play in August Wilson's . . . ten-play cycle chronicling African American life during the twentieth century. . . . This bittersweet drama of assimilation and alienation in nineties America traces the forces of change on a neighborhood and its people caught between history and the twenty-first century." Publisher's note
"A play that could well be Mr. Wilson's most provocative." N Y Times

Seven guitars. Dutton 1996 107p hardcover o.p. pa $12   812
ISBN 978-0-452-27692-5; 0-452-27692-6 (pa)
LC 95-50536
Also available in hardcover from Theatre Communications Group
Characters: 4 men, 3 women. 2 acts, 9 scenes. First produced at the Goodman Theater, Chicago, January 21, 1995
"Pittsburgh, summer 1948. Five of his friends gather after the funeral of Floyd Barton, mysteriously murdered at 35, just as his first blues record had become a hit. The sixth play in Wilson's cycle concerned with twentieth-century African American lives is mostly a flashback. We learn what happened to Floyd, but before that horrifying climax, Wilson steeps us in the pathos that Floyd glimpsed a way to escape. . . . As powerful as modern drama gets." Booklist

Two trains running; foreword by Laurence Fishburne. Theatre Communications Group 2007 99p $25   812
ISBN 978-1-55936-303-7   LC 2007-22095
First published 1992 by Dutton
Characters: 6 men, 1 woman. 2 acts 8 scenes. First produced at the Yale Repertory Theatre, New Haven, Ct., March 27, 1990
Drama set in Pittsburgh's Hill District. Explores the uncertain future promised by the Civil Rights movement of the 1960s from the perspective of urban blacks.

Wilson, Lanford, 1937-
21 short plays. Smith & Kraus 1993 268p pa $19.95   812
ISBN 1-880399-31-8   LC 93-34434

Wilson, Lanford, 1937——*Continued*
"Contemporary playwrights series"
Contents: Home free!; The madness of Lady Bright; Ludlow fair; This is the rill speaking; Days ahead; Wandering; Stoop; Sextet (yes); Ikke, Ikke, nye, nye, nye; Victory on Mrs, Dandywine's island; The Great Nebula in Orion; The family continues; Brontosaurus; Thymus vulgaris; Breakfast at the track; Say de Kooning; A betrothal; Abstinence; A poster of the cosmos; The moonshot tape; Eukiah

"The plays range in form from finely crafted one-act plays to short 'skits' written for various benefits. They are arranged in chronological order and the collection spans the years from 1963 to 1991. Wilson's dramatic style has been characterized by such phrases as 'lyric realism' and 'poetic realism,' but these short plays represent a far greater range of styles." Voice Youth Advocates

The Talley trilogy. Smith & Kraus 1999 272p (Collected works, v3) *   **812**
This volume includes Fifth of July, Talley's folly and Talley & son (1986). A tale told (1981), an early version of Talley & son is also included

"Wilson didn't begin what became, ultimately, a tetralogy with the idea of creating a play cycle. He just wanted to write a play set in the late 1970s that reflected in some way the post-Vietnam, post-Watergate letdown much of young America was feeling. . . . The resultant four-play cycle captures the Talley's foibles and follies as thoroughly—and as entertainingly—as J.D. Salinger's set of stories and short novels did the Glass family." Booklist

Zindel, Paul
The effect of gamma rays on man-in-the-moon marigolds; a drama in two acts; drawings by Dong Kingman. Harper & Row 1971 108p il pa $6.99 hardcover o.p.   **812**
ISBN 0-06-075738-8 (pa)
Also available in paperback from Dramatists Play Service
Characters: 5 women. First produced at the Mercer-O'Casey Theatre, New York City, April 7, 1970
"The play, in the naturalistic tradition, deals with a widow and her two daughters, the imagination of one of whom has been captured by the atom and the possibilities it offers of producing mutations." McGraw-Hill Ency of World Drama

812.008   American drama—Collections

The **Best** American short plays; edited by Howard Stein and Glenn Young. Applause Theatre Bk. Pubs. $32.95; pa $18.95   **812.008**
1. Drama—Collections 2. One act plays
ISSN 1062-7561
This series of annual collections was begun in 1937 under the editorship of Margaret Mayorga with title: Best one-act plays, and published by Dodd, Mead through 1955 (starting in 1953 title changed to The best short plays). Beacon Press published the volumes from 1956

through 1961 when publication was suspended. Resumed 1968 under the editorship of Stanley Richards. From 1981 through 1989 edited by Ramon Delgado. Changed to current title and editors with 1990/1991 volume. Volumes prior to 1988 o.p. Apply to publisher for availability and price of retrospective annuals

In addition to the plays each annual contains brief biographical and bibliographical data about dramatists represented

812.009   American drama—History and criticism

Abbotson, Susan C. W., 1961-
Critical companion to Arthur Miller; a literary reference to his life and work. Facts on File 2006 518p il (Facts on File library of American literature) $75   **812.009**
1. Miller, Arthur, 1915-2005
ISBN 0-8160-6194-7; 978-0-8160-6194-5
LC 2006-22902
This book "covers Miller's entire canon, including plays, screenplays, fiction, short stories, and poetry, as well as many of his important essays and critical pieces. Also included are . . . entries on literary, theatrical, and personal figures important to Miller; key terms and topics connected to his work; and various theatrical companies and places with which he has been associated." Publisher's note
Includes bibliographical references

Heintzelman, Greta
Critical companion to Tennessee Williams; [by] Greta Heintzelman, Alycia Smith Howard. Facts on File 2005 436p il (Facts on File library of American literature) $65; pa $19.95
812.009
1. Williams, Tennessee, 1911-1983
ISBN 0-8160-4888-6; 0-8160-6429-6 (pa)
LC 2004-7362
"The first comprises a 14-page biography with recommendations for further reading. The second and largest section includes entries for each of Williams's plays, stories, and miscellaneous publications. . . . The third section consists of brief entries on subjects relating to Williams and his work, covering, for example, awards, the Dramatists Guild, Truman Capote, and Washington University. The final section includes a chronology of Williams's life, a bibliography of his work, and a bibliography of secondary sources." Libr J
The authors "offer an excellent resource for those studying Williams's life and extensive body of work." Choice
Includes bibliographical references

Playwrights at work; Paris review; edited by George Plimpton. Modern Lib. 2000 411p il pa $14.95 *   **812.009**
1. Dramatists
ISBN 0-679-64021-5   LC 99-44064
"Interviews with: Albee, Beckett, Guare, Hellman, Ionesco, Mamet, Miller, Pinter, Shepard, Simon, Stoppard, Wasserstein, Wilder, Williams, Wilson"--Cover

Playwrights at work—*Continued*

"This is an excellent gathering of brilliant minds in the theater, and these interviews provide significant insight into the works of the writers." Libr J

813.009 American fiction—History and criticism

Brave new words; the Oxford dictionary of science fiction; edited by Jeffrey Prucher; introduction by Gene Wolfe. Oxford University Press 2007 xxxi, 342p $29.95   **813.009**
1. Science fiction—Dictionaries
ISBN 978-0-19-530567-8; 0-19-530567-1
                     LC 2006-37280
This is a "dictionary of the language of science fiction based on historical principles. . . . Entries include part of speech, etymology, definition with cross references to related terms, usage status (e.g., historical, jocular, derogatory, obsolete), variant forms, and . . . dated citations and quotations illustrating the usage of the word over time." Libr J
"This new science fiction lexicon . . . is an important and entertaining reference source for any science fiction writer, magazine editor, fan, neophyte reader, or librarian." Choice
Includes bibliographical references

The **Columbia** companion to the twentieth-century American short story; Blanche H. Gelfant, editor. Columbia Univ. Press 2000 660p $83.50; pa $24.50 *   **813.009**
1. Short stories—History and criticism 2. American fiction—Bio-bibliography
ISBN 0-231-11098-7; 0-231-11099-5 (pa)
                     LC 00-31610
"The first 100 pages are devoted to thematic essays that focus on the form of the short story, the development of the genre, several distinct subject types (e.g., short stories of the Holocaust or of the working class), and four different ethnic groups (African American, Asian American, Chicano Latino American, and Native American). . . . The remainder of the book is devoted to over 100 individual author essays that focus on reading for pleasure and understanding rather than critical interpretation. Entries discuss the development of each author and the content and meaning of his or her major short stories." Libr J
Includes bibliographical references

Contemporary Jewish-American novelists; a bio-critical sourcebook; edited by Joel Shatzky and Michael Taub; with a foreword by Daniel Walden. Greenwood Press 1997 xxxi, 506p $105   **813.009**
1. American fiction—Jewish authors 2. American fiction—Bio-bibliography
ISBN 0-313-29462-3   LC 96-37047
This "reference work 'includes alphabetically arranged entries for more than 75 Jewish-American novelists whose major works were largely written after World War II.' While major canonical figures such as Norman Mailer and Saul Bellow are profiled, lesser-known novel-

ists—including Judith Katz, Lev Raphael, and Steve Stern—are covered as well. One of the editors' goals is to show the diversity of Jewish-American literature. . . . Each entry includes a biographical section, a cogent discussion of major works and themes, an overview of each novelist's critical reception, and a bibliography of both primary and secondary sources." Booklist

The **Facts** on File companion to the American novel; edited by Abby H.P. Werlock; assistant editor, James P. Werlock. Facts on File 2005 3v (Facts on File library of American literature) set $195 *   **813.009**
1. American fiction—Encyclopedias 2. American fiction—Bio-bibliography
ISBN 0-8160-4528-3; 978-0-8160-4528-0
                     LC 2005-12437
"This A-to-Z reference contains 450 biographical overviews of American and foreign-born authors living in the United States and 500 signed analytical essays on their novels. . . . Libraries will value this compact set for including classics as well as hard-to-find contemporary authors." SLJ
Includes bibliographical references

Fargnoli, A. Nicholas
Critical companion to William Faulkner; a literary reference to his life and work; [by] A. Nicholas Fargnoli, Michael Golay, Robert W. Hamblin. Facts On File 2008 562p il (Facts on File library of American literature) $75
                     813.009
1. Faulkner, William, 1897-1962
ISBN 978-0-8160-6432-8   LC 2007-32361
First published 2001 with title: William Faulkner A to Z
"Coverage includes: Faulkner's major works, including novels, short stories, poetry, and nonfiction; descriptions of characters in Faulkner's fiction, such as Benjy and Quentin from *The Sound and the Fury*; details about Faulkner's family, friends, colleagues, and critics; real and fictional places important to Faulkner's life and literary development, from Yoknapatawpha County, Mississippi to Hollywood; interviews and speeches given by Faulkner; [and] ideas and events that influenced his life and works, including slavery, the Civil War, World War I, and civil rights." Publisher's note
Includes bibliographical references

Gillespie, Carmen
Critical companion to Toni Morrison; a literary reference to her life and work. Facts On File 2008 484p il (Facts on File library of American literature) $75   **813.009**
1. Morrison, Toni, 1931-
ISBN 978-0-8160-6276-8   LC 2006-38231
This book "examines Morrison's life and writing, featuring critical analyses of her work and themes, as well as . . . entries on related topics and relevant people, places, and influences." Publisher's note
Includes bibliographical references

Gunn, James E., 1923-

Isaac Asimov; the foundations of science fiction; by James Gunn. rev ed. Scarecrow Press 1996 276p hardcover o.p. pa $42   **813.009**

1. Asimov, Isaac, 1920-1992 2. Science fiction—History and criticism

ISBN 0-8108-3129-5; 0-8108-5420-1 (pa); 978-0-8108-5420-8 (pa)   LC 96-21068

First published 1982 by Oxford Univ. Press

The author "focuses on Asimov's robots and on the Foundation trilogy, emphasizing throughout Asimov's limited use of background, style, and characterization, and his constantly recurring theme of the rational solution of a problem. The Lucky Starr juveniles get comparatively cursory treatment, but otherwise this is a very fine book indeed—well informed, clearly written, and judicious." Booklist {review of 1982 edition}

Includes bibliographical references

Kirk, Connie Ann, 1951-

Critical companion to Flannery O'Connor. Facts on File 2008 415p il (Facts on File library of American literature) $75   **813.009**

1. O'Connor, Flannery

ISBN 978-0-8160-6417-5   LC 2007-6512

This book examines O'Connor's "life and works, and includes critical analyses of some of the themes in her writing, as well as entries on related topics and relevant people, places, and influences." Publisher's note

Includes bibliographical references

L'Amour, Louis, 1908-1988

The Sackett companion; a personal guide to the Sackett novels. Bantam Bks. 1988 341p il maps pa $14.95 hardcover o.p.   **813.009**

ISBN 0-553-37102-9 (pa)   LC 88-47530

"Each individual profile of the 17 Sackett novels contains a map, a cover painting, brief plot synopsis, and an annotated list of characters. Sackett enthusiasts will also welcome the inclusion of a detailed Sackett genealogy and family tree." Booklist

Oliver, Charles M.

Critical companion to Ernest Hemingway; a literary reference to his life and work. Facts on File 2006 630p il (Facts on File library of American literature) $75   **813.009**

1. Hemingway, Ernest, 1899-1961

ISBN 0-8160-6418-0; 978-0-8160-6418-2
          LC 2006-7970

First published 1999 with title: Ernest Hemingway A to Z

"This volume features entries on all of Hemingway's major and minor works, places and events related to his works, major figures in his life, and more. Appendixes include a complete list of Hemingway's works; a chronology; a genealogy; a . . . map for readers of Islands in the Stream; a list of film, stage, and radio adaptations; and a bibliography of secondary sources." Publisher's note

Includes filmography and bibliographical references

Pritchard, William H.

Updike. University of Massachusetts Press 2005 350p pa $24.95   **813.009**

ISBN 978-1-55849-507-4; 1-55849-507-X

First published 2000 by Steerforth Press

This study examines Updike's "novels, short stories, poetry, memoirs, and literary criticism, tracing themes, influences, and literary relations, as well as describing characters and situating the works into the larger context of contemporary American literature." Libr J

"All in all, Pritchard's book is a gentle and intelligent request for a little more thought and a little less cranky let'smoveon speed in judging the work of one of America's pre-eminent writers." N Y Times Book Rev

Includes bibliographical references

Rehak, Melanie

Girl sleuth; Nancy Drew and the women who created her. Harcourt 2005 364p il $25; pa $14
          813.009

1. Wirt, Mildred A. (Mildred Augustine), 1905- 2. Keene, Carolyn 3. Stratemeyer, Edward, 1862-1930 4. Drew, Nancy (Fictitious character)

ISBN 0-15-101041-2; 0-15-603056-X (pa)
          LC 2005-9129

This is an account of "the writers and editors who constituted Carolyn Keene, the pseudonymous author of the [Nancy Drew] series." N Y Times Book Rev

"Packed with revealing anecdotes, Rehak's meticulously researched account of the publishing phenomenon that survived the Depression and WWII . . . will delight fans of the beloved gumshoe whose gumption guaranteed that every reprobate got his due." Booklist

Includes bibliographical references

Rollyson, Carl

Critical companion to Herman Melville; a literary reference to his life and work; [by] Carl Rollyson, Lisa Paddock, and April Gentry. Facts on File 2006 394p il (Facts on File library of world literature) $75   **813.009**

1. Melville, Herman, 1819-1891

ISBN 0-8160-6461-X; 978-0-8160-6461-8
          LC 2005-36733

First published 2000 with title: Herman Melville A to Z

Entries in this "volume examine the characters and settings of Melville's novels and short stories, the critics and scholars who commented on his work, and his friends and associates, including such prominent literary figures as Oliver Wendell Holmes and Nathaniel Hawthorne." Publisher's note

Includes bibliographical references

Schultz, Jeffrey D., 1966-

Critical companion to John Steinbeck; a literary reference to his life and work; [by] Jeffrey Schultz, Luchen Li. Facts on File 2005 406p il (Facts on File library of American literature) $65; pa $19.99   **813.009**

1. Steinbeck, John, 1902-1968

ISBN 0-8160-4300-0; 0-8160-4301-9 (pa)
          LC 2004-26100

Schultz, Jeffrey D., 1966-—*Continued*

This "resource is divided into three parts: Biography, Works A-Z, and Related People, Places, and Topics. The first and shortest section provides a summary of Steinbeck's birth, early childhood, education, and career. The bulk of the book offers descriptions of all of his works—published and unpublished." SLJ

"Useful, succinct, and reasonably priced, it packs an abundance of information into one compact resource." Libr J

Includes bibliographical references

Smiley, Jane, 1949-

Thirteen ways of looking at the novel. Knopf 2005 591p $26.95   **813.009**

1. Fiction—History and criticism 2. Authorship

ISBN 1-4000-4059-0   LC 2005-45181

"The book is roughly divided into three sections: the first classifies the novel, beginning with the most simple of definitions (e.g., it's long, in prose, has a protagonist), and adds moral and aesthetic complexity as it moves along. The second section consists of a primer for fledgling novelists. . . . The result is a thorough reflection on the art and craft of the novel from one of its best-known contemporary practitioners." Publ Wkly

Includes bibliographical references

Tate, Mary Jo

Critical companion to F. Scott Fitzgerald; a literary reference to his life and work; foreword by Matthew J. Bruccoli. Facts on File 2006 464p il (Facts on File library of American literature) $75   **813.009**

1. Fitzgerald, F. Scott (Francis Scott), 1896-1940

ISBN 0-8160-6433-4; 978-0-8160-6433-5   LC 2006-11393

First published 1998 with title: F. Scott Fitzgerald A to Z

This book "studies the legacy of this writer, highlighting significant themes and historical references of his various works." Publisher's note

Includes bibliographical references

A **Theodore** Dreiser encyclopedia; edited by Keith Newlin. Greenwood Press 2003 xxiii, 431p il $99.95 *   **813.009**

1. Dreiser, Theodore, 1871-1945

ISBN 0-313-31680-5   LC 2003-40841

This is a "guide to the essential facts surrounding this prolific author's life and works. Dreiser's novels and short stories are covered, as are his plays, which are far less known. Front matter includes a list of entries, a chronology, and a preface that analyzes prior contributions to Dreiser scholarship. Alphabetically arranged essays on his books, short stories, and magazine and newspaper pieces make up the book's core. . . . The book ends with a bibliography arranged by category (books by Dreiser, critical studies, biographies, etc.). Highly recommended." Choice

Includes bibliographical references and index

Wright, Sarah Bird

Critical companion to Nathaniel Hawthorne; a literary reference to his life and work. Facts on File 2006 392p il (Facts on File library of American literature) $75   **813.009**

1. Hawthorne, Nathaniel, 1804-1864

ISBN 0-8160-5583-1; 978-0-8160-5583-8   LC 2005-34648

This book "offers critical entries on Hawthorne's novels, short stories, travel writing, criticism, and other works, as well as portraits of characters, including Hester Prynne and Roger Chillingworth. This . . . reference also provides entries on Hawthorne's family, friends—ranging from Herman Melville to President Franklin Pierce—publishers, and critics, as well as periodicals that published his work and important places and events in his life." Publisher's note

Includes bibliographical references

814   American essays

Angelou, Maya

Even the stars look lonesome. Random House 1997 145p $18; pa $10   **814**

1. African American authors 2. Women authors

ISBN 0-375-50031-6; 0-553-37972-0 (pa)   LC 97-17317

Angelou "touches on a number of topics in this brief collection of essays, including aging, fame, sensuality, art, and violence. Her opening piece, about the ending of a long marriage and the beginning of a new life in a new home, is a winner. Her take on aging is downright amusing; her tribute to sensuality, enlightening; and her salute to black women, a treasure." Libr J

Wouldn't take nothing for my journey now. Random House 1993 141p $17; pa $13   **814**

ISBN 0-679-42743-0; 0-553-38017-6 (pa)   LC 93-5904

Also available in paperback from Bantam Bks.

The author "shares her thoughts about humankind: how to respect others of different cultures, opinions, and values as taught by universal philosophies. . . . Angelou's prose is brisk, fluid, and entrancing. This work will provide a taste of wisdom to all who read it." Libr J

Atwood, Margaret, 1939-

Writing with intent; essays, reviews, personal prose, 1983-2005. Carroll & Graf Publishers 2005 427p $26   **814**

ISBN 0-7867-1535-9   LC 2005-42086

Some of the essays in this volume were first published 2004 in Canada with title: Moving targets

In these essays, the author "comments on world events, fellow writers, and her own development. She reviews books by John Updike, Italo Calvino, Antonia Fraser, and Dashiell Hammett, as well as the lesser-known Robert Bringhurst, Hilary Mantel, and H. Rider Haggard. . . . This collection will not disappoint Atwood fans as her analyses both challenge and entertain." Libr J

Includes bibliographical references

Baldwin, James, 1924-1987

Collected essays. Library of Am. 1998 869p $35

*   **814**

ISBN 1-883011-52-3   LC 97-23496

The essays in this volume were selected by Toni Morrison. "Morrison has reprinted all of the material contained in Baldwin's previous collected essays, The Price of the Ticket (1985). She has added eleven pieces, the earliest of which dates from 1947—Baldwin's first published review, of a biography of Frederick Douglass, in the Nation—and the latest from 1984." Times Lit Suppl

The **beholder's** eye; a collection of America's finest personal journalism; edited and with an introduction by Walt Harrington. Grove Press 2005 xxii, 256p pa $14   **814**

ISBN 0-8021-4224-5   LC 2005-46242

"Each writer takes a unique approach to the subject, drawing the reader into the experience of pit-bull fighting or hunting with the Inuit. Among the collection: Harrington, who is married to a black woman, explores his evolving attitudes on race through the lens of his relationship with his in-laws, Pete Earley returns to his hometown in search of the meaning of a sister's death in their youth, Ron Rosenbaum explores his own outlook on life in a philosophical discourse with then-New York governor Mario Cuomo, Davis Miller is unabashedly starstruck in a comfortable and closeup look at Muhammad Ali at the home of Ali's mother, and Stephen S. Hall is personally probing in his exploration, via MRI, of his own brain and its functioning. These stories are amusing, insightful, and touching in a way that only something personal can be." Booklist

The **best** American essays, 2008; edited and with an introduction by Adam Gopnik ; Robert Atwan, series editor. Houghton Mifflin 2008 xxiii, 293p il $28; pa $14 *   **814**

ISSN 0888-3742

ISBN   978-0-618-98331-5;   0-618-98331-7; 978-0-618-98322-3 (pa); 0-618-98322-8 (pa)

Annual. First published 1986 by Ticknor & Fields. Editors vary

Editors select essays from general interest magazines that touch on topics political, scientific, historical, religious, and sociological, in addition to the personal and literary.

The **Best** American essays of the century; Joyce Carol Oates, editor; Robert Atwan, coeditor; with an introduction by Joyce Carol Oates. Houghton Mifflin 2000 596p hardcover o.p. pa $18 *   **814**

ISBN 0-618-04370-5; 0-618-15587-2 (pa)

This anthology includes essays "that contemplate diverse worlds, from nature to courtrooms, war and family memories. Race is a pervasive theme, explored with candor and insight by many, including James Baldwin, Zora Neale Hurston, and, in a jolting 1912 condemnation of a Coatesville, Pennsylvania, lynching, John Jay Chapman." Booklist

"Oates has assembled a provocative collection of masterpieces reflecting both the fragmentation and surprising cohesiveness of various American identities." Publ Wkly

Includes bibliographical references

Bradbury, Ray, 1920-

Bradbury speaks; too soon from the cave, too far from the stars. William Morrow 2005 243p hardcover o.p. pa $14.95   **814**

ISBN 0-06-058568-4; 0-06-058569-2 (pa)

                          LC 2005-41489

In this collection of essays, the author "weighs in on a medley of topics, including the allure of Paris, his enthusiasm for trains, the genesis of his most popular novels, and his reasons for remaining a diehard optimist. . . . By turns whimsical, insightful, and unabashedly metaphoric, his prose is immediately accessible as well as thought-provoking. Fans and nonfans alike should enjoy." Booklist

Brodsky, Joseph, 1940-1996

Less than one; selected essays. Farrar, Straus & Giroux 1986 501p pa $18 hardcover o.p.

                           814

ISBN 0-374-52055-0 (pa)   LC 85-15900

The essays in this volume "begin and end with autobiographical pieces; in between there are alternate homages to favorite poets, both Russian and non-Russian, as well as substantial discussions of such topics as geography and history, political force and ethical choice, and literary tradition." N Y Times Book Rev

On grief and reason; essays. Farrar, Straus & Giroux 1996 484p pa $18 hardcover o.p.

                           814

ISBN 0-374-52509-9 (pa)   LC 94-10872

This volume "collects twenty-one essays, all but one written since 1986." N Y Rev Books

For an "essay on Frost, for an equally probing one on four poems by Thomas Hardy, for an 'Homage to Marcus Aurelius,' for half a hundred pages on an English translation of a poem Rainer Maria Rilke wrote in German 90 years ago, and for many scattered felicities, this collection is occasion for gratitude. It is rare for someone so advantageously situated, within poetry but both within and outside of American speech, culture and experience, to confide in us with such pedagogic confidence." N Y Times Book Rev

Capote, Truman, 1924-1984

Portraits and observations; the essays of Truman Capote. Random House 2007 518p $28.95 *

                           814

ISBN 978-1-4000-6661-2; 1-4000-6661-1

                        LC 2007-36624

This is a collection of 42 essays written by Capote from 1946 to 1984.

"The featured works cover the artist's interests in travel, celebrities, the arts—both visual and literary—crimes of passion, and himself. . . . This collection offers the highest quality of writing from a genuine American stylist." Libr J

Chabon, Michael

Maps and legends; reading and writing along the borderlands. McSweeney's 2008 222p $24

                           814

Chabon, Michael—*Continued*
1. Authorship
ISBN 978-1-932416-89-3; 1-932416-89-7
"In 16 essays, Chabon maps his enthusiasms. . . . Although in part a fragmentary memoir—we receive revealing glimpses of Chabon's family, boyhood home of Columbia, Md., and personal history—'Maps and Legends' is also a manifesto, a declaration of literary principles that asserts the value, even necessity, of genre. Especially in the book's first half, Chabon makes this argument through example, by closely examining and celebrating Arthur Conan Doyle's Sherlock Holmes tales, Philip Pullman's 'His Dark Materials' series, M.R. James' ghost stories, and the comics of Howard Chaykin, Ben Katchor and Will Eisner. . . . However disparately engaging you find the ruminations on other writers, the book's concluding quintet of pieces on the inspirations behind Chabon's major work will prove an illuminating delight for those of us who have the same fannish devotion to his work as he does to Conan Doyle's." St. Louis Post-Dispatch

Connell, Evan S., 1924-
The Aztec treasure house; new and selected essays. Counterpoint 2001 470p pa $17.50 hardcover o.p. *   **814**
ISBN 1-58243-253-8 (pa)   LC 2001-28899
Connell "writes about polar exploration; linguistic research; astronomy; preposterous, unkillable fantasies like El Dorado and Prester John; inspired travelers like Ibn Batuta and Mary Kingsley; the insane and tragic Children's Crusade—any subject that illustrates the human urge to strain against physical and mental boundaries. Connell is skeptical, clearheaded and a sworn enemy of all dogma." N Y Times Book Rev
Includes bibliographical references

Davenport, Guy, 1927-2005
The geography of the imagination; forty essays. 1st Nonpareil ed. David R. Godine 1997 384p (Nonpareil book) pa $19.95   **814**
ISBN 1-567-92080-2   LC 97-17831
First published 1981 by North Point Press
In addition to essays on modern and classical literature the author also discusses archaeology, biology, lexicography, music and photography. Among his subjects are: Poe, Agassiz, Pound, Ives, Zukofsky, Meatyard, Tchelitchew and Joyce.
Includes bibliographical references

The Hunter Gracchus, and other papers on literature and art. Counterpoint 1996 339p il hardcover o.p. pa $19.95   **814**
ISBN 978-1-887178-55-6; 1-887178-55-4
LC 96-43090
The author "announces blithely that this collection of essays and comments 'has for a semblance of unity only their being written on the same typewriter'. . . . Davenport is what the ancient Greek poet Antolochus would call a fox, or one who knows many things, rather than a hedgehog, who has a single central vision. These writings on Kafka, Darwin, Picasso, Shakers, and snake handlers have more in common than their means of production, however, because each is in its own way brilliant, the stylish work of a master stylist." Libr J

Didion, Joan
We tell ourselves stories in order to live; collected nonfiction; with an introduction by John Leonard. Knopf 2006 1122p $30   **814**
ISBN 978-0-307-26487-9; 0-307-26487-4
LC 2006-41043
This volume "contains seven books of journalism—all of [Didion's] nonfiction except her 2005 memoir of new widowhood, 'The Year of Magical Thinking.' Didion's writing was from the beginning startlingly individual. . . . Say what you will about her somewhat self-centered style; America needs more courageous thinkers who will write about life as it is lived—not as elites on all sides seek to manufacture it." Nat Rev
Includes bibliographical references

Dirda, Michael, 1948-
Classics for pleasure. Harcourt 2007 341p $25   **814**
1. Literature—History and criticism
ISBN 978-0-15-101251-0; 0-15-101251-2
LC 2007-03029
In these essays, Dirda discusses some 90 books, including "fantasy and science fiction, horror and adventure, as well as epics, history, essay, and children's literature." Publisher's note
This book is "a pleasure to dip into any time. Like the key that opens up the door to *The Secret Garden*, it provides easy entry to a colorful array of literary gems." America

Doctorow, E. L., 1931-
Creationists: selected essays, 1993-2006. Random House 2006 176p $24.95   **814**
1. Creation (Literary, artistic, etc.) 2. Literature—History and criticism
ISBN 978-1-4000-6495-3; 1-4000-6495-3
"In 16 essays adapted from reviews, book introductions and public lectures, Doctorow explores the theme of literary and scientific creation, considering how creators shape, and are shaped by, the culture that surrounds them." Publ Wkly
"Doctorow chose his gallery with what may seem a generous dash of whimsy. Many of his writers and other 'creationists' are not exactly habitues of the canon. Standing alongside the likes of Mark Twain, Sinclair Lewis, Scott Fitzgerald and John Dos Passos are Harriet Beecher Stowe; W. G. Sebald; the anonymous translators of Genesis into the King James version; Harpo Marx; Albert Einstein; [and] the makers of the atomic bomb. . . . And yet the writers assembled here efficiently serve the critic's intentions. Each yields in robustly illustrative ways to 'the voice of the book,' a voice more protean than the artist's own; a voice that soars into conjunction with the voice of the region, the nation, the times." N Y Times Book Rev

Ellison, Ralph

The collected essays of Ralph Ellison; edited with an introduction by John F. Callahan; preface by Saul Bellow. Modern Lib. 1995 xxix, 856p hardcover o.p. pa $18 **814**

1. Jazz music—History and criticism

ISBN 978-0-8129-6826-2 (pa); 0-8129-6826-3 (pa)

          LC 95-4719

This book "includes posthumously discovered reviews, criticism, and interviews, as well as the essay collections *Shadow and Act* (1964) . . . and *Going to the Territory* (1986), an exploration of literature and folklore, jazz and culture, and the nature and quality of lives that black Americans lead." Publisher's note

Emerson, Ralph Waldo, 1803-1882

Essays & lectures. Library of Am. 1983 1321p $35 **814**

ISBN 0-940450-15-1   LC 83-5447

Edited by Joel Porte

Contents: Nature; Addresses and lectures; Essays, first and second series; Representative men; English traits; The conduct of life; Uncollected prose

Includes bibliographical references

Ephron, Nora

I feel bad about my neck; and other thoughts on being a woman. Knopf 2006 137p $21.95; pa $12.95 **814**

ISBN 978-0-307-26455-8; 0-307-26455-6; 978-0-307-27682-7 (pa); 0-307-27682-1 (pa)

         LC 2005-57780

In this collection of essays, Ephron looks "at women who are getting older and dealing with the tribulations of maintenance, menopause, empty nests, and life itself." Publisher's note

"While very little in the book is meant to be taken seriously, it is clever enough to qualify as more than just an assemblage of one-liners. Whether you agree with her observations or not, Ephron's perspective as an admittedly high-maintenance, New York-dwelling, successful screenwriter will keep you entertained." Christ Sci Monit

Epstein, Joseph, 1937-

In a cardboard belt! essays personal, literary, and savage. Houghton Mifflin 2007 xxii, 410p $26 **814**

ISBN 978-0-618-72193-1; 0-618-72193-2

         LC 2007-8515

In this compendium Epstein includes "essays on his father's passing, movies, travel, dining, editing, writer's block, and the strangely gratifying unhappiness of academics; there are moving appreciations of W.H. Auden, Marcel Proust, and John Keats, and fierce depreciations of Edmund Wilson, Mortimer Adler, and poetry prizes. The result is an unusually broad portrait of a thinking man doing his stuff. Epstein is one of the handful of writers in America today whom one can pleasurably read both for substance and style. His writing sparkles with observation and humor." Claremont Rev Books

Fiedler, Leslie A.

Fiedler on the roof; essays on literature and Jewish identity; by Leslie Fiedler. Godine 1990 184p $19.95; pa $11.95 * **814**

1. Jews in literature

ISBN 0-87923-859-3; 0-87923-949-2 (pa)

         LC 90-55282

This volume is a collection of the literary critic's "essays and book reviews since 1970 on more or less Jewish topics. These include: anti-Semitism, the Holocaust, the Book of Job, Isaac Bashevis Singer, Bernard Malamud, . . . and Jewish consciousness in (J.) Joyce's Ulysses." Commentary

"Disturbing, provocative, and brilliant." Libr J

Fraser, Kennedy

Ornament and silence; essays on women's lives. Knopf 1996 247p pa $13 hardcover o.p.

            814

ISBN 0-375-70112-5 (pa)   LC 96-11479

A collection of fourteen profiles, personal reminiscences and extended reviews of books.

"A 'daughter of the paternal old *New Yorker*' in her youth, Fraser . . . has moved on with time, taking for her more mature role models Nina Berberova, Edith Wharton, and Germaine Greer. Fraser's essays are quiet, thorough, and beautifully paced." Libr J

The **Fun** of it; stories from The talk of the town, The New Yorker; edited by Lillian Ross; introduction by David Remnick. Modern Lib. 2001 xxi, 478p pa $16.95 **814**

1. New Yorker (Periodical)

ISBN 0-375-75649-3   LC 00-68237

A "selection of stories from 'Talk' in chronologically arranged sections that begin with the 1920s and end in 2000. Many of the early contributions were unsigned, but through archival research Ross ferrets out and reveals the authors of many of those initial pieces. Included in this lively collection are pieces by writers—some of whom became *New Yorker* regulars—such as Robert Benchley, James Thurber, E. B. White, A. J. Liebling, John Updike, Garrison Keillor, Ann Beattie, Bill McKibben, Roger Angell, Steve Martin, and Susan Orlean." Libr J

Gass, William H., 1924-

Finding a form: essays. Cornell University Press 1997 354p pa $21 **814**

1. Pulitzer Prizes 2. Biography as a literary form

ISBN 0-8014-8489-8

First published 1996 by Knopf

Gass "is 'as obdurate as nails' when it comes to the best possible use of the written word. Each essay in this wide-ranging book (be it titled 'Ezra Pound,' 'Nietzche: The Polemical Philosopher,' 'Robert Walser,' 'Nature, Culture, and Cosmos,' 'Pulitzer, The People Prize,' or 'The Music of Prose') offers evidence for such a conclusion. Gass is concerned with how best to use a phrase or word and believes we should be tough-minded when it comes to reading. He reveals a sardonic sense of humor as well, for example, in discussing the winners of the Pulitzer prize, and he dislikes the fact that anyone would enjoy his/her own writing." Libr J

Ginsberg, Allen, 1926-1997

Deliberate prose; selected essays, 1952-1995. HarperCollins Pubs. 2000 xxiv, 536p pa $17 hardcover o.p. *   **814**

ISBN 0-06-093081-0 (pa)   LC 99-41360

This collection of over 100 prose pieces "organizes the material under several general topics: 'Politics and Prophecies,' 'Drug Culture,' 'Manifestations and Spirituality,' 'Censorship and Sex Laws,' 'Autobiographical Fragments,' 'Literary Techniques and the Beat Generation,' 'Writer,' and 'Further Appreciations,' tributes to artistic collaborators and cultural heroes such as Robert Frank, Philip Glass, Andy Warhol, and the Beatles. . . . Taken together, they provide a rare glimpse into Ginsberg's creative practice, a key to sources and influences, and a good overview of his life and art." Libr J

Includes bibliographical references

Hamill, Pete

Piecework; writings on men and women, fools and heroes, lost cities, vanished friends, small pleasures, large calamities, and how the weather was; foreword by Jimmy Breslin. Little, Brown 1996 432p $32; pa $16   **814**

ISBN 0-316-34104-5; 0-316-34098-7 (pa)

LC 95-4738

This is a collection of previously-published essays by the New York newspaper reporter and columnist

"These essays are opinionated, hard-hitting, passionate, and sometimes disturbing. Writing for magazines ranging from Esquire to Art & Antiques, Hamill's writings show readers the decay of New York and other cities, the violence and heartbreak of Lebanon and Nicaragua, and the unraveling of civil life in many parts of our society." Libr J

Hampton, Howard, 1958-

Born in flames; termite dreams, dialectical fairy tales, and pop apocalypses. Harvard University Press 2007 473p $28.95 *   **814**

1. Motion pictures 2. Rock music 3. Popular culture
ISBN 978-0-674-02317-8; 0-674-02317-X

LC 2006-43680

"In these essays, written for alternative newspapers and art magazines, Hampton charts a freewheeling path through Hong Kong cinema, riot grrl albums and Buffy the Vampire Slayer." Publ Wkly

"The torrent of allusions presupposes an Olympian level of cultural indoctrination, and some sentences are so dense that they require a little thoughtful chewing, but Hampton offers something that grows scarcer as today's media bombardment grows in volume: fresh thinking. Knee-jerk intellectuals may find it easy to lampoon someone who takes pop this seriously, but Hampton is a writer—possibly the only one—who can analyze Buffy the Vampire Slayer in the context of D. H. Lawrence . . . and make it work." Booklist

Includes bibliographical references

Hoagland, Edward

Tigers & ice; reflections on nature and life. Lyons Press 1999 206p $22; pa $16.95   **814**

ISBN 1-55821-742-8; 1-58574-182-5 (pa)

LC 98-36477

"Edward Hoagland entered his 60's captivated by sight. After three years of legal blindness, a surgeon restored both his vision and his delight for the tableaux of the natural world. . . . In the 11 essays collected in 'Tigers and Ice,' he considers subjects as varied as suicide, friendship, cowardice, man-made ponds, Indian tigers and Antarctic penguins—all colored by his renewed view of the world." N Y Times Book Rev

Johnson, Charles Richard, 1948-

Turning the wheel; essays on Buddhism and writing; [by] Charles Johnson. Scribner 2003 187p hardcover o.p. pa $15.95   **814**

1. Johnson, Charles Richard, 1948- 2. African Americans in literature 3. Buddhism
ISBN   0-7432-4324-2;   978-1-4165-7243-5; 1-4165-7243-0   LC 2002-44666

Contents: Reading the Eightfold Path; The elusive art of "mindfulness"; Accepting the invitation; A sangha by another name; On the Book of Proverbs; A poet of being; Toro Nagashi; The role of the black intellectual in the twenty-first century; Uncle Tom's cabin; The singular vision of Ralph Ellison; On Kingsblood royal; Progress in literature; The beginner's mind; A phenomenology of On moral fiction; "Lift ev'ry voice and sing"; An American milk bottle

"The central leitmotifs of the lucid, fervently reasoned essays collected in 'Turning the Wheel' are 'enlightenment and liberation.'" N Y Times Book Rev

Includes bibliographical references

Kosinski, Jerzy N., 1933-1991

Passing by; selected essays, 1962-1991; [by] Jerzy Kosinski. Grove Press; Distributed by Publishers Group West 1995 256p pa $12   **814**

ISBN 0-8021-3423-8   LC 95-19519

First published 1992 by Random House

"A collection of essays, never published in book form, from the author whose 1991 suicide shocked the literary world." Libr J

"While the selections would be improved by contextualizing introductions, they portray a man who was impassioned about literature and who saw his role as confronting 'life's threatening encounters.'" Publ Wkly

Includes bibliographical references

Liebling, A. J. (Abbott Joseph), 1904-1963

Just enough Liebling; classic work by the legendary New Yorker writer; introduction by David Remnick. North Point Press 2004 xxvi, 534p $27.50 *   **814**

ISBN 0-374-10443-3   LC 2004-50056

"The book is divided into six sections, with a brief epilogue—pieces about Paris and about food; articles on

Liebling, A. J. (Abbott Joseph), 1904-1963—
Continued
the press; dispatches from World War II; excerpts from his writing about New York; some boxing stories; [and] excerpts from 'The Earl of Louisiana,' . . . about Gov. Earl Long, Huey's brother." N Y Times Book Rev
"This captivating and appropriately plump . . . collection will bring renewed attention to a master of the man-on-the-street, narrative nonfiction form and celebrate the centenary of Liebling's birth." Booklist

McPhee, John A.
Irons in the fire; [by] John McPhee. Farrar, Straus & Giroux 1997 215p $22; pa $14
                814
  ISBN 0-374-17726-0; 0-374-52545-5 (pa)
            LC 96-32358
The title essay of this "collection of *New Yorker* pieces is . . . [an] account of cattle rustling in Nevada that harks back to the Wild West. In California, McPhee ponders an environmental disaster in the making as he inspects the world's largest mountain of scrapped automobile tires. Other pieces deal with a blind professor of English who uses a talking computer and forensic geologists who sift sand, pebbles, microfossils and mineral grains to solve murders, track down terrorists and pinpoint remote geographies." Publ Wkly
"John McPhee's essays are proof that the kind of journalism that can effortlessly put a topic into perfect perspective will never go out of style." N Y Times Book Rev

Miller, Arthur, 1915-2005
Echoes down the corridor; collected essays, 1947-1999; edited by Stephen R. Centola. Viking 2000 332p pa $15 hardcover o.p.   **814**
  ISBN 0-14-200005-1 (pa)   LC 00-40427
"The 50 essays collected here range from atmospheric reminiscences of his childhood in Brooklyn and studies at the University of Michigan, to accounts of visits to China, the Soviet Union and Turkey as an advocate for victims of governmental persecution. Deeply influenced by the radical culture of the 1930s and by his youth during the depression, Miller has always been firmly on the political left." Publ Wkly
"This collection is not to be missed." Libr J

Ozick, Cynthia
The din in the head; essays. Houghton Mifflin Co. 2006 243p il $24 *   **814**
  1. Literature—History and criticism
  ISBN 978-0-618-47050-1; 0-618-47050-6
          LC 2005-16102
These essays investigate "the works of Leo Tolstoy, Saul Bellow, Helen Keller, Isaac Babel, Sylvia Plath, Susan Sontag, and others." Publisher's note
The author is "not only one of the finest novelists of our time but an essayist of startling spiritual verve and range." Christ Century

Quarrel & quandary; essays. Knopf 2000 247p pa $13 hardcover o.p. *   **814**
  1. Literature—History and criticism
  ISBN 0-375-72445-9 (pa)   LC 99-89889

Among the topics discussed in this collection of personal and literary essays are Henry James, Anne Frank, Kafka, poetry, and public intellectuals.
"All the essays collected here began life elsewhere as reviews and higher journalism. This kind of gathering of literary leftovers is usually not worth reprinting. Ozick's work is an exception. Her pieces have genuine durability. They are great essays." N Y Times Book Rev

Remnick, David
Reporting; writings from The New Yorker. Knopf 2006 483p $27.95   **814**
  ISBN 0-307-26358-4; 978-0-307-26358-2
          LC 2005-44709
This is a collection of "twenty-three New Yorker articles from the magazine's editor, David Remnick. . . . The earliest article dates from 1994; the latest was reported from Israel and Gaza within days of the Hamas victory in the January 2006 elections." N Y Times Book Rev
The author "is an ideal reporter, combining erudition, curiosity, wit, an eye for the telling anecdote and empathy." Publ Wkly

Said, Edward W.
Reflections on exile and other essays. Harvard Univ. Press 2000 xxxv, 617p (Convergences) $36.95; pa $19.95   **814**
  1. Melville, Herman, 1819-1891. Moby Dick
  2. Conrad, Joseph, 1857-1924. Nostromo 3. Politics in literature 4. Literature—History and criticism 5. Criticism
  ISBN 0-674-00302-0; 0-674-00997-5 (pa)
          LC 00-44996
"Written between 1967 and the present by a literary critic and advocate for the Palestinian cause, these pieces often deal with the self-deceiving fictions of the colonizers about the people they oppress; others deplore some fashionable critical theories as unengaged with real life and history." N Y Times Book Rev
Includes bibliographical references

Sontag, Susan, 1933-2004
At the same time; essays and speeches; edited by Paolo Dilonardo and Anne Jump; with a foreword by David Rieff. Farrar, Straus & Giroux 2007 235p $23 *   **814**
  ISBN 0-374-10072-1; 978-0-374-10072-8
          LC 2006-31179
This is a "collection of 16 essays written toward the end of . . . [Sontag's] life. . . . Every public and academic library should crave to own this." Libr J

Styles of radical will. Picador USA 2002 274p pa $15 *   **814**
  ISBN 0-312-42021-8   LC 2001-58071
  First published 1969 by Farrar, Straus & Giroux
"The book contains essays, some previously published, arranged in groups. The first group of three is aesthetic and philosophical; three deal with film; and the last set is . . . a reply to a Partisan Review questionnaire about America and an . . . essay on a trip to North Vietnam." Libr J

Sontag, Susan, 1933-2004—*Continued*

Where the stress falls; essays. Farrar, Straus & Giroux 2001 351p $25; pa $14 **814**
1. Gombrowicz, Witold. Ferdydurke 2. Zagajewski, Adam, 1945-. Another beauty 3. Wescott, Glenway, 1901-1987. The pilgrim hawk
ISBN 0-374-28917-4; 0-312-42131-1 (pa)
LC 2001-33704
The essays in this collection "are organized into three categories. 'Reading' encompasses Sontag's erudite, critical renderings on autobiography and the works and influence of international literary figures such as Machado de Assis, Roland Barthes, Danilo Kiš, Marina Tsvetaeva, and Robert Walser. In the middle section, 'Seeing,' Sontag is more approachable, expressing her perceptive and provocative opinions on cinema, garden history, photography, painting, opera, drama, and dance. Finally, in 'There and Now,' Sontag recounts her experiences in Sarajevo and her feelings regarding travel, activism, writing, and translations." Libr J

Updike, John
Due considerations; essays and criticism. Alfred A. Knopf 2007 xxii, 703p il $40 **814**
ISBN 978-0-307-26640-8; 0-307-26640-0
LC 2007-18665
"Updike's sixth collection of essays and literary criticism opens with . . . [an] overview of literary biographies, proceeds to five essays on topics ranging from China and small change to faith and late works, and takes up, under the heading 'General Considerations,' books, pokers, cars, and the American libido." Publisher's note
"A lush book to be savored over a long period of time." Booklist

Vidal, Gore, 1925-
The selected essays of Gore Vidal; edited by Jay Parini. Doubleday 2008 458p $27.50
814
ISBN 978-0-385-52484-1; 0-385-52484-6
LC 2008-13517
"Regardless of what one thinks of Vidal, what Vidal thinks is never in doubt in these 24 essays, divided here into two groups: literary criticism and historical or cultural commentary. His writing is clear, sharp, and disciplined, and his approbation of William Dean Howells and Italo Calvino are as finely tuned as his excoriation of John Updike and Herman Wouk." Libr J
Includes bibliographical references

Vonnegut, Kurt, 1922-2007
A man without a country; edited by Daniel Simon. Seven Stories Press 2005 146p il $23.95 *
814
ISBN 1-58322-713-X LC 2005-14967
The author discusses politics, human nature, and other topics "in this collection of articles written over the last five years, many from the alternative magazine In These Times." Publ Wkly

Wallace, David Foster
Consider the lobster; and other essays. Little, Brown 2005 343p il $25.95 **814**
ISBN 0-316-15611-6 LC 2005-10886
This "is a collection of literary essays and reportage pieces written for assorted magazines." N Y Times (Late N Y Ed)
"Wallace's complex essays are written, and rightfully so, to be read more than once." Booklist
Includes bibliographical references

White, E. B. (Elwyn Brooks), 1899-1985
Essays of E.B. White. Perennial Classics 1999 364p il pa $14.95 * **814**
ISBN 0-06-093223-6 LC 98-56019
Also available in hardcover from P. Smith
First published 1977
Most of the essays first appeared in The New Yorker. "They range from a 1934 piece on the St. Nicholas Magazine 'League' and the distinguished writers who were members of it as children, to a 1975 report from Allen Cove, Maine, where White had retreated from the bedlam of the city." Publ Wkly

Williams, William Carlos, 1883-1963
In the American grain. New Directions 1956 235p pa $13.95 hardcover o.p. **814**
ISBN 0-8112-0230-5 (pa) LC 56-13360
First published 1925 by A. & C. Boni
Williams portrays "the developing American conscience in sketches of such major figures as Columbus, Cotton Mather, Washington, Franklin, and Poe, and such minor ones as Champlain, Thomas Morton, Père Sebastian Rasles, and Jacataqua. He sought the grain of American character especially in homely, rather than heroic, incidents of national history." Benet's Reader's Ency of Am Lit

Wilson, Edmund, 1895-1972
Literary essays and reviews of the 1920s & 30s. Library of America 2007 958p $40 **814**
1. Literature—History and criticism 2. Modernism (Aesthetics)
ISBN 978-1-59853-013-1 LC 2007-928898
This volume collects The Shores of Light (1952), a collection of his early reviews and other writings; and Axel's Castle (1931), a book of literary criticism discussing modernism. It also includes several previously uncollected reviews.
"Anyone wishing to revisit the intellectual and literary passions of the period will be well advised to do so in the company of someone who could be a Virgil as well as recommend the reading of him. Edmund Wilson came as close as anybody has to making the labor of criticism into an art." Atl Mon
Includes bibliographical references

Literary essays and reviews of the 1930s & 40s; [Lewis M. Dabney, editor] Library of America 2007 979p $40 **814**
1. Literature—History and criticism 2. Modernism (Aesthetics)
ISBN 978-1-59853-014-8 LC 2007-928899

Wilson, Edmund, 1895-1972—*Continued*

This volume gathers together The Triple Thinkers (1938, revised 1948), The Wound and The Bow (1941), Classics and Commercials (1950), along with a selection of uncollected reviews.

"This is a required purchase for all libraries, public and academic—even for those collections already having these texts in separate volumes." Libr J

Includes bibliographical references

815.008 American speeches— Collections

American speeches. Library of America 2006 2v ea $35 *   **815.008**
1. American speeches
ISBN 1-931082-97-9 (v1); 1-931082-98-7 (v2)
LC 2006-40928

Contents: pt. 1. Political oratory from the Revolution to the Civil War—pt. 2. Political oratory from Abraham Lincoln to Bill Clinton

This is a collection of over 120 historical speeches delivered between 1761 and 1997.

Includes bibliographical references

816 American letters

Letters of the century; America, 1900-1999; edited by Lisa Grunwald and Stephen J. Adler. Dial Press (NY) 1999 741p il $35   **816**
1. American letters 2. United States—Civilization
ISBN 0-385-31590-2   LC 99-16808

This anthology "contains four hundred and twelve letters arranged chronologically to demonstrate the effects of war, the Depression, demographic change, scientific innovation, medical discovery, and artistic experimentation on American life." New Yorker

Among the letter writers gathered are "Carl Van Doren, Huey Long, Franklin D. Roosevelt, Lillian Hellman and a Vietnam soldier named Dusty. This is one of the most original literary tributes to the closing century." Publ Wkly

Includes bibliographical references

817 American humor and satire

Allen, Woody

Side effects. Ballantine 1987 213p pa $6.99
                                              817
ISBN 978-0-345-34335-2; 0-345-34335-2
First published 1980 by Random House

"The sixteen sketches—which are concerned with themes of love and death, angst and despair, bagels and lox—appeared originally in magazines." Commonweal

Without feathers. Ballantine 1983 221p pa $6.99
                                              817
ISBN 0-345-33697-6; 978-0-345-33697-2
First published 1975 by Random House

A collection of sixteen satirical sketches, most of which previously appeared in The New Yorker and other periodicals, and two one-act plays: God, and Death. The sketches include "takeoffs on other writers (Kafka, Bellow, Strindberg), and several 'intellectual' dissertations on such topics as the Irish genius, the origins of slang, the lesser ballets, psychic phenomena, etc." Libr J

Carlin, George, 1937-2008

Napalm & silly putty. Hyperion 2001 269p $22.95; pa $12.95   **817**
ISBN 0-7868-6413-3; 0-7868-8758-3 (pa)
LC 00-54055

The comedian "covers a wide range of issues from rape and religion to the homeless. . . . And any topic is fair game: abortion, airport security, cars, funerals, language, organ donors, sports, technology, TV and war. . . . Over 100 scintillating short pieces are interrupted by loony lists and hundreds of clever one-liners." Publ Wkly

Frazier, Ian

Coyote v. Acme. Picador USA 2002 117p pa $11   **817**
ISBN 0-312-42058-7; 978-0-312-42058-1
LC 2001-50067

First published 1996 by Farrar, Straus & Giroux

This collection "contains 22 pieces spoofing a wide range of subjects from Wylie Coyote to Joseph Stalin, from aggressive New Yorkers to the all-powerful Internal Revenue Service." Libr J

"The title essay, with its exposition, in deadly legalese, of one Wile E. Coyote's complaints against a generic purveyor of explosive devices, shows Frazier's great comic range, however trite the subject. Although this book is not Frazier at full-bore, readers of his generation will find an occasional cultural reference long thought lost, and find themselves oddly beholden to a fellow who can resurrect Billy Joe McCallister from beneath the Tallahatchie Bridge." Publ Wkly

Martin, Steve, 1945-

Pure drivel. Hyperion 1998 104p $19.95; pa $10.95   **817**
ISBN 0-7868-6467-2; 0-7868-8505-X (pa)
LC 98-28739

"The short essays, conversations, and proclamations collected here are relayed in a slyly deadpan Valley voice that belies the coiled craziness of their content. Martin also brings his gift for comedic timing to these creations, setting a quirky beat that perfectly sets off their ironic wiles." Booklist

Mirth of a nation; the best contemporary humor; edited by Michael J. Rosen. HarperPerennial 2000 619p pa $15.95   **817**
1. American wit and humor
ISBN 0-06-095321-7   LC 99-44293

An anthology of more than 50 contributors, "most represented by two or three short works. Included are veterans like Dave Barry, Roy Blount Jr., and Fran Lebowitz, and rising stars like David Sedaris, Sandra Tsing Loh, Patricia Marx, and David Rakoff. Though many of the pieces have been published or broadcast previously, some appear in this volume for the first time." Booklist

Nilsen, Alleen Pace

Encyclopedia of 20th century American humor; [by] Alleen Pace Nilsen and Don L. F. Nilsen. Oryx Press 2000 360p il $73.95 **817**

ISBN 1-57356-218-1 LC 99-47257

This "is a 98-entry reference work. A bibliography that includes scholarly works on humor, biographies, and joke books stretches over 20 pages and rounds out the text. Arranged alphabetically, articles vary in length from one to five pages. A few are illustrated with cartoons and photographs. Some longer articles are broken down into subtopics." Booklist

Includes bibliographical references

Sedaris, David

Dress your family in corduroy and denim. Little, Brown 2004 257p $24.95 **817**

ISBN 0-316-14346-4 LC 2003-65673

In this collection of essays, the author focuses on "the gentle dementia of the Sedaris clan; his many years wandering in obscurity; [and] his life in France with his boyfriend, Hugh." N Y Times Book Rev

The author "has a unique ability to supply exactly the right details to bring every funny, awkward, ludicrous, painful, horrible real-life moment into harrowingly crisp focus." Booklist

Me talk pretty one day. Little, Brown 2000 272p $22.95; pa $14.95 **817**

ISBN 0-316-77772-2; 0-316-77696-3 (pa)
LC 00-25052

"In this collection of 27 fairly short essays, some of which appeared in *Esquire* and *The New Yorker*, Sedaris gives the impression of ease and naturalness. Whether he is writing about overcoming a lisp, learning to play the guitar, trying to master French, or taking an IQ test, whether the locales are North Carolina, New York, or France, the author is both amused and amusing." Libr J

When you are engulfed in flames. Little, Brown 2008 323p $25.99 **817**

ISBN 978-0-316-14347-9; 0-316-14347-2
LC 2007-49021

This collection "gets its title from a booklet with tips for 'Disaster Damage Prevention' that Sedaris found in a Hiroshima hotel room when he moved to Japan for three months to quit smoking. . . . [His stay] provides fresh material aplenty for the longest piece, 'The Smoking Section,' which is destined to become a quit-lit (or quitterature) classic. The draw, as always, is Sedaris's utter lack of sanctimony and his use of humor as a portal to deeper feelings. Instead of insufferably touting his new purity, Sedaris recalls all those nasty habits he's overcome—alcohol, marijuana, cigarettes—with wistful fondness. His honesty is refreshing." Christ Sci Monit

817.008 American humor and satire—Collections

Mark Twain's library of humor; illustrated by E.W. Kemble; Steve Martin, series ed.; introduction by Roy Blount. Modern Library 2000 xl, 560p il pa $17 **817.008**

1. American wit and humor
ISBN 978-0-679-64036-3 LC 00-25971

"Beginning with the piece that made Mark Twain famous—'The Notorious Jumping Frog of Calaveras County'—and ending with his fanciful 'How I Edited an Agricultural Paper,' this . . . anthology, an abridgment of the 1888 original, collects twenty of Twain's own pieces, in addition to tall tales, fables, and satires by forty-three of Twain's contemporaries, including Washington Irving, Harriet Beecher Stowe, Ambrose Bierce, William Dean Howells, Joel Chandler Harris, Artemus Ward, and Bret Harte." Publisher's note

818 American miscellany

Alcott, Louisa May, 1832-1888

The sketches of Louisa May Alcott; with an introduction by Gregory Eiselein. Ironweed Press 2001 283p (Ironwood American classics) pa $22.95 **818**

ISBN 0-9655309-8-1 LC 00-57259

"Grouped into five categories ('Hospital sketches,' 'Letters from the Mountains,' 'Sketches of Europe,' 'Concord, Massachusetts,' and 'From *The Youth's Companion* and *Merry's Museum*),' these by turns frank, witty, ironic, charming and pensive pieces were almost all written when Alcott was between the ages of 28 and 43." Publ Wkly

Includes bibliographical references

Baraka, Imamu Amiri, 1934-

The LeRoi Jones/Amiri Baraka reader; by Amiri Baraka; edited by William Harris in collaboration with Amiri Baraka. 2nd ed. Thunder's Mouth Press 2000 xxxiii, 586p pa $16.95 **818**

1. Blues music
ISBN 1-56025-238-3 LC 99-32364
First published 1991

A collection of Baraka's poems, plays, and other writings. "The selections included are arranged chronologically in four distinct periods: The Beat Period (1957-62), The Transitional Period (1963-65), The Black Nationalist Period (1965-74), and The Third World Marxist Period (1974-present)." Libr J [review of 1991 edition]

Includes bibliographical references

Bishop, Elizabeth, 1911-1979

The collected prose; edited, with an introduction, by Robert Giroux. Farrar, Straus & Giroux 1984 xxii, 278p pa $16 hardcover o.p.
818

ISBN 0-374-51855-6 (pa) LC 83-16418

A collection of Bishop's autobiographical sketches and short stories

"Whether she is discussing the sensuous joys and dark fears of childhood or diamond mining and the preparation of food in Brazil, Elizabeth Bishop provides warm, unforced revelations on an array of topics. . . . A book to relish as well as to read." Choice

Includes bibliographical references

Capote, Truman, 1924-1984

Music for chameleons; new writing. Random House 1980 262p pa $13 hardcover o.p.

818

ISBN 0-679-74566-1 (pa)   LC 79-5532

"There are three sections: one of short stories, or something like; one consisting of the 'In cold blood'-like 'short novel, Handcarved coffins;' and one called 'Conversational portraits,' which is precisely that." Choice

Carson, Anne, 1950-

Decreation; poetry, essays, opera. Knopf 2005 245p $24.95   **818**

ISBN 1-4000-4349-2   LC 2004-63367

In 13 interrelated works of prose and poetry, the author "takes on the meaning and function of sleep; the art and attitudes of Samuel Beckett; the last days of an elderly mother; guns; a solar eclipse; 'Longing, a Documentary'; the films of Michelangelo Antonioni; and the vexing, paradoxical projects of women mystics, among them Simone Weil and the medieval heretic Marguerite Porete." Publ Wkly

"Carson's inquiry into the paradoxical 'decreation' of the self in the quest for the divine exemplifies her gift for joining erudition with feeling, insight with wit, and a sense of cosmic continuity with personal liberation." Booklist

Cather, Willa, 1873-1947

Stories, poems, and other writings. Library of Am. 1992 1039p $35 *   **818**

ISBN 0-940450-71-2   LC 91-62294

This volume contains the novels Alexander's bridge (1912) and My mortal enemy (1926); the poetry collection April twilights, and other poems (1923); the essay collection Not under forty (1936); and the following short story collections: Youth and the bright Medusa (1920); Obscure destinies (1932); The old beauty, and others (1948); and uncollected stories from 1892-1929

Crane, Stephen, 1871-1900

Prose and poetry. Library of Am. 1984 1379p $40; pa $15.95   **818**

1. Short stories

ISBN 0-940450-17-8; 1-883011-39-6 (pa)

LC 83-19908

Contents: Maggie: a girl of the streets; The red badge of courage; George's mother; The third violet; The monster; Stories, sketches, and journalism, by place and time; Poems

"This collection also includes both Crane's collections of epigrammatic free verses—'The Black Riders' and 'War is kind'—and selections from his uncollected poems." Publisher's note

Dillard, Annie

The Annie Dillard reader. HarperCollins Pubs. 1994 455p pa $15.95 hardcover o.p. *

818

ISBN 0-06-092660-0 (pa)   LC 94-19482

This reader includes Holy the firm; excerpts from Pilgrim at Tinker Creek, An American childhood, and Teaching a stone to talk; and a reworked version of the 1978 short story The living

"This selection of writings, chosen by Dillard herself, provides a perfect sampling of her incisive, versatile, and impeccable achievements." Booklist

Pilgrim at Tinker Creek. Harper & Row 1974 271p hardcover o.p. pa $14.95   **818**

1. Natural history—Virginia

ISBN 0-06-123332-3 (pa); 978-0-06-123332-6 (pa)

Also available in hardcover from Buccaneer Bks.

Starting with January, Dillard "records the seasons as they come and go at Tinker Creek in Virginia." Time

This work is "in an honored tradition of literature, not quite environmentalism and not the philosophy of science, it is rather the refraction of natural philosophy through the prismatic conscience of art. Highly recommended for the general reader—any general reader, anywhere—who wishes to deepen his awareness of his yard of world and to reflect upon it more profoundly." Choice

Teaching a stone to talk; expeditions and encounters. Harper & Row 1982 177p pa $13 hardcover o.p.   **818**

1. Natural history

ISBN 0-06-091541-2 (pa)   LC 82-47520

"In the fourteen pensées that make up this book {the author} bears witness, reflects on her observations of the order and disorder, the splendor and horror of the natural world." New Yorker

Du Bois, W. E. B. (William Edward Burghardt), 1868-1963

Writings. Library of Am. 1986 1334p $40; pa $15.95 *   **818**

ISBN 0-940450-33-X; 1-883011-31-0 (pa)

LC 86-10565

Edited by Nathan Huggins

Contents: The suppression of the African slave-trade; The souls of black folk; Dusk of dawn; Essays; Articles from The crisis

Includes bibliographical references

Einstein, Albert, 1879-1955

Ideas and opinions; with an introduction by Alan Lightman; based on Mein weltbild, edited by Carl Seelig, and other sources; new translations and revisions by Sonja Bargmann. Modern Lib. 1994 418p $16.95; pa $13   **818**

ISBN 0-679-60105-8; 0-517-88440-2 (pa)

LC 94-2115

A reissue of the title first published 1954 by Crown

This is a collection of the scientist's general writings on such subjects as freedom, education, religion, politics and government, the Jewish people, and Germany

Eiseley, Loren C., 1907-1977

The night country; [by] Loren Eiseley; illustrations by Leonard Everett Fisher; introduction to the Bison Books edition by Gale E. Christianson. University of Nebraska Press 1997 240p il pa $19.95   **818**

Eiseley, Loren C., 1907-1977—*Continued*
ISBN 0-8032-6735-5; 978-0-8032-6735-0
First published 1971 by Scribner
"First Bison Books printing" Verso of title page
These poetically expressed reflections "evoke a sense
of wonder and appreciation of nature and man's place in
the universe. The striking black-and-white illustrations
preceding each chapter contribute to the mood and tone."
Booklist
   Includes bibliographical references

The star thrower. Harcourt 1979 319p pa $15
818
ISBN 978-0-15-684909-8; 0-15-684909-7
First published 1978 by Times Bks.
A collection of the late scientist's essays and poems.
"The materials are arranged in three categories, 'Nature
and Autobiography,' 'Early Poems,' and 'Science and
Humanism.'" Christ Sci Monit
   "To read this collection is to see the things he points
out to us refracted, transmuted, and clarified through the
prism of his poetic imagination and literate style." Libr
J

Ellison, Ralph
   Going to the territory. Random House 1986
338p pa $14.95 hardcover o.p. *   **818**
ISBN 978-0-679-76001-6 (pa); 0-679-76001-6 (pa)
                LC 85-28117
   "This collection of essays, addresses, and reviews
deals with topics in literature, music, and race relations.
. . . Ellison tries to view American culture as a cloth of
one piece. His analysis of the growth of the culture, and
of the dynamic interaction of the diverse elements within
it, is perceptive and convincing." Libr J

Franklin, Benjamin, 1706-1790
   Autobiography, Poor Richard, and later writings;
letters from London, 1757-1775, Paris, 1776-1785,
Philadelphia, 1785-1790, Poor Richard's almanack,
1733-1758, The autobiography. Library of America
1997 816p $30 *   **818**
ISBN 1-883011-53-1   LC 97-21611
   "J.A. Leo Lemay wrote the notes and selected the
texts for this volume" Prelim. paging
   "This collection of Franklin's works begins with letters sent from London (1757-1775) describing the events
and diplomacy preceding the Revolutionary War. The
volume also contains political satires, bagatelles, pamphlets, and letters written in Paris (1776-1785), where he
represented the revolutionary United States at the court
of Louis XVI, as well as his speeches given in the Constitutional Convention and other works written in Philadelphia (1785-1790), including his last published article,
a . . . satire against slavery. Also included are the . . .
prefaces to Poor Richard's Almanack (1733-1758). . . .
[The] Autobiography, Franklin's last word on his greatest
literary creation—his own invented personality—is presented here in a new edition." Publisher's note
   Includes bibliographical references

Frost, Robert, 1874-1963
   Collected poems, prose, & plays. Library of
Am. 1995 1036p $35 *   **818**
   1. Poetry—By individual authors
ISBN 1-883011-06-X   LC 94-43693
This volume contains "all of the plays, a generous selection of prose, all collected poems, and 94 uncollected
poems, as well as 17 poems that were previously unpublished." Libr J

Gibran, Kahlil, 1883-1931
   The collected works; with eighty-four
illustrations by the author. Everyman's Library
2007 880p il $27.50   **818**
   ISBN 978-0-307-26707-8; 0-307-26707-5
              LC 2007-28736
   "Everyman's library"
   This anthology of writings by the Syrian poet includes
*The Madman, The Forerunner, The Prophet, Sand and
Foam, Jesus the Son of Man, Earth Gods, The Wanderer,
The Garden of the Prophet, Prose Poems, Spirits Rebel-
lious, Nymphs of the Valley*, and *A Tear and a Smile*.

Hurston, Zora Neale, 1891-1960
   Folklore, memoirs, and other writings. Library
of Am. 1995 1001p il $35 *   **818**
   ISBN 0-940450-84-4   LC 94-21384
   Companion volume to Novels and stories (1995)
   "This is the first time the unexpurgated version of
Hurston's 1942 autobiography, *Dust Tracks on the Road*,
is being published; sections deemed too provocative
(dealing with politics, race, and sex) have been restored.
Mules and Men (1935) is a collection of African Ameri-
can folklore she gleaned on travels in the South, while
Tell My Horse (1938) tenders her personal findings on
African-based religion in Jamaica and Haiti. Additionally,
22 magazine and book articles with anthropological
themes . . . that have never been gathered into book
form are corralled here." Booklist

Jefferson, Thomas, 1743-1826
   Writings. Library of Am. 1984 1600p $35 *
                     818
   ISBN 0-940450-16-X   LC 83-19917
   Edited by Merrill D. Peterson
   "Autobiography—A summary view of the rights of
British America—Notes on the State of Virginia—Public
papers—Addresses, messages, and replies—Miscellany—
Letters." Title page
   This is "the largest and most skillfully edited single-
volume Jefferson ever published." N Y Times Book Rev
   Includes bibliographical references

Kingston, Maxine Hong
   The fifth book of peace. Knopf 2003 401p $26;
pa $14.95   **818**
   1. Peace 2. Vietnam War, 1961-1975
   ISBN 0-679-44075-5; 0-679-76063-6 (pa)
                LC 2002-34103
   When "Kingston embarked on a sequel to her delightful novel 'Tripmaster Monkey,' she called it 'The Fourth

Kingston, Maxine Hong—*Continued*

Book of Peace,' echoing a half-remembered Chinese legend about Three Books of Peace. But the manuscript was destroyed in a fire—a suggestive occurrence to Kingston, because the books in the legend were also burned. Here she recreates her lost fictional narrative and sets it alongside an account of her life after the fire. . . . The book is rich in empathy and moral conviction." New Yorker

Matthiessen, Peter

The Peter Matthiessen reader; nonfiction 1959-1991; edited with an introduction by McKay Jenkins. Vintage Bks. 2000 359p pa $14

818

ISBN 0-375-70272-5   LC 99-35246

"A Vintage original"

Excerpts and essays highlighting the spiritual, literary, and political aspects of Matthiessen's work from Wildlife in America to Men's lives

Mencken, H. L. (Henry Louis), 1880-1956

A second Mencken chrestomathy; a new selection from the writings of America's legendary editor, critic, and wit; selected, revised, and annotated by the author; edited and with an introduction by Terry Teachout. Johns Hopkins University Press 2006 528p (Maryland paperback bookshelf) pa $35   **818**

ISBN 0-8018-8549-3   LC 2006-11581

First published 1995 by Knopf

"Mencken edited the first Chrestomathy himself in 1948. He called it 'a sort of Mencken Encyclopedia,' but noted that he had 'an excess of copied material about equal in bulk to the matter now in the book.' Mr. Teachout . . . has organized the unused material into discrete sections and provided titles and chapter headings—as well as performing a substantial amount of copy editing." Booklist

Miller, Henry, 1891-1980

Henry Miller on writing; selected by Thomas H. Moore from the published and unpublished works of Henry Miller. New Directions 1964 216p pa $11.95 *   **818**

ISBN 0-8112-0112-0

The author discusses the art and practice of writing with insights on how he set his goals, how he discovered the excitement of using words, how the books he read influenced him, and how he learned to draw on his own experiences

Oliver, Mary, 1935-

Winter hours; prose, prose poems, and poems. Houghton Mifflin 1999 109p $22; pa $14

818

1. Poetry—By individual authors

ISBN 0-395-85084-3; 0-395-85087-8 (pa)

LC 99-19141

"Oliver has set aside the frames of form and the mask of her poetic persona to share memories and meditations

in essays made of both poetry and prose. Writing with the knowingness born of many years of devotion to observation and expression, Oliver declares her unceasing love of nature, the source of her art, and her willingness to embrace what most people resent: the shift in tone and meter age brings." Booklist

The **Oxford** companion to Mark Twain; editor, Gregg Camfield. Oxford Univ. Press 2003 xxi, 767p il $75 *   **818**

1. Twain, Mark, 1835-1910

ISBN 0-19-510710-1   LC 2002-151880

Contents: Censorship, by N. Hentoff; Critical reception, by D. L. Smith; The dream of domesticity, by S. K. Harris; Etiquette, by J. Martin; Performance, by A. Miller; Realism, by F. Pohl; Mark Twain's reputation, by L. J. Budd; Technology, by B. Michelson; Researching Mark Twain; A bibliography of works, by S. L. Clemens; A chronology of Samuel Clemens's life, work, and times

This volume "begins with 300 alphabetically arranged entries of varying lengths devoted to all [Twain's] works, places and people related to his life, and analyses of his views on a variety of topics, from animals to spiritualism. Next come a bibliography of his published works collated from other bibliographies, a chronology, and a general index." Choice

Includes bibliographical references

Parker, Dorothy, 1893-1967

The portable Dorothy Parker; with a new introduction by Brendan Gill. rev and enl ed. Viking 1973 xxvii, 610p pa $18 hardcover o.p.

818

ISBN 978-0-14-303953-2; 0-14-303953-9

"The Viking portable library"

First published 1944 with title: Dorothy Parker

This collection contains: thirty-two short stories; poems; drama reviews; book reviews, including the entire text of Constant reader; and miscellaneous articles

"It is hard to imagine a library that would not want this book." Choice

Percy, Walker, 1916-1990

Lost in the cosmos; the last self-help book. Picador 2000 262p pa $14   **818**

ISBN 0-312-25399-0   LC 99-87846

A reissue of the title first published 1983 by Farrar, Straus & Giroux

"The book consists of a mock self-help quiz. Percy poses 20 questions with didactic overtones. . . . Lost in the Cosmos contains essays, science fiction, one-liners, charts, a script for 'The Last Donahue Show,' and letters to 'Dear Abby.'" Christ Today

"The whole is brought off with that sly humor and intellectual verve that have made the author's novels exceptional." Natl Rev

Signposts in a strange land; edited with an introduction by Patrick Samway. Picador 2000 428p pa $15   **818**

ISBN 0-312-25419-9   LC 99-89573

A reissue of the title first published 1991 by Farrar, Straus & Giroux

Percy, Walker, 1916-1990—*Continued*

This collection's "speeches, interviews, and essays (some published for the first time) investigate various aspects of Percy's lifelong interests: the South; science, language, and literature; and morality and religion." Booklist

Includes bibliographical references

Poe, Edgar Allan, 1809-1849

Essays and reviews. Library of Am. 1984 1544p $40 * **818**

ISBN 0-940450-19-4   LC 83-19923

Edited by G. R. Thompson

This volume is divided into six main divisions: Theory of poetry, Reviews of British and Continental authors; Reviews of American authors and American criticism; Magazines and criticism; The literary and social scene; and Articles and marginalia

Includes bibliographical references

Poetry and tales. Library of Am. 1984 1408p $37.50 * **818**

ISBN 0-940450-18-6   LC 83-19931

Edited by Patrick F. Quinn

This volume contains 70 stories and Poe's poetic work in its entirety

Includes bibliographical references

Rasmussen, R. Kent

Critical companion to Mark Twain; a literary reference to his life and work; with critical commentary by John H. Davis and Alex Feerst. Rev ed. Facts on File 2007 2v il map (Facts on File library of American literature) set $125 **818**

1. Twain, Mark, 1835-1910

ISBN 0-8160-5398-7; 978-0-8160-5398-8

     LC 2004-46910

First published 1995 in one volume with title: Mark Twain A to Z

Contents: v1. Part I: Biography; Part II: Works A-Z v2. Part III: Related people, places, and topics; Part IV: Appendices

This companion to the life and works of Mark Twain includes a biography, synopses and critical commentaries on each of his works, discussions about major characters and places in his works, and entries on important people, places, and other aspects of his life.

Includes glossary, filmography and bibliographical references

Rich, Adrienne

Arts of the possible; essays and conversations. Norton 2001 190p $23.95; pa $13.95 **818**

ISBN 0-393-05045-9; 0-393-32312-9 (pa)

     LC 00-51522

This volume "collects Rich's best-known prose from the 1970s and 1980s, with new writing that extends through the 1990s. In letters such as 'Why I Refused the National Medal for the Arts,' and through complaints about feminism as the cult of the personal and a renewed call for a collective global vision, she delights, and is by turns lyrical and polemical." Ms

Silko, Leslie, 1948-

Storyteller. Arcade Publishing 1989 278p pa $17.95 **818**

ISBN 978-1-55970-005-4; 1-55970-005-X

First published 1981 by Seaver Books

This "consists of short stories, anecdotes, folktales, poems, historical and autobiographical notes, and photographs." N Y Times Book Rev

"Memory and invention are the stuff of Silko's storytelling. Although many of her stories traverse familiar territory—the dislocation of a disinherited people—her perceptions are acute, and her style reflects the breadth, the texture, the mortality of her subjects." Saturday Rev

Sova, Dawn B.

Critical companion to Edgar Allan Poe; a literary reference to his life and work. Facts on File 2007 458p il (Facts on File library of American literature) $75 **818**

1. Poe, Edgar Allan, 1809-1849

ISBN 0-8160-6408-3; 978-0-8160-6408-3

     LC 2006-29466

First published 2001 with title: Edgar Allan Poe, A-Z

"Biographical, historical, and critical material on Poe's life and work is presented in alphabetical order in three sections. The entries on Poe's works each provide a synopsis, a publication history, and character descriptions, while major works such as 'The Cask of Amontillado' and 'The Purloined Letter' have . . . [a] commentary and . . . further-reading suggestions." SLJ

Includes bibliographical references

Stein, Gertrude, 1874-1946

Writings, 1903-1932. Library of Am. 1998 941p $40 **818**

ISBN 978-1-883011-40-6; 1-883011-40-X

     LC 97-28915

In Stein's "early works, she sought a new kind of realism exemplified here by Q.E.D. (written 1903, published posthumously), a novel about lesbian entanglements at college, and the modern classic Three Lives (1909), a set of novellas about the lives of three ordinary women, described in the simplest and most direct of prose. In her . . . abstract 'portraits' Stein uses an extraordinary array of verbal techniques to evoke those friends and collaborators—Matisse, Picasso, Apollinaire, Juan Gris, Satie, Mabel Dodge, Carl Van Vechten, Sherwood Anderson, Virgil Thomson—with whom she shared decades of revolutionary ferment in the arts. Her play Four Saints in Three Acts (1927), which became the basis for an opera by Virgil Thomson, is written for a free-wheeling theater of the mind where everything becomes possible. In 'Lifting Belly' and other works she joyously celebrates her lifelong relationship with Alice B. Toklas, one of the most famous domestic partnerships of that century. The Autobiography of Alice B. Toklas (1933), Stein's oblique and playful memoir, became an immediate bestseller and sealed Stein's international celebrity." Publisher's note

Writings, 1932-1946. Library of Am. 1998 844p $40 * **818**

ISBN 1-883011-41-8   LC 97-28916

Stein, Gertrude, 1874-1946—*Continued*

Contents: Stanzas in meditation; Lectures in America; The geographical history of America; Ida; Brewsie and Willie; Other works

In addition to theater pieces, fiction, and poetry "memoir, philosophical speculation, literary criticism and theory, all sorts of briefer forms that are hard to account for but easy to marvel at and even to delight in, pack these volumes, and constitute, as the editors surely intended us to discover, the most consistently achieved representation of new ways of responding to life and new possibilities of getting experience into words that American literature has to show." N Y Times Book Rev

Thompson, Hunter S., 1937-2005

The great shark hunt; strange tales from a strange time. Summit Bks. 1979 602p pa $16 hardcover o.p.   **818**

ISBN 0-7432-5045-1 (pa)   LC 79-831

"A Rolling Stone Press book"

"A retrospective in journalistic theater, this gathers together excerpts from Thompson's 'Fear and Loathing in Las Vegas' and 'Fear and Loathing on the Campaign Trail,' plus his reportage from such diverse journals as 'Rolling Stone,' 'Playboy,' 'The New York Times,' etc., going back to 1962." Publ Wkly

Includes bibliographical references

Thoreau, Henry David, 1817-1862

Collected essays and poems. Library of Am. 2001 703p $35 *   **818**

ISBN 1-883011-95-7   LC 00-46234

Edited by Elizabeth Hall Witherell

Among the 27 essays included are Civil disobedience, Walking, Martyrdom of John Brown, A Yankee in Canada, and Life without principle. Many of the poems were taken from Thoreau's journals and manuscripts

Includes bibliographical references

Walden, or, Life in the woods; with an introduction by Verlyn Klinkenborg. Knopf : Distributed by Random House 1992 xxxi, 295p $19 *   **818**

ISBN 0-679-41896-2   LC 92-54444

Hardcover and paperback editions also available from other publishers

"Everyman's library"

First published 1854

"Philosophy of life and observations of nature drawn from the author's solitary sojourn of two years in a cabin on Walden Pond near Concord, Massachusetts." Pratt Alcove

Includes bibliographical references

A week on the Concord and Merrimack rivers; Walden, or, Life in the woods; The Maine woods; Cape Cod. Library of Am. 1985 1114p il $35   **818**

ISBN 0-940450-27-5   LC 85-5175

Edited by Robert F. Sayre

"Politically the most conscious of the Transcendentalists, an acute observer of natural and social facts, Thoreau was an outstanding prose stylist." Reader's Ency

Includes bibliographical references

Trillin, Calvin

Too soon to tell. Farrar, Straus & Giroux 1995 292p hardcover o.p. pa $22   **818**

ISBN 0-374-27846-6; 978-0-374-52986-4 (pa); 0-374-52986-8 (pa)   LC 94-24629

"In this collection of nearly 100 syndicated columns, Calvin Trillin holds forth on everything from the animal kingdom . . . to the possibility of being labeled a member of the cultural elite. . . . 'Too Soon to Tell' abounds with Mr. Trillin's self-deprecating humor and slyly acerbic insights, not to mention invaluable homespun wisdom." N Y Times Book Rev

Twain, Mark, 1835-1910

The wit and wisdom of Mark Twain; edited by Alex Ayres. Harper & Row 1987 265p pa $13.95 hardcover o.p.   **818**

ISBN 978-0-06-075104-3 (pa); 0-06-075104-5 (pa)   LC 87-45020

The editor "provides systematic access to plenty of Twain's bon mots by arranging them in a dictionary of topics from *Adam* to *youth*. . . . Where background is needed, Ayres supplies it succinctly and, as an afterword, proffers 'What Mark Twain might say today' on such ponderables as communism, extraterrestrial intelligence, the national debt, terrorism, and the unborn. Much to Ayres' credit, many of these approximations sound markedly Twainian." Booklist

Includes bibliographical references

820.3 English literature— Encyclopedias and dictionaries

The **Continuum** encyclopedia of British literature; Steven R. Serafin and Valerie Grosvenor Myer, editors. Continuum 2003 1184p $175 *   **820.3**

1. English literature—Encyclopedias

ISBN 0-8264-1456-7   LC 2002-9231

"Most of the encyclopedia's 1,700 entries are devoted to writers. . . . The 69 topical articles provide . . . historical overviews of specific genres, themes, literary periods, and geographical areas. Among these are *Caribbean literature in English*, *Feminism*, *Old English*, and *War and literature*. With the exception of brief author entries of approximately 300 words or less, articles are signed and include bibliographical references." Booklist

"This reference work provides a fascinating current take on the canon. . . . The historical/literary time line and the lists of prize titles alone will keep researchers happy." SLJ

Includes bibliographical references

The **Oxford** companion to English literature; edited by Margaret Drabble. 6th ed., rev. Oxford University 2006 1172p $60 *   **820.3**

1. English literature—Dictionaries 2. English literature—Bio-bibliography 3. American literature—Dictionaries

ISBN 0-19-861453-5; 978-0-19-861453-1

LC 2006-49353

First published 1932 under the editorship of Sir Paul Harvey

The Oxford companion to English literature—
Continued

Entries "cover authors, literary movements and terms, critical theories, genres, publishers, plot summaries, and characters. . . . [This] is the best available one-volume reference on English literature." Libr J

820.8 English literature— Collections

The **Norton** anthology of English literature; Stephen Greenblatt, general editor; M.H. Abrams, founding editor emeritus. 8th ed. W.W. Norton 2006 2v il map v1; v1 pa; v2; v2 pa Apply to publisher for price **820.8**
1. English literature—Collections
ISBN 0-393-92713-X (v1); 0-393-92531-5 (v1 pa); 0-393-92715-6 (v2); 0-393-92532-3 (v2 pa)
LC 2005-52313
Also available in six paperback volumes
First published 1962. Periodically revised
Contains representative writings of authors which convey the tone and trends of specific literary movements and periods. Both volumes contain explanatory footnotes, selected bibliographies, notes on literary forms and usage, an author-title index, and marginalia glossaries.
Includes bibliographical references

820.9 English literature—History and criticism

The **Cambridge** guide to literature in English; edited by Dominic Head. 3rd ed. Cambridge University Press 2006 xxiii, 1241p il $50 *
820.9
1. English literature—Dictionaries 2. English literature—Bio-bibliography 3. American literature—Dictionaries
ISBN 978-0-521-83179-6; 0-521-83179-2
LC 2006-271458
First published 1988 under the editorship of Ian Ousby
"The scope of material covered . . . extends to the literature of the United Kingdom and well beyond: Africa, Asia, Australia, Canada, the Caribbean, India, New Zealand, and the U.S. are all well represented. . . . Literary terms are explained, literary movements are summarized, and literary magazines are sketched in unsigned entries ranging in length from a few lines to a few paragraphs or more. . . . With its broad coverage, clearly written and accessible text, and relatively modest price, this is a must purchase for most reference collections." Booklist

The **Cambridge** guide to women's writing in English; [edited by] Lorna Sage; advisory editors, Germaine Greer, Elaine Showalter. Cambridge Univ. Press 1999 696p il $80; pa $29 **820.9**
ISBN 0-521-49525-3; 0-521-66813-1 (pa)
LC 98-50778
A "guide to women writers in the English language. The coverage is thorough, crossing historical, national, and generic boundaries as it ranges from Julian of Nor-

wich to Terry Macmillan {sic}, from M.F.K. Fisher to Pauline Kael, from Ghanaian playwright Ama Ata Aidoo to Native American writer Mourning Dove. There are also articles on selected titles and themes. The entries, which range from 160 to 500 words, are informative, critical, and jargon-free." Libr J

Donoghue, Denis
Speaking of beauty. Yale University Press 2003 209p $24.95; pa $15 **820.9**
1. English literature—History and criticism
2. Aesthetics
ISBN 0-300-09893-6; 0-300-10593-2 (pa)
LC 2002-12243
The author "discusses Kant, Schiller, Keats, Hawthorne, Dickinson, Ruskin, Henry James, Proust, Yeats, Housman, Woolf, [and] T. S. Eliot. . . . He considers some of the main theories of beauty and their terms of reference and appreciation. And he examines the relation of beauty to form." Publisher's note
This book "is an eloquent reflection on the language beauty inspires and a careful critique of its place in literary criticism and cultural theory." N Y Times Book Rev
Includes bibliographical references

Lee, Hermione
Virginia Woolf's nose; essays on biography. Princeton University Press 2005 141p $19.95 **820.9**
1. Biography as a literary form
ISBN 0-691-12032-3
LC 2004-58457
In four essays, the author discusses "the difficulties that must be overcome when tackling a literary biography." Libr J
"Lee's immensely enjoyable study will energize debate among thoughtful readers and should become essential reading for aficionados of literary biography." Publ Wkly
Includes bibliographical references

The **Oxford** companion to Irish literature; edited by Robert Welch, assistant editor, Bruce Stewart. Oxford Univ. Press 1996 xxv, 614p maps $55 **820.9**
1. Irish literature—Dictionaries
ISBN 0-19-866158-4
LC 95-44943
Encompassing "Ireland's literary heritage from the bardic poets and Celtic sagas to twentieth-century authors like Brian Friel, Edna O'Brien, and Nuala Ni Dhomhnaill, the more than 2,000 unsigned entries cover writers, titles of major works, literary genres and motifs, folklore, mythology, periodicals, associations, and historical figures and events." Booklist

The **Oxford** guide to literature in English translation; edited by Peter France. Oxford Univ. Press 2000 xxii, 656p pa $29.95 hardcover o.p. * **820.9**
1. Literature—History and criticism 2. Translating and interpreting
ISBN 0-19-924784-6 (pa)
LC 99-28791
This "guide emphasizes 'high-culture' books in translation that have had the most lasting impact on English-

The Oxford guide to literature in English translation—*Continued*

speaking culture since the Middle Ages. . . . The first 116 pages cover translation theory and history, while the heart of this guide is the 17 geographic sections that follow, starting with African languages, moving through Latin, and ending with the West Asian languages. There are excellent bibliographies and an author index." Libr J

Includes bibliographical references

Sanders, Andrew, 1946-

The short Oxford history of English literature. 3rd ed. Oxford University Press 2004 756p pa $45
820.9

1. English literature—History and criticism
ISBN 978-0-19-926338-7; 0-19-926338-8
LC 2004-49555

First published 1994

"The History provides detailed discussion of Old and Middle English literature, the Renaissance, Shakespeare, the seventeenth and eighteenth centuries, the Romantics, Victorian and Edwardian literature, Modernism, and postwar writing. Discussions of key writers and works are combined with analysis of the impact on literature of contemporary political, social, and intellectual developments. The book includes Scottish, Irish, and Welsh writers, and it asks about the future of the canon in the light of the fragmented condition of British writing in the post-imperial period." Publisher's note

Includes bibliographical references

Vendler, Helen Hennessy

Coming of age as a poet; Milton, Keats, Eliot, Plath; [by] Helen Vendler. Harvard Univ. Press 2003 174p il $22.95
820.9

1. English poetry—History and criticism 2. American poetry—History and criticism
ISBN 0-674-01024-8
LC 2002-27287

Contents: John Milton: the elements of happiness; John Keats: perfecting the sonnet; T.S. Eliot: inventing Prufrock; Sylvia Plath: reconstructing the Colossus

"Milton's *L'Allegro*, Keats's *On First Looking into Chapman's Homer*, Eliot's *The Love Song of J. Alfred Prufrock*, and Plath's *The Colossus* are the poems that Helen Vendler considers, exploring each as an accession to poetic confidence, mastery, and maturity." Publisher's note

Vendler "succeeds in revealing the aesthetic power and technical beauty of great poetry." N Y Times Book Rev

Includes bibliographical references

821 English poetry

Adamson, Robert, 1943-

The goldfinches of Baghdad. Flood Editions 2006 103p pa $13.95 *
821

1. Poetry—By individual authors
ISBN 0-9746902-8-7

Adamson "lives on the Hawksbury River in New South Wales. . . . To give an overview of his poetry is

difficult, but it is largely concerned with where he is: the river, the natural environment and creatures, his life and history, his neighbours, love and death. It has little of the 'pastoral' feel about it, being obsessively attached to the present condition, and it never gives any sense of a contented settled existence free from urban cares, quite the reverse. There is indication indeed of a quite fraught personal existence, both past and present, without the poetry ever for a moment becoming 'confessional'. It is to objective for that and too poetic." Shearsman

Adcock, Fleur

Poems 1960-2000. Bloodaxe Books 2000 287p $54.95; pa $24.95 *
821

1. Poetry—By individual authors
ISBN 1-85224-529-8; 1-85224-530-1 (pa)

"Poems 1960-2000 reprints or selects from [Adcock's] previous twelve volumes, beginning with The Eye of the Hurricane (1964). Included are the five books and pamphlets published since her Selected Poems (1983), along with a few new pieces." World Lit Today

Adcock's "imagination thrives on what threatens her peace of mind, and only when she is unguarded can these threats have their full creative effect. . . . Throughout her writing life, she has made a fine art from holding on to principles of orderliness and good clear sense; but she has made an even finer one from loosening her grip on them." Times Lit Suppl

Auden, W. H. (Wystan Hugh), 1907-1973

Collected poems; edited by Edward Mendelson. Modern Library 2007 928p $40 *
821

1. Poetry—By individual authors
ISBN 978-0-679-64350-0; 0-679-64350-8
LC 2006-47163

Also available in paperback from Vintage Bks.

Originally published in different form by Random House in 1976

A compilation of all the poems Auden wished to preserve, in his final revisions. Previous collected editions and later shorter poems are included. There is also an absurdist play written 1928: Paid on both sides.

Blake, William, 1757-1827

The complete poetry and prose of William Blake; edited by David V. Erdman; with a new foreword and commentary by Harold Bloom. Newly revised edition. University of California Press 2008 xxviii, 990p il $70
821

1. Poetry—By individual authors
ISBN 978-0-520-04473-9
LC 81-40323

First published 1965 with title: Poetry and prose of William Blake

In addition to all of Blake's poetry, this volume also includes miscellaneous prose, marginalia, and letters

"The crucial preliminary problem [in establishing Blake's text] is simply to make out what Blake wrote. . . . Erdman has used modern aids such as infrared photography and microphotography. . . but his real achievement has been to look at Blake's text more closely and intelligently than any previous editor." N Y Rev Books

Boland, Eavan

New collected poems. W.W. Norton 2008 c2005
320p $27.95 **821**

1. Poetry—By individual authors

ISBN 978-0-393-06579-4; 0-393-06579-0

LC 2007-42554

First published 2005 in the United Kingdom

"Boland's resilient braid of outspoken feminism with Irish identity has given her a following on both sides of the Atlantic. Here is the recent Boland whose rapid verse celebrates women's courage and women's work, both public (several poems acknowledge Mary Robinson, the former president of the Irish Republic) and unsung: the poet remembers herself, when young, asking a statue in Dublin to 'Make me a heroine.' Here is the poet who learned from Adrienne Rich, among others, how to tackle big topics of loyalty, rebellion, descent and dissent." Publ Wkly

Brontë, Emily, 1818-1848

The complete poems of Emily Jane Brontë; edited from the manuscripts by C. W. Hatfield. Columbia Univ. Press 1941 xxi, 262p $65; pa $20 * **821**

1. Poetry—By individual authors

ISBN 0-231-01222-5; 0-231-10347-6 (pa)

A re-editing of the complete poems of Emily Brontë, based on all the known manuscripts. About half of the 193 poems are those belonging to the so-called Gondal cycle

Browning, Elizabeth Barrett, 1806-1861

Sonnets from the Portuguese; a celebration of love. St. Martin's Press 1986 [63]p il $9.95 * **821**

1. Poetry—By individual authors

ISBN 0-312-74501-X LC 86-13755

Hardcover and paperback editions also available from other publishers

A series of sonnets which "were written during a period of seven years and are considered by some scholars to have been inspired by her love for her husband poet Robert Browning." New Century Handb of Engl Lit

Browning, Robert, 1812-1889

Robert Browning; the major works; edited with notes by Adam Roberts; with an introduction by Daniel Karlin. Oxford University Press 2005 xxxii, 828p pa $18.95 **821**

1. Poetry—By individual authors

ISBN 978-0-19-280626-0; 0-19-280626-2

LC 2006-277696

First published 1997

This "selection includes over eighty of [Browning's] shorter poems, amongst them his most famous and best-loved dramatic monologues, as well as the complete text of many of his longer poems. It contains three books from The Ring and the Book and Browning's critical writing, Essay on Shelley. This edition also selects generously from the love letters between Browning and Elizabeth Barrett." Publisher's note

Includes bibliographical references

Robert Browning's poetry; authoritative texts, criticism; selected and edited by James F. Loucks and Andrew M. Stauffer. 2nd ed. W. W. Norton & Co. 2007 689p (A Norton critical edition) pa $14.50 * **821**

1. Poetry—By individual authors

ISBN 978-0-393-92600-2; 0-393-92600-1

LC 2006-47308

First published 1980

This collection of Browning's poetry, which includes Pauline, "reprints the texts of the seventeen-volume 'Fourth and complete edition' (Smith, Elder), of which all but the final volume were approved by Browning before his death. The poems are ordered chronologically according to their first appearance in book form." Publisher's note

Bunting, Basil

Complete poems; associate editor, Richard Caddel. New Directions Books 2003 239p pa $16.95 **821**

1. Poetry—By individual authors

ISBN 978-0-8112-1563-3; 0-8112-1563-6

LC 2003-15465

This volume "offers adventure, a confident voice, neat takes on history (both recent and archaic), an attractively careworn secular ethics and an even more attractive combination of archaic and vernacular English models. It also offers superb verbal command, chiseling every stanza to the fewest, densest possible words, giving each an aural shape. Those shapes are not always mellifluous—sometimes they are harsh, a mouthful—but each demonstrates Bunting's mastery, proving itself on the page as well as in the ear, where all good poems find their place." Nation

Burns, Robert, 1759-1796

Burns; poems; edited and introduced by Gerard Carruthers. Alfred A. Knopf 2007 255p (Everyman's library pocket poets) $12.50 **821**

1. Poetry—By individual authors

ISBN 978-0-307-26616-3; 0-307-26616-8

LC 2006-47299

"A pioneer of the Romantic movement, Burns wrote in a light Scots dialect with brio, emotional directness, and wit, drawing on classical and English literary traditions as well as Scottish folklore. . . . All of his most famous lyrics and poems are here, from 'A Red, Red Rose,' 'To a Mouse,' and 'To a Louse' to Tam o'Shanter, 'Holy Willie's Prayer,' and 'Auld Lang Syne.'" Publisher's note

Byron, George Gordon Byron, 6th Baron, 1788-1824

Selected poetry of Lord Byron; edited by Leslie A. Marchand; introduction by Thomas Disch; notes by Jeffrey Vail. Modern Library 2001 745p (The Modern Library classics) pa $16 **821**

1. Poetry—By individual authors

ISBN 978-0-375-75814-0; 0-375-75814-3

LC 2001-42771

Byron, George Gordon Byron, 6th Baron, 1788-1824—*Continued*

"From 'Manfred,' with its evocation of the figure that came to be called the 'Byronic hero,' to the melancholy 'Childe Harold,' to the satirical masterpiece 'Don Juan' (presented here in judiciously selected form), this . . . [selection seeks to include] the essential Byron." Publisher's note

Chaucer, Geoffrey, d. 1400

The complete poetry and prose of Geoffrey Chaucer; edited by John H. Fisher. 2nd ed. Harcourt Brace & Co. 1989 1040p il $105.95 *

821

1. Poetry—By individual authors
ISBN 0-03-028612-3   LC 88-29400
First published 1977
Contents: Canterbury tales; Troylus and Criseyde; Book of the Duchess; Parliament of fowls; House of fame; Legend of good women; Short poems; Romaunt of the rose; Boece; Treatise on the astrolabe, and Equatorie of the planets
Includes bibliographical references

Coleridge, Samuel Taylor, 1772-1834

The complete poems; edited by William Keach. Penguin 1997 xxx, 626p (Penguin classics) pa $18

821

1. Poetry—By individual authors
ISBN 978-0-14-042353-2
This edition "contains the final texts of all the poems published in the poet's lifetime, together with a substantial selection from the verse still in manuscript on his death. William Keach's notes draw attention to significant variants, and important earlier versions of 'Monody on the Death of Chatterton', 'The Eolian Harp', 'The Rime of the Ancient Mariner' and 'Dejection: An Ode' are included in full. The poems are arranged in chronological order of composition." Publisher's note

Constantine, David, 1944-

Collected poems. Bloodaxe Books 2005 c2004 384p pa $31.95   821
1. Poetry—By individual authors
ISBN 1-85224-667-7
"From the first line on this book's first page ('As our bloods separate the clock resumes') to the first sentence on its last ('When the kingfisher flitted/ Under the hazels I entered again into boyhood') Constantine declares himself a Romantic, in almost all the loaded, unfashionable and daring senses that once-omnipresent term can bear. In his elaborate lines, intelligence and strong emotion are collaborators, not competitors; he knows how to let them spur each other on." Times Lit Suppl

Davie, Donald, 1922-

Collected poems; edited by Neil Powell. Carcanet 2002 xxi, 634p (Poetry pléiade) $49.95; pa $24.95   821

ISBN   978-1-85754-579-1;   1-85754-579-6; 978-1-85754-406-0 (pa); 1-85754-406-4 (pa)
"Davie's poetic output, which abundantly stretches from Hardyesque lyrics ('Bride of Reason,' 'A Winter Talent,' 'The Battered Wife') to cognitively powerful long poems ('Six Epistles to Eva Hesse,' 'The Forests of Lithuania'), from translations of Pasternak and Mandelstam to lyrically brutal political commentary ('August, 1968'), evinces a kind of wide sweep and committed imagination that doesn't necessarily close itself off to confrontation and experiential risk, nor resign itself to failure as the phenomenological and lyrical refusal of further inquiry. In this sense, Davie has always seemed to be a poet working in the very high art of his eighteenth-century forebears." Jacket

Davis, Dick, 1945-

Belonging; poems. Swallow Press 2002 54p $24.95; pa $14.95   821
1. Poetry—By individual authors
ISBN 0-8040-1042-0; 0-8040-1043-9 (pa)
                                   LC 2002-17749
Davis' "poems are full of fine emotion, intelligence, wit, and multinational culture. He lithely celebrates the legendary rake Casanova; poignantly conjures 'Kipling's Kim, Thirty Years On'; economically reports a father's aching futility in comforting his child ('A Bit of Paternity'); deftly valorizes the power of art ('Just So'); and often muses on the shortness of life and the limitations of being human, so cogently that a single quatrain can take one's breath away." Booklist

Day Lewis, C. (Cecil), 1904-1972

The complete poems of C. Day Lewis; [edited by] Jill Balcon. Stanford Univ. Press 1992 745p hardcover o.p. pa $32.95   821
1. Poetry—By individual authors
ISBN 978-0-8047-2585-9; 0-8047-2585-3
                                   LC 91-68076
"The still lively fascination of his verse seems to depend on the variety of tones [Day Lewis] could pick up, change, and discard at will. . . . His modesty was genuine and profound, giving his verse texture its winning versatility, its air that 'tenure is not for me.' . . . Nothing that Day Lewis wrote is lacking its own sort of ephemeral though rediscoverable effectiveness. He was well aware of this, and it was a part of his modesty, as Jill Balcon points out in her thoughtful and sensitive introduction. . . . For anyone who likes poetry there is real interest here in [this] complete record." N Y Rev Books

Donne, John, 1572-1631

The complete poetry and selected prose of John Donne; edited by Charles M. Coffin; introduction by Denis Donoghue; notes by W. T. Chmielewski. Modern Lib. 2001 xxxii, 697p pa $14.95 *

821

1. Poetry—By individual authors
ISBN 0-375-75734-1   LC 2001-30077
A reissue of the Modern Library edition published 1994
This volume contains Donne's love poetry, satires, epigrams, verse letters and holy sonnets. Also includes selected prose and a sampling of private letters.

Donne, John, 1572-1631—*Continued*

Poems and prose. A.A. Knopf 1995 256p
(Everyman's library pocket poets) $12.50
821
1. Poetry—By individual authors
ISBN 978-0-679-44467-1; 0-679-44467-X
LC 95-15330
Edited by Peter Washington
"Contains Songs and Sonnets, Letters to the Countess
of Bedford, The First Anniversary, Holy Sonnets, Divine
Poems, excerpts from Paradoxes and Problems, Ignatius
His Conclave, The Sermons, Essays and Devotions, and
an index of first lines." Publisher's note

Dryden, John, 1631-1700

John Dryden; the major works; edited with an
introduction and notes by Keith Walker. Oxford
University Press 2003 xviii, 967p pa $18.95
821
1. Poetry—By individual authors
ISBN 978-0-19-284077-6; 0-19-284077-0
LC 2003-270051
This "edition brings together a unique combination of
Dryden's poetry and prose—all the major poems in full,
literary criticism, and translations—to give the essence of
his work and thinking. The collection includes the poems, MacFlecknoe and Absalom and Achitophel as well
as Dryden's classical translations; his versions of Homer,
Horace, and Ovid are reproduced in full. There are also
substantial selections from Dryden's Virgil, Juvenal, and
other classical writers. Fables, Ancient and Modern, tak-
en from Chaucer, Ovid, Boccaccio, and Homer, his last
and possibly greatest work, also appears in full." Publisher's note
Includes bibliographical references

**Gawain and the Grene Knight (Middle English
poem).**

Sir Gawain and the Green Knight; a new verse
translation; [translated by] Simon Armitage. W. W.
Norton & Company 2007 198p $25.95; pa $14.95
821
1. Arthurian romances
ISBN   978-0-393-06048-5;   0-393-06048-9;
978-0-393-33415-9 (pa); 0-393-33415-5 (pa)
LC 2007-28520
Armitage "clearly feels a special kinship with the Gawain poet. He captures his dialect and his landscape and
takes great pains to render the tale's alliterative texture
and drive. . . . His vernacular translation isn't literal—
sometimes he alliterates different letters, sometimes he
foreshortens the number of alliterations in a line, sometimes he changes lines altogether and so forth—but his
imitation is rich and various and recreates the gnarled
verbal texture of the Middle English original, which is
presented in a parallel text." N Y Times Book Rev

Gunn, Thom

Boss Cupid. Farrar, Straus & Giroux 2000 111p
pa $13 hardcover o.p.   **821**
1. Poetry—By individual authors
ISBN 0-374-52771-7 (pa)   LC 99-57739

"Boss Cupid offers a splendid introduction for the uninitiated. Almost all of Gunn's virtues are on display
here: his playful, metrical dexterity, his unflinching celebration both of beauty and of transience. . . . Advancing
age and the AIDS-related deaths of friends—'my
everpresent dead'—figure prominently in these poems,
but so does Gunn's humorous touch." Time

Collected poems. Farrar, Straus & Giroux 1994
495p pa $20   **821**
1. Poetry—By individual authors
ISBN 978-0-374-52433-3; 0-374-52433-5
LC 93-74183
There is a "a unity of purpose that extends throughout
the work, from the watchful early metrics through the
syllabics, the reach and skill of the free verse and, in
much of the latest work, a return to strong form that
might be termed triumphant had it not been called into
the service of matter so saddening." Times Lit Suppl

Hardy, Thomas, 1840-1928

Thomas Hardy; the complete poems; edited by
James Gibson. Palgrave 2001 xxxvi, 1003p il pa
$33.95   **821**
1. Poetry—By individual authors
ISBN 978-0-333-94929-0; 0-333-94929-3
LC 2001-32732
First published 1976
This collection "includes Hardy's more than 900 po-
ems, complemented by detailed notes. Collected here are
his eight books of verse, all the uncollected poems,
Domicilium, and the songs from The Dynasts. This edi-
tion contains an additional poem, The Sound of Her."
Publisher's note
Includes bibliographical references

Heaney, Seamus

District and circle. Farrar, Straus and Giroux
2006 78p $20   **821**
1. Poetry—By individual authors
ISBN 0-374-14092-8; 978-0-374-14092-2
LC 2005-44687
This "collection of robust lyrics celebrates work,
memory, and the physicality of existence. Brimming with
anvils, hammers, shovels, and pumps, these poems are
scored into the page with Heaney's signature accentual
and alliterative force." Libr J

Electric light. Farrar, Straus & Giroux 2001 98p
$20; pa $13   **821**
1. Poetry—By individual authors
ISBN 0-374-14683-7; 0-374-52841-1 (pa)
LC 00-67278
Heaney's "book of poems is a compendium of poetic
genres set in an array of forms and tuned to many kinds
of experience, the work of a mature poet and world citizen, aware of his cultural authority as a public man and
of the rights and responsibilities that go with it." N Y
Times Book Rev

Opened ground; selected poems, 1966-1996.
Farrar, Straus & Giroux 1998 443p pa $16
hardcover o.p.   **821**
1. Poetry—By individual authors
ISBN 0-374-52678-8 (pa)   LC 98-4331

Heaney, Seamus—*Continued*

"The best of nobel laureate Heaney's poems, gathered from 12 previous collections, create a substantial volume that charts the course of one man's thoroughly examined personal life and reflects a volatile era in the life of his troubled country, Northern Ireland, though the particulars Heaney renders so vibrantly become archetypal and unbounded in their tragedy and bliss." Booklist

Herbert, George, 1593-1633

Herbert: poems. Alfred A. Knopf 2004 253p (Everyman's library pocket poets) $12.50

821

ISBN 978-1-4000-4329-3; 1-4000-4329-8
LC 2005-273574

Poems selected by Peter Washington

Herbert experimented with a variety of forms, "from hymns and sonnets to 'pattern poems,' the shape of which reveal their subjects. Such technical agility never seems ostentatious, however, for precision of language and expression of genuine feeling were the primary concerns of this poet who admonished his readers to 'dare to be true.' An Anglican priest who took his calling with deep seriousness, he brought to his work a religious reverence richly allied with a playful wit and with literary and musical gifts of the highest order." Publisher's note

Hill, Geoffrey

The orchards of Syon. Counterpoint 2002 72p $24 *

821

1. Poetry—By individual authors
ISBN 1-58243-166-3   LC 2001-47245

"Cast as a sequence of 72 uniform blank-verse soliloquies compounded out of a dissonant amalgam of demotic jabber and oracular utterance, 'The Orchards of Syon' confirms that Hill, for all his newfound volubility, can be as refractory as ever. . . . But for readers with the patience and stamina to stick with it, Hill's brooding meditations on his ancestral countryside's 'wintry swampthickets, brush-heaps of burnt light' or 'the burring air of the fell' carry the haunting force of a last will and testament." N Y Times Book Rev

The triumph of love. Houghton Mifflin 1998 82p pa $13 hardcover o.p.   **821**

1. Poetry—By individual authors
ISBN 0-618-00183-2 (pa)   LC 98-19502

This book-length poem "ends up so much more satisfying than much of Hill's recent work because there is so much more of Hill in it. . . . When we have read [the book] a few times (no one should read it just once) we know, more than we could from his previous work, what vexes and distresses, what heartens and cheers Hill, what gives him his grim satisfactions and how." Yale Rev

Without title. Yale University Press 2007 81p $26; pa $16   **821**

1. Poetry—By individual authors
ISBN   978-0-300-12176-6;   0-300-12176-8;
0-300-12157-1 (pa); 978-0-300-12157-5 (pa)
LC 2006-926124

First published 2006 in the United Kingdom

"For much of Hill's five-decade career, his forbiddingly allusive and elliptical style, his sometimes peevish tone, his interest in English church history, and his rapt pastoralism have made him an unfashionable figure, but also a highly individual one. His latest collection exhibits typical erudition: who else would name-drop the Jesuit theologian Karl Rahner or describe Jimi Hendrix as an 'exquisite player of neumes' ('neumes' being an archaic form of musical notation)? Though the method is a magpie one, the impression that emerges is of absolute control and single-mindedness. And while Hill's outlook can seem willfully bleak . . . there is genuine grace in his descriptions of natural beauty." New Yorker

Hopkins, Gerard Manley, 1844-1889

Poems and prose. Alfred A. Knopf 1995 256p (Everyman's library pocket poets) $13.50

821

1. Poetry—By individual authors
ISBN 978-0-679-44469-5; 0-679-44469-6
LC 95-15331

This volume "contains a full selection of Hopkins's work, including selected verse, prose, and letters, and an index of first lines." Publisher's note

Housman, A. E. (Alfred Edward), 1859-1936

The collected poems of A. E. Housman. Holt & Co. 1965 254p pa $16 *   **821**

1. Poetry—By individual authors
ISBN 0-8050-0547-1

This anthology "constitutes the authorized canon of A. E. Housman's verse as established in 1939." Note on the text

Hughes, Ted, 1930-1998

Collected poems; edited by Paul Keegan. Farrar, Straus and Giroux 2003 1376p $50; pa $25

821

1. Poetry—By individual authors
ISBN   978-0-374-12538-7;   0-374-12538-4;
978-0-374-52965-9 (pa); 0-374-52965-5 (pa)
LC 2003-59938

"Paul Keegan has taken Hughes's New Selected Poems of 1995 as his model, and intercalated the expected and familiar Faber texts with uncollected or small press works like a Viennese layer cake—in astonishing quantity and quality." Poetry (Modern Poetry Association)

Jonson, Ben, 1573?-1637

The complete poems; edited by George Parfitt. Penguin Books 1988 634p (Penguin classics) pa $17   **821**

1. Poetry—By individual authors
ISBN 978-0-14-042277-1; 0-14-042277-3
LC 88-196178

"As well as the entire body of Jonson's nondramatic verse, extensively annotated, this edition contains many of the songs from his plays and masques and his translation of 'Horace, of the Art of Poetry'. His 'Conversations with Drummond', which adds much to our sense of the man, appears as an Appendix, as does 'Discoveries'; together they shed valuable light on Jonson's poetic theory and practice." Publisher's note

Keats, John, 1795-1821

The complete poems of John Keats. Modern Lib. 1994 398p $19.95 *   **821**
1. Poetry—By individual authors
ISBN 0-679-60108-2   LC 94-4339
The works in this compilation include Lamia, Isabella, The Eve of St. Agnes', Endymion, and La Belle Dame sans Merci

Poems. Knopf 1994 253p (Everyman's library pocket poets) $12.50   **821**
1. Poetry—By individual authors
ISBN 0-679-43319-8   LC 94-2495
A representative collection by the influential English romantic.

Includes bibliographical references

Kipling, Rudyard, 1865-1936

Complete verse; definitive edition. Doubleday 1989 c1940 850p pa $20 hardcover o.p. *
     821
1. Poetry—By individual authors
ISBN 0-385-26089-X (pa)   LC 88-7364
Replaces Rudyard Kipling's verse: definitive edition, published 1940
This edition includes all of Kipling's published poetry and, in addition, more than 20 poems which have not previously appeared in the inclusive edition of his verse

Langland, William, 1330?-1400?

Piers Plowman; the Donaldson translation, Middle English text, sources and backgrounds, criticism; edited by Elizabeth Robertson and Stephen H.A. Shepherd. Norton 2006 xxviii, 644p pa $15   **821**
1. Poetry—By individual authors
ISBN 978-0-393-97559-8; 0-393-97559-2
     LC 2004-57578
This Middle English poem is "written in 'Alliterative Verse' like Old English poetry and uses a deliberately rustic and archaic dialect. It is an allegorical moral and social satire, written as a 'vision' of the common medieval type." Reader's Ency. 4th edition

Larkin, Philip

Collected poems; edited with an introduction by Anthony Thwaite. Farrar, Straus & Giroux 1989 330p pa $15 hardcover o.p. *   **821**
1. Poetry—By individual authors
ISBN 978-0-374-52920-8 (pa); 0-374-52920-5 (pa)
     LC 88-83528
"'Larkin's poetry is a bit too easily resigned to grimness don't you think?' Elizabeth Bishop once wrote to Robert Lowell. It is true that his range is narrow, but within its confines is a beguiling variety of tones and forms. He never repeats himself to make the same point, and his poems are more readily memorized than those of almost any other postwar poet. . . . And when most of the flashier, more blustery contemporary literature has passed away, his poetry—ghostly, heartbreaking, exhilarating—will continue to haunt." N Y Times Book Rev

Collected poems; edited and with an introduction by Anthony Thwaite. Farrar, Straus and Giroux 2004 218p pa $15 *   **821**
1. Poetry—By individual authors
ISBN 978-0-374-52920-8; 0-374-52920-5
     LC 2003-60846
First published 2003 in the United Kingdom
"Thwaite has gathered all the poems Larkin wrote between 1946 and 1985, the year of his death; he also includes a generous selection of work written earlier, before Larkin found his characteristic voice. In all, there are some 240 poems, 83 of them never published before. The unpublished work comes from every period of Larkin's career and increases by half the number of poems in his canon. The poet we now have is considerably more prolific than the one who issued only three small, mature collections in his lifetime. With or without the new poems, Larkin is a major postwar British writer, and this is the best available collection of his poetry." Libr J

Lawrence, D. H. (David Herbert), 1885-1930

The complete poems; collected and edited with an introduction and notes by Vivian de Sola Pinto and Warren Roberts. Penguin Books 1993 1079p (Penguin twentieth-century classics) pa $24.95
     821
1. Poetry—By individual authors
ISBN 978-0-14-018657-4; 0-14-018657-3
First published 1964 by Viking
This "collection of Lawrence's poems, with appendices containing juvenilia, variants, and early drafts, and Lawrence's own critical introductions to his poems, also includes full textual and explanatory notes, glossary, and index." Publisher's note

Lear, Edward, 1812-1888

The complete verse and other nonsense; compiled and edited with an introduction and notes by Vivien Noakes. Penguin Books 2002 li, 566p il pa $20   **821**
ISBN 978-0-14-200227-8; 0-14-200227-5
     LC 2002-28998
This compilation "presents all of Lear's verse and other nonsense writings, including stories, letters, and illustrated alphabets, as well as previously unpublished material. [Features] Lear's own line drawings throughout and an introduction by leading Lear authority Vivien Noakes." Publisher's note
Includes bibliographical references

MacDiarmid, Hugh, 1892-1978

Selected poetry; introduction by Eliot Weinberger; edited by Alan Riach & Michael Grieve. New Directions 1993 289p $30.95
     821
1. Poetry—By individual authors
ISBN 978-0-8112-1248-9; 0-8112-1248-3
     LC 93-5312
"The preface by the poet's son Michael Grieve, 'Recalling Hugh MacDiarmid,' includes major biographical facts which shaped the poet's work. . . . Alan Riach's

MacDiarmid, Hugh, 1892-1978—*Continued*

'Reading Hugh MacDiarmid' provides a scholarly look at MacDiarmid's importance to the Scottish Renaissance and the themes that informed his poetry. . . . In addition to the two introductory essays, the volume also contains a chronology of MacDiarmid's life, illustrating both his private maturation and the public events that influenced him. The real reason to purchase the volume, however, is for the exceptional overview and easy accessibility it provides to a major poetic voice not only in Scotland but in the world." World Lit Today

Marvell, Andrew, 1621-1678

Poems; [selected by Peter Washington] A. A. Knopf 2004 256p (Everyman's library pocket poets) $12.50 **821**

1. Poetry—By individual authors
ISBN 978-1-4000-4252-4; 1-4000-4252-6

The "metaphysical poet Andrew Marvell was one of the chief wits and satirists of his time as well as a passionate defender of individual liberty. Today, however, he is known chiefly for his brilliant lyric poems, including 'The Garden,' 'The Definition of Love,' 'Bermudas,' 'To His Coy Mistress,' and the 'Horatian Ode' to Cromwell." Publisher's note

Muldoon, Paul

Horse latitudes. Farrar, Straus and Giroux 2006 107p $22 * **821**

1. Poetry—By individual authors
ISBN 978-0-374-17305-0; 0-374-17305-2

LC 2006-306

"Beginning with a sequence of sonnets whose titles start with the letter B, to a series of instant messages formatted as haiku, to an ending that tributes rocker Warren Zevon, readers are in for a lively ride." Libr J

Moy sand and gravel. Farrar, Straus & Giroux 2002 107p $22; pa $12 * **821**

1. Poetry—By individual authors
ISBN 0-374-21480-8; 0-374-52884-5 (pa)

LC 2002-20129

This collection "shimmers with play, the play of mind, the play of recondite information over ordinary experience, the play of observation and sensuous detail, of motion upon custom, of Irish and English languages and landscapes, of meter and rhyme. Sure enough, everything Muldoon thinks of makes him think of something else, and poem after poem takes the form of linked association." N Y Times Book Rev

Poems, 1968-1998. Farrar, Straus & Giroux 2001 479p $35; pa $19 * **821**

1. Poetry—By individual authors
ISBN 0-374-12543-0; 0-374-52844-6 (pa)

LC 00-45607

"Language is heightened, experimental, and also utterly mundane, even coarse. His subjects match the language, what with trips on mescaline chockablock with bucolic landscapes. The luck of this collection is that it is long and dense enough to show the poet wrestling not only with craft—his intricate and often hidden rhymes show, right from the start, his obsession with form—but also with the reason for poetry in a technological age." Booklist

Murray, Les A., 1938-

The biplane houses. Farrar, Straus and Giroux 2007 c2006 99p $23 **821**

1. Poetry—By individual authors
ISBN 978-0-374-11548-7; 0-374-11548-6

LC 2006-31763

First published 2006 in Australia

"Murray's poems, never exactly intimate and often patrolled by details and place-names nearly indecipherable to an outsider, reflect a life lived self-consciously and rather flamboyantly off the beaten track. . . . Pastoral is a sophisticated game pitting poets against earlier poets, like a chess match played across time. No poet writing about the natural world entirely opts out of the game, but Murray's poetry of elk and emus, bougainvillea and turmeric dust, comes close." New Yorker

Conscious and verbal; [by] Les Murray. Farrar, Straus & Giroux 2001 94p $23; pa $13 * **821**

1. Poetry—By individual authors
ISBN 0-374-12882-0; 0-374-52860-8 (pa)

LC 2001-40222

"The poet became a minor celebrity when he awoke from a three-week coma and was pronounced 'conscious and verbal,' but this new volume is more concerned with his familiar Australian topography: dead dogs, the 'Internationale,' oysters, soil, the color yellow. Murray sticks to the cheerfully formal lines that distinguish his work while letting his voice shift between chestnuts of local dialect and a brawny but humble standard English." New Yorker

Poems the size of photographs; [by] Les Murray. Farrar, Straus & Giroux 2003 128p $20 **821**

1. Poetry—By individual authors
ISBN 0-374-23520-1 LC 2002-192520

First published in 2002 in the United Kingdom

"Murray concentrates his muscular style, passion for landscape, and satirical humor into short and pithy poems. Tightly framed, most can be taken in at a glance, and yet, like developing photographs, they fully disclose their finer details and nuances more slowly. Murray begins with a mischievous tribute to the 'new hieroglyphics,' the international symbols of airports and restaurants, pictographs of the forbidden and the required. The contrasts between words and images intrigue Murray and inform his sly, sometimes startling, always colorful and animated lyrics, yarns, and epigrams." Booklist

Pickard, Tom, 1946-

Hole in the wall; new & selected poems. Flood Editions 2004 139p pa $15 * **821**

1. Poetry—By individual authors
ISBN 0-9710059-3-1

"In the Objectivist tradition, paring words down to broaden their sound and register meaning, Pickard's work here is of compact, dazzling, Bunting-esque musicality. It also bursts with a fluid sensual appeal reminiscent of D.H. Lawrence." Skanky Possum

Pope, Alexander, 1688-1744

Selected poetry; edited with an introduction and notes by Pat Rogers. Oxford Univ. Press 1998 xxiii, 226p pa $11.95 *   **821**

1. Poetry—By individual authors
ISBN 0-19-283494-0   LC 98-230887
"Oxford world's classics"
The works in this compilation of poems by the 18th century satirist include The Rape of the Lock, An Essay on Criticism, Windsor Forest, and The Dunciad
Includes bibliographical references

Selected poetry; edited with an introduction and notes by Pat Rogers. Oxford University Press 1998 xxiii, 226p (Oxford world's classics) pa $12.95
                                      821

ISBN 978-0-19-283494-2; 0-19-283494-0
                                LC 98-230887
Pope achieved "success with his first published work at the age of twenty-one. A succession of brilliant poems followed, including An Essay on Criticism (1711), Windsor Forest (1715), and his masterpiece, The Rape of the Lock. A second period of great poetry was begun in 1728 with the appearance of the first Dunciad. All these works . . . are included in this selection of his poetry." Publisher's note
Includes bibliographical references

Presley, Frances

Myne; new & selected poems and prose 1976-2005. Shearsman Books 2006 199p $20
                                      821

1. Poetry—By individual authors
ISBN 0-907562-87-6 (pa)
"Myne is a survey of Frances Presley's career to date, as well as a new collection of her poems. It begins with two recent cycles: the title sequence inspired by the Somerset landscape, and 'Stone Settings' which retraces the enigmatic patterns of prehistoric stones on Exmoor. Also here are the entire Somerset Letters, and Linocut, both originally published by Oasis Books, plus substantial selections from the author's first two books, The Sex of Art and Hula Hoop." Publisher's note

Raine, Kathleen, 1908-2003

The collected poems of Kathleen Raine. Counterpoint 2001 368p $30   **821**
ISBN 978-1-58243-135-2; 1-58243-135-3
                                LC 00-64448
"Here is a signature collection of [Raine's] work that will delight many and introduce her to many others. She deserves a very wide audience, as she has much to teach us. . . . Her personal religious journey was from a strict Protestant upbringing through conversion to Roman Catholicism to Eastern Vedic belief. From first to last, her poetry is unified by a tone of transcendental belief in visions, presence, angels, and oracles rooted in her Scottish mother's experience of nature." World Lit Today

Robinson, Edwin Arlington, 1869-1935

Poems; selected and edited by Scott Donaldson. A. A. Knopf 2007 553p (Everyman's library pocket poets) $12.50   **821**

1. Poetry—By individual authors
ISBN 978-0-307-26576-0; 0-307-26576-5
                                LC 2006-48269
"Wisely concentrating on poems of short and middling length, Donaldson . . . admits extracts only from Captain Craig and the ending of Lancelot. . . . [He] gives us whole texts of 'Rembrandt to Rembrandt,' 'Isaac and Archibald,' 'Aunt Imogen,' 'John Brown,' and 'Ben Jonson Entertains a Man from Stratford'— major poems all. For texts, he draws entirely from the Collected Poems, save for 'Romance' and four poems given as they appeared in magazines." New Criterion

Rossetti, Christina Georgina, 1830-1894

Christina Rossetti; the complete poems; text [edited] by R.W. Crump; notes and introduction by Betty S. Flowers. Penguin 2001 1v, 1221p (Penguin Classics) pa $20   **821**

1. Poetry—By individual authors
ISBN 978-0-14-042366-2; 0-14-042366-4
                                LC 2002-281810
This "fully annotated collection, based on the definitive texts, brings together fantasy poems such as 'Goblin Market,' terrifyingly vivid verses for children, love lyrics, sonnets, hymns, and ballads, as well as the vast body of her devotional poetry. . . . [This edition] incorporates contextual notes as well as notes on the text and language, an introduction, and a chronology of Rossetti's life and work." Publisher's note
Includes bibliographical references

Shelley, Percy Bysshe, 1792-1822

Poems. Knopf 1993 250p (Everyman's library pocket poets) $12.50   **821**

1. Poetry—By individual authors
ISBN 978-0-679-42909-8; 0-679-42909-3
                                LC 93-78335
"Among the English Romantics, [Shelley] has recovered his position as an undoubted major figure: the poet of volcanic hope for a better world, of fiery inspirations shot upward through bitter gloom." Oxford Companion to Engl Lit. 6th edition rev.

Shelley's poetry and prose; authoritative texts, criticism; selected and edited by Donald H. Reiman and Neil Fraistat. 2nd ed. Norton 2002 c2001 xxii, 786p il pa $18.75   **821**

1. Poetry—By individual authors
ISBN 0-393-97752-8   LC 2001-30903
"A Norton critical edition"
First published 1977
"This edition includes all of Shelley's greatest poetry and other poems frequently taught or discussed . . . as well as three of his most important prose works." Preface
Includes bibliographical references

Sisson, C. H. (Charles Hubert), 1914-2003

Selected poems; foreword by M.L. Rosenthal. New Directions 1996 94p pa $9.95   **821**

1. Poetry—By individual authors

ISBN 978-0-8112-1327-1; 0-8112-1327-7

LC 95-47599

"C.H. Sisson's Christianity is an austere, rural form that forbids pity for a newborn duckling that will obviously not survive. Yet Sisson, like Frost, sees death and old age as part of a design, not so much insidious as inexorable and thus no occasion for tears. Like Donne, whom he commemorates in 'A Letter to John Donne,' Sisson understands probably better than any contemporary poet the struggle between the call of the flesh and the love of God, and he knows, like Donne, that their reconciliation can only occur in art. . . . The poems [collected here] are sardonic, elegiac, but not despairing." World Lit Today

Smith, Stevie, 1902-1971

Collected poems; edited with a preface by James MacGibbon. New Directions 1983 591p il pa $19.95 *   **821**

1. Poetry—By individual authors

ISBN 0-8112-0882-6   LC 83-43008

First published 1975 in the United Kingdom

Smith "wrote three novels, but has been more widely recognized for her witty, caustic, and enigmatic verse, much of it illustrated by her own comic drawings." Concise Oxford Companion to Engl Lit

Spark, Muriel

All the poems of Muriel Spark. New Directions 2004 130p pa $13.95   **821**

1. Poetry—By individual authors

ISBN 978-0-8112-1576-3; 0-8112-1576-8

LC 2004-948

"As one might expect from a novelist who has always made use of the full range of fictional genres and devices, All the Poems does not come in a straightforward, chronological package or arrangement; from the outset, the book, like so much else written by Spark, is amusingly perverse. Beginning with 'A Tour of London' (c1950-51), it then immediately skips, in terms of both time and place, to 'The Dark Music of the Rue du Cherche-Midi' (2000), comes right up to date with 'The Creative Writing Class' (2003), travels back to 'The Victoria Falls' (c1948) and 'Shipton-under-Wychwood' (c1950), before regressing finally to a series of translations from Latin (c1949). The reader is therefore encouraged to search for the persistent themes and obvious connections. There is clearly a concern and interest in certain technical forms; there is a ballad, an ode, a couple of villanelles. There's the sharp intelligence and wry wit demonstrated in poems that function mainly as conundrums, unanswered questions and, possibly, as skipping rhymes. . . . But the most memorable parts of the book are those that give some clue to Spark's lifelong determination and dedication to her craft." Guardian (UK)

Spenser, Edmund, 1552?-1599

The faerie queene; edited by Thomas P. Roche, Jr., with the assistance of C. Patrick O'Donnell, Jr. Penguin Books 1987 1246p (Penguin classics) pa $20 *   **821**

1. Poetry—By individual authors

ISBN 978-0-14-043307-8; 0-14-042207-2

"The greatest work of Spenser, of which the first three books were entrusted to the printer in Nov. 1589, and the second three were published in 1596." Oxford Companion to Engl Lit

"An epic to compare with the great epics of the classical world and of Renaissance Italy, *The Faerie Queene* is simultaneously a nationalistic paean to the greatness of Elizabeth and her England, an imaginative romance, and a moral allegory of the soul in quest of salvation." Reader's Ency. 4th edition

Stevenson, Anne, 1933-

Poems, 1955-2005. Bloodaxe Books 2005 413p $64.95; pa $29.95 *   **821**

1. Poetry—By individual authors

ISBN 1-85224-721-5; 1-85224-699-5 (pa)

"Stevenson was born in England, raised and educated in the US, and has been living in various parts of Britain since the sixties. Poems 1955-2005 draws from thirteen publications since 1965, as well as from some early and late uncollected work. The poems are arranged thematically rather than chronologically." Poetry

"While Anne Stevenson is most certainly, and rightly, regarded as one of the major poets of our period, it has never been by virtue of this or that much anthologised poem, but by the work or mind as a whole. It is not so much a matter of the odd lightning-struck tree as of an entire landscape, and that landscape is always humane, intelligent and sane, composed of both natural and rational elements, and amply furnished with patches of wit and fury, which only serve to bring out the humanity." London Magazine

Tennyson, Alfred Tennyson, Baron, 1809-1892

Poems. A. A. Knopf 2004 255p (Everyman's library pocket poets) $12.50   **821**

1. Poetry—By individual authors

ISBN 978-1-4000-4187-9; 1-4000-4187-2

LC 2003-49505

"This collection includes such famous poems as 'The Lady of Shalott' and 'The Charge of the Light Brigade.' There are extracts from all the major masterpieces— Idylls of the King, The Princess, In Memoriam—and several complete long poems, such as 'Ulysses' and 'Demeter and Persephone,' that demonstrate his narrative grace. Finally, there are many of the short lyrical poems, such as 'Come into the Garden, Maud' and 'Break, Break, Break,' for which he is justly celebrated." Publisher's note

Thomas, Dylan, 1914-1953

The poems of Dylan Thomas; edited with an introduction and notes by Daniel Jones; with a preface by Dylan Thomas. rev ed. New Directions 2003 xxix, 320p il $34.95 **821**

1. Poetry—By individual authors

ISBN 978-0-8112-1541-1; 0-8112-1541-5

LC 2002-155790

Includes CD of the poet reading his work

First published 1971

"To the 90 poems Thomas published in Collected Poems, 1934-1952 Jones has added 102 and placed the total, as far as he could determine, in the chronological order of their composition. Some of the poems were still in manuscript form when Thomas died; others had been published in periodicals and anthologies. In an appendix, Jones offers Thomas' early poems—including one written when the poet was 12." Libr J [review of 1971 edition]

Includes bibliographical references

Tomlinson, Charles, 1927-

Selected poems; 1955-1997. New Directions 1997 226p pa $13.95 **821**

1. Poetry—By individual authors

ISBN 978-0-8112-1369-1; 0-8112-1369-2

LC 97-25373

"These poems are a fine achievement; they are the work of a consciousness mostly at ease with its dwelling in this world, and unabashed by a lack of inclination to dwell unduly on shadows rather than light. The sunniness of disposition, both geographically and psychologically, combined with Tomlinson's canny ability to metrically heighten what still sounds to the ear like the language of common day, give a tone that might be rationally described as Tomlinsonian. This . . . [is] a book essential to any collection of the best poetry of the postwar years." Am Book Rev

Skywriting and other poems. Ivan R. Dee 2003 96p $18.95 **821**

1. Poetry—By individual authors

ISBN 978-1-566-63541-7; 1-556-63541-1

LC 2003-55504

"Mr Tomlinson is an eloquent poet of place—in this collection he moves through Mexico, Italy, Japan, and his home county of Gloucestershire—whose work combines visual exactitude with an uncommon gracefulness of expression." Economist

Turnbull, Gael, 1928-2004

There are words; collected poems. Shearsman Books 2006 495p pa $30 * **821**

1. Poetry—By individual authors

ISBN 0-90756-289-2

"Restlessly experimental—but never for its own sake—Turnbull was constantly doing what Ezra Pound asked of poets at the beginning of the twentieth century, namely to make it new. His range is very wide. He employed the long line before C.K. Williams or Ciaran Carson; he experimented with prose-poems, found-poems; he wrote ballads, poems meant to be read out loud, poems that deftly rhyme and ones that deftly don't; he shaped poems on the page with varying line-lengths and indent-

ings; he used the spaces between lines and verses functionally; the touch is sometimes light, sometimes profoundly earnest. . . . In the almost 500pp of this superb Collected Poems there isn't one dud piece, one poem that doesn't have genuine poetic power and resonance." Stride (UK)

Wordsworth, William, 1770-1850

Selected poetry of William Wordsworth; edited by Mark Van Doren; introduction by David Bromwich. Modern Lib. 2001 xxii, 687p $24.95; pa $11.95 * **821**

1. Poetry—By individual authors

ISBN 0-679-64224-2; 0-375-75941-7 (pa)

LC 00-66444

This collection "represents Wordsworth's prolific output, from the poems first published in Lyrical Ballads in 1798 . . . to the late 'Yarrow Revisited.' Wordsworth's poetry is celebrated for its deep feeling, its use of ordinary speech, the love of nature it expresses, and its representation of commonplace things and events." Publisher's note

Yeats, W. B. (William Butler), 1865-1939

The collected poems of W.B. Yeats; edited by Richard J. Finneran. Rev. 2nd ed. Scribner Paperback Poetry 1996 xxv, 544p pa $20

821

1. Poetry—By individual authors

ISBN 978-0-684-80731-7; 0-684-80731-9

LC 96-23314

First published 1989 by Collier Books

This volume "includes all of the poems authorized by Yeats for inclusion in his standard canon. . . . Revised and corrected, this edition includes Yeats's own notes on his poetry, complemented by explanatory notes from . . .Yeats scholar Richard J. Finneran." Publisher's note

821.008 English poetry—Collections

100 essential modern poems; selected and introduced by Joseph Parisi. Ivan R. Dee 2005 305p $24.95 * **821.008**

1. English poetry—Collections 2. American poetry—Collections

ISBN 1-56663-612-4 LC 2005-9897

"Each of the 70 individuals whose work is represented receives a short, readable introduction that includes pertinent biographical information, a description of the poet's place in modern literary history, and an analysis of the writer's style. One to three representative poems follow each entry." SLJ

"Preceded by wonderfully conversational and expertly appreciative biocritical essays about each poet, his choices are superb as he lingers over Yeats and Stevens and includes often-overlooked witty and satirical poets, among them Dorothy Parker, Ogden Nash, Kay Ryan, Frank O'Hara, and Billy Collins." Booklist

100 great poems of the twentieth century; [edited by] Mark Strand. Norton 2005 320p $24.95 *
821.008
1. English poetry—Collections 2. American poetry—Collections
ISBN 0-393-05894-8　　　　　　　　LC 2005-2150
The editor "has selected works by poets of Europe and North and South America, and because there are so many gifted American poets, he restricted himself to those born before 1927. The result is a marvelously graceful, shimmering cosmos of poems by the likes of Anna Akhmatova, A. R. Ammons, Amy Clampit, Robert Desnos, Robert Frost, Nazim Hikmet, Kenneth Koch, Edna St. Vincent Millay, Gabriela Mistral, Eugenio Montale, Octavio Paz, and Derek Walcott." Booklist

The **Best** poems of the English language; from Chaucer through Robert Frost; selected and with commentary by Harold Bloom. HarperCollins Publishers 2004 xxviii, 972p $34.95; pa $19.95 *
821.008
1. English poetry—Collections 2. American poetry—Collections
ISBN 0-06-054041-9; 0-06-054042-7 (pa)
　　　　　　　　　　　　　　　LC 2003-51104
"Arranged chronologically by author, the poems are preceded by commentaries that extol their specific virtues and place them in historical context. Taken together, they provide an overview of Bloom's own theories of writing, such as his notion that the greatest poems manifest an 'inevitability' of phrasing . . . Bloom rarely bores, and at his best he achieves a cogency . . . worthy of the poets he so deeply admires." Libr J
Includes bibliographical references

British women poets of the Romantic era; an anthology; edited by Paula R. Feldman. Johns Hopkins Univ. Press 1997 xxxvi, 879p pa $29.95 hardcover o.p.
821.008
ISBN 0-8018-6640-5 (pa)　　　　　　LC 96-47417
An "anthology of works by 62 British women poets writing between 1770 and 1840. . . . The poets are presented in alphabetical order, with each entry including a brief biography with birth and death dates, sample poems, major works, selected works, and the source of the poetry. The result is a singular resource providing information found in no other reference work." Libr J
Includes bibliographical references

Christmas poems; selected and edited by John Hollander and J.D. McClatchy. Knopf 1999 254p (Everyman's library pocket poets) $12.50
821.008
1. Christmas—Poetry 2. English poetry—Collections 3. American poetry—Collections
ISBN 0-375-40789-8　　　　　　　　LC 99-36265
Contributors to this collection of Christmas poetry include Milton, Tennyson, Rossetti, Thackeray, Eliot, McGinley, Morris, Bishop and Geoffrey Hill

The **Columbia** anthology of British poetry; edited by Carl Woodring and James Shapiro. Columbia Univ. Press 1995 xxxi, 891p $41
821.008
1. English poetry—Collections
ISBN 0-231-10180-5　　　　　　　　LC 94-46333

This anthology "contains major British poetry from Beowulf to the present day. Poets receive a short biographical introduction along with their poetry. . . . It includes more female poets than most comparable anthologies, and is conducive to browsing. Major poems such as Coleridge's 'Rime of the Ancient Mariner,' Britain's best-loved poems, and newly rediscovered poems are part of this collection." SLJ

The **Making** of a poem; a Norton anthology of poetic forms; edited by Mark Strand and Eavan Boland. Norton 2000 xxxi, 366p pa $15.95 hardcover o.p.
821.008
1. English poetry—Collections 2. American poetry—Collections
ISBN 0-393-32178-9 (pa)　　　　　　LC 99-55233
A "collection of villanelles, sestinas, sonnets, elegies, pastorals, ballads, pantoums, odes, and other familiar structures that have shaped English poetry since Beowulf. Each chapter focuses on a single form. . . . Most useful are the selections themselves, which illustrate how particular forms have been employed over time, from canonical classics by Chaucer, Shelley, and Elizabeth Bishop through newer pieces by Hayden Carruth, Michael Palmer, and Thylias Moss." Libr J
Includes bibliographical references

The **New** Oxford book of Irish verse; edited, with translations, by Thomas Kinsella. Oxford Univ. Press 2001 xxx, 423p pa $16.95 *
821.008
1. Irish poetry—Collections
ISBN 0-19-280192-9　　　　　　　　LC 2001-278442
Replaces The Oxford Book of Irish verse, XVIIth century-XXth century, chosen by Donagh MacDonagh and Lennox Robinson (1958); this is a reissue of the 1986 edition
"This selection is divided into three parts. Book I opens with the earliest pre-Christian poetry in Old Irish and ends in the fourteenth century with the first Irish poetry in the English language. Book II covers the fourteenth to the eighteenth centuries and Book III the nineteenth and twentieth centuries." Publisher's note

The **New** Oxford book of Victorian verse. Oxford Univ. Press 1987 xxxiv, 654p pa $19.95 hardcover o.p. *
821.008
1. English poetry—Collections
ISBN 0-19-284084-3 (pa)　　　　　　LC 86-23701
Replaces The Oxford book of Victorian verse, edited by Sir Arthur Quiller-Couch (1912)
An anthology of 19th century English poetry. Among the poets prominently featured are: Clough, Morris, Arnold, the Decadents, Emily Brontë, Clare, Barnes, and Christina Rossetti
"While general collections should all add Ricks, those retaining {the Quiller-Couch edition} should dust him off and keep him available in order to represent fully Victorian verse and changing attitudes toward it." Libr J

The **Norton** anthology of modern and contemporary poetry; edited by Jahan Ramazani, Richard Ellmann, Robert O'Clair. 3rd ed. Norton 2003 2v pa set $75 *

821.008

1. English poetry—Collections 2. American poetry—Collections

ISBN 0-393-32429-X   LC 2002-37990

Volumes 1 and 2 also available separately in paperback each $55

First published 1973 with title: The Norton anthology of modern poetry

Contents: v1 Modern poetry; v2 Contemporary poetry

This volume includes "1596 poems by 195 poets. . . . The anthology includes the works of such masters as Walt Whitman, Ezra Pound, Dylan Thomas, Langston Hughes, Gertrude Stein, Lucille Clifton, Louise Erdrich, and Allen Ginsberg. . . . Extensive, and beautifully composed introductions provide insight, observations, and historical context for the selections. . . . This ambitious, highly successful work is a veritable tribute to the enduring power of literature and language." SLJ

Includes bibliographical references

The **Oxford** book of comic verse; edited by John Gross. Oxford Univ. Press 1994 xxxiv, 512p pa $16.95 hardcover o.p. *   **821.008**

1. English poetry—Collections 2. American poetry—Collections 3. Humorous poetry—Collections

ISBN 0-19-284086-X (pa)   LC 94-656

The editor "defines comic verse as primarily meant to amuse. From this bland definition he delves his principles of inclusion: funny poems that do not exceed the boundaries of good taste. No bawdy lyrics, no skewering satire here. Within these limits, he surveys the field from Chaucer to Glyn Maxwell (1962-)." Publ Wkly

Includes bibliographical references

The **Oxford** book of English verse; edited by Christopher Ricks. Oxford Univ. Press 1999 xxxii, 690p $39.95 *   **821.008**

1. English poetry—Collections

ISBN 0-19-214182-1   LC 99-20831

First published 1900 under the editorship of Sir Arthur Quiller-Couch with title: The Oxford book of English verse, 1250-1900. Present edition replaces The New Oxford book of English verse, 1250-1950, edited by Helen Gardner published 1972

This collection "starts with anonymous 13th-century lyric and ends with Seamus Heaney; in between are seven centuries' worth of poems in English from Britain and Ireland. . . . Ricks brings in plenty of dialect verse, excerpts from long poems and verse plays, and a few translations into English. . . . Long after reviewers stop debating how Ricks chose each item, readers will keep returning to these pages to find yet another good poem they've not before seen." Publ Wkly

The **Oxford** book of sonnets; edited by John Fuller. Oxford Univ. Press 2000 xxxiv, 362p $25; pa $15.95   **821.008**

1. English poetry—Collections 2. American poetry—Collections

ISBN 0-19-214267-4; 0-19-280389-1 (pa)   LC 00-36757

"Indisputable masterpieces appear plentifully, but Fuller's determination to present a large number of distinguished practitioners assures that there are also many superb poems by virtual unknowns. And Fuller's introduction is a sharp-witted miracle of concise comprehensiveness." Booklist

Includes bibliographical references

The **Penguin** book of the sonnet; 500 years of a classic tradition in English; edited by Phillis Levin. Penguin Bks. 2001 419p pa $18

821.008

1. English poetry—Collections 2. American poetry—Collections

ISBN 0-14-058929-5   LC 00-62350

In an introductory essay, Levin "discusses the sonnet's origins, history, traditions, and possibilities. . . . Interwoven with the history are approaches to interpreting and criticizing this poetic form. The bulk of the text is an anthology of over 600 sonnets composed by more than 230 poets. Over 150 of the poets represented wrote during the 20th century." Libr J

Includes bibliographical references

821.009   English poetry—History and criticism

The **Oxford** companion to Chaucer; edited by Douglas Gray. Oxford University Press 2003 xxiii, 526p il map $95   **821.009**

1. Chaucer, Geoffrey, d. 1400

ISBN 0-19-811765-5   LC 2004-270323

This reference includes "more than 2,000 signed entries on various aspects of Chaucer and his works as well as their larger cultural and literary context." Choice

Includes bibliographical references

Rossignol, Rosalyn

Critical companion to Chaucer; a literary reference to his life and work. Facts on File 2006 648p il $85   **821.009**

1. Chaucer, Geoffrey, d. 1400

ISBN 0-8160-6193-9; 978-0-8160-6193-8

    LC 2006-99

First published 1999 with title: Chaucer A to Z

This book on the works of Chaucer includes a biography of Chaucer, synopses and critical commentary on his works (including the Canterbury Tales), and lists of related people, places and topics.

Includes bibliographical references

Schmidt, Michael, 1947-

Lives of the poets. Knopf 1999 975p pa $20 hardcover o.p. *   **821.009**

1. English poetry—History and criticism 2. American poetry—History and criticism

ISBN 0-375-70604-6 (pa)   LC 98-51913

First published 1998 in the United Kingdom

In this "survey of poetry in English, Schmidt . . . enthuses about more than 250 poets whose work dates from the 14th century to 1998. More than a critical essay, this

Schmidt, Michael, 1947-—*Continued*
friendly and accessible history embodies the life of poetry and conveys its changeable, subjective beauty." Libr J

Includes bibliographical references

822 English drama

Behan, Brendan, 1923-1964
The complete plays; introduced by Alan Simpson; with a bibliography by E. H. Mikhail. Grove Weidenfeld 1991 384p pa $15 *

822

ISBN 0-8021-3070-4   LC 78-53931
"An Evergreen book"
First published 1978
Contents: The quare fellow; The hostage; Richard's cork leg; Moving out; A garden party; The big house

Bennett, Alan, 1934-
The history boys. Faber and Faber 2006 xxvii, 109p pa $13   **822**
ISBN 978-0-571-22464-7; 0-571-22464-4
                                          LC 2005-936593
First published 2004 in the United Kingdom
Characters: 11 men, 1 woman extras. First produced at the Lyttleton Theatre, London, May 18, 2004
"At a boys' grammar school in Sheffield, eight boys are being coached for the Oxbridge entrance exams. It is the mid-eighties, and the main concern of the unruly bunch of bright teenagers is getting out, starting university and starting life. At the heart of The History Boys are four characters, each with contrasting outlooks on teaching and school: Hector, an eccentric English teacher with no interest in exams; Irwin, a young teacher who sees history as 'entertainment'; Mrs Lintott, a traditionalist, who teaches 'history, not histrionics'; and a Headmaster obsessed with results." Publisher's note
"Nothing could diminish the incendiary achievement of this subtle, deep-wrought and immensely funny play about the value and meaning of education. . . . In short, a superb, life-enhancing play." Guardian

Bolt, Robert
A man for all seasons; a play in two acts. Random House 1962 xxv, 163p il pa $9.50 hardcover o.p. *   **822**
1. More, Sir Thomas, Saint, 1478-1535—Drama
2. Great Britain—History—1485-1603, Tudors—Drama
ISBN 0-679-72822-8 (pa)
Characters: 11 men, 2 women. First produced in the United States at the ANTA Theatre, New York City, November 22, 1961
A play set in sixteenth century England about Sir Thomas More, a devout Catholic, and his conflict with Henry VIII.

Christie, Agatha, 1890-1976
The mousetrap and other plays. New American Library 2000 742p hardcover o.p. pa $7.99
                                          822
ISBN 0-451-20118-3; 0-451-20114-0 (pa)
                                          LC 00-64727
First published 1978 by Dodd, Mead
Contents: Ten little Indians — Appointment with death — The hollow — The mousetrap — Witness for the prosecution — Towards zero — Verdict — Go back for murder
"The noted mystery writer composed adaptations of seven novels and stories into arresting plays as well as creating one original theater piece ('Verdict'). . . . All are as delightful to read for pleasure as Christie's mystery novels, especially since some that earlier appeared in the latter form have been intriguingly altered." Booklist

Churchill, Caryl
Mad forest; a play from Romania. Theatre Communications Group 1996 87p pa $13.95
                                          822
ISBN 1-55936-114-X; 978-1-55936-114-9
                                          LC 96-12875
First published 1991 in the United Kingdom
Large mixed cast. 3 acts. First performed at the New York Theater Workshop, New York, December 4, 1991
This play "explores the reactions of two ordinary families to the confused events of the Romanian revolution: the dreadful damage done to people's lives by years of repression, and the painful difficulties of sudden but lasting change." Publisher's note

Coward, Noel
Three plays; Blithe spirit, Hay fever, Private lives; introduction by Philip Hoare. Vintage Bks. 1999 254p pa $13 *   **822**
ISBN 0-679-78179-X   LC 98-47414
First published 1965 by Dell
Contents: Blithe spirit; Hay fever; Private lives

Dryden, John, 1631-1700
All for love; edited by David M. Vieth. University of Neb. Press 1972 xxxiv, 146p (Regents Restoration drama series) pa $24.95 hardcover o.p. *   **822**
1. Cleopatra, Queen of Egypt, d. 30 B.C.—Drama
ISBN 0-8032-5379-6 (pa)
Also available in paperback from Methuen
An English Restoration tragedy which is an adaptation of Shakespeare's "Antony and Cleopatra" done in blank verse

Fugard, Athol
Blood knot and other plays. Theatre Communications Group 1991 202p hardcover o.p. pa $15   **822**
ISBN 978-1-55936-019-7; 1-55936-019-4
                                          LC 90-29029

Fugard, Athol—*Continued*

"The brothers of Blood Knot—one dark-skinned, one light—betray their dream of a better future with the impossible wish of passing for white. In Hello and Goodbye, a poor white brother and sister churn through their once-promising past to comprehend their bleak present. Boesman and Lena, black husband and wife, tramp homelessly through a severe and unforgiving landscape, discovering strength and delivering devotion through an encounter with a mysterious old African." Publisher's note

"Master Harold"— and the boys. Penguin Books 1984 60p pa $11 *   **822**

1. South Africa—Race relations—Drama
ISBN 0-14-048187-7   LC 84-1008
First published 1982 by Random House
Characters: 3 men. 1 act. First produced at the Yale Repertory theatre, New Haven, Connecticut, 1982.

Drama with racial overtones set in Port Elizabeth tea room focuses on precocious white South African teenager's relationship with two black men who work for his family, both old enough to be his father.

Gay, John, 1685-1732

The beggar's opera; edited by Edgar V. Roberts; music edited by Edward Smith. University of Neb. Press 1969 xxix, 238p music (Regents Restoration drama series) hardcover o.p. pa $21.95

822

ISBN 978-0-8032-5361-2 (pa); 0-8032-5361-3 (pa)
First published 1728
A ballad opera, this is a rogues' comedy satirizing corrupt politics in 18th century England

Heaney, Seamus

The burial at Thebes; a version of Sophocles' Antigone. Farrar, Straus and Giroux 2004 79p $18

822

ISBN 0-374-11721-7   LC 2004-43986

"During the War of the Seven Against Thebes, Antigone, the daughter of Oedipus, learns that her brothers have killed each other, having been forced onto opposing sides of the battle. When Creon, king of Thebes, grants burial of one but not the 'treacherous' other, Antigone defies his order, believing it her duty to bury all of her close kin." Publisher's note

"There are many translations of Sophocles' Antigone but few with the understated power and spare beauty of . . . Heaney's version. . . . Written in a muscular but lively style, the translation, like Heaney's best poetry, finds music in the language of the streets and reveals the raw, primal power in the most carefully constructed rhetorical tropes." Booklist

Jonson, Ben, 1573?-1637

Volpone and other plays; edited by Michael Jamieson. Penguin 2004 496p (Penguin classics) pa $12   **822**

ISBN 978-0-14-144118-4; 0-14-144118-6
LC 2004-275516
First published 1966 in the United Kingdom with title: Three comedies

Contents: Volpone; The Alchemist; Bartholomew Fair

"Ben Jonson created in Volpone and The Alchemist hilarious portraits of cupidity and chicanery, while in Bartholomew Fair he portrays his fellow Londoners at their most festive—and most bawdy." Publisher's note

Marlowe, Christopher, 1564-1593

The complete plays; edited by Frank Romany and Robert Lindsey. Penguin Books 2003 xliv, 702p (Penguin classics) pa $15   **822**

ISBN 978-0-14-043633-4; 0-14-043633-2
LC 2004-268858
Contents: Dido, queen of Carthage; Tamburlaine the Great, part one; Tamburlaine the Great, part two; The Jew of Malta; Doctor Faustus; Edward the Second; The massacre at Paris
Includes bibliographical references

Orton, Joe

The complete plays; introduced by John Lahr. Grove Weidenfeld 1990 448p pa $15   **822**

ISBN 978-0-8021-3215-4   LC 90-3069
First published 1976 in the United Kingdom
Contents: The ruffian on the stair; Entertaining Mr Sloane; The good and faithful servant; Loot; The Erpingham camp; Funeral games; What the butler saw

Osborne, John, 1929-1994

Look back in anger. Penguin 1982 96p (Penguin Plays) pa $12 *   **822**

ISBN 0-14-048-175-3; 978-0-14-048-175-4
LC 82-9144
First published 1957 by Criterion Books
Characters: 3 men, 2 women. First produced at the Royal Court Theatre, London, May 8, 1956

This play "introduced a new strain of realism to British theatre and set the tone for the generation of anti-Establishment writers who became known as the Angry Young Men. Osborne described his own parents as 'impoverished middle class,' but his play deals with the frustrations, crude language, and squalid conditions of working-class life." Reader's Ency. 4th edition

Pinter, Harold, 1930-

Complete works; with an introduction, Writing for the theatre. Grove Weidenfeld 1990 4v v1 pa $14.50; v2 pa $13.50; v3 pa $14; v4 pa $13.50

822

ISBN 0-8021-5096-9 (v1); 0-8021-3237-5 (v2); 0-8021-5049-7 (v3); 0-8021-5050-0 (v4)
LC 90-13933
"An Evergreen book"
First Grove Press edition published 1977-1981
Contents: v1 The birthday party; The room; The dumb waiter; A slight ache; A night out; v2 The caretaker; The dwarfs; The collection; The lover; Night school; Trouble in the works; The black and white {revue sketch}; Request stop; Last to go; Special offer; v3 The homecoming; Tea party; The basement; Landscape; Silence; Night; That's your trouble; That's all; Applicant; Interview; Dialogue for three; v4 Old times; No man's land; Betrayal; Monologue; Family voices

Shaffer, Peter

Equus. Scribner 2005 112p pa $12 *

822

ISBN 0-7432-8730-4; 978-0-7432-8730-2

LC 2005-51600

First published 1973 in the United Kingdom

Characters: 5 men, 4 women. 1 act, 35 scenes. First produced by the National Theater, London, July 26, 1973

Drama about "a jolting confrontation between a psychiatrist and a 17-year-old boy who has blinded six horses from the stable where he is employed. As the probe into the boy's attitudes and behavior deepens, this criminal act is revealed to have been a result of his notions of a sexual/religious spirit in horses." Booklist

Peter Shaffer's Amadeus; with an introduction by the director Sir Peter Hall and a wholly new preface by the author. Perennial Bks. 2001 xxxiv, 124p pa $15 *

822

1. Mozart, Wolfgang Amadeus, 1756-1791—Drama
2. Salieri, Antonio, 1750-1825—Drama

ISBN 0-06-093549-9

LC 2001-278382

First published 1980 in the United Kingdom

Characters: 9 men, 1 woman, extras. 2 acts. First produced at the National Theater of Great Britain, November 1979

Explores relationship between Autrian court composer Antonio Salieri and the divinely gifted young Wolfgang Amadeus Mozart.

Shaw, Bernard, 1856-1950

Arms and the man; a pleasant play; [by] Bernard Shaw; introduction by Rodelle Weintraub; definitive text under the editorial supervision of Dan H. Laurence. Penguin Books 2006 xxvi 73p (Penguin classics) pa $9

822

ISBN 978-0-14-303976-1; 0-14-303976-8

LC 2005-56724

First produced 1894. Comedy set in Bulgaria satirizing romantic attitudes about war.

Heartbreak House; a fantasia in the Russian manner on English themes; definitive text under the editorial supervision of Dan H. Laurence; with an introduction by David Hare. Penguin Books 2000 160p il (Penguin Classics) pa $10

822

ISBN 978-0-14-043787-4; 0-14-043787-8

LC 2001-266517

Written in 1913, first produced 1920

"A complex allegorical work in which Shaw indicts apathy, confusion, and lack of purpose as the causes of the world's problems. The characters—all larger than life and with symbolic names—are gathered at the home of an eccentric sea captain; they each represent an evil in the modern world. Into their midst comes young Ellie Dunn, whose search for a husband Shaw treats as a new generation searching for a way of life." Benet's Reader's Ency. 4th edition

Includes bibliographical references

Major Barbara; definitive text under the editorial supervision of Dan H. Laurence; with an introduction by Margery Morgan. Penguin Books 2000 156p (Penguin classics) pa $11

822

1. Salvation Army 2. Father-daughter relationship
3. Crime

ISBN 978-0-14-043790-4; 0-14-043790-8

LC 2002-275028

In this "comedy, originally staged in 1905, Andrew Undershaft, a millionaire armaments dealer, loves money and despises poverty. His energetic daughter Barbara, however, is a devout major in the Salvation Army. She sees her father as just another soul to be saved. But when the Salvation Army needs funds to keep going, it is Undershaft who saves the day." Publisher's note

Man and Superman; a comedy and a philosophy; definitive text under the editorial supervision of Dan H. Laurence; introduced by Stanley Weintraub. Penguin 2000 264p (Penguin classics) pa $11

822

ISBN 978-0-14-043788-1; 0-14-043788-6

"In Man and Superman, Shaw combined seriousness with comedy to create a satirical and buoyant exposé of the eternal struggle between the sexes. . . . This volume includes Shaw's Preface of 1903 and his appendix, 'The Revolutionist's Handbook', the cast list from the first production of Man and Superman and a list of his principal works." Publisher's note

Pygmalion . . . and My fair lady; [Pygmalion] by George Bernard Shaw; and My fair lady/based on Shaw's Pygmalion; adaptation and lyrics by Alan Jay Lerner; music by Frederick Loewe. 50th anniversary ed. Signet Classic 2006 219p pa $5.95 *

822

ISBN 0-451-53009-8

"This is an authorized original paperback edition published by New American Library" Verso of title page

This volume includes the complete texts of Shaw's Pygmalion and Lerner's musical adaptation My fair lady.

Saint Joan; a chronicle play in six scenes and an epilogue; definitive text under the editorial supervision of Dan H. Laurence; with 'On playing Joan' by Imogen Stubbs; and an introduction by Joley Wood. Penguin 2003 xx, 168p (Penguin classics) pa $12

822

1. Joan, of Arc, Saint, 1412-1431—Drama

ISBN 978-0-14-043791-6; 0-14-04379-1

First produced 1923

Chronicle play in "which Joan of Arc, the young girl who led France to victory over the English, emerges as an unlettered country girl gifted with masterful will and innate intelligence." McGraw-Hill Ency World Drama

Sheridan, Richard Brinsley, 1751-1816

The school for scandal and other plays; edited with an introduction by Eric S. Rump. New ed. Penguin 2004 288p (Penguin classics) pa $12

822

1. Great Britain—Social life and customs

ISBN 978-0-14-043240-4

First published 1988

Sheridan, Richard Brinsley, 1751-1816—Continued

Contents: The rivals; The critic; The school for scandal

"In The Rivals, Captain Absolute becomes his own rival for the hand of Lydia Languish wooing her under another name, while her aunt, the verbally inept Mrs Malaprop, wishes her to marry the real Captain. The Critic, featuring the pompous Puff and the arrogant Sneer, is a mocking depiction of the theatre, playwrights and, of course, critics. And The School for Scandal continues the theme of imposture when Sir Oliver Surface tests his nephews by appearing before them in disguise, and learns that reputation and the approval of society are of little value. In his introduction, Eric S. Rump places the plays in their historical and dramatic context and examines their enduring popularity." Publisher's note

Stoppard, Tom

Arcadia. Faber & Faber 1993 97p pa $14 hardcover o.p. *   **822**
ISBN 0-571-16934-1 (pa)   LC 94-103754
Awarded the New York Drama Critics Circle Award for Best Play, 1995
Characters: 8 men, 3 women. 2 acts, 7 scenes. First produced at the Royal National Theatre, London, 1993. In the U.S., first produced at the Lincoln Center Theater, New York City, March 30, 1995
Dramatic comedy set in English country house concurrently in present day and 1809. Landscape gardening, poetry, chaos theory, sex, and the end of the world are among topics discussed in exploration of clash between classical order and romantic ardor.

The invention of love. Grove Press 1998 102p pa $12   **822**
1. Housman, A. E. (Alfred Edward), 1859-1936—Drama
ISBN 0-8021-3581-1   LC 98-28331
Characters: 19 men, 1 woman, extras. 2 acts. First performed at the American Conservatory Theater, San Francisco, January 14, 2000
Scenes from life of homosexual poet and classical scholar A. E. Housman.

Rosencrantz and Guildenstern are dead. Grove Press 1967 126p pa $12 hardcover o.p. *
822
1. Shakespeare, William, 1564-1616—Parodies, imitations, etc.
ISBN 0-8021-3275-8 (pa)
Characters: 13 men, 2 women, extras. First produced in this form April 11, 1967 in London
This play "took the theatre world on both sides of the Atlantic by storm. The originality of the idea which put Hamlet's two insignificant friends centerstage was matched by the brilliance of the dialogue between these bewildered nonentities." Reader's Ency. 4th edition

Travesties. Grove Press 1975 99p pa $13 *
822
ISBN 0-8021-5089-6
Characters: 5 men, 2 women. Prologue, 2 acts. First produced at the Aldwych Theatre, London, June 10,
1974
Satire on politics, literature and art. James Joyce, Lenin, and Dadist Tristan Tzara come together in memories of obscure English diplomat in Zurich. Song and dance routines.

Synge, J. M. (John Millington), 1871-1909

The complete plays. Vintage Bks. 1960 268p pa $10 *   **822**
ISBN 0-394-70178-X
Contents: In the shadow of the glen; Riders to the sea; The tinker's wedding; The well of the saints; The playboy of the Western world; Deirdre of the sorrows

Thomas, Dylan, 1914-1953

Under milk wood; a play for voices. New Directions 1954 107p music pa $8.95 *
822
ISBN 0-8112-0209-7
"A radio play for voices. Written in poetic, inventive prose, this play is full of humor, a joyful sense of the goodness of life and love, and a strong Welsh flavor. It is an impression of a spring day in the lives of the people of Llareggub, a Welsh village situated under Milk Wood. It has no plot, but a wealth of characters who dream aloud, converse with one another, and speak in choruses of alternating voices." Reader's Ency. 4th edition

Wilde, Oscar, 1854-1900

The importance of being earnest and other plays; introduction by Terrence McNally; notes by Michael F. Davis. Modern Library 2003 257p pa $9.95 *   **822**
ISBN 0-8129-6714-3   LC 2003-44566
Contents: Lady Windermere's fan —An ideal husband—The importance of being earnest
The title play, written in 1895, is a drawing room comedy exposing quirks and foibles of Victorian society with plot revolving around amorous pursuits of two men who face social obstacles when they woo young ladies of quality. The book also features Lady Windermere's fan (1893), a four act comedy about a woman who has an affair when she suspects her husband of adultery, and An ideal husband (1895), a comedy about a blackmail scheme involving a lord's investment in the Suez Canal days before the British government's purchase of it, and his wife's reaction to her husband's past misdeeds.

822.008   English drama—Collections

Everyman, and medieval miracle plays; edited by A. C. Cawley; with a new preface and bibliography by Anne Rooney. Tuttle 1993 256p pa $6.95 hardcover o.p. *   **822.008**
1. Mysteries and miracle plays
ISBN 0-460-87280-X (pa)
"Everyman's library"
First Everyman's library edition published 1909 with title: Everyman, with other interludes including eight miracle plays

Everyman, and medieval miracle plays—_Continued_

In addition to Everyman, this collection includes plays from the Towneley, Coventry, York and Chester cycles.

Includes bibliographical references

822.3   William Shakespeare

Bloom, Harold, 1930-
Hamlet: poem unlimited. Riverhead Bks. 2003 154p hardcover o.p. pa $13   **822.3**
1. Shakespeare, William, 1564-1616. Hamlet
ISBN 1-57322-233-X; 1-57322-377-8 (pa)
         LC 2002-31691
This "is Bloom's attempt to uncover the mystery of both Prince Hamlet and the play itself. . . . Bloom takes us through the major soliloquies, scenes, characters, and action of the play, to explore the enigma at the heart of the drama." Publisher's note
"Far superior to existing theories of performance and worth yards of criticism for each well-wrought page." Libr J

Shakespeare: the invention of the human. Riverhead Bks. 1998 xx, 745p pa $18 hardcover o.p.   **822.3**
1. Shakespeare, William, 1564-1616—Criticism
ISBN 1-57322-751-X (pa)   LC 98-21325
In this critical study, Bloom argues "that the plays and poems of Shakespeare are not just 'the center of the Western canon'; they are nothing less than 'secular scripture.'. . . Bloom's book proceeds through genre groupings in rough chronological order." Commentary
"The passion and obsessiveness of Bloom's approach are its greatest recommendation." N Y Rev Books

Boyce, Charles
Critical companion to William Shakespeare; a literary reference to his life and work. Rev. ed. Facts on File 2005 2v il (Facts on File library of world literature) set $104.50   **822.3**
1. Shakespeare, William, 1564-1616—Criticism
ISBN 0-8160-5373-1   LC 2004-25769
First published 1990 with title: Shakespeare A to Z
"The first two-thirds [of this set] covers the plays. Arranged alphabetically by title, the 3000 entries generally consist of a scene-by-scene summary, a commentary, sources, theatrical history, and character sketches. The last one-third features entries for actors, composers, musicians, places that figured in the plays, and miscellaneous items." Libr J
Includes bibliographical references

Bryson, Bill
Shakespeare; the world as stage. Atlas Books/HarperCollins 2007 199p (Eminent lives) $19.95   **822.3**
1. Shakespeare, William, 1564-1616
ISBN 978-0-06-074022-1; 0-06-074022-1
         LC 2007-21647

In this biography, the author marshals "the usual little facts that others might overlook—for example, that in Shakespeare's day perhaps 40% of women were pregnant when they got married—to paint a portrait of the world in which the Bard lived and prospered. . . . Bryson is a pleasant and funny guide to a subject at once overexposed and elusive—as Bryson puts it, he is a kind of literary equivalent of an electron—forever there and not there." Publ Wkly
Includes bibliographical references

Butler, Colin
The practical Shakespeare; the plays in practice and on the page. Ohio University Press 2005 205p $39.95; pa $19.95   **822.3**
1. Shakespeare, William, 1564-1616—Dramatic production
ISBN 0-8214-1621-9; 0-8214-1622-7 (pa)
         LC 2004-30580
"Notes on staging, acting behaviors, scenes not shown, entrances, exits, characterizations, prologues, choruses, and staging are each featured in the text. References to specific scenes in the plays are used to illustrate and support the material. Any group preparing a production of one of the plays should find this a useful reference." Univ Press Books for Public and Second Sch Libr, 2006
Includes bibliographical references

Dunton-Downer, Leslie
Essential Shakespeare handbook; [by] Leslie Dunton-Downer, Alan Riding. DK Pub. 2004 480p il pa $25   **822.3**
1. Shakespeare, William, 1564-1616—Criticism
ISBN 0-7894-9333-0   LC 2004-274586
This is an "illustrated guide to every play in the Shakespeare canon, as well as a portrait of the Bard's life and the world of Elizabethan and Jacobean theater." Publisher's note
"This is an excellent basic tool for gaining insight into the Bard's poetic genius. . . . It is an informative, visually enticing introduction to the world's most famous dramatist." SLJ

Frye, Northrop
Northrop Frye on Shakespeare; edited by Robert Sandler. Yale Univ. Press 1986 186p pa $17 hardcover o.p.   **822.3**
1. Shakespeare, William, 1564-1616—Criticism
ISBN 0-300-04208-6 (pa)   LC 86-50485
Shakespeare scholar Frye provides in-depth analyses of ten plays.
"Frye's work is completely accessible, its style crisp and engaging. Most of all, it is full of basic 'good sense' about our most abused literary figure." Libr J

Garber, Marjorie
Shakespeare after all. Pantheon Books 2004 989p hardcover o.p. pa $20   **822.3**
1. Shakespeare, William, 1564-1616—Criticism
ISBN 0-375-42190-4; 0-385-72214-1 (pa)
         LC 2004-40063

Garber, Marjorie—_Continued_

The author "provides a handbook on Shakespeare's plays. After an introduction supplying standard overviews of the Renaissance theater and Shakespeare's life, she offers a critical essay on each play, complete with bibliographies and filmographies. The strength of this work is that Garber shows how the plays are interrelated by recurring language, characters, and themes, how each era has interpreted Shakespeare for itself, and how Shakespeare continues to shape today's culture." Libr J

Includes bibliographical references

Greenblatt, Stephen J. (Stephen Jay)

Will in the world; how Shakespeare became Shakespeare; [by] Stephen Greenblatt. Norton 2004 430p il $26.95 **822.3**

1. Shakespeare, William, 1564-1616

ISBN 0-393-05057-2   LC 2004-11512

The author discusses "the importance of probable early encounters with Marlowe, Watson, Nashe, and other prominent dramatists, and at the other end of Shakespeare's meteoric career, Greenblatt discerns the alchemy that converted fears of old age into the fury of _King Lear_ and transformed mingled pride and misgivings over a lifetime's work into the autumnal poise of _The Tempest._" Booklist

"Greenblatt is at his best when he merges his gifts as a literary critic and scholar with his instincts as a biographer. He writes with real subtlety and skill about the sonnets. . . . He also writes very well about the climate of fear and the use of public punishment and torture in Elizabethan and early Jacobean England, and how this enters into the very spirit of Shakespeare's work." N Y Times Book Rev

Includes bibliographical references

The **Greenwood** companion to Shakespeare; a comprehensive guide to students; edited by Joseph Rosenblum. Greenwood Press 2005 4v set $299.95 * **822.3**

1. Shakespeare, William, 1564-1616—Criticism

ISBN 0-313-32779-3   LC 2004-28690

"Each of the set's four volumes relates to a specific genre—Overviews and the History Plays (Vol. 1), The Comedies (Vol. 2), The Tragedies (Vol. 3), and The Romances and Poetry (Vol. 4)—and is organized in 'Cliff Notes' fashion, devoting each entry to a single play, long poem, sonnet, or sonnet pair. . . . A great introduction to the Bard." Libr J

Includes bibliographical references

Kermode, Frank, 1919-

Shakespeare's language. Farrar, Straus & Giroux 2000 324p pa $15 hardcover o.p. **822.3**

1. Shakespeare, William, 1564-1616—Language

ISBN 0-374-52774-1 (pa)   LC 99-55846

Kermode "devotes particular attention to the four great tragedies written at the height of Shakespeare's powers: _Hamlet, Othello, King Lear_ and _Macbeth._ While Kermode's concern is with the Bard's verse, he betrays no simplistic notions about literary language operating in a vacuum. A careful, close analysis of passages in each play is informed by a breathtaking knowledge of Elizabe-

than history and culture, as well as by the entire history of Shakespeare criticism from Coleridge to Eliot and the new historicists." Publ Wkly

Includes bibliographical references

Lamb, Charles, 1775-1834

Tales from Shakespeare; by Charles & Mary Lamb; with an introduction by Marina Warner. Penguin Books 2007 304p (Penguin classics) pa $12 **822.3**

1. Shakespeare, William, 1564-1616—Adaptations

ISBN 978-0-14-144162-7; 0-14-144162-3

First published 1807

A now classic collection of twenty plays by Shakespeare adapted as prose stories—the comedies by Mary Lamb, the tragedies by Charles Lamb

"The _Tales_ were the first version of 'Shakespeare' to be published specifically for children. They are written in a clear, vigorous style, not often encumbered by the attempt to make the language resemble that of the original. A lot is left out. . . . But the literary quality of the _Tales_ makes them outshine almost every other English children's book of this period, and they proved an immediate and lasting success." Oxford Companion to Child Lit

Norwich, John Julius, 1929-

Shakespeare's kings; the great plays and the history of England in the Middle Ages, 1337-1485. Scribner 2000 401p il pa $16 hardcover o.p.
822.3

1. Shakespeare, William, 1564-1616—Histories

ISBN 0-7432-0031-4 (pa)   LC 99-58271

The author offers "overviews of _Edward III; Richard II; Henry IV,_ parts 1 and 2; _Henry V; Henry VI,_ parts 1, 2, and 3; and _Richard III,_ examining each play through the lens of history. In addition to providing the necessary historical commentary, he also fills in the gaps between the plays, enabling readers to thoroughly comprehend the entire series in the proper historical context." Booklist

Nuttall, A. D. (Anthony David)

Shakespeare the thinker. Yale University Press 2007 428p $30 **822.3**

1. Shakespeare, William, 1564-1616—Criticism

ISBN 978-0-300-11928-2; 0-300-11928-3

LC 2006-35179

The author "traces ideas about motivation, identity, speech, and symbol in Shakespeare's plays. His study is rich in unexpected juxtapositions: Hippolyta, of 'A Midsummer Night's Dream,' finds herself in casual conversation with David Hume, and Titus Andronicus is seen in the context of 'Goodfellas.' The analysis never pulls too far away from the action onstage; indeed, Nuttall painstakingly shows Shakespeare's skill at negotiating abstract ideas through suspense, conflict, and character." New Yorker

Includes bibliographical references

Olsen, Kirstin
All things Shakespeare; an encyclopedia of Shakespeare's world. Greenwood Press 2002 2v il maps set $150 **822.3**
1. Shakespeare, William, 1564-1616—Criticism
ISBN 0-313-31503-5   LC 2002-69732
This "encyclopedia describes Shakespeare's physical environment, including common objects, daily activities, and popular beliefs and attitudes. Information is grouped into general topic clusters such as 'Behavior,' 'Clothing and Dress,' 'Furniture,' 'Fire,' and 'War and Peace.' . . . Within the 200-plus entries, references are made to the play, act, and scene in which Shakespeare mentions the item or activity being discussed." Libr J

The **Oxford** companion to Shakespeare; general editor, Michael Dobson; associate general editor, Stanley Wells. Oxford Univ. Press 2001 xxix, 541p il maps $60 * **822.3**
1. Shakespeare, William, 1564-1616—Encyclopedias
ISBN 0-19-811735-3   LC 2001-277478
This volume "illuminates not only Shakespeare's life and works but also the many forms that interpretation of Shakespeare has taken in the centuries since his death." Booklist
Includes bibliographical references

Rosenbaum, Ron
The Shakespeare wars; clashing scholars, public fiascoes, palace coups. Random House 2006 601p $35 **822.3**
1. Shakespeare, William, 1564-1616—Criticism
ISBN 0-375-50339-0; 978-0-375-50339-9
     LC 2006-42541
The author "conveys the impassioned arguments of leading directors and scholars concerning how Shakespeare should be printed and performed. . . . Balancing academic reportage with his own lively observations, Rosenbaum wrestles with the weightiest issues of Shakespeare studies in a down-to-earth manner that readers will applaud." Publ Wkly
Includes bibliographical references

Shakespeare, William, 1564-1616
The Columbia dictionary of quotations from Shakespeare; [selected by] Mary and Reginald Foakes. Columbia Univ. Press 1998 516p $63 * **822.3**
1. Shakespeare, William, 1564-1616—Quotations
2. Quotations
ISBN 0-231-10434-0   LC 97-44894
"The book is organized by topics ('Age,' 'Duplicity,' 'Fish'), followed by passages of about five or six lines. After each selection, the citation, the character, and usually the context of the lines are given. If a reference is obscure, the explanation is more elaborate. Indexes provide access by play and poem, by character, and by keyword." SLJ

The complete works; general editors, Stanley Wells and Gary Taylor; editors, Stanley Wells . . . [et al.]; with introductions by Stanley Wells. 2nd ed. Clarendon Press; Oxford University Press 2005 lxxv, 1344p il $40 * **822.3**
ISBN 0-19-926717-0   LC 2005-47272
First published 1986
On cover: The Oxford Shakespeare
This anthology "features a brief introduction to each work as well as [a] General Introduction. . . . [The volume includes] essay on language, a list of contemporary allusions to Shakespeare, an index of Shakespearean characters, a glossary, a consolidated bibliography, and an index of first lines of the Sonnets." Publisher's note

Shapiro, James
A year in the life of William Shakespeare, 1599. HarperCollins Publishers 2005 394p il map $27.95 **822.3**
1. Shakespeare, William, 1564-1616
ISBN 0-571-21448-0   LC 2005-43342
The author "offers a critical examination of four plays Shakespeare wrote in the seminal year of 1599—Henry V, Julius Caesar, As You Like It, and Hamlet—and of the events that influenced the Bard at the time of their writing. . . . This work gives the reader a realistic sense of the multilayered and complex political, social, and literary pressures that influenced Shakespeare as a citizen of England, as a business partner in the Globe Theatre, and as a writer." Libr J
Includes bibliographical references

Wells, Stanley W., 1930-
Shakespeare: for all time; [by] Stanley Wells. Oxford Univ. Press 2003 xxi, 442p il $40 * **822.3**
1. Shakespeare, William, 1564-1616
ISBN 0-19-516093-2   LC 2002-27412
First published 2002 in the United Kingdom
"Chapters on Shakespeare's life in Stratford and in London offer a . . . view of the development of the writer's career and personality. At the core of the book lies a . . . study of the writings themselves—how Shakespeare set about writing a play, his relationships with the company of actors with whom he worked, his developing mastery of the literary and rhetorical skills that he learned at the Stratford grammar school, the essentially theatrical quality of the structure and language of his plays. Subsequent chapters trace the fluctuating fortunes of his reputation and influence." Publisher's note
Includes bibliographical references

Wood, Michael, 1948-
Shakespeare. Basic Bks. 2003 352p il map $29.95; pa $17.95 **822.3**
1. Shakespeare, William, 1564-1616
ISBN 0-465-09264-0; 0-465-09265-9 (pa)
Published in the United Kingdom with title: In search of Shakespeare
This biography of the English dramatist and poet was written as "a complement to a BBC series." America
"Wood has crafted a book of substance and originali-

Wood, Michael, 1948-—*Continued*

ty. Combining a wealth of scholarship and a bit of his own sleuthing, Wood presents a portrait of Shakespeare as very much a child of Stratford, a poet for whom the people of the village and countryside of his youth were always a part of his conscious, creative life. . . . A highly readable, informative, and artfully illustrated volume for bardolaters and common readers alike." Booklist

823.009 English fiction—History and criticism

Baker, William, 1944-

Critical companion to Jane Austen; a literary reference to her life and work. Facts on File 2008 644p il (Facts on File library of world literature) $75 **823.009**
1. Austen, Jane, 1775-1817
ISBN 978-0-8160-6416-8   LC 2006-102848
This book examines Jane Austen's "life and works, and includes critical analyses of the themes within her writing, as well as entries on related topics and relevant people, places, and influences." Publisher's note
"Janeites (and others) will find . . . [this book] a useful and accessible one-stop resource." Booklist
Includes bibliographical references

The **Cambridge** companion to Jane Austen; edited by Edward Copeland and Juliet McMaster. Cambridge Univ. Press 1997 251p (Cambridge companions to literature) $65; pa $23
823.009
1. Austen, Jane, 1775-1817
ISBN 0-521-49517-2; 0-521-49867-8 (pa)
LC 96-23387
Scholars assess "Jane Austen's works in the contexts of her contemporary world, and of present-day critical discourse. Besides discussions of Austen's novels and letters, there are essays on religion, politics, class consciousness, publishing practices, domestic economy, style in the novels and the significance of her juvenile works. A chronology provides biographical information." Publisher's note

Davis, Paul B. (Paul Benjamin), 1934-

Critical companion to Charles Dickens; a literary reference to his life and work. Rev ed. Facts on File 2007 676p il (Facts on File library of world literature) $75 * **823.009**
1. Dickens, Charles, 1812-1870
ISBN 0-8160-6407-5; 978-0-8160-6407-6
LC 2006-3026
First published 1998 with title: Charles Dickens A-Z
This "reference contains entries on this writer's works, including the characters in each work, . . . historical and thematic information, and critical discussion. It also includes entries on related people, places, themes, topics, and influences. Additional features include 116 illustrations, a chronology, a bibliography of primary and secondary sources, and much more." Publisher's note
Includes bibliographical references

The **Facts** on File companion to the British novel. Facts on File 2005 2v (Facts on File library of world literature) set $140 * **823.009**
1. English fiction—History and criticism
ISBN 0-8160-6377-X; 978-0-8160-6377-2
LC 2004-20914
Contents: v. 1. Beginnings through the 19th century / Virginia Brackett—v. 2. 20th century / Victoria Gaydosik
"This two-volume companion to the British novel contains more than 1000 A-to-Z entries (each averaging several pages in length) on English-writing authors hailing from either the British Isles or the Commonwealth as well as on novels, pertinent literary terms, themes, concepts, influential periodicals, and subgenres." Libr J
"With more than one thousand entries, each with a selected bibliography and a set of very usable appendixes, this work accomplishes much in a compact set." Ref & User Services Quarterly
Includes bibliographical references

Fargnoli, A. Nicholas

Critical companion to James Joyce; a literary companion to his life and work; [by] A. Nicholas Fargnoli, Michael Patrick Gillespie. Rev ed. Facts On File 2006 450p il (Facts on File library of world literature) $65; pa $19.95 **823.009**
1. Joyce, James, 1882-1941
ISBN   0-8160-6232-3;   978-0-8160-6232-4; 0-8160-6689-2 (pa); 978-0-8160-6689-6 (pa)
LC 2005-15721
First published 1995 with title: James Joyce A to Z
The authors "divide this reference to the writer's life and work into four parts. Part 1 is a brief biography. Part 2 focuses on individual works (e.g., Dubliners), including its publication date, a brief history, a synopsis, early critical reception, contemporary perspectives, and one or two recommended titles for further reading. The entries in Part 3 cover people (including friends and relatives), places, and ideas related to Joyce. Part 4 contains an appendix, a bibliography of the writer's work, a bibliography of secondary sources, chronologies, family trees, and more. . . . [This is] a great primer for those needing a detailed introduction into Joyce's world." Libr J
Includes bibliographical references

Ford, Paul F.

Companion to Narnia; a complete guide to the magical world of C.S. Lewis's The chronicles of Narnia; foreword by Madeleine L'Engle; illustrated by Lorinda Bryan Cauley. Rev and expanded. HarperSanFrancisco 2005 xxvi, 530p il map pa $16.95 **823.009**
1. Lewis, C. S. (Clive Staples), 1898-1963. Chronicles of Narnia
ISBN 0-06-079127-6
First published 1980
C. S. Lewis wrote seven books of fantasy that are collectively called The Chronicles of Narnia. This book "is an encyclopedia of Narnian names and terms and related matters, with . . . footnoted articles, page references to American and British hardcover editions, cross-references, and a running footline for quick location of materials in the alphabet." Choice
Includes bibliographical references

Head, Dominic
The Cambridge introduction to modern British fiction, 1950-2000. Cambridge Univ. Press 2002 307p $65; pa $22 *   **823.009**
1. English fiction—History and criticism
ISBN 0-521-66014-9; 0-521-66966-9 (pa)
LC 2001-43261
This study "includes chapters on the state and the novel, class and social change, gender and sexual identity, national identity, and multiculturalism." Publisher's note
"Anyone with an interest in the contemporary novel, not just British fiction, will appreciate this outstanding survey and analysis. . . . The quality of discussion is admirably consistent within and between each chapter, the prose as carefully crafted as the judgments are measured. . . . This book should become a standard reference work for its subject." Choice
Includes bibliographical references

Horror: another 100 best books; edited by Stephen Jones and Kim Newman; with a foreword by Peter Straub. Carroll & Graf Publishers 2005 456p pa $16.95 *
823.009
1. Horror fiction—History and criticism 2. Best books
ISBN 0-7867-1577-4
First published 1988
This book "features one hundred of the top names in the horror field discussing one hundred of the most spine-chilling novels ever written. Each entry includes a synopsis of the work as well as publication history, biographical information about the author of each title, and recommended reading and biographical notes on the contributor." Publisher's note
"Horror fans seeking what to read next will not only find out here; they'll also have their taste and appreciative capacity refined by the intelligent, passionate commentary of the 100 writers who selected these 100 books." Booklist

Maunder, Andrew
The Facts on File companion to the British short story. Facts on File 2006 528p (Facts on File library of world literature) $75   **823.009**
1. Short stories—History and criticism
ISBN 0-8160-5990-X; 978-0-8160-5990-4
LC 2006-6897
More than 450 alphabetically arranged entries cover authors, characters, and major short stories. Literary terms, themes, and motifs are covered. Winners of prizes and awards are noted.
Includes glossary and bibliographical references

Olsen, Kirstin
All things Austen; an encyclopedia of Austen's world. Greenwood Press 2005 2v il maps set $149.95   **823.009**
1. Austen, Jane, 1775-1817
ISBN 0-313-33032-8   LC 2004-28664
This Jane Austen encyclopedia contains "more than 150 well-designed and well-written A-to-Z articles on such topics as clothing, education, politics, religion, sci-

ence, business, society, and the military of 18th- and 19th-century England." Libr J
"This well-written and meticulously researched work provides a convenient means for general readers, students, and scholars to gain a better understanding of the social, cultural, and political climate of Austen's time." Booklist

824   English essays

Carlyle, Thomas, 1795-1881
Sartor resartus; edited with an introduction and notes by Kerry McSweeney and Peter Sabor. Oxford Univ. Press 1987 xlii, 273p (The World's classics) pa $11.95 *   **824**
ISBN 0-19-283673-0   LC 87-5753
First published 1833-1834, Sartor resartus contains the germ of Carlyle's philosophy. It purports to be an interpretation of the work of an erudite German professor but is really the story of Carlyle's own fierce spiritual conflict between doubt and faith. It presents a philosophy of clothes, or the outward forms of things
Includes bibliographical references

De Quincey, Thomas, 1785-1859
The confessions of an English opium-eater and other writings. Penguin Books 2003 xliv, 296p pa $14   **824**
1. Drug abuse
ISBN 978-0-14-043901-4; 0-14-043901-3
"Confessions forged a link between artistic self-expression and addiction, paving the way for later generations of literary drug-users from Baudelaire to Burroughs, and anticipating psychoanalysis with its insights into the subconscious. This edition is based on the original serial version of 1821, and reproduces the two 'sequels', 'Suspiria de Profundis' (1845) and 'The English Mail-Coach' (1849). It also includes a critical introduction discussing the romantic figure of the addict and the tradition of confessional literature, and an appendix on opium in the nineteenth century." Publisher's note

Hazlitt, William, 1778-1830
Selected writings; edited with an introduction and notes by Jon Cook. Oxford University Press 1998 xlvi, 423p (Oxford world's classics) pa $13.95   **824**
ISBN 978-0-19-283800-1; 0-19-283800-1
Hazlitt "developed a variety of identities as a writer: essayist, philosopher, critic of literature, drama and art, biographer, political commentator, and polemicist. Praised for his eloquence, he was also reviled by conservatives for his radical politics. This edition, thematically organized for ease of access, contains some of his best-known essays, such as 'The Indian Jugglers' and 'The Fight,' as well as more obscure pieces on politics, philosophy, and culture." Publisher's note

James, Clive, 1939-
As of this writing; the essential essays, 1968-2002. Norton 2003 619p $35   **824**

James, Clive, 1939-—*Continued*
ISBN 0-393-05180-3

This collection of "essays dealing with poetry and literature feature{s} pieces on Robert Lowell, D.H. Lawrence, and Solzhenitsyn, while a section on culture and criticism comments on the life and works of Lillian Hellman, Evelyn Waugh and Betrand Russell." Publ Wkly

"James writes with fluent wit, remarkable warmth, deep knowledge, and an exhilarating sense of mission." Booklist

Kermode, Frank, 1919-
Pieces of my mind; essays and criticism, 1958-2002. Farrar, Straus & Giroux 2003 466p $26; pa $16 * **824**
ISBN 0-8090-7601-2; 0-374-52936-1 (pa)
LC 2003-54727

This collection of essays samples the author's "interests from opera to modern dance, from the New Testament to the English novelist Ian McEwan. It includes chapters from Kermode's most famous books, freestanding academic pieces and lectures, essay-reviews . . . and four substantial unpublished essays." Publ Wkly

The author "parses complicated, even esoteric aspects of story and text, metaphysics and poetry, and the link between social change and the evolution of the novel, yet he is unfailingly clear and cheerfully engaging, classy, and stimulating." Booklist

Includes bibliographical references

Orwell, George, 1903-1950
Essays; selected and introduced by John Carey. Alfred A. Knopf 2002 c1996 xlv, 1369p (Everyman's library) $35 **824**
ISBN 978-0-375-41503-6; 0-375-41503-3

"Included among the more than 240 essays in this volume are Orwell's famous discussion of pacifism, 'My Country Right or Left'; his scathingly complicated views on the dirty work of imperialism in 'Shooting an Elephant'; and his very firm opinion on how to make 'A Nice Cup of Tea.'" Publisher's note

"The real reason we read Orwell is because his own fault-line, his fundamental schism, his hybridity, left him exceptionally sensitive to the fissure—which is everywhere apparent–between what ought to be the case and what actually is the case. He says the unsayable." Financial Times

Swift, Jonathan, 1667-1745
A tale of a tub, and other work; edited with an introduction by Angus Ross and David Woolley. Oxford Univ. Press 1986 xxviii, 237p (The World's classics) pa $8.95 **824**
ISBN 0-19-283593-9 LC 85-5072

Includes the Battle of the books and the Mechanical operation of the spirit

A tale of a tub, The battle of the books, and A discourse concerning the mechanical operation of the spirit, were first published together in 1704. The first is an allegorical satire ridiculing the corruptions of religion and learning by extremists and pedants. The second is a mock heroic satire on squabbles concerning the relative merits of ancient and modern authors presented as an account of the battle between ancient and modern books in St James Library. The third ridicules the manner of worship and preaching of religious enthusiasts of the period

Wilde, Oscar, 1854-1900
The artist as critic; critical writings of Oscar Wilde; edited by Richard Ellmann. University of Chicago Press 1982 xxviii, 446p pa $36.50
824
1. Literature—History and criticism 2. Criticism
ISBN 978-0-226-89764-6; 0-226-89764-8
LC 82-13361

First published 1969 by Random House

Included in this collection of Wilde's criticism "is a wide selection of Wilde's book reviews as well as such famous longer works as 'The Portrait of Mr. W.H.,' 'The Soul Man under Socialism,' and the four essays which make up Intentions." Publisher's note

Wilde's "book reviews and occasional pieces prove that while Wilde could be superbly malicious with fatheads, he was a generous and painstaking critic, quick to find merit and delighted to announce the discovery. It is easy to damn a book amusingly. Wilde could praise amusingly, a rare and difficult trick." Atlantic

826 English letters

The **Oxford** book of letters; edited by Frank and Anita Kermode. Oxford Univ. Press 1995 559p pa $16.95 hardcover o.p. * **826**
1. English letters 2. American letters
ISBN 0-19-280490-1 (pa) LC 94-36412

"This volume includes more than 300 letters that document the concerns of writers, political leaders, and ordinary citizens over the period 1535-1985. Each letter is accompanied by an explanatory note identifying the writer and establishing the context. The correspondents, some more skilled than others, pursue a range of topics, including an account of a public execution, gossip about friends and relatives, and the hardships of moving to a new land in search of a better life." Libr J

827 English humor and satire

The **Oxford** book of humorous prose; William Caxton to P.G. Wodehouse: a conducted tour; [chosen and edited] by Frank Muir. Oxford Univ. Press 1990 xxxiv, 1162p pa $21.50 hardcover o.p. * **827**
1. English wit and humor 2. American wit and humor
ISBN 0-19-280379-4 (pa) LC 89-9242

"A sprinkling of American contributors join British humorists in this selection of pieces ranging from the gently witty to the irreverent, the bawdy, and the sexy." Booklist

"Selections are generally very short, with bridges, often fairly humorous of themselves, by Muir. The humor ranges from the broad to the subtle and, in fact, in any other way that humor might range; there's something in here for everyone." Libr J

828   English miscellaneous writings

Achebe, Chinua, 1930-
Home and exile. Anchor Bks. 2001 115p pa $11
   828
ISBN 978-0-385-72133-2; 0-385-72133-1
   LC 2001-22599
First published 2000 by Oxford University Press
Based on the 1998 McMillan-Stewart Lectures at Harvard University
This volume consists of "Achebe's ruminations (both serious and humorous) on empire, post-colonialism, Western writers (e.g., Joseph Conrad, Graham Greene, and Elspeth Huxley) on Africa, universal culture, and expatriation and exile." Libr J
"This slim volume—told in Achebe's subtle, witty and gracious style—is one of those small gems of literary and historical analysis that readers will treasure and re-read over the years." Publ Wkly
Includes bibliographical references

DeGategno, Paul J.
Critical companion to Jonathan Swift; a literary reference to his life and works; [by] Paul J. DeGategno, R. Jay Stubblefield. Facts on File 2006 474p il (Facts on File library of world literature) $75   **828**
1. Swift, Jonathan, 1667-1745
ISBN 0-8160-5093-7; 978-0-8160-5093-2
   LC 2005-25470
This "work is divided into five parts. These parts consist of a ten-page biography of satirist Jonathan Swift (1667-1745); a 'Works A-Z' section that includes synopses and commentaries that generally run to several hundred words on virtually all of Swift's poems, essays, and books; a 'Related Entries' section with similar brief articles on persons, topics, and places relevant to Swift studies; appendixes that include a chronology of Swift's life; a . . . bibliography of primary and secondary works; and an index." Libr J
For a fuller review, see: Booklist, Feb. 1, 2007
Includes bibliographical references

Heaney, Seamus
Finders keepers; selected prose 1971-2001. Farrar, Straus & Giroux 2002 452p $30; pa $15 *
   828
1. Poetry—History and criticism
ISBN 0-374-15496-1; 0-374-52878-0 (pa)
This collection "gathers Heaney's occasional prose from four decades, much of it meditating upon other poets who have moved him, including familiar members of the canon, such as Eliot and Yeats and Auden, and lesser-known and newer moderns, such as Hugh MacDiarmid, Thomas Kinsella, and Norman MacCaig, whose work draws his interest. Not surprisingly for a poet from a war-wracked land, Heaney comes back again and again to the question of how poetry can matter against human savagery." Booklist

Johnson, Samuel, 1709-1784
Samuel Johnson; the major works; edited with an introduction and notes by Donald Greene. Oxford University Press 2000 xxvii, 840p (Oxford world's classics) pa $18.95   **828**
ISBN 978-0-19-284042-4; 0-19-284042-8
   LC 83-17280
"This volume celebrates Johnson's astonishing talent by selecting widely across the full range of his work. It includes 'London' and 'The Vanity of Human Wishes' among other poems, and many of his essays for the Rambler and Idler. The prefaces to his edition of Shakespeare and his famous Dictionary, together with samples from the texts, are given, as well as selections from A Journey to the Western Islands of Scotland, the Lives of the Poets, and Rasselas in its entirety. There is also a substantial representation of lesser-known prose, and of his poetry, letters, and journals." Publisher's note
Includes bibliographical references

The **New** Oxford book of literary anecdotes. Oxford University Press 2006 385p il $29.95 *
   828
1. English literature—Anecdotes 2. Authors, English—Anecdotes 3. Authors, American—Anecdotes
ISBN 0-19-280468-5; 978-0-19-280468-6
   LC 2005-33698
First published 1975 under the editorship of James Sutherland with title: The Oxford book of literary anecdotes
The editor "has compiled more than 700 anecdotes about English-language writers, from Geoffrey Chaucer to J.K. Rowling. The brief, chronologically-arranged (by subject's birth date) entries offer a glimpse into the personalities and times of these authors." Libr J
Includes bibliographical references

Sisman, Adam
Boswell's presumptuous task; the making of the life of Dr. Johnson. Penguin 2002 351p il pa $15
   828
1. Boswell, James, 1740-1795
ISBN 978-0-14-200175-2; 0-14-200175-9
First published 2000 in the United Kingdom
James Boswell's The Life of Samuel Johnson was published in 1791, six years after the death of its subject. In this book, Sisman chronicles Boswell's motives for writing his biography and the techniques he adopted.
"Mr. Sisman's book is illuminating both of Boswell's character and of all aspects of his authorship." Economist
Includes bibliographical references

Thomas, Dylan, 1914-1953
A child's Christmas in Wales; with woodcuts by Ellen Raskin. New Directions 2007 51p il pa $9.95   **828**
1. Christmas—Wales
ISBN 978-0-8112-1731-6; 0-8112-1731-0
   LC 2007-24727
First published 1954
The Welsh poet Dylan Thomas recalls the celebration of Christmas with his family and the feelings it evoked in him as a child.

Thomas, Dylan, 1914-1953—*Continued*
For any season of the year "the language is enchanting and the poetry shines with an unearthly radiance." N Y Times Book Rev

Woolf, Virginia, 1882-1941
The Virginia Woolf reader; edited by Mitchell A. Leaska. Harcourt Brace Jovanovich 1984 371p pa $16 hardcover o.p. **828**
   ISBN 0-15-693590-2 (pa)   LC 84-4478
   "A Harvest book"
   Excerpts from Woolf's "novels form less than 20 percent of a reader whose selections of short stories, essays, letters, and diary entries are excellent. This collection will be useful to those already familiar with Woolf's novels and seeking an introductory selection of her other writings." Libr J

829   Old English (Anglo-Saxon) literature

Beowulf.
Beowulf; [translated by] Seamus Heaney. Farrar, Straus & Giroux 1999 220p $25 *   **829**
   ISBN 0-374-11119-7   LC 99-23209
   This edition also available in paperback from Norton; other verse and prose translations available from various publishers
   "Much that seemed off-putting about Beowulf to modern readers becomes, in Heaney's retelling, eerily intriguing instead. . . . Beowulf may, by modern standards, seem bloodthirsty and deluded, but Heaney's poetry makes eloquently persuasive the hero's tragic stature." Time

830.3   German literature— Encyclopedias and dictionaries

Encyclopedia of German literature; Matthias Konzett, editor. Fitzroy Dearborn Pubs. 2000 2v set $175 *   **830.3**
   1. German literature—Encyclopedias 2. German literature—Bio-bibliography
   ISBN 1-57958-138-2
   "Essay-like entries cover three main categories: authors, works (novels, books of poetry, and essays), and topics, the last encompassing everything from literary terms and movements, artistic forums, cities, and historical eras to the key legacy of the Frankfurt School and its members. Rather lengthy lists for further reading are provided with each essay." Libr J
   Includes bibliographical references

Garland, Henry B. (Henry Burnand)
The Oxford companion to German literature; by Henry and Mary Garland. 3rd ed, by Mary Garland. Oxford Univ. Press 1997 951p maps $95 *   **830.3**
   1. German literature—Dictionaries 2. German literature—Bio-bibliography
   ISBN 0-19-815896-3   LC 96-53309

First published 1976
   Entries include biographies, synopses of important works, literary terms and movements, historical events and figures, and material relevant to the social and intellectual background of German literature from the earliest records to the present.

830.9   German literature—History and criticism

The **Cambridge** history of German literature; edited by Helen Watanabe-O'Kelly. Cambridge Univ. Press 1997 613p $90; pa $32 *   **830.9**
   1. German literature—History and criticism
   ISBN 0-521-43417-3; 0-521-78573-1 (pa)
       LC 95-52412
   This work provides a history of German literature "up to the Unification of Germany in 1990. It is a history for our times: well-known authors and movements are set in a wider literary, cultural and political context, standard judgments are reexamined where appropriate, and a new prominence is given to writing by women. . . . Titles and quotations are translated, and there is an extensive bibliography." Publisher's note
   A "briskly written survey of German literature that grounds literary practice in the social and historical context of each period and yet does not shortchange the aesthetic qualities of the representative works discussed." Choice

831   German poetry

Celan, Paul
Poems of Paul Celan; translated by Michael Hamburger. Rev and expanded. Persea Bks. 2002 xxxiv, 366p $35; pa $18.95 *   **831**
   1. Poetry—By individual authors
   ISBN 0-89255-275-1; 0-89255-276-X (pa)
       LC 2001-59341
   "A Karen and Michael Braziller book"
   First published 1980 with title: Paul Celan: poems
   "This bilingual German-English selection culled from [the poet's] nine collections reveals that his is a poetry of darkness: anguish over what life offers and denies; the ever-present shadow of death that shades each breath. . . . Yet it also expresses an undefined, perhaps undefinable, joy." Booklist [review of 1989 edition]

Goethe, Johann Wolfgang von, 1749-1832
Selected poetry; translated with an introduction and notes by David Luke. Penguin Books 2005 xliv, 283p (Penguin classics) pa $16   **831**
   1. Poetry—By individual authors
   ISBN 978-0-14-042456-0; 0-14-042456-3
   First published 1999 in the United Kingdom
   "The introduction gives a thoughtful summary of Goethe's fascinating and problematic life. . . . What Luke triumphantly does is not only to stay close to the original, but also to create a total structure that gives a convincing sense of the overall movement of the poem. . . .

Goethe, Johann Wolfgang von, 1749-1832—*Continued*

Goethe made no secret of his huge debt to Shakespeare; perhaps the English tradition might celebrate the new millennium by learning something from him in return. David Luke's selection makes an excellent starting point." Times Lit Suppl

Heine, Heinrich, 1797-1856

Poetry and prose; edited by Jost Hermand and Robert C. Holub; foreword by Alfred Kazin. Continuum 1982 299p (German library) hardcover o.p. pa $29.95   **831**

1. Poetry—By individual authors
ISBN 978-0-8264-0255-3 (pa); 0-8264-0265-8
LC 82-7981

This volume contains "some 47 poems in a . . . distribution of examples from all periods of Heine's lyric work, presented in German with facing English versions by various translators, new and old. A second part, 'Narrative Prose,' offers 'The Harz Journey' and 'Ideas: Book Le Grand' in translations by F.T. Wood and C.G. Leland, respectively, adapted here by R.C. Holub and M. Humphreys. Aaron Kramer's translation of 'Germany: A Winter's Tale' represents 'Epic Poetry.'" Choice

Mörike, Eduard Friedrich, 1804-1875

Mozart's journey to Prague and a selection of poems; [by] Eduard Mörike; translated and with an introduction and notes by David Luke; Scots translations by Gilbert McKay. rev ed. Penguin Books 2003 xl, 216p (Penguin Classics) pa $14
    831

1. Poetry—By individual authors
ISBN 978-0-14-044737-8; 0-14-044737-7
LC 2004-298957

First published 1997 in the United Kingdom

A selection of Mörike's most popular romantic and classical folk and fairy-tale poems. Also includes the 1855 novella Mozart's journey to Prague, an imaginary recreation of the journey Mozart made from Vienna to Prague in 1787 to conduct the first performance of Don Giovanni.

Includes bibliographical references

Rilke, Rainer Maria, 1875-1926

Ahead of all parting; the selected poetry and prose of Rainer Maria Rilke; edited and translated by Stephen Mitchell. Modern Library 1995 615p $24.95   **831**

1. Poetry—By individual authors
ISBN 978-0-679-60161-6; 0-679-60161-9
LC 94-43917

This collection "contains representative poems from [Rilke's] early collections The Book of Hours and The Book of Pictures; many selections from the revolutionary New Poems, which drew inspiration from Rodin and Cezanne; the hitherto little-known 'Letter to a Friend'; and a generous selection of the late uncollected poems. . . . Included too are passages from Rilke's influential novel, The Notebooks of Malte Laurids Brigge, and nine of his uncollected prose pieces. Finally the book presents the poet's two greatest masterpieces in their entirety: the Duino Elegies and The Sonnets of Orpheus." Publisher's note

Duino elegies; translated by David Young; with an introduction and commentary. W. W. Norton 2006 202p pa $13.95 *   **831**

1. Poetry—By individual authors
ISBN 978-0-393-32884-4; 0-393-32884-8
LC 2006-9872

First English translation published 1939; this translation was originally published in Field, Contemporary Poetry and Poetics, issues 5 through 9 and as a Norton paperback edition in 1992

"These elegies, the last great work of the poet, were named for the castle of Duino on the Adriatic, where they were first conceived." New Statesman (1913)

New poems; selected and translated by Edward Snow. rev bilingual ed. North Point Press 2001 329p pa $15   **831**

1. Poetry—By individual authors
ISBN 0-86547-612-8   LC 2001-42714

"The translations in this book were originally published in two separate volumes: New poems (Neue Gedichte) in 1984 and New poems: the other part (Der neuen Gedichte anderer Teil) in 1987." Preface

In this "translation, Edward Snow renders into believable English the complete text of Rilke's work of early maturity. . . . Maintaining fidelity to Rilke's idiosyncratic and problematic German, Snow does not reproduce his formal structures but does capture the rhythms, tone shifts, and overall feel of the poems to an admirable degree. Bilingual edition." Booklist [review of 1984 edition of New poems (1907)]

Sonnets to Orpheus; translated by M.D. Herter Norton. W. W. Norton 2006 c1942 160p pa $13.95 *   **831**

1. Poetry—By individual authors
ISBN 0-393-32885-6

First English translation 1936 in the United Kingdom; this translation first published 1942

"Deeply rooted in the symbolist tradition, the 'Sonnets' collapse the barriers that exist between the inner and the outer world and celebrate the inherently musical quality of language. In his masterful translation of the 'Sonnets', Young captures the fluidity of the original with sensitivity and precision." Libr J

Uncollected poems; selected and translated by Edward Snow. Bilingual ed. North Point Press 1995 265p pa $15 hardcover o.p.   **831**

1. Poetry—By individual authors
ISBN 0-86547-513-X (pa)   LC 94-24438

This volume includes poems "written between 1908, the year Rilke published New Poems, and 1923, when Duino Elegies and Sonnets to Orpheus appeared." Libr J

"Snow is particularly adept at capturing what one might call the non-Orphic side of Rilke's voice. Even in the most complex and rhetorically charged pieces, however, Snow is careful never to simplify Rilke. . . . Most important of all, these translations . . . let us get beyond the simplifications of the Rilke legend with its cycles of transcendent inspiration and imaginative paralysis." New Repub

831.008 German poetry—Collections

Twentieth-century German poetry; an anthology; edited by Michael Hofmann. Farrar, Straus and Giroux 2006 xxvii, 511p $40; pa $25

831.008

1. German poetry—Collections
ISBN 978-0-374-10535-8; 0-374-10535-9; 978-0-374-53093-8 (pa); 0-374-53093-9 (pa)

LC 2006-6873

This "duel-language volume will vastly expand what most American readers know of contemporary German poetry: maybe some Rilke, Celan or Brecht and probably little else. From a whimsy by the artist Paul Klee to a strange piece by young poet Jan Wagner . . ., this anthology's pleasures are many. Well-known poet and translator Hofman gathers a varied range of poems from the German canon—better-known poets and writers like Rilke, Georg Trakl, Brecht, Celan and Günter Grass, meet many poets who deserve a larger following outside Germany, like Hans Magnus Enzensberger and Durs Grünbein." Publ Wkly

Includes bibliographical references

832 German drama

Dürrenmatt, Friedrich
The visit; a tragi-comedy; translated from the German by Patrick Bowles. Grove Press 1962 109p pa $12 *

832

ISBN 0-8021-3066-6
"An Evergreen original"
Characters: 28 men, 6 women, extras. 3 acts. First produced in the United States at the Lunt-Fontaine Theatre, New York City, May 5, 1958

This play "concerns millionaire Claire Zachanassian's return to her small home town where, in her youth, she was seduced and abandoned by III. She seeks revenge and, to get it, she bribes the entire population: every man, woman and child will be rich for the rest of their lives if they agree to put III to death. After a feeble moral struggle and a travesty of a trial, the people of Güllen condemn and execute the erstwhile lover. In so doing they condemn themselves and Dürrenmatt condemns society as a whole." Cambridge Guide to World Theatre

Goethe, Johann Wolfgang von, 1749-1832
Goethe's Faust; the original German and a new tr. and introduction by Walter Kaufmann; part one and sections from part two. Anchor Books 1962 c1961 503p pa $10.95 *

832

ISBN 978-0-385-03114-1; 0-385-03114-9
Part I first published 1808; Part II 1832
In this epic drama "Mephistopheles makes a bargain with the aged Faust. If Faust is granted one moment of complete contentment, he loses his soul. Faust regains his youth and with Mephistopheles he travels about enjoying every form of earthly pleasure." Haydn. Thesaurus of Book Dig

Lessing, Gotthold Ephraim, 1729-1781
Nathan the Wise, Minna von Barnhelm, and other plays and writings; edited by Peter Demetz; foreword by Hannah Arendt. Continuum 1991 xxvii, 335p (German library) hardcover o.p. pa $29.95

832

ISBN 0-8264-0706-4; 0-8264-0707-2 (pa)

LC 91-19344

Contents: Minna von Barnhelm, translated by Kenneth J. Northcott; Emilia Galotti, translated by Anna Johanna Gode von Aesch; The Jews, translated by Ingrid Walsøe-Engel; Nathan the Wise, translated by Bayard Quincy Morgan; Ernst and Falk, translated by William L. Zwiebel; Selections from Lessing's philosophical, theological writings, translated by Henry Chadwick

Schiller, Friedrich, 1759-1805
Don Carlos and Mary Stuart; translated with notes by Hilary Collier Sy-Quia; adapted in verse drama by Peter Oswald; with an introduction by Lesley Sharpe. Oxford University Press 2008 xxx, 359p il pa $13.95

832

1. Carlos, Prince of Asturias, 1545-1568—Drama 2. Mary, Queen of Scots, 1542-1587—Drama
ISBN 978-0-19-954074-7

LC 2008-275155

First published 1996
This volume contains Don Carlos and Mary Stuart, two German historical dramas. "Dating from 1787 and 1800 respectively, one play was written immediately before the French Revolution, the other in its aftermath. These new translations into blank verse are accurate, elegant, and playable. The Introduction, Notes, and Chronology set the plays in their cultural and intellectual background, while a family tree explains the historical relationship between Don Carlos and Mary Stuart." Publisher's note

Includes bibliographical references

The robbers [and] Wallenstein; translated with an introduction by F. J. Lamport. Penguin Books 1979 472p (Penguin classics) pa $16

832

ISBN 978-0-14-044368-4; 0-14-044368-1
In The robbers (1782) a man, cheated out of his inheritance by his brother, forms a band of thieves. The Wallenstein trilogy, based on the fall of the German general Count Albrecht von Wallenstein, is comprised of: Wallenstein's camp (1798), The Piccolominis (1799), and Wallenstein's death (1799).

834 German essays

Sebald, Winfried Georg, 1944-2001
On the natural history of destruction; with essays on Alfred Andersch, Jean Améry, and Peter Weiss; {by} W.G. Sebald; translated by Anthea Bell. Random House 2003 202p $23.95; pa $12.95 *

834

1. World War, 1939-1945—Literature and the war
2. German literature—History and criticism
ISBN 0-375-50484-2; 0-375-75657-4 (pa)

LC 2002-75187

Original German edition, 1999

Sebald, Winfried Georg, 1944-2001—*Continued*
Contents: Air war and literature; Between the devil
and the deep blue sea: on Alfred Andersch; Against the
irreversible: on Jean Amery; The remorse of the heart:
on memory and cruelty in the work of Peter Weiss

838   German miscellaneous writings

Kleist, Heinrich von, 1777-1811
Selected writings; edited and translated by
David Constantine. Hackett Pub. 2004 xxvii, 442p
$44; pa $14.95   **838**
  ISBN   978-0-87220-744-8;   0-87220-744-7;
978-0-87220-743-1 (pa); 0-87220-743-9 (pa)
                                  LC 2004-54378
First published 1997 in the United Kingdom
"This volume includes the majority of Kleist's writings in English translation. An outstanding representation
of his work, this selection offers three plays, eight short
stories, five anecdotes, and three essays. Kleist's dramas
and stories resonate with complex circumstances and obscure consequences that the characters struggle to sail
through. Things are not always what they seem to be;
intriguingly, the guilty can look innocent and the innocent guilty. The play The Broken Jug, as well as the stories 'Michael Kohlhaas' and 'The Chilean Earthquake,'
depict predicaments of the falsely accused who are denied justice. Constantine . . . does an outstanding job of
conveying the beauty of Kleist's literary style while allowing himself some liberties in translation." Libr J
Includes bibliographical references

839   Other Germanic literatures

The **Sagas** of Icelanders; a selection; preface by
Jane Smiley; introduction by Robert Kellogg.
Viking 2000 lxvi, 782p il maps (World of the
sagas) pa $20 hardcover o.p. *   **839**
1. Sagas 2. Old Norse literature
ISBN 0-14-100003-1 (pa)   LC 99-44111
A selection from the 5 volume Complete sagas of Icelanders, published 1997 in the United Kingdom
"The Icelandic Sagas are among the masterpieces of
world literature whose composition stretches from about
the year 1000 to 1500. Presenting the adventures of
Norse and Viking heroes, the sagas are told with ritual
simplicity and a realism that anticipate the modern novel." Libr J
Includes bibliographical references

839.7   Swedish literature

Hammarskjöld, Dag, 1905-1961
Markings; translated from the Swedish by Leif
Sjöberg & W. H. Auden; with a foreword by W.
H. Auden. Knopf 1964 xxiii, 221p hardcover o.p.
pa $13.95   **839.7**
1. Spiritual life
  ISBN   0-394-43532-X;   0-307-27742-9   (pa);
978-0-307-27742-8 (pa)
Original Swedish edition, 1963

The author described this account as a sort of white
book concerning his negotiations with himself and with
God. A record of his inner life, it opens with a poem he
wrote around 1925; most of the entries were made during
the nineteen forties and fifties—and the book ends with
a poem written only a few weeks before his plane
crashed.

Strindberg, August, 1849-1912
Strindberg: five plays; translated, with an
introduction by Harry G. Carlson. University of
Calif. Press 1983 297p pa $21.95 hardcover o.p.
                                                839.7
  ISBN 978-0-520-04698-6 (pa)   LC 82-15882
  Contents: The father; Miss Julie; The dance of death;
A dream play; The ghost sonata

Tranströmer, Tomas, 1931-
The great enigma; new collected poems;
translated from the Swedish by Robin Fulton. New
Directions 2006 xxi, 262p pa $16.95
                                                839.7
  ISBN 978-0-8112-1672-2; 0-8112-1672-1
                                  LC 2006-22551
This volume "offers the most generous collection of
Tranströmer's poems to date. . . . Lean and uncluttered,
Fulton's translations in The Great Enigma neither preach
nor moralize. They refuse staged psychology and let inte-
riority take shape as mysterious judgments, made by the
selection of detail and the juxtaposition of things and
times and experiences." Boston Rev

839.8   Danish and Norwegian
literatures

Ibsen, Henrik, 1828-1906
The complete major prose plays; translated
[from the Norwegian] and introduced by Rolf
Fjelde. New American Library 1978 1143p pa $28
*   **839.8**
  ISBN 978-0-452-26205-8; 0-452-26205-4
                                  LC 78-50714
  First published 1978 by Farrar, Straus & Giroux
  Contents: Pillars of society; A doll house; Ghosts; An
enemy of the people; The wild duck; Rosmersholm; The
lady from the sea; Hedda Gabler; The master builder;
Little Eyolf; John Gabriel Borkman; When we dead
awaken
  Includes bibliographical references

Jacobsen, Rolf, 1907-1994
The roads have come to an end now; selected
and last poems of Rolf Jacobsen; translated by
Robert Bly, Roger Greenwald, and Robert Hedin.
Copper Canyon Press 2001 168p pa $16
                                                839.8
  ISBN 1-55659-165-9   LC 2001-4488
  "A Kage-an book"

Jacobsen, Rolf, 1907-1994—*Continued*
"This bilingual (Norwegian-English) edition of 73 poems demonstrates a poet whose vision of the natural world and humanity's place in it is cosmically penetrative. Jacobsen regards the world as filled with an essential energy, animated by what must be God, and reading his work induces a certain calm ecstasy about everyday existence." Booklist

840.3 French literature— Encyclopedias and dictionaries

The **New** Oxford companion to literature in French; edited by Peter France. Oxford Univ. Press 1995 li, 865p maps $80 *
840.3
1. French literature—Dictionaries 2. French literature—Bio-bibliography
ISBN 0-19-866125-8
First published 1959 with title: The Oxford companion to French literature
"This work views literature from the perspective of its greater cultural context. Accordingly, topics discussed go beyond the poets, novelists, and dramatists of the traditional French canon, and include philosophy, science, art, history, linguistics, and cinema. Even strip cartoons and pamphlets are treated. . . . The more than 3,000 entries are written by approximately 130 international experts. In addition to brief entries, there are long articles on general topics, such as Québec, feminism, Occitan literature, and the history of the French language." Am Ref Books Annu, 1996

841 French poetry

Baudelaire, Charles, 1821-1867
Les fleurs du mal; the complete text of The flowers of evil; in a new translation by Richard Howard; illustrated with nine original monotypes by Michael Mazur. Godine 1982 xxxii, 365p il hardcover o.p. pa $18.95 **841**
1. Poetry—By individual authors
ISBN 978-0-87923-462-1 (pa); 0-87923-462-8 (pa)
LC 81-13283
Original French edition, 1857
"Howard puts the original's rhymed alexandrines primarily into iambic pentameter blank verse, which allows him to capture the immediate, concrete, visceral quality of Baudelaire's imagery." Choice

Poems. Knopf 1993 256p (Everyman's library pocket poets) $12.50 * **841**
1. Poetry—By individual authors
ISBN 0-679-42910-7
LC 93-14363
A representative selection of poetry by the French symbolist.

Beckett, Samuel, 1906-1989
Collected poems in English and French. Grove Press 1977 147p pa $13.95 hardcover o.p. *
841
1. Poetry—By individual authors
ISBN 978-0-8021-3096-9 (pa)
LC 77-77855
This work contains poems written by Beckett in English and French along with his translations and bilingual versions of poems by Eluard, Rimbaud, Apollinaire, and Chamfort

Chanson de Roland.
The song of Roland; translated, with an introduction, by W.S. Merwin. Modern Library 2001 137p pa $11.95 * **841**
1. Roland (Legendary character)
ISBN 0-375-75711-2
LC 00-48989
Also available in paperback from Penguin Classics
"This heroic poem celebrates the mighty feats of Roland, the great French hero in the time of Charlemagne. The medieval legend has replaced and transformed the actual facts of history to a great extent but the epic poem has continued in popularity." Bookman's Manual
Includes bibliographical references

Hugo, Victor, 1802-1885
Selected poems of Victor Hugo; a bilingual edition; translated by E. H. and A. M. Blackmore. University of Chicago Press 2001 631p il $35; pa $22.50 **841**
1. Hugo, Victor 2. Poetry—By individual authors
ISBN 978-0-226-35980-9; 0-226-35980-8; 978-0-226-35981-6 (pa); 0-226-35981-6 (pa)
LC 00-61989
Hugo "stretched the rules of French verse and the reach of French vocabulary as did no other poet, which makes him very difficult to translate. There are also the problems of Hugo's voluminousness and his integrity. Even excluding his verse plays, this book contains only four percent of his total poetic output, and he insisted that to select from his work was to betray it. A yea-sayer of the first order, he felt that a poet, a person, or the world, for that matter, must be taken whole, the bad with the good, to be appreciated. That said, it must also be affirmed that the Blackmores, by exploiting the metrical diversity of nineteenth-century English verse, have fashioned highly readable versions of Hugo from every volume of his poetry." Booklist
Includes bibliographical references

Mallarmé, Stéphane, 1842-1898
Collected poems and other verse; translated with notes by E.H. and A.M. Blackmore; with an introduction by Elizabeth McCombie. Oxford University Press 2006 xxxvii, 282p pa $15.95
841
1. Poetry—By individual authors
ISBN 978-0-19-280362-7; 0-19-280362-X
This collection presents Mallarme's "Poesies in the last arrangement known to have been approved by the author. Prose poems, uncollected verse, and the unique, unclassifiable Un Coup de des. . . (A Dice Throw. . .)

Mallarmé, Stéphane, 1842-1898—*Continued*
are also present, including over 20 items that have never previously been translated. Original spelling, punctuation, and lineation have been preserved throughout." Publisher's note

Rimbaud, Arthur, 1854-1891
    Poems; Rimbaud ;[selected by Peter Washington] Knopf 1994 288p (Everyman's library pocket poets) $12.50   **841**
    1. Poetry—By individual authors
    ISBN 978-0-679-43321-7; 0-679-43321-X
                       LC 94-2496
    A collection of work by the French Symbolist known for his daring images and pioneering prose poems

Verlaine, Paul, 1844-1896
    Selected poems; translated by C. F. MacIntyre. University of Calif. Press 1948 xx, 228p il pa $15.95 *   **841**
    1. Poetry—By individual authors
    ISBN 0-520-01298-4
    Eighty poems, chosen from Verlaine's first six books. French originals and translations are on facing pages. Contains a preface by the translator
    The translator "has done Verlaine a gracious courtesy, and American readers a great kindness. The charm, verbal fireworks, sympathy and nostalgia of this major French poet are Englished with color and convictions." Chicago Sunday Trib
    Includes bibliographical references

Villon, François, b. 1431
    The poems of François Villon; translated with an introduction and notes by Galway Kinnell. New ed. University Press of New England 1982 xxiii, 246p pa $19.95   **841**
    1. Poetry—By individual authors
    ISBN 0-87451-236-0; 978-0-87451-236-6
                       LC 81-71907
    This translation first published 1965 by New American Library
    French text (based on the Longnon-Foulet edition of 1932) and English translation on facing pages. Includes a critical introduction and explanatory notes.
    "Using standard academic texts of the medieval French poet, Kinnell exceeds a transliteration of the originals. . . . Villon's ribaldry and humorous despair sparkle throughout." Booklist
    Includes bibliographical references

841.008   French poetry—Collections

French poetry, 1820-1950, with prose translations; selected, translated, and introduced by William Rees. Penguin Books 1994 c1990 xli, 854p (Penguin classics) pa $22   **841.008**
    1. French poetry—Collections
    ISBN 978-0-14-042385-3; 0-14-042385-0
                       LC 91-127343
    First published 1990 in the United Kingdom

    "While this anthology contains . . . generous selections from the established giants—Baudelaire, Rimbaud, Mallarmé, Valéry, Apollinaire, Michaux—it also draws attention to interesting 'minor' poets, such as Claudel or Cendrars, whose writing has been vital to the evolution of poetry in France. William Rees gives us an introduction to each poet, his or her life, affinities and aesthetics, and the significant literary movements Romanticism, the Parnassian Movement, Symbolism, Cubism, Surrealism and 'Négritude' are signposted and discussed." Publisher's note

The **Random** House book of twentieth-century French poetry; with translations by American and British poets; edited by Paul Auster. Random House 1982 xlix, 635p hardcover o.p. pa $26   **841.008**
    1. French poetry—Collections
    ISBN 978-0-394-71748-7 (pa); 0-394-71748-1 (pa)
                       LC 82-280
    This bilingual edition collects the verse of forty-eight poets as translated by eighty-four poets. The volume opens with a section of poems by Guillaume Apollinaire and closes with a group of poems by Philippe Denis. The original and translation appear on facing pages
    "This excellent anthology undertakes a double task: to provide a comprehensive view of French poetry in the twentieth century and to show, in the range of translators it offers, the influences of that poetry on American and British poets. . . . Paul Auster has done an excellent job of matching poets and translators." Nation
    Includes bibliographical references

842   French drama

Beckett, Samuel, 1906-1989
    Dramatic works; Paul Auster, series editor; introduction by Edward Albee. Grove Press 2006 509p (Samuel Beckett: the Grove centenary edition) $24.95   **842**
    ISBN 978-0-8021-1819-0; 0-8021-1819-4
                       LC 2005-55078
    Contents: Waiting for Godot; Endgame; All that fall; Act without words I; Embers; Act without words II; Krapp's last tape; Rough for theatre I; Rough for theatre II; The old tune; Happy days; Rough for radio I; Rough for radio II; Words and music; Cascando; Play; Film; Come and go; Eh Joe; Breath; Not I; That time; Footfalls; Ghost trio; . . . but the clouds . . . ; A piece of monologue; Rockaby; Ohio impromptu; Quad; Catastrophe; Nacht und Träume; What where

Camus, Albert, 1913-1960
    Caligula & three other plays; translated from the French by Stuart Gilbert; with a preface written specially for this edition and translated by Justin O'Brien. Knopf 1958 302p hardcover o.p. pa $13 *   **842**
    ISBN 978-0-394-70207-0 (pa); 0-394-70207-7 (pa)
    "Four of the author's best-known plays, written between 1938 and 1950. 'Caligula,' about the infamous emperor's self-destroying rebellion against fate; 'The

Camus, Albert, 1913-1960—*Continued*
Misunderstanding,' about the murder of a man by his ghoulish mother and sister,' 'The Just Assassins,' on the self-questionings of terrorists; and 'State of Siege,' an allegory about the refusal of one individual in a plague-stricken city to compromise with evil." Publ Wkly

Genet, Jean, 1910-1986
The blacks: a clown show; translated from the French by Bernard Frechtman. Grove Press 1960 128p pa $13 *   **842**
  ISBN 0-8021-5028-4
  "An Evergreen book"
  Original French edition, 1958
  "Drama in which a group of bizarrely dressed Negroes give a performance for another group of Negroes who wear white masks and represent the major figures of white society's established authority." McGraw-Hill Ency of World Drama

The maids [and] Deathwatch; two plays; with an introduction by Jean-Paul Sartre; translated from the French by Bernard Frechtman. Grove Press 1954 166p hardcover o.p. pa $14 *   **842**
  ISBN 978-0-8021-5056-1 (pa); 0-8021-5056-X (pa)
  Deathwatch, a one-act play written 1947 and first produced 1949 "deals with an insignificant criminal who tries to assume the highly desirable and prestigious role of murderer. . . . In 'The Maids (Les bonnes),' produced in 1947, . . . two servant girls have created an elaborate ritual in which they impersonate their mistress and finally murder her symbolically." McGraw-Hill Ency of World Drama

Ionesco, Eugène
Rhinoceros, and other plays; translated by Derek Prouse. Grove Press 1960 141p pa $10 *   **842**

  ISBN 0-8021-3098-4
  Also available in hardcover from P. Smith
  "An Evergreen book"
  Contents: Rhinoceros; The future is in eggs; The leader
  Three satirical comedies by a leading dramatist of the "theater of the absurd." In Rhinoceros, one man resists the pressure to conform as everyone about him accepts their transformation into rhinoceroses and he finds himself socially isolated. In The future is in eggs, a couple must produce eggs destined to become intellectuals. The leader is a satire on the mass adulation of political figures in which the leader turns out to be a headless figure

Molière, 1622-1673
The misanthrope and other plays; translated, and with an introduction by Donald M. Frame; and a new afterword by Lewis C. Seifert. Signet Classics 2005 524p pa $7.95   **842**
  ISBN 0-451-52987-1; 978-0-451-52987-9
          LC 2006-276841
  Contents: The misanthrope; The doctor in spite of himself; The miser; The would-be gentleman; The mischievous machinations of Scapin; The learned women; The imaginary invalid

Tartuffe and other plays; translated and with an introduction by Donald M. Frame; and a new foreword by Virginia Scott. Signet Classics 2007 xxiv, 408p pa $7.95 *   **842**
  ISBN 978-0-451-53033-2   LC 2007-275593
  Contents: The ridiculous precieuses; The school for husbands; The school for wives; The critique of the school for wives; The Versailles impromptu; Tartuffe; Don Juan
  Includes bibliographical references

Rostand, Edmond, 1868-1918
Cyrano de Bergerac; translated and adapted for the modern stage by Anthony Burgess. Applause Theatre & Cinema Bks. 1998 175p pa $6.95   **842**
  1. Cyrano de Bergerac, 1619-1655—Drama
  ISBN 1-55783-230-7   LC 96-2545
  A reissue of the title first published 1971 by Knopf
  This version was commissioned for production at the Tyrone Guthrie Theater in Minneapolis. It is adapted and translated from the French play originally produced in 1897. Cyrano, the hero, a Gascon poet and swordsman notorious for his long nose, is in love with Roxana

Sartre, Jean Paul, 1905-1980
No exit, and three other plays. Vintage Bks. 1989 275p pa $12 *   **842**
  ISBN 0-679-72516-4   LC 89-40097
  Contents: No exit; The flies; Dirty hands; The respectful prostitute
  No exit is a modern morality play; The flies is a reworking of the Orestes-Electra story. The third play concerns a young Communist intellectual's attempt to maintain his integrity as party line changes and personal relationships alter perceptions of his murder of a party boss who had fallen out of favor, but whose memory is later rehabilitated. The last play concerns a prostitute's involvement in false charges of rape against a murdered black man and his companion in a town in the American South

843.009   French fiction—History and criticism

Severson, Marilyn S.
Masterpieces of French literature. Greenwood Press 2004 186p (Greenwood introduces literary masterpieces) $45 *   **843.009**
  1. French literature—History and criticism
  ISBN 0-313-31484-5   LC 2003-59635
  Among the novels discussed are Albert Camus's *The stranger* and *The plague*, Gustave Flaubert's *Madame Bovary*, Victor Hugo's *The hunchback of Notre Dame* and *Les Miserables*, and Alexander Dumas's *The three musketeers*
  "Students and general readers seeking a thorough understanding of these influential novels will benefit greatly from this outstanding guide." Libr J
  Includes bibliographical references

Shattuck, Roger

Proust's way; a field guide to In search of lost time. Norton 2000 xxiv, 290p pa $16.95 hardcover o.p. **843.009**

1. Proust, Marcel, 1871-1922

ISBN 0-393-32180-0 (pa) LC 99-58472

Shattuck "explains the major settings of the work, summarizes character and plot, and discusses central themes. Shattuck acknowledges that there is no one right interpretation of *In Search of Lost Time* but succeeds in providing a framework to help readers get through it. He addresses readers coming to the work for the first time." Libr J

Includes bibliographical references

844 French essays

Camus, Albert, 1913-1960

The myth of Sisyphus, and other essays; translated from the French by Justin O'Brien. Knopf 1955 212p pa $12.95 hardcover o.p. * **844**

ISBN 0-679-73373-6 (pa)

Personal reflections on the meaning of life and the philosophical questions surrounding suicide

Resistance, rebellion, and death; translated from the French and with an introduction by Justin O'Brien. Knopf 1961 c1960 271p hardcover o.p. pa $13.95 **844**

ISBN 978-0-679-76401-4 (pa); 0679764011 (pa)

"A selection of forthright essays on contemporary world politics, on capital punishment and the relations of the state and the individual, and on art, chosen from the three volumes of 'Actuelles,' published in France between 1950 and 1958." Publ Wkly

848 French miscellaneous writings

Rimbaud, Arthur, 1854-1891

Rimbaud; complete works, selected letters: a bilingual edition; translated with an introduction and notes by Wallace Fowlie; updated, revised and with a foreword by Seth Whidden. University of Chicago Press 2005 xxxvi, 458p il $50; pa $19 **848**

ISBN 978-0-226-71976-4; 0-226-71976-6; 978-0-226-71977-1 (pa); 0226719774 (pa)

LC 2005-41859

First published 1966

In this bilingual edition of Rimbaud's work the original French texts are accompanied by English prose translations. In addition to the complete poetic works there are two prose fragments, a short story in the form of a seminarian's journal, and a selection of letters chosen to illustrate biographical details and Rimbaud's credo as a poet.

Includes bibliographical references

Valéry, Paul, 1871-1945

Selected writings. New Directions 1950 256p pa $12.95 hardcover o.p. * **848**

ISBN 0-8112-0213-5 (pa)

"Seventeen poems are translated by eighteen translators, including Denis Devlin, Léonie Adams, and C. Day Lewis. . . . The rest of the book is composed of the French love miscellanies, essays, dialogues, and critiques." New Yorker

Voltaire, 1694-1778

The portable Voltaire; edited, and with an introduction by Ben Ray Redmen. Viking 1949 569p pa $17 hardcover o.p. * **848**

ISBN 0-14-015041-2 (pa)

"The Viking portable library"

The selections from Voltaire's works include: Candide, part one; Three stories: Zadig, Micromegas, and Story of a good Brahmin; Letters, and selections from the Philosophical Dictionary and other works. The editor's introduction gives a biographical sketch of Voltaire.

850.3 Italian literature— Encyclopedias and dictionaries

The **Oxford** companion to Italian literature; edited by Peter Hainsworth and David Robey. Oxford Univ. Press 2002 xli, 644p maps $95 * **850.3**

1. Italian literature—Dictionaries 2. Italian literature—Bio-bibliography

ISBN 0-19-818332-1 LC 2001-59301

This reference work features "assessments of Italy's writers, famous and not-so-famous, from 1200 to 2000. It covers writers who wrote in Italian, dialect, or Latin, and offers . . . background information on historical events, regional culture, and the other arts." Publisher's note

"A magisterial addition to the Oxford companions to literature, this volume goes far beyond its core subject of Italian literature to cover its substrate and context. . . . An excellent ready-reference companion for readers seeking less an introduction to the summits of the literature . . . but a reminder of relevant details." Choice

Includes bibliographical references

850.9 Italian literature—History and criticism

The **Cambridge** history of Italian literature; edited by Peter Brand and Lino Pertile. rev ed. Cambridge Univ. Press 1999 xxii, 699p map pa $33 **850.9**

1. Italian literature—History and criticism

ISBN 0-521-66622-8 LC 00-265436

First published 1996

Scholars analyze and describe the works of writers who have added to Italy's literary tradition from its origins to today. The editors provide translations, maps, bibliographies, and chronological charts.

"Contemporary readers will no doubt be delighted to learn more about such topics as the evolution of opera, compositions by Italian women writers, and the development of feminism." Choice

Ruud, Jay
Critical companion to Dante; a literary reference to his life and work. Facts on File 2008 566p il (Facts on File library of world literature) $75
850.9
1. Dante Alighieri, 1265-1321
ISBN 978-0-8160-6521-9   LC 2007-33473
This title covers the works of Dante, including The Divine Comedy, La Vita Nuova, and his philosophical works.
Includes bibliographical references

851   Italian poetry

Ariosto, Lodovico, 1474-1533
Orlando Furioso/The frenzy of Orlando, part 1; a romantic epic; by Ludovico Ariosto; translated with an introduction by Barbara Reynolds. Penguin Books 1975 827p map (Penguin classics) pa $18
851
1. Poetry—By individual authors
ISBN 978-0-14-044311-0; 0-14-044311-8
LC 75-327748
An English verse translation in the original meter of the epic poem by the sixteenth-century Italian poet, courtier, and statesman, which is based on the adventures of Roland and other knights of Charlemagne in the wars against the Saracens
This translation is "lucid, lively, and eminently readable. . . . The first volume contains one-half (23) of the cantos plus invaluable aids for the reader: a lengthy, informative introduction, a list of characters and devices, maps and genealogical tables, notes for each canto and an index of proper names." Choice

Orlando Furioso/The frenzy of Orlando, part 2; a romantic epic; [by] Ludovico Ariosto; translated with an introduction by Barbara Reynolds. Penguin Books 1977 794p (Penguin Classics) pa $18
851
1. Poetry—By individual authors
ISBN 978-0-14-044310-3; 0-14-044310-X
"The value of this faithful translation is primarily that it helps you with the Italian. It lets you make your way painlessly into the poem. . . . It does not . . . draw attention to itself. Modestly, it points across, to the things going on in the original." Times Lit Suppl

Dante Alighieri, 1265-1321
The divine comedy; translated by Allen Mandelbaum; with an introduction by Eugenio Montale; and notes by Peter Armour. Alfred A. Knopf 1995 798p il (Everyman's library) $25 *
851
1. Poetry—By individual authors
ISBN 978-0-679-43313-2; 0-679-43313-9
LC 95-75206
An epic poem, completed in 1321, in which the poet describes his visionary spiritual journey through Hell, Purgatory and Paradise—guided first by the classical poet Vergil and then by his beloved Beatrice—which results in a purification of his religious faith.

The Inferno; translated by Robert Hollander and Jean Hollander; introduction & notes by Robert Hollander. Doubleday 2000 704p hardcover o.p. pa $16.95
851
1. Poetry—By individual authors
ISBN 978-0-385-49698-8 (pa); 0-385-49698-2 (pa)
LC 00-34531
A translation of Dante's poem, in which the Roman poet Virgil guides Dante through the underworld.
"The heart of the Hollanders' edition is the translation itself, which nicely balances the precision required for a much-interpreted allegory and the poetic qualities that draw most readers to the work. The result is a terse, lean Dante with its own kind of beauty. . . . The Hollanders' lines will satisfy both the poetry lover and scholar; they are at once literary, accessible and possessed of the seeming transparence that often characterizes great translations. The Italian text is included on the facing page for easy reference, along with notes drawing on some 60 Dante scholars, several indexes, a list of works cited and an introduction by Robert Hollander." Publ Wkly
Includes bibliographical references

Paradiso; a verse translation by Robert & Jean Hollander; introduction & notes by Robert Hollander. Doubleday 2007 915p $40; pa $19.95
851
1. Poetry—By individual authors
ISBN   978-0-385-50678-6;   0-385-50678-3; 978-1-4000-3115-3 (pa); 1-4000-3115-X (pa)
LC 2007-18070
This is a verse translation of the third volume of Dante's Divine Comedy with the original Italian text on facing pages and an introduction and notes.
"Dante's terza rima is impossible to recreate satisfactorily in English, but the Hollanders have produced a fine verse substitute. . . . Splendid as this new translation is, the endlessly valuable notes are what make this edition supplant all others. The commentary here has evolved not only from extensive research but also from the famous Dante Seminar Hollander has taught at Princeton for many years." Natl Rev

The portable Dante; translated, edited, and with an introduction and notes by Mark Musa. Penguin Bks. 1995 xliii, 654p pa $17
851
1. Poetry—By individual authors
ISBN 0-14-243754-9   LC 94-15988
First published 1947
This book "contains complete verse translations of Dante's two masterworks, The Divine Comedy and La Vita Nuova, as well as a bibliography, notes, and an introduction by . . . Mark Musa." Publisher's note
Contains complete verse translations of The Divine comedy and La vita nuova
Includes bibliographical references

Purgatorio; a verse translation by Jean and Robert Hollander; introduction and notes by Robert Hollander. Doubleday 2003 xxiv, 742p pa $18.95 hardcover o.p.
851
1. Poetry—By individual authors
ISBN 978-0-385-49700-8 (pa)   LC 2002-67100
"To enter Dante's Purgatorio is to step into a charmed world, balanced by the rhythmic interplay of sleep,

Dante Alighieri, 1265-1321—*Continued*
dreams, light, shadows, smiles, tears, and the reverberations of both solo and choral song. This is the most aesthetically vibrant of Dante's three realms, the one in
which the artisanal gestures of poet, painter, and musician prevail. . . . The Hollanders have rendered both the
supple lyricism and the rich imagery of the Purgatorio
with an admirably informed expertise, preserving the
stately economy of Dante's Italian throughout." Literary
Rev (Madison, N. J.)
Includes bibliographical references

Montale, Eugenio, 1896-1981
Collected poems, 1920-1954; translated and
annotated by Jonathan Galassi. rev ed. Farrar,
Straus & Giroux 2000 625p pa $18 *
          851
1. Poetry—By individual authors
ISBN 0-374-52625-7   LC 00-35456
First published 1997
Contents: Ossi di seppia = Cuttlefish bones; Le
occasioni = The occasions; La bufera e altro = The
storm, etc
"It is generally agreed that the core of Montale's work
consists of three major collections: Cuttlefish Bones
(1925), The Occasions (1939), and The Storm, etc.
(1956). Galassi chooses to publish all three together, separating them from a body of work of almost equal length
that came later. He defends this decision in a brilliant
afterword that offers the best short account I have yet
come across of the nature, import, and elusive content of
Montale's work." N Y Rev Books {review of 1997 edi-
tion}
Includes bibliographical references

854   Italian essays

Eco, Umberto
How to travel with a salmon & other essays;
translated from the Italian by William Weaver.
Harcourt Brace & Co. 1994 248p il hardcover o.p.
pa $15   **854**
ISBN 978-0-15-600125-0 (pa); 0-15-600125-X (pa)
                LC 94-10340
"A Helen and Kurt Wolff book"
"In this collection of parodies, satires and whimsical
mini-essays written over the last 30 years, Italian novel-
ist/critic Eco . . . takes readers on a delightful romp
through the absurdities of modern life." Publ Wkly

860.3   Spanish literature— Encyclopedias and dictionaries

Concise encyclopedia of Latin American literature;
editor, Verity Smith. Fitzroy Dearborn Pubs.
2000 xxi, 678p $75 *   **860.3**
1. Latin American literature—Encyclopedias 2. Latin
American literature—Bio-bibliography
ISBN 1-57958-252-4
Based on the Encyclopedia of Latin American literature (1997)

Contains entries on 50 leading writers and 50 important works of Latin American and Caribbean literature.
Also includes survey articles on the literature of individual countries and topical essays. Bibliographies of primary and secondary sources are listed
Includes bibliographical references

860.9   Spanish literature—History and criticism

The **Cambridge** history of Latin American
literature; edited by Roberto González
Echevarría and Enrique Pupo-Walker.
Cambridge Univ. Press 1996 3v ea $180
              860.9
1. Latin American literature—History and criticism
ISBN 0-521-34069-1 (v1); 0-521-34070-5 (v2);
0-521-41035-5 (v3)   LC 93-37750
Contents: v1 Discovery to modernism; v2 The twentieth century; v3 Brazilian literature. Bibliographies
"These volumes span from pre-Columbian times to the
present and include chapters on Latin American writing
in the United States. Some 40 international scholars trace
the development of Latin American literature in essay
form. The bibliography in Volume 3 consumes 455
pages." Libr J
"The editors have added an interdisciplinary dimension to their work by incorporating the materials and
methodologies proper to history. . . . [This] will become
a classic in the field." Choice

The **Cambridge** history of Spanish literature;
edited by David T. Gies. Cambridge University
Press 2004 863p $160 *   **860.9**
1. Spanish literature—History and criticism
ISBN 0-521-80618-6   LC 2004-45601
"The classics of the canon of eleven centuries of
Spanish literature are covered, from Berceo, Cervantes
and Calderón to García Lorca and Martín Gaite, but attention is also paid to lesser-known writers and works.
. . . The volume concludes with a consideration of the
influences of film and new media on modern Spanish literature." Publisher's note
Includes bibliographical references

861   Spanish poetry

Aleixandre, Vicente, 1898-1984
A longing for the light; selected poems of
Vicente Aleixandre; edited by Lewis Hyde. 2nd
ed. Copper Canyon Press 2007 xxi, 279p pa $18
              861
1. Poetry—By individual authors
ISBN 978-1-55659-254-6; 1-55659-254-X
                LC 2007-992
First published 1979 by Harper & Row
This "is the only available bilingual Spanish-English
translation of the poetry of Nobel Laureate Vicente
Aleixandre. The collection spans the entirety of
Aleixandre's career—from early surrealist work to his
complex and fascinating 'dialogues.' It also contains
prose interludes, an introduction by editor Lewis Hyde,
and a descriptive bibliography." Publisher's note

Borges, Jorge Luis, 1899-1986
Selected poems; edited by Alexander Coleman. Viking 1999 477p pa $20 hardcover o.p. *

861

1. Poetry—By individual authors
ISBN 0-14-058721-7 (pa)   LC 99-10318
"Poetry is the heart of Borges' metaphysical, mythical, and cosmopolitan oeuvre. . . . Editor Coleman commissioned a wealth of new translations for this unprecedented and invaluable collection, and the roster of translators includes such luminaries as Robert S. Fitzgerald, W.S. Merwin, Mark Strand, and John Updike." Booklist

Cid, ca. 1043-1099
The poem of the Cid; translated by Rita Hamilton and Janet Perry; with an introduction and notes by Ian Michael. Penguin 1984 c1975 242p map pa $14 *   **861**

1. Poetry—By individual authors
ISBN 0-14-044446-7
Parallel Spanish text and English translation, with English introduction and notes
"The poem is based on the exploits of Rodrigo or Ruy Diaz de Bivar (c.1043-1099), who was known as 'el Cid.' . . . Similar in form to the 'Chanson de Roland,' the poem is notable for its simplicity and directness and for its exact, picturesque detail. Despite the inclusion of much legendary material, the figure of the Cid who is depicted as the model Castilian warrior, is not idealized to an extravagant degree." Reader's Ency. 4th edition

García Lorca, Federico, 1898-1936
Collected poems; edited and with an introduction and notes by Christopher Maurer; translated by Francisco Aragon [et al.] Farrar, Straus & Giroux 1991 893p (Poetical works) hardcover o.p. pa $25   **861**

1. Poetry—By individual authors
ISBN 978-0-374-52691-7; 0-374-52691-5 (pa)
Volume 1 of Poetical works published 1988 with title: Poet in New York
This bilingual edition of Garcia Lorca's poetry, "which modestly claims not to be 'definitive,' includes every poem written by the acclaimed Spanish poet except *Poet in New York*. Assembled in the light of recent scholarship, its contents have been rendered into English by newer translators such as Alan S. Trueblood, Catherine Brown, Will Kirkland, and Greg Simon; older translators such as Stephen Spender, Langston Hughes, and Ben Belitt are not represented. Generally, rhyme and assonance are sacrificed to the 'silent counterpoint of poetic meaning,' and old-fashioned diction is avoided." Libr J

Poet in New York; edited and with an introduction and notes by Christopher Maurer; translated by Greg Simon and Steven F. White. Farrar, Straus & Giroux 1988 xxx, 275p il pa $18   **861**

1. New York (N.Y.)—Poetry
ISBN 978-0-374-52540-8; 0-374-52083-4
          LC 87-33154
Poems in English and Spanish; introd. and critical matter in English

This "is one of the perplexing classics of twentieth-century poetry. It is a difficult, sometimes bewildered, often hermetic work. It is elusive and enigmatic, mysterious, tortured—a book, to borrow one of the poet's own phrases, 'that can baptize in dark water all who look at it.' Reading it in [this] convincing new translation, . . . one feels the anguished authority and the demonic force and impact of the original. For all its strangeness, Lorca's testament may well be one of the greatest books of poems ever written about New York City." New Yorker
Includes bibliographical references

Juana Inés de la Cruz, 1651-1695
A Sor Juana anthology; translated by Alan S. Trueblood; with a foreword by Octavio Paz. Harvard Univ. Press 1988 248p pa $23 hardcover o.p. *   **861**

1. Poetry—By individual authors
ISBN 0-674-82121-1 (pa)   LC 87-27693
This volume "offers a useful sampling and English rendition of Sor Juana's work. Poetry predominates among the selections. . . . Given the difficulty of Mr. Trueblood's task—attempting to capture in English the voice of a poet who herself mastered many poetic languages—his translations are admirable." N Y Times Book Rev
Includes bibliographical references

Neruda, Pablo, 1904-1973
The poetry of Pablo Neruda; edited and with an introduction by Ilan Stavans. Farrar, Straus and Giroux 2003 996p hardcover o.p. pa $20 *

861

1. Poetry—By individual authors
ISBN 0-374-29995-1; 0-374-52960-4 (pa)
          LC 2002-32548
This volume contains translations of nearly 600 poems. "Arranged chronologically and often newly translated, the poems are sometimes accompanied by the Spanish original." Libr J
"Stavans has assembled the most complete anthology of Neruda yet available in English, drawing evenhandedly from the various stages of the poet's long and complex career. Neruda was, it seems, at least half a dozen poets, many of them in competition with the others. Needless to say, there are wonders in these pages that will delight readers unfamiliar with the tumultuously varied planet known as Neruda." Nation
Includes bibliographical references

Paz, Octavio, 1914-1998
The collected poems of Octavio Paz, 1957-1987; edited & translated by Eliot Weinberger; with additional translations by Elizabeth Bishop [et al.] New Directions 1987 669p il hardcover o.p. pa $26.95 *   **861**

1. Poetry—By individual authors
ISBN 978-0-8112-1173-4 (pa); 0-8112-1173-8 (pa)
          LC 87-23989
"Dense, weighty, and miraculous, this bilingual edition compresses into one volume all the poems published in book form since 1957. Nearly 200 poems, some newly

Paz, Octavio, 1914-1998—*Continued*
translated, many new to an English-language edition,
conclusively demonstrate Paz's power." Libr J
Includes bibliographical references

Twentieth century Latin American poetry; a
bilingual anthology; edited by Stephen Tapscott.
University of Tex. Press 1996 xxii, 418p il
(Texas Pan American series) pa $26.95
hardcover o.p.   **861**
1. Latin American poetry—Collections
ISBN 0-292-78140-7 (pa)   LC 95-40288
This anthology "samples the works of more than 75
poets, including such giants as Neruda, Dario, Reyes,
Vallejo, Borges and Paz. With original-language versions
and translations set side by side, the collection is arranged in order of the poets' dates of birth from José
Marti, born in Cuba in 1853, to Marjorie Agosin, born
in the U.S. 102 years later. Tapscott's well-conceived
and lucid introduction is expanded in concise individual
introductions that provide basic information and some
evaluation." Publ Wkly
Includes bibliographical references

Vallejo, César Abraham, 1892-1938
The complete poetry; a bilingual edition; edited
and translated by Clayton Eshleman; with a
foreword by Mario Vargas Llosa; an introduction
by Efraín Kristal; and a chronology by Stephen M.
Hart. University of California Press 2007 717p il
$49.95 *   **861**
1. Poetry—By individual authors
ISBN 978-0-520-24552-5; 0-520-24552-0
    LC 2006-45620
"Less famous than Neruda or Lorca, the Peruvian Vallejo (1892–1938) may stand as their equal among the
great Spanish language modernists. At times more demanding than both—and just as devoted to 'eternal love,'
'animal purity' and 'the absolute Encounter'—Vallejo
has inspired devotion and imitation across continents.
. . . Decades in the making, this faithful and forceful
complete text from poet and essayist Eshleman . . . deserves as much notice as any poetic translation can get."
Publ Wkly

861.008   Spanish poetry—Collections

The **Penguin** book of Spanish verse; introduced
and edited by J.M. Cohen; with plain prose
translations of each poem. 3rd ed. Penguin 1988
xliii, 596p pa $18   **861.008**
1. Spanish poetry—Collections
ISBN 978-0-14-058570-4; 0-14-058570-2
    LC 88-166999
First published 1956
Parallel text in English and Spanish
More than 300 works by 100 poets reflect nine centuries of poetry in Spain.

Reversible monuments; contemporary Mexican
poetry; edited by Mónica de la Torre and
Michael Wiegers. Copper Canyon Press 2002
675p pa $20   **861.008**
1. Mexican poetry—Collections
ISBN 1-55659-159-4   LC 2002-6189
This bilingual anthology includes 31 contributors,
"most writing in Spanish but some in indigenous languages. Spacious and accommodating, this work presents
a generous number of gracefully translated poems by
each poet, a felicitous in-depth approach that makes this
much more than a sampler, and a sound decision given
the poet's propensity for long, dreamy poems. Sensuality
is ever-present, as is an intimate connection with nature.
. . . This is without doubt a landmark volume." Booklist

862   Spanish drama

Calderón de la Barca, Pedro, 1600-1681
Life's a dream; a prose translation and critical
introduction by Michael Kidd. University Press of
Colorado 2004 159p pa $13.95 hardcover o.p.
    862
ISBN 978-0-87081-777-9 (pa)   LC 2004-10260
17th century Spanish verse play in prose translation.
King of Poland tests son, imprisoned from birth because
of prophecy, to see if he will become tyrant. Savage at
first, Prince later shows true nobility, exposing actual
meaning of prophecy.
"Michael Kidd advances the work of two often-
exclusive camps of comediantes: scholarship and performance. While his introduction provides ample criticism
for the scholar, he successfully presents an accessible
script for theatre practitioners looking to enact the story
of the play." Bulletin of Hispanic Studies
Includes bibliographical references

García Lorca, Federico, 1898-1936
Four major plays; translated by John Edmunds;
introduction by Nicholas Round; notes by Ann
MacLaren. Oxford University Press 1999 xli, 234p
(Oxford world's classics) pa $11.95   **862**
ISBN 978-0-19-283938-1   LC 00-703215
Contents: Blood wedding; Yerma; The house of
Bernarda Alba; Doña Rosita the spinster
"The ill-fated lovers of Blood Wedding, the desolate
Yerma, the fading spinster Rosita, and Bernarda Alba's
abused household of women all inhabit a familiar Anda-
lusia. Their predicaments are starkly plotted, with a
stagecraft rooted in classical theatrical tradition." Publisher's note
Edmunds's "versions are accurate . . . faithful . . .
fluent and idiomatic; they look like utterances of English.
. . . Readers can be sure that the texts will not lead
them astray, but they will also be grateful for the quite
excellent introductory essay by Nick Round. This is a
characteristically gritty display of erudition and common
sense." Times Lit Suppl
Includes bibliographical references

Vega, Lope de, 1562-1635

Three major plays; translated with an introduction and notes by Gwynne Edwards. Oxford University Press 2008 c1999 xli, 300p (Oxford world's classics) pa $14.95 **862**
    ISBN 978-0-19-954017-4; 0-19-954017-9
                      LC 98-26991
    Reissue of a title first published 1999
    Contents: Fuente Ovejuna; The knight from Olmedo; Punishment without revenge
    "Fuente Ovejuna, based on Spanish history, and revealing how tyranny leads to rebellion, is perhaps [Vega's] best-known play. The Knight from Olmedo is a moving dramatization of impetuous and youthful passion which ends in death. Punishment without Revenge, Lope's most powerful tragedy, centres on the illicit relationship of a young wife with her stepson and the revenge of a dishonoured husband." Publisher's note
    Includes bibliographical references

864   Spanish essays

Borges, Jorge Luis, 1899-1986

Selected non-fictions; edited by Eliot Weinberger; translated by Esther Allen, Suzanne Jill Levine & Eliot Weinberger. Viking 1999 559p hardcover o.p. pa $20 * **864**
    ISBN 978-0-14-029011-0 (pa); 0-14-029011-7 (pa)
                      LC 99-12386
    "Shifting effortlessly from Homer to Hitler, from Kafka to King Kong, these hundred and sixty-one essays, appreciations, prologues, and philosophical investigations are dizzying in scope and dazzling in execution. But it is Borges's dogged pursuit of familiar themes—infinity and eternity, reflexivity and recurrence—which gives this collection its unusual unity and depth." New Yorker
    Includes bibliographical references

Fuentes, Carlos, 1928-

Myself with others; selected essays. Farrar, Straus & Giroux 1988 214p $19.95; pa $18
                            864
    ISBN 0-374-21750-5; 0-374-52237-5 (pa)
                      LC 87-7448
    Essays by the Mexican writer on subjects ranging from the cinema of Buñuel to the literary output of Cervantes, Borges and Garcia Marquez

Paz, Octavio, 1914-1998

The labyrinth of solitude; The other Mexico, Return to the labyrinth of solitude, Mexico and the United States, The philanthropic ogre. Grove Press 1985 398p hardcover o.p. pa $14.50 *
                            864
    1. Mexico—Civilization 2. Mexican national characteristics
    ISBN 978-0-8021-5042-4 (pa); 0-8021-5042-X (pa)
                      LC 82-47999
    The labyrinth of solitude and The other Mexico were first published 1961 and 1972 respectively
    In this collection of essays and one interview, Paz explorers the cultural and historical influences on the social behavior of his countrymen

Vargas Llosa, Mario, 1936-

The language of passion; translated by Natasha Wimmer. Farrar, Straus & Giroux 2003 292p $24; pa $14 **864**
    ISBN 0-374-18326-0; 0-312-42254-7 (pa)
                      LC 2002-37909
    "This collection focuses on the essays that appeared during the 1990s, most of which are imbued with a wit and an intellect that make them instantly engaging." Libr J
    Includes bibliographical references

869   Portuguese literature

Camões, Luís de, 1524?-1580

Selected sonnets; edited and translated by William Baer. Bilingual ed. University of Chicago Press 2005 199p il $26 * **869**
    1. Poetry—By individual authors
    ISBN 0-226-09266-6   LC 2004-58521
    Camões "is Portugal's great sonneteer. He published only one sonnet in his lifetime, and many of doubtful authorship crept into the canon during their first century of great popularity. Baer presents 70 in Portuguese and his own English versions, formally faithful to the originals except that in the octaves Baer uses four (abba, cddc) rather than Camoes' two (abba, abba) rhymes. A sketch of Camoes' amazingly adventurous and colorful life, his works, and his reputation precedes the poems." Booklist

Lispector, Clarice, 1925-1977

Selected cronicas; translated by Giovanni Pontiero. New Directions 1996 212p pa $12.95 *
                            869
    ISBN 0-8112-1340-4   LC 96-23768
    "In these crônicas—part anecdote, memoir, observation, essay—the late avante-garde writer shows herself to have been as adept at short nonfiction as she was at short fiction. Based on a column she began writing at the behest of Brazil's leading newspaper in 1967, these pieces bring together the lyricism of poetry to everyday reality." Publ Wkly

Pessoa, Fernando, 1888-1935

Fernando Pessoa & Co.; selected poems; edited and translated from the Portuguese by Richard Zenith. Grove Press 1998 290p hardcover o.p. pa $14 * **869**
    1. Poetry—By individual authors
    ISBN 978-0-8021-3627-5 (pa); 0-8021-3627-3 (pa)
                      LC 97-50201
    "Pessoa developed his poetic opus through the mouthpieces of distinct and separate literary personalities called heteronyms. . . . This collection includes selections from three of those alter egos—the bucolic pagan Caeiro, the Epicurean classicist Reis, and the sensational modernist Campos—plus the 'real' Pessoa." Libr J
    Includes bibliographical references

870.8 Latin literature—Collections

The **Portable** Roman reader; edited, and with an
introduction by Basil Davenport. Viking 1951
656p pa $18 hardcover o.p. *   **870.8**
1. Latin literature—Collections
ISBN 0-14-015056-0 (pa)
"The Viking portable library"
This anthology includes selections from Plautus, Terence, Caesar, Virgil, Seneca, Juvenal as well as complete
plays by Plautus and Terence and the anonymous poem
Vigil of Venus

871 Latin poetry

Horace
The epistles of Horace; [translated by] David
Ferry. Farrar, Straus, and Giroux 2001 203p
hardcover o.p. pa $19   **871**
1. Poetry—By individual authors
ISBN 978-0-374-52852-7 (pa); 0-374-52852-7 (pa)
          LC 00-52746
Parallel text in English and Latin
"Horace's hexameter verse letters to his patron Maece-
nas, the Emperor Augustus, and his friends, including the
famous 'To the Pisos' (Ars Poetica), a classic statement
on Roman poetics, are masterpieces of wit and wry wisdom." Libr J
"Ferry takes his bearings from the great blank verse
poets of the last two hundred years, especially Frost, and
while he manages to be faithful to the meaning, substance and shades, of the Latin original, Ferry achieves
through his historical, cultural, and linguistic cross-
pollination something more important and lasting than
mere translation: he brings to life new as well as old
possibilities for poetry in America now." Harvard Rev
Includes bibliographical references

Lucretius Carus, Titus
On the nature of things: De rerum natura; [by]
Lucretius; edited and translated by Anthony M.
Esolen. Johns Hopkins Univ. Press 1995 296p pa
$25   **871**
1. Poetry—By individual authors
ISBN 978-0-8018-5055-4; 0-8018-5055-X
          LC 94-25165
"Writing in the waning days of the Roman Republic—
as Rome's politics grew individualistic and treacherous,
its high-life wanton, its piety introspective and morbid—
Lucretius sets forth a rational and materialistic view of
the world which offers a retreat into a quiet community
of wisdom and friendship." Publisher's note
"Ensolen has focused on the poet, translating the Latin
hexameters into accented pentameter in order to capture
the dynamics, rhythms, and syntax of the original. The
results are both satisfying and readable. Ensolen includes
an elegant introduction on Lucretius, as well as useful
notes. A valuable contribution to students of literature as
well as philosophy." Libr J

Virgil
The eclogues of Virgil; a translation by David
Ferry. Farrar, Straus & Giroux 1999 101p
hardcover o.p. pa $14   **871**
1. Poetry—By individual authors
ISBN 978-0-374-52696-2 (pa); 0-374-52696-6 (pa)
          LC 98-52547
Parallel text in English and Latin
The Eclogues "comprise not much more than 800
lines in total, but they may be the most influential collection of short poems by one author ever written. . . . It
is a conspicuous merit of Ferry's translations that they
have a kind of transparency; he does not intrude his style
or his personality between the reader and himself. His
versions are rather plain, unfussy, and usually of a quiet
dignity." New Republic

871.008 Latin poetry—Collections

The **Roman** poets; selected and edited by Peter
Washington. Knopf 1997 253p il (Everyman's
library pocket poets) $12.50 *   **871.008**
1. Latin poetry—Collections
ISBN 0-375-40071-0   LC 98-124022
A representative selection of classical Latin verse.

872 Latin dramatic poetry and drama

Plautus, Titus Maccius
The pot of gold, and other plays; [by] Plautus;
tr. by E. F. Watling. Penguin Books 1965 267p
(Penguin Classics) pa $12   **872**
ISBN 978-0-14-044149-9; 0-14-044149-2
          LC 65-8577
Contents: The pot of gold (Aulularia); The prisoners
(Captivi); The brothers Menaechmus (Menaechmi); The
swaggering soldier (Miles Gloriosus); and Pseudolus
Plautus "romanized many of the plots and characters
of New Greek Comedy. Through his plays, he introduced
to the non-Greek world characters which have since become part of traditional western European comedy,
among them the braggard soldier (in his Miles Gloriosus)
and the sly servant (in his Pseudolus)." Benet's Reader's
Ency. 4th edition

The rope, and other plays; [by] Plautus; tr. by
E. F. Watling. Penguin Books 1964 284p (Penguin
Classics) pa $12   **872**
ISBN 978-0-14-044136-9; 0-14-044136-0
          LC 63-2117
Contents: The ghost (Mostellaria); The rope (Rudens);
A three-dollar day (Trinummus); and Amphitruo

Terence

Terence, the comedies; translations by Palmer Bovie, Constance Carrier, and Douglass Parker; edited by Palmer Bovie. Johns Hopkins Univ. Press 1992 xxi, 398p (Complete Roman drama in translation) hardcover o.p. pa $25 **872**
ISBN 978-0-8018-4354-9 (pa); 0-8018-4354-5 (pa)
LC 91-33984
First published 1974 by Rutgers University Press with title: The complete comedies of Terence
Includes the following plays: The brothers (Adelphoe); The eunuch (Eunouchus); The girl from Andros (Andria); Her husband's mother (Hecyra); Phormio; The self-tormentor (Heautontimorumenos)

Virgil

The Georgics of Virgil; a translation; a translation [translated] by David Ferry. Farrar, Straus and Giroux 2005 xx, 202p hardcover o.p. pa $14 **872**
ISBN 978-0-374-16131-0 (pa); 0-374-16131-9 (pa)
LC 2004-20023
Parallel text in English and Latin
"The Georgics celebrates the crops, trees, and animals, and, above all, the human beings who care for them. It takes the form of teaching about this care: the tilling of fields, the tending of vines, the raising of the cattle and the bees." Publisher's note
"Ferry shows tremendous skill with his taut yet pliant pentameter. He also employs demotic and high lyrical diction with equal finesse. His version contains all the freshness of American speech and all the classical poise of the original: it comes across neither as a curatorial act of conservation nor as a modish remake. . . . This is the best poetry of Ancient Rome, rendered by the best translator of modern America." Poetry (Modern Poetry Association)

873 Latin epic poetry and fiction

Ovid, 43 B.C.-17 or 18

Tales from Ovid; [translated by] Ted Hughes. Farrar, Straus & Giroux 1997 257p pa $14 hardcover o.p. * **873**
1. Poetry—By individual authors
ISBN 0-374-52587-0 (pa)
LC 97-36061
Hughes retells 24 Greco-Roman myths from Ovid's Latin epic *Metamorphoses*.
This is "an inspired act of translation that stands as vigorous poetry in its own right." N Y Times Book Rev
Includes bibliographical references

Virgil

The Aeneid; translated by Robert Fitzgerald. Knopf 1992 xxvii,483p (Everyman's library) $20 **873**
1. Poetry—By individual authors
ISBN 978-0-679-41335-6; 0-679-41335-9
LC 91-58698
This translation first published 1983 by Random House

This is a translation of the Latin narrative poem whose twelve "books tell of the forced wanderings of the Trojan hero Aeneas (son of the goddess Venus and the mortal Anchises) after the fall of Troy; how he survived the wrath of the goddess Juno (who favored Troy's enemies, the Achaeans), and, after a series of demanding adventures, fulfilled a prophecy that he would lead his uprooted people to a new home and there found an empire-what would become the home of Augustus." Christ Sci Monit

"Fitzgerald's is so decisively the best modern Aeneid that it is unthinkable anyone will want to use any other version for a long time to come. Latinists, as they read it, will be led to consider their original afresh. Those without Latin are going to find, to their surprise, and I hope their pleasure, that the poem is still as good as anyone ever said it was." N Y Rev Books

The Aeneid; translated by Robert Fagles; introduction by Bernard Knox. Viking 2006 486p map $40 * **873**
1. Poetry—By individual authors
ISBN 0-670-03803-2
LC 2006-47220
Also available in paperback from Vintage and Cambridge Univ. Press
"The Aeneid is in twelve books: the first six in imitation of the Odyssey; the last six, of the Iliad. The Trojan hero is led to Italy, where he is to be the father of a race and of an empire supreme among nations. On his way thither he tarries at Carthage, whose queen, Dido, loves him as with the first love of a virgin. To her he tells the story of Troy. For love of him she slays herself when the gods lead him from her shores. Arrived in Italy he seeks the underworld, under the protection of the Sibyl of Cumae. He emerges thence to overcome his enemies." Keller. Reader's Dig of Books

874 Latin lyric poetry

Catullus, Gaius Valerius, 84-54 B.C.

The poems of Catullus; translated by Charles Martin. Johns Hopkins Univ. Press 1990 181p hardcover o.p. pa $19.95 **874**
1. Poetry—By individual authors
ISBN 978-0-8018-3926-9 (pa); 0-8018-3926-2 (pa)
LC 89-45486
First published 1979 in limited edition by Abattoir Editions, the University of Nebraska at Omaha
"The introduction ranges through Martin's observations on Catullus' place among Roman lyricists, his virtuosity, acuity, irony, and appeal to modern poets. The translations themselves, while open to inevitable quibbling among Latinists, are remarkably true to the versification, denotations, and connotations of the original texts. Martin is particularly adept at shaping the English into approximations of the Latin meters." Choice

The poems of Catullus; a bilingual edition; translated, with commentary by Peter Green. University of California Press 2005 339p (Joan Palevsky imprint in classical literature) $24.95 * **874**
1. Poetry—By individual authors
ISBN 0-520-24264-5
LC 2004-13920

Catullus, Gaius Valerius, 84-54 B.C.—*Continued*

This is "a translation of the complete poems of Catullus, with facing Latin original and extensive notes. . . . Green's translation should encourage readers of all kinds to read or reread Catullus, one of the greatest and most influential of all classical poets." New Repub

Horace

Odes and epodes; edited and translated by Niall Rudd. Harvard University Press 2004 350p (Loeb classical library) $24 * **874**

1. Poetry—By individual authors

ISBN 0-674-99609-7   LC 2003-65236

Originally published 1918; this is a reprint of the 1927 edition

English prose translations of the Odes and Epodes, opposite the original Latin. There is a short introductory chapter on the life and works of Horace, followed by a chapter on the meters he used. An index of proper names refer to the Latin originals by number and line

The odes of Horace; a translation by David Ferry. Farrar, Straus & Giroux 1997 343p hardcover o.p. pa $28   **874**

1. Poetry—By individual authors

ISBN 978-0-374-52572-9 (pa); 0-374-52572-2 (pa)
     LC 97-9483

Parallel text in English and Latin

"The foremost technician of Rome's Golden Age, Horace (658 B.C.) revolutionized Latin verse. He imported intricate Greek meters, invented the poet as a jeweller of words and left behind some of the most enduring models of what a short poem should address." Publ Wkly

Ferry "wisely does not try to reproduce Horace's meters in English. . . . And he often rearranges Horace's material to fit the run of his own verse, sometimes to stunning effect. . . . This is a Horace for our times." N Y Rev Books

875 Latin speeches

Cicero, Marcus Tullius, 106-43 B.C.

Political speeches; [by] Cicero; translated with introductions and notes by D.H. Berry. Oxford University Press 2006 xl, 345p map pa $13.95
     875

1. Speeches 2. Rome—History

ISBN 978-0-19-283266-5; 0-19-283266-2
     LC 2005-20919

"Cicero (106-43 BC) was the greatest orator of the ancient world and a leading politician of the closing era of the Roman republic. This book presents nine speeches which reflect the development, variety, and drama of his political career,among them two speeches from his prosecution of Verres, a corrupt and cruel governor of Sicily; four speeches against the conspirator Catiline; and the Second Philippic, the famous denunciation of Mark Antony which cost Cicero his life. Also included are On the Command of Gnaeus Pompeius, in which he praises the military successes of Pompey, and For Marcellus, a panegyric in praise of the dictator Julius Caesar." Publisher's note

Includes bibliographical references

Selected works; [by] Cicero; translated with an introduction by Michael Grant. Penguin Books 2004 272p (Penguin classics) pa $15   **875**

ISBN 978-0-14-044099-7; 0-14-044099-2

First published 1960

"Divided into two parts—'Against Tyranny' and 'How to Live'—this selection of Cicero's work reveals the private and public sides of his liberal personality and his opposition to oppressive and unparliamentary methods of government." Publisher's note

877 Latin satire and humor

Erasmus, Desiderius, 1466?-1536

Praise of folly; and, Letter to Maarten Van Dorp, 1515; [by] Erasmus of Rotterdam; translated by Betty Radice; with an introduction and notes by A.H.T. Levi. Penguin Books 1993 lvi, 188p (Penguin classics) pa $13 *   **877**

ISBN 978-014-044608-1; 0-14-044608-7
     LC 94-142502

A "satirical monologue in Latin. . . . Folly praises herself and proclaims her superiority over Wisdom. The author's argument, of course, is 'that it is folly not to see things as they really are; scholars should not abandon ideals just because they cannot be fully realized but should apply their learning and reason as best they can to daily living.'" Reader's Adviser

Juvenal

The sixteen satires; translated with an introduction and notes by Peter Green. 3rd ed. Penguin Books 1999 c1998 lxviii, 252p (Penguin classics) pa $13 *   **877**

ISBN 978-0-14-044704-0; 0-14-044704-0
     LC 99-987049

First published 1967

"The sixteen 'Satires' of Juvenal, which contain a vivid picture of contemporary Rome under the Empire, have seldom been equalled as biting diatribes. . . . Juvenal's invectives in powerful hexameters, exact and epigrammatic, were aimed at lax and luxurious society, tyranny, criminal excesses, and the immorality of women." Reader's Adviser

878 Latin miscellaneous writings

Caesar, Julius, 100-44 B.C.

The Gallic War; with an English translation by H. J. Edwards. Harvard Univ. Press 1958 xxii, 616p il maps $21.50 *   **878**

1. Rome—History

ISBN 0-674-99080-3

"The Loeb classical library"

Caesar's account of his campaign (58-50 B.C.) to bring the province of Gaul (France) under his control.

Cicero, Marcus Tullius, 106-43 B.C.

On the good life; translated with an introduction by Michael Grant. Penguin Books 1971 382p map (Penguin classics) pa $16   **878**

   1. Ethics

   ISBN 978-0-14-044244-1; 0-14-044244-8

                      LC 77-30399

For "Roman orator and statesman Cicero, 'the good life' was at once a life of contentment and one of moral virtue and the two were inescapably intertwined. This volume brings together a wide range of his reflections upon the importance of moral integrity in the search for happiness. . . . Cicero presents his views upon the significance of friendship and duty to state and family, and outlines a clear system of practical ethics." Publisher's note

Martial

Epigrams; selected and translated by James Michie; introduction by Shadi Bartsch. Modern Library 2002 xxxiv, 199p (Modern Library classics) pa $14.95   **878**

   1. Epigrams

   ISBN 978-0-375-76042-6; 0-375-76042-3

                      LC 2002-22343

First published 1972

Michie "has translated a selection of the epigrams—about one tenth of what Martial wrote. He has the text on the facing page—a great advantage if you can read Latin—an Introduction [and] Notes. . . . [He] uses rhyme, and makes his Martial much more like the English idea of an epigram than like the epigrams in the Greek Anthology. There isn't much pure humor in Latin literature (as opposed to waspishness and scurrility) but Martial is often very funny." Encounter (London, England)

Includes bibliographical references

Suetonius Tranquillus, C., ca. 69-ca. 122

The twelve Caesars; {by} Gaius Suetonius Tranquillus; translated by Robert Graves; revised with an introduction by Michael Grant. Penguin Bks. 2003 363p maps pa $14 *   **878**

   1. Emperors—Rome 2. Rome—History

   ISBN 0-14-044921-3   LC 2003-267782

A reissue with new Chronology and updated further reading of the translation published 1957

"A detailed account of the life and times of the first twelve emperors from Caesar to Domitian." Reader's Ency. 4th edition

Includes bibliographical references

Tacitus, Cornelius

Complete works of Tacitus; translated from the Latin by Alfred John Church and William Jackson Brodribb; edited and with an introduction by Moses Hadas. McGraw-Hill 1964 773p il pa $14.75 *   **878**

   1. Agricola, Gnaeus Julius, 40-93 2. Rome—History 3. Germany—History—0-1517

   ISBN 0-07-553639-0; 978-0-07-553639-0

First published 1942 by Modern Lib.

Contains: The annals; The history; The life of Cnaeus Julius Agricola; Germany and its tribes; A dialogue on oratory

880.3 Classical Greek literature—Encyclopedias and dictionaries

The **Oxford** companion to classical literature; edited by M. C. Howatson. 2nd ed. Oxford Univ. Press 1989 615p il maps $65; pa $29.95 *   **880.3**

   1. Classical literature—Dictionaries

   ISBN 0-19-866121-5; 0-19-860081-X (pa)

                      LC 88-27330

First published 1937 under the editorship of Sir Paul Harvey

This work "covers classical literature from the appearance of the Greeks, around 2200 B.C., to the close of the Athenian philosophy schools in A.D. 529. It includes articles on authors, major works, historical notables, mythological figures, and topics of literary significance. Short summaries of major works, chronologies, charts, and maps are special features." Nichols. Guide to Ref Books for Sch Media Cent. 4th edition

Thorburn, John E., Jr.

The Facts on File companion to classical drama. Facts on File 2005 680p map (Facts on File library of world literature) $71.50 *   **880.3**

   1. Classical drama—Encyclopedias

   ISBN 0-8160-5202-6   LC 2004-16803

This "compendium covers ancient Greek and Roman drama from the 500s B.C.E. through 100 C.E. Approximately 400 alphabetical entries, ranging in length from one sentence to several pages, delve into plays, authors, characters, settings, genres, themes, theatrical terms, historical events, etc." SLJ

"It is difficult to think of any other resource quite this thorough that combines all of Greek and Roman drama into a convenient single-volume publication." Libr J

Includes bibliographical references

880.8 Classical Greek literature—Collections

The **classical** Greek reader; edited by Kenneth J. Atchity; associate editor, Rosemary McKenna. Oxford University Press 1998 xxxiv, 442p il pa $24.95 *   **880.8**

   1. Greek literature—Collections 2. Greece—Civilization

   ISBN 0-19-512303-4   LC 98-12978

First published 1996 by Holt & Co.

This reader provides excerpts from the works of classical Greek writers.

"Across the centuries, ranging from the Homeric poets to Graeco-Roman writers of the third century A.D., we find ourselves in the company of physicians and storytellers, herbalists and romance writers—and women. Atchity is mining a tradition of inexhaustible riches: the voices we encounter here offer passage to the literary, ar-

The classical Greek reader—*Continued*
tistic, social, political, religious, scientific and philosophical texts that underlie Western intellectual tradition." Smithsonian

Includes bibliographical references

The **Norton** book of classical literature; edited by Bernard Knox. Norton 1993 866p $29.95 *
880.8

1. Greek literature—Collections
ISBN 0-393-03426-7   LC 92-10378
"A comprehensive volume of more than 300 pieces of classical literature, primarily Greek but also some Roman." Booklist

881   Classical Greek poetry

Apollonius, of Rhodes
The voyage of Argo: the Argonautica; translated with an introd. by E.V. Rieu. 2nd ed. Penguin Books 1971 213p map (Penguin Classics) pa $14
881

1. Argonauts (Greek mythology) 2. Poetry—By individual authors
ISBN 978-0-14-044085-0; 0-14-044085-0
This translation first published 1959
An epic account of Jason's voyage in quest of the Golden Fleece written in the third century B.C.

Hesiod, fl. ca. 700 B.C.
Works and days; and Theogony; translated by Stanley Lombardo; with introduction, notes, and glossary by Robert Lamberton. Hackett 1993 128p hardcover o.p. pa $10.95   881

1. Poetry—By individual authors
ISBN 978-0-87220-179-8 (pa); 0-87220-179-1 (pa)
LC 93-24545
This is a translation of two ancient Greek poems. "Theogony is a genealogy of the Greek gods and some of their myths, and the Works and Days is a meditation on work, justice, and the gods, together with a farmer's almanac of the ancient agricultural year. . . . For a literal rendition of the Greek, readers should turn elsewhere, but those who want a translation that captures something of the spirit of an ancient Greek poetic voice and its cultural milieu and transmits it in an appealing, lively, and accessible style will now turn to Lombardo." Choice

881.008   Classical Greek poetry— Collections

7 Greeks; translations by Guy Davenport. New Directions 1995 241p pa $16.95
881.008

1. Greek literature—Collections
ISSN 0-8112-1288-2
ISBN 978-0-8112-1288-5; 0-8112-1288-2
LC 95-4227
Davenport has translated a sampling of seventh- to third-century B.C.E. Greek poetry. "Included among the poems and fragments are lyrics by Archilochos, Sappho, Alkman, and Anakreon; philosophical verse by Herakleitos and Diogenes; and comic dramatic verse by Herondas. Arguing that no translation is final and occasionally offering several versions of the same work, Davenport attempts to capture the tone of the original rather than offering a literal or formal rendition." Libr J

The **Oxford** book of classical verse in translation; edited by Adrian Poole and Jeremy Maule. Oxford University Press 1995 xlix, 606p $45 *
881.008

1. Classical poetry—Collections
ISBN 0-19-214209-7
A "collection of classical verse from Homer to Boethius. Translations, modern and older, are brought together in a rich blending of Greek and Latin writings. Some of the greatest poets in the English language—Dryden, Pope, Tennyson, Poe, Byron, Yeats, Browning, Houseman, Wilde, Shelley, and Pound are among the translators. They emphasize the debt English poetry owes to the classics." SLJ

882   Classical Greek dramatic poetry and drama

Aeschylus
Aeschylus; edited by David Grene and Richmond Lattimore. University of Chicago Press 1992 c1991 352p (Complete Greek tragedies) $55
882

ISBN 978-0-226-30764-0; 0-226-30764-6
"Centennial edition"
Contents: Agamemnon; Libation bearers; Eumenides; Suppliant maidens; Persians; Seven against Thebes; Prometheus bound

The Oresteia; translated by Alan Shapiro and Peter Burian. Oxford University Press 2003 285p (The Greek tragedy in new translations) hardcover o.p. pa $11.95   882

ISBN 978-0-19-513592-3 (pa); 0-19-513592-X (pa)
LC 2002-66272
The only extant Greek dramatic trilogy. "It begins with Agamemnon, which describes Agamemnon's return from the Trojan War and his murder at the hands of his wife Clytemnestra, continues with her murder by their son Orestes in Libation Bearers, and concludes with Orestes' acquittal at a court founded by Athena in Eumenides." Publisher's note
"The collaboration of poet and scholar . . . produces a language that is easy to read and easy to speak." Libr J

Includes bibliographical references

Aristophanes
The complete plays; the new translations by Paul Roche. New American Library 2005 715p pa $17   882

ISBN 978-0-451-21409-6; 0-451-21409-9
LC 2004-56681

Aristophanes—*Continued*
Contents: Acharnians; Knights; Clouds; Wasps; Peace; Birds; Lysistrata; Women at Thesmophoria festival; Frogs; A parliament of women; Plutus (Wealth)

Euripides, ca. 485-ca. 406 B.C.
Euripides; edited by David Grene and Richmond Lattimore. University of Chicago Press 1992 c1942 665p (Complete Greek tragedies) $65
882

ISBN 978-0-226-30766-4; 0-226-30766-2
First published 1942
"Centennial edition"
Contents: Alcestis; Medea; Heracleidae; Hippolytus; Cyclops; Heracles; Iphigenia in Tauris; Helen; Hecuba; Andromache; The Trojan women

Euripides [2]; edited by David Grene and Richmond Lattimore. University of Chicago Press 1992 c1958 314p (Complete Greek tragedies) $44
882

ISBN 978-0-226-30767-1; 0-226-30767-0
First published 1958
"Centennial edition"
Contents: Ion; Rhesus; The suppliant women; Orestes; Iphigenia in Aulis; Electra; The Phoenician women; The Bacchae

Seneca, Lucius Annaeus, the Younger, 4 B.C.-65 A.D.
Four tragedies, and Octavia; [by] Seneca; tr. with an introduction by E. F. Watling. Penguin Books 1966 318p (Penguin Classics) pa $14
882

ISBN 978-0-14-044174-1; 0-12-044174-3
LC 66-8618
Contents: Phaedra; Oedipus; Thyestes; The Trojan women; Octavia
"Although their themes are borrowed from Greek drama, these exuberant and often macabre plays focus on action rather than moral concerns and are strikingly different in style from Seneca's prose writing." Publisher's note

Sophocles
Sophocles; edited by David Grene and Richmond Lattimore. University of Chicago Press 1992 c1991 466p (Complete Greek tragedies) $50
882

ISBN 978-0-226-30765-7; 0-226-30765-4
"Centennial edition"
Contents: Oedipus the King; Oedipus at Colonus; Antigone; Ajax; The women of Trachis; Electra; Philoctetes

The Theban plays of Sophocles; translated by David R. Slavitt. Yale University Press 2007 237p $28
882

ISBN 978-0-300-11776-9; 0-300-11776-0
LC 2006-26965
Contents: Antigone; Oedipus tyrannos; Oedipus at Colonus

"This version is meant to be an updated one, and the easy currency of its diction is a great virtue. The natural cadences of its free verse slide smoothly and sometimes beautifully into the ear." Claremont Rev Books
Includes bibliographical references

883 Classical Greek epic poetry and fiction

Homer
Iliad; translated by Stanley Lombardo; introduction by Sheila Murnaghan. Hackett 1997 516p $37.95; pa $12.95
883
1. Poetry—By individual authors
ISBN 978-0-87220-353-2; 0-87220-353-0; 978-0-87220-352-5 (pa); 0-87220-352-2 (pa)
LC 96-53368
This is a translation from the Greek of the epic poem on the Trojan War
"Lombardo manages to be respectful of Homer's dire spirit while providing on nearly every page some wonderfully fresh refashioning of his Greek. The result is a vivid and sometimes disarmingly hard-bitten reworking of a great classic. . . . Not all of Lombardo's gambles pay off, and his attention-grabbing colloquialisms sometimes undermine the force of the original. . . . Still, the success of so many of Lombardo's choices more than makes up for the false notes." N Y Times Book Rev

The Iliad; translated by Robert Fitzgerald. Knopf 1992 xxi, 594p (Everyman's library) $22
883
1. Poetry—By individual authors
ISBN 978-0-679-41075-1; 0-679-41075-9
LC 91-53222
This translation first published 1974 by Anchor Press/Doubleday
Homer's epic of the Trojan War in blank verse
"Fitzgerald has solved virtually every problem that has plagued translators of Homer. The narrative runs, the dialogue speaks, the military action is clear, and the repetitive epithets become useful text rather than exotic relics. Aside from the ability to write poetry, which is basic to the undertaking, Mr. Fitzgerald's success derives from the use of a predominantly Anglo-Saxon vocabulary, a concentration on specific meanings, and an occasional arbitrary, but highly effective, substitution of implication for literal sense." Atlantic

The Iliad; translated by Robert Fagles; introduction and notes by Bernard Knox. Viking 1990 683p $40; pa $15.95
883
1. Poetry—By individual authors
ISBN 978-0-670-83510-2; 978-0-14-027536-0 (pa)
LC 89-70695

Homer's epic of the Trojan War.
"Fagles gives us a stark and terrible poem, an Iliad about, as its first word announces, rage. He conveys, far better than either Lattimore or Fitzgerald, the psychological experience of combat and war." Classical World

Homer—*Continued*

Odyssey; translated by Stanley Lombardo; introduction by Sheila Murnaghan. Hackett 2000 414p il $37.95; pa $12.95   **883**

1. Poetry—By individual authors
ISBN 978-0-87220-485-0; 0-87220-485-5; 978-0-87220-484-3 (pa); 0-87220-484-7 (pa)
LC 99-54175

A retelling of Homer's epic that describes the wanderings of Odysseus after the fall of Troy.

Lombardo "has brought his laconic wit and love of the ribald, as well as his clever use of idiomatic American slang, to his version of the 'Odyssey.' His carefully honed syntax gives the narrative energy and a whirlwind pace. The lines, rhythmic and clipped, have the tautness and force of Odysseus' bow." N Y Times Book Rev

Includes bibliographical references

The Odyssey; translated by Robert Fitzgerald; with an introduction by Seamus Heaney. Knopf 1992 xxvii, 509p (Everyman's library) $21
   883

1. Poetry—By individual authors
ISBN 978-0-679-41047-8; 0-679-41047-3
LC 92-52903

This translation first published 1961 by Anchor Press/Doubleday

"An epic poem in Greek hexameters. . . . The 'Odyssey' is a sequel to the 'Iliad' and narrates the ten years' adventures of Ulysses during his return journey from Troy to his own kingdom, the island of Ithaca." Keller. Reader's Dig of Books

"Fitzgerald's new Odyssey . . . deserves to be singled out for what it is—a masterpiece." Nation

Includes bibliographical references

The Odyssey; translated by Robert Fagles; introduction and notes by Bernard Knox. Viking 1996 541p $35; pa $16   **883**

1. Poetry—By individual authors
ISBN 978-0-670-82162-4; 978-0-14-026886-7 (pa)
LC 96-17280

This is a verse translation of Homer's epic poem.

"Fagles' *Odyssey* is the one to put into the hands of younger, first-time readers, not least because of its paucity of notes, which, though sometimes frustrating, is a sign that translation has been used to do the work of explanation. Altogether, an outstanding piece of work." Booklist

Includes bibliographical references

Manguel, Alberto

Homer's The Iliad and The Odyssey; a biography. Atlantic Monthly Press 2008 c2007 285p (Books that changed the world) $19.95
   883

1. Homer. Iliad—About 2. Homer. Odyssey—About 3. Epic poetry
ISBN 978-0-87113-976-4; 0-87113-976-6

First published 2007 in the United Kingdom

A "study of the influence of The Iliad and The Odyssey on Western literature. First describing the two epics and the Homer question, Manguel then compares various translations in English, Spanish, French, and German, a move that brings out the complexities and richness of Homer's language. Does the poet sing of the rage, wrath, anger, rancor, or mania of Achilles? Then, following a more or less chronological progression, Manguel surveys the various shifting interpretations of the epics from Plato and Virgil to the present, including extended discussions of Derek Walcott, Timothy Findley, and Jorge Luis Borges. Highly recommended for general readers." Libr J

884   Classical Greek lyric poetry

Pindar

The complete odes of Pindar; translated by Anthony Verity; with an introduction and notes by Stephen Instone. Oxford University Press 2007 xxvii, 186p (Oxford world's classics) pa $15.95 *
   884

1. Poetry—By individual authors
ISBN 978-0-19-280553-9; 0-19-280553-3
LC 2006-39673

The Odes (Epinicia) celebrated victories in the great national games, and were accompanied by music, which is lost to us. The fragments represent almost every kind of lyric poem.

"Since Pindar's Epinicia are generally concerned with mythical subjects, reserving praise of the mortal victor for the end of the ode, his works are a fine source of legend." Reader's Ency. 4th edition

Sappho

If not, winter; fragments of Sappho; translated by Anne Carson. Knopf 2002 397p $27.50; pa $14 *   **884**

1. Poetry—By individual authors
ISBN 0-375-41067-8; 0-375-72451-6 (pa)
LC 2001-50247

"Carson's translation follows Sappho's diction and form . . . closely and includes the Greek original on the facing page. Much of what survives of Sappho are fragments, often just a stray word, phrase, or even a few letters. Like many modern poets, Carson deploys these on the blank page, letting their suggestiveness fill the gaps and create whole lyrics in the imagination of the readers." Libr J

Includes bibliographical references

888   Classical Greek miscellaneous

Aristotle, 384-322 B.C.

The basic works of Aristotle; edited, and with an introduction by Richard McKeon. Random House 1941 xxxix, 1487p $49.95; pa $19.95 *
   888

ISBN 0-394-41610-4; 0-375-75799-6 (pa)

Follows the Oxford translation of 1931

Contains entire texts of the following: Physica; De generatione et corruptione; De anima; Parva naturalia; Metaphysica; Ethica Nicomachea; Politica; De poetica

Includes bibliographical references

Plato

The collected dialogues of Plato, including the letters; edited by Edith Hamilton and Huntington Cairns. With introd. and prefatory notes. Princeton University Press 1961 xxv, 1743p (Bollingen series) $49.50   **888**
    ISBN 978-0-691-09718-3; 0-691-09718-6
    "All the writings of Plato generally considered to be authentic are here presented. . . . The editors set out to choose the contents of this collected edition from the work of the best British and American translators of the last 100 years, ranging from Jowett (1871) to scholars of the present day. The volume contains prefatory notes to each dialogue, by Edith Hamilton; an introductory essay on Plato's philosophy and writings, by Huntington Cairns; and a comprehensive index which seeks, by means of cross references, to assist the reader with the philosophical vocabulary of the different translators." Publisher's note
    "This elegant edition contains many of the best and most readable English translations of the Dialogues and Letters. . . . Judiciously edited, beautifully printed." Rev of Metaphysics

The republic; edited by G.R.F. Ferrari; translated by Tom Griffith. Cambridge Univ. Press 2000 xlviii, 382p (Cambridge texts in the history of political thought) $38; pa $11   **888**
    1. Utopias 2. Political science
    ISBN 0-521-48173-2; 0-521-48443-X (pa)
                                      LC 00-24471
    Translation from the Ancient Greek
    Griffith's "aim was to translate the Greek text as if it were a conversation, and he has succeeded admirably. The text does indeed flow like a conversation, with the entire back-and-forth interaction that such exchanges involve. . . . [He] has also written a very useful introduction that places the work in a historical context and provides a glossary that will help readers identify individuals and places mentioned in the work." Libr J
    Includes bibliographical references

889 Modern Greek literature

Cavafy, Constantine P., 1863-1933

The collected poems; [by] C.P. Cavafy; translated by Evangelos Sachperoglou; Greek text edited by Anthony Hirst; with an introduction by Peter Mackridge. Oxford University Press 2007 238p pa $12.95   **889**
    1. Poetry—By individual authors
    ISBN 978-0-19-921292-7; 0-19-921292-9
                                     LC 2007-15833
    "Cavafy writes about people on the periphery, whose religious, ethnic and cultural identities are blurred, and he was one of the pioneers in expressing a specifically homosexual sensibility. His poems present brief and vivid evocations of historical scenes and sensual moments, often infused with his distinctive sense of irony. . . . This volume presents the most authentic Greek text of the 154 authorized poems ever published, together with a new English translation." Publisher's note
    Includes bibliographical references

Elytēs, Odysseus, 1911-1996

The collected poems of Odysseus Elytis; translated by Jeffrey Carson and Nikos Sarris; introduction and notes by Jeffrey Carson. Rev and expanded ed. Johns Hopkins University Press 2005 $60   **889**
    1. Poetry—By individual authors
    ISBN 0-8018-8045-9   LC 2004-13496
    First published 1997
    "The work of 1979 Nobel Prize winner Elytis (1911-96) has the quality of a cathedral or epic—vast in scope yet richly decorated. This excellent 'complete' collected edition (it omits unpublished poems) testifies to the bountiful, sincere nature of Elytis's voice as patriot and poet. . . . Containing informative annotations, a chronology, an autobiographical essay, and the author's Nobel address, this work is a valuable resource on international poetry." Libr J
    Includes bibliographical references

Seferis, George, 1900-1971

Collected poems; translated, edited, and introduced by Edmund Keeley and Philip Sherrard. rev ed. Princeton Univ. Press 1995 296p (Lockert library of poetry in translation) pa $24.95 hardcover o.p. *   **889**
    ISBN 978-0-691-01491-3 (pa); 0-691-01491-4 (pa)
                                     LC 92-10552
    First published 1967
    Nobel laurete Seferis' "verse is spare, hernetic, and characterized by a profound knowledge of Greek history and classical mythology and a deep understanding of Greece's past and its relevance to her present and future." Reader's Ency. 4th edition
    Includes bibliographical references

891 East Indo-European and Celtic literatures

Firdawsī

Shahnameh; the Persian book of kings; [by] Abolqasem Ferdowsi; translated by Dick Davis; with a foreword by Azar Nafisi. Viking 2006 xxxvii, 886p il $45 *   **891**
    ISBN 0-670-03485-1   LC 2005-42352
    "Unlike Western epics that grasp the events of a single generation, whether of men or angels, Persia's Book of Kings encompasses whole ages of the world, chronicling the stratagems of Kings and heroes as real as Alexander the Great and as legendary as Rostam. . . . Action, myth, and history fairly fly off the page, for Davis renders Ferdowsi's 50,000 sesquipedalian lines of poetry as a prose narrative that here and there erupts into sonnet-sized snatches of verse. The scheme works brilliantly. Repeated for pages on end, Ferdowsi's lines, each longer than an heroic couplet, breed longueurs, but Davis's carefully rendered snatches of the best classic Farsi poetry illuminate the English text like so many Persian miniatures." New Criterion

Hāfiz, 14th cent.
The gift; poems by the great Sufi master; translated by Daniel James Ladinsky. Penguin/Arkana 1999 333p pa $16   **891**
1. Poetry—By individual authors
ISBN 978-0-14-019581-1; 0-14-019581-5
        LC 99-10920
"Less well known in the U.S. than his Sufi predecessor, Rumi, Hafiz (Shams-ud-din Muhammad) is also worthy of attention, and Ladinsky's free translations should help see that he gets it. Hafiz is so beloved in Iran that he outsells the Koran. Many know his verses by heart and recite them with gusto. And gusto is appropriate to this passionate, earthy poet who melds mind, spirit, and body in each of his usually brief pensees. Ladinsky has deliberately chosen a loose and colloquial tone for this collection, which might grate on the nerves of purists but makes Hafiz come vividly alive for the average reader." Booklist

Jalāl al-Dīn Rūmī, Maulana, 1207-1273
The essential Rumi; translated by Coleman Barks, with John Moyne, A.A. Arberry, Reynold Nicholson. Harper 1995 302p $23.95; pa $14.95   **891**
1. Poetry—By individual authors
ISBN   978-0-06-250958-1;   0-06-250958-6; 978-0-06-250959-8 (pa); 0-06-250959-4 (pa)
        LC 94-44995
A collection of ecstatic verse by the 13th-century Sufi mystic

Mahabharata.
The Mahābhārata; an English version based on selected verses; [translated by] Chakravarthi V. Narasimhan. rev ed, with a new preface. Columbia University Press 1998 xxix, 254p (Translations from the Asian classics) hardcover o.p. pa $25.50 *   **891**
ISBN 0-231-02624-2; 0-231-11055-3 (pa)
Also available in an illustrated paperback edition from the University of California Press
"One of the two great epic poems of ancient India (the other being the 'Ramayana'), about eight times as long as the 'Iliad' and 'Odyssey' together. It is a great compendium, added to as late as AD 600, although it had very nearly acquired its present form by the 4th century. Covering an enormous range of topics, the Mahabharata, with its famous interpolation, the 'Bhagavadgita', has as its central theme the great war between the sons of two royal brothers, in a struggle for succession." Reader's Ency. 4th edition

Mahabharata. Bhagavadgita.
Bhagavad Gita; a new translation; [translated by] Stephen Mitchell. Harmony Bks. 2000 223p hardcover o.p. pa $13.95 *   **891**
ISBN 0-609-60550-X; 0-609-81034-0 (pa)
        LC 00-28286
Hardcover and paperback editions also available from other publishers

"An eighteen-part discussion between the god Krishna, an avatar of Vishnu appearing as a charioteer, and Arjuna, a warrior about to enter battle, on the nature and meaning of life. Sometimes called the New Testament of Hinduism, it is an interpolation in the great Hindu epic the Mahabharata." Reader's Ency. 4th edition

Narayan, R. K., 1906-2001
The Ramayana; a shortened modern prose version of the Indian epic (suggested by the Tamil version of Kamban); introduction by Pankaj Mishra. Penguin Books 2006 157p (Penguin classics) pa $13 *   **891**
ISBN 0-14-303967-9   LC 2006-45201
First published 1972
A retelling of Prince Rama's courtship of the fourteen-year-old Sita, their exile, Sita's abduction, the search, and the great battle with her abductor Ravana, involving a pantheon of gods, heroes, and evil spirits.

Omar Khayyam
Rubáiyát of Omar Khayyám; rendered into English verse by Edward FitzGerald; with illustrations by Edmund J. Sullivan. St. Martin's Press 1983 75p il $9.95 *   **891**
ISBN 0-312-69527-6   LC 83-9767
Hardcover and paperback editions also available from other publishers
"The Rubaiyat' (Quatrains) of Omar the Tentmaker, of Persia, is composed of a series of stanzas forming 'a medley of love and tavern songs, tinged with Sufi mysticism, and with the melancholy of Eastern fatalism.'" Dickinson. Best Books Ser

Persian poets; selected and edited by Peter Washington. Knopf 2000 254p (Everyman's library pocket poets) $12.50   **891**
1. Persian poetry—Collections
ISBN 978-0-375-41126-7
Includes works by Omar, Sanai, Attar, Rumi, Saadi, Hafez, and Jami

Tagore, Sir Rabindranath, 1861-1941
Selected poems; translated by William Radice. Penguin Books 2005 202p (Penguin classics) pa $14   **891**
1. Poetry—By individual authors
ISBN 978-0-14-044988-4
"This collection offers a wide array of Tagore's poems from 1882 to 1941, plus textual notes and other scholarly extras." Libr J

891.6   Celtic literatures

Tain bo Cuailnge.
The Táin; translated from the Irish epic Táin Bó Cúailnge; [translated] by Thomas Kinsella; with brush drawings by Louis le Brocquy. Oxford University Press 2002 282p il map pa $19.95   **891.6**
ISBN 0-19-280373-5   LC 2002-726950

Tain bo Cuailnge.—*Continued*

This translation first published 1969

This Irish epic is the "centerpiece of the eighth-century Ulster cycle of heroic tales. . . . [This] translation is based on the partial texts in two medieval manuscripts, with elements from other versions. This edition includes a group of related stories which prepare for the action of the Tain." Publisher's note

Includes bibliographical references

891.7   East Slavic literatures. Russian

Akhmatova, Anna Andreevna, 1889-1966

The complete poems of Anna Akhmatova; {by} Anna Akhmatova; translated by Judith Hemschemeyer; edited and with an introduction by Roberta Reeder. Zephyr Press (Somerville) 1990 c1989 2v il pa $29 hardcover o.p. *

891.7

1. Poetry—By individual authors

ISBN 0-939010-27-5 (pa)   LC 88-51831

"Anna Akhmatova—the high priestess of Russian poetry—saw her husband shot, her son imprisoned twice by Stalin, her work banned in the 1930's and late 40's. . . . Sonorous, calm, deliberate in movement, her Russian has no English equivalent, but in this admirably restrained and accurate translation, sense and message strike with all the weight of the original." N Y Times Book Rev

Poems; [by] Akhmatova; translated by D.M. Thomas. New expanded ed. Knopf 2006 256p (Everyman's library pocket poets) $12.50

891.7

1. Poetry—By individual authors

ISBN 978-0-307-26424-4; 0-307-26424-6
                                          LC 2006-297217

First published 1985 in the United Kingdom with title: You will hear thunder

A representative selection of material from all her major works—including "Requiem" commemorating the victims of Stalin's terror.

Brodsky, Joseph, 1940-1996

Collected poems in English, 1972-1999; edited by Ann Kjellberg. Farrar, Straus & Giroux 2000 539p $30; pa $18 *

891.7

1. Poetry—By individual authors

ISBN 0-374-12545-7; 0-374-52838-1 (pa)
                                          LC 00-21059

This volume "gathers all the poetry in English Brodsky originally saw through to press in books (or had earmarked for eventual publication), including Russian poems he translated or co-translated. Originally Russian verse from the '60s and '70s gives way to the later, sometimes lighter, work of his last two decades, when he found a second home in the speech of his adoptive country." Publ Wkly

The **Cambridge** history of Russian literature; edited by Charles A. Moser. rev ed. Cambridge Univ. Press 1992 709p pa $55 hardcover o.p.

891.7

1. Russian literature—History and criticism

ISBN 0-521-42567-0 (pa)   LC 91-38275

This volume presents "a survey of Russian literature from the beginnings to this decade, in sufficient but not overwhelming detail.' Ten chapters by specialists elucidate this history from 988 to approximately 1980, with a lengthy bibliography at the end of the volume." Sheehy. Guide to Ref Books. 10th edition. suppl

Chekhov, Anton Pavlovich, 1860-1904

Chekhov; the four major plays; in new translations by Curt Columbus. Ivan R. Dee 2005 294p pa $15.95

891.7

ISBN 978-1-56663-626-1; 1-56663-626-4
                                          LC 2004-48612

Contents: Seagull; Uncle Vanya; Three sisters; Cherry orchard

"Columbus's translation triumphs through its clarity and consistent use of the active voice." Chicago Reader

The complete plays; [by] Anton Chekhov; translated, edited, and annotated by Laurence Senelick. W. W. Norton 2006 lx, 1060p hardcover o.p. pa $22.95

891.7

ISBN   978-0-393-04885-8;   0-393-04885-3; 978-0-393-33069-4 (pa); 0-393-33069-9 (pa)
                                          LC 2005-24362

Contents: Untitled play (without patrimony [disinherited] or Platonov); Along the highway; The power of hypnotism, by Anton Chekhov and Ivan Shcheglov; The fool, or, The retired captain; A young man; Unclean tragedians and leprous playwrights; An ideal examination; 'Chaos-vile in Rome;' A mouth as big as all outdoors; Honorable townsfolk; At the sickbed; The case of the year 1884; A drama; Before the eclipse; The sudden death of a steed, or, The magnanimity of the Russian people!; Swan song (calchas); The evils of tobacco, first version; Ivanov, first version; The bear; The proposal; Ivanov, final version; Tatyana Repina; An involuntary tragedian (from the life of vacationers); The wedding; The wood goblin; The celebration; The eve of the trial; The seagull; Uncle Vanya; Sisters; The evils of tobacco, final version; The cherry orchard

"This volume contains work never previously translated, including the newly discovered farce The Power of Hypnotism, the first version of Ivanov, Chekhov's early humorous dialogues, and a description of lost plays and those Chekhov intended to write but never did." Publisher's note

"The most complete collection of the Russian playwright's repertoire." Vogue

The portable Chekhov; edited and with an introduction by Avrahm Yarmolinsky. Viking 1947 631p pa $17 hardcover o.p.

891.7

ISBN 0-14-015035-8 (pa)

"The Viking portable Library"

This collection contains "two plays, 'The Cherry Orchard' and 'The Boor,' 28 short stories and selections from Chekhov's letters." Publ Wkly

Malcolm, Janet
Reading Chekhov; a critical journey. Random
House 2001 209p hardcover o.p. pa $13.95
            891.7
1. Chekhov, Anton Pavlovich, 1860-1904
ISBN 0-375-50668-3; 0-375-76106-3 (pa)
            LC 2001-19585
"The author's pilgrimage to Chekhov's Russia—Moscow, St. Petersburg, the gardens of his villa in Yalta—is
a reunion with this most reticent of literary fathers. Malcolm analyzes the transformations that Chekhov grants
his redeemable roués and guileless heroines, and illuminates the hidden surreality and waywardness of his realism." New Yorker
Includes bibliographical references

Mandelstam, Osip, 1891-1938
The selected poems of Osip Mandelstam;
translated by Clarence Brown and W.S. Merwin.
New York Review Books 2004 167p (New York
Review Books classics) pa $14.95   **891.7**
1. Poetry—By individual authors
ISBN 978-1-59017-091-1; 1-59017-091-1
            LC 2004-14656
First published 1974 by Atheneum
From Stone; From Tristia; From Poems (1928); Poems
of the thirties; Conversation about Dante
"The Brown/Merwin versions represent a sensitive and
sensible selection of Mandelstam's poetry. The translations do not attempt to imitate Mandelstam's fluid syntax
or subtle sound play. But they are honest representations
of Mandelstam's themes and recurrent imagery and many
of them, particularly certain of the poems in the section
'Poems of the Thirties,' come across as fine English poems." Libr J

Mayakovsky, Vladimir, 1893-1930
Listen! early poems; translated by Maria
Enzensberger; with a foreward [sic] by Elaine
Feinstein. City Lights Bks. 1991 60p pa $9.95
            891.7
1. Poetry—By individual authors
ISBN 978-0-87286-255-5; 0-87286-255-0
            LC 91-10330
First published 1987 in the United Kingdom
This collection of the Russian poet's early work has
parallel text in Russian and English and is illustrated
with some of Mayakovsky's art.

Nabokov, Vladimir Vladimirovich, 1899-1977
Lectures on Russian literature; edited with an
introduction by Fredson Bowers. Harcourt Brace
Jovanovich 1981 324p il pa $16 hardcover o.p.
            891.7
1. Russian literature—History and criticism
ISBN 0-15-602776-3 (pa)
Companion volume Lectures on literature
This book is "derived from notes Nabokov made for
his literature classes at Wellesley and Cornell. Included
are chapters on Gogol, Turgenev, Dostoevsky, Tolstoy,
Chekhov, and Gorki, as well as several miscellaneous es-
says on censorship and the art of translation." Libr J

Pushkin, Aleksandr Sergeevich, 1799-1837
Eugene Onegin and other poems; translated by
Charles Johnston. Knopf 1999 240p (Everyman's
library pocket poets) $12.50   **891.7**
1. Poetry—By individual authors
ISBN 978-0-375-40672-0; 0-375-40672-7
Contents: Eugene Onegin; Onegin's journey; The
bronze horseman
Tale in verse of a rich, bored young man who rather
offhandedly destroys his chance at love by killing a
friend in a duel and alienating his would-be beloved

Reference guide to Russian literature; editor, Neil
Cornwell; associate editor, Nicole Christian.
Fitzroy Dearborn Pubs. 1998 xl, 972p $160
            891.7
1. Russian literature—Dictionaries 2. Russian literature—Bio-bibliography
ISBN 1-88496-410-9   LC 97-169924
A guide to approximately 270 writers and their works
"author entries include telegraphic biographical sketches,
detailed bibliographies of Russian- and English-language
sources and critical studies, and, in many cases, 1000-
word entries for specific novels, plays, and stories. There
are alphabetical and chronological lists, 13 introductory
essays on various aspects of Russian literature, and a
Russian/English title index." Libr J
Includes bibliographical references

Terras, Victor
A history of Russian literature. Yale Univ. Press
1991 654p $37   **891.7**
1. Russian literature—History and criticism
ISBN 978-0-300-04971-8; 0-300-04971-4
            LC 91-13337
This history of Russian literature begins with a chapter
on folklore and then presents a chronological account
covering Old Russian literature (eleventh to sixteenth
centuries); the seventeenth century; the eighteenth century; the Romantic period; the age of the novel; the Silver
Age, and the Soviet period
"The book's minor shortcomings are overshadowed by
its numerous merits; its accuracy, keenness of observation, subtle comments, vivid quotations, erudition. . . .
Almost every page of the book invites one to read and
re-read Russian literature." Times Lit Suppl
Includes bibliographical references

Tolstaia, Tat´iana, 1951-
Pushkin's children; writings on Russia and
Russians; [by] Tatyana Tolstaya; translated by
Jamey Gambrell. Houghton Mifflin 2003 242p pa
$15   **891.7**
1. Russia—Politics and government
ISBN 0-618-12500-0   LC 2002-27610
"A Mariner original"
"A collection from a decade of vehement witness to
the radical transformations of Russia, with frequent re-
considerations of rulers and people." N Y Times Book
Rev
"Tolstaya's essays in this compact, historically signifi-
cant volume offer a fascinating, highly intelligent analy-
sis of Russian society and politics." Publ Wkly

Tsvetaeva, Marina Ivanovna, 1892-1941

Selected poems; [by] Marina Tsvetayeva; translated and introduced by Elaine Feinstein; with literal versions provided by Angela Livingstone . . . [et al.] Penguin Books 1994 131p (Penguin twentieth-century classics) pa $15 **891.7**

ISBN 978-0-14-018759-5; 0-14-018759-6

First published 1971 by Oxford Univ. Press

"As a poet Tsvetayeva impresses with her psychic energy, she is on fire with poetry, and nothing is put in perspective, everything is immediate, emotional in the best sense." N Y Times Book Rev

Yevtushenko, Yevgeny Aleksandrovich, 1933-

Selected poems; [by] Yevgeni Yevtushenko; translated by Robin Milner-Gulland and Peter Levi; with an introduction by Robin Milner-Gulland. Penguin Books 2008 90p il (Penguin Classics) pa $14 **891.7**

1. Poetry—By individual authors

ISBN 978-0-14-042477-5; 0-14-042477-6

First published 1961

With a "poetic voice that moves effortlessly between social and personal themes, [Yevtushanko] describes his idyllic childhood in Serbia, his impressions of home after a long absence in Moscow, his joy upon discovering the unexpected in a lover, his chance meeting with Hemingway in Copenhagen, and his impressions of war." Publisher's note

"These poems beat and tumble and thrash with life." Daily Telegraph

891.8 Slavic (Slavonic) literatures

Čapek, Karel, 1890-1938

R.U.R. and The insect play; by the Brothers Čapek. Oxford Univ. Press 1961 179p pa $15.95 * **891.8**

ISBN 0-19-281010-3

Translated from the Czech by Paul Selver

"R.U.R." is a fantasy in which robots revolt against their human masters. In "The insect play," a dying tramp dreams about insect life

Havel, Václav

The garden party and other plays. Grove Press 1993 273p $13.00; pa $14 **891.8**

ISBN 978-0-8021-3307-6; 0-8021-3307-X

LC 93-8656

Contents: Garden party; Memorandum; Increased difficulty of concentration; Audience (Conversation); Unveiling (Private view); Protest; Mistake

"Gathered together here for the first time are seven plays that span Havel's career from his early days at the Theater of the Balustrade through the Prague Spring, Charter 77, and the repeated imprisonments that made Havel's name into a rallying cry and propelled him to the leadership of his country." Publisher's note

Herbert, Zbigniew

The collected poems, 1956-1998; translated and edited by Alissa Valles; with additional translations by Czesław Miłosz and Peter Dale Scott; introduction by Adam Zagajewski. Ecco Press 2007 600p $34.95 **891.8**

1. Poetry—By individual authors

ISBN 978-0-06-078390-7; 0-06-078390-7

LC 2006-40856

This volume "contains the nine collections of poetry that Herbert published in his lifetime, most of them put into English by Alissa Valles with the exception of seventy-nine poems translated by Czeslaw Milosz and Peter Dale Scott, which were first published as Selected Poems in the Penguin Modern European Poets series in 1968." N Y Rev Books

Herbert is a "titan of not only Polish poetry, but of twentieth-century European poetry. His celebrated alter ego, Mr. Cogito, ranks as the one of the most original characters in modern poetry. . . . Herbert lived through the Nazi occupation of 1941 and the Soviet occupations of 1939 and 1944 and was an active member of Poland's underground resistance. Decades later, after marshal law was declared in Poland in 1981, Herbert supported the underground opposition to communism and was an important figure in the Solidarity movement. . . . If Herbert is a political poet, he's political in the way Don Quixote is political. He doesn't make us more aware. He makes us more human." Brooklyn Rail

Miłosz, Czesław, 1911-2004

Legends of modernity; essays and letters from occupied Poland, 1942-1943; translated from the Polish by Madeline G. Levine; introduction by Jaroslaw Anders. Farrar, Straus and Giroux 2005 266p $25 **891.8**

ISBN 0-374-18499-2 LC 2005-40950

Original Polish edition, 1996

"Written to the young intellectual Jerzy Andrejewski, the letters reveal Milosz's concern about the political climate of the era and the deterioration of religious influence owing to the chaos all across Europe and the rest of the world. . . . The essays explore the ideas of William James, André Gide, Stendhal (Henri Beyle), Honoré de Balzac, and others as they relate to religious faith, reason and rationalism, contradictions, doubting, and believing in a civilized world and its religious institutions. . . . Reading Milosz is a demanding, rewarding, and ultimately powerful experience for the mind and the soul." Libr J

Milosz's ABCs; translated from the Polish by Madeline G. Levine. Farrar, Straus & Giroux 2001 313p pa $14 hardcover o.p. * **891.8**

ISBN 0-374-52795-4 (pa) LC 00-42176

"The short prose entries in this quiet book take note of some of the people and places and ideas that contributed to the making of Milosz. The subjects of his sketches range from Alchemy and Curiosity to Rimbaud and Whitman, from childhood friends to Polish intellectuals little known in the West. But what could have been no more than a light memory work becomes almost a registry of gratitude: a meditation on the obligations of having lived a life and the responsibilities inherent in its particulars." New Yorker

Includes bibliographical references

Miłosz, Czesław, 1911-2004—*Continued*

New and collected poems 1931-2001.
HarperCollins Pubs. 2001 xxi, 776p $45; pa
$19.95 * **891.8**
1. Poetry—By individual authors
ISBN 0-06-019667-X; 0-06-051448-5 (pa)
LC 2001-50123
"Milosz has stated repeatedly in his poems his belief
in the power of language to rescue from the void all he
has seen and all the people he has known in a long life.
But beneath this belief, it now appears, was the deeper
belief that none of this was possible because of the inad-
equacy of language to capture reality, though he maintains this always has to be the poet's goal. . . . Throughout his career and throughout this vast collection, Milosz
argues with himself about his poetics." N Y Times Book
Rev

A roadside dog. Farrar, Straus & Giroux 1998
208p pa $14 hardcover o.p. * **891.8**
ISBN 0-374-52623-0 (pa) LC 98-14026
This "book is a collection of reflections, a few
dreams, some poems, and . . . 'Subjects to Let'—ideas
and plots that Milosz, at 87, feels he will never develop
and presents for others to flesh out. Two themes recur in
many of these little writings: the opposition of the inner
life of the mind and emotions and the outer life of the
body and communication; and the occasionally paradoxical nature of personality." Booklist
"Milosz makes a wise, wryly humane fin de siècle
companion." Publ Wkly

To begin where I am; selected essays; edited
and with an introduction by Bogdana Carpenter
and Madeline G. Levine. Farrar, Straus & Giroux
2001 462p pa $15 hardcover o.p. **891.8**
ISBN 0-374-52859-4 (pa) LC 2001-33356
A retrospective of Milosz's "prose works, in which he
weaves autobiography and portraits of people, famous
and otherwise, who have influenced him into graceful
and provocative musings on time, history, religion, science, and art." Booklist
Includes bibliographical references

Szymborska, Wisława, 1923-
Monologue of a dog; new poems; translated
from the Polish by Clare Cavanagh and Stanislaw
Baranczak; [foreword by Billy Collins] Harcourt
2005 96p $22 * **891.8**
ISBN 0-15-101220-2 LC 2005-16084
Original Polish edition, 2002
In this volume, Nobel laureate Szymborska "invites
readers to linger over moments small, earthly, and sometimes life-altering. With characteristically simple language and imagery, wit and irony, she shows us how life
can change at any moment. Hers are the politics of the
everyday, little observations on the value of life." Libr J

Poems, new and collected, 1957-1997; translated
from the Polish by Stanisław Baranczak and Clare
Cavanagh. Harcourt Brace & Co. 1998 273p $27;
pa $17 * **891.8**
ISBN 0-15-100353-X; 0-15-601146-8 (pa)
LC 97-32277

This career-spanning collection by the 1996 Nobel
Prize winner includes her Nobel lecture
Szymborska's "work is ultimately wisdom literature,
written in a first person that expresses a universal humanity that American poets—lockstep individualists all—
haven't dared essay since early in this century." Booklist

View with a grain of sand; selected poems;
translated from the Polish by Stanisław Baranczak
and Clare Cavanagh. Harcourt Brace & Co. 1995
214p $20; pa $14 **891.8**
ISBN 0-15-100153-7; 0-15-600216-7 (pa)
LC 94-36112
This collection by Poland's Nobel laureate "selects
work from seven volumes of poetry that span nearly 40
years. Her eye is sharp and her wit wonderfully wicked.
. . . It is about time more readers found the poetry of
Szymborska, and this collection gives them the opportunity." Libr J

Zagajewski, Adam, 1945-
Eternal enemies; translated from the Polish by
Clare Cavanagh. Farrar, Straus and Giroux 2008
116p $24 **891.8**
1. Poetry—By individual authors
ISBN 978-0-374-21634-4; 0-374-21634-7
LC 2007-42855
This collection "features the usual assortment of
Zagajewski poems—stunning, imagistic remembrances of
childhood; elegies to poets; glancing snapshots of life on
the move, the poet's internal eye-roving, yet always returning to the past. As in Proust, this journey is far more
than a ritual. It is a metaphysical meditation so yearning
it feels like prayer. . . . Zagajewski is a superb
phrasemaker, his lines full of arresting similes and compact metaphors." Newcitychicago.com
"Cavanagh's supple translations let the verse sing in
American English without making this Polish poet sound
too American." Publ Wkly

Without end; new and selected poems;
translations by Clare Cavanagh [et al.] Farrar,
Straus & Giroux 2002 285p $30; pa $15 *
891.8
ISBN 0-374-22096-4; 0-374-52861-6 (pa)
LC 2001-40252
Translated from Polish
"Zagajewski's poetic evolution is clearly charted in
'Without End,' a new anthology of his work that is made
up of his three English-language collections—'Tremor'
(1985), 'Canvas' (1991) and 'Mysticism for Beginners'
(1997)—as well as his most recent work and new translations of some early poems. . . . Zagajewski's poems
pull us from whatever routine threatens to dull our
senses, from whatever might lull us into mere existence.
This is an astonishing book." N Y Times Book Rev

892   Afro-Asiatic literatures. Semitic literatures

Amichai, Yehuda
Open closed open; poems; translated from the Hebrew by Chana Bloch and Chana Kronfeld. Harcourt Brace & Co. 2000 184p $25

892

1. Poetry—By individual authors
ISBN 0-15-100378-5   LC 00-23537
Original Hebrew edition, 1998
"Constructing a lineage in which to place himself, Amichai begins these verses of personal and cultural history with a stone from a destroyed Jewish graveyard; and moves on to enact the story of David, recall poems by Ibn Ezra, and even consider Jesus as an instance of 'Jewish Travel.' Within this vast context, the 25 longish poems of the collection, originally written in Hebrew, offer everyday acts of alternately joyous and sober reverence for God." Publ Wkly
Amichai "writes with the casual wisdom and generous humor of a master." Booklist

Poems of Jerusalem; and, Love poems; a bilingual edition. Sheep Meadow Press 1992 265p pa $16.95

892

1. Poetry—By individual authors
ISBN 1-87881-819-8   LC 92-31558
Poems of Jerusalem first published 1988 by Perennial Lib.; Love poems first published 1981 by Harper & Row
This work is "actually drawn from eight previous works and boasts an even larger array of translators (including Stephen Mitchell, David Rosenberg, Ted Hughes, and the poet himself). The thematic arrangement deftly emphasizes the Israeli poet's constant preoccupation with both Jerusalem and love." Libr J

The selected poetry of Yehuda Amichai; edited and translated from the Hebrew by Chana Bloch and Stephen Mitchell. newly rev & expanded ed. University of Calif. Press 1996 195p pa $16.95

892

1. Poetry—By individual authors
ISBN 0-520-20538-3   LC 96-18580
First published 1986
"Although much of Amichai's poetry focuses on war, he is able to describe its horrors by maintaining a clear distance between himself and his subject. The result is a finely controlled emotional pitch that allows the poet to convey his sense of pain and outrage without pathos or sentimentality. He writes colloquially, in language that is always commensurate with emotional experience." Reader's Ency. 4th edition

Gilgamesh.
Gilgamesh; a new English version [by] Stephen Mitchell. Free Press 2004 290p $25; pa $14 *

892

ISBN 0-7432-6164-X; 0-7432-6169-0 (pa)
LC 2004-50072
"Relying on existing translations (and in places where there are gaps, on his own imagination), Mitchell seeks

language that is as swift and strong as the story itself. . . . This wonderful new version of the story of Gilgamesh shows how the story came to achieve literary immortality—not because it is a rare ancient artifact, but because reading it can make people in the here and now feel more completely alive." Publ Wkly
Includes bibliographical references

892.7   Arabic literature

Anthology of modern Palestinian literature; edited and introduced by Salma Khadra Jayyusi. Columbia Univ. Press 1992 xxxiii, 744p hardcover o.p. pa $30.50   **892.7**
1. Arabic literature—Collections
ISBN 0-231-07508-1; 0-231-07509-X (pa)
LC 92-5189
"Presented here are translations of poems, stories, and excerpts from novels, as well as works by Palestinian poets who write in English. Also included are personal narratives by Palestinian writers depicting the varied aspects of Palestinian life from the turn of the century to the present. . . . Biographical sketches introduce the authors, and a chronology of modern Palestinian history provides background for some of the events and places referred to in the selections. The introduction by the editor provides a concise but comprehensive political history of Palestinian literature during the twentieth century." Publisher's note

Includes bibliographical references

Darwish, Maḥmūd, 1942-2008
Unfortunately, it was paradise; selected poems; translated and edited by Munir Akash and Carolyn Forche, with Sinan Antoon and Amira El-Zein. University of California Press 2003 191p pa $18.95   **892.7**
1. Poetry—By individual authors
ISBN 978-0-520-23754-4   LC 2002-68454
"As the Palestinian poet Mahmoud Darwish has observed, Palestine is a metaphor for the loss of Eden, for the sorrows of dispossession and exile, for the declining power of the Arab world in its dealings with the West. Mr. Darwish, who is widely considered the Palestinian national poet, has developed this metaphor to richly lyrical effect . . . . Like Yehuda Amichai, the Israeli poet he read in Hebrew as a young man, Mr. Darwish has given expression to his people's ordinary longings and desires." N Y Times Book Rev

Night and horses and the desert; an anthology of classical Arabic literature; edited by Robert Irwin. Anchor Books 2001 462p pa $16
892.7
1. Arabic literature—Collections 2. Arabic literature—History and criticism
ISBN 0-385-72155-2   LC 2001-53721
First published 2000 by Overlook Press
This "anthology presents a wide range of classical Arabic poetry and prose, covering the fifth to the 16th centuries from Afghanistan to Andalusia, Spain." Libr J
"The chapter on the Qur'an is perhaps the most essential as it examines just how vital the dogma of Islam has

Night and horses and the desert—*Continued*
been for the Arabic understanding of culture and art.
. . . This persuasive work will surely fill in the gap in
the study of Arabic literature in this country." Publ Wkly

Includes bibliographical references

The **Poetry** of Arab women; a contemporary
anthology; edited by Nathalie Handal. Interlink
Bks. 2000 xxi, 355p pa $22   **892.7**
1. Arabic poetry—Collections
ISBN 978-1-56656-374-1; 1-56656-374-7
                                          LC 00-58054
An anthology of "over 80 poets writing in Arabic,
French, English and other languages, and living in Syria,
Saudi Arabia, Lebanon, Yemen, Gaza and the U.S.
[Handal provides an] introduction, along with biographi-
cal notes on the poets and many translators." Booklist
  "Handal deserves high praise for producing an anthol-
ogy that mirrors faithfully Arab women's creative role
throughout the last century." Multicultural Rev

895.1   Chinese literature

An **Anthology** of Chinese literature; beginnings to
1911; edited and translated by Stephen Owen.
Norton 1996 xlviii, 1212p pa $59.65 hardcover
o.p.   **895.1**
1. Chinese literature—Collections
ISBN 0-393-97106-6 (pa)   LC 95-11409
  "In a book that moves roughly chronologically
through the tradition, Owen gathers texts according to
genres, themes, forms, and other groupings to show the
way essential texts build off each other and how the tradition echoes itself. Included are a range of forms . . .
presented . . . {with} commentary to provide a . . .
view of the interplay between Chinese literature, culture,
and history." Publisher's note

Includes bibliographical references

Anthology of modern Chinese poetry; edited and
translated by Michelle Yeh. Yale Univ. Press
1993 245p pa $21 hardcover o.p.   **895.1**
1. Chinese poetry—Collections
ISBN 0-300-05947-7 (pa)   LC 92-16322
Published with assistance from Mary Cady Tew Memorial Fund
  "Arranged chronologically, this selection of twentieth-
century poetry from China and Taiwan offers a few poems by each of 67 poets born between 1891 and 1963.
Its scope is enormous, its range impressive. Editor Yeh's
translations are accessible and fluid; her introduction and
notes are helpful without being overbearingly scholarly."
Booklist

Includes bibliographical references

The **Columbia** book of Chinese poetry; from early
times to the thirteenth century; translated and
edited by Burton Watson. Columbia Univ. Press
1984 385p il (Translations from the Oriental
classics) $69; pa $27   **895.1**
1. Chinese poetry—Collections
ISBN 0-231-05682-6; 0-231-05683-4 (pa)
                                          LC 83-26182

This anthology's "arrangement is historical, beginning
with selections from a first millenium BC collection of
Chinese verse (the Shih ching), and ending with tz'u lyrics from the Sung period (AD 960-1279). The 12 selections [are] each prefaced with a two- or three-page introduction." Choice

Includes bibliographical references

The **Columbia** history of Chinese literature; Victor
H. Mair, editor. Columbia Univ. Press 2001 xx,
1342p $78   **895.1**
1. Chinese literature—History and criticism
ISBN 0-231-10984-9   LC 2001-28236
This "history explores a wide range of Chinese literature, from the classics to humor to folk tales to oral traditions, and moves from ancient times to the end of the
20th century. . . . Mair has overseen a host of excellent
scholars writing on a vast subject." Libr J

Includes bibliographical references

Mountain home; the wilderness poetry of ancient
China; selected and translated by David Hinton.
New Directions Pub. 2005 xxi, 295p map pa
$17.95   **895.1**
1. Chinese poetry—Collections
ISBN 978-0-8112-1624-1   LC 2005-869
First published 2002 by Counterpoint
  "Translator and scholar Hinton ensures that Western
readers will experience this supreme collection of Chinese rivers-and-mountains (shan-shui) poetry at the deepest possible level by succinctly explaining the cosmology
inherent in this vital and profoundly influential tradition.
The keys to understanding the elegant poetry of such
masters as T'ao Ch'ien (365-427), Li Po (701-762), and
Lu Yu (1125-1210) are realizing that they perceive no
divide between the human and what we call nature, or
between being and nonbeing. . . . Oneness with life at
its purest is the desired mode for these thoughtful, yet
often playful, poets, and dwelling within these meditative
pages is the first step on the way there." Booklist

The **New** Directions anthology of classical chinese
poetry; edited by Eliot Weinberger; translations
by William Carlos Williams . . . [et al.] New
Directions 2003 xxvii, 242p $24.95; pa $16.95
                                                   895.1
1. Chinese poetry—Collections
ISBN   978-0-8112-1540-4;   0-8112-1540-7;
978-0-8112-1605-0 (pa); 0-8112-1605-5 (pa)
                                          LC 2002-156731
The poems are "translated into English by four of the
best-known American poets of the 20th century—Ezra
Pound, William Carlos Williams, Kenneth Rexroth and
Gary Snyder—and an academic scholar/translator called
David Hinton, who deserves to be as well known as the
others. It is not often that an anthology really demands
attention. . . . This poetry means what it says. It feels
companionable, and even sexy. It is not excessively—or
confusingly—metaphorical. It is not foggy with abstract
philosophising. It lacks the shriek of rhetoric; it seems to
move, so often, at an agreeable walking pace. It feels
spacious. In fact, there seems to be space between the
words themselves. It mixes the high and the low with
seeming ease. Its temper suggests that there is no unsuit-
able subject matter for poetry at all." New Statesman

The **Shorter** Columbia anthology of traditional Chinese literature; Victor H. Mair, editor. Columbia Univ. Press 2000 xxx, 741p map (Translations from the Asian classics) $65; pa $26 **895.1**

1. Chinese literature—Collections
ISBN 0-231-11998-4; 0-231-11999-2 (pa)

LC 00-35878

Abridged version of Columbia anthology of traditional Chinese literature, published 1994

Texts translated from the Chinese

This "abridged volume, which, like the original includes selections of Chinese literature from the beginnings to 1919 . . . retains the characteristics of the original in that it is arranged according to genre rather than chronology and interprets 'literature' very broadly to include not just literary fiction, poetry, and drama, but folk and popular literature, lyrics and arias, elegies and rhapsodies, biographies, autobiographies and memoirs, letters, criticism and theory, and travelogues and jokes. It also contains fresh translations by newer voices in the field." Publisher's note

Includes bibliographical references

895.6 Japanese literature

Keene, Donald, 1922-
Five modern Japanese novelists. Columbia Univ. Press 2002 113p $26 **895.6**

1. Japanese literature—History and criticism
ISBN 0-231-12610-7 LC 2002-73412

Contents: Preface; Tanizaki Jun'ichiro (1886-1965); Kawabata Yasunari (1899-1972); Mishima Yukio (1925-1970); Abe Kobo (1924-1993); Shiba Ryotaro (1923-1996); Supplemental Readings; Index

In this discussion of the lives and works of five 20th century Japanese novelists, the author recounts personal "anecdotes, telling the stories of their first meetings, and sharing his initial impressions. . . . He [also] mentions their best-known works and discusses some of the controversies surrounding them." Libr J

The author's essays, "part memoir and part literary evaluation, are ideal introductions to their subjects." Booklist

Includes bibliographical references

The pleasures of Japanese literature. Columbia Univ. Press 1988 133p il (Companion to Asian studies) $60; pa $19.50 **895.6**

1. Japanese literature—History and criticism
ISBN 0-231-06736-4; 0-231-06737-2 (pa)

LC 88-18069

The author discusses Japanese aesthetics, poetry, fiction and drama, focusing on works of the premodern period

"If your library has no other introduction to the Japanese classics, nor any need for another, this is the one it ought to include." Booklist

Includes bibliographical references

Seeds in the heart; Japanese literature from earliest times to the late sixteenth century; with a new preface by the author, Donald Keene. Columbia University Press 1999 1265p (History of Japanese literature) pa $37 **895.6**

1. Japanese literature—History and criticism
ISBN 0-231-11441-9 LC 99-25990

First published 1993 by Holt & Co.

This volume completes the author's history of Japanese literature begun with: World within walls (1977) and Dawn to the West (1984).

"The first half of 'Seeds in the Heart' encompasses everything from the myths, legends, songs and poems of the eighth-century 'Kojiki' ('Record of Ancient Matters') and 'Manyoshu,' a collection of 4,500 poems, to the 'The Tale of Genji' and later works of fiction. . . . During Japan's middle ages (1185-1600), Buddhism and popular (rather than aristocratic) forms of storytelling and theater generated a repertory of characters and genres that would eventually form the country's first broadly based, national culture. The literature of these centuries has rarely attracted the scholarly attention paid to the earlier 'high' classical tradition. So Mr. Keene's attention to this period makes the second half of 'Seeds in the Heart' especially valuable." N Y Times Book Rev

Includes bibliographical references

Modern Japanese literature; an anthology; compiled and edited by Donald Keene. Grove Press 1960 c1956 440p pa $15.95 hardcover o.p. **895.6**

1. Japanese literature—Collections
ISBN 0-8021-5095-0 (pa)

"The selections give a representative sampling of the poetry, prose, and drama from the 1870's through the 1940's. Short enlightening notes on the writers or background for the text are added unobtrusively." Booklist

One hundred poems from the Japanese; {edited and translated} by Kenneth Rexroth. New Directions 1956 143p pa $11.95 hardcover o.p. **895.6**

1. Japanese poetry—Collections
ISBN 0-8112-0181-3 (pa)

Also available: One hundred more poems from the Japanese pa $8.95 (ISBN 0-8112-0619-X)

A bilingual collection of poems drawn chiefly from the traditional Manyōshu, Kokinshū, and Hyakunin Isshu collections and also containing examples of haiku and other later forms. The translator's introduction provides background information on the history and nature of Japanese poetry

Includes bibliographical references

Waley, Arthur, 1889-1966
The Nō plays of Japan; an anthology. Dover Publications 1998 270p pa $12.95 **895.6**

1. Nō plays
ISBN 978-0-486-40156-0 LC 97-46053

First published 1921 in the United Kingdom; first United States edition published 1922 by Knopf

Contains translation of 20 No plays and summaries of 16 more. In his introduction Mr. Waley gives a brief history of the No drama, its origin, the text of the plays,

Waley, Arthur, 1889-1966—*Continued*

and the chief playwrights. He also tells about the stage settings, costumes and properties used in the production of these plays. The greatest representation is given to the works of Seami and Zenchiku Ujinobu

896   African literatures

The **New** African poetry; an anthology; edited by Tanure Ojaide, Tijan M. Sallah. Lynne Rienner Pubs. 1999 253p hardcover o.p. pa $19.95 *

        896

1. African poetry—Collections
ISBN 978-0-89410-891-4; 0-89410-891-3

        LC 99-29889

"A Three continents book"

In this anthology the editors "group poets by region. . . . Most of these 62 well-educated postcolonial poets more willingly embrace the ancestral 'oratory' tradition of the African continent than poets with a Western literary orientation of the era of Leopold Senghor and Wole Soyinka. Instead of anti-colonialism, these poets focus on women's roles, rural life, and the need for creativity despite economic hardships. Realistic criticism of patriarchies and traditional taboos arises from a strong attachment to homeland. Overall, regional diversity seems to have replaced defensiveness of Pan-African unity." Libr J

The **Penguin** book of modern African poetry; edited by Gerald Moore and Ulli Beier. 4th ed. Penguin Books 2007 c1998 xxvi, 448p pa $17

        896

1. African poetry—Collections
ISBN 978-0-14-042472-0; 0-14-042472-5

First published 1963 in the United Kingdom with title: Modern poetry from Africa

This anthology includes over 200 poems by 67 poets from 23 countries.

Includes bibliographical references

897   Literatures of North American native languages

The **Cambridge** companion to Native American literature; edited by Joy Porter and Kenneth M. Roemer. Cambridge University Press 2005 343p il map hardcover o.p. pa $26.95   **897**

1. Native American literature—History and criticism
ISBN 978-0-521-52979-2 (pa); 0-521-52979-4 (pa)

        LC 2005-44298

Essays organized "by historical and cultural context, by genre, and according to individual authors. Particularly insightful and informative are the tightly written essays on the eight currently best-known Indian writers. Also included are maps, a time line, suggested readings, and a brief series of 40 biobibliographies of notable Native American writers. . . . Readers of this volume should probably already have a working knowledge of the main figures in this increasingly important and respected segment of American literature." Libr J

900   HISTORY

901   Philosophy and theory of history

Berlin, Sir Isaiah

The sense of reality; studies in ideas and their history; edited by Henry Hardy; with an introduction by Patrick Gardiner. Farrar, Straus & Giroux 1997 xx, 278p pa $13 hardcover o.p. *

        901

1. History—Philosophy
ISBN 0-374-52569-2 (pa)   LC 96-39829

First published 1996 in the United Kingdom

Berlin maintains that "the great goods of human life are diverse and conflicting. . . . Values like self-realization and social cohesion, economic progress and settled communities cannot always be made compatible. Sometimes we must choose between them. In the nine seminal essays collected in 'The Sense of Reality' ranging over such diverse subjects as the Romantic movement, Marxism, Kant's influence on nationalism and the thought of Rabindranath Tagore, Berlin argues with rare wisdom and passion that every such choice entails a loss." N Y Times Book Rev

Includes bibliographical references

Hobsbawm, E. J. (Eric J.), 1917-

On history. New Press (NY) 1997 305p $25; pa $15.95   **901**

1. Historiography
ISBN 1-56584-393-2; 1-56584-468-8 (pa)

"In these collected pieces—articles, lectures and reviews—Eric Hobsbawm surveys the writings of modern historians with the magisterial gaze of a man who has seen both the rise of Hitler and the fall of Communism. He notes how the discipline has changed in the last century: how social history and economic history have come of age, how modern historians speak of change and forces where Victorians spoke of ideas and progress. He rejects postmodernist claims that history can be freely revised because all facts are merely intellectual constructions." N Y Times Book Rev

Spengler, Oswald, 1880-1936

The decline of the West, volume one; Form and actuality; authorized translation with notes by Charles Frances Atkinson. A. Knopf 1996 various paging $45   **901**

1. History—Philosophy 2. Civilization—History
ISBN 0-394-42179-5

Volumes one and two also available in one abridged paperback edition both from Vintage Bks. (ISBN: 1-4000-9700-2) and from Oxford Univ. Press

First published 1926

Volume one of a two-volume set; v2 o.p.

The first volume of a work that "reflects the pessimistic atmosphere in Germany after World War I. Spengler maintained that history has a natural development, in which every culture is a distinct organic form that grows, matures, and decays." Reader's Ency. 4th edition

Includes bibliographical references

902 Miscellany of history

Grun, Bernard, 1901-1972
The timetables of history; a historical linkage of people and events. 4th ed. Simon & Schuster 2005 835p $25 *   **902**
1. Historical chronology
ISBN 0-7432-7003-7; 978-0-7432-7003-8
    LC 2005-49766
"A Touchstone book"
Original German edition, 1946; first published in the United States 1975
"Based on Werner Stein's Kulturfahrplan"
This chronology "includes material from 4500 BCE to 2004. . . . The information is listed by year in seven columns labeled 'History, Politics', 'Literature, Theater', 'Religion, Philosophy, Learning', 'Visual Arts', 'Music', 'Science, Technology, Growth', and 'Daily Life.' . . . This work is an excellent chronological tool, and should be found in all libraries." Choice

National Geographic concise history of the world; an illustrated timeline; edited by Neil Kagan. National Geographic Society 2005 416p il map $40 *   **902**
1. Historical chronology
ISBN 0-792-28364-3   LC 2005-52248
This history is organized in time line format and broken up into eight historical eras. Includes maps, sidebars, and illustrations.
Includes bibliographical references

National Geographic visual history of the world; [authors, Klaus Berndl . . . et al.] National Geographic Society 2005 656p il $35
    902
1. World history
ISBN 0-7922-3695-5   LC 2005-541553
"Over 4,000 illustrations and photographs cover individuals and events from prehistory (the beginning to ca. 4000 BCE) to the contemporary world (1945 to the present). . . . This educational and entertaining volume of social, cultural, and military history will appeal to a wide readership." Choice

Stewart, Robert, 1941-
Mysteries of history; [by] Robert Stewart, with Clint Twist and Edward Horton. National Geographic Society 2003 191p il $29.95
    902
1. History—Miscellanea
ISBN 0-7922-6232-8   LC 2003-11268
"A Marshall ed"
Examines part, but not all, of the evidence surrounding some of history's unsolved mysteries, from why the pyramids were built to whether or not there was a conspiracy to kill President John F. Kennedy.
"Attractive enough for browsing, this volume is a good starting place for exploring any of the questions raised, and the extensive bibliography suggests books for further reading on each topic." Booklist

Teeple, John B., 1928-
Timelines of world history. DK Pub. 2002 666p il map hardcover o.p. pa $30   **902**
1. Historical chronology
ISBN 0-7894-8926-0; 0-7566-1703-0 (pa)
    LC 2002-73896
"This volume uses time lines to provide 'a visual chronicle of human history and development' from 10,000 B.C.E. to the present. Time lines appear in four columns—one each for Asia, Africa, Europe, and the Americas and Australasia—and are accompanied by gorgeous illustrations and maps. The outer column of each page has sidebars containing summaries of key events, condensed biographies, or descriptions of places." Booklist
"This superb reference tool will be especially appreciated in smaller libraries." Voice Youth Advocates

The **timetables** of American history; Laurence Urdang, editor; with an introduction by Henry Steele Commager and a new foreword by Arthur Schlesinger, Jr. Simon & Schuster [2001] c1996 534p il pa $24   **902**
1. Historical chronology
ISBN 0-7432-0261-9
"A Touchstone book"
First published 1982
"A Laurence Urdang reference book" Verso of title page
Presents information chronologically in tabular form. Each double-page spread has columns for history and politics, the arts, science and technology, and miscellaneous.

Williams, Hywel
Cassell's chronology of world history; dates, events and ideas that made history. Weidenfeld & Nicolson 2005 752p $39.95 *   **902**
1. Historical chronology
ISBN 0-304-35730-8
"Starting with the earliest human fossils, discovered in Ethiopia, the book settles into a sequential listing of the leading events of world history through the early 21st century. The text is arranged into four major sections—'The Ancient and Medieval Worlds, 135,000 B.P.–1449,' 'The Early Modern World, 1450-1799,' 'The Nineteenth Century World, 1800-1899,' and 'The Modern World, 1900-2004'—each of which is subdivided by continent and such categories as 'Economy and Society,' 'Science and Technology,' and 'Arts and Humanities.'" Libr J

The **Wilson** calendar of world history; edited by John Paxton and Edward W. Knappman; contributors: Rodney Carlisle [et al.] Wilson, H.W. 1999 460p il $100   **902**
1. Historical chronology 2. Calendars
ISBN 0-8242-0937-0   LC 98-50998
"A New England Publishing Associates book"
"Based on S.H. Steinberg's Historical table." Title page
This successor to Steinberg's chronology reports on 25,000 historical events and includes expanded coverage of the arts and sciences as well as events in Latin America, Asia, and Africa. Includes index for people, places,

The Wilson calendar of world history—*Continued*
events, concepts, inventions, discoveries, and titles of works.

Includes bibliographical references

903   Dictionaries, encyclopedias, concordances of history

Berkshire encyclopedia of world history; William H. McNeill, senior editor; Jerry H. Bentley [et al.] editorial board. Berkshire Pub. Group 2004 5v set $525   **903**
1. World history—Encyclopedias
ISBN 0-97430-910-9
This encyclopedia traces "the development of human history—with a focus on area studies, global history, anthropology, geography, science, arts, literature, economics, women's studies, African-American studies, and cultural studies related to all regions of the world." Publisher's note
For a review see: Booklist, Jan. 1 & 15, 2005

Encyclopedia of world history. Facts on File 2000 524p il maps $93.50   **903**
1. World history—Encyclopedias 2. History—Outlines, syllabi, etc.
ISBN 0-8160-4249-7   LC 00-34721
Editorial Board: Patrick K. O'Brien
"The 6,500 entries are alphabetical with cross-references and include colored maps, paintings, photographs, charts, and tables. Difficult-to-find topics, such as regions of Russia and the Balkans, Africa, and Oceania, are covered through the year 2000. The article on former President Bill Clinton discusses his full term. Interesting quotes from famous people accompany the articles, usually with illustrations." Voice Youth Advocates

904   Collected accounts of events

Davis, Lee Allyn
Man-made catastrophes; [by] Lee Davis. rev ed. Facts on File 2002 402p il $60   **904**
1. Disasters
ISBN 0-8160-4418-X   LC 2001-54324
"Facts on File science library"
First published 1993
This describes man-made disasters "from the burning of Babylon in 538B.C. to the 2001 terrorist attack on the World Trade Center in New York City. . . . [The entries] are organized by disaster type: air crashes, civil unrest and terrorism, explosions, maritime disasters, nuclear and industrial accidents, railway disasters, and space disasters." Publisher's note
Includes bibliographical references

Hanson, Victor Davis
Carnage and culture; landmark battles in the rise of Western power. Doubleday 2001 492p il pa $16 hardcover o.p.   **904**
1. Battles 2. Military history
ISBN 0-385-72038-6 (pa)   LC 00-65582

Published in the UK with title: Why the west has won
The author analyzes nine battles and "maintains that Western nations are the world's best when it comes to waging war. From Salamis in 480 B.C.E. to the Tet offensive in 1968, Western forces have prevailed." Libr J
"This provocative work is likely to engender controversy." Booklist
Includes bibliographical references

907   Education, research, related topics of history

Hamilton, Nigel, 1944-
Biography; a brief history. Harvard University Press 2007 345p il $21.95 *   **907**
1. Biography as a literary form
ISBN 978-0-674-02466-3; 0-674-02466-4
                                            LC 2006-51132
This book traces the "historical evolution of biography from the ancient world to the present." Publisher's note
"Hamilton has given readers a thoughtprovoking look at biography in its various forms; a fascinating and handy reference book for anyone wishing to know more about the history and art of biography." Libr J
Includes bibliographical references

Mills, Elizabeth S.
Evidence explained; citing history sources from artifacts to cyberspace; [by] Elizabeth Shown Mills. Genealogical Pub. Co. 2007 885p $49.95
                                            907
1. History—Sources 2. History—Research
ISBN 978-0-8063-1781-6   LC 2007-19749
This is a "guide to citing and analyzing historical records of all types. . . . It outlines foundational issues of evidence and citation analysis and then details the citation of specific types of materials. These include archival records and artifacts; business and organizational records; census information; local and national governmental records; property and probate records; books, compact discs, leaflets, and videos; miscellaneous legal documents; and periodicals, media broadcasts, and Web-based materials." Choice
"This is an essential resource for family historians; highly recommended for all libraries." Libr J
Includes bibliographical references

Schama, Simon
Dead certainties; unwarranted speculations. Knopf 1991 333p pa $16 hardcover o.p.
                                            907
1. Wolfe, James, 1727-1759 2. Parkman, Francis, 1823-1893 3. Parkman, George, 1790-1849 4. Historiography
ISBN 0-679-73613-1 (pa)   LC 90-52902
This exploration of the nature of historical writing consists of two stories. The first one "is concerned with the battlefield death of James Wolfe, British commander in the North American campaign of the Seven Years' War; the second with the murder ninety years later of a Harvard Medical School professor, George Parkman." New Repub

Tuchman, Barbara Wertheim
Practicing history; selected essays; by Barbara
W. Tuchman. Knopf 1981 306p pa $14.95
hardcover o.p. **907**
1. Historiography 2. Modern history
ISBN 0-345-30363-6 (pa)   LC 81-47509
A collection of essays on the nature, methodology and
writing of history

909   World history

Africana: the encyclopedia of the African and
African American experience; editors, Kwame
Anthony Appiah, Henry Louis Gates, Jr. 2nd ed.
Oxford University Press 2005 5v set $550 *
                                              909
1. Blacks—Encyclopedias 2. African diaspora—Ency-
clopedias 3. African Americans—Encyclopedias
4. Africa—Encyclopedias
ISBN 978-0-19-517055-9; 0-19-517055-5
                                    LC 2004-20222
First published 1999 by Basic Civitas Bks.
This encyclopedia covers "prominent individuals,
events, trends, places, political movements, art forms,
business and trade, religions, ethnic groups, organizations, and countries on both sides of the ocean. . . .
There are articles on contemporary nations of sub-
Saharan Africa, ethnic groups from various regions of
Africa, African American Academy award winners, Ca-
ribbean musical styles, African religions in Brazil, and
European colonial powers." Booklist [review of 1999
edition]
Includes bibliographical references

Boorstin, Daniel J., 1914-2004
The creators. Random House 1992 811p il
hardcover o.p. pa $18.95   **909**
1. Civilization 2. Arts 3. Creation (Literary, artistic,
etc.)
ISBN 0-394-54395-5; 0-679-74375-8 (pa)
                                    LC 91-39948
In this volume "Boorstin undertakes an interpretive
history of creativity in Western civilization. Packed with
shrewd, entertaining profiles of Dante, Goethe, Benjamin
Franklin and dozens of others, this stimulating synthesis
sets the achievements of individual geniuses into a coherent narrative of humanity's advance from ignorance."
Publ Wkly
Includes bibliographical references

Brenner, Frédéric, 1959-
Diaspora: homelands in exile. HarperCollins
2003 2v il map set $100   **909**
1. Jews—Pictorial works
ISBN 0-06-008778-1   LC 2003-42328
Contents: v1: Photographs -- v2: Voices
This is a "collection of photographs, taken over the
course of 25 years, chronicling Jewish lives, often in de-
clining communities, in every corner of the world, from
Azerbaijan and Uzbekistan to Ethiopia and Las Vegas.
For anyone, Jewish or otherwise, who generally thinks of
Jews in terms of Israel and the United States, the book
will be a revelation." Publ Wkly
Includes bibliographical references

Britain and the Americas; culture, politics, and
history: a multidisciplinary encyclopedia; edited
by Wil Kaufman and Heidi Slettedahl
Macpherson. ABC-CLIO 2005 3v il
(Transatlantic relations series) set $270
                                              909
1. America—History—Encyclopedias 2. Great Britain—History—Encyclopedias
ISBN 1-85109-431-8   LC 2004-24655
Also available as an e-book
"Included in the scope of this interdisciplinary work
are historical events (Boston Tea Party, Falklands War,
Yalta Conference); places (Brazil, Jamestown, Ontario);
and economic, social, political, and cultural forces (Fur
trade; Nuclear weapons; Reggae; Slave trade, Atlantic;
Treaties, Britain-U.S.). . . . There are more than 400
signed entries in alphabetical order, and each includes
see also's and references. The entries average about two
pages, with the longest, Cold War and Explorers, British
in the Americas, at seven pages each. There is one combined subject and person index in volume 3. While the
references are helpful and well researched, the work
could benefit from one comprehensive bibliography. Well
written and engaging enough to be used for research or
to be read on its own for enjoyment's sake." Booklist

Brown, Cynthia Stokes
A big history; from the Big Bang to the present.
Distributed by W.W. Norton 2007 288p il map
$25.95   **909**
1. World history 2. Human ecology
ISBN 978-1-59558-196-9; 1-59558-196-0
                                    LC 2007-6741
"In a multidisciplinary narrative subtly emphasizing
the mutual impact of people and planet, Brown covers
Earth's history from the big bang through the development of life and the growth of civilization. . . . This exciting saga crosses space and time to illustrate how humans, born of stardust, were shaped—and how they in
turn shaped the world we know today." Publ Wkly

Cahill, Thomas, 1940-
The gifts of the Jews; how a tribe of desert
nomads changed the way everyone thinks and
feels. Talese 1998 291p (Hinges of history)
$23.50; pa $14   **909**
1. Bible. O.T. —History of Biblical events
2. Judaism—History 3. Jews—History
ISBN 0-385-48248-5; 0-385-48249-3 (pa)
                                    LC 97-45139
In this colloquial look at the influence of the Hebrew
Bible on civilization, the author gives "the Jews credit
for revolutionizing the concepts of democracy, universal
law, monotheism, linear time, personal vocation, destiny,
self-improvement and the belief in the equality of all humans. He stumbles on the odd aside and occasionally is
surprisingly insensitive. . . Still, his passion and breadth
of knowledge are admirable." N Y Times Book Rev
Includes bibliographical references

Cahill, Thomas, 1940-—*Continued*
Sailing the wine-dark sea; why the Greeks matter. Talese 2003 304p (Hinges of history) $27.50; pa $14.95   **909**
1. Greece—Civilization
ISBN 0-385-49553-6; 0-385-49554-4 (pa)
                                        LC 2003-50725
This author "begins with a discussion of Homer's *Iliad* and *Odyssey* and how these two epic poems relate to the history of Greece. He then focuses on such themes as the Greek alphabet, literature, and political system, and its playwrights, philosophers, and artists. A final chapter examines the effects that Greco-Roman and Judeo-Christian traditions had on each other." Booklist
Includes bibliographical references

The **Cambridge** illustrated history of the Islamic world; edited by Francis Robinson. Cambridge Univ. Press 1996 xxiii, 328p il maps hardcover o.p. pa $36.99   **909**
1. Islamic countries—History
ISBN 0-521-43510-2; 0-521-66993-6 (pa)
                                        LC 95-37562
"Facts about Islam's history and practice are presented, along with its economic, societal, and intellectual structures. Excellent graphics support the text. Maps are extensive and exact." SLJ
Includes bibliographical references

Cultures of the Jews; a new history; edited with an introduction by David Biale. Schocken Bks. 2002 xxxiii, 1196p il $45 *   **909**
1. Jews—History 2. Jewish civilization
ISBN 0-8052-4131-0   LC 2002-23008
"The book is split into three main sections: 'Ancient Mediterranean Origins,' 'Diversities of Diaspora,' and 'Modern Encounters.' Within this framework, leading scholars such as Isaiah Gafni, Aron Rodrigue, and Stephen Whitfield contribute broad essays examining the development of Jewish culture in different contexts. Interactions between Jewish and non-Jewish cultures form an important subtext for the essays, as scholars outline the latest thinking about gender, language, religion, drama, and literature in Jewish history. The book pays equal attention to the Sephardic and Ashkenazic experiences and finishes with significant essays on American, European, and non-European Jewries." Choice
"The book is truly one of the most important works on the subject ever published." Booklist
Includes bibliographical references

Encyclopedia of Islam and the Muslim world; edited by Richard C. Martin. Macmillan Reference USA 2004 2v il map set $295   **909**
1. Islam—Encyclopedias
ISBN 0-02-865603-2   LC 2003-9964
This encyclopedia "provides an interdisciplinary examination of the 1400-year-old tradition, which began with prophet Mohammed's revelation. It not only addresses core tenets of Islamic beliefs but also broaches how the Muslim vision interacts with or relates to other major world religions." Libr J
"A solid choice for libraries needing a general treatment of Islam in sufficient detail." Choice
Includes bibliographical references

Encyclopedia of the developing world; Thomas M. Leonard, editor. Routledge 2005 3v set $625   **909**
1. Developing countries—Encyclopedias
ISBN 1-57958-388-1   LC 2005-49976
The entries "detail developments from 1945 forward. In addition to basic statistical and geographical information, country-focused entries detail history, economy, and political situation. Thematic entries cover people (e.g., Jomo Kenyatta), historical topics (e.g., colonialism), economic and government models (e.g., communism), the environment (e.g., water) and organizations (e.g., WTO)." Libr J
Includes bibliographical references

Fargues, Philippe
The atlas of the Arab world; [by] Philippe Fargues & Rafic Boustani. Facts on File 1991 144p il maps $55   **909**
1. Arab countries
ISBN 0-8160-2346-8   LC 89-675447
"Translation by Darla Rudy," "Copyright 1990 by Bordas S.A., Paris; translation copyright 1991 by Facts on File" Verso of title page
"A wealth of information presented in colorful maps, graphs, diagrams, and charts. Arranged by broad cultural topics such as ethnic groups and religions, society, cities, oil and industry, facts not readily available in standard resources are presented and compared." SLJ
Includes bibliographical references

Ferguson, Niall
Empire: the rise and demise of the British world order and the lessons for global power. Basic Books 2003 392p il map pa $17.95 hardcover o.p.   **909**
1. Imperialism 2. Great Britain—Colonies 3. Great Britain—Foreign relations 4. Commonwealth countries
ISBN 0-465-02329-0 (pa)   LC 2003-41469
First published 2002 in the United Kingdom
The author "sees America as both the offspring of and heir to Britain's global domination and traces key features of the modern world—capitalism, education, parliamentary democracy—to four centuries of British expansion." N Y Times Book Rev
This book "is ambitious, provocative, and entertaining—a rare hat trick in the genre of historical writing—in its meticulous charting of the rise and fall of the world's largest empire. . . . Ferguson makes a subtle, but impressive, argument that free trade, the English language, and superior education helped improve the lot of those under colonial rule." Natl Rev
Includes bibliographical references

Freeman, Charles, 1947-
Egypt, Greece, and Rome; civilizations of the ancient Mediterranean. 2nd ed. Oxford Univ. Press 2004 688p $29.95 *   **909**
1. Mediterranean civilization
ISBN 0-19-926364-7   LC 2004-41505
First published 1996

Freeman, Charles, 1947-—*Continued*

Freeman's "introduction to the ancient Mediterranean adds Egypt to the standard Greco-Roman nexus. Covering an immense variety of material with competence and sensitivity to nuance, Freeman relates the familiar parts of the classical story, but his is no mere rehash of the Persian War or the fall of the Roman Republic. He analytically recounts political events, religious movements, and society, with steady awareness of the fragmented character of the surviving evidence." Booklist [review of 1996 edition]

Includes bibliographical references

Great events from history, The 17th century, 1601-1700; editor, Larissa Juliet Taylor. Salem Press 2005 2v il map set $160   **909**
1. World history—17th century
ISBN 1-58765-225-0; 978-1-58765-225-7
LC 2005-17362
Also available online
Companion volume to Great lives from history, The 17th century, 1601-1700
Some of the essays in this work were originally published in Chronology of European history, 15,000 B.C. to 1997 (1997) and Great events from history: North American series. Rev. ed. (1997)
This set "offers two to three-page essays that detail the major milestones of the century as well as social developments that were reflective of daily life during the period. The perspective here is international and spans a variety of categories, including religion and theology, cultural and intellectual history, expansion and land acquisition, and natural disasters. A list of key figures involved in each event is provided." SLJ
Includes bibliographical references

Great events from history, The Renaissance & early modern era, 1454-1600; editor, Christina J. Moose. Salem Press 2005 2v il map set $160
   909
1. Renaissance 2. World history—15th century 3. World history—16th century
ISBN 1-58765-214-5; 978-1-58765-214-1
LC 2004-28878
Also available online
Companion volume to Great lives from history, The Renaissance & early modern era, 1454-1600
Some of the essays were previously published in various works
This collection of essays covers events in the scientific, intellectual, literary, sociological, political and military disciplines that happened worldwide during the Renaissance.
Includes bibliographical references

A **Historical** atlas of the Jewish people; from the time of the patriarchs to the present; general editor, Eli Barnavi; English edition editor, Miriam Eliav-Feldon; cartography, Michel Opatowski; new edition revised by Denis Charbit. new ed. Schocken Bks. 2002 321p il maps $45 *   **909**
1. Jews—History—Maps
ISBN 0-8052-4226-0   LC 2003-279553
First published 1992 by Knopf

"Covering three millennia of Jewish history and culture through a combination of concise text, accurate and well-drawn maps, and a sumptuous array of photographs, diagrams, and reproductions of paintings, this atlas succeeds in covering all the main themes of the Jewish experience. The material is arranged chronologically and systematically. . . . The result is a reference that will profit both scholars and lay readers." Libr J [review of 1992 edition]

A **History** of private life; Paul Veyne, editor; Arthur Goldhammer, translator [Philippe Ariès and Georges Duby, general editors] v1: From Pagan Rome to Byzantium. Belknap Press 1987 670p il map $62.50; pa $28   **909**
1. Civilization 2. Manners and customs 3. Family life
ISBN 0-674-39975-7; 0-674-39974-9 (pa)
LC 86-18286
This first volume of a five-volume history contains essays by five contributors, Paul Veyne, Peter Brown, Yvon Thebert, Michel Rouche, and Evelyne Patlagean, "on the Roman Empire, Late Antiquity, Roman Africa, the early Middle Ages in the west, and Byzantium in the tenth and eleventh centuries." Atlantic
"An extraordinarily rich compendium of information on virtually all aspects of life in all social classes. . . . The lucid style should appeal to the general reader, for whom the book is intended." Libr J
Includes bibliographic references

A **History** of private life; [Philippe Ariès and Georges Duby, general editors; translated by] Arthur Goldhammer. v2: Revelations of the medieval world. Belknap Press 1988 650p il pa $28 hardcover o.p.   **909**
1. Medieval civilization 2. Manners and customs 3. Family life
ISBN 0-674-40001-1   LC 86-18286
"Spanning the period from the 11th century to the Renaissance and focusing on France and Tuscan Italy, this [second volume] continues the . . . five-volume history of private life from the Roman world to the present. 'Private' is here defined as what medieval people considered intimate, familial, domestic." Libr J
Includes bibliographical references

A **History** of private life; [Philippe Ariès and Georges Duby, general editors]; Roger Chartier, editor; Arthur Goldhammer, translator. v3: Passions of the Renaissance. Belknap Press 1989 645p il col il pa $28 hardcover o.p.
   909
1. Renaissance 2. Manners and customs 3. Family life
ISBN 0-674-40002-X   LC 86-18286
This third volume of a five-volume "series conceived by the late Philippe Aries . . . [contains fourteen] essays on the shifting boundaries between public and private life in the period 1500-1800." Choice
Includes bibliographical references

A **History** of private life; [Philippe Ariès and Georges Duby, general editors]; Michelle Perrot, editor; Arthur Goldhammer, translator. v4: From the fires of revolution to the Great War. Belknap Press 1990 713p il $48.95; pa $28 **909**
1. France—Civilization 2. Manners and customs 3. Family life
ISBN 0-674-39978-1; 0-674-40003-8 (pa)
LC 86-18286
This is the fourth volume in a five-volume series conceived by Philippe Aries. The contributors include Michelle Perrot, Roger-Henri Guerrand and Alain Corbin. "All the essays except one on England offer sociological studies of private life in 19th-century France combined with . . . critical judgments of that life." NY Times Book Rev
Includes bibliographical references

A **History** of private life; Antoine Prost and Gérard Vincent, editors; translated by Arthur Goldhammer; [Philippe Ariès and Georges Duby, general editors] v5: Riddles of identity in modern times. Belknap Press 1991 630p il $62.50; pa $19.95 **909**
1. Modern civilization 2. Manners and customs 3. Family life
ISBN 0-674-39979-X; 0-674-40004-6 (pa)
LC 86-18286
This is the last volume of a five-volume "work on private life in Western civilization from Greco-Roman times to the present. . . . The editors and authors pursue [the theme of personal identity] . . . in the workplace and the city; . . . in the home and family; . . . and in middle groups between state and individual-such as church, or mosque, or party-where more and more personal dramas are acted out in a world of cultural diversity." Choice
Includes bibliographical references

Hourani, Albert Habib
A history of the Arab peoples; with a new afterword by Malise Ruthven. 2nd ed. Belknap Press 2002 xx, 565p il maps $39.95 **909**
1. Arab civilization
ISBN 0-674-01017-5
LC 2003-269357
First published 1991
This history of the Arab peoples is divided into five parts: The making of a world (seventh-tenth century); Arab Muslim societies (eleventh-fifteenth century); The Ottoman age (sixteenth-eighteenth century); The age of European empires (1800-1939); The age of nation-states (since 1939). Includes a 2002 afterword, genealogies and dynasties
Includes bibliographical references

Johnson, Paul, 1928-
A history of the Jews. Harper & Row 1987 644p pa $17 hardcover o.p. **909**
1. Jews—History
ISBN 0-06-091533-1 (pa)
LC 85-42575
This narrative attempts to cover the "interplay between Jewish history and Western history, and between the philosophical, ethical, religious, social and political no-tions of Judaic culture and those of Western culture." Publisher's note
This "is an absorbing, provocative, well-written, often moving book, an insightful and impassioned blend of history and myth, story and interpretation." Christ Sci Monit
Includes bibliographical references

Kennedy, Hugh, 1947-
The great Arab conquests; how the spread of Islam changed the world we live in. Da Capo 2007 421p $27.95 * **909**
1. Islamic civilization 2. Islam—History
ISBN 0-306-81585-0; 978-0-306-81585-0
LC 2008-297360
The author "has produced an extremely readable work chronicling the early Arab conquests to 750 CE. In the flowing narrative style for which he has become known, Kennedy brings together Arab, Byzantine, Armenian, Coptic, and Persian histories, legends, and anecdotes related to Arab expansion into the lands stretching from the Iberian Peninsula to the Sind. . . . Each chapter details the conquest of a given region, intertwining historic reality with legendary tales to provide for very colorful reading." Choice
Includes bibliographical references

Lamb, David
The Arabs; journeys beyond the mirage. 2nd Vintage Books ed, rev and updated. Vintage Bks. 2002 348p map pa $15 * **909**
1. Arab countries
ISBN 1-4000-3041-2
LC 2002-524048
First published 1987 by Random House
The author "explores the Arabs' religious, political, and cultural views, noting the differences and key similarities between the many segments of the Arab world. He explains Arab attitudes and actions toward the West, including the growth of terrorism, and situates current events in a larger historical backdrop that goes back more than a thousand years." Publisher's note
"Intelligent and incisive . . . Mr. Lamb has the first-rate reporter's tools, and he uses them to relate, with compelling detail, who the Arabs are." N Y Times Book Rev
Includes bibliographical references

Murray, Charles A.
Human accomplishment; the pursuit of excellence in the arts and sciences, 800 B.C. to 1950; [by] Charles Murray. HarperCollins Pubs. 2003 xx, 668p il map pa $24.95 **909**
1. Civilization—History 2. Genius
ISBN 0-06-019247-X; 978-0-06-092964-0 (pa); 0-06-092964-2 (pa)
LC 2003-47820
This is an "account of human excellence, from the age of Homer to our own time. . . . Murray compiles inventories of the people who have been [considered] essential to the stories of literature, music, art, philosophy, and the sciences—a total of 4,002 men and women from around the world, ranked according to their eminence. The heart of [the book] is a series of . . . descriptive chapters: on

Murray, Charles A.—*Continued*
the giants in the arts and what sets them apart from the merely great; on the differences between great achievement in the arts and in the sciences; on the meta-inventions, 14 crucial leaps in human capacity to create great art and science; and on the patterns and trajectories of accomplishment across time and geography." Publisher's note
Includes bibliographical references

Ortega y Gasset, José, 1883-1955
The revolt of the masses; translated, annotated, and with an introduction by Anthony Kerrigan; edited by Kenneth Moore; with a foreword by Saul Bellow. University of Notre Dame Press 1985 xxxi, 192p pa $13.95 hardcover o.p.   **909**
1. Civilization 2. Europe—Civilization 3. Proletariat
ISBN 0-393-31095-7   LC 81-40457
Original Spanish edition, 1930; first English translation, 1932
A collection of essays by the Spanish intellectual in which he analyzes the dangers of control of government by the masses. He sees Bolshevism and Fascism as particularly threatening to civilization

Pagden, Anthony
Peoples and empires; a short history of European migration, exploration, and conquest from Greece to the present. Modern library ed. Modern Lib. 2001 xxv, 206p hardcover o.p. pa $10.95 *   **909**
1. World history 2. Colonies 3. Immigration and emigration
ISBN 0-679-64096-7; 0-8129-6761-5 (pa)
                        LC 00-66204
"A Modern chronicles book"
This "overview of European empire building and colonization commences with the diffusion of Greek civilization and traces the subsequent evolution of the ensuing Roman, Spanish, French, and British empires. More interesting than how those empires physically expanded is the insightful discussion on what motivated individual men and entire nations to migrate and conquer." Booklist
Includes bibliographical references

Roberts, Callum
The unnatural history of the sea. Island Press/Shearwater Books 2007 435p il map $28
                        909
1. Ocean 2. Commercial fishing 3. Human influence on nature
ISBN 978-1-59726-102-9; 1-59726-102-5
                        LC 2007-1841
"Starting with the eighteenth-century voyages of Vitus Bering, Roberts leads the reader through a wealth of maritime history revealing countless examples of overfishing. . . . Thoughtful, inspiring, devastating, and powerful, Roberts' comprehensive, welcoming, and compelling approach to an urgent subject conveys large problems in a succinct and involving manner. Readers won't be able to put it down." Booklist
Includes bibliographical references

Roberts, J. M. (John Morris), 1928-2003
The new history of the world. {4th rev ed}. Oxford Univ. Press 2003 1232p il map $40
                        909
1. World history
ISBN 0-19-521927-9   LC 2003-270110
First published 1976 in the United Kingdom with title: The Hutchinson history of the world; first published 1976 in the United States in a slightly different form by Knopf with title: History of the world; this edition first published 2002 in the United Kingdom with title: The New Penguin history of the world
This overview of history from prehistoric times to the effects of the September 11, 2001 attacks is divided into eight sections: Before history--beginnings; The first civilizations; The classical Mediterranean; The age of diverging traditions; The making of the European age; The great acceleration; The end of the Europeans' world; The latest age

Sachar, Howard Morley, 1928-
A history of the Jews in the modern world; [by] Howard M. Sachar. 1st ed. Knopf 2005 831p $40
                        909
1. Jews—History
ISBN 0-375-41497-5   LC 2004-48814
The author begins "with an account of the European Jews and anti-Semitism they faced as early as the sixteenth century. . . . He goes on to describe such events as their life in western Europe during the seventeenth and eighteenth centuries, the French Revolution and Jewish questions, the Jews of czarist Russia, their struggle for civil rights in the 1830s and 1840s, and their place in what Sachar labels an emancipated economy." Booklist
This book "relates an immensely complex story with precision and learning." N Y Times Book Rev
Includes bibliographical references

909.07   World history—ca. 500-1450/1500

Andrea, Alfred J., 1941-
Encyclopedia of the crusades. Greenwood Press 2003 xxiii, 356p il, maps $75   **909.07**
1. Crusades—Encyclopedias 2. Europe—Church history—Encyclopedias
ISBN 0-313-31659-7   LC 2003-48544
This encyclopedia includes "more than 200 entries, each one between approximately 10 lines and four pages in length. . . . The introduction gives the entries some historical context and defines the term *crusade* for the reader. The entries are in alphabetical order and include cross-references in bold type to other entries in the book. Many entries also include suggested readings, both primary sources and historical studies. At the end of the work, the author has included a chronology of important dates and events, a 'Basic Crusade Library' of further readings in bibliographic essay style, and a general index. . . . This encyclopedia is recommended for high-school, undergraduate, and public libraries." Booklist
Includes bibliographical references

Burns, Thomas S.

A history of the Ostrogoths. Indiana Univ. Press 1984 299p il pa $19.95 hardcover o.p.

909.07

1. Medieval civilization 2. Teutonic peoples

ISBN 0-253-20600-6 (pa)   LC 83-49286

This "study of the Ostrogoths . . . explores the interaction between Rome and her eastern Germanic neighbors with the focus on the Ostrogothic experience. Traditional literary sources are looked at with a fresh eye, and new archaeological materials are thoroughly explored." Libr J

Includes bibliographical references

The **Crusades**; an encyclopedia; Alan V. Murray, editor. ABC-CLIO 2006 4v il map set $385 *

909.07

1. Crusades—Encyclopedias

ISBN 1-57607-862-0; 978-1-57607-862-4

LC 2006-19410

This encyclopedia "surveys all aspects of the crusading movement from its origins in the 11th century to its decline in the 16th century." Publisher's note

For a fuller review, see: Booklist, Dec. 1, 2006

Includes bibliographical references

Great events from history, The Middle Ages, 477-1453; editor, Brian A. Pavlac; consulting editors, Byron Cannon, . . . [et al.] Salem Press 2005 2v il map set $160   **909.07**

1. Middle Ages 2. Medieval civilization

ISBN 1-58765-167-X; 978-1-58765-167-0

LC 2004-16640

Also available online

Companion volume to Great lives from history, The Middle Ages, 477-1453

Some essays were previously published in Great events from history (1972-1980), Chronology of European history: 15,000 B.C. to 1997 (1997), Great events from history: North American series, revised edition (1997), Great events from history: ancient and medieval series (1972), and Great events from history: modern European series (1973)

This set "offers 322 essays, beginning with Confucianism arrives in Japan (fifth or sixth century) and ending with Fall of Constantinople (May 29, 1453)." Booklist

Includes bibliographical references

The **Oxford** illustrated history of the Crusades; edited by Jonathan Riley-Smith. Oxford Univ. Press 1995 436p il maps hardcover o.p. pa $26.50   **909.07**

1. Crusades

ISBN 0-19-820435-3; 0-19-285428-3 (pa)

LC 94-24229

Also available non-illustrated edition with title: The Oxford history of the Crusades pa $18.95 (ISBN: 0-19-280312-3)

Scholars explore the complex religious, economic, and military aspects of the Crusades.

Includes bibliographical references

909.08   Modern history, 1450/1500-

Garton Ash, Timothy

Free world; America, Europe, and the surprising future of the West. Random House 2004 286p il map $24.95; pa $14.95 *   **909.08**

1. World politics—1991-

ISBN 1-400-06219-5; 1-400-07646-3 (pa)

LC 2004-53862

The author "traces the gradual unravelling of the Atlantic alliance back through the destruction of the Twin Towers in 2001, America's 9/11, to the fall of the Berlin Wall on November 9, 1989, Europe's 9/11. He writes with great insight, balance and yet with passion, too." Times Lit Suppl

Includes bibliographical references

Herman, Arthur, 1956-

The idea of decline in Western history. Free Press 1996 521p pa $23.95   **909.08**

1. Western civilization

ISBN 0-684-82791-3; 978-1-4165-7633-4 (pa); 1-4165-7633-9 (pa)   LC 96-36285

"Herman recaps the two-century-long tradition of criticism of Western civilization. . . . He covers two historians most closely identified with predicting decline, Oswald Spengler and Arnold Toynbee, and also brings forth less famous prognosticators of the doom of the West. . . . An accessible survey for the serious nonacademic." Booklist

Includes bibliographical references

Jasanoff, Maya, 1974-

Edge of empire; lives, culture, and conquest in the East, 1750-1850. Knopf 2005 404p il $27.95

909.08

1. Great Britain—Colonies 2. Collectors and collecting

ISBN 1-4000-4167-8   LC 2004-60221

The author "challenges the idea that the British Empire imposed its own culture on its colonies, arguing instead that the empire thrived because it was able to 'find ways of accommodating difference.' As evidence, she traces the history of objects collected in India and Egypt by 'border-crossers.'" Publ Wkly

"In graceful prose and with evocative illustrations, Jasanoff scores her points about conquest, collecting, and cultural crossing, offering a thoughtful and highly subtle study." Libr J

Includes bibliographical references

Kennedy, Paul M., 1945-

The rise and fall of the great powers; economic change and military conflict from 1500 to 2000; [by] Paul Kennedy. Random House 1988 xxv, 677p maps pa $17 hardcover o.p.   **909.08**

1. Modern history 2. Economic conditions 3. Balance of power

ISBN 0-679-72019-7 (pa)   LC 87-9690

The author "assesses the interaction between economics and strategy of the past five centuries; the correlation between productive and revenue-sharing capacities on the

Kennedy, Paul M., 1945-—*Continued*
one hand and military strength on the other." Publ Wkly
"Kennedy's great achievement is that he makes us see our current international problems against a background of empires that have gone under because they were unable to sustain the material cost of greatness; and he does so in a universal historical perspective." N Y Rev Books
Includes bibliographical references

Tuchman, Barbara Wertheim
The march of folly; from Troy to Vietnam; [by] Barbara W. Tuchman. Knopf 1984 447p il pa $16.95 hardcover o.p. * **909.08**
1. Modern history
ISBN 0-345-30823-9 (pa)   LC 83-22206
The author analyzes examples of governmental bumbling including the Trojan horse, the U.S. involvement in Vietnam, and the British loss of the American colonies.
Includes bibliographical references

909.7 World history—18th century, 1700-1799

Great events from history, The 18th century, 1701-1800; editor John Powell. Salem Press 2006 2v il map set $160 **909.7**
1. World history—18th century
ISBN 978-1-58765-279-0; 1-58765-279-X
LC 2006-5406
Also available online
Companion volume to Great lives from history, The 18th century, 1701-1800
Some essays previously published in Great events from history: North American series (1997) and Chronology of European history (1997)
"Topics include geopolitical events, social and intellectual issues, scientific developments, philosophy, and the arts. The global coverage emphasizes turning points that redirected and shaped history and helped create the modern world. Essays have an average length of 1600 words. Each one begins with a short summary of the topic and includes dates, locales, categories, key figures, text, significance, further reading, see-also references, and cross-referencing to other essays in this set and in the rest of the series. . . . An informative resource." SLJ
Includes bibliographical references

Winik, Jay, 1957-
The great upheaval; America and the birth of the modern world, 1788-1800. Harper 2007 xx, 659p il map $29.95 **909.7**
1. Modern civilization 2. Modern history 3. United States—History—1783-1809
ISBN 0-06-008313-1; 978-0-06-008313-7
This narrative history of the concluding decade of the eighteenth century focuses primarily on "the new political world being born in the wake of the American and French revolutions." N Y Times (Late NY Ed)
"An outstandingly wide-ranging account of this vital era in world history." Booklist
Includes bibliographical references

909.81 World history—19th century, 1800-1899

Great events from history, The 19th century, 1801-1900; editor, John Powell. Salem Press 2006 4v il map set $360 **909.81**
1. World history—19th century
ISBN 978-1-58765-297-4; 1-58765-297-8
LC 2006-19789
Also available online
Companion volume to Great lives from history, The 19th century, 1801-1900
Some of the essays in this work appeared in various other Salem Press sets
"These volumes cover the world's most important events and developments from 1801 through 1900. . . . Essays address important social and cultural developments in daily life: major literary movements, significant developments in art and music, trends in immigration, and progressive social legislation." Publisher's note
Includes bibliographical references

909.82 World history—20th century, 1900-1999

The **Columbia** history of the 20th century; {edited by} Richard W. Bulliet. Columbia Univ. Press 1998 651p $62; pa $29 **909.82**
1. World history—20th century
ISBN 0-231-07628-2; 0-231-07629-0 (pa)
LC 97-39426
Scholars contribute chapters on topics ranging "from 'Ethnicity and Racism,' to 'Nationalism,' 'Communications,' 'Industry and Business,' and others. The idea is for readers to peruse those chapters that appeal to them. Articles average under 25 pages, so content is quite broad. While the level of scholarship varies a bit, overall quality is good." Libr J
Includes bibliographical references

Encyclopedia of conflicts since World War II; edited by James Ciment. 2nd ed. M.E. Sharpe 2007 4v set $439 **909.82**
1. World politics—1945-—Encyclopedias
ISBN 978-0-7656-8005-1; 0-7656-8005-X
LC 2006-14011
First published 1999
This "reference presents descriptions and analyses of more than 170 significant post-World War II conflicts around the globe." Publisher's note
"The illustrations are strong and the maps helpful, and the thumbnail biographies and glossary are useful. A valuable resource for most school and public libraries." SLJ
Includes bibliographical references

Encyclopedia of the Cold War; a political, social, and military history; Spencer C. Tucker, editor. ABC-CLIO 2007 5v il map set $495 **909.82**
1. Cold war—Encyclopedias 2. World politics—1945-—Encyclopedias
ISBN 978-1-85109-701-2   LC 2007-9681

Encyclopedia of the Cold War—*Continued*

This is a "five-volume reference on the defining conflict of the second half of the 20th century, covering all aspects of the Cold War as it influenced events around the world." Publisher's note

"The content gives a broad global view of an anxious period and provides useful background for some of today's conflicts." Booklist

Includes bibliographical references

Gilbert, Martin, 1936-

History of the twentieth century. Morrow 2001 783p maps pa $19.95 hardcover o.p.

909.82

1. World history—20th century

ISBN 0-06-050594-X (pa)   LC 2001-32612

Condensed version of the three-volume work first published 1997-1999

The author "chronicles world events year by year, from the dawn of aviation to the flourishing technology age, taking us through World War I to the inauguration of Franklin Roosevelt as president of the United States and Hitler as chancellor of Germany. He continues on to document wars in South Africa, China, Ethiopia, Spain, Korea, Vietnam, and Bosnia, as well as apartheid, the arms race, the moon landing, and the beginnings of the computer age, while interspersing the influence of art, literature, music, and religion." Publisher's note

Great events from history: The 20th century, 1901-1940; editor, Robert F. Gorman. Salem Press 2007 6v il map set $495   909.82

1. World history—20th century

ISBN 978-1-58765-324-7; 1-58765-324-9

LC 2007-1930

Also available online

Some of the essays in this work originally appeared in various Salem Press publications

This work "identifies key events that helped to shape the course of the history of the world from 1901 to 1940. In more than 1,000 essays, a plethora of topics are presented, including Canada claiming the Arctic Islands (1901); the plague killing 1.2 million in India (1907); Gertrude Ederle swimming the English Channel (1926); Stalin beginning the Purge Trials (1934); and Germany hosting the 1936 Olympics." Booklist

"This set provides access to clear, objective information, especially on topics in the sciences and mathematics." Libr J

Includes bibliographical references

Great events from history: The 20th century, 1941-1970; editor, Robert F. Gorman. Salem Press 2008 6v il map set $495   909.82

1. World history—20th century

ISBN 978-1-58765-331-5; 1-58765-331-1

LC 2007-37204

Also available online

Some of the essays in this work originally appeared in various Salem Press publications

The articles in this set "cover everything from the bombing of Pearl Harbor to the celebration of the First Earth Day. Each article lists a locale, key figures, categories, and a summary of events; readers can search for ad-

ditional information based on categories or key figures. The sixth volume contains a bibliography, personage, subject, category, and geographical indexes and a chronological list of entries. . . . An excellent cross-reference tool." Libr J

Includes bibliographical references

Great events from history: The 20th century, 1971-2000; editor, Robert F. Gorman. Salem Press 2008 6v il map set $495   909.82

1. World history—20th century

ISBN 978-1-58765-338-4; 1-58765-338-9

LC 2007-51351

Also available online

Some of the essays originally appeared in other Salem Press sets

This set "provides extended coverage of 1,083 major events between 1971 and 2000." Publisher's note

Includes bibliographical references

Hillstrom, Kevin

The Cold War; foreward by Christian Ostermann. Omnigraphics 2006 xx, 536p il (Primary sourcebook series) $65 *

909.82

1. Cold war 2. World politics—1945-1991

ISBN 0-7808-0934-3; 978-0-7808-0934-5

LC 2006-15330

"Examines the Cold War and its impact on America, the Soviet Union, and the world. Features include narrative overviews of key events and trends, 100+ primary source documents, chronology, glossary, bibliography, and subject index." Publisher's note

"The wide-ranging scope of documents compiled in this volume will provide AP history and social studies classes with a wealth of information for research and analysis." Libr Media Connect

Includes glossary and bibliographical references

Huntington, Samuel P.

The clash of civilizations and the remaking of world order. Simon & Schuster 1996 367p il maps pa $17 hardcover o.p.   909.82

1. World politics—1965- 2. Modern civilization—1950-

ISBN 0-684-84441-9 (pa)   LC 96-31492

Huntington posits "a paradigm for post-Cold War international politics in which the principal source of conflict will be cultural divisions among competing civilizations. Prophesying an assault on Western interests, values, and power from a Confucian-Islamic connection, he . . . {enjoins} Western governments to reconcile themselves to new global realities and {offers} recommendations for prescriptive action." Libr J

"The Huntington argument that the West should stop intervening in civilizational conflicts it doesn't understand makes a powerful claim that internationalists cannot easily ignore." N Y Times Book Rev

Judt, Tony

Reappraisals; reflections on the forgotten twentieth century. Penguin Press 2008 448p $29.95 **909.82**

1. Modern history 2. World history—20th century
ISBN 978-1-59420-136-3; 1-59420-136-6
LC 2007-30297

Judt writes about subjects ranging "from the history of the neglect and recovery of the Holocaust and the challenge of 'evil' in the understanding of the European past to the rise and fall of the 'state' in public affairs and the displacement of history by 'heritage.'" Publisher's note

The author "writes informatively about Manes Sperber, tenderly about Primo Levi, enthusiastically about Hannah Arendt. . . . [Tony Judt is] not only a historian of the first rank but (in a word we need an equivalent for) a politicologue who gives engagement a good name." N Y Times Book Rev

Includes bibliographical references

Junger, Sebastian

Fire. Norton 2001 224p $24.95 **909.82**
1. Disasters 2. World politics—1991- 3. Terrorism
4. War
ISBN 0-393-01046-5 LC 2001-45236

This is a collection of previously published magazine articles. "Two [pieces] deal with the dangerous work of firefighting . . . in the American West. . . . [Another] chronicles the author's travels with the anti-Taliban forces in northern Afghanistan a year or so ago, and contains a . . . portrait of Gen. Ahmed Shah Massoud, the Northern Alliance's longtime military leader, who was assassinated . . . by agents reportedly linked to Osama bin Laden." N Y Times (Late N Y Ed)

The stories are "all told with Junger's unfailing eye for detail, which often lends the pieces a disturbing authenticity." Libr J

Kurlansky, Mark

1968; the year that rocked the world. Ballantine 2004 xx, 441p il $26.95 **909.82**
1. Radicalism 2. Insurgency
ISBN 0-345-45581-9 LC 2004-299128

This is an account "of the global, social, and political upheaval, warfare, and assassinations that define one year in a tumultuous decade." Booklist

Includes bibliographical references

National Geographic eyewitness to the 20th century. National Geographic Soc. 1998 400p il pa $22.95 hardcover o.p. **909.82**
1. World history—20th century
ISBN 0-7922-8063-6 (pa) LC 98-22756

"Chapters are arranged thematically by decade and open with a six-page essay discussing each era. . . . Most useful of all are the double-page spreads for each year presenting events, people, and themes in short paragraph entries. Brief trends and trivia are listed vertically. A time line appears along the bottom of the pages. Photographs bring the discussions to life and sidebars present interesting developments and people." SLJ

The **Oxford** history of the twentieth century; edited by Michael Howard and Wm. Roger Louis. Oxford Univ. Press 1998 xxii, 458p il pa $26.50 hardcover o.p. **909.82**
1. World history—20th century
ISBN 978-0-19-280378-8 (pa); 0-19-280378-6 (pa)
LC 98-12861

"Besides global wars hot and cold, population explosion and urbanization impacted the entire century, as one of 27 articles in *Twentieth Century* underscores. Embracing nonpolitical topics in areas such as physics, modernism in art, and international economics, this work exposes the interested reader to developments that have affected most people." Booklist

Includes bibliographical references

Reynolds, David, 1952-

One world divisible; a global history since 1945. Norton 2000 861p il (Global century series) $35; pa $19.95 **909.82**
1. World history—1945-
ISBN 0-393-04821-7; 0-393-32108-8 (pa)
LC 99-33903

This world history focuses on the "concept of statebuilding, within the contexts of the competing trends of globalization and fragmentation. Writing with great economy but without compromising essential insights, Reynolds brings forth the forces at work—as often as not determined or fanatical individuals—in shaping a country's government and foreign policy. Whether assessing Nasser in Egypt, Jinnah in Pakistan, or Mao in China, Reynolds injects the account with fresh explanations of events." Booklist

Includes bibliographical references

Summits; six meetings that shaped the twentieth century. Basic Books 2007 544p il map $35 **909.82**
1. Diplomacy 2. World politics 3. World history—20th century
ISBN 978-0-465-06904-0; 0-465-06904-5

The author provides a "retelling of six pivotal meetings of world leaders in an effort to capture the larger and evolving significance of this diplomatic art form. He argues that modern summitry came of age with Chamberlain and Hitler at Munich in 1938 and was carried forward at Yalta in 1945 and into the Cold War with Kennedy and Khrushchev in 1961, Nixon and Brezhnev in 1972, and Reagan and Gorbachev in 1985." Foreign Affairs

"The author's thorough mastery of his subject is reflected in the fluency and assurance of the writing." Publ Wkly

Includes bibliographical references

Tuchman, Barbara Wertheim

The proud tower; a portrait of the world before the war, 1890-1914; [by] Barbara W. Tuchman. 1st Ballantine Books ed. Ballantine Books 1996 528p il pa $15.95 **909.82**
1. World history—20th century 2. World history—19th century 3. Europe—Social conditions 4. United States—Social conditions
ISBN 0-345-40501-3 LC 96-96511

Tuchman, Barbara Wertheim—*Continued*
First published 1966 by Macmillan
The author describes prewar social conditions in the U.S., France, England and Germany.
Includes bibliographical references

909.83   World history—21st century, 2000-2099

The **21st** century; edited by Hilary D. Claggett. Wilson, H.W. 1999 185p (Reference shelf) pa $50   **909.83**
1. Reference shelf 2. Millennium 3. Forecasting
ISBN 0-8242-0966-4   LC 99-462343
A collection of articles focusing on the millenial years 1000 and 2000. The Y2K scare is discussed and contributors speculate on the future of the planet
Includes bibliographical references

910   Geography & travel

De Porti, Andrea, 1968-
Explorers; the most exciting voyages of discovery, from the African expeditions to the lunar landing; [English translation, Paul Holberton] Firefly Books 2005 56p il $49.95   **910**
1. Explorers 2. Exploration
ISBN 1-55407-101-1
This book "details 58 expeditions from the past 150 years—from Robert Peary and Matthew Henson's trek to the North Pole in 1909 to Edmund Hillary's 1953 climb up Everest (called by Tibetans 'the mother goddess of the world') to Neil Armstrong's 'one small step' onto the moon in 1969. . . . The creative way these journeys are presented will impress armchair adventurers." Publ Wkly
Includes bibliographical references

Fleming, Fergus, 1959-
Off the map; tales of endurance and exploration; as told by Fergus Fleming. Atlantic Monthly Press 2005 518p il maps $24.95; pa $16   **910**
1. Explorers 2. Exploration
ISBN 0-8711-3899-9; 0-8021-4272-9 (pa)
                                      LC 2005-47849
First published 2004 in the United Kingdom
This book "consists of 45 biographical essays divided into three parts. 'The Age of Reconnaissance' begins in the 13th century with Marco Polo's wanderings in the Mongol Empire. 'The Age of Inquiry' takes the reader through the 18th century and halfway into the 19th, concluding with the . . . search for Sir John Franklin in the high Arctic. 'The Age of Endeavour' proceeds from the crossing of the Australian continent by Robert Burke and William Wills in 1861 to Umberto Nobile's . . . 1928 flight to the North Pole." N Y Times Book Rev
"Almost comprehensive enough to serve as a reference, this densely packed tome supplies a bewildering wealth of information about some of humanity's most compelling adventures." Publ Wkly
Includes bibliographical references

Points unknown; a century of great exploration; edited by David Roberts. Norton 2000 608p $29.95   **910**
1. Voyages and travels 2. Explorers 3. Adventure and adventurers
ISBN 0-393-05000-9   LC 00-32915
"An Outside book"
"Collection of excerpts from mostly first-person narratives of adventure travel and exploration from the beginning of the century until today. Each selection is preceded by a short introductory passage written by well-known writers and adventurers . . . as well as the lesser known. . . . At times the narratives focus on the challenge of the individual vs. nature, at others on the difficulty of teamwork when the struggle becomes overwhelming." Libr J
"A mesmerizing display of the pull adventure exerts." Booklist

The **travel** book; a journey through every country in the world. Lonely Planet 2004 444p il $50; pa $30   **910**
1. Travel
ISBN 1-74104-451-0; 1-74104-629-7 (pa)
This book covers "230 countries, including some not technically countries at all, like Greenland, Hong Kong, and various Caribbean islands. . . . Lonely Planet's editors have . . . managed to distill something essential about each location, in 1200 dancing images of its people and places and brief but spot-on suggestions of what to eat, drink, listen to, and watch. Entries are arranged alphabetically rather than geographically. . . . A dearth of historical facts or statistics—although capital, population, area, and official language information is included—make this not a reference work but rather, in the turning of the pages, a suggestive, provocative, loving portrait of our gorgeous, haunting planet, not lonely at all." Libr J

910.2   Geography—Miscellany. Travel guides

Hasbrouck, Edward
The practical nomad; how to travel around the world. 4th ed.; Updated ed. Avalon Travel 2007 601p il pa $21.95 *   **910.2**
1. Travel
ISBN 978-1-56691-828-2; 1-56691-828-6
First published 1997 by Moon Publications, Inc.
This guide "to independent world travel . . . [features] tips on finding the time and money for your trip, the best airfares, new security rules, travel documents, budgeting, and more. Excellent list of resources for novice and experienced globe-trotters." Libr J
Includes bibliographical references

Lopes, Rosaly M. C., 1957-
The volcano adventure guide; [by] Rosaly Lopes. Cambridge University Press 2005 352p il map $55   **910.2**
1. Volcanoes 2. Travel
ISBN 0-521-55453-5; 978-0-521-55453-4
This is a travel "guide to world-class volcanoes. Readers are first introduced to the different types of volcanoes

Lopes, Rosaly M. C., 1957-—*Continued*
and the various dynamic processes and eruption styles
that produce them. . . . The second part of the book is
packed with information and guidance to 20 select examples of volcanoes from around the world, coupled with
more information on additional volcanoes in each area
that could easily be visited. . . . Spectacular color photos, geologic and geographic maps, and schematic interpretive illustrations provide excellent support for a beautifully written text." Choice
Includes bibliographical references

Stellin, Susan
How to travel practically anywhere; the ultimate
travel guide. Houghton Mifflin Co. 2006 321p pa
$15.95 **910.2**
1. Travel
ISBN 978-0-618-60753-2; 0-618-60753-6
LC 2005-22728
This "guide to travel planning that covers the ins and
outs (and ups and downs) of do-it-yourself travel. . . .
[The author] offers information and advice on topics that
traditional travel guides discuss only minimally: solo
travel, travel insurance, last-minute planning, government
travel advisories, web fares, home-exchange information,
and more; she also includes a helpful section on what to
do in an emergency—when you need a doctor or have
lost your passport. . . . This comprehensive and well-
researched guide is useful for both new and seasoned
travelers and is highly recommended for all libraries with
travel collections." Libr J

910.3 Geography—Dictionaries,
encyclopedias, concordnces,
gazetteers

The **Columbia** gazetteer of the world; edited by
Saul B. Cohen. 2nd ed. Columbia University
Press 2008 3v set $595 * **910.3**
1. Gazetteers
ISBN 978-0-231-14554-1 LC 2008-9181
Also available online
First published 1952 with title: The Columbia
Lippincott gazetteer of the world
"The 170,000-plus entries cover political, physical,
and special places, including monuments and historic
sites. . . . Historically accurate, this title can be consid-
ered a reference standard." Libr J

Firefly geography dictionary. Firefly Books 2003
256p il map pa $14.95 **910.3**
1. Geography—Dictionaries
ISBN 1-55297-838-9 LC 2003-273971
First published 1995 in the United Kingdom with title:
Philip's geography dictionary
This dictionary "provides more than 1,500 entries and
130 illustrations for words and concepts in physical, human, and environmental geography. . . . Entries, arranged alphabetically, are defined in complete sentences.
. . . Despite its small size, this dictionary lives up to its
claim to be comprehensive. It would be valuable for
readers of elementary to advanced textbooks and journal
articles." Choice

Merriam-Webster's geographical dictionary. 3rd
ed. Merriam-Webster 1997 1361p maps $32.95
910.3
1. Geography—Dictionaries
ISBN 0-87779-546-0 LC 96-52365
First published 1949 with title: Webster's geographical
dictionary
This guide contains data about countries, cities, and
physical features. More than 48,000 entries and over 250
maps provide population, size, economic data and historical notes. Pronunciations are included and a table of foreign terms used in English is provided.

The **Oxford** companion to world exploration;
David Buisseret, editor in chief. Oxford
University Press 2007 2v il map set $250
910.3
1. Exploration
ISBN 0-19-514922-X; 978-0-19-514922-7
LC 2006-27968
"Published in association with the Newberry Library"
"The entries are presented in alphabetical order and
cover not only individual explorers, but also some geo-
graphic regions, wars, commercial operations, and reli-
gious organizations. . . . This work will become the first
stop for students and general readers who seek either ba-
sic information or a starting point for further reading."
Sci Books Films
Includes bibliographical references

Waldman, Carl
Encyclopedia of exploration; [by] Carl Waldman
and Alan Wexler. Facts on File 2004 2v il map
(Facts on File library of world history) set $225
910.3
1. Exploration 2. Explorers 3. Voyages and travels
ISBN 0-8160-4678-6 LC 2004-10625
Vol. 2 by Carl Waldman and Jon Cunningham
Contents: v. 1. The explorers -- v. 2. Places, technologies, and culture trends
"The first volume is all biographical entries with accompanying appendixes that list explorers by occupation,
area(s) explored, chronology, and the respective explorers' nationality. The second volume has topical entries
about all things related to exploration, such as specific
areas, technologies, and routes." Am Ref Books Annu,
2005
"This set is well organized and very readable."
Booklist
Includes bibliographical references

Worldmark encyclopedia of the nations; [Timothy
L. Gall and M. Hobby, editors] 12th ed.
Thomson Gale 2007 c2006 5v set il map $535
* **910.3**
1. United Nations 2. Geography—Encyclopedias
3. World history—Encyclopedias 4. World politics—
Encyclopedias
ISBN 1-414410-89-1
First published 1960
"Factual and statistical information on the countries of
the world, exhibited in uniform format under such ru-
brics as topography, population, public finance, language,
and ethnic composition. Country articles appear in vol-

Worldmark encyclopedia of the nations—*Continued*

umes 2 through 5, arranged geographically by continent. Volume 1 is devoted to the United Nations and its affiliated agencies. Illustrations, maps." Ref Sources for Small & Medium-sized Libr. 6th edition

910.4 Accounts of travel and facilities for travelers

Bathurst, Bella

The wreckers; a story of killing seas and plundered shipwrecks, from the eighteenth century to the present day. Houghton Mifflin 2005 326p il maps $25   **910.4**

1. Shipwrecks 2. Great Britain—Local history
ISBN 0-618-41677-3   LC 2005-45951

The author "explains that 'wreckers' were people who watched for a ship in distress and stole everything on board of any value, sometimes also drowning the crew and burning the boats. . . . Bathurst traveled to eight wrecking 'hot spots' in Britain in researching the history of wrecking over the last 300 years, its heyday occurring in the eighteenth and nineteenth centuries. . . . The result is an exceptional chronicle of knavery." Booklist

Includes bibliographical references

Bellec, François

Unknown lands; the log books of the great explorers; translated by Lisa Davidson and Elizabeth Ayre. Overlook Press 2002 c2000 213p il map $55   **910.4**

1. Explorers 2. Voyages and travels
ISBN 1-58567-201-7   LC 2001-36800

"Weaving together logs, correspondence, and stories of the 'ordinary and extraordinary men' who explored the oceans and unknown lands over five centuries, Bellec offers a . . . snapshot of the cultural and political circumstances that set the stage for maritime adventures and New World discoveries. Eyewitness accounts retold alongside maps and drawings contribute to an enlightening view of the minds, hearts, and talents of adventurers such as Columbus, Vasco de Gama, and James Cook. . . . This is simply a stunning book." Libr J

Includes bibliographical references

Bergreen, Laurence

Over the edge of the world; Magellan's terrifying circumnavigation of the globe. Morrow 2003 458p il maps hardcover o.p. pa $15.95   **910.4**

1. Magellan, Ferdinand, 1480?-1521 2. Voyages around the world
ISBN 0-06-621173-5; 0-06-093638-X (pa); 978-0-06-093638-9 (pa)   LC 2003-50143

This book "follows the voyagers who sailed west from Spain in 1519 in search of the Spice Islands. They returned in 1522 with a better understanding of the Pacific, but only after losing their captain, Magellan, most of their 260-member crew and four of their five ships." N Y Times Book Rev

The author "tells a well-rounded story of Magellan, not just that of the romanticized hero but also that of the explorer's darker side. . . . Fascinating reading for history buffs, and a great story that rivals any seagoing adventure." Booklist

Includes bibliographical references

The Best American travel writing 2007. Houghton Mifflin 2007 xx, 307p $28; pa $14 *   **910.4**

1. Travel
ISSN 1530-1516
ISBN 978-0-618-58217-4; 0-618-58217-7; 978-0-618-58218-1 (pa); 0-618-58218-5 (pa)
Annual. First published 2000
Editors vary

A selection of travel writing from various American publications

"The book's loose definition of the travel genre means it will appeal to any reader who enjoys high-quality nonfiction." Publ Wkly {review of 2003 edition}

Butler, Daniel Allen

Unsinkable: the full story of the RMS Titanic. Stackpole Bks. 1998 292p il $19.95   **910.4**

1. Titanic (Steamship) 2. Shipwrecks
ISBN 0-8117-1814-X   LC 98-9294
Also available in paperback from Da Capo Press

This is a history "of the disaster and aftermath, drawing on first-person accounts and solid secondary sources." Libr J

Includes bibliographical references

Cordingly, David, 1938-

Under the black flag; the romance and the reality of life among the pirates. Random House 1996 296p maps hardcover o.p. pa $15   **910.4**

1. Pirates
ISBN 0-679-42560-8; 978-0-8129-7722-6 (pa); 0-8129-7722-X (pa)   LC 95-41414

"This succinct history is full of unexpected revelations about the facts and myths of piracy; a typical seventeenth-century Western pirate vessel, for example, was run democratically long before the French Revolution, and one of the most successful pirates of all time was a nineteenth-century Chinese woman who controlled some fifty thousand seagoing outlaws." New Yorker

Includes bibliographical references

Women sailors and sailors' women; an untold maritime history. Random House 2001 286p il pa $14.95 hardcover o.p.   **910.4**

1. Voyages and travels 2. Adventure and adventurers 3. Women
ISBN 0-375-75872-0 (pa)   LC 00-62762

A look at "the lives of the intrepid women who went to sea during the great age of sail. Countless females set sail for reasons of adventure, romance, or duty in the seventeenth, eighteenth, and nineteenth centuries. Included among their numbers were the wives or mistresses of ships' officers, prostitutes, female pirates, and women disguised as male sailors. . . . A significant contribution

Cordingly, David, 1938- —*Continued*
to both women's history and maritime scholarship."
Booklist

Includes bibliographical references

Dana, Richard Henry, 1815-1882
Two years before the mast; a personal narrative
of life at sea; introduction by Gary Kinder; notes
by Duncan Hasell. Modern Library 2001 xxiv,
516p il pa $12.95 * **910.4**
 1. Seafaring life 2. Voyages and travels
 ISBN 0-375-75794-5   LC 2001-31243
First published anonymously in 1840
The author "shipped out of Boston in 1834 on the Pilgrim and sailed around the Horn to California on a hide-
trading expedition. The book is based on the journal he
kept during the voyage. Horrified by the brutal captain's
mistreatment of the sailors, and shocked by their lack of
legal redress, Dana wrote with a burning indignation that
did much to rouse the public to the mariners' plight."
HarperCollins Reader's Ency of Am Lit. 2d edition

Dodson, James
The road to somewhere; travels with a young
boy through an old world. Dutton 2003 292p
hardcover o.p. pa $15   **910.4**
 1. Voyages and travels 2. Father-son relationship
 ISBN 0-525-94762-0; 978-0-452-28657-3 (pa);
 0-452-28657-3 (pa)   LC 2003-2257
The author "recounts an ambitious journey through
England, Holland, Belgium, France, Italy and Greece
. . . with his 10-year-old son, Jack." Publ Wkly
 "The book is both educational and funny, but what
makes it special is the tender, charming relationship that
develops between its two principal characters. It is enchanting to watch man and boy learn from one another,
to see the man become a little more childlike and the
boy start his journey to manhood. There's plenty of
laughter here, but there are also a few gentle tears."
Booklist

García Márquez, Gabriel, 1928-
The story of a shipwrecked sailor; who drifted
on a life raft for ten days without food or water,
was proclaimed a national hero, kissed by beauty
queens, made rich through publicity, and then
spurned by the government and forgotten for all
time; translated from the Spanish by Randolph
Hogan. Knopf 1986 106p pa $11 hardcover o.p.
          910.4
 1. Velasco, Luis Alejandro, d. 2000 2. Survival after
 airplane accidents, shipwrecks, etc.
 ISBN 0-679-72205-X (pa)   LC 85-45673
Original Spanish edition, 1970
 "In 1955 Garcia Marquez was working as a reporter
in Colombia. One of his stories was a serialized account
of a sailor who was swept overboard with seven other
crew members of a Colombian destroyer and who was
the only one to survive. This book presents Garcia
Marquez' version of the sailor's first-person narrative."
Booklist

Greenberg, Peter
The complete travel detective bible; the
consummate insider tells you what you need to
know in an increasingly complex world! Rodale
2007 624p il pa $17.95 *   **910.4**
 1. Travel
 ISBN 978-1-59486-708-8; 1-59486-708-9
          LC 2007-30599
This guide features "insider secrets . . . on airfares,
ground transportation, hotels, cruises, frequent flyer programs (including how to earn miles when not flying), security, and online booking, as well as baggage, passports,
and travel and health insurance." Libr J

Heyerdahl, Thor
Kon-Tiki; across the Pacific by raft; translated
by F.H. Lyon. Washington Square Press 1984
240p map (Enriched classics series) pa $5.99
          910.4
 1. Kon-Tiki Expedition (1947) 2. Pacific Ocean
 3. Ethnology—Polynesia
 ISBN 0-671-72652-8   LC 84-42785
Original Norwegian edition, 1948
The "story of the six men who crossed the Pacific
from Peru to the Polynesians on a primitive balsa-log raft
such as Peruvian natives of the fifth century used, to
prove that it was possible that the legendary race that
came to Easter Island and the Polynesians could have
come from Peru." Wis Libr Bull

Jacobson, Mark, 1948-
12,000 miles in the nick of time; a
semi-dysfunctional family circumnavigates the
globe; with additional commentary by Rae
Jacobson. Atlantic Monthly Press 2003 271p il
maps pa $13 hardcover o.p.   **910.4**
 1. Voyages around the world
 ISBN 0-8021-4138-2 (pa)   LC 2003-41821
 "A few years ago, the Jacobsons . . . spent the summer touring Asia, the Middle East, and part of Europe on
the cheap. It wasn't easy to take three middle-class
American kids, ages 9 to 16, to Cambodia's Killing
Fields, India's Burning Gat, or the sex-shop strewn thor-
oughfares of Thailand. The book recounts the many trials, tribulations, and ironies of the trip as well as its
more usual wonders." SLJ
 "The book is very funny—the trip doesn't go exactly
as the parents plan—but it is also hugely educational,
history presented as a grand adventure. The kids learned
a lot, and so do we." Booklist
 Includes bibliographical references

Junger, Sebastian
The perfect storm; a true story of men against
the sea. Norton 1997 226p il map $23.95 *
          910.4
 1. Storms 2. Shipwrecks
 ISBN 0-393-04016-X   LC 96-42412
Also available in paperback from HarperCollins Pubs.
 "With waves as high as a hundred feet and winds so
strong that anemometers were torn from their moorings,
the storm of the title struck unsuspecting mariners off the

Junger, Sebastian—*Continued*
coast of Nova Scotia in October, 1991. Junger traces the last voyage of the Andrea Gail—a commercial sword-fishing boat that was lost, with all six hands, in the storm—and his account is relentlessly suspenseful." New Yorker

Konstam, Angus
The history of pirates. Lyons Press 1999 192p il maps pa $19.95 hardcover o.p.   **910.4**
1. Pirates
ISBN 1-58574-516-2 (pa)
The author "chronicles the evolution of piracy from antiquity to the present. . . . Konstam profiles individual pirates, explores infamous vessels, and compares and contrasts various pirate regions and eras. He does a commendable job of separating fact from fiction." Booklist

Literature of travel and exploration; an encyclopedia; Jennifer Speake, editor. Fitzroy Dearborn 2003 3v il map set $495
      910.4
1. Voyages and travels
ISBN 1-57958-247-8   LC 2003-5352
"Speake's encyclopedia covers from the classical world to the present and contains over 600 entries, international in scope, in alphabetical order, ranging in length from 1,000 to 5,000 words. Most entries are devoted to the history of people and places related to travel, but some treat travel-related topics, such as trains and airplanes. Entries about people include a brief biography." Choice
"This is a rich introduction to primary sources . . . and an excellent source for further research." Booklist
Includes bibliographical references

Lord, Walter, 1917-2002
A night to remember. Holt & Co. 1955 209p il hardcover o.p. pa $14 *   **910.4**
1. Titanic (Steamship) 2. Shipwrecks
ISBN 0-03-027615-2; 0-8050-7764-2 (pa)
A detailed account of "the tragic drama of that terrible night—April 4, 1912—when the 'Titanic,' the unsinkable ship, struck an iceberg and went down in the icy waters of the Atlantic." Libr J

McPhee, John A.
Looking for a ship. Farrar, Straus & Giroux 1990 241p $18.95; pa $15   **910.4**
1. Stella Lykes (Freighter) 2. Seafaring life
ISBN 0-374-19077-1; 0-374-52319-3 (pa)
                  LC 90-3311
In this book McPhee focuses on the "plight of the U.S. merchant marine. Accompanying Second Mate Andy Chase on a 42-day run down the west coast of South America aboard the S.S. *Stella Lykes,* McPhee provides the reader with stories and tales of modern seafaring life and the problems of making a living as a merchant mariner. . . . An engrossing tale of the sea, with excellent detail and humanity." Libr J

National Geographic expeditions atlas; foreword by Peter H. Raven. National Geographic Soc. 2000 310p il maps $40 *   **910.4**
1. Voyages and travels
ISBN 0-7922-7616-7   LC 99-86883
"Organized into seven topical sections, this book . . . includes time lines, more than 220 vibrant photographs and illustrations, 60 maps recounting National Geographic's 112-year history of exploration, and first-hand accounts that introduce the reader to some of the bravest adventurers of our time, such as Jacques Cousteau, Richard Byrd, Amelia Earhart, Jane Goodall, and many more." Libr J
Includes bibliographical references

Netzley, Patricia D.
Encyclopedia of women's travel and exploration. Oryx Press 2000 259p il $88.95   **910.4**
1. Voyages and travels—Encyclopedias 2. Women—Travel—Encyclopedias
ISBN 1-573-56238-6; 978-1-57356-238-6
               LC 00-10720
"The 315 entries, arranged alphabetically, focus on a wide variety of women explorers, adventurers, and travelers throughout history and across continents. Most entries are biographical, but some examine related topics such as accommodations, solo travel, guide books, and mountaineering, occasionally offering perceptive insights into women's travel experiences and motivations." Choice
Includes bibliographical references

Read, Piers Paul, 1941-
Alive; sixteen men, seventy-two days, and insurmountable odds—the classic adventure of survival in the Andes. Harper Perennial 2005 398p il pa $13.95 *   **910.4**
1. Survival after airplane accidents, shipwrecks, etc. 2. Andes
ISBN 0-06-077866-0
First published 1974 by Lippincott
The author describes the extraordinary hardships endured by the survivors of a horrific plane crash in the Andes.

Williams, Glyn, 1932-
Voyages of delusion; the quest for the Northwest Passage. Yale Univ. Press 2003 xx, 467p il maps $29.95   **910.4**
1. Northwest Passage 2. Arctic regions—Exploration
ISBN 0-300-09866-9   LC 2002-109284
First published 2002 in the United Kingdom
"Williams chronicles the ill-advised expeditions of several eighteenth-century explorers attempting to find the Northwest Passage." Booklist
"Students of maritime exploration and 18th-century British politics will find this work engrossing, especially the detailed notes on sources." Publ Wkly

Worlds to explore; classic tales of travel & adventure from National Geographic; edited by Mark Jenkins. National Geographic Society 2006 xxv, 438p il map $23   **910.4**
1. Voyages and travels
ISBN 0-7922-5487-2; 978-0-7922-5487-4

LC 2005-58392

"Culled from early issues of National Geographic by editor Jenkins . . . these riveting narratives transport the reader to distinctive geographical areas all over the globe. The narrators share a common quest for adventure and travel as they recount tales of natural disasters, early air travel, primitive exploration, and summit quests. . . . These stories are like potato chips; one is never enough, and they're all but impossible not to devour in rapid succession." Libr J

910.5   Geography—Serial publications

United States. Central Intelligence Agency
The CIA world factbook 2008. Skyhorse Publishing 2007 xxx, 801p map pa $12.95
910.5
1. Geography—Handbooks, manuals, etc. 2. World politics—Handbooks, manuals, etc. 3. Political science—Handbooks, manuals, etc.
ISBN 978-1-60239-080-5; 1-60239-080-0
Also available online

"First issued as a classified document in 1962, this public, annually published resource profiles over 270 recognized countries, oceanic regions, and wildlife refuges. When applicable, A-to-Z entries note significant historical developments, geographical characteristics, population and economic figures, governmental structure, media and transportation methods, enlisted military data, and major international disputes. . . . This is a practical, at-a-glance resource for both researchers and curious lay people." Libr J

911   Historical geography

Atlas of world history; Patrick O'Brien, general editor. Oxford Univ. Press 1999 367p il maps $85   **911**
1. Historical atlases
ISBN 0-19-521567-2
Also available concise edition $45 (ISBN 0-19-521921-X)

Published in the United Kingdom with title: Philip's atlas of world history

"The volume is divided into five main chronological sections, from 'The Ancient World' to 'The Twentieth Century.' Each of these sections contains numerous two-page spreads featuring maps and accompanying essays. Following the maps are a 24-page 'Timechart,' a 32-page section called 'Events, People and Places' that features brief entries on major subjects within the maps, a 24-page index, and a 4-page bibliography." Booklist

Beck, Warren A.
Historical atlas of the American West; by Warren A. Beck and Ynez D. Haase. University of Okla. Press 1989 xlii, 78p maps pa $24.95 hardcover o.p.   **911**
1. West (U.S.)—Historical geography 2. Historical atlases
ISBN 0-8061-2456-3   LC 88-40540

"Defining the West as that part of the United States lying west of the 100th meridian, Beck and Haase provide a cartographic survey of the history of the region. In addition to maps illustrating such standard themes as natural resources, exploration and travel routes, the growth of the transportation network, and Indian tribal lands, the authors have included detailed maps on such topics as the Spanish-Mexican land grants and the Mt. St. Helens's eruption. . . . This atlas is an essential purchase for most libraries." Libr J

Fisher, Ronald M., 1938-
National Geographic historical atlas of the United States; text adapted by Ron Fisher. National Geographic 2004 240p il map $40 *
911
1. United States—Historical geography—Maps
ISBN 0-7922-6131-3   LC 2004-50421

"Beginning in 1450 and leading up to the capture of Saddam Hussein by U.S. Forces, the atlas highlights the landmark events of our nation's history in chronological order." Publisher's note

Gilbert, Martin, 1936-
The Routledge atlas of American history. 5th ed. Routledge 2006 156p map $100; pa $29.95
911
1. United States—Historical geography—Maps
ISBN   978-0-415-35902-3;   0-4153-5902-3;
978-0-415-35903-0 (pa); 0-415-35903-1 (pa)

First published 1968 by Weidenfeld & Nicolson. Variant titles: American history atlas; Dent atlas of American history

This includes 157 maps relating to American political, military, social, transport, and economic history.

Hellmann, Paul T., 1949-
Historical gazetteer of the United States. Routledge 2005 865p $150 *   **911**
1. United States—Gazetteers 2. United States—Historical geography—Dictionaries 3. United States—Local history—Dictionaries
ISBN 0-415-93948-8   LC 2004-11421

This reference provides "historical records of U.S. cities and towns. Arrangement is alphabetical by state, including the District of Columbia. Each state chapter contains a brief description of major cities, date of incorporation into the U.S., the number of counties, and a rough breakdown of how the state categorizes municipalities, towns, townships, and cities. This is followed by alphabetical entries for significant places. Inclusion is determined more by historical importance (national or regional) than by population. All county seats are included. Entries are in paragraph form and typically begin by noting

Hellmann, Paul T., 1949-—*Continued*
the country and the part of the state in which the place is located as well as its approximate distance from the state's most important city. Events are listed chronologically ." Booklist

Historical atlas of the United States; [edited by] Mark C. Carnes; cartography, Malcolm A. Swanston. Routledge 2003 304p maps $125
911

1. United States—Historical geography—Maps
ISBN 0-415-94111-3   LC 2002-31764
"More than 300 maps divided into 21 chronologically arranged parts cover the history of the U.S. from the formation of the North American continent to the September 11, 2001, attacks. There are special sections for presidential elections and territorial growth. . . . Overall, this atlas is a useful companion to the study of American history." Booklist

Magocsi, Paul R.
Historical atlas of Central Europe; [by] Paul Robert Magocsi. rev and expanded ed. University of Wash. Press 2002 274p maps (History of East Central Europe) pa $45 hardcover o.p.
911

1. Central Europe—Historical geography—Maps
ISBN 0-295-98146-6   LC 2001-27907
First published 1993 with title: Historical atlas of East Central Europe
"The volume is arranged chronologically, with coverage beginning about A.D. 400 (roughly the time of the demise of the Roman Empire) and continuing through the end of the 20th century. The maps and tables provide information on military affairs; population and population movements; economy; ethnolinguistic distributions; and religious, cultural, and educational institutions. All are extremely well done." SLJ

912 Atlases. Maps

Aczel, Amir D.
The riddle of the compass; the invention that changed the world. Harcourt 2001 178p il maps hardcover o.p. pa $13   **912**
1. Compass
ISBN 0-15-100506-0; 0-15-600753-3 (pa)
                          LC 00-47153
This book tracks "down the roots of the compass and tells the story of navigation through the ages." Publisher's note
Includes bibliographical references

Atlas of North America; H.J. de Blij, editor; [cartography by Philip's] Oxford University Press 2004 320p il map $125   **912**
1. Atlases
ISBN 0-19-516993-X   LC 2004-45005
This "atlas of the three largest countries of North America . . . [features a] thematic section covering physical, historic, economic, urban, social, and cultural topics ranging from environmental change to religious

practice and from indigenous peoples to migration patterns." Publisher's note
"This exhaustive, authoritative resource presents a dynamic view of Canada, the U.S., and Mexico." SLJ

Atlas of the world; [prepared by National Geographic Maps for the Book Division] 8th ed. National Geographic Society 2005 various paging il map $165 *   **912**
1. Atlases
ISBN 0-7922-7543-8   LC 2004-45002
First published 1963
At head of title: National Geographic
This edition features 60 political maps, 17 thematic maps, and 10 panoramic satellite views of the world. Also includes views of all five ocean floors and both polar regions, the latest imagery from the Hubble Space Telescope, and new information from Mars. A world-thematic section addressing such global concerns as biodiversity, the world economy, and terrorism is also provided. The Web site that accompanies the atlas includes interactive maps
For a review see: Booklist, Feb. 15, 2005

Atlas of the world; [cartography by Philip's] 14th ed. Oxford University Press 2007 448p il map $80 *   **912**
1. Atlases
ISBN 978-0-19-533400-5   LC 2007-61603
First published 1992
At head of title: Oxford
This atlas "contains 179 pages of full-color, computer-generated political and topographical maps by Philips of the world, continents, and regions. . . . More than 70 world and regional thematic maps with illustrations and text explore topics from demographics to the environment, while a special city-map section covers 69 major international metropolitan areas with 42 closeup maps of city centers." Libr J

DK complete atlas of the world. Dorling Kindersley Publishing 2007 432p il map $75
912
1. Atlases
ISBN 978-0-7566-2859-8   LC 2008-627142
"The atlas begins with the usual information on the solar system (with Pluto and Eris noted as dwarf planets). Thematic world maps, charts, and tables are divided by subject—climate, health, language, economics, communications, etc. . . . For each continent, in addition to physical and political maps, there is a double-page satellite image ringed with small images of different cities or geographical examples keyed to the large map." Booklist

Firefly atlas of North America; United States, Canada & Mexico. Firefly Books 2006 272p il map $55   **912**
1. Atlases
ISBN 978-1-55407-207-1; 1-55407-207-7
This atlas is "divided into three sections covering the United States (including Puerto Rico and the U.S. Pacific Territories), Canada and Mexico. . . . Each country section opens with a map and a color-coded legend to the regional maps that follow. All 50 U.S. states (plus Washington, D.C.), the 13 Canadian provinces and territories

Firefly atlas of North America—*Continued*
(including Nunavut) and Mexico's 32 states are illustrated." Publisher's note

Goode, J. Paul, 1862-1932
Goode's world atlas; Howard Veregin, editor. 21st ed. Rand McNally 2005 371p il map $49.95

912

1. Atlases
ISBN 0-528-85339-2
First published 1922 with title: Goode's school atlas
At head of title: Rand McNally
"Contains thematic maps and tables showing distribution of population, minerals, manufacturing, and other subjects. Also included are metropolitan-area maps, physical-political maps of regions, geographic tables, and ocean-floor maps showing earth movement. Pronouncing index included." N Y Public Libr Book of How & Where to Look It Up
Includes bibliographical references

Hammond world atlas. 5th ed. Hammond World Atlas Corporation 2008 346p il map $59.95 *

912

1. Atlases
ISBN 978-0-8437-0967-4; 0-8437-0967-7
First published 1992 with title: Hammond atlas of the world
This atlas includes an "illustrated 64-page 'Thematic Section,' a 48-page 'Satellite Section' with more than 40 color photos and a commentary, and 228 pages of . . . full-color physical and political maps representing the world, continents, and regions with detailed . . . computer-generated terrain modeling." Libr J

Rand McNally commercial atlas & marketing guide 2008. 139th ed. Rand McNally 2007 2v maps set $395

912

1. Atlases
ISSN 0361-9723
ISBN 978-0-52894-193-1; 0-52894-193-3
Annual. First published 1876
"Primarily an atlas of the United States, with large, detailed, clear maps. Includes many statistical tables of population, business and manufacturers, agriculture, and other commercial features, such as indicators of market potential." Ref Sources for Small & Medium-sized Libr. 6th edition

World atlas of the oceans; more than 200 maps and charts of the ocean floor; edited by Manfred Leier. Firefly Bks. 2001 264p il maps $50 *

912

1. Ocean—Maps 2. Marine biology
ISBN 1-55209-585-1
"This work begins with several sections about oceans in general, including relief maps as well as chapters on 'How the Oceans Were Formed' and 'The Ocean as a Habitat and Commercial Area.' The section that follows contains bathymetric charts documenting the levels of individual oceans and basins. . . . The habitats and commerce section is extensive and covers many fascinating topics such as ocean currents and tides, hurricane formation, sea life, sea trade, oil and mineral deposits, and ca-

nals and ports. There is even information on sunken ships and treasure and shipwrecks of the twentieth century. Each topic warrants a two-page spread with photographs, maps, tables, or all of the above." Booklist

913 Geography of and travel in ancient world

Freeman, Philip, 1961-
The philosopher and the Druids; a journey among the ancient Celts. Simon & Schuster 2006 221p il maps $25

913

1. Posidonius, 1st cent. B.C. 2. Celtic civilization 3. Europe—History—To 476
ISBN 0-7432-6280-8   LC 2005-54150
The author "aims to piece together the lost account of the first-century B.C.E. journey of the Stoic philosopher Posidonius from Rhodes into the wild Celtic northlands in Gaul (now parts of Spain and France). . . . In examining ancient Celtic history and culture in tandem with Greek and Roman attitudes, Freeman has turned out an engrossing study that both students and lay readers will enjoy." Libr J
Includes bibliographical references

914 Geography of and travel in Europe

Mayes, Frances
A year in the world; journeys of a passionate traveller. Broadway Books 2006 xx, 420p map hardcover o.p. pa $15

914

1. Europe—Description and travel
ISBN   0-7679-1005-2;   978-0-7679-1005-7; 978-0-7679-1006-4 (pa); 0-7679-1006-0 (pa)
LC 2005-50831
The trips described in this book "are arranged in calendar order, beginning with a January visit to Andalucia and concluding with a year-end trip to Mantova, Italy. In the months between, Mayes takes a sweltering trip to Greece, reunites with friends in Scotland, and journeys to Fez, Naples, Sicily, Burgundy, Portugal, and more." Libr J
"Befitting her gifts as a poet, Mayes' prose shines with evocative imagery, bringing life to every subject she encounters across her peripatetic year." Booklist
Includes bibliographical references

914.1 Geography of and travel in the British Isles

Bryson, Bill
Notes from a small island. Morrow 1996 324p pa $14 hardcover o.p.

914.1

1. Great Britain—Civilization 2. Great Britain—Description and travel
ISBN 0-380-72750-1 (pa)   LC 95-43437

Bryson, Bill—_Continued_

"Before his return to the U.S. after a 20-year residence in England, journalist Bryson . . . embarked on a farewell tour of his adopted homeland. His trenchant, witty and detailed observations of life in a variety of towns and villages will delight Anglophiles." Publ Wkly

914.11 Geography of and travel in Scotland

Boswell, James, 1740-1795

The journal of a tour to the Hebrides with Samuel Johnson. Kessinger Publishing 2004 277p pa $28.95   **914.11**

1. Johnson, Samuel, 1709-1784 2. Hebrides (Scotland)—Description

ISBN 978-1-4191-6794-2; 1-4191-6794-4

Also available in a combined edition with Samuel Johnson's Journey to the Western Islands of Scotland from Everyman's Library $23 (ISBN 978-0-375-41418-3) and Penguin Classics $18 (ISBN 978-0-14-043221-3)

First published 1785

The renowned biographer here recounts the daily events of a tour which he took in 1773 with Johnson

914.5 Geography of and travel in Italy

Goethe, Johann Wolfgang von, 1749-1832

Italian journey; [by] J. W. Goethe; translated with an introduction by W.H. Auden and Elizabeth Mayer. Penguin 2004 (Penguin classics) pa $17
                                                     914.5

1. Italy—Description and travel

ISBN 978-0-14-044233-5; 0-14-044233-2

First published 1816; this translation first published 1962 in the United Kingdom

"In 1786 Goethe set out on his journey to Italy, hoping to fulfil a personal and artistic quest he had anticipated for years. During his trip he kept a journal and wrote many letters, and it was upon these sources that he based his Italian Journey." Publisher's note

"This rather free translation is beautifully transparent and fluent." N Y Times Book Rev

915 Geography of and travel in Asia

Stewart, Rory

The places in between. Harcourt, Inc. 2006 299p pa $14   **915**

1. Afghanistan—Description and travel

ISBN 0-15-603156-6; 978-0-15-603156-1
                                        LC 2005-32213

"A Harvest original"

First published 2004 in the United Kingdom

The author "decided to explore Afghanistan by walking across the country. This book is the resulting narra-

tive of what turned out to be a 20-month trek from Herat to Afghanistan's capital, Kabul, a journey that Stewart began in January 2002 after he had spent 16 months walking across Iran, Pakistan, India, and Nepal." Libr J

This book is "more than great journalism. It's a great travel narrative." N Y Times Book Rev

Theroux, Paul

The great railway bazaar; by train through Asia. Houghton Mifflin 1975 342p pa $14.95 hardcover o.p.   **915**

1. Asia—Description and travel 2. Railroads—Asia

ISBN 0-618-65894-7 (pa)

The author "took a four-month solitary lecture tour of Asia in 1973, traveling by train wherever possible. His route was through Turkey, Iran, India, Southeast Asia, Japan, and back to London via the Soviet Union. He writes of conversations and impressions of the people encountered." Libr J

Thubron, Colin, 1939-

Shadow of the Silk Road. Harper Collins 2007 363p map $25.95   **915**

1. Asia—Description and travel

ISBN 978-0-06-123172-8; 0-06-123172-X
                                        LC 2006-52142

First published 2006 in the United Kingdom

The author "follows the course—or at least the general drift—of the ancient network of trade routes that connected central China with the Mediterranean Coast, traversing along the way several former Soviet republics, war-torn Afghanistan, Iran and Turkey." Publ Wkly

"An illuminating account of a breathtaking journey." Booklist

915.1 Geography of travel in China and adjacent areas

Cabot, Mabel H.

Vanished kingdoms; a woman explorer in Tibet, China & Mongolia, 1921-1925; preface by Rubie Watson. Farrar, Straus & Giroux 2003 190p il map $35   **915.1**

1. Wulsin, Janet 2. China—Description and travel 3. Tibet (China)—Description and travel

ISBN 1-931788-08-1   LC 2002-110404

The author "explores the life of her mother, Janet Wulsin. . . . With an unrelenting enthusiasm, Wulsin accompanied her husband on scientific pursuits abroad and helped collect, catalog, preserve, and prepare specimens. . . . The most outstanding feature of the book is the expedition's photographic collection, which makes the work not only an informative study but also a visual joy." Libr J

Includes bibliographical references

Ma Jian, 1953-

Red dust; a path through China; translated from the Chinese by Flora Drew. Pantheon Bks. 2001 324p maps pa $14 hardcover o.p.   **915.1**

1. China—Description and travel

ISBN 0-385-72023-8 (pa)   LC 2001-21575

Ma Jian, 1953-—*Continued*

"Faced with imprisonment, Jian fled to the Chinese countryside, eventually making his way to Tibet. His journey is presented as a combination travelogue and a narrative of sheer poetry and spirituality." Booklist

Salzman, Mark

Iron & silk. Random House 1987 c1986 211p hardcover o.p. pa $12.95   **915.1**

1. China—Description and travel 2. Martial arts
ISBN 0-394-55156-7; 0-394-75511-1 (pa)

LC 86-11846

The author tells of his two years teaching English to medical students in China's Hunan Province following his graduation from Yale University in 1982.

This book is "not so much a treatise on modern Chinese mores as a series of telling vignettes. . . . [The author] describes his encounter with Pan Qingfu, the country's foremost master of wushu, the traditional Chinese martial art." Time

Theroux, Paul

Riding the iron rooster; by train through China; Paul Theroux. 1st Mariner Books ed. Houghton Mifflin 2006 480p map pa $7.50   **915.1**

1. Railroads 2. China—Description and travel
ISBN 978-0-6186-5897-8   LC 2006028745
First published 1988 by Putnam's

This is an account of the author's yearlong rail journey through China. "For Theroux, traveling is both about people—their thoughts, customs, and peculiarities-and a form of autobiography, and here we learn as much about his own quirks and fancies as we do about the intriguing world of contemporary China." Libr J

915.4   Geography of and travel in South Asia. India

Matthiessen, Peter

The snow leopard. Viking 1978 338p pa $15 hardcover o.p.   **915.4**

1. Natural history—Himalaya Mountains 2. Zen Buddhism
ISBN 0-14-025508-7 (pa)   LC 78-5
Companion volume Nine-headed dragon river (1986)

This book "is based on the journal Matthiessen kept during his trek with the field biologist George Schaller to the Crystal Mountain, in upper Nepal, in 1973. The trek took them 250 miles to the Land of Dolpo, on the Tibetan plateau. . . . The purpose: to observe the November rut of the Himalayan blue sheep in order to determine whether this little-known species is related to the extinct common ancestor of the goat and the sheep." Saturday Rev

Includes bibliographical references

915.6   Geography of and travel in the Middle East

Elliot, Jason, 1965-

Mirrors of the unseen; journeys in Iran. St. Martin's Press 2006 415p il $26.95   **915.6**

1. Iran—Description and travel
ISBN 978-0-312-30191-0; 0-312-30191-X

LC 2006-42918

The author discusses his travels in Iran.

"With Iran so central in the news, this is a good read for the armchair traveler and amateur geopolitical strategist alike." Publ Wkly

Feiler, Bruce S.

Walking the Bible; a journey by land through the five books of Moses; by Bruce Feiler. Morrow 2001 451p $26; pa $14.95   **915.6**

1. Bible. O.T. Pentateuch—Geography
ISBN 0-380-97775-3; 0-380-80731-9 (pa)

LC 00-56076

Maps of the Biblical World from c. 2000-1200 B.C.E. and of the Middle East on endpapers

"Determined to connect more deeply with his religious roots, Feiler joined an archaeologist in a trek through the Middle East, visiting the sites mentioned in the Pentateuch, the first five books of the Hebrew Bible. A book full of wonder and awe and personal enlightenment." Booklist

Includes bibliographical references

Horwitz, Tony, 1958-

Baghdad without a map, and other misadventures in Arabia. Dutton 1991 276p map pa $16 hardcover o.p.   **915.6**

1. Middle East—Description and travel
ISBN 0-452-26745-5 (pa)   LC 90-46653

This is an account of the author's travels in Egypt, Libya, the Sudan, Lebanon, Iraq, Iran and other countries in the Middle East. Horwitz accompanied his wife to the region "in the late 1980s and returned to Baghdad in August 1990 following the invasion of Kuwait." Libr J

"Horwitz mixes insight and humor in these observations that illustrate on an everyday level both the contradictions and the idiosyncrasies of the Arab world." Booklist

915.9   Geography of and travel in Southeast Asia

Gargan, Edward A.

A river's tale; a year on the Mekong. Knopf 2002 332p il maps pa $14.95 hardcover o.p.

    915.9

1. Southeast Asia—Description and travel
ISBN 0-375-70559-7 (pa)   LC 2001-38056

"A chronicle of a year-long journey along the nearly 3,000 miles of the Mekong River as it descends from the Tibetan plateau through southern Asia, Gargan's book is

Gargan, Edward A.—*Continued*
a vivid look at the disparate peoples [that] settled the length of the river's path." Publ Wkly

Includes bibliographical references

916   Geography of and travel in Africa

Campbell, James T.
Middle passages; African American journeys to Africa, 1787-2005; [by] James Campbell. Penguin Press 2006 513p il (The Penguin history of American life) $29.95   **916**

1. Africa—Description and travel
ISBN 1-59420-083-1; 978-1-59420-083-0
LC 2005-58672

The author "traces the travels and travails of diverse African-Americans—missionary, settler, journalist, tourist, immigrant—who journeyed to Africa over 200-plus years." Publ Wkly

"From the repatriation of former slaves in the early years of the United States to the recent heritage tourism featuring Goree Island and other slave-trading sites, Campbell provides an artful reconstruction of the often bittersweet experience of return and reunion." N Y Times Book Rev

Matthiessen, Peter
African silences. Random House 1991 225p maps pa $13 hardcover o.p. *   **916**

1. Natural history—Africa
ISBN 0-679-73102-4 (pa)   LC 90-52893

"In this account of three trips to Central and Western Africa, Matthiessen reports on the almost total devastation of wildlife in Senegal, Gambia, and the Ivory Coast and describes an expedition searching for the rare Congo peacock and gorillas in the Virunga Mountains of Zaire." Libr J

Theroux, Paul
Dark star safari; overland from Cairo to Cape Town. Houghton Mifflin 2003 472p maps $28   **916**

1. Africa—Description and travel
ISBN 0-618-13424-7   LC 2002-32710
First published 2002 in the United Kingdom

This book's "itinerary is Africa, from Cairo to Cape Town: down the Nile, through Sudan and Ethiopia, to Kenya, Uganda, and ultimately to the tip of South Africa." Publisher's note

"Where Theroux sees Africa uncluttered by preconceived notions, his writing can be brilliant. . . . But where Theroux has traveled before—40 years ago, as first a Peace Corps teacher, then a lecturer at Uganda's Makerere University in the golden years just after the country's independence—he sees Africa not for what it is, but for what it might have been." Christ Sci Monit

916.6   West Africa and offshore islands

Benanav, Michael
Men of salt; across the Sahara with the caravan of white gold. Lyons Press 2006 220p il map $23.95   **916.6**

1. Sahara Desert—Description and travel 2. Salt
ISBN 1-59228-772-7; 978-1-59228-772-7
LC 2005-23205

The author describes his experiences after he "joined what is known as the Caravan of White Gold—so-called because the salt was once literally worth its weight in gold—on its mission into the deadly heart of the Sahara to haul back gleaming slabs of solid salt for sale at market." Publisher's note

"Even if readers don't find the idea of spending 40 harrowing days with a caravan crossing some of the world's most unforgiving desert as enticing as Benanav does, that doesn't mean they won't quickly devour his thrilling account of that otherworldly journey." Publ Wkly

Includes bibliographical references

Tayler, Jeffrey
Angry wind; through Muslim Black Africa by truck, bus, boat, and camel. Houghton Mifflin 2005 252p map $25   **916.6**

1. Sahel—Description and travel
ISBN 0-618-33467-X   LC 2004-54066

Tayler "undertook a journey through the Sahel, the southern region of the Sahara Desert. His journey took him through some of the most dangerous regions of countries such as Chad, Nigeria, and Niger, as he sought out Africans of Muslim faith in particular. Tayler encountered many generous people along the way, as well as plenty of bureaucracy and even danger when he traversed territory rife with land mines. Along the way, he talked to Africans of both Muslim and Christian faiths, learning how deep the division between the two groups is." Booklist

"This substantial and informative work is no mere travel tale—it is a firsthand account of the author's deeply personal quest for knowledge and understanding of a people and a region that continues to struggle with extreme poverty and unrest." Libr J

917   Geography of and travel in North America

Cohan, Tony
Mexican days; journeys into the heart of Mexico. Broadway 2006 275p map $24.95   **917**

1. Mexico—Description and travel
ISBN 0-7679-2090-2; 978-0-7679-2090-2
LC 2005-52705

This is an "overview of Mexico's diverse culture, history, food, and customs. Those who know Mexico will gain new perspective on familiar tourist attractions and a glimpse into parts of Mexico travelers rarely visit." Libr J

The **Columbia** gazetteer of North America; edited by Saul B. Cohen. Columbia Univ. Press 2000 1157p il $156 **917**

1. North America—Gazetteers

ISBN 0-231-11990-9   LC 00-27512

"This work includes more than 50,000 entries covering every incorporated place and country in the United States, along with many unincorporated places and physical features throughout North America. Arranged alphabetically, each entry includes a pronunciation guide, location information, and longitude and latitude where appropriate. If the listing is a municipality, brief population figures are provided as well. . . . Color maps of the physical regions of North America, along with political maps of the region, are included as reference points." Am Ref Books Annu, 2001

Gimlette, John, 1963-

Theatre of fish; travels through Newfoundland and Labrador. Alfred A. Knopf 2005 xxii, 360p il map $25 **917**

1. Atlantic Coast (North America)

ISBN 1-4000-4322-0   LC 2005-44149

This book describes a "journey through Newfoundland and Labrador, where fishing villages are being abandoned." N Y Times Book Rev

"Readers will be fascinated by Newfoundland's and Labrador's bizarre, often tragic pasts and equally strange presents, and they will be glad it was the eloquent Gimlette who made the trip so they don't have to." Publ Wkly

Includes bibliographical references

917.3   Geography of and travel in the United States

Beatty, Michael A., 1935-

County name origins of the United States. McFarland & Co. 2001 665p $195 **917.3**

1. Geographic names—United States 2. United States—Local history

ISBN 0-7864-1025-6   LC 2001-18034

Arranged alphabetically by state, this study shows "how each county in the United States was named. Dates and circumstances under which counties were named or renamed are provided, including brief biographical, geographical, and other relevant historical information. In cases where name derivations are unknown or disputed, an informed discussion gives probable origins." Libr J

Includes bibliographical references

Conaway, James, 1941-

Vanishing America; in pursuit of our elusive landscapes. Shoemaker & Hoard 2007 275p map $24.95; pa $15.95 **917.3**

1. United States—Description and travel 2. United States—Local history 3. American national characteristics

ISBN 978-1-59376-128-8; 978-1-58243-442-1 (pa)

LC 2007-10643

The author "details aspects of the country's natural and cultural history that are steadily being destroyed." Booklist

"This is a powerful book, a thinking man's road trip that puts its finger on the flaw in our national character." Orion

Cronkite, Walter

Around America; a tour of our magnificent coastline; drawings by David Canright. Norton 2001 211p il maps $23.95; pa $13.95 **917.3**

1. United States—Description and travel 2. United States—Local history

ISBN 0-393-04083-6; 0-393-32335-8 (pa)

LC 00-69563

In this "rumination on the people and places along America's seashores, Cronkite shows his reverence for the country's coastal means of travel. Starting in the Northeast, working south, then circling around to the West Coast, the book reads like a lively but laid-back cruise." Publ Wkly

Curtis, Nancy C.

Black heritage sites; an African American odyssey and finder's guide. American Lib. Assn. 1996 677p il $75 **917.3**

1. Historic sites 2. African Americans—History

ISBN 0-8389-0643-5   LC 95-5788

Also available in a two volume paperback edition from New Press

This "guide locates significant places in African-American history and supplies . . . recent addresses, phone numbers, and visitors' information. . . . Organized by region, a historical essay introduces each section, presenting the culture and history in that area." Publisher's note

Ferris, Gary W.

Presidential places; a guide to the historic sites of U.S. presidents; [by] Gary Ferris. Blair 1999 284p il pa $15.95 **917.3**

1. Presidents—United States—Homes 2. Historic sites 3. United States—Description and travel

ISBN 0-89587-176-9   LC 98-50395

This is a "guide to historic places of interest relating to all the American presidents. Included are, among other things, presidential birthplaces, where they lived, where they went to school, the churches they attended, where they are buried, and the monuments, museums, and libraries dedicated to their lives and administrations." Libr J

Includes bibliographical references

Heat Moon, William Least

Blue highways; a journey into America; photographs by the author; with a new afterword by the author. Back Bay Bks. 1999 429p il $29.95; pa $14.95 **917.3**

1. United States—Description and travel

ISBN 0-316-35391-4; 0-316-35329-9 (pa)

LC 00-265444

Heat Moon, William Least—*Continued*
A reissue of the title first published 1982 by Little, Brown

An account of the author's journey across the U.S. in a van taking only secondary roads

River-horse; the logbook of a boat across America. Penguin Books 2001 506p il map pa $14
917.3
1. Inland navigation 2. Boats and boating 3. United States—Description and travel
ISBN 978-0-14-029860-4; 0-14-029860-6

First published 1999 by Houghton Mifflin

The author sets out across the United States "propelled chiefly by a dual-outboard dubbed Nikawa, 'River Horse' in Osage. In this hardy craft, he and a small crew attempt to travel more than 5000 miles by inland waterways from the Atlantic to the Pacific in a single season." Publ Wkly

Heat-Moon's "journey becomes a living history of the U.S. as the well-read author refers to numerous historical events that took place along his route, quoting at length from other writers and adventurers who preceded him." Booklist

Home ground; language for an American landscape; Barry Lopez, editor; Debra Gwartney, managing editor. Trinity University Press 2006 xxiv, 449p il $29.95   **917.3**
1. Geographic names—Encyclopedias
2. Americanisms—Encyclopedias
ISBN 978-1-59534-024-5; 1-59534-024-6
          LC 2006-19942

This is a "collection of geographical terms from every region of the United States. The 45 contributors, among them Jon Krakauer and Barbara Kingsolver, chose words that Americans use to describe landscape features where they live, then enriched their definitions with literary quotes, comments, irony, and humor. The result is a readable A-to-Z geological and geographical dictionary that surpasses other dictionaries in both scope and coverage." Libr J

Includes bibliographical references

Jenkins, Peter, 1951-
A walk across America. Morrow 1979 288p il maps pa $6.99 hardcover o.p.   **917.3**
1. United States—Description and travel
ISBN 0-06-095955-X (pa)   LC 78-10320

This book chronicles the author's journey with his dog from New York to the Gulf of Mexico

Kane, Joseph Nathan, 1899-2002
Nicknames and sobriquets of U.S. cities, states, and counties. 3rd ed, {by} Joseph Nathan Kane & Gerard L. Alexander. Scarecrow Press 1979 429p hardcover o.p. pa $53   **917.3**
1. Geographic names—United States 2. Nicknames
ISBN 0-8108-1255-X; 978-0-8108-4704-0 (pa);
0-8108-4704-3 (pa)   LC 79-20193

First published 1965 with title: Nicknames of cities and states of the U.S.

An enlargement of a section of Kane's "1000 facts worth knowing" plus Alexander's "Nicknames of American cities, towns and villages (past and present)"

"Comprehensive listing of nicknames of cities, counties, and states. Indexed geographically by city and state, and alphabetically by nickname." Ref Sources for Small & Medium-sized Libr. 6th edition

Lévy, Bernard Henri, 1948-
American vertigo; traveling America in the footsteps of Tocqueville; [by] Bernard-Henri Lévy; translated by Charlotte Mandell. Random House 2006 308p $24.95   **917.3**
1. Tocqueville, Alexis de 2. United States—Description and travel 3. American national characteristics 4. United States—Social conditions
ISBN 1-4000-6434-1   LC 2005-44782

The French journalist describes his experiences after *The Atlantic Monthly* "asked him to hit the road and observe the United States, just as his fellow countryman Alexis de Tocqueville did 173 years ago." N Y Times (Late N Y Ed)

This is "an engaging but often-disturbing portrait of our nation from an eloquent, brutally honest foreigner who wishes our country well." Booklist

McMurtry, Larry
Roads; driving America's great highways. Simon & Schuster 2000 206p pa $13 hardcover o.p.   **917.3**
1. United States—Description and travel 2. Roads
ISBN 0-684-86885-7 (pa)   LC 00-27889

In this volume McMurtry provides "reminiscence and commentary on whatever pops up in the windows or in his mind as he crisscrosses the country: enigmatic glances at the Western past, salutes to hundreds of literary and historical figures." N Y Times Book Rev

National Geographic guide to the national parks of the United States. 5th ed. National Geographic Society 2006 480p il pa $25 *
     917.3
1. National parks and reserves—United States
ISBN 0-7922-5322-1

First published 1989

This guide provides information on each of the fifty national parks, including things to do, campgrounds and accommodations, and facilities for the disabled.

National Geographic guide to the state parks of the United States; prepared by the Book Division, National Geographic Society. 2nd ed. National Geographic Soc. 2004 384p il maps pa $24   **917.3**
1. Parks—United States
ISBN 0-7922-6628-5   LC 2003-61515

First published 1997

A guide to more than 200 parks in all 50 states. Each entry provides information on: outstanding scenery and nature; historic and cultural sites; recreational activities; wildlife watching; camping and lodging. 32 maps and 250 color photographs accompany the text.

The **official** guide to America's national parks; [by the] National Park Foundation. 12th ed. Fodor's Travel Publs. 2004 528p il map pa $19
     917.3

The official guide to America's national parks—
Continued
1. National parks and reserves—United States
ISBN 978-1-4000-1375-3; 1-4000-1375-5
New edition in preparation
First published 1979 with title: The Complete guide to America's national parks. Periodically revised. Publisher varies
"Complete coverage of all 388 national parks" Cover
This park visitors' guide also covers national monuments, military parks, seashores and lakeshores, historic sites, and battlefields. Entries are listed by State, and include contact information, activities and facilities, travel directories, and nearby attractions and points of interest.

Parks directory of the United States; Darren L. Smith, Kay Gill, editors. Omnigraphics 2007 1101p maps $216   **917.3**
1. Parks—United States 2. Historic sites
ISBN 978-0-7808-0932-1; 0-7808-0932-7
First published 1992. Frequently revised
"A guide to more than 5,270 national and state parks, historic sites, battlefields, monuments, forests, preserves, memorials, seashores, trails, heritage areas, scenic byways, marine sanctuaries, wildlife refuges, urban parks and other designated recreation areas in the United States administered by national and state park agencies. Also includes Canadian national parks." Title page

Sandoval-Strausz, A. K.
Hotel; an American history. Yale University Press 2007 375p il map $37.50 *   **917.3**
1. Hotels and motels
ISBN 978-0-300-10616-9; 0-300-10616-5
LC 2007-10239
"This book recounts the . . . history of the hotel in America. . . . [It] explores why the hotel was invented, how its architecture developed, and the many ways, [according to the author], it influenced the course of United States history." Publisher's note
The author "develops social, moral, economic, legal and political connections with originality and insight. His impassioned reading of our 'built environment' is fascinating, his research prodigious. And the subject merits his talent as a historian." N Y Times Book Rev
Includes bibliographical references

Stone, Nathaniel
On the water; discovering America in a rowboat; illustrations by Elizabeth Stone. Broadway Bks. 2002 323p il $21.95; pa $12.95
917.3
1. Boats and boating 2. United States—Description and travel
ISBN 0-7679-0841-4; 0-7679-0842-2 (pa)
LC 2002-18489
"Pushing off from New York City's Hudson River, [the author] rowed up the Erie Canal, down to Ohio, onward to the Mississippi, across the Gulf to Key West, and back up along the coastline of the Atlantic to Maine. It was a 6,000-mile journey, and it took him 10 months to complete. This is the chronicle of his adventure, his voyage into and around America, the story of the people he met and the places he saw. . . . It's a straightforward, crisply written memoir." Booklist

917.4 Geography of and travel in New England

Bryson, Bill
A walk in the woods; rediscovering America on the Appalachian Trail. Broadway Bks. 1998 276p hardcover o.p. pa $14.95   **917.4**
1. Appalachian region—Description and travel
ISBN 0-7679-0251-3; 0-7679-0252-1 (pa)
LC 97-32627
"After living abroad, Bryson decided to reacquaint himself with America by walking the famed Appalachian Trail, which traverses 14 states and stretches 2,100 miles." Booklist
"Bryson's breezy, self-mocking tone may turn off readers who hanker for another 'Into Thin Air' or 'Seven Years in Tibet.' Others, however, may find themselves turning the pages with increasing amusement and anticipation as they discover that they're in the hands of a satirist of the first rank, one who writes (and walks) with Chaucerian brio." N Y Times Book Rev
Includes bibliographical references

917.41 Geography of and travel in Maine

Thoreau, Henry David, 1817-1862
The Maine woods; introduction by Edward Hoagland. Penguin Books 1988 xxxiii, 442p (Penguin nature library) pa $16   **917.41**
1. Maine—Description and travel
ISBN 0-14-017013-8   LC 88-3644
First published 1864 by Ticknor & Fields
This account of the author's rambles around the lakes and woods of Maine "records three different excursions: Thoreau's trip to Mount Katahdin (which he called 'Ktaadn'), published in the 'Union Magazine' in 1848; 'Chesuncook,' which appeared in the 'Atlantic Monthly' in the same year; and 'The Allegash and the East Branch,' which is a marvel of precise observation." Herzberg. Reader's Ency of Am Lit

917.44 Geography of and travel in Massachusetts

Thoreau, Henry David, 1817-1862
Cape Cod; photographs by Scot Miller. Ill. ed. of the American classic. Houghton Mifflin Co. 2008 255p il $35 *   **917.44**
1. Cape Cod (Mass.)—Description and travel
ISBN 978-0-618-75845-6; 0-618-75845-3
LC 2007-42952
Also available in hardcover and paperback from Princeton Univ. Press
"Published in cooperation with the Walden Woods Project"
First published 1865
This "account is based on the author's experiences during the three short visits to Cape Cod (Oct. 1849;

Thoreau, Henry David, 1817-1862—*Continued*
June 1850; July 1855), and includes ten essays on the history and character of the inhabitants, 'The Highland Light,' Nantucket, the sea, the beach, and other aspects of the Cape." Oxford Companion to Am Lit

917.47   Geography of and travel in New York

Gopnik, Adam
Through the children's gate; a home in New York. Alfred A. Knopf 2006 318p $25
917.47
1. New York (N.Y.)—Description and travel
ISBN 1-4000-4181-3; 978-1-4000-4181-7
LC 2006-45260
"Gopnik writes about returning to New York after five years in Paris." N Y Times Book Rev
"You don't have to be a New Yorker or even necessarily an enthusiast of the city to be alternately amused, touched, and charmed by Gopnik's well-crafted pieces." Christ Sci Monit

917.8   Geography of and travel in Western United States

Wallis, Michael, 1945-
Route 66: the mother road. St. Martin's Griffin 2001 276p il maps $35; pa $19.95
917.8
1. West (U.S.)—Description and travel
ISBN 0-312-28167-6; 0-312-28161-7 (pa)
LC 2001-31944
This is a reissue of the title first published 1990
"75th anniversary edition"
The author examines the highway's history, roadside diners, towns, motels, and people
Includes bibliographical references

917.91   Geography and travel in Arizona

Fletcher, Colin, 1922-2007
The man who walked through time. Vintage Bks. 1989 247p il pa $14.95
917.91
1. Grand Canyon (Ariz.)
ISBN 0-679-72306-4; 978-0-679-72306-6
LC 72-4082
First published 1967 by Knopf
An account of the author's journey on foot through the Grand Canyon National Park.

918   Geography of and travel in South America. Latin America

Theroux, Paul
The old Patagonian express; by train through the Americas. Houghton Mifflin 1979 404p pa $15 hardcover o.p.
918
1. Railroads—Latin America
ISBN 0-395-52105-X (pa)
LC 79-15353
The author describes his journey from Boston to Patagonia by train

918.1   Geography of and travel in Brazil

Millard, Candice
The river of doubt; Theodore Roosevelt's darkest journey. Doubleday 2005 416p il map $26
918.1
1. Roosevelt, Theodore, 1858-1919
2. Roosevelt-Rondon Scientific Expedition (1913-1914) 3. Amazon River valley
ISBN 0-385-50796-8
LC 2005-46541
This is an account of the Amazon expedition Theodore Roosevelt undertook in 1912, with his son Kermit and the Brazilian explorer Col. Candido Rondon.
The author "turns this incredible story into one that easily matches an Indiana Jones screen adventure." Libr J
Includes bibliographical references

918.2   Geography of and travel in Argentina

Chatwin, Bruce
In Patagonia; introduction by Nicholas Shakespeare. Penguin Books 2003 204p il map (Penguin classics) pa $15
918.2
1. Patagonia (Argentina and Chile)—Description and travel
ISBN 0-14-243719-0; 978-0-14-243719-3
LC 2002-45038
First published 1977 in the United Kingdom
This travelogue "captures the exotic characters and scenery Chatwin encountered in the southern tip of South America on a search for an important prehistoric artifact." Booklist

919 Geography of and travel in other parts of world and on extraterrestrial worlds. Geography of and travel in Pacific Ocean Islands

Theroux, Paul
The happy isles of Oceania; paddling the Pacific. Houghton Mifflin Co. 2006 528p map pa $15.95   **919**
1. Oceania—Description and travel
ISBN 978-0-618-65898-5; 0-618-65898-X
LC 2006-28742
First published 1992 by Putnam
The author "spent 18 months in a one-man collapsible kayak exploring such exotic Pacific islands as New Zealand, Australia, the Soloman and Cook Islands, Fiji, Samoa, Tahiti, Easter Island, and Hawaii. . . . A brilliant storyteller with an eye for the absurd, Theroux takes the reader to little-known places where time seems to have stood still and people lead simple lives totally unrelated to 20th-century America." Libr J

919.4 Geography of and travel in Australia

Chatwin, Bruce
The songlines. Viking 1987 293p pa $13.95 hardcover o.p.   **919.4**
ISBN 0-14-009429-6 (pa)   LC 86-40512
"An Elisabeth Sifton book"
The author's travels in this book were organized around the concept of "'Songlines'—the invisible pathways along which aboriginal Australians travel to perform their central cultural activities." Publ Wkly
"This is an important book and a challenging one. . . . It is full of odd characters, bizarre incidents, moments of poetry—some of them comic—that spring as much from the writer's own generosity of spirit as from the richness of things." Times Lit Suppl

920 Biography & genealogy

Books of biography are arranged as follows: 1. Biographical collections (920) 2. Biographies of individuals alphabetically by name of biographee (92)

Abdul-Jabbar, Kareem, 1947-
Black profiles in courage; a legacy of African American achievement; [by] Kareem Abdul-Jabbar and Alan Steinberg; foreword by Henry Louis Gates, Jr. Morrow 1996 xxiv, 232p il hardcover o.p. pa $13   **920**
1. African Americans—Biography
ISBN 0-688-13097-6; 0-380-81341-6 (pa)
LC 96-26245
This book "profiles the historical achievements of 11 historical black figures from Estevanico de Dorantes to Rosa Parks." Libr J
The authors have provided "interesting and nuanced accounts of heroic African Americans whose accomplishments changed U.S. history. . . . Although Abdul-Jabbar is highly critical of past and present racism in the U.S., he gives credit to the abolitionist movement and leaders such as William Lloyd Garrison for their efforts toward ending slavery." Publ Wkly
Includes bibliographical references

Acocella, Joan Ross
Twenty-eight artists and two saints; essays; [by] Joan Acocella. Pantheon Books 2007 524p il $30   **920**
1. Artists 2. Art—20th century
ISBN 978-0-375-42416-8; 0-375-42416-4
LC 2006-47266
Collected essays originally published in The New Yorker and The New York review of books
The author presents essays on such subjects as Joan of Arc and Mary Magdalene, "Italo Svevo, Stefan Zweig, Simone de Beauvoir, Marguerite Yourcenar, Joseph Roth, Vaslav Nijinsky, Lincoln Kirstein, Jerome Robbins, Martha Graham, Bob Fosse, H.L. Mencken, Dorothy Parker, Susan Sontag, and Philip Roth." Publisher's note
"Like every great critic, Acocella is subjective, uncompromising. She has a distinct point of view, a refreshingly not-fashionable one—she salutes Sunday-school virtues!—and writes from her conviction that beneath its hectic, irresponsible, even intoxicated surface, art makes singularly unglamorous demands: integrity, sacrifice, discipline." N Y Times Book Rev

Adams, Maureen B.
Shaggy muses; the dogs who inspired Virginia Woolf, Emily Dickinson, Edith Wharton, Elizabeth Barrett Browning, and Emily Brontë. Ballantine Books 2007 299p il   **920**
1. Woolf, Virginia, 1882-1941 2. Dickinson, Emily, 1830-1886   3.   Wharton,   Edith,   1862-1937 4. Browning, Elizabeth Barrett, 1806-1861 5. Brontë, Emily, 1818-1848 6. Dogs
ISBN 978034548406-2; 0-345-48406-1
LC 2006-101291
"Despite their different personalities and backgrounds, these writers all had in common dogs that provided stability and consistency in their lives. Each chapter is a minibiography of an author emphasizing and offering anecdotes about the deep bond she shared with her dog. By using diaries, letters, illustrations, and sometimes passages from these women's writings, Adams provides a unique perspective of her subjects as pet owners. A recurrent theme is the comfort the dogs provided. . . . From this unusual vantage point, Adams succeeds in linking these writers' lives in various ways." Libr J
Includes bibliographical references

African American lives; edited by Henry Louis Gates, Jr. and Evelyn Brooks Higginbotham. Oxford University Press 2004 xxvi, 1025p $55   **920**
1. African Americans—Biography
ISBN 0-19-516024-X   LC 2003-23640

African American lives—*Continued*

This compilation offers "biographies of 611 African-Americans over more than four centuries, beginning with Esteban, the first African known to have set foot in North America, up through writers, academics, artists, activists and more of today. A few of these profiles have been written by notable names—Gerald Early on Muhammad Ali, Clayborne Carson on Martin Luther King Jr. and Malcolm X, John Szwed on Miles Davis—though most are by lesser-known contributors." Publ Wkly

"This work opens multiple fresh vistas on proper African American history. . . . Essential for any serious African American collection." Libr J

Includes bibliographical references

Angelo, Bonnie

First families; the impact of the White House on their lives. Morrow 2005 336p il $25.95; pa $15.95 *   **920**

1. White House (Washington, D.C.) 2. Presidents—United States—Family

ISBN 0-06-056356-7; 0-06-056358-3 (pa)

LC 2005-41474

The author "takes readers inside the lives of the presidential families." Libr J

"Relying heavily on the recollections and memoirs of presidential family members, White House staff, and D.C. journalists, this chatty slice of Americana is chock-full of fun First Family facts." Booklist

Includes bibliographical references

Anthony, Carl Sferrazza

America's first families; an inside view of 200 years of private life in the White House. Touchstone 2000 411p il pa $18 hardcover o.p.

920

1. White House (Washington, D.C.) 2. Presidents—United States—Family

ISBN 0-684-86442-8 (pa)   LC 00-64936

"A Lisa Drew book"

"Anthony's book records the behind-the-scene lives of American presidents and their families with photographs, drawings, and letters from newspapers, library archives, and private collections." Booklist

"This close-up look at the lives of White House residents offers an intimate and objective perspective on the fish-bowl life most First Families have experienced." Libr J

Includes bibliographical references

Ball, Edward, 1959-

The sweet hell inside; the rise of an elite Black family in the segregated South. Perennial 2002 384p il pa $13.95   **920**

1. Harleston family 2. African Americans—Biography

ISBN 978-0-06-050590-5; 0-06-050590-7

First published 2001 by Morrow

"The Harlestons of South Carolina were descended from a slave woman and her master, the start of a line of fair-skinned blacks who rose to prominence in the state through commerce, social service, and the arts. . . . [The author] was approached by Edwina Harleston

Whitlock, a distant black relative (a sixth cousin, twice removed), to take a storehouse of genealogical material she had about her family and to write its history. The result is a stunning look at a fascinating family and the history of blacks in the U.S. from the 1800s to the 1960s." Booklist

Includes bibliographical references

Barrett, Paul M.

American Islam; the struggle for the soul of a religion. Farrar, Straus & Giroux 2006 304p $25

920

1. Muslims—United States 2. Islam

ISBN 978-0-374-10423-8; 0-374-10423-9

LC 2006-11404

The author "provides portraits of individual Muslims living in the United States. . . . [These include] a black imam, an activist, a webmaster, a publisher, two mystics, a scholar, and a feminist." Libr J

"In the post-9/11 world Muslims have frequently been stereotyped as monolithically murderous. . . . The heated debates among Muslims themselves about violence committed under the banner of Islam are often drowned out in the fray. Paul M. Barrett's timely and engaging new book brings some of those voices in the United States to life." N Y Times (Late N Y Ed)

Includes bibliographical references

Bell, Eric Temple, 1883-1960

Men of mathematics; [by] E. T. Bell. Simon & Schuster 1937 xxi, 592p il *   **920**

1. Mathematicians

ISBN 0-671-62818-6 (pa)

This volume looks at the lives and contributions of 35 pioneers of modern mathematics.

Boller, Paul F.

Presidential wives; [by] Paul F. Boller, Jr. 2nd, rev ed. Oxford Univ. Press 1998 553p pa $17.95

920

1. Presidents' spouses—United States

ISBN 0-19-512142-2   LC 98-3480

First published 1988

This collection covers every First Lady from Martha Washington to Hillary Rodham Clinton. The author devotes a chapter to each of his subjects featuring a biographical essay followed by anecdotes

Includes bibliographical references

Booknotes: life stories; notable biographers on the people who shaped America; {complied by} Brian Lamb. Times Bks. 1999 xxiii, 471p il pa $16.95 hardcover o.p.   **920**

1. Biography

ISBN 0-8129-3339-7 (pa)   LC 98-41374

"Lamb, host of C-SPAN's *Booknotes,* has compiled an anthology of interviews focusing on the lives of 75 prominent people from the 1700s to the present. The result is chatty and informal." Libr J

Brennan, Richard P.

Heisenberg probably slept here; the lives, times, and ideas of the great physicists of the 20th century. Wiley 1997 274p il (Wiley popular science) $22.95; pa $14.95 **920**

1. Physicists

ISBN 0-471-15709-0; 0-471-29585-X (pa)

LC 96-42935

The author "offers biographical sketches of physicists Isaac Newton, Albert Einstein, Max Planck, Ernest Rutherford, Niels Bohr, Werner Heisenberg, Richard Feynman, and Murray Gell-Mann, along with an explanation of the contribution each made to physics." Libr J

"Brennan provides an accessible view of some tough areas of science by knowing what to leave out, and the way he links the continuing quest of physics through the century is admirable." New Sci

Includes bibliographical references

Brightman, Carol

Sweet chaos; the Grateful Dead's American adventure. Pocket 1999 356p il pa $17

920

1. Grateful Dead (Musical group)

ISBN 0-671-01117-0

First published 1998 by Clarkson Potter

The author "explores the Grateful Dead's place in American culture, considering the influence of the beat generation, the 'acid tests' of Ken Kesey's Merry Pranksters, the student protest movement, and the ever-present drug culture." Libr J

"Brightman's is an engrossing treatment of the Dead and their times. . . . She offers fresh perspectives and insights and captures the flavor of the band." Booklist

Includes bibliographical references

Brookhiser, Richard

America's first dynasty; the Adamses, 1735-1918. Free Press 2002 244p il $25; pa $14

920

1. Adams family 2. Adams, John, 1735-1826 3. Adams, John Quincy, 1767-1848 4. Adams, Charles Francis, 1807-1886 5. Adams, Henry, 1838-1918

ISBN 0-684-86881-4; 0-684-86864-4 (pa)

LC 2001-51276

An "account of the lives of John, John Quincy, Charles Francis and Henry, four generations of men often brilliant but often shortsighted as well: two presidents, one diplomat and, finally, a historian who felt he had failed the ancestors." N Y Times Book Rev

Includes bibliographical references

Brynner, Rock, 1946-

Empire & odyssey; the Brynners in Far East Russia and beyond. Steerforth Press 2006 331p il map $29.95 * **920**

1. Bryner, Julius Josef, 1849-1920 2. Bryner, Boris Julievitch, 1889-1948 3. Brynner, Yul, 1920-1985

ISBN 1-58642-102-6; 978-1-58642-102-1

LC 2005-36507

The author "chronicles the lives of four generations of his own family, beginning with his great-grandfather,

Jules Bryner, a Swiss who eventually settled in Vladivostok, where he was greatly responsible for establishing its importance in the Russian Far East. Next, he covers Jules's son Boris, a major industrialist, and then Boris's son, the author's father, actor Yul Brynner. He concludes, full circle, with his own odyssey to Vladivostok in 2003. . . . [This is] a fascinating tale of a fascinating family." Libr J

Includes bibliographical references

Burt, Daniel S.

The biography book; a reader's guide to nonfiction, fictional, and film biographies of the 500 most fascinating individuals of all time. Oryx Press 2001 629p $83.95 **920**

1. Biography—Bibliography

ISBN 1-57356-256-4

LC 00-10116

This "book provides annotated bibliographies of works on international historical figures. Entries are arranged alphabetically by person and begin with a paragraph on the individual's life and significance. Each entry contains a birth and death date, and recommended autobiographical and biographical studies. Primary sources include letters, memoirs, diaries, interviews, etc. Biographical novels, fictional portraits, films, documentaries, and theatrical performances are also identified. . . . A wonderful resource for students, biography lovers, and librarians." SLJ

Includes bibliographical references

Carey, Charles W.

American inventors, entrepreneurs, and business visionaries; {by} Charles W. Carey, Jr. Facts on File 2002 xx, 410p il (American biographies) $65

920

1. Inventors 2. Businesspeople 3. United States—Biography

ISBN 0-8160-4559-3

LC 2001-53252

"More than 280 individuals from the seventeenth through twentieth centuries who helped change the American economy are profiled here. . . . Each entry provides birth date (and death date where applicable), followed by a page or two on the person's life and innovations, and concludes with a brief further reading list. . . . This volume is worthy of inclusion in reference collections of public, academic, and high-school libraries. Its content is wide-ranging and its entries provide interesting reading." Booklist

Includes bibliographical references

Chernow, Ron

The Warburgs; the twentieth-century odyssey of a remarkable Jewish family. Random House 1993 820p il pa $21 hardcover o.p. **920**

1. Warburg family

ISBN 0-679-74359-6 (pa)

LC 93-16599

The author "chronicles the saga of {one} of the world's most powerful and oldest banking families. In telling this monumental tale of the Warburgs, Chernow offers a panoramic view of nearly 500 years of world history, concentrating on the role of Jews in German business, culture, and politics from the time of Kaiser

Chernow, Ron—*Continued*
Wilhelm to that of Adolf Hitler. He also explains how the Warburgs extended their influence to America by marrying into two influential families." Booklist
Includes bibliographical references

Clay, Catrine
King, Kaiser, Tsar; three royal cousins who led the world to war. Walker & Company 2007 416p il $26.95 **920**
1. George V, King of Great Britain, 1865-1936 2. William II, German Emperor, 1859-1941 3. Nicholas II, Emperor of Russia, 1868-1918 4. World War, 1914-1918 5. Kings and rulers
ISBN 0-8027-1623-7; 978-0-8027-1623-1
This is a "biography of not one but three significant men. King George V of England, Kaiser Wilhelm II of Germany, and Tsar Nicholas II of Russia (familiarly known as Georgie, Willy, and Nicky) were more than just the leaders of three of the most powerful countries in the world in the early 20th century—they were cousins who had grown up together, played together, and attended family functions together. . . . [The author] provides an intimate look inside the lives of these boys as they grew into manhood and became king, kaiser, and tsar, bringing new pleasures and details to a well-known subject." Libr J
Includes bibliographical references

Cohen, Rich
Sweet and low; a family story. Farrar, Straus and Giroux 2006 272p il $25 **920**
1. Eisenstadt, Benjamin, 1906-1996 2. Cumberland Packing Corporation
ISBN 0-374-27229-8; 978-0-374-27229-6
LC 2005-15730
The author tells the "story of an American family and its patriarch, a short-order cook named Ben Eisenstadt who, in the years after World War II, invented the sugar packet and Sweet'N Low, converting his Brooklyn cafeteria into a factory and amassing the great fortune that would destroy his family." Publisher's note
This "is a story peopled with eccentrics and naifs and scoundrels, and a story recounted with uncommon acuity and wit." N Y Times (Late N Y Ed)

Coll, Steve
The Bin Ladens; an Arabian family in the American century. Penguin Press 2008 671p il $35
920
1. Bin Laden family 2. Saudi Arabia—History
ISBN 978-1-59420-164-6 LC 2007-42748
The author tells "the rags-to-riches story of the Arabian Peninsula's house of Bin Laden." Libr J
This "book not only gives us the most psychologically detailed portrait of the brutal 9/11 mastermind yet, but in telling the epic story of Osama bin Laden's extended family, it also reveals the crucial role that his relatives and their relationship with the royal house of Saud played in shaping his thinking, his ambitions, his technological expertise and his tactics." N Y Times (Late N Y Ed)
Includes bibliographical references

Contemporary black biography, v68; profiles from the international black community. Gale Res. 2008 275p il $124 **920**
1. African Americans—Biography
ISSN 1058-1316
ISBN 978-1-4144-3275-5; 1-4144-3275-5
Also available eBook version
Started publication 1992. Editors vary
"Included in each volume are biographies of innovators in the black global community who are currently living and/or who have had a lasting impact on society. Every field of endeavor imaginable is represented, from science, politics, and creative arts to sports. . . . This . . . title will be useful for its coverage of current people in the news who are not as easy to find elsewhere." Booklist

Craughwell, Thomas J., 1956-
Saints behaving badly; the cutthroats, crooks, trollops, con men, and devil-worshippers who became saints. Doubleday 2006 190p $15.95
920
1. Christian saints
ISBN 0-385-51720-3; 978-0-385-51720-1
LC 2006-299594
The author presents a "review of 32 less-than-perfect saints, among them St. Olga, St. Mary of Egypt, and Thomas a Becket. Relying on a wide range of sources—including his own expertise—he writes concise and informative profiles of these holy people that chronicle their respective rises to sainthood and end with what inspired them to abandon their wicked ways." Libr J
Includes bibliographical references

Dance, Stanley
The world of Count Basie. Da Capo Press 1985 c1980 xxi, 399p il pa $18 **920**
1. Jazz musicians
ISBN 0-306-80245-7 LC 85-12901
A reprint of the title first published 1980 by Scribner
This book "consists of numerous tape-recorded and edited interviews with musicians and vocalists associated with Basie, and each gets to tell his own story. Many overlap and there are interesting confirmations and disputes over details. The language has been polished (and no doubt in some cases cleaned up), but Dance does not noticeably impose his own views on others. There are good photographs." Choice
Includes discography and bibliographical references

Davis, Peter G.
The American opera singer; the lives and adventures of America's great singers in opera and concert, from 1825 to the present. Doubleday 1997 626p il pa $19.95 hardcover o.p. **920**
1. Singers
ISBN 0-385-42174-5 (pa) LC 97-9123
"This book records the emergence of American opera singers and the development of musical institutions to train and support them. It also traces the evolution of musical styles, which from 1825 on have placed new demands on the voice." New Yorker

Davis, Peter G.—*Continued*

"Davis tells anecdotes and presents essential details of his subjects' personal lives in biographical sketches ranging from a paragraph to several pages in length." Booklist

Includes bibliographical references

Denlinger, Elizabeth Campbell

Before Victoria; extraordinary women of the British Romantic era; by Elizabeth Campbell Denlinger; foreword by Lyndall Gordon. Columbia University Press 2005 188p il $41.50   **920**

1. Women—Great Britain 2. Great Britain—History—19th century

ISBN 0-231-13630-7   LC 2004-59267

"Published on the occasion of the exhibition, Before Victoria: extraordinary women of the British Romantic era, presented at the New York Public Library, Humanities and Social Sciences Library, D. Samuel and Jeane H. Gottesman Exhibition Hall, April 8-July 30, 2005" Verso of title page

This book "offers portraits of a group of women who were scientists, artists, writers, poets, philanthropists and reformers during the Romantic Era and details how their accomplishments changed the social and economic landscape for women." Univ Press Books for Public and Second Sch Libr, 2006

Includes bibliographical references

Dinnage, Rosemary

Alone! alone!: lives of some outsider women. New York Review Books 2004 296p $24.95 *
          920

1. Women—Biography

ISBN 1-590-17069-5   LC 2003-27805

The subjects of this volume of biographical essays include: Gwen John, Stevie Smith, Barbara Pym, Simone Weil, Clementine Churchill, Ottoline Morrell, Dora Russell, Giuseppina Verdi, Olive Schreiner, Helena Blavatsky and Annie Besant; Marie Stopes, Enid Blyton, Angela Brazil, Isak Dinesen, Rebecca West, Margaret Oliphant, Alice James and Katherine Mansfield

"The book is dutifully footnoted and academically solid yet is also beautifully written, marked with great feeling and vivid flashes of insight. It cannot fail to enrich a collection." Libr J

Englehart, Murray

AC/DC; maximum rock and roll; [by] Murray Engleheart with Arnaud Durieux. Morrow 2007 488p il $25.95   **920**

1. AC/DC (Musical group) 2. Rock musicians

ISBN 0-06-113391-4; 978-0-06-113391-6
          LC 2007-295661

This is a "biography of the wildly successful Australian rockers. Covering everything from guitarist Angus Young's first record purchase (*Club A Go-Go* by the Yardbirds) to the band's induction into the Rock and Roll Hall of Fame and all points in between, this book is a godsend for fans." Publ Wkly

Includes discography

Evans, Harold

They made America; [by] Harold Evans, with Gail Buckland and David Lefer. Little, Brown 2004 496p $40; pa $18.95   **920**

1. Inventors 2. Inventions

ISBN 0-316-27766-5; 0-316-01385-4 (pa)
          LC 2003-65954

The author "profiles 70 of America's leading inventors, entrepreneurs and innovators, some better known than others. Along with such obvious choices as Henry Ford, Thomas Edison and the Wright brothers, Evans profiles Lewis Tappan (an abolitionist who dreamed up the idea of credit ratings), Gen. Georges Doriot (pioneer of venture capital) and Joan Ganz Cooney, of the Children's Television Workshop." Publ Wkly

Feather, Leonard

From Satchmo to Miles; new foreword by the author. Da Capo Press 1984 c1972 258p il (Roots of jazz) pa $16 hardcover o.p.   **920**

1. Jazz musicians 2. African American musicians

ISBN 0-306-80302-X (pa)   LC 83-15223

First published 1972 by Stein & Day

A collection of profiles of jazz musicians including Count Basie, Lester Young, Oscar Peterson, Ray Charles, Don Ellis, Duke Ellington, Billie Holiday, Ella Fitzgerald, Louis Armstrong, Dizzy Gillespie, Norman Granz, Miles Davis and Charlie Parker.

Feldman, Burton

112 Mercer Street; Einstein, Russell, Gödel, Pauli, and the end of innocence in science; edited and completed by Katherine Williams. Arcade Pub. 2007 243p $26   **920**

1. Einstein, Albert, 1879-1955 2. Russell, Bertrand, 1872-1970 3. Gödel, Kurt 4. Pauli, Wolfgang, 1900-1958 5. Scientists

ISBN 978-1-55970-704-6; 1-55970-704-6
          LC 2007-1194

"During the winter of 1943–1944, Albert Einstein met weekly with three other aging geniuses—philosopher Bertrand Russell, mathematician Kurt Gödel and physicist Wolfgang Pauli—in the study of his home at 112 Mercer Street in Princeton, N.J. . . . What the authors present are illuminating biographical sketches of these men and their earlier, groundbreaking work." Publ Wkly

Includes bibliographical references

Finkbeiner, Ann K., 1943-

The Jasons; the secret history of science's postwar elite; [by] Ann Finkbeiner. Viking 2006 304p $27.95   **920**

1. Jason (Organization) 2. Scientists 3. Physicists

ISBN 978-0-670-03489-5; 0-670-03489-4
          LC 2005-43471

"The Jasons is a small and elite group of scientists—once consisting almost exclusively of physicists, but now more ecumenical—who since 1960 have helped the government find solutions to particularly difficult technical problems, mostly having to do with defense. During the Cold War, the Jasons were a hush-hush organization, much like the National Security Agency. Today, they la-

Finkbeiner, Ann K., 1943-—*Continued*
bor not so much in secret as in obscurity-which, one
learns from Finkbeiner's book, is the way most Jasons
prefer it. . . . By focusing on some of the more colorful
Jasons, Finkbeiner shines a spotlight on the activities of
the group as a whole." American Scientist

Flanders, Judith
A circle of sisters; Alice Kipling, Georgiana
Burne-Jones, Agnes Poynter and Louisa Baldwin.
W.W. Norton & Co. 2005 xxiii, 392p $27.95
920
1. McDonald family 2. Baldwin, Louisa, 1845-1925
3. Burne-Jones, Georgiana, Lady, 1840-1920
4. Kipling, Alice, 1837-1910 5. Poynter, Agnes, 1843-
1906
ISBN 0-393-05210-9   LC 2004-65415
This is a collective biography of the McDonald sisters,
two of whom grew up to marry Edward Burne-Jones and
Edward Poynter, while the other two became the mothers
of Rudyard Kipling and prime minister Stanley Baldwin.
"Offering perceptive commentary on the prescribed
role of women in Victorian society to be mere help-
meets, Flanders' attentive, scholarly accuracy is enhanced
by piquant observations that demonstrate both her professional talent and personal take on the lives of these remarkable, but unremarked upon, women." Booklist
Includes bibliographical references

Fox, James, 1945-
Five sisters; the Langhornes of Virginia. Simon
& Schuster 2000 496p il $30; pa $16
920
1. Langhorne family 2. Astor, Nancy Witcher
Langhorne, Viscountess, 1879-1964 3. Brand, Phyllis,
1880-1937
ISBN 0-684-80812-9; 0-7432-0042-X (pa)
LC 99-41815
First published 1998 in the United Kingdom with title:
The Langhorne sisters
"Irene Langhorne, the last great Southern belle, moved
North in 1895, when she married Charles Dana Gibson,
creator of the Gibson girl. In her wake, three younger
sisters (her elder, Lizzie, was already married) burst onto
the glittering society stage. Nancy, the most famous,
married Waldorf Astor and threw herself into English political activism; Phyllis, the author's grandmother, was
more introverted; Nora, with 'a heart like a hotel,' repeatedly led the family to the brink of scandal. Fox
brings intimacy to these semi-public personalities, elevat-
ing a century's gossip and legend into absorbing history." New Yorker
Includes bibliographical references

Fraser, Antonia, 1932-
The wives of Henry VIII. Knopf 1993 c1992
479p il hardcover o.p. pa $18.95   **920**
1. Henry VIII, King of England, 1491-1547 2. Great
Britain—History—1485-1603, Tudors
ISBN 978-0-394-58538-3; 978-0-679-73001-9 (pa);
0-679-73001-X (pa)   LC 92-52950
First published 1992 in the United Kingdom with title:
The six wives of Henry VIII

This work examines the lives of the six women—
Catherine of Aragon, Anne Boleyn, Jane Seymour, Anna
of Cleves, Katherine Howard, and Catherine Parr—who
became Queens of England between 1509 and 1547. The
author discusses their marriages to Henry VIII
"Fraser's readable style, empathy for her subjects, and
piquant use of historical details and anecdotes make this
a satisfying addition to the history shelves." Libr J
Includes bibliographical references

Fraser, Flora
Princesses; the six daughters of George III.
Knopf 2005 478p il hardcover o.p. pa $16.95
920
1. Great Britain—Kings and rulers
ISBN 0-679-45118-8; 1-4000-9669-5 (pa)
First published 2002 in the United Kingdom
The author "depicts royals who attempted to live a
rather homey life, but were torn both by the king's fa-
mous madness and by complex political and affectionate
alliances within the family itself." Publ Wkly
This "is a rich and richly hued Regency tale. . . . Fra-
ser is splendidly at home in the 18th century, adroit at
teasing history out from between guarded lines." N Y
Times Book Rev
Includes bibliographical references

Gates, Henry Louis
The African-American century; how Black
Americans have shaped our country; {by} Henry
Louis Gates, Jr. and Cornel West. Free Press 2000
414p il hardcover o.p. pa $16 *   **920**
1. African Americans—Biography 2. African Americans—Intellectual life
ISBN 0-684-86414-2; 0-684-86415-0 (pa)
LC 00-63596
"Gates and West have listed and written biographies
of their choices of the 100 most important and influential
[African Americans] of the . . . twentieth century. In
their opinion the subjects that they have selected have
made significant impacts and contributions to American
society. . . . The entries are arranged by decade and by
the person's period of prominence in society, 1900-1909
through 1990-1999. Profiles include Madame C.J. Walker, Langston Hughes, Carter G. Woodson, Paul Robeson,
Thurgood Marshall, and Colin Powell." MultiCult Rev
Includes bibliographical references

Thirteen ways of looking at a black man.
Random House 1997 xxvii, 226p $12 hardcover
o.p.   **920**
1. African Americans—Biography
ISBN 0-679-77666-4 (pa)   LC 96-33138
A "collection of essays about contemporary African
Americans. . . . Each essay focuses on a noted cultural
figure: James Baldwin, Albert Murray, Bill T. Jones, Colin Powell, O. J. Simpson, Louis Farrakhan, Harry Bela-
fonte, and Anatole Broyard; however, the effect of each
essay goes beyond its primary subject by illuminating society at large." Booklist
"Mr. Gates's strong suit is finding the common man
in uncommon figures, without losing sight of the ways
in which race, class and personal experience have shaped
each life." N Y Times Book Rev

Gilbert, Pat

Passion is a fashion; the real story of The Clash. Da Capo Press 2005 404p il map pa $18.95

920

1. Clash (Musical group) 2. Punk rock music
ISBN 0-306-81434-X   LC 2005-48403
First published 2004 in the United Kingdom
Gilbert chronicles the life and times of the English rock band The Clash.

"This is a heartbreaking and heartening story of punks growing up and growing old, the real story indeed. Essential for all popular music collections." Libr J
Includes discography and bibliographical references

Glover, Jane, 1949-

Mozart's women; the man, the music, and the loves of his life. HarperCollins 2006 406p il $27.95; pa $15.95   **920**

1. Mozart, Wolfgang Amadeus, 1756-1791 2. Mozart family
ISBN   0-06-056350-8;   978-0-06-056350-9; 0-06-056351-6 (pa); 978-0-06-056351-6 (pa)
LC 2005-52699
This "biography focuses on Mozart's mother, sister and wife." N Y Times Book Rev
The author "writes perceptively and knowledgeably about the theatrical genius of Mozart's operas, . . . and her expertise contributes significantly to the pleasures afforded by this volume." Christ Sci Monit
Includes bibliographical references

Gould, Jonathan, 1951-

Can't buy me love; the Beatles, Britain, and America. Harmony Books 2007 661p il $27.50

920

1. Beatles 2. Rock musicians
ISBN 978-0-307-35337-5; 0-307-35337-0
LC 2007-13240
Also available in paperback by Crown
The author "mixes biography with social commentary and musical and lyrical analysis, illustrating how the band crafted its groundbreaking songs and how its achievements impacted, and were impacted by, the tumultuous 1960s." Libr J
"Gould's combination group biography, cultural history, and musical criticism artfully places the Beatles in their time and social context while examining with great skill how they became an international phenomenon comparable only to themselves." Booklist
Includes bibliographical references

Green, Stanley, 1923-1990

The world of musical comedy; the story of the American musical stage as told through the careers of its foremost composers and lyricists. 4th ed rev and enl. Da Capo Press 1984 c1980 480p il
pa $35   **920**

1. Composers—United States 2. Librettists 3. Musicals
ISBN 0-306-80207-4   LC 83-26340
First published 1960 by Ziff-Davis; this is a reprint of the 1980 edition published by A. S. Barnes supplemented with author corrections

"From Victor Herbert to Marvin Hamlisch, Green gives us a classic history of the genre. . . . Thirty-one chapters tell the tale of some 70 individuals or teams that have had a lasting effect on the musical theater. . . . The appendix gives the vitals on every major production of the past 85 years." Booklist

Greenstein, George, 1940-

Portraits of discovery; profiles in scientific genius. Wiley 1997 c1998 232p il $24.95

920

1. Scientists
ISBN 0-471-19138-8   LC 97-6048
The author examines the interaction between the personal and professional in the lives of: Annie Jump Cannon, Cecilia Helena Payne Gaposchkin, Ludwig Boltzman, George Gamow, Homi Jehangir Bhaba, Luis W. Alvarez, Richard Phillips Feynman, Martin L. Perl, Margaret J. Geller, and John Huchra
Greenstein's "portraits are at least as interesting in what they reveal about the blemishes on the face of great scientists: The eccentricities and idiosyncrasies that energize many scientists' work also may accentuate their human flaws." Sci Books & Film
Includes bibliographical references

Halberstam, David, 1934-2007

The teammates. Hyperion 2003 217p il $22.95

920

1. Boston Red Sox (Baseball team) 2. Baseball—Biography
ISBN 1-401-30057-X   LC 2003-42334
This is an "account of the lives and friendships of four legendary Boston Red Sox: Ted Williams, Dominic DiMaggio, Johnny Pesky and Bobby Doerr; the story unfolds in a series of flashbacks as DiMiggio and Pesky drive 1,300 miles to Florida to visit the ailing Williams." N Y Times Book Rev
"This account of good people living full lives and appreciating the experience will move readers." Booklist

Haley, Alex, 1921-1992

Roots; the saga of an American family: the 30th anniversary edition. Vanguard Books 2007 899p
pa $15.95 *   **920**

1. Haley family 2. Kinte family
ISBN 978-1-59315-449-3; 1-59315-449-6
LC 2007-8822
First published 1976 by Doubleday
This book details Haley's "search for the genealogical history of his family. He describes his trip to Gambia, the African homeland of his ancestors, and recounts the lives of his forebears." Benet's Reader's Ency of Am Lit

Hargittai, István

The Martians of science; five physicists who changed the twentieth century. Oxford University Press 2006 xxiv, 313p il map $34.50   **920**

1. Von Kármán, Theodore, 1881-1963 2. Szilard, Leo 3. Wigner, Eugene P., 1902-1995 4. Von Neumann, John, 1903-1957 5. Teller, Edward, 1908-2003 6. Physicists
ISBN 978-0-19-517845-6; 0-19-517845-9
LC 2005-29427

Hargittai, István—*Continued*

This is a "presentation of the lives of five scientists (physicists and engineers) from Hungary who went to Germany and then to the United States. They . . . [are] Theodore von Karman, Leo Szilard, Eugene P. Wigner, John von Neumann, and Edward Teller. . . . [This book is an] extremely valuable account of the lives of these five brilliant and interesting Hungarian physicists." Sci Books Films

Includes bibliographical references

Haskins, James, 1941-2005

African American religious leaders; [by] Jim Haskins and Kathleen Benson. Wiley 2008 162p il (Black stars) lib bdg $24.95   **920**

1. African Americans—Biography 2. African Americans—Religion

ISBN 978-0-471-73632-5 (lib bdg); 0-471-73632-5 (lib bdg)   LC 2007-27347

This is a collective biography of "black religious leaders who helped shape the African American experience—from colonial to modern times." Publisher's note

"It's great to have all these figures between two covers, and even a sampling of the entries captures the importance of religion, and its leaders, in African American life." Booklist

Includes bibliographical references

Hastings, Max

Warriors; portraits from the battlefield. Knopf 2006 xxiii, 354p il maps $27.50   **920**

1. Soldiers 2. Military history

ISBN 1-4000-4441-3; 978-1-4000-4441-2
                                      LC 2005-44302

The author "selects memoirs and biographies about 15 combatants (one of them a woman) and distills accounts of their lives and trenchant observations about their personalities. . . . Filled with poignant psychological insight, Hastings' remarkable sketches will provoke greater-than-average demand from the military affairs readership." Booklist

Includes bibliographical references

Heller, Nancy

Women artists; an illustrated history. 4th ed. Abbeville Press 2003 312p il $39.95   **920**

1. Women artists

ISBN 978-0-7892-0768-5; 0-7892-0768-0
                                    LC 2004-269241

First published 1987

"Organized in six chapters by century, the survey provides brief biographical information, some critical analysis and context, and at least one color plate of the work of 125 women artists who lived and worked in Europe or North America. . . . An excellent resource." SLJ

Includes bibliographical references

Hibbert, Christopher, 1924-

The House of Medici; its rise and fall. Morrow 1975 c1974 364p il maps pa $16 hardcover o.p.
                                              920

1. House of Medici 2. Florence (Italy)—History

ISBN 0-688-05339-4 (pa)

First published 1974 in the United Kingdom with title: The rise and fall of the House of Medici

This book is concerned with "heads of the Medici family {who} directed the government of the Florentine state from 1434, with Cosimo's return from exile, until the death of the Grand Duke Giovanni Gastone in 1737." Times Lit Suppl

Includes bibliographical references

Hutchison, Kay Bailey

American heroines; the spirited women who shaped our country. 1st ed. William Morrow 2004 384p il $24.95; pa $14.95   **920**

1. Women—United States—Biography

ISBN 0-06-056635-3; 0-06-056636-1 (pa)
                                       LC 2004-56677

The author "presents female pioneers in fields as varied as government, business, education and healthcare, who overcame the resistance and prejudice of their times and accomplished things that no woman—and sometimes no man—had done before." Publisher's note

"Hutchinson's lively, personal writing makes this an accessible and important volume." Booklist

James, Clive, 1939-

Cultural amnesia; necessary memories from history and the arts. W.W. Norton & Co. 2007 xxxii, 876p il $35   **920**

1. Western civilization 2. Intellectual life 3. Intellectuals 4. Artists 5. Musicians 6. Philosophers

ISBN 978-0-393-06116-1; 0-393-06116-7
                                      LC 2006-36398

"Containing over 100 original essays, organized by quotations from A to Z, Cultural Amnesia . . . [covers] thinkers, humanists, musicians, artists, and philosophers of the twentieth century." Publisher's note

The author "not only preserves culture and nurtures humanism but also revitalizes the beauty and power of the English language." Booklist

Kane, Joseph Nathan, 1899-2002

Facts about the presidents; Janet Podell & Steven Anzovin {editors}. 7th ed. Wilson, H.W. 2001 721p il $140   **920**

1. Presidents—United States

ISBN 0-8242-1007-7   LC 2001-26261

First published 1959

The main part of this work provides an individual chapter on each President, from Washington through George W. Bush, presenting such information as family, education, election, Vice President, main events and accomplishments of his administration, and First Lady. Part two contains tables and lists presenting comparative data on all the Presidents

Includes bibliographical references

Kennedy, John F. (John Fitzgerald), 1917-1963

Profiles in courage. HarperCollins Pubs. 2003 xxii, 245p $19.95; pa $13.95 *   **920**

1. Politicians—United States 2. Courage

ISBN 0-06-053062-6; 0-06-085493-6 (pa)
                                      LC 2003-40676

Kennedy, John F. (John Fitzgerald), 1917-1963—*Continued*

A reissue of the title first published 1956

This series of profiles of Americans who took courageous stands at crucial moments in public life includes John Quincy Adams, Daniel Webster, Thomas Hart Benton, Sam Houston, Edmund G. Ross, Lucius Q. C. Lamar, George Norris, Robert A. Taft and others.

Includes bibliographical references

Kingston, Maxine Hong

China men. Knopf 1980 308p pa $13.95 hardcover o.p. **920**

1. Chinese Americans—Biography

ISBN 0-679-72328-5 (pa)   LC 79-3469

This book "paints a rich picture of the writer's male family members, but those portraits of her grandfathers, father, and brothers are interspersed with fascinating bits of historical data. . . . The whole is held together by pieces of folklore that one feels compelled to go back to and reread." Libr J

Leamer, Laurence

The Kennedy men; 1901-1963: the laws of the father. Perennial 2002 882p il pa $19.95

920

1. Kennedy family 2. Kennedy, Joseph P., 1888-1969 3. Kennedy, John F. (John Fitzgerald), 1917-1963

ISBN 978-0-06-050288-1; 0-06-050288-6

First published 2001 by Morrow

This is a biography of Joseph P. Kennedy and his sons from the beginning of the last century through the assassination of John F. Kennedy.

"Leamer's writing is impressive throughout, regularly catching the reader up with a felicitous phrase or a surprising insight." Booklist

Includes bibliographical references

Lee, Helie

In the absence of sun; a Korean American woman's promise to reunite three lost generations of her family. Harmony Bks. 2002 342p il maps pa $18.95 hardcover o.p. **920**

1. Lee family 2. Korean Americans 3. Korea (North)

ISBN 0-449-91171-3 (pa)   LC 2002-1680

"Lee's *Still Life with Rice* (1996) was a novelized account of her grandmother's life and escape from what would become North Korea. As she now recounts her and her father's struggles to get other people out of the North, she continues to wrestle with her own Korean heritage—in particular, the paternalistic and patronizing attitudes toward women." Booklist

Lees, Gene

You can't steal a gift; Dizzy, Clark, Milt, and Nat; foreword by Nat Hentoff. Yale Univ. Press 2001 269p il $27.95 **920**

1. Jazz musicians

ISBN 0-300-08965-1   LC 2001-3444

Lees discusses the lives and careers of four jazz musicians: Dizzy Gillespie, Terry Clark, Milt Hinton, and Nat

King Cole. A theme of the book is how these artists were affected by race relations in the United States

The author "has a natural ease with words and a graceful prose style that captures the reader's attention." Booklist

Life stories; profiles from The New Yorker; edited by David Remnick. Random House 2000 480p hardcover o.p. pa $15.95 **920**

1. United States—Biography

ISBN 0-375-50355-2; 0-375-75751-1 (pa)

LC 99-53712

An assemblage of 25 biographical profiles spanning the years 1927 to 1999 "with subjects ranging from Ernest Hemingway and Marlon Brando to a fake prince, a pair of eccentric mathematicians, and Biff the show dog." Booklist

Louvish, Simon

Monkey business; the lives and legends of the Marx brothers: Groucho, Chico, Harpo, Zeppo with added Gummo. St. Martin's Press 2000 471p il pa $13.95 hardcover o.p. **920**

1. Marx Brothers

ISBN 0-312-28382-2 (pa)   LC 00-302623

First published 1999 in the United Kingdom

In addition to Groucho, the author "expands the canvas to appraise the contributions of the other brothers, plus Margaret Dumont, a regular target of the brothers' mayhem. . . . Louvish does a solid job of separating fact from fiction and includes a family tree and a discussion of the FBI's file on the group." Libr J

Malone, John Williams

It doesn't take a rocket scientist; great amateurs of science; {by} John Malone. Wiley 2002 232p $24.95 **920**

1. Scientists

ISBN 0-471-41431-X   LC 2003-269159

This examines the lives and work of ten amateur scientists, including Gregor Mendel, David H. Levy, Henrietta Swan Leavitt, Joseph Priestley, Michael Faraday, Grote Reber, Arthur C. Clarke, Thomas Jefferson, Susan Hendrickson, and Felix d'Herelle

Includes bibliographical references

Marías, Javier, 1951-

Written lives; translated from the Spanish by Margaret Jull Costa. New Directions 2006 200p il $22.95 * **920**

1. Authors

ISBN 0-8112-1611-X   LC 2005-15033

Original Spanish edition, 2000

This book features "portraits of Rimbaud, Turgenev, Rilke, Giuseppe Tomasi di Lampedusa, Robert Louis Stevenson, Isak Dinesen, Djuna Barnes and a dozen other literary eminences. . . . [Though the author] acknowledges the artistic greatness of his chosen writers, he prefers to point out and relish their personal oddities, all those quirks, eccentricities and obsessions that make them neurotically and sometimes pitiably human. . . . This is a delightful volume." Washington Post Book World

Martin, James
My life with the saints. Loyola Press 2006 411p
$22.95   **920**
1. Christian saints
ISBN 0-8294-2001-0   LC 2005-28466
The author "relates how he discovered various 'saints'
and how each has affected his life. . . . Despite a theme
built on a particular facet of Catholic belief, Martin's animated style and wide-ranging experiences make this a
book readers of diverse backgrounds will enjoy." Publ
Wkly
Includes bibliographical references

Marton, Kati
The great escape; nine Jews who fled Hitler and
changed the world. Simon & Schuster 2006 271p
il $27   **920**
1. Jews—Hungary 2. Jewish refugees
ISBN 978-0-7432-6115-9; 0-7432-6115-1
                                          LC 2006-49162
"Cast out of the cafes of cosmopolitan Budapest by
the war, each of the nine extraordinary and ambitious
men portrayed in this account would become a household
name by the end of the twentieth century: Manhattan
Project physicists Leo Szilard, Edward Teller, and Eugene Wigner; computer inventor John von Neuman; writer Arthur Koestler . . . ; filmmakers Alexander Korda
(The Third Man) and Michael Curtiz (Casablanca); New
York photographer Andre Kertesz; and D-Day photographer Robert Capa." Booklist
"By looking at these nine lives—salvaged, and crucial—Marton provides a moving measure of how much
was lost." New Yorker
Includes bibliographical references

Hidden power; presidential marriages that
shaped our recent history. Pantheon Bks. 2001
414p il pa $14 hardcover o.p.   **920**
1. Presidents—United States 2. Presidents' spouses—
United States
ISBN 0-385-72188-9 (pa)
This book provides a "survey of a dozen First Couples, from Edith and Woodrow Wilson to Laura and
George Bush. Marton mixes some good history with a
lot of pop marriage psychology to show the part that patience, tolerance, insight, determination, sex and occasionally even love have played in the pursuit and exercise of presidential power." Time
Includes bibliographical references

Matuz, Roger
Reconstruction era: biographies; Lawrence W.
Baker, project editor. UXL 2004 xxiv, 246p il
(Reconstruction Era reference library) $60
                                                         920
1. Reconstruction (1865-1876)
ISBN 0-7876-9218-2   LC 2004-17300
This "volume covers political and military leaders as
well as activists, artists, writers, and more. Among them
are Louisa May Alcott, Frederick Douglass, Ulysses S.
Grant, and Zebulon Vance. Within each biographical en-
try are cross-references to other individuals covered in
this volume." Booklist
Includes bibliographical references

McBrien, Richard P.
Lives of the popes; the pontiffs from St. Peter
to John Paul II. HarperOne 2006 522p il pa $19.95
                                                         920
1. Popes 2. Papacy
ISBN 978-0-06-087807-8; 0-06-087807-X
A reissue of the title first published 1997
On cover: Recently updated to include Benedict XVI
The author provides biographical sketches of all the
popes since the Apostle Peter. He also offers an
"overview of the evolution of the Roman Catholic
Church, ponders the probable future of the papacy, reviews the rules governing both the election and the removal of a pope, furnishes . . . outlines of key papal en-
cyclicals, rates the popes, and includes a time line of significant papal, ecclasiastical, and secular events."
Booklist
McBrien offers "plenty of historical facts and sobering, valuable judgments." N Y Times Book Rev
Includes bibliographical references

Lives of the saints; from Mary and Francis of
Assisi to John XXIII and Mother Teresa.
HarperSanFrancisco 2001 xxiii, 646p il pa $19.95
hardcover o.p.   **920**
1. Christian saints
ISBN 0-06-123283-1 (pa)   LC 00-53933
"This work goes beyond the Roman Catholic Church's
list of saints to include those of the Orthodox, Anglican,
and Lutheran churches. Concise and well-researched biographical sketches are arranged by feast days, with access provided by indexes for saints, personal names, and
subjects. Complementing the biographies are thoughtful
essays on the history of saints, their place in religious
history, and canonization; a series of seven tables on
feast days, patron saints, iconography, and papal canonization." Libr J
Includes bibliographical references

McNally, Dennis
A long strange trip; the inside history of the
Grateful Dead. Broadway Bks. 2002 684p il $30;
pa $18.95   **920**
1. Grateful Dead (Musical group)
ISBN 0-7679-1185-7; 0-7679-1186-5 (pa)
                                          LC 2002-25561
A history of the rock music group led by Jerry Garcia
which first became popular in the 1960's
"As the Dead's publicist for more than 20 years,
McNally packs this . . . full of intimate details otherwise
unavailable. . . . The most exhaustively researched book
on the band to date." Publ Wkly
Includes bibliographical references

The **Mitfords**; letters between six sisters; edited
by Charlotte Mosley. Harper 2007 xxi, 834p il
$39.95   **920**
1. Mitford family
ISBN 978-0-06-137364-0; 0-06-137364-8
"The lost art of letter writing is splendidly portrayed
in this massive volume of correspondence among the six
Mitford sisters: Nancy, Pamela, Diana, Unity, Jessica,
and Deborah. . . . Arranged chronologically covering the
years 1925-2002, they include footnotes identifying peo-

The Mitfords—*Continued*

ple, places, and activities. In introductions to each of the nine sections of letters, Mosley provides a synopsis of the major events in each sister's life as well as thoughtful commentary and analysis." Libr J

Includes bibliographical references

Morrow, Lance

The best year of their lives; Kennedy, Johnson, and Nixon in 1948: learning the secrets of power. Basic Books 2005 xl, 312p $26   **920**
  1. Kennedy, John F. (John Fitzgerald), 1917-1963
  2. Johnson, Lyndon B. (Lyndon Baines), 1908-1973
  3. Nixon, Richard M. (Richard Milhous), 1913-1994
  4. United States—Politics and government—1945-1953
  ISBN 0-465-04723-8   LC 2005-1836
The author describes "three future presidents as young congressmen standing at the seductive threshold of power. Morrow also depicts the sowing of the seeds of the corruption that thrives alongside authority and success." Publ Wkly

"The book succeeds in drawing together three fascinating characters into an illuminating historical intersection. You don't have to agree with all of Morrow's interpretations to be entertained by his lively treatment of three crucial figures during an important time in American history." N Y Times Book Rev

Includes bibliographical references

Mortimer, Gavin

The great swim. Walker & Company 2008 325p il map $24.95   **920**
  1. Women athletes 2. Marathon swimming 3. United States—History—1919-1933
  ISBN 978-0-8027-1595-1; 0-8027-1595-8
                  LC 2008-256
Draws on primary sources, diaries, and family interviews to document the story of four American athletes who in 1926 became the first women to swim the English Channel, in an account that also cites the media frenzy that surrounded their achievement.

"The book can be read as the story of a sporting competition or as an exploration of our timeless fascination with celebrity. Either way, it's an absorbing and inspirational saga in the Seabiscuit mold." Booklist

Includes bibliographical references

Nachman, Gerald

Seriously funny; the rebel comedians of the 1950s and 1960s. Pantheon Bks. 2003 659p il $29.95 *   **920**
  1. Comedians 2. Wit and humor
  ISBN 0-375-41030-9   LC 2002-30713
Also available in paperback from Back Stage Bks.

Nachman examines American comedians, including "Mort Sahl, Sid Caesar, Tom Lehrer, Steve Allen, Stan Freberg, Ernie Kovacs, Phyllis Diller, Jonathan Winters, Shelley Berman, Nichols and May, Bob & Ray, Bob Newhart, Lenny Bruce, the Smothers Brothers, Mel Brooks, Dick Gregory, Woody Allen, Bill Cosby, [and] Joan Rivers. . . . 'Taken together, [Nachman writes],

they made up the faculty of a new school of vigorous, socially aware satire, a dazzling group of voices that reigned roughly from 1953 to 1965.'" N Y Times Book Rev

Includes bibliographical references

New York Times Company

Sultans of swat; the four great sluggers of the New York Yankees; as originally reported by The New York Times; with an introduction by Yogi Berra. St. Martin's Press 2006 345p il $29.95
                  920
  1. Ruth, Babe, 1895-1948 2. Mantle, Mickey, 1931-1995 3. Gehrig, Lou, 1903-1941 4. DiMaggio, Joe 5. New York Yankees (Baseball team) 6. Baseball—Biography
  ISBN 0-312-34014-1; 978-0-312-34014-8
                  LC 2005-52039
"Babe Ruth, Lou Gehrig, Joe DiMaggio, and Mickey Mantle were four of the greatest hitters in the history of baseball. . . . This volume uses sports reporting—game accounts, features, sidebars, photographs, and box scores—to recreate the four sluggers' careers. . . . To peruse these pages is to hop aboard a baseball time machine and experience the highlights of four great careers much as fans did at the time." Booklist

The **Norton** book of American autobiography; edited and introduced by Jay Parini and with a preface by Gore Vidal. Norton 1999 711p $32.50 *   **920**
  1. United States—Biography 2. Autobiography
  ISBN 0-393-04677-X   LC 98-43398
"Parini has compiled over 60 selections from autobiographies and memoirs published since the 17th century. . . . {He} includes works by such diverse writers as Henry David Thoreau, U.S. Grant, Gertrude Stein, Malcom X, Mary McCarthy, and Richard Rodriguez. . . . The selections are arranged chronologically, and each is prefaced by an introduction on its author and its merit." Libr J

Includes bibliographical references

Plutarch, ca. 46-ca. 120

Plutarch: the lives of the noble Grecians and Romans; the Dryden translation; edited and revised by Arthur Hugh Clough. Modern Lib. 1992 2v ea $23.95   **920**
  1. Greece—Biography 2. Rome—Biography
  ISBN 0-679-60008-6 (v1); 0-679-60009-4 (v2)
                  LC 92-50223
First Modern Library edition published 1932

This work is "arranged mainly in pairs in which a Greek and a Roman are contrasted. His subjects, who include Demosthenes and Cicero, were statesmen or generals. In the process of writing about them, he invents dialogue and describes the emotions of the personages involved." Reader's Ency. 4th edition

Reynolds, Moira Davison
American women scientists; 23 inspiring biographies, 1900-2000. McFarland & Co. 1999 149p il hardcover o.p. pa $24.95   **920**
  1. Women scientists
  ISBN 0-7864-0649-6; 0-7864-2161-4 (pa)
                         LC 99-14603
"Four-to-six page profiles of 23 of the century's premier women scientists, representing a wide variety of disciplines. The entries are arranged chronologically beginning with Cornelia Clapp (1849-1934) and ending with Mary Good (1931-). . . . Each entry includes a black-and-white portrait." SLJ
  Includes bibliographical references

Ritter, Lawrence S.
The glory of their times; the story of the early days of baseball told by the men who played it. new enl ed. Morrow 1984 360p il pa $14.95 hardcover o.p.   **920**
  1. Baseball—Biography
  ISBN 0688112730 (pa)   LC 84-221549
  First published 1966 by Macmillan
A collection of 26 oral histories of baseball's early days by veteran players

Roberts, Cokie
Founding mothers; the women who raised our nation. William Morrow 2004 xx, 359p il $24.95; pa $14.95 *   **920**
  1. Women—United States—History
  ISBN 0-06-009025-1; 0-06-009026-X (pa)
                        LC 2004-042873
"Focusing mainly on the wives, daughters, sisters, and mothers of the Founding Fathers, this . . . title chronicles the adventures and contributions of numerous women of the era between 1740 and 1797." SLJ
"In addition to telling wonderful stories, Roberts also presents a very readable, serviceable account of politics—male and female—in early America. If only our standard history textbooks were written with such flair!" Publ Wkly

Roe, Sue, 1956-
The private lives of the impressionists. HarperCollins Publishers 2006 356p il map $29.95   **920**
  1. Impressionism (Art) 2. Artists, French
  ISBN 0-06-054558-5; 978-0-06-054558-1
                        LC 2006-43621
This is a "group portrait of the revolutionary artists dubbed the impressionists for their atmospheric landscapes and forthright depictions of everyday life. Here, masterfully set against a panoramic rendering of their turbulent times, are Manet, Pissarro, Degas, Monet, Renoir, Cezanne, Sisley, Morisot, and Cassatt, each incisively defined as an individual and in terms of their complex interactions as they devoted themselves to paintings that met only with derision." Booklist
  Includes bibliographical references

Roiphe, Katie
Uncommon arrangements; seven portraits of married life in London literary circles, 1910-1939. Dial Press 2007 343p il $26   **920**
  1. Authors, English 2. Women authors 3. Marriage
  ISBN 978-0-385-33937-7; 0-385-33937-2
                        LC 2007-11798
"Seven 'modern' partnerships move through the book, all in (or near) the world of art and letters, including those of Vanessa and Clive Bell, Katherine Mansfield and John Middleton Murry, H.G. and Jane Wells, Radclyffe Hall and Una Troubridge, Vera Brittain and George Catlin. In different but always striking ways, each looked to transform the terms of intimacy." Salon.com
"Roiphe is at her most insightful—and funniest—in showing us where the declared credo of her characters collides with reality. . . . Often these unorthodox unions endured only because someone was willing to knuckle under." N Y Times Book Rev

Rubin, Louis Decimus, 1923-
My father's people; a family of Southern Jews; {by} Louis D. Rubin Jr. Louisiana State Univ. Press 2002 139p il $22.50   **920**
  1. Rubens family
  ISBN 0-8071-2808-2   LC 2002-454
The author "tells the stories of Hyman and Fannie Rubin, his grandparents, and their seven children. . . . Rubin's descriptions are affectionate, yet he doesn't gloss over their flaws, and as a result, those he knows best come alive for readers." Publ Wkly

Salley, Columbus
The black 100; a ranking of the most influential African-Americans, past and present; Columbus Salley. rev ed. Kensington Publishing Corp. 1999 384p il pa $18.95   **920**
  1. African Americans—Biography
  ISBN 978-0-8065-1550-2; 0-8065-1550-3
                        LC 98-47713
"A Citadel Press book"
A reprint of the title first published 1993 by Carol Publishing Group
The author profiles 100 black men and women and ranks them, based upon his subjective evaluation of their contributions to black American society. They include Dr. Martin Luther King, Jr., Malcolm X, Zora Neale Hurston, Paul Robeson, Muhammad Ali, Arthur Ashe, Toni Morrison, Oprah Winfrey, and August Wilson
  Includes bibliographical references

Schiff, Karenna Gore
Lighting the way; nine women who changed modern America. Miramax Books/Hyperion 2006 528p il $25.95; pa $17.95   **920**
  1. Women—United States—Biography
  ISBN 1-4013-5218-9; 1-4013-6015-7 (pa)
                        LC 2005-56247
The author "profiles nine women who helped change the course of history by overcoming injustice in their own lives." Libr J

Schiff, Karenna Gore—*Continued*

"This is an inspirational collection of biographies of women of various social, ethnic, and racial backgrounds fighting for social justice." Booklist

Includes bibliographical references

Schonberg, Harold C.

The great pianists. rev and updated. Simon & Schuster 1987 525p il pa $18 hardcover o.p.
    920
1. Pianists
ISBN 0-671-63837-8 (pa)   LC 87-341
"A Fireside book"
First published 1963
Beginning with the Bach family, the author describes the personal lives and careers of outstanding pianists from the eighteenth century to the present

The lives of the great composers. 3rd ed. Norton 1997 653p il $35 *   **920**
1. Composers
ISBN 0-393-03857-2   LC 96-13308
First published 1970
This book traces the lives of important musical figures from Monteverdi to Ives and includes information on the serialists, minimalist composers and the new tonalists of the 1990s

"Schonberg writes for the lay reader. His intention is to humanize the composers and the writing, always highly readable, emphasizes biographical information rather than musical analysis." Libr J

Includes bibliographical references

Sifters: Native American women's lives; edited by Theda Perdue. Oxford Univ. Press 2001 260p (Viewpoints on American culture) $55; pa $19.95   **920**
1. Native American women
ISBN 0-19-513080-4; 0-19-513081-2 (pa)
    LC 00-39950
"From Pocahontas, a Powhatan woman of the seventeenth century, to Ada Deer, the Menominee woman who headed the Bureau of Indian Affairs in the 1990s, the essays span four centuries. Each one recounts the experiences of women from vastly different cultural traditions. . . . Contributors focus on the ways in which different women have fashioned lives that remain firmly rooted in their identity as Native women." Publisher's note

Includes bibliographical references

Singer, Mark

Character studies; encounters with the curiously obsessed. Houghton Mifflin 2005 256p pa $13.95 hardcover o.p.   **920**
1. Eccentrics and eccentricities
ISBN 0-618-77363-0 (pa) LC 2004-62757
This is a "mix of . . . [the author's] portraits from The New Yorker, gathered in book form for the first time. In the essays he trains his skills on the likes of Martin Scorsese and Donald Trump; The Wednesday Group, the self-selected intelligentsia of El Paso; well-known bibliophile Michael Zinman; high-powered women who decide to quit the fast track; and Richard

Seiverling, a Tom Mix fan determined to preserve the memory of the movie cowboy. It's quite a cast of characters, and Singer lavishly gives them all their due." Libr J

Smith, Andrew

Moondust; in search of the men who fell to earth. Fourth Estate 2005 372p il $24.95; pa $14.95   **920**
1. Apollo project 2. Astronauts
ISBN 0-00-71554-17; 978-0-00-715541-5; 0-00-715542-5 (pa); 978-0-00-715542-2 (pa)
    LC 2005-40081
This book describes the lives of nine astronauts after they walked on the moon.

"In an artful blend of memoir and popular history, Smith makes flesh-and-blood people out of icons and reveals the tenderness of his own heart." Publ Wkly

Includes bibliographical references

Spitz, Bob

The Beatles: the biography. Little, Brown 2005 983p il $29.95 *   **920**
1. Beatles 2. Rock musicians
ISBN 0-316-80352-9   LC 2005-3838
"Calling on books, articles, radio programs and primary interviews, Spitz follows the band from each member's family origins in working-class Liverpool to the band's agonizing final days." Publ Wkly

This "beautifully written chronicle breathes new life into the familiar story of the Liverpool boys who conquered the world and became . . . the most influential entertainers of the past century. The author's passion for his subject, and for every nuance of every scene, electrifies even the most familiar moments in the legend." N Y Times Book Rev

Includes discography and bibliographical references

Stark, Steven D.

Meet the Beatles; a cultural history of the band that shook youth, gender, and the world. HarperEntertainment 2005 344p il $26.95; pa $14.95   **920**
1. Beatles 2. Rock musicians
ISBN 0-06-000892-X; 0-06-000893-8 (pa)
    LC 2004-59794
In this biography of the Beatles, the author focuses "as much on the cultural trends that produced the Beatles—and the trends they created—as on the Fab Four themselves. . . . Throughout, Stark is sharp and insightful, even when he wades into the psychoanalytic waters of the John/Yoko and Paul/Linda relationships." Publ Wkly

Starkey, David

Six wives: the queens of Henry VIII. HarperCollins Pubs. 2003 xxvii, 852p il hardcover o.p. pa $16.95   **920**

Starkey, David—*Continued*
1. Great Britain—History—1485-1603, Tudors
2. Queens
ISBN 0-694-01043-X; 0-06-000550-5 (pa)
The author covers each of Henry's six wives, "their personalities, their place in the family networks and religious currents at court and the overall patterns of the king's infatuations and disillusionments." Publ Wkly
"Solidly researched and delightfully told, this is highly recommended." Libr J
Includes bibliographical references

Stolen voices; young people's war diaries from World War I to Iraq; edited with commentaries by Zlata Filipovic and Melanie Challenger; foreword by Olara A. Otunnu. Penguin 2007 xxiii, 293p il pa $14 **920**
1. Children and war
ISBN 978-0-14-303871-9; 0-14-303871-0
"A Penguin original"
The editors have "compiled 14 diaries that were kept by children during wartime, from World War I to Iraq. Their poignant voices will break your heart." Libr J

Terkel, Studs, 1912-2008
My American century. New Press 1997 xxiii, 532p pa $14.95 hardcover o.p. * **920**
1. United States—Biography
ISBN 1-56584-469-6 (pa) LC 96-52779
This volume gathers "the introductions Terkel wrote for his eight oral-history books (and the fiftieth anniversary edition of Steinbeck's *The Grapes of Wrath*) with 40-odd interviews: Terkel's conversations with gangsters and grandmothers, authors and executives, photographers and farmers, cabbies and crusaders. . . . A superb introduction to Terkel's work (or to oral history) and a trip down memory lane for his fans." Booklist

Thomas, Robert McG., Jr.
52 McGs; the best obituaries from legendary New York Times writer Robert McG. Thomas Jr.; edited by Chris Calhoun; foreword by Thomas Mallon. Scribner 2001 192p il pa $14.95 hardcover o.p. **920**
1. Obituaries
ISBN 1-4165-9827-8 (pa) LC 2001-42952
Thomas chose "as his subjects unsung characters who had died in unremarkable ways. His obituaries, which became known simply as McG.s, focused on such marginal celebrities as the inventor of Kitty Litter, a traveling goat man, and a champion duckpins player." Libr J
"This highly browsable collection of 52 obits shows Thomas at his deadline best." Publ Wkly

Tillyard, Stella K.
A royal affair; George III and his scandalous siblings; [by] Stella Tillyard. Random House 2006 xxiv, 352p il $26.95 **920**
1. George III, King of Great Britain, 1738-1820
2. Great Britain—Kings and rulers
ISBN 978-1-4000-6371-0; 1-4000-6371-X
LC 2006-45130

This biography examines the life of King George III of Great Britain and his siblings.
"This riveting account reminds us that in the past, the misdemeanors of royals had serious, not simply gossip-rag, implications." Booklist
Includes bibliographical references

Tinniswood, Adrian, 1954-
The Verneys; a true story of love, war, and madness in seventeenth-century England. Riverhead Books 2007 569p il map $35
920
1. Verney family 2. Great Britain—History—1603-1714, Stuarts
ISBN 978-1-59448-948-8; 1-59448-948-3
LC 2007-911
"The letters of the Verney family survive as the largest and most continuous collection of personal correspondence from seventeenth-century Britain, and Tinniswood draws on them to produce a lively, almost novelistic account of an aristocratic family. . . Their stories range from the outrageous—Sir Francis Verney, who 'turned Turk' and became a pirate along the Barbary Coast; 'Mad' Mary Verney, whose husband's philandering drove her to zelotypia, or morbid jealousy—to the more familiar and heartrending: a father and son separated by political allegiances during civil war; a patriarch who worries about his children's financial security. Tinniswood's portraits are intimate, compelling, and deftly situated within the broader historical period, so that the turbulence of the seventeenth century is rendered as a human drama." New Yorker
Includes bibliographical references

To the best of my ability; the American presidents; James McPherson, editor. DK Pub. 2000 480p il map hardcover o.p. pa $20
920
1. Presidents—United States
ISBN 0-7894-5073-9; 0-7566-0777-9 (pa)
LC 00-21569
The first half of this book summarizes the "lives and administrations of the 42 men who have held the presidency. Each has a chapter generally running between six to eight pages . . . written by one of 32 contributing historians or biographers. . . . The second half of the book contains chapters on each election campaign, including very short essays describing issues, tables of results, and the full text of each president's inaugural address." Libr J

Vare, Ethlie Ann
Patently female; from AZT to TV dinners: stories of women inventors and their breakthrough ideas; [by] Ethlie Ann Vare, Greg Ptacek. Wiley 2002 220p il $27.95 **920**
1. Women inventors
ISBN 0-471-02334-5 LC 2001-26950
Sequel to: Mothers of invention (1988)
The authors "detail how women's ideas like the cotton gin, automatic sewing machine and even the Brooklyn Bridge have often been attributed to men and how history books and museums like the Smithsonian and the Na-

Vare, Ethlie Ann—*Continued*
tional Inventors Hall of Fame have ignored women's achievements." Publ Wkly
Includes bibliographical references

Vowell, Sarah, 1969-
Assassination vacation. Simon & Schuster 2005 258p il hardcover o.p. pa $14 **920**
1. Presidents—United States—Assassination 2. United States—Description and travel 3. United States—Local history
ISBN 0-7432-6003-1; 0-7432-6004-X (pa)
LC 2004-59134
The author "takes readers on a pilgrimage of sorts to the sites and monuments that pay homage to Lincoln, Garfield and McKinley, visiting everything from grave sites and simple plaques (like the one in Buffalo that marks the place where McKinley was shot) to places like the National Museum of Health and Medicine, where fragments of Lincoln's skull are on display." Publ Wkly
"[Vowell] has done her homework, providing lucid descriptions of the murders and agile summations of the scholarly assessments of each era." America

Walker-Hill, Helen
From spirituals to symphonies; African-American women composers and their music. Greenwood Press 2002 401p il $94.95
920
1. African American women 2. Composers
ISBN 0-313-29947-1 LC 2001-40600
Also available in paperback by University of Illinois Press
This profiles the lives and works of Undine Smith Moore, Julia Perry, Margaret Bonds, Irene Britton Smith, Dorothy Rudd Moore, Valerie Capers, Mary Watkins, and Regina Harris Baiocchi
This is "an accessible, thoughtful, and humanist study. . . . Detailed works lists and an appendix enumerating other black women composers add reference value." Libr J
Includes bibliographical references

Walsh, Jim, 1959-
The Replacements: all over but the shouting; an oral history. MBI Pub. Co. and Voyageur Press 2007 304p il $21.95 **920**
1. Replacements (Musical group) 2. Rock musicians
ISBN 978-0-7603-3062-3; 0-7603-3062-X
LC 2007-22576
"In this loving, appropriately ramshackle tribute to one of the most beloved rock-and-roll bands of the 1980s, Walsh gives his subjects the oral history treatment, assembling a wide range of associates, friends and famous fans to put their memories on the record." Publ Wkly
Includes bibliographical references

Ward-Royster, Willa, 1922-
How I got over; Clara Ward and the world-famous Ward Singers; {by} Willa Ward-Royster; as told to Toni Rose; foreword by Horace Clarence Boyer. Temple Univ. Press 1997 263p hardcover o.p. pa $24.95 **920**
1. Clara Ward Singers 2. Gospel music
ISBN 1-56639-489-9; 978-1-56639-490-1 (pa); 1-56639-490-2 (pa) LC 96-5943
"Ward-Royster relates the rise of her family's world-renowned gospel group, formed by her mother and headlined by her sister. . . . The book contains details on everything from successful performances on the stage of the Apollo, major TV variety shows, and international tours to top sales of hit recordings and friendships with such luminaries as Mahalia Jackson." Libr J

Ware, Susan, 1950-
Letter to the world; seven women who shaped the American century. Norton 1998 xxiv, 344p il $25.95 **920**
1. Women—Biography
ISBN 0-393-04652-4 LC 97-45923
Also available in paperback from Harvard Univ. Press
The author "considers the lives of seven women who had an exceptional impact on 20th-century American culture and society's perception of the role of women: Eleanor Roosevelt, Dorothy Thompson, Margaret Mead, Katharine Hepburn, Babe Didrikson Zaharias, Martha Graham, and Marian Anderson. In addition to focusing on outstanding achievements in their chosen fields, Ware looks at their often unconventional private lives." Libr J
Includes bibliographical references

Warner, Ezra J.
Generals in blue; lives of the Union commanders. Louisiana State Univ. Press 1964 xxiv, 679p il $39.95 * **920**
1. Generals 2. United States—History—1861-1865, Civil War—Biography
ISBN 0-8071-0822-7
This book contains biographical sketches of the 583 men who attained the rank of general during the Civil War years. A photograph of each man is also included
Includes bibliographical references

Generals in gray; lives of the Confederate commanders. Louisiana State Univ. Press 1959 xxvii, 420p il $39.95 **920**
1. Generals 2. United States—History—1861-1865, Civil War—Biography
ISBN 0-8071-0823-5
"Biographical sketches of the Confederate generals; concise outlines of their military careers, also giving dates of birth and death and places of burial. The product of ten years of research, much of it done in interviews with descendants. Illustrated with 425 portraits." Publ Wkly
Includes bibliographical references

Waugh, Alexander
Fathers and sons; the autobiography of a family.
Nan A. Talese 2007 472p il $27.50   **920**
1. Waugh family 2. Authors, English
ISBN 978-0-385-52150-5; 0-385-52150-2
LC 2007-5239
First published 2004 in the United Kingdom
"The scion of an illustrious—and fabulously eccentric—English literary dynasty referees four generations of father-son antagonisms in this scintillating family memoir. Waugh . . . focuses on the fraught relationship between his great-grandfather, prominent critic and publisher Arthur Waugh, and Arthur's son, the famous novelist Evelyn. . . . If this tome were merely an excuse to reprint some of Evelyn's hilarious jottings, it would be well worth the price, but it's also an absorbing study of how writers process their most painfully formative experiences." Publ Wkly
Includes bibliographical references

Waxman, Sharon
Rebels on the backlot; six maverick directors and how they conquered the Hollywood studio system. 1st ed. W. Morrow 2005 386p il $25.95; pa $14.95   **920**
1. Anderson, Paul Thomas 2. Fincher, David, 1963- 3. Jonze, Spike 4. Russell, David O. 5. Soderbergh, Steven 6. Tarantino, Quentin 7. Motion pictures—Production and direction
ISBN 0-06-054017-6; 0-06-054018-4 (pa)
LC 2004-59269
This is the author's "study of six boundary-breaking young directors who revolutionized 1990s filmmaking and still represent a refreshing alternative to 'cookie cutter scripts and cheap MTV imagery.' Her full-blooded profiles introduce Quentin Tarantino (Pulp Fiction), Paul Thomas Anderson (Boogie Nights), David Fincher (Fight Club), Steven Soderbergh (Traffic), David O. Russell (Three Kings) and Spike Jonze (Being John Malkovich). . . . Their stories make for compelling reading." Publ Wkly
Includes bibliographical references

Weir, Alison
The six wives of Henry VIII. Grove Weidenfeld 1992 643p il pa $15 hardcover o.p.   **920**
1. Henry VIII, King of England, 1491-1547 2. Great Britain—History—1485-1603, Tudors
ISBN 0-8021-3683-4 (pa)   LC 91-29522
First published 1991 in the United Kingdom
This is a collective biography of the wives of the Tudor king of England
"Wonderfully detailed, extensively researched. . . . The narrative is free flowing, humorous, informative, and readable." SLJ
Includes bibliographical references

920.003   Dictionaries, encyclopedias, concordances of biography as a discipline

Abrams, Irwin
The Nobel Peace Prize and the laureates; an illustrated biographical history, 1901-2001. Centennial ed. Science Hist. Publs. 2001 350p il pa $35   **920.003**
1. Nobel Prizes 2. Biography—Dictionaries
ISBN 0-88135-388-4   LC 2001-49554
First published 1988 by G.K. Hall & Co.
This reference work "provides a biography with bibliographic references (and a photograph) of each individual winner of the Nobel Peace Prize from its inception in 1901 through the 2001 award. . . . The introductory material and all the biographical entries are concise, well-written, meet high academic standards, and are enjoyable as well." Choice
Includes bibliographical references

Adamson, Lynda G.
Notable women in American history; a guide to recommended biographies and autobiographies. Greenwood Press 1999 450p $52.95   **920.003**
1. Women—Biography—Dictionaries
ISBN 0-313-29584-0   LC 98-55350
Companion volume to Notable women in world history
This volume "concentrates on women who made contributions to U.S. history from the colonial period through 1998. The 500 women covered were born in America or became naturalized citizens; had a full-length biography or autobiography published since 1970; and, in the case of twentieth-century actors, authors, and poets, have been recognized by their peers." Booklist

Notable women in world history; a guide to recommended biographies and autobiographies. Greenwood Press 1998 401p $52.95   **920.003**
1. Women—Biography—Dictionaries
ISBN 0-313-29818-1   LC 97-33136
Companion volume to Notable Women in American History
"The entries are arranged alphabetically by last name with appropriate cross-references for alternative designations. Each contains the woman's name, key dates, occupation or avocation, and birthplace. A short biographical sketch about parents, education, general achievement, and recognition or awards follows. Women of all time periods are included. . . . Because it includes only those born outside the U.S., it complements sources on American women. *Notable Women in World History* is a useful addition to academic, public, and high-school libraries. It would be especially useful for women's studies collections." Booklist

The **African** American national biography; editors in chief, Henry Louis Gates, Jr., Evelyn Brooks-Higginbotham. Oxford University Press 2008 8v il set $995 * **920.003**

1. African Americans—Biography—Dictionaries
ISBN 978-0-19-516019-2   LC 2007-44671

Also available online

Companion volume to African American lives (2004)

"A supplement to the 24-volume *American National Biography* . . . [this biographical encyclopedia] records the contributions of more than 4,000 African Americans—slaves, architects, entertainers, dentists, political leaders, artists, poets, and activists. . . . [This] is a major . . . standard reference work that most libraries of any size will want to have." Booklist

Includes bibliographical references

American authors, 1600-1900; a biographical dictionary of American literature; edited by Stanley J. Kunitz and Howard Haycraft. Wilson, H.W. 1938 846p il (Authors series) $120 **920.003**

1. Authors, American—Dictionaries 2. American literature—Bio-bibliography
ISBN 0-8242-0001-2

"Complete in one volume with 1300 biographies and 400 portraits." Title page

"This volume contains biographies of 1,300 authors who contributed to the development of American literature, from the founding of Jamestown (1607) to the end of the nineteenth century. Each essay describes the author's life, discusses past and present significance, and evaluates principal works." Safford. Guide to Ref Materials for Sch Media Cent. 5th edition

American men & women of science; a biographical directory of today's leaders in physical, biological and related sciences. 25th ed. Gale Group 2008 8v set $1530.75 **920.003**

1. Scientists—Dictionaries
ISSN 0192-8570
ISBN 1-4144-3291-7; 978-1-4144-3291-5

Also available eBook version

Irregular. First published 1906 by Science Press with title: American men of science. Some editions were divided into two sections: Physical and biological sciences and Social sciences

"Brief biographical sketches of . . . scientists and engineers active in the United States and Canada. Arranged alphabetically, with discipline index." Ref Sources for Small & Medium-sized Libr. 6th edition

American national biography; general editors, John A. Garraty, Mark C. Carnes. Oxford Univ. Press 1999 24v set $795 * **920.003**

1. United States—Biography—Dictionaries
ISBN 0-19-520635-5   LC 98-20826

Also available online; Also available Supplement 1 published 2002 $150 (ISBN 0-19-515063-5) and Supplement II published 2005 $150 (0-19-522202-4), the first two in an ongoing series of Supplements

Conceived as the successor to the Dictionary of American biography, first published between 1926 and 1937;

Published under the auspices of the American Council of Learned Societies

"ANB defines 'American' broadly as a person whose significance, achievement, fame, or influence occurred during residence within what is now the US, or whose life or career directly influenced the course of US history. Subjects must have died before 1996. . . . Subjects are arranged alphabetically. The typical entry, 750 to 7,500 words in length, proceeds chronologically, following the major personal and professional events of the subject's life, birth to death. The concluding paragraph attempts to assess the subject's contributions from today's perspective. A brief bibliography after each entry, not meant to be comprehensive, lists major sources, including locations of archives and collections of personal papers." Choice

Includes bibliographical references

American statesmen; secretaries of state from John Jay to Colin Powell; edited by Edward S. Mihalkanin. Greenwood Press 2004 xxxv, 571p $99.95 **920.003**

1. Statesmen—United States—Dictionaries
ISBN 0-313-30828-4   LC 2004-10871

This biographical dictionary features "65 biographical essays on each of the secretaries of state plus two important interim secretaries. . . . Each essay blends biographical information, early life, education, and influences; career information, appointment, and relations with the president and Congress; and a review of the major issues and accomplishments during the secretary's tenure in office." Am Ref Books Annu, 2005

For a fuller review, see: Booklist, Feb. 15, 2005

Includes bibliographical references

American writers; a collection of literary biographies; Leonard Unger, editor in chief. Scribner 1974-1998 4v + supplement I-IV (in 8v) + retrospective supplement 1 set $1845 **920.003**

1. Authors, American—Dictionaries 2. American literature—History and criticism
ISBN 0-684-80586-3

Continued by ongoing series of supplementary volumes each $145

"Signed essays on the life and works of selected American authors; selective bibliographies by and about each author. The basic set (1974. 4 v.) contains 97 essays originally published in the University of Minnesota pamphlets on American writers series; some have been revised and updated. Each of the 2-v. supplements covers 29 writers not included in the parent series; the supplements give greater attention to women and minorities." Guide to Ref Books. 11th edition

American writers: selected authors; a three volume set containing sixty-four essays from the parent publication is available $325 (ISBN 0-684-80604-5)

Ancell, R. Manning, 1942-
The biographical dictionary of World War II
generals and flag officers; the U.S. Armed Forces;
{by} R. Manning Ancell with Christine M. Miller.
Greenwood Press 1996 706p $130.95

   920.003
1. World War, 1939-1945—Biography
ISBN 0-313-29546-8   LC 95-50450
"The nearly 2,400 entries, which, according to the
preface, represent 99 percent of the total number who
served, are listed in alphabetical order in six chapters:
'Army,' 'Army Air Force,' 'National Guard,' 'Navy,'
'Marine Corps,' and 'Coast Guard.' . . . The volume
concludes with two appendixes (state-by-state and ser-
vice-by-service summary of birthplaces and birth dates;
generals and flag officers who died during World War II)
and an alphabetical index to all biographees." Booklist
Includes bibliographical references

Attwater, Donald, 1892-1977
The Penguin dictionary of saints; [by] Donald
Attwater, with Catherine Rachel John. 3rd ed.
Penguin Bks. 1995 381p pa $15.95

   920.003
1. Christian saints—Dictionaries
ISBN 0-14-051312-4   LC 96-165638
First published 1965
"Information includes classification of saints (martyr,
confessor, and so on); date of existence; their circumstances in becoming a saint; and their feast day. It also
provides a glossary and lists of further reading, some patron saints, some emblems that identify specific saints,
and feast days in the order that they arrive within the
calendar year." Am Ref Books Annu, 1997

Bader, Philip
African-American writers. Facts on File 2004
294p (A to Z of African Americans) $44 *

   920.003
1. American literature—African American authors—
Bio-bibliography 2. African American authors—Dictionaries
ISBN 0-8160-4860-6   LC 2003-8699
"This volume features biographical entries on 145 African American authors. Emphasizing writers whose
works are still in print and are regularly part of high
school and college curricula, it covers novelists, poets,
journalists, children's and young adult authors, nonfiction
writers, and critics. Among them are well-known figures
like Ralph Ellison and Countee Cullen and contemporary
voices like Suzan-Lori Parks and Edwidge Danticat. . . .
All of the entries are clear and focused and manage to
be comprehensive. . . . This volume's longer entries, illustrations, and indexes make it a worthwhile addition to
high school, public, and academic libraries." Libr J
Includes bibliographical references

Baker's biographical dictionary of popular
musicians since 1990; introduction by David
Freeland. Schirmer Ref. 2003 2v il set $195

   920.003
1. Popular music—Dictionaries
ISBN 0-02-865799-3   LC 2003-13956

This dictionary includes more than 500 artists and
groups active from 1990-2000. Rock, rhythm and blues,
rap, country, classical, and jazz are among the popular
styles covered. Select discographies, bibliographies, and
a glossary of musical terms are provided
"An excellent companion to the 2001 expansion of
Baker's Biographical Dictionary of Musicians. . . . Giv-
en the broad spectrum of musical styles covered here,
this would make an excellent reference for public and academic libraries." Libr J
Includes bibliographical references and discographies

Biographical encyclopedia of artists; Sir Lawrence
Gowing, general editor. Facts on File 2005 4v
il set $260

   920.003
1. Artists—Biography—Encyclopedias
ISBN 0-8160-5803-2   LC 2005-40500
First published 1983 by Prentice-Hall as volume two
of Encyclopedia of visual art
At head of title: Facts on File
"The artists covered include Laurie Anderson, Frank
Gehry, Anselm Kiefer, Jan Vermeer, and Andy Warhol.
. . . A visual chronology of artists by country and era
functions as an index to artists, and an alphabetical art-
ist/subject index concludes the work." Libr J
For a fuller review, see: Booklist, Jan. 1 & 15, 2006
Includes bibliographical references

Black women in America; Darlene Clark Hine,
editor in chief. 2nd ed. Oxford University Press
2005 3v il set $325 *

   920.003
1. African American women—Dictionaries
ISBN 0-19-515677-3   LC 2005-1532
First published 1993 by Carlson Pub.
This set features over 300 "profiles of women from
the 1800s to the present, including writers, activists, entrepreneurs, educators, ambassadors, and many others, interspersed with the roles they played in Islam, the Left,
librarianship, journalism, the labor movement, and more."
Libr J
"The essays offer fascinating glimpses into black
women's economic, social, and political contributions,
even at the grassroots level, and explore issues such as
spirituality, domestic servitude, and mixed-race identity
in terms of how they have shaped history." SLJ
Includes bibliographical references

British authors of the nineteenth century; edited
by Stanley J. Kunitz; associate editor: Howard
Haycraft; complete in one volume with 1000
biographies and 350 portraits. Wilson, H.W.
1936 677p il (Authors series) $105

   920.003
1. Authors, English—Dictionaries 2. English literature—Bio-bibliography
ISBN 0-8242-0007-1
"More than a thousand authors of the British Empire
(including Canada, Australia, South Africa, and New
Zealand) are represented by sketches varying in length
from approximately 100 to 2500 words, roughly propor-
tionate to the importance of the subjects." Preface

Butler, Alban, 1711-1773

Butler's Lives of the saints. Christian Classics 1956 4v set $149.95; pa $109.95 *

920.003

1. Christian saints—Dictionaries

ISBN 0-87061-045-7; 0-87061-137-2 (pa)

Also available in concise editions in paperback from HarperSanFrancisco (edited by Michael Walsh) and in hardcover from Liturgical Press (edited by Paul Burns)

A reprint of the four volume set published 1956 by Kenedy; New edition of a work first published 1756-1759. The calendar arrangement is retained, but the number of entries has almost doubled and many of the entries have been rewritten in whole or part

"The biographies of the saints and beati are arranged by their feast days with each of the four volumes containing three months. . . . Each volume has a table of contents arranged by the days of the month with a list of the feasts for each day." Booklist

The **Cambridge** dictionary of scientists; [by] David Millar [et al.] 2nd ed. Cambridge Univ. Press 2002 464p il $99 hardcover o.p.; pa $34.99 *

920.003

1. Scientists—Dictionaries

ISBN 0-521-80602-X; 0-521-00062-9 (pa)

LC 2002-512240

First published 1996 as a revision of: Chambers concise dictionary of scientists

"The alphabetically organized, illustrated biographical dictionary . . . [covers] over 1,500 key scientists . . . from 40 countries. Physics, chemistry, biology, geology, astronomy, mathematics, medicine, meteorology and technology are all represented and special attention is paid to pioneer women." Publisher's note

Carlin, Richard

Country music; a biographical dictionary. Routledge 2003 497p il $125

920.003

1. Country music—Dictionaries

ISBN 0-415-93802-3

LC 2002-3451

"Portions of this book originally appeared as The big book of country music: a biographical encyclopedia, by Richard Carlin (Penguin, 1995)." Verso of title page

The author "presents an authoritative and acerbically opinionated A-Z guide to 700 country western solo artists and groups. Each article consists of a brief biography, career highs and lows, and select discographies." Libr J

Includes bibliographical references

Contemporary artists; editors, Sara Pendergast and Tom Pendergast; advisers, Jean-Christophe Ammann [et al.] 5th ed. St. James Press 2001 2v il set $265

920.003

1. Artists—Dictionaries

ISBN 1-55862-407-4

LC 2001-48443

First one volume edition published 1977

In this reference "nearly 850 prominent artists (those who have exhibited works in major galleries or museums) are listed. . . . Alphabetic entries provide biographical information (e.g., nationality, education, address), individual and select group exhibitions, collections in which the artist's work is contained, publications by or

about the individual, a critical essay or essays, and occasionally a statement by the artist. The essays highlight the artist's achievements and offer insight into their work. . . . As a reference tool, this publication remains a classic, indispensable part of every art library's collection and is highly recommended." Am Ref Books Annu, 2003

Contemporary poets; editor, Thomas Riggs; with a preface by Diane Wakoski. 7th ed. St. James Press 2001 xxiii, 1443p (Contemporary writers series) $230 *

920.003

1. Poets, English—Dictionaries 2. Poets, American—Dictionaries 3. American poetry—Bio-bibliography

ISBN 1-55862-349-3

LC 00-45882

First published 1970 with title: Contemporary poets of the English language

"A biographical handbook of contemporary poets, arranged alphabetically. Entries consist of a short biography, full bibliography, comments by many of the poets, and a signed critical essay." Ref Sources for Small & Medium-sized Libr. 6th edition

Includes bibliographical references

Contemporary women artists; editors, Laurie Collier Hillstrom, Kevin Hillstrom; with a preface by Lucy R. Lippard. St. James Press 1999 760p $175

920.003

1. Women artists—Dictionaries

ISBN 1-558-62372-8

LC 99-10053

This work "covers 350 women artists, mostly US painters and sculptors. Entries are helpfully indexed by nationality and medium and include photographers, performance and video artists, ceramicists, filmmakers, textile artists, and weavers from countries in Latin America and western and eastern Europe." Choice

Includes bibliographical references

Current biography yearbook, 2007; editor, Clifford Thompson; senior editors, Miriam Helbok, Mari Rich. 68th annual cumulation. Wilson, H.W. 2007 730p il $175

920.003

1. Biography—Periodicals

ISSN 0084-9499

ISBN 978-0-8242-1084-7

Also available online; Current biography: cumulated index, 1940-2005 available $90 (ISBN 0-8242-1054-9)

Annual. First published 1940 with title: Current biography

Also issued monthly except December at a subscription price of $175 per year (ISSN 0011-3344). Yearbooks 1940-2003 available ea $160; yearbooks 2004-2006 available ea $175

"Biographies of prominent people written in lively, popular prose. Emphasis is on entertainers, star athletes, politicians, and other celebrities. Series is cumulative, with biographies revised and updated occasionally. Each volume has seven-year index." N Y Public Libr Book of How & Where to Look It Up

Dictionary of women artists; editor, Delia Gaze; picture editors, Maja Mihajlovic, Leanda Shrimpton. Fitzroy Dearborn Pubs. 1997 2v il set $310   **920.003**
1. Women artists—Dictionaries
ISBN 1-88496-421-4   LC 97-206872
Vol. 1, Introductory surveys. Artists, A-I; Vol. 2, Artists, J-Z

"The chronological coverage extends from 975 A.D. to artists born in 1945. Each of the alphabetically arranged entries includes a brief biography, information about the genre of art produced, and an example of the artist's work. These volumes also present 20 introductory surveys on such topics as 'Court Artists' and 'Training and Professionalism,' and include an overview of women's art in the 19th and 20th centuries by country. Together with their chronological list of artists, the volumes include a range of information not ordinarily found in a resource of this type." Am Libr

Drew, Bernard A. (Bernard Alger), 1950-
100 most popular nonfiction authors; biographical sketches and bibliographies. Libraries Unlimited 2007 438p il (Popular authors series) $65   **920.003**
1. Authors—Dictionaries 2. Literature—Bio-bibliography
ISBN 978-1-59158-487-2   LC 2007-19949
"The authors, chosen by means of consultations with librarians, are those whose impact has been seen mostly in the last half century, among them Diane Ackerman, John Krakauer, David McCullough, and Cornel West. Entries are headed by author's birth year and birthplace, and, if applicable, date of death, and by signature work and primary genres." Booklist
Includes bibliographical references

Encyclopedia of American war heroes; Bruce H. Norton, editor and compiler. Facts on File 2002 xxvii, 292p il $60; pa $19.95   **920.003**
1. Heroes and heroines 2. United States—Military history
ISBN 0-8160-4637-9; 0-8160-4638-7 (pa)
LC 2001-57517
"This volume includes almost 400 entries featuring men and women who fought and, in most cases, died during military service to the U.S. Many of the individuals profiled were awarded one or more citations for their heroic achievements. . . . An introduction, which describes the criteria the editor used for selecting entrants, is followed by a section explaining the different citations. Coverage is extensive, going back to 1675 and extending to the present." Booklist
Includes bibliographical references

Encyclopedia of artists; [consulting editor, William Vaughan; contributors, Christopher Ackroyd, et al.] Oxford Univ. Press 2000 6v il set $195   **920.003**
1. Artists—Dictionaries 2. Art—Dictionaries
ISBN 0-19-521572-9   LC 00-27167
"The first five volumes of this set alphabetically profile more than two hundred artists, covering western art from the Middle Ages to the present. Each artist is accorded a two-page spread consisting of three parts. The main introductory section details the artist's life and work. . . . Each entry then provides a data file that lists the major facts about each artist: nationality, style, dates, key works with dates, things to look for in the art, comparable artists, and related glossary terms. . . . Volume six consists of articles on art movements and styles mentioned in the other volumes." Voice Youth Advocates
"This set is beautifully written and illustrated. It will not only provide reliable information for researchers but will also entertain the interested browser." Am Ref Books Annu, 2001

Encyclopedia of women's autobiography; edited by Victoria Boynton and Jo Malin; Emmanuel S. Nelson, advisory editor. Greenwood Press 2005 2v set $249.95   **920.003**
1. Autobiography 2. Women—Biography—Encyclopedias
ISBN 0-313-32737-8   LC 2005-8526
The contents "range from autobiographies of individuals (e.g., Adrienne Rich, Sojourner Truth, Isak Dinesen) to those of specific ethnicities or nationalities (e.g., African American Women's Autobiography) to important genres and terms (e.g., Captivity/Prison Narrative, Diary, Feminism, and Voice)." Choice
This set's "encyclopedic and culturally diverse nature should appeal to a wide audience and provide a valuable starting point for further research." Libr J
Includes bibliographical references

Encyclopedia of world biography. 2nd ed. Gale Res. 1998 17v il set $1485 *   **920.003**
1. Biography—Dictionaries
ISBN 0-7876-2221-4   LC 97-42327
Kept up-to-date by yearly supplements. Volumes available 1998-2007 designated volumes 18-27 at $150 ea
First published 1973 with title: McGraw-Hill encyclopedia of world biography
Presents brief biographical sketches which provide vital statistics as well as information on the importance of the person listed. Volumes 1-16 are arranged alphabetically; volume 17 is the index

European authors, 1000-1900; a biographical dictionary of European literature; edited by Stanley J. Kunitz and Vineta Colby; complete in one volume with 967 biographies and 309 portraits. Wilson, H.W. 1967 1016p il (Authors series) $115   **920.003**
1. Literature—Bio-bibliography
ISBN 0-8242-0013-6
Includes continental European writers born after the year 1000 and dead before 1925. Nearly a thousand major and minor contributors to thirty-one different literatures are discussed.
"These biographies provide quick, satisfactory introductions to a staggering variety of authors and literatures." Choice

Ewen, David, 1907-1985
American songwriters; an H. W. Wilson biographical dictionary. Wilson, H.W. 1987 489p il $105　**920.003**
1. Composers—United States—Dictionaries
ISBN 0-8242-0744-0　LC 86-24654
Replaces Popular American composers and Popular American composers: First supplement, published 1962 and 1972 respectively
Arranged alphabetically, this reference volume includes 146 biographical entries on American lyricists and composers. Ragtime, minstrel, Tin Pan Alley, Broadway, rock, jazz, blues, folk, country and western, and soul are among the styles represented. Biographies range from Eubie Blake, George Gershwin and George M. Cohan to Chuck Berry, Carole King and Bob Dylan

Farmer, David Hugh
The Oxford dictionary of saints. 5th ed. Oxford University Press 2004 xxiv, 579p map pa $16.95　**920.003**
1. Christian saints—Dictionaries
ISBN 978-0-19-860949-0; 0-19-860949-3 (pa)　LC 2005-272790
A reissue of the title first published 1978
This biographical dictionary profiles the lives, cults, and artistic associations of over 1,000 saints, from the famous to the obscure. An appendix on pilgrimage sights in Europe is also included
"Even those who do not believe in the saints . . . will be able to enjoy and to profit from this splendid book." Economist
Includes bibliographical references

Feather, Leonard
The biographical encyclopedia of jazz; [by] Leonard Feather and Ira Gitler, with the assistance of Swing journal, Tokyo. Oxford Univ. Press 1999 xx, 718p hardcover o.p. pa $29.95　**920.003**
1. Jazz musicians
ISBN 0-19-507418-1; 978-0-19-532000-8 (pa); 0-19-532000-X (pa)　LC 98-15485
This book is based in part on Leonard Feather's Encyclopedia of jazz, The new encyclopedia of jazz, The encyclopedia of jazz in the sixties, and on a subsequent work by Mr. Feather and Ira Gitler, The encyclopedia of jazz in the seventies
This reference source "is made up of more than 3,000 biographies, listed in alphabetical order. Musicians, singers, songwriters, and producers are included. Each entry begins with birth and death information, instruments played, and music-education information. This is followed by a listing of groups each individual played with for significant periods of time. Concluding each entry are lists of recordings, broadcast appearances, and record labels. . . . An indispensable reference source for its comprehensiveness and quality of scholarship." Booklist
Includes discographies

Fredriksen, John C.
American military leaders; from colonial times to the present. ABC-CLIO 1999 2v il set $175　**920.003**
1. United States—Military history
ISBN 1-57607-001-8　LC 99-27929
"Prominent men and women of the military are the scope of this reference work. Coverage includes the most famous of leaders such as Grant, Patton, and Schwarzkopf; but what makes the source so outstanding is its inclusion of forgotten leaders such as Native American Stand Watie, aviator Jackie Cochran, and army educator Alden Partridge. Biographies range from two to three pages, concluding with a bibliography. Photographs and illustrations are included, and both a subject index and a list of leaders organized by their military titles can be found at the end of volume two." Am Libr
Includes bibliographical references

Friedman, Ian C.
Latino athletes. Facts on File 2007 278p il (A to Z of Latino Americans) $44　**920.003**
1. Hispanic Americans—Dictionaries 2. Athletes—Dictionaries
ISBN 978-0-8160-6384-0; 0-8160-6384-2　LC 2006-16901
"Gymnast Trent Dimas, mountain biker Juli Furtado, and speed skater Derek Parra are among the 176 athletes profiled in this volume. . . . Following the entries, athletes are listed by sport, year of birth, and ethnicity or country of origin." Booklist
Includes bibliographical references

Gates, Alexander E.
A to Z of earth scientists. Facts on File 2002 336p il (Notable scientists) $45　**920.003**
1. Earth sciences 2. Scientists—Dictionaries
ISBN 0-8160-4580-1　LC 2002-14616
This "profiles the lives of 192 people who devoted their careers to the disciplines and subdisciplines of the earth sciences during the 18th century to the present. . . . Entries appear in alphabetic order under the name by which the scientist is most commonly known. Also included are birth date, date of death (if applicable), nationality, and earth science specialty. An essay containing more personal data, including an emphasis on the scientist's main work and contributions to the field follows this information." Am Ref Books Annu, 2003
Includes bibliographical references

Grant, Michael, 1914-2004
Greek and Latin authors, 800 B.C.-A.D. 1000; a biographical dictionary. Wilson, H.W. 1980 490p il (Authors series) $105 *　**920.003**
ISBN 0-8242-0640-1　LC 79-27446
Covers more than 370 classical authors. Each entry includes "the pronunciation of the author's name, biographical background, an overview of major works with critical commentary on the nature and quality of those works, and, where relevant, a brief discussion of the influence of the author's works on later literature." Ref Sources for Small & Medium-sized Libr. 5th edition

Great lives from history: Notorious lives; editor, Carl L. Bankston III. Salem Press 2007 3v il set $252   **920.003**
1. Biography—Dictionaries 2. Criminals 3. Terrorists 4. War criminals 5. Dictators 6. Political corruption
ISBN 978-1-58765-320-9   LC 2006-32935
Also available online
This set "is made up of 637 essays by 248 scholars presenting the backstories of historically infamous figures, from ancient times to the present and worldwide, with an emphasis on North America and the West." Libr J
"The scope and depth of coverage make it a valuable resource for not just biographies but for criminal justice and popular culture as well." Booklist
Includes bibliographical references

Great lives from history, The 17th century, 1601-1700; editor, Larissa Juliet Taylor. Salem Press 2005 2v il set $160   **920.003**
1. Biography—Dictionaries 2. World history—17th century
ISBN 1-58765-222-6; 978-1-58765-222-6
    LC 2005-17804
Also available online
Companion volume to Great events from history, The 17th century, 1601-1700
First published as part of the Great lives from history series, published 1987-1995 under the editorship of Frank N. Magill; previously published as half of volume 4 of Dictionary of world biography, published 1998-1999
This "is a collection of biographical essays, ranging from three to five pages in length and documenting the lives of those individuals who helped to shape the history of the 17th century. The coverage is also global and includes both well-known and lesser-known figures." SLJ
Includes bibliographical references

Great lives from history, The 18th century, 1701-1800; editor, John Powell; editor, first edition, Frank N. Magill. Salem Press 2006 2v il map set $160   **920.003**
1. Biography—Dictionaries 2. World history—18th century
ISBN 978-1-58765-276-9; 1-58765-276-5
    LC 2006-5336
Also available online
Companion volume to Great events from history, The 18th century, 1701-1800
First published as part of the Great lives from history series, published 1987-1995 under the editorship of Frank N. Magill; previously published as half of volume 4 of Dictionary of world biography, published 1998-1999
"The alphabetically listed subjects encompass 36 areas of expertise and include John Newbery, Pontiac, Qianlong, Hannah More, Pius IV, Paul Revere, and Shah Wali Allah, among others. Each article is approximately three pages long and lists the subject's major accomplishments, important dates, and areas of achievement. . . . A well-written, useful set." SLJ
Includes bibliographical references

Great lives from history, The 19th century, 1801-1900; editor, John Powell. Salem Press 2006 4v il map set $360   **920.003**
1. Biography—Dictionaries 2. World history—19th century
ISBN 978-1-58765-292-9; 1-58765-292-7
    LC 2006-20187
Also available online
Companion volume to Great events from history, The 19th century, 1801-1900
First published as part of the Great lives from history series, published 1987-1995 under the editorship of Frank N. Magill; previously published as volumes 5 and 6 of Dictionary of world biography, published 1998-1999
"A total of 737 essays covering 757 major figures including 123 on women make up the set. . . . Major world leaders appear here, as well as the giants of religious faith who dominated the century: monarchs, presidents, popes, philosophers, writers, social reformers, educators, and military leaders who left their imprint on political as well as spiritual institutions." Publisher's note
Includes bibliographical references

Great lives from history: the 20th century, 1901-2000; editor, Robert F. Gorman. Salem Press 2008 10v il set $795   **920.003**
1. Biography—Dictionaries 2. World history—20th century
ISBN 978-1-58765-345-2   LC 2008-17125
Also available online
First published as part of the Great lives from history series, published 1987-1995 under the editorship of Frank N. Magill; previously published as volumes 7-9 of Dictionary of world biography, published 1998-1999
"This ten-volume set offers 1,330 . . . biographies of major personages in world history (many still living) from 1901-2000. . . . The personages covered are identified with one or more of the following regions: Africa, Asia, Australia, Caribbean, Europe, Latin America, Middle East, North America, South America, and Southeast Asia." Publisher's note
Includes bibliographical references

Great lives from history, The ancient world, prehistory-476 C.E; editor, Christina A. Salowey. Salem Press 2004 2v il, maps set $160   **920.003**
1. Biography—Dictionaries 2. Ancient history
ISBN 1-587-65152-1; 978-1-58765-164-9
    LC 2004-705
Also available online
Companion volume to Great events from history, The ancient world, prehistory-476 C.E
First published as part of the Great lives from history series, published 1987-1995 under the editorship of Frank N. Magill; previously published as volume 1 of Dictionary of world biography, published 1998-1999
This "set provides three-to-six-page biographies on major personages from the ancient world. Arranged alphabetically, each article gives basic information such as when and where the individual was born and also where and when he or she died, a description of his or her early life and life's work, the significance of the individual, an annotated bibliography, and related entries in both this set and in the . . . [Great events from history] set." Ref

Great lives from history, The ancient world, prehistory-476 C.E—*Continued*
& User Services Quarterly
Includes bibliographical references

Great lives from history, the Middle Ages, 477-1453; editor, Shelley Wolbrink. Salem Press 2005 2v il map set $160   **920.003**
1. Biography—Dictionaries 2. Middle ages—Biography
ISBN 1-58765-164-5; 978-1-58765-164-9
LC 2004-16696
Also available online
Companion volume to Great events from history, the Middle Ages, 477-1453
First published as part of the Great lives from history series, published 1987-1995 under the editorship of Frank N. Magill; previously published as volume 2 of Dictionary of world biography, published 1998-1999
These "volumes focus on the people throughout the world from after the Fall of Rome, in 476 C.E., to 1453. Coverage is worldwide. . . . Each entry begins with ready-reference information, followed by a summary of the person's life, a paragraph or two on 'Significance,' a list of further readings, and cross-references to entries both within the set and within the [Great events in history] companion set." Booklist
Includes bibliographical references

Great lives from history, the Renaissance & early modern era, 1454-1600; editor, Christina J. Moose. Salem Press 2005 2v il map set $160
920.003
1. Biography—Dictionaries 2. Renaissance
ISBN 1-58765-211-0; 978-1-58765-211-0
LC 2004-28875
Also available online
Companion volume to Great events from history, the Renaissance & early modern era, 1454-1600
First published as part of the Great lives from history series, published 1987-1995 under the editorship of Frank N. Magill; previously published as volume 3 of Dictionary of world biography, published 1998-1999
"This two-volume work offers biographies of 338 historical figures in entries that range from two to five pages in length. A publisher's note in volume 1 explains the set's format and use. All the biographies include name, nationality or ethnicity, historical role, dates, and area(s) of achievement; description of early life, work, and significance; an annotated bibliography; and cross-references." Choice
Includes bibliographical references

Gubert, Betty Kaplan, 1934-
Distinguished African Americans in aviation and space science; {by} Betty Kaplan Gubert, Miriam Sawyer, and Caroline M. Fannin. Oryx Press 2002 319p il (Distinguished African Americans series) $64.95   **920.003**
1. African American pilots 2. Astronauts
ISBN 1-57356-246-7   LC 2001-34821
This profiles 80 men and 20 women in aviation and space science covering 80 years of the 20th century

"Libraries should not hesitate to add this title to their collections." Booklist
Includes bibliographical references

Guiley, Rosemary Ellen
The encyclopedia of saints. Facts on File 2001 419p il $82.50; pa $24.95   **920.003**
1. Christian saints—Dictionaries
ISBN 0-8160-4133-4; 0-8160-4134-2 (pa)
LC 00-69176
This volume offers "accounts of the lives and experiences of more than 400 principal saints, from early martyrs such as Lucy of Syracuse to recently canonized saints such as Katherine Drexel. Entries provide a biographical overview, a record of the saint's religious journeys and mystical experiences, a discussion of personal philosophies and important theological influences, as well as his or her patronage, feast days and popular role within the Church." Publisher's note

Hall, Timothy L.
American religious leaders. Facts on File 2003 430p il (American biographies) $65 *
920.003
1. Religious biography
ISBN 0-8160-4534-8   LC 2002-2454
"Facts on File library of American history"
This reference "traces the history of American religion through the lives of its leaders. More than 250 entries explore America's religious and spiritual leaders from colonial times to today. The book focuses on those who have occupied the spotlight of historical attention in one way or another: the founders, the pioneers, the heretics, and the saints, among others. . . . Notable figures and leaders from many of the major churches and religious groups in America are covered, including Episcopalians, Presbyterians, Methodists, Catholics, Black Muslims, Jews, and Mormons along with leaders from smaller and lesser-known but no less important religions." Publisher's note
"This is a perfect source for fast, basic information for anyone who wishes a two-minute reading synopsis on an American religious leader. It should be within arms reach of any reference librarian working an information desk or a telephone." Am Ref Books Annu, 2003
Includes bibliographical references

Supreme Court justices; a biographical dictionary. Facts on File 2001 566p $65
920.003
1. United States. Supreme Court 2. Judges—Dictionaries
ISBN 0-8160-4194-6   LC 00-65415
"Facts on File library of American history"
This work offers "sketches of the lives of members of the Court through the Clinton presidency. . . . Includes a wide array of appendixes that would be valuable at a reference desk. . . . Of greatest interest is the excellent bibliography, grouped by general works, then by justice in alphabetical order. . . . This book would be useful in any public or academic library." Choice
Includes bibliographical references

Hamilton, Neil A., 1949-
Presidents: a biographical dictionary. 2nd ed.
Facts on File 2005 480p il (Facts on File library
of American history) $70; pa $19.95
920.003
1. Presidents—United States—Dictionaries
ISBN   0-8160-5733-8;   978-0-8160-5733-7;
0-8160-6424-5 (pa); 978-0-8160-6424-3 (pa)
LC 2005-6683
First published 2001
"The entries, arranged chronologically and including
black-and-white portraits, chronologies, and references,
are focused on policy but also reveal the characters of
the men as well as their accomplishments and shortcomings in the political arena. An appendix provides tables
that show each man's election results, administration,
family data, and 'Unusual Facts.' . . . The readability of
this title makes it appealing as well as informative."
Booklist
Includes bibliographical references

The **Harvard** biographical dictionary of music;
edited by Don Michael Randel. Belknap Press
1996 1013p il $39.95   **920.003**
1. Music—Bio-bibliography
ISBN 0-674-37299-9   LC 96-16456
Companion volume to The New Harvard dictionary of
music
"International in scope and covering all eras of music
from the ancient to the present, this important new reference source has information concerning 5,500 individuals. Most are associated with classical concert music, although prominent jazz, rock, folk, and popular personalities are also represented: Madonna, Mozart, Zoot Sims,
Mick Jagger, and Dolly Parton are included. Musicologists, educators, teachers, and reviewers, no matter how
influential, are excluded. Entries consist of brief to long
paragraphs that may include a bibliography or a list of
compositions. . . . This is an authoritative and significant new reference work which all libraries must purchase." Choice

Havlice, Patricia Pate
Index to artistic biography. Scarecrow Press
1973 2v set $135   **920.003**
1. Artists—Biography 2. Biography—Indexes
ISBN 0-8108-0540-5
First supplementary volume (published 1981) available
for $115.50 (ISBN 0-8108-1446-3); second supplementa-
ry volume (published 2002 in two volumes) available for
set $195 (ISBN 0-8108-4062-6)
The first two volumes list some 70,000 artists' biographies found in sixty-four reference works. The first supplement covers seventy titles and lists around 47,000
names. The second supplement covers 131 titles published from 1980 through 1999

Holy people of the world; a cross-cultural
encyclopedia; Phyllis G. Jestice, editor.
ABC-CLIO 2004 3v il set $285 *
920.003
1. Religious biography
ISBN 1-576-07355-6   LC 2004-22606

"More than 1,000 of the 1,183 entries are biographical
sketches of men and women from a variety of religious
traditions, including African religions, Amerindian religions, Bahaism, Buddhism, Christianity, Hinduism, Islam, Judaism, Shinto, and Sikhism. There are also survey
articles that address aspects of holy people across religious traditions." Booklist
"This edition deserves to become well-worn by the
time a second appears." Libr J
Includes bibliographical references

The **International** who's who. 71st ed. Europa
Publs. 2460p (Europa biographical reference
series) $650   **920.003**
1. Biography—Dictionaries
ISSN 0074-9613
ISBN 978-1-85743-415-6; 1-85743-415-3
Also available online with title: World who's who
Annual. First published 1935
"Offers brief biographical data on prominent persons
throughout the world." Guide to Ref Books. 11th edition

Jewish women in America; an historical
encyclopedia; edited by Paula E. Hyman and
Deborah Dash Moore. Routledge 1997 2v xxxi,
1770p set $275   **920.003**
1. Jewish women—Dictionaries
ISBN 0-415-91936-3   LC 97-26842
This work contains 800 "biographies and 110 topical
essays on subjects ranging from cookbooks to vaudeville.
. . . [It provides] encyclopedic coverage of the many
varied roles that Jewish women have occupied in America, from the earliest days until the present. All articles
are signed and written with attention to detail by noted
scholars; 500 period photographs are well-chosen and
supplement the text." Am Libr

Kelly, J. N. D. (John Norman Davidson)
The Oxford dictionary of Popes; with new
material by Michael Walsh. Updated [ed] Oxford
University Press 2006 349p pa $21.43
920.003
1. Popes—Dictionaries
ISBN 978-0-19-861433-3; 0-19-861433-0
LC 2006-277841
First published 1986
"An excellent source of information, arranged
chronologically with an alphabetical index. Includes
popes, antipopes, and an appendix on Pope Joan." Ref
Sources for Small & Medium-sized Libr. 6th edition
Includes bibliographical references

Kort, Carol
A to Z of American women in the visual arts;
[by] Carol Kort and Liz Sonneborn. Facts on File
2002 258p il (Facts on File library of American
history) $44   **920.003**
1. American art—Dictionaries 2. Women artists—Dictionaries
ISBN 0-8160-4397-3   LC 2001-40231
At head of title: A to Z of women
This "profiles 130 American women artists who work
in a variety of visual mediums, among them painting,

Kort, Carol—*Continued*
sculpture, printmaking, graphic arts, architecture, and quilting." Booklist
A "handy, well-written volume. . . . The biographical entries are filled with interesting personal and career details that make for absorbing reading." Voice Youth Advocates
Includes bibliographical references

Krismann, Carol
Encyclopedia of American women in business; from colonial times to the present; [by] Carol H. Krisman. Greenwood Press 2004 2v 692p set $175
*　　　　**920.003**
1. Businesswomen—Encyclopedias 2. Women executives—Encyclopedias
ISBN 0-313-32757-2　　　　LC 2004-56065
The author "presents the stories of 327 businesswomen who have succeeded as entrepreneurs, executives, or business owners in profit-making enterprises from Colonial times to this day. . . . In addition to the biographies, the book contains entries for work-related issues like old-boys network, office romance, and diversity as well as profiles of agencies related to women. . . . This excellent reference book is wonderfully readable and should encourage readers to conduct further research of the women profiled." Libr J
Includes bibliographical references

Kuhlman, Erika A., 1961-
A to Z of women in world history; [by] Erika Kuhlman. Facts on File 2002 452p il (Facts on File library of world history) $49.50
　　　　920.003
1. Women—Biography—Dictionaries
ISBN 0-8160-4334-5　　　　LC 2001-54327
"The 260 women who are profiled here have not only made a mark on their own cultures but have also 'influenced other women from diverse cultures and different historical periods pursuing the same goals.'. . . Entries are organized first under 14 areas of accomplishment, from 'Adventurers and Athletes' to 'Writers.'. . . Entries are generally around two pages in length, and each offers suggestions for further reading. . . . *A to Z of Women in World History* is a good place to start for researchers who are taking a sphere-of-activity approach to women's history. This highly readable volume is recommended." Booklist
Includes bibliographical references

Latin American writers; Carlos A. Solé, editor in chief; Maria Isabel Abreu, associate editor. Scribner 1989 3v set $350　　　　**920.003**
1. Authors, Latin American 2. Latin American literature—History and criticism
ISBN 0-684-18463-X　　　　LC 88-35481
Also available Supplement 1 $130 (ISBN 0-684-80599-5)
This work "provides a scholarly overview of Latin American literature from the colonial period to the present. Entries are lengthy and cover 176 writers of Spanish America and Brazil and include a signed biographical and critical essay, followed by a selected bibliography of primary and secondary sources." Ref Sources for Small & Medium-sized Libr. 6th edition

Leaders of the American Civil War; a biographical and historiographical dictionary; edited by Charles F. Ritter and Jon L. Wakelyn. Greenwood Press 1998 xxxiv, 465p $85
　　　　920.003
1. United States—History—1861-1865, Civil War—Biography—Dictionaries
ISBN 0-313-29560-3　　　　LC 98-12156
This dictionary "includes 47 articles on outstanding military and civilian Union and Confederate leaders as well as entries for other significant figures, including Frederick Douglass, Clara Barton, Dorothea Dix, and even Walt Whitman." Libr J
Includes bibliographical references

Leiter, Darryl J.
A to Z of physicists; {by} Darryl J. Leiter, with Sharon L. Leiter. Facts on File 2003 388p il (Notable scientists) $45　　　　**920.003**
1. Physicists
ISBN 0-8160-4798-7　　　　LC 2002-14709
This volume "contains basic biographies ranging from 500 to 2000 words describing major works of over 150 physicists throughout the world." Sci Books Films
"The essays are well written, but the book's greatest strength is the space it devotes to currently active physicists." Choice
Includes bibliographical references

Martinez Wood, Jamie
Latino writers and journalists. Facts on File 2007 294p il (A to Z of Latino Americans) $44
　　　　920.003
1. Hispanic Americans—Dictionaries 2. American literature—Hispanic American authors—Bio-bibliography
ISBN 0-8160-6422-9; 978-0-8160-6422-9
　　　　LC 2006-17394
This book "brings together 150 writers identified as Latino Americans. Approximately one-third of the profiles are accompanied by photographs." Booklist
Includes bibliographical references

Meier, Matt S.
Notable Latino Americans; a biographical dictionary; {by} Matt S. Meier with Conchita Franco Serri and Richard A. Garcia. Greenwood Press 1997 431p il $73.95　　　　**920.003**
1. Hispanic Americans—Dictionaries
ISBN 0-313-29105-5　　　　LC 96-27392
This dictionary "offers 127 biographies of men and women of Latino descent who were born in or immigrated to the United States and have made a noteworthy impact. The majority of those profiled are writers, sports figures, actors, or political activists, though some lesser-known personalities in the sciences, education, and the arts are also included. The entries average three pages and generally include a picture and a short bibliography of additional sources." Libr J

Modern Japanese writers; Jay Rubin, editor.
Scribner 2000 434p $130   **920.003**
1. Authors, Japanese 2. Japanese literature—History
and criticism
ISBN 0-684-80598-7   LC 00-63505
"This handbook is a collection of alphabetically arranged articles on 23 twentieth-century Japanese writers
and one literary genre, written by noted scholars in the
field. Entries are generally around 18 pages in length.
Each author entry treats a writer's life and work and is
accompanied by a selected bibliography of primary and
secondary sources. Most of the writers included have
been translated into English, and two of them, Kawabata
Yasunari and Oe Kenzaburo, are Nobel Prize winners."
Booklist
Includes bibliographical references

Monush, Barry
Screen world presents the encyclopedia of
Hollywood film actors; edited by Barry Monush.
v1: From the silent era to 1965. Applause Theatre
and Cinema Bks. 2003 1200p il $35 *
    920.003
1. Actors—Dictionaries 2. Motion pictures—Biography—Dictionaries
ISBN 1-557-83551-9   LC 2002-152728
Contents: v1 The silent era to 1965
"The first of a projected two-volume set, this encyclopedia provides biographical profiles of actors who
worked in Hollywood between 1915 and 1965 . . . .
[The author] includes all Oscar-winning actors as well as
performers who became prominent in film before the late
1960s. . . . Entries are arranged in alphabetical order
(Bud Abbott and Lou Costello to George Zucco), include
vital statistics, and note any higher-education institution
the actor attended. . . . This is an item that academic libraries and specialized film libraries will want to add. It
would also no doubt find an audience in public libraries." Booklist

Musicians since 1900; performers in concert and
opera; compiled and edited by David Ewen.
Wilson, H.W. 1978 974p il $120
    920.003
1. Musicians—Dictionaries
ISBN 0-8242-0565-0   LC 78-12727
"Replaces 'Living musicians' and its supplement
(1940-57). Gives 'detailed biographical, critical and personal information about 432 of the most distinguished
performing musicians in concert and opera since
1900.'—Introd.' . . . A few bibliographical references
are given at the end of each biography; a classified list
of musicians concludes the volume." Sheehy. Guide to
Ref Books. 10th edition

New dictionary of scientific biography; Noretta
Koertge, editor in chief. Scribner's 2008 8v il
set $995   **920.003**
1. Scientists—Dictionaries
ISBN 978-0-684-31320-7   LC 2007-31384
First published 1970-1980 in 16 volumes with title:
Dictionary of scientific biography
Published under the auspices of the American Council
of Learned Societies

This biographical dictionary "contains thousands of biographies of mathematicians and natural scientists from
all countries and from all historical periods." Publisher's
note
Includes bibliographical references

Newton, David E.
Latinos in science, math, and professions. Facts
on File 2007 274p il (A to Z of Latino Americans)
$44   **920.003**
1. Hispanic Americans—Dictionaries 2. Scientists—
Dictionaries 3. Mathematicians—Dictionaries
ISBN 978-0-8160-6385-7; 0-8160-6385-0
    LC 2006-16769
Among the figures profiled in this biographical dictio-
nary "are sociology expert Maxine Baca Zinn; Ellen
Ochoa, the first Latina in space; and research entomolo-
gist Fernando E. Vega." Libr J
Includes bibliographical references

Nobel Prize winners; an H.W. Wilson biographical
dictionary; editor, Tyler Wasson; consultants,
Gert H. Brieger [et al.] Wilson, H.W. 1987
xxxiv, 1165p il $145   **920.003**
1. Nobel Prizes 2. Biography—Dictionaries
ISBN 0-8242-0756-4   LC 87-16468
Also available 1987-1991 supplement $60 (ISBN 0-
8242-0834-X) and 1992-1996 supplement $60 (ISBN 0-
8242-0906-0); 1997-2001 supplement $70 (ISBN 0-8242-
1018-2)
This reference book "begins with an alphabetical listing of winners, a listing of prize categories (broken down
chronologically by years), an article on Alfred Nobel,
and another on the process by which the prizes are
awarded. . . . Included are all winners (persons and institutions) from 1901-1986 in entries of 1200-1500
words." SLJ

The **Norton/Grove** dictionary of women
composers; edited by Julie Anne Sadie & Rhian
Samuel. Norton 1995 xliii, 548p il $45
    920.003
1. Women composers—Dictionaries
ISBN 0-393-03487-9
First published 1994 in the United Kingdom with title:
The New Grove dictionary of women composers
This "provides detailed biographies of more than
1,000 creators of Western classical music. In signed articles, the Dictionary chronicles the lives and works of
women composers from all corners of the world." Publisher's note
"This important volume does not merely recycle material from the 1980 New Grove but collects 900 newly
written articles, the longer ones signed." Libr J

Notable American women; a biographical
dictionary completing the twentieth century;
Susan Ware, editor; Stacy Braukman, assistant
editor. Belknap Press 2004 xxx, 729p $45
    920.003
1. Women—United States—Biography 2. United
States—Biography—Dictionaries
ISBN 0-674-01488-X   LC 2004-48859

Notable American women—*Continued*

This volume includes "stars of the golden ages of radio, film, dance, and television; scientists and scholars; politicians and entrepreneurs; authors and aviators; civil rights activists and religious leaders; Native American craftspeople and world-renowned artists. Women from a broad spectrum of ethnic, class, political, religious, and sexual identities are all acknowledged." Publisher's note

Includes bibliographical references

Notable American women: the modern period; a biographical dictionary; edited by Barbara Sicherman {et al.}. Harvard Univ. Press 1980 xxii, 773p pa $41.50 hardcover o.p.

920.003

1. Women—United States—Biography 2. United States—Biography—Dictionaries

ISBN 0-674-62733-4 (pa)   LC 80-18402

Also available Notable American women, 1607-1950 pa $57.50 (ISBN 0-674-62734-2)

This set provides "1 1/2- to 2-page biographies and references for 442 American women. Women were chosen from science, business, and engineering as well as from such traditional fields as education, entertainment, and social work, with a wide variety of @career patterns, philosophical outlooks and personal styles' represented. . . . Entries describe the life and personality of the individual, evaluate her career, and place it in an historical context. Special emphasis is given to the conflicting demands of her public and personal lives." Choice

Notable black American men, book I; Jessie Carney Smith, editor. Gale Res. 1998 xxxiv, 1365p il $150   **920.003**

1. African Americans—Biography—Dictionaries 2. United States—Biography—Dictionaries

ISBN 0-7876-0763-0   LC 98-38166

Companion to Notable black American women

This work, the first volume of a two-volume biographical dictionary, "profiles 500 men, from poet Jupiter Hammon (b. 1711) to Tiger Woods. . . . Each entry begins with birth and death dates and a few words describing the subject's major fields of endeavor, followed by a biographical essay, a list of references, and, in some cases, a note on collections of source material." Booklist

Includes bibliographical references

Notable black American men, book II; Jessie Carney Smith, editor. Thomson Gale 2007 xxiv, 827p il $193   **920.003**

1. African Americans—Biography—Dictionaries 2. United States—Biography—Dictionaries

ISBN 0-7876-6493-6; 978-0-7876-6493-0

LC 2006-21193

Covering "prominent newsmakers as well as lesser-known individuals, . . . [this second volume of a two-volume work] offers full biographical entries, portraits, addresses for living listees and recommended sources for further study." Publisher's note

Includes bibliographical references

Notable black American scientists; Kristine M. Krapp, editor. Gale Res. 1999 xxvi, 349p il $125   **920.003**

1. Scientists—Dictionaries 2. African Americans—Biography—Dictionaries

ISBN 0-7876-2789-5   LC 98-36338

The "contributors to this compilation of 254 bibliographic profiles emphasize the achievements of black scientists and physicians, men and women, from Colonial times to the present, in the territory that is now the US. . . . Each entry begins with basic information about each subject—name, year of birth and death (if deceased), and specialty. A biographical essay follows." Choice

Includes bibliographical references

Notable black American women, book I; Jessie Carney Smith, editor. Gale Res. 1992 xlvii, 1334p il $203   **920.003**

1. African American women—Dictionaries 2. United States—Biography—Dictionaries

ISBN 0-8103-4749-0   LC 91-35074

Companion to Notable black American men

This first volume of a three-volume biographical encyclopedia "documents the achievements of 500 African-American women who have made significant contributions to American culture from the colonial era to the present. . . . Subjects include women active in all fields of endeavor, from education, science, and the arts, to business, law and politics. . . . Authoritative and entertaining at the same time." Am Libr

Notable black American women, Book III; Jessie Carney Smith, editor. Gale 2003 lxxviii, 881p il $165   **920.003**

1. African American women—Dictionaries 2. United States—Biography—Dictionaries

ISBN 0-7876-6494-4

In this third volume of a three-volume biographical dictionary, "narrative biographical essays . . . discuss each woman's significant achievements and the public response to those achievements. . . . [This book] features 300 contemporary and historical women, including Sarah Allen, Alicia Keys, Ruth Simmons and . . . more." Publisher's note

Includes bibliographical references

Notable Latino writers; from the editors of Salem Press. Salem Press 2005 3v il (Magill's choice) set $207 *   **920.003**

1. American literature—Hispanic American authors—History and criticism

ISBN 1-58765-243-9; 978-1-58765-243-1

LC 2005-17567

These volumes feature "122 essays about Latino novelists, short-story writers, poets, and playwrights of the Western Hemisphere who write in English, Spanish, or Portuguese. . . . This set may prove to be a useful research tool for students, teachers, and librarians." Libr J

Includes bibliographical references

Notable mathematicians; from ancient times to the present; Robyn V. Young, editor; Zoran Minderovic, associate editor. Gale Res. 1998 xxi, 612p il $120   **920.003**

1. Mathematicians—Dictionaries

ISBN 0-7876-3071-3   LC 97-33662

Notable mathematicians—*Continued*

This work profiles "300 mathematicians chosen for their historical importance, discoveries, familiarity to the public, awards and prizes, and involvement in mathematics education. . . . Female and minority mathematicians have been expressly represented." Libr J

Includes bibliographical references

Notable native Americans; Sharon Malinowski, editor; George H.J. Abrams, consulting editor and author of foreword. Gale Res. 1995 xliv, 492p il $105	**920.003**
1. Native Americans—Dictionaries
ISBN 0-8103-9638-6	LC 94-36202
This is a "compilation of biographical and bibliographical information on more than two hundred and sixty-five notable Native North American men and women throughout history, from all fields of endeavor. . . . Approximately thirty percent of the entries focus on historical figures and seventy percent on contemporary or twentieth-century individuals. Signed narrative essays, ranging from one to three pages in length, include Indian names and their English translations as well as name variants." Preface

Notable U.S. ambassadors since 1775; a biographical dictionary; edited by Cathal J. Nolan. Greenwood Press 1997 430p $109.95
920.003
1. Diplomats—Dictionaries 2. United States—Foreign relations—Dictionaries
ISBN 0-313-29195-0	LC 96-50291
This work contains historical-biographical profiles of 58 architects of U.S. foreign policy.
"Following a preface that describes the editor's selection criteria, each entry begins with full birth and death dates and locations, education, family background, and career progression. The larger issues during diplomatic assignments are described fully, as well as the difficulties in achieving success." Booklist

Notable women in mathematics; a biographical dictionary; edited by Charlene Morrow and Teri Perl. Greenwood Press 1998 302p il $52.95
920.003
1. Women mathematicians—Dictionaries
ISBN 0-313-29131-4	LC 97-18598
"This book features five-to-six page profiles of 59 mathematicians and scientific computing researchers from around the world. Each profile describes the woman's major life events and educational and career milestones, includes a discussion of her areas of mathematical research in nontechnical terms, and lists works by and about that person. All entries have an accompanying black-and-white photograph. The majority of essays are based on interviews by the authors." SLJ

Notable women in the physical sciences; a biographical dictionary; edited by Benjamin F. Shearer and Barbara S. Shearer. Greenwood Press 1997 479p il $55	**920.003**
1. Women scientists—Dictionaries
ISBN 0-313-29303-1	LC 96-9024
"Featuring biographical essays on 96 world and U.S. women scientists, this volume includes women who

made a significant contribution to the physical sciences from antiquity to the present, though the emphasis is on 20th-century women. . . . Disciplines include astronomy, astrophysics, biochemistry, chemistry, and physics. The essays average five pages in length and describe obstacles encountered and achievements experienced by each scientist. Each entry provides a chronology, a descriptive essay, and a bibliography." Choice

Oakes, Elizabeth H., 1951-
A to Z of chemists. Facts on File 2002 276p il $45 *	**920.003**
1. Chemists 2. Scientists—Dictionaries
ISBN 0-8160-4579-8	LC 2002-68685
"Facts on File science library"
At head of title: Notable scientists
"This title includes 152 biographies of chemists, including 23 women. . . . The entries run between 750 and 1200 words (one to one and one-half pages apiece). They all begin with a summary of the subject's major contribution, followed by a chronological biography of their personal and professional life. Appendixes list the birthplace and country of activity of the chemists as well as a chart of their life spans." Libr J
Includes bibliographical references

American writers. Facts on File 2004 430p il (American biographies) $65	**920.003**
1. American literature—Bio-bibliography 2. Authors, American—Dictionaries
ISBN 0-8160-5158-5	LC 2003-15743
"The volume has alphabetically arranged entries for approximately 260 authors from a variety of genres—poetry, fiction, drama, essay, and autobiography. Each . . . entry contains a short biography, critical analysis, and a bibliography of works about the author in both printed and Web formats. . . . [This book] offers a convenient introduction and is a worthwhile purchase." Booklist
Includes bibliographical references

International encyclopedia of women scientists. Facts on File 2002 448p il $82.50 *
920.003
1. Women scientists—Dictionaries
ISBN 0-8160-4381-7	LC 2001-23100
This volume "covers more than 500 scientists. Dating back to 400 BCE, it treats current, historical, and minority women scientists. The entries . . . include biographical information that provides detailed descriptions of education, research, and notable accomplishments. Oakes also supplies an impressive, expansive set of indexes: general alphabetical, field of specialization, country of birth, country of major scientific activity, and year of birth." Choice
Includes bibliographical references

Otfinoski, Steven, 1949-
Latinos in the arts. Facts on File 2007 277p il (A to Z of Latino Americans) $44
920.003
1. Hispanic Americans—Dictionaries 2. Artists—Dictionaries 3. Actors—Dictionaries 4. Musicians—Dictionaries
ISBN 978-0-8160-6394-9; 0-8160-6394-X
LC 2006-16900

Otfinoski, Steven, 1949-—*Continued*
"This volume profiles more than 178 individuals in the performing and visual arts 'who were born in the United States or who settled here permanently,' among them Marc Anthony, Cameron Diaz, Carmen Miranda, Tito Punete, and Shakira. Each entry concludes with a list of 'Further Reading' . . . and, in many cases, 'Further Listening' and 'Further Viewing.'" Booklist
Includes bibliographical references

Pendergast, Tom, 1964-
U-X-L graphic novelists; [by] Tom Pendergast and Sara Pendergast; Sarah Hermsen, project editor. U-X-L/Thomson Gale 2007 3v lxii, 634p il set $181 *   **920.003**
1. Graphic novels—Dictionaries 2. Cartoonists—Dictionaries
ISBN 1-4144-0440-9; 978-1-4144-0440-0
                                         LC 2006-13711
The three volumes include 75 alphabetically-arranged articles that profile authors, illustrators, and author-illustrators, and include European, American, and Japanese creators. The introduction provides some history of graphic novels, and there is a separate essay on manga.
"This accessible and readable survey of a timely topic should generate considerable attention in school library media center and public library collections. Well researched and documented, with subject and language appropriate for its intended audience, this set is highly recommended." Booklist
Includes bibliographical references

Popular contemporary writers; editor, Michael D. Sharp. Marshall Cavendish Reference 2005 11v il set $657.07   **920.003**
1. Authors—Dictionaries 2. Literature—Bio-bibliography
ISBN 0-7614-7601-6   LC 2005-42005
"This alphabetically arranged encyclopedia offers information on 96 contemporary writers, primarily British and North American, whose works tend to mine populist as well as artistic veins—usually with bestselling results. Each extensive, readable entry opens with stage-setting biographical and critical comments, then goes on in successive sections to describe the writers life and career to date, examine his or her dominant themes in a critical light, summarize and evaluate major works, and close with leads to Web-based resources of interest." SLJ
Includes bibliographical references

Rittner, Don
A to Z of scientists in weather and climate. Facts on File 2003 256p il (Notable scientists) $45
                                         920.003
1. Scientists 2. Meteorology
ISBN 0-8160-4797-9   LC 2002-152435
This reference "includes 115 biographical sketches of individuals throughout history, around the world, and working in a variety of disciplines, who have contributed to an understanding of climate and weather. Entries, informative and clearly written . . . consist of a text of 750 to 2,000 words that includes the subject's early history, educational background, positions held, prizes and awards, and major contributions to weather and climate studies." Choice
Includes bibliographical references and index

Schneider, Dorothy
First ladies; a biographical dictionary; [by] Dorothy Schneider, Carl J. Schneider. 2nd ed. Facts on File 2005 420p il (Facts on File library of American history) $70 *   **920.003**
1. Presidents' spouses—United States
ISBN 0-8160-5752-4   LC 2005-6682
First published 2001
"The entries, arranged chronologically and including black-and-white portraits, chronologies, and lists of further reading, show how . . . [the first ladies'] backgrounds and personal strengths and abilities influenced the women's approach to their times 'in office' and how the public's expectations changed through the years. . . . The readability of this volume makes it appealing as well as informative." Booklist
Includes bibliographical references

The **Scribner** encyclopedia of American lives; Kenneth T. Jackson, editor in chief; Karen Markoe, general editor; Arnold Markoe, executive editor. Scribner 1998-2003 6v il set $540   **920.003**
1. United States—Biography—Dictionaries
ISBN 0-684-31292-1   LC 98-33793
Individual volumes also available ea $140
Contents: v1 1981-1985; v2 1986-1990; v3 1991-1993; v4 1994-1996; v5 1997-1999; v6 2000-2002; v7 2003-2005
"Scribner envisions SEAL as the continuation of the *Dictionary of American Biography* (DAB). . . . Selection criteria are that the biographees made significant contributions to American life and culture. . . . An appreciable number of women and people of color are recognized. All biographies are signed contributions by 332 scholars." Libr J {review of first two volumes}

The **Scribner** encyclopedia of American lives, The 1960s; William L. O'Neill, volume editor. Scribner 2003 2v il set $250   **920.003**
1. United States—Biography—Dictionaries
ISBN 0-684-80666-5   LC 2002-12581
"Thematic series." Cover
"The two alphabetically arranged volumes in SEAL 1960s contain biographical sketches, usually between 1,000 and 2,000 words, of 647 figures who 'defined the decade, or who were influential at the time.' Americans from different races, socioeconomic groups, classes, and regions of the U.S. are included, along with the occasional person of another nationality who had long periods of residence in the U.S. and was an influence on American culture. The signed entries, written by scholars, begin with a brief summary of the person's chronology and important accomplishments. This is followed by a narrative of the subject's life. . . . In many cases, a black-and-white photograph accompanies the narrative, which concludes with an assessment of the subject's overall contribution and a brief bibliography listing a few key sources. . . . Recommended for all high-school, public, and academic libraries wanting complete SEAL coverage

**The Scribner encyclopedia of American lives,
The 1960s**—*Continued*

or libraries wanting to supplement their collection of
1960s resources with a purely biographical approach."
Booklist

Includes bibliographical references

Shipp, Steve, 1937-
Latin American and Caribbean artists of the
modern era; a biographical dictionary of more than
12,700 persons. McFarland & Co 2002 864p il
$115   **920.003**
1. Artists—Dictionaries 2. Latin American art
ISBN 0-7864-1057-4   LC 2002-13828
"All entries include expected information such as birth
date and place and artist's medium, and longer entries
also feature biographical sketches, including education
and influences, as well as lists of collections, exhibits,
and titles. . . . A good starting point for further research." Libr J

Includes bibliographical references

Sonneborn, Liz
A to Z of American women in the performing
arts. Facts on File 2001 264p il $44
         920.003
1. Entertainers 2. Women—United States—Biography
ISBN 0-8160-4398-1   LC 2001-23580
This "book profiles 150 female performers, with entries for performing categories that range from actresses,
dancers, and singers to circus and Wild West show performers. The book covers women of numerous ethnic
groups from the early 1800s to the present. The women
are listed alphabetically by their professional names and
entries average about a page in length. . . . Each entry
concludes with suggestions for further reading and research, and a list of recommended performances available on tape or disc." Book Rep

Includes bibliographical references

St. James guide to Hispanic artists; profiles of
Latino and Latin American artists; editor,
Thomas Riggs. St. James Press 2002 xx, 682p
il $195   **920.003**
1. Hispanic American art 2. Artists—United States
ISBN 1-55862-470-8   LC 2001-41935
"Published in association with the Association of Hispanic Arts, Association for Latin American Art"
This "guide profiles some 375 of the most prominent
Hispanic artists of the past century. The entries include
basic biographical information, critical commentary, and
lists of exhibitions, publications, and collections holding
their works." Libr J

Includes bibliographical references

The **Supreme** Court justices: a biographical
dictionary; edited by Melvin I. Urofsky. Garland
1994 570p il (Garland reference library of the
humanities) $85   **920.003**
1. United States. Supreme Court 2. Judges—Dictionaries
ISBN 0-8153-1176-1   LC 94-10028

"Alphabetically arranged, each entry begins with life
dates, the date of nomination to the Court, the name of
the president who nominated the justice, and the date he
or she was seated. The contributors . . . provide facts
and context along with analysis of the important cases in
the individual justice's career." Libr J

Waldrup, Carole Chandler, 1925-
The vice presidents; biographies of the 45 men
who have held the second highest office in the
United States. McFarland & Co. 1996 271p il
hardcover o.p. pa $39.95   **920.003**
1. Vice-presidents—United States
ISBN 0-7864-0179-6; 978-0-7864-2611-9 (pa);
0-7864-2611-X (pa)   LC 96-30538
This work "presents biographical portraits of the 45
individuals who have theoretically been 'a heartbeat from
the presidency.' These portraits are presented in chronological order of service, from John Adams to Albert
Gore Jr." Am Ref Books Annu, 1997
"Well-written with clear, precise language and vocabulary, this informative book will be useful in either the
reference section or with the collective biographies."
Book Rep

Includes bibliographical references

Who was who in America; with world notables.
Marquis Who's Who 1942-2006 18v & Index
set $999.95 v1-13 ea $90; v14-16 ea $95; v17
$98; v17 & Index $155.95   **920.003**
1. United States—Biography—Dictionaries
ISBN 0-8379-0254-1
Also available online; Also available historical volume
1607-1896 $90 (ISBN 0-8379-0236-3)
Contents: v1 1897-1942 (ISBN 0-8379-0201-0); v2
1943-1950 (ISBN 0-8379-0206-1); v3 1951-1960 (ISBN
0-8379-0203-7); v4 1961-1968 (ISBN 0-8379-0204-5);
v5 1969-1973 (ISBN 0-8379-0205-3); v6 1974-1976
(ISBN 0-8379-0207-X); v7 1977-1981 (ISBN 0-8379-
0210-X); v8 1982-1985 (ISBN 0-8379-0214-2); v9 1985-
1989 (ISBN 0-8379-0217-7); v10 1989-1993 (ISBN 0-
8379-0220-7); v11 1993-1996 (ISBN 0-8379-0225-8);
v12 1996-1998; v13 1998-2000; v14 2000-2002 (ISBN
0-8379-0245-2); v15 2002-2004 (ISBN 0-8379-0247-
9);v16 2004-2005 (0-8379-0251-7); v17 2005-2006 0-
8379-0255-X)
"Includes sketches removed from 'Who's who in
America' because of death of the biographee; date of
death and, often, interment location is added. With the
'Historical volume' these volumes form a series entitled
'Who's who in American history.'" Guide to Ref Books.
11th edition

Who's who 2008; an annual biographical
dictionary. 160th ed. A. & C. Black 2007 2574p
$325 *   **920.003**
1. Great Britain—Biography—Dictionaries
ISSN 0083-937X
ISBN 978-0-7136-8555-8; 0-7136-8555-7
Annual. First published 1849
"The pioneer work of the who's who type and still
one of the most important. Until 1897, it was the handbook of titled and official classes and included lists of
names rather than biographical sketches. . . . It is princi-

Who's who 2008—*Continued*
pally British, but a few prominent names of other nationalities are included. Biographies are reliable and fairly detailed; they give main facts, addresses, often telephone numbers and in case of authors, lists of works." Guide to Ref Books. 11th edition

Who's who among African Americans. 21st ed. Gale Res. 2008 1477p $275   920.003
1. African Americans—Biography—Dictionaries
ISSN 1081-1400
ISBN 978-1-4144-0020-4; 1-4144-0020-9
First published 1976 by Educational Communications with title: Who's who among black Americans. Biennial schedule after 5th edition
New edition in preparation
"Short entries focusing on career achievements and positions. Indexes list entries by place of birth and profession." N Y Public Libr Book of How & Where to Look It Up

Who's who in America, 2008. 62nd ed. Marquis Who's Who 2007 2v set $710.10
                                         920.003
1. United States—Biography—Dictionaries
ISSN 0083-9396
ISBN 978-0-8379-7011-0; 0-8379-7011-3
Also available online
Annual. First published 1899
"The standard dictionary of contemporary biography, containing concise biographical data, prepared according to established practices, with addresses and, in the case of authors, lists of works. . . . Each edition is thoroughly revised, new biographies added, and others dropped. For names of persons dropped because of death, see 'Who was who in America'." Guide to Ref Books. 11th edition

Who's who in American art, 2008. 28th ed. Marquis Who's Who 2007 1550p $267.30 *
                                         920.003
1. Artists—United States—Dictionaries
ISSN 0000-0191
ISBN 978-0-8379-6307-5; 0-8379-6307-9
Also available online
Companion volume to American art directory
Biennial. First published 1936 by American Federation of Arts as part of American art annual
"Profiles representatives of all segments of the art world including artists, administrators, and librarians. Entries give vital statistics, professional education and training, commissions and exhibitions, and membership in art societies. Includes geographic and professional classification indexes and cumulative necrology." N Y Public Libr Book of How & Where to Look It Up

Who's who in American politics 2007-2008; [prepared by Marquis Who's Who] 21st ed. Marquis Who's Who 2007 xxxvi, 1960p $314.10   920.003
1. Politicians—United States—Dictionaries
ISSN 0000-0205
ISBN 978-0-8379-6918-3
Biennial. First published 1967 by Bowker

"Biographical directory of political leaders in the Congress, the executive branch of the federal government, state legislatures, state executive branches, mayors of cities with populations over 50,000, national and state party chairs, national party committee members, county chairs, and state supreme court justices. Entries are arranged by state, then alphabetically by name. Indexed by name." Ref Sources for Small & Medium-sized Libr. 6th edition

Who's who in art; Charles Baile de Laperrière, editor. 33rd ed. Hilmarton Manor Press 2008 1128p $175   920.003
1. Artists, British—Dictionaries
ISBN 978-0-9047-2242-0; 0-9047-2242-2
Biennial. First published 1927 by Art Trade Press. Subtitle varies
"Includes primarily British artists, designers, craftsmen, critics, writers, teachers, collectors, and curators, with appendixes of monograms and signatures, and obituary, and acronyms. Includes a list of academies, groups, and societies." Guide to Ref Books. 11th edition

Who's who in British history; beginnings to 1901; general editor, Geoffrey Treasure; authors and contributors, Ian Dawson {et al.}. Fitzroy Dearborn Pubs. 1998 2v maps set $325
                                         920.003
1. Great Britain—Biography—Dictionaries
ISBN 1-884964-90-7
"The length of entries varies from many pages (Henry VIII) to a column for most persons. . . . The choice of entries (ending with 1901) reflects the traditional emphasis of history teaching, with heavy representation of statemen, royalty, military persons, diplomats, major writers, and leading ladies of the stage and aristocracy." Choice
Includes bibliographical references

Who's who in finance and business 2008-2009. 36th ed. Marquis Who's Who 2007 1,100p $349 *   920.003
1. Business—Biography—Dictionaries
ISSN 1930-3262
ISBN 978-0-8379-0356-9
Also available online
Biennial. First published 1936 with title: Who's who in commerce and industry. Continues Who's who in finance and industry
"Gives international coverage of businessmen. Includes index of firms with references to personnel for whom sketches are included." Guide to Ref Books. 11th edition

Who's who of American women 2007. 26th ed. Marquis Who's Who 2006 1,700p $305 *
                                         920.003
1. Women—United States—Biography 2. United States—Biography—Dictionaries
ISSN 0083-9841
ISBN 0-8379-0434-X
Also available online
Biennial. First published for 1958/1959
"This title provides information on women who are successful in a variety of professions, including business,

Who's who of American women 2007—*Continued*

government, education, art and culture, and those who have received prestigious honors or have been selected for honorary institutions. The biographical data are provided by the women themselves so the quality varies. In general it includes name, occupation, birth date, education, career history, publications, professional activities, awards, and home and office addresses. This has long been a standard source in many public and academic libraries." Am Ref Books Annu, 2003

Women in world history; a biographical encyclopedia; Anne Commire, editor, Deborah Klezmer, associate editor. Gale Res. 1999-2002 17v set $1,495   **920.003**
1. Women—History—Encyclopedias 2. Women—Biography
ISBN 0-7876-3736-X   LC 99-24692
"The editors researched wives, daughters, mothers, and other women who were not documented in traditional, male-oriented sources, especially history books. . . . Some entries are only a sentence or two because of lack of information, but the majority include most or all of the following: dates, if known, or time of flourishing; an identifying summary of life and achievements; a personal profile with vital statistics and names of family members; events in the life of the biographee; vitae listing such things as works for authors or winning records for athletes; a quotation by or about the individual; and bibliographical references." Booklist
Includes bibliographical references

World artists, 1950-1980; an H.W. Wilson biographical dictionary; {edited} by Claude Marks. Wilson, H.W. 1984 912p il $130
          920.003
1. Artists—Dictionaries
ISBN 0-8242-0707-6   LC 84-13152
"The 312 painters, sculptors, and graphic artists in this biographical dictionary were selected from the outstanding artistic figures in the US, Europe, and Latin America. . . . The biographical information includes family, working background, and aesthetic beliefs. There are many quotations from the artist and from critics. Also included is a list of significant collections and a bibliography." Choice

World artists, 1980-1990; an H.W. Wilson biographical dictionary; edited by Claude Marks. Wilson, H.W. 1991 413p il $95 *
          920.003
1. Artists—Dictionaries
ISBN 0-8242-0827-7   LC 91-13183
This volume contains brief biographies of 118 artists from around the world who have been influential in the 1980's

World authors, 1950-1970; a companion volume to Twentieth century authors; edited by John Wakeman; editorial consultant: Stanley J. Kunitz. Wilson, H.W. 1975 1594p il (Authors series) $160   **920.003**

1. Authors—Dictionaries 2. Literature—Bio-bibliography
ISBN 0-8242-0419-0
This volume includes 959 "authors who came into prominence between 1950 and 1970. . . . Authors were chosen for literary importance or outstanding popularity." Wilson Libr Bull

World authors, 1970-1975; editor, John Wakeman; editorial consultant, Stanley J. Kunitz. Wilson, H.W. 1980 894p il (Authors series) $140 *
          920.003
1. Authors—Dictionaries 2. Literature—Bio-bibliography
ISBN 0-8242-0641-X   LC 79-21874
This volume provides biographical or autobiographical sketches for 348 of the most influential and popular men and women of letters who have come into prominence between 1970 and 1975

World authors, 1975-1980; editor, Vineta Colby. Wilson, H.W. 1985 829p il (Authors series) $140   **920.003**
1. Authors—Dictionaries 2. Literature—Bio-bibliography
ISBN 0-8242-0715-7   LC 85-10045
This work profiles the lives and works of 379 writers

World authors, 1980-1985; editor, Vineta Colby. Wilson, H.W. 1990 938p il (Authors series) $140 *   **920.003**
1. Authors—Dictionaries 2. Literature—Bio-bibliography
ISBN 0-8242-0797-1   LC 90-49782
This volume covers 320 contemporary writers

World authors, 1985-1990; a volume in the Wilson authors series; editor, Vineta Colby. Wilson, H.W. 1995 970p il (Authors series) $140   **920.003**
1. Authors—Dictionaries 2. Literature—Bio-bibliography
ISBN 0-8242-0875-7   LC 95-41656
This volume covers 345 novelists, playwrights, poets, and other authors who have risen to prominence in the late 1980s

World authors, 1990-1995; editor, Clifford Thompson. Wilson, H.W. 1999 863p il (Authors series) $155 *   **920.003**
1. Authors—Dictionaries 2. Literature—Bio-bibliography
ISBN 0-8242-0956-7   LC 99-48161
The 317 authors treated in this volume include novelists, playwrights, and poets who have published significant work in the early 1990s. Also covers essayists, historians, biographers, critics, philosophers, and social scientists who have made exceptional contributions to the literature of our time.
Includes bibliographical references

World authors, 1995-2000; editors, Clifford Thompson, Mari Rich [et al.] Wilson, H.W. 2003 872p il (Authors series) $160

920.003

1. Authors—Dictionaries 2. Literature—Bio-bibliography

ISBN 0-8242-1032-8   LC 2003-45062

This reference includes 320 novelists, poets, dramatists, essayists, social scientists, and biographers who have published significant works from 1995 through 2000. Each profile details the author's life and career, the circumstances under which their works were produced, and their literary significance.

Includes bibliographical references

World authors, 2000-2005; editors, Jennifer Curry, David Ramm, Mari Rich, Albert Rolls. Wilson, H. W. 2007 800p il (Authors series) $170 *

920.003

1. Authors—Dictionaries 2. Literature—Bio-bibliography

ISBN 978-0-8242-1077-9

This book "covers some 300 novelists, poets, dramatists, essayists, scientists, biographers, and other authors whose books [were] published 2000 through 2005." Publisher's note

World explorers and discoverers; editor, Richard E. Bohlander; consultants, John L. Allen {et al.}. Macmillan 1991 531p il maps $110

920.003

1. Explorers—Dictionaries

ISBN 978-0-02-897445-3; 0-02-897445-X

LC 91-23156

"Over 300 explorers and discoverers are featured in this attractive compilation that covers exploration from ancient times to the present and includes such notable moderns as Jacques Cousteau and Edmund Hillary." Am Libr

World musicians; edited by Clifford Thompson; staff contributors: Denise Bonilla {et al.}; consultants: Justin Dello Joio, Lewis Porter. Wilson, H.W. 1999 1181p il $115

920.003

1. Musicians—Dictionaries

ISBN 0-8242-0940-0   LC 98-29205

International in coverage, this volume profiles "contemporary musicians whose specialties range from classical to pop, opera to rap, bluegrass to rock. . . . Written in a lively style and ranging in length from 500 to 3,500 words, the articles cover each musician's personal and professional life and are frequently spiced with quotations from published interviews with the subject and excerpts from critical commentary. Many entries include a black-and-white photo of the musician, and all conclude with a selected bibliography of additional publications and recordings." Booklist

World poets; Ron Padgett, editor in chief. Scribner 2000 3v il set $295   **920.003**

ISBN 0-684-80591-X   LC 00-24801

"This resource examines the lives and works of . . . poets. The individuals included represent writers from all over the world, from prehistory to the present time. . . . Following the entries on the individual poets are 15 thematic essays covering such topics as the troubadours, the poetry of the Harlem Renaissance, and Asian-American poetry. Appendixes include information on poetic meter and lists of major prizewinners. This useful set concludes with a comprehensive index." SLJ

Yount, Lisa

A to Z of biologists. Facts on File 2003 390p il (Notable scientists) $45 *   **920.003**

1. Biologists 2. Scientists—Dictionaries

ISBN 0-8160-4541-0   LC 2002-13816

"Facts on File science library"

"Each profile focuses on a particular biologist's research and contributions to the field and his or her effect on scientists whose work followed. Their lives and personalities are also discussed through incidents, quotations, and photographs. The profiles are culturally inclusive and span a range of biologists from ancient times to the present day." Publisher's note

Includes bibliographical references

92   Individual biography

Abdul-Jabbar, Kareem, 1947-

Abdul-Jabbar, Kareem. On the shoulders of giants; my journey through the Harlem Renaissance; [by] Kareem Abdul-Jabbar with Raymond Obstfeld. Simon & Schuster 2007 274p il $26 *   **92**

1. Harlem Renaissance

ISBN 1-4165-3488-1; 978-1-4165-3488-4

LC 2006-51776

The author "shares his life story, beginning with his childhood in Harlem, moving on to show how he was influenced by the Harlem Renaissance, and including contributions from celebrities like Magic Johnson, Quincy Jones, and Spike Lee." Libr J

"By mixing personal anecdotes with traditional research and reporting, . . . [Abdul-Jabbar] acts as a knowledgeable, passionate tour guide through the artistic and social history of one America's most dynamic creative eras." N Y Times Book Rev

Includes bibliographical references

Acheson, Dean, 1893-1971

Chace, James. Acheson; the Secretary of State who created the American world. Simon & Schuster 1998 512p pa $20 hardcover o.p.

92

1. United States—Foreign relations

ISBN 978-1-416-54865-2; 1-416-54865-3

LC 98-3801

Also available in paperback by Harvard Univesity Press

"Dean Acheson was Truman's Secretary of State from 1949 to 1953, and today's world, as Chace shows in this lucid biography, was shaped in no small degree by his efforts." New Yorker

Includes bibliographical references

Adams, Abigail, 1744-1818

Adams, John. My dearest friend. See entry under Adams, John, 1735-1826

Adams, Ansel, 1902-1984

Adams, Ansel. Ansel Adams, an autobiography; {by} Ansel Adams with Mary Street Alinder. Little, Brown 1985 400p il $65; pa $14.95

92

ISBN 0-8212-1596-5; 0-8212-2241-4 (pa)

LC 85-8135

"A New York Graphic Society book."

The American photographer's "autobiography moves from family reminiscences to his experiences with Edward Weston, Paul Strand, Dorothea Lange, the Newhalls, Georgia O'Keefe, Steiglitz, and Steichen, giving Adams's perspective on developments in the visual arts." Libr J

"Consisting of an almost perfect mix of interacting text and images, including some unexpected candid snapshops of Adams himself, this work is an outstanding document of 20th-century American photography." Choice

Includes bibliographical references

Alinder, Mary Street. Ansel Adams; a biography. Holt & Co. 1996 xx, 489p il pa $17.95 hardcover o.p.   92

ISBN 0-8050-5835-4 (pa)   LC 95-44741

"As Alinder traces the straightforward course of Adams' dazzling career . . . she emphasizes the connection between his stunning landscape photography and his zealous work with the Sierra Club. Alinder is as lucid on the topic of Adams' technical mastery as on his environmentalism and aesthetics, and she also tackles the muddle of his contentious private life with aplomb and candor." Booklist

Includes bibliographical references

Adams, Henry, 1838-1918

Adams, Henry. The education of Henry Adams; an autobiography; with a new introduction by Donald Hall. Houghton Mifflin 2000 517p pa $12

92

ISBN 0-618-05666-1   LC 00-26235

Also available in paperback from Oxford Univ. Press and Modern Library

"A Mariner book"

First published 1918

"Henry Adams was the son of Charles Francis Adams, U.S. Minister to Britain during the Civil War, and a grandson of John Quincy Adams. His 'education' consists of everything that happened to him or about him from his birth to his death." St. Louis Public Libr

"The book omits any mention of the thirteen years of Adams's marriage and the seven years following his wife's suicide. It does, however, present a vivid picture of the people and places the author knew." Reader's Ency. 4th edition

Adams, John, 1735-1826

Adams, John. My dearest friend; letters of Abigail and John Adams; edited by Margaret A. Hogan and C. James Taylor. Belknap Press of Harvard University Press 2007 508p il map $35 *

92

1. Adams, Abigail, 1744-1818 2. Presidents—United States 3. Presidents' spouses—United States

ISBN 978-0-674-02606-3; 0-674-02606-3

LC 2007-4380

This collection of correspondence between John and Abigail Adams includes "selection from the entire body of the Adams' correspondence, from their courtship . . . until Abigail left the White House near the end of John's presidential term, reminding him, 'I want to see the list of judges.' . . . This is a treasure, for general readers and scholars alike." Booklist

Grant, James. John Adams; party of one; [by] James L. Grant. Farrar, Straus and Giroux 2005 530p il $30 *   92

1. Presidents—United States

ISBN 0-374-11314-9   LC 2004-10863

"Going from his beginnings on a hardscrabble Massachusetts farm to the Continental Congress to the Court of St. James and the White House, Grant traces the words and deeds of one of our most learned but politically star-crossed leaders." Publisher's note

The author "is excellent at developing Adams' devotion to liberty, honed by British policies that affronted him and turned him into a revolutionary. In Grant's fine synthesis, Adams on the page is the pious, ambitious, and loving man he was in life." Booklist

Includes bibliographical references

McCullough, David G. John Adams; {by} David McCullough. Simon & Schuster 2001 751p il maps $35; pa $18.95   92

1. United States—Politics and government—1775-1783, Revolution

ISBN 0-684-81363-7; 0-7432-2313-6 (pa)

LC 2001-27010

"In tracing Adam's life from childhood through his many critical, heroic, and selfless acts during the Revolution, his vice presidency under Washington, and his own term as president, the full measure of Adams—a man widely regarded in his time as the equal of Jefferson, Hamilton, and all of the other Founding Fathers—is revealed." Libr J

"This is a wonderfully stirring biography; to read it is to feel as if you are witnessing the birth of a country firsthand." Booklist

Includes bibliographical references

Adams, John Quincy, 1767-1848

Nagel, Paul C. John Quincy Adams; a public life, a private life. Harvard University Press 1999 432p il map pa $18.95   92

1. Presidents—United States

ISBN 0-674-47940-8

First published 1997 by Knopf

The author traces the life and career of the sixth president of the United States "utilizing diary entries to provide keen insight into this extraordinary man, who often

Adams, John Quincy, 1767-1848—*Continued*
suffered from severe depression. The result is a fascinating psychobiography." Libr J
Includes bibliographical references

Remini, Robert Vincent. John Quincy Adams; [by] Robert V. Remini. Times Bks. 2002 172p (American presidents series) $20 **92**
1. Presidents—United States 2. United States—Politics and government—1783-1865
ISBN 0-8050-6939-9   LC 2002-24210
"Remini focuses on important incidents throughout Adams's life, demonstrating that he was not the failure he would have been if judged only by his presidential years." Libr J
The author's "judicious, eloquent survey of the sixth president's life and career intends not to proffer new and explosive ideas but to fashion recent scholarship into a highly readable overview for the general reader." Booklist
Includes bibliographical references

Addams, Jane, 1860-1935
Elshtain, Jean Bethke. Jane Addams and the dream of American democracy; a life. Basic Bks. 2001 xxii, 329p il pa $20 hardcover o.p. **92**
ISBN 0-465-01913-7 (pa)   LC 2001-43493
In this biography of the founder of the settlement-house movement, "Elshtain gives a moving account of a stunningly creative woman occupied cognitively, emotionally and spiritually with the ways an elite in a cosmopolitan society riven by inequality might offer succor to others." N Y Times Book Rev
Includes bibliographical references

Agee, James, 1909-1955
Wranovics, John. Chaplin and Agee; the untold story of the tramp, the writer, and the lost screenplay. Palgrave Macmillan 2005 256p il $24.95 **92**
1. Chaplin, Charlie, 1889-1977
ISBN 1-403-96866-7   LC 2004-62807
A "double biography of two of the 20th century's most talented artists. Wranovic's hook is a lost screenplay titled The Tramp's New World, which Agee wrote for Chaplin after the detonation of the atomic bomb over Hiroshima. . . . Using personal correspondence and critical reviews, Wranovics re-creates the fascinating historical backdrop of the Agee/Chaplin friendship, interweaving into the stunning tapestry the colorful lives of such luminaries as Brecht, Auden, Ed Sullivan, and John Huston." Choice

Akhmatova, Anna Andreevna, 1889-1966
Feinstein, Elaine. Anna of all the Russias; the life of Anna Akhmatova. Knopf 2006 331p il $27.50 * **92**
ISBN 1-4000-4089-2; 978-1-4000-4089-6
LC 2005-44542
First published 2005 in the United Kingdom

This is a "biography of the Russian Anna Akhmatova (1889-1966), whom she describes as 'a poet of womanly feeling in a brutal world.'" Libr J
"In her superb and concise biography, Feinstein brings to life the complex interplay between poetic truth and the ordinary truth of experience in the poet's life and work. . . . Feinstein's poetic sensibility gives her book a distinctive quality, setting it apart from previous biographies." N Y Rev Books
Includes bibliographical references

Albee, Edward, 1928-
Gussow, Mel. Edward Albee; a singular journey: a biography. Applause 2001 448p il pa $16.95 **92**
1. Dramatists, American
ISBN 978-1-55783-447-8; 1-55783-447-4
First published 1999 by Simon & Schuster
"Albee regained his position as one of America's greatest playwrights with the 1994 production of 'Three Tall Women,' achieving a level of theatrical mastery and critical acclaim that he hadn't seen since 'Who's Afraid of Virginia Woolf' and 'A Delicate Balance,' almost two decades earlier. The years in between were marked by excessive drinking, outrageous behavior, inferior work, and a diminished career, but Gussow, with a light and generous touch, shows us the strengths of an artist whose core of resilience ultimately insured his survival." New Yorker
Includes bibliographical references

Alcott, Amos Bronson, 1799-1888
Matteson, John. Eden's outcasts. See entry under Alcott, Louisa May, 1832-1888

Alcott, Louisa May, 1832-1888
Matteson, John. Eden's outcasts; the story of Louisa May Alcott and her father. W.W. Norton 2007 497p il $29.95 **92**
1. Alcott, Amos Bronson, 1799-1888 2. Authors, American
ISBN 978-0-393-05964-9   LC 2007-13707
"In his account of Louisa May Alcott and her father, Bronson Alcott, . . . [the author] relies heavily on the journals, letters, and works of both authors to portray their unique lives, also quoting extensively from the writings of famous friends and neighbors like Ralph Waldo Emerson." Libr J
"Matteson's lucid, commanding biography casts new light on an unusual father-daughter bond and a new land at war with itself." Booklist
Includes bibliographical references

Alexander, the Great, 356-323 B.C.
Foreman, Laura. Alexander the Conqueror; the epic story of the warrior king. Da Capo Press 2004 211p il map $35 **92**
1. Greece—History 2. Kings and rulers
ISBN 0-306-81293-2   LC 2003-62573
"A Tehabi book"

Alexander, the Great, 356-323 B.C.—*Continued*
This illustrated biography of the Macedonian ruler
"follows the progression of his conquests through the
Near East and Central Asia to the Indus Valley, and introduces Alexander's family, the personalities of his generals, and the cultures of the lands he conquered. Foreman examines the complex character of Alexander as
student, friend, lover, military genius, and emperor."
Publisher's note
This is "a lively, engrossing account of the life of one
of the world's greatest military commanders." SLJ
Includes bibliographical references

**Alexandra, Empress, consort of Nicholas II,
Emperor of Russia, 1872-1918**
Massie, Robert K. Nicholas and Alexandra. See
entry under Nicholas II, Emperor of Russia,
1868-1918

Ali, Khaliah
Ali, Khaliah. Fighting weight; how I achieved
healthy weight loss with "banding," a new
procedure that eliminates hunger—forever; [by]
Khaliah Ali; George Fielding, Christine Ren,
Lawrence Lindner. HarperCollins 2007 241p il
$22.95   **92**
1. Stomach—Surgery 2. Weight loss
ISBN 0-06-117094-1; 978-0-06-117094-2
                                    LC 2007-60870
The author "describes her own lifelong battle with
obesity and the effect of her own gastric-banding surgery. . . . Coauthor George Fielding, M.D., who performed Ali's surgery, explains the process and how it
differs from other bariatric surgeries. . . . A good combination of scientific information and personal narrative,
this title belongs in all public libraries." Libr J

Ali, Muhammad, 1942-
Kindred, Dave. Sound and fury; two powerful
lives, one fateful friendship. Free Press 2006 368p
il $27   **92**
1. Cosell, Howard, 1918-1995
ISBN 0-7432-6211-5; 978-0-7432-6211-8
                                    LC 2005-55217
This is an account of the friendship of Muhammad Ali
and Howard Cosell.
"Even if the shelves are sagging with books about Ali,
room should be made for this approachable, touching,
and altogether fascinating buddy comedy." Booklist
Includes bibliographical references

Remnick, David. King of the world: Muhammad
Ali and the rise of an American hero. Random
House 1998 326p il hardcover o.p. pa $14
                                                   92
1. African American athletes
ISBN 0-375-50065-0; 0-375-70229-6 (pa)
                                    LC 98-24539
This book focuses on Ali's career "in the early sixties—roughly, late 1962 to late 1965. . . . Five heavyweight title fights are dealt with in depth: the first Patter-
son-Liston fight on September 25, 1962, and their re-

match on July 22, 1963: the first Liston-Ali fight on February 25, 1964, and their rematch on May 25, 1965: and
the first Ali-Patterson fight on November 22, 1965." Nation
"This is the best book ever on Muhammad Ali and
one of the best on America in the 1960s." Booklist
Includes bibliographical references

Allen, Richard, 1760-1831
Newman, Richard S. Freedom's prophet; Bishop
Richard Allen, the AME Church, and the Black
founding fathers. New York University Press 2008
359p il $34.95   **92**
1. African Methodist Episcopal Church
ISBN 978-0-8147-5826-7; 0-8147-5826-6
                                    LC 2007-43259
This is a "biography of Allen that casts him as a black
founder who profoundly impacted the cause of abolition
and black community building as well as a peer to the
white Founding Fathers." Libr J
"Newman's beautifully written study is not only a
first-rate social history of the early Republic and African-
American culture and religion, it provides a detailed
sketch of Allen that is sure to become the definitive biography of the leader." Publ Wkly
Includes bibliographical references

Allende, Isabel
Allende, Isabel. My invented country; a
nostalgic journey through Chile; translated from
the Spanish by Margaret Sayers Peden.
HarperCollins Pubs. 2003 199p map $23.95; pa
$13.95   **92**
1. Chile 2. Authors, Chilean
ISBN 0-06-054564-X; 0-06-054567-4 (pa)
                                    LC 2002-191267
Also available Spanish language edition
"In this memoir-cum-study of her 'home ground,' the
author delves into the history, social mores and idiosyncrasies of Chile, where she was raised, showing, in the
process, how that land has served as her muse. . . . This
is a reflective book, lacking the pull of Allende's fiction
but unearthing intriguing elements of the author's captivating history." Publ Wkly

Allende, Isabel. Paula; translated from the
Spanish by Margaret Sayers Peden. HarperCollins
Pubs. 1995 330p hardcover o.p. pa $13.95 *
                                                   92
1. Allende family
ISBN 0-06-017252-5; 0-06-092721-6 (pa)
                                    LC 95-2452
Allende "interweaves the story of her own life with
the slow dying of her 28-year-old daughter, Paula." Publ
Wkly
This "is a deeply affecting tale, written in the rich, lu-
minous prose typical of Allende's novels, that investi-
gates the sources of her writing as it paints a vivid portrait of Chile." Libr J

Allende, Isabel—_Continued_

Allende, Isabel. The sum of our days; translated from the Spanish by Margaret Sayers Peden. HarperCollins 2008 320p $26.95   **92**

1. Authors, Chilean

ISBN 978-0-06-155183-3; 0-06-155183-X

LC 2007-33251

"In this sequel to her memoir Paula (1995), about the yearlong coma suffered by her daughter, Chilean novelist Allende tells of the difficult years following Paula's death. . . . Surprisingly candid, frequently funny, and highly aware of her own failings, Allende is a person fully engaged in life, and readers will find her eloquent memoir inspirational reading." Booklist

Amis, Kingsley, 1922-1995

Amis, Martin. Experience. See entry under Amis, Martin

Bradford, Richard. Lucky him: the life of Kingsley Amis. Owen, P.; distributed by Dufour Eds. 2001 432p il $44.95   **92**

ISBN 0-7206-1117-2   LC 2001-431013

This is a biography of the English novelist, best known for such works as Lucky Jim, The old devils, and Difficulties with girls

"The writing is consistently clear and the insights—literary and biographical—are formidable." Publ Wkly

Includes bibliographical references

Leader, Zachary. The life of Kingsley Amis. Pantheon Books 2007 c2006 996p $39.95

92

ISBN 978-0-375-42498-4; 0-375-42498-9

LC 2006-35012

First published 2006 in the United Kingdom

This "biography of novelist, poet, essayist, and journalist Kingsley Amis (1922-95) was authorized by the subject's son, Martin Amis. . . . Leader examines chronologically the life and works of this major British novelist, emphasizing how Amis incorporated episodes from his life and aspects of his family and friends' personalities into his writing. Amis lived his life with gusto, and Leader details the author's excesses in regard to alcohol and sex." Libr J

The "great virtue of Leader's biography of Amis is that you do not have to share his high opinion of the subject to benefit from the book's prodigious research and wealth of information so well presented." San Francisco Chronicle

Includes bibliographical references

Amis, Martin

Amis, Martin. Experience. Hyperion 2000 406p il $23.95; pa $14   **92**

1. Amis, Kingsley, 1922-1995

ISBN 0-7868-6652-7; 0-375-72683-7 (pa)

LC 00-699777

This is an "account of a literary life with an extraordinary father. Even by English standards Kingsley Amis, whom his son rightly sees as the finest comic novelist of his generation, was a highly eccentric figure." Publ Wkly

This is a "portmanteau of personal history, ancestor worship and promiscuous opinionizing, and a piñata of literary gossip that Amis beats with a stick, causing many names to drop. . . . And if we stay put till the last 100 pages, it will break our heart." N Y Times Book Rev

Andersen, Hans Christian, 1805-1875

Andersen, Jens. Hans Christian Andersen: a new life; translated from the Danish by Tiina Nunnally. Overlook Press 2005 624p il hardcover o.p. pa $22.95   **92**

1. Authors, Danish

ISBN 1-58567-642-X; 1-58567-737-X (pa)

LC 2004-65985

The author examines Andersen's "considerable gifts as an oral storyteller; his eccentric, often annoying public habits; his ambivalent sexuality; his bouts of narcissism; his painfully slow transformation from rough-hewn provincial and awkward melodramatist into brilliant, internationally famous writer-celebrity. The biography is best and most moving when it is frank about formerly suppressed aspects of Andersen's life." Booklist

Includes bibliographical references

Wullschläger, Jackie. Hans Christian Andersen; the life of a story teller. University of Chicago Press 2002 489p il map pa $19   **92**

1. Authors, Danish

ISBN 0-226-91747-9; 978-0-226-91747-4

LC 2002-18010

First published 2000 in the United Kingdom

This is a biography of the "Danish fairy-tale writer, who came out of more impoverished circumstances than did any other literary titan, retained peasantlike gaucheness and servility throughout his life, and whose neuroses and repressed bisexuality influenced his stories as much as his ugly-duckling success." Booklist

"Wullschlager succeeds brilliantly at portraying Andersens inner mind and uncovering his hopes and fears and details the historical context that served to produce such a grand body of literature. . . . [This biography] will be a standard study for years to come." Libr J

Includes bibliographical references

Anderson, Marian, 1897-1993

Keiler, Allan. Marian Anderson; a singer's journey. University of Illinois Press 2002 447p hardcover o.p. pa $21.95   **92**

1. African American singers 2. African American women

ISBN 0-684-80711-4; 0-252-07067-4 (pa)

LC 99-43319

"A Lisa Drew book"

"Keiler offers an assessment of the great contralto, the first African American soloist at the Metropolitan Opera." Libr J

The author's "clear, succinct prose, initially lacking narrative coherence, gains strength and momentum as his subject matures from a young and struggling artist into one of the enduring voices of our century." Publ Wkly

Includes discography and bibliographical references

Andoe, Joe

Andoe, Joe. Jubilee city; a memoir at full speed. William Morrow 2007 207p il $22.95 **92**

ISBN 978-0-06-124031-7; 0-06-124031-1

In this "memoir, Andoe narrates his journey from his Tulsa childhood through redneck, hard-partying teen years to a highly successful career as a (hard-partying redneck) painter in New York City. While Andoe may not be a professional writer, his humor and offbeat artistic sensibility make up for any lack of prose-writing chops. Through discrete anecdotes that seldom run longer than two pages, Andoe assembles vivid portraits of his family and friends and of the various environments he inhabited-the working-class Tulsa neighborhoods of the 1960s, the high school and college drug culture at the end of the hippie era, and the New York art scene of the 1980s." Publ Wkly

Andrews, Julie

Andrews, Julie. Home; a memoir of my early years. Hyperion 2008 339p il $26.95 **92**

1. Singers 2. Actors

ISBN 978-0-7868-6565-9; 0-7868-6565-2

LC 2007-48830

"Spanning events from her 1935 birth to the early 1960s, . . . [the author] covers her rise to fame and ends with Walt Disney casting her in Mary Poppins (1963). . . . The heart of her book documents the rehearsals, tryouts and smash 1956 opening of My Fair Lady. Readers will rejoice, since Andrews is an accomplished writer who holds back nothing while adding a patina of poetry to the antics and anecdotes throughout this memoir of bittersweet backstage encounters and theatrical triumphs." Publ Wkly

Angell, Roger

Angell, Roger. Let me finish. Harcourt 2006 302p $25 **92**

ISBN 0-15-101350-0; 978-0-15-101350-0

LC 2005-33067

This is a collection of autobiographical essays from the *New Yorker* columnist. "The topics of the individual essays range from baseball in the 1930s (Gehrig and Ruth in Yankee Stadium, Mel Ott and Bill Terry at the Polo Grounds) to friends, family, and colleagues at the New Yorker, where Angell, now in his eighties, has worked for 40 years and where his mother, Katherine, and stepfather, E. B. White, worked before him." Booklist

"The assembled pieces add up to a fine memoir." Publ Wkly

Angelou, Maya

Angelou, Maya. I know why the caged bird sings. Random House 2002 281p $21.95 * **92**

1. African American authors 2. Women authors

ISBN 0-375-50789-2 LC 2001-41914

Also available in paperback from Bantam Bks.

First published 1969

The first volume in the author's autobiographical series covers her childhood and adolescence in rural Ar-

kansas, St. Louis, and San Francisco.

"Angelou is a skillful writer; her language ranges from beautifully lyrical prose to earthy metaphor, and her descriptions have power and sensitivity." Libr J

Followed by Gather together in my name (1974); Singin' and swingin' and gettin' merry like Christmas (1976); The heart of a woman (1981); All God's children need traveling shoes (1986); A song flung up to heaven (2002)

Angelou, Maya. A song flung up to heaven. Random House 2002 212p $23.95; pa $13 **92**

ISBN 0-375-50747-7; 0-553-38203-9 (pa)

LC 2001-34914

"This sixth installment in Angelou's autobiographical works begins in 1964 as Angelou returned to the U.S. from Ghana. . . . She worked in Watts at the time of the riots, and Malcolm X and Martin Luther King Jr. were both assassinated just before she was to begin working with them. . . . She moved to New York, where she rejoined a vibrant group of famous writers, intellectuals, and friends; worried about her young-adult son; and understood the humor and heartache of a painful love affair. . . . Spiced with her mother's aphorisms, her often-poetic prose is best at the end, as she muses on the condition of black women and sitting at her mother's table, begins to write *I Know Why the Caged Bird Sings*." Booklist

Gillespie, Marcia Ann. Maya Angelou; a glorious celebration; [by] Marcia Ann Gillespie, Rosa Johnson Butler and Richard A. Long; foreword by Oprah Winfrey. Doubleday 2008 191p il $30 **92**

1. African American authors 2. Women authors

ISBN 978-0-385-51108-7 LC 2007-31301

This look at Maya Angelou's life as well as her myriad interests and accomplishments by the people who know her best (longtime friends Marcia Ann Gillespie and Richard Long and niece Rosa Johnson Butler) features over 150 sepia portraits, family photographs, and letters. Includes a bibliography of her works.

"A loving tribute to one of the most renowned authors today, this work is highly recommended." Libr J

Anthony, Susan B., 1820-1906

Anthony, Susan B. Failure is impossible; Susan B. Anthony in her own words; [edited by] Lynn Sherr. Times Bks. 1995 xxviii, 384p il pa $23 hardcover o.p. * **92**

1. Feminism

ISBN 0-8129-2718-4 LC 94-29913

This is a collection of Susan B. Anthony's journal entries, correspondence, speeches, interviews, and published writings. The author has arranged the selections by topic and chronologically within topics

Includes bibliographical references

Ward, Geoffrey C. Not for ourselves alone: the story of Elizabeth Cady Stanton and Susan B. Anthony. See entry under Stanton, Elizabeth Cady, 1815-1902

Antonia, Mother

Jordan, Mary. The prison angel; Mother Antonia's journey from Beverly Hills to a life of service in a Mexican jail; [by] Mary Jordan and Kevin Sullivan. Penguin Press 2005 237p il $24.95
92
ISBN 1-59420-056-4   LC 2004-60238
The authors describe the "journey of a woman who, at the age of 50, left the comforts of suburban L.A. to begin a charity mission in Mexico. . . . This is an inspiring story of one woman's compassion and her own journey of spiritual growth." Booklist

Arana, Marie

Arana, Marie. American chica; two worlds, one childhood. Dial Press (NY) 2001 309p pa $12.95 hardcover o.p.   **92**
ISBN 0-385-31963-0 (pa)   LC 00-47529
The author, born to a Peruvian father and an American mother, writes of her childhood in Peru
Arana "blends a journalist's dedication to research with a style that sings with humor. Her memoir is an outstanding contribution to the growing shelf of Latina literature." Publ Wkly

Armstrong, Karen

Armstrong, Karen. The spiral staircase; my climb out of darkness. Knopf 2004 xxii, 305p $24; pa $14   **92**
ISBN 0-375-41318-9; 0-385-72127-7 (pa)
LC 2003-47550
This "is the story of Armstrong's personal spiritual quest, which led her at age 17 to join a convent. However, she found that her own skeptical nature and the physical constraints of convent life crippled her intellectually and spiritually. . . . After seven years, Armstrong left the convent." SLJ

Armstrong, Lance

Armstrong, Lance. Every second counts; [by] Lance Armstrong, with Sally Jenkins. Broadway Books 2003 272p $24.95; pa $14   **92**
1. Athletes
ISBN 0-385-50871-9; 0-7679-1448-1 (pa)
LC 2003-55580
Companion volume to It's not about the bike
"The book is the story of a family man, world-class athlete, and cancer survivor who is determined to get every single drop of enjoyment and excitement out of life. It's a joyous, triumphant book, a celebration of all the things that make life good. It's also, for cyclists, a detailed look at the Tour de France, as seen through the eyes of one of its top competitors. Fascinating and inspiring." Booklist

Armstrong, Lance. It's not about the bike; my journey back to life; [by] Lance Armstrong with Sally Jenkins. Putnam 2000 275p il $24.95; pa $14
*   **92**
1. Athletes
ISBN 0-399-14611-3; 0-425-17961-3 (pa)
LC 00-35612

Armstrong describes his early years growing up in Plano, Texas, his rise through the sports world as a champion American cyclist, his diagnosis and recovery from testicular cancer and his triumph in the 1999 Tour de France.
"Readers will respond to the inspirational recovery story, and they will appreciate the behind-the-scenes cycling information." Booklist

Coyle, Daniel. Lance Armstrong's war; one man's battle against fate, fame, love, death, scandal, and a few other rivals on the road to the Tour de France. HarperCollins Publishers 2005 326p il $25.95   **92**
1. Athletes
ISBN 0-06-073497-3   LC 2005-279702
This biography focuses particular attention on the American cyclist's preparation for and participation in the 2004 Tour de France, an event that Armstrong won for the sixth time in as many years.
"This work is honest, personal and passionate, with plenty to chew on for fans and novices alike." Publ Wkly

Armstrong, Louis, 1900-1971

Armstrong, Louis. Louis Armstrong, in his own words; selected writings; edited and with an introduction by Thomas Brothers; annotated index by Charles Kinzer. Oxford Univ. Press 1999 xxvii, 255p il pa $14.95 hardcover o.p.   **92**
ISBN 0-19-514046-X   LC 99-17040
In this collection Armstrong "recounts episodes from his childhood in New Orleans, pays tribute to other musicians, and extolls the virtues of marijuana, laxatives, and rice and beans while speaking candidly about race relations, the music business, and his extramarital affairs. The joy he took in expressing himself on paper is abundantly evident." New Yorker
Includes bibliographical references

Collier, James Lincoln. Louis Armstrong, an American genius. Oxford Univ. Press 1983 383p il pa $21.50 hardcover o.p.   **92**
ISBN 0-19-503727-8 (pa)   LC 83-11378
The author tells the story of Armstrong's life and evaluates his musical contributions
"Collier's scholarship is impeccable, his note-by-note musical analysis razor sharp, and his conclusions about Armstrong's place in American music expertly defended. In all respects, a biography worthy of its subject." Booklist

Atkins, Vera, 1908-2000

Helm, Sarah. A life in secrets; Vera Atkins and the missing agents of WWII. Nan A. Talese 2006 493p il map hardcover o.p. pa $16   **92**
1. World War, 1939-1945—Secret service
ISBN 0-385-50845-X; 978-1-4000-3140-5 (pa); 1-4000-3140-0 (pa)   LC 2005-56870
First published 2005 in the United Kingdom
This is a biography of "the highest-ranking female official in the French section of a WWII British intelligence unit that aided the resistance. Atkins sent 400

Atkins, Vera, 1908-2000—*Continued*

agents into France, including 39 women she'd personally recruited and supervised. . . . Helm has produced a memorable portrait of a woman who knowingly sent other women to their deaths and a searing history of female courage and suffering during WWII." Publ Wkly

Includes bibliographical references

Atlas, Teddy

Atlas, Teddy. Atlas; from the streets to the ring: a son's struggle to become a man; [by] Teddy Atlas and Peter Alson. Ecco 2006 278p il $24.95
                                                                    92
ISBN 0-06-054240-3; 978-0-06-054240-5
                                            LC 2005-52104
The author "traces his circuitous route from Staten Island street thug, emotionally ignored by his doctor father, to renowned [boxing] trainer. . . . It's all here—the good, the bad and the ugly of Teddy Atlas, often rendered in a crude but convincing street language, captured so faithfully and so forcefully by his collaborator, Peter Alson." N Y Times Book Rev

Audubon, John James, 1785-1851

Rhodes, Richard. John James Audubon; the making of an American. Knopf 2004 528p il $30; pa $16   **92**
1. Artists—United States 2. Naturalists
ISBN 0-375-41412-6; 0-375-71393-X (pa)
                                            LC 2003-69489
The author "chronicles Audubon's ineluctable sense of mission, phenomenal skills, and triumph over adversity. . . . Rhodes sets Audubon's engrossing tale within the context of the War of 1812, the Louisiana Purchase, the wars against Native Americans (whom Audubon profoundly admired), and the rapid decimation of the American wilderness. . . . Full of passion and discovery, hardship and transcendence, Audubon's story is at once intimate and mythic, and Rhodes' fresh, comprehensive biography will capture the imagination of readers everywhere." Booklist

Includes bibliographical references

Augustine, Saint, Bishop of Hippo

Wills, Garry. Saint Augustine. Viking 1999 xx, 152p (Penguin lives series) $19.95   **92**
ISBN 0-670-88610-6   LC 98-50317
Wills begins "by addressing centuries of misconceptions. Though his admiration for the saint is occasionally tainted by defensiveness, his account of Augustine's search for a faith and a philosophy engages our sympathy. He also conveys the turbulence of the era, when the Roman Empire was beleaguered by barbarians and the Catholic Church by heretics, and shows how Augustine's responses to the troubles of his time have shaped Christianity down to our own." New Yorker

Includes bibliographical references

Augustus, Emperor of Rome, 63 B.C.-14 A.D.

Everitt, Anthony. Augustus; the life of Rome's first emperor. Random House 2006 377p il map $26.95 *   **92**
1. Rome—History
ISBN 1-4000-6128-8; 978-1-4000-6128-0
                                            LC 2006-41735
This is a "biography of Caesar Augustus (Octavian), first emperor of Rome." Libr J
The author's "writing is so crisp and so lively he brings both Rome and Augustus to life in this magnificent work, a must-read for anyone interested in classical times." Booklist

Includes bibliographical references

Aung San Suu Kyi

Wintle, Justin. Perfect hostage; a life of Aung San Suu Kyi, Burma's prisoner of conscience. Skyhorse Pub. 2008 464p il map $27.95
                                                                    92
1. National League for Democracy (Burma)
2. Women political activists 3. Political prisoners
4. Myanmar—Politics and government
ISBN 978-1-60239-266-3; 1-60239-266-8
                                            LC 2007-51031
This is a biography of the Burmese human rights activist.
The author "writes with a snarling wit, firm grasp of Burma's horrors, and penetrating respect for this tenacious and composed prisoner of conscience, detailing her genius for connecting with people, the threats against her life, and her devotion to peace." Booklist

Includes bibliographical references

Austen, Jane, 1775-1817

Nokes, David. Jane Austen; a life. University of Calif. Press 1998 577p il pa $24.95   **92**
1. Authors, English 2. Women authors
ISBN 0-520-21606-7; 978-0-520-21606-8
                                            LC 98-15785
First published 1997 by Farrar, Straus & Giroux
"Eschewing the biographer's usual perspective of omniscient foreknowledge in favor of a novelistic perspective of ambiguous immediacy, Nokes allows us to see Austen's talent as a mystery unfolding, not a fact explained. We thus witness the emergence of a personality sufficiently subtle and complex to produce Sense and Sensibility, Pride and Prejudice, and Emma. Readers of Austen's fiction will rejoice at having a biography so carefully nuanced, so refreshingly candid." Booklist

Includes bibliographical references

Shields, Carol. Jane Austen. Viking 2001 185p (Penguin lives) hardcover o.p. pa $13   **92**
1. Authors, English 2. Women authors
ISBN 0-670-89488-5; 0-14-303516-9 (pa)
                                            LC 00-43807
"In chronicling her subject's life and personality, Shields emphasizes Austen's keen ability to listen, observe, and capture clearly the social mores of her time and explore human nature in her writing. Shields contends that historical references are behind many of the scenes and characters in Austen's novels, and as a way

Austen, Jane, 1775-1817—*Continued*
of more clearly personalizing Austen's experiences or feelings, she interjects commentary regarding writing and publishing that is presumably based on personal experience." Libr J

Tomalin, Claire. Jane Austen; a life. Knopf 1997 341p il pa $14 hardcover o.p.   **92**
1. Authors, English 2. Women authors
ISBN 0-679-76676-6 (pa)   LC 97-36887
Tomalin's "biography of the great novelist reveals that Austen developed her skill in creating fascinating fictional lives while living a life that was more eventful—and far more traumatic—than her official biographers have previously acknowledged." Booklist
The author "has produced a portrait of remarkable subtlety. The light Ms. Tomalin casts on her subject is strong but oblique: the profile of the novelist appears surrounded by her friends and neighbours and by her energetic and beloved family." Economist

Autry, Gene, 1907-1998
George-Warren, Holly. Public cowboy no. 1; the life and times of Gene Autry. Oxford University Press 2007 406p il $28   **92**
1. Actors 2. Singers
ISBN 978-0-19-517746-6; 0-19-517746-0
     LC 2006-36369
This is a biography of the radio performer, singer and actor who performed in rodeos and appeared in such movies as Public Cowboy No.1 (1937) and The Phantom Empire (1935).
"This colorful study is much more than a biography of Autry; it also tells the story of country-western music, singing cowboys, radio and early television, and celebrity." Choice
Includes filmography, discography, and bibliographical references

Ayers, Nathaniel Anthony
Lopez, Steve. The soloist; a lost dream, an unlikely friendship, and the redemptive power of music. G. P. Putnam's Sons 2008 273p $25.95 *   **92**
1. Violinists 2. Homeless persons
ISBN 978-0-399-15506-2; 0-399-15506-6
     LC 2007-46314
The true story of Nathaniel Ayers, a musician who becomes schizophrenic and homeless, and his friendship with Steve Lopez, the Los Angeles columnist who discovers and writes about him in the newspaper.
"With self-effacing humor, fast-paced yet elegant prose and unsparing honesty, Lopez tells an inspiring story of heartbreak and hope." Publ Wkly

Baartman, Saartjie
Holmes, Rachel. African queen; the real life of the Hottentot Venus. Random House 2007 161p il $23.95 *   **92**
ISBN 978-1-4000-6136-5; 1-4000-6136-9
     LC 2006-45166

This is a biography of Saartjie Baartman. "Baartman was twenty-one years old when she was taken from her native South Africa and shipped to London. Within weeks, . . . [she] was the talk of the social season of 1810—hailed as 'the Hottentot Venus.'" Publisher's note
"This is a probing look at historical racism and sexual exploitation presented through the life of an extraordinary woman." Booklist
Includes bibliographical references

Bacall, Lauren, 1924-
Bacall, Lauren. By myself and then some. HarperEntertainment 2005 506p il $26.95
     92
ISBN 0-06-075535-0   LC 2005-40256
First published 1979 by Knopf with title: Lauren Bacall by myself
In this memoir, the actress describes how she got her start in acting and her relationships with other actors, including Humphrey Bogart.
"Certainly more intelligently written than your average celebrity autobiography, this memoir tells a fascinating story of one woman's journey through life with an intimacy that's sure to engage legions of readers." Booklist

Bach, Johann Sebastian, 1685-1750
Geck, Martin. Johann Sebastian Bach; life and work; translated from the German by John Hargraves. Harcourt 2006 738p il $40 *
     92
ISBN 978-0-15-100648-9; 0-15-100648-2
     LC 2006-12390
The author "follows the course of Bach's career, . . . from his humble beginnings as an organ tuner and self-taught court musician to his role as Kapellmeister and cantor of St. Thomas's Church in Leipzig." Publisher's note
This book "adds original scholarship to an exhaustive study of other studies of Bach. And although it is often dense with information, it is just as often entertaining: rich in anecdotes and scintillating in its conjectures." N Y Times (Late N Y Ed)
Includes bibliographical references

Wolff, Christoph. Johann Sebastian Bach; the learned musician. Norton 2000 599p il hardcover o.p. $21.95   **92**
ISBN 9780393322569; 0393322564   LC 99-54364
"Bach's professional life and continual development as a composer are described in chronological order; a separate chapter discusses his domestic life." Libr J
This work "is likely to be the standard one-volume Bach biography for some time to come. It is a solid, richly informative treatment, presenting the copious details of Bach's life in a coherent, readable narrative." N Y Rev Books
Includes bibliographical references

Baer, Max, 1909-1959
Schaap, Jeremy. Cinderella Man. See entry under Braddock, James J., 1906-1974

Baker, Russell, 1925-

Baker, Russell. Growing up. New American Library 1983 c1982 278p pa $15   **92**

1. Journalists

ISBN 0-452-25550-3

Also available in paperback from Signet Bks.

"A Plume book"

First published 1982 by Congdon & Weed

This book "recounts the first 24 years of [Baker's] life as the son of an independent and deep-rooted Virginian family." Natl Rev

Balanchine, George, 1904-1983

Gottlieb, Robert Adams. George Balanchine: the ballet maker. HarperCollins\Atlas Books 2004 224p (Eminent lives) $19.95   **92**

1. Choreographers 2. Ballet

ISBN 0-06-075070-7   LC 2004-48856

This biography tells Balanchine's life story "from his near-accidental enrollment, at the age of nine, in St. Petersburg's Imperial School of Ballet, through the deprivation and hunger of Bolshevik Russia, to Diaghilev's Ballets Russes, and finally, in 1933, to the United States and eventually to the New York City Ballet, to which his reputation is forever tied." Publisher's note

"This loving tribute captures Balanchine's legacy: his energy, confidence, lack of pretension and, most important, his joy in creation." Publ Wkly

Includes bibliographical references

Teachout, Terry. All in the dances: a brief life of George Balanchine. Harcourt 2004 208p $22 *
          92

1. Choreographers 2. Ballet

ISBN 0-15-101088-9   LC 2004-9226

Teachout tells the "story of George Balanchine, a Russian émigré who fell in love with American culture, married four times and kept a mistress on the side, and transformed the art of ballet forever." Publisher's note

"Balanchine's ballets are modern masterpieces, and Teachout, moving chronologically from work to work, uses them as stepping stones to tell Balanchine's own story. This is highly recommended as a first book on the life and art of George Balanchine for students and the general reader." Publ Wkly

Includes bibliographical references

Ball, Lucille, 1911-1989

Kanfer, Stefan. Ball of fire; the tumultuous life and comic art of Lucille Ball. Knopf 2003 361p il $25.95; pa $15   **92**

ISBN 0-375-41315-4; 0-375-72771-X (pa)
          LC 2002-43090

This is a biography of the comedian and star of the television shows I Love Lucy, The Lucy Show, and Here's Lucy

"A fine accumulation of research . . . balanced by Kanfer's insight into what Ball's contribution means in the context of entertainment history, this is the first study to examine all aspects of Ball's life, work, and business acumen." Libr J

Includes bibliographical references

Balzac, Honoré de, 1799-1850

Robb, Graham. Balzac; a life. Norton 1994 521p il pa $15 hardcover o.p.   **92**

ISBN 0-393-31387-5 (pa)   LC 94-18614

This is a biography of the nineteenth-century French novelist whose work includes the "nearly 100 interlinked novels and stories grouped under the collective heading 'La Comédie Humaine.'" Christ Sci Monit

"Balzac's life was more cause for incredulity than anything he wrote, and Robb compellingly sets out the documentable facts against and within the world Balzac created from them. . . . The result is nearly a novel, although Robb does not fictionalize with re-created dialogs and hypothetical events. He has in fact produced an extensive traditional biography . . . not a critical reassessment." Libr J

Includes bibliographical references

Barkley, Charles, 1963-

Barkley, Charles. I may be wrong but I doubt it; edited and with an introduction by Michael Wilbon. Random House 2002 245p $22.95; pa $12.95   **92**

ISBN 0-375-50883-X; 0-8129-6628-7 (pa)
          LC 2002-29169

The retired NBA champion "explores a wide range of interests. Each chapter has a theme, and Barkley has no problem speaking his mind on any topic, whether it is politics . . . or lack of minority control in sports. . . . In between these chapters are other sections that retell some of the great and not-so-great moments in his career. . . . This is a very entertaining look at one of the most intelligent minds in pro sports, and like Barkley's career, it's bound to produce fierce arguments." Publ Wkly

Barnum, P. T. (Phineas Taylor), 1810-1891

Saxon, A. H. P. T. Barnum: the legend and the man. Columbia Univ. Press 1989 437p il pa $22.50 hardcover o.p.   **92**

ISBN 0-231-05687-7 (pa)   LC 89-982

"Working primarily from Barnum's letters, business papers, family members' and associates' diaries, and legal documents, Saxon has pieced together a picture of the legendary circus owner. Saxon's detailed coverage of Barnum's life . . . is rich with anecdotes yet scholarly enough to please any researcher. Saxon succeeds admirably in capturing the essence of Barnum." Booklist

Includes bibliographical references

Barr, Nevada

Barr, Nevada. Seeking enlightenment—hat by hat; a skeptic's path to religion. Putnam 2003 222p $21.95; pa $13   **92**

ISBN 0-399-15057-9; 0-425-19603-8 (pa)
          LC 2003-43101

The author "charts the course of her spiritual evolution, how she sought to understand the many aspects of spiritual life, from forgiveness ('a sigh of relief on which the memory of evil is breathed out') to pain ('it is a duty to relieve our own pain') to commitment ('not a contract with the world but with the self'). Barr's account of her

Barr, Nevada—*Continued*

transformation from nonbeliever to committed churchgoer—but one who maintains a healthy sense of doubt even as she prays and attends Bible studies—is moving but never saccharine." Booklist

Barthelme, Frederick

Barthelme, Frederick. Double down; reflections on gambling and loss; {by} Frederick and Steven Barthelme. Houghton Mifflin 2000 198p hardcover o.p. pa $15   **92**

1. Barthelme, Steve
ISBN 0-395-95429-0; 978-0-15-601070-2 (pa); 0-15-601070-4 (pa)   LC 99-23957

"In the space of a couple of . . . years, the brothers Frederick and Steven Barthelme . . . managed to {lose} more than a quarter of a million dollars in the Mississippi gambling boats. Double Down is their account of how this happened, what led up to it and spurred them on, and how it ended in tears when . . . the casino which had taken their money charged them with conspiracy to cheat." N Y Rev Books

"Beautifully evoking the gamblers' addiction, their mesmerizing account is best read as a novel Camus might have imagined, with the writer/protagonists as their own lost characters. A work of high art; enthusiastically recommended." Libr J

Barthelme, Steve

Barthelme, Frederick. Double down. See entry under Barthelme, Frederick

Barton, Clara, 1821-1912

Oates, Stephen B. A woman of valor: Clara Barton and the Civil War. Free Press 1994 527p il map hardcover o.p. pa $16.95   **92**

1. United States—History—1861-1865, Civil War
ISBN 0-02-923405-0; 0-02-874012-2 (pa)
    LC 93-38830

The author "uses both primary and secondary sources in addressing the Civil War career of Clara Barton. . . . An 'angel of the battlefield' who succored the wounded while under fire, Barton also raised funds and supplies through a network of women's support groups, while challenging the conventional belief that nursing was inappropriate for respectable women." Publ Wkly

"This is a carefully written and researched work that brings to life both the Civil War and a period of Barton's life that was to affect her forever." Libr J

Includes bibliographical references

Basie, Count, 1904-1984

Basie, Count. Good morning blues: the autobiography of Count Basie; as told to Albert Murray. Da Capo Press 1995 399p il pa $17.95   **92**

1. Jazz musicians 2. African American musicians
ISBN 0-306-81107-3   LC 94-44697

First published 1985 by Random House

"Basie pays tribute to his colleagues and managers (and to John Hammond for 'discovering' him), but does not hesitate to discuss their weaknesses and shortcomings; his language is direct and earthy. Although some of the book reads more like a catalogue or itinerary than an autobiography, it will have strong appeal for jazz buffs and fans of the late bandleader." Publ Wkly

Bayley, John, 1925-

Bayley, John. Elegy for Iris. St. Martin's Press 1999 275p il pa $13 hardcover o.p.   **92**

1. Murdoch, Iris 2. Alzheimer's disease
ISBN 0-312-42111-7 (pa)   LC 98-40895

"Iris Murdoch is best known for her novels, which are filled with characters embroiled in philosophical conflicts. In this memoir, her husband, a renowned literary critic, presents his insights into her creativity, her personality, and their relationship. . . . Reminiscences of the past are juxtaposed with the reality of the present, in which Bayley tries to cope with the daily frustrations of caring for Murdoch now that she has Alzheimer's disease." Libr J

"This splendid book enlarges our imagination of the range and possibilities of love." N Y Times Book Rev

Beah, Ishmael

Beah, Ishmael. A long way gone; memoirs of a boy soldier. Farrar, Straus & Giroux 2007 229p map $22 *   **92**

1. Sierra Leone—History—Civil War, 1991-
ISBN 978-0-374-10523-5; 0-374-95191-8
    LC 2006-17101

"Sarah Crichton Books"

"In 1993, when the author was twelve, rebel forces attacked his home town, in Sierra Leone, and he was separated from his parents. For months, he straggled through the war-torn countryside, starving and terrified, until he was taken under the wing of a Shakespeare-spouting lieutenant in the government army. Soon, he was being fed amphetamines and trained to shoot an AK-47. . . . Beah's memoir documents his transformation from a child into a hardened, brutally efficient soldier who high-fived his fellow-recruits after they slaughtered their enemies—often boys their own age—and who 'felt no pity for anyone.'" New Yorker

Beauvoir, Simone de, 1908-1986

Bair, Deirdre. Simone de Beauvoir; a biography. Summit Bks. 1990 718p il pa $31.95 hardcover o.p.   **92**

ISBN 0-671-74180-2 (pa)   LC 89-22029

"Bair's biography of the French author, philosopher, and feminist aims to restore the balance between interest in de Beauvoir's personal life—as the lifelong companion of Jean-Paul Sartre and sometime lover of Nelson Algren—and the question of her achievements as a writer and thinker." Booklist

Includes bibliographical references

Bechdel, Alison, 1960-

Bechdel, Alison. Fun home; a family tragicomic. Houghton Mifflin 2006 232p il $19.95   **92**

1. Graphic novels 2. Autobiographical graphic novels
ISBN 978-0-618-47794-4; 0-618-47794-2
    LC 2005-30304

Bechdel, Alison, 1960-—*Continued*

This is a memoir in graphic novel format about the author's "childhood, her father's death and their shared homosexuality. . . . The death was deemed an accident—a truck hit [Mr. Bechdel] as he crossed a road with an armful of garden brush—but Ms. Bechdel suspects suicide." N Y Times (Late N Y Ed)

This "is one of the very best graphic novels ever." Booklist

Becker, Suzy

Becker, Suzy. I had brain surgery, what's your excuse? an illustrated memoir. Workman Pub 2003 282p il $19.95   **92**

ISBN 0-7611-2478-0   LC 2003-60039

Becker "was suffering seizures but didn't tell anyone until a friend witnessed an incident. Eventually, she was scheduled for brain surgery to remove a tumor. Writing with the dry sense of humor that some of us rely on to make it through situations, Becker recalls her reactions to her medical problems, from liking the first doctor who gave her no bad news ('just stress') to the terror of the eventual diagnosis. Her descriptions of the surgery and its dreadful, but temporary, effects on her ability to speak, read, write, and draw make for especially compelling reading. . . . Becker has turned one person's experience into a universal story of family, healing, and the return to creativity." Libr J

Beckett, Samuel, 1906-1989

Gordon, Lois G. The world of Samuel Beckett, 1906-1946; {by} Lois Gordon. Yale Univ. Press 1996 250p il $50; pa $16.95   **92**

ISBN 0-300-06409-8; 0-300-07495-6 (pa)
                                         LC 95-22851

Gordon "examines the first 40 years of the playwright/novelist's 83-year life, which includes periods in Ireland, where he was born; in Paris, where he spent much of his life; and in London, Germany, and other parts of France. . . . Gordon has been thorough in her research and careful in her presentation." Choice

Includes bibliographical references

Beckwith, Jonathan R., 1935-

Beckwith, Jonathan R. Making genes, making waves; a social activist in science; [by] Jon Beckwith. Harvard Univ. Press 2002 242p il $27.95   **92**

ISBN 0-674-00928-2   LC 2002-22747

"The text traces Beckwith's development as both a scientist and an activist, essentially in a chronological narrative form, with a few chapters providing expanded coverage of specific examples of the interaction between scientific research and societal effects. Those working in scientific fields or students who plan to pursue such a career would enjoy this book." Sci Books Films

Includes bibliographical references

Beecher, Henry Ward, 1813-1887

Applegate, Debby. The most famous man in America; the biography of Henry Ward Beecher. Doubleday 2006 529p il map $27.95 *
                                          92

ISBN 0-385-51396-8; 978-0-385-51396-8
                                          LC 2005-54842

This is a biography of the American clergyman.

"By illuminating Beecher's position in history, Applegate has produced a biography worthy of its subject." N Y Times Book Rev

Includes bibliographical references

Beethoven, Ludwig van, 1770-1827

Lockwood, Lewis. Beethoven: the music and the life. Norton 2002 c2003 604p il music $39.95
                                          92

ISBN 0-393-05081-5   LC 2002-75397

The author "concentrates primarily on his subject's music and development as a composer before dedicating separate chapters to biography and the historical, political, and cultural milieus. . . . All of Lockwood's narrative, including the discussion of specific compositions, will be accessible to serious music lovers with only a modest technical background. This results partly from an interesting innovation . . . 100 additional musical examples are available on a companion web site. . . . Lockwood's study offers a new and authoritative interpretation of a prodigiously gifted and complex man and artist." Libr J

Includes bibliographical references

Morris, Edmund. Beethoven: the universal composer. HarperCollins Publishers 2005 243p (Eminent lives) $21.95   **92**

1. Composers
ISBN 0-06-075974-7; 978-0-06-075974-2
                                          LC 2006-274925

This is a biography of the German composer.

The author "clearly admires his subject not only for the work but also for his constant fight against the odds, and he has written an ideal biography for the general reader." Publ Wkly

Includes bibliographical references

Solomon, Maynard. Beethoven. 2nd rev ed. Schirmer Bks. 1998 554p hardcover o.p. pa $19.95
                                          92

1. Composers
ISBN 978-0-8256-7268-2 (pa); 0-8256-7268-6 (pa)
                                          LC 97-51363

First published 1977

In this revision, "Solomon approaches his subject from myriad different angles—historical, psychological, sociological, and aesthetic—to treat the reader to a view of Beethoven, his music, and his era that answers longstanding questions and reveals new ways of considering the composer, his works, and his motivation." Libr J

Beland, Tom, 1962-

Beland, Tom. True story swear to God archives, vol. 1. Image Comics 2008 528p il pa $19.99
                                          92

Beland, Tom, 1962-—_Continued_
1. Graphic novels 2. Romance graphic novels
3. Autobiographical graphic novels
ISBN 978-1-58240-881-1
They met at a bus stop at Disneyworld, by chance: he
was a cartoonist from Napa, California, and she was a
radio personality from Puerto Rico. Their chance meeting
blossomed into a romance that survived a long-distance
separation, a Category 5 hurricane, his leaving home to
move to a new world. Tom Beland writes candidly about
the ups and downs of his relationship with Lily, with his
family, and all the slings and arrows of life one has to
deal with daily. He originally self-published these comics, and they were collected in several trade paperbacks
from AiT/PlanetLar. The book includes occasional harsh
language (including s-bombs and f-bombs), sexual situations, and frank talk about sex.

Bell, Alexander Graham, 1847-1922
Gray, Charlotte. Reluctant genius; Alexander
Graham Bell and the passion for invention. Arcade
Pub. 2006 466p il map $29.95 *   92
1. Inventors
ISBN 1-55970-809-3; 978-1-55970-809-8
                                        LC 2005-29609
The author "recounts both the inventor of the telephone's creation of the device and the projects he pursued once his future was secured. . . . Combining the
household history of the Bells with that of Alexander's
successive enthusiasms (Helen Keller, kites, airplanes,
hydrocraft), Gray fairly portrays the attractions and exas-
perations of Bell's life." Booklist
Includes bibliographical references

Bell, Gertrude Margaret Lowthian, 1868-1926
Howell, Georgina. Gertrude Bell; queen of the
desert, shaper of nations. Farrar, Straus and Giroux
2007 481p il map $27.50   92
1. Archeologists 2. Women—Travel
ISBN 978-0-374-16162-0; 0-374-16162-3
                                        LC 2006-29994
First published 2006 in the United Kingdom with title:
Daughter of the desert
This is a biography of the British archaeologist and
author of Desert and the Sown (1907) and Persian Pictures (1928).
"Bell's role in the creation of Iraq and the placement
of Faisal upon the throne, is fully detailed. . . . But the
strength and delight of Howell's superb biography is in
the fullness with which Bell's character is drawn." Publ
Wkly
Includes bibliographical references

Wallach, Janet. Desert queen; the extraordinary
life of Gertrude Bell: adventurer, adviser to kings,
ally of Lawrence of Arabia. Talese 1996 xxv,
419p hardcover o.p. pa $15.95   92
1. Archeologists 2. Women—Travel
ISBN 0-385-47408-3; 978-1-4000-9619-0 (pa);
1-4000-9619-7 (pa)   LC 95-44868
"High-spirited, outspoken, and self-reliant, . . . {Bell}
was the first woman to earn a degree in history at Oxford, a skilled mountain climber and equestrienne, and an

avid and fearless traveler who found her spiritual home
in the deserts of Iraq and Arabia. . . . Fluent in Arabic
and on good terms with powerful men, Bell became an
invaluable asset to British intelligence and was drafted as
a spy during World War I. . . . Wallach . . . brings the
resolute Bell and her complex world vividly to life."
Booklist
Includes bibliographical references

Bellow, Saul, 1915-2005
Atlas, James. Bellow; a biography. Random
House 2000 686p il pa $29 hardcover o.p.
                                        92
1. Authors, American
ISBN 0-375-75958-1 (pa)   LC 00-42529
The author "traces Bellow's life from his birth in
1915 through his student years to his mature develop-
ment as a novelist." Libr J
"Atlas shares his subject's devotion to literature, inti-
macy with Chicago (the city Bellow immortalized), and
Jewishness, and he succeeds brilliantly in chronicling and
interpreting Bellow's very full life, difficult personality,
and powerful work." Booklist
Includes bibliographical references

Benedict, Saint, Abbot of Monte Cassino
Butcher, Carmen Acevedo. Man of blessing; a
life of St. Benedict. Paraclete Press 2006 180p
map $21.95   92
ISBN 1-55725-485-0; 978-1-55725-485-6
                                        LC 2005-35827
This is the "story of the life of St. Benedict of Nursia,
who founded Western monasticism in the sixth century
and later became the patron saint of Europe. . . . The
book's readability will make it easy for patrons to escape
into late Roman culture and find peace in a monastic
simplicity." Libr J
Includes bibliographical references

Bergman, Ingrid, 1915-1982
Spoto, Donald. Notorious; the life of Ingrid
Bergman. Da Capo Press 2001 474p il pa $22
                                        92
1. Actors
ISBN 978-0-306-81030-5; 0-306-81030-1
First published 1997 by HarperCollins
Spoto traces Bergman's life "from her difficult childhood in Sweden . . . through her early career as a Swedish film star, to her ascension to Hollywood stardom as
the leading lady of such actors as Spencer Tracy, Humphrey Bogart and Cary Grant. Particular attention is giv-
en to her work with Alfred Hitchcock." Publ Wkly
The author's "perceptions about Bergman personally
and professionally are keen, and the narrative reads like
a full-bodied story, not just a listing of professional credits and personal landmarks." Booklist
Includes bibliographical references

Berlin, Irving, 1888-1989

Hamm, Charles. Irving Berlin; songs from the melting pot: the formative years, 1907-1914. Oxford Univ. Press 1996 292p il $42.50
      92

ISBN 0-19-507188-3   LC 96-6335

"Hamm explores the influence of pre-World War I culture on Berlin's output as it changed from ethnic novelty songs to songs for the stage influenced by European styles." Booklist

The author "shows an informed sensitivity for the social and historical atmosphere in which these songs were produced, and . . . makes effective use of period recordings . . . in an effort to understand how they were meant to play to their first listeners." N Y Times Book Rev

Includes discography and bibliographical references

Berlioz, Hector, 1803-1869

Holoman, D. Kern. Berlioz. Harvard Univ. Press 1989 687p il $36
      92

ISBN 0-674-06778-9   LC 88-35788

This is a biography of the nineteenth-century composer, conductor, and music critic

"There may be aspects of Berlioz's life which Holoman has not fathomed, but he paints as full a picture as has yet been attempted." New Statesman (1913)

Includes bibliographical references

Bernhardt, Sarah, 1844-1923

Bernhardt, Sarah. My double life: the memoirs of Sarah Bernhardt; translated by Victoria Tietze Larson. State Univ. of N.Y. Press 1999 345p $26.50; pa $25.95
      92

ISBN 0-7914-4053-2; 0-7914-4054-0 (pa)
       LC 98-30036

This is a newly translated abridgment of Bernhardt's autobiography originally published 1907

"The most tempestuous and possibly the most famous actress of her time, Bernhardt . . . is presented as both melodramatic and frustratingly discreet." Publ Wkly

Includes bibliographical references

Betjeman, Sir John, 1906-1984

Wilson, A. N. (Andrew Norman). Betjeman; a life. Farrar, Straus & Giroux 2006 375p il $27
      92

ISBN 978-0-374-11198-4; 0-374-11198-7
       LC 2006-930677

Wilson's biography of the British Poet Laureate "is a sharp-edged triumph of honest hero worship. Amazingly, he has found a real-life character whom he can love and admire. . . . Brushing aside hundreds of chatty anecdotes and conversations that might have happened, Wilson has tied his primary source material around a subtle analysis of the ultimate first sources, the poems themselves. This, it is safe to say, should be the final biography." Times Lit Suppl

Bewick, Thomas, 1753-1828

Uglow, Jennifer S. Nature's engraver; a life of Thomas Bewick. Farrar, Straus and Giroux 2007 458p il map $30
      92

1. Woodcuts

ISBN 978-0-374-11236-3; 0-374-11236-3
       LC 2006-31878

First published 2006 in the United Kingdom

This work "chronicles the life of the wood engraver acclaimed for exquisite little vignettes of the Northumbrian countryside and its people. . . . A naturalist as well as an artist, he rose to national fame with illustrations for three books, A General History of Quadrupeds, A History of British Birds and an edition of Aesop's Fables." Publ Wkly

"Biographies rarely afford a glimpse behind the office door, and it is the image of Bewick at work that is so valuable here. . . . It is hard to imagine a better biographer for this subject than Uglow, with her background in publishing and her knowledge of the North of England and the eighteenth century. It is also hard to imagine a more beautifully produced and illustrated book: scores of Bewick's frameless vignettes float frame-free and captionless throughout, appearing as they would have done in his own time, tale pieces every one." Times Lit Suppl

Includes bibliographical references

Bhutto, Benazir

Bhutto, Benazir. Reconciliation; Islam, democracy, and the West. HarperCollins 2008 328p $27.95 *
      92

1. Prime ministers—Pakistan 2. Islam and politics 3. Pakistan—Politics and government

ISBN 978-0-06-156758-2; 0-06-156758-2

In this posthumous work, Bhutto, the former Pakistani Prime Minister who was assassinated in December 2007, recounts "her final months in Pakistan and offers a . . . new agenda for how to stem the tide of Islamic radicalism." Publisher's note

This "is a book of enormous intelligence, courage and clarity. . . . Washington should arrange to have the portions of the book about Islam republished as a separate volume and translated into several languages. It would do more to win the battle of ideas within Islam than anything an American president could ever say." N Y Times Book Rev

Includes bibliographical references

Bierce, Ambrose, 1842-1914?

Morris, Roy. Ambrose Bierce; alone in bad company. Oxford University Press 1998 306p pa $19.95
      92

1. Authors, American

ISBN 0-19-512628-9   LC 98-33467

First published 1995 by Crown

This "study of Bierce (1842-1914), a journalist and short-story writer, draws a parallel between the sardonic writer's dark vision and his unhappy life. According to Morris the depression Bierce developed during a lonely and unhappy Indiana childhood intensified after his Civil War experiences." Publ Wkly

"Mr. Morris's disturbing, vividly realized biography brings to life a haunted writer whose private torments

Bierce, Ambrose, 1842-1914?—*Continued*
mirrored a turbulent era." NY Times Book Rev
Includes bibliographical references

Billy, the Kid
Utley, Robert Marshall. Billy the Kid; a short
and violent life; {by} Robert M. Utley. University
of Neb. Press 1989 302p il pa $16 hardcover o.p.
92

ISBN 0-8012-9558-8 (pa)   LC 89-30022
Examines the career of the young outlaw whose life
and death were an expression of the violence prevalent
on the American frontier
"Robert M. Utley does what countless books, movies,
television shows, musical compositions, and paintings
have failed to do: he successfully strips off the veneer of
legendry to expose the reality of Billy the Kid." Univ
Press Books for Public Libr
Includes bibliographical references

Wallis, Michael. Billy the Kid; the endless ride.
W.W. Norton & Co. 2007 328p il map $25.95 *
92

ISBN 978-0-393-06068-3; 0-393-06068-3
LC 2006-101364
"The boy who would become Billy the Kid (1859-
1881) was born Henry McCarty, perhaps in the Irish immigrant wards of New York City. Not much is known
about his parents, and it's difficult to trace his whereabouts until his family turned up in Silver City, Colo., in
the early 1870s. Both the facts and the legend pick up
in 1877, when Henry—already known to some under the
alias Kid—shot a man who was bullying him and began
a life on the run." Publ Wkly
"Drawing on archival sources and interviews as well
as documents and secondary works, Wallis digs beneath
the surface, clearly identifying what is known or probable and presenting the reasonable alternatives for what is
conjecture." Libr J
Includes bibliographical references

Black Elk, 1863-1950
Black Elk. Black Elk speaks; being the life story
of a holy man of the Oglala Sioux; [as told
through] John G. Neihardt; foreword by Vine
Deloria, Jr.; with illustrations by Standing Bear;
essays by Alexis N. Petri and Lori Utecht.
University of Nebraska Press 2004 xxix, 270p il
map pa $14.95   **92**
1. Oglala Indians
ISBN 0-8032-8385-7   LC 2004-12692
A reprint of the title first published 1932 by Morrow
The Indian whose life story this is, was born in 1863.
He was a famous warrior and hunter in his youth, and
became a practicing medicine man among his people. Of
him Neihardt says, "As an indubitable seer, he seemed
to represent the consciousness of the Plains Indian more
fully than any other I had ever known."
This "is about as near as you can get to seeing life
and death, war and religion, through an Indian's eyes."
Outlook

Steltenkamp, Michael F. Black Elk, holy man of
the Oglala. University of Okla. Press 1993 xxiii,
211p il maps pa $17.95 hardcover o.p.   **92**
1. Oglala Indians
ISBN 0-8061-2988-3 (pa)   LC 93-22089
This "is the story of Black Elk's later years, when the
holy man converted to Roman Catholicism and worked
actively as a catechist, converting the Lakota to his new
religion." Antioch Rev
Includes bibliographical references

Blackburn, Lucie, d. 1895
Smardz Frost, Karolyn. I've got a home in glory
land. See entry under Blackburn, Thornton, 1813
or 14-1890

Blackburn, Thornton, 1813 or 14-1890
Smardz Frost, Karolyn. I've got a home in glory
land; a lost tale of the Underground Railroad.
Farrar, Straus & Giroux 2006 450p il map $30 *
92
1. Blackburn, Lucie, d. 1895 2. Underground railroad
ISBN 978-0-374-16481-2; 0-374-16481-9
LC 2006-64
"Following escaped slaves Lucie and Thornton Blackburn from Louisville, KY, to Detroit and then to safety
in Canada in 1833, Frost details U.S. blacks' determined
resistance and the diplomatic problems cross-border fugitives created in U.S.-Canada relations." Libr J
The author's "fascination with her subject and love of
detailed historical documentation are evident in this engrossing look at a couple who defied slavery with their
escape and their assistance to other fugitive slaves."
Booklist
Includes bibliographical references

Blackjack, Ada, 1898-1983
Niven, Jennifer. Ada Blackjack; a true story of
survival in the Arctic. Hyperion 2003 431p il map
$24.95   **92**
1. Arctic regions—Exploration 2. Wrangel Island
(Russia)—Exploration
ISBN 0-7868-6863-5   LC 2003-50826
"In September 1921, four young men and Ada Blackjack, a . . . 25-year-old Eskimo woman, ventured deep
into the Arctic in a secret attempt to colonize desolate
Wrangel Island for Great Britain. Two years later, Ada
Blackjack emerged as the sole survivor of this ambitious
polar expedition. . . . Blackjack refused to speak to anyone about her horrific two years in the Arctic. Only on
one occasion—after charges were published falsely ac-
cusing her of causing the death of one of her companions—did she speak up." Publisher's note
The book "is exhilarating reading." Booklist
Includes bibliographical references

Blackmun, Harry A.
Greenhouse, Linda. Becoming Justice
Blackmun; Harry Blackmun's Supreme Court
journey. Times Books 2005 268p il $25
92
1. United States. Supreme Court
ISBN 0-8050-7791-X   LC 2004-63772

Blackmun, Harry A.—*Continued*

This is a "biography of Justice Harry Blackmun, from his childhood to his service on the Supreme Court. . . . Central to the narrative is Blackmun's involvement in Roe v. Wade, subsequent abortion litigation, and capital punishment litigation." Libr J

The author's "achievement in her meticulous narrative history is to provide new ammunition for Justice Blackmun's critics as well as his admirers. And readers who are unfamiliar with the inner workings of the court could not hope for a more engrossing introduction." N Y Times (Late N Y Ed)

Blackwell, Unita, 1933-

Blackwell, Unita. Barefootin'; life lessons from the road to freedom; [by] Unita Blackwell, with JoAnne Prichard Morris. Crown Publishers 2006 258p $23 * **92**

1. African American women 2. African Americans—Civil rights
ISBN 0-609-61060-0; 978-0-609-61060-2
LC 2005-34953

"This memoir by activist, organizer, politician and sage Unita Blackwell is valuable chronicle of one woman's heroism in the face of the brutality that was Jim Crow-era Mississippi." Ms.

Includes bibliographical references

Blake, William, 1757-1827

Bentley, G. E. (Gerald Eades). The stranger from paradise: a biography of William Blake. Yale Univ. Press 2001 xxvii, 532p il maps $39.95; pa $24.95 **92**

ISBN 0-300-08939-2; 0-300-10030-2 (pa)
The author "traces Blake from his natal landscape, youth, marriage, and apprenticeship through to his later years as a working engraver, poet, and radical visionary. Bentley is academic and thorough, and this is more of a straight biography than an analysis." Libr J

Includes bibliographical references

Blount, Roy

Blount, Roy. Be sweet; a conditional love story; [by] Roy Blount, Jr. Harcourt Brace & Co. 1999 329p pa $17 **92**

1. Humorists
ISBN 0-15-600682-0; 978-0-15-600682-8
LC 99-15146

First published 1998 by Knopf

"Blount figures that at age 57 he has lived long enough to hunt for life-defining moments among sundry episodes, including his stint as coeditor of his college paper with presidential wanna-be Lamar Alexander, his days smokin' dope with '70s slugger Richie Allen when Blount was a Sports Illustrated reporter, and a slew of childhood memories." Booklist

Blount, Anthony, 1907-1983

Carter, Miranda. Anthony Blunt: his lives. Farrar, Straus & Giroux 2001 590p il $30; pa $18 **92**

ISBN 0-374-10531-6; 0-312-42146-X (pa)
LC 2001-50135

In 1979 "the noted British art expert Anthony Blunt was revealed to have been a spy for the Soviet Union. This meticulous book traces Blunt's career: his early school days, his association with the Bloomsbury group, his membership in a 'secret debating society' known as the Apostles, his recruitment into the spy game as a 'talent spotter,' his time spent in MI5 (he started passing documents to the Russians in 1941), and beyond." Booklist

"Thoroughly researched and carefully crafted, this is sure to be the definitive biography." Publ Wkly

Blunt, Judy, 1954-

Blunt, Judy. Breaking clean. Knopf 2002 303p pa $13 hardcover o.p. **92**

ISBN 0-375-70130-3 (pa)
LC 2001-29861

The author chronicles the hardships she endured as a ranch wife, mother, and laborer in rural Montana, and how she left it all, including her marriage, to get herself a college education and become a writer

Blunt has a "keen and poetic awareness, steely candor, and commanding storytelling skills." Booklist

Boone, Daniel, 1734-1820

Faragher, John Mack. Daniel Boone; the life and legend of an American pioneer. Holt & Co. 1992 429p il maps pa $18 hardcover o.p. **92**

1. Frontier and pioneer life
ISBN 0-8050-3007-7 (pa)
LC 92-21873

"The popular image of Daniel Boone is that of an unlettered backwoodsman, skilled hunter and Indian fighter. But evidence argues that he was reasonably well educated for his time and place, that he was a landowner, businessman and a respected leader of frontier society. Faragher . . . has sifted through folklore and fact to reconstruct a realistic portrait of Boone and the expanding frontier. . . . Faragher has written an absorbing, definitive biography." Publ Wkly

Includes bibliographical references

Morgan, Robert. Boone; a biography. Algonquin Books of Chapel Hill 2007 538p il map $29.95 **92**

1. Frontier and pioneer life
ISBN 978-1-56512-455-4; 1-56512-455-3
LC 2007-14204

"A Shannon Ravenel book"

A biography of the American pioneer scout.

This is an "absorbing and stirring chronicle of the great frontiersman." Booklist

Includes bibliographical references

Borges, Jorge Luis, 1899-1986

Williamson, Edwin. Borges, a life. Viking 2004 416p $34.95 **92**

ISBN 0-670-88579-7
LC 2004-41290

The author "pieces together the life of Argentina's elusive literary master against a backdrop of the country's history and the author's oeuvre. While Borges was known as a rebel of narrative form and a crusader against conservative politics, Williamson argues that in

Borges, Jorge Luis, 1899-1986—*Continued*
spite of his ultracerebral writing style, he lived and died with very ordinary regrets." Publ Wkly

This "is a richly psychological, dynamically intellectual, and deeply affecting portrait of an often anguished and inhibited man who, through heroic perserverance and spiritual conviction, found salvation in writing and transformed literature for all time." Booklist

Includes bibliographical references

Borgia, Lucrezia, 1480-1519
Bradford, Sarah. Lucrezia Borgia; life, love, and death in Renaissance Italy. Viking 2004 xxiv, 421p il map $27.95; pa $16   **92**
    ISBN 0-670-03353-7; 0-14-303595-9 (pa)
                    LC 2004-54881
The author "presents Lucrezia as an intelligent noblewoman, powerless to defy her family's patriarchal order, yet an enlightened ruler in her own right as Duchess of Ferrara. . . . As a project designed to distinguish the historical Lucrezia Borgia from the legend, Bradford's readable biography resoundingly succeeds." Publ Wkly

Includes bibliographical references

Born, Max, 1882-1970
Greenspan, Nancy Thorndike. The end of the certain world; the Nobel physicist who ignited the quantum revolution. Basic Books 2005 374p il $26.95   **92**
    ISBN 0-7382-0693-8   LC 2004-21809
This "biography integrates the development of modern physics and its social and political concomitants in Europe, on the one hand, with the life and science of Max Born, on the other." Sci Books Films

"This empathetic work . . . lifts a deserving figure out of semi-obscurity and adds a valuable perspective on the origin of modern physics." Publ Wkly

Includes bibliographical references

Boswell, James, 1740-1795
Martin, Peter. A life of James Boswell. Yale Univ. Press 2000 613p $35; pa $18.95 *   **92**

    ISBN 0-300-08489-7; 0-300-09312-8 (pa)
This is a biography of the diarist and author of The life of Samuel Johnson

"Martin has written the best biography of the greatest biographer in the English language. . . . One of the many virtues of Martin's work is his successful synthesis of Boswell's life story with a keen analysis of Boswell's artistry." Atl Mon

Includes bibliographical references

Boylan, Jennifer Finney, 1958-
Boylan, Jennifer Finney. I'm looking through you; growing up haunted. Broadway Books 2008 270p il $23.95   **92**
    1. Authors, American 2. Ghosts 3. Transsexualism
    ISBN 978-0-7679-2174-9; 0-7679-2174-7
                    LC 2007-19199

The author, a male-to-female transgendered person, "uses the metaphor of 'being haunted' throughout to illustrate not only her boyhood experiences but also the memories that have shaped her as a person as she struggled with her gender identity throughout most of her life. . . . Her writing style is witty, self-deprecating, entertaining, and often poignant, especially when describing family and friends who have passed away. An adventure to read, this is highly recommended for all libraries." Libr J

Bradbury, Ray, 1920-
Weller, Sam. The Bradbury chronicles; the life of Ray Bradbury. William Morrow 2005 384p il $26.95; pa $15.95   **92**
    1. Authors, American
    ISBN 0-06-054581-X; 0-06-054584-4 (pa)
                    LC 2004-59491
The author "surveys Bradbury's ancestors and family, his boyhood move to Hollywood, his introduction to science fiction and fantasy and his early writing attempts." Publ Wkly

"Weller's research—based on interviews with Bradbury as well as family members and colleagues—is almost exhaustive in its detail, and he does a fine job of presenting the facts of his subject's unique life. The lively, conversational prose brings out the writer's winning personality and turns his struggles and successes into a highly readable story." SLJ

Includes bibliographical references

Braddock, James J., 1906-1974
Schaap, Jeremy. Cinderella Man; James J. Braddock, Max Baer, and the greatest upset in boxing history. Houghton Mifflin 2005 324p il $24   **92**
    1. Baer, Max, 1909-1959
    ISBN 0-618-55117-4   LC 2004-66085
    Also available Random House large print edition
The author goes into "detail on the brawny, reserved Braddock, who, at his lowest moments, was reduced to living off government relief and doing grueling work on the Hoboken, N.J., docks. But the story is as much about Max Baer, the lovably clownish and handsome heavyweight Braddock defeated as a 10-to-one underdog. . . . Boxing enthusiasts will be more than satisfied by Schaap's meticulous account, which includes round-by-round details of the fight, as well as profiles of other fighters of the era." Publ Wkly

Includes bibliographical references

Bradstreet, Anne, 1612?-1672
Gordon, Charlotte. Mistress Bradstreet; the untold life of America's first poet. Little, Brown and Co. 2005 337p il map $27.95   **92**
    1. Women poets
    ISBN 0-316-16904-8   LC 2004-22702
This is a biography of the colonial poet.

"Written with maximal clarity and communicativeness, this is a vibrant, engaging, realistic portrayal of early colonial Massachusetts and of its fascinating biographical subject." Booklist

Includes bibliographical references

Brady, Mathew B., ca. 1823-1896

Panzer, Mary. Mathew Brady and the image of history; with an essay by Jeana K. Foley. Smithsonian Institution Press 1997 xxiii, 232p il hardcover o.p. pa $19.95   **92**
   ISBN 1-56098-793-6; 978-1-58834-143-3 (pa); 1-58834-143-7 (pa)   LC 97-9493

In this reassessment of the life and work of the iconic 19th-century photographer, the author "points out that Brady seldom stood behind the camera, preferring the role of studio chief executive officer and entrepreneur to that of a mere 'operator.' . . . Moreover, Brady was an incompetent businessman, often leaving his creditors in the lurch, and ended his career in bankruptcy. This is enough to make us think twice about Brady, but Panzer's most audacious assertion is that we also need to think twice about the meaning of the pictures attributed to him." N Y Times Book Rev

Includes bibliographical references

Bragg, Rick

Bragg, Rick. All over but the shoutin'. Pantheon Bks. 1997 xxii, 329p hardcover o.p. pa $14 *
   92
1. Journalists
ISBN 0-679-44258-8; 0-679-77402-5 (pa)
   LC 97-9918

"Honest, unsentimental, and so elegantly spare it nearly hurts to read, this memoir by Pulitzer Prize-winning journalist Bragg recounts a dirt-poor childhood in Alabama and the debt he owes his mother." Libr J

Bragg, Rick. The prince of Frogtown. Alfred A. Knopf 2008 255p $24   **92**
1. Father-son relationship 2. Stepfathers 3. Journalists
ISBN 978-1-4000-4040-7; 1-4000-4040-X
   LC 2007-38884

The author "merges his father's history of severe hardships and simple joys with a tale from the present: his own relationship with his 10-year-old stepson. . . . [This book] is lush with narratives about manhood, fathers and sons, families and the changing face of the rural South." Publ Wkly

Brahms, Johannes, 1833-1897

Swafford, Jan. Johannes Brahms; a biography. Knopf 1997 xxii, 699p il hardcover o.p. $20
   92
ISBN 978-0-679-74582-2; 0-679-74582-3
   LC 97-29308

This book traces the composer's "early life playing piano in the brothels of Hamburg, through his middle years performing his chamber music and conducting his choral works, to his late years directing Vienna's Gesellschaft der Musikfreunde in his orchestral music." Booklist

"Swafford's study, clearly a labor of profound affection, is a model biography: eloquent, clear-sighted and often moving." Publ Wkly

Includes bibliographical references

Brando, Marlon, 1924-2004

Bosworth, Patricia. Marlon Brando. Viking 2001 228p il (Penguin lives series) $21.95   **92**
ISBN 0-670-88236-4   LC 00-68591

This biography presents "the personal and professional highlights of Brando's life, including his disastrous marriage to Anna Kashfi and its effect on his son, and how he resurrected his career (which had barely survived 10 flops) with Francis Ford Coppola's *The Godfather*." Publ Wkly

"Bosworth, a gifted writer, has a clean, spare, but witty style, which helps her pack much more than one might expect into this tiny volume." Booklist

Includes filmography

Brasillach, Robert, 1909-1945

Kaplan, Alice Yaeger. The collaborator: the trial & execution of Robert Brasillach; [by] Alice Kaplan. University of Chicago Press 2000 308p $25; pa $15   **92**
ISBN 0-226-42414-6; 0-226-42415-4 (pa)
   LC 99-48291

Kaplan details "the life of Robert Brasillach, a prolific and controversial French critic who was executed for treason, at age 35, after France's liberation from the Nazis. A fascist-leaning writer known for his defense of Nazi crimes . . . Brasillach was the only distinguished writer put to death by the postwar French government." Publ Wkly

This "is one of the best-written, most absorbing pieces of literary history in years." N Y Times Book Rev

Includes bibliographical references

Brecht, Bertolt, 1898-1956

Fuegi, John. Brecht and company; sex, politics, and the making of the modern drama. Grove Press 1994 xx, 732p il pa $20 hardcover o.p.
   92
ISBN 0-8021-3910-8 (pa)   LC 93-23051

The author "believes Brecht wrote very little in the dramas that made him famous; rather, he systematically plagiarized and 'collaborated' with lovers and colleagues by signing his name to plays they essentially wrote. . . . Fuegi's massive effort examines every aspect of Brecht's career and personality, and ranges from his childhood in Augsburg through his early successes and his exile to his return to East Germany." Booklist

Includes bibliographical references

Breslin, Jimmy

Breslin, Jimmy. I want to thank my brain for remembering me; a memoir. Little, Brown 1996 219p pa $12.95 hardcover o.p.   **92**
ISBN 0-316-11879-6 (pa)   LC 96-10488

"Confronting the possibility of death just past age 65 . . . Breslin memory-surfs through a troubled childhood and a lifetime in various journalistic trenches, from copyboy to columnist. . . . The book is full of family stories, political stories, and classic Breslin street stories, plus lots of details about brain operations from both patient's and surgeon's point of view." Booklist

Brinkley, John Richard, 1885-1942

Brock, Pope. Charlatan; America's most dangerous huckster, the man who pursued him, and the age of flimflam. Crown Publishers 2008 324p il $24.95 **92**

1. Quacks and quackery
ISBN 978-0-307-33988-1; 0-307-33988-2
LC 2007-10074

Tells the story of the little-known Dr. John Brinkley and his unquenchable thirst for fame and fortune and Morris Fishbein, a quackbuster extraordinaire who relentlessly pursued the greatest charlatan of the 1920s and 1930s.

"Presentation is everything in telling this elaborate, many-faceted story. And Mr. Brock's has three outstanding virtues. First of all, he has a terrific ear for singling out quotations. . . . Second, he is selective. This fast-moving, light-stepping book takes care not to throw in extraneous detail. Third, his own voice is wry enough to compete with the actual Brinkley material, which is saying a great deal." N Y Times (Late N Y Ed)

Includes bibliographical references

Brokaw, Tom, 1940-

Brokaw, Tom. A long way from home; growing up in the American heartland. Random House 2002 272p $24.95; pa $12.95 **92**

1. Journalists
ISBN 0-375-50763-9; 0-375-75935-2 (pa)
LC 2002-31865

News anchor Brokaw "shares the events, tone, and tenor of his midwestern upbringing." Booklist

"Peppered with photographs . . . this tribute to an idyllic childhood should please Brokaw's loyal fans." Publ Wkly

Brontë, Charlotte, 1816-1855

Gaskell, Elizabeth Cleghorn. The life of Charlotte Brontë; [by] Elizabeth Gaskell; edited with an introduction and notes by Angus Eason. Oxford University Press 2001 xxxvi, 587p (Oxford world's classics) pa $13.95 **92**

1. Authors, English 2. Women authors
ISBN 0-19-283805-9
First published 1857

"Mrs. Gaskell was herself a popular novelist, who commanded a very wide audience. She brought to bear upon the biography of Charlotte Bronte all those literary gifts which had made the charm of her seven volumes of romance. . . . It is quite certain that Charlotte Bronte would not stand on so splendid a pedestal today but for the single-minded devotion of her accomplished biographer." Clement K. Shorter

Includes bibliographical references

Gordon, Lyndall. Charlotte Brontë; a passionate life. Norton 1995 418p il pa $17 hardcover o.p. **92**

1. Authors, English 2. Women authors
ISBN 0-393-31448-0 (pa)
First published 1994 in the United Kingdom

The author "dismantles once and for all the image of Charlotte Brontë as a figure of pathos and presents, instead, a courageous survivor, a determined writer, and a woman of volcanic emotion. . . . Gordon, as skilled at literary analysis as at chronicling a life, approaches Brontë's tragic and enduringly relevant story from several angles, carefully identifying all the autobiographical elements of her novels and contrasting her commitment to writing and her independent spirit to her era's strict and pitiless code of behavior for women." Booklist

Includes bibliographical references

Brown, Claude, 1937-2002

Brown, Claude. Manchild in the promised land. Touchstone 1999 415p pa $14.95 **92**

1. African Americans—Biography 2. African Americans—Harlem (New York, N.Y.)
ISBN 0-684-86418-5
First published 1965 by Macmillan

This is "the autobiography of a young black man raised in Harlem. It is a realistic description of life in the ghetto. . . . The core of the book concerns the 'plague' of heroin addiction that swept through Harlem in the 1950s taking the lives of many of Brown's contemporaries." Publ Wkly

Brown, James

Brown, James. James Brown, the godfather of soul; by James Brown with Bruce Tucker; new introduction by Bruce Tucker; epilogue by Dave Marsh. Thunder's Mouth Press 1997 352p il pa $14.95 **92**

1. African American singers
ISBN 978-1-56025-115-6; 1-56025-115-8
LC 90-31961

First published 1986 by Macmillan

"Brown's musical career spans four decades and his style defines the genre called soul. He has chronicled his life, from his birth in 1933 through a troubled youth, prison, and the ups and downs of a spiraling career." Libr J

This "is a solid, informative autobiography, and fans will welcome its vast discography." N Y Times Book Rev

Includes discography

Brown, James, 1957-

Brown, James. The Los Angeles diaries; a memoir. Morrow 2003 200p $21.95; pa $12.95 **92**

ISBN 0-06-052151-1; 0-06-052152-X (pa)
LC 2003-48779

This is the author's "memoir of growing up with an emotionally disturbed mother and then drifting with his brother and sister into addiction even as he crafted award-winning stories. Looking back from the uncertain shore of sobriety, Brown alternates between his troubled childhood and even more troubling adulthood." Booklist

"Brown's revelations have no smugness or self-congratulation; they reek of remorse and desire, passion and futility. . . . The result is a grimly exquisite memoir that reads like a noir novel but grips unrelentingly like the hand of a homeless drunk begging for help." Publ Wkly

Brown, John, 1800-1859

Reynolds, David S. John Brown, abolitionist; the man who killed slavery, sparked the Civil War, and seeded civil rights. Alfred A. Knopf 2005 578p il $35   **92**
1. Abolitionists
ISBN 0-375-41188-7   LC 2004-48864

This biography contends "that Brown's most violent acts—his slaughter of unarmed citizens in Kansas, his liberation of slaves in Missouri, and his . . . raid in October 1859, on the federal arsenal at Harpers Ferry, Virginia—were inspired by the slave revolts, guerrilla warfare, and revolutionary Christianity of the day." Publisher's note

"Almost every page forces you to think hard, and in new ways, about American violence, American history, and what used to be called the American character." New Yorker

Includes bibliographical references

Brown, Carolyn

Brown, Carolyn. Chance and circumstance; twenty years with Cage and Cunningham. Alfred A. Knopf 2007 645p il $37.50 *   **92**
1. Cage, John 2. Cunningham, Merce
ISBN 978-0-394-40191-1; 0-394-40191-3
LC 2006-48799

The author "traces the trajectory of her modern dance career with that organization during its crawling stages in the 1950s and 1960s, when composer John Cage was musical director and artist Robert Rauschenberg was set and costume designer. Brown documents the company's early struggles for acceptance (it was considered avant-garde), various tours, and eventual world recognition. . . . This book will appeal to modern dance buffs and memoir readers." Libr J

Bryan, William Jennings, 1860-1925

Kazin, Michael. A godly hero; the life of William Jennings Bryan. Knopf 2006 374p il hardcover o.p. pa $16.95   **92**
ISBN 0-375-41135-6; 978-0-385-72056-4 (pa); 0-385-72056-4 (pa)   LC 2005-44105

The author "attempts a revisionist portrait of Bryan (1860-1925), whom scholars have long dismissed as a rabid white supremacist, bullying fundamentalist and braying pacifist/isolationist." Publ Wkly

"Kazin is not the first biographer to tackle the Great Commoner, but he is definitely the best writer among them. 'A Godly Hero' is a richly textured narrative with an excellent pace." Christ Sci Monit

Includes bibliographical references

Bryant, Bear

Barra, Allen. The last coach: a life of Paul "Bear" Bryant. W. W. Norton & Co. 2005 xxix, 546p il $26.95   **92**
ISBN 0-393-05982-0   LC 2005-14609

The author "focuses on Paul (Bear) Bryant, the legendary head coach at the University of Alabama from 1958 to 1982 and the winner of six national championships with the Crimson Tide." N Y Times Book Rev

"Readers will experience an array of emotions—humor, sadness, inspiration, awe—as Barra reveals his subject's contributions to college football and ability to touch and inspire people long after their associations with Bryant ended." Libr J

Includes bibliographical references

Bryson, Bill

Bryson, Bill. The life and times of the thunderbolt kid; a memoir. Broadway Books 2006 270p il $25   **92**
ISBN 0-7679-1936-X; 978-0-7679-1936-4
LC 2006-43859

The author "recounts the world of his younger self, buried in comic books in the Kiddie Corral at the local supermarket, resisting civil defense drills at school, and fruitlessly trying to unravel the mysteries of sex. . . . The larger world of 1950s America emerges through the lens of 'Billy's' world, including the dark underbelly of racism, the fight against communism, and the advent of the nuclear age." Libr J

"This affectionate portrait wistfully recalls the bygone days of Burns and Allen and downtown department stores but with a good-natured elbow poke to the ribs." Booklist

Includes bibliographical references

Buber, Martin, 1878-1965

Friedman, Maurice S. Encounter on the narrow ridge: a life of Martin Buber; [by] Maurice Friedman. Paragon House 1991 496p il $22.95; pa $18.95   **92**
ISBN 1-55778-453-1; 1-55778-596-1 (pa)
LC 90-44502

This biography (based on the author's three volume Martin Buber's life and work) "traces Buber's career showing the pivotal events in his life as well as the influences of Judaism, Christianity, general philosophical thought, and linguistics on his writings and lectures. Friedman analyzes succinctly, but with great care, Buber's responses to the important events of the 20th century." Libr J

Includes bibliographical references

Buckley, William F., 1925-2008

Buckley, William F. Miles gone by; a literary autobiography; [by] William F. Buckley Jr. Regnery Pub. 2004 594p il $29.95; pa $18.95   **92**
ISBN 0-89526-089-1; 0-89526-004-2 (pa)
LC 2004-7170

Includes computer optical disk

This autobiography consists of "a selection of 50 essays between a brief preface and epilogue. The extracts range in subject from his silver-spoon boyhood and boarding-school days to the lives and deaths of the many prominent people he has known." Publ Wkly

This "is an elegant book, one of Buckley's best, and the man the reader meets in these pages is the Platonic ideal of a dinner companion, a raconteur whose pomposity is calculated and whose self-deprecation charms." N Y Times Book Rev

Buckley, William F., 1925-2008—*Continued*
Buckley, William F. Nearer, my God; an autobiography of faith. Harcourt Brace & Co. 1998 xx, 313p il pa $14 * **92**
  ISBN 0-15-600618-9   LC 98-16194
  "A Harvest book"
  First published 1997 by Doubleday
  Buckley's book is "part memoir, part commentary on religious issues past and present." Time
  "As we might expect, Nearer My God is rich in anecdote, witty, and animated by what Buckley refers to as his 'polemical inclinations.'. . . But what gives it unity as a book, and not just a loose collection of pieces bound in cloth, is the warmth and the depth of Buckley's faith, at once complex and many-sided." Christ Today

Buffalo Bill, 1846-1917
Carter, Robert A. Buffalo Bill Cody; the man behind the legend. Wiley 2000 496p il hardcover o.p. pa $18.95 **92**
  1. Entertainers 2. Frontier and pioneer life—West (U.S.)
  ISBN 0-471-31996-1; 0-471-07780-1 (pa)
                                   LC 00-20368
  The author "explores Buffalo Bill's life, moving from his childhood to his marriage to his years as a scout, expert marksman, peerless Buffalo hunter, and, finally, entrepreneur-entertainer to the world." Libr J
  This is "a stolid sifting of facts from fiction." Booklist
  Includes bibliographical references

Warren, Louis S. Buffalo Bill's America; William Cody and the Wild West Show. Alfred A. Knopf 2005 652p il $30 **92**
  1. Entertainers 2. Frontier and pioneer life
  ISBN 0-375-41216-6   LC 2004-63280
  This is a biography of the American showman.
  This book "is well written and exhaustively researched, the weightiest and surely the most ambitious book ever published about Cody and his times." N Y Times Book Rev
  Includes bibliographical references

Bundrum, Charlie, d. 1958
Bragg, Rick. Ava's man. Knopf 2001 259p $25; pa $13 **92**
  ISBN 0-375-41062-7; 0-375-72444-3 (pa)
                                   LC 2001-32677
  In this account of his maternal grandfather's life as a roofer and bootlegger in Appalachia, the author "creates a soulful, poignant portrait of working-class Southern life." Publ Wkly

Bundy, Ted
Rule, Ann. The stranger beside me. Updated 20th anniversary ed. Signet 2001 548p il pa $7.99 **92**
  1. Criminals
  ISBN 0-451-20326-7; 978-0-451-20326-7
  "A Signet book"
  First published 1980 by Norton
  This is a biography of Ted Bundy, written by someone who "worked a suicide hotline in Seattle with Ted Bundy, not knowing he was a serial killer." Libr J

Burroughs, Augusten
Burroughs, Augusten. Running with scissors; a memoir. St. Martin's Press 2002 304p $23.95; pa $14 * **92**
  ISBN 0-312-28370-9; 0-312-42227-X (pa)
                                   LC 2001-58857
  In this memoir the author recalls his youth with a mentally ill mother, living with his mother's psychiatrist in a chaotic household, and his early homosexual experiences
  "Burroughs tempers the pathos with sharp, riotous humor in stories that are self-deprecating, raunchy, sexually explicit." Booklist

Burton, Isabel, Lady, 1831-1896
Lovell, Mary S. A rage to live: a biography of Richard and Isabel Burton. See entry under Burton, Sir Richard Francis, 1821-1890

Burton, Sir Richard Francis, 1821-1890
Lovell, Mary S. A rage to live: a biography of Richard and Isabel Burton. Norton 1998 910p il pa $19.95 hardcover o.p. **92**
  1. Burton, Isabel, Lady, 1831-1896
  ISBN 0-393-32039-1 (pa)   LC 98-29886
  This is a "dual biography of Victorian explorer/author Richard Burton and his equally adventurous wife, Isabel, using research materials not previously available." Libr J
  This is "a readable narrative of great verve and passion." N Y Rev Books
  Includes bibliographical references

Bush, Barbara, 1925-
Bush, Barbara. Barbara Bush; a memoir. Scribner 1994 575p il $25; pa $16 **92**
  1. Bush, George, 1924-
  ISBN 0-02-519635-9; 0-7432-5447-3 (pa)
                                   LC 94-13829
  Also available in paperback from St. Martin's Press
  "A Lisa Drew book"
  The former "First Lady, one of the most popular in modern history, gives the reader a tour through her life story and the parallel universe of the political spouse." NY Times Book Rev

Bush, George, 1924-
Bush, Barbara. Barbara Bush. See entry under Bush, Barbara, 1925-

Bush, George. All the best, George Bush; my life in letters and other writings. Scribner 1999 640p il $30; pa $16 **92**
  1. Presidents—United States
  ISBN 0-684-83958-X; 0-7432-0041-1 (pa)
                                   LC 99-40440
  "A Lisa Drew book"
  The former president presents his autobiography in the form of annotated letters, memos, journal entries, and speeches written between 1942 and March 1999
  This work "is refreshing and, in many ways, will shed

Bush, George, 1924-—*Continued*
more light on the man's personal character and public persona than any memoir or biography could. It offers an intriguing picture of a man who takes fierce pride in his modesty." Publ Wkly

Parmet, Herbert S. George Bush; the life of a Lone Star Yankee; with a new introduction by the author. Transaction Pubs. 2001 576p il (American presidents) pa $29.95   **92**
1. Presidents—United States
ISBN 0-7658-0730-0; 978-0-7658-0730-4
LC 00-42597
First published 1997 by Scribner
This biography of the forty-first president of the United States details his "climb up the business and political ladder in Texas . . . [then focuses on his] first runs for office, in 1964, when he faced a problem that dogged him his entire career: convincing right-wing Republicans that he was a true-blue Goldwater conservative. But he wasn't, and Parmet astutely analyzes both the contributors to and the forces within the Republican Party with which the unideological Bush had to contend." Booklist
Includes bibliographical references

Bush, George W.
Bruni, Frank. Ambling into history: the unlikely odyssey of George W. Bush. HarperCollins Pubs. 2002 278p pa $12.95 hardcover o.p.   **92**
1. Presidents—United States
ISBN 0-06093782-3 (pa)
The author, who covered Bush's 2000 presidential campaign for the New York Times, focuses on Bush's personality and mannerisms as well as his basic interactions with family, friends, and the public.
"Given [Bruni's] familiarity with Bush, one would expect his book to contain revealing insights, and this superb, incisive, and surprising account does not disappoint." Booklist
Includes bibliographical references

Minutaglio, Bill. First son: George W. Bush and the Bush family dynasty. Times Bks. 1999 371p il pa $14 hardcover o.p.   **92**
1. Presidents—United States
ISBN 0-609-80867-2 (pa)   LC 99-16462
In this political biography the "author traces the Bush family history from Prescott to George to First Son. This family dynasty has been of great assistance to George W. as he is called, in his rise in business and politics. While giving surprisingly little attention to George W.'s performance as governor of Texas . . . the author focuses on his development as a young man and emergence into the national political limelight." Libr J

Byron, George Gordon Byron, 6th Baron, 1788-1824
Eisler, Benita. Byron—child of passion, fool of fame. Knopf 1999 837p il pa $18 hardcover o.p.   **92**
ISBN 0-679-74085-6 (pa)   LC 98-35261
Eisler's "biography portrays Byron as a restless, brilliant man in thrall: he is, in her view, the puppet of his own extravagant passions and even in his lifetime was so fictionalized and mythologized by others that he found it hard to maintain his own sense of self." Publ Wkly
"This is a splendidly readable biography of a perpetually fascinating genius." Atl Mon
Includes bibliographical references

Caesar, Julius, 100-44 B.C.
Goldsworthy, Adrian Keith. Caesar; life of a colossus; [by] Adrian Goldsworthy. Yale University Press 2006 583p il map $35 *
     92
1. Rome—History
ISBN 978-0-300-12048-6; 0-300-12048-6
LC 2006-922060
This biography draws "together Julius Caesar's personal, political, and military history into a single volume. . . . This is an engaging and well-drawn resource for those who wish to be introduced to the man who was Caesar." Libr J
Includes bibliographical references

Cagney, James, 1899-1986
McCabe, John. Cagney. Carroll & Graf Pub. 1999 439p il pa $18.95   **92**
1. Actors
ISBN 978-0-7867-0580-1; 0-7867-0580-9
First published 1997 by Knopf
"The author traces Cagney's life from his poor beginnings with an alcoholic father but fiercely determined mother through his unexpected drift into vaudeville and the theater to his slow but inevitable rise to film stardom." Libr J
This work "exceeds the typical standards of celebrity biography because McCabe is fully attentive to the many dimensions of his subject's artistry." Commonweal
Includes filmography and bibliographical references

Callas, Maria, 1923-1977
Gage, Nicholas. Greek fire; the story of Maria Callas and Aristotle Onassis. Knopf 2000 xxi, 422p il $26.95; pa $7.99   **92**
1. Onassis, Aristotle Socrates, 1906-1975
ISBN 0-375-40244-6; 0-446-61076-3 (pa)
LC 00-40553
The author traces "Onassis's and Callas's pasts, their relationship, and the Jackie Kennedy years." Libr J
This "biography is perhaps the most understanding of La Callas yet to be published, and its appeal will extend beyond opera lovers to anyone with an interest in the lives of the rich and famous." Booklist
Includes bibliographical references

Scott, Michael. Maria Meneghini Callas. Northeastern Univ. Press 1992 372p il $29.95
     92
ISBN 1-55553-146-6   LC 92-17103
The author "traces the career of the controversial diva from her teenage appearances as a budding prima donna through the triumphs of the early 1950s to later years when Callas's voice was increasingly frail." Publ Wkly
"We come away from this critical biography with a

Callas, Maria, 1923-1977—*Continued*
sound understanding of Callas' complicated personal life
and her total commitment to her instrument and career."
Booklist

Includes bibliographical references

Camus, Albert, 1913-1960
Todd, Olivier. Albert Camus; a life; translated
by Benjamin Ivry. abr & ed English version.
Knopf 1997 434p il $30   **92**
1. Authors, French
ISBN 0-679-42855-0   LC 97-2991
Also available in paperback from Carroll & Graf
Pubs.
"A Borzoi Bk."
Original French edition, 1996
This is a biography of the French novelist, playwright,
literary editor, and philosopher.
"Todd's exhaustive biography, which aims—and suc-
ceeds—in presenting 'the man' and not just the writer,
has been shortened for its English translation, which re-
fers readers to the French edition for notes, sources and
bibliography." Publ Wkly

Capone, Al, 1899-1947
Bergreen, Laurence. Capone; the man and the
era. Simon & Schuster 1994 701p il pa $19
hardcover o.p.   **92**
ISBN 0-684-82447-7 (pa)   LC 94-5941
Bergreen "traces Capone's childhood in Brooklyn, his
entry into organized crime and his violent rise to the top
of the Chicago crime world. He focuses on Capone's
battles with law-enforcement agencies that eventually resulted, in 1931, in his conviction on tax evasion charges
and imprisonment at Alcatraz." Publ Wkly
"Mr. Bergreen has written a book objective and rigorous enough to meet scholarly standards, yet colorful
enough to engross the general reader." N Y Times Book
Rev

Includes bibliographical references

Capote, Truman, 1924-1984
Capote, Truman. Too brief a treat; the letters of
Truman Capote; edited by Gerald Clarke. Random
House 2004 487p il $27.95; pa $16 *
                                                92
ISBN 0-375-50133-9; 0-375-70241-5 (pa)
                                        LC 2004-50313
The author's letters "center on his daily life and the
life shared with Jack Dunphy (the man who anchored
Capote's entire adult life) and their work—especially the
time and effort invested in Capote's most publicized
book, In Cold Blood." Libr J
"Capote's untrammeled personality fairly falls off the
pages of these letters, and rather than being irritating, his
disregard of reticence is especially poignant in this day
of sterile e-mailing. Ideal for devotees to dip into here
and there instead of reading from start to finish."
Booklist

Includes bibliographical references

Plimpton, George. Truman Capote; in which
various friends, enemies, acquaintances, and
detractors recall his turbulent career. Talese 1997
498p il pa $16.95 hardcover o.p.   **92**
ISBN 0-385-49173-5 (pa)   LC 97-14792
This book of recollections of the American writer
"proceeds more or less chronologically, from Capote's
Alabama childhood in the 1920s to his . . . death in Los
Angeles in 1984." Times Lit Suppl
"The book is an intoxicating swirl of contradictory
stories, serious analysis and rumors, adroitly edited in
chapters arranged like those of a picaresque novel." Publ
Wkly

Caravaggio, Michelangelo Merisi da, 1573-1610
Langdon, Helen. Caravaggio; a life. Westview
Press 2000 436p il map pa $22   **92**
1. Artists, Italian
ISBN 0-8133-3794-1; 978-0-8133-3794-4
First published 1998 in the United Kingdom
In this study of the Renaissance painter, "Langdon's
masterly achievement is to integrate Caravaggio's art and
life in a convincing and vividly delineated recreation of
his world." Libr J

Includes bibliographical references

Prose, Francine. Caravaggio; painter of miracles.
Atlas Books/HarperCollins 2005 149p il (Eminent
lives) $21.95   **92**
1. Artists, Italian
ISBN 0-06-057560-3   LC 2005-40203
"A contemporary of Shakespeare, Caravaggio was
'belligerent, contemptuous, and competitive,' a revered
artist and a notorious street fighter wanted for murder
who died at 39 under tragic circumstances. Much has
been written about Caravaggio and his dramatic paintings, especially his daringly earthy depictions of biblical
scenes, but somehow Prose's concentrated interpretation
has a stronger impact. Not only does she cover all the
biographical essentials but she also more clearly and descriptively explicates the pioneering painter's unique perception of the miraculous in everyday life. Prose also reveals, with both subtlety and flourish, how Caravaggio's
frank interpretations of violence and pain, fear and grief,
dignity and transcendence are matched with a brilliant
subversion of our sense of reality." Booklist

Robb, Peter. M: the man who became
Caravaggio. Holt & Co. 2000 570p il pa $20
                                                92
1. Artists, Italian
ISBN 0-8050-6356-0; 978-0-312-27474-0 (pa);
0-312-27474-2 (pa)   LC 99-43576
"A John Macrae book"
First published 1998 in Australia
The author examines the life and work of the Italian
painter
Robb's "mettlesome assertions regarding M's ruthless-
ness, 'hairtriggered touchiness,' resiliency, and homosexuality, as well as his confident theories regarding his
crimes and punishments, make for great narrative vitality
and drama." Booklist

Includes bibliographical references

Carmichael, Hoagy, 1899-1982

Sudhalter, Richard. Stardust melody: the life and music of Hoagy Carmichael; [by] Richard M. Sudhalter. Oxford Univ. Press 2002 432p il hardcover o.p. pa $18.95 **92**
1. Jazz musicians
ISBN 0-19-513120-7; 0-19-516898-4 (pa)
LC 2001-34612
"Among the legends of American popular music, Carmichael, composer of such standards as 'Star Dust' and 'Skylark,' is not getting his due, argues the author, who intends to rectify this injustice. The result is a thorough and engaging profile of the great American composer and performer." Booklist
Includes bibliographical references

Carnegie, Andrew, 1835-1919

Krass, Peter. Carnegie. Wiley 2002 612p il $35; pa $19.95 **92**
ISBN 0-471-38630-8; 0-471-46883-5 (pa)
LC 2002-10162
"From bobbin boy in a cotton mill to one of American history's most famous characters, Carnegie's life was one of contradictions. In his lifetime, Carnegie gave away a staggering $350 million, setting a standard for social conscience. Krass used original sources such as letters, diaries, and other writings by primary and peripheral characters in Carnegie's life to penetrate the public persona and show the man who crusaded for universal literacy and world peace." Booklist
Includes bibliographical references

Nasaw, David. Andrew Carnegie. Penguin Press 2006 878p il $35; pa $20 **92**
ISBN 1-59420-104-8; 0-14-311244-9 (pa)
LC 2006-44840
This is a biography of the Scottish-born businessman and philanthropist. Carnegie was the founder of the Carnegie Steel Company which later became U.S. Steel.
"Highly readable despite it's length, 'Andrew Carnegie' shows signs of prodigious original research on almost every page." N Y Times (Late N Y Ed)
Includes bibliographical references

Wall, Joseph Frazier. Andrew Carnegie. University of Pittsburgh Press 1989 1137p il pa $22.50 hardcover o.p. **92**
ISBN 0-8229-5904-6 (pa)
LC 88-38160
A reissue of the title first published 1970 by Oxford University Press
This biography follows Carnegie from his boyhood in Scotland through his emigration to America, his rise in the business world, and his early ventures in oil, railroads, telegraphy, and the iron and steel industries
Includes bibliographical references

Carroll, Lewis, 1832-1898

Cohen, Morton Norton. Lewis Carroll; a biography; by Morton N. Cohen. Knopf 1995 xxiii, 577p il pa $14.36 hardcover o.p. *
92
ISBN 0-679-74562-9 (pa)
LC 95-2663

Cohen begins by "tracing Dodgson's early years up through his most productive decade, the 1860s, . . . then retraces his steps in order to examine Dodgson's achievements and personality." Booklist
"Delightfully illustrated with photographs and Carroll's drawings woven throughout, this extraordinary, meticulous biography gives us a sharper and deeper picture of Carroll than any before, presenting a many-sided man." Publ Wkly

Carson, Rachel, 1907-1964

Lear, Linda J. Rachel Carson; witness for nature; [by] Linda Lear. Holt & Co. 1997 634p il pa $20 hardcover o.p. **92**
1. Environmental movement
ISBN 0-8050-3428-5 (pa)
LC 97-8324
"Lear traces the path of Carson's determined, self-sacrificing life from her nature-struck youth to her dream of becoming a writer, her focus on science instead of literature in college, her unusual career as a government scientist, and, coming full circle, her transformation into a 'literary sensation.'" Booklist
This "is the most exhaustive account so far of Carson's private, professional and public lives." N Y Times Book Rev
Includes bibliographical references

Lytle, Mark H. The gentle subversive; Rachel Carson, Silent spring, and the rise of the environmental movement. Oxford University Press 2007 277p il $23; $12.95 **92**
1. Environmental movement
ISBN 978-0-19-517246-1; 0-19-517246-9; 978-0-19-517247-8 (pa); 0-19-517247-7 (pa)
LC 2006-49350
The author "examines the life of Rachel Carson, founder of today's environmental movement and antithesis of the stereotypical 1950s woman. Carson was educated in the sciences, worked full time, and was her family's primary provider and caregiver. Genteel in appearance, she was firmly committed to her goal of preserving nature. Using a lyrical, narrative style, Lytle probes Carson's interests and her purposes in writing a series of wellknown books that include The Sea Around Usand her most famous, Silent Spring." Libr J
Includes bibliographical references

Carter, Jimmy, 1924-

Carter, Jimmy. Everything to gain; making the most of the rest of your life; [by] Jimmy and Rosalynn Carter. University of Arkansas Press 1995 176p pa $21.95 **92**
1. Presidents—United States
ISBN 978-1-55728-388-7; 1-55728-388-5
First published 1987 by Random House
"The former president and First Lady alternate first-person reminiscences with sections written jointly to tell the story of their lives after leaving the White House in 1980. Frankly acknowledging the trauma of the lost election, the Carters record their efforts to overcome the difficulties of making a fresh start while deeply in debt, adjusting to life in a small house in Plains, Ga., and other challenges." Publ Wkly

Carter, Jimmy, 1924-—*Continued*

Carter, Jimmy. An hour before daylight; memories of my rural boyhood. Simon & Schuster 2001 284p il hardcover o.p. pa $15   **92**
  1. Carter family 2. Georgia—Social life and customs 3. Presidents—United States
  ISBN 0-7432-1193-6; 0-7432-1199-5 (pa)
                         LC 00-48248

In this memoir, the thirty-ninth president of the United States remembers his childhood in rural Georgia.

This "is social and agricultural history as plain and honest as one of the tables the author makes in his workshop—an American classic." New Yorker

Carter, Jimmy. Keeping faith: memoirs of a president. University of Ark. Press 1995 633p il pa $34.95   **92**
  1. Presidents—United States
  ISBN 1-55728-330-3   LC 95-9691

A reissue of the title first published 1982 by Bantam Bks.

These memoirs treat such matters as "improving relations with China; enacting energy legislation; negotiating the second Strategic Arms Limitation treaty (SALT II); concluding the Panama Canal treaties; and convincing Menachem Begin and Anwar Sadat to reach agreement at Camp David. Carter also devotes more than a quarter of the book to the frustrations arising from the capture of hostages in Tehran." N Y Rev Books

Carter, Jimmy. Living faith. Times Bks. 1996 256p pa $13 hardcover o.p.   **92**
  1. Presidents—United States
  ISBN 0-8129-3034-7 (pa)   LC 96-20993

In this "spiritual autobiography, the former president . . . traces the growth and development of his faith through his career in the Navy and various political offices, and through his work with Habitat for Humanity (which builds housing for poor Americans) and the Carter Center (an international peacemaking organization). Carter also discusses the impact that Soren Kierkegaard and Reinhold Niebuhr have had on his life." Publ Wkly

Carter, Jimmy. Sharing good times. Simon & Schuster 2004 174p $21; pa $13   **92**
  1. Presidents—United States
  ISBN 0-7432-7033-9; 0-7432-7068-1 (pa)
                    LC 2004-51351

The author "recalls various occasions in his life that became 'lasting sources of pleasure.' . . . [These remembrances] include his personal reasons for seeing his father as a hero, watching minor and major-league baseball games growing up, his days in the navy, road trips with his wife and children, his entry into politics, taking vacations while in the White House, his famous volunteer work, and even his hobbies." Booklist

Morris, Kenneth Earl. Jimmy Carter, American moralist; {by} Kenneth E. Morris. University of Ga. Press 1996 397p il $29.95; pa $19.95
                               92
  1. Presidents—United States
  ISBN 0-8203-1862-0; 0-8203-1949-X (pa)
                    LC 96-6350

The author asserts that "the Carter family is not quite the downhome, folksy clan of campaign advertising; they were actually rural gentry perched atop their county's segregated social pyramid. Members of the family were internally estranged, according to Morris, and Jimmy was a loner—a persona confirmed at Annapolis, where he left no discernible impression besides good grades. Yet Carter surmounted these aspects of himself and his background to become a gregarious integrationist, an indefatigable campaigner, and after a 1966 electoral defeat, a born-again Christian." Booklist

Includes bibliographical references

Carter, Robert, 1728-1804

Levy, Andrew. The first emancipator; the forgotten story of Robert Carter, the founding father who freed his slaves. Random House 2005 310p $25.95   **92**
  ISBN 0-375-50865-1   LC 2004-54054

The author "examines the unique life of Robert Carter III, one of the wealthiest men in 18th-century America, and his monumental 'Deed of Gift.' This legal document, recorded in 1791, allowed for the largest single emancipation of slaves until the Emancipation Proclamation." Libr J

"This well-written and thoroughly engaging book will certainly appeal to readers interested in the history of 18th- and 19th-century Virginia, but also to those interested in the history of slavery and racism in America and in historical biography." Publ Wkly

Includes bibliographical references

Carter, Rubin

Hirsch, James S. Hurricane: the miraculous journey of Rubin Carter. Houghton Mifflin 2000 358p il $25; pa $14   **92**
  ISBN 0-395-97985-4; 0-618-08728-1 (pa)
                    LC 99-52703

"In 1967, Rubin 'Hurricane' Carter, a black boxing champion and high-profile citizen of Paterson, New Jersey, and his friend John Artis were falsely convicted of the triple murders of three white people in a local bar. Each man spent almost 20 years in prison before being exonerated. . . . [This biography] briefly recounts Carter's youth and his boxing career before settling into the nightmare that began on that fateful night in 1967." Booklist

"Scrupulously researched and expertly crafted, Hirsch's updated account of Carter's life is both a rich portrait of a complex man and a clear-eyed telling of a remarkable life." Publ Wkly

Carver, Raymond

Halpert, Sam. Raymond Carver; an oral biography. University of Iowa Press 1995 196p $32.95; pa $17.95   **92**
  ISBN 0-87745-502-3; 0-87745-503-1 (pa)
                    LC 94-46555

This is a "remembrance of Carver by his family, friends, and fellow writers. . . . These reminiscences include many insights into the sources and literary qualities of his writings. This highly readable oral biography is an expanded and rearranged version of *When We Talk About Raymond Carver* (Gibbs Smith, 1991)." Libr J

Cash, Johnny
Streissguth, Michael. Johnny Cash; the biography. Da Capo Press 2006 334p il $26
                                    92
   ISBN 0-306-81368-8   LC 2006-101191
   This is a biography of the country singer and song-writer.
   The author "leaves us mightily impressed with the volume of Cash's work and the convictions that animate it, and perhaps even more impressed by Cash's endurance of his own self-destructiveness. . . . Streissguth gives everyone interested in Cash a very satisfying book about him." Booklist
   Includes bibliographical references

Cassady, Neal
Sandison, David. Neal Cassady; the fast life of a beat hero; [by] David Sandison and Graham Vickers. Chicago Review Press 2006 340p il $24.95 *   **92**
   1. Beat generation
   ISBN 978-1-55652-615-2; 1-55652-615-6
                           LC 2006-9112
   "Drawing on Cassady's correspondence, interviews with those who knew him, and previous works by memoirist Carolyn Cassady (the subject's widow), biographer Tom Christopher, and others, Sandison and Vickers portray Cassady as all too human—a desperate, lost soul who was plagued by contradictions and sought personal fulfillment and spiritual salvation. Debunking the mythology that grew up around Cassady as a result of his appearance in works by Kerouac, Ken Kesey, and Tom Wolfe, the authors attempt to separate the life from the legend. They present Cassady as someone who wanted to be a good husband and father but was unable to conquer his demons, which included sex, drugs, gambling, and an innate restlessness. Ironically, it was these very demons that ensured Cassady's place in American literature." Libr J
   Includes bibliographical references

Cassatt, Mary, 1844-1926
Mathews, Nancy Mowll. Mary Cassatt; a life. Yale Univ. Press 1998 383p il pa $21   **92**
   1. Artists—United States
   ISBN 0-300-07754-8   LC 98-8028
   First published 1994 by Villard Bks.
   "Mathews presents the little-known facts of Cassatt's very private life and answers the question: Why did Cassatt, single and childless, choose to make motherhood her 'signature theme'?" Publ Wkly
   This "is an evenly written, well-documented, and sympathetic—but not patronizing—biography that should be acquired by most libraries." Libr J
   Includes bibliographical references

Cassavetes, John
Fine, Marshall. Accidental genius; how John Cassavetes invented the American independent film. Miramax Books 2006 482p il $27.95
                                      92

   ISBN 1-4013-5249-9
   The author "argues that mainstream moviegoers ought to care about maverick director Cassavetes (1929-89) as the progenitor of today's American independent film movement." Booklist

Casso, Gaspipe, 1942-
Carlo, Philip. Gaspipe; confessions of a Mafia boss. William Morrow 2008 346p il $25.95
                                      92
   1. Mafia 2. Criminals 3. Organized crime
   ISBN 978-0-06-142984-2   LC 2008-2683
   The author "chronicles the extraordinary life of Lucchese family underboss Anthony 'Gaspipe' Casso." Kirkus
   "This powerful story is required reading for anyone with a yen for the Mafia, the criminal underworld and a law enforcement system struggling to keep up." Publ Wkly

Castro, Fidel, 1926-
Castro, Fidel. Fidel Castro: my life; a spoken autobiography; [by] Fidel Castro and Ignacio Ramonet; translated by Andrew Hurley. Scribner 2008 723p il map $40 *   **92**
   1. Cuba—Politics and government 2. Cuba—History—1958-1959, Revolution
   ISBN 978-1-4165-5328-1; 1-4165-5328-2
   Original Spanish edition, 2006
   Ramonet "sat down with Castro over the course of many hours, engaging him in long, involved discussions about his revolutionary life (and little about his personal life). The result is, in the words of the interviewer, Castro's 'political testament, an oral summoning-up of Fidel Castro's life by Fidel himself at almost eighty.' That rather simple description does not begin to cover the magnitude and significance of this major document. . . . By itself an incomplete history of the Cuban Revolution, to be sure, but an important—the ultimate insider view—contribution to the *complete* picture." Booklist
   Includes bibliographical references

   Coltman, Sir Leycester. The real Fidel Castro; with a foreword by Julia E. Sweig. Yale Univ. Press 2003 335p il map $30; pa $20   **92**
   1. Cuba—Politics and government
   ISBN 0-300-10188-0; 0-300-10760-9 (pa)
                            LC 2003-12942
   This biography "offers a fresh assessment of the revolutionary leader. . . . It chronicles the events of Castro's extraordinary life and explores the contradiction between the private character and the public reputation." Univ Press Books for Public and Second Sch Libr, 2004
   Includes bibliographical references

   Quirk, Robert E. Fidel Castro. Norton 1993 898p il maps pa $19.95 hardcover o.p.   **92**
   1. Cuba—Politics and government
   ISBN 0-393-31327-1 (pa)   LC 92-39300
   The author provides "a historian's interpretation of the Cuban leader's complex life and times. . . . Quirk offers detailed interpretations of Castro's personal rise to power, the failures of the Cuban Revolution, and the re-

Castro, Fidel, 1926-—*Continued*
gime's recent difficulties." Libr J

"Quirk's richly detailed, psychologically acute portrait reveals more about Castro's unique personality and character than do previous biographies." Publ Wkly

Includes bibliographical references

Szulc, Tad. Fidel; a critical portrait. Post Road Press 2000 703p map pa $18.95   **92**
1. Cuba—Politics and government
ISBN 978-0-380-80888-5; 0-380-80888-9
"An Avon book"
First published 1986 by Morrow
The author "devotes the greater part of this book to Castro's early, formative years and the forging and triumph of his revolutionary movement. The years of Castro's rule after the Bay of Pigs invasion receive briefer treatment. Well written and very readable." Choice

Includes bibliographical references

Cather, Willa, 1873-1947
Lee, Hermione. Willa Cather; double lives. Pantheon Bks. 1989 410p il pa $23 hardcover o.p.
    92
ISBN 0-679-73649-2 (pa)   LC 89-43233
"This interpretive biography . . . examines the relationship between Cather's work and her personal life." Booklist
The author's "discussion of Cather's 12 novels and numerous stories is so absorbing that it provokes a rereading of the work, which makes it a valuable critical study." N Y Times Book Rev

Includes bibliographical references

Woodress, James Leslie. Willa Cather; a literary life; {by} James Woodress. University of Neb. Press 1987 xx, 583p il pa $29.95 hardcover o.p.
    92
ISBN 0-8032-9708-4 (pa)   LC 86-30894
The author "does a fine job of describing Willa Cather's colorful public life and of piecing together the puzzle of her unconventional private life. . . . Mr. Woodress does not try to superimpose on Cather's life any theories—feminist, Freudian, Lacanian, or otherwise. Instead, he recounts in straightforward and lively prose the life of a remarkable woman." N Y Times Book Rev

Includes bibliographical references

Catherine II, the Great, Empress of Russia, 1729-1796
Catherine II, the Great, Empress of Russia. The memoirs of Catherine the Great; a new translation by Mark Cruse and Hilde Hoogenboom. Modern Library 2005 xc, 247p il map $26.95 *
    92
1. Russia—History 2. Russia—Kings and rulers
ISBN 0-679-64299-4   LC 2004-61107
Original French edition, 1859
"The memoirs cover the years before Catherine (1729-1796) became empress in 1762." Publ Wkly
This is "a source of major importance and every serious library should own it." Choice

Erickson, Carolly. Great Catherine. St. Martin's Griffin 1995 392p pa $18.95   **92**
1. Russia—History 2. Russia—Kings and rulers
ISBN 0-312-13503-3   LC 95-22619
First published 1994 by Crown
The author portrays Catherine as "a shrewd, headstrong, cultivated woman, a political reformer and supporter of education and the arts, who codified laws, built schools and asserted her independence in a land where women had low status." Publ Wkly
"Erickson's fluid, captivating portrait of Catherine the Great reads like a first-rate historical novel." Booklist

Rounding, Virginia. Catherine the Great; love, sex and power. St. Martin's Press 2007 566p il $29.95   **92**
1. Russia—History 2. Russia—Kings and rulers
ISBN 978-0-312-32887-0; 0-312-32887-7
    LC 2006-47084
First published 2006 in the United Kingdom
The author "relies on memoirs, private letters and previous monographs as she details how, after dissolution of the unhappy marriage that brought Catherine (1729-1798) to Russia from Germany, the empress juggled her relationships with men as she attempted to thrust Russia into the modern era and make it a European power. . . . [This] work will appeal to Catherine-philes and those interested in women's history." Publ Wkly

Includes bibliographical references

Troyat, Henri. Catherine the Great; translated by Joan Pinkham. Dutton 1980 377p il pa $16.95 hardcover o.p.   **92**
1. Russia—History 2. Russia—Kings and rulers
ISBN 0-452-01120-5 (pa)   LC 79-25613
Original French edition, 1977
"Relying heavily on Catherine's own memoirs, plus her correspondence with her Western idolaters-publicists, such as Friedrich Grimm, Voltaire and Diderot, Troyat gives us a portrait the Empress herself might have decreed for posterity." Publ Wkly

Includes bibliographical references

Cayce, Edgar, 1877-1945
Kirkpatrick, Sidney. Edgar Cayce; an American prophet. Riverhead Bks. 2000 564p il pa $16 hardcover o.p.   **92**
ISBN 1-57322-896-6 (pa)   LC 00-27975
"Born in 1877 in rural Christian County, Kentucky, Cayce became a professional portrait photographer, but he regularly gave 'trance readings' for the sick on the side. These readings, in which he made accurate medical diagnoses and prescribed effective treatments for thousands of patients, eventually made him famous." New Yorker
This is a "fair, fascinating, and well-researched biography of one of 20th-century America's most famous psychics." Libr J

Cézanne, Paul, 1839-1906
Rewald, John. Cezanne; a biography. Abrams 2006 288p il $75   **92**

Cézanne, Paul, 1839-1906—*Continued*
1. Artists, French
ISBN 978-0-8109-0775-1; 0-8109-0775-5
This biography of the French painter is a revised and expanded version of the author's 1936 Sorbonne doctoral dissertation. An English translation was published in 1948 by Simon & Schuster under the title: Paul Cezanne: a biography
"The artist's character is revealed in his own words and in those of his friends . . . making Cezanne accessible in a way simple narrative cannot. Adding greatly to our understanding of Cezanne's development as a painter are the 270 illustrations." Libr J [review of 1986 edition]
Includes bibliographical references

Chambers, Whittaker
Chambers, Whittaker. Witness; forewords by William F. Buckley and Robert D. Novak. 50th annivesary ed. Regnery Pub. 2001 808p pa $19.95
92
1. Communism—United States
ISBN 978-0-89526-789-4; 0-89526-789-6
First published 1952 by Random House
Whittaker Chambers' own account of his life, his connection with the Communist Party and his repudiation of it, and his role in the Hiss-Chambers trial.

Chandler, Raymond, 1888-1959
Hiney, Tom. Raymond Chandler; a biography. Atlantic Monthly Press 1997 310p il pa $14 hardcover o.p. **92**
ISBN 0-8021-3637-0 (pa)   LC 97-264
"Hiney traces the writer's nomadic childhood from pre-Mafia Chicago to pre-telephone Nebraska, from Quaker Ireland and Edwardian England to his education south of London at Dulwich College and his 1913 arrival in the 'mean streets' of Los Angeles, the later setting for his crime fiction. . . . Living at over 100 addresses, he sustained no long friendships, and was 'variously rich, poor, drunk, teetotal, sacked, married and suicidal.'. . . No rough edges have been filed off for this revealing, well-written biography." Publ Wkly
Includes bibliographical references

Chaplin, Charlie, 1889-1977
The essential Chaplin; perspectives on the life and art of the great comedian; edited with an introduction by Richard Schickel. I.R. Dee 2006 315p $27.50; pa $16.95   **92**
1. Actors 2. Motion picture producers and directors—Biography
ISBN   978-1-56663-682-7;   1-56663-682-5; 978-1-56663-701-5 (pa); 1-56663-701-5 (pa)
LC 2005-37250
"This collection of some 30 essays by such renowned figures as journalist Alistair Cooke, film critics Dilys Powell and André Bazin, statesman Winston Churchill, and novelist Graham Greene offers a . . . look into Chaplin's life and oeuvre. Each of the book's six sections explores a different period in the silent film star's career, from his earliest days to his latest features." Libr J

"The book's best feature is its organized cacophony, its trace of this astonishingly long and rich body of work and personal travail . . . in some several dozen voices of fading or lasting memory, and with countless aesthetic and ideological grudges beyond the narrow province of the movies. There is much to savor in these essays; and the book might also serve as a worthy companion to a reader's return to Chaplin's films themselves." Va Q Rev

Lynn, Kenneth S. Charlie Chaplin and his times. Cooper Square Press 2003 604p il pa $19.95 *
92
1. Actors 2. Motion picture producers and directors—Biography
ISBN 0-8154-1255-X; 978-0-8154-1255-7
LC 2002-31420
First published 1997 by Simon & Schuster
The author "interweaves Chaplin's life with the events and personalities of his era, including British music hall impresario Fred Karno, silent screen star and pal Douglas Fairbanks, numerous lovers and wives, brother Sydney, and Adolf Hitler. . . . Lynn addresses his subject's leftist views and makes sense of the House Committee on Un-American Activities investigations of 1947 that led to Chaplin's European exile until 1973. All a biography should be, this is enthusiastically recommended." Libr J
Includes bibliographical references

Scovell, Jane. Oona. See entry under Chaplin, Oona

Wranovics, John. Chaplin and Agee. See entry under Agee, James, 1909-1955

Chaplin, Oona
Scovell, Jane. Oona; living in the shadows: a biography of Oona O'Neill Chaplin. Warner Bks. 1998 354p il pa $14.99 hardcover o.p.   **92**
1. Chaplin, Charlie, 1889-1977
ISBN 0-446-67541-5 (pa)   LC 98-21592
A "biography of Oona O'Neill Chaplin, daughter of playwright Eugene O'Neill and wife of film legend Charlie Chaplin." Publ Wkly
Includes bibliographical references

Chapman, Eddie, 1914-1997
Macintyre, Ben. Agent Zigzag; a true story of Nazi espionage, love, and betrayal. Harmony Books 2007 364p il $25.95   **92**
1. World War, 1939-1945—Secret service
ISBN 978-0-307-35340-5   LC 2006-101603
This is a biography of Eddie Chapman, a British double agent during World War II.
"Meticulously researched—relying extensively on recently released wartime files of Britain's Secret Intelligence Service—Macintyre's biography often reads like a spy thriller." Publ Wkly
Includes bibliographical references

Charlemagne, Emperor, 742-814

Sypeck, Jeff. Becoming Charlemagne; Europe, Baghdad, and the empires of 800 A.D. ECCO 2006 284p il map $25.95   **92**
1. Kings and rulers
ISBN 978-0-060-79706-5; 0-06-079706-1
LC 2006-46460
"This is the story of how one medieval king named Karl was shaped and guided to become the profoundly important Emperor Charlemagne." Libr J
"An inspired, instantly readable work of popular history." Booklist
Includes bibliographical references

Wilson, Derek A. Charlemagne. Doubleday 2006 226p il map $26; pa $14.95   **92**
1. Kings and rulers
ISBN 0-385-51670-3; 0-307-27480-2 (pa)
LC 2005-48483
This biography of the Frankish emperor "demonstrates how the empire he built led to the development of the European identity." SLJ
The author "writes with clarity and passion, and his thesis is food for thought for both general readers and students." Libr J
Includes bibliographical references

Chatwin, Bruce

Shakespeare, Nicholas. Bruce Chatwin. Talese 2000 618p il $35; pa $18   **92**
ISBN 0-385-49829-2; 0-385-49830-6 (pa)
LC 99-36474
"This life of the author of 'The Songlines', who died of AIDS in 1989, portrays a man, beset with an almost biological lust for loneliness, whose singular genius was for passionate transitory connection." N Y Times Book Rev
Includes bibliographical references

Chaucer, Geoffrey, d. 1400

Ackroyd, Peter. Chaucer; Peter Ackroyd. 1st ed in the U.S.A. Nan A. Talese/Doubleday 2005 188p il (Ackroyd's brief lives) $19.95   **92**
ISBN 0-385-50797-6   LC 2004-49796
This "account of the life of Geoffrey Chaucer (1343?-1400) [is also] a consideration of his role in shaping England's national identity. The poet is hailed as the 'progenitor of a national style,' and deft literary analysis explicates Chaucer's innovations while acknowledging the influence of other poets. . . . Much is made of Chaucer's position in the royal court, which provided the financial means to live comfortably while writing his verse." Publ Wkly
Includes bibliographical references

West, Richard. Chaucer, 1340-1400; the life and times of the first English poet. Carroll & Graf Pubs. 2000 302p il map pa $14 hardcover o.p.
   92
1. Great Britain—History—1154-1399, Plantagenets
ISBN 0-7867-0925-1 (pa)   LC 00-712752
West's biography "combines history and literary criticism. He places Chaucer within his historical context and examines his life and writings." Libr J

Chekhov, Anton Pavlovich, 1860-1904

Callow, Philip. Chekhov, the hidden ground; a biography. Dee, I.R: 1998 428p il $30; pa $18.95
   92
ISBN 1-56663-187-4; 1-56663-395-8 (pa)
LC 97-46679
"Callow sees Chekhov as distant in virtually all his relationships, with romantic disillusionment and the search for intimacy recurring themes in his writing. He argues persuasively that while Chekhov's art is resplendent with human emotion, his own life was strangely cold and remote. . . . Not strictly a literary biography, this book is particularly effective in discussing Chekhov's work as it relates to his life." Libr J
Includes bibliographical references

Chekhov, Anton Pavlovich. Anton Chekhov's life and thought; selected letters and commentary; translated from the Russian by Michael Henry Heim, in collaboration with Simon Karlinsky; selection, introduction, and commentary by Simon Karlinsky. Northwestern Univ. Press 1997 494p pa $39.95   **92**
ISBN 978-0-8101-1460-9; 0-8101-1460-7
LC 96-41240
First published 1973 by Harper & Row with title: Letters of Anton Chekhov
"Out of the more than four thousand published letters of Anton Chekhov we have tried to select those that give a comprehensive picture of his literary, social and scientific interests and views." Foreword
"Karlinsky's extended commentary and detailed notes amount to a first-rate critical biography, with much unfamiliar information and arrows pointing us toward further investigation." Newsweek

Chen, Da, 1962-

Chen, Da. Colors of the mountain. Random House 1999 310p pa $13 hardcover o.p.
   92
1. China—History—1949-
ISBN 0-385-72060-2 (pa)
This is a memoir of the author's childhood. "Chen, 38, was born in a tiny village on the southeastern tip of China during the 'Year of the Great Starvation.' Because his grandfather was a wealthy landowner, his family was a prime target during the Cultural Revolution." Newsweek
"Despite the devastating circumstances of his childhood and adolescence, Chen recounts his coming of age with arresting simplicity." Publ Wkly

Chen, Da. Sounds of the river; a memoir. HarperCollins Pubs. 2002 307p pa $12.95 hardcover o.p.   **92**
1. China—History—1949-
ISBN 0-06-095872-3 (pa)   LC 2001-39215
"This book begins where Chen's . . . memoir, *Colors of the Mountain* left off. Coming from the small town of Yellow Stone in the southern province of Fujian, 16-year-old Chen moves to early 1980's Beijing to study English at the university." Publ Wkly
"Da Chen once again describes his past with fondness and buoyancy." N Y Times Book Rev

Chen, Pauline W.

Chen, Pauline W. Final exam; a surgeon's reflections on mortality. Alfred A. Knopf 2007 267p $23.95 * **92**

1. Terminal care—Ethical aspects

ISBN 978-0-307-26353-7; 0-307-26353-3

LC 2006-49361

This collection of essays "follows [the author] over the course of her education, training, and practice as she grapples at . . . with the problem of mortality, and struggles to reconcile the lessons of her training with her innate knowledge of shared humanity, and to separate her ideas about healing from her fierce desire to cure." Publisher's note

"A graceful, precise, and empathetic writer enthralled by her work, Chen imparts much about medical schooling and surgery, too." Booklist

Includes bibliographical references

Cheng, Nien, 1915-

Cheng, Nien. Life and death in Shanghai. Grove Press 1987 c1986 547p pa $16 hardcover o.p. **92**

1. China—History—1949-

ISBN 0-14-010870-X (pa)   LC 86-45254

First published 1986 in the United Kingdom

"For six and a half years, from 1966 until 1973, Nien Cheng, an upper-class Chinese widow . . . was held in solitary confinement at Shanghai Detention House No. 1, charged with espionage, but never tried. Her book . . . {is an} account of that experience and its aftermath." Ms

This "is a volume that belongs on the shelf alongside the writings of Primo Levi, Elie Wiesel, Dith Pran, and other chroniclers of ideological fanaticism, its dehumanizing consequences, and its all too rare resisters." Christ Sci Monit

Chiang, Mei-ling, 1898-2003

Li, Laura Tyson. Madame Chiang Kai-Shek; China's eternal first lady. Atlantic Monthly 2006 557p il map $30 **92**

ISBN 0-87113-933-2; 978-0-87113-933-7

LC 2005-58858

This is a biography of the wife of former Chinese president Chiang Kai-Shek.

"With access to newly opened files, fluent insights into China's convulsive transformation, and a phenomenal gift for elucidating intricate politics and complicated psyches, Li brilliantly analyzes a fearless and profoundly conflicted woman of extraordinary force." Booklist

Includes bibliographical references

Child, Julia

Child, Julia. My life in France; [by] Julia Child with Alex Prud'homme. Knopf 2006 317p il $25.95 **92**

ISBN 1-4000-4346-8; 978-1-4000-4346-0

LC 2005-44727

This is a "memoir of the famous chef's first, formative sojourn in France with her new husband, Paul Child, in 1949. . . . This is a valuable record of gorgeous meals in bygone Parisian restaurants, and the secret arts of a culinary genius." Publ Wkly

Fitch, Noel Riley. Appetite for life; the biography of Julia Child. Doubleday 1997 569p il pa $16.95 hardcover o.p. **92**

ISBN 0-385-49383-5 (pa)   LC 97-11061

This biography details the private life and professional career of PBS' The French chef, whose Mastering the art of French cooking (1961) revolutionized the American kitchen

"Fitch not only richly details Child's personal life but also effectively places her writing and television shows within the context of work by other cooking luminaries of the time. Entertaining and informative." Libr J

Includes bibliographical references

Chopin, Frédéric, 1810-1849

Eisler, Benita. Chopin's funeral. Knopf 2003 230p il $23; pa $13.95 **92**

ISBN 0-375-40945-9; 0-375-70868-5 (pa)

LC 2002-73097

"Seeking to untangle the paradoxical relationship between the shy, fragile pianist and the passionate sexual outlaw and novelist George Sand, Eisler's book underscores Chopin's illness and Sand's nursing skills, and sees a mutual attraction arising from their voracious appetite for work." N Y Times Book Rev

"Eisler is a compelling storyteller, sweeping the reader into the exhilarating milieu of Paris in the 1820s and 1830s." Libr J

Includes bibliographical references

Churchill, Sir Winston, 1874-1965

Herman, Arthur. Gandhi and Churchill; the epic rivalry that destroyed an empire and forged our age. Bantam Book 2008 721p il map $30 **92**

1. Gandhi, Mahatma, 1869-1948 2. Great Britain—Foreign relations—India 3. India—Foreign relations—Great Britain

ISBN 978-0-553-80463-8; 0-553-80463-4

LC 2008-149

This dual biography of Mahatma Gandhi and Winston Churchill focuses "on two of the most universally recognizable icons of the twentieth century, and reveals how their forty-year rivalry sealed the fate of India and the British Empire." Publisher's note

"A well-wrought historical narrative that adds significantly to our understanding of both figures." Kirkus

Includes bibliographical references

Manchester, William. The last lion, Winston Spencer Churchill; alone, 1932-1940. Little, Brown 1988 xxvi, 756p il map $50 **92**

1. Prime ministers—Great Britain 2. Great Britain—Politics and government—20th century

ISBN 0-316-54512-0   LC 82-24972

Also available in paperback from Delta

This second volume of a projected three-volume biography of the British statesman "covers the years leading up to the outbreak of World War II." Time

Includes bibliographical references

Churchill, Sir Winston, 1874-1965—*Continued*

Manchester, William. The last lion, Winston Spencer Churchill; visions of glory, 1874-1932. Little, Brown 1983 973p il maps $50 **92**
1. Prime ministers—Great Britain 2. Great Britain—Politics and government—20th century
ISBN 0-316-54503-1 LC 82-24972
Also available in paperback from Delta
This first volume of a projected three-volume biography of Churchill covers the life of the British statesman from his birth up to his split with the Conservative party over its policy regarding Indian self-rule.
Includes bibliographical references

Cicero, Marcus Tullius, 106-43 B.C.

Everitt, Anthony. Cicero; the life and times of Rome's greatest politician. Random House 2002 c2001 359p il maps pa $14.95 hardcover o.p.
92
1. Rome—History
ISBN 0-375-75895-X (pa) LC 2001-48531
The author presents the Roman orator as "a product of his age. . . . {He} scrutinizes Roman society in discussing events of the orator's life and, when describing Cicero's marriage, acquaints the reader with various aspects of that institution and the home of the era." Libr J
This "masterful biography draws on Cicero's letters to his friend Atticus to give a clear picture of the famous Roman orator, noting both his brilliance and his faults." Booklist
Includes bibliographical references

Clapton, Eric

Clapton, Eric. Clapton; the autobiography. Broadway Books 2007 343p il $26 **92**
1. Rock musicians
ISBN 978-0-385-51851-2; 0-385-51851-X
LC 2007-15482
"As he retraces every step of his career, from the early stints with the Yardbirds and Cream to his solo successes, Clapton also devotes copious detail to his drug and alcohol addictions, particularly how they intersected with his romantic obsession with Pattie Boyd. . . . Both the youthful excesses and the current calm state are narrated with an engaging tone that nudges Clapton's story ahead of other rock 'n' roll memoirs." Publ Wkly

Schumacher, Michael. Crossroads; the life and music of Eric Clapton. Citadel Press 2003 420p il pa $15.95 **92**
1. Rock musicians
ISBN 978-0-8065-2466-5; 0-8065-2466-9
First published 1995 by Hyperion
The author "chronicles the life and career of the reclusive British blues performer. . . . Schumacher covers a tale of unhappy personal relationships, a failed marriage, drug and alcohol addiction and the tragic death of the performer's infant son, while giving full account of Clapton's significant accomplishments as guitarist and vocalist, his forays into rock and his performances and recordings." Publ Wkly

Clare, John, 1793-1864

Bate, Jonathan. John Clare: a biography. Farrar, Straus & Giroux 2003 648p il map $40
92
ISBN 0-374-17990-5 LC 2003-44063
This is a "biography of the farm laborer who is now considered the peer of his fellow second-generation British Romantic poets, Byron, Shelley, and Keats." Booklist
This biography "succeeds splendidly . . . not only making generous use of Clare's own wonderful prose and verse but adding historical perspective and a constant, intelligent probing which amount almost to a dialogue with Clare's view of himself." Times Lit Suppl
Includes bibliographical references

Clark, James H., 1944-

Lewis, Michael. The new new thing; a Silicon Valley story. Norton 1999 268p $25.95
92
ISBN 0-393-04813-6 LC 99-43412
Also available in paperback from Penguin Bks.
The author offers a "look at the life and career of Dr. Jim Clark, the eccentric but brilliant visionary who thus far has created three multi-billion-dollar ground-breaking enterprises—Silicon Graphics, Netscape, and Healtheon." Libr J
This "is a splendid, entirely satisfying book, intelligent and fun and revealing and troubling in the correct proportions, resolutely skeptical but not at all cynical, brimming with fabulous scenes as well as sharp analysis." NY Times Book Rev

Cleaver, Eldridge, 1935-1998

Cleaver, Eldridge. Target zero; a life in writing; edited by Kathleen Cleaver; foreword by Henry Louis Gates, Jr.; afterword by Cecil Brown. Palgrave Macmillan 2005 xxvi, 336p $27.95; pa $16.95 **92**
ISBN 978-1-4039-6237-9; 1-4039-6237-5; 978-1-4039-7657-4 (pa); 1-4039-7657-0 (pa)
LC 2005-51252
"The book's four parts chart Cleaver's life trhough his essays, short stories, letters, interviews, and poems, many previously unpublished. . . . This well-crafted reader . . . is a rich experience." Choice
Includes bibliographical references

Clemente, Roberto, 1934-1972

Maraniss, David. Clemente; the passion and grace of baseball's last hero. Simon & Schuster 2006 401p il maps $26; pa $15 **92**
1. Baseball—Biography
ISBN 0-7432-1781-0; 978-0-7432-1781-1; 0-7432-9999-X; 978-0-7432-9999-2 (pa)
LC 2006-42235
This is a "biography of the first Latin American player named to the Baseball Hall of Fame." Libr J
The author "has produced a baseball-savvy book sensitive to the social context that made Clemente, a black Puerto Rican, a leading indicator of baseball's future." N Y Times Book Rev
Includes bibliographical references

Cleveland, Grover, 1837-1908

Graff, Henry F. (Henry Franklin). Grover Cleveland. Times Bks. 2002 154p il (American presidents series) $20   **92**
1. Presidents—United States
ISBN 0-8050-6923-2   LC 2002-20315
A biography of the only American president to serve two nonconsecutive terms
This "volume is a valuable addition to the literature on the Presidency and is a compelling argument for taking Cleveland seriously as a President." Libr J
Includes bibliographical references

Clinton, Bill, 1946-

Clinton, Bill. My life. Knopf 2004 957p il $35   **92**
1. Presidents—United States 2. United States—Politics and government—1989-
ISBN 0-375-41457-6   LC 2004-107564
In this memoir the former president traces his life from his childhood in Arkansas through his time as governor of Arkansas and then focuses on his White House years
"Clinton's memoir has the raw material for a blockbuster book." Publ Wkly

Felsenthal, Carol. Clinton in exile; a president out of the White House. William Morrow 2008 386p il $25.95   **92**
1. Presidents—United States 2. United States—Politics and government—1989-
ISBN 978-0-06-123159-9; 0-06-123159-2
This book follows President Clinton from his "last hours in office, through his . . . humanitarian efforts, to his front-of-camera and behind-the-scenes coordination of his wife's presidential campaign." Publisher's note
"Anyone curious, but especially those who remain fans, will enjoy Felsenthal's look at Clinton's post-presidency." Publ Wkly

Maraniss, David. First in his class: a biography of Bill Clinton. Simon & Schuster 1995 512p il pa $15 hardcover o.p. *   **92**
1. Presidents—United States
ISBN 0-684-81890-6 (pa)   LC 94-48245
The author "offers a heavily documented (nearly 400 interviews), unauthorized biography that ends with Clinton's announcement for the presidency. Maraniss writes, 'My goal was for this book to be neither pathography nor hagiography, but a fair-minded examination of a complicated human being and the forces that shaped him and his generation.' He has achieved his goal. . . . All in all, *First in His Class* is solid journalism that thoughtfully evokes the tumultuous times—desegregation, assassinations, Vietnam—that shaped Clinton." Booklist
Includes bibliographical references

McDougal, Susan. The woman who wouldn't talk. See entry under McDougal, Susan

Clinton, Hillary Rodham, 1947-

Bernstein, Carl. A woman in charge; the life of Hillary Rodham Clinton. Alfred A. Knopf 2007 628p il $27.95   **92**
ISBN 978-0-375-40766-6; 0-375-40766-9
      LC 2007-17472
The author "offers a three-dimensional portrait of a person with enduring strengths (discipline, tenacity, a sustaining religious faith) and weaknesses (excessive secrecy, a tendency to self-righteousness and a habit of nursing grudges). . . . Bernstein almost always finds new facts and telling details. [His] account benefits enormously from remarkably candid on-the-record assessments of both Clintons by intimates such as close friend Jim Blair and Betsey Wright, Clinton's gubernatorial chief of staff in Arkansas." Los Angeles Times Book Rev
Includes bibliographical references

Clinton, Hillary Rodham. Living history. Simon & Schuster 2003 562p il $28; pa $16   **92**
ISBN 0-7432-2224-5; 0-7432-2225-3 (pa)
      LC 2003-276264
This is the former First Lady's "memoir of life through the White House years. It is also her chronicle of living history with Bill Clinton." Publisher's note
"This book is important not because of the history Senator Clinton records, but because of the history she doesn't record, and what that airbrushing tells us about the history she aspires to shape." N Y Times Book Rev

Cobain, Kurt, 1967-1994

Cross, Charles R. Heavier than heaven: a biography of Kurt Cobain. Hyperion 2001 381p il $24.95; pa $14.95   **92**
1. Nirvana (Musical group)
ISBN 0-7868-6505-9; 0-7868-8402-9 (pa)
      LC 2001-24187
This is a biography of Kurt Cobain, the lead singer of the rock group Nirvana, who committed suicide in 1994 at the age of 27
"Cross followed the Nirvana juggernaut from the beginning, and though he nearly bludgeons the reader with tales of Cobain's debauched excesses, one is still drawn to the artist's forceful personality." Libr J

Cobb, Ty, 1886-1961

Stump, Al. Cobb; a biography; with a foreword by Jimmie Reese. Algonquin Bks. 1994 436p il pa $15.95 hardcover o.p.   **92**
ISBN 1-56512-144-9 (pa)   LC 94-26122
The author, who collaborated with Cobb on his 1961 autobiography (My life in baseball), here presents his own version of the life and times of the baseball player
"Emphasizing Cobb's bitter final days, Stump's portrait of the splenetic Hall of Famer is both chilling and oddly moving." Am Libr
Includes bibliographical references

Cole, Nat King, 1919?-1965

Epstein, Daniel Mark. Nat King Cole. Northeastern University Press 2000 437p il pa $20
*   92

1. African American singers 2. Jazz musicians
ISBN 1-555-53469-4; 978-1-555-53469-1
LC 00-42727

First published 1999 by Farrar, Straus & Giroux

This biography of the African American vocalist, jazz pianist and composer "depicts a multitalented musician who–whether contending with racism, with black leaders criticizing his lack of activism or with jazz critics who believed he had 'sold out'–maintained an implacable, dignified demeanor." Publ Wkly

"The biographer sometimes digs too deep into esoterica, spending pages analyzing the lyrics of Straighten Up and Fly Right, for example. But when he recounts the singer's personal struggles, including a shocking 1956 onstage kidnapping attempt by Alabama racists, the human drama is, well unforgettable." Time

Includes bibliographical references

Cole, Natalie

Cole, Natalie. Angel on my shoulder; an autobiography; written with Digby Diehl. Warner Bks. 2000 353p il $38   92
ISBN 978-0-446-52746-0; 0-446-52746-7
LC 00-61455

In this memoir by the daughter of the late Nat King Cole, the Grammy Award-winning songstress recalls her childhood, her personal battle and victory over drugs and alcohol, and the legal battles with her mother and siblings over her father's estate

"Although she concentrates mostly on the good times, Cole isn't shy about the bad times, which makes this intriguing, engaging, and inspirational life story worthy of attention." Booklist

Colette, 1873-1954

Thurman, Judith. Secrets of the flesh: a life of Colette. Knopf 1999 592p il pa $18.95 hardcover o.p.   92
ISBN 0-345-37103-8 (pa)   LC 99-18959

Thurman focuses on the "morally subversive Colette in the social milieu of early-20th-century Paris. . . . {She} does not hesitate to expose the dishonest, selfish, exploitive facets of the feminist icon who wrote articles for Occupation newspapers and sometimes behaved heartlessly toward lovers. Nevertheless, her Colette comes off as an appealing, even heroic, figure." Publ Wkly

Includes bibliographical references

Columbus, Christopher

Morison, Samuel Eliot. Admiral of the ocean sea: a life of Christopher Columbus; maps by Erwin Raisz; drawings by Bertram Greene. Little, Brown 1942 xx, 680p il maps pa $28.99 hardcover o.p.   92
1. Explorers
ISBN 0-316-58478-9 (pa)
"An Atlantic Monthly Press book"
A condensation of the author's two-volume work with same title also published in 1942 but now o.p.

"An authoritative . . . biography of Columbus which is also decidedly original in its emphasis on the ability of Columbus as seaman and navigator and in the amount of space given to tracing the routes of the voyages and landings." Libr J

Conroy, Pat

Conroy, Pat. My losing season. Talese 2002 402p $27.95; pa $14.95   92
1. Authors, American
ISBN 0-385-48912-9; 0-553-38190-3 (pa)
LC 2002-66212

"Novelist Conroy ruminates on the profound effect of his final year as a point guard for the Citadel's basketball team, interweaving stories about the years leading up to college, his abusive father, his love-hate relationship with his school, and his growing fondness for books and writing." Booklist

"A wonderfully rich, informative, and well-researched reminiscence." Libr J

Conway, Jill K., 1934-

Conway, Jill K. True north; a memoir. Knopf 1994 250p pa $13 hardcover o.p.   92
ISBN 0-679-74461-4 (pa)   LC 93-45302

This continuation of the author's memoir begun in The road from Coorain covers "the period from her departure from Australia for the U.S. to enter graduate school in 1960 through her appointment as Smith College president in 1975." Publ Wkly

"Conway analyzes her own experiences in the U.S. and Canada just as thoughtfully and penetratingly as her academic work investigates the lives of several previous generations of American women." Booklist

Cook, James, 1728-1779

Hough, Richard Alexander. Captain James Cook; {by} Richard Hough. Norton 1995 398p il pa $18.95 hardcover o.p.   92
ISBN 0-393-31519-3 (pa)   LC 94-35998

Available in hardcover from Replica Bks.

First published 1994 in the United Kingdom

This is a "narrative of the life of the great 18th-century navigator, explorer, and cartographer." Libr J

"Hough's easygoing, thorough treatment . . . spotlights a proud, determined man." Booklist

Includes bibliographical references

Thomas, Nicholas. Cook; the extraordinary voyages of Captain James Cook. Walker & Company 2003 xxxvii, 467p il map $28; pa $18.95   92
ISBN 0-8027-1412-9; 0-8027-7711-2 (pa)
LC 2003-57648

Published in the United Kingdom with title: Discoveries: the voyages of Captain James Cook

This biography focuses "on the anthropological and scientific research carried out during Cook's three voyages, as evidenced in Cook's and the other scientists' journals." Libr J

"Rich, vivid and deeply provocative, Thomas's work combines premiere adventure story with thorough history and intensive sociology." Publ Wkly

Includes bibliographical references

Cooke, Sam

Guralnick, Peter. Dream boogie; the triumph of Sam Cooke. Little, Brown 2005 750p il $27.95 *
                               92

ISBN 0-316-37794-5   LC 2005-77

This is a biography of the American singer.

"For those who only know the singer through his pop hits—'You Send Me'; 'Twistin' the Night Away'—the extensive account of his childhood background in gospel music will prove fascinating, and the evocation of the harsh realities faced by African-American musicians touring the South a powerful reminder of just how explosive this music could be." Publ Wkly

Includes discography and bibliographical references

Cooper, James Fenimore, 1789-1851

Franklin, Wayne. James Fenimore Cooper; the early years. Yale University Press 2007 708p il map $40   **92**

1. Authors, American

ISBN 978-0-300-10805-7; 0-300-10805-2
                    LC 2006-31247

"Published with assistance from the Louis Stern Memorial Fund."

In this first of a projected two-volume work, the author gives an "account of how Cooper ran afoul of a crew of duplicitous businessmen while embarking on his writing career and ends the volume in 1826, as the 36-year-old Cooper, having wrapped up his worrisome financial affairs and written some dozen chapters of his soon-to-be-fabulously successful The Last of the Mohicans, leaves America for a seven-year sojourn in Europe." Libr J

"This volume profoundly enriches our understanding of how the young writer helped forge our national mythology in works such as The Last of The Mohicans and The Pioneers." Booklist

Includes bibliographical references

Copernicus, Nicolaus, 1473-1543

Repcheck, Jack. Copernicus' secret; how the scientific revolution began. Simon & Schuster 2007 239p il map $25   **92**

1. Astronomers

ISBN 978-0-7432-8951-1; 0-7432-8951-X
                    LC 2007-24649

This biography "concentrates on the last 12 years of the astronomer's life." N Y Times Book Rev

"The book is fascinating reading, even to those who may be familiar with much of its contents." Choice

Includes bibliographical references

Vollmann, William T. Uncentering the Earth; Copernicus and "The Revolutions of the Heavenly Spheres". Norton 2006 295p il (Great discoveries) $22.95   **92**

1. Astronomers

ISBN 0-393-05969-3   LC 2005-25864

"Atlas books."

This is a "meditation on the life and work of astronomer Nicolaus Copernicus (1473-1543). The writer reflects on Copernicus's achievement in pursuing and publishing a heliocentric view of the universe." Libr J

"Readers who want to understand the significance of Copernicus's book in both his own time and ours will find this the next best thing to reading it." Publ Wkly

Cosell, Howard, 1918-1995

Kindred, Dave. Sound and fury. See entry under Ali, Muhammad, 1942-

Cox, Lynne

Cox, Lynne. Swimming to Antarctica; tales of a long-distance swimmer. Knopf 2004 323p $24.95
                                92

1. Women athletes

ISBN 0-375-41507-6   LC 2003-47577

Also available in paperback from Harvest Bks.

The author "has swum the Mediterranean, the three-mile Strait of Messina, under the ancient bridges of Kunning Lake, [and] below the old summer palace of the emperor of China in Beijing. . . . She writes about the ways in which these swims . . . became vehicles for personal goals." Publisher's note

"Cox is a pleasure. . . . Many passages are grip-the-page exciting, whether she's dodging Antarctic icebergs or Nile River sewage." Booklist

Coxeter, H. S. M. (Harold Scott Macdonald), 1907-2003

Roberts, Siobhan. King of infinite space; Donald Coxeter, the man who saved geometry. Walker & Co. 2006 399p il $27.95 *   **92**

ISBN 0-8027-1499-4; 978-0-8027-1499-2
                    LC 2006-497355

This is the story of geometer H. S. M. "Donald" Coxeter's "life, his work, and his interactions with mathematicians, scientists, and artists of his time. . . . The author carefully weaves a lot of mathematical details into her work, but not so much that it becomes burdensome to the historical focus of the book." Sci Books Films

Includes bibliographical references

Crane, Hart, 1899-1932

Mariani, Paul L. The broken tower: a life of Hart Crane; [by] Paul Mariani. Norton 1999 492p il pa $15.95 hardcover o.p.   **92**

ISBN 0-393-32041-3 (pa)   LC 98-37726

"Using unpublished letters, manuscripts, and photographs [Mariani] pieces together the life and passions of this brilliant yet tormented man whose creative genius left us 'The Bridge' and whose influence still reverberates among poets today." Libr J

Includes bibliographical references

Crane, Kathleen, 1951-

Crane, Kathleen. Sea legs; tales of a woman oceanographer. Westview Press 2003 318p il map hardcover o.p. pa $16   **92**

1. Oceanography 2. Women scientists

ISBN 0-8133-4004-7; 0-8133-4285-6 (pa)
                    LC 2003-1690

Crane, Kathleen, 1951-—*Continued*

"Crane chronicles the relentless adversity she faced in becoming a world-class oceanographer with a modest matter-of-factness that almost camouflages the high caliber of her achievements. . . . She was the first to postulate the existence of the now famous deep-sea hot springs. . . . Crane's experiences are diverse, dramatic, and important; her understanding of international affairs and environmental realities laudable and moving; and her triumphs over personal sorrows and illness impressive and inspiring." Booklist

Includes bibliographical references

Crazy Horse, Sioux Chief, ca. 1842-1877

McMurtry, Larry. Crazy Horse. Viking 1999 148p (Penguin lives series) $19.95; pa $13

92

1. Dakota Indians
ISBN 0-670-88234-8; 0-14-303480-4 (pa)

LC 98-26644

"Though essentially a loner and devoid of political ambition, Crazy Horse was a respected military tactician, equally feared and admired for the strength and the intensity of his convictions. Rather than merely attempting to sort out fact from fiction, McMurtry incorporates conjecture and legend into this philosophical portrait of both the man and the myth." Booklist

Crick, Francis, 1916-2004

Ridley, Matt. Francis Crick; discoverer of the genetic code. Atlas Books 2006 213p (Eminent lives) $19.95

92

1. Scientists 2. Genetics
ISBN 0-06-082333-X; 978-0-06-082333-7

LC 2005-55878

This "biography examines the paired strands of Crick's life and work." N Y Times Book Rev

"A briskly written essential for the DNA shelf." Booklist

Includes bibliographical references

Cronkite, Walter

Cronkite, Walter. A reporter's life. Knopf 1997 384p il $26.95; pa $15

92

ISBN 0-394-57879-1; 0-345-41103-X (pa)

LC 96-21053

A Borzoi Bk.

In this memoir the news broadcaster writes "about his midwestern childhood, marriage, and family and . . . {the} stories he's covered." Booklist

Cronkite's "memoir is a short course on the flow of events in the second half of this century—events the world knows more about because of Walter Cronkite's work, and some of which might not have happened without it." N Y Times Book Rev

Crosby, Bing, 1904-1977

Giddins, Gary. Bing Crosby: a pocketful of dreams: the early years, 1903-1940. Little, Brown 2001 728p il $30; pa $17.95

92

ISBN 0-316-88188-0; 0-316-88645-9 (pa)

LC 00-44403

This "work chronicles Crosby's life as well as his singing, recording, radio, and film careers up to 1940, the year of the first of his popular 'Road' movies with Bob Hope." Libr J

"Giddins has contributed a landmark study of popular singing in the first half of the twentieth century." Booklist

Includes bibliographical references

Cummings, E. E. (Edward Estlin), 1894-1962

Sawyer-Lauçanno, Christopher. E.E. Cummings; a biography. Sourcebooks 2004 606p il $29.95; pa $16.95 *

92

ISBN 1-570-71775-3; 1-4022-0594-5 (pa)

LC 2004-12234

This biography of poet and artist e.e. cummings draws parallels between cummings' private life and his work.

This "is a responsible, adept, and necessary contribution to the body of secondary work about one of America's greatest poets." Christ Sci Monit

Curie, Marie, 1867-1934

Brian, Denis. The Curies; a biography of the most controversial family in science. Wiley 2005 438p il $30

92

1. Curie, Pierre, 1859-1906
ISBN 0-471-27391-0

LC 2005-7001

This book "follows five generations of the Sklodowska-Curie-Joliot family. Beginning before Marie Sklodowska and Pierre Curie meet, Brian details their courtship and 11-year marriage, bringing the reader to the Curie dinner table and into the converted garden shed (replete with a leaking roof) where the Curies' work on polonium and radium transformed physics and won them two Nobel prizes. . . . Extremely well-done and highly recommended." Publ Wkly

Includes bibliographical references

Dry, Sarah. Curie; with an essay by Sabine Seifert. Haus 2003 170p il (Life & times) pa $15.95

92

1. Women scientists
ISBN 1-904341-29-2

This is a biography of the first woman to win two Nobel Prizes, one for physics and the other for chemistry

"Concise and engaging, this amply illustrated history of Madame Curie . . . makes an excellent introduction to the feminist icon and scientific pioneer. Dry does an excellent job of delineating the major events of Curie's life, including her early education in the underground schools of the 19th-century Polish resistance movement, her heady intellectual courtship with Pierre Curie in France, and later their discovery of radioactivity in 1898. Sidebars on topics such as the invention of the laboratory, and the inclusion of Seifert's essay on Irène Joliot-Curie, Marie Curie's less famous daughter and coworker, make this pocket sized book especially comprehensive, and a wonderful introduction to a fascinating and inspiring career." Publ Wkly

Includes bibliographical references

Curie, Marie, 1867-1934—*Continued*
Quinn, Susan. Marie Curie; a life. Addison-Wesley 1996 509p il pa $21   **92**
1. Women scientists
ISBN 0-201-88794-0; 978-0-201-88794-5

LC 96-167

"A Merloyd Lawrence book"

First published 1995 by Simon & Schuster

This a biography of the Polish-born scientist who was twice the recipient of the Nobel Prize for her work with radium.

"A well-written, evenhanded story of dedication, disappointment, tragedy, and extraordinary achievement." Booklist

Includes bibliographical references

Curie, Pierre, 1859-1906
Brian, Denis. The Curies. See entry under Curie, Marie, 1867-1934

Custer, George Armstrong, 1839-1876
Wert, Jeffry D. Custer; the controversial life of George Armstrong Custer. Simon & Schuster 1996 462p il maps hardcover o.p. pa $20   **92**
1. Generals
ISBN 0-684-81043-3; 0-684-83275-5 (pa)

LC 96-7290

"Focusing on Custer's Civil War actions, Wert methodically examines a man often considered an enigma in American history. Clear writing and excellent use of primary source materials demonstrate how history should be written." Booklist

Da Ponte, Lorenzo, 1749-1838
Bolt, Rodney. The librettist of Venice; the remarkable life of Lorenzo Da Ponte, Mozart's poet, Casanova's friend, and Italian opera's impresario in America. Bloomsbury Pub. 2006 428p il $29.95   **92**
ISBN 1-59691-118-2   LC 2006-5713

This is a biography of "Lorenzo Da Ponte, Mozart's collaborator and the librettist for 'The Marriage of Figaro,' 'Don Giovanni' and 'Cosi Fan Tutte.'" N Y Times (Late NY Ed)

"Reading Bolt's lively narrative of Da Ponte's life from the ghetto of Venice to the sparkling opera houses of Europe is pure pleasure." Publ Wkly

Dalai Lama XIV, 1935-
Dalai Lama XIV. Freedom in exile; the autobiography of the Dalai Lama. HarperCollins Pubs. 1990 288p il maps pa $15 hardcover o.p. *   **92**
ISBN 0-06-098701-4   LC 89-46523
"A Cornelia & Michael Bessie book"

"The Dalai Lama's story is, in part, a chapter in the 2,500-year history of Buddhism as well as a testament to the 'mendacity and barbarity' of Communist China. He shares the details of his amazing life, a glimpse at some of the mysteries of Tibetan Buddhism, and his unshakable belief in the basic good of humanity." Booklist

Iyer, Pico. The open road; the global journey of the fourteenth Dalai Lama. Bloomsbury 2008 288p $24 *   **92**
ISBN 978-0-307-26760-3; 0-307-26760-1

LC 2007-43991

In this biography of the 14th Dalai Lama, "Iyer organizes his observations by smart descriptions of aspects of the Dalai Lama's work and character: icon, monk, philosopher, politician." Publ Wkly

"The combination of Iyer's exacting observations, incisive analysis, and frank respect for the unknowable results in a uniquely internalized, even empathic portrait of one of the world's most embraced and least understood guiding lights." Booklist

Includes bibliographical references

Daley, Richard J., 1902-1976
Cohen, Adam. American pharaoh: Mayor Richard J. Daley: his battle for Chicago and the nation; {by} Adam Cohen and Elizabeth Taylor. Little, Brown 2000 614p map pa $16.95 hardcover o.p.   **92**
1. Chicago (Ill.)—Politics and government
ISBN 0-316-83489-0 (pa)   LC 99-42157

This is a biography of the man who was "mayor of Chicago from 1955 until his death in 1976. His command extended far beyond the boundaries of Cook County, where he greatly influenced such decisive events as the Sixties as Kennedy's election in 1960, Martin Luther King's ill-fated Chicago campaign for civil rights, and the notorious '68 Democratic Convention." Libr J

"Penetrating, nonsensationalistic and exhaustive, this is an impressive and important biography." Publ Wkly

Includes bibliographical references

Dampier, William, 1652-1715
Preston, Diana. A pirate of exquisite mind: explorer, naturalist, and buccaneer: the life of William Dampier; {by} Diana and Michael Preston. Walker & Company 2004 372p il map $27   **92**
1. Voyages around the world
ISBN 0-8027-1425-0   LC 2003-62197

This is a biography of the English pirate William Dampier who was "a pioneering navigator, naturalist and hydrographer." N Y Times Book Rev

"Dampier's adventures and observations ignited the imagination of a generation, but today his name is largely unknown. This exhaustive biography . . . won't make Dampier famous again, but it will give readers a clear understanding of one of the most well-traveled men in history." Publ Wkly

Includes bibliographical references

Danticat, Edwidge, 1969-
Danticat, Edwidge. Brother, I'm dying. Alfred A. Knopf 2007 272p $23.95 *   **92**
1. Women authors
ISBN 978-1-4000-4115-2; 1-4000-4115-5

LC 2007-06887

"A Borzoi book"

Danticat, Edwidge, 1969-—*Continued*
This family memoir by the author of The Dew Breaker (2004) centers on the experiences of "her father, Mira, and his older brother, Joseph." Publisher's note
The author "has written a fierce, haunting book about exile and loss and family love, and how that love can survive distance and separation, loss and abandonment and somehow endure, undented and robust." N Y Times (Late NY Ed)

Darnley, Henry Stewart, Lord, 1545-1567
Weir, Alison. Mary, Queen of Scots, and the murder of Lord Darnley. See entry under Mary, Queen of Scots, 1542-1587

Darwin, Charles, 1809-1882
Browne, Janet. Charles Darwin. v2: The power of place. Knopf 2002 591p il $37.50 **92**
1. Naturalists
ISBN 0-679-42932-8
Also available in paperback from Princeton Univ. Press
"A Borzoi book"
This second volume of Browne's biography of Darwin begins "a year before the publication of On the Origin of Species, with the arrival of a package from Alfred Russel Wallace, whose own ideas on natural selection virtually mirrored Darwin's, forcing him to go public. . . . Browne's subject is monumental, but her writing style is never overburdened by the weight. Rather, her prose is elegant in its clarity of thought, her craftsmanship impeccable in the way it weaves a coherent whole from the innumerable threads of thought, experience and persona that comprised this colossal life." Publ Wkly
Includes bibliographical references

Browne, Janet. Charles Darwin; a biography. v1: Voyaging. Princeton Univ. Press 1996 605p il pa $25.95 **92**
1. Naturalists
ISBN 0-691-02606-8 LC 95-53319
First published 1995 by Knopf
This first volume of a two-part biography of Darwin focuses on his early years, leading up to his marriage and his moving out of London to the countryside of Kent.
The author "captures the spirit of a quietly revolutionary scientist whose ingrained Victorian prejudices were at odds with his radical ideas." Publ Wkly
Includes bibliographical references
Followed by Charles Darwin: The power of place (2002)

Desmond, Adrian J. Darwin; [by] Adrian Desmond & James Moore. W.W. Norton & Co. 1994 808p il pa $23.95 **92**
1. Naturalists
ISBN 0-393-31150-3; 978-0-393-31150-1
First published 1991 in the United Kingdom
The authors portray "Darwin as a freethinking agnostic fearful of being labeled an anarchist, a scientific titan trapped on a literary treadmill, a voyager on the Beagle appalled at 'low' races of savages, and a paterfamilias

who subordinated women but was completely dependent on his wife." Publ Wkly
"No other biography of Darwin has anywhere near the density of detail this book has. This rich tapestry, supplemented with 91 fine illustrations, is intended to provide the basis for relating Darwin the creative scientist to his social and political milieu." N Y Times Book Rev
Includes bibliographical references

Quammen, David. The reluctant Mr. Darwin; an intimate portrait of Charles Darwin and the making of his theory of evolution. Atlas Books/Norton 2006 304p (Great discoveries) $22.95; pa $14.95 * **92**
1. Naturalists
ISBN 0-393-05981-2; 978-0-393-05981-6; 0-393-32995-X (pa); 978-0-393-32995-7 (pa)
LC 2006-9864
The author "concentrates on how Darwin privately developed his theory of evolution and reluctantly made his ideas public when [Alfred] Wallace began to publish similar theories." Libr J
"This often slyly witty book stands out among the flood of books being published for Darwin's bicentenary." Publ Wkly
Includes bibliographical references

David, King of Israel
Pinsky, Robert. The life of David. Schocken 2005 209p (Jewish encounters) $19.95 **92**
ISBN 0-8052-4203-1 LC 2005-41696
The author "considers the peculiarities, paradoxes, and timeless significance of David's often baffling story from his golden days as a handsome upstart confronting King Saul in 'gangsterish' encounters to David's wild years as a desert Robin Hood and ascension to the throne. . . . Witty, frank, skeptical, and clearly moved by mercurial David's chutzpah and losses, Pinsky brings remarkable lucidity, depth, and creativity to his dynamic and poetic reading of a legendary figure who has become emblematic of both destructive and heroic aspects of human nature." Booklist

Davis, Jefferson, 1808-1889
Cooper, William J. Jefferson Davis, American. Knopf 2000 757p il maps $35; pa $18 **92**
1. United States—History—1861-1865, Civil War
ISBN 0-394-56916-4; 0-375-72542-3 (pa)
LC 00-62006
In this biography of the president of the Confederacy, the author traces Davis' political career and personal life, including his days at West Point, as Secretary of War in the Mexican War, and as U.S. senator from Mississippi
"In the already cluttered field of Civil War history, Cooper's is the definitive biography; readers will be particularly pleased to discover the compelling power of his narrative." Publ Wkly
Includes bibliographical references

Davis, Miles

Cook, Richard. It's about that time; Miles Davis on and off record. Oxford University Press 2007 373p il $27   **92**

1. Jazz musicians 2. African American musicians
ISBN 978-0-19-532266-8; 0-19-532266-5
LC 2006-50694

"Coming at the trumpeter from the perspective of 14 important recordings—e.g., *Birth of the Cool, Kind of Blue*—. . . [the author] concentrates on the music and the musicians who made them, creating a portrait of Miles the musician in the context of the contributions of such sidemen and collaborators as John Coltrane and Gil Evans." Libr J

"Cook's thoughtful, illuminating criticism and boundless knowledge of his subject make this a rich and satisfying read for jazz aficionados and novices alike." Publ Wkly

Includes discography and bibliographical references

Davis, Miles. Miles, the autobiography; {by} Miles Davis with Quincy Troupe. Simon & Schuster 1989 431p il pa $15 hardcover o.p.
    92

1. Jazz musicians 2. African American musicians
ISBN 0-671-72582-3 (pa)   LC 89-19652

"The legendary jazz musician Miles Davis . . . takes us on a historical journey that begins with his growing up in the mid-1920s in East St. Louis, then moves on to New York City in the 1940s, where he was a student at the Julliard School of Music, and to his encounters with other jazz greats like Charlie Parker, Dizzy Gillespie, Billie Holiday, Herbie Hancock, and George Duke." Libr J

This book "is profusely detailed, exceedingly candid and eminently readable—by any criterion a major addition to the literature of jazz." N Y Times Book Rev

Troupe, Quincy. Miles and me: biography of Miles Davis. University of Calif. Press 2000 189p il $25; pa $12.95   **92**

1. Jazz musicians 2. African American musicians
ISBN 0-520-21624-5; 0-520-23471-5 (pa)
LC 99-54370

"In the late 1970s, Troupe met Davis in New York, became friends with him, and eventually collaborated with him on Miles' autobiography. This slim memoir tells the intimate story of their unlikely friendship. . . . This is both a revealing look at a musical genius and a tender, surprisingly sweet remembrance of a good but demanding friend." Booklist

Dawidoff, Nicholas

Dawidoff, Nicholas. The crowd sounds happy; a story of love, madness, and baseball. Pantheon Books 2008 271p $24.95   **92**

1. Baseball—Biography
ISBN 978-0-375-40028-5; 0-375-40028-1
LC 2007-30525

In this memoir, the author describes how his love of baseball helped him through rough periods of his youth, including his father descent into mental illness.

"Essential reading for anyone who wishes a balm for heartbreaks in youth, torn family life, love, and seventh-game losses." Libr J

De Kooning, Willem, 1904-1997

Stevens, Mark. De Kooning: an American master; [by] Mark Stevens and Annalyn Swan. Knopf 2004 731p il $35   **92**

ISBN 1-4000-4175-9   LC 2004-48297

This is a biography of the twentieth-century painter and a study of his work

This is a "sweeping, authoritative biography. . . . The elusiveness of its subject makes the achievements of 'De Kooning' that much more dazzling. This is a book that traces de Kooning's history, puts him on Freud's couch, plumbs the mysteries of his cryptic and ever-changing work and follows the arc of modern art through much of the 20th century, fusing all these elements into a remarkably lucid narrative." N Y Times (Late N Y ed)

Includes bibliographical references

Dean, James, 1931-1955

Alexander, Paul. Boulevard of broken dreams; the life, times, and legend of James Dean. Plume 1997 312p il pa $16   **92**

1. Actors
ISBN 978-0-452-27840-0; 0-452-27840-6
First published 1994 by Viking

"The interesting thing about James Dean is the fact that, almost 40 years after his death, he remains an icon of American pop culture. In the last chapter of this tell-all biography, Alexander takes a stab at accounting for Dean's continuing popularity, but his real interest throughout the book is in the actor's sex life. Although he devotes some attention to Dean's work as an actor and to his heterosexual liaisons, Alexander's contribution to the Dean legend is to label him as homosexual." Booklist

Gehring, Wes D. James Dean: rebel with a cause. Indiana Historical Society Press 2005 303p il (Indiana biography series) $19.95 *
    92

1. Actors
ISBN 0-87195-181-9   LC 2005-41440

This is a "study of Dean's entire life and an appreciation of his rightful place in film history. Gehring makes the point that audiences have confused the actor with his troubled-teenager roles, and he counters that misimpression with a fuller portrait." Booklist

Includes filmography and bibliographical references

Deen, Paula H., 1947-

Deen, Paula H. Paula Deen: it ain't all about the cookin'; [by] Paula Deen, with Sherry Suib Cohen. Simon & Schuster 2007 287p il $25   **92**
   1. Cooks 2. Southern cooking   LC 2006-53501
   ISBN 978-0-7432-9285-6; 0-7432-9285-5
"Deen talks about everything from her decades-long battle with agoraphobia and her troubled first marriage to the hard work that went into building her first business, The Bag Lady, and the professional and personal successes that followed. A few of Deen's recipes (almost all new) are sprinkled among her stories, which offer a sample of the distinctively Southern cooking that is the foundation of Deen's life and career. This wonderfully nourishing book will have readers laughing, crying, and hungry for more." Libr J

Delany, Bessie
Delany, Sadie. Having our say. See entry under Delany, Sadie

Delany, Sadie
Delany, Sadie. Having our say; the Delany sisters' first 100 years; [by] Sarah and A. Elizabeth Delany; with Amy Hill Hearth. Kodansha Int. 1993 210p il $20   **92**
   1. Delany, Bessie 2. Delany family
   ISBN 1-56836-010-X   LC 93-23890
   Also available in paperback from Dell
"The Delany sisters' story is a collective meditation on American life since Sadie's birth in 1889 and Bessie's in 1891 in Raleigh, North Carolina. . . . The sisters migrated to New York City's Harlem in the 1910s and in the 1950s to the suburb of Mt. Vernon, New York. The assertive Bessie battled racism and sexism as the only black female member of her Columbia University Dental School class in the 1920s. The more reticent Sadie became the first black domestic science teacher in the New York City high schools." Libr J
"The combination of the two voices, beautifully blended by Ms. Hearth, evokes an epic history, often cruel and brutal, but always deeply humane in their spirited telling of it." N Y Times Book Rev

Delbridge, Melissa J.
Delbridge, Melissa J. Family Bible. University of Iowa Press 2008 143p (Sightline books: the Iowa series in literary nonfiction) $23.95   **92**
   1. Tuscaloosa (Ala.)
   ISBN 978-1-58729-651-2; 1-58729-651-9
        LC 2007-43968
A collection of autobiographical essays about growing up in 1960s Tuscaloosa, Alabama
"Melissa's daddy was a charmer, a Kirk Douglas look-alike who loved to fish and hunt and to go away for the weekend pretending to be fishing and hunting at the 'River Bend Hunting Club' while actually seeing other women. This naturally drove Momma crazy and, sadly, she took it out on Melissa. Momma took her kids from the house in the middle of the night, moved across town,

and, when she left Melissa's father for good, 'remarried fast enough to cause a lot of high talk.' . . . The relationship between Delbridge's parents and then the toxic mess that constituted her home with her stepdad, identified as a local exterminator magnate and ex-Marine, are staples in memoir, but the story is gracefully told, without self-pity. . . . Much of this volume is, as one might expect, about Delbridge's own sexual awakening, and you know it will be out of the ordinary, even melodramatic." Tuscaloosa News

Dempsey, Jack, 1895-1983
Kahn, Roger. A flame of pure fire: Jack Dempsey and the roaring '20s. Harcourt Brace & Co. 1999 474p il pa $15 hardcover o.p.
                                       92
   ISBN 0-15-601414-9 (pa)   LC 99-15382
   This biography details the life and career of heavyweight boxer William Harrison "Jack" Dempsey
"In graceful and fluid prose, Kahn presents the con men, gangsters, prostitutes and starlets who inhabited the turbulent, Prohibition-era story of Jack Dempsey." Publ Wkly
   Includes bibliographical references

Descartes, René, 1596-1650
Grayling, A. C. Descartes: the life and times of a genius. Walker 2006 303p il map $27
                                       92
   ISBN 978-0-8027-1501-2; 0-8027-1501-X
   First published 2005 in the United Kingdom with title: Descartes : the life of René Descartes and its place in his times
"As Newton was to physics, so Descartes was to philosophy, moving it from superstition and religion to science and reason. They are the founding fathers of the modern world. Grayling's life of Descartes is set firmly in the age of the Counter-Reformation and the Thirty Years War, which are evoked in a lively, almost novelistic style of which Descartes would certainly have approved. This propels the narrative forward and illuminates the philosophy for a lay readership." Times (London)

Watson, Richard A. Cogito ergo sum: the life of René Descartes; {by} Richard Watson. Godine 2002 375p $35 *   **92**
   ISBN 1-56792-184-1   LC 2001-40858
   In this biography the author "is less interested in the revered philosopher and mathematician than in the diminutive, arrogant Frenchman who fathered a child out of wedlock, probably dabbled in drugs, and practiced vivisection on animals." New Yorker
"For all of his puckish delight in a juicy anecdote, Watson recognizes and carefully explicates the cultural centrality of Descartes' intellectual legacy. That legacy ensures numerous readers sure to praise a biographer who delivers both the philosopher's cerebral doctrines and his unmistakably human conduct." Booklist
   Includes bibliographical references

Devonshire, Georgiana Spencer Cavendish, Duchess of, 1757-1806

Foreman, Amanda. Georgiana, Duchess of Devonshire. Random House 2000 454p pa $15.95 hardcover o.p.   **92**

ISBN 0-375-75383-4 (pa)   LC 99-23580

Publication date from CIP data; Genealogical chart on endpapers

Georgiana "was the society leader of her day. Daughter of the fabulously wealthy Earl Spencer (and ancestor of the late princess of Wales) and married to the even more wealthy duke of Devonshire, Georgiana was watched, adored, and imitated. But she evolved herself into more than just a fashionable hostess; she got involved in Whig politics, to an extent unprecedented for women. . . . The tenor of the subject's time and place—in this instance, aristocratic Britain in the late 1700s and early 1800s—is both colorfully and meaningfully realized." Booklist

Includes bibliographical references

Diana, Princess of Wales, 1961-1997

Brown, Tina. The Diana chronicles. Doubleday 2007 542p $27.50 *   **92**

1. Princesses
ISBN 978-0-385-51708-9; 0-385-51708-4

This is a biography of Diana, Princess of Wales.

"Like scraping barnacles off an old hulk, Tina Brown has taken the story of Princess Diana, hosed off layers of hearsay and myth, sifted through tons of accumulated legend, and presented us with a fresh and vividly perceptive portrait." Times Lit Suppl

Includes bibliographical references

Dickens, Charles, 1812-1870

Smiley, Jane. Charles Dickens. Viking 2002 212p (Penguin lives series) $19.95   **92**

1. Authors, English
ISBN 0-670-03077-5   LC 2001-45607

"A Penguin life; A Lipper\Viking book"

This "biography examines Dickens' life through his work, starting not with his birth but rather the beginnings of his literary career. After writing short essays for a monthly magazine, Dickens began the serialization of his first novel, The Pickwick Papers. Dickens quickly became both a best-selling novelist and a famous man, who had to contend with both the envy of other authors and, much later on, the very public dissolution of his marriage. . . . Smiley's superb and thoughtful analysis should appeal to anyone familiar with the great author's work." Booklist

Dickinson, Emily, 1830-1886

Habegger, Alfred. My wars are laid away in books; the life of Emily Dickinson. Random House 2001 764p il pa $16.95 hardcover o.p.
                    92

ISBN 0-8129-6601-5 (pa)   LC 2001-19429

The author "traces Dickinson's evolution as a writer from her early childhood in the 1830s to her poetry of sex, isolation, and death in the 1860s and 1870s." Libr J

"Weaving together a chronologically integrated reading of Emily Dickinson's poetry and correspondence, Habegger has written the most complete and satisfying biography to date of a poet long shrouded in myth and illusion." Booklist

Includes bibliographical references

Didion, Joan

Didion, Joan. The year of magical thinking. Knopf 2005 227p $23.95 *   **92**

1. Dunne, John Gregory, 1932-2003
ISBN 1-4000-4314-X   LC 2005-45132

The author "chronicles the year following the death of her husband, fellow writer John Gregory Dunne, from a massive heart attack on December 30, 2003, while the couple's only daughter, Quintana, lay unconscious in a nearby hospital suffering from pneumonia and septic shock. . . . This is an indispensable addition to Didion's body of work and a lyrical, disciplined entry in the annals of mourning literature." Publ Wkly

Dierker, Larry, 1946-

Dierker, Larry. This ain't brain surgery; how to win the pennant without losing your mind. Simon & Schuster 2003 289p il $25   **92**

1. Houston Astros (Baseball team)
ISBN 0-7432-0400-X   LC 2003-52809

"Dierker, a pitcher and then radio commentator for the Houston Astros, stepped out of the announcer's booth to become the Astros' manager in 1997. . . . Baseball and the Houston Astros have been Dierker's professional adult life, but unlike many baseball lifers, he has a healthy perspective about the game and his role in it, as reflected in the title of this literate, humorous, and entertaining memoir." Booklist

Dillard, Annie

Dillard, Annie. An American childhood. Harper & Row 1987 255p pa $14 hardcover o.p.
                    92

ISBN 0-06-091518-8 (pa)   LC 87-45042

In this autobiography, Dillard presents as account of her life from her childhood in Pittsburgh until her entrance into college

"Dillard's luminous prose painlessly captures the pain of growing up in this wonderful evocation of childhood. . . . The events of childhood often loom larger than life; the magic of Dillard's writing is that she sets down typical childhood happenings with their original immediacy and force." Publ Wkly

Dillard, Annie. The writing life. Harper & Row 1989 111p pa $11 hardcover o.p.   **92**

ISBN 0-06-091988-4 (pa)   LC 89-45034

The author "probes the sorcery that levitates her own writing, discussing with clear eye and wry wit how, where and why she writes." Publ Wkly

Diller, Phyllis, 1917-

Diller, Phyllis. Like a lampshade in a whorehouse; my life in comedy; [by] Phyllis Diller with Richard Buskin. J.P. TarcherPenguin 2005 266p il $24.95; pa $14.95   **92**

ISBN 1-585-42396-3; 1-585-42476-5 (pa)

LC 2004-58520

This is an autobiography by the American comedian. "Brash comedy and a surprising bitterness fuel this unsparing account of Diller's drive to make it big." Publ Wkly

DiMaggio, Joe

Cramer, Richard Ben. Joe DiMaggio; the hero's life. Simon & Schuster 2000 546p $28; pa $16   **92**

ISBN 0-684-85391-4; 0-684-86547-5 (pa)

LC 00-49232

In this biography of the baseball player, "Cramer taps every plank in the wall that DiMaggio erected around himself and that protected him from inquiry. In the wall's hollow spots, Cramer locates the girls, finds the Mob guys, and behind the legend of grace and elegance on and off the field discovers a legend who in reality was more often than not graceless and inelegant." New Yorker

Dinesen, Isak, 1885-1962

Thurman, Judith. Isak Dinesen; the life of a storyteller. St. Martin's Press 1982 495p il pa $18 hardcover o.p. *   **92**

ISBN 0-312-13525-4 (pa)   LC 82-5573

This biography traces Dinesen's life from her childhood in Denmark through her years in Kenya and her return to Denmark to focus on her literary career

"With great insight and a novelist's gift for nuance and narrative sweep, Thurman shows the extraordinary degree to which Dinesen's life and art meshed. In addition, Thurman's sensitive criticism of Dinesen's work reveals exceptional artistry in its own right." Booklist

Includes bibliographical references

Doctorow, E. L., 1931-

Doctorow, E. L. Reporting the universe. Harvard Univ. Press 2003 125p (The William E. Massey Sr. lectures in the history of American civilization, 2000) $22.95; pa $13.95   **92**

ISBN 0-674-00461-2; 0-674-01628-9 (pa)

LC 2002-32742

"In the 14 essays . . . Doctorow recalls his boyhood during the Depression in his culturally rich Brooklyn home and reflects on his intellectual development at Kenyon College under the tutelage of the poet John Crowe Ransom. He also explores the complex relationship between literature and religion." N Y Times Book Rev

"This potent collection of elegantly distilled essays offers a fresh perspective on our species' capacity for both the sublime and the horrific." Booklist

Domino, Fats, 1928-

Coleman, Rick. Blue Monday; Fats Domino and the lost dawn of rock 'n' roll. Da Capo 2006 364p il map hardcover o.p. pa $15.95   **92**

1. African American musicians 2. Rock musicians

ISBN 0-306-81491-9; 978-0-306-81531-7 (pa); 0-306-81531-1 (pa)

Coleman has crafted a "biography of Fats Domino, drawing on new interviews with the pianist himself. From his childhood in New Orleans through the early days of rock'n'roll, when he endured travel difficulties in the segregated South and frequent riots at his concerts, Fats remained a shy but demanding performer and personality. A homesick father who seemed to cherish his family, Fats was also a hard-drinking womanizer, and Coleman tells his story with compassion and honesty up to Fats's survival of Hurricane Katrina in his Ninth Ward home. His argument that rock'n'roll sprung from Fats and the New Orleans sound is hard to dispute, as Fats was playing long before others now credited with starting the revolution. Despite the occasional slips into fandom, this is an essential purchase for any library collecting the history of rock'n'roll." Libr J

Includes bibliographical references

Doolittle, James Harold, 1896-1993

Doolittle, James Harold. I could never be so lucky again; an autobiography; by General James H. "Jimmy" Doolittle, with Carroll V. Glines. Bantam Bks. 1991 574p il hardcover o.p. pa $7.99   **92**

1. Air pilots

ISBN 0-553-07807-0; 0-553-58464-2 (pa)

LC 91-3353

In this "memoir, World War II flying ace Doolittle . . . recalls his sterling military career and the importance of his family." Booklist

"The book recalls vividly Doolittle's days as an aviation pioneer—and retells the exciting story of the Tokyo raid." Publ Wkly

Includes bibliographical references

Dornstein, David Scott, 1963-1988

Dornstein, Ken. The boy who fell out of the sky; a true story. Random House 2006 304p il $23.95; pa $13.95   **92**

1. Pan Am Flight 103 Bombing Incident, 1988

ISBN 0-375-50359-5; 0-375-70769-7 (pa)

LC 2005-42683

"On December 21, 1988, Dornstein's older brother, David, went down with Pan Am Flight 103 over Lockerbie, Scotland. Shattered, Dornstein returned to college and tried to move on. But eight years later, he started reading the papers left behind by his brother, who was an unpublished but prolific writer. . . . This memoir cobbles together the author's memories, past news accounts and David's . . . journal entries and letters." Publ Wkly

"Dornstein's account of his relationship with his brother and of his own self-examination is a startlingly honest, completely absorbing look at loss and brotherly love." Booklist

Includes bibliographical references

Dostoyevsky, Fyodor, 1821-1881

Frank, Joseph. Dostoevsky. v1: The seeds of revolt, 1821-1849. Princeton University Press 1976 401p il hardcover o.p. pa $24.95   **92**
1. Authors, Russian
ISBN 0-691-06260-9; 0-691-01355-1 (pa)

This first volume of a five volume biography of Dostoyevsky traces his life from his boyhood to 1849. His writings are discussed in relation to influences and themes which recur in his greatest works.
Includes bibliographical references

Frank, Joseph. Dostoevsky. v2: The years of ordeal, 1850-1859. Princeton Univ. Press 1983 320p il hardcover o.p. pa $24.95   **92**
1. Authors, Russian
ISBN 0-691-06576-4; 0-691-01422-1 (pa)
LC 83-11216

In this second of a five-volume biography of Dostoyevsky, Frank focuses on the Russian author's arrest, imprisonment, and exile for his socialist activities. Special attention is given to his book, *The House of The Dead*.
Includes bibliographical references

Frank, Joseph. Dostoevsky. v3: The stir of liberation, 1860-1865. Princeton Univ. Press 1986 395p il hardcover o.p. pa $24.95   **92**
1. Authors, Russian
ISBN 0-691-06652-3; 0-691-01452-3 (pa)
LC 85-43280

In this third volume of a five-volume biography of the writer, Frank "describes the influence of the social and political background of Dostoyevsky's Russia on his intellectual and artistic development." Natl Rev
Includes bibliographical references

Frank, Joseph. Dostoevsky. v4: The miraculous years, 1865-1871. Princeton Univ. Press 1995 523p il hardcover o.p. pa $24.95   **92**
1. Authors, Russian
ISBN 0-691-04364-7; 0-691-01587-2 (pa)
LC 94-43403

"This fourth installment in Frank's acclaimed . . . five-volume biography presents an astonishingly vivid, uncanny portrait of Dostoevsky's spiritual, emotional and artistic development during his crucial years abroad." Publ Wkly
Includes bibliographical references

Frank, Joseph. Dostoevsky. v5: The mantle and the prophet, 1871-1881. Princeton Univ. Press 2002 784p il $60; pa $24.95   **92**
1. Authors, Russian
ISBN 0-691-08665-6; 0-691-11569-9 (pa)
LC 2001-38749

This is the fifth and final volume of Frank's biography of Dostoevsky.
Includes bibliographical references

Doty, Mark

Doty, Mark. Dog years; a memoir. HarperCollins Publishers 2007 215p $23.95   **92**
ISBN 0-06-117100-X; 978-0-06-117100-0
LC 2006-46491

The author "celebrates the 16 lovely years his two beloved 70-pound Labs, Beau and Arden, gave him. . . . Against a backdrop of devastating human loss, both personal (the death of his partner) and public (9/11), Doty bears witness to the inexorable decline of his beloved retrievers. . . . Poignant, intelligent, and quite simply superb." Libr J

Douglas, Kirk, 1916-

Douglas, Kirk. My stroke of luck. Morrow 2002 196p il pa $12.95 hardcover o.p.   **92**
ISBN 0-06-001404-0 (pa)
LC 2002-727755

"Douglas reflects on his 1995 stroke, the flubbed suicide attempt that followed, and celebrity friends who have had battles of their own." Libr J

"Entertaining and uplifting, Douglas's story is a lesson in survival, one that will entice readers whether or not they have had similar illnesses. . . . This book is a natural for the 65-plus crowd." Publ Wkly

Douglass, Frederick, 1817?-1895

Douglass, Frederick. Autobiographies. Library of Am. 1994 1126p $35; pa $13.95 *   **92**
1. Abolitionists 2. African Americans—Biography
ISBN 0-940450-79-8; 1-883011-30-2 (pa)
LC 93-24168

Contents: Narrative of the life of Frederick Douglass, an American slave; My Bondage and my freedom; Life and times of Frederick Douglass

"This one volume containing Douglass's seminal works is highly recommended for black history collections." Libr J
Includes bibliographical references

Douglass, Frederick. My bondage and my freedom; edited with an introduction and notes by John David Smith. Penguin Bks. 2003 lx, 366p (Penguin Classics) pa $12   **92**
1. Abolitionists 2. African Americans—Biography
ISBN 0-14-043918-8
LC 2002-28992

First published 1855 by Orton & Mulligan
In this autobiography Douglass tells of his life as a slave and his early years in the abolitionist movement.
Includes bibliographical references

Douglass, Frederick. Narrative of the life of Frederick Douglass, an American slave; written by himself; edited with an introduction by Houston A. Baker, Jr. Penguin Bks 1982 159p il pa $10   **92**
1. Abolitionists 2. African Americans—Biography
ISBN 0-14-039012-X
LC 82-5371

Originally published 1845 by the Boston Anti-slavery office

"Frederick Douglass became famous as a slave who escaped to the North and spent his lifetime in the aboli-

Douglass, Frederick, 1817?-1895—*Continued*
tionist movement. His 'Narrative,' one of three autobiographical works written by the self-taught slave, is the story of his life up to his escape to freedom." Libr J
Includes bibliographical references

Doyle, Sir Arthur Conan, 1859-1930
Doyle, Sir Arthur Conan. Arthur Conan Doyle; his life in letters; edited by Jon Lellenberg, Daniel Stashower & Charles Foley. Harper Press 2007 706p il $37.95 *   **92**
1. Authors, Scottish
ISBN 978-1-59420-135-6; 1-59420-135-8
           LC 2007-14692
This volume presents the selected correspondence of the British author at various points during his life.
"This will be essential reading for all fans of Conan Doyle and his sleuth." Publ Wkly

Stashower, Daniel. Teller of tales: the life of Arthur Conan Doyle. Holt & Co. 1999 472p il pa $16 hardcover o.p.   **92**
1. Authors, Scottish
ISBN 0-8050-6684-5 (pa)   LC 98-35059
"Best known for creating Sherlock Holmes, Sir Arthur Conan Doyle . . . led a turbulent life as a doctor, playwright, avid sportsman, and crusader for hopeless or unpopular causes." Libr J
"Stashower has done an admirable job in creating both a general, well-researched biography of a complex literary giant and in providing insights into the origins and apparent contradictions of his later beliefs." Publ Wkly
Includes bibliographical references

Du Bois, W. E. B. (William Edward Burghardt), 1868-1963
Lewis, David Levering. W.E.B. DuBois; biography of a race, 1868-1919. Holt & Co. 1993 735p il pa $20 hardcover o.p. *   **92**
1. African Americans—Civil rights
ISBN 0-8050-3568-0 (pa)   LC 93-16617
In this first volume of a two-volume set, "the first 50 years of DuBois's life are detailed, not only on a personal level but also in the context of American history. This exhaustive study includes an in-depth analysis of the civil rights movement of the 19th and early 20th centuries. . . . A magnificent resource." SLJ
Includes bibliographical references

Du Pré, Jacqueline, 1945-1987
Wilson, Elizabeth. Jacqueline du Pré; her life, her music, her legend. Arcade Pub. 1999 466p il $27.95; pa $14.95   **92**
ISBN 1-55970-490-X; 1-55970-519-1 (pa)
           LC 98-49664
This is a biography of "the classical cellist, who flourished briefly as the brightest young star in the firmament in the 1960s and early '70s, only to see her career ended before she was 30 by multiple sclerosis." Publ Wkly
"Wilson, a professional cellist, has given priority to the music. Her method is discreet, methodical, informed and accurate. Above all it is measured in its tone." N Y Times Book Rev
Includes bibliographical references

Duchamp, Marcel, 1887-1968
Tomkins, Calvin. Duchamp; a biography. Holt & Co. 1996 550p il map pa $20 hardcover o.p.
    92
1. Artists, French
ISBN 0-8050-5789-7   LC 96-3080
"A John Macrae book"
"Tomkins organizes the facts of Duchamp's life and work into a sober, coherent whole, and for this alone his book makes valuable reading for anyone seeking to understand how art's cutting edge was honed." New Repub
Includes bibliographical references

Dukakis, Olympia
Dukakis, Olympia. Ask me again tomorrow; a life in progress; [by] Olympia Dukakis with Emily Heckman. HarperCollins Pubs. 2003 211p il $25.95; pa $13.95   **92**
ISBN 0-06-018821-9; 0-06-093409-3 (pa)
           LC 2003-49909
In this "autobiography, the first-generation Greek-American recounts her life and work." Publ Wkly
"Students of the theater will be interested in her views on acting. All in all, this is a satisfying look into the personal and professional life of a theater actor." Libr J
Includes bibliographical references

Dulles, Allen Welsh, 1893-1969
Grose, Peter. Gentleman spy; the life of Allen Dulles. University of Mass. Press 1996 641p il pa $19.95   **92**
1. United States. Central Intelligence Agency
ISBN 1-55849-044-2; 978-1-55849-044-4
           LC 96-19010
First published 1994 by Houghton Mifflin
This biography of the CIA director under Eisenhower and Kennedy "renders the interplay of person and public event and allows readers to enter the dark world of US-sponsored terror and covert paramilitary operations. . . . Grose sets forth in fascinating and often unfamiliar detail the spectacular CIA covert operations: in Iran, Guatemala, Indonesia; the U2 incident; the Bay of Pigs." Choice

Duncan, Isadora, 1878-1927
Kurth, Peter. Isadora; a sensational life. Little, Brown 2001 652p il $29.95; pa $17.95
    92
ISBN 0-316-50726-1; 0-316-05713-4 (pa)
           LC 2001-38064
The author recounts the life and career of the modern dance legend through "her own writings, recollections of her contemporaries and press coverage of the day." Libr J
Kurth "diligently tracks Duncan's every triumph and tragedy . . . and sets her entire complex milieu in motion." Booklist
Includes bibliographical references

Durrell, Gerald M., 1925-1995

Botting, Douglas. Gerald Durrell; the authorized biography. Carroll & Graf Pubs. 1999 xx, 644p il $29.95; pa $16.95   **92**

ISBN 0-7867-0655-4; 0-7867-0796-8 (pa)

LC 00-268642

A biography of the naturalist, writer, and founder of the Jersey Zoo

"Given full access to Durrell's personal and professional papers, Botting clearly admires his subject yet presents an evenhanded account." Libr J

Includes bibliographical references

Dylan, Bob, 1941-

Dylan, Bob. Chronicles. v1. Simon & Schuster 2004 293p il $24   **92**

1. Rock musicians

ISBN 0-7432-2815-4   LC 2004-564

This is the first installment of a projected three-volume autobiography by the American singer and songwriter

"This book will stand as a record of a young man's self-education, as contagious in its frank excitement as the letters of John Keats and as sincere in its ramble as Jack Kerouac's On the Road, to which Dylan frequently refers. A person of Dylan's stature could have gotten away with far less; that he has been so thoughtful in the creation of this book is a measure of his talents, and a gift to his fans." Publ Wkly

Sounes, Howard. Down the highway: the life of Bob Dylan. Grove Press 2001 527p il $27.50; pa $16   **92**

1. Rock musicians

ISBN 0-8021-1686-8; 0-8021-3891-8 (pa)

LC 00-69463

This biography traces Dylan's "career: the early days as a struggling folksinger, the rise to the forefront of the early-'60s folk scene, the controversial switch to rock, the motorcycle accident and the subsequent retreat from public view, and the latter-day de-emphasis of recording and concentration on the concert series known as the Never Ending Tour." Booklist

"Through extensive interviews Sounes aptly captures the contradictory facets of an American folk legend." Publ Wkly

Includes bibliographical references

Spitz, Bob. Dylan; a biography; with a discography by Jeff Friedman. Norton 1991 664p il pa $19.95   **92**

1. Rock musicians

ISBN 0-393-30769-7   LC 88-12912

First published 1989 by McGraw-Hill

"Lamenting the impenetrable mythology that surrounds singer/songwriter Bob Dylan . . . Spitz accomplishes his demystification through a sometimes fanciful reconstruction of Dylan's life, replete with sordid examples of his reputedly capricious personality. Although the relevance of such treatment is questionable and his often lurid prose will be objectionable to some, Spitz gives a fascinating portrayal of one of the most influential and complex figures in popular music." Choice

Includes discography and bibliographical references

Eakins, Thomas, 1844-1916

Kirkpatrick, Sidney. The revenge of Thomas Eakins; [by] Sidney D. Kirkpatrick. Yale University Press 2006 565p il (The Henry McBride series in modernism and modernity) $39.95   **92**

ISBN 0-300-10855-9   LC 2005-27935

This is a "portrait of Thomas Eakins, the controversial Philadelphia portrait artist whose 'failure to abide by the artistic trends that defined his times' resulted in work that was richly interesting and highly controversial. . . . Kirkpatrick gives Eakins convincing depth that reminds readers of the ways biography can enhance appreciation of art." Publ Wkly

Includes bibliographical references

Earhart, Amelia, 1898-1937

Butler, Susan. East to the dawn; the life of Amelia Earhart. Da Capo Press 1999 489p il map pa $19.95   **92**

1. Women air pilots

ISBN 0-306-80887-0; 978-0-306-80887-6

LC 98-47717

First published 1997 by Addison-Wesley

In this biography of the pilot and women's rights advocate "Butler shows a mastery of aviation history, and considerable sophistication about the technology of flight and navigation . . . The mountain of new material it marshals guarantees 'East to the Dawn' a permanent place on the shelf of Amelia Earhart references." N Y Times Book Rev

Includes bibliographical references

Rich, Doris L. Amelia Earhart; a biography. Smithsonian Institution Press 1989 321p il pa $16.95 hardcover o.p.   **92**

1. Women air pilots

ISBN 1-56098-725-1 (pa)   LC 89-32181

"Rich emphasizes Earhart's flying career and the stories and personalities behind her accomplishments. It is a scholarly account of her life, highlighting her goals, enthusiasm, and competitive pioneer spirit." Libr J

A "fast-paced, richly detailed biography." Publ Wkly

Includes bibliographical references

Earp, Wyatt, 1848-1929

Barra, Allen. Inventing Wyatt Earp; his life and many legends. Carroll & Graf Pubs. 1998 432p pa $15.95 hardcover o.p. paperback available $15.95

92

ISBN 0-7867-0685-6 (pa)

This is a "biographical and historical study of the legend of Wyatt Earp as it occurs in text and film." Libr J

"Barra is at his best in describing the efforts of assorted Hollywood icons, including John Ford, John Sturges, and Kevin Costner, to depict the 'real' Earp." Booklist

Tefertiller, Casey. Wyatt Earp; the life behind the legend. Wiley 1997 403p $45; pa $19.95

92

ISBN 0-471-18967-7; 0-471-28362-2 (pa)

LC 97-2932

Earp, Wyatt, 1848-1929—_Continued_

This is an account "of the storied life of lawman Wyatt Earp—a villain and a hero in Tombstone, Arizona, both before and after his death in 1929. Portrayed by novelists, historians, and filmmakers, the Earp brothers—especially Wyatt—became the stuff of legends. Attempting to uncover what really happened in Tombstone, Tefertiller draws on newspaper articles and personal accounts by Earp's friends, enemies, and acquaintances." Libr J

"An engrossing, satisfying inspection of a quintessential figure in American popular culture." Booklist

Includes bibliographical references

Eastwood, Clint

Schickel, Richard. Clint Eastwood; a biography. Knopf 1996 557p il pa $15 hardcover o.p.

92

ISBN 0-679-74991-8 (pa)   LC 96-32836
A Borzoi Bk.

Schickel examines the life and career of the actor-director

"No mere celebrity bio, this is a beautifully written, comprehensive and astonishingly insightful study of a man who, seemingly against all odds, has achieved world renown as both a pop culture icon and an accomplished film artist." Publ Wkly

Includes bibliographical references

Ebadi, Shirin

Ebadi, Shirin. Iran awakening; a memoir of revolution and hope; [by] Shirin Ebadi with Azedeh Moaveni. Random House 2006 232p il map hardcover o.p. pa $14.95   92
1. Iran—History—1979-
ISBN   1-4000-6470-8;   978-1-4000-6470-0;
978-0-8129-7528-4 (pa); 0-8129-7528-6 (pa)
LC 2005-55255

This is a memoir by the Iranian lawyer and human right activist.

This book "offers the chance to understand Iran's tumultuous recent history, seen through the eyes of a supremely courageous Islamic woman." Christ Sci Monit

Includes bibliographical references

Eddy, Mary Baker, 1821-1910

Gill, Gillian. Mary Baker Eddy. Perseus Bks. 1998 xxxv, 713p il pa $24 hardcover o.p.

92

1. Christian Science
ISBN 0-7382-0227-4 (pa)   LC 98-86397
A Merloyd Lawrence book

This "biography of Christian Science's founder offers detailed depictions of her early years of obscurity, her multiple marriages, the controversies she endured, and the inspiration that sustained her." Libr J

Includes bibliographical references

Edelman, Marian Wright, 1939-

Edelman, Marian Wright. Lanterns; a memoir of mentors. HarperPerennial 2000 xxi, 208p il pa $14

92

ISBN 0-06-095859-6   LC 00-33430

First published 1999 by Beacon Press

This is "Edelman's account of how a diverse group of mentors, ranging from Martin Luther King Jr. and Robert Kennedy to the women of her South Carolina hometown, influenced her to dedicate her life to securing a future for America's children. Upon graduating from Yale Law School in the 1960's, Edelman became an attorney at the NAACP Legal Defense and Educational Fund Inc., . . . where she fought to integrate the schools." NY Times Book Rev

"Throughout this absorbing memoir, Edelman's voice resounds with spirituality, a reliance on her faith, and a belief in equality." Booklist

Includes bibliographical references

Edison, Thomas A. (Thomas Alva), 1847-1931

Israel, Paul. Edison; a life of invention. Wiley 1998 552p il $50; pa $18.95 *   92
ISBN 0-471-52942-7; 0-471-36270-0 (pa)
LC 98-10105

This biography focuses on Edison's technical work, experiments, and business dealings

"Dozens of facsimiles of his original drawings are reproduced, which fortify the impression of Edison's meticulousness, as do Israel's accounts of his business ventures." Booklist

Includes bibliographical references

Edwards, Jonathan, 1703-1758

Marsden, George M. Jonathan Edwards; a life. Yale Univ. Press 2003 xx, 615p $35; pa $19.95

92

ISBN 0-300-09693-3; 0-300-10596-7 (pa)
LC 2002-013611

"In the first full critical biography of Edwards in 60 years, the author humanizes America's greatest colonial clergyman." Booklist

"Clearly sympathetic to his subject without ever becoming an outright apologist for either his character or his theology, Marsden . . . writes with such verve that he has given us not only the definitive biography but also a narrative that reads like a novel—that most appropriate art form for examining the interior drama of the soul." Commonweal

Includes bibliographical references

Ehrlich, Gretel

Ehrlich, Gretel. A match to the heart. Penguin Books 1995 200p pa $15   92
1. Lightning
ISBN 0-14-017937-2   LC 93-34981

First published 1994 by Pantheon Bks.

"Hit by lightning on a stormy August afternoon in 1991, Ms. Ehrlich was left with damage to her nervous system that resulted in constant fainting spells. . . . This eclectic chronicle of recovery offers excursions into neurobiology, cardiology, the lore and science of lightning, and the medical literature of lightning injury, as well as musings on the Tibetan Book of the Dead and the healing power of the ocean." N Y Times Book Rev

Einstein, Albert, 1879-1955

Fölsing, Albrecht. Albert Einstein; a biography; translated from the German by Ewald Osers. Viking 1997 882p il pa $20 hardcover o.p.

92

ISBN 0-14-023719-4 (pa)   LC 96-26341

This biography traces "Einstein's life from early childhood through his final years at Princeton's Institute for Advanced Study. It gives equal detail to his technical accomplishments and personal life, including his role as an international spokesman for Zionism and pacifism. It also includes a more honest picture of his relationships with women." Libr J

Includes bibliographical references

Isaacson, Walter. Einstein: his life and universe. Simon & Schuster 2007 xxii, 675p il $32 *

92

ISBN 978-0-7432-6473-0; 0-7432-6473-8

LC 2006-51264

This book tells the story of the German-American physicist's life.

"This is a warm, insightful, affectionate portrait with a human and immensely charming Einstein at its core." N Y Times (Late N Y Ed)

Includes bibliographical references

Eire, Carlos M. N.

Eire, Carlos M. N. Waiting for snow in Havana; confessions of a Cuban boy; {by} Carlos Eire. Free Press 2003 383p il hardcover o.p. pa $15

92

ISBN   0-7432-1965-1;   978-0-7432-4641-5; 0-7432-4641-1 (pa)   LC 2002-73875

"From 1960 through 1962, some fourteen thousand Cuban children were airlifted—unaccompanied—to the United States by Operation Pedro (Peter) Pan. Once here, they were farmed out to CIA-funded refugee camps, then to foster homes. Many never saw their island parents again. Carlos Eire, now a Yale professor of history and religious studies, was a Peter Pan. {This memoir} tells mostly of Eire's privileged boyhood during the pre-Castro 1950s." Commonweal

The author "looks beyond the literal to see the mythological themes inherent in the epic struggle for identity that each of our lives represents. . . . As painful as Eire's journey has been, his ability to see tragedy and suffering as a constant source of redemption is what makes this book so powerful." Publ Wkly

Eisenhower, Dwight D. (Dwight David), 1890-1969

Ambrose, Stephen E. Eisenhower; soldier and president. Simon & Schuster 1990 635p il pa $18 hardcover o.p.   **92**

1. Presidents—United States
ISBN 0-671-74758-4 (pa)   LC 90-9701

Condensed version of a two volume work published 1983-1984

"Tracing Eisenhower's family background, education, military and political careers, and influence as elder statesman, the author chronicles Eisenhower's triumphs and failures and at the same time provides a vivid pic-

ture of the off-duty Ike. . . . This is the definitive one-volume biography of Eisenhower." Publ Wkly

Includes bibliographical references

Korda, Michael. Ike: an American hero. HarperCollins 2007 779p il map $34.95

92

1. Presidents—United States
ISBN 978-0-06-075665-9; 0-06-075665-9

LC 2006-52856

This is a biography of the American president and World War II general.

"With a sure touch on Ike's Kansas boyhood, marriage to Mamie, and prewar army mentors, Korda . . . successfully reintroduces the Eisenhower personality that was so popular privately, militarily, and politically." Booklist

Includes bibliographical references

Wicker, Tom. Dwight D. Eisenhower. Times Bks. 2002 158p (American presidents series) $20

92

1. United States—Politics and government—1953-1961 2. Presidents—United States
ISBN 0-8050-6907-0   LC 2002-20397

This volume "holds Eisenhower's accomplishments up against the two major issues of his time: the cold war and civil rights. Wicker . . . likes the man more than his policies." N Y Times Book Rev

This work "captures the key events of the Eisenhower presidency in a way that is highly accessible and intellectually compelling." Libr J

Includes bibliographical references

Eisenhower, Mamie Doud, 1896-1979

Eisenhower, Susan. Mrs. Ike; memories and reflections on the life of Mamie Eisenhower. Capital Bks. 2002 398p il (Capital classics) pa $16.95   **92**

1. Presidents' spouses—United States
ISBN 1-931868-04-2; 978-1-931868-04-4

LC 2002-31378

First published 1996 by Farrar, Straus & Giroux

This biography "follows Mamie Doud from the proper, functional, socially conscious family environment into which she was born, to her early married years to Ike Eisenhower . . . to the war years as home-front wife of the Allied commander, and to her years in the White House, where she functioned as the perfect 1950s First Lady." Booklist

"Enhanced by unpublished letters . . . this work is a good attempt at exploring a woman of another time who lived in a different state of grace." Libr J

Includes bibliographical references

Eisner, Will, 1917-2005

Andelman, Bob. Will Eisner, a spirited life. M Press 2005 375p il pa $14.95   **92**
ISBN 1-59582-011-6   LC 2005-26326

This is a biography of the American cartoonist and comic book publisher.

"Besides verifying Eisner's impact on nearly every artist who drew comics in his wake, Andelman shows that Eisner's influence extends to such film directors as Spielberg and Tarantino." Booklist

Eleanor, of Aquitaine, Queen, consort of Henry II, King of England, 1122?-1204

Weir, Alison. Eleanor of Aquitaine; a life. Ballantine Bks. 2000 xxi, 441p il maps $28; pa $15.95 **92**

ISBN 0-345-40540-4; 0-345-43487-0 (pa)

LC 99-54785

First published 1999 in the United Kingdom with title Eleanor of Aquitaine: by the wrath of God, Queen of England

A biography of the twelfth-century queen, first of France, then of England, the consort of Henry II and mother of Richard the Lionhearted

"In approaching as complex a subject as feudalism, Weir wears her learning lightly and has a pleasant habit of anticipating all the questions of a curious reader." Publ Wkly

Includes bibliographical references

Elijah Muhammad, 1897-1975

Evanzz, Karl. The messenger: the rise and fall of Elijah Muhammad. Pantheon Bks. 1999 667p pa $18 hardcover o.p. **92**

ISBN 0-679-77406-8 (pa)   LC 99-11826

A "critical biography of one of America's leading black nationalists of the 20th century. One of the founders of the Nation of Islam (NOI), Muhammad helped convert thousands of African Americans to the religion popularly known as the Black Muslims. Evanzz concludes that Muhammad was essentially a con man who used his considerable powers of persuasion to get rich and seduce women. Especially fascinating is Evanzz's extensive use of FBI files to make his case." Libr J

Includes bibliographical references

Eliot, George, 1819-1880

Hughes, Kathryn. George Eliot; the last Victorian. Cooper Square Press 2001 383p il pa $19.95 **92**

1. Authors, English

ISBN 0-8154-1121-9; 978-0-8154-1121-5

LC 2001-28024

First published 1998 in the United Kingdom

In this biography Hughes "shows how George Eliot (nee Mary Anne Evans, 1819-80), in spite of her outwardly anti-Victorian lifestyle, was in fact a true Victorian. . . . A solitary, ascetic child and young woman, she was raised in an upwardly mobile country family. . . . In 1852 she met the married writer and editor George Henry Lewes, with whom she lived until his death in 1878." Libr J

Includes bibliographical references

Eliot, T. S. (Thomas Stearns), 1888-1965

Gordon, Lyndall. T.S. Eliot; an imperfect life. Norton 1999 721p $35; pa $18.95 * **92**

ISBN 0-393-04728-8; 0-393-32093-6 (pa)

LC 98-46864

First published 1998 in the United Kingdom

"The present volume combines material from Gordon's previous award-winning works, *Eliot's Early Years* [1977] and *Eliot's New Life* [1988], with extensive addi-

tional research. Subjects covered in depth include Eliot's complex relationships with women and the Americanness of his work despite his near-obsession with things British." Libr J

"Gordon's book is the most authoritative life of Eliot thus far, and is certain to spark new controversies." Publ Wkly

Includes bibliographical references

Elizabeth I, Queen of England, 1533-1603

Hibbert, Christopher. The virgin queen: Elizabeth I, genius of the Golden Age. Perseus Books 1992 287p il map pa $22 **92**

1. Great Britain—Kings and rulers 2. Great Britain—History—1485-1603, Tudors

ISBN 978-0-201-60817-5; 0-201-60817-0

First published 1990 in the United Kingdom; First United States edition published 1991 by Addison-Wesley

This "biography is essentially personal rather than political history. . . . There are many biographies of Elizabeth, and more than a few good ones, but Hibbert's is solid and sure to charm. . . . A reliable and highly readable choice." Libr J

Includes bibliographical references

Strachey, Lytton. Elizabeth and Essex; a tragic history. Harcourt Brace & Co. 1928 296p il pa $14 hardcover o.p. **92**

1. Essex, Robert Devereux, 2nd Earl of, 1566-1601
2. Great Britain—Kings and rulers 3. Great Britain—History—1485-1603, Tudors

ISBN 0-15-602761-5 (pa)

The story "begins where the conventional biography recedes, when the queen at fifty-three falls in love with a lad of twenty—a favorite whom she forgives again and again and sends at last to the scaffold." Chicago Public Libr

Includes bibliographical references

Weir, Alison. The life of Elizabeth I. Ballantine Bks. 1998 532p il pa $15.95 hardcover o.p.

92

1. Great Britain—History—1485-1603, Tudors

ISBN 0-345-42550-2 (pa)   LC 98-34917

This is a biography of "Elizabeth Tudor, the second of the three surviving children of the great English king Henry VIII." Booklist

"Weir brings a fine sense of selection and considerable zest to her portrait of the self-styled Virgin Queen." Publ Wkly

Includes bibliographical references

Elizabeth II, Queen of Great Britain, 1926-

Pimlott, Ben. The Queen: a biography of Elizabeth II. Wiley 1997 651p il pa $24.95 hardcover o.p. **92**

1. Great Britain—History—1952-

ISBN 0-471-28330-4 (pa)   LC 97-21270

First published 1996 in the United Kingdom

The author explores "the role of the queen and how the events of the past few decades have changed it. Is the monarch just a figurehead, or are there specific governmental actions she can take? How did the royal fami-

Elizabeth II, Queen of Great Britain, 1926-
Continued

ly lose its privacy, along with much public respect? Pimlott tackles these questions and other historical, psychological, and sociological issues surrounding the queen and her family." Libr J

"One of the many merits of Ben Pimlott's superbly judicious biography of Elizabeth II is that it understands this connection between monarchy and masses, and carefully evokes its political importance." N Y Times Book Rev

Includes bibliographical references

Ellison, Ralph

Rampersad, Arnold. Ralph Ellison; a biography. Alfred A. Knopf 2007 657p il $35 * **92**

ISBN 978-0-375-40827-4; 0-375-40827-4

LC 2006-26464

Rampersad depicts the author's "early life in Oklahoma; his love of music, whisch led to a scholarship at the Tuskegee Institute; his complex relationships with his wives and mentors; and, finally, his years as a fixture in the New York literary scene." Bookmarks Magazine

"As the first scholar granted complete access to the Ellison papers, Rampersad introduces us to people and places that reveal the total range of Ellison's sensibilities. . . . Through elegant and lively prose, Rampersad reveals sides of Ellison that are disturbing and instructive." Charlotte Observer

Includes bibliographical references

Emerson, Ralph Waldo, 1803-1882

Richardson, Robert D. Emerson; the mind on fire: a biography; by Robert D. Richardson, Jr.; with a frontispiece by Barry Moser. University of Calif. Press 1995 671p il $50; pa $21.95

92

ISBN 0-520-08808-5; 0-520-20689-4 (pa)

LC 94-36008

"A Centennial book"

"Richardson focuses principally on his subject's inner life, the life of his mind and spirit. But in this subtle portrayal of Emerson the thinker, the reader also sees the clearly limned portrait of Emerson the social activist. . . . A masterful work, this biography will attract the attention of scholars and serious general readers for decades." Booklist

Includes bibliographical references

Eminem

Bozza, Anthony. Whatever you say I am; the life and times of Eminem. Crown Pubs. 2003 278p il $23; pa $12.95 **92**

1. Rap music

ISBN 1-400-05059-6; 1-400-05380-3 (pa)

LC 2003-8923

Bozza "first charts his subject's rags-to-riches rise to superstardom in concert, on CD, and in the film *8 Mile*, continuing with the press reaction to his outrageous public persona and a . . . history of hip-hop . . . The author ends with an examination of Eminem's homophobia and misogyny, the latter exemplified in part by his strained relationships with his mother and ex-wife." Libr J

"It is Bozza's relationship with Eminem that lends credibility to this bio, as well as his ability to fold personal reminiscence into longer analytical sections on Eminem's life, the Detroit rap scene and pop culture. Bozza's unprecedented access to Mathers then and now has given rise to one of the only fully honest accounts of the now brilliant star." Publ Wkly

Includes bibliographical references

Equiano, Olaudah, 1745-1797

Carretta, Vincent. Equiano, the African; biography of a self-made man. University of Georgia Press 2005 xxiv, 436p il map $29.95 *

92

ISBN 0-8203-2571-6   LC 2005-11898

This "biography tells the story of the former slave Olaudah Equiano. . . . [Equiano authored the] 1789 autobiography, The Interesting Narrative of the Life of Olaudah Equiano, or Gustavus Vassa, the African. . . . [The Narrative] includes the earliest firsthand description by a slave of the . . . Middle Passage from Africa to the Americas." Publisher's note

"This is a thoroughly rich, engrossing, and well-researched portrait of an exceptional man and the cause he championed." Booklist

Includes bibliographical references

Erdrich, Louise

Erdrich, Louise. Books and islands in Ojibwe country. National Geographic Soc. 2003 143p il map (National Geographic directions) $20

92

1. Ojibwa Indians

ISBN 0-7922-5719-7   LC 2003-45906

"Fans of Erdrich's bestselling fiction will recognize her signature combination of the sacred and the ordinary in this lively traveler's memoir, and many will enjoy the rare glimpse of her personal life as well as the physical facts of her journey from her home in Minneapolis to the lakes and islands of her Ojibwe ancestors in Ontario and Minnesota." Booklist

Erikson, Erik H. (Erik Homburger), 1902-1994

Friedman, Lawrence Jacob. Identity's architect; a biography of Erik H. Erikson. Harvard University Press 2000 592p il pa $19.95

92

ISBN 978-0-674-00437-5; 0-674-00437-X

First published 1999 by Scribner

The author "portrays Erikson as an artistic, somewhat insecure, courageous, upbeat, wise, and perhaps tragic figure. Trained in Vienna by Anne Freud, Erikson had no academic degree yet became a professor at Harvard." Libr J

"Friedman's biography is lucidly written, extensively researched and covers both Erikson's rise to celebrity in the 1950s and 1960s and the attacks on his reputation from feminist and New Left critics in the 1970s." Publ Wkly

Includes bibliographical references

Essex, Robert Devereux, 2nd Earl of, 1566-1601
Strachey, Lytton. Elizabeth and Essex. See entry under Elizabeth I, Queen of England, 1533-1603

Evans, Walker, 1903-1975
Rathbone, Belinda. Walker Evans; a biography. Houghton Mifflin 1995 358p il pa $15 hardcover o.p. **92**
ISBN 0-6180-5672-6 (pa)   LC 95-3711
This is a biography of the photographer whose "documentary studies of the rural South during the Depression evoke the dark side of the American dream." Publ Wkly
"Rathbone does a superb job of describing Evans' elusive personality and unique vision." Booklist
Includes bibliographical references

Evers, Medgar Wiley, 1925-1963
Evers, Medgar Wiley. The autobiography of Medgar Evers: a hero's life and legacy revealed through his writings, letters, and speeches; edited by Myrlie Evers-Williams and Manning Marable. Basic Civitas Books 2005 xxiv, 352p il $26; pa $14 **92**
ISBN 0-465-02177-8; 0-465-02178-6 (pa)
LC 2006-296327
This is a collection of "Evers's unpublished papers and personal collections as well as [his widow] Evers-Williams's recollections. The resulting text resurrects the life, intellectual output, and creative legacy of the slain civil rights hero." Libr J
Includes bibliographical references

Evert, Chris
Howard, Johnette. The rivals; Chris Evert vs. Martina Navratilova: their epic duels and extraordinary friendship. Broadway Books 2005 296p il $24.95 **92**
1. Navratilova, Martina, 1956- 2. Tennis—Biography
ISBN 0-7679-1884-3   LC 2004-61918
"In sixteen years, Chris Evert and Martina Navratilova met on the tennis court eighty times—sixty times in finals. . . . [This book examines] the intertwined lives of these [athletes]." Publisher's note
"This work makes a fine contribution to the history of women in sports." Publ Wkly

Fanon, Frantz, 1925-1961
Macey, David. Frantz Fanon; a biography. Picador 2001 640p maps $40; pa $20 **92**
ISBN 0-312-27550-1; 0-312-30042-5 (pa)
LC 2001-21807
A biography "of the psychiatrist from Martinique who propagandized for Algerian independence in the 1950's and sought to justify violence not only as a tactic but also as therapy for the oppressed." N Y Times Book Rev
"Macey's writing and research is rich with historical context and personal information that both Fanon loyalists and general readers will appreciate." Libr J
Includes bibliographical references

Faraday, Michael, 1791-1867
Hirshfeld, Alan. The electric life of Michael Faraday. Walker & Co. 2006 258p il $24
92
1. Physicists
ISBN 0-8027-1470-6   LC 2005-25533
In this biography of the English scientist, the author "explains Faraday's status as one of the most inspirational and significant figures of science. . . . A vibrant portrayal that emphasizes Faraday's qualities of wonder, acuity, and diligence, which propelled him to greatness." Booklist
Includes bibliographical references

Farmer, Paul, 1959-
Kidder, Tracy. Mountains beyond mountains. Random House 2003 336p $25.95; pa $14.95
92
1. Physicians
ISBN 0-375-50616-0; 0-8129-7301-1 (pa)
LC 2003-41253
This is a "portrait of Paul Farmer (MacArthur 'genius' grant, 1993), a driven, dedicated, rigidly idealistic doctor who commutes between Harvard and Haiti, where he works . . . to relieve the suffering of some of the poorest people on earth." N Y Times Book Rev
"This story is remarkable, and Kidder's skill in sequencing both dramatic and understated elements into a reflective commentary is unsurpassed." SLJ
Includes bibliographical references

Farrakhan, Louis, 1933-
Levinsohn, Florence Hamlish. Looking for Farrakhan. Dee, I.R. 1997 305p $25   **92**
1. Black Muslims
ISBN 1-56663-157-2   LC 97-11335
Levinsohn's "biography, which reflects on the black experience and how it changed young Eugene Walcott into Louis Farrakhan, leader of the Nation of Islam, attempts to make sense of this prominent figure in American politics." Libr J

Faulkner, William, 1897-1962
Parini, Jay. One matchless time; a life of William Faulkner. HarperCollins Publishers 2004 492p il $29.95; pa $14.95 *   **92**
ISBN 0-06-621072-0; 0-06-093555-3 (pa)
LC 2004-42891
The author "offers a portrait of a man always trying to invent a new mask for himself as well as the portrait of an artist consumed by a desire to tell about the South and its class struggles, its depravity, and its captivity to the double bonds of land and history. Parini examines each of Faulkner's novels, from *Soldier's Pay* to *The Reivers*, and connects the Snopses, Sutpens, and Compsons of Faulkner's mythic Yoknapatawpha County foibles, his insecurities, and his inestimable literary achievement." Libr J
Includes bibliographical references

Feige, David

Feige, David. Indefensible; one lawyer's journey into the inferno of American justice. Little, Brown and Co. 2006 276p $24.95 **92**

1. Administration of criminal justice

ISBN 978-0-316-15623-3; 0-316-15623-X

LC 2006-1283

The author "takes us through a typically harrowing day as a public defender, dealing with arbitrary judges and clients who are often victims of the judicial system. . . . Feige skillfully shares his wisdom and his humanity and sheds light on a justice system that too often works irrationally." Publ Wkly

Feynman, Richard Phillips, 1918-1988

Gleick, James. Genius: the life and science of Richard Feynman. Pantheon Bks. 1992 532p pa $16 hardcover o.p. **92**

ISBN 0-679-74704-4 (pa)   LC 92-6577

"Although it would be hard to relate personal stories about Feynman more engagingly than Feynman himself did in *What Do You Care What Other People Think?* the late Nobelist could not hope for better than his biographer here delivers—a portrait in which the physicist remains a person and is not reduced to an icon of science." Publ Wkly

Includes bibliographical references

Mlodinow, Leonard. Feynman's rainbow; a search for beauty in physics and life. Warner Bks. 2003 171p il $21; pa $13.95 **92**

ISBN 0-446-53045-X; 0-446-69251-4 (pa)

LC 2002-31137

In this memoir "of a stint as a postdoctoral colleague of Feynman's at Caltech, the aging physicist . . . cracks wise, crashes parties, works on his physics at a strip joint and needles stuffed-shirt academics. . . . Mlodinow's accessible style manages to convey Feynman's cantankerous appeal as well as some of the weirdness of theoretical physics without overtaxing lay readers." Publ Wkly

Fisher, Eddie

Fisher, Eddie. Been there, done that; {by} Eddie Fisher, with David Fisher. St. Martin's Press 1999 341p il $24.95; pa $7.99 **92**

ISBN 0-312-20972-X; 0-312-87558-9 (pa)

LC 99-27236

"Thomas Dunne books"

"Fisher tells the story of his rise from poverty to 1950s crooner stardom and beyond." Publ Wkly

"What makes this memoir engaging is Fisher's sharp, often self-deprecating wit and his willingness to dish about his cohorts and conquests." N Y Times Book Rev

Fitzgerald, F. Scott (Francis Scott), 1896-1940

Fitzgerald, F. Scott (Francis Scott). A life in letters; edited by Matthew J. Bruccoli; with the assistance of Judith S. Baughman. Scribner 1994 xxiii, 503p $30; pa $18 **92**

1. Authors, American

ISBN 0-684-19570-4; 0-684-80153-1 (pa)

LC 93-31011

"Early letters to his editor, Maxwell Perkins, and friends, Edmund Wilson and Ernest Hemingway, document Fitzgerald's devotion to craft, exemplified by *The Great Gatsby* (1925), as well as the novelist's ever-present financial problems. . . . Letters to his wife, Zelda—when she was hospitalized for mental illness—detail the destruction of their marriage." Publ Wkly

"Essential reading for a full understanding of Fitzgerald as an artist and a man." Libr J

Flaubert, Gustave, 1821-1880

Brown, Frederick. Flaubert; a biography. Little, Brown 2006 628p il $35 **92**

ISBN 0-316-11878-8   LC 2005-17036

This is a biography of the nineteenth-century French novelist.

The author "has put together a judicious work that sticks to the record and relies on expertly chosen passages from Flaubert's brilliant letters and the works of his contemporaries to develop a convincing portrait, brushstroke by brushstroke." N Y Times (Late N Y Ed)

Includes bibliographical references

Flynn, Nick, 1960-

Flynn, Nick. Another bullshit night in Suck City; a memoir. W.W. Norton & Co 2004 347p il $23.95 **92**

ISBN 0-393-05139-0   LC 2004-11796

This "memoir describes the years poet Flynn . . . spent, in his late 20s, working at one of the city's homeless shelters, where his path crisscrossed with his down-and-out father's. . . . Although it's depressing, the book never seems hopeless, because readers know the author has succeeded at doing what his father only pretended to do: write, and write well." Publ Wkly

Foner, Moe, 1915-2002

Foner, Moe. Not for bread alone; a memoir; by Moe Foner with Dan North; foreword by Ossie Davis. Cornell Univ. Press 2002 142p $25 **92**

ISBN 0-8014-4061-0   LC 2002-5100

This memoir focuses on Foner's work on behalf of "the union of New York City hospital and healthcare workers, best known by its number—1199." Nation

Foner's "memoir is a unique window into the evolution of 1199 SEIU from its origins as a tiny conglomeration of drugstore employees into the country's largest healthcare union." Libr J

Includes bibliographical references

Foote, Horton

Foote, Horton. Beginnings; a memoir. Scribner 2001 270p il $24; pa $14 **92**

ISBN 0-7432-1115-4; 0-7432-1116-2 (pa)

LC 2001-47088

Sequel to Farewell

Foote "chronicled his Wharton, TX, childhood in *Farewell*. . . . Now he continues his story where he left off, leaving Wharton at 17 to study to become an actor. He travels to theater school in Pasadena but eventually

Foote, Horton—*Continued*

makes it to New York by way of Martha's Vineyard, where he soon discovers his talent for writing and hobnobs with the likes of Martha Graham, Tennessee Williams, and Agnes de Mille." Libr J

Ford, Henry, 1863-1947

Baldwin, Neil. Henry Ford and the Jews; the mass production of hate. PublicAffairs 2001 416p il $27.50; pa $16 *   **92**
1. Antisemitism
ISBN 1-891620-52-5; 1-58648-163-0 (pa)
                                       LC 2001-41679
"Baldwin reveals the complex tale of how 'Heinrich' Ford promoted a virulent brand of antisemitism, disseminating his point of view through a privately-published newspaper, *The Dearborn Independent*—and how the Jewish American community responded with alarm and courage." Publisher's note
"The strength of this biography lies in context: by emphasizing Ford's background, influences and the world around the auto manufacturer, Baldwin . . . brings a fresh approach to what has long been known about one of America's most famous anti-Semites." Publ Wkly
Includes bibliographical references

Watts, Steven. The people's tycoon; Henry Ford and the American century. Knopf 2005 614p il $30   **92**
1. Antisemitism
ISBN 0-375-40735-9   LC 2004-48594
The author "traces Ford's rise to fame and the innovations, such as the 'five-dollar' workday, which doubled factory workers' salaries, that he brought to the workplace, while a chapter titled 'Bigot' delineates his notorious anti-Semitism." Publ Wkly
"Steven Watts is intelligent, thorough and engaging . . . in telling the story of an American who not only was influential but remains unavoidable to this day." N Y Times Book Rev
Includes bibliographical references

Ford, John, 1894-1973

Davis, Ronald L. John Ford; Hollywood's old master. University of Okla. Press 1995 383p il (Oklahoma western biographies) pa $21.95 hardcover o.p.   **92**
1. Motion picture producers and directors—Biography
ISBN 0-8061-2916-6 (pa)   LC 94-25178
In this study of the influential filmmaker, "Davis draws on the recollections of the actors who worked frequently with Ford, including John Wayne, Henry Fonda and Maureen O'Hara, to document Ford's tyranny on the set, which intimidated his cast but wrung brilliant performances from them." Publ Wkly
Includes bibliographical references

Eyman, Scott. Print the legend; the life and times of John Ford. Johns Hopkins Univ. Press 2000 656p il pa $23.50   **92**
1. Motion picture producers and directors—Biography
ISBN 0-8018-6560-3; 978-0-8018-6560-2
                                       LC 00-33044
First published 1999 by Simon & Schuster

This is a biography chronicling the life and career of the director of "such classics as The grapes of wrath, The searchers and The man who shot Liberty Valance. . . . Eyman has written a quietly magnificent biography of an American original who has shaped our perception of movies as serious art." Publ Wkly
Includes bibliographical references

Forten, James, 1766-1842

Winch, Julie. A gentleman of color: the life of James Forten. Oxford Univ. Press 2002 501p il hardcover o.p. pa $18.95   **92**
1. African Americans—Biography 2. Abolitionists
ISBN 0-19-508691-0; 0-19-516340-0 (pa)
                                       LC 2001-36215
This is "a life-and-times biography of James Forten (1766-1842), an entrepreneur, social reformer, Revolutionary War patriot, and gentleman, who stood as one of the most influential and well-known African Americans of his day." Libr J
The author "has done a masterful job of researching and piecing together Forten's life. . . . But the strength of the book—aside from rediscovering Forten—is the careful and often surprising research into the complexity of African-American life in the 18th and early 19th centuries." Publ Wkly
Includes bibliographical references

Fossey, Dian

Mowat, Farley. Woman in the mists: the story of Dian Fossey and the mountain gorillas of Africa. Warner Bks. 1987 380p il pa $19.95 hardcover o.p.   **92**
1. Gorillas
ISBN 0-446-38720-7 (pa)   LC 87-40166
The author has "organized Fossey's journals into a biography that quotes her writings so heavily as to be autobiographical. Much of the text parallels material in Fossey's Gorillas in the Mist but provides additional insights into her personal life, difficulties in maintaining funding, and the continuation of her work up to her death in 1985. This gripping, action-packed story is essential reading for all who understand the sacrifice of self for the preservation of other species." Libr J

Foster, Stephen Collins, 1826-1864

Emerson, Ken. Doo-dah!: Stephen Foster and the rise of American popular culture. Da Capo Press 1998 400p il pa $16.50   **92**
ISBN 0-306-80852-8   LC 98-15480
First published 1997 by Simon & Schuster
The author "explores the roots of early popular music while tracing the tragic life of composer Stephen Collins Foster. . . . He also aims his spotlight at other musical personalities of the period, and provides further illumination of how Foster's songs have been incorporated into popular contemporary melodies. . . . Emerson's exhaustive research . . . has been meticulously worked into a vivid portrait of 19th-century America." Publ Wkly
Includes discography and bibliographical references

Fox, Michael J.

Fox, Michael J. Lucky man; a memoir. Hyperion 2002 304p $22.95; pa $12.95

92

ISBN 0-7868-6764-7; 0-7868-8874-1 (pa)

In this autobiography the actor discusses his professional career in feature films and television. He also "writes of the last 10 years, during which--with the unswerving support of his wife, family, and friends--he has dealt with his illness. He talks about what Parkinson's has given him: the chance to appreciate a wonderful life and career, and the opportunity to help search for a cure and spread public awareness of the disease." Publisher's note

Francis, of Assisi, Saint, 1182-1226

Martin, Valerie. Salvation: scenes from the life of St. Francis. Knopf 2001 268p pa $13 hardcover o.p.

92

ISBN 0-375-70883-9 (pa)   LC 00-44361

"This is a series of 31 frescolike word panels on the radical popular stigmatist and founder of the Franciscan Order. . . . The scenes begin with Francis's death and end with his encounter with a leper. The use of the present tense draws one into the joy and suffering of Francis and the barbarity of his age." Libr J

"This portrait will be most interesting to readers who are already familiar with the basic facts of Francis's life and remain open to exploring a new, gritty interpretation of them." Publ Wkly

Includes bibliographical references

Frank, Anne, 1929-1945

Frank, Anne. The diary of a young girl: the definitive edition; edited by Otto H. Frank and Mirjam Pressler; translated by Susan Massotty. Doubleday 1995 340p $27.50; pa $6.99 *

92

1. World War, 1939-1945—Jews 2. Netherlands—History—1940-1945, German occupation 3. Jews—Netherlands 4. Holocaust, 1933-1945

ISBN 0-385-47378-8; 0-553-57712-3 (pa)

LC 94-41379

"This new translation of Frank's famous diary includes material about her emerging sexuality and her relationship with her mother that was originally excised by Frank's father, the only family member to survive the Holocaust." Libr J

Frank, Anne. The diary of Anne Frank: the critical edition. rev Critical ed. Doubleday 2003 851p il $75

92

1. World War, 1939-1945—Jews 2. Netherlands—History—1940-1945, German occupation 3. Jews—Netherlands 4. Holocaust, 1933-1945

ISBN 0-385-50847-6   LC 2003-269527

First published 1989

"Prepared by the Netherlands State Institute for War Documentation; introduced by Harry Paape, Gerrold van der Stroom, and David Barnouw; with a summary of the report by the Netherlands Forensic Institute; compiled by H.J.J. Hardy; edited by David Barnouw and Gerrold van der Stroom; translated by Arnold J. Pomerans, B.M. Mooyaart-Doubleday and Susan Massotty." Title page

This volume brings together "the three known versions of Frank's diary—the original, a self-edited version . . . {and} another edited by her father. It also contains . . . handwriting and paper analyses, new documentation regarding the Frank family's arrest, and . . . information about the diary's troubled publication history." Libr J {review of 1989 edition}

Includes bibliographical references

Müller, Melissa. Anne Frank; the biography; translated by Rita and Robert Kimber. Holt & Co. 1998 330p hardcover o.p. pa $14   **92**

1. World War, 1939-1945—Jews 2. Netherlands—History—1940-1945, German occupation 3. Jews—Netherlands 4. Holocaust, 1933-1945

ISBN 0-8050-5996-2; 0-8050-5997-0 (pa)

LC 98-22923

This biography covers Anne Frank's life from her childhood to her last days in Bergen-Belsen concentration camp

"Müller includes a family tree; a family history; and considerable insight into the character, personality, and quality of life of Anne's parents, relatives, and friends. Interviews with many of these surviving people give a clearer idea of the situation and Anne's reactions to it." SLJ

Frank, Otto, 1889-1980

Lee, Carol Ann. The hidden life of Otto Frank. Morrow 2003 411p il pa $13.95 hardcover o.p.

92

1. Holocaust, 1933-1945

ISBN 0-06-052083-3 (pa)   LC 2002-38941

Lee offers a portrait of Anne Frank's father and seeks to settle the question of who betrayed the Frank family to the Nazis

Includes bibliographical references

Frankl, Viktor E.

Frankl, Viktor E. Man's search for meaning; part one translated by Ilse Lasch; foreword by Harold S. Kushner; afterword by William J. Winslade. Beacon Press 2006 165p pa $13 *

92

1. Holocaust, 1933-1945—Personal narratives 2. Psychologists

ISBN 0-8070-1427-3; 978-0-8070-1427-1

LC 2006-287144

Original German edition, 1946

"Between 1942 and 1945 Frankl labored in four different camps, including Auschwitz, while his parents, brother, and pregnant wife perished. Based on his own experience and the experiences of others he treated later in his practice, Frankl argues that we cannot avoid suffering but we can choose how to cope with it, find meaning in it, and move forward with renewed purpose. Frankl's theory—known as logotherapy, from the Greek word logos ('meaning')—holds that our primary drive in life is not pleasure, as Freud maintained, but the discovery and pursuit of what we personally find meaningful." Publisher's note

Franklin, Benjamin, 1706-1790

Brands, H. W. The first American: the life and times of Benjamin Franklin. Doubleday 2000 759p pa $17 hardcover o.p.   **92**
1. Statesmen—United States
ISBN 0-385-49540-4 (pa)   LC 00-27930
"Brands fills in disparate pockets of history (the importance of Cotton Mather in Boston, the intellectual enthusiasms of the Royal Society in London) with readable, unobtrusive scholarship. Perhaps he took as his model his unassuming subject, who treated his extraordinary achievements in fields as diverse as science and diplomacy as if they were ordinary. Franklin emerges as a man with a passion to add to human happiness." New Yorker
Includes bibliographical references

Franklin, Benjamin. The autobiography of Benjamin Franklin; introduction by Lewis Leary. Simon & Schuster 2004 143p pa $10.95 *
                                                   92
1. Statesmen—United States
ISBN 0-7432-5506-2   LC 2003-54477
"A Touchstone book"
Written between 1771 and 1788
"Franklin's account of his life, written for his son William. . . . During the Revolutionary War, the manuscript was put aside. . . . Franklin later more than doubled the length . . . but still took the story only to 1757-1759, ending before the period of his greatest public service. Still, the book remains the first undisputed classic of American literature and one of the most interesting autobiographies in English." Benet's Reader's Ency of Am Lit

Franklin, Benjamin. Not your usual founding father; selected readings from Benjamin Franklin; edited by Edmund S. Morgan. Yale University Press 2006 303p il map $26 *   **92**
1. Statesmen—United States
ISBN 0-300-11394-3; 978-0-300-11394-5
                          LC 2006-45706
The editor "explains that this anthology differs from the typical selections of writings by founders, which showcase themes of revolution, war, and political philosophy. Here Morgan pursues the man himself, particularly Franklin's fascination with the curiosities of human behavior. . . . Franklin's humane solicitude and observational acuity surface in varied places (on ship, in Parisian salons) and in varied formats (personal letters, published satires) in such a way that readers encounter directly Franklin's seeming simplicity, which actually masked a deep complexity and which continually makes him the most interesting founder." Booklist

Isaacson, Walter. Benjamin Franklin; an American life. Simon & Schuster 2003 590p il $30; pa $16.95   **92**
1. Statesmen—United States
ISBN 0-684-80761-0; 0-7432-5807-X (pa)
                          LC 2003-50463
The author "considers the social activist and historical actor, focusing on Franklin as 'a civic-minded man' who expressed the virtues and values of a rising middle class, America's new ruling class of ordinary citizens. He also highlights Franklin's personal relations with numerous individuals—including his common-law wife, Deborah Read—his famous moments and achievements, e.g., the kiteflying electricity experiment, and his evolving social thought on a range of issues, including slavery." Libr J
This "is a thoroughly researched, crisply written, convincingly argued chronicle that is also studded with little nuggets of fresh information." N Y Times Book Rev
Includes bibliographical references

Morgan, Edmund Sears. Benjamin Franklin; {by} Edmund S. Morgan. Yale Univ. Press 2002 339p il $24.95; pa $16   **92**
1. Statesmen—United States
ISBN 0-300-09532-5; 0-300-10162-7 (pa)
                          LC 2002-1143
"Morgan adopts a chronological approach from which he often departs for expansive discussions of Franklin's occupational arenas—printing, morals, science, politics, and diplomacy—through which Franklin expressed his attitude toward life." Booklist
"The general reader will find this book to be a well-written, thoughtful appreciation of one of the Founding Fathers who did the most to shape his era and our own." Libr J
Includes bibliographical references

Franklin, Rosalind, 1920-1958

Maddox, Brenda. Rosalind Franklin: the dark lady of DNA. HarperCollins Pubs. 2002 380p il $29.95; pa $15.95   **92**
ISBN 0-06-018407-8; 0-06-098508-9 (pa)
                          LC 2002-68898
This "biography elucidates the vital role that Franklin played in the discovery of DNA's structure and the evolution of virology, and dispels the myths that surround this gifted biophysicist, who fought sexism for most of her all-too-brief life." Booklist
The author "does an excellent job of revisiting Franklin's scientific contributions . . . while revealing Franklin's complicated personality." Libr J
Includes bibliographical references

Franzen, Jonathan

Franzen, Jonathan. The discomfort zone; a personal history. Farrar, Straus & Giroux 2006 195p $22   **92**
ISBN 978-0-374-29919-4; 0-374-29919-6
                          LC 2006-2700
This is a memoir by the author of The Corrections.
"For those who admire the razor-sharp jabs Franzen makes at himself and anyone else standing too close, 'The Discomfort Zone' is both a delicious read and a clever showcase for Franzen's talents." Christ Sci Monit

Frederick II, King of Prussia, 1712-1786

MacDonogh, Giles. Frederick the Great; a life in deed and letters. St. Martin's Press 2000 436p il pa $16.95 hardcover o.p.   **92**
ISBN 0-312-27266-9 (pa)   LC 00-24799
First published 1999 in the United Kingdom
This biography portrays Frederick II of Prussia "as a sensitive young man who plots an escape from his fa-

Frederick II, King of Prussia, 1712-1786—*Continued*

ther's tyrannical control, and later . . . as an accomplished diplomat, strategist and military leader." Publ Wkly

"Both general readers and those with a strong background in European history will find great value in this outstanding biography." Booklist

Includes bibliographical references

Freeman, Walter J.

El-Hai, Jack. The lobotomist; a maverick medical genius and his tragic quest to rid the world of mental illness. J. Wiley 2005 362p il $27.95; pa $16.95 *   **92**

ISBN 0-471-23292-0; 0-470-09830-9 (pa)
LC 2004-14946

El-Hai chronicles the life and professional career of the American neuroscientist who pioneered the use of lobotomy in the treatment of mental illness.

"This is a well-written, thoroughly researched book, a fascinating story that deserves to be considered as the definitive biography of a physician who went from fame to infamy as 'the most scorned physician of the twentieth century.'" Sci Books Films

Includes bibliographical references

Freud, Sigmund, 1856-1939

Gay, Peter. Freud; a life for our time; with a new foreword. Norton 2006 810p il pa $21.95
                                                          92

ISBN 0-393-32861-9   LC 2006-283026
First published 1988

This biography provides an "updating of our knowledge of the life of the founder of psychoanalysis . . . and it also delineates the continuing impact of Freud's thought on modern endeavors in a number of fields." Sci Books Films

"The book is beautifully written. Gay's approach is to try to understand Freud and his alliances and environment rather than to worship or challenge him." Choice

Includes bibliographical references

Friedan, Betty, 1921-2006

Friedan, Betty. Life so far. Simon & Schuster 2000 399p il hardcover o.p. pa $17   **92**
ISBN 0-684-80789-0; 978-0-7432-9986-2 (pa);
0-7432-9986-8 (pa)   LC 00-23920

In this memoir, "Friedan reminisces over a life of social activism that has included helping to found the National Organization for Women, the National Abortion and Reproductive Rights Action League, and the National Women's Political Caucus, as well as writing the pivotal *The Feminine Mystique*." Libr J

Friedman, Milton, 1912-2006

Ebenstein, Alan O. Milton Friedman; a biography; [by] Lanny Ebenstein. Palgrave Macmillan 2007 286p $27.95   **92**
1. Economists
ISBN 1-4039-7627-9; 978-1-4039-7627-7
LC 2006-52023

The author "creates a picture of Milton Friedman, one of the leading economists and political philosophers of the twentieth century, as not just a revered economic theorist but also a public intellectual. Ebenstein begins with Friedman's childhood and early career, moving through his long tenure as an economist at the University of Chicago, and completes the book with a picture of Friedman as a renowned public figure. . . . Ebenstein's attention to detail and copious quotes from others who knew Friedman well make for an engaging picture of one of America's most important economic theorists." Booklist

Includes bibliographical references

Frost, Robert, 1874-1963

Parini, Jay. Robert Frost; a life. Holt & Co. 1999 514p il $35; pa $16 *   **92**
ISBN 0-8050-3181-2; 0-8050-6341-2 (pa)
LC 98-26690

This biography of the American poet has "its focus on the internal realm where, in Frost's case, creativity and madness fought a battle royal." Publ Wkly

"Rarely has Frost's story been told this dexterously, or with a better understanding of the relation of Frost's personal crises to his accomplishment as a poet." Publ Wkly

Includes bibliographical references

Fuller, Alexandra, 1969-

Fuller, Alexandra. Don't let's go to the dogs tonight; an African childhood. Random House 2002 301p il $24.95; pa $13.95   **92**
ISBN 0-375-50750-7; 0-375-75899-2 (pa)
LC 2001-41752

"Fuller grew up in Rhodesia (now Zimbabwe) during the civil war, and she watched her parents fight against the local Africans to keep their farm. In a memoir powerful in its frank straightforwardness, she neither apologizes for nor champions her family's views and actions. Instead she gives us an honest, moving portrait of one family struggling to survive tumultuous times." Booklist

Fuller, Margaret, 1810-1850

Von Mehren, Joan. Minerva and the muse: a life of Margaret Fuller. University of Mass. Press 1995 398p il $40; pa $20.95   **92**
ISBN 0-87023-941-4; 1-55849-015-9 (pa)
LC 94-18663

The author "details Fuller's evolution from child prodigy to leading New England intellectual." Publ Wkly

"Von Mehren is sympathetic to Fuller's lifelong struggle to achieve fame and public acclamation for her views on Transcendentalism and feminism, but she balances her sympathy with objectivity and distance." Libr J

Includes bibliographical references

Fulton, Robert, 1765-1815

Sale, Kirkpatrick. The fire of his genius: Robert Fulton and the American dream. Free Press 2001 242p il $24; pa $13   **92**
ISBN 0-684-86715-X; 0-7432-2321-7 (pa)
LC 2001-23064

Fulton, Robert, 1765-1815—*Continued*

Sale examines the life of the American inventor, "explaining how his North River steamboat opened up the North American continent to settlement and how it became the key factor that influenced the beginnings of the American industrial revolution. . . . This is an informative, moving story that personalizes the relatively obscure life of a self-taught tinkerer who had a genius for self-promotion and exploiting the discoveries of others." Libr J

Includes bibliographical references

Galento, Tony, 1910-1979

Monninger, Joseph. Two Ton; one fight, one night: Tony Galento vs. Joe Louis. Steerforth Press 2006 208p il $19.95   92

ISBN 978-1-58642-115-1; 1-58642-115-8

LC 2006-12828

Th author offers a detailed "description of the 1939 heavyweight title fight between Joe Louis and Orange, New Jersey native 'Two Ton' Tony Galento. Monninger's real achievement is not the tale of the fight itself, but rather of the circumstances that lead up to it, and its explanation of how one chunky, heavyset bartender with a far-from-average left hook could rise to fight for the world championship." BrickCityBoxing.com

Galilei, Galileo, 1564-1642

Shea, William R. Galileo in Rome; the rise and fall of a troublesome genius; [by] William R. Shea and Mariano Artigas. Oxford University Press 2003 226p il hardcover o.p. pa $15.95   92

1. Astronomers 2. Religion and science

ISBN 0-19-516598-5; 0-19-517758-4 (pa)

LC 2003-4247

In recounting the story of Galileo's conflict with the Roman Catholic Church over his heliocentric theory, this book "promotes the idea that Galileo himself contributed to his fate. . . . Structuring their narrative around the several journeys Galileo made from Florence to Rome, Shea and Artigas identify numerous friendly suggestions given to him by supporters to tone things down. . . . In recounting the actual people with whom Galileo fenced, as well as the theological doctrines involved, the authors demythologize the man. Their criticism makes Galileo as interesting a figure as ever." Booklist

Includes bibliographical references

Sobel, Dava. Galileo's daughter. See entry under Maria Celeste, 1600-1634

Gandhi, Mahatma, 1869-1948

Chadha, Yogesh. Gandhi; a life. Wiley 1998 c1997 546p il pa $19.95 hardcover o.p.

92

1. India—Politics and government

ISBN 0-471-35062-1 (pa)   LC 97-37406

First published 1997 in the United Kingdom with title: Rediscovering Gandhi

"Chadha reexamines Gandhi's life with an eye to restoring its complications and contradictions, noting that 'to suppress his weaknesses would be to undermine his strengths.' And he succeeds in his mission, presenting the great leader not as a holy man but as a humanist and politician." Booklist

Includes bibliographical references

Gandhi, Rajmohan. Gandhi; the man, his people, and the empire. University of California Press 2008 xv, 738p il map $34.95   92

1. India—Politics and government

ISBN 978-0-520-25570-8; 0-520-25570-4

LC 2007-40986

First published 2006 in India with title: Mohandas: a true story of a man, his people, and an empire

"A biography of the political and spiritual leader, written by his grandson. . . . It tells of Gandhi's campaigns against racial discrimination in South Africa and untouchability in India, tracks the momentous battle for India's freedom, explores the evolution of Gandhi's strategies of nonviolent resistance, and examines relations between Muslims and non-Muslims." Publisher's note

The author exhibits a deep "understanding of the social and political landscape of India, of the cleavages of caste and religion, and of the dynamics of the dominant Congress Party (to which Gandhi had a lifelong allegiance). Rajmohan takes us at a leisurely pace through the broad sweep of Gandhi's personal and public life." Times Lit Suppl

Includes bibliographical references

Herman, Arthur. Gandhi and Churchill. See entry under Churchill, Sir Winston, 1874-1965

Wolpert, Stanley A. Gandhi's passion; the life and legacy of Mahatma Gandhi; [by] Stanley Wolpert. Oxford Univ. Press 2001 308p il hardcover o.p. pa $17.95 *   92

1. India—Politics and government

ISBN 0-19-513060-X; 0-19-515634-X (pa)

LC 00-45298

"From his pampered childhood to his ascetic final years, the text follows the Mahatma ('Great Soul') on a paradoxical pilgrimage in which the deliberate acceptance of suffering endowed him with the power he needed to challenge the leading politicians of Europe, Africa, and Asia." Booklist

"This accessible account of Gandhi's life is an excellent introduction to the work of the most compelling of 20th-century leaders." Christ Century

Includes bibliographical references

Garcia, Jerry

Jackson, Blair. Garcia; an American life. Viking 1999 497p hardcover o.p. $18   92

1. Grateful Dead (Musical group)

ISBN 978-0-14-029199-5; 0-14-029199-7

LC 99-28775

"As the front man for the Grateful Dead, the band that epitomized the '60s hippie counterculture, Jerry Garcia's place in music history is assured. Yet, Jackson asserts in this . . . biography, Garcia's genius as a guitarist and songwriter has often been overlooked." Publ Wkly

"Jackson has written a wonderful account of the beginnings of the band . . . in the mid-1960's, their relationship with Ken Kesey and his Merry Pranksters, their embrace of psychedelic drugs and the adoration and obsession of Deadheads throughout the country." N Y Times Book Rev

Includes bibliographical references

García Lorca, Federico, 1898-1936

Gibson, Ian. Federico García Lorca: a life. Pantheon Bks. 1989 xxii, 551p il pa $18 hardcover o.p. **92**

　　ISBN 0-679-77401-7 (pa)　　　　LC 88-28871

Loosely based on the two-volume Spanish work published 1985-1987

This is a biography of the Spanish writer who was assassinated during the Spanish Civil War

"Gibson's sense of place is equalled by his sense of person. His re-creation of the teeming artistic talent and the café life of Spain in the 1930s is superb. So effective is Gibson's account of Lorca's vitality and fecundity that along with admiration for the poet's opulent talent, he provokes a fierce outrage at his ultimate fate." Times Lit Suppl

Includes bibliographical references

García Márquez, Gabriel, 1928-

García Márquez, Gabriel. Living to tell the tale; translated by Edith Grossman. Knopf 2003 483p maps $26.95; pa $14.95 **92**

　ISBN 1-4000-4134-1; 1-4000-3454-X (pa)

　　　　　　　　　　　　　　　LC 2003-58924

"Garcia Márquez tells the entrancing story of his remarkable family, chronicles the turbulence of his troubled country, Colombia, and offers a piquant portrait of himself as a struggling young writer. A resplendent memoir written with compassion and artistry." Booklist

Gardner, Ava, 1922-1990

Server, Lee. Ava Gardner; "love is nothing". St. Martin's Press 2006 551p il $29.95 **92**

　ISBN 0-312-31209-1; 978-0-312-31209-1

　　　　　　　　　　　　　　　LC 2005-51697

This is a biography of the actress.

"No matter how objective Server tries to appear in detailing the highs and lows of [Gardner's] 67 years—the three marriages, the numerous affairs, the binges, the nightlong cruising of low-life byways and bordellos, the mainly poor movies she was in—he cannot really hide his essential fondness for her. It is the kind of affection virtually every one of the more than 100 people he interviewed felt and spoke of with enthusiasm, the kind a reader too will find hard to resist." N Y Times Book Rev

Includes filmography and bibliographical references

Gardner, Chris

Gardner, Chris. The pursuit of happyness; [by] Chris Gardner with Quincy Troupe and Mim Eichler Rivas. Amistad 2006 302p il map $25.95 **92**

　ISBN 978-0-06-074486-1; 0-06-074486-3

　　　　　　　　　　　　　　　LC 2005-57203

The author "recounts his 'long walk to Wall Street,' a journey that took him from a childhood in the ghettos of Milwaukee to an enormously successful career as a stockbroker in New York city." Libr J

Garland, Judy

Clarke, Gerald. Get happy: the life of Judy Garland. Random House 2000 510p il pa $15.95 hardcover o.p. **92**

　　ISBN 0-385-33515-6 (pa)　　　　LC 99-36285

Clarke reexamines the life of the singer and actress who "began her career as a toddler in vaudeville, went on to movies, radio, TV, and concert tours, and experienced more than the average number of reversals, love affairs, and suicide attempts." New Yorker

"This exhaustively researched and illuminating biography . . . is as compassionate as it is wrenching." Publ Wkly

Includes bibliographical references

Gates, Henry Louis

Gates, Henry Louis. Colored people; a memoir; [by] Henry Louis Gates, Jr. Knopf 1994 216p pa $13 hardcover o.p. **92**

　　ISBN 0-679-73919-X (pa)　　　　LC 93-12256

The author presents a "memoir of growing up in a West Virginia mill town during the 1950s and '60s." Time

"As Gates traces his evolution from 'Negro' to Afro-wearing 'black,' he also traces the evolution of Piedmont (and, by extension, of much of America) at a time when the relationship between the races was being redefined." Newsweek

Gatzoyiannis, Eleni

Gage, Nicholas. Eleni. Random House 1983 470p hardcover o.p. pa $14.95 * **92**

　　ISBN 0-394-52093-9; 978-0-345-41043-6 (pa);
0-345-41043-2 (pa)　　　　　　　LC 82-42803

"On August 28, 1948, a Greek peasant woman, Eleni Gatzoyiannis, was executed by guerrillas in her village of Lia. Some 30 years later, her son . . . wrote this book . . . weaving together three stories: World War II and the civil war in Greece; Eleni's life and how the catastrophic events in Greece smashed her world; and his own search for vengeance." Libr J

"The separate strands lead to an intensely moving climax, making Eleni one of the rare books in which the power of art re-creates the full historical truth." NY Rev Books

An account of Nicholas Gage's life in America, A place for us, is entered above.

Gauguin, Paul, 1848-1903

Gayford, Martin. The yellow house. See entry under Gogh, Vincent van, 1853-1890

Thomson, Belinda. Gauguin. Thames & Hudson 1987 215p il (World of art) pa $14.95 **92**

　　ISBN 0-500-20220-6　　　　　　LC 87-50203

This "covers the artist's private life and professional development in great detail and captures the dramatic appeal inherent in both these areas. Some of the controversies of Gauguin's life are also clarified." Booklist

Includes bibliographical references

Gaulle, Charles de, 1890-1970

Williams, Charles. The last great Frenchman; a life of General de Gaulle. Wiley 1995 544p il $30; pa $19.95 **92**

ISBN 0-471-11711-0; 0-471-18071-8 (pa)

LC 94-42881

The author offers "appraisals of de Gaulle's career as soldier, politician and head of state. Williams contrasts the infuriatingly obstinate public figure with the private man, emotional and affectionate in the bosom of his family. Especially interesting is the account of de Gaulle's tender relationship with his retarded daughter. . . . The author also sheds light on de Gaulle's determined anti-Americanism during his final years." Publ Wkly

Includes bibliographical references

Gautama Buddha

Armstrong, Karen. Buddha. Viking 2001 xxix, 205p map (Penguin lives series) hardcover o.p. pa $13 **92**

ISBN 0-670-89193-2; 0-14-303436-7 (pa)

LC 00-43808

"A Penguin life"

"Armstrong interprets the mythologized story of the Buddha's abandonment of his life of comfort and privilege; commitment to practicing advanced forms of yoga and nearly fatal asceticism; enlightenment beneath a bodhi tree; and 45 years of wandering and teaching until his death in 483. And as she does so, she lucidly explains his revelations and influence." Booklist

Includes bibliographical references

Gay, Peter, 1923-

Gay, Peter. My German question; growing up in Nazi Berlin. Yale Univ. Press 1998 208p il $40; pa $11.95 **92**

1. Jews—Germany 2. Jews—Persecutions

ISBN 0-300-07670-3; 0-300-08070-0 (pa)

LC 98-26686

Gay writes of his childhood in pre-World War II Berlin. He reflects that "his family was fortunate to emigrate from Germany to America shortly after the 1938 Kristallnacht, the 'Night of Broken Glass' when Nazi-sponsored riots destroyed synagogues and Jewish stores. But Gay . . . takes issue with the suggestion that German Jews should have fled when Hitler came to power in 1933." Libr J

"A searching, sensitive portrait of Gay's youth, as crystalline as memory can be made." Booklist

Gehrig, Lou, 1903-1941

Eig, Jonathan. Luckiest man; the life and death of Lou Gehrig. Simon & Schuster 2005 420p il $26; pa $15 **92**

1. Baseball—Biography

ISBN 0-7432-4591-1; 0-7432-6893-8 (pa)

LC 2004-59137

This is a biography of the first baseman for the New York Yankees.

The author "has done a superb job of digging out the real Gehrig from behind the legend, and the mask of his own modesty." N Y Times Book Rev

Includes bibliographical references

Robinson, Ray. Iron horse: Lou Gehrig in his time. Norton 1990 300p il pa $14.95 o.p.

92

1. Baseball—Biography

ISBN 978-0-393-32882-0 (pa); 0-393-32882-1 (pa)

LC 89-29272

"Playing in the considerable shadow of Babe Ruth, Lou Gehrig's accomplishments as baseball's 'Iron Horse' include a legendary record of 2,130 consecutive games played. . . . Robinson's narrative not only traces Gehrig's life and career but also provides an insightful look at baseball in the 1920s and the Depression years." Libr J

Gelb, Arthur, 1924-

Gelb, Arthur. City room. Putnam 2003 664p $29.95; pa $17.95 **92**

1. New York Times Company

ISBN 0-399-15075-7; 0-425-19831-6 (pa)

LC 2003-43154

"A Marian Wood book"

This is a "memoir of life at The New York Times by one who spent nearly 50 years there, rising from copy boy to managing editor; [the author] has the power to evoke whole generations of change in the news business, reaching back to the glorious postwar years of manual typewriters, chain smokers, and all-nighters." N Y Times Book Rev

Gell-Mann, Murray, 1929-

Johnson, George. Strange beauty: Murray Gell-Mann and the revolution in twentieth-century physics. Knopf 1999 434p il pa $15 hardcover o.p.

92

ISBN 0-679-75688-4 (pa)

LC 99-19952

This is a biography of the American physicist who was awarded the Nobel prize in 1969 for his work on the interaction of elementary particles and their classification

"While it is necessarily dense in parts, this book is free of mathematics and is accessible to the advanced lay reader." Libr J

Includes bibliographical references

Geronimo, Apache Chief, 1829-1909

Debo, Angie. Geronimo; the man, his time, his place. University of Okla. Press 1976 xx, 480p il maps (Civilization of the American Indian series) hardcover o.p. pa $24.95 **92**

1. Apache Indians

ISBN 0-8061-1333-2; 0-8061-1828-8 (pa)

LC 76-13858

The author "interviewed people who knew Geronimo, who fought with him and lived with him in captivity. She has written a colorful narrative of revenge and raids, of escape, pursuit and surrender. . . . Her portrait of Geronimo the old celebrity is touching, and a tribute to an exceptional leader." Publ Wkly

Includes bibliographical references

Gershwin, George, 1898-1937

Gilbert, Steven E. The music of Gershwin. Yale Univ. Press 1995 255p music (Composers of the twentieth century) $47   **92**

ISBN 0-300-06233-8   LC 95-12086

This book analyzes major musical works of George Gershwin including Rhapsody in Blue, Concerto in F, An American in Paris, Porgy and Bess, and some of his popular songs and lesser known works

"With this book, Gershwin's music finally gets the attention it deserves. . . . Gilbert's book is not for the casual reader, since it requires an understanding of music theory and notation." Libr J

Includes bibliographical references

Hyland, William G. George Gershwin; a new biography. Praeger Pubs. 2003 312p il $39.95   **92**

ISBN 0-275-98111-8   LC 2003-46303

The author "explores Gershwin's complex personality and his pioneering music. . . . Hyland explains how Gershwin became the first composer to apply popular music to classical forms and how his compositions reflected the restlessness of our country during the Jazz Age." Booklist

"This fresh and well-researched biography of one of America's great composers is highly recommended for all libraries." Libr J

Includes bibliographical references

Pollack, Howard. George Gershwin; his life and work. University of California Press 2006 884p il $39.95 *   **92**

ISBN 978-0-520-24864-9; 0-520-24864-3
        LC 2006-17926

"In part one, a study of popular music trends serves as an overture to Gershwin's musical influences, his childhood and Tin Pan Alley years, followed by a look at Gershwin as a pianist and conductor through his death from a brain tumor at the age of 38. The book's second half, titled 'Work,' . . . [attempts] to document Gershwin's entire output, from orchestral works to theater, radio and films, including the role of lyricist Ira Gershwin in reworking his brother's tunes." Publ Wkly

"This engaging biography is also a tour de force of scholarship." Booklist

Includes bibliographical references

Ghahramani, Zarah, 1981-

Ghahramani, Zarah. My life as a traitor; [by] Zarah Ghahramani, with Robert Hillman. Farrar, Straus and Giroux 2008 242p $23   **92**

1. Women—Iran 2. Political prisoners
ISBN 978-0-374-21730-3; 0-374-21730-0
        LC 2007-17983

"Zarah Ghahramani wrote 'My Life as a Traitor' soon after fleeing Iran for Australia. Born in 1981, she never knew a prerevolutionary Iran. . . . In 2001, when she was 20, Ghahramani was tortured and imprisoned at Evin for her role in a protest at Tehran University." N Y Times Book Rev

"This compelling book is a coming-of-age story in which the author examines her beliefs and emotions while she tells of a country in turmoil." SLJ

Gielgud, Sir John, 1904-2000

Croall, Jonathan. Gielgud; a theatrical life, 1904-2000. Continuum 2001 579p il $35; pa $24.95   **92**

ISBN 0-8264-1333-1; 0-8264-1403-6 (pa)
        LC 2001-28019

Croall examines the life and career of the British actor, director, and producer

"Witty and well-written as well as well-researched, Croall's fine and complete portrait of the man and his endearing charm often reads more like a novel than like nonfiction." Booklist

Includes bibliographical references

Gielgud, Sir John. An actor and his time. Applause Theatre Bk. Pubs. 1997 333p $21.95; pa $16.95   **92**

ISBN 1-55783-299-4; 1-55783-415-6 (pa)
        LC 97-31701

First published 1979 in the United Kingdom

This autobiography chronicles Gielgud's work in the theatre and motion pictures. Includes his personal reminiscences of Ellen Terry, Sarah Bernhardt, Mrs. Patrick Campbell, Bernard Shaw and Ralph Richardson, among others

Gielgud "proves himself to be a storyteller of the highest order, making this essential reading for theater lovers." Libr J

Gilbert, Elizabeth, 1969-

Gilbert, Elizabeth. Eat, pray, love; one woman's search for everything across Italy, India and Indonesia. Viking 2006 334p $24.95   **92**

ISBN 0-670-03471-1   LC 2005-42435

"Plagued with despair after a nasty divorce, the author, in her early 30s, divides a year equally among three dissimilar countries, exploring her competing urges for earthly delights and divine transcendence." Publ Wkly

"A probing, thoughtful title with a free and easy style, this work seamlessly blends history and travel for a very enjoyable read." Libr J

Ginsberg, Allen, 1926-1997

Ginsberg, Allen. Spontaneous mind; selected interviews, 1958-1996; with a preface by Václav Havel; edited by David Carter. HarperCollins Pubs. 2001 601p pa $17.95 hardcover o.p.
        92

1. Beat generation
ISBN 0-06-093082-9 (pa)   LC 00-40849

"The bulk of the collection [of interviews] dates from 1965-72, Ginsberg's years as countercultural symbol and spokesman: dialogues at demonstrations and on the road, transcripts from 'Firing Line' and the Chicago Seven trial." N Y Times Book Rev

Includes bibliographical references

Morgan, Bill. I celebrate myself; the somewhat private life of Allen Ginsberg. Viking 2006 702p il $29.95   **92**

1. Beat generation
ISBN 0-670-03796-6   LC 2006-50045

Ginsberg, Allen, 1926-1997—*Continued*

"Relying heavily on Ginsberg's journals and letters, as well as interviews with close friends, [Morgan] creates here a detailed, revealing portrait of Ginsberg as a gifted poet and flawed human being driven by a fierce hunger for love and an insatiable thirst for fame. This most exhaustive biography to date chronicles Ginsberg's life from cradle to grave, but a major theme is Ginsberg's love life especially his relationship with Peter Orlovsky. Although he became an icon for gay liberation, Ginsberg tended to fall in love with straight men like Jack Kerouac, Neal Cassady, and Orlovsky, which, of course, led to a good deal of rejection and frustration. Morgan's is the first life of Ginsberg to explore this curious paradox in any depth. Cleverly designed, his book includes marginal references to the poems Ginsberg was working on at the time. A monumental work." Libr J

Giuliani, Rudolph W.

Kirtzman, Andrew. Rudy Giuliani; emperor of the city. Morrow 2000 333p il pa $13.95 hardcover o.p.   **92**
1. New York (N.Y.)—Politics and government
ISBN 0-06-009389-7 (pa)
This political biography follows Giuliani from 1989 when he first set out to capture New York's City's mayoralty to his withdrawal from the 2000 senate race for medical and personal reasons

Siegel, Frederick F. The prince of the city; Giuliani, New York, and the genius of American life; [by] Fred Siegel, with Harry Siegel. Encounter Books 2005 386p $26.95   **92**
1. New York (N.Y.)—Politics and government
ISBN 1-594-03084-7   LC 2005-40127
This is a "narrative of Giuliani's eight years (1994-2001) as New York's chief elected executive. The account engagingly portrays how Giuliani made things happen, ranging from Giuliani the man to Giuliani the politician to Giuliani the policy innovator." Choice
Includes bibliographical references

Gladstone, W. E. (William Ewart), 1809-1898

Jenkins, Roy, Baron. Gladstone; a biography. Random House 1997 xxvii, 698p il pa $16.95 hardcover o.p.   **92**
ISBN 0-8129-6641-4 (pa)   LC 96-49632
First published 1995 in the United Kingdom
The author provides "insights into Gladstone's political achievements, failures, and personal eccentricities. . . . Jenkins is at his best tracing the major issues Gladstone attempted to ameliorate in his four premierships—extending the franchise, giving home rule to Ireland, and opposing imperialism." Booklist
This "book is a very decent try at an immensely difficult subject, encompassing an enormous amount of material. Lord Jenkins goes through the sources with commendable zeal. He also writes well." N Y Times Book Rev
Includes bibliographical references

Glavine, Tom, 1966-

Feinstein, John. Living on the black; two pitchers, two teams, one season to remember. Little, Brown 2008 525p il $26.99   **92**
1. Mussina, Mike, 1968- 2. New York Mets (Baseball team) 3. New York Yankees (Baseball team) 4. Baseball—Biography
ISBN 978-0-316-11391-5; 0-316-11391-3
LC 2007-50618
The author presents a yearlong look at the lives of pitchers Mike Mussina of the New York Yankees and Tom Glavine of the New York Mets during the 2007 MLB season.
"Feinstein achieves a double play fans should savor for its scrupulous look at what life is like for the 21st-century major leaguer." Christ Sci Monit

Glenn, John, 1921-

Glenn, John. John Glenn; a memoir; [by] John Glenn with Nick Taylor. Bantam Bks. 1999 422p il $27; pa $7.99   **92**
1. United States. Congress. Senate 2. Astronauts
ISBN 0-553-11074-8; 0-553-58157-0 (pa)
LC 99-42672
This is Glenn's account of how a "small-town Ohio boy weathers the Depression nurtured by conservative patriotic values, marries his high school sweetheart, flies combat missions in two wars, is selected as one of the original Mercury astronauts, becomes an instant national hero as the first American to orbit the earth, is elected to the Senate, and, after serving for four terms . . . returns to space aboard the Shuttle at age 77." Libr J

Goddard, Robert Hutchings, 1882-1945

Clary, David A. Rocket man; Robert H. Goddard and the birth of the space age. Hyperion 2003 324p il $24.95 *   **92**
1. Rocketry
ISBN 0-7868-6817-1   LC 2002-27321
In this biography Goddard emerges "as a paradoxical man who relentlessly promoted his work, winning hundreds of thousands of dollars in Guggenheim grants, while shunning offers to collaborate with other scientists. Clary presents a clear and relatively straightforward narrative of his subject's life. . . . Readers who come to this generally well-written biography with some knowledge of Goddard's significance will find much of interest to fill out their knowledge of this complex and fascinating scientist for whom NASA's Goddard Space Center is named." Publ Wkly
Includes bibliographical references

Gödel, Kurt

Goldstein, Rebecca. Incompleteness; the proof and paradox of Kurt Godel; Rebecca Goldstein. W.W. Norton 2005 296p il (Great discoveries) $22.95   **92**
ISBN 0-393-05169-2   LC 2004-23052
The author "explains the philosophical vision that inspired Gödel's mathematics, and reveals the ironic twist that led to radical misinterpretations of his theorems by the trendier intellectual fashions of the day, from positiv-

Gödel, Kurt—*Continued*

ism to postmodernism." Publisher's note

This "is a stimulating exploration of both the power and the limitations of the human intellect." Publ Wkly

Includes bibliographical references

Godwin, Gail, 1937-

Godwin, Gail. The making of a writer; journals, 1961-1963; edited by Rob Neufeld. Random House 2006 333p $25.95   **92**

    ISBN 1-4000-6432-5   LC 2005-44929

"The text begins in 1961 after Godwin, 24, has departed North Carolina for a job at the Miami Herald—a job from which she is soon fired. At the same time, she is married and divorced. She records her relationships and observations throughout with humor and humility, which results in a vivid portrait of Godwin's daily life and her relentless pursuit of a career as a writer." Libr J

Includes bibliographical references

Godwin, Peter

Godwin, Peter. When a crocodile eats the sun; a memoir of Africa. Little, Brown and Co. 2007 344p il map $24.99   **92**

    1. Zimbabwe

    ISBN 978-0-316-15894-7; 0-316-15894-1

            LC 2006-27973

First published 2006 in South Africa

"In 1996 when his father suffers a heart attack, Godwin returns to Africa and sparks the central revelation of the book—the father is Jewish and has hidden it from Godwin and his siblings. As his father's health deteriorates, so does Zimbabwe. [Robert] Mugabe, self-proclaimed president for life, institutes a series of ill-conceived land reforms that throw the white farmers off the land they've cultivated for generations and consequently throws the country's economy into free fall. . . . This is a tour de force of personal journalism and not to be missed." Publ Wkly

Includes bibliographical references

Goethe, Johann Wolfgang von, 1749-1832

Armstrong, John. Love, life, Goethe; lessons of the imagination from the great German poet. 1st American ed. Farrar, Straus and Giroux 2007 482p il $30   **92**

    1. Poets

    ISBN 978-0-374-29968-2; 0-374-29968-4

            LC 2006-34072

First published 2006 in the United Kingdom

In this biography, the author "seeks to analyze the works and life of Johann Wolfgang von Goethe (1749-1832) from a generalist's viewpoint." Choice

"Armstrong's thoughtful analysis of Goethe's life and works enables readers to fully appreciate the great German poet as an eminently human genius striving for growth and wholeness." Booklist

Includes bibliographical references

Gogh, Vincent van, 1853-1890

Gayford, Martin. The yellow house; Van Gogh, Gauguin, and nine turbulent weeks in Arles. Little, Brown and Co. 2006 339p il $24.99   **92**

    1. Gauguin, Paul, 1848-1903

    ISBN 978-0-316-76901-3; 0-316-76901-0

            LC 2006-10538

Also available in paperback from Houghton Mifflin

This is a "retelling of the famous events of late 1888, when Vincent van Gogh and Paul Gauguin shared a studio in a small town in southern France." Booklist

"Though it is impossible to entirely understand what motivated these two great artists during their weeks together in Arles, these pages deliver as close and vivid an image as may be possible." Publ Wkly

Includes bibliographical references

Goldberg, Jeffrey

Goldberg, Jeffrey. Prisoners; a Muslim and a Jew across the Middle East divide. Knopf 2006 316p $25 *   **92**

    1. Hijazi, Rafiq 2. Israel-Arab conflicts

    ISBN 0-375-41234-4; 978-0-375-41234-9

            LC 2006-41026

This is a "memoir of the author, an American-bred Zionist, and his 15-year relationship with a Palestinian insurgent. . . . Goldberg lived in Israel as a college student, sharpening the contradictory emotions shared by many of his American peers and eventually watching his former certainty crumble under the weight of military service at Ketziot, an Israeli prison. Grounded in his relationship with a prisoner, Goldberg's book travels from Long Island to Afghanistan as he struggles to understand Israeli-Palestinian violence. . . . Like the warring nationalisms it presents, his book is complex and deeply affecting." Publ Wkly

Goldman, Emma, 1869-1940

Rudahl, Sharon. A dangerous woman; the graphic biography of Emma Goldman. The New Press 2007 115p il $17.95   **92**

    1. Graphic novels 2. Biographical graphic novels 3. Anarchism and anarchists—Graphic novels

    ISBN 978-1-59558-064-1   LC 2007-15415

Emma Goldman was a revolutionary activist, speaker, writer, and feminist and anarchist. An immigrant to the U.S., she spoke out against inhumane working conditions, taught contraception, and opposed conscription for World War I. She founded the Free Speech League (a precursor to the ACLU), and the magazine Mother Earth. When she was deported to Russia just after the Bolshevik Revolution, she became disillusioned with the authoritarianism she found there, and she ended up supporting the fight against fascism in the Spanish Civil War. Rudahl based her graphic novel on Goldman's autobiography. The book includes nudity, sexual situations, and some violence.

Goodall, Jane, 1934-

Goodall, Jane. Beyond innocence; an autobiography in letters: the later years; edited by Dale Peterson. Houghton Mifflin 2001 418p il $28; pa $15 * **92**
1. Women scientists
ISBN 0-618-12520-5; 0-618-25734-9 (pa)
LC 00-54124
This second volume of Goodall's correspondence follows Africa in my blood
In this "volume of Goodall's letters, a lively portrait is formed through her missives as the young woman rose to the height of her scientific contributions and fame. She became a mother, divorced her first husband, married her second, and lost him to cancer. She was also the first to observe cannibalism in chimps, lost many of her study troop during a polio epidemic, and weathered the kidnapping of a group of her students. . . . This illuminating glimpse into the mind, emotions, and philosophy of an important scientist who also happens to be a celebrated figure will be requested in all libraries." Booklist

Goodall, Jane. Reason for hope; a spiritual journey; {by} Jane Goodall with Phillip Berman. Warner Bks. 1999 282p $26.95; pa $14.95 **92**
1. Women scientists
ISBN 0-446-52225-2; 0-446-67613-6 (pa)
LC 99-25611
Primatologist Goodall "offers this autobiography as a meditation on how her spiritual beliefs evolved in response to major events of her lifetime, including her childhood in World War II-era England; early days at Gombe with the chimpanzees; rearing her only child, Grub; divorce, remarriage, and the loss of her second husband to cancer, and the turning point in her career when she dedicated herself to the plight of chimpanzees held in captivity for biomedical research." Libr J

Peterson, Dale. Jane Goodall: the woman who redefined man. Houghton Mifflin 2006 740p il $24.95 **92**
1. Women scientists
ISBN 978-0-395-85405-1; 0-395-85405-9
LC 2006-6050
The author "details the life of the woman who revolutionized primate studies." Publ Wkly
Peterson "vividly and significantly enriches our understanding of Goodall as a scientist, spiritual thinker, and humanist." Booklist
Includes bibliographical references

Goodwin, Doris Kearns

Goodwin, Doris Kearns. Wait till next year; a memoir. Simon & Schuster 1997 261p il pa $14 hardcover o.p. **92**
ISBN 0-684-84795-7 (pa) LC 97-39766
The author, a Brooklyn Dodger fan, discusses "the remarkable '50s in New York baseball, together with the rituals of her church and the universal preoccupations of childhood." Booklist
"For self-esteem-building female role models, for baseball lore and inning-by-inning action and for a lively trip into the recent American past, you could hardly do better." N Y Times Book Rev

Goodyear, Charles, 1800-1860

Korman, Richard. The Goodyear story; an inventor's obsession and the struggle for a rubber monopoly. Encounter Bks. 2002 230p il $25.95; pa $16.95 **92**
1. Goodyear Tire & Rubber Company 2. Rubber
ISBN 1-89355-437-6; 1-89355-482-1 (pa)
LC 2001-55635
"Charles Goodyear began his obsessive quest to find the recipe for making rubber in the 1830s and ended up becoming an American industrial legend. Besides tracing the life of this inspiring entrepreneur, Korman's social history of factory life and debtors prison in the early to mid-1800s is exceedingly well drawn." Booklist
Includes bibliographical references

Slack, Charles. Noble obsession; Charles Goodyear, Thomas Hancock, and the race to unlock the greatest industrial secret of the nineteenth century. Hyperion 2002 274p il $24.95; pa $14.95 **92**
1. Hancock, Thomas, 1786-1865 2. Goodyear Tire & Rubber Company 3. Rubber
ISBN 0-7868-6789-2; 0-7868-8856-3 (pa)
LC 2002-68932
This is the story of how Charles Goodyear discovered the process of vulcanization of rubber, making possible the manufacture of rubber tires carried out by Thomas Hancock and the company which bears Goodyear's name
"Slack brings Charles Goodyear back to life and redeems the man who gave up everything to give his gift to the world." Booklist
Includes bibliographical references

Gordimer, Nadine, 1923-

Gordimer, Nadine. Conversations with Nadine Gordimer; edited by Nancy Topping Bazin and Marilyn Dallman Seymour. University Press of Miss. 1990 xxiv, 321p (Literary conversations series) $46 **92**
ISBN 0-87805-444-8 LC 90-12556
This is a collection of interviews in which Gordimer talks "about her life as a white South African, about her fiction, and about writers she admires." Booklist
Includes bibliographical references

Gordon, Anna, d. 2002

Gordon, Mary. Circling my mother. See entry under Gordon, Mary, 1949-

Gordon, Mary, 1949-

Gordon, Mary. Circling my mother. Pantheon Books 2007 254p $24 **92**
1. Gordon, Anna, d. 2002 2. Authors, American
ISBN 978-0-375-42456-4; 0-375-42456-3
LC 2006-102286
Mary Gordon's "memoir centers on her mother's . . . religious life and her deep respect for priests." N Y Times Book Rev
This is "is a moving, affecting work on the tug-of-war between mother and daughter, between women and the changing world around them." Publ Wkly

Gore, Al, 1948-
Zelnick, Bob. Gore: a political life. Regnery
Pub. 1999 384p $29.95; pa $16.95 **92**
ISBN 0-89526-326-2; 0-89526-241-X (pa)
LC 99-194035
Zelnick examines the life and career of Al Gore, the
former senator from Tennessee and Vice President of the
United States
The author provides "a useful and comprehensive sur-
vey of the highs and lows of Gore's political career."
NY Times Book Rev

Gorey, Edward, 1925-2000
Ross, Clifford. The world of Edward Gorey; by
Clifford Ross and Karen Wilkin. Abrams 1996
190p il pa $19.95 hardcover o.p. **92**
ISBN 0-8109-9083-0 (pa) LC 95-47900
This book includes an "interview with Mr. Ross, {in
which} Edward Gorey speaks of his likes and dislikes
and aspects of his career. . . . Ms. Wilkin discusses
Gorey's work as illustrator, author, stage designer, and
miscellaneous creator." Atl Mon
Includes bibliographical references

Gorky, Arshile, 1904-1948
Spender, Matthew. From a high place; a life of
Arshile Gorky. University of California Press 2000
417p il pa $21.95 **92**
1. Artists—United States
ISBN 0-520-22548-1; 978-0-520-22548-0
LC 00-28715
First published 1999 by Knopf
"Spender, a sculptor and writer and the husband of
Gorky's daughter, provides a personal and intimate biog-
raphy of the Armenian American abstract expressionist."
Libr J
Includes bibliographical references

Goya, Francisco, 1746-1828
Blackburn, Julia. Old man Goya. Pantheon Bks.
2002 239p il $23; pa $13 **92**
ISBN 0-375-40611-5; 0-375-70579-1 (pa)
LC 2002-280534
The author "focuses on the second half of Goya's
long and amazingly productive life, beginning with the
devastating illness that left him deaf at age 47. . . .
[She] not only empathetically imagines the sea change
caused by Goya's abrupt sensory loss, and convincingly
assesses its impact on his work, she also conjures up the
artists's mise-en-scène, from the frenetic streets of Madrid to the sanctuary of the studio, the bizarreness of the
court of Charles IV, the horrors of famine and war,
Goya's long marriage, and, after his wife's death, late-
life relationship with a much younger woman. . . . [This
is a] vital, inventively participatory portrait of a master
portraitist and observer of life." Booklist
Includes bibliographical references

Hughes, Robert. Goya. Knopf 2003 429p il $40
* **92**
ISBN 0-394-58028-1 LC 2002-43281

This is the "story of an artist whose life and work
bridged the transition from the eighteenth-century reign
of the old masters to the early days of the nineteenth-
century moderns. . . . Hughes tracks Goya's development, as man and artist . . . from the early works commissioned by the Church, through his long, productive,
and tempestuous career at court, to the darkly sinister
and cryptic work he did at the end of his life." Publisher's note
This is "a remarkably vital, delectably discursive, and
deeply affecting study." Booklist
Includes bibliographical references

Graham, Billy, 1918-
Graham, Billy. Just as I am; the autobiography
of Billy Graham. HarperSanFrancisco 1997 xxiii,
760p il maps hardcover o.p. pa $18 **92**
1. Clergy
ISBN 0-06-063387-5; 0-06-063392-1 (pa)
LC 97-605
"In this memoir, Graham looks back at age 78 on his
lifetime of personal relationships, ministry, leadership,
and experiences. He chronicles such events and stories as
his boyhood in North Carolina, his first steps in ministry,
details of evangelistic trips and revivals, and meetings
with world and local leaders. . . . All libraries would do
well to stock this readable title by an important national
figure." Libr J

Graham, Katharine
Graham, Katharine. Personal history. Knopf
1997 642p il $35; pa $15.95 **92**
1. Washington post
ISBN 0-394-58585-2; 0-375-70104-4 (pa)
LC 96-49638
"In 1963, Graham took over as publisher of the *Washington Post* as a classic grieving widow. Her husband,
Phil, had shot himself at their country estate. . . . The
first half of her story centers around life with Phil, the
second on three pivotal events at the *Post*: the publication of the Pentagon Papers, the Watergate scandal and
the prolonged pressman's strike of 1975." Publ Wkly
"Throughout this easy-to-read story, Graham writes
about her personal life and the lives of others, ranging
from presidents to household help, with sympathy and
grace." Libr J

Grant, Cary, 1904-1986
McCann, Graham. Cary Grant; a class apart.
Columbia Univ. Press 1997 346p il pa $19.95
hardcover o.p. **92**
ISBN 0-231-10885-0 (pa) LC 96-38577
First published 1996 in the United Kingdom
"McCann's biography shows how working-class Ar-
chie Leach transformed himself into Cary Grant. Unlike
many self-made successes, Grant never renounced his
humble origins but incorporated them into his persona.
As a result, he became, McCann says, a 'democratic gen-
tleman,' at ease in any element, who shone in both serious dramas and screwball comedies and, unlike most
male stars, appealed equally to men and women."
Booklist
Includes bibliographical references

Grant, Ulysses S. (Ulysses Simpson), 1822-1885

Bunting, Josiah. Ulysses S. Grant; [by] Josiah
Bunting III. Times Books 2004 xx, 180p
(American presidents series) $20   **92**

ISBN 0-8050-6949-6   LC 2004-47889

The author's "goal is a re-examination of one of the
most vilified presidents in American history." SLJ

"This superb book should support those who are gradually moving Grant from the lower to the upper half of
rankings of chief executives." Publ Wkly

Includes bibliographical references

Catton, Bruce. Grant moves south; with maps
by Samuel H. Bryant. Little, Brown 1960 564p
maps pa $24.99 hardcover o.p. *   **92**

1. United States—History—1861-1865, Civil War—
Campaigns

ISBN 0-316-13244-6 (pa)

"Grant's development as a man and leader is brilliantly shown in this reconstruction of his Mississippi campaign." Booklist

Includes bibliographical references

Catton, Bruce. Grant takes command; with maps
by Samuel H. Bryant. Little, Brown 1969 556p
maps pa $24.99 hardcover o.p.   **92**

1. United States—History—1861-1865, Civil War—
Campaigns

ISBN 0-316-13240-3 (pa)

This sequel to Grant moves south "takes up Ulysses
S. Grant's career just after his capture of Vicksburg in
1863. . . . It carries the action right up to Richmond and
Lee's surrender at Appomattox." Publ Wkly

Includes bibliographical references

Flood, Charles Bracelen. Grant and Sherman;
the friendship that won the Civil War. Farrar,
Straus and Giroux 2005 460p il map $27

92

1. Sherman, William T. (William Tecumseh), 1820-
1891 2. United States—History—1861-1865, Civil
War

ISBN 0-374-16600-5   LC 2005-04170

The author "underscores the powerful bond formed
between Ulysses S. Grant and William Tecumseh Sherman and tells the story of a friendship that would influence both the politics and the military operations of the
Civil War. . . . One of the big-profile history books of
the season and highly recommended for all history-
minded readers." Booklist

Includes bibliographical references

Grant, Ulysses S. (Ulysses Simpson). Memoirs
and selected letters; personal memoirs of U.S.
Grant, selected letters, 1839-1865. Library of Am.
1990 2v in 1 il maps $35 *   **92**

1. United States—History—1861-1865, Civil War

ISBN 0-940450-58-5   LC 90-60013

This volume includes Grant's personal memoirs, first
published in 1885 and 175 letters written between 1839
and 1865

Includes bibliographical references

Korda, Michael. Ulysses S. Grant: the unlikely
hero. Atlas Books\HarperCollins 2004 161p
(Eminent lives) $19.95   **92**

1. United States—History—1861-1865, Civil War

ISBN 0-06-059015-7   LC 2004-46125

This book features "anecdotes that reveal Grant as a
man of unprepossessing presence in peace, cool temperament in war, bad luck in business, innocence and pre-
science in politics, and good fortune in marriage." Libr
J

The author "freshly characterizes his man without psy-
chologizing an unpromising subject. . . . This is a highly
readable, accurate study of the man." Publ Wkly

Includes bibliographical references

Simpson, Brooks D. Ulysses S. Grant; triumph
over adversity, 1822-1865. Houghton Mifflin 2000
533p $35 *   **92**

1. United States—History—1861-1865, Civil War

ISBN 0-395-65994-9   LC 99-43518

In this first volume of a planned two-volume biography, Simpson's main focus is on Grant's Civil War
years. He had resigned from the army in 1854, charged
with drunkenness. "The outbreak of war in 1861 found
the thirty-nine-year-old Grant working as a salesman in
his father's leather store at Galena, Illinois. . . . {Simp-
son analyzes} Grant's rise in three years from store clerk
to commander of the armies of the United States." New
Repub

"A detailed and exciting narrative of how one man
succeeded, where so many others had failed, in pinning
the Union back together again, albeit with a bloody bay-
onet." N Y Times Book Rev

Includes bibliographical references

Smith, Jean Edward. Grant. Simon & Schuster
2001 781p il $35; pa $20   **92**

1. United States—History—1861-1865, Civil War

ISBN 0-684-84926-7; 0-684-84927-5 (pa)

LC 00-53794

This biography surveys the career and achievements of
the 18th U.S. president, from his days at West Point to
the Civil War campaigns and his subsequent elevation to
the presidency

"While he acknowledges Grant's failure to rein in his
'friends' and cabinet members as president, Smith convincingly illustrates how Grant's backbone and political
skills were used to advance the cause of former slaves
in the South. This is an outstanding and long overdue
reevaluation of the life and career of a great American."
Booklist

Includes bibliographical references

Grealy, Lucy, 1963-2002

Patchett, Ann. Truth & beauty; a friendship.
HarperCollins Publishers 2004 257p $23.95; pa
$13.95   **92**

1. Women authors

ISBN 0-06-057214-0; 0-06-057215-9 (pa)

LC 2003-67586

"As young writers. Patchett and Lucy Grealy began an
intense friendship that lasted until Grealy's tragic death.
With intimacy, gracy, and humor, Patchett's memoir captures Lucy's exuberance and her roller-coaster struggles
with disfigurement and depression." Booklist

Greene, Belle da Costa, 1883-1950

Ardizzone, Heidi. An illuminated life; Belle da Costa Greene's journey from prejudice to privilege. W. W. Norton & Co. 2007 580p il $35

92

1. Morgan Library & Museum (New York, N.Y.) 2. African American librarians 3. African American women

ISBN 978-0-393-05104-9; 0-393-05104-8

LC 2007-04967

This is a biography of the first director of the Morgan Library.

"Ardizzone more than succeeds in portraying a vivid figure who rose to the top in a segregated, paternalistic world yet suffered loneliness and was haunted by personal demons. A valuable work for students of early 20th-century culture as well as for librarians, feminists, and students of race relations." Libr J

Includes bibliographical references

Greene, Graham, 1904-1991

Sherry, Norman. The life of Graham Greene. v3: 1955-1991. Viking 2004 800p $39.95

92

ISBN 0-670-0342-9

Also available in paperback by Penguin

"In the final volume of this definitive life of Greene . . . {Sherry} chronicles years during which Greene turned almost everything—politics, romance, literature, and religion—into reasons for conflict. . . . Nor did Greene's religious faith—eaten away by doubt and self-accusation—provide much late-life serenity or assurance. In narrating Greene's unending struggles, Sherry candidly confronts the author's deplorable lapses in craft and judgment. But, in the end, he delivers a writer who triumphed in his truth-seeking artistry and who even experienced the unexpected final beauty of peace on his Swiss deathbed. Greene's many readers will cherish this poignant and detailed concluding volume to a masterful portrait." Booklist

Greenspan, Alan

Greenspan, Alan. The age of turbulence; adventures in a new world. Penguin Press 2007 531p il $35

92

1. Economists

ISBN 978-1-59420-131-8   LC 2007-13169

"The former U. S. Federal Reserve Board chair relates his life story, focusing on lessons learned in government service, particularly post-9/11. He also includes political anecdotes, asserts his faith in market capitalism, and shares his predictions for the world of 2030." Libr J

Includes bibliographical references

Martin, Justin. Greenspan; the man behind money. Perseus Bks. 2000 284p il pa $17.50 hardcover o.p.

92

1. Economists

ISBN 0-7382-0524-9 (pa)

In this biography the author "shows how Alan Greenspan's early experiences have shaped his tenure as chairman of the Federal Reserve Board." N Y Times Book Rev

Includes bibliographical references

Gregorian, Vartan

Gregorian, Vartan. The road to home; my life and times. Simon & Schuster 2003 354p il hardcover o.p. pa $15

92

ISBN 0-684-80834-X; 978-0-7432-5565-3; 0-7432-5565-8 (pa)   LC 2003-45566

In this "memoir, Gregorian explains how he went from a childhood in a poor section of Tabriz, Iran, to become president of the New York Public Library and, later, the president of Brown University." Publ Wkly

Grey, Zane, 1872-1939

Pauly, Thomas H. Zane Grey; his life, his adventures, his women. University of Illinois Press 2005 385p il map $34.95

92

ISBN 978-0-252-03044-4; 0-252-03044-3

LC 2005-9413

This is a biography of the "author of westerns like 'Riders of the Purple Sage,' 'The Light of Western Stars' and 'Code of the West.'" N Y Times Book Rev

The author "offers an honest exploration of the complex author. . . . A solid, entertaining read." Choice

Includes bibliographical references

Grove, Andrew S., 1936-

Tedlow, Richard S. Andy Grove; the life and times of an American. Portfolio 2006 512p $29.95

92

1. Intel Corp.

ISBN 978-1-591-84139-5; 1-591-84139-9

LC 2006-49829

The author "presents the story of Andy Grove, a penniless Hungarian immigrant who became an icon of twentieth-century corporate America. Grove joined Intel in 1968 at its founding, and while he was CEO from 1987 to 1998, 'market capitalization increased from $4.3 billion to $197.6 billion, a compound annual growth rate of 42% and a total increase of almost 4,500%.' Grove led the company with Intel's 386 microprocessor, which became the industry standard. Tedlow describes Grove, Time magazine's 1997 man of the year, as an extraordinary manager, author, and significant player in the fights against prostate cancer and Parkinson's disease. With unique access to Grove and Intel's internal resources and documents, Tedlow claims objectivity, telling the truth as he sees it in this laudatory narrative, although he also confirms his close ties to the subject." Booklist

Groves, Leslie R., 1896-1970

Norris, Robert S. Racing for the bomb: General Leslie R. Groves, the Manhattan Project's indispensable man. Steerforth Press 2002 xxi, 722p pa $24.95 hardcover o.p.

92

1. Manhattan Project

ISBN 1-58642-067-4 (pa)   LC 2001-57629

This is a biography of the military engineer in charge of the Manhattan Project, which developed the atomic bomb

This "work will not only serve scholars and general readers equally well but also take its place among the handful of best books about the birth of the atomic age." Booklist

Includes bibliographical references

Guevara, Ernesto, 1928-1967

Anderson, Jon Lee. Che Guevara; a revolutionary life. Grove Press 1997 814p il maps pa $20 hardcover o.p. **92**

ISBN 0-8021-3558-7 (pa)   LC 97-3993

This is a "biography of the life and death of the larger-than-life revolutionary Ernesto 'Che' Guevara, the Argentine doctor who joined with Castro to overturn Fulgencio Batista's reign in Cuba. . . . This book, with its 89 photographs, will be an invaluable addition to the literature of American revolutionaries." Booklist

Includes bibliographical references

Guggenheim, Peggy, 1898-1979

Gill, Anton. Art lover; a biography of Peggy Guggenheim. HarperCollins Pubs. 2002 480p il $29.95; pa $15.95 * **92**

ISBN 0-06-019697-1; 0-06-095681-X (pa)
LC 2001-51731

A biography of the art collector who "championed the work of Kandinsky, Tanguy, Pollock, Rothko and the New York School. Gill traces her evolution from 'belle-laide' to 'grande dame' of the modern art world." N Y Times Book Rev

Guggenheim "was known as much for her sexual exploits as for her championing of modern art, a fact Gill . . . examines with candor, sensitivity, and mellifluous grace." Booklist

Includes bibliographical references

Gunther, John, 1929-1947

Gunther, John. Death be not proud; a memoir. Harper & Row 1949 261p il pa $13.95 hardcover o.p. **92**

ISBN 0-06-123097-9 (pa)

Also available in hardcover from Buccaneer Bks.

A memoir of John Gunther's seventeen-year-old son, who died after a series of operations for a brain tumor. Not only a tribute to a remarkable boy but an account of a brave fight against disease

Gutierrez, Eduardo, 1978-1999

Breslin, Jimmy. The short sweet dream of Eduardo Gutierrez. Crown 2002 213p pa $12 hardcover o.p. **92**

ISBN 1-400-04682-3 (pa)   LC 2001-47283

"A true-life account of an illegal Mexican immigrant who died on a New York construction site, and of the dreary lives and modest ambitions common to Mexicans in this country." N Y Times Book Rev

Haffner, Sebastian

Haffner, Sebastian. Defying Hitler; a memoir; translated from the German by Oliver Pretzel. Farrar, Straus & Giroux 2002 309p il $24; pa $14 **92**

1. Germany—History—1918-1933
ISBN 0-374-16157-7; 0-312-42113-3 (pa)
LC 2002-17058

"In August 1938 a young German lawyer and journalist with the . . . name of Raimund Pretzel arrived in England. . . . Pretzel, a non-Jew, was fleeing to join and marry a Jewish woman pregnant with their first child. . . . Choosing a new name—Sebastian Haffner—to keep the Nazis from retaliating against his relatives, he went on to a . . . career as a journalist and historian in England, where he died in 1999. Afterward, while perusing his father's papers, Oliver Pretzel . . . found a . . . typescript in German. It was Haffner's unfinished memoir about his early years, begun in 1939, that sought through autobiography to understand how Hitler came to power." New Leader

"This is a small masterpiece." Booklist

Hamilton, Alexander, 1757-1804

Brookhiser, Richard. Alexander Hamilton, American. Free Press 1999 240p il pa $14 hardcover o.p. **92**

1. United States—Politics and government—1783-1809
ISBN 0-684-86331-6 (pa)   LC 98-46846

This is a biography of the Secretary of the Treasury. Brookhiser discusses Hamilton's life, from his "teenage years in St. Croix and youth in Manhattan, through his formative years as Washington's aide during the Revolutionary War, to his role in the writing of the Constitution and the Federalist Papers, to his later careers as Secretary of the Treasury, lawyer, politician, and journalist." Natl Rev

Includes bibliographical references

Chernow, Ron. Alexander Hamilton. Penguin Press 2004 818p il $35 * **92**

1. United States—Politics and government—1783-1809
ISBN 1-594-20009-2   LC 2003-65641

The author "makes the case for {Hamilton} as one of the most important Founding Fathers, arguing that America is heir to the Hamiltonian vision of the Modern economic state." Libr J

"Chernow makes fresh contributions to Hamiltoniana: no one has discovered so much about Hamilton's illegitimate origins and harrowed youth; few have been so taken by Hamilton's long-suffering, loving wife, Eliza. . . . This is a fine work that captures Hamilton's life with judiciousness and verve." Publ Wkly

Includes bibliographical references

Randall, Willard Sterne. Alexander Hamilton; a life. HarperCollins Pubs. 2003 476p il map $32.50; pa $15.95 **92**

1. United States—Politics and government—1783-1809
ISBN 0-06-019549-5; 0-06-095466-3 (pa)
LC 2002-68674

The author focuses on "Hamilton's fortune-marked rise to fame, which was sealed when the ambitious aide-de-camp of Washington pleaded for, and got, the assignment to lead the final assault at the Battle of Yorktown. . . . Randall's vigorous prose captures shows the compass of Hamilton's life and his role in making the U.S. a going concern." Booklist

Includes bibliographical references

Hammer, Armand, 1898-1990

Epstein, Edward Jay. Dossier; the secret history of Armand Hammer. Carroll & Graf 1999 418p il pa $15.95   **92**

ISBN 978-0-7867-0677-8; 0-7867-0677-5

First published 1996 by Random House

"Epstein follows Hammer from his dealings with Lenin in the 1920s to his rise to the top of the corporate world in the 1970s. Along the way, Epstein provides many lurid details, concerning Hammer's dealings with wives, lovers, family members, fellow board members, foreign heads of state, and every president since FDR." Libr J

The author employs a "wealth of primary sources he tapped in Soviet archives and elsewhere. . . . It is hard to imagine a sharper picture of how a tycoon is both born and made and how the power game is played." N Y Times Book Rev

Includes bibliographical references

Hammond, John, 1910-1987

Prial, Dunstan. The producer; John Hammond and the soul of American music. Farrar, Straus and Giroux 2006 347p il $27   **92**

ISBN 978-0-374-11304-9; 0-374-11304-1

LC 2005-12666

This is a "portrait of the famed 20th-century critic, journalist and producer." Publ Wkly

The author "brings Hammond to life in clear, insightful prose and places him and figures such as Dylan, Franklin, and Springsteen in the proper historical context." Libr J

Includes discography and bibliographical references

Hancock, Thomas, 1786-1865

Slack, Charles. Noble obsession. See entry under Goodyear, Charles, 1800-1860

Handel, George Frideric, 1685-1759

Hogwood, Christopher. Handel; chronological table by Anthony Hicks. Rev ed. Thames & Hudson 2007 324p map pa $21.95   **92**

ISBN 978-0-500-28681-4; 0-500-28681-7

LC 2006-909559

First published 1984 in the United Kingdom

The author "addresses his book to the serious layman. The composer's comings and goings are documented as accurately as possible, and Mr. Hogwood has added terse critical commentary about the music in sophisticated language but without musical examples." N Y Times Book Rev

Includes bibliographical references

Hansberry, Lorraine, 1930-1965

Hansberry, Lorraine. To be young, gifted, and Black; Lorraine Hansberry in her own words; adapted by Robert Nemiroff; with drawings and art by Lorraine Hansberry; introduction by James Baldwin; and a new preface by Jewell Handy Gresham Nemiroff. 1st Vintage Books ed. Vintage Books 1995 xxx, 261p il pa $13.95   **92**

1. African American women 2. Dramatists, American

ISBN 0-679-76415-1   LC 96-119999

First published 1969 by Prentice-Hall

Work on this book and on the script for the play of the same title, which was presented at New York's Cherry Lane Theatre in 1969, "proceeded concurrently, each drawing upon the experiences and creative discoveries of the other, but ultimately diverging quite drastically." Postscript

Hardy, Thomas, 1840-1928

Tomalin, Claire. Thomas Hardy. Penguin Group 2006 xxv, 486p il map $35   **92**

ISBN 1-59420-118-8; 978-1-59420-118-9

LC 2007-295886

In this "biography of Hardy, . . . [the author] gives full treatment to the novels but is especially interested in how Hardy's poetry reflects the events of his life and how small incidents and emotions recollected over time come back to inform the moments of his poetry." Libr J

"A priceless resource for the general reader and the Victorian scholar." Booklist

Includes bibliographical references

Hari, Daoud

Hari, Daoud. The translator; a tribesman's memoir of Darfur. Random House 2008 204p $23   **92**

1. Sudan—History—Darfur conflict, 2003-

ISBN 978-1-4000-6744-2; 1-4000-6744-8

LC 2007-42308

In this memoir, the author recounts his life in Darfur, Sudan before and after the conflict in 2003.

"Those with the courage to join Hari's odyssey may find this a life-changing read." Publ Wkly

Harrington, Michael, 1928-1989

Isserman, Maurice. The other American: the life of Michael Harrington. PublicAffairs 2000 449p $28.50; pa $14   **92**

ISBN 1-89162-030-4; 1-58648-036-7 (pa)

LC 99-56654

This biography of the leftist social critic and author of the influential The other America (1962) is "also a veritable Zagat's guide through the left sectarian factions of the last three-quarters of the 20th century." N Y Times Book Rev

Includes bibliographical references

Harrison, Benjamin, 1833-1901

Calhoun, Charles W. (Charles William). Benjamin Harrison. Times Books 2005 206p il (American presidents series) $20   **92**

1. Presidents—United States

ISBN 0-8050-6952-6; 978-0-8050-6952-5

LC 2004-63778

The author "dusts off an almost thoroughly forgotten chief executive, known primarily for serving between Cleveland's two terms, to disclose a harbinger of the modern, activist president. . . . One of the most revelatory entries in the American Presidents series." Booklist

Includes bibliographical references

Harrison, Jim, 1937-

Harrison, Jim. Off to the side; a memoir.
Atlantic Monthly Press 2002 313p $25; pa $14
92

ISBN 0-87113-860-3; 0-8021-4030-0 (pa)
LC 2002-26051

"Harrison reflects on how childhood tragedies and a
profound involvement with nature gave rise to . . . [his]
passion for writing. . . . A mesmerizing storyteller and
down-to-earth philosophizer, Harrison explicates his 'sev-
en obsessions,' which include alcohol, strip clubs, hunting, fishing, and dogs, and offers compelling ruminations
on the splendor of nature and the crimes of man, the
mysteries of spirit and the revelations of art." Booklist

Hart, Moss, 1904-1961

Bach, Steven. Dazzler; the life and times of
Moss Hart. Da Capo 2002 462p il pa $20
92

1. Dramatists, American
ISBN 0-306-81135-9; 978-0-306-81135-7
First published 2001 by Knopf

This biography of the actor, director, and playwright
chronicles "Hart's life, his early successes, his artistic
missteps in middle age, and his later-life triumphs in the
1950s and 1960s." Booklist

"In narrating its subject's life, Dazzler is both gossipy
and credible, a relatively rare and laudable combination."
New Leader

Includes bibliographical references

Haskins, Don, 1930-2008

Haskins, Don. Glory road; my story of the 1966
NCAA basketball championship and how one team
triumphed against the odd and changed America
forever; [by] Don Haskins with Daniel Wetzel.
Hyperion 2006 254p il pa $14.95 *   **92**

ISBN 1-4013-0791-4   LC 2005-50349

This is an "autobiography of Don Haskins, Texas college basketball icon and inadvertent civil rights pioneer."
Publ Wkly

"This is one of the best sports autobiographies in
many years." Booklist

Havel, Václav

Havel, Václav. To the castle and back;
translated from the Czech by Paul Wilson. Knopf
2007 383p $27.95; pa $15.95   **92**

1. Czechoslovakia—Politics and government
2. Czech Republic—Politics and government
ISBN   978-0-307-26641-5;   0-307-26641-9;
978-0-307-33845-2 (pa); 0-307-38845-X (pa)
LC 2007-4413

Original Czech edition, 2006

The book "gives Havel's account of his journey from
dissident-in-chief to head of state during the Velvet Revolution of 1989—and the turmoil that followed. Hardly
a conventional memoir, its three intermixed narratives are
at first as disorienting as his role reversal—which dismayed his wife Olga as much as himself. . . . These selections are by turns obscure, funny, insightful, poignant,
and peevish. . . . Living in truth was what [Havel]

preached as a dissident, and it is what he preached as
president. . . . Whatever his political shortcomings in office, at least in this, the Czechs were privileged to have
Havel as president." Commonweal

Hawking, Stephen W., 1942-

White, Michael. Stephen Hawking; a life in
science; {by} Michael White and John Gribbin.
New updated ed. Joseph Henry Press 2002 348p
pa $17.95   **92**

1. Astrophysics
ISBN 0-309-08410-5   LC 2002-11961
First published 1992 by Dutton

This book "sets out to show how natural talent combined with immense willpower have enabled Hawking to
live a surprisingly active and interesting life and at the
same time be a distinguished astrophysicist. It tries hard
to express abstract concepts in ordinary language and
tells enough about Hawking's relations with the world
for readers to grasp that living close to such determination is not always easy. . . . Highly recommended."
Choice

Includes bibliographical references

Hawthorne, Nathaniel, 1804-1864

Miller, Edwin Haviland. Salem is my dwelling
place: a life of Nathaniel Hawthorne. University of
Iowa Press 1991 596p il hardcover o.p. pa $24.95
92

ISBN 0-87745-332-2; 0-87745-381-0 (pa)
LC 91-14543

This is a biography of the 19th century American novelist

"Psychologically probing (but free of all jargon), Miller's elegantly written study gives us a fresh, sympathetic
picture of an immensely complex, repressed man. . . . A
masterful work, wholly satisfying." Libr J

Includes bibliographical references

Wineapple, Brenda. Hawthorne: a life. Alfred A.
Knopf 2003 509p il $30   **92**

ISBN 0-375-40044-3   LC 2002-192485

In this biography Wineapple discusses the "public
controversies that shaped [Hawthorne's] world: the Whig
triumphs that cost him his customhouse job and forced
him into writing; the critical exchanges that heartened
him with praise for his work . . . and wounded him with
disparagement; and the Civil War battles that drove him
to despair—and into political disrepute as a copperhead."
Booklist

Includes bibliographical references

Haydn, Joseph, 1732-1809

Geiringer, Karl. Haydn: a creative life in music;
by Karl Geiringer in collaboration with Irene
Geiringer. 3rd rev & enl ed. University of Calif.
Press 1982 403p il pa $21.95 hardcover o.p.
92

ISBN 0-520-04317-0 (pa)   LC 82-2821
First published 1946

The author is "one of the few scholars who have devoted themselves almost exclusively to the study of this

Haydn, Joseph, 1732-1809—*Continued*
great master. He has not only collected all the new data
that have cast light on Haydn research . . . he has also
contributed many valuable observations and ideas." Saturday Rev
Includes bibliographical references

Haydn; edited by David Wyn Jones; consultant
editor Otto Biba. Oxford Univ. Press 2002 xxi,
515p il map (Oxford composer companions) $75
92
ISBN 0-19-866216-5   LC 2002-510033
This Haydn encyclopedia features over 900 "articles
by 41 contributors on the surroundings (Eszterháza, Vienna), people (family, teachers, composers, performers,
patrons), in-the-air ideas (Josephinism, Freemasonry), and
musical genres (mass, quartet, symphony) that informed
the composer, along with entries on his compositions and
the long-range influence of his inventions (on everything
from Brahms to the name of a pastry)." Libr J
"This volume will be useful to persons who need
quick, specific information about Haydn, his works, and
18th-century style." Choice

Hearst, William Randolph, 1863-1951
Nasaw, David. The chief: the life of William
Randolph Hearst. Houghton Mifflin 2000 687p il
$35; pa $16   **92**
ISBN 0-395-82759-0; 0-618-15446-9 (pa)
LC 99-462122
"Few publishers have loomed as large in their life-
times, or cast as long a shadow after death, as William
Randolph Hearst. . . . Nasaw's judicious and compre-
hensive biography sensibly seeks to understand its sub-
ject, not to judge him." New Yorker
Includes bibliographical references

Hellman, Lillian, 1906-1984
Hellman, Lillian. Pentimento. Little, Brown
1973 297p pa $14.95 hardcover o.p.   **92**
1. Dramatists, American
ISBN 0-316-35288-8 (pa)
This continuation of An unfinished woman—a memoir
(1969) offers sketches of events and people from the author's past. She reminisces about her childhood in the
South, some of her eccentric relatives including Cousin
Bethe and Uncle Willy, Julia, her childhood friend who
was trapped by the Nazis, Dashiell Hammett, who was
her lover, and her experiences in the theater
"Pentimento is valuable as a picture of a woman and
writer in the making." New Repub

Martinson, Deborah. Lillian Hellman; a life with
foxes and scoundrels. Counterpoint 2005 448p il
$27.95   **92**
1. Dramatists, American
ISBN 1-58243-315-1   LC 2005-16616
The author describes the details of the playwright's
"life, from her demanding temperament to her gutsy poli-
tics and legendary relationship with Dashiel Hammett."
Booklist
This is "a richly thorough, sometimes somber, and
fairly objective portrait of an enigmatic individual." Libr
J
Includes bibliographical references

Hemingway, Ernest, 1899-1961
Lynn, Kenneth S. Hemingway. Harvard
University Press 1995 702p il pa $27   **92**
1. Authors, American 2. Journalists
ISBN 0-674-38732-5; 978-0-674-38732-4
LC 95-129513
First published 1987 by Simon and Schuster
"Taking as his premise Hemingway's glib assertion
that the only analyst he relied upon was his 'portable
Corona Number 3,' Lynn tracks the exploration of a dis-
ordered inner world as Hemingway sought to find some
sort of resolution to the agony of his personal conflicts
through 'his cunningly wrought fiction.' The man who
emerges from Lynn's biography is a vastly more complex and compelling figure than the white-bearded, pon-
tificating 'Papa' of myth." Publ Wkly
Includes bibliographical references

Mellow, James R. Hemingway; a life without
consequences. Addison-Wesley 1994 704p il pa
$15   **92**
1. Authors, American 2. Journalists
ISBN 0-201-62620-9; 978-0-201-62620-9
LC 93-24497
First published 1992 by Houghton Mifflin
"In sheer number of pages, Mr. Mellow's version of
the life is most heavily weighed toward the years 1921
to 1930, when Hemingway lived in Paris during his first
two marriages and published the novels and stories that
built his early reputation as one of this country's most
important writers. Mr. Mellow seems in a hurry to get
through the rest of the story, but he does dutifully summarize Hemingway's childhood, adolescence and the major events of the later years. . . . Mr. Mellow takes careful note of Hemingway's publications in the context of
his life and gives sensitive readings, both biographical
and critical, to them all." N Y Times Book Rev
Includes bibliographical references

Reynolds, Michael S. Hemingway: the 1930's;
[by] Michael Reynolds. Norton 1997 360p il maps
hardcover o.p. pa $15.95   **92**
1. Authors, American 2. Journalists
ISBN 0-393-04093-3; 0-393-31778-1 (pa)
LC 96-43113
"This fourth volume in Reynold's ongoing series finds
Hemingway setting up a home base in Key West, Florida, while also following the bullfights—and later the civil war—in Spain, going on safari in Africa, and fishing
off Cuba." Libr J
"Filled with fascinating details and anecdotes, this fine
biography illuminates our understanding of this crucial
decade." Publ Wkly
Includes bibliographical references

Reynolds, Michael S. Hemingway: the
homecoming; [by] Michael Reynolds. W.W.
Norton 1999 xxiii, 264p il map pa $14.95
92
1. Authors, American 2. Journalists
ISBN 0-393-31981-4
First published 1992 by Blackwell with title: Hemingway: the American homecoming
This third volume of a five-volume study of Hemingway's life begun with The young Hemingway (1998) and

Hemingway, Ernest, 1899-1961—*Continued*

Hemingway: the Paris years (1999) "covers 1926-29, a transitional period that marked the conclusion of Hemingway's artistic apprenticeship and the cooling of many literary friendships; the end of one marriage and the beginning of another; the suicide of his father; and the writing of The Sun Also Rises, Men Without Women, A Farewell to Arms, and an ultimately abandoned novel." Libr J

Includes bibliographical references

Reynolds, Michael S. Hemingway: the Paris years; [by] Michael Reynolds. W.W. Norton 1999 402p il map pa $18.95 **92**
1. Authors, American 2. Journalists
ISBN 0-393-31879-6
First published 1989 by Blackwell
In this second volume of a five-volume biography of Hemingway begun with The young Hemingway (1998), the author "locates Hemingway in an American sociocultural context wherein he rejects middle-class restraints and aspires to identity as hero and self-reliant frontiersman (soldier, bullfighter, hunter, lover). The genius of the book lies in a graceful and informative linkage between literary creation and biographical incident." Libr J

Includes bibliographical references

Reynolds, Michael S. The young Hemingway; [by] Michael Reynolds. W. W. Norton 1998 291p il pa $15.95 **92**
1. Authors, American 2. Journalists
ISBN 0-393-31776-5
First published 1986 in the United Kingdom
This first volume of a five-volume biography of Hemingway is a "study of Hemingway from his early youth to the time just before his expatriate years." N Y Times Book Rev
"This incisive, well-written biography . . . will prove useful at almost every readership level, from general reader to scholar." Choice

Includes bibliographical references

Hendrix, Jimi

Cross, Charles R. Room full of mirrors; a biography of Jimi Hendrix. Hyperion 2005 384p il $24.95 * **92**
ISBN 1-401-30028-6   LC 2005-46362
The author's "narrative, based on more than 300 interviews, describes Hendrix as thoughtful and craving some semblance of order to his life, even as it became steeped in drug use." Publ Wkly
"Admirably comprehensive and well referenced, this is the Hendrix biography to acquire if you can acquire only one." Booklist

Includes bibliographical references

Murray, Charles Shaar. Crosstown traffic: Jimi Hendrix and the post-war rock'n'roll revolution. St. Martin's Press 1990 c1989 247p il pa $12 hardcover o.p. **92**
ISBN 0-312-06324-5 (pa)   LC 89-77681
First published 1989 in the United Kingdom
Engl. title: Crosstown traffic: Jimi Hendrix and post-war pop

"The book is a broad-based study of African-American music—blues, jazz, rhythm and blues, and soul—and how the music influenced, and was influenced by, Hendrix." Libr J
"This informed, textured account will be irresistible to devotees of Hendrix and psychedelic rock as well as fans of blues, funk, jazz and rock 'n' roll." Booklist

Includes discography and bibliographical references

Henry VIII, King of England, 1491-1547

Weir, Alison. Henry VIII; the king and his court. Ballantine Bks. 2001 632p il $28; pa $16.95 **92**
ISBN 0-345-43659-8; 0-345-43708-X (pa)
                                    LC 2001-116042
In this biography of the Tudor king, the author "examines the minutiae of his daily life and gives prominence to the background players of his court. . . . At times, the weighty detail and numerous characters will make the work inaccessible; however, as a scholarly study it is a significant achievement." Libr J

Includes bibliographical references

Hepburn, Audrey, 1929-1993

Walker, Alexander. Audrey; her real story. St. Martin's Press 1995 319p il pa $16.95 hardcover o.p. **92**
ISBN 0-312-18046-2 (pa)   LC 94-33716
The author "recounts his subject's childhood in war-torn Europe and her early stage and film career. . . . Both the narrative and the writing itself become more lively as he discusses the heyday of her career, her sometimes turbulent love life and her work with Third World children for UNICEF." Publ Wkly

Hepburn, Katharine, 1907-2003

Berg, A. Scott (Andrew Scott). Kate remembered. Putnam 2003 370p il $25.95; pa $15 **92**
ISBN 0-399-15164-8; 0-425-19909-6 (pa)
                                    LC 2003-545232
In this posthumous biography, the author reveals "details about such pivotal events as the death of her brother by hanging, her relationships with powerful men like Howard Hughes and John Ford, and her slow, sad decline. . . . Berg's writing is so intimate that readers may feel they are hiding behind a curtain as they listen to the stories he elicits from his subject. Kate herself comes across pretty much the way she did on screen: bossy, courageous, and self-involved." Booklist

Hepburn, Katharine. Me; stories of my life. Knopf 1991 420p il pa $15.95 hardcover o.p. **92**
ISBN 0-345-41009-2   LC 90-50805
This book "sounds just like its author—lots of cropped sentences, dashes, Hepburnian phrasing. But it's not a full-dress autobiography; as the subtitle proclaims, this is a collection of stories. . . . Still, fans will not be disappointed. Beginning with her early years . . . and concluding with her relationship with Tracy, Hepburn delivers all kinds of wry moments and, of course, a most interesting cast of characters." Booklist

Hepburn, Katharine, 1907-2003—*Continued*

Leaming, Barbara. Katharine Hepburn. Limelight Eds. 2000 549p il $23.95   **92**
ISBN 0-87910-293-4   LC 00-25227

A reissue of the title first published 1995 by Crown

This biography begins with a "portrait of the entire Hepburn clan, stressing the effect of the suicides that ran through Kate's maternal and paternal families. This is, in fact, a family biography, with at least half the book devoted to Hepburn's grandmother and mother. . . . By the time Kate enters the story, readers will be thoroughly caught up in a tale that already has delivered a full measure of intrigue, romance, and scandal. The book has been prodigiously researched (Leaming's source notes make fascinating reading on their own), and her access to various, previously unavailable papers not only makes possible the family history, but also paves the way for startling new revelations about Hepburn's life." Booklist [review of 1995 edition]

Mann, William J. Kate: the woman who was Hepburn. H. Holt 2006 xxviii, 621p il $30
92
ISBN 978-0-8050-7625-7; 0-8050-7625-5

This is a biography of the American actress.

"This will surely be the definitive version of Hepburn's life for decades to come, as it is an outstanding example of painstaking research matched with splendid writing." Publ Wkly

Includes bibliographical references

Herbert, Frank, 1920-1986

Herbert, Brian. Dreamer of Dune; the biography of Frank Herbert. TOR Bks. 2003 576p il $27.95; pa $16.95 *   **92**
ISBN 0-7653-0646-8; 0-7653-0647-6 (pa)
LC 2002-42951

"A Tom Doherty Associates book"

"Though subtitled a 'biography,' this is more of a personal memoir of the author's father, the well-known sf writer Frank Herbert." Libr J

"This moving, sometimes painfully obsessive biography is an impressive testament of family loyalty and love. A must-read for Herbert fans (both senior and junior), it includes family photos and a bibliography." Publ Wkly

Herriot, James

Herriot, James. All creatures great and small. 20th anniversary ed. St. Martin's Press 1992 442p $21.95; pa $13.95   **92**
1. Veterinary medicine
ISBN 0-312-08498-6; 0-312-33085-5 (pa)
LC 92-18975

First published 1972

The first volume of Herriot's autobiographical account of the practice of veterinary medicine in Yorkshire, England in the 1930s

Followed by All things bright and beautiful (1974), All things wise and wonderful (1977), and The Lord God made them all (1981)

Hershey, Milton Snavely, 1857-1945

D'Antonio, Michael. Hershey; Milton S. Hershey's extraordinary life of wealth, empire, and utopian dreams. Simon & Schuster 2006 305p il $25   **92**
ISBN 0-7432-6409-6   LC 2005-51581

This is a "look at the man who brought America the five-cent chocolate bar and founded a utopian village." Publ Wkly

"While some look at Hershey and see either a beneficent angel or a willful tyrant, it is the great charm of D'Antonio's book that he will not plunk entirely for one judgment or the other. It's the man he's after, not the god." N Y Times Book Rev

Includes bibliographical references

Hewitt, Don, 1922-

Hewitt, Don. Tell me a story; 50 years and 60 minutes in television. PublicAffairs 2001 272p il $26; pa $15   **92**
ISBN 1-58648-017-0; 1-58648-141-X (pa)
LC 2001-16222

"Beginning in 1948 as producer-director of [CBS Television's] first nightly newscast with Douglas Edwards and then with Walter Cronkite, [Hewitt] also worked with Edward R. Murrow. . . . He has presided over '60 Minutes' since he developed the program in 1968. . . . [This book] traces Hewitt's life and provides observations on news, politics and his signature show." N Y Times Book Rev

"Hewitt has positive things to say about most of the reporters and anchors he discusses, but his comments about the several generations of CBS executives and owners for whom he has worked are less consistently sunny. At 78, Hewitt remains blunt, opinionated, and full of ideas about where TV news has been and where it's going. His life may be one of the more interesting stories the veteran newsman has ever told." Booklist

Hickam, Homer H., 1943-

Hickam, Homer H. The Coalwood way; by Homer H. Hickam, Jr. Delacorte Press 2000 318p pa $6.99 hardcover o.p.   **92**
ISBN 0-440-23716-5   LC 00-35884

This sequel to Rocket boys "continues the author's life story with his senior year in high school, 1959, in the declining West Virginia mining town of Coalwood. The rocket club, featured in the last book, is pushed to the periphery, and the focus shifts to Hickam's teenage problems, which include his parents, girls, and a sadness whose cause he cannot divine." Booklist

Hickam, Homer H. Rocket boys; a memoir; {by} Homer H. Hickam, Jr. Delacorte Press 1998 368p $25.95; pa $14 *   **92**
ISBN 0-385-33320-X; 0-385-33321-8 (pa)
LC 98-19304

"Raised in Appalachian coal country, Homer H. Hickam, Jr., might well have followed his father and grandfather into the mine. But when he was 14, his life was changed by a space launch on the other side of the world. Hickam's story of how a teenage boy's handmade rockets lifted the hopes of a hardscrabble town is told in

Hickam, Homer H., 1943-—_Continued_
his {memoir}." Smithsonian
"Even if Hickam stretched the strict truth to metamorphose his memories into Stand By Me-like material for Hollywood . . . the embellishing only converts what is a good story into an absorbing, rapidly readable one that is unsentimental but artful about adolescence, high school, and family life." Booklist

Hijazi, Rafiq
Goldberg, Jeffrey. Prisoners. See entry under Goldberg, Jeffrey

Hilleman, Maurice R., 1919-2005
Offit, Paul A. Vaccinated; one man's quest to defeat the world's deadliest diseases. Smithsonian Books/Collins 2007 254p $26.95   **92**
  1. Biologists 2. Vaccination
  ISBN 978-0-06-122795-0; 0-06-122795-1
                                         LC 2006-53054
The author "traces the history of vaccines in what is largely a biography of Hilleman, who appears at the center of most of the stories and controversies." Libr J
"This book leaves one with a great appreciation for the work of the Salks and Sabins of the world, and it makes one want to lead a movement to enshrine Maurice Hilleman in the pantheon of American pop heroes." Choice
Includes bibliographical references

Hillerman, Tony
Hillerman, Tony. Seldom disappointed; a memoir. HarperCollins Pubs. 2001 341p il pa $13.95 hardcover o.p.   **92**
  1. Authors, American
  ISBN 0-06-050586-9 (pa)   LC 2001-24160
In this memoir Hillerman "relates his childhood in Oklahoma during the Depression, his service in World War II, his university education, his career in journalism and academia, and his eventual turn to writing mysteries. The entire book will appeal to his fans, but the first half is intensely gripping." Libr J
Includes bibliographical references

Him, Chanrithy, 1965-
Him, Chanrithy. When broken glass floats; growing up under the Khmer Rouge. Norton 2000 330p il map pa $13.95 hardcover o.p.   **92**
  ISBN 0-393-32210-6 (pa)   LC 99-58417
Him "was 10 in 1975 when the Khmer Rouge overtook her country in what she calls the time of broken glass. Feeling a survivor's responsibility to do so, Him vividly recalls the brutality of the camps, the strict social control, and alienation from family that the Khmer Rouge enforced." Booklist

Himes, Chester, 1909-1984
Sallis, James. Chester Himes; a life. Walker & Co. 2000 368p il $28; pa $18.95   **92**
  ISBN 0-8027-1362-9; 0-8027-7639-6 (pa)
                                         LC 00-63328

This is a biography of the African-American crime novelist. "Sentenced to 25 years in prison for armed robbery when he was 19, he turned to writing while behind bars and, when released after serving eight years, published two novels. Their poor reception by the white establishment only confirmed Himes's beliefs about racism in America. He eventually moved to Paris, spending most of the rest of his life abroad. . . . The author succeeds splendidly in fleshing Himes out in this riveting biography." Libr J
Includes bibliographical references

Himmler, Heinrich, 1900-1945
Breitman, Richard. The architect of genocide; Himmler and the final solution. University Press of New England 1992 335p (The Tauber Institute for the Study of European Jewry) pa $30   **92**
  1. Hitler, Adolf, 1889-1945 2. National socialism 3. Germany—Politics and government—1933-1945
  ISBN 0-87451-596-3; 978-0-87451-596-1
                                         LC 92-53857
"Brandeis University Press"
First published 1991 by Knopf
The author "focuses on Himmler's role in the decision making of the final solution, on how Himmler and the SS gained control of Nazi Germany's Jewish policy, and on other related World War II activities." Booklist
"This engrossing, detailed study constitutes a powerful refutation of revisionist scholars who claim that Hitler did not plan the Final Solution in advance but instead improvised it out of either military or political frustration." Publ Wkly
Includes bibliographical references

Hirohito, Emperor of Japan, 1901-1989
Bix, Herbert P. Hirohito and the making of modern Japan. HarperCollins Pubs. 2000 800p il maps pa $18 hardcover o.p. *   **92**
  1. Japan—Politics and government
  ISBN 0-06-093130-2 (pa)   LC 99-89427
"In 1945, fearing that the Japanese would resist American occupation unless the Emperor ordered them to obey, General MacArthur colluded with Hirohito in maintaining that the sovereign had been powerless to control Japan's military leaders. . . . {Bix}, uses newly available sources to argue that Hirohito was a war criminal. An imperialist whose policies reflected his belief in the racial superiority of the Japanese, Hirohito governed by manipulation for almost two decades, and used the threat of Soviet Communism to justify domestic repression and soaring military budgets. The author's virtuoso scholarship and accessible narrative invite us into Hirohito's world." New Yorker
Includes bibliographical references

Hirsi Ali, Ayaan, 1969-
Hirsi Ali, Ayaan. Infidel. Free Press 2007 353p il $26; pa $15   **92**
  1. Muslim women 2. Refugees
  ISBN 0-7432-8968-4;   978-0-7432-8968-9;
  0-7432-8969-2 (pa); 978-0-7432-8969-6 (pa)
                                         LC 2006-49762

Hirsi Ali, Ayaan, 1969- —*Continued*

"A Somali by birth and a recently elected member of the Dutch Parliament, Ms. Hirsi Ali had waged a personal crusade to improve the lot of Muslim women. Her warnings about the dangers posed to the Netherlands by unassimilated Muslims made her Public Enemy No. 1 for Muslim extremists, a feminist counterpart to Salman Rushdie. The circuitous, violence-filled path that led Ms. Hirsi Ali from Somalia to the Netherlands is the subject of 'Infidel,' her brave, inspiring and beautifully written memoir." N Y Times (Late N Y Ed)

Hiss, Alger

Hiss, Tony. The view from Alger's window. See entry under Hiss, Alger

Hiss, Tony

Hiss, Tony. The view from Alger's window; a son's memoir. Knopf 1999 241p il pa $13 hardcover o.p.   **92**
1. Hiss, Alger
ISBN 0-375-70128-1 (pa)   LC 98-50911
Companion volume to the author's Laughing last (1977)
A Borzoi Bk.
This memoir "revolves around the 445 previously unpublished letters that 'Alger'. . . wrote home from federal prison in Lewisburg, Pa., where he served nearly four years for perjury." Publ Wkly
"A poignant, wonderfully written and deeply troubling memoir." N Y Times Book Rev

Hitchcock, Alfred, 1899-1980

Chandler, Charlotte. It's only a movie; Alfred Hitchcock, a personal biography. Simon & Schuster 2005 349p il $26   **92**
ISBN 0-7432-4508-3   LC 2004-52559
The author reveals "several insights into Hitchcock's technical genius, creative worldview and personality. . . . Chandler allows her sources to reminisce at great length, and they tend to tell fascinating stories." Publ Wkly
Includes filmography

Spoto, Donald. The dark side of genius; the life of Alfred Hitchcock; {with a new introduction by the author}. Centennial ed. Da Capo Press 1999 594p il pa $22   **92**
ISBN 0-306-80932-X   LC 99-37941
This is a reissue of the title first published 1983 by Little, Brown
This is a biography of the director of such films as The man who knew too much, The thirty-nine steps, The lady vanishes, Rebecca, Spellbound, Strangers on a train, Rear window, and Psycho
This "is a vivid and perceptive portrait of a man whose character was as strange and shadowed as his films. . . . Hitchcock's final obsession was secretiveness, but he has been well served by a knowledgeable and revealing biography." Time
Includes bibliographical references

Hitler, Adolf, 1889-1945

Bullock, Alan. Hitler and Stalin; parallel lives. Knopf 1992 c1991 1081p il maps pa $25 hardcover o.p.   **92**
1. Stalin, Joseph, 1879-1953 2. Germany—Politics and government—1933-1945 3. Soviet Union—Politics and government
ISBN 0-679-72994-1 (pa)   LC 91-52711
First published 1991 in the United Kingdom
This biography of Hitler and Stalin "places the lives of the dictators side by side and follows them from beginning to end." Christ Sci Monit
"The twentieth century cannot be understood without close examination of the work of Stalin and Hitler. It is particularly important to note what their regimes and aims had in common and where they differed. Alan Bullock has put us all in his debt by placing their actions side by side, in enormous detail, and in chronological sequence to make the comparison easy." Times Lit Suppl
Includes bibliographical references

Hitler, Adolf. Mein Kampf; translated by Ralph Manheim. Houghton Mifflin 1943 xxi, 694p $40; pa $22 *   **92**
1. National socialism 2. Germany—Politics and government—1918-1933
ISBN 0-395-95105-4; 0-395-92503-7 (pa)
"Hitler's steady rise to power was interrupted only by the Beer Hall Putsch (1923), an unsuccessful attempt to overthrow the Weimar Republic. . . . During the nine months of imprisonment that followed he wrote 'Mein Kampf' (1924; tr. 'My struggle,' 1940). This book contained autobiographical and reflective passages, rife with hysterical anti-Semitism and paranoia, as well as the program he intended to implement; for the West it was a warning that went unheeded." Reader's Ency. 3d edition

Kershaw, Ian. Hitler, 1889-1936: hubris. Norton 1999 xxx, 845p il $35; pa $21.95   **92**
1. Germany—Politics and government—1918-1933 2. Germany—Politics and government—1933-1945
ISBN 0-393-04671-0; 0-393-32035-9 (pa)
           LC 98-29569
This first volume of a two-volume biography of the Nazi leader spans the years from his birth in 1889 to 1936 when Nazi power was completely established
"Kershaw provides an examination based on a number of archival sources not used by previous biographers. . . . More than a chronicle of Hitler's life, this is an analysis of the major historiographical issues, the circumstances that shaped his personality, and the historical events that enabled Hitler to rise to power." Libr J
Includes bibliographical references

Toland, John. Adolf Hitler. Anchor Bks. (NY) 1992 xx, 1035p il pa $24   **92**
1. Germany—Politics and government—1933-1945 2. National socialism
ISBN 0-385-42053-6   LC 91-31242
A reissue of the title first published 1976
This biography is based on more than 250 interviews with people acquainted with Hitler and materials from U.S. and British archives
"In the course of detailed and painstaking investigations [Toland] has disposed of a number of myths." N Y Times Book Rev
Includes bibliographical references

Ho, Chí Minh, 1890-1969

Duiker, William J. Ho Chi Minh; by William Duiker. Hyperion 2000 695p il maps $35; pa $16.95 **92**

ISBN 0-7868-6387-0; 0-7868-8701-X (pa)

LC 00-26757

In this biography the author "examines Ho's life primarily in the context of his political activity in Paris, Moscow, southern China, and Vietnam, occasionally spiced with anecdotes of Ho's highly secretive personal life. . . . Duiker handles the complicated political and diplomatic issues with ease, and his narrative, though it sometimes strays from Ho's life to fill in the bigger picture, never bogs down." Booklist

Includes bibliographical references

Hoffa, Jimmy, b. 1913

Russell, Thaddeus. Out of the jungle; Jimmy Hoffa and the remaking of the American working class. Temple University Press 2003 272p il (Labor in crisis) pa $21.95 **92**

1. International Brotherhood of Teamsters, Chauffeurs, Warehousemen and Helpers of America

ISBN 1-592-13027-5; 978-1-592-13027-6

LC 2002-43556

First published 2001 by Knopf

In this chronicle of the life and career of Hoffa, "the author presents new interpretations of how the Depression, the New Deal, World War II, and Robert F. Kennedy's crusade against organized crime affected not only Hoffa and the Teamsters but also the American labor movement as a whole." Publisher's note

"Russell makes good use of a range of primary-source materials plus period newspaper accounts and other materials to highlight this story." Libr J

Includes bibliographical references

Hogan, Linda

Hogan, Linda. The woman who watches over the world; a native memoir. Norton 2001 224p $24.95; pa $13.95 **92**

1. Native Americans

ISBN 0-393-05018-1; 0-393-32305-6 (pa)

LC 00-49005

In this memoir the author chronicles "her difficult childhood, alcoholism, the anguish of her two psychologically damaged adopted children, and struggles with a neuromuscular disease. She also expresses a lacerating yet crucial vision of the tragic legacies of the U.S. government's brutal war on Native Americans." Booklist

Holiday, Billie, 1915-1959

Blackburn, Julia. With Billie. Pantheon Books 2005 354p $25 * **92**

1. African American singers

ISBN 0-375-40610-7

LC 2004-58661

This "oral biography of Billie Holiday is based on interviews that researcher Linda Kuehl did in the late 1970s with more than 150 people who knew and worked with the singer. . . . Rather than her recordings, the emphasis is on the events and issues surrounding the music. . . . This is in many ways a joyful portrait of a woman

determined to go her own way but, in the end, unable to fulfill her own dreams." Libr J

Includes bibliographical references

Clarke, Donald. Billie Holiday; wishing on the moon. Da Capo 2002 468p il pa $21 **92**

1. African American singers

ISBN 0-306-81136-7; 978-0-306-81136-4

First published 1994 by Viking with title: Wishing on the moon: the life and times of Billie Holiday

This biography "not only chronicles every phase of Holiday's ascent from the streets of Baltimore to the stages of New York's hottest nightclubs and most prestigious concert halls, but also documents every significant recording session, performance, and tour. . . . Clarke's portrait embraces every facet of Holiday's paradoxical nature, from her fierceness to her vulnerability, her childlikeness to her innate elegance and amazing strength." Booklist

Griffin, Farah Jasmine. If you can't be free, be a mystery; in search of Billie Holiday. Ballantine Books 2002 240p il pa $14.95 **92**

1. African American singers

ISBN 978-0-345-44973-3; 0-345-44973-8

First published 2001 by Free Press

In this biography Griffin places Billie Holiday "in the musical and political context of her time and explores the myths she and others manufactured about her life." Booklist

"While Griffin's book isn't the last word on Holiday, it does prove to be an excellent antidote to the often ridiculous material that has been written about Lady Day over the years." Libr J

Includes bibliographical references

Holiday, Billie. Lady sings the blues; [Billie Holiday with William Dufty] 50th anniversary ed., 1st Harlem Moon trade pbk. ed. Harlem Moon 2006 231p il pa $15.95 * **92**

1. African American singers

ISBN 978-0-7679-2386-6; 0-7679-2386-3

LC 2007-271682

First published 1956 by Doubleday

Includes audio CD

"A hard, bitter and unsentimental book, written with brutal honesty and having much to say not only about Billie Holiday, the person, but about what it means to be poor and black in America." N Y Her Trib Books

Includes discography

Nicholson, Stuart. Billie Holiday. Northeastern Univ. Press 1995 311p il $42.50; pa $18.95 **92**

1. African American singers

ISBN 1-55553-248-9; 1-55553-303-5 (pa)

LC 95-16155

"Nicholson's fact-filled biography conveys not only the details of African American jazz singer Holiday's stormy life, but also a sense of the musical and social environments that produced her." Booklist

Includes discography and bibliographical references

Holiday, Billie, 1915-1959—*Continued*

O'Meally, Robert G. Lady Day; the many faces of Billie Holiday; [by] Robert O'Meally; produced by Toby Byron/Multiprises. Da Capo Press 1991 207p il pa $20   **92**

1. African American singers

ISBN 978-0-306-80959-0; 0-306-80959-1

First published 1991 by Arcade

"Narcotics, jail, sexual abuse, and prejudice are often our first associations concerning the life of the great jazz singer, but this biography recalls only Holiday as artist. O'Meally . . . puts her tragedy and talent into perspective, and what emerges is a critique of a singer. The book's first section is outstanding in this regard, employing stories, quotes, and interviews in describing Holiday's technique." Libr J

Includes discography and bibliographical references

Holman, James, 1786-1857

Roberts, Jason. A sense of the world; how a blind man became history's greatest traveler. HarperCollins Publishers 2006 382p il $26.95; pa $14.95   **92**

1. Blind

ISBN 0-00-716106-9; 978-0-00-716106-5; 0-00-716126-3 (pa); 978-0-00-716126-3 (pa)

LC 2005-58166

The author "narrates the life of a 19th-century British naval officer who was mysteriously blinded at 25, but nevertheless became the greatest traveler of his time. . . . Roberts does Holman justice, evoking with grace and wit the tale of this man once lionized as 'The Blind Traveler.'" Publ Wkly

Includes bibliographical references

Homes, A. M.

Homes, A. M. The mistress's daughter. Viking 2007 238p il $24.95   **92**

ISBN 978-0-670-03838-1; 0-670-03838-5

LC 2006-41354

"Before A. M. Homes was born, she was put up for adoption. Her birth mother was a twenty-two-year-old single woman who was having an affair with a much older married man with children of his own. The Mistress's Daughter is the story of what happened when, thirty years later, her birth parents came looking for her." Publisher's note

"Though the quest seems, at times, overwrought as Homes searches for meaning and connection where there may not be any, the writing is consistently controlled and knowing. . . . Though Homes gives away some of her mystery with this book, she will gain further respect as a writer." Seattle Times

Hood, Ann, 1956-

Hood, Ann. Comfort; a journey through grief. W. W. Norton & Co. 2008 188p $19.95   **92**

1. Loss (Psychology)

ISBN 978-0-393-06456-8   LC 2008-1310

"Ann Hood has written about her little girl's death. Grace died on April 18, 2002, from a virulent form of

strep. She was 5 years old. One morning she was there and the next she was gone, leaving her tights on the floor and her leopard-print rain boots in the hall and her hat with the pompom on a hook by the door. . . . What makes this book so different from other such memoirs is that it seems to be taking place in real time. Hood doesn't cut us any slack. Even Joan Didion, grieving the loss of her husband and her daughter's illness in 'The Year of Magical Thinking,' held back from the brink, retreated into her vast intellect. Hood will not retreat." Los Angeles Times Book Rev

Hooks, Bell

Hooks, Bell. Wounds of passion; a writing life. Holt & Co. 1997 xxiii, 260p pa $13 hardcover o.p.   **92**

ISBN 0-8050-5722-6 (pa)   LC 97-23506

In this continuation of the author's autobiography, Hooks chronicles "her rigorous education, both in a long, complicated relationship with a fellow writer and as a college and graduate student, experiences that led her away from poetry (her first literary love) to groundbreaking prose that expressed her feminist convictions and views on the status of black women in America." Booklist

Hoover, J. Edgar (John Edgar), 1895-1972

Gentry, Curt. J. Edgar Hoover; the man and the secrets. Norton 1991 846p il pa $17.95 hardcover o.p.   **92**

1. United States. Federal Bureau of Investigation

ISBN 0-393-32128-2 (pa)   LC 90-30576

The author "has based his account of Hoover on more than 300 interviews and on access to previously classified FBI documents. . . . Gentry paints a portrait of Hoover as the 'indispensable man,' with many provocative revelations about his political dealings." Libr J

Includes bibliographical references

Hope, Bob, 1903-2003

Quirk, Lawrence J. Bob Hope: the road well-traveled. Applause Theatre Bk. Pubs. 1998 327p il hardcover o.p. pa $14.95   **92**

1. Actors 2. Comedians

ISBN 1-55783-353-2; 1-55783-450-4 (pa)

LC 98-87957

"Quirk recaps Hope's life and surveys his relationships with myriad entertainment personalities. . . . This is a good, solid Hollywood bio by a veteran Tinseltown observer." Booklist

Includes filmography and bibliographical references

Houdini, Harry, 1874-1926

Brandon, Ruth. The life and many deaths of Harry Houdini. Random House 1994 355p il pa $14.95 hardcover o.p.   **92**

1. Magicians

ISBN 0-8129-7042-X (pa)   LC 94-4080

The author provides a psychological "portrait of the great and enigmatic escape artist Harry Houdini. She not only reveals Houdini's impressive technical secrets but

Houdini, Harry, 1874-1926—*Continued*
also identifies the sources of his unabashed melodramatics and puzzling innocence. . . . Houdini was one of the most compelling 'idols of popular culture' in the early years of this mass-appeal century, and he still works his magic through the medium of Brandon's bold and magnetic interpretation." Booklist
Includes bibliographical references

House, Callie, 1861-1928
Berry, Mary Frances. My face is black is true; Callie House and the struggle for ex-slave reparations. Knopf 2006 314p il $26.95; pa $14.95
92
1. African American women 2. African Americans—Reparations
ISBN 1-4000-4003-5 (Knopf); 0-307-27705-4 (pa, Vintage); 978-0-307-27705-3 (pa, Vintage)
LC 2004-51330
The author "unearths the intriguing story of Callie House (1861–1928), a Tennessee washerwoman and seamstress become activist, and the organization she led, the National Ex-Slave Mutual Relief, Bounty and Pension Association. . . . Students and scholars of African-American history, as well as those engaged in the current reparations debates, will be deeply informed by the rise and fall of the Ex-Slave Association." Publ Wkly
Includes bibliographical references

Houze, David, 1965-
Houze, David. Twilight people; one man's journey to find his roots. University of California Press 2006 329p il $24.95 *
92
1. African Americans—Civil rights 2. Apartheid
ISBN 0-520-24398-6; 978-0-520-24398-9
LC 2005-35322
"The George Gund Foundation imprint in African American studies"
"The 1960s U.S. civil rights movement, South Africa's antiapartheid struggle, and the ramifications of mixed-race identity resonate personally with South African-born, Mississippi-raised Houze." Booklist
This "graceful memoir is a sensitive look into racial history in Africa and America, as well as a riveting personal narrative." Publ Wkly
Includes bibliographical references

Hoyle, Fred
Mitton, Simon. Conflict in the cosmos; Fred Hoyle's life in science. Joseph Henry Press 2005 401p il $27.95
92
ISBN 0-309-09313-9
LC 2004-30638
The author "sheds light on both the scientist and the science through research and his own experiences with Hoyle's colleagues, students, and the man himself. . . . This excellent biography brings Hoyle to life while explaining, in language clear enough for the amateur enthusiast, the work that made him great." Libr J
Includes bibliographical references

Hughes, Langston, 1902-1967
Hughes, Langston. I wonder as I wander; an autobiographical journey; introd. by Arnold Rampersad. 2nd Hill and Wang ed. Hill & Wang 1993 xxii, 405p (American century series) pa $16
*
92
1. African American authors 2. Poets, American
ISBN 0-8090-1550-1
LC 92-39307
First published 1956 by Rinehart
Continuing the autobiography begun in The big sea (1940), this volume contains an account of Hughes' journeys through Russia, Spain, China, and Japan, as well as some incidents of his poetry readings in this country

Rampersad, Arnold. The life of Langston Hughes Volume I: 1902-1941; I, too, sing America. 2nd ed. Oxford University Press 2002 478p il hardcover o.p. pa $33
92
1. African American authors 2. Poets, American
ISBN 0-19-515160-7; 0-19-514642-5 (pa)
First published 1986
This is the first volume of a two-volume set chronicling the life of the Harlem Renaissance poet and author.
Includes bibliographical references

Rampersad, Arnold. The life of Langston Hughes Volume II: 1941-1967; I dream a world. 2nd ed. Oxford Univ. Press 2002 576p il hardcover o.p. pa $33 *
92
1. African American authors 2. Poets, American
ISBN 0-19-515161-5; 0-19-514643-3 (pa)
LC 2001-58766
First published 1988
This second volume of a two-volume biography of the Harlem Renaissance poet and author "finds Hughes rooting himself in Harlem, receiving stimulation from his rich cultural surroundings. Here he rethought his view of art and radicalism, and cultivated relationships with younger, more militant writers such as Richard Wright, Ralph Ellison, James Baldwin, and Amiri Bakara." Publisher's note
Includes bibliographical references

Hughes, Robert
Hughes, Robert. Things I didn't know; a memoir. Knopf 2006 395p $27.95 *
92
ISBN 1-4000-4444-8; 978-1-4000-4444-3
LC 2006-40968
This is a memoir by the author of *Heaven and Hell in Western Art* (1968), *The Shock of the New*, and *The Culture of Complaint* (1993).
"Hughes's vivid ruminations and sharp-eyed insights combine in bold, definitive strokes to yield a rich portrait of the art expert." Publ Wkly

Hughes, Ted, 1930-1998
Feinstein, Elaine. Ted Hughes; the life of a poet. Norton 2001 273p il $29.95; pa $15.95
92
ISBN 0-393-04967-1; 0-393-32362-5 (pa)
LC 2001-44925

Hughes, Ted, 1930-1998—*Continued*
This biography of the English poet examines Hughes's relationship with "his first wife, Sylvia Plath, who committed suicide in 1963 during the acrimonious breakup of their marriage, . . . [and with] Assia Wevill, the woman for whom Hughes left Plath, and who later killed herself and their child." Economist
Includes bibliographical references

Hurston, Zora Neale, 1891-1960
Boyd, Valerie. Wrapped in rainbows; the life of Zora Neale Hurston. Scribner 2003 527p il $30
                                         92
1. African American authors 2. African American women
ISBN 0-684-84230-0   LC 2002-17011
"A Lisa Drew book"
This is a biography of the folklorist and author of Their Eyes Were Watching God (1937), Tell My Horse (1938), Dust Tracks on a Road (1942) and Seraph on the Suwanee (1948)
"As the author adeptly and passionately analyzes Hurston's revolutionary books, intense spirituality, and myriad adventures, Hurston emerges in all her splendor—not only smarter, tougher, and more dazzlingly alive than most people but also freer." Booklist
Includes bibliographical references

Hurston, Zora Neale. Dust tracks on a road; an autobiography; with a foreword by Maya Angelou. 1st Harper Perennial Modern Classic ed. Harper Perennial Modern Classics 2006 308p il pa $13.95
*   **92**
1. African American authors 2. African American women
ISBN 0-06-085408-1; 978-0-06-085408-9
                                LC 2005-52616
"The restored text established by The Library of America"
First published 1942 by Lippincott
On cover: P.S. insights, interviews & more
The author describes her wanderings in and out of schools and jobs as a young girl, finishing her course work at Barnard, and beginning her life's work.
Includes bibliographical references

Hurston, Zora Neale. Zora Neale Hurston: a life in letters; collected and edited by Carla Kaplan. Doubleday 2002 880p il $40; pa $19.95
                                        92
1. African American authors 2. African American women
ISBN 0-385-49035-6; 0-385-49036-4 (pa)
                                LC 00-65671
A collection of over 500 letters by the Harlem Renaissance author
These letters reveal "a gifted yet complex personality at once humorous, cynical, and analytical." Libr J
Includes bibliographical references

Huxley, Elspeth, 1907-1997
Huxley, Elspeth. The flame trees of Thika; memories of an African childhood. Penguin Bks. 2000 280p pa $15
                                        92
1. Kenya
ISBN 0-14-118378-0; 978-0-14-118378-7
                                LC 99-47965
First published 1959 by Morrow
This is an account of the author's childhood on a coffee plantation in Kenya. She describes the landscape, the Kikuya peoples, the European settlers and the difficulties her parents faced adjusting to life in' the bush.

Hyde, James Hazen, 1876-1959
Beard, Patricia. After the ball; Gilded Age secrets, boardroom betrayals, and the party that ignited the great Wall Street scandal of 1905. HarperCollins 2003 402p il $25.95; pa $14.95
                                        92
1. Equitable Life Insurance Co. 2. Wall Street (New York, N.Y.)
ISBN 0-06-019939-3; 0-06-095892-8 (pa)
                                LC 2003-44987
The author "details the great Equitable Life Assurance scandal of 1905 that captured the national spotlight and shook Wall Street. The death in 1899 of Equitable's president and founder, Henry Hyde, created a power vacuum in one of the era's richest and most powerful companies. Hyde's chosen successor, his son James Hazen Hyde, quickly became embroiled in a struggle for control of the company with the 'old guard.' James's extravagant lifestyle and expensive tastes came to be used against him. . . . The saga is complete with betrayal, romance, accounting fraud, sneaky backroom deals, and connections to some of the most powerful men of the era, including President Theodore Roosevelt. Well written and documented, this fast-paced book reads like a novel." Libr J
Includes bibliographical references

Ishi
Kroeber, Theodora. Ishi in two worlds; a biography of the last wild Indian in North America. University of Calif. Press 1976 262p il $50; pa $16.95 *   **92**
1. Yana Indians
ISBN 0-520-00674-7; 0-520-22940-1 (pa)
First published 1961
An account "of the life of the sole survivor of a California Indian tribe. The author, wife of the famed anthropologist, reconstructs the decimation of Ishi's {Yana} people and his reluctant entry in 1911 into the world of his conquerors." Booklist

Ivan IV, the Terrible, Czar of Russia, 1530-1584
De Madariaga, Isabel. Ivan the Terrible; first tsar of Russia. Yale University Press 2005 xxi, 484p il map $35   **92**
ISBN 0-300-09757-3   LC 2004-29807
This is a biography of the Russian tsar.
This "is a persuasively argued, widely researched and

Ivan IV, the Terrible, Czar of Russia, 1530-1584—*Continued*
impressively authoritative work that casts new light on the Tsar, his reign, and Russia in the sixteenth century." Times Lit Suppl
Includes bibliographical references

Ives, Charles Edward, 1874-1954
Swafford, Jan. Charles Ives; a life with music. Norton 1996 525p il hardcover o.p. $18.95
92

ISBN 978-0-393-31719-0; 0-393-31719-6
LC 95-22549
"Ives was a professional organist, a successful insurance executive, a political idealist, and an immensely prolific composer. The author believes that Ives's transcendentalism was central to his identity, ceaselessly inspiring him while also spurring him on to an inevitable physical collapse. Swafford—a composer himself—intersperses his biography with valuable 'entr'actes' of approachable musical analysis, and ends with a ringing endorsement of Ives as an ideal composer for a democratic society." New Yorker
Includes bibliographical references

Jackson, Andrew, 1767-1845
Brands, H. W. Andrew Jackson; his life and times. Doubleday 2005 620p il map $35 *
92

ISBN 0-385-50738-0; 978-0-385-50738-7
LC 2005-42178
This is a biography of the seventh president of the United States.
This book "is a bracing, human portrait of both a remarkable man and of American democracy as it was transformed from a 'government of the people' into a 'government by the people.'" Publ Wkly
Includes bibliographical references

Burstein, Andrew. The passions of Andrew Jackson. Knopf 2003 xxi, 292p il map $25; pa $15
92

1. Presidents—United States
ISBN 0-375-41428-2; 0-375-71404-9 (pa)
LC 2002-16258
Burstein "explains his subject's imperious personality in relation to the uncertainties of frontier life in the Old Southwest and guides the reader through the 'politics of memory,' or what people have chosen to remember. The author succeeds in illuminating the strengths and weakness of his subject, whose forceful, at times bullying personality represented the temperament of many early 19th-century Americans. This captivating, richly documented work fills a niche even within the crowded field of Jackson studies. A worthwhile purchase for academic and large public libraries." Libr J
Includes bibliographical references

Wilentz, Sean. Andrew Jackson. Times Books 2005 195p (American presidents series) $20
92

1. Presidents—United States
ISBN 0-8050-6925-9
LC 2005-52857

The author "shows that our complicated seventh president was a central figure in the development of American democracy. . . . It is rare that historians manage both Wilentz's deep interpretation and lively narrative." Publ Wkly
Includes bibliographical references

Jackson, Joe, 1888-1951
Fleitz, David L. Shoeless; the life and times of Joe Jackson. McFarland & Co. 2001 314p il pa $29.95
92

1. Chicago White Sox (Baseball team)
ISBN 0-7864-0978-9
LC 2001-18318
"Shoeless Joe Jackson, banned from baseball for his alleged involvement in the 1919 World Series gambling scandal, is viewed by many as an illiterate phenom hustled by city slickers. Fleitz shows it ain't so, Joe, in this provocative biography." Booklist
Includes bibliographical references

Jacobs, Harriet A., 1813-1897
Yellin, Jean Fagan. Harriet Jacobs: a life. Basic Civitas Books 2004 394p il map $27.50; pa $16.95
92

ISBN 0-465-09288-8; 0-465-09289-6 (pa)
LC 2003-17256
Yellin "presents the first full biography of a woman who began life in slavery and survived the Civil War to become a politically and socially active citizen." Booklist
"This scholarly account, woven in a reader friendly fashion, restores 'an heroic woman who lived in an heroic time' to history and to us." Publ Wkly
Includes bibliographical references

Jaffrey, Madhur
Jaffrey, Madhur. Climbing the mango trees; a memoir of a childhood in India. Knopf 2006 297p il $25
92

ISBN 1-4000-4295-X; 978-1-4000-4295-1
LC 2006-45255
First published 2005 in the United Kingdom
This is the memoir by the Indian actress and cookbook author.
The author's "taste memories sparkle with enthusiasm, and her talent for conveying them makes the book relentlessly appetizing." N Y Times Book Rev

James, Etta, 1938-
James, Etta. Rage to survive; the Etta James story; [by] Etta James with David Ritz. Da Capo Press 2003 288p il pa $18
92

ISBN 0-306-81262-2; 978-0-306-81262-0
First published 1995 by Villard Books
"Born to a 14-year-old mother and raised by surrogate parents, blues and R&B star James started singing gospel in church at five, was discovered at 14 and had a rapid rise to fame. Nevertheless, her story is a disturbing saga of drug addiction, jail sentences for writing bad checks and stealing prescription drugs, involvements with the wrong men and anger at a disruptive and unstable mother who has refused to reveal who her daughter's father is."

James, Etta, 1938-—*Continued*
Publ Wkly
"With a supporting cast resembling the roster of the Rock Hall of Fame, this autobiography reads as its author sings-rough, gritty, and brutally honest." Libr J
Discography

James, Jesse, 1847-1882
Stiles, T. J. Jesse James; last rebel of the Civil War. Knopf 2002 510p il maps $27.50; pa $16 *
92
ISBN 0-375-40583-6; 0-375-70558-9 (pa)
LC 2002-25493
This is a "revisionist biography of Jesse James, one that takes issue with the traditional image of the Wild West outlaw . . . and with the folk-hero notion of James as a prairie Robin Hood. . . . Mr. Stiles presents James as a Confederate terrorist caught up in the wild political turbulence of his times." N Y Times Book Rev
"This is a well-written and often surprising reinterpretation of the life of a legendary and enigmatic figure." Booklist
Includes bibliographical references

James, P. D.
James, P. D. Time to be in earnest; a fragment of autobiography. Knopf 2000 269p pa $12.95 hardcover o.p.
92
ISBN 0-345-44212-1 (pa)
LC 99-57603
"In 1997, on the eve of her 77th birthday noted mystery novelist James . . . decided to keep a diary for the first time ever, recording one year in her life. The result is this 'fragment of autobiography,' a mix of memoir, ruminations on everything from her writing career to Princess Diana's death, and literary criticism." Libr J

James, William, 1842-1910
Richardson, Robert D. William James; in the maelstrom of American modernism: a biography. Houghton Mifflin 2006 622p il $30
92
ISBN 978-0-618-43325-4; 0-618-43325-2
LC 2005-37776
This is a biography of the psychologist and philosopher.
The author's "enthusiasm for what he calls 'the matchless incandescent spirit' of William James is contagious." Publ Wkly
Includes bibliographical references

Jefferson, Thomas, 1743-1826
Bernstein, Richard B. Thomas Jefferson; [by] R.B. Bernstein. Oxford University Press 2003 253p il hardcover o.p. pa $15.95
92
1. Presidents—United States
ISBN 0-19-516911-5; 978-0-19-518130-2 (pa); 0-19-518130-1 (pa)
LC 2003-5556
The author "provides a . . . view not of Jefferson the politician, but of the man whose ideas changed the world and provided the US with a sense of purpose. This short biography provides a judicious synthesis of the prevailing scholarship on the third president and explores more

deeply his views on government and union, slavery (revealing what is known about the Sally Hemings affair and what cannot yet be determined), and debt. . . . Its concise form, limited notes, and evenhanded style will appeal to general readers seeking insight into an incredibly complex historical figure." Choice
Includes bibliographical references

Hitchens, Christopher. Thomas Jefferson: author of America. HarperCollins Publishers 2005 188p (Eminent lives) $19.95
92
ISBN 0-06-059896-4
LC 2005-296593
"Beginning with his aristocratic upbringing, . . . this biography explores both the public and private aspects of Jefferson's life, from his political philosophies to his affair with his slave Sally Hemings. . . . This opinionated, lively narrative sheds light not only on Jefferson's complex personality but on the politics of his time, making it both a fascinating character study and an excellent review of early American history." Publ Wkly

Randall, Willard Sterne. Thomas Jefferson; a life. HarperPerennial 1994 708p pa $20
92
1. Presidents—United States
ISBN 0-06-097617-9
LC 94-14363
First published 1993 by Holt & Co.
This biography focuses on Jefferson's "youthful lawyering on the frontier, his political eclipse as Virginia's ineffectual war governor, and his ambassadorship to France." Booklist
"Randall's substantial, balanced biography will be valuable for general readers who seek a one-volume work on one of the leading Founding Fathers." Libr J
Includes bibliographical references

Joan, of Arc, Saint, 1412-1431
Gordon, Mary. Joan of Arc. Viking 2000 xxv, 180p (Penguin lives series) $19.95 *
92
1. Christian saints 2. France—History—1328-1589, House of Valois
ISBN 0-670-88537-1
LC 99-55678
"A Lipper/Viking book"
"A Penguin life."
"This biography rehearses the well-known highlights in Joan's short life: the voices she heard who charged her with the mission to save France, her participation in the Battle of Orléans and the coronation of King Charles VII; her trial by an ecclesiastical court, where she was charged with witchcraft, heresy and idolatry. . . . The strength of this 'biographical meditation' lies in the penultimate chapter, in which Gordon investigates the numerous re-creations of Joan on stage and screen." Publ Wkly
Includes bibliographical references

Pernoud, Régine. Joan of Arc: her story; Régine Pernoud, Marie-Véronique Clin; translated and revised by Jeremy duQuesnay Adams; edited by Bonnie Wheeler. St. Martin's Griffin 1999 xxii, 304p il map hardcover o.p. pa $16.95
92
1. Christian saints 2. France—History—1328-1589, House of Valois
ISBN 0-312-21442-1; 0-312-22730-2 (pa)
LC 98-45059

Joan, of Arc, Saint, 1412-1431—*Continued*

Original French edition, 1986

This work "traces the appearance of Joan as a documented historical character rather than adhering to a standard chronological sequence. Informing the narrative is a novel interpretation of Joan as a political prisoner. Moving beyond the narrative, the American translator . . . has added a series of appendixes containing valuable contextual material. . . . These materials discuss key historical events, provide biographical information on Joan's contemporaries, and discuss Joan's afterlife in history, literature, folklore, art, and iconography." Libr J

Includes bibliographical references

John Paul II, Pope, 1920-2005

Buttiglione, Rocco. Karol Wojtyła; the thought of the man who became Pope John Paul II; translated by Paolo Guietti and Francesca Murphy. Eerdmans 1997 384p $35   **92**

ISBN 0-8028-3848-0   LC 97-23188

Original Italian edition, 1982

The author traces the Pope's "intellectual development, offering a critique of his literary works and a detailed analysis of how he was influenced by Thomism and phenomenology, which he sought to reconcile while emphasizing individual freedom of conscience. . . . Recommended for general collections for its broad sweep complementary to other biographies on the pope." Libr J

Cornwell, John. The pontiff in winter; triumph and conflict in the reign of John Paul II. Doubleday 2004 336p il $24.95; pa $14.95

92

ISBN 0-385-51484-0; 0-385-51485-9 (pa)

LC 2004-58306

Published in the United Kingdom with title: The Pope in winter: the dark face of John Paul's papacy

The author "argues that John Paul's mystical view of history and conviction that his mission has been divinely established are central to understanding his pontificate." Publisher's note

Includes bibliographical references

Flynn, Raymond. John Paul II; a personal portrait of the pope and the man. St. Martin's Press 2001 204p il pa $14.95 hardcover o.p.

92

ISBN 0-312-28328-8 (pa)   LC 00-45965

Flynn, the "former mayor of Boston and ex-ambassador to the Vatican, tells us . . . what his book is not: It is not a biography, or an analysis. . . . Flynn views it, rather, as a profile based on his own experiences with Pope John Paul II, dating back to a 1969 visit to Boston of then-Cardinal Karol Wojtyla." Natl Rev

O'Connor, Garry. Universal Father: a life of John Paul II. Bloomsbury 2005 436p il map $24.95   **92**

ISBN 1-59691-096-8

"The text is divided into four distinct phases of Pope John Paul II's life: '1920-1946,' '1946-1978,' '1978-1990,' and '1990-2005.' Each phase balances fact with

anecdotal evidence, which lends the biography both credibility and charm. . . . This timely and remarkable biography will be sought after by serious readers." Libr J

Weigel, George. Witness to hope: the biography of Pope John Paul II. Cliff St. Bks. 1999 992p il $35; pa $20   **92**

ISBN 0-06-018793-X; 0-06-093286-4 (pa)

LC 99-26340

Weigel "focuses on John Paul's trademark ideas: Christian humanism, the inner connection between freedom and truth, and culture as the driving force of history. As a guide to the pope's thought, *Witness to Hope* is invaluable." Publ Wkly

Includes bibliographical references

Johnson, Harriet McBryde

Johnson, Harriet McBryde. Too late to die young; nearly true tales from a life. Henry Holt and Co. 2005 261p $23; pa $14   **92**

ISBN 0-8050-7594-1; 0-312-42571-6 (pa)

LC 2004-54007

In this memoir, the wheelchair-bound lawyer and activist describes her battles for disability rights.

"From her first demonstration against the MDA telethon to her celebrated debate with Peter Singer of Harvard, who has stated that killing a disabled infant is not morally equivalent to killing a person, this lady pulls no punches. An entertaining look at an activist who insists on living life her way, disability or no." Libr J

Johnson, Jack, 1878-1946

Ward, Geoffrey C. Unforgivable blackness; the rise and fall of Jack Johnson. Knopf 2004 492p il $26.95 *   **92**

ISBN 0-375-41532-7   LC 2004-48524

This is "a life of the first black heavyweight champ, who drove white America nuts." N Y Times Book Rev

The author "brings us back into Johnson's life and times with exquisitely rendered details, and the fight scenes themselves are gripping: fights so bloody that referees have to change shirts midbout, for instance, and a manager who pulls a gun on his fighter to keep him from quitting. The authoritative biography of Johnson for sure, but also one of the best boxing books in recent memory." Booklist

Includes bibliographical references

Johnson, Joyce, 1935-

Kerouac, Jack. Door wide open. See entry under Kerouac, Jack, 1922-1969

Johnson, Lyndon B. (Lyndon Baines), 1908-1973

Caro, Robert A. Master of the senate. Knopf 2002 xxiv, 1167p il (The years of Lyndon Johnson) $35; pa $19.95   **92**

1. Presidents—United States 2. United States—Politics and government—20th century

ISBN 0-394-52836-0; 0-394-72095-4 (pa)

LC 2002-282796

Johnson, Lyndon B. (Lyndon Baines), 1908-1973—*Continued*

The third entry in Mr. Caro's multi-volume biography of the thirty-sixth president of the United States, this installment covers Johnson's Senate career.

"Mr. Caro has written a panoramic study of how power plays out in the legislative arena. Combining the best techniques of investigative reporting with majestic storytelling ability, he has created a vivid, revelatory institutional history as well as a rich hologram of Johnson's character." N Y Times (Late N Y Ed)

Includes bibliographical references

Caro, Robert A. Means of ascent. Knopf 1990 xxxiv, 506p il (The years of Lyndon Johnson) $45; pa $20   **92**
1. Presidents—United States 2. United States—Politics and government—20th century
ISBN 0-394-52835-2; 0-679-73371-X (pa)
LC 90-201544

This second volume of Caro's multi-volume biography covers the life of the future president "from 1941 until the 1948 Texas Democratic senatorial primary that Johnson won by 87 votes." N Y Times Book Rev

"Caro has written a brilliant but disturbing book that Johnson admirers will intensely dislike. It throws a merciless spotlight on its subject. Readers are asked to reexamine the distinction between political means and ends. Caro examines what he perceives to be Johnson's deepest weaknesses: his lust for power and wealth; his mean spiritedness; his perversity to exploit the difficulties of others and then revel in his own brazen dishonesty. One looks in vain for a redeeming sign of decency in the LBJ of this volume." Christ Sci Monit

Includes bibliographical references

Caro, Robert A. The path to power. Knopf 1982 xxiii, 882p il (The years of Lyndon Johnson) $49.95; pa $19.95   **92**
1. Presidents—United States 2. United States—Politics and government—20th century
ISBN 0-394-49973-5; 0-679-72945-3 (pa)
LC 90-201781

This volume, the first volume of a projected four-volume biography of Lyndon B. Johnson, "follows him from the Hill Country to New Deal Washington, from his boyhood through the years of the Depression to his debut as Congressman, his . . . defeat in his first race for the Senate, and his attainment, nonetheless, at age 31, of the national power for which he hungered." Publisher's note

Includes bibliographical references

Woods, Randall Bennett. LBJ; architect of American ambition; [by] Randall B. Woods. Free Press 2006 1007p il $35   **92**
1. Presidents—United States 2. United States—Politics and government—20th century
ISBN 978-0-684-83458-0; 0-684-83458-8
LC 2006-41259

This is a biography of the 36th president of the United States.

The author "has produced an excellent biography that fully deserves a place alongside the best of the Johnson studies yet to appear." N Y Times Book Rev

Includes bibliographical references

Johnson, Robert, 1911-1938

Wald, Elijah. Escaping the delta; Robert Johnson and the invention of the blues. Amistad 2004 342p $24.95; pa $14.95 *   **92**
1. Blues music 2. African American musicians
ISBN 0-06-052423-5; 0-06-052427-8 (pa)
LC 2003-52287

"In this combination history of blues music and biography of Robert Johnson, Wald . . . explores Johnson's rise from a little known guitarist who died in 1938 to one of the most influential artists in rock and roll. From the blues' meager beginning in the early 1900s to its '30s heyday and its 1960s revival, Wald gives a revisionist history of the music, which he feels, in many instances, has been mislabeled and misjudged." Publ Wkly

The author "writes better than anyone else ever has about the blues. If you read only one book about blues—maybe ever—read this one." Booklist

Includes bibliographical references

Johnson, Samuel, 1709-1784

Boswell, James. The life of Samuel Johnson; with an introduction by Claude Rawson. Random House 1992 liii, 127p il (Everyman's library) $30   **92**
ISBN 0-679-41717-6   LC 92-52915
Also available in paperback from Penguin Books
First published 1791
Variant title: The life of Johnson

"The most famous biography in the English language. It is an intimate and minute delineation of the great lexicographer's life, character and person, enlivened with small-talk, gossip and bits of familiar correspondence. It is also an admirable portrayal of the society of which Johnson was the outstanding figure." Pratt Alcove

Includes bibliographical references

Jones, Mother, 1830-1930

Gorn, Elliott J. Mother Jones; the most dangerous woman in America. Hill & Wang 2001 408p il pa $14 hardcover o.p.   **92**
ISBN 0-8090-7094-4 (pa)   LC 00-44997

This is a biography of union organizer and labor leader Mary Harris Jones, known more popularly as Mother Jones

Gorn "has successfully separated fact from myth . . . situating Jones's story within a wider cultural frame." Publ Wkly

Includes bibliographical references

Jones, John Paul, 1747-1792

Morison, Samuel Eliot. John Paul Jones; a sailor's biography; with an introduction by James C. Bradford; charts and diagrams by Erwin Raisz. Naval Inst. Press 1989 xxvi, 537p il (Classics of naval literature) pa $24.95 hardcover o.p.   **92**
1. United States—Naval history
ISBN 1-55750-410-5 (pa)   LC 89-13423

A reissue with a new introduction of the title first published 1959 by Little, Brown

Jones, John Paul, 1747-1792—*Continued*
This "documented chronicle of the American sea captain's life . . . is particularly concerned with his ability as a seaman and with the naval engagements in which he took part." Booklist
"Morison has destroyed the myth of John Paul Jones but has left us a more human, more understandable character." Best Sellers
Includes bibliographical references

Thomas, Evan. John Paul Jones; sailor, hero, father of the American Navy. Simon & Schuster 2003 383p il hardcover o.p. pa $16 *
92
1. United States—Naval history
ISBN 0-7432-0583-9; 978-0-7432-5804-3;
0-7432-5804-5 (pa) LC 2003-42411
This is a biography of the Revolutionary War admiral known for his victory at sea in the "battle between Jones's frigate, the Bonhomme Richard, and a British man-of-war, the Serapis." N Y Times (Late NY Ed)
"The complex portrait is rendered with nautical precision—the author knows his topsail from his topgallant—and a lively eye for such details as the Enlightenment virtues espoused by Freemasonry or the proper way to kiss a French lady in the eighteenth century." Publ Wkly
Includes bibliographical references

Jones, Judith
Jones, Judith. The tenth muse; my life in food. Alfred A. Knopf 2007 290p il $24.95 **92**
1. Cooks
ISBN 0-307-26495-5; 978-0-307-26495-4
LC 2007-6789
This is a memoir of the author's career in publishing. "Judith Jones is senior editor and vice president at Alfred A. Knopf, where she has worked since 1957." Publisher's note
The author "recounts experiences that food and book lovers will admire and envy." Booklist
Includes bibliographical references

Jones, Quincy, 1933-
Jones, Quincy. Q: the autobiography of Quincy Jones. Doubleday 2001 412p il $26; pa $15.95
92
ISBN 0-385-48896-3; 0-7679-0510-5 (pa)
LC 2001-28151
"With some chapters written by Jones, and others by his family and friends . . . this (auto)biography full of behind-the-scenes anecdotes has an improvisational feel that suits its subject: a jazz musician and superstar composer. . . . Jones has composed a life story that gives much more than the typical celebrity memoir." Publ Wkly
Includes discography and filmography

Joplin, Scott, 1868-1917
Berlin, Edward A. King of ragtime: Scott Joplin and his era. Oxford Univ. Press 1994 334p il pa $21.50 hardcover o.p. **92**
ISBN 0-19-510108-1 (pa) LC 93-28318

The author "shows how Joplin launched his career in the black social clubs of Sedalia, Mo.; achieved success with the *Maple Leaf Rag*; and went on to win the respect of whites as well as his fellow African Americans, composing numerous rags and two operas." Publ Wkly
"Essential in any library concerned with American music." Booklist
Includes bibliographical references

Curtis, Susan. Dancing to a black man's tune: a life of Scott Joplin. University of Mo. Press 1994 xx, 265p il (Missouri biography series) $29.95
92
ISBN 0-8262-0949-1 LC 93-46116
A "study of the life and world of ragtime creator Scott Joplin (1868-1917). Lapsing only occasionally into academic jargon, the author ably places Joplin in the context of an emerging biracial society and culture as a man who was denied rights because of his color yet applauded as a musician." Publ Wkly
Includes bibliographical references

Jordan, Michael, 1963-
Halberstam, David. Playing for keeps: Michael Jordan and the world he made. Random House 1999 426p pa $16.95 hardcover o.p. **92**
1. Chicago Bulls (Basketball team) 2. African American athletes 3. Basketball—Biography
ISBN 0-7679-0444-3 (pa) LC 98-49964
Halberstam presents a biography of basketball player Michael Jordan.
"What's particularly effective about Halberstam's storytelling is that he follows Jordan's athletic trajectory, not in chronological order but through juxtaposed images of a hot-blooded college player with an as-yet unpolished game and an even-tempered 30-year-old at the height of his career. Jordan was not born a flawless pro, but developed his gifts by working tirelessly and intensely." Natl Rev

Joyce, James, 1882-1941
Ellmann, Richard. James Joyce. new and rev ed. Oxford Univ. Press 1982 887p il pa $27.50 hardcover o.p. **92**
ISBN 0-19-503381-7 (pa) LC 81-22455
First published 1959
This biography describes "Joyce's working methods, views on life and literature, political opinions, familial relationships and problems, and incessant struggle against poverty and threatening blindness." Publ Wkly
This "is a vast undertaking and continuing achievement—massive, masterly, and definitive, rich in anecdote and detail. It is also extremely readable; the easy, often sympathetic style communicates gracefully not only facts but analysis." Choice
Includes bibliographical references

O'Brien, Edna. James Joyce. Viking 1999 179p (Penguin lives series) $19.95 * **92**
ISBN 0-670-88230-5 LC 99-23214
"A Lipper/Viking book"
O'Brien "tells the story of the aspiring young writer and his downwardly mobile family, his escape to Europe,

Joyce, James, 1882-1941—*Continued*
the constant struggle to scrape together enough money to
live on, and finally his relative comfort, thanks to patrons, once *Ulysses* was published. She also provides
thoughtful appreciations of Joyce's major works."
Booklist
Includes bibliographical references

Joyner-Kersee, Jackie, 1962-
Joyner-Kersee, Jackie. A kind of grace; the
autobiography of the world's greatest female
athlete; [by] Jackie Joyner-Kersee with Sonja
Steptoe. Warner Bks. 1997 310p il $28
92
1. African American athletes
ISBN 0-446-52248-1   LC 97-14966
This memoir recounts the Olympic gold medalist's
"triumphs over poverty, family tragedy, and near-fatal
asthma attacks." Libr J
"A competent account of an admirable life." Booklist

Juan Carlos I, King of Spain, 1938-
Preston, Paul. Juan Carlos; steering Spain from
dictatorship to democracy. W. W. Norton 2004
608p $35   **92**
1. Spain—History—1975-
ISBN 0-393-05804-2   LC 2004-47435
This biography explores the life of the Spanish monarch
Preston "supplies a much-needed, serious, comprehensive, and absolutely dynamic biography of *el rey*, impressively researched and deeply probing." Booklist
Includes bibliographical references

Jung, C. G. (Carl Gustav), 1875-1961
Hayman, Ronald. A life of Jung. Norton 2001
xxi, 522p il pa $18.95 hardcover o.p.   **92**
ISBN 0-393-32322-6 (pa)   LC 00-54802
First published 1999 in the United Kingdom
In this exploration of the life and career of the Swiss
psychologist, "Hayman ferrets out the childhood beginnings of schizophrenic tendencies, chronicles his descent
into near insanity, documents his flirtation with fascism,
and details his abusive treatment of women." Booklist
"One of the many strengths of this candid and discerning biography is that Hayman enlists . . . provocative, alarming material to build a careful, nuanced portrait of his subject that neither excuses nor excoriates his
actions and words." Publ Wkly
Includes bibliographical references

Jung, C. G. (Carl Gustav). Memories, dreams,
reflections; recorded and edited by Aniela Jaffé;
translated from the German by Richard and Clara
Winston. rev ed. Vintage Bks. 1989 c1963 430p
pa $14   **92**
ISBN 0-679-72395-1   LC 88-37040
First published 1963 by Pantheon Bks.
"This volume of recollections reveals the intellectual
and spiritual development of an eminent Swiss psychologist and psychiatrist while only touching upon the outward events of his long and productive life. . . . An im-

portant, firsthand document for readers who wish to understand this seminal writer and thinker." Booklist
Includes bibliographical references

Kafka, Franz, 1883-1924
Murray, Nicholas. Kafka. Yale University Press
2004 440p il $30   **92**
ISBN 0-300-10631-9   LC 2004-107048
This biography "relates Kafka's brief life, trying val-
iantly to depict a more normal Kafka, a man who lived
in society with good friends, enjoyed sex, had wide-
ranging intellectual interests and became enamored of Judaism. In Murray's account, Kafka's employer valued
him highly, and under the imprint of no less a figure
than Kurt Wolff, he experienced some literary success.
Despite Murray's best efforts to contain Kafka's idiosyncrasies, though, the writer remains the tormented soul
who created out of his personal anxieties and agonies
some of the most acclaimed works of the 20th century."
Publ Wkly
Includes bibliographical references

Stach, Reiner. Kafka, the decisive years; the
decisive years; translated from the German by
Shelley Frisch. 1st U.S. ed. Harcourt 2005 581p il
$35 *   **92**
ISBN 0-15-100752-7   LC 2005-14554
Original German edition, 2002
This first of a projected three-volume biography focus-
es on Kafka's life from 1910 to 1915, during which he
wrote "The Metamorphosis" and The Trial.
"Essential reading for all Kafka devotees." Booklist
Includes bibliographical references

Kahlo, Frida, 1907-1954
Herrera, Hayden. Frida: a biography of Frida
Kahlo. Harper & Row 1983 507p il pa $24.95
hardcover o.p.   **92**
1. Artists, Mexican
ISBN 0-06-008589-4 (pa)   LC 80-8688
This biography of the Mexican painter and wife of Diego Rivera "is a mesmerizing story of radical art, romantic politics, bizarre loves and physical suffering. . . .
Herrera resolves Kahlo the public figure and Kahlo the
artist in a perceptive portrait of a woman who rose above
a circumscribed content with a grand style." Time
Includes bibliographical references

Kahlo, Frida. The diary of Frida Kahlo; an
intimate self-portrait; introduction by Carlos
Fuentes; essay and commentaries by Sarah M.
Lowe; [project director, Claudia Madrazo; editor,
Phyllis Freeman; translators, Barbara Crow de
Toledo and Ricardo Pohlenz] 2005 ed. Harry N.
Abrams 2005 295p il $24.95   **92**
1. Artists, Mexican
ISBN 0-8109-5954-2   LC 2006-284768
First published 1995
This is "a facsimile of a journal [the artist Frida
Kahlo] wrote in longhand in the last decade of her life.
The diary [is] supplemented by a translation of her Span-
ish entries. . . . [It includes] drawings and watercolors."

Kahlo, Frida, 1907-1954—*Continued*
N Y Times Book Rev
"Sprinkled with irony, black humor, even gaiety . . . this volume is a testament to Kahlo's resilience and courage." Publ Wkly
Includes bibliographical references

Zamora, Martha. Frida Kahlo; the brush of anguish; abridged and translated by Marilyn Sode Smith. Chronicle Bks. 1990 143p il pa $24.95 hardcover o.p.   **92**
1. Artists, Mexican
ISBN 0-8118-0485-2 (pa)   LC 90-33874
This biography of the Mexican painter is an abridgment and translation of a title originally published in Mexico in 1987
Most "important here is the collection of 75 color plates of the artist's original works. Of interest to the initiated because they comprise largely seldom-seen works in various Mexican collections, these plates represent the best collection now available of Kahlo's work." Libr J
Includes bibliographical references

Kandel, Eric R.
Kandel, Eric R. In search of memory; the emergence of a new science of mind. W. W. Norton & Company 2006 510p il $29.95 *
                                                          92
1. Memory 2. Nervous system
ISBN 0-393-05863-8; 978-0-393-05863-5
                                    LC 2005-28565
The author "recounts his own revolutionary research in establishing the molecular chemistry of short-term memory and the cellular dynamics of long-term memory, highlighting particularly the potential of his findings for the treatment of Alzheimer's and other mental disorders. But even as he outlines the biomechanics of memory, Kandel shares his personal reminiscences of the years during which he unraveled those mysteries. . . . An autobiography of exceptional substance." Booklist
Includes bibliographical references

Karajan, Herbert von
Osborne, Richard. Herbert von Karajan; a life in music. Northeastern Univ. Press 2000 851p il $37.50   **92**
ISBN 1-55553-425-2   LC 99-59108
First published 1998 in the United Kingdom
"Because Karajan's career developed in Nazi Germany, Osborne dwells at length . . . on Karajan's involvement with the regime and his postwar exoneration. Drawing on a vast variety of source materials and quoting some in full, Osborne takes us on the enthralling musical journey that was the life of one of the greatest of conductors." Booklist
Includes bibliographical references

Kazan, Elia
Schickel, Richard. Elia Kazan; a biography. HarperCollins 2005 xxxi, 510p il $29.95
                                                          92
ISBN 0-06-019579-7   LC 2005-43344

This is "the life story of the distinguished stage and screen director. No mere page turner, this is a page devourer, generating the kind of suspense that is usually the province of the playwright or novelist." N Y Times Book Rev
Includes bibliographical references

Keaton, Buster, 1895-1966
Meade, Marion. Buster Keaton; cut to the chase. 1st Da Capo Press ed. Da Capo Press 1997 440p il pa $18   **92**
1. Actors
ISBN 0-306-80802-1   LC 97-17745
First published 1995 by HarperCollins
The author "paints a moving and loving portrait of a comic genius, mechanical thinker, and superb athlete. The book provides the context of family and friends, (including Charlie Chaplin and Fatty Arbuckle) behind Keaton's career, and in doing so adds flesh and humanity to the funny bones and gags that have entertained and marveled audiences for decades. A remarkably gentle and insightful story of a silent comic riddle." Choice
Includes filmography and bibliographical references

Keats, John, 1795-1821
Motion, Andrew. Keats. University of Chicago Press 1999 636p il pa $18   **92**
1. Poets, English
ISBN 0-226-54240-8; 978-0-226-54240-9
                                    LC 98-41014
First published 1997 in the United Kingdom
"Motion emphasizes that Keats was no otherworldly creature of exquisite sensibilities but a man whose liberal politics and commitment to medicine animated his aesthetics and enlightened his poetry." Booklist
Includes bibliographical references

Keller, Helen, 1880-1968
Herrmann, Dorothy. Helen Keller; a life. University of Chicago Press 1999 394p il pa $22
                                                          92
1. Blind 2. Deaf
ISBN 0-226-32763-9; 978-0-226-32763-1
                                    LC 99-23242
First published 1998 by Knopf
The author "takes us beyond the image of Helen Keller portrayed in The Miracle Worker to unearth a passionate, politically radical woman whose inspiration and teacher, Annie Sullivan, is equally fiery and brilliant. Herrmann brings us into the every day lives of the famous pair, but the story is hardly mundane. . . . Herrmann gives us fascinating details via archives and unpublished memoirs to show how society's view of disabled people was greatly shaped by Keller and Sullivan." Libr J
Includes bibliographical references

Keller, Helen. Helen Keller: selected writings; edited by Kim E. Nielsen; consulting editor, Harvey J. Kaye. New York University Press 2005 317p il (History of disability series) $35
                                                          92
1. Blind 2. Deaf
ISBN 0-8147-5829-0   LC 2004-28974

Keller, Helen, 1880-1968—*Continued*
"Published in conjunction with the American Foundation for the Blind"
This is a collection "of Keller's personal letters, political writings, speeches, and excerpts of her published materials from 1887 to 1968." Univ Press Books for Public and Second Sch Libr, 2006
Includes bibliographical references

Keller, Helen. The story of my life; edited and with a preface by James Berger. The restored ed. Modern Library 2003 xlvi, 343p il hardcover o.p. pa $9.95 *   **92**
1. Blind 2. Deaf
ISBN 0-679-64287-0; 0-8129-6886-7 (pa)
LC 2002-40971
First published 1903
This biography of the inspirational Keller contains accounts of her home life and her relationship with her devoted teacher Anne Sullivan.
Includes bibliographical references

Kemble, Fanny, 1809-1893
Clinton, Catherine. Fanny Kemble's civil wars. Oxford Univ. Press 2001 302p il pa $24
92
1. Actors 2. Abolitionists
ISBN 0-19-514815-0   LC 2001-21405
First published 2000 by Simon & Schuster
This is the biography of the English actress, author, and abolitionist who "commanded center stage in the American drama over slavery and in her much-publicized personal civil wars of marriage to one of America's wealthiest slaveholders, bitter divorce, and publication of her private letters and her antislavery journal describing life on a Georgia plantation." Libr J
"This biography is every bit as sharp, evocative and eloquent as Kemble's Journal." Publ Wkly
Includes bibliographical references

Kennan, George Frost, 1904-2005
Kennan, George Frost. Sketches from a life. W. W. Norton 2000 365p pa $14.95   **92**
1. United States—Foreign relations
ISBN 978-0-393-32139-5; 0-393-32139-8
First published 1989 by Pantheon
"This is a collection of very private reflections spanning some 60 years of foreign service in Nazi Germany, the Baltic states, the Low Countries, the Soviet Union, as well as nonofficial travels covering the entire globe. Kennan has marvelous insight into his ever-changing surroundings—an insight that is always sharp, sometimes melancholy, and punctuated frequently by dry, Midwestern wit." Libr J
Includes bibliographical references

Kennedy, Dan, 1967-
Kennedy, Dan. Rock on. Algonquin Books 2008 224p pa $14.95   **92**
1. Music industry
ISBN 978-1-565-12509-4; 1-565-12509-6
LC 2007-17025
Subtitle on cover: An office power ballad

This is a memoir of the author's experiences in the music industry.
"Kennedy's style—hilarious, paranoid and vulnerable—captures wonderfully the absurdity of the corporate music industry." Publ Wkly

Kennedy, John F. (John Fitzgerald), 1917-1963
Dallek, Robert. Let every nation know; John F. Kennedy in his own words; [by] Robert Dallek and Terry Golway. Sourcebooks MediaFusion 2006 289p il $29.95; pa $19.95   **92**
1. Presidents—United States 2. United States—Politics and government—1961-1974
ISBN   1-4022-0647-X;   978-1-4022-0647-4; 1-4022-0922-3 (pa); 978-1-4022-0922-2 (pa)
LC 2005-37973
This book gives "brief analyses of 31 of JFK's speeches and debates, presented in audio selections on the accompanying CD-ROM. The results reveal Kennedy's eloquence, humor, and grace under pressure. . . . This work illuminates the importance of public address to the success and reputation of presidents and shows that Kennedy mastered this art." Libr J
Includes bibliographical references

Dallek, Robert. An unfinished life: John F. Kennedy, 1917-1963. Little, Brown 2003 838p il $30; pa $17.95   **92**
1. Presidents—United States 2. United States—Politics and government—1961-1974
ISBN 0-316-17238-3; 0-316-90792-8 (pa)
LC 2002-116388
Published in the UK with the title: John F. Kennedy
This is a biography of the thirty-fifth president of the United States
The author "has written the most accessible, balanced, and scholarly biography yet of JFK. . . . It is the Kennedy biography against which others will be measured." Libr J
Includes bibliographical references

Kenney, Charles. John F. Kennedy; the presidential portfolio: history as told through the collection of the John F. Kennedy Library and Museum; introduction by Michael Beschloss. PublicAffairs 2000 241p il $35   **92**
1. Presidents—United States 2. United States—Politics and government—1961-1974
ISBN 1-891620-36-3   LC 00-57581
Includes computer optical disc
This volume features approximately 250 photos and documents and highlights "the many remarkable events of Kennedy's life and his presidency." Publisher's note
"The text is less detailed (and less focused on controversy) than a full-scale biography, but it emphasizes what most would consider the key elements of JFK's presidency . . . while also devoting chapters to Jacqueline and Robert F. Kennedy. Likely to appeal to Kennedy fans and to others seeking a sense of the period." Booklist

Kennedy, John F. (John Fitzgerald), 1917-1963—*Continued*

Mahoney, Richard D. Sons and brothers: the days of Jack and Bobby Kennedy. Arcade Pub. 1999 441p il $27.95; pa $14.95   **92**

1. Kennedy, Robert F., 1925-1968 2. Kennedy, Joseph P., 1888-1969 3. United States—Politics and government—1961-1974

ISBN 1-55970-480-2; 1-55970-534-5 (pa)

LC 99-25681

This study "of the brothers' relationship chronicles its evolution, its mutual dependencies, and the wide-ranging effect that the actions of the brothers' father, Joe, had on Jack's and Bobby's political lives." Booklist

"Writing in a steady, almost relentlessly elegiac tone, Mahoney proves that the lives and deaths of John F. and Robert F. Kennedy remain as compelling now as they were throughout the turbulent 1960s." Publ Wkly

Includes bibliographical references

Reeves, Richard. President Kennedy; profile of power. Simon & Schuster 1993 798p il pa $22 hardcover o.p.   **92**

1. Presidents—United States 2. United States—Politics and government—1961-1974

ISBN 0-671-89289-4 (pa)   LC 93-24805

This is an account "of John F. Kennedy's three years as president, with an emphasis on leadership techniques." Choice

"Reeves doesn't try to soft-pedal the distasteful, but his account of the Kennedy presidency is resolutely matter of fact and not an indictment." Time

Includes bibliographical references

Kennedy, Robert F., 1925-1968

Mahoney, Richard D. Sons and brothers: the days of Jack and Bobby Kennedy. See entry under Kennedy, John F. (John Fitzgerald), 1917-1963

Schlesinger, Arthur M. Robert Kennedy and his times; {by} Arthur M. Schlesinger, Jr. Houghton Mifflin 1978 1066p il pa $17.95 hardcover o.p.   **92**

1. United States—Politics and government—20th century

ISBN 978-0-618-21928-5 (pa); 0-618-21928-5 (pa)

LC 78-8469

"A highly sympathetic and readable political biography covering in depth Robert Kennedy's tenure in public life. At times extremely partisan, at times dispassionate, Schlesinger's study effectively captures Kennedy's impact on national politics and the main currents of American politics during the 1950s and 1960s." Choice

Includes bibliographical references

Thomas, Evan. Robert Kennedy; his life. Simon & Schuster 2000 509p il pa $15 hardcover o.p. *

92

ISBN 0-7432-0329-1 (pa)   LC 00-41995

This biography "reveals a very human Kennedy struggling to come to terms with his brother's assassination, his role in wiretapping Martin Luther King Jr., and his fatal decision to take on Eugene McCarthy and Hubert Humphrey in the 1968 Democratic primary." Libr J

"A solid, judicious life of a politician whose tragic death inspired a generation of what-if history." Booklist

Includes bibliographical references

Kerouac, Jack, 1922-1969

Kerouac, Jack. Door wide open; a beat love affair in letters, 1957-1958; {by} Jack Kerouac and Joyce Johnson; with introduction and commentary by Joyce Johnson. Viking 2000 xxvi, 182p pa $13 hardcover o.p.   **92**

1. Johnson, Joyce, 1935-

ISBN 0-14-100187-9 (pa)   LC 99-53219

"In a hip, literate correspondence marked by high diction and '50s slang, 21-year-old Johnson (born Glassman) and 35-year-old Kerouac chart the flowering of the Beats and their complicated love affair." Publ Wkly

Includes bibliographical references and index

Kerouac, Jack. Selected letters, 1940-1956; edited with an introduction and commentary by Ann Charters. Viking 1995 xxvi, 629p pa $16.95 hardcover o.p.   **92**

ISBN 0-14-023444-6 (pa)   LC 94-12911

"These letters, addressed to the likes of William Burroughs, Allen Ginsberg, and publisher Robert Giroux, take Kerouac from his early years up to the publication of *On the Road*." Libr J

The editor "made two very wise decisions here: she supplied continuity and context for the letters, and she included significant letters from the correspondents. The frustration of the long-rejected writer is doubly felt by the reader, since this selection ends on the eve of the big Beat breakthrough." Choice

Includes bibliographical references

Kerouac, Jack. Selected letters, 1957-1969; edited with an introduction and commentary by Ann Charters. Viking 1999 xxvii, 514p pa $17 hardcover o.p.   **92**

ISBN 0-14-029615-8 (pa)   LC 99-17374

This volume "starts with the publication of *On the Road* and continues almost to the day Kerouac died. The years 1957-1960, the height of Kerouac's career, occupy more than half the volume. Later letters record his struggle to care for his ailing mother, his efforts to finish his later books and his troubles with money and health. . . . Frequent addressees and subjects include Gary Snyder, Philip Whalen, Lawrence Ferlinghetti, William Burroughs and Allen Ginsberg." Publ Wkly

Khrushchev, Nikita Sergeevich, 1894-1971

Nikita Khrushchev; edited by William Taubman, Sergei Khrushchev, and Abbott Gleason; translated by David Gehrenbeck, Eileen Kane, and Alla Bashenko. Yale Univ. Press 2000 391p $45

92

1. Soviet Union—Politics and government

ISBN 0-300-07635-6   LC 99-51323

A collection of essays re-evaluating aspects of Khrushchev's political career. Topics include his rise to power and his domestic, foreign, and military policy. Two essays compare Khrushchev and Gorbachev

Khrushchev, Nikita Sergeevich, 1894-1971—
Continued

Taubman, William. Khrushchev; the man and his era. Norton 2003 p. cmp   **92**
  ISBN 0-393-05144-7
                                                LC 2002-26404
Includes bibliographical references and index

King, B. B.
King, B. B. Blues all around me; the autobiography of B.B. King; [by] B.B. King with David Ritz. Avon Bks. 1996 336p il hardcover o.p. pa $14 *   **92**
  1. Blues music 2. African American musicians
  ISBN 0-380-97318-9; 0-380-80760-2 (pa)
                                                LC 96-27773
King recounts his humble beginnings and his career as a prominent blues guitarist.
  "This is one of the best recent pop-music bios. King speaks straight from the soul, it seems, just like he plays the guitar." Booklist

King, Martin Luther, Jr., 1929-1968
Dyson, Michael Eric. I may not get there with you: the true Martin Luther King, Jr. Free Press 2000 404p $25; pa $15   **92**
  1. African Americans—Biography 2. African Americans—Civil rights
  ISBN 0-684-86776-1; 0-684-83037-X (pa)
                                                LC 99-40478
In this work of biocriticism, the author "argues that we have tarnished King's true legacy by translating it into a cliché." N Y Times Book Rev
  Dyson "believes that the ministry fostered King's rhetorical gifts but also encouraged his authoritarian personality. We learn much about his flaws, and about conflict, dissent, and generational differences within the black community, as Dyson insists that King, properly understood, remains a controversial figure." New Yorker
  Includes bibliographical references

King, Martin Luther, Jr. The autobiography of Martin Luther King, Jr; edited by Clayborne Carson. Warner Bks. 1998 400p il $25; pa $15.95   **92**
  1. African Americans—Biography 2. African Americans—Civil rights
  ISBN 0-446-52412-3; 0-446-67650-0 (pa)
                                                LC 98-35704
"Carson, director of Martin Luther King Jr. Papers Project, brings together selections from King's writings, speeches, and recordings to create this fascinating 'autobiography' of the famed civil rights leader and Nobel Peace Prize winner. The writings trace King's struggles with religion, philosophy, and the racial politics of the U.S." Booklist
  Includes bibliographical references

King, Stephen, 1947-
King, Stephen. On writing; a memoir of the craft. Scribner 2000 288p $25; pa $14.95   **92**
  1. Authors, American 2. Authorship
  ISBN 0-684-85352-3; 0-671-02425-6 (pa)
                                                LC 00-30105
The author recounts "his life from early childhood through the aftermath of the 1999 accident that nearly killed him. Along the way, King touts the writing philosophies of William Strunk and Ernest Hemingway, advocates a healthy appetite for reading, expounds upon the subject of grammar, critiques a number of popular writers, and offers the reader a chance to try out his theories. . . . Recommended for anyone who wants to write and everyone who loves to read." Libr J

Kinkade, Thomas, 1958-
Kinkade, Thomas. The Thomas Kinkade story; a 20-year chronology of the artist; [by] Thomas Kinkade; text by Rick Barnett. Bulfinch Press 2003 224p il $24.95   **92**
  1. Artists—United States
  ISBN 978-0-8212-6179-8; 0-8212-6179-7
                                                LC 2003-052256
This book provides a "look at the artists life and work. Each period in Kinkade's career is examined." Publisher's note

Kipling, Rudyard, 1865-1936
Gilmour, David. The long recessional: the imperial life of Rudyard Kipling. Farrar, Straus & Giroux 2002 351p il maps $26; pa $15   **92**
  ISBN 0-374-18702-9; 0-374-52896-9 (pa)
                                                LC 2002-100585
This biography focuses on Kipling's social and political views in relation to the British Empire, especially as expressed in his fiction and poetry
  The author "offers a brief, sympathetic, well-informed, and highly readable account of Kipling." Libr J
  Includes bibliographical references

Ricketts, Harry. Rudyard Kipling; a life. Carroll & Graf Pubs. 2000 c1999 434p il pa $16 hardcover o.p.   **92**
  ISBN 0-7867-0830-1 (pa)
First published 1999 in the United Kingdom with title: The unforgiving minute: a life of Rudyard Kipling
  This work "succeeds in disentangling some of the political muddle of Kipling's life. Ricketts' literary analysis is competent, if unsophisticated. Most valuably, he traces the debt to Browning and the many other resonant literary allusions in Kipling's work, thus undermining the charges of philistinism . . . levelled against it." New Statesman (Engl)

Kissinger, Henry, 1923-
Dallek, Robert. Nixon and Kissinger. See entry under Nixon, Richard M. (Richard Milhous), 1913-1994

Kissinger, Henry, 1923-—*Continued*

Kissinger, Henry. Years of renewal. Simon & Schuster 1999 1151p il maps pa $24 hardcover o.p.   **92**
     1. United States—Foreign relations
     ISBN 0-684-85572-0 (pa)   LC 98-41038
This concluding volume of Kissinger's memoirs "starts with Nixon's resignation and continues through the two years of the Ford administration. . . . As Kissinger explains China policy, Soviet policy, Middle East diplomacy and various crises (in Cyprus, Angola and elsewhere), his insight extends not only to explanations of policy but also to accounts of bureaucratic infighting and turf battles—as well as to relations between the executive branch and Congress." Publ Wkly

"Statecraft defies simple solutions, and one of the merits of Kissinger's memoir—especially this somber and reflective third volume—is that he so rarely provides them." N Y Times Book Rev

Includes bibliographical references

Klemperer, Victor, 1881-1960

Klemperer, Victor. I will bear witness; a diary of the Nazi years, 1933-1941; translated by Martin Chalmers. Random House 1998 556p pa $15.95 hardcover o.p. *   **92**
     1. Germany—History—1933-1945
     ISBN 0-375-75378-8 (pa)   LC 98-15429
Also available volume covering years 1941-1945 pa $15.95 (ISBN 0-375-75697-3)
"Klemperer, a professor at the University of Dresden, was a Jew by birth. He managed to survive the war, living relatively unscathed with his Aryan wife in Dresden. After his death in 1960, a former student discovered his wartime diaries, and this is the first volume to be published in the U.S." Booklist

"Never has the isolation of living in a world that wishes one's people dead been rendered with greater pathos. Every act of cruelty as well as every gesture of kindness is scrupulously recorded." Nation

Knight, Bobby

Knight, Bobby. Knight: my story; [by] Bob Knight with Bob Hammel. Thomas Dunne Bks. 2002 387p il $25.95; pa $14.95   **92**
     1. Basketball—Biography
     ISBN 0-312-28257-5; 0-312-31117-6 (pa)
     LC 2001-48990
Knight, fired after 29 years as the basketball coach of Indiana University, "displays here his palpable affection for his players and his reverence for the game and the great coaches who preceded him—Joe Lapchick and Henry Iba, among others." Booklist

"College hoops fans can learn more about the game from this book than from most instructional guides." Publ Wkly

Koppel, Ted, 1940-

Koppel, Ted. Off camera; private thoughts made public. Knopf 2000 320p pa $14 hardcover o.p.   **92**
     ISBN 0-375-72708-6 (pa)   LC 00-34919

The television journalist of *Nightline* presents a daily diary for 1999 chronicling "the controversial events from the century's last year, such as the Clinton impeachment trial and the Columbine High School shootings. . . . The subtitle of the book may lead some readers to expect a bit of muckraking, but they will be disappointed. . . . Yet one does not get the sense that Koppel is restraining himself or hiding anything, merely that this is a person who lives his life with integrity so that his private thoughts are full of the same." Libr J

Koufax, Sandy, 1935-

Gruver, Ed. Koufax; by Edward Gruver. Taylor Pub. Co. 2000 264p il $24.95; pa $16.95   **92**
     ISBN 0-87833-157-3; 0-87833-294-4 (pa)
     LC 99-56763
"This is the biography of legendary L.A. Dodgers pitcher Sandy Koufax, who for half a decade mesmerized hitters as few have ever done. . . . Drawing on childhood friends, teammates, opponents, journalists, and Dodger management, Gruver has written a compelling story, complete with appendix of notable statistics." Libr J

Leavy, Jane. Sandy Koufax; a lefty's legacy. HarperCollins Pubs. 2002 xxii, 282p $23.95; pa $13.95   **92**
     ISBN 0-06-019533-9; 0-06-093329-1 (pa)
     LC 2002-68722
In this biography of the Dodgers pitcher "Levy also uses his career to examine the changes baseball has undergone in the last four decades." Booklist

The author "delivers an honest and exquisitely detailed examination of a complex man." Publ Wkly

Kübler-Ross, Elisabeth

Kübler-Ross, Elisabeth. The wheel of life; a memoir of living and dying. Scribner 1997 286p il pa $13 hardcover o.p.   **92**
     ISBN 0-684-84631-4 (pa)   LC 97-6435
In this autobiography "Kübler-Ross describes her growing-up years in Switzerland as one of a set of triplet sisters, her fight to become a doctor, and later, the even stronger opposition she met when she began her research on death and dying. Despite the weightiness inherent in working with and writing about mortality, the book has a light, almost airy feel to it, which goes along with the author's central theme that death is merely a transformation." Booklist

Kubrick, Stanley

LoBrutto, Vincent. Stanley Kubrick; a biography. Da Capo Press 1999 579p pa $20   **92**
     1. Motion picture producers and directors—Biography
     ISBN 0-306-80906-0   LC 98-47434
First published 1996 by Fine, D.I.
"LoBrutto traces Kubrick's career from his highschool days as a photographer for Look magazine to the decade of inactivity since Full Metal Jacket." Booklist

"For the true film buff, there's an astonishing amount

Kubrick, Stanley—*Continued*
of technical information, but there's also a good deal of illuminating backstage human interest." Publ Wkly
Includes filmography and bibliographical references

Walker, Alexander. Stanley Kubrick, director; a visual analysis by Sybil Taylor and Ulrich Ruchti. rev and expanded. Norton 1999 376p il $35; pa $25   **92**
ISBN 0-393-04601-X; 0-393-32119-3 (pa)
                                          LC 98-24086
First published 1998 in the United Kingdom
"Walker describes Kubrick as a guarded, suspicious, obsessive, controlling, paranoid workaholic, and makes us feel that he's bestowing a compliment. Each movie is given a thorough analysis, reinforced by the extensive use of stills in each case." Publ Wkly
Includes bibliographical references

Kurosawa, Akira, 1910-1998
Kurosawa, Akira. Something like an autobiography; translated by Audie E. Bock. Knopf 1982 205p il pa $15 hardcover o.p.
                                          92
1. Motion picture industry
ISBN 0-394-71439-3 (pa)   LC 81-48100
These are the memoirs of the Japanese filmmaker, covering his life up to 1951-52, when his film Rashōmon won international awards
This "is a fascinating, moving record of one man's pursuit of excellence in a single art." N Y Times Book Rev

Kurson, Robert, 1963-
Kurson, Robert. Crashing through; a story of risk, adventure, and the man who dared to see. Random House 2007 306p il $25.95   **92**
ISBN 978-1-4000-6335-2; 1-4000-6335-3
                                          LC 2007-3092
"Blinded at age three, Michael May became a champion skier, CIA analyst, entrepreneur, and more, but his biggest challenge was deciding whether to go through with an operation that could restore his sight." Libr J
The book "becomes most interesting when the flaws in Mr. May's new eyesight become apparent. He makes wondrous discoveries of things blind people never hear about—shadows, freckles, the movement and transparency of running water—but has more difficulty with the cognitive aspects of pattern recognition. He can see facial features but cannot decipher facial expressions. . . . Eventually the joy of sight fades for him and the investigatory challenges begin." N Y Times (Late N Y Ed)

Lafayette, Marie Joseph Paul Yves Roch Gilbert du Motier, marquis de, 1757-1834
Gaines, James R. For liberty and glory. See entry under Washington, George, 1732-1799

Laffite, Jean, 1780?-1825?
Davis, William C. The pirates Laffite; the treacherous world of the corsairs of the Gulf. Harcourt 2005 706p il map $28   **92**
1. Laffite, Pierre, d. 1826?
ISBN 0-15-100403-X   LC 2004-29150
This is a study of "Jean and Pierre Laffite, [brothers whose] lives were intertwined with . . . [a] colorful period in New Orleans' history, the era from just after the Louisiana Purchase through the War of 1812. Labeled as corsairs and buccaneers for methods that bordered on piracy, the brothers ran a privateering cooperative that provided contraband goods to a hungry market." Publisher's note
"This is an excellent examination of interesting, tough men who knew how to survive in an interesting, tough age." Booklist
Includes bibliographical references

Laffite, Pierre, d. 1826?
Davis, William C. The pirates Laffite. See entry under Laffite, Jean, 1780?-1825?

Lancaster, Burt, 1913-1994
Buford, Kate. Burt Lancaster; an American life. Da Capo Press 2001 447p il pa $20   **92**
1. Actors
ISBN 978-0-306-81019-0; 0-306-81019-0
First published 2000 by Knopf
"Lancaster's decades-long political involvement with liberal causes (and his constant run-ins with the House Un-American Activities Committee in the 1950s) are a central theme in this well-researched and engaging biography, which also details the artist's acting career, his turns as a producer and his personal life." Publ Wkly
Includes filmography and bibliographical references

Lardner, Ring, 1915-2000
Lardner, Ring. I'd hate myself in the morning; a memoir; {by} Ring Lardner, Jr. Thunder's Mouth Press 2000 198p il $22.95; pa $14.95
                                          92
ISBN 1-56025-296-0; 1-56025-338-X (pa)
                                          LC 00-44298
"Lardner was a two-time Academy Award winner . . . and a member of the 'Hollywood Ten,' the group of writers and directors who went to jail rather than name names to the House Un-American Activities Committee (HUAC). In this book, he easily blends sketches of his famous father . . . with those of his student days in Moscow and anecdotes of his Hollywood and blacklist years." Booklist
"Of interest to cultural historians as well as general readers, this book belongs in both academic and public libraries." Libr J

Larsen, Nella
Hutchinson, George. In search of Nella Larsen; a biography of the color line. Belknap Press of Harvard University Press 2006 611p il $39.95
                                          92
ISBN 0-674-02180-0; 978-0-674-02180-8
                                          LC 2005-58129

Larsen, Nella—*Continued*
This is a biography of the author of Quicksand (1928) and Passing (1929).

The author "has produced what must be the definitive biography of Larsen. It's hard to think of a stone he hasn't looked under in his quest to establish the facts, correct mistakes and trace her private life. But Hutchinson's biography also manages to be an insightful reconsideration of a much-studied period in American literature and black cultural history." Nation

Includes bibliographical references

Latus, Amy, 1965-2002
Latus, Janine. If I am missing or dead. See entry under Latus, Janine, 1959-

Latus, Janine, 1959-
Latus, Janine. If I am missing or dead. Simon & Schuster 2007 309p il $25 **92**
1. Latus, Amy, 1965-2002 2. Abused women
ISBN 978-0-7432-9653-3; 0-7432-9653-2
LC 2006-52313
"When journalist Latus's younger sister Amy vanishes at age 37 in 2002, authorities find a chiller of a note in Amy's desk: 'If I am missing or dead . . . question Ron.' Ron Ball is Amy's ex-con boyfriend, and when Amy's body is found, something shatters in Latus. A victim of abuse herself, Latus tunnels back to her difficult suburban childhood to decode why two smart, talented sisters might be so starving for love that they would risk their lives to get it. Latus's book unfolds like a gripping novel, getting at the brutal heart of darkness that underscores domestic violence." People

Laveau, Marie, 1794-1881
Ward, Martha Coonfield. Voodoo queen; the spirited lives of Marie Laveau; by Martha Ward. University Press of Mississippi 2004 246p il map $26 **92**
1. Voodooism
ISBN 1-578-06629-8
LC 2003-18292
"Spiritual leaders Marie Laveau, mother and daughter, reigned in New Orleans between the 1820s and 1880s. Through their story, Ward offers fresh perspective on Creole culture and voodoo." Booklist
Including bibliographical references

Lawrence, D. H. (David Herbert), 1885-1930
Worthen, John. D.H. Lawrence; the life of an outsider. Counterpoint 2005 xxvi, 518p il $29.95 **92**

ISBN 1-58243-341-0
"Using as a unifying theme Lawrence's perpetual status as an outsider, both in working-class Nottinghamshire and in the English literary world, Worthen gives us the full sweep of this groundbreaking writer's utterly unconventional, often torturous, and occasionally rhapsodic life." Booklist
Includes bibliographical references

Worthen, John. D.H. Lawrence, the early years, 1885-1912. Cambridge Univ. Press 1991 626p il (The Cambridge biography—D.H. Lawrence, 1885-1930) pa $30 hardcover o.p. **92**
ISBN 0-521-43772-5 (pa)
LC 90-23423
This "first volume of Cambridge's three-volume life of Lawrence, . . . takes the young writer through his elopement with Frieda. . . . This persuasive biography is compulsive good reading from cover to cover. A major event in modern literary studies." Libr J
Includes bibliographical references

Lawrence, T. E. (Thomas Edward), 1888-1935
Brown, Malcolm. T.E. Lawrence. New York University Press 2003 160p il map (Historic lives) $21.95 * **92**
ISBN 0-8147-9920-5
LC 2003-51387
This biography is part "adventure story, part modern morality tale, and places special emphasis on the years of the desert war the period that both made Lawrence and broke him. It also shows how the once haloed figure surrounded by hero-worship has increasingly come to be seen as a man of our time, to whom countless people can relate, not because he acquired what we now call celebrity status, but because he was prepared to relinquish it." Publisher's note
"The book is a major literary work." Publ Wkly
Includes bibliographical references

Leadbelly, 1885-1949
Wolfe, Charles K. The life and legend of Leadbelly; [by] Charles Wolfe and Kip Lornell. Da Capo Press 1999 333p il pa $16.95 **92**
1. Blues music 2. African American musicians
ISBN 978-0-306-80896-8; 0-306-80896-X
First published 1992 by HarperCollins
"Drawing on a variety of primary and secondary sources, including numerous interviews, Wolfe and Lornell attempt to separate fact from fiction. . . . Photographs, informative notes, and a full discography are valuable additions." Choice
Includes discography and bibliographical references

Leary, Timothy, 1920-1996
Greenfield, Robert. Timothy Leary; a biography. Harcourt, Inc. 2006 689p il $28 **92**
ISBN 0-15-100500-1; 978-0-15-100500-0
LC 2005-30154
"A James H. Silberman book"
This is a biography of LSD guru and counterculture icon Timothy Leary.
"A veritable who's who of the age of Aquarius and a real page-turner, Greenfield's cornerstone portrait of the acidhead who would be king brilliantly illuminates the paradoxes of the psychedelic age." Booklist

Leavitt, Henrietta Swan, 1868-1921
Johnson, George. Miss Leavitt's stars; the untold story of the woman who discovered how to measure the universe. W. W. Norton 2005 162p il (Great discoveries) $22.95 **92**
ISBN 0-393-05128-5
LC 2005-02823

Leavitt, Henrietta Swan, 1868-1921—*Continued*

This is a biography of the American astronomer whose research concerned the measuring of distance in space.

This book is "a fine tribute to a remarkable woman of science." Publ Wkly

Includes bibliographical references

Ledyard, John, 1751-1789

Gifford, Bill. Ledyard; in search of the first American explorer. Harcourt 2007 331p il map $25   **92**

ISBN 978-0-15-101218-3; 0-15-101218-0

LC 2006-17064

"Long before Lewis and Clark, American explorer John Ledyard planned an audacious cross-country journey to explore the uncharted interior of North America. Starting in 1786, he intended to travel on foot from west to east, first crossing Russia and then the Bering Strait to Alaska and continuing across the continent toward Virginia. Sadly, his plan failed after he was expelled from Russia, and his fame as an explorer dimmed over time. Journalist Gifford attempts to revive Ledyard's place in history with this . . . biography." Libr J

This book "makes an important contribution to the existing literature through its personal approach to Ledyard's life. Few of Ledyard's letters and journals remain . . . but, by using most of what's available and tracking down details through his own travels, the author paints a fascinating portrait of the man he calls the 'archetype of the restless American wanderer.'" N Y Times Book Rev

Lee, Robert E. (Robert Edward), 1807-1870

Blount, Roy. Robert E. Lee; a Penguin life; [by] Roy Blount, Jr. Lipper/Viking Bk. 2003 210p (Penguin lives series) $19.95; pa $13 *   **92**

1. Generals 2. United States—History—1861-1865, Civil War

ISBN 0-670-03220-4; 0-14-303866-4 (pa)

LC 2002-32423

This is a biography of "the famous Southern general admired for his military leadership but also scorned for defending the Confederacy. Blount's concise writing keeps his biography trim and succinct, and his admiration for the subject allows for enjoyable reading." Booklist

Includes bibliographical references

Fellman, Michael. The making of Robert E. Lee. Johns Hopkins Univ. Press 2003 360p il pa $19.95   **92**

1. Generals 2. United States—History—1861-1865, Civil War

ISBN 0-8018-7411-4   LC 2002-43290

First published 2000 by Random House

"Struggling to subdue his ambitions and passions in a peacetime military career whose monotony was only momentarily breached by the Mexican American War and at Harpers Ferry, Lee found in the Civil War a chance to express himself fully. In a study rich with discussions of Lee's religious beliefs and political opinions, the author skewers previous efforts to detach Lee from slavery, racism, and the mentality of the Lost Cause. Sure to arouse debate, this book challenges and delights." Libr J

Includes bibliographical references

Freeman, Douglas Southall. Lee; an abridgment in one volume, by Richard Harwell, of the four-volume R. E. Lee; with a new foreword by James M. McPherson. Scribner 1991 xxiii, 601p il maps pa $18 hardcover o.p.   **92**

1. United States—History—1861-1865, Civil War 2. Generals

ISBN 0-684-82953-3 (pa)   LC 91-20088

First published 1961

"Students of history will continue to want and to use the original four-volume work but most general readers will find this abridgment more convenient and adequate to their interest. All footnotes and all of the appendix have been omitted as well as details of Civil War action that are not necessary to show the main course of Lee's life and action." Booklist

Nolan, Alan T. Lee considered; General Robert E. Lee and Civil War history. University of N.C. Press 1991 231p il $29.95; pa $16.95   **92**

1. United States—History—1861-1865, Civil War 2. Generals

ISBN 0-8078-1956-5; 0-8078-4587-6 (pa)

LC 90-48296

In this biography of the Confederate Civil War general, the author contends "that Lee the slaveholder was not antislavery, that the reluctant secessionist endorsed Southern independence, that the general lost the war by his repeated offensive thrusts and provincial vision—and more." Libr J

"Nolan uses sources cleverly to build his case and adroitly pits this new 'truth' against the words of Lee's historically staunchest promoters." Booklist

Includes bibliographical references

Thomas, Emory M. Robert E. Lee; a biography. Norton 1995 472p il maps pa $17.95   **92**

1. Generals

ISBN 0-393-31631-9 (pa)   LC 95-10522

"Civil War historian Thomas presents Lee as neither an icon nor a flawed figure, but rather as a man who made the best of his lot, whose comic vision of life ultimately shaped him into an individual who was both more and less than his legend." Publ Wkly

Includes bibliographical references

Lelyveld, Joseph

Lelyveld, Joseph. Omaha blues; a memory loop. Farrar, Straus and Giroux 2005 226p il $22; pa $14   **92**

ISBN 0-374-22590-7; 0-312-42510-4 (pa)

LC 2004-12362

In this autobiographical narrative, the American newspaper editor reflects on his childhood.

This "is a worldly, graceful book; there is a great deal to admire in it and to be moved by." New Leader

Lenin, Vladimir Il´ich, 1870-1924

Service, Robert. Lenin—a biography. Harvard Univ. Press 2000 xxv, 561p il maps $38.95; pa $19.95 **92**

ISBN 0-674-00330-6; 0-674-00828-6 (pa)

LC 00-21394

This biography focuses "on Lenin the man. It draws on a wealth of new material to provide a subtle and complex portrait. . . . In particular, Service's account adds much to our knowledge of Lenin's early years and his final years as a man cut down by a series of strokes. . . . It is lucidly written, sharply observed, full of good sense, packed with vivid anecdote and, above all, succeeds—where so many have failed—in creating a Lenin who is believably human." Hist Today

Includes bibliographical references

Volkogonov, Dmitriĭ Antonovich. Lenin; a new biography; [by] Dmitri Volkogonov; translated and edited by Harold Shukman. Free Press 1994 xxxix, 529p il $30 **92**

ISBN 0-02-933435-7 LC 94-31752

A condensed English version of the two-volume Russian edition published in 1994

The author argues "that Lenin, far from having laid the foundations for a more liberal form of socialism, was the true progenitor of Stalinism; and . . . that in his personality and philosophy Lenin was hostile to the interests of Russia." Economist

"The author draws heavily on newly declassified KGB archives that he oversees as special assistant to President Boris Yeltsin. . . . Volkogonov's narrative is indispensable for understanding the Bolshevik coup, their crushing of the democratic opposition and the tragic aftermath." Publ Wkly

Includes bibliographical references

Leonardo, da Vinci, 1452-1519

Aquino, Lucia. Leonardo Da Vinci; preface by Mario Pomilio; [translation, Miriam Hurley] Rizzoli 2005 173p il (Art classics) pa $9.95 **92**

1. Artists, Italian

ISBN 978-0-8478-2677-3; 0-8478-2677-5

LC 2004-099908

"Originally published in Italian by Rizzoli Libri Illustrati" verso of title page

This book "features a literary introduction and . . . description of a selection of the artist's masterpieces. . . . [It also includes] a visual chart with captions as to the whereabouts of each painting and a . . . bibliography." Publisher's note

Includes bibliographical references

Bramly, Serge. Leonardo; the artist and the man; translated by Sian Reynolds. Penguin Bks. 1994 493p il pa $25 **92**

1. Artists, Italian

ISBN 0-14-023175-7; 978-0-14-023175-5

Original French edition, 1988

In this account Bramly "sheds light on the more personal aspects of Leonardo. . . . As he follows da Vinci's often frustrating career and ever-widening sphere of inquiries, inventions, and discoveries, he also patches to-

gether overlooked clues about his private life, causing us to marvel anew at Leonardo's fertile and versatile mind while acquiring a sharper image of Leonardo the man. A richly detailed, expansive, and thoroughly enjoyable portrait." Booklist

Includes bibliographical references

Nuland, Sherwin B. Leonardo da Vinci. Viking 2000 170p il (Penguin lives series) pa $13 **92**

1. Artists, Italian

ISBN 0-670-89391-9; 978-0-14-303510-7 (pa); 0-14-303510-X (pa) LC 00-32061

"A Lipper/Viking book"

"Nuland devotes the first 120 pages . . . to Leonardo's pursuit of life as what we would call a scientist. The remaining 50 pages are focused specifically on his works as an anatomist. Nuland chronicles Leonardo's insights and mistakes and discusses his place in the history of anatomical studies." Libr J

"Nuland . . . elegantly sketches Leonardo's life of constant employment by noblemen eager to enjoy the prestige he reflected on them and of even more constant curiosity, which drove him to become the greatest anatomist before Vasari. . . . A scintillating addition." Booklist

White, Michael. Leonardo; the first scientist. St. Martin's Press 2000 370p il $27.95; pa $16.95 **92**

1. Artists, Italian

ISBN 0-312-20333-0; 0-312-27026-7 (pa)

The author "focuses on the scientific creations of da Vinci, emphasizing his notebooks, which had been lost for 200 years and only portions of which have been recovered. White describes how da Vinci's personal life affected his scientific discoveries and predictions, and vice versa." Booklist

Leonowens, Anna Harriette, 1834-1914

Landon, Margaret. Anna and the King of Siam; illustrated by Margaret Ayer. Harper & Row 1944 391p il map pa $14.95 hardcover o.p. **92**

1. Mongkut, King of Siam, 1804-1868 2. Thailand—Social life and customs

ISBN 0-06-095488-4 (pa)

Also available in hardcover from Buccaneer Bks.

Anna Leonowens' experiences at the Siamese court in the 1860's. From her experiences she wrote two books, "The English governess at the Siamese court," and "The romance of the harem." The author has put these two books into one story with additions to make a complete tale.

Lessing, Doris May, 1919-

Lessing, Doris May. Under my skin; volume one of my autobiography, to 1949; {by} Doris Lessing. HarperCollins Pubs. 1994 419p il pa $15 hardcover o.p. * **92**

ISBN 0-06-092664-3 (pa) LC 94-20051

This autobiography "covers the first 30 years of Doris Lessing's life, from her birth to British expatriate parents then living in Persia, through her girlhood growing up on

Lessing, Doris May, 1919-—*Continued*
a farm in Southern Rhodesia, up until 1949, the year she
departed for England." Christ Sci Monit

"In this immediate, vivid, beautifully paced memoir,
Doris Lessing sets the individual against history, the personal against the general, and shows, by the example of
her own life set down honestly, how biography and fiction mesh, how fiction transmutes the personal to the
general, how the particular experience illuminates the
universe." London Rev Books

Levi, Primo, 1919-1987
Angier, Carole. The double bond: Primo Levi, a
biography. Farrar, Straus & Giroux 2002 xxvi,
898p il $40; pa $20   **92**
ISBN 0-374-11315-7; 0-374-52898-5 (pa)

This is a biography of the Italian Jewish chemist and
writer. Levi was the author of The Periodic Table, Survival in Auschwitz, The Drowned and the Saved and
Other People's Trades

"Angier's long, gripping narrative of Levi's time in
Auschwitz synthesizes the best of his memoirs, poetry,
fiction, essays, and scientific writing. . . . A compelling
biography and a must for all Holocaust collections."
Booklist

Includes bibliographical references

Anissimov, Myriam. Primo Levi; tragedy of an
optimist. Overlook Press 1998 452p il $37.95; pa
$18.95   **92**
1. Auschwitz (Poland: Concentration camp)
ISBN 0-87951-806-5; 1-58567-020-0 (pa)
     LC 97-9904

"A serious, lively, conscientiously researched biography of the distinguished Italian writer whose optimism
and rationalism were not totally suppressed by his experience as an inmate of Auschwitz." N Y Times Book
Rev

Includes bibliographical references

Levi, Primo. The periodic table; translated from
the Italian by Raymond Rosenthal. Schocken Bks.
1984 233p pa $12 hardcover o.p.   **92**
ISBN 0-8052-1041-5 (pa)   LC 84-5453
Available in hardcover from Random House
Original Italian edition, 1975

"This curious memoir, organized in 21 chapters from
Argon to Zinc, ransacks the periodic table of the elements for strained metaphors as it traces one adolescent's
search for identity. Levi ironically portrays himself as a
young aspiring chemist eager to fathom nature's secrets."
Publ Wkly

Lewis, C. S. (Clive Staples), 1898-1963
Wilson, A. N. (Andrew Norman). C.S. Lewis; a
biography. Norton 1990 334p il pa $15.95
hardcover o.p.   **92**
ISBN 0-393-32340-4 (pa)   LC 89-27361

This biography "brings to light the most important episodes and aspects of Lewis' life: for instance, his curious and longstanding relationship with Janie 'Minto'
Moore, his troubled friendship with J. R. R. Tolkien, his
secret marriage to Joy Gresham, his conversion to Chris-

tianity, and his unending and increasingly subtle scrutiny
of what it meant to be a Christian." Booklist

"The mixture presented in Wilson's biography of the
life of learning, the college life at Magdalen where he
taught, of domestic drama and bad temper, religion, and
sex, is irresistible." N Y Rev Books

Includes bibliographical references

Lewis, Jerry, 1926-
Lewis, Jerry. Dean & me; a love story.
Doubleday 2005 340p il $26.95   **92**
1. Martin, Dean
ISBN 0-7679-2086-4   LC 2005-49682

The author "recounts his professional and personal relationship with his former show business partner, the late
Dean Martin." Libr J

"This is a wild, joyous book, but also a heartbreaking
one." N Y Times Book Rev

Li, Charles N., 1940-
Li, Charles N. The bitter sea; coming of age in
a China before Mao. HarperCollins Publishers
2008 283p il $25.95   **92**
1. China—History—1949-
ISBN 978-0-06-134664-4; 0-06-134664-0
     LC 2007-25697

The author, "who had an extraordinary life growing
up in pre-Communist China, shares his story of betrayal,
loss, hope, and triumph in this lyrical account. . . . This
brilliant memoir is as much about modern Chinese history as it is about familial relationships." Libr J

Li, Leslie, 1945-
Li, Leslie. Daughter of heaven; a memoir with
earthly recipes. Arcade Pub. 2005 274p $25; pa
$13.95   **92**
1. Chinese cooking
ISBN 1-55970-768-2; 1-55970-800-X (pa)
     LC 2004-23452

The book centers on the author's "relationship with
both her father and Nai-nai, her grandmother, who lands
in New York City for an extended visit. In stories
and in the nearly 20 recipes (including Drunken Chicken
and Cantonese Fried Rice), Li reveals the tale of an
Asian woman caught between many different worlds and
times and places." Booklist

Lincoln, Abraham, 1809-1865
Carwardine, Richard. Lincoln: a life of purpose
and power. Knopf 2006 394p il map $27.50
     92
1. Presidents—United States 2. United States—History—1861-1865, Civil War
ISBN 1-4000-4456-1   LC 2005047230
First published 2003 in the United Kingdom

The author "traces Lincoln's political struggles and
machinations from his early days as an Illinois state leg-
islator through his final days in the presidency." Libr J

This book "is not only analytical and smart, it's also
delightfully readable—and it will surely emerge as one
of the most important Lincoln books to be published this
decade." Publ Wkly

Includes bibliographical references

Lincoln, Abraham, 1809-1865—*Continued*

Donald, David Herbert. Lincoln. Simon & Schuster 1995 714p il maps hardcover o.p. pa $20
92

1. Presidents—United States
ISBN 0-684-80846-3; 0-684-82535-X (pa)
LC 95-4782
This biography examines: "Lincoln's relationship with his father; his romance with Ann Rutledge; his bouts of 'hypo,' which amounted at times almost to clinical depression; his marriage; his political ambition; his attitudes toward slavery and black people; his relations with radical Republicans during the Civil War; the mistakes and successes of his wartime leadership." Atl Mon
Includes bibliographical references

Gienapp, William E. Abraham Lincoln and Civil War America; a biography. Oxford Univ. Press 2001 239p il maps hardcover o.p. pa $24.95
92

1. Presidents—United States 2. United States—History—1861-1865, Civil War
ISBN 0-19-515099-6; 0-19-515100-3 (pa)
LC 2001-50056
This biography focuses on the American president's leadership during the Civil War.
"In spite of the book's size, its discriminating history of Lincoln's life is surprisingly rich, and the narrative of his presidency and the unfolding of the war is crisp and coherent." Bookmarks
Includes bibliographical references

Goodwin, Doris Kearns. Team of rivals; the political genius of Abraham Lincoln. Simon & Schuster 2005 916p il map $35 *
92
1. United States—Politics and government—1861-1865 2. Presidents—United States
ISBN 0-684-82490-6
LC 2005-44615
In this biography of the sixteenth president of the United States, the author sets out "to look at Lincoln through his relationships with his former political rivals turned cabinet members: Sen. William H. Seward of New York (who became Lincoln's secretary of state), Gov. Salmon P. Chase of Ohio (who became secretary of the treasury), and Missouri's elder statesman, Edward Bates (who became attorney general)." N Y Times (Late NY Ed)
"The knowledge gained here about these three significant figures who well attended Lincoln gain for the reader an even keener appreciation of the rare individual that he was." Booklist
Includes bibliographical references

Keneally, Thomas. Abraham Lincoln. Viking 2003 183p (Penguin lives series) $19.95
92

1. Presidents—United States 2. United States—History—1861-1865, Civil War
ISBN 0-670-03175-5
LC 2003-268078
"Keneally's Lincoln is a self-actuated farm boy made good by self-discipline, savvy instincts, wit, the wisdom acquired from courtrooms, friendships, and political huckstering—and luck . . . [The author] recounts Lincoln's early missteps in romance, business, and politics

and his self-doubts and depression as his star dimmed several times, and he concedes Lincoln's erratic course toward emancipation and a successful strategy for Union victory during the Civil War . . . This is an epic compressed into a tightly written biography that all Americans might read with profit. Keneally's occasional tendency to let folklore stand as fact notwithstanding, there is no better brief introduction to Lincoln and his American dream." Libr J

Lind, Michael. What Lincoln believed; the values and convictions of America's greatest president. Doubleday 2005 358p $27.95
92

1. Presidents—United States
ISBN 0-385-50739-9
LC 2004-41333
This intellectual biography examines "Lincoln's public philosophy and [seeks to] place his ideals and presidential decisions within the context of his times." Publisher's note
"Some readers may not recognize their own cherished Lincoln in Lind's well-researched and reasoned book. Yet it adds a valuable perspective to the vast arena of Lincoln scholarship." Christ Sci Monit
Includes bibliographical references

McPherson, James M. Tried by war; Abraham Lincoln as commander in chief. Penguin Press 2008 329p il map $35
92
1. United States—History—1861-1865, Civil War 2. United States—Politics and government—1861-1865 3. Presidents—United States
ISBN 978-1-594-20191-2; 1-594-20191-9
LC 2008-25229
Evaluates Lincoln's talents as a commander in chief in spite of limited military experience, tracing the ways in which he worked with, or against, his senior commanders to defeat the Confederacy and reshape the presidential role.
This book "is a perfect primer, not just for Civil War buffs or fans of Abraham Lincoln, but for anyone who wishes to understand the evolution of the president's role as commander in chief." N Y Times Book Rev
Includes bibliographical references

Pinsker, Matthew. Lincoln's sanctuary; Abraham Lincoln and the Soldiers' Home. Oxford University Press 2003 256p il maps hardcover o.p. pa $17.95
92
1. United States Soldiers' and Airmen's Home (Washington, D.C.) 2. Presidents—United States
ISBN 0-19-516206-4; 978-0-19-517985-9 (pa); 0-19-517985-4 (pa)
LC 2003-1215
"National Trust for Historic Preservation"
The author "follows the War President to his 'retreat' at the Soldiers' Home away from the daily noise, posturing, and politicking of the capital and finds there a serenity that allowed Lincoln to relax with his family, think through issues, conduct secret meetings with allies and enemies, and reinvigorate his resolve. . . . Through Pinsker's probing inquiry into sources heretofore surprisingly underused, the ever elusive private Lincoln comes into new light. A book for our time and for all libraries." Libr J

Lincoln, Abraham, 1809-1865—*Continued*

Sandburg, Carl. Abraham Lincoln: The prairie years and The war years. illustrated ed. Harcourt Brace Jovanovich 1970 c1954 640p il maps pa $26 hardcover o.p.   **92**
1. Frontier and pioneer life 2. United States—History—1861-1865, Civil War 3. Presidents—United States
ISBN 0-15-602752-6 (pa)
First published 1954
A condensation of the two volumes of "The prairie years" (1926) and the four volumes of "The war years" (1939). The author has taken advantage of material made available since the original volumes were published to include in this edition of his lifetime study of Lincoln
"A biography that as a whole is superior to the longer life. This one volume has a form which the six lacked. It is a tighter and tidier book. It retains the superb qualities of the original work without the faults of the latter." Saturday Rev
Includes bibliographical references

Shenk, Joshua Wolf. Lincoln's melancholy; how depression challenged a president and fueled his greatness. Houghton Mifflin 2005 350p $25   **92**
1. Presidents—United States
ISBN 0-618-55116-6   LC 2005-9653
This book "argues that Abraham Lincoln's lifelong depression was responsible for his becoming one of America's greatest presidents." N Y Times Book Rev
"An estimable contribution to the Lincoln literature." Booklist
Includes bibliographical references

White, Ronald C. (Ronald Cedric). The eloquent president: a portrait of Lincoln through his words; [by] Ronald C. White, Jr. Random House 2005 xxiii, 448p il $26.95; pa $15.95   **92**
1. Presidents—United States
ISBN 1-400-06119-9; 0-8129-7046-2 (pa)
     LC 2004-50766
The author "traces Lincoln's evolving rhetoric over the course of his presidency in a series of highly detailed critical essays. He follows Lincoln from the cautious, lawyerly text of the First Inaugural to the soaring, triumphant poetics of the Gettysburg Address." Publ Wkly
Includes bibliographical references

Lincoln, Mary Todd, 1818-1882
Baker, Jean H. Mary Todd Lincoln; a biography. Norton 1987 429p il pa $17.95 hardcover o.p.   **92**
1. Spouses of the presidents
ISBN 0-393-30586-4 (pa)   LC 86-23757
The author "portrays Mrs. Lincoln as a woman tortured by a series of family bereavements and thwarted from developing her natural talents by a patriarchal society that branded as 'unwomanly' her involvement in her husband's political career. Ms. Baker establishes her first argument with a lengthy investigation of Mary Todd's early family history in Lexington, Ky., and sustains the second by enlarging upon such topics as 19th-century domesticity, childbirth, mourning customs, spiritualism and

America's deplorable insanity laws." NY Times Book Rev
Includes bibliographical references

Lindbergh, Anne Morrow, 1906-2001
Hertog, Susan. Anne Morrow Lindbergh; a biography. Talese 1999 561p il pa $17 hardcover o.p.   **92**
ISBN 0-385-72007-6 (pa)   LC 99-28759
After her marriage to Charles Lindbergh, Anne Morrow "soon recognized the difficulty of reconciling her literary ambitions with accompanying her husband as copilot, navigator and radio operator. After the tragic kidnapping and death of their first child, which they blamed in part on dogged press coverage of their personal life, the Lindberghs moved abroad. They became embroiled with the leaders of Nazi Germany, according to Hertog, because Charles believed that the democratic system was weak and ineffectual. . . . This sympathetic portrayal of Anne as a wife, mother, poet and feminist may well find a readership more interested in a talented woman's creative struggle than in the oft-told Lindbergh story." Publ Wkly
Includes bibliographical references

Winters, Kathleen C. Anne Morrow Lindbergh; first lady of the air. Palgrave Macmillan 2006 241p il map $24.95   **92**
ISBN 978-1-4039-6932-3; 1-4039-6932-9
     LC 2006-43290
This book focuses on Anne Morrow Lindbergh's career as an aviator. "She was one of the earliest female pilots, as well as the first American female glider pilot, and a radio operator. . . . Winters shows in great detail that Lindbergh accomplished this under the glare of an unremitting spotlight, and in the company of an often-demanding spouse. That the author is able to bring something new to the Lindbergh story is impressive, and she does it through both technical explanations of Lindbergh's accomplishments and Anne's own words about her flying exploits, marriage, and writing." Booklist
Includes bibliographical references

Lindbergh, Charles, 1902-1974
Berg, A. Scott (Andrew Scott). Lindbergh. Putnam 1998 628p il $30; pa $16 *   **92**
1. Air pilots
ISBN 0-399-14449-8; 0-425-17041-1 (pa)
     LC 98-18548
"The first biographer to be granted unfettered access to Lindbergh's private papers, Berg provides enough fresh detail to trace the roots of Lindbergh's personality, its strengths as well as its maddening flaws, all the way back to his turbulent boyhood." N Y Times Book Rev
Includes bibliographical references (p. {569}-612) and index

Lindbergh, Reeve
Lindbergh, Reeve. Under a wing; a memoir. Delta Trade Paperbacks 1999 223p il pa $15   **92**

Lindbergh, Reeve—_Continued_
1. Lindbergh, Charles, 1902-1974 2. Lindbergh, Anne
Morrow, 1906-2001 3. Air pilots
ISBN 978-0-385-33444-0; 0-385-33444-3
First published 1998 by Simon & Schuster
From the "perspective of a woman in her early fifties,
the youngest child of aviator and American hero Charles
Lindbergh and beloved writer Anne Morrow Lindbergh
tellingly reflects on the foibles, as well as the strength of
character of those two well-known figures." Booklist
"A rare memoir whose goal is not to expose but final-
ly to understand." Libr J

Linné, Carl von, 1707-1778
Blunt, Wilfrid. Linnaeus, the compleat naturalist;
with an introduction by William T. Stearn.
Princeton Univ. Press 2002 264p il maps $35
92
ISBN 0-691-09636-8
First published 1971 by Viking with title: The
compleat naturalist: a life of Linnaeus
This biography traces the Swedish scientist's life from
his days as a poor student at Lund University through his
scientific achievements and academic career at Uppsala
Includes bibliographical references

Lively, Penelope, 1933-
Lively, Penelope. A house unlocked. Grove
Press 2002 c2001 225p il $23; pa $13   **92**
ISBN 0-8021-1712-0; 0-8021-4007-6 (pa)
LC 2001-55745
First published 2001 in the United Kingdom
"The British novelist Penelope Lively spent her early
childhood in Egypt, but it was her school holidays at
Golsoncott—a manor house that her grandparents bought
in the wilds of Somerset, in 1923—that shaped her life.
In this slim, beguiling book, Lively describes the con-
tents and customs of the house. . . . By meticulously
tracing the provenance of these objects, she re-creates the
life they once furnished." New Yorker
Includes bibliographical references

Lloyd Webber, Andrew, 1948-
Citron, Stephen. Sondheim and Lloyd-Webber.
See entry under Sondheim, Stephen

Lombardi, Vince
Maraniss, David. When pride still mattered: a
life of Vince Lombardi. Simon & Schuster 1999
541p il pa $16 hardcover o.p.   **92**
ISBN 0-684-77018-5 (pa)   LC 99-37859
"From Lombardi's formative years as a player and
coach at Fordham University through assistantships with
West Point and the Giants and, finally, to his tenure as
head coach of the Packers, Maraniss presents a portrait
of a complicated human being who was a great teacher
but a mediocre listener, an effective psychologist despite
being rife with flaws." Publ Wkly
Includes bibliographical references

Long, Huey Pierce, 1893-1935
Hair, William Ivy. The Kingfish and his realm:
the life and times of Huey P. Long. Louisiana
State Univ. Press 1991 406p il map pa $21.95
hardcover o.p.   **92**
1. Louisiana—Politics and government
ISBN 0-8071-2124-X (pa)   LC 91-18546
This is a biography of the man who was governor of
Louisiana from 1928 to 1932 and senator from 1932 un-
til his assassination in 1935
"Written with passion and mordant wit, the book is
literally hard to put down; the Kingfish seems to stimu-
late good writing. Overall, {this} is one of the more convincing negative biographies of recent years." Rev Am
Hist
Includes bibliographical references

Longworth, Alice Roosevelt, 1884-1980
Cordery, Stacy A. Alice; Alice Roosevelt
Longworth, from White House princess to
Washington power broker. Viking 2007 590p il
$32.95   **92**
ISBN 978-0-670-01833-8   LC 2006-103087
This is a biography of Alice Roosevelt Longworth, the
Washington hostess and author of Crowded Hours
(1933).
The author "pens an authoritative, intriguing portrait
of a first daughter who broke the mold." Publ Wkly
Includes bibliographical references

Loomis, Alfred Lee, 1887-1975
Conant, Jennet. Tuxedo Park; a Wall Street
tycoon and the secret palace of science that
changed the course of World War II. Simon &
Schuster 2002 330p il $26; pa $14   **92**
1. Atomic bomb
ISBN 0-684-87287-0; 0-684-87288-9 (pa)
LC 2002-21001
In 1928 Alfred Loomis, a wealthy financier and ama-
teur physicist, "established a premier research facility in
Tuxedo Park, N.Y., that attracted such brilliant minds as
Einstein, Bohr and Fermi and became instrumental in the
Allies' WWII victory. Conant . . . draws on studies,
family papers and interviews with Loomis's friends, family and colleagues . . . to trace the story of the tycoon's
professional and social life." Publ Wkly
"Conant displays a real feel for the personal lives and
sensibilities of the era's leading scientists and industrialists in a fascinating, never-before-told bit of American
history." Booklist
Includes bibliographical references

Louis XIV, King of France, 1638-1715
Fraser, Antonia. Love and Louis XIV; the
women in the life of the Sun King. Nan A.
Talese/Doubleday 2006 xxviii, 388p il $32.50
92
ISBN 978-0-38550984-8; 0-385-50984-7
LC 2006-44674
This is an account of Louis XIV's relationships with
his wife and his mistresses.
"One of the most enveloping popular histories of the
current publishing season." Booklist
Includes bibliographical references

Lowell, Robert, 1917-1977

Mariani, Paul L. Lost puritan: a life of Robert Lowell. Norton 1994 527p il pa $15 hardcover o.p.
*   **92**

     ISBN 0-393-31374-3 (pa)   LC 93-48018
This biography "of a protean confessional poet uses letters and diaries to reveal a writer whose fascination with preachers, statesmen and generals hints at restlessness with his own art." N Y Times Book Rev
"Mariani, for all his moment-by-moment acuteness and lucidity, offers no radically new insights into Lowell's life or art, nor does he provide those powerfully developed thematic and narrative lines that distinguish the greatest literary biographies. Still, this remains an impressive piece of writing and documentation." Choice

Lowman, Margaret

Lowman, Margaret. Life in the treetops; adventures of a woman in field biology; [by] Margaret D. Lowman. Yale Univ. Press 1999 219p il maps $37.50; pa $13.95   **92**
     1. Botanists 2. Women scientists
     ISBN   0-300-07818-8;   978-0-300-07818-3;
     0-300-08464-1 (pa); 978-0-300-08464-1 (pa)
                              LC 98-48691
The author is a botanist who studies canopies, the uppermost layers of forests. "Interwoven with her narrative of field work is the story of how she balanced the needs of marriage, housewifery, children, and eventual single parenthood with college teaching and research trips to locales such as Panama, Australia, and Cameroon." Booklist
Lowman "gives a funny, unassuming and deeply idiosyncratic chronicle of her trials and triumphs as a field biologist of tree canopies and other ecosystems in Australia, New England, Belize, Panama and elsewhere." N Y Times Book Rev
     Includes bibliographical references
     Followed by It's a jungle up there! (2006)

Luce, Clare Boothe, 1903-1987

Morris, Sylvia Jukes. Rage for fame: the ascent of Clare Boothe Luce. Random House 1997 561p il pa $27 hardcover o.p.   **92**
     ISBN 0-8129-9249-0 (pa)   LC 96-43084
This first of a projected two-volume biography "describes how the future congresswoman and second wife of *Time* magazine founder Henry Luce, bedded her way upward while career-climbing in New York journalism and writing a stage mega-hit, *The Women*. . . . By 1942—at age 39—she turned to politics and was elected a Republican representative from Connecticut." Publ Wkly
     Includes bibliographical references

Luther, Martin, 1483-1546

Bainton, Roland Herbert. Here I stand: a life of Martin Luther. Abingdon Press 1950 422p il music pa $7 hardcover o.p.   **92**
     1. Europe—Church history 2. Reformation
     ISBN 0-687-16895-3 (pa)
     Also available paperback from NAL/Dutton

This biography of Martin Luther interprets his work, writings, and lasting contributions. It recreates the spiritual setting of the sixteenth century and shows Luther's place within it
     Includes bibliographical references

Erikson, Erik H. (Erik Homburger). Young man Luther; a study in psychoanalysis and history. Norton 1958 288p pa $13.95 hardcover o.p.
                               92
     1. Reformation 2. Europe—Church history
     ISBN 0-393-31036-1 (pa)
"This study of Martin Luther as a young man was planned as a chapter in a book on emotional crises in late adolescence and early adulthood. But Luther proved too bulky a man to be merely a chapter." Preface

Oberman, Heiko Augustinus. Luther: man between God and the Devil; {by} Heiko A. Oberman;   translated   by   Eileen Walliser-Schwarzbart. Yale Univ. Press 1990 c1989 xx, 380p il pa $20 hardcover o.p.
                               92
     1. Europe—Church history 2. Reformation
     ISBN 978-0-300-10313-7 (pa); 0-300-10313-1 (pa)
                               LC 89-5747
     Original German edition, 1982
The author "posits that to understand Luther the reformer is to first realize he was a medieval man for whom Satan was as real as God and human. By placing Luther back into the context of his own age, Oberman strips away any simplistic, post-Enlightenment notions of Luther as the savior of humanity from the darkest obscurantism of the Catholic Church. . . . A triumph of scholarship that brings Luther to life in all of his furious, outspoken, and violent passion." Booklist
     Includes bibliographical references

Wilson, Derek A. Out of the storm; the life and legacy of Martin Luther; [by] Derek Wilson. St. Martin's Press 2008 399p il $29.95   **92**
     1. Europe—Church history 2. Reformation
     ISBN 978-0-312-37588-1; 0-312-37588-3
                              LC 2007-39331
This is a "biography of the man who, more than any other, precipitated the Protestant Reformation." Libr J
"A nuanced portrait of a perplexing titan." Booklist
     Includes bibliographical references

Lynn, Loretta

Lynn, Loretta. Still woman enough; a memoir; {by} Loretta Lynn with Patsi Bale Cox. Hyperion 2002 244p il $24.95; pa $7.99   **92**
     ISBN 0-7868-6650-0; 0-7868-8987-X (pa)
In this sequel to Coal miner's daughter, "Lynn mostly focuses on her marriage and the trials and pleasures of Nashville stardom, including fond recollections of friends like Conway Twitty and Tammy Wynette. . . . Though her grammar may make purists flinch . . . Lynn's literary voice is as natural and endearing as her songs." Publ Wkly

Maathai, Wangari, 1940-
Maathai, Wangari. Unbowed; a memoir; [by] Wangari Muta Maathai. Knopf 2006 314p il $24.95   **92**
    ISBN 0-307-26348-7; 978-0-307-26348-3
                  LC 2006-44729
    "Nobel Peace Prize winner Maathai tells the unforgettable story of her Kenya girlhood, struggles as a biologist and professor, and founding of the Green Belt Movement to restore Kenya's decimated forests and provide women with work." Booklist

MacArthur, Douglas, 1880-1964
Frank, Richard B. MacArthur; foreword by Wesley K. Clark. Palgrave Macmillan 2007 224p (Great generals series) $21.95   **92**
    1. Generals
    ISBN 1-4039-7658-9; 978-1-4039-7658-1
    This biography of the World War II general is an "assessment of both the man and the soldier, covering the failures and triumphs in an assured and dispassionate tone. . . . A good starting point for generalists." Libr J

Machiavelli, Niccolò, 1469-1527
Viroli, Maurizio. Niccolò's smile: a biography of Machiavelli; translated from the Italian by Antony Shugaar. Farrar, Straus & Giroux 2000 271p maps pa $13 hardcover o.p.   **92**
    ISBN 0-374-52800-4 (pa)   LC 00-29380
    This biography of the Italian political philosopher traces his life "from respected secretary of the Florentine republic, dispatched on crucial diplomatic missions to Europe's most illustrious courts, to forgotten commoner. . . . Viroli provides a detailed, historical background for Machiavelli's personal triumphs and woes. But the strength of this work lies in his ceaseless concentration on Machiavelli the man, who comes alive on each page." Publ Wkly
    Includes bibliographical references

MacLeish, Archibald, 1892-1982
MacLeish, Archibald. Archibald MacLeish: reflections; edited by Bernard A. Drabeck and Helen E. Ellis; foreword by Richard Wilbur. University of Mass. Press 1986 291p il $40; pa $18.95   **92**
    ISBN 0-87023-511-7; 0-87023-623-7 (pa)
                  LC 85-28912
    "In these long interviews, conducted during the last five years of his life, a noted writer talks about his professional life as a poet, playwright, lawyer, editor of 'Fortune,' Librarian of Congress and Harvard professor." Publ Wkly
    "In this genial, relaxed book we have a golden view of the candidly retrospective statesman-poet in his old age as he really was, with most pretension and all rhetoric abandoned." N Y Times Book Rev
    Includes bibliographical references

Madison, Dolley, 1768-1849
Allgor, Catherine. A perfect union; Dolley Madison and the creation of the American nation. Henry Holt & Co. 2006 493p il $30   **92**
    ISBN 0-8050-7327-2; 978-0-8050-7327-0
                  LC 2005-55127
    The author "makes the case that not only was Dolley Madison incredibly popular with the American people . . . [but that] the wife of America's fourth president was also a 'master politician.'" Publ Wkly
    "In this evocative study a remarkable woman, creator of the 'first lady' role, comes vividly to life. " N Y Times Book Rev
    Includes bibliographical references

Madison, James, 1751-1836
Wills, Garry. James Madison. Times Bks. 2002 xx, 184p (American presidents series) $20   **92**
    1. Presidents—United States
    ISBN 0-8050-6905-4   LC 2002-19692
    The author "maintains that Madison possessed qualities that served him well early in his career but proved to be a handicap during his Presidency. . . . Written with flair, this clear and balanced account is based on a sure handling of the material." Libr J
    Includes bibliographical references

Mah, Adeline Yen, 1937-
Mah, Adeline Yen. Falling leaves; a true story of an unwanted Chinese daughter. Wiley 1998 278p il $22.95   **92**
    ISBN 0-471-24742-1   LC 97-40144
    Also available in paperback from Broadway Bks.
    First published 1997 in the United Kindgom with title: Falling leaves return to their roots
    "Although the focus of this memoir is the author's struggle to be loved by a family that treated her cruelly, it is more notable for its portrait of the domestic affairs of an immensely wealthy, Westernized Chinese family in Shanghai as the city evolved under the harsh strictures of Mao and Deng. . . . In recounting this painful tale, Yen Mah's unadorned prose is powerful, her insights keen and her portrait of her family devastating." Publ Wkly

Mailer, Norman, 1923-2007
Dearborn, Mary V. Mailer; a biography. Houghton Mifflin 1999 478p il hardcover o.p. pa $15   **92**
    1. Authors, American
    ISBN 0-395-73655-2; 0-618-15460-4 (pa)
                  LC 99-32214
    "Dearborn supplies a close reading of one of the most controversial American writers of the postwar era. Mailer's body of work, beginning with his career-defining first novel, *The Naked and the Dead* (1948), is analyzed with remarkable insight. Mailer's notorious personal life is also examined, as Dearborn sorts through the various preoccupations that have obsessed the writer over five decades in the literary spotlight." Booklist
    Includes bibliographical references

Malamud, Bernard, 1914-1986

Smith, Janna Malamud. My father is a book; a memoir of Bernard Malamud. Houghton Mifflin 2006 292p $24   **92**

ISBN 0-618-69166-9; 978-0-618-69166-1

LC 2005-24736

"On the twentieth anniversary of Bernard Malamud's death, Janna Malamud Smith explores her father's private, unpublished letters and journals to remember the life of [the writer]." Publisher's note

"Analytical without being acrimonious, honest without wallowing in self-preening exposure, this is a wise, generous book full of insights on what it's like to be a writer and to be a writer's daughter." Christ Sci Monit

Includes bibliographical references

Malcolm X, 1925-1965

Carson, Clayborne. Malcolm X: the FBI file; introduction by Spike Lee; edited by David Gallen. Carroll & Graf Pubs. 1991 514p il pa $13.95 hardcover o.p.   **92**

ISBN 0-88184-758-5 (pa)   LC 91-26697

"This is a collection of declassified documents from the FBI surveillance of the orator and religious (later political) leader that, with historian Carson's studious commentary, focuses less on Malcolm's relation to the FBI and more on that to the larger civil rights movement. These excerpts . . . follow his travels and speeches, media interviews and FBI interviews, oftentimes including transcripts as written or summarized by Gallen and Carson." Booklist

Malcolm X. The autobiography of Malcolm X; with the assistance of Alex Haley; introduction by M. S. Handler; epilogue by Alex Haley; afterword by Ossie Davis. Ballantine Bks. 1992 500p $25; pa $15 *   **92**

1. African Americans—Biography 2. Black Muslims

ISBN 0-345-37975-6; 0-345-37671-4 (pa)

LC 92-52659

Also available in hardcover from Amereon

First published 1965 by Grove Press

Based on tape-recorded conversations with Alex Haley, this account of the life of the Black Muslim leader was completed shortly before his murder

Alex Haley "did his job with sensitivity and with devotion. . . . {The book} will have a permanent place in the literature of the Afro-American struggle." N Y Rev Books

Perry, Bruce. Malcolm; the life of a man who changed black America. Station Hill Press 1991 542p il pa $14.95 hardcover o.p.   **92**

ISBN 0-88268-121-4 (pa)   LC 90-23350

"Perry traces Malcolm X's footsteps from birth in 1925 to death in 1965, using several hundred interviews to fill in detail and correct the autobiography Alex Haley edited. Probing what he labels as the deep-seated and hidden causes that made Malcolm who and what he was, Perry produces a portrait of an emotionally abused and abandoned boy who grew to manipulate his fearful helplessness into emotional and political power." Libr J

Includes bibliographical references

Mandela, Nelson

Mandela, Nelson. In his own words; edited by Kader Asmal, David Chidester, [and] Wilmot James. Little, Brown 2003 558p il $28.95   **92**

1. South Africa—Race relations 2. South Africa—Politics and government

ISBN 0-316-11019-1   LC 2004-107807

This book "presents the Nobel laureate's speeches on a wide variety of subjects. The book is organized topically; each section—on struggle, freedom, reconciliation, nation building, development, education and culture—is introduced with an essay by a leading spokesperson for the respective field (e.g., Bill Cosby, Desmond Tutu). Together, the speeches chart Mandela's evolution from freedom fighter . . . to president to secular icon." Publ Wkly

"This collection of Mandela's speeches shows why he remains a universal hero. . . . This volume will be in great demand for the personal drama, the history, and, yes, for the inspiring moral values." Booklist

Mandela, Nelson. Long walk to freedom: the autobiography of Nelson Mandela. Little, Brown 1994 558p il pa $16.95 hardcover o.p.   **92**

1. South Africa—Politics and government 2. South Africa—Race relations

ISBN 0-316-54818-9 (pa)   LC 94-79980

This is an account of Nelson "Mandela's life from his 'country childhood' following his birth on July 18, 1918 to his inauguration as president of South Africa on May 10, 1994." Libr J

This book "provides important new evidence to the forty-year story of apartheid, as seen by its most formidable opponent. And there is enough candour to provide insights into the nature of leadership." Times Lit Suppl

Mandela, Nelson. Mandela; an illustrated autobiography. Little, Brown 1996 208p il map $29.95 *   **92**

1. South Africa—Race relations 2. South Africa—Politics and government

ISBN 0-316-55038-8   LC 96-77497

"This is an illustrated and abridged edition of Long walk to freedom: the autobiography of Nelson Mandela." Verso of title page

"The photos, from a variety of archives and journalistic sources, ably illustrate Mandela and, even more so, the South Africa around him." Libr J

Sampson, Anthony. Nelson Mandela; the authorized biography. Knopf 1999 xxvi, 672p pa $19 hardcover o.p.   **92**

1. South Africa—Race relations 2. South Africa—Politics and government

ISBN 0-679-78178-1 (pa)   LC 99-18498

Sampson traces "the course of Nelson Mandela's life, from his birth in 1918 in the Transkei region of South Africa, to his retirement from the presidency in 1999, at the end of his first and only term." Commonweal

"While not neglecting the personality of the man, Mr. Sampson has concentrated on the politics, and, for an authorised life, it can be treated as definitive." Economist

Includes bibliographical references

Mandelstam, Nadezhda, 1899-1980

Mandelstam, Nadezhda. Hope against hope; a memoir; translated from the Russian by Max Hayward; with an introduction by Clarence Brown and: Nadezhda Mandelstaum (1899-1980): an obituary, by Joseph Brodsky. Modern Lib. 1999 442p pa $23   **92**
   ISBN 978-0-375-75316-9; 0-375-75316-8
                        LC 98-47833
"Mandelstam tells the story of her family's experiences of hardship in Soviet Russia under Stalin. What is remarkable about the book is not just its content but also its authorial voice, which, in Max Hayward's deft translation, is so unique and consistent that the reader can get a sense of it by opening the book at random and reading almost any paragraph. Although Hope Against Hope is a painful book to read, one of the things that makes it bearable, apart from its sheer beauty, is a kind of unquenchable spirit and optimism that keeps rising to the surface, compounding the more mysterious consolations of art." Harper's

Manet, Édouard, 1832-1883

Brombert, Beth Archer. Edouard Manet; rebel in a frock coat. University of Chicago Press 1997 505p il pa $19.95   **92**
   1. Artists, French
   ISBN 0-226-07544-3; 978-0-226-07544-0
                        LC 97-3321
   First published 1996 by Little, Brown
This biography of the French painter discusses "Manet's world and the importance of 19th-century Paris to the formation of Manet's personal and artistic life." Libr J
"To recount Manet's life, as Brombert has done in this elegant biography, is to tell the story of an enormously influential artist struggling to paint what he called 'the spirit of contemporaneity' while remaining committed to the conservative institutions of civil life—the very same institutions that shunned him." New Yorker
   Includes bibliographical references

Mankiller, Wilma

Mankiller, Wilma. Mankiller: a chief and her people; {by} Wilma Mankiller and Michael Wallis. St. Martin's Press 1993 xxiv, 292p il pa $14.95 hardcover o.p.   **92**
   1. Cherokee Indians
   ISBN 0-312-20662-3 (pa)   LC 93-25698
This "account of the first woman principal chief of the Cherokee Nation describes . . . {her} childhood spent on an allotment farm in Mankiller Flat, Oklahoma, her teenage years in the 1960s as an 'urban Indian,' a near brush with death, and a life of solid accomplishment in service and tribal leadership rooted in Cherokee culture." Libr J
"A must-read for everyone interested in, specifically, the history of Native Americans and women and, in general, tales of exceptional people." Booklist

Mann, Thomas, 1875-1955

Kurzke, Hermann. Thomas Mann; life as a work of art: a biography; translated by Leslie Willson. Princeton Univ. Press 2002 581p il $35
                            92
   ISBN 0-691-07069-5   LC 2002-23665
   Translated from the German
This biography of the German author focuses on "Mann's homosexuality, his relations to Jews and Judaism, the canny construction of the persona of Great Author, and how Mann transformed everything around him into art." Libr J
"A major achievement in literary biography." Booklist

Mao Zedong, 1893-1976

Chang, Jung. Mao: the unknown story; [by] Jung Chang, Jon Halliday. Knopf 2005 814p il $35   **92**
   1. China—Politics and government
   ISBN 0-679-42271-4   LC 2004-63826
The author "aims to uncover Mao's further cruelties (beyond those commonly known) by debunking claims made by the Communist Party in his service." Publ Wkly
"This is a magisterial work. . . . This biography supplies substantial . . . information and presents it all in a stylish way that will put it on bedside tables around the world." N Y Times Book Rev
   Includes bibliographical references

Short, Philip. Mao; a life. Holt & Co. 2000 782p il maps pa $20 hardcover o.p.   **92**
   1. China—Politics and government
   ISBN 0-8050-6638-1 (pa)   LC 99-41839
   "A John Macrae book"
This biography "takes Mao from his 1893 birth in the village of Shaoshan to school in Changsha, where he trained to be a teacher, and then into revolutionary activity, the long fight with Chiang Kai-shek, and leadership of the most populous nation on Earth." Booklist
   Includes bibliographical references

Spence, Jonathan D. Mao Zedong; [by] Jonathan Spence. Viking 1999 188p map (Penguin lives series) $19.95   **92**
   1. China—Politics and government
   ISBN 0-670-88669-6   LC 99-27739
   "A Lipper/Viking book"
"This specialist's book for nonspecialists concisely recounts the life of the Communist leader who revolutionized China. Ideas travel fast: Mao, a peasant son born in 1893, was able to read Darwin and Marx in translation and add Western ideas to his heritage of classical Chinese thought, and Spence helps us understand why he eventually embraced Communism. What is less clear is why a gifted, high-minded youth became a ruthless, crackpot tyrant." New Yorker
   Includes bibliographical references

Maravich, Pete, 1947-1988
Kriegel, Mark. Pistol; the life of Pete Maravich.
Free Press 2007 381p il $27; pa $15 *
92

ISBN   978-0-7432-8497-4;   0-7432-8497-6;
978-0-7432-8498-1 (pa); 0-7432-8498-4 (pa)
LC 2006-51526
This is a biography of the basketball player who
played at Louisiana State University before joining the
N.B.A.
The author "skillfully pulls off the balancing act required of good sports biography. It plays large historical
forces (segregation, the rise of televised sports) against
the individual magic of its subject." New York
Includes bibliographical references

Maria Celeste, 1600-1634
Sobel, Dava. Galileo's daughter; a historical
memoir of science, faith, and love. Walker & Co.
1999 420p $27
92
1. Galilei, Galileo, 1564-1642
ISBN 0-8027-1343-2   LC 99-23885
Also available in paperback from Penguin Bks.
This book "is organized around a series of letters that
Suor Maria Celeste wrote to Galileo from May 1623,
when Galileo was 59 and already celebrated throughout
Europe, until April 1634, when she died of dysentary.
. . . For the most part they deal with the daughter's concern for her father's constant illnesses and difficulties
with his enemies, expressions of love and devotion, requests for money, details of the brutally spare life in the
convent of San Matteo and routine household matters
while Galileo was on trial in Rome." N Y Times Book
Rev
"Sobel has a remarkable ability to explain technical
subjects without being simplistic or pedantic. There is a
tremendous amount of fascinating detail in this work,
and yet it reads as smoothly and compellingly as fiction." Libr J
Includes bibliographical references

Marie Antoinette, Queen, consort of Louis XVI, King of France, 1755-1793
Fraser, Antonia. Marie Antoinette; the journey.
Talese 2001 xxii, 512p il $35; pa $16.95
92
1. Queens 2. France—History—1589-1789, Bourbons
ISBN 0-385-48948-X; 0-385-48949-8 (pa)
LC 2001-23493
The author portrays the Austrian-born Queen consort
of Louis XVI of France as "neither heroine nor villain,
but a young wife and mother who, in her journey into
maturity, finds herself caught in a deadly vise." Publ
Wkly
"A well-researched biography that may cause one to
rethink the role in which history has cast Marie Antoinette." Libr J
Includes bibliographical references

Lever, Evelyne. Marie Antoinette; the last queen
of France; translated from the French by Catherine
Temerson. Farrar, Straus & Giroux 2000 357p il
pa $16.95 hardcover o.p.
92
1. Queens 2. France—History—1589-1789, Bourbons
ISBN 0-312-08333-4 (pa)   LC 00-28763

The author examines "the opulent Versailles subculture and the queen whose royal excesses served as a major catalyst for the revolutionary upheaval of 1789.
Through the skillful use of memoirs and other primary
documents, Lever creates an empathic picture of Louis
XVI's headstrong wife." Libr J
Includes bibliographical references

Markham, Beryl, 1902-1986
Trzebinski, Errol. The lives of Beryl Markham;
Out of Africa's hidden free spirit and Denys Finch
Hatton's last great love. Norton 1993 396p il maps
pa $12 hardcover o.p.   **92**
ISBN 0-393-31252-6 (pa)   LC 93-9919
This is a biography of the aviator who was the first
woman to fly solo across the Atlantic. "Markham was
born in 1902 to British parents and grew up on her fa-
ther's farm in Kenya." Libr J
The author offers "confirmation of the rumor that Ber-
yl's third husband actually wrote her best-selling memoir,
West with the Night." Booklist
Includes bibliographical references

Marlowe, Christopher, 1564-1593
Honan, Park. Christopher Marlowe; poet & spy.
Oxford University Press 2005 421p il $32.50 *
92
1. Dramatists, English 2. Great Britain—History—
1485-1603, Tudors
ISBN 0-19-818695-9   LC 2005-19761
This is a biography of the sixteenth-century English
dramatist.
The author "sheds light on the much-speculated (and
previously erroneously reported) aspects of Marlowe's
life without neglecting its more ordinary features (his sta-
ble two-parent upbringing, his diligent scholarship at
Cambridge) or destroying the poet's aura of intrigue."
Publ Wkly
Includes bibliographical references

Nicholl, Charles. The reckoning; the murder of
Christopher Marlowe. University of Chicago Press
1995 413p il pa $33   **92**
1. Dramatists, English 2. Great Britain—History—
1485-1603, Tudors
ISBN 0-226-58024-5; 978-0-226-58024-1
First published 1992 in the United Kingdom
The author argues that the Elizabethan playwright,
who is believed to have been stabbed in a dispute over
the bill ('recknynge') at Eleanor Bull's victualling house
in 1593, was in fact murdered with government complicity as part of a plot against Sir Walter Raleigh.
"A remarkable piece of scholarship, this work carefully reconstructs the events leading up to the murder with
all the excitement and suspense of a modern mystery
novel; at the same time it vividly conveys the energy and
color of Elizabethan England." Libr J
Includes bibliographical references

Marshall, John, 1755-1835

Smith, Jean Edward. John Marshall; definer of a nation. Holt & Co. 1996 736p il pa $22 hardcover o.p. **92**

    1. United States. Supreme Court
ISBN 0-8050-5510-X (pa)   LC 96-15072
"A Marian Wood book"
A Marian Wood Bk.

Smith presents a "portrait of the most significant and influential jurist in U.S. history. Appointed chief justice of the Supreme Court in 1801, John Marshall, farmer, soldier, lawyer, diplomatic envoy, and politician, served as the nation's premier legal authority and moral barometer for 35 years." Booklist

"Mr. Smith's splendid biography deserves a large readership mostly because it has recovered Marshall the man." N Y Times Book Rev

Includes bibliographical references

Marshall, Thurgood, 1908-1993

Marshall, Thurgood. Thurgood Marshall; his speeches, writings, arguments, opinions, and reminiscences; edited by Mark Tushnet; foreword by Randall Kennedy. Hill Bks. 2001 xxvi, 548p (Library of Black America) $40; pa $24.95

    92

    1. United States. Supreme Court 2. African Americans—Biography 3. African Americans—Civil rights
ISBN 1-55652-385-8; 1-55652-386-6 (pa)
    LC 2001-16793

"In a career ranging from his trial and appellate work for the NAACP to his tenure as an associate justice of the Court, Marshall wrought revolutionary changes in U.S. law and politics, and this collection of his legal briefs, writings, speeches, and judicial opinions, plus a never-before-published oral interview, gives us a superior analysis of the advocate, the democrat, the dissenter, and the unflagging fighter for equality." Libr J

Includes bibliographical references

Rowan, Carl Thomas. Dream makers, dream breakers; the world of Justice Thurgood Marshall; [by] Carl T. Rowan. Welcome Rain 2002 475p il pa $18.95 **92**

    1. United States. Supreme Court 2. National Association for the Advancement of Colored People 3. Judges
ISBN 978-1-56649-235-5; 1-56649-235-1

First published 1993 by Little, Brown

The author "offers a no-holds barred account of one of the most influential and controversial figures in American law and jurisprudence of this century. His work brings to life Marshall, the Supreme Court, U.S. law and modern America itself. Particularly effective is Rowan's account of the innovative legal arguments Marshall and his colleagues employed to win the now-famous Brown v. Board of Education case of 1954." Libr J

Includes bibliographical references

Williams, Juan. Thurgood Marshall; American revolutionary. Times Bks. 1998 459p il pa $16 hardcover o.p. **92**

    1. United States. Supreme Court 2. African Americans—Biography 3. African Americans—Civil rights
ISBN 0-8129-3299-4 (pa)   LC 98-9735

"Williams presents Marshall as a revolutionary 'of grand vision,' but this well-rounded portrait of the man also addresses his vanities and warts, from his ascension to his deflation and subsequent redemption. This is a must read for all Americans concerned with the struggle for civil and individual rights." Booklist

Includes bibliographical references

Martin, Dean

Lewis, Jerry. Dean & me. See entry under Lewis, Jerry, 1926-

Martin, Steve, 1945-

Martin, Steve. Born standing up; a comic's life. Scribner 2007 209p il $25 **92**

    1. Actors 2. Comedians
ISBN 978-1-4165-5364-9; 1-4165-5364-9
    LC 2007-27143

This is an autobiography by the comedian and author of Shopgirl (2000).

This book "does a sharp-witted job of breaking down the step-by-step process that brought [the author] from Disneyland, where he spent his version of a Dickensian childhood as a schoolboy employee, to both the pinnacle of stardom and the brink of disaster. . . . Even for readers already familiar with Mr. Martin's solemn side, [this] is a surprising book: smart, serious, heartfelt and confessional without being maudlin." N Y Times (Late NY Ed)

Marx, Groucho, 1891-1977

Kanfer, Stefan. Groucho: the life and times of Julius Henry Marx. Knopf 2000 465p il pa $15 hardcover o.p. **92**

    ISBN 0-375-70207-5 (pa)   LC 99-54002

"Plagued by nagging financial insecurities, partly realized literary ambitions, and difficult, unsatisfying relations with his wives, lovers, and daughters, Groucho was a 'depressive clown,' notes Kanter. . . . The book also details Groucho's ambivalent relations with his son, Arthur; his brothers; New Deal liberals; intellectuals and collaborators like S. J. Perelman; and his custodian, Erin Fleming." Libr J

Includes bibliographical references

Marx, Karl, 1818-1883

Wheen, Francis. Karl Marx; a life. Norton 2000 431p il $27.95; pa $14.95 **92**

    1. Communism
ISBN 0-393-04923-X; 0-393-32157-6 (pa)
    LC 99-87466

First published 1999 in the United Kingdom

"Following Marx from his childhood in Trier, Germany, through his exile in London, Wheen . . . takes readers from hovel to grand house, from the International Working Man's Association to *Capital*, from obscurity to notoriety and back again." Publ Wkly

Includes bibliographical references

Mary, Blessed Virgin, Saint

Hazleton, Lesley. Mary: a flesh-and-blood biography of the Virgin Mother. Bloomsbury 2004 246p $24.95 **92**

    ISBN 1-582-34236-9   LC 2003-17403

Mary, Blessed Virgin, Saint—*Continued*

The author "helps us to see who the mother of Jesus might have been, places her in context socially and religiously, and shows how the figure she became absorbed goddess myths." Booklist

Hazleton "takes readers through an impressive array of historical, cultural, literary, and spiritual topics. . . . This book is an easy read, and Hazleton's stream-of-consciousness style is intriguing." Libr J

Includes bibliographical references

Mary, Queen of Scots, 1542-1587

Fraser, Antonia. Mary Queen of Scots. illustrated abridged ed. Delacorte Press 1978 208p il pa $19.95 hardcover o.p.   **92**
    1. Great Britain—History—1485-1603, Tudors
    2. Scotland—History—16th century
ISBN 0-380-31129-X (pa)   LC 78-703

A condensation of the title first published 1969

A look at the tragic life of Mary Stuart, the 16th century Catholic ruler of Protestant Scotland, and her incessant struggle with political and religious opponents

Includes bibliographical references

Weir, Alison. Mary, Queen of Scots, and the murder of Lord Darnley. Ballantine Bks. 2003 670p il map $27.95; pa $16.95   **92**
    1. Darnley, Henry Stewart, Lord, 1545-1567
    2. Scotland—History—16th century
ISBN 0-345-43658-X; 0-8129-7151-5 (pa)
    LC 2002-34467

The author "sets out to prove that contrary to supposition Mary, Queen of Scots, was innocent of the murder of her husband, Lord Darnley." Libr J

"No stone is left unturned in {Weir's} investigation, and despite its detail, her book is as dramatic as witnessing firsthand the most riveting court case." Booklist

Mason, George, 1725-1792

Broadwater, Jeff. George Mason, forgotten founder. University of North Carolina Press 2006 329p il $34.95 *   **92**
ISBN 978-0-8078-3053-6; 0-8078-3053-4
    LC 2006-10729

"Mason played a key role in the Stamp Act Crisis, the American Revolution, and the drafting of Virginia's first state constitution. He is perhaps best known as author of the Virginia Declaration of Rights, often hailed as the model for the Bill of Rights." Publisher's note

"Because Mason left little evidence of his private life, there are blurred edges in the portrait that Broadwater paints, but overall this is an exemplary biography: sympathetic but dispassionate, thorough but not cluttered, convincing in its interpretations and arguments. It leaves no doubt that Mason deserves to be returned to the esteem and reputation he enjoyed during his lifetime, but in no way is it hagiography." Washington Post Book World

Includes bibliographical references

Matisse, Henri

Spurling, Hilary. Matisse the master; a life of Henri Matisse, the conquest of colour, 1909-1954. Knopf 2005 xxi, 511p il $40   **92**
    ISBN 0-679-43429-1   LC 2004-51074

Companion volume to The unknown Matisse

This second volume of the author's biography of the French artist "covers the years from Matisse's emergence as a mature artist to his death at age 85." Libr J

"Spurling's rich, flexible style is well attuned to the rigors and flights of Matisse's creative life." Publ Wkly

Includes bibliographical references

Spurling, Hilary. The unknown Matisse; a life of Henri Matisse. v1: The early years, 1869-1908. Knopf 1998 xxv, 480p il $40   **92**
    ISBN 0-679-43428-3   LC 97-46816

Also available in paperback from University of Calif. Press

Companion volume to Matisse the master

In this first volume of the author's biography of the French artist, Spurling focuses on Matisse's training as an art student in Paris

This volume "makes for a gripping read and reveals much about the artist's early development." Publ Wkly

Includes bibliographical references

Mauldin, Bill, 1921-2003

DePastino, Todd. Bill Mauldin; a life up front. W.W. Norton 2008 370p il $27.95   **92**
    1. Cartoonists
ISBN 978-0-393-06183-3; 0-393-06183-3
    LC 2007-40494

This is a biography of the author of What's Got Your Back Up? (1961), I've Decided I Want My Seat Back (1965), and The Brass Ring (1971). During World War II, Mauldin was a cartoonist who depicted the daily lives of soldiers for the G.I. newspaper Stars and Stripes.

"Thoroughly researched and sprightly written, DePastino's balanced biography is a solid introduction to an American original. Classic Mauldin cartoons are an entertaining bonus." Publ Wkly

Includes bibliographical references

Mayakovsky, Vladimir, 1893-1930

Night wraps the sky; writings by and about Mayakovsky; edited by Michael Almereyda. Farrar, Straus and Giroux 2008 xxvii, 272p il $27
    92
ISBN 978-0-374-28135-9; 0-374-28135-1
    LC 2007-46662

This is a collection of Vladimir Mayakovksy's poems, newly translated, älongside memoirs, artistic appreciations, and eyewitness accounts." Publisher's note

"The book further explores Mayakovsky's relationships with Lili Brik and Tatiana Yakovleva, explains his propaganda work, and addresses his mixture of the surreal, the lyric, and the sarcastic; the text is generously illustrated with photographs of Mayakovsky's friends and contemporaries and artworks of the times." Libr J

Mayer, Louis B. (Louis Burt), 1885-1957

Eyman, Scott. Lion of Hollywood; the life and legend of Louis B. Mayer. Simon & Schuster 2005 596p il $35 *   **92**

ISBN 0-7432-0481-6   LC 2005-42472

This is a "biography of Louis B. Mayer, the chief of Metro-Goldwyn-Mayer—MGM—the biggest and most successful film studio of Hollywood's Golden Age." Publisher's note

"Eyman's extensive knowledge of old Hollywood, his scrupulous research and his refusal to indict the often-pilloried Mayer make this biography an often revelatory delight." Publ Wkly

Includes bibliographical references

McBride, James

McBride, James. The color of water. See entry under McBride-Jordan, Ruth, 1921-

McBride-Jordan, Ruth, 1921-

McBride, James. The color of water; a black man's tribute to his white mother. Riverhead Bks. 1996 228p il $23.95; pa $14   **92**

1. McBride, James
ISBN 1-57322-022-1; 1-57322-578-9 (pa)
                                        LC 95-37243

This volume combines accounts of McBride's childhood in a mixed-race family and of his mother's life history, in alternating chapters. "Ruth McBride recounts fleeing the rural South and her Orthodox Jewish family to live in Harlem, cofound a Baptist church, and twice survive widowhood to raise 12 children." Booklist

"Told with humor and clear-eyed grace, McBride's memoir is not only a terrific story, it's a subtle contribution to the current debates on race and identity. . . . The sheer strength of spirit, pain and humor of McBride and his mother as they wrestled with different aspects of race and identity is vividly told." Nation

McCain, John S., 1936-

McCain, John S. Faith of my fathers; {by} John McCain with Mark Salter. Random House 1999 349p $25   **92**

1. McCain, John Sidney
ISBN 0-375-50191-6   LC 99-13496
Also in paperback from HarperPerennial

"McCain examines the lives of his grandfather and father—both four-star admirals—and shows how their lessons helped him through his years as a prisoner of war in Vietnam." Booklist

This is a "serious, utterly engrossing account of faith, fathers and military tradition." Publ Wkly

McCall, Nathan

McCall, Nathan. Makes me wanna holler; a young black man in America. Random House 1994 404p pa $14.95 hardcover o.p.   **92**

1. African Americans—Biography
ISBN 0-679-74070-8 (pa)   LC 93-30654

The author relates the "story of his rise from poverty to success as a journalist at the *Washington Post*. He

uses graphic language, blunt descriptions, honest expression, introspection, and careful observation to describe his early years in Portsmouth, Virginia, as a young black male, the recipient of a 12-year prison sentence for armed robbery, whose life was dangerously out of control. Insensitivity, alienation, racial hatred, drugs (especially crack), guns, rape, robbery, the black American as an endangered species—McCall covers it all in a depressing yet spellbinding documentary." Libr J

McCarthy, Joseph, 1908-1957

Wicker, Tom. Shooting star: the brief arc of Joe McCarthy. Harcourt 2006 212p $22   **92**

ISBN 978-0-15-101082-0; 0-15-101082-X
                                        LC 2005-20990

This is a biography of the Senator from Wisconsin who led the House Committee on Un-American Activities and was censured by the Senate in 1954.

"This perceptive, well-written book should have wide appeal." Choice

Includes bibliographical references

McCarthy, Mary, 1912-1989

Kiernan, Frances. Seeing Mary plain: a life of Mary McCarthy. Norton 2000 845p il $35; pa $25
                                                  92

ISBN 0-393-03801-7; 0-393-32307-2 (pa)
                                        LC 99-41098

Kiernan uses "her interviews with more than 200 sources to provide multiple points of view on McCarthy's life and work. McCarthy knew most of her generation's literary leading lights, from the *Partisan Review* crowd to anti-Vietnam activists. . . . Each chapter includes commentary by McCarthy, friends, ex-lovers, admirers, and adversaries." Booklist

Includes bibliographical references

McClellan, George Brinton, 1826-1885

Sears, Stephen W. George B. McClellan; the young Napoleon. Da Capo Press 1999 482p il map pa $16.95   **92**

1. Generals 2. United States—History—1861-1865, Civil War
ISBN 0-306-80913-3   LC 98-33277
First published 1988 by Ticknor & Fields

This biography of the Civil War general "covers both the awkward character traits that led to McClellan's incompetence and the battlefield actions that he regularly bungled. In addition to its merit as Civil War history, the book is of great interest as the portrait of an intelligent man working at what he failed to realize was the wrong profession." Atlantic

Includes bibliographical references

McCourt, Frank

McCourt, Frank. Angela's ashes; a memoir. Scribner 1996 364p il $25; pa $14 *   **92**

1. Irish Americans
ISBN 0-684-87435-0; 0-684-84267-X (pa)
                                        LC 96-5335

McCourt, Frank—*Continued*

"Frank McCourt, a teacher, grandfather and occasional actor, was born in New York City, but grew up in the Irish town of Limerick during the grim 1930's and 40's before he came back here as a teen-ager. His recollections of childhood are mournful and humorous, angry and forgiving." N Y Times Book Rev

McCourt, Frank. Teacher man; a memoir. Scribner 2005 258p $26   **92**
1. Irish Americans
ISBN 0-7432-4377-3   LC 2005-54113
The author presents an account of his teaching career. "Frank McCourt spent three decades teaching in New York City, conducting, by his count, at least 33,000 classes and instructing some 12,000 students. He taught days and nights and summers. He taught basic English to immigrants and creative writing to the college-bound." N Y Times (Late N Y Ed)
"Full of gritty specifics, never preachy, often hilarious, McCourt's . . . book thrusts you right into the hormones-and-catcalls chaos of the classroom—where learning is not just a mystery but a flat-out miracle." Newsweek

McCourt, Frank. 'Tis; a memoir. Scribner 1999 367p pa $14 hardcover o.p.   **92**
1. Irish Americans
ISBN 0-684-86574-2 (pa)   LC 99-31280
Sequel to Angela's ashes
This volume "takes McCourt from his arrival in America and subsequent service in the Korean War through the mid-1980s. . . . This memoir features a mesmerizing narrative fraught with sufferings. It triumphs by effecting a genuinely comic meditation upon human frailty, grace and possibility." Publ Wkly

McCourt, Malachy, 1931-

McCourt, Malachy. A monk swimming. Hyperion 1998 290p $23.95; pa $14   **92**
ISBN 0-7868-6398-6; 0-7868-8414-2 (pa)
LC 97-46720
The author recounts stories of his "serendipitous success as an actor and a bar owner after arriving in New York penniless and uneducated." Booklist
"The memoir, which covers ground through 1963, will have readers smiling and laughing constantly." Publ Wkly

McCourt, Malachy. Singing my him song. HarperCollins Pubs. 2000 242p pa $14 hardcover o.p.   **92**
ISBN 0-06-095548-1 (pa)   LC 00-59774
In this sequel to A monk swimming, "McCourt tells us the rest of his story; how he got from there to here, how he went from living the headlong and heedless life of a world-class drunk to becoming a sober, loving father and grandfather, still happily married after thirty-five years." Publisher's note

McCullers, Carson, 1917-1967

Savigneau, Josyane. Carson McCullers; a life; translated by Joan E. Howard. Houghton Mifflin 2001 370p il $30   **92**
ISBN 0-395-87820-9   LC 00-46547

In this biography the author explores "McCuller's life as a writer and on the 'adolescent spirit' that she says not only permeated McCuller's work but also characterized her personal relationships with fellow writers like Tennessee Williams and Truman Capote as well as with members of her family." N Y Times Book Rev
This is a "heartfelt, honest portrait of one of the great novelists of the American South." Libr J
Includes bibliographical references

McDaniel, Hattie, 1895-1952

Jackson, Carlton. Hattie: the life of Hattie McDaniel. Madison Bks. 1989 220p il pa $12.95 hardcover o.p.   **92**
ISBN 1-56833-004-9 (pa)   LC 89-30903
"For those of us who knew her only as 'Mammy' in *Gone with the Wind,* Hattie McDaniel's life story holds lots of surprises. She was also a singer, songwriter, and radio, stage, and TV performer. With an anecdotal style, the author clears up a lot of errors concerning her career." Booklist
Includes bibliographical references

Watts, Jill. Hattie McDaniel; black ambition, white Hollywood. Amistad 2005 352p il $27.95   **92**
ISBN 0-06-051490-6   LC 2005-42126
This biography "tracks the career of the actress who, in 1940, became the first African-American ever to win an Oscar (for her role as Mammy in 'Gone With the Wind')." N Y Times Book Rev
"Watts is both sympathetic and honest: we pity McDaniel and her unenviable position, but at the same time, see how her intense careerism drove her often to accommodate rather than challenge film industry racism. . . . Watts' research is extensive, her writing clear and accessible, and her book a thorough, engaging, intelligent piece of historical scholarship." Women's Rev of Books

McDermott, Mickey, 1928-2003

McDermott, Mickey. A funny thing happened on the way to Cooperstown; {by} Mickey McDermott with Howard Eisenberg. Triumph 2003 270p il $24.95   **92**
1. Baseball—Biography
ISBN 1-57243-532-1   LC 2002-45573
McDermott "won 18 games for the Boston Red Sox in 1951 and seemed a sure thing, but he finished a lackluster career with 69 wins and 69 losses. . . . After leaving baseball, McDermott struggled at various jobs until, unbelievably, he won $7 million in the Arizona state lottery in 1991. With the help of coauthor Eisenberg, he tells the story of his life and wild times in this thoroughly engaging memoir." Booklist

McDougal, Susan

McDougal, Susan. The woman who wouldn't talk; {by} Susan McDougal with Pat Harris; introduction by Helen Thomas. Carroll & Graf Pubs. 2003 384p il $25; pa $14   **92**
1. Clinton, Bill, 1946-—Impeachment
ISBN 0-7867-1128-0; 0-7867-1302-X (pa)
LC 2002-192705

McDougal, Susan—*Continued*

Includes index

"In the 1996 Whitewater investigation, McDougal was indicted for fraud over a $300,000 loan, claiming that only her ex-husband, Jim McDougal, knew the money's intended purpose. Kenneth Starr, head of the Office of the Independent Counsel investigating Whitewater, offered her leniency if she would implicate President Clinton and Hillary Clinton. McDougal refused to testify, she writes, because she didn't want her statements about the Clintons' innocence twisted into perjury by the Starr Commission. She spent the next 21 months in prison on a charge of civil contempt. McDougal has written an engaging, sometimes gossipy, insightful biography, notable for its accounts of her different trials and more so for the depiction of life in women's prisons." Libr J

McEnroe, John

McEnroe, John. You cannot be serious; {by} John McEnroe with Jams Kaplan. Putnam 2002 342p il $25.95; pa $14   **92**

ISBN 0-399-14858-2; 0-425-19008-0 (pa)

LC 2002-23875

Tennis star McEnroe's "recollections fall into three categories: accounts of key matches, life as a jet-setting celebrity, and reflections on the emotional roller coaster that has been his personal life." Booklist

McKinley, William, 1843-1901

Phillips, Kevin P. William McKinley; {by} Kevin Phillips. Times Bks. 2003 188p (American presidents series) $20 *   **92**

1. United States—Politics and government—1898-1919

ISBN 0-8050-6953-4   LC 2003-50701

Phillips portrays a "'surprisingly modern McKinley' who honored Booker T. Washington and competently directed the Spanish-American War by cable and telephone; 'the egalitarian who ran with the Grangers and promoted women's rights, the "people's candidate" who beat the Eastern bosses, the man who wouldn't have a lobbyist in his cabinet, the cautious reformer who was on the verge of leading a fight to curb the trusts, reform the tariff system and reenact a progressive income tax.'" N Y Times Book Rev

"This little work of rehabilitation should help set McKinley's reputation right." Publ Wkly

Includes bibliographical references

McMurtry, Larry

McMurtry, Larry. Walter Benjamin at the Dairy Queen; reflections at sixty and beyond. Simon & Schuster 1999 204p il pa $12 hardcover o.p.

   92

ISBN 0-684-87019-3 (pa)   LC 99-19346

"When McMurtry recalls reading 'Don Quixote' as a thirteen-year-old on a Texas ranch and imagining himself as a character in the novel, other obsessional readers will immediately feel a kinship with this author. His appealing ruminations about his life and work as a reader, writer, and bookseller explore the differences between 'dense and empty, open and closed, new country and old cities,

no society and old society'—the bare land in which he was reared and the crowded universe of literature." New Yorker

McPherson, Aimee Semple, 1890-1944

Epstein, Daniel Mark. Sister Aimee: the life of Aimee Semple McPherson 1993 475p il pa $18 hardcover o.p.   **92**

ISBN 0-15-600093-8 (pa)   LC 92-23324

This is a biography of the American evangelist and faith healer

"Any secular treatment of a subject who claims divine inspiration must sooner or later confront The Question: did God actually speak to her? Epstein's hedge is that Sister Aimee believed He did. . . . On the whole, however, the book is a lively read. That it is neither hagiography nor exposé is its strength as well as its weakness. Sister Aimee emerges as an unlikely yet compelling heroine." Natl Rev

Includes bibliographical references

Mead, Margaret, 1901-1978

Mead, Margaret. Blackberry winter; my earlier years; with a new introduction by Nancy Lutkehaus. Kodansha International 1995 305p il (Kodansha globe) pa $15   **92**

1. Anthropologists

ISBN 1-568-36069-X; 978-1-568-36069-0

LC 95-13302

First published 1972 by Morrow

"About one-third of Mead's autobiography covers the years before she became an anthropologist and another third her field work in Samoa, in New Guinea, among the Omaha Indians, and in Bali. . . . The concluding chapters . . . describe in subjective detail her role as mother and grandmother." Choice

Includes bibliographical references

Meegeren, Han van, 1889-1947

Dolnick, Edward. The forger's spell; a true story of Vermeer, Nazis, and the greatest art hoax of the twentieth century. HarperCollins 2008 349p il $26.95   **92**

1. Vermeer, Johannes, 1632-1675 2. Art—Forgeries 3. World War, 1939-1945—Art and the war

ISBN 978-0-06-082541-6; 0-06-082541-3

LC 2007-36578

This is an account of the Vermeer forgeries done by the Dutch painter Han van Meegeren during the late 1930s and early 1940s.

"Dolnick's zesty, incisive, and entertaining inquiry illuminates the hidden dimensions and explicates the far-reaching implications of this fascinating and provocative collision of art and ambition, deception and war." Booklist

Includes bibliographical references

Meiji, Emperor of Japan, 1852-1912

Keene, Donald. Emperor of Japan: Meiji and His world, 1852-1912. Columbia Univ. Press 2002 922p il $82.50; pa $27.95   **92**

1. Japan—History—1868-1945

ISBN 0-231-12340-X; 0-231-12341-8 (pa)

LC 2001-28826

This is a "biography-cum-history of Emperor Meiji and his times. . . . Meiji's reign saw Japan become fully industrialized under a brand new constitution, and with new economic and educational systems adopted. Despite the book's massive scale, Keene's graceful writing holds the reader's interest throughout." Booklist

Includes bibliographical references

Mellon, Andrew William, 1855-1937

Cannadine, David. Mellon; an American life. A.A. Knopf 2006 779p il $35 *   **92**

ISBN 0-679-45032-7; 978-0-679-45032-0

LC 2006-45116

This is a "biography of Andrew Mellon, the powerful American financier, secretary of the treasury, and art collector. . . . Cannadine's recounting of Mellon's public career make this a worthy contribution to our understanding of the man and his era." Booklist

Includes bibliographical references

Melville, Herman, 1819-1891

Delbanco, Andrew. Melville; his world and work. Knopf 2005 xxiii, 415p il map $30
          92

1. Authors, American

ISBN 0-375-40314-0   LC 2005-40919

This book "places the great novelist . . . in his time and delves into his works' continuing significance." Publ Wkly

"This is sure to elicit new appreciation for Melville's work and could well be the best one-volume biography for some time to come." Libr J

Includes bibliographical references

Hardwick, Elizabeth. Herman Melville. Viking 2000 161p (Penguin lives series) $19.95
          92

1. Authors, American

ISBN 0-670-89158-4   LC 00-36510

"A Lipper/Viking book"

"Interweaving critical readings of his fiction and poetry with events in Melville's life, Hardwick offers glimpses into his tortured writing career, his sometimes difficult family life, and his ambivalent relationship with his friend Nathaniel Hawthorne." Libr J

Includes bibliographical references

Parker, Hershel. Herman Melville; a biography. v1: 1819-1851. Johns Hopkins Univ. Press 1996 942p il maps $50; pa $29.95   **92**

1. Authors, American

ISBN 0-8018-5428-8; 0-8018-8185-4 (pa)

LC 96-18984

This, the first volume of a two-volume "biography of Melville, ends in 1851, when the author presented to his . . . friend Nathaniel Hawthorne an inscribed pre-publication copy of Moby-Dick." Atl Mon

Includes bibliographical references

Parker, Hershel. Herman Melville; a biography. v2: 1851-1891. Johns Hopkins Univ. Press 2002 1,184p il maps $50; pa $29.95   **92**

1. Authors, American

ISBN 0-8018-6892-0; 0-8018-8186-2 (pa)

"This second volume opens with American readers' hostile reaction to . . . [Moby Dick] for not being like his earlier successes, Typee and Omoo. With immense sympathy, Parker relates how Melville's intellectual growth resulted in his writing novels that were increasingly obscure to his ever-diminishing readership, and how, in his early 30s, as a husband and a father of four, his repeated failures curdled his spirit and caused him to withdraw into himself." Libr J

"A magnificent achievement . . . Hershel Parker's magnum opus is a magisterial work of retrieval and un-flagging scholarship." Times Lit Suppl

Includes bibliographical references

Robertson-Lorant, Laurie. Melville; a biography. University of Massachusetts Press 1998 710p il pa $29.95   **92**

1. Authors, American

ISBN 1-55849-145-7; 978-1-55849-145-8

LC 98-4899

First published 1996 by Potter

"With access to more than 500 recently discovered Melville family letters, which show Melville to have been a functioning member of a problem-torn extended family, Robertson-Lorant corrects our traditional view of the older Melville as isolato. Instead, he appears here to represent the social consciousness of 19th century America. Together with jargon-free, user-friendly commentary on all Melville's major works. Robertson-Lorant offers an array of historical phenomena . . . that provide an invaluable context for Melville's life and art." Libr J

Includes bibliographical references

Mencken, H. L. (Henry Louis), 1880-1956

Mencken, H. L. (Henry Louis). My life as author and editor; edited and with an introduction by Jonathan Yardley. Knopf 1993 xxi, 449p $30; pa $25 *   **92**

ISBN 0-679-41315-4; 0-679-74102-X (pa)

LC 92-4496

Mencken's "memoir, which he set aside in 1948 following a severe stroke and ordered locked away for 35 years after his death, covers his literary apprenticeship, his co-editorship of The Smart Set and his feuds and friendships with Theodore Dreiser, Sinclair Lewis, F. Scott Fitzgerald, Ezra Pound, Alfred Knopf and others." Publ Wkly

An "absorbing memoir that anyone who cares about modern American literature will want to read." N Y Times Book Rev

Rodgers, Marion Elizabeth. Mencken; the American iconoclast. Oxford University Press 2005 662p il $35   **92**

ISBN 0-19-507238-3   LC 2005-47786

The author offers a "look at the 'bad boy of Baltimore' who grew to international fame and influence." Booklist

"This is a meticulous portrait of one of the most origi-

Mencken, H. L. (Henry Louis), 1880-1956—
Continued
nal and complicated men in American letters." Publ
Wkly
   Includes bibliographical references

Teachout, Terry. The skeptic: the life of H.L.
Mencken. HarperCollins Pubs. 2002 410p il
$29.95; pa $15.95 **92**
   ISBN 0-06-050528-1; 0-06-050529-X (pa)
                              LC 2002-24953
   "This biography copes with Mencken's crankiness, his
provinciality and his inability to believe Germany was
doing wrong in the 20th century by placing them in con-
temporary contexts." N Y Times Book Rev
   This is "an engrossing, sympathetic biography."
Booklist
   Includes bibliograpical references

Mendel, Gregor, 1822-1884
Henig, Robin Marantz. The monk in the garden:
how Gregor Mendel and his pea plants solved the
mystery of inheritance. Houghton Mifflin 2000
292p il $24; pa $14 **92**
   ISBN 0-395-97765-7; 0-618-12741-0 (pa)
                              LC 00-24341
   The author explores "Mendel's personality and experiments. The latter lasted but a few years in the 1850s and
1860s, ending when Mendel became the abbot of his
monastery in what is now Brno in the Czech Republic.
Henig crisply conveys how the laws of inheritance that
Mendel derived from his statistical analysis remained unnoticed until several botanists who discovered them inde-
pendently in 1900 also learned that Mendel found them
first. This biography itself rediscovers a scientist often
mentioned but insufficently known." Booklist

Mendeleev, Dmitri I.
Gordin, Michael D. A well-ordered thing:
Dmitrii Mendeleev and the shadow of the periodic
table. Basic Books 2004 364p il $30 *
                                          92
   1. Periodic law
   ISBN 0-465-02775-X   LC 2003-25533
   This is an account of the "man who organized chemistry into the periodic table—and of how he tried to organize Imperial Russia." Publisher's note
   "This is not a chronological biography of the man;
rather, it is a work that shows Mendeleev as an important part of the changes that occurred in Russia during
the days between the freeing of the serfs in 1861 and the
crumbling of tsarist power in 1905." Sci Books & Films
   Includes bibliographical references

Mendelsohn, Daniel, 1960-
Mendelsohn, Daniel. The lost; a search for six
of six million; photographs by Matt Mendelsohn.
HarperCollins Publishers 2006 512p il $27.95
                                          92
   1. Holocaust, 1933-1945
   ISBN 0-06-054297-7   LC 2006-41096

The author describes his efforts to find out what happened to his uncle Shmiel Jager, his wife and four
daughters, who lived in the Polish town of Bolechow,
and perished during the Holocaust.
   "Mr. Mendelsohn, an evocative, ruminative writer,
brings to life the vanished world not just of prewar Poland but also of his childhood and his extended family."
N Y Times (Late N Y Ed)

Mendelssohn, Felix, 1809-1847
Mercer-Taylor, Peter Jameson. The life of
Mendelssohn; [by] Peter Mercer-Taylor.
Cambridge Univ. Press 2000 238p il (Musical
lives) hardcover o.p. pa $34.99 **92**
   1. Composers
   ISBN 0-521-63025-8; 0-521-63972-7 (pa)
                              LC 99-58441
   A study of "the composer and his music, family history, cultural setting, and creative aspirations. . . . The
book contains no musical examples but plentiful allusions to monumental works in the Western art music tradition. . . . The author describes pieces in ways music
lovers can appreciate and places the composer in the
context of his times for historians who seek breadth in
biographies. The bibliographic essay . . . guides readers
to other sources." Libr J
   "The book is well written, carefully produced, and a
pleasure to read." Choice

Merton, Thomas, 1915-1968
Merton, Thomas. Intimate Merton; his life from
his journals; edited by Patrick Hart and Jonathan
Montaldo. HarperSanFrancisco 1999 374p il pa
$16 hardcover o.p. **92**
   ISBN 0-06-251629-9 (pa)   LC 99-33239
   Includes index
   "This is a one-volume condensation of Merton's journals, which have been published over the last few years;
its seven chapters correspond to the seven volumes of
Merton's complete journals. . . . {The editors} have
maintained all of Merton's central themes—including
controversial ones, like the relationship with the nurse
identified as 'M.' and Merton's doubts about his vocation." Libr J

Merton, Thomas. The seven storey mountain.
Fiftieth anniversary edition. Harcourt Brace & Co.
1998 467p $35; pa $16 * **92**
   ISBN 0-15-100413-7; 0-15-601086-0 (pa)
                              LC 98-198169
   First published 1948. This edition "includes an introduction by Merton's editor, Robert Giroux, and a reader's note by biographer and Thomas Merton Society
Founder Fr. William Shannon." Libr J
   "The autobiography of a poet who became a convert
to Catholicism and at the age of 26 after a full and traveled world career as student and teacher, entered a Trap-
pist monastery." Publ Wkly

Micheaux, Oscar, 1884-1951

McGilligan, Patrick. Oscar Micheaux; the great and only; the life of America's first great Black filmmaker. HarperCollins Publishers 2007 402p il $29.95 **92**

ISBN 978-0-06-073139-7; 0-06-073130-7

LC 2007-60735

"One of the fascinating side streets in American film is the history of 'race pictures,' celluloid productions by black artists for black audiences during those decades when Jim Crow laws enforced segregation. The mainstay of race pictures was Oscar Micheaux (18841951), an intrepid filmmaker-novelist-entrepreneur whose career spanned four decades and who made more than 40 movies. . . . McGilligan's prose style may be pedestrian, but he organizes his biographical materials into a lively, readable tale." N Y Times Book Rev

Mill, John Stuart, 1806-1873

Mill, John Stuart. Autobiography; edited with an introduction by John M. Robson. Penguin Bks. 1989 234p pa $8.95 * **92**

1. Philosophers

ISBN 0-14-043316-3 LC 91-103446

Written 1873

"A human document of unusual interest. Mill, a noble spirit educated by a narrow-minded pedant, shut off from all normal contact, developed an egotism that makes this book so completely an autobiography that besides his father and [his] wife he seems to exist alone in a world of which he has both center and circumference." Pratt Alcove

Includes bibliographical references

Millay, Edna St. Vincent, 1892-1950

Milford, Nancy. Savage beauty: the life of Edna St. Vincent Millay. Random House 2001 550p il $29.95; pa $14.95 **92**

ISBN 0-394-57589-X; 0-375-76081-4 (pa)

LC 2001-18598

"In 1923, Edna St. Vincent Millay became the first woman to win the Pulitzer Prize for poetry. To write her biography, Milford . . . persuaded Millay's younger sister and sole heir, Norma, to give her access to hundreds of Millay's personal papers, letters, and notebooks. Selecting from 'this extraordinary collection,' Milford meticulously integrates Millay's major poems, letters received and sent, reactions of friends, and comments from extensive interviews with Norma into an orderly and affecting narrative." Libr J

Includes bibliographical references

Miller, Arthur, 1915-2005

Gottfried, Martin. Arthur Miller; his life and work. Da Capo Press 2003 484p il hardcover o.p. pa $18 **92**

ISBN 0-306812-14-2; 0-306813-77-7 (pa)

LC 2004-298989

This biography "portrays Miller as a representative of the 20th century and establishes him among the giants of US, perhaps world, drama. . . . [The author] discusses the importance of Miller's marriages, his immense and

uninterrupted popularity in Great Britain, the erosion and resurrection of his reputation in the US, his involvement with Hollywood, and his political activities, especially with the director Elia Kazan and the House Committee on Un-American Activities." Choice

This is "an uncomfortable, challenging work, forbidding us any bien-pensant ease, and we should be grateful for it." Times Lit Suppl

Includes bibliographical references

Miller, Emmett

Tosches, Nick. Where dead voices gather. Little, Brown 2001 330p $24.95; pa $14.95 **92**

ISBN 0-316-89507-5; 0-316-89537-7 (pa)

LC 2001-18608

This book "attempts to rescue from obscurity the blackface performer and minstrel singer Emmett Miller, who gained brief fame in the twenties and thirties, and who left behind only a handful of recordings at his death, in 1962." New Yorker

"As engrossing as a great mystery novel, this is essential for libraries with a focus on American popular culture." Libr J

Miller, Lee, 1907-1977

Burke, Carolyn. Lee Miller; a life. Knopf 2005 426p il $35 * **92**

ISBN 0-375-40147-4 LC 2004-43844

This is a biography of the model and photographer.

This "sympathetic tribute sheds further light on the lives of this highly original, often misunderstood woman." Economist

Includes bibliographical references

Miller, Sue

Miller, Sue. The story of my father; a memoir. Knopf 2003 173p il $22.50; pa $12.95 **92**

ISBN 0-375-41479-7; 0-345-45544-4 (pa)

LC 2002-69460

This is the author's "remembrance of her relationship with her father, especially during his later years, when his memory loss caused by Alzheimer's became apparent. It is also a meditation on the meaning of writing in her life." Libr J

"A familiar but still touching story of a parent's descent into Alzheimer's disease; the deeper Miller's father sinks into confusion, the more powerfully candid her writing becomes." N Y Times Book Rev

Millner, Caille, 1979-

Millner, Caille. The golden road; notes on my gentrification. Penguin Press 2007 248p $22.95

92

ISBN 978-1-59420-109-7; 1-59420-109-9

LC 2006-51010

The author "uses her own story to explore geographic and personal notions of place and the effects of change on both. The product of a troubled family and raised in Latino and Caucasian neighborhoods, she searches for her identity as a black woman, a search complicated by her parents' efforts to succeed in white America and

Millner, Caille, 1979-—*Continued*

their determination that their children do the same. . . . In quietly mesmerizing prose informed throughout by an attitude of wry objectivity, Millner makes her life thus far compelling reading and an outstanding addition to a crowded field." Libr J

Min, Anchee, 1957-

Min, Anchee. Red Azalea. Anchor Books 2006 306p pa $13   **92**

1. China—History—1949-
ISBN 978-1-4000-9698-5; 1-4000-9698-7
                                          LC 2006-271433
First published 1994 by Pantheon Bks.

"In this memoir of growing up in China during the Cultural Revolution, sexual freedom becomes a powerful political as well as literary statement." N Y Times Book Rev

Mingus, Charles, 1922-1979

Santoro, Gene. Myself when I am real: the life and music of Charles Mingus. Oxford Univ. Press 2000 452p hardcover o.p. pa $17.95   **92**
ISBN 0-19-509733-5; 0-19-514711-1 (pa)
                                          LC 99-46734
The author "has attempted not only to capture the complex, contradictory character of jazz bassist and composer Mingus, but also to assert his music's towering significance in American culture as a whole." Publ Wkly
Includes discography and bibliographical references

Mitchell, Andrea

Mitchell, Andrea. Talking back—to presidents, dictators, and assorted scoundrels. Viking 2005 414p il $25.95   **92**
ISBN 0-670-03403-7   LC 2005-42279
In this "memoir, Mitchell recalls her climb to the top of her profession, including stints at NBC Nightly News, Today, and Meet the Press." Booklist
This "is a collection of good stories, inside dope and real-life quandaries, all from someone still eager enough to compare herself to Nancy Drew and Brenda Starr." Am Journalism Rev

Moaveni, Azadeh, 1976-

Moaveni, Azadeh. Lipstick jihad; a memoir of growing up Iranian in America and American in Iran. Public Affairs 2005 249p $25; pa $13
                                                  92
1. Iran
ISBN 1-58648-193-2; 1-58648-378-1 (pa)
                                          LC 2004-43184
"Moaveni, an Iranian-American who grew up in California, decided to embark on a journey in spring 2000 to rediscover her Iranian heritage. In this account, she . . . conveys the tensions she observed between the fundamentalist mullahs and younger Iranians, who are pushing for a more Westernized, modern Iran. . . . A charming and informative memoir." Libr J

Mongkut, King of Siam, 1804-1868

Landon, Margaret. Anna and the King of Siam. See entry under Leonowens, Anna Harriette, 1834-1914

Monroe, Bill, 1911-1996

Smith, Richard D. Can't you hear me callin': the life of Bill Monroe, father of bluegrass. Little, Brown 2000 365p il $25.95   **92**
ISBN 0-316-80381-2   LC 99-54372
Also available in paperback from Da Capo Press
The author traces Monroe's "life from a music-rich but isolated childhood in the pastoral backroads of Kentucky to his early years as a struggling professional musician to his well-deserved status as an acclaimed elder statesman and musical ambassador. . . . A sensitive, tasteful, well-balanced portrait of a complicated man." Booklist
Includes discography, videography and bibliographical references

Monroe, Marilyn, 1926-1962

Leaming, Barbara. Marilyn Monroe. Crown 1998 464p il pa $16 hardcover o.p.   **92**
ISBN 0-609-80553-3 (pa)   LC 98-18738
In this biography the film star "emerges as a smart perfectionist riddled with self-doubt and self-destructive tendencies. . . . The story of Monroe's life reads tragically from day one. . . . It was a life that despite the bright light of fame shining on it for many years could only be described as one long downward spiral." Booklist
Learning "has a sure dramatic instinct for illuminating overlooked material and re-examining the most interesting episodes." N Y Times Book Rev

Mooney, Jonathan

Mooney, Jonathan. The short bus; a journey beyond normal. H. Holt 2007 272p $25
                                                  92
1. Handicapped students
ISBN 978-0-8050-7427-7; 0-8050-7427-9
                                          LC 2006-52588
"Considered learning disabled as a child, Mooney still managed to graduate with honors from Brown. Here he recounts a four-month cross-country trip to meet children and adults who have similarly triumphed." Libr J
The author's "target audience is not policy makers but his fellow misfits, and his boundless empathy will surely console those who also face the worst that cruel schoolchildren and the educational bureaucracy have to offer." N Y Times Book Rev

Moore, Honor, 1945-

Moore, Honor. The bishop's daughter; a memoir. W. W. Norton & Co. 2008 365p il $25.95   **92**
1. Moore, Paul, 1919-2003
ISBN 978-0-393-05984-7   LC 2008-01337
This is a memoir by Paul Moore's daughter. Moore "retired in 1989 as the Episcopal bishop of the Diocese

Moore, Honor, 1945-—*Continued*
of New York." N Y Times Book Rev
This is "a generous and thought-provoking chronicle
of public altruism and private betrayal, high ideals and
forbidden desire, love and forgiveness." Booklist
Includes bibliographical references

Moore, Marianne, 1887-1972
Molesworth, Charles. Marianne Moore; a
literary life. Northeastern University Press 1991
xxii, 472p il pa $16.95   **92**
1. Poets, American
ISBN 1-555-53115-6   LC 91-13570
First published 1990 by Atheneum Pubs.
"Molesworth charts the growth of a major modernist
through careful critical readings of her poetry and prose,
her work as an editor of the Dial, and an examination of
Moore as an active, social New York literary figure
whose colleagues and admirers included T.S. Eliot and
Ezra Pound." Publ Wkly
Includes bibliographical references

Moore, Michael
Rapoport, Roger. Citizen Moore; the life and
times of an American iconoclast. RDR 2006 310p
il $15.95   **92**
1. Motion picture producers and directors—Biography
ISBN 1-57143-163-2; 9781571431639 (pa)
In this biography of the controversial filmmaker, the
author "compares Moore to Upton Sinclair and Ralph
Nader, chronicling the filmmaker's early activism, community organizing, radio and theater career, and involvement in alternative journalism. . . . In this engaging profile, Rapoport portrays the quirks and complexities of a
man whose life is as fascinating as his films." Booklist

Moore, Paul, 1919-2003
Moore, Honor. The bishop's daughter. See entry
under Moore, Honor, 1945-

Morgan, J. Pierpont (John Pierpont), 1837-1913
Strouse, Jean. Morgan; American financier.
HarperPerennial 2000 796p il pa $18   **92**
1. Businesspeople
ISBN 0-06-095589-9; 978-0-06-095589-2
                                      LC 99-87598
First published 1999 by Random House
This biography "focuses on the accomplishments and
failures of Morgan as financier, art collector, and American." Libr J
"Strouse is in full command of Pierpont Morgan's personal life, his financial operations, his collecting, and his
benefactions, and presents a rich, vivid picture of the
background against which they took place. . . . She has
written a magnificent biography, which illuminates her
subject and his world." N Y Rev Books
Includes bibliographical references

Morris, Tom, 1821-1908
Cook, Kevin. Tommy's honor. See entry under
Morris, Tom, 1851-1875

Morris, Tom, 1851-1875
Cook, Kevin. Tommy's honor; the story of old
Tom Morris and young Tom Morris, golf's
founding father and son. Gotham Books 2007
327p il $27.50   **92**
1. Morris, Tom, 1821-1908 2. Golf
ISBN 978-1-59240-297-7; 1-59240-297-6
                                      LC 2007-8165
"In Cook's telling, the story of Tom Morris, winner of
golf's first Open Championship in 1860, and his son,
Tommy, who won the Open three years in a row, be-
comes a compelling saga of near-Homeric proportions."
Booklist
Includes bibliographical references

Morris, Willie
Morris, Willie. My dog Skip. Random House
1995 122p il pa $10 hardcover o.p.   **92**
1. Dogs
ISBN 0-679-76722-3 (pa)   LC 94-41637
"Morris remembers back to the boy-and-his-dog days
in his small hometown in the Deep South, where Skip
was involved in all of his pranks and escapades. Poignancy rather than humor is the pervading tone of this
ode to a steadfast presence." Booklist

Morrison, Jim, 1943-1971
Hopkins, Jerry. No one here gets out alive; by
Jerry Hopkins and Daniel Sugerman. Warner Bks.
1980 387p il pa $7.99 hardcover o.p.   **92**
1. Doors (Musical group)
ISBN 0-446-60228-0 (pa)   LC 79-26611
This biography of rock musician Jim Morrison gives
"an idea of how profoundly Morrison, as lyricist and
lead singer of the Doors, affected the youth of America
in the late 1960s. . . . The book includes a list of the
Doors' records, books, and films." Booklist

Riordan, James. Break on through: the life and
death of Jim Morrison; [by] James Riordan and
Jerry Prochnicky. Morrow 1991 544p il pa $15
hardcover o.p.   **92**
1. Doors (Musical group)
ISBN 0-688-11915-8 (pa)   LC 90-26580
This look at the life and work of Jim Morrison is
"well documented and avoids unfounded speculation and
unnecessary tales of debauchery common to many other
rock 'n' roll biographies. . . . An excellent biography of
a true rock icon." Choice
Includes discography and bibliographical references

Morse, Samuel Finley Breese, 1791-1872
Silverman, Kenneth. Lightning man; the
accursed life of Samuel F.B. Morse. Knopf 2003
503p il $35 *   **92**
ISBN 0-375-40128-8   LC 2002-43613
Also available in paperback from Da Capo Press
This is a "biography of Samuel F.B. Morse, the inven-
tor of the Morse code and the disputed inventor of the
electromagnetic telegraph. . . . Silverman shows how
Morse's never-ending battle with negative self-image, a

Morse, Samuel Finley Breese, 1791-1872—*Continued*

result of his strict Calvinist upbringing, was the common thread that tied together the disparate events of his life. And Silverman's well-paced, character-driven storytelling brings Morse's raw, emotional persona to life. Strongly recommend for public libraries and for academic library collections at all levels." Libr J

Moses, Robert, 1888-1981

Caro, Robert A. The power broker: Robert Moses and the fall of New York. Knopf 1974 1246, xxxivp il $50; pa $21.95   **92**
ISBN 0-394-48076-7; 0-394-72024-5 (pa)

This is a biographical critique of the man who in four decades as a public official "built most of the parks, bridges and highways in and around New York City." Newsweek

Includes bibliographical references

Mowat, Farley

King, James. Farley: the life of Farley Mowat. Steerforth Press 2002 397p il $27.95   **92**
ISBN 1-58642-055-0   LC 2002-151149

The author "recounts Mowat's life from his experience in college to his service in World War II and his work in the Northwest Territories as a student biologist. The emerging portrait is of a man whose evolution as both an environmentalist and an artist was profound, an activist who has never backed away from a controversy. The exploration of Mowat's life is detailed but never boring." Libr J

Includes bibliographical references

Mowat, Farley. Born naked. Houghton Mifflin 1994 c1993 256p il maps pa $13 hardcover o.p.
                                                  92
ISBN 0-395-73528-9 (pa)   LC 93-23702

"A Peter Davison book"

First published 1993 in Canada

The "renowned naturalist and writer gives us a glimpse of his parents, his growing up in Canada, and the roots of his love for animals." Booklist

"There are no dull pages here; every man, woman, child, and animal mentioned even casually makes an impression. . . . Highly recommended to all those who like good writing." Libr J

Moyers, William C.

Moyers, William C. Broken: my story of addiction and redemption; [by] William Cope Moyers with Katherine Ketcham. Viking 2006 372p il $25.95   **92**
ISBN 0-670-03789-3; 978-0-670-03789-6
                                  LC 2006-41378

This is an autobiography of "the prodigal son of Bill Moyers, the exemplary broadcast journalist, [who] wrecked a bright career at CNN and deserted his family in 1994, hitting bottom as a 'thirty-five-year-old crack addict.'" Publ Wkly

The author's "gripping account of his struggles with alcohol and crack addiction will have readers rooting for him from the very beginning." Libr J

Moynihan, Daniel Patrick, 1927-2003

Hodgson, Godfrey. The gentleman from New York: Daniel Patrick Moynihan: a biography. Houghton Mifflin 2000 452p il $38   **92**
ISBN 0-395-86042-3   LC 00-38921

"A cold war liberal, more of a regular Democrat than a reformer, Moynihan will no doubt be remembered as one of the smarter, more thoughtful elected officials of the late twentieth century. Others will probably produce more critical biographies, but, for now, Hodgson has supplied a fairly balanced overview." Booklist

Includes bibliographical references

Mozart, Wolfgang Amadeus, 1756-1791

Einstein, Alfred. Mozart; his character, his work; translated by Arthur Mendel and Nathan Broder. Oxford Univ. Press 1945 492p il music pa $22.50 hardcover o.p.   **92**
1. Composers
ISBN 0-19-500732-8 (pa)

The author's "examination of the events of Mozart's life in relation to his character, and even more, his analysis of the sources, models, and methods of the musician's creative processes are penetrating and illuminating." Christ Sci Monit

Gutman, Robert W. Mozart; a cultural biography. Harcourt Brace & Co. 1999 839p hardcover o.p. pa $25   **92**
1. Composers
ISBN 978-0-15-601171-6 (pa); 0-15-601171-9 (pa)
                                  LC 99-31953

The author interweaves "the chronology of Mozart's life and musical compositions with essays on the social, political, and religious fabrics of the 18th century, offering extended discourses on the Enlightenment, *Sturm und Drang*, Freemasonry, and other movements that influenced the composer both personally and in his works." Libr J

Includes bibliographical references

Mozart, Wolfgang Amadeus. Mozart's letters, Mozart's life; selected letters; edited and newly translated by Robert Spaethling. Norton 2000 479p il $35; pa $19.95   **92**
1. Composers
ISBN 978-0-393-04719-6; 978-0-393-32830-1 (pa)
                                  LC 00-25530

"For this collection, Robert Spaethling has carefully chosen letters written by Mozart over a span of almost twenty-two years—from his first journey to Italy as a shy teenager to the final months of his life in Vienna. The letters, together with the accompanying introductions, chronicle the composer's life, personal development, and artistic growth." Publisher's note

This is a "wonderful collection that gives Mozart a voice as a son, husband, brother and friend. Mozart's main subjects were his composing and performing, but he usually digresses into love for his parents, his sister and his wife, Constanze. And there was a bawdy side, too, to the composer of such elegant music." N Y Times Book Rev

Includes bibliographical references

Mozart, Wolfgang Amadeus, 1756-1791—*Continued*

Solomon, Maynard. Mozart; a life. HarperCollins Pubs. 1995 640p il hardcover o.p. pa $22.95   **92**

1. Composers
ISBN 0-06-019046-9; 978-0-06-088344-7 (pa); 0-06-088344-8 (pa)   LC 94-42277

"The author explores Mozart's life and works with a wealth of facts that were culled from 18th-century sources as well as from the most recent scholarship. Mozart and his family emerge in a new light from this mass of well-chosen detail through Solomon's own convincing interpretation of events and relationships. Appropriate musical and pictorial examples, which will appeal to both scholarly and casual readers, accompany the text." Libr J

Includes bibliographical references

Muḥammad, d. 632

Armstrong, Karen. Muhammad; a prophet for our time. Atlas Books/HarperCollins Publishers 2006 249p map (Eminent lives) $21.95; pa $14.95   **92**

ISBN   0-06-059897-2;   978-0-06-059897-6; 0-06-115577-2 (pa); 978-0-06-115577-2 (pa)
                                         LC 2006-45864

First published 1991 in the United Kingdom with subtitle: A Western attempt to understand Islam; Original American edition published 1992 with subtitle: A biography of the prophet

This is a biography of the founder of Islam.

"Readers of these pages cannot escape the genius of Muhammad and his aim for peace and compassion among nations and among Muslims themselves. . . . Recommended for all libraries." Libr J

Includes bibliographical references

Muir, John, 1838-1914

Ehrlich, Gretel. John Muir; nature's visionary. National Geographic Soc. 2000 240p il map $35   **92**

1. Naturalists
ISBN 0-7922-7954-9   LC 00-60944

The author chronicles Muir's "life—from his self-education as a boy in Scotland and Wisconsin to his solitary cross-country treks, fruitful mountain hermitage, and cofounding of the Sierra Club. . . . Ehrlich beautifully captures Muir's essence and clearly defines the ongoing significance of his accomplishments. Lynn Johnson's gorgeous landscape photography and a wealth of wonderful archival images provide the perfect accompaniment." Booklist

Muir, John. Nature writings; the story of my boyhood and youth, my first summer in the Sierra, the mountains of California, Stickeen, selected essays. Library of Am. 1997 888p il $35   **92**

1. Naturalists
ISBN 1-88301-124-8   LC 96-9664

This compilation of Muir's writings "combines The Story of My Boyhood and Youth, My First Summer in

the Sierra, The Mountains of California, Stickeen, and a number of his essays along with illustrations, a chronology of his life, and scholarly notes." Libr J

Muir "is at his best . . . when he is looking intently at something, walking around it, sniffing the air, looking again. As a writer he is a kind of visionary sensualist, a seer who reveals what lies in plain sight." Commentary

Muir, John. The story of my boyhood and youth; with a foreword by Vernon Carstensen. University of Wisconsin Press 1965 227p pa $17.95 hardcover o.p.   **92**

1. Naturalists
ISBN 0-299-03654-5 (pa)   LC 65-14539

First published 1913 by Houghton Mifflin

"The naturalist's childhood in a strict Presbyterian home in Scotland, his boyhood experiences of the privations and out-of-door delights of pioneer life on a Wisconsin farm, and his shifts and contrivances while earning his way through the state university." Cleveland Public Libr

Wilkins, Thurman. John Muir; apostle of nature. University of Okla. Press 1995 xxvii, 302p il maps (Oklahoma western biographies) pa $21.95 hardcover o.p.   **92**

1. Naturalists
ISBN 0-8061-2797-X (pa)   LC 95-11426

"Wilkins follows Muir from his Scottish boyhood, clouded by a harsh, fundamentalist father, to an adolescence of arduous farmwork in Wisconsin to a lifelong career of exploration and study of wildernesses, particularly those of the western U.S., and vividly relates some of Muir's more perilous adventures on cliffside and snowfield. . . . An affectionate, uncluttered tale of an American folk hero." Booklist

Includes bibliographical references

Mullane, R. Mike, 1945-

Mullane, R. Mike. Riding rockets; the outrageous tales of a space shuttle astronaut; [by] Mike Mullane. Scribner 2006 368p il hardcover o.p. pa $15   **92**

ISBN 978-0-7432-7682-5; 978-0-7432-7683-2 (pa); 0-7432-7683-3 (pa)   LC 2005-56123

This is a memoir by the American astronaut.

"A strong addition to science and space collections of any size." Booklist

Munch, Edvard, 1863-1944

Prideaux, Sue. Edvard Munch; behind the Scream. Yale University Press 2005 391p il map $35   **92**

ISBN 0-300-11024-3   LC 2005-12040

The author "explores the events of . . . [Munch's] turbulent life and . . . places his experiences in their intellectual, emotional, and spiritual contexts." Publisher's note

Prideaux's "treatment is very effective and her writing, cohesive, clear, and often compelling." Libr J

Includes bibliographical references

Murdoch, Iris

Bayley, John. Elegy for Iris. See entry under Bayley, John, 1925-

Conradi, Peter. Iris Murdoch; a life; {by} Peter J. Conradi. Norton 2001 xxix, 706p il $35; pa $19.95 **92**

ISBN 0-393-04875-6; 0-393-32401-X (pa)

LC 2001-32972

Originally published: London : HaprerCollins Publishers, 2001

The author chronicles the personal, professional, and literary life of the philosopher and novelist, "documenting Murdoch's eccentricities and legendary kindnesses." Publ Wkly

"Rich footnoting leads the reader to expansions on the narrative as well as to the authority behind the biographer's statements. Scholars need this text, but it will also intrigue lay readers." Libr J

Includes bibliographical references

Murphy, Gerald, 1888-1964

Vaill, Amanda. Everybody was so young; Gerald and Sara Murphy, a lost generation love story. Broadway Bks. 1999 470p il pa $16.95 **92**

1. Murphy, Sara, 1883-1975 2. Artists—United States

ISBN 0-7679-0370-6; 978-0-7679-0370-7

LC 99-10416

First published 1998 by Houghton Mifflin

"Often considered minor Lost Generation celebrities, the Murphys were in fact much more than legendary party givers. Vaill's compelling biography unveils their role in the European avant-garde movement of the 1920s." Libr J

Includes bibliographical references

Murphy, Sara, 1883-1975

Vaill, Amanda. Everybody was so young. See entry under Murphy, Gerald, 1888-1964

Murrow, Edward R.

Edwards, Bob. Edward R. Murrow and the birth of broadcast journalism; [by] Robert A. Edwards. Wiley 2004 174p (Turning points) $19.95

92

1. Journalists

ISBN 0-471-47753-2   LC 2003-21223

"The author chronicles Murrow's innovations in radio and television broadcasting, including live radio reports of the war in progress in Europe in 1940; exposure of the despotism of Senator Joseph McCarthy on CBS in 1953; the powerful television documentary *Harvest of Shame* on the deplorable conditions of migrant workers in the U.S.; and the first in-depth television news program, *See It Now*. . . . Edwards brings to life the early days of radio and television and the innovations that Murrow sparked. . . . Readers interested in journalism will enjoy this slim book." Booklist

Includes bibliographical references

Sperber, Ann M. Murrow, his life and times; {by} A. M. Sperber; with a preface by Neil Hickey. Fordham Univ. Press 1998 xxvi, 795p il $35; pa $25 **92**

1. Journalists

ISBN 0-8232-1881-3; 0-8232-1882-1 (pa)

LC 98-52507

A reissue of the title first published 1986 by Freundlich Bks.

This "is the biography of America's foremost broadcast journalist, Edward R. Murrow. At twenty-nine, he was the prototype of a species new to communications—an eyewitness to history with power to reach millions. His wartime radio reports from London rooftops brought the world into American homes for the first time. His legendary television documentary See it Now exposed us to the scandals and injustices within our own country." Publisher's note

This "ambitious exploration of Murrow's life places his story in the foreground of what is, as well, a panorama of the years 1935-65." N Y Times Book Rev

Includes bibliographical references

Mussina, Mike, 1968-

Feinstein, John. Living on the black. See entry under Glavine, Tom, 1966-

Mussolini, Benito, 1883-1945

Bosworth, R. J. B. (Richard J. B.). Mussolini. Oxford Univ. Press 2002 584p il hardcover o.p. pa $14.95 **92**

1. Fascism—Italy 2. Italy—Politics and government

ISBN 0-340-73144-3; 0-340-80988-4 (pa)

LC 2002-283267

"While Bosworth does not demonize Mussolini, he views him as an extreme example of an ego-driven personality incapable of divorcing his own self-gratifying impulses from the best interests of his people. . . . The author also . . . asserts that, as a political force, Mussolini was not an aberration." Booklist

This is "the definitive study of the Italian dictator and belongs in every public and academic library with a strong European history collection." Libr J

Includes bibliographical references

Nabokov, Vladimir Vladimirovich, 1899-1977

Boyd, Brian. Vladimir Nabokov: the American years. Princeton Univ. Press 1991 783p il hardcover o.p. pa $49 **92**

1. Authors, Russian

ISBN 0-691-06797-X; 0-691-02471-5 (pa)

LC 90-26374

This volume, which completes the biography begun with Vladimir Nabokov: The Russian Years (1990), is an account of the writer's life from 1940, when he arrived in the United States.

Includes bibliographical references

Boyd, Brian. Vladimir Nabokov: the Russian years. Princeton Univ. Press 1990 607p il hardcover o.p. pa $49 **92**

1. Authors, Russian

ISBN 0-691-06794-5; 0-691-02470-7 (pa)

LC 90-8040

Nabokov, Vladimir Vladimirovich, 1899-1977—
Continued

First volume of a two-volume biography of Nabokov, followed by Vladimir Nabokov: the American years (1991)

The author aims to "describe the liberal milieu of the aristocratic Nabokovs, their escape from Russia [after the Revolution], Nabokov's education at Cambridge, and the murder of his father in Berlin. Boyd then turns to the years that Nabokov spent, impoverished, in Germany and France, until the coming of Hitler forced him to flee, with wife and son, to the United States." Publisher's note

Includes bibliographical references

Nabokov, Vladimir Vladimirovich. Speak, memory; an autobiography revisited; {by} Vladimir Nabokov; with an introduction by Brian Boyd. Knopf 1999 xxxv, 268p il map $17; pa $14 *   **92**
1. Authors, Russian
ISBN 0-375-40553-4; 0-679-72339-0 (pa)
                                            LC 98-49237
A revised version of the memoir first published 1951 in the United States with title: Conclusive evidence

A Borzoi Bk.

These recollections of the author's youthful years give an account of a vanishing world. They offer a picture of the author's family, their flight from Russia, education in England, and émigré life in Paris and Berlin

Includes bibliographical references

Nafisi, Azar

Nafisi, Azar. Reading Lolita in Tehran; a memoir in books. Random House 2003 347p $23.95; pa $11.16   **92**
1. Women—Iran 2. Books and reading
ISBN 0-375-50490-7; 0-8129-7106-X (pa)
                                            LC 2002-36724
"In 1997 Iran, Nafisi formed an illicit book group whose syllabus provided the perfect framework for appraising life before and after the Islamic Revolution— and afforded her female students what little freedom they knew. Through impassioned discussions of Nabokov, James, and Fitzgerald, she details her teaching career and the obstacles her students faced. Her seamless blend of literary criticism and memoir begets a whole new genre." Libr J

Naipaul, V. S. (Vidiadhar Surajprasad), 1932-

Naipaul, V. S. (Vidiadhar Surajprasad). Between father and son; selected correspondence of V.S. Naipaul and his family, 1949-1953; edited by Gillon Aitken. Knopf 2000 297p $26; pa $13
                                                    92
ISBN 0-375-40730-8; 0-375-70726-3 (pa)
                                            LC 99-31089
"In 1950, at the age of 17, famous-writer-in-the-making V. S. Naipaul ventured to Oxford University in England on a scholarship supplied by the government of his native Trinidad. He and his father maintained a rich, full correspondence during his time away, and these letters fortunately have been gathered into book form." Booklist

Include bibliographical references

Naipaul, V. S. (Vidiadhar Surajprasad). Reading & writing; a personal account. New York Review of Bks. 2000 64p $16.95   **92**
ISBN 0-940322-38-2   LC 99-49615
Naipaul writes about his experiences growing up as an Indian living in Trinidad, his travels in India, his education at Oxford, and his struggles as a young writer in London

The author "elegantly expresses hard-earned wisdom about literature and culture, the political stakes of history and the relationship between the writer and the world." N Y Times Book Rev

Napoleon I, Emperor of the French, 1769-1821

Johnson, Paul. Napoleon. Viking 2002 190p (Penguin lives series) hardcover o.p. pa $13 *
                                                    92
1. France—Kings and rulers
ISBN 0-670-03078-3; 0-14-303745-5 (pa)
                                            LC 2001-45605
"A Lipper\Viking book"

Johnson "presents a concise appraisal of Napoleon's career and a precise understanding of his enigmatic character. The author views Napoleon, not as an 'idea man' whose ideology was the ladder by which he propelled himself to heights of power, but as an opportunist who took advantage of a series of events and situations he could manipulate into achieving supreme control." Booklist

Includes bibliographical references

Schom, Alan. Napoleon Bonaparte; a life. HarperCollins Pubs. 1997 xxii, 888p pa $23.95 hardcover o.p.   **92**
1. France—Kings and rulers
ISBN 0-06-092958-8 (pa)   LC 97-5805
The author's aim in this study of Napoleon's life is to offer a "one-volume biography in English covering all aspects of his life." N Y Times Book Rev

"Schom's judgments have all the more impact for being brief and infrequent. What really interests him is telling the story of the man who made universal rules for others but recognized none for himself. He tells it straightforwardly and well; and not, thankfully, at the multi-volume length he believes the subject still really requires." Times Lit Suppl

Includes bibliographical references

Nasdijj

Nasdijj. The blood runs like a river through my dreams; a memoir. Houghton Mifflin 2000 216p $23; pa $13   **92**
ISBN 0-618-04892-8; 0-618-15448-5 (pa)
                                            LC 00-38916
"Born on the Navajo reservation in 1950 to migrant workers (a Navajo storytelling mother and a white cowboy father) . . . Nasdijj writes about the life and death of his son, Tommy Nothing Fancy, their fishing trips, his travails as a committed but unpublished writer, life on the reservation, homelessness, ethnic cleansing in America, love, survival, hope. Illuminating both the comic and the tragic, his writing is a striking blend of 'tell it like it is' truths that hit right between the eyes and sensuous,

Nasdijj—*Continued*

expressive, poetic passages that urgently bid the reader to reread, linger, share, and appreciate. The stories and their implications are heartbreaking; but more importantly, they are heart expanding." Booklist

Nash, Ogden, 1902-1971

Parker, Douglas M. Ogden Nash; the life and work of America's laureate of light verse; with a foreword by Dana Gioia. Ivan R. Dee 2005 316p il $27.50 **92**

    ISBN 1-566-63637-X   LC 2004-59912

This is a biography of New Yorker writer Ogden Nash, who published "more than two dozen books of verse as well as screenplays, lyrics and scripts for the theater, children's stories, and essays." Publisher's note

"Parker's is a useful, highly readable biography of one of America's best-loved poets." Publ Wkly

Includes bibliographical references

Navasky, Victor S.

Navasky, Victor S. A matter of opinion. Farrar, Straus and Giroux 2005 458p $27   **92**

    1. Nation (Periodical)

    ISBN 0-374-29997-8   LC 2004-59395

This is the author's "memoir of a quarter-century at the Nation—first as its editor and, since 1994, its publisher and part owner." Time

"Anybody who has ever dreamed of starting a magazine, or worried that the country is losing the ability to speak seriously to itself, should read 'A Matter of Opinion.'" N Y Times Book Rev

Navratilova, Martina, 1956-

Howard, Johnette. The rivals. See entry under Evert, Chris

Needham, Joseph, 1900-1995

Winchester, Simon. The man who loved China; the fantastic story of the eccentric scientist who unlocked the mysteries of the Middle Kingdom. HarperCollins Publishers 2008 316p il map $27.95 *   **92**

    1. Scientists 2. Science—China—History

    ISBN 978-0-06-088459-8; 0-06-088459-2

                  LC 2007-40516

The author "explores Needham's fascinating and sometimes controversial personal life, his travels to China, and especially the significance and topicality of his scholarship on the early accomplishments of Chinese science and technology. . . . Essential for all libraries." Libr J

Includes bibliographical references

Nehru, Jawaharlal, 1889-1964

Brown, Judith M. (Judith Margaret). Nehru: a political life. Yale University Press 2003 407p il $35   **92**

    1. Prime ministers—India

    ISBN 0-300-09279-2   LC 2003-5807

This biography "focuses upon the challenges to Nehru as father of Indian independence. Although Nehru's family ties and friendships do not escape scrutiny, it is the political side of Nehru that dominates the book." Publ Wkly

"This compelling biography, the most complete and penetrating account of Nehru yet written, casts new light on both the public and private man. It also offers insights into the history of India's nationalist movement and the complexities of constructing a new nation state in the aftermath of imperial rule." Univ Press Books for Public and Second Sch Libr, 2004

Includes bibliographical references

Tharoor, Shashi. Nehru: the invention of India. Arcade Pub 2003 282p $24.95; pa $13.95

                          92

    1. Prime ministers—India

    ISBN 1-559-70697-X; 1-559-70737-2 (pa)

                  LC 2003-58274

The author touches "on key points in Nehru's life: his English education, the importance of guidance he received from his father and Gandhi, his prison years during the drive for independence, and his administration of the new Indian republic. He neatly pulls together the essence of Nehru's beliefs in democratic institution building, pan-Indian secularism, Socialist democratic economy, and the foreign policy of nonalignment. . . . If readers could choose only one narrative about Nehru, this would suffice." Libr J

Includes bibliographical references

Nelson, Horatio Nelson, Viscount, 1758-1805

Hibbert, Christopher. Nelson; a personal history. Addison-Wesley 1994 472p il pa $22 hardcover o.p.   **92**

    1. Admirals

    ISBN 0-201-40800-7 (pa)   LC 94-39545

This biography of Horatio Nelson concentrates mostly on the "admiral's life ashore, especially his liaison with Emma, Lady Hamilton." Choice

The book "succeeds admirably in presenting a vivid and intimate picture of Nelson and Lady Hamilton together, helped by numerous and apt illustrations, half of them in colour. . . . The result is essentially a book of domestic detail, told with charm and perception." Times Lit Suppl

Includes bibliographical references

Sugden, John. Nelson: a dream of glory, 1758-1797. Henry Holt 2004 943p il map $35

                          92

    1. Admirals

    ISBN 0-8050-7757-X   LC 2004-54057

"A John Macrae book"

First volume of a projected two volume biography of Lord Nelson

"This first of a projected two-volume study covers the least familiar period of Nelson's life, from childhood through his rise to international fame in 1797. . . . Sugden's account of Nelson's early career certainly bids fair to fill the gaps, ranging from the future admiral's first years to the disastrous action off Tenerife. . . . Sugden has done well here." Libr J

Includes bibliographical references

Nelson, Horatio Nelson, Viscount, 1758-1805—
Continued

Vincent, Edgar. Nelson; love & fame. Yale
Univ. Press 2003 640p il map $35; pa $19.95
92
1. Great Britain. Royal Navy 2. Admirals
ISBN 0-300-09797-2; 0-300-10260-7 (pa)
LC 2002-14566
The author "has interwoven two separate strands—the
professional and the emotional—of Horatio Nelson's life
into [this] biography of the man and the hero. While
Nelson's military exploits are all well-documented, and
his infamous affair with Lady Emma Hamilton common
knowledge, the author probes beneath the surface of the
obvious, plumbing the depths of a man with an insatiable
desire for admiration and attention." Booklist
"Nelson is a masterly biography, cool and sharp in
long shots, intimately persuasive in close focus, at all
times difficult to put down and as timely as it is suggestive in its implications." N Y Times Book Rev
Includes bibliographical references

Nelson, Willie
Patoski, Joe Nick. Willie Nelson; an epic life.
Little, Brown 2008 567p il $27.99 *   **92**
1. Country musicians
ISBN 978-0-316-01778-7; 0-316-01778-7
LC 2007-44984
A biography of the country music singer and song-
writer.
"This impressive, entertaining chronicle of Willie Nel-
son's life is replete with exactly what you'd expect—
honky-tonk, long nights on the open road, whiskey,
womanizing and weed—but . . . [the author] looks be-
yond country music trappings to find the funny, talented,
determined man who became an unlikely icon." Publ
Wkly
Includes discography and bibliographical references

Nemat, Marina
Nemat, Marina. Prisoner of Tehran; a memoir.
Free Press 2007 306p $26   **92**
1. Political prisoners 2. Iran—History—1979-
ISBN 1-4165-3742-2; 978-1-4165-3742-7
LC 2006-50191
Nemat was sixteen when she was arrested in Iran in
early 1982 for political protests against the new fundamentalist regime. This is an account of her prison experiences.
The author's "story is not so much a political history
lesson than it is a memoir of faith and love, a protest
against violence that cannot be silenced. . . . Her persistence in standing for goodness is a lesson for us all."
Christ Sci Monit

Neruda, Pablo, 1904-1973
Feinstein, Adam. Pablo Neruda; a passion for
life. Bloomsbury 2004 497p il $32.50; pa $18.95
*   **92**
ISBN 1-582-34410-8; 1-582-34594-5 (pa)
LC 2004-715

The author "recounts Neruda's efforts during the
Spanish Civil War and resistance to two Chilean dictators, but he also attempts to clarify Neruda's controversial views of Stalinist communism." Libr J
"Feinstein undoubtedly researched every existent
source and found new ones, and the result is a detailed
and accurate biography. . . . This is a necessary book,
with many beautiful photos." Publ Wkly
Includes bibliographical references

Urrutia, Matilde. My life with Pablo Neruda;
{translated by} Alexandria Giardino. Stanford
University Press 2004 318p $27.95   **92**
ISBN 0-8047-5009-2   LC 2004-8535
Original Spanish edition, 1986
"Urrutia, Neruda's third wife, provides a . . . biography from her particular vantage. Her purpose is twofold:
to present her Pablo as the exuberant, warm, and loving
individual he was and to inform readers of the menace
imposed by Chilean dictator Pinochet, who was responsible for the assassination of elected president Allende,
Neruda's close friend. Urrutia's account is highly selective but well worth reading for another perspective on
this great man." Libr J

Newton, Sir Isaac, 1642-1727
Fara, Patricia. Newton: the making of genius.
Columbia Univ. Press 2002 347p il $83.50; pa $23
92
1. Scientists
ISBN 0-231-12806-1; 0-231-12807-X (pa)
LC 2003-265510
This "social history examines the reasons behind Isaac
Newton's canonization as scientific genius. . . . Fara
contributes to Newton's biography by focusing on the
roots of Newton's apotheosis. She examines how idealized portraits propagated Newton's public image, and
how the marketing of Newtonian images outside academic circles commercialized science in the same way Einstein's face sells today. Throughout, Fara, . . . effectively employs the words and imagery of religious discourse
to characterize the idealization and commercialization of
Newton in the service of emerging secular politics and
culture." Publ Wkly
Includes bibliographical references

Gleick, James. Isaac Newton. Pantheon Bks.
2003 272p il hardcover o.p. pa $13   **92**
1. Scientists
ISBN 0-375-42233-1; 1-4000-3295-4 (pa)
LC 2002-192696
In this biography Gleick presents "his subject in his
scientific glory and in his less well known roles of heretic, alchemist, and recluse; he also reveals how Newton's
mathematical ideas were instrumental in creating what
we now call the scientific worldview." Libr J
This "is now the biography of choice for the interested layman. Gleick copes with the complex tapestry of
Newton's interests by teasing them apart into individual
chapters, assembled into a smooth chronological flow.
. . . Newton the man emerges from the shadows." N Y
Times Book Rev
Includes bibliographical references

Newton, Sir Isaac, 1642-1727—*Continued*

Westfall, Richard S. The life of Isaac Newton. Cambridge Univ. Press 1993 328p il pa $16 hardcover o.p. **92**

1. Scientists

ISBN 0-521-47737-9 (pa)   LC 92-33777

In this book the author has "reduced his longer 1980 biography of Newton *(Never at Rest)* to a size that is more suitable for general audiences. The result is a work whose faults lie only in the paucity of source materials that all Newton biographers face. . . . Westfall's book comes as close to presenting the man as the impersonal evidence allows without undue extrapolation." Sci Books Films

Includes bibliographical references

Nicholas II, Emperor of Russia, 1868-1918

Ferro, Marc. Nicholas II; the last of the tsars; translated by Brian Pearce. Oxford Univ. Press 1993 305p il map pa $19.95 hardcover o.p. **92**

1. Russia—History 2. Russia—Kings and rulers

ISBN 0-19-509382-8 (pa)   LC 92-41440

"The last Tsar, as this fluently written biography makes abundantly clear, was largely to blame for the demise of the monarchy. Ferro is concerned to illuminate the personality of the Tsar, his relationship with his wife and Rasputin and to look again at the circumstances surrounding his death." Hist Today

Includes bibliographical references

Massie, Robert K. Nicholas and Alexandra. Ballantine Books 2000 613p il map pa $18.95 **92**

1. Alexandra, Empress, consort of Nicholas II, Emperor of Russia, 1872-1918 2. Rasputin, Grigoriĭ Efimovich, 1871-1916 3. Russia—History 4. Russia—Kings and rulers

ISBN 0-345-43831-0; 978-0-345-43831-7

     LC 99-91507

First published 1967 by Atheneum

This study provides an intimate account of the Romanov family and the coming of the Russian Revolution. Kerensky, Lenin and Rasputin are among the personalities profiled.

This book, "solid with research, reads as lightly as a novel, as authoritatively as a textbook. Dialogue and lively description lend a sense of immediacy, but his notes, discreetly relegated to the back of the book, show how carefully he has avoided slipping into fiction." Christ Sci Monit

Includes bibliographical references

Nicklaus, Jack

Nicklaus, Jack. Jack Nicklaus; my story; with Ken Bowden. Simon & Schuster 1997 505p il $30; pa $24.95 * **92**

ISBN 0-684-83628-9; 0-684-83870-2 (pa)

     LC 97-3824

This "is both Nicklaus's autobiography and a history of modern golf, for the subjects are wholly intertwined. The book begins with Nicklaus's first national accomplishment, winning the United States Amateur at the age of 19 in 1959. It concludes with Nicklaus winning the Masters for the sixth time in 1986." N Y Times Book Rev

"What comes across most forcibly in this fine book is Nicklaus' respect for the complexity of golf and the never-ending challenges it affords players at every level." Booklist

Nietzsche, Friedrich Wilhelm, 1844-1900

Safranski, Rüdiger. Nietzsche; a philosophical biography; translated by Shelley Frisch. Norton 2001 409p $29.95; pa $18.95 **92**

ISBN 0-393-05008-4; 0-393-32380-3 (pa)

     LC 2001-52130

This biography of the German philosopher focuses "on the temporal course of Nietzsche's inner life and his self-transformation through thought and writing." New Rep

"With brilliant insights and impressive scholarship, Safranski . . . here makes a major contribution to understanding and appreciating the lasting significance of Friedrich Nietzsche." Libr J

Includes bibliographical references

Nixon, Richard M. (Richard Milhous), 1913-1994

Black, Conrad M. Richard M. Nixon; a life in full; [by] Conrad Black. PublicAffairs 2007 1152p il $40 **92**

1. Presidents—United States

ISBN 978-1-58648-519-1; 1-58648-519-9

     LC 2007-34530

This is a biography of the thirty-seventh president.

"Black's superb volume, incorporating much new research, is an important and worthy addition to the literature." Publ Wkly

Includes bibliographical references

Dallek, Robert. Nixon and Kissinger; partners in power. HarperCollins Publishers 2007 740p il $32.50 **92**

1. Kissinger, Henry, 1923- 2. United States—Foreign relations

ISBN 978-0-06-072230-2; 0-06-072230-4

     LC 2006-52100

A look "behind the scenes at this quintessential pair of power brokers and their lasting influence, for good and ill, on the political stage." Bookmarks Magazine

Includes bibliographical references

Reeves, Richard. President Nixon; alone in the White House. Simon & Schuster 2001 702p il $35; pa $16 **92**

1. United States—Politics and government—1961-1974 2. Presidents—United States

ISBN 0-684-80231-7; 0-7432-2719-0 (pa)

     LC 2001-34417

This narrative "is chronological, from Nixon's inauguration in January 1969 to April 1973, when he realized that he had lost control over the Watergate scandals. . . . In between are Vietnam and crime in the streets, affirmative action and the end of the gold standard, Chile and the antiballistic missile treaty, the opening to China and, of course, Watergate. A fascinating study of the brilliant,

Nixon, Richard M. (Richard Milhous), 1913-1994—*Continued*

profoundly flawed man elected to lead the nation through a troubled time." Booklist

Includes bibliographical references

Novacek, Michael J.

Novacek, Michael J. Time traveler; in search of dinosaurs and ancient mammals from Montana to Mongolia; [by] Michael Novacek. Farrar, Straus & Giroux 2002 368p il $26; pa $15   **92**

ISBN 0-374-27880-6; 0-374-52876-4 (pa)

LC 2001-40438

"The author first describes the youthful experiences that inspired him to become a paleontologist. . . . Then Novacek launches into his various expeditions. . . . Interweaving his adventures with explanations of where his finds fit into the geologic past, Novacek has combined the comedic with the informative in this entertaining survey of his career." Booklist

Includes bibliographical references

Nudelman, Meyer

Nuland, Sherwin B. Lost in America. See entry under Nuland, Sherwin B.

Nuland, Sherwin B.

Nuland, Sherwin B. Lost in America; a journey with my father. Knopf 2003 209p $24; pa $12   **92**

1. Nudelman, Meyer
ISBN 0-375-41294-8; 0-375-75722-1 (pa)

LC 2002-40795

This is a "memoir about becoming an assimilated second-generation American from a home dominated by his angry, altogether unassimilable Orthodox Jewish father." N Y Times Book Rev

"Written with enormous empathy, yet without a hint of sentimentality, Nuland's memoir is both heartbreaking and breathtaking." Publ Wkly

Nureyev, Rudolf, 1938-1993

Kavanagh, Julie. Nureyev; the life. Pantheon Books 2007 782p il $37.50 *   **92**

1. Ballet dancers
ISBN 978-0-375-40513-6; 0-375-40513-5

LC 2006-38137

Published in the UK with the title Rudolf Nureyev

In this biography of the Russian ballet dancer, the author "chronicles Nureyev's many tempestuous relationships, including his legendary work with Margot Fonteyn and his formative affair with the outstanding Danish dancer Erik Bruhn. . . . Kavanagh's consummate biography will stand as a pillar in dance history." Booklist

Includes bibliographical references

Nusseibeh, Sari

Nusseibeh, Sari. Once upon a country; a Palestinian life; [by] Sari Nusseibeh, with Anthony David. Farrar, Straus and Giroux 2007 542p il $27.50   **92**

1. Palestinian Arabs 2. Israel-Arab conflicts
ISBN 978-0-374-29950-7; 0-374-29950-1

LC 2006-13272

"Nusseibeh is head of the only Arab university in Jerusalem. His ancient family roots in Palestine go back 1,300 years. . . . [This] insider's account blends Nusseibeh's personal experience as son, husband, father, intellectual, and activist leader with the raging politics of his homeland over the last 40 years. Striving for a two-state solution, he calls for civil disobedience against the Israeli Occupation, never for violence. He is close to the Israeli Peace Now movement, always believing that Palestinians and Jews are natural allies." Booklist

"This is a rare book, one written by a partisan in the struggle over Palestine who nevertheless recognizes—and bravely records—the moral and political failures of his own people." Los Angeles Times

Includes bibliographical references

Oakley, Annie, 1860-1926

Kasper, Shirl. Annie Oakley. University of Okla. Press 1992 288p il $29.95; pa $19.95   **92**

1. Frontier and pioneer life—West (U.S.)
ISBN 0-8061-2418-0; 0-8061-3244-2 (pa)

LC 91-50864

This biography of the legendary sharpshooter "not only paints a picture of a woman with an unusual occupation for her time; it also colors the whole era of Wild West performers from Buffalo Bill to Will Rogers." Booklist

Includes bibliographical references

Riley, Glenda. The life and legacy of Annie Oakley. University of Okla. Press 1994 252p il (Oklahoma western biographies) hardcover o.p. pa $19.95   **92**

1. Frontier and pioneer life—West (U.S.)
ISBN 0-8061-2656-6; 978-0-8061-3506-9 (pa)

LC 94-10260

"To provide a factual and intimate biography of Annie Oakley, the legendary female sharpshooter and star of Buffalo Bill Cody's Wild West Show, Riley attempts to place her seemingly mythical subject firmly into historical, cultural, and sociological contexts. . . . What emerges is a multidimensional portrait of an entertainer and a businesswoman whose enduring fame and popularity both reflected and defied the conventions of her era." Booklist

Includes bibliographical references

Oates, Joyce Carol, 1938-

Oates, Joyce Carol. The journal of Joyce Carol Oates: 1973-1982; edited by Greg Johnson. Ecco 2007 509p il $29.95 *   **92**

1. Authors, American 2. Women authors
ISBN 978-0-06-122798-1; 0-06-122798-6

LC 2007-29378

Oates, Joyce Carol, 1938—*Continued*

This is a collection of diaries from the period when Oates published *Do With Me What You Will* (1973), *Bellefleur* (1980), and other works.

"This journal immerses the reader in a complex, searching, imaginative personality—an artist who continues to refine her search for literary expression." Publ Wkly

Includes bibliographical references

Obama, Barack, 1961-

Mendell, David. Obama; from promise to power. Amistad 2007 406p il $25.95 **92**

1. United States. Congress. Senate 2. African Americans—Biography

ISBN 978-0-06-085820-9; 0-06-085820-6

This is a biography of Barack Obama, junior senator from Illinois and US presidential candidate.

The author "draws on interviews with Obama, his wife, family, friends, aides, and rivals, as well as his own extensive coverage since Obama's days in the Illinois Senate, to offer a nuanced, compelling look at a man of idealism and ambition intent on making history." Booklist

Includes bibliographical references

O'Brian, Patrick

King, Dean. Patrick O'Brian; a life revealed. Holt & Co. 2000 397p il pa $15 hardcover o.p.

92

ISBN 0-8050-5977-6 (pa) LC 99-48495

"This is exactly the sort of literary biography that O'Brian, the author of the celebrated Aubrey/Maturin naval novels, hoped to avoid. Reluctant to provide facts about himself, and often untruthful when he did so, O'Brian . . . had much in his past that he wanted buried. He walked away from his first marriage, changed his name from Russ to O'Brian, and pretended Anglo-Irish ancestry. King's diligent research yields pleasing details." New Yorker

Includes bibliographical references

O'Connor, Flannery

Cash, Jean W. Flannery O'Connor: a life. University of Tenn. Press 2002 356p il $30; pa $24.95 **92**

ISBN 1-572-33192-5; 1-572-33305-7 (pa)

LC 2002-250

Contents: Savannah, 1925-1938 -- Milledgeville, 1938-1942 -- Milledgeville, 1942-1945 -- Iowa, 1945-1948 -- Yaddo, New York City, and Connecticut, 1948-1950 -- Return to Milledgeville and a pivotal decision -- Regina and Flannery -- Milledgeville, early friendships -- Later friendships -- Last friendships -- Lectures and travel outside Milledgeville, 1955-1959 -- Lectures, 1960-1963 -- Reviews, 1956-1964 -- Illness, death, and legacy

"Cash analyzes the woman behind the myth, introducing an extraordinarily intelligent human being noted for her keen sense of humor, intellectual versatility, and tremendous capacity for friendship. This intimate chronicle of a major literary talent will appeal to both students and scholars." Booklist

Includes bibliographical references

O'Connor, Flannery. The habit of being; letters; edited and with an introduction by Sally Fitzgerald. Farrar, Straus & Giroux 1979 617p pa $20 hardcover o.p. **92**

ISBN 0-374-52104-2 (pa) LC 78-11559

This collection includes letters to friends in the literary establishment: Robert Lowell and Elizabeth Hardwick, Caroline Gordon Tate, Robert and Sally Fitzgerald and others

O'Connor, Sandra Day

Biskupic, Joan. Sandra Day O'Connor; how the first woman on the Supreme Court became its most influential justice. Ecco 2005 419p il $26.95

92

ISBN 0-06-059018-1 LC 2005-52103

This book "explores the life and influence of Justice Sandra Day O'Connor." N Y Times Book Rev

The author "offers an insightful biography of perhaps the most influential associate justice in recent history." Libr J

Includes bibliographical references

O'Faolain, Nuala

O'Faolain, Nuala. Almost there; the onward journey of a Dublin woman. Riverhead Bks. 2003 275p $24.95; pa $14 **92**

ISBN 1-57322-241-0; 1-57322-374-3 (pa)

LC 2002-36722

In this autobiography the author "reveals the emotional damage she still suffers from being raised in a large family by an alcoholic mother and a remote father." Booklist

This "is a thought-provoking work that differs markedly from the self-serving memoirs we frequently see." Libr J

O'Faolain, Nuala. Are you somebody; the accidental memoir of a Dublin woman. Holt & Co. 1998 c1996 215p pa $13 hardcover o.p.

92

ISBN 0-8050-5664-4 (pa) LC 97-29725

First published 1996 in Ireland

In this memoir O'Faolain "describes growing up in the kind of poverty that had her mother raiding the gas meter for shillings while her father ignored his nine children and kept a mistress on the other side of town. The nascent women's movement and O'Faolain's expansive love of reading kept her afloat: she made it to college, rubbed elbows with literary Dublin, and became a BBC producer in London." New Yorker

This is a "moving and painfully honest memoir." Libr J

Oher, Michael, 1986-

Lewis, Michael. The blind side; evolution of a game. W.W. Norton 2006 299p $24.95 *

92

1. Football—Biography 2. College sports

ISBN 978-0-393-06123-9; 0-393-06123-X

LC 2006-23509

Oher, Michael, 1986-—_Continued_
The author "describes the NFL's ever-growing obsession with left tackles as a means to counter defenders who seem to grow bigger, stronger, and more vicious each season. He juxtaposes that narrative with the unlikely story of [football player] Michael Oher. . . . The book works on three levels. First as a shrewd analysis of the NFL; second, as an expose of the insanity of big-time college football recruiting; and, third, as a moving portrait of the positive effect that love, family, and education can have in reversing the path of a life that was destined to be lived unhappily and, most likely, end badly." Booklist

O'Keeffe, Georgia, 1887-1986
Drohojowska-Philp, Hunter. Full bloom; the art and life of Georgia O'Keeffe. W.W. Norton 2004 630p $35 **92**
ISBN 0-393-05853-0   LC 2003-26071
This is a biography of the American painter
"O'Keeffe lived a long, adventurous, and profoundly productive life, and Drohojowska-Philp charts her triumphs over adversity in an involving, revelatory biography that attains the grand scope and depth her subject deserves." Booklist
Includes bibliographical references

Robinson, Roxana. Georgia O'Keeffe: a life. University Press of New England 1999 639p il pa $22.95 * **92**
ISBN 0-87451-906-3   LC 98-30944
A reissue of the title first published 1989 by Harper & Row
"This biography, the first to draw on sources unavailable during O'Keeffe's lifetime—and the first to be granted her family's cooperation—offers a persuasive feminist analysis of the life and work of an iconic figure in American art. . . . [The author's] detailed, sensitive critique of O'Keeffe's work . . . alternates with an absorbing, intimate narrative of O'Keeffe's personal life." Publ Wkly
Includes bibliographical references

Olivier, Laurence, 1907-1989
Lewis, Roger. The real life of Laurence Olivier. Applause Theatre Bk. Pubs. 1997 272p il $25.95; pa $18.95 **92**
ISBN 1-55783-298-6; 1-55783-413-X (pa)
LC 97-31702
First published 1996 in the United Kingdom
This is a life of the English stage and screen actor
"Lewis enjoys exploring the details that make up such a rich life—Olivier seemed to have met everyone, known everyone, and played every major role in existence. The indexing and photographs are quite good." Libr J

Olmsted, Frederick Law, 1822-1903
Rybczynski, Witold. A clearing in the distance: Frederick Law Olmsted and America in the nineteenth century. Scribner 1999 480p il $28; pa $15.95 **92**
ISBN 0-684-82463-9; 0-684-86575-0 (pa)
LC 99-18094

"A portrait of Olmsted not just as landscape architect but as cultural figure." Libr J
"Rybczynski, celebrated for his sparkling prose as well as for his deep knowledge of architectural history, adeptly chronicles the life of the man who 'was a landscape architect before that profession was founded.'" Booklist
Includes bibliographical references

Onassis, Aristotle Socrates, 1906-1975
Gage, Nicholas. Greek fire. See entry under Callas, Maria, 1923-1977

Onassis, Jacqueline Kennedy, 1929-1994
Bowles, Hamish. Jacqueline Kennedy; the White House Years: selections from the John F. Kennedy Library and Museum; {compiled and edited by} Hamish Bowles; with essays by Arthur Schlesinger, Jr., Hamish Bowles, and James Wagner. Bulfinch Press 2001 198p il $50 **92**
ISBN 0-8212-2745-9   LC 00-66237
Also available in hardcover and paperback from the Metropolitan Museum of Art
This "book accompanies a summer 2001 Metropolitan Museum of Art exhibition of the same name, curated by Bowles. . . . The focus here is Jackie's famous and much emulated wardrobe. Each gown, suit, and accessory has an informational entry that includes a photograph of Jackie wearing the item." Libr J
The selections "examine in detail different aspects of Jackie's life, including the inauguration, her White House style, her travels, and her hats, as well as other topics. . . . Viewers can expect a sense of nostalgia, a swelling of pride, and a tightening of the throat. A time line of Jackie's life is appended." Booklist

Davis, John H. Jacqueline Bouvier; an intimate memoir; [by] John Davis. Wiley 1996 208p il $24.95; pa $14.95 **92**
ISBN 0-471-12945-3; 0-471-24944-0 (pa)
LC 96-4332
This "book by the late Mrs. Onassis's cousin is as much a nostalgic look at a vanished way of life as it is a memoir of Jacqueline Bouvier from her birth in 1929 until her marriage to Senator John F. Kennedy in September 1953. The author's access to family papers helped fill in the details of an enormously privileged yet often unhappy childhood." Libr J
"Davis is an engaging writer, and although many of the facts of his story will be known by Kennedy aficionados, there is a wistful sweetness to his writing that captures both the woman and the era of privileged upbringings." Booklist

Leaming, Barbara. Mrs. Kennedy; the missing history of the Kennedy years. Free Press 2001 406p il $25; pa $14 **92**
ISBN 0-684-86209-3; 0-7432-2749-2 (pa)
LC 2001-40442
"Asserting that Jacqueline Kennedy's role in shaping her husband's presidency has been under-examined, Leaming . . . offers a corrective in this intimate look at

Onassis, Jacqueline Kennedy, 1929-1994—Continued
a very private woman. Initially inclined to keep herself as much in the background as possible, says Leaming, Jacqueline Kennedy became an increasingly visible and vocal first lady as she realized how effective she could be as an image maker. It's in this capacity that Leaming convincingly depicts her as being instrumental in shaping the course of her husband's administration." Publ Wkly

Includes bibliographical references

O'Neill, Eugene, 1888-1953
Black, Stephen A. (Stephen Ames). Eugene O'Neill; beyond mourning and tragedy. Yale Univ. Press 1999 xxiv, 543p $45; pa $17.95   **92**
    ISBN 0-300-07676-2; 0-300-09399-3 (pa)
                    LC 99-33897
When Black "tracks down correspondences between O'Neill's life and art he adds zip to the life but depersonalizes the art. Still, as he brings the life and the art into apposition, new coloring is cast on a number of the plays. His observations will prove enlightening." New Leader

Includes bibliographical references

Oppenheimer, J. Robert, 1904-1967
Bernstein, Jeremy. Oppenheimer; portrait of an enigma. Dee, I.R. 2004 223p il $25   **92**
    ISBN 1-566-63569-1   LC 2003-66652
The author "recounts Oppenheimer's eclectic life as it evolved in the US through his education and service at several prestigious institutions. . . . The book is not a review of Oppenheimer's contributions to physics or the development of the atomic bomb; rather, it provides insight into the human side of a brilliant individual, all things considered. Of course, his leadership of the Manhattan Project, and his persecution by Congress for alleged communist sympathies, defined Oppenheimer's career. Bernstein provides personalized insights into both." Choice

Includes bibliographical references

Bird, Kai. American Prometheus; the triumph and tragedy of J. Robert Oppenheimer; [by] Kai Bird and Martin J. Sherwin. Knopf 2005 721p il $35   **92**
    ISBN 0-375-41202-6   LC 2004-61535
The authors explore Oppenheimer's life "from his youth as a child prodigy through his radical political activities in the 1930s, and on to the Manhattan Project and its political fallout. The humanity of the troubled man behind the porkpie hat emerges on every page of this unquestionably definitive account." Booklist

Includes bibliographical references

Ormes, Jackie, 1911-1985
Goldstein, Nancy. Jackie Ormes; the first African American woman cartoonist. University of Michigan Press 2008 225p il $35   **92**
    1. Cartoonists 2. African American women
    ISBN 978-0-472-11624-9; 0-472-11624-X
                    LC 2007-35395

This book covers the life and career of Jackie Ormes, who was the first African American woman cartoonist. She wrote and drew comic strips that ran in Black newspapers such as the Pittsburgh Courier and the Chicago Defender. She was part of the Black elite in Chicago and knew other luminaries such as singer Eartha Kitt and musician/composer/conductor Duke Ellington. She was also investigated by the FBI because of her Leftist political ideas and activities. While she did such things as create Torchy paper dolls, based on her beautiful and sexy cartoon character, and cute Patty-Jo dolls, Ormes also used her comic strips to put forth her political views. This book reproduces some of her cartoons and comic strips, in both black and white and in color.

Includes bibliographical references

Orwell, George, 1903-1950
Meyers, Jeffrey. Orwell; wintry conscience of a generation. Norton 2000 380p il maps pa $16.95 hardcover o.p.   **92**
    ISBN 0-393-32263-7 (pa)   LC 00-38020
In this biography Meyers "writes about the aristocratic air Orwell cultivated at Eton; his devotion to social justice and instinct for self-punishment (which led him to live with the destitute and take a bullet in the Spanish Civil War); his steadfast socialism and hatred of totalitarianism; his mix of politeness and prickliness; his sadistic streak . . . and his desperate need for love, exhibited in his various affairs." Publ Wkly

"With wit and acumen, Meyers portrays a complex, eccentric, intelligent, and unbending man hard on family and friends, a writer of singular gifts, and a 'prophetic moralist' whose vision continues to illuminate society's dark side." Booklist

Includes bibliographical references

Taylor, David J. Orwell: the life; {by} D.J. Taylor. Holt & Co. 2003 466p il $30; pa $17 ***
                               92
    ISBN 0-8050-7473-2; 0-8050-7693-X (pa)
                    LC 2003-41747
"Starting with a . . . description of Orwell's funeral in 1950, Taylor . . . presents the years in India, the 'down and out' adventures, fighting in Spain, Orwell's work with the BBC during the war, and his final great novels. Taylor breaks the chronological flow with nine brief, interpretive essays (e.g., on Orwell's face, voice, and paranoia). . . . Taylor's book is a fresh and compelling life of the man he calls 'a light glinting in the darkness.'" Libr J

Includes bibliographical references

Osama bin Laden
Randal, Jonathan C. Osama: the making of a terrorist; {by} Jonathan Randal. Knopf 2004 339p $26.95   **92**
    1. Terrorism
    ISBN 0-375-40901-7   LC 2004-46522
This is an "account of Osama bin Laden's role in the rise of terrorism in the Middle East. Randal . . . {depicts} how Osama's life epitomizes the fatal collision between twenty-first-century Islam and the West, and he describes the course of Osama's estrangement from both

Osama bin Laden—*Continued*

the West and the Saudi petro-monarchy of which his family is a part." Publisher's note

The author's "meticulous account of the emergence and spread of the terror virus is less a biography of the strange, desiccated Saudi Arabian terrorist who heads Al Qaeda than a map of the world that produced him and his fellow Islamists. This is the biography of a hatred: deep, detailed, and depressing." N Y Times Book Rev

Includes bibliographical references

Osborne, John, 1929-1994

Heilpern, John. John Osborne; the many lives of the angry young man. Alfred A. Knopf 2007 527p il $35 **92**

ISBN 978-0-375-40315-6; 0-375-40315-9

LC 2006-46575

First published 2006 in the United Kingdom

"Heilpern draws on Osborne's bleak private notebooks to generate acute readings of his often autobiographical plays. Sympathy for the man and admiration for the work don't blind Heilpern to his subject's outsized flaws. Osborne had a talent for invective and could be cruelly intolerant in matters large and small. He threatened theatre critics with physical violence by way of anonymous seaside postcards. Stung by his teenage daughter's indifference to high culture, he damned her as 'criminally commonplace' and never spoke to her again. Without excusing such 'breathtaking abuse,' Heilpern makes a compelling case for Osborne as a necessary 'truthteller' and 'unyielding advocate of individualism in conformist times.'" New Yorker

Includes bibliographical references

Owens, Jesse, 1913-1980

Schaap, Jeremy. Triumph; the untold story of Jesse Owens and Hitler's Olympics. Houghton Mifflin 2007 272p il $24; pa $14.95 **92**

1. Olympic games, 1936 (Berlin, Ger.)

ISBN 978-0-618-68822-7; 0-618-68822-6; 978-0-618-91910-9 (pa); 0-618-91910-4 (pa)

LC 2006-26926

"As Jeremy Schaap points out in his evocative new study of Owens and the Berlin Olympics, writers and human rights advocates debated whether the United States should even participate in the games, which were a calculated showcase for Adolf Hitler's Third Reich. Owens himself tepidly endorsed an Olympic boycott, but . . . he also knew the Olympics would be his ultimate international stage. When the games began in August 1936, the 22-year-old Owens was seen as the living repudiation of Hitler's credo of Aryan supremacy. . . . If that seemed a heavy responsibility for a 160-pound sprinter, Owens proved equal to the task. . . . [Schaap] keeps one eye on the track and another on Hitler's official box, gauging the effect of Owens's triumphs and those of America's other black athletes on the Nazi brass." Washington Post Book Rev

Includes bibliographical references

Oz, Amos

Oz, Amos. A tale of love and darkness; translated from the Hebrew by Nicholas de Lange. Harcourt 2004 538p $26 **92**

ISBN 0-15-100878-7

LC 2004-7302

This is "the story of a boy growing up in the wartorn Jerusalem of the forties and fifties, in a small apartment crowded with books in twelve languages and relatives speaking nearly as many. . . . When Oz was twelve and a half years old, his mother committed suicide, a tragedy that was to change his life. He leaves the constraints of the family and the community of dreamers, scholars, and failed businessmen and joins a kibbutz, changes his name, marries, has children, and finally becomes a writer as well as an active participant in the political life of Israel." Publisher's note

"A powerful story of the making of a writer . . . Oz's panoramic memoir enhances the history of literature and of Israel, and the literature of examined lives." Booklist

Paige, Satchel, 1906-1982

Fox, William Price. Satchel Paige's America. University of Alabama Press 2005 142p pa $16.95 **92**

1. Baseball—Biography

ISBN 0-8173-5189-2

LC 2004-18911

This biography is based upon the author's conversations with the legendary baseball pitcher as he spent a week following him around Kansas City, MO, in 1970.

This is "a lively, moving, and often hilarious tale of an encounter 30 years ago and of a life richly led." Libr J

Paine, Thomas, 1737-1809

Collins, Paul. The trouble with Tom: the strange afterlife and times of Thomas Paine. Bloomsbury 2005 278p map $24.95 **92**

ISBN 1-58234-502-3

LC 2005-45240

The author "traces the bizarre story of Thomas Paine's remains through nearly two centuries of American and English history. . . . Part travelogue, part memoir and part historical mystery, this book reads like a wry, witty novel and offers a delicious twist at the end." Publ Wkly

Includes bibliographical references

Palmer, Arnold, 1929-

Palmer, Arnold. A golfer's life; {by} Arnold Palmer with James Dodson. Ballantine Bks. 1999 420p il pa $15 hardcover o.p. **92**

ISBN 0-345-41482-9 (pa)

LC 98-51681

Palmer's "immense popularity is widely credited with rescuing professional golf in the late 1950s and 1960s. Written with humor and candor, the book recounts Palmer's friendships and rivalries with the greats of the game, his enduring marriage to Winnie Palmer, his legendary triumphs and disasters, and his battle against cancer." Libr J

Paracelsus, 1493-1541

Ball, Philip. The devil's doctor; Paracelsus and the world of Renaissance magic and science. Farrar, Straus and Giroux 2006 430p il map $27 **92**

ISBN 0-374-22979-1

LC 2005-19848

This biography "illuminates the life of alchemist, physician, theologian, and astrologer Paracelsus (1493-1541),

Paracelsus, 1493-1541—*Continued*
placing him . . . in the context of the Reformation. . . .
Ball captures and explains all of Paracelsus's idiosyncrasies and contradictions in writing that is clear and enjoyable." Libr J
Includes bibliographical references

Parker, Dorothy, 1893-1967
Meade, Marion. Dorothy Parker; what fresh hell
is this? Penguin 1989 459p il pa $20   **92**
1. Authors, American
ISBN 0-14-011616-8; 978-0-14-011616-8
                                      LC 88-23782
First published 1988 by Villard Books
"The author has written a disturbing story of a writer
whose life was marked by endless disturbances and self-
depreciation, and who left behind no correspondence,
manuscripts, or private papers. Under the circumstances,
Ms. Meade has brilliantly reconstructed her subject's life.
. . . The book is a tribute to a woman who left her mark
on the literary history of her times and whose coruscat-
ing wit is still remembered." West Coast Rev Books
Includes bibliographical references

Parks, Rosa, 1913-2005
Brinkley, Douglas. Rosa Parks. Viking 2000
246p (Penguin lives series) $19.95; pa $13
                                              92
1. African American women 2. African Americans—
Civil rights
ISBN 0-670-89160-6; 0-14-303600-9 (pa)
                                      LC 00-35916
"A Lipper/Viking book"
"Rosa Parks' story takes readers from rural Alabama
to the Montgomery Industrial School for Girls, marriage
to barber Raymond Parks, quiet activism in the '30s and
'40s, a first experience of integration at the Highlander
Folk School, arrest in 1955 and the bus boycott, a move
to Detroit, and more than 20 years on the staff of Rep.
John Conyers (D-Mich.)." Booklist
Includes bibliographical references

Parks, Rosa. Quiet strength; the faith, the hope,
and the heart of a woman who changed a nation;
reflections by Rosa Parks with Gregory J. Reed.
Zondervan 1994 93p il pa $9.99 hardcover o.p.
                                              92
1. African American women 2. African Americans—
Civil rights
ISBN 0-310-23587-1 (pa)   LC 94-46141
"Parks, one of the U.S.' authentic living legends, is
the black lady who on December 1, 1955, refused to surrender her bus seat to a white man, was arrested under
the Jim Crow law that required blacks to make way for
whites, and thereby launched the yearlong bus boycott by
blacks in Birmingham, Alabama, which led to the national overturning of that city's and similar segregation laws
across the nation. In this tiny collection of what seem
like outtakes from oral-history tapes, she rehearses her
great day." Booklist
Includes bibliographical references

Parsons, Jack, 1914-1952
Pendle, George. Strange angel; the otherworldly
life of rocket scientist John Whiteside Parsons.
Harcourt 2005 350p il $25; pa $15   **92**
ISBN 0-15-100997-X; 0-15-603179-5 (pa)
                                      LC 2004-10666
This is a biography of "John Whiteside Parsons, the
self-taught rocket expert who helped found the Jet Pro-
pulsion Laboratory." N Y Times Book Rev
"Marshaling a cast of characters ranging from Robert
Millikan to L. Ron Hubbard, Pendle offers a fascinating
glimpse into a world long past, a story that would make
a compelling work of fiction if it weren't so
astonishingly true." Publ Wkly
Includes bibliographical references

Pascal, Blaise, 1623-1662
Connor, James A. Pascal's wager; the man who
played dice with God. HarperSanFrancisco 2006
224p il $24.95   **92**
ISBN 978-0-06-076691-7; 0-06-076691-3
                                      LC 2006-43489
This biography of the mathematician and theologian
focuses on his Jansenist religious beliefs.
This book "should interest readers drawn to the cross-
roads of religion and science." Booklist
Includes bibliographical references

Patton, George S. (George Smith), 1885-1945
D'Este, Carlo. Patton; a genius for war.
HarperCollins Pubs. 1995 977p il maps pa $21
hardcover o.p.   **92**
ISBN 0-06-092762-3 (pa)   LC 95-38433
In this biography of the World War II general the author "provides new information from family archives and
other sources about Patton's ancestry, childhood and pre-
WW II military career. . . . The account of Patton's
campaigns from North Africa through Sicily, Normandy
and the Ardennes enables the reader to understand why
the general is regarded as one of the great military leaders. This is a major biography of a major American military figure." Publ Wkly
Includes bibliographical references

Hirshson, Stanley P. General Patton: a soldier's
life. HarperCollins Pubs. 2002 xxii, 826p il maps
$34.95; pa $18.95   **92**
ISBN 0-06-000982-9; 0-06-000983-7 (pa)
                                      LC 2002-68881
The author attempts "to round out the unknown familial aspects of Patton's life and [provide a] . . . context
for understanding the enigmatic commander. . . . Those
interested in Patton will find Hirshson's book valuable
reading." Libr J
Includes bibliographical references

Showalter, Dennis E. Patton and Rommel; men
of war in the twentieth century; [by] Dennis
Showalter. Berkley Caliber 2005 441p $24.95 *
                                              92
1. Rommel, Erwin, 1891-1944 2. World War, 1939-
1945
ISBN 0-425-19346-2   LC 2004-57464

Patton, George S. (George Smith), 1885-1945—
Continued

This is a "parallel biography of George Patton and Erwin Rommel. The research is thorough, the quality of the writing superb. . . . [The author] ranks as a scholar who has done them justice, making two complex men and a vast panorama of military history remarkably accessible for experts and lay readers alike." Publ Wkly

Paul, the Apostle, Saint

Murphy-O'Connor, J. (Jerome). Paul; a critical life; {by} Jerome Murphy-O'Connor. Clarendon Press 1996 416p maps pa $21 hardcover o.p.

92

ISBN 01-9-285342-2 (pa)   LC 95-49173

This biography of the apostle Paul is based on an "analysis of his letters. . . . The first chapter of the book, 'The Chronological Framework,' compares evidence from the Pauline corpus with that of Luke's Acts and extant extrabiblical archaeological evidence. . . . The remaining 13 chapters, based on information extracted from the authentic Pauline letters, discuss in more detail specific events in Paul's life. . . . In addition to Paul's biography, Murphy-O'Connor also treats the development in Paul's theological thought." Libr J

"This is likely to become the standard work on Paul's life for the next generation and is warmly recommended as such." Choice

Includes bibliographical references

Wilson, A. N. (Andrew Norman). Paul: the mind of the Apostle. Norton 1997 273p pa $16.95 hardcover o.p.

92

ISBN 0-393-31760-9 (pa)   LC 96-47834

The author gives "an explanation of the abiding influence of the apostle Paul in Western culture. He accomplishes this . . . by profiling Paul against the social context of the Greco-Roman world in which the apostle lived." Choice

"Wilson's insights fascinate and provoke. Even as rich and incisive a portrait as this one cannot provide a complete understanding of Paul or the turbulent time in which he lived, but readers will come away seeing the enigmatic apostle as an imaginative transformer who shaped a worldwide religious movement." Booklist

Includes bibliographical references

Pauling, Linus C., 1901-1994

Pauling, Linus C. Linus Pauling in his own words; selections from his writings, speeches, and interviews; edited by Barbara Marinacci; introduction by Linus Pauling. Simon & Schuster 1995 320p pa $20 hardcover o.p.   **92**

ISBN 0-6848-1387-4 (ps)   LC 95-31123

"A Touchstone book"

This book "attempts to follow the life and career of Dr. Pauling through his own writings, interspersed with narrative by the editor. The book succeeds wonderfully. Linus Pauling is unique among modern scientists, both for winning two Nobel Prizes and for his political and social views. Through his writings, the breadth and depth of his work become clear to the reader." Sci Books Films

Includes bibliographical references

Pearl, Daniel, 1963-2002

Pearl, Mariane. A mighty heart; the brave life and death of my husband, Danny Pearl; [by] Mariane Pearl, with Sarah Crichton. Scribner 2003 278p $25; pa $13 *   **92**

ISBN 0-7432-4442-7; 0-7432-6237-9 (pa)

LC 2003-60143

"On January 23, 2002, Danny Pearl, the South Asia bureau chief of the *Wall Street Journal* stationed in Pakistan, left his Karachi home to go to some meetings. It was the last time his wife, fellow journalist Mariane, saw him alive. . . . This memoir, written by his widow, begins the morning of his abduction and takes us through the confirmation of his abduction, the efforts to free him, and his assassination. . . . Plenty of words have been written about the Pearl abduction, but these are by far the most personal and most poignant." Booklist

Pépin, Jacques

Pépin, Jacques. The apprentice: my life in the kitchen. Houghton Mifflin 2003 318p il $26

92

ISBN 0-618-19737-0   LC 2002-192158

"Pépin recounts his journey from the kitchen of his mother's humble restaurant in rural France after World War II to his current position as author of 21 cookbooks, star of 13 PBS cooking shows and dean of special programs at the French Culinary Institute in New York City. . . . Each chapter concludes with one or two recipes." Publ Wkly

"Pépin relates how his interest in food and culinary techniques developed into passions for cooking and teaching. He does this deftly, neatly capturing personalities and events with clear, concise writing." Libr J

Pepys, Samuel, 1633-1703

Pepys, Samuel. The diary of Samuel Pepys; edited and with a preface by Richard Le Gallienne; introduction by Robert Louis Stevenson. Modern Lib. 2001 xxxv, 310p $22; pa $15.95 *

92

ISBN 0-679-64221-8; 0-8129-7071-3 (pa)

LC 00-54817

An abridged edition of Pepys' eleven-volume diary, originally written between 1660 and 1669.

Tomalin, Claire. Samuel Pepys; the unequalled self. Knopf 2002 xxiii, 470p il $30; pa $16.95

92

1. Great Britain—History—1603-1714, Stuarts
2. Great Britain—Social life and customs
ISBN 0-375-41143-7; 0-375-72553-9 (pa)

LC 2002-75701

"Tomalin mines the diary, and she also expands upon the characters and events, great and small, that affected Pepys' life and livelihood to bring the man and his milieu to life—pungently as well as vibrantly." Booklist

Includes bibliographical references

Pham, Thong Van

Pham, Andrew X. The eaves of heaven; a life in three wars; by Andrew X. Pham, on behalf of my father, Thong Van Pham. Harmony Books 2008 301p $24.95 *   **92**

1. Vietnamese Americans 2. Refugees 3. Vietnam—History

ISBN 978-0-307-38120-0; 0-307-38120-X

LC 2007-33894

"In a narrative set between the years of 1940 and 1976, Pham . . . recounts the story of his once wealthy father, Thong Van Pham, who lived through the French occupation of Indochina, the Japanese invasion during WWII, and the Vietnam War. . . . For those not familiar with Vietnamese history, Pham does an admirable job of recounting the complex cast of characters and the political machinations of the various groups vying for power over the years. In the end, he also gracefully delivers a heartfelt family history." Publ Wkly

Includes bibliographical references

Philip II, King of Spain, 1527-1598

Kamen, Henry. Philip of Spain. Yale Univ. Press 1997 384p il maps hardcover o.p. pa $18.95

92

1. Spain—History

ISBN 0-300-07081-0; 0-300-07800-5 (pa)

LC 96-52421

The author "offers the most favorable major assessment of Philip ever written in English. . . . The reason he has fared so badly until lately, Kamen . . . suggests, is that he 'failed to project his image', disdaining the visual and literary propaganda mastered by his rivals, especially Elizabeth of England." Atl Mon

"Kamen's prose is lucid, succinct, and thorough. . . . In humanizing a man too often viewed as a cardboard tyrant, Kamen has made a valuable contribution to European historiography." Booklist

Includes bibliographical references

Picasso, Pablo, 1881-1973

Léal, Brigitte. The ultimate Picasso; {by} Brigitte Léal, Christine Piot, Marie-Laure Bernadac; preface by Jean Leymarie. Abrams 2000 535p il pa $ hardcover o.p.   **92**

ISBN 0-8109-9114-4 (pa)

Translated from the French

These "essays detail events in Picasso's life and the circumstances surrounding the creation of his art, his influences, and world events. This lavish, handsome book contains more than 1200 reproductions, nearly 800 in full color." SLJ

Includes bibliographical references

Penrose, Sir Roland. Picasso: his life and work. 3rd ed. University of Calif. Press 1981 517p il pa $21.95 hardcover o.p. *   **92**

ISBN 0-520-04207-7 (pa)

LC 80-54015

First published 1958 by Harper

The author "has produced a painstaking, comprehensive biography . . . and, what is more, a popular biography, assuming neither knowledge of nor sympathy with twentieth-century art on the part of the reader." Times Lit Suppl {review of 1958 edition}

Includes bibliographical references

Pickford, Mary, 1893-1979

Whitfield, Eileen. Pickford; the woman who made Hollywood. University Press of Ky. 1997 441p il $27.50   **92**

ISBN 0-8131-2045-4   LC 97-29312

"Silent screen star Mary Pickford was 'America's Sweetheart,' capturing the imagination of the public as 'Little Mary,' the adolescent with spunk. She married swashbuckler Douglas Fairbanks, and with Charlie Chaplin and D.W. Griffith they formed United Artists, the first production company run by people who acted and directed. . . . Though it does include delicious anecdotes from those who were there, this is not simply a typical celebrity biography but a 'biography' of the times." Libr J

Includes bibliographical references

Pinchot, Gifford, 1865-1946

Miller, Char. Gifford Pinchot and the making of modern environmentalism. Island Press (Washington, D.C.) 2001 458p il $28   **92**

ISBN 1-55963-822-2   LC 2001-5665

"Charismatic, progressive, and controversial, Gifford Pinchot (1865-1946) established and directed the Forest Service under Theodore Roosevelt, lobbied hard for responsible logging practices, expressed prescient warnings about pollution, and called for sustainable energy. Miller's animated biography portrays Pinchot in all his fervor, and environmentalism in all its complexity." Booklist

Includes bibliographical references

Pinkerton, Allan, 1819-1884

Mackay, James A. (James Alexander). Allan Pinkerton; the first private eye; [by] James Mackay. Wiley 1997 256p il $35   **92**

1. Pinkerton's National Detective Agency

ISBN 0-471-19415-8   LC 97-21271

"Though Pinkerton started the first U.S. detective agency after successfully uncovering a counterfeit ring, little was known about him. The author does an excellent job of tracing Pinkerton's early life and his arrival in the United States from Scotland. Then he examines better-known aspects of Pinkerton's career—his part in Lincoln's train ride through Baltimore, investigation of the Confederate spy Rose Greenhow, and association with Gen. George McClellan, his mentor and hero." Libr J

Includes bibliographical references

Pirsig, Robert M., 1928-

Pirsig, Robert M. Zen and the art of motorcycle maintenance; an inquiry into values. Morrow 1974 412p $26; pa $13.95   **92**

ISBN 0-688-00230-7; 0-06-083987-2 (pa)

A collection of the author's philosophical musings inspired by a motorcycle trip with his son

Pius XII, Pope, 1876-1958

Cornwell, John. Hitler's pope: the secret history of Pius XII. Viking 1999 430p il pa $15 hardcover o.p.   **92**

ISBN 0-14-029627-1 (pa)   LC 99-28311

Pius XII, Pope, 1876-1958—*Continued*
"Relying on exclusive access to Vatican and Jesuit archives, . . . {the author} argues that through a 1933 Concordat with Hitler, Pope Pius XII facilitated the dictator's rise—and, ultimately, the Holocaust." Libr J
Includes bibliographical references

Plath, Sylvia
Plath, Sylvia. The unabridged journals of Sylvia Plath, 1950-1962; edited by Karen V. Kukil. Anchor Press 2000 732p il pa $18　　　　**92**
　ISBN 0-385-72025-4　　　　LC 00-42024
First published 2000 in the United Kingdom with title: Journals of Sylvia Plath, 1950-1962
"Transcribed from the original manuscripts at Smith College."; Originally published: Journals of Sylvia Plath, 1950-1962. London : Faber and Faber, 2000
Kukil presents diaries written by the poet Sylvia Plath. "This edition includes two journals written between August 1957 and November 1959 that {her husband Ted} Hughes ordered to be unsealed in 1997 shortly before his death." Christ Sci Monit
"This is essential for anyone engaged in Plath studies." Libr J
Includes bibliographical references

Wagner-Martin, Linda. Sylvia Plath; a literary life. St. Martin's Press 1999 172p (Literary lives) $45; pa $19.95　　　　**92**
　ISBN 0-312-22323-4; 1-40391-653-5 (pa)
　　　　　　　　　　　　　LC 99-12184
First published 1998 in the United Kingdom
The author "begins by summarizing Plath's childhood, which was marked by her educator parents' deep involvement with books, and her father's unexpected death when she was eight. . . . Wagner-Martin works strictly by the light of Plath's writings as she spins the oft-told tale of Plath's blazing creativity and fatal despair, and what emerges is a tragic tale of an artist envied and mistreated by those closest to her, and of a poet far more artistic than her reputation for being confessional implies." Booklist
Includes bibliographical references

Poe, Edgar Allan, 1809-1849
Silverman, Kenneth. Edgar A. Poe; mournful and never-ending remembrance. HarperCollins Pubs. 1991 564p il pa $18 hardcover o.p.
　　　　　　　　　　　　　　92
　ISBN 0-06-092331-8 (pa)　　　　LC 90-56397
The author explains "how Poe's early life influenced his work. He details Poe's turbulent career as poet, short story writer, and editor . . . and traces his literary development through bouts of alcoholism and hallucinations and disputes with literary rivals. An excellent addition to the literature that furthers understanding of America's gothic tale-teller." Libr J
Includes bibliographical references

Walsh, John Evangelist. Midnight dreary; the mysterious death of Edgar Allan Poe. St. Martin's Minotaur 2000 199p il pa $14.95　　　　**92**
　ISBN 0-312-22732-9; 978-0-312-22732-6
　　　　　　　　　　　　　LC 00-25571

First published 1998 by Rutgers Univ. Press
This is an account of the "circumstances leading to Poe's death in Baltimore, in October 1849." Publ Wkly
Walsh "has undertaken a superbly informed speculation on the week proceeding the mysterious death of Edgar Allan Poe 150 years ago." Libr J
Includes bibliographical references

Poitier, Sidney
Goudsouzian, Aram. Sidney Poitier; man, actor, icon. University of North Carolina Press 2004 480p il $29.95　　　　**92**
　ISBN 0-8078-2843-2　　　　LC 2003-19372
The author "traces Poitier's journey from life as the son of a poor Bahamian farmer to celebrity status in the States as a trailblazing actor who has received as much criticism as praise for his portrayal of dignified and stoical black men." Booklist
Includes bibliographical references

Poitier, Sidney. The measure of a man; a spiritual autobiography. HarperSanFrancisco 2007 c2000 299p il $25.95; pa $14.95 *　　　　**92**
　ISBN　978-0-06-135791-6;　0-06-135791-X; 978-0-06-135790-9 (pa); 0-06-135790-1 (pa)
A reissue of the title first published 2000
"Poitier attempts to unravel for himself his own remarkable life story, looking at early life experiences, his family, and various themes that he believes have contributed to his success. *Measure* is not a chronological autobiography; the book emphasizes themes that have shaped his life. . . . Poitier's tale is an affirmation of the value of morality and personal integrity in leading a successful, fulfilling life." Booklist

Polk, James K. (James Knox), 1795-1849
Borneman, Walter R. Polk; the man who transformed the presidency and America. Random House 2008 422p il map $30　　　　**92**
　1. Presidents—United States
　ISBN 978-1-4000-6560-8　　　　LC 2007-14040
The author "presents a birth-death biography of Polk. . . . Borneman has a pleasing style and makes fine use of primary sources that all demonstrate why Polk is habitually ranked as one of the ten best presidents by historians." Libr J
Includes bibliographical references

Dusinberre, William. Slavemaster president; the double career of James Polk. Oxford Univ. Press 2003 258p il map $35　　　　**92**
　1. Slavery—United States 2. Presidents—United States
　ISBN 0-19-515735-4　　　　LC 2002-74852
This book focuses on "Polk's management of his slaves and his public positions on slavery and related issues. The author suggests that Polk's policies were critical to the development of the secessionist movement in the South and that these policies derived from his personal financial interests. . . . Dusinberre's research also expands our understanding of the management of plantations. Essential reading for anyone wanting greater insight into the factors that led to the Civil War, this work is highly recommended." Libr J
Includes bibliographical references

Pollock, Jackson, 1912-1956
Solomon, Deborah. Jackson Pollock; a biography. Cooper Square Press 2001 287p il pa $17.95   **92**
1. Abstract expressionism 2. Artists—United States
ISBN 978-0-8154-1182-6; 0-8154-1182-0
         LC 2001-28915
First published 1987 by Simon and Schuster
A biography of the American abstract expressionist painter.
"A concisely written biography; the footnotes indicate solid research." Libr J
Includes bibliographical references

Polo, Marco, 1254-1323?
Bergreen, Laurence. Marco Polo; from Venice to Xanadu. Knopf 2007 415p il map $28.95
    92
1. Voyages and travels 2. Explorers 3. China—Description and travel
ISBN 978-1-4000-4345-3; 1-4000-4345-3
         LC 2007-21860
This is a biography of the Venetian explorer.
The author "gives a full-blooded rendition of Polo's astonishing journey. It is richly researched and vividly conveyed." Washington Post Book World
Includes bibliographical references

Pompadour, Jeanne Antoinette Poisson, marquise de, 1721-1764
Lever, Evelyne. Madame de Pompadour; translated from the French by Catherine Temerson. Farrar, Straus & Giroux 2002 310p il $26; pa $16.95   **92**
1. France—History—1589-1789, Bourbons
ISBN 0-374-11308-4; 0-312-31050-1 (pa)
         LC 2002-22811
Original French edition, 2000
This is a biography of "Madame de Pompadour, official 'favorite' of France's handsome but moody Louis XV." Booklist
"Lever has crafted a detailed and fascinating portrait of the woman who pretty well ran France from 1745 to 1764." Publ Wkly
Includes bibliographical references

Pomus, Doc, 1925-1991
Halberstadt, Alex E. Lonely avenue; the unlikely life and times of Doc Pomus. Da Capo Press 2007 254p il $26   **92**
ISBN 978-0-306-81300-9; 0-306-81300-9
"One of America's most popular songwriters was Jerome Felder, better known as 'Doc Pomus.' For decades he wrote big hits ('Save the Last Dance for Me,' 'This Magic Moment,' 'A Teenager in Love') for such artists as Dion, Fabian, the Drifters, Elvis and Dr. John. . . . The son in a New York working-class Jewish family, Pomus contracted polio when he was seven and lost the use of his legs. From then on, his life was all about music; he started bands, wrote music and promoted artists until the day he died." Publ Wkly
"Throughout this book Halberstadt sketches a broad canvas of characters, Pomus's friends and enemies along with a gallery of rogues, malcontents, hustlers, knaves, acquaintances, colleagues, and hangers-on. . . . There's some guesswork here; Halberstadt had access to Pomus' notebooks and done interviews with some of Doc's contemporaries, but there are also moments of revelation and introspection that can only be ventured. Halberstadt exercises this license faithfully and believably." PopMatters

Ponzi, Charles, d. 1949
Zuckoff, Mitchell. Ponzi's scheme; the true story of a financial legend. Random House 2005 390p il $25.95; pa $14.95   **92**
ISBN 1-400-06039-7; 0-8129-6836-0 (pa)
         LC 2004-46770
The author "chronicles Ponzi's mercurial rise and fall as he conjured up one get-rich-quick scheme after another. . . . Zuckoff provides not only a definitive portrait of Ponzi's life but also insights into immigrant life and the social world of early 20th-century Boston." Publ Wkly
Includes bibliographical references

Pop, Iggy, 1947-
Trynka, Paul. Iggy Pop; open up and bleed. Broadway Books 2007 371p il $23.95; pa $14.95
    92
1. Punk rock music 2. Rock musicians
ISBN 978-0-7679-2319-4; 978-0-7679-2320-0 (pa)
         LC 2006-30216
"Drawing from original interviews with Iggy (né James Newell Osterberg Jr.) and his countless accomplices over the years, Trynka . . . has constructed a comprehensive portrait of the seemingly indestructible rock provocateur, one that touches all the familiar bases in recounting Iggy's riotous ascent from suburban Michigan schoolboy to frontman of the Stooges to solo artist with an intermittently transcendent career to composer of a drug-inspired hit song that became the jingle for a luxury cruise line." N Y Times Book Rev
Includes bibliographical references

Porter, Cole, 1891-1964
McBrien, William. Cole Porter; a biography. Knopf 1998 459p il hardcover o.p. $16
    92
ISBN 978-0-679-72792-7; 0-679-72792-2
         LC 97-46116
In this biography of the American songwriter, the author "weaves a complex and groundbreaking portrait of Porter, interspersed with lyrics and 72 illustrations, recounting his affluent upbringing in Peru, Ind., and his emergence in the 1930s as the musical theater's reigning sophisticate. . . . This astute biography will help to create a standard-setting portrait of Porter as a homosexual artist in a heterosexual world." Publ Wkly
Includes bibliographical references

Potter, Beatrix, 1866-1943
Lear, Linda J. Beatrix Potter; a life in nature; [by] Linda Lear. Allen Lane/Penguin 2007 583p il $30 *   **92**
ISBN 9780312369347; 0-312-36934-4
         LC 2006-51245

Potter, Beatrix, 1866-1943—*Continued*
This is a biography of the children's author.
This "is a meticulously researched and brilliantly rec-
reated life that . . . is endlessly fascinating and often il-
luminating. It is altogether a remarkable achievement."
Booklist
Includes bibliographical references

Pound, Ezra, 1885-1972
Tytell, John. Ezra Pound; the solitary volcano.
Anchor Press 1987 368p il pa $19 hardcover o.p.
                                                        92
ISBN 0-385-19870-1 (pa)   LC 86-25912
"In this incisive interpretative biography, based on in-
terviews with those who knew him and a mass of pub-
lished and unpublished Poundiana, Tytell examines the
circumstances behind the poems and thereby generates
new understanding of the man." Publ Wkly
Includes bibliographical references

Powell, Colin L., 1937-
De Young, Karen. Soldier: the life of Colin
Powell. Knopf 2006 610p il $28.95   **92**
1. Statesmen—United States
ISBN 1-400-04170-8   LC 2006-45288
This biography ranges "from Powell's Bronx childhood and meteoric rise through the military ranks to his
formative roles in Washington's corridors of power and
his controversial tenure as secretary of state." Publisher's
note
This is a "diligent, sympathetic, but not uncritical full-
scale biography." N Y Rev Books
Includes bibliographical references

Powell, Colin L. My American journey; [by]
Colin L. Powell, with Joseph E. Persico. Random
House 1995 643p il $26.95; pa $14.95   **92**
1. Statesmen—United States
ISBN 0-679-43296-5; 0-345-46641-1 (pa)
                                          LC 95-17119
"This is the 'story so far,' as General Powell tells it,
from the Bronx to Vietnam to the White House, from the
common to the regal. His account is one of . . . extremes, tales that span from peeling potatoes with the Soviet General Staff to conversing with the Queen of England." Libr J
This "is an endearing and well-written book. It will
make you like Colin Powell." N Y Times Book Rev

Presley, Elvis, 1935-1977
Guralnick, Peter. Careless love: the unmaking of
Elvis Presley. Little, Brown 1999 767p il $27.95;
pa $17.95 *   **92**
1. Rock musicians
ISBN 0-316-33222-4; 0-316-33297-6 (pa)
                                          LC 98-25778
This second and concluding volume of Guralnick's biography of the rock star covers "Elvis's hitch in the
army through his death in 1977. . . . The breadth of
Guralnick's research is nothing short of amazing, and his
lyrical narrative presents an empathetic portrait of a man
struggling with drugs, sex, family, personal eccentricities,

money, and the delicate web of relationships surrounding
any famous figure." Libr J
Includes bibliographical references

Guralnick, Peter. Last train to Memphis: the rise
of Elvis Presley. Little, Brown 1994 560p il
$27.95; pa $17.95   **92**
1. Rock musicians
ISBN 0-316-33220-8; 0-316-33225-9 (pa)
                                          LC 94-10763
The first of a two volume biography of the rock pioneer
The author "depicts Elvis as a naive yet extremely talented boy whose dream of stardom came true, leaving
him a virtual prisoner of his own success. . . . Taking
pains to keep the story fresh and flowing and refraining
from foreshadowing and editorializing, Guralnick lets the
facts speak for themselves." Booklist
Includes bibliographical references

Mason, Bobbie Ann. Elvis Presley. Viking 2002
178p (Penguin lives series) $19.95; pa $13
                                          92
1. Rock musicians
ISBN 0-670-03174-7; 0-14-303889-3 (pa)
                                     LC 2002-28873
"A Lipper/Viking book"
The author "chronicles Elvis' sad story: humble origins, 1954 breakthrough, adoption by 'the Colonel'
(manager Tom Parker), early TV appearances, army
hitch, the death of his mother, marriage to Priscilla, Hollywood, 1968 'comeback', Las Vegas headliner, prescription drug abuse, meeting with Nixon, and death at 42 in
1977." Booklist
Includes discography, filmography and bibliographical
references

Price, Reynolds, 1933-
Price, Reynolds. A whole new life. Atheneum
Pubs. 1994 213p $23; pa $13   **92**
ISBN 0-684-87255-2; 0-7432-3854-0 (pa)
                                          LC 93-35967
Price gives an "account of his 'mid-life collision with
cancer and paralysis.' In 1984, he was found to have a
malignant tumor of the spinal cord, and three surgeries
and radiation therapy arrested the growth but left him unable to walk. Although he has not written an essay on
illness per se, he embraces elements of an essay as he
pauses to ponder nature's systemic breakdowns, the importance of friendships in times of stress, or how to handle pain psychologically. His book is primarily a chronological narrative of events in the treatment of his disease
and his rehabilitation." Booklist

Pritchett, V. S. (Victor Sawdon), 1900-1997
Treglown, Jeremy. V.S. Pritchett: a working life.
Random House 2005 334p $25.95   **92**
ISBN 0-375-50853-8   LC 2004-53857
This biography follows the life and career of the En-
glish writer, who for most of the century ennobled the
ordinary and whose two tumultuous marriages fueled his
art
"Treglown's genial and sympathetic biography effec-

Pritchett, V. S. (Victor Sawdon), 1900-1997—
Continued
tively expands . . . awareness of the life and career of
this greatly accessible and warmhearted writer of fiction,
travel literature, and criticism. . . . This is a biography
as open-minded and unpretentious as Pritchett's own
writing." Booklist
Includes bibliographical references

Prokofiev, Sergey, 1891-1953
Nice, David. Prokofiev: from Russia to the
West, 1891-1935. Yale Univ. Press 2003 390p il
music $35 *   **92**
ISBN 0-300-09914-2
First of a projected two volume work
"Part 1 chronicles Prokofiev's childhood, family rela-
tionships, and training at the St. Petersburg Conserva-
toire, while Part 2 covers his concert tours in America,
France, and Germany and prodigious compositional out-
put, beginning with the fairy tale opera, *The Love of
Three Oranges*. . . . Nice embeds many musical examples in the body of the text and writes cogently about
them. . . . Overall, the writing is fluid and unencumbered by excessive analytical detail, and at times witty.
. . . Throughout, the composer's outsized personality and
compositional brilliance shine through." Libr J
Includes discography and bibliographical references

Proust, Marcel, 1871-1922
Carter, William C. Marcel Proust; a life. Yale
Univ. Press 2000 946p $45; pa $18.95   **92**
ISBN 0-300-08145-6; 0-300-09400-0 (pa)
                LC 99-53701
"Excavating biographic details out of such material as
untranslated memoirs and recently collected letters, Car-
ter . . . accounts for the daily affairs of this social but-
terfly-turned-hypochondriac and shut-in. Proust's ro-
mances and infatuations, his political action during the
Dreyfus affair, and his literary runs-ins with Anatole
France and André Gide, as well as larger issues such as
his homosexuality, all receive lengthy treatment." Publ
Wkly
Includes bibliographical references

Puccini, Giacomo, 1858-1924
Berger, William. Puccini without excuses; a
refreshing reassessment of the world's most
popular composer. Vintage Books 2005 471p pa
$16   **92**
1. Opera
ISBN 978-1-4000-7778-6; 1-4000-7778-8
                LC 2005-46157
The author "sets Puccini within his times before discussing the circumstances of each opera's premiere and
famous interpreters of the roles, providing character lists
and synopses and fleshing all this out with musical commentary. Chapters on opera production and the genre's
relation to film are useful. . . Berger's lucid yet hardly
dispassionate views are designed to elicit strong reactions, so this is not the first place one should go for an
unbiased introduction to the composer's oeuvre. But the
author's grounding information is helpful for the novice,
and he refers to some of the current authoritative
sources." Libr J

Pushkin, Aleksandr Sergeevich, 1799-1837
Binyon, T. J. Pushkin: a biography. Knopf 2003
xxix, 727p il maps $35; pa $20 *   **92**
ISBN 1-4000-4110-4; 1-4000-7652-8 (pa)
              LC 2003-112113
The author argues that Pushkin's "political views and
rebellious temper were a continual source of trouble, inviting criticism and condemnation his entire life and
eventually ending it in 1837 when he was fatally wounded in a duel with George D'Anthes. . . . A stunning
achievement, this thorough biography is sure to become
the definitive account of Pushkin's life for years to come
and will appeal to the scholar and general reader alike."
Libr J
Includes bibliographical references

Putin, Vladimir
Putin, Vladimir. First person: an astonishingly
frank self-portrait; by Russia's president Vladimir
Putin with Nataliya Gevorkyan, Natalya Timakova,
and Andrei Kolesnikov; translated by Catherine A.
Fitzpatrick. PublicAffairs 2000 206p il pa $15
                       92
ISBN 1-58648-018-9   LC 00-132549
This volume is "the product of some 24 hours of interviews with Putin conducted by three Russian journalists, with brief comments from other sources, including
Putin's family, friends, teachers, and some associates.
. . . The approach is chronological, describing Putin as
son, schoolboy, university student, young intelligence
specialist, spy, democrat, family man, and
politician." Booklist

Pyle, Ernie, 1900-1945
Tobin, James. Ernie Pyle's war; America's
eyewitness to World War II. Free Press 1997 312p
il pa $15   **92**
ISBN 0-684-83642-4; 978-0-7432-8476-9 (pa);
0-7432-8476-3 (pa)   LC 97-6165
"This is the portrait of a complex, enormously gifted
but tortured writer, entrapped and ultimately driven to
death by a sense of obligation to the image he inadver-
tently created of himself." N Y Times Book Rev
"Living and working among the troops he so vividly
chronicled, Pyle offered a unique insider's perspective of
the harsh reality experienced by the common soldier during World War II. . . . A respectful and insightful biography of a giant among journalists." Booklist
Includes bibliographical references

Qazwini, Hassan
Qazwini, Hassan. American crescent; A Muslim
cleric on the power of his faith, the struggle
against prejudice, and the future of Islam and
America. Random House 2007 282p il $26.95
                       92
1. Muslims—United States
ISBN 978-1-4000-6454-0; 1-4000-6454-0
              LC 2007-10345
This is a memoir by "the religious leader of the Islamic Center of America in Dearborn, Michigan." Publisher's note

Qazwini, Hassan—*Continued*

This "a useful book, especially for American readers who are unfamiliar with Islam or who wonder how Muslim Americans and Arab-Americans can be integrated into American life." N Y Times Book Rev

Includes bibliographical references

Rabin, Yitzhak, 1922-1995

Shalom, friend: the life and legacy of Yitzhak Rabin; the Jerusalem Report staff; edited by David Horovitz; prologue by Hirsch Goodman. Newmarket Press 1996 314p il maps $24.95

92

ISBN 1-55704-287-X   LC 96-5146

"This is a collaborative effort by more than a dozen writers and editors of the *Jerusalem Report,* a prestigious Israeli newsmagazine, all of whom had close personal and professional knowledge of the former prime minister, assassinated in November 1995. Their views are supplemented by numerous, interviews with knowledgeable people." Libr J

Includes bibliographical references

Ramanujan Aiyangar, Srinivasa, 1887-1920

Kanigel, Robert. The man who knew infinity; a life of the genius Ramanujan. Washington Sq. Press 1992 438p map il pa $15   **92**

1. Hardy, Grahame H. 2. Mathematicians

ISBN 0-671-75061-5; 978-0-671-75061-9

LC 91-37763

First published 1991 by Charles Scribner's Sons

This biography traces the life of the Indian mathematician. "Working alone in relative obscurity and lacking the usual academic credentials [Ramanujan] could easily have passed unnoticed. However, with the help of a handful of friends and the ultimate support of renowned English mathematician G.H. Hardy, his work was brought to the attention of the world." Libr J

"Kanigel deserves high praise for a work of arduous research and rare insight." Booklist

Includes bibliographical references

Rand, Ayn, 1905-1982

Rand, Ayn. Journals of Ayn Rand; edited by David Harriman; foreword by Leonard Peikoff. Dutton 1997 727p il pa $22 hardcover o.p.

92

ISBN 0-452-27887-2 (pa)   LC 97-12737

"This work offers almost everything the author ever wrote to herself. As intriguing yet sometimes numbing as her fiction, the book, which covers the years from 1927 to the mid-1970s, contains her first philosophical stabs, notes on her novels, HUAC testimony against alleged Hollywood communists, and her unfinished projects." Publ Wkly

Rand, Ayn. Letters of Ayn Rand; edited by Michael S. Berliner; introduction by Leonard Peikoff. Dutton 1995 xxi, 681p il pa $20 hardcover o.p. paperback available $20   **92**

ISBN 0-452-27404-4 (pa)   LC 94-23646

"Sprinkled with critiques of liberals, leftists and others whom she saw as corrupted by collectivist thinking, the voluminous correspondence reflects Rand's desperate concerns for her parents and sisters, trapped under Stalinism in her native Russia (which she left for Hollywood in 1926), and includes her analyses of her novels' plots as well as pessimistic cultural commentary on an America she considered to be in decline." Publ Wkly

"Imbued with her fiercely held beliefs, the letters most devoted to politics and philosophy fairly blaze off the page. . . . Regardless of one's opinion of her thinking, her letters add greatly to our understanding of a most exceptional woman of letters." Booklist

Ray, Man, 1890-1976

Lottman, Herbert R. Man Ray's Montparnasse. Abrams 2001 261p il $29.95   **92**

ISBN 0-8109-4333-6   LC 2001-633

Lottman presents a "snapshot of Man Ray between the two world wars, emphasizing the 1920s, with the developing Montparnasse section of Paris as the backdrop. Here are the cutting-edge dadaists and surrealists flanking Man Ray and his unerring camera eye, along with poets and artists, collectors, lovers, and other assorted characters. . . . Lottman's vivid exploration of 20th-century art events will serve the art historian and student of Paris very well in documenting an essential epoch and place." Libr J

Includes bibliographical references

Reagan, Ronald, 1911-2004

D'Souza, Dinesh. Ronald Reagan; how an ordinary man became an extraordinary leader. Free Press 1997 292p pa $13 hardcover o.p.

92

1. United States—Politics and government—1974-1989 2. Presidents—United States

ISBN 0-684-84823-6 (pa)   LC 97-31396

In this study of the fortieth president of the United States, D'Souza "argues that Reagan earned presidential stature comparable with that of Washington, Lincoln, and Roosevelt." Booklist

The author's "provocative argument for Reagan's greatness opens a necessary and complicated debate." Commentary

Includes bibliographical references

Reagan, Ronald. Reagan; a life in letters; edited, with an introduction and commentary by Kiron K. Skinner, Annelise Anderson, {and} Martin Anderson; with a foreword by George P. Shultz. Free Press 2003 934p $35; pa $18.95 *

92

1. Presidents—United States

ISBN 0-7432-1966-X; 0-7432-1967-8 (pa)

LC 2003-49249

"This volume consists of a sampling of the former president's copious outpouring of personal letters, from his childhood to the onset of Alzheimer's after the presidency. The editors . . . arrange the letters thematically, introduce each chapter with a brief commentary, and introduce each letter with a sentence or two of explanation. The editors have done an admirable job in compiling

Reagan, Ronald, 1911-2004—*Continued*
these documents. Their commentary is exactly as it might have been had Ronald Reagan been able to produce this volume himself." Choice

Includes bibliographical references

Reagan, Ronald. The Reagan diaries; edited by Douglas Brinkley. HarperCollins 2007 767p il $35
92
1. United States—Politics and government—1974-1989 2. Presidents—United States
ISBN 978-0-06-087600-5; 0-06-087600-X
"During his two terms as the fortieth president of the United States, Ronald Reagan kept a daily diary in which he recorded, by hand, his innermost thoughts and observations on the extraordinary, the historic, and the routine day-today occurrences of his presidency." Publisher's note
"There is a kind of touching banality to many of the entries, as though Reagan were just another CEO writing about corporate life at the top, albeit corporate life that revolved around nuclear and hostage negotiations. Edited by Douglas Brinkley . . ., the book shows a Reagan almost sweetly amazed by small trappings of office. . . . Reading these diaries, Americans will find it easier to understand how Reagan did what he did for so long: by steady work, and a steadfast commitment to the job at hand." Newsweek

Reeve, Christopher, 1952-2004
Reeve, Christopher. Still me. Random House 1998 309p il pa $7.99 hardcover o.p. **92**
1. Actors 2. Physically handicapped
ISBN 0-345-43241-X (pa)   LC 98-10223
This autobiography begins with Reeve's "riding accident and relates in almost slow-motion detail what happened before and after the near-fatal spill in 1995. His remembrances then move back and forth in time. Reeve's early life, his complex relationships, and his career are juxtaposed against the life he leads now as filmmaker, husband and father, and spokesman for those with spinal-cord injuries." Booklist

Reichl, Ruth
Reichl, Ruth. Comfort me with apples; more adventures at the table. Random House 2001 302p $24.95; pa $13.95   **92**
ISBN 0-375-50195-9; 0-375-75873-9 (pa)
LC 00-53355
Sequel to Tender at the bone (1998)
"In this second installment of her memoirs, {Reichl} retraces her route from married life on a commune in late-seventies Berkeley to her first job as a food critic, dining at expensive restaurants in Los Angeles with her glamorous editor. . . . Reichl writes with gusto, and her story has all the ingredients of a modern fairy tale: hard work, weird food, and endless curiosity." New Yorker

Reichl, Ruth. Garlic and sapphires. Penguin Press 2005 333p $24.95   **92**
ISBN 1-594-20031-9   LC 2004-51362
This is "an account of the various disguises [the author] donned so she would not be recognized as restaurant critic of the New York Times." Libr J
"Reichl's ability to experience meals in such a dramatic way brings an infectious passion to her memoir. Reading this work . . . ensures that the next time readers sit down in a restaurant, they'll notice things they've never noticed before." Publ Wkly

Reinhardt, Django, 1910-1953
Dregni, Michael. Django: the life and music of a Gypsy legend. Oxford University Press 2004 326p il $35; pa $16.95   **92**
ISBN 0-19-516752-X; 0-19-530448-9 (pa)
LC 2004-6214
This "biography does its complex subject justice. And even when Dregni dallies overlong on some byways, his immersion in the period's history enriches his storytelling and our understanding. The panoramic results present Django Reinhardt as he has never been seen." N Y Times Book Rev
Includes bibliographical references

Rembrandt Harmenszoon van Rijn, 1606-1669
Schama, Simon. Rembrandt's eyes. Knopf 1999 640p il $50; pa $35   **92**
ISBN 0-679-40256-X; 0-375-70981-9 (pa)
LC 99-19971
Schama's prose unfurls the life of Rembrandt in all its pathos. From prodigy to pauper, the troubled genius of 17th century Dutch painting is intricately conceived as he rises and falls in a world of war, plague and stolid bourgeois comfort. . . . Schama's book is a marvel of storytelling: sometimes heart pounding, always sympathetic and coolly reasoned. Seamlessly joining social history and art, what a triumph of scholarship and imagination. Time

Remington, Frederic, 1861-1909
Dippie, Brian W. The Frederic Remington Art Museum collection. Abrams 2000 264p il $49.50
92
1. West (U.S.) in art
ISBN 0-8109-6711-1   LC 00-49339
This biography examines the artist's life and work and follows his evolution from illustrator to artist
"Photographs and comparative images enhance the author's discussions of Remington himself and of the individual paintings, drawings, and sculptures." Libr J
Includes bibliographical references

Renoir, Auguste, 1841-1919
Renoir, Jean. Renoir: my father; introduction by Robert Herbert; translated by Randolph and Dorothy Weaver. New York Review of Bks. 2001 437p il pa $17.95   **92**
ISBN 0-940322-77-3   LC 2001-2539
First published 1962 by Little, Brown
The author "tells the life story of his father, Pierre Auguste Renoir, the great Impressionist painter. Recounting Pierre-Auguste's extraordinary career, beginning as a painter of fans and porcelain, recording the rules of thumb by which he worked, and capturing his unpretentious and wonderfully engaging talk and personality. . . . {This volume} includes 12 pages of color plates and 18 pages of black and white images." Publisher's note

Richardson, John, 1924-

Richardson, John. The sorcerer's apprentice; Picasso, Provence, and Douglas Cooper. University of Chicago Press 2001 318p il pa $17   **92**

1. Cooper, Douglas, 1911-1984

ISBN 0-226-71245-1

First published 1999 by Knopf

Picasso biographer John Richardson "has written a concise account of the first half of his own life and notably of his long relationship as a young man with the Cubist art historian and collector Douglas Cooper. The account concentrates on the dozen years, from early 1949 to the end of 1960, when Richardson lived with Cooper, visiting museums and monuments all over Europe, meeting the great artists and other personalities of the day, and restoring the colonnaded Chateau de Castille in the south of France." NY Times Book Rev

Includes bibliographical references

Richter, Charles F., 1900-1985

Hough, Susan Elizabeth. Richter's scale; measure of an earthquake, measure of a man. Princeton University Press 2007 335p il $27.95   **92**

1. Scientists

ISBN 978-0-691-12807-8; 0-691-12807-3

LC 2006-16480

"In this biography, [the author] interweaves the stories of Richter's life with the history of earthquake exploration and seismology." Publisher's note

"The discussions of the effects of earthquakes on land, structures, and people and the intense search for an understanding of the complex, underlying science will be of interest to many. Readers with substantially different levels of scientific knowledge will find the book comprehensible and interesting." Sci Books Films

Includes bibliographical references

Riefenstahl, Leni, 1902-2003

Bach, Steven. Leni: the life and work of Leni Riefenstahl. A.A. Knopf 2007 368p il $30   **92**

ISBN 978-0-375-40400-9; 0-375-40400-7

LC 2006-49323

This is a biography of the filmmaker.

This "is a lively, incisive look at a compelling and somewhat appalling figure who demonstrated that beauty isn't always truth." Publ Wkly

Includes bibliographical references

Trimborn, Jürgen. Leni Riefenstahl; translated from the German by Edna McCown. Faber & Faber 2007 351p il $30   **92**

ISBN 978-0-374-18493-3; 0-374-18493-3

LC 2006-13263

Original German edition, 2002

This is a biography of the German filmmaker whose work includes Triumph of the Will, a propaganda film for Hitler, and Olympia, a documentary of the 1936 Olympics in Berlin

Trimborn "interviewed Riefenstahl in 1997, when he was twenty-five, having already spent six years of 'intensive labor' on the project, and he briefly entertained the quixotic hope of writing a definitive book with her blessing and collaboration. Unwilling to misrepresent himself as a hagiographer, he was doomed to fail, though his disappointment does not seem to have warped his fair-mindedness. . . . [The author's] aim was to correct the murky published record and the 'attitudes' of his compatriots. One has to admire the sniperlike precision with which he takes out fugitive falsehoods that have lived under cover for a century." New Yorker

Rilke, Rainer Maria, 1875-1926

Rilke, Rainer Maria. Diaries of a young poet; translated and annotated by Edward Snow and Michael Winkler. Norton 1997 xxi, 306p il pa $15.95 hardcover o.p.   **92**

ISBN 0-393-31850-8 (pa)

"Three diaries reveal three Rilkes. The Florence Diary, which he began at twenty-two, is a kind of open letter to his then love, Lou Andreas-Salomé, full of youthful ardor and sublime observations of art and nature. . . . The Schmargendorf Diary reveals the virtuoso at play, with slender fragments of stories, fairy tales, and poems following each other in dazzling succession. The last diary, written during his stay in Worpswede, is the most rewarding, for the chance to watch Rilke's rich friendships with other artists ripen alongside the growing authority of his poetic voice." New Yorker

Ripken, Cal, Jr.

Ripken, Cal, Jr. The only way I know; [by] Cal Ripken, Jr., and Mike Bryan. Viking; distributed by Penguin Putnam 1997 326p il hardcover o.p. pa $12.95   **92**

1. Baseball—Biography

ISBN 0-670-87193-1; 0-14-026626-7 (pa)

LC 97-9159

"Cal Junior chronicles his moves through the minor leagues and into the majors in great detail, always pointing out what he learned at each step of the journey and who taught it to him. There are some great baseball anecdotes—especially involving fiery Oriole skipper Earl Weaver—and plenty of the behind-the-scenes detail." Booklist

Ritchie, Jean, 1922-

Ritchie, Jean. Singing family of the Cumberlands. University Press of Ky. 1988 c1955 258p il $35; pa $20   **92**

1. Folk music—United States 2. Appalachian region 3. Singers

ISBN 978-0-8131-1679-2; 0-8131-1679-1; 978-0-8131-0186-6 (pa); 0-8131-0186-7 (pa)

LC 88-17337

First published 1955 by Oxford University Press

The youngest of the Ritchies, a Cumberland mountain family, whose singing was the order of the day, writes about her own life and that of her family. The Ritchies still sing the songs and ballads brought from Virginia in 1768, by Jean's three times great grandfather. Words and music of 42 songs are included.

"Ritchie writes as she sings—naturally and with an instinctive sense for rhythms. Her story of her rearing in the hill-circled town of Viper is simple, vivid, and moving. . . . A beautiful story of American living." NY Herald Tribune

Rivera, Diego, 1886-1957

Hamill, Pete. Diego Rivera. Abrams 1999 207p il $49.50; pa $24.95 **92**
1. Artists, Mexican
ISBN 0-8109-3234-2; 0-8109-9082-2 (pa)
LC 99-28100
The author examines "Rivera's work and diverse styles. He also describes the pivotal role Rivera's art played in Mexico's development." N Y Times Book Rev
Includes bibliographical references

Marnham, Patrick. Dreaming with his eyes open; a life of Diego Rivera. University of California Press 2000 350p il pa $29.95 **92**
1. Artists, Mexican
ISBN 0-520-22408-6; 978-0-520-22408-7
LC 99-44964
First published 1998 by Knopf
"Retracing the steps of writers who've tackled Rivera's life and times before him, Marnham attempts to separate the facts from the fables surrounding the man." Publ Wkly
"For the browsing public as well as specialists in European, Latin American, and American modern art, this book is not to be overlooked." Libr J
Includes bibliographical references

Robbins, Jerome

Vaill, Amanda. Somewhere; the life of Jerome Robbins. Broadway Books 2006 675p il $40 * **92**
ISBN 0-7679-0420-6; 978-0-7679-0420-9
LC 2006-48960
This is a biography of the choreographer of such works as Afternoon of a Faun, On the Town, Gypsy, West Side Story, and Fiddler on the Roof.
"The book is essential reading for lovers of theater and dance." Publ Wkly
Includes bibliographical references

Robeson, Paul, 1898-1976

Robeson, Paul. Here I stand; with a preface by Lloyd L. Brown and a new introduction by Sterling Stuckey. Beacon Press 1988 xxxvi, 121p pa $14 hardcover o.p. **92**
1. African Americans—Civil rights
ISBN 0-8070-6445-9 (pa)
LC 87-47882
First published 1958 by Othello Associates
"Combining a narrative of his life and travels with commentary on history and the events of his time, [the author] relates the fight against segregation to social progress for all Americans, white and black, claiming that 'white supremacy' disenfranchises and impoverishes white workers and white farmers as well as black." Libr J

Robeson, Paul, Jr. The undiscovered Paul Robeson; the early years (1898-1939). Wiley 2001 383p il $30 **92**
1. African Americans—Biography
ISBN 0-471-24265-9
LC 2001-17656

This is the first volume of a biography of the African American actor, singer and political activist by his son. It covers the years from Robeson's birth in Princeton, N.J., through the 1930s
"Extensively illustrated with personal photographs, this is a unique account of a brilliant but troubled man." Libr J
Includes bibliographical references

Robespierre, Maximilien, 1758-1794

Scurr, Ruth. Fatal purity; Robespierre and the French Revolution. Metropolitan Books 2006 408p il map $30 **92**
1. France—History—1789-1799, Revolution
ISBN 978-0-8050-7987-6; 0-8050-7987-4
LC 2005-57694
This is a biography of the French revolutionary.
This "is quite the calmest and least abusive history of the Revolution you will ever read. It works well as a general history of the years 1789-94, besides being a succinct guide to one of its dominant figures." London Rev Books
Includes bibliographical references

Robinson, Jackie, 1919-1972

Falkner, David. Great time coming: the life of Jackie Robinson, from baseball to Birmingham. Simon & Schuster 1995 382p il pa $18.95 hardcover o.p. * **92**
ISBN 0-684-82348-9 (pa)
LC 94-44876
This is a biography of the baseball player and civil rights activist. In addition to covering Robinson's professional career, the book focuses attention on his life after baseball
"Falkner has written a very balanced account—neither muckraking nor fawning—of a fascinating and complex figure, one whose importance and interest reaches well beyond his exploits as an athlete." Christ Sci Monit
Includes bibliographical references

Robison, John Elder, 1957-

Robison, John Elder. Look me in the eye; my life with Asperger's. Crown Publishers 2007 288p $25.95 **92**
1. Asperger's syndrome
ISBN 978-0-307-39598-6; 0-307-39598-7
LC 2007-13139
In this memoir, the author describes growing up with Asperger's syndrome (which went undiagnosed until he was 40 years old), dealing with an alcoholic father and a mentally unstable mother, and developing an affinity for machines that would eventually lead him to a career restoring classic cars.
"Robison's memoir is must reading for its unblinking (as only an Aspergian can) glimpse into the life of a person who had to wait decades for the medical community to catch up with him." Booklist
Includes bibliographical references

Rockefeller, David, 1915-
Rockefeller, David. Memoirs. Random House
2002 517p $35; pa $17.95　　　**92**
1. Chase Manhattan Bank, N.A.
ISBN 0-679-40588-7; 0-8129-6973-1 (pa)
　　　　　　　　　　　　LC 2002-24800
"This autobiography by the youngest son of John D.
Rockefeller Jr. and Abby Aldrich Rockefeller is also a
history of 20th-century America and its influence in the
world order." Libr J
"Rockefeller's style is restrained and self-deprecating;
the account of his attempts to modernize and globalize
Chase makes for excellent business history, and his
sketch of his complicated relationship with his brother is
especially convincing." New Yorker

Rockefeller, John D. (John Davison), 1839-1937
Chernow, Ron. Titan: the life of John D.
Rockefeller, Sr. Random House 1998 xxii, 774p il
$30; pa $18　　　**92**
ISBN 0-679-43808-4; 0-679-75703-1 (pa)
　　　　　　　　　　　　LC 97-33117
This is a biography of the industrialist who created
Standard Oil. "Chernow presents Rockefeller as a princi-
pled, enterprising monopolist whose philanthropic abili-
ties rivaled his knack for making money." Publ Wkly
"This book is a triumph of the art of biography.
Unflaggingly interesting, it brings John D. Rockefeller
Sr. . . to life through sustained narrative portraiture of
the large-scale, 19th-century kind." N Y Times Book
Rev
Includes bibliographical references

Rockne, Knute, 1888-1931
Robinson, Ray. Rockne of Notre Dame; the
making of a football legend. Oxford Univ. Press
1999 290p il pa $16.95 hardcover o.p.　　　**92**
ISBN 0-19-515792-3 (pa)　　　LC 99-13712
"After a childhood sketch, Robinson briefly touches
on Rockne's playing career before devoting most of the
book to a game-by-game description of Rockne's 12
years as coach, during which his Notre Dame teams,
with the help of Rockne's motivational techniques and
coaching tactics, won an astounding 105 games while
losing only 12. To Robinson's credit, the book is cleanly
written and mainly free of sports jargon." Publ Wkly

Rodgers, Richard, 1902-1979
The Richard Rodgers reader; edited by Geoffrey
Block. Oxford Univ. Press 2002 356p il music
(Readers on American musicians) $55; pa $38
　　　　　　　　　　　　92
1. Composers—United States
ISBN 0-19-513954-2; 0-19-531343-7 (pa)
　　　　　　　　　　　　LC 2001-37505
"This reader depicts Rodgers as methodical, versatile,
outgoing, and a family man—the most successful, productive, diverse, and influential American composer for
the musical stage of the twentieth century." Booklist
"A fine combination of anecdote, music criticism, and
biography, this is recommended for all libraries interested
in American popular culture and American musical theater." Libr J
Includes bibliographical references

Rodriguez, Richard, 1944-
Rodriguez, Richard. Hunger of memory; the
education of Richard Rodriguez: an autobiography.
Bantam trade pbk. ed. Bantam Books 2004 212p
pa $15　　　**92**
1. Mexican Americans
ISBN 0-553-38251-9　　　LC 2004-269979
First published 1982 by Godine
An account "of the coming of age of a person of
Mexican descent and culture in American society and the
inevitable transition in the private life of his family. Rodriguez focuses on his educational experiences, from his
parochial elementary school . . . to his university years
and subsequent experience as an educator." Libr J

Rogers, Will, 1879-1935
Robinson, Ray. American original: a life of Will
Rogers. Oxford Univ. Press 1996 288p il $34
　　　　　　　　　　　　92
1. Entertainers
ISBN 0-19-508693-7　　　LC 95-31578
In this biography of the American humorist, Robinson
attempts "to separate fact from legend and build up a
composite portrait of the man. As such, the book is so
complete and thorough that until, if ever, new material
comes to light, it can scarcely be superseded. Robinson's
admiration for Rogers is evident on every page, but that
does not blind him to Rogers's faults." Libr J

Yagoda, Ben. Will Rogers; a biography. Knopf
1993 409p il pa $24.95　　　**92**
1. Entertainers
ISBN 0-8061-3238-8　　　LC 92-40177
This is a biography of "the rope-twirling vaudeville
monologist, salty political commentator, silent film actor
and *New York Times* columnist. . . . [This is] a resonant
portrait imbued with Rogers's irreverent spirit, yet attuned to both the strengths and limitations of his
commonsense, crackerbarrel world view." Publ Wkly
Includes bibliographical references

Roiphe, Anne Richardson, 1935-
Roiphe, Anne Richardson. 1185 Park Avenue; a
memoir; [by] Anne Roiphe. Free Press 1999 257p
il hardcover o.p. pa $14.95　　　**92**
1. Authors, American
ISBN 0-684-85731-6; 0-684-85732-4 (pa)
　　　　　　　　　　　　LC 98-51939
The author "dissects her childhood family, depicting
as well a grim view of growing up rich and Jewish on
Upper Park Avenue in the 1940s and 1950s. The daughter of a wealthy, frightened, chain-smoking mother and
a handsome, philandering, cold, immigrant father who rejected his past, Roiphe watched her parents savage each
other daily." Libr J
"Roiphe's devastating memoir fully engages the reader
in her painful story of hatred and betrayal." Publ Wkly

Rommel, Erwin, 1891-1944
Fraser, David. Knight's cross: a life of Field
Marshal Erwin Rommel. HarperCollins Pubs. 1994
c1993 601p il maps pa $21.95 hardcover o.p.
　　　　　　　　　　　　92
ISBN 0-06-092597-3 (pa)　　　LC 93-43832

Rommel, Erwin, 1891-1944—_Continued_

First published 1993 in the United Kingdom

This is a biography of the general who commanded German troops in World War II

"Fraser presents what definitely will become the standard biography . . . as the author astutely traces the qualities of leadership which Rommel embodied." Booklist

Includes bibliographical references

Showalter, Dennis E. Patton and Rommel. See entry under Patton, George S. (George Smith), 1885-1945

Rooney, Andrew A.

Rooney, Andrew A. My war; [by] Andy Rooney. PublicAffairs 2000 333p il $20; pa $14
92

ISBN 1-58648-010-3; 1-58648-159-2 (pa)

LC 00-59228

First published 1995 by Random House

The author "relates how he became a notable combat journalist in WW II, a war he calls 'the ultimate experience for anyone in it.' For the Army newspaper _Stars and Stripes,_ he covered the air war over Germany, the D-Day invasion of Normandy and the Allied drive into Germany. Rooney's simple, ruminative style . . . grips the reader as he describes famous events of the war." Publ Wkly

Roosevelt, Eleanor, 1884-1962

Cook, Blanche Wiesen. Eleanor Roosevelt. v1: 1884-1933. Penguin Bks. 1993 587p il pa $18
92

1. Presidents' spouses—United States

ISBN 0-14-009460-1

LC 87-40632

First published 1992

This first volume of a two-volume biography of Eleanor Roosevelt "spans the years from Eleanor's birth to her husband Franklin Delano's inauguration." Publisher's note

"A feminist biography that regards its subject not only as a mostly 19th-century woman who invented her own life with very little help, but also as a self-created political figure of considerable significance." N Y Times Book Rev

Includes bibliographical references

Cook, Blanche Wiesen. Eleanor Roosevelt. v2: 1933-1938, the defining years. Viking 1999 686p pa $20 hardcover o.p.
92

1. Presidents' spouses—United States

ISBN 0-14-017894-5 (pa)

"This second volume covering the Depression years focuses equally on Roosevelt's emotional life and her public role." Libr J

"Cook is unafraid to take on difficult issues . . . thus rendering the biography not simply a riveting read but also a profoundly moving and wise account of how history has been shaped by the intricacies of the human heart, mind and spirit." Publ Wkly

Includes bibliographical references

Goodwin, Doris Kearns. No ordinary time. See entry under Roosevelt, Franklin D. (Franklin Delano), 1882-1945

Roosevelt, Franklin D. (Franklin Delano), 1882-1945

Davis, Kenneth Sydney. FDR, into the storm, 1937-1940; a history; {by} Kenneth S. Davis. Random House 1993 691p pa $29 hardcover o.p.
92

1. United States—Politics and government—1933-1945 2. Presidents—United States

ISBN 0-8129-8205-9 (pa)

LC 92-21640

This is the fourth volume of a five-volume biography begun with FDR, the beckoning destiny, 1882-1928 (1972); FDR, the New York years, 1928-1933 (1985); FDR, the New Deal years, 1933-1937 (1986)

In this study "particular emphasis is laid on Roosevelt's attempt to 'pack' the Supreme Court, his response to the growing threat of fascism in Europe, and the unexpectedly strong challenge by Republican Wendell Wilkie in the 1940 presidential campaign." Publ Wkly

Includes bibliographical references

Fried, Albert. F.D.R. and his enemies. St. Martin's Press 1999 261p pa $15.95 hardcover o.p.
92

1. United States—Politics and government—1933-1945 2. Presidents—United States

ISBN 0-312-23827-4 (pa)

LC 98-56141

The author "examines Roosevelt's conflict with and victory over varied critics, including Al Smith, Huey Long, Charles Lindbergh, and Charles Coughlin. Fried convincingly asserts that Roosevelt defeated his critics primarily because he was a superb pragmatist who refused to be hindered by an ideological straightjacket." Booklist

Includes bibliographical references

Goodwin, Doris Kearns. No ordinary time; Franklin and Eleanor Roosevelt: the home front in World War II. Simon & Schuster 1994 759p il pa $18 hardcover o.p. *
92

1. Roosevelt, Eleanor, 1884-1962 2. World War, 1939-1945—United States 3. United States—History—1933-1945

ISBN 0-684-80448-4 (pa)

LC 94-28565

"This is a nearly day-by-day account of the doings of Franklin and Eleanor Roosevelt during the Second World War. While Eleanor was championing the rights of female munitions workers and of Negroes in segregated Army barracks, her husband was making and breaking policy." New Yorker

Includes bibliographical references

Jackson, Robert Houghwout. That man: an insider's portrait of Franklin D. Roosevelt; [by] Robert H. Jackson; edited and introduced by John Q. Barrett; with a foreword by William E. Leuchtenburg. Oxford University Press 2003 xxviii, 290p il hardcover o.p. pa $17.95
92

1. Presidents—United States 2. United States—Politics and government—1933-1945

ISBN 0-19-516826-7; 0-19-517757-6 (pa)

LC 2003-9275

"While conducting research for a biography on Robert H. Jackson, Franklin D. Roosevelt's solicitor general, at-

Roosevelt, Franklin D. (Franklin Delano), 1882-1945—*Continued*

torney general, and appointee to the U.S. Supreme Court, Barrett . . . discovered Jackson's unfinished manuscript on the president dating from the early 1950s. Here, he supplements that text with excerpts from Jackson's unpublished autobiography and oral interviews." Libr J

This "is a lively, revealing and suddenly relevant book. Jackson's memoir sheds new light—not always flattering—on important events and on a president who too often appears only in silhouette." N Y Times Book Rev

Includes bibliographical references

Smith, Jean Edward. FDR. Random House 2007 858p il $35   **92**
1. Presidents—United States
ISBN 978-1-4000-6121-1; 1-4000-6121-0
LC 2006-43087
Smith's "FDR is at once a careful, intelligent synopsis of the existing Roosevelt scholarship (the sheer bulk of which is huge) and a meticulous reinterpretation of the man and his record. Smith pays more attention to Roosevelt's personal life than have most previous biographers. He is openly sympathetic yet ready to criticize when that is warranted, and to do so in sharp terms; he conveys the full flavor and import of Roosevelt's career without ever bogging down in detail." Washington Post Book World

Includes bibliographical references

Roosevelt, Theodore, 1858-1919

Cooper, John Milton. The warrior and the priest: Woodrow Wilson and Theodore Roosevelt. See entry under Wilson, Woodrow, 1856-1924

McCullough, David G. Mornings on horseback; {by} David McCullough. Simon & Schuster 1981 445p il pa $16 hardcover o.p.   **92**
1. Roosevelt family 2. Presidents—United States
ISBN 0-671-44754-8 (pa)   LC 81-1697
This biography follows Theodore Roosevelt from his childhood to his defeat for mayor of New York and marriage to Edith Carow in 1886.

"Based on diligent and thorough research, with emphasis on family, physical ailments, and friends, and written with verve and color, this is a stimulating book that will appeal to the general reader." Libr J

Includes bibliographical references

Morris, Edmund. The rise of Theodore Roosevelt. Modern Library pa. ed. Modern Lib. 2001 xxxiv, 920p il pa $17.95   **92**
1. Presidents—United States
ISBN 0-375-75678-7   LC 2001-30520
A reissue of the title first published 1979 by Coward, McCann & Geoghegan

"Revised and updated." Cover

This first volume of a projected three volume study of the life and times of Theodore Roosevelt "covers Roosevelt's life up to the age of 42, when an assassin's bullet elected him the youngest president in the nation's history." Booklist

Includes bibliographical references

Morris, Edmund. Theodore Rex. Random House 2001 772p il map $35; pa $16.95   **92**
1. Presidents—United States
ISBN 0-394-55509-0; 0-8129-6600-7 (pa)
LC 2001-19366
Sequel to: The rise of Theodore Roosevelt

"The second entry in Morris's projected three-volume life of Theodore Roosevelt focuses on the presidential years 1901 through early 1909." Publ Wkly

"Morris excels at placing TR in the context of his time, showing how he out maneuvered powerful but ossified opponents from the Gilded Age and trumped isolationists by averting war, in the process winning the first Nobel Peace Prize." Libr J

Includes bibliographical references

O'Toole, Patricia. When trumpets call; Theodore Roosevelt after the White House. Simon & Schuster 2005 494p il $30   **92**
1. Presidents—United States
ISBN 0-684-86477-0   LC 2004-62590
O'Toole narrates the "facts of TR's growing dissatisfaction with his hand-chosen successor, William Howard Taft; his own failed bid to return to the White House as a progressive candidate in 1912, and his nearly fatal 1914 exploration of Brazil's River of Doubt." Publ Wkly

The author "adeptly revisits this story, uncovering previously unexploited material and presenting a fuller and more sympathetic account. . . . O'Toole has written the definitive account of TR's postpresidential years." Libr J

Includes bibliographical references

Ross, Barney, 1909-1967

Century, Douglas. Barney Ross. Schocken Books 2006 215p il (Jewish encounters) $19.95   **92**
ISBN 0-8052-4223-6; 978-0-8052-4223-2
LC 2005-49939
This is a biography of the American boxer.

"This is an excellent story of a man and his times. And proof positive that time does not relinquish its hold over men or monuments." N Y Times Book Rev

Includes bibliographical references

Ross, Lillian, 1927-

Ross, Lillian. Here but not here; a love story. Counterpoint 2001 240p il pa $15   **92**
1. Shawn, William, 1907-1992 2. New Yorker (Periodical) 3. Authors, American
ISBN 1-582-43110-8; 978-1-582-43110-9
LC 00-65948
First published 1998 by Random House

"New Yorker writer Ross on her intimate relationship with the magazine's famed editor, William Shawn." Libr J

"Ross writes directly and with great feeling about her years with Shawn. . . . It is a remarkable and very moving love story, composed like most great love stories of both passion and regret." Booklist

Rossini, Gioacchino, 1792-1868

Servadio, Gaia. Rossini; a life. Carroll & Graf Publishers 2003 244p il $26   **92**
ISBN 0-7867-1195-7   LC 2003-43563

Rossini, Gioacchino, 1792-1868—*Continued*

The author "traces the history of Rossini—a man who exchanged ideas with Richard Wagner and in Paris salons kept company with Victor Hugo, Honore de Balzac, and Eugene Delacroix—from a difficult, impoverished childhood through his complicated relationships with his divas, to his battles with nervous illnesses. She sets Rossini's life, too, against the sweep of European history in an age defined and betrayed by Napoleon." Publisher's note

"This is a deeply rewarding book, written with real personality and much scholarship." Publ Wkly

Includes bibliographical references

Roth, Henry, 1906-1995

Kellman, Steven G. Redemption: the life of Henry Roth. W.W. Norton 2005 371p il $25.95

92

ISBN 0-393-05779-8   LC 2005-11979

The author "traces Roth's fascinating career from his birth in Galicia, Austria-Hungary, to his final years in New Mexico. He focuses on his experience of New York's Lower East Side and Jewish and Irish Harlem. . . . This biography should be included in all public library and academic collections." Libr J

Includes bibliographical references

Roth, Herman, 1901-1989

Roth, Philip. Patrimony; a true story. Vintage Bks. 1996 238p pa $12   **92**

ISBN 0-679-75293-5; 978-0-679-75293-6

LC 95-43453

First published 1991 by Simon & Schuster

This "is an account of how Roth cared for his eighty-six-year-old father during the last stages of the parent's incurable brain tumor." Time

This "ordinary, crucial story is well suited to a comic master, and Mr. Roth brings to the tale his gift for attention, his worldly, vernacular heart and the tremendous inventive force that here he keeps largely in check." N Y Times Book Rev

Roth, Philip

Roth, Philip. The facts; a novelist's autobiography. Vintage Bks. 1997 195p pa $14

92

1. Authors, American
ISBN 0-679-74905-5; 978-0-679-74905-9

LC 96-28807

First published 1988 by Farrar, Straus & Giroux

Following a prologue about his parents, Roth recounts "five stages of his life: his New Jersey youth; his college days at Bucknell; meeting his wife-to-be while an instructor at the University of Chicago; his early writing days, including [his conflict with] . . . the Jewish community; and his life in the sixties." Libr J

"The Facts is a lively and serious version of a novelist's life, but it seems even more interesting as a new way of formulating the questions about the imagination that Roth has been pursuing with increasing complication in the Zuckerman novels." N Y Rev Books

Rothko, Mark, 1903-1970

Breslin, James E. B. Mark Rothko; a biography. University of Chicago Press 1993 700p il $45; pa $27.50   **92**

ISBN 0-226-07405-6; 0-226-07406-4 (pa)

LC 93-14966

This biography covers "Rothko's personal and artistic relationships, as well as the changing cultural and philosophical forces that shaped his life and art. Breslin also considers Rothko's attitude toward the role of the self in the paintings." Libr J

This book "is painstakingly researched, fluently written and unfailingly intelligent in tracing the tragic course of its subject's tormented character." N Y Times Book Rev

Includes bibliographical references

Rothschild, Charlotte, 1819-1884

Weintraub, Stanley. Charlotte and Lionel. See entry under Rothschild, Lionel Nathan, Baron, 1808-1879

Rothschild, Lionel Nathan, Baron, 1808-1879

Weintraub, Stanley. Charlotte and Lionel; a Rothschild love story. Free Press 2003 316p il hardcover o.p. pa $22.95   **92**

1. Rothschild, Charlotte, 1819-1884
ISBN   0-7432-2686-0;   978-1-4165-7332-6;
1-4165-7332-1 (pa)   LC 2002-29994

The author profiles one of the Victorian era's "oddly (given their Jewishness and British anti-Semitism) quintessential couples. Lionel Rothschild, scion of the British branch of the famed banking family, married his beautiful German wife, Charlotte, in 1836, when she was 16 (he was a decade older). The bride was, following family custom, also Lionel's cousin and would mature into a sparkling saloniste and hostess whose dinner invitations, Weintraub notes, were preferred over those from Buckingham Palace. . . . Weintraub offers an enticing inside look at a storied family that played a central public role in Victorian England." Publ Wkly

Includes bibliographical references

Rousseau, Jean-Jacques, 1712-1778

Cranston, Maurice. Jean-Jacques: the early life and work of Jean-Jacques Rousseau, 1712-1754. University of Chicago Press 1991 382p il map pa $23   **92**

ISBN 0-226-11862-2   LC 90-45994

First published 1983 by Norton

This first volume of Cranston's biographical study of the life and work of the French philosopher "traces the evolution of Rousseau's attitudes through the influence of that . . . Calvinist citystate, Geneva, his refuge in Catholic Savoy, and his introduction to the new 'scientific' ideology of the French Enlightenment." Publisher's note

"Cranston presents Rousseau's work in the context of his life. He proceeds impartially but not dispassionately; his scholarship is impeccable but not obtrusive. The result is a most readable narrative that has something for readers at all levels of sophistication." Choice

Includes bibliographical references

Rousseau, Jean-Jacques, 1712-1778—*Continued*

Cranston, Maurice. The noble savage: Jean-Jacques Rousseau, 1754-1762. University of Chicago Press 1991 399p il $45; pa $20
        92
  ISBN 0-226-11863-0; 0-226-11864-9 (pa)
        LC 90-28111
This second volume of the trilogy "covers the most productive, turbulent, and controversial eight years of Rousseau's life. His *Discourse on Inequality, Letter to Voltaire on Providence, Letter to d'Alembert, La Nouvelle Héloïse, The Social Contract*, and *Emile* emerge from this period." Choice
"Cranston offers the finest and most richly detailed portrait ever assembled of these vagabond years." New Statesman Soc
Includes bibliographical references

Cranston, Maurice. The solitary self: Jean-Jacques Rousseau in exile and adversity; with a foreword by Sanford Lakoff. University of Chicago Press 1997 247p il $35; pa $20
        92
  ISBN 0-226-11865-7; 0-226-11866-5 (pa)
        LC 96-12922
"This final volume in Cranston's definitive trilogy chronicles Rousseau's last turbulent years as an outcast in England and Neuchatel, after the burning of *Émile* and the order for his arrest. . . . This is a scholarly yet ingratiating portrayal of a man whose last years found him battling sciatica and Voltaire, enjoying botany and Boswell. Cranston's authoritative work has given us an invaluable account of the paradoxical life of an emotionally devoted yet tactlessly demanding man." Booklist
Includes bibliographical references

Damrosch, Leopold. Jean-Jacques Rousseau; restless genius; [by] Leo Damrosch. Houghton Mifflin 2005 566p il map $30 *   **92**
  ISBN 0-618-44696-6   LC 2005-13579
This is a biography of the author of *The Social Contract, Emile,* and the *Confessions.*
"A delight to read, Damrosch comes as close to Rousseau's authentic self as we are likely to get." N Y Times Book Rev
Includes bibliographical references

Rousseau, Jean-Jacques. Confessions; edited and introduced by P. N. Furbank. Knopf 1992 2v in 1 $20   **92**
  ISBN 0-679-40998-X   LC 91-53194
Also available in paperback from Penguin Bks. and Oxford Univ. Press
"Everyman's library"
First Everyman's library edition, 1931
"An autobiography by Jean-Jacques Rousseau. The twelve volumes, written between 1766 and 1770, were published posthumously (I-VI, 1781; VII-XII, 1788). In this work, Rousseau 'frankly and sincerely' reveals the details of his erratic and rebellious life. Scholars find, however, that his unconscious motivation was to justify himself in the eyes of his supposedly numerous persecutors." Reader's Ency. 4th edition

Routledge, Katherine, 1866-1935
Van Tilburg, JoAnne. Among stone giants; the life of Katherine Routledge and her remarkable expedition to Easter Island; foreword by Andrew Tatham. Scribner 2003 351p il $26   **92**
  1. Easter Island
  ISBN 0-7432-4480-X   LC 2002-42751
"A Lisa Drew book"
This is a "biography of Katherine Routledge, an Englishwoman who was the first to attempt a methodical archaeological study of Easter Island." N Y Times Book Rev
Includes bibliographical references

Ruth, Babe, 1895-1948
Creamer, Robert W. Babe; the legend comes to life. Simon & Schuster 1974 443p il pa $14 hardcover o.p.   **92**
  1. Baseball—Biography
  ISBN 0-671-76070-X (pa)
This biography covers Babe Ruth's personal life and his sports career.

Rutherford, Ernest, 1871-1937
Reeves, Richard. A force of nature; the frontier genius of Ernest Rutherford. W. W. Norton & Co. 2008 207p il (Great discoveries) $23.95
        92
  1. Physicists
  ISBN 978-0-393-05750-8; 0-393-05750-X
        LC 2007-33184
"Atlas books"
The author "re-introduces Ernest Rutherford, one of the founding geniuses of nuclear physics. . . . This biography does an outstanding job of capturing the excitement and almost breathless pace of physics research in the 20th century's first four decades." Publ Wkly
Includes bibliographical references

Ryan, Evelyn, d. 1998
Ryan, Terry. The prize winner of Defiance, Ohio; how my mother raised 10 kids on 25 words or less; foreword by Suze Orman. Simon & Schuster 2001 351p il $24; pa $13   **92**
  1. Ryan family
  ISBN 0-7432-1122-7; 0-7432-1123-5 (pa)
        LC 2001-18379
The author recounts the life of her mother, "a small-town Ohio housewife in the nineteen-fifties who lived on the brink of dire poverty, thanks to a brood of ten kids and an ineffectual drunk of a husband. Since Evelyn couldn't work outside her home, she worked inside it, penning hundreds of product jingles and entering them in the national contests that drove the advertising industry of the day." New Yorker

Sacagawea, b. 1786
Clark, Ella Elizabeth. Sacagawea of the Lewis and Clark expedition; {by} Ella E. Clark and Margot Edmonds. University of Calif. Press 1979 171p il pa $16.95 hardcover o.p. * **92**
  1. Lewis and Clark Expedition (1804-1806)
  ISBN 0-520-05060-6 (pa)   LC 78-65466

Sacagawea, b. 1786—*Continued*

"Sacagawea, the Shoshone Indian woman who accompanied the Lewis and Clark expedition, has been a regional heroine and a feminist celebrity for most of this century. But, as these writers show, her role as 'the guide' was more fictive than actual. . . . Based on careful interpretation of the explorer's journals, this revisionist study does a good job of redefining her actual contributions." Booklist

Includes bibliographical references

Sacks, Oliver W.

Sacks, Oliver W. Uncle Tungsten; memories of a chemical boyhood; [by] Oliver Sacks. Knopf 2001 337p il hardcover o.p. pa $14   **92**

1. Physicians

ISBN 0-375-40448-1; 0-375-70404-3 (pa)

LC 2001-33738

"Sacks' first scientific love was chemistry, and he presents an avid history of the field within a memoir that pays tribute to his uncle, who welcomed Sacks into his lab, thus encouraging his passion for chemistry and learning." Booklist

Sagan, Carl, 1934-1996

Davidson, Keay. Carl Sagan; a life. Wiley 1999 xx, 540p pa $24.95 hardcover o.p.   **92**

ISBN 0-471-39536-6 (pa)   LC 99-36206

The author profiles the life and scientific career of the influential American astronomer

"Sagan is presented in such a way that readers can decide whether to view him admirably or with a dose of skepticism." Booklist

Includes bibliographical references

Sagan, Carl. Conversations with Carl Sagan; edited by Tom Head. University Press of Mississippi 2006 xxv, 167p (Literary conversations series) $50; pa $20   **92**

ISBN 1-57806-735-9; 1-57806-736-7 (pa)

LC 2005-48747

The editor "has selected 16 engaging conversations from such popular venues as Rolling Stone, Psychology Today, The Charlie Rose Show, and NPR, and it's a boon to connect with Sagan's knowledge, wisdom, and generosity . . . after his early death at 62." Booklist

Includes bibliographical references

Said, Edward W.

Said, Edward W. Out of place; a memoir. Knopf 1999 295p il $26.95; pa $14   **92**

ISBN 0-394-58739-1; 0-679-73067-2 (pa)

LC 99-31106

In this memoir Said offers an "account of his intellectual and moral development. At the heart of Said's story is the sense of dislocation experienced by a boy whose father was a Palestinian-born American citizen, whose mother was Lebanese, and who was raised in Egypt under the colonial rule of the British. This is the moving tale of a man who is always an outsider." Publ Wkly

Said, Kurban, 1905-1942

Reiss, Tom. The Orientalist; solving the mystery of a strange and a dangerous life. Random House 2005 xxvii, 433p il $25.95; pa $14.95   **92**

ISBN 1-4000-6265-9; 0-8129-7276-7 (pa)

LC 2004-50928

This is a biography of Lev Nussimbaum, a Jew from Baku who wrote in Germany under the pseudonyms Essad Bey and Kurban Said.

The author "takes the reader through his own search for the truth; through the twists of 20th-century history in Russia and Germany, and hence though the life-story itself. This would be hard work if the interweaving of biography, investigation and geopolitics were not so elegant." Economist

Includes bibliographical references

Sakharov, Andreĭ Dmitrievich, 1921-1989

Lourie, Richard. Sakharov; a biography. University Press of New England 2002 465p il $35   **92**

ISBN 1-58465-207-1   LC 2001-5246

A biography "of Andrei Sakharov, the nuclear physicist who developed into an authentic apostle of humanity and democracy in the former Soviet Union." N Y Times Book Rev

"Utilizing newly accessible KGB files as well as Sakharov's personal correspondence, Lourie provides a revealing portrait of an extraordinary man to whom the world owes a great debt." Booklist

Includes bibliographical references

Salk, Jonas, 1914-1995

Kluger, Jeffrey. Splendid solution: Jonas Salk and the conquest of polio. G.P. Putnam's Sons 2004 373p il hardcover o.p. pa $15   **92**

1. Poliomyelitis

ISBN 0-399-15216-4; 0-425-20570-3 (pa)

LC 2004-50527

The author "tells how polio was beaten 50 years ago in one of the triumphs of modern medicine. The narrative naturally centers on Jonas Salk, whose lab developed the first polio vaccine." Publ Wkly

"Can't-put-it-down medical-science history." Booklist

Includes bibliographical references

Salzman, Mark

Salzman, Mark. Lost in place; growing up absurd in suburbia. Random House 1995 273p pa $13 hardcover o.p.   **92**

ISBN 0-679-76778-9 (pa)   LC 95-7847

In this "memoir about his 'existential angst' as a slightly off-center teenager, . . . writer Salzman vividly recalls his unconventional friends, frugal parents, and other memorable characters from his freewheeling, Connecticut youth." Booklist

Sampson, Deborah, 1760-1827

Young, Alfred Fabian. Masquerade: the life and times of Deborah Sampson, Continental soldier; [by] Alfred F. Young. Knopf 2004 417p il map $26.95; pa $16 *   **92**

1. Women soldiers 2. United States—History—1775-1783, Revolution

ISBN 0-679-44165-4; 0-679-76185-3 (pa)

LC 2003-47549

This is a biography of a woman "who fought in the American Revolution as Robert Shurtliff. . . . [Deborah Sampson served] for seventeen months during the period between the British surrender at Yorktown and the signing of the final treaty." Publisher's note

This book "makes a valuable contribution to American women's history. It offers nuggets of insight about an array of historical topics. . . . What's more, it tells a terrific story." Rev Am Hist

Includes bibliographical references

Sand, George, 1804-1876

Eisler, Benita. Naked in the marketplace; the lives of George Sand. Counterpoint 2006 308p $26.95   **92**

ISBN 978-1-58243-349-3; 1-58243-349-6

LC 2006-21684

This is a biography of the French writer.

"Eisler's portrait of this woman of many firsts brings Sand and her boldly improvised life forward more vividly than ever before." Booklist

Includes bibliographical references

Harlan, Elizabeth. George Sand. Yale University Press 2004 376p il $35   **92**

ISBN 0-300-10417-0   LC 2004-10315

"Sand, née, Aurore Dupin, left her husband and two children in provincial France and successfully launched herself as a self-supporting writer in Paris, donning men's clothing to ease passage into the professional world and taking a pseudonym to protect her aristocratic family's name. Sand took on many lovers, among them poet Alfred de Musset and composer Frédéric Chopin. Yet despite Sand's outward daring, as Harlan shows, she obsessed over her identity, as both a woman and an aristocrat. . . . Harlan sensitively analyzes the gaps and idiosyncrasies in her subject's heavily self-edited correspondence, autobiography and novels to uncover a fresh portrait of this volatile, imaginative woman of letters." Publ Wkly

Includes bibliographical references

Jack, Belinda Elizabeth. George Sand; a woman's life writ large; {by} Belinda Jack. Knopf 2000 395p il pa $16 hardcover o.p.   **92**

ISBN 0-679-77918-3 (pa)   LC 99-40857

"Prodigious author, cross-dresser, lover of Chopin and Alfred de Musset, intimate of (among others) Liszt, Balzac, Dumas (*père* and *fils*), Turgenev, and Flaubert (who cried twice at her funeral), Sand was both before her time and quintessentially of it. Jack's nuanced, moving assessment of the writer's early years . . . is the strongest section of this packed life. When Sand moves onto a larger stage, Jack's style becomes breathless, as if she could barely keep up with her flamboyant subject." New Yorker

Sanders, Scott R. (Scott Russell), 1945-

Sanders, Scott R. (Scott Russell). A private history of awe; [by] Scott Russell Sanders. North Point Press 2006 322p hardcover o.p. pa $15   **92**

ISBN 0-86547-693-4; 978-0-86547-693-6; 978-0-86547-734-6 (pa); 0-86547-734-5 (pa)

LC 2005-14236

The author "uses autobiography as a vehicle for far-reaching reflections on nature and humankind. . . . Sanders' thoughtful reflections on the cycles of life, the flashpoints of awe, and our quest for meaning are quietly revelatory." Booklist

Includes bibliographical references

Sanger, Margaret, 1879-1966

Reed, Miriam. Margaret Sanger: her life in her words; foreword by Margaret Sanger Lampe. Barricade Bks. 2003 288p il $29.95; pa $16.95 *   **92**

1. Birth control 2. Women's rights

ISBN 1-56980-255-6; 1-56980-246-7 (pa)

LC 2003-40416

Reed "seeks to revitalize our appreciation for Sanger in this invaluable collection of her seminal, intelligent, and compassionate writings, which are accompanied by Reed's vibrant and illuminating commentary and a charming introduction by Sanger's granddaughter, Margaret Sanger Lampe." Booklist

Includes bibliographical references

Sartre, Jean Paul, 1905-1980

Sartre, Jean Paul. The words; translated from the French by Bernard Frechtman. Vintage 1981 255p pa $11.95   **92**

1. Authors, French

ISBN 0-394-74709-7; 978-0-394-74709-5

First published 1964 by Braziller

The French existentialist writer "examines the formation of his character during his childhood years, which were passed in a completely adult world between his widowed mother and her parents. The central event of his childhood was the discovery of the world of words, of language." Libr J

Satrapi, Marjane, 1969-

Satrapi, Marjane. Persepolis. Pantheon Bks. 2003 153p il $17.95; pa $11.95   **92**

1. Iran—Graphic novels 2. Graphic novels 3. Autobiographical graphic novels

ISBN 0-375-42230-7; 0-375-71457-X (pa)

LC 2002-190806

This is an "autobiography in . . . comic book form by a woman born to the leftish secular bourgeoisie of 1960's Iran; she was 10 when the shah fell and his tyranny was replaced by the ayatollah version. The book ends when she is 14 and her parents put her on a plane for some safer place (she now lives in France)." N Y Times Book Rev

"Satrapi's cursive, geometrical drawing style . . . eloquently conveys her ingenuousness and fervor as a child." Booklist

Satrapi, Marjane, 1969-—*Continued*

Satrapi, Marjane. Persepolis 2; [the story of a return] Pantheon Books 2004 187p il $17.95; pa $12.95 *   **92**

1. Graphic novels 2. Autobiographical graphic novels
ISBN 0-375-42288-9; 0-375-71466-9 (pa)
LC 2003-70699

Sequel to: Persepolis

This continuation of Satrapi's memoir-in-comics begins "in the areligious West. There Satrapi endured initiations into sex, drugs, and partying, and travails over peer and love relationships that mirrored those of her Western fellow students. . . . After breaking up with her first love . . . she became homeless for three months and, after hospitalization for exposure, returned to Tehran, where the second half of this book transpires. . . . Satrapi's high-contrast, bold-lined, stencil-ish artwork remains very much at the service of one of the most compelling youth memoirs of recent years." Booklist

Savonarola, Girolamo, 1452-1498

Martines, Lauro. Fire in the city; Savonarola and the struggle for Renaissance Florence. Oxford University Press 2006 336p il map $30
92

1. Florence (Italy)—History
ISBN 0-19-517748-7; 978-0-19-517748-0
LC 2005-31802

The author investigates "the tumultuous political life of late 15th-century Florence. His focus is the short-lived Florentine republic (1494-98), when the dominant voice belonged to a charismatic Dominican friar, Girolamo Savonarola." Libr J

"This absorbing account . . . captures Savonarola's brilliance as well as the exciting and dangerous days of Renaissance Florence." Publ Wkly
Includes bibliographical references

Scheeres, Julia, 1967-

Scheeres, Julia. Jesus land; a memoir. Counterpoint 2005 356p $23; pa $14   **92**
ISBN 1-58243-338-0; 1-58243-354-2 (pa)
LC 2005-14816

The author writes about her "bond with the boy her fundamentalist family adopted and abused." N Y Times Book Rev

"Tinged with sadness yet pervaded by a sense of triumph, Scheeres's book is a crisply written and earnest examination of the meaning of family and Christian values." Publ Wkly

Schiff, Dorothy, 1903-1989

Nissenson, Marilyn. The lady upstairs; Dorothy Schiff and the New York Post. St. Martin's Press 2007 500p il $29.95   **92**
1. New York post
ISBN 978-0-312-31310-4; 0-312-31310-1
LC 2006-53087

This is a biography of newspaper owner "Dorothy Schiff. From 1939 to 1976, Schiff owned The New York Post." N Y Times Book Rev

This "is Marilyn Nissenson's carefully documented and revealing account of Schiff's nearly four decades of ownership. It's an admiring but not uncritical story of a woman who at her best 'was feisty rather than cowed, personally diffident but professionally forceful,' and who, although married four times, ended up wedded mainly to the paper itself." Columbia J Rev
Includes bibliographical references

Schindler, Oskar, 1908-1974

Crowe, David. Oskar Schindler; the untold account of his life, wartime activities, and the true story behind the list; [by] David M. Crowe. Westview Press 2004 766p il $30   **92**
ISBN 0-8133-3375-X   LC 2004-13879

This biography of the businessman who saved over 1100 Jews during the Holocaust "covers both the prewar and the postwar periods through Schindler's death and the death of his wife." Libr J

This book "is essential in understanding one of the most extraordinary figures from the Holocaust." Booklist
Includes bibliographical references

Schlesinger, Arthur M., 1917-2007

Schlesinger, Arthur M. Journals: 1952-2000; edited by Andrew Schlesinger and Stephen Schlesinger. Penguin Press 2007 894p $40
92

1. Historians—United States 2. United States—History—1945-
ISBN 978-1-594-20142-4

The distinguished political historian's journals provide an intimate history of postwar America, the writer's contributions to multiple presidential administrations, and his relationships with numerous cultural and intellectual figures.

This book "contains juicy morsels on every one of its [pages]. . . . The book contains not just his witty apercus, but those of hundreds of A-list friends, some of whom are still alive and will blanch at seeing private lunches in print. The presidential scuttlebutt is prime. . . . The private score-settling is fun reading." Newsweek

Schlesinger, Arthur M. A life in the twentieth century; innocent beginnings, 1917-1950; [by] Arthur M. Schlesinger, Jr. Houghton Mifflin 2000 557p il $28.95; pa $15   **92**
1. Historians—United States
ISBN 0-395-70752-8; 0-618-21925-0 (pa)
LC 00-61322

This first volume of Schlesinger's autobiography covers the author's life through the publication of The Age of Jackson and The Vital Center.

Schlesinger's "autobiography, skillfully interweaving the personal and the historical, is elegantly simple and marvellously clear. Complex thoughts are set forth with a lucidity that conceals the depth of the intellectual analysis. Wit, humour and the resources of a natural storyteller sweep the reader along." Economist

Schoen, Douglas E., 1953-

Schoen, Douglas E. The power of the vote; electing presidents, overthrowing dictators, and promoting democracy around the world. William Morrow 2007 396p pa $25.95   **92**

1. Democratic Party (U.S.) 2. United States—Politics and government

ISBN 978-0-06-123188-9; 0-06-123188-6

LC 2006-52877

The author presents an account of his work as a politcal strategist.

Includes bibliographical references

Schorr, Daniel, 1916-

Schorr, Daniel. Staying tuned; a life in journalism. Pocket Bks. 2001 354p il pa $14 hardcover o.p.   **92**

ISBN 0-671-02088-9 (pa)   LC 2001-21014

Schorr tells of his life as a reporter for CBS, CNN and National Public Radio.

"Schorr's memoir is as much an inside look at the famous world figures of the latter half of the twentieth century as it is the story of one man's life and career." Booklist

Schulz, Charles M.

Michaelis, David. Schulz and Peanuts; a biography. Harper 2007 655p il $34.95 *

92

1. Peanuts (Comic strip) 2. Cartoonists

ISBN 978-0-06-621393-4; 0-06-621393-2

This is a biography of the cartoonist and author of Happiness is a Warm Puppy (1962), The Charlie Brown Dictionary (1973), Peanuts Jubilee (1975), Snoopy's Tennis Book (1979), and Things I Learned After It Was Too Late (1981).

"It is Mr. Michaelis's achievement in these pages that he leaves us with both a shrewd appreciation of Schulz's minimalist art and a sympathetic understanding of Schulz the man." N Y Times (Late N Y Ed)

Includes bibliographical references

Schwartz, Morris

Albom, Mitch. Tuesdays with Morrie; an old man, a young man, and life's greatest lesson. Doubleday 1997 192p $22.95; pa $12.95

92

ISBN 0-385-48451-8; 0-7679-0592-X (pa)

LC 96-52535

"As a student at Brandeis University in the late 1970s, Albom was especially drawn to his sociology professor, Morris Schwartz. On graduation he vowed to keep in touch with him, which he failed to do until 1994, when he saw a segment about Schwartz on the TV program *Nightline*, and learned that he had just been diagnosed with Lou Gehrig's disease. By then a sports columnist for the *Detroit Free Press* . . . Albom was idled by the newspaper strike in the Motor City and so had the opportunity to visit Schwartz in Boston every week until the older man died. Their dialogue is the subject of this moving book." Publ Wkly

Schwarzkopf, H. Norman

Schwarzkopf, H. Norman. It doesn't take a hero: General H. Norman Schwarzkopf; the autobiography; written with Peter Petre. Bantam Bks. 1992 530p il maps pa $7.99 hardcover o.p.

92

1. Persian Gulf War, 1991

ISBN 0-553-56338-6 (pa)   LC 92-20762

"The whole book is a description of General Schwarzkopf's relations with people. It is remarkably emotional. To an unusual degree he sees events as secondary to the personalities he has been affected by. He emphasizes his sensitive side. . . . 'It Doesn't Take a Hero' is not a military record. . . . It covers the gulf war, of course, but General Schwarzkopf devotes so much space to his life before that event that he has produced two books in one." N Y Times Book Rev

Includes bibliographical references

Schweitzer, Albert, 1875-1965

Schweitzer, Albert. Out of my life and thought; an autobiography; translated by Antje Bultmann Lemke; foreword by Jimmy Carter; preface by Rhena Schweitzer Miller and Antje Bultmann Lemke. Johns Hopkins Univ. Press 1998 272p il (Albert Schweitzer library) pa $18.95   **92**

ISBN 0-8018-6097-0   LC 98-28166

First English translation by C. T. Campion published 1933; this translation first published 1990 by Holt

This is "the autobiography of the world-famous missionary doctor, organist, philosopher, theologian, and Nobel Peace Prize winner." Booklist

Includes bibliographical references

Seeger, Pete

Dunaway, David King. How can I keep from singing: Pete Seeger. Da Capo Press 1990 388p il pa $17   **92**

ISBN 0-306-80399-2   LC 89-71394

A reprint with a new preface of the title first published 1981 by McGraw-Hill

"The focus of Seeger's life has been on using music as a force for social change. . . . But he is perhaps best known as the major banjo-playing folksinger who pioneered the folk music revival that flowered in the 1960s. This excellent book provides a well-written and extensively researched account, not only of Seeger's life, but also of the social and political movements of the times in which he lived. An extensive bibliography and discography add to the book's usefulness." Libr J

Includes Discography

Semmelweis, Ignác Fülöp, 1818-1865

Nuland, Sherwin B. The doctors' plague; germs, childbed fever, and the strange story of Ignác Semmelweis. Norton 2003 191p il (Great discoveries) $21.95; pa $13.95   **92**

ISBN 0-393-05299-0; 0-393-32625-X (pa)

LC 2003-11412

This is an account of the work of the 19th-century obstetrician Ignas Semmelweis. "Semmelweis is remembered for the now-commonplace notion that doctors must

Semmelweis, Ignác Fülöp, 1818-1865—*Continued*
wash their hands before examining patients. . . . With
deaths from childbed fever exploding, Semmelweis discovered that doctors themselves were spreading the disease." Publisher's note
Includes bibliographical references

Seuss, Dr.
Morgan, Judith. Dr. Seuss & Mr. Geisel; a
biography; [by] Judith & Neil Morgan. Da Capo
Press 1996 345p il pa $18.50 *   **92**
1. Authors, American
ISBN 0-306-80736-X; 978-0-306-80736-7
                                    LC 96-19313
First published 1995 by Random House
"Fans of The Cat in the Hat, The Grinch Who Stole
Christmas and other classics may be surprised to learn
that Dr. Seuss was terrified of children and had none of
his own, and that writing verse was a supreme effort for
him. While children's literature is Ted Geisel's principal
claim to fame, his creative life was multifarious, including an apprenticeship with film director and army major
Frank Capra during WWII and stints in advertising. The
authors deftly evoke the settings where Geisel lived and
worked." Publ Wkly

Sewall, Samuel, 1652-1730
LaPlante, Eve. Salem witch judge; the life and
repentance of Samuel Sewall. HarperSanFrancisco
2007 352p il map $25.95   **92**
1. Massachusetts—History—1600-1775, Colonial period
ISBN 978-0-06-078661-8; 0-06-078661-2
                                    LC 2007-18392
"In 1692, Salem magistrate Samuel Sewall (1652-
1730), along with several others, presided over the conviction and execution of 20 people accused of witchcraft.
Five years and much soul-searching later, Sewall publicly
repented of his part in the witch trials. . . . [The author]
richly narrates his life in its cultural and religious setting." Publ Wkly
Includes bibliographical references

Sexton, Anne
Middlebrook, Diane Wood. Anne Sexton; a
biography. Vintage Bks. 1992 xxiii, 498p il pa $14
                                            92
1. Poets, American
ISBN 0-679-74182-8   LC 92-50093
First published 1991 by Houghton Mifflin
For this biography of the troubled American confessional poet the author "plumbed psychiatric records, including tapes made of therapy sessions; interviewed family members, fellow poets, friends and lovers; and closely read the poems themselves to reconstruct Sexton's
life—its interior sequences and external chronology."
Publ Wkly
"Ms. Middlebrook has written a wonderful book: just,
balanced, insightful, complex in its sympathies and in its
judgment of Sexton both as a person and as a writer."
NY Times Book Rev
Includes bibliographical references

Shabazz, Betty
Rickford, Russell John. Betty Shabazz: a
remarkable story of survival and faith before and
after Malcolm X; foreword by Myrlie
Evers-Williams. Sourcebooks 2003 xxii, 633p il
$35   **92**
1. African Americans—Civil rights
ISBN 1-4022-0171-0   LC 2002-003447
"Just as the achievements of her husband, Malcolm X,
were overshadowed by those of Martin Luther King Jr.,
Betty Shabazz's accomplishments have been overshadowed by those of King's widow. {The author} corrects
that imbalance with this penetrating biography." Booklist
Includes bibliographical references

Shakur, Tupac
Dyson, Michael Eric. Holler if you hear me:
searching for Tupac Shakur. Basic Bks. 2001 292p
il hardcover o.p. pa $15   **92**
1. African American musicians 2. Rap music
ISBN 0-465-01755-X; 0-465-01728-2 (pa)
                                    LC 2001-36564
In this biography of the late rapper, Dyson "examines
Tupac both culturally and spiritually through a loosely
organized series of meditations that begin in Tupac's
childhood . . . and move through his manhood." New
Yorker
"Dyson's discussion goes beyond slogans and poses to
the actualities of 'thug life' and the consequences of
Shakur's passions and allegiances. Piquant and analyti-
cal." Booklist
Includes bibliographical references

Sharon, Ariel
Hefez, Nir. Ariel Sharon; a life; [by] Nir Hefez
and Gadi Bloom; translated from the Hebrew by
Mitch Ginsburg. Random House 2006 490p il
$29.95   **92**
ISBN 1-4000-6587-9; 978-1-4000-6587-5
                                    LC 2006-49144
This is a biography of the Israeli prime minister.
"This revealing and engrossing biography adds a great
deal to our understanding of the man." Booklist
Includes bibliographical references

Shaw, Bernard, 1856-1950
Peters, Sally. Bernard Shaw; the ascent of the
superman. Yale Univ. Press 1996 328p il
hardcover o.p. pa $22   **92**
1. Dramatists, English
ISBN 0-300-06097-1; 0-300-07500-6 (pa)
                                    LC 95-37248
An "exploration of the ambiguities and passions that
formed this great playwright and thinker. Shaw's sexuality, always a good topic of speculation, is studied here,
but one wishes for more insights and in-depth analysis.
Peters does devote a chapter to Shaw's close relationship
with the actor and playwright Harley Granville Barker,
mainly from Shaw's point of view. One may not agree
with Peter's conclusions, but they will prove to be of interest to anyone studying Shaw." Libr J
Includes bibliographical references

Shawn, Allen

Shawn, Allen. Wish I could be there; notes from a phobic life. Viking 2007 267p $24.95

92

1. Agoraphobia

ISBN 0-670-03842-3; 978-0-670-03842-8

LC 2006-41368

The author "probes the causes of his long struggle with agoraphobia—a fear of certain spaces which makes it difficult to 'move forward in the world without knowing already what lies ahead'—in this vividly written combination of memoir and scientific inquiry." New Yorker

Includes bibliographical references

Shawn, William, 1907-1992

Ross, Lillian. Here but not here. See entry under Ross, Lillian, 1927-

Shelley, Mary Wollstonecraft, 1797-1851

Seymour, Miranda. Mary Shelley. Grove Press 2001 655p il $35; pa $20   **92**

1. Women authors 2. Authors, English

ISBN 0-8021-1702-3; 0-8021-3948-5 (pa)

LC 2001-35094

First published 2000 in the United Kingdom

"Born to two of the most famous parents in 19th-century England—philosopher and novelist William Godwin and political activist Mary Wollstonecraft, who died ten days after giving birth to Mary—the young girl inherited their intellectual perspicacity. When she was 16, she eloped with Percy Bysshe Shelley, and by the time she was 24, she had been widowed, lost three of her four children in infancy, and written what was to become her most famous book, *Frankenstein*." Libr J

"A convincing and memorable portrait." Booklist

Includes bibliographical references

Sunstein, Emily W. Mary Shelley; romance and reality. Johns Hopkins Univ. Press 1991 478p il pa $20.95   **92**

1. Women authors 2. Authors, English

ISBN 0-8018-4218-2; 978-0-8018-4218-4

LC 90-23541

First published 1989 by Little, Brown

A "revisionist account of a woman who 'literally embodies the English Romantic movement'. . . . Sunstein provides substantial documentation of the breadth of Shelley's education and the extent of her writing. . . . Most rewarding, perhaps, are Sunstein's astute insights into Shelley's emotional life." Choice

Includes bibliographical references

Sherman, William T. (William Tecumseh), 1820-1891

Fellman, Michael. Citizen Sherman; a life of William Tecumseh Sherman. University Press of Kansas 1997 486p il pa $19.95   **92**

1. Generals 2. United States—History—1861-1865, Civil War

ISBN 978-0-7006-0840-9; 0-7006-0840-0

First published 1995 by Random House

"Using Sherman's personal correspondence as well as that of his friends and family, Fellman . . . examines the private thoughts and life of the Union general." Libr J

"This superb biography gives as full a portrait of nineteenth-century family dynamics as of the dynamics of the battlefield. Fellman's Sherman is not a lovable man, but he is a complete one." New Yorker

Includes bibliographical references

Flood, Charles Bracelen. Grant and Sherman. See entry under Grant, Ulysses S. (Ulysses Simpson), 1822-1885

Kennett, Lee B. Sherman; a soldier's life; [by] Lee Kennett. HarperCollins Pubs. 2001 426p il maps pa $14.95 hardcover o.p.   **92**

1. Generals 2. United States—History—1861-1865, Civil War

ISBN 0-06-093074-8 (pa)   LC 2001-16687

The author presents a "consideration of Sherman's personality and character . . . as well as a thoughtful reconsideration of Sherman's views on a number of issues (including his relationship with Ulysses S. Grant) and his wartime performance." Libr J

This is a "well-balanced analytical biography." Publ Wkly

Includes bibliographical references

Sickles, Daniel E., 1825-1914

Keneally, Thomas. American scoundrel: the life of the notorious Civil War General Dan Sickles. Talese 2002 397p $27.50; pa $15 *   **92**

ISBN 0-385-50139-0; 0-385-72225-7 (pa)

LC 2001-43078

A "biography of Tammany politician and Civil War general Dan Sickles. Sickles was famous in his time both as the cold-blooded killer of his wife's lover, the son of Francis Scott Key, and as the insubordinate commander who defied orders at Cemetery Ridge." Publ Wkly

"A frequently spellbinding recitation of the career of a totally awful politician, crook, adulterer and murderer who was no good as a general either." N Y Times Book Rev

Simon, Neil

Simon, Neil. The play goes on; a memoir. Simon & Schuster 1999 348p il pa $14 hardcover o.p.   **92**

ISBN 0-684-86980-2 (pa)   LC 99-36449

Sequel to Rewrites

This memoir "recounts the second half of Simon's life, starting with the life-shattering impact of the death of his first wife, Joan, of cancer at 40, and proceeding through the ensuing 30 years, during which Simon had periods of incredible fertility and others in which his creativity dried up and he feared he would never write again." Booklist

Simon, Neil. Rewrites; a memoir. Simon & Schuster 1996 397p pa $14 hardcover o.p.   **92**

ISBN 0-684-83562-2 (pa)   LC 96-13691

This first volume of the dramatist's memoirs focuses on his career as it evolved from writing high school skits

Simon, Neil—*Continued*

to TV programs to Broadway

"This is a gentleman's autobiography, and Simon never stoops to dishing the dirt on his show biz cronies." Libr J

Simpson, Colton

Simpson, Colton. Inside the Crips; life inside L.A.'s most notorious gang; [by] Colton Simpson with Ann Pearlman. St. Martin's Press 2005 xxiii, 323p $24.95; pa $14.95   **92**

1. Crips (Gang)
ISBN 0-312-32929-6; 0-312-30930-X (pa)
         LC 2005-42704

The author "provides an insider's perspective on day-to-day life in the Crips, the gang's history (including quite a bit about its rival, the Bloods), and the plight of growing up in the 'hood while wanting a better life. . . . This unvarnished portrayal of gang life is enlightening and even inspiring about a subject badly in need of illumination." Booklist

Sinatra, Frank, 1915-1998

Friedwald, Will. Sinatra! the song is you; a singer's art. Da Capo Press 1997 559p il pa $18.50 *   **92**

ISBN 0-306-80742-4   LC 96-43855

A reprint of the title first published 1995 by Scribner

This work "details Sinatra's musical legacy, from his start as a big band vocalist and his early Columbia recordings, through his Capital Records triumphs of the 1950s and his not always successful 1960s and 1970s experiments on the Reprise label, to his commercial pinnacle but aesthetic nadir, the recent *Duets*." Booklist

Friedwald's "commentary is alert and perceptive, and even more valuable is the wealth of pointed reminiscence drawn from interviews he has done with musicians who worked closely with Mr. Sinatra." N Y Times Book Rev

Includes discography and bibliographical references

Singer, Isaac Bashevis, 1904-1991

Singer, Isaac Bashevis. More stories from my father's court; translated by Curt Leviant. Farrar, Straus & Giroux 2000 216p pa $12 hardcover o.p.   **92**

1. Jews—Poland
ISBN 0-374-52798-9 (pa)   LC 00-37583
Sequel to In my father's court

These pieces were first published in Yiddish in the Jewish daily Forward from 1955-1960

These autobiographical sketches depict the workings of the beth din, the rabbinical court that met in the Singer's Warsaw home

"This book is a portrait of the artist as a voyeuristic yeshiva boy, someone who assimilated into his soul the weird contradictions of modern Jewish life and, half chronicler and half creator, spun them into lasting stories." N Y Times Book Rev

Sitting Bull, Dakota Chief, 1831-1890

Utley, Robert Marshall. Sitting Bull: the life and times of an American patriot; by Robert M. Utley. Henry Holt 2008 464p il pa $18   **92**

ISBN 978-0-8050-8830-4; 0-8050-8830-X
"A John Macrae book"
A reissue with a new preface by the author of the title first published 1993

"Born in 1831 on the great Plains, son of a chief, Sitting Bull was a seasoned warrior by the age of 15; at 26, he was tribal war chief. As the conflicts with the U.S. Army began in the 1850s, Sitting Bull represented the spirit of resistance among his people. Utley follows the increasing hostilities of succeeding years and gives a vivid account of the Battle of the Little Big Horn in 1876." Publ Wkly

"This book is well written, strongly documented, and fairly reasoned to satisfy even specialists within the field. It surpasses all previous biographies of Sitting Bull." Choice

Includes bibliographical references

Skinner, B. F. (Burrhus Frederic), 1904-1990

Bjork, Daniel W. B.F. Skinner; a life. American Psychological Assn. 1997 298p il pa $19.95   **92**

ISBN 1-55798-416-6   LC 96-40385
A reissue of the title first published 1993 by Basic Bks.

This is a biography of the psychologist known for his utopian novel Walden Two, his book Beyond freedom and dignity, and his behaviorist theories

"Bjork places Skinner squarely in the context of the US social, technological, and political history. . . . Although heavily documented, Bjork's book is very readable because documentation is in endnotes. A handsome, well-indexed work, with an excellent bibliography." Choice

Smith, Alfred Emanuel, 1873-1944

Finan, Christopher M. Alfred E. Smith, the happy warrior. Hill & Wang 2002 396p il $26; pa $16   **92**

1. United States—Politics and government
ISBN 0-8090-3033-0; 0-8090-1632-X (pa)
         LC 2002-19476

This is a biography of the "governor of New York and the first Catholic candidate for president, trounced by Herbert Hoover in the 1928 election amidst a torrent of anti-Catholic bigotry." Booklist

"Finan writes well, but for an occasional lapse into anachronism." NY Times Book Rev

Includes bibliographical references

Smith, Joseph, 1805-1844

Brodie, Fawn McKay. No man knows my history: the life of Joseph Smith, the Mormon prophet; by Fawn M. Brodie. 2nd ed rev and enl. Knopf 1971 499, xxp il pa $18 hardcover o.p.   **92**

1. Mormons
ISBN 0-679-73054-0 (pa)
First published 1945

Taking as her title a phrase from a sermon by Joseph Smith himself, the author has attempted to discover as much of the truth concerning Joseph Smith and the be-

Smith, Joseph, 1805-1844—*Continued*
ginnings of Mormonism, as can be found in an intensive
research into documents, diaries, unpublished manuscripts, etc.
Includes bibliographical references

Bushman, Richard L. Joseph Smith; rough stone
rolling; [by] Richard Lyman Bushman, with the
assistance of Jed Woodworth. Knopf 2005 740p il
map $35; pa $18.95   **92**
    1. Mormons
    ISBN 1-4000-4270-4; 1-4000-7753-2 (pa)
                   LC 2004-61613
In this biography of the founder of the Mormon
church, the author "stresses the boy seer's thoroughly ordinary origins—born to a hard-pressed New England
farm family and denied all but the rudiments of a formal
education—to emphasize the marvel of the religious revolution he brought about. . . . A deft portrait of a deeply
controversial figure." Booklist
Includes bibliographical references

Remini, Robert Vincent. Joseph Smith. Viking
2002 190p (Penguin lives series) $19.95
                          92
    1. Mormons
    ISBN 0-670-03083-X   LC 2001-56762
In this biography of the founder of the Mormon
Church, the author "places Smith in the context of his
time in terms of the broader social, political, and eco-
nomic events that influenced him and his church." Libr
J
"A masterful evenhanded précis that will engross his-
tory and religion readers alike." Booklist
Includes bibliographical references

Smith, William, 1769-1839
Winchester, Simon. The map that changed the
world; William Smith and the birth of modern
geology; illustrations by Soun Vannithone.
HarperCollins Pubs. 2001 329p il map $26; pa
$13.95   **92**
    1. Stratigraphic geology
    ISBN 0-06-019361-1; 0-06-093180-9 (pa)
                   LC 2001-16603
"In the early years of the nineteenth century, William
Smith created the first geological map of Great Britain,
a time-consuming, solitary project that helped establish
geology as one of the 'fundamental fields of study.' . . .
Winchester tells Smith's story, including the dramatic
ups and downs of his personal life. . . . This is just the
kind of creative nonfiction that elevates a seemingly arcane topic into popular fare." Booklist

Smithson, James, 1765-1829
Ewing, Heather P. The lost world of James
Smithson; science, revolution, and the birth of the
Smithsonian; [by] Heather Ewing. Bloomsbury
2007 432p il map $29.95   **92**
    1. Smithsonian Institution—History 2. Scientists
    ISBN 978-1-59691-029-4; 1-59691-029-1
This is a biography of the British chemist who
founded the Smithsonian Institution in Washington, DC.

The author "provides a readable and informative perspective on late Enlightenment chemistry, backing it up
with extensive archival research and forays into secondary literature on science." Times Lit Suppl
Includes bibliographical references

Snyder, Don J.
Snyder, Don J. The cliff walk; a memoir of a
lost job and a life found. Little, Brown 1997 265p
$23.95; pa $12.95   **92**
    ISBN 0-316-80308-1; 0-316-80348-0 (pa)
                   LC 96-51163
"When the author is fired by Colgate University, he
never doubts that his brilliance and charm will soon gain
him entrance to a new ivory tower. Instead, he is forced
to move his family of five to Maine in the off season.
With his pride and his checking account steadily eroding,
he concocts wild schemes—stealing golf balls from a
nearby course with his son, and secretly contemplating
selling his unborn child. Finally, Snyder gives his last
seventeen hundred dollars to a dying woman so she can
take her children to Disney World. This dire act propels
him into a real job—building a house—and toward a vision of self that depends more on strength than on prestige." New Yorker

Solomon, Dorothy Allred
Solomon, Dorothy Allred. Predators, prey, and
other kinfolk; growing up in polygamy. Norton
2003 399p $24.95   **92**
    1. Mormons 2. Polygamy
    ISBN 0-393-04946-9   LC 2003-1044
This is the memoir of "the only daughter of a polyga-
mous, fundamentalist Mormon. . . . The twenty-eighth
of 48 children, she was instilled, as were her many
brothers, by her father with the sense of the family's difference, which the world beyond its circle, even most
other Mormons (the church officially abolished polygamy
in 1890), wouldn't welcome." Booklist
The author "provides a remarkably balanced account
of the contradictions and pressures she experienced both
from within her family and from the surrounding culture." Libr J
Includes bibliographical references

Sondheim, Stephen
Citron, Stephen. Sondheim and Lloyd-Webber;
the new musical. Oxford Univ. Press 2001 425p il
$39.95   **92**
    1. Lloyd Webber, Andrew, 1948-
    ISBN 0-19-509601-0   LC 2001-31408
In this volume Citron profiles the two composers,
highlighting their personal lives and tracing "their creative development from tentative neophytes to much-
feted giants, integrating the various directions that musical theater has taken." Libr J
Includes bibliographical references

Sonnenberg, Susanna
Sonnenberg, Susanna. Her last death; a memoir.
Scribner 2008 273p $24   **92**
    ISBN 978-0-7432-9108-8; 0-7432-9108-5
                   LC 2007-3515

Sonnenberg, Susanna—*Continued*

Sonnenberg's memoir illuminates her resolve to forge her independence, to become a woman capable of trust and to be a good mother to her own children after being raised by a mother who was a compulsive liar and a drug user.

"A heartbreaking yet wickedly entertaining portrait of a magically seductive, immensely flawed mother who fails dramatically as a parent and of a daughter who learns to trust and love others despite an orphanlike upbringing marked by disillusion." Libr J

Sontag, Susan, 1933-2004

Rollyson, Carl E. (Carl Edmund). Susan Sontag; the making of an icon; {by} Carl Rollyson and Lisa Paddock. Norton 2000 370p il $29.95
92

ISBN 0-393-04928-0   LC 00-20402
The authors "have unearthed a deluge of information on Sontag's personal life—on her early years and family life, her lesbianism. . . her relationship with son David Rieff and her battles with breast cancer. While the authors provide an intelligent, though not strikingly original, analysis of her work, they are best at detailing how Sontag and her publishers have marketed her image as much as her thought." Publ Wkly

Includes bibliographical references

Sorensen, Theodore C., 1928-

Sorensen, Theodore C. Counselor; a life at the edge of history; [by] Ted Sorensen. HarperCollins 2008 556p il $27.95   **92**
1. Kennedy, John F. (John Fitzgerald), 1917-1963
ISBN 978-0-06-079871-0; 0-06-079871-8
  LC 2007-47328
This is a memoir by President Kennedy's advisor and speechwriter.

"This book is instantly essential for any student of the period. It fills gaps in the historical record; it vividly conveys life inside the administration; and it generously dishes anecdotes." Washington Post Book World

Soto, Hernando de, ca. 1500-1542

Duncan, David Ewing. Hernando de Soto; a savage quest in the Americas. University of Okla. Press 1997 570p map il pa $29.95   **92**
1. Explorers
ISBN 0-8061-2977-8; 978-0-8061-2977-8
  LC 97-10455
First published 1995 by Crown
This is a "biography of the conquistador who from 1539 to his death in 1543 was 'the first European to penetrate deeply into the interior of our continent.'" Libr J

"Duncan's scholarship and documentation are impeccable, and his chronology unfolds like a superbly crafted novel." Booklist

Includes bibliographical references

Soyinka, Wole

Soyinka, Wole. You must set forth at dawn; a memoir. Random House 2006 499p map $26.95 *
  92

ISBN 0-375-50365-X; 978-0-375-50365-8
"This memoir covers Soyinka's life from young manhood to the present." N Y Times Book Rev

"By turns panoramic and intimate, ruminative and politically resolute, Soyinka's memoir is a dense but intriguing conversation between a writer and his times." Publ Wkly

Speaker, Tris, 1888-1958

Gay, Timothy M. Tris Speaker; the rough-and-tumble life of a baseball legend. University of Nebraska Press 2005 314p il $27.95
  92

ISBN 0-8032-2206-8   LC 2005-16975
This is a "look at the Hall of Fame center fielder, whose colorful personality and remarkable talent were overshadowed by contemporaries like Ty Cobb and Cy Young. . . . Gay has insured the righting of history with this biography. A worthwhile read for any sports fan." Publ Wkly

Spector, Phil

Brown, Mick. Tearing down the wall of sound; the rise and fall of Phil Spector. Knopf 2007 452p il $26.95; pa $16.95 *   **92**
1. Record producers
ISBN   978-1-4000-4219-7;   1-400-04219-4; 978-1-4000-7661-1 (pa); 1-4000-7661-7 (pa)
  LC 2007-4819
This is a biography of the record producer and songwriter.

"Stacked with incredible anecdotes, Brown's entertaining and nuanced portrait lifts the fog of myth and outright falsehood (including Spector's own) that have obscured the celebrity producer (like an enormous, gravity-defying wig) through the years." Publ Wkly

Includes bibliographical references

Speer, Albert, 1905-1981

Fest, Joachim C. Speer: the final verdict; {by} Joachim Fest; translated from the German by Ewald Osers and Alexandra Dring. Harcourt 2002 419p il $30; pa $15   **92**
ISBN 0-15-100556-7; 0-15-602874-3 (pa)
  LC 2002-6074
One of the "defendants at Nuremberg . . . was armaments minister Albert Speer. . . . {He projected} the image of himself as the apolitical 'outsider' at the heart of the Nazi regime—as the person who accepted moral responsibility for its crimes but first came to hear of them at the end of the war. . . . {This is a} biographical study {of Speer}." Hist Today

"This is a valuable, important biography, but perhaps it is an effort to explain the unexplainable." Booklist

Includes bibliographical references

Sereny, Gitta. Albert Speer; his battle with truth. Knopf 1995 757p il pa $25 hardcover o.p.
  92
1. National socialism 2. Germany—Politics and government—1933-1945
ISBN 0-679-76812-2 (pa)   LC 94-19764

Speer, Albert, 1905-1981—*Continued*

The author of this biography of the Nazi war criminal "conducted intensive and protracted interviews with Speer . . . and many of the people who were close to him. Along with the interviews and analysis are good descriptions of what was happening in Germany throughout the Third Reich. Sereny's clear and concise prose makes this book suitable for both the scholar and the lay reader. She has produced what will become one of the standard works in Holocaust studies." Libr J

Includes bibliographical references

Spender, Stephen, 1909-1995

Sutherland, John. Stephen Spender; a literary life. Oxford University Press 2005 627p il $40
92

ISBN 0-19517-816-5　　　　LC 2004-09727

"Stephen Spender was one of a generation of Oxford-educated English writers, including W. H. Auden and Christopher Isherwood, who sought to revolutionize literature in the 1930s. In this official account of his life . . . emphasis is appropriately placed on the 1930s, when Spender came to prominence writing prose, short stories, criticism, and journalism in addition to his politically charged poetry. He was as experimental in life as in art, as evidenced by his bisexuality and his loyalty to left-wing Socialist causes." Libr J

Stalin, Joseph, 1879-1953

Bullock, Alan. Hitler and Stalin. See entry under Hitler, Adolf, 1889-1945

Conquest, Robert. Stalin; breaker of nations. Viking 1991 346p il pa $14.95 hardcover o.p.
92
1. Soviet Union—Politics and government
2. Dictators
ISBN 0-14-016953-9 (pa)　　　　LC 91-28782

The author "portrays the Soviet dictator as an insufferably rude husband, a Georgian who hated his roots and Russified himself, a crude boor who yearned to be a backslapping man to the people." Publ Wkly

"Intended for the general reader, [this work] provides a superb portrait of the man who terrorized his country for 30 years. . . . Briskly written, authoritative yet not pedantic, filled with interesting incidents and anecdotes, [it] makes for fascinating reading." N Y Times Book Rev

Includes bibliographical references

Montefiore, Sebag. Stalin: the court of the red tsar; by Simon Sebag Montefiore. Knopf 2004 xxvii, 785p il map $30 *
92
1. Dictators 2. Soviet Union—History
ISBN 1-400-04230-5　　　　LC 2003-27390
First published 2003 in the United Kingdom

"An intimate portrait of the Soviet dictator and his henchmen." N Y Times Book Rev

"In the relentless detail, the mood-setting descriptions of the leader's surroundings, the sketches of the people around him and in Stalin's own words, pranks and tempers, Montefiore gives us not only the most intimate view of the general secretary that we have to date but a rounded and complex portrait of a man who could go from charming to lethal in the space of a few seconds." Nation

Includes bibliographical references

Montefiore, Sebag. Young Stalin; [by] Simon Sebag Montefiore. Knopf 2007 xxxii, 460p il map $30 *
92
1. Dictators 2. Soviet Union—History
ISBN 1-4000-4465-0; 978-1-4000-4465-8
LC 2007-29220

This is a "biography of Stalin's early years. . . . Mr. Montefiore offers a . . . picture of Stalin's childhood and youth, his shadowy career as a revolutionary in Georgia and his critical role during the October Revolution." N Y Times (Late N Y Ed)

Stalin "is brilliantly brought to life in this superb biography." Hist Today

Includes bibliographical references

Pringle, Peter. The murder of Nikolai Vavilov. See entry under Vavilov, N. I. (Nikolaĭ Ivanovich), 1887-1943

Radzinsky, Edvard. Stalin; the first in-depth biography based on explosive new documents from Russia's secret archives; translated by H.T. Willetts. Doubleday 1996 607p il pa $16.95 hardcover o.p.
92
1. Dictators 2. Soviet Union
ISBN 0-385-47954-9 (pa)　　　　LC 95-4495

For this biography of the Soviet ruler the author "has examined mountains of rare archival sources and interviewed many who lived through decades of Stalinist (mis)rule. The result is the best general biography of Stalin to date. Radzinsky strips away layer after layer of myth, falsehood, and enigma to produce a riveting portrait of a man whose primary role model was Ivan the Terrible." Libr J

Includes bibliographical references

Service, Robert. Stalin; a biography. Belknap Press of Harvard University Press 2005 715p il map $29.95
92
1. Soviet Union—History 2. Dictators
ISBN 0-674-01697-1　　　　LC 2004-61115

This book covers Stalin's life "from his early, troubled years in a small town in Georgia to the pinnacle of power in the Kremlin. . . . By providing such a rich and complex portrait of the dictator and the Soviet system, Service humanizes Stalin without ever diminishing the extent of the atrocities he unleashed upon the Soviet population." Publ Wkly

Includes bibliographical references

Stanley, Henry M. (Henry Morton), 1841-1904

Jeal, Tim. Stanley; the impossible life of Africa's greatest explorer. Yale University Press 2007 570p il map $38
92
1. Explorers
ISBN 978-0-300-12625-9; 0-300-12625-5
LC 2007-923548

This is a biography of the explorer.

"There have been many biographies of Stanley, but

Stanley, Henry M. (Henry Morton), 1841-1904—*Continued*

Jeal's is the most felicitous, the best informed, the most complete and readable and exhaustive." N Y Times Book Rev

Includes bibliographical references

Stanton, Elizabeth Cady, 1815-1902

Ward, Geoffrey C. Not for ourselves alone: the story of Elizabeth Cady Stanton and Susan B. Anthony; an illustrated history; based on a documentary film by Ken Burns, written by Geoffrey C. Ward; with a preface by Ken Burns; introduction by Paul Barnes; and contributions by Martha Saxton, Ann D. Gordon, Ellen Carol DuBois. Knopf 1999 240p $35; pa $19.95 *

92

1. Anthony, Susan B., 1820-1906 2. Feminism
ISBN 0-375-40560-7; 0-375-70969-X (pa)

LC 99-31056

This biographical study of Cady and Anthony, leaders of the women's rights movement in the United States, was published to accompany a television film by Ken Burns.

"Ward writes beautifully, and he knows how to weigh evidence and how to assess the salience of events. He quotes shrewdly from the words of his protagonists. Although the interpretation is far from exciting or original, he freshens his material by including new essays by scholars." New Repub

Includes bibliographical references

Stanton, Tom

Stanton, Tom. Road to Cooperstown; a father, two sons, and the journey of a lifetime. Thomas Dunne Bks. 2003 260p il $24.95; pa $13.95

92

1. National Baseball Hall of Fame and Museum
2. Baseball—Biography
ISBN 0-312-30350-5; 0-312-33118-5 (pa)

LC 2003-40862

Companion volume to The final season

The author "examines family, fatherhood, life and, of course, baseball while on a road trip that was a lifetime in the making." Publ Wkly

Steffens, Lincoln, 1866-1936

Steffens, Lincoln. The autobiography of Lincoln Steffens; foreword by Thomas C. Leonard. Heyday Books 2005 882p il (California legacy book) pa $21.95

92

1. Journalists
ISBN 1-59714-016-3

LC 2005-27009

First published 1931 by Harcourt Brace & Co.

The life of an American reporter, journalist, student of ethics and politics.

"Here is a textbook on journalism; a treasure house for the historian of that wave of social idealism that shook the United States from 1900 to 1917; a casebook for the psychologist of political types. Above all it is the vivid diary of a bold and humane pilgrim." Survey

Stein, Gertrude, 1874-1946

Malcolm, Janet. Two lives; Gertrude and Alice. Yale University Press 2007 229p il $25

92

1. Toklas, Alice B. 2. Authors, American
ISBN 978-0-300-12551-1; 0-300-12551-8

LC 2007-12085

This book examines the "relationship between Gertrude Stein and Alice B. Toklas." N Y Times Book Rev

"This is a vital addition to Stein criticism as well as an important work that critiques the political responsibility of the artist (even a genius) to the larger world." Publ Wkly

Includes bibliographical references

Stein, Gertrude. The autobiography of Alice B. Toklas. Modern Lib. 1993 342p $15.50; pa $13

92

1. Toklas, Alice B. 2. Paris (France)—Intellectual life
3. Authors, American
ISBN 0-679-60081-7; 0-679-72463-X (pa)

LC 93-15339

First published 1933 by Harcourt Brace & Co.

"The book is really Stein's autobiography, presented as though written by her secretary, Alice Toklas. The book provoked a rejoinder from various Parisian artists and writers, *Testimony Against Gertrude Stein* (1935). . . . For the average reader, however, Stein's book holds much fascination in its views of Parisian life and personalities, and the whole is offered in a genuinely witty style." Benet's Reader's Ency of Am Lit

Steinem, Gloria

Heilbrun, Carolyn G. The education of a woman; the life of Gloria Steinem. Ballantine Books 1996 450p il pa $23

92

1. Feminism
ISBN 0-345-40621-4; 978-0-345-40621-7

First published 1995 by Dial Press

The author "offers a study of Steinem that takes into account both her feminine and feminist appeal." Libr J

"The portrait that results is nuanced and thoughtful. . . . Heilbrun's goal is at once to understand how Steinem became the woman she is, and what her life can teach us about childhood and family, self and society. Slow at the start, but Heilbrun soon captures readers' interest and imagination." Booklist

Includes bibliographical references

Steinke, Darcey

Steinke, Darcey. Easter everywhere; a memoir. Bloomsbury USA 2007 225p $24.95

92

ISBN 978-1-582-34530-7; 1-582-34530-9

LC 2006-31637

"A scrappy kid with a violent stutter, novelist Steinke . . . is the oldest child of an aloof Lutheran minister and a clinically depressed former Miss Albany. The household is steeped in the word of God; Steinke grows up brewing her own communion wine, baptizing the neighborhood cats and craving, even at age six, spiritual transcendence. It's a wish that never leaves her, and she's tireless in her pursuit of this elusive state of oneness, first seeking it in a sexually obsessive relationship with

Steinke, Darcey—*Continued*

a man who turns out to be gay, and then in her doomed marriage." Publ Wkly

"This book is an excellent account of a writer going head-to-head with the divine and finding some inner quiet—even in the darkest corners of her imagination." Time Out New York

Stengel, Casey

Creamer, Robert W. Stengel; his life and times. University of Neb. Press 1996 349p il pa $18.95 **92**

ISBN 0-8032-6367-8   LC 95-40143

First published 1984 by Simon & Schuster

"Casey Stengel is remembered as either the shrewd, innovative New York Yankee manager who won 10 pennants and seven World Series from 1949 to 1960 or as the seemingly senile, aged master of malaprop who (mis)-managed the legendarily inept New York Mets in the early 1960s. Creamer . . . dissolves the apparently disparate images and melds them into an inclusive vision of an unexpectedly complex man." Booklist

Stone, I. F. (Isidor Feinstein), 1907-1989

MacPherson, Myra. All governments lie; the life and times of rebel journalist I.F. Stone. Scribner 2006 564p il $35 * **92**

ISBN 978-0-684-80713-3; 0-684-80713-0

LC 2006-42389

"A Lisa Drew book"

This is a look "at I. F. Stone—one of America's most independent and revered journalists." Publisher's note

"This biography interweaves his life and journalism within the context of the social and political era, providing an engaging overview of a complex man who challenged his contemporaries. Many of the political issues Stone confronted will resonate with today's readers." Libr J

Includes bibliographical references

Stone, Robert, 1937-

Stone, Robert. Prime green; remembering the sixties. Ecco 2007 229p il $25.95 **92**

1. United States—History—1961-1974

ISBN 0-06-019816-8; 978-0-06-019816-9

LC 2006-46351

"From the New York City of Kline and De Kooning to the jazz era of New Orleans's French Quarter to Ken Kesey's psychedelic California, [the book] explores the 1960s. . . . An account framed by two wars, it begins with [the author's] last year in the Navy, when he took part in an Antarctic expedition navigating the globe, and ends in Vietnam, where he was a correspondent in the days following the invasion of Laos." Publisher's note

The author "is a born storyteller, with a wonderful feel for place and character that vividly evokes the cultural gulf America crossed in that decade." Publ Wkly

Stowe, Harriet Beecher, 1811-1896

Hedrick, Joan D. Harriet Beecher Stowe; a life. Oxford Univ. Press 1994 507p il pa $19.95 hardcover o.p. **92**

ISBN 0-19-509639-8 (pa)   LC 93-16610

This biography "brings to life not just the complex and fascinating woman and writer but also the 19th-century America that shaped her and was in turn shaped by her. Hedrick manages to weave into his immensely readable biography a history teeming with the domestic detail of the famous Beecher clan, the settling of the West, and the impact of the Civil War and the abolition movement." Libr J

Includes bibliographical references

Stravinsky, Igor, 1882-1971

Joseph, Charles M. Stravinsky inside out. Yale Univ. Press 2001 xx, 320p il $29.95 **92**

ISBN 0-300-07537-5   LC 2001-913

This study "reveals a . . . flawed and fragile human being, who craved approval, dealt ungenerously with colleagues, loved James Bond movies, and tried hard to further his son's musical career. Although the aged Stravinsky's eagerness to play the role of celebrity composer for the golden age of television . . . was an embarrassment, most of these episodes testify to the protean survival skills of an artist whose sense of identity was always in flux and whose cunning was commensurate with his talent." New Yorker

Includes bibliographical references

Walsh, Stephen. Stravinsky: a creative spring; Russia and France, 1882-1934. University of California Press 2002 698p il pa $25.95 **92**

ISBN 978-0-520-22749-1; 0-520-22749-2

LC 2002-23256

First published 1999 by Knopf

"In this reference-oriented biography, Walsh uses diaries, press clippings, and other materials to probe in detail the life of a man kept very busy with effectively dividing his time between performance, composition, family, and mistress." Booklist

Includes bibliographical references

Walsh, Stephen. Stravinsky: the second exile; France and America, 1934-1971; Stephen Walsh. Alfred A. Knopf 2006 709p il $40 **92**

ISBN 0-375-40752-9   LC 2005-47231

Sequel to Stravinsky: a creative spring

"In tracing the artist's path from a Paris study in 1934 to a Lenox Hill deathbed, readers see the same composer who incited an audience to riot in 1913 eventually boring his listeners in the late 1930s with neoclassical works of sterile harmony." Booklist

"This is essential reading for musicologists and other music enthusiasts who wish to delve into the life and mind of perhaps the greatest composer of the 20th century." Libr J

Includes bibliographical references

Stringer, Caverly

Stringer, Caverly. Sleepaway school; stories from a boy's life; [by] Lee Stringer. A Seven Stories Press 1st ed. Seven Stories Press 2004 227p $21.95; pa $13.95 **92**

1. African Americans—Biography

ISBN 1-58322-478-5; 1-58322-701-6 (pa)

LC 2004-3610

Stringer, Caverly—*Continued*

"In more than 30 connected true stories, Stringer portrays his boyhood as a poor, black foster child coincidentally growing up in a wealthy white neighborhood after he was sent to a school for troubled boys—mostly white, middle-class boys." Booklist

The author "deftly tells a believable, candid and vivid tale of a person scarred by his past." Publ Wkly

Sullivan, Ed, 1902-1974

Maguire, James. Impresario; the life and times of Ed Sullivan. Billboard Books 2006 344p il $24.95   92

ISBN 0-8230-7962-7; 978-0-8230-7962-9 (ISBN-13)

This is a "portrait of Sullivan as a tough-minded micromanager who tightly controlled every aspect of his show, even telling Ella Fitzgerald what to sing." N Y Times Book Rev

The author "has written a fascinating biography and meticulously recorded the birth of TV, the heyday of newspaper columnists and the glamour of New York." Publ Wkly

Taft, Helen Herron, 1861-1943

Anthony, Carl Sferrazza. Nellie Taft; the unconventional first lady of the ragtime era. 1st ed. William Morrow 2005 534p il $29.95; pa $15.95   92

ISBN 0-06-051382-9; 0-06-051383-7 (pa)

LC 2004-52553

This is a "biography of Helen Herron Taft, the unconventional wife of the twenty-seventh President of the United States who, in an era before Eleanor Roosevelt, was overt about her power and saw to it that her husband both aspired to, and won, the highest office in the land." Publisher's note

"This lively biography provides an illuminating glimpse into the life of an until-now underappreciated First Lady." Booklist

Includes bibliographical references

Tallchief, Maria

Tallchief, Maria. Maria Tallchief; America's prima ballerina; [by] Maria Tallchief with Larry Kaplan. University Press of Florida 2005 368p pa $19.95   92

ISBN 0-8130-2846-9; 978-0-8130-2846-0

LC 2005-42211

First published 1997 by Henry Holt

In this memoir Tallchief focuses "on her remembrances of her years with choreographer George Balanchine. . . . She met Balanchine at the start of her career, when she was with the Ballet Russe de Monte Carlo and Balanchine was about to form a company that would become a precursor to the New York City Ballet. Tallchief subsequently became Balanchine's wife, muse, and prima ballerina, and, though the marriage was short-lived, their artistic partnership endures in Balanchine's works created for Tallchief. She also writes about other stars, but the memoir sparkles when she recalls the subtlety and detail of a movement or the beauty of a musical phrase." Libr J

Tammet, Daniel, 1979-

Tammet, Daniel. Born on a blue day; inside the extraordinary mind of an autistic savant: a memoir. Free Press 2007 226p il $24; pa $14   92

1. Autism 2. Asperger's syndrome 3. Savants (Savant syndrome)

ISBN 1-4165-3507-1; 978-1-4165-3507-2; 1-4165-4901-3 (pa); 978-1-4165-4901-7 (pa)

LC 2006-41331

First published 2006 in the United Kingdom

This "first-person account offers a window into the mind of a high-functioning, 27-year-old British autistic savant with Asperger's syndrome." Publ Wkly

This "autobiography is as fascinating as Benjamin Franklin's and John Stuart Mill's, both of which are, like his, about the growth of a mind." Booklist

Tan, Amy

Tan, Amy. The opposite of fate; a book of musings. Putnam 2003 398p il $24.95; pa $15   92

ISBN 0-399-15074-9; 0-14-200489-8 (pa)

LC 2003-47190

This autobiography contains the author's "musings on topics as varied as rock'n'roll, the film adaptation of *The Joy Luck Club*, her reactions to the Cliff Notes' analysis of her work and life, her recent health problems, and other autobiographical observations. The selections are culled from essays, speeches, interviews, and a commencement address." Libr J

"No matter how much readers already revere Tan, their appreciation for her will grow tenfold after experiencing these provocative and unforgettable revelations." Booklist

Taylor, Major, 1878-1932

Balf, Todd. Major; a Black athlete, a White era, and the fight to be the world's fastest human being. Crown Publishers 2008 306p il $24   92

1. African American athletes 2. Bicycle racing

ISBN 978-0-307-23658-6   LC 2007-20747

The author "chronicles the life of the unlikeliest of stars in the early years of cycling: Marshall 'Major' Taylor. Taylor was an incomparable athlete, poet and celebrity, but he was also a black man living during a time when the scars of the Civil War and slavery were still fresh in the minds of Americans. Balf . . . does great work presenting the complex nature of Taylor's life, including his upbringing in poverty in Indianapolis, the years he was treated as a son by a rich white family, the fans who both worshipped and vilified him and his close relationships with his white trainer and promoter." Publ Wkly

Includes bibliographical references

Tecumseh, Shawnee Chief, 1768-1813

Eckert, Allan W. A sorrow in our heart: the life of Tecumseh. Bantam Bks. 1992 862p maps pa $7.99 hardcover o.p.   92

1. Shawnee Indians

ISBN 0-553-56174-X (pa)   LC 91-31858

Tecumseh, Shawnee Chief, 1768-1813—*Continued*

This is a "narrative biography of Tecumseh, the remarkable Shawnee warrior and statesman who succeeded in organizing a group of disparate tribes into a cohesive confederacy of nations. . . . Eckert places his subject firmly within his proper social and historical context by providing a tremendous amount of meticulously researched and authenticated background information, including illuminating details of tribal life and Shawnee culture." Booklist

Includes bibliographical references

Teferra, Haregewoin

Greene, Melissa Fay. There is no me without you; one woman's odyssey to rescue Africa's children. Bloomsbury Pub. 2006 472p il $25.95
                                                            92

1. AIDS (Disease) 2. Ethiopia 3. Orphans
ISBN 978-1-59691-116-1; 1-59691-116-6
                                        LC 2006-14088
This book chronicles "the odyssey of Haregewoin Teferra, who took in AIDS orphans. . . . In telling her story, journalist Greene who had adopted two Ethiopian children before meeting Teferra, juggles political history, medical reportage and personal memoir. . . . Greene takes a very close look at what appears to be the fringe of an important social event and illuminates the entire subject." Publ Wkly

Includes bibliographical references

Teller, Edward, 1908-2003

Goodchild, Peter. Edward Teller, the real Dr Strangelove. Harvard University Press 2004 xxv, 469p il $29.95 *   **92**
ISBN 0-674-01669-6   LC 2004-54257
This is a biography of "the 'father of the hydrogen bomb,' a witness against J. Robert Oppenheimer in the latter's security hearing, and, finally, an ardent promoter of the Cold War arms race. . . . {The author} studied a wide range of primary and secondary sources and interviewed many people on both sides of the controversies that swirled around Teller. The result is a remarkably well-balanced study of a notoriously prickly and opinionated person." Libr J

Includes bibliographical references

Teller, Edward. Memoirs; a twentieth-century journey in science and politics; {by} Edward Teller with Judith Shoolery. Perseus Bks. 2001 628p il pa $18.95 hardcover o.p.   **92**
ISBN 0-7382-0778-0 (pa)
This memoir, by the nuclear physicist who worked to develop the hydrogen bomb, recounts his origins in the scientific community in Germany prior to the Nazi takeover and describes his "work on safe proliferation of nuclear energy, the so-called Stars Wars defense system and the early detection of earth-crossing objects. . . . Readers can enjoy these panoramic and beautifully written recollections of one of the great scientific, if controversial, figures of all time." Publ Wkly

Includes bibliographical references

Teresa, Mother, 1910-1997

Spink, Kathryn. Mother Teresa; a complete authorized biography. HarperSanFrancisco 1997 306p il pa $15.95 hardcover o.p.   **92**
1. Missionaries of Charity 2. Missions—India
ISBN 0-06-251553-5 (pa)   LC 97-41349
"Spink's biography benefits from her own 18-year involvement with the work of the Missionaries of Charity Order as well as from the intimate relationship she developed over the years with Mother Teresa. . . . A final chapter in the book provides glimpses of Mother Teresa's affection for Princess Diana, a brief description of Mother Teresa's funeral and a short account of the election of Sister Nirmal as her successor." Publ Wkly

Teresa, of Avila, Saint, 1515-1582

Medwick, Cathleen. Teresa of Avila; the progress of a soul. Knopf 1999 282p pa $12.95 hardcover o.p.   **92**
1. Christian saints
ISBN 0-385-50129-3 (pa)   LC 99-18921
"This is a Borzoi bk."
In this biography of the sixteenth-century Spanish nun, "Medwick traces Teresa's early years, her entrance into the genteel life of the Convent of the Incarnation in Avila, her second conversion as a person of prayer, and her subsequent trials as a founder of reformed monasteries of women under the austere rule of Mount Carmel." Commonweal

Includes bibliographical references

Terkel, Studs, 1912-2008

Terkel, Studs. Touch and go; a memoir; [by] Studs Terkel, with Sydney Lewis. New Press 2007 269p il $24.95   **92**
1. Authors, American
ISBN 978-1-59558-043-6; 1-59558-043-3
                                        LC 2007-18673
"Terkel's memoir is . . . a medley of all the extraordinary characters he's encountered through his career, from the adult loners of his youth in Chicago's Wells-Grand Hotel, to New Deal politicians. Terkel details his long journey through law school, the air force, theater, radio, early television, sports commentary, jazz criticism and oral history. . . . Americans might get to know their collective past a lot better if all history lessons were as absorbing and entertaining as this one." Publ Wkly

Thomas, Abigail, 1941-

Thomas, Abigail. A three dog life. Harcourt 2006 182p $22   **92**
ISBN 978-0-15-101211-4; 0-15-101211-3
                                        LC 2005-33782
In this memoir, the author focuses on her "third husband, Rich, who flounders in a miasmic present after a hit-and-run in their Manhattan neighborhood shatters his skull, destroys his short-term memory and consigns him to permanent brain trauma." Publ Wkly
"Thomas has elevated what could be, at best, an overemotional sermon or, at worst, a grim romp in self-pity to a high plain of true inspiration." Booklist

Thomas, Dylan, 1914-1953

Lycett, Andrew. Dylan Thomas: a new life. Overlook Press 2004 434p il $35   92
ISBN 1-58567-541-5
First published 2003 in the United Kingdom
This biography of the Welsh poet and dramatist "analyzes Thomas' difficult family life, including his volatile marriage to wild-hearted Caitlin, his soulful poetry and stories, and his tragic self-destructiveness." Booklist
"Other biographies . . . have ably recounted the essential details of Thomas's life, but Lycett here provides a wealth of useful detail, bringing the Welsh poet's life story up to date." Libr J
Includes bibliographical references

Thompson, Hunter S., 1937-2005

Thompson, Hunter S. Fear and loathing in America; the brutal odyssey of an outlaw journalist, 1968-1976; foreword by David Halberstam; edited by Douglas Brinkley. Simon & Schuster 2000 xxv, 756p il $30; pa $15 *   92
1. Journalists
ISBN 0-684-87315-X; 0-684-87316-8 (pa)
                                        LC 00-47012
This is the second volume of a projected three volume edition of Thompson's letters; earlier volume The proud highway published 1997 by Villard Books
"During the period covered in this collection, Thompson was a vital, deliriously erratic force in journalism, covering the turbulent 1968 Democratic National Convention in Chicago, the 1968 election of Richard M. Nixon, the 1972 campaign, Watergate, the falls of Nixon and Saigon." N Y Times Book Rev

Thompson, Hunter S. The kingdom of fear; loathsome secrets of a star-crossed child in the final days of the American century. Simon & Schuster 2003 xx, 354p il hardcover o.p. pa $16   92
ISBN   0-684-87323-0;   978-0-684-87324-4;
0-684-87324-9 (pa)   LC 2002-191228
In this book the American journalist writes about his life and career experiences
"Just as Thompson paved his own way in writing about politics, sports, news and culture throughout the 1960s and '70s, he now offers an autobiography that is typically unorthodox in style but still revealing previously unknown facts about its subject. Wavering between the uproarious and the lunatic, it's vintage Thompson through and through." Publ Wkly

Wenner, Jann S. Gonzo; the life of Hunter S. Thompson; by Jann S. Wenner & Corey Seymour; introduction by Johnny Depp. Little, Brown 2007 467p il $28.99 *   92
1. Journalists
ISBN 978-0-316-00527-2; 0-316-00527-4
                                        LC 2007-11693
This oral biography is a "look at the turbulent life of Gonzo journalism pioneer Hunter S. Thompson (1937-2005). . . . This fine, fond biography amuses, inspires, outrages and haunts at all the right moments—and sometimes all at once." Publ Wkly

Thorpe, Jim, 1888-1953

Crawford, Bill. All American; the rise and fall of Jim Thorpe. John Wiley & Sons, Inc 2004 284p il $24.95 *   92
1. Athletes
ISBN 0-471-55732-3   LC 2004-14376
This "terse, punchy biography of sports legend Thorpe (1888–1953) illuminates the current debate over the exploitation of unpaid college athletes by moneymaking, headline-grabbing educational institutions." Publ Wkly
Includes bibliographical references

Timerman, Jacobo, 1923-1999

Timerman, Jacobo. Prisoner without a name, cell without a number; translated from the Spanish by Toby Talbot. University of Wisconsin Press 2002 164p (The Americas) pa $17.95   92
1. Political prisoners
ISBN 978-0-299-18244-1; 0-299-18244-4
First published 1981 by Knopf
The author, "an outspoken Zionist and formerly a newspaper publisher in Buenos Aires, relates his 30-month political incarceration—torture and isolation in a clandestine prison, then detention in an official penal institution—which preceded his expulsion from Argentina in 1979." Publ Wkly

Tiptree, James, 1916-1987

Phillips, Julie. James Tiptree, Jr.; the double life of Alice B. Sheldon. St. Martin's Press 2006 469p il $27.95   92
ISBN 0-312-20385-3; 978-0-312-20385-6
                                        LC 2006-40095
This is a biography of the American science fiction writer.
The author "has achieved a wonder: an evenhanded, scrupulously documented, objective yet sympathetic portrait of a deliberately elusive personality." Publ Wkly
Includes bibliographical references

Tirone Smith, Mary-Ann, 1944-

Tirone Smith, Mary-Ann. Girls of tender age; a memoir. Free Press 2006 285p il map $24 *   92
ISBN 0-7432-7977-8   LC 2005-51376
This memoir, an "unsentimental view of life in a post-World War II working-class family, is interspersed with the story of Bob Malm, a serial pedophile who brutally murdered a fifth-grade classmate of hers in December 1953. . . . This poignant memoir belongs in all collections." Libr J
Includes bibliographical references

Tito, Josip Broz, 1892-1980

West, Richard. Tito; and the rise and fall of Yugoslavia. Carroll & Graf Pubs. 1995 436p il pa $15.95 hardcover o.p.   92
1. Yugoslavia—Politics and government
ISBN 0-7867-0332-6 (pa)   LC 95-10404
First published 1994 in the United Kingdom

Tito, Josip Broz, 1892-1980—*Continued*

This biography "describes Tito's rise to power, his creation of the Partisan Army during the Axis occupation, his consolidation of southern Slavs after the war and establishment of a Communist Yugoslavia, the break with Stalin in 1948, Tito's subsequent rivalry with the Soviet bloc and his leadership of nonaligned states. . . . The book also clarifies the present three-way conflict among Serbs, Croats and Muslims." Publ Wkly

"This combination of history and biography is based on a sympathetic attitude toward its subject, a relaxed style of writing, and a good command of published sources." Libr J

Includes bibliographical references

Tocqueville, Alexis de

Epstein, Joseph. Alexis De Tocqueville; democracy's guide. Atlas Books 2006 208p (Eminent lives) $21.95   **92**

ISBN 0-06-059898-0; 978-0-06-059898-3

LC 2006-47175

The author provides an "examination of the man, his works, his influence, his times and what we can learn from Democracy in America. . . . As an introduction to the man and a primer for his works, Epstein's book is admirable." Publ Wkly

Toklas, Alice B.

Malcolm, Janet. Two lives. See entry under Stein, Gertrude, 1874-1946

Stein, Gertrude. The autobiography of Alice B. Toklas. See entry under Stein, Gertrude, 1874-1946

Tolkien, J. R. R. (John Ronald Reuel), 1892-1973

Hammond, Wayne G. J.R.R. Tolkien, artist & illustrator; {by} Wayne G. Hammond, Christina Scull. Houghton Mifflin 1995 207p il pa $25 hardcover o.p.   **92**

ISBN 0-618-08361-8 (pa)   LC 96-105237

Along with biographical material and text describing his artwork, this book reproduces more than 200 drawings, sketches and paintings Tolkien made throughout his life. Included are the "Father Christmas" letters to his children and images created in connection with The Hobbit and The Lord of the Rings

"The open and inviting format and the reproductions of his art make this a Tolkien lover's dream, and the insightful text will quickly capture attention as well." Booklist

Includes bibliographical references

Toulouse-Lautrec, Henri de, 1864-1901

Frey, Julia. Toulouse-Lautrec; a life. Phoenix 1995 597p il pa $27.50   **92**

1. Artists, French

ISBN 1-85799-363-2; 978-1-85799-363-9

First published 1994 by Viking

"The author chronicles Toulouse-Lautrec's transformation from a pampered invalid into one of the most radical of the fin de siecle artists. . . . Her sensitive, eloquent, and richly illustrated biography has brought the real Toulouse-Lautrec out from behind the scrim of myth." Booklist

Includes bibliographical references

Toussaint Louverture, 1743?-1803

Bell, Madison Smartt. Toussaint Louverture; a biography. Pantheon Books 2007 333p map $27 *
92

ISBN 978-0-375-42337-6; 0-375-42337-0

LC 2006-45848

This is a biography of the Haitian leader.

"This is the best biography of Toussaint yet, in large part because Bell does not shy away from the man's contradictions." N Y Times Book Rev

Includes bibliographical references

Trillin, Alice, 1938-2001

Trillin, Calvin. About Alice. Random House 2007 78p $14.95   **92**

ISBN 1-4000-6615-8; 978-1-4000-6615-5

LC 2006-45573

This book is a "love letter to Trillin's wife, Alice, who died in 2001 at the age of 63 while awaiting a heart transplant, after a battle with lung cancer 25 years previously had left her heart weakened by radiation." N Y Times Book Rev

"This succinct account of Alice's upbringing, their meeting, their romance, their family, and her career beyond that of Trillin's helpmeet, offers glimpses into a multifaceted character." Booklist

Truman, Harry S., 1884-1972

McCullough, David G. Truman; {by} David McCullough. Simon & Schuster 1992 1117p il $40; pa $22   **92**

ISBN 0-671-45654-7; 0-671-86920-5 (pa)

LC 92-5245

This biography of the 33rd president "not only conveys in rich detail Truman's accomplishments as a politician and statesman, but also reveals the character and personality of this constantly-surprising man—as schoolboy, farmer, soldier, merchant, county judge, senator, vice president and chief executive. The book relates how Truman overcame the stigma of business failure and debt . . . and acquired a reputation for honesty, reliability and common sense." Publ Wkly

Includes bibliographical references

Trump, Donald J.

Slater, Robert. No such thing as over-exposure; inside the life and celebrity of Donald Trump. Prentice Hall 2005 xxiv, 247p $24.95   **92**

ISBN 0-13-149734-0   LC 2004-116294

This "biography outlines Trump's deals, business strategies, leadership style, and ability to craft his own image in the media." Libr J

Donald Trump "is not so easily understood, but this book goes a long way toward defining him." Booklist

Includes bibliographical references

Truth, Sojourner, d. 1883

Painter, Nell Irvin. Sojourner Truth; a life, a symbol. Norton 1996 370p il hardcover o.p. pa $15.95 * 92

1. Abolitionists 2. Feminism

ISBN 0-393-02739-2; 0-393-31708-0 (pa)

LC 95-47595

"Sojourner Truth's remarkable career as a powerful, impassioned speaker and advocate of abolitionism and women's rights spanned more than 30 years. Painter . . . traces Truth's life and legacy using a variety of sources, including her many photographs." Libr J

"Painter persuasively offers us the real woman behind the myth." Publ Wkly

Includes bibliographical references

Tubman, Harriet, 1820?-1913

Clinton, Catherine. Harriet Tubman: the road to freedom. Little, Brown 2004 272p hardcover o.p. pa $14.95 92

1. Abolitionists 2. African American women 3. Underground railroad

ISBN 0-316-14492-4; 0-316-15594-2 (pa)

LC 2003-56185

The author "places Tubman's life within its times, describing, among other things, the history of the abolitionist movement and the impact of the Fugitive Slave Law of 1850." N Y Times Book Rev

"Clinton turns sobriquets into meaningful descriptors of a unique person. In her hands, a familiar legend acquires human dimension with no diminution of its majesty and power." Publ Wkly

Includes bibliographical references

Humez, Jean McMahon. Harriet Tubman; the life and the life stories; [by] Jean M. Humez. University of Wisconsin Press 2004 c2003 471p il (Wisconsin studies in autobiography) $45

92

1. Abolitionists 2. African American women 3. Underground railroad

ISBN 0-299-19120-6

LC 2003-5676

In this volume the author "includes a collection of Tubman's autobiographical stories culled from rare early publications and manuscript sources. This book will become an important resource for scholars, historians, and general readers interested in slavery, the Underground Railroad, the Civil War, and African American women." Univ Press Books for Public and Second Sch Libr, 2004

Includes bibliographical references

Larson, Kate Clifford. Bound for the promised land; Harriet Tubman, portrait of an American hero. Ballantine Bks. 2003 xxi, 402p il map $26.95; pa $14.95 92

1. Abolitionists 2. African American women 3. Underground railroad

ISBN 0-345-45627-0; 0-345-45628-9 (pa)

LC 2004-297886

"Using a clear writing style, Larson does an excellent job of placing Tubman in the context of her times." SLJ

Includes bibliographical references

Turing, Alan Mathison, 1912-1954

Leavitt, David. The man who knew too much; Alan Turing and the invention of the computer. W. W. Norton 2006 319p il (Great discoveries) $22.95

92

ISBN 0-393-05236-2 LC 2005-18034

"Atlas books"

This is a biography of the British mathematician.

The author "succeeds in drawing a wonderfully vivid picture of his shy, dry, brilliant hero." Natl Rev

Includes bibliographical references

Turnage, Wallace, d. 1916

Blight, David W. A slave no more. See entry under Washington, John, d. 1918

Turner, Ted, 1938-

Auletta, Ken. Media man; Ted Turner's improbable empire. Norton 2004 205p il $22.95

92

ISBN 0-393-05168-4 LC 2004-12215

"Atlas books"

The author "describes how Turner's upbringing by a domineering father and his marriage to and later divorce from actress and radical Jane Fonda influenced his life and career. He also shows how Turner revolutionized TV by turning a tiny Atlanta station into a national cable powerhouse." Libr J

Includes bibliographical references

Turner, Tina

Turner, Tina. I, Tina; {by} Tina Turner, with Kurt Loder. Morrow 1986 236p il pa $6.99 o.p.

92

ISBN 0-380-70097-2 (pa) LC 86-16455

"Born Anna Mae Bullock in 1939 in Nut Bush, Tennessee, Tina Turner is now—after a fantastic comeback—one of the hottest acts in rock music. . . . The path that Tina . . . followed to pull herself out of sleepy Nut Bush and eventually to gain international stardom is traced here." Booklist

"Kurt Loder has edited I, Tina nicely, letting {Turner's} narrative take center stage, punctuating it with the voices of friends, colleagues, and family." Nation

Twain, Mark, 1835-1910

Powers, Ron. Mark Twain; a life. Free Press 2005 722p il $35 92

ISBN 0-7432-4899-6 LC 2005-48816

The author "develops topics neglected by other Twain biographers: the writer's genuinely mean late treatment of his bumbling brother, Orion; the negative impact of advancing technology on Twain's capacity for visual description; and his principled determination, late in life, to repay every cent he owed his creditors." Libr J

"A masterful biography of interest to both general readers and academics." Booklist

Includes bibliographical references

Twain, Mark. The autobiography of Mark Twain; as arranged and edited with an introduction and notes, by Charles Neider. Harper & Row 1959 xxvi, 388p il pa $15 hardcover o.p. 92

Twain, Mark, 1835-1910—*Continued*
1. Authors, American
ISBN 0-06-095542-2 (pa)
The editor "has arranged the selections in coordinated chronological order, ending with the death of Clemens' daughter Jean in December, 1909." Booklist

Tyler, John, 1790-1862
Crapol, Edward P. John Tyler; the accidental president. University of North Carolina Press 2006 332p il map $37.50 *   **92**
ISBN 978-0-8078-3041-3; 0-8078-3041-0
LC 2005-37963
In this biography of the former U.S. president, the author "argues that Tyler was in fact a terrifically strong president who helped strengthen the executive branch. . . . This balanced, fascinating volume will introduce a new generation of readers to an oft-ignored president." Publ Wkly
Includes bibliographical references

Tynan, Kenneth, 1927-1980
Tynan, Kenneth. The diaries of Kenneth Tynan; edited by John Lahr. Bloomsbury Press 2001 439p il $32.95; pa $16.95   **92**
ISBN 1-58234-160-5; 1-58234-245-8 (pa)
LC 2001-35274
Tynan "was one of Britain's foremost drama critics; here, he spent two seasons as theater critic for the *New Yorker.* Along with Laurence Olivier, he helped found London's National Theater, where he functioned as literary manager for 10 years. Not surprisingly, Tynan dissects theatrical foibles and politicking with a keen inside perspective; he can also discourse on the European common market, Spaniards' attitudes toward homosexuality, cricket, French cuisine, Ethel Merman and much more. . . . Celebrated names are not merely dropped (from Katharine Hepburn and Princess Margaret to W.H. Auden and Jerry Lewis), but integral to his revelatory anecdotes." Publ Wkly

Typhoid Mary, d. 1938
Bourdain, Anthony. Typhoid Mary; an urban historical. Bloomsbury Pub. 2001 148p $19.95
92
ISBN 1-58234-133-8   LC 2001-18444
The subject of Bourdain's book is the cook "Mary Mallon, who became known as Typhoid Mary after infecting 33 people with typhoid fever . . . in turn-of-the-century New York." N Y Times Book Rev
"Investing a tragic tale with a new twist, Bourdain plays historical detective, providing an entertaining and suspenseful evocation of turn-of-the-century New York." Booklist
Includes bibliographical references

Ung, Loung, 1970-
Ung, Loung. Lucky child; a daughter of Cambodia reunites with the sister she left behind. HarperCollins Publishers 2005 268p il $24.95; pa $13.95 *   **92**
1. Ung, Chou 2. Cambodian Americans
3. Cambodia—History—1975-
ISBN 0-06-073394-2; 0-06-073395-0 (pa)
LC 2004-54346
Sequel to First they killed my father
In this "memoir, Ung picks up where her first . . . left off, with the author escaping a devastated Cambodia in 1980 at age 10 and flying to her new home in Vermont. . . . She and her eldest brother, with whom she escaped, left behind their three other siblings. This book is alternately heart-wrenching and heartwarming, as it follows the parallel lives of Loung Ung and her closest sister, Chou, during the 15 years it took for them to reunite." Publ Wkly
Includes bibliographical references

Valentino, Rudolph, 1895-1926
Leider, Emily Wortis. Dark lover: the life and death of Rudolph Valentino; [by] Emily W. Leider. Farrar, Straus & Giroux 2003 514p il $35; pa $16   **92**
ISBN 0-374-28239-0; 0-571-21114-3 (pa)
LC 2002-29779
This is a "study of the movie star and his era, and of how he altered forever the electric charges of both men and women in 1921 with 'The Sheik.'" N Y Times Book Rev
"A comprenhensive . . . portrait of the great screen lover." Booklist
Includes bibliographical references

Van Buren, Martin, 1782-1862
Widmer, Edward L. Martin Van Buren; [by] Ted Widmer. Times Bks. 2005 189p (American presidents series) $20   **92**
1. Presidents—United States
ISBN 0-8050-6922-4   LC 2004-53652
This is a "portrait of our eighth president, who, Widmer says, created the modern political party system." Publ Wkly
The author "keenly evokes the environment that enabled Van Buren to thrive. . . . Widmer also lends a certain dignity to Van Buren's post-presidential attempts to resolve the sectional crisis." N Y Times Book Rev
Includes bibliographical references

Van Zandt, Townes, 1944-1997
Kruth, John. To live's to fly; the ballad of the late, great Townes Van Zandt. Da Capo 2007 326p il $26   **92**
ISBN 978-0-306-81553-9; 0-306-81553-2
This is "the first biography of legendary Texas singer/songwriter Townes Van Zandt (1944-97). In his struggle for recognition among a wider public, Van Zandt wrestled for years with depression and alcoholism while writing songs—e.g., 'Pancho and Lefty' and 'Be Here To Love Me'—that today are revered by the elite of Texas

Van Zandt, Townes, 1944-1997—*Continued*
and Nashville songwriters as well as by a cult group of fans. Through access to Van Zandt's friends, family members, and fellow musicians, Kruth provides an intimate and unflinching look at the singer's life." Libr J

Vavilov, N. I. (Nikolaĭ Ivanovich), 1887-1943
Pringle, Peter. The murder of Nikolai Vavilov; the story of Stalin's persecution of one of the great scientists of the twentieth century. Simon & Schuster 2008 370p il $26 **92**
1. Stalin, Joseph, 1879-1953 2. Botanists
ISBN 978-0-7432-6498-3; 0-7432-6498-3
LC 2008-03510
This is a biography of the Russian botanist and geneticist who was starved to death in a Soviet prison in 1943.
This "is a must-read to grasp the ultimate, disasterous effect of politics trumping science." Sci Books Films
Includes bibliographical references

Verdi, Giuseppe, 1813-1901
Berger, William. Verdi with a vengeance; an energetic guide to the life and complete works of the king of opera. Vintage Bks. 2000 497p il pa $15 **92**
ISBN 0-375-70518-X LC 00-42261
The author "provides a brief overview of the composer's life and times and examines the connections between contemporary politics and Verdi's creative output. . . . A glossary and recommended recordings, films, and soundtracks are included. Informative and eminently readable for the novice and scholar alike." Libr J
Includes bibliographical references

Vespucci, Amerigo, 1451-1512
Fernández-Armesto, Felipe. Amerigo; the man who gave his name to America. Random House 2007 231p il map $24.95 **92**
1. America—Exploration
ISBN 978-1-4000-6281-2; 1-4000-6281-0
LC 2006-51739
First published 2006 in the United Kingdom
The author chronicles the life and times of the explorer and navigator Amerigo Vespucci
"A well-connected Florentine wheeler-dealer who settled in Seville, Vespucci began by outfitting Columbus's ships and later made voyages of his own. . . . Fernandez-Armesto accepts that Amerigo Vespucci made two voyages to north eastern South America, one in 1499 and another in 1501-02. But the evidence is maddeningly vague on exactly where he went, what he did, and even in what capacity he served (he is unlikely to have been the commander, as he claimed). Faced by such unreliable sources, Fernandez-Armesto sticks to what can be said of Vespucci with confidence, and wisely opts to paint a rich portrait of the times rather than speculate about details that may never be known." Times Lit Suppl

Victoria, Queen of Great Britain, 1819-1901
Erickson, Carolly. Her little majesty: the life of Queen Victoria. Simon & Schuster 1997 304p il pa $19.95 hardcover o.p. **92**
1. Great Britain—History—19th century
ISBN 0-7432-3657-2 (pa) LC 96-35041
This is a biography of the British monarch
"Erickson has a knack for plucking pithy quotes, and the essentials of the queen's life are often deftly set out." Publ Wkly
Includes bibliographical references

Hibbert, Christopher. Queen Victoria; a personal history. Basic Bks. 2000 557p il pa $21 hardcover o.p. **92**
1. Great Britain—History—19th century
ISBN 0-306-81085-9 (pa) LC 2001-269136
Hibbert explores the life and reign of the British monarch based on "primary sources, particularly the 60 million words of Victoria's letters and journals. As a result, he renders Victoria and her familial and political relationships with deliciously gossipy and often touching intimacy." N Y Times Book Rev
Includes bibliographical references

Vallone, Lynne. Becoming Victoria. Yale Univ. Press 2001 256p il $26.95 **92**
1. Great Britain—History—19th century
ISBN 0-300-08950-3 LC 00-68561
"Analyzing Victoria's girlhood diaries, drawings and fiction, as well as records of her education and scores of accounts of her childhood, Valone . . . constructs a revisionist account of the princess's youthful persona but also traces the process by which Victoria was molded into the 'right' kind of adult: capable of assuming the throne and also a clear embodiment of all that was womanly and pure. . . . Well-researched, and with sophisticated cultural criticism, this sound scholarship will engage the interest of academics and nonacademics alike." Publ Wkly
Includes bibliographical references

Vidal, Gore, 1925-
Vidal, Gore. Point to point navigation; a memoir, 1964 to 2006. Doubleday 2006 277p il $26 **92**
ISBN 0-385-51721-1; 978-0-385-51721-8
LC 2006-11644
This memoir by the novelist and essayist is a continues the narrative begun in Palimpsest (1995). Among the "notables to be found in these pages . . . are Jack and Jacqueline Kennedy, Tennessee Williams ('the Glorious Bird'), Eleanor Roosevelt, Orson Welles, Johnny Carson, Greta Garbo, Federico Fellini, Rudolf Nureyev, Elia Kazan, and Francis Ford Coppola." Publisher's note
"The memoir is a perfect encapsulation of Vidal's outsized personality—and readers' reactions will be determined by how they already feel about him." Publ Wkly

Vieira de Mello, Sergio, 1948-2003
Power, Samantha. Chasing the flame; Sergio Vieira de Mello and the fight to save the world. Penguin Press 2008 622p il $32.95 **92**
1. United Nations 2. Diplomats
ISBN 978-1-594-20128-8 LC 2007-30978

Vieira de Mello, Sergio, 1948-2003—*Continued*

This is a biography of the career diplomat who "died in a terrorist attack on UN Headquarters in Iraq in 2003." Publisher's note

"Strongly argued, lacerating, and utterly human, this invaluable history will be a catalyst for soul searching and debate." Booklist

Includes bibliographical references

Villa, Pancho, 1878-1923

Katz, Friedrich. The life and times of Pancho Villa. Stanford Univ. Press 1998 985p pa $30.95 hardcover o.p.   **92**

1. Mexico—History

ISBN 0-8047-3046-6 (pa)   LC 97-47271

The author "traces Pancho Villa's rise from relatively obscure outlaw to national leader of the Mexican Revolution (1910-20) and his subsequent decline to guerrilla leader. . . .{This} is likely to be the definitive account of Villa for years to come." Libr J

Includes bibliographical references

Volpe, Joseph

Volpe, Joseph. The toughest show on earth; my rise and reign at the Metropolitan Opera; [by] Joseph Volpe with Charles Michener. Knopf 2006 304p il $25.95   **92**

1. Metropolitan Opera (New York, N.Y.)

ISBN 0-307-26285-5; 978-0-307-26285-1

LC 2005-57932

This is a memoir by the "general manager of New York's Metropolitan Opera since 1990. . . . This enthralling book provides an insider's view of a complex and fascinating institution." Libr J

Includes bibliographical references

Voltaire, 1694-1778

Pearson, Roger. Voltaire almighty; a life in pursuit of freedom. Bloomsbury 2005 xxxii, 447p il $35 *   **92**

ISBN 978-1-58234-630-4; 1-58234-630-5

LC 2005-53027

This is a biography of the French philosopher.

The author "has composed a lively and thorough account of the illustrious philosophe's chaotic life." Choice

Includes bibliographical references

Von Braun, Wernher, 1912-1977

Neufeld, Michael J. Von Braun; dreamer of space, engineer of war. A.A. Knopf 2007 587p il $35   **92**

1. Rocketry 2. Scientists

ISBN 978-0-307-26292-9; 0-307-26292-8

LC 2007-5711

This is a "biography of Wernher von Braun, chief rocket engineer of the Third Reich—creator of the . . . V2 rocket—who became one of the fathers of the U.S. space program." Publisher's note

This "is a meticulously researched and technically accurate biography of von Braun." N Y Rev Books

Includes bibliographical references

Wagner, Richard, 1813-1883

Berger, William. Wagner without fear; learning to love—and even enjoy—opera's most demanding genius. Vintage Bks. 1998 454p maps pa $15.95   **92**

1. Opera

ISBN 978-0-375-70054-5; 0-375-70054-4

LC 98-19825

The author's goal is to make Richard Wagner's operas accessible to the uninitiated. "After a breezy summary of the composer's life, he devotes a chapter to each of his mature works, interspersing plot outlines with chatty commentary. There is a bit of performance history, as well as advice on how to pronounce names, get through the rough spots at the notoriously long performances and when to eat, drink and visit the restroom. . . . Chapters on Wagner CDs and the best books to read on the composer and his operas are useful." Publ Wkly

Walker, Alice, 1944-

Walker, Alice. The same river twice; honoring the difficult: a meditation on life, spirit, art, and the making of the film The color purple, ten years later. Scribner 1996 302p il pa $14 hardcover o.p.   **92**

1. Color purple (Motion picture)

ISBN 0-671-00377-1 (pa)   LC 95-30056

This "book finds the Pulitzer Prize-winning author still grappling with criticism of the film version of her novel *The Color Purple*. . . . Walker's memoir pieces together assorted journal entries, magazine clippings, occasional photographs and even her original screenplay to form an intimate scrapbook of the period." Publ Wkly

Includes bibliographical references

Wallace, Alfred Russel, 1823-1913

Slotten, Ross A. The heretic in Darwin's court; the life of Alfred Russel Wallace. Columbia University Press 2004 602p il maps $77.50; pa $25   **92**

ISBN 0-231-13010-4; 0-231-13011-2 (pa)

LC 2003-68833

"Slotten explains why Wallace, who also discovered natural selection, was relegated to footnote status while Darwin ascended to the scientific pantheon; he analyzes Wallace's complex relationship with his fellow biologist, and offers fresh insight into this unpredictable genius." Booklist

"With a narrative of almost 500 pages, the biography was clearly a labor of love for the author, who is a medical doctor and a Wallace enthusiast. Although some readers may find the amount of material overwhelming, it is quite accessible to general audiences." Sci Books Films

Includes bibliographical references

Wallach, Eli, 1915-

Wallach, Eli. The good, the bad, and me; in my anecdotage. Harcourt 2005 312p il $25; pa $16   **92**

ISBN 0-15-101189-3; 0-15-603169-8 (pa)

LC 2004-23121

Wallach, Eli, 1915-—*Continued*
The author "tells his story, from a Brooklyn childhood as the only Jew in an Italian neighborhood, through Actors Studio days with Brando and others, and on to his long and illustrious career on both stage and screen. . . . This compelling memoir shows the full range of a remarkable actor's life." Booklist

Walls, Jeannette
Walls, Jeannette. The glass castle; a memoir. Scribner 2005 288p $25; pa $14 *   92
ISBN 0-7432-4753-1; 0-7432-4754-X (pa)
LC 2004-58907
The author "describes a childhood spent careering across the country, from California to West Virginia, in a succession of ever more rattletrap cars, in pursuit of increasingly implausible get-rich-quick schemes." Time
"Shocking, sad, and occasionally bitter, this gracefully written account speaks candidly, yet with surprising affection, about parents and about the strength of family ties—for both good and ill." Booklist

Walters, Barbara, 1931-
Walters, Barbara. Audition; a memoir. Alfred A. Knopf 2008 612p il $29.95   92
1. Women journalists
ISBN 978-0-307-26646-0; 0-307-26646-X
LC 2008-05843
This is a memoir by the television newscaster.
"Alternating between tales of her personal struggles, professional achievements and insider anecdotes about the celebrities and world leaders she's interviewed, this mammoth memoir's energy never flags." Publ Wkly

Walton, Sam
Walton, Sam. Sam Walton, made in America; my story; by Sam Walton with John Huey. Bantam Books 1992 346p il pa $7.99   92
1. Wal-Mart Stores, Inc. 2. Businessmen
ISBN 0-553-56283-5; 978-0-553-56283-5
First published 1992 by Doubleday
The founder of Wal-Mart Stores, the largest retail chain in the world, recounts how he made his fortune.
"Readers will enjoy the folksy narrative of the small-town millionaire who revolutionized retail distribution. . . . Coauthor Huey does a fine job of incorporating candid testimonials from family members and associates." Libr J

Wareham, Dean
Wareham, Dean. Black postcards; a rock & roll romance. Penguin Press 2008 324p il $25.95
          92
1. Galaxie 500 (Musical group) 2. Luna (Musical group) 3. Rock musicians
ISBN 978-1-59420-155-4; 1-59420-155-2
LC 2007-35280
"In this collection of over 50 sequential autobiographical essays, . . . [the author] takes us from his childhood in New Zealand, through his formative years exploring New York City's punk scene, to his adult life in Cam-

bridge, MA, where he becomes a notable figure in the alternative music scene. Wareham documents in great detail the history of his two bands, Galaxy 500 and Luna. . . . Fans of Wareham's bands and such bands as Bongwater, Cocteau Twins, R.E.M., and the Velvet Underground, as well as anyone with an interest in American and European alternative music, will find this to be an insightful and entertaining read." Libr J

Washington, Booker T., 1856-1915
Harlan, Louis R. Booker T. Washington: the making of a black leader, 1856-1901. Oxford Univ. Press 1972 379p il pa $21.50 hardcover o.p.
          92
1. African Americans—Biography
ISBN 0-19-501915-6 (pa)
This book "covers Washington's life from his birth as a slave in western Virginia up to [the year 1901, when he dined] with Theodore Roosevelt at the White House, an event signifying white recognition of Washington as the chief spokesman for black interests in the period before World War I." Libr J

Harlan, Louis R. Booker T. Washington: the wizard of Tuskegee, 1901-1915. Oxford Univ. Press 1983 548p il pa $24.95 hardcover o.p.
          92
1. Tuskegee Institute 2. African Americans—Biography
ISBN 0-19-504229-8 (pa)   LC 82-14547
This is the second and concluding volume of a life of the black educator and founder of Tuskegee Institute.
"Having avoided the pitfalls of white guilt and black rage and the temptation to judge the past by standards of the present, Mr. Harlan deserves honors for his remarkable achievement." N Y Times Book Rev
Includes bibliographical references

Uncle Tom or new Negro; African Americans reflect on Booker T. Washington and Up from slavery one hundred years later; edited by Rebecca Carroll. Broadway Books/Harlem Moon 2006 320p pa $15.95   92
1. African Americans—Biography
ISBN 0-7679-1955-6; 978-0-7679-1955-5
LC 2005-50161
"This collection of 20 commentaries by contemporary writers offers new perspectives on Booker T. Washington's autobiography and his place in the struggle for racial equality. Among the commentators are Debra Dickerson, Julianne Malveaux, Bill Ethanson, Ronald Walkers, Earl Ofari Hutchinson, and John McWhorter. The book also includes the complete text of *Up from Slavery*." Booklist
Includes bibliographical references

Washington, Booker T. Up from slavery; with a new introduction by Ishmael Reed. New American Library 2000 xxii, 228p (Edwards Black Heritage Collection) pa $4.95 *   92
1. Tuskegee Institute 2. African Americans—Biography
ISBN 0-451-52754-2   LC 99-34954
First published 1901

Washington, Booker T., 1856-1915—*Continued*
"The classic autobiography of the man who, though born in slavery, educated himself and went on to found Tuskegee Institute." N Y Public Libr

Includes bibliographical references

Washington, George, 1732-1799
Brookhiser, Richard. Founding father: rediscovering George Washington. Free Press 1996 230p pa $14 hardcover o.p.   **92**
1. Presidents—United States
ISBN 0-684-83142-2 (pa)   LC 95-50650
The author presents what he calls a "'moral biography' of the first president. He explores Washington's role as a general, his part in the writing of the Constitution, and his years as president. Brookhiser then turns to Washingon's private life, examining his character, his strong sense of duty, and his constant struggle to hold his temper in check so he could be an effective leader. Finally, the author describes Washington's role as the father of his country." Libr J
"Brookhiser's slim, graceful volume is readable in one sitting. His style is muscular and discursive, yet unaffectedly erudite." Christ Sci Monit

Includes bibliographical references

Ellis, Joseph J. His Excellency; George Washington. Knopf 2004 320p il $26.95; pa $15
*   **92**
1. Presidents—United States
ISBN 1-4000-4031-0; 1-4000-3253-9 (pa)
LC 2004-46576
This is a "look at America's premier Founding Father, revealing a man with incredible energy, stamina, integrity, and vision as well as one who could be quite insecure, controlling, and shortsighted. Ellis examines the evolution of Washington's personality and challenges conventional scholarship. . . . He also determines that Washington's decisions on slavery were driven more by economics and posterity than purely by morality." Libr J
The author "offers a magisterial account of the life and times of George Washington, celebrating the heroic image of the president whom peers like Jefferson and Madison recognized as 'their unquestioned superior' while acknowledging his all-too-human qualities." Publ Wkly

Includes bibliographical references

Flexner, James Thomas. George Washington and the new nation, 1783-1793. Little, Brown 1969 466p il map (His George Washington) $42
92
1. Presidents—United States
ISBN 0-316-28600-1   LC 78-117042
This third volume of a four-volume biography of Washington focuses on the period between the end of the Revolutionary War through his first term as president.
Includes bibliographical references

Flexner, James Thomas. George Washington: anguish and farewell 1793-1799. Little, Brown 1972 554p il (His George Washington) $45
92
1. Presidents—United States
ISBN 0-316-28602-8   LC 72-6875

This final volume of a four-volume biography of Washington covers his second term as president, his retirement, and death.

Includes bibliographical references

Flexner, James Thomas. George Washington: the forge of experience, 1732-1775. Little 1965 390p il map (His George Washington) $40
92
1. Presidents—United States
ISBN 0-316-28597-8   LC 65-21361
The author "covers forty-three years of Washington's life in this volume, the first in a series of four . . . [that carries] Washington through the Revolutionary War and on to the end of his life." Publisher's note

Includes bibliographical references

Gaines, James R. For liberty and glory; Washington, Lafayette, and their revolutions. W.W. Norton & Co. 2007 533p il map $29.95
92
1. Lafayette, Marie Joseph Paul Yves Roch Gilbert du Motier, marquis de, 1757-1834 2. United States—History—1775-1783, Revolution 3. France—History—1789-1799, Revolution
ISBN 978-0-393-06138-3; 0-393-06138-8
LC 2007-22449
Gaines examines the relationship between George Washington and the Marquis de Lafayette.
This is a "fresh and engaging new look at the pair. . . . Gaines has a dry sense of humor and an appreciation for human foibles. . . . The American founding fathers, in particular, come across as extraordinary men with ordinary obsessions and—surprise!—senses of humor." Christ Sci Monit

Includes bibliographical references

Johnson, Paul. George Washington: the Founding Father. HarperCollins Publishers 2005 126p (Eminent lives) $19.95   **92**
1. Presidents—United States
ISBN 0-06-075365-X   LC 2004-52907
This is a biography of the first president of the United States.
The author "submits a beautifully cogent, enthrallingly perceptive, and . . . startlingly fresh take on the ultimate American icon." Booklist

Includes bibliographical references

Randall, Willard Sterne. George Washington; a life. Holt & Co. 1997 548p pa $18 hardcover o.p.
92
1. United States—History 2. Presidents—United States
ISBN 0-8050-5992-X (pa)   LC 97-19125
"A John Macrae book"
"Chronicling less the adaptive leader of the struggling rebellion or the persuasive conciliator of the infant republic, Randall . . . portrays instead the vain, restless, ambitious provincial who got 'tremendously lucky'. . . . Altogether human, Randall's demythologized Washington comes vividly to life." Publ Wkly

Includes bibliographical references

Washington, George, 1732-1799—*Continued*

Washington, George. George Washington's diaries; an abridgment; Dorothy Twohig, editor. University Press of Va. 1999 xxxi, 453p il $65; pa $22.95 * **92**
1. Presidents—United States
ISBN 0-8139-1856-1; 0-8139-1857-X (pa)
LC 98-11681
"Culled from the six volumes of *The Diaries of George Washington* completed in 1979, this selection of entries . . . reveals the lifelong preoccupations of the public and private man." Publisher's note
Includes bibliographical references

Wiencek, Henry. An imperfect god; George Washington, his slaves, and the creation of America. Farrar, Straus and Giroux 2003 404p il map $26; pa $15 * **92**
1. Presidents—United States
ISBN 0-374-17526-8; 0-374-52951-5 (pa)
LC 2003-6984
"This work of stylish scholarship and genealogical investigation makes Washington an even greater and more human figure than he has seemed before." Publ Wkly
Includes bibliographical references

Washington, John, d. 1918

Blight, David W. A slave no more; two men who escaped to freedom: including their own narratives of emancipation. Harcourt 2007 307p il map **92**
1. Turnage, Wallace, d. 1916 2. African Americans—Biography 3. Slavery—United States
ISBN 978-0-15-101232-9; 0-15-101232-6
LC 2007-14467
Three "works are packaged here: two unpublished manuscripts by former slaves Wallace Turnage (1846-1916) and John Washington (1838-1918), and . . . [the author's] analysis of them." Publ Wkly
"Required reading for scholars or even casual students, this signal [sic] contribution is essential for any collection on slavery, emancipation, or African American or U.S. history and literature." Libr J
Includes bibliographical references

Washington, Martha, 1731-1802

Brady, Patricia. Martha Washington; an American life. Viking 2005 276p il $24.95; pa $15 **92**
1. Presidents' spouses—United States
ISBN 0-670-03430-4; 0-14-303713-7 (pa)
LC 2004-61242
In this book, the original first lady "is depicted as a very human but true heroine who remained steadfast through personal adversity and the uncertainties of war and revolution." Libr J
"Brady's splendid biography offers a compelling new portrait of this passionate, committed founding mother who has unjustly been obscured by others, such as Abigail Adams." Publ Wkly
Includes bibliographical references

Wasserman, Lew R., 1913-2002

Bruck, Connie. When Hollywood had a king; the reign of Lew Wasserman, who leveraged talent into power and influence. Random House 2003 512p il hardcover o.p. pa $16.95 **92**
ISBN 0-375-50168-1; 978-0-8129-7217-7 (pa); 0-8129-7217-1 (pa) LC 2003-41418
Includes index
The author "shows how Lew Wasserman managed both to end the era of movie moguls (by freeing the stars of the 1940s from their studio contracts) and then to become the greatest mogul of them all (by realizing that television was an opportunity not a threat)." Booklist
"Those who are interested in comprehensive details about the inner workings of the entertainment industry—its history, business, customs, people, and gossip—will find this a fascinating read and a solid resource." Libr J
Includes bibliographical references

Waters, Muddy, 1915-1983

Gordon, Robert. Can't be satisfied: the life and times of Muddy Waters. Little, Brown 2002 xx, 408p il $25.95; pa $15.95 **92**
ISBN 0-316-32849-9; 0-316-16494-1 (pa)
LC 2001-50473
In this biography of the blues musician "Gordon details the gritty life reflected in Muddy's lyrics. . . . He makes Muddy the musician, Muddy the man, Muddy the parent, and Muddy the tool of the (not so) sainted Chess brothers come alive. . . . Packed with facts, copiously referenced, and featuring a foreword by . . . Keith Richards, this book is absolutely essential for any popular music collection worthy of the name." Booklist
Includes bibliographical references

Watson, James D., 1928-

Watson, James D. Avoid boring people; lessons from a life in science. Alfred A. Knopf 2007 347p il $26.95 **92**
1. Scientists
ISBN 978-0-375-41284-4; 0-375-41284-0
LC 2007-15675
"In this memoir, Watson shows by example how to get to the top and stay there. Spanning his boyhood interest in birds to his resignation from Harvard University in 1976 to his leadership of Cold Spring Harbor Laboratory, Watson's reminiscences encompass his claim to fame—cocredit for deducing DNA's structure in 1953—but focus on his ambition and his conduct of academic politics. . . . In angular and opinionated prose, Watson proves as engaging as ever." Booklist
Includes bibliographical references

Watson, James D. Genes, girls, and Gamow; after the double helix. Knopf 2002 xxix, 259p il $26; pa $14 **92**
ISBN 0-375-41283-2; 0-375-72715-9 (pa)
LC 2001-38543
"A Borzoi book"--T.p. verso; Includes index
"In 1953, Watson, then 25, and colleague Francis Crick discovered the structure of DNA. . . . Here Watson . . . gives a detailed, journal-writer's account of the aftermath, recalling . . . his younger self's professional

Watson, James D., 1928-—*Continued*
and—equally pressing—amorous ambitions. . . . Reading
Watson is a delight, an opportunity to breathe the rarefied air of his generation's greatest scientists and to
crash a faculty cocktail party or two along the way."
Publ Wkly

Webb, James E., 1906-1992
Bizony, Piers. The man who ran the moon;
James E. Webb and the secret history of Project
Apollo. Thunder's Mouth 2006 242p il $24.95
                                                    92
1. United States. National Aeronautics and Space Ad-
ministration 2. Apollo project
ISBN 1-56025-751-2; 9781560257512
                                    LC 2006-298038
"An imprint of Avalon Publishing Group, Inc."
The author looks "at how James Webb, a North Caro-
lina farm boy turned Washington insider, ran his end of
the space race as NASA's administrator under presidents
Kennedy and Johnson." Publ Wkly
"Emerging from the bureaucratic thickets with an ultimately praiseworthy portrait of Webb, this should circu-
late with the space program set." Booklist
Includes bibliographical references

Webster, Daniel, 1782-1852
Remini, Robert Vincent. Daniel Webster; the
man and his time; {by} Robert V. Remini. Norton
1997 796p il $26; pa $14 *   **92**
1. United States—Politics and government—1815-
1861
ISBN 0-393-04552-8; 0-375-72715-9 (pa)
                                    LC 97-24371
This work explores the life and times of the influential
politician and statesman of antebellum America
"Remini tends to exaggerate Webster's personal pec-
cadilloes, but it cannot be said that he underestimates his
subject's importance to American political culture. For
Remini, Webster's muscular nationalism, embroidered
with Lincoln's democratic eloquence, provided the foundation for a strong and enduring union." Choice
Includes bibliographical references

Weil, Simone, 1909-1943
Gray, Francine du Plessix. Simone Weil. Viking
2001 248p il (Penguin lives series) $19.95
                                                    92
ISBN 0-670-89998-4   LC 00-51367
The author "recounts the chronology of Weil's short
life, all the while interweaving Weil's emerging political,
philosophical, and spiritual ideas into the biographical
narrative." Libr J
"Part intellectual primer and part case study, this slim,
sympathetic biography makes us question whether we
value Weil's thinking despite the example of her punish-
ing, courageous, profoundly exasperating life, or because
of it." New Yorker
Includes bibliographical references

Weill, Kurt, 1900-1950
Schebera, Jürgen. Kurt Weill; an illustrated life;
translated by Caroline Murphy. Yale Univ. Press
1995 381p il $55; pa $38   **92**
1. Composers
ISBN 0-300-06055-6; 0-300-07284-8 (pa)
                                    LC 94-41444
Original German edition, 1990
"Published with the assistance of the Kurt Weill Foundation for Music"
"Schebera makes wonderful use of archival illustrations: concert programs, advertisements, photos, even a
few record labels from the Twenties and Thirties. This is
a scholarly work, but the appealing subject, complete
with the drama of Nazi persecution and flight from prewar Germany, makes it a good choice for most music
collections." Libr J
Includes discography and bibliographical references

Weisskopf, Michael
Weisskopf, Michael. Blood brothers; among the
soldiers of Ward 57. H. Holt 2006 301p il $25
                                                    92
1. Iraq War, 2003—Personal narratives
ISBN 978-0-8050-7860-2; 0-8050-7860-6
                                    LC 2006-43382
The author, "an embedded journalist on assignment
for Time magazine, was riding through the streets of
Baghdad in the back of a Humvee when a small, dark
object landed on the seat beside him. For reasons he still
finds inexplicable, he picked it up. He was trying to toss
it away when it exploded, obliterating his right hand and
inflicting serious shrapnel wounds on him and several
men riding with him. . . . He recounts the struggles of
three other amputees, as well as his own, as they try to
put their lives back together. " N Y Times Book Rev
"Weisskopf recognizes his own experience in that of
the soldiers, making for a wonderful story of tragedy and
recovery." Libr J
Includes bibliographical references

Weldon, Fay
Weldon, Fay. Auto da Fay. Grove Press 2003
366p il $25; pa $14   **92**
ISBN 0-8021-1750-3; 0-8021-4142-0 (pa)
                                    LC 2002-44685
First published 2002 in the United Kingdom
This "autobiography primarily focuses on her peripatetic childhood and difficult years of single parenthood,
concluding in the 1960s with her second marriage and
the beginning of her writing career. . . . Filled with
warmth, wit, and her trademark irreverence, Weldon's
memoir is a vivid and engaging account of a brave and
brainy 'lost girl' who found her way." Booklist

Welles, Orson, 1915-1985
Thomson, David. Rosebud: the story of Orson
Welles. Knopf 1996 463p il pa $16 hardcover o.p.
                                                    92
ISBN 0-679-77283-9 (pa)   LC 95-44216
In this examination of Welles, "Thomson trots out the
myths and reinterprets them in Welles' favor, which he

Welles, Orson, 1915-1985—*Continued*

fits into his ingenious conceit of Welles as the antihero Kane. . . . Throughout, Thomson is engaging and humorous, particularly in working with another masterful conceit. On a controversial interpretation or on an exquisite insight, the publisher enters the narrative and converses with the author. Prettily done. Thomson summarizes that Welles was, at once, 'magnificent *and* a poor bastard.' And this is, at once, a brilliant and maddening inquiry." Booklist
Includes bibliographical references

Wellington, Arthur Wellesley, Duke of, 1769-1852

Hibbert, Christopher. Wellington; a personal history. Perseus Books 1999 460p il map pa $22 * **92**
1. Great Britain—History—19th century
ISBN 0-7382-0148-0; 978-0-7382-0148-1
First published 1997 in the United Kingdom by HarperCollins
In this biography of Arthur Wellesley, the author "emphasizes the duke of Wellington's personality, family, and friendships." Booklist
"Altogether, Wellington does not quite pass the 'niceness' test. . . . He was a difficult man, a major military figure, a minor Prime Minister and in sum a historically important legend. Hibbert skillfully brings out all these characteristics." N Y Times Book Rev
Includes bibliographical references

Wells-Barnett, Ida B., 1862-1931

Giddings, Paula. Ida: a sword among lions; Ida B. Wells and the campaign against lynching. Amistad 2008 800p il $35 * **92**
1. African Americans—Civil rights 2. African American women 3. Women political activists 4. Lynching
ISBN 978-0-06-051921-6; 0-06-051921-5
"An iconic figure in American history, Wells was not always celebrated by her contemporaries for her groundbreaking activism because of her assertive politics and difficult personality. . . . Giddings offers a look at how Wells' own self-assertion affected her relationships with family, friends, colleagues, and the broader American public as she evolved as a woman and an activist. . . . With meticulous research, including Wells' own diary, Giddings brings to life one of the most fascinating women in American history, giving readers a real feel for the texture and context of Wells' life." Booklist
Includes bibliographical references

Welty, Eudora, 1909-2001

Marrs, Suzanne. Eudora Welty: a biography. Harcourt 2005 652p il $28 **92**
1. Authors, American
ISBN 0-15-100914-7   LC 2004-30490
The author traces "Welty's life from her roots in Jackson, Mississippi, to her rise to international stature." Publisher's note
This book "belongs on the shelf beside its subject's own work. Neither hagiography nor pathography, it is, you feel, the thoroughly respectful and straightforward

biography its honest, modest, intensely private subject would have wanted." N Y Times Book Rev
Includes bibliographical references

Waldron, Ann. Eudora; a writer's life. Doubleday 1998 398p il pa $23 hardcover o.p. **92**
1. Authors, American
ISBN 0-385-47648-5 (pa)   LC 98-5708
This is a biography of the writer from Mississippi
"Waldron's biography of Welty is the first to be written and, until the definitive treatment arrives, will satisfy readers curious to know details about the life of this much loved figure." Booklist
Includes bibliographical references

Welty, Eudora. One writer's beginnings. Harvard Univ. Press 1984 104p il (William E. Massey, Sr. lectures in the history of American civilization) $20.95; pa $12 **92**
1. Authors, American
ISBN 0-674-63925-1; 0-674-63927-8 (pa)
          LC 83-18638
A series of lectures in which the author reflects on her Southern heritage and her early artistic influences.

Wesley, John, 1703-1791

Tomkins, Stephen. John Wesley; a biography. Eerdmans 2003 208p pa $20 * **92**
1. Methodist Church
ISBN 0-8028-2499-4   LC 2003-54328
In this biography of the founder of the Methodist religion "Tomkins presents a keenly engaging portrait of a great man full of contradictoriness. Wesley insisted he was loyal to the Church of England yet consented to his followers setting up establishments and engaging in practices that flouted Anglican authority. . . . He altered the face of Christianity in the West by inspiring modern evangelicalism and Pentecostalism. A fascinating figure, fascinatingly limned." Booklist
Includes bibliographical references

West, Mae, 1892-1980

Leider, Emily Wortis. Becoming Mae West. Farrar, Straus & Giroux 1997 431p il hardcover o.p. pa $18.95 **92**
ISBN 978-0-374-10959-2; 978-0-306-80951-4 (pa); 0-306-80951-6 (pa)   LC 96-43803
This exploration of the West persona "focuses on the first four decades of West's career, up to 1938. Yet Leider's biography is also a portrait of an era: she devotes a great deal of the book to rendering the historical context, particularly the moral landscape, of the early 1900's, in order to more clearly define West's place in it and ultimately her mastery of it." N Y Times Book Rev

Wharton, Edith, 1862-1937

Lee, Hermione. Edith Wharton. Alfred A. Knopf 2007 869p il $35 * **92**
ISBN 978-0-375-40004-9; 0-375-40004-4
          LC 2006-48795

Wharton, Edith, 1862-1937—*Continued*

"Highlighting Wharton's later years in France, Hermione Lee's biography illuminates the prolific—if late-blooming—Pulitzer Prize winner . . . against the cultural and social upheaval of the early 20th century. She also explores Wharton's affair with Morton Fullerton, her divorce, her friendship with Henry James, and their subsequent effects on her writing." Bookmarks Magazine

"Marked by an elegant literary style that does justice to its subject and a clear, compassionate eye for detail, [this] is not only the best book on its subject, but one of the finest literary biographies to appear in recent years." Atlanta Journal-Constitution

Includes bibliographical references

White, E. B. (Elwyn Brooks), 1899-1985

Elledge, Scott. E. B. White; a biography. Norton 1984 400p il pa $21.95 hardcover o.p.   **92**

1. Authors, American

ISBN 0-393-30305-5 (pa)   LC 83-4032

This biography "follows White from his birth in Mount Vernon, N.Y. to his . . . octogenarian retreat in Maine." Libr J

The author is "fair, respectful, thorough, entertaining, skillful and unpedantic. He has performed a splendid exercise in scholarship and literary analysis, and the result is fun." N Y Times Book Rev

Includes bibliographical references

White, E. B. (Elwyn Brooks). Letters of E.B. White; originally collected and edited by Dorothy Lobrano Guth. Rev. ed., revised and updated by Martha White. Harper Collins 2006 713p il $35   **92**

1. Authors, American

ISBN 978-0-06-075708-3; 0-06-075708-6

LC 2006-43490

First published 1976

This collection of letters by the essayist, poet, novelist and author of several classic children's books is chronologically arranged. Written between the years 1908 when White was nine and 1985 when he died, they concern his relationships with his wife, Katherine White and his family and friends, which include Harold Ross, James Thurber, Robert Benchley, Alexander Woollcott and others.

White, Edmund, 1940-

White, Edmund. My lives. Ecco 2006 356p il $25.95 *   **92**

ISBN 0-06-621397-5; 978-0-06-621397-2

LC 2005-49506

First published 2005 in the United Kingdom

This is an autobiography by "an award-winning author and leader of the gay liberation movement of the 1960s. . . . The stories of his mother's egotism and incessant chatter, struggle to master the French language, obsession with European culture, literary associates, and work as a novelist, teacher, and essayist are largely overshadowed by graphic and explicit tales of the men in his life. . . . White's writing is amusing, descriptive, shocking, and, ultimately, thought-provoking." Libr J

Whitman, Walt, 1819-1892

Callow, Philip. From noon to starry night: a life of Walt Whitman. Dee, I.R. 1992 394p il $28.50; pa $14.95   **92**

ISBN 0-929587-95-2; 1-56663-133-5 (pa)

LC 92-5311

The author "attempts to illuminate Walt Whitman's life . . . by focusing primarily on the poet's experiences before the Civil War. . . . Callow adds a historical sketch of early-19th-century America to show how the nation Whitman celebrated so eloquently in *Leaves of Grass* formed his complex personality." Publ Wkly

"Infused with tenderness and respect, this fine biography deciphers the complexity of Whitman's sexuality and passionate creativity while celebrating his abiding compassion and grandeur of spirit." Booklist

Includes bibliographical references

Wideman, John Edgar

Wideman, John Edgar. Hoop roots. Houghton Mifflin 2001 242p $24; pa $13   **92**

ISBN 0-395-85731-7; 0-618-25775-6 (pa)

LC 2001-26455

Wideman "examines his lifelong relationship with basketball. He argues that basketball first allowed him to set his own standard in a white world that often imposes definitions of success on black people. A poignant, thought-provoking memoir." Booklist

Wiesel, Elie, 1928-

Wiesel, Elie. All rivers run to the sea; memoirs. Knopf 1995 432p il $35; pa $15   **92**

1. Holocaust, 1933-1945—Personal narratives

ISBN 0-679-43916-1; 0-8052-1028-8 (pa)

LC 95-17607

Original French edition, 1994

A Borzoi Bk.

Wiesel "begins with his boyhood in the Carpathian Mountains of Central Europe and his uprooting and transport by cattle car to the barbed wire infernos of Auschwitz and Buchenwald. Here Wiesel describes the horror of being among Jews bound for the death camps as the war was drawing to a close. . . . He describes in following chapters his schooling in postwar France, his decision to become a journalist, and his travels to Israel and throughout the world." Libr J

"Wiesel's immensely moving, unforgettable memoir has the searing intensity of his novels and autobiographical tales." Publ Wkly

Wiesel, Elie. And the sea is never full; memoirs, 1969-; translated from the French by Marion Wiesel. Knopf 1999 429p pa $15 hardcover o.p. *   **92**

1. Holocaust, 1933-1945—Personal narratives

ISBN 0-8052-1029-6 (pa)   LC 99-15604

Continues the author's memoirs begun in All the rivers run to the sea

Original French edition, 1996

"This concluding volume begins when the author is age 40. He continues his travels . . . and he continues to write, his books including *Souls on fire, Four Hasidic Masters, Twilight*, and more. . . . Wiesel is the most sig-

Wiesel, Elie, 1928-—*Continued*
nificant writer to have made the Holocaust the major
theme of his work, just as it has been of major importance to his life. The horror of the Holocaust can be felt
in this memoir with an intensity beyond words." Booklist

Wiesenthal, Simon
Pick, Hella. Simon Wiesenthal; a life in search
of justice. Northeastern Univ. Press 1996 349p il
$35 **92**
    ISBN 1-55553-273-X   LC 96-11808
"Simon Wiesenthal, a survivor of Auschwitz, Gross-
Rosen, and Mauthausen concentration camps, has spent
his life searching for Nazis suspected of participation in
the Holocaust. Pick, who lost close relatives in the Holocaust, {interviewed} . . . Wiesenthal and was allowed
unrestricted access to . . . his archives and files."
Booklist
This biography "has interesting things to say about
forgiveness, including an extraordinary hallucinogenic
encounter with a dying SS officer, and conveys a broadly
sympathetic picture of a man capable of distinguishing
between individuals and their political rhetoric." Times
Lit Suppl
    Includes bibliographical references

Wilde, Oscar, 1854-1900
Ellmann, Richard. Oscar Wilde. Knopf 1988
c1987 680p il pa $19.95 hardcover o.p.
92
    ISBN 0-394-75984-2 (pa)   LC 87-45354
    First published 1987 in the United Kingdom
"Wilde's life epitomizes the classic formula for a tragic history, the man who, by hubris, falls from greatness.
In Mr. Ellmann's hands, the story becomes as compelling
as fiction while never deviating from the facts. Humour
and elegance illuminate the accounts of Wilde's family,
his friends and the enemies he earned." Economist
    Includes bibliographical references

Wilder, Billy, 1906-2002
Sikov, Ed. On Sunset Boulevard: the life and
times of Billy Wilder. Hyperion 1998 675p il pa
$17.95 hardcover o.p. **92**
    ISBN 0-7868-8503-3 (pa)   LC 98-23504
This biography of the filmmaker concentrates "on
Wilder's movies and their humorous cynicism and sullied
idealism about life and love." Booklist
"Sikov has painted as good a portrait of Billy Wilder,
the man, the artist, the showman, the self-promoter, the
profitably prescient art collector and the successful businessman, as we are likely to get from the outside." N Y
Times Book Rev
    Includes filmography

Wilder, Laura Ingalls, 1867-1957
Anderson, William T. Laura Ingalls Wilder
country; text by William Anderson; color
photography by Leslie A. Kelly. HarperPerennial
1990 119p il pa $24.95 hardcover o.p. **92**
    1. Literary landmarks—United States
    ISBN 0-06-097346-3 (pa)   LC 89-46512

Cover subtitle: The people and places in Laura Ingalls
Wilder's life and books
"Contemporary and period photographs of the places
in the Laura Ingalls Wilder books have been combined
with a narrative about the actual historical settings."
Horn Book

Williams, Hank, 1923-1953
Escott, Colin. Hank Williams; the biography;
{by} Colin Escott with George Merritt and
William MacEwen. Little, Brown 1994 307p il pa
$19.99 hardcover o.p. **92**
    ISBN 0-316-24938-6 (pa)   LC 93-48092
A look at the career of the influential country sing-
er/songwriter. Williams' self-destructive behavior and
turbulent personal life are also examined
    Includes discography and bibliographical references

Hemphill, Paul. Lovesick blues; the life of Hank
Williams. Viking 2005 207p $23.95 *
92
    ISBN 0-670-03414-2   LC 2004-65113
    This is a biography of the country singer.
"This is the finest work of literature about Williams
yet written." Booklist

Williams, Roger, 1604?-1683
Gaustad, Edwin Scott. Roger Williams; [by]
Edwin S. Gaustad. Oxford University Press 2005
150p il (Lives and legacies) $17.95 **92**
    ISBN 0-19-518369-X   LC 2004-25246
This is a biography of "the founder of Rhode Island
and of the first Baptist Church in America." Publisher's
note
The author "provides not just an excellent introduction
to the man but a deep analysis of his largely unacknowl-
edged influence on our political and cultural life." Reason

Williams, Ted, 1918-2002
Linn, Edward. Hitter: the life and turmoils of
Ted Williams; {by} Ed Linn 1993 437p il pa $16
hardcover o.p. **92**
    1. Boston Red Sox (Baseball team)
    ISBN 0-15-600091-1 (pa)   LC 92-41870
"Linn's book is not a typical game-by-game baseball
biography, but a series of snapshots of Williams's career.
The {author} . . . touches on the many high points, but
does not neglect Williams's warts, including his constant
battle with Boston baseball writers. The product of an
unhappy childhood, Williams formed close friendships
with the 'underdogs,' and gave unsparingly of himself to
a charity for combatting cancer in children." Libr J

Williams, Ted. Ted Williams; my life in
pictures; [by] Ted Williams with David Pietrusza.
Total Sports 2001 201p il $45 **92**
    ISBN 1-930844-07-7   LC 2001-23360
Featuring over 300 photographs, this pictorial autobiography recounts Williams's life on and off the field,
"many from his personal collection and never before
published." Publisher's note

Williams, Tennessee, 1911-1983
  Leverich, Lyle. Tom; the unknown Tennessee Williams. Norton 2007 644p il pa $35   **92**
    1. Dramatists, American
    ISBN 978-0-393-31663-6; 0-393-31663-7
    First published 1995 by Crown
    This is the first installment of a projected two-volume biography of the American dramatist. Coverage begins with Williams' birth in 1911 and extends to the opening of The Glass Menagerie in 1945.
    "The book is a tremendous accomplishment, and Leverich is an appealing biographer: modest, thorough, balanced, and passionate. In prose that is clear—if not scintillating—he bushwhacks a path through a morass of gossip and myth, and prepares the way for a more subtle interpretation of the man and his plays." New Yorker

  Spoto, Donald. The kindness of strangers: the life of Tennessee Williams. Da Capo Press 1997 409p il pa $18.50   **92**
    ISBN 0-306-80805-6   LC 97-8428
    First published 1985 by Little, Brown
    "Based on hundreds of interviews with those who knew him and on other previously unpublished material, {the author} presents a portrait of Tennessee Williams which is both respectful and sensitive." Wilson Libr Bull
    Includes bibliographical references

Wilson, Diane
  Wilson, Diane. An unreasonable woman; a true story of shrimpers, politicos, polluters and the fight for Seadrift, Texas; foreword by Kenny Ausubel. Chelsea Green 2005 400p map $27.50; pa $18   **92**
    ISBN   1-931498-88-1;   978-1-931498-88-3; 1-933392-27-4 (pa); 978-1-933392-27-1 (pa)
                                LC 2005-9894
    "With the discovery that her 'piddlin' little county on the Gulf Coast' led the nation in toxic emissions, shrimper Wilson, a mother of five, found herself embarking on a voyage of discovery and activism that would strain her marriage and stretch her horizons. A David up against big-time chemical Goliaths, Wilson is a gifted storyteller, rendering dialogue and pacing plot turns as a novelist might." Publ Wkly

Wilson, Woodrow, 1856-1924
  Brands, H. W. Woodrow Wilson. Times Books 2003 169p il (American presidents series) $20 *   **92**
    1. Presidents—United States
    ISBN 0-8050-6955-0   LC 2002-41393
    The author "presents Wilson as a moralistic, idealistic intellectual who came to the presidency well versed in domestic policy but sadly lacking in knowledge and experience of international affairs, a leader who ultimately sacrificed his health and his presidential legacy in a doomed battle with Sen. Henry Cabot Lodge to have the League of Nations ratified. . . . Brands's brief, skillful life of the President is recommended for all public libraries." Libr J
    Includes bibliographical references

  Cooper, John Milton. The warrior and the priest: Woodrow Wilson and Theodore Roosevelt; [by] John Milton Cooper, Jr. Belknap Press 1983 442p il pa $20.95 hardcover o.p.   **92**
    1. Roosevelt, Theodore, 1858-1919 2. Presidents—United States 3. United States—Politics and government—1898-1919
    ISBN 0-674-94751-7 (pa)   LC 83-6021
    This "book is divided into four sections dealing respectively with the origins and early careers of both men, the parallel presidencies of Theodore Roosevelt (US) and Woodrow Wilson (Princeton), the election of 1912, and WW I." Choice
    The author's "distinctions are sharp, his insights original, his judgments balanced and his narrative unfailingly graceful." N Y Times Book Rev
    Includes bibliographical references

Winchell, Walter, 1897-1972
  Gabler, Neal. Winchell; gossip, power, and the culture of celebrity. Knopf 1994 681p il pa $17 hardcover o.p.   **92**
    ISBN 0-679-76439-9 (pa)   LC 93-44259
    A Borzoi Bk.
    "At the peak of his career during the 1930s and 1940s, Walter Winchell was America's most powerful and feared journalist; when he died in 1972, he had been long forgotten. Gabler's biography brings back to life the man credited with inventing the gossip column and with creating today's celebrity culture." Libr J
    Includes bibliographical references

Winkfield, Jimmy, 1882-1974
  Drape, Joe. Black maestro; the epic life of an American legend. Morrow 2006 280p il $24.95   **92**
    ISBN 0-06-053729-9; 978-0-06-053759-6
                                LC 2006-41939
    This is a biography of "Jimmy Winkfield, the last black jockey to win the Kentucky Derby. . . . This well-researched biography of Jimmy Winkfield and the larger chapter of America his life highlights is a valuable and entertaining read." Publ Wkly

Winters, Richard
  Alexander, Larry. Biggest brother; the life of Major D. Winters, the man who led the Band of Brothers. NAL Caliber 2005 287p il $24.95   **92**
    ISBN 0-451-21510-9   LC 2004-27330
    This is "the story of what distinguished Easy Company from other first-class field units: its leadership, in the person of Major Richard Winters, its commander. . . . Alexander is especially good at showing how Winters' sense of responsibility developed as a student, an enlistee, in OCS, and as an officer. He also gives a detailed picture of the army of 60-plus years ago, and the process that turned thousands of young civilians into the men who beat the Germans." Booklist

Winthrop, John, 1588-1649

Bremer, Francis J. John Winthrop; America's forgotten founding father. Oxford University Press 2003 478p il hardcover o.p. pa $21.95   **92**

ISBN 0-19-514913-0; 978-0-19-517981-1 (pa); 0-19-517981-1 (pa)   LC 2002-38143

This biography provides a "background of the lives of Winthrop's grandfather, father, and uncles; a review of Winthrop's youth, education, and rise to a position of governmental responsibility in England; and . . . the more familiar story of Winthrop's role in the founding and shaping of Massachusetts." Libr J

"Bremer's definitive biography gracefully portrays Winthrop as a man of his time, whose influence in the new colony grew out of his own struggles to establish his identity before he left England." Publ Wkly

Includes bibliographical references

Wodehouse, P. G. (Pelham Grenville), 1881-1975

McCrum, Robert. Wodehouse; a life. Norton 2004 530p il $27.95   **92**

ISBN 0-393-05159-5   LC 2004-18562

The author "takes the reader from Wodehouse's school days at Dulwich to his successful work as a Broadway lyricist and a master storyteller of Edwardian times who gave us Bertie Wooster and Jeeves to his darkest hour during World War II and final years of semi-exile in America. He offers his most spirited and convincing analysis in countering accusations that Wodehouse knowingly collaborated with the Nazis. . . . This work is thoroughly researched and well written; it will please Wodehouse aficionados and general readers alike." Libr J

Includes bibliographical references

Wolff, Tobias, 1945-

Wolff, Tobias. This boy's life: a memoir. Atlantic Monthly Press 1989 288p hardcover o.p. pa $14 *   **92**

1. Authors, American

ISBN 0-871-13248-6; 0-8021-3668-0 (pa)
   LC 88-17600

The novelist and short story writer "offers an engrossing and candid look into his childhood and adolescence in his first book of nonfiction. In unaffected prose he recreates scenes from his life that sparkle with the immediacy of narrative fiction. The result is an intriguingly guileless book, distinct from the usual reflective commentary of autobiography." Libr J

Wollstonecraft, Mary, 1759-1797

Gordon, Lyndall. Vindication; a life of Mary Wollstonecraft. HarperCollins 2005 562p il $29.95   **92**

ISBN 0-06-019802-8   LC 2005-40237

Published in the United Kingdom with title: Mary Wollstonecraft

This biography of the eighteenth century feminist covers "her difficult childhood . . . her struggle to support herself as a writer, her ill-fated romance with American adventurer Gilbert Imlay, the birth of her first daughter, her marriage to writer William Godwin, and her death following the birth of her second daughter, Mary." Libr J

The author "tackles this formidable woman with grace, clarity and much new research. . . . Gordon relates Wollstonecraft's story with the same potent mixture of passion and reason her subject personified." N Y Times Book Rev

Includes bibliographical references

Woodhull, Victoria C., 1838-1927

Goldsmith, Barbara. Other powers; the age of suffrage, spiritualism, and the scandalous Victoria Woodhull. HarperPerennial 1999 531p il pa $16   **92**

1. Feminism 2. Women—Suffrage 3. Spiritualism

ISBN 0-06-095332-2   LC 98-33315

First published 1998 by Knopf

"Victoria Woodhull was a charismatic and notorious figure in the struggle for women's rights in the years following the Civil War. She was the first woman to address Congress and the first woman to run for president. Goldsmith . . . has successfully woven together a history of Woodhull's life with the lives of the powerful she touched." Libr J

Includes bibliographical references

Woods, Tiger, 1975-

Callahan, Tom. In search of Tiger; a journey through golf with Tiger Woods. Crown 2003 245p il $23.95; pa $14   **92**

ISBN 0-609-60943-2; 1-4000-5140-1 (pa)
   LC 2002-11350

The author "examines Tiger's early years, how he got to the top of his game and his vision for the future. Anecdotes and insider insights highlight portraits of major Tiger victories. . . . This is a comprehensive examination of the man, his talent, his competition and the world of professional golf, a must-read for fans and players alike." Publ Wkly

Woolf, Leonard, 1880-1969

Glendinning, Victoria. Leonard Woolf; a biography. Simon & Schuster 2006 498p il $30 *   **92**

ISBN 978-0-7432-4653-8; 0-7432-4653-5
   LC 2006-49784

This is a biography of the publisher and author of Empire and Commerce in Africa (1920), Village in the Jungle (1926), After the Deluge (1931), Quack, Quack! (1935), Barbarians Within and Without (1939), Sowing (1960), Growing (1961), Beginning Again (1964), Downhill All the Way (1967), and The Journey Not the Arrival Matters (1969).

"Glendinning's generous biography does not ignore that Woolf could be grumpy and was too often cheeseparing, but her account does justice to his range of passions, his literary and political contributions and, above all, his human goodness—he was a man who knew how to live." New Statesman

Includes bibliographical references

Woolf, Virginia, 1882-1941

Briggs, Julia. Virginia Woolf: an inner life. Harcourt 2005 527p il $30 **92**

ISBN 0-15-101143-5 LC 2005-16048

"Each chapter is devoted to one of Woolf's works and concludes with a . . . discussion of its critical reception." Libr J

"That this book is a must for Woolf fans goes without saying, but it is also a must for anyone interested in the nature of female consciousness at its most self-aware and the workings of artistic sensibility at their most illuminating." Publ Wkly

Includes bibliographical references

Gordon, Lyndall. Virginia Woolf, a writer's life. Norton 1985 c1984 341p il pa $14.95 hardcover o.p. **92**

ISBN 0-393-32205-X (pa) LC 84-25424

First published 1984 in the United Kingdom

"Gordon combines literary criticism with biographical investigation in her life of Virginia Woolf. . . . Using the major novels *To the Lighthouse* and *The Waves,* Gordon explores in detail the autobiographical ramifications of these works as she traces Woolf's childhood, marriage, and literary career." Booklist

Includes bibliographical references

Lee, Hermione. Virginia Woolf. Knopf 1997 893p il pa $20 hardcover o.p. * **92**

ISBN 0-375-70136-2 (pa) LC 97-71155

First published 1996 in the United Kingdom

A Borzoi Bk.

Lee "re-creates the world Woolf was born into in 1882, a maze of formalities and reticences, and then leads us through changes that, slow in coming but shocking in effect, made all that seem light-years away by the time Woolf was 50. She convinces us that Woolf, contrary to previous assumptions, reveled in a deep intimacy with her husband, Leonard. Finally, she makes a persuasive case for the underlying sanity of this woman as she battled her own madness and shows the brilliant literary uses she made of her instability." N Y Times Book Rev

Includes bibliographical references

Woolf, Virginia. A moment's liberty: the shorter diary; abridged and edited by Anne Olivier Bell; introduction by Quentin Bell. Harcourt Brace Jovanovich 1990 516p $22.95; pa $20 **92**

ISBN 0-15-161894-1; 0-15-661912-1 (pa)

LC 90-33428

An abridged edition of the five volumes of Woolf's Diary, published 1977-1984

"The diaries here may appeal to a larger audience, not least because each year represented is prefaced by a wonderfully succinct overview. Here are Woolf's superbly drawn portraits of Max Beerbohm, T.S. Eliot, John Maynard Keynes, Katherine Mansfield—and her occasionally acerbic remarks on what they said and did. But the diaries are also a repository for luminous thoughts on birds and weather, the pleasures of walking or listening to music." Publ Wkly

Woolf, Virginia. Moments of being; edited, with an introduction and notes, by Jeanne Schulkind. 2nd ed. Harcourt Brace Jovanovich 1985 230p pa $14 **92**

ISBN 0-15-661918-0 LC 85-8521

"A Harvest/HBJ book"

First published 1976

This volume consists of unpublished autobiographical writings, including several "Reminiscences" written at the start of Woolf's career, a piece entitled "A sketch of the past" written shortly before her suicide, and papers read to the Memoir Club

Includes bibliographical references

Woolman, John, 1720-1772

Slaughter, Thomas P. The beautiful soul of John Woolman, apostle of abolition. Hill and Wang 2008 464p il map $30 **92**

1. Abolitionists

ISBN 978-0-8090-9514-8; 0-8090-9514-9

LC 2008-22765

This is a "biography of the Quaker ascetic who refused all involvement with slavery, preached abolition throughout the colonies, and wrote a classic of religious literature." Booklist

"Any understanding of the history of social reform in America begins with Woolman, and understanding Woolman begins here." Kirkus

Includes bibliographical references and index

Wordsworth, William, 1770-1850

Johnston, Kenneth R. The hidden Wordsworth; poet, lover, rebel, spy. Norton 1998 965p il $45; pa $24.95 **92**

ISBN 0-393-04623-0; 0-393-32159-2 (pa)

LC 97-40317

Maps on lining papers

This "volume focuses on the poet's first thirty-six years, the tumultuous decades immortalized in 'The Prelude.' Johnston's spacious, absorbing argument—that Wordsworth's moments of emotion recollected in tranquillity were themselves rather less than tranquil—is amply supported by a thorough documentation of the multifarious life and times of the young poet, at Hawkshead, at Cambridge, in Grasmere, and abroad." New Yorker

Includes bibliographical references

Wright, Frank Lloyd, 1867-1959

Huxtable, Ada Louise. Frank Lloyd Wright. Lipper\Viking 2004 251p il (Penguin lives series) $19.95 * **92**

ISBN 0-670-03342-1 LC 2004-46477

The author "pairs a critique of Wright's architecture with . . . {a} narrative of his scandalous private life, including his abandonment of his first family, the murder of a mistress and her children by a deranged servant, and other tempestuous relationships with artistic, high-strung women." Publ Wkly

"The eventfulness of the extraordinary life and the refreshing intelligence and craft of the author make this book a pleasure to read. That I found myself on occasion arguing with the text only proves the provocative quality of Huxtable's exploration." N Y Times Book Rev

Wright, Frank Lloyd, 1867-1959—*Continued*

Secrest, Meryle. Frank Lloyd Wright; a biography. University of Chicago Press 1998 634p il pa $20   **92**

ISBN 0-226-74414-0   LC 97-51590

First published 1992 in the United Kingdom; first United States edition published 1993 by Knopf

A portrait of a "complex, often contradictory architect. . . . Secrest writes with authority and compassion about Wright's long and turbulent career. Her exhaustive scholarship provides fresh insights into Wright's personality." Libr J

Includes bibliographical references

Wright, Orville, 1871-1948

Wright, Orville. How we invented the airplane; an illustrated history; edited with an introduction and commentary by Fred C. Kelly; additional text by Alan Weissman. Dover Publs. 1988 c1953 87p il pa $9.95   **92**

1. Wright, Wilbur, 1867-1912 2. Aeronautics—History

ISBN 0-486-25662-6   LC 87-33037

First published 1953 by D. McKay

This "account by the two inventors . . . covers experiments, discovery of aeronautical principles, construction of planes and motors, first flights, and much more. Also included is a later account written by both brothers." Publisher's note

Includes bibliographical references

Wright, Richard, 1908-1960

Rowley, Hazel. Richard Wright; the life and times. Holt & Co. 2001 626p il pa $18 hardcover o.p.   **92**

ISBN 0-8050-7088-5 (pa)   LC 00-54249

"A John Macrae book."

In this biography Rowley chronicles Wright's "journey from the South to Chicago, New York, and Paris—and from *Native Son,* the novel that made him famous, to his scorchingly honest books about Africa and Spain." Booklist

"The strength of {this book} is {the} painstaking research. Rowley . . . has a daunting dedication to primary sources and her documentation is meticulous." N Y Times Book Rev

Includes bibliographical references

Wright, Richard. Black boy; (American hunger): a record of childhood and youth; foreword by Edward P. Jones. 60th anniversary ed., 1st ed. HarperCollinsPublishers 2005 419p $24.95; pa $14.95 *   **92**

1. African American authors 2. African Americans—Social conditions

ISBN   0-06-083400-5;   978-0-06-083400-5; 0-06-113024-9 (pa); 978-0-06-113024-3 (pa)

     LC 2005-52698

First published 1945 by World Publishing Company

"The restored text established by the Library of America"

This autobiographical work concludes with Wright "newly arrived in Chicago in 1927 as a fugitive from the white South that never knew him. [It] relates his nomadic life in Tennessee, Arkansas, and Mississippi, abandoned by his father and with his mother working at menial jobs or incapacitated by illness." Benet's Reader's Ency of Am Lit

Includes bibliographical references

Wright, Wilbur, 1867-1912

Wright, Orville. How we invented the airplane.
See entry under Wright, Orville, 1871-1948

Wyeth, Andrew, 1917-

Wyeth, Andrew. Andrew Wyeth; autobiography; [by] Andrew Wyeth and Thomas Hoving. Bulfinch Press 1999 168p il $29.99   **92**

1. Artists—United States

ISBN 978-0-8212-2569-1; 0-8212-2569-3

First published 1995

This "volume reproduces 138 tempera, drybrush & watercolor paintings & pencil studies by Andrew Wyeth." Publisher's note

"Each painting is accompanied by commentary from the artist that lends insight into his life and character. Several nude studies are included." Booklist [review of 1995 edition]

Includes bibliographical references

Wyeth, N. C. (Newell Convers), 1882-1945

Michaelis, David. N.C. Wyeth; a biography. Perennial 2003 555p il pa $27.95   **92**

1. Artists—United States

ISBN 0-06-008926-1; 978-0-06-008926-9

     LC 2003-42876

First published 1998 by Knopf

This biography "explores not only the destiny of a ferociously disciplined and conflicted patriarch but the lives of four generations of an American artistic dynasty." New Yorker

"Michaelis's work is an outstanding example of the biographer's art. Integrating Wyeth's complex personal and psychological life with his artistic oeuvre, Michaelis creates a portrait of both the artist and the man." Libr J

Includes bibliographical references

Yang, Kao Kalia, 1980-

Yang, Kao Kalia. The latehomecomer; a Hmong family memoir. Coffee House Press 2008 277p il pa $14.95   **92**

1. Hmong Americans 2. Refugees

ISBN 978-1-56689-208-7   LC 2007-46386

The author, "of the Southeast Asian Hmong people, was born in a refugee camp in Thailand in 1980. Her family was forced to flee the Pathet Lao, of Laos, who singled out the Hmong in retribution for their aiding the Americans during the Vietnam War. With no homeland to return to and not necessarily welcome in Thailand, Yang's family took the opportunity to come to the United States and make a new life. . . . Yang chronicles her family's journey." Libr J

"By the end of this moving, unforgettable book . . . readers will delight at how intimately they have become part of this formerly strange culture." Publ Wkly

Yates, Richard, 1926-1992

Bailey, Blake. A tragic honesty: the life and work of Richard Yates. Picador 2003 671p $35; pa $18 **92**

ISBN 0-312-28721-6; 0-312-42375-6 (pa)
LC 2002-42525

This biography of the novelist discusses his "unhappy Greenwich Village childhood and his struggles to write while teaching and working as a business writer, Hollywood screenwriter, and speechwriter for Robert Kennedy. As Bailey meticulously and perceptively chronicles Yates' arduous translation of experience into art, he exposes the anguish and transcendence of the writing life and the tragedy of mental illness." Booklist

Yeats, W. B. (William Butler), 1865-1939

Brown, Terence. The life of W.B. Yeats; a critical biography. Blackwell 1999 410p il (Blackwell critical biographies) $66.95; pa $29.95
* **92**

1. Poets, Irish
ISBN 0-631-18298-5; 0-631-22851-9 (pa)
LC 99-28388

In this biography Brown places "Yeats's work as poet and dramatist in its political and social—as well as personal and erotic—context." N Y Times Book Rev
Includes bibliographical references

Foster, R. F. (Robert Fitzroy). W.B. Yeats: a life. v1: The apprentice mage, 1865-1914. Oxford Univ. Press 1997 xxxi, 640p il hardcover o.p. pa $29.95 **92**

1. Poets, Irish
ISBN 0-19-211735-1; 0-19-288085-3 (pa)
LC 96-31671

This is the first installment of a two-volume biography of the Irish poet.

Foster, R. F. (Robert Fitzroy). W.B. Yeats: a life. v2: The arch-poet, 1915-1939. Oxford Univ. Press 2003 xxiv, 798p il $47.50 **92**

1. Poets, Irish
ISBN 0-19-818465-4

This second volume of a two-volume biography covers Yeats's final decades, from his 50th year to his death in 1939.

Includes bibliographical references

Young, Neil

McDonough, Jimmy. Shakey: Neil Young's biography. Villard Bks. 2002 786p il $29.95; pa $16.95 **92**

ISBN 0-679-42772-4; 0-679-75096-7 (pa)
LC 2001-43528

Includes index

This biography of the rock musician "follows Mr. Young from his Canadian childhood through the nearly 50 albums he has made." N Y Times (Late N Y Ed)

"When Young talks, the book sparkles and offers a warm, engaging portrait of the man who keeps on rockin' in the free world." Libr J

Zappa, Frank

Zappa, Frank. The real Frank Zappa book; {by} Frank Zappa, with Peter Occhiogrosso. Poseidon Press 1989 352p il pa $14 hardcover o.p.
92

ISBN 0-671-70572-5 (pa) LC 89-3470

"The outspoken Zappa, one of the most inventive and controversial artists of the past 20 years, is frank, often disgusting, and always entertaining in describing his life. . . . Zappa also relates his opinions about the music performing and recording industries, but then rattles on about a myriad of things: church, drugs, yuppies, politics." Libr J

Zevon, Warren

Zevon, Crystal. I'll sleep when I'm dead; the dirty life and times of Warren Zevon; foreword by Carl Hiassen. Ecco Press 2007 452p il $26.95; pa $15.95 **92**

1. Rock musicians
ISBN 978-0-06-076345-9; 0-06-076345-0; 978-0-06-076349-7 (pa); 0-06-076349-3 (pa)
LC 2006-52138

"Interweaving the remembrances of Zevon's many friends with entries from his own journals, Crystal, his widow, presents an intimate look at Zevon's wild life of drugs, women, and music. Among others, Jackson Browne, Linda Ronstadt, Bruce Springsteen, Carl Hiaasen, Stephen King, and the Everly Brothers, with whom Zevon got his start, share reminiscences. . . . All pop music collections need this book." Libr J

929 Genealogy, names, insignia

Baxter, Angus, 1912-

In search of your European roots; a complete guide to tracing your ancestors in every country in Europe. 3rd ed. Genealogical 2001 315p pa $18.95 **929**

1. Genealogy
ISBN 0-8063-1657-8 LC 00-136383
First published 1985

This work covers the various types of genealogical records available in approximately 30 European countries. Archival resources from the national to local level are described. Also included are telephone numbers, e-mail addresses, fax numbers, and URL's for various European archives and organizations
Includes bibliographical references

Bentley, Elizabeth Petty

Directory of family associations; [by] Elizabeth Petty Bentley, & Deborah Ann Carl. 4th ed. Genealogical 2001 320p $34.95 **929**

1. Genealogy
ISBN 0-8063-1679-9 LC 2001-131456
First published 1991

Contains information on approximately 6,000 family name associations in the United States; lists addresses, phone numbers, contact persons, and publications (if any)

Bentley, Elizabeth Petty—*Continued*

The genealogist's address book. 5th ed. Genealogical 2005 783p pa $49.99 *

929

1. Genealogy
ISBN 0-8063-1757-4; 978-0-8063-1757-1
Also available CD-ROM version
First published 1991. Periodically revised
A "source for names, addresses, phone numbers, hours, and publications for national and state genealogical institutions and organizations. Included are ethnic and religious organizations that can help with genealogical research, as well as research centers and lineage societies. Special sections address adoption research and the use of computers." Libr J [review of 1992 edition]

Croom, Emily Anne

The genealogist's companion and sourcebook. 2nd ed. Betterway Bks. 2003 454p il map pa $19.99
929
1. Genealogy
ISBN 1-55870-651-8   LC 2003-50017
First published 1994
This how-to genealogy handbook seeks to explore "collections and libraries within the U.S. and the records that may be found within them. . . . In addition to covering government records, cemetery records, newspapers, city directories, and other sources, there are chapters of African American and Native American genealogy. . . . Because the volume is easy reading and instructive at the same time, it will be a very popular choice for public libraries." Booklist {review of 1994 edition}
Includes bibliographical references

Franklin, John Hope, 1915-

In search of the promised land; a Black family and the Old South; [by] John Hope Franklin, Loren Schweninger. Oxford University Press 2005 286p il map (New narratives in American history) $23; pa $13.95 *
929
1. Slavery—United States 2. African Americans—Southern States 3. United States—Race relations
ISBN 0-19-516087-8; 0-19-516088-6 (pa)
LC 2004-61666
The authors trace "the history of the Thomas-Rapier family during the antebellum and Civil War eras. Starting with matriarch Sally Thomas, born a slave in 1787, the book enables readers to distinguish the various complex modes within which slavery operated. The resulting family history also traces the evolution of race relations in diverse locations from New Orleans to New York City, Canada, Minnesota, and the Caribbean." Libr J
Includes bibliographical references

Greenwood, Val D.

The researcher's guide to American genealogy. 3rd ed. Genealogical 2000 662p il $29.95
929
1. Genealogy 2. Archives—United States
ISBN 0-8063-1621-7   LC 99-73349
First published 1973

"This classic textbook for the more experienced researcher gives detailed answers to questions about primary records, including vital, census, probate, land, court (including adoption), church, military, cemetery, and wills. Completely updated, it remains the outstanding text and reference book in American genealogy and the benchmark against which others must be judged." Libr J [review of 1990 edition]
Includes bibliographical references

Kemp, Thomas Jay

Virtual roots 2.0; a guide to genealogy and local history on the World Wide Web. rev and updated. Scholarly Resources 2003 311p $75; pa $29.95
929
1. Genealogy 2. World Wide Web
ISBN 0-8420-2922-2; 0-8420-2923-0 (pa)
LC 2002-154366
First published 1997
Accompanied by computer laser optical disc
The more than 1,000 "Web sites in this directory are arranged into four primary categories—general subjects, U.S., international, and family associations—each of which is further subdivided by topic, state, country, or family name. Web site entries include organization name, address, telephone number(s), Internet and e-mail addresses, and, where appropriate, other Web links that open even more doorways." Booklist [review of 1997 edition]
Includes bibliographical references

Kovacs, Diane K.

Genealogical research on the Web. Neal-Schuman 2002 194p (Neal-Schuman netguide series) pa $59.95
929
ISBN 1-55570-430-1   LC 2001-59644
"The first section of this book . . . addresses the basics of using the Internet for genealogical research. Next is a discussion of the top 10 genealogical tools on the Internet, followed by a chapter on networking with other genealogists. . . . Each chapter ends with a tutorial composed of several activities, typically involving visits to Web sites. . . . This is one work that serves a variety of users as well as uses and should be of interest wherever genealogists are to be found." Booklist
Includes bibliographical references

Melnyk, Marcia Yannizze, 1951-

Family history 101; a beginner's guide to finding your ancestors; [by] Marcia D. Yannizze Melnyk. Family Tree Books 2005 138p il pa $16.99
929
1. Genealogy
ISBN 1-558-70706-9   LC 2004-58111
"The author provides information on recording data, surfing the Web in search of relevant information, separating facts from fiction, and accessing the most likely places to locate records. . . . Novices wondering where and how to undertake the task will appreciate having the fundamentals succinctly laid out for them." Booklist
Includes bibliographical references

Moore, Dahrl Elizabeth

The librarian's genealogy notebook; a guide to resources. American Lib. Assn. 1998 142p il map pa $35   **929**

1. Genealogy
ISBN 0-8389-0744-X   LC 98-19110

"Moore shows librarians how to mine their own libraries for reference sources that might already be available, offers useful advice on obtaining information from external sources, and also includes general sources to which libraries may want to provide access or own." Publisher's note

Includes bibliographical references

Printed sources; a guide to published genealogical records; edited by Kory L. Meyerink. Ancestry 1998 840p $49.95   **929**

1. United States—History—Bibliography
ISBN 0-916489-70-1   LC 98-10852

The book opens with an "introductory chapter that highlights categories of research, the evaluation of records, interlibrary loan, and even the Dewey Decimal system. Editor Meyerink then divides the book into four sections encompassing background information (how-to-books, atlases), finding aids, printed original records, and compiled records (family histories, periodicals)." Libr J

Roberts, Ralph, 1945-

Genealogy via the Internet; tracing your family roots quickly and easily: computerized genealogy in plain English. 2nd ed. Alexander Bks. 2003 288p il $24.95   **929**

ISBN 1-57090-129-5
First published 1998

The author "explains about personal computers, the basics of genealogy and how to go about combining the two for online searching. He provides several pages of possible web sites a searcher might explore, and an index for easy location of topics." Book Rep [review of 1998 edition]

Includes bibliographical references

929.4   Personal names

Delahunty, Andrew

Oxford dictionary of nicknames. Oxford University Press 2003 229p $29.95; pa $24
                 929.4

1. Nicknames
ISBN 0-19-860539-0; 0-19-860948-5 (pa)
             LC 2004-273526

This book "covers not only individual historical figures, politicians, sports people, actors, and entertainers, but also place-names. Arrangement is alphabetical by nickname, rather than proper name; a general index cites the proper names and matching nicknames." Choice

"This volume is a treasure trove of popular linguistic creativity. From the Hanging Judge to Hanoi Jane, and from Queen Dick to the Queen of Hearts, it makes for delightful bathroom browsing with just a dab of history and culture." Publ Wkly

Dictionary of American family names; Patrick Hanks, editor. Oxford Univ. Press 2003 3v set $295 *   **929.4**

1. Personal names—United States
ISBN 0-19-508137-4   LC 2003-3844

This is a "guide to 70,000 of the most frequently found surnames in the United States. Based on an 88.7 million-name sample culled from a commercial telephone database, the entries indicate the frequency of the name within the sample, plus an explanation of the name." Libr J

"This set will be useful for genealogists, historians, and others curious about their family roots." SLJ

Includes bibliographical references

Latham, Edward

A dictionary of names, nicknames, and surnames of persons, places, and things. Omnigraphics 1990 334p $48   **929.4**

1. Nicknames 2. Personal names—Dictionaries
ISBN 1-55888-901-9   LC 89-26513

A reissue of the title first published 1904 by Dutton

Compiled as a supplement to the "ordinary dictionaries of biography, geography, mythology, etc. [wherein] a person or place is often alluded to by means of a surname or nickname without any clue being given to the reader, who does not happen to be aware of the actual name of the person or place." Preface

Shankle, George Earlie

American nicknames; their origin and significance. 2nd ed. Wilson, H.W. 1955 524p $85
                 929.4

1. Nicknames 2. Personal names—United States
3. Geographic names—United States
ISBN 0-8242-0004-7
First published 1937

"Not limited to nicknames of persons, but includes also those applied to places, institutions, or objects, arranged by real names with cross-references from nicknames. Information under the real names includes some explanation of the nicknames and their origin, and gives references to sources of information in footnotes." Guide to Ref Books. 11th edition

Twentieth century American nicknames; edited by Laurence Urdang; compiled by Walter C. Kidney and George C. Kohn; with a foreword by Leslie Alan Dunkling. Wilson, H.W. 1979 398p $70   **929.4**

1. Nicknames 2. Personal names—United States
3. Geographic names—United States
ISBN 0-8242-0642-8   LC 79-23390

"Nicknames and the real names of persons, places, etc., are listed in a single alphabet. Includes variant nicknames. Editor attempted to avoid duplication of nicknames appearing in Shankle's *American nicknames*." Ref Sources for Small & Medium-sized Libr. 5th edition

929.9 Flags. Forms of insignia and identification

Leepson, Marc, 1945-
Flag: an American biography. Thomas Dunne Books/St. Martin's Press 2005 334p il $24.95; pa $14.95 **929.9**
1. Flags—United States
ISBN 978-0-312-32308-0; 0-312-32308-5; 978-0-312-32309-7 (pa); 0-312-32309-3 (pa)
LC 2004-65920
"Chronicling the two-centuries-plus history of the U.S. flag, Leepson considers the abundant stories that purport to be the truth about Old Glory." Booklist
"From reverence to kitsch, Americans' attitudes to their flag and its mythology have changed over the years, and Leepson does a creditable job of recounting those changes." Publ Wkly
Includes bibliographical references

Shearer, Benjamin F.
State names, seals, flags, and symbols; a historical guide. 3rd ed, rev and expanded. Greenwood Press 2001 495p il $73.95
929.9
1. Geographic names—United States 2. Seals (Numismatics) 3. Flags—United States
ISBN 0-313-31534-5 LC 2001-23525
First published 1987
"Chapters on mottoes, flowers, trees, birds, songs, holidays, and license plates are just a sampling of what is covered, and the format is such that the concisely written material can be found as expeditiously as possible. Even though the book is touted predominantly as a reference tool, the information provided makes fascinating and enlightening reading." Libr J {review of 1994 edition}
Includes bibliographical references

930 History of ancient world (to ca.499)

The **Cambridge** ancient history. Cambridge Univ. Press 1970-2005 il maps set $3500 **930**
1. Ancient history
ISBN 978-0-521-85073-5
Volumes also available separately; contact publisher for pricing
Original 12 volume set published 1923-1939 with 5 volumes of plates
Contents: v1, pt 1 Prolegomena and prehistory 3rd ed. 1970; v1, pt 2 Early history of the Middle East 3rd ed. 1971; v2, pt 1 History of the Middle East and the Aegean Region c. 1800-1380 B.C 3rd ed. 1973; v2, pt 2 History of the Middle East and the Aegean region, c. 1380-1000 B.C. 3rd ed. 1975; v3, pt 1 The prehistory of the Balkans; and the Middle East and the Aegean World, tenth to eighth centuries B.C. 2nd ed. 1982; v3, pt 2 The Assyrian and Babylonian empires and other states of the Near East, from the eighth to the sixth centuries, B.C. 2nd ed. 1992; v3, pt 3 The expansion of the Greek World, eighth to sixth centuries B.C. 2nd ed. 1988; v4

Persia, Greece, and the western Mediterranean, c. 525 to 479 B.C. 2nd ed. 1992; v5 The Fifth Century B.C. 2nd ed. 1992; v6 The Fourth Century B.C. 2nd ed. 1994; v7, pt 1 The Hellenistic World 2nd ed. 1984; v7, pt 2 The rise of Rome to 220 B.C. 2nd ed. 1990; v8 Rome and the Mediterranean to 133 B.C. 2nd ed. 1990; v9 The last age of the Roman Republic, 146-43 B.C. 2nd ed. 1994; v10 The Augustinian Empire, 43 B.C.-A.D. 69 2nd ed. 1996; v11 The High Empire, A.D. 70-192 2nd ed. 2000; v12 The crisis of empire, AD 193-337 2nd ed. 2005; v13 The late empire, A.D. 337-425 1998; v14 Late antiquity: empire and successors, A.D. 425-600 2001
"An excellent reference history. Each chapter has been written by a specialist, with full bibliographies at the end of each volume." Guide to Ref Books. 11th edition

Cantor, Norman F., 1929-2004
Antiquity: the civilization of the ancient world. HarperCollins Pubs. 2003 240p map $24.95; pa $13.95 **930**
1. Ancient civilization
ISBN 0-06-017409-9; 0-06-093098-5 (pa)
LC 2003-42317
The author offers an "introductory survey of the major empires of the ancient world, divided into two parts. The first provides a basic narrative of Hellenistic culture, the Roman Empire and Christianity. . . . In the second part, he offers a more detailed exploration of the development of each of these ancient cultures, as well as ancient Judaism and Egypt." Publ Wkly
"Cantor's work provides the beginning classicist with an enticing yet sturdy foundation for further exploration." Booklist
Includes bibliographical references

Encyclopedia of the ancient world; editor, Thomas J. Sienkewicz. Salem Press 2002 3v il maps set $341 * **930**
1. Ancient civilization—Encyclopedias
ISBN 0-89356-038-3 LC 2001-49896
This reference work encompasses "not only Greece and Rome but also 'the civilizations, cultures, traditions, monuments and artifacts, significant wars and battles, and important personages of the rest of the world: Europe (outside Greece and Rome), Africa, the Americas, Asia, and Oceania.' The time span is from prehistory to approximately 700 C.E." Booklist
Includes bibliographical references

Great events from history, The ancient world, prehistory-476 C.E.; editor, Mark W. Chavalas; consulting editors, Mark S. Aldenderfer . . . [et al.] Salem Press 2004 2v il map set $160
930
1. Ancient history
ISBN 1-58765-155-6; 978-1-58765-155-7
LC 2004-1360
Also available online
Companion volume to Great lives from history, The ancient world, prehistory-476 C.E.
Some essays previously published in Great events from history (1972-1980), Chronology of European history, 15,000 B.C. to 1997 (1997), and Great events from history, North American series (1997)

Great events from history, The ancient world, prehistory-476 C.E.—*Continued*

"Articles are arranged chronologically, beginning around 25,000 B.C.E. with the San Peoples, who created the first discernible art in Africa, and ends on September 4, 476 C.E. with the fall of Rome, when the last Roman emperor, Romulus Augustulus, was deposed. Articles cover the entire world, with special attention paid to non-European areas. . . . All articles maintain the same structure and give the locale of the event, its category, a summary of the event, its significance, an annotated list of further readings, and cross references to related events." Ref & User Services Quarterly

Includes bibliographical references

Kapuscinski, Ryszard, 1932-2007

Travels with Herodotus; translated from the Polish by Klara Glowczewska. Alfred A. Knopf 2007 275p $25   **930**

1. Herodotus 2. Voyages and travels
ISBN 9781400043385; 1-400-04338-5

LC 2006-39565

Original Polish edition, 2004

The late author offers an "account of his beginnings as a journalist and an homage to the ancient-Greek historian whom Cicero dubbed the 'father of history.' . . . Kapuscinski was working for a Polish newspaper in the mid-1950s when his editor dispatched him to India and, as a parting gift, gave him a copy of Herodotus's Histories. The book spurred the young Kapuscinski's imagination and virtually altered his view of time, space, and the contours of the past. It would become a decisive influence, he tells us, an introduction to politics, foreign places, the nature of tyranny, and the savagery of conflict between peoples, the stuff that became his subject matter." Bookforum

"A work of art: so eloquent, so simple, that you find yourself marveling at its prose, its gentle observation and the rhythm of the words. And you find yourself applauding such good translation as well." Washington Post Book World

Ryan, William B. F.

Noah's flood; the new scientific discoveries about the event that changed history; [by] William Ryan and Walter Pitman; illustrations by Anastasia Sotiropoulos; maps by William Haxby. Simon & Schuster 1999 319p il maps hardcover o.p. pa $14   **930**

1. Floods
ISBN 0-684-81052-2; 0-684-85920-3 (pa)

LC 98-45384

The authors present "evidence that there really was a flood of biblical proportions 7000 years ago, one that destroyed a civilization and doubled the capacity of the Black Sea." Libr J

This is "an interesting and provocative story . . . that incorporates archeology, oceanography, biblical studies, anthropology (not to mention archeobotany, paleopathology and archeozoology) and, one must conclude, a healthy portion of imagination." N Y Times Book Rev

Includes bibliographical references

930.1 Archaeology

Beneath the seven seas; adventures with the Intitute of Nautical Archaeology; edited by George F. Bass. Thames & Hudson 2005 256p il maps $39.95   **930.1**

1. Underwater exploration 2. Archeology
3. Shipwrecks
ISBN 978-0-500-05136-8; 0-500-05136-4

LC 2005-900862

This book features "accounts by many distinguished archaeologists associated with the INA [Institute of Nautical Archaeology]. They tell of the discovery, excavation, and preservation of more than 40 shipwrecks—and one sunken city—the world over, from ancient times through the Byzantine, medieval, and Renaissance eras and on through World War II. . . . This book will appeal to general readers and specialists alike in nautical archaeology." Libr J

Includes bibliographical references

Ceram, C. W., 1915-1972

Gods, graves, and scholars; the story of archaeology; translated from the German by E. B. Garside and Sophie Wilkins. 2nd rev and substantially enl ed. Knopf 1967 441p il maps pa $11.16 hardcover o.p.   **930.1**

1. Archeology
ISBN 0-394-74319-9 (pa)

Original German edition, 1949; first English language edition, 1951

"The story of Champollion and the reading of the Rosetta Stone, the decipherment of the inscriptions on the monument of Darius the Great, Leonard Woolley's famous excavations at Ur, and John Lloyd Stephens' discovery of the ruins of a great Mayan city are . . . told in this book." Doors to More Mature Read

Includes bibliographical references

Encyclopedia of underwater and maritime archaeology; edited by James P. Delgado. Yale Univ. Press 1998 493p il $75   **930.1**

1. Underwater exploration—Encyclopedias
ISBN 0-300-07427-1   LC 97-61536

First published 1997 in the United Kingdom with title: British Museum encyclopaedia of underwater and maritime archaeology

"The volume's 450 alphabetically arranged entries cover sites from prehistory to the modern era (including Titanic), legislation and legal issues, organizations, nations and regions, research themes, and technology and techniques. . . . More than 100 illustrations in color are complemented by more than 200 black-and-white drawings and photos." Booklist

Includes bibliographical references

Hunt, Patrick

Ten discoveries that rewrote history. Plume 2007 226p pa $27.95   **930.1**

1. Archeology—History 2. Antiquities 3. Ancient civilization
ISBN 978-0-452-28877-5; 0-452-28877-0

LC 2007-19808

Hunt, Patrick—_Continued_

"This book allots one chapter to each of ten key discoveries: the Rosetta stone, Troy, the Assyrian Library at Nineveh, Tutankhamen's Tomb, Machu Picchu, Pompeii, the Dead Sea Scrolls, Akrotiri on Thera, the Olduvai Gorge, and the Tomb of 10,000 Warriors. These discoveries are examined 'in the context of the evolving discipline of archaeology since the eighteenth century.'" Libr J

The author "has produced a wonderful volume of of archaeological history. In doing so, he has provided a seldom seen look at some of the most important scientific developments in the field." Sci Books Films

Includes bibliographical references

The **Oxford** companion to archaeology; editor in chief, Brian M. Fagan; editors, Charlotte Beck {et al.}. Oxford Univ. Press 1996 xx, 844p il maps $75   **930.1**

ISBN 0-19-507618-4   LC 96-30792

"In addition to broad discussions of specific civilizations such as Islamic, Olmec, and African, there are entries on theories (post processual), ethics, processes (lithics), dating techniques, pop culture (archaeology in film and television), specific sites and site management, plantation archaeology, and human evolution." Booklist

932   Egypt to 640 A.D.

Aldred, Cyril, 1914-1991

Akhenaten: King of Egypt. Thames & Hudson 1988 320p il pa $26.95 hardcover o.p.
    932

1. Akhenaton, King of Egypt, fl. ca. 1388-1358 B.C.
2. Egypt—Antiquities

ISBN 0-500-27621-8 (pa)   LC 87-51153

The author "relates the archaeological processes whereby Akhenaten's existence and his impact on Egyptian life were reconstructed through unearthed physical evidence." Booklist

Aldred "ranges over archaeology, art-history, morbid pathology, social and political history and the evolution of ideas. This is a book to which one will return, and gain each time one does so." Times Lit Suppl

Includes bibliographical references

Brier, Bob

The murder of Tutankhamen; a true story. Berkley Books 2005 xx, 264p il pa $14
    932

1. Tutankhamen, King of Egypt 2. Egypt—History

ISBN 0-425-20690-4; 978-0-425-20690-4
     LC 2005-41085

First published 1998 by Putnam

By "combining known historical events with evidence gathered by advanced technologies, Brier has recreated the suspenseful story of religious upheaval and political intrigue that likely resulted in the murder of the teenage King Tutankhamen." Booklist

"Brier obviously knows his subject and is impassioned by it. Readers who enjoy history or true-crime stories will be intrigued by this work." SLJ

Includes bibliographical references

Bunson, Margaret R.

Encyclopedia of ancient Egypt. rev ed. Facts on File 2002 462p il maps $70   **932**

1. Egypt—Civilization—Encyclopedias

ISBN 0-8160-4563-1   LC 2002-3550

First published 1991

This work consists of "alphabetically arranged entries covering Egypt from around 3200 B.C. to the fall of the New Kingdom in 1070 B.C. There are several broad entries such as _Egypt, Agriculture, and Religion_. The bulk of the book, however, consists of specific entries for kings and queens, gods and goddesses, cities, important documents, etc." Booklist [review of 1991 edition]

David, A. Rosalie (Ann Rosalie)

Handbook to life in ancient Egypt; [by] Rosalie David. rev ed. Facts on File 2003 417p il maps (Facts on File library of world history) $50
    932

1. Egypt—Civilization

ISBN 0-8160-5034-1   LC 2002-35229

First published 1998

This covers such topics as the geography of Ancient Egypt, society and government, religion, funerary beliefs and customs, architecture, trade and transport, the army and navy, economy and industry, and everyday life.

Includes bibliographical references

Hatshepsut: from queen to Pharaoh; edited by Catharine H. Roehrig with Renée Dreyfus and Cathleen A. Keller. Yale University Press 2005 339p il map $65   **932**

1. Hatshepsut, Queen of Egypt 2. Egypt—Civilization 3. Egypt—History

ISBN 0-300-11139-8   LC 2005-20286

Catalogue to an exhibition at the MH de Young Memorial Museum, San Francisco, from October 15, 2005, to February 5, 2006; at The Metropolitan Museum of Art, New York, from March 21 to July 9, 2006; and at the Kimbell Art Museum, Fort Worth, August 24 to December 31, 2006.

The editors "offer a magnificent portrait of this remarkable woman and all aspects of Egyptian life in the 18th Dynasty, from religion and politics to art and jewelry." Publ Wkly

Includes bibliographical references

Hawass, Zahi A.

Hidden treasures of ancient Egypt; unearthing the masterpieces of Egyptian history; [by] Zahi Hawass; photographs by Kenneth Garrett. National Geographic Society 2004 256p il $35   **932**

1. Excavations (Archeology)—Egypt 2. Egyptian art 3. Egypt—Antiquities

ISBN 0-7922-6319-7   LC 2004-44845

The author "narrates the past 150 years of excavation, from the colonial period—when Westerners overwhelmed the ranks of those recovering the nation's treasures—through Egypt's independence and the present era of international cooperation. . . . This breathtaking glimpse at the country's archeological wealth should excite curious and adventurous minds worldwide." Publ Wkly

Hawass, Zahi A.—*Continued*
Tutankhamun and the golden age of the pharaohs; [by] Zahi Hawass; photographs by Kenneth Garrett. National Geographic Books 2005 285p il map $35 *   **932**
1. Tutankhamen, King of Egypt 2. Egypt—Antiquities
ISBN 0-7922-3873-7   LC 2005-41678
This companion to an exhibition displaying about 130 items found in the tombs of Tutankhamun and other kings from the same dynasty "describes the physical and symbolic attributes of each object and explains its purpose in the afterlife. . . . An arrestingly visual album destined for high demand." Booklist
Includes bibliographical references

Lepre, J. P.
The Egyptian pyramids; a comprehensive, illustrated reference. McFarland & Co. 1990 341p il hardcover o.p. pa $35   **932**
1. Egypt—Antiquities 2. Pyramids
ISBN 0-89950-461-2; 0-7864-2955-0 (pa)
LC 89-43623
This "study of the pyramids built during the reigns of 42 different pharaohs, incorporates details pertaining to the history of each of the pharaohs who constructed a pyramid, concise chronological listings of the pyramids, relevant textual studies from the ancient Egyptian sources, and a review of the material remains associated with the pyramids." Choice
Includes bibliographical references

Mertz, Barbara, 1927-
Temples, tombs, & hieroglyphs; a popular history of ancient Egypt. 2nd ed., 1st William Morrow ed. William Morrow 2007 xxvi, 324p il map $26.95   **932**
1. Egypt—Antiquities 2. Egypt—Civilization
ISBN 978-0-06-125276-1; 0-06-125276-X
LC 2007-29118
First published 1964 by Coward-McCann
This is an "introduction to the history of ancient Egypt and Egyptology. . . . Mertz gives special attention to such topics as the kingship (yes) of Queen Hatshepsut, the exploits of Thutmose III, and the Amarna Period with its intriguing players Akhenaten, Nefertiti, and Tutankhamen. Presenting both pros and cons of current theories, Mertz also explains in simple language archaeological techniques such as carbon 14 dating and historical chronology. . . . [This is] an excellent introduction for patrons interested in the land of the pharaohs." Libr J

The **Oxford** encyclopedia of ancient Egypt; Donald B. Redford, editor in chief. Oxford Univ. Press 2001 3v set $450   **932**
1. Egypt—Civilization—Encyclopedias 2. Egypt—Antiquities—Encyclopedias
ISBN 0-19-510234-7   LC 99-54801
This reference work covers "archaeology, biography, history, language, social history, and more. . . . [It features] essays from more than 250 contributors from various countries and scholarly pursuits, all with solid academic credentials. . . . One is not likely to encounter another work of this magnitude on a subject of such universal interest for some time." Booklist
Includes bibliographical references

Tyldesley, Joyce A.
Nefertiti; Egypt's sun queen; [by] Joyce Tyldesley. Viking 1999 232p il $27.95; pa $14.95   **932**
1. Egypt—History
ISBN 0-670-86998-8; 0-14-025820-5 (pa)
LC 98-35469
"Born in approximately 1350 B.C., Nefertiti was the wife of Akhenaten, an eighteenth-dynasty pharaoh who initiated a radical religious revolution in his kingdom. . . . Adored by the masses, Nefertiti was elevated to semidivine status and adopted a dynamic political and cultural role. . . . Tyldesley manages to do an admirable job re-creating the exquisite opulence of palace life and piecing together Nefertiti's early public years." Booklist
Includes bibliographical references

Verner, Miroslav
The pyramids; the mystery, culture, and science of Egypt's great monuments; translated from the German by Steven Rendall. Grove Press 2001 495p il map pa $17.50 hardcover o.p.
932
1. Pyramids 2. Egypt—Antiquities
ISBN 0-8021-3935-3 (pa)   LC 2001-35084
In this study, the author "focuses on research of the last decade and excavations over the past 20 years. Verner divides his book into chapters according to pharaonic dynasty, spotlighting individual pharaohs' pyramids. He not only explains the layout of each pyramid but also presents various theories on how each pyramid was built and tells stories about the people that were buried there." Booklist
Includes bibliographical references

933   Palestine to 70 A.D.

Goodman, Martin, 1953-
Rome and Jerusalem; the clash of ancient civilizations. Alfred A. Knopf 2007 598p il map $35   **933**
1. Jews—Rome 2. Jews—History
ISBN 978-0-375-41185-4; 0-375-41185-2
LC 2007-5267
This is a "history of the titanic struggle between the Roman and Jewish worlds that led to the destruction of Jerusalem." Publisher's note
"For scholars of Roman and Jewish history as well as well-informed general readers, this work provides a definitive account." Booklist
Includes bibliographical references

936   Europe north and west of Italian peninsula to ca. 499 A.D.

Ancient Europe 8000 B.C.-A.D. 1000; encyclopedia of the Barbarian world; Peter Bogucki & Pam J. Crabtree, editors-in-chief. Thomson/Gale 2004 2v il, maps set $280 *
936
1. Europe—History—Encyclopedias 2. Ancient history
ISBN 0-684-80668-1   LC 2003-15251

Ancient Europe 8000 B.C.-A.D. 1000—*Continued*

Contents: v. 1. The Mesolithic to Copper Age (c. 8000-2000 B.C.) -- v. 2. Bronze Age to Early Middle Ages (c. 3000 B.C.-A.D. 1000)

"The 212 articles are arranged in seven sections. The first provides a general overview, while the remainder cover major periods from Mesolithic hunters to the Middle Ages." Libr J

"Any public and academic library that has a clientele interested in European archeology or the featured historical period covered will find this a valuable purchase." Booklist

Includes bibliographical references

Cunliffe, Barry, 1939-
The ancient Celts. Penguin Books 1999 324p il map pa $21.95   **936**
1. Celts
ISBN 0-14-025422-6
First published 1997 by Oxford Univ. Press
This is a "survey of the origins of the Celts and their expansion during the Iron Age through their largely successful subjection by the Romans. . . . [Cunliffe] has written a readable and informative book with many attractive illustrations." Libr J
Includes bibliographical references

937 Roman Empire

Allan, Tony, 1946-
Life, myth, and art in Ancient Rome. J. Paul Getty Museum 2005 144p il pa $19.95
937
1. Roman art 2. Roman mythology 3. Rome—Civilization 4. Rome—Antiquities
ISBN 0-89236-821-7   LC 2004-114326
This is an "illustrated guide to the cultural and political heritage of ancient Rome, including the enduring legacy of its art and architecture, the engineering innovations of its vast system of roads and aqueducts, the . . . myths of its gods and goddesses, and the power of its emperors and legions." Publisher's note
Includes bibliographical references

Berry, Joanne, 1971-
The complete Pompeii. Thames & Hudson 2007 256p il map $40   **937**
1. Pompeii (Extinct city)
ISBN 978-0-500-05150-4; 0-500-05150-X
LC 2007-922095
This book "covers the origins and evolution of the city, the daily life of its residents, the geography of the region, and the eruption of Mt. Vesuvius, as well as a history of the excavation of the site. Easy to read and with full color pictures of the excavation, along with maps, time lines, diagrams, and vivid art reproductions, this book gives a broad and comprehensive introduction to the Pompeian world. . . . High school libraries should be advised that there is a section on eroticism that contains visually and verbally explicit sexual material." Libr J
Includes bibliographical references

Bunson, Matthew
Encyclopedia of the Roman Empire. rev ed. Facts on File 2002 636p il maps $75   **937**
1. Rome—History—Encyclopedias
ISBN 0-8160-4562-3   LC 2001-53253
First published 1994
This reference work provides information on the key places, people, events, and culture of Roman history, from the reign of Julius Caesar to the fall of the last Roman emperor in 476 A.D.
"An excellent ready-reference source." Booklist [review of 1994 edition]
Includes bibliographical references

Cambridge illustrated history of the Roman world; edited by Greg Woolf. Cambridge University Press 2003 384p il map (Cambridge illustrated history) $45   **937**
1. Rome—History
ISBN 0-521-82775-2   LC 2004-298480
This book explores such topics as "religion, Rome's relationship with Greece, warfare and Empire, and science and culture." Publisher's note
Includes bibliographical references

Connolly, Peter, 1935-
The ancient city; life in classical Athens & Rome; [by] Peter Connolly, Hazel Dodge. Oxford Univ. Press 1998 256p il maps hardcover o.p. pa $21.95   **937**
1. Classical civilization 2. Rome—Civilization 3. Athens (Greece) 4. Greece—Civilization
ISBN 0-19-917242-0; 0-19-521582-6 (pa)
LC 98-201131
The authors "focus specifically on city life in two 'golden ages' of ancient times: Athens in fifth-century B.C. and Rome in second-century A.D. [They] place each city in its historical and geographical perspective, and then highlight how people really lived in those times and places. Detailed color drawings, cutaways, photographs, and maps make this an extremely useful as well as an outstandingly attractive book." Voice Youth Advocates
Includes bibliographical references

Fowler, Brenda
Iceman; uncovering the life and times of a prehistoric man found in an alpine glacier. University of Chicago Press ed. University of Chicago Press 2001 315p il pa $15   **937**
1. Mummies 2. Italy—Antiquities 3. Prehistoric peoples
ISBN 0-226-25823-8   LC 2001-27805
First published 2000 by Random House
"In September 1991, hikers in the Alps discovered a well-preserved frozen corpse; nearby lay a stone ax and swatches of leather and fur. The man turned out to have died in the early Bronze Age, making him an incalculable treasure for students of early human beings. Fowler . . . offers a brisk and easy-to-follow narrative, first of the great discovery, then of the personal and political struggles for control of the frozen body." Publ Wkly
Includes bibliographical references

Gibbon, Edward, 1737-1794

The decline and fall of the Roman empire; Edward Gibbon; edited, abridged, and with a critical introduction by Hans-Friedrich Mueller; introduction by Daniel J. Boorstin; illustrations by Giovanni Battista Piranesi. Modern Library paperback ed. Modern Library 2003 xxxvii, 1258p il map pa $15.95 *			**937**

1. Rome—History 2. Byzantine Empire

ISBN 0-375-75811-9			LC 2002-32585

Hardcover and paperback editions also available from other publishers

First published 1776-1788 in the United Kingdom with title: The history of the decline and fall of the Roman Empire

"In this substantial history of the Roman Empire, Gibbon bridges the abyss between the ancient and the modern world. It is the one historical work of the eighteenth century that is still accepted as authoritative. It covers thirteen centuries of history, during which time paganism was breaking down and Christianity was taking its place." Reader's Adviser

Includes bibliographical references

Grant, Michael, 1914-2004

Collapse and recovery of the Roman Empire. Routledge 1999 123p $34.95			**937**

1. Emperors—Rome 2. Rome—History

ISBN 0-415-17323-X			LC 98-8222

"Grant examines the causes for the near disintegration of the empire in the mid-third century A.D., including the problems of imperial succession, Germanic encroachments on the frontiers, and chronic conflicts with the Persians in the East. . . . This work is a worthy and necessary addition to both academic and public library collections on classical history." Booklist

Includes bibliographical references

The **Oxford** history of the Roman world; edited by John Boardman, Jasper Griffin, Oswyn Murray. Oxford Univ. Press 1991 518p il maps pa $17.95 hardcover o.p.			**937**

1. Rome—History

ISBN 0-19-280203-8			LC 91-11763

"The text ... first published 1986 ... in The Oxford history of the classical world." Verso of title page

This "work tells the story of the rise of Rome from its origins as a cluster of villages to the foundation of the Roman Empire by Augustus, to its consolidation in the first two centuries CE. It also discusses aspects of the later Empire and its influence on Western civilization." Publisher's note

Includes bibliographical references

Pellegrino, Charles R.

Ghosts of Vesuvius; a new look at the last days of Pompeii, how the towers fell, and other strange connections; [by] Charles Pellegrino. 1st ed. W. Morrow 2004 489p il map $25.95; pa $15.95 *			**937**

1. Excavations (Archeology)—Italy 2. Pompeii (Extinct city)

ISBN 0-380-97310-3; 0-06-075100-2 (pa)

LC 2003-71055

"In August A.D. 79, Mt. Vesuvius erupted and famously buried the city of Pompeii and, less famously, the city of Herculaneum. From this node of history, Pellegrino goes off on a . . . search for the connections and ruptures that have shaped not only human civilization but the very course of life on Earth and the universe at large. . . . This is a book to be savored, reread and passed along to future generations." Publ Wkly

Includes bibliographical references

938   Greece to 323 A.D.

Adkins, Lesley

Handbook to life in ancient Greece; [by] Lesley Adkins and Roy A. Adkins. Updated ed. Facts on File 2005 514p il map (Facts on File library of world history) $70			**938**

1. Greece—Civilization

ISBN 0-8160-5659-5			LC 2004-47105

First published 1997

This book covers "all aspects of ancient Greek life—from the beginnings of the Minoan civilization in Crete to the final defeat by the Roman world in 30 BCE." Publisher's note

Includes bibliographical references

Burckhardt, Jacob, 1818-1897

The Greeks and Greek civilization; translated by Sheila Stern; edited with an introduction by Oswyn Murray. St. Martin's Press 1998 449p pa $16.95 hardcover o.p.			**938**

1. Greece—Civilization

ISBN 0-312-24447-9 (pa)			LC 98-30107

Translation of selected lectures on ancient Greece delivered by the German cultural historian in the 1870s

"These lectures provide not only a rich overview of Burckhardt's learning but a precious glimpse into the intellectual world of the late nineteenth century. . . . Here his topics range from the importance of the 'agon' in forging individualism to the pessimism and violence that underlay much of Greek culture." New Yorker

Includes bibliographical references

Green, Peter, 1924-

The Hellenistic age; a history. Modern Library 2007 xxxiii, 199p map (Modern Library chronicles) $21.95			**938**

1. Mediterranean region—History 2. Greece—History 3. Hellenism

ISBN 978-0-679-64279-4; 0-679-64279-X

LC 2006-46657

Tis study "traces the unfolding of Hellenistic civilization in a linear fashion, while at the same time drawing connections between successive alterations in the political, economic and social landscape of the Hellenistic East and the appearance of new cultural and intellectual perspectives. . . . [The book] provides an interesting and well-written overview of a historical period that Green aptly describes as covering 'some of the most crucial and transformational history of the ancient world. . . . The changes are lasting and fundamental.' If only for this, students of world history are in Green's debt." Philadelphia Inquirer

Includes bibliographical references

Herodotus

The landmark Herodotus; the Histories: a new translation; a new translation by Andrea L. Purvis with maps, annotations, appendices, and encyclopedic index; edited by Robert B. Strassler; with an introduction by Rosalind Thomas. Pantheon Books 2007 lxiv, 953p il map $45 *

938

1. Greece—History
ISBN 978-0-375-42109-9; 0-375-42109-2

LC 2007-24149

"A major theme of the Histories is the way in which time can effect surprising changes in the fortunes and reputations of empires, cities, and men; all the more appropriate, then, that Herodotus' reputation has once again been riding very high. In the academy, his technique, once derided as haphazard, has earned newfound respect, while his popularity among ordinary readers will likely get a boost from the publication of perhaps the most densely annotated, richly illustrated, and user-friendly edition of his Histories ever to appear: 'The Landmark Herodotus,' edited by Robert B. Strassler and bristling with appendices, by a phalanx of experts, on everything from the design of Athenian warships to andent units of liquid measure." New Yorker

Includes bibliographical references

Kagan, Donald

The Peloponnesian War. Viking 2003 xxvii, 511p il map $29.95; pa $15 **938**
1. Greece—History—431-404 B.C., Peloponnesian War
ISBN 0-670-03211-5; 0-14-200437-5 (pa)

LC 2002-193377

This is a study of "the conflict between Athens and Sparta in the fifth century B.C.E. . . . {Kagan's} primary source is, of course, Thucydides' epic history, but {he} draws on Aristotle, Xenophon, and others to provide an objective, nuanced perspective on the military drama. And it's quite a drama: the clash of democracy and oligarchy, the testing of great leaders, the innovative military tactics, and the unprecedented human cost." Booklist

Includes bibliographical references

Lane Fox, Robin

The classical world; an epic history from Homer to Hadrian. Basic Books 2006 656p il map $35

938

1. Classical civilization 2. Greece—Civilization 3. Rome—Civilization
ISBN 978-0-465-02496-4; 0-465-02496-3

LC 2006-20247

First published 2005 in the United Kingdom

A "portrait of Greek and Roman culture over a period of roughly 900 years. Although he utilizes a broadly chronological approach, Fox goes well beyond the usual, dreary narrative of battles, dynastic changes, and political conflicts that often characterize surveys of the period. Instead, Fox focuses on the gradual development and transformation of various cultural aspects of Greek and Roman societies, and he discusses in often fascinating detail topics that are normally given short shrift in general histories." Booklist

Thucydides

The history of the Peloponnesian War. Rev ed. Penguin Group 1954 648p map (Penguin classics) pa $15 **938**
1. Greece—History—431-404 B.C., Peloponnesian War
ISBN 978-0-14-044039-3; 0-14-044039-9
Variant title: The Peloponnesian War

Thucydides' "chosen subject was the Peloponnesian War, which covered 27 years of his own lifetime, 431-404 B.C., and in which he fought as a commander of the Athenian troops in Thrace. His ideal of history is said to have been first accuracy, and then relevancy. . . . He rarely digressed. His history is unfinished, breaking off in the middle of the year 411 B.C." Reader's Adviser

The landmark Thucydides; a comprehensive guide to the Peloponnesian War; edited by Robert B. Strassler; introduction by Victor Davis Hanson. A newly revised edition of the Richard Crawley translation with maps, annotations, appendices, and encyclopedic index. Free Press 1996 xxxiii,713p $45; pa $25 **938**
1. Greece—History—431-404 B.C., Peloponnesian War
ISBN 978-1-416-59087-3; 0-684-82790-5

LC 96-24555

"Strassler, an unaffiliated scholar of classical studies, has remedied many of the flaws of Richard Crawley's 1874 translation of The Peloponnesian War. He has added descriptive paragraph-by-paragraph synopses, topic headers on every page, numerous maps keyed to the adjoining text, explanatory footnotes, an extensive index, an excellent introduction by Victor Davis Hanson . . ., and 11 appendixes (by various scholars) on politics, warfare, and society in the Greece of the fifth century B.C.E." Libr J

938.003   Classical dictionaries

Ancient Greece; edited by Thomas J. Sienkewicz. Salem Press 2007 3v il map (Magill's choice) set $207 * **938.003**
1. Greece—History—Encyclopedias
ISBN 1-58765-281-1; 978-1-58765-281-3

LC 2006-16525

Some of the essays in this work appeared in various other Salem Press sets

This is a "comprehensive examination of Greek civilization and its impact on Western history, 'from its earliest archaeological remains until the Battle of Actium in 31 B.C.E.' . . . [The essays included] cover art, daily life and customs, government, literature, medicine and science, war, the role of women, and mythology. Biographical entries profile statesmen, artists, writers, scientists, and philosophers, and relevant entries probe battles, philosophical movements, and types of literature." SLJ

Includes bibliographical references

The **Cambridge** dictionary of classical civilization;
edited by Graham Shipley . . . [et al.]
Cambridge University Press 2006 xliv, 966p il
map $180 *   **938.003**
1. Classical civilization—Dictionaries
ISBN 0-521-48313-1; 978-0-521-48313-1
LC 2006-299203
The "entries and more than 500 illustrations focus on
social, economic, and cultural aspects of these civilizations from the mid-eighth century BCE to the end of the
fifth century." Booklist
Includes bibliographical references

Grant, Michael, 1914-2004
A guide to the ancient world; a dictionary of
classical place names. Wilson, H.W. 1986 728p
maps $105   **938.003**
1. Classical dictionaries
ISBN 0-8242-0742-4   LC 86-15785
"This dictionary provides background for about nine
hundred places important to an understanding of the cultures of the ancient Greeks, Etruscans, and Romans. . . .
The time period covered is from the first millennium
B.C. until the fall of the Roman empire in the fifth century A.D. Depending on the subject, a typical entry includes information about history, geography, archaeology, and sometimes art and mythology." Am Ref Books
Annu, 1987

The **Oxford** classical dictionary; edited by Simon
Hornblower and Antony Spawforth. 3rd rev ed.
Oxford Univ. Press 2003 lv, 1640p $110
938.003
1. Classical dictionaries
ISBN 0-19-860641-9
First published 1949 under the editorship of M. Cary
and others
This reference includes over 6,000 entries about the
ancient Greco-Roman world, covering such topics as politics, government and economy, religion and mythology,
law and philosophy, science and geography, languages,
literature, art and architecture, archeology, historical writing, military history, social history, sex, and gender
"This is a work that makes a fascinating world of
learning accessible to a broad audience." Booklist
Includes bibliographical references

Sacks, David
Encyclopedia of the ancient Greek world;
editorial consultant, Oswyn Murray; revised by
Lisa R. Brody. Rev ed. Facts on File 2005 xx,
412p il map (Facts on File library of world
history) $75   **938.003**
1. Greece—History—Encyclopedias
ISBN 0-8160-5722-2   LC 2004-56429
First published 1995
This encyclopedia covers "ancient Greece, from the
dawning of Minoan civilization to the conquest of
Rome—2000 years of a remarkable civilization that left
an indelible imprint on human history. . . . This is a
first-rate purchase for libraries on a topic of endless inquiry and fascination." SLJ
Includes bibliographical references

939   Other parts of ancient world to ca. 640

Civilizations of the Ancient Near East; Jack M.
Sasson, editor in chief; John Baines, Gary
Beckman, Karen S. Rubinson, associate editors.
Hendrickson Publishers 2000 4v in 2 il map set
$169.95 *   **939**
1. Middle East—Civilization
ISBN 1-56563-607-4   LC 00-63144
First published 1995 by Scribner
This "work concentrates on the Near East, broadly de-
fined to include a region from Northeast Africa to India,
Pakistan, and Burma, with principal focus on the core ar-
eas of Egypt, Syro-Palestine, Mesopotamia, and Anatolia.
The time span ranges from the third millennium B.C.E.,
when writing was invented, to 330 B.C.E., when Alexander triumphed over the Persian Empire. The 189 contributors from five continents and 16 countries include some
of the world's finest scholars." Libr J [review of 1995
edition]
Includes bibliographical references

Wood, Michael, 1948-
In search of the Trojan War. University of Calif.
Press 1998 288p il pa $19.95   **939**
1. Trojan War 2. Troy (Extinct city) 3. Bronze Age
ISBN 0-520-21599-0   LC 98-4958
First published 1985 by Facts on File
The author "outlines the path the legend took through
medieval, Renaissance and modern society. The bulk of
this . . . book is devoted to archeological efforts to
prove the truth of Homer's epic and confirm that Troy
was actually at Hissarlik. Mr. Wood also describes the
history and archeology of Mycenae." N Y Times Book
Rev [review of 1985 edition]
"This is a first-rate book. . . . The book makes a
readable and clear approach to some of the knottiest
problems of Bronze Age archaeology." Choice [review of
1985 edition]
Includes bibliographical references

940   History of Europe

Sachar, Howard Morley, 1928-
Dreamland; Europeans and Jews in the
aftermath of the Great War; {by} Howard M.
Sachar. Knopf 2002 385p map pa $15 hardcover
o.p.   **940**
1. Jews—Europe 2. Europe—History—1918-1945
ISBN 0-375-70829-4 (pa)   LC 2001-38471
An overview of Jewish life in Europe during the three
decades before the Holocaust
"This scholarly analysis provides a completely original
slant on the much-studied interwar period." Booklist
Includes bibliographical references

940.1 Europe—Early history to 1453

Dictionary of the Middle Ages; Joseph R. Strayer, editor in chief. Scribner 1982-1989 12v + index il maps set $1,625 * **940.1**
ISBN 0-684-19073-7   LC 82-5904
Also available supplement published 2003 $130 (ISBN 0-684-80642-8)

"Authoritative and modern, this interdisciplinary dictionary spans the years from A.D. 500 to 1500, taking cognizance of the Byzantine, Islamic, and Jewish contributions to medieval life as well as the European. . . . The contents are in alphabetical sequence, some articles providing brief definitions or identifications, others offering extensive background and analysis." Ref Sources: a brief guide

English, Edward D.
Encyclopedia of the medieval world. Facts on File 2004 2v il map (Facts on File library of world history) set $150   **940.1**
1. Middle Ages—Encyclopedias
ISBN 0-8160-4690-5   LC 2003-27825
This encyclopedia "covers the time period from the late antique world to about 1500 C.E and includes events, people, institutions, and culture in western and eastern Europe, Scandinavia, North Africa, Byzantium, and the Near East. The 2,000 entries discuss significant people, art, politics, literature, religion, economics, law, science, and warfare in an A-Z format." Booklist
Includes bibliographical references

Freeman, Charles, 1947-
The closing of the Western mind; the rise of faith and the fall of reason. Knopf 2003 xxiii, 432p il map $32.50; pa $16.95   **940.1**
1. Western civilization 2. Church history—30-600, Early church 3. Hellenism 4. Europe—History—476-1492 5. Europe—Intellectual life
ISBN 1-400-04085-X; 1-400-03380-2 (pa)
     LC 2002-44821
The author contends that "when the Emperor Constantine converted to Christianity in 312 AD, he changed the course of European history in a way that continues to have repercussions to the present day. Adopting those aspects of the religion that suited his purposes, he turned Rome on a course from the relatively open, tolerant and pluralistic civilisation of the Hellenistic world, towards a culture that was based on the rule of fixed authority, whether that of the Bible, or the writings of Ptolemy in astronomy and of Galen and Hippocrates in medicine. Only a thousand years later, with the advent of the Renaissance and the emergence of modern science, was Europe to begin to free itself from the effects." Publisher's note

"This is one of the best books to date on the development of Christianity. . . . Beautifully written and impressively annotated, this is an indispensable read for anyone interested in the roots of Christianity and its implications for our modern worldview." Choice
Includes bibliographical references

Gies, Frances
Life in a medieval village; [by] Frances and Joseph Gies. Harper & Row 1990 257p il maps hardcover o.p. pa $14.95 *   **940.1**
1. Medieval civilization 2. Middle Ages
ISBN 0-06-016215-5; 0-06-092046-7 (pa)
     LC 89-33759
"Elton, England, is the focal point of the authors' efforts to portray the everyday life and social structure of the High Middle Ages. After giving a brief summary of Elton's origins and development in the Roman and Anglo-Saxon periods, the book examines just how the residents lived and worked within the feudal structure at the beginning of the fourteenth century." Booklist
Includes bibliographical references

Gies, Joseph
Life in a medieval city; [by] Joseph and Frances Gies. HarperPerennial 1981 c1969 274p il map pa $13.95   **940.1**
1. Middle Ages 2. Medieval civilization
ISBN 0-06-090880-7
First published 1969 by Crowell
"A portrait of a medieval city [Troyes], a flourishing settlement of a type not known in Europe before the Middle Ages." Cincinnati Public Libr
Includes bibliographical references

Herlihy, David, 1930-1991
The black death and the transformation of the west; edited and with an introduction by Samuel K. Cohn, Jr. Harvard Univ. Press 1997 117p pa $12 hardcover o.p.   **940.1**
1. Plague 2. Europe—History—476-1492 3. Medieval civilization 4. Renaissance
ISBN 0-674-07613-3 (pa)   LC 96-54637
These "essays redefine the historical study of the Black Death. . . . Herlihy's contention is that we can learn from this 'devastating natural disaster': for example, parallels can be drawn to today's pandemic of AIDS, especially in the resultant bigotries that both engendered. Cohn introduces the lectures, admirably setting the scene. This book, which opens a new chapter on the history and implications of the plague, is essential for all readers of medieval history." Libr J
Includes bibliographical references

The **New** Cambridge medieval history; edited by Paul Fouracre . . . [et al.] Cambridge Univ. Press 2005 7v in 8 il maps set $1600   **940.1**
1. Middle Ages 2. Medieval civilization
ISBN 978-0-521-85360-6; 0-521-85360-5
Volumes also available separately ea $205
This set replaces the Cambridge medieval history, published 1929-1967
Volume 4 published in 2 parts
Contents: v1 c. 500-c. 700 / edited by Paul Fouracre — v2 c. 700-c. 900 / edited by Rosamond McKitterick — v3 c. 900-c. 1024 / edited by Timothy Reuter — v4, pts. 1-2. 1024-c. 1198 / edited by David Luscombe and Jonathan Riley-Smith — v5 c. 1198-c. 1300 / edited by David Abulafia — v6 c. 1300-c. 1415 / edited by Michael Jones — v7 c. 1415-c. 1500 / edited by Christopher Allmand

The New Cambridge medieval history—*Continued*

"An excellent reference history, written by specialists, with full bibliographies at the end of each volume." Guide to Ref Books. 11th edition [entry for Cambridge medieval history]

The **Oxford** history of medieval Europe; edited by George Holmes. Oxford Univ. Press 2001 395p il maps pa $16.95 *   **940.1**
1. Europe—History—476-1492
ISBN 0-19-280133-3   LC 2002-281715
This is an abridged edition of The Oxford illustrated history of medieval Europe, published 1988

This compact edition covers such subjects as the chivalric code of knights, popular festivals, new art forms, the Black Death, the fall of Rome, and the emergence of the Reformation

Includes bibliographical references

Reston, James, Jr.
The last apocalypse; Europe at the year 1000 A.D. Doubleday 1998 299p il map pa $14.95 hardcover o.p.   **940.1**
1. Europe—History—476-1492
ISBN 0-385-48336-8 (pa)   LC 97-18812
The author "theorizes that the year A.D. 999 . . . was a turning point in history, marking the Christian West's joining of forces against the triple heathen threat of Vikings, Hungarian Magyar tribes and the Moors in Spain." Publ Wkly

"Reston's seemingly encyclopedic knowledge of the tenth century, combined with his disarming interpretations of the period's events, makes for fascinating reading." Booklist
Includes bibliographical references

Slotkin, Richard, 1942-
Lost battalions; the Great War and the crisis of American nationality; Richard Slotkin. H. Holt 2005 639p il maps   **940.1**
1. United States. Army. Infantry Regiment, 369th 2. World War, 1914-1918—United States 3. African American soldiers
ISBN 0-8050-4124-9   LC 2005-46312
"A John Macrae book."
This is a "history of the African-American 369th Infantry, known as the 'Harlem Hellfighters,' and the 77th Division, dubbed the 'Melting Pot' for its ranks of Italians, Jews and other eastern Europeans. . . . Slotkin smoothly telescopes from the trenches to the political and social implications for decades to come in this insightful, valuable account." Publ Wkly

940.2 Europe—1453-

Adkin, Mark
The Trafalgar companion; a guide to history's most famous sea battle and the life of Admiral Lord Nelson. Aurum Press 2005 560p il map $75
940.2

1. Nelson, Horatio Nelson, Viscount, 1758-1805 2. Trafalgar (Spain), Battle of, 1805
ISBN 1-84513-018-9
"Beginning with a prologue that describes the wounding and death of Vice-Admiral Horatio Nelson, the book introduces readers to the history of the campaign from 1802 to 1805 and to . . . information about the men and ships of the Royal Navy, in alternate chapters. . . . It will long stand as the definitive one-volume study of Great Britain's foremost naval hero and his times." Choice

Includes bibliographical references

Barbero, Alessandro, 1959-
The Battle; a new history of Waterloo. Walker & Company 2005 340p il map $28; pa $16
940.2
1. Waterloo, Battle of, 1815
ISBN   0-8027-1453-6;   978-0-8027-1453-4; 0-8027-1500-1 (pa); 978-0-8027-1500-5 (pa)
Original Italian edition, 2003
This is a "narrative of one of the most significant battles in European history." Booklist
The author's "narrative flows smoothly, making readers feel part of the battle's events. The chapters are short—never more than a few pages—and they pull the reader along with the action." Choice
Includes bibliographical references

Barzun, Jacques, 1907-
From dawn to decadence; 500 years of Western cultural life, 1500 to the present. HarperCollins Pubs. 2000 877p pa $20 hardcover o.p.
940.2
1. Western civilization 2. Europe—Intellectual life 3. Europe—Civilization
ISBN 0-06-092883-2 (pa)   LC 99-16194
"Barzun recounts the religious, political, artistic, and social revolutions that shaped Western culture." Booklist
"Encyclopedic without being discontinuous, the book hardly seems as long, as carefully constructed or as densely packed as it is. Though the ideas it explains are often complicated, the explanations it offers are limpidly clear, sparkling with biographical anecdote and counter-canonical observations." N Y Times Book Rev
Includes bibliographical references

Blanning, T. C. W.
The pursuit of glory; Europe, 1648-1815; [by] Tim Blanning. Viking 2007 xxvii, 707p il map (The Penguin history of Europe) $39.95 *
940.2
1. Europe—History—1492-1789 2. Europe—History— 1789-1815 3. Europe—Civilization
ISBN 978-0-670-06320-8; 0-670-06320-7
LC 2006-37324
This is an "account of Europe from the end of the Thirty Years' War to the Battle of Waterloo." Publisher's note
The author "thoroughly covers the politics and endless wars of the period. . . . 'The Pursuit of Glory' is history writing at its glorious best." N Y Times (Late N Y Ed)
Includes bibliographical references

Coote, Stephen
Napoleon and the Hundred Days. DaCapo Press 2005 308p il $27.50 **940.2**
1. Napoleon I, Emperor of the French, 1769-1821
2. France—History—1799-1815
ISBN 0-306-81408-0 LC 2004-65505
First published 2004 in the United Kingdom
This history "of the 100 days between Napoleon's escape from Elba and his capitulation after Waterloo uses the period as a lens through which to examine his character in general. . . . This accessible work is reminiscent of the finest classical Roman histories and biographies." Publ Wkly
Includes bibliographical references

Encyclopedia of the Renaissance; Paul F. Grendler, editor in chief. Scribner 1999 6v set $750 * **940.2**
1. Renaissance—Encyclopedias
ISBN 0-684-80514-6 LC 99-48290
"Published in association with the Renaissance Society of America."
This set covers "aspects of the Renaissance from the origins of humanism in Italy (ca. 1350) through 1750. . . . The encyclopedia's strength lies in its scholarship and in the comprehensiveness and diversity of its scope." Booklist

Europe 1789 to 1914; encyclopedia of the age of industry and empire; Merriman and Jay Winter, editors in chief. Charles Scribner's Sons 2006 5v il map (Scribner library of modern Europe) set $595 **940.2**
1. Europe—History—1789-1900—Encyclopedias
2. Europe—History—1871-1918—Encyclopedias
3. Europe—Civilization—Encyclopedias
ISBN 0-684-31359-6; 978-0-684-31359-7
LC 2006-7335
This encyclopedia covers "the time period between the onset of the French Revolution to the outbreak of World War I." Publisher's note
Includes bibliographical references

Gies, Joseph
Life in a medieval castle; [by] Joseph and Frances Gies. Harper & Row 1979 c1974 272p il pa $14.95 **940.2**
1. Castles 2. Middle Ages
ISBN 0-06-090674-X LC 79-103901
First published 1974 by Crowell
Using Chepstow Castle on the Welsh border as a model, the authors provide "descriptions of the medieval world where the castle was household, feudal center, and military target, and by concentrating on Anglo-Norman examples illustrate what existence was like as the dark ages began to brighten." Booklist
Includes glossary and bibliographical references

Hobsbawm, E. J. (Eric J.), 1917-
The age of revolution 1789-1848. Vintage Books 1996 356p il map pa $15.95 **940.2**
1. Europe—History—1789-1900 2. Industries—History
ISBN 978-0-679-77253-8; 0-679-77253-7
First published 1962 by World Pub. Co.

"This book traces the transformation of the world between 1789 and 1848 insofar as it was due to what is here called the 'dual revolution'—the French Revolution of 1789 and the contemporaneous (British) Industrial Revolution." Preface
Includes bibliographical references

King, David, 1970-
Vienna, 1814; how the conquerors of Napoleon made love, war, and peace at the Congress of Vienna. Harmony Books 2008 434p il $27.50
940.2
1. Congress of Vienna (1814-1815) 2. Europe—History—1789-1815 3. Europe—Politics and government
ISBN 978-0-307-33716-0; 0-307-33716-2
LC 2007-24680
"The conquerors of Napoleon were in a festive mood when they met in Vienna in the fall of 1814 to decide the fate of Europe. . . . [The author] does a superb job of evoking the bedazzling social scene that served as the backdrop to the Congress of Vienna. His characterizations of such luminaries as Czar Alexander, Metternich, Talleyrand, and Castlereagh are lucid and thoroughly grounded in primary sources. . . . This is a worthy contribution to the study of a critical historical event long neglected by historians." Libr J
Includes bibliographical references

Manchester, William
A world lit only by fire; the medieval mind and the Renaissance: portrait of an age. Little, Brown 1992 318p il maps pa $15.95 hardcover o.p.
940.2
1. Renaissance
ISBN 0-316-54556-2 (pa) LC 91-39928
The author covers "the tumultuous span from the Dark Ages to the dawn of the Renaissance. He delineates an age when invisible spirits infested the air, when tolerance was seen as treachery and 'a mafia of profane popes desecrated Christianity.' Besides re-creating the arduous lives of ordinary people, . . . {Manchester} peoples his tapestry with such figures as Leonardo, Machiavelli, Lucrezia Borgia, Erasmus, Luther, Henry VIII and Anne Boleyn." Publ Wkly
Includes bibliographical references

Pocock, Tom
The terror before Trafalgar; Nelson, Napoleon and the secret war. Naval Institute Press 2005 255p il map pa $16.95 **940.2**
1. Nelson, Horatio Nelson, Viscount, 1758-1805 2. Napoleon I, Emperor of the French, 1769-1821 3. Europe—History—1789-1815
ISBN 978-1-5911-4681-0; 1-5911-4681-X
LC 2004-58185
First published 2003 by Norton
The author "retells the story of the four years in which the French confidently prepared to invade Britain, overrun its army, take out its armaments and replace the government with something easier to control. . . . Pocock's little book . . . gives a chilling insight into ineffectual undercover operations and groundbreaking

Pocock, Tom—*Continued*

weaponry: rockets, torpedos, submarines, airships and the construction of an undersea tunnel, all so far ahead of their time that none turned out in the end to be much use in practical terms to either side." N Y Times Book Rev
Includes bibliographical references

Pope, Stephen

Dictionary of the Napoleonic wars. Facts on File 2000 572p $71.50 *   **940.2**
ISBN 0-8160-4243-8   LC 99-48829
Pope "has produced more than 1000 alphabetical entries, supplemented by 30 maps, detailing nearly every aspect of Napoleonic warfare. From broad subjects such as strategy, tactics, diplomacy, and propaganda to specific battles, treaties, weapons, naval warfare, and myriad colorful personalities, the book offers a wealth of succinct information." Libr J

The **Renaissance**; an encyclopedia for students; [edited by] Paul F. Grendler. Charles Scribner's Sons 2003 4v set $395   **940.2**
1. Renaissance—Encyclopedias
ISBN 0-684-31281-6   LC 2003-15672
Adaptation of Encyclopedia of the Renaissance, published 1999
This encyclopedia includes articles on various aspects of social, cultural, and political history such as literature, government, warfare, and technology, plus maps, charts, definitions, and chronology
"Researchers should find their needs more than satisfied by this appealing and student-friendly resource." SLJ

Roberts, Andrew, 1963-

Waterloo: June 18, 1815; the battle for modern Europe. HarperCollins 2005 143p il maps (Making history) $21.95; pa $12.95   **940.2**
1. Waterloo, Battle of, 1815
ISBN 0-06-008866-4; 0-06-076215-2 (pa)
                                    LC 2005-282517
This is a study of the defeat of Napoleon's army at the Battle of Waterloo in June, 1815.
The author "instills an appreciation for Waterloo as a horrific experience saturated with alternative possible outcomes. A must for the military shelf." Booklist
Includes bibliographical references

Wells, Colin

Sailing from Byzantium; how a lost empire shaped the world; Colin Wells. Delacorte Press 2006 xxx, 335p map $22   **940.2**
1. Byzantine Empire
ISBN 0-553-80381-6   LC 2006-42665
The author "considers how Byzantium, the Eastern, Greek-language Roman Empire of the Middle Ages, influenced three successor civilizations Western Europe, Islam, and the eastern Slavic world of the Balkans and Russia. . . . This history is a needed reminder of the debt that three of our major civilizations owe to Byzantium." Libr J
Includes bibliographical references

Wilson, Ellen Judy

Encyclopedia of the Enlightenment; Peter Hanns Reill, consulting editor; Ellen Judy Wilson, principal author. rev ed. Facts on File 2004 670p $75 *   **940.2**
1. Enlightenment—Encyclopedias 2. Philosophy—Encyclopedias 3. Europe—Intellectual life
ISBN 0-8160-5335-9   LC 2003-22973
First published 1996
This reference provides a "review of the important ideas, people, and events that shaped the world during the Enlightenment. [It] covers the major changes in science, education, philosophy, art and architecture, and politics which took place during the 17th and 18th centuries and led to the birth of the modern era. . . . The biographical entries cover such notables as Robespierre, Schiller, Fielding, Kant, and Voltaire. . . . Larger public, school, and academic libraries looking for a comprehensive overview of the subject for the student or interested reader will find this a valuable and accessible resource." Libr J
Includes bibliographical references

Zamoyski, Adam

Rites of peace; the fall of Napoleon and the Congress of Vienna. HarperCollins 2007 634p il map $29.95   **940.2**
1. Congress of Vienna (1814-1815) 2. Europe—History—1789-1815
ISBN 0-06-077518-1; 978-0-06-077518-6
"This sequel to Zamoyski's . . . Moscow 1812 (2004) shifts from military to diplomatic affairs surrounding the defeat of Napoleonic France and the disposal of its empire. Zamoyski narrates their course from 1813, when Russia's Alexander I decided to continue the war rather than settle with Napoleon, to 1815 and the latter's final Waterloo." Booklist
This "book is old-fashioned, impressively detailed diplomatic history." Economist
Includes bibliographical references

940.3   World War I, 1914-1918

Audoin-Rouzeau, Stéphane

14-18, understanding the Great War; {by} Stéphane Audoin-Rouzeau and Annette Becker; translated from the French by Catherine Temerson. Hill & Wang 2002 280p $24; pa $14
                                    940.3
1. World War, 1914-1918
ISBN 0-8090-4642-3; 0-8090-4643-1 (pa)
                                    LC 2002-111422
Original French edition, 2000
"The authors take an anthropological approach to the cataclysm that engulfed Europe in 1914 and examine three significant aspects of the war: violence, crusade, and mourning. . . . Supported by contemporary documentation, this unique work will become a classic study." Libr J
Includes bibliographical references

Burg, David F.

Almanac of World War I; [by] David F. Burg and L. Edward Purcell; introduction by William Manchester. University Press of Ky. 1998 320p il maps hardcover o.p. pa $22 **940.3**

1. World War, 1914-1918

ISBN 0-8131-2072-1; 0-8131-9087-8 (pa)

LC 98-26625

"The bulk of the text is arranged chronologically by year and date, listing almost daily occurrences from 1914 through 1918. . . . The work is international in scope, covering political and military happenings from around the world. . . . There is really nothing comparable to this volume." Booklist

Includes bibliographical references

The **Encyclopedia** of World War I; a political, social, and military history. ABC-CLIO 2005 5v il map set $485 **940.3**

1. World War, 1914-1918—Encyclopedias

ISBN 1-85109-420-2 LC 2005-22937

This set opens with "four essays discussing the origins, outbreak, overview, and legacy of the war. They are followed by alphabetical entries on virtually every aspect of the conflict, including battles, people, military equipment and strategies, and social and political changes associated with it." SLJ

Includes bibliographical references

Gilbert, Martin, 1936-

The First World War; a complete history. Holt & Co. 1994 xxiv, 615p il maps hardcover o.p. pa $22.50 **940.3**

1. World War, 1914-1918

ISBN 0-8050-1540-X; 0-8050-4734-4 (pa)

LC 94-27268

This work "covers WW I on all major fronts—domestic, diplomatic, military—as well as such bloody preludes as the Armenian massacre of 1915." Publ Wkly

"What Mr. Gilbert seeks to do, and frequently succeeds in doing, is to humanize, indeed to personalize, World War I. His effort and accomplishment make this a rewarding and significant book." N Y Times Book Rev

Includes bibliographical references

Keegan, John, 1934-

An illustrated history of the First World War. Knopf 2001 429p il $50 **940.3**

1. World War, 1914-1918

ISBN 0-375-41259-X LC 2001-41410

The text is an abridgment of the author's The First World War

The text is an abridgment of the author's The First World War. For this illustrated volume the text is complemented by "almost 500 photographs, posters, drawings and maps, a cross-section of material produced by all the major combatants and clarified by Keegan's extensive captions." Publ Wkly

Includes bibliographical references

MacMillan, Margaret

Paris 1919; six months that changed the world. Random House 2002 560p $35; pa $16.95 **940.3**

1. Wilson, Woodrow, 1856-1924 2. Paris Peace Conference (1919-1920) 3. World War, 1914-1918—Peace 4. Germany—History—1918-1933

ISBN 0-375-50826-0; 0-375-76052-0 (pa)

LC 2002-23707

First published 2001 in the United Kingdom with title: Peacemakers

The author examines the Paris Peace Conference of 1919. Economist John Maynard Keynes blamed "the failure of the conference on the vindictiveness of the French in general and of Clemenceau in particular. Margaret MacMillan . . . argues that the conference has been blamed for many disasters that were, in fact, determined either by events that took place before it began or by later troubles." Economist

"MacMillan's lucid prose brings her participants to colorful and quotable life, and the grand sweep of her narrative encompasses all the continents the peacemakers vainly carved up." Publ Wkly

Includes bibliographical references

Strachan, Hew

The First World War. Viking 2004 364p il maps hardcover o.p. pa $16 **940.3**

1. World War, 1914-1918

ISBN 0-670-03295-6; 0-14-303518-5 (pa)

LC 2003-62191

The author details the "factors behind World War I, covers the major ground and naval campaigns and battles, and assesses the roles of leading officers and statesmen while simultaneously highlighting the home fronts and the non-European aspects of this cataclysmic event." Libr J

"Readers already familiar with the sequence of events in strict order will benefit most. But all readers will eventually be gripped, and even the most seasoned ones will praise the insights and the original choice of illustrations." Publ Wkly

Includes bibliographical references

Tuchman, Barbara Wertheim

The guns of August; [by] Barbara W. Tuchman; [with a new foreword by Robert K. Massie] 1st Ballantine Books ed. Ballantine 1994 xxiv, 511p il, maps pa $14 * **940.3**

1. World War, 1914-1918

ISBN 0-345-38623-X LC 93-90461

First published 1962 by Macmillan

A history of the negotiations that preceded World War I and the course of the war's first month.

Includes bibliographical references

The Zimmermann telegram. Ballantine Books [1985] c1966 244p il pa $14 **940.3**

1. World War, 1914-1918—Causes

ISBN 0-345-32425-0 LC 84-91737

First published 1958 by Macmillan

The author discusses the German plan to induce Mexico to attack the U.S. during World War I.

Includes bibliographical references

The **United** States in the First World War; an
encyclopedia; editor, Anne Cipriano Venzon;
consulting editor, Paul L. Miles. Garland 1995
xx, 830p maps (Garland reference library of the
humanities) $155; pa $45   **940.3**
1. World War, 1914-1918
ISBN 0-8240-7055-0; 0-8153-3353-6 (pa)
       LC 95-1782
"Biography, economics, civil rights, women's issues,
foreign relations, battles, armaments, and conferences are
among the topics included. Arrangement is alphabetical,
and most articles are brief—between one column and a
page. . . . Most articles include brief bibliographies.
There are six maps, but no other illustrations." Libr J

World War I; a history; edited by Hew Strachan.
Oxford Univ. Press 1999 356p il maps
hardcover o.p. pa $28.95   **940.3**
1. World War, 1914-1918
ISBN 0-19-820614-3; 978-0-19-289325-3 (pa);
0-19-289325-4 (pa)   LC 97-44997
First published 1998 in the United Kingdom with title:
The Oxford illustrated history of the First World War
Paperback published with title: The Oxford illustrated
history of the First World War
"Strachan has commissioned 20 historians to summarize present thought about the July 1914 crisis, the military course of the war, the social and economic strains
it exerted in all the belligerents, and its conclusion in
revolutions and treaties. . . . Readers will find this comprehensive work a captivating introduction to the Great
War." Booklist
Includes bibliographical references

940.4   Military history of World War I

Dallas, Gregor
1918: war and peace. Overlook Press 2001 616p
$40; pa $19.95   **940.4**
1. World War, 1914-1918—Peace
ISBN 1-58567-157-6; 1-58567-319-6 (pa)
       LC 2001-21104
The author discusses how the First World War ended.
He examines "how the ceasefire was arranged, who the
major participants were, and how the general population
learned about the armistice." Libr J
Dallas "provides a meticulously detailed and intensive
study of the years 1918-1919." Publ Wkly
Includes bibliographical references

Eisenhower, John S. D., 1922-
Yanks: the epic story of the American Army in
World War I; {by} John S. D. Eisenhower with
Joanne Thompson Eisenhower. Free Press 2001
353p il maps hardcover o.p. pa $16   **940.4**
1. United States. Army 2. World War, 1914-1918—
Campaigns
ISBN 0-684-86304-9; 0-7432-2385-3 (pa)
       LC 2001-23124

"This history focuses entirely on the challenges, victo-
ries, sacrifices . . . and long-term consequences of the
American Expeditionary Force (AEF) in Europe during
World War I." Libr J
"This is an important work that should help alter the
historical picture of the American role in the conflict."
Booklist
Includes bibliographical references

Farwell, Byron
Over there; the United States in the Great War,
1917-1918. Norton 1999 336p $27.95; pa $15.95
     940.4
1. World War, 1914-1918—United States
ISBN 0-393-04698-2; 0-393-32028-6 (pa)
       LC 98-35705
This history of American intervention in World War
I focuses primarily on the military aspects of the war but
also discusses its social and economic impact
"This title does provide good coverage on the inter-
vention in Russia and the role of women in the war, no-
tably the 'Hello Girls.' " Libr J
Includes bibliographical references

Harries, Meirion, 1951-
The last days of innocence; America at war,
1917-1918; {by} Meirion and Susie Harries.
Random House 1997 573p il pa $16 hardcover
o.p.   **940.4**
1. World War, 1914-1918—United States
ISBN 0-679-74376-6 (pa)   LC 96-21756
The authors first "treat the details of America's entrance into the war and the agonizing months of war
preparation; they then visit the fighting and the peace efforts." Libr J
"This is an excellent study of US participation in
WWI. The research is in far greater depth than the usual
'popular history,' the analysis is sharp and informative,
and the writing is clear and a pleasure to read. The authors strike an even balance between necessity for condensation and the accuracy that comes from detailed
treatment." Choice
Includes bibliographical references

Lawrence, T. E. (Thomas Edward), 1888-1935
Seven pillars of wisdom; a triumph. Doubleday
1935 672p il maps pa $19.95 hardcover o.p.
     940.4
1. World War, 1914-1918—Middle East 2. Arabs
3. Bedouins 4. Wahhabis
ISBN 0-385-41895-7 (pa)
"Not only a history of the Arab revolt during the
{First} World War, but a commentary on the national
characteristics, and political policies of Arabs, Turks and
British." Cleveland Public Libr

Liddell Hart, Sir Basil Henry, 1895-1970
The real war, 1914-1918; with twenty-five
maps; by B. H. Liddell Hart. Little, Brown 1930
508p maps pa $23.99 hardcover o.p.
     940.4

Liddell Hart, Sir Basil Henry, 1895-1970—*Continued*
1. World War, 1914-1918
ISBN 0-316-52505-7 (pa)
A short history of World War I in which the action of the book ranges wherever Germany and the Allies locked in combat: Poland, Mesopotamia, Gallipoli, Caporetto, Baghdad, the North Sea, and the Mediterranean
Includes bibliographical references

Massie, Robert K., 1929-
Castles of steel; Britain, Germany, and the winning of the Great War at sea. Random House 2003 865p il map $35; pa $17.95   **940.4**
1. Great Britain. Royal Navy 2. Germany. Kriegsmarine 3. World War, 1914-1918—Naval operations
ISBN 0-679-45671-6; 0-345-40878-0 (pa)
LC 2003-41373
"Drawing on excerpts from official sources, contemporary accounts, and personal memoirs, the author . . . chronicles the action between the British and German navies during 1914-18, offering his analysis of the period's various battles, ships, policies, and commanders." Libr J
The author "makes a coherent if long narrative out of a sequence of events familiar to students of naval history but probably not to many other potential readers." Publ Wkly

Millman, Chad, 1971-
The detonators; the secret plot to destroy America and an epic hunt for justice. Little, Brown 2006 330p il map $24.99   **940.4**
1. World War, 1914-1918—United States 2. Sabotage
ISBN 978-0-316-73496-7; 0-316-73496-9
LC 2005-24401
"In 1916, a group of German agents blew up an ammunition warehouse on Black Tom Island in New York Harbor near the Jersey shore. The explosion destroyed thousands of tons of munitions destined for France, shattered windows all over lower Manhattan, and triggered a 23-year legal battle. . . . [The author describes] the sabotage ring's effects. His story then shifts to the legal battle, after World War I, to assess the damages and determine whether Germany's Weimar Republic was responsible." Libr J
"With its obvious contemporary resonance, Millman's able account of an earlier foreign attack on America should draw the espionage audience and more." Booklist
Includes bibliographical references

Mosier, John, 1944-
The myth of the Great War; a new military history of World War I. HarperCollins Pubs. 2001 381p il hardcover o.p. pa $14.95   **940.4**
1. World War, 1914-1918—Campaigns
ISBN 0-06-019676-9; 0-06-008433-2 (pa)
LC 00-46103
"After dissecting the major campaigns on the western front, Mosier concludes that Germany's ultimate defeat was the direct result of the influx of American soldiers into France in 1917 and 1918. . . . This is revisionist

history that convincingly smashes the myths that Allied governments, leaders, and propagandists worked so hard to promulgate. Mosier's masterful account is a welcome addition." Booklist
Includes bibliographical references

Neiberg, Michael
Fighting the Great War; a global history; [by] Michael S. Neiberg. Harvard University Press 2005 xx, 395p il map $27.95 *   **940.4**
1. World War, 1914-1918
ISBN 0-674-01696-3   LC 2004-54330
In this history of World War I, the author "develops military explanations for its continuation in the face of apparent futility." Booklist
"Readers interested in a general overview of WW I can do no better than Neiberg's excellent account." Choice
Includes bibliographical references

Ousby, Ian
The road to Verdun; World War I's most momentous battle and the folly of nationalism. Doubleday 2002 393p il maps $30; pa $16   **940.4**
1. World War, 1914-1918—Campaigns
ISBN 0-385-50393-8; 0-385-72173-0 (pa)
LC 2002-19475
This is a study of the Battle of Verdun which "killed 700,000 French and German soldiers, 10% of all those killed in the war. Yet a sense of glory was maintained, however inappropriately, amid the gore: the road leading to the battlefield was called the Sacred Way, and the French General Neville gained immortality by his brave statement, 'They {the Germans} shall not pass.'" Publ Wkly

940.5   Europe—1918-

Europe since 1914; encyclopedia of the age of war and reconstruction; John Merriman and Jay Winter, editors in chief. Charles Scribner's Sons/Thomson Gale 2006 5v il map (Scribner library of modern Europe) set $595   **940.5**
1. Europe—History—20th century—Encyclopedias 2. Europe—Civilization—Encyclopedias
ISBN 0-684-31365-0; 978-0-684-31365-8
LC 2006-14427
This encyclopedia "details European history from the Bolshevik Revolution to the European Union, linking it to the history of the rest of the world." Publisher's note
Includes bibliographical references

Linenthal, Edward Tabor, 1947-
Preserving memory; the struggle to create America's Holocaust Museum; [by] Edward T. Linenthal. Columbia University Press 2001 xxiv, 336p il pa $18.50   **940.5**
1. United States Holocaust Memorial Museum 2. Holocaust, 1933-1945
ISBN 0-231-12407-4   LC 2001-37168

Linenthal, Edward Tabor, 1947—*Continued*
First published 1995 by Viking
The author "describes the 15-year effort to create a national museum commemorating the Holocaust. He begins with the creation in May 1978 of the President's Commission on the Holocaust during the Carter administration. He then covers issues related to the location, design, and construction of the museum building. Linenthal's most significant contribution is the chapter on defining and representing the horror of the Holocaust." Libr J
Includes bibliographical references

Mak, Geert
In Europe; travels through the twentieth century; translated from the Dutch by Sam Garrett. Pantheon 2007 876p map $35 *   **940.5**
1. Europe—History—20th century 2. Europe—Description and travel
ISBN 0-375-42495-4; 978-0-375-42495-3
LC 2007-9260
Original Dutch edition, 2004
This book recounts the author's travels through Europe and examines the history of European countries, particularly focusing on the the effects of the Treaty of Rome.
"Mak's brilliant compendium is difficult to define—is it a history book, a travelogue, a memoir?—but stands out as a remarkable, insightful, exhilarating exposition on that peculiar continent across the Atlantic." Publ Wkly

940.53   World War II, 1939-1945

Ackerman, Diane
The zookeeper's wife. W.W. Norton 2007 368p il $24.95 *   **940.53**
1. Jews—Poland 2. Holocaust, 1933-1945 3. World War, 1939-1945—Jews—Rescue 4. Zoos
ISBN 978-0-393-06172-7; 0-393-06172-8
LC 2007-12635
This is an account of how the director of the Warsaw Zoo and his wife, Jan and Antonina Zabinski, respectively, saved 300 Jews during World War II.
"An exemplary work of scholarship and an 'ecstasy of imagining,' Ackerman's affecting telling of the heroic Zabinskis' dramatic story illuminates the profound connection between humankind and nature, and celebrates life's beauty, mystery, and tenacity." Booklist
Includes bibliographical references

Berenbaum, Michael, 1945-
The world must know; the history of the Holocaust as told in the United States Holocaust Memorial Museum; Arnold Kramer, editor of photographs. 2nd ed. United States Holocaust Memorial Museum 2006 xxi, 250p il pa $29.95
940.53
1. United States Holocaust Memorial Museum 2. Holocaust, 1933-1945
ISBN 0-8018-8358-X
First published 1993 by Little, Brown

This book documents the "stories of the Holocaust as told in the renowned permanent exhibition of the United States Holocaust Memorial Museum in Washington, D.C." Publisher's note
"Visually evocative and unsettling, the book, supplemented with a useful bibliography, is an excellent choice for those with little acquaintance of the subject or those needing a concise synopsis." Libr J [review of 1993 edition]
Includes bibliographical references

Berthon, Simon
Warlords; an extraordinary recreation of World War II through the eyes and minds of Hitler, Roosevelt, Churchill, and Stalin; [by] Simon Berthon and Joanna Potts. Da Capo Press 2006 358p il $24.95   **940.53**
1. Hitler, Adolf, 1889-1945 2. Churchill, Sir Winston, 1874-1965 3. Roosevelt, Franklin D. (Franklin Delano), 1882-1945 4. Stalin, Joseph, 1879-1953 5. World War, 1939-1945—Diplomatic history
ISBN 0-306-81467-6   LC 2005-432583
First published 2005 in the United Kingdom
This book focuses "on the day-to-day actions of Hitler, Stalin, Churchill, and Roosevelt as they grapple with the war's events and plot strategy. . . . For anyone interested in how these four leaders engaged in the war, here is a great place to start." Libr J
Includes bibliographical references

Beschloss, Michael R., 1955-
The conquerors: Roosevelt, Truman, and the destruction of Hitler's Germany, 1941-1945; {by} Michael Beschloss. Simon & Schuster 2002 377p il maps $26.95; pa $15 *   **940.53**
1. Roosevelt, Franklin D. (Franklin Delano), 1882-1945 2. Truman, Harry S., 1884-1972 3. World War, 1939-1945—Germany 4. Reconstruction (1939-1951) 5. United States—Foreign relations—Germany 6. Germany—Foreign relations—United States
ISBN 0-684-81027-1; 0-7432-4454-0 (pa)
LC 2002-30331
"As German forces were driven back in 1943-45, American leaders were anxious that in 20 years, just as it had done after its defeat in 1918, a vengeful Germany would start another world war. To prevent this, two schools of thought flowed through DC's salons of power: punishment or rehabilitation. . . . Beschloss covers the meeting-by-meeting, memo-by-memo political battle between the two approaches. . . . Beschloss' comprehensive research and narration into every nuance opens a significant perspective on bureaucratic politics' effect on the Germany that eventually formed in the early cold war." Booklist
Includes bibliographical references

The **Buchenwald** report; translated, edited, and with an introduction by David A. Hackett; foreword by Frederick A. Praeger. Westview Press 1995 397p map hardcover o.p. pa $29
940.53
1. Holocaust, 1933-1945—Personal narratives 2. Buchenwald (Germany: Concentration camp)
ISBN 0-8133-1777-0; 0-8133-3363-6 (pa)
LC 94-39714

The Buchenwald report—*Continued*

"This seminal document, published here in its entirety for the first time, is a report compiled for the Allied Army from interviews with the inmates of the Buchenwald concentration camp, located near Weimar, Germany in April 1945, shortly after the camp's liberation. . . . It is immediate, direct, and, as the product of the testimony of many people, more inclusive and wide-ranging than any single individual's personal testament. A classic of Holocaust literature that should be in any library that covers European history." Libr J

Includes bibliographical references

Carley, Michael Jabara, 1945-

1939; the alliance that never was and the coming of World War II. Dee, I.R. 1999 xxv, 321p maps $28.95 **940.53**
  1. World War, 1939-1945—Diplomatic history 2. World War, 1939-1945—Causes
  ISBN 1-56663-252-8 LC 99-24873
Carley "asserts that reflexive and extreme anti-Communist paranoia on the part of British and French politicians and diplomats prevented a very achievable alliance against Hitler." Booklist

The author "provides a detailed and fascinating perspective on one of the major causes of World War II." Libr J

Includes bibliographical references

Churchill, Sir Winston, 1874-1965

Closing the ring. Houghton Mifflin 1951 749p maps (Second World War, v5) pa $18 hardcover o.p. **940.53**
  1. World War, 1939-1945 2. World War, 1939-1945—Great Britain
  ISBN 0-395-41059-2 (pa)
"'Closing the Ring' sets forth the year of conflict from June 1943 to June 1944. Aided by the command of the oceans, the mastery of the U-boats, and our ever growing superiority in the air, the Western Allies were able to conquer Sicily and invade Italy, with the result that Mussolini was overthrown and the Italian nation came over to our side." Preface

The gathering storm. Houghton Mifflin 1948 784p maps (Second World War, v1) pa $19 hardcover o.p. **940.53**
  1. World War, 1939-1945 2. World War, 1939-1945—Great Britain
  ISBN 0-395-41055-X (pa)
The first volume of Churchill's monumental history of the Second World War describes the days between the false peace and Hitler's near-victory just before Dunkirk

The grand alliance. Houghton Mifflin 1950 903p maps (Second World War, v3) pa $18 hardcover o.p. **940.53**
  1. World War, 1939-1945 2. World War, 1939-1945—Great Britain
  ISBN 0-395-41057-6 (pa)
This volume begins with the German drive in the East, covers the War in Africa and describes the entrance into the war of Russia and, after Pearl Harbor, the United States

The hinge of fate. Houghton Mifflin 1950 1000p maps (Second World War, v4) pa $18 hardcover o.p. **940.53**
  1. World War, 1939-1945 2. World War, 1939-1945—Great Britain
  ISBN 0-395-41058-4 (pa)
Describing events leading to the invasion of Sicily, warfare in Africa, the discouragingly slow job of reconquest in Europe, meetings with Roosevelt, and efforts at collaboration with Stalin, this volume covers the period from January 1942 to May 1943

Their finest hour. Houghton Mifflin 1949 751p maps (Second World War, v2) pa $19 hardcover o.p. **940.53**
  1. World War, 1939-1945 2. World War, 1939-1945—Great Britain
  ISBN 0-395-41056-8 (pa)
This volume starts with the problems confronting Churchill as he assumed the office of Prime Minister in 1940 and continues with accounts of the Battle of Britain, the Battle of France and Dunkirk

Triumph and tragedy. Houghton Mifflin 1953 800p maps (Second World War, v6) pa $18 hardcover o.p. **940.53**
  1. World War, 1939-1945 2. World War, 1939-1945—Great Britain
  ISBN 0-395-41060-6 (pa)
The concluding volume of Churchill's history of World War II begins with D-Day and covers campaigns leading to the defeat of Germany and Japan

Clendinnen, Inga

Reading the Holocaust. Cambridge Univ. Press 1999 227p il map $69; pa $19.99 **940.53**
  1. Holocaust, 1933-1945—Historiography
  ISBN 0-521-64174-8; 0-521-01269-4 (pa)
  LC 98-53636
In this reexamination of the Holocaust Clendinnen "first considers the problematic nature of eyewitness accounts, then turns to an unflinching inquiry into the Nazi mentality and finally takes on the tough question of artistic representation. . . . This slim, powerful book forces a reader to re-examine almost all the assumptions we've accepted since the Holocaust occurred." N Y Times Book Rev

Includes bibliographical references

Cohen, Rich

The avengers. Knopf 2000 261p il pa $13 hardcover o.p. **940.53**
  1. Kovner, Abba, 1918-1987 2. Korczak-Marla, Rozka, 1921-1988 3. Kempner, Vitka 4. World War, 1939-1945—Underground movements 5. Holocaust, 1933-1945
  ISBN 0-375-70529-5 (pa) LC 00-21062
Cohen chronicles the resistance efforts of a small group of European Jews during the Second World War. Attention is focused primarily on the activities of three individuals: Rozka Korczak, Vitka Kempner, and Abba Kovner

"Cohen is a skilled writer. His language is spare and muscular, his descriptions evocative, his technique suspenseful." N Y Times Book Rev

Cooke, Alistair, 1908-2004

American home front, 1941-1942. Atlantic Monthly 2006 xx, 327p il $24 **940.53**

1. World War, 1939-1945—United States 2. United States—Social life and customs 3. United States—Social conditions 4. United States—Description and travel

ISBN 978-0-87113-939-9; 0-87113-939-1

LC 2005-58860

This book was written "during the early days of World War II. . . . Shortly after the bombing of Pearl Harbor in 1941, Cooke, a newly naturalized American citizen, set out to see his country." Publisher's note

"Crisscrossing the American continent from east to west and north to south, stopping in diners and bus stations and newly humming industrial plants, Mr. Cooke brings to life an America stepping into the unknown, committing its muscle and blood to an enterprise that most citizens could barely articulate, in places most of them had never heard of." N Y Times (Late N Y Ed)

Dallas, Gregor

1945; the war that never ended. Yale University Press 2005 xx, 739p il map $40; pa $22

940.53

1. World War, 1939-1945

ISBN 0-300-10980-6; 978-0-300-10980-1; 0-300-11988-7 (pa); 978-0-300-11988-6 (pa)

LC 2005-926051

"The book begins with the death of Adolf Hitler, followed by a history of WW II in Europe, omitting the struggle in Asia. The author argues that the movement of armies determined European life for the next two generations. . . . Dallas's history is not for beginners, but it will be a very important addition to every collection on WW II in Europe." Choice

Includes bibliographical references

Daniels, Roger

Prisoners without trial; Japanese Americans in World War II. Rev. ed. Hill and Wang 2004 162p il (Critical issue series) pa $12 **940.53**

1. Japanese Americans—Evacuation and relocation, 1942-1945 2. World War, 1939-1945—United States

ISBN 0-8090-7896-1 LC 2004-47328

First published 1993

An account of "the relocation of Japanese Americans during World War II, an injustice prompted not by military necessity but by political and racial motivations. The purpose of this volume is to tell the story in light of the redress legislation enacted in 1988." Libr J [review of 1993 edition]

Includes bibliographical references

Dawidowicz, Lucy S.

The war against the Jews, 1933-1945. 10th anniversary ed. Bantam Books 1986 xxxx, 466p il pa $19 **940.53**

1. Holocaust, 1933-1945 2. Jews—Europe

ISBN 978-0-553-34532-2; 0-553-34532-X

LC 85-48051

A reissue with new introduction and supplementary bibliography of the title first published 1975 by Holt, Rinehart & Winston

"One of the best histories of the mass murder of Jews in World War II. Argues for the centrality of anti-Semitism in Hitler's program." Reader's Adviser

Includes bibliographical references

Dwork, Deborah

Holocaust: a history; {by} Deborah Dwork, Robert Jan Van Pelt. Norton 2002 xx, 444p il $27.95; pa $15.95 * **940.53**

1. Holocaust, 1933-1945 2. Jews—Germany 3. Germany—Politics and government—1933-1945

ISBN 0-393-05188-9; 0-393-32524-5 (pa)

LC 2002-23565

"The authors examine such issues as the historic relationship between Jews, gentiles, and Germans; World War I and its consequences; National Socialism in the Weimar Republic; the Third Reich and its anti-Semitic measures; worldwide refugee policies that became a disaster for the Jews; and Jewish and gentile life under German occupation. They also examine the efforts by Allied nations to help the Jews. . . . This is a monumental work of impeccable scholarship." Booklist

Includes bibliographical references

Encyclopedia of Jewish life before and during the Holocaust; edited by Shmuel Spector and Geoffrey Wigoder. New York Univ. Press 2001 3v il maps set $99 **940.53**

1. Jews—Europe 2. Holocaust, 1933-1945—Encyclopedias

ISBN 0-8147-9356-8

"These three volumes are an abridgment of the multi-volume Encyclopedia of Jewish Communities published in Hebrew by Yad Vashem" Verso of title page

"Each entry provides vital information on the town's Jewish inhabitants on the eve of German occupation, gives the dates of Jewish roundups and mass executions and estimates how many Jews from that community survived the war." Publ Wkly

Encyclopedia of the Holocaust; Israel Gutman, editor in chief. complete and unabridged ed. Macmillan Lib. Ref. USA 1995 c1990 2v set $295 **940.53**

1. Holocaust, 1933-1945

ISBN 0-0286-4527-8

A reissue of the 1990 edition

"This set provides a wealth of information about a major event in the history of Western civilization. More than 1,000 entries treat countries, people, reflections in the arts and theology, sites of camps and massacres, and contemporary documentation centers." Ref Sources for Small & Medium-sized Libr. 6th edition

Encyclopedia of the Holocaust; Schmuel Spector, Robert Rozett, editors. Facts on File 2000 528p il $93.50 **940.53**

1. Holocaust, 1933-1945—Encyclopedias

ISBN 0-8160-4333-7 LC 00-30917

Following several introductory essays are "alphabetical entries on people, places, events, organizations, laws, and concepts. The language is clear, but more important is the authenticity of the information and the refusal to surrender to a simplification of issues. There are ample

Encyclopedia of the Holocaust—*Continued*
good-quality, black-and-white photographs, some unfamiliar, and also maps and tables. A detailed chronology and a thematic bibliography conclude the volume." SLJ
Includes bibliographical references

Encyclopedia of World War II; a political, social and military history; Spencer C. Tucker, editor, Priscilla Mary Roberts, editor volume 5. ABC-CLIO 2004 5v il map set $485 *
940.53
1. World War, 1939-1945—Encyclopedias
ISBN 1-576-07999-6   LC 2004-23745
"The 1,465 alphabetically arranged articles provide an international perspective on people; key battles, campaigns, and events; military equipment and strategy; countries; and other relevant topics. . . . Country entries not only cover the main Allied and Axis powers but also such countries as Afghanistan, Brazil, Estonia, Iraq, Mexico, New Zealand, and Somalia as well as world regions. . . . An excellent resource for high-school, public, and academic libraries." Booklist
Includes bibliographical references

Epstein, Eric Joseph, 1959-
Dictionary of the Holocaust; biography, geography, and terminology; [by] Eric Joseph Epstein and Philip Rosen; foreword by Henry R. Huttenbach. Greenwood Press 1997 416p $67.95
940.53
ISBN 0-313-30355-X   LC 97-8779
The nearly 2,000 alphabetically arranged entries cover people, places and events related to the Holocaust. "Among the personalities profiled here are Dietrich Bonhoeffer, Anne Frank, Primo Levi, Oskar Schindler, Harry S. Truman, and Elie Wiesel. Place entries include references to well-known locations, the number of prewar Jewish inhabitants, the date of liberation, and the number of Jews left after liberation. Entries dealing with concentration camps are generally the longest and identify camps by location, type, when opened and liberated, nationalities incarcerated, numbers murdered, other victimization, and camp commandants. Among the terms that are defined are many foreign expressions." Booklist

Evans, Richard J.
Lying about Hitler; history, Holocaust, and the David Irving trial; [by] Richard Evans. Basic Bks. 2001 318p hardcover o.p. pa $16.95
940.53
1. Irving, David John Cawdell, 1938- 2. Lipstadt, Deborah E. 3. Trials 4. Holocaust, 1933-1945—Historiography
ISBN 0-465-02152-2; 0-465-02153-0 (pa)
LC 00-140130
Evans writes of the unsuccessful libel suit brought by English historian "David Irving against Deborah Lipstadt. . . . In her book, 'Denying the Holocaust,' Lipstadt called Irving 'one of the most dangerous spokespersons for Holocaust denial.'" New Yorker
Evans's "superb [book], . . . is never less than absorbing. A sure-footed writer, he allows the story to tell itself, eschewing rhetorical flourishes in favor of a clini-

cal dissection of Irving's works and statements." Natl Rev
Includes bibliographical references

Friedländer, Saul, 1932-
Nazi Germany and the Jews. vl: The years of persecution, 1933-1939. HarperCollins Pubs. 1997 436p hardcover o.p. pa $19.95   **940.53**
1. Jews—Germany   2. Jews—Persecutions
3. Holocaust, 1933-1945 4. Germany—History—1933-1945
ISBN 0-06-019042-6; 0-06-092878-6 (pa)
LC 96-21915
This is the first of a projected two volume study, continued with The years of extermination: Nazi Germany and the Jews, 1939-1945 (2006)
The author examines "the segregation of the Jewish communities in both Germany and Austria in the period between 1933-1939. The author argues that Hitler was driven by a fanatical hatred of Jews, which he labeled 'redemptive anti-Semitism.' . . . Friedländer argues, however, that Hitler's fanaticism was not shared by most Germans, although antisemitism was endemic throughout Germany." Choice
"Not the least impressive aspect of Friedländer's book is the skill with which he juxtaposes different levels of reality within an overall chronological frame, moving from high-level Nazi debates on Jewish policy to the routine brutalities of the SA and SS, and from the perceptions of the average German citizen to those of the victims." N Y Rev Books
Includes bibliographical references

The years of extermination; Nazi Germany and the Jews, 1939-1945. HarperCollins Publishers 2007 xxvi, 870p $39.95   **940.53**
1. Jews—Germany   2. Jews—Persecutions
3. Holocaust, 1933-1945 4. Germany—History—1933-1945
ISBN 0-06-019043-4; 978-0-06-019043-9
LC 2006-48982
The second part of a two-part series starting with Nazi Germany and the Jews: vl: The years of persecution, 1933-1939 (1997)
"The book describes and interprets the persecution and murder of the Jews throughout occupied Europe." Publisher's note
"This is a masterful synthesis that draws on a lifetime of learning and research." Publ Wkly
Includes bibliographic references

Gies, Miep, 1909-
Anne Frank remembered; the story of the woman who helped to hide the Frank family; [by] Miep Gies with Alison Leslie Gold. Simon & Schuster 1987 252p il maps hardcover o.p. pa $14
940.53
1. Frank family 2. Netherlands—History—1940-1945, German occupation 3. Holocaust, 1933-1945
ISBN 0-671-54771-2; 0-671-66234-1 (pa)
LC 86-25991
"A memoir by the courageous Dutch woman who helped hide the Frank family, this book augments the

Gies, Miep, 1909-—*Continued*

Anne Frank story. Perceptive characterizations, with insight into life in Amsterdam during the Nazi occupation." SLJ

Gilbert, Martin, 1936-

Holocaust journey; traveling in search of the past. Columbia Univ. Press 1997 480p il $60; pa $20.95   **940.53**

1. Holocaust, 1933-1945 2. Concentration camps 3. Jews—Europe

ISBN 0-231-10964-4; 0-231-10965-2 (pa)

LC 97-15895

The author chronicles "a tour of Holocaust sites that he conducted with a dozen students and friends; the text of documents they studied at each stop is included. Gilbert not only describes their itinerary and the problems of conducting a tour but integrates the history of European Jewry into his narrative. He then details the specific events of the Holocaust associated with each location." Libr J

Includes bibliographical references

Kristallnacht; prelude to destruction. HarperCollins Publishers 2006 314p il map (Making history) $21.95   **940.53**

1. Jews—Persecutions 2. Germany—History—1933-1945

ISBN 0-06-057083-0; 978-0-06-057083-5

LC 2005-58169

This is "an account of the Night of Broken Glass, which was unleashed against the Jewish communities across Germany on November 10, 1938. . . . A powerful account of the helplessness of the Jews." Booklist

Includes bibliographical references

The Routledge atlas of the Holocaust. 3rd ed. Routledge 2002 282p il maps hardcover o.p. pa $19.95 *   **940.53**

1. Holocaust, 1933-1945

ISBN 0-415-28145-8; 0-415-28146-6 (pa)

First published 1982 in the United Kingdom with title: The Dent atlas of the Holocaust

New edition in preparation

The author "uses 317 maps, text, and photographs to document Hitler's attempt to destroy Europe's Jews. . . . Commentary offers statistical information, historical background, and something about the people of the area. Archival photographs bring the events to life. . . . This small but effective work demonstrates the magnitude of the Nazi terror by bringing it down to a personal level." Am Ref Books Annu, 2003

Includes bibliographical references

The Second World War; a complete history. Holt & Co. 1989 846p il maps pa $25 hardcover o.p.   **940.53**

1. World War, 1939-1945

ISBN 0-8050-1788-7 (pa)

LC 89-11129

The author begins this study "with the invasion of Poland. Gilbert's flowing narrative is spiced with anecdotal details culled from diaries, memoirs and official documents. He is especially skillful at interweaving summaries of military strategy with vignettes of civilian

suffering—the genocide of the Jews is never far from view." Newsweek

Includes bibliographical references

Glass, James M.

Life unworthy of life; racial phobia and mass murder in Hitler's Germany. Basic Bks. 1997 252p pa $23 hardcover o.p.   **940.53**

1. Holocaust, 1933-1945 2. Antisemitism 3. Eugenics

ISBN 0-465-09846-0 (pa)

LC 97-20118

The author's "thesis is that the Holocaust was possible because the German scientific community supported the genocidal actions against the Jews. {According to Glass}, the German public health profession {taught} . . . that Jews possessed innate criminal tendencies. . . . It also disseminated the belief that Jewish flesh and blood polluted the health of the German nation, its genes, and its culture." Choice

"Forcefully argued and well documented, this work is a must for any Holocaust collection." Booklist

Includes bibliographical references

Goldhagen, Daniel

Hitler's willing executioners; ordinary Germans and the Holocaust; {by} Daniel Jonah Goldhagen. Knopf 1996 622p il maps $35; pa $16

940.53

1. Holocaust, 1933-1945 2. Germany—History—1933-1945 3. Antisemitism 4. National socialism

ISBN 0-679-44695-8; 0-679-77268-5 (pa)

LC 95-38591

The author "endeavors to show that the common apologia for the Germans—that Hitler 'brainwashed' them—is nonsense and that most Germans gave their active assent to genocide. An ordinary German commander, for example, might feel himself bound by a strict code of conduct yet not be at all averse to murdering Jews. The book ends with a detailed notes section and an appendix that explains the correct methodology for studying the Nazi period." Libr J

A moral reckoning; the role of the Catholic Church in the Holocaust and its unfulfilled duty of repair; [by] Daniel Jonah Goldhagen. Knopf 2002 362p il hardcover o.p. pa $16   **940.53**

1. Pius XII, Pope, 1876-1958 2. Catholic Church—Relations—Judaism 3. Holocaust, 1933-1945 4. Antisemitism

ISBN 0-375-41434-7; 0-375-71417-0 (pa)

LC 2002-16264

The author "addresses a series of questions about the behavior of the Roman Catholic Church during the Holocaust." N Y Times (Late N Y Ed)

This is "a landmark work. . . . This volume is recommended for all libraries and essential for those supporting a Holocaust studies program." Libr J

Includes bibliographical references

Goldsmith, Martin
The inextinguishable symphony; a true story of
music and love in Nazi Germany. Wiley 2000
346p il hardcover o.p. pa $15.95   **940.53**
1. Goldsmith, George 2. Goldsmith, Rosemarie, 1917-
1984 3. Jews—Germany 4. Holocaust, 1933-1945
ISBN 0-471-35097-4; 0-471-07864-6 (pa)
LC 00-25955
The author "tells the story of his parents, musicians
who played in the orchestra of the Jewish Kulturbund,
which was established by the Nazis as a propaganda
tool." Libr J
Goldsmith's "weaving together of cultural and personal history constitutes a gripping tale of persecution, intrigue, and love and an insider's—or two insiders'—view
of a dark time." Booklist
Includes bibliographical references

Groom, Winston, 1944-
1942; the year that tried men's souls. Atlantic
Monthly Press 2005 459p il maps $27.50 *
940.53
1. World War, 1939-1945
ISBN 0-8711-3889-1   LC 2004-62779
In this military history of one year during World War
II, the author "delivers the traditional worshipful portrait
of General MacArthur while admitting he made several
key blunders that doomed the Philippines in the year's
early months. . . . He adds that brains and luck win
more battles than courage, providing a perfect illustration
in Midway, fought in June 1942. . . . Groom has written
a page-turner; readers needing an introduction will love
it." Publ Wkly
Includes bibliographical references

Guttenplan, D. D.
The Holocaust on trial. Norton 2001 328p il pa
$15.95 hardcover o.p.   **940.53**
1. Irving, David John Cawdell, 1938- 2. Lipstadt,
Deborah E. 3. Trials 4. Holocaust, 1933-1945—Historiography
ISBN 0-393-32292-0 (pa)   LC 2001-30370
The author chronicles the "libel trial in Britain brought
by historian David Irving. Irving, widely viewed as an
apologist for Hitler, sued American scholar Deborah
Lipstadt, whose *Denying the Holocaust* (1993) had labeled Irving as a right-wing extremist. . . . Interspersing
essayistic diversions, the author presents a thoughtful
work as well as a courtroom thriller." Booklist
Includes bibliographical references

Hoffman, Eva
After such knowledge; memory, history and the
legacy of the Holocaust. Public Affairs 2004 301p
$25; pa $14   **940.53**
1. Holocaust, 1933-1945
ISBN 1-586-48046-4; 0-586-48304-8 (pa)
LC 2003-66443
The author "focuses on the consciousness and experience of the Holocaust's second generation—the children
of survivors. . . . The book considers such diverse concepts as how the 'trauma' of the Holocaust is construct-

ed, the role of emigration and national identity in shap-
ing the second generation's narratives of their lives. . . .
Hoffman writes with a subdued but vibrant passion."
Publ Wkly
Includes bibliographical references

The **Holocaust** and history; the known, the
unknown, the disputed, and the reexamined;
edited by Michael Berenbaum and Abraham J.
Peck. Indiana Univ. Press 1998 836p $58.71; pa
$35   **940.53**
1. Holocaust, 1933-1945
ISBN 0-253-33374-1; 0-253-21529-3 (pa)
LC 97-40030
Published in association with the United States Holocaust Memorial Museum, Washington, D.C.
"Papers collected here originated at a 1993 conference
organized by the US Holocaust Memorial Museum's Research Institute. . . . The 50 contributors treat the subject
from every conceivable angle: the role of antisemitism
and racism; the politics of 'racial hygiene'; Nazi leadership and bureaucracy; the complicity of 'ordinary' people; the experiences of Gypsies, homosexuals, and
blacks; the concentration camps; the Holocaust as reflected in international relations; the response of Jews, rescuers, and survivors. Recognizing the passionately controversial nature of the field, the editors have opted for variety over unanimity." Choice

The **Holocaust** encyclopedia; Walter Laqueur,
editor; Judith Tydor Baumel, associate editor.
Yale Univ. Press 2001 xxxix, 765p il maps $60
940.53
1. Holocaust, 1933-1945—Encyclopedias
ISBN 0-300-08432-3   LC 00-106567
This "encyclopedia provides fresh and lengthy articles
on such topics as antisemitism, historiography, Jewish
women, memorials, and resistance, just to brush the surface." Choice
Includes bibliographical references

Huchthausen, Peter A., 1939-
Shadow voyage; the extraordinary wartime
escape of the legendary SS Bremen. Wiley 2005
260p il $24.95   **940.53**
1. World War, 1939-1945—Naval operations
ISBN 0-471-45758-2   LC 2004-14948
The author describes "the Bremen's extraordinary
flight to Germany, which became a life-and-death race
with British warships and submarines intent on intercept-
ing her." Publisher's note
"This book will interest not only World War II buffs
but also anyone drawn to tales of the sea." Libr J
Includes bibliographical references

Japanese Americans, from relocation to redress;
edited by Roger Daniels, Sandra C. Taylor,
Harry H.L. Kitano; contributions by Leonard J.
Arrington {et al.}. rev & updated ed. University
of Wash. Press 1991 xxi, 242p il pa $25
940.53
1. Japanese Americans—Evacuation and relocation,
1942-1945 2. World War, 1939-1945—Reparations
ISBN 0-295-97117-7   LC 91-2892
First published 1986 by University of Utah Press

Japanese Americans, from relocation to redress—*Continued*

A collection of essays on Japanese Americans focusing on their wartime relocation and their efforts to seek reparations.

Includes bibliographical references

Keegan, John, 1934-

The Second World War. Penguin Books 2005 608p il map pa $22   **940.53**

1. World War, 1939-1945

ISBN 0-14-303573-8; 978-0-14-303573-2

LC 2005-274899

First published 1989 in the United Kingdom

This military and stategic history contains sections covering the Eastern and Western fronts and the war in the Pacific.

"Keegan accompanies his narrative with a series of set battlepieces, of strategic analyses, and of 'themes of war'. . . . The book is beautifully ordered and . . . a pleasure to read." New Statesman Soc

Includes bibliographical references

Kruk, Herman, 1897-1944

The last days of the Jerusalem of Lithuania; chronicles from the Vilna ghetto and the camps, 1939-1944; edited and introduced by Benjamin Harshav; translated by Barbara Harshav. Yivo Inst. for Jewish Res. 2002 732p il maps $45

940.53

1. Jews—Lithuania 2. Holocaust, 1933-1945 3. World War, 1939-1945—Underground movements

ISBN 0-300-04494-1   LC 2002-16736

Published in collaboration with the YIVO Institute for Jewish Research; Translated from the Yiddish

This a collection of Kruk's journals and other writings from the Jewish ghetto of Vilna and a labor camp in Estonia

This "is a major addition to Holocaust literature and Jewish history. In 1961 a Yiddish edition of the Vilna diaries was published. This larger new edition has been painstakingly assembled from those diaries and other documents and writings by Kruk that were widely scattered and only found since the 1961 edition; Harshav has also added a wealth of new footnotes." Publ Wkly

Includes bibliographical references

Langer, Lawrence L.

Admitting the Holocaust; collected essays. Oxford Univ. Press 1995 202p pa $14.95 hardcover o.p.   **940.53**

1. Malamud, Bernard, 1914-1986 2. Appelfeld, Aron 3. Kafka, Franz, 1883-1924 4. Bellow, Saul, 1915-2005 5. Styron, William, 1925-2006 6. Holocaust, 1933-1945 7. Holocaust, 1933-1945, in literature

ISBN 0-19-510648-2 (pa)   LC 94-13368

In these essays Langer examines how "Western intellectuals and writers have sought to come to terms with the Holocaust. He argues that they have created, in their novels, stories, and films, a morally manageable version of the Holocaust rather than an unadorned yet honest view of mass murder without historical parallel." Libr J

"A horribly bleak, undeniably important book." Booklist

Includes bibliographical references

Levi, Primo, 1919-1987

The drowned and the saved; translated from the Italian by Raymond Rosenthal. Vintage International 1989 203p pa $12.95   **940.53**

1. Holocaust, 1933-1945—Personal narratives 2. Auschwitz (Poland: Concentration camp)

ISBN 0-679-72186-X; 978-0-679-72186-4

LC 88-40375

Original Italian edition, 1986

Auschwitz survivor Levi, an Italian Jewish chemist from Turin, wrote this final contemplation of the Holocaust before his suicide in 1987.

"If the unending tragedy of the Holocaust can ever be said to make sense, then it does so in these pages." New Yorker

Survival in Auschwitz; the Nazi assault on humanity; translated from the Italian by Stuart Woolf ; including "A conversation with Primo Levi by Philip Roth". Collier Books; Maxwell Macmillan Canada 1993 187p hardcover o.p. pa $13   **940.53**

1. World War, 1939-1945—Personal narratives 2. Holocaust, 1933-1945—Personal narratives 3. Auschwitz (Poland: Concentration camp)

ISBN 0-02-029192-2; 0-684-82680-1 (pa)

LC 86-13656

Originally published 1958 in Italy; first United States editon published 1959 by Orion Press with title: If this is a man

This volume tells of the Italian Jewish chemist's ten months as a concentration camp inmate

Lewy, Guenter, 1923-

The Nazi persecution of the gypsies. Oxford Univ. Press 2000 306p il hardcover o.p. pa $24.95
*   **940.53**

1. Gypsies 2. World War, 1939-1945—Atrocities 3. National socialism

ISBN 0-19-512556-8; 0-19-514240-3 (pa)

LC 98-52545

The author "begins with a brief history of the maltreatment of Gypsies all over Europe, from the fifteenth century onward; then, by dint of exhaustive research, Lewy documents the horrors of their expulsions, detentions, deportations, and deaths during the systematic madness of the Holocaust." Booklist

Includes bibliographical references

Life: World War 2; history's greatest conflict in pictures; edited by Richard B. Stolley. Little, Brown 2001 351p il hardcover o.p. pa $29.95

940.53

1. World War, 1939-1945—Pictorial works 2. World history—20th century—Pictorial works

ISBN 0-8212-2771-8; 0-8212-5713-7 (pa)

LC 2001-93633

"A Bulfinch Press book"

Life: World War 2—*Continued*

This "album of 665 photographs taken from the archives of *Life* magazine and other collections begins with the years 1919 to 1939, the two decades leading up to World War II. Editor Stolley then proceeds to chronicle the war, year by year through 1945, and ends with what he calls 'the war's aftermath,' 1946 to 2001. . . . For World War II buffs, the book is a natural treasure." Booklist

Lifton, Robert Jay, 1926-

The Nazi doctors; medical killing and the psychology of genocide. Basic Bks. 1986 561p pa $23 hardcover o.p. **940.53**
1. Holocaust, 1933-1945 2. World War, 1939-1945—Atrocities 3. Concentration camps
ISBN 0-465-04905-2 (pa)   LC 85-73874
"How could German physicians trained as scientist-healers carry out Nazi orders for mass killings? . . . Lifton, an American Jewish physician, seeks answers through interviews with surviving doctors, family members, and victims and by painstakingly gleaning Holocaust archives." Sci Books Films
Includes bibliographical references

Lipstadt, Deborah E.

Denying the Holocaust; the growing assault on truth and memory; with a new preface by the author. Plume 1994 278p pa $16   **940.53**
1.   Holocaust,   1933-1945—Historiography
2. Antisemitism
ISBN 0-452-27274-2; 978-0-452-27274-3
                                            LC 93-45586
First published 1993 by Free Press
This is an "account of the antecedents, origins, and development of the . . . movement to deny that the [Nazi] destruction of European Jewry ever took place at all." Commentary
"Lipstadt has written a disturbing book that deserves a wide readership." Libr J
Includes bibliographical references

History on trial; my day in court with David Irving. Ecco 2005 xxi, 346p il $25.95; pa $14.95
*   **940.53**
1. Irving, David John Cawdell, 1938- 2. Holocaust, 1933-1945—Historiography 3. Trials
ISBN 0-06-059376-8; 0-06-059377-6 (pa)
                                            LC 2004-57533
"One of the first attempts to systematically address Holocaust denial, Lipstadt's 1993 book Denying the Holocaust grabbed headlines when she was sued for libel by David Irving for calling the deeply controversial Hitler biographer a Holocaust denier and right-wing extremist. Lipstadt here narrates her lengthy legal battle with Irving." Booklist
"No one who cares about historical truth, freedom of speech or the Holocaust will avoid a sense of triumph from Gray's decision—or a sense of dismay that British libel laws allowed such intimidation by Irving of a historian and a publisher in the first place." Publ Wkly
Includes bibliographical references

Lukacs, John, 1924-

Five days in London, May 1940. Yale Univ. Press 1999 236p $19.95; pa $11.95
                                            940.53
1. Halifax, Edward Frederick Lindley Wood, 1st Earl of, 1881-1959 2. Churchill, Sir Winston, 1874-1965 3. World War, 1939-1945—Diplomatic history 4. World War, 1939-1945—Great Britain 5. Great Britain—Politics and government—20th century
ISBN 0-300-08030-1; 0-300-08466-8 (pa)
                                            LC 99-27583
This work focuses on the "chaotic few days during which, according to the author, Hitler came closest to winning the war. . . . Lukacs concentrates on the struggle within the British War Cabinet, which pitted the Prime Minister, Winston Churchill, against the Foreign Secretary, Lord Halifax, a Tory idol and a friend of the King. The point of contention was Halifax's belief that England should attempt to negotiate a general European settlement with Hitler. Churchill's stubborn refusal won out. The author's equally stubborn digging uncovered a stunning amount of defeatism and intrigue against Churchill by contemporary statesmen." New Yorker
Includes bibliographical references

Mortimer, Gavin

The longest night; the bombing of London on May 10, 1941. Berkley Caliber 2005 356p il $24.95   **940.53**
1. World War, 1939-1945—Great Britain 2. World War, 1939-1945—Aerial operations
ISBN 0-425-20557-6   LC 2005-45281
This is an "account of the deadliest night of the 1940–1941 London Blitz." Publ Wkly
"This account is given special power and poignancy by using the recollections of surviving men and women who endured that terrible night. An outstanding addition to World War II collections." Booklist

Ng, Wendy L.

Japanese American internment during World War II; a history and reference guide; [by] Wendy Ng. Greenwood Press 2002 xxvi, 204p $45
                                            940.53
1. Japanese Americans—Evacuation and relocation, 1942-1945
ISBN 0-313-31375-X   LC 00-69128
Contents: Chronology of events in Japanese American history: The Japanese in America before World War II; Evacuation; Life within barbed wire; The question of loyalty: Japanese Americans in the military and draft resisters; Legal challenges to the evacuation and internment; After the war: Resettlement and redress; Photographic essay
"The combination of historical facts as presented in the essays and the ideas and sentiments expressed in the primary documents gives readers a vivid sense of this period in history. This readable book would be a solid addition to high school, public, and academic libraries." Voice Youth Advocates
Includes bibliographical references

Nicholas, Lynn H.
Cruel world; the children of Europe in the Nazi web. A.A. Knopf 2005 632p il maps $35; pa $17.95 * **940.53**
1. World War, 1939-1945—Children 2. Children and war 3. Holocaust, 1933-1945
ISBN 0-679-45464-0; 0-679-77663-X (pa)
LC 2004-57745
This is an account of the lives of children in Europe during the Holocaust and World War II.
The author "has put together a well-written, compelling history that makes us look at the war era anew." Publ Wkly
Includes bibliographical references

Overy, R. J. (Richard James), 1947-
Why the Allies won; {by} Richard Overy. Norton 1996 396p il maps pa $17.95 hardcover o.p. **940.53**
1. World War, 1939-1945 2. Strategy
ISBN 0-393-31619-X (pa) LC 95-52444
"Eschewing the belief that the Allies won solely because of their prodigious production of weapons and equipment, Mr. Overy points out that in the early stages of the war, before the Allies were fully mobilized, the Axis countries held the production advantage, yet failed to achieve victory because Germany's management of supply logistics was far inferior to that of the Allies—frequently as a result of Hitler's wrongheaded interference. . . . Assiduously researched and concisely written, this is a highly perceptive study." N Y Times Book Rev
Includes bibliographical references

The **Oxford** companion to World War II; general editor, I.C.B. Dear; consultant editor, M.R.D. Foot. New ed. Oxford University Press 2005 1072p il map $75 **940.53**
1. World War, 1939-1945—Encyclopedias
ISBN 0-19-280670-X; 978-0-19-280670-3
First published 1995
Entries in this companion include "surveys of the countries involved in the conflict; politics and strategy; domestic and economic issues; resistance and intelligence; campaigns and battles; warfare and weapons; wartime leaders and influential people; [and] slogans and slang." Publisher's note
Includes bibliographical references

Rees, Laurence, 1957-
Auschwitz: a new history; Laurence Rees. Public Affairs 2005 xxii, 327p il $30; pa $16 **940.53**
1. Auschwitz (Poland: Concentration camp) 2. Holocaust, 1933-1945
ISBN 1-586-48303-X; 1-586-48357-9 (pa)
LC 2004-43196
For this history of the concentration camp, the author "interviewed 100 former Nazi perpetrators and survivors from the camp and drew on hundreds of interviews conducted for his previous research on the Third Reich, many with former members of the Nazi Party. . . . This is a significant contribution to our understanding of the intricacies of Nazi racial and ethnic policy that resulted in this ultimate abomination." Booklist
Includes bibliographical references

Reporting World War II. Library of Am. 1995 2v ea $35 **940.53**
1. World War, 1939-1945 2. Reporters and reporting
ISBN 1-883011-04-3 (v1); 1-883011-05-1 (v2)
LC 94-45463
Contents: v1 American journalism, 1938-1944; v2 American journalism, 1944-1946
This "collection of some 200 entries by nearly 90 writers, drawn from newspapers, magazine articles, broadcast transcripts and book excerpts, recalls WW II campaigns and battles in all theaters but pays attention to the home front as well. It begins with an excerpt from William L. Shirer's *Berlin Diary* and ends with one from John Hersey's *Hiroshima*. . . . This is a treasure trove of war reporting, featuring writing of the highest order." Publ Wkly

Reynolds, David, 1952-
In command of history; Churchill fighting and writing the Second World War; by David Reynolds. Random House 2005 xxiv, 631p il $35 **940.53**
1. Churchill, Sir Winston, 1874-1965 2. World War, 1939-1945—Historiography
ISBN 0-679-45743-7 LC 2004-51087
The author subjects "Winston Churchill's monumental six-volume work The Second World War (1948-53) to historical scrutiny." Booklist
"Packed with detail and vivid characterizations . . . [this book is] a different take on one of the few men capable of both making history and writing it." Publ Wkly
Includes bibliographical references

Rosenfeld, Oskar, 1884-1944
In the beginning was the ghetto; 890 days in Łódz; edited and with an introduction by Hanno Loewy; translated from the German by Brigitte M. Goldstein. Northwestern Univ. Press 2002 xxxviii, 313p $40 **940.53**
1. Jews—Poland 2. Holocaust, 1933-1945—Personal narratives 3. Łódz (Poland)
ISBN 0-8101-1488-7 LC 2001-6691
Original German edition, 1994
These entries from Rosenfeld's diary "contain vivid descriptions of daily life in the ghetto, including details about deportations, forced labor, hunger, diseases, cold, terror, and the struggle to maintain human dignity. . . . This book is one of the most important and lasting works documenting the horrors of the Holocaust." Booklist
Includes bibliographical references

Smith, Lyn, 1934-
Remembering, voices of the holocaust; a new history in the words of the men and women who survived; [foreword by Laurence Rees] Carroll & Graf 2006 351p il map $27 **940.53**
1. Holocaust, 1933-1945—Personal narratives
ISBN 0-7867-1640-1 LC 2006-284769
First published 2005 in the United Kingdom
The author, "who has recorded the experiences of survivors for London's Imperial War Museum, weaves together more than 100 accounts to construct a narrative of

Smith, Lyn, 1934---_Continued_
Nazi persecutions from the first anti-Semitic measures in 1933 through the liberation of the concentration camps. . . . This is an extraordinary work of scholarship and a reminder of the power of individual stories, which can bring home the horrors of WWII more forcefully than abstract numbers." Publ Wkly
Includes bibliographical references

Spiegelman, Art
Maus; a survivor's tale. Pantheon Bks. 1996 2v in 1 il $35   **940.53**
1. Spiegelman, Vladek—Graphic novels 2. Holocaust, 1933-1945—Graphic novels 3. Graphic novels 4. Biographical graphic novels
ISBN 0-679-40641-7   LC 96-32796
Also available CD-ROM version,The complete Maus; available paperback boxed set edition $28 (ISBN 0-679-74840-7)
A combined edition of Maus (1986) and Maus II (1991)
Contents: My father bleeds history; And here my troubles began
In this work "Spiegelman takes the comic book to a new level of seriousness, portraying Jews as mice and Nazis as cats. Depicting himself being told about the Holocaust by his Polish survivor father, Spiegelman not only explores the concentration-camp experience, but also the guilt, love, and anger between father and son." Rochman. Against borders

Stargardt, Nicholas
Witnesses of war; children's lives under the Nazis. Distributed by Random House 2006 493p il map $30; pa $16.95   **940.53**
1. World War, 1939-1945—Children
ISBN 1-4000-4088-4; 978-1-4000-4088-9; 1-4000-3379-9 (pa); 978-1-4000-3379-9 (pa)
LC 2005-50409
First published 2005 in the United Kingdom
The author "divides this work into chapters following the rise, escalation, and defeat of Nazism, concentrating on how children (Jews, patients at mental hospitals, inmates in juvenile homes, 'regular' Germans, and conquered nationalities) coped with this existence." Libr J
This is "a sharp and taut account of misery." Publ Wkly
Includes bibliographical references

Takaki, Ronald T., 1939-
Double victory; a multicultural history of America in World War II; [by] Ronald Takaki. Little, Brown 2000 282p il $28; pa $19.99
940.53
1. World War, 1939-1945—United States 2. United States—Race relations
ISBN 0-316-83155-7; 0-316-83156-5 (pa)
LC 99-40374
"Takaki discusses the experiences of African Americans, Indians, Chicanos, Asian Americans from several nations, German and Italian Americans, and Jewish Americans. . . . Despite Jim Crow, internment camps, neglected slums, barrios, reservations, and rejection of

Jewish refugees, the nation's not-quite-Americans fought bravely in World War II." Booklist
Includes bibliographical references

Weinberg, Gerhard L.
A world at arms; a global history of World War II. 2nd ed. Cambridge University Press 2005 xxix, 1178p map $65; pa $25.99 *   **940.53**
1. World War, 1939-1945
ISBN 0-521-85316-8; 978-0-521-85316-3; 0-521-61826-6 (pa); 978-0-521-61826-7 (pa)
LC 2005-41954
First published 1994
"Beginning with the German invasion of Poland and concluding with the Japanese surrender, this . . . overview of WW II concentrates on the tactical decisions made by Allied and Axis leaders and the interrelationship among the various theaters." Publ Wkly [review of 1994 edition]
"Weinberg's unrivaled command of archival sources combine with a smooth writing style to produce a definitive one-volume history of World War II." Libr J [review of 1994 edition]
Includes bibliographical references

Weyr, Thomas
The setting of the pearl; Vienna under Hitler; by Thomas Weyr. Oxford University Press 2005 352p il map $30   **940.53**
1. Vienna (Austria) 2. World War, 1939-1945—Austria
ISBN 0-19-514679-4   LC 2004-18295
In this "chronicle of the destruction of the city's cultural and political life, [the author] shows that most Austrians happily accepted the 1938 union with Germany and the benefits of the pillaging of Europe in the war's first years. . . . For Weyr, Nazi domination led to the destruction of the glittering culture of Vienna, the city of Freud, Klimt, Loos and so many other intellectual and artistic luminaries." Publ Wkly
"This is a superbly written work and an excellent addition to World War II collections." Booklist
Includes bibliographical references

Witness; voices from the Holocaust; edited by Joshua M. Greene and Shiva Kumar in consultation with Joanne Weiner Rudof; foreword by Lawrence L. Langer; in association with the Fortunoff Video Archive for Holocaust Testimonies, Yale University. Free Press 2000 xxx, 270p il $26; pa $15   **940.53**
1. Holocaust, 1933-1945—Personal narratives
ISBN 0-684-86525-4; 0-684-86526-2 (pa)
LC 99-58401
In this companion to the PBS series the editors "have woven together the testimonies of 27 individuals into an unforgettable narrative of the Holocaust: starting with pre-WWII Jewish life, they go on to describe the war's out-break, ghettos, resistance and hiding, death camps, death marches, liberation and life after the Holocaust." Publ Wkly
Includes bibliographical references

A **woman** in Berlin; eight weeks in the conquered city: a diary; by Anonymous; translated by Philip Boehm. Metropolitan Books/Henry Holt 2005 261p $23   **940.53**
1. Berlin, Battle of, 1945 2. World War, 1939-1945—Personal narratives 3. World War, 1939-1945—Women
ISBN 0-8050-7540-2   LC 2005-41984
Original German edition, 2003; Expurgated edition translated by James Stern published 1954 by Harcourt, Brace

"The author of this diary was a 34-year-old journalist, now deceased, who consistently refused to reveal her identity publicly. . . . [This] account covers the period from late April to mid-June 1945, beginning with the massive Soviet bombardment of Berlin and ending with the opening weeks of the Soviet occupation." Booklist

This "is one of the most important documents to emerge from World War II." N Y Times Book Rev

The **World** reacts to the Holocaust; David S. Wyman, editor; Charles H. Rosenzveig, project director. Johns Hopkins Univ. Press 1996 xxiii, 981p $80 *   **940.53**
1. Holocaust, 1933-1945
ISBN 0-8018-4969-1   LC 96-15395
This is a "country-by-country chronicle of the impact of the Holocaust on world history. Covering 22 countries and the United Nations, the volume carefully traces the contentions and controversies involved in coming to terms with the events leading up to the Holocaust, from prewar attitudes and perceptions to the political, economic, and cultural legacies in the 1990s." Univ Press Books for Public and Second Sch Libr

Includes bibliographical references

World War II; an encyclopedia of quotations; compiled and edited by Howard J. Langer. Greenwood Press 1999 449p il $83.95
                    940.53
1. Quotations
ISBN 0-313-30018-6   LC 98-26436
This is a collection of 1,554 "quotations dealing with World War II. . . . The first 12 chapters are arranged by type of person quoted . . . and then alphabetically by name. A typical entry has a short introductory paragraph providing biographical and historical information including birth and death years of persons. The remaining chapters cover other sources, including movies and songs." Booklist

World War II; Douglas Brinkley, general editor ; edited and with chapter introductions by David Rubel. Times Books 2003-2004 2v il (New York Times living history) $30 ea
                    940.53
1. World War, 1939-1945
ISBN 0-8050-7246-2 (v1); 0-8050-7247-0 (v2)
                    LC 2003-59658
"The diaries, documents, speeches, and newspaper reports that defined World War II." On cover
Contents: v1 The Axis assault, 1939-1942 ; v2 The Allied counteroffensive, 1942-1945

Yellin, Emily, 1961-
Our mothers' war; American women at home and at the Front during World War II. Free Press 2004 447p il hardcover o.p. pa $14
                    940.53
1. World War, 1939-1945—Women
ISBN 0-7432-4514-8; 0-7432-4516-4 (pa)
                    LC 2004-40496
"Yellin reveals all of the responsibilities held by women, including helping to manufacture aircraft, ships, and other munitions; and, in the process, outproducing all of America's allies and enemies, by far. Readers see war brides who worked hard to maintain the morale of their husbands while surviving long separation, fear, and shortages of virtually everything necessary to support a family. . . . [This book] is an important book because the role played by women in World War II has been regularly ignored." SLJ
Includes bibliographical references

Zuccotti, Susan, 1940-
Under his very windows; the Vatican and the Holocaust in Italy. Yale Univ. Press 2000 408p il $29.95; pa $16.95   **940.53**
1. Pius XII, Pope, 1876-1958 2. Jews—Italy 3. Holocaust, 1933-1945 4. Catholic Church—Relations—Judaism
ISBN 0-300-08487-0; 0-300-09310-1 (pa)
                    LC 00-43307
Zuccotti's "aim is to show that whatever help was given to the Jews by the Catholic Church during the war resulted almost entirely from spontaneous acts by courageous individuals—priests, monks and nuns, and occasionally prelates—and not from any interventions by the Vatican. . . . Zuccotti makes her case strongly. . . . This is a serious and well-researched book." N Y Times Book Rev
Includes bibliographical references

940.54   Military history of World War II

Alperovitz, Gar
The decision to use the atomic bomb and the architecture of an American myth; {by} Gar Alperovitz with the assistance of Sanho Tree {et al.}. Knopf 1995 843p pa $18 hardcover o.p.
                    940.54
1. World War, 1939-1945—United States 2. Hiroshima (Japan)—Bombardment, 1945 3. United States—Foreign relations
ISBN 0-679-76285-X (pa)   LC 95-8778
"Alperovitz is the dean of revisionist scholars who argue that the nuclear bombing of Japan was unnecessary and that America bears a hefty responsibility for the cold war. . . . His main and probably most controversial contention is that certain documents pertaining to the decision were doctored, some by none other than Truman himself. Further, Alperovitz sees James Byrnes, Truman's Mephistophelian secretary of state, as a furtive player who nixed such alternative plans as modifying the unconditional-surrender demand and encouraging a Russian declaration of war." Booklist
Includes bibliographical references

Ambrose, Stephen E.

Band of brothers; E Company, 506th Regiment, 101st Airborne from Normandy to Hitler's Eagle's Nest; [by] Stephen Ambrose. Simon & Schuster 2001 333p il maps $25; pa $16 *

940.54

1. United States. Army. Parachute Infantry Regiment, 506th. Company E 2. World War, 1939-1945—Europe
ISBN 0-7432-1638-5; 0-7432-2454-X (pa)

LC 2001-20134

A reissue of the title first published 1992

"Here is the story of the daring E Company, which began the war by parachuting into France on D-Day and ended it by capturing Eagle's Nest, Hitler's outpost in Bavaria." Libr J

"Moving, poignant, and uplifting, this book is highly recommended for medium and large World War II collections." Booklist

Includes bibliographical references

Citizen soldiers; the U.S. Army from the Normandy beaches to the Bulge to the surrender of Germany, June 7, 1944-May 7, 1945. Simon & Schuster 1997 512p il maps pa $17 hardcover o.p.

940.54

1. World War, 1939-1945—Campaigns—France
ISBN 0-684-84801-5 (pa)   LC 97-23876

This continuation of D-Day focuses on the front-line experiences of American soldiers who fought in northwestern Europe in the war's last years

"These events have all been well documented, but in Ambrose's capable hands, the bloody and dramatic battles fought in northwest Europe in 1944-45 come alive as never before." N Y Times Book Rev

Includes bibliographical references

D-Day, June 6, 1944; the climactic battle of World War II. Simon & Schuster 1994 655p il maps $30; pa $17   **940.54**

1. World War, 1939-1945—Campaigns—France
2. Normandy (France), Attack on, 1944
ISBN 0-671-88403-4; 0-684-80137-X (pa)

LC 93-40353

This is an account of the Allied invasion of Normandy in 1944. The author argues "that the invasion represented a triumph of the old United States Army, whose officers had transformed millions of civilians into a cohesive, highly trained and motivated mass army that, backed by a united nation, won with relative ease." Christ Sci Monit

"Mr. Ambrose wonderfully illuminates the mind of the very young soldier of any nation anywhere who has never been in fighting before." N Y Times Book Rev

Includes bibliographical references

The victors; Eisenhower and his boys, the men of World War II. Simon & Schuster 1998 396p pa $16 hardcover o.p.   **940.54**

1. Eisenhower, Dwight D. (Dwight David), 1890-1969
2. United States. Army 3. World War, 1939-1945—Campaigns
ISBN 0-684-85629-8 (pa)   LC 98-37808

This work "follows the World War II Allied campaign in Europe from the appointment of Gen. Dwight D. Eisenhower as commander of the European Theater of Op-

erations to the final surrender of Germany, seven days after Hitler's suicide." N Y Times Book Rev

"The author is a master of letting his subjects tell the story, of standing back and allowing the large lessons to unfold. The result is history with lasting impact." SLJ

Includes bibliographical references

The wild blue; the men and boys who flew the B-24s over Germany 1944-45. Simon & Schuster 2001 299p il $26; pa $16   **940.54**

1. McGovern, George S. (George Stanley), 1922-
2. B-24 bomber 3. Air pilots 4. World War, 1939-1945—Aerial operations
ISBN 0-7432-0339-9; 0-7432-2309-8 (pa)

LC 2001-20563

Ambrose presents profiles of American pilots who flew B-24 bombers focusing on the Dakota Queen piloted by future senator and presidential candidate George McGovern

"Ambrose's narrative flows smoothly, even as he manages to cover each man's story." Libr J

Includes bibliographical references

Atkinson, Rick

An army at dawn; the war in North Africa, 1942-1943. Holt & Co. 2002 681p il maps (The liberation trilogy) $30; pa $16 *   **940.54**

1. World War, 1939-1945—Campaigns—North Africa
2. World War, 1939-1945—North Africa
ISBN 0-8050-6288-2; 0-8050-7448-1 (pa)

LC 2002-24130

This is the first volume of a projected World War II trilogy.

This "volume covers the conception of Operation Torch through the German surrender in Tunisia in May 1943. . . . An exemplary work that feeds anticipation of the succeeding volumes." Booklist

Includes bibliographical references

Followed by The day of battle (2007)

The day of battle; the war in Sicily and Italy, 1943-1944. H. Holt 791p il map (The liberation trilogy) $35 *   **940.54**

1. World War, 1939-1945—Campaigns—Italy
ISBN 978-0-8050-6289-2; 0-805-06289-0

LC 2007-7653

"The second volume of . . . [the author's] 'Liberation' trilogy, which began with the Pulitzer Prizewinning An Army at Dawn: The War in North Africa, 1942–1943, this is probably the most eagerly awaited World War II book of the year. Atkinson's clear prose, perceptive analysis, and grasp of the personalities and nuances of the campaigns make his book an essential purchase." Libr J

Includes bibliographical references

Ballard, Robert D., 1942-

Return to Midway; {by} Robert D. Ballard and Rick Archbold; principal photography by David Doubilet. . . . National Geographic Soc. 1999 191p il maps $40   **940.54**

1. Midway, Battle of, 1942 2. Shipwrecks 3. World War, 1939-1945—Naval operations
ISBN 0-7922-7500-4   LC 99-10831

Ballard, Robert D., 1942--*Continued*

In this narrative, Ballard "intersperses chapters on the Battle of Midway with a fascinating account of his search for the U.S.S. *Yorktown*, which was sunk by a Japanese destroyer on June 7, 1942. Period photographs from the battle are combined with those of the *Yorktown* as she rests today, and paintings by marine artist Ken Marschall add detail to complete the record. The lively narrative is punctuated with two Japanese and two American oral history accounts of the battle." Libr J

Includes bibliographical references

Bayly, C. A. (Christopher Alan)

Forgotten armies; the fall of British Asia, 1941-1945; [by] Christopher Bayly and Tim Harper. Belknap Press of Harvard University Press 2005 xxxiii, 555p il maps $29.95; pa $18.95
                940.54

1. World War, 1939-1945—Asia 2. Great Britain—Colonies—Asia

ISBN 0-674-01748-X; 0-674-02219-X (pa)

                LC 2004-54300

This is an account of "the birth of modern south and southeast Asia and the death of British rule." Publisher's note

This "study is by far the most comprehensive to date, an excellent survey for those interested in both WW II and the denouement of British imperialism in Asia." Choice

Includes bibliographical references

Beevor, Antony, 1946-

The fall of Berlin 1945. Viking 2002 xxxvii, 489p il maps $29.95; pa $16   **940.54**

1. Berlin, Battle of, 1945 2. World War, 1939-1945—Germany

ISBN 0-670-03041-4; 0-14-200280-1 (pa)

                LC 2002-510674

Engl. title: Berlin; the downfall, 1945

This narrative covers "the months from January to May in 1945, as Soviet and other Allied troops advanced to Berlin." Publ Wkly

The author "relies on material from American, German, British, French, and Swedish archives and documents from former Soviet files, making the book an invaluable and meticulous account." Booklist

Includes bibliographical references (p. 466-475) and index

Blair, Clay, 1925-1998

Hitler's U-boat war; the hunted, 1942–1945. Random House 1998 2v xxviii, 909p il map pa $19.95 hardcover o.p.   **940.54**

1. World War, 1939-1945—Naval operations—Submarine 2. World War, 1939-1945—Atlantic Ocean

ISBN 0-6794-5742-9   LC 96-2275

This is a history of the German submarine campaign against Allied forces during the Second World War

This is "the most thorough study of the U-Boat campaign available; it includes a massive amount of detailed statistics." Libr J {review of volume 1}

Includes bibliographical references

Bradley, James

Flags of our fathers; [by] James Bradley with Ron Powers. Bantam Bks. 2000 376p $24.95; pa $14   **940.54**

1. Rosenthal, Joe, 1911-2006 2. United States. Marine Corps 3. Iwo Jima, Battle of, 1945

ISBN 0-553-11133-7; 0-553-38415-5 (pa)

                LC 00-25803

This is the "story of the most famous photograph to come out of World War II, the flag-raising on Mount Suribachi during the Battle of Iwo Jima in February 1945. Bradley is the son of one of the six men immortalized in that remarkable photo, and his gripping narrative, vivid descriptions, and heartfelt style make this a powerful story of courage, humility, and tragedy." Libr J

Includes bibliographical references

Breitman, Richard, 1947-

Official secrets; what the Nazis planned, what the British and Americans knew. Hill & Wang 1998 325p hardcover o.p. pa $22   **940.54**

1. World War, 1939-1945—Atrocities 2. Holocaust, 1933-1945 3. Germany—Politics and government—1933-1945

ISBN 0-8090-3819-6; 0-8090-0184-5 (pa)

                LC 98-7997

Breitman sheds new light on "evidence that Britain's top intelligence analysts knew, as early as September 1941, that the Germans were systematically carrying out mass murder of Jews in Nazi-occupied Soviet territories and planning their liquidation in the lands they conquered." Publ Wkly

This "is a remarkable study, concise yet carefully nuanced." N Y Times Book Rev

Includes bibliographical references

Brokaw, Tom, 1940-

An album of memories; personal histories from the greatest generation. Random House 2001 314p il maps $29.95; pa $14.95   **940.54**

1. World War, 1939-1945—Personal narratives

ISBN 0-375-50581-4; 0-375-76041-5 (pa)

                LC 2001-273436

This volume "gathers letters written to Brokaw by Americans who lived through the Depression and World War II and, in some cases, letters written by their children. Brokaw provides a brief introduction and a time line for each chapter; these cover the Depression, the war in Europe and in the Pacific, and the wartime 'home front,' closing with 'Reflections.' The book is lavishly illustrated with reproductions of photographs, drawings, documents, and other memorabilia of the era." Booklist

The greatest generation. Random House 1998 412p il $24.95; pa $13.95   **940.54**

1. World War, 1939-1945—Personal narratives

ISBN 0-375-50202-5; 0-385-33462-1 (pa)

                LC 98-44267

Brokaw presents profiles of some fifty men and women who came of age during the Depression and World War II, focusing particularly on their experiences of the war.

"If not the greatest, all Brokaw's heroes—tall and

Brokaw, Tom, 1940———*Continued*
short, famous and obscure—are part of the great generation that turned the old Chinese curse 'May you live in
interesting times' into a blessing." Time

Costello, John, 1943-1995
The Pacific War. Quill 1982 742p il $21.95
940.54
1. World War, 1939-1945—Pacific Ocean
ISBN 0-688-01620-0; 978-0-688-01620-3
LC 82-15054
First published 1981 by Rawson, Wade
A "history of World War II as it was played out in
the Pacific theater. . . . Emphasizing the role played by
Allied intelligence sources during the early period of the
war, Costello analyzes the actual battles from Pearl Har-
bor to the atomic bombing of Japan." Booklist
Includes bibliographical references

Daws, Gavan
Prisoners of the Japanese; POWs of World War
II in the Pacific. Morrow 1994 462p il map
hardcover o.p. pa $19.95 * **940.54**
1. World War, 1939-1945—Prisoners and prisons
2. Prisoners of war 3. World War, 1939-1945—Pacific
Ocean
ISBN 0-688-11812-7; 0-688-14370-9 (pa)
LC 93-49363
This is an "account of the treatment that more than
140,000 American, Australian, British and Dutch prison-
ers of war . . . [received] at the hands of the Japanese
in World War II." N Y Times Book Rev
"Daws offers a well-written thoroughly researched account of these POWs. . . . An exceptionally worthwhile
addition to the literature on the war in the Pacific."
Booklist
Includes bibliographical references

Dunnigan, James F.
The Pacific War encyclopedia; {by} James F.
Dunnigan and Albert A. Nofi. Facts on File 1998
2v il maps set $137.50 **940.54**
1. World War, 1939-1945—Encyclopedias
ISBN 0-8160-3439-7 LC 97-15634
"Entries are arranged alphabetically and include . . .
(military personnel and politicos from all sides, as well
as persons such as Charles Lindbergh and Ernie Pyle),
places (Manchukuo, Melbourne, Nagasaki, Timor, etc.)
and events (Battle of Iwo Jima, Port Chicago mutiny)."
Booklist
This work "is lively as well as informative, and . . .
will be attractive to military buffs while still useful to
more serious researchers." Libr J

Frank, Richard B.
Downfall; the end of the Imperial Japanese
Empire. Penguin 2001 484p il map pa $18 *
940.54
1. World War, 1939-1945—Japan 2. World War,
1939-1945—Aerial operations 3. Japan—History—
1868-1945
ISBN 0-14-100146-1
First published 1999 by Random House

"Weaving together the strands of military and diplomatic events, Frank contends that absent the bombings of
Hiroshima and Nagasaki the war would have continued
for at least several more months, at a cost in Japanese
and Allied civilian and combatant lives far in excess of
the admittedly awful toll that the atomic bombs exacted.
A powerful work of history." Libr J
Includes bibliographical references

Fussell, Paul, 1924-
Wartime: understanding and behavior in the
Second World War. Oxford Univ. Press 1989 330p
il $35; pa $16.95 **940.54**
1. World War, 1939-1945—United States 2. World
War, 1939-1945—Great Britain 3. World War, 1939-
1945—Propaganda
ISBN 0-19-503797-9; 0-19-506577-8 (pa)
LC 89-2875
In this book Fussell "seeks to evoke the psychological
and emotional culture of Americans and Britons during
the Second World War." Newsweek
"Fussell's version of the war doesn't, perhaps, exactly
'balance the scales,' but it is a useful corrective. Nobody
who reads it will come away thinking about the war
complacently." New Repub
Includes bibliographical references

The **good** war; an oral history of World War Two;
[edited by] Studs Terkel. New Press 1997 589p
pa $16.95 **940.54**
1. World War, 1939-1945—Personal narratives
ISBN 1-56584-343-6 LC 2003-389322
First published 1984 by Pantheon Bks.
In a series of interviews Terkel depicts how WWII affected the lives of average Americans.

Grayling, A. C.
Among the dead cities; the history and moral
legacy of the WWII bombing of civilians in
Germany and Japan. Walker & Co. 2006 361p il
maps $25.95 **940.54**
1. World War, 1939-1945—Aerial operations
2. World War, 1939-1945—Ethical aspects
ISBN 0-8027-1471-4 LC 2005-58597
"Was it wrong for the Allies to bomb German and
Japanese civilians in World War II? In this book, . . .
[the author] attends to one of the twentieth-century's
largest unexploded moral conundrums. . . . Grayling's
book builds careful, generous cases for and against the
bombing, admitting as evidence both the experience of
the bombed as well as the bombers." Booklist
Includes bibliographical references

Hastings, Max
Armageddon: the battle for Germany, 1944-45.
A.A. Knopf 2004 584p il maps $30
940.54
1. World War, 1939-1945
ISBN 0-375-41433-9 LC 2004-46468
The author "tells the grim tale of the final collapse of
the Third Reich. It does so from the viewpoints of the
upper millstone (the Western Allies), the lower millstone

Hastings, Max—*Continued*
(the Russians) and the grain being ground in between
(the Germans). The research includes previously untapped Russian archives (particularly in the accounts of
Soviet veterans) and leads to a gripping and horrifying
story that serious students of military history will find almost impossible to put down." Publ Wkly
Includes bibliographical references

Retribution; the battle for Japan, 1944-45.
Alfred A. Knopf 2008 615p il map $35
940.54
1. World War, 1939-1945—Japan
ISBN 978-0-307-26351-3; 0-307-26351-7
LC 2007-34202
First published 2007 in the United Kingdom with title:
Nemesis
This chronicle of the final year of the Pacific war dis-
cusses such topics as the events leading to Allied victory,
Japan's war against China, and the decision to bomb Hi-
roshima and Nagasaki.
"Encompassing the British, Chinese, and Soviet roles
in vanquishing Japan, Hastings is both comprehensive
and finely acute in this masterful interpretive narrative."
Booklist
Includes bibliographical references

Hersey, John, 1914-1993
Hiroshima; a new edition with a final chapter
written forty years after the explosion. Knopf 1985
196p il $26; pa $6.50
940.54
1. Hiroshima (Japan)—Bombardment, 1945
2. Atomic bomb 3. World War, 1939-1945—Japan
ISBN 0-394-54844-2; 0-679-72103-7 (pa)
LC 85-40346
First published 1946
An account of the aftermath of the first atomic bomb
as reflected in the lives of six survivors

Hicks, George, 1936-
The comfort women; Japan's brutal regime of
enforced prostitution in the Second World War.
Norton 1995 c1994 303p il maps hardcover o.p. pa
$14.95 *
940.54
1. Comfort women 2. World War, 1939-1945—Wom-
en 3. Sino-Japanese Conflict, 1937-1945
ISBN 0-393-03807-6; 0-393-31694-7 (pa)
LC 95-2162
The author begins his "report with a historical survey
of wartime sexual exploitation of women, then narrows
the focus to the 'comfort women' system developed by
the Japanese. The copious testimony of victims is shock-
ingly graphic. . . . This significant addition to 'the poor
record of mankind to womankind, especially in war,'
properly approaches the subject as a human-rights issue
tied to the rise of feminism in Asia." Publ Wkly
Includes bibliographical references

Hornfischer, James D.
Ship of ghosts; the story of the USS Houston,
FDR's legendary lost cruiser, and the epic saga of
her survivors. Bantam Books 2006 530p il map
$26
940.54
1. Houston (Cruiser) 2. World War, 1939-1945—Naval operations
ISBN 0-553-80390-5; 978-0-553-80390-7
LC 2006-47530
This book "recounts the exploits of the Houston,
mainstay of the skimpy Allied fleet opposing the Japanese onslaught in the war's early days, until her sinking
in a desperate battle with overwhelming Japanese forces
in the Java Sea in 1942. . . . The narrative then shifts
gears to follow the Houston's several hundred survivors
through Japanese POW camps in Southeast Asia, focusing on the labor camps on the Burma-Thailand railway
(glamorized in the movie Bridge on the River Kwai).
. . . [This is] a gripping, well-told memorial to Greatest
Generation martyrdom." Publ Wkly
Includes bibliographical references

Kaplan, Alice Yaeger
The interpreter; [by] Alice Kaplan. University of
Chicago Press 2007 240p il map pa $15
940.54
1. Hendricks, James E. 2. Whittington, George P.,
1913-1996 3. Guilloux, Louis, 1899-1980 4. African
American soldiers 5. World War, 1939-1945—African
Americans 6. Trials (Homicide)
ISBN 978-0-226-42425-5; 0-226-42425-1
LC 2006-35822
First published 2005 by Free Press
This is an "account of the trials of two American soldiers accused of murdering French citizens in the waning
days of World War II. One of the accused soldiers, a
black man named James Hendricks, was sentenced to
death, while the other, George Whittington, a white who
had been proclaimed a war hero, was acquitted. French
political novelist Louis Guilloux served as an interpreter
at these trials, and Kaplan draws from Guilloux's diaries
as well as from a novel he based upon the trials. . . . Inventive, moving, and beautifully written, this is a major
contribution to investigative history." Libr J
Includes bibliographical references

Katz, Robert, 1933-
The battle for Rome; the Germans, the allies,
the partisans and the Pope, September 1943-June
1944. Simon & Schuster 2003 418p il map $28;
pa $16
940.54
1. World War, 1939-1945—Italy
ISBN 0-7432-1642-3; 0-7432-5808-8 (pa)
LC 2003-45677
"This narrative history describes the Eternal City at a
key time of struggle—the dark year of German occupation between the overthrow of Mussolini in 1943 and liberation by the Allies in 1944. Four parties wrestle for
Rome: the ruthless yet wary German occupiers, the Holy
See in self-preservation mode, a gutsy band of patriotic
students with homemade explosives, and the U.S. Fifth
Army under Mark Clark. . . . This is challenging research presented fluidly, and Katz's fascination with a
key moment for a fascinating city shines through."

Katz, Robert, 1933——_Continued_
Booklist
Includes bibliographical references

Keuning-Tichelaar, An, 1922-
Passing on the comfort; the war, the quilts, and the women who made a difference; [by] An Keuning-Tichelaar and Lynn Kaplanian-Buller. Good Books 2005 186p il pa $14.95
940.54
1. World War, 1939-1945—Personal narratives 2. Quilts
ISBN 1-561484-82-2   LC 2005-01932
This is the "narrative of a Dutch resistance operation during WWII conducted by Keuning-Tichelaar and her husband, Herman, a Mennonite minister. With the support of their townspeople, the two young newlyweds sheltered and saved the lives of Jewish adults and children, and others in danger from the Nazis. As part of a relief effort, quilts were created by women in North American Mennonite circles and sent to the Netherlands. Beautifully illustrated with 19 color photographs of the quilts, this book describes in an understated voice the harrowing events and the daily acts of courage that Keuning-Tichelaar undertook. When, decades later, coauthor Kaplanian-Buller, a U.S. citizen living in Amsterdam, found the old quilts, she persuaded An to share her story." Publ Wkly
Includes bibliographical references

Knox, Donald, 1936-
Death march; the survivors of Bataan. Harcourt Brace Jovanovich 1981 xxv, 482p il maps hardcover o.p. pa $18   **940.54**
1. World War, 1939-1945—Prisoners and prisons 2. World War, 1939-1945—Campaigns—Philippines 3. Prisoners of war
ISBN 0-15-124094-9; 0-15-602784-4 (pa)
LC 81-47555
The author records "recollections of some 68 survivors of the Japanese capture of Bataan. . . . Some of these soldiers, nurses, pilots, sailors, and others went to prison camp, some escaped to join guerrilla bands, some ended the war working in Japan and Manchuria as slave labor." Libr J

Leckie, Robert
Okinawa; the last battle of World War II. Viking 1995 220p il hardcover o.p. pa $13.95
940.54
1. World War, 1939-1945—Campaigns—Okinawa Island
ISBN 0-670-84716-X; 0-14-017389-7 (pa)
LC 94-39145
In this history of the Battle of Okinawa "Leckie supplies an accessible historical overview of a perplexing war tactic, the kamikaze attack." Booklist

Lee, Bruce
Marching orders; the untold story of World War II. Da Capo Press 2001 608p map pa $24
940.54

1. World War, 1939-1945—Secret service 2. Cryptography 3. World War, 1939-1945—Japan
ISBN 978-0-306-81036-7; 0-306-81036-0
First published 1995 by Crown
This "study argues that the U.S. breaking of Japanese diplomatic and military codes played a major role as well in the defeat of Nazi Germany. Lee . . . suggests that intercepts expressing Germany's commitment to world conquest helped determine the Allied policy of unconditional surrender." Publ Wkly
"Many of the mysteries that have eluded historians since the end of the war are much clarified. . . . This is the most significant publication about World War II since the recent series of books on the Ultra revelations and should be purchased by all libraries." Libr J
Includes bibliographical references

Liebling, A. J. (Abbott Joseph), 1904-1963
World War II writings. Library of America 2008 1089p map (The library of America) $40
940.54
1. World War, 1939-1945—Campaigns 2. World War, 1939-1945—Personal narratives
ISBN 978-1-59853-018-6   LC 2007-938791
This volume "brings together three books along with 26 uncollected New Yorker pieces and two excerpts from The Republic of Silence (1947), Liebling's collection of writing from the French Resistance. The Road Back to Paris (1944) narrates Liebling's experiences from September 1939 to March 1943, including his shock at the fall of France and dismay at isolationist indifference in the United States. . . . Mollie and Other War Pieces (1964) brings together Liebling's portrait of a legendary nonconformist American soldier in North Africa with his eyewitness account of Omaha beach on D-Day, evocative reports from Normandy, and investigation of a German atrocity in rural France. In Normandy Revisited (1958) Liebling writes about his return to France in 1955 and recalls the joyous liberation of his beloved Paris while exploring with bittersweet perception how wartime experience is transformed into memory." Publisher's note
"The war brought out the best in [Liebling]. Here he . . . relied on straightforward observation, delivered in a style less mannered than Hemingway's, less sentimental than Ernie Pyle's, less excitable than Michael Herr's. It's the kind of writing that looks easy, except that very few war correspondents have ever done it so well." N Y Times Book Rev
Includes bibliographical references

Lifton, Robert Jay, 1926-
Hiroshima in America; a half century of denial; [by] Robert Jay Lifton & Greg Mitchell; with a new afterword by the authors. Avon Books 1996 427p il pa $18.95   **940.54**
1. Atomic bomb 2. Hiroshima (Japan)—Bombardment, 1945
ISBN 978-0-380-72764-3; 0-380-72764-1
First published 1995 by Putnam with title: Hiroshima in America: fifty years of denial
Lifton and Mitchell examine "the reaction of the American people to the bombing of Hiroshima in 1945 and its domestic aftermath. The authors examine what they perceive to be a conspiracy by the government to

Lifton, Robert Jay, 1926——*Continued*
mislead and suppress information about the actual bombing, Truman's decision to drop the bomb, and the birth and mismanagement of the beginning of the nuclear age." Libr J
Includes bibliographical references

Manchester, William
Goodbye, darkness; a memoir of the Pacific War. Little, Brown 1980 401p il pa $16.95 hardcover o.p. **940.54**
1. World War, 1939-1945—Pacific Ocean 2. World War, 1939-1945—Personal narratives
ISBN 0-316-50111-5 (pa)　　　　LC 80-17310
This memoir arises from a 1978 trip the author made "to Pacific battlefields, seeking to exorcise three decades of nightmares dating to wartime days as a Marine Corps sergeant. . . . First tracing his family background, youth, enlistment, training, and embarkation from San Diego, Manchester unravels a memoir featuring historical reconstruction, disjointed flash-forwards, shocking vignettes, {and} redoubtable vocabulary." Choice

Megellas, James
All the way to Berlin; a paratrooper at war in Europe. Presidio Press 2003 xxi, 309p il maps $25.95 **940.54**
1. World War, 1939-1945—Personal narratives 2. World War, 1939-1945—Campaigns 3. World War, 1939-1945—Europe
ISBN 0-89141-784-2　　　　LC 2002-192563
This is the author's account of "the September 1944 assault across the Waal River. . . . The attrition Megellas witnessed over months on the front line, at Anzio and in the Battle of the Bulge, shapes his narrative, but his observations about the craft of killing lend it a distinctive tone. . . . Strongly put and unsentimental, this memoir is a must for the World War II collection." Booklist

Merridale, Catherine, 1959-
Ivan's war; life and death in the Red Army, 1939-1945. Metropolitan Books 2006 426p il map $30 * **940.54**
1. Soviet Union. Red Army 2. World War, 1939-1945—Soviet Union
ISBN 0-8050-7455-4　　　　LC 2005-50457
The author discusses the life of the ordinary Russian soldier during World War II.
Merridale "succeeds admirably in fashioning a compelling portrait, helped immensely by her talent as a writer." Foreign Affairs
Includes bibliographical references

Miller, Nathan, 1927-
War at sea; a naval history of World War II. Oxford University Press 1996 592p il map pa $29.95 **940.54**
1. World War, 1939-1945—Naval operations
ISBN 0-19-511038-2　　　　LC 96-31787
"A Lisa Drew book"
First published 1995 by Scribner

The author "relates the history of the last great sea war for the general reader, from the sinking of the passenger ship Athenia on September 2, 1939, to the surrender ceremony aboard the USS Missouri on September 2, 1945." Publ Wkly
"Miller's research—primarily on the Royal Navy—and a reading of hundreds of pertinent monographs has enabled him to fashion a briskly paced narrative that will both inform and entertain." Choice
Includes bibliographical references

Moses, Sam
At all costs; how a crippled ship and two American merchant mariners turned the tide of World War II. Random House 2006 335p il $25.95 **940.54**
1. World War, 1939-1945—Mediterranean Sea 2. World War, 1939-1945—Naval operations
ISBN 1-4000-6318-3　　　　LC 2006-40425
This is a "retelling of the story of Operation Pedestal, one of the most desperate convoy battles of World War II." Booklist
"The remarkable heroism that won the day, as well as Moses' thorough retelling, makes this an exciting, imperative read for anyone interested in WWII." Publ Wkly
Includes bibliographical references

Murphy, David E., 1921-
What Stalin knew; the enigma of Barbarossa. Yale University Press 2005 xxii, 310p il maps $30; pa $18 **940.54**
1. Stalin, Joseph, 1879-1953 2. World War, 1939-1945—Campaigns—Soviet Union 3. Soviet Union—Politics and government
ISBN 0-300-10780-3; 0-300-11981-X (pa)
　　　　　　　　　LC 2004-65916
This is an account of Soviet intelligence regarding the German invasion in 1941.
"Murphy's well-researched account offers both a meticulous reconstruction of an intelligence epic and a window into the tragedy of Stalin's despotism." Publ Wkly
Includes bibliographical references

Nelson, Craig
The first heroes; the extraordinary story of the Doolittle Raid—America's first World War II victory. Viking 2002 430p il $27.95; pa $15 **940.54**
1. Doolittle, James Harold, 1896-1993 2. United States. Army Air Forces 3. World War, 1939-1945—Japan 4. World War, 1939-1945—Aerial operations
ISBN 0-670-03087-2; 0-14-200341-7 (pa)
　　　　　　　　　LC 2002-28092
"The Doolittle Raid in April 1942 consisted of 16 B-25 bombers, crewed by 80 volunteers, who made the first air raid on the home islands of Japan. Four months after Pearl Harbor, they struggled off the USS *Hornet*, flew halfway across the Pacific, bombed Tokyo, and carried on into China." Libr J
"The most interesting part of the book is the harrowing story of survival as crew members are forced to ditch their planes on the Asian mainland. This is a thrilling real-life saga that both informs and inspires." Booklist
Includes bibliographical references

Nossiter, Adam

The Algeria Hotel; France, memory, and the Second World War. Houghton Mifflin 2001 302p il maps $26 *   **940.54**

1. World War, 1939-1945—France 2. France—History—1940-1945, German occupation

ISBN 0-395-90245-2   LC 00-69458

Maps on inside covers

"The rationalizations that let the French dispose of the past are the subject of this sensitive book, which covers the trial of a former cabinet minister, the Vichy memory hole and the interpretation of a Nazi atrocity." N Y Times Book Rev

"This is a powerfully revealing and important contribution to a continuing controversy." Booklist

Includes bibliographical references

The **Pacific** war companion; from Pearl Harbor to Hiroshima; editor, Daniel Marston. Osprey 2005 272p il map $29.95; pa $12.95   **940.54**

1. World War, 1939-1945—Campaigns—Pacific Ocean

ISBN   1-84176-882-0;   978-1-84176-882-3; 1-84603-212-1 (pa); 978-1-84603-212-7 (pa)

"These essays on the Pacific theater of WW II, written by a group of international scholars representing Australia, Great Britain, Japan, and the US, cover the wellknown events at Pearl Harbor, the Coral Sea, and Midway; MacArthur's push to the Philippines; Nimitz's island campaign in the central Pacific; Okinawa; and the dropping of the atomic bomb on Hiroshima and Nagasaki. . . . A chronology, detailed maps, and photographs greatly enhance this excellent volume on the Pacific phase of WW II." Choice

Includes bibliographical references

Patton, George S. (George Smith), 1885-1945

War as I knew it; by George S. Patton, Jr.; annotated by Paul D. Harkins. Houghton Mifflin 1947 425p il maps pa $18 hardcover o.p.
940.54

1. World War, 1939-1945—Campaigns

ISBN 0-395-73529-7 (pa)

Edited by Beatrice Ayer Patton

An account of the General's WWII European campaigns from the fight for Sicily to the conquest of Germany based on a series of "open letters" written to his wife

Pleshakov, Konstantin

Stalin's folly; the tragic first ten days of World War II on the Eastern Front; [by] Constantine Pleshakov. Houghton Mifflin 2005 326p il map $26 *   **940.54**

1. Stalin, Joseph, 1879-1953 2. World War, 1939-1945—Europe

ISBN 0-618-36701-2   LC 2004-65133

This is an account of the German invasion of the Soviet Union in 1941.

This book "belongs in every World War II collection." Libr J

Includes bibliographical references

Prange, Gordon William, 1910-1980

At dawn we slept; the untold story of Pearl Harbor; [by] Gordon W. Prange in collaboration with Donald M. Goldstein and Katherine V. Dillon. Viking 1991 889p il   **940.54**

1. Pearl Harbor (Oahu, Hawaii), Attack on, 1941

LC 91-50176

First published 1981 by McGraw-Hill

The author "offers a comprehensive account of Japanese preparations for the attack, the origins and extent of American unpreparedness, and the aftermath of the attack on both sides." Booklist

Includes bibliographical references

Read, Anthony

The fall of Berlin; [by] Anthony Read and David Fisher. Da Capo Press 1995 513p il map pa $18.50   **940.54**

1. Berlin, Battle of, 1945 2. World War, 1939-1945—Germany 3. Germany—History—1933-1945

ISBN 0-306-80619-3; 978-0-306-80619-3

LC 94-47998

First published 1992 in the United Kingdom

A description of "the bombing of Berlin by the British and Americans and how the Russian Army fought its way toward and through Berlin in 1945. The authors intend no startling new interpretations or profound analysis. Instead, they offer vignettes, often based on diaries, to describe life in Berlin late in the war. They also retell the story of fanatical Nazi leaders and of the Wehrmacht's desperate efforts to defend the city. The result is a highly readable and, at the same time, sophisticated and reliable narrative history." Libr J

Includes bibliographical references

Scott-Clark, Cathy

The Amber Room; the fate of the world's greatest lost treasure; [by] Catherine Scott-Clark & Adrian Levy. Walker & Co. 2004 386p il $26
940.54

1. Art thefts 2. World War, 1939-1945—Destruction and pillage

ISBN 0-8027-1424-2   LC 2004-49625

"One of the more enduring mysteries of lost treasures has been that of the Amber Room—a room in the Catherine Palace in Pushkin, outside of Leningrad (St. Petersburg), that was lined with amber panels given to Peter the Great in 1717 by Frederick I of Prussia. The panels disappeared during the 1941 Nazi invasion and have never been seen since. Levy and Scott-Clark . . . present the . . . story of what they believe happened to this 'eighth wonder of the world.'" Libr J

The authors "tell an exciting, intense, and surprising story. It is filled with episodes of cold-war intrigue, cynicism, amoral betrayal, and bureaucratic stalling that degenerates into absurdity." Booklist

Includes bibliographical references

Sebag-Montefiore, Hugh

Enigma: the battle for the code. Wiley 2000
422p il hardcover o.p. pa $16.95   **940.54**
1. Cryptography 2. World War, 1939-1945—Secret
service

ISBN 0-471-40738-0; 0-471-49035-0 (pa)
          LC 00-43920

This is the story of the German Enigma code.
"Describing the breaking of the German naval code
during World War II, is both engrossing and exciting.
Much of the information presented here is based on recently declassified documents." Booklist

Includes bibliographical references

Sheftall, Mordecai G.

Blossoms in the wind; the human legacy of the
Kamikaze; [by] M.G. Sheftall. NAL Caliber 2005
480p il $24.95   **940.54**
1. Kamikaze airplanes 2. World War, 1939-1945—Aerial operations

ISBN 0-451-21487-0   LC 2004-27356

This account of the "design, training, and execution
[of Japanese suicide missions] includes interviews with
the families of dead pilots and, harder to reach, pilots
who survived the missions." Booklist

The author "has produced a superior addition to the
literature on Japan's tokko, or suicide, warriors." Publ
Wkly

Includes bibliographical references

Sides, Hampton, 1962-

Ghost soldiers; the forgotten epic story of World
War II's most dramatic mission. Doubleday 2001
342p il maps $24.95   **940.54**
1. United States. Army. Ranger Battalion, 6th
2. World War, 1939-1945—Campaigns—Philippines
3. World War, 1939-1945—Prisoners and prisons

ISBN 0-385-49564-1   LC 2001-17337

Sides presents an account of a military operation in
the Pacific during World War II. "A force of 121 soldiers from the invading United States Army's Sixth
Ranger Battalion was ordered to liberate a prisoner of
war camp near the town of Cabanatuan. With the aid of
a group of Filipino guerrillas, the mission was accomplished." N Y Times Book Rev

"The author's excellent grasp of human emotions and
bravery makes this a compelling book hard to put
down." Publ Wkly

Spector, Ronald

Eagle against the sun; the American war with
Japan; {by} Ronald H. Spector. Free Press 1985
589p il pa $18 hardcover o.p.   **940.54**
1. World War, 1939-1945—Campaigns—Pacific
Ocean 2. World War, 1939-1945—United States
3. World War, 1939-1945—Japan

ISBN 0-394-74101-3 (pa)   LC 84-47888

Also available in paperback from Vintage Bks.

This is a "one-volume history of the American-
Japanese conflict during WW II." Choice

While "policy, strategy and military operations are
emphasized . . . Mr. Spector makes a real attempt to

give readers some idea of what the war was like for the
men and women who fought it. It is here that the book
is at its best." N Y Times Book Rev

Includes bibliographical references

Stinnett, Robert B.

Day of deceit; the truth about FDR and Pearl
Harbor. Free Press 1999 386p il maps pa $16
hardcover o.p.   **940.54**
1. Roosevelt, Franklin D. (Franklin Delano), 1882-
1945 2. Pearl Harbor (Oahu, Hawaii), Attack on, 1941
3. Intelligence service—United States

ISBN 0-7432-0129-9 (pa)   LC 99-38402

The author addresses the question of whether the U.S.
had knowledge of the impending Japanese attack on
Pearl Harbor

"Although Stinnett's accusatory light doesn't definitively fall on FDR, it illuminates fishy aspects of the
case. . . . Whether the result of simple dereliction or sinister dereliction of duty, Pearl Harbor holds fewer secrets
because of Stinnett's research." Booklist

Includes bibliographical references

Takaki, Ronald T., 1939-

Hiroshima; why America dropped the atomic
bomb; [by] Ronald Takaki. Little, Brown 1995
193p il $28; pa $14.95   **940.54**
1. World War, 1939-1945—United States 2. Atomic
bomb 3. Hiroshima (Japan)—Bombardment, 1945

ISBN 0-316-83122-0; 0-316-83124-7 (pa)
          LC 95-13546

This study of the bombings of Hiroshima and Nagasaki focuses on the psychological motivations of the American decision-makers, especially Harry Truman.

"Right or wrong, the study is a provocative addition
to the unresolved debate over the dropping of the atomic
bombs." Publ Wkly

Includes bibliographical references

Thomas, Evan

Sea of thunder; four commanders and the last
great naval campaign, 1941-1945. Simon &
Schuster 2006 415p il map $27 *
     940.54
1. World War, 1939-1945—Naval operations
2. World War, 1939-1945—Campaigns—Pacific
Ocean

ISBN 978-0-7432-5221-8; 0-7432-5221-7
          LC 2006-47511

This is an "account of the Battle of Leyte Gulf, October 1944, one of history's largest naval battles, where
Admiral William 'Bull' Halsey, the commander of the
U.S. Third Fleet, and his commander, Ernest Evans, met
the forces of Japanese admirals Takeo Kurita and
Matome Ugaki. . . . Thomas paints compelling portraits
of these men, offering insight into their characters and
actions throughout the war in the Pacific." Libr J

Includes bibliographical references

Thompson, Robert Smith
Empires on the Pacific; World War II and the struggle for the mastery of Asia. Basic Bks. 2001 434p $30; pa $18.95 **940.54**
1. World War, 1939-1945—Asia
ISBN 0-465-08575-X; 0-465-08576-8 (pa)
LC 2001-36561
In this study, Thompson asserts that "the U.S. had strong political and economic interests in East Asia and saw Japan as a danger to those interests. . . . The author makes his points by telling only one side of the story, but his alternate view of our 'last good war' is bound to attract attention and may generate controversy." Booklist
Includes bibliographical references

940.55 Europe—1945-

Judt, Tony
Postwar; a history of Europe since 1945. Penguin Press 2005 878p il maps $39.95
940.55
1. Europe—History—1945-
ISBN 1-59420-065-3 LC 2005-52126
This is an "historical overview of today's Europe from the end of World War II through the economic, social, cultural, and political changes and continuities of the last 60 years." Libr J
"This is the best history we have of Europe in the postwar period and not likely to be surpassed for many years." Publ Wkly
Includes bibliographical references

Mazower, Mark
Dark continent: Europe's twentieth century. Knopf 1999 487p il maps pa $16 hardcover o.p.
940.55
1. Europe—History—20th century
ISBN 0-679-75704-X (pa) LC 98-15886
Mazower shapes his "history of Europe's 20th century as a struggle among liberal democracy, communism and fascism." Publ Wkly
The author's "relative unconcern with international and great-power politics probably accounts for a rather intra-European perspective . . . just as it contributes to some exaggeration of the points of comparison and convergence in East and West European economic history. . . . But these are minor defects, the price to be paid for a confident and unconventional work of historical interpretation." N Y Times Book Rev
Includes bibliographical references

941 British Isles

The **Columbia** companion to British history; edited by Juliet Gardiner & Neil Wenborn. Columbia Univ. Press 1997 840p maps $63
941
1. Great Britain—History—Encyclopedias
ISBN 0-231-10792-7 LC 96-23774
First published 1995 in the United Kingdom with title: The History today companion to British history
Engl. title: The History Today companion to British history

This reference work contains "more than 4,500 dictionary entries that not only cover political and constitutional history, but also provide information on social, economic, religious, military, naval, legal, and cultural history. . . . The entries . . . [cover topics such as] blasphemy, divorce, and homosexuality, as well as the historical events and rulers that are standard for any encyclopedia. In addition, the encyclopedia seems to be strong on entries for Scotland and Ireland." Booklist

Fraser, Rebecca
The story of Britain; from the Romans to the present: a narrative history. Norton 2005 829p il map $35 * **941**
1. Great Britain—History
ISBN 0-393-06010-1 LC 2004-26049
First published 2003 in the United Kingdom with title: A people's history of Britain
The author's "narrative advances with the emphasis on the roles of a litany of historical icons, from Queen Boudica to Margaret Thatcher. For those readers who are primarily interested in the 'who, what, when, where, why' of British history, this is a valuable general study." Booklist
Includes bibliographical references

Lacey, Robert
Great tales from English history; the truth about King Arthur, Lady Godiva, Richard the Lionheart, and more. Little, Brown and Co. 2004 254p maps $22.95 **941**
1. Great Britain—History
ISBN 0-316-10910-X LC 2003-115660
First published 2003 in the United Kingdom
"This volume begins in 7150 BC with the life and death of Cheddar Man and ends in 1381 with Wat Tyler and the Peasants' Revolt." Publisher's note
Includes bibliographical references

Great tales from English history [2]; Joan of Arc, the princes in the Tower, Bloody Mary, Oliver Cromwell, Sir Isaac Newton, and more. Little, Brown and Co. 2005 271p il map $23.95
941
1. Great Britain—History
ISBN 0-316-10924-X LC 2004-63351
First published 2004 in the United Kingdom
The author's "second volume on English history opens in 1348, the year of the Black Plague, which wiped out half of England's five million people, and proceeds through the astonishing scientific discoveries of Sir Isaac Newton in 1687. . . . Lacey's animated prose, energetic storytelling and spirited approach to British history bring the past to life." Publ Wkly
Includes bibliographical references

Great tales from English history [3]; Captain Cook, Samuel Johnson, Queen Victoria, Charles Darwin, Edward the Abdicator, and more. Little, Brown and Co. 2006 305p $23.99 *
941
1. Great Britain—History
ISBN 978-0-316-11459-2; 0-316-11459-6
LC 2006-931723

Lacey, Robert—*Continued*

"The third volume in Lacey's series of edifying and entertaining stories from English history abounds in fascinating profiles. Industrial and agricultural pioneers such as Jethro Tull, James Hargreaves and Isambard Kingdom Brunel abide alongside human rights protestors such as Thomas Clarkson, who founded the British antislavery movement; feminist philosopher Mary Wollstonecraft; and journalist Annie Besant, who initiated a successful 1888 match girls' strike." Publ Wkly

Includes bibliographical references

The **Oxford** history of Britain; edited by Kenneth O. Morgan. rev ed, updated ed. Oxford Univ. Press 2001 780p maps pa $18.95　　**941**
1. Great Britain—History
ISBN 0-19-280135-X　　　　LC 2001-271568
Also available The Oxford illustrated history of Britain $26.50 (ISBN 0-19-289326-2)

Text based on: The Oxford illustrated history of Britain, published 1984

"Covering two thousand years of British history, the book tells the story of Britain and her peoples from the coming of the Roman legions to the present day. Here ten . . . contributors including Peter Salway, John Blair, John S. Morrill, and Paul Langford offer essays on everything from the Anglo-Saxon period to the Stuarts to the Liberal Age and the twentieth century." Publisher's note

Includes bibliographical references

Schama, Simon

A history of Britain. Hyperion 2000-2003 3v ea $40　　　　　　　　　　　　　　　**941**
1. Great Britain—History
ISBN 0-7868-6675-6 (v1); 0-7868-6752-3 (v2); 0-7868-6899-6 (v3)　　　　LC 00-61442
"Talk Miramax books"

Contents: [v1] At the edge of the world, 3500 B.C.-1603 A.D.; v2 The wars of the British, 1603-1776; v3 The fate of empire, 1776-2000

Schama "writes wonderfully, in an easygoing yet elegant manner, with an eye for the telling aesthetic detail, and throughout brimming with intelligence and passion." N Y Times Book Rev

Includes bibliographical references

Tompson, Richard S.

Great Britain: a reference guide from the Renaissance to the present. Facts on File 2003 552p il (European nations series) $85 *
　　　　　　　　　　　　　　　　　　941
1. Great Britain—History
ISBN 0-8160-4474-0　　　　　LC 200219

This guide contains "an introductory overview of British history, Renaissance to the present; a narrative history; a historical dictionary, topical and biographical; a chronology; appendixes (maps, genealogies of English royal houses, lists of English sovereigns from 899, and prime ministers from 1721). The work concludes with an unannotated bibliography, arranged in sections for bibliogaphies, dictionaries and encyclopedias, general works, surveys, and topics." Choice

941.07　British Isles—Period of House of Hanover, 1714-1837

Brewer, John, 1947-

The pleasures of the imagination; English culture in the eighteenth century. University of Chicago Press 2000 721p il pa $20
　　　　　　　　　　　　　　　　　　941.07
1. Great Britain—Civilization 2. Great Britain—Social life and customs 3. Great Britain—Intellectual life
ISBN 0-226-07419-6; 978-0-226-07419-1
　　　　　　　　　　　　　　　LC 99-57059

First published 1997 by Farrar, Straus and Giroux

The author "examines the evolution of the visual arts, literature, music and theater in 18th-century England." Publ Wkly

"A remarkable feat of scholarship, this volume will quickly establish itself as an indispensable reference." Booklist

Includes bibliographical references

McLynn, Frank

1759: the year Britain became master of the world. Atlantic Monthly Press 2004 c2005 422p il map $26　　　　　　　　　**941.07**
1. Seven Years' War, 1756-1763 2. Great Britain—Foreign relations 3. Great Britain—Colonies
ISBN 0-87113-881-6　　　　LC 2004-57397

First published 2004 in the United Kingdom

1759 "was the fourth [year] in the Seven Years War, a struggle between France and England for global dominance that was fought worldwide. McLynn focuses on the deadly conflict, contrasting the two nations' differing wartime policies and showing how the combination of Britain's maritime prowess and sheer good luck helped it emerge triumphant, albeit by a narrow margin. . . . Splendidly narrated, with balanced insights into the Native American aspect of the French and Indian Wars, McLynn's book will enthrall all lovers of history told well." Publ Wkly

Includes bibliographical references

941.08　British Isles—Period of Victoria and House of Windsor, 1837-

The **Cambridge** illustrated history of the British Empire; edited by P.J. Marshall. Cambridge Univ. Press 1996 400p il maps $55; pa $35 *
　　　　　　　　　　　　　　　　　　941.08
1. Great Britain—Colonies 2. Commonwealth countries—History 3. Imperialism
ISBN 0-521-43211-1; 0-521-00254-0 (pa)
　　　　　　　　　　　　　　　LC 95-14535

"This book examines the experience of colonialism in North America, India, Africa, Australia and the Caribbean, giving a brief history of the British imperial territories and looking at slavery, trade, religion, art, transportation, and the development of new ideas." Book Rep

Includes bibliographical references

McKillop, A. B., 1946-
The spinster & the prophet; H.G. Wells, Florence Deeks, and the case of the plagiarized text. Four Walls Eight Windows 2002 477p il $26.95   **941.08**
1. Wells, H. G. (Herbert George), 1866-1946 2. Deeks, Florence Amelia 3. Plagiarism 4. Historiography
ISBN 1-56858-236-6   LC 2002-71292
"When, in 1920, Florence Deeks finally received her rejected manuscript—a feminist history of the world—from Macmillan after eight months, she couldn't understand why it appeared in such bad condition. . . . Later that year, when she read H.G. Wells's new book, *The Outline of History*, published by Macmillan, she felt a chill. There were so many similarities to her own work: shared themes, organization, word choice, even the same mistakes. Florence made a dramatic decision—she would sue Wells and his publisher for plagiarism. . . . The author handles the dual story line brilliantly, weaving together two opposing characters into one altogether gripping tale of literary theft." Publ Wkly
Includes bibliographical references

941.081 British Isles—Reign of Victoria, 1837-1901

Encyclopedia of the Victorian era; James Eli Adams, editor in chief; Tom Pendergast, Sara Pendergast, editors. Grolier Academic Reference 2004 4v il map set $499   **941.081**
1. Great Britain—History—19th century 2. Great Britain—Civilization
ISBN 0-7172-5860-2   LC 2003-57101
"Entries ranging in length from a few paragraphs to several pages are written by experts, treat topics from William Acton to zoological gardens, and seek to encompass the important issues, people, and events of the Victorian era. . . . While predictable figures such as Queen Victoria and Benjamin Disraeli appear, so too do social history topics such as the sporting life, penny dreadfuls, and cholera." Choice
Includes bibliographical references

Wilson, A. N. (Andrew Norman), 1950-
The Victorians. Norton 2003 724p il $35; pa $17.95   **941.081**
1. Great Britain—History—19th century 2. Great Britain—Civilization
ISBN 0-393-04974-4; 0-393-32543-1 (pa)
    LC 2002-33809
First published 2002 in the United Kingdom
This history begins with the burning of the Houses of Parliament in 1834 and ends with the death of Queen Victoria. It is a "cultural, political, intellectual, economic, literary, and social history." N Y Rev Books
"Even to fastidious readers, Wilson's failings are minor, and the colorful tapestry he presents of a smoky world peopled with the likes of Carlyle, Mill, Marx, Ruskin, and Darwin can hardly fail to enthrall. Both professional scholars and laypeople will love to relax with this book, although some knowledge of the age is a must." Choice
Includes bibliographical references

941.085 British Isles—1945-

Junor, Penny
The Firm: the troubled life of the House of Windsor. Thomas Dunne Books 2005 xxi, 442p il $25.95   **941.085**
1. House of Windsor 2. Great Britain—Kings and rulers
ISBN 0-312-35274-3   LC 2005-45528
The author "considers the British royal family's continuation into the 21st century in this . . . account, covering Diana's death to the present day." Publ Wkly
"Readers of this interesting and occasionally jaw-dropping look at the world's most famous dysfunctional family will find plenty to engage them." Libr J
Includes bibliographical references

941.1 Scotland

Devine, T. M. (Thomas Martin)
The Scottish nation 1700-2000. Viking 1999 xxiii, 695p il maps pa $20 hardcover o.p.
    941.1
1. Scotland—History
ISBN 0-14-100234-4 (pa)   LC 99-29866
"The author divides the book into chronological periods to cover Scottish economic, military, and social history; regional differences in the Highlands and Lowlands; and the development of Scottish identity." Libr J
Includes bibliographical references

Herman, Arthur, 1956-
How the Scots invented the modern world; the true story of how western Europe's poorest nation created our world & everything in it. Crown 2001 392p $25.95; pa $14.95   **941.1**
1. Scotland—Civilization 2. Scottish national characteristics
ISBN 0-609-60635-2; 0-609-80999-7 (pa)
    LC 2001-28951
The author discusses Scottish "contributions to education, science, history, and political thought." Libr J
"This is a worthwhile book for the general reader." Publ Wkly
Includes bibliographical references

Nicolson, Adam, 1957-
Sea room: an island life in the Hebrides. North Point Press 2002 391p il maps $27; pa $14
    941.1
ISBN 0-86547-636-5; 0-86547-667-5 (pa)
    LC 2002-19816
First published 2001 in the United Kingdom
The author is the owner "of three remote Scottish islands, the Shiants, located in the Hebrides and purchased by Nicolson's father through a 1937 newspaper advertisement. . . . Nicolson's book offers as much information about the geological origins of the islands, the seasonal details of the flora and fauna, and the melding of Norse language into the culture as it does about the au-

Nicolson, Adam, 1957- —*Continued*
thor's solitary boat rides and peaceful beachcombing adventures." Libr J
"Magnificent and poetic, this is a literary and ecological masterpiece." Booklist
Includes bibliographical references

941.5   Ireland

Cahill, Thomas, 1940-
How the Irish saved civilization; the untold story of Ireland's heroic role from the fall of Rome to the rise of medieval Europe; [by] Thomas Cahill. Talese 1995 246p il maps $27.50; pa $12.95   **941.5**
1. Ireland—Civilization 2. Learning and scholarship 3. Medieval civilization
ISBN 0-385-41848-5; 0-385-41849-3 (pa)
                                          LC 94-28130
This book describes the part played by Irish scribal scholars during the Dark Ages "in preserving and transmitting the classical literature of both Greece and Rome." Booklist
"Highly literate and affectionate, if somewhat rambling and indulgent. . . . As a freewheeling, witty popular history of Irish Christianity in the Dark Ages, this will amuse and enlighten." Libr J
Includes bibliographical references

The **Encyclopedia** of Ireland; edited by Brian Lalor; foreword by Frank McCourt. Yale University Press 2003 xxxvii, 1218p il map $65
                                          941.5
1. Ireland—Encyclopedias
ISBN 0-300-09442-6   LC 2003-103834
This encyclopedia contains alphabetically arranged entries from Abbey Theatre to Zozimus, a nineteenth-century balladeer. Coverage includes art, cinema, current events, fashion, food, history, Irish language, literature, music, politics, religion, sports, and biographies of a wide range of famous people of Irish descent, including St. Brigid, Éamon de Valera, John F. Kennedy, Bono, Eugene O'Neill, Mary Robinson, and William Butler Yeats
"This wonderful reference work will delight researchers and lovers of Ireland and the Irish." Choice

Encyclopedia of Irish history and culture; James S. Donnelly Jr., editor in chief; Karl S. Bottigheimer . . . [et al.], associate editors. Macmillan Reference USA 2004 2v il map set $270 *   **941.5**
1. Ireland—Encyclopedias
ISBN 0-02-865902-3   LC 2004-5353
"The A-Z entries are preceded by a chronology and followed by a selection of almost 150 primary documents ranging from the Confession of St. Patrick (c. 450) to the Belfast/Good Friday Agreement (1998). . . . Providing the latest in scholarship, entries are well written and cover the gamut of historical, social, and cultural topics." Booklist
Includes bibliographical references

Ferriter, Diarmaid, 1972-
The transformation of Ireland. Overlook Press 2005 884p $37.50   **941.5**
1. Ireland—History
ISBN 1-58567-681-0   LC 2005-49849
First published 2004 in the United Kingdom
"This book isn't a political history of 20th-century Ireland; it's more a chronicle of the social reaction to the events that shaped that century. . . . [The author] has written an informative, funny, at times derisive book that takes a fresh approach to 20th-century Ireland." Publ Wkly
Includes bibliographical references

The **Oxford** illustrated history of Ireland; edited by R.F. Foster. Oxford Univ. Press 1989 382p il maps hardcover o.p. pa $24.95   **941.5**
1. Ireland—History
ISBN 0-19-822970-4; 0-19-285245-0 (pa)
                                          LC 89-16168
Also available non-illustrated edition with title: The Oxford history of Ireland pa $17.95 (ISBN: 0-19-280202-X)
This illustrated history includes "six essays by Irish scholars, five covering chronological periods in Irish history and the sixth a . . . discussion of the interplay between Irish literature and history." Libr J
"A thoughtful and highly informative volume that manages to underscore the ancient and rooted aspects of Irish culture, even while it explores in depth the mobility and shifting of the Irish people into 'fractured and sometimes unexpected patterns.'" Booklist
Includes bibliographical references

941.6   Ulster. Northern Ireland

Coogan, Tim Pat, 1935-
The troubles; Ireland's ordeal, 1966-1996, and the search for peace. Palgrave 2002 589p il map pa $22.95   **941.6**
1. Northern Ireland
ISBN 978-0-312-29418-2; 0-312-29418-2
First published 1995 in the United Kingdom
In this political history the author "examines all parties to the struggle. . . . He reconstructs the past 30 years, from the 1969 marching and riots to the H-Block protests, the MacBride Principles, the Anglo-Irish agreement, and the recent paramilitary cease-fire. Coogan traces the current peace process, stalled by Great Britain's insistence that the IRA hand in its weapons, to the 1979 visit of Pope John Paul II." Libr J
Includes bibliographical references

942   England and Wales

Medieval England; an encyclopedia; editors: Paul E. Szarmach, M. Teresa Tavormina, Joel T. Rosentha. Garland 1998 lxiv, 882p il maps $155
                                          942
1. Great Britain—History—Encyclopedias 2. Medieval civilization—Encyclopedias
ISBN 0-8240-5786-4   LC 97-35523

Medieval England—*Continued*
"Containing more than 700 entries by more than 300 international scholars, the volume encompasses the fields of Old English and Middle English language and literature, music and liturgy, history, and history of art. . . . The A-Z entries are supported by lists of kings and queens of England, archbishops of Canterbury and York, and popes, 590-1502, as well as a glossary of musical and liturgical terms." Booklist

942.01   England—Early history to 1066

Goodrich, Norma Lorre
King Arthur. Harper & Row 1989 406p il map pa $17   **942.01**
1. Arthur, King 2. Great Britain—History—0-1066
ISBN 0-06-097182-7; 978-0-06-097182-3
LC 85-22558
"Perennial Library"
First published 1986 by Watts
The author examines historical and literary materials relating to Arthur as both an actual and legendary figure.
Includes bibliographical references

King Arthur in legend and history; edited by Richard White; foreword by Allan Massie. Routledge 1998 xxv, 570p il maps pa $34.95 hardcover o.p.   **942.01**
1. Arthur, King 2. Great Britain—History—0-1066
ISBN 0-415-92063-9 (pa)   LC 97-47726
First published 1997 in the United Kingdom
"This book is a compilation of source material excerpted primarily from longer works. . . . The documents themselves are arranged in roughly chronological and geographical order, ranging from *Gildas* (c. 548) to *The Buik of the Chronicles of Scotland* (1535). The anthology presents both historical and literary works and draws from French and German as well as English sources." Libr J
Includes bibliographical references

942.04   England—Period of Houses of Lancaster and York, 1399-1485

Weir, Alison
The Wars of the Roses. Ballantine Bks. 1995 462p il hardcover o.p. pa $15.95   **942.04**
1. Great Britain—History—1455-1485, War of the Roses
ISBN 0-345-39117-9; 0-345-40433-5 (pa)
This is an account "of the first phase of the War of the Roses. Accepting the Tudor view that the conflict originated with Richard II's deposition, [the author] devotes half of the book to relations between Lancaster and York from 1399 to 1455. The second half deals with the period from the first Battle of St. Albans (1455) to the Battle of Tewkesbury (1471)." Libr J
"No history collection should do without this perfectly focused and beautifully unfolded account." Booklist

942.06   England—Stuart and Commonwealth periods, 1603-1714

Fraser, Antonia, 1932-
Faith and treason; the story of the Gunpowder Plot. Doubleday 1996 xxxv, 347p il pa $16 hardcover o.p. *   **942.06**
1. Fawkes, Guy, 1570-1606 2. Gunpowder plot, 1605 3. Great Britain—History—1603-1714, Stuarts
ISBN 0-385-47190-4 (pa)   LC 96-21709
"A Nan A. Talese book"
Engl. title: The gunpowder plot
"A small group of Roman Catholics planned to blow up Parliament on its opening day in 1605, when the Protestant King James and his older son would be present, and to proclaim the nine-year-old princess Elizabeth queen, raise her as a Catholic, and so restore Catholicism as the state religion. . . . The Gunpowder Plot was both cruel and crackpot, but Fraser does a wonderful job of conveying to the modern reader just why a few Catholics felt that it was justified and also was likely to succeed." New Yorker
Includes bibliographical references

Trevelyan, George Macaulay, 1876-1962
The English Revolution, 1688-1689; [by] G. M. Trevelyan. Oxford University Press 1965 136p pa $30   **942.06**
1. Great Britain—History—1688, Revolution
ISBN 978-0-19-500263-8; 0-19-500263-6
First published 1938 in the United Kingdom
This study covers not only the revolution itself but also the events of the reign of James II, which led up to it and the political changes which followed.
Includes bibliographical references

942.08   England—Period of Victoria and House of Windsor, 1837-

Taylor, A. J. P. (Alan John Percivale), 1906-1990
English history, 1914-1945. Oxford Univ. Press 1965 xxvii, 708p maps (Oxford history of England) $194.50 *   **942.08**
1. Great Britain—History—20th century
ISBN 0-19-821715-3
A study of the political, economic, and social changes in England over a thirty year span.

942.1   London

Ackroyd, Peter
London: the biography. Talese 2001 c2000 xxvi, 801p il $45; pa $18.95   **942.1**
1. London (England)—History
ISBN 0-385-49770-9; 0-385-49771-7 (pa)
LC 2001-27153
First published 2000 in the United Kingdom

Ackroyd, Peter—*Continued*

Ackroyd's social history of London is organized thematically with "essays on such topics as drinking, natural history, suicide, crowds, ghosts, rivers, prostitution, theatres, murder, sounds and children." London Rev Books

"A sweeping, highly readable account of London's colorful and complicated history." Libr J

Includes bibliographical references

942.9   Wales

Morris, Jan, 1926-

A writer's house in Wales. National Geographic Soc. 2002 143p (National Geographic directions) $25   **942.9**

1. Wales

ISBN 0-7922-6523-8   LC 2001-44731

The author "reflects on her home in Wales, its beautiful setting and the nature of being Welsh. . . . This slim and charming volume offers a crisp account of the turbulent history of the Welsh and their battle to maintain their language and culture in the shadow of their more powerful neighbor." Publ Wkly

943   Central Europe. Germany

Craig, Gordon Alexander, 1913-2005

The Germans; [by] Gordon A. Craig. Meridian 1991 361p il pa $18   **943**

1. Hitler, Adolf, 1889-1945 2. Germany—Civilization 3. Germany—History 4. Antisemitism

ISBN 0-452-01085-3; 978-0-452-01085-7

LC 91-12814

First published 1982 by Putnam

This work examining the social history of Germany contains "chapters on religion, money, Germans and Jews, women, professors and students, romantics, literature and society, soldiers, Berlin—and an appendix called 'The Awful German Language.'" Publisher's note

Includes bibliographical references

Fulbrook, Mary, 1951-

A concise history of Germany. 2nd ed. Cambridge University Press 2004 277p il, maps (Cambridge concise histories) hardcover o.p. pa $22 *   **943**

1. Germany—History

ISBN 0-521-83320-5; 0-521-54071-2 (pa)

LC 2004-271599

First published 1990 in the United Kingdom

This history of Germany "spans the early Middle Ages to the present day. . . . Mary Fulbrook explores the interrelationships between social, political and cultural factors in the light of the latest scholarly controversies." Publ Wkly

Includes bibliographical references

Gay, Ruth

The Jews of Germany; a historical portrait; with an introduction by Peter Gay. Yale Univ. Press 1992 297p il maps hardcover o.p. pa $35

943

1. Jews—Germany

ISBN 0-300-05155-7; 0-300-06052-1 (pa)

LC 91-30235

This is a history of Germany's Jews from the first century to the Holocaust.

"Illustrated sumptuously with paintings, photographs and excerpts from letters and historical documents, . . . this affirming history survives the sad end of the centuries-old German Jewish way of life." N Y Times Book Rev

Gorra, Michael Edward, 1957-

The bells in their silence; travels through Germany; {by} Michael Gorra. Princeton University Press 2004 211p $24.95   **943**

1. Germany—Description and travel

ISBN 0-691-11765-9

Gorra's "account of his travels through Germany is shaped—perhaps even haunted—by figures from the past: historical, literary, personal. A captivating, unique work of synthesis." Booklist

Includes bibliographical references

Schulze, Hagen

Germany; a new history; translated by Deborah Lucas Schneider. Harvard Univ. Press 1998 356p il maps pa $16.95 hardcover o.p.   **943**

1. Germany—History

ISBN 0-674-00545-7 (pa)   LC 98-23629

Schulze provides "a concise overview of 2,000 years of German history. . . . This is a fast-moving survey that manages to touch most of the critical bases—from Charlemagne to Frederick the Great to Hitler—without concentrating on any one particular historical era." Booklist

Includes bibliographical references

943.08   Germany since 1866

Craig, Gordon Alexander, 1913-2005

Germany, 1866-1945; by Gordon A. Craig. Oxford Univ. Press 1978 825p (Oxford history of modern Europe) pa $41.95 hardcover o.p.

943.08

1. Germany—History

ISBN 0-19-502724-8 (pa)   LC 78-58471

"A Clarendon Press book"

A "predominantly military and political history of modern Germany." Libr J

"An impressive . . . survey of modern German history, this book is an indispensable reference." New Statesman (1913)

Includes bibliographical references

Evans, Richard J.
The coming of the Third Reich; a history; Richard J. Evans. Penguin Press 2004 622p il map $34.95; pa $18 *   943.08
1. National socialism 2. Germany—History—1866-1918 3. Germany—History—1918-1933
ISBN 1-594-20004-1; 0-14-303469-3 (pa)
LC 2003-63205
First published 2003 in the United Kingdom
First volume of a projected three volume set on the history of the Third Reich; followed by The Third Reich in power
This "volume covers the period from the founding of modern Germany (1871) through Hitler's coming to power (1933)." Libr J
"This is a first-rate narrative history that informs and educates and may inspire readers to delve even deeper into the subject." Booklist
Includes bibliographical references

Smith, Helmut Walser, 1962-
The butcher's tale; murder and anti-semitism in a German town. Norton 2002 270p il maps $25.95; pa $14.95   943.08
1. Antisemitism 2. Homicide 3. Germany—Ethnic relations
ISBN 0-393-05098-X; 0-393-32505-9 (pa)
LC 2002-22883
"In 1900, in Konitz, a small town in the Eastern reaches of the German Empire, a Christian boy was found murdered. . . . Though the Konitz police never caught their killer, they scrupulously recorded each indictment, . . . [including] the long disclosure, published in a local newspaper, of Gustav Hoffmann, the town's Christian butcher, in which he accused his next-door neighbor, the Jewish butcher Adolph Lewy, of conspiring with other Jews of the town to commit the crime. . . . [Smith reconstructs the] crime, the ensuing investigation, and the anti-Semitic mob violence that obscured the identity of the real killer." Publisher's note
The author "does a masterful job exploring the history of the blood libel . . . as well as of community and how people band together to bring about great good or in the case of Konitz genuine evil. . . . Although classed by the publisher as history/Judaica, this powerful volume will also appeal to true-crime readers and anyone interested in the dynamics that can turn a peaceful community into a place of hatred and violence." Publ Wkly
Includes bibliographical references

Stern, Fritz Richard, 1926-
Five Germanys I have known; [by] Fritz Stern. Farrar, Straus & Giroux 2006 546p il map $30
943.08
1. Germany—History
ISBN 978-0-374-15540-7; 0-374-15540-2
LC 2006-60
In this "memoir, Stern looks back over the 'five Germanys' his generation has seen—the Weimar Republic, Nazi tyranny, the post-1945 Federal Republic, the Soviet-controlled German Democratic Republic and, lastly, the reunited Germany of the present—and explains how he came to reconcile himself with his birth country (which his Jewish family fled in 1938) as it has come to terms

with its new place in today's more cohesive and peaceful Europe. . . . The book's intriguing structure makes it a wonderful combination of history, memoir, analysis and even poetry." Publ Wkly

943.086   Germany—Period of Third Reich, 1933-1945

Ayçoberry, Pierre
The social history of the Third Reich; 1933-1945; translated from the French by Janet Lloyd. New Press 2000 380p $30; pa $15.95
943.086
1. National socialism 2. Germany—Politics and government—1933-1945
ISBN 1-56584-549-8; 1-56584-635-4 (pa)
LC 99-14059
Translated from the French
"In examining the actions of individuals and social groups, [the author] illustrates that German citizens' response to the Nazi regime varied wildly. Some resisted bravely; others saw an opportunity for advancement. Most people sought merely to survive. In fact, what is extremely unsettling is how so many could maintain a semblance of normalcy in their lives. Ayçoberry does not attempt to answer the unanswerable questions posed by the Nazi era, but his disturbing, brutally honest, and scrupulously fair work may be a landmark in the field." Booklist
Includes bibliographical references

Burleigh, Michael, 1955-
The Third Reich; a new history. Hill & Wang 2000 xxv, 965p il maps pa $18 hardcover o.p.
943.086
1. Germany—History—1933-1945
ISBN 0-8090-9326-X (pa)   LC 00-31838
This account of Germany under National Socialism "focuses on the moral breakdown that gave Hitler control of an industrial society, which then, along with the rest of the world, suffered the catastrophic consequences." Publ Wkly
"This brilliant and unique view of a great tyranny is an important addition to our understanding of the first half of the twentieth century." Booklist
Includes bibliographical references

Evans, Richard J.
The Third Reich in power, 1933-1939; Richard J. Evans. Penguin Press 2005 941p il map $37.95 *   943.086
1. National socialism 2. Germany—History—1933-1945
ISBN 1-594-20074-2   LC 2005-52128
Second volume of a projected three volume set on the history of the Third Reich; volume one is The coming of the Third Reich
This book focuses "on the nine years after Hitler's appointment as chancellor. His main thesis is that the basic goal of the Nazi state from its inception was the renewal of war, and every Nazi policy was tied into that desire."

Evans, Richard J.—*Continued*

Libr J

This "is a major achievement. No other recent synthetic history has quite the range and narrative power of Evans's work." Publ Wkly

Includes bibliographical references

Fischer, Klaus P., 1942-

Nazi Germany; a new history. Continuum 1995 734p il pa $32.95 hardcover o.p.   **943.086**

1. Hitler, Adolf, 1889-1945 2. National socialism 3. Germany—History—1933-1945

ISBN 0-8264-0906-7 (pa)   LC 94-41796

This is an "analysis of the Third Reich from its late-19th-century origins to its apocalyptic collapse." Libr J

"An indispensable, compellingly readable political, military and social history of the Third Reich." Publ Wkly

Includes bibliographical references

Fleming, Gerald

Hitler and the final solution; with an introduction by Saul Friedlander. University of Calif. Press 1984 xxxvi, 219p il pa $18.95 hardcover o.p.   **943.086**

1. Hitler, Adolf, 1889-1945 2. Holocaust, 1933-1945

ISBN 0-520-06022-9 (pa)   LC 83-24352

Original German edition, 1982

This work attempts to prove "that the Final Solution was deliberately designed and personally willed and ordered by Hitler. Fleming reveals the elaborate precautions taken not only to disguise the nature of the operation but also to ensure that it could not be connected with Hitler." Publisher's note

Includes bibliographical references

Hay, Jeff

A history of the Third Reich; by Jeff T. Hay; Christopher R. Browning, consulting editor. Greenhaven Press 2003 4v il maps set $299.80   **943.086**

1. National socialism 2. Germany—History—1933-1945

ISBN 0-7377-1283-X   LC 2002-33900

"Combines A-Z articles, biographical profiles, and primary source material to help high-school students understand the social and political forces that shaped, or were shaped by, the Third Reich. An accessible, reliable source." Booklist

Johnson, Eric A. (Eric Arthur), 1948-

What we knew; terror, mass murder and everyday life in Nazi Germany: an oral history; [by] Eric A. Johnson and Karl-Heinz Reuband. Basic Books 2005 xxiii, 434p $27.50   **943.086**

1. Germany—History—1933-1945 2. Holocaust, 1933-1945

ISBN 0-465-08571-7

"The authors posit that 'far from living in a state of constant fear and discontent, most Germans led happy and even normal lives in Nazi Germany.' They believe that the Holocaust could not have been possible without the complicity of the majority of the German population. . . . This scholarly work is a major contribution to the understanding of life in Nazi Germany and a compelling narrative that is certain to be the standard work on the subject." Booklist

Includes bibliographical references

Parssinen, Terry M.

The Oster conspiracy of 1938; the unknown story of the military plot to kill Hitler and avert World War II; [by] Terry Parssinen. HarperCollins Pubs. 2003 xxii, 232p il map $27.95; pa $13.95   **943.086**

1. Oster, Hans, 1888-1945 2. Hitler, Adolf, 1889-1945 3. Germany—Politics and government—1933-1945

ISBN 0-06-019587-8; 0-06-095525-2 (pa)

LC 2002-68896

This is the "story of an aborted coup and a plan to eliminate Hitler. . . . Knowing Hitler was bent on war with Czechoslovakia by October 1, 1938, at the latest, military intelligence officer Hans Oster organized disquieted German generals to overthrow the dictator *if* he gave the invasion order *and* the British promised to go to war. Chamberlain's accession to Hitler's demands invalidated both prerequisites of Oster's plan." Booklist

"A fascinating, blow-by-blow account of a seemingly feasible but failed attempt to prevent World War II. . . . Even knowing the outcome, readers feel suspense and hope as events unfold; alternate history buffs and history students alike will gain new insight into the past and into human character from this tragic story." SLJ

Includes bibliographical references

Pool, James, 1948-

Hitler and his secret partners; contributions, loot and rewards, 1933-1945. Pocket Bks. 1997 415p il pa $14 hardcover o.p.   **943.086**

1. Hitler, Adolf, 1889-1945 2. Germany—Politics and government—1933-1945 3. World War, 1939-1945—Destruction and pillage

ISBN 0-671-76082-3 (pa)   LC 97-15506

The author examines the way German industrialists and financiers backed Hitler and how the Nazis received material support from abroad. Pool alleges that Henry Ford, Edward VIII and Joe Kennedy assisted the Nazi regime

This book "is a reminder that the worst-kept secret of WWII is that so many malefactors emerged little the worse." Publ Wkly

Includes bibliographical references

Rempel, Gerhard

Hitler's children; the Hitler youth and the SS. University of N.C. Press 1989 354p il pa $24.95 hardcover o.p. *   **943.086**

1. Germany—History—1933-1945 2. National socialism

ISBN 0-8078-4299-0 (pa)   LC 88-28036

The author examines the alliance between the Nazi SS and the Hitler Youth

Rempel, Gerhard—*Continued*
"Rempel's objective work brings into focus one aspect of the sordid history of the Third Reich." Booklist
Includes bibliographical references

Rosenbaum, Ron
Explaining Hitler; the search for the origins of his evil. HarperPerennial 1999 444p pa $16
943.086
1. Hitler, Adolf, 1889-1945 2. National socialism 3. Germany—Politics and government—1933-1945
ISBN 0-06-095339-X; 978-0-06-095339-3
LC 99-25965
First published 1998 by Random House
This book examines interpretations of Hitler made by his contemporaries and by historians.
"In this brilliantly skeptical inventory of the world's Hitler-thinking, Rosenbaum analyzes not only the multiple Hitler theories but also the agendas and fantasies that the theorizers bring to their subject." Time
Includes bibliographical references

Shirer, William L. (William Lawrence)
The rise and fall of the Third Reich; a history of Nazi Germany; with a new afterword by the author. Simon & Schuster 1990 1249p pa $25 hardcover o.p.
943.086
1. Germany—History—1933-1945
ISBN 0-671-72868-7 (pa)
LC 90-221762
"A Touchstone book"
First published 1960
This is a comprehensive, documented history of Germany from the beginning of the Nazi party in 1918 to the World War II defeat of Germany in 1945. Here is a detailed account of the events, and the leading figures of the Nazi era, especially Adolf Hitler
Includes bibliographical references

Speer, Albert, 1905-1981
Inside the Third Reich; memoirs; translated from the German by Richard and Clara Winston; introduction by Eugene Davidson. Simon & Schuster 1997 596p il pa $18 *
943.086
1. Hitler, Adolf, 1889-1945 2. Germany—History—1933-1945 3. World War, 1939-1945—Germany
ISBN 0-684-82949-5; 978-0-684-82949-4
Original German edition, 1969
The author, Hitler's "architect and later his armaments minister, was in the dictator's inner circle for almost 12 years. . . . After the war Speer used the enforced leisure of his 20 prison years as a war criminal to plan and write these memoirs." Libr J
Includes bibliographical references

Turner, Henry Ashby
Hitler's thirty days to power; January 1933; {by} Henry Ashby Turner, Jr. Addison-Wesley 1996 255p il pa $16 hardcover o.p.
943.086
1. Hitler, Adolf, 1889-1945 2. National socialism 3. Germany—Politics and government—1918-1933
ISBN 0-201-32800-3 (pa)
LC 96-20012

The author explores "the fateful 30 days before Hitler became chancellor of Germany in January 1933. Although many of the facts are known, this study reveals that the Nazi dictator did not come to power as the result of 'impersonal forces.' The slender, analytical volume indicates that rather, at a time of mortal peril for Germany—and the world—intrigue was the order of the day in Berlin. . . . Students of German history and extremist movements should enjoy this fast-paced narrative." Publ Wkly
Includes bibliographical references

943.087 Germany—1945-1990

Brenner, Michael
After the Holocaust; rebuilding Jewish lives in postwar Germany; translated from the German by Barbara Harshav. Princeton Univ. Press 1997 196p il $47.50; pa $19.95
943.087
1. Jews—Germany 2. Holocaust survivors 3. Germany—History—1945-1990
ISBN 0-691-02665-3; 0-691-00679-2 (pa)
LC 97-1149
Original German edition, 1995
This introduction to German Jewry since 1945 consists of two essays by Brenner and 15 short autobiographical statements by Jewish communal, religious, and cultural leaders
"If the middle section of interviews seems redundant, it is only because Brenner has covered the material so well and so succinctly elsewhere." Publ Wkly
Includes bibliographical references

Darnton, Robert
Berlin journal, 1989-1990. Norton 1991 352p il pa $12.95 hardcover o.p.
943.087
1. Germany (East)—Politics and government 2. Berlin (Germany)
ISBN 0-393-31018-3 (pa)
LC 90-19745
"Darnton spent parts of 1989 and 1990 in Germany, witnessing the end of that country's division into East and West as the Berlin Wall fell. . . . {He} focuses more on events and aftereffects in East Germany as experienced by ordinary citizens, rather than trying to write a definitive study. Darnton talks with workers, bureaucrats, and government officials and describes what was happening and what the people understood about these momentous events." Booklist

943.7 Czech Republic and Slovakia

Demetz, Peter, 1922-
Prague in black and gold; scenes from the life of a European city. Hill & Wang 1997 411p maps pa $15 hardcover o.p.
943.7
ISBN 0-8090-1609-5 (pa)
LC 96-52216
The author presents an "account of the city's history and culture by focusing on epic events as well as heroes, villains and martyrs throughout the millennia of its existence. . . . A highly literate panorama of a focal point of European culture." Publ Wkly
Includes bibliographical references

943.8   Poland

The **Chronicle** of the Łódz ghetto, 1941-1944; edited by Lucjan Dobroszycki; translated by Richard Lourie {et al.}. Yale Univ. Press 1984 lxviii, 551p il pa $37 hardcover o.p.

        943.8

1. Jews—Poland 2. Holocaust, 1933-1945 3. Lodz (Poland)—Social conditions

ISBN 0-300-03924-7 (pa)   LC 84-3614

"This English edition comprises about one fourth of the original surviving German and Polish manuscript. Day-by-day entries of one to ten pages recorded events and living conditions from January 1941 to the ghetto's liquidation in July 1944. The chronicle was composed by a team of writers, employees of the Jewish ghetto administration." Libr J

"The record is made more profoundly melancholic by the restrained archivist style employed by the chroniclers." New Statesman (1913)

943.9   Hungary

Michener, James A., 1907-1997

    The bridge at Andau. Fawcett Crest 1983 277p pa $6.99   **943.9**

1. Hungary—History—1956, Revolution 2. Hungarian refugees

ISBN 978-0-449-21050-5; 0-449-21050-2

First published 1957 by Random House

"The heroism, horror and tragedy of the 1956 Hungarian revolt is revealed through interviews with many refugees who crossed the bridge at Andau to freedom." Cleveland Public Libr

944   France and Monaco

Horne, Alistair

    La belle France; a short history. Knopf 2005 485p il map $30 *   **944**

1. France—History

ISBN 1-4000-4140-6   LC 2004-42329

First published 2004 in the United Kingdom with title: Friend or foe: an Anglo-Saxon history of France

"Beginning with Julius Caesar's division of Gaul into three parts, Horne leads us . . . through the ages: from Charlemagne, Philippe-Auguste and the Sun King, Louis XIV, to Cardinal Richelieu and Napoleon Bonaparte, Charles de Gaulle and Jacques Chirac." Publisher's note

"This compelling narrative belongs in any public library needing an excellent, current one-volume history of France." Booklist

Includes bibliographical references

    Seven ages of Paris. Knopf 2002 448p $35; pa $16   **944**

1. Paris (France)

ISBN 0-679-45481-0; 1-4000-3446-9 (pa)

         LC 2002-29653

The author traces "the history of Paris through seven periods, beginning in the 12th century and ending with the death of Charles de Gaulle in 1969. . . . Each section includes fascinating insights into the social and cultural life of the age, fashions in clothing, architectural developments, leading personalities, and lifestyles of rich and poor alike. With the verve of a master storyteller, Horne captures Parisians' 'zest for living.'" Libr J

Includes bibliographical references

Jones, Colin, 1947-

    Paris; biography of a city; Colin Jones. Viking 2005 xxv, 566p il map $29.95   **944**

1. Paris (France)

ISBN 0-670-03393-6   LC 2004-53608

First published 2004 in the United Kingdom

"Moving from prehistoric tribal habitation through Roman times, medieval uncertainty and splendor, early modern religious wars, Enlightenment, revolution, and two world wars, Jones examines how rulers, economy, religion and violence have shaped the city. . . . Anyone who loves Paris will find connections and revelations here, a Paris of the mind that resonates through the centuries." Publ Wkly

Includes bibliographical references

Karnow, Stanley

    Paris in the fifties; illustrations by Annette Karnow. Times Bks. 1997 352p il pa $14 hardcover o.p.   **944**

1. French national characteristics 2. France—Politics and government

ISBN 0-8129-3137-8 (pa)   LC 97-18521

"Karnow chronicles his early years in Paris, where he worked as a young reporter for Time magazine (1950-59). . . . {His book} closes with the collapse of the Fourth Republic in 1958 and the recall to power of Charles de Gaulle." Libr J

"Not content with simply ensconcing himself in the *Time* bureau offices, . . . Karnow created a personal life for himself and took in all that Paris and the provinces had to offer. And now he offers this succulent book, which Francophiles will devour." Booklist

Tuchman, Barbara Wertheim

    A distant mirror; the calamitous 14th century; {by} Barbara W. Tuchman. Knopf 1978 xx, 677p il maps pa $17.95 hardcover o.p.   **944**

1. Coucy, Enguerrand de, 1340-1397 2. France—History—1328-1589, House of Valois 3. World history—14th century 4. Medieval civilization

ISBN 0-345-34957-1 (pa)   LC 78-5985

The author traces the history of the fourteenth century by following the career of a "feudal lord, Enguerrand de Coucy VII, the seigneur of some 150 towns and villages in Picardy. He was born in 1340, and he died in captivity in 1397, having been made a prisoner by the Turks." Time

Includes bibliographical references

White, Edmund, 1940-

    The flaneur; a stroll through the paradoxes of Paris. Bloomsbury Pub. 2001 211p maps $16.95   **944**

1. Paris (France)—Description and travel

ISBN 1-58234-135-4   LC 00-46812

White, Edmund, 1940-—*Continued*
"White defines the *flâneur* of his title as an 'aimless stroller who loses himself in the crowd, who has no destination and goes wherever caprice or curiosity direct his or her step.' White assumes the role of *flâneur* to perambulate the narrow streets and grand boulevards of Paris, to gather impressions of people and places." Booklist
"White is richly informed, and his evocative writing should appeal to both armchair travelers and visitors to Paris." Libr J

944.04   France—Revolutionary period, 1789-1804

Burke, Edmund, 1729?-1797
Reflections on the Revolution in France; edited by J.C.D. Clark. Stanford Univ. Press 2001 446p $65; pa $29.95 *   **944.04**
  1. France—History—1789-1799, Revolution
  ISBN   0-8047-3923-4;   978-0-8047-3923-8;
  0-8047-4205-7 (pa); 0-8047-4205-4 (pa)
                                         LC 00-63732
  First published 1790
  "A treatise by Edmund Burke, written in the form of a letter to a Frenchman. It attacks the leaders and principles of the French Revolution for their violence and excesses, and urges reform, rather than rebellion, as a means of correcting social and political abuses." Benet's Reader's Ency. 4th edition
  Includes bibliographical references

Lefebvre, Georges, 1874-1959
The French Revolution. Columbia Univ. Press 1962-1964 2v v1 pa $32 hardcover o.p.; v2 pa $32
                                         944.04
  1. France—History—1789-1799, Revolution
  ISBN 0-231-08598-2 (v1 pa); 0-231-08599-0 (v2 pa)
  Original French edition, 1930; this translation is based on 1957 reprintings
  Contents: v1 From its origins to 1793, translated by Elizabeth Moss Evanson; v2 From 1793 to 1799, translated by John Hall Stewart and James Friguglietti
  An account of the political, military, social, economic and intellectual aspects of the French Revolution.
  Includes bibliographical references

944.05   France—Period of First Empire, 1804-1815

Schom, Alan
One hundred days; Napoleon's road to Waterloo. Oxford University Press 1993 398p pa $45   **944.05**
  1. Napoleon I, Emperor of the French, 1769-1821
  2. Waterloo, Battle of, 1815
  ISBN 978-0-19-508177-0; 0-19-508177-3
                                         LC 93-11787
  First published 1992 by Atheneum
  This is an account of "Napoleon's escape from Elba in February 1815 and his return . . . to France. Rallying

the nation behind him, he mustered his army and marched off to meet Wellington at Waterloo. . . . This is a first-class reconstruction of Napoleon's final campaign." Publ Wkly
  Includes bibliographical references

944.081   France—Period of Third Republic, 1870-1945

Bredin, Jean-Denis
The affair; the case of Alfred Dreyfus; translated from the French by Jeffrey Mehlman. Braziller 1986 628p il pa $19.95 hardcover o.p.
                                         944.081
  1. Dreyfus, Alfred, 1859-1935 2. Antisemitism
  3. France—Politics and government—1815-1914
  ISBN 0-8076-1175-1 (pa)   LC 85-22374
  Original French edition, 1983
  Translation of: L'affaire
  In his examination of the case, the author seeks to "set the affair within the . . . currents of French history and the rising tide of anti-Semitism." Choice
  "That Bredin manages to be both passionate and exact is his first outstanding virtue. He is admirably free of the baroque conspiracy theories that sprout so luxuriantly on both sides of this case." N Y Rev Books
  Includes bibliographical references

Derfler, Leslie
The Dreyfus affair. Greenwood Press 2002 xxii, 167p il (Greenwood guides to historic events, 1500-1900) $44.95 *   **944.081**
  1. Dreyfus, Alfred, 1859-1935 2. France—Politics and government—1815-1914 3. Antisemitism
  ISBN 0-313-31791-7   LC 2001-38365
  "Following a chronology is a 'Historical Overview' containing several chapters of background and analysis. These chapters provide context for what is commonly known as the Dreyfus affair, discuss how anti-Semitism and socialism played into and were affected by the affair, and summarize how the affair has been viewed through history. The next section is an A-Z collection of biographies of almost 20 key individuals. . . . Primary documents comprise the next chapter and most documents are accompanied by short explanations. . . . This guide is useful for researchers who need more information than they can find in an encyclopedia." Booklist
  Includes bibliographical references

944.083   France—Period of Fifth Republic, 1958-

Mayle, Peter
Encore Provence; new adventures in the south of France. Knopf 1999 226p $23; pa $12
                                         944.083
  1. Provence (France)
  ISBN 0-679-44124-7; 0-679-76269-8 (pa)
                                         LC 99-62335
  Companion volume to Toujours Provence (1991) and A year in Provence (1995)

Mayle, Peter—*Continued*

Mayle's "book is all about the renewal of his acquaintance with the land he so loves. Essays range widely over Provençal life. . . . His observations and commentaries are laced with humor but encompass true respect and admiration for his adopted homeland." Booklist

945 Italian Peninsula and adjacent islands. Italy

Berendt, John

The city of falling angels; a Venice story. Penguin Press 2005 414p $25.95; pa $15

945

1. Venice (Italy)—Social life and customs
ISBN 1-59420-058-0; 1-59420-061-0 (pa)

LC 2005-47661

The author describes some of his encounters with contemporary Venetians. The starting point for his travels was the investigation of the fire which destroyed La Fenice opera house in 1996.

Berendt "delivers an urbane, beautifully fashioned book with much exotic charm. . . . [The author] makes erudite, inquisitive, nicely skeptical company as he leads the reader through the shadows of what was heretofore better known as a tourist attraction." N Y Times (Late N Y Ed)

Bosworth, R. J. B. (Richard J. B.), 1943-

Mussolini's Italy; life under the dictatorship, 1915-1945. Penguin 2006 xxvi, 692p il map $35

945

1. Mussolini, Benito, 1883-1945 2. Fascism—Italy 3. Italy—History—1914-1945
ISBN 1-59420-078-5

LC 2005-52127

First published 2005 in the United Kingdom

The author "investigates how fascistic Italian society became under the ministrations of Il Duce." Booklist

Bosworth "combines prodigious research with a clear writing style that will appeal to all readers interested in the Italy of Il Duce." Libr J

Includes bibliographical references

Levey, Sir Michael, 1927-

Florence; a portrait. Harvard Univ. Press 1996 xxix, 498p il pa $22.95 hardcover o.p.

945

1. Florence (Italy)—History
ISBN 0-674-30658-9 (pa)

LC 95-31215

This is an analysis of "Florence's political and artistic history from earliest times through the nineteenth century." Booklist

"If at times the detail overwhelms the big picture, the 150 illustrations (50 in color) and Levey's excellent artistic counsel make this a worthy guide for anyone seriously seeking Florence." Publ Wkly

Includes bibliographical references

Mayes, Frances

Under the Tuscan sun; at home in Italy. Chronicle Bks. 1996 280p $22.95 *

945

1. Tuscany (Italy)—Social life and customs 2. Italian cooking
ISBN 0-8118-0842-4

LC 96-15137

Also available in paperback from Broadway Bks.

The author "recounts the purchase and renovation of an abandoned Tuscan villa." Libr J

"Casual and conversational, {Ms. Mayes's} chapters are filled with craftsmen and cooks, with exploratory jaunts into the countryside—but what they all boil down to is an intense celebration of what she calls 'the voluptuousness of Italian life.' Occasionally, this leads to the sort of gushy observations you might expect from a besotted lover. But more often it produces an appealing and very vivid snapshot imagery." N Y Times Book Rev

946 Iberian Peninsula and adjacent islands. Spain

Kurlansky, Mark

The Basque history of the world. Penguin 2001 387p il map pa $15

946

1. Basque Provinces (France and Spain)
ISBN 978-0-14-029851-2; 0-14-029851-7

First published 1999 by Walker & Co.

"This book traces the history of the Basques from their mysterious origins to their politically fraught existence in this century. . . . Kurlansky shows how Basques, famed for their geographic and linguistic isolation, have played significant roles in world history-as mercenaries in ancient Greece, whalers in the Middle Ages, explorers in the Americas, and even cautious supporters of modern European integration." New Yorker

Lowney, Chris

A vanished world; medieval Spain's golden age of enlightenment. Free Press 2005 320p il map $26

946

1. Spain—Civilization
ISBN 0-7432-4359-5

LC 2004-56362

This is a history of Spain between the Muslim conquest in 711 and the driving of Muslims from Iberia in 1492, during which the author argues there was a tentative peace between Christians, Muslims, and Jews.

The author "successfully brings the story of medieval Spain to a wider audience and draws out of this rich history important lessons for the post-9/11 world." Christ Sci Monit

Includes bibliographical references

Spain: a history; edited by Raymond Carr. Oxford Univ. Press 2000 318p il hardcover o.p. pa $19.95

946

1. Spain—History
ISBN 0-19-820619-4; 978-0-19-280236-1 (pa); 0-19-280236-4 (pa)

LC 99-42639

The essays in this volume present a journey through Spain's "entire history: from its prehistoric settlement through Roman, Visigothic, and Islamic rule, and from its golden age of exploration to the Spanish Civil War in

Spain: a history—*Continued*
the 1930s, Franco's resulting rule, the monarchy's reestablishment, Basque separatists, and modern Spain's political unrest." Booklist

Includes bibliographical references

Stewart, Chris
Driving over lemons; an optimist in Andalucia. Pantheon Bks. 2000 248p il maps hardcover o.p. pa $13.95   **946**
ISBN 978-0-375-41028-4; 978-0-375-70915-9 (pa); 0-375-70915-0 (pa)   LC 99-56675
"Stewart, one of the founders and the first drummer of the rock band Genesis . . . sets out for Spain from England. He buys a sheep farm in the Alpujarra Mountains in Andalucia, and, accompanied by wife Ana and his young daughter, learns to survive without running water, electricity, or roads. Along the way, Stewart forges some solid friendships with neighboring peasants and farmers, travelers, and expatriates." Libr J
"The ability to write hilarious travelogues featuring excruciating scenes of discomfort may well be a {British} national characteristic. It's certainly possessed by Chris Stewart." N Y Times Book Rev

Tremlett, Giles
Ghosts of Spain; travels through Spain and its secret past. Walker 2007 386p $26.95
    946
1. Spain—Description and travel 2. Spain—Social life and customs
ISBN 0-8027-1574-5; 978-0-8027-1574-6
First published 2006 in the United Kingdom
An "examination of the Franco years and their legacy make a somber backdrop for an otherwise cheery tale. Having summoned the ghosts, [the author] moves along to offer a guided tour of modern Spain, making stops at the usual journalistic destinations. The educational system, politics, health care, child rearing and the national character are dealt with in well-organized chapters that move the reader briskly along. . . . A highly informative, well-written introduction to post-Franco Spain." N Y Times (Late N Y Ed)

Vincent, Mary
Cultural atlas of Spain and Portugal; {by} Mary Vincent and R.A. Stradling. Facts on File 1994 240p il maps $45   **946**
1. Spain 2. Portugal
ISBN 0-8160-3014-6   LC 94-31211
This volume explores the cultural history of the Iberian peninsula. "The text and maps are complemented by 240 beautiful color photographs that highlight many important historical and cultural events. These encompass features on art, palaces, buildings, artists, posters, food, and even Expo'92 in Seville. A chronology, dynastic chart, glossary, short bibliography, and gazetteer complete the volume." Am Ref Books Annu, 1996

946.081   Spain—Period of Second Republic, 1931-1939

Lewis, Norman, 1908-2003
The tomb in Seville; crossing Spain on the brink of civil war; introduction by Julian Evans. Carroll & Graf 2005 150p $20; pa $14.95
    946.081
1. Spain—Description and travel
ISBN 0-7867-1439-5; 0-7867-1687-8 (pa)
First published 2003 in the United Kingdom
The author "recounts traveling through Spain in 1934 with his brother-in-law Eugene Corvaja to find the Corvaja family tomb in Seville. Their plans for a straightforward north-to-south journey, beginning in San Sebastián, are altered by uprisings foretelling the impending Spanish Civil War." Publ Wkly
"Reading the author's account of his travels in a country on the brink of war is almost as satisfying as being there." Booklist

947   Eastern Europe. Russia

Borrero, Mauricio, 1959-
Russia: a reference guide from the Renaissance to the present. Facts on File 2004 497p il map (European nations series) $85 *   **947**
1. Russia—History—Dictionaries
ISBN 0-8160-4454-6   LC 2003-60547
Alphabetically arranged entries cover "influential individuals, significant places, important policies . . . {and} various moments that have profoundly impacted the historical development of the country and its people." Publisher's note
"Readers will find an authoritative reference work distinguished by readability throughout and by wise decision making regarding what information to include and how it might best be presented. . . . It is a splendid resource, which is designed to serve the needs of students . . . as well as academic specialists and general readers." Booklist
Includes bibliographical references

Drakulic, Slavenka
Café Europa; life after communism. Penguin Books 1999 213p pa $14   **947**
1. Eastern Europe—Social conditions 2. Eastern Europe—Politics and government
ISBN 978-0-14-027772-2; 0-14-027772-2
First published 1996 in the United Kingdom; first United States edition published 1997 by Norton
The author of these pieces is "at once critical of a culture that remains bleakly conformist in the aftermath of Communist rule and empathetic for its having known nothing else. With consistent equanimity, she examines the frustrating plight of the novice Balkan democracies. On a more quotidian level, too, she finds that much is wanting, measured against Western standards of richesse, congeniality, and even taxi service. Owing largely to Drakulic's knack for drawing humor from an abundance of anecdotes—whether about a toothpaste monopoly or the bureaucratic cartwheels required to purchase a vacuum cleaner—these essays read like stories." New Yorker

Eastern Europe; an introduction to the people, lands, and culture; edited by Richard Frucht. ABC-CLIO 2004 3v set $285   **947**
1. Eastern Europe 2. Central Europe 3. Balkan Peninsula
ISBN 1-57607-800-0   LC 2004-22300
Contents: v. 1. The northern tier: Poland \ Piotr Wrobel. Estonia \ Mel Huang. Latvia \ Aldis Purs. Lithuania \ Terry D. Clark -- v. 2. Central Europe: Czech Republic \ Daniel E. Miller. Slovakia \ June Alexander. Hungary \ Andras Boros-Kazai. Croatia \ Mark Biondich. Slovenia \ Brigit Farley -- v. 3. Southeastern Europe: Serbia and Montenegro \ Nicholas T. Miller. Macedonia \ Aleksandar Panev. Bosnia-Hercegovina \ Katherine McCarthy. Albania \ Robert Austin. Romania \ James P. Niessen. Bulgaria \ Richard Frucht. Greece \ Alexandros K. Kyrou
For a review see: Booklist, March 15, 2005
Includes bibliographical references

Encyclopedia of Russian history; James R. Millar, editor in chief. Macmillan Reference USA 2004 4v il map set $475   **947**
1. Russia—History—Encyclopedias
ISBN 0-02-865693-8
This reference set "includes historical events; documents, declarations, or treaties; military campaigns or battles; the arts, literature, philosophy, or science; economic developments or strategies; ethnic groups; geographical regions; political or territorial units; countries prominent in Russian history; government policies or programs; organizations, movements, or political parties; influential individuals; basic terms or phrases. Entries vary in length from less than one column . . . to several pages for major topics or individuals." Choice
"Rarely has an encyclopedia come along at such a historical juncture as to make it an imperative of the modern library. . . . This is an impressive work recommended for school, undergraduate academic, and public libraries." Libr J

Hosking, Geoffrey A., 1942-
Russia and the Russians; a history; {by} Geoffrey Hosking. Belknap Press 2001 718p il map $35; pa $18.95 *   **947**
1. Russia—History 2. Soviet Union—History
ISBN 0-674-00473-6; 0-674-01114-7 (pa)
LC 00-65085
Hosking argues "that Russia was far more successful in constructing an imperial identity than in envisioning a nation evolving from its diversity." New Leader
"This is a high-quality overview, suitable for all libraries." Booklist

Russia: people and empire, 1552-1917; [by] Geoffrey Hosking. Harvard Univ. Press 1997 548p maps $33; pa $15.16   **947**
1. Russian national characteristics 2. Russia—History
ISBN 0-674-78118-X; 0-674-78119-8 (pa)
LC 97-5069
The author explores the question "of how and why the Russians never developed a sense of nation. He argues that the Russian monarchy and aristocracy were always more interested in building an expansive empire than in

promoting the belief in nationhood, something understood by the powerless peasantry. The expensive and inefficient bureaucracy that emerged over the centuries weighed against any possibility of community, and in the end this tottering edifice was unable to withstand the cataclysm of World War I. Hosking has brought a powerful intellect and great erudition to this work." Libr J
Includes bibliographical references

Massie, Suzanne
Land of the firebird; the beauty of old Russia. Hearttree 1980 493p il pa $32   **947**
1. Russia—Civilization 2. Russian art
ISBN 978-0-9644184-1-7; 0-9644184-1-X
First published 1980 by Simon & Schuster
The author's intent "is to give 'a sense of the whole, now-vanished culture of old Russia . . . to describe that beauty which the Russians once knew how to create, what they loved, and admired and how they once lived and rejoiced.'" N Y Times Book Rev
Includes bibliographical references

Milner-Gulland, R. R.
Cultural atlas of Russia and the former Soviet Union; by Robin Milner-Gulland with Nikolai Dejevsky. rev ed. Checkmark Bks. 1998 240p il maps $50   **947**
1. Russia—Civilization 2. Former Soviet republics
ISBN 0-8160-3815-5   LC 98-29263
"An Andromeda book"
First published 1989 with title: Cultural atlas of Russia and the Soviet Union
This survey of the civilizations of Russia and the former Soviet republics is divided into three parts: The geographical background, History, and Regions and countries of the former Soviet Union
"Aimed at the general reader, the atlas is easy to use, informative, and entertaining." Choice {review of 1989 edition}
Includes bibliographical references

Riasanovsky, Nicholas Valentine, 1923-
A history of Russia; [by] Nicholas V. Riasanovsky, Mark D. Steinberg. 7th ed. Oxford University Press 2005 2v il map set $56   **947**
1. Russia—History 2. Soviet Union—History
ISBN 0-19-515394-4; 978-0-19-515394-1
LC 2004-49594
First published 1963
This narrative history includes discussions of economics, social organization, religion, and culture.
Includes bibliographical references

Stokes, Gale
The walls came tumbling down; the collapse of communism in Eastern Europe. Oxford Univ. Press 1993 319p hardcover o.p. pa $31.95   **947**
1. Communism 2. Eastern Europe—Politics and government
ISBN 0-19-506644-8; 0-19-506645-6 (pa)
LC 92-44862

Stokes, Gale—*Continued*

The author "deals with all the formerly Communist countries in Eastern Europe except Albania, and he traces the history of the collapse of the Soviet-type regimes rather than concentrating . . . on their evolution since the collapse." N Y Times Book Rev

This book "can be recommended as a coherent, well-written history that defines its time frame well, provides sound coverage, makes prudent judgments, and wears its analysis lightly. . . . Stokes's overview traces the ebb and flow of personalities and events in a manner that is both accessible to lay readers and informative to scholars." Libr J

Volkov, Solomon

St. Petersburg; a cultural history; translated by Antonina W. Bouis. Free Press 1995 598p il pa $26.50 hardcover o.p. **947**

1. Akhmatova, Anna Andreevna, 1889-1966 2. Brodsky, Joseph, 1940-1996 3. Balanchine, George, 1904-1983 4. Shostakovich, Dmitriĭ Dmitrievich, 1906-1975

ISBN 0-684-83296-8 (pa) LC 95-24116

The author offers an "overview of the traditions and individuals responsible for the great cultural evolution of St. Petersburg (Leningrad) and its ever-shifting mythos—from Pushkin to Chagall, from Gogol to Stravinsky and on to the cultural diaspora of the late 20th century." Libr J

Four of Volkov's "six very long chapters revolve around figures representative of certain periods or trends in the evolution of the St. Petersburg myth: Akhmatova, Balanchine, Shostakovich and Brodsky. Aspects of these central biographical and cultural portraits lead him . . . into countless mini-biographies of related figures." N Y Times Book Rev

Warnes, David

Chronicle of the Russian tsars; the reign-by-reign record of the rulers of imperial Russia. Thames & Hudson 1999 224p il $34.95 **947**

1. Russia—Kings and rulers 2. Russia—History

ISBN 0-500-05093-7 LC 98-61289

The introduction provides a "historical overview of how Tsarism came into being. The succeeding chapters are divided by major political events and social upheaval. . . . The reign of each tsar is analyzed within this framework, highlighting major events, but also giving abundant personal details such as marriages, children, etc." SLJ

Includes bibliographical references

947.08 Russia—1855-

Kurth, Peter

Tsar: the lost world of Nicholas and Alexandra; photographs by Peter Christopher. Little, Brown 1995 229p il hardcover o.p. pa $29.95 **947.08**

1. Nicholas II, Emperor of Russia, 1868-1918 2. Alexandra, Empress, consort of Nicholas II, Emperor of Russia, 1872-1918 3. Russia—History

ISBN 0-316-50787-3; 0-316-55788-9 (pa)

LC 95-12820

In text and photographs, this volume examines the lives of Tsar Nicholas II, the Empress Alexandra, and the Russian Imperial family.

"A large format and a profusion of illustrations ostensibly mark it a picture book; instead it is a remarkably comprehensive overview of the reign of the last czar and his consort. . . . Kurth sensitively documents the imperial family's suffering as prisoners of the Bolsheviks and their eventual execution." Booklist

Includes bibliographical references

Massie, Robert K., 1929-

The Romanovs; the final chapter. Random House 1995 308p il hardcover o.p. pa $14.95 * **947.08**

1. Nicholas II, Emperor of Russia, 1868-1918 2. House of Romanov 3. Russia—Kings and rulers

ISBN 0-394-58048-6; 0-345-40640-0 (pa)

LC 95-4718

This book "is divided into three major parts. The first segment—by far the most fascinating and original—focuses on the complex scientific process used in identifying the Romanovs' remains. . . . The second part concerns the various impostors who have claimed to be members of the Russian imperial family. . . . [The] third segment [is] a report on those Romanov émigrés—close relatives of the Czar's—who survived the Bolsheviks' persecution." N Y Times Book Rev

Includes bibliographical references

Pipes, Richard

A concise history of the Russian Revolution. Knopf 1995 431p il maps pa $16 hardcover o.p. **947.08**

1. Russia—History

ISBN 0-679-74544-0 (pa) LC 95-3127

A one volume condensation of the author's The Russian Revolution and Russia under the Bolshevik regime

"Forcefully showing why the 70-year-old Communist experiment failed {Pipes} provides the nonacademic reader with accurate historical events in a highly readable format." Libr J

Includes bibliographical references

The Russian Revolution. Knopf 1990 xxiv, 944p il maps pa $25 hardcover o.p. **947.08**

1. Russia—History

ISBN 0-679-73660-3 (pa) LC 89-35129

The author provides a "history of great turmoil, from the last decade of the nineteenth century, when student

Pipes, Richard—_Continued_

ferment reached troublesome proportions, to the Bolshevik takeover in October 1917 and the party's subsequent establishment of its own authoritarian regime." Booklist

This is a "massive, wonderfully vivid, gripping chronicle. . . . No other book so brilliantly clarifies the inner dynamics of the Russian Revolution." Publ Wkly

Includes bibliographical references

947.084   Russia (Soviet Union)—1917-1991

Amis, Martin

Koba the dread; laughter and the twenty million. Hyperion 2002 306p il $24.95   **947.084**
1. Stalin, Joseph, 1879-1953 2. Soviet Union—Politics and government
ISBN 0-7868-6876-7

Also available in paperback from Vintage Bks.

This book "evokes a terrible crime, in fact several million crimes. Koba is Joseph Stalin, the 20 million his victims. Interwoven with [the author's] impressionistic narrative . . . are details of Amis's family history, along with his sparring with the memory of his late father, Kingsley, and a close friend, the English journalist Christopher Hitchens, both one-time defenders of Soviet rule." Libr J

"Amis create[s] a compelling narrative, summarizing vast amounts of information and presenting it in a lucid, accessible form." New York Times

Brent, Jonathan

Stalin's last crime; the plot against the Jewish doctors, 1948-1953; {by} Jonathan Brent and Vladimir P. Naumov. HarperCollins 2003 399p $26.95; pa $14.95   **947.084**
1. Stalin, Joseph, 1879-1953 2. Jews—Persecutions
ISBN 0-06-019524-X; 0-06-093310-0 (pa)
LC 2002-191930

"This book points out suspicious inconsistencies in official accounts of Stalin's death and fingers chief of secret police Beria as a likely assassin. . . . Brent and Naumov link Stalin's famously anti-Semitic 'Doctors' Plot,' in which Jewish doctors were unjustly accused of conspiring to murder important politicians, to the ridiculous 'plan of the internal blow,' another alleged conspiracy of officials supposedly aiding an American plan to nuke the Kremlin itself. The authors argue that these Stalin-engineered plots were to be used by the paranoid dictator as justification for nuclear war. Tales of Stalin's paranoia are nothing new, but rarely are his subtle, yet relentless, machinations laid out in such intricate detail." Booklist

Includes bibliographical references

Figes, Orlando

A people's tragedy; the Russian Revolution, 1891-1924. Viking 1997 xx, 923p pa $25 hardcover o.p.   **947.084**
1. Soviet Union—History—1917-1921, Revolution
ISBN 0-14-024364-X (pa)   LC 96-36761
First published 1996 in the United Kingdom

This is a "history of the Russian Revolution from 1917 to Lenin's death in 1924." Choice

The author has "produced an engagingly written and well-researched book that will leave few readers with any doubts that the Bolsheviks, and especially their leader, Lenin, were ruthless killers, willing to sacrifice millions of lives for the sake of power and their own personal ambitions." N Y Times Book Rev

Includes bibliographical references

The whisperers; private life in Stalin's Russia. Metropolitan Books 2007 xxxviii, 739p il map $35
*   **947.084**
1. Soviet Union—Social conditions 2. Communism—Soviet Union
ISBN 978-0-8050-7461-1; 0-8050-7461-9
LC 2007-24223

The author describes "the inner world of ordinary Soviet citizens as they struggled to survive." Publisher's note

"This is a humbling monument to the evil and endurance of Russia's Soviet past and, implicitly, a guide to its present." Economist

Includes bibliographical references

Hochschild, Adam, 1942-

The unquiet ghost; Russians remember Stalin. Houghton Mifflin 2003 304p il map pa $14.95
947.084
1. Stalin, Joseph, 1879-1953 2. Soviet Union—History
ISBN 978-0-618-25747-8; 0-618-25747-0
"A Mariner book"
First published 1994 by Viking

In this look at Stalin's legacy the author "visits the ruins of the old prison camps of Kazakhstan and Kolyma, digs through the K.G.B. archives and spends a night at Stalin's seaside retreat. Most important, he interviews camp survivors, camp guards and the children of both. The questions he asks are of universal significance. . . . By asking these questions while traveling through today's Russia, Mr. Hochschild effectively places Stalinism in a modern context." N Y Times Book Rev

Includes bibliographical references

Medvedev, Roy Aleksandrovich, 1925-

Let history judge; the origins and consequences of Stalinism; {by} Roy Medvedev. rev and expanded ed, edited and translated by George Shriver. Columbia Univ. Press 1989 xxi, 903p $104; pa $35 *   **947.084**
1. Stalin, Joseph, 1879-1953 2. Soviet Union—Politics and government
ISBN 0-231-06350-4; 0-231-06351-2 (pa)
LC 89-758

Original Russian edition copyrighted 1967; first United States edition published 1972 by Knopf

"Never have Stalin's crimes against humanity been more forcefully or more thoroughly documented than in . . . {this book, which} distills firsthand testimonies of the mass arrests, torture, imprisonment and executions that befell millions of innocent Soviet citizens." Publ Wkly

Includes bibliographical references

Pipes, Richard
Russia under the Bolshevik regime. Vintage
Books 1995 587p il map pa $21   **947.084**
1. Lenin, Vladimir Il´ich, 1870-1924 2. Soviet
Union—History
ISBN 978-0-679-76184-6; 0-679-76184-5
First published 1994 by Knopf
"In this sequel to The Russian Revolution Pipes persuasively argues that Lenin's one-party dictatorship,
through its terrorizing, suppression of the press, censorship and monopolistic control of cultural organizations,
set the stage for Stalin's genocidal totalitarianism. . . .
Pipes shows how both Hitler and Mussolini drew on Lenin's tyrannical methods, and he perceptively analyzes
the mindset of Western fellow-travelers who wove fantasies of the U.S.S.R. as an egalitarian Eden while rational-
izing its evils." Publ Wkly
Includes bibliographical references

Reed, John, 1887-1920
Ten days that shook the world. Penguin Books
2007 368p (Penguin classics) pa $12
                                    947.084
1. Soviet Union—History—1917-1921, Revolution
ISBN 978-0-14-144212-9; 0-14-144212-3
First published 1919 by International Pubs.
"A reportorial, firsthand, and sympathetic account of
the November Revolution in Russia (1917). . . . After
prefatory explanation of political groups and other organizations, and of the background of the uprising, the
work tells with graphic detail of the fall of the provisional government, the revolution and counterrevolution, the
solidifying of power, and the resultant congress." Oxford
Companion to Am Lit. 5th edition

947.085   Russia (Soviet Union)—
1953-1991

Gorbachev, Mikhail
On my country and the world; [by] Gorbachev.
Columbia Univ. Press 1999 300p $50; pa $17.95
                                    947.085
1. World politics—1965- 2. Soviet Union—Politics
and government 3. Russia (Federation)—Politics and
government
ISBN 0-231-11514-8; 0-231-11515-6 (pa)
                            LC 99-31273
The former Soviet leader presents an analysis of his
country's Communist past and an account of his role in
government in the 1980s. Gorbachev also includes ideas
for political change
Gorbachev is "fresh and candid in its initial section on
the pluses and minuses of the Revolution of 1917." Nation

Remnick, David
Lenin's tomb; Russia and the fall of
Communism. Random House 1993 576p pa $15.95
hardcover o.p. *   **947.085**
1. Soviet Union—Politics and government
ISBN 0-679-75125-4 (pa)   LC 92-56841

"This book is a record of almost four years beginning
in 1988 when David Remnick, a Washington Post reporter, was assigned to Moscow. . . . He argues convincingly that what did in the old Soviet leadership, right down
through Mikhail Gorbachev, was its unending assault not
only on people but on memory. By making a secret of
history, it made its people increasingly distracted, and
desperate, until they overthrew it." N Y Times Book Rev

Satter, David, 1947-
Age of delirium; the decline and fall of the
Soviet Union. Yale University Press 2001 424p pa
$30   **947.085**
1. Soviet Union—History
ISBN 0-300-08705-5; 978-0-300-08705-5
First published 1996 by Knopf
The author "appraises the Russians by writing about
the travails of average people in the last decade of Soviet
rule. Objects of the Communist ideology's enforced unanimity, his subjects include dissidents sent to psychiatric
wards, persecuted religious people, a TASS journalist
learning how to write the party line, and miners exploited by the workers' state. . . . An insightful from-the-
ground-up view of typical Russians whom the top-down
politicians are now courting." Booklist

947.086   Russia—1991-

Baker, Peter
Kremlin rising; Vladimir Putin's Russia and the
end of revolution; [by] Peter Baker and Susan
Glasser. Scribner 2005 453p il $27.50
                                    947.086
1. Russia (Federation)—Politics and government
ISBN 0-743-26431-2   LC 2005-44157
"A Lisa Drew book"
The authors chronicle the transformation of contempo-
rary Russia under President Vladimir Putin.
"Well written, well reported and well organized, the
book consists of freestanding chapters that touch on the
most important events and trends in contemporary Rus-
sia, from the war in Chechnya to the spread of AIDS and
the dire state of the Russian judicial system." N Y Times
(Late N Y Ed)
Includes bibliographical references

Lieven, Anatol
Chechnya; tombstone of Russian power; with
photographs by Heidi Bradner. Yale Univ. Press
1998 436p il $55; pa $28   **947.086**
1. Chechnya (Russia)
ISBN 0-300-07398-4; 0-300-07881-1 (pa)
                            LC 98-84479
This is an account of "Chechnya's strategic and symbolic significance, the breakdown of legitimacy, mismanagement and pervasive corruption within the Russian
state, from Yeltsin down, which destroyed public and
military morale." Publ Wkly
"The book is a great, ostentatiously erudite festival of
ideas, sometimes brilliant, sometimes dubious, but never
less than interesting." N Y Times Book Rev

Meier, Andrew

Black earth; a journey through Russia after the fall. Norton 2003 511p il map $28.95; pa $15.95

947.086

1. Russia (Federation)

ISBN 0-393-05178-1; 0-393-32641-1 (pa)

LC 2003-6562

"The author recounts his travels crisscrossing post-Soviet Russia. . . . Apart from brief sections devoted to Moscow at the beginning and end, the bulk of the book is devoted to the South (Chechnya), the North (Norilsk), the East (Sakhalin Island) and the West (St. Petersburg)." N Y Times Book Rev

"After talking to scores of people—from survivors of the Aldy massacre to a harrowed Russian lieutenant colonel who runs the body-collection point closest to the Chechen battleground—Meier paints in this heartbreaking book a devastating picture of contemporary life in a country where, as one man put it, people have 'lived like the lowest dogs for more than eighty years.'" Publ Wkly

Includes bibliographical references

Politkovskaya, Anna

A Russian diary; a journalist's final account of life, corruption, and death in Putin's Russia; translated by Arch Tait; foreword by Scott Simon. Random House 2007 369p map $25.95

947.086

1. Putin, Vladimir 2. Russia (Federation)—Politics and government

ISBN 1-4000-6682-4; 978-1-4000-6682-7

LC 2007-296943

These are the journals kept by the Russian journalist who was killed in Moscow in 2006.

This is a "brilliant . . . portrayal of Russian life during the middle years of Putin's rule." New York Rev Books

Remnick, David

Resurrection; the struggle for a new Russia. Random House 1997 398p pa $15 hardcover o.p.
*

947.086

1. Russia (Federation)—Politics and government

ISBN 0-375-75023-1 (pa)   LC 96-47360

In this companion volume to Lenin's tomb, "Remnick concentrates on the post-Soviet scene and its prospects. . . . Chaotic uncertainty, massive corruption, and crime are notoriously present, yet the possibility of a different, better life also beckons. . . . This is an interesting, highly informative portrait of a country struggling toward a fateful future." Libr J

Includes bibliographical references

Service, Robert

A history of twentieth-century Russia. Harvard Univ. Press 1998 xxxiii, 653p il maps $32.50; pa $20.95

947.086

1. Soviet Union—History

ISBN 0-674-40347-9; 0-674-40348-7 (pa)

LC 97-37440

First published 1997 in the United Kingdom

In this "survey of recent Russian history, Robert Service spans the . . . era from the rise of communism in the first decade of this century to the aftermath of its collapse in 1991." Economist

"A perceptive, judicious appraisal." Booklist

Includes bibliographical references

947.5   Caucasus

Baiev, Khassan

The Oath; a surgeon under fire; [by] Khassan Baiev; with Ruth and Nicholas Daniloff. Walker & Co. 2003 376p il $26   **947.5**

1. Chechnya (Russia)

ISBN 0-8027-1404-8   LC 2003-52502

This "memoir tells the story of a surgeon in Chechnya who, through two invasions of his homeland, refused to take up arms, choosing instead to treat civilians and soldiers on both sides, even as he was targeted for death by both Russian and Chechen leaders." Booklist

The author "is modest, which only adds to his heroism. But more than that, he has humanized the Chechens, whom others have portrayed as terrorists. Russian president Vladimir Putin has tried to equate Russia's fight against the Chechens with the U.S. battle against al-Qaida. Those who read this stirring memoir will be hard-pressed to see the situation so simply." Publ Wkly

Seierstad, Åsne

The angel of Grozny; orphans of a forgotten war; translated by Nadia Christensen. Basic Books 2008 340p $25.95   **947.5**

1. Chechnya (Russia)—History—1994- (Civil War)

ISBN 978-0-465-01122-3; 0-465-01122-5

LC 2008-925222

In the early hours of New Year's 1994, Russian troops invaded the Republic of Chechnya, plunging the country into a prolonged and bloody conflict that continues to this day. A foreign correspondent in Moscow at the time, Åsne Seierstad traveled regularly to Chechnya to report on the war, describing its affects on those trying to live their daily lives amidst violence.

"Seierstad's searing, evocative recounting brings Chechnya to life, especially the unimaginable suffering and strength of the Chechen people. Powerful, painful, and raw, . . . [this] is essential reading." Booklist

948   Scandinavia

The **Oxford** illustrated history of the Vikings; edited by Peter Sawyer. Oxford Univ. Press 1997 298p il maps hardcover o.p. pa $27.50

948

1. Vikings

ISBN 0-19-820526-0; 0-19-285434-8 (pa)

LC 97-16649

This illustrated collection of articles includes discussion of the Vikings' impact on England, Iceland, Greenland, Russia, and the Frankish and Danish Empires; Viking ships and ship-building; Viking religion; and the ways in which Vikings have been portrayed throughout history. Significant archaeological finds are featured.

Includes bibliographical references

Roesdahl, Else

The Vikings; translated by Susan M. Margeson and Kirsten Williams. 2nd ed. Penguin Books 1998 324p il map pa $17 **948**

1. Vikings

ISBN 0-14-025282-7; 978-0-14-025282-8

Original Danish edition, 1987

A survey of Viking civilization from c.750-c.1050.

"About one-third of the book deals with Viking expansion into Russia, Normandy, the British Isles, Iceland, Greenland, etc. . . . . Most of the book surveys the geography, people, society, religion, art, etc., of the Vikings' Scandinavian homelands." Libr J

Includes bibliographical references

948.97 Finland

Beach, Hugh

A year in Lapland; guest of the reindeer herders; with a new afterword by the author. University of Washington Press 2001 242p il map pa $25 **948.97**

1. Lapland 2. Sami (European people)

ISBN 0-295-98037-0; 978-0-295-98037-9

LC 00-47936

First published 1993 by Smithsonian Institution Press

The author "tells of his first year among the Saami reindeer herders of Swedish Lapland. His narrative interweaves adventure, descriptions of the harsh beauty of the landscape, supernatural tales and ancient myths. Beach also explores topics of change in the lives of the herders brought on by laws requiring village groups to move and by adaptations to new items such as rubber boots, seaplanes, and appliances." Libr J

949.2 Netherlands

Schama, Simon

The embarrassment of riches; an interpretation of Dutch culture in the Golden Age. Knopf 1987 698p il maps pa $23 hardcover o.p. **949.2**

1. Netherlands—Civilization

ISBN 0-679-78124-2 (pa)

LC 86-45418

A Borzoi Bk.

The author aims to show "how, in the seventeenth century, a modest assortment of farming, fishing and shipping communities, without shared language, religion or government, transformed themselves into a formidable world empire—the Dutch Republic." Publisher's note

"Delving into customs, beliefs, popular art and quirks of behavior, Schama has fashioned a tour de force, a profound, unconventional and rewarding portrait of a people." Publ Wkly

Includes bibliographical references

949.5 Greece

Clogg, Richard, 1939-

A concise history of Greece. 2nd ed. Cambridge Univ. Press 2002 291p il maps (Cambridge concise histories) $53; pa $19 **949.5**

1. Greece—History

ISBN 0-521-80872-3; 0-521-00479-9 (pa)

LC 2002-725551

First published 1992

This is an illustrated introduction to the history of modern Greece from the late eighteenth century to the present

Includes bibliographical references

Mazower, Mark

Salonica, city of ghosts; Christians, Muslims, and Jews, 1430-1950. Knopf 2005 490p il maps $35 **949.5**

1. Thessalonike (Greece)

ISBN 0-375-41298-0

LC 2004-57690

First published 2004 in the United Kingdom

This is a history of the Greek city.

The author's "graceful, evocative prose, his deft attention to details and his empathetic presentation of all sides of the story add up to a magnificent tale of this unique city." Publ Wkly

Includes bibliographical references

Norwich, John Julius, 1929-

Byzantium: the apogee. Knopf 1991 xxiv, 389p il map $49.95 **949.5**

1. Byzantine Empire

ISBN 0-394-53779-3

LC 91-53119

"A Borzoi Bk."

This is the second volume of a three-volume narrative history of the Byzantine Empire. "Beginning with Charlemagne's coronation in 800 A.D. and the resulting split in the Christian world, Norwich traces the return of iconoclasm, political intrigues, military campaigns, atrocities, and alliances, ending with the fateful battle at Nanzikert from which the Empire never recovered. . . . [The author] deftly brings to life the frozen icons of the history books." Libr J

Includes bibliographical references

Byzantium: the decline and fall. Knopf 1995 xxxvii, 488p il maps $49.95 **949.5**

1. Byzantine Empire

ISBN 0-679-41650-1

This final volume of the author's three volume narrative history chronicles the last four centuries of the Byzantine Empire.

Includes bibliographical references

Byzantium: the early centuries. Knopf 1989 407p il $49.95 **949.5**

1. Byzantine Empire

ISBN 0-394-53778-5

LC 88-45508

"A Borzoi Bk."

First published 1988 in the United Kingdom

Norwich, John Julius, 1929-—*Continued*

This is the first of a three-volume narrative history of the Byzantine Empire. It traces Byzantium's history "from the birth of Constantine c.274 to the coronation of Charlemagne on Christmas Day 800." Libr J

Includes bibliographical references

A short history of Byzantium. Knopf 1997 430p
il maps pa $17.95 hardcover o.p. *

949.5

1. Byzantine Empire
ISBN 0-679-77269-3 (pa)   LC 96-44458

"In his shorter telling of the history between the founding of Constantinople in 330 and its fall in 1453, Lord Norwich has sacrificed none of the virtues of the longer work: lively narration and a taste for the eccentric anecodote and revelatory detail." N Y Times Book Rev

949.6   Balkan Peninsula

Pamuk, Orhan, 1952-

Istanbul; memories and the city; translated from the Turkish by Maureen Freely. Knopf 2005 384p
il $26.95   **949.6**

1. Istanbul (Turkey)
ISBN 1-400-04095-7   LC 2004-61537
Original Turkish edition, 2003

The novelist writes about his life as a resident of Istanbul.

"The author mingles 'personal memoir with cultural history', and a fascinating read it is too for anyone who has even the slightest acquaintance with this fabled bridge between east and west." Economist

949.7   Serbia and Montenegro, Croatia, Slovenia, Bosnia and Hercegovina, Macedonia

Clark, Wesley K.

Waging modern war; Bosnia, Kosovo, and the future of combat. PublicAffairs 2001 xxxi, 479p il
map pa $18 hardcover o.p. *   **949.7**

1. Yugoslav War, 1991-1995
ISBN 1-58648-139-8 (pa)   LC 01-19717

This is an account of the former Supreme Allied Commander's experiences during the Kosovo crises. "Clark tells a story of frustration with NATO allies, who had to approve each operation and target selection, and with U.S. policymakers as he tried to formulate a strategy that would achieve his military goals." Libr J

Di Giovanni, Janine

Madness visible; a memoir of war. Knopf 2003
285p map hardcover o.p. pa $14   **949.7**

1. Kosovo (Serbia)
ISBN 0-375-41073-2; 978-0-375-72455-8 (pa);
0-375-72455-9 (pa)   LC 2002-44820

This "narrative of the 1999 war in Kosovo, NATO's campaign against Serbia, and the ouster of Milosevic of-

fers an unbiased view of the enormous suffering of Yugoslav Albanians and Serbs following the genocidal rage of the Belgrade regime against the Kosovo Liberation Army's (KLA) drive for an independent Kosovo. . . . This exciting work is highly recommended for all libraries." Libr J

Includes bibliographical references

Maass, Peter, 1960-

Love thy neighbor; a story of war. Knopf 1996
305p pa $14 hardcover o.p.   **949.7**

1. Yugoslav War, 1991-1995 2. Bosnia and Hercegovina
ISBN 0-679-76389-9 (pa)   LC 95-39250

This book on the Yugoslav conflict is based on Maass's experiences as the Washington Post's reporter in Bosnia

"Maass was only in Bosnia for about a year, from 1992 to 1993, but he saw a great deal. And he displays extraordinary sensitivity to the ambiguities of his position." Nation

Includes bibliographical references

McAllester, Matthew, 1969-

Beyond the Mountains of the Damned; the war inside Kosovo. New York Univ. Press 2002 227p
il $30; pa $17.95   **949.7**

ISBN 0-8147-5660-3; 0-8147-5661-1 (pa)
LC 2001-4370

This is an account of the war in Kosovo. McAllester "tells the story of Pec, Kosovo's most destroyed city and the site of the earliest and worst atrocities of the war, through the lives of two men—one Serb and one Kosovar." Publisher's note

"McAllester's spare, understated prose . . . is potent, as is his exploration of the human side of geopolitics and war." Publ Wkly

Includes bibliographical references

Rieff, David

Slaughterhouse; Bosnia and the failure of the West. Simon & Schuster 1995 240p pa $18.95
hardcover o.p.   **949.7**

1. Yugoslav War, 1991-1995 2. Bosnia and Hercegovina
ISBN 0-684-81903-1 (pa)   LC 94-40148

This account of the war in the former Yugoslavia grew out of Rieff's travels in the region from 1992 through 1994

"*Slaughterhouse* is perhaps the most powerful, passionate, and penetrating dissection of a Westerner of the ongoing Bosnian tragedy." Booklist

Rohde, David, 1967-

Endgame; the betrayal and fall of Srebrenica, Europe's worst massacre since World War II. Westview Press 1998 450p il pa $20

949.7

1. Yugoslav War, 1991-1995 2. Srebrenica (Bosnia and Hercegovina)
ISBN 0-8133-3533-7; 978-0-8133-3533-9

LC 98-26127

Rohde, David, 1967-—*Continued*

First published 1997 by Farrar, Straus & Giroux

This "is an account of the capture of the small Bosnian town of Srebrenica in July 1995 and the subsequent killing by the conquering Serbs of around 7,000 of its people. The massacre gnaws at the Western conscience not just because of its coldbloodedness and size, but because in April 1993 Srebrenica had become the first place in the world to be declared a 'safe area' by the United Nations." N Y Times Book Rev

"Rohde argues that the fall of Srebrenica could have been prevented, but he is ultimately unable to explain the 'collective failure' of the United States, the United Nations, and NATO in stopping the massacre. His investigation is carefully documented by over 300 footnotes. This is an important and revealing book." Libr J

Includes bibliographical references

Silber, Laura

Yugoslavia; death of a nation; {by} Laura Silber and Allan Little. rev and updated ed. Penguin Bks. 1997 403p il maps pa $15 * **949.7**

1. Yugoslav War, 1991-1995 2. Yugoslavia—Politics and government

ISBN 0-14-026263-6   LC 96-36086

First published 1995 in the United Kingdom with title: The death of Yugoslavia; first United States edition published 1996 by TV Books

This book, a companion volume to a BBC television series called The Death of Yugoslavia, chronicles the disintegration of the Socialist Federal Republic of Yugoslavia in 1991 and charts the development of the ensuing conflict

This is "an impressive achievement. Strong on characters, regional nuances, and the 'inner' diplomatic game, 'Yugoslavia' is a work of depth and breadth that will be hard to eclipse. It answers many perplexities left from five years of Balkan intrigues and war." Christ Sci Monit {review of 1996 edition}

950   History of Asia

Fallows, James M.

Looking at the sun; {by} James Fallows. Pantheon Bks. 1994 517p pa $15 hardcover o.p. **950**

1. East Asia

ISBN 0-679-76162-4 (pa)   LC 93-38367

The author discusses the "culture, government and economic development of 11 East Asian nations. . . . Mr. Fallows's central thesis is that Western societies, especially the United States, 'have been using the wrong mental tools to classify, shape and understand the information they receive about Asia.'" N Y Times Book Rev

"A fascinating, fresh, and potentially controversial contemplation of the global market." Booklist

Higham, Charles

Encyclopedia of ancient Asian civilizations; [by] Charles F.W. Higham. Facts on File 2004 xxi, 440p il map (Facts on File library of world history) $85 **950**

1. Asia—Civilization—Encyclopedias

ISBN 0-8160-4640-9   LC 2003-48513

This "volume 'concentrates on civilizations that arose east of the Caspian Sea,' from modern Afghanistan and the Aral Sea south to India and Sri Lanka and east to Japan, Korea, and the islands of Southeast Asia. The years covered range from 3000 B.C.E. through the 15th century." SLJ

"This is a good beginning point for research, especially in regard to archaeological excavations." Booklist

Includes bibliographical references

Levinson, David, 1947-

Encyclopedia of modern Asia; {by} David Levinson, Karen Christensen. Scribner 2002 6v il maps set $695 **950**

ISBN 0-684-80617-7   LC 2002-8712

This "set is alphabetically arranged by topic. Volume 6 provides the index for the set. . . . The topics cover the 33 Asian countries' geography, economics, politics, human rights, cultures and languages, and biographies. Sidebars derived from primary source materials and black-and-white illustrations are interspersed throughout the text." Am Ref Books Annu, 2003

Includes bibliographical references

951   China and adjacent areas

The **Cambridge** history of China; general editors, Denis Twitchett and John K. Fairbank. Cambridge Univ. Press 1978-2002 12v v1 $205; v3 $205; v6 $178; v7 $205; v8 $178; v9 $178; v10 $195; v11 $205; v12 $205; v13 $205; v14 $180; v15 $195 * **951**

1. China—History

ISBN 0-521-24327-0 (v1); 0-521-21446-7 (v3); 0-521-24331-9 (v6); 0-521-24332-7 (v7); 0-521-24333-5 (v8); 0-521-24334-3 (v9); 0-521-21447-5 (v10); 0-521-22029-7 (v11); 0-521-23541-3 (v12); 0-521-24338-6 (v13); 0-521-24336-X (v14); 0-521-24337-8 (v15)

      LC 76-29852

Twelve volumes of a projected fifteen volume set

Contents: v1 The Ch'in and Han Empires, 221 B.C.-A.D. 220; v3 Sui and T'ang China, 589-906, pt.1 (ISBN 0-521-21446-7); v6 Alien regimes and border states, 907-1368; v7 The Ming Dynasty, 1368-1644, pt.1; v8 The Ming Dynasty, 1368-1644, pt.2; v9 The Ch'ing Empire to 1800, pt.1; v10 Late Ch'ing, 1800-1911, pt.1; v11 Late Ch'ing, 1800-1911, pt.2; v12 Republican China, 1912-1949, pt.1; v13 Republican China, 1912-1949, pt.2; v14 The People's Republic, pt.1; v15 The People's Republic, pt.2: Revolutions within the Chinese Revolution, 1966-1982

"An important series for scholars, this is also a valuable reference tool for general collections." Libr J

Includes bibliographical references

Chetham, Deirdre

Before the deluge; the vanishing world of the Yangtze's Three Gorges. Palgrave 2002 xxiii, 296p il map pa $17.95 hardcover o.p.   **951**

    1. Yangtze River valley (China)

    ISBN 1-4039-6428-9 (pa)   LC 2002-16939

"What will be the world's largest hydroelectric dam is under construction in the remote Three Gorges area of China's Upper Yangtze River. Of the nearly 1500 towns that will be submerged when the project is complete, the author focuses on a handful. . . . She describes their residents involved in their daily affairs—working, worshiping, getting by—even as the flood waters ineluctably rise around them." Libr J

The author "paints a pulsating picture of the great river, the countryside, the people and their occupations, the amazingly fluid political philosophies and the sheer endurance of all parties, past and present, involved with the overwhelming project." Publ Wkly

Includes bibliographical references

Dalai Lama XIV, 1935-

My Tibet; text by His Holiness the fourteenth Dalai Lama of Tibet; photographs and introduction by Galen Rowell. University of Calif. Press 1990 162p il pa $34.95 hardcover o.p.   **951**

    ISBN 0-520-08948-0 (pa)   LC 90-10868

"A Mountain Light Press book"

This is "a volume of photographs taken in recent years by Galen Rowell, with a text drawn from interviews with the Dalai Lama or essays written previously by him." N Y Times Book Rev

"Nowhere has the logic of merging Buddhist philosophy and environmentalism received a clearer and more compelling expression than in My Tibet. . . . It is a model of the kind of chemistry that can develop when both a wonderful photographer and a thoughtful writer care deeply about their subject." Nat Hist

DeWoskin, Rachel

Foreign babes in Beijing; behind the scenes of a new China. W. W. Norton 2005 332p $24.95; pa $13.95   **951**

    1. China—Social life and customs

    ISBN 0-393-05902-2; 0-393-32859-7 (pa)

                        LC 2005-939

The author recounts her experiences living in China in the 1990s, where she had a starring role in the soap opera "Foreign Babes in Beijing."

"Ms DeWoskin's portrait of the complexities of urban China is not uncritical. But her book is written with enormous warmth for its people. And it is all the better for avoiding neat conclusions." Economist

Dong, Stella

Shanghai, 1842-1949; the rise and fall of a decadent city. Morrow 2000 318p il pa $15 hardcover o.p.   **951**

    1. Shanghai (China)

    ISBN 0-06-093481-6 (pa)   LC 99-41902

An "account of a city legendary for decadence, violence, and greedy imperialism. Dong meticulously details

the European commercial interests that deliberately promoted opium trafficking and exploited the land and people of Shanghai with every conceivable vice for nearly 100 years." Booklist

Facts about China; edited by Xiao-bin Ji; contributors, Eric Dalle. Wilson, H.W. 2003 751p map $105   **951**

    1. China

    ISBN 0-8242-0961-3   LC 2001-45510

This "reference source covers all major topics regarding the People's Republic of China. Part 1 includes chapters on its geography and climate, peoples and language, systems of thought and belief, health and medicine, arts, entertainment and sports, literature, science and technology, economy and trade, and institutions (government and other) of Chinese society. Part 2 provides a chronology of important events in Chinese history; part 3, an alphabetical list of common Chinese concepts, important figures and events; and part 4, information and advice for future travelers." Choice

Includes bibliographical references

Fairbank, John King, 1907-1991

China; a new history; {by} John King Fairbank and Merle Goldman. enl ed. Belknap Press 1998 546p il maps pa $19.95 hardcover o.p. *   **951**

    1. China—History

    ISBN 0-674-11673-9 (pa)   LC 98-9474

First published 1992

Fairbank covers the history of China from paleolithic cultures of 400,000 B.C. up to 1989. Goldman adds a chapter on events in the post-Mao period and a new preface and epilogue

Includes bibliographical references

The great Chinese revolution: 1800-1985. Harper & Row 1986 396p maps hardcover o.p. pa $16   **951**

    1. China—History

    ISBN 0-06-039057-3; 0-06-039076-X (pa)

                        LC 86-665

"A Cornelia & Michael Bessie book"

Contents: Late imperial China: growth and change, 1800-1895; The transformation of the late imperial order, 1895-1911; The era of the first Chinese Republic, 1912-1949; The Chinese People's Republic, 1949-1985

"The book is never pedantic, but gathers together a lifetime of scholarship plus a true gift for presentation of complex issues and a fine eye for telling illustration." Libr J

Includes bibliographical references

Hessler, Peter, 1969-

Oracle bones; a journey between China's past and present. HarperCollins 2006 491p il $26.95 *   **951**

    1. China—Description and travel 2. China—Civilization

    ISBN 0-06-082658-4   LC 2005-52607

Hessler, Peter, 1969——*Continued*

This book explores "the interaction of China with the West, [as] told through craftily interwoven vignettes with cultural, political, and social resonance." Libr J

The author "has a marvelous sense of the intonations and gestures that give life to the moment; he knows when to join in the action and when simply to wait for things to happen. Today's China could have been made for him." N Y Times Book Rev

Includes bibliographical references

Kemenade, Willem van

China, Hong Kong, Taiwan, Inc.; translated from the Dutch by Diane Webb. Knopf 1997 444p pa $16 hardcover o.p.   **951**
1. China—Politics and government 2. Hong Kong (China) 3. Taiwan
ISBN 0-679-77756-3 (pa)   LC 97-71923

This is an "analysis of China's recent past and reflections on its future direction. Van Kemenade explores the anticipated political and economic fallout from the mainland's absorption of capitalist Hong Kong . . . and the possibility of its eventual takeover of Taiwan. He projects a foreseeable confrontation with Japan over Asian hegemony, ethnic and economic upheavals on China's 'wild' western border that abutts former Soviet republics and a political backlash from the fast-growing middle class, which in its pursuit of wealth seems no longer loyal to socialist ideals." Publ Wkly

Prager, Emily

Wuhu diary; on taking my adopted daughter back to her hometown in China. Random House 2001 238p il pa $13 hardcover o.p.   **951**
1. China—Description and travel 2. Adoption
ISBN 0-385-72199-4 (pa)   LC 2001-19104

Prager discusses bringing her adopted daughter on a visit back to China. The book "chronicles mother and daughter's seven-week journey to Wuhu, a small city in the southern Chinese province of Anhui, where LuLu eventually celebrates her fifth birthday." Christ Sci Monit

"For anyone considering multicultural adoption or already involved in one, this compelling work offers encouragement and an example of how to help an adopted child get acquainted with her roots and build her sense of self. For others, it provides a wonderful view of a part of China seldom written about." Libr J

Preston, Diana

The Boxer Rebellion; the dramatic story of China's war on foreigners that shook the world in the summer of 1900. Walker & Co. 2000 xxvii, 436p il maps $28   **951**
1. China—History
ISBN 0-8027-1361-0   LC 00-39243
Also available in paperback from Berkley Pub. Group

"The Boxers, Chinese peasants who blamed foreigners for the dislocation of their lives, began by murdering missionaries and converts and destroying railroad and telegraph lines in the countryside. Gaining strength, they besieged the foreign quarters of Tientsin and Peking until European and Japanese troops came to the rescue." New

Yorker

"Preston's account, compiled from the many letters, diaries, and memoirs by European survivors of the siege, captures an odd strain of mordant humor." N Y Times Book Rev

Includes bibliographical references

Schell, Orville

Virtual Tibet; searching for Shangri-la from the Himalayas to Hollywood. Metropolitan Bks. 2000 340p $26; pa $15   **951**
1. Tibet (China)
ISBN 0-8050-4381-0; 0-8050-4382-9 (pa)
    LC 99-88146

"Metropolitan books."

Schell examines romanticized visions of Tibet in Western travel accounts and films

The author is a "seasoned traveler in China, . . . and his book has the bracing air about it of disenchantment. The fact that he was a bit of a seeker once himself, mesmerized by the idea of Tibet, and of Communist China, makes him the perfect chronicler of such afflictions in others." N Y Rev Books

Spence, Jonathan D.

The Chan's great continent; China in Western minds. Norton 1998 279p pa $14.95 hardcover o.p.
    951
1. China—Civilization
ISBN 0-393-31989-X (pa)   LC 98-10823

"Spence follows the ways that China has been 're-fracted over time in Western minds.' . . . In analyzing Western reactions to China from the thirteenth century to the present, reactions ranging from imaginative to stereotypical to informed, Spence {covers} . . . diplomatic reports, correspondence, travelogues, novels, drama, poetry, and film." Booklist

"Spence's book will appeal not only to those interested in history and literature, but to anyone looking for a perspective on contemporary discourse about China." Publ Wkly

Includes bibliographical references

God's Chinese son; the Taiping Heavenly Kingdom of Hong Xiuquan. Norton 1996 400p il maps pa $15.95 hardcover o.p.   **951**
1. Hung, Hsiu-ch'üan, 1814-1864 2. China—History—1850-1864, Taiping Rebellion
ISBN 0-393-31556-8 (pa)   LC 95-17245

"In 1836, twenty-two-year-old Hong Xiuquan failed the civil-service examinations in Canton and came across some Christian tracts. When he later fell sick and had visions, he became convinced that he was the Christian God's second son, destined to rule a 'heavenly kingdom' on earth. Many were attracted to Hong's egalitarian policies—despite his enforced separation of the sexes—and his sect prospered. But its attempts to overthrow the Qing dynasty resulted in unprecedented bloodshed: twenty million people died before the uprising was defeated, in 1864. Spence's present-tense narrative is riveting." New Yorker

Includes bibliographical references

Spence, Jonathan D.—*Continued*
The search for modern China. Norton 1990 xxv, 876p il maps pa $27.70 hardcover o.p.

951

1. China—History
ISBN 0-393-30780-8 (pa)   LC 89-9241
"Beginning with the decline of the Ming dynasty and ending with the Tiananmen Square massacre, Spence chronicles the cultural and social transformations of the country, concentrating on the many wars and rebellions." Booklist

Spence's "own sense of China's past is so vivid, his understanding so sure and his writer's skill so powerful that the reader apprehends distant events as if they were contemporary." New Statesman (1913)

Includes bibliographical references

Treason by the book; [by] Jonathan Spence. Viking 2001 300p map $24.95; pa $14

951

1. Tseng, Ch'ing, 1568-1650 2. China—History 3. China—Politics and government
ISBN 0-670-89292-0; 0-14-200041-8 (pa)
LC 00-43805
"In early-eighteenth-century China, Emperor Yongzheng deployed his vast bureaucracy to ferret out the origins of certain slanderous statements. The gossip proved to be part of a disinformation campaign run by rebels bent on overthrowing his dynasty. He quashed it by publishing a volume of some of the rebellious writings that had inspired the malcontents, along with rebuttals by a team of scholars, and then distributed it throughout his enormous empire as compulsory reading." New Yorker

"Spence's story of emperor, officials, and conspirators is both rousingly unlikely and highly informative." Libr J

Tsering Shakya
The dragon in the land of snows; a history of modern Tibet since 1947. Columbia Univ. Press 1999 574p il $32.50

951

1. Tibet (China)
ISBN 0-231-11814-7   LC 99-14020
Also available in paperback from Penguin Bks.
This history "explains what has happened to Tibet since the Chinese military invasion of 1950." Publ Wkly

"Drawing on Tibetan, Chinese, British, Indian and American sources, Shakya weaves an authoritative and easily readable narrative. 'The Dragon in the Land of Snows' is likely to be the definitive history of modern Tibet for a generation or more." N Y Times Book Rev

Includes bibliographical references

951.04   China—Period of Republic, 1912-1949

Chang, Iris, 1968-2004
The rape of Nanking; the forgotten holocaust of World War II. Penguin 1998 290p il pa $16 *

951.04

1. Nanjing (Jiangsu Province, China) massacre, 1937 2. Sino-Japanese Conflict, 1937-1945
ISBN 0-14-027744-7; 978-0-14-027744-9
LC 97-24137
First published 1997 by Basic Books
This is an account of the massacre in Nanking "of at least 250,000 Chinese civilians by invading Japanese troops in 1937." Libr J

"Chang's book is a memorial to the victims of Nanking, a damning indictment of Japanese political historiography, a valuable addition to Pacific war literature, and a literary model of how to speak about the unspeakable." Booklist

Includes bibliographical references

Sun Shuyun, 1963-
The Long March; the true history of Communist China's founding myth. Doubleday 2007 c2006 270p il map $26

951.04

1. Mao Zedong, 1893-1976 2. China—History—1912-1949
ISBN 978-0-385-52024-9; 0-385-52024-7
First published 2006 in the United Kingdom
"In 1934, surrounded by Chiang Kai-shek's forces in the south, Mao's Red Army marched more than eight thousand miles to a new base, in the northwest. The march, completed by only a fifth of the original army, was a defeat in all ways but one: it returned Mao from the political wilderness to power. Mao transformed the march into the founding myth of modern China and, in doing so, created a new narrative around victories that never happened. Shuyun, a Chinese-born BBC documentary producer, retraces the route and interviews the few remaining survivors, in an account that shows the human cost of Mao's revisionism." New Yorker

951.05   China—Period of People's Republic, 1949-

August, Oliver, 1971-
Inside the red mansion; on the trail of China's most wanted man. Houghton Mifflin Company 2007 268p map $26

951.05

1. Lai Changxing 2. China—Description and travel
ISBN 978-0-618-71498-8; 0-618-71498-7
LC 2006-26930
"In 1999, China's Public Enemy No. 1 was 'Fatty' Lai Changxing, an illiterate rice farmer turned real-estate and shipping mogul who fled the country, accused of heading a multibillion-dollar smuggling ring. This account . . . casts Lai's rise and fall as a cautionary tale of boomtown China. The author tours the remains of Lai's empire—a film studio built as a replica of the For-

August, Oliver, 1971-—*Continued*

bidden City; a posh brothel where he bribed Party officials with the company of 'Miss Temporarys'—but he reserves his most vivid prose for the 'fakers and fortune seekers, oddballs and outlaws' he meets along the way." New Yorker

Becker, Jasper

The Chinese. Oxford University Press 2002 493p il map pa $21.95　　　　**951.05**

1. China—Economic conditions 2. China—Social conditions

ISBN 0-19-514940-8

First published 2000 by Free Press

This account of China and the Chinese "conveys the sense of a country out of control: political corruption endangers economic development, ecological disaster looms, and a chasm grows between the powerful rich and the underrepresented poor. As Becker shows, China today is emerging from its Maoist past, which created a new nation and a Leninist bureaucracy but not a democracy, and from Deng Xiaoping's reforms, which unleashed market forces without waiting for the development of a legal system, public culture, or institutional transformation." Libr J [review of 2000 edition]

This "is a captivating and enlightening read for anyone interested in Asian or cultural studies." Booklist [review of 2000 edition]

Includes bibliographical references

Buruma, Ian

Bad elements; Chinese rebels from Los Angeles to Beijing. Random House 2001 xxv, 367p pa $15 hardcover o.p.　　　　**951.05**

1. Dissent 2. Human rights 3. China—Politics and government

ISBN 0-679-78136-6 (pa)　　　　LC 2001-19365

The author interviews Chinese dissidents in the United States, Asia, and Europe "to find out what happened to them and how they feel about the future of human rights in China. Buruma's study is both engaging and deeply informed." Libr J

Includes bibliographical references

Chang, Jung, 1952-

Wild swans; three daughters of China. Simon & Schuster 1991 524p il pa $15 hardcover o.p.

　　　　951.05

1. China—History 2. Women—China

ISBN 0-7432-4698-5 (pa)　　　　LC 91-20696

Also available in paperback from Anchor Bks.

The author "tells the harrowing life stories of her maternal grandmother, her mother, and herself. Their tales span a period of radical change in China that has touched every aspect of life." Booklist

Fang Lizhi

Bringing down the Great Wall; writings on science, culture, and democracy in China; introduction by Orville Schell; editor and principal translator, James H. Williams. Norton 1992 336p pa $10.95　　　　**951.05**

1. Human rights 2. China—Politics and government

ISBN 0-393-30885-5; 978-0-393-30885-3

　　　　LC 90-53064

First published 1990 by Knopf

"A comprehensive selection of the written (and spoken) words of the witty, passionate, tenacious and articulate Chinese scientist and dissident who at present is living in the United States." N Y Times Book Rev

Includes bibliographical references

Lord, Bette Bao

Legacies: a Chinese mosaic. Knopf 1990 245p pa $19 hardcover o.p.　　　　**951.05**

1. China—Social life and customs 2. China—Politics and government

ISBN 0-449-90620-5 (pa)　　　　LC 89-43452

The author lived in China from 1985 to 1989. Her book is based on interviews with Chinese people, including an actress, a teacher, a veteran of the Long March, an artist, a journalist, a peasant, an entrepreneur and a Communist Party cadre, who recount their experiences of persecution during the Cultural Revolution. The author also describes her own experiences and her family history

"A vivid and startling mosaic of the political struggles that foreshadowed the Tiananmen Square uprising." Time

Pomfret, John

Chinese lessons; five classmates and the story of the new China. H. Holt 2006 315p il map $26

　　　　951.05

1. China

ISBN 978-0-8050-7615-8; 0-8050-7615-8

　　　　LC 2006-41211

"As a twenty-year-old exchange student from Stanford University, John Pomfret spent a year at Nanjing University in China. His fellow classmates were among those who survived the twin tragedies of Mao's rule—the Great Leap Forward and the Cultural Revolution. . . . Pomfret went on to a career in journalism, spending the bulk of his time in China. After attending the twentieth reunion of his class, he decided to reacquaint himself with some of his classmates. Chinese Lessons is their story and his own." Publisher's note

This "is a highly personal, honest, funny and well-informed account of China's hyperactive effort to forget its past and reinvent its future." N Y Times Book Rev

Schoppa, R. Keith, 1943-

The Columbia guide to modern Chinese history. Columbia Univ. Press 2000 356p il map (Columbia guides to Asian history) $49

　　　　951.05

1. China—History

ISBN 0-231-11276-9　　　　LC 99-53420

Schoppa, R. Keith, 1943——*Continued*
This narrative overview of Chinese history focuses on five areas: domestic politics, society, the economy, culture, and relations with the outside world. Contains approximately 500 annotated entries for further research in English as well as electronic resources and films. A chronology, excerpts from primary documents, and numerous graphs and tables are appended
Includes bibliographical references

Wu, Harry
Bitter winds; a memoir of my years in China's Gulag; [by] Harry Wu and Carolyn Wakeman. Wiley 1993 290p il $35; pa $19.95
951.05
1. Political prisoners 2. China—Politics and government
ISBN 0-471-55645-9; 0-471-11425-1 (pa)
LC 93-15799
"A Robert L. Bernstein book."
In this "memoir, Wu recalls his 19 years in Chinese labor camps. Though a middle-class college student, he was initially a patriotic Communist, but he soon ran afoul of the thought police. Hoping to flee the country in 1959, he was denounced as an 'enemy of the revolution.' The book . . . focuses primarily on Wu's first decade as a prisoner struggling against starvation, seeing others succumb and learning a brutal survival ethic from fellow inmates. It is an intimate story of bravery and tragedy." Publ Wkly

Troublemaker; one man's crusade against China's cruelty; [by] Harry Wu, with George Vecsey. NewsMax.com Book 2002 326p il pa $24.95
951.05
1. China—Politics and government 2. Human rights 3. Political prisoners
ISBN 0-9704029-9-6; 978-0-9704029-9-8
LC 2004-273145
First published 1996 by Times Books
Wu "chronicles his recent campaign to expose China's slave-labor camp system—six to eight million inmates in 1155 camps rife with beatings, torture, murders and near starvation conditions. He also presents shocking evidence that China is executing prisoners to harvest their organs for transplants, and that China's prison-made goods—everything from shoes to tea to tools—are exported to the U.S." Publ Wkly
"Denounced in China as a 'traitor' and 'spy,' Wu is hailed as a hero in the West and has received many human rights awards. This book meticulously unveils the dramatic story of his 'crusade' against the Chinese government. . . . An interesting but disturbing book." Libr J

951.7 Mongolia

Atwood, Christopher Pratt, 1964-
Encyclopedia of Mongolia and the Mongol empire; [by] Christopher P. Atwood. Facts on File 2004 678p il map (Facts on File library of world history) $85
951.7
1. Mongolia
ISBN 0-8160-4671-9
LC 2003-61696

"In about 1800 A-Z entries, the book covers everything from the Abbasid Caliphate to the yurt." Libr J
"Coverage is good for all time periods, and the encyclopedia as a whole makes a sound case for the enormous influence of Mongolian civilization on the history of the Far East, the Indian subcontinent, and Eastern Europe." Booklist
Includes bibliographical references

951.9 Korea

Brady, James, 1928-
The coldest war; a memoir of Korea. St. Martin's Griffin 2000 248p il map pa $15.95
951.9
1. Korean War, 1950-1953—Personal narratives
ISBN 978-0-312-26511-3; 0-312-26511-5
"Thomas Dunne books"
First published 1990 by Orion Bks.
"From November 1951 to July 1952, the author was a marine lieutenant who frequently found himself called upon to fight and kill Chinese and North Korean soldiers on the battlefields of Korea. His memoir of that experience is a well-crafted piece told in a voice that skillfully mixes the sardonic insight of an older man looking back on a highly extraordinary episode of his past with the naivete of the young warrior he once was." Booklist

Breen, Michael, 1952-
The Koreans; who they are, what they want, where their future lies. St. Martin's Press 1999 276p pa $14.95 hardcover o.p.
951.9
1. Korean national characteristics 2. Korea—History
ISBN 0-312-32609-2 (pa)
LC 99-45599
First published 1998 in the United Kingdom
In this survey of Korea's culture, the author "probes such diverse topics as the status of civil liberties, generational social strains within families, and the massive corruption that permeates Korean society. He writes with a snappy, readable style." Booklist
Includes bibliographical references

Cumings, Bruce, 1943-
Korea's place in the sun; a modern history. Updated ed. W. W. Norton 2005 542p il map pa $16.95
951.9
1. Korea—History
ISBN 0-393-32702-7; 0-393-31681-5
LC 2006-276040
First published 1997
This history of Korea from 1860 focuses primarily on the post-1945 period
"Mr. Cumings has pored over the historical documents and he argues intelligently. His book is important precisely because he marshals considerable evidence to challenge conventional understanding." N Y Times Book Rev
Includes bibliographical references

Edwards, Paul M., 1933-

The Korean War; a historical dictionary. Scarecrow Press 2003 xxxix, 367p il maps (Historical dictionaries of war, revolution, and civil unrest) $75 **951.9**

1. Korean War, 1950-1953—Dictionaries
ISBN 0-8108-4479-6   LC 2002-70848

"This reference is designed to provide brief . . . information about all aspects of the war including units involved, the United Nations, political and military actions, significant sites and operations, and weapons used." Publisher's note

Includes bibliographical references

Korean War almanac. Facts on File 2006 592p il map (Almanacs of American wars) $85

951.9

1. Korean War, 1950-1953
ISBN 0-8160-6037-1   LC 2005-9374

First published 1990 under the authorship of Harry G. Summers

This book "contains a day-by-day chronology of the events and the people involved in this important war." Publisher's note

Includes bibliographical references

Encyclopedia of the Korean War; a political, social, and military history; Spencer C. Tucker, editor; Jinwung Kim . . . [et al.], assistant editors; [foreword by John S. D. Eisenhower] Checkmark Books 2002 xlii, 851p il map pa $29.95 **951.9**

1. Korean War, 1950-1953—Encyclopedias
ISBN 0-8160-4682-4   LC 2001-37155

First published 2000 as volumes 1 and 2 in a 3-volume set by ABC-CLIO

This reference work covers "personalities, events, technical and military information, political and social background, and battles and campaigns." Libr J [review of 2000 edition]

Includes bibliographical references

Halberstam, David, 1934-2007

The coldest winter; America and the Korean War. Hyperion 2007 719p map $35 *

951.9

1. Korean War, 1950-1953
ISBN 1-401-30052-9; 978-1-401-30052-4

     LC 2007-1635

In this history of the Korean War, the author presents a "narrative of the political decisions and miscalculations on both sides. . . . At the heart of the book are the individual stories of the soldiers on the front lines who were left to deal with the consequences of the dangerous misjudgements and competing agendas of powerful men." Publisher's note

"Alive with the voices of the men who fought, Halberstam's telling is a virtuoso work of history." Publ Wkly

Includes bibliographical references

Hickey, Michael, 1929-

The Korean War; the West confronts communism. Overlook Press 2000 397p il maps pa $19.95 hardcover o.p. **951.9**

1. United Nations—Armed Forces—Korea 2. Korean War, 1950-1953
ISBN 1-58567-179-7 (pa)   LC 00-27692

First published 1999 in the United Kingdom

An "analysis of both the military and political factors that caused the war and the conduct on all sides. . . . The author does not mince words when criticizing General MacArthur and other UN commanders. Using declassified documents as well as regimental and personal diaries, he wades through political intrigue and military disasters and triumphs to give us a memorable account." Libr J

Includes bibliographical references

Oberdorfer, Don

The two Koreas; a contemporary history. New ed. Basic Bks. 2001 521p il map pa $21

951.9

ISBN 0-465-05162-6   LC 2001-43486

First published 1997 by Addison-Wesley

This is a study of North and South Korean politics and an analysis of U.S. policy from the 1970s to the present

Includes bibliographical references

951.93   North Korea (People's Democratic Republic of Korea)

Delisle, Guy, 1966-

Pyongyang: a journey in North Korea; translated by Helge Dascher. Drawn & Quarterly 2005 176p il map $19.95; pa $14.95 **951.93**

1. Korea (North)—Graphic novels 2. Graphic novels
ISBN 1-896597-89-0; 1-897299-21-4 (pa)

This book "documents the two months French animator Delisle spent overseeing cartoon production in North Korea. . . . He records everything from the omnipresent statues and portraits of dictators Kim Il-Sung and Kim Jong-Il to the brainwashed obedience of the citizens." Booklist

"Pyongyang will appeal to multiple audiences: current events buffs, Persepolis fans and those who just love a good yarn." Publ Wkly

952   Japan

The **Cambridge** encyclopedia of Japan; editors, Richard Bowring, Peter Kornicki. Cambridge Univ. Press 1993 400p il maps $70

952

1. Japan
ISBN 0-521-40352-9   LC 92-8167

This volume is divided "into eight categories: geography, history, language, thought and religion, arts and crafts, society, politics, and the economy. Each of these categories is further divided into 7-11 subjects that deal with numerous topics, such as the physical structure of

The Cambridge encyclopedia of Japan—*Continued*
the country, climate, education, family, judicial system, cinema, products, foreign policy, and important historical figures." Am Ref Books Annu, 1994

Downer, Lesley
Women of the pleasure quarters; the secret history of the geisha. Broadway Bks. 2001 288p il pa $14.95 hardcover o.p.   **952**
1. Geishas 2. Japan—Social life and customs
ISBN 0-7679-0490-7 (pa)   LC 00-49409
Downer's "book is a combination of the history of the geisha and a study of the contemporary world of the geisha." Booklist
The author "skillfully intertwines her profiles of Kyoto personalities and tea-house customs with a fluidly written geisha history that's unabashedly aimed at a Western audience. . . . Written in dynamic, highly readable prose, the book is supported by exhaustive research and a lengthy bibliography." Publ Wkly
Includes bibliographical references and index

Gordon, Andrew, 1952-
The modern history of Japan. Oxford University Press 2003 384p il $35; pa $29.95   **952**
1. Japan—History
ISBN 0-19-511060-9; 0-19-511061-7 (pa)
     LC 2002-70916
The author examines "Japan's political, economic, social, and cultural inventions of its modernity in evolving international contexts, incorporating inside viewpoints and debates. Beyond identifying the national stages (feudalism, militarism, democracy), the author innovatively emphasizes how labor unions, cultural figures, and groups in society (especially women) have been affected over time and have responded." Libr J
Includes bibliographical references

Jansen, Marius B.
The making of modern Japan. Belknap Press 2000 871p il maps $35; pa $18.95 *
     952
1. Japan—History
ISBN 0-674-00334-9; 0-674-00991-6 (pa)
     LC 00-41352
"Roughly a third of the book deals with Tokugawa politics, culture, and society before the 'opening to the world' in the mid-19th century; fewer than 100 pages cover the period since 1945; and the balance treats the crucial 1868-1945 period of modernization and war." Libr J
"Jansen has produced what is sure to become the standard narrative history of modern Japan. . . . In every way this is a remarkable book . . . and no reference collection on Japan can pretend to be complete without it." Choice
Includes bibliographical references

McClain, James L., 1944-
Japan, a modern history. Norton 2001 632p il maps $35; pa $31.25   **952**
1. Japan—History
ISBN 0-393-04156-5; 0-393-97720-X (pa)
     LC 2001-34545
In this study McClain "analyzes major trends in politics, the economy, society, culture and the arts, foreign affairs, and almost every other conceivable aspect of Japanese society." Libr J
"This is a well-written, well-researched, and easily readable survey of the modern history of a fascinating and important nation." Booklist
Includes bibliographical references

Nathan, John
Japan unbound; a volatile nation's quest for pride and purpose. Houghton Mifflin 2004 271p $25   **952**
1. Japan—Civilization
ISBN 0-618-13894-3   LC 2003-60559
The author "explores the dynamics of cultural continuity and change in Japan driven in part by economic stagnation. . . . The author also confronts the reader with the links between a loss of personal pride and purpose as a result of economic uncertainty, and the search for a new basis of pride and purpose in the form of heightened nationalism. . . . This book is a must for general and specialized library collections." Choice
Includes bibliographical references

Perez, Louis G.
The history of Japan. Greenwood Press 1998 244p maps (Greenwood histories of the modern nations) $45   **952**
1. Japan—History
ISBN 0-313-30296-0   LC 97-45657
This history covers prehistoric and early feudal Japan through 1997. Cultural aspects examined include theater and cinema, marriage customs as well as the women's movement and political scandals. Includes chronology, glossary of selected terms, and a bibliographic essay.
Includes bibliographical references

Reischauer, Edwin O. (Edwin Oldfather), 1910-1990
Japan; the story of a nation. 4th ed. McGraw-Hill 1990 401p il map pa $68.75 $15.00
     952
1. Japan—History
ISBN 0-07-557074-2; 978-0-07-557074-5
     LC 89-12418
First published 1970 by Knopf
This history of the Japanese people from their origins to the present examines their civilization, cultural heritage, militarism, and economy.
Includes bibliographical references

The Japanese today; change and continuity. Belknap Press 1988 426p il maps $25; pa $12.50
     952
1. Japan
ISBN 0-674-47181-4; 0-674-47182-2 (pa)
     LC 87-14904

Reischauer, Edwin O. (Edwin Oldfather), 1910-1990—*Continued*

First published 1977 with title: The Japanese

The author "shows how change within continuity has been the most enduring characteristic of the Japanese experience—throughout the nation's history. He analyzes and explains in detail the government, education, business, and social structure of the country in modern times." Christ Sci Monit

Includes bibliography

Seagrave, Sterling

The Yamato dynasty; the secret history of Japan's Imperial family. Broadway Bks. 2000 394p il pa $23 hardcover o.p. **952**

1. Japan—Politics and government 2. Japan—Kings and rulers

ISBN 0-7679-0497-4 (pa)   LC 99-49888

This "history of Japan from the mid-19th century to the present weaves together an iconoclastic historical narrative with a mostly caustic view of Japan's imperial family. The Seagraves depict modern Japan as a country consistently dominated by a closed financial oligarchy in league with politicians, bureaucrats, the imperial family, and underworld bosses." Libr J

Includes bibliographical references

Smith, Patrick L.

Japan; a reinterpretation. Pantheon Bks. 1997 385p pa $14 hardcover o.p. **952**

1. Japan—Civilization 2. Japan—History

ISBN 0-679-74511-4 (pa)   LC 96-39220

This study focuses on events after World War II. Smith examines the U.S. role in post-war Japan, and the social structure of Japanese society

"In his sweeping analysis of the country's history, economy, politics and culture, Smith has produced a new startlingly clear-sighted vision of the often misunderstood Japanese." Publ Wkly

Includes bibliographical references

952.03   Japan—1868-1945

Buruma, Ian

Inventing Japan, 1853-1964. Modern Lib. 2003 194p hardcover o.p. pa $12.95 **952.03**

1. Japan—History

ISBN 0-679-64085-1; 0-8129-7286-4 (pa)

LC 2002-26346

"A Modern Library chronicles book"

"Buruma traces the remarkable metamorphosis that transformed an isolated island shogunate into an expansive military empire and then into a pacified and prosperous democracy. . . . An excellent introductory study." Booklist

Includes bibliographical references

Pleshakov, Konstantin

The Tsar's last armada; the epic journey to the Battle of Tsushima; {by} Constantine Pleshakov. Basic Bks. 2002 xx, 396p il maps pa $17.50 hardcover o.p. **952.03**

1. Russo-Japanese War, 1904-1905

ISBN 0-465-05792-6 (pa)   LC 2001-52532

This is an account of events leading to the Russo-Japanese War and the defeat of the Russian fleet in the Tsushima Straits in 1905

"A compulsively readable account told from the Russian viewpoint." Booklist

Includes bibliographical references

952.04   Japan—1945-

Dower, John W.

Embracing defeat; Japan in the wake of World War II; by John Dower. Norton 1999 676p il $29.95; pa $17.95 **952.04**

1. Japan—History—1945-1952, Allied occupation

ISBN 0-393-04686-9; 0-393-32027-8 (pa)

LC 98-22133

This "account of Japan between August 1945 and April 1952 assesses the impact of Allied activity on modern Japanese history." N Y Times Book Rev

"Dower demonstrates an impressive mastery of voluminous sources, both American and Japanese, and he deftly situates the political story within a rich cultural context." Publ Wkly

Includes bibliographical references

Encyclopedia of contemporary Japanese culture; edited by Sandra Buckley. Routledge 2001 xxix, 634p $140 * **952.04**

1. Japan—Civilization—Encyclopedias

ISBN 0-415-14344-6   LC 2001-19655

New edition in preparation

This reference includes "more than 750 topical and biographical entries exploring the 'lived experience of everyday Japanese life' for the postwar period. . . . [It includes] articles on minorities in Japan and the Japanese Diaspora in the Americas. Most notably . . . [this] features excellent coverage of Japanese women and consistently introduces critical feminist perspectives that are rarely seen in other reference works on Japan. . . . [This] is eminently readable . . . an ideal reference tool." Am Ref Books Annu, 2003

Includes bibliographical references

Richie, Donald, 1924-

The Japan journals, 1947-2004; edited by Leza Lowitz. Stone Bridge Press 2004 494p il $29.95 **952.04**

1. Japan—Civilization

ISBN 1-88065-691-4   LC 2004-16239

"The material in this volume was extracted and organized by Lowitz from previously unpublished sporadic diaries and jottings. They give a running commentary on Japan's rise from wartime destitution into the rich society of the 1980s boom, then its development into overbuilt and washed out postmodern complacency. There is some

Richie, Donald, 1924-—*Continued*
personal trivia, but most entries are alert and sometimes surprising glimpses of modern Japanese writers and filmmakers." Libr J

953 Arabian Peninsula and adjacent areas

Theroux, Peter
Sandstorms: days and nights in Arabia. Norton 1990 281p pa $13.95 hardcover o.p. **953**
ISBN 0-393-30797-2 (pa) LC 89-28609
The author "recounts his experiences in the Middle East of the 1980s. The author went to Egypt to teach English and wound up chronicling the disappearance of Lebanon's Shia Iman Moussa Sadr. But *Sandstorms* is the human side of an American in Arabia. . . . Theroux's Arabia is rough but undeniably real, poignant and elemental." Libr J

954 South Asia. India

Dalrymple, William
White Mughals; love and betrayal in the eighteenth-century India. Viking 2003 xlvii, 459p il map $34.95; pa $16 **954**
1. Kirkpatrick, James Achilles, 1764-1805 2. British—India
ISBN 0-670-03184-4; 0-14-200412-X (pa)
LC 2002-191082
First published 2002 in the United Kingdom
James Kirkpatrick was the Resident of the East India Company in Hyderabad. This book documents his marriage to Khair-un-Nissa, a Mughal aristocrat
This "book, ambitious in scope and rich in detail, demonstrates that a century before Kipling's 'never the twain'—and two centuries before neocons and radical Islamists trumpeted the clash of civilizations—the story of the Westerner in Muslim India was one not of conquest but of appreciation, adaptation, and seduction." New Yorker
Includes bibliographical references

Lapierre, Dominique
The City of Joy. Warner Books 1991 528p il pa $7.99 **954**
1. Calcutta (India)—Social conditions
ISBN 0-446-35556-9
Original French edition, 1985
An account of life in the most squalid of Calcutta's slums, Anand Nagar (The City of Joy). The author focuses on the lives of a rickshaw driver, a Polish Catholic priest, an American doctor and an Assamese nurse.

McLeod, John, 1963-
The history of India. Greenwood Press 2002 xx, 223p (Greenwood histories of the modern nations) $39.95 **954**
1. Mogul Empire 2. India—History—1526-1765
ISBN 0-313-31459-4 LC 2002-276829

The author presents "in broad outlines some of the major events and episodes that make up India's history. . . . This is a useful compilation of important facts relating to Indian history. Its strength lies primarily in the last six chapters in which brief narratives of the struggle for independence and post-independence India down to the close of the twentieth century are nicely presented. All in all, this is a book that all libraries should have." Recomm Ref Books for Small & Medium-sized Libr & Media Cent, 2003
Includes bibliographical references

Mehta, Suketu
Maximum city; Bombay lost and found. Alfred A. Knopf 2004 542p $27.95 * **954**
1. Bombay (India)
ISBN 0-375-40372-8 LC 2004-48969
The author "explores various aspects of Bombay life, from setting up residence to exploring the hugely successful domestic film industry; from detailing Bombay's sex industry to profiling the reasons behind India's own 'September 11,' the 1993 riots and bombings that exposed a vast enmity between extremist Hindus and Muslims. . . . Mehta delivers a fresh and unblinking look at contemporary Bombay." Booklist

Sen, Amartya Kumar
The argumentative Indian; writings on Indian history, culture, and identity; [by] Amartya Sen. Farrar, Straus and Giroux 2006 xx, 409p il **954**
1. India—Civilization
ISBN 0-374-10583-9 LC 2005-49460
The author "addresses the many aspects of Indian identity, from the Vedas (the sacred Hindu scriptures) to nuclear weapons, in order to build evidence for an inclusive, humane vision of India's potential." Libr J
"Sen's lucid reasoning and thoroughgoing humanism . . . ensure a lively and commanding defense of diversity and dialogue." Publ Wkly
Includes bibliographical references

Singh, Patwant, 1925-
The Sikhs. Knopf 2000 276p il $27.50; pa $14 **954**
1. Sikhs
ISBN 0-375-40728-6; 0-385-50206-0 (pa)
LC 99-31807
The author "traces Sikh history from its origins in the 15th century through Indira Gandhi's 1984 storming of the Golden Temple. . . . Sikhs, he argues, have for centuries been an embattled people because their culture and religion defy the predominant religions in the region, as well as the Indian caste system with its ruling elite." Publ Wkly
Includes bibliographical references

Tharoor, Shashi, 1956-
India; from midnight to the millennium. Arcade Pub. 1997 392p map hardcover o.p. pa $15.95 **954**
1. India—History
ISBN 1-55970-384-9; 978-1-55970-803-6 (pa); 1-55970-803-4 (pa) LC 97-8376

Tharoor, Shashi, 1956-—*Continued*

This is an "economic, political, and sociological study of India since independence in 1947, considering such issues as centralization vs. federalism and pluralism vs. fundamentalism." Libr J

"Each telling anecdote illuminates some aspect of Indian culture, from politics to religion, creating a mosaic that reflects India's endless variations on the theme of life." Booklist

Wolpert, Stanley A., 1927-

A new history of India. 7th ed. Oxford University Press 2004 c2003 530p il map $63.95; pa $43 **954**

1. Mogul Empire

ISBN 0-19-516677-9; 0-19-516678-7 (pa)

LC 2003-53589

First published 1977. Periodically revised

A comprehensive survey of Indian history from its early beginnings to the present. Includes discussion of the assassination of Rajiv Gandhi; violence in Kashmir, Punjab, and Assam; and the effects of rural development

Includes bibliographical references

954.04 India—1947-1971

Guha, Ramachandra

India after Gandhi; the history of the world's largest democracy. Ecco 2007 893p il map $34.95 **954.04**

1. India—History—1947-

ISBN 978-0-06-019881-7; 0-06-019881-8

LC 2006-52180

This book documents India's transformation from a colonial state to independence.

The author "builds his story by making us witnesses of events as they occur, drawing on contemporary accounts. His voluminous account may seem daunting, but it is crucial for the understanding of modern India. . . . Guha is patient in his approach, gentle in his criticism, exasperated by what he does not like, and eclectic in drawing on evidence that supports his argument." New Statesman

Includes bibliographical references

954.05 India—1971-

Bumiller, Elisabeth

May you be the mother of a hundred sons; a journey among the women of India. Random House 1990 306p il pa $13.95 hardcover o.p. **954.05**

1. Women—India 2. India—Social life and customs

ISBN 0-449-90614-0 (pa) LC 89-27120

"In addition to the usual discussion of arranged marriages, movie stars, and Indira Gandhi, India's late prime minister, Bumiller portrays a wide cross section of Indian society. Her discussion of bride burning, family planning, village health programs, the outlook of village women, and female infanticide will generate much comment and discussion. Essential for libraries with women's studies and Third World collections." Libr J

Includes bibliographical references

Mishra, Pankaj

Temptations of the West; how to be modern in India, Pakistan, Tibet, and beyond. Farrar, Straus & Giroux 2006 323p $25 * **954.05**

1. South Asia—Description and travel

ISBN 0-374-17321-4; 978-0-374-17321-0

LC 2006-11987

Essays first appearing in slightly different forms in The New York Review of Books, Granta, The New York Times Magazine, and the Guardian Weekend Magazine.

This book examines the "contradictory relationship between South Asia and the West." N Y Times Book Rev

"It is impossible in a short form to do justice to the density and complexity of . . . [the author's] arguments, to his comprehensive illustrations, to his scathing demolition of the comfort zones of both East and West, and to the intrepid and endlessly questioning spirit which lies behind his book." N Y Rev Books

955 Iran

Follett, Ken, 1949-

On wings of eagles. New American Library 1984 415p il pa $7.99 **955**

1. Iran hostage crisis, 1979-1981

ISBN 0-451-16353-2; 978-0-451-16353-0

"A Signet book"

First published 1983 by Morrow

The author "recounts the efforts of successful Texas industrialist Ross Perot to rescue from a Teheran jail two senior corporate executives arrested during the anti-American and revolutionary period in Iran in 1979." Libr J

Mackey, Sandra, 1937-

The Iranians; Persia, Islam, and the soul of a nation; W. Scott Harrop, research assistant. Dutton 1996 xxii, 426p maps pa $15.95 hardcover o.p. **955**

1. Iran—Politics and government

ISBN 04-522-7563-6 (pa) LC 95-44135

The author presents "information on Iranian civilization from Cyrus the Great to the present. Throughout this turbulent history of invasions and conquerors, the Persian soul, with its foundations in the Zoroastrian concept of justice overlaid with Shia Islam, has steadfastly endured. Since many Westerners had little familiarity with Iran until the overthrow of the Shah in 1979, this very readable book provides a perspective on what led up to those events, what is happening in Iran today, and how the current situation is likely to affect the future of Iran and its relationship with the West." Libr J

My sister, guard your veil; my brother guard, your eyes; uncensored Iranian voices; Lila Azam Zanganeh, editor. Beacon Press 2006 132p il pa $12 **955**

1. Iran—Social conditions 2. Women—Iran

ISBN 0-8070-0463-4; 978-0-8070-0463-0

LC 2005-27496

This "volume features frank interviews with an array of reputable Iranians—intellectuals, artists, and writers,

My sister, guard your veil; my brother guard, your eyes—*Continued*

some of whom live in exile. Their compelling personal experiences, views, and opinions answer some persistent questions about the lives of ordinary people in Iran and challenge established myths and stereotypes. . . . This volume opens a window on the irrepressible talents, aspirations, and energy of Iranians both at home and abroad, despite their adverse conditions" MultiCult Rev

Satrapi, Marjane, 1969-

Embroideries. Pantheon Books 2005 134p il $16.95   **955**

1. Iran—Graphic novels 2. Women—Iran—Graphic novels 3. Graphic novels

ISBN 0-375-42305-2   LC 2004-58660

This book "explores the lives of Iranian women young and old. The book begins with Satrapi arriving for afternoon tea at her grandmother's house. There, her mother, aunt and their group of friends tell stories about their lives as women, and, more specifically, the men they've lived with and through." Publ Wkly

"Discussions of sex are frank and explicit and laced with high humor. . . . Satrapi's simple black-and-white cartooning style is tremendously effective, expertly portraying emotional nuances with just a few lines." Libr J

Wright, Robin

The last great revolution; turmoil and transformation in Iran. Knopf 2000 xxiv, 339p il hardcover o.p. pa $14   **955**

1. Iran—Politics and government

ISBN 0-375-40639-5; 0-375-70630-5 (pa)

      LC 99-27798

The author "talks to journalists, educators, politicians, entertainers, and others to present a picture of the cultural and political changes in Iran: the softening of cultural restrictions, the empowerment of women, and the modernization of industry and the economy." Booklist

Includes bibliographical references

956 Middle East

Akçam, Taner, 1953-

A shameful act; the Armenian genocide and the question of Turkish responsibility; translated by Paul Bessemer. Metropolitan Books 2006 483p map $30   **956**

1. Armenian massacres, 1915-1923 2. Genocide

ISBN 0-8050-7932-7; 978-0-8050-7932-6

      LC 2005-58401

Original Turkish edition, 1999

This is a study of the killing of some one million Armenians in 1915. The author "follows the chain of events leading up to the killing and then reconstructs [what he sees as] its systematic orchestration by coordinated departments of the Ottoman state, the ruling political parties, and the military. He also probes the . . . question of how Turkey succeeded in evading responsibility." Publisher's note

"This groundbreaking and lucid account by a prominent Turkish scholar speaks forcefully to all." Publ Wkly

Includes bibliographical references

Balakian, Peter, 1951-

The burning Tigris; the Armenian genocide and America's response. HarperCollins 2003 xx, 475p il $26.95; pa $14.95 *   **956**

1. Armenian massacres, 1915-1923 2. Genocide

ISBN 0-06-019840-0; 0-06-055870-9 (pa)

      LC 2003-44986

This is a "narrative of the massacres of the Armenians in the 1890s and genocide in 1915 at the hands of the Ottoman Turks." Publisher's note

"The book's real power derives from the eyewitness accounts of the genocide itself. The sheer volume of outsiders' testimony that Balakian compiles, and the horrifying similarity of their observations of men, women and children beaten, tortured, burned to death in churches or sent out into the desert to starve, is an overwhelmingly convincing retort to genocide deniers." N Y Times Book Rev

Includes bibliographical references

The **Continuum** political encyclopedia of the Middle East; Avraham Sela, editor. rev and updated ed. Continuum 2002 944p maps $175   **956**

1. Middle East—Politics and government 2. Middle East—History

ISBN 0-8264-1413-3   LC 2001-8542

First published 1999 with title: The political encyclopedia of the Middle East

This "contains entries on countries ranging from Afghanistan to Yemen; political movements and leaders; major foreign nations that impact this area, such as the United States and Russia; religions and religious movements; and regional topics of concern including 'Oil,' 'Terrorism,' 'Water Politics,' and 'Women, Gender and Politics.'. . . Alphabetical entries range from a few paragraphs to lengthy commentaries. . . . Large libraries serving older students will find this a useful . . . source of objective information on the history and issues affecting the contemporary Middle East." SLJ

Includes bibliographical references

Encyclopedia of the modern Middle East & North Africa; Philip Mattar, editor in chief. 2nd ed. Macmillan Reference USA 2004 4v il map set $475   **956**

1. Middle East—Encyclopedias 2. North Africa—Encyclopedias

ISBN 0-02-865769-1   LC 2004-5650

First published 1996

"The set covers the modern history of the Middle East and North Africa, with major sections on Colonialism and Imperialism, the World Wars, the Israeli-Palestinian conflict and the United Nations involvement in the region. Each country in the region is reviewed, detailing its population, economy and government." Publisher's note

"For current, accurate, and non-partisan information on the Middle East and North Africa, this excellent reference set . . . will answer basic questions and serve as a starting point for research on the region." Libr Media Connect

Includes bibliographical references

Finkel, Caroline

Osman's dream; the story of the Ottoman Empire, 1300-1923. Basic Books 2006 660p il map $35 * **956**

1. Turkey—History

ISBN 0-465-02396-7; 978-0-465-02396-7

First published 2005 in the United Kingdom

This is a history "of the Ottoman Empire from its origins in the thirteenth century through its destruction on the battlefields of World War I." Publisher's note

"This history makes a riveting and enjoyable read for all audiences." Publ Wkly

Includes bibliographical references

Friedman, Thomas L.

From Beirut to Jerusalem. Farrar, Straus & Giroux c1990 541p il maps $32 **956**

1. Middle East—Politics and government 2. Jewish-Arab relations 3. Lebanon—History 4. Israel—Politics and government

ISBN 0-374-15895-9   LC 92-148666

Also available in paperback from Anchor Bks.

First published 1989

The author presents an account of the political situation in the Middle East as he witnessed it in his years as a reporter in Lebanon and Jerusalem

"When recounting his frequently harrowing experiences in that troubled region, Friedman can be absolutely riveting; similarly, his historical insights, his explanation of the root causes of the Arab-Israeli conflict, and his impressions of people and places in the Holy Land never fail to fascinate." Booklist

Herzog, Chaim, 1918-1997

The Arab-Israeli wars; war and peace in the Middle East from the 1948 War of Independence to the present; updated by Shlomo Gazit; introduction by Isaac Herzog and Michael Herzog. 2nd ed, rev and updated. Vintage Books 2005 476p il pa $16.95 **956**

1. Jewish-Arab relations

ISBN 1-4000-7963-2   LC 2005-280207

First published 1982 by Random House

This book traces "the Arab-Israeli wars and military conflicts from the 1948 War of Independence through the 1973 Yom Kippur War." Libr J

Includes bibliographic references

Hiro, Dilip

The essential Middle East; a comprehensive guide; Dilip Hiro. 1st Carroll & Graf ed. Carroll & Graf 2003 639p il map pa $17.95 **956**

1. Middle East

ISBN 0786712694   LC 2003055293

First published 1996 by St. Martin's Press with title: A dictionary of the Middle East

"In more than 1,000 alphabetically arranged entries, varying in length from a few lines to a few pages, Hiro covers more than 150 personalities in politics, business, culture, and religion; places of religious and cultural significance; oil and other minerals; political and religious sects; economic infrastructure; and political and religious ideologies." Booklist

Lewis, Bernard

The Middle East; a brief history of the last 2,000 years. Scribner 1995 433p il $30; pa $16 **956**

1. Middle East—History

ISBN 0-684-80712-2; 0-684-83280-1 (pa)

LC 96-4384

"Lewis has chosen to accentuate the social, economic, and cultural changes that have occurred over 20 centuries. He ranges from seemingly trivial concerns (changes in dress and manners in an Arab coffeehouse) to earth-shaking events (the Mongol conquest of Mesopotamia) in painting a rich, varied, and fascinating portrait of a region that is steeped in traditionalism while often forced by geography and politics to accept change." Booklist

Includes bibliographical references

What went wrong? Western impact and Middle Eastern response. Oxford Univ. Press 2002 180p il $23 **956**

1. Middle East—History

ISBN 0-19-514420-1   LC 2001-36214

Also available in paperback from HarperCollins Pubs.

Subtitle of paperback edition varies: The clash between Islam and modernity

The author's "fundamental argument is that Muslims became accustomed in the early centuries of their history to perceiving themselves as the bearers of the final and true faith, and so never came to understand or accept the Christian civilization of Western Europe that he maintains has surpassed and humbled them." N Y Times (Late N Y Ed)

"Like many of Lewis's previous writings on this subject . . . this book will undoubtedly generate significant debate and disagreement among scholars regarding the author's analysis of Islamic responses to modernity and Westernization." Libr J

Includes bibliographical references

The **Middle** East. 11th ed. CQ Press 2007 xix, 663p il map $70; pa $46.95 * **956**

1. Middle East—Politics and government

ISBN   978-0-87289-368-9;   0-87289-368-5; 978-0-87289-369-6 (pa); 0-87289-369-3 (pa)

LC 2007-19956

First published 1974. Periodically revised

Covers topics such as oil, Islam, the Arab-Israeli conflict, the Persian Gulf, and the arms trade in the Middle East. Also presents profiles of Middle Eastern nations and twentieth-century leaders and includes documents such as UN resolutions and peace treaties

Includes bibliographical references

Morris, Benny, 1948-

Righteous victims; a history of the Zionist-Arab conflict, 1881-1998. Knopf 1999 751p pa $18 hardcover o.p. **956**

1. Israel-Arab conflicts 2. Jewish-Arab relations

ISBN 0-679-74475-4 (pa)   LC 98-42774

Morris traces the history of Arab-Israeli conflicts and examines major events and their aftereffects

"The author displays a remarkable grasp of the history of the Zionist-Arab conflict and an analytical style that is devoid of the polemics that have characterized so

Morris, Benny, 1948-—*Continued*
many books on this subject." Libr J
Includes bibliographical references

Said, Edward W.
The end of the peace process; Oslo and after.
Pantheon Bks. 2000 345p $27.50; pa $14
956
1. Israel-Arab conflicts 2. Jewish-Arab relations
ISBN 0-375-40930-0; 0-375-72574-1 (pa)
LC 99-44765
The author provides "analysis of the pitfalls of the
Oslo agreement. Most of the essays in this collection
have appeared in Cairo's *al-Ahram Weekly* and *al-Hayat*,
London's Arabic-language daily. Each essay is Said's re-
flection on a dimension of the Palestinian predicament.
. . . He is as critical of the corruption, incompetence,
and authoritarianism of the Palestinian Authority as he is
of American and Israeli postures." Libr J

956.04 Middle East—1945-1980

Oren, Michael
Six days of war; June 1967 and the making of
the modern Middle East; [by] Michael B. Oren.
Oxford Univ. Press 2002 446p il $30
956.04
1. Israel-Arab War, 1967
ISBN 0-19-515174-7
LC 2001-58823
Also available in paperback from Presidio Press
This is a history of the June 1967 Arab-Israeli War
"What makes this book important is the breadth and
depth of the research. Oren draws on archives, newly de-
classified documents, memoirs and interviews from Isra-
el, America, Britain and what was then the Soviet
Union." N Y Times Book Rev
Includes bibliographical references

956.05 Middle East—1980-

Wright, Robin
Dreams and shadows; the future of the Middle
East. Penguin Press 2008 464p map $26.95
956.05
1. Middle East—Politics and government
ISBN 1-59420-111-0; 978-1-59420-111-0
LC 2007-46267
The author presents a "tour d'horizon of the new Middle East, with on-the-ground reportage of the ideas and
movements driving change across the region—and the
obstacles they confront." Publisher's note
"Absorbing accounts of brave activists are interwoven
with relevant context and history in clear, vivid language.
These elements make the book an engaging read, and a
useful one for people who want to better understand this
important part of the world." Christ Sci Monit
Includes bibliographical reference

956.1 Turkey

Goodwin, Jason, 1964-
Lords of the horizons; a history of the Ottoman
Empire. Holt & Co. 1999 351p il map pa $15
hardcover o.p. **956.1**
1. Turkey—History
ISBN 0-312-42066-8 (pa)
LC 98-41601
"A John Macrae book"
In this study of the Ottoman Empire, the chapters
"each have a theme: the importance of the annual campaign to capture new territory, for example, and the part
played in the Ottoman psyche by the concept of borderlands, the absence of clock-time, {and} the role of the
city or of the sea." Natl Rev
"A history of distinctive originality, Goodwin's account imbibes deeply of traveler's impressions and seeks
to see and describe, rather than explain and judge. A
valuable synthesis." Booklist
Includes bibliographical references

Kinzer, Stephen
Crescent and star; Turkey between two worlds.
Farrar, Straus & Giroux 2001 252p pa $14
hardcover o.p. **956.1**
1. Turkey—Politics and government
ISBN 0-374-52866-7 (pa)
LC 2001-23298
The author "gives a concise introduction to Turkey:
Kemal Atatürk's post-WWI establishment of the modern
secular Turkish state; the odd makeup of contemporary
society, in which the military enforces Atatürk's reforms.
In stylized but substantive prose, he devotes chapters to
the problems he sees plaguing Turkish society: Islamic
fundamentalism, frictions regarding the large Kurdish minority and the lack of democratic freedoms." Publ Wkly

Mango, Andrew, 1926-
The Turks today; Andrew Mango. 1st ed.
Overlook Press 2004 292p map $29.95; pa $17.95
956.1
1. Turkey—History
ISBN 1-585-67615-2; 1-585-67756-6 (pa)
LC 2004-58339
"The first four chapters provide a general political history of Turkey since Atatürk, weaving the account
around the roles of the successive leaders, from Atatürk
to Recep Tayyip Erdogan. Mango then turns to thematic
topics, including the economy, education, the Kurds, and
Turkish efforts to join the European Union." Foreign Affairs
"This fascinating and timely survey is both a political
history and a cultural examination of a diverse, dynamic
society." Booklist
Includes bibliographical references

Pope, Hugh
Turkey unveiled; a history of modern Turkey;
[by] Hugh and Nicole Pope. Overlook Press 1998
373p il maps $29.95; pa $16.95 **956.1**
1. Turkey—Politics and government
ISBN 0-87951-898-7; 1-58567-096-0 (pa)
LC 98-16616

Pope, Hugh—*Continued*

The authors present a study of "Turkish governments and political leaders over the past seventy years, with particular emphasis on the . . . reforms of . . . President Turgut Özal." Times Lit Suppl

"The Popes have written a deeply revealing guide to modern Turkish culture and politics that fills a wide gap in our cultural knowledge." N Y Times Book Rev

Includes bibliographical references

956.7 Iraq

Anderson, Jon Lee

The fall of Baghdad. Penguin Press 2004 389p $24.95   **956.7**

1. Hussein, Ṣaddām 2. Iraq War, 2003 3. Iraq—Politics and government

ISBN 1-594-20034-3   LC 2004-46421

These are the author's "memoirs of residing in Saddam Hussein's Iraq from 2000 and experiencing both the approach of war in March 2003 and the country's continuing chaos and violence in April 2004. . . . Rendered in compelling and lucid prose, this story of deceit, terror, death, and searing religious hatred evokes a great sense of despair and a deep sadness." Libr J

Atkinson, Rick

Crusade; the untold story of the Persian Gulf War. Houghton Mifflin 1993 575p il maps pa $17 hardcover o.p.   **956.7**

1. Persian Gulf War, 1991

ISBN 0-395-71083-9 (pa)   LC 93-14388

The author provides an "account of the actions and utterances of those who directed and fought in the Persian Gulf War. He also provides a thorough analysis of diplomatic and political aspects of the conflict. Rich in pertinent details, the powerful narrative leaps nimbly from Washington to Riyadh, from Baghdad to Kuwait City, and to various battle sites across the sands. Expectedly, the book's dominant personality is General H. Norman Schwarzkopf." Publ Wkly

Includes bibliographical references

In the company of soldiers; a chronicle of combat. H. Holt 2004 319p il maps $25; pa $14   **956.7**

1. United States. Army. Airborne Division, 101st 2. Iraq War, 2003

ISBN 0-8050-7561-5; 0-8050-7773-1 (pa)

LC 2003-67607

This is an eyewitness account of the war in Iraq. "In the spring of 2003, the author accompanied combat units to Iraq. He spent two months embedded with the 101st Airborne Division's headquarters staff, sharing their daily experiences from initial deployment out of Fort Campbell, KY, to overseas staging areas in Kuwait, and ultimately bearing witness to the unit's march on Baghdad. His view of the war was from a vantage point that permitted scrutiny of strategy, planning, and decision making at the senior command level." SLJ

Bogdanos, Matthew

Thieves of Baghdad; one marine's passion for ancient civilizations and the journey to recover the world's greatest stolen treasures; [by] Matthew Bogdanos with William Patrick. Bloomsbury 2005 302p il map $25.95; pa $15.95   **956.7**

1. Iraq War, 2003—Destruction and pillage 2. Iraq—Antiquities

ISBN 1-58234-645-3; 1-59691-146-8 (pa)

LC 2005-27652

The author describes the events that took place after he "and several colleagues volunteered to investigate the theft of treasures from Baghdad's Iraq Museum in 2003." Booklist

Bogdanos "cuts through politics and hyperbole to tell an engrossing story abundant with history, colored by stories of brave Iraqis and Americans, and shaded with hope for the future." Publ Wkly

Includes bibliographical references

Carlisle, Rodney P.

Iraq war; [by] Rodney P. Carlisle; John S. Bowman, general editor. Updated ed. Facts on File 2007 198p il map (America at war) $35

956.7

1. Iraq War, 2003 2. Iraq—History

ISBN 978-0-8160-7129-6   LC 2006-35763

First published 2004

This book "explains how coalition forces destroyed the Iraqi army and defeated the regime of Saddam Hussein. The . . . narrative describes such later events as the capture of Saddam Hussein by U.S. forces while also addressing the aftermath of the military campaign and the continuing unrest in the country." Publisher's note

Includes bibliographical references

Chandrasekaran, Rajiv

Imperial life in the emerald city; inside Iraq's green zone. Alfred A. Knopf 2006 320p map $25.95; pa $14.95   **956.7**

1. Iraq. Coalition Provisional Authority 2. Iraq War, 2003 3. Political corruption

ISBN 1-4000-4487-1;   978-1-4000-4487-0; 0-307-27883-2 (pa); 978-0-307-27883-8 (pa)

LC 2006-41014

The author "brings to life the small world of the roughly 1,500 individuals (overwhelmingly American, with a few British and others) who manned the Coalition Provisional Authority, which was lodged in the Green Zone—a seven-square-mile enclave in the heart of Baghdad—during that critical first year of the U.S. presence. Those living in the Green Zone made of it an Oz-like Emerald City, physically and psychologically removed from the Iraqis whose state they were charged with rebuilding." Foreign Affairs

"This is a clearly written, blessedly undidactic book. It should be read by anyone who wants to understand how things went so badly wrong in Iraq." N Y Times Book Rev

Includes bibliographical references

Clancy, Tom, 1947-

Into the storm; a study in command; {by} Tom Clancy with Fred Franks, Jr. Putnam 1997 531p il maps pa $16.95 hardcover o.p. **956.7**
1. Persian Gulf War, 1991
ISBN 0-425-16308-3 (pa) LC 96-38068
This history of the Persian Gulf War focuses on the command of General Frederick M. Banks
Includes bibliographical references

Cockburn, Patrick

The occupation. Norton 2006 229p map $24.95 **956.7**
1. Iraq War, 2003
ISBN 1-84467-100-3; 978-1-84467-100-7
LC 2006-19472
The author "takes the reader through the often bewildering array of forces and personalities that are shaping developments in post-Saddam Iraq and makes them comprehensible to Western readers. . . . Cockburn's account of the evolving conflict, the emergence of the resistance movement, the increasingly sectarian nature of the conflict, and the jockeying for power among the Shia, Sunni, and Kurdish communities is informed by his keen personal observations and understanding of the complexities and horrors of daily life in Iraq." Libr J
Includes bibliographical references

Danner, Mark

Torture and truth; America, Abu Ghraib, and the war on terror. New York Review Books 2004 580p il pa $19.95 **956.7**
1. Abu Ghraib (Baghdad, Iraq: Prison) 2. Political prisoners
ISBN 1-590-17152-7 LC 2004-22408
Contents: Torture and truth; The logic of torture; The secret road to Abu Ghraib; Iraq: the new war; Delusions in Baghdad
This is "a book of permanent value for the study of the Iraq war and of how apparently reasonable policies can be swept away by intense pressure, political or military, to produce a particular result." Publ Wkly

Etherington, Mark

Revolt on the Tigris; the Al-Sadr uprising and the governing of Iraq. Cornell University Press 2005 252p il maps $25 **956.7**
ISBN 0-8014-4451-9 LC 2005-49675
This "firsthand account of post-conflict Iraq describes the turmoil visited on the country by outside intervention and the difficulties faced by the Coalition in fashioning a new political and civil apparatus." Publisher's note
"Anyone seriously interested either in the future of that beleaguered nation or the possibilities of intelligent diplomacy would do well to read this firsthand account." Publ Wkly
Includes bibliographical references

Feuer, Alan

Over there; from the Bronx to Baghdad. Counterpoint 2005 283p $24 **956.7**
1. Iraq War, 2003—Personal narratives
ISBN 1-58243-327-5; 978-1-58243-327-1
LC 2004-27149
The author describes the events that occured after he "was bustled off to the Middle East to cover the invasion of Iraq. . . . This is one war memoir that demands to be read." Booklist

Ghareeb, Edmund

Historical dictionary of Iraq; [by] Edmund A. Ghareeb; with the assistance of Beth K. Dougherty. Scarecrow Press 2004 lxxvi, 459p map (Historical dictionaries of Asia, Oceania, and the Middle East, no. 44) $85 **956.7**
1. Iraq—History
ISBN 0-8108-4330-7 LC 2003-11526
This book "provides an overview of Iraq's economy, politics, ecology, major ethnic groups, and historical and current conflicts. Entries range from a quarter page to one page long, with a few longer entries for more detailed topics." Libr J
"This work should be a required purchase in academic, public, and even some high-school libraries." Booklist
Includes bibliographical references

Gordon, Michael R.

The generals' war; the inside story of the conflict in the Gulf; by Michael R. Gordon and Bernard E. Trainor. Little, Brown 1994 551p il map pa $18.95 hardcover o.p. **956.7**
1. Persian Gulf War, 1991
ISBN 0-316-32100-1 (pa) LC 94-27144
This book examines the strategy of "U.S. command officers in the conflict with Iraq. . . . {It asks the question} Why didn't the generals press on to dismantle the Republican Guard of Saddam Hussein, and what were the consequences of their decision against such an act?" Booklist
"This cogent analysis provides several disturbing answers worthy of our attention." Libr J
Includes bibliographical references

Iraq Study Group

The Iraq Study Group report; James A. Baker, III, and Lee H. Hamilton, co-chairs; [by] Lawrence S. Eagleburger . . . [et al.] Vintage Books 2006 142p map pa $10.95 * **956.7**
1. Iraq War, 2003 2. War on terrorism 3. Military policy—United States
ISBN 0-307-38656-2; 978-0-307-38656-4
LC 2006-474152
Also available online and in hardcover from Filibust
Contents: I. Assessment -- Assessment of the current situation in Iraq -- Consequences of continued decline in Iraq -- Some alternative courses in Iraq -- Achieving our goals -- II. The way forward: a new approach -- The external approach: building an international consensus -- The internal approach: helping Iraqis help themselves

Iraq Study Group—*Continued*

This book was "delivered by the Iraq Study Group to the Bush administration and simultaneously and inexpensively published for the general public. And there is no excuse for any public library, large or small, not to own a copy." Booklist

Kelly, Michael, 1957-2003

Martyrs' Day; chronicle of a small war. 2nd Vintage Books ed, {with a new foreword and afterword}. Vintage Bks. 2001 365p pa $14

956.7

ISBN 1-4000-3036-6   LC 2002-524049

First published 1993 by Random House

"This eyewitness account differs from the many other books on the Persian Gulf War in that it deals primarily with the human-interest elements rather than military matters. Kelly, a journalist who traveled extensively in the countries that were affected by the Gulf conflict, chronicles the vagaries of the war and its impact on the lives of the people in a revealing and disturbing text." Libr J

Kennedy, Hugh, 1947-

When Baghdad ruled the Muslim world; the rise and fall of Islam's greatest dynasty. Da Capo Press 2005 xxv, 326p il map $26; pa $17.95

956.7

1. Baghdad (Iraq) 2. Islamic civilization
ISBN   0-306-81435-8;   978-0-306-81435-8;
0-306-81480-3 (pa)   LC 2006-295518

First published 2004 in the United Kingdom with title: The Court of the Caliphs

"Baghdad was founded in 762 by the Abbasid caliphate, which, claiming its legitimacy from lineage to the family of the prophet Muhammad, had overthrown the Umayyad caliphate. Chronicling the first two of the Abbasids' five centuries of rule, historian Kennedy acquaints nonspecialists with an important segment of Islamic history." Booklist

The author "has written an informative and sobering lesson for those who idolize the past." Choice

Includes bibliographical references

La Guardia, Anton

War without end; Israelis, Palestinians, and the struggle for a promised land. St. Martin's Griffin 2003 xxii, 436p il map pa $16.95   **956.7**

1. Israel-Arab conflicts 2. Israeli national characteristics 3. Palestinian Arabs 4. Zionism
ISBN 0-312-31633-X   LC 2003-41288

First published 2001 in the United Kingdom with title: Holy Land, unholy war: Israelis and Palestinians

"This is fundamentally an examination of two wounded peoples, neither of whom seems capable of surmounting national myths and past hatreds to forge a new future. La Guardia is evenhanded in his criticism of both Israeli and Palestinian leaders, but he does not spare ordinary people. . . . This is an absorbing but heartbreaking examination of a seemingly endless tragedy that continues to unfold before our eyes." Booklist [review of 2002 edition]

Includes bibliographical references

Mackey, Sandra, 1937-

The reckoning; Iraq and the legacy of Saddam Hussein. Norton 2002 415p il maps $27.95; pa $16.95   **956.7**

1. Hussein, Ṣaddām 2. Iraq—Politics and government
ISBN 0-393-05141-2; 0-393-32428-1 (pa)

LC 2002-16611

The author offers a "history of Iraq and its early Mesopotamian civilization with . . . biographies of all of its historical figures through the ages, shedding perspective on the current regime of Saddam Hussein and looking ahead to what an Iraq without Hussein might resemble. . . . An extremely thorough appraisal." Booklist

Includes bibliographical references

Miller, T. Christian

Blood money; wasted billions, lost lives, and corporate greed in Iraq. Little, Brown 2006 334p il map $24.99   **956.7**

1. Bush, George W. 2. Iraq War, 2003 3. United States—Politics and government—2001-
ISBN 0-316-16627-8; 978-0-316-16627-0

LC 2006-15074

This is an "account of how the Bush administration has mismanaged the Iraq war and reconstruction. Miller focuses on the bungling of government spending and private contracts, some $30 billion committed to rebuilding Iraq, a greater sum than for the Marshall Plan. . . . Readers interested in understanding the political and economic dynamics behind the faltering campaign in Iraq will appreciate this investigation." Booklist

Includes bibliographical references

Murray, Williamson

The Iraq war; a military history; by Williamson Murray and Robert H. Scales, Jr. Belknap Press of Harvard University Press 2003 312p il map $29.95

956.7

1. United States—Armed forces
ISBN 0-674-01280-1

This is a military history of the 2003 American-led war against Iraq

"Williamson Murray and Robert Scales, both American military academics, have produced a superlative record of the invasion—part history, part critique and part doctrinal template for the future. Technical and operational aspects are explained clearly without losing the depth required to make this a serious study." Economist

Includes bibliographical references

Newell, Clayton R., 1942-

Historical dictionary of the Persian Gulf War, 1990-1991. Scarecrow Press 1998 lix, 363p maps (Historical dictionaries of war, revolution, and civil unrest) $65   **956.7**

1. Persian Gulf War, 1991
ISBN 0-8108-3511-8   LC 98-18944

The author attempts "to help the reader understand the Gulf War and its background. He includes several pages of abbreviations and acronyms along with pages of maps, all . . . describing what happened and why during the 1991 conflict. There is . . . a 30-page introduction that

Newell, Clayton R., 1942——*Continued*

describes the political developments that led up to the
war and a much-needed chronology of events. . . . The
dictionary entries average about a paragraph and cover
the war's personalities as well as its combat equipment."
Libr J

Operation homecoming; Iraq, Afghanistan, and
the Home Front, in the words of U.S. troops
and their families; edited by Andrew Carroll;
preface by Dana Gioia. Random House 2006
xxviii, 386p il $26.95   **956.7**
1. Iraq War, 2003—Personal narratives 2. Afghan
War, 2001—Personal narratives
ISBN 978-1-4000-6562-2; 1-4000-6562-3
           LC 2006-45838
"National Endowment for the Arts"

This book was created as part of a National Endowment for the Arts-funded project that "brought together
some of the nation's most distinguished writers, including Tobias Wolff and Marilyn Nelson, and the men and
women (and their spouses) fighting in the Middle East.
The result is an incredibly wide range of opinions and
emotions about U.S. policy in the Middle East, the war
on terrorism, and the duties and responsibilities of citizens and the military. In 100 pieces of poetry, essays,
letters, e-mails, plays, and journal entries, soldiers recall
the awful thrill in the threat of killing or being killed, the
deaths of buddies, and the cultural and psychological adjustments to a strange land." Booklist

Packer, George

The assassins' gate; America in Iraq. Farrar,
Straus & Giroux 2005 467p $26   **956.7**
1. Iraq War, 2003 2. United States—Politics and government—2001- 3. Iraq—Politics and government
ISBN 0-374-29963-3   LC 2005-11521
This "book rests on three main pillars: analysis of the
intellectual origins of the Iraq war, summary of the political argument that preceded and then led to it, and firsthand description of the consequences on the ground. . . .
The Iraq debate has long needed someone who is both
tough-minded enough, and sufficiently sensitive, to register all its complexities. In George Packer's work, this
need is answered." Publ Wkly
Includes bibliographical references

Polk, William Roe, 1929-

Understanding Iraq; the whole sweep of Iraqi
history, from Genghis Khan's Mongols to the
Ottoman Turks to the British mandate to the
American occupation; [by] William R. Polk.
HarperCollins 2005 221p map $22.95; pa $13.95
*   **956.7**
1. Iraq—History
ISBN 0-06-076468-6; 0-06-076469-4 (pa)
           LC 2005-281319
The author presents an account of the history of Iraq,
from the Dark Ages to the American occupation that began in 2003.
This is "a sober and informed account of Iraq's history, culminating in a compelling critique of the U.S. inter-
vention there." Foreign Affairs
Includes bibliographical references

Raddatz, Martha

The long road home; a story of war and family.
Putnam 2007 310p il map $24.95; pa $15
                  956.7
1. United States. Army. Cavalry, 1st 2. Soldiers—
United States
ISBN   0-399-15382-9;   978-0-399-15382-2;
0-425-21934-8 (pa); 978-0-425-21934-8 (pa)
           LC 2006-37332
Raddatz seeks to reconstruct the events of a battle in
Iraq as she addresses "the effects of war not just on the
soldiers but also on the families waiting back at home."
Publisher's note
This "account has grit and high drama. . . . Some-
times the level of detail is astonishing." N Y Times (Late
N Y Ed)

Reporting Iraq; an oral history of the war by the
journalists who covered it; edited by Mike Hoyt,
John Palattella, and the staff of the Columbia
Journalism Review. Melville House 2007 191p
il pa $21.95 *   **956.7**
1. Iraq War, 2003—Personal narratives 2. Reporters
and reporting
ISBN 978-1-93363-334-3; 1-93363-334-4
"44 reporters casually and directly discuss all angles
of the War in Iraq, including their own shock, fear and
incomprehension, in this compilation of interviews conducted by The Columbia Journalism Review. . . . This
vital, breathtaking collection may be the closest contemporary reporting gets to cutting through the fog of war."
Publ Wkly

Ricks, Thomas E.

Fiasco: the American military adventure in Iraq.
Penguin Press 2006 482p il map $27.95
                  956.7
1. Iraq War, 2003
ISBN 1-59420-103-X; 978-1-59420-103-5
           LC 2006-45357
The author critically assesses "the Bush administration's decision to invade Iraq and its management of the
war and the occupation." N Y Times (Late NY Ed)
This book is "not a political rant nor is it shrill. But
in its low-key, extraordinarily well-sourced, highly-
detailed portrait of the run-up to and conduct of the war
it is devastating." Christ Sci Monit
Includes bibliographical references

Schwartz, Richard Alan, 1951-

Encyclopedia of the Persian Gulf War.
McFarland & Co. 1998 216p il maps $45
                  956.7
1. Persian Gulf War, 1991
ISBN 0-7864-0451-5   LC 97-51886
"Beginning with a seven-page overview, this encyclopedia presents alphabetically arranged entries that describe the conflict, including key figures, places, battles,
diplomacy, and more." SLJ
Includes bibliographical references

Seierstad, Åsne
A hundred and one days; a Baghdad journal; translated by Ingrid Christophersen. Basic Books 2005 321p il maps $22.95   **956.7**
1. Iraq War, 2003
ISBN 0-465-07600-9
First published 2005 in the United Kingdom
The author "writes about her stay as a reporter for Scandinavian, Dutch, and German media in Baghdad in the days before the war in Iraq through the fall of Baghdad. . . . Seierstad puts a human face to and provides insight into the mosaic of the people of Iraq, the Bath party supporters, the dissidents, and the average person caught in the nightmare of the Saddam regime and the horrors of war." SLJ

Shadid, Anthony
Night draws near; Iraq's people in the shadow of America's war. Holt & Co. 2005 424p il $26
                                                         956.7
1. Iraq War, 2003
ISBN 0-8050-7602-6   LC 2005-40348
This book presents a "portrait of life in postwar Iraq and the fallout that the American war has had on ordinary Iraqi civilians." N Y Times (Late N Y Ed)
"Even-handed and keenly observed, containing just enough (and no more) of the author to suggest a decent man worthy of our trust, . . . [this book] is written for the inexpert but has fresh material for scholars." Economist
Includes bibliographical references

Skiba, Katherine M.
Sister in the Band of Brothers; embedded with the 101st Airborne in Iraq. University Press of Kansas 2005 257p il (Modern war studies) $29.95
                                                         956.7
1. United States. Army. Airborne Division, 101st
2. Iraq War, 2003—Personal narratives
ISBN 0-7006-1382-X   LC 2004-26475
The author "was the only woman embedded with the 101st Airborne when the United States invaded Iraq in 2003. She has written a fascinating memoir of her time within the training with other reporters, waiting to invade Iraq and spending the first few months of the war with soldiers in Iraq." Univ Press Books for Public and Second Sch Libr, 2006

Stewart, Rory
The prince of the marshes; and other occupational hazards of a year in Iraq. Harcourt, Inc. 2006 396p il $25 *   **956.7**
1. Iraq—Politics and government
ISBN 978-0-15-101235-0; 0-15-101235-0
                                        LC 2006-06905
"In 2003, Stewart, a former British diplomat, joined the Coalition Provisional Authority in Iraq and was posted to the southern province of Maysan, where he found himself the de-facto governor of a restive populace whose allegiances were split among fifty-four political parties, twenty major tribes, and numerous militias. Stewart's account of his attempts to placate the various local figures who continually threaten to kill each other, or him, is both shrewd and self-deprecating." New Yorker

Swofford, Anthony
Jarhead: a Marine's chronicle of the Gulf War and other battles. Scribner 2003 260p $25; pa $15
                                                         956.7
1. United States. Marine Corps
ISBN 0-7432-3535-5; 0-7432-4491-5 (pa)
                                        LC 2002-30866
The author, "who served in a United States Marine Corps Surveillance and Target Acquisition/Scout-Sniper platoon during the [1991 Gulf War] operation known as Desert Storm [presents an account of his experiences]." N Y Times (Late NY Ed)
This book offers "an unflinching portrayal of the loneliness and brutality of modern warfare and sophisticated analyses of—and visceral reactions to—its politics." Publ Wkly

Tripp, Charles
A history of Iraq. 3rd ed. Cambridge University Press 2007 xxiii, 357p il map $70; pa $24.99
                                                         956.7
1. Iraq—History
ISBN 978-0-521-87823-4; 978-0-521-70247-8 (pa)
                                        LC 2007-282451
First published 2000
This book traces the political history of Iraq from the Ottoman Empire to the fall of Saddam Hussein and the American occupation.
Includes bibliographical references

What was asked of us; an oral history of the Iraq War by the soldiers who fought it; [compiled by] Trish Wood. Little, Brown and Co. 2006 xxii, 309p il map $25.99   **956.7**
1. Iraq War, 2003—Personal narratives
ISBN 0-316-01670-5; 978-0-316-01670-4
                                        LC 2006-930963
This is "a collection of 41 interviews conducted by Canadian investigative journalist Wood with veterans of the current war in Iraq." Libr J
"Colloquial, coarse and compelling, these narratives flash with humor, horror, nihilism and poesy." Publ Wkly

Woodward, Bob, 1943-
Plan of attack. Simon & Schuster 2004 467p il map $28; pa $14 *   **956.7**
1. Iraq War, 2003 2. United States—Politics and government—2001-
ISBN 0-7432-5547-X; 0-7432-5548-8 (pa)
                                        LC 2004-351204
This is a "behind-the-scenes look at the two years of debate and maneuvering within the administration that led to its defining moment: the march to war against Iraq." N Y Times Book Rev
The author "delivers an engrossing blow-by-blow of the run-up to war in Iraq. . . . With this book, Woodward . . . has delivered his most important and impressive work in years. Ultimately, this first-class work of contemporary history will be remembered for shedding needed light on the Iraq War." Publ Wkly

Wright, Evan

Generation kill; Devil Dogs, Iceman, Captain America, and the new face of American war. G.P. Putnam's Sons 2004 354p il maps $24.95; pa $14

956.7

ISBN 0-399-15193-1; 0-425-20040-X (pa)

LC 2004-44682

The author discusses his experiences when embedded with the First Marine Division in Iraq. This book is based on a series of articles that originally appeared in *Rolling Stone*.

This "account is a personality-driven, readable and insightful look at the Iraq War's first month from the Marine grunt's point of view." Publ Wkly

956.94   Palestine. Israel

Armstrong, Karen

Jerusalem; one city, three faiths. Knopf 1996 xxi, 471p il maps hardcover o.p. pa $17.95

956.94

ISBN 0-679-43596-4; 0-345-39168-3 (pa)

LC 96-75888

Armstrong's "overarching theme, that Jerusalem has been central to the experience and 'sacred geography' of Jews, Muslims and Christians and thus has led to deadly struggles for dominance, is a familiar one, yet she brings to her sweeping, profusely illustrated narrative a grasp of sociopolitical conditions seldom found in other books." Publ Wkly

Bregman, Ahron

A history of Israel. Palgrave Macmillan 2002 xx, 320p map (Palgrave essential histories) $70; pa $21.95

956.94

1. Israel—History

ISBN 0-333-67631-9; 0-333-67632-7 (pa)

LC 2002-72304

This book "examines Israel's turbulent history from the first Zionist Congress in 1897 to the present day. The driving themes of this . . . account are Jewish immigration, war, and attempts to forge peace between Israelis, Arabs, and Palestinians. " Publisher's note

"Bregman takes into account all the major issues involving Israel's history." Booklist

Includes bibliographical references

Collins, Larry, 1929-2005

O Jerusalem! {by} Larry Collins and Dominique Lapierre. Simon & Schuster 1972 637p il maps pa $17 hardcover o.p.

956.94

1. Jerusalem—History—1948, Siege 2. Israel-Arab War, 1948-1949

ISBN 0-671-66241-4 (pa)

This is an account of the struggle for the city of Jerusalem during the Israel-Arab War of 1948

Includes bibliographical references

Farsoun, Samih K.

Palestine and the Palestinians; {by} Samih K. Farsoun with Christina E. Zacharia. Westview Press 1997 375p maps pa $29 hardcover o.p.

956.94

1. Palestinian Arabs 2. Israel-Arab conflicts

ISBN 0-8133-2773-3 (pa)

LC 97-21954

This study of the Palestinian peoples covers their economic and social conditions, their political activity and national aspirations

"This is an excellent introduction to the modern history of the Palestinians, the transformations of their troubled land, and the prospects of both." Choice

Includes bibliographical references

Gilbert, Martin, 1936-

Jerusalem in the twentieth century. Wiley 1996 412p il maps $30; pa $16.95

956.94

1. Jerusalem

ISBN 0-471-16308-2; 0-471-28328-2 (pa)

LC 96-18458

This political, social and military history of Jerusalem "concentrates on the return of the Jews to Jerusalem in the 20th century. They find a squalid city badly governed by the Turks and inaugurate the cultural, intellectual, social (hospitals, etc.), and economic rejuvenation in the city. What ensues is a continual record of conflict among the inhabitants of the region." Libr J

"Gilbert's history is heavily Zionist. . . . Nonetheless, despite his tilt, Gilbert is well worth reading. He has an unrivalled ability to tell a story through the eyes of (some of) those taking part and his book is good popular history." London Rev Books

Includes bibliographical references

Gorenberg, Gershom

The accidental empire; Israel and the birth of the settlements, 1967-1977. Times Books 2006 454p il map $30

956.94

1. West Bank 2. Gaza Strip 3. Israel—Politics and government

ISBN 0-8050-7564-X; 978-0-8050-7564-9

LC 2005-52988

This is an account of the settler movement in Israel, beginning with the aftermath of the 1967 war.

This is "an absorbing narrative with extensive references to archives, private papers, oral histories, books and articles." Nation

Includes bibliographical references

Hazony, Yoram

The Jewish state; the struggle for Israel's soul. Basic Bks. 2000 433p pa $18 hardcover o.p.

956.94

1. Zionism 2. Israel—Politics and government

ISBN 0-465-02902-7 (pa)

LC 00-21814

The author "asserts that 'the idea of the Jewish state'—and the future of the state—is under fervent attack from its own intellectual and cultural establishment. These 'post-Zionists' advocate, for example, the dejudaization of the public school curriculum and the repeal the Law of Return . . . in order to create a more

Hazony, Yoram—*Continued*
secular and equitable 'post-Jewish' state." Publ Wkly
"An extremely well-thought-out treatise, *The Jewish State* screams out for attention and is strongly recommended for anyone interested in contemporary Israeli politics." Libr J

Horovitz, David Phillip
A little too close to God; the thrills and panic of a life in Israel; [by] David Horovitz. Knopf 2000 311p $27.50 **956.94**
 1. Israel—Politics and government 2. Israeli national characteristics
 ISBN 0-375-40381-7
The author, editor of the Jerusalem Report, argues "that in recent years the conservative Netanyahu government and the continued influence of extreme Orthodox Jews have done little except complicate daily life in Israel and prevent serious peace negotiations from taking place. He presents a highly informative history and current-events narrative in a manner that makes it personal and relevant to Jews and non-Jews alike." Libr J

How Israelis and Palestinians negotiate; a cross-cultural analysis of the Oslo peace process; edited by Tamara Cofman Wittes. United States Institute of Peace Press 2005 160p $40; pa $12 * **956.94**
 1. Israel-Arab conflicts 2. Cross-cultural studies 3. Israeli national characteristics 4. Palestinian Arabs
 ISBN 1-929223-64-1; 1-929223-63-3 (pa)
 LC 2004-65759
"Five essays by leading scholars focus on the concept of culture and the role it plays in the success and failure of the Middle East peace process. Both Israeli and Palestinian cultures are assessed and explained as a context to understand snags and successes from Oslo II to the Camp David accords. This small volume is very accessible to high school readers and should generate interest in understanding the larger issues which continue to add to the instability of the region." Univ Press Books for Public and Second Sch Libr, 2006
Includes bibliographical references

Laqueur, Walter, 1921-
A history of Zionism; with a new preface by the author. Schocken Bks. 1989 xxii, 639p il pa $16.95 hardcover o.p. **956.94**
 1. Zionism
 ISBN 0-8052-1149-7 (pa) LC 88-38221
A reissue with new introduction of the title first published 1972 by Holt, Rinehart & Winston
The author examines the history of Zionism over the past three centuries from its European roots to the establishment of the state of Israel
Includes bibliographical references

LeBor, Adam
City of oranges; an intimate history of Arabs and Jews in Jaffa. W.W. Norton 2007 xxxviii, 424p il map pa $14.95 **956.94**
 1. Israel-Arab conflicts
 ISBN 0-393-32984-4; 978-0-393-32984-1
 LC 2007-2389

First published 2006 in the United Kingdom
LeBor presents interviews with Arab and Jewish families in Jaffa, Israel.
"Those looking for a well-rounded and truly human insight into the conflict will enjoy this account." Publ Wkly
Includes bibliographical references

Lozowick, Yaacov
Right to exist; a moral defense of Israel's wars. Doubleday 2003 326p map $26; pa $15
 956.94
 1. Israel-Arab conflicts
 ISBN 0-385-50905-7; 1-4000-3243-1 (pa)
 LC 2003-48477
The author "asserts that Israel is now, as before, struggling against opponents whose goal is the eventual destruction of the Jewish state. In examining the entire history of the Zionist enterprise, he illustrates both the moral justification of that enterprise and of the wars Israelis have been compelled to fight to preserve their independence. . . . {This} is an eloquent and necessary justification of Israel's right to defend itself." Booklist

Miller, Jennifer, 1980-
Inheriting the Holy Land; an American's search for hope in the Middle East. Ballantine Books 2005 xxxiii, 261p map $24.95; pa $14.95 * **956.94**
 1. Israel-Arab conflicts
 ISBN 0-345-46924-0; 978-0-345-46924-3; 0-345-46925-9 (pa); 978-0-345-46925-0 (pa)
 LC 2004-66349
The author "is the daughter of one of the chief American negotiators in the Israeli-Palestinian conflict and a longtime participant in the Seeds of Peace program, bringing together Israeli and Palestinian children. Using the many contacts that she has made, from the highest leaders to the children on the street, Miller explores . . . the many different viewpoints and preconceptions of the people involved in the conflict, not excluding her own. . . . This is a superb book on a crucial issue of our time." SLJ
Includes bibliographical references

Peres, Shimon, 1923-
The imaginary voyage; with Theodor Herzl in Israel; in collaboration with Patrick Girard. Arcade Pub. 1999 256p $23.95 **956.94**
 1. Herzl, Theodor, 1860-1904 2. Zionism 3. Israel—History
 ISBN 1-55970-468-3 LC 99-24365
Peres "takes the reader on an imaginary journey around present-day Israel with Theodor Herzl (1860-1904), the father of modern Zionism. The imaginary Herzl proves a good foil to whom Peres explains concisely how Israel has evolved." Publ Wkly

Sachar, Howard Morley, 1928-
A history of Israel; from the rise of Zionism to
our time; [by] Howard M. Sachar. 3rd ed, rev and
updated. Knopf 2007 xxii, 1270p map pa $39.95
956.94
1. Israel—History 2. Zionism
ISBN 978-0-375-71132-9; 0-375-71132-5
LC 2006-101970
First published in two volumes 1976-1987
This is a history of the state of Israel. "When first
published in 1976, this truly monumental history was
hailed as a definitive work. . . . As extraordinarily
stimulating as the first edition." Booklist
Includes bibliographical references

Shipler, David K.
Arab and Jew; wounded spirits in a promised
land. rev ed. Penguin Bks. 2002 xxxix, 565p maps
pa $17   **956.94**
1. Jewish-Arab relations 2. Israel-Arab conflicts
3. Palestinian Arabs
ISBN 0-14-200229-1   LC 2001-54862
First published 1986 by Times Bks.
The author examines the stereotypes that Arabs and
Jews have of one another and "the origins of the prejudices that have been intensified by war, terrorism, and
nationalism. . . . Shipler examines the process of indoctrination that begins in schools; he discusses the far-
ranging effects of socioeconomic differences, historical
conflicts between Islam and Judaism, attitudes about the
Holocaust, and much more." Publisher's note
Includes bibliographical references

Shlaim, Avi
The iron wall; Israel and the Arab world since
1948. Norton 1999 704p il pa $17.95 hardcover
o.p.   **956.94**
1. Israel-Arab conflicts 2. Jewish-Arab relations
3. Israel—Foreign relations
ISBN 0-393-32112-6 (pa)   LC 99-23121
"The title of Shlaim's book is an allusion to an article
called 'On the Iron Wall' by Zeev Jabotinsky. . . .
Jabotinsky argued, the only path forward for the Zionist
project was the path of force: to erect an 'iron wall' in
the form of a Jewish battalion in the British army. . . .
{Shlaim uses} the concept of the 'iron wall' as an organizing paradigm to explain the evolution of the politics
of the Yishuv and the state of Israel from the 1920s to
the 1980s." New Repub
"A thorough analysis of Israel's relationships with the
West as well as its neighbors from a controversial but
thoughtful point of view." Booklist
Includes bibliographical references

Timmerman, Kenneth R.
Preachers of hate; Islam and the war on
America. Crown Publishers 2003 370p $25.95; pa
$14.95   **956.94**
1. Israel-Arab conflicts
ISBN 1-4000-4901-6; 1-4000-5373-0 (pa)
LC 2003-11455

Contents: "The Jews did it!" -- Horror at Passover --
"They have a plan" -- The elements of hate -- Hitler and
the mufti -- The house of war -- Arafat's reign of terror
-- The big lie -- The "new" anti-Semitism in Europe --
The Islamic repubic of America -- Islam on the march:
on the trail of Osama bin Laden
The author "examines the politics that demonize Isra-
el—and, increasingly, the U.S.—for failures of domestic
policy in many Arab nations." Booklist
Includes bibliographical references

Tolan, Sandy
The lemon tree; an Arab, a Jew, and the heart
of the Middle East. Bloomsbury Pub. 2006 362p
$24.95   **956.94**
1. Israel-Arab conflicts
ISBN 1-58234-343-8; 978-1-58234-343-3
LC 2005-30360
The author "captures the Arab-Israeli struggle in this
story of a house and the two families, first Palestinian
and then Jewish, who successively lived in it. . . . This
wonderful human story vividly depicts the depths of attachment to contested ground." Libr J

956.95   Jordan and West Bank

Grossman, David
The yellow wind; translated from the Hebrew
by Haim Watzman; {with a new afterword by the
author}. Picador 2002 222p map pa $13
956.95
1. Palestinian Arabs 2. West Bank 3. Jewish-Arab relations
ISBN 0-312-42098-6   LC 2002-67325
Original Hebrew edition, 1987; this translation first
published 1988
"Grossman was assigned to report for a weekly newspaper on life for both occupied and occupier on the West
Bank during the 20th anniversary of its conquest. With
an eye and ear for revealing detail, he argues that the
Jews are now doing to Palestinians what has been done
to them through the ages." Libr J

Shehadeh, Raja, 1951-
Palestinian walks; forays into a vanishing
landscape. Scribner 2008 xxii, 200p il map pa $15
956.95
1. Israel-Arab conflicts 2. West Bank—Description
and travel
ISBN 978-1-4165-6966-4; 1-4165-6966-9
First published 2007 in the United Kingdom
The author "spent most of his adult life as a lawyer
trying to prevent Jewish settlement development in the
West Bank. In this work, he recounts his thoughts during
six walks into the surrounding Ramallah wilderness between 1978 and 2006. . . . He reveals his anger and
pain as he muses on history, his life, his failures, political turmoil, and the unique natural beauty of a beloved
land that is succumbing to development and access restrictions. . . . This compelling but unsettling story,
which provides insight into the endless woes of a troubled region, is highly recommended for general libraries
and Middle Eastern collections." Libr J

Winslow, Philip C.
Victory for us is to see you suffer; in the West Bank with the Palestinians and the Israelis. Beacon Press 2007 xxiii, 224p map $24.95
956.95

1. West Bank 2. Israel-Arab conflicts
ISBN 978-0-8070-6906-6; 0-8070-6906-X
LC 2007-13411

The author "depicts the universal cost of Israel's occupation of Palestinian lands in excruciatingly human terms in a memoir detailing 30 months spent on the West Bank with the United Nations Relief and Works Agency (UNRWA)." Publ Wkly

Includes bibliographical references

957 Siberia (Asiatic Russia)

Thubron, Colin, 1939-
In Siberia. HarperCollins Pubs. 2000 287p pa $14 hardcover o.p. 1. Siberia (Russia) **957**
ISBN 0-06-095373-X (pa) LC 99-41346

The author "traverses all points of the compass in Russia's vast, sparsely settled Wild East. Thubron journeys into what 'seems less a country than a region in people's minds,' encountering people in search of explanations for past atrocities and ways to live through current hardships—all the while finding solace in science or religion." Libr J

"Thubron elegantly encompasses both awe-inspiring landscapes and their dark histories as well as immersing himself in local eccentricities." Times Lit Suppl

958 Central Asia

Hanks, Reuel R.
Central Asia; a global studies handbook. ABC-CLIO 2005 xvii, 467p il map (Global studies) $55 * **958**
1. Central Asia
ISBN 1-85109-656-6 LC 2005-14716

This book covers Uzbekistan, Kazakhstan, and Kyrgyzstan. "Each part of the book is divided into a narrative and a reference section. The narrative portion covers the geography and history of each country, along with essays on current economic, social, and cultural trends. The reference section contains a historical chronology; encyclopedic entries on significant people, places, and events in each country; an overview of typical food and drink consumption; basic etiquette; a directory of country-related organizations; and a short, annotated bibliography." Choice

"The superb text makes accessible, whether for reports or general reading, former Silk Road lands that may play increasingly important roles—think of oil-rich Kazakhstan—in the world's economy." SLJ

Includes bibliographical references

958.1 Afghanistan

Akbar, Said Hyder
Come back to Afghanistan; a California teenager's story; [by] Said Hyder Akbar and Susan Burton. Distributed to the trade by Holtzbrinck Publishers 2005 339p map $24.95; pa $14.95
958.1

1. Afghanistan
ISBN 1-58234-520-1; 1-59691-068-2 (pa)
LC 2005-9249

The author "provides a firsthand account of his trips back home balancing his observations and experiences of Afghanistan's sources of instability, such as tribalism and narcotics, with personal notations on American failures, such as a tortured detainee, unfulfilled promises, and a security detail that leaves President Karzai a 'virtual prisoner.'" Libr J

"This is required reading for anyone seeking a better understanding of Afghanistan and of what it feels like to be a bicultural young person pulled between continents." Booklist

Anderson, Jon Lee
The lion's grave; dispatches from Afghanistan; photographs by Thomas Dworzak. Grove Press 2002 244p il $23; pa $13 **958.1**
1. Afghanistan
ISBN 0-8021-1723-6; 0-8021-4025-4 (pa)
LC 2002-70659

In this "account, which includes his diary entries. Anderson recounts the arduous task of developing sources and reporting on the complexities of a nation caught up in its own ethnic and religious conflicts and its place in the new war on terrorism." Booklist

"The author's reporting reflects an astute understanding of the constellation of sociopolitical forces in today's Afghanistan. Anderson's penetrating observations and his ability to bring life to his subject—the fall of Kandahar and Kunduz, the dangerous search of the Tora Bora caves—are admirable." Libr J

Ansary, Mir Tamim
West of Kabul, East of New York; an Afghan American story. Farrar, Straus & Giroux 2002 292p hardcover o.p. pa $13 **958.1**
1. Afghanistan—Social conditions 2. Islamic civilization
ISBN 0-374-28757-0; 0-312-42151-6 (pa)

The author, an Afghan American, reflects on his dual heritage. In light of the events of September 11, he focuses particular attention on the relationship between Islam and the West.

"While Ansary's political insights can be detached or perhaps purposefully aloof his descriptions of having lived in and identified alternately with the West and the Islamic world are utterly compelling." Publ Wkly

Bergen, Peter L.

Holy war, Inc.; inside the secret world of Osama bin Laden. Free Press 2001 242p hardcover o.p. pa $14   **958.1**
1. Terrorism
ISBN 0-7432-0502-2; 0-7432-3495-2 (pa)
LC 2001-54732

The author was a member of the CNN team that interviewed Saudi terrorist Osama bin Laden in 1997. Here he discusses "the history of Al Qaeda as a terrorist organization, profiles its leaders and more prominent members and examines its evolution as a global network." NY Times

"Although it may be impossible to fully understand bin Laden, Bergen does an admirable job of portraying him as a person, not just the face of terrorism. Readers will come away from this book understanding why bin Laden has been successful and how difficult it will be to dismantle his organization of terror." Booklist

Includes bibliographical references

Chayes, Sarah, 1962-

The punishment of virtue; inside Afghanistan after the Taliban. Penguin Press 2006 386p il map hardcover o.p. pa $16 *   **958.1**
1. Afghan War, 2001-
ISBN 1-59420-096-3; 978-0-14-311206-8 (pa); 0-14-311206-6 (pa)   LC 2006-43499

This is an eyewitness account of conditions "in Afghanistan in the wake of the defeat of the Taliban." Publisher's note

The author's "hands-on experience as a deeply immersed reporter and activist gives her lucid analysis and prescriptions a practical scope and persuasive authority." Publ Wkly

Includes bibliographical references

Coll, Steve

Ghost wars; the secret history of the CIA, Afghanistan, and bin Laden, from the Soviet invasion to September 10, 2001. Penguin Press 2004 695p maps $29.95; pa $16   **958.1**
1. Osama bin Laden 2. United States. Central Intelligence Agency 3. Afghanistan
ISBN 1-594-20007-6; 0-14-303466-9 (pa)
LC 2003-58593

This is a "history of the CIA's role in Afghanistan, including its covert program against Soviet troops from 1979 to 1989, and examines the rise of the Taliban, the emergence of bin Laden, and the secret efforts by CIA officers and their agents to capture or kill bin Laden in Afghanistan after 1998." Publisher's note

The author "has given us what is certainly the finest historical narrative so far on the origins of Al Qaeda in the post-Soviet rubble of Afghanistan." N Y Times Book Rev

Includes bibliographical references

Corwin, Phillip

Doomed in Afghanistan; a UN officer's memoir of the fall of Kabul and Najibullah's escape, 1992. Rutgers Univ. Press 2003 xx, 241p il $28
958.1
1. Najibullah, Mohammed 2. United Nations—Afghanistan 3. Afghanistan—History—Soviet occupation, 1979-1989
ISBN 0-8135-3171-3   LC 2002-24831

This book "focuses on the period after the Soviets left the country in 1988, when the UN was given the task of establishing a broad-based regime that would have included the communists. Thanks to the intrigues of the US and its clients, Pakistan and Saudi Arabia, the UN team, of which the author was a member, failed to effect the escape of Najibullah, the leftist president of Afghanistan, from Kabul. As a result, there could be no broad-based coalition that might have prevented the rise of the Taliban and the country's decline into barbarism. . . . This engaging and sympathetic essay enables readers to understand the country's tragic recent past and the failure of diplomacy . . . which paved the way for civil war and the rise of 'Islamic fundamentalism.'" Choice

Includes bibliographical references

Elliot, Jason, 1965-

An unexpected light; travels in Afghanistan. St. Martin's Press 2001 473p map pa $18 hardcover o.p. 1. Afghanistan—Description   **958.1**
ISBN 0-312-28846-8 (pa)   LC 2001-50036

This "is an account of Elliot's two visits to Afghanistan. The first occurred when he joined the mujaheddin circa 1979 and was smuggled into Soviet-occupied Afghanistan; the second happened nearly ten years later, when he returned to the still war-torn land. The skirmishes that Elliot painstakingly describes here took place between the Taliban and the government of Gen. Ahmad Shah Massoud in Kabul. . . . Elliot traveled widely in the hinterland, visiting Faizabad in the north and Herat in the west. The result is some of the finest travel writing in recent years." Libr J

Ewans, Martin

Afghanistan; a short history of its people and politics. HarperCollins Pubs. 2002 244p il maps pa $13.95 hardcover o.p.   **958.1**
1. Afghanistan—History
ISBN 0-06-050508-7 (pa)   LC 2002-17342

"Ewans shows how centuries of invasions, fierce tribal rivalries, and powerful dynasties led to the creation of an Afghan empire during the eighteenth century. . . . The ruling Afghan dynasty was overthrown by a communist coup in the 1970s, which was answered in turn by a Soviet invasion in 1979. Roughly a decade later, the Soviet Union was forced to withdraw and left Afghanistan with a civil war that was to tear apart the nation's last remnants of religious and ethnic unity. It was into this climate that the Taliban was born." Publisher's note

"This is a fascinating story and the best book-length examination of Afghanistan's history we're likely to have for some time." Booklist

Includes bibliographical references

Rashid, Ahmed
Taliban: militant Islam, oil, and fundamentalism in Central Asia. Yale Univ. Press 2000 274p maps $40; pa $14.95 **958.1**
1. Taliban (Afghanistan) 2. Afghanistan—Politics and government 3. Islamic fundamentalism
ISBN 0-300-08340-8; 0-300-08902-3 (pa)
LC 99-68718
The author "covers the origin and rise of the Taliban, its concepts of Islam on questions of gender roles and drugs, and the importance of the country to the development of energy resources in the region. . . . A lucid and thoroughly researched account." Libr J

Schroen, Gary C.
First in; an insider's account of how the CIA spearheaded the war on terror in Afghanistan. Presidio Press/Ballantine Books 2005 $25.95; pa $14.95 **958.1**
1. United States. Central Intelligence Agency 2. Afghanistan
ISBN 0-89141-872-5; 0-89141-875-X (pa)
LC 2005-43171
The author describes his experiences after he "was tapped to lead the effort to establish contact with the Northern Alliance in the days following 9/11; the 35-year CIA veteran commanded the first American team on the ground in Afghanistan. . . . Schroen delivers what he advertises: a powerful account that takes the reader inside war councils and 19th-century- style cavalry charges in the months just after 9/11." Publ Wkly

Seierstad, Åsne
The bookseller of Kabul; translated by Ingrid Christophersen. Little, Brown 2003 287p $19.95; pa $12.95 **958.1**
1. Khan family 2. Afghanistan
ISBN 0-316-73450-0; 0-316-15941-7 (pa)
LC 2003-54643
The author "entered Kabul with Northern Alliance soldiers after they ousted the Taliban. She took the rare opportunity to live with and write a book about the extended family of Sultan Khan, bookseller and entrepreneur. The result, organized around events in the lives of individual members of Khan's large clan . . . provides appropriate information about recent Afghani history, a glimpse from the inside at an Islamic family, and an understanding of the harshness and difficulty of the daily grind in Afghanistan—both under the Taliban and after the U.S. antiterrorist campaign." Booklist

Shah, Saira
The storyteller's daughter. Knopf 2003 253p $24; pa $13.95 **958.1**
1. Afghanistan
ISBN 0-375-41531-9; 1-4000-3147-8 (pa)
LC 2004-295126
The author "weaves oral traditions with history to describe life as an Afghani raised in the West but with solid roots in the East. . . . We learn about Shah's documentary work in Afghanistan, the power of myth through which Afghanistan's tradition is born, the brave work of

peoples and organizations such as the Revolutionary Association of the Women of Afghanistan (RAWA), and the West's (and even East's) misconceptions regarding Muslim teachings. . . . This rare personal and historic account of the region is a great addition to public and academic libraries." Libr J

Wahab, Shaista
A brief history of Afghanistan; [by] Shaista Wahab and Barry Youngerman. Facts On File 2006 308p il map $45 * **958.1**
1. Afghanistan—History
ISBN 0-8160-5761-3; 978-0-8160-5761-0
LC 2006-43979
This is "a synoptic view of Afghanistan from prehistory to 2006. . . . Wahab covers the Great Game between the Russian and British empires, the unrest of the 20th century, the Soviet occupation of the 1980s, the rise of the mujahideen, and the Taliban era and the civil war that followed, and concludes with a chapter summarizing the current status of her native county." SLJ
Includes bibliographical references

Zoya
Zoya's story; an Afghan woman's struggle for freedom; {by} Zoya with John Follain and Rita Cristofari. HarperCollins Pubs. 2002 239p $24.95; pa $12.95 **958.1**
1. Afghanistan
ISBN 0-06-009782-5; 0-06-009783-3 (pa)
"After both her parents were killed by the Mujahideen, Zoya took up her mother's work in the Revolutionary Association of the Women of Afghanistan and, with her grandmother, journeyed to Pakistan, where she could receive an education. A few years later, Zoya returned to Afghanistan, where she witnessed public executions but also saw heartening displays of courage. A stirring memoir by an uncompromisingly brave woman." Booklist

958.4 Turkestan

Robbins, Christopher, 1946-
Apples are from Kazakhstan; the land that disappeared. Atlas Books 2008 296p il map $24 **958.4**
1. Kazakhstan
ISBN 0-9777433-8-1; 978-0-9777433-8-4
LC 2008-299516
First published 2007 in the United Kingdom with the title: In search of Kazakhstan
A "delightful and masterful travelog reveals . . . a country rich in history, natural beauty, and, perhaps most important, tolerance. . . . [The author] manages to make this an overall hopeful book by combining grave topics with less grave ones and adding a good dose of wit." Libr J

959 Southeast Asia

Somers Heidhues, Mary F.

Southeast Asia: a concise history. Thames & Hudson 2000 192p il maps pa $18.95 hardcover o.p. 1. Southeast Asia—History **959**

ISBN 0-500-28303-6 (pa) LC 99-66014

This "history ranges from Southeast Asia's prehistoric times to the most recent political developments in Indonesia. Heidhues . . . divides her study into seven well-balanced chapters, touching on the political history, economics, society, and culture of Burma, Thailand, Cambodia, Vietnam, Malaysia, Singapore, Brunei, Indonesia, and the Philippines." Libr J

Southeast Asia; a historical encyclopedia from Angkor Wat to East Timor; edited by Ooi Keat Gin. ABC-CLIO 2004 3v il map set $285 *
959

1. Southeast Asia

ISBN 1-576-07770-5 LC 2004-4813

The countries covered in this book include "Myanmar (Burma), Thailand (Siam), Laos, Cambodia, Vietnam, Malaysia, Singapore, Brunei, the Philippines, Indonesia, and East Timor. This A-Z aims to help students and researchers grasp the fragmented region through 800 detailed articles on archaeology, politics, culture, economic transformation, and more." Libr J

Includes bibliographical references

959.1 Myanmar

Aung San Suu Kyi

Freedom from fear, and other writings; edited with an introduction by Michael Aris; foreword to the first edition by Vaclav Havel, foreword to the second edition by Archbishop Desmond Tutu. rev ed. Penguin Bks. 1995 xxxi, 374p il pa $14.95
959.1

1. Myanmar—Politics and government

ISBN 0-14-025317-3 LC 96-902734

First published 1991

This is a collection of essays, letters, speeches, and other writings by the Burmese opposition leader, Winner of the 1991 Nobel Peace Prize

"Mrs. Aung San Suu Kyi's excellent book offers inspiration to many other peoples in the region as much as it reflects Myanmar's own desire for change." N Y Times Book Rev [review of 1991 edition]

Includes bibliographical references

Marshall, Andrew

The trouser people; a story of Burma—in the shadow of the Empire. Counterpoint 2002 307p il maps pa $16 hardcover o.p. paperback available $16 **959.1**

1. Scott, Sir James George, 1851-1935 2. Myanmar

ISBN 1-58243-242-2 (pa) LC 2001-47246

"Marshall recounts his adventures in Burma over a five-year period, inspired by the diaries of late-19th-

century Scottish adventurer Sir George Scott. . . . Scott furthered the interests of the British colonials (aka the trouser people) by mapping and photographing remote areas of Burma. . . . This is a valuable firsthand look at areas and living conditions in a country relatively unknown in the West." Publ Wkly

Thant Myint-U, 1966-

The river of lost footsteps; histories of Burma. Farrar, Straus & Giroux 2006 361p il map $25
959.1

1. Myanmar

ISBN 978-0-374-16342-6; 0-374-16342-1

LC 2006-09199

The author "tells the story of modern Burma, in part through a telling of his own family's history." Publisher's note

"This readable, reflective history will support revived interest in Burma." Booklist

Includes bibliographical references

959.3 Thailand

Krauss, Erich, 1971-

Wave of destruction; the stories of four families and history's deadliest tsunami. Rodale 2006 244p il map $24.95 **959.3**

1. Tsunamis 2. Thailand 3. Survival after airplane accidents, shipwrecks, etc.

ISBN 1-59486-378-4 LC 2005-24531

The author provides an "account of four families in a Thai village devastated by the tsunami of December 26, 2004. . . . Passionately told, this tragic story portrays the full human cost of natural devastation." Publ Wkly

Wyatt, David K., 1937-2006

Thailand: a short history. 2nd ed. Yale Univ. Press 2003 352p il maps pa $20 *

1. Thailand—History **959.3**

ISBN 0-3000-8475-7

First published 1984

This volume provides a general history of Thailand beginning with the migrations of the Tai peoples from southern China, examining the social and economic changes to the present

Includes bibliographical references

959.6 Cambodia

Bizot, François

The gate; translated from the French by Euan Cameron; with a preface by John Le Carré. Knopf 2003 275p $24; pa $14 **959.6**

1. Bizot, François

ISBN 0-375-41293-X; 0-375-72723-X (pa)

LC 2002-69428

Original French edition, 2000

The author, who was "seized by Cambodian rebels in 1971, recalls peculiar daily chat sessions over politics

Bizot, François—*Continued*
and philosophy with his chief captor, an obviously dangerous man who later ran one of the Khmer Rouge's ghastliest killing fields." N Y Times Book Rev

Bizot's "tale of his experiences, both in the camp and as translator at the gate of the French embassy, leaves readers with haunting images of the doomed." Booklist

Dunlop, Nic, 1969-
The lost executioner; a journey to the heart of the killing fields. Walker & Co. 2006 326p il map $24   **959.6**
1. Kang, Kek Ieu 2. Khmer Rouge 3. Cambodia—History—1975-
ISBN 0-8027-1472-2
First published 2005 in the United Kingdom
This is an "account of the Khmer Rouge, the Cambodian Communist regime responsible for more than two million deaths between 1975 and 1979. Armed with a black-and-white photograph of Comrade Duch—Pol Pot's chief executioner—Dunlop traveled to the war-ravaged country to probe the dark depths of a once-studious young boy and dedicated teacher who became one of the twentieth-century's most notorious mass murderers. . . . Dunlop's interviews with former Khmer Rouge members are both wrenching and revelatory." Booklist
Includes bibliographical references

Kamm, Henry
Cambodia: report from a stricken land. Arcade Pub. 1998 xxiv, 262p il maps $25.95
1. Cambodia—History   **959.6**
ISBN 1-55970-433-0   LC 98-22707
This is an account of events in Cambodia since the 1970s. Kamm argues that these "events were man-made and avoidable, the consequence of cynical and callous decisions by rival Cambodian leaders and by foreign powers, including the United States. . . . Guiltiest by far were the Khmer Rouge, who made Cambodia a killing field while their . . . regime under Pol Pot held power between 1975 and 1979." N Y Times Book Rev
"Sober yet passionate, Kamm's well-informed survey is an excellent introduction to a country that the world has all but abandoned." Libr J

Kiernan, Ben
The Pol Pot regime; race, power, and genocide in Cambodia under the Khmer Rouge, 1975-79. 2nd ed. Yale Univ. Press 2002 xxiii, 477p il map (Yale Nota bene) pa $19.95   **959.6**
1. Communism—Cambodia   2. Atrocities
3. Cambodia—Politics and government
ISBN 0-300-09649-6   LC 2002-100979
First published 1996
This is an account of "the Cambodian catastrophe; the significant internal resistance to the Khmer Rouge; and the racialist and totalitarian attitudes by which Pol Pot's regime justified the death, by starvation and disease as well as torture and murder, of some 1.5 million of their 8 million countrymen." Booklist {review of 1996 edition}
Includes bibliographical references

Ung, Loung, 1970-
First they killed my father; a daughter of Cambodia remembers. HarperCollins Pubs. 2000 240p il hardcover o.p. pa $13.95   **959.6**
1. Cambodia—History—1975-
ISBN 0-06-019332-8; 0-06-085626-2 (pa)
LC 99-34707
The author's father was a "high-ranking government official in Phnom Penh. She was only five when the Khmer Rouge stormed the city and her family was forced to flee. They sought refuge in various camps, hiding their wealth and education, always on the move and ever fearful of being betrayed. After 20 months, Ung's father was taken away, never to be seen again. Her story of starvation, forced labor, beatings, attempted rape, separations, and the deaths of her family members is one of horror and brutality." SLJ

959.7   Vietnam

Prochnau, William W., 1937-
Once upon a distant war. Vintage Bks. 1996 546p il pa $15   **959.7**
1. Sheehan, Neil 2. Halberstam, David, 1934-2007
3. Browne, Malcolm W. 4. Vietnam War, 1961-1975—Journalists
ISBN 0-679-77265-0
First published 1995 by Times Books
This is a study of American journalists who reported on the Vietnam War, focusing on the years between 1961 and 1963. The author discusses the activities of reporters and photographers such as Peter Arnett, Homer Bigart, Malcolm Browne, Horst Fass, David Halberstam, Marguerite Higgins, Charley Mohr, and Neil Sheehan.
Prochnau's "thesis is hardly new—Vietnam has long been seen as the lesson that taught reporters to stop automatically believing government handout—but Prochnau illustrates it in fresh, interesting ways." Time

Sachs, Dana
The house on Dream Street; memoir of an American woman in Vietnam. Seal Press 2003 357p pa $15.95   **959.7**
1. Vietnam—Description and travel
ISBN 1-580-05100-6   LC 2003-57299
First published by Algonquin Bks in 2000
This is an American journalist's account of her visits to Vietnam. "Her memoir covers the time from her initial plunge into the country, as a touring backpacker in 1989, to her triumphant return in 1998 with . . . [her] husband and son." Publ Wkly

959.704   Vietnam—1949-

Anderson, David L.
The Columbia guide to the Vietnam War. Columbia Univ. Press 2002 308p maps (Columbia guides to American history and cultures) $47; pa $22.50 *   **959.704**
1. Vietnam War, 1961-1975
ISBN 0-231-11492-3; 0-231-11493-1 (pa)
LC 2002-20143

Anderson, David L.—*Continued*

"The first part of the book contains a historical narrative. The rest consists of a 'mini-encyclopedia' listing events, individuals, and military operations; a brief chronology; an annotated bibliography of books, feature films, documentaries, and electronic resources; a collection of mostly excerpted documents; and an appendix of pertinent statistics." Booklist

"Anderson's guide successfully compresses the copiously documented, labyrinthine history of the Vietnamese conflict into a single economical volume. In five parts, the guide's narrative and encyclopedia sections provide a fascinating survey of the war, while the remaining elements of the work link modern researchers to a host of richly documented resources. . . . The guide will become an important resource for those seeking a historical overview as well as direction for further research. Strongly recommended." Choice

Includes bibliographical references

Berman, Larry

No peace, no honor; Nixon, Kissinger, and betrayal in Vietnam. Free Press 2001 334p $27.50; pa $14   **959.704**

1. Nixon, Richard M. (Richard Milhous), 1913-1994 2. Kissinger, Henry, 1923- 3. Vietnam War, 1961-1975 4. United States—Politics and government—1961-1974

ISBN 0-684-84968-2; 0-7432-2349-7 (pa)
      LC 2001-23904

Berman "navigates recently declassified records to show that Nixon never sought a peaceful solution to the war. Instead, the Paris Peace Treaty, which ended U.S. involvement in 1973 after five years of tortured negotiations between Kissinger and his North Vietnam counterpart Le Duc Tho, was so deliberately ambiguous that Nixon believed he would be able to return with U.S. air power to avoid being blamed for the loss of the war." Libr J

"In the endless flow of assessments, reassessments and re-reassessments of the war in Vietnam, a study occasionally appears that goes beyond a rehash of the polemics that have marked that tragic experience. Larry Berman's 'No Peace, No Honor' belongs in that select category." N Y Times Book Rev

Includes bibliographical references

Bissell, Tom, 1974-

The father of all things; a Marine, his son, and the legacy of Vietnam. Pantheon Books 2007 407p il $25   **959.704**

1. Bissell, John 2. Vietnam War, 1961-1975 3. Vietnam—Description and travel

ISBN 978-0-375-42265-2; 0-375-42265-X
      LC 2006-49427

"In 2003, Bissell travelled to Vietnam with his father, who had fought there nearly four decades before. Their relationship was uneasy: as a child, Bissell once reported his father to an abuse hotline (after an unusually physical game of rock, paper, scissors) and, at the age of twenty-nine, he still felt 'diminished' in the man's presence; meanwhile, his father, only half joking, called him a Communist. In this ambitious, uneven book, Bissell chronicles their pilgrimage to former battlefields and

seeks to reconcile his personal 'mythology,' as the son of a Vietnam veteran, with the larger context of 'the only war in which the United States failed to enact its will.' Bissell writes with conviction, and his prose, if sometimes swashbuckling, has moments of startling beauty." New Yorker

Includes bibliographical references

Burrows, Larry, 1926-1971

Vietnam; introduction by David Halberstam. Knopf 2002 243p il $50   **959.704**
ISBN 0-375-41102-X   LC 2002-19100

This volume presents the work of Larry Burrows, who "photographed the conflict in Vietnam from 1962, the earliest days of American involvement, until 1971, when he died in a helicopter shot down on the Vietnam/Laos border. . . . [It includes] unpublished images from the Burrows archive." Publisher's note

This "confirms that [Burrows] was an artist as well as a journalist, capable of arousing the great tragic emotions, pity and terror." Booklist

Includes bibliographical references

Caputo, Philip

A rumor of war; with a twentieth anniversary postscript by the author. Henry Holt and Co. 1996 xxi, 356p pa $15 *   **959.704**

1. Vietnam War, 1961-1975—Personal narratives
ISBN 0-8050-4965-X   LC 96-19314

"An Owl book"

First published 1977 by Holt, Rinehart & Winston

These are "the combat recollections of a very young Marine officer in Vietnam in 1965-1966. Caputo later became a newspaperman. . . . He remembers himself as a patriotic youngster, eager to prove his manhood, and then . . . he takes us through his step-by-step discovery that war and manhood and their interrelation are more complicated than he had dreamed." New Yorker

Ellsberg, Daniel, 1931-

Secrets: a memoir of Vietnam and the Pentagon papers. Viking 2002 498p il $29.95; pa $16   **959.704**

1. Pentagon Papers 2. Vietnam War, 1961-1975
ISBN 0-670-03030-9; 0-14-200342-5 (pa)
      LC 2002-16874

Ellsberg recalls how he leaked "the Pentagon Papers, which documented U.S. foreign-policy failures and deceit in Vietnam from 1945 to 1968. . . . Ellsberg's autobiographical account provides insight into the disturbing abuses of presidential power that plagued the Vietnam/Watergate era." Libr J

Includes bibliographical references

FitzGerald, Frances, 1940-

Fire in the lake; the Vietnamese and the Americans in Vietnam. Little, Brown 1972 491p maps pa $16.95 hardcover o.p.   **959.704**

1. Vietnam War, 1961-1975 2. Vietnam—Politics and government
ISBN 0-316-15919-0 (pa)

"An Atlantic Monthly Press book"

FitzGerald, Frances, 1940-—*Continued*
This book looks at the effects American intervention had on the Vietnamese social and intellectual landscape.
Includes bibliographical references

Glasser, Ronald J.
365 days. Braziller 1971 292p pa $14.95 hardcover o.p.   **959.704**
1. Vietnam War, 1961-1975—Personal narratives
2. Vietnam War, 1961-1975—Medical care
ISBN 0-8076-1527-7 (pa)
The author, a military doctor who was stationed in Japan, recounts his experiences treating wounded American military personnel during the Vietnam War

Goldstein, Donald M.
The Vietnam War: the story and photographs; by Donald M. Goldstein, Katherine V. Dillon, and J. Michael Wenger. Brassey's 1997 179p il maps pa $19.95 hardcover o.p.   **959.704**
1. Vietnam War, 1961-1975
ISBN 1-57488-210-4 (pa)   LC 97-11574
This history of the Vietnam War "proceeds both chronologically and thematically, beginning with the French colonial era and the Indochina War, then covering successive stages of the U.S. involvement. The text is sufficiently detailed, clear, and balanced to serve as a narrative introduction to the subject, but the real strength lies in the photographs. They cover the subject with admirable thoroughness. . . . They do not include too many chestnuts, and they adequately cover the Vietnamese, the navy, and other subjects relatively neglected in the literature thus far." Booklist
Includes bibliographical references

Hendrickson, Paul
The living and the dead; Robert McNamara and five lives of a lost war. Knopf 1996 427p il pa $15 hardcover o.p.   **959.704**
1. McNamara, Robert S., 1916- 2. Vietnam War, 1961-1975
ISBN 0-679-7811-X (pa)   LC 96-7445
In this look at the Vietnam War, the author "probes the histories of several men and women whose lives were irreversibly altered by the war: an Army nurse, a Quaker protester who immolated himself outside the Pentagon, a Marine helicopter gunner, and a Vietnamese politician. But the main exhibit here is the life and conscience of Robert McNamara." New Yorker
"Exhaustively researched, probing, important contribution to the annals of American history." Publ Wkly
Includes bibliographical references

Inside the Pentagon papers; edited by John Prados and Margaret Pratt Porter. University Press of Kansas 2004 248p (Modern war studies) $29.95   **959.704**
1. Pentagon Papers 2. Vietnam War, 1961-1975
ISBN 0-7006-1325-0   LC 2004-1961
The editors "reexamine the secret government papers that blew the whistle on the Vietnam War, led to the federal attempts to restrain the press and ultimately resulted

in President Richard Nixon's resignation. . . . Volumes about these issues abound, but Prados and Porter offer a concise look at those pivotal events and their long-term effects." Publ Wkly
Includes bibliographical references

Isaacs, Arnold R.
Vietnam shadows; the war, its ghosts, and its legacy. Johns Hopkins Univ. Press 1997 236p pa $19.95 hardcover o.p.   **959.704**
1. Vietnam War, 1961-1975 2. United States—Civilization
ISBN 0-8018-6344-9 (pa)   LC 97-10823
This overview of the Vietnam War explores the political, social, cultural and military dimensions of the conflict
The author's "range is impressive. He comments on everything from the moral opacity of Robert McNamara to American 'escape-goating'—his neologism for the impulse to produce counterfactual histories in which we win the war after all. Isaacs's basic judgments are sound, and his exquisite nose for detecting self-deception leads him to some awkward truths about the wartime mythologies that have become encased in middle-aged amber." NY Times Book Rev
Includes bibliographical references

Kaiser, David E., 1947-
American tragedy; Kennedy, Johnson, and the origins of the Vietnam War; [by] David Kaiser. Harvard Univ. Press 2000 566p il $36; pa $18.95   **959.704**
1. Kennedy, John F. (John Fitzgerald), 1917-1963
2. Johnson, Lyndon B. (Lyndon Baines), 1908-1973
3. Vietnam War, 1961-1975 4. United States—Politics and government—1961-1974
ISBN 0-674-00225-3; 0-674-00672-0 (pa)
     LC 99-52925
The author argues that "a cautious President Kennedy consistently resisted the entreaties of State and Defense Department professionals (many of them Eisenhower holdovers) to dramatically expand our commitment in Vietnam. Unfortunately, Kaiser asserts, President Johnson was far more willing to accept the advice of those same men." Booklist
"The first-rate research is complemented by an intriguing model of intergenerational policy-making." Libr J
Includes bibliographical references

Karnow, Stanley
Vietnam; a history. 2nd rev & updated ed. Penguin Bks. 1997 768p il maps pa $17.95   **959.704**
1. Vietnam War, 1961-1975 2. Vietnam—History
ISBN 0-14-026547-3
First published 1983
A summation "of over two centuries of conflict in Indochina. Chronicling a tragic history, Karnow presents a balanced and sympathetic view of Vietnamese aspirations and the mishaps that led to American involvement in a 'war nobody won.'" Voice Youth Advocates [review of 1983 edition]
Includes bibliographical references

Kissinger, Henry, 1923-

Ending the Vietnam War; a history of America's involvement in and extrication from the Vietnam War. Touchstone 2002 640p map pa $18

959.704

1. Vietnam War, 1961-1975

ISBN 0-7432-1532-X   LC 2002-17996

The former national security advisor "culls his Vietnam diplomatic record from his three-volume memoirs and his bestselling book, *Diplomacy*. . . . Kissinger provides . . . accounts of the 1970 Cambodia incursion, the failed 1971 Laos campaign, and Hanoi's 1972 Spring Offensive." Libr J

"Readers interested in the Vietnam period but unfamiliar with Kissinger's previous books will find this new volume worthwhile. . . . Kissinger's account of America's venture in Vietnam and his role in that shipwreck is factually accurate, eminently informed and masterfully crafted." Publ Wkly

Includes bibliographical references

Langguth, A. J., 1933-

Our Vietnam; the war, 1954-1975. Simon & Schuster 2000 766p il maps pa $20 hardcover o.p.

959.704

1. Vietnam War, 1961-1975

ISBN 0-7432-1231-2 (pa)   LC 00-57384

The author tells the story of the Vietnam War "mainly through the actions of key personalities. Each of his chapters is titled for one of the principal characters, . . . among them presidents and other . . . American officials of the era, as well as figures like Daniel Ellsberg, who leaked the Pentagon Papers. The list also includes the names of . . . Vietnamese leaders on both sides." N Y Times Book Rev

This book "is unique in its perspective of the major players on both sides." Booklist

Includes bibliographical references

Lind, Michael, 1962-

Vietnam, the necessary war; a reinterpretation of America's most disastrous military conflict. Free Press 1999 314p $25; pa $14   959.704

1. Vietnam War, 1961-1975 2. United States—Foreign relations

ISBN 0-684-84254-8; 0-684-87027-4 (pa)

LC 99-28449

The author "argues that the war in Vietnam, however horrifying, had to be fought not to extend ideology but to preserve the military and diplomatic credibility of the United States." Libr J

"Lind's arguments, if not always persuasive, are always provocative." Publ Wkly

Includes bibliographical references

Mann, Robert, 1958-

A grand delusion; America's descent into Vietnam. Basic Bks. 2000 821p il $35; pa $22

959.704

1. Vietnam War, 1961-1975 2. Vietnam—Politics and government 3. United States—Politics and government—20th century

ISBN 0-465-04369-0; 0-465-04370-4 (pa)

LC 00-49824

This account of the United States involvement in the Vietnam War focuses on the political causes and "collision of personalities throughout the White House, Congress, and elsewhere during that era. Mann's history concentrates on seven American leaders in the halls of power rather than on the battlefield." Libr J

Includes bibliographical references

Maraniss, David

They marched into sunlight; war and peace in Vietnam and America, October 1967. Simon & Schuster 2003 592p il map $29.95; pa $16

959.704

1. Vietnam War, 1961-1975

ISBN 0-7432-1780-2; 0-7432-6104-6 (pa)

LC 2003-52885

This is a "narrative by a reporter who juxtaposes a ghastly little battle in Vietnam with an antiwar and anti-Dow demonstration at the University of Wisconsin, Madison, on the same day; it captures moral ambiguity everywhere, without stereotyping or condescension." N Y Times Book Rev

Includes bibliographical references

McCloud, Bill, 1948-

What should we tell our children about Vietnam? University of Okla. Press 1989 155p pa $14.95 hardcover o.p.   959.704

1. Vietnam War, 1961-1975

ISBN 0-8061-3240-X (pa)   LC 89-40218

"President Bush, William Westmoreland, Gary Trudeau, and Philip Caputo are among some of the best known of 128 individuals who gave their views when McCloud, a junior high school teacher and veteran, wrote to ask them what young people should understand about the war." Booklist

Includes bibliographical references

McNamara, Robert S., 1916-

In retrospect; the tragedy and lessons of Vietnam. Vintage Bks. 1996 518p il map pa $16.95   959.704

1. Vietnam War, 1961-1975

ISBN 0-679-76749-5; 978-0-679-76749-7

First published 1995 by Times Books

"Former defense secretary McNamara seeks 'to put Vietnam in context' and counter 'the cynicism and even contempt with which so many people view our political institutions and leaders.' . . . He identifies 'eleven major causes for our disaster in Vietnam' and six points when the U.S. could legitimately have withdrawn. Certainly not the last word on this still-controversial subject but an essential acquisition for most libraries." Booklist

Includes bibliographical references

Moore, Harold G., 1922-
We were soldiers once—and young; Ia Drang: the battle that changed the war in Vietnam; [by] Harold G. Moore and Joseph L. Galloway. Random House 1992 412p il maps $26.95; pa $7.50   **959.704**
  1. Vietnam War, 1961-1975—Personal narratives
  ISBN 0-679-41158-5; 0-345-47264-0 (pa)
                  LC 92-53642
  "On Nov. 14, 1965, the 1st Battalion of the 7th Cavalry, commanded by Col. Moore and accompanied by UPI reporter Galloway, helicoptered into Vietnam's remote Ia Drang Valley and found itself surrounded by a numerically superior force of North Vietnamese regulars. Moore and Galloway here offer a detailed account, based on interviews with participants and on their own recollections, of what happened during the four-day battle." Publ Wkly
  Includes bibliographical references

Reporting Vietnam. Library of Am. 1998 2v il maps v1-v2 ea $35; v2 pa $17.95 *   **959.704**
  1. Vietnam War, 1961-1975 2. Reporters and reporting
  ISBN 1-88301-158-2 (v1); 1-88301-159-0 (v2); 1-88301-190-6 (v2 pa)   LC 98-12267
  Contents: Pt.1 American journalism, 1959-1969; pt.2 American journalism, 1969-1975
  This collection includes "newspaper, magazine, book excerpts, and one TV commentary, Walter Cronkite's post-Tet report concluding that the United States should quickly negotiate its way out." Commonweal
  "This book will help readers understand better what it was like to live through that tumultuous period of American history." Publ Wkly
  Includes bibliographical references

Sallah, Michael
Tiger Force; a true story of men and war; [by] Michael Sallah and Mitch Weiss. Little, Brown 2006 403p il map $25.95   **959.704**
  1. United States. Army. Infantry Regiment, 327th. Battalion, 1st 2. Vietnam War, 1961-1975
  ISBN 0-316-15997-2; 978-0-316-15997-5
               LC 2005-20921
  "In 1967, the Tiger Force platoon of the 101st Airborne went on a seven-month-long rampage through South Vietnam's central highlands that left dead more than 325 civilians, mostly children, women, and old men. . . . [This] is a searing narrative, difficult to read yet difficult to put down, about Tiger Force's descent into a leaderless and ruthless unit, in which, as one of the ex-soldiers puts it to the authors, the objective was to 'kill anything that moves.'" Libr J
  Includes bibliographical references

Sheehan, Neil
A bright shining lie: John Paul Vann and America in Vietnam. Random House 1988 861p il pa $18 hardcover o.p.   **959.704**
  1. Vann, John Paul 2. Vietnam War, 1961-1975
  ISBN 0-679-72414-1 (pa)   LC 87-43330
  The author "tells the story of the war through the focus of John Paul Vann, an army officer who faced down

South Vietnamese politicians and American generals to expose the corruption that undermined our efforts and later was President Nixon's civilian adviser in Vietnam until he was killed in a helicopter crash in 1972. It is a dramatic device that lets Mr. Sheehan bring the very palpable feel of the war to us with passionate power." N Y Times Book Rev
  Includes bibliographical references

Shultz, Richard H., 1947-
The secret war against Hanoi; Kennedy and Johnson's use of spies, saboteurs, and covert warriors in North Vietnam; {by} Richard H. Shultz, Jr. HarperCollins Pubs. 1999 408p il pa $15 hardcover o.p.   **959.704**
  1. United States. Military Assistance Command, Vietnam. Studies and Observations Group 2. Vietnam War, 1961-1975—Secret service 3. Subversive activities 4. United States—Politics and government—1961-1974
  ISBN 0-06-093253-8 (pa)   LC 99-44524
  "Organized in a military entity euphemistically named the Studies and Observation Group (SOG), the covert war, it was hoped, would annoy Hanoi enough to force it to scale back its war in the south. . . . Schultz was given access to SOG archives and veterans and has produced a professional volume on how SOG originated and operated over its eight-year existence." Booklist
  Includes bibliographical references

The **Vietnam** War; editor, Mark Lawrence; introduction by David K. Shipler. Fitzroy Dearborn Pubs. 2001 2v il maps (New York Times 20th century in review) set $150   **959.704**
  1. Vietnam War, 1961-1975
  ISBN 1-57958-368-7   LC 2002-726953
  Articles and photos from The New York Times trace "the origins, the strategies, the successes, the failures, and the bitter legacy of this war for the United States, Vietnam, and the world." Publisher's note
  "A must-have for all libraries." Recomm Ref Books for Small & Medium-sized Libr & Media Cent, 2003

959.8   Indonesia and East Timor

Taylor, Jean Gelman, 1944-
Indonesia: peoples and histories. Yale University Press 2003 420p il maps $45; pa $20 *   **959.8**
  1. Indonesia
  ISBN 0-300-09709-3; 0-300-09710-7 (pa)
              LC 2002-152348
  Contents: Early beginnings; Communities and kingdoms; Sultans and states; Monarchs, mentors, and mobile men; Newcomers in the Muslim circle; Inside Indonesian sultanates; New and old states; Maps and mentality; Many kingdoms, one colony; Breaking dependence on foreign powers; Rearranging map and mind; Majapahit visions
  This is "an account of Indonesia from the earliest migrations and settlements in the archipelago to the col-

Taylor, Jean Gelman, 1944-—*Continued*
lapse of yet another government just a few years ago.
While basically historical in design, this is no ordinary
history. The book is one great historical essay . . . that
allows the historian's search for the past to wander into
social, religious, artistic, and anthropological byways."
Choice
Includes bibliographical references

959.9   Philippines

Karnow, Stanley
In our image; America's empire in the
Philippines. Random House 1989 494p il maps pa
$27 hardcover o.p.   **959.9**
    ISBN 0-345-32816-7 (pa)   LC 88-42676
    A history of American involvement in the Philippines
from 1898 to the present
    The author's "treatment of the indecisiveness of Presi-
dent McKinley over the issue of empire and of the ego-
tistical General MacArthur make the work a definite purchase for libraries. . . . Those who love swashbuckling
history will enjoy this work." Libr J
    Includes bibliographical references

960   History of Africa

Africa: an encyclopedia for students; John
Middleton, editor. Scribner 2002 4v il maps set
$395   **960**
    1. Africa—Encyclopedias
    ISBN 0-684-80650-9   LC 2001-49348
    A comprehensive look at the continent of Africa and
the countries that comprise it, including peoples and cultures, the land and its history, art and architecture, and
daily life

Cultural atlas of Africa; edited by Jocelyn
Murray. rev ed. Checkmark Bks. 1998 240p il
maps $50   **960**
    1. Africa—Civilization
    ISBN 0-8160-3813-9
    "An Andromeda book"
    First published 1981
    This survey of African civilization is divided into
three parts. Part One: The physical background, describes
the geography of the continent. Part Two: The Cultural
background, includes such topics as languages, religions,
early man, history, the arts, and education. Part Three:
The Nations of Africa, offers information about individual countries divided by region
    This "is an important contribution to our understand-
ing of the African continent." Booklist {review of 1981
edition}
    Includes bibliographical references

Encyclopedia of African history; Kevin
Shillington, editor. Fitzroy Dearborn 2004 3v il
map set $395   **960**
    1. Africa—Encyclopedias
    ISBN 1-579-58245-1   LC 2004-16779

"The scope of the coverage encompasses the entire
continent, including North Africa, and features all historical periods, with special attention to recent events. Most
entries are given 1000 words, though major topics, such
as regional surveys, stretch to 3000-4000 words. Topics
range from art to anthropology to economics, but emphasis is placed on biographies and country studies, both
pre- and postcolonial. . . . Simply put, this is an essential reference resource for students of African history."
Libr J
    Includes bibliographical references

Encyclopedia of African history and culture;
Willie F. Page, editor. rev ed, by R. Hunt Davis,
Jr. Facts on File 2005 5v il map set $425 *
                                                           960
    1. Africa—Encyclopedias
    ISBN 0-8160-5199-2   LC 2004-22929
    "A Learning Source Book"
    First published 2001
    This encyclopedia's "arrangement is chronological,
with each of the five volumes representing a major era
of African history: 'Ancient Africa,' 'African Kingdoms,'
'From Conquest to Colonization,' 'The Colonial Era,'
and 'Independent Africa.'" Choice
    This set "fulfills its information and education goals
and is highly recommended for high-school, public, and
academic libraries." Booklist
    Includes bibliographical references

Falola, Toyin, 1953-
Key events in African history; a reference guide.
Greenwood Press 2002 xxiii, 347p il maps $64.95
*   **960**
    1. Africa—History
    ISBN 0-313-31323-7   LC 2001-58644
    "An Oryx book"
    "Falola surveys the . . . history of the African conti-
nent by focusing on 36 pivotal events that either caused
or led to significant changes and developments in African social, political, and cultural life from around 40,000
B.C.E. to the collapse of apartheid in the 1990s. . . .
Following a detailed time line of historical events, each
topic is highlighted in an individual chapter including
cross-references, historical and political maps, illustrations, a notes section, and a suggested list for further
reading." Booklist
    Includes bibliographical references

Gates, Henry Louis
Wonders of the African world; [by] Henry
Louis Gates, Jr. Knopf 1999 275p il map
hardcover o.p. pa $24.95   **960**
    1. Africa—Civilization
    ISBN 0-375-40235-7; 0-375-70948-7 (pa)
                                              LC 99-18496
    "In conjunction with the PBS television series of the
same title, Gates offers a 12-nation reprise of the magnif-
icence of ancient African civilizations . . . [moving] in
clusters—from the black gods and kings of Nubia, to
Ethiopia's links to the Holy Land and the Lost Ark of
the Covenant, to Timbuktu's commercial and intellectual
center, to the slave kingdoms, and to the Lost Cities of

Gates, Henry Louis—*Continued*
Great Zimbabwe." Libr J
"Gates writes with concentration and clarity, and anticipates the questions that arise in the wary reader's mind, delivering the answers at just the right time." N Y Times Book Rev
Includes bibliographical references

Lefkowitz, Mary R., 1935-
Not out of Africa; how Afrocentrism became an excuse to teach myth as history; [by] Mary Lefkowitz. Basic Bks. 1996 222p il map hardcover o.p. pa $19 **960**
1. Africa—Historiography 2. History—Study and teaching
ISBN 0-465-09837-1; 0-465-09838-X (pa)
LC 95-49109
"A New Republic book"
"Those classicists who believe there are Egyptian antecedents for Greek philosophy are known as Afrocentrists. . . . Lefkowitz claims that the Afrocentrists are perpetuating myths and that they protect their claims by labeling those who question those claims as narrow-minded or racist." Libr J
"The book is a case study in historical methods, the value and limits of scholarship, and the preciousness of hard-bitten reason and objectivity. The book is also lucid and accessible." Christ Sci Monit
Includes bibliographical references

New encyclopedia of Africa; John Middleton, editor in chief; Joseph C. Miller, editor. Charles Scribner's Sons 2008 5v il map set $625
960
1. Africa—Encyclopedias
ISBN 978-0-684-31454-9 LC 2007-21746
First published 1997 with title: Encyclopedia of Africa, south of the Sahara
This encyclopedia "covers the entire continent, from the Europe-facing shores of the Mediterranean to the commercial bustle of Cape Town. The set addresses the . . . history of African cultures from the pharaohs and the ancient civilizations of the south through the colonial era to the emergence of 53 independent countries." Publisher's note
Includes bibliographical references

Pakenham, Thomas, 1933-
The scramble for Africa; the White man's conquest of the dark continent from 1876 to 1912. Avon 1992 xxv, 738p il map pa $22.95
960
1. Africa—History
ISBN 0-380-71999-1
First published 1991 by Random House
This book is an account of the colonization and conquest of Africa by five European nations—Great Britain, France, Belgium, Germany, and Italy.
This is a "sweeping narrative, refreshingly old fashioned in its appreciation of the fact that imperialism did have some virtues, which offers as good an introduction to the 'scramble' as has ever been written." Libr J
Includes bibliographical references

962.4 Sudan

Deng, Benson
They poured fire on us from the sky; the true story of three lost boys from Sudan; [by] Benson Deng, Alephonsion Deng, Benjamin Ajak; with Judy Bernstein. Public Affairs 2005 xxiii, 311p map hardcover o.p. pa $13.95 **962.4**
1. Refugees 2. Sudan
ISBN 1-58648-269-6; 1-58648-388-9 (pa)
LC 2005-42566
"Three young refugees in California—Alephonsion Deng, Benson Deng, and Benjamin Ajak, two brothers and a cousin—remember how they were driven from their homes in southern Sudan in the ethnic and religious conflicts that have left two million dead." Booklist
"This collection is moving in its depictions of unbelievable courage." Publ Wkly

963 Ethiopia and Eritrea

Shah, Tahir
In search of King Solomon's mines. Little, Brown 2003 c2002 240p il map $24.95; pa $13.95
963
1. Ethiopia—Description and travel
ISBN 1-55970-641-4; 1-55970-724-0 (pa)
First published in 2002 in the United Kingdom
This is an account of the author's search for "the mysterious mines of Ophir, where King Solomon, the Bible's wisest king, was supposed to have buried a fortune in gold. . . . According to his reckoning, the mines should be in modern-day Ethiopia, so he set out on an adventure of a lifetime with a shifty bookseller named (no kidding) Ali Baba. Along the way, readers are treated to his accounts of everything from the California gold rush to a sadistic Sultan." Libr J
Includes bibliographical references

964 Northwest African coast and offshore islands. Morocco

Shah, Tahir
The Caliph's house; Tahir Shah. Bantam Books 2006 349p il $22 **964**
1. Morocco—Description and travel
ISBN 0-553-80399-9 LC 2005-53656
This is the author's "story of his family's move from the gray skies of London to the sun-drenched city of Casablanca, where Islamic tradition and African folklore converge." Publisher's note
"Shah's picture of Moroccan society, its deeply held Islamic faith, its primitive superstition, and its raucous economy makes for endlessly fascinating reading." Booklist

965   Algeria

Morgan, Ted, 1932-
My battle of Algiers; by Ted Morgan.
Collins/Smithsonian 2006 284p maps $24.95
965
1. Algeria—History—1954-1962, Revolution
ISBN 0-06-085224-0   LC 2005-52160
The author "recalls his service as a young officer in
France's bitter war in Algeria. . . . Anyone interested in
the origins of modern terrorist tactics will benefit from
his recollections." Publ Wkly

966   West Africa and offshore islands

Langewiesche, William
Sahara unveiled; a journey across the desert.
Pantheon Bks. 1996 301p il pa $14 hardcover o.p.
966
1. Sahara Desert
ISBN 0-679-75006-1 (pa)   LC 95-48864
"Besides evoking the Sahara's power, majesty, emptiness, heat, beauty and terrors and describing its ecology
and meteorology, Langewiesche adds details that may astonish armchair travelers who still think of the desert as
populated by camels and Bedouins. . . . He is knowledgeable about the imprint of French colonialism on
North African economy and politics, and about Muslim
beliefs in practice. Throughout this vivid account, he
scatters many charming native folktales." Publ Wkly

966.4   Sierra Leone

Campbell, Greg
Blood diamonds; tracing the deadly path of the
world's most precious stones. Westview Press
2002 xxv, 251p maps hardcover o.p. pa $15.95
966.4
1. Diamonds 2. Sierra Leone
ISBN 0-8133-3939-1; 0-8133-4220-1 (pa)
LC 2002-4931
"Campbell explores the significance of the diamond
trade in Sierra Leone. . . . He recounts the horrors of
this war-torn nation. . . . The underlying motivation for
the violence and strife of Sierra Leone is centered in the
diamond trade, much of it illegal smuggling sanctioned
by the cartel DeBeers." Booklist
"This focused study of the catastrophic effect of blood
diamonds on Sierra Leone belongs in all libraries." Libr
J

Includes bibliographical references

966.68   Ivory Coast

Erdman, Sarah
Nine hills to Nambonkaha; two years in the
heart of an African village. Holt & Co. 2003 322p
$23; pa $14   **966.68**
1. Peace Corps (U.S.) 2. Ivory Coast
ISBN 0-8050-7381-7; 0-312-42312-8 (pa)
LC 2003-44955
The author "spent two years as a Peace Corps worker
in the small town of Nambonkaha, Ivory Coast, at the
end of the last decade. Erdman, who acted as a healthcare worker and instructor, is surprised to find herself
called upon to help women in labor, surrounded by curious children who want to learn to read, and honored with
gifts from the chief. She also faces the challenge of trying to meld medical knowledge with traditional sorcery,
as the village denizens believe most illness and misfortune is caused by witchcraft rather than infection."
Booklist
"This is an engrossing, well-told tale certain to appeal
to armchair travelers and to anyone—especially wom-
en—considering international volunteer work." Publ
Wkly

966.9   Nigeria

Maier, Karl
This house has fallen; midnight in Nigeria.
PublicAffairs 2000 xxxvii, 327p pa $18 hardcover
o.p.   **966.9**
1. Nigeria—Politics and government
ISBN 0-8133-4045-4 (pa)   LC 00-28199
The author "explores the promise and paradox of Nigeria. {He} . . . recounts the history of this nation cob-
bled together from British colonial interests in its formative years and dominated by international oil interests in
more recent years." Booklist
Includes bibliographical references

967.5   Democratic Republic of the Congo, Rwanda, Burundi

Hochschild, Adam, 1942-
King Leopold's ghost; a story of greed, terror,
and heroism in Colonial Africa. Houghton Mifflin
1998 366p il map hardcover o.p. pa $15 *
967.5
1. Belgium—Colonies 2. Atrocities
ISBN 0-395-75924-2; 0-618-00190-5 (pa)
LC 98-16813
The author "focuses on King Leopold's reign of terror
in the Belgian Congo and the unswerving efforts by human rights activists (Sir Roger Casement, E.D. Morel,
and others) and the Congo Reform Association to raise
awareness of the enslavement, mutilation, and murder of
millions of Congolese." Libr J
"Hochschild's impressively researched history records
the roles of the famous and obscure, missionaries, journalists, opportunists, politicians, and royalty in this long-
forgotten drama." Booklist
Includes bibliographical references

967.571   Rwanda

Gourevitch, Philip
We wish to inform you that tomorrow we will be killed with our families; stories from Rwanda. Farrar, Straus & Giroux 1998 355p hardcover o.p. pa $15   **967.571**
1. Rwanda—Politics and government 2. Genocide
ISBN 0-374-28697-3; 0-312-24335-9 (pa)
LC 98-22132
"In 1994, the world was informed of the inexplicable mass killings in Rwanda, in which over 800,000 were killed in 100 days. Gourevitch . . . spent over three years putting together an oral history of the mass killing that occurred in this small country." Libr J
This work is "readable and moving, Gourevitch is an impassioned and thoughtful observer. But this is not a work that gives much pleasure or comfort. Nor are its arguments fool-proof, its evidence complete, or its documentation thorough. . . . Still Gourevitch does struggle to come close to a great mystery of evil, and he makes us attend to great crimes." Commonweal

Hatzfeld, Jean
Machete season; the killers in Rwanda speak: a report; translated from the French by Linda Coverdale; preface by Susan Sontag. Farrar, Straus and Giroux 2005 253p il maps $24; pa $14
967.571
1. Tutsi (African people) 2. Hutu (African people) 3. Rwanda 4. Genocide
ISBN 0-374-28082-7; 0-312-42503-1 (pa)
LC 2004-61600
Original French edition, 2003
"In April-May 1994, 800,000 Rwandan Tutsis were massacred by their Hutu fellow citizens—about 10,000 a day, mostly being hacked to death by machete. In Machete Season, the . . . foreign correspondent Jean Hatzfeld reports on the results of his interviews with nine of the Hutu killers." Publisher's note
"Steering clear of politics, this important book succeeds in offering the reader some grasp of how such unspeakable acts unfolded." Publ Wkly

967.6   Uganda and Kenya

Beard, Peter H., 1938-
The end of the game; the last word from paradise; [by] Peter Beard; [foreword by Paul Theroux] Taschen 2008 280p il $39.99
967.6
1. Hunting 2. East Africa—Description and travel
ISBN 978-3-83650-530-7; 3-83650-530-4
First published 1965 by Viking; updated 1977 and published by Doubleday
"This landmark book, with a chilling (and acerbic) new introduction by travel writer and novelist Paul Theroux, contains photographs many of them shocking that reveal the sad situation of African wildlife, and most particularly the elephant. Beard mourns the end of a continent from a diverse and interdependent ecosystem to a land suffocated by cement, wire, walls and ditches (not to mention war)." Stuart News (Stuart, Florida)

Chrétien, Jean-Pierre
The great lakes of Africa; two thousand years of history; translated by Scott Straus. Zone Books 2003 504p map $36 *   **967.6**
1. East Africa
ISBN 1-89095-134-X   LC 2002-191001
This is an "historical account of the Great Lakes region of Eastern Africa, {an area} which encompasses Burundi, eastern Congo, Rwanda, western Tanzania, and Uganda." Publisher's note
"This is an impressive and important book surveying 2,000 years of history. . . . The preeminence accorded Rwanda and Burundi . . . leads to the book's most significant contribution: to demonstrate that the region's recent interrelated conflicts claiming over four million lives are not based on ancient, unchanging 'ethnic' cleavages, most notably between Tutsi and Hutu." Choice
Includes bibliographical references

967.62   Kenya

Anderson, David M. (David McBeath), 1957-
Histories of the hanged; the dirty war in Kenya and the end of the empire; [by] David Anderson. Norton 2005 406p il map $25.95; pa $15.95
967.62
1. Mau Mau 2. Kenya 3. Great Britain—Colonies—Africa
ISBN 0-393-05986-3; 0-393-32754-X (pa)
LC 2004-24804
This "history of the last days of the British Empire in Kenya focuses on the colonial judicial system, which sent over 1,000 native Kenyans to the gallows between 1952 and 1959, during the state of emergency triggered by the Mau Mau insurrection. . . . This is vital reading for any student of British colonial and African history." Publ Wkly
Includes bibliographical references

Dinesen, Isak, 1885-1962
Out of Africa and Shadows on the grass. Vintage Bks. 1989 462p pa $13.95 *
967.62
1. Kenya
ISBN 0-679-72475-3   LC 89-40144
Out of Africa is a recording of the author's life on a Kenya coffee plantation. Shadows on the grass consists of four short essays which present the author's recollections of her servants in Africa

967.73   Somalia

Bowden, Mark, 1951-
Black Hawk down; a story of modern war. Atlantic Monthly Press 1999 386p il maps $25; pa $13.95
967.73
1. Somalia
ISBN 0-87113-738-0; 0-14-028850-3 (pa)
LC 98-46688
"Portions of this book were originally published as a series in The Philadelphia inquirer."

Bowden, Mark, 1951-—*Continued*

The author describes "both sides of the October 1993 raid into the heart of Mogadishu, Somalia, a raid that quickly became the most intensive close combat Americans have engaged in since the Vietnam War. But Bowden's gripping narrative of the fighting is only a framework for an examination of the internal dynamics of America's elite forces and a critique of the philosophy of sending such high-tech units into combat with minimal support." Publ Wkly

968   Southern Africa. Republic of South Africa

Thompson, Leonard Monteath

A history of South Africa; {by} Leonard Thompson. 3rd ed. Yale Univ. Press 2001 xxiv, 358p il maps pa $17.95 hardcover o.p.

968

1. South Africa—History
ISBN 0-300-08776-4 (pa)   LC 00-32101
First published 1990

This is an exploration of South Africa's "history, from the earliest known human inhabitation of the region to the present, focusing primarily on the experiences of its black inhabitants." Publisher's note

Includes bibliographical references

968.04   Southern Africa—1814-1910

Meredith, Martin

Diamonds, gold, and war; the British, the Boers, and the making of South Africa. PublicAffairs 2007 570p il map $35   **968.04**

1. South African War, 1899-1902 2. South Africa—History 3. Great Britain—Colonies—Africa
ISBN 978-1-58648-473-6; 1-58648-473-7

LC 2007-34540

A history of the tumultuous period leading up to the 1910 founding of the modern state of South Africa explores how the discovery of vast diamond and gold deposits led to a fierce struggle between the British and the Boers for control of the region.

"Meredith thoroughly involves us in this gripping history. Highly recommended for all libraries." Libr J

Includes bibliographical references

968.06   Period as Republic, 1961-

Carlin, John

Playing the enemy; Nelson Mandela and the game that made a nation. Penguin 2008 274p il $24.95   **968.06**

1. Mandela, Nelson
ISBN 978-1-59420-174-5; 1-59420-174-9

LC 2008-298721

This book focuses on Nelson Mandela's advocacy of "the national rugby team, the Springboks, who would host the sport's World Cup in 1995." Publisher's note

"Deftly sketched characters make up both an audience for the big game and a gallery of South Africa, through which Carlin will recount the absorbing story of a country emerging from its cruelly absurd racist experiment." N Y Times Book Rev

Includes bibliographical references

Duke, Lynne

Mandela, Mobutu, and me; a newswoman's African journey. Doubleday 2003 294p $24

968.06

1. Mandela, Nelson 2. Mobutu Sese Seko, 1930-1997 3. South Africa—Politics and government
ISBN 0-385-50398-9   LC 2002-73365

The author covers "some of the bloodier postcolonial wars of southern Africa as well as one of the most constructive struggles: the shaping of a postapartheid government. Her interviews with Mandela and Mobutu 'bookend' . . . conversations with common folk: township women struggling for clean water, AIDS nurses battling superstitious villagers and even a quiet old Zulu man impressed to meet his 'first foreign black folk.' A consummate journalist, Duke gives readers concise but thorough background briefings on a country's relevant history before cutting to the chase: who's taken control now, why, and what that means for the balance of power. . . . She deftly combines solid information and personal perspective to produce a powerful, readable chronicle." Publ Wkly

Tutu, Desmond

No future without forgiveness; [by] Desmond Mpilo Tutu. Doubleday 1999 287p pa $15.95 hardcover o.p. *   **968.06**

1. South Africa. Commission for Truth and Reconciliation 2. South Africa—Race relations
ISBN 0-385-49690-7 (pa)   LC 99-34451

The author reflects on his role "as chairman of the Truth and Reconciliation Commission. Tutu speaks frankly of . . . the struggle that preceded it and of the betrayals and jubilations of this unique commission. The TRC's work was unprecedented not only in its emphasis on restorative over retributive justice but in the spirituality that permeated its work, the bulk of which constituted hearings from the 'victims' and 'perpetrators' of apartheid." Publ Wkly

Includes bibliographical references

The rainbow people of God; the making of a peaceful revolution; edited by John Allen. Doubleday 1994 xxii, 281p il pa $15.95 hardcover o.p.   **968.06**

1. South Africa—Race relations 2. Sermons
ISBN 0-385-48374-0 (pa)   LC 94-16011

This collection of Tutu's "speeches, letters, and sermons—from the time of the 1976 Soweto Uprising, through the long years of repression and defiance, up to the triumph of the democratic election—serves as an immediate contemporary history of South Africa. Tutu's media secretary, John Allen, provides a general historical introduction and a connecting narrative that places the individuals pieces in dramatic context." Booklist

Includes bibliographical references

Waldmeir, Patti

Anatomy of a miracle; the end of apartheid and the birth of the new South Africa. Rutgers University Press 1998 289p pa $22.95

968.06

1. South Africa—Politics and government 2. South Africa—Race relations

ISBN 0-8135-2582-9; 978-0-8135-2582-2

LC 98-15628

First published 1997 by W.W. Norton

Waldmeir traces the political and personal struggles that ultimately contributed to the dismantling of apartheid in South Africa

"Although Mandela attributes greatness to de Klerk for his courage, it is Mandela's own character that dominates this history. . . . Engrossing in its sweep, this account also describes the obstacles facing the regime." Publ Wkly

Includes bibliographical references

968.91 Zimbabwe

Lamb, Christina

House of stone; the true story of a family divided in war-torn Zimbabwe. Lawrence Hill Books 2007 290p il map **968.91**

1. Hough, Nigel 2. Aqui, 1962- 3. Zimbabwe—Race relations

ISBN 978-1-55652-735-7; 1-55652-735-7

LC 2007-19814

"Through the parallel accounts of two people in Zimbabwe, one a poor black maid, one a rich white farmer, . . . Lamb tells the compelling story of a country ravaged first by colonial settlers and now by brutal civil war. . . . The anguished personal detail, true to the changing viewpoints, makes for a gripping read." Booklist

970 History of North America

Morgan, Ted, 1932-

Wilderness at dawn; the settling of the North American continent. Simon & Schuster 1993 541p il maps pa $20 hardcover o.p. **970**

1. United States—History—1600-1775, Colonial period 2. Canada—History—0-1763 (New France)

ISBN 0-671-88237-6 (pa)

LC 93-2628

The author discusses "movements of people into what is today the US, from the arrival of the earliest hunters approximately 15,000 years ago to the colonists of the late 18th century." Choice

Morgan "tells a good story, emphasizing the ordinary people who did the actual settlement. . . . A useful survey of the colonial frontier." Libr J

Includes bibliographical references

Purcell, L. Edward

Encyclopedia of battles in North America, 1517 to 1916; [by] L. Edward Purcell and Sarah J. Purcell. Facts on File 2000 383p maps (Facts on File library of American history) $66 *

970

1. Battles 2. United States—Military history 3. Canada—Military history

ISBN 0-8160-3350-1

LC 99-38634

"Entries are in alphabetical order by battle name, from Adobe Walls to Yorktown, each one with bibliographic references. Many were from wars that are vaguely remembered today, if at all (e.g., the Pequot War of 1637 or the Russian-Indian War of 1804 in Alaska). There are cross references to alternate names, a comprehensive bibliography, a glossary, 50 maps, and indexes by war, year, and geographic area." Libr J

Includes bibliographical references

970.004 North American native peoples

American Indians; consulting editor, Harvey Markowitz. Salem Press 1995 3v il maps (Ready reference) set $331 **970.004**

1. Native Americans—Encyclopedias

ISBN 0-89356-757-4

LC 94-47633

"A Magill book"

"This set contains 1,129 articles ranging in length from 200 to 3,000 words. The entries cover a wide range of persons, tribes, organizations, cultural and historical events, and contemporary issues of U.S., Canadian, and some Mesoamerican Indian groups. Individual entries appear for 275 North American tribes. Entries are arranged alphabetically and are illustrated with 250 black-and-white photographs, maps, charts, tables, and drawings." Booklist

Boyer, Ruth McDonald, 1918-

Apache mothers and daughters; four generations of a family. University of Okla. Press 1992 xx, 393p il maps pa $19.95 hardcover o.p.

970.004

1. Apache Indians

ISBN 0-8061-2922-0 (pa)

LC 92-54149

A family history of four generations of Chiricahua Apache women. "Woven into this account are factual details about the Apaches." Publisher's note

"The voice throughout the narrative is an Apache one, emphasizing the continuation of Chiricahua culture. . . . It's a treat for anyone interested in cultural change and persistence." Libr J

Includes bibliographical references

Bragdon, Kathleen J.

The Columbia guide to American Indians of the Northeast. Columbia Univ. Press 2001 292p il maps (Columbia guides to American Indian history and culture) $53.50; pa $25.50 **970.004**

1. Native Americans

ISBN 0-231-11452-4; 0-231-11453-2 (pa)

LC 2001-47341

Bragdon, Kathleen J.—*Continued*
This handbook "includes not only a broad overview of
the history of Native Americans in the Northeast but also
a partially annotated listing of materials for further research including published primary sources, oral traditions, films, and Internet sites." Libr J
Includes bibliographical references

Brown, Dee Alexander
Bury my heart at Wounded Knee; an Indian
history of the American West; [by] Dee Brown.
Thirtieth anniversary ed. Holt & Co. 2001 487p il
$35; pa $16 *   **970.004**
1. Native Americans—West (U.S.) 2. Native Ameri-
cans—Wars 3. West (U.S.)—History
ISBN 0-8050-6634-9; 0-8050-6669-1 (pa)
                                              LC 00-40958
First published 1970
This is an account of the experience of the American
Indian during the white man's expansion westward
Includes bibliographical references

Bruchac, Joseph, 1942-
Our stories remember; American Indian history,
culture, & values through storytelling. Fulcrum
2003 192p map pa $16.95   **970.004**
1. Native Americans—History 2. Storytelling
ISBN 1-555-91129-3   LC 2002-151236
"Synthesizes the stories of many different Indian nations, including Navajo, Abenaki, Cherokee, Cree, Sioux,
and Tlingit in order to illustrate core values, which are
pivotal to them all." Booklist
"This important volume includes a wealth of traditional stories and solid information." SLJ
Includes bibliographical references

Deloria, Vine
Custer died for your sins; an Indian manifesto;
by Vine Deloria, Jr. University of Oklahoma Press
1988 278p pa $19.95 *   **970.004**
1. Native Americans
ISBN 0-8061-2129-7   LC 87-40561
First published 1969 by Macmillan
The author examines how anthropologists,
missionaries, and government agencies have mistreated
American Indians.

Documents of American Indian diplomacy;
treaties, agreements, and conventions,
1775-1979; [compiled by] Vine Deloria, Jr., and
Raymond J. DeMallie; with a foreword by
Daniel K. Inouye. University of Okla. Press
1999 2v (Legal history of North America) set
$125   **970.004**
1. Native Americans—Government relations
2. Treaties
ISBN 0-8061-3118-7   LC 98-45365
This is a collection of hundreds of treaties and agreements made by American Indian nations with the Continental Congress, England, Spain, and other foreign countries, the Confederacy, the Republic of Texas, railroad

companies, other Indian nations, and the U.S. government, with chapter introductions which put them in historical and political context
"A must for all libraries." Libr J
Includes bibliographical references

Encyclopedia of Native American wars and
warfare; general editors, William B. Kessel,
Robert Wooster. Facts on File 2005 398p il map
$75; pa $21.95   **970.004**
1. Native Americans—Wars—Encyclopedias
ISBN 0-8160-3337-4; 0-8160-6430-X (pa)
                                              LC 00-56200
"More than 600 entries provide access to information
about the persons, tribes, treaties, battles, places, weaponry, and concepts related to armed conflicts between Native Americans and those of European descent, for the
years between 1599 and 1890 and primarily the geographic locations now within the borders of the U.S."
Booklist
"This encyclopedia offers readers a wide range of information about Native American history in North America after 1492." Choice
Includes bibliographical references

Fenton, William Nelson, 1908-2005
The Great Law and the Longhouse; a political
history of the Iroquois Confederacy; {by} Willam
N. Fenton. University of Okla. Press 1998 xxii,
786p il map (Civilization of the American Indian
series) $75   **970.004**
1. Iroquois Indians—History
ISBN 0-8061-3003-2   LC 97-19842
This is a history of the Iroquois Confederacy of the
Six Nations "from the mid-sixteenth century to the Can-
andaigua treaty of 1794." Publisher's note
"If a library has only one book about the Iroquois
. . . it should be this title." Libr J
Includes bibliographical references

Fowler, Loretta, 1944-
The Columbia guide to American Indians of the
Great Plains. Columbia Univ. Press 2003 283p il
maps (Columbia guides to American Indian history
and culture) $53.50; pa $26.50   **970.004**
1. Native Americans—Great Plains
ISBN 0-231-11700-0; 0-231-11701-9 (pa)
                                              LC 2002-73708
"This work is divided into four parts: a general survey
of the history and cultures of the native peoples of the
region; alphabetically arranged entries focusing on individuals, places, and events; a chronology; and a listing
of resources for further research that includes published
primary sources, oral traditions, films, and Internet sites.
. . . Highly recommended." Libr J
Includes bibliographical references

Handbook of North American Indians; William C. Sturtevant, general editor. Smithsonian Institution Press 1978- il maps v3 $72; v4 $62; v5 $63; v6 $62; v7 $62; v8 $62; v9 $59.50; v10 $63; v11 $63; v12 $67; v13 pts. 1 & 2 set $106; v14 $72; v15 $64; v17 $89.50 *

970.004

1. Native Americans
ISBN 978-0-16-077511-6 (v3); 0-16-004583-5 (v4); 0-16-004580-0 (v5); 0-16-004578-9 (v6); 0-16-020390-2 (v7); 0-16-004574-6 (v8); 0-16-004577-0 (v9); 0-16-004579-7 (v10); 0-16-004581-9 (v11); 0-16-049514-8 (v12); 0-16-050400-7 (v13 pts. 1 & 2); 978-0-16-072300-1 (v14); 0-16-004575-4 (v15); 0-16-048774-9 (v17)

LC 77-17162

Also available in hardcover from U.S. Government Printing Office, Superintendent of Documents

Volumes published to date are: v3 Environment, origins, and population; Douglas H. Ubelaker, volume editor; v4 History of Indian-white relations; Wilcomb E. Washburn, volume editor; v5 Arctic; David Damas, volume editor; v6 Subarctic; June Helm, volume editor; v7 Northwest coast; Wayne Suttles, volume editor; v8 California; Robert F. Heizer, volume editor; v9-10 Southwest; Alfonso Ortiz, volume editor; v11 Great Basin; Warren L. D'Azevedo, volume editor; v12 Plateau; Deward E. Walker, Jr., volume editor; v13 Plains; Raymond J. Demallie, volume editor; v14 Southeast; Raymond D. Fogelson, volume editor; v15 Northeast; Bruce G. Trigger, volume editor; v17 Languages; Ives Goddard, volume editor

"This projected twenty-one volume set . . . gives an encyclopedic summary of current historical-cultural knowledge of North American Indians. Extensively researched, readable essays are accompanied by illustrations, maps, and bibliographies." Ref Sources for Small & Medium-sized Libr. 6h edition

Harmon, Alexandra, 1945-
Indians in the making; ethnic relations and Indian identities around Puget Sound. University of Calif. Press 1998 393p il maps (American crossroads) pa $21.95 hardcover o.p.

970.004

1. Native Americans—Northwest Coast of North America
ISBN 0-520-22685-2 (pa)   LC 98-17665
The author "examines how both the federal government and the native peoples of western Washington were constantly redefining Indian identity to their advantage over a 150-year period. Harmon's examination of the native fishing rights controversy of the 1960s and 1970s is particularly useful." Libr J
Includes bibliographical references

Hendricks, Steve
The unquiet grave; the FBI and the struggle for the soul of Indian country. Thunder's Mouth Press 2006 490p il map $27.95   **970.004**

1. Aquash, Anna Mae, 1945-1976 2. American Indian Movement 3. United States. Federal Bureau of Investigation 4. Native Americans—Government relations
ISBN 1-56025-735-0; 978-1-56025-735-6
The author tells "the story of the American Indian Movement (AIM) to reclaim civil and treaty rights. . . . Bracketed by the 1976 murder of AIM activist Anna Mae Aquash and the 2004 trial related to it, Hendricks's swift narrative is riddled with judicial travesties, coverups, vigilantism, COINTELPRO-style tactics, mounting paranoia and lawlessness on both sides, as activists and ordinary American Indians confront the devastating neglect and outright hostility of government authorities." Publ Wkly
Includes bibliographical references

Iverson, Peter
We are still here; American Indians in the twentieth century. Davidson, H. 1998 255p il (American history series) pa $14.95

970.004

1. Native Americans
ISBN 0-88295-940-9   LC 97-38321
The author "begins at Wounded Knee and tells the stories of Indian communities throughout the United States, including not only political leaders and activists, but also professionals, artists, soldiers and athletes." Publisher's note
Includes bibliographical references

Johansen, Bruce E. (Bruce Elliott), 1950-
The Native peoples of North America; a history. Praeger 2005 2v il set $99.95   **970.004**
1. Native Americans—History
ISBN 0-275-98159-2   LC 2004-28732
This is a history of "cultures indigenous to North America from their earliest origins to the present. . . . Encompassing not only traditional historical records but also oral histories and biographical sketches, these two volumes will undoubtedly become an integral part of Native American history, an increasingly popular field." Booklist
Includes bibliographical references

Johnson, Michael, 1937-
Encyclopedia of native tribes of North America; color plates by Richard Hook. 3rd ed. Firefly Books 2007 320p il map $49.95   **970.004**
1. Native Americans—Encyclopedias
ISBN 978-1-55407-307-8; 1-55407-307-3
First published 1993 in the United Kingdom with title: The native tribes of North America
"The volume is organized into ten regionally based culture areas (Northwestern Woodlands, Southeastern Woodlands, Plains and Prairie, Plateau, Great Basin, California, Southwest, Northwest Coast, Subarctic, and Arctic); each area is introduced with general information on language, subsistence, religion, culture, and history. . . . The rich illustrations and supplemental sections make this volume worthwhile." Choice
Includes bibliographical references

Josephy, Alvin M., 1915-2005

The Nez Perce Indians and the opening of the Northwest; {by} Alvin M. Josephy, Jr. Houghton Mifflin 1997 xx, 705p il map pa $19

970.004

1. Nez Percé Indians 2. Pacific Northwest
ISBN 0-395-85011-8   LC 96-54278
"A Mariner book"
First published 1965 by Yale University Press
This history of the Nez Perce tribe traces its contact with white settlers from Lewis and Clark to Chief Joseph and war in 1877
Includes bibliographical references

Now that the buffalo's gone; a study of today's American Indians. University of Okla. Press 1984 300p pa $24.95 *   970.004
1. Native Americans
ISBN 0-8061-1915-2; 978-0-8061-1915-1
First published 1982 by Knopf
This look at American Indians focuses primarily on the Seminoles, the Pequots, the Senecas, and the Taos Pueblo Indians.

Keoke, Emory Dean

Encyclopedia of American Indian contributions to the world; 15,000 years of inventions and innovations; {by} Emory Dean Keoke and Kay Marie Porterfield. Facts on File 2002 384p il $65

970.004

1. Native Americans—Encyclopedias 2. Inventions
ISBN 0-8160-4052-4   LC 00-49034
This "volume describes more than 450 inventions and innovations that originated with indigenous peoples of North, Middle, and South America." Booklist
"This volume provides comprehensive coverage of the often-underreported contributions and achievements of the Indians of the western hemisphere." Book Rep
Includes bibliographical references

McLoughlin, William Gerald

After the Trail of Tears; the Cherokees' struggle for sovereignty, 1839-1880; {by} William G. McLoughlin. University of N.C. Press 1993 439p maps pa $21.95 hardcover o.p.   970.004
1. Ross, John, Cherokee Chief, 1790-1866
2. Cherokee Indians
ISBN 0-8078-4433-0 (pa)   LC 93-18532
The author "recounts the tragedy that continued to afflict the Cherokee Nation after their forced removal from their traditional home to Oklahoma during the 1820s and 1830s. In Oklahoma the Cherokee Nation set out to reconstruct their society, reestablishing their newspaper, which published in the Cherokee language, and governing themselves according to a constitution modeled on that of the United States. . . . McLoughlin vividly depicts the conflicts between 'full-bloods,' who sought to live by more traditional ways, and Cherokees of mixed ancestry who favored assimilation into the dominant culture." Publ Wkly
Includes bibliographical references

McReynolds, Edwin C.

The Seminoles. University of Okla. Press 1957 397p il maps (Civilization of the American Indian series) pa $21.95 hardcover o.p.   970.004
1. Seminole Indians
ISBN 0-8061-1255-7 (pa)
"This is almost strictly a military and political history, in great detail, spiced with a few incidents which reveal the courageous character of the Seminoles, and stressing their relations with the Creeks." Libr J
Includes bibliographical references

Nagel, Joane

American Indian ethnic renewal; Red power and the resurgence of identity and culture. Oxford Univ. Press 1996 298p il pa $21.95 hardcover o.p.

970.004

1. Native Americans
ISBN 0-19-512063-9 (pa)   LC 94-23948
The author "argues that American Indian political activism, especially the Red Power movement of the 1970s, was directly responsible for both a cultural renaissance among Indian peoples and major changes in federal Indian policy." Libr J
Includes bibliographical references

Native America in the twentieth century; an encyclopedia; edited by Mary B. Davis; assistant editors, Joan Berman, Mary E. Graham, Lisa A. Mitten. Garland 1994 xxxvii, 787p il maps (Garland reference library of social science) pa $50 hardcover o.p.   970.004
1. Native Americans—Encyclopedias
ISBN 0-8153-2583-5 (pa)   LC 94-768
This volume offers "tribal-specific information on the art, daily life, economic development, and religion of 20th-century American Indians and Alaskan Natives and the government policy that affects them." Libr J

Native American testimony; a chronicle of Indian-white relations from prophecy to the present, 1492-2000; edited by Peter Nabokov; with a foreword by Vine Deloria, Jr. Rev and updated ed. Penguin Bks. 1999 xxiii, 506p il maps pa $16.95 *   970.004
1. Native Americans—Government relations
2. Native Americans—History—Sources
ISBN 0-14-028159-2
First published 1978 by Crowell with subtitle: An anthology of Indian and white relations, first encounter to dispossession
"A collection of primary-source material, grouped by key issues that arose during 500 years of Indian and white encounters in North America. Nabokov uses traditional narratives, old government transcripts, reservation newspapers, and firsthand interviews to highlight this chronological volume. Photographs appear throughout." SLJ {review of 1991 edition}
Includes bibliographical references

Perdue, Theda, 1949-
The Columbia guide to American Indians of the
Southeast; [by] Theda Perdue and Michael D.
Green. Columbia Univ. Press 2001 325p il maps
(Columbia guides to American Indian history and
culture) $53.50; pa $27.50 **970.004**
1. Native Americans—Southern States
ISBN 0-231-11570-9; 0-231-11571-7 (pa)
LC 2001-35338
"The first half of the text focuses on the history and
culture of the region's native groups. This includes not
only the Mississippian Moundbuilder cultures that arose
between 800 and 1000 C.E. but also well-known native
groups such as the Cherokee and Creeks. . . . Immediately following the survey are alphabetically arranged entries focusing on individuals, places, and events. The final two sections are a chronology and a listing of resources for further research, which include published primary sources, oral traditions, films, and Internet sites.
. . . An essential purchase for all libraries collecting
books about Native Americans." Libr J
Includes bibliographical references

Philip, Neil
The great circle; a history of the First Nations;
foreword by Dennis Hastings. Clarion Books 2006
153p il map $25 **970.004**
1. Native Americans
ISBN 978-0-618-15941-3; 0-618-15941-X
LC 2005032743
"Philip takes on a huge challenge here: to present a
unified narrative that explains the complex and
confrontational relationships between Native Americans
and white settlers. . . . He pulls it off, however, thanks
to solid research, an engaging writing style, and a talent
for making individual stories serve the whole. . . . Top
marks, too, for the volume's photographs and historical
renderings, which so intensely illustrate the pages."
Booklist
Includes bibliographical references

Pritzker, Barry
A Native American encyclopedia; history,
culture, and peoples; [by] Barry M. Pritzker.
Oxford Univ. Press 2000 591p il hardcover o.p. pa
$29.95 **970.004**
1. Native Americans—Encyclopedias
ISBN 0-19-513897-X; 0-19-513877-5 (pa)
LC 99-53677
First published 1998 by ABC-CLIO as a two-volume
set with title: Native Americans
"Organized geographically, each section begins with
an introduction to the area and its original inhabitants.
Tribal entries follow, with some smaller related groups
discussed together. Each article includes sections on location, population, language, history, religion, government,
customs, dwellings, diet, key technology, trade, notable
arts, transportation, dress, and war/weapons. A contemporary section follows, with information on govern-
ment/reservations, economy, legal status, and daily life."
Libr J [review of 1998 edition]
Includes bibliographical references

Prucha, Francis Paul
The great father; the United States government
and the American Indians. University of Neb.
Press 1984 2v il pa $60 hardcover o.p.
970.004
1. Native Americans—Government relations
ISBN 0-8032-8734-8 (pa) LC 83-16837
"Beginning with the American Revolution and continuing to 1980, Prucha . . . brilliantly chronicles the history of relations between the federal government and Native Americans, in a work that belongs in all public and
academic libraries." Libr J
Includes bibliographical references

Rajtar, Steve, 1951-
Indian war sites; a guidebook to battlefields,
monuments, and memorials, state by state with
Canada and Mexico. McFarland & Co. 1999 330p
$39.95 **970.004**
1. Native Americans—Wars
ISBN 0-7864-0710-7 LC 99-25893
This is a "reference to hundreds of conflicts, both major and minor, between American Indians and Europeans.
Divided alphabetically by state and then chronologically
within each, entries include name and date, a nonspecific
location (e.g., Spring River), a brief description, and bibliographic sources. If the battle was a part of a larger
war Rajtar also gives the name of the war; and if there
is a monument, he tells its location and briefly describes
what's there." Libr J
Includes bibliographical references

Richter, Daniel K.
Facing east from Indian country; a Native
history of early America. Harvard Univ. Press
2001 317p il maps $27.50; pa $15.95
970.004
1. Native Americans
ISBN 0-674-00638-0; 0-674-01117-1 (pa)
LC 2001-24997
The author "recasts early American history from the
Native American point of view and in doing so illuminates as much about the Europeans as about the original
Americans. . . . Exploring the varying complexities of
different native people's relationships with England,
France and Spain, he argues that the Native Americans
were safer during the colonial era than after the Revolution. . . . Gracefully written and argued, Richter's compelling research and provocative claims make this an important addition to the literature for general readers of
both Native American and U.S. studies." Publ Wkly
Includes bibliographical references

Roberts, David, 1943-
Once they moved like the wind; Cochise,
Geronimo, and the Apache wars. Simon &
Schuster 1993 368p il hardcover o.p. pa $22
970.004
1. Cochise, Apache Chief, d. 1874 2. Geronimo,
Apache Chief, 1829-1909 3. Apache Indians
4. Native Americans—Wars
ISBN 0-671-70221-1; 0-671-88556-1 (pa)
LC 93-7112

Roberts, David, 1943---_Continued_

The author "tells the story of the Chiricahua Apache resistance to the encroachments of the whites in post-Civil War frontier America. Using contemporary letters and reminiscences, he relates the story from the Apache point of view, focusing on the leadership of Cochise and Geronimo." Libr J

"The book is history at its most engrossing." Publ Wkly

Includes bibliographical references

Waldman, Carl

Atlas of the North American Indian; illustrations by Molly Braun. rev ed. Facts on File 2000 385p maps hardcover o.p. pa $21.95   **970.004**

1. Native Americans
ISBN 0-8160-3974-7; 0-8160-3975-5 (pa)
LC 99-23678

First published 1985

New edition in preparation

"Details the migration of prehistoric tribes to North America from Asia. A unique section on 'Lifeways' provides information on all socioeconomic and religious aspects of Native American cultures, both pre- and post-contact with European Americans. Covers the Indian Wars, the Land Cessions, and contemporary Native American conditions." N Y Public Libr. Book of How & Where to Look It Up

Includes bibliographical references

Encyclopedia of Native American tribes. 3rd rev ed. Facts on File 2006 xxiv, 360p il map (Facts on File library of American history) $75; pa $21.95
970.004

1. Native Americans—Encyclopedias
ISBN   0-8160-6273-0;   978-0-8160-6273-7;
0-8160-6274-9 (pa); 978-0-8160-6274-4 (pa)
LC 2006-12529

First published 1988

This book discusses "more than 200 American Indian tribes of North America, as well as prehistoric peoples and civilizations. . . . [The] text summarizes the historical record—locations, migrations, contacts with non-Indians, wars, and more—and includes present-day tribal affairs and issues. The book also covers traditional Indian lifeways, including diet, housing, transportation, tools, clothing, art, and rituals, as well as language families." Publisher's note

"This well-written and easily accessible encyclopedia of a good starting point for research on Native American tribes." Libr Media Connect

Includes bibliographical references

Wallace, Anthony F. C., 1923-

The long bitter trail; Andrew Jackson and the Indians; consulting editor, Eric Foner. Hill & Wang 1993 143p maps (Critical issue series) pa $11 hardcover o.p.   **970.004**

1. Jackson, Andrew, 1767-1845 2. Native Americans—Government relations
ISBN 0-8090-1552-8 (pa)   LC 92-32609

A "retelling of the story of the Trail of Tears. This refers to the forced removal in the 1830s of thousands of Indians, particularly the Cherokee and the Choctaw, from the American east to west of the Mississippi River. The author expands his focus to examine the relocation of numerous Indian groups. Central to the story is Andrew Jackson, who assumed the presidency confronted with a government divided over the question of Indian removal and who soon became one of its major proponents." Publ Wkly

Weatherford, J. McIver

Native roots; how the Indians enriched America; [by] Jack Weatherford. Fawcett 1992 310p il map pa $13.95   **970.004**

1. Native Americans
ISBN 978-0-449-90713-9; 0-449-90713-9

First published 1991 by Crown

The author "writes about some 20 different aspects of the material and intellectual culture of Native Americans, in . . . [an attempt] to show how present-day America was built on Indian foundations." Voice Lit Suppl

"A valuable corrective to the sentimentality with which we regard the first U.S. settlers and developers." Booklist

Includes bibliographical references

Wilson, James, 1949-

The earth shall weep; the history of Native Americans. Atlantic Monthly Press 1999 xxix, 466p maps pa $16 hardcover o.p.   **970.004**

1. Native Americans
ISBN 0-8021-3680-X (pa)   LC 99-13098

"Wilson begins with the first English settlements on the Atlantic coast in the 1500s and moves from century to century, focusing on various geographic areas through the massacre at Wounded Knee in 1890. He then addresses today's social, political, and economic issues while trying to examine the legacy of ignorance and misunderstanding." Libr J

"Employing elegiac prose and steady narrative momentum, Wilson has written a richly informative history that places Native Americans 'at the center of the historical stage.'" Publ Wkly

Includes bibliographical references

970.01   North America—Early history to 1599

Adovasio, J. M. (James M.), 1944-

The first Americans; in pursuit of archaeology's greatest mystery; {by} J.M. Adovasio with Jake Page. Random House 2002 328p il maps pa $14.95 hardcover o.p.   **970.01**

1. Native Americans—Origin 2. America—Antiquities
ISBN 0-375-75704-X (pa)   LC 2002-69766

"In 1974, Adovasio stepped into a roiling debate about the first human presence in the Americas when he unearthed materials suggesting that we were here 4000 years earlier than commonly believed." Libr J

"Readers get a lively, close-up view of how archaeologists study America's original discoverers." Booklist

Includes bibliographical references

America in 1492; the world of the Indian peoples before the arrival of Columbus; edited and with an introduction by Alvin Josephy, Jr.; developed by Frederick E. Hoxie. Knopf 1992 477p il maps hardcover o.p. pa $20 **970.01**
1. Native Americans—History 2. Native Americans—Antiquities 3. America—Exploration 4. America—Antiquities
ISBN 0-394-56438-3; 0-679-74337-5 (pa)
LC 90-26222
These essays depict "the diverse lives of the approximately 75 million people living in the Americas around the turn of the fifteenth century. Geography guides the first section. . . . Another section focuses on languages, spiritual beliefs and customs, art, and 'systems of knowledge.'" Booklist
Includes bibliographical references

Archaeology of prehistoric native America; an encyclopedia; editor, Guy Gibbon; associate editors, Kenneth M. Ames [et al.] Garland 1998 lxxvii, 941p il map (Garland reference library of the humanites) $205 **970.01**
1. Native Americans—Antiquities—Encyclopedias 2. North America—Antiquities—Encyclopedias
ISBN 0-8153-0725-X LC 98-11443
This encyclopedia includes alphabetically arranged entries covering North American prehistory and archaeology.
"This superb reference source . . . has no equal in its coverage of Native American cultures in North America prior to European contact." Libr J
Includes bibliographical references

Dillehay, Tom D.
The settlement of the Americas; a new prehistory; {by} Thomas D. Dillehay. Basic Bks. 2000 xxi, 371p il pa $22 hardcover o.p. *
970.01
1. America—Exploration 2. America—Antiquities
ISBN 0-465-07669-6 (pa) LC 00-27572
Dillehay "pushes back by at least 1,000 years our estimates of when the New World was first settled. He challenges a long-held belief—that the first inhabitants of the Americas were the so-called Clovis people, a big-game-hunting culture who came through North America starting 11,200 years ago and reached South America even later. Drawing on his 20-plus years of research at Monte Verde, in Chile, he argues that South America was inhabited by 12,500 years ago." Publ Wkly
This "is a seminal work in the field that is accessible to lay readers." Libr J
Includes bibliographical references

Horwitz, Tony, 1958-
A voyage long and strange; rediscovering the new world. Henry Holt and Co. 2008 445p il map $27.50 * **970.01**
1. America—Exploration 2. Explorers
ISBN 978-0-8050-7603-5; 0-8050-7603-4
LC 2007-45883

"Realizing that his knowledge of American history between Columbus's discovery and Plymouth Rock over 100 years later was sketchy at best, . . . [the author] sets out to educate himself with his own explorations. He intertwines his experiences retracing the early conquistadors, adventurers, and entrepreneurs through such regions as Newfoundland, the Dominican Republic, and the American South, Southwest, and New England with thoroughly researched accounts of the territories themselves, the natives who were historically affected, and the motives of the explorers. . . . This readable and vastly entertaining history travelog is highly recommended for public libraries." Libr J
Includes bibliographical references

Mann, Charles C.
1491; new revelations of the Americas before Columbus. Knopf 2005 465p il maps $30; pa $14.95 **970.01**
1. Native Americans—History 2. America—Antiquities
ISBN 1-4000-4006-X; 1-4000-3205-9 (pa)
LC 2005-42178
U.S. title: Ancient Americans
The author "demonstrates that long before any European explorers set foot in the New World, Native American cultures were flourishing with a high degree of sophistication." Publ Wkly
"Mann navigates adroitly through the controversies. He approaches each in the best scientific tradition, carefully sifting the evidence, never jumping to hasty conclusions, giving everyone a fair hearing—the experts and the amateurs; the accounts of the Indians and their conquerors. And rarely is he less than enthralling." N Y Times Book Rev
Includes bibliographical references

Schobinger, Juan
The ancient Americans; a reference guide to the art, culture, and history of pre-Columbian North and South America; translation, Carys Evans-Corrales; consultant, Susan Kart. Sharpe, M.E. 2000 2v il maps set $159 *
970.01
1. Native Americans—Antiquities 2. America—Antiquities
ISBN 0-7656-8034-3 LC 00-56280
Original Spanish language edition, 1997
This reference "surveys the entire Western Hemisphere prior to the arrival of Europeans in the Americas. This copiously illustrated work is especially notable for its numerous full-color plates of Native American rock art." Libr J
Includes bibliographical references

Vikings: the North Atlantic saga; edited by William W. Fitzhugh and Elisabeth I. Ward. Smithsonian Institution Press 2000 432p il maps $60; pa $34.95 **970.01**
1. Vikings 2. America—Exploration
ISBN 1-56098-970-X; 1-56098-995-5 (pa)
LC 99-57983
Catalog of an exhibition at the National Museum of Natural History, Smithsonian Institution, Washington, D.C., April 29, 2000-September 5, 2000

Vikings: the North Atlantic saga—*Continued*

"While the book concentrates on the New World, there are also chapters on the Vikings in Iceland, Greenland, and France and along the coasts of Britain and the rivers of Russia. The contributors discuss the Viking saga from the perspectives of natural science, archaeology, history, oral tradition, and early writings." Libr J

This book is "well designed, heavily illustrated and almost encyclopedic in scope and detail." Publ Wkly

Includes bibliographical references

971   Canada

Riendeau, Roger E., 1950-

A brief history of Canada; [by] Roger Riendeau. 2nd ed. Facts on File 2007 444p il map $45 *

971

1. Canada—History

ISBN 978-0-8160-6335-2   LC 2006-47130

First published 2000

This is a history of Canada "beginning with the exploration of the Northern American frontier and continuing through the rise and fall of the French and British empires to the foundations of Canadian nationhood and the present day." Publisher's note

Includes bibliographical references

Weihs, Jean Riddle

Facts about Canada, its provinces and territories; [by] Jean Weihs; illustrations by Cameron Riddle. Wilson, H.W. 1995 246p il maps $60

971

1. Canada

ISBN 0-8242-0864-1   LC 94-23275

Coverage includes "geography and climate, parks and historic sites, demography, government and politics, financial and economic information, history, culture and education, motor vehicle use statistics, trivia about the 'first, biggest and best,' information sources and a selected bibliography. Weihs provides very current information and has clearly researched her topic extensively." Voice Youth Advocates

971.6   Nova Scotia

MacDonald, Laura M., 1963-

Curse of the Narrows. Walker & Co. 2005 355p il maps $26

971.6

1. Explosions 2. Halifax (N.S.)

ISBN 0-8027-1458-7   LC 2005-44255

This is an account of "how a boat collision led to the destruction of Halifax, Nova Scotia, in 1917." N Y Times Book Rev

This "book captures in vivid detail the history of this catastrophe." Booklist

Includes bibliographical references

971.9   Northern territories of Canada

Mowat, Farley

High latitudes; an Arctic journey; foreword by Margaret Atwood. Steerforth Press 2003 300p map pa $15.95   **971.9**

1. Arctic regions 2. Natural history—Canada

ISBN 1-58642-061-5   LC 2002-151151

First published 2002 in Canada

"In 1966, Mowat's publisher, Jack McClelland, sent Mowat into northern Canada to research an illustrated volume on the region. This book is the tale of that journey. Hopscotching by creaky plane from one isolated settlement to another, Mowat witnesses the devastation being wrought on the native peoples by encroaching white men, lured by a mirage of the north's supposedly limitless minerals and the raw beauty of the land and its people. A cavalcade of vivid, fiction-worthy characters fills these pages. . . . Voiced with a passionate sense of justice, this work is stirring reading from the bard of the Canadian north." Publ Wkly

972   Middle America. Mexico

Coe, Michael D.

The Maya; Michael D. Coe. 7th ed fully rev and expanded. Thames and Hudson 2005 272p il map (Ancient peoples and places) pa $22.50

972

1. Mayas

ISBN 978-0-500-28505-3; 0-500-28505-5

First published 1966 by Praeger

An illustrated survey of the Maya civilization, focusing on the achievements of the Classic Period, A.D. 300-900

Includes bibliographical references

Díaz del Castillo, Bernal, 1496-1584

The discovery and conquest of Mexico, 1517-1521; translated by A.P. Maudslay. Da Capo Press 2003 478p il map pa $24   **972**

1. Mexico—History

ISBN 0-306-81319-X; 978-0-306-81319-1

First published 1956 by Farrar, Straus & Giroux

"Edited from the only exact copy of the original MS (and published in Mexico) by Genaro García; translated with an introduction and notes by A.P. Maudslay, and a new introduction by Hugh Thomas." Title page

"The memoirs of an old man, who began to write of his experiences half a century after they occurred and completed his account at the age of 84, they are not free from minor inaccuracies, but they are the most reliable narrative that exists." Chicago Sunday Trib

Foster, Lynn V.

A brief history of Mexico. Updated ed. Facts on File 2007 304p il map $45 *   **972**

1. Mexico—History

ISBN 978-0-8160-7170-8; 0-8160-7170-5

LC 2006-52531

Foster, Lynn V.—*Continued*
First published 1997
An overview of Mexican history covering pre-Columbian civilizations and contemporary indigenous cultures. Language, art, religion, politics and economics are discussed. A chronology and bibliography are included.
Includes bibliographical references

Kirkwood, Burton
The history of Mexico. Greenwood Press 2000 245p (Greenwood histories of the modern nations) $45   **972**
1. Mexico—History
ISBN 0-313-30351-7   LC 99-33688
Also available in paperback from Palgrave Macmillan
A historical survey of Mexico and its people from the arrival of the first humans in the Western Hemisphere to the end of the 20th century. Topics range from Mexico's cultural past to current issues such as the war on drugs and the North American Free Trade Agreement.
Includes bibliographical references

Meyer, Michael C.
The course of Mexican history; [by] Michael C. Meyer, William L. Sherman, Susan M. Deeds. 8th ed. Oxford University Press 2007 688p il map hardcover o.p. pa $64.95 *   **972**
1. Mexico—History
ISBN   0-19-517835-1;   978-0-19-517835-7;
0-19-517836-X (pa); 978-0-19-517836-4 (pa)
LC 2006-51741
First published 1979. Periodically revised
A chronologically arranged survey of the political, economic, social, and cultural history of Mexico, ranging from the pre-Columbian period to the present.
Includes bibliographical references

The **Oxford** history of Mexico; edited by Michael C. Meyer and William H. Beezley. Oxford Univ. Press 2000 709p il maps $45
972
1. Mexico—History
ISBN 0-19-511228-8   LC 99-56044
The editors "have compiled 20 previously unpublished essays by experts who explore Mexico from precolonial times to the present. . . . Examining the country with new and different approaches, the contributors challenge traditional historical concepts on a variety of issues." Libr J
Includes bibliographical references

Prescott, William Hickling, 1796-1859
History of the conquest of Mexico. Modern Lib. 1998 xxvi, 1005p pa $17.95 hardcover o.p.
972
1. Cortés, Hernán, 1485-1547 2. Mexico—History 3. Aztecs
ISBN 0-375-75803-8 (pa)   LC 98-10173
Also available in edition with History of the conquest of Peru from Cooper Sq. Press
First published 1843 in three volumes

This is a history of the subjugation of the Aztec people by Hernan Cortez and his soldiers between 1519 and 1522.

Smith, Michael Ernest, 1953-
The Aztecs; [by] Michael E. Smith. 2nd ed. Blackwell 2003 c2002 367p il maps (Peoples of America) hardcover o.p. pa $29.95   **972**
1. Aztecs 2. Mexico—Antiquities
ISBN 0-631-23015-7; 0-631-23016-5 (pa)
LC 2001-6950
First published 1996
The author "summarizes the results of archaeological research conducted largely in the past 30 years into the everyday lives of ordinary people in the villages, hamlets, and farmsteads from many regions of central Mexico. His method permits a fresh view of such topics as agricultural methods, population size, market system, relations between city-states and the empire, and even human sacrifice. Smith carries his social account of these people through transformation under Spanish rule and their legacy in modern Mexico." Libr J [review of 1996 edition]
Includes bibliographical references

Townsend, Richard F.
The Aztecs. rev ed, 2nd ed. Thames & Hudson 2000 232p il maps (Ancient peoples and places) pa $18.95   **972**
1. Aztecs
ISBN 0-500-28132-7   LC 99-70847
First published 1992
"In addition to analyzing the advancement and eventual dissolution of the extensive Aztec empire, the author also provides a fascinating record of the minutiae of daily life. . . . A compact introduction to the historical and sociological evolution of a prominent Meso-American civilization." Booklist {review of 1992 edition}
Includes bibliographical references

972.08   Mexico since 1867

Fuentes, Carlos, 1928-
A new time for Mexico; translated from the Spanish by Marina Gutman Castañeda and the author. University of Calif. Press 1997 226p pa $16.95   **972.08**
1. Mexico—Politics and government
ISBN 0-520-21183-9   LC 97-8427
First published 1996 by Farrar, Straus, & Giroux
In these essays "Fuentes calls on Mexican president Ernesto Zedillo to take definitive steps toward a full democracy—electoral reform; equal access of candidates to the media; independent, aggressive labor unions; and, above all, true separation between the ruling party and the government. . . . Offering lapidary, lyrical meditations on Mexico as a land of continual metamorphosis, Fuentes nostalgically reminisces about his home in Veracruz, whose port his father defended against a Yankee invasion in 1914." Publ Wkly

Lewis, Oscar, 1914-1970

The children of Sánchez; autobiography of a Mexican family. Random House 1961 xxxi, 499p pa $17 hardcover o.p. *   **972.08**

1. Poor—Mexico City (Mexico) 2. Family

ISBN 0-394-70280-8 (pa)

"First-person autobiographical narratives by the members of a poor family in Mexico City. One by one, the father and his four grown children told the anthropologist author their stories of fights, sex, struggles for jobs, bitterness, hate, sickness, death, and only a little happiness." Publ Wkly

"Oscar Lewis has made something brilliant and of singular significance, a work of such unique concentration and sympathy." N Y Times Book Rev

Womack, John

Zapata and the Mexican Revolution. Knopf 1969 c1968 435p il pa $17 hardcover o.p.
972.08

1. Zapata, Emiliano, 1879-1919 2. Mexico—History

ISBN 0-394-70853-9 (pa)

The author reconstructs the "history of the agrarian revolution in southern Mexico from the late Diaz period to about 1920. The work is well written {and} carefully conceived." Choice

972.8   Central America

Pérez-Brignoli, Héctor

A brief history of Central America; translated by Ricardo B. Sawrey A. and Susana Stettri de Sawrey. University of Calif. Press 1989 223p maps pa $18.97 hardcover o.p.   **972.8**

1. Central America—History

ISBN 0-520-06832-7 (pa)   LC 89-31889

This book presents the economic, political and cultural history of Guatemala, Honduras, El Salvador, Nicaragua and Costa Rica, the five national states of Central America

"For interested laypersons, this is an excellent introduction with an accurate sense of the region." Libr J

Includes bibliographical references

972.81   Guatemala

Goldman, Francisco

The art of political murder; who killed the Bishop? Grove Press 2007 396p il map $25
972.81

1. Gerardi, Juan, d. 1998—Assassination 2. Trials (Homicide) 3. Guatemala—Politics and government

ISBN 978-0-8021-1828-8; 0-8021-1828-3

This "is the story of the murder investigation of a Guatemalan bishop. . . . [Bishop Juan Gerardi] was bludgeoned to death in his garage on a Sunday night in 1998, two days after the presentation of a . . . church-sponsored report implicating the military in the murders and disappearances of some two hundred thousand civilians." N Y Times (Late N Y Ed)

This book "is a tour de force, not just for . . . [the author's] reportorial tenacity . . . but because his novelist's eye and his deep understanding of Guatemalan society take you places no other reporter could." Nation

Includes bibliographical references

972.87   Panama

McCullough, David G., 1933-

The path between the seas; the creation of the Panama Canal, 1870-1914; [by] David McCullough. Simon & Schuster 1977 698p il maps pa $18 hardcover o.p. *   **972.87**

1. Panama Canal

ISBN 0-671-24409-4   LC 76-57967

This is a "history of the canal project, beginning with de Lesseps' bold and ultimately disastrous investment and ending with the triumph of American enterprise in 1914." Libr J

"Not only is this a well-told story of the building of the Panama Canal but it also supplies welcome background for the . . . debate on the canal's role in inter-American relations." Booklist

Includes bibliographical references

972.91   Cuba

Encyclopedia of Cuba; people, history, culture; edited by Luis Martinez-Fernández {et al.}. Greenwood Press 2003 2v il maps set $174.95
972.91

1. Cuba—Encyclopedias

ISBN 1-57356-334-X   LC 2002-70030

"An Oryx book"

"The editors intend this work to be a non-politicized look at Cuban people, politics, history, and culture. Chapters cover topics such as history, government, and popular culture. Within each chapter, entries are in alphabetical order. An excellent introduction to a colorful and important nation." Booklist

Includes bibliographical references

Gimbel, Wendy

Havana dreams; a story of Cuba. Knopf 1998 234p il pa $13 hardcover o.p.   **972.91**

1. Revuelta, Naty, 1925- 2. Cuba—History

ISBN 0-679-75070-3 (pa)   LC 98-14571

"A Borzoi Bk."

At the center of this personal "history of modern Cuba is a brief affair between a married Havana socialite named Naty Revuelta and Fidel Castro, carried out mostly in love letters written in 1953-54 while the future dictator was in jail. The affair fizzled, but not before Castro supposedly left his paramour with a daughter, Alina." Publ Wkly

Gimbel "succeeds in showing the complexity of family relationships resulting from the Cuban revolution, which extends into two countries." Libr J

Includes bibliographical references

Guillermoprieto, Alma, 1949-
Dancing with Cuba; a memoir of the revolution; translated from the Spanish by Esther Allen. Pantheon 2004 290p $25; pa $13   **972.91**
  1. Cuba—Description and travel
  ISBN 0-375-42093-2; 0-375-72581-4 (pa)
                              LC 2003-44200
The author "revisits the six months in 1970 she spent teaching modern dance in Cuba. . . . Her intense commitment to art . . . provides a jumping-off point for her book about dance, which is really about Cuba and a political coming-of-age." Publ Wkly
"Guillermoprieto vividly and purposefully recounts her acute discomfort with the strained and ludicrous rhetoric of the revolution, her sorrow over Castro's catastrophic failures, her astonishment at the great valor of Cuba's people, and her gradual recognition of her true calling as a journalist." Booklist

Harvey, David Alan, 1944-
Cuba; photographs by David Alan Harvey; essays by Elizabeth Newhouse. National Geographic Soc. 1999 215p il $50   **972.91**
  1. Cuba—Pictorial works
  ISBN 0-7922-7501-2   LC 99-32488
This collection of Harvey's photographs depicts "the effects of Cuba's totalitarian government and dire economy upon its remarkably resilient population. . . . These images are matched with staff writer Newhouse's historical overview, which discusses the country's rich architectural heritage, culture, and social conditions. Together these add up to a sympathetic understanding of what the island is like today." Libr J

Pérez, Louis A., 1943-
Cuba; between reform and revolution. Oxford University Press 2006 442p il map (Latin American histories) $77.95; pa $34.95
                                    972.91
  1. Cuba—History
  ISBN   0-19-517911-0;   978-0-19-517911-8; 0-19-517912-9 (pa); 978-0-19-517912-5 (pa)
                              LC 2004-65477
  First published 1988
"A narrative history that emphasizes the antecedents of the Cuban revolution and concludes with an analysis of Fidel Castro's successes and failures." N Y Public Libr Book of How & Where to Look It Up [entry for 1988 edition]
  Includes bibliographical references

Suchlicki, Jaime
Cuba; from Columbus to Castro and beyond; {by} Jaime Suchlicki. 5th ed. Brassey's 2002 285p pa $24.95   **972.91**
  1. Cuba—History
  ISBN 1-57488-436-0   LC 2002-3953
  First published 1997
A summary of Cuba's development, with emphasis on the twentieth century and the factors that led to the Cuban revolution
  Includes bibliographical references

Symmes, Patrick, 1964-
The boys from Dolores; Fidel Castro's schoolmates from revolution to exile. Pantheon Books 2007 352p $26.95   **972.91**
  1. Castro, Fidel, 1926- 2. Colegio de Dolores (Cuba) 3. Cuba—Description and travel
  ISBN 978-0-375-42283-6; 0-375-42283-8
                              LC 2006-30323
"The author writes of Castro's schoolmates from Dolores, the private Jesuit academy in Santiago de Cuba on the island's eastern end, and he visits several of them. . . . Among the Dolores students were Castro's brothers Raul and Ramon and a future star in North American television, Desi Arnaz. But it is Cuban intellectuals like Lundy Aguilar to whom Symmes turns for insights into Cuba before and after Castro's revolution. The result is a remarkable account of the country and its people." Libr J

972.97   Leeward Islands

Kincaid, Jamaica
A small place. Farrar, Straus & Giroux 1988 81p pa $11 hardcover o.p.   **972.97**
  1. Antigua and Barbuda
  ISBN 0-374-52707-5 (pa)   LC 88-376
Antiguan Kincaid addresses foreign visitors to her country. In this essay, she discusses the poverty and political corruption of the island, which she views as a legacy of British colonialism and also as a result of an economy controlled by tourism

973   United States

American eras. Gale Res. 1997-1998 8v il set $950 *   **973**
  1. United States—Civilization 2. United States—History
  ISBN 0-7876-1477-7
  Also available separately for $130
This reference set "provides information on U.S. history, including social history, prior to the twentieth century. Each era-specific volume includes an introductory essay describing the time period to provide context and an overview, 150 illustrations, an index of photographs, a bibliography, a subject index and a list of contributors." Publisher's note

The **American** presidency; edited by Alan Brinkley and Davis Dyer. Houghton Mifflin Co 2004 572p il pa $19.95   **973**
  1. Presidents—United States 2. United States—Politics and government
  ISBN 0-618-38273-9   LC 2003-62513
An updated version of The reader's companion to the American presidency (2000)
This work assesses "how presidents shape and define culture and society and, at the same time, reflect them. . . . {This} can serve as a beginning point for research and should engage casual readers as well as students of the American presidency." Choice
  Includes bibliographical references

Americans at war; society, culture, and the homefront; John P. Resch, Editor in Chief. Macmillan Reference USA 2005 4v il set $395
973
1. War and civilization 2. United States—Military history 3. United States—Civilization
ISBN 0-02-865806-X LC 2004-17314
Contents: v. 1. 1500-1815 -- v. 2. 1816-1900 -- v. 3. 1901-1945 -- v. 4. 1946-present
This book "delivers well-written articles and would make an excellent addition to high-school, academic, and public libraries." Booklist
Includes bibliographical references

Anzovin, Steven, 1954-
Famous first facts about American politics; [by] Steven Anzovin & Janet Podell. Wilson, H.W. 2001 756p $180 *
973
1. United States—Politics and government 2. United States—History
ISBN 0-8242-0971-0 LC 00-49960
This offers over 5,000 entries of firsts in national, state, and local U.S. politics from the founding of the nation through the 2000 election and includes five indexes: subject, name, year, day, and place.
Includes bibliographical references

Appleby, Joyce Oldham
Inheriting the revolution; the first generation of Americans; [by] Joyce Appleby. Belknap Press 2000 322p il $28.50; pa $16
973
1. United States—History—1783-1865 2. United States—Social conditions
ISBN 0-674-00236-9; 0-674-00663-1 (pa)
LC 99-49787
The author "deals with two themes in this book: the historical experience of the generation after the American Revolution and conflicts within American identity." N Y Times Book Rev
"This book provides a splendid introduction to the period for students and general readers." Libr J
Includes bibliographical references

Boller, Paul F.
Presidential inaugurations; {by} Paul F. Boller, Jr. Harcourt 2001 298p $25; pa $14
973
1. Presidents—United States—Inauguration 2. Washington (D.C.)—Social life and customs
ISBN 0-15-100546-X; 0-15-600759-2 (pa)
LC 00-49893
The author "examines the events and controversies surrounding Presidential inaugurations. . . . Written with elegance and wit, this is a wonderful addition to the very thin literature available on Presidential inaugurations." Libr J
Includes bibliographical references

Boorstin, Daniel J., 1914-2004
The Americans: The democratic experience. Random House 1973 717p pa $19 hardcover o.p.
973

1. United States—Civilization 2. United States—Social conditions 3. United States—Economic conditions
ISBN 0-394-71011-8 (pa)
Concluding volume of the author's trilogy which began with The Americans: The colonial experience and continued with The Americans: The national experience
This volume is concerned with the democratization of the national character over the past hundred years and the growth of technology
Includes bibliographical references

The Americans: The national experience. Random House 1965 517p pa $16 hardcover o.p.
973
1. United States—Civilization 2. American national characteristics 3. United States—Intellectual life
ISBN 0-394-70358-8 (pa)
This is the second volume of the author's trilogy
A cultural interpretation of American history, this book traces "the roots of contemporary American life to the years between the Revolution and the Civil War." Booklist
Includes bibliographical references

Hidden history; selected and edited by Daniel J. Boorstin and Ruth F. Boorstin. Vintage Books 1989 332p pa $15
973
1. United States—Civilization
ISBN 978-0-679-72223-6; 0-679-72223-8
First published 1987 by Harper & Row
"A collection of essays and abridgments from [Boorstin's] books that investigates certain overlooked or disregarded corners of history. . . . History engagingly written, deeply felt, widely appealing." Booklist

Churchill, Sir Winston, 1874-1965
The great republic; a history of America; edited by Winston S. Churchill. Random House 1999 454p hardcover o.p. pa $15.95
973
1. United States—History
ISBN 0-375-50320-X; 978-0-375-75440-1 (pa); 0-375-75440-7 (pa) LC 99-28511
"The first half of the volume offers an old-fashioned narrative history of America's political development, from the age of exploration to the 1880s. The second half reprints articles that Churchill penned for English publications on such themes as Prohibition, the muckracking of Upton Sinclair, and the death of Franklin Delano Roosevelt." Libr J
Includes bibliographical references

Commager, Henry Steele, 1902-1998
The American mind; an interpretation of American thought and character since the 1880's. Yale Univ. Press 1950 476p pa $14.95 hardcover o.p.
973
1. United States—Civilization 2. United States—Intellectual life
ISBN 0-300-00046-4 (pa)
Partial contents: John Fiske and the evolutionary philosophy; William James and the impact of pragmatism; Determinism in literature; Religious thought and practice; Lester Ward and the science of society; Thorstein Veblen

Commager, Henry Steele, 1902-1998—*Continued*
and the new economics; Innovators in historical interpretation; Applications of political theory; Evolution of American law; Architecture and society; Bibliography

Eyewitness to America; 500 years of America in the words of those who saw it happen; edited by David Colbert. Pantheon Bks. 1997 xxx, 599p hardcover o.p. pa $16.95 * **973**
1. United States—History—Sources
ISBN 0-679-44224-3; 0-679-76724-X (pa)
LC 96-24150
This volume contains a "panorama of first-person accounts of moments in the country's story that stretch from an October 10, 1492, diary entry by one of Columbus's crewmen to a 1994 e-mail message from Bill Gates. The nearly 300 entries tend to be short, preceded by informative introductions. The result is a feeling for history that is both immediate and dramatic." Publ Wkly
Includes bibliographical references

Facts about the states; editors, Joseph Nathan Kane, Janet Podell, Steven Anzovin. 2nd ed. Wilson, H.W. 1994 c1993 624p il $115
973
1. United States—Local history 2. State governments
ISBN 0-8242-0849-8 LC 93-30328
First published 1989
Provides geographic, demographic, economic, political, and cultural facts about the fifty states, Puerto Rico, and the District of Columbia. Part I presents state entries in alphabetical order. Part II provides comparative tables that rank states in categories such as population, geography, education, and finance.

The **Greenwood** library of American war reporting; David A. Copeland, general editor. Greenwood Press 2005 8v il set $995
973
1. United States—Military history—Sources
ISBN 0-313-33435-8 LC 2005-10122
"Beginning with 1753 and ending in April 2004 with photographs depicting the mistreatment of Iraqi prisoners at Abu Ghraib, these volumes offer primary documents, mainly newspaper and magazine articles and radio and television transcripts. Indispensable to the study of war reporting and the most definitive . . . reference work available on the subject." Booklist
Includes bibliographical references

Hofstadter, Richard, 1916-1970
The American political tradition, and the men who made it; with a foreword by Christopher Lasch. 25th anniversary ed. Knopf 1973 xxxiii, 378p pa $14 hardcover o.p. **973**
1. United States—Politics and government
ISBN 0-679-72315-3 (pa)
First published 1948
This volume contains twelve essays, ten of which analyze the political careers of Lincoln, Jefferson, Jackson, Calhoun, Wendell Phillips, Bryan, Theodore Roosevelt, Wilson, Hoover and Franklin D. Roosevelt.
Includes bibliographical references

Kammen, Michael G.
In the past lane; historical perspectives on American culture; {by} Michael Kammen. Oxford Univ. Press 1997 277p il pa $25 hardcover o.p.
973
1. United States—Civilization 2. Popular culture—United States 3. United States—Historiography
ISBN 0-19-513091-X (pa) LC 97-21613
These essays "range from the influence of the personal experiences of prominent historians on their work to the changing attitudes toward the 'unique' aspects of American history as reflected in the views of historians, past and present. For professional historians or serious students of history, Kammen's essays provide an excellent opportunity to gauge how those who chronicle our past both influence and are influenced by national and personal experiences." Booklist
Includes bibliographical references

Keegan, John, 1934-
Fields of battle; the wars for North America. Knopf 1996 c1995 348p il maps hardcover o.p. pa $15 * **973**
1. North America—Military history
ISBN 0-679-42413-X; 0-679-74664-1 (pa)
LC 96-154385
First published 1995 in the United Kingdom with title: Warpaths: travels of a military historian in North America
The author "demonstrates how North America's geography has influenced its history: how its mountain chains and river systems have determined where people fought, and fought repeatedly. For example, the defenses that Cornwallis built at Yorktown to deter American forces were improved and reused by the Confederates almost a century later. Keegan's tour of the continent skips the Mexican War, and his book is atypically discursive. For Americans, the charm is the familiarity of its sites—Brooklyn, Pittsburgh, Laramie, and other home towns." New Yorker

Loewen, James W.
Lies across America; what our historic sites get wrong. Simon & Schuster 2007 464p pa $16
973
1. Historic sites 2. Monuments
ISBN 978-0-7432-9629-8; 0-7432-9629-X
First published 1999 by New Press
"The book consists of 95 brief commentaries on specific sites from Alaska to Florida to Maine, sandwiched between essays that offer advice on how to interpret what you read or are told at historic sites." N Y Times Book Rev [review of 1999 edition]

Marcus, Greil
The shape of things to come; prophecy and the American voice. Farrar, Straus & Giroux 2006 320p $25 **973**
1. American national characteristics 2. Nationalism—United States 3. United States—Civilization
ISBN 978-0-374-10438-2; 0-374-10438-7
LC 2005-33139

Marcus, Greil—*Continued*

Marcus "posits that the United States of America is a cultural construction, grounded in the Declaration of Independence and the Constitution. Without those bedrocks, Marcus believes, the nation would be 'little more than a collection of buildings and people who have no special reason to speak to each other, and nothing to say.' Marcus builds his own erudite vision upon John Winthrop's 1630 speech 'A Modell of Christian Charity,' Abraham Lincoln's second inaugural address in 1865, Martin Luther King Jr.'s 1963 exhortation from the steps of the Lincoln Memorial in Washington, the later novels of Philip Roth, the films of David Lynch and the music of David Thomas with his band Pere Ubu. More than most books, Marcus's latest tour de force is quite likely to divide readers into two camps: those who find it brilliant and those who find it baffling." Publ Wkly

Morison, Samuel Eliot, 1887-1976

A concise history of the American Republic; {by} Samuel Eliot Morison, Henry Steele Commager, William E. Leuchtenburg. 2nd ed. Oxford Univ. Press 1983 765p il maps pa $58.95 hardcover o.p.   **973**
1. United States—History
ISBN 0-19-503180-6 (pa)   LC 82-3621
Also available in a two volume paperback edition, each $39.95: v1 To 1877 (ISBN 0-19-503181-4); v2 Since 1865 (ISBN 0-19-503182-2)
First published 1977
"An abbreviated and revised edition of The growth of the American Republic." Title page
Includes bibliographical references

The growth of the American Republic; [by] Samuel Eliot Morison, Henry Steele Commager, and William E. Leuchtenburg. 7th ed. Oxford Univ. Press 1980 2v il maps ea $59.95
973
1. United States—History
ISBN 0-19-502593-8 (v1); 0-19-502594-6 (v2)
LC 79-52432
First published 1930 in a single volume
A history of the United States that deals with military, political, economic, social, literary and spiritual aspects of the nation's development
"A good general history, well-written." Sheehy. Guide to Ref Books. 10th edition

Osborn, William M.

The wild frontier; atrocities during the American-Indian War from Jamestown Colony to Wounded Knee. Random House 2000 363p pa $19 hardcover o.p.   **973**
1. Native Americans—Wars 2. Native Americans—Government relations 3. Frontier and pioneer life
ISBN 0-375-75856-9 (pa)   LC 00-27171
"Characterizing the years between 1622 and 1890 as the era of the American-Indian War, Osborn provides a balanced analysis of the vicious atrocities committed by white settlers and Native Americans during the prolonged period of westward expansion. . . . Laden with stark, unsparing descriptions . . . the detailed narrative retains an admirable objectivity." Booklist
Includes bibliographical references

Schlesinger, Arthur M., 1917-2007

The cycles of American history; {by} Arthur M. Schlesinger, Jr. Houghton Mifflin 1986 498p pa $16 hardcover o.p.   **973**
1. United States—History 2. United States—Foreign relations 3. United States—Politics and government
ISBN 0-395-95793-1 (pa)   LC 86-7706
"For this volume, Schlesinger has revised and updated papers, reviews, and essays that have appeared in various forms over the past quarter-century. . . . Each of the 14 essays that make up the book offers a fresh, demanding, and lively argument about important issues in American intellectual, political, or diplomatic history." Choice
Includes bibliographical references

The disuniting of America; reflections on a multicultural society. rev & enl ed. Norton 1998 208p $21.95; pa $12.95   **973**
1. Multiculturalism 2. Multicultural education 3. United States—Historiography 4. United States—Civilization
ISBN 0-393-04580-3; 0-393-31854-0 (pa)
LC 97-25124
First published 1992
The author argues against radical multiculturalism, bilingual education, and the influence of ethnic, political, and religious pressure groups on the teaching of history. Includes an epilogue that assesses the impact of radical multiculturalism and radical monoculturalism on the Bill of Rights and concludes with an annotated reading list of titles essential for understanding the American experience
Includes bibliographical references

Steinbeck, John, 1902-1968

Travels with Charley; in search of America. Viking 1962 246p hardcover o.p. pa $14
973
1. United States—Civilization 2. United States—Description and travel
ISBN 0-670-72508-0; 0-14-200070-1 (pa)
The Nobel laureate recounts his impressions and observations of America gathered during a trip through forty states in the company of his French poodle Charley

Virga, Vincent

Eyes of the nation; a visual history of the United States; by Vincent Virga and curators of the Library of Congress; historical commentary by Alan Brinkley. Knopf 1997 399p il $75
973
ISBN 0-679-44330-4   LC 97-36603
Also available in paperback from Bunker Hill
This visual history "showcases more than 500 illustrations, manuscripts, engravings, prints, movie stills and other artifacts stretching back to the 15th century. The accompanying text by the historian Alan Brinkley rolls through the high and low points of the nation's history, but it is the captions that sparkle the brightest, adding context while offering surprising information." N Y Times Book Rev

Wetterau, Bruce
Congressional Quarterly's desk reference on the Presidency. CQ Press 2000 311p il (Desk reference series) $49.95 **973**
1. Presidents—United States
ISBN 1-56802-589-0   LC 00-63024
Over 500 questions and answers on the organization, procedures, and history of the office and on the presidents and their wives. Topics covered include scandals, elections, the White House, and the executive branch
Includes bibliographical references

Wills, Garry, 1934-
A necessary evil; a history of American distrust of government. Simon & Schuster 1999 365p pa $15 hardcover o.p. **973**
1. United States—Politics and government
2. Resistance to government
ISBN 0-684-87026-6 (pa)   LC 99-35879
This "analysis of the distorted mythology that has grown up around government in the U.S. takes on hot-button issues from the Second Amendment and term limits to the idea that the Founders sought to create an inefficient government. Provocative and enlightening." Booklist
Includes bibliographical references

Zimmermann, Warren, 1934-2004
First great triumph; how five Americans made their country a world power. Farrar, Straus & Giroux 2002 562p il $30; pa $15 **973**
1. United States—History—1898-1919
2. Spanish-American War, 1898
ISBN 0-374-17939-5; 0-374-52893-4 (pa)
     LC 2002-25015
The author credits five men "for the vision, determination and political skill that first gave the United States its global ambition. His book is a history of the American rise to power and a collective biography of [his] five heroes: Theodore Roosevelt, the assistant secretary of the Navy and later president; Alfred T. Mahan, the naval strategist; Senator Henry Cabot Lodge of Massachusetts; Secretary of State John Hay; and the first American colonial administrator, Elihu Root." N Y Times (Late N Y Ed)
Includes bibliographical references

973.02   United States—History— Miscellany. Chronologies

The **New** encyclopedia of American scandal; George Childs Kohn, editor. Facts on File 2001 455p il (Facts on File library of American history) $71.50; pa $24.95 **973.02**
ISBN 0-8160-4225-X; 0-8160-4420-1 (pa)
1. United States—History—Miscellanea LC 00-34099
First published 1989 under the authorship of George C. Kohn with title: Encyclopedia of American scandal
This compendium includes "more than 450 people and incidents from the 1600s to the present, surveying episodes of graft, bribery, deception, and outrage by people in high places. Although the tragic, career-derailing im-

pact of historic humiliations cannot be denied, this frank book entertains as well as informs." Choice
Includes bibliographical references

The **New** York Public Library American history desk reference. 2nd ed. Hyperion 2003 576p il maps pa $21.95 **973.02**
1. United States—History—Dictionaries
ISBN 0-7868-6847-3   LC 2003-56655
"A Stonesong Press book"
First published 1997 by Macmillan
This book includes "information on a variety of topics from military and foreign affairs to education and science. Information is organized into . . . timelines highlighting events throughout America's history, along with numerous sidebars, photos, maps, brief biographies, and trivia tidbits." Publisher's note
"{This is a} well-designed, convenient-size volume filled with lists, charts, tables, and short articles. . . . {This} volume should be {a} useful ready-reference compilation for public and academic libraries." Booklist {review of 1997 edition}
Includes bibliographical references

Shenkman, Richard
Legends, lies & cherished myths of American history. HarperPerennial 1989 213p il pa $13 **973.02**
1. United States—History 2. Legends—United States
ISBN 978-0-06-097261-5; 0-06-097261-0
First published 1988 by Morrow
The author "debunks a host of popular myths associated with U.S. history. From the Founding Fathers to the Reagan presidency, heretofore undisputed facts are exposed as fiction. Misquotes, misinterpretations, and downright fabrications are all duly recorded in an amusing and illuminating fashion. An irresistible browsing item." Booklist
Includes bibliographical references

973.03   United States—History— Encyclopedias and dictionaries

Cornelison, Pam
The great American history fact-finder; the who, what, where, when, and why of American history; [by] Pam Cornelison and Ted Yanak. 2nd ed, updated and expanded. Houghton Mifflin 2004 608p il, maps pa $14.95 * **973.03**
1. United States—History—Dictionaries
ISBN 0-618-43941-2   LC 2004-47480
First published 1993 with authors' names in reverse order
This book provides "information about significant persons as well as political, legal, sporting, and cultural events in American history. Entries are alphabetically arranged, and related entries cross-referenced. . . . Besides an index, there are suggested readings and information on the states, presidents, vice presidents, population, Supreme Court, Articles of Confederation, Declaration of Independence, and US Constitution (with signers and nonsigners). This is a good quick reference." Choice

Dictionary of American history; Stanley I. Kutler, editor in chief. 3rd ed. Scribner 2003 10v il map set $1,050   **973.03**
1. United States—History—Dictionaries
ISBN 0-684-80533-2   LC 2002-12433
First published 1940 in 5 volumes edited by James Truslow Adams
"This set provides 4,434 entries pertaining to American history. . . . Volumes 1-8 provide an alphabetic listing of key events, while volume 9 offers primary documents and archival maps and volume 10 offers a research guide and index to the set. Each article runs several paragraphs to several pages in length and each have a bibliography and *see also* references." Am Ref Books Annu, 2003
Includes bibliographical references

Encyclopedia of American cultural and intellectual history; edited by Mary Kupiec Cayton and Peter W. Williams. Scribner 2000 3v il set $400   **973.03**
1. United States—Civilization—Encyclopedias
2. United States—Intellectual life—Encyclopedias
ISBN 0-684-80561-8   LC 2001-20005
Art movements, education and academia, the counterculture, the sciences, domestic life, social classes, Hollywood, and post-structuralism are among the topics covered. Each article includes illustrations, boxed biographies, or documentary excerpts

Encyclopedia of American historical documents; edited by Susan Rosenfeld. Facts on File 2004 3v (Facts on File library of American history) set $300 *   **973.03**
1. United States—History—Sources
ISBN 0-8160-4995-5   LC 2003-51610
"Each section begins with an overview of the period and each document is introduced with commentary on when and why it was created and its significance, then and now. Entries include material 'with resonance for the 21st century' that represents turning points in U.S. history, and documents of a controversial nature. Students can read Supreme Court justices' opinions, presidential announcements and inaugural addresses, excerpts from noteworthy books that influenced American thought and action, and speeches of women and people of color. . . . Students and teachers will welcome this mammoth resource." SLJ
Includes bibliographical references

Encyclopedia of American history; Gary B. Nash, general editor. Facts on File 2003 11v il maps set $935   **973.03**
1. United States—History—Encyclopedias
ISBN 0-8160-4371-X   LC 2001-51278
"The volumes are organized chronologically, but the entries within each volume are alphabetical. Each book begins with a contents list, and there are copious see and cross-references. Essays of varying length cover events; 'major categories of the American experience' (education, urbanization, etc.); people, places, concepts, and more. At the end of each entry, one or more suggestions for further reading (generally adult titles) are offered. . . . This encyclopedia is a valuable resource for students of American history and can be used to support any classroom text, offering students ample opportunity for fuller exploration of topics of interest." SLJ

The **Encyclopedia** of American political history; edited by Paul Finkelman, Peter Wallenstein. CQ Press 2001 xxxii, 494p il map $140   **973.03**
1. United States—Politics and government—Encyclopedias
ISBN 1-56802-511-4   LC 00-66812
This reference tool covers "significant events, people {and} concepts in U.S. political history. Organized alphabetically, the 225 entries vary in length from a few paragraphs to several pages. The book opens with a descriptive time line of political events and ends with an appendix of acronyms and abbreviations used in U.S. history." Libr J
Includes bibliographical references

Encyclopedia of American studies; edited by George T. Kurian [et al.] Grolier Educ. 2001 4v il set $399   **973.03**
1. United States—Civilization—Encyclopedias
ISBN 0-7172-9222-3   LC 2001-23415
"Published under the sponsorship of the American Studies Association"
This work "brings together a range of topics related to the culture of the US, from political movements, arts, and religion to wars, landmark legal rulings, and technology. The preface explains the concept and discipline of 'American studies.' A table of contents groups by subject the 660 entries, nearly all written by academics. . . . Entries are clearly written with . . . interesting detail." Choice
Includes bibliographical references

Encyclopedia of rural America; the land and people; Gary A. Goreham, editor. 2nd ed. Grey House Pub. 2008 2v il map set $250   **973.03**
1. Country life—United States—Encyclopedias
2. United States—Rural conditions—Encyclopedias
3. United States—Geography—Encyclopedias
ISBN 978-1-59237-115-0; 1-59237-115-9
First published 1997 by ABC-CLIO
"This encyclopedia covers a broad range of topics, such as agriculture, the arts, economics, the environment, health, humanities, and political and social science. The . . . alphabetically arranged entries, from addiction to worker's compensation, are listed in the front of each volume for handy reference." Booklist [review of 1997 edition]
Includes bibliographical references

Encyclopedia of the new American nation; the emergence of the United States, 1754-1829; Paul Finkelman, editor in chief. Thomson Gale 2005 3v il map set $395   **973.03**
1. United States—History—1600-1775, Colonial period—Encyclopedias 2. United States—History—1775-1783, Revolution—Encyclopedias 3. United States—History—1783-1865—Encyclopedias
ISBN 0-684-31346-4   LC 2005-17783
The timeframe covered in this encyclopedia of major political events and figures "is roughly from 1754 (be-

Encyclopedia of the new American nation—
Continued
ginning of the Seven Years' War) to the inauguration of President Andrew Jackson (1829). Woven among this set of political markers and milestones are entries outlining the cultural development of the new nation, including entries on art, music, literature, dress and daily life." Publisher's note

The editor and contributors "have produced a wonderful reference source." Ref & User Services Quarterly

Includes bibliographical references

The **Greenwood** encyclopedia of American regional cultures; William Ferris, consulting editor. Greenwood Press 2004 8v il map set $699.95 * **973.03**

1. United States—Social life and customs—Encyclopedias 2. United States—Civilization—Encyclopedias
ISBN 0-313-33266-5

This "set explores the history and culture of U.S. regions from the Atlantic to the Pacific. The essay-long articles examine at length each region's art, ethnicity, fashion, film, folklore, food, literature, religion, sports, and more." Libr J

Includes bibliographical references

Olson, James Stuart, 1946-
Encyclopedia of the industrial revolution in America; {by} James S. Olson; technical editor: Robert L. Shadle. Greenwood Press 2002 xxv, 313p il $69.95 **973.03**

1. Industrial revolution—Encyclopedias
ISBN 0-313-30830-6 LC 00-52129

This encyclopedia offers "coverage of the economic, political, and social developments of the Industrial Revolution in the United States from 1750 to 1920. . . . Highlights of the work include . . . entries on developments in water and rail transportation, agriculture, manufacturing, mass production, the labor movement, big government, and the key inventions that changed the American economy." Publisher's note

"A well-organized and comprehensive ready reference." Voice Youth Advocates

Includes bibliographical references

The **Oxford** companion to United States history; editor in chief, Paul S. Boyer; editors, Melvyn Dubofsky {et al.}. Oxford Univ. Press 2001 xliv, 940p il maps $75 **973.03**

1. United States—History—Dictionaries
ISBN 0-19-508209-5 LC 00-55801

First published 1966 under the authorship of Thomas A. Johnson with title: The Oxford companion to American history

This reference work contains 1,400 alphabetically arranged signed entries. See and see also references are provided. Coverage starts with the colonial period and examines notable men and women and major events in U.S. history

Includes bibliographical references

973.06 United States—History— Organizations

American Association for State and Local History
Directory of historical organizations in the United States and Canada. 15th ed. American Assn. for State & Local Hist. 2002 1358p pa $149.95 **973.06**

1. United States—History—Societies—Directories
ISBN 0-7591-0002-0

First published 1956 with title: Directory of historical societies and agencies in the United States and Canada. Periodically revised

This publication "lists historical societies geographically, giving mailing address, number of members, museums, hours and size of library, publication program, etc." Ref Sources for Small & Medium-sized Libr. 5th edition

973.1 United States—Early history to 1607

Schneider, Paul
Brutal journey: the epic story of the first crossing of North America. Holt 2006 366p il maps $26 **973.1**

1. Narváez, Pánfilo de, d. 1528 2. America—Exploration
ISBN 978-0-8050-6835-1; 0-8050-6835-X
LC 2005-50246

"A John McRae book"

This is an account of a "failed expedition to the New World. . . . In 1527, Panfilo de Narvaez led some 400 men on an expedition to Florida. Four survived." N Y Times Book Rev

"Equally able in his dramatizations of the privations and brutalities suffusing this extraordinary tale, Schneider scores big with fans of historical (mis)adventure." Booklist

Includes bibliographical references

973.2 United States—Colonial period, 1607-1775

Anderson, Fred, 1949-
The crucible of war; the Seven Years' War and the fate of empire in British North America, 1754-1766; with illustrations from the William L. Clements Library. Knopf 2000 862p il pa $21 hardcover o.p. **973.2**

1. Seven Years' War, 1756-1763 2. United States—History—1600-1775, Colonial period
ISBN 0-375-70636-4 (pa) LC 99-18512

The author "demonstrates that the conflict was more than just a peripheral squabble that anticipated the American Revolution. Not only did the war decisively alter relations among the French, the English and the Native American allies of the two powers, who for decades had played the English and French off one another to their

Anderson, Fred, 1949——*Continued*

own advantage, but just as critical, argues Anderson, the war also changed the character of British imperialism, with the mother country trying to reshape the terms of empire and the colonists' place in it." Publ Wkly

The dominion of war; empire and liberty in North America, 1500-2000; [by] Fred Anderson and Andrew Cayton. Viking 2005 520p il maps $27.95; pa $16   **973.2**
1. United States—Military history 2. United States—Territorial expansion
ISBN 0-670-03370-7; 0-14-303651-3 (pa)
The authors provide an "account of the U.S. rise to global preeminence over five centuries. Central to their thesis is the assertion that military conflict has been essential in determining the cultural and political evolution of North America. . . . Anderson and Cayton have provided a well-written and important reinterpretation of our past." Booklist
Includes bibliographical references

Bailyn, Bernard

The peopling of British North America; an introduction. Knopf 1986 177p pa $12 hardcover o.p.   **973.2**
1. United States—History—1600-1775, Colonial period
ISBN 0-394-75779-3 (pa)   LC 85-82144
In this introductory volume of a projected multivolume work, the author "gives first airing to his overall argument on settling patterns in history. Though designed to introduce the subsequent volumes, this superbly articulate study is understandable on its own." Booklist
Includes bibliographical references

Boorstin, Daniel J., 1914-2004

The Americans: The colonial experience. Random House 1958 434p pa $15 hardcover o.p.   **973.2**
1. United States—Civilization 2. United States—History—1600-1775, Colonial period 3. American national characteristics 4. United States—Intellectual life
ISBN 0-394-70513-0 (pa)
The first volume of the author's trilogy entitled: The Americans
"This study of colonial America attempts to show that it was not merely an offshoot of the mother country, but a new civilization. . . . The author centers his highly informative work on colonial education, the special qualities of American speech, and the growth of a distinct culture." Booklist
Includes bibliographical references

Demos, John, 1937-

The unredeemed captive; a family story from early America. Knopf 1994 315p maps pa $14 hardcover o.p.   **973.2**
1. Williams, Eunice, 1696-1786 2. Williams family 3. Williams, John, 1664-1729 4. Mohawk Indians 5. Massachusetts—History—1600-1775, Colonial period
ISBN 0-679-75961-1 (pa)   LC 93-23907

John Williams, "a Puritan minister, and his family were captured in 1704 in their Massachusetts home by a group of Frenchmen and Native Americans, and forced to march to Canada. Although he and four of his children were later released, his wife died on the march and his daughter, Eunice, became a convert to Catholicism and married a Native American. Despite the ongoing attempts of her father and brother to persuade Eunice to return to Massachusetts, she would agree only to brief visits and lived in a Native American settlement until her death at the age of 95." Publ Wkly
This "is a lively introduction to an authentically multicultural colonial North America." N Y Times Book Rev

Fowler, William M., 1944-

Empires at war; the French & Indian War and the struggle for North America, 1754-1763; [by] William M. Fowler, Jr. Walker & Company 2005 xxv, 332p il maps $27; pa $15   **973.2**
1. United States—History—1755-1763, French and Indian War
ISBN 0-8027-1411-0; 0-8027-7737-6 (pa)
      LC 2004-43064
In this history of the French and Indian War, the author "glances occasionally at the European and Caribbean theaters of this 'first world war,' but concentrates on the North American operations that determined Britain's victory over France in the struggle for imperial supremacy. . . . The result is a judicious, well-paced and engaging introduction to a turning point in American and world history." Publ Wkly
Includes bibliographical references

Hawke, David Freeman

Everyday life in early America. Harper & Row 1988 195p il (Everyday life in America) pa $13 hardcover o.p.   **973.2**
1. United States—History—1600-1775, Colonial period 2. United States—Social life and customs
ISBN 0-06-091251-0 (pa)   LC 87-17667
The author "provides enlightening and colorful descriptions of early Colonial Americans and debunks many widely held assumptions about 17th century settlers." Publ Wkly
Includes bibliographical references

Lepore, Jill, 1966-

The name of war; King Philip's War and the origins of American identity. Knopf 1998 xxviii, 337p il maps pa $15 hardcover o.p.   **973.2**
1. King Philip's War, 1675-1676 2. Native Americans—Wars 3. Great Britain—Colonies—America
ISBN 0-375-70262-8 (pa)   LC 97-2820
"Lepore's history of King Philip's War, deals with what happened in New England and what sense the participants and their heirs have made of it over the years." N Y Times Book Rev
"This is a powerful book that doesn't shy away from depicting the sheer horror of what must be termed a race war." Booklist
Includes bibliographical references

Philbrick, Nathaniel
Mayflower; a story of courage, community, and war. Viking 2006 461p il $29.95 *
973.2
1. Pilgrims (New England colonists) 2. Massachusetts—History—1600-1775, Colonial period
ISBN 0-670-03760-5; 978-0-670-03760-5
LC 2005-58470
This is the "story of the Plymouth Colony." Publisher's note
The author "has written a judicious, fascinating work of revisionist history. 'Mayflower' is a surprise-filled account of what are supposed to be some of the best-known events in this country's past but are instead an occasion for collective amnesia." N Y Times (Late N Y Ed)
Includes bibliographical references

Schultz, Eric B., 1957-
King Philip's War; the history and legacy of America's forgotten conflict; {by} Eric B. Schultz, Michael J. Tougias. Countryman Press 1999 416p il maps pa $18.95 hardcover o.p.
973.2
1. King Philip's War, 1675-1676 2. Native Americans—Government relations 3. New England—History—1600-1775, Colonial period
ISBN 0-88150-483-1 (pa)
LC 99-23481
The first part of this volume provides a "chronological retelling of the war. The second part, organized geographically and the heart of the volume, takes readers through New England to various sites associated with the conflict. . . . The third part offers three contemporary narratives reflecting the significance of the war on the people of the era. Useful maps assist the reader throughout." Libr J
Includes bibliographical references

973.3 United States—Periods of Revolution and Confederation, 1775-1789

The **American** Revolution; writings from the War of Independence. Library of Am. 2001 878p $40
973.3
1. United States—History—1775-1783, Revolution
ISBN 1-88301-191-4
LC 00-45373
This collection includes "over 120 pieces by more than 70 Revolution-era writers from both sides of the War of Independence. The book begins with Paul Revere's personal account of his famous ride in April 1775 and ends with a description of George Washington's resignation from the command of the Continental Army in December 1783. . . . At the book's end one can find a long section that includes a chronology, biographical sketches of the authors, and other notes on the texts." Libr J
"This work will serve as a marvelous research tool for specialists, but general readers with an interest in American history will also find fascinating gems." Booklist
Includes bibliographical references

Becker, Carl, 1873-1945
The Declaration of Independence; a study in the history of political ideas. Knopf 1942 286p pa $11 hardcover o.p.
973.3
1. Jefferson, Thomas, 1743-1826 2. United States. Declaration of Independence 3. United States—Politics and government—1775-1783, Revolution
ISBN 0-394-70060-0 (pa)
A reprint, with a new preface, of a book first published 1922 by Harcourt Brace & Co.
"A study of the Declaration, the philosophy that lay behind it, the history of its several drafts, an estimate of its literary quality." Wis Libr Bull
Includes bibliographical references

Blumrosen, Alfred W.
Slave nation; how slavery united the colonies & sparked the American Revolution; [by] Alfred W. Blumrosen and Ruth G. Blumrosen; introduction by Eleanor Holmes Norton. Sourcebooks 2005 336p il map $24.95
973.3
1. Slavery—United States 2. United States—History—1775-1783, Revolution—Causes
ISBN 1-4022-0400-0
LC 2004-27271
The authors "use the Somerset case of 1772, which freed all slaves in Britain, to illustrate how the price of freedom from English rule ensured continued bondage for slaves in the American South. The Blumrosens argue that Southerners feared that the ruling might be extended to the entire empire and therefore joined the move to win independence from Britain. . . . This well-researched book is sure to be controversial." Libr J
Includes bibliographical references

Bobrick, Benson, 1947-
Angel in the whirlwind; the triumph of the American Revolution. Penguin Bks. 1998 553p map pa $18
973.3
1. United States—History—1775-1783, Revolution
ISBN 0-14-027500-2; 978-0-14-027500-1
LC 97-11320
First published 1997 by Simon & Schuster
This survey of the American Revolution ranges "from the end of the French and Indian War to the end of the Revolutionary War, with brief coverage of the framing of the Constitution and the inauguration of Washington." Libr J
"Many of the stories are familiar—Paul Revere's ride, Arnold's descent into infamy—but the book's strength lies in its many lesser-known details on the battlefield and beyond. . . . Though the format demands only brief treatment of complicated issues, what emerges is a highly impressive show of exhaustive research and engaging storytelling." Publ Wkly
Includes bibliographical references

Cohen, I. Bernard, 1914-2003

Science and the founding fathers; science in the political thought of Jefferson, Franklin, Adams and Madison. Norton 1995 368p il pa $15.95 hardcover o.p.   **973.3**

1. Franklin, Benjamin, 1706-1790 2. Jefferson, Thomas, 1743-1826 3. Madison, James, 1751-1836 4. Adams, John Quincy, 1767-1848 5. Political science 6. Science—United States—History

ISBN 0-393-31510-X (pa)   LC 94-26731

The author "analyzes how Thomas Jefferson, Benjamin Franklin, John Adams, and James Madison incorporated their scientific beliefs and knowledge into their political lives. Cohen examines each man's scientific education and then searches for examples of how that knowledge was expressed in their published works. He looks closely at phrases from the Declaration of Independence and the Constitution and shows that they have a Newtonian basis." Libr J

Davis, William C., 1946-

Battle at Bull Run; a history of the first major campaign of the Civil War. Louisiana State University Press 1981 298p il map pa $19.95
                                             973.3
1. Bull Run, 1st Battle of, 1861

ISBN 978-0-8071-0867-3; 0-8071-0867-7

First published 1977 by Doubleday

In this account of the war's first major engagement Davis' "sketches of the commanders, which will particularly delight Civil War enthusiasts, delve into the officer's backgrounds and unusual characteristics and include critical appraisals of their leadership capabilities. In addition, Davis includes fascinating human interest stories about the troops." Libr J

Includes bibliographical references

Draper, Theodore, 1912-2006

A struggle for power; the American Revolution. Times Bks. 1996 544p pa $13.56 hardcover o.p.
                                             973.3
1. United States—History—1775-1783, Revolution

ISBN 0-679-77642-7 (pa)   LC 95-11605

The author "maintains that the Revolution was really a power struggle spawned by the British system of chartering colonies, which placed fiscal control of public funds with the colonial assemblies." Libr J

This is an "elegantly written, masterful study. . . . Drawing freely on period pamphlets, letters, petitions, travelogues and assembly minutes, [the author] vividly evokes the populist discontent, intellectual gymnastics and mob violence that led to revolution." Publ Wkly

Includes bibliographical references

Dunn, Susan, 1945-

Sister revolutions; French lightning, American light. Faber & Faber 1999 258p il pa $14 hardcover o.p.   **973.3**
1. United States—History—1775-1783, Revolution 2. France—History—1789-1799, Revolution

ISBN 0-571-19989-5 (pa)   LC 99-18178

"The American Revolution, according to Dunn, was more peaceful and practical, in part because its leaders were both intellectuals and men of political experience. The French Revolution, on the other hand, veered into extravagant abstractions because its leaders were intellectuals with litttle or no previous political experience. This book is clearly written and should appeal particularly to undergraduate students and members of the general public." Choice

Includes bibliographical references

Ellis, Joseph J.

American creation; triumphs and tragedies at the founding of the republic. A. A. Knopf 2007 283p
                                             973.3
1. United States—History—1775-1783, Revolution 2. United States—History—1783-1809 3. United States—Politics and government—1775-1783, Revolution 4. United States—Politics and government—1783-1809

ISBN 978-0-307-26369-8; 0-307-26369-X

                                        LC 2007-5273

The author "selects 'certain propitious moments' from the American Revolution and early republic, dramatizes them, and analyzes their crucial ramifications for America's future. . . . A history bound for phenomenal popularity." Booklist

Includes bibliographical references

Ferling, John E.

Setting the world ablaze; Washington, Adams, and Jefferson and the American Revolution; {by} John Ferling. Oxford Univ. Press 2000 xxiv, 392p il maps pa $19.95 hardcover o.p.   **973.3**
1. Washington, George, 1732-1799 2. Adams, John, 1735-1826 3. Jefferson, Thomas, 1743-1826 4. United States—History—1775-1783, Revolution

ISBN 0-19-515084-8 (pa)   LC 99-89686

In this history Ferling profiles "the three men who were, in his view, the most important leaders of the American Revolution. Thomas Jefferson was the 'pen,' John Adams the 'tongue,' and George Washington the 'sword.' Ferling's command of the material is surefooted, though not everyone will agree with his views." Libr J

Includes bibliographical references

Fischer, David Hackett

Paul Revere's ride. Oxford Univ. Press 1994 445p il maps $37.50; pa $19.95   **973.3**
1. Revere, Paul, 1735-1818 2. Lexington (Mass.), Battle of, 1775 3. Concord (Mass.), Battle of, 1775

ISBN 0-19-508847-6; 0-19-509831-5 (pa)

                                        LC 93-25739

"Fischer's solid study of Paul Revere and his infamous ride debunks the myths surrounding the event, reconstructing the circumstances leading to the Battle of Lexington and Concord. Fischer's extensive use of primary sources affords an intimate glimpse of the participants' thoughts and feelings." Booklist

Includes bibliographical references

Fischer, David Hackett—*Continued*

Washington's crossing. Oxford University Press 2004 564p il maps (Pivotal moments in American history) $35; pa $16.95   **973.3**
   1. Washington, George, 1732-1799 2. United States—History—1775-1783, Revolution—Campaigns
   ISBN 0-19-517034-2; 0-19-518159-X (pa)
                  LC 2003-19858
   The author describes how "Washington, his officers, and their men turn the early military defeats of Long Island and New York City into victory at Trenton and Princeton. The opening chapter is devoted to the painting *Washington Crossing the Delaware*. Then the author discusses the British, Hessian, and American military units that were involved in these campaigns and gives background on their officers. This is Fischer's strong suit: he tells stories and gives details that bring history alive. . . . In the hands of such a thorough researcher and talented writer, this is powerful stuff." SLJ
   Includes bibliographical references

Fleming, Thomas J., 1927-

Washington's secret war; the hidden history of Valley Forge; [by] Thomas Fleming. Smithsonian Books/Collins 2005 384p il map $27.95; pa $14.95
                          973.3
   1. Washington, George, 1732-1799—Military leadership 2. United States. Continental Army 3. United States—History—1775-1783, Revolution—Campaigns
   ISBN 0-06-082962-1; 0-06-087293-4 (pa)
                  LC 2005-52157
   The author "writes of the trials and tribulations of George Washington as he led the Continental Army during the infamous Valley Forge winter of 1777-78. . . . Fleming's point is that he was not simply fighting the elements and attacks by the nearby British; he was also reckoning with members of the Continental Congress and fellow army officers who deemed him inadequate." Libr J
   "Fleming has provided an original and provocative reinterpretation of a critical period in the struggle for independence." Booklist
   Includes bibliographical references

Foner, Eric

Tom Paine and Revolutionary America. Updated ed. Oxford University Press 2005 xxxvi, 326p $71.50; pa $34.95   **973.3**
   1. Paine, Thomas, 1737-1809 2. United States—Politics and government—1775-1783, Revolution 3. United States—Economic conditions—1775-1783, Revolution 4. United States—Social conditions
   ISBN 0-19-517486-0; 0-19-517485-2 (pa)
                  LC 2004-54799
   First published 1976
   The author examines the roots of Paine's thought within the social, economic and political context of colonial America
   Includes bibliographical references

Hibbert, Christopher, 1924-

Redcoats and rebels; the American Revolution through British eyes. Norton 1990 xx, 375p il maps hardcover o.p. pa $18.95 *   **973.3**
   1. United States—History—1775-1783, Revolution
   ISBN 0-393-02895-X; 0-393-32293-9 (pa)
                  LC 90-31753
   Beginning with the Stamp Act of 1765 "the author interprets the War for Independence as viewed by the mother country: more a dirty insurrection than the sacred pursuit of liberty." Booklist
   "Mr. Hibbert has an eye for the telling anecdote and the graphic quotation, and his bibliography indicates that he has consulted a wealth of manuscript material as well as research published during the last 30 years that illuminates what lay behind the British defeat." N Y Times Book Rev

Howard, Hugh

Houses of the founding fathers; original photography by Roger Straus III. Artisan 2007 354p il $50   **973.3**
   1. Statesmen—United States 2. Politicians—United States 3. Historic buildings—United States 4. United States—Local history
   ISBN 978-1-57965-275-3; 1-57965-275-1
                  LC 2006-48015
   "A prolific and popular architecture writer specializing in Colonial and early American historic preservation, teams up with veteran architecture photographer . . . to offer a sumptuously illustrated American history primer-cum-historic house tour. . . . A pleasantly flowing text interweaves historic events, details of daily life, personal anecdotes, and architectural insights into descriptions of the homes built and occupied by the era's upper social stratum." Libr J
   Includes bibliographical references

Ketchum, Richard M., 1922-

Saratoga; turning point of America's Revolutionary War. Holt & Co. 1997 545p il maps pa $18 hardcover o.p.   **973.3**
   1. Saratoga Campaign, 1777
   ISBN 0-8050-6123-1 (pa)   LC 97-2773
   A "narrative account of the Saratoga campaign of 1777. . . . Ketchum provides the full political context within which the fighting took place while penning dozens of colorful portraits of the principal characters. The author also succeeds in his goal of telling the story from the perspective of the participants, illustrating what the American Revolution in upstate New York meant for soldiers and civilians alike." Libr J
   Includes bibliographical references

Maier, Pauline, 1938-

American scripture; making the Declaration of Independence. Knopf 1997 xxi, 304p pa $14 hardcover o.p.   **973.3**
   1. United States. Declaration of Independence 2. United States—Politics and government—1775-1783, Revolution
   ISBN 0-679-77908-6 (pa)   LC 97-2769

Maier, Pauline, 1938---*Continued*

"In the spring of 1776, with a British invasion fleet on its way, the Second Continental Congress appointed a committee to compose a statement explaining America's decision to seek independence. Thomas Jefferson was the principal drafter of the statement, but Maier makes it clear that his task was to express the sentiments of the Congress, not his personal views, and she shows that when the congressmen edited his draft they improved it greatly (rather than 'mangling' it, as Jefferson ever after maintained). The Declaration of Independence is, she argues, a profoundly collective document, both in its origins and in our still-evolving interpretation of its self-evident truths." New Yorker

McCullough, David G., 1933-

1776; [by] David McCullough. Simon & Schuster 2005 386p il map $32   **973.3**
1. United States—History—1775-1783, Revolution
ISBN 0-7432-2671-2   LC 2005-42505
The author provides "account of the year that began with the humiliating British abandonment of Boston and ended with Washington's small but symbolically important triumph at Trenton. In between, McCullough recounts the American disaster at Brooklyn and the demoralizing retreat across New Jersey." Booklist
"This is a narrative tour de force, exhibiting all the hallmarks the author is known for: fascinating subject matter, expert research and detailed, graceful prose." Publ Wkly
Includes bibliographical references

Middlekauff, Robert

The glorious cause; the American Revolution, 1763-1789. Rev. and expanded ed. Oxford University Press 2004 736p il map (Oxford history of the United States) $37.50 *   **973.3**
1. United States—History—1775-1783, Revolution
ISBN 0-19-516247-1   LC 2004-16295
First published 1982
"Beginning with the French and Indian War and continuing to the election of George Washington as first president, Robert Middlekauff offers a . . . history of the conflict between England and America." Publisher's note
"This is narrative history at its best, written in a conversational and engaging style." Libr J
Includes bibliographical references

Morgan, Edmund Sears

The birth of the Republic, 1763-89. 3rd ed. University of Chicago Press 1992 206p (Chicago history of American civilization) hardcover o.p. pa $13 *   **973.3**
1. United States—History—1775-1783, Revolution
2. United States—History—1783-1809
ISBN 0-226-53756-0; 0-226-53757-9 (pa)
    LC 92-8871
First published 1956
A brief study of the American revolutionary period from 1763 to 1789.
Includes bibliographical references

Raphael, Ray

A people's history of the American Revolution; how common people shaped the fight for independence. 1st Perennial ed. Perennial 2002 506p pa $13.95 *   **973.3**
1. United States—History—1775-1783, Revolution
ISBN 0-06-000440-1   LC 2002-16992
First published 2001 by New Press
This volume "collects the experiences of ordinary people during the American Revolution and sutures them into a story. And that story is that the rebellion and war inescapably influenced everyone—farmers, townspeople, women, Indians, free blacks and enslaved blacks, plutocrats and proletarians." Booklist
"Moving from broad overviews to stories of small groups or individuals, Raphael's study is impressive in both its sweep and its attention to the particular." Publ Wkly
Includes bibliographical references

Tuchman, Barbara Wertheim

The first salute; [by] Barbara W. Tuchman. Knopf 1988 347p il maps hardcover o.p. pa $16.95   **973.3**
1. United States—History—1775-1783, Revolution
ISBN 0-394-55333-0; 0-345-33667-4 (pa)
    LC 88-45216
"'The first salute' accorded to the striped flag of the thirteen States was given by a Dutch colony, St. Eustatius, in November, 1776. The subject of this study is the contribution of the Dutch and the French, to the independence of the United States." West Coast Rev Books
"The book is a tightly woven narrative, ingeniously structured. It is not a blow-by-blow account of the conflict; familiarity with issues and events is assumed. Instead, Tuchman takes a specific incident and through it elucidates the course and outcome of the war." Christ Sci Monit
Includes bibliographical references

Weintraub, Stanley

Iron tears; America's battle for freedom, Britain's quagmire, 1775-1783. Free Press 2005 375p il maps $28   **973.3**
1. United States—History—1775-1783, Revolution
ISBN 0-7432-2687-9   LC 2004-56363
The author "examines the possibility that the British lost the war because of protest and lack of support at home. . . . The British failure to win a war against ill-trained but determined guerrilla forces in often unpredictable circumstances and weather appears now as an eerie harbinger of modern conflicts such as the Vietnam War. Weintraub's fast-paced narrative and impeccable historical research provide a stimulating challenge to conventional histories of the Revolutionary War that focus exclusively on the heroism of American forces." Publ Wkly
Includes bibliographical references

Wood, Gordon S.

The radicalism of the American Revolution. Knopf 1992 447p pa $16 hardcover o.p.

973.3

1. United States—Politics and government—1775-1783, Revolution 2. United States—History—1775-1783, Revolution 3. United States—Social life and customs

ISBN 0-679-73688-3 (pa) LC 91-19719

"Under the broad categories of monarchy, republicanism, and democracy, Wood explains how the US was transformed from a society that took for granted a non-working elite and a dependent servile underclass to one in which the free-standing individualist, who worked for a living, became the norm. . . . {A} readable book based on hundreds of primary and secondary sources." Choice

Includes bibliographical references

973.4   United States—Constitutional period, 1789-1809

Cerami, Charles A.

Jefferson's great gamble; the remarkable story of Jefferson, Napoleon and the men behind the Louisiana Purchase. Sourcebooks 2003 309p il $22.95; pa $14.95 **973.4**

1. Jefferson, Thomas, 1743-1826 2. Napoleon I, Emperor of the French, 1769-1821 3. Louisiana Purchase

ISBN 1-57071-945-4; 1-40220-240-7 (pa)

LC 2002-153440

In this history of the Louisiana Purchase, the author gives a "retelling of the long and tangled negotiations between a team of Americans (chiefly Thomas Jefferson, Robert Livingston, James Madison, and James Monroe) and a rival team of Frenchmen (chiefly Napoleon and his adviser, Talleyrand)." Libr J

"Anyone wanting to read the story of a momentous turning point in American history, a story of diplomatic maneuvering and international politics, will be hard-pressed to find a better version than this." Publ Wkly

Includes bibliographical references

Ellis, Joseph J.

American sphinx: the character of Thomas Jefferson. Knopf 1997 365p $29.95; pa $15

973.4

ISBN 0-679-44490-4; 0-679-76441-0 (pa)

1. Jefferson, Thomas, 1743-1826 LC 96-26171

This biography focuses on "various important junctures of Jefferson's life (his tenures as minister to France, secretary of state, and, of course, president, among others) and major aspects of his personal consciousness (from his conduct of romance to his attitude toward slavery)." Booklist

"Penetrating Jefferson's placid, elegant facade, this extraordinary biography brings the sage of Monticello down to earth without either condemning or idolizing him." Publ Wkly

Founding brothers; the revolutionary generation. Knopf 2000 288p $26.95; pa $14 **973.4**

1. United States—History—1783-1809 2. United States—Politics and government—1783-1809 3. Presidents—United States 4. United States—Biography

ISBN 0-375-40544-5; 0-375-70524-4 (pa)

LC 99-59304

This study looks at the intertwined lives of "Benjamin Franklin, Thomas Jefferson, John Adams, Alexander Hamilton, James Madison and Aaron Burr. . . . As Ellis sees it, the founding brethren not only 'created the American republic' but 'held it together throughout the volatile and vulnerable early years by sustaining their presence until national habits and customs took root.'" NY Times Book Rev

"Ellis' essays are angled, fascinating, and perfect for general-interest readers." Booklist

Includes bibliographical references

Freeman, Joanne B.

Affairs of honor; national politics in the new republic. Yale Univ. Press 2001 xxiv, 376p $29.95; pa $16.95 **973.4**

1. United States—Politics and government—1783-1865

ISBN 0-300-08877-9; 0-300-09755-7 (pa)

LC 2001-915

According to Freeman, an "honor culture" structured the American founders' "political status before political parties developed. In those early years, she argues, 'the culture of honor met with a burgeoning democracy and an ambiguous egalitarian ethic of republicanism; the former questioned assumptions about political leadership, the latter renounced the trappings of aristocracy without offering a defined alternative.' . . . [Freeman describes] national politics in the new nation, devotes chapters to three major techniques wielded by political players—political gossip, 'a paper war,' and dueling—and then examines, as a case study, the 1800 presidential election." Booklist

"Freeman's prose is lively, and she balances entertaining narrative with sharp analysis." Publ Wkly

Includes bibliographical references

Gordon-Reed, Annette

Thomas Jefferson and Sally Hemings; an American controversy. University Press of Va. 1997 xx, 288p pa $14.95 hardcover o.p.

973.4

1. Hemings, Sally, 1773-1835

ISBN 0-8139-1833-2 (pa) LC 96-34550

"Hemings, a slave who was one-quarter African, was also a half sister of Jefferson's deceased wife, and she lived at Monticello for many years. In this understated, brilliant study an African-American law professor examines the allegation that Jefferson was the father of Hemings' children." New Yorker

Includes bibliographical references

Hamilton, Alexander, 1757-1804
Writings. Library of Am. 2001 1108p $40
                        973.4
1. United States—Politics and government—1775-1783, Revolution 2. United States—Politics and government—1783-1809
ISBN 1-931082-04-9   LC 2001-23043
"The text consists of more than 170 letters, speeches, essays, reports, and memoranda written between 1769 and 1804, including all of Hamilton's material presented in The Federalist. This additionally sports several conflicting eyewitness accounts of Hamilton's lethal duel with Aaron Burr." Libr J
Includes bibliographical references

Hogeland, William
The Whiskey Rebellion; George Washington, Alexander Hamilton, and the frontier rebels who challenged America's newfound sovereignty. Scribner 2006 302p map $26.95 *   **973.4**
1. Whiskey Rebellion, Pa., 1794
ISBN 978-0-7432-5490-8; 0-7432-5490-2
                        LC 2005-56340
"A Lisa Drew book"
"Soon after Americans ousted inequitable British taxation, Secretary of Finance Alexander Hamilton, hatched a plan to put the new nation on steady financial footing by imposing the first American excise tax, on whiskey makers. The tax favored large distillers over small farmers with stills in the mountains of Pennsylvania, Maryland and Virginia, and the farmers fomented their own new revolution—a challenge to the sovereignty of the new government and the power of the wealthy eastern seaboard. In a fast-paced, blow-by-blow account of this 'primal national drama,' journalist Hogeland energetically chronicles the skirmishes that made the Whiskey Rebellion from 1791 to 1795 a symbol of the conflict between republican ideals and capitalist values." Publ Wkly
Includes bibliographical references

Kukla, Jon, 1948-
A wilderness so immense; the Louisiana Purchase and the destiny of America. Knopf 2003 430p il map $30; pa $16   **973.4**
1. Louisiana Purchase
ISBN 0-375-40812-6; 0-375-70761-1 (pa)
                        LC 2002-27395
Kukla discusses the "struggles in the 1780's and 90's for unimpeded use of the {Mississippi} river and its southernmost port {New Orleans}. . . . So alarmed by westward expansion were some new Englanders in the 1780's that they started a separatist movement. . . . After the {Louisiana} Purchase in {1803}, Jeffersonian Republicans rejoiced in the ties that would bind East and West." N Y Times Book Rev
"This judicious, aptly illustrated work will gratify all its readers. Rarely does a work of history combine grace of writing with such broad authority." Publ Wkly
Includes bibliographical references

The **Louisiana** Purchase; a historical and geographical encyclopedia; Junius P. Rodriguez, editor. ABC-CLIO 2002 xxxv, 513p il maps $95
                        973.4
1. Louisiana Purchase 2. United States—History—1783-1809
ISBN 1-57607-188-X   LC 2002-3228
"The reasons for as well as the immediate and historical repercussions of the purchase are explored in nearly 300 articles written by 85 distinguished scholars. Coverage includes native peoples, noteworthy personalities, and geographical areas associated with a land acquisition that nearly doubled the size of our nation. An extensive bibliography, 49 pertinent documents, a chronology, and an index round out this excellent volume." Libr J
Includes bibliographical references

Miller, John Chester, 1907-1991
The Federalist era, 1789-1801; by John C. Miller. Waveland Press 1998 304p il pa $16.95
                        973.4
1. Hamilton, Alexander, 1757-1804 2. Jefferson, Thomas, 1743-1826 3. Federal Party (U.S.) 4. United States—History—1783-1809
ISBN 978-1-57766-031-6; 1-57766-031-5
First published 1960 by Harper & Row
A chronicle of the administrations of George Washington and John Adams, concentrating on the politics and diplomacy.
Includes bibliographical references

Purcell, Sarah J.
The early national period; [by] Sarah Purcell. Facts on File 2004 420p il map (Eyewitness history) $75   **973.4**
1. United States—History—1783-1865
ISBN 0-8160-4769-3   LC 2003-14969
Contents: Post-revolutionary change: 1783-1786; Making a new Constitution: 1787-1788; A new nation: 1789-1792; Federalist order: 1793-1796; Federalist disorder: 1797-1800; Jeffersonian America: 1801-1803; Rising conflict: 1804-1807; Commercial crisis and the clamor for war: 1808-1811; The War of 1812: 1812-1815; The era of good feelings?: 1816-1819; Economic crisis, political stability: 1820-1823; Democracy: 1824-1828
"The introduction to each section summarizes major events and provides excerpts from primary resources including speeches, letters, newspaper accounts, diary entries, and advertisements." SLJ
"A serious history student will find this book invaluable." Libr Media Connect
Includes bibliographical references

Staloff, Darren, 1961-
Hamilton, Adams, Jefferson; the politics of enlightenment and the American founding. Hill & Wang 2005 419p $30   **973.4**
1. Hamilton, Alexander, 1757-1804 2. Adams, John, 1735-1826 3. Jefferson, Thomas, 1743-1826 4. Enlightenment
ISBN 0-8090-7784-1; 978-0-8090-7784-7
                        LC 2005-40433

Staloff, Darren, 1961-—*Continued*
The author "provides a biographical and intellectual comparison among three major early American statesmen. He shows how the personal experiences and regional cultural traditions of each man shaded his interpretation of the European Enlightenment." Libr J
"Staloff has created a work that is a must-read for any serious scholar of US history." Choice
Includes bibliographical references

Vidal, Gore, 1925-
Inventing a nation: Washington, Adams, Jefferson. Yale University Press 2003 224p $22; pa $14   **973.4**
1. Washington, George, 1732-1799 2. Adams, John, 1735-1826 3. Jefferson, Thomas, 1743-1826
ISBN 0-300-10171-6; 0-300-10592-4 (pa)
LC 2003-015612
"Mr. Vidal covers roughly the period from the making of the Constitution through Washington's two presidencies and Adams's single . . . one, to Jefferson's first great presidential move: the . . . acquisition in 1803 of a huge expanse of western territory—the Louisiana Purchase—from Napoleon." NY Times (Late N Y Ed)
Vidal offers "characteristically brilliant and acerbic reflections on power and personality. . . . This entertaining and enlightening reappraisal of the Founders is a must for buffs of American civilization and its discontents." Booklist

Washington, George, 1732-1799
Writings. Library of Am. 1997 xxiii, 1149p $40
*   **973.4**
1. Virginia—History 2. United States—Politics and government—1775-1783, Revolution 3. United States—Politics and government—1783-1809
ISBN 1-883011-23-X   LC 96-9665
This "selection of Washington's letters, speeches, diary entries, maxims and military orders reveals a writer of surprising versatility and a statesman consciously involved with the forging of our national character." Publ Wkly

Wills, Garry, 1934-
Henry Adams and the making of America. Houghton Mifflin 2005 467p hardcover o.p. pa $15.95   **973.4**
1. Adams, Henry, 1838-1918 2. United States—Historiography
ISBN 0-618-13430-1; 0-618-87266-3 (pa)
LC 2005-40305
The author examines "the nine volumes of Henry Adams's little-studied history of the United States from 1800 to 1817 and proclaims it to be both 'a prose masterpiece' and a model for how to research and write history." Publ Wkly
"Those unfamiliar with Adams' historical writings will find Wills a helpful and accessible guide; those who know Adams already will enjoy revisiting his histories with this knowledgeable and learned companion." Foreign Affairs
Includes bibliographical references

Zacks, Richard
The pirate coast; Thomas Jefferson, the first marines, and the secret mission of 1805. Hyperion 2005 432p il map $25.95; pa $15.95
973.4
1. Eaton, William, 1764-1811 2. Jefferson, Thomas, 1743-1826 3. United States—History—1801-1805, Tripolitan War
ISBN 1-401-30003-0; 1-401-30849-X (pa)
LC 2004-60635
The focus of this book "is on the long-forgotten William Eaton, dispatched by Jefferson to lead a column of troops, including eight U.S. marines, overland from Egypt to Tripoli to overthrow the Bashaw, or Pasha." Libr J
"This is the book that Captain Eaton has long deserved." Publ Wkly
Includes bibliographical references

973.5   United States—1809-1845

Encyclopedia of the United States in the nineteenth century; Paul Finkelman, editor in chief. Scribner 2001 3v il maps set $400
973.5
1. United States—History—19th century—Encyclopedias
ISBN 0-684-80500-6   LC 00-45811
In this historical overview: "population, politics and government, economy and work, society and culture, religion, social problems and reform, everyday life, and foreign policy are explored in more than 600 A-to-Z articles. Complete with more than 400 illustrations and maps, this set includes . . . {a} year-by-year chronology, original documents {and} tables." Publisher's note

Groom, Winston, 1944-
Patriotic fire; Andrew Jackson and Jean Laffite at the Battle of New Orleans. Alfred A. Knopf 2006 xxiv, 292p il map $26   **973.5**
1. Jackson, Andrew, 1767-1845 2. Laffite, Jean, 1780?-1825? 3. New Orleans (La.), Battle of, 1815
ISBN 1-4000-4436-7; 978-1-4000-4436-8
LC 2005-51001
This is an "account of the last battle in the War of 1812, which actually took place in January 1815, a couple of weeks after the Treaty of Ghent had been signed but before news of the treaty had crossed the ocean." Libr J
"This is a beautifully written and exciting work of popular history." Booklist
Includes bibliographical references

Howe, Daniel Walker
What hath God wrought; the transformation of America, 1815-1848. Oxford University Press 2007 904p il map (Oxford history of the United States) $35   **973.5**
1. United States—History—1815-1861
ISBN 9780195078947; 0-19-507894-2
LC 2007-12370

Howe, Daniel Walker—*Continued*

The author "narrates a crucial period in U.S. history—a time of territorial growth, religious revival, booming industrialization, a recalibrating of American democracy and the rise of nationalist sentiment. . . . Supported by engaging prose, Howe's achievement will surely be seen as one of the most outstanding syntheses of U.S. history published this decade." Publ Wkly

Includes bibliographical references

Lincoln, Abraham, 1809-1865

Speeches and writings, 1832-1858; speeches, letters, and miscellaneous writings: the Lincoln Douglas debates. Library of Am. 1989 898p $35
*   **973.5**

1. United States—Politics and government—1815-1861 2. Lincoln-Douglas debates, 1858

ISBN 0-940450-43-7   LC 88-82723

Based on the "eight volumes of 'The Collected Works of Abraham Lincoln,' edited by Roy P. Basler, Marion Dolores Pratt and Lloyd A. Dunlap, the present . . . [volume contains] all seven of the Lincoln-Douglas debates, as well as the . . . speeches, before and after the debates, that attacked the repeal of the Missouri Compromise of 1820 and 'squatter sovereignty' in the territories." N Y Times Book Rev

Includes bibliographical references

Miller, William Lee

Arguing about slavery; the great battle in the United States Congress. Knopf 1996 577p pa $17 hardcover o.p.   **973.5**

1. Adams, John Quincy, 1767-1848 2. United States. Congress 3. Slavery—United States 4. United States—Politics and government—1815-1861

ISBN 0-679-76844-0 (pa)   LC 95-35075

A Borzoi Bk.

"In tracing the growing hostility between North and South over the extension of slavery into the Western territories, Miller pays special attention to the so-called gag rule, in force from 1834 to 1844, which blocked discussion of antislavery proposals in the House of Representatives. The central figure in Miller's study is John Quincy Adams, in his second career as U.S. representative from Massachusetts, and his heroic fight for repeal of the gag rule and for the right to petition Congress for the abolition of slavery." Publ Wkly

"Miller lays out the arcane workings of the proceedings with admirable detail, clarity, and verve." Christ Sci Monit

Includes bibliographical references

Oates, Stephen B., 1936-

The approaching fury; voices of the storm, 1820-1861; Buz Wyeth, editor. HarperCollins Pubs. 1997 495p pa $15 hardcover o.p.
                                                    973.5

1. United States—History—1815-1861 2. United States—History—1861-1865, Civil War—Causes

ISBN 0-06-092885-9 (pa)   LC 96-31965

Companion volume to The whirlwind of war

This work consists of a "series of dramatic autobiographical monologs relating 13 different voices and viewpoints on the coming of the Civil War, from Jefferson Davis's and Lincoln's agonizing over disunion in 1860-61. Turner, Harriet Beecher Stowe, Frederick Douglass, Mary Chestnut, and others make cameo appearances, but Henry Clay, John Calhoun, Stephen A. Douglas, Davis, and Lincoln dominate the discussion." Libr J

"Taken on its own terms, this book powerfully recreates some of the momentous events that produced the catastrophe of 1861. Mr. Oates succeeds in bringing his characters alive and in creating highly dramatic scenes for them to act out." N Y Times Book Rev

Includes bibliographical references

Remini, Robert Vincent, 1921-

The Battle of New Orleans; {by} Robert V. Remini. Viking 1999 226p il maps pa $14 hardcover o.p. *   **973.5**

1. New Orleans (La.), Battle of, 1815

ISBN 0-14-100179-8 (pa)   LC 99-19837

This "book establishes the War of 1812 historically as our second War of Independence, and describes its climactic battle in the maze of cypress swamps and bayous along the winding Mississippi. Remini, . . . unforgettably portrays individuals on both sides, and provides good maps to help us follow the action." New Yorker

Includes bibliographical references

Tocqueville, Alexis de, 1805-1859

Democracy in America; with an introduction by Alan Ryan. Knopf 1994 lxxii, 434, xi, 394p (Everyman's library) $27   **973.5**

1. United States—Social conditions 2. United States—Politics and government 3. Democracy 4. American national characteristics

ISBN 978-0-679-43134-3; 0-679-43134-9
                                                LC 94-1752

Also available in paperback from Penguin Classics

First part originally published in France, 1835; the second in 1840

Based partly on the French author's observations of American political and social conditions during a visit in 1831-1832. "It remains the best philosophical discussion of Democracy illustrated by the experience of the United States, up to the time when it was written, which can be found in any language." Pratt Alcove

Includes bibliographical references

Wilentz, Sean

The rise of American democracy; Jefferson to Lincoln. Norton 2005 xxiii, 1044p il $35
                                                    973.5

1. Democracy 2. United States—Politics and government—1783-1865

ISBN 0-393-05820-4   LC 2004-29466

The author traces the evolution of democratic principles in the United States from the American Revolution to the Civil War.

This "is a magnificent chronicle, the life of an idea that, although it is mentioned nowhere in the Constitution, nevertheless slowly elbowed its way into the heart

Wilentz, Sean—*Continued*
of American life. . . . Wilentz shows what [the] fight
has cost, and why it's worth it." Newsweek
Includes bibliographical references

973.6 United States—1845-1861

Guelzo, Allen C.
Lincoln and Douglas; the debates that defined
America. Simon & Schuster 2008 xxvii, 383p il
map $26   **973.6**
   1. Lincoln, Abraham, 1809-1865 2. Douglas, Stephen
Arnold, 1813-1861 3. Lincoln-Douglas debates, 1858
4. United States—Politics and government—1815-
1861
   ISBN 978-0-7432-7320-6; 0-7432-7320-6
                    LC 2007-44254
This is an "account of the celebrated Lincoln-Douglas
debates of 1858." Publ Wkly
"This Lincoln-Douglas rendition will engage every interest in Civil War and black history." Booklist
Includes bibliographical references

973.7 United States— Administration of Abraham Lincoln, 1861-1865. Civil War

Blanton, DeAnne, 1964-
They fought like demons; women soldiers in the
American Civil War; [by] DeAnne Blanton and
Lauren M. Cook. Louisiana State Univ. Press 2002
277p il (Conflicting worlds) $29.95   **973.7**
   1. Women soldiers 2. United States—History—1861-
1865, Civil War
   ISBN 0-8071-2806-6   LC 2002-4441
Also available in paperback from Vintage Bks.
"The authors reconstruct the reasons why women entered the armed forces: many were simply patriotic,
while others followed their husbands or lovers and yet
others yearned to break free from the constraints that
Victorian society had laid on them as women. Blanton
and Cook detail women soldiers in combat, on the
march, in camp and in the hospital, where many were
discovered after getting sick. Some even wound up in
grim prisons kept by both sides, while a few hid pregnancies and were only discovered after giving birth. . . .
Solid research by the authors, including a look at the careers of a few women soldiers after the war, makes this
a compelling book that belongs in every Civil War library." Publ Wkly
Includes bibliographical references

Boatner, Mark Mayo, 1921-
The Civil War dictionary; by Mark Mayo
Boatner III; maps and diagrams by Allen C.
Northrop and Lowell I. Miller. 1st Vintage Civil
War Library ed. Vintage Civil War Library 1991
974p il map pa $24   **973.7**
   1. United States—History—1861-1865, Civil War—
   Encyclopedias
   ISBN 0-679-73392-2; 978-0-679-73392-8
                    LC 91-50013

First published 1959 by McKay
"With more than 4,000 entries . . . this dictionary remains the most comprehensive and consistently accurate
reference tool on the American Civil War. In addition to
the biographical sketches there are entries relating to
campaigns and battles, naval engagements, weapons, issues and incidents, military terms and definitions, politics, literature, and statistics." Choice
Includes bibliographical references

Bordewich, Fergus M.
Bound for Canaan; the epic story of the
underground railroad, America's first integrated
civil rights movement; Fergus M. Bordewich.
Amistad 2005 540p il map $27.95; pa $14.95 *
                     973.7
   1. Underground railroad 2. Slavery—United States
   ISBN 0-06-052430-8; 0-06-052431-6 (pa)
                  LC 2004-52082
The author "covers six decades of the Underground
Railroad, from its inchoate beginnings to its height, when
it boasted a complex network of individuals determined
to eliminate slavery from a nation proclaiming to be the
land of liberty." Libr J
"The men and women of this remarkable account will
remain with readers for a long time to come." Publ Wkly
Includes bibliographical references

Boritt, G. S., 1940-
The Gettysburg gospel; the Lincoln speech that
nobody knows. Simon & Schuster 2006 415p il
$28   **973.7**
   1. Lincoln, Abraham, 1809-1865
   ISBN 978-0-7432-8820-0; 0-7432-8820-3
                  LC 2006-50578
"The author sets the speech in its contemporary context and, most interestingly, demonstrates that it was not
only minimally noticed by Lincoln's peers and the press
at the time but was virtually forgotten to history until the
20th century. He addresses many of the myths surrounding the address, such as that Lincoln wrote it in haste on
the train to Gettysburg. In fact, it went through a number
of careful revisions. He includes images of the known
copies of the handwritten address, broadsides and programs relating to the dedication ceremony at Gettysburg,
selections of photos from the era, and a line-byline analysis of the various drafts of the address. Boritt's narrative style will appeal to lay readers . . ., while his extensive research and insightful conclusions will appeal to
scholars." Libr J

Catton, Bruce, 1899-1978
A stillness at Appomattox. Doubleday 1953
438p maps pa $14.95 hardcover o.p.
                     973.7
   1. Appomattox Campaign, 1865 2. United States—
   History—1861-1865, Civil War—Campaigns
   ISBN 0-385-04451-8 (pa)
Concluding volume of trilogy which began with Mr.
Lincoln's army (1951) and Glory road (1952). This final
volume of the author's study of the Army of the Poto-
mac covers the period from early 1864 to April, 1865

Catton, Bruce, 1899-1978—*Continued*

The author's "approach is judicious, his interpretation unbiased and his coverage comprehensive." N Y Times Book Rev

Includes bibliographical references

The **Causes** of the Civil War; edited by Kenneth M. Stampp. 3rd rev ed. Simon & Schuster 1991 255p pa $14   **973.7**

1. United States—History—1861-1865, Civil War—Causes 2. United States—History—1861-1865, Civil War—Sources

ISBN 0-671-75155-7   LC 91-36819

"A Touchstone book"

First published 1959 by Prentice-Hall

This book integrates the conclusions of various postwar historians with the thoughts of contemporary commentators like Jefferson Davis, Horace Greeley, and Lincoln. Political, cultural and economic aspects are emphasized

Includes bibliographical references

Colaiaco, James A., 1945-

Frederick Douglass and the Fourth of July. Palgrave Macmillan 2006 247p $24.95
     973.7

1. Douglass, Frederick, 1817?-1895 2. Slavery—United States

ISBN 1-4039-7033-5   LC 2005-51520

The author "offers a critical evaluation of the magisterial address that Frederick Douglass, the preeminent African American abolitionist and orator, gave in observance of Independence Day on July 5, 1852, in Rochester, NY." Libr J

"Colaiaco's careful study recaptures Douglass' reputation as one of America's greatest orators." Booklist

Includes bibliographical references

Craughwell, Thomas J., 1956-

Stealing Lincoln's body. Belknap Press of Harvard University Press 2007 250p il $24.95
     973.7

1. Lincoln, Abraham, 1809-1865—Tomb 2. Grave robbing 3. Counterfeits and counterfeiting

ISBN 978-0-674-02458-8; 0-674-02458-3

     LC 2006-50842

The author "investigates the 1876 attempt to steal Abraham Lincoln's body from Oak Ridge Cemetery in Springfield, IL. On the night of the presidential election, three men with criminal records as counterfeiters sought to break into the Lincoln Monument. The plan was to then hold the body for ransom, but Secret Service detective Patrick Tyrrell had been tipped off and thwarted the plot, catching the criminals in the act with the help of Lincoln Monument custodian John Carroll Power." Libr J

"Summoning the raw spirit of crime novels and horror stories, as well as the forensic detail of a coroner's inquest, Thomas J. Craughwell has turned the eerie final chapter of the Lincoln story into a guilty pleasure." Washington Post Book World

Includes bibliographical references

Daniel, Larry J., 1947-

Shiloh; the battle that changed the Civil War. Simon & Schuster 1997 430p il map pa $14 hardcover o.p.   **973.7**

1. Shiloh (Tenn.), Battle of, 1862

ISBN 0-684-83857-5 (pa)   LC 96-51539

"Before Antietam, Shiloh stood as the bloodiest engagement of the Civil War. The April 1862 battle did not decide the war, as Daniel . . . recognizes, but it almost ruined Gen. U.S. Grant, shook up the commands of both Union and Confederate armies, and left the West open to Union advances." Libr J

The author "has crafted a superbly researched volume that will appeal to both the beginning Civil War reader as well as those already familiar with the course of fighting in the wooded terrain bordering the Tennessee River." Publ Wkly

Includes bibliographical references

Davis, Burke, 1913-

Sherman's march. Random House 1980 335p il maps pa $14 hardcover o.p.   **973.7**

1. Sherman, William T. (William Tecumseh), 1820-1891 2. United States—History—1861-1865, Civil War—Campaigns

ISBN 0-394-75763-7 (pa)   LC 79-5550

The author "reconstructs Sherman's infamous, but vastly consequential march through Georgia and the Carolinas, which sent the Confederacy into its death throes. Basing his narrative on eyewitness accounts, Davis brings the event down to a personal level." Booklist

Includes bibliographical references

To Appomattox; nine April days, 1865. Burford Books 2002 433p map pa $18.95   **973.7**

1. Appomattox Campaign, 1865 2. United States—History—1861-1865, Civil War

ISBN 1-580-80097-1; 978-1-580-80097-6

     LC 2001-56744

First published 1959 by Rinehart

"The story of the last nine days of the Civil War from the march on Richmond to the surrender at Appomattox. Quotations from diaries, letters, newspapers and military reports create a sense of immediacy as the reader follows each day's events in the city, in the Confederate camp, and with the Union Army." Publ Wkly

Includes bibliographical references

Davis, William C., 1946-

An honorable defeat; the last days of the Confederate government. Harcourt 2001 496p il maps $30; pa $16   **973.7**

1. Davis, Jefferson, 1808-1889 2. Breckinridge, John Cabell, 1821-1875 3. Confederate States of America

ISBN 0-15-100564-8; 0-15-600748-7 (pa)

     LC 00-46143

Maps on lining paper

This is an account of "the contentious relationship of two men . . . Jefferson Davis, the stubborn, imperious, and delusional leader of the Rebel forces, and the sensible and personable John C. Breckenridge, Davis's Secretary of War." Libr J

Davis "knows his two principal players well, and a

Davis, William C., 1946-—*Continued*
marvelous supporting cast of politicians and soldiers
helps him to fashion a story rich in pathos and humor."
N Y Times Book Rev
Includes bibliographical references

Eicher, David J., 1961-
The longest night; a military history of the Civil
War; foreword by James M. McPherson; maps by
Lee Vande Visse. Simon & Schuster 2001 990p
maps $40; pa $22   **973.7**
1. United States—History—1861-1865, Civil War—
Campaigns
ISBN 0-684-84944-5; 0-684-84945-3 (pa)
LC 2001-34153
An account of battles and military strategies in the
Civil War
"Civil War buffs and military history scholars will
find Eicher's superb analyses and original insights into
oft-neglected theaters of operations extremely valuable.
An important work that will be an essential component
of Civil War collections." Booklist
Includes bibliographical references

Encyclopedia of the American Civil War; a
political, social, and military history; David S.
Heidler and Jeanne T. Heidler, editors; foreword
by James W. McPherson; David J. Coles,
associate editor; Gary W. Gallagher, James M.
McPherson, Mark E. Neely, Jr., editorial board.
ABC-CLIO 2000 5v il maps set $425 *
973.7
1. United States—History—1861-1865, Civil War—
Encyclopedias
ISBN 1-57607-066-2   LC 00-11195
Also available in a one-volume edition from Norton
"The editors have compiled a comprehensive source
that provides a first-stop reference on broad areas or specific topics on the Civil War. The contemporary photographs and lithographs bring the human element into the
encyclopedia, a type of reference known more for facts
and figures than emotions. The primary-source-
documents volume brings obscure resources together,
which will further illumine the period for students."—
"Outstanding Reference Sources." American Libraries,
May 2001
Includes bibliographical references

Faust, Drew Gilpin
Mothers of invention; women of the
slaveholding South in the American Civil War.
University of N.C. Press 1996 326p il $37.50; pa
$19.95   **973.7**
1. United States—History—1861-1865, Civil War—
Women 2. Women—Southern States
ISBN 0-8078-2255-8; 0-8078-5573-1 (pa)
LC 95-8896
Based on journals, letters and memoirs, this is an
"analysis of the impact of secession, invasion and conquest on Southern white women. Antebellum images
based on helplessness and dependence were challenged
as women assumed an increasing range of social and
economic responsibilities. . . . Faust's provocative analy-

sis of a complex subject merits a place in all collections
of U.S. history." Publ Wkly
Includes bibliographical references

This republic of suffering; death and the
American Civil War. Alfred A. Knopf 2008 346p
il $27.95   **973.7**
1. United States—History—1861-1865, Civil War
2. Death
ISBN 978-0-375-40404-7; 0-375-40404-X
LC 2007-14658
The author "surveys the many ways the Civil War
generation coped with the trauma: the concept of the
Good Death—conscious, composed and at peace with
God; the rise of the embalming industry; the sad attempts
of the bereaved to get confirmation of a soldier's death,
sometimes years after war's end; the swelling national
movement to recover soldiers' remains and give them decent burials; the intellectual quest to find meaning—or its
absence—in the war's carnage. . . . The result is an
insightful, often moving portrait of a people torn by
grief." Publ Wkly
Includes bibliographical references

Ferguson, Andrew, 1956-
Land of Lincoln; adventures in Abe's America.
Atlantic Monthly Press 2007 279p il $24
973.7
1. Lincoln, Abraham, 1809-1865—Influence
2. United States—Description and travel
ISBN 978-0-871-13967-2; 0-871-13967-7
LC 2006-52634
An "offbeat tour of Lincoln shrines, statues, cabins
and museums. The 16th president comes in many forms,
and every one, it seems, has a following, right down to
Lincoln the chief executive officer, dispenser of corporate leadership tips. . . . Along with the silly statues, the
bogus exhibits and Abe's get-rich-quick tips, Mr. Ferguson includes some genuinely touching, if strange, examples of Lincoln love. . . . The Land of Lincoln turns out
to be a big place: bigger than Illinois, bigger even than
the United States, stranger than anyone would have
thought. Mr. Ferguson maps it expertly, with an understated Midwestern sense of humor that Lincoln, master
of the funny story, would have been the first to appreciate." N Y Times (Late N Y Ed)

Foote, Shelby, 1916-2005
The Civil War; a narrative. Random House
1958-1974 3v maps set $165; pa $75
973.7
1. United States—History—1861-1865, Civil War
ISBN 0-394-49517-9; 0-394-74913-8
Volumes also available separately
Contents: v1 Fort Sumter to Perryville; v2 Fredericks-
burg to Meridian; v3 Red River to Appomattox
"In objectivity, in range, in mastery of detail, in beau-
ty of language and feeling for the people involved, this
work surpasses anything else on the subject." New
Repub
Includes bibliographical references

Fredrickson, George M., 1934-2008
Big enough to be inconsistent; Abraham Lincoln confronts slavery and race. Harvard University Press 2008 156p (The W.E.B. Du Bois lectures) $19.95   **973.7**
1. Lincoln, Abraham, 1809-1865 2. Slavery—United States 3. African Americans—Civil rights
ISBN 978-0-674-02774-9; 0-674-02774-4
LC 2007-34018
The author "wades into a controversial arena: was Lincoln a heroic emancipator or a racist who didn't care about slaves at all? Stating that in between 'pathological' racism and egalitarianism lies a spectrum of possibilities, Fredrickson says that Lincoln is not easily classified. . . . This brief book will be widely discussed by historians and will provide nonacademic readers a lucid introduction to some of the most heated debates about the 16th president." Publ Wkly
Includes bibliographical references

Fredriksen, John C.
Civil War almanac. Facts on File, Inc. 2007 858p il map (Almanacs of American wars) $85
973.7
1. United States—History—1861-1865, Civil War
ISBN 0-8160-6459-8; 978-0-8160-6459-5
LC 2006-29985
First published 1983 under the editorship of John Stewart Bowman
This book contains a "day-by-day chronology of the events and people of this monumental war, along with an A-to-Z dictionary offering biographical information on leading military and political figures involved in the conflict." Publisher's note
Includes bibliographical references

Furgurson, Ernest B., 1929-
Chancellorsville, 1863; the souls of the brave. Knopf 1992 405p il maps pa $16 hardcover o.p.
973.7
1. Chancellorsville (Va.), Battle of, 1863
ISBN 0-679-72831-7 (pa)   LC 91-47059
Furgurson presents an account of "the battle's separate phases, the strategic thinking on both sides, the confusion and hesitation in Richmond and Washington, and the events surrounding Stonewall Jackson's death." Choice
"Mr. Furgurson has written what should become the standard account of the battle. He is especially good at discussing both larger tactical issues and the experiences of ordinary soldiers. He is also evenhanded." N Y Times Book Rev
Includes bibliographical references

Freedom rising; Washington in the Civil War. Knopf 2004 463p il $30; pa $16   **973.7**
1. Washington (D.C.) 2. United States—History—1861-1865, Civil War
ISBN 0-375-40454-6; 0-375-70409-4 (pa)
LC 2004-40820
This is an "account of how the Civil War transformed the nation's capital from the debating forum for a loose union of states into the seat of a forceful central government." Publisher's note

"Furgurson paints a compelling portrait of a dynamic, rapidly evolving city on edge. . . . This is a well-written and informative account of a city and its citizens passing through a traumatic national ordeal." Booklist
Includes bibliographical references

Not war but murder; Cold Harbor, 1864. Knopf 2000 328p il maps pa $14 hardcover o.p.
973.7
1. Cold Harbor (Va.), Battle of, 1864
ISBN 0-679-78139-0 (pa)   LC 99-37147
"On June 3, 1864, the Union Second, Sixth, and Eighteenth Corps assaulted Confederate breastworks at Cold Harbor outside Richmond, VA. The resulting bloodbath amounted to U.S. Grant's worst defeat and 'Bobby' Lee's final great victory. . . . {Furgurson} retells the well-known story of how the friction between Grant and his insecure direct subordinate, George Meade, poisoned the Army of the Potomac's whole chain of command." Libr J
The author's "engagement with the people he writes about comes through in every line, making one of the most wrenching incidents of the war grimly immediate." Publ Wkly
Includes bibliographical references

Gallagher, Gary W.
The Confederate War. Harvard Univ. Press 1997 218p il *   **973.7**
1. United States—History—1861-1865, Civil War 2. Confederate States of America
LC 97-2495
This is a "historiographical study of the arguments over why the South lost the Civil War. {Gallagher} addresses various explanations—lack of a sense of nationality, guilt over slavery, low morale (especially among women), and the heavy casualties caused by Lee's offensive strategy." Booklist
This book "is the best thing that has happened to Confederate historiography in many years. Gallagher has a more thorough command of the sources for Confederate history than any other historian I have read and he brings that mastery to bear in a concise, hard-hitting book." NY Rev Books
Includes bibliographical references

Harper, Judith E., 1953-
Women during the Civil War; an encyclopedia. Routledge 2003 472p il map $170; pa $59.95
973.7
1. United States—History—1861-1865, Civil War—Women
ISBN 0-415-93723-X; 0-415-95574-2 (pa)
LC 2003-7181
"The 128 entries range in length from 400 to 4000 words, and include biographies of women from all regions of the U.S. Well-known figures such as Harriet Tubman, Clara Barton, Louisa May Alcott, and Mary Todd Lincoln are represented but so too are African-American sculptor Edmonia Lewis, poet Lucy Larcom, and Emma LeConte. . . . As well as biographies, there are superb thematic entries on women living in the West, prostitutes, industrial workers, family life, and invasion and occupation. . . . This encyclopedia is a welcomed

Harper, Judith E., 1953-—*Continued*
addition to reference collections." SLJ
Includes bibliographical references

Horwitz, Tony, 1958-
Confederates in the attic; dispatches from the unfinished Civil War. Pantheon Bks. 1998 406p map pa $14.95 hardcover o.p.   **973.7**
   1. United States—History—1861-1865, Civil War
   ISBN 0-679-75833-X (pa)   LC 97-26759
According to Horwitz's "chronicle of his tour of the Old South, many people have yet to make peace with the past. In a South Carolina town, whites relate to Horwitz their pride in the 'lost cause,' even equating southern valor with the courage of Martin Luther King; a black preacher explains that affection for the 'cause' strikes him as an endorsement of slavery. Esteemed Civil War scholar Shelby Foote strives to explain the origins of the Klan as the reaction to a perceived foreign occupation." Booklist
This "is the work of a skilled journalist looking at how—and why—the War Between the States continues to live in so many issues still with us." Libr J

Klein, Maury, 1939-
Days of defiance; Sumter, secession, and the coming of the Civil War. Knopf 1997 496p il pa $16 hardcover o.p.   **973.7**
   1. United States—History—1861-1865, Civil War
   ISBN 0-679-76882-3 (pa)   LC 96-39156
This is "a study of the months between Abraham Lincoln's election and the outbreak of hostilities at Fort Sumter on April 12, 1861." New Leader
"With a novelist's skill, Klein has crafted an engrossing portrait of the nation's descent into chaos and war." Publ Wkly
Includes bibliographical references

Leonard, Elizabeth D.
All the daring of the soldier; women of the Civil War armies. Norton 1999 368p il hardcover o.p. pa $22.95   **973.7**
   1. Women soldiers 2. United States—History—1861-1865, Civil War
   ISBN 978-0-393-04712-7; 978-0-393-33547-7 (pa); 0-393-33547-X (pa)   LC 98-52304
The author presents "stories of dozens of women who served in both the Union and Confederacy during the Civil War. Some were spies, but many more adopted men's names, dressed in men's clothes and lived and fought and died alongside mostly unsuspecting men." Publ Wkly
Includes bibliographical references

Lincoln, Abraham, 1809-1865
Speeches and writings, 1859-1865; speeches, letters, and miscellaneous writings, presidential messages and proclamations. Library of Am. 1989 xxxiii, 787p $35 *   **973.7**
   1. United States—Politics and government—1861-1865
   ISBN 0-940450-63-1   LC 89-45349

This volume is based upon The Collected Works of Abraham Lincoln. It includes public statements, business letters, "poems, personal letters, telegrams to generals in the field, and other [writings]." Libr J
Includes bibliographical references

Marten, James, 1956-
Civil War America; voices from the home front. ABC-CLIO 2003 346p il $85   **973.7**
   1. United States—History—1861-1865, Civil War—Personal narratives
   ISBN 1-576-07237-1   LC 2002-154377
Also available in paperback from Fordham University Press
"Marten offers a view of the war through the eyes of diverse noncombatants. Four parts of this five-part work each deal with Southerners, Northerners, children, and African Americans . . . Part five, 'Aftermaths,' includes descriptions of the postwar lives of veterans, orphans, and ex-slaves, and concludes with a chapter on the Civil War stories by Ambrose Bierce. Readers will find Marten's overarching theme of change—both immediate and long-range—revelatory and instructional." SLJ
Includes bibliographical references

McPherson, James M.
Abraham Lincoln and the second American Revolution. Oxford Univ. Press 1991 173p pa $16.95 hardcover o.p.   **973.7**
   1. Lincoln, Abraham, 1809-1865 2. United States—History—1861-1865, Civil War
   ISBN 0-19-507606-0 (pa)   LC 90-6885
The author "examines Lincoln's role in the transformation wrought by the Civil War—the liberation of four million slaves, the overthrow of the social and political order of the South." Publ Wkly
Includes bibliographical references

Battle cry of freedom; the Civil War era. Oxford Univ. Press 1988 904p il maps (Oxford history of the United States) $47.50; pa $18.95
                         973.7
   1. United States—History—1861-1865, Civil War
   ISBN 0-19-503863-0; 0-19-516895-X (pa)
                         LC 87-11045
A narrative history of events from the Mexican War through Appomattox. The author describes military campaigns, tactics and leaders. How the war changed the American political, social and economic landscape is explored
This volume "is comprehensive yet succinct, scholarly without being pedantic, eloquent but unrhetorical. It is compellingly readable." N Y Times Book Rev
Includes bibliographical references

Drawn with the sword; reflections on the American Civil War. Oxford Univ. Press 1996 258p $45; pa $18.95 *   **973.7**
   1. Lincoln, Abraham, 1809-1865 2. United States—History—1861-1865, Civil War
   ISBN 0-19-509679-7; 0-19-511796-4 (pa)
                         LC 95-38107

McPherson, James M.—*Continued*

A collection of "essays on some of the most thought-provoking questions of the Civil War. All of the essays were published earlier but have been updated and revised for this compilation. The topics deal with such subjects as the origins of the Civil War, the slavery question in both North and South, why the North won the war and why the South lost, President Abraham Lincoln, and the change in historical writing." Libr J

"These pieces provide a lively reminder that the best scholarship is also often a pleasure to read." N Y Times Book Rev

For cause and comrades; why men fought in the Civil War. Oxford Univ. Press 1997 237p $25; pa $15.95   **973.7**
1. Soldiers—United States 2. United States—History—1861-1865, Civil War
ISBN 0-19-509023-3; 0-19-512499-5 (pa)
LC 96-24760

"Volumes have been written on the causes of the Civil War, but less has been written on what caused soldiers to risk their lives on the battlefield. McPherson . . . fills the gap. After studying thousands of letters and diaries, he discusses what really led soldiers to enlist, what kept them in the army, and what led them to the front lines." Libr J

Includes bibliographical references

Hallowed ground; a walk at Gettysburg. Crown Publishers 2003 144p map (Crown Journeys series) $16   **973.7**
1. Gettysburg (Pa.), Battle of, 1863
ISBN 0-609-61023-6   LC 2002-35154

In this study of the Battle of Gettysburg, "McPherson walks readers over its presently hallowed ground, with monuments numbering into the hundreds." Publ Wkly

"If it were only a pointer to the physical ground and commemorative markers, this guide would be ordinary, but McPherson so articulately injects reminders—as of a free black farmer who fled the approaching battle lest Confederates enslave him—of what the Civil War was about as to display the crystalline style that has made him one of our finest Civil War historians." Booklist

This mighty scourge; perspectives on the Civil War. Oxford University Press 2007 260p $28 *
                                             973.7
1. Lincoln, Abraham, 1809-1865 2. United States—History—1861-1865, Civil War
ISBN 0-19-531366-6   LC 2006-35523

In this collection of essays "McPherson sheds light on topics large and small, from the average soldier's avid love of newspapers to the postwar creation of the mystique of a Lost Cause in the South. Readers will find . . . pieces on such intriguing figures as Harriet Tubman, John Brown, Jesse James, and William Tecumseh Sherman, and on such vital issues such as Confederate military strategy, the failure of peace negotiations to end the war, and the realities and myths of the Confederacy." Publisher's note

These essays "stand as a remarkably elegant and clarifying narrative exploration of the most basic questions concerning the Civil War, issues over which scholars and activists still contend. . . 'This Mighty Scourge,' in fact, is an exemplary exercise in the contribution a great histo-

rian and eloquent writer can make to a people's understanding of themselves." Los Angeles Times

Paludan, Phillip S., 1938-2007

The presidency of Abraham Lincoln; [by] Phillip Shaw Paludan. University Press of Kan. 1994 xx, 384p (American presidency series) $29.95; pa $15.95   **973.7**
1. Lincoln, Abraham, 1809-1865 2. United States—Politics and government—1861-1865
ISBN 0-7006-0671-8; 0-7006-0745-5 (pa)
LC 93-46830

The author "traces the year-by-year chronology of a Presidency engaged with recruiting, placating, appeasing and coercing the various and competing factions of the war years, and sees in Lincoln 'a commitment to the political-constitutional system that would itself move the nation toward its highest ambitions.' . . . Equally interesting is Mr. Paludan's depiction of how the war transformed the national Government, not only establishing the foundations for the Gilded Age but more subtly strengthening and enriching the role of government." NY Times Book Rev

Includes bibliographical references

Perry, James M.

Touched with fire; five presidents and the Civil War battles that made them. PublicAffairs 2003 335p il map $26; pa $16   **973.7**
1. Presidents—United States 2. United States—History—1861-1865, Civil War
ISBN 1-586-48114-2; 1-586-48290-4 (pa)
LC 2003-46625

"All chief executives during the Gilded Age volunteered for the Union in the Civil War (excluding Grover Cleveland, who paid for a substitute). Perry here recounts their war records with an eye to the subsequent electoral advertising of their bravery and patriotism. . . . Perry, a wry storyteller, delivers the regimental-level detail that buffs crave while dusting events with the skepticism that presidential electoral campaigning invites." Booklist

Includes bibliographical references

Sears, Stephen W.

Chancellorsville. Houghton Mifflin 1996 593p pa $17 hardcover o.p. *   **973.7**
1. Chancellorsville (Va.), Battle of, 1863
ISBN 0-395-87744-X (pa)   LC 96-31220

In this history of the campaign that ended in Chancellorsville, the author argues that "a chain of errors, assumptions, and communications failures combined with the genuine brilliance and good luck of the Confederates to lead to a stinging if indecisive Union defeat." Booklist

Includes bibliographical references

Gettysburg. Houghton Mifflin 2003 623p il map $30; pa $17   **973.7**
1. Gettysburg (Pa.), Battle of, 1863
ISBN 0-395-86761-4; 0-618-48538-4 (pa)
LC 2002-191259

This is an "assessment of the battle of Gettysburg and the events leading up to it. . . . Sears examines several

Sears, Stephen W.—*Continued*
turning points during the battle's buildup and three-day
duration. The resulting insights add to the excellent and
dramatic narrative flow. . . . For all Civil War collections and academic libraries." Libr J
Includes bibliographical references

Landscape turned red; the Battle of Antietam.
Houghton Mifflin 2003 431p il pa $17
973.7
1. Antietam (Md.), Battle of, 1862
ISBN 978-0-618-34419-2; 0-618-34419-5
"A Mariner book"
First published 1983 by Ticknor & Fields
This "account of the Battle of Antietam, the bloodiest
day of the Civil War, is wide-ranging, detailed, and copiously documented. Stephen Sears . . . describes the ten-
sion-filled days preceding September 17, 1862, especially
the political climate of Union pessimism and Confederate
optimism. . . . The battle itself is then exhaustively recounted." Booklist

To the gates of Richmond; the peninsula
campaign. Mariner 2001 468p il map pa $17 *
973.7
1. Peninsular Campaign, 1862
ISBN 978-0-618-12713-9; 0-618-12713-5
First published 1992 by Ticknor & Fields
"The campaign on the peninsula between the James
and York rivers in Virginia in the spring of 1862 was
McClellan's major strategic effort and the first major
Union offensive in the East. . . . Sears does an outstanding job in making intelligible an extremely complex campaign." Booklist
Includes bibliographical references

Stout, Harry S.
Upon the altar of the nation : a moral history of
the American Civil War. Viking 2006 552p il
$29.95 **973.7**
1. United States—History—1861-1865, Civil War
ISBN 0-670-03470-3 LC 2005-42420
The author "examines the evolving rhetoric of warfare,
both Northern and Confederate, within the rubric of 'the
just war' theory of conflict." Publ Wkly
"Impeccably sourced and highly engaging, the book
will surely be controversial—the best histories often are."
Booklist
Includes bibliographical references

Swanson, Mark, 1951-
Atlas of the Civil War, month by month; major
battles and troop movements; maps by Mark
Swanson, with Jacqueline D. Langley. University
of Georgia Press 2004 141p il map $39.95
973.7
1. United States—History—1861-1865, Civil War—
Maps
ISBN 0-8203-2658-5 LC 2004-12264
This Civil War atlas depicts "multiple aspects of the
war's action in a month-by-month sequence from April
1861 to June 1865. . . . An absolute must for Civil War

studies." Univ Press Books for Public and Second Sch
Libr, 2006
Includes bibliographical references

Tobin, Jacqueline, 1950-
From Midnight to Dawn; the last tracks of the
underground railroad; [by] Jacqueline Tobin with
Hettie Jones. Doubleday 2006 272p il $24.95 *
973.7
1. Underground railroad 2. Abolitionists 3. Slavery—
United States
ISBN 978-0-385-51431-6; 0-385-51431-X
LC 2006-46304
"In the mid-nineteenth century, the city of Detroit
bore the code name Midnight on the Underground Railroad. Its sister city of Windsor, Ontario, was code-named
Dawn. Tobin tells the story of the journey of slaves from
Midnight to Dawn as they traveled to freedom in Canada
and established settlements with churches, schools, businesses, farms, and factories to sustain themselves."
Booklist
"There's an enlightening portrait of Josiah Henson
(the model for Stowe's Uncle Tom) as a political activist, a fascinating look at the pioneering journalist and
early feminist Mary Ann Shadd and an intriguing section
on the deep 'Canadian connection to Harpers Ferry,' as
John Brown meets with the fugitives in Chatham. Accessible and fluidly written, the book will appeal to general
readers." Publ Wkly
Includes bibliographical references

Hidden in plain view; the secret story of quilts
and the underground railroad; [by] Jacqueline L.
Tobin and Raymond G. Dobard. Doubleday 1999
208p il map hardcover o.p. pa $14 **973.7**
1. Underground railroad 2. Ciphers 3. Quilts
ISBN 0-385-49137-9; 0-385-49767-9 (pa)
LC 98-49804
The authors present the "theory that slaves created
quilts coded with patterns to help one another flee to
freedom." N Y Times Book Rev
This is "a needed and valuable contribution to the literature of African American culture." Libr J
Includes bibliographical references

Trudeau, Noah Andre, 1949-
Like men of war; black troops in the Civil War,
1862-1865. Little, Brown 1998 xxii, 548p il maps
$29; pa $18 **973.7**
1. African American soldiers 2. United States—History—1861-1865, Civil War
ISBN 0-316-85325-9; 0-316-85344-5 (pa)
LC 97-15380
A "study of the battlefield experiences of black Union
regiments. Some 60 maps help the reader make sense of
famous engagements (Fort Wagner and the Crater) and
notorious incidents (Fort Pillow) in which black soldiers
fought, as well as scores of lesser-known clashes. Rich
archival research is integrated into a lively narrative that
places the raising and deployment of black regiments in
broader contexts. This book will become a basic source
of information on the subject." Libr J
Includes bibliographical references

Ward, Andrew, 1946-
The slaves' war; the Civil War in the words of
former slaves. Houghton Mifflin Co. 2008 386p il
$28 *   **973.7**
1. United States—History—1861-1865, Civil War—
Personal narratives 2. Slavery—United States
ISBN 978-0-618-63400-2; 0-618-63400-2
               LC 2008-1532
The author "has provided a . . . narrative that gives
voice to the experiences and attitudes of slaves who endured the conflict. Ward utilizes testimonials, diaries, and
letters, and organizes them in chronological order from
the months before the commencement of hostilities to the
aftermath of the surrender at Appomattox. . . . This is
a work that will interest both scholars and general readers." Booklist
Includes bibliographical references

Ward, Geoffrey C.
The Civil War; an illustrated history; [by]
Geoffrey C. Ward with Ken Burns and Ric Burns.
Knopf 1990 425p il maps $75; pa $29.95
                      973.7
1. United States—History—1861-1865, Civil War
ISBN 0-394-56285-2; 0-679-74277-8 (pa)
               LC 89-43475
The authors aim to "present the war as the central defining event of American history and of the lives of
those Americans caught up in it. In four separate, additional essays, professional historians briefly discuss the
causes of the war, emancipation, the politics of the war,
and its long-term meaning." Libr J
"A companion to a nine-part Public Broadcasting System documentary, this superbly designed book easily
stands on its own." N Y Times Book Rev
Includes bibliographical references

Wert, Jeffry D.
Mosby's Rangers. Simon & Schuster 1990 384p
il pa $14 hardcover o.p.   **973.7**
1. Confederate States of America. Army. Virginia
Cavalry Battalion, 43rd 2. United States—History—
1861-1865, Civil War
ISBN 0-671-74745-2 (pa)   LC 90-37917
In this "history of Mosby's Rangers, one of the most
successful irregular army units to operate during the Civil War, Wert details the guerrilla group's exploits which
provided Jeb Stuart and Robert E. Lee with valuable intelligence on the enemy's movements." Booklist
"Well-researched, objectively written, this is a first-
class history." Publ Wkly
Includes bibliographical references

White, Ronald C. (Ronald Cedric), 1939-
Lincoln's greatest speech; the second inaugural;
{by} Ronald C. White Jr. Simon & Schuster 2002
254p il pa $14 hardcover o.p. *   **973.7**
1. Lincoln, Abraham, 1809-1865 2. Presidents—United
States—Inaugural addresses
ISBN 0-7432-1299-1 (pa)   LC 2001-54234
"White breaks down the speech phrase by phrase, then
integrates it according to its rhetorical framework of past,

present, and future. He seeks sources for the speech's
ideas in Lincoln's ambiguous stance toward organized religion, in the sermons of preachers he listened to, and in
his Bible-reading habit. . . . Must-have Lincolnalia."
Booklist
Includes bibliographical references

Wiley, Bell Irvin, 1906-
The life of Billy Yank; the common soldier of
the Union; with a foreword by James I. Robertson,
Jr. Updated ed. Louisiana State University Press
2008 454p il pa $21.95   **973.7**
1. United States. Army—Military life 2. United
States—History—1861-1865, Civil War
ISBN 978-0-8071-3375-0; 0-8071-3375-2
              LC 2008-24243
First published 1952 by Bobbs-Merrill
"The soldiers' own writings—their letters and diaries—are . . . used as chief source for a picture of the
response of the Union men to the call to arms, their
training, army life, reactions to Southerners they encountered, opinions of Negroes, and comments on their Reb
counterparts." Booklist
Includes bibliographical references

The life of Johnny Reb; the common soldier of
the Confederacy. Updated ed. Louisiana State
University Press 2008 444p il pa $21.95
                      973.7
1. Confederate States of America. Army—Military life
2. United States—History—1861-1865, Civil War
ISBN 978-0-8071-3325-5   LC 2007-33859
First published 1943 by Bobbs-Merrill
"Composite biography of the ordinary soldier of the
Confederacy—his behavior in camp and under fire, his
food, clothing, weapons, religion, amusements, attitude
toward women, and so on. Taken mostly from firsthand
accounts in letters, diaries, and records." New Yorker
Includes bibliographical references

Wills, Garry, 1934-
Lincoln at Gettysburg; the words that remade
America. Simon & Schuster 1992 317p pa $14
hardcover o.p.   **973.7**
1. Lincoln, Abraham, 1809-1865
ISBN 0-671-86742-3 (pa)   LC 92-3546
The author "argues that in the Gettysburg Address
Abraham Lincoln, with consummate skill, changed the
Constitution from within, making the hope it embodies
triumph over its words by insinuating the ringing affir-
mation of equality from the Declaration of Independence
into people's minds as the foundation of the American
Government." N Y Times Book Rev
This is a "tour de force that will cause much discus-
sion and argument." Libr J
Includes bibliographical references

Woodworth, Steven E.

Atlas of the Civil War; by Steven Woodworth and Kenneth J. Winkle; foreword by James M. McPherson. Oxford University Press 2004 400p il map $75 **973.7**

1. United States—History—1861-1865, Civil War—Maps

ISBN 0-19-522131-1   LC 2004-53112

"Each of five major chapters is devoted to a single year from 1861 to 1865. In addition to every important battle, there is coverage of nonmilitary topics, such as population, the economy, transportation, elections, and the home front. . . . The work ends with a list of major battle sites, a chronology, a glossary, a short bibliography, and an index, which provides access to illustrations and maps as well as names." Booklist

"Richly illustrated, this publication will be wanted by all types of libraries. . . . The text entries are useful, while the maps and illustrations are both informative and eye-catching." Choice

973.8 United States—Reconstruction period, 1865-1901

Connell, Evan S., 1924-

Son of the Morning Star. North Point Press 1984 441p il hardcover o.p. pa $18 *
973.8

1. Custer, George Armstrong, 1839-1876 2. Little Bighorn, Battle of the, 1876

ISBN 0-86547-160-6; 0-86547-510-5 (pa)

LC 84-60681

The author "explores the whole context of the defeat of General Custer at the Battle of the Little Bighorn." Booklist

This book is "impressive in its massive presentation of information, and in the conclusions it draws about the probable events that led to the fracas on the banks of the Little Bighorn. But its strength lies in the way the author has shaped his material." N Y Times Book Rev

Includes bibliographical references

Diner, Steven J., 1944-

A very different age; Americans of the progressive era. Hill & Wang 1997 320p pa $14 hardcover o.p. **973.8**

1. Progressivism (United States politics) 2. United States—History—20th century

ISBN 0-8090-1611-7 (pa)   LC 97-3801

The author examines the "social, economic, political, and other changes experienced by Americans during the first two decades of the 20th century. . . . The writing is succinct and fluid. . . . This rewarding social history is an excellent book for both experienced historians and novices." Libr J

Includes bibliographical references

Donovan, Jim, 1954-

A terrible glory; Custer and the Little Bighorn—the last great battle of the American West; [by] James Donovan. Little, Brown and Co. 2008 528p il map $26.99 **973.8**

1. Custer, George Armstrong, 1839-1876 2. Little Bighorn, Battle of the, 1876

ISBN 978-0-316-15578-6; 0-316-15578-0

LC 2007-26156

The author "collects the multiple threads that led to the 1876 massacre at Little Big Horn. . . . Exhaustive research, lively prose and fresh interpretation make for a valuable addition to literature on this otherwise well-trodden historical event." Publ Wkly

Includes bibliographical references

Foner, Eric

Forever free; the story of emancipation and Reconstruction; illustrations edited and with commentary by Joshua Brown. Knopf 2005 xxx, 268p il $27.50; pa $15 **973.8**

1. Reconstruction (1865-1876) 2. Slavery—United States 3. United States—Politics and government—1865-1898

ISBN   0-375-40259-4;   978-0-375-40259-3; 0-375-70274-1 (pa); 978-0-375-70274-7 (pa)

LC 2005-40706

"Forever Free project: Stephen B. Brier, Peter O. Almond, executive editors/producers; Christine Doudna, editor."

This "examination of the years of Emancipation and Reconstruction during and immediately following the Civil War emphasizes the era's political and cultural meaning for today's America." Publisher's note

This "is an invaluable and timely book about a subject central to U.S. history and still of obvious significance today—slavery, the Civil War, emancipation, Reconstruction, and both the immediate aftermath and longer-term consequences of those things." Rev Am Hist

Includes bibliographical references

Reconstruction; America's unfinished revolution, 1863-1877. HarperCollins Pubs. 1988 xxvii, 690p il maps pa $23.95 hardcover o.p. *
973.8

1. Reconstruction (1865-1876) 2. United States—History—1865-1898

ISBN 0-06-093716-5 (pa)   LC 87-45615

Also available in hardcover from P. Smith

"Incorporating much eyewitness material, this book emphasizes the centrality of the Black experience. The book also examines the themes of race and class, the remodeling of Southern society, and the national context. A complete, modern, scholarly text." N Y Public Libr Book of How & Where to Look It Up

Includes bibliographical references

Franklin, John Hope, 1915-
Reconstruction after the Civil War. 2nd ed.
University of Chicago Press 1994 265p (Chicago
history of American civilization) pa $16 hardcover
o.p. **973.8**
   1. Reconstruction (1865-1876) 2. United States—History—1865-1898
   ISBN 0-226-26079-8 (pa)   LC 94-27366
   First published 1961
   This is an "account of American life in a time of great
challenge, unfamiliar problems, and uncertain leadership.
Discusses the Radicals' effort to secure racial justice in
the South, the fact that corruption existed not only in the
South, and that some worthwhile measures emerged from
'carpetbag' legislatures." Guide to Read in Am Hist {review of 1961 edition}
   Includes bibliographical references

Grumet, Bridget Hall
Reconstruction era: primary sources; Lawrence
W. Baker, project editor. UXL 2004 xxv, 228p il
(Reconstruction Era reference library) $60
     973.8
   1. Reconstruction (1865-1876)
   ISBN 0-7876-9219-0   LC 2004-17309
   This book "contains 19 complete or partial documents,
such as the Fourteenth Amendment of the U.S. Constitution and Rutherford B. Hayes' inaugural address. Each
document is accompanied by an introduction, keys to
reading the document, a discussion of subsequent events
related to the document, and other material." Booklist
   Includes bibliographical references

Howes, Kelly King
Reconstruction era: almanac; Lawrence W.
Baker, project editor. UXL 2004 xxxvii, 228p il
map (Reconstruction Era reference library) $60
     973.8
   1. Reconstruction (1865-1876)
   ISBN 0-7876-9217-4   LC 2004-17301
   This book "covers the political and social aspects of
Reconstruction, including carpetbaggers and scalawags,
amnesty for white Southerners, 'Black Codes,' the impeachment of President Johnson, the rise of the Ku Klux
Klan, attempts to restore the old order in the South and
much more." Publisher's note
   Includes bibliographical references

Rauchway, Eric, 1979-
Murdering McKinley; the making of Theodore
Roosevelt's America. Hill & Wang 2003 250p il
$25; pa $14   **973.8**
   1. McKinley, William, 1843-1901—Assassination
2. Czolgosz, Leon F., 1873?-1901 3. Roosevelt, Theodore, 1858-1919 4. United States—Politics and government—1898-1919
   ISBN 0-8090-7170-3; 0-8090-1638-9 (pa)
            LC 2003-40666
   The author "uses a search for the motive of President
William McKinley's assassin as a means to comment on
the Progressive Era and show how Theodore Roosevelt
manipulated the emotions of rage and despair after the

tragic event to give it meaning, thereby advancing his
own political vision. . . . Novel in its conception and
well written, the book is appropriate for public as well
as academic libraries." Choice
   Includes bibliographical references

Sandoz, Mari, 1896-1966
The Battle of the Little Bighorn. Lippincott
1966 191p maps (Great battles of history series)
hardcover o.p. pa $12.95 *   **973.8**
   1. Custer, George Armstrong, 1839-1876 2. Little Bighorn, Battle of the, 1876
   ISBN 0-397-00410-9; 0-8032-9100-0 (pa)
   "An account of the United States Army expedition
against the Sioux Nation with emphasis on the political
motives and ambitions of General Custer." Publ Wkly
   Includes bibliographical references

Schlereth, Thomas J.
Victorian America; transformations in everyday
life, 1876-1915. HarperCollins Pubs. 1991 363p
(Everyday life in America) pa $15 hardcover o.p.
     973.8
   1. United States—Social life and customs
   ISBN 0-06-092160-9 (pa)   LC 89-46555
   The author surveys the objects, events, experiences,
products and tastes that comprised what he terms America's Victorian culture (1876-1915) and shows how its
values shaped modern life.
   "What a wonderful book. . . . Schlereth is no wry
compiler of trivia. His analysis of social context reveals
truly profound, intangible transformations in how and
where Americans spent their time during four pivotal
decades." Booklist
   Includes bibliographical references

Utley, Robert Marshall, 1929-
Custer: cavalier in buckskin; {by} Robert M.
Utley. rev ed. University of Okla. Press 2001 176p
il map $29.95; pa $17.95   **973.8**
   1. Custer, George Armstrong, 1839-1876 2. Native
Americans—Wars 3. West (U.S.)—History
   ISBN 0-8061-3347-3; 0-8061-3387-2 (pa)
            LC 2001-27356
   First published 1988 with title: Cavalier in buckskin
   The author offers theories and facts regarding the mythology surrounding Custer, telling how he promoted
himself as an American hero in an effort to increase his
rank in the army
   This "is a fair and full-bodied account that cogently
interprets the facts, provides the proper psychological
analysis, and offers solid grounding for the development
of the considerable myth." Booklist {review of 1988 edition}
   Includes bibliographical references

Welch, James, 1940-2003
Killing Custer; the Battle of the Little Bighorn and the fate of the Plains Indians; by James Welch with Paul Stekler. Norton 1994 320p il pa $14.95 hardcover o.p. **973.8**
1. Little Bighorn, Battle of the, 1876 2. Native Americans—Wars
ISBN 0-393-32939-9 (pa)   LC 94-5617
"Welch produced this history of the Indian wars of the northern plains as a by-product of his work scripting a television documentary on the Battle of the Little Bighorn. In addition to military history, it contains long sections describing the life of the Plains Indians, accounts of contemporary Indian radical groups, and Welch's reactions while visiting the various historic sites in the area." Libr J
Includes bibliographical references

973.9   United States—1901-

American decades. Gale Res. 1994-2000 10v set $995 **973.9**
1. United States—Civilization 2. United States—History—20th century
ISBN 0-7876-5076-5
Also available American decades primary sources ten volume companion set $995 (ISBN 0-7876-6587-8)
"A Manly, Inc. book"
The set is divided as follows: 1900-1909 (ISBN 0-8103-5722-4); 1910-1919 (ISBN 0-8103-5723-2); 1920-1929 (ISBN 0-8103-5724-0); 1930-1939 (ISBN 0-8103-5725-9); 1940-1949 (ISBN 0-8103-5726-7); 1950-1959 (ISBN 0-8103-5727-5); 1960-1969 (ISBN 0-8103-8883-9); 1970-1979 (ISBN 0-8103-8882-0); 1980-1989 (ISBN 0-8103-8881-2); 1990-1999 (ISBN 0-7876-4030-1)
"A series of volumes covering the twentieth century by decades. . . . Fun to browse, each volume is divided into 13 sections covering topics such as the arts, government and politics, lifestyles and social trends, medicine and health, and sports. Each section opens with a chronology and overview and closes with short biographies, deaths, and a bibliography of important books published in the decade. Sidebars highlight events and prominent individuals." Am Libr

American decades primary sources; Cynthia Rose, project editor. Gale 2004 10v il map set $1,055 **973.9**
1. United States—Civilization 2. United States—History—20th century—Sources
ISBN 0-7876-6587-8   LC 2002-8155
Companion set to American decades published 1994-2000
Contents: [1] 1900-1909 -- [2] 1910-1919 -- [3] 1920-1929 -- [4] 1930-1939 -- [5] 1940-1949 -- [6] 1950-1959 -- [7] 1960-1969 -- [8] 1970-1979 -- [9] 1980-1989 -- [10] 1990-1999
"A treasure trove of more than 2,000 primary sources on U.S. history and culture, ranging from speeches and literary works to graphs and architectural drawings. Although many of the sources might be found on the Internet, they lack the organization and context provided here." Booklist

Cooke, Alistair, 1908-2004
Letter from America, 1946-2004. Knopf 2004 xx, 503p il $35 **973.9**
1. United States—Social life and customs
ISBN 1-4000-4402-2   LC 2004-304550
This is a collection of radio essays originally broadcast on the BBC which "showcased Cooke's . . . impressions of the American scene, its players and victims, its edges and contours, its movers, shakers and fools." Publ Wkly
"Arranged into chapters by decades, these commentaries reveal not only Cooke's mastery of clear prose but also the range of American topics that caught his interest, from politics to culture. . . . A book for appreciators of American culture in the second half of the previous century as well as those who relish the essay in either oral or written form." Booklist

Evans, Harold
The American century; by Harold Evans with Gail Buckland and Kevin Baker. Knopf 1998 xxiii, 710p il hardcover o.p. pa $35 **973.9**
1. United States—History—20th century 2. United States—Politics and government—20th century
ISBN 0-679-41070-8; 0-375-70938-X (pa)
LC 96-7449
This narrative history of the United States spans the years 1889-1989
This "compilation is a family album for all Americans to ponder; it smartly emphasizes the contributions of men and women other than presidents and top politicians, although these leaders are not slighted. The chapters are thematic, forthrightly exploring such overarching ideas as capitalism vs. communism, the contributions of immigrants, the struggle for civil rights, and the rise of conservatism at the century's close. Accompanying the text are 900 unforgettable (and many rarely seen) photographs." Libr J
Includes bibliographical references

Galbraith, John Kenneth, 1908-2006
Name-dropping; from F.D.R. on. Houghton Mifflin 1999 194p $26; pa $14 **973.9**
1. Politicians—United States 2. United States—Politics and government—20th century
ISBN 0-395-82288-2; 0-618-15453-1 (pa)
LC 99-20070
The author "reminisces about important figures with whom he has been involved in his long and distinguished life in the public arena. Among the brief portraits are those of Franklin and Eleanor Roosevelt, Harry Truman, JFK, LBJ, Nehru, and others. More than the self-effacing title indicates, this book offers important insights into the people and times on which its author reflects. Galbraith writes with a wit, style, and elegance few can match." Libr J

Gould, Lewis L.
The modern American presidency; foreword by Richard Norton Smith. University Press of Kansas 2003 301p il $29.95; pa $15.95 **973.9**
1. Presidents—United States
ISBN 0-7006-1252-1; 0-7006-1330-7 (pa)
LC 2002-154108

Gould, Lewis L.—*Continued*

Contents: The age of Cortelyou : William McKinley and Theodore Roosevelt -- The lawyer and the professor : William Howard Taft and Woodrow Wilson -- The modern presidency recedes : Warren G. Harding, Calvin Coolidge, and Herbert Hoover -- The modern presidency revives and grows : Franklin D. Roosevelt -- The presidency in the Cold War era : Harry S. Truman and Dwight D. Eisenhower -- The souring of the modern presidency : John F. Kennedy and Lyndon B. Johnson -- The rise of the continuous campaign : Richard Nixon -- The modern presidency under siege : Gerald Ford and Jimmy Carter -- The modern presidency in a Republican era : Ronald Reagan and George H.W. Bush -- Perils of the modern presidency : Bill Clinton

The author "does a solid job of reviewing the modern presidents, covering the high and low points of each administration, and giving a general audience a readable, engaging text." Libr J

Includes bibliographical references

Menand, Louis

The Metaphysical Club. Farrar, Straus & Giroux 2001 546p il $30; pa $15   **973.9**

1. Holmes, Oliver Wendell, 1841-1935 2. James, William, 1842-1910 3. Peirce, Charles S. (Charles Sanders), 1839-1914 4. Dewey, John, 1859-1952 5. United States—Intellectual life 6. Metaphysics

ISBN 0-374-19963-9; 0-374-52849-7 (pa)

LC 00-66279

In this book Menand "provides a panorama of American post-Civil War thought . . . focusing on the lives and thinking of 'four giants': William James, Charles Sanders Peirce, Oliver Wendell Holmes Jr., and John Dewey. . . . The 'club' of the title, with the four giants as its core, actually only existed for about nine months in 1872, but its members influenced the culture for decades to come." Booklist

"Menand brings rare common sense and graceful, witty prose to his richly nuanced reading of American intellectual history." N Y Times Book Rev

Includes bibliographical references

Morgan, Ted, 1932-

Reds: McCarthyism in twentieth-century America. Random House 2003 685p $35; pa $16.95   **973.9**

1. McCarthy, Joseph, 1908-1957 2. Anticommunist movements 3. Communism—United States 4. United States—Politics and government—20th century

ISBN 0-679-44399-1; 0-812-97302-X (pa)

LC 2003-46509

Morgan "defines McCarthyism both as 'publicizing accusations of disloyalty and subversion with insufficient regard to evidence' and as 'dubious methods of investigation in order to suppress opposition.' He {aims to} show that unreliable witnesses, forged documents and indiscriminate campaigns against subversives, real and imagined, date back to 1917. And he argues that McCarthyism persists long past the Wisconsin senator's death in 1957." Newsweek

"Senator Joseph McCarthy's demagogic career is just part of this sweeping account of anti-Communist purges and Communist espionage." N Y Times Book Rev

Includes bibliographical references

Slotkin, Richard, 1942-

Gunfighter nation; the myth of the frontier in twentieth-century America. University of Oklahoma Press 1998 850p pa $32.95   **973.9**

1. Frontier and pioneer life—West (U.S.) 2. Popular culture—United States

ISBN 0-8061-3031-8; 978-0-8061-3031-6

LC 97-32043

First published 1992 by Atheneum

This is the final volume of Slotkin's trilogy on the influence of the frontier on the American character begun with Regeneration through violence (1973) and The fatal environment (1985)

"On the premise that myth is spread by mass media, Slotkin examines numerous elements of popular culture ranging from James Fenimore Cooper's Hawkeye in The last of the Mohicans to John Wayne's Green Berets film to demonstrate how the myth affects American perceptions regarding foreign and domestic issues." Libr J

Includes bibliographical references

St. James encyclopedia of popular culture; editors, Tom Pendergast and Sara Pendergast; with an introduction by Jim Cullen. St. James Press 1999 c2000 5v il set $695   **973.9**

1. Popular culture—United States—Encyclopedias 2. United States—Civilization—Encyclopedias

ISBN 1-55862-400-7   LC 99-46540

This is an "overview of popular culture in twentieth-century America with a particular emphasis on the second half of the century. In more than 2,700 entries, the nearly 450 contributors attempt to cover the major personalities, productions, products, events, and developments from film, music, print culture, social life, sports, television and radio, art, and performances (which include theater, dance, stand-up comedy, and other live performances). . . . The entries seldom sink to trivialization. They are generally thoughtful and well written, providing information and insight. . . . The editors have done a masterful job of providing something for nearly everyone." Am Ref Books Annu, 2001

Includes bibliographical references

973.91   United States—1901-1953

Allen, Frederick Lewis, 1890-1954

Only yesterday; an informal history of the 1920's. Wiley 1997 285p (Wiley investment classics) $21.95   **973.91**

1. United States—History—1919-1933 2. United States—Social conditions 3. United States—Economic conditions—1919-1933

ISBN 0-471-18952-9   LC 97-19930

Also available in paperback from HarperCollins Pubs.

A reissue of the title first published 1931 by Harper and Brothers

"An account of the years from the spring of 1919 to . . . {1931}. It is a kaleidoscopic picture of American politics, society, manners, morals, and economic conditions." Booklist

Includes bibliographical references

Burns, James MacGregor

The three Roosevelts; patrician leaders who transformed America; by James MacGregor Burns & Susan Dunn. Atlantic Monthly Press 2001 678p il $37.50; pa $18 **973.91**

1. Roosevelt, Theodore, 1858-1919 2. Roosevelt, Franklin D. (Franklin Delano), 1882-1945 3. Roosevelt, Eleanor, 1884-1962 4. United States—Politics and government—20th century

ISBN 0-87113-780-1; 0-8021-3872-1 (pa)

LC 00-60896

Burns and Dunn "present an analysis of the Roosevelts that [aims to] establish the connections among their careers, ideas and values. . . . Theodore, Franklin and Eleanor not only changed the very nature of American society, [the authors argue], they also altered the history of the rest of the world." America

Burns and Dunn "succeed in approaching their subjects with grace, respect and insight. In the end, they do great justice to three remarkable lives." Publ Wkly

Includes bibliographical references

Hagedorn, Ann

Savage peace; hope and fear in America, 1919. Simon & Schuster 2007 543p il $30 **973.91**

1. United States—History—1919-1933 2. United States—Race relations

ISBN 978-0-7432-4371-1; 0-7432-4371-4

LC 2006-51258

An "account of America in upheaval in the wake of WWI. In 1919, both the world and the U.S. were in need of reconstruction: soldiers returning from war needed jobs, and the influenza epidemic wasn't quite under control. Two threads Hagedorn follows are middle-class Americans' fear of Bolshevism, and the struggles of black Americans." Publ Wkly

Hagedorn "weaves numerous threads of history together to provide a clear vision of American society at the dawn of the modern age. This is not the dull history of academia: Her writing is concise, colorful and compelling." PopMatters

Includes bibliographical references

Hofstadter, Richard, 1916-1970

The age of reform from Bryan to F.D.R. Knopf 1955 328, xxp pa $12.95 hardcover o.p. **973.91**

1. United States—Politics and government—20th century

ISBN 0-394-70095-3 (pa)

This analysis of the reform movements in American politics from 1890-1940 reviews: The agrarian uprising that found its expression in the Populist movement of the 1890's; The Progressive movement from about 1900-1914; The New Deal of the 1930's. Emphasis is placed upon the ideas of the leading political reformers.

Includes bibliographical references

Kennedy, David M., 1941-

Freedom from fear; the American people in depression and war, 1929-1945. Oxford Univ. Press 1999 936p il maps (Oxford history of the United States) $39.95; pa $22.50 * **973.91**

1. United States—History—1919-1933 2. United States—History—1933-1945

ISBN 0-19-503834-7; 0-19-514403-1 (pa)

LC 98-49580

Also available in a two-volume paperback edition

This narrative history of the United States spans the period from the Great Depression to the end of the Second World War

"Rarely does a work of historical synthesis combine such trenchant analysis and elegant writing. For its scope, its insight and its purring narrative engine, Kennedy's book will stand for years to come as the definitive account of the critical decades of the American century." Publ Wkly

Includes bibliographical references

Miller, Nathan, 1927-

New world coming; the 1920s and the making of modern America. Da Capo Press 2004 433p pa $19.95 **973.91**

1. Fitzgerald, F. Scott (Francis Scott), 1896-1940 2. United States—History—1919-1933

ISBN 978-0-306-81379-5; 0-306-81379-3

LC 2004-56140

First published 2003 by Scribner

The author "illuminates the United States as it existed under presidents Harding, Coolidge and Hoover, using the life of F. Scott Fitzgerald, with all its peaks and valleys during the 1920s, as the backbone of his narrative. . . . In addition to events in the arts and sciences, Miller details bitter labor struggles, the rise of the reconstituted Ku Klux Klan and Prohibition. . . . This volume comprises an excellent chronicle of that turbulent, troubled and tempestuous decade called 'the roaring '20s.'" Publ Wkly

Includes bibliographical references

Pietrusza, David, 1949-

1920: the year of the six presidents. Carroll & Graf 2007 533p il $28.95 **973.91**

1. Presidents—United States—Election—1920

ISBN 978-0-78671-622-7; 0-7867-1622-3

"Six men—a sitting president, former president, and four eventual presidents—competed in the 1920 presidential election. . . . [The author] contends that this election marked the birth of modern American politics. . . . The many issues and forces that swirled during that time, from the fear of Communists and Socialists and the terrorism they allegedly perpetrated to technological advances and Prohibition, make for a fascinating and compelling tale of an often-overlooked election in our history." Libr J

Includes bibliographical references

Schlesinger, Arthur M., 1917-2007
The crisis of the old order, 1919-1933; [by] Arthur M. Schlesinger, Jr. Houghton Mifflin 2003 557p (Age of Roosevelt) pa $17   **973.91**
    1. Roosevelt, Franklin D. (Franklin Delano), 1882-1945 2. United States—History—1919-1933
    ISBN 0-618-34085-8   LC 2003-47884
    "A Mariner book"
    First published 1957
    This is the first of three volumes which interpret the political, economic, social, and intellectual life of the United States during the time when Franklin D. Roosevelt was in office. This volume covers the years preceding his first term
    Includes bibliographical references
    Followed by The coming of the New Deal, and The politics of upheaval

Shlaes, Amity
The forgotten man; a new history of the Great Depression. HarperCollins Publishers 2007 464p il $26.95   **973.91**
    1. Great Depression, 1929-1939 2. New Deal, 1933-1939
    ISBN 978-0-06-621170-1; 0-06-621170-0
              LC 2006-49761
    "Reminding readers that the reputedly do-nothing Hoover pulled hard on the fiscal levers (raising tariffs, increasing government spending), Shlaes nevertheless emphasizes that his enthusiasm for intervention paled against the ebullient FDR's glee in experimentation. She focuses closely on the influence of his fabled Brain Trust, her narrative shifting among Raymond Moley, Rexford Tugwell, and other prominent New Dealers. Businesses that litigated their resistance to New Deal regulations attract Shlaes' attention, as do individuals who coped with the despair of the 1930s through self-help, such as Alcoholics Anonymous cofounder Bill Wilson. The book culminates in the rise of Wendell Willkie, and Shlaes' accent on personalities is an appealing avenue into her skeptical critique of the New Deal." Booklist
    Includes bibliographical references

Terkel, Studs, 1912-2008
Hard times; an oral history of the great depression. Norton 2000 462p pa $14.95 *   **973.91**
    1. Great Depression, 1929-1939 2. United States—Social conditions 3. United States—Economic conditions—1919-1933 4. United States—Economic conditions—1933-1945
    ISBN 1-56584-656-7   LC 2003-389318
    A reissue of the title first published 1970 by Pantheon Bks.
    "Persons of all ages, occupations, and classes scattered across the U.S. remember what they experienced or were told about the economic crisis of the 1930's. The result is a social document of immense interest." Booklist

Watkins, T. H. (Tom H.), 1936-2000
The hungry years; a narrative history of the Great Depression in America. Holt & Co. 1999 587p il pa $17 hardcover o.p.   **973.91**
    1. Great Depression, 1929-1939 2. United States—Economic conditions—1919-1933 3. United States—Economic conditions—1933-1945
    ISBN 0-8050-6506-7 (pa)   LC 99-10391
    "A Marian Wood book"
    "This book explores how everyday Americans across the country coped with economic disaster." Libr J
    "The vignettes Watkins selects are gritty, visceral, and seamlessly sutured to the federal programs that rolled out in the course of the decade, making this a signal addition to the rich historiography of the Depression." Booklist
    Includes bibliographical references

973.917   United States—Administration of Franklin D. Roosevelt, 1933-1945

Leuchtenburg, William Edward, 1922-
Franklin D. Roosevelt and the New Deal, 1932-1940; {by} William E. Leuchtenburg. Harper & Row 1963 393p il (New American nation series) pa $16 hardcover o.p.   **973.917**
    1. Roosevelt, Franklin D. (Franklin Delano), 1882-1945 2. New Deal, 1933-1939 3. United States—History—1933-1945
    ISBN 0-06-133025-6 (pa)
    This treatment of Roosevelt's first two terms in office emphasizes the economic crisis and New Deal reforms. The author shows how social forces influenced government action: the San Francisco strike in 1934, the careers of Huey Long and Father Coughlin, the sharecroppers' revolt, and unemployment
    This book "is comprehensive, logically organized, and written with clarity and detachment." Am Hist Rev
    Includes bibliographical references

Schlesinger, Arthur M., 1917-2007
The coming of the New Deal, 1933-1935; {by} Arthur M. Schlesinger, Jr. Houghton Mifflin 2003 669p (Age of Roosevelt) pa $17   **973.917**
    1. Roosevelt, Franklin D. (Franklin Delano), 1882-1945 2. New Deal, 1933-1939 3. United States—History—1933-1945
    ISBN 0-618-34086-6   LC 2003-47859
    "A Mariner book"
    First published 1959
    "This second volume of 'The Age of Roosevelt' continues the work begun with 'The Crisis of the Old Order, 1919-1933'. . . . The dramatic story of how representative democracy began the battle to conquer economic collapse is followed through the first two years of the New Deal." Libr J
    Includes bibliographical references
    Followed by The politics of upheaval

Schlesinger, Arthur M., 1917-2007—*Continued*

The politics of upheaval, 1935-1936; {by} Arthur M. Schlesinger, Jr. Houghton Mifflin 2003 749p (Age of Roosevelt) pa $17   **973.917**
1. Roosevelt, Franklin D. (Franklin Delano), 1882-1945 2. New Deal, 1933-1939 3. United States—History—1933-1945
ISBN 0-618-34087-4   LC 2003-47889
"A Mariner book"
First published 1960
This third volume of The age of Roosevelt "concentrates on the turbulent concluding years of Franklin D. Roosevelt's first term." Publisher's note
Includes bibliographical references

973.92   United States—1953-2001

Atlas of American politics, 1960-2000; [by] Fred M. Shelley [et al.] CQ Press 2002 242p maps $156.25 *   **973.92**
ISBN 1-56802-665-X   LC 2001-18267
This work "examines U.S. government and politics at the congressional district, state, and national levels from a combined historical, geographical, and political perspective. More than 200 maps from a variety of government and private sources show the relationship between the nation's geography and its political life. . . . This book provides a unique look at U.S. politics during the last 40 years and will be useful to students and researchers from the high-school level up." Booklist
Includes bibliographical references

Bloom, Allan David

The closing of the American mind. Simon & Schuster 1987 392p pa $14 hardcover o.p.
    973.92
1. Higher education 2. United States—Intellectual life
ISBN 0-671-65715-1 (pa)   LC 86-24768
This is the author's assessment of liberal arts education today. "In essence, he argues that over the last 25 years the academy has all but abandoned the intellectual and moral principles that have traditionally informed and given substance to liberal education, becoming prey to the enthusiasms—increasingly politicized—of the moment." N Y Times Book Rev

Bryson, Bill

I'm a stranger here myself; notes on returning to America after 20 years away. Broadway Bks. 1999 288p pa $14.95 hardcover o.p.   **973.92**
1. United States—Description and travel 2. United States—Social life and customs
ISBN 0-7679-0382-X (pa)   LC 99-18074
The author collects "columns on America he wrote weekly, while living in New Hampshire in the mid-to-late 1990s, for a British Sunday newspaper. Although he happily describes himself as dazzled by American ease, friendliness and abundance, Bryson has no trouble finding comic targets, among them fast food, computer efficiency and, ironically, American friendliness and putative convenience." Publ Wkly

The **Columbia** guide to America in the 1960s; David Farber and Beth Bailey, editors. Columbia Univ. Press 2001 508p il map (Columbia guides to American history and cultures) $60; pa $25   **973.92**
1. United States—History—1961-1974 2. United States—Social conditions
ISBN 0-231-11372-2; 0-231-11373-0 (pa)
    LC 00-65577
This reference work includes "a dictionary, an extensive annotated bibliography, a chronology of the era, and statistical information [and] two extraordinary bonuses: a section 'Debating the Sixties,' which includes ten essays by prominent historians . . . and an excellent 77-page history of the 1960s. This book is a fine addition to any library's collection." Choice
Includes bibliographical references

Frum, David, 1960-

How we got here; the 70's: the decade that brought you modern life (for better or worse). Basic Bks. 2000 xxiv, 418p il pa $18.95 hardcover o.p.   **973.92**
1. United States—Civilization—1970-
ISBN 0-465-01496-5 (pa)
The author "aims 'to describe—and to judge' the transformation of American values during the '70s. Surveying politics, legal cases and opinion polls as well as popular culture, he links what he sees as America's loss of faith in government, the rise of 'sourness and cynicism' and the culture of licentiousness and divorce, among other social changes, to events in that decade." Publ Wkly
Includes bibliographical references

Gitlin, Todd

The sixties; years of hope, days of rage. Bantam Bks. 1987 513p pa $19.95 hardcover o.p. *
    973.92
1. United States—History—1961-1974 2. United States—Social conditions 3. Students—Political activity
ISBN 0-553-37212-2 (pa)   LC 87-47575
"Though ex-SDS leader Gitlin occasionally falls prey to the self-indulgence that snares most sixties' commentators, his analysis of the decade's politics is thought-provoking and clearheaded. Rather than singing the familiar hymn of praise to youthful idealism, Gitlin carefully dissects why the activist spirit developed when it did and what its legacy has been." Am Libr
Includes bibliographical references

Gregory, Ross

Cold War America, 1946 to 1990; Richard Balkin, general editor. Facts on File 2003 670p il map (Almanacs of American life) $105
    973.92
1. Cold war 2. United States—History—1945- 3. United States—Social conditions
ISBN 0-8160-3868-6   LC 2001-51136
"This is a treasure trove of statistical information documenting the enormous changes in American life from

Gregory, Ross—*Continued*

1945 to 1990. . . . Found herein are data on everything from the population by sex . . . region, and race, business formations and failures, bull and bear markets, and operations of the postal service to the federal debt, high school seniors and drugs, executions by gender and race, and recipients of National Book Awards and Pulitzer Prizes. . . . Enhancing the work's appeal are photographs throughout the text and an exhaustive index." Am Ref Books Annu, 2003

Includes bibliographical references

Halberstam, David, 1934-2007

The fifties. Villard Bks. 1993 800p il pa $17.95 hardcover o.p.   **973.92**

1. United States—Social life and customs 2. United States—Politics and government—20th century 3. Popular culture—United States

ISBN 0-449-90933-6 (pa)   LC 92-56815

This is a social history of the United States during the 1950s

The author's "sources are secondary and derivative, but his instinct for the revealing anecdote, his ear for the memorable quote, and his awesome powers of organization add up to a variegated overview that moves seamlessly between the serious shenanigans of Chief Justice Earl Warren and the frivolous ones of . . . Grace Metalious." Natl Rev

Includes bibliographical references

Huchthausen, Peter A., 1939-

America's splendid little wars; a short history of U.S. military engagements, 1975-2000. Viking 2003 254p il, maps $25.95; pa $15

973.92

1. Intervention (International law) 2. United States—Military history

ISBN 0-670-03232-8; 0-14-200465-0 (pa)

LC 2002-38025

This is "a review of America's conflicts since the fall of Saigon in 1975. Each of the 15 chronologically arranged conflicts has its own chapter, and they are also grouped by presidential administration, with the author demonstrating how U.S. foreign policy changed during each administration. The author does an excellent job of describing the circumstances surrounding the different conflicts, including eyewitness testimony and solid research to tell each story. . . . This book should appeal to subject specialists and casual readers alike." Libr J

Includes bibliographical references

Kort, Michael

The Columbia guide to the Cold War. Columbia Univ. Press 1998 366p (Columbia guides to American history and cultures) $60; pa $19.50 *

973.92

1. Cold war 2. United States—Foreign relations 3. United States—History—1945-

ISBN 0-231-10772-2; 0-231-10773-0 (pa)

LC 98-7154

The author begins "with a narrative survey of the Cold War which explains some of the historiographical

debates that have occupied historians for more than 50 years. Following this section is a mini-encyclopedia consisting of one- or two-page essays on a wide range of Cold War topics. The book concludes with a concise chronology and a comprehensive bibliography of books, films, novels, journal articles, and archival sources. Finally . . . Kort points out some of the relevant current websites and CD-ROM products." Libr J

Kuralt, Charles, 1934-1997

Charles Kuralt's America. Anchor Books 1996 279p il pa $14.95   **973.92**

1. United States—Description and travel 2. United States—Social life and customs

ISBN 0-385-48510-7; 978-0-385-48510-4

LC 96-18992

First published 1995 by Putnam

"After serving 37 years as a reporter at CBS, Kuralt retired and set out on a trip to see his favorite American locations. . . . In this journal, the author records the people, places, and pets he encountered." Libr J

"Kuralt is not in search of crises or epiphanies; he values nature and good food, neighborliness and craftsmanship, quaintness and quirkiness. Though no literary match for American chroniclers like Calvin Trillin, the effable Kuralt does, in un-fancy style, convey his enthusiasm and his engagement." Publ Wkly

On the road with Charles Kuralt. Fawcett 1986 363p il pa $19   **973.92**

1. United States—Social life and customs 2. United States—Description and travel

ISBN 0-449-00740-5; 978-0-449-00740-2

First published 1985 by Putnam

"As a CBS reporter specializing in 'soft' news, Kuralt has been roaming around the U.S. since 1967 in search of 'just plain folks.' Some 100 of the television interviews that resulted from that search have been transcribed for this collection. Loosely organized by themes emphasizing the individuality, altruism, and humor that characterize small town and rural Americans, the interviews and anecdotes are consistently entertaining." Booklist

Marling, Karal Ann

As seen on TV; the visual culture of everyday life in the 1950s. Harvard Univ. Press 1994 328p il map $27.50; pa $20.50   **973.92**

1. Television broadcasting 2. Popular culture—United States 3. United States—Social life and customs

ISBN 0-674-04882-2; 0-674-04883-0 (pa)

LC 94-2814

"Marling highlights the impact of television's first influential decade. From Mamie Eisenhower's apparel to the aesthetics of food advertising and cookbooks, she [aims to] demonstrate the extent to which Americans began to measure their personal lives against what was seen on television." Christ Sci Monit

"A nostalgic, informative and sometimes funny view of 1950's American culture." Publ Wkly

Includes bibliographical references

Morrow, Lance

Second drafts of history; essays; Lance Morrow. Basic Books 2006 323p $26.95   **973.92**

1. United States—Politics and government—1989-
2. United States—Social conditions

ISBN 0-4650-4750-5   LC 2005-17092

"Loosely arranged by subject, these essays cover the gamut of human experience, seen through Morrow's practiced yet unjaundiced point of view. Whether offering a fact-laden piece on the AIDS epidemic or a personal meditation on the Jonesboro, Ark., school shootings, Morrow manages—without becoming sentimental—to evoke the spirit of a collective America. . . . Since Morrow is a weekly columnist, the news of the day is often the primary subject." Publ Wkly

Phillips, Kevin P.

Arrogant capital; Washington, Wall Street, and the frustration of American politics; {by} Kevin Phillips. Little, Brown 1994 231p pa $18.99 hardcover o.p.   **973.92**

1. United States—Politics and government—20th century 2. Political corruption

ISBN 0-316-70602-7 (pa)   LC 94-10035

This book "suggests that Bill Clinton's early successes and later failures were both symptoms of a deeper political and economic shift. That shift . . . is the collapse of the capacity of the US economy to sustain growth in jobs and income for the middle class. The 'arrogant capital' of Phillips's title means both Washington, DC, with its lobbyists and warring interest groups, and the financial capital that flows through brokerages and investment banks without creating an adequate base for middle-class employment." N Y Rev Books

Phillips "makes a convincing case that voters see Washington as the enemy because they can't crack the interlock between interest-group power and the political system." N Y Times Book Rev

Includes bibliographical references

Postwar

Postwar America; an encyclopedia of social, political, cultural, and economic history; James Ciment, editor. M.E. Sharpe 2006 4v il set $399   **973.92**

1. United States—Civilization—Encyclopedias

ISBN 0-7656-8067-X; 978-0-7656-8067-9

LC 2004-13120

"A-Z entries address specific persons, groups, concepts, events, geographical locations, organizations, and cultural and technological phenomena. Sidebars highlight primary source materials, items of special interest, statistical data, and other information; and Cultural Landmark entries chronologically detail the music, literature, arts, and cultural history of the era. Bibliographies covering literature from the postwar era and about the era are also included, as well as illustrations and specialized indexes." Publisher's note

Includes bibliographical references

Rather, Dan

The American dream; stories from the heart of our nation. Morrow 2001 xxii, 266p hardcover o.p. pa $12.95   **973.92**

1. American national characteristics 2. United States—Social life and customs 3. United States—Social conditions

ISBN 0-688-17892-8; 0-06-093770-X (pa)

LC 2001-30031

In this book Rather tells stories of individual Americans and their dreams. He "groups his material into chapters that focus on elements of our national aspirations: liberty, enterprise, pursuit of happiness, family, fame, education, innovation, and 'giving back.' The Americans that Rather describes are a diverse group but, he urges, their stories are an inspirational reminder of the power of the nation's fundamental ideas to motivate a wide range of people." Booklist

Schwartz, Richard Alan, 1951-

The 1990s; [by] Richard A. Schwartz. Facts on File 2006 496p il (Eyewitness history) $75   **973.92**

1. United States—History—1989- 2. United States—Politics and government—1989-

ISBN 0-8160-5696-X   LC 2004-28884

This book "provides hundreds of firsthand accounts of the 1990s—including diary entries, letters, speeches, and newspaper accounts—that illustrate how historical events appeared to those who lived through them. Each chapter provides an introductory essay and a chronology of events." Publisher's note

Includes bibliographical references

Cold War culture; media and the arts, 1945-1990; [by] Richard A. Schwartz. Facts on File 1998 376p il (Cold War America) $60.50; pa $24.95   **973.92**

1. Popular culture—United States 2. United States—Civilization

ISBN 0-8160-3104-5; 0-8160-4264-0 (pa)

LC 96-29642

At head of title: Cold War America

This work "covers the various influences on American culture during the years 1945 to 1990. Schwartz organizes Cold War culture alphabetically within the following broad categories: art, cartoons, consumer goods, dance, film, games and toys, television and theater. . . . This reference source is easy to read and hard to put down as a browsing item." SLJ

Includes bibliographical references

Smith, Hedrick

The power game; how Washington works. Random House 1988 xxii, 793p pa $16.95 o.p.   **973.92**

1. United States—Politics and government—1974-1989 2. Power (Social sciences)

ISBN 0-345-41048-3 (pa)   LC 87-42669

The author "relies primarily on anecdotes and case studies from the Reagan era to illustrate how the use of power determines the effectiveness of government." Libr J

Smith, Hedrick—*Continued*

Smith "has an insider's awareness of the alliances, machinations and turf-battles that make the capital work; he knows what he is talking about." Economist

Includes bibliographical references

Witcover, Jules

The year the dream died; revisiting 1968 in America. Warner Bks. 1997 544p $25; pa $16

973.92

1. United States—History—1961-1974

ISBN 0-446-51849-2; 0-446-67471-0 (pa)

LC 96-42017

Political columnist Witcover reviews "the tumultuous year in which the nation came 'unglued.' Nixon and Agnew vie for the villain's role, although neither would have been significant, contends the author, had LBJ not eroded his Kennedy legacy by escalating American involvement in Vietnam. . . . This backward look is enriched by the 20/20 hindsight of surviving participants, some still prominent in public life." Publ Wkly

Woodward, Bob, 1943-

Shadow; five presidents and the legacy of Watergate. Simon & Schuster 1999 592p il pa $16 hardcover o.p.   **973.92**

1. Presidents—United States 2. Watergate Affair, 1972-1974 3. United States—Politics and government—1974-1989 4. United States—Politics and government—1989-

ISBN 0-684-85263-2 (pa)   LC 99-37045

Woodward examines the long-term effect of the Watergate Affair on the presidencies of Gerald Ford, Jimmy Carter, Ronald Reagan, George Bush, and Bill Clinton

The author is an "effective investigative journalist. These skills are on full display in Shadow. . . . {The book} is most interesting as a reconstruction of the many scandals that have troubled the Clinton Administration." Nation

Includes bibliographical references

973.921 United States— Administration of Dwight D. Eisenhower, 1953-1961

Branch, Taylor

Parting the waters: America in the King years, 1954-63. Simon & Schuster 1988 1064p il hardcover o.p. pa $22 *   **973.921**

1. King, Martin Luther, Jr., 1929-1968 2. United States—History—1953-1961 3. African Americans—Civil rights

ISBN 0-671-46097-8; 0-671-68742-5 (pa)

LC 88-24033

This history of the American civil rights movement from 1954 to 1963 focuses on the life of Dr. Martin Luther King.

The author "has searched out the hidden reality and often tragic human drama of the King years. On his best pages, the past, miraculously, seems to spring back to

life. King himself appears human, all too human. Yet when the reader is done, his remarkable virtues and ordinary vices seem of a piece, the component parts of a coherent, towering personality." Newsweek

Includes bibliographical references

Johnson, Haynes Bonner, 1931-

The age of anxiety; McCarthyism to terrorism; [by] Haynes Johnson. Harcourt 2005 609p il $26

973.921

1. McCarthy, Joseph, 1908-1957 2. Anticommunist movements 3. War on terrorism

ISBN 0-15-101062-5; 978-0-15-101062-2

LC 2005-13117

"A James H. Silberman book"

"Most of the volume is devoted to an account of the history and effects of the McCarthy era. . . . [According to the author], fears following September 11, 2001 . . . parallel those of the cold war." Christ Century

The author "offers an engrossing account of the career of red-baiting demagogue Joseph McCarthy and a chilling description of his legacy for today." Publ Wkly

Includes bibliographical references

973.922 United States— Administration of John F. Kennedy, 1961-1963

Benson, Michael

The encyclopedia of the JFK assassination. Facts on File 2002 348p il map (Facts on File library of American history) $75; pa $21.95

973.922

1. Kennedy, John F. (John Fitzgerald), 1917-1963—Assassination

ISBN 0-8160-4476-7; 0-8160-4477-5 (pa)

LC 2001-53212

"This volume provides a listing of people, places, and events related (however slightly) to November 22 to 24, 1963. Following an introduction that describes the events and summarizes conspiracy theories are hundreds of entries. . . . These range from a paragraph to identify people and groups . . . to 4 or 5 pages. . . . This volume is readable and intriguing." Booklist

Branch, Taylor

Pillar of fire; America in the King years, 1963-65. Simon & Schuster 1998 746p il pa $17 hardcover o.p. *   **973.922**

1. King, Martin Luther, Jr., 1929-1968 2. United States—History—1961-1974 3. African Americans—Civil rights

ISBN 0-684-84809-0 (pa)   LC 97-46076

Second volume in the author's proposed trilogy about the civil rights movement, begun with: Parting the waters: America in the King years, 1954-1963

This volume covers "the years of Birmingham, Freedom Summer, the Nobel Peace Prize award to Martin Luther King Jr., and countless other public and private campaigns, conflicts, episodes, and incidents." Libr J

"Branch's research is impeccable and his knowledge

Branch, Taylor—*Continued*
of his material solid. . . . The book is significant for
marshaling so much information, particularly the profiles
of all the many individuals involved in the race issues of
that time." Booklist
Includes bibliographical references

Bugliosi, Vincent
Reclaiming history; the assassination of
President John F. Kennedy. W.W. Norton & Co.
2007 xlv, 1612p il $49.95   **973.922**
1. Kennedy, John F. (John Fitzgerald), 1917-1963—
Assassination 2. Oswald, Lee Harvey, 1939-1963
3. Conspiracies
ISBN 978-0-393-04525-3; 0-393-04525-0
                                LC 2007-01545
The author argues that Lee Harvey Oswald was the
lone assassin of John F. Kennedy.
"Destined to be the most significant challenge (save
the Warren Report) to conspiracy theories, Bugliosi's
study will provoke controversy and debate." Booklist
Includes bibliographical references

Dobbs, Michael, 1950-
One minute to midnight; Kennedy, Khrushchev,
and Castro on the brink of nuclear war. Alfred A.
Knopf 2008 426p $28.95 *   **973.922**
1. Cuban Missile Crisis, 1962
ISBN 978-1-4000-4358-3; 1-4000-4358-1
                                LC 2007-52250
The author discusses the Cuban Missile Crisis of
1962.
This book "is filled with . . . insights that will change
the views of experts and help inform a new generation
of readers." N Y Times Book Rev
Includes bibliographical references

Freedman, Lawrence
Kennedy's wars; Berlin, Cuba, Laos, and
Vietnam. Oxford Univ. Press 2000 xx, 528p il
hardcover o.p. pa $18.95   **973.922**
1. Kennedy, John F. (John Fitzgerald), 1917-1963
2. United States—Foreign relations 3. Military policy—United States
ISBN 0-19-513453-2; 0-19-515243-3 (pa)
                                LC 99-87898
The author examines how President Kennedy's "time
in office was occupied with a series of confrontations
with communism. . . . {He contends that} in each of the
four cases under review Kennedy resisted pressure from
his staff and advisers, not to mention from the Pentagon,
to take drastic action, . . . and that he left the cold war
in a far less dangerous state than he found it." Economist
"Lawrence's book is an excellent treatment of U.S.
foreign policy during this dynamic era and an insightful
portrait of John F. Kennedy as a leader." Libr J
Includes bibliographical references

Fursenko, A. V. (Aleksandr Vasil´evich)
"One hell of a gamble"; Khrushchev, Castro,
and Kennedy, 1958-1964; {by} Aleksandr
Fursenko and Timothy Naftali. Norton 1997 420p
il pa $15.95 hardcover o.p.   **973.922**
1. Cuban Missile Crisis, 1962 2. United States—Foreign relations—Soviet Union 3. Soviet Union—Foreign relations—United States
ISBN 0-393-31790-0 (pa)   LC 97-1022
For this diplomatic history of the Cuban Missile Crisis, the authors were granted "permission to review
Krushchev's papers; they were also able to draw on archival material from other official Soviet sources." N Y
Times Book Rev
Includes bibliographical references

Halberstam, David, 1934-2007
The best and the brightest; foreword by John
McCain. Modern Library ed. Modern Lib. 2001
xxviii, 780p $24.95; pa $16,95   **973.922**
1. United States—Politics and government—1961-
1974 2. United States—Foreign relations—Vietnam
3. Vietnam—Foreign relations—United States
ISBN 0-679-64099-1; 0-449-90870-4 (pa)
                                LC 2001-31261
A reissue of the title first published 1972
"The author describes analytically rather than narra-
tively, how the Kennedy-Johnson intellectual (McNamara, Bundy, Rusk, Ball, Taylor, et al.) men praised as
'the best and the brightest' men of this century, became
the architects of the disastrous American policy of Indochina." Libr J
Includes bibliographical references

Kaiser, David E., 1947-
The road to Dallas; the assassination of John F.
Kennedy; [by] David Kaiser. Belknap Press of
Harvard University Press 2008 509p il map $35
                                973.922
1. Kennedy, John F. (John Fitzgerald), 1917-1963—
Assassination
ISBN 978-0-674-02766-4; 0-674-02766-3
                                LC 2007-27305
The author argues that "the events of November 22,
1963, cannot be understood without fully grasping the
two larger stories of which [he believes] they were a
part: the U.S. government's campaign against organized
crime, which began in the late 1950s and accelerated
dramatically under Robert Kennedy; and the . . . quest
of two administrations—along with a cadre of private interest groups—to eliminate Fidel Castro." Publisher's
note
"This is a deeply disturbing look at a national tragedy,
and Kaiser's sober tone and reasoned analysis may well
convince some in the Oswald-was-alone-nut camp." Publ
Wkly
Includes bibliographical references

Kennedy, Robert F., 1925-1968

Make gentle the life of this world; the vision of Robert F. Kennedy; edited and with an introduction by Maxwell Taylor Kennedy. Broadway Books 1999 188p il pa $15

973.922

1. Quotations

ISBN 0-7679-0371-4   LC 98-55988

First published 1998 by Harcourt Brace & Co.

This is a collection of quotations by Robert F. Kennedy and the authors who inspired him

"Chapters are arranged by issues that were most important to Kennedy and remain timely today—the responsibilities of citizens to their government, the tragedy of poverty in the midst of plenty, the importance of dissent in a democratic society, and work as the solution for the welfare crises. The book's haunting photos convey Kennedy's spirit as successfully as the words." Libr J

Includes bibliographical references

Thirteen days; a memoir of the Cuban missile crisis; with introductions by Robert S. McNamara and Harold Macmillan. Norton 1969 224p il pa $12.95 hardcover o.p.   **973.922**

1. Cuban Missile Crisis, 1962 2. United States—Politics and government—1961-1974 3. United States—Foreign relations—Soviet Union 4. Soviet Union—Foreign relations—United States

ISBN 0-393-31834-6 (pa)

A behind-the-scenes account of the Cuban Missile Crisis of 1962. Includes reproductions of pertinent documents and speeches by both President Kennedy and Nikita Khrushchev.

Matthews, Chris, 1945-

Kennedy & Nixon; the rivalry that shaped postwar America; {by} Christopher Matthews. Simon & Schuster 1996 377p il pa $14 hardcover o.p.   **973.922**

1. Kennedy, John F. (John Fitzgerald), 1917-1963 2. Nixon, Richard M. (Richard Milhous), 1913-1994 3. United States—Politics and government—20th century

ISBN 0-684-83246-1 (pa)   LC 96-15677

This exploration of the rift between Kennedy and Nixon "shows how these two anti-New Dealers, anti-Communists, and freshmen members of Congress in 1946 became enemies as their political careers advanced." Libr J

Includes bibliographical references

Posner, Gerald L.

Case closed; Lee Harvey Oswald and the assassination of JFK; [by] Gerald Posner. Anchor Books 2003 608p il pa $17.95   **973.922**

1. Kennedy, John F. (John Fitzgerald), 1917-1963—Assassination 2. Oswald, Lee Harvey, 1939-1963

ISBN 1-400-03462-0; 978-1-400-03462-8

LC 2003-283539

First published 1993

In this book Posner argues that Lee Harvey Oswald was solely responsible for the assassination of President Kennedy and that none of the theories alleging conspira-

cy is valid.

"One of the strongest and most important features of the book, indeed, is Posner's painstaking dissection of each and every one of the competing conspiracy theories. None of them stands up under scrutiny." Natl Rev

Includes bibliographical references

973.923   United States— Administration of Lyndon B. Johnson, 1963-1969

Branch, Taylor

At Canaan's edge; America in the King years, 1965-68. Simon & Schuster 2006 1039p il $35 *

973.923

1. King, Martin Luther, Jr., 1929-1968 2. United States—History—1961-1974 3. African Americans—Civil rights

ISBN 0-684-85712-X   LC 2005-40177

Third volume in the author's trilogy about the civil rights movement, begun with: Parting the waters: America in the King years, 1954-1963

In this history that follows the life of Martin Luther King "from the protest at Selma and the 1966 Meredith March through King's expanding political concern for the poor to his 1968 assassination in Memphis, Tenn., Branch gives us not only the civil rights leader's life but also the rapidly changing pulse of American culture and politics. . . . This magisterial book is a fitting tribute to a magisterial man." Publ Wkly

Includes bibliographical references

Busby, Horace W., d. 2000

The thirty-first of March; an intimate portrait of Lyndon Johnson's final days in office; [by] Horace Busby; with a preface by Scott Busby and an introduction by Hugh Sidey. Farrar, Straus and Giroux 2005 250p il $24; pa $14   **973.923**

1. Johnson, Lyndon B. (Lyndon Baines), 1908-1973 2. United States—Politics and government—1961-1974

ISBN 0-374-27574-2; 0-374-53021-1 (pa)

This book "covers the 20 years during which Busby served as a trusted advisor and speechwriter for Johnson. This previously unpublished manuscript was discovered by Busby's son after his father's death in 2000. . . . This is an engrossing and important contribution to our understanding of a compelling political personality." Booklist

Taking charge; the Johnson White House tapes, 1963-1964; edited and with commentary by Michael R. Beschloss. Simon & Schuster 1997 591p il pa $16 hardcover o.p.   **973.923**

1. Johnson, Lyndon B. (Lyndon Baines), 1908-1973 2. United States—Politics and government—1961-1974

ISBN 0-684-84792-2 (pa)   LC 97-26749

This book is a "selection of conversations taped by Lyndon B. Johnson during the first nine months of his Presidency—beginning on the day of the Kennedy assas-

Taking charge—*Continued*

sination and continuing through the close of the Democratic National Convention in 1964. . . . There are no stunning revelations and no recorded moments of epochal importance. But 'Taking Charge' is a riveting book nevertheless. This is partly because it has been superbly edited and annotated by the historian Michael R. Beschloss, who has made everything—even the most arcane references—accessible to ordinary readers." N Y Times Book Rev

The **Times** were a changin'; the sixties reader; edited by Irwin Unger and Debi Unger. Three Rivers Press (NY) 1998 355p pa $16 hardcover o.p. **973.923**
1. United States—History—1961-1974
ISBN 0-609-80337-9 (pa)   LC 97-39844
The Ungers have compiled "an anthology illustrating the social, cultural, and political events that made the 1960s distinctive in American history. {They} present nearly 60 letters, manifestos, reports, speeches, essays, articles, and court decisions . . . arranged in 12 chapters." Libr J
"The broad range of viewpoints and the easy access to such an array of primary sources make the book a powerful adjunct for study of the sixties, as well as an interesting book for browsing." Book Rep

973.924 United States— Administration of Richard Nixon, 1969-1974

Abuse of power; the new Nixon tapes; edited with an introduction and commentary by Stanley I. Kutler. Free Press 1997 xxiii, 675p pa $30.95 hardcover o.p. * **973.924**
1. Nixon, Richard M. (Richard Milhous), 1913-1994 2. Watergate Affair, 1972-1974 3. United States—Politics and government—1961-1974
ISBN 0-684-85187-3 (pa)   LC 97-32096
"This is an edited collection of transcripts of President Nixon's Watergate-related conversations made available under a 1974 Congressional directive covering tapes related to 'abuse of governmental power.' More than 90 percent of the volume covers the year after the June 1972 break-in and focuses on Watergate." Choice

Bernstein, Carl
All the president's men; {by} Carl Bernstein, Bob Woodward. Simon & Schuster 1999 349p il hardcover o.p. pa $14 **973.924**
1. Washington post 2. Watergate Affair, 1972-1974
ISBN 0-684-86355-3; 0-671-89441-2 (pa)
            LC 98-54773
A reissue of the title first published 1974
The two Washington Post reporters whose investigative journalism first revealed the Watergate scandal tell the way it happened from the first suspicions, through the trail of false leads, lies, secrecy, and high-level pressure, to the final moments when they were able to put the pieces of the puzzle together and write the series that won the Post a Pulitzer Prize

Caputo, Philip
13 seconds; a look back at the Kent State shootings. Chamberlain Bros. 2005 198p $21.95
            973.924
1. Kent State University 2. Vietnam War, 1961-1975—Protest movements
ISBN 1-59609-080-4   LC 2005-41328
Includes DVD
The author reconstructs "the events of May 4, 1970, when National Guard troops in Ohio opened fire on Kent State University students during an antiwar rally, killing four and wounding nine." Publ Wkly
"The book is packaged with a DVD containing the 2001 documentary Kent State: The Day the War Came Home. Together, the images and Caputo's words serve as a powerful antidote to the romanticization of an era." Booklist

Emery, Fred
Watergate; the corruption of American politics and the fall of Richard Nixon. Touchstone 1994 xvi, 559p il pa $25.95 **973.924**
1. Nixon, Richard M. (Richard Milhous), 1913-1994 2. Watergate Affair, 1972-1974
ISBN 0-684-81323-8   LC 95-12511
First published 1994 by Times Bks.
"In addition to an introductory section on the cast of characters involved, Emery provides a detailed examination of the Committee To Reelect the President (CRP) and its dirty tricks: wiretapping, money laundering campaigns, and the infamous burglary of Democratic National Committee headquarters. Unlike much of the psychopersonal material that has come out on Nixon, Emery's book focuses on the tough political problems, documenting the need for impeachment and ultimately endorsing it. Riveting reading that is based on an unprecedented combing of the primary sources." Libr J
Includes bibliographical references

Killen, Andreas
1973 nervous breakdown; Watergate, Warhol, and the birth of post-sixties America. Bloomsbury 2006 312p $24.95 **973.924**
1. United States—Civilization—1970-
ISBN 1-59691-059-3; 978-1-59691-059-1
            LC 2005-23661
This book is a "portrait of the year that delivered Roe v. Wade, Watergate, the winding down of the Vietnam War, the Arab oil embargo, the completion of the World Trade Center, repeated hijackings, and an outbreak of cults." Booklist
This "is a high-definition snapshot, both nostalgic and perceptive, of a transitional time." Libr J
Includes bibliographical references

Olson, Keith W., 1931-
Watergate; the presidential scandal that shook America. University Press of Kansas 2003 220p il $35; pa $15.95 **973.924**
1. Watergate Affair, 1972-1974
ISBN 0-7006-1250-5; 0-7006-1251-3 (pa)
            LC 2002-38058

Olson, Keith W., 1931-—Continued
The author describes "the White House-approved break-in at Democratic National Committee headquarters in Washington's Watergate complex and its aftermath—most importantly, the dramatic proceedings of the Senate Watergate Committee. . . . {This} book provides an excellent, compact narrative of a crucial moment in the history of the American presidency." Publ Wkly
Includes bibliographical references

Reston, James, Jr., 1941-
The conviction of Richard Nixon; the untold story of the Frost/Nixon interviews. Harmony Books 2007 207p $22   **973.924**
1. Nixon, Richard M. (Richard Milhous), 1913-1994
2. Frost, David 3. Presidents—United States
4. Watergate Affair, 1972-1974
ISBN 978-0-307-39420-0; 0-307-39420-4
LC 2007-1238
"In 1977, three years after his resignation, Richard Nixon returned to the public eye in a series of interviews with British television journalist David Frost, for which Nixon received $1 million. Figuring his political and lawyerly skills were more than a match for Frost's interrogation, Nixon instead found himself doing exactly what his successor, Gerald Ford, had tried to prevent with a presidential pardon: publicly admitting that he had broken the law. Reston Jr. was one of the aides Frost hired to help him plan his line of attack; this book, written at the time of the interviews, is being published for the first time now. . . . Reston's passion for finding the chinks in Nixon's armor makes for fascinating reading." Publ Wkly

Woodward, Bob, 1943-
The final days; {by} Bob Woodward, Carl Bernstein. Simon & Schuster 1976 476p il pa $16 hardcover o.p. *   **973.924**
1. Nixon, Richard M. (Richard Milhous), 1913-1994
2. Watergate Affair, 1972-1974 3. United States—Politics and government—1961-1974
ISBN 0-7432-7406-7 (pa)
The title refers to the final days of the Nixon Presidency. The authors have "constructed a two-part narrative, the first half covering the period from April 30, 1973—the day John Dean was fired as White House counsel—until late July 1974, and the second half covering the last two weeks in detail." N Y Times Book Rev

973.925 United States— Administration of Gerald R. Ford, 1974-1977

Schulman, Bruce J.
The seventies; the great shift in American culture, society, and politics. Da Capo 2002 334p pa $17.95   **973.925**
1. United States—Civilization—1970-
ISBN 0-306-81126-X; 978-0-306-81126-5
First published 2001 by Free Press

Schulman explores developments in American politics and culture during "the years between Woodstock and Reagan. . . . 'The great shift' [he sees] is away from the public-spirited universalism that gave America the New Deal and the civil rights movement, and toward the sovereignty of the free market and private life." N Y Times Book Rev
"This is an important contribution to modern American social history and the literature of popular culture." Publ Wkly
Includes bibliographical references

973.927 United States— Administration of Ronald Reagan, 1981-1989

FitzGerald, Frances, 1940-
Way out there in the blue; Reagan, Star Wars, and the end of the Cold War. Simon & Schuster 2000 592p pa $17 hardcover o.p.   **973.927**
1. Reagan, Ronald, 1911-2004 2. Strategic Defense Initiative 3. Cold war 4. United States—Politics and government—1974-1989
ISBN 0-7432-0023-3 (pa)   LC 99-59913
Fitzgerald offers a history of U.S. missile-defense programs over the last two decades, focusing particular attention on the Strategic Defense Initiative (SDI) supported by President Reagan
"Explaining the Star Wars saga, Fitzgerald delivers all the information that any nonexpert could absorb." Booklist
Includes bibliographical references

The **Iran-Contra** scandal; the declassified history; edited by Peter Kornbluh and Malcolm Byrne. New Press 1993 xxxiii, 412p pa $24.95 hardcover o.p.   **973.927**
1. Iran-Contra Affair, 1985-1990
ISBN 1-56584-047-X (pa)   LC 92-53732
"A National Security Archive Documents reader"
This volume contains "one hundred documents concerning the Iran-Contra Scandal, covering the period from Reagan's original presidential finding of Dec. 1, 1981 to Bush's grant of executive clemency of Dec. 24, 1992. With a helpful chronology of key events and a glossary of major participants, the volume sets forth with contextual introductions the documents, the paper trail of this major controversy in contemporary American politics." Libr J
Includes bibliographical references

Johnson, Haynes Bonner, 1931-
Sleepwalking through history; America in the Reagan years; {by} Haynes Johnson. Norton 1991 524p il pa $15.95 hardcover o.p.   **973.927**
1. Reagan, Ronald, 1911-2004 2. United States—Politics and government—1974-1989 3. United States—History—1974-1989
ISBN 0-393-32434-6 (pa)   LC 90-38623
This is a study of American politics, history, and culture during the 1980s
The author "concentrates on major events like the

Johnson, Haynes Bonner, 1931- —*Continued*
Iran-contra affair and the Wall street scene, and briefly touches on other domestic scandals. . . . Not the definitive history of the 1980s, but recommended as an important book by an important author." Libr J

Includes bibliographical references

Reagan, Ronald, 1911-2004
Reagan, in his own hand; edited, with an introduction and commentary by Kiron K. Skinner, Annelise Anderson, Martin Anderson; with a foreword by George P. Schultz. Free Press 2001 xxvi, 549p il $30; pa $16   **973.927**
    1. United States—Politics and government—1989-
    ISBN 0-7432-0123-X; 0-7432-1938-4 (pa)
                        LC 00-66304
    Subtitle on jkt.: The writings of Ronald Reagan that reveal his revolutionary vision for America
    "A collection of . . . manuscripts is presented here, just as Reagan wrote them, including his corrections and notes. With a few exceptions, they are very short radio commentaries delivered during the pre-presidential period (1975-1979), focusing mostly on foreign policy and the economy." Publ Wkly
    This collection provides "an excellent glimpse into Reagan the man and the thinker." Libr J

Reeves, Richard
President Reagan: the triumph of imagination. Simon & Schuster 2005 571p il $30
                              973.927
    1. Reagan, Ronald, 1911-2004 2. United States—Politics and government—1974-1989
    ISBN 0-7432-3022-1   LC 2005-54198
    This is an examination of the Reagan presidency.
    This book "is a compelling read, fast-paced and scrupulously fair. . . . Anybody who is interested in Reagan's extraordinary presidency needs to reckon with Reeves." N Y Times Book Rev
    Includes bibliographical references

973.928 United States— Administration of George Bush, 1989-1993

Schell, Jonathan, 1943-
Writing in time; a political chronicle. Moyer Bell 1997 303p pa $14.95 hardcover o.p.
                              973.928
    1. United States—Politics and government—1989-
    ISBN 1-55921-295-0 (pa)   LC 96-8516
    This volume "traces the 1992 Presidential campaign, the election and President Clinton's first term through Jonathan Schell's columns for Newsday. This chronicle is a distinctly partisan one: Schell's views of the White House and its wannabes are seen strictly from the left. But the author's eye for issues and motives is so sure that even those who detest his opinions will find 'Writing in Time' a lively refresher course on five years of American history." N Y Times Book Rev

Woodward, Bob, 1943-
The commanders. Simon & Schuster 1991 398p il hardcover o.p. pa $16 *   **973.928**
    1. Bush, George, 1924- 2. United States. Dept. of Defense 3. United States—Foreign relations 4. Persian Gulf War, 1991
    ISBN 0-671-41367-8; 0-7432-3475-8 (pa)
                        LC 91-13037
    This book discusses "top-level White House [and] Pentagon decisionmaking, first in the attack on Panama, and then in the $5\frac{1}{2}$ months of diplomatic and especially military maneuvering that preceded the [1991] war with Iraq." Christ Sci Monit

973.929 United States— Administration of Bill Clinton, 1993- 2001

Applebome, Peter
Dixie rising; how the South is shaping American values, politics, and culture. Harcourt Brace 1997 393p il pa $14   **973.929**
    1. Southern States—Politics and government 2. Southern States—Civilization
    ISBN 0-15-600550-6; 978-0-15-600550-0
                        LC 97-27787
    First published 1996 by Times Books
    The author explores the "contradictions of the modern South. Not only does the South exercise disproportionate political power (Dixie now claims leadership of Congress as well as the White House); most of our serious conflicts over race and religion continue to play out dramatically in the old Confederacy. Applebome's unusual historical literacy helps him understand a region drenched in the tradition and legends of the Civil War, racist demagoguery and the battles over integration." Publ Wkly
    Includes bibliographical references

Halpern, Jake, 1975-
Braving home; dispatches from the Underwater Town, the Lava-Side Inn, and other extreme locales. Houghton Mifflin 2003 240p il $23; pa $13   **973.929**
    1. Halpern, Jake, 1975- 2. Home 3. United States—Local history 4. United States—Description and travel
    ISBN 0-618-15548-1; 0-618-44662-1 (pa)
                      LC 2002-191262
    "The author tells the stories of individuals who refused to evacuate their property in the face of impending disasters." SLJ
    "The book is like a stay-at-home adventure, with all the excitement but none of the hardship. . . . This is the perfect book for armchair travelers interested in virtual visits to 'extreme locations.'" Booklist
    Includes bibliographical references

Reich, Robert B.
Locked in the cabinet. Knopf 1997 338p pa $15 hardcover o.p.   **973.929**
    1. United States. Dept. of Labor 2. United States—Politics and government—1989-
    ISBN 0-375-70061-7 (pa)   LC 97-71921

Reich, Robert B.—*Continued*

The author writes about his tenure as Secretary of Labor in the first Clinton administration

"Reich has an acid pen, and he is by turns witty, churlish, and plain vulgar. . . . The specificity of detail in this book adds up not only to an absorbing accounting of failed service in the Cabinet but also to a powerful indictment of the Clinton Presidency." New Leader

Stephanopoulos, George

All too human; a political education. Little, Brown 1999 456p $32; pa $14.95

973.929

1. Clinton, Bill, 1946- 2. Presidents—United States 3. United States—Politics and government—1989-
ISBN 0-316-92919-0; 0-316-93016-4 (pa)

LC 99-13817

This is a political memoir by a former senior advisor to President Clinton

"A fascinating if controversial insiders account of life inside the Clinton pressure cooker administration during its early years." Libr J

Includes bibliographical references

Toobin, Jeffrey R.

A vast conspiracy; the real story of the sex scandal that nearly brought down a president. 1st Touchstone ed. Simon & Schuster 2000 422p pa $20

973.929

1. Clinton, Bill, 1946- 2. United States—Politics and government—1989-
ISBN 0-7432-0413-1; 978-0-7432-0413-2

LC 00-59524

"A Touchstone book"

First published 1999 by Random House

"Toobin's thesis is that the real vast conspiracy wasn't the right-wing one . . . [Hillary Clinton] charged was behind the scandal, but a more subtle attempt by the legal system to circumvent the political process through an 'after the fact election.'" Time

"Even for those who disagree with [Toobin's] assessment, the book is still hugely entertaining. There are plenty of scandal pellets to be found scattered throughout the analysis." Christ Sci Monit

Includes bibliographical references

Will, George F.

The woven figure; conservatism and America's fabric, 1994-1997. Scribner 1997 384p pa $21.95 hardcover o.p.

973.929

1. Conservatism 2. United States—Politics and government—1989-
ISBN 0-684-84820-1 (pa)

LC 97-34731

This is a collection of previously published newspaper columns presenting the author's views on such topics as affirmative action, abortion, welfare reform, the Clinton administration, multiculturalism, and campaign finance reform

973.93 United States—2001-

Brookhiser, Richard

What would the Founders do? our questions, their answers. Basic Books 2006 261p $26

973.93

1. Presidents—United States 2. Statesmen—United States 3. United States—Politics and government—2001-
ISBN 0-465-00819-4; 978-0-465-00819-3

The author "uses the Founders' written and oral statements to imagine their thoughts concerning contemporary issues ranging from stem cells and terrorism to censorship and gay marriage. The short answers he gives for each question can be serious or witty and are often infused with interesting historical facts." Libr J

Includes bibliographical references

Shorris, Earl, 1936-

The politics of heaven; America in fearful times. Norton 2007 371p $25.95

973.93

1. United States—Politics and government—2001- 2. Christianity and politics 3. Christian fundamentalism 4. Conservatism
ISBN 978-0-393-05963-2; 0-393-05963-4

LC 2007-12726

The author "offers a historical perspective on religion in the U.S., from Calvinist doctrine marrying religion and capitalism to the conservative modern-day gospels as preached by Billy Graham and Jerry Falwell. Drawing on research and interviews with political figures and advisors, academics, and theologians, Shorris examines the confluence of history, philosophy, experiences, and 'elemental feelings' that have gained enough momentum to become a movement of the fearful . . . Shorris eloquently offers a penetrating and unsettling look at American fear birthed by the horrors of the atom bomb and nurtured by 9/11 that promises to have an enduring impact on global and domestic policy for generations to come." Booklist

973.931 United States— Administration of George W. Bush, 2001-

Bernstein, Richard

Out of the blue; the story of September 11, 2001, from Jihad to Ground Zero; {by} Richard Bernstein and the staff of the New York Times. Times Bks. 2002 287p il hardcover o.p. pa $15

973.931

1. September 11 terrorist attacks, 2001 2. Terrorism
ISBN 0-8050-7240-3; 0-8050-7410-4 (pa)

LC 2002-20396

This account of the September 11, 2001 terrorist attacks focuses "on the personal—the victims, the perpetrators and heroes whose lives became tangled in catastrophe. . . . It uses these stories as a jumping-off point for a comprehensive look at the terror attacks—the reactions of New Yorkers, the nation and the world; the criticism

Bernstein, Richard—*Continued*
of U.S. government agencies; the lingering effects of the tragedy. While some of this information has been published elsewhere, it has not been gathered so comprehensively—nor has it been written so well." Publ Wkly

Brill, Steven
After: how America confronted the September 12 era. Simon & Schuster 2003 723p $29.95; pa $16   **973.931**
1. September 11 terrorist attacks, 2001
ISBN 0-7432-3709-9; 0-7432-3710-2 (pa)
LC 2003-42727
The author presents a "narrative of how Americans responded to personal, social, political, and economic upheavals during the year following {September 11th, 2001}. . . . Stories of selected ordinary people serve as examples of the traumas and life-altering experiences endured by so many Americans." Libr J
This "book gives a sophisticated demonstration of the strengths and weaknesses of 21-century commercial democracy under pressure." N Y Times Book Rev
Includes bibliographical references

Buchanan, Patrick
Where the right went wrong; how neoconservatives subverted the Reagan revolution and hijacked the Bush presidency; [by] Patrick J. Buchanan. Thomas Dunne Books 2004 264p $24.95; pa $14.95   **973.931**
1. Conservatism 2. United States—Politics and government—2001- 3. Economic policy—United States
ISBN 0-312-34115-6; 0-312-34116-4 (pa)
LC 2004-558171
This is a critique of the present-day conservative movement in the United States
"Whether or not one agrees with [his] conclusions, Buchanan's book is provocative and will certainly ruffle feathers on both sides of the party line." Publ Wkly

Clarke, Richard A.
Against all enemies; inside America's war on terror. Free Press 2004 304p $27; pa $14
    973.931
1. Al Qaeda (Organization) 2. War on terrorism
ISBN 0-7432-6024-4; 0-7432-6045-7 (pa)
LC 2004-273844
The author, "the U.S.'s former terrorism czar, offers a . . . look into the successes and failures of the nation's security apparatus." Publ Wkly
"Richard A. Clarke knows too much, and 'Against All Enemies' is too good to be ignored. . . . It is a rarity among Washington-insider memoirs—it's a thumping good read." N Y Times Book Rev

Corn, David
The lies of George W. Bush; mastering the politics of deception. Crown 2003 337p $24; pa $12.95   **973.931**
1. Bush, George W. 2. United States—Politics and government—2001-
ISBN 1-4000-5066-9; 1-400-05067-7 (pa)
LC 2003-18347

The author chronicles "the lies, falsehoods, and misrepresentations of President George W. Bush. . . . He also shows that Bush committed them for a reason, engaging in 'strategic lying' in an effort to cover up his past and pave his way to governance. . . . From lies about his arrest and National Guard records, to environmental and energy concerns, to the war against Iraq, Corn has painstakingly unearthed a bill of particulars against the President that is as damaging as it is thorough." Libr J

Dowd, Maureen
Bushworld; enter at your own risk. G.P. Putnam's Sons 2004 523p $25.95; pa $15
    973.931
1. Bush, George W. 2. United States—Politics and government—2001-
ISBN 0-399-15258-X; 0-425-20276-3 (pa)
LC 2004-48798
This is a "collection of 145 of [the author's] *New York Times* columns about George W. Bush, father, and family." Libr J
The author "is scorching in her analysis of the Bushes, putting them 'on the couch,' as they have contemptuously labeled efforts to delve into their relationship. . . . Bush detractors will love Dowd's sharp analysis, but even his fans should acknowledge her wit." Booklist

Draper, Robert
Dead certain; the presidency of George W. Bush. Free Press 2007 463p il $28 *
    973.931
1. Presidents—United States
ISBN 978-0-7432-7728-0; 0-7432-7728-7
LC 2007-23471
The author sets out to tell "the story of the Bush White House from the inside, with a special emphasis on how the very personality of this strong-willed president has affected the outcome of events." Publisher's note
This book gives "the reader an intimate sense of the president's personality and how it informs his decision making." N Y Times (Late N Y Ed)
Includes bibliographical references

Franks, Tommy, 1945-
American soldier; [by] Tommy Franks, with Malcolm McConnell. Regan Bks. 2004 590p il map $27.95; pa $16.95   **973.931**
ISBN 0-06-073158-3; 0-06-077954-3 (pa)
LC 2004-558617
In this "memoir, General Franks retraces his journey from a small-town boyhood in Oklahoma and Midland, Texas, through a lifetime of military service—including his heroic tour as an Artillery officer in Vietnam, where he was wounded three times. . . . [Also, Franks offers an] insider's account of the war on terrorism that has changed the world since September 11, 2001." Publisher's note
"The real value of 'American Soldier' . . . is not what it says about the war on terror, but what it reveals about Tommy Franks. . . . The chapter on Vietnam, where Franks spent a year in brutal combat as a field artillery officer, is a cleareyed, mordant memoir." N Y Times Book Rev

Friedman, Thomas L.

Longitudes and attitudes; exploring the world after September 11. Farrar, Straus & Giroux 2002 383p $23   **973.931**

1. September 11 terrorist attacks, 2001 2. Terrorism 3. United States—Politics and government—1989- 4. United States—Foreign relations

ISBN 0-374-19066-6   LC 2002-74321

Also available in paperback from Anchor Bks.

This is a collection "of Friedman's *New York Times* columns from September 2001 through June 2002, with a lengthy postscript describing Friedman's travels and interviews throughout this period." Booklist

"Unapologetically pro-American, Friedman's deliberation on what changed on September 11 outside of the U.S. ultimately centers on the strength of American society and our place in the world." Publ Wkly

Includes bibliographical references

Hersh, Seymour M.

Chain of command; the road from 9/11 to Abu Ghraib. HarperCollins 2004 394p map $25.95 *
    973.931

1. Abu Ghraib (Baghdad, Iraq: Prison) 2. War on terrorism 3. Iraq War, 2003 4. September 11 terrorist attacks, 2001

ISBN 0-06-019591-6

The author writes "about why the United States went from leading an international coalition, united in horror at the attacks of 9/11, to fighting alone in Iraq and, in Abu Ghraib, to violating the very human rights it said it had come to restore." N Y Times Book Rev

"This sobering book is the closest anyone without a security clearance will get to operatives in the inner sanctums of America's intelligence, military, political and diplomatic worlds." Publ Wkly

Jacobson, Sidney

The 9/11 report; a graphic adaptation; by Sid Jacobson and Ernie Colón; [with a foreword by Thomas H. Kean and Lee H. Hamilton] Hill and Wang 2006 133p il $30; pa $16.95
    973.931

1. September 11 terrorist attacks, 2001—Graphic novels 2. Graphic novels

ISBN   0-8090-5738-7;   978-0-8090-5738-2; 0-8090-5739-5 (pa); 978-0-8090-5739-9 (pa)

On cover: Based on the final report of the National Commission on Terrorist Attacks upon the United States

"The book aims to make . . . [The 9/11 Commission Report] more accessible to all readers and draw in young adults. . . . This graphic adaptation is an important and necessary part of any collection." Libr J

Kaplan, Robert D.

Imperial grunts; the American military on the ground. Random House 2005 421p maps $27.95
    973.931

1. Soldiers—United States 2. Military policy—United States

ISBN 1-4000-6132-6   LC 2004-61466

The author argues that "America is no less an imperial power than Britain and Rome in their times . . . one that is backed by the same sort of enforcers. To illustrate, he travels to seven nations and describes how American troops are, if not ruling the world, working to persuade it to follow our lead." Publ Wkly

Kaplan's "on-the-ground reportage makes for riveting reading." N Y Times (Late N Y Ed)

Includes bibliographical references

Kessler, Ronald

The CIA at war; inside the secret campaign against terror. St. Martin's Press 2003 362p il $27.95; pa $15.95   **973.931**

1. United States. Central Intelligence Agency 2. War on terrorism

ISBN 0-312-31932-0; 0-312-31933-9 (pa)

       LC 2003-58487

The author "takes us from the formation of the CIA as an outgrowth of World War II OSS intelligence activities, when most agents were East Coast Ivy League elites focused on cold war scrimmages, through the current war on terror, where the enemy is often unknown and the agency elite are somewhat more diverse. Through numerous interviews with both agents and operatives, Kessler brings to life a world generally described only in fiction." Booklist

Includes bibliographical references

Miller, John

The cell: inside the 9/11 plot and why the FBI and CIA failed to stop it; {by} John Miller and Michael Stone, with Chris Mitchell. Hyperion 2002 336p $24.95; pa $13.95   **973.931**

1. September 11 terrorist attacks, 2001 2. Terrorism 3. Intelligence service—United States

ISBN 0-7868-6900-3; 0-7868-8782-6 (pa)

       LC 2002-27322

The authors analyze the circumstances inside and outside the United States that culminated in the September 11 terrorist attack. Included is an account of Miller's face-to-face meeting with Osama bin Laden in Afghanistan in 1998.

This is a "frightening and important book." Publ Wkly

National Commission on Terrorist Attacks Upon the United States

The 9/11 Commission report; final report of the National Commission on Terrorist Attacks Upon the United States. Norton 2004 567p il $19.95; pa $10 *   **973.931**

1. Al Qaeda (Organization) 2. September 11 terrorist attacks, 2001 3. Terrorism 4. War on terrorism 5. National security—United States

ISBN 0-393-06041-1; 0-393-32671-3 (pa)

       LC 2004-57564

Also available in paperback from St. Martin's Press

"Authorized edition"

This work aims to describe how the terrorist attacks of September 11, 2001 occurred and to provide recommendations for the prevention of future attacks.

This book "reads like a Shakespearean drama. . . .

National Commission on Terrorist Attacks Upon the United States—*Continued*
This multi-author document produces an absolutely compelling narrative intelligence, one with clarity, a sense of shared mission and an overriding desire to *do* something about the situation." Publ Wkly

Includes bibliographical references

Noonan, Peggy
A heart, a cross & a flag; America today. Free Press 2003 270p (Wall Street journal book) hardcover o.p. pa $19.95   **973.931**
1. United States—Politics and government—2001-
2. September 11 terrorist attacks, 2001 3. American national characteristics 4. War on terrorism
ISBN   0-7432-5005-2;   978-0-7432-5048-1;
0-7432-5048-6   LC 2003-48336
Collection of articles published in the Wall Street journal from Sept. 2001 to Sept. 2002
"Noonan's essays are thoughtful, introspective, and deeply patriotic. Although she is devastated by the horror of 9/11, her spirits are lifted by the heroism and kindness she sees in her fellow New Yorkers, from the firemen who bravely raced into the doomed towers to the people who turned out to cheer on the rescue workers and firemen who toiled in the wreckage." Booklist

Spiegelman, Art
In the shadow of no towers. Pantheon Books 2004 various paging il $19.95   **973.931**
1. September 11 terrorist attacks, 2001—Graphic novels 2. Graphic novels
ISBN 0-375-42307-9   LC 2004-43870
This is a "memoir of the attacks on the World Trade Center, which Spiegelman witnessed from close range, a rant on their effects on the world at large and within the author, and a monograph on the Sunday newspaper comic strips of the early 20th century." N Y Times Book Rev
The author "provides a hair-raising and wry account of his family's frantic efforts to locate one another on September 11 as well as a morbidly funny survey of his trademark sense of existential doom. . . . This is a powerful and quirky work of visual storytelling by a master comics artist." Publ Wkly

Suskind, Ron
The one percent doctrine; deep inside America's pursuit of its enemies since 9/11. Simon & Schuster 2006 367p $27   **973.931**
1. War on terrorism 2. Terrorism 3. United States—Politics and government—2001-
ISBN 0-7432-7109-2; 978-0-7432-7109-7
LC 2006-279373
"Relying on . . . access to former and current government officials, this book [seeks to] . . . reveal for the first time how the U.S. government—from President Bush on down—is frantically improvising to fight a new kind of war." Publisher's note
"Suskind's powerful, uncompromising criticism of Bush, combined with his incisive analysis of a deeply flawed policy, makes this book indispensable to understanding the current administration's mistakes and triumphs in its 'war on terror.'" Commonweal

The **torture** papers; the road to Abu Ghraib; edited by Karen J. Greenberg, Joshua L. Dratel; introduction by Anthony Lewis. Cambridge University Press 2005 xxxiv, 1249p il $50
973.931
1. Abu Ghraib (Baghdad, Iraq: Prison)
ISBN 0-521-85324-9
This work "consists of the so-called 'torture memos' and reports that . . . U.S. government officials wrote to authorize and to document coercive interrogation and torture [of prisoners] in Afghanistan, Guantanamo, and Abu Ghraib." Publisher's note
"A gripping and alarming read about the use of government power." Choice

Includes bibliographical references

Woodward, Bob, 1943-
State of denial. Simon & Schuster 2006 560p il $30   **973.931**
1. Bush, George W. 2. Iraq War, 2003
ISBN 0-7432-7223-4; 978-0-7432-7223-0
LC 2006-285190
Subtitle on cover: Bush at war, part III
This is a critique of the Bush administration's handling of the war in Iraq.
"If journalism is the first page of history, then Woodward's opus will be required reading for any would-be historians of the time." Publ Wkly

Includes bibliographical references

Wright, Lawrence
The looming tower; Al Qaeda and the road to 9/11. Knopf 2006 469p map $27.95
973.931
1. Al Qaeda (Organization) 2. September 11 terrorist attacks, 2001 3. Terrorism
ISBN 0-375-41486-X   LC 2006-41032
The author "goes back—way back—to 1948 to dissect the personal influences and political radicalization that would lead to al Qaeda's attack on America." Libr J
This book "is not just a detailed, heart-stopping account of the events leading up to 9/11, written with style and verve, and carried along by villains and heroes that only a crime novelist could dream up. It's an education, too . . . a thoughtful examination of the world that produced the men who brought us 9/11, and of their progeny who bedevil us today." N Y Times Book Rev
Includes bibliographical references

974 Northeastern United States

The **Encyclopedia** of New England; the culture and history of an American region; edited by Burt Feintuch and David H. Watters; foreword by Donald Hall. Yale University Press 2005 xxiii, 1564p il map $65 *   **974**
1. New England—Encyclopedias
ISBN 0-300-10027-2   LC 2005-10353
"A project of the Center for the Humanities at the University of New Hampshire"
This "work aims to serve as an authoritative resource of information about people, places, events, culture, and

The Encyclopedia of New England—*Continued*
ideas of the region. . . . [This is] a valuable tool for students, researchers, and casual readers alike." Libr J
For a fuller review, see: Booklist, Nov. 15, 2005
Includes bibliographical references

974.4　Massachusetts

Bradford, William, 1590-1657
Of Plymouth Plantation, 1620-1647; the complete text, with notes and an introduction by Samuel Eliot Morison. Knopf 1952 xliii, 448p maps $25　　　　　　　　　　　　　　　**974.4**
1. Massachusetts—History—1600-1775, Colonial period 2. Pilgrims (New England colonists)
ISBN 0-394-43895-7
Also available in paperback from McGraw-Hill
Written between 1630 and 1650; first published 1856 with title: History of Plymouth Plantation
First ed. published in 1856 under title: History of Plymouth Plantation; Includes index
"The opening book sketches the origin of the Separatist movement, the flight from England to Holland, the settlement at Leiden, the plans for the settlement in New England, and the *Mayflower* voyage. The second book, which includes the major part of the history, is in the form of annals from 1620 to 1646, and describes every aspect of the life of the Pilgrims. Besides being a primary historical source, the work has artistic value because of its dignified, sonorous style, deriving from the Geneva Bible." Oxford Companion to Am Lit. 5th edition

Cliff, Nigel
The Shakespeare riots; revenge, drama, and death in nineteenth-century America. Random House 2007 312p il $26.95　　　　　　　　**974.4**
1. Forrest, Edwin, 1806-1872 2. Macready, William Charles, 1793-1873 3. Shakespeare, William, 1564-1616—Stage history 4. Riots—New York (N.Y.) 5. Astor Place (New York, N.Y.) 6. New York (N.Y.)—Social life and customs
ISBN 9780345486943; 0-345-48694-3
LC 2006-49139
"During the evening of May 10, 1849, a massive riot broke out in Astor Place in New York City, involving at least 20,000 rioters, causing scores of fatalities, and leading to the use of the military in quelling the violence. . . . The rival gangs were fighting on behalf of two unlikely antagonists, both of them prominent Shakespearean actors. William Macready was an aristocratic, foppish actor acclaimed by elites in New York and London; Edwin Forrest was the darling of working-class theater fans." Booklist
"Cliff argues persuasively that 'the Astor Place riot,' as it came to be known, marked a turning point in America's search for a national identity. . . . [This] is an intriguing, thought-provoking book." Washington Post Book World
Includes bibliographical references

Kidder, Tracy
Home town. Washington Square Press 2000 432p pa $14.95　　　　　　　　　　　　**974.4**

1. Northampton (Mass.) 2. City and town life
ISBN 978-0-671-78521-5; 0-671-78521-4
First published 1999 by Random House
Kidder presents a portrait of the town of Northampton, Massachusetts. He "surveys Northampton through several sets of eyes. . . . But the observer who tells most of the story . . . [is a] town cop named Tommy O'Connor. . . . O'Connor was born in town-his father Bill was the county treasurer-played Little League here, has seen jobs dry up and the downtown decay, and then . . . has seen the . . . town center yuppified." Time
This "acutely observed, crisply written, and utterly absorbing documentary proves that there is nothing on this spinning earth more amazing and full of grace than everyday life." Booklist
Includes bibliographical references

Masur, Louis P.
The soiling of Old Glory; the story of a photograph that shocked America. Bloomsbury Press 2008 224p il $24.95　　　　　　　**974.4**
1. Boston (Mass.)—Race relations 2. Photojournalism 3. Demonstrations 4. Busing (School integration)
ISBN 978-1-59691-364-6; 1-59691-364-9
LC 2007-31215
"On April 5, 1976, an antibusing rally in Boston grew violent when African American lawyer Ted Landsmark was attacked by some of the protesters. News photographer Stanley Forman captured the ruckus on film; one photo gained international attention and is the subject of this . . . study by Masur. . . . Masur writes descriptively about the photo while creating an ethnographic history of 1970s Boston, with diversions into the political and cultural uses of the American flag and the history of photojournalism in the United States. He also describes the aftermath of the photo's front-page publication. . . . A compelling story; highly recommended for all high school, public, and academic libraries." Libr J
Includes bibliographical references

974.7　New York

Bloom, Ken
Broadway; its history, people, and places: an encyclopedia. 2nd ed. Routledge 2003 679p il $95
974.7
1. Theater—New York (N.Y.)
ISBN 0-415-93704-3　　　　　　LC 2003-2692
First published 1991
"Following a brief historical overview, . . . [the author] presents 394 alphabetical entries with multiple cross references for easy browsing. The most substantial entries cover theaters, playwrights, composers, directors, performers, and producers, with a special emphasis on composers and lyricists. . . . Bloom adds a touch of atmosphere with entries on critics, restaurants, publicity stunts, nightclubs, and other periphery characters and incidents that are so much a part of the Great White Way. As much a storyteller as a chronicler, he uses anecdotes and a plethora of black-and-white photographs, many never before published, to produce an entertaining as well as an informative work. Highly recommended for all theater collections." Libr J
Includes bibliographical references

Burns, Cherie
The great hurricane–1938. Atlantic Monthly Press 2005 240p il $24   **974.7**
1. Hurricanes 2. Northeastern States
ISBN 0-8711-3893-X   LC 2005-41211
The author discusses the hurricane of September 1938, which affected the northeastern United States from Long Island to Providence, Rhode Island.
The author "has dug up old newspaper accounts and local histories to reconstruct the terror and destruction that accompanied the 1938 hurricane. Those who suffered the most, of course, did not survive to tell their tales. Nearly 700 people died, and about 63,000 were left homeless. . . . Survivor's stories, however, give ample feeling for the power of the rain, tide, and wind." Nat Hist

Burrows, Edwin G., 1943-
Gotham; a history of New York City to 1898; {by} Edwin G. Burrows and Mike Wallace. Oxford Univ. Press 1998 xxiv, 1383p il maps pa $29.95 hardcover o.p.   **974.7**
1. New York (N.Y.)—History
ISBN 0-19-514049-4 (pa)   LC 97-39308
This history "begins with the Indian settlements and the subsequent seizure of the city by the Dutch in 1626 and continues up to the consolidation of the five boroughs in 1898. The authors . . . cover an extraordinary range of topics, including religion, race, gender and class, architecture, society and the arts, noted personalities, sports and the special customs immigrants brought with them." America
Includes bibliographical references

Dwyer, Jim, 1957-
102 minutes; the untold story of the fight to survive inside the Twin Towers; [by] Jim Dwyer and Kevin Flynn. Times Books 2005 322p il $26; pa $15   **974.7**
1. World Trade Center terrorist attack, 2001
2. September 11 terrorist attacks, 2001
ISBN 0-8050-7682-4; 0-8050-8032-5 (pa)
LC 2004-55321
The authors "take us into the 102 minutes of hell experienced by those in the World Trade Center between the time the first jet crashed into the north tower and the last standing tower toppled. While other accounts have focused on the members of NYFD and NYPD who responded to the catastrophe, this book tells the stories of scores of civilians." Libr J
Dwyer and Flynn have "given us a fitting tribute to the people caught up in one of the great dramas of our time. And for people still haunted by the events of that day, reading '102 Minutes' provides a cathartic release." N Y Times Book Rev

The **Encyclopedia** of New York City; edited by Kenneth T. Jackson. Yale Univ. Press 1995 1350p il $65   **974.7**
ISBN 0-300-05536-6   LC 95-2811
This volume "serves up 4,300 articles by 680 authors, along with tables, lists, charts, and 688 illustrations. . . . Survey-articles take on the large conceptual subjects, like

government and politics, architecture, education, immigration and science. Major articles are devoted to the history of each borough. Smaller entries deal with neighborhoods past and present, institutions (banks, advertising agencies, churches, labor unions, charities), historical events, local foods and folkways, ethnic groups, religions, newspapers, magazines, writers, [and] painters." NY Times Book Rev

The **encyclopedia** of New York State; editor in chief, Peter Eisenstadt; managing editor, Laura-Eve Moss; foreword by Carole F. Huxley. 1st ed. Syracuse University Press 2005 xxviii, 1921p il map $95 *   **974.7**
1. New York (State)—Encyclopedias
ISBN 0-8156-0808-X   LC 2005-1032
"The alphabetically arranged entries include all cities, towns, and counties (more than 1,500), with an additional 3,000-plus entries for information on a wide range of topics. . . . This ambitious project is a definite success." Booklist
Includes bibliographical references

Friend, David, 1955-
Watching the world change; the stories behind the images of 9/11. Farrar, Straus and Giroux 2006 435p il $30   **974.7**
1. World Trade Center (New York, N.Y.)
2. September 11 terrorist attacks, 2001—Pictorial works 3. Documentary photography
ISBN 978-0-374-29933-0; 0-374-29933-1
LC 2005-36158
In this "analysis of how images of 9/11 and the 'war on terror' have altered our understanding of power, world politics, religion and identity, . . . [the author] successfully merges reportage and analysis as he interprets the images of falling towers, panic in Manhattan streets and prisoners at Abu Ghraib that have been burned into our brains." Publ Wkly
Includes bibliographical references

Homberger, Eric
The historical atlas of New York City; a visual celebration of nearly 400 years of New York City's history; Alice Hudson, cartographic consultant. Holt & Co. 1994 192p il maps (Henry Holt reference book) pa $22 hardcover o.p.
974.7
1. New York (N.Y.)—History
ISBN 0-8050-6004-9 (pa)   LC 94-18992
This is an "encyclopedic overview of the history of New York City. . . . Detailed color maps abound, accompanied by a running commentary of major historical and cultural eras. Many of the most detailed maps are rendered schematically for easier reading. Each period treated features historical photos and illustrations along with accompanying map(s). . . . A visual delight." Libr J

Langewiesche, William
American ground, unbuilding the World Trade
Center. North Point Press 2002 205p $22; pa $13
        974.7
1. World Trade Center (New York, N.Y.)
2. September 11 terrorist attacks, 2001
ISBN 0-86547-582-2; 0-86547-675-6 (pa)
        LC 2002-75153
First published as a three part series of articles in Atlantic Monthly
This is an account "of the cleanup operation at ground
zero—the 'unbuilding,' as he puts it, of the World Trade
Center." N Y Times (Late N Y Ed)
"This is a genuinely monumental story, told without
melodrama, an intimate depiction of ordinary Americans
reacting to grand-scale tragedy at their best—and sometimes their worst." Publ Wkly

Lepore, Jill, 1966-
New York burning; liberty, slavery, and
conspiracy in an eighteenth-century Manhattan.
Alfred A. Knopf 2005 323p il maps $26.95
        974.7
1. Slavery—United States 2. New York (N.Y.)—History
ISBN 1-4000-4029-9   LC 2004-57625
The author "offers new analysis of an episode in Colonial New York that revealed the city's racism, the so-
called New York Conspiracy, or Negro Plot, of 1741."
Libr J
"In this first-rate social history, Lepore not only
adroitly examines the case's travesty, questioning whether such a conspiracy ever existed, but also draws a splendid portrait of the struggles, prejudices and triumphs of
a very young New York City in which fully 'one in five
inhabitants was enslaved.'" Publ Wkly
Includes bibliographical references

New York September 11; by Magnum
photographers; introduction by David
Halberstam. PowerHouse Bks. 2001 140p il
$29.95   **974.7**
1. World Trade Center terrorist attack, 2001
2. Documentary photography
ISBN 1-57687-130-4   LC 2001-52330
This collection of photographs documents the attack
on the World Trade Center on September 11, 2001. The
book is organized essentially as a series of picture essays
by individual photographers

Schecter, Barnet
The devil's own work; the Civil War draft riots
and the fight to reconstruct America; Barnet
Schecter. Walker & Co. 2005 434p il $28 *
        974.7
1. United States—History—1861-1865, Civil War—
Draft resisters 2. Riots
ISBN 0-8027-1439-0   LC 2005-18089
This "book explores immediate antebellum and post-
bellum economic and social relationships that buttressed
antidraft riots in New York and other cities." Libr J
"Copiously researched and highlighted with a wealth
of period commentary, his lucid narrative colorfully rec-

reates a historical watershed and offers a rich exploration
of the Civil War's unfinished business." Publ Wkly
Includes bibliographical references

Schneider, Paul
The Adirondacks; a history of America's first
wilderness. Holt & Co. 1997 368p il maps pa $16
hardcover o.p.   **974.7**
ISBN 0-8050-5990-3 (pa)   LC 96-39844
"A John Macrae book"
The author presents a "history of New York State's
Adirondack region. He relates here the life and lore of
these scenic mountains and lakes (Whiteface, Mt. Marcy,
Fulton Chain Lakes) from the region's earliest inhabi-
tants (Haudenosaunce/Iroquois) through the advent of
Henry Hudson (1609), the Revolutionary War, abolition-
ists (John Brown), 19th-century homesteaders, Hudson
River School artists, tuberculosis patients to Melville
Dewey's Lake Placid Club, the Adirondack Mountain
Club, and the present environmental conservation ef-
forts." Libr J

Taylor, Alan, 1955-
The divided ground; Indians, settlers and the
northern borderland of the American Revolution.
Alfred A. Knopf 2006 542p il maps $35; pa
$16.95   **974.7**
1. Iroquois Indians—History 2. United States—History—1775-1783, Revolution 3. New York (State)—History
ISBN 0-679-45471-3; 1-4000-7707-9 (pa)
        LC 2005-43582
The author "explores how the Iroquois used their political and military alliance with the British to maintain
their sovereignty, a strategy that worked well until the
outbreak of the American Revolution." Libr J
"Taylor's exquisite writing and thorough research in
both Canadian and US archives and manuscript collections make this a major work." Choice
Includes bibliographical references

Von Drehle, Dave
Triangle: the fire that changed America. Atlantic
Monthly Press 2003 340p il $25; pa $14 *
        974.7
1. Triangle Shirtwaist Company, Inc. 2. Fires 3. New
York (N.Y.) 4. Clothing industry 5. Factories
ISBN 0-87113-874-3; 0-8021-4151-X (pa)
        LC 2003-41835
"The tragic conflagration at the Triangle Shirtwaist
Factory in March 1911 resulted in the deaths of 123
women (most of them young immigrants), caused widespread public outrage, and set in motion a wave of reform. Drehle's vivid retelling of this horrifying event begins with the strike that immediately preceded it and then
examines the terrible fire, the unsuccessful prosecution of
the factory owners, and the fight to prevent similar tragedies in the future." Libr J
"Von Drehle's engrossing account, which emphasizes
the humanity of the victims and the theme of social justice, brings on of the pivotal and most shocking episodes
of American labor history to life." Publ Wkly
Includes bibliographical references

White, Shane

Stories of freedom in Black New York. Harvard Univ. Press 2002 260p il $27.95   **974.7**

1. African Company (Theater company) 2. African Americans—New York (N.Y.) 3. New York (N.Y.)—Race relations 4. New York (N.Y.)—Intellectual life

ISBN 0-674-00893-6   LC 2002-68540

"The early nineteenth century was turbulent in New York, as the state dealt with the end of slavery. Focusing especially on a black theater group, its leading actor, and a Jewish newspaper editor, White examines the black theater, balls, cotillions, and other social expressions that provoked virulent attacks and editorials from whites." Booklist

The author "makes a persuasive case for the company's cultural importance, particularly as a forerunner of the Harlem Renaissance that was still a century away." Publ Wkly

Includes bibliographical references

974.8   Pennsylvania

Longman, Jere

Among the heroes; United Flight 93 and the passengers and crew who fought back. HarperCollins Pubs. 2002 288p il $24.95; pa $13.95   **974.8**

1. Hijacking of airplanes 2. September 11 terrorist attacks, 2001

ISBN 0-06-009908-9; 0-06-009909-7 (pa)

LC 2002-68530

This is an account of the United Airlines flight which was hijacked on September 11, 2001 and crashed in Pennsylvania before reaching its intended target

This book "gives us an incredibly detailed and personal tale of that horrific episode." Booklist

Includes bibliographical references

Pennsylvania: a history of the Commonwealth; edited by Randall M. Miller and William Pencak. Pennsylvania State Univ. Press 2002 xxxi, 654p il maps $49.95; pa $29.95

    974.8

1. Pennsylvania—History

ISBN 0-271-02213-2; 0-271-02214-0 (pa)

LC 2002-5457

"A Keystone book"

"More than half of this book is an unusual and inspired hybrid of history and nine other disciplines from geography to literature. . . . The editors profess to discover the sources of Pennsylvania's greatness and significance but also expose its faults and declining significance in the 20th century. They succeed at both." Choice

974.9   New Jersey

Wolff, Daniel

4th of July, Asbury Park; a history of the promised land. Bloomsbury 2005 277p hardcover o.p. pa $14.95   **974.9**

1. Springsteen, Bruce 2. Asbury Park (N.J.)

ISBN 1-58234-509-0; 1-59691-114-X (pa)

LC 2004-26965

This is a "history of the New Jersey resort town where [Bruce] Springsteen, after graduating from Freehold High School and briefly attending Ocean County Community College, served his rock 'n' roll apprenticeship." N Y Times Book Rev

The author "creates popular history at its best. Springsteen fans will love it, and so will anyone interested in American social history." Booklist

Includes bibliographical references

975   Southeastern United States. Southern States

Blount, Roy

Long time leaving; dispatches from up South; [by] Roy Blount, Jr. Knopf 2007 383p $25

    975

1. Southern States—Civilization 2. Southern States—Humor

ISBN 978-0-307-26618-7; 0-307-26618-4

LC 2007-6799

In this collection of essays, the author "focuses on his own dueling loyalties across [what he sees as] the great American divide, North vs. South." Publisher's note

"This delightful collection is not only fun and funny but insightful as well." Libr J

Cash, Wilbur Joseph, 1900-1941

The mind of the South; with a new introduction by Bertram Wyatt-Brown. Vintage Bks. 1991 xliv, 444p pa $16   **975**

1. Southern States—Civilization

ISBN 0-679-73647-6   LC 91-50042

First published 1941 by Knopf

A psychological, cultural, and social history of the old South

Dent, Tom, 1932-1998

Southern journey; a return to the civil rights movement. University of Georgia Press 2001 400p pa $18.95   **975**

1. Southern States—Race relations 2. African Americans—Civil rights

ISBN 0-8203-2291-1; 978-0-8203-2291-9

LC 00-61990

First published 1997 by Morrow

This book examines race relations in the American South. "To collect impressions of what has changed, and what hasn't since the 1960s, Dent traveled the back roads of a half-dozen Southern states for nearly a year, talking with 140 Southerners, black and white." Christ Sci Monit

"Dent compellingly reveals that ordinary Southerners fundamentally changed the region and are poised to make more substantive changes." Libr J

Includes bibliographical references

Lemann, Nicholas
Redemption: the last battle of the Civil War.
Farrar, Straus and Giroux 2006 257p $24
    975
1. African Americans—Segregation 2. Southern
States—Race relations
ISBN 978-0-374-24855-0; 0-374-24855-9
    LC 2006-91
"Focusing on the 1873-75 race war that ex-
Confederate vigilante White Leaguers waged in Louisi-
ana and Mississippi, . . . [the author] illustrates the Civil
War's meaning as a black-and-white lived experience in
the postwar South." Libr J
This book "offers a vigorous, necessary reminder of
how racist reaction bred an American terrorism that sup-
pressed black political activity and crushed Reconstruc-
tion in the South." N Y Times Book Rev
Includes bibliographical references

Wiencek, Henry
The Hairstons; an American family in black and
white. St. Martin's Press 1999 xx, 361p il map pa
$14.95 hardcover o.p. paperback available $14.95
    975
1. Hairston family 2. African Americans—Southern
States 3. Slavery—United States 4. United States—
Race relations
ISBN 0-312-25393-1 (pa)   LC 98-44014
Wiencek tells the "story of the Hairston family, the
largest slaveholders in the South and one of the wealthiest families in the U.S. Wiencek details the race mixing
that occured between master and slave and the family's
efforts to keep its dark-skinned members enslaved and to
maintain wealth only for its white members. A fascinating book that explores the complexity of family and racial relationships in the U.S." Booklist
Includes bibliographical references

975.3   District of Columbia (Washington)

Katharine Graham's Washington; {compiled by}
Katharine Graham. Knopf 2002 813p il $30; pa
$16.95   **975.3**
1. Washington (D.C.)
ISBN 0-375-41471-1; 1-4000-3059-5 (pa)
    LC 2002-111640
"The late newspaper publisher's posthumous legacy is
a delightful and insightful anthology of writings on the
city that formed so much of her personality and her professional life. She draws from her personal collection of
writings by a range of writers, many of them personal
friends." Booklist

Monkman, Betty C.
The White House; its historic furnishings and
first families; principal photography by Bruce
White. Abbeville Press 2000 320p il $65 *
    975.3
1. White House (Washington, D.C.)
ISBN 0-7892-0624-2   LC 00-27085
Published "with the support of the Hon. Walter H.
Annenberg White House Publication Fund."

"Monkman, the White House curator, documents the
furnishings and decorative objects as well as the metamorphoses of White House interiors. The impact of the
presidents and first ladies is particularly intriguing." Libr
J
Includes bibliographical references

The **White** House; actors and observers; edited by
William Seale. Northeastern Univ. Press 2002
xxii, 214p il $40   **975.3**
1. White House (Washington, D.C.) 2. Presidents—
United States
ISBN 1-55553-547-X   LC 2002-9087
Essays derived from papers delivered at a 200th anniversary symposium sponsored by the White House Historical Association
This is "a pictorial history of the presidential residence. Accompanied by a succession of essays presented
at a symposium honoring the 200th anniversary of the
White House, this stunning collection of paintings, drawings, and photographs chronicles two centuries of presidential life. . . . This irresistible gallery of pictures will
appeal to scholars and browsers alike." Booklist
Includes bibliographical references

975.5   Virginia

Furgurson, Ernest B., 1929-
Ashes of glory; Richmond at war. Knopf 1996
419p il maps pa $16 hardcover o.p.   **975.5**
1. Richmond (Va.)—History 2. United States—History—1861-1865, Civil War—Campaigns
ISBN 0-679-74660-9 (pa)   LC 95-49591
The author "tells the story of a city that between 1861
and 1865 epitomized the experience of the Civil War as
a revolutionary one. Capital of a state that had long opposed secession, Richmond now became the symbol of
Southern independence. It also remained a center of clandestine Unionism that hosted a struggle between espionage networks matching anything seen in Cold War Berlin." Publ Wkly
Includes bibliographical references

Horn, James P. P.
A land as God made it; Jamestown and the birth
of America; [by] James Horn. Basic Books 2005
337p il maps $26   **975.5**
1. Jamestown (Va.)—History
ISBN 0-465-03094-7   LC 2005-13054
The author "writes an account of the Jamestown Colony, founded in 1607—the first permanent English settlement in North America, predating the Mayflower's arrival at Plymouth by 13 years." Libr J
"Possessing Jamestown's inherent drama, this is a solid rendition of the saga." Booklist
Includes bibliographical references

Milton, Giles, 1966-
Big Chief Elizabeth; the adventures and fate of the First English Colonists in America. Farrar, Straus & Giroux 2000 358p il maps pa $14 hardcover o.p. **975.5**
1. Elizabeth I, Queen of England, 1533-1603 2. Virginia—History 3. Great Britain—Colonies—America 4. Native Americans 5. America—Exploration
ISBN 0-312-42018-8 (pa) LC 00-31522
"Nearly 500 years ago, a small group of white men landed on the shores of North America and named it Virginia (for the Virgin Queen [Elizabeth]). Their purpose was to capture some natives and bring them to England to learn their language and everything else they could about the country they wished to colonize. . . . [Milton] chronicles the century-long battle to establish a permanent settlement in Virginia." Christ Sci Monit
Includes bibliographical references

Noël Hume, Ivor, 1927-
The Virginia adventure; Roanoke to James Towne: an archaeological and historical odyssey. University Press of Va. 1997 xxviii, 491p il map pa $19.95 **975.5**
1. United States—History—1600-1775, Colonial period 2. Roanoke Island (N.C.)—History 3. Jamestown (Va.)—History
ISBN 0-8139-1758-1 LC 97-16651
First published 1994 by Knopf
The author discusses "the historical archaeology of the Roanoke and James Fort (later James Towne) settlements. Drawing extensively on firsthand accounts and other textual sources, he conjures up the feel of the Elizabethan experience that gave life to these settlements. . . . Hume also includes masterly and generous accounts of the history of the excavation of these sites and offers his well-informed views on where future work needs to be done. Written with wit, compassion, and tremendous attention to detail, this is historical archaeology at its best." Libr J

Price, David, 1961-
Love and hate in Jamestown; John Smith, Pocahontas, and the heart of a new nation; {by} David A. Price. Knopf 2003 305p maps $25.95; pa $14.95 * **975.5**
1. Smith, John, 1580-1631 2. Pocahontas, d. 1617 3. Jamestown (Va.)—History
ISBN 0-375-41541-6; 1-4000-3172-9 (pa)
 LC 2002-43437
This is a "history of the founding and development of Jamestown, the first permanent English settlement in North America. Spanning Jamestown's establishment in 1606 to the revocation of the Virginia Company's charter in 1624, Price examines the interaction among the colonists and their relation to the native tribes, focusing on Capt. John Smith and Pocahontas." Libr J
"For those general readers who wish to move beyond the myths and obtain a better understanding of them and the early years of the colony, this book will be an enjoyable and valuable tool." Booklist
Includes bibliographical references

975.7 South Carolina

Ball, Edward, 1959-
Slaves in the family. Ballantine Books 1999 505p il map pa $17.95 **975.7**
1. Ball family 2. Plantation life 3. Slavery—United States 4. South Carolina 5. United States—Race relations
ISBN 978-0-345-43105-9; 0-345-43105-7
First published 1998 by Farrar, Straus & Giroux
"For nearly a hundred and seventy years before the Civil War, members of the Ball family owned a string of plantations worked by slaves along South Carolina's Cooper River. After the war, the author's ancestors lost or sold their land and scattered to make new lives, but he wondered what happened to the slaves. This book, a brilliant blend of archival research and oral history, tells what he found." New Yorker
Includes bibliographical references

975.8 Georgia

Berendt, John
Midnight in the garden of good and evil; a story of Savannah. Random House 1994 388p $25; pa $14 **975.8**
1. Savannah (Ga.)
ISBN 0-679-42922-0; 0-679-75152-1 (pa)
 LC 93-3955
On one level, this book is a "travelog, recounting former *New York* magazine editor Berendt's eight years in Savannah, Georgia, that beautifully preserved hothouse of a Southern city where eccentric characters like black drag queen Lady Chablis and charming con man Joe Odom blossom in rich profusion. It is also a tale of true crime, the saga of antiques dealer Jim Williams whose 1981 shooting of his sometime lover Danny Hansford in the historic Mercer House obsesses Savannah denizens." Libr J
"Berendt has fashioned a Baedeker to Savannah that, while it flirts with condescension, is always contagiously affectionate. Few cities have been introduced more seductively." Newsweek

Foxfire 40th anniversary book; faith, family, and the land; edited by Angie Cheek, Lacy Hunter Nix, and Foxfire students. Anchor Books 2006 xxxix, 512p il pa $17.95 * **975.8**
1. Country life—Georgia 2. Appalachian region—Social life and customs 3. Handicraft
ISBN 0-307-27551-5; 978-0-307-27551-6
 LC 2006-45311
"Drawing on the magazine's published talks by local high school students with elderly rural inhabitants, the books have explored the crafts, cooking, music, gardening and stories that have been passed down through the generations. The focus in this anniversary volume is on devotion to religion, family and the land. Collecting pieces from 40 years' worth of the magazine, the book inevitably covers topics covered in previous Foxfire collections, including snake handling, childhood toys and recipes. But the spoken words remain captivating, eloquent if plainspoken." Publ Wkly

975.9   Florida

Grunwald, Michael

The swamp; the Everglades, Florida, and the politics of paradise. Simon & Schuster 2005 450p il map hardcover o.p. pa $15   **975.9**

1. Everglades (Fla.)

ISBN   0-7432-5105-9;   978-0-7432-5105-1; 978-0-7432-5107-5 (pa); 0-7432-5107-5 (pa)

LC 2005-56329

This is a "chronicle of the history of the Everglades. . . . [This] is a riveting tale of ambition versus ecological reality, politics versus science, and, on the upside, our gradual awakening to the true nature of nature." Booklist

Includes bibliographical references

Roberts, Diane, 1959-

Dream state; eight generations of swamp lawyers, conquistadors, Confederate daughters, banana Republicans, and other Florida wildlife. Free Press 2004 355p il $25   **975.9**

1. Florida

ISBN 0-7432-5206-3   LC 2004-56276

"From Ponce de Leon to the Seminole wars to the hanging chads of the 2000 election, Roberts tells the story of Florida through her relatives and ancestors." Booklist

"With hurricane-force prose, . . . Roberts hits the land of orange groves, theme parks and mobile homes with a torrential outpouring of love and hate, affection and disgust." Publ Wkly

Includes bibliographical references

976.1   Alabama

Agee, James, 1909-1955

Let us now praise famous men; [by] James Agee, Walker Evans; with an introduction to the new edition by John Hersey. Houghton Mifflin il $30; pa $18   **976.1**

1. Alabama—Social conditions 2. Farm tenancy

ISBN   978-0-395-95771-4;   0-395-95771-0; 978-0-618-12749-8 (pa); 0-618-12749-6 (pa)

First published 1941

This republication of the classic work based on a 1936 journalistic assignment contains "about twice as many photographs by Evans as the original contained." Best Sellers

This work documents "the ways of life of three Alabama tenant-farming families. . . . It is a unique and complex book, deeply honest and compassionate, and remarkable for its extraordinary descriptive, lyric, and meditative prose." Benet's Reader's Ency of Am Lit

McWhorter, Diane

Carry me home; Birmingham, Alabama: the climactic battle of the civil rights revolution. Simon & Schuster 2001 701p il $35; pa $17

976.1

1. African Americans—Civil rights 2. Birmingham (Ala.)—Race relations

ISBN 0-684-80747-5; 0-7432-1772-1 (pa)

LC 00-53827

Maps on lining papers

McWhorter presents an account of the struggle for civil rights in Birmingham, Ala., both from a personal and societal perspective

"A daughter of Birmingham's privileged elite, McWhorter weaves a personal narrative through this startling account of the history, events, and major players on both sides of the civil rights battle in that city." Booklist

Includes bibliographical references

976.2   Mississippi

Rubin, Richard

Confederacy of silence; a true tale of the new old South. Atria Bks. 2002 438p $26; pa $14

976.2

1. Mississippi—Race relations

ISBN 0-671-03666-1; 0-671-03667-X (pa)

LC 2002-510321

"Rubin, an Ivy League-educated New Yorker, went to work as a sportswriter in Greenwood, Mississippi. Almost in spite of himself, he came to love Greenwood, even as he remained aware of the ways in which the New South resembled the old. He also befriended a black high-school quarterback who he believed would become an N.F.L. star. Five years after Rubin left town, though, he heard that the player had been indicted for murder, and he returned to find out what had gone wrong." New Yorker

"Rubin's memoir exposes the racial polarity of the Delta in clear, effective prose." Publ Wkly

Welty, Eudora, 1909-2001

One time, one place; Mississippi in the Depression : a snapshot album. rev ed. University Press of Miss. 1996 115p il $35   **976.2**

ISBN 0-87805-866-4   LC 95-46057

First published 1971 by Random House

This is a "collection of photographs of Mississippians that Welty took in the 1930s, when she worked for the Works Progress Administration (WPA). This Silver Anniversary Edition contains a great foreword by William Maxwell that absolutely nails the importance of the book for many readers." Booklist

976.3 Louisiana

After the storm; black intellectuals explore the meaning of Hurricane Katrina; edited by David Dante Troutt. New Press 2006 xxvii, 164p il $22.95 * **976.3**
1. Hurricane Katrina, 2005 2. African Americans—Social conditions
ISBN 978-1-59558-116-7; 1-59558-116-2
LC 2006-8883
The contributors "assess why Katrina was handled as it was (and still is), how inevitable future crises should be handled differently, and how redevelopment of New Orleans should occur. Angry, learned, focused, readable, essential." Libr J
Includes bibliographical references

Brinkley, Douglas
The great deluge; Hurricane Katrina, New Orleans, and the Mississippi Gulf Coast. Morrow 2006 716p il $29.95 **976.3**
1. Hurricane Katrina, 2005 2. Disaster relief
ISBN 0-06-112423-0 LC 2006-43338
This is an account of Hurricane Katrina, which ravaged the Gulf Coast in late summer 2005.
The author "captures the human toll of Katrina as graphically as the most vivid newspaper and television accounts did, and by pulling together a huge, choral portrait of what happened during that first week of havoc and distress (from Saturday, Aug. 27, through Saturday, Sept. 3), he gives the reader a richly detailed timeline of disaster—a timeline in which the sheer cumulative power of details impresses upon us, again, just how abysmally inept relief efforts were on every level, from FEMA to the Red Cross to the New Orleans police department, from the federal government to state and local authorities." N Y Times (Late N Y Ed)

Clark, Joshua, 1975-
Heart like water; surviving Katrina and life in its disaster zone. Free Press 2007 356p map $25 **976.3**
1. Hurricane Katrina, 2005
ISBN 978-1-4165-3763-2; 1-4165-3763-5
LC 2007-5157
"Clark was among the few hearty or hapless souls who remained in New Orleans during Hurricane Katrina. . . . In this riveting first-person account, Clark recalls the static in the air as the hurricane approached; the unnerving silence afterwards without even the sound of birds; and 'shopping' for supplies at a local store where the owner had apparently given permission before fleeing. . . . This is a raw, revealing, and highly personal look at surviving Hurricane Katrina." Booklist

Codrescu, Andrei, 1946-
New Orleans, mon amour; by Andrei Codrescu. Algonquin Books of Chapel Hill 2006 273p pa $14 **976.3**
1. New Orleans (La.)—Social life and customs
ISBN 1-56512-505-3 LC 2005-53599

In this collection of short essays Codrescu sketches "portraits of a fabled city and its equally fabled inhabitants. The author, who has called the Big Easy home for two decades, shows how, like some gigantic bohemian magnet, New Orleans attracts some of the world's most talented, self-indulgent freaks. Codrescu finds himself quite at home there. He expertly weaves pages of New Orleans history through his stories of personal discovery and debauchery. The last few essays, written post-Katrina, radiate simultaneous anger and clarity. Full of pride and defensiveness, Codrescu closes the collection ruminating about rebuilding the city and his longing to return to its rhythms and eccentricities. Despite Codrescu's frustrations, this collection is, in the end, gentle and sweet." Publ Wkly

Dyson, Michael Eric, 1958-
Come hell or high water; Hurricane Katrina and the color of disaster. Basic Civitas 2006 258p $23; pa $14.95 **976.3**
1. Hurricane Katrina, 2005 2. Disaster relief 3. African Americans—Social conditions
ISBN 978-0-465-01761-4; 0-465-01761-4; 978-0-465-01772-0 (pa); 0-465-01772-X (pa)
LC 2007-310210
This book on Hurrican Katrina "not only chronicles what happened when, it also argues that the nation's failure to offer timely aid to Katrina's victims indicates deeper problems in race and class relations. . . . [The author's] contention that Katrina exposed a dominant culture pervaded not only by 'active malice' toward poor blacks but also by a long history of 'passive indifference' to their problems is both powerful and unsettling." Publ Wkly
Includes bibliographical references

Horne, Jed, 1948-
Breach of faith; Hurricane Katrina and the near death of a great American city. Random House 2006 412p map $25.95 * **976.3**
1. Hurricane Katrina, 2005 2. New Orleans (La.)—Description and travel 3. Disaster relief
ISBN 978-1-4000-6552-3; 1-4000-6552-6
LC 2006-46468
According to the author, "Hurricane Katrina shredded one of the great cities of the South, and as levees failed and the federal relief effort proved lethally incompetent, a natural disaster became a manmade catastrophe. As an editor of New Orleans' daily newspaper, the Times-Picayune, Horne has had [access] . . . to the unfolding drama of the city's collapse into chaos and its continuing struggle to survive." Publisher's note
This book does "an admirable job of detailing the design flaws that left New Orleans underwater." New Repub
Includes bibliographical references

Lane, Charles, 1961-
The day freedom died; the Colfax massacre, the Supreme Court, and the betrayal of Reconstruction. Henry Holt and Co. 2008 326p il map $27
976.3
1. United States. Supreme Court 2. Louisiana—Race relations 3. African Americans—History 4. Massacres 5. Reconstruction (1865-1876) 6. Trials (Homicide)
ISBN 978-0-8050-8342-2; 0-8050-8342-1
LC 2007-37514
"The Colfax Massacre . . . took place on an Easter Sunday afternoon in 1873. Within four hours, at least eighty black American men had been brutally murdered by white vigilantes in Colfax, La. Journalist Lane's groundbreaking and persuasive work illustrates this 'pivotal event in the political and constitutional history of post-Civil War America' and its social, political and judicial aftermath. . . . Students of American and African-American history will find it particularly valuable; fans of American history will find it a moving and instructive drama." Publ Wkly
Includes bibliographical references

Van Heerden, Ivor Ll., 1950-
The storm; what went wrong and why during Hurricane Katrina; [by] Ivor van Heerden and Mike Bryan. Viking 2006 308p il map $25.95
976.3
1. Hurricane Katrina, 2005 2. Disaster relief
ISBN 0-670-03781-8   LC 2006-44727
This book focuses on public mismanagement relating to Hurricane Katrina.
"This serious, scientific explanation of what exactly happened in the hours—and years—leading up to Hurricane Katrina's devestation of New Orleans brings a fresh perspective to a tragedy that has generated remarkably similar news accounts over the past eight months." Publ Wkly
Includes bibliographical references

976.4   Texas

Davis, William C., 1946-
Three roads to the Alamo; the lives and fortunes of David Crockett, James Bowie and William Barret Travis. HarperCollins Pubs. 1998 791p il pa $20 hardcover o.p. *   **976.4**
1. Crockett, Davy, 1786-1836 2. Bowie, Jim, 1796-1836 3. Travis, William Barret, 1809-1836 4. Texas—History 5. Alamo (San Antonio, Tex.)
ISBN 0-06-093094-2 (pa)   LC 97-43815
Davis provides portraits of the three frontiersmen "showing both the differences and similarities that propelled them into a remote Spanish mission in Mexican Texas for a fatal confrontation with the Mexican President, Santa Anna and his troops in March 1836." N Y Times Book Rev
This "is a readable, stimulating, and exceptionally well-researched narrative history." Libr J
Includes bibliographical references

976.6   Oklahoma

Hirsch, James S.
Riot and remembrance; the Tulsa race war and its legacy. Houghton Mifflin 2002 358p il $25; pa $14   **976.6**
1. African Americans—Tulsa (Okla.) 2. Riots 3. Tulsa (Okla.)—Race relations
ISBN 0-618-10813-0; 0-618-34076-9 (pa)
LC 2001-51615
"James S. Hirsch's history of the Tulsa, Okla., race riot in 1921 places the incident in a national debate on race and reparations." N Y Times Book Rev
"Hirsch unearths an important episode in U.S. history with verve, intelligence and compassion." Publ Wkly
Includes bibliographical references

977   North Central United States. Lake states

Barry, John M.
Rising tide; the great Mississippi flood of 1927 and how it changed America. Simon & Schuster 1997 524p il maps pa $16 hardcover o.p.
977
1. Floods—Mississippi River 2. Mississippi River valley—History
ISBN 0-684-84002-2 (pa)   LC 96-40077
This is the "story of human defeat by a savage, unpredictable river. . . . The flood of 1927, three times greater than the flood of 1993, was an unprecedented disaster that spurred a political innovation. Congress's agreement to rebuild the Mississippi's shattered flood-control system marked the federal government's first assumption of full financial responsibility for a regional calamity. Much of the book recounts how the greed of New Orleans bankers and Delta planters increased the sufferings of the rural poor. . . . Barry's book is a virtuoso piece of exposition." New Yorker
Includes bibliographical references

Dennis, Jerry
The living Great Lakes; searching for the heart of the inland seas. Thomas Dunne Bks. 2003 296p il maps $25.95   **977**
1. Great Lakes
ISBN 0-312-25193-9   LC 2002-32500
The author offers a "description of being a crew member on the schooner *Malabar* on a six-week trip through the waters of Lakes Huron, Ontario, Michigan, Erie and Superior. . . . Dennis weaves anecdotes from his childhood, such as a family-fishing trip on Lake Michigan, together with informed commentary on the natural history of the lakes and the people who live there." Publ Wkly
Includes bibliographical references

Laskin, David, 1953-
The children's blizzard; . HarperCollins 2004 307p map $24.95; pa $13.95   **977**
1. Blizzards
ISBN 0-06-052075-2; 0-06-052076-0 (pa)
LC 2005-295018

Laskin, David, 1953-—_Continued_

The author describes the events of the School Children's Blizzard, when "in 1888, a sudden, violent blizzard swept across the American plains, killing hundreds of people, many of them children on their way home from school." Publ Wkly

"An adroit, sensitive drama and a skillful addition to a popular genre." Booklist

Includes bibliographical references

977.1 Ohio

Frazier, Ian

Family. Farrar, Straus & Giroux 1994 386p il maps pa $16 hardcover o.p. **977.1**
1. Frazier family 2. City and town life
ISBN 0-312-42059-5 (pa)   LC 94-14730
"An extraordinary history of an ordinary family, in which the author plays the roles of gossip, pedant and loyal member, yielding a reunion strangers are welcome—and fortunate—to attend." N Y Times Book Rev

977.3 Illinois

Abbott, Karen, 1973-

Sin in the Second City; madams, ministers, playboys, and the battle for America's soul. Random House 2007 xxiv, 356p il $25.95
977.3
1. Everleigh, Ada, 1876-1960 2. Everleigh, Minna, 1878-1948 3. Everleigh Club (Chicago, Ill.) 4. Prostitution 5. Chicago (Ill.)—Social life and customs
ISBN 978-1-4000-6530-1; 1-4000-6530-5
LC 2006-51878
This is an account of "the Everleigh Club, which opened in Chicago in 1900 and lasted 11 years as the self-proclaimed grandest whorehouse in America." N Y Times (Late N Y Ed)
"Lavish in her details, nicely detached in her point of view, [and with] scrupulous concern for historical accuracy, Ms. Abbott has written an immensely readable book. Sin in the Second City offers much in the way of reflection for those interested in the unending puzzle that goes by the name of human nature." Wall Street Journal
Includes bibliographical references

The **Encyclopedia** of Chicago; edited by James R. Grossman, Ann Durkin Keating, Janice L. Reiff; cartographic editor, Michael P. Conzen. University of Chicago Press 2004 xxix, 1117p il map $65   **977.3**
1. Chicago (Ill.)—Encyclopedias
ISBN 0-226-31015-9   LC 2004-3487
"The main alphabetical section of the _Encyclopedia,_ comprising more than 1,400 entries, covers . . . Chicago's neighborhoods, suburbs, and ethnic groups, as well as the city's cultural institutions, technology and science, architecture, religions, immigration, transportation, business history, labor, music, health and medicine, and hundreds of other topics." Publisher's note

Miller, Donald L., 1944-

City of the century; the epic of Chicago and the making of America; {by} Donald Miller. Simon & Schuster 1996 704p il maps pa $18 hardcover o.p.
977.3
1. Chicago (Ill.)—History
ISBN 0-684-83138-4 (pa)   LC 96-4018
In this account of Chicago's history in the nineteenth century "Miller tells of Chicago's historical and literary figures, reform leaders, architects, industrialists, and entrepreneurs." Libr J

Tintori, Karen

Trapped: the 1909 Cherry Mine disaster. Simon & Schuster 2002 273p il $25; pa $14
977.3
1. Coal mines and mining—Accidents
ISBN 0-7434-2194-9; 0-7434-2195-7 (pa)
LC 2002-104596
"On November 13, 1909, a fire trapped 480 coal miners . . . 400 feet below ground in a mine at Cherry, Illinois. Only 221 escaped. . . . Tintori describes the life-and-death struggle of the miners below ground and the terror of the women and children gathered at the mine's entrance. . . . Tintori's graphic account of this tragedy is a sad but gripping story." Booklist

978   Western United States

Ambrose, Stephen E.

Lewis & Clark; voyage of discovery; [photographs by] Sam Abell. National Geographic Soc. 2002 255p il maps $35 *   **978**
1. Lewis and Clark Expedition (1804-1806) 2. West (U.S.)—Exploration 3. West (U.S.)—Description and travel
ISBN 0-7922-6473-8   LC 2002-727771
First published 1998
Bicentennial edition
"Ambrose, drawing on his hikes and canoe trips to all the monuments between St. Louis and Fort Clatsop associated with the explorers, melds his memories and own journal entries with `a . . . Lewis and Clark narrative spiced by entries from their journals." Booklist
"In addition to the superb writing, the book has stunning, full-color photographs of the places that Lewis and Clark so vividly described. . . . This combination of easy-to-read writing, high-quality photographs, and period artwork makes this book appealing to a wide range of readers." SLJ
Includes bibliographical references

Undaunted courage; Meriwether Lewis, Thomas Jefferson, and the opening of the American West. Simon & Schuster 1996 511p il maps $30; pa $17
978
1. Lewis, Meriwether, 1774-1809 2. Lewis and Clark Expedition (1804-1806) 3. West (U.S.)—Exploration
ISBN 0-684-81107-3; 0-684-82697-6 (pa)
LC 95-37146
This treatment of the Lewis and Clark Expedition "is essentially a biography of Lewis, although the bulk of it

Ambrose, Stephen E.—*Continued*

is a lively retelling of the journey of the two captains—together with their party of soldiers and frontiersmen, Clark's black slave, York, and the legendary Shoshone Indian woman, Sacagawea, and her infant son—conveyed with passionate enthusiasm by Mr. Ambrose and sprinkled liberally with some of the most famous and vivid passages from the travelers' journals." N Y Times Book Rev

Includes bibliographical references

Brown, Dee Alexander

The American West; photos edited by Martin F. Schmitt. Scribner 1994 461p il maps pa $17 hardcover o.p.   **978**

1. West (U.S.)—History
ISBN 0-684-80441-7 (pa)   LC 94-37444
"This narrative history of westward expansion paints a vivid portrait of the settlers, pioneers, entrepreneurs, and Native Americans of the old West. Useful as collateral research material and for recreational reading." Booklist

Includes bibliographical references

Calloway, Colin G. (Colin Gordon), 1953-

One vast winter count; the Native American West before Lewis and Clark. University of Nebraska Press 2003 631p il (History of the American West) $39.95   **978**

1. Native Americans—West (U.S.) 2. West (U.S.)—History
ISBN 0-8032-1530-4   LC 2003-44757
"Calloway concentrates on the Indian experience from the Appalachians to the Pacific, in a time frame from prehistory to the 18th century. The scope is staggering, but Calloway masters it, demonstrating a remarkable command of a broad spectrum of historical, ethnographic and archeological sources including printed material and oral traditions." Publ Wkly

Includes bibliographical references

Dary, David

The Oregon Trail; an American saga. Knopf 2004 414p il map $35 *   **978**

1. Oregon Trail 2. Frontier and pioneer life—West (U.S.)
ISBN 0-375-41399-5   LC 2004-46512
The author "looks at the men and women who trekked the trouble-strewn paths to the nation's northwest coast. . . . Dary opens with 18th-century maritime explorers and carries us into the late 19th century, when the trail west from Independence, Mo., had ceded its importance to the railroads. . . . His closing chapter on the Oregon Trail's rebirth as a tourist draw in the 20th century is a real contribution to modern western lore. It's hard to imagine a more informative introduction to the westering itch along the Oregon Trail and to those who responded to it." Publ Wkly

Includes bibliographical references

The Santa Fe Trail; its history, legends, and lore. Knopf 2000 368p il maps $30 *
                                                    978
1. Santa Fe Trail
ISBN 0-375-40361-2   LC 00-23276
Also available in paperback from Penguin Bks.
This is a history of the Santa Fe Trail, a route in the Southwestern United States "employed for commercial and emigrant traffic for nearly six decades, beginning in 1822, . . . after New Spain declared independence from Spain and renamed itself Mexico." N Y Times Book Rev
"This is a solid account, grounded in available original sources. . . . Far from writing a dry business history, Dary has an engaging style that allows him to relate some of the lore and legends and show that they are just lore and legends." Libr J

Includes bibliographical references

Duncan, Dayton

Lewis & Clark; the journey of the Corps of Discovery; based on a documentary film by Ken Burns, written by Dayton Duncan; with a preface by Ken Burns and conributions by Stephen E. Ambrose, Erica Funkhouser, William Least Heat-Moon. Knopf 1997 248p il maps $45; pa $25
                                                    978
1. Lewis and Clark Expedition (1804-1806) 2. West (U.S.)—Exploration
ISBN 0-679-45450-0; 0-375-70652-6 (pa)
                                     LC 97-73823
This is a companion volume to PBS television film 'Lewis and Clark: The journey of the Corps of Discovery,' by Ken Burns
An "attractive book with a well-written text and an excellent presentation of historic paintings, photographs, maps, and original quotations from various of Lewis and Clark's journals." Sci Books Films

Egan, Timothy

The worst hard time; the untold story of those who survived the great American dust bowl. Houghton Mifflin Co. 2005 340p il map $28
                                                    978
1. Dust storms 2. Great Plains—History
ISBN 0-618-34697-X   LC 2005-08057
The author focuses "on the plight of a handful of families from the hardest-hit bottom of the Dust Bowl, the western edge of the Oklahoma Panhandle known as No Man's Land; Dallam County due south in the Texas Panhandle; and Baca County in southeastern Colorado." N Y Times (Late N Y Ed)
"With characters who seem to have sprung from a novel by Sinclair Lewis or Steinbeck, and Egan's powerful writing, this account will long remain in readers' minds." Publ Wkly

Includes bibliographcial references

Frazier, Ian

Great Plains. Farrar, Straus & Giroux 1989 290p il maps pa $13 hardcover o.p.   **978**
ISBN 0-312-27850-0 (pa)   LC 88-31106

Frazier, Ian—*Continued*

The author recounts his experiences and observations traveling in the Western United States

"This is a colorful and engaging blend of travelogue, local color, geography and folklore." Publ Wkly

The **Lewis** and Clark journals; an American epic of discovery: the abridgment of the definitive Nebraska edition; [by] Meriwether Lewis, William Clark, and members of the Corps of Discovery; edited and with an introduction by Gary E. Moulton. University of Neb. Press 2003 lviii, 413p il maps $29.95 **978**

1. Lewis, Meriwether, 1774-1809 2. Lewis and Clark Expedition (1804-1806) 3. West (U.S.)—Exploration

ISBN 0-8032-2950-X LC 2002-28526

"Moulton presents an abridged version of the Journals of the Lewis and Clark Expedition . . . that celebrates the Corps of Discovery's landmark journey 200 years ago. What makes this single volume of journal selections more powerful than its contemporaries is the use of other corps members' diaries to provide further details about the journey. Major themes include anthropological observations about the Native Americans the corps encountered, their relations with these tribes, and the natural history work of Lewis and Clark. The expedition is broken down into 12 chronological chapters, and notes defining 19th-century vocabulary, shifting geographic place names, and events requiring editorial explanation are included alongside the text. This book will bring the expedition alive to a new generation of readers. Recommended for all libraries." Libr J

"This is a very smooth abridgment of the 13-volume edition of the explorers' journals. Suited to the general reader, this edition is an invaluable and easily digested account of the epic journey." Booklist

Luchetti, Cathy, 1945-

Children of the West; family life on the frontier. Norton 2001 253p il $39.95 * **978**

1. Children—West (U.S.) 2. Frontier and pioneer life—West (U.S.) 3. West (U.S.)—Social life and customs

ISBN 0-393-04913-2 LC 00-53287

"In the nineteenth and early twentieth centuries, the children who resided in the sparsely populated plains and prairies of the western U.S. were subject to a unique variety of hardships and joys. . . . Utilizing more than 100 vintage photographs and excerpts from letters, diaries, and journals, Luchetti examines aspects of childbearing, child rearing, childhood, and adolescence on the American frontier." Booklist

Includes bibliographical references

McLynn, Frank

Wagons west; the epic story of America's overland trails. Grove Press 2002 509p il maps $32.50; pa $16.50 **978**

1. Overland journeys to the Pacific 2. Frontier and pioneer life—West (U.S.)

ISBN 0-8021-1731-7; 0-8021-4063-7 (pa)

LC 2002-33859

This "account of the westward migration covers the years 1840-49, spanning the time between the eclipse of the mountain men and the beginning of the gold rush. . . . Relying on original diaries and memoirs, McLynn eloquently illustrates how diverse groups of people, including midwestern farmers, Native Americans, Mormons, and missionaries, played their parts in transforming the West while being transformed by it. This work will be a valuable addition to western history collections." Booklist

Includes bibliographical references

Morgan, Ted, 1932-

A shovel of stars; the making of the American West, 1800 to the present. Simon & Schuster 1995 559p il maps pa $25 hardcover o.p. **978**

1. West (U.S.)—History 2. Frontier and pioneer life—West (U.S.)

ISBN 0-684-81492-7 (pa) LC 94-43838

Companion volume Wilderness at dawn

Morgan "looks at the settlement of each state during its territorial period from the Louisiana Purchase in 1803 to the admission of Alaska and Hawaii in 1959." Libr J

"This grandly inspired work—a completely satisfying read—embraces the texture and the drama of the West in all its heartbreak and heroism." Booklist

Includes bibliographical references

Parkman, Francis, 1823-1893

The Oregon trail; The conspiracy of Pontiac. Literary Classics of the United States, Distributed to the trade in the U.S. and Canada by the Viking Press 1991 951p il $40 **978**

1. Oregon Trail 2. West (U.S.)—Description and travel 3. Frontier and pioneer life—West (U.S.) 4. Native Americans 5. Pontiac's Conspiracy, 1763-1765

ISBN 0-940450-54-2 LC 90-62264

The Oregon Trail was originally published serially in Knickerbocker Magazine; first published in book form, 1849, with title: The California and Oregon Trail.

In *The Conspiracy of Pontiac* (1851), the author describes Native American resistance to white expansion in the Northeast after the French's loss of the Seven Years' War. *The Oregon Trail* is "an account of a trip made in 1846 by the author and his cousin Quincy Adams Shaw. They traveled together from St. Louis to Fort Laramie; there they separated, Parkman going to live for some weeks with a tribe of Sioux Indians. *The Oregon Trail* provides valuable descriptions of the prairies at the most fascinating period of their history and a remarkable ethnological study of the Indians." Benet's Reader's Ency of Am Lit

Includes bibliographical references

Raban, Jonathan

Bad land; an American romance. Pantheon Bks. 1996 324p pa $14 hardcover o.p. **978**

1. Frontier and pioneer life—West (U.S.) 2. West (U.S.)—History

ISBN 0-679-75906-9 (pa) LC 96-13432

This "book about Montana examines the present remains and historical origins of the last great wave of American western settlement, the migration of home-

Raban, Jonathan—*Continued*

steaders to eastern Montana in the first decade of this century." London Rev Books

Raban "turns Montana into a profound symbol for America's sense of displacement; for its tragic romance with rootlessness, its search for identity under that big blue sky." New Statesman (1913)

Schlissel, Lillian

Far from home; families of the westward journey; [by] Lillian Schlissel, Byrd Gibbens, Elizabeth Hampsten; foreword by Robert Coles. University of Nebraska Press 2002 264p il pa $14.95   **978**

1. Frontier and pioneer life—West (U.S.) 2. West (U.S.)—Social life and customs

ISBN 0-8032-9295-3

First published 1989 by Schocken Bks.

"The authors relate the story of three pioneering families—largely through the words of mothers and daughters preserved in old correspondence and later autobiographical writings." Christ Sci Monit

"An immensely readable book that peers closely into the lives of ordinary American frontier families." Booklist

Includes bibliographical references

Schmidt, Thomas, 1959-

The Lewis & Clark Trail; foreword by Stephen E. Ambrose. Bicentennial ed completely rev. National Geographic Soc. 2002 192p il maps pa $16   **978**

1. Lewis and Clark Expedition (1804-1806) 2. West (U.S.)—Description and travel

ISBN 0-7922-6471-1   LC 2001-7003

First published 1998

"An official guide of the National Council of the Lewis & Clark Bicentennial"

Color photographs and maps provide a guide to the Lewis and Clark National Historic Trail

Sides, Hampton, 1962-

Blood and thunder; an epic of the American West. Doubleday 2006 460p il $26.95   **978**

1. Carson, Kit, 1809-1868 2. West (U.S.)—History 3. United States—Territorial expansion 4. Frontier and pioneer life—West (U.S.) 5. Navajo Indians

ISBN 978-0-385-50777-6; 0-385-50777-1

LC 2006-16579

The author's "main focus is the virtual decimation of the Navajo nation from the 1820s to the late 1860s. Sides depicts the complex role of whites in the subjugation of the Navajos through his portrait of Kit Carson— an illiterate trapper, soldier and scout who knew the Native Americans intimately, married two of them and, without blinking, participated in the Indians' slaughter." Publ Wkly

This book "will surely capture readers, and it ought to. It's a riveting account of a vast swath of history with which few Americans are familiar." New Yorker

Includes bibliographical references

Slaughter, Thomas P.

Exploring Lewis and Clark; reflections on men and wilderness. Knopf 2003 231p il maps $24; pa $14   **978**

1. Lewis, Meriwether, 1774-1809 2. Clark, William, 1770-1838 3. Sacagawea, b. 1786 4. York, ca. 1775-ca. 1815 5. Lewis and Clark Expedition (1804-1806) 6. West (U.S.)—Exploration

ISBN 0-375-40078-8; 0-375-70071-4 (pa)

LC 2002-69376

The author "utilizes the journals of explorers Lewis and Clark to investigate their epic journey and its subsequent mythical status. What becomes quickly apparent is that these were imperfect men who have become legends." Libr J

"It may be easy to dismiss as a nitpicking revisionist potshot at our beloved heroes, but as the expedition's bicentennial approaches, this book's perspective will help keep our understanding well nuanced and grounded in fact." Booklist

Includes bibliographical references

Tubbs, Stephenie Ambrose

The Lewis and Clark companion; an encyclopedic guide to the voyage of discovery; {by} Stephenie Ambrose Tubbs, with Clay Straus Jenkinson. Holt & Co. 2003 345p il maps $30; pa $16 *   **978**

1. Lewis and Clark Expedition (1804-1806) 2. West (U.S.)—Exploration 3. West (U.S.)—Description and travel

ISBN 0-8050-6725-6; 0-8050-6726-4 (pa)

LC 2002-37992

"An Owl book"

"Arranged alphabetically, the more than 500 entries vary from concise, one-sentence descriptions to multipage treatises for principle corps members, major events, important geographic features, and significant flora and fauna. References follow each entry, and a considerable bibliography is included." Libr J

"This alphabetical primer on all things Lewis and Clark is comprehensive but not exhaustive. Both novices and scholars will benefit from the cogent entries." Publ Wkly

Ward, Geoffrey C.

The West; an illustrated history; narrative by Geoffrey C. Ward; based on a documentary film script by Geoffrey C. Ward and Dayton Duncan; with a preface by Stephen Ives and Ken Burns; and contributions by Dayton Duncan {et al.}. Little, Brown 1996 445p il pa $24.95 hardcover o.p.   **978**

1. West (U.S.)—History

ISBN 0-316-73589-2 (pa)   LC 96-4323

"The book's eight chapters, each written by a different historian, are arranged according to the corresponding PBS series. Beginning with Western America in the 1500s, the work presents all aspects of Western culture from the reality to the myth, moving chronologically from the Spanish exploration of the West, Native Americans, Hispanic Westerners, women in the West, and the Gold Rush, and ending with Buffalo Bill's Wild West

Ward, Geoffrey C.—*Continued*

Show. If one is looking for an in-depth, comprehensive history of the westward movement, this is not it, but as an introduction, this work is an enjoyable and interesting place to start." Libr J

Woodger, Elin

Encyclopedia of the Lewis and Clark Expedition; [by] Elin Woodger, Brandon Toropov; foreword by Ned Blackhawk. Facts on File 2004 xxv, 438p il (Facts on File library of American history) $65.00; pa $21.95   **978**

1. Lewis and Clark Expedition (1804-1806) 2. West (U.S.)—Exploration

ISBN 0-8160-4781-2; 0-8160-4782-0 (pa)

LC 2003-6120

"Coverage includes information about the people in the expedition party and those encountered, the conditions under which they traveled, the land they traversed, and the plants and animals they observed." Lib Media Connect

"This is a complete, authoritative overview of a fascinating landmark in American history and will be a first purchase for most libraries." SLJ

Includes bibliographical references

978.03 Western United States— Encyclopedias and dictionaries

Encyclopedia of the Great Plains; David J. Wishart, editor. University of Nebraska Press 2004 919p il map $75   **978.03**

1. Great Plains—Encyclopedias

ISBN 0-8032-4787-7   LC 2003-21037

The author "presents 1,316 signed entries, written by some 1000 scholars and divided according to 27 topics that range from the Paleo-Indians to the 2000 census. The contents of each topic are outlined with an introductory essay, followed by specific articles arranged alphabetically within the topic. Historical figures are listed under their common names rather than their formal names." Libr J

"Here is a unique reference book that cuts a broad swath through parts of the U.S. and Canada, the region known as the heartland. The book's topical arrangement perfectly suits the cross-boundary approach." Booklist

The New encyclopedia of the American West; edited by Howard R. Lamar. Yale Univ. Press 1998 1324p il maps $60   **978.03**

1. Frontier and pioneer life—West (U.S.)—Encyclopedias

ISBN 0-300-07088-8   LC 98-6231

First published 1977 by Crowell with title: The Reader's encyclopedia of the American West

This reference work covers "the history, geography, culture, literature, art, and natural history of both the real and the imaginary West. . . . {Coverage spans} prehistory to the present, and . . . {includes} events in the history of the trans-Mississippi West . . . {as well as} the frontier or 'western' stage of all 50 American states. Entries range from important events in the expansion of the U.S. . . . to the first European and American discover-

ers, among them Coronado, LaSalle, and Lewis and Clark." Publisher's note

Includes bibliographical references

Slatta, Richard W., 1947-

The cowboy encyclopedia. Norton 1996 474p il pa $17   **978.03**

1. Cowhands—Encyclopedias

ISBN 0-393-31473-1   LC 94-19824

First published 1994 by ABC-CLIO

"Focusing on the cowboy experience in North and South America, *The Cowboy Encyclopedia* provides history, definitions, and commentary in an A-to-Z arrangement with major topics such as saddles and cowboy films receiving longer topical entries. Excellent cross-references and an extensive index provide easy access to all aspects of a topic. Appendixes cover cowboy films and videotape sources, museums, periodicals, and western cultural happenings." Am Libr

978.1   Kansas

Frank, Thomas

What's the matter with Kansas? how conservatives won the heart of America. Metropolitan Books 2004 306p map $24; pa $14   **978.1**

1. Kansas 2. Conservatism

ISBN 0-8050-7339-6; 0-8050-7774-X (pa)

LC 2004-44824

The author "turns his eye on what he calls the 'thirty-year backlash'—the populist revolt against a supposedly liberal establishment. . . . [Frank asks] 'what's the matter with Kansas?'—how a place famous for its radicalism became one of the most conservative states in the union." Publisher's note

This is "a brilliant book, one of the best so far this decade on American politics." Nation

Includes bibliographical references

Stratton, Joanna L.

Pioneer women; voices from the Kansas frontier; introduction by Arthur M. Schlesinger, Jr. Simon & Schuster 1981 319p il $15 hardcover o.p.   **978.1**

1. Women—Kansas 2. Frontier and pioneer life—Kansas 3. Kansas—History

ISBN 0-671-44748-3 (pa)   LC 80-15960

"A unique book based on the memoirs of nearly 800 pioneer women who lived in Kansas between 1854 and 1890. . . . The book presents personal and detailed accounts of life inside homes, the schools, and the social organizations of early Kansas." Choice

Includes bibliographical references

978.7   Wyoming

Meyer, Judith L., 1956-
The spirit of Yellowstone; the cultural evolution
of a national park; photographs by Vance Howard.
Roberts Rinehart 2003 145p il pa $19.95
978.7
1. Yellowstone National Park 2. Human influence on
nature
ISBN 1-570-98395-X   LC 2002-156320
First published 1996 by Rowman & Littlefield
The author "pays tribute to the park and all its glories,
covering the park's history, its prime landmarks, and its
prominence in art. The photographs are truly striking and
not the typical landscape fare. Howard plays with light
and texture to capture images that will amaze even those
already familiar with the park's unprecedented beauty."
Libr J
Includes bibliographical references

978.9   New Mexico

Childs, Craig Leland
House of rain; tracking a vanished civilization
across the American Southwest; [by] Craig Childs.
Little, Brown and Co. 2006 496p il map $24.99
978.9
1. Chaco Culture National Historical Park (N.M.)
2. Southwestern States—Antiquities 3. Pueblo Indians
ISBN 978-0-316-60817-6; 0-316-60817-3
LC 2006-19112
"Beginning at the monumental cultural center of Chaco Canyon, where the Anasazi flourished, Childs's quest
to understand their apparent disappearance leads him to
the numerous great houses of New Mexico, such as
Pueblo Bonito, to the Four Corners area of northeastern
Arizona, southern Colorado and Utah, and beyond to
northern Mexico. In these places, he identifies features
that had not appeared prior to the apparent abandonment
of Chaco (thus implying that the Anasazi migrated to
these areas). Childs' vividly weaves his personal narrative, imbued with a deep respect for the geography and
cultural landscape, with scientific research and numerous
interactions with foremost scholars." Libr J

979   Great Basin and Pacific Slope region of the United States. Pacific Coast states

Durham, Michael S., 1935-
Desert between the mountains; Mormons,
miners, padres, mountain men, and the opening of
the Great Basin, 1772-1869. University of
Oklahoma Press 1999 336p il map pa $19.95
979
1. Frontier and pioneer life—West (U.S.)
2. Mormons 3. Great Basin
ISBN 0-8061-3186-1; 978-0-8061-3186-3
LC 99-23572
First published 1997 by Holt & Co.

This is a history of the settlement of the Great Basin
area in what is now Utah and Nevada.
"This is well-written history at its most easygoing."
Publ Wkly
Includes bibliographical references

979.1   Arizona

Dolnick, Edward, 1952-
Down the great unknown; John Wesley Powell's
1869 journey of discovery and tragedy through the
Grand Canyon. HarperCollins Pubs. 2001 367p il
maps $27.50; pa $13.95   **979.1**
1. Powell, John Wesley, 1834-1902 2. Grand Canyon
(Ariz.) 3. Colorado River (Colo.-Mexico)
ISBN 0-06-019619-X; 0-06-095586-4 (pa)
LC 2001-24819
This book recounts "the adventures of the 19th-
century explorer. Powell, who had lost an arm during the
Civil War, set out in early 1869 with a team of nine oth-
er men in the first endeavor to map the Green and Colo-
rado Rivers, along with the canyons that cradle them."
NY Times Book Rev
"Dolnick, a science journalist who has rafted down the
Grand, turns in a most estimable rendition of that storied
expedition. It skillfully integrates the notes and journals
of expedition members with technical insight about the
perils of roiling whitewater." Booklist
Includes bibliographical references

979.2   Utah

Walker, Ronald W., 1939-
Massacre at Mountain Meadows; an American
tragedy; by Ronald W. Walker, Richard E. Turley,
Jr., Glen M. Leonard. Oxford University Press
2008 430p il map $29.95 *   **979.2**
1. Mountain Meadows Massacre, 1857
ISBN 978-0-19-516034-5   LC 2008-14451
The authors tell the story of "the titular 1857 tragedy
in which 157 emigrants traveling to California were
killed by local Mormons. With its understated prose, an
essential purchase." Libr J
Includes bibliographical references

979.3   Nevada

Denton, Sally
The money and the power; the making of Las
Vegas and its hold on America, 1947-2000; by
Sally Denton and Roger Morris. Knopf 2001 479p
pa $15 hardcover o.p.   **979.3**
1. Las Vegas (Nev.) 2. Organized crime 3. Political
corruption
ISBN 0-375-70126-5 (pa)   LC 00-62011
The authors contend that "modern Las Vegas enjoys
a thriving economy dependent on gambling, greed, political corruption, and drugs that mirrors what is practiced
throughout America." Libr J

Denton, Sally—*Continued*

"The idea of Las Vegas as the epitome of crass American pop culture has become at least a surface truism in most circles. But Denton and Morris . . . go much deeper than the surface in this sobering account of the famous Nevada resort town." Booklist

Includes bibliographical references

979.4   California

Cannon, Lou

Official negligence; how Rodney King and the riots changed Los Angeles and the LAPD. Westview Press 1999 706p il pa $27

         979.4

1. King, Rodney 2. Riots 3. Los Angeles (Calif.)—Race relations

ISBN 978-0-8133-3725-8; 0-8133-3725-9

First published 1997 by Times Books

This is an account of the riots in Los Angeles in 1992 that were the aftermath of the beating "of a black motorist, Rodney King, by four white police officers." Economist

This work represents "the best kind of reportage—meticulous, unbiased and complete." Publ Wkly

Didion, Joan

Where I was from. Knopf 2003 226p $23; pa $13.95

         979.4

1. American national characteristics 2. California—History 3. California—Social conditions

ISBN 0-679-43332-5; 0-679-75286-2 (pa)

         LC 2002-43325

In this "assessment of her home and her opinions, Didion gives up on California and its inhabitants, including her own pioneer family; she now sees the state's history as a fiasco, a saga of advancement with other people's money, chiefly the government's spent on behalf of business interests." N Y Times Book Rev

This "is a complex and challenging memoir, difficult to enter into but just as difficult to put down. . . . Those who have long admired the clarity and precision of her prose will not be disappointed with this partly autobiographical, partly historical, but fully engrossing account." Libr J

Muir, John, 1838-1914

The Yosemite; the original John Muir text; illustrated with photographs by Galen Rowell; each photograph accompanied by an excerpt from the works of John Muir and an annotation by Galen Rowell; introduction by the photographer. Sierra Club Bks. 1989 218p il pa $14.95 hardcover o.p.

         979.4

1. Yosemite National Park (Calif.)

ISBN 0-87156-782-2 (pa)   LC 88-34919

"A Yolla Bolly Press book"

New photographs complement Muir's classic 1912 natural history of the national park

Includes bibliographical references

Winchester, Simon

A crack in the edge of the world; America and the great California earthquake of 1906. HarperCollins; distributed by us 2005 462p il maps $27.95 *

         979.4

1. Earthquakes—California

ISBN 0-06-057199-3   LC 2005-46009

The author "writes about the earthquake and fire that destroyed San Francisco almost 100 years ago." N Y Times Book Rev

"In this brawny page-turner, . . . [the author] has crafted a magnificent testament to the power of planet Earth and the efforts of humankind to understand her." Publ Wkly

Includes bibliographical references

979.7   Washington

Harden, Blaine

A river lost; the life and death of the Columbia. Norton 1996 271p maps $25; pa $14.95

         979.7

1. Columbia River

ISBN 0-393-03936-6; 0-393-31690-4 (pa)

         LC 95-38618

In this look at the development of Columbia River region, the author "examines the changes—sociological, environmental, economic and aesthetic—that the taming of this great river wrought. His wonderful account touches on the destruction of Native American cultures dependent on the river and its salmon, and on the near extinction of the salmon themselves. Also fairly portrayed are the people and industries currently dependent on both the managed river and massive government subsidies." Publ Wkly

Includes bibliographical references

Krist, Gary

The white cascade; the Great Northern Railway disaster and America's deadliest avalanche. Henry Holt and Company 2007 315p il map $26

         979.7

1. Avalanches 2. Railroad accidents

ISBN 978-0-8050-7705-6; 0-8050-7705-7

         LC 2006-49047

Krist tells the "story of one of the worst rail disasters in U.S. history in which two trains full of people, trapped high in the Cascade Mountains, are hit by a devastating avalanche." Publisher's note

"This is a tale in which snow falls, a mountain looms, and most of the protagonists simply sit. The outcome is predetermined. Mr. Krist does wonders with this unpromising material, however. Adopting a restrained, documentary tone, he slowly builds a picture of massing natural forces and helpless humanity, brought closer and closer to catastrophe with each tick of the clock. The pacing is expertly judged, and the potentially confusing narrative threads, involving multiple actors in scattered locations, are tied together neatly." N Y Times (Late N Y Ed)

Includes bibliographical references

979.8   Alaska

Borneman, Walter R., 1952-
Alaska: saga of a bold land. HarperCollins Pubs.
2003 608p il maps $34.95; pa $16.95 *
979.8

1. Alaska—History
ISBN 0-06-050306-8; 0-06-050307-6 (pa)
LC 2002-27271
"Separated into nine chronologically based chapters,
the text explores a recurring theme in Alaska's development: conflict among disparate groups over how the land
would be used for personal enrichment. . . . Engaging
chapters detail the important events and those who
helped shape Alaska's history. . . . This expansive, comprehensive history is recommended for all libraries." Libr
J

Includes bibliographical references

Jenkins, Peter, 1951-
Looking for Alaska. St. Martin's Press 2002
434p il $25.95; pa $14.95   **979.8**
1. Alaska—Description and travel
ISBN 0-312-26178-0; 0-312-30289-4 (pa)
LC 2001-48871
This is the author's "account of eighteen months spent
traveling over twenty thousand miles in tiny bush planes,
on snow machines and snowshoes, in fishing boats and
kayaks, on the Alaska Marine Highway and the Haul
Road, searching for what defines Alaska." Publisher's
note
This book "sparkles with adventure, quirky characters,
unbelievable hardships, and indescribable beauty." Libr J

McPhee, John A.
Coming into the country; {by} John McPhee.
Farrar, Straus & Giroux 1977 438p maps pa $15
hardcover o.p.   **979.8**
1. Alaska—Description and travel
ISBN 0-374-52287-1 (pa)   LC 77-12249
This book "is actually three lengthy bulletins about
Alaska. . . . The first describes a canoe trip that McPhee
and four companions took. . . . Second, McPhee tells of
a helicopter ride with a committee looking for a site on
which to build a new state capital. The last and longest
section covers some wintry months spent in Eagle, a tiny
settlement on the Yukon River." Time

Raban, Jonathan
Passage to Juneau; a sea and its meanings.
Pantheon Bks. 1999 435p $26.50; pa $15
979.8
1. Alaska—Description and travel
ISBN 0-679-44262-6; 0-679-77614-1 (pa)
LC 99-28777
"Long fascinated by the Inside Passage (the protected
waterway that runs from Washington State up to Alaska),
Raban casts off in his 35'ketch from his home port in
Seattle to follow in the wake of generations of salmon
fishermen. He draws a rather dark portrait of the region
as he fills out its history, through the cranky journals of

Captain Vancouver and others, and meditates on the
beautiful but threatening and lonesome landscape, with
its struggling communities, submerged mountains, tricky
waters, and names like Deception Pass and Desolation
Sound." Libr J

980   History of South America

The **Cambridge** history of Latin America; edited
by Leslie Bethell. Cambridge Univ. Press
1984-1995 10v in 11 v1 $205; v2 $236; v3
$225; v4 $205; v5 $236; v6 pt. 1 $162; v6 pt.
2 $162; v7 $205; v8 $205; v10 $162; v11 $178
980

1. Latin America—History
ISBN 0-521-23223-6 (v1); 0-521-24516-8 (v2);
0-521-23224-4   (v3);   0-521-23225-2   (v4);
0-521-24517-6 (v5); 0-521-23226-0 (v6 pt. 1);
0-521-46556-7 (v6 pt. 2); 0-521-24518-4 (v7);
0-521-26652-1   (v8);   0-521-49594-6   (v10);
0-521-39525-9 (v11)   LC 83-19036
First ten volumes of a projected eleven volume set
Contents: v1-2 Colonial Latin America; v3 From independence to c.1870; v4-5 c.1870 to 1930; v6 pt1-pt 2
Latin America Since 1930: Economy, society, and politics pt1 Economy and society, pt2 Politics and society;
v7 Latin America since 1930, Mexico, Central America
and the Caribbean; v8 Latin America since 1930; v10
Latin America since 1930: Ideas, culture, and society;
v11 Bibliographical essays
"History of the areas south of the United States from
just prior to the European invasions to the present. . . .
Covers general themes in Latin American history with
chronological accounts of the individual countries. Bibliographical essays are appended to each chapter." NY
Public Libr Book of How & Where to Look It Up

Chasteen, John Charles, 1955-
Born in blood and fire; a concise history of
Latin America. 2nd ed. W.W. Norton 2006 372p
il map pa $43.25   **980**
1. Latin America—History
ISBN 978-0-393-92769-6; 0-393-92769-5
LC 2005-48248
First published 2000
"Chasteen focuses on major political, social and eco-
nomic topics and trends that helped shape Latin America,
including liberalism, the caste system, the mixing of
races, nationalism and the Western notion of 'Progress';
he also examines the role that Europe and the United
States played in the development of these phenomena.
Also refreshing is Chasteen's examination of the periods
he covers from the perspective of women." Publ Wkly
[review of 2000 edition]
Includes bibliographical references

Encyclopedia of Latin American history and
culture; Jay Kinsbruner, editor in chief; Erick D.
Langer, senior editor. 2nd ed. Gale 2008 6v il
map set $695 *   **980**
1. Latin America—Encyclopedias
ISBN 978-0-684-31270-5   LC 2008-3461
First published 1996

Encyclopedia of Latin American history and culture—*Continued*

"This reference set covers the Western Hemisphere from Mexico to the tip of South America. . . . [This is] an outstanding encyclopedia that will serve a wide range of users from high school students to Latin American scholars." Libr J

Includes bibliographical references

Thomas, Hugh, 1931-

Rivers of gold; the rise of the Spanish Empire, from Columbus to Magellan. Random House 2003 xxi, 696p il map $35 **980**

1. Spain—Colonies 2. America—Exploration

ISBN 0-375-50204-1   LC 2003-69316

The author "concentrates here on the mere 30 years between Columbus' first contact and Magellan's circumnavigation to address the extraordinary speed and scope of Spain's imperial expansion as part of Europe's amazing rise to world power in the Renaissance." N Y Times Book Rev

"Engagingly presented, this book clearly shows the author's passion for his subject." Booklist

Includes bibliographical references

Williamson, Edwin

The Penguin history of Latin America. Penguin Books 1992 631p map pa $18 **980**

1. Latin America—History

ISBN 0-14-012559-0   LC 2005-412242

"The book is organized topically, rather than by country, and the author wisely selected regional examples of his major themes, rather than attempting a detailed analysis of each country. The work ends with an unusual exploration of literature and culture in relation to identity and modernization, followed by a helpful bibliographic essay." Libr J

Includes bibliographical references

981 Brazil

Page, Joseph A.

The Brazilians. Addison-Wesley 1995 540p il map pa $22.50 hardcover o.p. **981**

1. Brazilian national characteristics 2. Brazil

ISBN 0-201-44191-8 (pa)   LC 94-45812

The author "probes deep into the layers of Spanish, Portuguese, Dutch, African and Indian heritage that make Brazil so alluring and paradoxical. . . . In this magnetizing study, Page also explores the meld of Catholicism and Pentecostalism, of native Indian healers and modern medicine, of African rhythms and Western music. He discusses the environmental and investment scenes as well as the addiction to soccer and to the *telenovelas* of the powerful Globus media empire." Publ Wkly

Includes bibliographical references

Skidmore, Thomas E.

Brazil; five centuries of change. Oxford Univ. Press 1999 254p maps pa $28.95 hardcover o.p. **981**

1. Brazil

ISBN 0-19-505810-0 (pa)   LC 98-23122

Skidmore explores the country's "history, its political and economic development, and social and racial relationships. . . . This is a well-researched look at a fascinating country." Booklist

Includes bibliographical references

Whitaker, Robert

The mapmaker's wife; a true tale of love, murder, and survival in the Amazon. Basic Books 2004 352p il maps $25 **981**

1. Godin des Odonais, Isabelle de Grandmaison, 1728-1792 2. Scientific expeditions 3. Amazon River valley

ISBN 0-7382-0808-6; 978-0-7382-0808-4

     LC 2003-26902

Also available in paperback by Bantam Books

"The harrowing journey of Isabel Godin across the Andes and down the Amazon to rejoin her husband after a 20-year separation is only a small part of the extended history of the Charles-Marie de la Condamine expedition, which in turn is set within its context of the history of Enlightenment science, 18th-century mapping methods, the debate over the shape of the earth, and the sorry history of the Spanish and Portuguese conquest of South America." Sci Books Films

Includes bibliographical references

982 Argentina

Brown, Jonathan C.

A brief history of Argentina. Facts on File 2002 324p il maps hardcover o.p. pa $19.95 **982**

1. Argentina—History

ISBN 0-8160-4959-9; 0-8160-5719-2 (pa)

     LC 2002-6459

Contents: Ancient Argentina and the European Encounter; The Colonial Rio de la Plata; Imperial Reform and Conflict in the Rio de la Plata; Crisis of the Colonial Order and Revolution; Agrarian Expansion and Nation Building, 1820-1880; The Liberal Age, 1880-1916; The Decline of Liberalism, 1916-1930; The Rise of Populism, 1930-1955; The Failure of De-Peronization, 1955-1983; The Neo-Liberal Age Begins

This "reference focuses on such key events as the arrival of European colonialists, the struggle for independence, the era of Juan and Eva Peron, and the period known as the Dirty War. Special attention is given to: the culture and history of Argentina's indigenous population; how the area became one of Spain's most commercially successful colonies; the historic, social, and political conditions that led to the Dirty War [and] the conflict of political power and economic privilege in modern Argentina." Publisher's note

Includes bibliographical references

Parrado, Nando, 1949-
Miracle in the Andes; 72 days on the mountain and my long trek home; [by] Nando Parrado with Vince Rause. Crown Publishers 2006 291p il map hardcover o.p. pa $13.95 *   **982**
1. Survival after airplane accidents, shipwrecks, etc. 2. Andes
ISBN   1-4000-9767-3;   978-1-4000-9767-8; 1-4000-9769-X (pa); 978-1-4000-9769-2 (pa)
LC 2005-21629
"In October 1972, a plane carrying an Uruguayan rugby team crashed in the Andes. Not immediately rescued, the survivors turned to cannibalism to survive and after 72 days were saved. Rugby team member Parrado has written a beautiful story of friendship, tragedy and perseverance." Publ Wkly

985   Peru

Bingham, Hiram, 1875-1956
Lost city of the Incas; the story of Machu Picchu and its builders; with an introduction by Hugh Thomson; photographs by Hugh Thomson. Sterling 2002 274p il $35; pa $12.95 *
985
1. Machu Picchu (Peru) 2. Peru—Antiquities 3. Incas
ISBN 0-2976-0759-6; 1-84212-585-0 (pa)
LC 2002-483039
A reissue of the title first published 1948 by Duell
"In 1911 Bingham, an American explorer, found the Inca city of Machu Picchu, which had been lost for 300 years. In this volume he tells of its origin, how it came to be lost and how it was finally discovered." Libr J
Includes bibliographical references

MacQuarrie, Kim
The last days of the Incas. Simon & Schuster 2007 522p il map $30; pa $16.95   **985**
1. Incas 2. Peru—History
ISBN   978-0-7432-6049-7;   0-7432-6049-X; 978-0-7432-6050-3 (pa); 0-7432-6050-3 (pa)
LC 2007-61700
This is an "exploration of Incan history, from first contact with Europeans in 1526 to the rediscovery of buried Incan historical artifacts to 2005. The story of the downfall and rediscovery of the Incan Empire is revealed by following the footsteps of influential individuals in the history of interactions between the Incan civilization and Europeans." Libr J
This "is a first-rate reference work of ambitious scope that will most likely stand as the definitive account of these people." Booklist
Includes bibliographical references

Moseley, Michael Edward
The Incas and their ancestors; the archaeology of Peru. rev ed. Thames & Hudson 2001 288p il maps $27.50 *   **985**
1. Incas 2. Peru—Antiquities
ISBN 0-500-28277-3   LC 00-108866
First published 1992

This account of Andean prehistory and archaeology takes us from the first settlement of 10,000 years ago to the Spanish conquest
"Clearly presented, with a generous ration of maps and illustrations, {the volume} is thoughtful and welcome." Times Lit Suppl {review of 1992 edition}
Includes bibliographical references

Thomson, Hugh
The white rock; an exploration of the Inca heartland. Overlook Press 2003 316p il map $27.95; pa $16.95   **985**
1. Incas
ISBN 1-585-67355-2; 1-585-67503-2 (pa)
LC 2002-34606
First published 2001 in the United Kingdom
The author "recounts a successful expedition he led in 1982 to 'refind' Llactapata, the 'lost city of the Incas,' and to explore other Inca sites spanning three countries." Libr J
"So entertaining and appealing is Thomson's story of his exploration of the Inca empire that readers will wish they could take off and follow in his footsteps. . . . Thomson's wit, eye for detail and reverence for humanity set him apart from the average travel-adventure writer—he is as good a companion as a traveler could hope for." Publ Wkly
Includes bibliographical references

986.6   Ecuador

Kane, Joe
Savages. Knopf 1995 273p il map pa $14 hardcover o.p. *   **986.6**
1. Waorani Indians 2. Amazon River valley 3. Human ecology
ISBN 0-679-74019-8 (pa)   LC 95-4258
"In the Ecuadorian Amazon the author befriends Moi, a Huaorani warrior who is learning new strategies in his fight to keep American oil companies from destroying his homeland. Moi not only smuggles Kane past Ecuadorian military check-points into Huaorani territory but also returns with him to confront the savages in the conference halls of Washington." New Yorker
Includes bibliographical references

990   History of other areas

Michener, James A., 1907-1997
Return to paradise. Random House 1951 437p pa $7.99 hardcover o.p.   **990**
1. Islands of the Pacific
ISBN 0-449-20650-5 (pa)
Essays included are: The atoll; Polynesia; Fuji; Guadalcanal; Espiritu Santo; New Zealand; Australia; New Guinea; Rabaul; What I learned. Short stories included are: Mr. Morgan; Povenaa's daughter; Mynah birds; The story; Good life; Until they sail; The jungle; The fossickers
"Alternate chapters describe each island followed by a short story set against the region described." Ont Libr Rev

994 Australia

The **Australian** people; an encyclopedia of the nation, its people and their origins; edited by James Jupp. Cambridge Univ. Press 2001 xx, 940p il maps $150   **994**
1. Australia—Race relations
ISBN 0-521-80789-1   LC 2001-37896
First published 1988 in Australia
This "documents the dramatic history of Australian settlement and describes the rich ethnic and cultural inheritance of the nation through the contributions of its people." Publisher's note
Includes bibliographical references

Bryson, Bill
In a sunburned country. Broadway Bks. 2000 307p il maps pa $14.95 hardcover o.p.
                    994
1. Australia—Description and travel
ISBN 0-7679-0386-2 (pa)   LC 00-25566
In this book, Bryson "chronicles his exploration of Australia, he introduces us to a town that went without electricity until the early 1990s, a former high-ranking politician who hawks his own autobiography to passersby, an assortment of coffee shops and restaurants, . . . a type of giant worm, and the world's most poisonous creature, the box jellyfish." Booklist
Includes bibliographical references

Clarke, F. G. (Francis Gordon)
The history of Australia. Greenwood Press 2002 236p (Greenwood histories of the modern nations) $45   **994**
1. Australia—History
ISBN 0-313-31498-5   LC 2001-54704
This volume "begins with a timeline of historical events. The first chapter is a very short overview of Australia (geography, climate, culture, and so on). The rest of the text is a chronological study in short, concise chapters beginning 60,000 years ago with Aboriginal Australia and ending with 2001 and beyond. Each chapter is broken down into smaller sections, with headings, covering such essential topics as colonization, war, government, and politics. The work ends with smaller sections for notable people, notes, a bibliographic essay, and an index." Recomm Ref Books for Small & Medium-sized Libr & Media Cent, 2003
Includes bibliographical references

Clendinnen, Inga
Dancing with strangers; Europeans and Australians at first contact; Inga Clendinnen. Cambridge University Press 2005 324p il map $60; pa $21.99   **994**
1. Aboriginal Australians 2. Australia—Race relations 3. Great Britain—Colonies—Australia
ISBN 0-5218-5137-8; 0-5216-1681-6 (pa)
                    LC 2005-11523
First published 2003 in Australia

"In January 1788, the First Fleet arrived in New South Wales, Australia and a thousand British men and women encountered the people who would be their new neighbors. . . . [This book] tells the story of what happened between the first British settlers of Australia and these Aborigines." Publisher's note
Includes bibliographical references

Hughes, Robert
The fatal shore. Knopf 1987 688p il maps pa $18 hardcover o.p. *   **994**
1. Australia—History 2. Penal colonies
ISBN 0-394-75366-6 (pa)   LC 86-45272
"This epic account chronicles the history of Australia during the 80 years (1788-1868) of England's convict transportation system, when some 160,000 convicts reached 'the fatal shore.' Interweaving his own lucid narrative with untapped original sources—including the diaries and letters of the prisoners themselves—Hughes shows the evolution of the system and of the fledgling nation that emerged from the brutal penal colony." Libr J
Includes bibliographical references

Keneally, Thomas, 1935-
A commonwealth of thieves; the improbable birth of Australia. Nan A. Talese/Doubleday 2006 385p map hardcover o.p. pa $15.95   **994**
1. Phillip, Arthur, 1738-1814 2. Australia—History 3. Frontier and pioneer life—Australia 4. Penal colonies
ISBN   0-385-51459-X;   978-0-385-51459-0;
1-4000-7956-X (pa); 978-1-4000-7956-8 (pa)
                    LC 2006-44470
First published 2005 in Australia
The author discusses the founding of New South Wales in 1788, originally established by the British as a penal colony. "At the book's center is the relationship between Arthur Phillip, the pragmatic first governor, and Woolawarre Bennelong, the Aborigine who eventually served as a liaison between the settlers and natives." Publ Wkly
This "book offers an engaging treatment of a subject which over the years has provoked a long and sometimes heated debate." Times Lit Suppl
Includes bibliographical references

995.3 Papua New Guinea. New Guinea region

Flannery, Tim F. (Tim Fridjof), 1956-
Throwim way leg; tree-kangaroos, possums, and penis gourds—on the track of unknown mammals in wildest New Guinea; [by] Tim Flannery. Atlantic Monthly Press 1998 326p il map pa $14 hardcover o.p.   **995.3**
1. Ethnology—New Guinea 2. New Guinea—Description
ISBN 0-8021-3665-6 (pa)   LC 98-38435
Flannery chronicles "his scientific and cross-cultural adventures during 15 expeditions of New Guinea—

Flannery, Tim F. (Tim Fridjof), 1956-—*Continued*

undertaken in order to research the many species of mammals that exist on this large island, which he refers to as 'one of the world's last frontiers.'" Publ Wkly

This "is more than an account of [the author's] fieldwork. It is an enthralling introduction to the mountain people of New Guinea." N Y Times Book Rev

996 Other parts of Pacific. Polynesia

Alexander, Caroline, 1956-

The Bounty: the true story of the mutiny on the Bounty. Viking 2003 491p il hardcover o.p. pa $17   **996**

1. Bligh, William, 1754-1817 2. Christian, Fletcher, 1764-1793 3. Bounty (Ship) 4. Oceania

ISBN   0-670-03133-X;   978-0-14-200469-2; 0-14-200469-3 (pa)   LC 2003-50158

Alexander reexamines the story of the 1789 mutiny on the Bounty during a voyage to the South Pacific. She explores "the Royal Navy's efforts to bring the mutineers who did not escape to Pitcairn [Island with Fletcher Christian] to justice, a proceeding complicated by the political, legal and social influence exerted to defend Christian's reputation in absentia and that of one of his well-born colleagues in mutiny. This was Peter Heywood." N Y Times Book Rev

"A rollicking sea adventure told with enormous confidence and style." Booklist

Includes bibliographical references

Severin, Timothy

In search of Robinson Crusoe. Basic Bks. 2002 333p il pa $16.95 hardcover o.p.   **996**

1. Selkirk, Alexander, 1676-1721 2. Defoe, Daniel, 1661?-1731. Robinson Crusoe 3. Survival after airplane accidents, shipwrecks, etc.

ISBN 0-465-07699-8 (pa)   LC 2002-71661

The author examines "the fictional Crusoe alongside the historic realities of colonization and human ingenuity. . . . Readers learn about the history of marooning among plunderers, blockade navies and other piratical sailors, as well as the ethnography of the so-called 'Moskito Man' (aka Man Friday) and all the ways to provide for oneself on a deserted island. . . . The work is energetic and Severin is an ideal guide to the world behind the word. This will surely appeal to the lovers of maritime history." Publ Wkly

Souhami, Diana

Selkirk's Island; the true and strange adventures of the real Robinson Crusoe. Harcourt 2002 c2001 246p $24; pa $13 *   **996**

1. Selkirk, Alexander, 1676-1721 2. Defoe, Daniel, 1661?-1731. Robinson Crusoe 3. Survival after airplane accidents, shipwrecks, etc. 4. Islands of the Pacific

ISBN 0-15-100526-5; 0-15-602717-8 (pa)

LC 01-24979

First published 2001 in the United Kingdom

"Daniel Defoe based his 1719 novel *Robinson Crusoe* on the trials and tribulations of Scottish seaman Alexander Selkirk. Souhami . . . draws on journals, maritime histories and ship and parish records to detail his . . . [story]. Complete with detailed comparisons between Defoe's novel and Selkirk's life, Souhami's account is a well-researched investigation of a forgotten anti-hero." Publ Wkly

Includes bibliographical references

998 Arctic islands and Antarctica

Alexander, Caroline, 1956-

The Endurance; Shackleton's legendary Antarctic expedition. Knopf 1998 211p il $29.95   **998**

1. Shackleton, Sir Ernest Henry, 1874-1922 2. Endurance (Ship) 3. Imperial Trans-Antarctic Expedition (1914-1917) 4. Antarctica—Exploration

ISBN 0-375-40403-1

Published in association with the American Museum of Natural History

In 1914, Sir Ernest Shackleton "sailed to Antarctica with 27 men in hopes of being the first human to transverse the continent. But his ship, the *Endurance,* was trapped, then crushed, by ice in the Weddell Sea, propelling the party into a nightmare of cold and near starvation. Alexander, relying extensively on journals by crew members, some never published, as well as on myriad other sources, delivers a spellbinding story of human courage. . . . What makes this book especially exciting, however, are the 170 previously unpublished photos by the expedition's photographer, Frank Hurley." Publ Wkly

Antarctica: an encyclopedia from Abbott Ice Shelf to zooplankton; edited by Mary Trewby. Firefly Bks. 2002 208p il maps $35   **998**

1. Antarctica—Encyclopedias

ISBN 1-55297-590-8   LC 2002-514992

This "guide to Antarctica features a true encyclopedia layout, with over 1000 concise, alphabetically arranged entries and 250 photographs that cover natural history, climate, geology, tourism, and more. . . . The entries in this book are easily accessible and particularly useful for quick reference." Libr J

Cookman, Scott, 1952-

Ice blink; the mysterious fate of Sir John Franklin's lost polar expedition. Wiley 2000 244p il maps $24.95; pa $15.95 *   **998**

1. Franklin, Sir John, 1786-1847 2. Northwest Passage 3. Arctic regions—Exploration

ISBN 0-471-37790-2; 0-471-40420-9 (pa)

LC 99-47620

In this "account of the fabled 1845 Franklin expedition in search of the Northwest Passage, Cookman inculpates a novel malefactor in the tragedy: botulism. In the 1980s, three frozen corpses of expedition members were found and exhumed. . . . Autopsies revealed lead, fingering lead-soldered cans from the provisions. . . . Adventure readers will flock to this fine regaling of the enduring mystery surrounding the best-known disaster in

Cookman, Scott, 1952-—*Continued*
Arctic exploration." Booklist
  Includes bibliographical references

Ehrlich, Gretel
  This cold heaven; seven seasons in Greenland.
Pantheon Bks. 2001 377p il maps hardcover o.p.
pa $14   **998**
    1. Greenland
    ISBN 0-679-44200-6; 0-679-75852-6 (pa)
                                              LC 00-69277
  "Ehrlich began traveling to Greenland during her recovery from a nearly fatal lightning strike, and her keen,
often poetic responses to the beauty of the frigid landscape and the warmth of Inuit families, combined with
a profound immersion in Greenland history, infuse her
captivating account with both drama and reflection."
Booklist
  Includes bibliographical references

Encyclopedia of the Arctic; Mark Nuttall, editor.
  Routledge 2005 3v il map set $525
                                                          998
    1. Arctic regions—Encyclopedias
    ISBN 1-57958-436-5   LC 2004-16694
  Nuttall "has put together a multidisciplinary work that
covers indigenous peoples, explorers, scientists, history,
environment, climate, plants and animals, geography, current research concerns, and more. The 1200 alphabetically arranged entries, all written by experts from 20 countries (a number of them native to the Arctic), range in
length from 500 to 5000 words." Libr J
  For a fuller review see: Booklist, Jan. 1 & 15, 2005

The **ends** of the earth; an anthology of the finest
  writing on the Arctic and the Antarctic.
  Bloomsbury 2007 2v in 1 map $29.95
                                                          998
    1. Polar regions 2. Arctic regions 3. Antarctica
    ISBN 1-59691-443-2; 978-1-59691-443-8
  Works bound back-to-back and inverted; titles tran-
scribed from individual title pages
  Contents: The Arctic / edited by Elizabeth Kolbert —
The Antarctic / edited by Francis Spufford
  The editors "present an anthology of writings about
the Arctic and Antarctic, which is actually two books in
one. Halfway through, readers can turn the book upside
down for writings about the opposite end of the earth.
. . . Included are primary-source accounts by early explorers such as Ernest Shackleton, John Franklin, and
Kund Rasmussen, nature writings by Barry Lopez and
Gretel Ehrlich, excerpts from novels by Jules Verne, Jack
London, and H.P. Lovecraft, and essays by journalists
and scientists. Each excerpt is just long enough to whet
the reader's appetite. Great reading for the armchair adventurer." Libr J

Fleming, Fergus, 1959-
  Ninety degrees North; the quest for the North
Pole. Grove Press 2002 c2001 xxi, 470p il maps
$26; pa $15   **998**
    1. Arctic regions—Exploration 2. North Pole
    ISBN 0-8021-1725-2; 0-8021-4036-X (pa)
                                              LC 2002-21469

Companion volume to Barrow's boys (2000)
  First published 2001 in the United Kingdom
  Fleming presents a historical "narrative of the late
19th-century Arctic exploration and the quest for the
North Pole." New Sci
  "The book is fascinating for how Fleming renders the
haughty, post-Enlightenment brio of the principal adven-
turers and the extreme, often fatal ends toward which it
pushed them." Publ Wkly
  Includes bibliographical references

Griffiths, Tom, 1957-
  Slicing the silence; voyaging to Antarctica.
Harvard University Press 2007 399p map $29.95
                                                          998
    1. Antarctica—Description and travel
    ISBN 978-0-674-02633-9; 0-674-02633-0
                                              LC 2007-06549
  Simultaneously published in Australia
  "Believing that to understand the experiences of explorers and the history of Antarctica one must experience
its mighty winds, cold, danger, and silence, the author,
in 2002, joined a ship delivering scientists and supplies
to Casey Station. This book is part diary of that voyage
and part history of that most southerly land. . . . This
enjoyable and highly readable book would be an excellent addition to any natural history, polar history, or adventure travel collection." Libr J
  Includes bibliographical references

Kavenna, Joanna
  The ice museum; in search of the lost land of
Thule. Viking 2006 294p il map $24.95; pa $15
                                                          998
    1. Arctic regions—Exploration
    ISBN 0-670-03473-8; 0-14-303846-X (pa)
  First published 2005 in the United Kingdom
  The author "chronicles her personal journey into the
myth and reality of the legendary Arctic land of Thule.
. . . [This book] transcends all genre description, and
holds its own as a journey into a world that somehow vi-
brantly exists on paper and nowhere else." Booklist

Kearns, David A.
  Where hell freezes over. Thomas Dunne Books
2005 286p il map $24.95   **998**
    1. Survival after airplane accidents, shipwrecks, etc.
    2. Antarctica—Exploration
    ISBN 0-312-34205-5   LC 2005-45526
  This is an "account of the crash of the Martin PBM
seaplane George 1 in Antarctica in December 1946. . . .
With intimate access to surviving sources, plus a depth
of personal commitment, the author makes a compelling
addition to survival literature." Publ Wkly
  Includes bibliographical references

Preston, Diana
  A first rate tragedy; Robert Falcon Scott and the
race to the South Pole. Houghton Mifflin 1998
269p il map pa $14 hardcover o.p.   **998**
    1. Scott, Robert Falcon, 1868-1912 2. British Antarctic
    ("Terra   Nova")   Expedition   (1910-1913)
    3. Antarctica—Exploration 4. South Pole
    ISBN 0-618-00201-4 (pa)   LC 98-47411

Preston, Diana—*Continued*

"In 1912, Robert Scott and four members of his Antarctic expedition reached the South Pole only to find a Norwegian flag planted by Roald Amundsen. The returning party of Englishmen perished, . . . failing in the attempt to be first to the Pole and sending their country into mourning but making a legend of Scott." Libr J

"A whole generation was brought up on the legend of Scott of the Antarctic. Diana Preston successfully explains why and how this came about. . . . {She} has written a first-rate book retelling the familiar tale in compulsive terms and adding a thoughtful twist of her own." Times Lit Suppl

Includes bibliographical references

Riffenburgh, Beau, 1955-

Shackleton's forgotten expedition; the voyage of the Nimrod; by Beau Riffenburgh. Bloomsbury, Distributed to the trade by Holtzbrinck Publishers 2004 xxiv, 358p il map $25.95; pa $15.95

998

1. Shackleton, Sir Ernest Henry, 1874-1922
2. Antarctica—Exploration

ISBN 1-58234-488-4; 1-58234-611-9 (pa)

LC 2004-11999

The author recounts Shackleton's "voyage to the Antarctic from 1907 to 1909, during which he led a small group of men to within 97 miles of the South Pole. . . . For those who thrilled to the Endurance saga, Riffenburgh offers an equally gripping adventure, which laid the foundations of Shackleton's capacity for brilliant leadership under pressure." Publ Wkly

Includes bibliographical references

Smith, Roff

Life on the ice; no one goes to Antarctica alone. National Geographic 2005 208p pa $16

998

1. Antarctica—Description and travel

ISBN 0-7922-9345-2   LC 2005-298454

First published 2002 in Australia

The author provides an "account of several trips to Antarctica, where he visited the South Pole, the large American base at McMurdo, and the smaller bases that other countries maintain. . . . Throughout, he encounters people with a passion for their work in Antarctica and a respect and appreciation for the continent." Libr J

"Smith is the most exceptional of travel writers: his portraits of people are deeply sympathetic, while his language is at once lyrical and knowledgeable. Not to be missed." Booklist

Solomon, Susan, 1956-

The coldest March. Yale Univ. Press 2001 xxii, 383p il maps $29.95; pa $16.95   **998**

1. Scott, Robert Falcon, 1868-1912 2. British Antarctic ("Terra Nova") Expedition (1910-1913) 3. Antarctica—Exploration 4. South Pole

ISBN 0-300-08967-8; 0-300-09921-5 (pa)

LC 00-54996

"In November 1911, Capt. Robert Falcon Scott and his British team set out to be the first to reach the South Pole. Battling the brutal weather of Antarctica, they reached the pole in January 1912 only to discover that a Norwegian team had beat them there by nearly a month. On their return from the Pole, Scott and four of his companions died in harsh conditions. Ever since, history has not known whether to label them heroes or bunglers. Solomon . . . analyzes all the factors present during Scott's expedition in an attempt to explain that his failure was due not to incompetence but to a combination of unpredictable weather, erroneous choices and bad luck." Libr J

Includes bibliographical references

AUTHOR, TITLE AND SUBJECT INDEX

This index to the books in the Classified Collection includes author, title and subject entries; added entries for joint authors and for editors of works entered under title; and name and subject cross-references; all arranged in one alphabet. The number in boldface type at the end of each entry refers to the Dewey Decimal Classification where the main entry for the book will be found.

For further directions for use of this index, see Directions for Use on page x.

Aliens—*Continued*
United States
See also United States—Immigration and emigration

Bray, I. M. How to get a green card   **342**

Alighieri, Dante *See* Dante Alighieri, 1265-1321

Alinder, Mary Street, 1946-
Ansel Adams   **92**
(jt. auth) Adams, A. Ansel Adams, an autobiography   **92**

Alinsky, Saul
Rules for radicals   **322.4**

Alire, Camila
Serving Latino communities   **027.6**

Alive. Read, P. P.   **910.4**

Alkoran *See* Koran

All about techniques in acrylics   **751.4**

All American [biography of Jim Thorpe] Crawford, B.   **92**

All creatures great and small. Herriot, J.   **92**

All for love. Dryden, J.   **822**

All God's children. Butterfield, F.   **364.1**

All governments lie [biography of I.F. Stone] MacPherson, M.   **92**

The **all-in-one** college guide. Nemko, M.   **378.1**

All in the dances: a brief life of George Balanchine. Teachout, T.   **92**

All is change. Sutin, L.   **294.3**

All music guide to classical music   **781.6**

All music guide to country   **781.642**

The **all-natural** diabetes cookbook. Newgent, J.   **641.5**

All-new hints from Heloise. Heloise   **640**

All of the women of the Bible. Deen, E.   **220.9**

All of us. Carver, R.   **811**

All over but the shoutin'. Bragg, R.   **92**

All rivers run to the sea. Wiesel, E.   **92**

All terrain cycling *See* Mountain biking

All the best, George Bush. Bush, G.   **92**

All the daring of the soldier. Leonard, E. D.   **973.7**

All the laws but one. Rehnquist, W. H.   **342**

All the money in the world   **305.5**

All the poems of Muriel Spark. Spark, M.   **821**

All the president's men. Bernstein, C.   **973.924**

All the Shah's men. Kinzer, S.   **327.73**

All the stops. Whitney, C. R.   **786.5**

All the way to Berlin. Megellas, J.   **940.54**

All things Shakespeare. Olsen, K.   **822.3**

All too human. Stephanopoulos, G.   **973.929**

Allaby, Michael, 1933-
The Facts on File weather and climate handbook   **551.6**

Allan, Tony, 1946-
Life, myth, and art in Ancient Rome   **937**

Allee, Nancy
(ed) The Medical Library Association encyclopedic guide to searching and finding health information on the Web. See The Medical Library Association encyclopedic guide to searching and finding health information on the Web   **025.04**

Allen, Arthur
Vaccine   **614.4**

Allen, Frederick Lewis, 1890-1954
Only yesterday   **973.91**

Allen, John
(jt. auth) Tutu, D. The rainbow people of God   **968.06**

Allen, Richard, 1760-1831
About
Newman, R. S. Freedom's prophet [biography of Richard Allen]   **92**

Allen, Stewart Lee
In the devil's garden   **641**

Allen, William Francis
Slave songs of the United States   **781.62**

Allen, Woody
Side effects   **817**
Without feathers   **817**
Woody Allen on Woody Allen   **791.43**
About
Lax, E. Conversations with Woody Allen   **791.43**

Allende, Isabel
My invented country   **92**
Paula   **92**
The sum of our days   **92**

Allende family
About
Allende, I. Paula   **92**

Allergies, Food *See* Food allergy

Allergies A-Z. See Lipkowitz, M. Encyclopedia of allergies   **616.97**

Allergy
See also Food allergy

Brody, J. E. Jane Brody's allergy fighter   **616.2**

Pescatore, F. The allergy and asthma cure   **616.97**

Walsh, W. E. Food allergies   **616.97**

The **allergy** and asthma cure. Pescatore, F.   **616.97**

Allgor, Catherine
A perfect union [biography of Dolley Madison]   **92**

Alligators, old mink, & new money. Houtte, A.   **746.9**

Allison, Graham T.
Nuclear terrorism   **363.32**

Allison, Jay
(ed) This I believe. See This I believe   **170**
(ed) This I believe II. See This I believe II   **170**

Allison, Nancy, 1954-
(ed) The Illustrated encyclopedia of body-mind disciplines. See The Illustrated encyclopedia of body-mind disciplines   **615.5**

Apache Indians—*Continued*
Debo, A. Geronimo   **92**
Roberts, D. Once they moved like the wind
    970.004
See/See also pages in the following book(s):
Brown, D. A. The American West   **978**
Josephy, A. M. Now that the buffalo's gone
    970.004
Apache mothers and daughters. Boyer, R. M.
    970.004
Apartheid
Houze, D. Twilight people   **92**
The **apartment** book. Spier, C.   **747**
The **apartment** book. See Michael, M. The new
  apartment book   **747**
Apartment houses
Michael, M. The new apartment book   **747**
Spier, C. The apartment book   **747**
The **ape** and the sushi master. Waal, F. d.
    156
Aperture (Periodical)
Photography past forward: Aperture at 50
    770.9
Apes
    See also Chimpanzees; Gorillas; Orangutan
World atlas of great apes and their conservation
    599.8
Apiculture *See* Beekeeping; Bees
Apocalypses. Weber, E.   **200**
Apollo Project *See* Project Apollo
Apollo project
Bizony, P. The man who ran the moon [biography of James E. Webb]   **92**
Chaikin, A. A man on the moon   **629.45**
French, F. In the shadow of the moon
    629.45
Schefter, J. L. The race   **629.45**
Smith, A. Moondust   **920**
Zimmerman, R. Genesis: the story of Apollo 8
    629.45
Apollonius, of Rhodes
The voyage of Argo: the Argonautica   **881**
Apollonius, Rhodius *See* Apollonius, of Rhodes
Apollo's fire. Sims, M.   **529**
Apologetics
Augustine, Saint, Bishop of Hippo. Concerning the city of God against the pagans   **239**
Collins, F. S. The language of God   **215**
John Paul, Pope. Crossing the threshold of hope
    282
Keller, T. J. The reason for God   **239**
Apologizing
Lazare, A. On apology   **155.9**
Apoplexy *See* Stroke
Apostolic Church *See* Church history—30-600, Early church
Appalachia. Wright, C.   **811**
Appalachian Mountain region *See* Appalachian region
Appalachian region
Kingsolver, B. Animal, vegetable, miracle
    641
Reece, E. Lost mountain   **622**

Ritchie, J. The dulcimer book   **787.9**
Ritchie, J. Singing family of the Cumberlands
    92
    Description and travel
Bryson, B. A walk in the woods   **917.4**
    Social life and customs
Foxfire 40th anniversary book   **975.8**
The **appearance** of impropriety. Morgan, P. W.
    306
Appelbaum, Judith
How to get happily published   **070.5**
Appelfeld, Aharon *See* Appelfeld, Aron
Appelfeld, Aron
    About
Langer, L. L. Admitting the Holocaust
    940.53
Appetite disorders *See* Eating disorders
Appetite for life. Fitch, N. R.   **92**
An **appetite** for poetry. Kermode, F.   **801**
Appetizers
Andrés, J. Tapas   **641.8**
Appiah, Anthony
(ed) Africana: the encyclopedia of the African and African American experience. See Africana: the encyclopedia of the African and African American experience   **909**
The **Applause/best** plays theater yearbook. See The best plays of 2006-2007   **808.82**
Applebaum, Anne, 1964-
Gulag   **365**
Applebaum, Wilbur
(ed) Encyclopedia of the scientific revolution. See Encyclopedia of the scientific revolution
    509
Applebome, Peter
Dixie rising   **973.929**
Appleby, Joyce Oldham
Inheriting the revolution   **973**
Appleby, R. Scott
(jt. auth) Almond, G. A. Strong religion
    200.9
Applegate, Debby
The most famous man in America [biography of Henry Ward Beecher]   **92**
Apples
See/See also pages in the following book(s):
Hubbell, S. Shrinking the cat   **660.6**
Pollan, M. The botany of desire   **581.6**
Apples are from Kazakhstan. Robbins, C.
    958.4
Applications for college *See* College applications
Applications for positions
The Adams resume almanac   **650.14**
Beatty, R. H. 175 high-impact cover letters
    650.14
Beatty, R. H. The interview kit   **650.14**
Bolles, R. N. What color is your parachute? 2008   **331.7**
Enelow, W. S. Cover letter magic   **650.14**
Jackson, T. The perfect resume   **650.14**
Resumes and cover letters that have worked
    650.14
Yate, M. J. Knock 'em dead 2008   **650.14**

Army Air Forces (U.S.) *See* United States. Army Air Forces

An **army** at dawn. Atkinson, R.   **940.54**

Army life *See* Soldiers

Arnell, Charles
(jt. auth) Bennett, J. The complete snowboarder   **796.9**

Arnold, Roseanne *See* Barr, Roseanne

Arnot, Bob
The breast health cookbook   **616.99**
Wear and tear   **616.7**

Arnot, Robert Burns *See* Arnot, Bob

Aronson, Amy, 1962-
(ed) Men and masculinities. See Men and masculinities   **305.31**

Aronson, Ronald
(ed) Sartre, J. P. Truth and existence   **121**

Arouet, François Marie *See* Voltaire, 1694-1778

Around America. Cronkite, W.   **917.3**

Arousal, the secret logic of sexual fantasies. Bader, M. J.   **306.7**

Arrington, Leonard J.
Japanese Americans, from relocation to redress. See Japanese Americans, from relocation to redress   **940.53**

The **ARRL** handbook for radio communications   **621.3841**

Arrogant capital. Phillips, K. P.   **973.92**

Arsenals of folly. Rhodes, R.   **355**

Arsenault, Raymond
Freedom riders   **323**

Arson
Wambaugh, J. Fire lover   **364.1**

Art
See also Artistic anatomy; Commercial art; Decoration and ornament; World War, 1939-1945—Art and the war
Kampen O'Riley, M. Art beyond the west   **709**

15th and 16th centuries
Adams, L. Italian Renaissance art   **709.02**
Campbell, G. Renaissance art and architecture   **709.02**
Graham-Dixon, A. Renaissance   **709.02**

19th century
See also Impressionism (Art)
Craske, M. Art in Europe, 1700-1830   **709.03**
Rosenblum, R. 19th century art   **709.03**

20th century
See also Computer art
Acocella, J. R. Twenty-eight artists and two saints   **920**
Barnitz, J. Twentieth-century art of Latin America   **709**
Fineberg, J. D. Art since 1940   **709.04**
Lucie-Smith, E. Art today   **709.04**

20th century—Encyclopedias
Dempsey, A. Art in the modern era   **709.04**

Dictionaries
The Concise Oxford dictionary of art and artists   **703**

Encyclopedia of artists   **920.003**
Frazier, N. The Penguin concise dictionary of art history   **703**
Langmuir, E. Yale dictionary of art and artists   **703**
Lucie-Smith, E. The Thames & Hudson dictionary of art terms   **703**

Directories
American art directory 2005-2006   **702.5**

Encyclopedias
Facts on File encyclopedia of art   **703**

Forgeries
Dolnick, E. The forger's spell   **92**
Hoving, T. False impressions   **702.8**

History
Beckett, W. Sister Wendy's American collection   **709**
Fenton, J. Leonardo's nephew   **709**
Gardner, H. Gardner's art through the ages   **709**
Gombrich, E. H. The story of art   **709**
Hoving, T. Art for dummies   **709**
Janson, H. W. Janson's history of art   **709**
Johnson, P. Art: a new history   **709**
Little, S. . . . isms: understanding art   **709**
Schama, S. The power of art   **709**

History—Maps
Atlas of world art   **709**

Marketing
Grant, D. Selling art without galleries   **708**
Michels, C. How to survive and prosper as an artist   **702**

Marketing—Directories
2008 artist's & graphic designer's market   **702.5**

Museums
See Art museums

Psychology
Jung, C. G. Man and his symbols   **150.19**

Study and teaching
Peterson's college guide for visual arts majors 2008   **700**

Technique
Smith, R. The artist's handbook   **702.8**

Art, African *See* African art

Art, African American *See* African American art

Art, American *See* American art

Art, Ancient *See* Ancient art

Art, Baroque *See* Baroque art

Art, Buddhist *See* Buddhist art

Art, Byzantine *See* Byzantine art

Art, Canadian *See* Canadian art

Art, Chinese *See* Chinese art

Art, Christian *See* Christian art

Art, Computer *See* Computer art

Art, Egyptian *See* Egyptian art

Art, French *See* French art

Art, Graphic *See* Graphic arts

Art, Greek *See* Greek art

Art, Hispanic American *See* Hispanic American art

Art, Indian *See* Native American art

Art, Islamic *See* Islamic art

Art, **Italian** *See* Italian art

Art, **Latin American** *See* Latin American art

Art, **Medieval** *See* Medieval art

Art, **Modern** *See* Modern art

Art, **Prehistoric** *See* Prehistoric art

Art, **Renaissance** *See* Art—15th and 16th centuries

Art, **Roman** *See* Roman art

Art, **Russian** *See* Russian art

The **art** & craft of hand lettering. Cicale, A. 745.6

The **art** & craft of making jewelry. Gollberg, J. 739.27

The **art** & elegance of beadweaving. Wells, C. W. 745.58

Art: a new history. Johnson, P. 709

Art and architecture in Italy, 1600-1750. Wittkower, R. 709.45

The **art** and architecture of ancient Egypt. Smith, W. S. 709.32

The **art** and architecture of Russia. Hamilton, G. H. 709.47

The **art** and architecture of the ancient Orient. Frankfort, H. 709.39

Art and mythology
Dictionaries
Impelluso, L. Gods and heroes in art 700

Art and religion
Bussagli, M. Angels 704.9
Silverman, D. Van Gogh and Gauguin 759.4

Art appreciation
Beckett, W. Sister Wendy's American collection 709
Hoving, T. Art for dummies 709

Art beyond the west. Kampen O'Riley, M. 709

Art criticism
Updike, J. Still looking 709.73

Art deco
Art deco 1910-1939 709.04
Art deco 1910-1939 709.04

Art for dummies. Hoving, T. 709

Art in Europe, 1700-1830. Craske, M. 709.03

Art in the modern era. Dempsey, A. 709.04

Art industries and trade *See* Decorative arts

Art Institute of Chicago
Impressionism and post-impressionism in the Art Institute of Chicago. See Impressionism and post-impressionism in the Art Institute of Chicago 759.05

Art lover. Gill, A. 92

Art museums
See also names of individual art museums
Loebl, S. America's art museums 708

Art nouveau
Escritt, S. Art Nouveau 709.03

The **art** of ancient Egypt. Robins, G. 709.32

The **art** of calligraphy. Harris, D. 745.6

The **art** of chemistry. Greenberg, A. 540.9

The **art** of enameling. Darty, L. 738.4

The **art** of fiction. Gardner, J. 808.3

The **art** of figure drawing. Robins, C. 743

The **art** of Frederick Sommer. Sommer, F. 779

The **art** of hand reading. Reid, L. 133.6

The **art** of loving. Fromm, E. 152.4

The **Art** of natural building 690

The **art** of Peter Max. Riley, C. A. 760

The **art** of political murder. Goldman, F. 972.81

The **art** of quick breads. See Hensperger, B. The best quick breads 641.8

The **art** of Ray Harryhausen. Harryhausen, R. 778.5

The **art** of simple food. Waters, A. 641.5

The **art** of spelling. Vos Savant, M. M. 421

The **art** of teaching. Parini, J. 371.1

Art of the Middle Ages. Snyder, J. 709.02

The **Art** of the personal essay 808.84

The **art** of the sports car. Adler, D. 629.222

The **art** of war. See Sun-tzu. The illustrated art of war 355

Art since 1940. Fineberg, J. D. 709.04

Art thefts
Atwood, R. Stealing history 364.1
Dolnick, E. The rescue artist 364.1
Harclerode, P. The lost masters 709
Petropoulos, J. The Faustian bargain 709
Scott-Clark, C. The Amber Room 940.54

Art today. Lucie-Smith, E. 709.04

Arthritis
Arnot, B. Wear and tear 616.7

Arthur, King
About
Goodrich, N. L. King Arthur 942.01
King Arthur in legend and history 942.01
Malory, Sir T. Le morte Darthur, or, The hoole book of Kyng Arthur and of his noble knyghtes of the Rounde Table 398.2

Arthur, Wallace
Creatures of accident 591.3

Arthurian romances
Gawain and the Grene Knight (Middle English poem). Sir Gawain and the Green Knight 821

Artificial flies
Fulsher, K. Thunder Creek flies 799.1
Schullery, P. The rise 799.1

Artificial intelligence
Brooks, R. A. Flesh and machines 629.8
Gutkind, L. Almost human 629.8
Kurzweil, R. The age of spiritual machines 006.3
Menzel, P. Robo sapiens: evolution of a new species 629.8
Wood, G. Edison's Eve 629.8
See/See also pages in the following book(s):
Devlin, K. J. Goodbye, Descartes 128

Artificial satellites
Brzezinski, M. Red moon rising 629.4
Dickson, P. Sputnik: the shock of the century 629.46

Asante, Molefi K., 1942-
The African-American atlas   **305.8**
(ed) Encyclopedia of Black studies. See Encyclopedia of Black studies   **305.8**
Asbury Park (N.J.)
Wolff, D. 4th of July, Asbury Park   **974.9**
The **ascent** of science. Silver, B. L.   **509**
Asch, Moses, 1905-1986
(ed) Leadbelly. The Leadbelly songbook
  782.42

Ashbery, John
Collected poems 1956-1987   **811**
Notes from the air   **811**
Selected poems   **811**
Where shall I wander   **811**
A worldly country   **811**
Ashby, Bonnie
(jt. auth) Turkington, C. The encyclopedia of infectious diseases   **616.9**
Ashenburg, Kathy
The dirt on clean   **391**
Ashes of glory. Furgurson, E. B.   **975.5**
Ashes to ashes. Kluger, R.   **394.1**
Ashin, Deborah
(jt. auth) Carlton, P. Take charge of your child's eating disorder   **618.92**
Ashley, Dwayne
(jt. auth) Williams, J. I'll find a way or make one   **378.73**
Asia
See also names of individual countries, e.g. China
Civilization—Encyclopedias
Higham, C. Encyclopedia of ancient Asian civilizations   **950**
Description and travel
Padel, R. Tigers in red weather   **599.75**
Theroux, P. The great railway bazaar   **915**
Thubron, C. Shadow of the Silk Road   **915**
Religion—Dictionaries
Leeming, D. A. A dictionary of Asian mythology   **201.03**
Asia, Central See Central Asia
Asia, East See East Asia
Asia, Southeast See Southeast Asia
Asian Americans
History
Avakian, M. Atlas of Asian-American history
  305.8
Takaki, R. T. Strangers from a different shore
  305.8
Asian architecture
Ruan Xing. New China architecture   **720.9**
Asian civilization See Asia—Civilization
Asian cooking
Trang, C. Essentials of Asian cuisine   **641.5**
See/See also pages in the following book(s):
Tsai, M. Blue Ginger   **641.5**
The **Asian** journal of Thomas Merton. Merton, T.
  248
Asian mythology
Yang Lihui. Handbook of Chinese mythology
  299.5

Dictionaries
Leeming, D. A. A dictionary of Asian mythology   **201.03**
Asian philosophy See Oriental philosophy
Asimov, Isaac, 1920-1992
About
Gunn, J. E. Isaac Asimov   **813.009**
Ask me again tomorrow. Dukakis, O.   **92**
Aslan, Reza
No god but God   **297**
Asleson, Robyn, 1961-
Albert Moore   **759.2**
Asma, Stephen T.
Stuffed animals & pickled heads   **508**
Asmal, Kader
(ed) Mandela, N. In his own words   **92**
ASPCA complete cat care manual. Edney, A. T. B.   **636.8**
ASPCA complete dog care manual. Fogle, B.
  636.7
ASPCA complete dog training manual. See Fogle, B. New complete dog training manual
  636.7
ASPCA complete guide to cats. Richards, J. R.
  636.8
Asperger's syndrome
Attwood, T. The complete guide to Asperger's syndrome   **616.85**
Bashe, P. R. The oasis guide to Asperger syndrome   **618.92**
Hewetson, A. The stolen child   **616.89**
Jackson, L. Freaks, geeks and asperger syndrome   **618.92**
Osborne, L. American normal   **616.89**
Robison, J. E. Look me in the eye   **92**
Tammet, D. Born on a blue day   **92**
Assassination vacation. Vowell, S.   **920**
The **assassins'** gate. Packer, G.   **956.7**
The **assist**. Swidey, N.   **796.323**
Assistance to developing areas See Foreign aid
Assisted suicide See Euthanasia
Associations
See also Societies
Associations, International See International agencies
Asteroids
Burrows, W. E. The survival imperative
  629.4
Peebles, C. Asteroids   **523.4**
Asthma
Adams, F. V. The asthma sourcebook   **616.2**
Fanta, C. H. The Harvard Medical School guide to taking control of asthma   **616.2**
Freedman, M. R. Living well with asthma
  616.2
Pescatore, F. The allergy and asthma cure
  616.97
See/See also pages in the following book(s):
Brazelton, T. B. To listen to a child   **155.4**
The **asthma** sourcebook. Adams, F. V.   **616.2**
Astin, Patty Duke See Duke, Patty

Astros (Baseball team) *See* Houston Astros (Baseball team)

Asunción, Josep

The complete book of papermaking   676

At all costs. Moses, S.   940.54

At Canaan's edge. Branch, T.   973.923

At dawn we slept. Prange, G. W.   940.54

At day's close. Ekirch, A. R.   306.4

At the edge of a dream. Epstein, L. J.   305.8

At the hands of persons unknown. Dray, P.
    364.1

At the same time. Sontag, S.   814

At war with ourselves. Hirsh, M.   327.73

Atchity, Kenneth John

(ed) The classical Greek reader. See The classical Greek reader   880.8

Ath, Rand Flem- *See* Flem-Ath, Rand

Atheism

> *See also* Agnosticism

Dawkins, R. The God delusion   211
Gay, P. A Godless Jew   150.19
Hitchens, C. God is not great   200
See/See also pages in the following book(s):
Turner, J. Without God, without creed   211

Athens, Lonnie H.

> **About**

Rhodes, R. Why they kill   364.3

Athens (Greece)

Connolly, P. The ancient city   937

Athletes

> *See also* African American athletes; Women athletes

Armstrong, L. Every second counts   92
Armstrong, L. It's not about the bike   92
Coyle, D. Lance Armstrong's war   92
Crawford, B. All American [biography of Jim Thorpe]   92

> **Dictionaries**

Friedman, I. C. Latino athletes   920.003

> **Drug use**

> *See also* Steroids

Bryant, H. Juicing the game   796.357
Kuhn, C. Pumped   617.1
Pampel, F. C. Drugs and sports   362.29

Athletic medicine *See* Sports medicine

Athletics

> *See also* Sports

Miller, S. G. Ancient Greek athletics   796.09

Atkins, Peter William, 1940-

The periodic kingdom   541

Atkins, Robert C.

Dr. Atkins' age-defying diet revolution   613
Dr. Atkins' new diet revolution   613.2

Atkins, Stephen E.

Encyclopedia of modern American extremists and extremist groups   322.4
Encyclopedia of modern worldwide extremists and extremist groups   320.5

Atkins, Vera, 1908-2000

> **About**

Helm, S. A life in secrets [biography of Vera Atkins]   92

Atkinson, Rick

An army at dawn   940.54
Crusade   956.7
The day of battle   940.54
In the company of soldiers   956.7

Atlanta (Ga.)

> **Race relations**

Brown, E. The condemnation of Little B
    364.1

Atlantic Coast (North America)

Gimlette, J. Theatre of fish   917

Atlantic Coast Conference

Feinstein, J. A march to madness   796.323

The **Atlantic** slave trade. Postma, J.   326

Atlantis

Ellis, R. Imagining Atlantis   001.9
Wilson, C. The Atlantis blueprint   001.9

The **Atlantis** blueprint. Wilson, C.   001.9

Atlas, James

Bellow   92

Atlas, Teddy

Atlas   92
See/See also pages in the following book(s):
Remnick, D. Reporting   814

Atlas of American politics, 1960-2000   973.92

Atlas of Asian-American history. Avakian, M.
    305.8

The **atlas** of bird migration   598

The **atlas** of climate change. Dow, K.   551.6

Atlas of global development   338.9

Atlas of human anatomy. Netter, F. H.   611

Atlas of North America   912

The **atlas** of the Arab world. Fargues, P.   909

Atlas of the Civil War. Woodworth, S. E.
    973.7

Atlas of the Civil War, month by month. Swanson, M.   973.7

Atlas of the North American Indian. Waldman, C.
    970.004

Atlas of the universe. See Firefly atlas of the universe   523

Atlas of the world   912

Atlas of the world's religions   201

Atlas of world art   709

Atlas of world history   911

Atlases

Atlas of North America   912
Atlas of the world   912
DK complete atlas of the world   912
Firefly atlas of North America   912
Goode, J. P. Goode's world atlas   912
Hammond world atlas   912
Rand McNally commercial atlas & marketing guide 2008   912
World atlas of great apes and their conservation
    599.8

Atlases, Historical *See* Historical atlases

Atmosphere

> *See also* Air

Walker, G. An ocean of air   551.5

Bach, Johann Sebastian, 1685-1750
About
Geck, M. Johann Sebastian Bach   92
Wolff, C. Johann Sebastian Bach   92
See/See also pages in the following book(s):
Grout, D. J. A history of western music
    780.9

Bach, Steven
Dazzler [biography of Moss Hart]   92
Leni: the life and work of Leni Riefenstahl
    92

Bach family
See/See also pages in the following book(s):
Schonberg, H. C. The great pianists   920

Bachman, Richard *See* King, Stephen, 1947-

Back
Encyclopedias
Sayler, M. H. The encyclopedia of the back and
spine systems and disorders   617

Back on the career track. Cohen, C. F.   650.14

Backbone *See* Spine

Backfire: Carly Fiorina's high-stakes battle for the
soul of Hewlett-Packard. Burrows, P.
    338.7

Backpacker and hiker's handbook. Kemsley, W.,
Jr.   796.51

Backpacking
Hart, J. Walking softly in the wilderness
    796.51
Kemsley, W., Jr. Backpacker and hiker's hand-
book   796.51

The **backyard** astronomer's guide. Dickinson, T.
    522

The **backyard** bird feeder's bible. Roth, S.
    598

Backyard giants. Warren, S.   635

Bacon, Francis, 1561-1626
See/See also pages in the following book(s):
Durant, W. J. The story of philosophy   109

Bacon, Tony
The ultimate guitar book   787.87

Bacteria
Bakalar, N. Where the germs are   616

Bacteriology
See also Germ theory of disease
See/See also pages in the following book(s):
Friedman, M. Medicine's 10 greatest discoveries
    610.9

The **bad** & the beautiful. Kashner, S.   791.43
Bad elements. Buruma, I.   951.05
The **bad** guys won. Pearlman, J.   796.357
Bad land. Raban, J.   978

Bade, Patrick
(jt. auth) Manca, J. 1000 sculptures of genius
    730.9

Bader, Michael J.
Arousal, the secret logic of sexual fantasies
    306.7

Bader, Philip
African-American writers   920.003

Badger, David
Snakes   597.96

Baer, Max, 1909-1959
About
Schaap, J. Cinderella Man [dual biography of
James J. Braddock and Max Baer]   92

Baer, William
(ed & tr) Camões, L. d. Selected sonnets
    869

Bagemihl, Bruce
Biological exuberance   591.56

Baghdad (Iraq)
Kennedy, H. When Baghdad ruled the Muslim
world   956.7

Baghdad without a map, and other misadventures
in Arabia. Horwitz, T.   915.6

Baghdad Zoo (Iraq)
Anthony, L. Babylon's ark   590.73

Bahn, Paul G.
The Cambridge illustrated history of prehistoric
art   709.01
(jt. auth) Lister, A. Mammoths   569

Baiev, Khassan
The Oath   947.5

Baig, Edward C.
Macs for dummies   004

Baigrie, Brian S. (Brian Scott)
(ed) History of modern science and mathematics. See History of modern science and mathematics   509

Bailey, Beth L., 1957-
(ed) The Columbia guide to America in the
1960s. See The Columbia guide to America
in the 1960s   973.92

Bailey, Blake
A tragic honesty: the life and work of Richard
Yates   92

Bailey, Covert
Smart exercise   613.7

Bailey, Frankie Y.
(ed) Famous American crimes and trials. See
Famous American crimes and trials   364

Bailey, Jill
(ed) The Facts on File dictionary of botany. See
The Facts on File dictionary of botany
    580

Bailey, R. A.
(jt. auth) Rittner, D. Encyclopedia of chemistry
    540.3

Bailey, Rebecca Anne, 1952-
Easy to love, difficult to discipline   649

Bailyn, Bernard
The peopling of British North America
    973.2

Bain, David Haward
Empire express   385

Bainbridge, David
Beyond the zonules of Zinn   611

Bainton, Roland Herbert, 1894-1984
Here I stand: a life of Martin Luther   92

Baiocchi, Regina A. Harris, 1956-
See/See also pages in the following book(s):
Walker-Hill, H. From spirituals to symphonies
    920

Baseball

See also Negro leagues

Angell, R. Game time: a baseball companion
796.357

Angell, R. Once more around the park
796.357

Barra, A. Clearing the bases   796.357

Baseball: a literary anthology   810.8

Block, D. Baseball before we knew it
796.357

Boston, T. 1939, baseball's tipping point
796.357

Bouton, J. Ball four   796.357

Bryant, H. Juicing the game   796.357

Bryant, H. Shut out   796.357

Costas, B. Fair ball   796.357

Deford, F. The old ball game   796.357

Dickson, P. The hidden language of baseball
796.357

Geist, B. Little League confidential   796.357

Giamatti, A. B. A great and glorious game
796.357

Gould, S. J. Triumph and tragedy in Mudville
796.357

Hample, Z. Watching baseball smarter
796.357

Hogan, L. D. Shades of glory   796.357

Joy in Mudville   796.357

Kahn, R. Beyond the boys of summer
796.357

Kahn, R. The boys of summer   796.357

Kahn, R. The head game   796.357

Kelly, J. Bushville   796.357

Lewis, M. Moneyball   796.357

Madden, B. Pride of October   796.357

McCarver, T. Tim McCarver's Baseball for brain surgeons and other fans   796.357

Murphy, C. Crazy '08   796.357

Pearlman, J. The bad guys won   796.357

Posnanski, J. The soul of baseball   796.357

Prager, J. The echoing green   796.357

Ripken, C., Jr. Play baseball the Ripken way
796.357

Shapiro, M. The last good season   796.357

Smith, R. Red Smith on baseball   796.357

Snyder, B. Beyond the shadow of the Senators
796.357

Sokolove, M. Y. The ticket out: Darryl Strawberry and the boys of Crenshaw   796.357

Tofel, R. J. A legend in the making
796.357

Tygiel, J. Baseball's great experiment
796.357

Vecsey, G. Baseball: a history of America's favorite game   796.357

Ward, G. C. Baseball: an illustrated history
796.357

Wendel, T. The new face of baseball
796.357

Will, G. F. Bunts: Curt Flood, Camden Yards, Pete Rose, and other reflections on baseball
796.357

Will, G. F. Men at work   796.35

Biography

Creamer, R. W. Babe [Ruth]   92

Dawidoff, N. The crowd sounds happy   92

Eig, J. Luckiest man [biography of Lou Gehrig]
92

Feinstein, J. Living on the black [dual biography of Tom Glavine and Mike Mussina]   92

Fox, W. P. Satchel Paige's America   92

Halberstam, D. The teammates   920

Maraniss, D. Clemente   92

McDermott, M. A funny thing happened on the way to Cooperstown   92

New York Times Company. Sultans of swat
920

Ripken, C., Jr. The only way I know   92

Ritter, L. S. The glory of their times   920

Robinson, R. Iron horse: Lou Gehrig in his time
92

Stanton, T. Road to Cooperstown   92

Encyclopedias

Light, J. F. The cultural encyclopedia of baseball   796.357

Statistics

Baseball register 2007   796.357

Baseball: a literary anthology   810.8

Baseball before we knew it. Block, D.
796.357

Baseball register 2007   796.357

Baseball's great experiment. Tygiel, J.   796.357

Basham, Arthur Llewellyn

The origins and development of classical Hinduism   294.5

Bashe, Patricia Romanowski

The oasis guide to Asperger syndrome
618.92

Bashe, Philip

(jt. auth) McFarlane, R. The complete bedside companion   649.8

Basic book repair methods. Schechter, A. A.
025.7

Basic crocheting. Silverman, S. H.   746.43

A **basic** guide to ice hockey   796.962

Basic Japanese-English dictionary   495.6

Basic rights *See* Civil rights; Human rights

Basic weight training for men and women. Fahey, T. D.   613.7

The **basic** works of Aristotle. Aristotle   888

Basic writings. Krell, D. F.   193

The **basic** writings of C. G. Jung. Jung, C. G.
150.19

Basic writings of Kant. Kant, I.   193

Basic writings of Nietzsche. Nietzsche, F. W.
193

The **basic** writings of Sigmund Freud. Freud, S.
150.19

Basie, Count, 1904-1984

Good morning blues: the autobiography of Count Basie   92

About

Dance, S. The world of Count Basie   920

See/See also pages in the following book(s):

Feather, L. From Satchmo to Miles   920

Murray, A. The blue devils of Nada   700

Basie, William *See* Basie, Count, 1904-1984

Basketball
Araton, H. Crashing the borders   **796.323**
Blais, M. In these girls, hope is a muscle
796.323
Bradley, B. Values of the game   **796.323**
D'Orso, M. Eagle blue   **796.323**
Feinstein, J. Last dance   **796.323**
Feinstein, J. A march to madness   **796.323**
Kent, R. G. Inside women's college basketball
796.323
Lazenby, R. The show   **796.323**
Swidey, N. The assist   **796.323**
Wolff, A. Big game, small world   **796.323**
Biography
Halberstam, D. Playing for keeps: Michael Jordan and the world he made   **92**
Knight, B. Knight: my story   **92**
Baskin, Elizabeth Cogswell
How to run your business like a girl   **658**
Baskin, Yvonne
A plague of rats and rubbervines   **577**
Basoalto, Ricardo Elizier Neftali Reyes See Neruda, Pablo, 1904-1973
Basque cooking
Barrenechea, T. The Basque table   **641.5**
The **Basque** history of the world. Kurlansky, M.
946
Basque Provinces (France and Spain)
Kurlansky, M. The Basque history of the world
946
The **Basque** table. Barrenechea, T.   **641.5**
Bass, Ellen
The courage to heal   **362.83**
Bass, George Fletcher, 1932-
(ed) Beneath the seven seas. See Beneath the seven seas   **930.1**
Bass, William M., 1928-
Death's acre   **614**
Bastianich, Lidia
Lidia's family table   **641.5**
Lidia's Italian-American kitchen   **641.5**
Lidia's Italian table   **641.5**
Batali, Mario
About
Buford, B. Heat   **641.5**
Bate, Jonathan
John Clare: a biography   **92**
Bateman, Robert, 1930-
(jt. auth) Matthiessen, P. The birds of heaven
598
Bathsheba's breast. Olson, J. S.   **616.99**
Bathurst, Bella
The wreckers   **910.4**
Batman (Fictional character)
Batman unauthorized   **741.5**
Batman unauthorized   **741.5**
Batson, Raymond M.
(jt. auth) Greeley, R. The compact NASA atlas of the solar system   **523.2**
Batstone, David B., 1958-
Saving the corporate soul & (who knows?) maybe your own   **658.4**
Battered children See Child abuse

Battered women See Abused women
The **batterer**. Dutton, D. G.   **362.82**
Battering of wives See Wife abuse
The **Battle**. Barbero, A.   **940.2**
Battle at Bull Run. Davis, W. C.   **973.3**
Battle cries and lullabies. De Pauw, L. G.   **355**
Battle cry of freedom. McPherson, J. M.
973.7
The **battle** for God. Armstrong, K.   **200**
The **battle** for Rome. Katz, R.   **940.54**
The **battle** for Social Security. Altman, N. J.
368.4
The **Battle** of New Orleans. Remini, R. V.
973.5
The **Battle** of the Little Bighorn. Sandoz, M.
973.8
Battle of Waterloo See Waterloo, Battle of, 1815
Battles
Hanson, V. D. Carnage and culture   **904**
Purcell, L. E. Encyclopedia of battles in North America, 1517 to 1916   **970**
Battleships See Warships
Baudelaire, Charles, 1821-1867
Les fleurs du mal   **841**
Poems   **841**
Baughman, Judith
(ed) Fitzgerald, F. S. A life in letters   **92**
Bauhaus
Gropius, W. The new architecture and the Bauhaus   **724**
Influence
Wolfe, T. From Bauhaus to our house
720.973
Baumann, Martin
(ed) Religions of the world. See Religions of the world   **200.3**
Baumfree, Isabella See Truth, Sojourner, d. 1883
Baumgardner, Jennifer, 1970-
Grassroots: a field guide for feminist activism
305.4
Baur, Gene
Farm Sanctuary   **179**
Bausch, Paul
(jt. auth) Dornfest, R. Google hacks   **025.04**
Bausell, R. Barker, 1942-
Snake oil science   **615.5**
Bawer, Bruce, 1956-
Stealing Jesus   **277.3**
While Europe slept   **305**
Baxandall, Rosalyn Fraad, 1939-
(ed) America's working women. See America's working women   **331.4**
Baxter, Angus, 1912-
In search of your European roots   **929**
Bayless, Deann Groen
(jt. auth) Bayless, R. Rick Bayless's Mexican kitchen   **641.5**
Bayless, Rick
Rick Bayless's Mexican kitchen   **641.5**
Bayley, Iris See Murdoch, Iris

The **Beaulieu** encyclopedia of the automobile
629.222

Beautiful child. Hayden, T. L. 371.9

The **beautiful** cigar girl. Stashower, D.
364.152

The **beautiful** soul of John Woolman, apostle of abolition. Slaughter, T. P. 92

Beauty, Personal *See* Personal grooming

The **beauty** myth. Wolf, N. 305.4

The **beauty** of the husband. Carson, A. 811

Beauty shops
Rodriguez, D. Kabul Beauty School 305.4

Beauty: the new basics. Berg, R. 646.7

Beauvoir, Simone de, 1908-1986
The second sex 305.4
About
Bair, D. Simone de Beauvoir 92

Because I said so 306.8

Bechdel, Alison, 1960-
Fun home 92

Beck, Jerry
The animated movie guide 016.79143

Beck, Simone
(jt. auth) Child, J. Mastering the art of French cooking 641.5

Beck, Warren A.
Historical atlas of the American West 911

Becker, Annette
(jt. auth) Audoin-Rouzeau, S. 14-18, understanding the Great War 940.3

Becker, Carl, 1873-1945
The Declaration of Independence 973.3

Becker, Charlotte B., 1944-
(ed) Encyclopedia of ethics. See Encyclopedia of ethics [Routledge] 170

Becker, Ethan
(jt. auth) Rombauer, I. v. S. Joy of cooking 641.5

Becker, Jasper
The Chinese 951.05

Becker, Lawrence C.
(ed) Encyclopedia of ethics. See Encyclopedia of ethics [Routledge] 170

Becker, Marion Rombauer, 1903-1976
(jt. auth) Rombauer, I. v. S. Joy of cooking 641.5

Becker, Norman
The complete book of home inspection 643

Becker, Patricia C.
(ed) Social change in America. See Social change in America 303.4

Becker, Suzy
I had brain surgery, what's your excuse? 92

Beckett, Kenneth A.
Gardening basics. See Gardening basics 635

Beckett, Samuel, 1906-1989
Collected poems in English and French 841
Dramatic works 842
About
Gordon, L. G. The world of Samuel Beckett, 1906-1946 92

See/See also pages in the following book(s):
Bloom, H. The Western canon 809
Playwrights at work 812.009

Beckett, Wendy
Sister Wendy's American collection 709
The story of painting 759

Beckman, James A.
(ed) Affirmative action. See Affirmative action 331.1

Beckwith, Jon *See* Beckwith, Jonathan R., 1935-

Beckwith, Jonathan R., 1935-
Making genes, making waves 92

Becoming. Allport, G. 155.2

Becoming a graphic designer. Heller, S. 741.6

Becoming a tiger. McCarthy, S. 591.5

Becoming Charlemagne. Sypeck, J. 92

Becoming Justice Blackmun. Greenhouse, L.
92

Becoming Mae West. Leider, E. W. 92

Becoming Mona Lisa. Sassoon, D. 759.5

Becoming Victoria. Vallone, L. 92

A **bed** for the night. Rieff, D. 361.2

Bedard, Claire
(jt. auth) Garbarino, J. Parents under siege
649

Bedick, Peter
Living with spina bifida 618.92

Bednar, Nancy
The encyclopedia of sewing machine techniques
646.2

Bedouins
Lawrence, T. E. Seven pillars of wisdom
940.4

The **Bedside** book of birds 598

Bee culture *See* Beekeeping

Beebe, Reta F.
Jupiter 523.4

Beebe, William, 1877-1962
About
Matsen, B. Descent 551.46

Beecher, Henry Ward, 1813-1887
About
Applegate, D. The most famous man in America [biography of Henry Ward Beecher] 92

Beekeeping
Ellis, H. Sweetness & light 595.7

Beekman, Scott
Ringside 796.8

Been there, done that. Fisher, E. 92

Beers, Diane L.
For the prevention of cruelty 179

Beers, Mark H.
(ed) The Merck manual of diagnosis and therapy. See The Merck manual of diagnosis and therapy 610.3
(ed) The Merck manual of medical information. See The Merck manual of medical information 616.02

Bees
See also Beekeeping
Ellis, H. Sweetness & light 595.7

The **big** book of soups & stews. Vollstedt, M.
641.8

Big-box swindle. Mitchell, S. **381**

Big Chief Elizabeth. Milton, G. **975.5**

Big coal. Goodell, J. **333.79**

Big enough to be inconsistent. Fredrickson, G. M.
973.7

Big game hunting *See* Hunting

Big game, small world. Wolff, A. **796.323**

A **big** history. Brown, C. S. **909**

The **big** necessity. George, R. **363.7**

Big pharma. Law, J. **338.4**

The **big** sort. Bishop, B. **305.8**

The **big** splat; or, How our moon came to be.
Mackenzie, D. **523.3**

Bigelow, Christopher Kimball
(jt. auth) Riess, J. Mormonism for dummies
289.3

The **biggest** bangs. Katz, J. I. **522**

Biggest brother. Alexander, L. **92**

Biggs, Emma, 1956-
The encyclopedia of mosaic techniques
738.5

Bigotry *See* Toleration

Bijlefeld, Marjolijn, 1960-
Encyclopedia of diet fads **613.2**

Bill, Buffalo *See* Buffalo Bill, 1846-1917

The **Bill** McKibben reader. McKibben, B.
333.72

The **Billboard** book of top 40 hits. Whitburn, J.
781.64

The **Billboard** illustrated encyclopedia of jazz &
blues **781.65**

Billiards
See also Pool (Game)
Byrne, R. Byrne's new standard book of pool
and billiards **794.7**

Billie Holiday. Clarke, D. **92**

Billig, Michael D., 1956-
(jt. auth) Cassel, G. H. The eye book **617.7**

Billions and billions. Sagan, C. **500**

Billy, the Kid
About
Utley, R. M. Billy the Kid **92**
Wallis, M. Billy the Kid **92**
See/See also pages in the following book(s):
Brown, D. A. The American West **978**

Bin Laden, Osama *See* Osama bin Laden

Bin Laden family
About
Coll, S. The Bin Ladens **920**
The **Bin** Ladens. Coll, S. **920**

Bing Crosby: a pocketful of dreams: the early
years, 1903-1940. Giddins, G. **92**

Binge-purge behavior *See* Bulimia

Bingham, Hiram, 1875-1956
Lost city of the Incas **985**

Binladen family *See* Bin Laden family

Binyon, T. J.
Pushkin: a biography **92**

Biochemistry
Dictionaries
The Facts on File dictionary of biochemistry
572
Research
Watson, J. D. The double helix **572.8**

Bioengineered foods *See* Food—Biotechnology

Bioethics
Clones and clones **174**
The Double-edged helix **599.93**
Fox, M. W. Beyond evolution **174**
Human cloning and human dignity **174**
Encyclopedias
Encyclopedia of bioethics **174**

Biogeography
World atlas of great apes and their conservation
599.8

The **biographical** dictionary of World War II generals and flag officers. Ancell, R. M.
920.003

Biographical directory of the American Congress,
1774-1996 **328.73**

Biographical encyclopedia of artists **920.003**

The **biographical** encyclopedia of jazz. Feather, L.
920.003

Biographical graphic novels
Rudahl, S. A dangerous woman [biography of
Emma Goldman] **92**
Spiegelman, A. Maus **940.53**

Biography
Booknotes: life stories **920**
Bibliography
Burt, D. S. The biography book **920**
Dictionaries
Abrams, I. The Nobel Peace Prize and the laure-
ates **920.003**
Encyclopedia of world biography **920.003**
Great lives from history: Notorious lives
920.003
Great lives from history, The 17th century,
1601-1700 **920.003**
Great lives from history, The 18th century,
1701-1800 **920.003**
Great lives from history, The 19th century,
1801-1900 **920.003**
Great lives from history: the 20th century, 1901-
2000 **920.003**
Great lives from history, The ancient world, pre-
history-476 C.E **920.003**
Great lives from history, the Middle Ages, 477-
1453 **920.003**
Great lives from history, the Renaissance & ear-
ly modern era, 1454-1600 **920.003**
The International who's who **920.003**
Nobel Prize winners **920.003**
Indexes
Havlice, P. P. Index to artistic biography
920.003
Periodicals
Current biography yearbook, 2007 **920.003**
Technique
See Biography as a literary form

Biography. Hamilton, N. **907**

Blues music—*Continued*
Poetry

Blues poems	**811.008**
Blues poems	**811.008**

Blum, Arlene, 1945-

Breaking trail	**796.522**

Blum, Deborah

Ghost hunters	**133.9**
Love at Goon Park	**150.19**
The monkey wars	**179**
Sex on the brain	**612.6**

Blumenthal, Betsy, 1943-

Hands on dyeing	**746.1**

Blumenthal, Eileen, 1948-

Puppetry	**791.5**

Blumrosen, Alfred W.

Slave nation	**973.3**

Blumrosen, Ruth Gerber

(jt. auth) Blumrosen, A. W. Slave nation
973.3

Blunt, Anthony, 1907-1983
About

Carter, M. Anthony Blunt: his lives	**92**

Blunt, Judy, 1954-

Breaking clean	**92**

Blunt, Wilfrid, 1901-1987

Linnaeus, the compleat naturalist	**92**

Bly, Robert

Eating the honey of words	**811**
Iron John	**305.31**
The night Abraham called to the stars	**811**

See/See also pages in the following book(s):

Gioia, D. Can poetry matter?	**809.1**
(tr) Jacobsen, R. The roads have come to an end now	**839.8**

BNA's directory of state and federal courts, judges, and clerks 2008 **347**

Boa constrictors

O'Shea, M. Boas and pythons of the world
597.96

Board games

Botermans, J. The book of games **794**

Board of Governors of the Federal Reserve System (U.S.) *See* Federal Reserve System (U.S.). Board of Governors

Boardman, John, 1927-

Greek art	**709.38**

(ed) The Oxford history of the Roman world. See The Oxford history of the Roman world
937

Boas and pythons of the world. O'Shea, M.
597.96

Boatbuilding
See also Shipbuilding

Boatner, Mark Mayo, 1921-

The Civil War dictionary	**973.7**

Boats, Submarine *See* Submarines

Boats and boating

Heat Moon, W. L. River-horse	**917.3**
Stone, N. On the water	**917.3**

The **Bob** Dylan encyclopedia. Gray, M. **782.42**

Bob Hope: the road well-traveled. Quirk, L. J.
92

Bob Vila's complete guide to remodeling your home. Vila, B. **643**

Bobbi Brown beauty evolution. Brown, B.
646.7

Bobbitt, Philip

The shield of Achilles	**327**
Terror and consent	**363.32**

Bobby Fischer teaches chess. Fischer, B.
794.1

Bobby Flay's grilling for life. Flay, B. **641.5**

Bobick, James E.

(ed) The Handy science answer book. See The Handy science answer book **500**

Bobrick, Benson, 1947-

Angel in the whirlwind	**973.3**

Bobrow, Jerry

Barron's comprehensive postal exam, 473/473-C
383

Bocij, Paul

Cyberstalking	**613.6**

Bodanis, David

E=mc2	**530.1**
Electric universe	**537**

Boden, E. (Edward)

(ed) Black's veterinary dictionary. See Black's veterinary dictionary **636.089**

Boden, Edward *See* Boden, E. (Edward)

Bodmer, W. F. (Walter Fred), 1936-

The book of man	**572.8**

Bodmer, Walter Fred *See* Bodmer, W. F. (Walter Fred), 1936-

Body and mind *See* Mind and body

Body brokers. Cheney, A. **617.9**

Body fluids

Arikha, N. Passions and tempers	**612.4**
The **body** hunters. Shah, S.	**362.1**

Body language *See* Nonverbal communication

Body piercing saved my life. Beaujon, A.
781.66

Bodybuilding (Weight lifting) *See* Weight lifting

Boehm, Arthur

(jt. auth) Tsai, M. Blue Ginger **641.5**

Boer, Jelle Zeilinga de *See* Zeilinga de Boer, Jelle

Boer War, 1899-1902 *See* South African War, 1899-1902

Boettcher, Jennifer C.

Industry research using the economic census
338

Bogard, Travis, 1918-1997

(ed) O'Neil, E. Complete plays **812**

Bogdanos, Matthew

Thieves of Baghdad	**956.7**

Bogdanov, Vladimir, 1965-

(ed) All music guide to country. See All music guide to country **781.642**

Bogira, Steve

Courtroom 302	**345**

Botulinum toxin
Mitchell, D. R. The Botox miracle   **615.8**

Bouchard, Sue
(jt. auth) Burns, E. Underground railroad sampler   **746.46**

Boucher, Bruce
Andrea Palladio   **720.9**

Bouknight, Joanne Kellar
The kitchen idea book   **643**

Boukreev, Anatoli, d. 1997
The climb   **796.522**

Boulder (Colo.). Police Dept.
Schiller, L. Perfect murder, perfect town   **364.1**

Boulevard of broken dreams [biography of James Dean] Alexander, P.   **92**

Boulter, Michael Charles
Extinction: evolution and the end of man   **576.8**

Boulware, Rick
(ed) Encyclopedia of American business. See Encyclopedia of American business   **338**

Bound by honor. Bonanno, B.   **364.1**

Bound for Canaan. Bordewich, F. M.   **973.7**

Bound for the promised land [biography of Harriet Tubman] Larson, K. C.   **92**

Bounty (Ship)
Alexander, C. The Bounty: the true story of the mutiny on the Bounty   **996**

Bourbaki, Nicolas
About
Aczel, A. D. The artist and the mathematician   **510**

Bourdain, Anthony
A cook's tour   **641**
Typhoid Mary   **92**

Bourgeoisie See Middle class

Bouricius, Ann
The romance readers' advisory   **016.8**

Boustani, Rafic
(jt. auth) Fargues, P. The atlas of the Arab world   **909**

Bouton, Jim
(jt. auth) Shecter, L. Ball four   **796.357**

Bovie, Smith Palmer
(ed & tr) Terence. Terence, the comedies   **872**

Bowden, John, 1935-
(ed) Encyclopedia of Christianity. See Encyclopedia of Christianity   **230.003**

Bowden, Ken
(jt. auth) Nicklaus, J. Golf my way   **796.352**
(jt. auth) Nicklaus, J. Jack Nicklaus   **92**

Bowden, Mark, 1951-
Black Hawk down   **967.73**

Bowe, John
Nobodies   **331.1**

Bowen, Mark
Thin ice   **551.51**

Bowers, Edgar
Collected poems   **811**

Bowie, James See Bowie, Jim, 1796-1836

Bowie, Jim, 1796-1836
About
Davis, W. C. Three roads to the Alamo   **976.4**

Bowker, John, 1935-
The complete Bible handbook   **220.6**
World religions   **200**
(ed) The Cambridge illustrated history of religions. See The Cambridge illustrated history of religions   **200.9**

The **Bowker** annual library and book trade almanac 2008   **020.5**

Bowles, Chester, 1901-1986
See/See also pages in the following book(s):
Galbraith, J. K. Name-dropping   **973.9**

Bowles, Hamish
Jacqueline Kennedy   **92**

Bowman, Carl F.
(jt. auth) Kraybill, D. B. On the backroad to heaven   **289.7**

Bowman, John Stewart, 1931-
(ed) Carlisle, R. P. Iraq war   **956.7**
(ed) Facts about the American wars. See Facts about the American wars   **355**

Bowman, Manoah
(jt. auth) Keaton, E. Buster Keaton remembered   **791.43**

Bown, Stephen R.
A most damnable invention   **174**

Bowring, Richard John, 1947-
(ed) The Cambridge encyclopedia of Japan. See The Cambridge encyclopedia of Japan   **952**

The **Boxer** Rebellion. Preston, D.   **951**

Boxing
Anasi, R. The gloves   **796.8**
Kram, M. The ghosts of Manila   **796.8**
Margolick, D. Beyond glory   **796.8**
Schulberg, B. Ringside   **796.8**
Schulberg, B. Sparring with Hemingway and other legends of the fight game   **796.8**

Boxshall, Geoffrey Allan
(jt. auth) Lincoln, R. J. The Cambridge illustrated dictionary of natural history   **508**

The **boy** genius and the mogul. Stashower, D.   **791.45**

The **boy** who cried freebird. Myers, M.   **781.64**

The **boy** who fell out of the sky [biography of David Scott Dornstein] Dornstein, K.   **92**

Boyatzis, Richard E.
(jt. auth) Goleman, D. Primal leadership   **658.4**

Boyce, Charles
Critical companion to William Shakespeare   **822.3**

Boyd, Brian, 1952-
Vladimir Nabokov: the American years   **92**
Vladimir Nabokov: the Russian years   **92**

Boyd, Heidi, 1966-
Simply beautiful beading   **745.58**

Boyd, Herb, 1938-
We shall overcome   **323.1**

Buhle, Paul, 1944-
(ed) Rudahl, S. A dangerous woman [biography of Emma Goldman] **92**

Build your dream home for less. Woodson, R. D. **690**

Building
See also Carpentry; House construction
The Art of natural building **690**
Eck, J. The distinctive home **728**
Scutella, R. M. How to plan, contract, and build your own home **690**
Woodson, R. D. Build your dream home for less **690**

Details
See Architecture—Details
Dictionaries
Dictionary of architecture & construction **720.3**
Means illustrated construction dictionary **690**
Building a character. See Stanislavsky, K. An actor's work **792**
Building a great résumé. Wendleton, K. **650.14**
Building and designing decks. Schuttner, S. **690**

Building failures
Levy, M. Why buildings fall down **690**
Building Jerusalem. Hunt, T. **307.7**

Building materials
The Art of natural building **690**
Building the Getty. Meier, R. **708**
Building the Titanic. Green, R. **623.82**

Buildings
See also Apartment houses; Church buildings; Garages; Historic buildings; Houses; Public buildings
Buildings, Public *See* Public buildings
Built for growth. Rubinfeld, A. **658.4**

Buisseret, David
(ed) The Oxford companion to world exploration. See The Oxford companion to world exploration **910.3**

Buker, Derek M.
The science-fiction and fantasy readers' advisory **025.5**

Bukiet, Melvin Jules
(ed) Nothing makes you free. See Nothing makes you free **808.8**

Bukowski, Charles
The pleasures of the damned **811**

Bukowski, Steven J.
Flooring instant answers **690**

Bulbs
Hill, L. Bulbs **635.9**

Bulfinch, Thomas, 1796-1867
Bulfinch's mythology **398.2**
Bulfinch's mythology. Bulfinch, T. **398.2**

Bulimia
Hornbacher, M. Wasted: a memoir of anorexia and bulimia **616.85**

Bull, John L.
The National Audubon Society field guide to North American birds, Eastern region **598**
Bull!: a history of the boom, 1982-1999. Mahar, M. **332.6**

Bull riding
Peter, J. Fried twinkies, buckle bunnies & bull riders **791.8**

Bull Run, 1st Battle of, 1861
Davis, W. C. Battle at Bull Run **973.3**

Bullard, Sara
Teaching tolerance **649**

Buller, Lynn Kaplanian- *See* Kaplanian-Buller, Lynn

Bullfights
Hemingway, E. The dangerous summer **791.8**
Hemingway, E. Death in the afternoon **791.8**
Lewine, E. Death and the sun **791.8**

Bulliet, Richard W.
(ed) The Columbia history of the 20th century. See The Columbia history of the 20th century **909.82**

Bullock, Alan
Hitler and Stalin **92**

Bulls (Basketball team) *See* Chicago Bulls (Basketball team)

Bull's-eye: unraveling the medical mystery of Lyme disease. Edlow, J. A. **616.9**

Bully for brontosaurus. Gould, S. J. **508**

Bülow, Hans von, 1830-1894
See/See also pages in the following book(s):
Schonberg, H. C. The great pianists **920**

Bumiller, Elisabeth
May you be the mother of a hundred sons **954.05**

Bunch, Bryan H.
The kingdom of infinite number **513**

Bundrum, Charlie, d. 1958
About
Bragg, R. Ava's man [Bundrum, Charlie] **92**

Bundy, McGeorge, 1919-1996
See/See also pages in the following book(s):
Halberstam, D. The best and the brightest **973.922**

Bundy, Ted
About
Rule, A. The stranger beside me [biography of Ted Bundy] **92**
Bundy, Theodore Robert *See* Bundy, Ted

Bungalow style. Crochet, T. **747**

Bunson, Margaret R.
Encyclopedia of ancient Egypt **932**

Bunson, Matthew
Encyclopedia of the Roman Empire **937**
The vampire encyclopedia **398**
(ed) Catholic Almanac, 2008. See Catholic Almanac, 2008 **282**

Bunting, Basil
Complete poems **821**

Bunting, Josiah, 1939-
Ulysses S. Grant **92**

Cancer

See also Breast cancer; Lung cancer; Ovaries—Cancer

Adrouny, A. R. Understanding colon cancer **616.99**

American Cancer Society's complete guide to prostate cancer **616.99**

American Cancer Society's Guide to complementary and alternative cancer methods **616.99**

Cancer sourcebook **616.99**

Caregiving: a step-by-step resource for caring for the person with cancer at home **649.8**

Davis, D. L. The secret history of the war on cancer **616.99**

Everyone's guide to cancer therapy **616.99**

Gordon, J. S. Comprehensive cancer care **616.99**

Harpham, W. S. Diagnosis, cancer **616.99**

Informed decisions **616.99**

Janes-Hodder, H. Childhood cancer **618.92**

Panno, J. Cancer: the role of genes, lifestyle, and environment **616.99**

Patt, R. B. The complete guide to relieving cancer pain and suffering **616.99**

Schwartz, A. Cancer fitness **616.99**

Silver, J. K. After cancer treatment **616.99**

Torrey, E. F. Surviving prostate cancer **616.99**

See/See also pages in the following book(s):
Gallo, R. C. Virus hunting **616.97**

Diet therapy

Arnot, B. The breast health cookbook **616.99**

Encyclopedias

Turkington, C. The encyclopedia of cancer **616.99**

Turkington, C. The encyclopedia of men's reproductive cancer **616.99**

Turkington, C. The encyclopedia of women's reproductive cancer **616.99**

Cancer fitness. Schwartz, A. **616.99**

Cancer sourcebook **616.99**

Cancer: the role of genes, lifestyle, and environment. Panno, J. **616.99**

Candelaria, Cordelia

(ed) Encyclopedia of Latino popular culture. See Encyclopedia of Latino popular culture **305.8**

Candlemaker's companion. Oppenheimer, B. **745.59**

Candles

Oppenheimer, B. Candlemaker's companion **745.59**

Candy

Almond, S. Candyfreak: a journey through the chocolate underbelly of America **338.4**

Candyfreak: a journey through the chocolate underbelly of America. Almond, S. **338.4**

Canfield, Jack, 1944-

The success principles **158**

Cannadine, David, 1950-

Mellon **92**

Cannan, Edwin, 1861-1935

(ed) Smith, A. The wealth of nations **330.1**

Canning and preserving

Costenbader, C. W. The big book of preserving the harvest **641.4**

Ziedrich, L. The joy of pickling **641.4**

Cannon, Annie Jump, 1863-1941

See/See also pages in the following book(s):
Greenstein, G. Portraits of discovery **920**

Cannon, Byron, 1940-

(ed) Great events from history, The Middle Ages, 477-1453. See Great events from history, The Middle Ages, 477-1453 **909.07**

Cannon, Lou

Official negligence **979.4**

Canoes and canoeing

Fredston, J. A. Rowing to latitude **797.1**

Mason, B. Path of the paddle **797.1**

The **canon**. Angier, N. **500**

Can't be satisfied: the life and times of Muddy Waters. Gordon, R. **92**

Can't buy me love. Gould, J. **920**

Can't remember what I forgot. Halpern, S. M. **616.8**

Can't stop, won't stop. Chang, J. **781.64**

Can't you hear me callin': the life of Bill Monroe, father of bluegrass. Smith, R. D. **92**

Cantor, Georg, 1845-1918

See/See also pages in the following book(s):
Bell, E. T. Men of mathematics **920**

Cantor, Norman F., 1929-2004

Antiquity: the civilization of the ancient world **930**

In the wake of the plague **614.5**

Cantor-Cooke, Robin

(jt. auth) Sotile, W. M. Thriving with heart disease **362.1**

Cantor Fitzgerald LP

Lutnick, H. On top of the world **332.6**

The **cantos** of Ezra Pound. Pound, E. **811**

Canzoneri, Jennifer

(ed) The Psychology of superheroes. See The Psychology of superheroes **741.5**

Capa, Robert, 1913-1954

See/See also pages in the following book(s):
Marton, K. The great escape **920**

Capablanca, José Raúl, 1888-1942

Chess fundamentals **794.1**

Capacity. McMichael, J. **811**

Capano, Thomas J., 1949-
About

Rule, A. —and never let her go **364.1**

Cape, Judith See Page, P. K. (Patricia Kathleen), 1916-

Cape Cod (Mass.)
Description and travel

Thoreau, H. D. Cape Cod **917.44**

Cape wind. Williams, W. **333.9**

Cape Wind Associates (Firm)

Williams, W. Cape wind **333.9**

Children—*Continued*
Institutional care
See/See also pages in the following book(s):
Bartholet, E. Nobody's children   **362.7**
Management
See Child rearing
Medical care
Johnson, C. M. Your critically ill child
    618.92
Nutrition
Sears, W. The family nutrition book   **613.2**
The Yale guide to children's nutrition   **613.2**
Pictorial works
Coles, R. When they were young   **779**
Psychology
See Child psychology
Religious life
Coles, R. The spiritual life of children   **204**
Socialization
See Socialization
Training
See Child rearing
Travel
Ryder, C. S. Take your pediatrician with you
    618.92
United States
Chudacoff, H. P. Children at play   **305.23**
Coles, R. Children of crisis   **305.23**
Medved, M. Saving childhood   **305.23**
Mintz, S. Huck's raft   **305.23**
West (U.S.)
Luchetti, C. Children of the West   **978**

Children, Emotionally disturbed *See* Emotionally disturbed children

The **children**. Halberstam, D.   **323.1**

Children and adults *See* Child rearing

Children and war
Nicholas, L. H. Cruel world   **940.53**
Stolen voices   **920**
See/See also pages in the following book(s):
Beah, I. A long way gone   **92**

Children at play. Chudacoff, H. P.   **305.23**

Children for hire. Levine, M. J.   **331.3**

Children of alcoholics
Black, C. Straight talk from Claudia Black
    362.29

Children of crisis. Coles, R.   **305.23**

Children of divorced parents
Wallerstein, J. S. Second chances   **306.89**

Children of drug addicts
Black, C. Straight talk from Claudia Black
    362.29

Children of narcotic addicts *See* Children of drug addicts

The **children** of Sánchez. Lewis, O.   **972.08**

Children of single parents *See* Single parent family

Children of the West. Luchetti, C.   **978**

Children with autism   **618.92**

Children with spina bifida   **618.92**

The **children's** blizzard. Laskin, D.   **977**

Children's catalog. 19th ed.   **011.6**

Children's diseases *See* Children—Diseases

The **Children's** Hospital guide to your child's health and development   **618.92**

Children's libraries
See also Young adults' libraries
Cullum, C. N. The storytime sourcebook II
    027.62
Fiore, C. D. Fiore's summer library reading program handbook   **027.62**

Children's literature
See also Fairy tales; Newbery Medal; Picture books for children
Bibliography
Children's catalog. 19th ed.   **011.6**
Silvey, A. 100 best books for children
    011.6
Trelease, J. The read-aloud handbook   **028.5**
Dictionaries
Helbig, A. Dictionary of American children's fiction, 1995-1999   **028.5**
Encyclopedias
The Cambridge guide to children's books in English   **028.5**
History and criticism
Gillespie, J. T. The Newbery/Printz companion
    028.5
Marcus, L. S. Minders of make-believe
    070.5
Technique
Aiken, J. The way to write for children
    808.06
Seuling, B. How to write a children's book and get it published   **808.06**
Shulevitz, U. Writing with pictures   **808.06**

Children's poetry
See also Nursery rhymes
The **Children's** song index, 1978-1993   **782.42**

Children's writer's & illustrator's market. See 2009 children's writer's & illustrator's market
    808

Childress, Alice, 1916 or 20-1994
See/See also pages in the following book(s):
Black women writers (1950-1980)   **810.9**

Childs, Craig Leland
House of rain   **978.9**

Childs, Lucinda
See/See also pages in the following book(s):
Sontag, S. Where the stress falls   **814**

A **child's** Christmas in Wales. Thomas, D.
    828

Chile
Allende, I. My invented country   **92**

Chiles, James R.
The god machine   **629.133**

Chilies to chocolate   **641.3**

Chilton, Bruce
The Cambridge companion to the Bible
    220.9
Mary Magdalene   **226**
Rabbi Jesus   **232.9**

Chilvers, Ian
(ed) The Concise Oxford dictionary of art and artists. See The Concise Oxford dictionary of art and artists   **703**

The **Complete** directory of large print books and serials 2008 **015.73**

The **complete** directory to prime time network and cable TV shows, 1946-present. Brooks, T. **791.45**

Complete do-it-yourself manual **643**

The **complete** dog book. American Kennel Club **636.7**

Complete dog training manual. See Fogle, B. New complete dog training manual **636.7**

Complete drug reference. See Consumer drug reference 2008 **615**

Complete encyclopedia of the saltwater aquarium. See Jennings, G. The new encyclopedia of the saltwater aquarium **639.34**

The **complete** gods and goddesses of ancient Egypt. Wilkinson, R. H. **299**

The **complete** golfer's handbook. Player, G. **796.352**

The **complete** guide to Alzheimer's-proofing your home. Warner, M. L. **362.1**

The **Complete** guide to America's national parks. See The official guide to America's national parks **917.3**

The **complete** guide to Asperger's syndrome. Attwood, T. **616.85**

Complete guide to building log homes. Burch, M. **694**

The **complete** guide to digital illustration. Caplin, S. **776**

The **complete** guide to digital photography. Freeman, M. **775**

The **complete** guide to embroidery stitches. Campbell, J. **746.44**

The **Complete** guide to mental health for women **616.89**

The **complete** guide to relieving cancer pain and suffering. Patt, R. B. **616.99**

Complete guide to sewing. See New complete guide to sewing **646.2**

The **complete** guitarist. Chapman, R. **787.87**

The **complete** history of costume and fashion. Cosgrave, B. **391**

Complete home how-to. See Jackson, A. Popular mechanics complete home how-to **643**

The **complete** home learning sourcebook. Rupp, R. **371.04**

The **complete** home veterinary guide. Pinney, C. C. **636.089**

The **complete** houseplant survival manual. Pleasant, B. **635.9**

The **complete** how to figure it. Huff, D. **640**

Complete idiot's guide to knitting and crocheting illustrated. Breiter, B. **746.43**

The **complete** illustrated guide to shaping wood. Bird, L. **684**

The **complete** lesbian & gay parenting guide. Lev, A. I. **649**

The **complete** major prose plays. Ibsen, H. **839.8**

The **complete** meat cookbook. Aidells, B. **641.6**

The **complete** motorcycle book. Bennett, J. S. **629.28**

The **complete** odes of Pindar. Pindar **884**

Complete office handbook. Jaderstrom, S. **651.8**

The **complete** operas of Mozart. Osborne, C. **792.5**

The **complete** operas of Puccini. Osborne, C. **792.5**

The **complete** operas of Richard Wagner. Osborne, C. **792.5**

The **complete** photo guide to window treatments **646.2**

The **complete** pig. Rath, S. **636.4**

The **complete** plays. Behan, B. **822**

The **complete** plays. Chekhov, A. P. **891.7**

The **complete** plays. Marlowe, C. **822**

The **complete** plays. Orton, J. **822**

The **complete** plays. Synge, J. M. **822**

Complete poems. Bunting, B. **821**

The **complete** poems. Jarrell, R. **811**

The **complete** poems. Jonson, B. **821**

The **complete** poems. Lawrence, D. H. **821**

Complete poems. Poe, E. A. **811**

The **complete** poems. Sexton, A. **811**

Complete poems, 1904-1962. Cummings, E. E. **811**

The **complete** poems and plays, 1909-1950. Eliot, T. S. **811**

Complete poems and selected letters. Crane, H. **811**

The **complete** poems of Anna Akhmatova. Akhmatova, A. A. **891.7**

The **complete** poems of C. Day Lewis. Day Lewis, C. **821**

The **complete** poems of Carl Sandburg. Sandburg, C. **811**

The **complete** poems of Emily Jane Brontë. Brontë, E. **821**

The **complete** poems of John Keats. Keats, J. **821**

The **complete** poems of Kenneth Rexroth. Rexroth, K. **811**

The **complete** poetry. Vallejo, C. A. **861**

Complete poetry and collected prose. Whitman, W. **811**

The **complete** poetry and prose of Geoffrey Chaucer. Chaucer, G. **821**

The **complete** poetry and prose of William Blake. Blake, W. **821**

The **complete** poetry and selected prose of John Donne. Donne, J. **821**

The **complete** Pompeii. Berry, J. **937**

The **complete** practical guide to stencilling and stamping. Ganderton, L. **745.7**

The **complete** RFID handbook. Ward, D. **025**

The **complete** serger handbook. James, C. **646.2**

The **complete** single mother. Engber, A. **306.8**

Cronin, Isaac, 1948-
(ed) Confronting fear. See Confronting fear
303.6

Cronkite, Walter
Around America 917.3
A reporter's life 92

Croom, Emily Anne
The genealogist's companion and sourcebook
929

Crops See Farm produce

Crosby, Bing, 1904-1977
About
Giddins, G. Bing Crosby: a pocketful of dreams: the early years, 1903-1940 92

Crosby, Molly Caldwell
The American plague 614.5

Cross, Charles R.
Heavier than heaven: a biography of Kurt Cobain 92
Room full of mirrors [biography of Jimi Hendrix] 92

Cross, F. L. (Frank Leslie), 1900-1968
(ed) The Oxford dictionary of the Christian Church. See The Oxford dictionary of the Christian Church 230.003

Cross, Gary S.
(ed) Encyclopedia of recreation and leisure in America. See Encyclopedia of recreation and leisure in America 790

Cross, Mary Ann Evans See Eliot, George, 1819-1880

Cross cultural conflict See Culture conflict

Cross-cultural studies
How Israelis and Palestinians negotiate
956.94

Cross-stitch
2001 cross stitch designs 746.44
The big book of cross-stitch designs 746.44
Greenoff, J. The cross stitcher's bible
746.44
Hasler, J. S. Native American cross stitch
746.44
The **cross** stitcher's bible. Greenoff, J. 746.44

Crossan, John Dominic
Excavating Jesus 225.9
Who killed Jesus? 232.9
(jt. auth) Borg, M. J. The last week 232.9

Crossing the blvd. Lehrer, W. 305.9

Crossing the danger water 810.8

Crossing the threshold of hope. John Paul, Pope
282

Crossroads [biography of Eric Clapton]
Schumacher, M. 92

Crosstown traffic: Jimi Hendrix and the post-war rock'n'roll revolution. Murray, C. S. 92

Crossword puzzles
Dictionaries
Merriam-Webster's crossword puzzle dictionary
793.73
Pulliam, T. The New York times crossword puzzle dictionary 793.73
Random House Webster's crossword puzzle dictionary 793.73

Croswell, Ken
The alchemy of the heavens 523.1

Crouch, Stanley
Considering genius 781.65

The **crowd** sounds happy. Dawidoff, N. 92

Crowds
Surowiecki, J. The wisdom of crowds 303.3

Crowe, David
Oskar Schindler 92

The **crucible** of war. Anderson, F. 973.2

Cruden, Alexander, 1701-1770
Cruden's Complete concordance 220.5

Cruden's Complete concordance. Cruden, A.
220.5

Cruel world. Nicholas, L. H. 940.53

Cruelty to animals See Animal welfare

Cruickshank, Duncan
(jt. auth) Player, G. The complete golfer's handbook 796.352

Crump, R. W. (Rebecca W.), 1944-
(ed) Rossetti, C. G. Christina Rossetti 821

Crump, Rebecca W. See Crump, R. W. (Rebecca W.), 1944-

Crusade. Atkinson, R. 956.7

Crusades
The Oxford illustrated history of the Crusades
909.07
See/See also pages in the following book(s):
Tuchman, B. W. A distant mirror 944
Encyclopedias
Andrea, A. J. Encyclopedia of the crusades
909.07
The Crusades 909.07
The **Crusades** 909.07

Cruz, Nilo
Anna in the tropics 812

Crying
Lutz, T. Crying 152.4

Cryogenics See Low temperatures

Cryptography
Lee, B. Marching orders 940.54
Sebag-Montefiore, H. Enigma: the battle for the code 940.54
Singh, S. The code book 652

Crystal, David, 1941-
The Cambridge encyclopedia of language
400
The Cambridge encyclopedia of the English language 420
A dictionary of language 410
English as a global language 420
How language works 401
Language and the internet 410
The stories of English 427

Crystallography See Crystals

Crystals
Holden, A. Crystals and crystal growing 548
Johnsen, O. Minerals of the world 549

Crystals and crystal growing. Holden, A. 548

Csikszentmihalyi, Mihaly
Creativity 153.3

Cunningham, Jon, 1965-
(jt. auth) Waldman, C. Encyclopedia of exploration **910.3**

Cunningham, Marion
(jt. auth) Farmer, F. M. The Fannie Farmer baking book **641.8**

Cunningham, Merce
About
Brown, C. Chance and circumstance **92**

Cunningham, Rosa Lee
About
Dash, L. Rosa Lee **305.8**

Cupcakes and kalashnikovs. See Journalistas **808.8**

The **cure** within. Harrington, A. **616**

Curie, Maria Sklodowska See Curie, Marie, 1867-1934

Curie, Marie, 1867-1934
About
Brian, D. The Curies **92**
Dry, S. Curie **92**
Quinn, S. Marie Curie **92**

Curie, Pierre, 1859-1906
About
Brian, D. The Curies **92**

The **Curies**. Brian, D. **92**

Curiosities and wonders
See also Eccentrics and eccentricities; Monsters
Clark, J. Unnatural phenomena **001.9**
Guinness book of records 2008 **032.02**
The Seventy wonders of the modern world **720.9**

Curl, James Stevens, 1937-
A dictionary of architecture and landscape architecture **720.3**

Curly girl. Massey, L. **646.7**

Curran, Brian
(jt. auth) Amery, C. Vanishing histories **363.6**

Current biography yearbook, 2007 **920.003**

Current surgical diagnosis & treatment **617**

Curricula (Courses of study) See Education—Curricula

Curriden, Mark
(jt. auth) Wecht, C. H. Tales from the morgue **614**

Currie, Philip J.
(ed) Encyclopedia of dinosaurs. See Encyclopedia of dinosaurs **567.9**

Curry, Jennifer
(ed) World authors, 2000-2005. See World authors, 2000-2005 **920.003**

Curry, Judith A.
(ed) Encyclopedia of atmospheric sciences. See Encyclopedia of atmospheric sciences **551.5**

Curry. Collingham, E. M. **394.1**

Curse of the Narrows. MacDonald, L. M. **971.6**

A **cursing** brain? Kushner, H. I. **616.8**

The **curtain**. Kundera, M. **801**

Curtains See Draperies

Curtan, Patricia
(jt. auth) Waters, A. The art of simple food **641.5**

Curtin, Sharon R.
(jt. auth) Gordon, J. S. Comprehensive cancer care **616.99**

Curtis, Adrian
(ed) Oxford Bible atlas. See Oxford Bible atlas **220.9**

Curtis, Brian, 1971-
Every week a season **796.332**

Curtis, Garniss H., 1919-
(jt. auth) Swisher, C. C. Java Man **599.93**

Curtis, Glade B.
Your pregnancy week by week **618.2**

Curtis, Nancy C.
Black heritage sites **917.3**

Curtis, Susan, 1956-
Dancing to a black man's tune: a life of Scott Joplin **92**

Curtis, William J. R.
Modern architecture since 1900 **724**

Curtiz, Michael, 1888-1962
See/See also pages in the following book(s):
Marton, K. The great escape **920**

Curzon, Susan Carol
Managing change **025.1**

Cushing, Robert G.
(jt. auth) Bishop, B. The big sort **305.8**

Cusick, Dawn
(ed) The Michaels book of paper crafts. See The Michaels book of paper crafts **745.54**

Cusick, Thomas W., 1943-
Mathematics made simple **510**

Cusk, Rachel, 1967-
A life's work **306.8**

Custer, George Armstrong, 1839-1876
About
Connell, E. S. Son of the Morning Star **973.8**
Donovan, J. A terrible glory **973.8**
Sandoz, M. The Battle of the Little Bighorn **973.8**
Utley, R. M. Custer: cavalier in buckskin **973.8**
Wert, J. D. Custer **92**

Custer died for your sins. Deloria, V. **970.004**

Customer relations
Phillips, E. H. Shocked, appalled, and dismayed! **651.7**

Customs, Social See Manners and customs

Cut flower industry
Stewart, A. Flower confidential **338.1**

Cutcliffe, Stephen H.
(ed) Technology & American history. See Technology & American history **609**

Cuthbertson, Yvonne, 1944-
Beginners' guide to herb gardening **635**

Cvetaeva, Marina Ivanovna See Tsvetaeva, Marina Ivanovna, 1892-1941

Cyber commerce See Electronic commerce

Damasio, Antonio R.
The feeling of what happens   **153**
Looking for Spinoza   **152.4**
The **damn** good resume guide. Parker, Y.
    650.14

Damon Lee Fowler's new southern baking. Fowler, D. L.   **641.8**
Dampier, William, 1652-1715
About
Preston, D. A pirate of exquisite mind: explorer, naturalist, and buccaneer: the life of William Dampier   **92**
Damrosch, Barbara
The garden primer   **635**
Damrosch, David
The buried book   **809**
Damrosch, Leopold, 1941-
Jean-Jacques Rousseau   **92**
Dana, Richard Henry, 1815-1882
Two years before the mast   **910.4**
Dance, Stanley
The world of Count Basie   **920**
Dance
See also Ballet; Belly dancing; Modern dance
Reynolds, N. No fixed points   **792.8**
Dictionaries
Craine, D. The Oxford dictionary of dance
    792.8
The **dance** of anger. Lerner, H. G.   **152.4**
The **dance** of deception. Lerner, H. G.   **155.3**
The **dance** of intimacy. Lerner, H. G.   **155.6**
The **dance** of molecules. Sargent, T.   **620**
Dancers
See also Ballet dancers
Danchin, Antoine
The Delphic boat   **572.8**
Dancing *See* Dance
Dancing at the Dead Sea. Mitchell, A.   **304.2**
The **dancing** girls of Lahore. Brown, L.   **306.7**
Dancing with Cuba. Guillermoprieto, A.
    972.91
Dancing with Rose. Kessler, L.   **362.1**
Dancing with strangers. Clendinnen, I.   **994**
Dando, Marc
(jt. auth) Compagno, L. J. V. Sharks of the world   **597**
Danger on peaks. Snyder, G.   **811**
Dangerous animals
See also Animal attacks; Poisonous animals
Quammen, D. Monster of God   **591.6**
Dangerous doses. Eban, K.   **363.1**
Dangerous nation. Kagan, R.   **327.73**
The **dangerous** summer. Hemingway, E.   **791.8**
A **dangerous** woman [biography of Emma Goldman] Rudahl, S.   **92**
Daniel, Jessica Henderson
(ed) The Complete guide to mental health for women. See The Complete guide to mental health for women   **616.89**

Daniel, Larry J., 1947-
Shiloh   **973.7**
Daniell, David
The Bible in English   **220.5**
Daniels, Cora
Black Power Inc.   **658.4**
Daniels, Les, 1943-
Marvel   **741.5**
Daniels, Roger
Coming to America   **325.73**
Prisoners without trial   **940.53**
(ed) Japanese Americans, from relocation to redress. See Japanese Americans, from relocation to redress   **940.53**
Danielsen, Anne
Presence and pleasure   **781.644**
Daniloff, Nicholas
(jt. auth) Baiev, K. The Oath   **947.5**
Daniloff, Ruth
(jt. auth) Baiev, K. The Oath   **947.5**
Danish authors *See* Authors, Danish
Danner, Mark
Torture and truth   **956.7**
Danson, Edwin, 1948-
Weighing the world   **526**
Dante Alighieri, 1265-1321
The divine comedy   **851**
The Inferno   **851**
Paradiso   **851**
The portable Dante   **851**
Purgatorio   **851**
About
Ruud, J. Critical companion to Dante   **850.9**
See/See also pages in the following book(s):
Bloom, H. The Western canon   **809**
Danticat, Edwidge, 1969-
After the dance   **394.25**
Brother, I'm dying   **92**
D'Antonio, Michael
Hershey   **92**
(jt. auth) Spielman, A. Mosquito   **595.7**
Dare to repair. Sussman, J.   **643**
Darion, Joe, 1917-2001
(jt. auth) Wasserman, D. Man of La Mancha
    812
Dark Ages *See* Middle Ages
Dark continent: Europe's twentieth century. Mazower, M.   **940.55**
Dark cosmos. Hooper, D.   **523.1**
Dark lover: the life and death of Rudolph Valentino. Leider, E. W.   **92**
Dark nature. Watson, L.   **111**
The **dark** side of genius [biography of Alfred Hitchcock] Spoto, D.   **92**
The **dark** side of the game. Green, T.   **796.332**
Dark star safari. Theroux, P.   **916**
Dark sun. Rhodes, R.   **623.4**
Dark tide. Puleo, S.   **363.1**
Darke, Rick
The American woodland garden   **635.9**
Darkness visible. Styron, W.   **616.85**

Dinosaurs—*Continued*
Larson, P. L. Rex appeal   **567.9**
Nothdurft, W. E. The lost dinosaurs of Egypt
    567.9
Powell, J. L. Night comes to the Cretaceous
    576.8
Rea, T. Bone wars   **560**
The Scientific American book of dinosaurs
    567.9

Encyclopedias
Encyclopedia of dinosaurs   **567.9**
Lambert, D. Dinosaur encyclopedia   **567.9**

Dinwiddie, R. (Robert)
Universe. See Universe   **523.1**

Dinwiddie, Robert *See* Dinwiddie, R. (Robert)

Dionne, E. J., Jr.
Stand up, fight back   **306**

Diplomacy
Kissinger, H. Diplomacy   **327.73**
Reynolds, D. Summits   **909.82**

Diplomats
Power, S. Chasing the flame [biography of Sergio Vieira de Mello]   **92**
Wright, J. The ambassadors   **327**
Dictionaries
Notable U.S. ambassadors since 1775
    920.003

Dippie, Brian W.
The Frederic Remington Art Museum collection
    92

Dirda, Michael, 1948-
Book by book   **028**
Classics for pleasure   **814**

Directed by desire. Jordan, J.   **811**

Direction (Motion pictures) *See* Motion pictures—Production and direction

Direction (Theater) *See* Theater—Production and direction

Direction sense
See also Navigation
The **directory** for exceptional children   **371.9**

Directory of family associations. Bentley, E. P.
    929

Directory of financial aids for women 2007-2009. Schlachter, G. A.   **378.3**

Directory of historical organizations in the United States and Canada. American Association for State and Local History   **973.06**

Directory of historical societies and agencies in the United States and Canada. See American Association for State and Local History. Directory of historical organizations in the United States and Canada   **973.06**

The **directory** of mail order catalogs 2008
    016.381

Directory of medical specialists. See The Official ABMS directory of board certified medical specialists   **610.69**

Directory of national trade and professional associations of the United States. See National trade and professional associations of the United States   **061.025**

Directory of online databases. See Gale directory of databases   **025.04**

Directory of physicians in the United States
    610.69

Directory of portable databases. See Gale directory of databases   **025.04**

Directory of special libraries and information centers, [2008]   **026**

Dirigible balloons *See* Airships

Dirr, Michael
Dirr's Hardy trees and shrubs   **635.9**
Dirr's trees and shrubs for warm climates
    635.9

Dirr's Hardy trees and shrubs. Dirr, M.   **635.9**

Dirr's trees and shrubs for warm climates. Dirr, M.   **635.9**

The **dirt** on clean. Ashenburg, K.   **391**

The **dirty** dozen: toxic chemicals and the earth's future. Johansen, B. E.   **363.7**

DiSabato-Aust, Tracy
The well-designed mixed garden   **712**
The well-tended perennial garden   **635.9**

Disabled *See* Handicapped

Disabled students *See* Handicapped students

Disadvantaged children *See* Socially handicapped children

The **disappearing** girl. Machoian, L.   **616.85**

Disappearing ink. Gioia, D.   **811**

Disarmament *See* Arms control

Disaster planning. Halsted, D. D.   **025.8**

Disaster relief
Brinkley, D. The great deluge   **976.3**
Dyson, M. E. Come hell or high water
    976.3
Halsted, D. D. Disaster planning   **025.8**
Horne, J. Breach of faith   **976.3**
Van Heerden, I. L. The storm   **976.3**

Disasters
See also Accidents; Natural disasters
Davis, L. A. Man-made catastrophes   **904**
Junger, S. Fire   **909.82**

Discipline of children *See* Child rearing

The **discomfort** zone. Franzen, J.   **92**

Discount stores
Wal-Mart   **381**

Discoveries (in geography) *See* Exploration

The **discoveries**. Lightman, A. P.   **509**

Discoveries: the voyages of Captain James Cook. See Thomas, N. Cook   **92**

The **discovery** and conquest of Mexico, 1517-1521. Díaz del Castillo, B.   **972**

The **discovery** of being. May, R.   **150.19**

The **discovery** of global warming. Weart, S. R.
    551.6

The **discovery** of God. Klinghoffer, D.   **222**

Discrimination
See also Hate crimes; Race discrimination; Sex discrimination

Discrimination in education
See also Segregation in education
Kozol, J. Death at an early age   **306.43**

Dobroszycki, Lucjan
 (ed) The Chronicle of the Łódz ghetto, 1941-
 1944. See The Chronicle of the Łódz ghetto,
 1941-1944 **943.8**

Dobson, Michael
 (ed) The Oxford companion to Shakespeare. See
 The Oxford companion to Shakespeare
 822.3

Doctor Atkins' new diet revolution. See Atkins, R.
 C. Dr. Atkins' new diet revolution **613.2**

Doctor Franklin's medicine. Finger, S. **610.9**

Doctorow, E. L., 1931-
 Creationists: selected essays, 1993-2006 **814**
 Reporting the universe **92**

Doctors See Physicians

The **Doctor's** book of home remedies for dogs and
 cats **636.7**

The **doctors'** plague [biography of Ignác Fülöp
 Semmelweis] Nuland, S. B. **92**

Doctors Without Borders (Organization) See
 Médecins Sans Frontières (Organization)

Doctrinal theology
 Davies, B. The thought of Thomas Aquinas
 230
 Holifield, E. B. Theology in America **230**

Documentaries (Motion pictures) See Documentary films

Documentary films
 Encyclopedia of the documentary film
 791.4303

Documentary photography
 Friend, D. Watching the world change **974.7**
 Lee, R. Russell Lee photographs **779**
 New York September 11 **974.7**
 Platinum anniversary collection **779**
 Sontag, S. Regarding the pain of others
 303.6
 Through the lens **779**

Documents of American Indian diplomacy
 970.004

DOD See United States. Dept. of Defense

Dodge, Hazel
 (jt. auth) Connolly, P. The ancient city **937**

Dodge, Norton T., 1927-
 About
 McPhee, J. A. The ransom of Russian art
 709.47

Dodgers (Baseball team) See Brooklyn Dodgers
 (Baseball team)

Dodgson, Charles Lutwidge See Carroll, Lewis,
 1832-1898

Dodman, Nicholas H.
 Dogs behaving badly **636.7**

Dodson, Bert
 (jt. auth) Hoagland, M. B. The way life works
 570

Dodson, Howard, 1939-
 Jubilee: the emergence of African-American culture **305.8**

Dodson, James
 The road to somewhere **910.4**
 (jt. auth) Palmer, A. A golfer's life **92**

Doerr, Bobby, 1918-
 See/See also pages in the following book(s):
 Halberstam, D. The teammates **920**

Does America need a foreign policy? Kissinger, H.
 327.73

Does God belong in public schools? Greenawalt,
 K. **379**

Does my child have a speech problem? Martin, K.
 L. **618.92**

Dog days. Katz, J. **636**

Dog owner's manual. Fogle, B. **636.7**

Dog racing
 See also Iditarod Trail Sled Dog Race,
 Alaska; Sled dog racing

Dog years. Doty, M. **92**

Dogs
 Adams, M. B. Shaggy muses **920**
 American Kennel Club. The complete dog book
 636.7
 Budiansky, S. The truth about dogs **636.7**
 Coppinger, R. Dogs **636.7**
 Coren, S. Why we love the dogs we do
 636.7
 Dibra, B. Dogspeak **636.7**
 The Doctor's book of home remedies for dogs
 and cats **636.7**
 Dodman, N. H. Dogs behaving badly **636.7**
 Dogs: the ultimate care guide **636.7**
 Fogle, B. ASPCA complete dog care manual
 636.7
 Fogle, B. Dog owner's manual **636.7**
 Geeson, E. Ultimate dog grooming **636.7**
 Healy, T. I have heard you calling in the night
 636.7
 Herriot, J. James Herriot's dog stories **636.7**
 Hugo, L. Where the trail grows faint **615.8**
 Katz, J. The new work of dogs **636.7**
 Kerasote, T. Merle's door **636.7**
 Lane, M. The Humane Society of the United
 States complete guide to dog care **636.7**
 McConnell, P. For the love of a dog **636.7**
 McGinnis, T. The well dog book **636.7**
 Morris, W. My dog Skip **92**
 The Original dog bible **636.7**
 Palika, L. K.I.S.S. guide to raising a puppy
 636.7
 Petspeak **636.089**
 Thomas, E. M. The social lives of dogs
 636.7
  Encyclopedias
 Coile, D. C. Encyclopedia of dog breeds
 636.7
 Fogle, B. The new encyclopedia of the dog
 636.7
  Training
 Fogle, B. New complete dog training manual
 636.7
 Katz, J. Katz on dogs **636.7**
 Monks of New Skete. How to be your dog's
 best friend **636.7**
 Taylor, D. Old dog, new tricks **636.7**

Dogs behaving badly. Dodman, N. H. **636.7**

Dogs that know when their owners are coming
 home. Sheldrake, R. **133.8**

Encyclopedia of the documentary film
791.4303

The **encyclopedia** of the dog. See Fogle, B. The new encyclopedia of the dog 636.7

Encyclopedia of the Enlightenment. Wilson, E. J. 940.2

Encyclopedia of the great Black migration 307

Encyclopedia of the Great Plains 978.03

The **encyclopedia** of the heart and heart disease. Randall, O. S. 612.1

Encyclopedia of the Holocaust [Facts on File] 940.53

Encyclopedia of the Holocaust [Macmillan] 940.53

The **encyclopedia** of the horse. See Edwards, E. H. The new encyclopedia of the horse 636.1

Encyclopedia of the industrial revolution in America. Olson, J. S. 973.03

Encyclopedia of the Jewish religion. See The Oxford dictionary of the Jewish religion 296.03

The **encyclopedia** of the JFK assassination. Benson, M. 973.922

Encyclopedia of the Korean War 951.9

Encyclopedia of the Lewis and Clark Expedition. Woodger, E. 978

Encyclopedia of the medieval world. English, E. D. 940.1

Encyclopedia of the modern Middle East & North Africa 956

The **encyclopedia** of the muscle and skeletal systems and disorders. Sayler, M. H. 616.7

Encyclopedia of the new American nation 973.03

Encyclopedia of the Persian Gulf War. Schwartz, R. A. 956.7

Encyclopedia of the piano. See Piano: an encyclopedia 786.2

Encyclopedia of the Renaissance 940.2

Encyclopedia of the Renaissance. See The Renaissance 940.2

Encyclopedia of the Roman Empire. Bunson, M. 937

Encyclopedia of the scientific revolution 509

Encyclopedia of the sea. Ellis, R. 551.46

The **encyclopedia** of the Supreme Court. Schultz, D. A. 347

Encyclopedia of the U.S. Census 304.6

Encyclopedia of the United Nations. Moore, J. A. 341.23

Encyclopedia of the United Nations and international agreements. Osmanczyk, E. J. 341.23

Encyclopedia of the United States Congress. Dewhirst, R. E. 328.73

Encyclopedia of the United States in the nineteenth century 973.5

Encyclopedia of the Victorian era 941.081

Encyclopedia of the world's minorities 305.8

Encyclopedia of twentieth-century photography 770.9

Encyclopedia of underwater and maritime archaeology 930.1

The **encyclopedia** of unsolved crimes. Newton, M. 364.1

The **Encyclopedia** of vitamins, minerals, and supplements 613.2

The **encyclopedia** of war movies. Davenport, R. 791.4303

Encyclopedia of wars. Phillips, C. 355

Encyclopedia of water. Newton, D. E. 553.7

Encyclopedia of water garden plants. Speichert, C. G. 635

The **encyclopedia** of westerns. Fagen, H. 791.43

The **encyclopedia** of witches and witchcraft. See Guiley, R. E. The encyclopedia of witches, witchcraft, and Wicca 133.4

The **encyclopedia** of witches, witchcraft, and Wicca. Guiley, R. E. 133.4

Encyclopedia of women in the American West 305.4

Encyclopedia of women's autobiography 920.003

Encyclopedia of women's health issues. Gay, K. 613

Encyclopedia of women's history in America. Cullen-DuPont, K. 305.4

The **encyclopedia** of women's reproductive cancer. Turkington, C. 616.99

Encyclopedia of women's travel and exploration. Netzley, P. D. 910.4

The **Encyclopedia** of wood 674

Encyclopedia of world biography 920.003

Encyclopedia of world history 903

The **Encyclopedia** of World War I 940.3

Encyclopedia of World War II 940.53

Encyclopedias and dictionaries

See also Picture dictionaries names of languages with the subdivision *Dictionaries* and subjects with the subdivision *Dictionaries* or *Encyclopedias*

Brahms, W. B. Notable last facts 031.02

The Encyclopedia Americana 031

Famous first facts, international edition 031.02

Kane, J. N. Famous first facts 031.02

The New Encyclopaedia Britannica 031

The New York Public Library desk reference 031.02

The New York times guide to essential knowledge 031.02

Webster's new explorer desk encyclopedia 031

The World Book encyclopedia 031

The **end** of education. Postman, N. 370

The **end** of physics. Lindley, D. 539.7

The **end** of poverty. Sachs, J. D. 339.4

The **end** of the certain world [the life and science of Max Born] Greenspan, N. T. 92

Ever since Darwin. Gould, S. J.   **576.8**

Everest: mountain without mercy. Coburn, B.   **796.522**

Everglades (Fla.)
Douglas, M. S. The Everglades   **577.6**
Grunwald, M. The swamp   **975.9**

Everitt, Anthony
Augustus   **92**
Cicero   **92**

Everitt, Brian
The Cambridge dictionary of statistics   **519.5**

Everleigh, Ada, 1876-1960
About
Abbott, K. Sin in the Second City   **977.3**

Everleigh, Minna, 1878-1948
About
Abbott, K. Sin in the Second City   **977.3**

Everleigh Club (Chicago, Ill.)
Abbott, K. Sin in the Second City   **977.3**

Evers, Medgar Wiley, 1925-1963
The autobiography of Medgar Evers: a hero's life and legacy revealed through his writings, letters, and speeches   **92**

Evers-Williams, Myrlie
(ed) Evers, M. W. The autobiography of Medgar Evers: a hero's life and legacy revealed through his writings, letters, and speeches   **92**

Everson, Landis, 1926-
Everything preserved: poems, 1955-2005   **811**

Evert, Chris
About
Howard, J. The rivals [dual biography of Chris Evert and Martina Navratilova]   **92**

Every book its reader. Basbanes, N. A.   **028**

Every drop for sale. Rothfeder, J.   **333.91**

Every employee's guide to the law. Joel, L. G.   **344**

Every landlord's legal guide. Stewart, M.   **346.04**

Every man a speculator. Fraser, S.   **332.6**

Every second counts. Armstrong, L.   **92**

Every shut eye ain't asleep   **811.008**

Every week a season. Curtis, B.   **796.332**

Every woman's guide to diabetes. Eisenstat, S. A.   **616.4**

Every woman's quick & easy car care. Kachur, B.   **629.28**

Everybody was so young [biography of Gerald and Sara Murphy] Vaill, A.   **92**

Everybody's guide to small claims court. Warner, R. E.   **347**

Everyday greatness. Covey, S. R.   **170**

Everyday life in early America. Hawke, D. F.   **973.2**

Everyman, and medieval miracle plays   **822.008**

Everyman's Talmud. Cohen, A.   **296.1**

Everyone's guide to cancer therapy   **616.99**

Everything bad is good for you. Johnson, S.   **306**

Everything conceivable. Mundy, L.   **176**

The **everything** guide to pregnancy over 35. Sember, B. M.   **618.2**

Everything preserved: poems, 1955-2005. Everson, L.   **811**

Everything to gain. Carter, J.   **92**

Everything you need to know about Lyme disease and other tick-borne disorders. Vanderhoof-Forschner, K.   **616.9**

Evidence explained. Mills, E. S.   **907**

Evidence of harm. Kirby, D.   **614.4**

Evil *See* Good and evil

Evil spirits *See* Demonology

Evolution
Arthur, W. Creatures of accident   **591.3**
Avise, J. C. Genetics in the wild   **591.3**
Ayala, F. J. Darwin's gift to science and religion   **576.8**
Bloom, H. The Lucifer principle   **128**
Boulter, M. C. Extinction: evolution and the end of man   **576.8**
The Cambridge encyclopedia of human evolution   **599.93**
Carroll, S. B. Endless forms most beautiful   **571.8**
Carroll, S. B. The making of the fittest   **572.8**
Darwin, C. The Darwin reader   **576.8**
Darwin, C. The origin of species by means of natural selection, or, The preservation of favored races in the struggle for life   **576.8**
Dawkins, R. The ancestor's tale   **576.8**
Dawkins, R. Climbing Mount Improbable   **576**
Dawkins, R. River out of Eden   **576**
Dawkins, R. The selfish gene   **576**
Dennett, D. C. Darwin's dangerous idea   **146**
Diamond, J. M. The third chimpanzee   **599.93**
Duve, C. d. Life evolving   **576.8**
Duve, C. d. Vital dust   **570.1**
Eiseley, L. C. The immense journey   **576.8**
Eldredge, N. Fossils   **560**
Fortey, R. A. Life   **576.8**
Fortey, R. A. Trilobite!   **560**
Gibbons, A. The first human   **599.93**
Goodwin, B. C. How the leopard changed its spots   **576.8**
Gould, S. J. Bully for brontosaurus   **508**
Gould, S. J. Ever since Darwin   **576.8**
Gould, S. J. Hen's teeth and horse's toes   **576.8**
Gould, S. J. Leonardo's mountain of clams and the Diet of Worms   **508**
Gould, S. J. The lying stones of Marrakesh   **508**
Gould, S. J. The panda's thumb   **576.8**
Gould, S. J. The richness of life   **508**
Gould, S. J. The structure of evolutionary theory   **576.8**
Gould, S. J. Wonderful life: the Burgess Shale and the nature of history   **560**
Greenspan, S. I. The first idea   **153.7**
Gribbin, J. R. The origins of the future   **523.1**

Flesch, Rudolf Franz, 1911-1986
Why Johnny can't read—and what you can do about it **372.4**

Flesh and machines. Brooks, R. A. **629.8**

Fletcher, Sir Banister Flight, 1866-1953
Sir Banister Fletcher's A history of architecture **720.9**

Fletcher, Colin, 1922-2007
The man who walked through time **917.91**

Les **fleurs** du mal. Baudelaire, C. **841**

Flexner, James Thomas, 1908-2003
George Washington and the new nation, 1783-1793 **92**
George Washington: anguish and farewell 1793-1799 **92**
George Washington: the forge of experience, 1732-1775 **92**

Fliedl, Gottfried, 1948-
Klimt **759.36**

Flies, Artificial See Artificial flies

Flight: 100 years of aviation. Grant, R. G. **629.13**

Flinn, Frank K.
Encyclopedia of Catholicism **282**

The **floating** brothel. Rees, S. **365**

Flood, Charles Bracelen
Grant and Sherman **92**

Floods
Ryan, W. B. F. Noah's flood **930**
Mississippi River
Barry, J. M. Rising tide **977**

Floods, droughts, and climate change. Collier, M. **551.6**

Flooring instant answers. Bukowski, S. J. **690**

Floors
Bollinger, D. Hardwood floors **694**
Bukowski, S. J. Flooring instant answers **690**

Flora, Joseph M.
(ed) The Companion to southern literature. See The Companion to southern literature **810.3**

Flora: a gardener's encyclopedia **635.9**

Florence (Italy)
History
Hibbert, C. The House of Medici **920**
Levey, Sir M. Florence **945**
Martines, L. Fire in the city [biography of Girolamo Savonarola] **92**
Parks, T. Medici money **332.1**

Florey, Howard, Baron Florey, 1898-1968
See/See also pages in the following book(s):
Friedman, M. Medicine's 10 greatest discoveries **610.9**

Florey, Kitty Burns
Sister Bernadette's barking dog **428**

Florida
Belleville, B. Losing it all to sprawl **307**
Roberts, D. Dream state **975.9**
Description and travel
See/See also pages in the following book(s):
White, E. B. Essays of E.B. White **814**

Flow: the psychology of optimal experience. Csikszentmihalyi, M. **155.2**

Flower arrangement
Heffernan, C. Flowers A to Z **635.9**
Hillier, M. Flowers **745.92**
Pryke, P. Flowers, flowers! **745.92**

Flower confidential. Stewart, A. **338.1**

Flower gardening
Ellis, B. W. Taylor's guide to annuals **635.9**
Ellis, B. W. Taylor's guide to perennials **635.9**
Heffernan, C. Flowers A to Z **635.9**

Flower industry See Cut flower industry

Flower shows
Scott, A. C. Otherwise normal people **635.9**

Flowering plant families of the world **582.13**

Flowering plants of the world. See Flowering plant families of the world **582.13**

Flowers, Charles
Instability rules **509**

Flowers
See also Perennials; Roses; Wild flowers
Burger, W. C. Flowers: how they changed the world **582.13**
Flora: a gardener's encyclopedia **635.9**
Flowering plant families of the world **582.13**
Heffernan, C. Flowers A to Z **635.9**
Wells, D. 100 flowers and how they got their names **582.13**

Flowers. Hillier, M. **745.92**

Flowers, flowers!. Pryke, P. **745.92**

Flowers in the dustbin. Miller, J. **781.66**

Flu See Influenza

Flu. Kolata, G. **614.5**

Fluent in fantasy. Herald, D. T. **016.8**

Fluid mechanics
See also Hydraulic engineering

Fluids and humors, Animal See Body fluids

Fly casting
Hafele, R. Nymph-fishing rivers and streams **799.1**
L.L. Bean ultimate book of fly fishing **799.1**

The **fly** in the cathedral. Cathcart, B. **539.7**

Flying at night. Kooser, T. **811**

The **flying** book. Blatner, D. **387.7**

Flynn, Kevin, 1956-
(jt. auth) Dwyer, J. 102 minutes **974.7**

Flynn, Nick, 1960-
Another bullshit night in Suck City **92**

Flynn, Raymond
John Paul II **92**

Flynn, Roger R., 1939-
(ed) Computer sciences. See Computer sciences **004**

FM: the rise and fall of free-form rock radio. Neer, R. **791.44**

Foa, Edna B.
If your adolescent has an anxiety disorder **618.92**

Food—*Continued*
Composition
Kraus, B. Barbara Kraus' calories and carbohydrates **613.2**
Mindell, E. Dr. Earl Mindell's unsafe at any meal **613.2**
Dictionaries
International dictionary of food & cooking **641.03**
Encyclopedias
Davidson, A. The Oxford companion to food **641.03**
Larousse gastronomique **641.03**
The Oxford encyclopedia of food and drink in America **641.3**
Rolland, J. L. The food encyclopedia **641.03**
History
The Cambridge world history of food **641.3**
Fernández-Armesto, F. Near a thousand tables **641.3**
Spencer, C. British food **394.1**
Law and legislation
Hilts, P. J. Protecting America's health **353.9**

Preservation
See also Canning and preserving
Food, Cost of *See* Cost and standard of living
Food, Natural *See* Natural foods
Food additives
See/See also pages in the following book(s):
Mindell, E. Dr. Earl Mindell's unsafe at any meal **613.2**
Dictionaries
Winter, R. A consumer's dictionary of food additives **664**
Food adulteration and inspection
Hilts, P. J. Protecting America's health **353.9**
Nestle, M. Safe food **363.1**
Food allergies. Walsh, W. E. **616.97**
Food allergy
Pescatore, F. The allergy and asthma cure **616.97**
Sicherer, S. H. Understanding and managing your child's food allergies **618.92**
Food and Drug Administration (U.S.) *See* United States. Food and Drug Administration
Food as medicine. Singh Khalsa, D. **613.2**
The **food** encyclopedia. Rolland, J. L. **641.03**
Food habits *See* Eating customs
Food, inc. Pringle, P. **363.1**
Food industry
Schlosser, E. Fast food nation **394.1**
Spurlock, M. Don't eat this book **614.5**
The **food** of Portugal. Anderson, J. **641.5**
Food plants of the world. Van Wyk, B.-E. **581.6**
Food preparation *See* Cooking
Food service
See also Restaurants
Food supply
See also Agriculture

See/See also pages in the following book(s):
Diamond, J. M. Guns, germs, and steel **303.4**
Fool for love, and other plays. Shepard, S. **812**
Football
See also Soccer
Anderson, L. Carlisle vs. Army **796.332**
Bissinger, H. G. Friday night lights **796.332**
Curtis, B. Every week a season **796.332**
Dent, J. The Junction boys **796.332**
Dent, J. The undefeated **796.332**
Feinstein, J. Next man up **796.332**
Green, T. The dark side of the game **796.332**
MacCambridge, M. America's game **796.332**
St. John, W. Rammer jammer yellow hammer **796.332**
See/See also pages in the following book(s):
Barra, A. The last coach: a life of Paul "Bear" Bryant **92**
Biography
Lewis, M. The blind side **92**
Foote, Horton
Beginnings **92**
Collected plays v2 **812**
Foote, Shelby, 1916-2005
The Civil War **973.7**
For cause and comrades. McPherson, J. M. **973.7**
For liberty and glory [dual biography of George Washington and Marie Joseph Lafayette] Gaines, J. R. **92**
For love of insects. Eisner, T. **595.7**
For the glory of God. Stark, R. **201**
For the love of a dog. McConnell, P. **636.7**
For the prevention of cruelty. Beers, D. L. **179**
For women only!. Null, G. **613**
Forbes, Peter, 1947-
The gecko's foot **600**
Forbush, Edward Howe, 1858-1929
Criticism
See/See also pages in the following book(s):
White, E. B. Essays of E.B. White **814**
Birds of Massachusetts and other New England states; criticism
In White, E. B. Essays of E.B. White **814**
Forbush, William Byron 1868-1927
(ed) Foxe, J. Fox's book of martyrs **272**
Force and energy
Bodanis, D. E=mc2 **530.1**
Bodanis, D. Electric universe **537**
The **force** of character. Hillman, J. **155.67**
A **force** of nature [biography of Ernest Rutherford] Reeves, R. **92**
A **force** upon the plain. Stern, K. S. **322.4**
Forced indoctrination *See* Brainwashing
Forced labor *See* Slavery
Forces of habit. Courtwright, D. T. **362.29**

Forché, Carolyn
Blue hour   811
(tr) Darwish, M. Unfortunately, it was paradise
                                             892.7
Ford, Betty
Healing and hope   362.29
Ford, Charlotte
Crash course in reference   025.5
Ford, Ford Madox, 1873-1939
See/See also pages in the following book(s):
Gass, W. H. Finding a form: essays   814
Ford, Gerald R., 1913-2006
See/See also pages in the following book(s):
Woodward, B. Shadow   973.92
Ford, Henry, 1863-1947
                    About
Baldwin, N. Henry Ford and the Jews   92
Brinkley, D. Wheels for the world   338.7
Watts, S. The people's tycoon [biography of
Henry Ford]   92
Ford, John, 1894-1973
                    About
Davis, R. L. John Ford   92
Eyman, S. Print the legend [biography of John
Ford]   92
Gallagher, T. John Ford   791.43
Ford, Mark, 1962-
(ed) O'Hara, F. Frank O'Hara: selected poems
                                          811
Ford, Paul F.
Companion to Narnia   823.009
Ford (Betty) Center *See* Betty Ford Center
Ford Motor Co.
Brinkley, D. Wheels for the world   338.7
Forecasting
        See also Economic forecasting; Weather
forecasting
The 21st century   909.83
Dyson, F. J. The sun, the genome, & the
Internet   303.4
Jenkins, P. The new faces of Christianity
                                          270
Foreign aid
Easterly, W. The white man's burden
                                        338.91
Sachs, J. D. The end of poverty   339.4
Foreign aid program *See* Foreign aid
Foreign babes in Beijing. DeWoskin, R.   951
Foreign economic relations *See* International economic relations
Foreign population *See* Immigrants
Foreign relations *See* International relations
Foreign trade *See* International trade
Foreigners *See* Immigrants
Foreman, Amanda, 1968-
Georgiana, Duchess of Devonshire   92
Foreman, Laura, d. 2001
Alexander the Conqueror   92
Forensic anthropology
Bass, W. M. Death's acre   614
Maples, W. R. Dead men do tell tales   614
Pringle, H. A. The mummy congress   393

See/See also pages in the following book(s):
Massie, R. K. The Romanovs   947.08
Forensic medicine *See* Medical jurisprudence
Forensic science. Brenner, J. C.   363.2
Forensic science glossary. See Brenner, J. C. Forensic science   363.2
Forensic sciences
Evans, C. The casebook of forensic detection
                                          614
Lee, H. C. Blood evidence   614
Wagner, E. J. The science of Sherlock Holmes
                                        363.2
Wecht, C. H. Tales from the morgue   614
Zugibe, F. T. Dissecting death   614
                  Dictionaries
Bell, S. The Facts on File dictionary of forensic
science   363.2
Brenner, J. C. Forensic science   363.2
                 Encyclopedias
Bell, S. Encyclopedia of forensic science
                                        363.2
Conklin, B. G. Encyclopedia of forensic science
                                        363.2
Forest ecology
        See also Rain forest ecology
Forest fires
Brown, D. Under a flaming sky   634.9
Taylor, M. A. Jumping fire   634.9
Forest plants
Darke, R. The American woodland garden
                                        635.9
Forest reserves
        See also National parks and reserves
Forests and forestry
        See also Trees
Forever free. Foner, E.   973.8
The **forger's** spell. Dolnick, E.   92
Forgery
        See also Literary forgeries
Innes, B. Fakes & forgeries   364.1
Worrall, S. The poet and the murderer
                                        364.1
Forgery of works of art *See* Art—Forgeries
The **forgetting:** Alzheimer's, portrait of an epidemic. Shenk, D.   616.8
Forgiveness
Kraybill, D. B. Amish grace   364.152
Wiesenthal, S. The sunflower   179.7
Forgotten armies. Bayly, C. A.   940.54
The **forgotten** fifth. Nash, G. B.   326
The **forgotten** man. Shlaes, A.   973.91
The **forgotten** pollinators. Buchmann, S.   577
Former Soviet republics
        See also Soviet Union
Milner-Gulland, R. R. Cultural atlas of Russia
and the former Soviet Union   947
Formica, Ronald J.
(ed) Famous first facts about the environment.
See Famous first facts about the environment
                                        363.7
Formosa *See* Taiwan

The **future** of the wild. Adams, J. S.　　333.95
Future shock *See* Culture conflict
Future shock. Toffler, A.　　303.4
Futurology *See* Forecasting

G

G.I.'s *See* Soldiers—United States
Gabler, Neal
　Winchell　　92
Gabriel, Philip
　(tr) Murakami, H. Underground　　364.1
Gachet, Paul, 1828-1909
　　　About
　Saltzman, C. Portrait of Dr. Gachet
　　　　759.9492
Gaddis, John Lewis
　Surprise, security, and the American experience
　　　355
Gaffers, grips, and best boys. Taub, E.　791.43
Gage, Nicholas
　Eleni [biography of Eleni Gatzoyiannis]　92
　Greek fire　　92
Gager, John G.
　The origins of anti-Semitism　　296.3
Gaia hypothesis
　Lovelock, J. The ages of Gaia　　570.1
　Margulis, L. Symbiotic planet　　576.8
Gaines, James R.
　For liberty and glory [dual biography of George
　Washington and Marie Joseph Lafayette]
　　　92
Gaines, Leonard M.
　(jt. auth) Boettcher, J. C. Industry research using
　the economic census　　338
Gaines, Patrice
　Moments of grace　　170
Gaius Caesar *See* Caligula, Emperor of Rome,
　12-41
Galaburda, Albert M., 1948-
　(jt. auth) Ratey, J. J. A user's guide to the brain
　　　612.8
Galassi, Jonathan
　(tr) Montale, E. Collected poems, 1920-1954
　　　851
Galaxie 500 (Musical group)
　Wareham, D. Black postcards　　92
Galaxy (Milky Way) *See* Milky Way
**Galba, Servius Sulpicius, Emperor of Rome, 3
B.C.-69**
　See/See also pages in the following book(s):
　Suetonius Tranquillus, C. The twelve Caesars
　　　878
Galbraith, John Kenneth, 1908-2006
　The affluent society　　330
　The Great Crash, 1929　　338.5
　Name-dropping　　973.9
Galdikas, Birutė
　Reflections of Eden　　599.8

Gale directory of databases　　025.04
Gale directory of publications. See Gale directory
　of publications and broadcast media
　　　070.025
Gale directory of publications and broadcast media
　　　070.025
The **Gale** encyclopedia of alternative medicine
　　　615.5
The **Gale** encyclopedia of children's health
　　　618.92
Gale encyclopedia of everyday law　　349
The **Gale** encyclopedia of medicine　　610.3
The **Gale** encyclopedia of mental disorders. See
　The Gale encyclopedia of mental health
　　　616.89
The **Gale** encyclopedia of mental health
　　　616.89
The **Gale** encyclopedia of psychology　　150.3
Gale encyclopedia of science　　503
Galens, David
　(ed) Literary movements for students. See Liter-
　ary movements for students　　809
Galento, Domenick Anthony *See* Galento, Tony,
　1910-1979
Galento, Tony, 1910-1979
　　　About
　Monninger, J. Two Ton　　92
Galilei, Galileo, 1564-1642
　　　About
　Shea, W. R. Galileo in Rome　　92
　Sobel, D. Galileo's daughter　　92
Galilei, Maria Celeste *See* Maria Celeste, 1600-
　1634
Galilei, Virginia *See* Maria Celeste, 1600-1634
Galileo *See* Galilei, Galileo, 1564-1642
Galileo in Rome. Shea, W. R.　　92
Galileo's daughter. Sobel, D.　　92
Galimberti Jarman, Beatriz
　(ed) The Oxford Spanish dictionary. See The
　Oxford Spanish dictionary　　463
Galison, Peter Louis
　Einstein's clocks and Poincaré's maps　　529
Gall, Gilbert J.
　(jt. auth) Zieger, R. H. American workers,
　American unions　　331.8
Gallagher, Gary W.
　The Confederate War　　973.7
Gallagher, Maggie
　(jt. auth) Waite, L. J. The case for marriage
　　　306.8
Gallagher, Tag
　John Ford　　791.43
Gallagher, Tess
　Dear ghosts,　　811
Gallagher, Tim
　The grail bird　　598
Gallaudet, T. H. (Thomas Hopkins), 1787-1851
　See/See also pages in the following book(s):
　Lepore, J. A is for American　　306.44
Gallaudet, Thomas Hopkins *See* Gallaudet, T. H.
　(Thomas Hopkins), 1787-1851

Garner, Abigail
Families like mine   **306.8**

Garner, Bryan A.
Garner's modern American usage   **423**
(ed) Black's law dictionary. See Black's law dictionary   **340.03**

Garner's modern American usage. Garner, B. A.
    423

Garratt, Richard
(il) Day, T. Oceans   **551.46**

Garraty, John Arthur, 1920-2007
(ed) American national biography. See American national biography   **920.003**

Garrett, Laurie
Betrayal of trust   **362.1**
The coming plague   **614.4**

Garrison, Lucy McKim
(jt. auth) Allen, W. F. Slave songs of the United States   **781.62**

Garten, Ina
Barefoot Contessa family style   **641.5**

Garton Ash, Timothy
The file   **327.12**
Free world   **909.08**

Gaskell, Elizabeth Cleghorn, 1810-1865
The life of Charlotte Brontë   **92**

Gaskin, Ina May, 1940-
Ina May's guide to childbirth   **618.4**

Gaskin, J. C. A. (John Charles Addison)
(ed) Hobbes, T. Leviathan   **320.1**

Gaskin, John Charles Addison See Gaskin, J. C. A. (John Charles Addison)

Gaspipe [biography of Anthony "Gaspipe" Casso] Carlo, P.   **92**

Gass, William H., 1924-
Finding a form: essays   **814**

Gasset, José Ortega y See Ortega y Gasset, José, 1883-1955

Gaster, Theodor Herzl, 1906-1992
(ed) Dead Sea scrolls. The Dead Sea scriptures
    229

Gastrointestinal system
Encyclopedias
Minocha, A. The encyclopedia of the digestive system and digestive disorders   **616.3**

The **gate**. Bizot, F.   **959.6**

The **gatekeepers**. Steinberg, J.   **378**

Gately, Iain
Tobacco   **394.1**

Gates, Alexander E.
A to Z of earth scientists   **920.003**
Encyclopedia of earthquakes and volcanoes
    551.2

Gates, Henry Louis
The African-American century   **920**
Colored people   **92**
The future of the race   **305.8**
Thirteen ways of looking at a black man
    920
Wonders of the African world   **960**
(ed) African American lives. See African American lives   **920**

(ed) The African American national biography.
See The African American national biography
    920.003
(ed) Africana: the encyclopedia of the African and African American experience. See Africana: the encyclopedia of the African and African American experience   **909**
(ed) The Norton anthology of African American literature. See The Norton anthology of African American literature   **810.8**

Gates, Robert M.
From the shadows   **327.73**

A **gathering** of wonders. Wallace, J.   **508**

The **gathering** storm. Churchill, Sir W.   **940.53**

Gatzoyiannis, Eleni
About
Gage, N. Eleni [biography of Eleni Gatzoyiannis]   **92**

Gaudynski, Diane
Guide to machine quilting   **746.46**

Gauguin, Paul, 1848-1903
About
Gayford, M. The yellow house [dual biography of Vincent Van Gogh and Paul Gauguin]
    92
Silverman, D. Van Gogh and Gauguin   **759.4**
Thomson, B. Gauguin   **92**

Gaulle, Charles de, 1890-1970
About
Williams, C. The last great Frenchman   **92**
See/See also pages in the following book(s):
Kissinger, H. Diplomacy   **327.73**

Gauss, Carl Friedrich, 1777-1855
See/See also pages in the following book(s):
Bell, E. T. Men of mathematics   **920**
Mlodinow, L. Euclid's window   **516**

Gaustad, Edwin Scott
New historical atlas of religion in America
    200.9
Roger Williams   **92**

Gautama Buddha
About
Armstrong, K. Buddha   **92**
Mishra, P. An end to suffering   **294.3**

Gawain, Shakti
Creative visualization   **153.3**

Gawain and the Grene Knight (Middle English poem)
Sir Gawain and the Green Knight   **821**

Gawande, Atul
Better   **616**

Gay, John, 1685-1732
The beggar's opera   **822**

Gay, Kathlyn, 1930-
Encyclopedia of women's health issues   **613**

Gay, Peter, 1923-
Freud   **92**
A Godless Jew   **150.19**
My German question   **92**
The rise of modern paganism   **190**
The science of freedom   **190**
(ed) Freud, S. The Freud reader   **150.19**

Gay, Ruth
The Jews of Germany   **943**

Georgano, George Nicolas *See* Georgano, G. N. (George Nicolas)

Georgano, Nick *See* Georgano, G. N. (George Nicolas)

George III, King of Great Britain, 1738-1820
About
Tillyard, S. K. A royal affair   920
See/See also pages in the following book(s):
Fraser, F. Princesses   920

George V, King of Great Britain, 1865-1936
About
Clay, C. King, Kaiser, Tsar   920

George, Henry, 1839-1897
See/See also pages in the following book(s):
Heilbroner, R. L. The worldly philosophers   330.1

George, John H.
(jt. auth) Boller, P. F. They never said it   808.88

George, Nelson
Hip hop America   781.64
(ed) Best music writing 2008. See Best music writing 2008   781.64

George, Rose, 1969-
The big necessity   363.7

George Gershwin. Hyland, W. G.   92

George Mason, forgotten founder. Broadwater, J.   92

George-Warren, Holly
Public cowboy no. 1 [biography of Gene Autry]   92
(ed) The Rolling Stone illustrated history of rock & roll. See The Rolling Stone illustrated history of rock & roll   781.66

Georgia
History
See/See also pages in the following book(s):
Boorstin, D. J. The Americans: The colonial experience   973.2
Social life and customs
Carter, J. An hour before daylight   92

Georgia O'Keeffe: a life. Robinson, R.   92

Georgiana, Duchess of Devonshire. Foreman, A.   92

The **Georgics** of Virgil. Virgil   872

Gerardi, Juan, d. 1998
Assassination
Goldman, F. The art of political murder   972.81

Gerasimo, Luisa
(comp) McGraw-Hill's big red book of resumes. See McGraw-Hill's big red book of resumes   650.14

Gerberg, Mort
(ed) Joy in Mudville. See Joy in Mudville   796.357

Gerding, Stephanie K.
Grants for libraries   025.1

Gerdts, William H.
American impressionism   759.13

Gerges, Fawaz A.
Journey of the Jihadist   322.4

Gerhards, Paul
How to sell what you make   658.8

Geriatrics *See* Elderly—Diseases; Elderly—Health and hygiene

Gerlach, Julia R.
(comp) Creative beading. See Creative beading   745.594

Germ theory of disease
Bakalar, N. Where the germs are   616
Biddle, W. A field guide to germs   616

Germ warfare *See* Biological warfare

German cooking
Anderson, J. The new German cookbook   641.5

German Democratic Republic *See* Germany (East)

German language
Dictionaries
Cassell's German dictionary   433
Oxford-Duden German dictionary   433
Random House Webster's German-English, English-German dictionary   433

German literature
Bio-bibliography
Encyclopedia of German literature   830.3
Garland, H. B. The Oxford companion to German literature   830.3
Dictionaries
Garland, H. B. The Oxford companion to German literature   830.3
Encyclopedias
Encyclopedia of German literature   830.3
History and criticism
The Cambridge history of German literature   830.9
Sebald, W. G. On the natural history of destruction   834

German poetry
Collections
Twentieth-century German poetry   831.008

Germano, William P., 1950-
Getting it published   070.5

The **Germans**. Craig, G. A.   943

Germany
Civilization
Craig, G. A. The Germans   943
Description and travel
Gorra, M. E. The bells in their silence   943
Ethnic relations
Smith, H. W. The butcher's tale   943.08
Foreign relations—United States
Beschloss, M. R. The conquerors: Roosevelt, Truman, and the destruction of Hitler's Germany, 1941-1945   940.53
History
Craig, G. A. The Germans   943
Craig, G. A. Germany, 1866-1945   943.08
Fulbrook, M. A concise history of Germany   943
Schulze, H. Germany   943
Stern, F. R. Five Germanys I have known   943.08
History—0-1517
Tacitus, C. Complete works of Tacitus   878

Handbook of computer networks   **004.6**

Handbook of death & dying   **306.9**

Handbook of denominations in the United States. Mead, F. S.   **280**

The **handbook** of knots. Pawson, D.   **623.88**

Handbook of model rocketry. Stine, G. H.   **629.47**

Handbook of North American Indians   **970.004**

The **Handbook** of private schools   **370.25**

Handbook of the best private schools of the United States and Canada. See The Handbook of private schools   **370.25**

Handbook of United States coins 2009   **737.4**

Handbook to life in ancient Egypt. David, A. R.   **932**

Handbook to life in ancient Greece. Adkins, L.   **938**

The **handbook** to wills, funerals, and probate. Hughes, T. E.   **346**

Handel, George Frideric, 1685-1759
About
Hogwood, C. Handel   **92**
See/See also pages in the following book(s):
Grout, D. J. A history of western music   **780.9**

Handicapped
See also Physically handicapped
Civil rights
Perritt, H. H., Jr. Americans with Disabilities Act handbook   **344**
Encyclopedias
Encyclopedia of disability   **362.4**

Handicapped children
See also Socially handicapped children
Brodey, D. The elephant in the playroom   **306.8**
Greenspan, S. I. The child with special needs   **362.1**

Handicapped students
Mooney, J. The short bus   **92**

Handicraft
See also Arts and crafts movement; Nature craft
Arendt, M. Altered art for the first time   **745.5**
Banker, S. M. 1001 full-size patterns, projects & ideas   **745.5**
Engelbreit, M. Mary Engelbreit's children's companion   **645**
Foxfire 40th anniversary book   **975.8**
Gerhards, P. How to sell what you make   **658.8**
Kilby, J. E. By hand   **745**
Ledoux, J. Abode à la mode   **747**
Lowell, C. Christopher Lowell's one-of-a-kind decorating projects   **747.2**
Ludens, R. Teach yourself visually scrapbooking   **745.593**
Marshall, M. H. Shell chic   **745.55**
Michaels book of wedding crafts   **745.594**
Stewart, M. Great American wreaths   **745.92**
Taylor, T. Altered art   **745.5**
Ultimate Christmas book   **745.5**

Ure, S. The altered book scrapbook   **745.593**

White, C. Uniquely felt   **746**

Handlin, Oscar, 1915-
The uprooted   **325.73**

Hands on dyeing. Blumenthal, B.   **746.1**

Hands to work. Hancock, L.   **361.6**

Handspring, Hiram *See* Laughlin, James, 1914-1997

The **handweaver's** pattern directory. Dixon, A.   **746.1**

Handwriting
See also Calligraphy

The **Handy** science answer book   **500**

The **handy** weather answer book. Lyons, W. A.   **551.6**

Haner, Jim, 1957-
Soccerhead   **796.334**

Haney, Eric L.
Inside Delta Force   **356**

Hanging Captain Gordon. Soodalter, R.   **326**

Hanks, Patrick
(ed) Dictionary of American family names. See Dictionary of American family names   **929.4**

Hanks, Reuel R.
Central Asia   **958**

Hanlan, James P.
(ed) Historical encyclopedia of American labor. See Historical encyclopedia of American labor   **331.8**

Hansberry, Lorraine, 1930-1965
A raisin in the sun   **812**
To be young, gifted, and Black   **92**

Hansen, Carol Rae
(jt. auth) Devine, C. Human rights   **323**

Hansen, Eric
Orchid fever   **635.9**

Hanson, Elizabeth, 1962-
Animal attractions   **590.73**

Hanson, Jon
Good debt, bad debt   **332.024**

Hanson, Victor Davis
Carnage and culture   **904**
The soul of battle   **355**

Hanssen, Robert Philip
About
Vise, D. A. The bureau and the mole   **327.12**
Wise, D. Spy: the inside story of how the FBI's Robert Hanssen betrayed America   **327.12**

Hanukkah
See/See also pages in the following book(s):
Strassfeld, M. The Jewish holidays   **296.4**

The **happiest** baby on the block. Karp, H.   **649**

Happily ever after: a guide to reading interests in romance fiction. See Ramsdell, K. Romance fiction   **016.8**

Happiness
Browne, J. The nine fantasies that will ruin your life and the eight realities that will save you   **158**

Historiography—*Continued*

Schama, S. Dead certainties 907

Tuchman, B. W. Practicing history 907

History

> *See also* Ancient history; Conspiracies; Military history; Naval history; World history

Miscellanea

Stewart, R. Mysteries of history 902

Outlines, syllabi, etc.

Encyclopedia of world history 903

Philosophy

Berlin, Sir I. The sense of reality 901

Bloom, H. The Lucifer principle 128

Spengler, O. The decline of the West, volume one 901

Research

Mills, E. S. Evidence explained 907

Sources

Mills, E. S. Evidence explained 907

Study and teaching

Lefkowitz, M. R. Not out of Africa 960

History, Ancient *See* Ancient history

History, Modern *See* Modern history

The **history** boys. Bennett, A. 822

History of AIDS. Grmek, M. D. 616.97

History of art. See Janson, H. W. Janson's history of art 709

A **history** of art in Africa. Visonà, M. B. 709.6

History of astronomy 520.3

The **history** of Australia. Clarke, F. G. 994

A **history** of Britain. Schama, S. 941

A **history** of Christianity. Chadwick, O. 270

A **history** of God. Armstrong, K. 200

The **history** of hell. Turner, A. K. 200

The **history** of India. McLeod, J. 954

A **history** of Iraq. Tripp, C. 956.7

A **history** of Israel. Bregman, A. 956.94

A **history** of Israel. Sachar, H. M. 956.94

The **history** of Japan. Perez, L. G. 952

A **history** of mathematics. Boyer, C. B. 510

The **history** of Mexico. Kirkwood, B. 972

History of modern science and mathematics 509

A **history** of molecular biology. Morange, M. 572.8

A **history** of narrative film. Cook, D. A. 791.43

The **history** of pirates. Konstam, A. 910.4

History of Plymouth Plantation. See Bradford, W. Of Plymouth Plantation, 1620-1647 974.4

A **History** of private life v1 909

A **History** of private life v2 909

A **History** of private life v3 909

A **History** of private life v4 909

A **History** of private life v5 909

A **history** of psychiatry. Shorter, E. 616.89

A **history** of Russia. Riasanovsky, N. V. 947

A **history** of Russian literature. Terras, V. 891.7

The **History** of science and religion in the western tradition 201

The **History** of science in the United States 509

A **history** of South Africa. Thompson, L. M. 968

The **history** of television, 1942 to 2000. Abramson, A. 621.388

A **history** of the Arab peoples. Hourani, A. H. 909

History of the conquest of Mexico. Prescott, W. H. 972

The **history** of the decline and fall of the Roman Empire. See Gibbon, E. The decline and fall of the Roman empire 937

A **history** of the devil. Messadié, G. 200

A **history** of the Federal Reserve v1. Meltzer, A. H. 332.1

A **history** of the French new wave cinema. Neupert, R. J. 791.43

The **history** of the Gulag. Khlevniuk, O. V. 365

History of the Internet: a chronology, 1843 to the present. See The Internet 004.6

A **history** of the Jews. Johnson, P. 909

A **history** of the Jews in America. Sachar, H. M. 305.8

A **history** of the Jews in the modern world. Sachar, H. M. 909

History of the mass media in the United States 302.23

A **history** of the Ostrogoths. Burns, T. S. 909.07

The **history** of the Peloponnesian War. Thucydides 938

History of the theatre. Brockett, O. G. 792.09

A **history** of the Third Reich. Hay, J. 943.086

History of the twentieth century. Gilbert, M. 909.82

History of the U.S. Navy. Love, R. W. 359

A **history** of the wife. Yalom, M. 306.8

A history of the world in 6 glasses. Standage, T. 394.1

A **history** of twentieth-century Russia. Service, R. 947.086

A **history** of Western architecture. Watkin, D. 720.9

A **history** of western music. Grout, D. J. 780.9

A **history** of Western philosophy. Russell, B. 109

A **history** of Zionism. Laqueur, W. 956.94

History on trial. Lipstadt, D. E. 940.53

The **History** today companion to British history. See The Columbia companion to British history 941

Hitchcock, Alfred, 1899-1980

About

Auiler, D. Vertigo 791.43

Chandler, C. It's only a movie [biography of Alfred Hitchcock] 92

Homes, A. M.
The mistress's daughter   **92**

Homestead Grays (Baseball team)
Snyder, B. Beyond the shadow of the Senators
          796.357

Homicide
See also Trials (Homicide)
Brown, E. The condemnation of Little B
          364.1
Bugliosi, V. Helter skelter   **364.1**
Burke, T. M. The Paradiso files   **364.152**
Buss, D. M. The murderer next door
          364.152
Capote, T. In cold blood   **364.1**
Carrère, E. The adversary   **364.1**
Diebel, L. Betrayed   **364.152**
Douglas, J. E. The cases that haunt us
          364.1
Gourevitch, P. A cold case   **364.1**
Jones, A. Women who kill   **364.1**
Junger, S. A death in Belmont   **364.152**
Kersten, J. Journal of the dead   **364.1**
King, J. Hate crime: the story of a dragging in
    Jasper, Texas   **364.1**
Larson, E. The devil in the white city   **364.1**
Larson, E. Thunderstruck   **364.152**
Leake, J. Entering Hades   **364.152**
Lévy, B. H. Who killed Daniel Pearl?   **364.1**
May, G. The informant   **364.152**
Maynard, J. Internal combustion   **364.152**
McGinniss, J. Fatal vision   **364.1**
Olsen, J. I: the creation of a serial killer
          364.1
Rivard, R. Trail of feathers: searching for Philip
    True   **364.152**
Rule, A. —and never let her go   **364.1**
Rule, A. Too late to say goodbye   **364.152**
Salamon, J. Facing the wind   **364.1**
Schiller, L. Perfect murder, perfect town
          364.1
Smith, H. W. The butcher's tale   **943.08**
Stashower, D. The beautiful cigar girl
          364.152
Stewart, J. B. Blind eye   **364.1**
Summerscale, K. The suspicions of Mr. Whicher
          364.152
The Ultimate Jack the Ripper companion
          364.1
Worrall, S. The poet and the murderer
          364.1
Encyclopedias
Newton, M. The encyclopedia of serial killers
          364.03

Homosexual marriage *See* Same-sex marriage

Homosexual parents *See* Gay parents

Homosexuality
See also Lesbianism
Bagemihl, B. Biological exuberance   **591.56**
Encyclopedia of lesbian and gay histories and
    cultures   **306.76**
Encyclopedia of lesbian, gay, bisexual, and
    transgender history in America   **306.76**
Faderman, L. Gay L.A.   **306.76**
Marcus, E. Is it a choice?   **306.76**

Mondimore, F. M. A natural history of homo-
    sexuality   **306.76**
Robb, G. Strangers: homosexual love in the
    nineteenth century   **306.76**
See/See also pages in the following book(s):
Pollack, W. S. Real boys   **305.23**

Homosexuality in motion pictures
Mann, W. J. Behind the screen   **791.43**

Homosexuals, Female *See* Lesbians

Homosexuals, Male *See* Gay men

Honan, Park
Christopher Marlowe   **92**

Honderich, Ted
(ed) The Oxford companion to philosophy. See
    The Oxford companion to philosophy   **103**

Honesty
See also Truthfulness and falsehood

Honey, Michael K.
Going down Jericho Road   **331.8**

Honeybee culture *See* Beekeeping

Hong, Tan Mew *See* Tan, Mew Hong

Hong Kong (China)
Kemenade, W. v. China, Hong Kong, Taiwan,
    Inc.   **951**

Hong Pen *See* Kang, Kek Ieu

Hong Xiuquan *See* Hung, Hsiu-ch'üan, 1814-1864

An **honorable** defeat. Davis, W. C.   **973.7**

Honour, Hugh
(ed) The Penguin dictionary of architecture and
    landscape architecture. See The Penguin dic-
    tionary of architecture and landscape architec-
    ture   **720.3**

Hood, Ann, 1956-
Comfort   **92**

Hooded Americanism: the history of the Ku Klux
    Klan. Chalmers, D. M.   **322.4**

Hooked on horror. Fonseca, A. J.   **016.8**

Hooker, Joseph, 1814-1879
See/See also pages in the following book(s):
Sears, S. W. Chancellorsville   **973.7**

Hooks, Bell
Remembered rapture   **808**
Salvation   **306.7**
Wounds of passion   **92**

Hoop roots. Wideman, J. E.   **92**

Hooper, Brad
The short story readers' advisory   **809.3**

Hooper, Dan, 1976-
Dark cosmos   **523.1**

Hooper, Judith
Of moths and men   **576.8**

Hoops. Jackson, M.   **811**

Hoover, Herbert, 1874-1964
See/See also pages in the following book(s):
Hofstadter, R. The American political tradition,
    and the men who made it   **973**

Hoover, J. Edgar (John Edgar), 1895-1972
About
From the secret files of J. Edgar Hoover
          363.2
Gentry, C. J. Edgar Hoover   **92**

Infection and infectious diseases *See* Communicable diseases

Infeld, Leopold, 1898-1968
(jt. auth) Einstein, A. The evolution of physics   **530**

The **Inferno**. Dante Alighieri   **851**

Infertility
    See also Childlessness; Sterilization (Birth control)
Bruce, D. F. Making a baby   **618.2**
Marrs, R. P. Dr. Richard Marrs' fertility book   **616.6**
Silber, S. J. How to get pregnant   **616.2**

Infidel. Hirsi Ali, A.   **92**

Infidelity, Marital *See* Adultery

Infinite
Barrow, J. D. The infinite book   **111**

The **infinite** book. Barrow, J. D.   **111**

The **infinite** gift. Yang, C.   **401**

Inflammatory bowel diseases
    See also Intestines—Diseases
Zonderman, J. Understanding Crohn disease and ulcerative colitis   **616.3**

The **inflationary** universe. Guth, A. H.   **523.1**

Influence: the psychology of persuasion. Cialdini, R. B.   **153.8**

Influenza
    See also Avian influenza
Barry, J. M. The great influenza   **614.5**
Kolata, G. Flu   **614.5**
See/See also pages in the following book(s):
Oldstone, M. B. A. Viruses, plagues, and history   **614.4**

The **informant**. May, G.   **364.152**

Information networks
    See also Computer networks; Internet

Information science
    See also Information theory

Information services
    See also Business—Information services; Electronic publishing; Health—Information services; Hotlines (Telephone counseling); Medicine—Information services

Information society
    See also Information technology
Friedman, T. L. The world is flat   **330.9**
Lessig, L. The future of ideas   **346.04**
Reich, R. B. The future of success   **306**

Information storage and retrieval systems *See* Information systems

Information systems
    See also Digital libraries
Mitchell, A. M. Cataloging and organizing digital resources   **025.3**
    Directories
Gale directory of databases   **025.04**

Information technology
Bolan, K. Technology made simple   **025**
Farkas, M. Social software in libraries   **025.5**

Information theory
Seife, C. Decoding the universe   **006.3**

Informed decisions   **616.99**

Inge, William, 1913-1973
4 plays   **812**

Ingenious pursuits. Jardine, L.   **509**

Ingram, Jay
The barmaid's brain and other strange tales from science   **500**

Inherit the wind. Lawrence, J.   **812**

Inheritance and succession
Clifford, D. Make your own living trust   **346.05**

Inheriting the Holy Land. Miller, J.   **956.94**

Inheriting the revolution. Appleby, J. O.   **973**

Inhuman bondage. Davis, D. B.   **326**

Inhumane society. Fox, M. W.   **179**

Initiation rites
    See also Circumcision

Initiative and referendum *See* Referendum

Injuries *See* Accidents; First aid

Inland navigation
Heat Moon, W. L. River-horse   **917.3**

Inner cities
Kozol, J. Amazing grace   **362.7**

Inner voices. Howard, R.   **811**

Innes, Brian, 1928-
Fakes & forgeries   **364.1**

Innovations, Technological *See* Technological innovations

Inns *See* Hotels and motels

Innuit *See* Inuit

Inoculation *See* Vaccination

An **inordinate** fondness for beetles. Evans, A. V.   **595.7**

An **inquiry** into the nature and causes of the wealth of nations. See Smith, A. The wealth of nations   **330.1**

Inquisition
Kamen, H. The Spanish Inquisition   **272**
Pérez, J. The Spanish Inquisition   **272**

Insane *See* Mentally ill

    Hospitals
    See Psychiatric hospitals

The **insanity** offense. Torrey, E. F.   **362.1**

Inscriptions
    See also Graffiti

Inscriptions, Cuneiform *See* Cuneiform inscriptions

Insect lives   **595.7**

Insect pests
Waldbauer, G. Insights from insects   **632**

Insect societies. Wilson, E. O.   **595.7**

Insects
    See also Ants; Butterflies; Grasshoppers; Moths
Alcock, J. In a desert garden   **595.7**
Alderton, D. Firefly encyclopedia of the vivarium   **639.3**
Eisner, T. For love of insects   **595.7**
Eisner, T. Secret weapons   **595.7**

Insects—*Continued*
The Firefly encyclopedia of insects and spiders
595.7
Insect lives **595.7**
Marshall, S. A. Insects: their natural history and diversity **595.7**
Milne, L. J. The Audubon Society field guide to North American insects and spiders **595.7**
Waldbauer, G. Millions of monarchs, bunches of beetles **595.7**
Waldbauer, G. What good are bugs? **595.7**
Wilson, E. O. Insect societies **595.7**
See/See also pages in the following book(s):
Waldbauer, G. Insects through the seasons
595.7

Encyclopedias
Encyclopedia of insects **595.7**

Insects, Injurious and beneficial *See* Insect pests

Insects through the seasons. Waldbauer, G.
595.7

Insecure at last. Ensler, E. **305.4**

Inside Delta Force. Haney, E. L. **356**

Inside Inside. Lipton, J. **792**

Inside Rikers. Wynn, J. **365**

Inside the Actors Studio (Television program)
Lipton, J. Inside Inside **792**

Inside the CIA. Kessler, R. **327.12**

Inside the Crips. Simpson, C. **92**

Inside the hurricane. Davies, P. **551.55**

Inside the Pentagon papers **959.704**

Inside the red mansion. August, O. **951.05**

Inside the Third Reich. Speer, A. **943.086**

Inside the Vatican. Reese, T. J. **282**

Inside the Victorian home. Flanders, J. **306**

Inside women's college basketball. Kent, R. G.
796.323

Insider's guide to book editors, publishers, and literary agents. See Herman, J. Jeff Herman's guide to book publishers, editors, & literary agents 2008 **070.5**

An **insider's** guide to the UN. Fasulo, L. M.
341.23

Insights from insects. Waldbauer, G. **632**

Insomnia
Greene, G. Insomniac **616.8**
Max, D. T. The family that couldn't sleep
616.8

Insomniac. Greene, G. **616.8**

Inspiration *See* Creation (Literary, artistic, etc.)

Instability rules. Flowers, C. **509**

Instinct
Menninger, K. A. Love against hate **150.19**

Institutions, Religious *See* Religious institutions

Instruction *See* Teaching

Instructional materials centers
See also School libraries

Instrumental music
See/See also pages in the following book(s):
Grout, D. J. A history of western music
780.9

Instrumentation and orchestration
Piston, W. Orchestration **784**

Instruments of science **502.8**

Insulin
Steward, H. L. The new sugar busters!
613.2

Insulin pump therapy demystified. Kaplan-Mayer, G. **616.4**

Insulin pumps
Kaplan-Mayer, G. Insulin pump therapy demystified **616.4**

Insurance, State and compulsory *See* Social security

Insurgency
Kurlansky, M. 1968 **909.82**

Integration in education *See* School integration

Integrity. Carter, S. L. **170**

Intel Corp.
Tedlow, R. S. Andy Grove **92**

Intellect
Arendt, H. The life of the mind **153**
Baars, B. J. In the theater of consciousness
153
Calvin, W. H. How brains think **153.9**
Goleman, D. Emotional intelligence **152.4**
Goleman, D. Social intelligence **158**
Johnson, S. Everything bad is good for you
306
Jolly, A. Lucy's legacy **599.93**
Sagan, C. The dragons of Eden **153**
See/See also pages in the following book(s):
Deacon, T. W. The symbolic species **153.6**
Glynn, I. An anatomy of thought **612.8**
Pinker, S. How the mind works **153**

Intellectual freedom
Intellectual freedom manual **323.44**

Intellectual freedom manual **323.44**

Intellectual life
James, C. Cultural amnesia **920**

Intellectual property. Wherry, T. L. **346.04**

Intellectuals
James, C. Cultural amnesia **920**
Soviet Union
Chamberlain, L. Lenin's private war **325**

Intelligence *See* Intellect

Intelligence, Artificial *See* Artificial intelligence

Intelligence of animals *See* Animal intelligence

Intelligence service
See also Espionage
Germany (East)
Garton Ash, T. The file **327.12**
Great Britain
Dorril, S. MI6 **327.12**
United States
Herrington, S. A. Traitors among us **327.12**
Kessler, R. Inside the CIA **327.12**
McCoy, A. W. A question of torture **323.4**
Miller, J. The cell: inside the 9/11 plot and why the FBI and CIA failed to stop it **973.931**
Prados, J. Presidents' secret wars **327.12**
Stinnett, R. B. Day of deceit **940.54**
Theoharis, A. G. Chasing spies **327.12**
Weiner, T. Legacy of ashes **327.12**

The **landmark** Thucydides. Thucydides   **938**

Landmarks, Literary *See* Literary landmarks

Landmarks in mechanical engineering   **621**

Landmarks in western science. Whitfield, P.
    509

Landon, Margaret, 1903-1993
  Anna and the King of Siam [biography of Anna
    Harriette Leonowens]   **92**

Landsberg, Brian K.
  (ed) Major acts of Congress. See Major acts of
    Congress   **348**

Landscape architecture
  The Oxford companion to the garden   **712**
  Step-by-step yard & garden basics   **635**
  Van Sweden, J. A. Architecture in the garden
    712

Dictionaries
  Curl, J. S. A dictionary of architecture and land-
    scape architecture   **720.3**

Landscape gardening
  See also Garden design
  Adam, J. Landscape planning   **635**
  Beginner's guide to gardening   **635**
  Buchanan, R. Taylor's master guide to landscap-
    ing   **712**
  Dirr, M. Dirr's Hardy trees and shrubs
    635.9
  Dirr, M. Dirr's trees and shrubs for warm cli-
    mates   **635.9**
  DiSabato-Aust, T. The well-designed mixed gar-
    den   **712**
  Hayward, G. Stone in the garden   **712**
  Joyce, D. Topiary and the art of training plants
    635.9
  King, M. Gardening with grasses   **635.9**
  The Oxford companion to the garden   **712**
  The plant finder   **635.9**
  Speichert, C. G. Encyclopedia of water garden
    plants   **635**
  Taylor's master guide to gardening   **635.9**

Landscape painting
  Wilton, A. American sublime   **759.13**

Landscape planning. Adam, J.   **635**

Landscape turned red. Sears, S. W.   **973.7**

Lane, Anthony
  Nobody's perfect   **791.43**

Lane, Charles, 1961-
  The day freedom died   **976.3**

Lane, Marion
  The Humane Society of the United States com-
    plete guide to dog care   **636.7**

Lane, Nancy E.
  The osteoporosis book   **616.7**

Lane Fox, Robin
  The classical world   **938**

Lang, Anthony E.
  (jt. auth) Weiner, W. J. Parkinson's disease
    616.8

Lang, Kenneth R.
  The Cambridge guide to the solar system
    523.2

Lang, Paul Henry, 1901-1991
  Music in Western civilization   **780.9**

Lang, Susan S.
  (jt. auth) Patt, R. B. The complete guide to re-
    lieving cancer pain and suffering   **616.99**

Langdon, Helen
  Caravaggio   **92**

Lange, Dianne
  (ed) Informed decisions. See Informed decisions
    616.99

Lange, Norbert Adolph, 1892-1970
  (ed) Lange's handbook of chemistry. See
    Lange's handbook of chemistry   **540**

Langer, Erick Detlef
  (ed) Encyclopedia of Latin American history
    and culture. See Encyclopedia of Latin Amer-
    ican history and culture   **980**

Langer, Howard J.
  (ed) World War II. See World War II
    940.53

Langer, Lawrence L.
  Admitting the Holocaust   **940.53**

Lange's handbook of chemistry   **540**

Langewiesche, William
  American ground, unbuilding the World Trade
    Center   **974.7**
  The atomic bazaar   **355**
  Sahara unveiled   **966**

Langguth, A. J., 1933-
  Our Vietnam   **959.704**

Langhorne family
About
  Fox, J. Five sisters   **920**
  The **Langhorne** sisters. See Fox, J. Five sisters
    920

Langland, William, 1330?-1400?
  Piers Plowman   **821**

Langley, Jacqueline D.
  (jt. auth) Swanson, M. Atlas of the Civil War,
    month by month   **973.7**

Langmuir, Erika
  Yale dictionary of art and artists   **703**

Langone, John, 1929-
  The new how things work   **600**

Language and languages
  See also Grammar; Semantics; Sign lan-
    guage; Sociolinguistics names of languages or
    groups of cognate languages
  Abram, D. The spell of the sensuous   **128**
  Crystal, D. How language works   **401**
  Crystal, D. Language and the internet   **410**
  Deacon, T. W. The symbolic species   **153.6**
  Dunbar, R. I. M. Grooming, gossip, and the
    evolution of language   **599.93**
  Kenneally, C. The first word   **400**
  Pinker, S. The language instinct   **400**
  Pinker, S. The stuff of thought   **401**
  Pinker, S. Words and rules   **401**
  Poole, S. Unspeak: how words become weap-
    ons, how weapons become a message, and
    how that message becomes reality   **306.44**
  Yang, C. The infinite gift   **401**
Dictionaries
  Crystal, D. A dictionary of language   **410**
  Dalby, A. Dictionary of languages   **410**

A **long** way gone. Beah, I.   92

Longe, Jacqueline L.
(ed) The Gale encyclopedia of alternative medicine. See The Gale encyclopedia of alternative medicine   **615.5**
(ed) The Gale encyclopedia of medicine. See The Gale encyclopedia of medicine   **610.3**

The **longest** night. Eicher, D. J.   **973.7**

The **longest** night. Mortimer, G.   **940.53**

Longevity

     See also Aging; Old age
Benecke, M. The dream of eternal life   **612.6**
Chopra, D. Ageless body, timeless mind   **612.6**
Friedman, D. M. The immortalists   **610.28**
Rowe, J. W. Successful aging   **612.6**

Longfellow, Henry Wadsworth, 1807-1882
Poems and other writings   **811**

A **longing** for the light. Aleixandre, V.   **861**

Longing to tell   **306.7**

Longitude
Raymo, C. Walking zero   **526**
Sobel, D. Longitude   **526**

Longitudes and attitudes. Friedman, T. L.   **973.931**

Longman, Jere
Among the heroes   **974.8**

Longshore, David
Encyclopedia of hurricanes, typhoons, and cyclones   **551.55**

Longworth, Alice Lee *See* Longworth, Alice Roosevelt, 1884-1980

Longworth, Alice Roosevelt, 1884-1980
About
Cordery, S. A. Alice [biography of Alice Roosevelt Longworth]   **92**

Lonier, Terri
Working solo   **658**

Look back in anger. Osborne, J.   **822**

Look me in the eye. Robison, J. E.   **92**

The **look** of architecture. Rybczynski, W.   **721**

Looking at the sun. Fallows, J. M.   **950**

Looking for a ship. McPhee, J. A.   **910.4**

Looking for Alaska. Jenkins, P.   **979.8**

Looking for Farrakhan. Levinsohn, F. H.   **92**

Looking for Spinoza. Damasio, A. R.   **152.4**

The **looming** tower. Wright, L.   **973.931**

Loomis, Alfred Lee, 1887-1975
About
Conant, J. Tuxedo Park [biography of Alfred Lee Loomis]   **92**

Loosestrife. Dunn, S.   **811**

Lopate, Phillip, 1943-
(ed) American movie critics. See American movie critics   **791.43**
(ed) The Art of the personal essay. See The Art of the personal essay   **808.84**

Lopes, Rosaly M. C., 1957-
The volcano adventure guide   **910.2**

Lopez, Barry Holstun, 1945-
Of wolves and men   **599.77**
(ed) Home ground. See Home ground   **917.3**

Lopez, Steve
The soloist [biography of Nathaniel Anthony Ayers]   **92**

Lorca, Federico García *See* García Lorca, Federico, 1898-1936

Lord, Bette Bao
Legacies: a Chinese mosaic   **951.05**

Lord, Gary, 1952-
It's faux easy by Gary Lord   **698**

Lord, Macauley
L.L. Bean ultimate book of fly fishing. See L.L. Bean ultimate book of fly fishing   **799.1**

Lord, Walter, 1917-2002
A night to remember   **910.4**

Lorde, Audre
The collected poems of Audre Lorde   **811**
See/See also pages in the following book(s):
Black women writers (1950-1980)   **810.9**

Lords of the harvest. Charles, D.   **664**

Lords of the horizons. Goodwin, J.   **956.1**

Loret, John
(ed) Experiment central. See Experiment central   **507.8**

Los Alamos National Laboratory
Security measures
Trulock, N. Code name Kindred Spirit   **327.12**

Los Alamos Scientific Laboratory
See also Los Alamos National Laboratory
Conant, J. 109 East Palace   **623.4**

Los Angeles (Calif.)
Faderman, L. Gay L.A.   **306.76**
Race relations
Cannon, L. Official negligence   **979.4**

The **Los** Angeles diaries. Brown, J.   **92**

Los Angeles Lakers (Basketball team)
Lazenby, R. The show   **796.323**

Lose your mother. Hartman, S. V.   **326**

Losing it all to sprawl. Belleville, B.   **307**

Losing the race. McWhorter, J. H.   **305.8**

Loss (Psychology)
Attig, T. The heart of grief   **155.9**
Attig, T. How we grieve   **155.9**
Edelman, H. Motherless daughters   **155.9**
Edelman, H. Motherless mothers   **155.9**
Finkbeiner, A. K. After the death of a child   **155.9**
Hood, A. Comfort   **92**
Levy, A. The orphaned adult   **155.9**

The **loss** of a pet. Sife, W.   **155.9**

The **lost**. Mendelsohn, D.   **92**

The **lost** art of healing. Lown, B.   **610**

Lost battalions. Slotkin, R.   **940.1**

The **lost** children of Wilder. Bernstein, N.   **362.7**

Lost city of the Incas. Bingham, H.   **985**

The **lost** dinosaurs of Egypt. Nothdurft, W. E.   **567.9**

Low-carbohydrate diet—*Continued*
Atkins, R. C. Dr. Atkins' new diet revolution
    613.2
Bernstein, R. K. The diabetes diet   **641.5**

Low-cholesterol diet
    See also Low-fat diet
The new American Heart Association cookbook
    641.5

Low-fat diet
Wenner, P. F. Garden cuisine   **613.2**

Low temperatures
    Research
Shachtman, T. Absolute zero and the conquest
of cold   **536**

Lowden, John
Early Christian & Byzantine art   **709.02**

Lowe, Doug
Networking for dummies   **004.6**

Lowell, Amy, 1874-1925
Selected poems   **811**

Lowell, Christopher
Christopher Lowell's one-of-a-kind decorating
projects   **747.2**

Lowell, Robert, 1917-1977
Collected poems   **811**
    About
Mariani, P. L. Lost puritan: a life of Robert
Lowell   **92**
See/See also pages in the following book(s):
Heaney, S. Finders keepers   **828**

Lowenstein, Roger
While America aged   **331.2**

Lowery, Charles D., 1937-
(ed) The Greenwood encyclopedia of African
American civil rights. See The Greenwood
encyclopedia of African American civil rights
    305.8

Lowitz, Leza
(ed) Richie, D. The Japan journals, 1947-2004
    952.04

Lowman, Margaret
Life in the treetops   **92**

Lown, Bernard
The lost art of healing   **610**

Lowney, Chris
A vanished world   **946**

Lozano, Luis-Martin
Frida Kahlo. See Frida Kahlo [critical essays]
    759.972

Lozowick, Yaacov
Right to exist   **956.94**

Lubrano, Alfred
Limbo: blue-collar roots, white-collar dreams
    305.5

Luce, Clare Boothe, 1903-1987
    About
Morris, S. J. Rage for fame: the ascent of Clare
Boothe Luce   **92**

Luce, Henry Robinson, 1898-1967
See/See also pages in the following book(s):
Life stories   **920**

Lucey, Donna M., 1951-
(jt. auth) Wiencek, H. National Geographic
guide to America's great houses   **728.8**

Luchetti, Cathy, 1945-
Children of the West   **978**

Lucie-Smith, Edward, 1933-
Art today   **709.04**
The Thames & Hudson dictionary of art terms
    703

Lucientes, Francisco José de Goya y *See* Goya,
Francisco, 1746-1828

The **Lucifer** effect. Zimbardo, P. G.   **155.9**
The **Lucifer** principle. Bloom, H.   **128**
Luck. Dolnick, B.   **130**
Luckiest man [biography of Lou Gehrig] Eig, J.
    92
Lucky. Sebold, A.   **362.883**
Lucky child. Ung, L.   **92**
Lucky him: the life of Kingsley Amis. Bradford,
R.   **92**

Lucretius Carus, Titus
On the nature of things: De rerum natura
    871

Lucy, Liza Prior
(jt. auth) Fassett, K. Glorious patchwork
    746.46
Lucy: the beginnings of humankind. Johanson, D.
C.   **599.93**
Lucy's legacy. Jolly, A.   **599.93**

Ludens, Rebecca
Teach yourself visually scrapbooking
    745.593

Ludlum, David M., 1910-1997
The Audubon Society field guide to North
American weather   **551.6**

Ludman, Mark D.
(jt. auth) Wynbrandt, J. The encyclopedia of genetic disorders and birth defects   **616**

Luhr, James
(ed) Earth. See Earth   **550**

Lukács, Georg *See* Lukács, György, 1885-1971

Lukács, György, 1885-1971
See/See also pages in the following book(s):
Said, E. W. Reflections on exile and other es-
says   **814**

Lukacs, John, 1924-
Five days in London, May 1940   **940.53**

Lukas, J. Anthony, 1933-1997
Common ground   **305.8**

Lukas, Tony *See* Lukas, J. Anthony, 1933-1997

Luke, David, 1921-
(tr) Mörike, E. F. Mozart's journey to Prague
and a selection of poems   **831**

Lukeman, Noah
The plot thickens   **808.3**

Lumber and lumbering
Peters, R. Woodworker's guide to wood   **684**

Lumet, Sidney
Making movies   **791.43**

Luna (Musical group)
Wareham, D. Black postcards   **92**

Malcolm, Janet
Reading Chekhov   **891.7**
Two lives [dual biography of Gertrude Stein and Alice B. Toklas]   **92**
Malcolm, Trisha, 1960-
(ed) Vogue knitting American collection. See Vogue knitting American collection   **746.43**

Malcolm X, 1925-1965
The autobiography of Malcolm X   **92**
About
Carson, C. Malcolm X: the FBI file   **92**
Perry, B. Malcolm   **92**
West, C. Race matters   **305.8**
The **male** body. Bordo, S.   **305.31**
Male circumcision See Circumcision
Male role See Sex role
Maleskey, Gale
Nature's medicines   **615.5**
Malin, Jo
(ed) Encyclopedia of women's autobiography. See Encyclopedia of women's autobiography   **920.003**

Malinowski, Sharon
(ed) Notable native Americans. See Notable native Americans   **920.003**
Maliszewski-Pickart, Margaret, 1963-
Architecture and ornament   **721**
Mallarmé, Stéphane, 1842-1898
Collected poems and other verse   **841**
Mallon, Mary See Typhoid Mary, d. 1938
Mallon, Thomas, 1951-
Mrs. Paine's garage and the murder of John F. Kennedy   **364.1**
Malnutrition
    See also Starvation
Malone, John Williams
It doesn't take a rocket scientist   **920**
Maloney, Robert K., 1958-
(jt. auth) Kornmehl, E. W. LASIK: a guide to laser vision correction   **617.7**
Malory, Sir Thomas, 15th cent.
Le morte Darthur, or, The hoole book of Kyng Arthur and of his noble knyghtes of the Rounde Table   **398.2**
Malseed, Mark
(jt. auth) Vise, D. A. The Google story   **338.7**
Malthus, T. R. (Thomas Robert), 1766-1834
See/See also pages in the following book(s):
Heilbroner, R. L. The worldly philosophers   **330.1**
Malthus, Thomas Robert See Malthus, T. R. (Thomas Robert), 1766-1834
Maltin, Leonard
Leonard Maltin's 2009 movie guide   **791.43**
Mamet, David
Bambi vs. Godzilla   **791.43**
Glengarry Glen Ross   **812**
On directing film   **791.43**
Speed-the-plow   **812**
True and false   **792**

See/See also pages in the following book(s):
Playwrights at work   **812.009**
Mamiya, Lawrence H.
(jt. auth) Lincoln, C. E. The black church in the African American experience   **277.3**
Mammal tracks & sign. Elbroch, M.   **599**
Mammals
    See also Fossil mammals groups of mammals; and names of mammals
Attenborough, D. The life of mammals   **599**
Mares, M. A. A desert calling   **599**
Nowak, R. M. Walker's mammals of the world   **599**
Tudge, C. The time before history   **599.93**
Whitaker, J. O., Jr. National Audubon Society field guide to North American mammals   **599**

See/See also pages in the following book(s):
Elbroch, M. Mammal tracks & sign   **599**
Mammals, Marine See Marine mammals
Mammoths
Lister, A. Mammoths   **569**
Man See Human beings
    Influence of environment
    See Environmental influence on humans
    Influence on nature
    See Human influence on nature
    Origin
    See Human origins
Man, Fossil See Fossil hominids
Man, Prehistoric See Prehistoric peoples
Man and camel. Strand, M.   **811**
Man and his symbols. Jung, C. G.   **150.19**
Man and microbes. Karlen, A.   **614.4**
Man and Superman. Shaw, B.   **822**
A **man** for all seasons. Bolt, R.   **822**
Man-made catastrophes. Davis, L. A.   **904**
Man o' War (Race horse)
Ours, D. Man o' War   **798.4**
Man of blessing. Butcher, C. A.   **92**
Man of La Mancha. Wasserman, D.   **812**
A **man** on the moon. Chaikin, A.   **629.45**
Man Ray See Ray, Man, 1890-1976
Man Ray's Montparnasse. Lottman, H. R.   **92**
The **man** who counted. Tahan, M.   **793.74**
The **man** who knew infinity. Kanigel, R.   **92**
The **man** who knew too much [biography of Alan Turing] Leavitt, D.   **92**
The **man** who loved China [biography of Joseph Needham] Winchester, S.   **92**
The **man** who mistook his wife for a hat and other clinical tales. Sacks, O. W.   **616.8**
The **man** who ran the moon [biography of James E. Webb] Bizony, P.   **92**
The **man** who walked through time. Fletcher, C.   **917.91**
A **man** without a country. Vonnegut, K.   **814**
Management
Barajas, L. Small business, big life   **658**

Mann, William J.
Behind the screen **791.43**
Kate: the woman who was Hepburn [biography of Katharine Hepburn] **92**

Manners *See* Etiquette

Manners and customs
 See also Country life names of ethnic groups, countries, cities, etc. with the subdivision *Social life and customs*
Dresser, N. Multicultural manners **395**
A History of private life v1 **909**
A History of private life v2 **909**
A History of private life v3 **909**
A History of private life v4 **909**
A History of private life v5 **909**
 Encyclopedias
The Greenwood encyclopedia of daily life **390**
Worldmark encyclopedia of cultures and daily life **306**

Manning, Richard, 1951-
Grassland **577.4**

A **man's** journey to simple abundance. Ban Breathnach, S. **158**

Man's search for meaning. Frankl, V. E. **92**

Manser, Martin H.
The Facts on File dictionary of foreign words and phrases **422.03**
The Facts on File dictionary of proverbs **398.9**
(ed) The Facts on File dictionary of classical and biblical allusions. See The Facts on File dictionary of classical and biblical allusions **809**

Manslaughter *See* Homicide

Manson, Charles, 1934-
 About
Bugliosi, V. Helter skelter **364.1**

Manspace. Martin, S. **729**

Mantle, Mickey, 1931-1995
 About
New York Times Company. Sultans of swat **920**

A **manual** for writers of dissertations. See Turabian, K. L. A manual for writers of research papers, theses, and dissertations **808**

A **manual** for writers of research papers, theses, and dissertations. Turabian, K. L. **808**

Manual of American dialects, for radio, stage, screen, and television. See Herman, L. American dialects **427**

Manual of style. See United States. Government Printing Office. Style manual **808**

Manual of Zen Buddhism. Suzuki, D. T. **294.3**

Manual workers *See* Working class

Many are called. Evans, W. **779**

The **many** faces of God. Campbell, J. **215**

The **Many** faces of Islam **297**

The **many** faces of philosophy **100**

Many worlds in one. Vilenkin, A. **523.1**

Mao, Tse-tung *See* Mao Zedong, 1893-1976

Mao Zedong, 1893-1976
 About
Chang, J. Mao: the unknown story **92**
MacMillan, M. Nixon and Mao **327.73**
Short, P. Mao **92**
Spence, J. D. Mao Zedong **92**
Sun Shuyun. The Long March **951.04**

The **map** that changed the world. Winchester, S. **92**

A **map** to the next world. Harjo, J. **811**

Maples, William R., 1937-1997
Dead men do tell tales **614**

Mapping human history. Olson, S. **599.9**

Mapping Mars. Morton, O. **523.4**

Mapping time. Richards, E. G. **529**

Maps
 See also Atlases
100 maps **526**

Maps and legends. Chabon, M. **814**

Marable, Manning, 1950-
Living Black history **305.8**
(ed) Evers, M. W. The autobiography of Medgar Evers: a hero's life and legacy revealed through his writings, letters, and speeches **92**
(ed) Freedom on my mind. See Freedom on my mind **305.8**

Marani, Pietro C.
Leonardo da Vinci—the complete paintings **759.5**

Maraniss, David
Clemente **92**
First in his class: a biography of Bill Clinton **92**
They marched into sunlight **959.704**
When pride still mattered: a life of Vince Lombardi **92**

Marasco, Ron
Notes to an actor **792**

Marathon running
Higdon, H. Marathon: the ultimate training guide **796.42**

Marathon swimming
Mortimer, G. The great swim **920**

Marathon: the ultimate training guide. Higdon, H. **796.42**

Maravich, Pete, 1947-1988
 About
Kriegel, M. Pistol **92**

Marcella cucina. Hazan, M. **641.5**

Marcella says . . . Hazan, M. **641.5**

The **march** of folly. Tuchman, B. W. **909.08**

A **march** to madness. Feinstein, J. **796.323**

Marchand, Leslie Alexis, 1900-1999
(ed) Byron, G. G. B., 6th Baron. Selected poetry of Lord Byron **821**

Marches (Demonstrations) *See* Demonstrations

Marching orders. Lee, B. **940.54**

Marconi, Guglielmo, 1874-1937
 About
Larson, E. Thunderstruck **364.152**

Martines, Lauro
Fire in the city [biography of Girolamo Savona-
rola]　92

Martínez, Rubén
The new Americans　305.9

Martínez Alemán, Ana M.
(ed) Women in higher education. See Women in
higher education　378

Martínez-Fernández, Luis, 1960-
(ed) Encyclopedia of Cuba. See Encyclopedia of
Cuba　972.91

Martinez Wood, Jamie
Latino writers and journalists　920.003

Martinson, Deborah, 1946-
Lillian Hellman　92

Marton, Kati
The great escape　920
Hidden power　920

Marty, Martin E., 1928-
Pilgrims in their own land　277.3

Martyrs
Foxe, J. Fox's book of martyrs　272

Martyrs' Day. Kelly, M.　956.7

Martz, Louis Lohr
(ed) H. D. Collected poems, 1912-1944　811

Marvel. Daniels, L.　741.5

Marvel comics (New York, N.Y.)
Daniels, L. Marvel　741.5

Marvell, Andrew, 1621-1678
Poems　821

Marx, Groucho, 1891-1977
About
Kanfer, S. Groucho: the life and times of Julius
Henry Marx　92

Marx, Julius H. *See* Marx, Groucho, 1891-1977

Marx, Karl, 1818-1883
Capital: an abridged edition　330.1
The Communist manifesto　335.4
About
Wheen, F. Karl Marx　92
See/See also pages in the following book(s):
Camus, A. The rebel　303.6
Heilbroner, R. L. The worldly philosophers
330.1

Marx Brothers
See also Marx, Groucho, 1891-1977
About
Louvish, S. Monkey business　920

Marxism
See also Communism; Socialism

Mary, Blessed Virgin, Saint
About
Hazleton, L. Mary: a flesh-and-blood biography
of the Virgin Mother　92
Pelikan, J. J. Mary through the centuries
232.91

Mary, Duchess of Gloucester, 1776-1857
See/See also pages in the following book(s):
Fraser, F. Princesses　920

**Mary, Princess, daughter of George III, King of
Great Britain, 1776-1857** See Mary, Duchess of
Gloucester, 1776-1857

Mary, Queen of Scots, 1542-1587
About
Fraser, A. Mary Queen of Scots　92
Weir, A. Mary, Queen of Scots, and the murder
of Lord Darnley　92
Drama
Schiller, F. Don Carlos and Mary Stuart
832

Mary: a flesh-and-blood biography of the Virgin
Mother. Hazleton, L.　92

Mary Engelbreit's children's companion.
Engelbreit, M.　645

Mary Gilliatt's great renovations and restorations.
Gilliatt, M.　747

Mary Magdalene, Saint
About
Chilton, B. Mary Magdalene　226
Ehrman, B. D. Peter, Paul, and Mary Magdalene
225.9

Mary Magdalene. Chilton, B.　226

Mary through the centuries. Pelikan, J. J.
232.91

Mary Wollstonecraft. See Gordon, L. Vindication
[biography of Mary Wollstonecraft]　92

Marzollo, Jean
Fathers & babies　649

Maslon, Laurence, 1959-
(jt. auth) Kantor, M. Broadway: the American
musical　792.6

Maslow, Abraham Harold
Toward a psychology of being　155.2

Mason, Bill, 1929-
Path of the paddle　797.1

Mason, Bobbie Ann
Elvis Presley　92

Mason, David, 1954-
(ed) Twentieth-century American poetry. See
Twentieth-century American poetry
811.008

Mason, George, 1725-1792
About
Broadwater, J. George Mason, forgotten founder
92

Mason, Julian D. (Julian Dewey), 1931-
(ed) Wheatley, P. The poems of Phillis
Wheatley　811

Mason, Michael Paul, 1971-
Head cases　617

Masons (Secret order) *See* Freemasons

Masquerade: the life and times of Deborah Sampson, Continental soldier. Young, A. F.　92

Mass communication *See* Communication; Telecommunication

Mass extinction of species
Boulter, M. C. Extinction: evolution and the end
of man　576.8
Glavin, T. The sixth extinction　333.95
Leakey, R. E. The sixth extinction　304.2
Mitchell, A. Dancing at the Dead Sea　304.2
Powell, J. L. Night comes to the Cretaceous
576.8
Raup, D. M. Extinction　560

Mass media
Bok, S. Mayhem   **302.23**
History of the mass media in the United States
     302.23
Jones, G. Killing monsters   **302.23**
McLuhan, M. The global village   **302.23**
Postman, N. Amusing ourselves to death
     302.23

Massachusetts
     History—1600-1775, Colonial period
Bradford, W. Of Plymouth Plantation, 1620-1647   **974.4**
Demos, J. The unredeemed captive   **973.2**
LaPlante, E. Salem witch judge [biography of Samuel Sewall]   **92**
Philbrick, N. Mayflower   **973.2**

Massacre at Mountain Meadows. Walker, R. W.
     979.2

Massacres
Lane, C. The day freedom died   **976.3**

Massey, Lorraine
Curly girl   **646.7**

Massie, Robert K., 1929-
Castles of steel   **940.4**
Nicholas and Alexandra   **92**
The Romanovs   **947.08**

Massie, Suzanne
Land of the firebird   **947**

Masson, J. Moussaieff (Jeffrey Moussaieff), 1941-
The pig who sang to the moon   **591.5**
When elephants weep   **591.5**

Masson, Jeffrey Moussaieff *See* Masson, J. Moussaieff (Jeffrey Moussaieff), 1941-

Mast, Gerald, 1940-1988
A short history of the movies   **791.43**

"Master Harold"— and the boys. Fugard, A.
     822

Master of the senate [biography of Lyndon B. Johnson] Caro, R. A.   **92**

Master the GED 2009   **373.1**

Mastering the art of French cooking. Child, J.
     641.5

Masterpieces of French literature. Severson, M. S.
     843.009

Masterpieces of world literature   **809**

Masterplots II, drama series   **809.2**

Masterplots II, poetry series   **809.1**

Masters, Virginia Johnson *See* Johnson, Virginia E.

Masters, William H.
Masters and Johnson on sex and human loving
     155.3

Masters. Sampson, C.   **796.352**

Masters and Johnson on sex and human loving. Masters, W. H.   **155.3**

Masters of American comics   **741.5**

Masur, Louis P.
The soiling of Old Glory   **974.4**
(ed) "The Real war will never get in the books". See "The Real war will never get in the books"   **810.8**

Mat, mount and frame it yourself. Logan, M. D.
     749

A **match** to the heart. Ehrlich, G.   **92**

Materia medica
     See also Drugs
The AARP guide to pills   **615**
Chevallier, A. Encyclopedia of herbal medicine
     615
Karch, S. B. The consumer's guide to herbal medicine   **615**
The Merck index   **615**
Physician's desk reference 2008   **615**

Materials
     Encyclopedias
Brady, G. S. Materials handbook   **620.1**

Materials handbook. Brady, G. S.   **620.1**

The **math** gene. Devlin, K. J.   **510**

Mathematical models
Baker, S. The numerati   **303.4**

Mathematical mysteries. Clawson, C. C.   **512.7**

A **mathematical** mystery tour. Dewdney, A. K.
     510

Mathematical recreations
Gardner, M. The colossal book of short puzzles and problems   **793.8**
Stewart, I. The magical maze   **793.74**
Tahan, M. The man who counted   **793.74**

The **mathematical** universe. Dunham, W.   **510**

A **mathematician** reads the newspaper. Paulos, J. A.   **510**

Mathematicians
     See also Women mathematicians
Aczel, A. D. The artist and the mathematician
     510
Bell, E. T. Men of mathematics   **920**
Dunham, W. The mathematical universe   **510**
God created the integers   **510**
Kanigel, R. The man who knew infinity   **92**
     Dictionaries
Newton, D. E. Latinos in science, math, and professions   **920.003**
Notable mathematicians   **920.003**

Mathematics
     See also Patterns (Mathematics); Pi
Acheson, D. J. 1089 and all that   **510**
Cole, K. C. The universe and the teacup
     510
Cusick, T. W. Mathematics made simple
     510
Devlin, K. J. The math gene   **510**
Dewdney, A. K. 200% of nothing   **510**
Dewdney, A. K. A mathematical mystery tour
     510
Dunham, W. The mathematical universe   **510**
Glazer, E. Real-life math   **510**
Guillen, M. Five equations that changed the world   **530.1**
Huff, D. The complete how to figure it   **640**
Kogelman, S. The only math book you'll ever need   **513**
Pasles, P. C. Benjamin Franklin's numbers
     510
Paulos, J. A. Beyond numeracy   **510**

Micheaux, Oscar, 1884-1951
About
McGilligan, P. Oscar Micheaux   92

Michelangelo & the Pope's ceiling. King, R.
759.5

Michelangelo Buonarroti, 1475-1564
About
King, R. Michelangelo & the Pope's ceiling
759.5

Micheli, Lyle J., 1940-
The sports medicine bible for young athletes
617.1

Michelli, Joseph A., 1960-
The Starbucks experience   658

Michels, Caroll
How to survive and prosper as an artist   702

Michener, Charles
(jt. auth) Volpe, J. The toughest show on earth
92

Michener, David
Taylor's guide to ground covers   635.9

Michener, James A., 1907-1997
The bridge at Andau   943.9
Return to paradise   990

Michie, James
(tr) Martial. Epigrams   878

Michigan
Race relations
Cox, A.-L. A stronger kinship   305.8

Michler, J. Marsha
Crazy quilting   746.46
The magic of crazy quilting   746.46

Micklethwait, Alicia
(jt. auth) Hamilton, S. Greed and corporate failure   338.6

Micklethwait, John
The company   338.7
The right nation   320.5

Micklewright, Keith, 1933-
Drawing: mastering the language of visual expression   741.2

Microbes See Bacteria

Microbes and people: an A-Z of microorganisms in our lives. Sankaran, N.   579

Microbiology
See also Biotechnology
Bakalar, N. Where the germs are   616
Biddle, W. A field guide to germs   616

Microchip: an idea, its genesis, and the revolution it created. Zygmont, J.   338.7

Microcomputers
Gookin, D. PCs for dummies   004
Lloyd, S. Programming the universe   530.1
Miller, M. Absolute beginner's guide to computer basics   004
White, R. How computers work   004
Maintenance and repair
Mueller, S. Upgrading and repairing PCs
621.39
Upgrading
Mueller, S. Upgrading and repairing PCs
621.39

Microelectronics
Zygmont, J. Microchip: an idea, its genesis, and the revolution it created   338.7

Microorganisms
See also Bacteria
Karlen, A. Biography of a germ   579.3

Microsoft Corporation
Buderi, R. Guanxi (The art of relationships)
338.8

Microsoft Excel (Computer program) *See* Excel (Computer program)

Mid-career changes *See* Career changes

Middle age
See also Aging
Kiss tomorrow hello   305.24
Levinson, D. J. The seasons of a man's life
155.6
Levinson, D. J. The seasons of a woman's life
155.6
Peck, B. The baby boomer body book   613
Sember, B. M. The everything guide to pregnancy over 35   618.2
Sheehy, G. New passages   305.24
Sheehy, G. Understanding men's passages
305.31

Middle Ages
See also Church history—600-1500, Middle Ages; Europe—History—476-1492; Medieval civilization; World history—14th century; World history—15th century
Adams, H. Mont-Saint-Michel and Chartres
726
Gies, F. Life in a medieval village   940.1
Gies, J. Life in a medieval castle   940.2
Gies, J. Life in a medieval city   940.1
Great events from history, The Middle Ages, 477-1453   909.07
The New Cambridge medieval history   940.1
Orme, N. Medieval children   305.23
Biography
Great lives from history, the Middle Ages, 477-1453   920.003
Encyclopedias
English, E. D. Encyclopedia of the medieval world   940.1
Women in the Middle Ages   305.4

Middle class
Frank, R. H. Falling behind   305.5
Whitaker, J. Service and style   381

Middle earth. Cole, H.   811

Middle East
See also Arab countries
Hiro, D. The essential Middle East   956
Antiquities
Frankfort, H. The art and architecture of the ancient Orient   709.39
Civilization
Civilizations of the Ancient Near East   939
Description and travel
Feiler, B. S. Where God was born   200.9
Horwitz, T. Baghdad without a map, and other misadventures in Arabia   915.6

Morris, Mary, 1913-
(jt. auth) Morris, W. Morris dictionary of word and phrase origins   **422.03**

Morris, Robert D.
The blue death   **614.4**

Morris, Roger
(jt. auth) Denton, S. The money and the power   **979.3**

Morris, Roy
Ambrose Bierce   **92**
Fraud of the century   **324**

Morris, Sylvia Jukes
Rage for fame: the ascent of Clare Boothe Luce   **92**

Morris, Tom, 1821-1908
About
Cook, K. Tommy's honor [dual biography of "Old Tom" Morris and Tommy Morris]   **92**

Morris, Tom, 1851-1875
About
Cook, K. Tommy's honor [dual biography of "Old Tom" Morris and Tommy Morris]   **92**

Morris, William, 1913-1994
Morris dictionary of word and phrase origins   **422.03**

Morris, Willie
My dog Skip   **92**

Morris dictionary of word and phrase origins. Morris, W.   **422.03**

Morrison, Gordon
(jt. auth) Leahy, C. W. The birdwatcher's companion to North American birdlife   **598**

Morrison, Jim, 1943-1971
About
Hopkins, J. No one here gets out alive [biography of Jim Morrison]   **92**
Riordan, J. Break on through: the life and death of Jim Morrison   **92**

Morrison, Joanna
(jt. auth) Charles, J. A. The mystery readers' advisory   **025.5**

Morrison, Phylis, 1927-
(jt. auth) Holden, A. Crystals and crystal growing   **548**

Morrison, Terri
Kiss, bow, or shake hands   **395**

Morrison, Toni, 1931-
About
Gillespie, C. Critical companion to Toni Morrison   **813.009**
See/See also pages in the following book(s):
Black women writers (1950-1980)   **810.9**

Morrow, Charlene, 1948-
(ed) Notable women in mathematics. See Notable women in mathematics   **920.003**

Morrow, Lance
The best year of their lives   **920**
Second drafts of history   **973.92**

Morse, Linda
Luxury knitting   **746.43**

Morse, Samuel Finley Breese, 1791-1872
About
Silverman, K. Lightning man [biography of Samuel Morse]   **92**
See/See also pages in the following book(s):
Lepore, J. A is for American   **306.44**

Le **morte** Darthur, or, The hoole book of Kyng Arthur and of his noble knyghtes of the Rounde Table. Malory, Sir T.   **398.2**

Mortgages
Fields, A. Your new house   **643**

Morthland, John
(ed) Bangs, L. Mainlines, blood feasts and bad taste   **781.66**

Morticians *See* Undertakers and undertaking

Mortimer, Gavin
The great swim   **920**
The longest night   **940.53**

Morton, Brian, 1954-
(jt. auth) Cook, R. The Penguin guide to jazz recordings   **781.65**

Morton, Oliver
Mapping Mars   **523.4**

Morton, R. L. (Ronald Lee)
Music of the earth   **550**

Morton, Ronald Lee *See* Morton, R. L. (Ronald Lee)

Mosaddeq, Mohammad, 1880-1967
About
Kinzer, S. All the Shah's men   **327.73**

Mosaics
Biggs, E. The encyclopedia of mosaic techniques   **738.5**

Mosby, John Singleton, 1833-1916
See/See also pages in the following book(s):
Wilson, E. Patriotic gore   **810.9**

Mosby, Rebekah Presson
(ed) Poetry speaks expanded. See Poetry speaks expanded   **811.008**

Mosby's diagnostic and laboratory test reference. Pagana, K. D.   **616.07**

Mosby's medical & nursing dictionary. See Mosby's medical dictionary   **610.3**

Mosby's medical dictionary   **610.3**

Mosby's medical, nursing, and allied health dictionary. See Mosby's medical dictionary   **610.3**

Mosby's Rangers. Wert, J. D.   **973.7**

Moseley, Michael Edward
The Incas and their ancestors   **985**

Mosenfelder, Donn
(jt. auth) Fischer, B. Bobby Fischer teaches chess   **794.1**

Moser, Charles A., 1935-2006
(ed) The Cambridge history of Russian literature. See The Cambridge history of Russian literature   **891.7**

Moses, Kate
(ed) Because I said so. See Because I said so   **306.8**

Mussolini, Benito, 1883-1945
        About
  Bosworth, R. J. B. Mussolini   **92**
  Bosworth, R. J. B. Mussolini's Italy **945**
Mussolini's Italy. Bosworth, R. J. B. **945**
Mutsuhito See Meiji, Emperor of Japan, 1852-1912
My American century. Terkel, S. **920**
My American journey. Powell, C. L. **92**
My battle of Algiers. Morgan, T. **965**
My Better Homes and Gardens cook book. See Better homes and gardens new cook book **641.5**
My bondage and my freedom. Douglass, F. **92**
My dearest friend [dual biography of John Adams and Abigail Adams] Adams, J. **92**
My dog Skip. Morris, W. **92**
My double life: the memoirs of Sarah Bernhardt. Bernhardt, S. **92**
My face is black is true [biography of Callie House] Berry, M. F. **92**
My father is a book [biography of Bernard Malamud] Smith, J. M. **92**
My father married your mother **306.8**
My father's people. Rubin, L. D. **920**
My fellow Americans **352.23**
My German question. Gay, P. **92**
My invented country. Allende, I. **92**
My life. Clinton, B. **92**
My life as a traitor. Ghahramani, Z. **92**
My life as author and editor. Mencken, H. L. **92**
My life in France. Child, J. **92**
My life with Pablo Neruda. Urrutia, M. **92**
My life with the saints. Martin, J. **920**
My lives. White, E. **92**
My losing season. Conroy, P. **92**
My mother/my self. Friday, N. **155.6**
My sister, guard your veil; my brother guard, your eyes **955**
My stroke of luck. Douglas, K. **92**
My Tibet. Dalai Lama **951**
My war. Rooney, A. A. **92**
My wars are laid away in books. Habegger, A. **92**

Myanmar
  Marshall, A. The trouser people **959.1**
  Thant Myint-U. The river of lost footsteps **959.1**
      Politics and government
  Wintle, J. Perfect hostage [biography of Aung San Suu Kyi] **92**
Mycology See Fungi
Myer, Valerie Grosvenor
  (ed) The Continuum encyclopedia of British literature. See The Continuum encyclopedia of British literature **820.3**
Myers, Allen C., 1945-
  (ed) Eerdmans dictionary of the Bible. See Eerdmans dictionary of the Bible **220.3**

Myers, Ann
  (jt. auth) Koestler, A. J. Understanding chronic pain **616**
Myers, David G.
  A quiet world **617.8**
Myers, Isabel Briggs
  Gifts differing **155.2**
Myers, Mitch
  The boy who cried freebird **781.64**
Myers, Peter B., 1926-
  (jt. auth) Myers, I. B. Gifts differing **155.2**
Myers, Tamara
  (ed) Mosby's medical dictionary. See Mosby's medical dictionary **610.3**
Myerson, Joel
  (ed) Transcendentalism. See Transcendentalism **810.8**
Myne. Presley, F. **821**
Myrdal, Gunnar, 1898-1987
  See/See also pages in the following book(s):
  Ellison, R. The collected essays of Ralph Ellison **814**
Myself when I am real: the life and music of Charles Mingus. Santoro, G. **92**
Myself with others. Fuentes, C. **864**
MySpace (Web site)
  Magid, L. J. MySpace unraveled **004.6**
MySpace unraveled. Magid, L. J. **004.6**
Mysteries and miracle plays
  Everyman, and medieval miracle plays **822.008**
Mysteries of history. Stewart, R. **902**
Mystery and detective stories See Mystery fiction
The **mystery** and meaning of the Dead Sea scrolls. Shanks, H. **296.1**
Mystery and suspense writers **809.3**
Mystery fiction
      Bibliography
  Bleiler, R. Reference and research guide to mystery and detective fiction **016.8**
  Charles, J. A. The mystery readers' advisory **025.5**
  Niebuhr, G. W. Make mine a mystery **809.3**
  Trott, B. Read on . . . crime fiction **016.8**
      History and criticism
  Critical survey of mystery and detective fiction **809.3**
  Niebuhr, G. W. Make mine a mystery **809.3**
  Symons, J. Bloody murder **809.3**
      Technique
  Roberts, G. You can write a mystery **808.3**
  Wheat, C. How to write killer fiction **808.3**
The **mystery** of capital. Soto, H. d. **330.1**
The **mystery** readers' advisory. Charles, J. A. **025.5**
Mysticism
  Armstrong, K. Visions of God **248.2**
  Downing, D. C. Into the region of awe **248.2**
  The Essential writings of Christian mysticism **248.2**
  Furlong, M. Visions & longings **248.2**

New Year
Gulevich, T. Encyclopedia of Christmas and New Year's celebrations   **394.26**
New York (N.Y.)
Von Drehle, D. Triangle: the fire that changed America   **974.7**
Description and travel
Gopnik, A. Through the children's gate   **917.47**
See/See also pages in the following book(s):
White, E. B. Essays of E.B. White   **814**
History
Burrows, E. G. Gotham   **974.7**
Homberger, E. The historical atlas of New York City   **974.7**
Kaiser, C. The gay metropolis   **306.76**
Lepore, J. New York burning   **974.7**
Intellectual life
White, S. Stories of freedom in Black New York   **974.7**
Poetry
García Lorca, F. Poet in New York   **861**
Politics and government
Kirtzman, A. Rudy Giuliani   **92**
Siegel, F. F. The prince of the city [biography of Rudolph W. Giuliani]   **92**
Population
Glazer, N. Beyond the melting pot   **305.8**
Race relations
White, S. Stories of freedom in Black New York   **974.7**
Social conditions
Canada, G. Fist, stick, knife, gun   **305.23**
Freeman, J. B. Working-class New York   **305.5**
Lehrer, W. Crossing the blvd   **305.9**
Lerner, M. A. Dry Manhattan   **363.4**
Social life and customs
Cliff, N. The Shakespeare riots   **974.4**
New York (N.Y.). Fire Dept.
Downey, T. The last men out   **363.34**
Golway, T. So others might live   **628.9**
Halberstam, D. Firehouse   **363.34**
Smith, D. Report from ground zero   **363.34**
New York (N.Y.). Metropolitan Opera *See* Metropolitan Opera (New York, N.Y.)
New York (N.Y.). World Trade Center *See* World Trade Center (New York, N.Y.)
New York (State)
Encyclopedias
The encyclopedia of New York State   **974.7**
History
Taylor, A. The divided ground   **974.7**
New York burning. Lepore, J.   **974.7**
New York Giants (Baseball team)
Deford, F. The old ball game   **796.357**
Prager, J. The echoing green   **796.357**
New York Mets (Baseball team)
Feinstein, J. Living on the black [dual biography of Tom Glavine and Mike Mussina]   **92**
Golenbock, P. Amazin'   **796.357**
Pearlman, J. The bad guys won   **796.357**
New York post
Nissenson, M. The lady upstairs [biography of Dorothy Schiff]   **92**

The **New** York Public Library African American desk reference   **305.8**
The **New** York Public Library American history desk reference   **973.02**
The **New** York Public Library business desk reference   **651**
The **New** York Public Library desk reference   **031.02**
New York September 11   **974.7**
New York Stock Exchange, Inc.
Weiner, E. J. What goes up   **332.6**
The **New** York times 1000 gardening questions & answers. Land, L.   **635**
The **New** York Times 2008 almanac   **031.02**
New York Times Company
Gelb, A. City room   **92**
Sultans of swat   **920**
The **New** York times crossword puzzle dictionary. Pulliam, T.   **793.73**
The **New** York Times essential library: Jazz. See Ratliff, B. Jazz: a critic's guide to the 100 most important recordings   **781.65**
The **New** York times guide to essential knowledge   **031.02**
The **New** York times guide to the best 1,000 movies ever made.   **791.43**
The **New** York Times Jewish cookbook   **641.5**
The **New** York times manual of style and usage. Siegal, A.   **808**
The **New** York Times Passover cookbook   **641.5**
The **New** York Times second book of science questions and answers. Ray, C. C.   **500**
The **New** York Times selective guide to colleges. See Fiske, E. B. Fiske guide to colleges 2009   **378.73**
New York world (Newspaper)
Baker, N. The World on Sunday   **071**
New York Yankees (Baseball team)
Bradley, R. The greatest game   **796.357**
Feinstein, J. Living on the black [dual biography of Tom Glavine and Mike Mussina]   **92**
Halberstam, D. Summer of '49   **796.357**
Kahn, R. October men   **796.357**
Madden, B. Pride of October   **796.357**
New York Times Company. Sultans of swat   **920**
Tofel, R. J. A legend in the making   **796.357**
New Yorker (Periodical)
The complete cartoons of the New Yorker   **741.5**
The Fun of it   **814**
Ross, L. Here but not here   **92**
See/See also pages in the following book(s):
Fraser, K. Ornament and silence   **814**
New Yorker Magazine, Inc.
The complete cartoons of the New Yorker   **741.5**
Steinberg, S. Steinberg at the New Yorker   **741.5**
The **Newbery/Printz** companion. Gillespie, J. T.   **028.5**

Newbery Medal
Gillespie, J. T. The Newbery/Printz companion
028.5

Newbury, Tim
20 best garden designs   712

Newcomb, Horace
(ed) Encyclopedia of television. See Encyclopedia of television   791.45

Newell, Clayton R., 1942-
Historical dictionary of the Persian Gulf War, 1990-1991   956.7

Newgent, Jackie
The all-natural diabetes cookbook   641.5

Newhouse, Elizabeth L.
(jt. auth) Harvey, D. A. Cuba   972.91

Newlin, Keith, 1956-
(ed) A Theodore Dreiser encyclopedia. See A Theodore Dreiser encyclopedia   813.009

Newman, Cathy
Women photographers at National Geographic
770.9

Newman, Joseph Dwight
See/See also pages in the following book(s):
Dance, S. The world of Count Basie   920

Newman, Katherine S., 1953-
The missing class   305.5

Newman, Kim, 1959-
(ed) Horror: another 100 best books. See Horror: another 100 best books   823.009

Newman, Richard S.
Freedom's prophet [biography of Richard Allen]
92

News broadcasting See Broadcast journalism

News photography See Photojournalism

Newspapers
See also Journalism; Periodicals
Directories
Gale directory of publications and broadcast media   070.025
United States
Burns, E. Infamous scribblers   071

Newton, David E.
Encyclopedia of air   551
Encyclopedia of water   553.7
Latinos in science, math, and professions
920.003
Stem cell research   616

Newton, Deborah
Designing knitwear   746.43

Newton, Francis, 1917- See Hobsbawm, E. J. (Eric J.), 1917-

Newton, Sir Isaac, 1642-1727
About
The Cambridge companion to Newton   530
Fara, P. Newton: the making of genius   92
Gleick, J. Isaac Newton   92
Westfall, R. S. The life of Isaac Newton   92
See/See also pages in the following book(s):
Bell, E. T. Men of mathematics   920
Brennan, R. P. Heisenberg probably slept here
920
Guillen, M. Five equations that changed the world   530.1

Horvitz, L. A. Eureka!: scientific breakthroughs that changed the world   509

Newton, Michael, 1951-
The encyclopedia of serial killers   364.03
The encyclopedia of unsolved crimes   364.1

Next man up. Feinstein, J.   796.332

Next of kin. Fouts, R.   156

Nexus: small worlds and the groundbreaking science of networks. Buchanan, M.   530

Nez Percé Indians
See/See also pages in the following book(s):
Brown, D. A. The American West   978
The **Nez** Perce Indians and the opening of the Northwest. Josephy, A. M.   970.004

NFL *See* National Football League

Ng, Wendy L.
Japanese American internment during World War II   940.53

Ngawang Lobsang Yishey Tenzing Gyatso *See* Dalai Lama XIV, 1935-

Nguyen, Dinh Hoa, 1924-
NTC's Vietnamese-English dictionary   495.9

Nguyen, Tram
We are all suspects now   323.1

Nguyen Dinh Hoa *See* Nguyen, Dinh Hoa, 1924-

Nguyen Tat Thành *See* Ho, Chí Minh, 1890-1969

NHL *See* National Hockey League

The **Niagara** River. Ryan, K.   811

Niccolò's smile: a biography of Machiavelli. Viroli, M.   92

Nice, David
Prokofiev: from Russia to the West, 1891-1935
92

Nicholas II, Emperor of Russia, 1868-1918
About
Clay, C. King, Kaiser, Tsar   920
Ferro, M. Nicholas II   92
Kurth, P. Tsar: the lost world of Nicholas and Alexandra   947.08
Massie, R. K. Nicholas and Alexandra   92
Massie, R. K. The Romanovs   947.08

Nicholas, Lynn H.
Cruel world   940.53

Nicholas and Alexandra. Massie, R. K.   92

Nicholl, Charles
The reckoning [biography of Christopher Marlowe]   92

Nichols, Peter M.
(ed). The New York times guide to the best 1,000 movies ever made   791.43

Nicholson, Stuart
Billie Holiday   92

Nichter, Mimi
Fat talk   613.2

Nickel and dimed. Ehrenreich, B.   305.5

Nicklaus, Jack
Golf my way   796.352
Jack Nicklaus   92

Nicknames
Delahunty, A. Oxford dictionary of nicknames
929.4

Nisqualli Indians
See/See also pages in the following book(s):
Josephy, A. M. Now that the buffalo's gone
    970.004

Nissenson, Marilyn, 1939-
The lady upstairs [biography of Dorothy Schiff]
    92

Niven, Jennifer
Ada Blackjack   **92**

Nix, Lacy Hunter, 1979-
(ed) Foxfire 40th anniversary book. See Foxfire
  40th anniversary book   **975.8**

Nixon, Richard M. (Richard Milhous), 1913-
1994

About
Abuse of power   **973.924**
Berman, L. No peace, no honor   **959.704**
Black, C. M. Richard M. Nixon   **92**
Dallek, R. Nixon and Kissinger   **92**
Emery, F. Watergate   **973.924**
MacMillan, M. Nixon and Mao   **327.73**
Matthews, C. Kennedy & Nixon   **973.922**
Morrow, L. The best year of their lives   **920**
Reeves, R. President Nixon   **92**
Reston, J., Jr. The conviction of Richard Nixon
    973.924
Woodward, B. The final days   **973.924**
See/See also pages in the following book(s):
Kissinger, H. Diplomacy   **327.73**
Mann, J. About face   **327.73**
Woodward, B. Shadow   **973.92**

Nixon and Kissinger. Dallek, R.   **92**
Nixon and Mao. MacMillan, M.   **327.73**
No applause, just throw money; or, The book that
  made vaudeville famous. Trav S. D.
    792.7
No crueler tyrannies. Rabinowitz, D.   **345**
No exit, and three other plays. Sartre, J. P.
    842
No fixed points. Reynolds, N.   **792.8**
No future without forgiveness. Tutu, D.   **968.06**
No god but God. Aslan, R.   **297**
No heaven. Ostriker, A.   **811**
No man knows my history: the life of Joseph
  Smith, the Mormon prophet. Brodie, F. M.
    92
No man's land. Tatum, D.   **658.4**
No nature. Snyder, G.   **811**
No ordinary time [biography of Franklin D. Roo-
  sevelt] Goodwin, D. K.   **92**
No other book. Jarrell, R.   **809**
No peace, no honor. Berman, L.   **959.704**
Nō plays
Waley, A. The Nō plays of Japan   **895.6**
The **Nō** plays of Japan. Waley, A.   **895.6**
No room for error. Carney, J. T.   **356**
No small courage   **305.4**
No such thing as over-exposure [biography of
  Donald Trump] Slater, R.   **92**
No turning back. Freedman, E. B.   **305.4**
No two alike. Harris, J. R.   **155.2**

No way home. Wilcove, D. S.   **591.56**
No way to pick a president. Witcover, J.   **324**
Noah, Mordecai Manuel, 1785-1851
See/See also pages in the following book(s):
White, S. Stories of freedom in Black New
  York   **974.7**
Noah's flood. Ryan, W. B. F.   **930**
Noakes, Vivien, 1937-
(ed) Lear, E. The complete verse and other non-
  sense   **821**
Nobel, Alfred Bernhard, 1833-1896
About
Bown, S. R. A most damnable invention
    174
The **Nobel** Peace Prize and the laureates. Abrams,
  I.   **920.003**
Nobel Prize winners   **920.003**
Nobel Prizes
Abrams, I. The Nobel Peace Prize and the laure-
  ates   **920.003**
Feldman, B. The Nobel Prize   **001.4**
Nobel Prize winners   **920.003**
Noble, David F.
The religion of technology   **261.5**
Noble obsession. Slack, C.   **92**
The **noble** savage: Jean-Jacques Rousseau, 1754-
  1762. Cranston, M.   **92**
Nobodies. Bowe, J.   **331.1**
Nobody's children. Bartholet, E.   **362.7**
Nobody's perfect. Lane, A.   **791.43**
Noël Hume, Ivor, 1927-
The Virginia adventure   **975.5**
Nofi, Albert A.
(jt. auth) Dunnigan, J. F. The Pacific War ency-
  clopedia   **940.54**
Noise
Kosko, B. Noise   **155.9**
Nokes, David
Jane Austen   **92**
Nolan, Alan T.
Lee considered   **92**
Nolan, Cathal J.
The Greenwood encyclopedia of international
  relations   **327**
(ed) Notable U.S. ambassadors since 1775. See
  Notable U.S. ambassadors since 1775
    920.003
Nolen, Stephanie
28: stories of AIDS in Africa   **614.5**
Noll, Richard, 1959-
The encyclopedia of schizophrenia and other
  psychotic disorders   **616.89**
Nolo's encyclopedia of everyday law   **340**
Nolo's essential guide to buying your first home.
  Bray, I. M.   **643**
Nolo's essential guide to divorce. Doskow, E.
    346.01
Nolt, Steven M., 1968-
(jt. auth) Kraybill, D. B. Amish grace
    364.152
Non-proliferation of nuclear weapons See Arms
  control

Nonbook materials *See* Audiovisual materials

Nonconformity *See* Dissent

Nonfiction films *See* Documentary films

Nonfiction readers' advisory **025.5**

Nonprescription drugs
Physicians desk reference for nonprescription drugs, dietary supplements, and herbs 2008 **615**

Nonrequired reading. Szymborska, W. **028.1**

Nonverbal communication
 See also Personal space
Dimitrius, J.-E. Reading people **155.2**
Pease, A. The definitive book of body language **153.6**

Noonan, John Thomas, Jr.
Narrowing the nation's power: the Supreme Court sides with the states **342**

Noonan, Peggy
A heart, a cross & a flag **973.931**

Noonan, Raymond J.
(ed) The Continuum complete international encyclopedia of sexuality. See The Continuum complete international encyclopedia of sexuality **306.7**

The **noonday** demon. Solomon, A. **616.85**

Nora, Élisabeth
(ed) Face to face. See Face to face **779**

Norgay, Jamling Tenzing *See* Jamling Tenzing Norgay

Norgay, Tenzing *See* Tenzing Norgay, 1914-1986

Norlin, Elaina
Usability testing for library websites **025.04**

Norman, Jill
Herbs & spices **641.3**
(jt. auth) David, E. Is there a nutmeg in the house? **641.5**

Norman, Marsha
Collected plays v1 **812**

Norman, Michael, 1947-
Haunted America **133.1**

Normandy (France), Attack on, 1944
Ambrose, S. E. D-Day, June 6, 1944 **940.54**

Norris, George William, 1861-1944
See/See also pages in the following book(s):
Kennedy, J. F. Profiles in courage **920**

Norris, Judith Stepan- *See* Stepan-Norris, Judith, 1957-

Norris, Kathleen, 1947-
The cloister walk **255**
Journey: new and selected poems, 1969-1999 **811**

Norris, Robert S.
Racing for the bomb: General Leslie R. Groves, the Manhattan Project's indispensable man **92**

Norse literature *See* Old Norse literature

Norse mythology
Hamilton, E. Mythology **292**

Norsemen *See* Vikings

North, Dan
(jt. auth) Foner, M. Not for bread alone **92**

North (U.S.) *See* Northeastern States

North Africa
 Encyclopedias
Encyclopedia of the modern Middle East & North Africa **956**

North America
 Antiquities—Encyclopedias
Archaeology of prehistoric native America **970.01**

North America
 Gazetteers
The Columbia gazetteer of North America **917**

 Military history
Keegan, J. Fields of battle **973**

 Natural history
 See Natural history—North America

North American Indians *See* Native Americans

North American women artists of the twentieth century **709**

North Korea *See* Korea (North)

North Pole
 See also Arctic regions
Fleming, F. Ninety degrees North **998**

Northampton (Mass.)
Kidder, T. Home town **974.4**

Northeastern States
Burns, C. The great hurricane–1938 **974.7**

Northern Ireland
Coogan, T. P. The troubles **941.6**
See/See also pages in the following book(s):
Conroy, J. Unspeakable acts, ordinary people **323.4**

Northmen *See* Vikings

Northrop Frye on Shakespeare. Frye, N. **822.3**

Northwest Passage
Cookman, S. Ice blink **998**
Williams, G. Voyages of delusion **910.4**
See/See also pages in the following book(s):
Connell, E. S. The Aztec treasure house **814**

Norton, B. H. (Bruce H.)
(ed) Encyclopedia of American war heroes. See Encyclopedia of American war heroes **920.003**

Norton, Richard C., 1953-
A Chronology of American musical theater **792.6**

The **Norton/Grove** dictionary of women composers **920.003**

The **Norton** anthology of African American literature **810.8**

The **Norton** anthology of American literature **810.8**

The **Norton** anthology of English literature **820.8**

The **Norton** anthology of modern and contemporary poetry **821.008**

The **Norton** anthology of modern poetry. See The Norton anthology of modern and contemporary poetry **821.008**

Norton anthology of western music **780.9**

Park, Jessy, 1958-
About
Park, C. C. Exiting nirvana   **616.89**
Park, Robert L.
Voodoo science   **500**
Park, Yeon Hwan
Black belt tae kwon do   **796.8**
Parker, Andrew, 1967-
In the blink of an eye   **576.8**
Parker, Barry R.
Albert Einstein's vision   **530.1**
Quantum legacy   **530.1**
Parker, Charlie, 1920-1955
See/See also pages in the following book(s):
Feather, L. From Satchmo to Miles   **920**
Parker, Derek
(jt. auth) Parker, J. Parkers' complete book of
dreams   **154.6**
Parker, Dorothy, 1893-1967
The portable Dorothy Parker   **818**
About
Meade, M. Dorothy Parker   **92**
Parker, Douglas M., 1935-
Ogden Nash   **92**
Parker, Douglass S.
(tr) Terence. Terence, the comedies   **872**
Parker, Ely Samuel, 1828-1895
See/See also pages in the following book(s):
Brown, D. A. Bury my heart at Wounded Knee
    970.004
Parker, Hershel
Herman Melville v1   **92**
v2   **92**
Parker, Julia, 1932-
Parkers' complete book of dreams   **154.6**
Parker, Yana
The damn good resume guide   **650.14**
Parker Brothers (Firm)
Orbanes, P. The game makers   **338.7**
Parkers' complete book of dreams. Parker, J.
    154.6

Parkes, Graham, 1949-
(tr) Nietzsche, F. W. Thus spoke Zarathustra
    193
Parkinson, Peter, 1942-
The artist blacksmith   **682**
Parkinson's disease
Cram, D. L. Answers to frequently asked questions in Parkinson's disease   **616.8**
Duvoisin, R. C. Parkinson's disease   **616.8**
Freed, C. Healing the brain   **616.8**
Hauser, R. A. Parkinson's disease: questions and
answers   **616.8**
Lieberman, A. 100 questions & answers about
Parkinson [sic] disease   **616.8**
Lieberman, A. Shaking-up Parkinson disease
    616.8
Sacks, O. W. The island of the colorblind
    617.7
Weiner, W. J. Parkinson's disease   **616.8**
When Parkinson's strikes early   **616.8**
Encyclopedias
Mosley, A. D. The encyclopedia of Parkinson's
disease   **616.8**

Personal narratives
Havemann, J. A life shaken   **362.1**
See/See also pages in the following book(s):
Fox, M. J. Lucky man   **92**
Parkman, Francis, 1823-1893
The Oregon trail; The conspiracy of Pontiac
    978
About
Schama, S. Dead certainties   **907**
Parkman, George, 1790-1849
About
Schama, S. Dead certainties   **907**
Parks, Rosa, 1913-2005
Quiet strength   **92**
About
Brinkley, D. Rosa Parks   **92**
See/See also pages in the following book(s):
Abdul-Jabbar, K. Black profiles in courage
    920
Parks, Suzan-Lori
Topdog/underdog   **812**
Parks, Tim
Medici money   **332.1**
Parks
    See also National parks and reserves
United States
National Geographic guide to the state parks of
the United States   **917.3**
Parks directory of the United States   **917.3**
Parks directory of the United States   **917.3**
Parkyn, Neil, 1943-
(ed) The Seventy wonders of the modern world.
See The Seventy wonders of the modern
world   **720.9**
Parliament (Musical group)
Danielsen, A. Presence and pleasure   **781.644**
The **parliament** of man. Kennedy, P. M.
    341.23
Parliamentary practice
Robert, H. M. Robert's Rules of order newly revised   **060.4**
Sturgis, A. The standard code of parliamentary
procedure   **060.4**
Webster's New World Robert's rules of order
    060.4
Parmet, Herbert S.
George Bush   **92**
Paroli, Emma Trenti
(jt. auth) Linden, D. W. Preemies   **618.92**
Parr, Katherine See Catharine Parr, Queen, consort of Henry VIII, King of England, 1512-
1548
Parrado, Nando, 1949-
Miracle in the Andes   **982**
Parrish, Thomas
The submarine   **359.9**
Parrots
Lantermann, W. The new parrot handbook
    636.6
Parrott, Andrew
(ed) The New Oxford book of carols. See The
New Oxford book of carols   **782.28**

Perry, Arthur W.
Straight talk about cosmetic surgery   **617.9**

Perry, Bruce
Malcolm   **92**

Perry, James M.
Touched with fire   **973.7**

Perry, Julia, 1924-1979
See/See also pages in the following book(s):
Walker-Hill, H. From spirituals to symphonies
   920

Perry, Michael, 1964-
Truck: a love story   **629.223**

Persecution
Foxe, J. Fox's book of martyrs   **272**
See/See also pages in the following book(s):
Conroy, J. Unspeakable acts, ordinary people
   323.4

Persepolis. Satrapi, M.   **92**
Persepolis 2. Satrapi, M.   **92**

Perseus (Greek mythology)
See/See also pages in the following book(s):
Hamilton, E. Mythology   **292**

Persia *See* Iran

Persian Gulf War, 1991
Atkinson, R. Crusade   **956.7**
Clancy, T. Into the storm   **956.7**
Gordon, M. R. The generals' war   **956.7**
Newell, C. R. Historical dictionary of the Persian Gulf War, 1990-1991   **956.7**
Schwartz, R. A. Encyclopedia of the Persian Gulf War   **956.7**
Schwarzkopf, H. N. It doesn't take a hero: General H. Norman Schwarzkopf   **92**
Woodward, B. The commanders   **973.928**

Persian poetry
Collections
Music of a distant drum   **808.81**
Persian poets   **891**

Persian poets   **891**

The **Persian** puzzle. Pollack, K. M.   **327.73**

Persico, Joseph E.
(jt. auth) Powell, C. L. My American journey
   92

Persistent pain *See* Chronic pain

Personal appearance
Berg, R. Beauty: the new basics   **646.7**
Brown, B. Bobbi Brown beauty evolution
   646.7
DuPriest, L. Natural beauty   **646.7**
Essence total makeover   **646.7**
Etcoff, N. L. Survival of the prettiest   **391**
Fornay, A. The African American woman's guide to successful makeup and skincare
   646.7
Hall, S. S. Size matters   **612.6**
Kashuk, S. Real beauty   **646.7**
Pedersen, S. K-I-S-S beauty   **646.7**
Peiss, K. L. Hope in a jar   **391**
Wolf, N. The beauty myth   **305.4**
See/See also pages in the following book(s):
Bordo, S. The male body   **305.31**

Personal conduct *See* Conduct of life

Personal finance
See also Consumer credit
Downes, J. Barron's finance & investment handbook   **332.6**
Glink, I. R. 50 simple things you can do to improve your personal finances   **332.024**
Hanson, J. Good debt, bad debt   **332.024**
Huff, D. The complete how to figure it   **640**
Quinn, J. B. Making the most of your money
   332.024
Schwab-Pomerantz, C. It pays to talk
   332.024
Tobias, A. P. The only investment guide you'll ever need   **332.024**

Personal grooming
Ashenburg, K. The dirt on clean   **391**
Gross, K. J. Woman's face   **646.7**

Personal history. Graham, K.   **92**

Personal hygiene *See* Hygiene

Personal loans
See also Mortgages

Personal names
Dictionaries
Latham, E. A dictionary of names, nicknames, and surnames of persons, places, and things
   929.4
United States
Dictionary of American family names   **929.4**
Shankle, G. E. American nicknames   **929.4**
Twentieth century American nicknames
   929.4

Personal space
Martin, S. Manspace   **729**

Personal time management *See* Time management

Personality
See also Eccentrics and eccentricities
Allport, G. Becoming   **155.2**
Dimitrius, J.-E. Reading people   **155.2**
Hamer, D. H. Living with our genes   **155.2**
Harris, J. R. No two alike   **155.2**
LeDoux, J. E. Synaptic self   **612.8**
Maslow, A. H. Toward a psychology of being
   155.2
Myers, I. B. Gifts differing   **155.2**
Whybrow, P. C. A mood apart   **616.89**

Personality disorders
See also Multiple personality
Kramer, P. D. Listening to Prozac   **616.85**
Whybrow, P. C. A mood apart   **616.89**

Personnel management
See also Employees—Dismissal
Giesecke, J. Fundamentals of library supervision
   023
Kelly, M. The dream manager   **658.3**
Lancaster, L. C. When generations collide
   658.3

Persuasion (Psychology)
Cialdini, R. B. Influence: the psychology of persuasion   **153.8**
Levine, R. The power of persuasion   **153.8**

Pert, Candace, 1946-
Molecules of emotion   **612.8**

Prostate
American Cancer Society's complete guide to prostate cancer   **616.99**
Torrey, E. F. Surviving prostate cancer   **616.99**

Prostitution
Abbott, K. Sin in the Second City   **977.3**
Brown, L. The dancing girls of Lahore   **306.7**

Protecting America's health. Hilts, P. J.   **353.9**

Protection of birds *See* Birds—Protection

Protection of environment *See* Environmental protection

Protection of wildlife *See* Wildlife conservation

Protestant Reformation *See* Reformation

Protestantism
McGrath, A. E. Christianity's dangerous idea   **280**
Encyclopedias
The encyclopedia of Protestantism   **280**

Protests, demonstrations, etc. *See* Demonstrations

Prothero, Stephen R.
Religious literacy   **200**
(jt. auth) Queen, E. L. The encyclopedia of American religious history   **200.9**

The **proud** tower. Tuchman, B. W.   **909.82**

Proust, Marcel, 1871-1922
About
Carter, W. C. Marcel Proust   **92**
Shattuck, R. Proust's way   **843.009**
See/See also pages in the following book(s):
Bloom, H. The Western canon   **809**
Swann's way; criticism
In Nabokov, V. V. Lectures on literature   **808.3**

Proust and the squid. Wolf, M.   **612.8**

Proust's way. Shattuck, R.   **843.009**

Provence (France)
Mayle, P. Encore Provence   **944.083**
The **Provence** cookbook. Wells, P.   **641.5**

Proverbs
Cordry, H. V. The multicultural dictionary of proverbs   **398.9**
A Dictionary of American proverbs   **398.9**
Manser, M. H. The Facts on File dictionary of proverbs   **398.9**

Providence and government of God
Kushner, H. S. When bad things happen to good people   **296.3**

Provincialism *See* Regionalism

Prozac backlash. Glenmullen, J.   **616.85**

Prozac diary. Slater, L.   **616.89**

Prucha, Francis Paul
The great father   **970.004**

Prucher, Jeff
(ed) Brave new words. See Brave new words   **813.009**

Prud'homme, Alex
(jt. auth) Child, J. My life in France   **92**

Prudhomme, Paul
Chef Paul Prudhomme's Louisiana tastes   **641.5**

Pruitt, David B.
(ed) Your adolescent. See Your adolescent   **155.5**

Pruning
Pruning & training   **635.9**

Pruning & training   **635.9**

Pryke, Paula
Flowers, flowers!   **745.92**

Pryor, Gale
Nursing mother, working mother   **649**

Pryor, Richard, 1940-2005
See/See also pages in the following book(s):
Life stories   **920**

Psoriasis
Cram, D. L. Coping with psoriasis   **616.5**

Psychiatric hospitals
Whitaker, R. Mad in America   **616.89**

Psychiatry
See also Child psychiatry
Kramer, P. D. Listening to Prozac   **616.85**
Porter, R. Madness   **616.89**
Scull, A. T. Madhouse   **616.89**
Shorter, E. A history of psychiatry   **616.89**
Stone, M. H. Healing the mind   **616.89**
Encyclopedias
The Gale encyclopedia of mental health   **616.89**
Kahn, A. P. The encyclopedia of mental health   **616.89**

Psychic healing *See* Mental healing

Psychical research *See* Parapsychology

Psychoactive drugs *See* Psychotropic drugs

Psychoanalysis
Alvarez, A. Night   **154.6**
Bettelheim, B. Freud and man's soul   **150.19**
Buhle, M. J. Feminism and its discontents   **150.19**
Freud, S. The basic writings of Sigmund Freud   **150.19**
Freud, S. The Freud reader   **150.19**
Freud, S. Interpretation of dreams   **154.6**
Freud, S. Totem and taboo   **306**
Freud: conflict and culture   **150.19**
Fromm, E. On being human   **150.19**
Gay, P. A Godless Jew   **150.19**
Horney, K. New ways in psychoanalysis   **150.19**
Jung, C. G. The basic writings of C. G. Jung   **150.19**
Jung, C. G. The essential Jung   **150.19**
Jung, C. G. The portable Jung   **150.19**
Menninger, K. A. Love against hate   **150.19**
Mitchell, S. A. Freud and beyond   **150.19**
Phillips, A. Going sane   **616.89**
Thurschwell, P. Sigmund Freud   **150.19**
See/See also pages in the following book(s):
Tillich, P. Theology of culture   **230**

Psychogenetics *See* Behavior genetics

Psychologists
Frankl, V. E. Man's search for meaning   **92**

The **quark** and the jaguar. Gell-Mann, M.
530.1

Quarrel & quandary. Ozick, C.   814

Queen, Billy *See* Queen, William

Queen, Edward L.
The encyclopedia of American religious history
200.9

Queen, William
Under and alone   364.1

The **Queen:** a biography of Elizabeth II. Pimlott,
B.   92

Queen Latifah
Ladies first   158

Queens
See also names of queens and countries
with the subdivision *Kings and rulers*
Fraser, A. Marie Antoinette   92
Lever, E. Marie Antoinette   92
Starkey, D. Six wives: the queens of Henry VIII
920

The **quest** for cosmic justice. Sowell, T.   303.3

The **quest** for life in amber. Poinar, G. O.
560

A **question** of choice. Weddington, S. R.
363.46

A **question** of torture. McCoy, A. W.   323.4

Questions and answers
Feldman, D. When do fish sleep? and other imponderables of everyday life   031.02
Feldman, D. Why do clocks run clockwise? and
other imponderables   031.02

Quick and easy cooking
Silverton, N. A twist of the wrist   641.5
Waters, A. The art of simple food   641.5

Quick-meal cookery *See* Quick and easy cooking

Quiet strength. Parks, R.   92

A **quiet** world. Myers, D. G.   617.8

Quigley, Eileen S.
(ed) International motion picture almanac. See
International motion picture almanac
791.43

Quilting
Beyer, J. Quiltmaking by hand   746.46
Brackman, B. Facts & fabrications: unraveling
the history of quilts and slavery   746.46
Burns, E. Underground railroad sampler
746.46
Causee, L. Quilts A to Z   746.46
Fassett, K. Glorious patchwork   746.46
Gaudynski, D. Guide to machine quilting
746.46
Hakala, S. Teach yourself visually quilting
746.46
Hargrave, H. Heirloom machine quilting
746.46
Kavaya, K. Community quilts   746.46
Michler, J. M. Crazy quilting   746.46
Michler, J. M. The magic of crazy quilting
746.46

Quiltmaking by hand. Beyer, J.   746.46

Quilts
Kavaya, K. Community quilts   746.46

Keuning-Tichelaar, A. Passing on the comfort
940.54
Tobin, J. Hidden in plain view   973.7

Quilts A to Z. Causee, L.   746.46

Quinine
Rocco, F. The miraculous fever tree   616.9

Quinine. See Rocco, F. The miraculous fever tree
616.9

Quinion, Michael, 1942-
Ballyhoo, buckeroo, and spuds   422

Quinlan, Karen Ann
See/See also pages in the following book(s):
Filene, P. G. In the arms of others   179.7

Quinn, Alice
(ed) Bishop, E. Edgar Allan Poe & the juke-box
811

Quinn, Elisabeth Lasch- *See* Lasch-Quinn, Elisabeth

Quinn, Jane Bryant
Making the most of your money   332.024

Quinn, Susan
Marie Curie   92

Quirk, Lawrence J.
Bob Hope: the road well-traveled   92

Quirk, Robert E.
Fidel Castro   92

Quit-smoking programs *See* Smoking cessation
programs

Quotations
See also Proverbs
Andrews, R. The Columbia dictionary of quota-
tions   808.88
Andrews, R. Famous lines   808.88
Bartlett, J. Bartlett's familiar quotations
808.88
Boller, P. F. They never said it   808.88
The Columbia Granger's dictionary of poetry
quotations   808.88
A Dictionary of quotations in mathematics
510
Guinagh, K. Dictionary of foreign phrases and
abbreviations   422.03
Kennedy, R. F. Make gentle the life of this
world   973.922
Nowlan, R. A. Born this day   808.88
The Oxford book of aphorisms   808.88
Oxford dictionary of humorous quotations
808.88
The Oxford dictionary of quotations   808.88
Oxford dictionary of scientific quotations
500
Quotations for all occasions   808.88
Shakespeare, W. The Columbia dictionary of
quotations from Shakespeare   822.3
World War II   940.53
The Yale book of quotations   808.88

Quotations for all occasions   808.88

Quran *See* Koran

The **Qur'an:** an encyclopedia   297.1

R

R. J. Reynolds Industries, Inc.
See also RJR Nabisco Inc.

R.U.R. and The insect play. Čapek, K.   **891.8**

Raab, Selwyn
Five families   **364.1**

Raban, Jonathan
Bad land   **978**
Passage to Juneau   **979.8**

Rabban, David M., 1949-
Free speech in its forgotten years   **342**

Rabbi Jesus. Chilton, B.   **232.9**

Rabin, Vivian Steir
(jt. auth) Cohen, C. F. Back on the career track   **650.14**

Rabin, Yitzhak, 1922-1995
   About
Shalom, friend: the life and legacy of Yitzhak Rabin   **92**

Rabindranath Tagore *See* Tagore, Sir Rabindranath, 1861-1941

Rabiner, Susan
Thinking like your editor   **808**

Rabinow, Paul
Making PCR   **572.8**

Rabinowitz, Dorothy
No crueler tyrannies   **345**

Race
Wolpoff, M. H. Race and human evolution   **599.97**

The **race**. Schefter, J. L.   **629.45**

Race. Terkel, S.   **305.8**

Race and human evolution. Wolpoff, M. H.   **599.97**

Race awareness
   See also African Americans—Race identity

Race discrimination
Bryant, H. Shut out   **796.357**
Cose, E. Color-blind   **305.8**
Katznelson, I. When affirmative action was white   **323.1**
Rhoden, W. C. $40 million slaves   **796**
Roediger, D. R. Working toward whiteness   **305.8**

Race experts. Lasch-Quinn, E.   **305.8**

The **race** for the Triple Crown. Drape, J.   **798.4**

Race matters. West, C.   **305.8**

Race psychology *See* Ethnopsychology

Race relations
   See also Culture conflict; Ethnic relations; Multiculturalism names of countries, cities, etc., with the subdivision *Race relations*
Sowell, T. The economics and politics of race   **305.8**

Race rules. Dyson, M. E.   **305.8**

Races of people *See* Ethnology

Rachel and her children. Kozol, J.   **362.5**

Rachmaninoff, Sergei, 1873-1943
See/See also pages in the following book(s):
Schonberg, H. C. The great pianists   **920**

Racial balance in schools *See* School integration

Racially mixed people
Lewis, E. Fade: my journeys in multiracial America   **305.8**
Morales, E. Living in Spanglish   **305.8**

Racing for the bomb: General Leslie R. Groves, the Manhattan Project's indispensable man. Norris, R. S.   **92**

Racism
   See also Race discrimination; White supremacy movements
Bushart, H. L. Soldiers of God   **322.4**
Ezekiel, R. S. The racist mind   **322.4**
Kennedy, R. Nigger   **305.8**
Reed, I. Another day at the front   **305.8**
Steele, S. White guilt   **305.8**
   Encyclopedias
Encyclopedia of racism in the United States   **305.8**

The **racist** mind. Ezekiel, R. S.   **322.4**

Radcliffe, Margaret
The knitting answer book   **746.43**

Raddatz, Martha
The long road home   **956.7**

Radford, Edwin, 1891-1973
Encyclopaedia of superstitions   **398.03**

Radford, Mona Augusta
(jt. auth) Radford, E. Encyclopaedia of superstitions   **398.03**

The **radical** center. Halstead, T.   **320.5**

The **Radical** reader   **303.4**

Radicalism
   See also Militia movements
Alinsky, S. Rules for radicals   **322.4**
Anderson, T. H. The movement and the sixties   **303.4**
Atkins, S. E. Encyclopedia of modern American extremists and extremist groups   **322.4**
Atkins, S. E. Encyclopedia of modern worldwide extremists and extremist groups   **320.5**
Hamilton, N. A. Rebels and renegades   **322.4**
Hoffman, A. The best of Abbie Hoffman   **303.4**
Kurlansky, M. 1968   **909.82**
The Radical reader   **303.4**
Ronson, J. Them: adventures with extremists   **322.4**
Stern, K. S. A force upon the plain   **322.4**

The **radicalism** of the American Revolution. Wood, G. S.   **973.3**

Radice, William, 1951-
(tr) Tagore, Sir R. Selected poems   **891**

Radio
Larson, E. Thunderstruck   **364.152**
   Handbooks, manuals, etc.
The ARRL handbook for radio communications   **621.3841**
   Repairing
Carr, J. J. Old time radios!   **621.384**

The **Radio** amateur's handbook. See The ARRL handbook for radio communications

621.3841

Radio authorship
Straczynski, J. M. The complete book of scriptwriting **808.2**

Radio broadcasting
Broadcasting & cable yearbook 2009 **384.54**
Fisher, M. Something in the air **384.54**
Heil, A. L., Jr. Voice of America **384.54**
Neer, R. FM: the rise and fall of free-form rock radio **791.44**
Encyclopedias
The Museum of Broadcast Communications encyclopedia of radio **384.54**
Sies, L. F. Encyclopedia of American radio, 1920-1960 **791.44**

Radio frequency identification systems
Ward, D. The complete RFID handbook **025**

Radio golf. Wilson, A. **812**

Radio industry See Radio broadcasting

Radio journalism See Broadcast journalism

Radio programs
Dunning, J. On the air **791.44**
Encyclopedias
Sies, L. F. Encyclopedia of American radio, 1920-1960 **791.44**

Radzinsky, Edvard
Stalin **92**

Rage See Anger

Rage for fame: the ascent of Clare Boothe Luce. Morris, S. J. **92**

A **rage** to live: a biography of Richard and Isabel Burton. Lovell, M. S. **92**

Rage to survive. James, E. **92**

Railroad accidents
Krist, G. The white cascade **979.7**

Railroads
Theroux, P. Riding the iron rooster **915.1**
Asia
Theroux, P. The great railway bazaar **915**
Latin America
Theroux, P. The old Patagonian express **918**
United States
Ambrose, S. E. Nothing like it in the world **385**
Bain, D. H. Empire express **385**

Rain forest ecology
London, M. The last forest **333.75**
Royte, E. The Tapir's morning bath **577.3**

Rain forests
London, M. The last forest **333.75**
Encyclopedias
Jukofsky, D. Encyclopedia of rainforests **578.7**
Pictorial works
Marent, T. Rainforest **578.7**

The **rainbow** people of God. Tutu, D. **968.06**

Raine, Kathleen, 1908-2003
The collected poems of Kathleen Raine **821**

A **raisin** in the sun. Hansberry, L. **812**

Raising a child with a neuromuscular disorder. Thompson, C. E. **618.92**

Raising a child with autism. Richman, S. **618.92**

Raising a happy, unspoiled child. White, B. L. **649**

Raising America. Hulbert, A. **649**

Raising baby green. Greene, A. R. **618.2**

Raising less corn, more hell. Pyle, G. **338.1**

Raising resilient children. Brooks, R. B. **649**

Raising the dead. Munson, R. **174**

Rajtar, Steve, 1951-
Indian war sites **970.004**
United States holidays and observances **394.26**

Râles, Sébastien See Rasles, Sébastien, 1657-1724?

Ralph Ellison. Rampersad, A. **92**

Ralston, John
(jt. auth) Port, D. The caveman's pregnancy companion **618.2**

Ramanujan Aiyangar, Srinivasa, 1887-1920
About
Kanigel, R. The man who knew infinity **92**

The **Ramayana**. Narayan, R. K. **891**

Ramazani, Jahan, 1960-
(ed) The Norton anthology of modern and contemporary poetry. See The Norton anthology of modern and contemporary poetry **821.008**

Rameses II, King of Egypt See Ramses II, King of Egypt

Ramey, Gene
See/See also pages in the following book(s):
Dance, S. The world of Count Basie **920**

Ramm, David
(ed) World authors, 2000-2005. See World authors, 2000-2005 **920.003**

Rammer jammer yellow hammer. St. John, W. **796.332**

Ramonet, Ignacio, 1943-
(jt. auth) Castro, F. Fidel Castro: my life **92**

Rampersad, Arnold
The life of Langston Hughes Volume I: 1902-1941 **92**
The life of Langston Hughes Volume II: 1941-1967 **92**
Ralph Ellison **92**
(ed) The Oxford anthology of African-American poetry. See The Oxford anthology of African-American poetry **811.008**

Ramsdell, Kristin, 1940-
Romance fiction **016.8**

Ramses II, King of Egypt
See/See also pages in the following book(s):
Mertz, B. Temples, tombs, & hieroglyphs **932**

Ramsey, John Bennett
About
Schiller, L. Perfect murder, perfect town **364.1**

Rasputin, Grigoriĭ Efimovich, 1871-1916
About
Massie, R. K. Nicholas and Alexandra 92

Rastafari movement
Chevannes, B. Rastafari: roots and ideology
299.6
Kebra Nagast. The Kebra Nagast 299.6
Rastafari: roots and ideology. Chevannes, B.
299.6

Ratey, John J., 1948-
A user's guide to the brain 612.8
(jt. auth) Hallowell, E. M. Delivered from distraction 616.85
(jt. auth) Hallowell, E. M. Driven to distraction
616.85

Rath, Sara
The complete pig 636.4

Rathbone, Belinda
Walker Evans 92

Rather, Dan
The American dream 973.92

Rationalism
See also Enlightenment

Ratliff, Ben
Jazz: a critic's guide to the 100 most important recordings 781.65

Rattlesnakes
Rubio, M. Rattlesnake 597.96

Ratzinger, Joseph *See* Benedict XVI, Pope, 1927-

Rauchway, Eric, 1979-
Murdering McKinley 973.8

Raup, David M.
Extinction 560

Rause, Vince
(jt. auth) Parrado, N. Miracle in the Andes
982

Ravago, Miguel
(jt. auth) Tausend, M. Cocina de la familia
641.5

Ravens
Heinrich, B. Mind of the raven 598

Ravens (Football team) *See* Baltimore Ravens (Football team)

Ravitch, Diane
The language police 371.3

Ray, C. Claiborne
The New York Times second book of science questions and answers 500

Ray, Man, 1890-1976
About
Lottman, H. R. Man Ray's Montparnasse 92

Raymo, Chet
An intimate look at the night sky 520
Walking zero 526

Razac, Olivier
Barbed wire 323.4

Rea, Tom, 1950-
Bone wars 560

Reaching up for manhood. Canada, G. 305.23

Reaction (Political science) *See* Right and left (Political science)

Read, Anthony
The fall of Berlin 940.54

Read, Piers Paul, 1941-
Alive 910.4

The **read-aloud** handbook. Trelease, J. 028.5

Read on . . . crime fiction. Trott, B. 016.8

Read on . . . fantasy fiction. Hollands, N.
016.8

The **readers'** advisory guide to nonfiction. Wyatt, N. 025.5

Readers' advisory service in the public library. Saricks, J. G. 025.5

A **Reader's** companion to the short story in English 809.3

Reader's Digest Association, Inc.
Foods that harm, foods that heal 613.2
Reader's Digest complete do-it-yourself manual. See Complete do-it-yourself manual 643
Reader's Digest complete guide to sewing. See New complete guide to sewing 646.2
Reader's digest complete guide to the Bible
220.7
Reader's Digest fix-it-yourself manual. See New fix-it-yourself manual 643
The **Reader's** encyclopedia of the American West. See The New encyclopedia of the American West 978.03
Reader's guide to Judaism 296.03
Reader's guide to military history 355
Reader's guide to the history of science 509

Reading
Flesch, R. F. Why Johnny can't read—and what you can do about it 372.4
Wolf, M. Proust and the squid 612.8
Phonetic method
See also Phonetics
Remedial teaching
Rosow, L. V. Accessing the classics 011

Reading & writing. Naipaul, V. S. 92

Reading Chekhov. Malcolm, J. 891.7

Reading disability
Shaywitz, S. E. Overcoming dyslexia 371.9

Reading interests of children *See* Children—Books and reading

Reading Judas. Pagels, E. H. 229

Reading like a writer. Prose, F. 808

Reading Lolita in Tehran. Nafisi, A. 92

Reading people. Dimitrius, J.-E. 155.2

Reading the Holocaust. Clendinnen, I. 940.53

Reading the rocks. Bjornerud, M. 551.7

Reagan, Leslie J.
When abortion was a crime 363.46

Reagan, Ronald, 1911-2004
Reagan 92
The Reagan diaries 92
About
D'Souza, D. Ronald Reagan 92
FitzGerald, F. Way out there in the blue
973.927
Johnson, H. B. Sleepwalking through history
973.927

Red Smith on baseball. Smith, R.   **796.357**

Red Sox (Baseball team) *See* Boston Red Sox (Baseball team)

Redcoats and rebels. Hibbert, C.   **973.3**

Redemption: the last battle of the Civil War. Lemann, N.   **975**

Redemption: the life of Henry Roth. Kellman, S. G.   **92**

Redesigning humans. Stock, G.   **176**

Redford, Donald B.
(ed) The Oxford encyclopedia of ancient Egypt. See The Oxford encyclopedia of ancient Egypt   **932**

Rediker, Marcus Buford
The slave ship   **326**

Rediscovering Gandhi. See Chadha, Y. Gandhi   **92**

Reds: McCarthyism in twentieth-century America. Morgan, T.   **973.9**

Reducing *See* Weight loss

Redwood
Preston, R. The wild trees   **577**

Reece, Erik
Lost mountain   **622**

Reed, Annette Gordon- *See* Gordon-Reed, Annette

Reed, Carol
Router joinery workshop   **684**

Reed, Gregory J.
(jt. auth) Parks, R. Quiet strength   **92**

Reed, Ishmael, 1938-
Another day at the front   **305.8**
New and collected poems, 1966-2006   **811**
(ed) From totems to hip-hop. See From totems to hip-hop   **811.008**

Reed, John, 1887-1920
Ten days that shook the world   **947.084**

Reed, Jonathan L.
(jt. auth) Crossan, J. D. Excavating Jesus   **225.9**

Reed, Miriam
Margaret Sanger: her life in her words   **92**

Reef, Catherine
Poverty in America   **362.5**
Working in America   **331**

Rees, Alan M.
(ed) Consumer health information source book. See Consumer health information source book   **016.613**

Rees, Dafydd
(jt. auth) Crampton, L. Rock & roll year by year   **781.66**

Rees, Laurence, 1957-
Auschwitz: a new history   **940.53**

Rees, Martin J., 1942-
Just six numbers   **523.1**
Our cosmic habitat   **523.1**
Our final hour   **303.49**

Rees, Siân, 1965-
The floating brothel   **365**

Reese, Thomas J.
Inside the Vatican   **282**

Reeve, Christopher, 1952-2004
Still me   **92**

Reeves, Bass
See/See also pages in the following book(s):
Abdul-Jabbar, K. Black profiles in courage   **920**

Reeves, Randall R.
National Audubon Society guide to marine mammals of the world. See National Audubon Society guide to marine mammals of the world   **599.5**

Reeves, Richard
President Kennedy   **92**
President Nixon   **92**
President Reagan: the triumph of imagination   **973.927**

Reeves, Richard, 1936-
A force of nature [biography of Ernest Rutherford]   **92**

Reference and research guide to mystery and detective fiction. Bleiler, R.   **016.8**

Reference books
Bibliography
American reference books annual 2008 edition, volume 39   **011**
Guide to reference books   **011**
Katz, W. A. Introduction to reference work   **025.5**
Recommended reference books for small and medium-sized libraries and media centers   **011**
Reference sources for small and medium-sized libraries   **011**
Reviews
Recommended reference books for small and medium-sized libraries and media centers   **011**

Reference books for small and medium-sized libraries. See Reference sources for small and medium-sized libraries   **011**

The **reference** guide to famous engineering landmarks of the world. Berlow, L. H.   **620**

Reference guide to mystery and detective fiction. See Bleiler, R. Reference and research guide to mystery and detective fiction   **016.8**

Reference guide to Russian literature   **891.7**

Reference guide to science fiction, fantasy, and horror. Burgess, M.   **016.8**

Reference guide to world literature   **809**

Reference services (Libraries)
Buker, D. M. The science-fiction and fantasy readers' advisory   **025.5**
Charles, J. A. The mystery readers' advisory   **025.5**
Cords, S. S. The real story   **025.5**
Ford, C. Crash course in reference   **025.5**
Katz, W. A. Introduction to reference work   **025.5**
Moyer, J. E. Research-based readers' advisory   **025.5**
Nonfiction readers' advisory   **025.5**
Saricks, J. G. Readers' advisory service in the public library   **025.5**
Spratford, B. S. The horror readers' advisory   **025.5**

Sanders, Andrew, 1946-
The short Oxford history of English literature
820.9

Sanders, Donald Theodore
(jt. auth) Zeilinga de Boer, J. Earthquakes in human history
363.34

Sanders, E. P.
The historical figure of Jesus
232.9

Sanders, Scott R. (Scott Russell), 1945-
A private history of awe
92

Sandford, Gina
Aquarium owner's manual
639.34

Sandison, David
Neal Cassady
92

Sandler, Adrian
(jt. auth) Bedick, P. Living with spina bifida
618.92

Sandler, Robert
(ed) Frye, N. Northrop Frye on Shakespeare
822.3

Sandoval-Strausz, A. K.
Hotel
917.3

Sandoz, Mari, 1896-1966
The Battle of the Little Bighorn
973.8

Sandra Betzina sews for your home. Betzina, S.
646.2

Sands, Matthew L. (Matthew Linzee)
(jt. auth) Feynman, R. P. Six easy pieces
530

Sandstorms: days and nights in Arabia. Theroux, P.
953

Sanger, Margaret, 1879-1966
About
Reed, M. Margaret Sanger: her life in her words
92

Sanitation
George, R. The big necessity
363.7
Honey, M. K. Going down Jericho Road
331.8

Sankaran, Neeraja
Microbes and people: an A-Z of microorganisms in our lives
579

Santa Fe Trail
Dary, D. The Santa Fe Trail
978

Santa Maria del Fiore (Cathedral: Florence, Italy)
King, R. Brunelleschi's dome
726

Santayana, George, 1863-1952
See/See also pages in the following book(s):
Durant, W. J. The story of philosophy
109

Santoro, Gene
Myself when I am real: the life and music of Charles Mingus
92

Sanzio, Raffaello *See* Raphael, 1483-1520

Sapolsky, Robert M.
A primate's memoir
599.8

Sappho
If not, winter
884

Sarajevo (Bosnia and Hercegovina)
See/See also pages in the following book(s):
Sontag, S. Where the stress falls
814

Saratoga. Ketchum, R. M.
973.3

Saratoga Campaign, 1777
Ketchum, R. M. Saratoga
973.3

Sardegna, Jill
(ed) The Encyclopedia of blindness and vision impairment. See The Encyclopedia of blindness and vision impairment
362.4

Sargent, Ted
The dance of molecules
620

Saricks, Joyce G.
Readers' advisory service in the public library
025.5

Sarmiento, Esteban
The last human
569.9

Sarna, Jonathan D.
American Judaism
296

Sarnoff, David, 1891-1971
About
Stashower, D. The boy genius and the mogul
791.45

Sarris, Nikos
(tr) Elytēs, O. The collected poems of Odysseus Elytis
889

SARS (Disease)
Greenfeld, K. T. China syndrome
614.5

Sarton, May, 1912-1995
Selected poems of May Sarton
811

Sartor resartus. Carlyle, T.
824

Sartore, Joel
(jt. auth) Chadwick, D. H. The company we keep
591.68

Sartre, Jean Paul, 1905-1980
Being and nothingness
142
Existentialism and human emotions
142
No exit, and three other plays
842
Truth and existence
121
The words
92
See/See also pages in the following book(s):
Bair, D. Simone de Beauvoir
92
Existentialism from Dostoevsky to Sartre
142

SAS survival handbook. Wiseman, J.
613.6

Sasha Kagan's country inspiration. Kagan, S.
746.43

Sasson, Jack M.
(ed) Civilizations of the Ancient Near East. See Civilizations of the Ancient Near East
939

Sassoon, Donald
Becoming Mona Lisa
759.5

SAT *See* Scholastic Assessment Test

Satan *See* Devil

Satellites
Leutwyler, K. The moons of Jupiter
523.4

Satellites, Artificial *See* Artificial satellites

Satinover, Jeffrey, 1947-
Cracking the Bible code
222

Satire
Lewis, C. S. The Screwtape letters
248

Satrapi, Marjane, 1969-
Embroideries
955
Persepolis
92
Persepolis 2
92

Satter, David, 1947-
Age of delirium   947.085
Sauces
    See also Tabasco sauce
Saudi Arabia
Simmons, M. R. Twilight in the desert
    338.2
     History
Coll, S. The Bin Ladens   920
     Kings and rulers
Unger, C. House of Bush, house of Saud
    327.73
Savage, Jon
Teenage   305.23
Savage beauty: the life of Edna St. Vincent Millay. Milford, N.   92
Savage inequalities. Kozol, J.   371.9
The **savage** mind. Lévi-Strauss, C.   155.8
Savage peace. Hagedorn, A.   973.91
Savageau, David
Places rated almanac   307.7
Retirement places rated   307.7
Savages. Kane, J.   986.6
Savannah (Ga.)
Berendt, J. Midnight in the garden of good and evil   975.8
Savants (Savant syndrome)
Tammet, D. Born on a blue day   92
Savastinuk, Laura C., 1979-
(jt. auth) Casey, M. E. Library 2.0   025.1
Saviano, Roberto, 1979-
Gomorrah   364.1
Savigneau, Josyane
Carson McCullers   92
Saving beauty from the beast. Crompton, V.
    362.88
Saving childhood. Medved, M.   305.23
Saving the corporate soul & (who knows?) maybe your own. Batstone, D. B.   658.4
Saving your brain. Victoroff, J. I.   612.8
Savonarola, Girolamo, 1452-1498
     About
Martines, L. Fire in the city [biography of Girolamo Savonarola]   92
Sawyer, Kathy
The rock from Mars   576.8
Sawyer, Miriam
(jt. auth) Gubert, B. K. Distinguished African Americans in aviation and space science
    920.003
Sawyer, P. H., 1928-
(ed) The Oxford illustrated history of the Vikings. See The Oxford illustrated history of the Vikings   948
Sawyer, R. Keith (Robert Keith)
Group genius   658.4
Sawyer-Lauçanno, Christopher, 1951-
E.E. Cummings   92
Saxon, A. H.
P. T. Barnum: the legend and the man   92
Say uncle. Ryan, K.   811

Sayler, Mary Harwell
The encyclopedia of the back and spine systems and disorders   617
The encyclopedia of the muscle and skeletal systems and disorders   616.7
Scalapino, Leslie
It's go in horizontal   811
Scales, Robert H., 1944-
(jt. auth) Murray, W. The Iraq war   956.7
The **scalpel** and the butterfly. Rudacille, D.
    179
Scandinavian literature
    See also Old Norse literature; Sagas
Scandinavians
    See also Vikings
Scarlet tanager. Mayer, B.   811
Scarlett, W. George
(ed) Encyclopedia of religious and spiritual development. See Encyclopedia of religious and spiritual development   200.3
Scarne, John, 1903-1985
Scarne's encyclopedia of card games   795.4
Scarne's encyclopedia of card games. Scarne, J.
    795.4
Scattered poems. Kerouac, J.   811
Scenarios *See* Motion picture plays
Scenic art and construction. Troubridge, E.
    792
Scenic photography 101. Drager, K.   770.2
The **scent** of desire. Herz, R. S.   152.1
Schaaf, Fred
The 50 best sights in astronomy and how to see them   520
Schaap, Dick, 1934-2001
(ed) Joy in Mudville. See Joy in Mudville
    796.357
Schaap, Jeremy, 1969-
Cinderella Man [dual biography of James J. Braddock and Max Baer]   92
Triumph [biography of Jesse Owens]   92
Schacter, Daniel L.
Searching for memory   153.1
The seven sins of memory   153.1
Schaller, George B.
A naturalist and other beasts   508
Schama, Simon
Dead certainties   907
The embarrassment of riches   949.2
A history of Britain   941
The power of art   709
Rembrandt's eyes   92
Rough crossings   326
Schappert, Phil, 1956-
The last Monarch butterfly   595.7
Schebera, Jürgen
Kurt Weill   92
Schechter, Abraham A.
Basic book repair methods   025.7
Scheck, Barry
(jt. auth) Dwyer, J. Actual innocence   347
Schecter, Barnet
The devil's own work   974.7

Seafaring life
Dana, R. H. Two years before the mast
910.4

McPhee, J. A. Looking for a ship   910.4
Music of the sea   781.62

Seafood
See also Cooking—Seafood; Fish as food
Brody, J. E. Jane Brody's good seafood book
641.6

Seagrave, Peggy
(jt. auth) Seagrave, S. The Yamato dynasty
952

Seagrave, Sterling
The Yamato dynasty   952

Seal, Graham, 1950-
Encyclopedia of folk heroes   398.03

Seale, William
(ed) The White House. See The White House
975.3

SEALs See United States. Navy. Sea Air Land
Team

Seals (Numismatics)
Shearer, B. F. State names, seals, flags, and
symbols   929.9

Seaman, Barbara
The greatest experiment ever performed on
women   615
(jt. auth) Null, G. For women only!   613

Seaman, Nancy

About
Maynard, J. Internal combustion   364.152

Seamen See Sailors

Search and rescue operations See Rescue work

The **search** for life on other planets. Jakosky, B.
M.   576.8

The **search** for modern China. Spence, J. D.
951

The **search** for superstrings, symmetry, and the
theory of everything. Gribbin, J. R.   539.7

The **search** for the giant squid. Ellis, R.   594

Searching for memory. Schacter, D. L.   153.1

Searching the internet See Internet searching

Sears, Martha
(jt. auth) Sears, W. Parenting the fussy baby and
high-need child   649

Sears, Robert, M.D.
The vaccine book   614.4

Sears, Stephen W.
Chancellorsville   973.7
George B. McClellan   92
Gettysburg   973.7
Landscape turned red   973.7
To the gates of Richmond   973.7

Sears, William
The family nutrition book   613.2
Parenting the fussy baby and high-need child
649
The Baby book. See The Baby book   649

Sears list of subject headings   025.4

Seashore
See also Coasts
Carson, R. The edge of the sea   577.7

Seashore ecology
Dean, C. Against the tide   333.91

A **season** in Dornoch. Rubenstein, L.   796.352

The **seasons** of a man's life. Levinson, D. J.
155.6

The **seasons** of a woman's life. Levinson, D. J.
155.6

A **seat** at the table. Smith, H.   323.44

Seaweeds See Algae

Sebag-Montefiore, Hugh
Enigma: the battle for the code   940.54

Sebald, W. G. See Sebald, Winfried Georg, 1944-
2001

Sebald, Winfried Georg, 1944-2001
On the natural history of destruction   834

Sebold, Alice
Lucky   362.883

Second Advent
See/See also pages in the following book(s):
Lewis, C. S. The world's last night, and other
essays   230

Second chances. Wallerstein, J. S.   306.89

The **second** creation. Wilmut, I.   174

Second drafts of history. Morrow, L.   973.92

The **second** family. Taffel, R.   306.8

A **second** Mencken chrestomathy. Mencken, H. L.
818

A **second** opinion. Relman, A.   362.1

Second opinions. Groopman, J. E.   610

The **second** sex. Beauvoir, S. d.   305.4

The **Second** World War. Gilbert, M.   940.53

The **Second** World War. Keegan, J.   940.53

Secondary school libraries See High school libraries

Secrecy. Moynihan, D. P.   352

Secrest, Meryle
Frank Lloyd Wright   92

Secret agents. Drexler, M.   614.4

Secret empire. Taubman, P.   327.12

The **secret** history of the war on cancer. Davis, D.
L.   616.99

Secret ingredients   641

Secret Intelligence Service (Great Britain) See
Great Britain. MI6

The **secret** language of eating disorders. Claude-
Pierre, P.   616.85

The **secret** of scent. Turin, L.   668

The **secret** pulse of time. Klein, S.   153.7

The **secret** room. Laughlin, J.   811

Secret service
See also Espionage; Intelligence service;
Spies

Secret societies
See also Freemasons

The **secret** war against Hanoi. Shultz, R. H.
959.704

Secret weapons. Eisner, T.   595.7

Secret writing See Cryptography

Shakespeare, Nicholas, 1957-
Bruce Chatwin   92
Shakespeare, William, 1564-1616
The Columbia dictionary of quotations from
Shakespeare   **822.3**
The complete works   **822.3**
About
Bryson, B. Shakespeare   **822.3**
Greenblatt, S. J. Will in the world [biography of
William Shakespeare]   **822.3**
Shapiro, J. A year in the life of William Shake-
speare, 1599   **822.3**
Wells, S. W. Shakespeare: for all time

                                            822.3
Wood, M. Shakespeare   **822.3**
Adaptations
Lamb, C. Tales from Shakespeare   **822.3**
Criticism
Bloom, H. Shakespeare: the invention of the hu-
man   **822.3**
Boyce, C. Critical companion to William Shake-
speare   **822.3**
Dunton-Downer, L. Essential Shakespeare hand-
book   **822.3**
Frye, N. Northrop Frye on Shakespeare

                                            822.3
Garber, M. Shakespeare after all   **822.3**
The Greenwood companion to Shakespeare

                                            822.3
Nuttall, A. D. Shakespeare the thinker   **822.3**
Olsen, K. All things Shakespeare   **822.3**
Rosenbaum, R. The Shakespeare wars   **822.3**
Dramatic production
Butler, C. The practical Shakespeare   **822.3**
Harold, M. An actor's guide to performing
Shakespeare   **792**
Encyclopedias
The Oxford companion to Shakespeare

                                            822.3

Histories
Norwich, J. J. Shakespeare's kings   **822.3**
Language
Kermode, F. Shakespeare's language   **822.3**
Parodies, imitations, etc.
Stoppard, T. Rosencrantz and Guildenstern are
dead   **822**
Quotations
Shakespeare, W. The Columbia dictionary of
quotations from Shakespeare   **822.3**
Stage history
Cliff, N. The Shakespeare riots   **974.4**
Hamlet; criticism
In Bloom, H. Hamlet: poem unlimited

                                            822.3
Shakespeare A to Z. See Boyce, C. Critical com-
panion to William Shakespeare   **822.3**
Shakespeare after all. Garber, M.   **822.3**
Shakespeare: for all time. Wells, S. W. **822.3**
The **Shakespeare** riots. Cliff, N.   **974.4**
Shakespeare the thinker. Nuttall, A. D. **822.3**
The **Shakespeare** wars. Rosenbaum, R.   **822.3**
Shakespeare's kings. Norwich, J. J.   **822.3**
Shakespeare's language. Kermode, F.   **822.3**
Shakey: Neil Young's biography. McDonough, J.
                                            92

Shaking-up Parkinson disease. Lieberman, A.
                                          616.8
Shakur, Tupac
About
Dyson, M. E. Holler if you hear me: searching
for Tupac Shakur   92
Shakya, Tsering *See* Tsering Shakya
Shalom, friend: the life and legacy of Yitzhak Ra-
bin   92
Shamanism
Encyclopedias
Shamanism   **201.03**
Shamanism   **201.03**
The **Shambhala** guide to Sufism. Ernst, C. W.
                                           297
The **shame** of the nation. Kozol, J.   **379**
A **shameful** act. Akçam, T.   **956**
Shamie, Arya Nick
(jt. auth) Sayler, M. H. The encyclopedia of the
back and spine systems and disorders   **617**
Shanghai (China)
Dong, S. Shanghai, 1842-1949   **951**
Shankar, Ravi, 1975-
(ed) Language for a new century. See Language
for a new century   **808.81**
Shanker, Stuart G.
(jt. auth) Greenspan, S. I. The first idea
                                           153.7
Shankle, George Earlie
American nicknames   **929.4**
Shanks, Hershel
The mystery and meaning of the Dead Sea
scrolls   **296.1**
(ed) Understanding the Dead Sea scrolls. See
Understanding the Dead Sea scrolls   **296.1**
Shannon, Joyce Brennfleck
(ed) Diet and nutrition sourcebook. See Diet and
nutrition sourcebook   **613.2**
(ed) Disease management sourcebook. See Dis-
ease management sourcebook   **616**
(ed) Transplantation sourcebook. See Transplan-
tation sourcebook   **617.9**
The **shape** of the journey. Harrison, J. **811**
The **shape** of things to come. Marcus, G. **973**
Shaping a nation. Wiseman, C.   **720.973**
Shapiro, Alan, 1952-
(tr) Aeschylus. The Oresteia   **882**
Shapiro, David, 1947-
New and selected poems (1965-2006)   **811**
Shapiro, Edward S., 1938-
A time for healing   **305.8**
Shapiro, Fred R., 1954-
(ed) The Yale book of quotations. See The Yale
book of quotations   **808.88**
Shapiro, Harvey, 1924-
(ed) Poets of World War II. See Poets of World
War II   **811.008**
Shapiro, Ian
(ed) Locke, J. Two treatises of government; and,
A letter concerning toleration   **320.1**

Sheler, Jeffery L.
Is the Bible true?   **220.1**

Shell chic. Marshall, M. H.   **745.55**

Shelley, Fred M., 1952-
Atlas of American politics, 1960-2000. See Atlas of American politics, 1960-2000   **973.92**

Shelley, Mary Wollstonecraft, 1797-1851
About
Seymour, M. Mary Shelley   **92**
Sunstein, E. W. Mary Shelley   **92**

Shelley, Percy Bysshe, 1792-1822
Poems   **821**
Shelley's poetry and prose   **821**
See/See also pages in the following book(s):
Lee, H. Virginia Woolf's nose   **820.9**

Shelley's poetry and prose. Shelley, P. B.   **821**

Shells
Marshall, M. H. Shell chic   **745.55**

Shelter from the storm. Hilden, J. M.   **618.92**

Shelton, Dinah
(ed) Encyclopedia of genocide and crimes against humanity. See Encyclopedia of genocide and crimes against humanity   **304.6**

Shelton, Nelda
(jt. auth) Burton, S. Office procedures for the 21st century   **651.3**

Shemel, Sidney, 1913-1992
(jt. auth) Krasilovsky, M. W. This business of music   **780**

Shenk, David, 1966-
The forgetting: Alzheimer's, portrait of an epidemic   **616.8**

Shenk, Joshua Wolf
Lincoln's melancholy   **92**

Shenkman, Richard
Legends, lies & cherished myths of American history   **973.02**

Shepard, Sam, 1943-
Fool for love, and other plays   **812**
Sam Shepard; seven plays   **812**
The unseen hand and other plays   **812**
See/See also pages in the following book(s):
Playwrights at work   **812.009**

Shepherd, Jesse See Grierson, Francis, 1848-1927

Shepherd, Margaret
Learn calligraphy   **745.6**

Shepherd, Stephen H. A.
(ed) Malory, Sir T. Le morte Darthur, or, The hoole book of Kyng Arthur and of his noble knyghtes of the Rounde Table   **398.2**

Sheppard, Rob
Kodak guide to digital photography   **775**

Sheridan, Judy
How to work with an interior designer   **747**

Sheridan, Richard Brinsley, 1751-1816
The school for scandal and other plays   **822**

Sherlock Holmes in Babylon   **510**

Sherman, Carol, 1944-
(jt. auth) Rolland, J. L. The food encyclopedia   **641.03**

Sherman, Joan R.
(ed) African-American poetry of the nineteenth century. See African-American poetry of the nineteenth century   **811.008**

Sherman, William L.
(jt. auth) Meyer, M. C. The course of Mexican history   **972**

Sherman, William T. (William Tecumseh), 1820-1891
About
Davis, B. Sherman's march   **973.7**
Fellman, M. Citizen Sherman [biography of William Tecumseh Sherman]   **92**
Flood, C. B. Grant and Sherman   **92**
Hanson, V. D. The soul of battle   **355**
Kennett, L. B. Sherman   **92**
See/See also pages in the following book(s):
Wilson, E. Patriotic gore   **810.9**

Sherman's march. Davis, B.   **973.7**

Shermer, Michael
Why people believe weird things   **001.9**

Sherr, Lynn
(ed) Anthony, S. B. Failure is impossible   **92**

Sherrard, Philip
(ed) Seferis, G. Collected poems   **889**

Sherrin, Ned
(ed) Oxford dictionary of humorous quotations. See Oxford dictionary of humorous quotations   **808.88**

Sherry, Norman
The life of Graham Greene v3   **92**

Sherwin, Martin J.
(jt. auth) Bird, K. American Prometheus [biography of J. Robert Oppenheimer]   **92**

Shestov, Lev, 1866-1938
See/See also pages in the following book(s):
Miłosz, C. To begin where I am   **891.8**

The **Shia** revival. Nasr, V.   **297**

Shi'ah
Nasr, V. The Shia revival   **297**

The **shield** of Achilles. Bobbitt, P.   **327**

Shields, Carol
Jane Austen   **92**

Shilling, Jane
The fox in the cupboard   **799.2**

Shillington, Kevin
(ed) Encyclopedia of African history. See Encyclopedia of African history   **960**

Shiloh (Tenn.), Battle of, 1862
Daniel, L. J. Shiloh   **973.7**

Shilts, Randy
And the band played on   **362.1**

Shim, Jae K.
(jt. auth) Siegel, J. G. Accounting handbook   **657**

Shimbo, Hiroko
The Japanese kitchen   **641.5**

Shintani, Terry
The good carbohydrate revolution   **613.2**

Shinto
See/See also pages in the following book(s):
Eastern religions   **200.9**

Ship of ghosts. Hornfischer, J. D.   **940.54**

Sies, Luther F.
Encyclopedia of American radio, 1920-1960
791.44

Sifakis, Carl
The mafia encyclopedia **364.1**

Sife, Wallace
The loss of a pet **155.9**

Sifters: Native American women's lives **920**

Sigerman, Harriet
(ed) The Columbia documentary history of American women since 1941. See The Columbia documentary history of American women since 1941 **305.4**

Sight *See* Vision

Sign language
Chambers, D. P. Communicating in sign **419**
Costello, E. Random House Webster's American sign language dictionary **419**
Grayson, G. Talking with your hands, listening with your eyes **419**
Proctor, C. O. NTC's multilingual dictionary of American sign language **419**
Sacks, O. W. Seeing voices **362.4**
Sternberg, M. L. A. American Sign Language **419**
Tennant, R. A. The American Sign Language handshape dictionary **419**
Dictionaries
The Gallaudet dictionary of American Sign Language **419**

Signposts in a strange land. Percy, W. **818**

Signs and symbols
See also Sign language
Biedermann, H. Dictionary of symbolism **302.2**
The Complete dictionary of symbols **302.2**
Stahl, D. Abbreviations dictionary **421.03**

Signs of the zodiac. Snodgrass, M. E. **133.5**

Sikhs
Singh, P. The Sikhs **954**

Sikov, Ed
On Sunset Boulevard: the life and times of Billy Wilder **92**

Silber, Laura
Yugoslavia **949.7**

Silber, Mark
Growing herbs and vegetables **635**

Silber, Sherman J.
How to get pregnant **616.2**

Silber, Terry, 1940-
(jt. auth) Silber, M. Growing herbs and vegetables **635**

Sildenafil
Loe, M. The rise of Viagra **616.6**

Silence
See/See also pages in the following book(s):
Sontag, S. Styles of radical will **814**

The **silent** deep. Koslow, J. A. **578.7**

The **silent** passage: menopause. Sheehy, G. **618.1**

A **silent** sorrow. Kohn, I. **618.3**

Silent spring. Carson, R. **363.7**

The **silent** treatment. Howard, R. **811**

Silk
See/See also pages in the following book(s):
Hubbell, S. Shrinking the cat **660.6**

Silko, Leslie, 1948-
Storyteller **818**

Sillett, Steve
About
Preston, R. The wild trees **577**

Silver, Brian L.
The ascent of science **509**

Silver, Daniel B., 1941-
Refuge in hell **362.1**

Silver, Julie K., 1965-
After cancer treatment **616.99**

Silver, Marc, 1951-
Breast cancer husband **616.99**

The **silver** spoon **641.5**

Silverman, Debora, 1954-
Van Gogh and Gauguin **759.4**

Silverman, Kathy Kirtland
(jt. auth) Marrs, R. P. Dr. Richard Marrs' fertility book **616.6**

Silverman, Kenneth
Edgar A. Poe **92**
Lightning man [biography of Samuel Morse] **92**

Silverman, Sharon Hernes
Basic crocheting **746.43**

Silverton, Nancy
A twist of the wrist **641.5**

Silvey, Anita
100 best books for children **011.6**

Simic, Charles, 1938-
Selected early poems **811**
That little something **811**
The voice at 3:00 a.m **811**

Simmons, Matthew R.
Twilight in the desert **338.2**

Simmons, Rachel, 1966-
Odd girl out **305.23**

Simon, Daniel, 1957-
(ed) Hoffman, A. The best of Abbie Hoffman **303.4**
(jt. auth) Vonnegut, K. A man without a country **814**

Simon, James F.
What kind of nation **342.73**

Simon, Neil
Brighton Beach memoirs **812**
The collected plays of Neil Simon **812**
Lost in Yonkers **812**
The play goes on **92**
Rewrites **92**
See/See also pages in the following book(s):
Playwrights at work **812.009**

Simon, Steven
(jt. auth) Benjamin, D. The age of sacred terror **303.6**

Simon and Schuster's guide to rocks and minerals **549**

Slack, Charles
Noble obsession   **92**

Slang!. Dickson, P.   **427**

Slann, Martin W.
(jt. auth) Combs, C. C. Encyclopedia of terrorism   **303.6**

Slater, Lauren
Prozac diary   **616.89**
(ed) The Complete guide to mental health for
women. See The Complete guide to mental
health for women   **616.89**

Slater, Robert, 1943-
No such thing as over-exposure [biography of
Donald Trump]   **92**

Slatta, Richard W., 1947-
The cowboy encyclopedia   **978.03**

Slaughter, Thomas P.
The beautiful soul of John Woolman, apostle of
abolition   **92**
Exploring Lewis and Clark   **978**

Slaughterhouse. Rieff, D.   **949.7**

Slave nation. Blumrosen, A. W.   **973.3**

A **slave** no more. Blight, D. W.   **92**

The **slave** ship. Rediker, M. B.   **326**

Slave songs of the United States. Allen, W. F.
     781.62

Slave trade
Gallay, A. The Indian slave trade   **326**
Hartman, S. V. Lose your mother   **326**
Johnson, W. Soul by soul   **326**
Postma, J. The Atlantic slave trade   **326**
Rediker, M. B. The slave ship   **326**
Segal, R. Islam's Black slaves   **326**
Soodalter, R. Hanging Captain Gordon   **326**

Slavemaster president [biography of James Polk]
Dusinberre, W.   **92**

Slavery
Hochschild, A. Bury the chains   **326**
Pybus, C. Epic journeys of freedom: runaway
slaves of the American Revolution and their
global quest for liberty   **323.3**
Rediker, M. B. The slave ship   **326**
Segal, R. Islam's Black slaves   **326**
Stark, R. For the glory of God   **201**
Wise, S. M. Though the heavens may fall
     342

History
Davis, D. B. Inhuman bondage   **326**

United States
See also Abolitionists
Ball, E. Slaves in the family   **975.7**
Berlin, I. Generations of captivity   **326**
Blight, D. W. A slave no more   **92**
Blumrosen, A. W. Slave nation   **973.3**
Bordewich, F. M. Bound for Canaan   **973.7**
Bowe, J. Nobodies   **331.1**
Brackman, B. Facts & fabrications: unraveling
the history of quilts and slavery   **746.46**
Colaiaco, J. A. Frederick Douglass and the
Fourth of July   **973.7**
Dusinberre, W. Slavemaster president [biogra-
phy of James Polk]   **92**
Foner, E. Forever free   **973.8**

Fox-Genovese, E. Within the plantation house-
hold   **305.4**
Franklin, J. H. From slavery to freedom
     305.8
Franklin, J. H. In search of the promised land
     929
Fredrickson, G. M. Big enough to be inconsis-
tent   **973.7**
Horton, J. O. Slavery and the making of Ameri-
ca   **326**
Johnson, C. R. Africans in America: America's
journey through slavery   **326**
Johnson, W. Soul by soul   **326**
Lepore, J. New York burning   **974.7**
Miller, W. L. Arguing about slavery   **973.5**
Nash, G. B. The forgotten fifth   **326**
Passages to freedom   **326**
Remembering slavery   **326**
Schama, S. Rough crossings   **326**
Schneider, D. Slavery in America   **326**
Soodalter, R. Hanging Captain Gordon   **326**
Tobin, J. From Midnight to Dawn   **973.7**
Ward, A. The slaves' war   **973.7**
White, S. The sounds of slavery   **326**
Wiencek, H. The Hairstons   **975**
Wills, G. 'Negro president'   **326**
See/See also pages in the following book(s):
The Causes of the Civil War   **973.7**
Foner, E. The story of American freedom
     323.44
Levy, A. The first emancipator [biography of
Robert Carter]   **92**

United States—Encyclopedias
Encyclopedia of slave resistance and rebellion
     326

United States—Songs
Allen, W. F. Slave songs of the United States
     781.62

Slavery and the making of America. Horton, J. O.
     326

Slavery in America. Schneider, D.   **326**

Slaves in the family. Ball, E.   **975.7**

The **slaves'** war. Ward, A.   **973.7**

Slavinski, Cindy Tate
(jt. auth) Hartman, G. R. Landmark Supreme
Court cases   **347**

Slavitt, David R., 1935-
(tr) Sophocles. The Theban plays of Sophocles
     882

Sled dog racing
See also Iditarod Trail Sled Dog Race,
Alaska
Paulsen, G. Winterdance   **798.8**

Sleep
Alvarez, A. Night   **154.6**
Dement, W. C. The promise of sleep   **612.8**
Ferber, R. Solve your child's sleep problems
     618.92
Goldman, B. Brain fitness   **153.1**
Lavie, P. The enchanted world of sleep
     612.8
Sleep disorders sourcebook   **616.8**
See/See also pages in the following book(s):
Brazelton, T. B. To listen to a child   **155.4**

Stout, Harry S.
Upon the altar of the nation : a moral history of
the American Civil War **973.7**

Stow, Dorrik A. V.
Oceans: an illustrated reference **551.46**

Stow, Josie
The African kitchen **641.5**

Stowe, Calvin Ellis, 1802-1886
See/See also pages in the following book(s):
Wilson, E. Patriotic gore **810.9**

Stowe, Harriet Beecher, 1811-1896
About
Hedrick, J. D. Harriet Beecher Stowe **92**
See/See also pages in the following book(s):
McPherson, J. M. Drawn with the sword
973.7
Wilson, E. Patriotic gore **810.9**
Uncle Tom's cabin; criticism
In McPherson, J. M. Drawn with the sword
973.7

Stowe, Harriet Elizabeth *See* Stowe, Harriet Beecher, 1811-1896

Strachan, Hew
The First World War **940.3**
(ed) World War I. See World War I **940.3**

Strachey, James
(ed) Freud, S. Totem and taboo **306**

Strachey, Lytton, 1880-1932
Elizabeth and Essex **92**

Straczynski, J. Michael, 1954-
The complete book of scriptwriting **808.2**

Stradling, R. A.
(jt. auth) Vincent, M. Cultural atlas of Spain and
Portugal **946**

Straight talk about cosmetic surgery. Perry, A. W.
617.9

Straight talk from Claudia Black. Black, C.
362.29

Strain (Psychology) *See* Stress (Psychology)

Strand, Mark, 1934-
Blizzard of one **811**
Chicken, shadow, moon and more **811**
Man and camel **811**
(ed) 100 great poems of the twentieth century.
See 100 great poems of the twentieth century
821.008
(ed) The Making of a poem. See The Making of
a poem **821.008**

Strange angel [biography of Jack Parsons] Pendle,
G. **92**

Strange beauty: Murray Gell-Mann and the revolution in twentieth-century physics. Johnson,
G. **92**

The **strange** career of Jim Crow. Woodward, C.
V. **305.8**

Strange piece of paradise. Jentz, T. **364.1**

The **stranger** beside me [biography of Ted Bundy]
Rule, A. **92**

The **stranger** from paradise: a biography of William Blake. Bentley, G. E. **92**

Strangers from a different shore. Takaki, R. T.
305.8

Strangers: homosexual love in the nineteenth century. Robb, G. **306.76**

Strassfeld, Michael
The Jewish holidays **296.4**

Strassler, Robert B., 1937-
(ed) Herodotus. The landmark Herodotus
938

Strategic business letters and e-mail. Lindsell-
Roberts, S. **651.7**

Strategic Defense Initiative
FitzGerald, F. Way out there in the blue
973.927

Strategic planning and management for library
managers. Matthews, J. R. **025.1**

Strategy
Overy, R. J. Why the Allies won **940.53**

Stratemeyer, Edward, 1862-1930
About
Rehak, M. Girl sleuth **813.009**

Stratigraphic geology
Fortey, R. A. Earth **551.7**
Hancock, G. Underworld: the mysterious origins
of civilization **551.7**
Macdougall, J. D. A short history of planet earth
551.7
Winchester, S. The map that changed the world
92

Stratton, Joanna L.
Pioneer women **978.1**

Stratton, Stephen E.
(jt. auth) Watstein, S. B. The encyclopedia of
HIV and AIDS **616.97**

Straus, Roger, III
(jt. auth) Howard, H. Houses of the founding fathers **973.3**

Strauss, Claude Lévi- *See* Lévi-Strauss, Claude

Strauss, Diane Wheeler
(jt. auth) Moss, R. W. Strauss's handbook of
business information **650**

Strauss, Joseph Baermann, 1870-1938
About
Petroski, H. Engineers of dreams **624.2**

Strauss, Richard, 1864-1949
See/See also pages in the following book(s):
Tuchman, B. W. The proud tower **909.82**

Strauss, Steven D., 1958-
Landlord and tenant **346.04**
Wills and trusts **346.05**

Strauss's handbook of business information. Moss,
R. W. **650**

Stravinsky, Igor, 1882-1971
About
Joseph, C. M. Stravinsky inside out **92**
Walsh, S. Stravinsky: a creative spring **92**
Walsh, S. Stravinsky: the second exile **92**
See/See also pages in the following book(s):
Gardner, H. Creating minds **153.3**

Stravinsky inside out. Joseph, C. M. **92**

Strawberry, Darryl
About
Sokolove, M. Y. The ticket out: Darryl Straw-
berry and the boys of Crenshaw **796.357**

Strayer, Joseph Reese, 1904-1987
(ed) Dictionary of the Middle Ages. See Dictionary of the Middle Ages **940.1**

Streatfeild, Dominic
Cocaine **362.29**

Street, Emmet *See* Behan, Brendan, 1923-1964

Street art
Ganz, N. Graffiti world **751**

Street gangs *See* Gangs

Street people *See* Homeless persons

Streets
New York (N.Y.)
See also Wall Street (New York, N.Y.)

Streiff, Fritz
(jt. auth) Waters, A. The art of simple food **641.5**

Streissguth, Michael
Johnny Cash **92**

Strength to love. King, M. L., Jr. **252**

Strength training for women. Pagano, J. **613.7**

Stress (Physiology)
Goldman, B. Brain fitness **153.1**
Kahn, A. P. The encyclopedia of stress and stress-related diseases **616.9**

Stress (Psychology)
See also Anxiety; Post-traumatic stress disorder
Kahn, A. P. The encyclopedia of stress and stress-related diseases **616.9**
Taylor, S. E. The tending instinct **304.5**

Stress A-Z. See Kahn, A. P. The encyclopedia of stress and stress-related diseases **616.9**

Strickland, Bonnie R., 1936-
(ed) The Gale encyclopedia of psychology. See The Gale encyclopedia of psychology **150.3**

Strictly science fiction. Herald, D. T. **016.8**

Strikes
United States
Honey, M. K. Going down Jericho Road **331.8**

Strindberg, August, 1849-1912
Strindberg: five plays **839.7**

String theory
Greene, B. R. The elegant universe **539.7**
Kaku, M. Parallel worlds **523.1**
Smolin, L. The trouble with physics **530.1**
Susskind, L. Cosmic landscape **523.1**

Stringer, Caverly
Sleepaway school **92**

Stringer, Christopher B., 1947-
African exodus **599.93**

Stringer, Lee *See* Stringer, Caverly

Stroke
Managing stroke **616.8**
Spence, J. D. How to prevent your stroke **616.8**

Strom, Yale
The book of Klezmer **781.62**

Stroman, James
Administrative assistant's & secretary's handbook **651.3**

Stromer, Ernst
About
Nothdurft, W. E. The lost dinosaurs of Egypt **567.9**

Strong, James, 1822-1894
The strongest Strong's exhaustive concordance of the Bible **220.5**

Strong, M. C. (Martin Charles), 1960-
The great rock discography **781.66**

Strong, Martin Charles *See* Strong, M. C. (Martin Charles), 1960-

Strong is your hold. Kinnell, G. **811**

Strong religion. Almond, G. A. **200.9**

Strong women eat well. Nelson, M. E. **613.2**

Strong women, strong bones. Nelson, M. E. **616.7**

A **stronger** kinship. Cox, A.-L. **305.8**

The **strongest** Strong's exhaustive concordance of the Bible. Strong, J. **220.5**

Strong's exhaustive concordance of the Bible. See Strong, J. The strongest Strong's exhaustive concordance of the Bible **220.5**

Stroom, Gerrold van der
(ed) Frank, A. The diary of Anne Frank: the critical edition **92**

Strouse, Jean
Morgan **92**

Struck by lightning. Rosenthal, J. **519.2**

Structural failures
Levy, M. Why buildings fall down **690**

The **structure** of evolutionary theory. Gould, S. J. **576.8**

A **struggle** for power. Draper, T. **973.3**

Strumpf, Michael
The grammar bible **428**

Strunk, William, 1869-1946
The elements of style **808**

Stuart, Henry *See* Darnley, Henry Stewart, Lord, 1545-1567

Stuart, P. G. Maxwell- *See* Maxwell-Stuart, P. G.

Stubblefield, R. Jay
(jt. auth) DeGategno, P. J. Critical companion to Jonathan Swift **828**

Stubenrecht, Werner Scholze- *See* Scholze-Stubenrecht, Werner

Student aid
See also Scholarships; Student loan funds
Scholarships, fellowships and loans **378.3**

Student busing *See* Busing (School integration)

Student loan funds
College money handbook 2008 **378.3**
Getting financial aid 2009 **378.3**
Scholarships, fellowships and loans **378.3**

Students
See also College students; High school students
Political activity
Gitlin, T. The sixties **973.92**

Students, Handicapped *See* Handicapped students

Theoharis, Athan G.—*Continued*
(ed) The FBI: a comprehensive reference guide.
See The FBI: a comprehensive reference
guide **363.2**
(ed) From the secret files of J. Edgar Hoover.
See From the secret files of J. Edgar Hoover
363.2

Theology
See also Doctrinal theology; Faith; Secularism
Bonhoeffer, D. A testament to freedom **230**
Great thinkers of the Western world **190**
Kierkegaard, S. The present age, and Of the difference between a genius and an apostle
230
Küng, H. Great Christian thinkers **230**
Teilhard de Chardin, P. Christianity and evolution **231.7**

Theology, Doctrinal *See* Doctrinal theology

Theology, Natural *See* Natural theology

Theology in America. Holifield, E. B. **230**

Theology of culture. Tillich, P. **230**

Theory of knowledge
Baars, B. J. In the theater of consciousness
153
Greenspan, S. I. The first idea **153.7**
Kant, I. Critique of pure reason **193**
Locke, J. An essay concerning human understanding **121**
Sartre, J. P. Truth and existence **121**
Wilson, E. O. Consilience **121**

Theory of systems *See* System theory

The **theory** of the leisure class. Veblen, T.
305.5

Therapeutics
See also Gene therapy; Pet therapy

Therapy, Gene *See* Gene therapy

Therapy, Psychological *See* Psychotherapy

There are words. Turnbull, G. **821**

There goes my everything. Sokol, J. **305.8**

There is no me without you [biography of
Haregewoin Teferra] Greene, M. F. **92**

Theresa, Saint *See* Teresa, of Avila, Saint, 1515-
1582

Thermageddon: countdown to 2030. Hunter, R.
363.7

Thermodynamics
Von Baeyer, H. C. Maxwell's demon **536**
See/See also pages in the following book(s):
Shachtman, T. Absolute zero and the conquest
of cold **536**

Theroux, Paul
Dark star safari **916**
The great railway bazaar **915**
The happy isles of Oceania **919**
The old Patagonian express **918**
Riding the iron rooster **915.1**

Theroux, Peter
Sandstorms: days and nights in Arabia **953**

Theroux, Phyllis
(ed) The Book of eulogies. See The Book of eulogies **808.8**

These are my rivers. Ferlinghetti, L. **811**

Theseus (Greek mythology)
See/See also pages in the following book(s):
Hamilton, E. Mythology **292**

Thessalonike (Greece)
Mazower, M. Salonica, city of ghosts **949.5**

They all laughed. Flatow, I. **609**

They all laughed at Christopher Columbus. Weil,
E. **621.43**

They fought like demons. Blanton, D. **973.7**

They made America. Evans, H. **920**

They marched into sunlight. Maraniss, D.
959.704

They never said it. Boller, P. F. **808.88**

They poured fire on us from the sky. Deng, B.
962.4

A **thief** of strings. Revell, D. **811**

Thieret, John W., 1926-2005
National Audubon Society field guide to North
American wildflowers: eastern region
582.13

Thieves of Baghdad. Bogdanos, M. **956.7**

Thieves of paradise. Komunyakaa, Y. **811**

Thin ice. Bowen, M. **551.51**

A **thing** that is. Lax, R. **811**

Things I didn't know. Hughes, R. **92**

Think: a compelling introduction to philosophy.
Blackburn, S. **100**

Think and grow rich. Hill, N. **650.1**

Think tanks *See* Group problem solving

Thinking *See* Thought and thinking

Thinking about the earth. Oldroyd, D. R. **551**

Thinking like your editor. Rabiner, S. **808**

The **third** chimpanzee. Diamond, J. M. **599.93**

The **Third** Reich. Burleigh, M. **943.086**

The **Third** Reich in power, 1933-1939. Evans, R.
J. **943.086**

The **third** wave. Toffler, A. **303.4**

Third World *See* Developing countries

Thirteen days. Kennedy, R. F. **973.922**

Thirteen seconds. See Caputo, P. 13 seconds
973.924

Thirteen ways of looking at a black man. Gates,
H. L. **920**

Thirteen ways of looking at the novel. Smiley, J.
813.009

The **thirty-first** of March. Busby, H. W.
973.923

The **Thirtymile** fire. Maclean, J. N. **634.9**

This ain't brain surgery. Dierker, L. **92**

This boy's life: a memoir. Wolff, T. **92**

This business of music. Krasilovsky, M. W.
780

This changes everything. Robb, C. **305**

This cold heaven. Ehrlich, G. **998**

This craft of verse. Borges, J. L. **809.1**

This far by faith. Williams, J. **200**

This house has fallen. Maier, K. **966.9**

Tibetan book of the dead
The Tibetan book of the dead   **294.3**

Tichelaar, An Keuning- *See* Keuning-Tichelaar, An, 1922-

The **ticket** out: Darryl Strawberry and the boys of Crenshaw. Sokolove, M. Y.   **796.357**

Ticks
> *See also* Lyme disease
> Vanderhoof-Forschner, K. Everything you need to know about Lyme disease and other tick-borne disorders   **616.9**

Tidal waves *See* Ocean waves

Tidal waves, Seismic *See* Tsunamis

Tiffin, Matthew *See* Harold, Madd, 1973-

Tiger Force. Sallah, M.   **959.704**

The **Tiger** Woods way. Andrisani, J.   **796.352**

Tigers
> Matthiessen, P. Tigers in the snow   **599.75**
> Padel, R. Tigers in red weather   **599.75**
> Thomas, E. M. The tribe of tiger   **599.75**

Tigers & ice. Hoagland, E.   **814**

Tigers in red weather. Padel, R.   **599.75**

Tigers in the snow. Matthiessen, P.   **599.75**

Tigges, Julie A.
> (ed) Women's legal guide. See Women's legal guide   **346.01**

Tilden, Samuel J., 1814-1886
> **About**
> Morris, R. Fraud of the century   **324**

Till, Emmett
See/See also pages in the following book(s):
> Abdul-Jabbar, K. Black profiles in courage   **920**

Tillich, Paul, 1886-1965
> The courage to be   **179**
> Dynamics of faith   **234**
> Theology of culture   **230**

Tillyard, Stella K.
> A royal affair   **920**

A **timbered** choir. Berry, W.   **811**

Time
> *See also* Geological time; Night
> Aveni, A. F. Empires of time   **529**
> Barnett, J. E. Time's pendulum   **529**
> Galison, P. L. Einstein's clocks and Poincaré's maps   **529**
> Gleick, J. Faster   **529**
> Gorst, M. Measuring eternity   **115**
> Klein, S. The secret pulse of time   **153.7**
> Richards, E. G. Mapping time   **529**
> Sims, M. Apollo's fire   **529**
> Von Baeyer, H. C. Maxwell's demon   **536**

Time almanac, 2008   **031.02**

Time and materials. Hass, R.   **811**

Time and space *See* Space and time

The **time** before history. Tudge, C.   **599.93**

A **time** for building. Sorin, G.   **305.8**

A **time** for gathering. Diner, H. R.   **305.8**

A **time** for healing. Shapiro, E. S.   **305.8**

A **time** for planting. Faber, E.   **305.8**

A **time** for searching. Feingold, H. L.   **305.8**

Time, love, memory. Weiner, J.   **591.5**

Time management
> Covey, S. R. First things first   **158**
> Heller, R. Essential manager's manual   **658.4**
> Klein, S. The secret pulse of time   **153.7**
> Nakone, L. Organizing for your brain type   **640**

Time of our lives. Kirkwood, T.   **612.6**

Time saving cookery *See* Quick and easy cooking

Time to be in earnest. James, P. D.   **92**

A **time** to die. McKhann, C. F.   **179.7**

Time travel in Einstein's universe. Gott, J. R.   **530.1**

Time traveler. Novacek, M. J.   **92**

The **timeline** book of the arts. See Ochoa, G. The Wilson chronology of the arts   **700**

Timelines of world history. Teeple, J. B.   **902**

Timerman, Jacobo, 1923-1999
> Prisoner without a name, cell without a number   **92**

Time's pendulum. Barnett, J. E.   **529**

The **Times** were a changin'   **973.923**

The **timetables** of African-American history. Harley, S.   **305.8**

The **timetables** of American history   **902**

The **timetables** of history. Grun, B.   **902**

Timetables of world literature. Kurian, G. T.   **809**

Timmerman, Kenneth R.
> Preachers of hate   **956.94**

Timmons, Stuart, 1957-
> (jt. auth) Faderman, L. Gay L.A.   **306.76**

Timucua Indians
See/See also pages in the following book(s):
> Josephy, A. M. Now that the buffalo's gone   **970.004**

The **Tin** Pan Alley song encyclopedia. Hischak, T.   **782.42**

Tinkering with Eden. Todd, K.   **591.6**

Tinniswood, Adrian, 1954-
> The Verneys   **920**

Tintori, Karen
> Trapped: the 1909 Cherry Mine disaster   **977.3**

Tiptree, James, 1916-1987
> **About**
> Phillips, J. James Tiptree, Jr.   **92**

Tiradritti, Francesco
> (ed) Egyptian treasures from the Egyptian Museum in Cairo. See Egyptian treasures from the Egyptian Museum in Cairo   **709.32**

Tirion, Wil
> The Cambridge star atlas   **523.8**
> (jt. auth) Chartrand, M. R. The Audubon Society field guide to the night sky   **523**

Tirnady, Frank
> (jt. auth) Lee, H. C. Blood evidence   **614**

Tirone Smith, Mary-Ann, 1944-
> Girls of tender age   **92**

'Tis. McCourt, F.   **92**

Tischler, Nancy M., 1931-
Men and women of the Bible   **220.9**

Tissue procurement *See* Procurement of organs, tissues, etc.

Titan: the life of John D. Rockefeller, Sr. Chernow, R.   **92**

Titanic (Steamship)
Butler, D. A. Unsinkable: the full story of the RMS Titanic   **910.4**
Green, R. Building the Titanic   **623.82**
Lord, W. A night to remember   **910.4**

Tito, Josip Broz, 1892-1980
About
West, R. Tito   **92**

Titus, Emperor of Rome, 40-81
See/See also pages in the following book(s):
Suetonius Tranquillus, C. The twelve Caesars   **878**

To Appomattox. Davis, B.   **973.7**

To be young, gifted, and Black. Hansberry, L.   **92**

To begin again. Levy, N.   **296.7**

To begin where I am. Miłosz, C.   **891.8**

To conquer the air. Tobin, J.   **629.13**

To die well. Wanzer, S. H.   **179.7**

To have or to be? Fromm, E.   **302**

To life!. Kushner, H. S.   **296**

To listen to a child. Brazelton, T. B.   **155.4**

To live's to fly. Kruth, J.   **92**

To the actor. Chekhov, M.   **792**

To the best of my ability   **920**

To the castle and back. Havel, V.   **92**

To the flag. Ellis, R.   **323.6**

To the gates of Richmond. Sears, S. W.   **973.7**

Toads
Beltz, E. Frogs: inside their remarkable world   **597.8**

Toasts
Toasts   **808.88**

Toasts   **808.88**

Tobacco
Gately, I. Tobacco   **394.1**
Encyclopedias
Tobacco in history and culture   **394.1**

Tobacco habit
See also Smoking cessation programs
Fisher, E. B. American Lung Association 7 steps to a smoke-free life   **616.86**
Kluger, R. Ashes to ashes   **394.1**

Tobacco in history and culture   **394.1**

Tobacco industry
Brandt, A. M. The cigarette century   **338.4**
Kluger, R. Ashes to ashes   **394.1**

Tobias, Andrew P.
The only investment guide you'll ever need   **332.024**

Tobias, Sheila
Overcoming math anxiety   **510**

Tobias, Steven E.
(jt. auth) Elias, M. J. Emotionally intelligent parenting   **649**

Tobin, Daniel R.
(jt. auth) Hilden, J. M. Shelter from the storm   **618.92**

Tobin, Jacqueline, 1950-
From Midnight to Dawn   **973.7**
Hidden in plain view   **973.7**

Tobin, James, 1956-
Ernie Pyle's war   **92**
Great projects   **620**
To conquer the air   **629.13**
Reporting America at war. See Reporting America at war   **070.4**

Tocqueville, Alexis de
About
Epstein, J. Alexis De Tocqueville   **92**
Lévy, B. H. American vertigo   **917.3**

Tocqueville, Alexis de, 1805-1859
Democracy in America   **973.5**

Todd, Kim, 1970-
Tinkering with Eden   **591.6**

Todd, Olivier
Albert Camus   **92**

Toerge, John E.
(ed) Managing stroke. See Managing stroke   **616.8**

Tofel, Richard J., 1957-
A legend in the making   **796.357**

Toffler, Alvin
Future shock   **303.4**
Powershift   **303.4**
Revolutionary wealth   **339**
The third wave   **303.4**

Toffler, Heidi
(jt. auth) Toffler, A. Revolutionary wealth   **339**

Toklas, Alice B.
About
Malcolm, J. Two lives [dual biography of Gertrude Stein and Alice B. Toklas]   **92**
Stein, G. The autobiography of Alice B. Toklas   **92**

The **Tokyo** gas attack and the Japanese psyche. See Murakami, H. Underground   **364.1**

Tolan, Sandy
The lemon tree   **956.94**

Toland, John
Adolf Hitler   **92**

Toleration
Bullard, S. Teaching tolerance   **649**
Locke, J. Two treatises of government; and, A letter concerning toleration   **320.1**

Tolkien, J. R. R. (John Ronald Reuel), 1892-1973
About
Hammond, W. G. J.R.R. Tolkien, artist & illustrator   **92**

Tolkien, John Ronald Reuel *See* Tolkien, J. R. R. (John Ronald Reuel), 1892-1973

Toll, Ian W.
Six frigates   **359**

Tolle, Eckhart, 1948-
A new earth   **158**
The power of now   **158**

The **unquiet** grave. Hendricks, S.   **970.004**

Unraveling the mystery of autism and pervasive developmental disorder. Seroussi, K.
618.92

An **unreasonable** woman. Wilson, D.   **92**

The **unredeemed** captive. Demos, J.   **973.2**

Unsafe at any meal. See Mindell, E. Dr. Earl Mindell's unsafe at any meal   **613.2**

The **unseen** hand and other plays. Shepard, S.
812

Unsinkable: the full story of the RMS Titanic. Butler, D. A.   **910.4**

Unspeak: how words become weapons, how weapons become a message, and how that message becomes reality. Poole, S.   **306.44**

Unspeakable acts, ordinary people. Conroy, J.
323.4

Unstrange minds. Grinker, R. R.   **616.85**

The **unsubscriber**. Knott, B.   **811**

The **unswept** room. Olds, S.   **811**

Unterweger, Jack, 1950-1994
About
Leake, J. Entering Hades   **364.152**

Untouchables. Jadhav, N.   **305.5**

Unweaving the rainbow. Dawkins, R.   **501**

The **unwritten** rules of friendship. Elman, N. M.
649

Up close & personal (Motion picture)
Dunne, J. G. Monster   **791.43**

Up from slavery. Washington, B. T.   **92**

Upchurch, Thomas Adams
(ed) The Greenwood encyclopedia of African American civil rights. See The Greenwood encyclopedia of African American civil rights
305.8

Updike, John
Americana and other poems   **811**
Collected poems, 1953-1993   **811**
Due considerations   **814**
Still looking   **709.73**
About
Pritchard, W. H. Updike   **813.009**
(ed) Shapiro, K. J. Selected poems   **811**

Upgrading and repairing PCs. Mueller, S.
621.39

Upholstery
Cone, S. Singer upholstery basics plus   **645**
Upholstery basics. See Cone, S. Singer upholstery basics plus   **645**

Upon the altar of the nation : a moral history of the American Civil War. Stout, H. S.
973.7

Upper atmosphere
Bowen, M. Thin ice   **551.51**

The **uprooted**. Handlin, O.   **325.73**

The **ups** and downs of raising a bipolar child. Lederman, J.   **618.92**

Upton, Clive
Oxford rhyming dictionary   **423**

Upton, Eben
(jt. auth) Upton, C. Oxford rhyming dictionary
423

Urban areas *See* Cities and towns

Urban development *See* Urbanization

Urban life *See* City and town life

Urban planning *See* City planning

Urban sociology
See also Urbanization

Urbanization
Belleville, B. Losing it all to sprawl   **307**

An **urchin** in the storm. Gould, S. J.   **570**

Urdang, Laurence
(ed) The timetables of American history. See The timetables of American history   **902**
(ed) Twentieth century American nicknames. See Twentieth century American nicknames
929.4

Ure, Susan
The altered book scrapbook   **745.593**
Scrapbooking your vacations   **745.593**

Urinary incontinence
Genadry, R. A woman's guide to urinary incontinence   **616.6**

Urofsky, Melvin I.
(jt. auth) Finkelman, P. Landmark decisions of the United States Supreme Court   **347**
(ed) The Supreme Court justices: a biographical dictionary. See The Supreme Court justices: a biographical dictionary   **920.003**

Urquhart, Rachel
(jt. auth) Gross, K. J. Woman's face   **646.7**

Urrutia, Matilde, 1912-1985
My life with Pablo Neruda   **92**

Ury, William
Getting past no   **158**

Us and them. Berreby, D.   **305**

Usability testing for library websites. Norlin, E.
025.04

USAF *See* United States. Air Force

Use of time *See* Time management

A **user's** guide to the brain. Ratey, J. J.   **612.8**

USMA *See* United States Military Academy

Ussama bin Laden *See* Osama bin Laden

Uterine fibroids
Goodwin, S. C. What your doctor may not tell you about fibroids   **616.99**

Utilitarianism
See also Secularism

Utley, Robert Marshall, 1929-
Billy the Kid   **92**
Custer: cavalier in buckskin   **973.8**
Sitting Bull: the life and times of an American patriot   **92**

Utopias
More, Sir T., Saint. Utopia   **321**
Plato. The republic   **888**
See/See also pages in the following book(s):
Heilbroner, R. L. The worldly philosophers
330.1

V

Wade, Henry, 1914-2001
About
Hull, N. E. H. Roe v. Wade   344

Wade, Josie
(jt. auth) Segen, J. C. The patient's guide to medical tests   **616.07**

Wade, Nicholas
Before the dawn   **599.93**

Wadyka, Sally
(jt. auth) Brown, B. Bobbi Brown beauty evolution   **646.7**

Wadzanai See Aqui, 1962-

Wages See Salaries, wages, etc.

Minimum wage
See Minimum wage

Waging modern war. Clark, W. K.   **949.7**

Wagner, E. J.
The science of Sherlock Holmes   **363.2**

Wagner, Linda Welshimer See Wagner-Martin, Linda

Wagner, Melissa
(jt. auth) Friedman, V. M. Field guide to stains   **648**

Wagner, Richard, 1813-1883
About
Berger, W. Wagner without fear   **92**
Osborne, C. The complete operas of Richard Wagner   **792.5**
See/See also pages in the following book(s):
Sontag, S. Where the stress falls   **814**

Wagner-Martin, Linda
Sylvia Plath   **92**
(ed) The Oxford book of women's writing in the United States. See The Oxford book of women's writing in the United States   **810.8**

Wagner without fear. Berger, W.   **92**

Wagons west. McLynn, F.   **978**

Wahab, Shaista
A brief history of Afghanistan   **958.1**

Wahhabis
Lawrence, T. E. Seven pillars of wisdom   **940.4**

Wait till next year. Goodwin, D. K.   **92**

Waite, Linda J.
The case for marriage   **306.8**

Waiting for Aphrodite. Hubbell, S.   **592**

Waiting for bebé. Alcañiz, L.   **618.2**

Waiting for snow in Havana. Eire, C. M. N.   **92**

Waiting for the macaws. See Glavin, T. The sixth extinction   **333.95**

Waiting 'til the midnight hour. Joseph, P. E.   **323.1**

Wake-up calls. Lunden, J.   **155.2**

Wakelyn, Jon L.
(ed) Leaders of the American Civil War. See Leaders of the American Civil War   **920.003**

Wakeman, Carolyn
(jt. auth) Wu, H. Bitter winds   **951.05**

Wakeman, John, 1928-
(ed) World authors, 1950-1970. See World authors, 1950-1970   **920.003**
(ed) World authors, 1970-1975. See World authors, 1970-1975   **920.003**

Wal-Mart   **381**

Wal-Mart Stores, Inc.
Featherstone, L. Selling women short   **331.4**
Wal-Mart   **381**
Walton, S. Sam Walton, made in America   **92**

Walcott, Derek
Collected poems, 1948-1984   **811**
Omeros   **811**
The prodigal   **811**

Wald, Elijah
Escaping the delta [biography of Robert Johnson]   **92**

Waldbauer, Gilbert
Insects through the seasons   **595.7**
Insights from insects   **632**
Millions of monarchs, bunches of beetles   **595.7**
What good are bugs?   **595.7**

Walden, or, Life in the woods. Thoreau, H. D.   **818**

Waldman, Anne, 1945-
In the room of never grieve   **811**

Waldman, Carl
Atlas of the North American Indian   **970.004**
Encyclopedia of exploration   **910.3**
Encyclopedia of Native American tribes   **970.004**

Waldman, Michael, 1960-
(comp) My fellow Americans. See My fellow Americans   **352.23**

Waldman, Murray
Dying for a hamburger   **614.5**

Waldman, Steven, 1962-
Founding faith   **342**

Waldmeir, Patti
Anatomy of a miracle   **968.06**

Waldron, Ann
Eudora [Welty]   **92**

Waldrup, Carole Chandler, 1925-
The vice presidents   **920.003**

Wales
Morris, J. A writer's house in Wales   **942.9**

Waley, Arthur, 1889-1966
The Nō plays of Japan   **895.6**
(tr) Confucius. The Analects   **181**

A **walk** across America. Jenkins, P.   **917.3**

A **walk** in the woods. Bryson, B.   **917.4**

Walker, Aidan
(ed) The Encyclopedia of wood. See The Encyclopedia of wood   **674**

Walker, Alan
The wisdom of the bones   **599.93**

Walker, Alexander
Audrey [Hepburn]   **92**
Stanley Kubrick, director   **92**

Walker, Alice, 1944-
The same river twice   **92**

Water wars. Ward, D. R. **333.91**

Watercolor painting
Technique
Crawshaw, A. You can paint watercolors
 751.42
Kunz, J. Painting beautiful watercolors from
 photographs **751.42**
MacKenzie, G. The watercolorist's essential
 notebook **751.42**
Taylor, J. Watercolor wisdom **751.42**
Watercolor wisdom. Taylor, J. **751.42**
The **watercolorist's** essential notebook. MacKenzie, G. **751.42**
Watergate. Olson, K. W. **973.924**
Watergate Affair, 1972-1974
Abuse of power **973.924**
Bernstein, C. All the president's men
 973.924
Emery, F. Watergate **973.924**
Olson, K. W. Watergate **973.924**
Reston, J., Jr. The conviction of Richard Nixon
 973.924
Woodward, B. The final days **973.924**
Woodward, B. Shadow **973.92**
Waterloo, Battle of, 1815
Barbero, A. The Battle **940.2**
Roberts, A. Waterloo: June 18, 1815 **940.2**
Schom, A. One hundred days **944.05**
Waters, Alice
The art of simple food **641.5**
Chez Panisse vegetables **641.6**
Waters, Muddy, 1915-1983
About
Gordon, R. Can't be satisfied: the life and times
 of Muddy Waters **92**
Watkin, David, 1941-
A history of Western architecture **720.9**
Watkins, Gloria Jean See Hooks, Bell
Watkins, Mary, 1939-
See/See also pages in the following book(s):
Walker-Hill, H. From spirituals to symphonies
 920
Watkins, S. Craig (Samuel Craig)
Hip hop matters **781.64**
Watkins, Samuel Craig See Watkins, S. Craig
 (Samuel Craig)
Watkins, T. H. (Tom H.), 1936-2000
The hungry years **973.91**
Watling, E. F.
(tr) Plautus, T. M. The pot of gold, and other
 plays **872**
(tr) Plautus, T. M. The rope, and other plays
 872
(tr) Seneca, L. A., the Younger. Four tragedies,
 and Octavia **882**
Watson, Bruce
Sacco and Vanzetti **345**
Watson, Burton, 1925-
(ed) The Columbia book of Chinese poetry. See
 The Columbia book of Chinese poetry
 895.1
Watson, James D., 1928-
Avoid boring people **92**

DNA: the secret of life **576.5**
The double helix **572.8**
Genes, girls, and Gamow **92**
See/See also pages in the following book(s):
Flowers, C. Instability rules **509**
Friedman, M. Medicine's 10 greatest discoveries
 610.9
Horvitz, L. A. Eureka!: scientific breakthroughs
 that changed the world **509**
Watson, John Broadus, 1878-1958
Behaviorism **150.19**
Watson, Lucy, 1968-
Life drawing class **743**
Watson, Lyall
Dark nature **111**
Jacobson's organ and the remarkable nature of
 smell **612.8**
Watson, Richard A., 1931-
Cogito ergo sum: the life of René Descartes
 92
Watson, Victor
(ed) The Cambridge guide to children's books
 in English. See The Cambridge guide to children's books in English **028.5**
Watstein, Sarah B.
The encyclopedia of HIV and AIDS **616.97**
Watters, David H.
(ed) The Encyclopedia of New England. See
 The Encyclopedia of New England **974**
Watters, James
(jt. auth) Howard, J. Jean Howard's Hollywood
 791.43
Watterson, Bill
The complete Calvin and Hobbes **741.5**
Watts, Alan, 1915-1973
The way of Zen **294.3**
Watts, Jill
Hattie McDaniel **92**
Watts, Steven, 1952-
The people's tycoon [biography of Henry Ford]
 92
Waugh, Alexander
Fathers and sons **920**
Waugh family
About
Waugh, A. Fathers and sons **920**
Wauson, Jennifer
(jt. auth) Stroman, J. Administrative assistant's
 & secretary's handbook **651.3**
Wave of destruction. Krauss, E. **959.3**
Waves
 See also Ocean waves
Waxman, Sharon
Rebels on the backlot **920**
Way, Lawrence W.
(ed) Current surgical diagnosis & treatment. See
 Current surgical diagnosis & treatment
 617
The **way** it is. Stafford, W. E. **811**
The **way** life works. Hoagland, M. B. **570**
Way more West. Dorn, E. **811**
A **way** of being. Rogers, C. R. **150.19**